**ST. MARY'S PARISH CHURCH
TWICKENHAM**

PRESENTED TO

MAQSOOD
Amaya

BY

................................VICAR

Fr. Plott A-S SCHOOL CHAPLAIN

with the
Prayers and blessing
of the whole church.

January 2018

INTERNATIONAL CHILDREN'S BIBLE

My child, pay attention to my words.
Listen closely to what I say.
Don't ever forget my words.
Keep them within your heart.
These words are the secret to life for those who find
them.

THE GREATEST COMMANDMENT

"'Love the Lord your God with all your heart, soul and
mind'. This is the first and most important command.
And the second command is like the first: 'Love your
neighbour as you love yourself'. All the law and the
writings of the prophets depend on these two
commands."

Holy Bible

INTERNATIONAL CHILDREN'S BIBLE

NEW CENTURY VERSION

Presented to

from

Date

Jesus said, "Those who hear the teaching of God and obey it – they are the ones who are truly blessed." *Luke 11:28*

THE OLD TESTAMENT

	Abbreviation		*Abbreviation*
Genesis	Gen	Ecclesiastes	Ecc
Exodus	Ex	Song of Songs	Song
Leviticus	Lev	Isaiah	Is
Numbers	Num	Jeremiah	Jer
Deuteronomy	Deut	Lamentations	Lam
Joshua	Josh	Ezekiel	Ezek
Judges	Judg	Daniel	Dan
Ruth	Ruth	Hosea	Hos
1 Samuel	1 Sam	Joel	Joel
2 Samuel	2 Sam	Amos	Amos
1 Kings	1 Kgs	Obadiah	Obad
2 Kings	2 Kgs	Jonah	Jon
1 Chronicles	1 Chr	Micah	Mic
2 Chronicles	2 Chr	Nahum	Nah
Ezra	Ezra	Habakkuk	Hab
Nehemiah	Neh	Zephaniah	Zeph
Esther	Esth	Haggai	Hag
Job	Job	Zechariah	Zech
Psalms	Ps	Malachi	Mal
Proverbs	Prov		

THE NEW TESTAMENT

	Abbreviation		*Abbreviation*
Matthew	Mt	1 Timothy	1 Tim
Mark	Mk	2 Timothy	2 Tim
Luke	Lk	Titus	Tit
John	Jn	Philemon	Phlm
Acts	Acts	Hebrews	Heb
Romans	Rom	James	Jas
1 Corinthians	1 Cor	1 Peter	1 Pet
2 Corinthians	2 Cor	2 Peter	2 Pet
Galatians	Gal	1 John	1 Jn
Ephesians	Eph	2 John	2 Jn
Philippians	Phil	3 John	3 Jn
Colossians	Col	Jude	Jude
1 Thessalonians	1 Thes	Revelation	Rev
2 Thessalonians	2 Thes		

CONTENTS
THE OLD TESTAMENT

Genesis	1	Ecclesiastes	748
Exodus	62	Song of Songs	760
Leviticus	112	Isaiah	767
Numbers	151	Jeremiah	854
Deuteronomy	196	Lamentations	940
Joshua	237	Ezekiel	949
Judges	266	Daniel	1010
Ruth	297	Hosea	1030
1 Samuel	302	Joel	1044
2 Samuel	339	Amos	1050
1 Kings	372	Obadiah	1061
2 Kings	410	Jonah	1063
1 Chronicles	447	Micah	1066
2 Chronicles	485	Nahum	1075
Ezra	527	Habakkuk	1079
Nehemiah	539	Zephaniah	1084
Esther	557	Haggai	1089
Job	567	Zechariah	1092
Psalms	610	Malachi	1103
Proverbs	709		

THE NEW TESTAMENT

Matthew	1109	1 Timothy	1393
Mark	1156	2 Timothy	1399
Luke	1185	Titus	1403
John	1233	Philemon	1406
Acts	1267	Hebrews	1407
Romans	1312	James	1422
1 Corinthians	1332	1 Peter	1427
2 Corinthians	1350	2 Peter	1433
Galatians	1362	1 John	1437
Ephesians	1369	2 John	1442
Philippians	1376	3 John	1443
Colossians	1381	Jude	1444
1 Thessalonians	1386	Revelation	1446
2 Thessalonians	1390		

THE I.C.B. FAMILY TREE

AMB	Amplified Bible	LIND	The Lindisfarne Gospels in Latin
ASV	American Standard Version	LVB	Living Bible
AV	The Authorised Version/King James Bible	MAT	Matthew's Bible
		MOF	Moffat Bible
BEDE	Part of John's Gospel in Anglo-Saxon	NAB	New American Bible
BISH	The Bishop's Bible	NASB	New American Standard Bible
COV	Coverdale. First printed English Bible	NEB	New English Bible
DOUAI	The Douai-Rheims Bible. Roman Catholic version	NIV	New International Version
		NJB	New Jerusalem Bible
GB	The Great Bible	NKJ	New King James Bible Revised Authorised Version
GNB/TEV	Good News Bible/Today's English Version	NRSV	New Revised Standard Version
GREEK/NT	Original Greek New Testament	REB	Revised English Bible
GVA	The Geneva Bible. First small edition in Roman type	RSV	Revised Standard Version
		RV	English Revised Version
HEBREW OT	Original Hebrew Old Testament	SEPT/OT	Septuagint Old Testament (Greek) – the first translation from Hebrew
I.C.B.	International Children's Bible	TNT	Translator's New Testament
JBP	JB Phillips' New Testament	TYND	Tyndale. First printed English New Testament
JER	Jerusalem Bible		
KNX	Knox. Roman Catholic Version	WB	William Barclay. New Testament
LATIN VUL	Translated by Jerome using Greek and Hebrew texts	WYC	Wycliffe. First Bible in English

Holy Bible

International
Children's Bible

Holy Bible

International
Children's Bible

Holy Bible

International
Children's Bible

PREFACE

The International Children's Bible (ICB), unlike all other editions, is neither a book of Bible stories nor a paraphrased version. This is the children's edition of the New Century Version, and is the only translation solely for children from the original Hebrew and Greek texts. This is the first time that a translation of God's Word has been specifically prepared for children. Children have either only had story books or have had to grapple with adult translations, leaving them flummoxed, confused and, at worst, with the wrong ideas. God spoke because he wanted everyone to understand him and his purposes. The earliest scriptures were spoken to and written for a fairly uneducated society. Words were short and simple and fully understandable. The New Testament was written by the likes of fishermen, in simple Greek phrases. Jesus used teaching ideas that were easily understood, parables of the land, and comparisons with everyday living.

An Accurate Translation?

This translation was put together by a team from the World Bible Translation Centre, and another twenty-one experienced scholars of the Bible were brought together to work on this project for thirteen years to ensure accuracy. These are people who have had experience translating texts to be used in the New International Version, the New American Standard Bible and the New King James Version. This International Children's Bible is based on the best available Greek and Hebrew texts and quality up-to-date scholarship.

A Clear Translation

One of the reasons for producing this Bible was to make the language easy enough for children to read and understand for themselves. Guidelines were drawn up to maintain simplicity, such as keeping sentences short, using appropriate children's vocabulary, and where the words are complicated, there are references, marked "d", to the dictionary which is at the back of the Bible. Otherwise, footnotes, marked "n", are provided at the bottom of the page.

The International Children's Bible helps a child by putting biblical concepts into modern terms. Measurements are now in metric units and the twenty-first-century versions of geographical names are now used, such as "Mediterranean Sea" instead of "Great Sea" or "Western Sea". Also, to prevent confusion, one name for one place is used consistently throughout. For instance, "Lake Galilee" is used throughout, rather than its variant forms, "Sea of Kinnereth" and "Sea of Tiberias".

Ambiguous words and phrases which would lead children into odd flights of fancy have been avoided to prevent potential misunderstandings.

Rhetorical questions are not understood by children, so rather than implying an answer, we state the meaning quite clearly. Thus, when the psalmist asks, "Who is equal to our God?" our translation states "No one is equal to God".

Hebrew idioms have been translated in order to communicate the same meaning to today's children. For example, the Hebrew idiom "he rested with his fathers" is translated as "he died". Wherever possible we have tried to retain the beauty and poetry of the original in English images.

This anglicised edition of this special Bible for children features colourful artwork, dynamically presenting biblical scenes. Full-colour maps of Bible lands and journeys have been provided, and flow charts, prayers, quotes, a dictionary and footnotes are included as study aids.

Our Prayer

Realising our own lack of knowledge, we have had to trust in the Lord to guide us throughout, honour him for his steadfastness and pray none of us forget his teaching.

We pray that God through his Spirit will teach and guide you in his truth, and that you will find his love for the whole of your life. To that end we give you his Word.

THE PUBLISHERS

WHAT IS THE BIBLE?

The Bible is God's holy Word, which he has spoken to help us to find out more about him, and the life he wants us to lead. The Bible is made up of 66 books, from Genesis through to Revelation. These books have an incredible way of fitting together to form a whole. Each book is special on its own, but put together, all these books give us the history of what God has done in our world and his message of love and hope through his Son Jesus Christ, who came to live, to die, and to save us.

The Bible is not just a book of amazing stories but also a personal guide for us to follow. God has not left us to struggle on our own; instead he has purposefully used history, writing, culture and people to talk to us. Inside you will find adventure, excitement, battles and mysteries. There is, though, some serious reading and learning – God is the authority and his Word should not ever be distorted, ignored or added to. There are no mistakes in what God has said, and we now have the chance to discover the Truth. The Holy Bible is a reliable book and worth reading all the way through! (More than once!)

This Bible was especially translated for children to read and understand.

There are two major sections in the Bible: the Old Testament and the New Testament.

There are 39 books in the Old Testament, mostly written by Jews, in their own language, Hebrew. It begins with the story of how God created the world, the sky, the earth, the animals, the trees, and human beings in his image, and proved his goodness to us through creation. The history continues through God's special people, the Jews. We learn about prophets and what God told them to tell us. They spoke a lot about a very special person, the Messiah. It really is quite surprising how accurate they were, and it is proof that God really told them what was to come in the future.

The New Testament has 27 books, written by Christians, mostly in Greek, which was the language they spoke. This second section starts with the birth of Jesus Christ, God's son. It tells us what Jesus said, how he was killed and then came back to life again. It also explains that one day he will come back. This testament tells us how Jesus' teaching led to the start and continued growth of the Christian Church and how we should continue with that today.

HOW DO I USE MY BIBLE?

Because the Bible has 66 books in it, sometimes it is very hard to find what you want. So here is a tip or two . . .

1. Open your Bible and see how at the top of each page there is a name and a number. These are called the books and the chapters.

1 JOHN 2

2. Now look down one page and you can see that there are lots of little numbers in each chapter. Each one is called a verse.

> him to do wrong. ¹¹But whoever hates his brother is in darkness. He lives in darkness and does not know where he is going. The darkness has made him blind.
> ¹²I write to you, dear children,
>   because your sins are forgiven
>   through Christ.
> ¹³I write to you, fathers,
>   because you know the One who

The chapter and verse numbers help you to find what you need quickly.

Sometimes though there are two books with exactly the same name. Where this happens they have a number first.

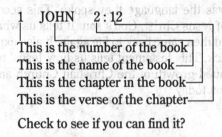

1   JOHN   2 : 12

This is the number of the book
This is the name of the book
This is the chapter in the book
This is the verse of the chapter

Check to see if you can find it?

It should say: I write to you dear children, because your sins are forgiven through Christ.

Everyone who has heard or reads the Gospel must either: accept Jesus and receive his power, or leave him behind. Who is Jesus to you? A name or a friend? If as yet you don't know, at least read and reply to the agreement below.

I ....
promise to read and try to understand that the Bible is from God. If I find that this book tells me the truth and that Jesus Christ is my Saviour and Lord, I will accept him and try to follow him my whole life.

Signed ....

Date ....

List of Maps

The Exodus

The Holy Land Today

Palestine in the Life of Jesus

Paul's Journeys 1 and 2

Paul's Journeys 3 and 4

God's World

THE OLD TESTAMENT

CONTENTS

THE OLD TESTAMENT

Genesis	1	Ecclesiastes	748
Exodus	62	Song of Songs	760
Leviticus	112	Isaiah	767
Numbers	151	Jeremiah	854
Deuteronomy	196	Lamentations	940
Joshua	237	Ezekiel	949
Judges	266	Daniel	1010
Ruth	297	Hosea	1030
1 Samuel	302	Joel	1044
2 Samuel	339	Amos	1050
1 Kings	372	Obadiah	1061
2 Kings	410	Jonah	1063
1 Chronicles	447	Micah	1066
2 Chronicles	485	Nahum	1075
Ezra	527	Habakkuk	1079
Nehemiah	539	Zephaniah	1084
Esther	557	Haggai	1089
Job	567	Zechariah	1092
Psalms	610	Malachi	1103
Proverbs	709		

GENESIS

The Beginning of All Things

The Beginning of the World

1 In the beginning God created the sky and the earth. ²The earth was empty and had no form. Darkness covered the ocean, and God's Spirit*d* was moving over the water.

³Then God said, "Let there be light!" And there was light. ⁴God saw that the light was good. So he divided the light from the darkness. ⁵God named the light "day" and the darkness "night". Evening passed, and morning came. This was the first day.

⁶Then God said, "Let there be something to divide the water in two!" ⁷So God made the air to divide the water in two. Some of the water was above the air, and some of the water was below it. ⁸God named the air "sky". Evening passed, and morning came. This was the second day.

⁹Then God said, "Let the water under the sky be gathered together so the dry land will appear." And it happened. ¹⁰God named the dry land "earth". He named the water that was gathered together "seas". God saw that this was good.

¹¹Then God said, "Let the earth produce plants. Some plants will make grain for seeds. Others will make fruit with seeds in it. Every seed will produce more of its own kind of plant." And it happened. ¹²The earth produced plants. Some plants had grain for seeds. The trees made fruit with seeds in it. Each seed grew its own kind of plant. God saw that all this was good. ¹³Evening passed, and morning came. This was the third day.

¹⁴Then God said, "Let there be lights in the sky to separate day from night. These lights will be used for signs, seasons, days and years. ¹⁵They will be in the sky to give light to the earth." And it happened.

¹⁶So God made the two large lights. He made the brighter light to rule the day. He made the smaller light to rule the night. He also made the stars. ¹⁷God put all these in the sky to shine on the earth. ¹⁸They are to rule over the day and over the night. He put them there to separate the light from the darkness. God saw that all these things were good. ¹⁹Evening passed, and morning came. This was the fourth day.

²⁰Then God said, "Let the water be filled with living things. And let birds fly in the air above the earth."

²¹So God created the large sea animals. He created every living thing that moves in the sea. The sea is filled with these living things. Each one produces more of its own kind. God also made every bird that flies. And each bird produces more of its own kind. God saw that this was good. ²²God blessed them and said, "Have many young ones and grow in number. Fill the water of the seas, and let the birds grow in number on the earth." ²³Evening passed, and morning came. This was the fifth day.

²⁴Then God said, "Let the earth be filled with animals. And let each produce more of its own kind. Let there be tame animals, small crawling animals and wild animals. And let each produce more of its kind." And it happened.

²⁵So God made the wild animals, the tame animals and all the small crawling animals to produce more of their own kind. God saw that this was good.

²⁶Then God said, "Let us make hu-

man beings in our image and likeness. And let them rule over the fish in the sea and the birds in the sky. Let them rule over the tame animals, over all the earth and over all the small crawling animals on the earth."

27So God created human beings in his image. In the image of God he created them. He created them male and female. 28God blessed them and said, "Have many children and grow in number. Fill the earth and be its master. Rule over the fish in the sea and over the birds in the sky. Rule over every living thing that moves on the earth."

29God said, "Look, I have given you all the plants that have grain for seeds. And I have given you all the trees whose fruits have seeds in them. They will be food for you. 30I have given all the green plants to all the animals to eat. They will be food for every wild animal, every bird of the air and every small crawling animal." And it happened. 31God looked at everything he had made, and it was very good. Evening passed, and morning came. This was the sixth day.

The Seventh Day — Rest

2 So the sky, the earth and all that filled them were finished. 2By the seventh day God finished the work he had been doing. So on the seventh day he rested from all his work. 3God blessed the seventh day and made it a holy day. He made it holy because on that day he rested. He rested from all the work he had done in creating the world.

The First People

4This is the story of the creation of the sky and the earth. When the Lord God made the earth and the sky, 5there were no plants on the earth. Nothing was growing in the fields.

The Lord God had not yet made it rain on the land. And there was no man to care for the ground. 6But a mist often rose from the earth and watered all the ground.

7Then the Lord God took dust from the ground and formed man from it. The Lord breathed the breath of life into the man's nose. And the man became a living person. 8Then the Lord God planted a garden in the East, in a place called Eden. He put the man he had formed in that garden. 9The Lord God caused every beautiful tree and every tree that was good for food to grow out of the ground. In the middle of the garden, God put the tree that gives life. And he put there the tree that gives the knowledge of good and evil.

10A river flowed through Eden and watered the garden. From that point the river was divided. It had four streams flowing into it. 11The name of the first stream is Pishon. It flows around the whole land of Havilah, where there is gold. 12That gold is good. Bdellium and onyx*n* are also there. 13The name of the second river is Gihon. It flows around the whole land of Cush. 14The name of the third river is Tigris. It flows out of Assyria toward the east. The fourth river is the Euphrates.

15The Lord God put the man in the garden of Eden to care for it and work it. 16The Lord God commanded him, "You may eat the fruit from any tree in the garden. 17But you must not eat the fruit from the tree which gives the knowledge of good and evil. If you ever eat fruit from that tree, you will die!"

The First Woman

18Then the Lord God said, "It is not good for the man to be alone. I will make a helper who is right for him."

bdellium and onyx Bdellium is an expensive, sweet-smelling resin like myrrh. Onyx is a gem.

¹⁹From the ground God formed every wild animal and every bird in the sky. He brought them to the man so the man could name them. Whatever the man called each living thing, that became its name. ²⁰The man gave names to all the tame animals, to the birds in the sky and to all the wild animals. But Adam*ⁿ* did not find a helper that was right for him. ²¹So the Lord God caused the man to sleep very deeply. While the man was asleep, God took one of the ribs from the man's body. Then God closed the man's skin at the place where he took the rib. ²²The Lord God used the rib from the man to make a woman. Then the Lord brought the woman to the man.

²³And the man said,

"Now, this is someone whose
   bones came from my bones.
Her body came from my body.
I will call her 'woman',
   because she was taken out of
      man."

²⁴So a man will leave his father and mother and be united with his wife. And the two people will become one body. ²⁵The man and his wife were naked, but they were not ashamed.

The Beginning of Sin

3 Now the snake was the most clever of all the wild animals the Lord God had made. One day the snake spoke to the woman. He said, "Did God really say that you must not eat fruit from any tree in the garden?"

²The woman answered the snake, "We may eat fruit from the trees in the garden. ³But God told us, 'You must not eat fruit from the tree that is in the middle of the garden. You must not even touch it, or you will die'."

⁴But the snake said to the woman, "You will not die. ⁵God knows that if you eat the fruit from that tree, you will learn about good and evil. Then you will be like God!"

⁶The woman saw that the tree was beautiful. She saw that its fruit was good to eat and that it would make her wise. So she took some of its fruit and ate it. She also gave some of the fruit to her husband, and he ate it.

⁷Then, it was as if the man's and the woman's eyes were opened. They realised they were naked. So they sewed fig leaves together and made something to cover themselves.

⁸Then they heard the Lord God walking in the garden. This was during the cool part of the day. And the man and his wife hid from the Lord God among the trees in the garden. ⁹But the Lord God called to the man. The Lord said, "Where are you?"

¹⁰The man answered, "I heard you walking in the garden. I was afraid because I was naked. So I hid."

¹¹God said to the man, "Who told you that you were naked? Did you eat fruit from that tree? I commanded you not to eat from that tree."

¹²The man said, "You gave this woman to me. She gave me fruit from the tree. So I ate it."

¹³Then the Lord God said to the woman, "What have you done?"

She answered, "The snake tricked me. So I ate the fruit."

¹⁴The Lord God said to the snake,
"Because you did this,
   a curse will be put on you.
You will be cursed more than
   any tame animal or wild
      animal.
You will crawl on your stomach,
   and you will eat dust all the days
      of your life.
¹⁵I will make you and the woman
   enemies to each other.
Your descendants*ᵈ* and her
   descendants
   will be enemies.
Her child will crush your head.

Adam This is the name of the first man. It also means "humans", including men and women.

And you will bite his heel."

16Then God said to the woman,
"I will cause you to have much
    trouble
when you are pregnant.
And when you give birth to
    children,
    you will have great pain.
You will greatly desire your
    husband,
    but he will rule over you."

17Then God said to the man, "You
listened to what your wife said. And
you ate fruit from the tree that I com-
manded you not to eat from.
"So I will put a curse on the
    ground.
    You will have to work very hard
        for food.
In pain you will eat its food
    all the days of your life.
18The ground will produce thorns
    and weeds for you.
And you will eat the plants of
    the field.
19You will sweat and work hard
    for your food.
Later you will return to the
    ground.
This is because you were taken
    from the ground.
You are dust.
    And when you die, you will
        return to the dust."
20The man named his wife Eve.*
This is because she is the mother of
everyone who ever lived.

21The Lord God made clothes from
animal skins for the man and his wife.
And so the Lord dressed them.
22Then the Lord God said, "Look, the
man has become like one of us. He
knows good and evil. And now we
must keep him from eating some of
the fruit from the tree of life. If he
does, he will live for ever." 23So the
Lord God forced the man out of the

garden of Eden. He had to work the
ground he was taken from. 24God
forced the man out of the garden.
Then God put angels on the east side
of the garden. He also put a sword of
fire there. It flashed around in every
direction. This kept people from getting to the tree of life.

The First Family

4 Adam had sexual relations with his
   wife Eve. She became pregnant
and gave birth to Cain.* Eve said,
"With the Lord's help, I have given
birth to a man." 2After that, Eve gave
birth to Cain's brother Abel. Abel took
care of sheep. Cain became a farmer.
3Later, Cain brought a gift to God.
He brought some food from the
ground. 4Abel brought the best parts
of his best sheep. The Lord accepted
Abel and his gift. 5But God did not accept Cain and his gift. Cain became
very angry and looked unhappy.
6The Lord asked Cain, "Why are
you angry? Why do you look so unhappy? 7If you do good, I will accept you.
But if you do not do good, sin is ready
to attack you. Sin wants you. But you
must rule over it."
8Cain said to his brother Abel,
"Let's go out into the field." So Cain
and Abel went into the field. Then
Cain attacked his brother Abel and
killed him.
9Later, the Lord said to Cain,
"Where is your brother Abel?"
Cain answered, "I don't know. Is it
my job to take care of my brother?"
10Then the Lord said, "What have
you done? Your brother's blood is on
the ground. That blood is like a voice
that tells me what happened. 11And
now you will be cursed in your work
with the ground. It is the same ground
where your brother's blood fell. Your
hands killed him. 12You will work the
ground. But it will not grow good

Eve This name sounds like the Hebrew word meaning "alive".
Cain This name sounds like the Hebrew word for "I have given birth".

crops for you any more. You will wander around on the earth."

¹³Then Cain said to the Lord, "This punishment is more than I can stand! ¹⁴Look! You have forced me to stop working the ground. And now I must hide from you. I will wander around on the earth. And anyone who meets me can kill me."

¹⁵Then the Lord said to Cain, "No! If anyone kills you, I will punish that person seven times more." Then the Lord put a mark on Cain. It was a warning to anyone who met him not to kill him.

Cain's Family

¹⁶Then Cain went away from the Lord. Cain lived in the land of Nod," east of Eden. ¹⁷Cain had sexual relations with his wife. She became pregnant and gave birth to Enoch. At that time Cain was building a city. He named it after his son Enoch. ¹⁸Enoch had a son named Irad. Irad had a son named Mehujael. Mehujael had a son named Methushael. And Methushael had a son named Lamech.

¹⁹Lamech married two women. One wife was named Adah, and the other was Zillah. ²⁰Adah gave birth to Jabal. He was the first person to live in tents and raise cattle. ²¹Jabal's brother was Jubal. Jubal was the first person to play the harp and flute. ²²Zillah gave birth to Tubal-Cain. He made tools out of bronze and iron. The sister of Tubal-Cain was Naamah.

²³Lamech said to his wives:
"Adah and Zillah, hear my voice!
You wives of Lamech, listen to what I say.
I killed a man for wounding me.
I killed a young man for hitting me.
²⁴Cain's killer may be punished seven times.

Then Lamech's killer will be punished 77 times."

Adam and Eve Have a New Son

²⁵Adam had sexual relations with his wife Eve again. And she gave birth to a son. She named him Seth." Eve said, "God has given me another child. He will take the place of Abel, who was killed by Cain." ²⁶Seth also had a son. They named him Enosh. At that time people began to pray to the Lord.

Adam's Family History

5 This is the family history of Adam. When God created human beings, he made them in God's likeness. ²He created them male and female. And on that day he blessed them and named them human beings.

³When Adam was 130 years old, he became the father of another son. He was in the likeness and image of Adam. Adam named him Seth. ⁴After Seth was born, Adam lived 800 years. During that time he had other sons and daughters. ⁵So Adam lived a total of 930 years. Then he died.

⁶When Seth was 105 years old, he had a son named Enosh. ⁷After Enosh was born, Seth lived 807 years. During that time he had other sons and daughters. ⁸So Seth lived a total of 912 years. Then he died.

⁹When Enosh was 90 years old, he had a son named Kenan. ¹⁰After Kenan was born, Enosh lived 815 years. During that time he had other sons and daughters. ¹¹So Enosh lived a total of 905 years. Then he died.

¹²When Kenan was 70 years old, he had a son named Mahalalel. ¹³After Mahalalel was born, Kenan lived 840 years. During that time he had other sons and daughters. ¹⁴So Kenan lived a total of 910 years. Then he died.

¹⁵When Mahalalel was 65 years old,

he had a son named Jared. [16]After Jared was born, Mahalalel lived 830 years. During that time he had other sons and daughters. [17]So Mahalalel lived a total of 895 years. Then he died.

[18]When Jared was 162 years old, he had a son named Enoch. [19]After Enoch was born, Jared lived 800 years. During that time he had other sons and daughters. [20]So Jared lived a total of 962 years. Then he died.

[21]When Enoch was 65 years old, he had a son named Methuselah. [22]After Methuselah was born, Enoch walked with God 300 years more. During that time he had other sons and daughters. [23]So Enoch lived a total of 365 years. [24]Enoch walked with God. One day Enoch could not be found, because God took him.

[25]When Methuselah was 187 years old, he had a son named Lamech. [26]After Lamech was born, Methuselah lived 782 years. During that time he had other sons and daughters. [27]So Methuselah lived a total of 969 years. Then he died.

[28]When Lamech was 182, he had a son. [29]Lamech named his son Noah.[n] Lamech said, "Noah will comfort us from the pain of our work. The pain is because God has cursed the ground." [30]After Noah was born, Lamech lived 595 years. During that time he had other sons and daughters. [31]So Lamech lived a total of 777 years. Then he died.

[32]After Noah was 500 years old, he became the father of Shem, Ham and Japheth.

The Human Race Becomes Evil

6 The number of people on earth began to grow. Daughters were born to these people. [2]The sons of God saw that these girls were beautiful. And they married any of them they chose. [3]The Lord said, "My Spirit[d] will not remain in human beings for ever. This is because they are flesh. They will live only 120 years."

[4]The Nephilim[d] were on the earth in those days and also later. That was when the sons of God had sexual relations with the daughters of men. These women gave birth to children, who became famous. They were the mighty warriors of long ago.

[5]The Lord saw that the human beings on the earth were very wicked. He also saw that their thoughts were only about evil all the time. [6]The Lord was sorry he had made human beings on the earth. His heart was filled with pain. [7]So the Lord said, "I will destroy all human beings that I made on the earth. And I will destroy every animal and everything that crawls on the earth. I will also destroy the birds of the air. This is because I am sorry that I have made them." [8]But Noah pleased the Lord.

Noah and the Great Flood

[9]This is the family history of Noah. Noah was a good man. He was the most innocent man of his time. He walked with God. [10]Noah had three sons: Shem, Ham and Japheth.

[11]People on earth did what God said was evil. Violence was everywhere. [12]And God saw this evil. All people on the earth did only evil. [13]So God said to Noah, "People have made the earth full of violence. So I will destroy all people from the earth. [14]Build a boat of cypress wood for yourself. Make rooms in it and cover it inside and outside with tar. [15]This is how big I want you to build the boat: 140 metres long, 23 metres wide and 13.5 metres high. [16]Make an opening around the top of the boat. Make it 0.5 metres high from the edge of the roof down. Put a door in the side of the boat. Make an upper, middle and lower deck in it. [17]I will bring a flood of water

---

Noah This name sounds like the Hebrew word for "rest".

on the earth. I will destroy all living things that live under the sky. This includes everything that has the breath of life. Everything on the earth will die. [18]But I will make an agreement with you. You, your sons, your wife and your sons' wives will all go into the boat. [19]Also, you must bring into the boat two of every living thing, male and female. Keep them alive with you. [20]There will be two of every kind of bird, animal and crawling thing. They will come to you to be kept alive. [21]Also gather some of every kind of food. Store it on the boat as food for you and the animals."

[22]Noah did everything that God commanded him.

The Flood Begins

7 Then the Lord said to Noah, "I have seen that you are the best man among the people of this time. So you and your family go into the boat. [2]Take with you seven pairs, each male with its female, of every kind of clean[d] animal. And take one pair, each male with its female, of every kind of unclean animal. [3]Take seven pairs of all the birds of the sky, each male with its female. This will allow all these animals to continue living on the earth after the flood. [4]Seven days from now I will send rain on the earth. It will rain 40 days and 40 nights. I will destroy from the earth every living thing that I made."

[5]Noah did everything that the Lord commanded him.

[6]Noah was 600 years old when the flood came. [7]He and his wife and his sons and their wives went into the boat. They went in to escape the waters of the flood. [8]The clean animals, the unclean animals, the birds and everything that crawls on the ground [9]came to Noah. They went into the boat in groups of two, male and female. This was just as God had commanded Noah. [10]Seven days later the flood started.

[11]Noah was now 600 years old. The flood started on the seventeenth day of the second month of that year. That day the underground springs split open. And the clouds in the sky poured out rain. [12]The rain fell on the earth for 40 days and 40 nights.

[13]On that same day Noah and his wife, his sons Shem, Ham and Japheth and their wives went into the boat. [14]They had every kind of wild animal and tame animal. There was every kind of animal that crawls on the earth. Every kind of bird was there. [15]They all came to Noah in the boat in groups of two. There was every creature that had the breath of life. [16]One male and one female of every living thing came. It was just as God had commanded Noah. Then the Lord closed the door behind them.

[17]Water flooded the earth for 40 days. As the water rose, it lifted the boat off the ground. [18]The water continued to rise, and the boat floated on the water above the earth. [19]The water rose so much that even the highest mountains under the sky were covered by it. [20]The water continued to rise until it was more than 6.9 metres above the mountains.

[21]All living things that moved on the earth died. This included all the birds, tame animals, wild animals and creatures that swarm on the earth. And all human beings died. [22]So everything on dry land died. This means everything that had the breath of life in its nose. [23]So God destroyed from the earth every living thing that was on the land. This was every man, animal, crawling thing and bird of the sky. All that was left was Noah and what was with him in the boat. [24]And the waters continued to cover the earth for 150 days.

The Flood Ends

8 But God remembered Noah and all the wild animals and tame animals with him in the boat. God made

a wind blow over the earth. And the water went down. [2]The underground springs stopped flowing. And the clouds in the sky stopped pouring down rain. [3-4]The water that covered the earth began to go down. After 150 days the water had gone down so much that the boat touched land again. It came to rest on one of the mountains of Ararat. [n] This was on the seventeenth day of the seventh month. [5]The water continued to go down. By the first day of the tenth month the tops of the mountains could be seen.

[6]Forty days later Noah opened the window he had made in the boat. [7]He sent out a raven. It flew here and there until the water had dried up from the earth. [8]Then Noah sent out a dove. This was to find out if the water had dried up from the ground. [9]The dove could not find a place to land because water still covered the earth. So it came back to the boat. Noah reached out his hand and took the bird. And he brought it back into the boat.

[10]After seven days Noah again sent out the dove from the boat. [11]And that evening it came back to him with a fresh olive leaf in its mouth. Then Noah knew that the ground was almost dry. [12]Seven days later he sent the dove out again. But this time it did not come back.

[13]Noah was now 601 years old. It was the first day of the first month of that year. The water was dried up from the land. Noah removed the covering of the boat and saw that the land was dry. [14]By the twenty-seventh day of the second month the land was completely dry. [15]Then God said to Noah, [16]"You and your wife, your sons and their wives should go out of the boat. [17]Bring every animal out of the boat with you—the birds, animals and everything that crawls on the earth. Let them have many young ones and let them grow in number."

[18]So Noah went out with his sons, his wife and his sons' wives. [19]Every animal, everything that crawls on the earth and every bird went out of the boat. They left by families.

[20]Then Noah built an altar to the Lord. Noah took some of all the clean[d] birds and animals. And he burned them on the altar as offerings to God. [21]The Lord was pleased with these sacrifices. He said to himself, "I will never again curse the ground because of human beings. Their thoughts are evil even when they are young. But I will never again destroy every living thing on the earth as I did this time. [22]"As long as the earth continues,
there will be planting and harvest.
Cold and hot,
summer and winter,
day and night
will not stop."

The New Beginning

9 Then God blessed Noah and his sons. He said to them, "Have many children. Grow in number and fill the earth. [2]Every animal on earth and every bird in the sky will respect and fear you. So will every animal that crawls on the ground and every fish in the sea respect and fear you. I have given them to you.

[3]"Everything that moves, everything that is alive, is yours for food. Earlier I gave you the green plants. And now I give you everything for food. [4]But you must not eat meat that still has blood in it, because blood gives life. [5]I will demand your blood for your lives. That is, I will demand the life of any animal that kills a person. And I will demand the life of anyone who takes another person's life.

[6]"Whoever kills a human being
will be killed by a human being.

Ararat The ancient land of Urartu, an area in eastern Turkey.

This is because God made humans in his own image.

7"Noah, I want you and your family to have many children. Grow in number on the earth and become many."

8Then God said to Noah and his sons, 9"Now I am making my agreement with you and your people who will live after you. 10And I also make it with every living thing that is with you. It is with the birds, the tame animals and the wild animals. It is with all that came out of the boat with you. I make my agreement with every living thing on earth. 11I make this agreement with you: I will never again destroy all living things by flood waters. A flood will never again destroy the earth."

12And God said, "I am making an agreement between me and you and every living creature that is with you. It will continue from now on. This is the sign: 13I am putting my rainbow in the clouds. It is the sign of the agreement between me and the earth. 14When I bring clouds over the earth, a rainbow appears in the clouds. 15Then I will remember my agreement. It is between me and you and every living thing. Flood waters will never again destroy all life on the earth. 16When the rainbow appears in the clouds, I will see it. Then I will remember the agreement that continues for ever. It is between me and every living thing on the earth."

17So God said to Noah, "That rainbow is a sign. It is the sign of the agreement that I made with all living things on earth."

Noah and His Sons

18The sons of Noah came out of the boat with him. They were Shem, Ham and Japheth. (Ham was the father of Canaan.) 19These three men were Noah's sons. And all the people on earth came from these three sons.

20Noah became a farmer and planted a vineyard. 21He drank wine made from his grapes. Then he became drunk and lay naked in his tent. 22Ham, the father of Canaan, looked at his naked father. Ham told his brothers outside. 23Then Shem and Japheth got a coat and carried it on both their shoulders. They walked backwards into the tent and covered their father. They turned their faces away. In this way they did not see their father without clothes.

24Noah was sleeping because of the wine. Later he woke up. Then he learned what his youngest son, Ham, had done to him. 25So Noah said,
"May there be a curse on Canaan!
  May he be the lowest slave to
    his brothers."
26Noah also said,
"May the Lord, the God of Shem,
    be praised!
  May Canaan be Shem's slave.
27May God give more land to
    Japheth.
  May Japheth live in Shem's
    tents,
  and may Canaan be their slave."
28After the flood Noah lived 350 years. 29He lived a total of 950 years. Then he died.

Nations Grow and Spread

10 This is the family history of the sons of Noah: Shem, Ham and Japheth. After the flood these three men had sons.

Japheth's Sons

2The sons of Japheth were Gomer, Magog, Madai, Javan, Tubal, Meshech and Tiras.

3The sons of Gomer were Ashkenaz, Riphath and Togarmah.

4The sons of Javan were Elishah, Tarshish, Kittim*n* and Rodanim.

Kittim His descendants were the people of Cyprus.

[5]Those who lived in the lands around the Mediterranean Sea came from these sons of Japheth. All the families grew and became different nations. Each nation had its own land and its own language.

Ham's Sons

[6]The sons of Ham were Cush, Mizraim,[n] Put and Canaan.

[7]The sons of Cush were Seba, Havilah, Sabtah, Raamah and Sabteca.

The sons of Raamah were Sheba and Dedan.

[8]Cush also had a descendant[d] named Nimrod. Nimrod became a very powerful man on earth. [9]He was a great hunter before the Lord. That is why people say someone is "like Nimrod, a great hunter before the Lord." [10]At first Nimrod's kingdom covered Babylon, Erech, Akkad and Calneh in the land of Babylonia. [11]From there he went to Assyria. There he built the cities of Nineveh, Rehoboth Ir and Calah. [12]He also built Resen, the great city between Nineveh and Calah.

[13]Mizraim was the father of the Ludites, Anamites, Lehabites, Naphtuhites, [14]Pathrusites, Casluhites and the people of Crete. (The Philistines came from the Casluhites.)

[15]Canaan was the father of Sidon his first son and of Heth. [16]Canaan was also the father of the Jebusites, Amorites, Girgashites, [17]Hivites, Arkites, Sinites, [18]Arvadites, Zemarites and Hamathites. The families of the Canaanites scattered. [19]The land of the Canaanites reached from Sidon to Gerar as far as Gaza. And it reached to Sodom, Gomorrah, Admah and Zeboiim, as far as Lasha.

[20]All these people were the sons of Ham. All these families had their own languages, their own lands and their own nations.

Shem's Sons

[21]Shem, Japheth's older brother, also had sons. One of his descendants[d] was the father of all the sons of Eber.

[22]The sons of Shem were Elam, Asshur, Arphaxad, Lud and Aram.

[23]The sons of Aram were Uz, Hul, Gether and Meshech.

[24]Arphaxad was the father of Shelah. Shelah was the father of Eber. [25]Eber was the father of two sons. One son was named Peleg[n] because the earth was divided during his life. Eber's other son was named Joktan.

[26]Joktan was the father of Almodad, Sheleph, Hazarmaveth, Jerah, [27]Hadoram, Uzal, Diklah, [28]Obal, Abimael, Sheba, [29]Ophir, Havilah and Jobab. All these people were the sons of Joktan. [30]These people lived in the area between Mesha and Sephar in the hill country in the East.

[31]These are the people from the family of Shem. They are arranged by families, languages, countries and nations.

[32]This is the list of the families from the sons of Noah. They are arranged according to their nations. From these families came all the nations who spread across the earth after the flood.

The Languages Confused

11 At this time the whole world spoke one language. Everyone used the same words. [2]As people moved from the East, they found a plain in the land of Babylonia. They settled there to live.

[3]They said to each other, "Let's make bricks and bake them to make them hard." So they used bricks instead of stones, and tar instead of mortar. [4]Then they said to each other, "Let's build for ourselves a city and a tower. And let's make the top of

---

Mizraim This is another name for Egypt.
Peleg This name sounds like the Hebrew word for "divided".

the tower reach high into the sky. We will become famous. If we do this, we will not be scattered over all the earth."

⁵The Lord came down to see the city and the tower that the people had built. ⁶The Lord said, "Now, these people are united. They all speak the same language. This is only the beginning of what they will do. They will be able to do anything they want. ⁷Come, let us go down and confuse their language. Then they will not be able to understand each other."

⁸So the Lord scattered them from there over all the earth. And they stopped building the city. ⁹That is where the Lord confused the language of the whole world. So the place is called Babel.ⁿ So the Lord caused them to spread out from there over all the whole world.

The Story of Shem's Family

¹⁰This is the family history of Shem. Two years after the flood, when Shem was 100 years old, his son Arphaxad was born. ¹¹After that, Shem lived 500 years and had other sons and daughters.

¹²When Arphaxad was 35 years old, his son Shelah was born. ¹³After that, Arphaxad lived 403 years and had other sons and daughters.

¹⁴When Shelah was 30 years old, his son Eber was born. ¹⁵After that, Shelah lived 403 years and had other sons and daughters.

¹⁶When Eber was 34 years old, his son Peleg was born. ¹⁷After that, Eber lived 430 years and had other sons and daughters.

¹⁸When Peleg was 30 years old, his son Reu was born. ¹⁹After that, Peleg lived 209 years and had other sons and daughters.

²⁰When Reu was 32 years old, his son Serug was born. ²¹After that, Reu

lived 207 years and had other sons and daughters.

²²When Serug was 30 years old, his son Nahor was born. ²³After that, Serug lived 200 years and had other sons and daughters.

²⁴When Nahor was 29 years old, his son Terah was born. ²⁵After that, Nahor lived 119 years and had other sons and daughters.

²⁶After Terah was 70 years old, his sons Abram, Nahor and Haran were born.

The Story of Terah's Family

²⁷This is the family history of Terah. Terah was the father of Abram, Nahor and Haran. Haran was the father of Lot. ²⁸Haran died while his father, Terah, was still alive. This happened in Ur in Babylonia, where he was born. ²⁹Abram and Nahor both married. Abram's wife was named Sarai. Nahor's wife was named Milcah. She was the daughter of Haran. Haran was the father of Milcah and Iscah. ³⁰Sarai was not able to have children.

³¹Terah took his son Abram, his grandson Lot (Haran's son) and his daughter-in-law Sarai (Abram's wife). They moved out of Ur of Babylonia. They had planned to go to the land of Canaan. But when they reached the city of Haran, they settled there.

³²Terah lived to be 205 years old. Then he died in Haran.

God Calls Abram

12 Then the Lord said to Abram, "Leave your country, your relatives and your father's family. Go to the land I will show you.
²I will make you a great nation,
and I will bless you.
I will make you famous.
And you will be a blessing to
others.
³I will bless those who bless you.

Babel This name sounds like the Hebrew word for "confused".

I will place a curse on those
who harm you.
And all the people on earth
will be blessed through you."
[4]So Abram left Haran as the Lord
had told him. And Lot went with him.
At this time Abram was 75 years old.
[5]Abram took his wife Sarai, his nephew Lot and everything they owned.
They took all the servants they had
gained in Haran. They set out from
Haran, planning to go to the land of
Canaan. In time, they arrived there.
[6]Abram travelled through that land.
He went as far as the great tree of
Moreh at Shechem. The Canaanites
were living in the land at that time.
[7]The Lord appeared to Abram. The
Lord said, "I will give this land to your
descendants."[d] So Abram built an altar there to the Lord, who had appeared to him. [8]Then Abram travelled
from Shechem to the mountain east of
Bethel. And he set up his tent there.
Bethel was to the west, and Ai was to
the east. There Abram built another
altar to the Lord and worshipped him.
[9]After this, he travelled on toward
southern Canaan.

Abram Goes to Egypt

[10]At this time there was not much
food in the land. So Abram went down
to Egypt to live because there was so
little food. [11]Just before they arrived
in Egypt, Abram said to his wife Sarai,
"I know you are a very beautiful woman. [12]When the Egyptians see you,
they will say, 'This woman is his wife'.
Then they will kill me but let you live.
[13]Tell them you are my sister. Then
things will go well with me. And I may
be allowed to live because of you."

[14]So Abram went into Egypt. The
people of Egypt saw that Sarai was
very beautiful. [15]Some of the Egyptian
officers saw her also. They told the
king of Egypt how beautiful she was.
They took her to the king's palace.
[16]The king was kind to Abram because
he thought Abram was Sarai's broth-

er. He gave Abram sheep, cattle and
male and female donkeys. Abram also
was given male and female servants
and camels.

[17]But the Lord sent terrible diseases on the king and all the people in
his house. This was because of
Abram's wife Sarai. [18]So the king sent
for Abram. The king said, "What have
you done to me? Why didn't you tell
me Sarai was your wife? [19]Why did
you say, 'She is my sister'? I made her
my wife. But now here is your wife.
Take her and leave!" [20]Then the king
commanded his men to make Abram
leave Egypt. So Abram and his wife
left with everything they owned.

Abram and Lot Separate

13 So Abram, his wife and Lot left
Egypt. They took everything
they owned and travelled to southern
Canaan. [2]Abram was very rich in cattle, silver and gold.

[3]He left southern Canaan and went
back to Bethel. He went where he had
camped before, between Bethel and
Ai. [4]It was the place where Abram had
built an altar before. So he worshipped the Lord there.

[5]During this time Lot was travelling
with Abram. Lot also had many
sheep, cattle and tents. [6]Abram and
Lot had so many animals that the land
could not support both of them together. [7]Abram's herders and Lot's
herders began to argue. The Canaanites and the Perizzites were living in
the land at this time.

[8]So Abram said to Lot, "There
should be no arguing between you and
me. Your herders and mine should not
argue either. We are brothers. [9]We
should separate. The whole land is
there in front of you. If you go to the
left, I will go to the right. If you go to
the right, I will go to the left."

[10]Lot looked all around and saw the
whole Jordan Valley. He saw that
there was much water there. It was
like the Lord's garden, like the land of

Egypt in the direction of Zoar. (This was before the Lord destroyed Sodom and Gomorrah.) ¹¹So Lot chose to move east and live in the Jordan Valley. In this way Abram and Lot separated. ¹²Abram lived in the land of Canaan. But Lot lived among the cities in the Jordan Valley. He moved very near to Sodom. ¹³Now the people of Sodom were very evil. They were always sinning against the Lord.

¹⁴After Lot left, the Lord said to Abram, "Look all around you. Look north and south and east and west. ¹⁵All this land that you see I will give to you and your descendants^d for ever. ¹⁶I will make your descendants as many as the dust of the earth. If anyone could count the dust on the earth, he could count your people. ¹⁷Get up! Walk through all this land. I am now giving it to you."

¹⁸So Abram moved his tents. He went to live near the great trees of Mamre. This was at the city of Hebron. There he built an altar to the Lord.

Lot Is Captured

14 Now Amraphel was king of Babylonia. Arioch was king of Ellasar. Kedorlaomer was king of Elam. And Tidal was king of Goiim. ²All these kings went to war against several other kings: Bera king of Sodom, Birsha king of Gomorrah, Shinab king of Admah, Shemeber king of Zeboiim and the king of Bela. (Bela is also called Zoar.)

³These kings who were attacked united their armies in the Valley of Siddim. (The Valley of Siddim is now the Dead Sea.^d) ⁴These kings had served Kedorlaomer for 12 years. But in the thirteenth year, they all turned against him. ⁵Then in the fourteenth year, Kedorlaomer and the kings with him came and defeated the Rephaites^d in Ashteroth Karnaim. They also defeated the Zuzites in Ham and the Emites in Shaveh Kiriathaim. ⁶And

they defeated the Horites in the mountains of Edom to El Paran. (El Paran is near the desert.) ⁷Then they turned back and went to En Mishpat (that is, Kadesh). They defeated all the Amalekites. They also defeated the Amorites who lived in Hazazon Tamar.

⁸At that time the kings of Sodom, Gomorrah, Admah, Zeboiim and Bela went out to fight in the Valley of Siddim. (Bela is called Zoar.) ⁹They fought against Kedorlaomer king of Elam, Tidal king of Goiim, Amraphel king of Babylonia, and Arioch king of Ellasar. So there were four kings fighting against five. ¹⁰There were many tar pits in the Valley of Siddim. The kings of Sodom and Gomorrah and their armies ran away. Some of the soldiers fell into the tar pits. But the others ran away to the mountains.

¹¹Now Kedorlaomer and his armies took everything the people of Sodom and Gomorrah owned. They also took all their food. ¹²They took Lot, Abram's nephew who was living in Sodom. The enemy also took everything he owned. Then they left. ¹³One of the men who was not captured went to Abram, the Hebrew. He told Abram what had happened. At that time Abram was camped near the great trees of Mamre the Amorite. Mamre was a brother of Eshcol and a brother of Aner. And they had all made an agreement to help Abram.

Abram Rescues Lot

¹⁴Abram learned that Lot had been captured. So he called out his 318 trained men who had been born in his camp. Abram led the men and chased the enemy all the way to the town of Dan. ¹⁵That night he divided his men into groups. And they made a surprise attack against the enemy. They chased them all the way to Hobah, north of Damascus. ¹⁶Then Abram brought back everything the enemy had stolen. Abram brought back the

women and the other people. And he also brought back Lot and everything Lot owned.

¹⁷After defeating Kedorlaomer and the kings who were with him, Abram went home. As Abram was returning, the king of Sodom came out to meet him in the Valley of Shaveh. (That is now called King's Valley.)

¹⁸Melchizedek king of Salem also went to meet Abram. Melchizedek was a priest for God Most High. He brought bread and wine. ¹⁹Melchizedek blessed Abram and said,

"Abram, may God Most High give
    you blessings.
God made heaven and earth.
²⁰And we praise God Most High.
    He has helped you to defeat
    your enemies."

Then Abram gave Melchizedek a tenth of everything he had brought back from the battle.

²¹Then the king of Sodom said to Abram, "You may keep all these things for yourself. Just give me my people who were captured."

²²But Abram said to the king of Sodom, "I make a promise to the Lord. He is the God Most High, who made heaven and earth. ²³I promise that I will not keep anything that is yours. I will not keep even a thread or a sandal strap. That way you cannot say, 'I made Abram rich'. ²⁴I will keep nothing but the food my young men have eaten. But give Aner, Eshcol and Mamre their share of what we won. They went with me into battle."

God's Agreement with Abram

15 After these things happened, the Lord spoke his word to Abram in a vision. God said, "Abram, don't be afraid. I will defend you. And I will give you a great reward."

²But Abram said, "Lord God, what can you give me? I have no son. So my slave Eliezer from Damascus will get everything I own after I die." ³Abram said, "Look, you have given me no

son. So a slave born in my house will inherit everything I have."

⁴Then the Lord spoke his word to Abram. He said, "That slave will not be the one to inherit what you have. You will have a son of your own. And your son will inherit what you have."

⁵Then God led Abram outside. God said, "Look at the sky. There are so many stars you cannot count them. And your descendants*ᵈ* will be too many to count."

⁶Abram believed the Lord. And the Lord accepted Abram's faith, and that faith made him acceptable to God.

⁷God said to Abram, "I am the Lord who led you out of Ur of Babylonia. I did that so I could give you this land to own."

⁸But Abram said, "Lord God, how can I be sure that I will own this land?"

⁹The Lord said to Abram, "Bring me a three-year-old cow, a three-year-old goat and a three-year-old male sheep. Also bring me a dove and a young pigeon."

¹⁰Abram brought them all to God. Then Abram killed the animals and cut each of them into two pieces. He laid each half opposite the other half. But he did not cut the birds in half. ¹¹Later, large birds flew down to eat the animals. But Abram chased them away.

¹²As the sun was going down, Abram fell into a deep sleep. While he was asleep, a very terrible darkness came. ¹³Then the Lord said to Abram, "You can be sure that your descendants will be strangers and travel in a land they don't own. The people there will make them slaves. And they will do cruel things to them for 400 years. ¹⁴But I will punish the nation where they are slaves. Then your descendants will leave that land, taking great wealth with them. ¹⁵Abram, you will live to be very old. You will die in peace and will be buried. ¹⁶After your great-great-grandchildren are born, your people will come to this land

again. It will take that long, because
the Amorites are not yet evil enough
to punish."

¹⁷The sun went down, and it was
very dark. Suddenly a smoking firepot
and a blazing torch passed between
the halves of the dead animals.ⁿ ¹⁸So
on that day the Lord made an agreement with Abram. The Lord said, "I
will give this land to your descendants. I will give them the land between the river of Egypt and the great
river Euphrates. ¹⁹This is the land of
the Kenites, Kenizzites, Kadmonites,
²⁰Hittites, Perizzites, Rephaites,ᵈ
²¹Amorites, Canaanites, Girgashites
and Jebusites."

Hagar and Ishmael

16 Sarai, Abram's wife, had no
children. She had a slave girl
from Egypt named Hagar. ²Sarai said
to Abram, "Look, the Lord has not allowed me to have children. So have
sexual relations with my slave girl. If
she has a child, maybe I can have my
own family through her."

Abram did what Sarai said. ³This
was after Abram lived ten years in Canaan. And Sarai gave Hagar to her
husband Abram. (Hagar was her slave
girl from Egypt.)

⁴Abram had sexual relations with
Hagar, and she became pregnant.
When Hagar learned she was pregnant, she began to treat her mistress
Sarai badly. ⁵Then Sarai said to
Abram, "This is your fault. I gave my
slave girl to you. And when she became pregnant, she began to treat me
badly. Let the Lord decide who is
right—you or me."

⁶But Abram said to Sarai, "You are
Hagar's mistress. Do anything you
want to her." Then Sarai was hard on
Hagar, and Hagar ran away.

⁷The angel of the Lord found Hagar
beside a spring of water in the desert.
The spring was by the road to Shur.
⁸The angel said, "Hagar, you are Sarai's slave girl. Where have you come
from? Where are you going?"

Hagar answered, "I am running
from my mistress Sarai."

⁹The angel of the Lord said to her,
"Go home to your mistress and obey
her." ¹⁰The angel of the Lord also
said, "I will give you so many descendantsᵈ they cannot be counted."

¹¹The angel also said to her,

"You are now pregnant,
    and you will have a son.
You will name him Ishmael,ⁿ
    because the Lord has heard
        your cries.
¹²Ishmael will be like a wild donkey.
    He will be against everyone.
    And everyone will be against
        him.
He will attack all his brothers."

¹³The slave girl gave a name to the
Lord who spoke to her. She said to
him, "You are 'God who sees me'."
This is because she said to herself,
"Have I really seen God who sees
me?" ¹⁴So the well there was called
Beer Lahai Roi.ⁿ It is between Ka-
desh and Bered.

¹⁵Hagar gave birth to a son for
Abram. And Abram named him Ish-
mael. ¹⁶Abram was 86 years old when
Hagar gave birth to Ishmael.

Proof of the Agreement

17 When Abram was 99 years old,
the Lord appeared to him. The
Lord said, "I am God All-Powerful.
Obey me and do what is right. ²I will
make an agreement between us. I will
make you the ancestor of many people."

³Then Abram bowed face down on

---

passed . . . animals This showed that God sealed the agreement between himself and
    Abram.
Ishmael The Hebrew words for "Ishmael" and "has heard" sound similar.
Beer Lahai Roi This means "the well of the Living One who sees me".

the ground. God said to him, [4]"I am making my agreement with you: I will make you the father of many nations. [5]I am changing your name from Abram[n] to Abraham.[n] This is because I am making you a father of many nations. [6]I will give you many descendants.[d] New nations will be born from you. Kings will come from you. [7]And I will make an agreement between me and you and all your descendants from now on: I will be your God and the God of all your descendants. [8]You live in the land of Canaan now as a stranger. But I will give you and your descendants all this land for ever. And I will be the God of your descendants."

[9]Then God said to Abraham, "You and your descendants must keep this agreement from now on. [10]This is my agreement with you and all your descendants: every male among you must be circumcised.[d] You must obey this agreement. [11]Cut away the foreskin to show that you follow the agreement between me and you. [12]From now on when a baby boy is eight days old, you will circumcise him. This includes any boy born among your people or any who is your slave. (He would not be one of your descendants.) [13]So circumcise every baby boy. Circumcise him whether he is born in your family or bought as a slave. Your bodies will be marked. This will show that you are part of my agreement that lasts for ever. [14]Any male who is not circumcised will be separated from his people. He has broken my agreement."

Isaac — the Promised Son

[15]God said to Abraham, "I will change the name of Sarai,[n] your wife. Her new name will be Sarah.[n] [16]I will bless her. I will give her a son, and you will be the father. She will be the mother of many nations. Kings of nations will come from her."

[17]Abraham bowed face down on the ground and laughed. He said to himself, "Can a man have a child when he is 100 years old? Can Sarah give birth to a child when she is 90?" [18]Then Abraham said to God, "Please let Ishmael be the son you promised."

[19]God said, "No. Sarah your wife will have a son, and you will name him Isaac.[n] I will make my agreement with him. It will be an agreement that continues for ever with all his descendants.[d]

[20]"You asked me about Ishmael, and I heard you. I will bless him. I will give him many descendants. And I will cause their numbers to grow very greatly. He will be the father of 12 great leaders. I will make him into a great nation. [21]But I will make my agreement with Isaac. He is the son whom Sarah will have at this same time next year." [22]After God finished talking with Abraham, God rose and left him.

[23]Then Abraham gathered Ishmael and all the males born in his camp. He also gathered the slaves he had bought. So that day Abraham circumcised every man and boy in his camp. This was what God had told him to do. [24]Abraham was 99 years old when he was circumcised. [25]And Ishmael, his son, was 13 years old when he was circumcised. [26]Abraham and his son were circumcised on that same day. [27]Also on that day all the men in Abraham's camp were circumcised. This

---

Abram This name means "honoured father".
Abraham The end of the Hebrew word for "Abraham" sounds like the beginning of the Hebrew word for "many".
Sarai An Aramaic name meaning "princess".
Sarah A Hebrew name meaning "princess".
Isaac The Hebrew words for "he laughed" (vs. 17) and "Isaac" sound the same.

included all those born in his camp and all the slaves he had bought from other nations.

The Three Visitors

18 Later, the Lord again appeared to Abraham near the great trees of Mamre. At that time Abraham was sitting at the door of his tent. It was during the hottest part of the day. ²He looked up and saw three men standing near him. When Abraham saw them, he ran from his tent to meet them. He bowed face down on the ground before them. ³Abraham said, "Sir, if you think well of me, please stay awhile with me, your servant. ⁴I will bring some water so all of you can wash your feet. You may rest under the tree. ⁵I will get some bread for you, so you can regain your strength. Then you may continue your journey."

The three men said, "That is fine. Do as you said."

⁶Abraham hurried to the tent where Sarah was. He said to her, "Hurry, prepare 22 litres of fine flour. Make it into loaves of bread." ⁷Then Abraham ran to his cattle. He took one of his best calves and gave it to a servant. The servant hurried to kill the calf and to prepare it for food. ⁸Abraham gave the three men the calf that had been cooked. He also gave them milk curds and milk. While the three men ate, he stood under the tree near them.

⁹The men asked Abraham, "Where is your wife Sarah?"

"There, in the tent," said Abraham.

¹⁰Then the Lord said, "I will certainly return to you about this time a year from now. At that time your wife Sarah will have a son."

Sarah was listening at the entrance of the tent which was behind him. ¹¹Abraham and Sarah were very old. Sarah was past the age when women normally have children. ¹²So she laughed to herself, "My husband and I are too old to have a baby."

¹³Then the Lord said to Abraham, "Why did Sarah laugh? Why did she say, 'I am too old to have a baby'? ¹⁴Is anything too hard for the Lord? No! I will return to you at the right time a year from now. And Sarah will have a son."

¹⁵Sarah was afraid. So she lied and said, "I didn't laugh."

But the Lord said, "No. You did laugh."

¹⁶Then the men got up to leave and started out toward Sodom. Abraham walked along with them a short time to send them on their way.

Abraham's Bargain with God

¹⁷The Lord said, "Should I tell Abraham what I am going to do now? ¹⁸Abraham's children will certainly become a great and powerful nation. And all nations on earth will be blessed through him. ¹⁹I have chosen him so he would command his children and his descendants*d* to live the way the Lord wants them to. I did this so they would live right and be fair. Then I, the Lord, will give Abraham what I promised him."

²⁰Then the Lord said, "I have heard many things against the people of Sodom and Gomorrah. They are very evil. ²¹So I will go down and see if they are as bad as I have heard."

²²So the men turned and went toward Sodom. But Abraham stood there before the Lord. ²³Then Abraham approached the Lord. Abraham asked, "Lord, do you plan to destroy the good persons along with the evil persons? ²⁴What if there are 50 good people in that city? Will you still destroy it? Surely you will save the city for the 50 good people living there. ²⁵Surely you will not destroy the good people along with the evil people. Then the good people and the evil people would be treated the same. You are the judge of all the earth. Won't you do what is right?"

²⁶Then the Lord said, "If I find 50

good people in the city of Sodom, I will save the whole city because of them."
²⁷Then Abraham said, "I am only dust and ashes. Yet I have been brave to speak to the Lord. ²⁸What if there are only 45 good people in the city? Will you destroy the whole city for the lack of five good people?"

The Lord said, "If I find 45 good people there, I will not destroy the city."

²⁹Again Abraham said to the Lord, "If you find only 40 good people there, will you destroy the city?"

The Lord said, "If I find 40 good people, I will not destroy the city."

³⁰Then Abraham said, "Lord, please don't be angry with me. Let me ask you this. If you find only 30 good people in the city, will you destroy it?"

The Lord said, "If I find 30 good people there, I will not destroy the city."

³¹Then Abraham said, "I have been brave to speak to the Lord. But what if there are 20 good people in the city?"

The Lord answered, "If I find 20 good people there, I will not destroy the city."

³²Then Abraham said, "Lord, please don't be angry with me. Let me bother you this one last time. What if you find ten good people there?"

The Lord said, "If I find ten good people there, I will not destroy it."

³³When the Lord finished speaking to Abraham, he left. And Abraham returned home.

Lot's Visitors

19 The two angels came to Sodom in the evening. Lot was sitting near the city gate and saw them. He got up and went to them and bowed face down on the ground. ²Lot said, "Sirs, please come to my house and spend the night. There you can wash your feet. Then tomorrow you may continue your journey."

The angels answered, "No, we will spend the night in the city's public square."

³But Lot begged them to come to his house. So they agreed and went to his house. Then Lot prepared a meal for them. He baked bread without yeast, and they ate it.

⁴Before bedtime, all the men of the city surrounded Lot's house. These men were both young and old and came from every part of Sodom. ⁵They called to Lot, "Where are the two men who came to you tonight? Bring them out to us. We want to have sexual relations with them."

⁶Lot went outside to them, closing the door behind him. ⁷He said, "No, my brothers! Do not do this evil thing. ⁸Look! I have two daughters. They have never slept with a man. I will give them to you. You may do anything you want with them. But please don't do anything to these men. They have come to my house, and I must protect them."

⁹The men around the house answered, "Move out of the way!" Then they said to each other, "This man Lot came to our city as a stranger. Now he wants to tell us what to do!" They said to Lot, "We will do worse things to you than to them." So they started pushing Lot back. They were ready to break down the door.

¹⁰But the two men staying with Lot opened the door and pulled him back inside the house. Then they closed the door. ¹¹The two men struck the men outside the door with blindness. So these men, both young and old, could not find the door.

¹²The two men said to Lot, "Do you have any other relatives in this city? Do you have any sons-in-law, sons, daughters or any other relatives? If you do, tell them to leave now. ¹³We are about to destroy this city. The Lord has heard of all the evil that is here. So he has sent us to destroy it."

¹⁴So Lot went out and spoke to his future sons-in-law. They were

pledged to marry his daughters. Lot said, "Hurry and leave this city! The Lord is about to destroy it!" But they thought Lot was joking.

¹⁵At dawn the next morning, the angels begged Lot to hurry. They said, "Go! Take your wife and your two daughters with you. Then you will not be destroyed when the city is punished."

¹⁶But Lot delayed. So the two men took the hands of Lot, his wife and his two daughters. The men led them safely out of the city. So the Lord was merciful to Lot and his family. ¹⁷The two men brought Lot and his family out of the city. Then one of the men said, "Run for your lives! Don't look back or stop anywhere in the valley. Run to the mountains or you will be destroyed."

¹⁸But Lot said to one of them, "Sir, please don't force me to go so far! ¹⁹You have been merciful and kind to me. You have saved my life. But I can't run to the mountains. The disaster will catch me, and I will die. ²⁰Look, that little town over there is not too far away. Let me run there. It's really just a little town. I'll be safe there."

²¹The angel said to Lot, "Very well, I will allow you to do this also. I will not destroy that town. ²²But run there fast. I cannot destroy Sodom until you are safely in that town." (That town is named Zoar,ⁿ because it is little.)

Sodom and Gomorrah Destroyed

²³The sun had already come up when Lot entered Zoar. ²⁴The Lord sent a rain of burning sulphur down from the sky on Sodom and Gomorrah. ²⁵So the Lord destroyed those cities. He also destroyed the whole Jordan Valley, everyone living in the cities and even all the plants.

²⁶At that point Lot's wife looked back. When she did, she became a pillar of salt.

²⁷Early the next morning, Abraham got up and went to the place where he had stood before the Lord. ²⁸Abraham looked down toward Sodom and Gomorrah and all the Jordan Valley. He saw smoke rising from the land. It was like smoke from a furnace.

²⁹God destroyed the cities in the valley. But he remembered what Abraham had asked. So God saved Lot's life. But he destroyed the city where Lot had lived.

Lot and His Daughters

³⁰Lot was afraid to continue living in Zoar. So he and his two daughters went to live in the mountains. They lived in a cave there. ³¹One day the older daughter said to the younger, "Our father is old. Everywhere on the earth women and men marry. But there are no men around here for us to marry. ³²Let's get our father drunk. Then we can have sexual relations with him. We can use our father to have children. That way we can continue our family."

³³That night the two girls got their father drunk. Then the older daughter went and had sexual relations with him. But Lot did not know when she lay down or when she got up.

³⁴The next day the older daughter said to the younger, "Last night I had sexual relations with my father. Let's get him drunk again tonight. Then you can go and have sexual relations with him, too. In this way we can use our father to have children to continue our family." ³⁵So that night they got their father drunk again. Then the younger daughter went and had sexual relations with him. Again, Lot did not know when she lay down or when she got up.

Zoar This name sounds like the Hebrew word for "little".

³⁶So both of Lot's daughters became pregnant by their father. ³⁷The older daughter gave birth to a son. She named him Moab. Moab is the ancestor of all the Moabite people who are still living today. ³⁸The younger daughter also gave birth to a son. She named him Ben-Ammi. He is the father of all the Ammonite people who are still living today.

Abraham and Abimelech

20 Abraham left Hebron and travelled to southern Canaan. He stayed awhile between Kadesh and Shur. Then he moved to Gerar. ²Abraham told people that his wife Sarah was his sister. Abimelech king of Gerar heard this. So he sent some servants to take her. ³But one night God spoke to Abimelech in a dream. God said, "You will die. That woman you took is married."

⁴But Abimelech had not slept with Sarah. So he said, "Lord, would you destroy an innocent nation? ⁵Abraham himself told me, 'This woman is my sister'. And she also said, 'He is my brother'. I am innocent. I did not know I was doing anything wrong."

⁶Then God said to Abimelech in the dream, "Yes, I know that you did not realise what you were doing. So I did not allow you to sin against me. I did not allow you to sleep with her. ⁷Give Abraham his wife back. He is a prophet.ᵈ He will pray for you, and you will not die. But if you do not give Sarah back, you will die. And all your family will surely die."

⁸So early the next morning, Abimelech called all his officers. He told them everything that had happened in the dream. They were very much afraid. ⁹Then Abimelech called Abraham to him. Abimelech said, "What have you done to us? What wrong did I do against you? Why did you bring this trouble to my kingdom? You should not have done these things to me. ¹⁰What were you thinking that caused you to do this?"

¹¹Then Abraham answered, "I thought no one in this place respected God. I thought someone would kill me to get Sarah. ¹²And it is true that she is my sister. She is the daughter of my father. But she is not the daughter of my mother. ¹³God told me to leave my father's house and wander in many different places. When that happened, I told Sarah, 'You must do a special favour for me. Everywhere we go tell people I am your brother'."

¹⁴Then Abimelech gave Abraham some sheep, cattle and male and female slaves. Abimelech also gave Sarah, his wife, back to him. ¹⁵And Abimelech said, "Look around you at my land. You may live anywhere you want."

¹⁶Abimelech said to Sarah, "I gave your brother Abraham 11.5 kilograms of silver. I did this to make up for any wrong that people may think about you. I want everyone to know that you are innocent."

¹⁷Then Abraham prayed to God. And God healed Abimelech, his wife and his servant girls. Now they could have children. ¹⁸The Lord had kept all the women in Abimelech's house from having children. This was God's punishment on Abimelech for taking Abraham's wife Sarah.

A Baby for Sarah

21 The Lord cared for Sarah as he had said. He did for her what he had promised. ²Sarah became pregnant. And she gave birth to a son for Abraham in his old age. Everything happened at the time God had said it would. ³Abraham named his son Isaac. Sarah gave birth to this son of Abraham. ⁴Abraham circumcisedᵈ Isaac when he was eight days old as God had commanded.

⁵Abraham was 100 years old when his son Isaac was born. ⁶And Sarah

said, "God has made me laugh."[n] Everyone who hears about this will laugh with me. [7]No one thought that I would be able to have Abraham's child. But I have given Abraham a son while he is old."

Hagar and Ishmael

[8]Isaac grew and became old enough to eat food. At that time Abraham gave a great feast. [9]But Sarah saw Ishmael making fun of Isaac. (Ishmael was the son of Abraham by Hagar, Sarah's Egyptian slave.) [10]So Sarah said to Abraham, "Throw out this slave woman and her son. When we die, our son Isaac will inherit everything we have. I don't want her son to inherit any of our things."

[11]This troubled Abraham very much because Ishmael was also his son. [12]But God said to Abraham, "Don't be troubled about the boy and the slave woman. Do whatever Sarah tells you. The descendants[d] I promised you will be from Isaac. [13]I will also make the descendants of Ishmael into a great nation. I will do this because he is your son, too."

[14]Early the next morning Abraham took some food and a leather bag full of water. He gave them to Hagar and sent her away. Hagar carried these things and her son. She went and wandered in the desert of Beersheba.

[15]Later, all the water was gone from the bag. So Hagar put her son under a bush. [16]Then she went away a short distance and sat down. Hagar thought, "My son will die. I cannot watch this happen." She sat there and began to cry.

[17]God heard the boy crying. And God's angel called to Hagar from heaven. He said, "What is wrong, Hagar? Don't be afraid! God has heard the boy crying there. [18]Help the boy up. Take him by the hand. I will make his descendants into a great nation."

[19]Then God showed Hagar a well of water. So she went to the well and filled her bag with water. Then she gave the boy a drink.

[20]God was with the boy as he grew up. Ishmael lived in the desert. He learned to shoot with a bow very well. [21]He lived in the Desert of Paran. His mother found a wife for him in Egypt.

Abraham's Bargain with Abimelech

[22]Then Abimelech came with Phicol, the commander of Abimelech's army. They said to Abraham, "God is with you in everything you do. [23]So make a promise to me here before God. Promise that you will be fair with me and my children and my descendants.[d] Be kind to me and to this land where you have lived as a stranger. Be as kind to me as I have been to you."

[24]And Abraham said, "I promise." [25]Then Abraham complained to Abimelech about Abimelech's servants. They had captured a well of water.

[26]But Abimelech said, "I don't know who did this. You never told me about this before today."

[27]Then Abraham gave Abimelech some sheep and cattle. And they made an agreement. [28]Abraham also put seven female lambs in front of Abimelech.

[29]Abimelech asked Abraham, "Why did you put these seven female lambs by themselves?"

[30]Abraham answered, "Accept these lambs from me. That will prove that you believe I dug this well."

[31]So that place was called Beersheba[n] because they made a promise to each other there.

[32]So Abraham and Abimelech made an agreement at Beersheba. Then Abimelech and Phicol, the commander

laugh The Hebrew words for "he laughed" and "Isaac" sound the same.
Beersheba This name means "well of the promise" or "well of seven".

of his army, went back to the land of the Philistines.

³³Abraham planted a tamarisk tree at Beersheba. There Abraham prayed to the Lord, the God who lives for ever. ³⁴And Abraham lived as a stranger in the land of the Philistines for a long time.

God Tests Abraham

22 After these things God tested Abraham's faith. God said to him, "Abraham!"

And he answered, "Here I am."

²Then God said, "Take your only son, Isaac, the son you love. Go to the land of Moriah. There kill him and offer him as a whole burnt offering. Do this on one of the mountains there. I will tell you which one."

³Early in the morning Abraham got up and saddled his donkey. He took Isaac and two servants with him. He cut the wood for the sacrifice. Then they went to the place God had told them to go. ⁴On the third day Abraham looked up and saw the place in the distance. ⁵He said to his servants, "Stay here with the donkey. My son and I will go over there and worship. Then we will come back to you."

⁶Abraham took the wood for the sacrifice and gave it to his son to carry. Abraham took the knife and the fire. So Abraham and his son went on together. ⁷Isaac said to his father Abraham, "Father!"

Abraham answered, "Yes, my son."

Isaac said, "We have the fire and the wood. But where is the lamb we will burn as a sacrifice?"

⁸Abraham answered, "God will give us the lamb for the sacrifice, my son."

So Abraham and his son went on together. ⁹They came to the place God had told him about. There, Abraham built an altar. He laid the wood on it. Then he tied up his son Isaac. And he laid Isaac on the wood on the altar.

¹⁰Then Abraham took his knife and was about to kill his son. ¹¹But the angel of the Lord called to him from heaven. The angel said, "Abraham! Abraham!"

Abraham answered, "Yes."

¹²The angel said, "Don't kill your son or hurt him in any way. Now I can see that you respect God. I see that you have not kept your son, your only son, from me."

¹³Then Abraham looked up and saw a male sheep. Its horns were caught in a bush. So Abraham went and took the sheep and killed it. He offered it as a whole burnt offering to God. Abraham's son was saved. ¹⁴So Abraham named that place The Lord Gives. Even today people say, "On the mountain of the Lord it will be given."

¹⁵The angel of the Lord called to Abraham from heaven a second time. ¹⁶The angel said, "The Lord says, 'You did not keep back your son, your only son, from me. Because you did this, I make you this promise by my own name: ¹⁷I will surely bless you and give you many descendants.^d They will be as many as the stars in the sky and the sand on the seashore. And they will capture the cities of their enemies. ¹⁸Through your descendants all the nations on the earth will be blessed. This is because you obeyed me'. "

¹⁹Then Abraham returned to his servants. They all travelled back to Beersheba, and Abraham stayed there.

²⁰After these things happened, someone told Abraham: "Your brother Nahor and his wife Milcah have children now. ²¹The first son is Uz. The second son is Buz. The third son is Kemuel (the father of Aram). ²²Then there are Kesed, Hazo, Pildash, Jidlaph and Bethuel." ²³Bethuel became the father of Rebekah. Milcah was the mother of these eight sons, and Nahor was the father. Nahor was Abraham's brother. ²⁴Also Nahor had four other

sons by his slave woman[d] Reumah. Their names were Tebah, Gaham, Tahash and Maacah.

Sarah Dies

23 Sarah lived to be 127 years old. [2]She died in Kiriath Arba (that is, Hebron) in the land of Canaan. Abraham was very sad and cried because of her. [3]After a while Abraham got up from the side of his wife's body. And he went to talk to the Hittites. He said, [4]"I am only a stranger and a foreigner here. Sell me some of your land so that I can bury my dead wife."

[5]The Hittites answered Abraham, [6]"Sir, you are a great leader among us. You may have the best place we have to bury your dead. You may have any of our burying places that you want. None of us will stop you from burying your dead wife."

[7]Abraham rose and bowed to the people of the land, the Hittites. [8]Abraham said to them, "If you truly want to help me bury my dead wife here, speak to Ephron for me. He is the son of Zohar. [9]Ask him to sell me the cave of Machpelah. It is at the edge of his field. I will pay him the full price. You can be the witnesses that I am buying it as a burial place."

[10]Ephron was sitting among the Hittites at the city gate. Ephron answered Abraham, [11]"No, sir. I will give you the land and the cave that is in it. I will give it to you with these people as witnesses. Bury your dead wife."

[12]Then Abraham bowed down before the Hittites. [13]He said to Ephron before all the people, "Please let me pay you the full price for the field. Accept my money, and I will bury my dead there."

[14]Ephron answered Abraham, [15]"Sir, the land is worth 4.5 kilograms of silver. But I won't argue with you

over the price. Take the land, and bury your dead wife."

[16]Abraham agreed and paid Ephron in front of the Hittite witnesses. Abraham weighed out the full price: 4.5 kilograms of silver. They counted the weight as the traders normally did.

[17-18]So Ephron's field in Machpelah, east of Mamre, was sold. Abraham became the owner of the field, the cave in it and all the trees that were in the field. The sale was made at the city gate, with the Hittites as witnesses. [19]After this, Abraham buried his wife Sarah in the cave. It was in that field of Machpelah, near Mamre. (Mamre was later called Hebron in the land of Canaan.) [20]Abraham bought the field and the cave on it from the Hittites. He used it as a burying place.

A Wife for Isaac

24 Abraham was now very old. The Lord had blessed him in every way. [2]Abraham's oldest servant was in charge of everything Abraham owned. Abraham called that servant to him and said, "Put your hand under my leg.[n] [3]Make a promise to me before the Lord, the God of heaven and earth. Don't get a wife for my son from the Canaanite girls who live around here. [4]Instead, go back to my country, to the land of my relatives. Get a wife for my son Isaac from there."

[5]The servant said to him, "What if this woman does not want to return with me to this land? Then, should I take your son with me back to your homeland?"

[6]Abraham said to him, "No! Don't take my son back there. [7]The Lord is the God of heaven. He brought me from the home of my father and the land of my relatives. But the Lord promised me, 'I will give this land to your descendants'.[d] The Lord will send his angel before you. The angel

---

Put . . . leg This showed that a person would keep the promise.

will help you get a wife for my son there. ⁸But if the girl won't come back with you, you will be free from this promise. But you must not take my son back there." ⁹So the servant put his hand under his master's leg. He made a promise to Abraham about this.

¹⁰The servant took ten of Abraham's camels and left. He carried with him many different kinds of beautiful gifts. He went to North West Mesopotamia to Nahor's city. ¹¹He made the camels kneel down at the well outside the city. It was in the evening when the women come out to get water.

¹²The servant said, "Lord, you are the God of my master Abraham. Allow me to find a wife for his son today. Please show this kindness to my master Abraham. ¹³Here I am, standing by the spring of water. The girls from the city are coming out to get water. ¹⁴I will say to one of the girls, 'Please put your jar down so I can drink'. Then let her say, 'Drink, and I will also give water to your camels'. If that happens, I will know she is the right one for your servant Isaac. And I will know that you have shown kindness to my master."

¹⁵Before the servant had finished praying, Rebekah came out of the city. She was the daughter of Bethuel. (Bethuel was the son of Milcah and Nahor, Abraham's brother.) Rebekah was carrying her water jar on her shoulder. ¹⁶She was very pretty. She was a virgin;ᵈ she had never had sexual relations with a man. She went down to the spring and filled her jar. Then she came back up. ¹⁷The servant ran to her and said, "Please give me a little water from your jar."

¹⁸Rebekah said, "Drink, sir." She quickly lowered the jar from her shoulder and gave him a drink. ¹⁹After he finished drinking, Rebekah said, "I will also pour some water for your camels." ²⁰So she quickly poured all the water from her jar into the drinking trough for the camels. Then she kept running to the well until she had given all the camels enough to drink.

²¹The servant quietly watched her. He wanted to be sure the Lord had made his trip successful. ²²After the camels had finished drinking, he gave Rebekah a gold ring weighing about 6 grams. He also gave her two gold arm bracelets weighing about 115 grams each. ²³The servant asked, "Who is your father? Is there a place in his house for me and my men to spend the night?"

²⁴Rebekah answered, "My father is Bethuel. He is the son of Milcah and Nahor." ²⁵Then she said, "And, yes, we have straw for your camels. We have a place for you to spend the night."

²⁶The servant bowed and worshipped the Lord. ²⁷He said, "Blessed is the Lord, the God of my master Abraham. The Lord has been kind and truthful to him. He has led me to my master's relatives."

²⁸Then Rebekah ran and told her mother's family about all these things. ²⁹She had a brother named Laban. He ran out to Abraham's servant, who was still at the spring. ³⁰Laban had heard what she had said. And he had seen the ring and the bracelets on his sister's arms. So he ran out to the well. And there was the man standing by the camels at the spring. ³¹Laban said, "Sir, you are welcome to come in. You don't have to stand outside. I have prepared the house for you and also a place for your camels."

³²So Abraham's servant went into the house. Laban unloaded the camels and gave them straw and food. Then Laban gave water to Abraham's servant so he and the men with him could wash their feet. ³³Then Laban gave the servant food. But the servant said, "I will not eat until I have told you why I came."

So Laban said, "Then tell us."

34He said, "I am Abraham's servant. 35The Lord has greatly blessed my master in everything. My master has become a rich man. The Lord has given him many flocks of sheep and herds of cattle. He has given Abraham silver and gold, male and female servants, camels and horses. 36Sarah, my master's wife, gave birth to a son when she was old. My master has given everything he owns to that son. 37My master had me make a promise to him. He said, 'Don't get a wife for my son from the Canaanite girls who live around here. 38Instead you must go to my father's people and to my family. There you must get a wife for my son'. 39I said to my master, 'What if the woman will not come back with me?' 40But he said, 'I serve the Lord. He will send his angel with you and will help you. You will get a wife for my son from my family and my father's people. 41Then you will be free from the promise. Or if they will not give you a wife for my son, you will be free from this promise'.

42"Today I came to this spring. I said, 'Lord, God of my master Abraham, please make my trip successful. 43Look, I am standing by this spring of water. I will wait for a young woman to come out to get water. Then I will say, "Please give me water from your jar to drink." 44Then let her say, "Drink this water. I will also get water for your camels." By this I will know the Lord has chosen her for my master's son'.

45"Before I finished my silent prayer, Rebekah came out of the city. She had her water jar on her shoulder. She went down to the spring and got water. I said to her, 'Please give me a drink'. 46She quickly lowered the jar from her shoulder. She said, 'Drink this. I will also get water for your camels'. So I drank, and she gave water to my camels also. 47Then I asked her, 'Who is your father?' She answered, 'My father is Bethuel son of Milcah and Nahor'. Then I put the ring in her nose and the bracelets on her arms. 48At that time I bowed my head and thanked the Lord. I praised the Lord, the God of my master Abraham. I thanked him because he led me on the right road to get the granddaughter of my master's brother for his son. 49Now, tell me, will you be kind and truthful to my master? And if not, tell me so. Then I will know what I should do."

50Laban and Bethuel answered, "This is clearly from the Lord. We cannot change what must happen. 51Rebekah is yours. Take her and go. Let her marry your master's son as the Lord has commanded."

52When Abraham's servant heard these words, he bowed face down on the ground before the Lord. 53Then the servant gave Rebekah gold and silver jewellery and clothes. He also gave expensive gifts to her brother and mother. 54The servant and the men with him ate and drank. And they spent the night there. When they got up the next morning, the servant said, "Now let me go back to my master."

55Rebekah's mother and her brother said, "Let Rebekah stay with us at least ten days. After that she may go."

56But the servant said to them, "Do not make me wait. The Lord has made my trip successful. Now let me go back to my master."

57Rebekah's brother and mother said, "We will call Rebekah and ask her what she wants to do." 58They called her and asked her, "Do you want to go with this man now?"

She said, "Yes, I do."

59So they allowed Rebekah and her nurse to go with Abraham's servant and his men. 60They blessed Rebekah and said,

"Our sister, may you be the
    mother of thousands of
    people.

And may your descendants[d]
capture the cities of their
enemies."

61Then Rebekah and her servant
girls got on the camels and followed
the servant and his men. So the servant took Rebekah and left.

62At this time Isaac had left Beer
Lahai Roi. He was living in southern
Canaan. 63One evening he went out to
the field to think. As he looked up, he
saw camels coming. 64Rebekah looked
and saw Isaac. Then she jumped down
from the camel. 65She asked the servant, "Who is that man walking in the
field to meet us?"

The servant answered, "That is my
master." So Rebekah covered her
face with her veil.

66The servant told Isaac everything
that had happened. 67Then Isaac
brought Rebekah into the tent of Sarah, his mother. And she became his
wife. Isaac loved her very much. So
he was comforted after his mother's
death.

Abraham's Family

25 Abraham married again. His
new wife was Keturah. 2She
gave birth to Zimran, Jokshan, Medan, Midian, Ishbak and Shuah. 3Jok-
shan was the father of Sheba and
Dedan. Dedan's descendants[d] were
the people of Assyria, Letush and
Leum. 4The sons of Midian were
Ephah, Epher, Hanoch, Abida and El-
daah. All these were descendants of
Keturah. 5Abraham left everything he
owned to Isaac. 6But before Abraham
died, he did give gifts to the sons of
his other wives. Abraham sent them
to the East to be away from Isaac.

7Abraham lived to be 175 years old.
8He breathed his last breath and died
at an old age. He had lived a long and
satisfying life. 9His sons Isaac and Ishmael buried him in the cave of Machpelah. This cave is in the field of
Ephron east of Mamre. Ephron was
the son of Zohar the Hittite. 10This is

the same field that Abraham had
bought from the Hittites. Abraham
was buried there with his wife Sarah.
11After Abraham died, God blessed
his son Isaac. Isaac was now living at
Beer Lahai Roi.

12This is the family history of Ishmael, Abraham's son. (Hagar, Sarah's
Egyptian servant, was Ishmael's
mother.) 13These are the names of
Ishmael's sons in the order they were
born. The first son was Nebaioth.
Then came Kedar, Adbeel, Mibsam,
14Mishma, Dumah, Massa, 15Hadad,
Tema, Jetur, Naphish and Kedemah.
16These were Ishmael's sons. And
these are the names of the tribal leaders. They are listed according to their
settlements and camps. 17Ishmael
lived 137 years. Then he breathed his
last breath and died. 18Ishmael's
descendants lived from Havilah to
Shur. This is east of Egypt stretching
toward Assyria. Ishmael's descendants often attacked the descendants
of his brothers.

Isaac's Family

19This is the family history of Isaac.
Abraham had a son named Isaac.
20When Isaac was 40 years old, he
married Rebekah. Rebekah was from
North West Mesopotamia. She was
Bethuel's daughter and the sister of
Laban the Aramean. 21Isaac's wife
could not have children. So Isaac
prayed to the Lord for her. The Lord
heard Isaac's prayer, and Rebekah became pregnant.

22While she was pregnant, the babies struggled inside her. She asked,
"Why is this happening to me?" Then
she went to get an answer from the
Lord.

23The Lord said to her,

"Two nations are in your body.
Two groups of people will be
taken from you.
One group will be stronger than
the other.

The older will serve the younger."

²⁴And when the time came, Rebekah gave birth to twins. ²⁵The first baby was born red. His skin was like a hairy robe. So he was named Esau.ⁿ ²⁶When the second baby was born, he was holding on to Esau's heel. So that baby was named Jacob.ⁿ Isaac was 60 years old when they were born.

²⁷When the boys grew up, Esau became a skilled hunter. He loved to be out in the fields. But Jacob was a quiet man. He stayed among the tents. ²⁸Isaac loved Esau. Esau hunted the wild animals that Isaac enjoyed eating. But Rebekah loved Jacob.

²⁹One day Jacob was boiling a pot of vegetable soup. Esau came in from hunting in the fields. He was weak from hunger. ³⁰So Esau said to Jacob, "Let me eat some of that red soup. I am weak with hunger." (That is why people call him Edom.ⁿ)

³¹But Jacob said, "You must sell me your rights as the firstborn son."ⁿ

³²Esau said, "I am almost dead from hunger. If I die, all of my father's wealth will not help me."

³³But Jacob said, "First, promise me that you will give it to me." So Esau made a promise to Jacob. In this way he sold his part of their father's wealth to Jacob. ³⁴Then Jacob gave Esau bread and vegetable soup. Esau ate and drank and then left. So Esau showed how little he cared about his rights as the firstborn son.

Isaac Lies to Abimelech

26 Once there was a time of hunger in the land. This was besides the time of hunger that happened during Abraham's life. So Isaac went to the town of Gerar. He went to see Abimelech king of the Philistines. ²The Lord appeared to Isaac and said, "Don't go down to Egypt. Live in the land where I tell you to live. ³Stay in this land, and I will be with you. I will bless you. I will give you and your descendantsᵈ all these lands. I will keep the agreement I made to Abraham your father. ⁴I will give you many descendants. They will be as hard to count as the stars in the sky. And I will give them all these lands. Through your descendants all the nations on the earth will be blessed. ⁵I will do this because your father Abraham obeyed me. He did what I said. He obeyed my commands, my teachings and my rules."

⁶So Isaac stayed in Gerar. ⁷Isaac's wife Rebekah was very beautiful. The men of that place asked Isaac about her. Isaac said, "She is my sister." He was afraid to tell them she was his wife. He thought they might kill him so they could have her.

⁸Isaac lived there a long time. One day as Abimelech king of the Philistines looked out his window, he saw Isaac. Isaac was holding his wife Rebekah tenderly. ⁹Abimelech called for Isaac and said, "This woman is your wife. Why did you say she was your sister?"

Isaac said to him, "I was afraid you would kill me so you could have her."

¹⁰Abimelech said, "What have you done to us? One of our men might have had sexual relations with your wife. Then we would have been guilty of a great sin."

¹¹So Abimelech warned everyone.

Esau This name may mean "hairy".
Jacob This name sounds like the Hebrew word for "heel". "Grabbing someone's heel" is a Hebrew saying for tricking someone.
Edom This name sounds like the Hebrew word for "red".
rights ... son Usually the firstborn son had a high rank in the family. The firstborn son usually became the new head of the family.

He said, "Anyone who touches this man or his wife will be put to death."

Isaac Becomes Rich

[12]Isaac planted seed in that land. And that year he gathered a great harvest. The Lord blessed him very much. [13]Isaac became rich. He gathered more wealth until he became a very rich man. [14]He had many slaves and many flocks and herds. The Philistines envied him. [15]So they stopped up all the wells the servants of Isaac's father Abraham had dug. (They had dug them when Abraham was alive.) The Philistines filled those wells with earth. [16]And Abimelech said to Isaac, "Leave our country. You have become much more powerful than we are."

[17]So Isaac left that place. He camped in the Valley of Gerar and lived there. [18]Long before this time Abraham had dug many wells. After Abraham died, the Philistines filled them with earth. So Isaac dug those wells again. He gave them the same names his father had given them. [19]Isaac's servants dug a well in the valley. From it a spring of water flowed. [20]But the men who herded sheep in Gerar argued with Isaac's servants. They said, "This water is ours." So Isaac named that well Argue because they argued with him. [21]Then Isaac's servants dug another well. The people also argued about it. So Isaac named that well Fight. [22]Isaac moved from there and dug another well. No one argued about this one. So he named that well Enough Room. Isaac said, "Now the Lord has made room for us. We will be successful in this land."

[23]From there Isaac went to Beersheba. [24]The Lord appeared to Isaac that night. The Lord said, "I am the God of your father Abraham. Don't be afraid because I am with you. I will

bless you and give you many descendants.[d] I will do this because of my servant Abraham." [25]So Isaac built an altar and worshiped the Lord there. He made a camp there, and his servants dug a well.

[26]Abimelech came from Gerar to see Isaac. Abimelech brought with him Ahuzzath, who advised him, and Phicol, the commander of his army. [27]Isaac asked them, "Why have you come to see me? You were my enemy. You forced me to leave your country."

[28]They answered, "Now we know that the Lord is with you. We will make a promise to you. And we would like you to make one to us. We would like to make an agreement with you. [29]We did not hurt you. So promise you will not hurt us. And we were good to you, and we sent you away in peace. Now the Lord has blessed you."

[30]So Isaac prepared food for them, and they all ate and drank. [31]Early the next morning the men made a promise to each other. Then Isaac sent them away, and they left in peace.

[32]That day Isaac's servants came and told him about the well they had dug. They said, "We found water in that well." [33]So Isaac named it Shibah.[n] And that city is still called Beersheba even now.

[34]When Esau was 40 years old, he married two Hittite women. One was Judith daughter of Beeri. The other was Basemath daughter of Elon. [35]These women brought much sorrow to Isaac and Rebekah.

Jacob Tricks Isaac

27 When Isaac was old, his eyes were not good. He could not see clearly. One day he called his older son Esau to him. Isaac said, "Son."

Esau answered, "Here I am."

[2]Isaac said, "I am old. I don't know when I might die. [3]So take your bow

Shibah This name sounds like the Hebrew words for "seven" and "promise".

and arrows, and go hunting in the field. Kill an animal for me to eat. [4]Prepare the tasty food that I love. Bring it to me, and I will eat. Then I will bless you before I die." [5]So Esau went out in the field to hunt.

Rebekah was listening as Isaac said this to his son Esau. [6]Rebekah said to her son Jacob, "Listen, I heard your father talking to your brother Esau. [7]Your father said, 'Kill an animal. Prepare some tasty food for me to eat. Then I will bless you before the Lord before I die'. [8]So obey me, my son. Do what I tell you. [9]Go out to our goats and bring me two fat, young ones. I will prepare them just the way your father likes them. [10]Then you will take the food to your father. And he will bless you before he dies."

[11]But Jacob said to his mother Rebekah, "My brother Esau is a hairy man. I am smooth! [12]If my father touches me, he will know I am not Esau. Then he will not bless me. He will place a curse on me because I tried to trick him."

[13]So Rebekah said to him, "If your father puts a curse on you, I will accept the blame. Just do what I said. Go and get the goats for me."

[14]So Jacob went out and got two goats and brought them to his mother. Then she cooked them in the special way Isaac enjoyed. [15]She took the best clothes of her older son Esau that were in the house. She put them on the younger son Jacob. [16]She took the skins of the goats. And she put them on Jacob's hands and neck. [17]Then she gave Jacob the tasty food and the bread she had made.

[18]Jacob went in to his father and said, "Father."

And his father said, "Yes, my son. Who are you?"

[19]Jacob said to him, "I am Esau, your first son. I have done what you told me. Now sit up and eat some meat of the animal I hunted for you. Then bless me."

[20]But Isaac asked his son, "How did you find and kill the animal so quickly?"

Jacob answered, "Because the Lord your God led me to find it."

[21]Then Isaac said to Jacob, "Come near so I can touch you, my son. If I can touch you, I will know if you are really my son Esau."

[22]So Jacob came near to Isaac his father. Isaac touched him and said, "Your voice sounds like Jacob's voice. But your hands are hairy like the hands of Esau." [23]Isaac did not know it was Jacob, because his hands were hairy like Esau's hands. So Isaac blessed Jacob. [24]Isaac asked, "Are you really my son Esau?"

Jacob answered, "Yes, I am."

[25]Then Isaac said, "Bring me the food. I will eat it and bless you." So Jacob gave him the food, and Isaac ate. Jacob gave him wine, and he drank. [26]Then Isaac said to him, "My son, come near and kiss me." [27]So Jacob went to his father and kissed him. Isaac smelled Esau's clothes and blessed him. Isaac said,

"The smell of my son
  is like the smell of the field
  that the Lord has blessed.
[28]May God give you plenty of rain
  and good soil.
Then you will have plenty of
  grain and wine.
[29]May nations serve you.
May peoples bow down to you.
May you be master over your
  brothers.
May your mother's sons bow
  down to you.
May everyone who curses you be
  cursed.
And may everyone who blesses
  you be blessed."

[30]Isaac finished blessing Jacob. Then, just as Jacob left his father Isaac, Esau came in from hunting. [31]Esau also prepared some tasty food and brought it to his father. He said, "Father, rise and eat the food that

your son killed for you. Then bless me."

³²Isaac asked, "Who are you?"

He answered, "I am your son — your firstborn^d son — Esau."

³³Then Isaac trembled greatly. He said, "Then who was it that hunted the animals and brought me food before you came? I ate it, and I blessed him. And it is too late now to take back my blessing."

³⁴When Esau heard the words of his father, he let out a loud and bitter cry. He said to his father, "Bless me — me, too, my father!"

³⁵But Isaac said, "Your brother came and tricked me. He has taken your blessing."

³⁶Esau said, "Jacobⁿ is the right name for him. He has tricked me these two times. He took away my share of everything you own. And now he has taken away my blessing." Then Esau asked, "Haven't you saved a blessing for me?"

³⁷Isaac answered, "I gave Jacob the power to be master over you. And all his brothers will be his servants. And I kept him strong with grain and wine. There is nothing left to give you, my son."

³⁸But Esau continued, "Do you have only one blessing, Father? Bless me, too, Father!" Then Esau began to cry out loud.

³⁹Isaac said to him,

"You will live far away from the
    best land,
    far from the rain.

⁴⁰You will live by using your sword
    and be a slave to your brother.
But when you struggle,
    you will break free from him."

⁴¹After that Esau hated Jacob because of the blessing from Isaac. Esau thought to himself, "My father will soon die, and I will be sad for him. After that I will kill Jacob."

⁴²Rebekah heard about Esau's plan to kill Jacob. So she sent for Jacob. She said to him, "Listen, your brother Esau is comforting himself by planning to kill you. ⁴³So, son, do what I say. My brother Laban is living in Haran. Go to him at once! ⁴⁴Stay with him for a while, until your brother is not so angry. ⁴⁵In time, your brother will not be angry. He will forget what you did to him. Then I will send a servant to bring you back. I don't want to lose both of my sons on the same day."

⁴⁶Then Rebekah said to Isaac, "I am tired of Hittite women. If Jacob marries one of these Hittite women here in this land, I will want to die."

Jacob Searches for a Wife

28 Isaac called Jacob and blessed him. Then Isaac commanded him, "You must not marry a Canaanite woman. ²Go to the house of Bethuel, your mother's father, in North West Mesopotamia. Laban, your mother's brother, lives there. Marry one of his daughters. ³May God All-Powerful bless you and give you many children. May you become the father of many peoples. ⁴May the Lord give you and your descendants^d the blessing of Abraham. Then you may own the land where you are now living as a stranger. This is the land God gave to Abraham." ⁵So Isaac sent Jacob to North West Mesopotamia. Jacob went to Laban, the brother of Rebekah. Bethuel, the Aramean, was the father of Laban and Rebekah. And Rebekah was the mother of Jacob and Esau.

⁶Esau learned that Isaac had blessed Jacob and sent him to North West Mesopotamia. Jacob went to find a wife there. Esau also learned that Isaac had commanded Jacob not to marry a Canaanite woman. ⁷And Esau learned that Jacob had obeyed his father and mother. He had gone to

Jacob This name sounds like the Hebrew word for "heel". "Grabbing someone's heel" is a Hebrew saying for tricking someone.

North West Mesopotamia. [8]So Esau saw that his father Isaac did not want his sons to marry Canaanite women. [9]Now Esau already had wives. But he went to Ishmael son of Abraham. And he married Mahalath, Ishmael's daughter. Mahalath was the sister of Nebaioth.

Jacob's Dream at Bethel

[10]Jacob left Beersheba and set out for Haran. [11]He came to a place and spent the night there because the sun had set. He found a stone there and laid his head on it to go to sleep. [12]Jacob dreamed that there was a ladder resting on the earth and reaching up into heaven. And he saw angels of God going up and coming down the ladder. [13]And then Jacob saw the Lord standing above the ladder. The Lord said, "I am the Lord, the God of Abraham, your grandfather. And I am the God of Isaac. I will give you and your descendants[d] the land on which you are now sleeping. [14]Your descendants will be as many as the dust of the earth. They will spread west and east, north and south. All the families of the earth will be blessed through you and your descendants. [15]I am with you, and I will protect you everywhere you go. And I will bring you back to this land. I will not leave you until I have done what I have promised you."

[16]Then Jacob woke from his sleep. He said, "Surely the Lord is in this place. But I did not know it." [17]Jacob was afraid. He said, "This place frightens me! It is surely the house of God and the gate of heaven."

[18]Jacob rose early in the morning. He took the stone he had slept on and set it up on its end. Then he poured olive oil on the top of it. [19]At first, the name of that city was Luz. But Jacob named it Bethel.[n]

[20]Then Jacob made a promise. He said, "I want God to be with me and protect me on this journey. I want God to give me food to eat and clothes to wear. [21]Then I will be able to return in peace to my father's house. If the Lord does these things, he will be my God. [22]This stone which I have set up on its end will be the house of God. And I will give God one-tenth of all he gives me."

Jacob Arrives in North West Mesopotamia

29 Then Jacob continued his journey. He came to the land of the people of the East. [2]He looked and saw a well in the field. Three flocks of sheep were lying nearby, because they drank water from this well. A large stone covered the mouth of the well. [3]All the flocks would gather there. The shepherds would roll the stone away from the well and water the sheep. Then they would put the stone back in its place.

[4]Jacob said to the shepherds there, "My brothers, where are you from?"

They answered, "We are from Haran."

[5]Then Jacob asked, "Do you know Laban grandson of Nahor?"

They answered, "We know him."

[6]Then Jacob asked, "How is he?"

They answered, "He is well. Look, his daughter Rachel is coming now with his sheep."

[7]Jacob said, "But look, it is still the middle part of the day. It is not time for the sheep to be gathered for the night. So give them water and let them go back into the pasture."

[8]But they said, "We cannot do that until all the flocks are gathered. Then we will roll away the stone from mouth of the well and water the sheep."

[9]While Jacob was talking with the shepherds, Rachel came with her father's sheep. It was her job to take care of the sheep. [10]Then Jacob saw

Bethel This name means "house of God".

Laban's daughter Rachel and Laban's sheep. So he went to the well and rolled the stone from its mouth. Then he watered Laban's sheep. Now Laban was the brother of Rebekah, Jacob's mother. [11]Then Jacob kissed Rachel and cried. [12]He told her that he was from her father's family. He said that he was the son of Rebekah. So Rachel ran home and told her father.

[13]When Laban heard the news about his sister's son Jacob, Laban ran to meet him. Laban hugged him and kissed him and brought him to his house. Jacob told Laban everything that had happened.

[14]Then Laban said, "You are my own flesh and blood."

Jacob Is Tricked

So Jacob stayed there a month. [15]Then Laban said to Jacob, "You are my relative. But it is not right for you to keep on working for me without pay. What would you like me to pay you?"

[16]Now Laban had two daughters. The older was Leah, and the younger was Rachel. [17]Leah had weak eyes, but Rachel was very beautiful. [18]Jacob loved Rachel. So he said to Laban, "Let me marry your younger daughter Rachel. If you will, I will work seven years for you."

[19]Laban said, "It would be better for her to marry you than someone else. So stay here with me." [20]So Jacob worked for Laban seven years so he could marry Rachel. But they seemed to him like just a few days. This was because he loved Rachel very much.

[21]After seven years Jacob said to Laban, "Give me Rachel so that I may marry her. The time I promised to work for you is over."

[22]So Laban gave a feast for all the people there. [23]That evening Laban brought his daughter Leah to Jacob. Jacob and Leah had sexual relations together. [24](Laban gave his slave girl Zilpah to his daughter to be her servant.) [25]In the morning Jacob saw that he had had sexual relations with Leah! He said to Laban, "What have you done to me? I worked hard for you so that I could marry Rachel! Why did you trick me?"

[26]Laban said, "In our country we do not allow the younger daughter to marry before the older daughter. [27]But complete the full week of the marriage ceremony with Leah. I will give you Rachel to marry also. But you must serve me another seven years."

[28]So Jacob did this and completed the week with Leah. Then Laban gave him his daughter Rachel as a wife. [29](Laban gave his slave girl Bilhah to his daughter Rachel to be her servant.) [30]So Jacob had sexual relations with Rachel also. And Jacob loved Rachel more than Leah. Jacob worked for Laban for another seven years.

Jacob's Family Grows

[31]The Lord saw that Jacob loved Rachel more than Leah. So the Lord made it possible for Leah to have children. But Rachel did not have any children. [32]Leah became pregnant and gave birth to a son. She named him Reuben,[n] because she said, "The Lord has seen my troubles. Surely now my husband will love me."

[33]Leah became pregnant again and gave birth to another son. She named him Simeon.[n] She said, "The Lord has heard that I am not loved. So he gave me this son."

[34]Leah became pregnant again and gave birth to another son. She named

---

Reuben This name sounds like the Hebrew word for "he has seen my troubles".
Simeon This name sounds like the Hebrew word for "has heard".

him Levi.[n] Leah said, "Now, surely my husband will be close to me. I have given him three sons."

[35]Then Leah gave birth to another son. She named him Judah.[n] Leah named him this because she said, "Now I will praise the Lord." Then Leah stopped having children.

30 Rachel saw that she was not giving birth to children for Jacob. So she envied her sister Leah. Rachel said to Jacob, "Give me children, or I'll die!"

[2]Jacob became angry with her. He said, "Can I do what only God can do? He is the one who has kept you from having children."

[3]Then Rachel said, "Here is my slave girl Bilhah. Have sexual relations with her so she can give birth to a child for me. Then I can have my own family through her."

[4]So Rachel gave Bilhah, her slave girl, to Jacob as a wife. And he had sexual relations with her. [5]She became pregnant and gave Jacob a son. [6]Rachel said, "God has declared me innocent. He has listened to my prayer and has given me a son." So Rachel named this son Dan.[n]

[7]Bilhah became pregnant again and gave Jacob a second son. [8]Rachel said, "I have struggled hard with my sister. And I have won." So she named that son Naphtali.[n]

[9]Leah saw that she had stopped having children. So she gave her slave girl Zilpah to Jacob as a wife. [10]Then Zilpah had a son. [11]Leah said, "I am lucky." So she named her son Gad.[n] [12]Zilpah gave birth to another son. [13]Leah said, "I am very happy! Now

women will call me happy." So she named that son Asher.[n]

[14]During the wheat harvest Reuben went into the field and found some mandrake[n] plants. He brought them to his mother Leah. But Rachel said to Leah, "Please give me some of your son's mandrakes."

[15]Leah answered, "You have already taken away my husband. Now you are trying to take away my son's mandrakes."

But Rachel answered, "If you will give me your son's mandrakes, you may sleep with Jacob tonight."

[16]When Jacob came in from the field that night, Leah went out to meet him. She said, "You will have sexual relations with me tonight. I have paid for you with my son's mandrakes." So Jacob slept with her that night.

[17]Then God answered Leah's prayer, and she became pregnant again. She gave birth to a fifth son. [18]Leah said, "God has given me what I paid for, because I gave my slave girl to my husband." So Leah named her son Issachar.[n]

[19]Leah became pregnant again and gave birth to a sixth son. [20]She said, "God has given me a fine gift. Now surely Jacob will honour me, because I have given him six sons." So Leah named the son Zebulun.[n]

[21]Later Leah gave birth to a daughter. She named her Dinah.

[22]Then God remembered Rachel and answered her prayer. God made it possible for her to have children. [23]She became pregnant and gave birth to a son. She said, "God has taken away my shame." [24]She named him

Levi This name sounds like the Hebrew word for "be close to".
Judah This name sounds like the Hebrew word for "praise".
Dan This name means "he has declared innocent".
Naphtali This name sounds like the Hebrew word for "my struggle".
Gad This name may mean "lucky".
Asher This name may mean "happy".
mandrake A plant which was believed to cause a woman to become pregnant.
Issachar This name sounds like the Hebrew word for "paid for".
Zebulun This name sounds like the Hebrew word for "honour".

Joseph.ⁿ Rachel said, "I wish the Lord would give me another son."

Jacob Tricks Laban

25After the birth of Joseph, Jacob said to Laban, "Now let me go to my own home and country. 26Give me my wives and my children, and let me go. I have earned them by working for you. You know that I served you well."

27Laban said to him, "If I have pleased you, please stay. I know the Lord has blessed me because of you. 28Tell me what I should pay you, and I will give it to you."

29Jacob answered, "You know that I have worked hard for you. Your flocks have grown while I cared for them. 30When I came, you had little. Now you have much. Every time I did something for you, the Lord blessed you. But when will I be able to do something for my own family?"

31Laban asked, "Then what should I give you?"

Jacob answered, "I don't want you to give me anything. Just do this one thing. Then I will come back and take care of your flocks. 32Today let me go through all your flocks of white sheep and black goats. I will take every spotted or speckled lamb. I will take every black lamb and every spotted or speckled goat. That will be my pay. 33In the future you can easily see if I am honest. You can come to look at my flocks. If I have any goat that isn't speckled or spotted or any sheep that isn't black, you will know I stole it."

34Laban answered, "Agreed! We will do what you ask." 35But that day Laban took away all the male goats that had streaks or spots. And he took all the speckled and spotted female goats (all those that had white on them). And he took all the black sheep. He told his sons to watch over them. 36Laban took these animals to a place that was three days' journey away from Jacob. Jacob took care of all the animals that were left.

37So Jacob cut green branches from poplar, almond and plane trees. He peeled off some of the bark so that the branches had white stripes on them. 38He put the branches in front of the flocks at the watering places. When the animals came to drink, they also mated there. 39So the goats mated in front of the branches. Then the young that were born were streaked, speckled or spotted. 40Jacob separated the young animals from the others. And he made them face the streaked and dark animals in Laban's flock. Jacob kept his animals separate from Laban's. 41When the stronger animals in the flock were mating, Jacob put the branches before their eyes. This was so the animals would mate near the branches. 42But when the weaker animals mated, Jacob did not put the branches there. So the animals born from the weaker animals were Laban's. And the animals born from the stronger animals were Jacob's. 43In this way Jacob became very rich. He had large flocks, many male and female servants, camels and donkeys.

Jacob Runs Away

31 One day Jacob heard Laban's sons talking. They said, "Jacob has taken everything our father owned. Jacob has become rich in this way." 2Then Jacob noticed that Laban was not as friendly as he had been before. 3The Lord said to Jacob, "Go back to the land where your ancestors lived. I will be with you."

4So Jacob told Rachel and Leah to meet him in the field where he kept his flocks. 5He said to them, "I have seen that your father is not as friendly with me as he used to be. But the God of my father has been with me. 6You both know that I have worked as hard

---

Joseph This name sounds like the Hebrew word for "he adds".

as I could for your father. ⁷But he cheated me. He has changed my pay ten times. But God has not allowed your father to harm me. ⁸At one time Laban said, 'You can have all the speckled goats as your pay'. After that, all the animals gave birth to speckled young ones. But then Laban said, 'You can have all the streaked goats as your pay'. After that, all the animals gave birth to streaked babies. ⁹So God has taken the animals away from your father. And God has given them to me.

¹⁰"I had a dream during the season when the animals were mating. I saw that the only male goats who were mating were streaked, speckled or spotted. ¹¹The angel of God spoke to me in that dream. He said, 'Jacob!' I answered, 'Yes!' ¹²The angel said, 'Look! Only the streaked, speckled or spotted goats are mating. I have seen all the wrong things Laban does to you. ¹³I am the God who appeared to you at Bethel. There you poured olive oil on the stone you set up on end. There you made a promise to me. Now I want you to leave here. Go back to the land where you were born'."

¹⁴Rachel and Leah answered Jacob, "Our father has nothing to give us when he dies. ¹⁵He has treated us like strangers. He sold us to you, and then he spent all of the money you paid for us. ¹⁶God took all this wealth from our father, and now it belongs to us and our children. So you do whatever God told you to do."

¹⁷So Jacob put his children and his wives on camels. ¹⁸Then they began their journey back to Isaac, his father. He lived in the land of Canaan. All the flocks of animals that Jacob owned walked ahead of them. He carried everything with him that he had gained while he lived in North West Mesopotamia.

¹⁹Laban had gone to cut the wool from his sheep. While he was away, Rachel stole the idols of false gods that belonged to him. ²⁰And Jacob tricked Laban the Aramean. He did not tell Laban he was leaving. ²¹Jacob and his family left quickly. They crossed the Euphrates River and travelled toward the mountains of Gilead.

²²Three days later Laban learned that Jacob had run away. ²³So Laban gathered his relatives and began to chase Jacob. After seven days Laban found him in the mountains of Gilead. ²⁴That night God came to Laban the Aramean in a dream. The Lord said, "Be careful! Do not say anything to Jacob, good or bad."

The Search for the Stolen Idols

²⁵So Laban caught up with Jacob. Now Jacob had made his camp in the mountains. So Laban and his relatives set up their camp in the mountains of Gilead. ²⁶Laban said to Jacob, "What have you done? Why did you trick me? You took my daughters as if you had captured them in a war. ²⁷Why did you run away without telling me? Why did you trick me? Why didn't you tell me? Then I could send you away with joy and singing. There would be the music of tambourines*d* and harps. ²⁸You did not even let me kiss my grandchildren and my daughters goodbye. You were very foolish to do this! ²⁹I have the power to harm you. But last night the God of your father spoke to me. He warned me not to say anything to you, good or bad. ³⁰I know you want to go back to your home. But why did you steal my idols?"

³¹Jacob answered Laban, "I left without telling you, because I was afraid! I thought you would take your daughters away from me. ³²If you find anyone here who has taken your idols, he will be killed! Your relatives will be my witnesses. You may look for anything that belongs to you. Take anything that is yours." (Now Jacob did not know that Rachel had stolen Laban's idols.)

33So Laban looked in Jacob's tent and in Leah's tent. He looked in the tent where the two slave women stayed. But he did not find his idols. When he left Leah's tent, he went into Rachel's tent. 34Rachel had hidden the idols inside her camel's saddle. And she was sitting on them. Laban looked through the whole tent, but he did not find them.

35Rachel said to her father, "Father, don't be angry with me. I am not able to stand up before you. I am having my monthly period." So Laban looked through the camp, but he did not find his idols.

36Then Jacob became very angry. He said, "What wrong have I done? What law have I broken to cause you to chase me? 37You have looked through everything I own. But you have found nothing that belongs to you. If you have found anything, show it to everyone. Put it in front of your relatives and my relatives. Then let them decide which one of us is right. 38I have worked for you now for 20 years. During all that time none of the lambs and kids died during birth. And I have not eaten any of the male sheep from your flocks. 39Any time a sheep was killed by wild animals, I did not bring it to you. I made up for the loss myself. You made me pay for any animal that was stolen during the day or night. 40In the daytime the sun took away my strength. At night I was cold and could not sleep. 41I worked like a slave for you for 20 years. For the first 14 years I worked to get your two daughters. The last 6 years I worked to earn your animals. And during that time you changed my pay ten times. 42But the God of my father was with me. He is the God of Abraham and the God of Isaac. If God had not been with me, you would have sent me away with nothing. But he saw the trouble I had and the hard work I did. And last night God corrected you."

Jacob and Laban's Agreement

43Laban said to Jacob, "These girls are my daughters. Their children belong to me, and these animals are mine. Everything you see here belongs to me. But I can do nothing to keep my daughters and their children. 44Let us make an agreement. Let us set up a pile of stones to remind us of our agreement."

45So Jacob took a large rock and set it up on its end. 46He told his relatives to gather rocks. So they took the rocks and piled them up. Then they ate beside the pile of rocks. 47Laban named that place in his language A Pile to Remind Us. And Jacob gave the place the same name in Hebrew.

48Laban said to Jacob, "This pile of rocks will remind us of the agreement between us." That is why the place was called A Pile to Remind Us. 49It was also called Mizpah.ⁿ This was because Laban said, "Let the Lord watch over us while we are separated from each other. 50Remember that God is our witness. This is true even if no one else is around us. He will know if you harm my daughters or marry other women. 51Here is the pile of rocks that I have put between us. And here is the rock I set up on end. 52This pile of rocks and this rock set on end will remind us of our agreement. I will never go past this pile to hurt you. And you must never come to my side of them to hurt me. 53The God of Abraham is the God of Nahor and the God of their fathers. Let God punish either of us if we break this agreement."

So Jacob made a promise in the name of God. This was the God of his father Isaac. 54Then Jacob killed an animal and offered it as a sacrifice on the mountain. And he invited his relatives

---

Mizpah This name sounds like the Hebrew word for "watch".

to share in the meal. After they had finished eating, they spent the night on the mountain. ⁵⁵Early the next morning Laban kissed his grandchildren and his daughters. He blessed them, and then he left to return home.

Jacob Meets Esau

32 When Jacob also went his way, the angels of God met him. ²When Jacob saw them, he said, "This is the camp of God!" So Jacob named that place Mahanaim.ⁿ

³Jacob's brother Esau was living in the area called Seir in the country of Edom. Jacob sent messengers to Esau. ⁴Jacob told the messengers, "Give this message to my master Esau: 'This is what Jacob, your servant, says: I have lived with Laban and have remained there until now. ⁵I have cattle, donkeys, flocks, and male and female servants. I send this message to you and ask you to accept us'."

⁶The messengers returned to Jacob and said, "We went to your brother Esau. He is coming to meet you. And he has 400 men with him."

⁷Then Jacob was very afraid and worried. He divided the people who were with him into two camps. He also divided all the flocks, herds and camels into two camps. ⁸Jacob thought, "Esau might come and destroy one camp. But the other camp can run away and be saved."

⁹Jacob said, "God of my father Abraham! God of my father Isaac! Lord, you told me to return to my country and my family. You said that you would do good to me. ¹⁰I am not worthy of the kindness and continual goodness you have shown me. The first time I travelled across the Jordan River, I had only my walking stick. But now I own enough to have two camps. ¹¹Please save me from my brother Esau. I am afraid he will come

and kill all of us, even the mothers with the children. ¹²You said to me, 'I will do good to you. I will make your children as many as the sand of the seashore. There will be too many to count'."

¹³Jacob stayed there for the night. He prepared a gift for Esau from what he had with him. ¹⁴It was 200 female goats and 20 male goats, 200 female sheep and 20 male sheep. ¹⁵There were 30 female camels and their young, 40 cows and ten bulls, 20 female donkeys and ten male donkeys. ¹⁶Jacob gave each separate flock of animals to one of his servants. Then he said to them, "Go ahead of me and keep some space between each herd." ¹⁷Jacob gave them their orders. To the servant with the first group of animals he said, "My brother Esau will come to you. He will ask you, 'Whose servant are you? Where are you going? Whose animals are these?' ¹⁸Then you will answer, 'These animals belong to your servant Jacob. He sent them as a gift to you my master, Esau. And Jacob also is coming behind us'."

¹⁹Jacob ordered the second servant, the third servant and all the other servants to do the same thing. He said, "Say the same thing to Esau when you meet him. ²⁰Say, 'Your servant Jacob is coming behind us'." Jacob thought, "If I send this gift ahead of me, maybe Esau will forgive me. Then when I see him, perhaps he will accept me." ²¹So Jacob sent the gift to Esau. But Jacob stayed that night in the camp.

Jacob Wrestles with God

²²During the night Jacob rose and crossed the Jabbok River at the crossing. He took his two wives, his two slave girls and his 11 sons with him. ²³He sent his family and everything he had across the river. ²⁴But Jacob stayed behind alone. And a man came

Mahanaim This name means "two camps".

and wrestled with him until the sun came up. [25]The man saw that he could not defeat Jacob. So he struck Jacob's hip and put it out of joint. [26]Then the man said to Jacob, "Let me go. The sun is coming up."

But Jacob said, "I will let you go if you will bless me."

[27]The man said to him, "What is your name?"

And he answered, "Jacob."

[28]Then the man said, "Your name will no longer be Jacob. Your name will now be Israel,[n] because you have wrestled with God and with men. And you have won."

[29]Then Jacob asked him, "Please tell me your name."

But the man said, "Why do you ask my name?" Then he blessed Jacob there.

[30]So Jacob named that place Peniel.[n] He said, "I have seen God face to face. But my life was saved." [31]Then the sun rose as he was leaving that place. Jacob was limping because of his leg. [32]So even today the people of Israel do not eat the muscle that is on the hip joint of animals. This is because Jacob was touched there.

Jacob Shows His Bravery

33 Jacob looked up and saw Esau coming. With him were 400 men. So Jacob divided his children among Leah, Rachel and the two slave girls. [2]Jacob put the slave girls with their children first. Then he put Leah and her children behind them. And he put Rachel and Joseph last. [3]Jacob himself went out in front of them. He bowed down flat on the ground seven times as he was walking toward his brother.

[4]But Esau ran to meet Jacob. Esau put his arms around him and hugged him. Then Esau kissed him, and they both cried. [5]Esau looked up and saw

the women and children. He asked, "Who are these people with you?"

Jacob answered, "These are the children God has given me. God has been good to me, your servant."

[6]Then the two slave girls and their children came up to Esau. They bowed down flat on the earth before him. [7]Then Leah and her children came up to Esau. They also bowed down flat on the earth. Last of all, Joseph and Rachel came up to Esau. And they, too, bowed down flat before him.

[8]Esau said, "I saw many herds as I was coming here. Why did you bring them?"

Jacob answered, "They were to please you, my master."

[9]But Esau said, "I already have enough, my brother. Keep what you have."

[10]Jacob said, "No! Please! If I have pleased you, then please accept the gift I give you. I am very happy to see your face again. It is like seeing the face of God because you have accepted me. [11]So I beg you to accept the gift I give you. God has been very good to me. And I have more than I need." And because Jacob begged, Esau accepted the gift.

[12]Then Esau said, "Let us get going. I will travel with you."

[13]But Jacob said to him, "My master, you know that the children are weak. And I must be careful with my flocks and their young ones. If I force them to go too far in one day, all the animals will die. [14]So, my master, you go on ahead of me, your servant. I will follow you slowly. I will let the animals and the children set the speed at which we travel. I will meet you, my master, in Edom."

[15]So Esau said, "Then let me leave some of my men with you."

"No, thank you," said Jacob. "I only

Israel This name means "he wrestles with God".
Peniel This name means "the face of God".

want to please you, my master." ¹⁶So that day Esau started back to Edom. ¹⁷But Jacob went to Succoth. There he built a house for himself. And he made shelters for his animals. That is why the place was named Succoth.ⁿ ¹⁸Jacob left North West Mesopotamia. And he arrived safely at the city of Shechem in the land of Canaan. He camped east of the city. ¹⁹He bought a part of the field where he had camped. He bought it from the sons of Hamor father of Shechem for 100 pieces of silver. ²⁰He built an altar there and named it after God, the God of Israel.

Dinah Is Attacked

34 Dinah was the daughter of Leah and Jacob. At this time Dinah went out to visit the women of that land. ²Shechem son of Hamor the Hivite, the ruler of that land, saw Dinah. He took her and forced her to have sexual relations with him. ³Shechem fell in love with Dinah, and he spoke kindly to her. ⁴He told his father, Hamor, "Please get this girl for me so I can marry her."

⁵Jacob learned how Shechem had disgraced his daughter. But Jacob's sons were out in the field with the cattle. So Jacob said nothing until they came home. ⁶And Hamor father of Shechem went to talk with Jacob.

⁷When Jacob's sons heard what had happened, they came in from the field. They were very angry, because Shechem had done such a wicked thing to Israel. It was wrong for him to have sexual relations with Jacob's daughter. A thing like this should not be done.

⁸But Hamor talked to the brothers of Dinah. He said, "My son Shechem is deeply in love with Dinah. Please let him marry her. ⁹Marry our people. Give your women to our men as wives. And take our women for your

men as wives. ¹⁰You can live in the same land with us. You will be free to own land and to trade here."

¹¹Shechem also talked to Jacob and to Dinah's brothers. He said, "Please accept my offer. I will give anything you ask. ¹²Ask as much as you want for the payment for the bride. I will give it to you. Just let me marry Dinah."

¹³The sons of Jacob answered Shechem and his father with lies. They were angry because Shechem had disgraced their sister Dinah. ¹⁴The brothers said to them, "We cannot allow you to marry our sister. You are not circumcised.ᵈ That would be a disgrace to us. ¹⁵But we will allow you to marry her if you do this one thing: every man in your town must be circumcised like us. ¹⁶Then your men can marry our women, and our men can marry your women. Then we will live in your land and become one people. ¹⁷If you refuse to be circumcised, we will take Dinah and leave."

¹⁸What they asked seemed fair to Hamor and Shechem. ¹⁹So Shechem went quickly to be circumcised because he loved Jacob's daughter.

Now Shechem was the most respected man in his family. ²⁰So Hamor and Shechem went to the gate of their city. They spoke to the men of their city. They said, ²¹"These people want to be friends with us. So let them live in our land and trade here. There is enough land for all of us. Let us marry their women. And we can let them marry our women. ²²But our men must agree to one thing. All our men must agree to be circumcised as they are. Then they will agree to live in our land. And we will be one people. ²³If we do this, their cattle and their animals will belong to us. Let us do what they say, and they will stay in our land." ²⁴All the men who had come to the city gate heard this. And they

Succoth This name means "shelters".

agreed with Hamor and Shechem. And every man was circumcised. [25]Three days later the men who were circumcised were still in pain. Two of Jacob's sons, Simeon and Levi (Dinah's brothers), took their swords. They made a surprise attack on the city. And they killed all the men there. [26]Simeon and Levi killed Hamor and his son Shechem. Then they took Dinah out of Shechem's house and left. [27]Jacob's sons went among the dead bodies and stole everything that was in the city. This was to pay them back for what Shechem had done to their sister. [28]So the brothers took the flocks, herds and donkeys. And they took everything in the city and in the fields. [29]They took every valuable thing those people owned. They even took the wives and children and everything that was in the houses. [30]Then Jacob said to Simeon and Levi, "You have caused me a lot of trouble. Now the Canaanites and the Perizzites who live in the land will hate me. There are only a few of us. If they join together to attack us, my people and I will be destroyed." [31]But the brothers said, "We will not allow our sister to be treated like a prostitute."[d]

Jacob in Bethel

35 God said to Jacob, "Go to the city of Bethel and live there. Make an altar to the God who appeared to you there. This was when you were running away from your brother Esau." [2]So Jacob said to his family and to all who were with him, "Put away the foreign gods you have. Make yourselves clean,[d] and change your clothes. [3]We will leave here and go to Bethel. There I will build an altar to God. He has helped me during my time of trouble. He has been with me everywhere I have gone." [4]So they gave Jacob all the foreign gods they had. And they gave him the earrings

they were wearing. He hid them under the great tree near the town of Shechem. [5]Then Jacob and his sons left there. But God caused the people in the nearby cities to be afraid. So they did not follow the sons of Jacob. [6]And Jacob and all the people who were with him went to Luz. It is now called Bethel. It is in the land of Canaan. [7]There Jacob built an altar. He named the place Bethel, after God, because God had appeared to him there. That was when he was running from his brother.

[8]Deborah, Rebekah's nurse, died and was buried under the oak tree at Bethel. They named that place Oak of Crying.

Jacob's New Name

[9]When Jacob came back from North West Mesopotamia, God appeared to him again. And God blessed him. [10]God said to him, "Your name is Jacob. But you will not be called Jacob any longer. Your new name will be Israel." So he called him Israel. [11]God said to him, "I am God All-Powerful. Have many children and grow in number as a nation. You will be the ancestor of many nations and kings. [12]I gave Abraham and Isaac land. I will give that same land to you and your descendants."[d] [13]Then God left him. [14]Jacob set up a stone on edge in that place where God had talked to him. And he poured a drink offering and olive oil on it to make it special for God. [15]And Jacob named the place Bethel.

Rachel Dies Giving Birth

[16]Jacob and his group left Bethel. Before they came to Ephrath, Rachel began giving birth to her baby. [17]But she was having a lot of trouble with this birth. When Rachel's nurse saw this, she said, "Don't be afraid, Rachel. You are giving birth to another son." [18]Rachel gave birth to the son, but she died. As she lay dying, she named the

boy Son of My Suffering. But Jacob called him Benjamin.[n]

[19]Rachel was buried on the road to Ephrath, a district of Bethlehem. [20]And Jacob set up a rock on her grave to honour her. That rock is still there today. [21]Then Israel, also called Jacob, continued his journey. He camped just south of Migdal Eder.

[22]While Israel was in that land Reuben had sexual relations with Israel's slave woman[d] Bilhah. And Israel heard about it.

The Family of Israel

Jacob had 12 sons. [23]He had six sons by his wife Leah. Reuben was his first son. Then Leah had Simeon, Levi, Judah, Issachar and Zebulun.

[24]He had two sons by his wife Rachel: Joseph and Benjamin.

[25]He had two sons by Rachel's slave girl Bilhah: Dan and Naphtali.

[26]And he had two sons by Leah's slave girl Zilpah: Gad and Asher.

These are Jacob's sons who were born in North West Mesopotamia.

[27]Jacob went to his father Isaac at Mamre near Hebron. This is where Abraham and Isaac had lived. [28]Isaac lived 180 years. [29]So Isaac breathed his last breath and died when he was very old. And his sons Esau and Jacob buried him.

Esau's Family

36 This is the family history of Esau (also called Edom).

[2]Esau married women from the land of Canaan. He married Adah daughter of Elon the Hittite. And he married Oholibamah daughter of Anah. Anah was the son of Zibeon the Hivite. And he married [3]Basemath, Ishmael's daughter, the sister of Nebaioth.

[4]Adah gave Esau one son, Eliphaz. Basemath gave Esau Reuel. [5]And Oholibamah gave Esau Jeush, Jalam and Korah. These were Esau's sons

who were born in the land of Canaan.

[6]Esau took his wives, his sons, his daughters and all the people who lived with him. He took his herds and other animals. And he took all the belongings he had gained in Canaan. And he went to a land away from his brother Jacob. [7]Esau's and Jacob's belongings were becoming too many for them to live in the same land. The land where they had lived could not support both of them. They had too many herds. [8]So Esau lived in the mountains of Edom. (Esau is also named Edom.)

[9]This is the family history of Esau. He is the ancestor of the Edomites, who live in the mountains of Edom.

[10]Esau's sons were Eliphaz son of Adah and Esau, and Reuel son of Basemath and Esau.

[11]Eliphaz had five sons: Teman, Omar, Zepho, Gatam and Kenaz. [12]Eliphaz also had a slave woman[d] named Timna. Timna and Eliphaz gave birth to Amalek. These were Esau's grandsons by his wife Adah.

[13]Reuel had four sons: Nahath, Zerah, Shammah and Mizzah. These were Esau's grandsons by his wife Basemath.

[14]Esau's third wife was Oholibamah. She was the daughter of Anah. (Anah was the son of Zibeon.) Esau and Oholibamah gave birth to Jeush, Jalam and Korah.

[15]These were the leaders that came from Esau. Esau's first son was Eliphaz. From him came these leaders: Teman, Omar, Zepho, Kenaz, [16]Korah, Gatam and Amalek. These were the leaders that came from Eliphaz in the land of Edom. They were the grandsons of Adah.

[17]Esau's son Reuel was the father of these leaders: Nahath, Zerah, Shammah and Mizzah. These were the leaders that came from Reuel in the land of Edom. They were the grandsons of Esau's wife Basemath.

Benjamin This name means "right-hand son" or "favourite son".

¹⁸Esau's wife Oholibamah gave birth to these leaders: Jeush, Jalam and Korah. These are the leaders that came from Esau's wife Oholibamah. She was the daughter of Anah. ¹⁹These were the sons of Esau (also called Edom), and these were their leaders.

²⁰These were the sons of Seir the Horite, who were living in the land: Lotan, Shobal, Zibeon, Anah, ²¹Dishon, Ezer and Dishan. These sons of Seir were the leaders of the Horites in Edom.

²²The sons of Lotan were Hori and Homam. (Timna was Lotan's sister.)

²³The sons of Shobal were Alvan, Manahath, Ebal, Shepho and Onam.

²⁴The sons of Zibeon were Aiah and Anah. Anah is the man who found the hot springs in the desert. He found them while he was caring for his father's donkeys.

²⁵The children of Anah were Dishon and Oholibamah daughter of Anah.

²⁶The sons of Dishon were Hemdan, Eshban, Ithran and Keran.

²⁷The sons of Ezer were Bilhan, Zaavan and Akan.

²⁸The sons of Dishan were Uz and Aran.

²⁹These were the names of the Horite leaders: Lotan, Shobal, Zibeon, Anah, ³⁰Dishon, Ezer and Dishan.

These men were the leaders of the Horite families. They lived in the land of Edom.

³¹These are the kings who ruled in the land of Edom before the Israelites ever had a king.

³²Bela son of Beor was the king of Edom. He came from the city of Dinhabah.

³³When Bela died, Jobab son of Zerah became king. Jobab was from Bozrah.

³⁴When Jobab died, Husham became king. He was from the land of the Temanites.

³⁵When Husham died, Hadad son of Bedad became king. Hadad had de-feated Midian in the country of Moab. Hadad was from the city of Avith.

³⁶When Hadad died, Samlah became king. He was from Masrekah.

³⁷When Samlah died, Shaul became king. He was from Rehoboth on the Euphrates River.

³⁸When Shaul died, Baal-Hanan son of Acbor became king.

³⁹When Baal-Hanan son of Acbor died, Hadad became king. He was from the city of Pau. His wife's name was Mehetabel daughter of Matred. Matred was the daughter of Me-Zahab.

⁴⁰These Edomite leaders came from Esau. They are listed by their families and regions. Their names were Timna, Alvah, Jetheth, ⁴¹Oholibamah, Elah, Pinon, ⁴²Kenaz, Teman, Mibzar, ⁴³Magdiel and Iram. These were the leaders of Edom. (Esau was the father of the Edomites.) The area where each of these families lived was named after that family.

Joseph the Dreamer

37 Jacob lived in the land of Canaan, where his father had lived. ²This is the family history of Jacob.

Joseph was a young man, 17 years old. He and his brothers cared for the flocks. His brothers were the sons of Bilhah and Zilpah, his father's wives. Joseph gave his father bad reports about his brothers. ³Joseph was born when his father Israel, also called Jacob, was old. So Israel loved Joseph more than his other sons. He made Joseph a special robe with long sleeves. ⁴Joseph's brothers saw that their father loved Joseph more than he loved them. So they hated their brother and could not speak to him politely.

⁵One night Joseph had a dream. When he told his brothers about it, they hated him even more. ⁶Joseph said, "Listen to the dream I had. ⁷We were in the field tying bundles of wheat together. My bundle stood up,

and your bundles of wheat gathered around mine. Your bundles bowed down to mine."

⁸His brothers said, "Do you really think you will be king over us? Do you truly think you will rule over us?" His brothers hated him even more now. They hated him because of his dreams and what he had said.

⁹Then Joseph had another dream. He told his brothers about it also. He said, "Listen, I had another dream. I saw the sun, moon and 11 stars bowing down to me."

¹⁰Joseph also told his father about this dream. But his father scolded him, saying, "What kind of dream is this? Do you really believe that your mother, your brothers and I will bow down to you?" ¹¹Joseph's brothers were jealous of him. But his father thought about what all these things could mean.

¹²One day Joseph's brothers went to Shechem to herd their father's sheep. ¹³Jacob said to Joseph, "Go to Shechem. Your brothers are there herding the sheep."

Joseph answered, "I will go."

¹⁴His father said, "Go and see if your brothers and the sheep are all right. Then come back and tell me." So Joseph's father sent him from the Valley of Hebron.

When Joseph came to Shechem, ¹⁵a man found him wandering in the field. He asked Joseph, "What are you looking for?"

¹⁶Joseph answered, "I am looking for my brothers. Can you tell me where they are herding the sheep?"

¹⁷The man said, "They have already gone. I heard them say they were going to Dothan." So Joseph went to look for his brothers and found them in Dothan.

Joseph Sold into Slavery

¹⁸Joseph's brothers saw him coming from far away. Before he reached them, they made a plan to kill him.

¹⁹They said to each other, "Here comes that dreamer. ²⁰Let's kill him and throw his body into one of the wells. We can tell our father that a wild animal killed him. Then we will see what will become of his dreams."

²¹But Reuben heard their plan and saved Joseph. He said, "Let's not kill him. ²²Don't spill any blood. Throw him into this well here in the desert. But don't hurt him!" Reuben planned to save Joseph later and send him back to his father. ²³So when Joseph came to his brothers, they pulled off his robe with long sleeves. ²⁴Then they threw him into the well. It was empty. There was no water in it.

²⁵While Joseph was in the well, the brothers sat down to eat. When they looked up, they saw a group of Ishmaelites. They were travelling from Gilead to Egypt. Their camels were carrying spices, balm*ᵈ* and myrrh.*ᵈ*

²⁶Then Judah said to his brothers, "What will we gain if we kill our brother and hide his death? ²⁷Let's sell him to these Ishmaelites. Then we will not be guilty of killing our own brother. After all, he is our brother, our own flesh and blood." And the other brothers agreed. ²⁸So when the Midianite traders came by, the brothers took Joseph out of the well. They sold him to the Ishmaelites for 0.2 kilograms of silver. And the Ishmaelites took him to Egypt.

²⁹Reuben was not with his brothers when they sold Joseph to the Ishmaelites. When Reuben came back to the well, Joseph was not there. Reuben tore his clothes to show he was sad. ³⁰Then he went back to his brothers and said, "The boy is not there! What shall I do?" ³¹The brothers killed a goat and dipped Joseph's long-sleeved robe in its blood. ³²Then they brought the robe to their father. They said, "We found this robe. Look it over carefully. See if it is your son's robe."

³³Jacob looked it over and said, "It is my son's robe! Some savage animal

has eaten him. My son Joseph has been torn to pieces!" [34]Then Jacob tore his clothes and put on rough cloth to show that he was sad. He continued to be sad about his son for a long time. [35]All of Jacob's sons and daughters tried to comfort him. But he could not be comforted. Jacob said, "I will be sad about my son until the day I die." So Jacob cried for his son Joseph.

[36]Meanwhile the Midianites who had bought Joseph had taken him to Egypt. There they sold him to Potiphar. Potiphar was an officer to the king of Egypt and captain of the palace guard.

Judah and Tamar

38 About that time, Judah left his brothers. He went to stay with a man named Hirah. Hirah was from the town of Adullam. [2]Judah met a Canaanite girl there and married her. (Her father was named Shua.) And Judah had sexual relations with her. [3]She became pregnant and gave birth to a son. Judah named him Er. [4]Later she gave birth to another son. She named him Onan. [5]Later she had another son. She named him Shelah. She was at Kezib when this third son was born.

[6]Judah chose a girl named Tamar to be the wife of his first son Er. [7]Er was Judah's oldest son. But he did what the Lord said was evil. So the Lord killed him. [8]Then Judah said to Er's brother Onan, "Go and have sexual relations with your dead brother's wife." [n] It is your duty to provide children for your brother in this way." [9]But Onan knew that the children would not belong to him. Onan was supposed to have sexual relations with Tamar. But he did not complete the sex act. This made it impossible for Tamar to become pregnant. So Er

could not have descendants. [d] [10]The Lord was displeased by this wicked thing Onan had done. So the Lord killed Onan also. [11]Then Judah said to his daughter-in-law Tamar, "Go back to live in your father's house. And don't marry until my young son Shelah grows up." Judah was afraid that Shelah also would die like his brothers. So Tamar returned to her father's home.

[12]After a long time Judah's wife, the daughter of Shua, died. After Judah had got over his sorrow, he went to Timnah. He went to his men who were cutting the wool from his sheep. His friend Hirah from Adullam went with him. [13]Tamar learned that Judah, her father-in-law, was going to Timnah to cut the wool from his sheep. [14]So she took off the clothes that showed she was a widow. Then she covered her face with a veil to hide who she was. She sat down by the gate of Enaim. It was on the road to Timnah. She did this because Judah's younger son Shelah had grown up. But Judah had not made plans for her to marry him.

[15]When Judah saw her, he thought she was a prostitute. [d] This was because she had covered her face with a veil. [16]So Judah went to her and said, "Let me have sexual relations with you." He did not know that she was Tamar, his daughter-in-law.

She asked, "What will you give me if I let you have sexual relations with me?"

[17]Judah answered, "I will send you a young goat from my flock."

She answered, "First give me something to keep as a deposit until you send the goat."

[18]Judah asked, "What do you want me to give you as a deposit?"

Tamar answered, "Give me your

Go ... wife It was a custom in Israel that if a man died without children, one of his brothers would marry the widow. If a child was born, it would be considered the dead man's child.

seal and its cord,[n] and give me your walking stick." So Judah gave these things to her. Then Judah and Tamar had sexual relations, and Tamar became pregnant. [19]Tamar went home. She took off the veil that covered her face. And she put on the clothes that showed she was a widow.

[20]Judah sent his friend Hirah with the young goat. Judah told Hirah to find the woman and get back his seal and the walking stick he had given her. But Hirah could not find her. [21]Hirah asked some of the men at the town of Enaim, "Where is the prostitute who was here by the road?" The men answered, "There has never been a prostitute here."

[22]So he went back to Judah and said, "I could not find the woman. The men who lived there said, 'There has never been a prostitute here'."

[23]Judah said, "Let her keep the things. I don't want people to laugh at us. I sent her the goat as I promised. But you could not find her."

[24]About three months later someone told Judah, "Tamar, your daughter-in-law, is guilty of acting like a prostitute. Now she is pregnant." Then Judah said, "Bring her out and let her be burned to death."

[25]When the men went to bring Tamar out, she sent a message to her father-in-law. She said, "The man who owns these things has made me pregnant. Look at this seal and its cord and this walking stick. Tell me whose they are."

[26]Judah recognised them. He said, "She is more in the right than I. She did this because I did not give her to my son Shelah as I promised." And Judah did not have sexual relations with her again.

[27]When the time came for Tamar to give birth, there were twins in her body. [28]While she was giving birth, one baby put his hand out. The nurse tied a red string on his hand. She said, "This baby came out first." [29]But he pulled his hand back in. So the other baby was born first. The nurse said, "So you are able to break out first." And they named him Perez.[n] [30]After this, the baby with the red string on his hand was born. They named him Zerah.

Joseph Is Sold to Potiphar

39 Now Joseph had been taken down to Egypt. An Egyptian named Potiphar was an officer to the king of Egypt. He was the captain of the palace guard. He bought Joseph from the Ishmaelites who had brought him down there. [2]The Lord was with Joseph, and he became a successful man. He lived in the house of his master, Potiphar the Egyptian.

[3]Potiphar saw that the Lord was with Joseph. He saw that the Lord made Joseph successful in everything he did. [4]So Potiphar was very happy with Joseph. He allowed Joseph to be his personal servant. He put Joseph in charge of the house. Joseph was trusted with everything Potiphar owned. [5]So Joseph was put in charge of the house. He was put in charge of everything Potiphar owned. Then the Lord blessed the people in Potiphar's house because of Joseph. And the Lord blessed everything that belonged to Potiphar, both in the house and in the field. [6]So Potiphar put Joseph in charge of everything he owned. Potiphar was not concerned about anything, except the food he ate.

---

seal . . . cord A seal was used like a rubber stamp. People ran a string through it to tie around the neck. They wrote a contract, folded it, put wax or clay on the contract, and pressed the seal onto it as a signature.
Perez This name means "breaking out".

Joseph Is Put into Prison

Now Joseph was well built and handsome. [7]After some time the wife of Joseph's master began to desire Joseph. One day she said to him, "Have sexual relations with me."

[8]But Joseph refused. He said to her, "My master trusts me with everything in his house. He has put me in charge of everything he owns. [9]There is no one in his house greater than I. He has not kept anything from me, except you. And that is because you are his wife. How can I do such an evil thing? It is a sin against God."

[10]The woman talked to Joseph every day, but he refused to have sexual relations with her or even spend time with her.

[11]One day Joseph went into the house to do his work as usual. He was the only man in the house at that time. [12]His master's wife grabbed his coat. She said to him, "Come and have sexual relations with me." But Joseph left his coat in her hand and ran out of the house.

[13]She saw what Joseph had done. He had left his coat in her hands and had run outside. [14]So she called to the servants in her house. She said, "Look! This Hebrew slave was brought here to shame us. He came in and tried to have sexual relations with me. But I screamed. [15]My scream scared him, and he ran away. But he left his coat with me." [16]She kept his coat until her husband came home. [17]And she told her husband the same story. She said, "This Hebrew slave you brought here came in to shame me! [18]When he came near me, I screamed. He ran away, but he left his coat."

[19]When Joseph's master heard what his wife said Joseph had done, he became very angry. [20]So Potiphar arrested Joseph and put him into prison. This prison was where the king's prisoners were put. And Joseph stayed there in the prison.

[21]But the Lord was with Joseph and showed him kindness. The Lord caused the prison warden to like Joseph. [22]The prison warden chose Joseph to take care of all the prisoners. He was responsible for whatever was done in the prison. [23]The warden paid no attention to anything that was in Joseph's care. This was because the Lord was with Joseph. The Lord made Joseph successful in everything he did.

Joseph Interprets Two Dreams

40 After these things happened, two of the king's officers displeased the king. These officers were the man who served wine to the king and the king's baker. [2]The king became angry with his officer who served him wine and his baker. [3]So he put them in the prison of the captain of the guard. This was the same prison where Joseph was kept. [4]The captain of the guard put the two prisoners in Joseph's care. They stayed in prison for some time.

[5]One night both the king's officer who served him wine and the baker had a dream. Each had his own dream with its own meaning. [6]When Joseph came to them the next morning, he saw they were worried. [7]Joseph asked the king's officers who were with him, "Why do you look so unhappy today?"

[8]The two men answered, "We both had dreams last night. But no one can explain the meaning of them to us."

Joseph said to them, "God is the only One who can explain the meaning of dreams. So tell me your dreams."

[9]So the man who served wine to the king told Joseph his dream. He said, "I dreamed I saw a vine. [10]On the vine there were three branches. I watched the branches bud and blossom, and then the grapes ripened. [11]I was hold-

Genesis 2:2
By the seventh day God had
finished all the work he had
been doing.

Genesis 9:16
"The rainbow (is) the
  agreement . . . between me and
every living thing on the earth."

ing the king's cup. So I took the grapes and squeezed the juice into the cup. Then I gave it to the king."

[12]Then Joseph said, "I will explain the dream to you. The three branches stand for three days. [13]Before the end of three days the king will free you. He will allow you to return to your work. You will serve the king his wine just as you did before. [14]But when you are free, remember me. Be kind to me. Tell the king about me so that I can get out of this prison. [15]I was taken by force from the land of the Hebrews. And I have done nothing here to deserve being put in prison."

[16]The baker saw that Joseph's explanation of the dream was good. So he said to Joseph, "I also had a dream. I dreamed there were three bread baskets on my head. [17]In the top basket there were all kinds of baked food for the king. But the birds were eating this food out of the basket on my head."

[18]Joseph answered, "I will tell you what the dream means. The three baskets stand for three days. [19]Before the end of three days, the king will cut off your head! He will hang your body on a pole. And the birds will eat your flesh."

[20]Three days later it was the king's birthday. So he gave a feast for all his officers. In front of his officers, he let the chief officer who served his wine and the chief baker out of prison. [21]The king gave his chief officer who served wine his old position. Once again he put the king's cup of wine into the king's hand. [22]But the king hanged the baker on a pole. Everything happened just as Joseph had said it would. [23]But the officer who served wine did not remember Joseph. He forgot all about him.

The King's Dreams

41 Two years later the king had a dream. He dreamed he was standing on the bank of the Nile River.

[2]He saw seven fat and beautiful cows come up out of the river. They stood there, eating the grass. [3]Then seven more cows came up out of the river. But they were thin and ugly. They stood beside the seven beautiful cows on the bank of the Nile. [4]The seven thin and ugly cows ate the seven beautiful fat cows. Then the king woke up. [5]The king slept again and dreamed a second time. In his dream he saw seven full and good heads of grain growing on one stalk. [6]After that, seven more heads of grain sprang up. But they were thin and burned by the hot east wind. [7]The thin heads of grain ate the seven full and good heads. Then the king woke up again. And he realised it was only a dream. [8]The next morning the king was troubled about these dreams. So he sent for all the magicians and wise men of Egypt. The king told them his dreams. But no one could explain their meaning to him.

[9]Then the chief officer who served wine to the king said to him, "I remember something I promised to do. But I had forgotten about it. [10]There was a time when you were angry with me and the baker. You put us in prison in the house of the captain of the guard. [11]In prison we each had a dream on the same night. Each dream had a different meaning. [12]A young Hebrew man was in the prison with us. He was a servant of the captain of the guard. We told him our dreams, and he explained their meanings to us. He told each man the meaning of his dream. [13]Things happened exactly as he said they would: I was given back my old position, and the baker was hanged."

[14]So the king called for Joseph. The guards quickly brought him out of the prison. He shaved, put on clean clothes and went before the king.

[15]The king said to Joseph, "I have had a dream. But no one can explain its meaning to me. I have heard that

you can explain a dream when someone tells it to you."

¹⁶Joseph answered the king, "I am not able to explain the meaning of dreams. God will do this for the king."

¹⁷Then the king said to Joseph, "In my dream I was standing on the bank of the Nile River. ¹⁸I saw seven fat and beautiful cows. They came up out of the river and ate the grass. ¹⁹Then I saw seven more cows come out of the river. They were thin and lean and ugly. They were the worst looking cows I have seen in all the land of Egypt. ²⁰And these thin and ugly cows ate the first seven fat cows. ²¹But after they had eaten the seven cows, no one could tell they had eaten them. They looked just as thin and ugly as they did in the beginning. Then I woke up.

²²"I had another dream. I saw seven full and good heads of grain growing on one stalk. ²³Then seven more heads of grain sprang up after them. But these heads were thin and ugly. They were burned by the hot east wind. ²⁴Then the thin heads ate the seven good heads. I told this dream to the magicians. But no one could explain its meaning to me."

Joseph Tells the Dreams' Meaning

²⁵Then Joseph said to the king, "Both of these dreams mean the same thing. God is telling you what he is about to do. ²⁶The seven good cows stand for seven years. And the seven good heads of grain stand for seven years. Both dreams mean the same thing. ²⁷The seven thin and ugly cows stand for seven years. And the seven thin heads of grain burned by the hot east wind stand for seven years of hunger. ²⁸This will happen as I told you. God is showing the king what he is about to do. ²⁹You will have seven years of good crops and plenty to eat in all the land of Egypt. ³⁰But after those seven years, there will come

seven years of hunger. All the food that grew in the land of Egypt will be forgotten. The time of hunger will eat up the land. ³¹People will forget what it was like to have plenty of food. This is because the hunger that follows will be so great. ³²You had two dreams which mean the same thing. This shows that God has firmly decided that this will happen. And he will make it happen soon.

³³"So let the king choose a man who is very wise and understanding. Let the king set him over the land of Egypt. ³⁴And let the king also appoint officers over the land. They should take one-fifth of all the food that is grown during the seven good years. ³⁵They should gather all the food that is produced during the good years that are coming. Under the king's authority they should store the grain in the cities and guard it. ³⁶That food should be saved for later. It will be used during the seven years of hunger that will come on the land of Egypt. Then the people in Egypt will not die during the seven years of hunger."

Joseph Is Made Ruler over Egypt

³⁷This seemed like a very good idea to the king. All his officers agreed. ³⁸And the king asked them, "Can we find a better man than Joseph to take this job? God's Spirit is truly in him!"

³⁹So the king said to Joseph, "God has shown you all this. There is no one as wise and understanding as you are. ⁴⁰I will put you in charge of my palace. All the people will obey your orders. Only I will be greater than you."

⁴¹Then the king said to Joseph, "Look! I have put you in charge of all the land of Egypt." ⁴²Then the king took off from his own finger his ring with the royal seal on it. And he put it on Joseph's finger. He gave Joseph fine linen clothes to wear. And he put a gold chain around Joseph's neck. ⁴³The king had Joseph ride in the sec-

Genesis 21:5-6
Abraham was 100 years old when
his son Isaac was born.   And Sarah
said, "God has made me laugh."

ond royal chariot. Men walked ahead of his chariot calling, "Bow down!" By doing these things, the king put Joseph in charge of all of Egypt. [44]The king said to him, "I am the king. And I say that no one in all the land of Egypt may lift a hand or a foot unless you say he may." [45]The king gave Joseph the name Zaphenath-Paneah. He also gave Joseph a wife named Asenath. She was the daughter of Potiphera, priest of On. So Joseph travelled through all the land of Egypt.

[46]Joseph was 30 years old when he began serving the king of Egypt. And he left the king's court and travelled through all the land of Egypt. [47]During the seven good years, the crops in the land grew well. [48]And Joseph gathered all the food which was produced in Egypt during those seven years of good crops. He stored the food in the cities. In every city he stored grain that had been grown in the fields around that city. [49]Joseph stored much grain, as much as the sand of the seashore. He stored so much grain that he could not measure it.

[50]Joseph's wife was Asenath daughter of Potiphera, the priest of On. Before the years of hunger came, Joseph and Asenath had two sons. [51]Joseph named the first son Manasseh.[n] Joseph said, "God has made me forget all the troubles I have had and all my father's family." [52]Joseph named the second son Ephraim.[n] Joseph said, "God has given me children in the land of my troubles."

[53]The seven years of good crops came to an end in the land of Egypt. [54]Then the seven years of hunger began, just as Joseph had said. In all the lands people had nothing to eat. But in Egypt there was food. [55]The time of hunger became terrible in all of Egypt. The people cried to the king for food.

He said to all the Egyptians, "Go to Joseph. Do whatever he tells you to do."

[56]The hunger was everywhere in that part of the world. And Joseph opened the storehouses and sold grain to the people of Egypt. This was because the time of hunger became terrible in Egypt. [57]And all the people in that part of the world came to Joseph in Egypt to buy grain. This was because the hunger was terrible everywhere in that part of the world.

The Dreams Come True

42 Jacob learned that there was grain in Egypt. So he said to his sons, "Why are you just sitting here looking at one another? [2]I have heard that there is grain in Egypt. Go down there and buy grain for us to eat. Then we will live and not die."

[3]So ten of Joseph's brothers went down to buy grain from Egypt. [4]But Jacob did not send Benjamin, Joseph's brother, with them. Jacob was afraid that something terrible might happen to Benjamin. [5]Along with many other people, the sons of Jacob, also called Israel, went to Egypt to buy grain. This was because the people in the land of Canaan were hungry also.

[6]Now Joseph was governor over Egypt. He was the one who sold the grain to people who came to buy it. So Joseph's brothers came to him. They bowed face down on the ground before him. [7]When Joseph saw his brothers, he knew who they were. But he acted as if he didn't know them. He asked unkindly, "Where do you come from?"

They answered, "We have come from the land of Canaan to buy food."

[8]Joseph knew they were his brothers. But they did not know who he was. [9]And Joseph remembered his dreams about his brothers bowing to

---

Manasseh This name sounds like the Hebrew word for "made me forget".
Ephraim This name sounds like the Hebrew word for "given me children".

him. He said to them, "You are spies! You came to learn where the nation is weak!"

¹⁰But his brothers said to him, "No, my master. We come as your servants just to buy food. ¹¹We are all sons of the same father. We are honest men, not spies."

¹²Then Joseph said to them, "No! You have come to learn where this nation is weak!"

¹³And they said, "We are ten of 12 brothers. We are sons of the same father. We live in the land of Canaan. Our youngest brother is there with our father right now. And our other brother is gone."

¹⁴But Joseph said to them, "I can see I was right! You are spies! ¹⁵But I will give you a way to prove you are telling the truth. As surely as the king lives, you will not leave this place until your youngest brother comes here. ¹⁶One of you must go and get your brother. The rest of you will stay here in prison. We will see if you are telling the truth. If not, as surely as the king lives, you are spies." ¹⁷Then Joseph put them all in prison for three days.

¹⁸On the third day Joseph said to them, "I am a God-fearing man. Do this thing, and I will let you live: ¹⁹if you are honest men, let one of your brothers stay here in prison. The rest of you go and carry grain back to feed your hungry families. ²⁰Then bring your youngest brother back here to me. If you do this, I will know you are telling the truth. Then you will not die."

The brothers agreed to this. ²¹They said to each other, "We are being punished for what we did to our brother. We saw his trouble. He begged us to save him, but we refused to listen. That is why we are in this trouble now."

²²Then Reuben said to them, "I told you not to harm the boy. But you refused to listen to me. So now we are being punished for what we did to him."

²³When Joseph talked to his brothers, he used an interpreter. So they did not know that Joseph understood what they were saying. ²⁴Then Joseph left them and cried. After a short time he went back and spoke to them. He took Simeon and tied him up while the other brothers watched. ²⁵Joseph told his servants to fill his brothers' bags with grain. They were to put the money the brothers had paid for the grain back in their bags. They were to give them things they would need for their trip back home. And the servants did this.

²⁶So the brothers put the grain on their donkeys and left. ²⁷When they stopped for the night, one of the brothers opened his sack. He was going to get food for his donkey. Then he saw his money in the top of the sack. ²⁸He said to the other brothers, "The money I paid for the grain has been put back. Here it is in my sack!"

The brothers were very frightened. They said to each other, "What has God done to us?"

The Brothers Return to Jacob

²⁹The brothers went to their father Jacob in the land of Canaan. They told him everything that had happened. ³⁰They said, "The master of that land spoke unkindly to us. He accused us of spying on his country. ³¹But we told him that we were honest men, not spies. ³²We told him that we were ten of 12 brothers—sons of one father. We said that one of our brothers was gone. And we said that our youngest brother was with our father in Canaan.

³³"Then the master of the land said to us, 'Here is a way I can know you are honest men: leave one of your brothers with me. Take back grain to feed your hungry families, and go. ³⁴And bring your youngest brother to me. Then I will know that you are not

spies but honest men. And I will give you back your brother whom you leave with me. And you can move about freely in our land'."

[35]Then the brothers emptied their sacks. And each of them found his money in his sack. When they and their father saw it, they were afraid.

[36]Their father Jacob said to them, "You are robbing me of all my children. Joseph is gone. Simeon is gone. And now you want to take Benjamin away, too. Everything is against me."

[37]Then Reuben said to his father, "You may put my two sons to death if I don't bring Benjamin back to you. Trust him to my care. I will bring him back to you."

[38]But Jacob said, "I will not allow Benjamin to go with you. His brother is dead. He is the only son left from my wife Rachel. I am afraid something terrible might happen to him during the trip to Egypt. Then I would be sad until the day I die."

The Brothers Go Back to Egypt

43 Still no food grew in the land of Canaan. [2]Jacob's family had eaten all the grain they had brought from Egypt. So Jacob said to them, "Go to Egypt again. Buy a little more grain for us to eat."

[3]But Judah said to Jacob, "The governor of that country strongly warned us. He said, 'Bring your brother back with you. If you don't, you will not be allowed to see me'. [4]If you will send Benjamin with us, we will go down and buy food for you. [5]But if you refuse to send Benjamin, we will not go. The governor of that country warned us. He said we would not see him if we didn't bring Benjamin with us."

[6]Jacob, also called Israel, said, "Why did you tell the man you had another brother? You have caused me a lot of trouble."

[7]The brothers answered, "He questioned us carefully about ourselves and our family. He asked us, 'Is your father still alive? Do you have another brother?' We just answered his questions. How could we know he would ask us to bring our other brother to him?"

[8]Then Judah said to his father Jacob, "Send Benjamin with me. Then we will go at once. Do this so that we, you and our children, may live and not die. [9]I will guarantee you that he will be safe. I will be personally responsible for him. If I don't bring him back to you, you can blame me all my life. [10]If we had not wasted all this time, we could have already made two trips."

[11]Then their father Jacob said to them, "If it has to be that way, then do this: take some of the best foods in our land in your packs. Give them to the man as a gift: some balm,[d] some honey, spices, myrrh,[d] pistachio nuts and almonds. [12]Take twice as much money with you this time. Take back the money that was returned to you in your sacks last time. Maybe it was a mistake. [13]And take Benjamin with you. Now leave and go to the man. [14]I pray that God All-Powerful will cause the governor to be merciful to you. I pray that he will allow Simeon and Benjamin to come back with you. If I am robbed of my children, then I am robbed of them!"

[15]So the brothers took the gifts. They also took twice as much money as they had taken the first time. And they took Benjamin. They hurried down to Egypt and stood before Joseph.

[16]In Egypt Joseph saw Benjamin with them. Joseph said to the servant in charge of his house, "Bring those men into my house. Kill an animal and prepare a meal. Those men will eat with me today at noon." [17]The servant did as Joseph told him. He brought the men to Joseph's house.

[18]The brothers were afraid when they were brought to Joseph's house. They thought, "We were brought here because of the money that was

put in our sacks on the first trip. He wants to attack us, make us slaves and take our donkeys." [19]So the brothers went to the servant in charge of Joseph's house. They spoke to him at the door of the house. [20]They said, "Sir, we came here once before to buy food. [21]While we were going home, we stopped for the night and opened our sacks. Each of us found all his money in his sack. We brought that money with us to give it back to you. [22]And we have brought more money. It is to pay for the food we want to buy this time. We don't know who put that money in our sacks."

[23]But the servant answered, "It's all right. Don't be afraid. Your God, the God of your father, must have put the money in your sacks. I got the money you paid me for the grain last time." Then the servant brought Simeon out to them.

[24]The servant led the men into Joseph's house. He gave them water, and they washed their feet. Then he gave their donkeys food to eat. [25]The men prepared their gift to give to Joseph when he arrived at noon. They had heard they were going to eat with him there.

[26]When Joseph came home, the brothers gave him the gift they had brought into the house. Then they bowed down to the ground to him. [27]Joseph asked them how they were doing. He said, "How is your aged father you told me about? Is he still alive?"

[28]The brothers answered, "Your servant, our father, is well. He is still alive." And they bowed low before Joseph to show him respect.

[29]Then Joseph saw his brother Benjamin, who had the same mother as he. Joseph asked, "Is this your youngest brother you told me about?" Then Joseph said to Benjamin, "God be good to you, my son!" [30]Then Joseph hurried off. He had to hold back the tears when he saw his brother Benjamin. So Joseph went into his room and cried there. [31]Then he washed his face and came out. He controlled himself and said, "Serve the meal."

[32]So they served Joseph at one table. They served his brothers at another table. And they served the Egyptians who ate with him at another table. This was because Egyptians did not like Hebrews and never ate with them. [33]Joseph's brothers were seated in front of him. They were in order of their ages, from oldest to youngest. And they looked at each other because they were so amazed. [34]Food from Joseph's table was taken to them. But Benjamin was given five times more food than the others. Joseph's brothers drank with him until they were very drunk.

Joseph Sets a Trap

44 Then Joseph gave a command to the servant in charge of his house. Joseph said, "Fill the men's sacks with as much grain as they can carry. And put each man's money into his sack with the grain. [2]Put my silver cup in the sack of the youngest brother. Also put his money for the grain in that sack." The servant did what Joseph told him.

[3]At dawn the brothers were sent away with their donkeys. [4]They were not far from the city when Joseph said to the servant in charge of his house, "Go after the men. When you catch up with them, say, 'Why have you paid back evil for good? [5]The cup you have stolen is the one my master uses for drinking. And he uses it for explaining dreams. You have done a very wicked thing!'"

[6]So the servant caught up with the brothers. He said to them what Joseph had told him to say.

[7]But the brothers said to the servant, "Why do you say these things? We would not do anything like that!

⁸We brought back to you the money we found in our sacks. We brought it back from the land of Canaan. So surely we would not steal silver or gold from your master's house. ⁹If you find that silver cup in the sack of one of us, then let him die. And we will be your slaves."

¹⁰The servant said, "We will do as you say. But only the man who has taken the cup will become my slave. The rest of you may go free."

¹¹Then every brother quickly lowered his sack to the ground and opened it. ¹²The servant searched the sacks, going from the oldest brother to the youngest. He found the cup in Benjamin's sack. ¹³The brothers tore their clothes to show they were sad. Then they put their sacks back on the donkeys. And they returned to the city.

¹⁴When Judah and his brothers went back to Joseph's house, Joseph was still there. The brothers bowed face down on the ground before him. ¹⁵Joseph said to them, "What have you done? Didn't you know that a man like me can learn things by signs and dreams?"

¹⁶Judah said, "Sir, what can we say? And how can we show we are not guilty? God has uncovered our guilt. So all of us will be your slaves, not just Benjamin."

¹⁷But Joseph said, "I will not make you all slaves! Only the man who stole the cup will be my slave. The rest of you may go back safely to your father."

¹⁸Then Judah went to Joseph and said, "Sir, please let me speak plainly to you. Please don't be angry with me. I know that you are as powerful as the king of Egypt himself. ¹⁹When we were here before, you asked us, 'Do you have a father or a brother?' ²⁰And we answered you, 'We have an old father. And we have a younger brother. He was born when our father was old. This youngest son's brother is dead.

So he is the only one of his mother's children left alive. And our father loves him very much'. ²¹Then you said to us, 'Bring that brother to me. I want to see him'. ²²And we said to you, 'That young boy cannot leave his father. If he leaves him, his father would die'. ²³But you said to us, 'You must bring your youngest brother. If you don't, you will not be allowed to see me again'. ²⁴So we went back to our father and told him what you had said.

²⁵"Later, our father said, 'Go again. Buy us a little more food'. ²⁶We said to our father, 'We cannot go without our youngest brother. Without our youngest brother, we will not be allowed to see the governor'. ²⁷Then my father said to us, 'You know that my wife Rachel gave me two sons. ²⁸One son left me. I thought, "Surely he has been torn apart by a wild animal." And I haven't seen him since. ²⁹Now you want to take this son away from me also. But something terrible might happen to him. Then I would be sad until the day I die'. ³⁰Now what will happen if we go home to our father without our youngest brother? He is the most important thing in our father's life. ³¹When our father sees that the young boy is not with us, he will die. And it will be our fault. We will cause the great sorrow that kills our father.

³²"I gave my father a guarantee that the young boy would be safe. I said to my father, 'If I don't bring him back to you, you can blame me all my life'. ³³So now, please allow me to stay here and be your slave. And let the young boy go back home with his brothers. ³⁴I cannot go back to my father if the boy is not with me. I couldn't stand to see my father that sad."

Joseph Reveals Who He Is

45 Joseph could not control himself in front of his servants any longer. He cried out, "Have everyone leave me." When only the brothers were left with Joseph, he told them who he was. [2]Joseph cried so loudly that the Egyptians heard him. And the people in the king's palace heard about it. [3]He said to his brothers, "I am Joseph. Is my father still alive?" But the brothers could not answer him, because they were very afraid of him.

[4]So Joseph said to them, "Come close to me." So the brothers came close to him. And he said to them, "I am your brother Joseph. You sold me as a slave to go to Egypt. [5]Now don't be worried. Don't be angry with yourselves because you sold me here. God sent me here ahead of you to save people's lives. [6]No food has grown on the land for two years now. And there will be five more years without planting or harvest. [7]So God sent me here ahead of you. This was to make sure you have some descendants[d] left on earth. And it was to keep you alive in an amazing way. [8]So it was not you who sent me here, but God. God has made me the highest officer of the king of Egypt. I am in charge of his palace. I am the master of all the land of Egypt.

[9]"So leave quickly and go to my father. Tell him, 'Your son Joseph says: God has made me master over all Egypt. Come down to me quickly. [10]Live in the land of Goshen. You will be near me. Also your children, your grandchildren, your flocks and herds and all that you have will be near me. [11]I will care for you during the next five years of hunger. In this way, you and your family and all that you have will not starve'.

[12]"Now you can see for yourselves. The one speaking to you is really Joseph. And my brother Benjamin can see this. [13]So tell my father about how powerful I have become in Egypt. Tell him about everything you have seen. Now hurry and bring him back to me." [14]Then Joseph hugged his brother Benjamin and cried. And Benjamin cried also. [15]Then Joseph kissed all his brothers. He cried as he hugged them. After this, his brothers talked with him.

[16]The king of Egypt and his officers learned that Joseph's brothers had come. And they were very happy about this. [17]So the king said to Joseph, "Tell your brothers to load their animals and go back to the land of Canaan. [18]Tell them to bring their father and their families back here to me. I will give them the best land in Egypt. And they will eat the best food we have here. [19]Tell them to take some wagons from Egypt for their children and their wives. And tell them to bring their father back also. [20]Tell them not to worry about bringing any of their things with them. We will give them the best of what we have in Egypt."

[21]So the sons of Israel did this. Joseph gave them wagons as the king had ordered. And he gave them food for their trip. [22]He gave each brother a change of clothes. But he gave Benjamin five changes of clothes. And Joseph gave him about 3.5 kilograms of silver. [23]Joseph also sent his father ten donkeys loaded with the best things from Egypt. And he sent ten female donkeys. They were loaded with grain, bread and other food for his father on his trip back. [24]Then Joseph told his brothers to go. As they were leaving, he said to them, "Don't quarrel on the way home."

[25]So the brothers left Egypt and went to their father Jacob in the land of Canaan. [26]They told him, "Joseph is still alive. He is the ruler over all the land of Egypt." Their father was shocked and did not believe them. [27]But the brothers told him everything Joseph had said. Then Jacob saw the wagons that Joseph had sent to carry him back to Egypt. Now Jacob felt better. [28]Jacob, also called Israel, said, "Now I believe you. My son Jo-

seph is still alive. I will go and see him before I die."

Jacob Goes to Egypt

46 So Jacob, also called Israel, took all he had and started his trip. He went to Beersheba. There he offered sacrifices to the God of his father Isaac. [2]During the night God spoke to Israel in a vision. He said, "Jacob, Jacob."

And Jacob answered, "Here I am."
[3]Then God said, "I am God, the God of your father. Don't be afraid to go to Egypt. I will make your descendants[d] a great nation there. [4]I will go to Egypt with you. And I will bring you out of Egypt again. Joseph's own hands will close your eyes when you die."

[5]Then Jacob left Beersheba. The sons of Israel loaded their father, their children and their wives. They put them in the wagons the king of Egypt had sent. [6]They also took their farm animals and everything they had gained in Canaan. So Jacob went to Egypt with all his descendants. [7]He took his sons and grandsons, his daughters and granddaughters. He took all his family to Egypt with him.

Jacob's Family

[8]Now these are the names of the children of Israel who went into Egypt. (They are Jacob and his descendants.[d])

Reuben was Jacob's first son. [9]Reuben's sons were Hanoch, Pallu, Hezron and Carmi.

[10]Simeon's sons were Jemuel, Jamin, Ohad, Jakin, Zohar and Shaul. (Shaul was Simeon's son by a Canaanite woman.)

[11]Levi's sons were Gershon, Kohath and Merari.

[12]Judah's sons were Er, Onan, Shelah, Perez and Zerah. (But Er and Onan had died in the land of Canaan.) Perez's sons were Hezron and Hamul.

[13]Issachar's sons were Tola, Puah, Jashub and Shimron.

[14]Zebulun's sons were Sered, Elon and Jahleel.

[15]These are the sons of Leah and Jacob born in North West Mesopotamia. His daughter Dinah was also born there. There were 33 people in this part of Jacob's family.

[16]Gad's sons were Zephon, Haggi, Shuni, Ezbon, Eri, Arodi and Areli.

[17]Asher's sons were Imnah, Ishvah, Ishvi and Beriah. Their sister was Serah. Beriah's sons were Heber and Malkiel.

[18]These are Jacob's sons by Zilpah. She was the slave girl whom Laban gave to his daughter Leah. There were 16 people in this part of Jacob's family.

[19]The sons of Jacob's wife Rachel were Joseph and Benjamin. [20]In Egypt, Joseph became the father of Manasseh and Ephraim by his wife Asenath. She was the daughter of Potiphera, priest of On.

[21]Benjamin's sons were Bela, Beker, Ashbel, Gera, Naaman, Ehi, Rosh, Muppim, Huppim and Ard.

[22]These are the sons of Jacob by his wife Rachel. There were 14 people in this part of Jacob's family.

[23]Dan's son was Hushim.

[24]Naphtali's sons were Jahziel, Guni, Jezer and Shillem.

[25]These are Jacob's sons by Bilhah. She was the slave girl whom Laban gave to his daughter Rachel. There were seven people in this part of Jacob's family.

[26]So the total number of Jacob's direct descendants who went to Egypt was 66. (The wives of Jacob's sons were not counted in this number.) [27]Joseph had two sons born in Egypt. So the total number in the family of Jacob in Egypt was 70.

Jacob Arrives in Egypt

[28]Jacob sent Judah ahead of him to see Joseph in Goshen. Then Jacob and

his people came into the land of Go-shen. ²⁹Joseph prepared his chariot and went to meet his father Israel in Goshen. As soon as Joseph saw his father, he hugged his neck. And he cried there for a long time.

³⁰Then Israel said to Joseph, "Now I am ready to die. I have seen your face. And I know that you are still alive."

³¹Joseph said to his brothers and his father's family, "I will go and tell the king you are here. I will say, 'My brothers and my father's family have left the land of Canaan. They have come here to me. ³²They are shepherds and take care of farm animals. And they have brought their flocks and their herds and everything they own with them'. ³³When the king calls you, he will ask, 'What work do you do?' ³⁴This is what you should tell him: 'We, your servants, have taken care of farm animals all our lives. Our ancestors did the same thing'. Then the king will allow you to settle in the land of Goshen. This is away from the Egyptians. They don't like to be near shepherds."

Jacob Settles in Goshen

47 Joseph went in to the king and said, "My father and my brothers have arrived from Canaan. They have their flocks and herds and everything they own with them. They are now in the land of Goshen." ²Joseph chose five of his brothers to introduce to the king.

³The king said to the brothers, "What work do you do?"

And they said to him, "We, your servants, are shepherds. Our ancestors were also shepherds." ⁴They said to the king, "We have come to live in this land. There is no grass in the land of Canaan for our animals to eat. The hunger is very terrible there. So please allow us to live in the land of Goshen."

⁵Then the king said to Joseph, "Your father and your brothers have come to you. ⁶You may choose any place in Egypt for them to live. Give your father and your brothers the best land. Let them live in the land of Goshen. And if any of them are skilled shepherds, put them in charge of my sheep and cattle."

⁷Then Joseph brought in his father Jacob and introduced him to the king. And Jacob blessed the king.

⁸Then the king said to Jacob, "How old are you?"

⁹Jacob said to him, "My life has been spent wandering from place to place. It has been short, filled with trouble. I have lived only 130 years. My ancestors lived much longer than I." ¹⁰Then Jacob blessed the king and left.

¹¹Joseph obeyed the king. He gave his father and brothers the best land in Egypt. It was near the city of Rameses. ¹²And Joseph gave his father, his brothers and everyone who lived with them the food they needed.

Joseph Buys Land for the King

¹³The hunger became worse, and there was no food anywhere in the land. The land of Egypt and the land of Canaan became very poor because of this. ¹⁴Joseph collected all the money that was to be found in Egypt and Canaan. People paid him this money for the grain they were buying. He brought that money to the king's palace. ¹⁵After some time, the people in Egypt and Canaan had no money left. So they went to Joseph and said, "Please give us food. Our money is gone. If we don't eat, we will die here in front of you."

¹⁶Joseph answered, "Since you have no money, give me your farm animals. I will give you food in return." ¹⁷So people brought their farm animals to Joseph. And he gave them food in exchange for their horses, sheep, cattle and donkeys. So he kept

them alive by trading food for their farm animals that year.

¹⁸The next year the people came to Joseph and said, "You know we have no money left. And all our animals belong to you. We have nothing left except our bodies and our land. ¹⁹Surely both we and our land will die here in front of you. Buy us and our land in exchange for food. And we will be slaves to the king, together with our land. Give us seed to plant. Then we will live and not die. And the land will not become a desert."

²⁰So Joseph bought all the land in Egypt for the king. Every Egyptian sold Joseph his field, because the hunger was very great. So the land became the king's. ²¹And Joseph made the people slaves from one end of Egypt to the other. ²²The only land he did not buy was the land the priests owned. They did not need to sell their land because the king paid them for their work. So they had money to buy food.

²³Joseph said to the people, "Now I have bought you and your land for the king. So I will give you seed. And you can plant your fields. ²⁴At harvest time you must give one-fifth to the king. You may keep four-fifths for yourselves. Use it as seed for the field and as food for yourselves, your families and your children."

²⁵The people said, "You have saved our lives. If you like, we will become slaves of the king."

²⁶So Joseph made a law in Egypt, which continues today: one-fifth of everything from the land belongs to the king. The only land the king did not get was the priests' land.

"Don't Bury Me in Egypt"

²⁷The Israelites continued to live in the land of Goshen in Egypt. There they got possessions. They had many children and grew in number.

²⁸Jacob, also called Israel, lived in Egypt 17 years. So he lived to be 147 years old. ²⁹Israel knew he soon would die. So he called his son Joseph to him. He said to Joseph, "If you love me, put your hand under my leg.ⁿ Promise me you will not bury me in Egypt. ³⁰When I die, carry me out of Egypt. Bury me where my ancestors are buried."

Joseph answered, "I will do as you say."

³¹Then Jacob said, "Promise me." And Joseph promised him that he would do this. Then Israel worshipped as he leaned on the top of his staff.

Blessings for Manasseh and Ephraim

48 Some time later Joseph learned that his father was very sick. So he took his two sons Manasseh and Ephraim and went to his father. ²When Joseph arrived, someone told Jacob, also called Israel, "Your son Joseph has come to see you." Jacob was weak. So he used all his strength and sat up on his bed.

³Then Jacob said to Joseph, "God All-Powerful appeared to me at Luz in the land of Canaan. God blessed me there. ⁴He said to me, 'I will give you many children. I will make you the father of many peoples. And I will give your descendantsᵈ this land for ever'. ⁵Your two sons were born here in Egypt before I came. They will be counted as my own sons. Ephraim and Manasseh will be my sons just as Reuben and Simeon are my sons. ⁶But if you have other children, they will be your own. But their land will be part of the land given to Ephraim and Manasseh. ⁷When I came from North West Mesopotamia, Rachel died in the land of Canaan. We were travelling toward Ephrath. This made me very sad. I buried her there beside the road to

put . . . leg This showed that a person would keep a promise.

Ephrath." (Today Ephrath is Bethlehem.)

⁸Then Israel saw Joseph's sons. He
said, "Who are these boys?"

⁹Joseph said to his father, "They are
my sons. God has given them to me
here in Egypt."

Israel said, "Bring your sons to me
so I may bless them."

¹⁰At this time Israel's eyesight was
bad because he was old. So Joseph
brought the boys close to him. Israel
kissed the boys and put his arms
around them. ¹¹He said to Joseph, "I
thought I would never see you alive
again. And now God has let me see
you and also your children." ¹²Then
Joseph moved his sons off Israel's lap.
Joseph bowed face down to the
ground. ¹³He put Ephraim on his right
side and Manasseh on his left. (So
Ephraim was near Israel's left hand,
and Manasseh was near Israel's right
hand.) Joseph brought the boys close
to Israel. ¹⁴But Israel crossed his
arms. He put his right hand on the
head of Ephraim, who was younger.
He put his left hand on the head of Manasseh. But he was the firstborn[d] son.

¹⁵And Israel blessed Joseph and said,
   "My ancestors Abraham and Isaac
       served our God.
   And like a shepherd God has led
       me all my life.
¹⁶He was the Angel who saved me
       from all my troubles.
   Now I pray that he will bless
       these boys.
   May my name be known through
       these boys.
   And may the names of my
       ancestors Abraham and Isaac
       be known through them.
   May they have many descendants[d]
       on the earth."

¹⁷Joseph saw that his father put his
right hand on Ephraim's head. Joseph
didn't like it. So he took hold of his father's hand. He wanted to move it
from Ephraim's head to Manasseh's

head. ¹⁸Joseph said to his father, "You
are doing it wrong, Father. Manasseh
is the firstborn son. Put your right
hand on his head."

¹⁹But his father refused and said, "I
know, my son, I know. Manasseh will
be great and have many descendants.
But his younger brother will be greater. And his descendants will be
enough to make a nation." ²⁰So Israel blessed them that day.
He said,
   "When a blessing is given in
       Israel, they will say:
   'May God make you like
       Ephraim and Manasseh'."
In this way he made Ephraim greater
than Manasseh.

²¹Then Israel said to Joseph, "Look
at me. I am about to die. But God will
be with you. He will take you back to
the land of your fathers. ²²I have given
you something that I did not give your
brothers. I have given you the land of
Shechem that I took from the Amorite
people. I took it with my sword and
my bow."

Jacob Blesses His Sons

49 Then Jacob called his sons to
him. He said, "Come here to
me. I will tell you what will happen to
you in the future.

²"Come together and listen, sons
       of Jacob.
   Listen to Israel, your father."
³"Reuben, my first son, you are
       my strength.
   Your birth showed I could be a
       father.
   You have the highest position
       among my sons.
   You are the most powerful.
⁴But you are uncontrolled like
       water.
   So you will no longer lead your
       brothers.
   This is because you got into your
       father's bed.

You shamed me by having
　　sexual relations with my
　　slave girl.
⁵"Simeon and Levi are brothers.
　　They used their swords to do
　　violence.
⁶I will not join their secret talks.
　　I will not meet with them to
　　plan evil.
They killed men because they
　　were angry.
　　And they crippled oxen just for
　　fun.
⁷May their anger be cursed,
　　because it is too violent.
May their violence be cursed,
　　because it is too cruel.
I will divide them up among the
　　tribes*ᵈ* of Jacob.
I will scatter them through all
　　the tribes of Israel.
⁸"Judah, your brothers will praise
　　you.
　　You will grab your enemies by
　　the neck.
Your brothers will bow down to
　　you.
⁹Judah is like a young lion.
　　You have returned from killing,
　　my son.
Like a lion, he stretches out and
　　lies down to rest.
　　No one is brave enough to wake
　　him.
¹⁰Men from Judah's family will be
　　kings.
　　Someone from Judah will always
　　be on the throne.
Judah will rule until the real king
　　comes.
　　And the nations will obey him.
¹¹He ties his donkey to a grapevine.
　　He ties his young donkey to the
　　best branch.
He can afford to use wine to wash
　　his clothes.
　　He even uses grape juice to
　　wash his robes.
¹²His eyes are bright from drinking
　　wine.

His teeth are white from
　　drinking milk.
¹³"Zebulun will live near the sea.
　　His shore will be a safe place for
　　ships.
　　His land will reach as far as
　　Sidon.
¹⁴"Issachar is like a strong donkey.
　　He lies down while carrying his
　　load.
¹⁵He will see his resting place is
　　good.
　　He will see how pleasant his
　　land is.
Then he will put his back to the
　　load.
　　He will become a slave.
¹⁶"Dan will rule his own people
　　like the other tribes in Israel.
¹⁷Dan will be like a snake by the
　　side of the road.
　　He will be like a dangerous
　　snake lying near the path.
That snake bites a horse's leg.
　　And the rider is thrown off
　　backwards.
¹⁸"Lord, I wait for your salvation.
¹⁹"Robbers will attack Gad.
　　But he will defeat them and
　　drive them away.
²⁰"Asher's land will grow much good
　　food.
　　He will grow food fit for a king.
²¹"Naphtali is like a female deer that
　　runs free.
　　She has beautiful fawns.
²²"Joseph is like a grapevine that
　　produces much fruit.
　　He is like a healthy vine watered
　　by a spring.
　　He is like a vine whose branches
　　grow over the wall.
²³Men attack him violently with
　　arrows.
　　They shoot at him angrily.
²⁴But he aims his bow well.
　　His arms are made strong.

He gets his power from the
   Mighty God of Jacob.
He gets his strength from the
   Shepherd, the Rock*d* of
   Israel.
25Your father's God helps you.
God All-Powerful blesses you.
He blesses you with rain from
   above.
He blesses you with water from
   springs below.
He blesses you with many babies
   born to your wives.
He blesses you with many
   young ones born to your
   animals.
26The blessings of your father are
   greater
than the blessings of the oldest
   mountains.
They are greater than the good
   things of the long-lasting
   hills.
May these blessings rest on the
   head of Joseph.
May they rest on the forehead
   of the one who was
   separated from his brothers.
27"Benjamin is like a hungry wolf.
In the morning he eats what he
   has caught.
In the evening he divides what
   he has taken."

28These are the 12 tribes of Israel.
And this is what their father said to
them. He gave each son the blessing
that was right for him. 29Then Israel
gave them a command. He said, "I am
about to die. Bury me with my ancestors in the cave in the field of Ephron
the Hittite. 30That cave is in the field
of Machpelah east of Mamre. It is in
the land of Canaan. Abraham bought
that field from Ephron the Hittite for
a burying place. 31Abraham and Sarah
his wife are buried there. Isaac and
Rebekah his wife are buried there. I
buried my wife Leah there. 32The field
and the cave in it were bought from
the Hittite people." 33After Jacob had

finished talking to his sons, he lay
down. He put his feet back on the bed,
took his last breath and died.

Jacob's Burial

50 When Jacob died, Joseph
hugged his father and cried
over him and kissed him. 2He commanded the doctors who served him
to prepare his father's body. So the
doctors prepared Jacob's body to be
buried. 3It took the doctors 40 days to
prepare his body. This was the usual
time it took. And the Egyptians had a
time of sorrow for Jacob. It lasted 70
days.
   4When this time of sorrow had ended, Joseph spoke to the king's officers. He said, "If you think well of me,
please tell this to the king: 5'When my
father was near death, I made a promise to him. I promised I would bury
him in a cave in the land of Canaan.
This is a burial place that he cut out for
himself. So please let me go and bury
my father. Then I will return'."
   6The king answered, "Keep your
promise. Go and bury your father."
   7So Joseph went to bury his father.
All the king's officers, the older leaders and all the leading men of Egypt
went with Joseph. 8Everyone who
lived with Joseph and his brothers
went with him. And everyone who
lived with his father also went. They
left only their children, their flocks
and their herds in the land of Goshen.
9Men in chariots and on horses also
went with Joseph. It was a very large
group.
   10They went to the threshing*d* floor
of Atad, east of the Jordan River.
There they cried loudly and bitterly
for Jacob, also called Israel. Joseph's
time of sorrow continued for seven
days. 11The people that lived in Canaan saw the sadness at the threshing
floor of Atad. They said, "Those
Egyptians are showing great sorrow!"
So now that place is named Sorrow of
the Egyptians.

¹²So Jacob's sons did what their father commanded. ¹³They carried his body to the land of Canaan. They buried it in the cave in the field of Machpelah near Mamre. Abraham had bought this cave and field from Ephron the Hittite. He bought the cave to use as a burial place. ¹⁴After Joseph had buried his father, he returned to Egypt. His brothers and everyone who had gone with him to bury his father also returned.

The Brothers Fear Joseph

¹⁵After Jacob died, Joseph's brothers said, "What if Joseph is still angry with us? We did many wrong things to him. What if he plans to pay us back?" ¹⁶So they sent a message to Joseph. It said, "Your father gave this command before he died. ¹⁷He said to us, 'You have done wrong. You have sinned and done evil to Joseph. Tell Joseph to forgive you, his brothers'. So now, Joseph, we beg you to forgive our wrong. We are the servants of the God of your father." When Joseph received the message, he cried.

¹⁸And his brothers went to him and bowed low before him. They said, "We are your slaves."

¹⁹Then Joseph said to them, "Don't be afraid. Can I do what only God can do? ²⁰You meant to hurt me. But God turned your evil into good. It was to save the lives of many people. And it is being done. ²¹So don't be afraid. I will take care of you and your children." So Joseph comforted his brothers and spoke kind words to them.

²²Joseph continued to live in Egypt with all his father's family. He died when he was 110 years old. ²³During Joseph's life Ephraim had children and grandchildren. And Joseph's son Manasseh had a son named Makir. Joseph accepted Makir's children as his own.

The Death of Joseph

²⁴Joseph said to his brothers, "I am about to die. But God will take care of you. He will lead you out of this land. He will lead you to the land he promised to Abraham, Isaac and Jacob." ²⁵Then Joseph had the sons of Israel make a promise. He said, "Promise me that you will carry my bones with you out of Egypt."

²⁶Joseph died when he was 110 years old. Doctors prepared his body for burial. Then they put him in a coffin in Egypt.

EXODUS

Escape from Egypt

Jacob's Family in Egypt

1 When Jacob, also called Israel, went to Egypt, he took his sons. And each son took his own family with him. These are the names of the sons of Israel: [2]Reuben, Simeon, Levi, Judah, [3]Issachar, Zebulun, Benjamin, [4]Dan, Naphtali, Gad and Asher. [5]There was a total of 70 people who were descendants[d] of Jacob. Jacob's son Joseph was already in Egypt.

[6]By some time later, Joseph and his brothers had died, along with all the people who had lived at that same time. [7]But the people of Israel had many children, and their number grew greatly. They became very strong, and the country of Egypt was filled with them.

Trouble for the People of Israel

[8]Then a new king began to rule Egypt. He did not know who Joseph was. [9]This king said to his people, "Look! The people of Israel are too many! And they are too strong for us to handle! [10]We must make plans against them. If we don't, the number of their people will grow even more. Then if there is a war, they might join our enemies. Then they could fight us and escape from the country!"

[11]So the Egyptians made life hard for the people of Israel. They put slave masters over the Israelites. The slave masters forced the Israelites to build the cities Pithom and Rameses for the king. These cities were supply centres in which the Egyptians stored things. [12]The Egyptians forced the Israelites to work even harder. But this made the Israelites grow in number and spread more. So the Egyptians

became more afraid of them. [13]They forced the Israelites to work even harder. [14]The Egyptians made life hard for the Israelites. They forced the Israelites to work very hard making bricks and mortar. They also forced them to do all kinds of hard work in the fields. The Egyptians were not merciful to them in all their hard work.

[15]There were two Hebrew nurses named Shiphrah and Puah. These nurses helped the Israelite women give birth to their babies. The king of Egypt said to the nurses, [16]"When you are helping the Hebrew women give birth to their babies, watch! If the baby is a girl, let the baby live. But if it is a boy, kill it!" [17]But the nurses feared God. So they did not do as the king told them. They let all the boy babies live. [18]Then the king of Egypt sent for the nurses. He said, "Why did you do this? Why did you let the boys live?"

[19]The nurses said to him, "The Hebrew women are much stronger than the Egyptian women. They give birth to their babies before we can get there." [20]God was good to the nurses. And the Hebrew people continued to grow in number. So they became even stronger. [21]Because the nurses feared God, he gave them families of their own.

[22]So the king commanded all his people: "Every time a boy is born to the Hebrews, you must throw him into the Nile River. But let all the girl babies live."

Baby Moses

2 There was a man from the family of Levi. He married a woman who

was also from the family of Levi. ²She became pregnant and gave birth to a son. She saw how wonderful the baby was, and she hid him for three months. ³But after three months, she was not able to hide the baby any longer. So she got a basket made of reeds and covered it with tar so that it would float. She put the baby in the basket. Then she put the basket among the tall grass at the edge of the Nile River. ⁴The baby's sister stood a short distance away. She wanted to see what would happen to him.

⁵Then the daughter of the king of Egypt came to the river. She was going to take a bath. Her servant girls were walking beside the river. She saw the basket in the tall grass. So she sent her slave girl to get it. ⁶The king's daughter opened the basket and saw the baby boy. He was crying, and she felt sorry for him. She said, "This is one of the Hebrew babies."

⁷Then the baby's sister asked the king's daughter, "Would you like me to find a Hebrew woman to nurse the baby for you?"

⁸The king's daughter said, "Yes, please." So the girl went and got the baby's own mother.

⁹The king's daughter said to the woman, "Take this baby and nurse him for me. I will pay you." So the woman took her baby and nursed him. ¹⁰After the child had grown older, the woman took him to the king's daughter. She adopted the baby as her own son. The king's daughter named him Moses,ⁿ because she had pulled him out of the water.

Moses Helps His People

¹¹Moses grew and became a man. One day he visited his people, the Hebrews. He saw that they were forced to work very hard. He saw an Egyptian beating a Hebrew man, one of Moses' own people. ¹²Moses looked all around and saw that no one was watching. So he killed the Egyptian and hid his body in the sand.

¹³The next day Moses returned and saw two Hebrew men fighting each other. He saw that one man was in the wrong. Moses said to that man, "Why are you hitting one of your own people?"

¹⁴The man answered, "Who made you our ruler and judge? Are you going to kill me as you killed the Egyptian?"

Then Moses was afraid. He thought, "Now everyone knows what I did."

¹⁵When the king heard about what Moses had done, he tried to kill Moses. But Moses ran away from the king and went to live in the land of Midian. There he sat down near a well.

Moses in Midian

¹⁶There was a priest in Midian who had seven daughters. His daughters went to that well to get water for their father's sheep. They were trying to fill the water troughs for their father's sheep. ¹⁷But some shepherds came and chased the girls away. Then Moses defended the girls and watered their sheep.

¹⁸Then they went back to their father, Reuel, also called Jethro. He asked them, "Why have you come home early today?"

¹⁹The girls answered, "The shepherds chased us away. But an Egyptian defended us. He got water for us and watered our sheep.

²⁰He asked his daughters, "Where is this man? Why did you leave him? Invite him to eat with us."

²¹Moses agreed to stay with Jethro. And Jethro gave his daughter Zipporah to Moses to be his wife. ²²Zipporah gave birth to a son, and Moses named him

Moses The name Moses sounds like the Hebrew word for "to pull out".

Gershom.ⁿ Moses named him this because Moses was a stranger in a land that was not his own.

23After a long time, the king of Egypt died. The people of Israel groaned because they were forced to work very hard. They cried for help. And God heard them. 24God heard their cries, and he remembered the agreement he had made with Abraham, Isaac and Jacob. 25God saw the troubles of the people of Israel, and he was concerned about them.

The Burning Bush

3 One day Moses was taking care of Jethro's sheep. Jethro was the priest of Midian and also Moses' father-in-law. Moses led the sheep to the west side of the desert. He came to Sinai, the mountain of God. 2There the angel of the Lord appeared to Moses in flames of fire coming out of a bush. Moses saw that the bush was on fire, but it was not burning up. 3So Moses said, "I will go closer to this strange thing. How can a bush continue burning without burning up?"

4The Lord saw Moses was coming to look at the bush. So God called to him from the bush, "Moses, Moses!"

And Moses said, "Here I am."

5Then God said, "Do not come any closer. Take off your sandals. You are standing on holy ground. 6I am the God of your ancestors. I am the God of Abraham, the God of Isaac and the God of Jacob." Moses covered his face because he was afraid to look at God.

7The Lord said, "I have seen the troubles my people have suffered in Egypt. And I have heard their cries when the Egyptian slave masters hurt them. I am concerned about their pain. 8I have come down to save them from the Egyptians. I will bring them

out of that land. I will lead them to a good land with lots of room. This is a land where much food grows. This is the land of these people: the Canaanites, Hittites, Amorites, Perizzites, Hivites and Jebusites. 9I have heard the cries of the people of Israel. I have seen the way the Egyptians have made life hard for them. 10So now I am sending you to the king of Egypt. Go! Bring my people, the Israelites, out of Egypt!"

11But Moses said to God, "I am not a great man! Why should I be the one to go to the king and lead the Israelites out of Egypt?"

12God said, "I will be with you. This will be the proof that I am sending you: you will lead the people out of Egypt. Then all of you will worship me on this mountain."

13Moses said to God, "When I go to the Israelites, I will say to them, 'The God of your fathers sent me to you'. What if the people say, 'What is his name?' What should I tell them?"

14Then God said to Moses, "I AM WHO I AM.ⁿ When you go to the people of Israel, tell them, 'I AM sent me to you'."

15God also said to Moses, "This is what you should tell the people: 'The Lord is the God of your ancestors. He is the God of Abraham, the God of Isaac and the God of Jacob. And he sent me to you'. This will always be my name. That is how people from now on will know me.

16"Go and gather the older leaders and tell them this: 'The Lord, the God of your ancestors, has appeared to me. The God of Abraham, Isaac and Jacob spoke to me. He says: I care about you, and I have seen what has happened to you in Egypt. 17I have decided that I will take you away from the troubles you are suffering in

---

Gershom This name sounds like the Hebrew word meaning "a stranger there".
I . . . I AM The Hebrew words are like the name "YAHWEH". This Hebrew name for God, usually called "Lord", shows that God always lives and is always with his people.

Egypt. I will lead you to the land of the Canaanites, Hittites, Amorites, Perizzites, Hivites and Jebusites. This land grows much food'.

18"The older leaders will listen to you. And then you and the older leaders of Israel will go to the king of Egypt. You will tell him, 'The Lord, the God of the Hebrews, appeared to us. Let us travel three days into the desert. There we must offer sacrifices to the Lord our God'.

19"But I know that the king of Egypt will not let you go. Only a great power will force him to let you go. 20So I will use my great power against Egypt. I will make miracles[d] happen in that land. After I do this, he will let you go. 21And I will cause the Egyptian people to think well of the people of Israel. So when you leave, they will give gifts to your people. 22Each Hebrew woman will ask her Egyptian neighbour and any Egyptian woman living in her house for gifts. Ask for silver, gold and clothing. You will put those gifts on your children when you leave Egypt. In this way you will take with you the riches of the Egyptians."

Proof for Moses

4 Then Moses answered, "What if the people of Israel do not believe me or listen to me? What if they say, 'The Lord did not appear to you'?"

2The Lord said to him, "What is that in your hand?"

Moses answered, "It is my staff."

3The Lord said, "Throw it on the ground."

So Moses threw it on the ground. And it became a snake. Moses ran from the snake. 4But the Lord said to him, "Reach out and grab the snake by its tail." So Moses reached out and took hold of the snake. When he did this, it again became a staff in his hand. 5The Lord said, "When this happens, the Israelites will believe that the Lord appeared to you. I am the

God of their ancestors. I am the God of Abraham, the God of Isaac and the God of Jacob."

6Then the Lord said to Moses, "Put your hand inside your coat." So Moses put his hand inside his coat. When he took his hand out, it was white with a harmful skin disease.

7Then the Lord said, "Now put your hand inside your coat again." So Moses put his hand inside his coat again. When he took it out, his hand was healthy again. It was like the rest of his skin.

8Then the Lord said, "The people may not believe you or be convinced by the first miracle.[d] They may believe you when you show them this second miracle. 9After these two miracles they still may not believe or listen to you. Then take some water from the Nile River. Pour it on the dry ground. The water will become blood when it touches the ground."

10But Moses said to the Lord, "But Lord, I am not a skilled speaker. I have never been able to speak well. And now, even after talking to you, I am not a good speaker. I speak slowly and can't find the best words."

11Then the Lord said to him, "Who made man's mouth? And who makes him deaf or not able to speak? Or who gives a man sight or makes him blind? It is I, the Lord. 12Now go! I will help you speak. I will tell you what to say."

13But Moses said, "Please, Lord, send someone else."

14The Lord became angry with Moses. He said, "Your brother Aaron, from the family of Levi, is a skilled speaker. He is already coming to meet you. And he will be happy when he sees you. 15I will tell you what to say. Then you will tell Aaron. I will help both of you know what to say and do. 16And Aaron will speak to the people for you. You will tell him what God says. And he will speak for you. 17Take your walking stick with you. Use it to do the miracles."

Moses Returns to Egypt

18Then Moses went back to Jethro, his father-in-law. Moses said to him, "Let me go back to my people in Egypt. I want to see if they are still alive."

Jethro said to Moses, "You may go. Have a safe trip."

19While Moses was still in Midian, the Lord said to him, "Go back to Egypt. The men who wanted to kill you are dead now."

20So Moses took his wife and his sons and put them on a donkey. Then he started back to Egypt. He took with him the staff of God.

21The Lord said to Moses, "When you get back to Egypt, do all the miracles.d I have given you the power to do them. Show them to the king of Egypt. But I will make the king very stubborn. He will not let the people go. 22Then say to the king: 'This is what the Lord says: Israel is my first-bornd son. 23And I told you to let my son go. Let him go so he may worship me. But you refused to let Israel go. So I will kill your firstborn son'."

24As Moses was on his way to Egypt, he stopped at a resting place for the night. The Lord met him there and tried to kill him. 25But Zipporah took a flint knife and circumcisedd her son. She took the skin and touched Moses' feet with it. Then she said to him, "You are a bridegroom of blood to me." 26Zipporah said this because she had to circumcise her son. So the Lord did not kill Moses.

27Meanwhile the Lord said to Aaron, "Go out into the desert to meet Moses." When Aaron went, he met Moses at Sinai, the mountain of God, and kissed him. 28Moses told Aaron everything the Lord had said to him when he sent him to Egypt. And Moses told him about the miracles which the Lord had commanded him to do. 29So Moses and Aaron gathered all the older leaders of the Israelites.

30Aaron told them everything that the Lord had told Moses. Then Moses did the miracles for all the people to see. 31So the Israelites believed. They heard that the Lord was concerned about them and had seen their troubles. Then they bowed down and worshipped him.

Moses and Aaron Before the King

5 After Moses and Aaron talked to the people, they went to the king of Egypt. They said, "This is what the Lord, the God of Israel says: 'Let my people go so they may hold a feast for me in the desert'."

2But the king of Egypt said, "Who is the Lord? Why should I obey him and let Israel go? I do not know the Lord. And I will not let Israel go."

3Then Aaron and Moses said, "The God of the Hebrews has talked with us. Now let us travel for three days into the desert. There we will offer sacrifices to the Lord our God. If we don't do this, he may kill us with a disease or in war."

4But the king said to them, "Moses and Aaron, why are you taking the people away from their work? Go back to your hard work! 5There are very many Hebrews. And now you want them to stop their hard work!"

6That same day the king gave a command to the slave masters and foremen. 7He said, "Don't give the people straw to make bricks as you used to do. Let them gather their own straw. 8But they must still make the same number of bricks as they did before. Do not accept fewer. They have become lazy. That is why they are asking me, 'Let us go to offer sacrifices to our God'. 9Make these people work harder. Keep them busy. Then they will not have time to listen to the lies of Moses."

10So the slave masters and foremen went to the Israelites and said, "This is what the king says: I will no longer give you straw. 11Go and get your

own straw wherever you can find it.
But you must make as many bricks as
you made before." ¹²So the people
went everywhere in Egypt looking for
dry stalks to use for straw. ¹³The
slave masters kept forcing the people
to work harder. They said, "You must
make just as many bricks as you did
when you were given straw." ¹⁴The
king's slave masters had chosen the
Israelite foremen. They had made
them responsible for the work the
people did. The Egyptian slave masters beat these men and asked them,
"Why aren't you making as many
bricks as you made in the past?"

¹⁵Then the Israelite foremen went
to the king. They complained and
said, "Why are you treating us, your
servants, this way? ¹⁶You give us no
straw. But we are commanded to
make bricks. Our slave masters beat
us. But it is your own people's fault."

¹⁷The king answered, "You are
lazy! You don't want to work! That is
why you ask to leave here and make
sacrifices to the Lord. ¹⁸Now, go back
to work! We will not give you any
straw. But you must make just as
many bricks as you did before."

¹⁹The Israelite foremen knew they
were in trouble. This was because the
king had told them: "You must make
just as many bricks each day as you
did before." ²⁰As they were leaving
the meeting with the king, they met
Moses and Aaron. Moses and Aaron
were waiting for them. ²¹So they said
to Moses and Aaron, "May the Lord
punish you. You caused the king and
his officers to hate us. You have given
them an excuse to kill us."

Moses Complains to God

²²Then Moses returned to the Lord
and said, "Lord, why have you
brought this trouble on your people?
Is this why you sent me here? ²³I
went to the king and said what you
told me to say. But ever since that
time he has made the people suffer.

And you have done nothing to save
them."

6 Then the Lord said to Moses,
"Now you will see what I will do to
the king of Egypt. I will use my great
power against him, and he will let my
people go. Because of my power,
he will force them out of his country."

²Then God said to Moses, "I am the
Lord. ³I appeared to Abraham, Isaac
and Jacob by the name, God All-
Powerful. But they did not know me
by my name, the Lord. ⁴I also made
my agreement with them to give them
the land of Canaan. They lived in that
land, but it was not their own land.
⁵Now I have heard the cries of the Israelites. The Egyptians are treating
them as slaves. And I remember my
agreement. ⁶So tell the people of Israel that I say to them, 'I am the Lord.
I will save you from the hard work the
Egyptians force you to do. I will make
you free. You will not be slaves to the
Egyptians. I will free you by my great
power. And I will punish the Egyptians terribly. ⁷I will make you my own
people, and I will be your God. You
will know that I am the Lord your
God. I am the One who saves you
from the hard work the Egyptians
force you to do. ⁸I will lead you to the
land that I promised to Abraham,
Isaac and Jacob. I will give you that
land to own. I am the Lord'."

⁹So Moses told this to the people of
Israel. But they would not listen to
him. They were discouraged, and
their slavery was hard.

¹⁰Then the Lord said to Moses,
¹¹"Go and tell the king of Egypt that he
must let the Israelites leave his land."

¹²But Moses answered, "The Israelites will not listen to me. So surely
the king will not listen to me, either.
I am not a good speaker."

¹³But the Lord told Moses and Aaron to talk to the king. He commanded
them to lead the Israelites out of
Egypt.

Families of Israel

[14]These are the leaders of the families of Israel:

Israel's first son, Reuben, had four sons. They were Hanoch, Pallu, Hezron and Carmi. These are the family groups of Reuben. [15]Simeon's sons were Jemuel, Jamin, Ohad, Jakin, Zohar and Shaul. Shaul was the son of a Canaanite woman. These are the family groups of Simeon. [16]Levi lived for 137 years. These are the names of his sons according to their family history: Gershon, Kohath and Merari. [17]Gershon had two sons, Libni and Shimei, with their families. [18]Kohath lived for 133 years. The sons of Kohath were Amram, Izhar, Hebron and Uzziel. [19]The sons of Merari were Mahli and Mushi.

These are the family groups of Levi, according to their family history. [20]Amram married his father's sister Jochebed. Jochebed gave birth to Aaron and Moses. Amram lived for 137 years. [21]Izhar's sons were Korah, Nepheg and Zicri. [22]Uzziel's sons were Mishael, Elzaphan and Sithri. [23]Aaron married Elisheba. She was the daughter of Amminadab and the sister of Nahshon. Elisheba gave birth to Nadab, Abihu, Eleazar and Ithamar. [24]The sons of Korah were Assir, Elkanah and Abiasaph. These are the family groups of the Korahites. [25]Eleazar son of Aaron married a daughter of Putiel. And she gave birth to Phinehas.

These are the leaders of the family groups of the Levites. [26]This was the Aaron and Moses to whom the Lord spoke. He said, "Lead my people out of Israel in their divisions." [27]Aaron and Moses are the ones who talked to the king of Egypt. They told him to let the people of Israel leave Egypt.

God Repeats His Call to Moses

[28]The Lord spoke to Moses in the land of Egypt. [29]He said, "I am the Lord. Tell the king of Egypt everything I tell you."

[30]But Moses answered, "I am not a good speaker. The king will not listen to me."

7 The Lord said to Moses, "I have made you like God to the king of Egypt. And your brother Aaron will be like a prophet[d] for you. [2]Tell Aaron your brother everything that I command you. Then let him tell the king of Egypt to let the Israelites leave his country. [3]But I will make the king stubborn. Then I will do many miracles[d] in Egypt. [4]But he will still refuse to listen. So then I will punish Egypt terribly. And I will lead my divisions, my people the Israelites, out of that land. [5]I will punish Egypt with my power. And I will bring the Israelites out of that land. Then they will know I am the Lord."

[6]Moses and Aaron did just as the Lord had commanded them. [7]Moses was 80 years old, and Aaron was 83, when they spoke to the king.

Aaron's Staff Becomes a Snake

[8]The Lord said to Moses and Aaron, [9]"The king will ask you to do a miracle.[d] When he does, Moses, you tell Aaron to throw his staff down in front of the king. It will become a snake."

[10]So Moses and Aaron went to the king as the Lord had commanded. Aaron threw his staff down in front of the king and his officers. And it became a snake.

[11]So the king called in his wise men and his magicians. With their tricks the Egyptian magicians were able to do the same thing. [12]They threw their

staffs on the ground, and their staffs became snakes. But then Aaron's staff swallowed theirs. [13]But the king was stubborn. He refused to listen to Moses and Aaron, just as the Lord had said.

The Water Becomes Blood

[14]Then the Lord said to Moses, "The king is being stubborn. He refuses to let the people go. [15]In the morning the king will go out to the Nile River. Go and meet him by the edge of the river. Take with you the staff that became a snake. [16]Tell him this: The Lord, the God of the Hebrews, sent me to you. He said, 'Let my people go to worship me in the desert'. Until now you have not listened. [17]This is what the Lord says: 'This is how you will know that I am the Lord. I will strike the water of the Nile River with this staff in my hand. And the water will change into blood. [18]Then the fish in the Nile will die, and the river will begin to stink. And the Egyptians will not be able to drink the water from the Nile'."

[19]The Lord said to Moses, "Tell Aaron to stretch the staff in his hand over the rivers, canals, ponds and pools in Egypt. The water will become blood everywhere in Egypt. There even will be blood in the wooden buckets and stone jars."

[20]So Moses and Aaron did just as the Lord had commanded. Aaron raised his staff and struck the water in the Nile River. He did this in front of the king and his officers. So all the water in the Nile changed into blood. [21]The fish in the Nile died, and the river began to stink. So the Egyptians could not drink water from it. Blood was everywhere in the land of Egypt.

[22]Using their tricks, the magicians of Egypt did the same thing. So the king was stubborn and refused to listen to Moses and Aaron. This happened just as the Lord had said. [23]The king turned and went into his palace. He ignored what Moses and Aaron had done. [24]The Egyptians could not drink the water from the Nile. So all of them dug along the bank of the river. They were looking for water to drink.

The Frogs

[25]Seven days passed after the Lord changed the Nile River.

8 Then the Lord told Moses, "Go to the king of Egypt and tell him, 'This is what the Lord says: Let my people go to worship me. [2]If you refuse, then I will punish Egypt with frogs. [3]The Nile River will be filled with frogs. They will come from the river and enter your palace. They will be in your bedroom and your bed. The frogs will enter the houses of your officers and your people. They will enter your ovens and your baking pans. [4]The frogs will jump up all over you, your people and your officers'."

[5]Then the Lord said to Moses, "Tell Aaron to hold his staff in his hand over the rivers, canals and ponds. Make frogs come up out of the water onto the land of Egypt."

[6]So Aaron held his hand over all the waters of Egypt. The frogs came up out of the water and covered the land of Egypt. [7]The magicians used their tricks to do the same thing. So even more frogs came up onto the land of Egypt.

[8]So the king called for Moses and Aaron. He said, "Pray to the Lord to take the frogs away from me and my people. I will let your people go to offer sacrifices to the Lord."

[9]Moses said to the king, "Please set the time that I should pray for you, your people and your officers. Then the frogs will leave you and your houses. They will remain only in the Nile."

[10]The king answered, "Tomorrow."

Moses said, "What you want will happen. By this you will know that there is no one like the Lord our God.

11The frogs will leave you, your houses, your officers and your people. They will remain only in the Nile."

12Moses and Aaron left the king. Moses asked the Lord about the frogs he had sent to the king. 13And the Lord did as Moses asked. The frogs died in the houses, in the yards and in the fields. 14The Egyptians put them in piles. The whole country began to stink. 15When the king saw that they were free of the frogs, he became stubborn again. He did not listen to Moses and Aaron, just as the Lord had said.

The Gnats

16Then the Lord said to Moses, "Tell Aaron to raise his staff and strike the dust on the ground. Then everywhere in Egypt the dust will change into gnats." 17They did this. Aaron raised the staff that was in his hand and struck the dust on the ground. Then everywhere in Egypt the dust changed into gnats. The gnats got on the people and animals. 18Using their tricks, the magicians tried to do the same thing. But they could not make the dust change into gnats. The gnats remained on the people and animals. 19So the magicians told the king that the power of God had done this. But the king was stubborn and refused to listen to them. This happened just as the Lord had said.

The Flies

20The Lord told Moses, "Get up early in the morning. Meet the king of Egypt as he goes out to the river. Tell him, 'This is what the Lord says: Let my people go so they can worship me. 21If you don't let them go, I will send swarms of flies. I will send them into your houses. The flies will be on you, your officers and your people. The houses of Egypt will be full of flies. And they will be all over the ground, too. 22But I will not treat the people of

Israel the same as the Egyptian people. There will not be any flies in the land of Goshen, where my people live. By this you will know that I, the Lord, am in this land. 23I will treat my people differently from your people. This miracle[d] will happen tomorrow'."

24So the Lord did as he had said. Great swarms of flies came into the king's palace and his officers' houses. All over Egypt flies were ruining the land. 25The king called for Moses and Aaron. He told them, "Offer sacrifices to your God here in this country."

26But Moses said, "It wouldn't be right to do that. The Egyptians hate the sacrifices we offer to the Lord our God. They will see us offer sacrifices they hate. Then they will throw stones at us and kill us. 27Let us make a three-day journey into the desert. We must offer sacrifices to the Lord our God there. This is what the Lord told us to do."

28The king said, "I will let you go. Then you may offer sacrifices to the Lord your God in the desert. But you must not go very far away. Now go and pray for me."

29Moses said, "I will leave and pray to the Lord. He will take the flies away from you, your officers and your people tomorrow. But do not try to trick us again. Do not stop the people from going to offer sacrifices to the Lord."

30So Moses left the king and prayed to the Lord. 31And the Lord did as Moses asked. He removed the flies from the king, his officers and his people. Not one fly was left. 32But the king became stubborn again and did not let the people go.

The Disease on the Farm Animals

9 Then the Lord told Moses, "Go to the king of Egypt. Tell him, 'This is what the Lord, the God of the Hebrews, says: Let my people go to worship me. 2You might refuse to let

them go and continue to hold them. ³Then the Lord will punish you. He will send a terrible disease on all your farm animals. He will cause all of your horses, donkeys, camels, cattle and sheep to become sick. ⁴But the Lord will treat Israel's animals differently from the animals of Egypt. None of the animals that belong to the Israelites will die. ⁵The Lord has set tomorrow as the time he will do this in the land'." ⁶The next day the Lord did as he promised. All the farm animals in Egypt died. But none of the animals belonging to the Israelites died. ⁷The king sent people to see what had happened to the animals of Israel. They found that not one of them had died. But the king was still stubborn. He did not let the people go.

The Boils

⁸The Lord said to Moses and Aaron, "Fill your hands with the ashes from a furnace. Moses, throw the ashes into the air in front of the king of Egypt. ⁹The ashes will spread like dust through all the land of Egypt. The dust will cause boils to break out and become sores on the skin. These sores will be on people and animals everywhere in the land."

¹⁰So Moses and Aaron took ashes from a furnace. Then they went and stood before the king. Moses threw ashes into the air. It caused boils to break out and become sores on people and animals. ¹¹The magicians could not stand before Moses. This was because all the Egyptians had boils, even the magicians. ¹²But the Lord made the king stubborn. So he refused to listen to Moses and Aaron. This happened just as the Lord had said.

The Hail

¹³Then the Lord said to Moses, "Get up early in the morning and go to the king of Egypt. Tell him, 'This is what the Lord, the God of the Hebrews, says: Let my people go to worship me. ¹⁴If you do not do this, this time I will punish you with all my power. I will punish you, your officers and your people. Then you will know that there is no one in the whole land like me. ¹⁵By now I could have used my power and caused a bad disease. It would have destroyed you and your people from the earth. ¹⁶But I have let you live for this reason: to show you my power. In this way my name will be talked about in all the earth. ¹⁷You are still against my people. You do not want to let them go. ¹⁸So at this time tomorrow, I will send a terrible hailstorm. It will be the worst in Egypt since it became a nation. ¹⁹Now send for your animals and whatever you have in the fields. Bring them into a safe place. The hail will fall on every person or animal that is still in the fields. If they have not been brought in, they will die'." ²⁰Some of the king's officers respected the word of the Lord. They hurried to bring their slaves and animals inside. ²¹But others ignored the Lord's message. They left their slaves and animals in the fields.

²²The Lord told Moses, "Raise your hand toward the sky. Then the hail will start falling over all the land of Egypt. It will fall on people, animals and on everything that grows in the fields of Egypt." ²³So Moses raised his staff toward the sky. And the Lord sent thunder and hail. And lightning flashed down to the earth. So he caused hail to fall upon the land of Egypt. ²⁴There was hail, and there was lightning flashing as it hailed. This was the worst hailstorm in Egypt since it had become a nation. ²⁵The hail destroyed everything that was in the fields in all the land of Egypt. The hail destroyed both people and animals. It also destroyed everything that grew in the fields. It broke all the trees in the fields. ²⁶The only place that it did not hail was in the land of Goshen. The people of Israel lived there.

²⁷The king sent for Moses and Aaron. He told them, "This time I have sinned. The Lord is in the right. And I and my people are in the wrong. ²⁸Pray to the Lord. We have had enough of God's thunder and hail. I will let you go. You do not have to stay here any longer."

²⁹Moses told the king, "When I leave the city, I will raise my hands to the Lord in prayer. And the thunder and hail will stop. Then you will know that the earth belongs to the Lord. ³⁰But I know that you and your officers do not yet fear the Lord God."

³¹The flax was in bloom, and the barley had ripened. So these crops were destroyed. ³²But both wheat crops ripen later. So they were not destroyed.

³³Moses left the king and went outside the city. He raised his hands to the Lord. And the thunder and hail stopped. The rain also stopped falling to the ground. ³⁴The king saw that the rain, hail and thunder had stopped. Then he sinned again. He and his officers became stubborn again. ³⁵The king became stubborn and refused to let the Israelites go. This happened just as the Lord had said through Moses.

The Locusts

10 The Lord said to Moses, "Go to the king of Egypt. I have made him and his officers stubborn. I did this so I could show them my powerful miracles.ᵈ ²I also did this so you could tell your children and your grandchildren. Tell them how I made fools of the Egyptians. Tell them about the miracles I did among them. Then all of you will know that I am the Lord."

³So Moses and Aaron went to the king. They told him, "This is what the Lord, the God of the Hebrews, says: 'How long will you refuse to be sorry for what you have done? Let my people go to worship me. ⁴If you refuse to let my people go, tomorrow I will bring locustsᵈ into your country. ⁵They will cover the land, and no one will be able to see the ground. They will eat anything that was left from the hailstorm. They will eat the leaves from every tree growing in the field. ⁶They will fill your palaces and all your officers' houses. They will fill the houses of all the Egyptian people. There will be more locusts than your fathers or ancestors have ever seen. There will be more locusts than there have been since people began living in Egypt'." Then Moses turned and walked away from the king.

⁷The king's officers asked him, "How long will this man make trouble for us? Let the Israelite men go to worship the Lord their God. Don't you know that Egypt is ruined?"

⁸So Moses and Aaron were brought back to the king. He said to them, "Go and worship the Lord your God. But tell me, just who is going?"

⁹Moses answered, "We will go with our young and our old people, our sons and daughters and sheep and cattle. This is because we are going to have a feast to honour the Lord."

¹⁰The king said to them, "The Lord really will have to be with you if ever I let you and all of your children leave Egypt. See, you are planning something evil. ¹¹No! Only the men may go and worship the Lord. That is what you have been asking for." Then the king forced Moses and Aaron out of his palace.

¹²The Lord told Moses, "Raise your hand over the land of Egypt, and the locusts will come. They will spread all over the land of Egypt. They will eat all the plants that the hail did not destroy."

¹³So Moses raised his staff over the land of Egypt. And the Lord caused a strong wind to blow from the east. It blew across the land all that day and night. When morning came, the east wind had brought the locusts.

14Swarms of locusts covered all the land of Egypt and settled everywhere. There were more locusts than ever before or after. 15The locusts covered the whole land so that it was black. They ate everything that was left after the hail. They ate every plant in the field and all the fruit on the trees. Nothing green was left on any tree or plant anywhere in Egypt.

16The king quickly called for Moses and Aaron. He said, "I have sinned against the Lord your God and against you. 17Now forgive my sin this time. Pray to the Lord your God. Ask him to stop this punishment that kills."

18Moses left the king and prayed to the Lord. 19So the Lord changed the wind. He made a very strong wind to blow from the west. It blew the locusts away into the Red Sea.d Not one locust was left anywhere in Egypt. 20But the Lord caused the king to be stubborn again. And he did not let the people of Israel go.

The Darkness

21Then the Lord told Moses, "Raise your hand toward the sky, and darkness will cover the land of Egypt. It will be so dark you will be able to feel it." 22So Moses raised his hand toward the sky. Then total darkness was everywhere in Egypt for three days. 23No one could see anyone else. And no one could go anywhere for three days. But the Israelites had light where they lived.

24Again the king of Egypt called for Moses. He said, "All of you may go and worship the Lord. You may take your women and children with you. But you must leave your sheep and cattle here."

25Moses said, "You must let us have animals to use as sacrifices and burnt offerings. We have to offer them to the Lord our God. 26So we must take our animals with us. Not a hoof will be left behind. We have to use some of the animals to worship the Lord our God. We do not yet know exactly what we will need to worship the Lord. We will know when we get there."

27But the Lord made the king stubborn again. So he refused to let them go. 28Then he told Moses, "Get out of here! Don't come here again! The next time you see me, you will die."

29Then Moses told the king, "I'll do what you say. I will not come to see you again."

The Death of the Firstborn

11 Now the Lord had told Moses, "I have one more way to punish the king and the people of Egypt. After this, the king will send all of you away from Egypt. When he does, he will force you to leave completely. 2Tell the men and women of Israel to ask their neighbours for things made of silver and gold." 3The Lord had caused the Egyptians to respect the Israelites. The king's officers and the Egyptian people already considered Moses to be a great man.

4So Moses said to the king, "This is what the Lord says: 'About midnight tonight I will go through all Egypt. 5Every firstbornd son in the land of Egypt will die. The firstborn son of the king, who sits on his throne, will die. Even the firstborn of the slave girl grinding grain will die. Also the firstborn farm animals will die. 6There will be loud crying everywhere in Egypt. It will be worse than any time before or after this. 7But not even a dog will bark at the Israelites or their animals'. Then you will know that the Lord treats Israel differently from Egypt. 8Then all your officers will come to me. They will bow face down to the ground before me. They will say, 'Leave and take all your people with you'. After that, I will leave." Then Moses very angrily left the king.

9The Lord had told Moses, "The king will not listen to you and Aaron. This is so that I may do many miracles*d* in the land of Egypt." ¹⁰Moses and Aaron did all these great miracles in front of the king. But the Lord made him stubborn. And the king would not let the people of Israel leave his country.

Passover

12 The Lord spoke to Moses and Aaron in the land of Egypt: ²"This month will be the first month of the year for you. ³Both of you are to tell the whole community of Israel: on the tenth day of this month each man must get one lamb. It is for the people in his house. ⁴There may not be enough people in his house to eat a whole lamb. Then he must share it with his closest neighbour. There must be enough lamb for everyone to eat. ⁵The lamb must be a one-year-old male. It must have nothing wrong with it. This animal can be either a young sheep or a young goat. ⁶Keep the animal with you to take care of it until the fourteenth day of the month. On that day all the people of the community of Israel will kill these animals. They will do this as soon as the sun goes down. ⁷The people must take some of the blood. They must put it on the sides and tops of the doorframes. These are the doorframes of the houses where they eat the lambs. ⁸On this night they must roast the lamb over a fire. Then they must eat it with bitter herbs and bread made without yeast. ⁹Do not eat the lamb raw or boiled in water. Roast the whole lamb over a fire — with its head, legs and inner organs. ¹⁰You must not leave any of it until morning. But if any of it is left over until morning, you must burn it with fire. ¹¹"This is the way you must eat it: you must be fully dressed as if you were going on a trip. You must have your sandals on, and you must have your staff in your hand. You must eat it in a hurry. This is the Lord's Passover.*d*

¹²"That night I will go through the land of Egypt. I will kill all the firstborn*d* of animals and people in the land of Egypt. I will punish all the gods of Egypt. I am the Lord. ¹³But the blood will be a sign on the houses where you are. When I see the blood, I will pass over you. Nothing terrible will hurt you when I punish the land of Egypt. ¹⁴"You are always to remember this day. Celebrate it with a feast to the Lord. Your descendants*d* are to honour the Lord with this feast from now on. ¹⁵For this feast you must eat bread made without yeast for seven days. On the first day of this feast, you are to remove all the yeast from your houses. No one should eat any yeast for the full seven days of the feast. If anyone eats yeast, then that person will be separated from Israel. ¹⁶You are to have holy meetings on the first and last days of the feast. You must not do any work on these days. The only work you may do on these days is to prepare your meals. ¹⁷You must celebrate the Feast*d* of Unleavened Bread. Do this because on this very day I brought your divisions of people out of Egypt. So all of your descendants must celebrate this day. This is a law that will last from now on. ¹⁸You are to eat bread made without yeast. Start this on the evening of the fourteenth day of the first month of your year. Eat this until the evening of the twenty-first day. ¹⁹For seven days there must not be any yeast in your houses. Anybody who eats yeast during this time must be separated from the community of Israel. This includes Israelites and non-Israelites. ²⁰During this feast you must not eat yeast. You must eat bread made without yeast wherever you live."

²¹Then Moses called all the older leaders of Israel together. He told them, "Get the animals for your families. Kill the animals for the Passover. ²²Take a branch of the hyssop plant and dip it into the bowl filled with

blood. Wipe the blood on the sides and tops of the doorframes. No one may leave his house until morning. ²³The Lord will go through Egypt to kill the Egyptians. He will see the blood on the sides and tops of the doorframes. Then the Lord will pass over that house. He will not let the one who brings death come into your houses and kill you.

²⁴"You must keep this command. This law is for you and your descendants from now on. ²⁵Do this when you go to the land the Lord has promised to give to you. ²⁶When your children ask you, 'Why are we doing these things?' ²⁷you will say, 'This is the Passover sacrifice to honour the Lord. When we were in Egypt, the Lord passed over the houses of Israel. The Lord killed the Egyptians, but he saved our homes'." So now the people bowed down and worshipped the Lord. ²⁸They did just as the Lord commanded Moses and Aaron.

²⁹At midnight the Lord killed all the firstborn sons in the land of Egypt. The firstborn of the king, who sat on the throne, died. Even the firstborn of the prisoner in jail died. Also all the firstborn farm animals died. ³⁰The king, his officers and all the Egyptians got up during the night. Someone had died in every house. So there was loud crying everywhere in Egypt.

Israel Leaves Egypt

³¹During the night the king called for Moses and Aaron. He said to them, "Get up and leave my people. You and your people may do as you have asked. Go and worship the Lord. ³²Take all of your sheep and cattle as you have asked. Go. And also bless me." ³³The Egyptians also asked the Israelites to hurry and leave. They said, "If you don't leave, we shall all die!"

³⁴The people of Israel took their dough before the yeast was added. They wrapped the bowls for making dough in clothing and carried them on their shoulders. ³⁵The people of Israel did what Moses told them to do. They asked their Egyptian neighbours for things made of silver and gold and for clothing. ³⁶The Lord caused the Egyptians to think well of the Israelites. So the Israelites took rich gifts from the Egyptians.

³⁷The Israelites travelled from Rameses to Succoth. There were about 600,000 men walking. This does not include the women and children. ³⁸Many other people who were not Israelites went with them. A large number of sheep, goats and cattle went with them. ³⁹The Israelites used the dough they had brought out of Egypt. They baked loaves of bread without yeast. The dough had no yeast in it because they had been rushed out of Egypt. So they had no time to get food ready for their trip.

⁴⁰The people of Israel had lived in Egypt for 430 years. ⁴¹On the day the 430 years ended, the Lord's divisions of people left Egypt. ⁴²That night the Lord kept watch to bring them out of Egypt. So on this same night the Israelites are to keep watch. They are to do this to honour the Lord from now on.

⁴³The Lord told Moses and Aaron, "Here are the rules for Passover:ᵈ no foreigner is to eat the Passover. ⁴⁴Suppose a person buys a slave and circumcisesᵈ him. Then the slave may eat the Passover. ⁴⁵But no one who lives for a short time in your country may eat it. No hired worker may eat it.

⁴⁶"The meal must be eaten inside the house. None of the meat is to be taken outside the house. Don't break any of the bones. ⁴⁷The whole community of Israel must take part in this feast. ⁴⁸A foreigner who lives with you may share in the Lord's Passover. But first all the males in his house must be circumcised. Then, since he will be like a citizen of Israel, he may

share in the meal. But a man who is not circumcised may not eat the Passover meal. ⁴⁹The same rules apply to an Israelite born in the country. And they apply to a foreigner living there." ⁵⁰So all the Israelites did just as the Lord had commanded Moses and Aaron. ⁵¹Then on that same day, the Lord led the Israelites out of Egypt. The people left by divisions.

The Law of the Firstborn

13 Then the Lord said to Moses, ²"Give every firstborn*ᵈ* male to me. Every firstborn male among the Israelites belongs to me, whether human or animal."

³Moses said to the people, "Remember this day, the day you left Egypt. You were slaves in that land. The Lord with his great power brought you out of it. You must not eat bread made with yeast. ⁴Today, in the month of Abib,*ᵈ* you are leaving Egypt. ⁵The Lord made a promise to your ancestors. The Lord promised to give you the land of these people: the Canaanites, Hittites, Amorites, Hivites and Jebusites. The Lord will lead you to this land where much food grows. There you must celebrate this feast during the first month of every year. ⁶For seven days you must eat bread made without yeast. On the seventh day there will be a feast to honour the Lord. ⁷So for seven days you must not eat any bread made with yeast. There must be no bread made with yeast anywhere in your land. ⁸On that day you should tell your son: 'We are having this feast because of what the Lord did for me when I came out of Egypt'. ⁹This feast will help you remember. It will be like a mark on your hand. It will be like a reminder on your forehead. This feast will remind you to speak the Lord's teachings. This is because the Lord used his great power to bring you out of Egypt. ¹⁰So celebrate this feast every year at the right time.

¹¹"The Lord will take you into the land of the Canaanites. He promised to give this land to you and your ancestors. ¹²Then you must give him every firstborn male. And every firstborn male animal must be given to the Lord. ¹³Buy back every firstborn donkey by offering a lamb. If you don't want to buy the donkey back, then break its neck. You must buy back from the Lord every firstborn of your sons.

¹⁴"From now on your son will ask you: 'What does this mean?' You will answer, 'With his great power, the Lord brought us out of Egypt. We were slaves in that land. ¹⁵In Egypt the king was stubborn. He refused to let us leave. But the Lord killed every firstborn male in Egypt, both human and animal. That is why I sacrifice every firstborn male animal to the Lord. And that is why I buy back each of my firstborn sons from the Lord'. ¹⁶This feast is like a mark on your hand. And it is like a reminder on your forehead. It will help you remember that the Lord brought us out of Egypt with his great power."

The Way Out of Egypt

¹⁷The king sent the people out of Egypt. God did not lead them on the road through the Philistine country. That road is the shortest way. But God said, "They might think they will have to fight. Then they might change their minds and go back to Egypt." ¹⁸So God led them through the desert toward the Red Sea.*ᵈ* The Israelites were dressed for fighting when they left the land of Egypt.

¹⁹Moses carried the bones of Joseph with him. Before Joseph died, he had made the sons of Israel promise to do this. He had said, "When God saves you, remember to carry my bones with you out of Egypt."

²⁰The people of Israel left Succoth and camped at Etham. Etham was on the edge of the desert. ²¹The Lord

showed them the way. During the day he went ahead of them in a pillar of cloud. And during the night the Lord was in a pillar of fire to give them light. They could travel during the day or night. ²²The pillar of cloud was always with them during the day. And the pillar of fire was always with them at night.

14 Then the Lord said to Moses, ²"Tell the Israelites to turn back to Pi Hahiroth. Tell them to camp for the night between Migdol and the Red Sea. This is near Baal Zephon. ³The king will think, 'The Israelites are lost, trapped by the desert'. ⁴I will make the king stubborn again so he will chase after them. But I will defeat the king and his army. This will bring honour to me. Then the people of Egypt will know that I am the Lord." The people of Israel did just as they were told.

The King Chases the Israelites

⁵The king of Egypt was told that the people of Israel had already left. Then he and his officers changed their minds about them. They said, "What have we done? We have let the people of Israel leave. We have lost our slaves!" ⁶So the king prepared his war chariot and took his army with him. ⁷He took 600 of his best chariots. He also took all the other chariots of Egypt. Each chariot had an officer in it. ⁸The Lord made the king of Egypt stubborn. So he chased the Israelites, who were leaving victoriously. ⁹The king of Egypt came with his horses, chariot drivers and army. And they chased the Israelites. They caught up with the Israelites while they were camped by the Red Sea.ᵈ This was near Pi Hahiroth and Baal Zephon.

¹⁰The Israelites saw the king and his army coming after them. They were very frightened and cried to the Lord for help. ¹¹They said to Moses, "What have you done to us? Why did you bring us out of Egypt to die in the

desert? There were plenty of graves for us in Egypt. ¹²We told you in Egypt, 'Let us alone! Let us stay and serve the Egyptians'. Now we will die in the desert."

¹³But Moses answered, "Don't be afraid! Stand still and see the Lord save you today. You will never see these Egyptians again after today. ¹⁴You will only need to remain calm. The Lord will fight for you."

¹⁵Then the Lord said to Moses, "Why are you crying out to me? Command the people of Israel to start moving. ¹⁶Raise your staff and hold it over the sea. The sea will split. Then the people can cross the sea on dry land. ¹⁷I have made the Egyptians stubborn so they will chase the Israelites. But I will be honoured when I defeat the king and all of his chariot drivers and chariots. ¹⁸I will defeat the king, his chariot drivers and chariots. Then Egypt will know that I am the Lord."

¹⁹The angel of God usually travelled in front of Israel's army. Now the angel of God moved behind them. Also, the pillar of cloud moved from in front of the people and stood behind them. ²⁰So the cloud came between the Egyptians and the people of Israel. The cloud made it dark for the Egyptians. But it gave light to the Israelites. So the cloud kept the two armies apart all night.

²¹Moses held his hand over the sea. All that night the Lord drove back the sea with a strong east wind. And so he made the sea become dry ground. The water was split. ²²And the Israelites went through the sea on dry land. A wall of water was on both sides.

²³Then all the king's horses, chariots and chariot drivers followed them into the sea. ²⁴Between two and six o'clock in the morning, the Lord looked down from the pillar of cloud and fire at the Egyptian army. He made them panic. ²⁵He kept the wheels of the chariots from turning.

This made it hard to drive the chariots. The Egyptians shouted, "Let's get away from the Israelites! The Lord is fighting for them and against us Egyptians."

²⁶Then the Lord told Moses, "Hold your hand over the sea. Then the water will come back over the Egyptians, their chariots and chariot drivers." ²⁷So Moses raised his hand over the sea. And at dawn the water became deep again. The Egyptians were trying to run from it. But the Lord swept them away into the sea. ²⁸The water became deep again. It covered the chariots and chariot drivers. So all the king's army that had followed the Israelites into the sea was covered. Not one of them survived.

²⁹But the people of Israel crossed the sea on dry land. There was a wall of water on their right and on their left. ³⁰So that day the Lord saved the Israelites from the Egyptians. And the Israelites saw the Egyptians lying dead on the seashore. ³¹When the people of Israel saw the great power that the Lord had used against the Egyptians, they feared the Lord. And they trusted the Lord and his servant Moses.

The Song of Moses

15 Then Moses and the Israelites sang this song to the Lord:

"I will sing to the Lord
    because he is worthy of great
        honour.
He has thrown the horse and its
        rider
    into the sea.
²The Lord gives me strength and
        makes me sing.
    He has saved me.
He is my God,
    and I will praise him.
He is the God of my fathers,
    and I will honour him.
³The Lord is a great warrior.
    The Lord is his name.

⁴The chariots and soldiers of the
        king of Egypt
    he has thrown into the sea.
The king's best officers
    are drowned in the Red Sea.ᵈ
⁵The deep waters covered them.
    They sank to the bottom like a
        rock.

⁶Your right hand, Lord,
    is amazingly strong.
Lord, your right hand
    broke the enemy into pieces.
⁷In your great victory
    you destroyed those who were
        against you.
Your anger destroyed them,
    like fire burning straw.
⁸Just a blast of your breath,
    and the waters were blown
        back.
The moving water stood up like a
        wall.
And the deep waters became
    solid in the middle of the
        sea.

⁹"The enemy boasted,
    'I'll chase them and catch them.
I'll take all their riches.
I'll take all I want.
I'll pull out my sword,
    and my hand will destroy them'.
¹⁰But you blew on them with your
        breath
    and covered them with the sea.
They sank like lead
    in the powerful water.

¹¹"Are there any gods like you,
        Lord?
    No! There are no gods like you.
You are wonderfully holy.
You are amazingly powerful.
You do great miracles.ᵈ
¹²You reached out with your right
        hand,
    and the earth swallowed our
        enemies.

¹³You keep your loving promise.
    You lead the people you have
        saved.

With your strength you will guide
  them
to your holy land.
14"The other nations will hear this
    and tremble with fear.
Terror will take hold of the
    Philistines.
15The leaders of the tribes[d] of
    Edom will be very
    frightened.
The powerful men of Moab will
    shake with fear.
The people of Canaan will lose all
    their courage.
16Those people will be filled with
    fear.
When they see your strength,
  they will be as still as a rock.
They will be still until your people
    pass by, Lord.
They will be still until the people
    you have bought from
    slavery pass by.
17You will lead your people and
    place them
on your very own mountain.
Lord, that is the place that you
    made for yourself to live.
Lord, that is the temple that
    your hands have made.
18The Lord will rule for ever!"

19The horses, chariot drivers and
chariots of the king of Egypt went into
the sea. And the Lord covered them
with water from the sea. But the Israelites walked through the sea on dry
land. 20Then Aaron's sister Miriam,
who was a prophetess,[d] took a tambourine[d] in her hand. All the women
followed her, playing tambourines and
dancing. 21Miriam told them:

"Sing to the Lord
  because he is worthy of great
    honour.
He has thrown the horse and its
    rider
  into the sea."

Marah This name means "bitter".

The Bitter Water

22Moses led the people of Israel
away from the Red Sea.[d] The people
went into the Desert of Shur. They
travelled for three days in the desert
but found no water. 23Then they came
to Marah, where there was water.
But they could not drink it because it
was too bitter. That is why the place
was named Marah.[n] 24The people
grumbled to Moses. They asked,
"What will we drink?"

25Moses cried out to the Lord. So
the Lord showed him a tree. Moses
threw the tree into the water. And the
water became good to drink.

There the Lord gave the people a
rule and a law to live by. There he also
tested their loyalty to him. 26He said,
"You must obey the Lord, your God.
You must do what the Lord said is
right. You must obey all his laws and
keep his rules. If you do these things,
I will not give you any of the sicknesses I gave the Egyptians. I am the
Lord. I am the Lord who heals you."

27Then the people travelled to Elim.
At Elim there were 12 springs of water and 70 palm trees. So the people
camped there near the water.

The People Demand Food

16 Then the whole Israelite community left Elim. They came to
the Desert of Sin. This place was between Elim and Sinai. They came to
this place on the fifteenth day of the
second month after they had left
Egypt. 2Then the whole Israelite community grumbled to Moses and Aaron
in the desert. 3The Israelites said to
them, "It would have been better if
the Lord had killed us in the land of
Egypt. There we had meat to eat. We
had all the food we wanted. But you
have brought us into this desert. You
will starve us to death here."

4Then the Lord said to Moses, "I

will cause food to fall like rain from the sky. This food will be for all of you. Every day the people must go out and gather what they need for that day. I will do this to see if the people will do what I teach them. ⁵On the sixth day of each week, they are to gather twice as much as they gather on other days. Then they are to prepare it."

⁶So Moses and Aaron said to all the Israelites: "This evening you will know that the Lord is the one who brought you out of Egypt. ⁷Tomorrow morning you will see the greatness of the Lord. He has heard you grumble against him. We are nothing. You are not grumbling against us, but against the Lord." ⁸And Moses said, "Each evening the Lord will give you meat to eat. And every morning he will give you all the bread you want. He will do this because he has heard you grumble against him. You are not grumbling against Aaron and me. You are grumbling against the Lord."

⁹Then Moses said to Aaron, "Speak to the whole community of the Israelites. Say to them, 'Meet together in front of the Lord because he has heard your grumblings'."

¹⁰So Aaron spoke to the whole community of the Israelites. While he was speaking, they looked toward the desert. There the greatness of the Lord appeared in a cloud.

¹¹The Lord said to Moses, ¹²"I have heard the grumblings of the people of Israel. So tell them, 'At twilight you will eat meat. And every morning you will eat all the bread you want. Then you will know I am the Lord, your God'."

¹³That evening, quail came and covered the camp. And in the morning dew lay around the camp. ¹⁴When the dew was gone, thin flakes like frost were on the desert ground. ¹⁵When the Israelites saw it, they asked each other, "What is that?" They asked this question because they did not know what it was.

So Moses told them, "This is the bread the Lord has given you to eat. ¹⁶The Lord has commanded, 'Each one of you must gather what he needs. Gather about 2 litres for every person in your family'."

¹⁷So the people of Israel did this. Some people gathered much, and some gathered little. ¹⁸Then they measured it. The person who gathered more did not have too much. The person who gathered less did not have too little. Each person gathered just as much as he needed.

¹⁹Moses said to them, "Don't keep any of it to eat the next day." ²⁰But some of the people did not listen to Moses. They kept part of it to eat the next morning. But it became full of worms and began to stink. So Moses was angry with these people.

²¹Every morning each person gathered as much food as he needed. But when the sun became hot, it melted away.

²²On the sixth day the people gathered twice as much food. They gathered 4.5 litres for every person. So all the leaders of the community came and told this to Moses. ²³Moses said to them, "This is what the Lord commanded. Tomorrow is the Sabbath,ᵈ the Lord's holy day of rest. Bake what you want to bake, and boil what you want to boil today. But save the rest of the food until tomorrow morning."

²⁴So the people saved it until the next morning, as Moses had commanded. And none of it began to stink or have worms in it. ²⁵Moses told the people, "Eat the food you gathered yesterday. Today is a Sabbath, the Lord's day of rest. So you will not find any out in the field today. ²⁶You should gather the food for six days. But the seventh day is a Sabbath day. On that day there will not be any food on the ground."

²⁷On the seventh day some of the people went out to gather food, but they couldn't find any. ²⁸Then the

Lord said to Moses, "How long will all you people refuse to obey my commands and teachings? [29]Look, the Lord has made the Sabbath a day of rest for all of you. So on the sixth day he will give you enough food for two days. But on the Sabbath each of you must stay where you are. Do not leave your house." [30]So the people rested on the Sabbath.

[31]The people of Israel called the food manna.[d] The manna was like small white seeds. It tasted like wafers made with honey.

[32]Then Moses said, "The Lord said, 'Save 2 litres of this food for your descendants.[d] Then they can see the food that I gave you to eat. I did this in the desert when I brought you out of Egypt'."

[33]Moses told Aaron, "Take a jar and fill it with 2 litres of manna. And save this manna for your descendants." [34]So Aaron did what the Lord had commanded Moses. Aaron put the jar of manna in front of the Ark[d] of God. He did this so it could be kept. [35]The Israelites ate manna for 40 years. They ate it until they came to the land where they settled. They ate manna until they came to the edge of the land of Canaan. [36]The measure they used for the manna was 2 litres. It was one-tenth of an ephah.[n]

Water from a Rock

17 The whole Israelite community left the Desert of Sin. They travelled from place to place as the Lord commanded. They camped at Rephidim. But there was no water there for the people to drink. [2]So they quarrelled with Moses. They said, "Give us water to drink."

But Moses said to them, "Why do you quarrel with me? Why are you testing the Lord?"

[3]But the people were very thirsty for water. So they grumbled against Moses. They said, "Why did you bring us out of Egypt? Was it to kill us, our children and our farm animals with thirst?"

[4]So Moses cried to the Lord, "What can I do with these people? They are almost ready to kill me with stones."

[5]The Lord said to Moses, "Go ahead of the people of Israel. And take some of the older leaders of Israel with you. Carry with you the staff that you used to strike the Nile River. Now go! [6]I will stand in front of you on a rock at Mount Sinai. Hit that rock with the staff, and water will come out of it. Then the people can drink." Moses did these things as the older leaders of Israel watched. [7]Moses named that place Massah[n] because the Israelites tested the Lord. They asked, "Is the Lord with us or not?" He also named it Meribah[n] because they quarrelled.

The Amalekites Fight Israel

[8]At Rephidim the Amalekites came and fought the Israelites. [9]So Moses said to Joshua, "Choose some men and go and fight the Amalekites. Tomorrow I will stand on the top of the hill. I will hold the staff God gave me to carry."

[10]Joshua obeyed Moses and went to fight the Amalekites. At the same time Moses, Aaron and Hur went to the top of the hill. [11]As long as Moses held his hands up, the Israelites would win the fight. But when Moses put his hands down, the Amalekites would win. [12]Later, Moses' arms became tired. So the men put a large rock under Moses, and he sat on it. Then Aaron and Hur held up Moses' hands. Aaron was on one side of Moses, and Hur was on the other side. They held

---

ephah An ephah was a measure that equalled 20 litres.
Massah This name sounds like the Hebrew word for "testing".
Meribah This name sounds like the Hebrew word for "quarrelled".

his hands up like this until the sun went down. 13So Joshua defeated the Amalekites in this battle.

14Then the Lord said to Moses, "Write about this battle in a book so people will remember. And be sure to tell Joshua. Tell him because I will completely destroy the Amalekites from the earth."

15Then Moses built an altar. He named it The Lord is my Banner. 16Moses said, "I lifted my hands toward the Lord's throne. The Lord will fight against the Amalekites for ever."

Jethro Visits Moses

18 Jethro, Moses' father-in-law, was the priest of Midian. He heard about everything that God had done for Moses and his people, the Israelites. Jethro heard how the Lord had led the Israelites out of Egypt. 2Moses had sent his wife Zipporah to Jethro, his father-in-law. 3Moses had also sent his two sons. The first son was named Gershom.ⁿ When he was born, Moses said, "I am a stranger in a foreign country." 4The other son was named Eliezer.ⁿ When he was born, Moses said, "The God of my father is my help. He saved me from the king of Egypt."

5So Jethro, Moses' father-in-law, went to Moses. Moses was camped in the desert near Sinai, the mountain of God. Moses' wife and his two sons came with Jethro. 6Jethro had sent a message ahead to Moses. He said, "I am Jethro, your father-in-law. I am coming to you with your wife and her two sons."

7So Moses went out to meet his father-in-law. Moses bowed down and then kissed him. The two men asked about each other's health. Then they went into Moses' tent. 8Moses told his father-in-law everything the Lord had done to the king and the Egyptians. The Lord had done these things to help Israel. Moses told of all the problems they had faced along the way. And Moses told him how the Lord had saved them.

9Jethro was very happy when he heard all the good things the Lord had done for Israel. He was happy because the Lord had saved them from the Egyptians. 10Jethro said, "Praise the Lord. He has saved all of you from the Egyptians and their king. He has saved the people from the power of the Egyptians. 11Now I know the Lord is greater than all gods. He did this to those who looked down on Israel." 12Then Jethro, Moses' father-in-law, gave a whole burnt offering and other sacrifices to God. Aaron and all the older leaders of Israel came to Moses' father-in-law. They ate the holy meal together before God.

13The next day Moses solved disagreements among the people. So the people stood around Moses from morning until night. 14Moses' father-in-law saw all that Moses was doing for the people. He asked, "What is all this you are doing for the people? Why are you the only one to solve disagreements? All the people are standing around you from morning until night!"

15Then Moses said to his father-in-law, "It is because the people come to me for God's help in solving their disagreements. 16When people have a disagreement, they come to me. I decide who is right. And I tell them God's laws and teachings."

17Moses' father-in-law said to him, "You are not doing this right. 18You and the people who come to you will get too tired. This is too much work for you. You can't do it by yourself. 19Now listen to me. I will give you some advice. I want God to be with you. You must talk to God for the peo-

Gershom This name sounds like the Hebrew word for "a stranger there".
Eliezer This name sounds like the Hebrew word for "my help".

ple. You must tell him about their disagreements. 20You should tell them the laws and teachings. Tell them the right way to live and what they should do. 21But choose some capable men from among the people. Choose men who respect God and who can be trusted. They will not change their decisions for money. Make these men officers over groups of 1,000, 100, 50 and ten people. 22Let these officers solve the disagreements among the people all the time. They can bring the hard cases to you. But they can decide the simple cases themselves. That will make it easier for you. These men will share the work with you. 23Do this if it is what God commands. Then you will be able to do your job. And all the people will go home with their disagreements solved."

24So Moses listened to his father-in-law and did everything he said. 25He chose capable men from all the Israelites. He made them leaders over the people. They were officers over groups of 1,000, 100, 50 and ten people. 26These officers solved disagreements among the people all the time. They brought the hard cases to Moses. But they decided the simple cases themselves.

27Then Moses let his father-in-law leave. And Jethro went back to his own home.

Israel at Sinai

19 Exactly three months after the Israelites had left Egypt, they reached the Desert of Sinai. 2They had left Rephidim and had come to the Desert of Sinai. The Israelites camped in the desert in front of Mount Sinai. 3Then Moses went up on the mountain to God. The Lord called to him from the mountain. The Lord said, "Say this to the family of Jacob. And tell this to the people of Israel: 4'Every one of you has seen what I did to the people of Egypt. You saw how I carried you out of Egypt. I did it as

an eagle carries her young on her wings. And I brought you here to me. 5So now obey me and keep my agreement. Do this, and you will be my own possession, chosen from all nations. Even though the whole earth is mine, 6you will be my kingdom of priests. You will be a nation that belongs to me alone'. You must tell the Israelites these words."

7So Moses went down and called the older leaders of the people together. He told them all the words the Lord had commanded him to say. 8And all the people answered together, "We will do everything he has said." Then Moses took their answer back to the Lord.

9And the Lord said to Moses, "I will come to you in a thick cloud. I will speak to you. The people will hear me talking to you. I will do this so the people will always trust you." Then Moses told the Lord what the people had said.

10The Lord said to Moses, "Go to the people and have them spend today and tomorrow preparing themselves. They must wash their clothes 11and be ready by the day after tomorrow. On that day I, the Lord, will come down on Mount Sinai. And all the people will see me. 12But you must set a limit around the mountain. The people are not to cross it. Tell the people not to go up on the mountain. Tell them not to touch the foot of it. Anyone who touches the mountain must be put to death. 13He must be put to death with stones or shot with arrows. No one is allowed to touch him. Whether it is a person or an animal, he will not live. But the trumpet will make a long blast. Only then may the people go up on the mountain."

14So Moses went down from the mountain to the people. He made them prepare themselves for service to God. And the people washed their clothes. 15Then Moses said to the people, "Be ready in three days. Do not have sexual relations during this time."

¹⁶It was the morning of the third day. There was thunder and lightning with a thick cloud on the mountain. And there was a very loud blast from a trumpet. All the people in the camp were frightened. ¹⁷Then Moses led the people out of the camp to meet God. They stood at the foot of the mountain. ¹⁸Mount Sinai was covered with smoke. This happened because the Lord came down on it in fire. The smoke rose from the mountain like smoke from a furnace. And the whole mountain shook wildly. ¹⁹The sound from the trumpet became louder. Then Moses spoke, and the voice of God answered him.

²⁰So the Lord came down on the top of Mount Sinai. Then he called Moses to come up to the top of the mountain. So Moses went up. ²¹The Lord said to Moses, "Go down and warn the people. They must not force their way through to see me. If they do, many of them will die. ²²Even the priests, who may come near me, must first prepare themselves. If they don't, I, the Lord, will punish them."

²³Moses told the Lord, "The people cannot come up Mount Sinai. You yourself told us to set a limit around the mountain. We made it holy."

²⁴The Lord said to him, "Go down and bring Aaron with you. But don't allow the priests or the people to force their way through. They must not come up to the Lord. If they do, I will punish them."

²⁵So Moses went down to the people and told them these things.

The Ten Commandments

20 Then God spoke all these words:

²"I am the Lord your God. I brought you out of the land of Egypt where you were slaves.

³"You must not have any other gods except me.

⁴"You must not make for yourselves any idols. Don't make something that looks like anything in the sky above or on the earth below or in the water below the land. ⁵You must not worship or serve any idol. This is because I, the Lord your God, am a jealous God. A person may sin against me and hate me. I will punish his children, even his grandchildren and great-grandchildren. ⁶But I will be very kind to thousands who love me and obey my commands.

⁷"You must not use the name of the Lord your God thoughtlessly. The Lord will punish anyone who is guilty and misuses his name.

⁸"Remember to keep the Sabbath*d* as a holy day. ⁹You may work and get everything done during six days each week. ¹⁰But the seventh day is a day of rest to honour the Lord your God. On that day no one may do any work: not you, your son or daughter, or your men or women slaves. Neither your animals nor the foreigners living in your cities may work. ¹¹The reason is that in six days the Lord made everything. He made the sky, earth, sea and everything in them. And on the seventh day, he rested. So the Lord blessed the Sabbath day and made it holy.

¹²"Honour your father and your mother. Then you will live a long time in the land. The Lord your God is going to give you this land.

¹³"You must not murder anyone.

¹⁴"You must not be guilty of adultery.*d*

¹⁵"You must not steal.

¹⁶"You must not tell lies about your neighbour in court.

¹⁷"You must not want to take your neighbour's house. You must not want his wife or his men or women slaves. You must not want his ox or his donkey. You must not want to take anything that belongs to your neighbour."

¹⁸The people heard the thunder and the trumpet. They saw the lightning

on the mountain and smoke rising from the mountain. They shook with fear and stood far away from the mountain. ¹⁹Then they said to Moses, "Speak to us yourself. Then we will listen. But don't let God speak to us, or we will die."

²⁰Then Moses said to the people, "Don't be afraid. God has come to test you. He wants you to respect him so you will not sin."

²¹The people stood far away from the mountain while Moses went near the dark cloud where God was. ²²Then the Lord told Moses to say these things to the Israelites: "You yourselves have seen that I talked with you from heaven. ²³You must not use gold or silver to make idols for yourselves. You must not worship these false gods in addition to me.

²⁴"Make an altar of earth for me. Offer your whole burnt offerings and fellowship offerings on this altar as a sacrifice to me. Use your sheep and your cattle to do this. Worship me in every place that I choose. Then I will come and bless you. ²⁵You may use stones to make an altar for me. But don't use stones that you have made smooth with tools. You must not use any tools on the stones. If you do, you make them unsuitable for use in worship. ²⁶And you must not make steps leading up to my altar. If you go up steps, people will be able to see under your clothes."

Laws for Living

21 Then God said to Moses, "These are the laws for living that you will give to the Israelites:

²"If you buy a Hebrew slave, he will serve you for six years. In the seventh year you are to set him free. And he will have to pay nothing. ³He might not be married when he becomes your slave. Then he must leave without a wife. The man might be married when he becomes your slave. Then he may take his wife with him. ⁴The slave's master might give him a wife, and she might give birth to sons or daughters. Then the woman and her children will belong to the master. When the slave is set free, only he may leave.

⁵"But the slave might say, 'I love my master, my wife and my children. I don't want to go free'. ⁶Then the slave's master will take him to God. The master will take him to a door or doorframe. And he will punch a hole through the slave's ear using a sharp tool. Then the slave will serve that master all his life.

⁷"A man might sell his daughter as a slave. There are rules for setting her free. They are different from the rules for setting the men slaves free. ⁸Maybe the master wanted to marry her but then decided he was not pleased with her. He must let one of her close relatives buy her back. He has no right to sell her to foreigners. This is because he has treated her unfairly. ⁹The man who bought her might promise to let the woman marry his son. Then he must treat her as a daughter. ¹⁰The man who bought her might marry another woman. Then he must not keep his slave woman from having food or clothing or sexual relations. ¹¹If he does not give her these three things, she may go free. She owes him no money.

Injuries

¹²"Anyone who hits a person and kills him must be put to death. ¹³But if a person kills someone accidentally, God allowed that to happen. So the person must go to a place I will choose. ¹⁴A person might plan and murder another person on purpose. Put him to death, even if he has run to my altar for safety.

¹⁵"Anyone who hits his father or his mother must be put to death.

¹⁶"A person might kidnap someone. Then he either sells him as a slave or still has him when he is caught. That person must be put to death.

¹⁷"Anyone who says cruel things to his father or mother must be put to death.

¹⁸"Two men might argue. And one might hit the other with a rock or with his fist. The hurt man might not be killed. But he might have to stay in bed. ¹⁹Later he might be able to get up. And he might be able to walk around outside with his staff. Then the one who hit him is not to be punished. But he must pay the injured man for the loss of his time. And he must support the injured man until he is completely healed.

²⁰"A man might beat his male or female slave with a stick. And the slave might die on the spot. Then the owner must be punished. ²¹But the slave might get well after a day or two. Then that owner will not be punished since the slave belongs to him.

²²"Two men might be fighting, and they might hit a pregnant woman so that the baby comes out. But there is no further injury. Then the man who caused the injury must pay money. He must pay what the woman's husband says and the court allows. ²³But if there is further injury, then the punishment is that life must be paid for life, ²⁴eye for eye, tooth for tooth. It is also hand for hand, foot for foot, ²⁵burn for burn, wound for wound and bruise for bruise.

²⁶"A man might hit his male or female slave in the eye. And the eye might be blinded. Then the man is to free the slave to pay for the eye. ²⁷A master might knock out a tooth of his male or female slave. Then the man is to free the slave to pay for the tooth.

²⁸"A man's bull might kill a man or woman. Then you must kill that bull with stones. You should not eat the bull. But the owner of the bull is not guilty. ²⁹But the bull might have hurt people in the past. The owner might have been warned. If he did not keep it in a pen and then it kills a man or woman, the bull must be killed with stones. And the owner must also be put to death. ³⁰But the family of the dead man might accept money. Then the man who owned the bull may buy back his life. But he must pay whatever is demanded. ³¹Use this same law if the bull kills a person's son or daughter. ³²But the bull might kill a male or female slave. Then the owner must pay the master the price for a new slave. That is 0.3 kilograms of silver. And the bull must also be killed with stones.

³³"A man might take the cover off a pit. Or he might dig one and not cover it. Another man's ox or donkey might come and fall into it. ³⁴The owner of the pit must pay the owner of the animal for his loss. The dead animal will belong to the one who pays.

³⁵"One man's bull might kill another man's bull. Then they must sell the bull that is alive. Both men get half of the money. And both men will also get half of the bull that was killed. ³⁶A man's bull might have hurt other animals in the past. But the owner might not have kept it in a pen. Then that owner must pay bull for bull. And the dead animal is his.

Property Laws

22 A man might steal a bull or a sheep and kill or sell it. Then he must pay back five bulls for the one bull he stole. Or he must pay back four sheep for the one sheep he stole.

²⁻⁴"The robber who is caught must pay back what he stole. He might own nothing. Then he must be sold as a slave to pay for what he stole. The stolen animal might be found alive with the robber. Then he must give the owner two animals for every animal he stole. He must pay, whether he stole a bull, donkey or sheep.

"A thief might be killed while breaking into a house at night. Then the one who killed him is not guilty of murder. But if this happens during the day, he is guilty of murder.

5"A person might let his farm animal graze in his field or vineyard. And it might wander into another person's field or vineyard. Then the owner of the animal must repay him for the loss. The payment must come from the best of his crop.

6"A man might start a fire that spreads through the thornbushes to his neighbour's field. The fire might burn his neighbour's growing grain or grain that has been stacked. Or it might burn his whole field. Then the person who started the fire must pay for what was burned.

7"A man might give his neighbour money or other things to keep for him. Those things might be stolen from the neighbour's house. And the thief might be caught. Then he must pay back twice as much as he stole. 8But it maybe that the thief is never found. Then the owner of the house must make a promise before God. He must promise that he has not stolen his neighbour's things.

9"Two men might disagree about who owns something. It might be an ox, donkey, sheep or clothing. Or it might be something else that is lost. Each says, 'This is mine'. Each man must bring his case to God. God's judges will decide who is guilty. Then he must pay the other man twice as much as the thing is worth.

10"A man might ask his neighbour to keep his animal for him. This animal might be a donkey, ox, sheep or some other animal. And that animal might die, be hurt or be taken away. And no one saw what happened. 11That neighbour must promise before the Lord that he did not harm or kill the other man's animal. The owner of the animal must accept his promise made before God. The neighbour does not have to pay the owner for the animal. 12But the animal might have been stolen from the neighbour. Then he must pay the owner for it. 13Wild animals might have killed the animal. Then the neighbour must bring the body as proof. He will not have to pay for the animal that was killed.

14"A man might borrow an animal from his neighbour. It might get hurt or die while the owner is not there. Then the one who borrowed it must pay the owner for the animal. 15The owner might be with the animal. Then the one who borrowed it does not have to pay. If the animal was rented, the rental price covers the loss.

Laws and Relationships

16"A man might find a woman who is not pledged to be married. She has never had sexual relations with a man. He might trick her into having sexual relations with him. Then he must give her family the payment to marry her. And she will be his wife. 17But her father might refuse to allow his daughter to marry him. Then the man must still give the payment for a bride. He must pay the usual charge for a woman who has never had sexual relations.

18"Put to death any woman who does evil magic.

19"Put to death anyone who has sexual relations with an animal.

20"Destroy completely any person who makes a sacrifice to any god except the Lord.

21"Do not cheat or hurt a foreigner. Remember that you were foreigners in the land of Egypt.

22"Do not cheat a widow or an orphan. 23If you do, they will cry out to me for help. I will certainly hear their cry. 24And I will be very angry and kill you in war. Then your wives will become widows, and your children will become orphans.

25"You might lend money to one of my people who is poor. Then do not treat him as a moneylender would. Charge him nothing for using your money. 26Your neighbour might give you his coat as a promise. He is promising to pay you the money he owes you. But you must give it back to him by sunset. 27That coat is the only cover to keep his body warm. He has nothing else to sleep in. If he cries out to me for help, I will listen because I am merciful.

28"You must not speak against God. You must not curse a leader of your people.

29"Do not hold back your offering from the first of your harvest. Give me the first grain that you harvest. Give me the first wine that you make. Also, you must give me your first-born*d* sons. 30You must do the same with your bulls and your sheep. Let the firstborn males stay with their mothers for seven days. On the eighth day you must give them to me.

31"You are to be my holy people. You must not eat the meat of any animal that has been killed by wild animals. Instead, give it to the dogs.

Laws About Fairness

23 "You must not tell lies. You might be a witness in court. Don't help a bad person by telling lies.

2"You must not do wrong just because everyone else is doing it. You might be a witness in court. Then you must not ruin a fair trial. You must not tell lies just because everyone else is.

3A poor man might be in court. You must not take his side just because he is poor.

4"You might see your enemy's ox or donkey wandering away. Then you must return it to him. 5You might see that your enemy's donkey has fallen because its load is too heavy. You must not leave it there. You must help your enemy get the donkey back on its feet.

6"You must not be unfair to a poor man when he is in court. 7You must not lie when you accuse someone in court. Never allow an innocent or honest person to be put to death as punishment. This is because I will not treat guilty people as if they were innocent.

8"You must not accept money from a person who wants you to lie in court. Such money will not let you see what is right. Such money makes good people tell lies.

9"You must not mistreat a foreigner. You know how it feels to be a foreigner. You were foreigners in Egypt.

Laws for the Sabbath

10"For six years you are to plant and harvest crops on your land. 11Then during the seventh year, do not plough or plant your land. If any food grows there, allow the poor people to have it. And let the wild animals eat what is left. You should do the same with your vineyards and your groves of olive trees.

12"You should work six days a week. But on the seventh day you must rest. This lets your ox and your donkey rest. This also lets the slave born in your house and the foreigner be refreshed.

13"Be sure to do all that I have said to you. You must not even say the names of other gods. The names of those gods must not come out of your mouth.

Three Yearly Feasts

14"Three times each year you must hold a feast to honour me. 15You must celebrate the Feast*d* of Unleavened Bread. Do this in the way I commanded you. For seven days you must eat bread that is made without yeast. You must do this at the set time during the month of Abib.*d* This is the month when you came out of Egypt. No one is to come to worship me without bringing an offering.

16"You must celebrate the Feast*d* of Harvest. Offer to God the first things you harvest. These are from the crops you planted in your fields.

"You must celebrate the Feast*d* of Tents in the fall. Do this when you

gather all the crops from your fields.
17"So three times during every year all men must come to worship the Lord God.
18"You must not offer animal blood along with anything that has yeast in it.
"You must not save any of the fat from the sacrifice for the next day.
19"You must bring the best of the firstfruits*d* of your land. Bring them to the Holy Tent*n* of the Lord your God.
"You must not cook a young goat in its mother's milk.

Promises

20"I am sending an angel ahead of you. He will protect you as you travel. He will lead you to the place I have prepared. 21Pay attention to the angel and obey him. Do not turn against him. He will not forgive such turning against him because my power is in him. 22You must listen carefully to all he says. You must do everything that I tell you. If you do this, I will be an enemy to your enemies. I will fight all who fight against you. 23My angel will go ahead of you. He will take you into the land of these people: the Amorites, Hittites, Perizzites, Canaanites, Hivites and Jebusites. And I will destroy them.
24"You must not bow down to their gods or worship those gods. You must not live the way those people live. You must destroy their idols. And you must break into pieces stone pillars they use in worship. 25You must worship the Lord your God. If you do, I will bless your bread and your water. I will take away sickness from you. 26None of your women will have her baby die before it is born. All women will have children. I will allow you to live long lives.
27"I will make your enemies afraid of me. I will confuse any people you fight against. I will make all your enemies

run away from you. 28I will send something like hornets ahead of you. They will force the Hivites, Canaanites and Hittites out of your way. 29But I will not force all those people out in only one year. If I did, the land would become a desert. Then the wild animals would become too many for you. 30Instead, I will force those people out of your land very slowly. I will wait until there are enough of you to take over the land.
31"I will give you the land from the Gulf of Aqaba to the Mediterranean Sea. And I will give you the land between the desert and the Euphrates River. I will give you power over the people who now live in the land. You will force them out ahead of you. 32You must not make an agreement with those people or with their gods. 33You must not let them live in your land. If they live there, they will make you sin against me. If you worship their gods, you will be like someone caught in a trap."

God and Israel Make Their Agreement

24 The Lord told Moses, "You, Aaron, Nadab, Abihu and 70 of the older leaders of Israel must come up to me. You must worship me from a distance. 2Then Moses alone must come near me. The other men must not come near. And the rest of the people must not come up the mountain with Moses."
3So Moses told the people all the Lord's words and laws for living. Then all of the people answered out loud together. They said, "We will do all the things that the Lord has said." 4So Moses wrote down all the words of the Lord. And he got up early the next morning. He built an altar near the bottom of the mountain. He set up 12 stones, one stone for each of the 12 tribes*d* of Israel. 5Then Moses sent

Holy Tent Literally, "house of the Lord your God". See Exodus 25:9.

young Israelite men to offer whole burnt offerings. They also sacrificed young bulls as fellowship offerings to the Lord. ⁶Moses took the blood of these animals. He put half of it in bowls. And he sprinkled the other half of the blood on the altar. ⁷Then Moses took the book with the agreement written in it. He read it so the people could hear him. And they said, "We will do everything that the Lord has said. We will obey."

⁸Then Moses took the blood from the bowls. He sprinkled it on the people. He said, "This is the blood that begins the agreement. This is the agreement which the Lord has made with you about all these things."

⁹Moses, Aaron, Nadab, Abihu and 70 of the older leaders of Israel went up the mountain. ¹⁰They saw the God of Israel. The ground he was standing on looked as if it were paved with blue sapphire stones. And it was as clear as the sky! ¹¹These leaders of the Israelites saw God. But God did not destroy them. Then they ate and drank together.

Moses Gets the Stone Tablets

¹²The Lord said to Moses, "Come up the mountain to me. Wait there, and I will give you two stone tablets. On these are the teachings and the commandments. I have written these to teach the people."

¹³So Moses and his helper Joshua set out. Moses went up Sinai, the mountain of God. ¹⁴Moses said to the older leaders, "Wait here for us until we come back to you. Aaron and Hur are with you. Anyone who has a disagreement with others can take it to them."

Moses Meets with God

¹⁵When Moses went up on the mountain, the cloud covered it. ¹⁶The greatness of the Lord came down on Mount Sinai. The cloud covered the mountain for six days. On the seventh day the Lord called to Moses from inside the cloud. ¹⁷The Israelites could see the greatness of the Lord. It looked like a fire burning on top of the mountain. ¹⁸Then Moses went into the cloud and went higher up the mountain. Moses was on the mountain for 40 days and 40 nights.

Gifts for the Lord

25 The Lord said to Moses, ²"Tell the Israelites to bring me gifts. Receive for me the gifts each man wants to give. ³These are the gifts that you should receive from them: gold, silver, bronze, ⁴blue, purple and red thread, and fine linen. Receive cloth made of goat hair. ⁵Receive the male sheep skins that are dyed red. Receive fine leather, acacia wood ⁶and olive oil to burn in the lamps. And receive spices for sweet-smelling incenseᵈ and the special olive oil poured on a person's head to make him a priest. ⁷Also accept onyx stones and other jewels to be put on the holy robeᵈ and the chest covering.

⁸"The people must build a holy place for me. Then I can live among them. ⁹Build this Holy Tentᵈ and everything in it by the plan I will show you.

Altar to the Ark of God

¹⁰"Use acacia wood and build a Holy Ark.ᵈ It must be 1.1 metres long, 0.7 metres wide and 0.7 metres high. ¹¹Cover the Holy Ark inside and out with pure gold. And put a gold strip all around it. ¹²Make four gold rings for the Holy Ark. Attach the gold rings to its four feet, two rings on each side. ¹³Then make poles from acacia wood and cover them with gold. ¹⁴Put the poles through the rings on the sides of the Ark. Use these poles to carry the Holy Ark. ¹⁵These poles must always stay in the rings of the Holy Ark. Do not take the poles out. ¹⁶Then put the two flat stones in the Holy Ark. I will give you these stones on which the commands are written.

17"Then make a lid of pure gold for the Holy Ark. This lid is the mercy seat.*d* Make it 1.1 metres long and 0.7 metres wide. 18Then hammer gold to make two creatures with wings. Put one on each end of the lid. 19Put one creature with wings on one end of the lid. And put the other creature with wings on the other end. Attach the creatures with wings to the lid so that they will all be one piece. 20The creatures' wings should be spread out over the lid. The creatures are to face each other across the lid. 21Put this lid on top of the Holy Ark. Also put in this Holy Ark the agreement which I will make with you. 22I will meet with you there, above the lid between the two creatures with wings. These are on the Ark of God. There I will give you all my commands for the Israelites.

The Table

23"Make a table out of acacia wood. It must be 0.9 metres long, 0.5 metres wide and 0.7 metres high. 24Cover it with pure gold. Put a gold strip around it. 25Then make a frame 8 centimetres high that stands up all around the edge. Put a gold strip around the frame. 26Then make four gold rings. Attach them to the four corners of the table where the four legs are. 27Put the rings close to the frame around the top of the table. These rings will hold the poles for carrying the table. 28Make the poles out of acacia wood and cover them with gold. Carry the table with these poles. 29Make the plates and bowls for the table out of pure gold. Make the jars and cups out of pure gold. They will be used for pouring out the drink offerings. 30On this table put the bread that shows you are in my presence. It must always be there in front of me.

The Lampstand

31"Hammer pure gold to make a lampstand. Its base, stand, flower-like cups, buds and petals must all be joined together in one piece. 32The lampstand must have three branches on one side and three branches on the other. 33Each branch must have three cups shaped like almond flowers on it. Each cup must have a bud and a petal. 34And there must be four more cups made like almond flowers on the lampstand itself. These cups must also have buds and petals. 35Put a bud under each pair of branches that goes out from the lampstand. 36The branches, buds and lampstand must be one piece of pure, hammered gold.

37"Then make seven small oil lamps and put them on the lampstand. They will give light to the area in front of the lampstand. 38The wick trimmers and trays must be made of pure gold. 39Use 34 kilograms of pure gold to make the lampstand and everything with it. 40Be very careful to make them by the plan I showed you on the mountain.

The Holy Tent

26 "Make the Holy Tent*d* with ten pieces of cloth. These pieces must be made of fine linen and blue, purple and red thread. Have a skilled craftsman sew designs of creatures with wings on the pieces of cloth. 2Make each piece the same size. Each piece should be 13 metres long and 1.8 metres wide. 3Sew five pieces of cloth together for one set. Sew the other pieces together for the second set. 4Make loops of blue cloth down the edge of the end piece of each set. 5Make 50 loops on the end piece of the first set. And make 50 loops on the end piece of the second set. These loops must be opposite each other. 6And make 50 gold hooks. Use these to join the two sets of cloth. This will make the Holy Tent one piece.

7"Then make another tent that will cover the Holy Tent. Make this tent of 11 pieces of cloth made from goat hair. 8All these pieces of cloth must be the same size. They must be 13.5

metres long and 1.8 metres wide.
⁹Sew five of the pieces together into
one set. Then sew the other six
pieces together into the second set.
Fold the sixth piece double over the
front of the Tent. ¹⁰Make 50 loops
down the edge of the end piece of one
set. Do the same for the end piece of
the other set. ¹¹Then make 50 bronze
hooks. Put these in the loops to join
the two sets of cloth. This will make
the covering one piece. ¹²Let the extra half piece of cloth hang over the
back of the Holy Tent. ¹³There will be
0.5 metres hanging over the sides of
the Holy Tent. This will protect the
Tent. ¹⁴Make two more coverings for
the Holy Tent. One should be made
from male sheep skins coloured red.
The outer covering should be from
fine leather.

¹⁵"Use acacia wood to make upright
frames for the Holy Tent. ¹⁶Each
frame must be 4.5 metres long and
0.7 metres wide. ¹⁷Every frame must
be made the same way. There must
be two pegs side by side in each
frame. ¹⁸Make 20 frames for the south
side of the Holy Tent. ¹⁹Each frame
must have two silver bases to go
under it. A peg fits into each silver
base. You must make 40 silver bases
for the frames. ²⁰Make 20 more frames
for the north side of the Holy Tent.
²¹Make 40 silver bases for them.
Make two bases for each frame. ²²You
must make six frames for the rear or
west end of the Holy Tent. ²³Make
two frames for each corner at the
rear. ²⁴The two frames at each corner
are to be joined together. Hold them
together from bottom to top with a
metal ring. Both corner frames must
be made this way. ²⁵So there will be a
total of eight frames at the rear of
the Tent. And there will be 16 silver
bases — two bases under each frame.

²⁶"Make crossbars of acacia wood
to connect the upright frames of the
Holy Tent. Make five crossbars to
hold the frames together on one side.

²⁷Also make five crossbars to hold the
frames together on the other side.
And make crossbars to hold the
frames together on the west end, at
the rear. ²⁸The middle crossbar is to
be set halfway up the frames. It is to
run along the entire length of each
side and rear. ²⁹Make gold rings on
the sides of the frames. Pass the
crossbars through the rings. Cover
the frames and the crossbars with
gold. ³⁰Set up the Holy Tent by the
plan shown to you on the mountain.

³¹"Make a curtain of fine linen and
blue, purple and red thread. Have a
skilled craftsman sew designs of creatures with wings on the curtain.
³²Hang the curtain by gold hooks on
four posts of acacia wood. Cover
these posts with gold and set them in
four silver bases. ³³Hang the curtain
from the hooks in the roof. Put the
Holy Ark*d* containing the two flat
stones behind the curtain. This curtain will separate the Holy Place from
the Most Holy Place. ³⁴Put the lid on
the Holy Ark in the Most Holy Place.

³⁵"Outside the curtain, put the table
on the north side of the Holy Tent.
And put the lampstand on the south
side of the Holy Tent. This will be
opposite the table.

The Entrance of the Holy Tent

³⁶"Then make a curtain for the entrance of the Tent.*d* Make it with fine
linen and blue, purple and red thread.
Someone who can sew well is to sew
designs on it. ³⁷Make five posts of
acacia wood covered with gold. Make
five gold hooks on which to hang the
curtain from the posts. And make five
bronze bases for the five posts.

The Altar

27 "Make an altar for burnt offerings out of acacia wood. Make
it 1.4 metres high. It should be
square: 2.3 metres long and wide.
²Make each of the four corners of the
altar stick out like a horn. The corners

with their horns must be all one piece. Then cover the whole altar with bronze.

3"Use bronze to make all the tools and dishes that will be used on the altar. Make pots to remove the ashes. Make shovels, bowls for sprinkling blood, meat forks and pans for carrying the burning wood. 4"Make a large, bronze screen to hold the burning wood. And put a bronze ring at each of the four corners of the screen. 5Put the screen inside the altar, under its rim, halfway up from the bottom. 6"Make poles of acacia wood for the altar. And cover them with bronze. 7Put the poles through the rings on both sides of the altar to carry it. 8Make the altar out of boards and leave the inside hollow. Make it as you were shown on the mountain.

The Courtyard of the Holy Tent

9"Make a wall of curtains to form a courtyard around the Holy Tent.d The south side should have a wall of fine linen curtains 46 metres long. 10Hang the curtain with silver hooks and bands. Put these on 20 bronze posts on 20 bronze bases. 11The north side must also be 46 metres long. Hang its curtains on silver hooks and bands. Put these on 20 bronze posts on 20 bronze bases. 12"The west end of the courtyard must have a wall of curtains 23 metres long. It must have ten posts and ten bases on that wall. 13The east end of the courtyard must also be 23 metres long. 14On one side of the entrance, there is to be a wall of curtains. It is to be 6.9 metres long. It is to be held up by three posts on three bases. 15On the other side of the entry, there is to be a wall of curtains. It is to be 6.9 metres long. It is to be held up by three posts on three bases. 16"The entry to the courtyard is to be a curtain 9 metres wide. It is to be made of fine linen with blue, purple

and red thread. Someone who can sew well is to sew designs on it. It is to be held up by four posts on four bases. 17All the posts around the courtyard must have silver bands and hooks and bronze bases. 18The courtyard must be 46 metres long and 23 metres wide. The wall of curtains around it should be 2.3 metres high. They must be made of fine linen. The bases in which the posts are set must be bronze. 19All the things used in the Holy Tent must be made of bronze. And all the tent pegs for the Holy Tent and the wall around the courtyard must be made of bronze.

Oil for the Lamp

20"Command the people of Israel to bring you pure olive oil. It is to be made from pressed olives. This is to keep the lamps on the lampstand burning. 21Aaron and his sons must keep the lamps burning before the Lord from evening till morning. This will be in the Meeting Tent.d It is outside the curtain which is in front of the Holy Ark.d The Israelites and their descendantsd must obey this rule from now on.

Clothes for the Priests

28 "Tell your brother Aaron to come to you. His sons Nadab, Abihu, Eleazar and Ithamar must come with him. Separate them from the other Israelites. These men must serve as priests. 2Make holy clothes for your brother Aaron to give him honour and beauty. 3Speak to all the people to whom I have given the ability to make clothes. Tell these skilled craftsmen to make the clothes for Aaron. Use these clothes to make him belong to me. Then he may serve me as a priest. 4These are the clothes they must make: a chest covering, a holy robe,d an outer robe, a woven inner robe, a turban and a cloth belt. The craftsmen must make these holy clothes. They are for your brother

Aaron and his sons. Then Aaron and his sons may serve me as priests. [5]The craftsmen must use gold and blue, purple and red thread, and fine linen.

The Holy Robe

[6]"Use gold and blue, purple and red thread, and fine linen to make the holy robe.[d] The craftsmen are to make this holy robe. [7]At each top corner of this holy robe there will be a pair of shoulder straps. These are to be tied together over each shoulder.

[8]"The craftsmen will very carefully weave a belt on the holy robe. Make the belt with gold and blue, purple and red thread, and fine linen.

[9]"Take two onyx stones. Write the names of the 12 sons of Israel on these jewels. [10]Write six names on one stone and six names on the other stone. Write the names in order, from the oldest son to the youngest. [11]Carve the names of the sons of Israel on these stones. Do this the same way a person carves words and designs on the seals.[d] Put gold around the stones to hold them on the holy robe. [12]Put the two stones on the two straps of the holy robe. These stones are reminders of the 12 sons of Israel. Aaron is to wear their names on his shoulders. They are before the Lord as reminders of the sons of Israel. [13]Make two gold pieces to hold the stones. [14]Then make two chains of pure gold. Twist them together like a rope. Attach the chains to the two gold pieces that hold the stones.

The Chest Covering

[15]"Make a chest covering to help in making decisions. The craftsmen should make it as they made the holy robe.[d] They must use gold and blue, purple and red thread, and fine linen. [16]The chest covering must be square. It should be 23 centimetres long and wide. Fold it double to make a pocket. [17]Put four rows of beautiful gems on the chest covering. The first row of jewels must have a ruby, a topaz and a yellow quartz. [18]The second row must have a turquoise, a sapphire and an emerald. [19]The third row must have a jacinth, an agate and an amethyst. [20]The fourth row must have a chrysolite, an onyx and a jasper. Put gold around these jewels to attach them to the chest covering. [21]There must be 12 jewels on the chest covering. That is one jewel for each of the names of the sons of Israel. Carve the name of one of the 12 tribes[d] on each of the stones. Carve them as you would carve a seal.[d]

[22]"Make chains of pure gold for the chest covering. Twist them together like rope. [23]Make two gold rings. Put them on the two upper corners of the chest covering. [24]Attach the two gold chains to the two rings. These are at the upper corners of the chest covering. [25]Attach the other ends of the two chains to the two gold pieces on the shoulder straps. This will tie the chains to the shoulder straps in the front of the holy robe.

[26]"Make two more gold rings. Put them at the two lower corners of the chest covering. Put them on the inside edge of the chest covering next to the holy robe. [27]Make two more gold rings. Attach them to the bottom of the shoulder straps in the front of the holy robe. Put the gold rings close to the seam above the woven belt of the holy robe. [28]Join the rings of the chest covering to the rings of the holy robe with blue ribbon. This will connect it to the woven belt. In this way the chest covering will not swing out from the holy robe.

[29]"When Aaron enters the Holy Place, he will wear the names of the sons of Israel over his heart. These names are on the chest covering that helps in making decisions. This will be a continual reminder before the Lord. [30]And put the Urim and Thummim[d] inside the chest covering. These things

will be on Aaron's heart when he goes before the Lord. They will help in making decisions for the Israelites. So Aaron will always carry them with him when he is before the Lord.

31"Make the outer robe to be worn under the holy robe, using only blue cloth. 32Make a hole in the centre for Aaron's head. And there must be a woven collar around the hole so it will not tear. 33Make balls like pomegranates*d* of blue, purple and red thread. Hang these pomegranate balls around the bottom of the outer robe. And hang gold bells between them. 34So all around the bottom of the outer robe there should be a gold bell and a pomegranate ball, a gold bell and a pomegranate ball. 35Aaron must wear this robe when he serves as priest. The ringing of the bells will be heard. They will ring when he enters and leaves the Holy Place before the Lord. This way Aaron will not be killed.

36"Make a strip of pure gold. Carve these words on the gold strip as you would carve on a seal:*d* 'Holy to the Lord'. 37Use blue ribbon to tie a strip of gold to the turban. Put it on the front of the turban. 38Aaron must wear this on his forehead. In this way, he will be blamed if anything is wrong with the gifts of the Israelites. Aaron must always wear this on his head so the Lord will accept the gifts of the people.

39"Make the woven inner robe of fine linen. Make the turban of fine linen, also. Make the cloth belt with designs sewn on it. 40Also make woven inner robes, cloth belts and headbands for Aaron's sons. This will give them honour and beauty. 41Put these clothes on your brother Aaron and his sons. Then pour olive oil on their heads to appoint them as priests. Make them belong to me so they may serve me as priests.

42"Make for them linen underclothes to cover them from the waist to the upper parts of the legs. 43Aaron and his sons must wear these underclothes when they enter the Meeting Tent.*d* And they must wear these clothes whenever they come near the altar to serve as priests in the Holy Place. If they do not wear these clothes, they will be guilty of wrong. And they will be killed. This will be a law that will last from now on for Aaron and all his descendants.*d*

Appointing the Priests

29 "This is what you must do to appoint Aaron and his sons. Then they may serve me as priests. Take one young bull and two male sheep that have nothing wrong with them. 2Use fine wheat flour without yeast to make bread and cakes mixed with olive oil. Also use wheat flour without yeast to make wafers brushed with olive oil. 3Put these in one basket. Bring them in the basket along with the bull and two male sheep. 4Bring Aaron and his sons to the entrance of the Meeting Tent.*d* Then wash them with water. 5Take the clothes. Dress Aaron in the inner robe and the outer robe of the holy robe.*d* Then put on him the holy robe and the chest covering. Then tie the holy robe on him with its skilfully woven belt. 6Put the turban on his head. Put the holy crown, the strip of gold, on the turban. 7Take the special olive oil and pour it on his head to make him a priest.

8"Then bring his sons and put the inner robes on them. 9Put the headbands on their heads. Then tie cloth belts around their waists. Aaron and his descendants*d* will be priests in Israel. This is by a rule that will continue from now on. This is how you will appoint Aaron and his sons as priests.

10"Bring the bull to the front of the Meeting Tent. Aaron and his sons must put their hands on the bull's head. 11Then kill the bull before the Lord at the entrance to the Meeting

Tent. ¹²Take some of the bull's blood and go to the altar. Use your finger to put some blood on the corners of the altar. Pour the blood that is left at the bottom of the altar. ¹³Then take all the fat that covers the inner organs. Take the best part of the liver, and take both kidneys and the fat around them. Burn these on the altar. ¹⁴Take the bull's meat, skin and intestines. Burn these things outside the camp. This is an offering to take away sin.

¹⁵"Take one of the male sheep. Have Aaron and his sons put their hands on its head. ¹⁶Then kill that male sheep. Take its blood and sprinkle it on all four sides of the altar. ¹⁷Then cut the male sheep into pieces. Wash its inner organs and its legs. Put them with its head and its other pieces. ¹⁸Burn the whole male sheep on the altar. It is a burnt offering made by fire to the Lord. Its smell is pleasing to the Lord.

¹⁹"Take the other male sheep. Have Aaron and his sons put their hands on its head. ²⁰Kill that male sheep and take some of its blood. Put it on the bottom of the right ears of Aaron and his sons. Also put it on the thumbs of their right hands. And put it on the big toes of their right feet. Then sprinkle the rest of the blood against all four sides of the altar. ²¹Then take some of the blood from the altar. Mix it with the special oil used in appointing priests. Sprinkle this on Aaron and his clothes. And sprinkle this on his sons and their clothes. This will show that Aaron and his sons and their clothes are given to my service.

²²"Then take the fat from the male sheep. Take the fat tail and the fat that covers the inner organs. Take the best part of the liver. Take both kidneys and the fat around them and the right thigh. This is the male sheep to be used in appointing priests.

²³"Then take the basket of bread that you made without yeast. This is the basket you put before the Lord. From it take a loaf of bread, a cake made with olive oil and a wafer. ²⁴Put these in the hands of Aaron and his sons. Tell them to present these things in their hands before the Lord. This will be an offering presented to the Lord. ²⁵Then take them from their hands. Burn them on the altar with the whole burnt offering. This is an offering made by fire to the Lord. Its smell is pleasing to the Lord. ²⁶Then take the breast of the male sheep used to appoint Aaron as priest. Present the breast of the male sheep before the Lord. It is an offering presented to the Lord. This part of the animal will be your share. ²⁷Then give to the service of the Lord the parts of the male sheep used to appoint the priests. They belong to Aaron and his sons. They are the breast and the right thigh. These were presented to the Lord. ²⁸This is to be the regular share which the Israelites will always give to Aaron and his sons. This is the gift the Israelites must give to the Lord from their fellowship offerings.

²⁹"The holy clothes made for Aaron will belong to his descendants. They must wear these clothes when they are appointed as priests. ³⁰Aaron's son will become high priest after Aaron. He will come to the Meeting Tent to serve in the Holy Place. He is to wear these clothes for seven days.

³¹"Take the male sheep used to appoint priests. Boil its meat in a place made holy for serving me. ³²Then Aaron and his sons must eat the meat of the male sheep. They must do that at the entrance of the Meeting Tent. And they must also eat the bread that is in the basket. ³³These offerings were used to remove their sins when they were made priests so they would belong to God. Now they should eat these offerings. But no one else is to eat these things because they are holy. ³⁴If any of the meat from that male sheep or any of the bread is left

the next morning, it must be burned. It shall not be eaten because it is holy. [35]"Do all these things that I commanded you to do to Aaron and his sons. You are to spend seven days appointing them. [36]Each day for seven days you are to offer a bull. This will remove the sins of Aaron and his sons so they will be given for service to the Lord. Make the altar ready for service to the Lord. Pour oil on it to make it holy. [37]Spend seven days making the altar ready for service to God and making it holy. Then the altar will become very holy. Anything that touches it must be holy.

The Daily Sacrifices

[38]"Every day from now on, offer on the altar two lambs that are one year old. [39]Offer one lamb in the morning and the other in the evening. [40]In the morning, when you offer the first lamb, offer also 2 litres of fine flour. Mix it with 1 litre of oil from pressed olives. Pour out a litre of wine as a drink offering. [41]Offer the second lamb in the evening. Also offer the same grain offering and drink offering as you did in the morning. This is an offering by fire to the Lord. And its smell is pleasing to the Lord.

[42]"You must burn these things as an offering to the Lord every day. Do this at the entrance of the Meeting Tent[d] before the Lord from now on. When you make the offering, I, the Lord, will meet you there and speak to you. [43]I will meet with the people of Israel there. And that place will be holy because of my greatness.

[44]"So I will make the Meeting Tent and the altar holy. And I will make Aaron and his sons holy so they may serve me as priests. [45]I will live with the people of Israel. I will be their God. [46]And they will know that I am the Lord their God. They will know that I am the one who led them out of Egypt. I did this so I could live with them. I am the Lord their God.

The Altar for Burning Incense

30 "Make an altar out of acacia wood for burning incense.[d] [2]Make it square — half a metre long and wide. It must be 0.9 metre high. Make the corners stick out like horns. These must be one piece with the altar. [3]Cover its top, its sides and its corners with pure gold. And put a gold strip all around the altar. [4]Make two gold rings beneath the gold strip on opposite sides of the altar. Slide poles through these gold rings to carry the altar. [5]Make the poles from acacia wood and cover them with gold. [6]Put the altar of incense in front of the curtain. This curtain is in front of the Ark[d] of God. Put the altar in front of the lid that covers that Holy Ark. There I will meet with you.

[7]"Aaron must burn sweet-smelling incense on the altar every morning. He will do this when he comes to take care of the oil lamps. [8]He must burn incense again in the evening when he lights the lamps. So incense will burn before the Lord every day from now on. [9]Do not use this altar for offering any other incense or burnt offering. Do not use this altar to offer any kind of grain offering or drink offering. [10]Once a year Aaron must make the altar ready for service to God. He will do it by putting blood on its corners. This is blood of the animal offered to remove sins. He is to do this once a year from now on. This altar belongs completely to God's service."

The Tax for the Meeting Tent

[11]The Lord said to Moses, [12]"Count the people of Israel. At that time every person must pay to buy back his life from the Lord. Then no terrible things will happen to the people when you number them. [13]Every person who is counted must pay 6 grams of silver. This is set by the Holy Place measure, which weighs 12 grams. This amount is a gift to the

Lord. ¹⁴Every person who is counted and is 20 years old or older must give this amount to the Lord. ¹⁵A rich person must not give more than 6 grams. And a poor person must not give less than 6 grams. You are paying this to the Lord to buy back your lives. ¹⁶Gather from the people of Israel this money paid to buy back their lives. Spend it to buy things for the service in the Meeting Tent.*ᵈ* This payment will remind the Lord that the Israelites' lives have been bought back."

The Bronze Bowl

¹⁷The Lord said to Moses, ¹⁸"Make a bronze bowl for washing. Build it on a bronze stand. Put the bowl and stand between the Meeting Tent*ᵈ* and the altar. Put water in the bowl. ¹⁹Aaron and his sons must wash their hands and feet with the water from this bowl. ²⁰Each time, before they enter the Meeting Tent, they must wash with water. This way they will not die. They approach the altar to serve as priests. They offer a sacrifice to the Lord by fire. ²¹Each time they do this, they must wash their hands and their feet so they will not die. This is a rule which Aaron and his descendants*ᵈ* are to keep from now on."

Oil for Appointing

²²Then the Lord said to Moses, ²³"Take the finest spices: 6 kilograms of liquid myrrh,*ᵈ* half that amount (that is, 3 kilograms) of sweet-smelling cinnamon, 3 kilograms of sweet-smelling cane ²⁴and 6 kilograms of cassia.*ᵈ* Weigh all these by the Holy Place measure. Also take 4 litres of olive oil. ²⁵Mix all these things like a perfume to make a holy olive oil. This special oil must be put on people and things. Do this to make them ready for service to God. ²⁶Put this oil on the Meeting Tent*ᵈ* and the Holy Ark*ᵈ* with my laws in it. ²⁷Put this oil on the table and all its dishes. And put this oil on the lampstand and all its tools. Put the oil

on the incense*ᵈ* altar. ²⁸Also, put the oil on the altar for burning offerings and all its tools. Put this oil on the bowl and the stand under the bowl. Put oil on all these things to prepare them for service to God. ²⁹You will give these things for service to God. They will be very holy. Anything that touches these things must also be holy.

³⁰"Put the oil on Aaron and his sons to make them priests. Give them for service to me. Then they may serve me as priests. ³¹Tell the Israelites, 'This is to be my holy olive oil from now on. It is to be put on people and things to make them ready for service to God. ³²Do not pour it on the bodies of ordinary people. Do not make perfume the same way you make this oil. It is holy, and you must treat it as holy. ³³Someone might make perfume like it. Or he might put it on someone who is not a priest. Then that person must be separated from his people'."

Incense

³⁴Then the Lord said to Moses, "Take these sweet-smelling spices: resin, onycha, galbanum and pure frankincense.*ᵈ* Be sure that you have equal amounts of each. ³⁵You must make incense*ᵈ* as a man who makes perfume would do. Add salt to it to keep it pure and holy. ³⁶Beat some of the incense into a fine powder. Put some of it in front of the Holy Ark*ᵈ* of God in the Meeting Tent.*ᵈ* There I will meet with you. You must use this incense powder only for its very special purpose. ³⁷Do not make incense for yourselves the same way you make this incense. Treat it as holy to the Lord. ³⁸Whoever makes incense like this to use as perfume must be separated from his people."

Bezalel and Oholiab

31 Then the Lord said to Moses, ²"See, I have chosen Bezalel son of Uri from the tribe*ᵈ* of Judah. Uri

was the son of Hur. ³I have filled Bezalel with the Spirit*ᵈ* of God. I have given him the skill, ability and knowledge to do all kinds of work. ⁴He is able to design pieces to be made from gold, silver and bronze. ⁵He is able to cut jewels and put them in metal. And he can carve wood. Bezalel can do all kinds of work. ⁶I have also chosen Oholiab son of Ahisamach from the tribe of Dan. Oholiab will work with Bezalel. I have given skills to all skilled craftsmen. They will be able to make all these things I have commanded you: ⁷the Meeting Tent,*ᵈ* the Ark*ᵈ* of God, the lid that covers the Holy Ark and everything in the Tent. ⁸This includes the table and everything on it, the pure gold lampstand and everything with it and the altar of incense.*ᵈ* ⁹It also includes the altar for burnt offerings and everything used with it, the bowl and the stand under it. ¹⁰They will make the woven clothes and the holy clothes for Aaron and the clothes for his sons to wear when they serve as priests. ¹¹They will also make the special olive oil used in appointing people and things to the service of the Lord, and the sweet-smelling incense for the Holy Place.

"These workers will make all these things just as I have commanded you."

The Day of Rest

¹²Then the Lord said to Moses, ¹³"Tell the Israelites, 'You must keep the rules about my Sabbaths.*ᵈ* This is because they will be a sign between you and me from now on. In this way you will know that I, the Lord, am making you holy.

¹⁴" 'Make the Sabbath a holy day. If anyone treats the Sabbath like any other day, that person must be put to death. Anyone who works on the Sabbath day must be separated from his people. ¹⁵There are six days for working. But the seventh day is a day of rest. It is a day holy for the Lord. Anyone who works during the Sabbath day must be put to death. ¹⁶The Israelites must remember the Sabbath day. It is an agreement between them and me that will continue from now on. ¹⁷The Sabbath day will be a sign between me and the Israelites for ever. This is because in six days I, the Lord, made the sky and the earth. And on the seventh day I did not work. I rested'."

¹⁸So the Lord finished speaking to Moses on Mount Sinai. Then the Lord gave him the two stone tablets with the agreement written on them. The finger of God wrote the commands on the stones.

The People Make a Gold Calf

32 The people saw that a long time had passed. And Moses had not come down from the mountain. So they gathered around Aaron. They said to him, "Moses led us out of Egypt. But we don't know what has happened to him. So make us gods who will lead us."

²Aaron said to the people, "Take off the gold earrings that your wives, sons and daughters are wearing. Bring them to me." ³So all the people took their gold earrings and brought them to Aaron. ⁴Aaron took the gold from the people. Then he melted it and made a statue of a calf. He finished it with a tool. Then the people said, "Israel! These are your gods who brought you out of the land of Egypt!"

⁵Aaron saw all this, and he built an altar before the calf. Then he made an announcement. He said, "Tomorrow there will be a special feast to honour the Lord." ⁶The people got up early the next morning. They offered whole burnt offerings and fellowship offerings. First the people sat down to eat and drink. Then they got up and sinned sexually.

⁷And the Lord said to Moses, "Go

down from this mountain. Your people, the people you brought out of the land of Egypt, have committed a terrible sin. [8]They have quickly turned away from the things I commanded them to do. They have made for themselves a calf of melted gold. They have worshipped that calf and offered sacrifices to it. The people have said, 'Israel, these are your gods who brought you out of Egypt'."

[9]The Lord said to Moses, "I have seen these people. I know that they are very stubborn people. [10]So now do not stop me. I am so angry with them that I am going to destroy them. Then I will make you and your descendants[d] a great nation."

[11]But Moses begged the Lord his God. Moses said, "Lord, don't let your anger destroy your people. You brought these people out of Egypt with your great power and strength. [12]Don't let the people of Egypt say, 'The Lord brought the Israelites out of Egypt. But he planned to kill them in the mountains and remove them from the earth'. So stop being angry. Don't destroy your people. [13]Remember the men who served you— Abraham, Isaac and Israel. You promised with an oath to them. You said, 'I will make your descendants as many as the stars in the sky. I will give your descendants all this land that I have promised them. It will be theirs for ever'." [14]So the Lord changed his mind. He did not destroy the people as he had said he might.

[15]Then Moses went down the mountain. In his hands he had the two stone tablets with the agreement on them. The commands were written on both sides of each stone, front and back. [16]God himself had made the stones. And God himself had written the commands on the stones.

[17]Then Joshua heard the noise of the people shouting. He said to Moses, "It sounds like war down in the camp."

[18]Moses answered:
"It is not an army's shout of victory.
It is not an army's cry of defeat.
It is the sound of singing that I hear."

[19]When Moses came close to the camp, he saw the gold calf and the dancing. He became very angry. He threw down the stone tablets which he was carrying. He broke them at the bottom of the mountain. [20]Then he took the calf that the people had made. He melted it in the fire. And he ground the gold until it became powder. He threw the powder into the water. And he forced the Israelites to drink that water.

[21]Moses said to Aaron, "What did these people do to you? Why did you cause them to do such a terrible sin?"

[22]Aaron answered, "Don't be angry, master. You know that these people are always ready to do wrong. [23]The people said to me, 'Moses led us out of Egypt. But we don't know what has happened to him. So make us gods who will lead us'. [24]So I told the people, 'Take off your gold jewellery'. So they gave me the gold. I threw it into the fire and out came this calf!"

[25]Moses saw that the people were acting wildly. He saw that Aaron had let them get out of control. Their enemies would laugh at them. [26]So Moses stood at the entrance to the camp. He said, "Let anyone who wants to follow the Lord come to me." And all the people from the family of Levi gathered around Moses.

[27]Then Moses said to them, "The Lord, the God of Israel, says this: 'Every man must put on his sword and go through the camp from one end to the other. Each man must kill his brother, his friend and his neighbour'." [28]The people from the family of Levi obeyed Moses. That day about 3,000 of the people of Israel died. [29]Then Moses said, "Today you

have been given for service to the Lord. You were willing to kill your own sons and brothers. And God has blessed you for this."

[30]The next day Moses told the people, "You have done a terrible sin. But now I will go up to the Lord. Maybe I can do something so your sins will be removed. Then you will belong to God again." [31]So Moses went back to the Lord and said, "How terrible it is! These people have sinned horribly. They have made for themselves gods from gold. [32]Now, forgive them of this sin. If you will not, then erase my name. Erase it from the book in which you have written the names of your people."

[33]But the Lord told Moses, "I will erase from my book the names of the people who sin against me. [34]So now, go. Lead the people where I have told you. My angel will lead you. When the time comes to punish, I will punish them for their sin."

[35]So the Lord caused terrible things to happen to the people. He did this because of what they did with the calf Aaron had made.

33 Then the Lord said to Moses, "You and the people you brought out of Egypt must leave this place. Go to the land that I promised in an oath to give to Abraham, Isaac and Jacob. I said, 'I will give that land to your descendants'. [2]I will send an angel to lead you. And I will force these people out of the land: the Canaanites, Amorites, Hittites, Perizzites, Hivites and Jebusites. [3]Go up to the land where much food grows. But I will not go with you. This is because I might destroy you on the way. You are such a stubborn people."

[4]The people heard this bad news, and they became very sad. None of them put on jewellery. [5]This was because the Lord had said to Moses, "Tell the Israelites, 'You are a stubborn people. If I were to go with you even for a moment, I would destroy

you. So take off all your jewellery. Then I will decide what to do with you'." [6]So the people of Israel took off their jewellery at Mount Sinai.

The Meeting Tent

[7]Moses used to take a tent and set it up a long way outside the camp. Moses called it the "Meeting Tent".[d] A person might want to ask the Lord about something. Then he would go to the Meeting Tent outside the camp. [8]Whenever Moses went out to the Tent, all the people would rise. They stood at the entrances of their tents and watched Moses until he entered the Meeting Tent. [9]When Moses went into the Tent, the pillar of cloud would always come down. It would stay at the entrance of the Tent while the Lord spoke with Moses. [10]The people saw the pillar of cloud at the entrance of the Tent. Then they stood and worshipped, each person at the entrance of his own tent.

[11]The Lord spoke to Moses face to face as a man speaks with his friend. Then Moses would return to the camp. But Moses' young helper, Joshua son of Nun, did not leave the Tent.

[12]Moses said to the Lord, "You have told me to lead these people. But you did not say whom you would send with me. You have said to me, 'I know you very well. I am pleased with you'. [13]If I have truly pleased you, show me your plans. Then I may know you and continue to please you. Remember that this nation is your people."

[14]The Lord answered, "I myself will go with you. And I will give you victory."

[15]Then Moses said to him, "If you yourself don't go with us, then don't send us away from this place. [16]If you don't go with us, no one will know that you are pleased with me and your people. These people and I would be no different from any other people on earth."

[17]Then the Lord said to Moses, "I

will do what you ask. This is because I know you very well, and I am pleased with you."

Moses and God's Greatness

¹⁸Then Moses said, "Now, please show me your greatness."

¹⁹The Lord answered, "I will cause all my goodness to pass in front of you. I will announce my name, the Lord, so you can hear it. I will show kindness to anyone I want to show kindness. I will show mercy to anyone I want to show mercy. ²⁰But you cannot see my face. No one can see me and stay alive.

²¹"There is a place near me where you may stand on a rock. ²²My greatness will pass that place. I will put you in a large crack in that rock. And I will cover you with my hand until I have passed by. ²³Then I will take away my hand, and you will see my back. But my face must not be seen."

Moses Gets New Stones

34 The Lord said to Moses, "Cut two more stone tablets like the first two. I will write the same words on them that were on the first two stones which you broke. ²Be ready tomorrow morning. Then come up on Mount Sinai. Stand before me there on the top of the mountain. ³No one may come with you. No one should even be seen in any place on the mountain. Not even the sheep or cattle may eat grass near that mountain."

⁴So Moses cut two stone tablets like the first ones. Then early the next morning he went up Mount Sinai. He did this just as the Lord had commanded him. Moses carried the two stone tablets with him. ⁵Then the Lord came down in the cloud and stood there with Moses. And the Lord called out his name, the Lord.

⁶The Lord passed in front of Moses and said, "I am the Lord. The Lord is a God who shows mercy and is kind. The Lord doesn't become angry quickly. The Lord has great love and faithfulness. ⁷The Lord is kind to thousands of people. The Lord forgives people for wrong and sin and turning against him. But the Lord does not forget to punish guilty people. The Lord will punish not only the guilty people. He will also punish their children, their grandchildren, their great-grandchildren and their great-great-grandchildren."

⁸Then Moses quickly bowed to the ground and worshipped. ⁹Moses said, "Lord, if you are pleased with me, please go with us. I know that these are stubborn people. But forgive our evil and our sin. Take us as your own people."

¹⁰Then the Lord said, "I am making this agreement with you. I will do miracles*d* in front of all your people. These things have never before been done for any other nation on earth. The people with you will see my work. I, the Lord, will do wonderful things for you. ¹¹Obey the things I command you today, and I will force your enemies to leave your land. I will force out the Amorites, Canaanites, Hittites, Perizzites, Hivites and Jebusites ahead of you. ¹²Be careful. Don't make any agreement with the people who live in the land where you are going. It will bring you trouble. ¹³But destroy their altars. Break their stone pillars. Cut down their Asherah*d* idols. ¹⁴Don't worship any other god. This is because I, the Lord, the Jealous One, am a jealous God.

¹⁵"Be careful. Don't make any agreements with the people who live in that land. They will worship their false gods. And they will invite you to join them. Then you will join them, and you will eat their sacrifices. ¹⁶You might choose some of their daughters as wives for your sons. Those daughters worship false gods. They might lead your sons to do the same thing. ¹⁷"Do not make gods of melted metal.

18"Celebrate the Feast[d] of Unleavened Bread. For seven days you must eat bread made without yeast as I commanded you. Do this during the month I have chosen, the month of Abib.[d] This is because in that month you came out of Egypt.

19"Every firstborn[d] cow or sheep that is born to each animal belongs to me. 20You may buy back a donkey by paying for it with a lamb. But if you don't want to buy back a donkey, you must break its neck. You must buy back all your firstborn sons.

"No one is to come before me without a gift.

21"You must work for six days. But on the seventh day you must rest. You must do this even during the planting season and harvest season.

22"Celebrate the Feast[d] of Weeks when you gather the first grain of the wheat harvest. And celebrate the Feast[d] of Harvest in the Autumn.

23"Three times each year all your men must come before the Master, the Lord, the God of Israel. 24I will force out nations ahead of you. I will expand the borders of your land. You will go before the Lord your God three times each year. And at that time no one will try to take your land from you.

25"Do not offer the blood of a sacrifice to me with anything containing yeast. And do not leave any of the sacrifice of the Feast[d] of Passover. It must not be left until the next morning.

26"Bring the best first crops that you harvest from your ground. Bring those things to the Tent[d] of the Lord your God.

"You must not cook a young goat in its mother's milk."

27Then the Lord said to Moses, "Write down these words. This is because with these words I have made an agreement with you and Israel."

28Moses stayed there with the Lord for 40 days and 40 nights. During that time he did not eat food or drink water. And Moses wrote the words of the agreement—the Ten Commandments—on the stone tablets.

The Face of Moses Shines

29Then Moses came down from Mount Sinai. In his hands he was carrying the two stone tablets of the agreement. But Moses did not know that his face was shining because he had talked with the Lord. 30Aaron and all the people of Israel saw that Moses' face was shining. So they were afraid to go near him. 31But Moses called to them. So Aaron and all the leaders of the people returned to Moses. Moses talked with them. 32After that, all the people of Israel came near him. And he gave them all the commands that the Lord had given him on Mount Sinai.

33When Moses had finished speaking to the people, he put a covering over his face. 34Any time Moses went before the Lord to speak with him, Moses took off the covering until he came out. Then Moses would come out and tell the people of Israel the things the Lord had commanded. 35The Israelites would see that Moses' face was shining. So he would cover his face again. He did this until the next time he went in to speak with the Lord.

Rules About the Sabbath

35 Moses gathered all the Israelite community together. He said to them, "These are the things the Lord has commanded you to do. 2You are to work for six days. But the seventh day will be a holy day, a Sabbath[d] of rest to honour the Lord. Anyone who works on that day must be put to death. 3On the Sabbath day you must not light a fire in any of your houses."

4Moses said to all the Israelites, "This is what the Lord has commanded: 5from what you have, take an offering for the Lord. Let everyone who is willing bring this offering to the Lord: gold, silver, bronze, [6]blue, purple and red thread, and fine linen, goat hair [7]and male sheep skins, coloured red. And they may bring fine leather and acacia wood. [8]They may also bring olive oil for the lamps, spices for the special olive oil used for appointing priests and for the sweet-smelling incense.[d] [9]And they may bring onyx stones and other jewels to be put on the holy robe[d] and chest covering of the priests.

[10]"Let all the skilled workers come and make everything the Lord commanded: [11]the Holy Tent,[d] its outer tent and its covering, the hooks, frames, crossbars, posts and bases; [12]the Ark[d] of God, its poles, lid and the curtain in front of it; [13]the table and its poles, all the things that go with the table and the bread that shows we are in God's presence; [14]the lampstand for the light and all the things that go with it, the lamps and olive oil for the light; [15]the altar of incense and its poles, the special oil and the sweet-smelling incense, the curtain for the entrance of the Meeting Tent; [16]the altar of burnt offering and its bronze screen, its poles and all its tools, the bronze bowl and its base; [17]the curtains around the courtyard, their posts and bases, and the curtain at the entrance to the courtyard; [18]the pegs of the Holy Tent and of the courtyard and their ropes; [19]the special clothes that the priest will wear in the Holy Place. These are the holy clothes for Aaron the priest and his sons to wear when they serve as priests."

[20]Then all the people of Israel went away from Moses. [21]Everyone who wanted to give came and brought a gift to the Lord. These gifts were used for making the Meeting Tent, all the things in the Tent and the special clothes. [22]All the men and women who wanted to give brought gold jewellery

of all kinds. They brought pins, earrings, rings and bracelets. They all presented their gold to the Lord. [23]Everyone who had blue, purple and red thread, and fine linen came and gave it to the Lord. Anyone who had goat hair or male sheep skins coloured red or fine leather brought them to the Lord. [24]Everyone who could give silver or bronze brought that as a gift to the Lord. Everyone who had acacia wood to be used in the work brought it. [25]Every skilled woman used her hands to make the blue, purple and red thread and fine linen. And they brought what they had made. [26]All the women who were skilled and wanted to help made thread of the goat hair. [27]The leaders brought onyx stones and other jewels. These stones and jewels were put on the holy robe and chest covering for the priest. [28]They also brought spices and olive oil. These were used for the sweet-smelling incense, the special oil and the oil to burn in the lamps. [29]All the men and women of Israel who wanted to help brought gifts to the Lord. They were used for all the work the Lord had commanded Moses and the people to do.

[30]Then Moses said to the people of Israel, "Look, the Lord has chosen Bezalel. He is the son of Uri the son of Hur, from the tribe[d] of Judah. [31]The Lord has filled Bezalel with the Spirit[d] of God. The Lord has given Bezalel the skill, ability and knowledge to do all kinds of work. [32]He is able to design pieces to be made of gold, silver and bronze. [33]He is able to cut stones and jewels and put them in metal. Bezalel can carve wood and do all kinds of work. [34]The Lord has given Bezalel and Oholiab the ability to teach others. Oholiab is the son of Ahisamach from the tribe of Dan. [35]The Lord has given them the skill to do all kinds of work. They are able to cut designs in metal and stone. They can plan and sew designs in the fine

linen with the blue, purple and red thread. And they are also able to weave things.

36 So Bezalel, Oholiab and every skilled person will do the work the Lord has commanded. The Lord gave these people the wisdom and understanding to do all the skilled work needed to build the Holy Tent."

²Then Moses called Bezalel, Oholiab and all the other skilled people to whom the Lord had given skills. And they came because they wanted to help with the work. ³They received from Moses everything the people of Israel had brought as gifts to build the Holy Tent. The people continued to bring gifts each morning because they wanted to. ⁴So all the skilled workers left the work they were doing on the Holy Tent. And they went to speak to Moses. They said, ⁵"The people are bringing more than we need to do the work the Lord commanded."

⁶Then Moses sent this command throughout the camp: "No man or woman should make anything else as a gift for the Holy Tent." So the people were kept from giving more. ⁷What they had was already more than enough to do all the work.

The Holy Tent

⁸Then the skilled workers made the Holy Tent.ᵈ They made the ten pieces of blue, purple and red cloth. And they sewed designs of creatures with wings on the pieces. ⁹Each piece was the same size. It was 13 metres long and 1.8 metres wide. ¹⁰Five of the pieces were fastened together to make one set. The other five were fastened together to make another set. ¹¹Then they made loops of blue cloth along the edge of the end piece on the first set of five. They did the same thing with the other set of five. ¹²There were 50 loops on one piece and 50 loops on the other piece. The loops were opposite each other. ¹³Then they made 50 gold hooks to join the two pieces together. So the Holy Tent was joined together as one piece.

¹⁴Then the workers made another tent of 11 pieces of cloth made of goat hair. This was to put over the Holy Tent. ¹⁵All 11 pieces were the same size. They were 13.5 metres long and 1.8 metres wide. ¹⁶The workers sewed five pieces together into one set. Then they sewed six together into another set. ¹⁷They made 50 loops along the edge of the outside piece of one set. And they made 50 loops along the edge of the outside piece of the other set. ¹⁸Then they made 50 bronze rings to join the two sets of cloth together and make the tent one piece. ¹⁹Then they made two more coverings for the outer tent. One covering was made of male sheep skin coloured red. The other covering was made of fine leather.

²⁰Then they made upright frames of acacia wood. ²¹Each board was 4.5 metres tall and 0.7 metres wide. ²²There were two pegs side by side on each frame. Every frame of the Holy Tent was made this same way. ²³They made 20 frames for the south side of the Tent. ²⁴Then they made 40 silver bases that went under the 20 frames. There were two bases for every frame—one for each peg of each board. ²⁵They also made 20 frames for the north side of the Holy Tent. ²⁶They made 40 silver bases—two to go under each frame. ²⁷They made six frames for the rear or west end of the Holy Tent ²⁸and two frames for the corners at the rear of the Holy Tent. ²⁹These two frames were joined together from the bottom to the top with a metal ring. They did this for each of these corners. ³⁰So there were eight frames and 16 silver bases—two bases under each frame.

³¹Then they made crossbars of acacia wood to connect the upright frames of the Holy Tent. Five crossbars held the frames together on one

side of the Tent. ³²Five crossbars held the frames together on the other side. And five crossbars held the frames together on the west end, at the rear of the Tent. ³³They made the crossbar run along the entire length of each side and rear of the Tent. It was set halfway up the frames. ³⁴They made gold rings on the sides of the frames. They passed the crossbars through the rings. They covered the frames and the crossbars with gold.

³⁵Then they made the curtain with blue, purple and red thread, and fine linen. A skilled craftsman sewed designs of creatures with wings on it. ³⁶They made four posts of acacia wood and covered them with gold. Then they made gold hooks for the posts. And they made four silver bases in which to set the posts. ³⁷Then they made a curtain for the entrance to the Tent. They used blue, purple and red thread, and fine linen. A person who sewed well sewed designs on it. ³⁸Then they made five posts and hooks for it. They covered the tops of the posts and their bands with gold. And they made five bronze bases for the posts.

The Ark

37 Bezalel made the Ark*ᵈ* of acacia wood. The Ark was 1.1 metres long, 0.7 metres high and wide. ²He covered the inside and outside of the Ark with pure gold. Then he put a gold strip around it. ³He made four gold rings for it and attached them to its four feet. There were two rings on each side. ⁴Then he made poles of acacia wood and covered them with gold. ⁵He put the poles through the rings on each side of the Ark to carry it. ⁶Then he made a lid of pure gold. It was 1.1 metres long and 0.7 metres wide. ⁷Then Bezalel hammered gold to make two creatures with wings. He attached them to each end of the lid. ⁸He made one creature with wings on one end of the lid. He made the other

creature with wings on the other end. He attached them to the lid so that it would be one piece. ⁹The creatures' wings were spread out over the lid. The creatures faced each other across the lid.

The Table

¹⁰Then he made the table of acacia wood. The table was 0.9 metres long, 0.5 metres wide and 0.7 metres high. ¹¹He covered the table with pure gold. He put a gold strip around it. ¹²Then he made a frame 8 centimetres high that stood up all around the edge. He put a gold strip around the frame. ¹³Then he made four gold rings for the table. He attached them to the four corners of the table, where the four legs were. ¹⁴The rings were put close to the frame around the top of the table. The rings held the poles that were used to carry the table. ¹⁵The poles for carrying the table were made of acacia wood. They were covered with gold. ¹⁶Then he made of pure gold all the things that were used on the table: the plates, bowls, cups and jars used for pouring the drink offerings.

The Lampstand

¹⁷Then he made the lampstand of pure gold. He hammered out its base and stand. Its flower-like cups, buds and petals were joined together in one piece with the base and stand. ¹⁸There were three branches on one side of the lampstand and three branches on the other. ¹⁹Each branch had three cups shaped like almond flowers. Each cup had a bud and a petal. ²⁰There were four more cups shaped like almond flowers on the lampstand itself. Each cup had its buds and petals. ²¹Three pairs of branches went out from the lampstand. A bud was under the place where each pair was attached to the lampstand. ²²The buds, branches and lampstand were all one piece of pure,

hammered gold. ²³He made seven pure gold lamps for this lampstand. Then he made pure gold wick trimmers and trays. ²⁴He used about 34 kilograms of pure gold to make the lampstand and all the things that go with it.

The Altar for Burning Incense

²⁵Then he made the altar for incense*d* of acacia wood. The altar was square. It was 0.5 metres long and wide and 0.9 metres high. Each corner stuck out like a horn. Each corner was joined into one piece with the altar. ²⁶He covered the top and all the sides and the corners with pure gold. Then he put gold trim around the altar. ²⁷He made two gold rings and put them below the trim on opposite sides of the altar. These rings held the poles for carrying the altar. ²⁸He made the poles of acacia wood and covered them with gold.

²⁹Then he made the holy olive oil for appointing the priests. He also made the pure, sweet-smelling incense. He made them like a person who mixes perfumes.

The Altar

38 Then he built the altar for burning offerings. He made the altar of acacia wood. The altar was square. It was 2.3 metres long and wide and 1.4 metres high. ²He made each corner stick out like a horn. The horns and the altar were joined together in one piece. Then he covered the altar with bronze. ³He made all the tools of bronze to use on the altar: the pots, shovels, bowls for sprinkling blood, meat forks and pans for carrying the fire. ⁴He made a large bronze screen to hold the burning wood for the altar. He put the screen inside the altar, under its rim, halfway up from the bottom. ⁵He made bronze rings for holding the poles for carrying the altar. He put the rings at the four corners of the screen. ⁶Then he made poles of acacia wood and covered them with bronze. ⁷He put the poles through the rings on both sides of the altar. They were used for carrying the altar. He made the altar of boards and left the inside hollow.

The Bronze Bowl

⁸He made the bronze bowl for washing. He built it on a bronze stand. He used the bronze of mirrors. These mirrors belonged to the women who served at the entrance to the Meeting Tent.*d*

The Courtyard of the Holy Tent

⁹Then he made a wall of curtains to form a courtyard around the Holy Tent.*d* On the south side the curtains were 46 metres long and were made of fine linen. ¹⁰The curtains hung on silver hooks and bands. These were on 20 bronze posts on 20 bronze bases. ¹¹On the north side the wall of curtains was also 46 metres long. It hung on silver hooks and bands on 20 posts with 20 bronze bases.

¹²On the west side of the courtyard, the wall of curtains was 23 metres long. It was held up by silver hooks and bands on ten posts and ten bases. ¹³The east side was 23 metres wide. ¹⁴On one side of the entry there was a wall of curtains that was 6.9 metres long. It was held up by three posts and three bases. ¹⁵On the other side of the entrance there was a wall of curtains 6.9 metres long. It was held up by three posts and three bases. ¹⁶All the curtains around the courtyard were made of fine linen. ¹⁷The bases for the posts were made of bronze. The hooks and the bands on the posts were made of silver. The tops of the posts were covered with silver also. All the posts in the courtyard had silver bands.

¹⁸The curtain for the entrance of the courtyard was made of blue, purple and red thread, and fine linen. It was sewn by a person who could sew well. The curtain was 9 metres long and 2.3

metres high. It was the same height as the curtains around the courtyard. [19]The curtain was held up by four posts and four bronze bases. The hooks and bands on the posts were made of silver. The tops on the posts were covered with silver. [20]All the tent pegs for the Holy Tent and for the curtains around the courtyard were made of bronze.

[21]This is a list of the metals used to make the Holy Tent. This is where the two flat stones with the Ten Commandments are kept. Moses ordered the Levites to make this list. Ithamar son of Aaron was in charge of keeping the list. [22]Bezalel son of Uri made everything the Lord commanded Moses. Uri was the son of Hur of the tribe[d] of Judah. [23]Oholiab son of Ahisamach of the tribe of Dan helped him. Oholiab could cut designs into metal and stone. He was a designer. He was also skilled at sewing the blue, purple and red thread, and fine linen.

[24]The total amount of gold used to build the Holy Tent was presented to the Lord. It weighed about 1 ton, as set by the Holy Place measure. [25]The silver was given by the members of the community who were counted. It weighed about 3.4 tons, as set by the Holy Place measure. [26]All the men 20 years old or older were counted. There were 603,550 men, and each man had to pay 6 grams of silver. This is the weight as set by the Holy Place measure. [27]Of this silver, about 3.4 tons was used to make the 100 bases. These bases were for the Holy Tent and for the curtain. There was about 34 kilograms of silver in each base. [28]The other about 20 kilograms of silver was used to make the hooks for the posts. It was also used to cover the tops of the posts and to make the bands on the posts.

[29]The bronze which was presented to the Lord weighed about about 2.4 tons. [30]They used the bronze to make the bases at the entrance of the Meeting Tent. They also used the bronze to make the altar and the bronze screen. And this bronze was used to make all the tools for the altar. [31]This bronze was also used to make bases for the wall of curtains around the courtyard. It was used for the bases for the curtains at the entrance to the courtyard. And this bronze was used to make the tent pegs for the Holy Tent and curtains that surrounded the courtyard.

Clothes for the Priests

39 They used blue, purple and red thread to make woven clothes for the priests. They were to wear these when they served in the Holy Place. They also made the holy clothes for Aaron as the Lord had commanded Moses.

[2]They made the holy robe[d] of gold and blue, purple and red thread, and fine linen. [3]They hammered the gold into sheets. Then they cut the gold into long, thin strips. They worked the gold into the blue, purple and red thread, and fine linen. This was done by a skilled craftsman. [4]They made the shoulder straps for the holy robe. These straps were attached to the top corners of the robe. Then the shoulder straps were tied together over each shoulder. [5]The skilfully woven belt was made in the same way. It was joined to the holy robe as one piece. It was made of gold and blue, purple and red thread, and fine linen. It was made the way the Lord commanded Moses. [6]They put gold around the onyx stones. Then they wrote the names of the sons of Israel on these gems. They did that as a person carves words and designs on a seal.[d] [7]Then they attached the gems on the shoulder straps of the holy robe. These gems are reminders of the 12 sons of Israel. This was done the way the Lord had commanded Moses.

[8]The skilled craftsmen made the chest covering. It was made like the

holy robe. It was made of gold and blue, purple and red thread, and fine linen. ⁹The chest covering was square, 23 centimetres long and 23 centimetres wide. It was folded double to make a pocket. ¹⁰Then they put four rows of beautiful jewels on it. In the first row there was a ruby, a topaz and a yellow quartz. ¹¹In the second row there was a turquoise, a sapphire and an emerald. ¹²In the third row there was a jacinth, an agate and an amethyst. ¹³In the fourth row there was a chrysolite, an onyx and a jasper. Gold was put around these jewels to attach them to the chest covering. ¹⁴The names of the sons of Israel were carved on these 12 jewels as a person carves a seal. Each jewel had the name of one of the 12 tribes*d* of Israel.

¹⁵They made chains of pure gold for the chest covering. They were twisted together like a rope. ¹⁶The workers made two gold pieces and two gold rings. They put the two gold rings on the two upper corners of the chest covering. ¹⁷Then they put two gold chains in the two rings. These are at the ends of the chest covering. ¹⁸They fastened the other two ends of the chains to the two gold pieces. Then they attached these gold pieces to the two shoulder straps in the front of the holy robe. ¹⁹They made two more gold rings and put them at the lower corners of the chest covering. They put them on the inside edge next to the holy robe. ²⁰Then they made two more gold rings on the bottom of the shoulder straps in front of the holy robe. These rings were near the seam, just above the woven belt of the holy robe. ²¹They used a blue ribbon and tied the rings of the chest covering to the rings of the holy robe. This connected it to the woven belt. In this way the chest covering would not swing out from the holy robe. They did all these things the way the Lord commanded.

²²Then they made the outer robe to be worn under the holy robe. It was woven of blue cloth. ²³They made a hole in the centre of the outer robe. A woven collar was sewn around this hole so it would not tear. ²⁴Then they made balls like pomegranates*d* of blue, purple and red thread, and fine linen. They hung them around the bottom of the outer robe. ²⁵They also made bells of pure gold. They hung these around the bottom of the outer robe between the balls. ²⁶So around the bottom of the outer robe there was a bell and a pomegranate ball, a bell and a pomegranate ball. The priest wore this outer robe when he served as priest, just as the Lord had commanded Moses.

²⁷They wove inner robes of fine linen for Aaron and his sons. ²⁸And they made turbans and underclothes of fine linen. ²⁹Then they made the cloth belt of fine linen and blue, purple and red thread. Designs were sewn onto the cloth. These things were made as the Lord had commanded Moses.

³⁰They made a strip of pure gold, which is the holy crown. They carved these words in the gold: "Holy to the Lord." They did it as one might carve on a seal. ³¹Then they tied this flat piece to the turban with a blue ribbon. This was done as the Lord had commanded Moses.

³²So all the work on the Meeting Tent*d* was finished. The Israelites did everything just as the Lord had commanded Moses. ³³Then they brought the Holy Tent to Moses: the Tent and all its furniture, hooks, frames, crossbars, posts and bases; ³⁴the covering made of male sheep skins coloured red, the covering made of fine leather and the curtain that covered the entrance to the Most Holy Place; ³⁵the Ark*d* of God, its poles and lid; ³⁶the table, all its containers and the bread that showed they were in God's presence; ³⁷the pure gold lampstand with its lamps in a row, all its tools and the olive oil for the light; ³⁸the gold altar,

the special olive oil used for appointing priests, the sweet-smelling incense,*d* and the curtain that covered the entrance to the Tent; [39]the bronze altar and its screen, its poles and all its tools, the bowl and its stand; [40]the curtains for the courtyard with their posts and bases, the curtain that covered the entrance to the courtyard, the cords, pegs and all the things in the Meeting Tent. [41]They brought the clothes for the priests to wear when they served in the Holy Tent: the holy clothes for Aaron the priest and the clothes for his sons. They wore these when they served as priests.

[42]The Israelites had done all this work just as the Lord had commanded Moses. [43]Moses looked closely at all the work. He saw they had done it just as the Lord had commanded. So Moses blessed them.

Setting Up the Holy Tent

40 Then the Lord said this to Moses: [2]"On the first day of the first month, set up the Holy Tent,*d* which is the Meeting Tent. [3]Put the Ark*d* of God in the Meeting Tent. Hang the curtain in front of the Ark. [4]Then bring in the table. Arrange everything on the table that should be there. Then bring in the lampstand and set up its lamps. [5]Put the gold altar for burning incense*d* in front of the Ark of God. Then put the curtain at the entrance to the Holy Tent.

[6]"Put the altar of burnt offerings in front of the entrance of the Holy Tent, the Meeting Tent. [7]Put the bowl between the Meeting Tent and the altar. Put water in the bowl. [8]Set up the courtyard around the Holy Tent. Then put the curtain at the entrance to the courtyard.

[9]"Use the special olive oil and pour it on the Holy Tent and everything in it. Give the Tent and all that is in it for service to the Lord. They will be holy. [10]Pour the special oil on the altar for burning offerings. Pour it on all its

tools. Give the altar for service to God. It will be very holy. [11]Then pour the special olive oil on the bowl and the base under it. When you do this, they will be given for service to God.

[12]"Bring Aaron and his sons to the entrance of the Meeting Tent. Wash them with water. [13]Then put the holy clothes on Aaron. Pour the special oil on him, and give him for service to God. Then he may serve me as a priest. [14]Bring Aaron's sons and put the inner robes on them. [15]Pour the special oil on them to make them priests. Do this the same way that you appointed their father as priest. Then they may also serve me as priests. Pouring oil on them will make them a family of priests. They and their descendants*d* will be priests from now on." [16]Moses did everything that the Lord commanded him.

[17]So the Holy Tent was set up. It was the first day of the first month during the second year after they left Egypt. [18]When Moses set up the Holy Tent, he put the bases in place. Then he put the frames on the bases. Next he put the crossbars through the rings of the frames and set up the posts. [19]After that, Moses spread the cloth over the Holy Tent. Then he put the covering over the Tent. He did these things just as the Lord commanded.

[20]Moses put the flat stones into the Ark of God. These had God's law written on them. Moses put the poles through the rings of the Ark. Then he put the lid on it. [21]Next Moses brought the Ark into the Tent. He hung the curtain to cover the Ark. Moses did these things just as the Lord commanded him.

[22]Moses put the table in the Meeting Tent. He put it on the north side of the Holy Tent in front of the curtain. [23]Then he put the bread on the table before the Lord. He did this just as the Lord commanded him. [24]Moses put the lampstand in the Meeting

Tent. He put it on the south side of the Holy Tent opposite the table. 25Then he put the lamps on the lampstand before the Lord. He did this just as the Lord commanded him.

26Moses put the gold altar for burning incense in the Meeting Tent. He put it in front of the curtain. 27Then he burned sweet-smelling incense on it, just as the Lord commanded him. 28Then he hung the curtain at the entrance to the Holy Tent.

29He put the altar for burning sacrifices at the entrance to the Holy Tent, the Meeting Tent. Then Moses offered a whole burnt offering and grain offerings on that altar. He did these things just as the Lord commanded him. 30Moses put the bowl between the Meeting Tent and the altar for burning sacrifices. Moses put water in the bowl for washing. 31Moses, Aaron and Aaron's sons used this water to wash their hands and feet. 32They washed themselves every time they entered the Meeting Tent. They also washed themselves every time they went near the altar for burning sacri-

fices. They did these things just as the Lord commanded Moses.

33Then Moses set up the courtyard around the Holy Tent. He put the altar for burning sacrifices in the courtyard. Then he put up the curtain at the entrance to the courtyard. So Moses finished the work.

The Cloud over the Holy Tent

34Then the cloud covered the Meeting Tent.d The greatness of the Lord filled the Holy Tent. 35Moses could not enter the Meeting Tent. This was because the cloud had settled on it. And this was because the greatness of the Lord filled the Holy Tent. 36When the cloud rose from the Holy Tent, the Israelites would begin to travel. 37But as long as the cloud stayed on the Holy Tent, the people did not travel. They stayed in that place until the cloud rose. 38So the cloud of the Lord was over the Holy Tent during the day. And there was a fire in the cloud at night. So all the Israelites could see the cloud while they travelled.

LEVITICUS

Rules for Worship and Living

The Burnt Offering

1 The Lord called to Moses and spoke to him from the Meeting Tent.ᵈ The Lord said, ²"Tell the people of Israel: 'When you bring an offering to the Lord, bring as your offering one of the cattle. Or you may bring one of the sheep or goats.

³" 'If anyone offers a whole burnt offering from the cattle, it must be a male. It must have nothing wrong with it. The person must take the animal to the entrance of the Meeting Tent. Then the Lord will accept the offering. ⁴The person must put his hand on the animal's head. Then the Lord will accept that burnt offering. It will remove the person's sin so he will belong to God. ⁵The person must kill the young bull before the Lord. Then the priests must bring its blood to the altar. They must sprinkle the blood on all sides of the altar. This is the altar at the entrance to the Meeting Tent. ⁶The person will cut the skin from that animal. Then he will cut the animal into pieces. ⁷The priests must put wood and fire on the altar. ⁸They must lay the head, the fat and other pieces on the wood. That wood is on the fire on the altar. ⁹The priest must wash the animal's inner organs and legs with water. Then the priest must burn all the animal's parts on the altar. It is a whole burnt offering, an offering made by fire. And its smell is pleasing to the Lord.

¹⁰" 'The burnt offering may be a sheep or goat. It must be a male animal that has nothing wrong with it. ¹¹The person must kill the animal on the north side of the altar. This is to be before the Lord. Then the priests must sprinkle its blood on the altar. They must sprinkle it on all sides. ¹²The person must cut the animal into pieces. Then the priest must lay the pieces with the head and fat on the wood. The wood is on the fire on the altar. ¹³The person must wash the animal's inner organs and legs with water. Then the priest must burn all its parts on the altar. It is a burnt offering, an offering made by fire. And its smell is pleasing to the Lord.

¹⁴" 'The whole burnt offering may be a bird. It must be a dove or a young pigeon. ¹⁵The priest will bring the offering to the altar. He will pull off the bird's head. Then he will burn it on the altar. The bird's blood must be drained out on the side of the altar. ¹⁶The priest must remove the bird's cropⁿ and its contents. He must throw them on the east side of the altar. This is where they put the ashes from the altar. ¹⁷Then the priest must tear the bird open by its wings. But he must not divide the bird into two parts. Then the priest must burn the bird on the altar. He must place it on the wood which is on the fire. It is a burnt offering, an offering made by fire. Its smell is pleasing to the Lord.

The Grain Offering

2 " 'When anyone offers a grain offering to the Lord, it must be made from fine flour. The person must pour oil on it and put incenseᵈ on it. ²Then he must take it to Aaron's sons and the priests. The priest must

---

crop A small bag inside a bird's throat. When a bird eats, its food goes into this part first. There, the food is made soft before it goes into the stomach.

Exodus 8:3
"Frogs . . . will enter your palace."

Exodus 12:13
"When I see the blood, I will pass over you."

Exodus 20:21
The people stood far away from the
mountain while Moses went near the
dark cloud where God was.

take a handful of the fine flour, with the oil and all the incense. He must burn it on the altar as a memorial portion. It is an offering made by fire. Its smell is pleasing to the Lord. ³The rest of the grain offering will belong to Aaron and the priests. This offering is a most holy part of the offerings made by fire to the Lord.

⁴" 'If you bring a grain offering that was baked in the oven, it must be made from fine flour. It may be loaves made without yeast and mixed with oil. Or it may be wafers made without yeast. They are to have oil poured over them. ⁵If your grain offering is cooked on a griddle, it must be made without yeast. It must be made of fine flour mixed with oil. ⁶Crumble it and pour oil over it. It is a grain offering. ⁷If your grain offering is cooked in a pan, it must be made from fine flour and oil. ⁸Bring the grain offering made of these things to the Lord. Give it to the priest. He will take it to the altar. ⁹He will take out the memorial portion from the grain offering. He will burn it on the altar. This is an offering made by fire. Its smell is pleasing to the Lord. ¹⁰The rest of the grain offering belongs to Aaron and the priests. It is a most holy part of the offerings made to the Lord by fire.

¹¹" 'Every grain offering you bring to the Lord must be made without yeast. You must not burn yeast or honey in an offering made by fire to the Lord. ¹²You may bring yeast and honey to the Lord as an offering from the first harvest. But yeast and honey must not be burned on the altar as a pleasing smell. ¹³You must also put salt on all your grain offerings. Salt stands for your agreement with God that will last for ever. Do not leave it out of your grain offering. You must add salt to all your offerings.

¹⁴" 'If you bring a grain offering from the first harvest to the Lord, bring crushed heads of new grain. They must be roasted in the fire. ¹⁵Put oil

and incense on the grain. It is a grain offering. ¹⁶The priest will burn the memorial portion of the crushed grain and oil. It will have incense on it. It is an offering by fire to the Lord.

The Fellowship Offering

3 " 'A person's fellowship offering to the Lord may be from the cattle. It may be a male or female animal. But it must have nothing wrong with it. ²The person must put his hand on the animal's head. He must kill it at the entrance to the Meeting Tent.ᵈ Then the priests must sprinkle the blood on all sides of the altar. ³This person must make a sacrifice from the fellowship offering. The sacrifice must be made by fire to the Lord. He must offer the fat of the animal's inner organs. This is both the fat that is in them and that covers them. ⁴He must also offer both kidneys and the fat on them. They are near the lower back muscle. He must also offer the best part of the liver. He will remove it with the kidneys. ⁵Then the priests will burn these parts on the altar. They will put them on the burnt offering that is on the wood on the fire. It is an offering made by fire. Its smell is pleasing to the Lord.

⁶" 'A person's fellowship offering to the Lord may be a lamb or a goat. He may offer a male or female animal. But it must have nothing wrong with it. ⁷If he offers a lamb, he must bring it before the Lord. ⁸He must put his hand on its head. Then he must kill the animal in front of the Meeting Tent. The priests will sprinkle its blood on all sides of the altar. ⁹Then the person must make a sacrifice from the fellowship offering. The sacrifice must be made by fire to the Lord. The person must bring the fat and the whole fat tail. The tail must be cut off close to the backbone. He must also offer the fat of the inner organs. This is both the fat that is in them and that covers them. ¹⁰He must offer both kidneys

and the fat on them. They are near the lower back muscle. And he must offer the best part of the liver. He will remove it with the kidneys. ¹¹Then the priest will burn these parts on the altar as food. It will be an offering made by fire to the Lord.

¹²" 'A person's fellowship offering may be a goat. He is to offer it before the Lord. ¹³He must put his hand on the goat's head. And he must kill it in front of the Meeting Tent. Then the priests must sprinkle its blood on all sides of the altar. ¹⁴From this fellowship offering the person must make a sacrifice. It will be an offering by fire to the Lord. The person must offer all the fat of the goat's inner organs. This is both the fat that is in them and that covers them. ¹⁵He must offer both kidneys and the fat on them. They are near the lower back muscle. And he must offer the best part of the liver. He will remove it with the kidneys. ¹⁶The priest will burn these parts on the altar as food. It is an offering made by fire. Its smell is pleasing to the Lord. All the fat belongs to the Lord.

¹⁷" 'This law will continue for people from now on, wherever you live: you must not eat fat or blood'."

The Sin Offering

4 The Lord said to Moses, ²"Tell the people of Israel this: 'A person might sin by accident. He might do some things the Lord has commanded not to be done. If so, that person must do these things:

³" 'It may be the appointed priest who has sinned. If so, he has brought guilt on the people. So he must offer a young bull to the Lord. It must have nothing wrong with it. This will be a sin offering for the sin he has done. ⁴He will bring the bull to the entrance of the Meeting Tent.ᵈ He must bring it in front of the Lord. Then he will put his hand on the bull's head. And he will kill the bull before the Lord. ⁵Then the appointed priest must bring some of

the bull's blood into the Meeting Tent. ⁶The priest is to dip his finger into the blood. He must sprinkle it seven times before the Lord in front of the curtain. This curtain is in front of the Most Holy Place. ⁷The priest must also put some of the blood on the corners of the altar of incense.ᵈ It stands before the Lord in the Meeting Tent. Then the priest must pour out the rest of the bull's blood. It must be poured at the bottom of the altar of burnt offering. That altar is at the door of the Meeting Tent. ⁸He must remove all the fat from the bull of the sin offering. He must remove the fat on and around the inner organs. ⁹He must remove both kidneys and the fat on them. They are near the lower back muscle. He must remove the best part of the liver with the kidneys. ¹⁰He must do this in the same way the fat is removed from the bull of the fellowship offering. Then the priest must burn the animal parts on the altar of burnt offering. ¹¹⁻¹²But the priest must carry out the skin of the bull and all its meat. He must take these with the rest of the bull—its head, legs, intestines and other inner organs. He must take it outside the camp to the special cleanᵈ place where the ashes are poured out. He must burn it on a wood fire on the pile of ashes.

¹³" 'The whole nation of Israel might sin without knowing it. They might do something the Lord has commanded not to be done. If this happens, they are guilty. ¹⁴When they learn about the sin they have done, a young bull must be offered. It is a sin offering for the whole nation. They must bring it and give it before the Meeting Tent. ¹⁵The older leaders of the group of people must put their hands on the bull's head. It must be done before the Lord. And the bull must be killed before the Lord. ¹⁶Then the appointed priest must bring some of the bull's blood into the Meeting Tent. ¹⁷The priest will dip his finger in the blood.

He must sprinkle it seven times before the Lord in front of the curtain. 18Then he must put some of the blood on the corners of the altar. The altar is before the Lord in the Meeting Tent. The priest must pour out the rest of the blood. He must pour it at the bottom of the altar of burnt offering. That altar is at the entrance to the Meeting Tent. 19The priest must remove all the fat from the animal. And he must burn it on the altar. 20He will do the same thing with this bull that he did with the first bull of the sin offering. In this way the priest removes the sins of the people so they will belong to the Lord. And the Lord will forgive them. 21Then the priest must carry the bull outside the camp and burn it. He must do this just as he did with the first bull. This is the sin offering for the whole community.

22" 'A ruler might sin by accident. He might do something the Lord his God has commanded must not be done. If he does, he is guilty. 23When he learns about his sin, he must bring a male goat. It must have nothing wrong with it. That will be his sin offering. 24The ruler must put his hand on the goat's head and kill it. This must be done where they kill the whole burnt offering before the Lord. The goat is a sin offering. 25The priest must take some of the blood of the sin offering on his finger. He must put it on the corners of the altar of burnt offering. He must pour out the rest of the blood at the bottom of the altar of burnt offering. 26He must burn all the goat's fat on the altar. He must burn it in the same way he burns the fat of the fellowship offerings. In this way the priest removes the ruler's sin so he belongs to the Lord. And the Lord will forgive him.

27" 'A person in the community might sin by accident. He might do something which the Lord has commanded must not be done. He is guilty of sin. 28When the person learns about

his sin, he must bring a female goat. It must have nothing wrong with it. That will be his sin offering. 29He must put his hand on the animal's head. He must kill it at the place of the whole burnt offering. 30Then the priest must take some of the goat's blood on his finger. He must put it on the corners of the altar of burnt offering. He must pour out the rest of the goat's blood at the bottom of the altar. 31Then the priest must remove all the goat's fat. He must do it in the same way the fat is removed from the fellowship offerings. He must burn it on the altar. Its smell is pleasing to the Lord. In this way the priest will remove that person's sin so he will belong to the Lord. And the Lord will forgive him.

32" 'This person may bring a lamb as his sin offering. If he does, he must bring a female. It must have nothing wrong with it. 33The person must put his hand on the animal's head. He must kill it as a sin offering. He must kill it where they kill the whole burnt offering. 34The priest must take some of the blood from the sin offering on his finger. He must put it on the corners of the altar of burnt offering. Then he must pour out the rest of the lamb's blood at the bottom of the altar. 35The priest must remove all the lamb's fat. He must do it in the same way that the lamb's fat is removed from the fellowship offerings. He must burn the pieces on the altar. They go on top of the offerings made by fire for the Lord. In this way the priest will remove that person's sins so he will belong to the Lord. And the Lord will forgive him.

Special Types of Accidental Sins

5 " 'These are things for which a sin offering must be made:
" 'A person might be ordered to tell in court what he has seen or what he knows. If he does not tell the court, he is guilty of sin.
2" 'Or someone might touch some-

thing unclean.*d* It might be the dead body of an unclean wild animal or an unclean farm animal or an unclean crawling animal. He might not know that he touched it. But he will still be unclean and guilty of sin.

³" 'Many things come from a person which are not clean. Someone might touch one of these unclean things from a person and not know it. But when he learns about it, he will be guilty.

⁴" 'Or someone might make a promise before the Lord without thinking. He might promise to do something bad or good. The promise might be about anything. He might even make a promise before the Lord and forget about it. But when he remembers, he will be guilty.

⁵" 'When anyone is guilty of any of these things, he must tell how he sinned. ⁶He must bring an offering to the Lord. It is a penalty for his sin. It must be a female lamb or goat from the flock. The priest will perform the acts to remove that person's sin so he will belong to the Lord.

⁷" 'But perhaps the person cannot afford a lamb. Then he must bring two doves or two young pigeons to the Lord. These will be the penalty for his sin. One bird must be for a sin offering. The other must be for a burnt offering. ⁸He must bring them to the priest. First the priest will offer the one for the sin offering. He will pull the bird's head from its neck. But he will not pull it completely off. ⁹He must sprinkle the blood from the sin offering on the side of the altar. Then he must pour the rest of the blood at the bottom of the altar. It is a sin offering. ¹⁰Then the priest must offer the second bird as a burnt offering. This is what the law says. In this way the priest will remove the person's sin so he will belong to the Lord. And the Lord will forgive him.

¹¹" 'The person might not be able to afford two doves or two pigeons. If

not, he must bring about 2 litres of fine flour. This will be an offering for his sin. He must not put oil on the flour. And he must not put incense*d* on it, because it is a sin offering. ¹²He must bring the flour to the priest. The priest will take a handful of the flour as a memorial offering. He will burn it on the altar. It goes on top of the offerings made by fire to the Lord. It is a sin offering. ¹³In this way the priest will remove the person's sins so he will belong to the Lord. And the Lord will forgive him. What is left of the sin offering belongs to the priest. This is like the grain offering'."

The Penalty Offering

¹⁴The Lord said to Moses, ¹⁵"A person might accidentally sin and do something against the holy things of the Lord. That person must bring a male sheep from the flock. It must have nothing wrong with it. This will be his penalty offering to the Lord. The value in silver of the male sheep must be correct. Use the proper value for silver as set by the Holy Place measure. ¹⁶That person must pay for the sin he did against the holy thing. He must add one-fifth to its value. Then he must give it all to the priest. In this way the priest will remove the person's sin so he will belong to the Lord. The priest does it by means of the male sheep of the penalty offering. And the Lord will forgive the person.

¹⁷"A person might sin and do something the Lord has commanded not to be done. It does not matter if that person knew or not. He is guilty. He is responsible for his sin. ¹⁸He must bring the priest a male sheep from the flock. It must have nothing wrong with it. It must be worth the correct amount. The male sheep will be a penalty offering. The person sinned without knowing it. But with this offering the priest will remove the sin so the person will belong to the Lord. And the Lord will forgive him. ¹⁹The per-

son is guilty of doing wrong against the Lord. So he must give the penalty offering to the Lord."

6 The Lord said to Moses, 2"A person might sin against the Lord by doing one of these sins: he might lie about what happened to something he was taking care of for someone else. Or he might lie about a promise he made. Or he might steal something or cheat someone. 3He might find something that had been lost and then lie about it. He might make a promise before the Lord about something and not mean it. Or he might do some other sin. 4If he does any of these things, he is guilty of sin. He must bring back whatever he stole. Or he must bring back what he took by cheating. Or he must bring back the thing he took care of for someone else. Or he must bring back what he found and lied about. 5Or he must bring back what he made a false promise about. He must pay the full price. Then he must pay an extra one-fifth of the value of what he took. He must give the money to the true owner. This must be done on the day he brings his penalty offering. 6He must pay a penalty to the priest. It must be a male sheep from the flock. It must not have anything wrong with it. And it must be worth the correct amount. It will be a penalty offering to the Lord. 7Then the priest will perform the acts to remove that person's sin so he will belong to the Lord. And the Lord will forgive him for the sins that made him guilty."

The Whole Burnt Offering

8The Lord said to Moses, 9"Give this command to Aaron and the priests: 'These are the teachings about the whole burnt offering. The burnt offering must stay on the altar all night until morning. The altar's fire must be kept burning. 10The priest must put on his linen robe. He must put on linen underclothes next to his body. Then he will remove the ashes

from the burnt offering on the altar. He will put these ashes beside the altar. 11Then he must take off those clothes and put on others. He must carry the ashes outside the camp to a special clean*d* place. 12But the fire must be kept burning on the altar. It must not be allowed to go out. The priest must put more firewood on the altar every morning. He must place the whole burnt offering on the fire. He must burn the fat of the fellowship offerings. 13The fire must be kept burning on the altar all the time. It must not go out.

The Grain Offering

14" 'These are the teachings about the grain offering: the priests must bring it to the Lord in front of the altar. 15The priest must take a handful of fine flour. The oil and incense*d* must be on it. The priest must burn the grain offering on the altar. It will be a memorial offering to the Lord. Its smell is pleasing to him. 16Aaron and the priests may eat what is left. It must be eaten without yeast in a holy place. The priests must eat it in the courtyard of the Meeting Tent.*d* 17It must not be cooked with yeast. I have given it as their share of the offerings made to me by fire. It is most holy, like the sin offering and the penalty offering. 18Any male descendant*d* of Aaron may eat it. It is his share of the offerings made to the Lord by fire. This will continue from now on. Whatever touches these offerings must be holy'."

19The Lord said to Moses, 20"This is the offering Aaron and the priests must bring to the Lord. They must do this on the day they appoint Aaron as high priest. They must bring 2 litres of fine flour for a grain offering. They must bring half of it in the morning and half in the evening. 21The fine flour must be mixed with oil and cooked on a griddle. Bring it when it is well mixed. You must break it into pieces.

It will be a smell that is pleasing to the Lord. [22]One of the priests will be appointed to take Aaron's place as high priest. He must make the grain offering to the Lord. It is a rule for ever. The grain offering must be completely burned to the Lord. [23]Every grain offering made by a priest must be completely burned. It must not be eaten."

The Sin Offering

[24]The Lord said to Moses, [25]"Tell Aaron and the priests: 'These are the teachings about the sin offering. The sin offering must be killed in front of the Lord. It must be killed in the same place the whole burnt offering is killed. It is most holy. [26]The priest who offers the sin offering must eat it. He must eat it in a holy place. It must be in the courtyard of the Meeting Tent.[d] [27]Whatever touches the meat of the sin offering must be holy. If the blood is sprinkled on any clothes, you must wash them in a holy place. [28]The clay pot the meat is cooked in must be broken. If a bronze pot is used, it must be scrubbed and rinsed with water. [29]Any male in a priest's family may eat the offering. It is most holy. [30]The blood of the sin offering may be taken into the Meeting Tent. It may be used to remove sin in the Holy Place. That sin offering must be burned with fire. It must not be eaten.

The Penalty Offering

7 "'These are the teachings about the penalty offering. It is most holy. [2]The penalty offering must be killed where the whole burnt offering is killed. Then the priest must sprinkle its blood on all sides of the altar. [3]He must offer all the fat from the penalty offering. He must offer the fat tail and the fat that covers the inner organs. [4]He must offer both kidneys and the fat on them. They are near the lower back muscle. And he must offer the best part of the liver. This is to be removed with the kidneys. [5]The priest must burn all these things on the altar. They will be an offering made by fire to the Lord. It is a penalty offering. [6]Any male in a priest's family may eat it. It is most holy. So it must be eaten in a holy place.

[7]"'The penalty offering is like the sin offering. The teachings are the same for both. The priest who offers the sacrifice to remove sins will get the meat for food. [8]The priest who offers the burnt offering may also have the skin from it. [9]Every grain offering belongs to the priest who offers it. This includes those baked in an oven, cooked on a griddle or baked in a dish. [10]The grain offerings belong to the priests. They may be dry or mixed with oil. All priests will share alike.

Fellowship Offerings

[11]"'These are the teachings about the fellowship offering a person may offer to the Lord: [12]he may bring the fellowship offering to show his thanks. If he does, he should also bring loaves of bread. They must be made without yeast, mixed with oil. And he should bring wafers made without yeast. They must have oil poured over them. He should also bring loaves of fine flour mixed with oil. [13]He must also offer loaves of bread made with yeast. These should be brought with his fellowship offering, which he gives to show thanks. [14]One of each kind of offering will be for the Lord. It will be given to the priest who sprinkles the blood of the fellowship offering. [15]The fellowship offering is to thank the Lord. The meat from it must be eaten the same day it is offered. None of it must be left until morning.

[16]"'A person might bring a fellowship offering just to give a gift to God. Or it may be done because of a special promise to God. Then, the sacrifice should be eaten the same day he offers it. If there is any left, it may be eaten the next day. [17]If any meat from this sacrifice is left on the third day, it

must be burned up. [18]Any meat of the fellowship offering eaten on the third day will not be accepted. The Lord will not count the sacrifice for the person who offered it. It will become unclean. [d] Anyone who eats the meat will be guilty of sin.

[19]" 'People must not eat meat that touches anything unclean. They must burn this meat with fire. But anyone who is clean may eat other meat. [20]But a person who is unclean might eat the meat from the fellowship offering that belongs to the Lord. If he does, he must be separated from his people.

[21]" 'Someone might touch something unclean that comes from people. Or the unclean thing might be an animal or some hated thing. Touching it will make him unclean. If he then eats meat from the fellowship offering that belongs to the Lord, he must be separated from his people'."

[22]The Lord said to Moses, [23]"Tell the people of Israel: 'You must not eat any of the fat from cattle, sheep or goats. [24]If an animal is found dead or torn by wild animals, you may use its fat for other things. But you must not eat it. [25]Someone might eat fat from an animal offering made by fire to the Lord. That person must be separated from his people. [26]It does not matter where you live. You must not eat blood from any bird or animal. [27]Anyone who eats blood must be separated from his people'."

The Priests' Share

[28]The Lord said to Moses, [29]"Tell the people of Israel: 'Someone may bring a fellowship offering to the Lord. He must give part of it as his sacrifice to the Lord. [30]He must carry that part of the gift in his own hands. It will be an offering made by fire to the Lord. He must carry the fat and the breast of the animal to the priest. The breast must be presented to the Lord as the priests' share. [31]Then the priest must

burn the fat on the altar. But the breast of the animal will belong to Aaron and the priests. [32]You must also give the right thigh from the fellowship offering to the priest as a gift. [33]It will belong to the priest who offers the blood and fat of the fellowship offering. [34]I have taken the breast and the thigh of the fellowship offering. And I have given these parts to Aaron and the priests as their share from the Israelites'."

[35]This is the portion that belongs to Aaron and his sons. It is from the offerings made by fire to the Lord. Aaron and his sons were given this share on the day they were presented to the Lord as priests. [36]On the day the Lord appointed the priests, he commanded Israel to give this share to them. It is to be given to the priests as their share from now on.

[37]These are the teachings about the whole burnt offering, the grain offering, the sin offering and the penalty offering. They are the teachings about the appointment of priests. And they are the teachings about the fellowship offerings. [38]The Lord gave these teachings to Moses on Mount Sinai. It was on the day he commanded the Israelites to bring their offerings to him in the Sinai Desert.

Aaron and His Sons Appointed

8 The Lord said to Moses, [2]"Bring Aaron and his sons and their clothes. Bring the special olive oil used in appointing people and things to the service of the Lord. Also bring the bull of the sin offering and the two male sheep. And bring the basket of bread made without yeast. [3]Then gather the people together at the entrance to the Meeting Tent."[d] [4]Moses did as the Lord commanded him. The people met together at the entrance to the Meeting Tent.

[5]Then Moses spoke to the people. He said, "This is what the Lord has commanded to be done." [6]Then Mo-

ses brought Aaron and his sons forward. He washed them with water. [7]He put the inner robe on Aaron. And he tied the cloth belt around Aaron. Then he put the outer robe on him. Next he put the holy robe[d] on Aaron. Then he tied the skilfully woven belt around him. So the holy robe was tied to Aaron. [8]Then Moses put the chest covering on him. And he put the Urim and the Thummim[d] in the chest covering. [9]He also put the turban on Aaron's head. He put the strip of gold on the front of the turban. This strip of gold is the holy crown. Moses did this as the Lord commanded him to do.

[10]Then Moses put the special oil on the Holy Tent[d] and everything in it. In this way Moses made them holy for the Lord. [11]He sprinkled some oil on the altar seven times. He sprinkled the altar and all its tools. He also sprinkled special oil on the large bowl and its base. In this way he made them holy for the Lord. [12]Then he poured some of the special oil on Aaron's head. In this way he made Aaron holy for the Lord. [13]Then Moses brought Aaron's sons forward. And he put the inner robes on them. He tied cloth belts around them. Then he put headbands on them. He did these things as the Lord had commanded him.

[14]Then Moses brought the bull for the sin offering. And Aaron and his sons put their hands on its head. [15]Moses killed the bull and took some of the blood. With his finger he put some of the blood on all the corners of the altar. In this way he made the altar pure. Then he poured out the rest of the blood at the bottom of the altar. So he made it holy and ready for service to God. [16]Moses took all the fat from the inner organs of the bull. He took the best part of the liver. And he took both kidneys and the fat on them. Then he burned them on the altar. [17]But he took the bull's skin, its meat and its intestines outside the camp.

He burned them in a fire outside the camp. Moses did all these things as the Lord had commanded him.

[18]Next Moses brought the male sheep of the burnt offering. Aaron and his sons put their hands on its head. [19]Then Moses killed it. He sprinkled the blood on all sides of the altar. [20]Moses cut the male sheep into pieces. And he burned the head, the pieces and the fat. [21]He washed the inner organs and legs with water. Then he burned the whole sheep on the altar. It was a burnt offering made by fire to the Lord. Its smell was pleasing to the Lord. Moses did these things as the Lord had commanded him.

[22]Then Moses brought the other male sheep. It was used in appointing Aaron and his sons as priests. They put their hands on its head. [23]Then Moses killed the sheep. He put some of its blood on the bottom of Aaron's right ear. He put some on the thumb of Aaron's right hand. And he put some on the big toe of his right foot. [24]Then Moses brought Aaron's sons close to the altar. He put some of the blood on the bottom of their right ears. He put it on the thumbs of their right hands. And he put it on the big toes of their right feet. Then he sprinkled blood on all sides of the altar. [25]He took the fat and the fat tail from the sheep. He took all the fat on the inner organs. He took the best part of the liver. He also took both kidneys, their fat and the right thigh. [26]A basket of bread made without yeast is put before the Lord each day. From the basket Moses took a loaf of bread. And he took a loaf made with oil and a wafer. He put these pieces of bread on the fat and right thigh of the male sheep. [27]He put all these things in the hands of Aaron and his sons. He presented the pieces as an offering before the Lord. [28]Then Moses took them from their hands. And he burned them on the altar on top of the burnt

offering. So this was the offering for appointing Aaron and his sons as priests. It was an offering made by fire to the Lord. Its smell was pleasing to the Lord. ²⁹Moses took the breast and presented it as an offering before the Lord. It was Moses' share of the male sheep used in appointing the priests. This was as the Lord had commanded Moses.

³⁰Moses took some of the special oil and some of the blood which was on the altar. He sprinkled some of the oil on Aaron and Aaron's clothes. He also sprinkled some on Aaron's sons and their clothes. In this way Moses made Aaron, his clothes, his sons and their clothes holy for the Lord.

³¹Then Moses said to Aaron and his sons, "I gave you a command. I said, 'Aaron and his sons will eat these things'. So take the meat and basket of bread from the offering for appointing priests. Boil the meat at the door of the Meeting Tent. Eat it there with the bread. ³²If any of the meat or bread is left, burn it. ³³The time of appointing will last seven days. You must not go outside the entrance of the Meeting Tent until that time is up. Stay there until the time of your appointing is finished. ³⁴The Lord commanded the things that were done today. He commanded these things to remove your sins so you will belong to him. ³⁵You must stay at the entrance of the Meeting Tent. Stay there day and night for seven days. If you don't obey the Lord's commands, you will die! The Lord has given me these commands."

³⁶So Aaron and his sons did everything the Lord had commanded through Moses.

Aaron and His Sons Offer Sacrifices

9 On the eighth day after the time of appointing, Moses called for Aaron and his sons. He also called for the older leaders of Israel. ²He said to

Aaron, "Take a bull calf and a male sheep. There must be nothing wrong with these animals. The calf will be a sin offering. And the male sheep will be a whole burnt offering. Offer these animals to the Lord. ³Tell the people of Israel, 'Take a male goat for a sin offering. And take a calf and a lamb for a whole burnt offering. The calf and the lamb must each be one year old. There must be nothing wrong with these animals. ⁴Take a bull and a male sheep for fellowship offerings. Take with these animals a grain offering mixed with oil. Offer these things to the Lord. This is because the Lord will appear to you today'."

⁵So all the people came to the front of the Meeting Tent.ᵈ They brought the things Moses had commanded them to bring. And they stood before the Lord. ⁶Moses said, "You have done what the Lord commanded. So you will see the Lord's glory."

⁷Then Moses told Aaron, "Go to the altar. There offer sin offerings and whole burnt offerings. Do this to remove your sins and the people's sins so you will belong to God. Offer the sacrifices for the people. And perform the acts to remove their sins for them so they will belong to the Lord. Do this as the Lord has commanded."

⁸So Aaron went to the altar. He killed the bull calf as a sin offering for himself. ⁹Then his sons brought the blood to him. Aaron dipped his finger in the blood and put it on the corners of the altar. Then he poured out the rest of the blood at the bottom of the altar. ¹⁰Aaron took the fat, the kidneys and the best part of the liver from the sin offering. He burned these things on the altar. He did this the way the Lord had commanded Moses. ¹¹Aaron burned the meat and skin outside the camp.

¹²Then Aaron killed the animal for the whole burnt offering. Aaron's sons brought the blood to him. And he sprinkled it on all sides of the altar.

¹³Aaron's sons gave the pieces and head of the burnt offering to Aaron. And he burned them on the altar. ¹⁴Aaron also washed the inner organs and the legs of the burnt offering. And he burned them on the altar.

¹⁵Then Aaron brought the offering that was for the people. He took the goat of the people's sin offering. He killed and offered the goat of the sin offering. He did this just as he had done the first sin offering.

¹⁶Then Aaron brought the whole burnt offering and offered it. He did it as the Lord had commanded. ¹⁷He also brought the grain offering to the altar. He took a handful of the grain and burned it on the altar. This was in addition to the morning's burnt offering.

¹⁸Aaron also killed the bull and the male sheep. These were the fellowship offerings for the people. Aaron's sons brought the blood from these animals to Aaron. He sprinkled it on all sides of the altar. ¹⁹Aaron's sons also brought to Aaron the fat of the bull and the male sheep. They brought the fat tail and the fat covering the inner organs. They also brought the kidneys and the best part of the liver. ²⁰Aaron's sons put these fat parts on the breasts of the bull and sheep. Then Aaron burned these fat parts on the altar. ²¹He presented the breasts and the right thigh before the Lord as the priests' share of the offering. He did this as Moses had commanded.

²²Then Aaron lifted up his hands toward the people and blessed them. Aaron had finished offering the sin offering, the burnt offering and the fellowship offering. Then he stepped down from the altar.

²³Moses and Aaron went into the Meeting Tent. Then they came out and blessed the people. Then the Lord's glory came to all the people. ²⁴Fire came out from the Lord. It burned up the burnt offering and fat on the altar. When the people saw this,

they shouted with joy. They bowed face down on the ground.

God Destroys Nadab and Abihu

10 Aaron's sons Nadab and Abihu took their pans for burning incense.ᵈ They put fire in them and added incense. But they did not use the special fire Moses had commanded them to use. ²So fire came down from the Lord and destroyed Nadab and Abihu. They died in front of the Lord. ³Then Moses said to Aaron, "This is what the Lord was speaking about when he said,

'I must be respected as holy
  by those who come near me.
Before all the people
  I must be given honour'."

So Aaron did not say anything about the death of his sons.

⁴Aaron's uncle Uzziel had two sons named Mishael and Elzaphan. Moses said to them, "Come here. Pick up your cousins' bodies. Carry them outside the camp away from the front of the Holy Place. ⁵So Mishael and Elzaphan obeyed Moses. They carried the bodies of Nadab and Abihu outside the camp. Nadab and Abihu were still wearing the special priest's inner robes.

⁶Then Moses spoke to Aaron and his other sons, Eleazar and Ithamar. Moses told them, "Don't show any sadness. Don't tear your clothes or leave your hair uncombed. If you do those things, you will die, and the Lord will be angry with all the people. All the people of Israel are your relatives. They may cry loudly about the Lord burning Nadab and Abihu. ⁷But you must not even leave the Meeting Tent.ᵈ If you go out of the entrance, you will die! This is because the Lord has appointed you to his service." So Aaron, Eleazar and Ithamar obeyed Moses.

⁸Then the Lord said to Aaron, ⁹"You and your sons must not drink wine or beer when you go into the

Meeting Tent. If you do, you will die! This law will continue from now on. [10]You must keep what is holy separate from what is not holy. You must keep what is clean[d] separate from what is unclean. [11]The Lord gave his laws to Moses. And Moses gave them to the people. You must teach the people all the laws."

[12]Moses talked to Aaron and his remaining sons, Eleazar and Ithamar. Moses said, "Some of the grain offering is left from the sacrifices offered by fire to the Lord. Eat that part of the grain offering. But do not add yeast to it. Eat it near the altar because it is most holy. [13]The Law I gave you says this part belongs to you and your sons. But you must eat it in a holy place. It is part of the offerings made by fire to the Lord. I have been commanded to tell you this.

[14]"Also, you, your sons and daughters may eat the breast and thigh of the fellowship offering. They were presented to the Lord. You must eat them in a clean place. They are your share of the fellowship offerings given by the Israelites. [15]The people must bring the fat from their animals. It is part of the offering made by fire. They must also bring the thigh and the breast of the fellowship offering. These will be presented to the Lord. They will be the regular share of the offerings for you and your children. The Lord has commanded it."

[16]Moses looked for the goat of the sin offering. But it had already been burned up. So he became very angry with Eleazar and Ithamar, Aaron's remaining sons. He said, [17]"You were supposed to eat that goat in a holy place before the Lord! It is most holy! He gave it to you to take away the guilt of the people. The goat was for removing the sins of the people so they will belong to the Lord. [18]You didn't bring the goat's blood inside the Holy Place. So you were supposed to eat the goat in a holy place, as I commanded!"

[19]But Aaron said to Moses, "Today they brought their sin offering and burnt offering before the Lord. But these terrible things have still happened to me today! Do you think the Lord would be any happier if I ate the sin offering today?" [20]When Moses heard this, he was satisfied.

Rules About What May Be Eaten

11 The Lord spoke to Moses and Aaron. [2]He said, "Tell the people of Israel this: 'These are the land animals you may eat: [3]you may eat any animal that has split hoofs completely divided and chews the cud.[d]

[4]"'Some animals only chew the cud or only have split hoofs. Don't eat these animals. The camel chews the cud but does not have a split hoof. It is unclean[d] for you. [5]The rock badger chews the cud but does not have a split hoof. It is unclean for you. [6]The rabbit chews the cud but does not have a split hoof. It is unclean for you. [7]Now the pig has a split hoof that is completely divided. But it does not chew the cud. It is unclean for you. [8]You must not eat the meat from these animals. Don't even touch their dead bodies. They are unclean for you.

[9]"'Some animals live in the sea or in a river. If the animal has fins and scales, you may eat it. [10]But some animals live in the sea or in a river and do not have fins and scales. This includes the things that fill the water. And it includes all other things that live in the water. You should hate them. [11]You must not eat any meat from them. Don't even touch their dead bodies. This is because you should hate them. [12]You must hate any animal in the water that does not have fins and scales.

[13]"'Also, some birds should not be eaten. They should be hated. You must not eat any of these birds: eagles, vultures, black vultures, [14]kites

or any kind of falcon. 15Don't eat any kind of raven, 16horned owls, screech owls, sea gulls or any kind of hawk. 17Don't eat little owls, cormorants, great owls, 18white owls, desert owls or ospreys. 19Don't eat storks, any kind of heron, hoopoes or bats.

20" 'Don't eat insects that have wings and walk on all four feet. They are also to be hated.

21" 'But you may eat certain insects that have wings and walk on four feet. You may eat those that have legs with joints above their feet so they can jump. 22These are the insects you may eat: all kinds of locusts, winged locusts, crickets and grasshoppers. 23But all other insects that have wings and walk on four feet are hated. 24Those insects will make you unclean. Anyone who touches the dead body of one of these insects will become unclean until evening. 25If someone picks up one of these dead insects, he must wash his clothes. He will be unclean until evening.

26" 'Some animals have split hoofs. But the hoofs are not completely divided. And some animals do not chew the cud. They are unclean for you. Anyone who touches the dead body of one of these animals will become unclean. 27Other animals do not have hoofs at all. They walk on their paws. These animals are unclean for you. Anyone who touches the dead body of one of these animals will become unclean. He will be unclean until evening. 28Anyone who picks up their dead bodies must wash his clothes. He will be unclean until evening. These animals are unclean for you.

29" 'These crawling animals are unclean for you: moles, rats, all kinds of great lizards, 30geckos, crocodiles, lizards, sand reptiles and chameleons. 31These crawling animals are unclean for you. Anyone who touches their dead bodies will be unclean until evening.

32" 'If an unclean animal dies and falls on something, that thing will also become unclean. The animal might fall on a thing made from wood, cloth, leather or rough cloth. It does not matter what the thing was used for. Whatever the animal falls on must be washed with water. It will be unclean until evening. Then it will become clean again. 33The dead, unclean animal might fall into a clay bowl. If it does, anything in the bowl will become unclean. And you must break the bowl. 34If water from the unclean clay bowl gets on any food, that food will become unclean. 35If any dead, unclean animal falls on something, that thing becomes unclean. The animal may fall on a clay oven or a clay baking pan. If so, it must be broken into pieces. These things will be unclean. They are unclean for you.

36" 'A spring or well that collects water will stay clean. But anyone who touches the dead body of any unclean animal will become unclean. 37A dead, unclean animal might fall on a seed to be planted. That seed is still clean. 38But you might put water on some seeds. If a dead, unclean animal falls on those seeds, they are unclean for you.

39" 'Also, an animal which you use for food may die. If it does, anyone who touches its body will be unclean until evening. 40Anyone who eats meat from this animal's dead body must wash his clothes. He will be unclean until evening. Anyone who picks up the animal's dead body must wash his clothes. He will be unclean until evening.

41" 'Every animal that crawls on the ground is one of the hated animals. It must not be eaten. Anyone who picks up the animal's dead body must wash his clothes. He will be unclean until evening. 42You must not eat any of the animals that crawl on the ground. This includes animals that crawl on their stomachs. And it includes animals that walk on all four feet or on many feet.

Those are hated animals to you. ⁴³Do not make yourself unclean by these hated animals. You must not become unclean by them. ⁴⁴I am the Lord your God. Keep yourselves holy for me because I am holy. Don't make yourselves unclean with these hated, crawling animals. ⁴⁵I am the Lord who brought you out of Egypt. I did it so I could be your God. You must be holy because I am holy.

⁴⁶" 'These are the teachings about all of the cattle, birds and other animals on earth. These are the teachings about the animals in the sea. And these are the teachings about the animals that crawl on the ground. ⁴⁷These teachings help people know the difference between unclean animals and clean animals. They help people know which animals may be eaten and which ones must not be eaten'."

Rules for New Mothers

12 The Lord said to Moses, ²"Tell the people of Israel this: 'If a woman gives birth to a son, she will become unclean*ᵈ* for seven days. This will be like her being unclean during her monthly period. ³On the eighth day the boy must be circumcised.*ᵈ* ⁴Then it will be 33 days before she becomes clean from her loss of blood. She must not touch anything that is holy. She must not enter the holy place until her time of cleansing is finished. ⁵But a woman may give birth to a daughter. Then the mother will be unclean for two weeks. This is like her being unclean during her monthly period. It will be 66 days before she becomes clean from her loss of blood.

⁶" 'After she has a son or daughter, she must have a time of cleansing. When it is over, the new mother must bring certain sacrifices to the Meeting Tent.*ᵈ* She must give the priest at the entrance a year-old lamb for a burnt offering. And she must bring a dove or young pigeon for a sin offering. ⁷He

will offer them before the Lord to make her clean so she will belong to the Lord again. Then she will be clean from her loss of blood. These are the teachings for a woman who gives birth to a boy or girl.

⁸" 'If she cannot afford a lamb, she is to bring two doves or two young pigeons. One bird will be for a burnt offering and one for a sin offering. In this way the priest will make her clean so she will belong to the Lord again. And she will be clean'."

Rules About Skin Diseases

13 The Lord said to Moses and Aaron, ²"Someone might have a swelling on his skin. Or he might have a scab or a bright spot on his skin. If the sore looks like a harmful skin disease, the person must be brought to Aaron the priest. Or he must be brought to one of Aaron's sons, the priests. ³The priest must look at the sore on the person's skin. The hair in the sore may have become white. And the sore may seem deeper than the person's skin. If so, it is a harmful skin disease. When he has finished looking at the person, the priest must announce that the person is unclean.*ᵈ*

⁴"Sometimes there is a white spot on a person's skin, but the spot does not seem deeper than the skin. If that is true, and if the hair from the spot has not turned white, the priest must separate that person from other people for seven days. ⁵On the seventh day the priest must look at the person again. He may see that the sore has not changed. It might not have spread on the skin. Then the priest must keep the person separated for seven more days. ⁶On the seventh day the priest must look at the person again. The sore may have faded. And it may not have spread on the skin. If that is true, the priest must announce that the person is clean. The sore is only a rash. The person must wash his

clothes. Then he will become clean again.

7"But the sore may have spread again after the priest has announced him clean. Then the person must come again to the priest. 8The priest must look at him. If the rash has spread on the skin, the priest must announce that person is unclean. It is a harmful skin disease.

9"If a person has a harmful skin disease, he must be brought to the priest. 10The priest must look at him. There might be a white swelling in the skin. And the hair may have become white. And the skin may look raw in the swelling. 11If these things are true, it is a harmful skin disease. It is one that he has had for a long time. The priest must announce that the person is unclean. He will not need to separate that person from other people. This is because everyone already knows that the person is unclean.

12"Sometimes skin disease spreads all over a person's body. The disease covers that person's skin from his head to his feet, as far as the priest can see. Then the priest must look at the person's whole body. 13The priest might see that the disease covers the whole body. It might have turned all of the person's skin white. Then the priest must announce that the person is clean.

14"But when the person has an open sore, he is not clean. 15When the priest sees the open sore, he must announce that the person is unclean. The open sore is not clean. It is a harmful skin disease. 16If the open sore becomes white again, the person must come to the priest. 17The priest must look at him. If the sores have become white, the priest must announce that the person with the sores is clean. Then he will be clean.

18"Someone may have a boil on his skin, but it is healed. 19In the place where the boil was, there might be a white swelling. Or there might be a bright red spot. This place on the skin must be shown to the priest. 20And the priest must look at it. The spot might seem deeper than the skin. And the hair on it might have become white. If these things are true, the priest must announce that the person is unclean. The spot is a harmful skin disease. It has broken out from inside the boil. 21But the priest must look at the spot. There might be no white hairs in it. The spot may not be deeper than the skin. And it may have faded. Then the priest must separate the person from other people for seven days. 22If the spot spreads on the skin, the priest must announce that the person is unclean. It is a disease that will spread. 23But the bright spot might not spread or change. Then it is only the scar from the old boil. Then the priest must announce that the person is clean.

24"A person might get a burn on his skin. If the open sore becomes white or red, 25the priest must look at it. The white spot might seem deeper than the skin. And the hair at that spot might have become white. If these things are true, it is a harmful skin disease. The disease has broken out in the burn. Then the priest must announce that the person is unclean. It is a harmful skin disease. 26But the priest must look at the spot. There might be no white hair in the bright spot. And the spot may be no deeper than the skin. It may have faded. Then the priest must separate the person from other people for seven days. 27On the seventh day the priest must look at him again. If the spot has spread on the skin, the priest must announce that the person is unclean. It is a harmful skin disease. 28But the bright spot may not have spread on the skin. It may have faded. Then it is the swelling from the burn. And the priest must announce that the person is clean. The spot is only a scar from the burn.

²⁹"Someone might get a sore on his scalp or on his chin. ³⁰A priest must look at the sore. It may seem to be deeper than the skin. And the hair around it may be thin and yellow. If these things are true, the priest must announce that the person is unclean. It is an itch, a harmful skin disease of the head or chin. ³¹But when the priest looks at it, the sore might not seem deeper than the skin. There might not be any black hair in it. If that is true, the priest must separate the person from other people for seven days. ³²On the seventh day the priest must look at the sore. It may not have spread. There may be no yellow hairs growing in it. And the sore may not seem deeper than the skin. ³³If these things are true, the person must shave himself. But he must not shave the sore place. The priest must separate that person from other people for seven more days. ³⁴On the seventh day the priest must look at the sore. The sore may not have spread on the skin. And it may not seem deeper than the skin. If that is true, the priest must announce that the person is clean. So the person must wash his clothes and become clean. ³⁵But the sore might spread on the skin after the person has become clean. ³⁶Then the priest must look at him again. If the sore has spread on the skin, the priest doesn't need to look for the yellowish hair. The person is unclean. ³⁷But the priest might think the sore has stopped spreading. And black hair may be growing in it. Then the sore has healed. The person is clean. And the priest must announce that he is clean.

³⁸"When a person has white spots on his skin, ³⁹a priest must look at them. If the spots on his skin are dull white, the disease is only a harmless rash. That person is clean.

⁴⁰"A man might lose hair from his head and be bald. He is clean. ⁴¹He might lose hair from the front of his head and have a bald forehead. He is clean. ⁴²But if there is a red-white sore on his scalp, it is a skin disease. ⁴³A priest must look at that person. The swelling of the sore might be red-white. It might look like a skin disease that spreads. ⁴⁴Then that person has a skin disease. He is unclean. And the priest must announce that the person is unclean because of the sore on his head.

⁴⁵"If a person has a skin disease that spreads, he must warn other people. He must shout, 'Unclean, unclean!' His clothes must be torn at the seams. He must let his hair stay uncombed. And he must cover his mouth. ⁴⁶That person will be unclean the whole time he has the disease. He is unclean. He must live alone outside the camp.

Rules About Mildew

⁴⁷"Some clothing might have mildew[d] on it. The cloth might be linen or wool. ⁴⁸It might be woven or knitted. The mildew might be on a piece of leather or on something made from leather. ⁴⁹The mildew might be in the clothing, leather or woven or knitted material. If the mildew is green or red, it is a spreading mildew. Then it must be shown to the priest. ⁵⁰The priest must look at the mildew. And he must put that thing in a separate place for seven days. ⁵¹On the seventh day he must look at the mildew. It doesn't matter if the mildew is on leather or cloth. It doesn't matter if the cloth is woven or knitted. It doesn't matter what it was used for. If the mildew has spread, it is a mildew that destroys. ⁵²The priest must burn it. It does not matter if it is woven or knitted, wool or linen or a leather article. The mildew is spreading. The thing must be burned.

⁵³"If the priest sees that the mildew has not spread, the cloth or leather must be washed. It does not matter if it is leather or cloth, knitted or woven. It must be washed. ⁵⁴The priest must

order the people to wash that piece of leather or cloth. Then he must separate the clothing for seven more days. ⁵⁵After that time the priest must look at it again. If the mildew still looks the same, that thing is unclean.ᵈ It does not matter if the mildew has not spread. You must burn that cloth or piece of leather.

⁵⁶"But when the priest looks at that piece of leather or cloth, the mildew might have faded. Then the priest must tear the mildew out of the piece of leather or cloth. It does not matter if the cloth is woven or knitted. ⁵⁷But the mildew might come back to that piece of leather or cloth. If that happens, the mildew is spreading. And that piece of leather or cloth must be burned. ⁵⁸The cloth, the woven or knitted material, or the leather may be washed. The mildew may then be gone. It must be washed again. Then it will be clean.

⁵⁹"These are the teachings about mildew on pieces of leather or cloth. It doesn't matter if the cloth is woven or knitted."

Rules for Cleansing from Skin Diseases

14 The Lord said to Moses, ²"These are the teachings for people who had a harmful skin disease and have become well. These teachings are for making that person clean.ᵈ

³"A priest must look at the person who had the skin disease. He must go to that person outside the camp. He must see if the skin disease is healed. ⁴If the person is healthy, the priest will tell him to do these things: he must get two living, clean birds. He must also get a piece of cedar wood, a piece of red cloth and a hyssop plant. These things are for cleansing the person with the skin disease.

⁵"The priest must order one bird to be killed in a clay bowl containing fresh water. ⁶Then he will take the other

bird that is still alive. He will take the piece of cedar wood, the red cloth and the hyssop. He will dip the living bird and other things into the blood. (This is the blood of the bird that was killed over the fresh water.) ⁷The priest will sprinkle the blood seven times on the person who had the skin disease. He must announce that the person is clean. Then the priest must go to an open field. He must let the living bird go free.

⁸"Next, that person must wash his clothes. He must shave off all his hair. And he must wash with water. Then he will be clean and may go into the camp. But at first he must stay outside his tent for seven days. ⁹On the seventh day he must shave off all his hair. He must shave off his hair, his beard and his eyebrows. He must wash his clothes and bathe his body in water. Then he will be clean.

¹⁰"On the eighth day the person who had the skin disease must take two male lambs. They must have nothing wrong with them. He must also take a year-old female lamb. It must have nothing wrong with it. The person must take 6.5 litres of fine flour mixed with oil. This is for a grain offering. He must also take 0.3 of a litre of olive oil. ¹¹A priest must announce that the person is clean. Then he must bring that person and his sacrifices before the Lord. This is at the entrance of the Meeting Tent.ᵈ ¹²The priest will take one of the male lambs. He will offer it and the olive oil as a guilt offering. And he will present them before the Lord as an offering. ¹³Then he will kill the male lamb in the holy place. He will kill it where they kill the sin offering and the whole burnt offering. The penalty offering is like the sin offering. It belongs to the priest. It is most holy.

¹⁴"The priest will take some of the blood of the penalty offering. He will put some of it on the bottom of the right ear of the person to be made

clean. He will put some of it on the thumb of the person's right hand. And he will put some on the big toe of the person's right foot. 15The priest will also take some of the oil and pour it into his own left hand. 16Then he will dip a finger of his right hand into the oil that is in his left hand. He will use his finger to sprinkle some of the oil seven times before the Lord. 17The priest will put some oil from his hand on the bottom of the right ear of the person to be made clean. He will put some of it on the thumb of the person's right hand. And he will put some of it on the big toe of the person's right foot. The oil will go on these places on top of the blood for the penalty offering. 18He will put the rest of the oil that is in his left hand on the head of the person to be made clean. In this way the priest will make that person clean so he can belong to the Lord again.

19"Next the priest will offer the sin offering. It will make that person clean so he can belong to the Lord again. After this the priest will kill the animal for the whole burnt offering. 20Then he will offer the burnt offering and grain offering on the altar. In this way he will make that person clean so he can belong to the Lord again.

21"But the person may be poor and unable to afford these offerings. Then he must take one male lamb for a penalty offering. It will be presented to the Lord so the priest can make that person clean. Then he can belong to the Lord again. The person must take 2 litres of fine flour mixed with oil. It will be used for a grain offering. He must also take 0.3 of a litre of olive oil. 22He must take two doves or two young pigeons, which he can afford. One bird will be a sin offering. The other will be a whole burnt offering. 23On the eighth day the person will bring them to the priest at the entrance of the Meeting Tent. The gifts will be offered before the Lord. This is so the person can become clean.

24The priest will take the lamb for the penalty offering and the oil. He will present them as an offering before the Lord. 25Then he will kill the lamb of the penalty offering. He will take some of the blood of the penalty offering. He will put it on the bottom of the right ear of the person to be made clean. The priest will put some of this blood on the thumb of the person's right hand. And he will put some on the big toe of the person's right foot. 26He will also pour some of the oil into his own left hand. 27Then with a finger of his right hand, he will sprinkle some of the oil from his left hand. He will sprinkle it seven times before the Lord. 28Then the priest will take some of the oil from his hand. He will put it on the bottom of the right ear of the person to be made clean. He will also put some of it on the thumb of the person's right hand. And he will put some on the big toe of the person's right foot. The oil will go on these places on top of the blood from the penalty offering. 29The priest must put the rest of the oil that is in his hand on the head of the person to be made clean. In this way the priest will make the person clean so he can belong to the Lord again. 30Then the priest will offer one of the doves or young pigeons. He must offer what the person can afford. 31He must offer one of the birds as a sin offering. And he must offer the other bird as a whole burnt offering. He must offer them with the grain offering. In this way the priest will make the person clean so he can belong to the Lord again. The person will become clean.

32"These are the teachings for making a person clean. This is done after he has become well from a skin disease. These teachings are for people who cannot afford the regular sacrifices for becoming clean."

Rules for Cleaning Mildew

33The Lord also said to Moses and

Aaron, ³⁴"I am giving the land of Canaan to your people. When they enter that land, I might cause mildewᵈ to grow in someone's house. ³⁵The owner of that house must come and tell the priest. He should say, 'I have seen something like mildew in my house'. ³⁶Then the priest must order the people to empty the house. They must do this before he goes in to look at the mildew. This is so he will not have to say that everything in the house is unclean.ᵈ After the people have emptied the house, the priest will go in to look at it. ³⁷He will look at the mildew. The mildew on the walls of the house might be green or red. It might go into the wall's surface. ³⁸If these things are true, he must go out and close up the house for seven days. ³⁹On the seventh day the priest must come back and check the house. The mildew may have spread on the walls of the house. ⁴⁰If it has, the priest must order the people to tear out the stones with the mildew on them. They should throw the stones away. They must put the stones at a certain unclean place outside the city. ⁴¹Then the priest must have all the inside of the house scraped. The people must throw away the plaster they scraped off the walls. They must put the plaster at a certain unclean place outside the city. ⁴²Then the owner must put new stones in the walls. And he must cover the walls with new clay plaster.

⁴³"A person may have taken away the old stones and plaster. He may have put in new stones and plaster. But mildew may again appear in his house. ⁴⁴If it does, the priest must come back and check the house again. If the mildew has spread in the house, it is a mildew that destroys things. So the house is unclean. ⁴⁵Then the owner must tear down the house. He must remove all its stones, plaster and wood. He must take them to the unclean place outside the city. ⁴⁶Anyone who goes into that house will be unclean until evening. ⁴⁷Anyone who eats in that house or lies down there must wash his clothes.

⁴⁸"After new stones and plaster have been put in a house, the priest must check it again. The mildew may not have spread in the house. Then the priest will announce that the house is clean. This is because the mildew is gone.

⁴⁹"Then, to make the house clean, the priest must take two birds. He must also take a piece of cedar wood, a piece of red cloth and a hyssop plant. ⁵⁰He will kill one bird in a clay bowl containing fresh water. ⁵¹Then he will take the other bird that is still alive. He will also take the cedar wood, the hyssop and the red cloth. He will dip the living bird and other things into the blood. (This is the blood of the bird that was killed over the fresh water.) Then the priest will sprinkle the blood on the house seven times. ⁵²He will use the bird's blood, the fresh water and the live bird. And he will use the cedar wood, the hyssop and the red cloth. With these things he will make the house clean. ⁵³The priest will go to an open field outside the city. And he will let the living bird go free. This is how the priest makes the house clean and ready for service to the Lord."

⁵⁴These are the teachings about any kind of skin disease. ⁵⁵These are the teachings for mildew on pieces of cloth or in a house. ⁵⁶These are also the teachings for swellings, rashes or bright spots on the skin. ⁵⁷They teach when things are unclean and when they are clean. These are the teachings about all these kinds of diseases.

Rules About a Man's Body

15 The Lord also said to Moses and Aaron, ²"Say to the people of Israel: 'When a fluid comes from a man's body, he is unclean.ᵈ ³It doesn't matter if the fluid flows freely or if it is blocked from flowing.

[4]" 'The man who discharges the body fluid may lie on a bed. If he does, that bed becomes unclean. Everything he sits on becomes unclean. [5]Also anyone who touches his bed must wash his clothes and bathe in water. This person will be unclean until evening. [6]Someone might sit on something that the man who discharges the fluid sat on. If he does, he must wash his clothes and bathe in water. He will be unclean until evening. [7]Anyone who touches the man who discharges the body fluid must wash his clothes and bathe in water. The person will be unclean until evening.

[8]" 'The man who discharges the body fluid might spit on a clean person. If so, the person who was clean must wash his clothes. He must bathe in water. The person will be unclean until evening. [9]Everything on which the man who is unclean has ridden will become unclean. [10]Someone might touch something that was under the man who discharges a body fluid. If he does, he will be unclean until evening. Someone might carry these things that were under the man who discharges a body fluid. This person must wash his clothes and bathe in water. He will be unclean until evening.

[11]" 'The man who discharges a body fluid may not have washed his hands in water. If he touches another person, that person must wash his clothes. That person must bathe in water. He will be unclean until evening.

[12]" 'A man who discharges a body fluid may touch a clay bowl. That bowl must be broken. If he touches a wooden bowl, that bowl must be washed in water.

[13]" 'A man who discharges a body fluid may be made clean. He must count seven days for himself for his cleansing. He must wash his clothes and bathe his body in fresh water. Then he will be clean. [14]On the eighth day he must take two doves or two young pigeons. He must come before the Lord at the entrance of the Meeting Tent.[d] He will give the two birds to the priest. [15]The priest will offer the birds. One bird is for a sin offering. The other is for a burnt offering. So the priest will make that man clean so he can belong to the Lord again.

[16]" 'If semen[n] goes out from a man, he must bathe in water. He will be unclean until evening. [17]If the fluid gets on any clothing or leather, it must be washed with water. It will be unclean until evening.

[18]" 'If a man has sexual relations with a woman and semen comes out, both people must bathe in water. They will be unclean until evening.

Rules About a Woman's Body

[19]" 'When a woman has her monthly period, she is unclean[d] for seven days. Anyone who touches her will be unclean until evening. [20]Anything she lies on during this time will be unclean. Everything she sits on during that time will be unclean. [21]Anyone who touches her bed must wash his clothes and bathe in water. That person will be unclean until evening. [22]Anyone who touches something she has sat on must wash his clothes and bathe in water. That person will be unclean until evening. [23]It does not matter if the person touched the woman's bed or something she sat on. That person will be unclean until evening.

[24]" 'A man may have sexual relations with a woman during her monthly period. If he does, he will be unclean for seven days. Every bed he lies on will also be unclean.

[25]" 'A woman might have a loss of blood for many days. It may not be during her regular monthly period. Or

---

semen A man's body fluid by which he can make a woman pregnant.

she may continue to have a loss of blood after her regular period. If she does, she will be unclean, as she is during her monthly period. She will be unclean for as long as she continues to bleed. ²⁶Any bed she lies on during all the time of her bleeding will be like her bed during her regular monthly period. Everything she sits on will be unclean. It will be as it is during her regular monthly period.

²⁷" 'If anyone touches those things, that person will be unclean. He must wash his clothes and bathe in water. He will be unclean until evening. ²⁸When the woman becomes clean from her bleeding, she must wait seven days. After this she will be clean. ²⁹Then on the eighth day she must take two doves or two young pigeons. She must bring them to the priest at the entrance of the Meeting Tent.ᵈ ³⁰Then the priest must offer one bird for a sin offering. He must offer the other bird for a whole burnt offering. So the priest will make her clean so she can belong to the Lord again.

³¹" 'So you must warn the people of Israel to stay separated from things that make them unclean. If you don't warn the people, they might make my Holy Tentᵈ unclean. And then they would have to die!' "

³²These are the teachings for the man who discharges a body fluid. These are the teachings for men who become unclean from semenⁿ coming out of their bodies. ³³These are the teachings for women who become unclean from their monthly period. These are the teachings for anyone who becomes unclean by having sexual relations with another person who is unclean.

The Day of Cleansing

16 Now two of Aaron's sons had died while offering incenseᵈ to the Lord. At that time the Lord spoke to Moses. ²He said, "Talk to your brother Aaron. Tell him there are times when he cannot go behind the curtain into the Most Holy Place where the Holy Arkᵈ is. If he goes in when I appear in a cloud over the lid on the Holy Ark, he will die.

³"Aaron may enter the Most Holy Place only on the Day of Cleansing. Before he enters, he must offer a bull for a sin offering. And he must offer a male sheep for a whole burnt offering. ⁴He must put on these clothes. He will put on the holy linen inner robe. The linen underclothes will be next to his body. His belt will be the cloth belt. And he will wear the linen turban. These are holy clothes. So he must wash his whole body with water before he puts them on.

⁵"Aaron must take from the people of Israel two male goats for a sin offering. And he must take one male sheep for a burnt offering. ⁶Then he will offer the bull for the sin offering. This sin offering is for himself. Then he will perform the acts to remove sins from him and his family so they will belong to the Lord.

⁷"Next Aaron will take the two goats. He will bring them before the Lord at the entrance to the Meeting Tent.ᵈ ⁸Aaron will throw lotsᵈ for the two goats. One lot will be for the Lord. The other lot will be for the goat that removes sin. ⁹Then Aaron will take the goat that was chosen for the Lord by throwing the lot. He must offer this goat as a sin offering. ¹⁰The other goat was chosen by lot to remove the sin. It must be brought alive before the Lord. The priest will use it to perform the acts to remove Israel's sin so they will belong to the Lord. Then this goat will be sent out into the desert.

¹¹"Then Aaron will offer the bull as a sin offering for himself. This will remove the sins of him and his family so

---

semen A man's body fluid by which he can make a woman pregnant.

they will belong to the Lord. He will kill the bull for the sin offering for himself. [12]Then he must take a pan full of burning coals from the altar before the Lord. Aaron must take two handfuls of sweet incense that has been ground into powder. He must bring it into the room behind the curtain. [13]He must put the incense on the fire before the Lord. Then the cloud of incense will cover the lid on the Holy Ark. Then when Aaron comes in, he will not die. [14]Also, Aaron must take some of the blood from the bull. He must sprinkle it with his finger on the front of the lid. Then, with his finger he will sprinkle the blood seven times in front of the lid.

[15]"Then Aaron must kill the goat of the sin offering for the people. He must bring this goat's blood into the room behind the curtain. He must do with the goat's blood as he did with the bull's blood. He must sprinkle the goat's blood on the lid and in front of it. [16]The people in Israel have been unclean.[d] So Aaron will perform the acts to make the Most Holy Place ready for service to the Lord. Then it will be clean from the sins and crimes of the people of Israel. He must do this because the Meeting Tent stays in the middle of unclean people. [17]When Aaron makes the Most Holy Place ready for service to the Lord, no one is allowed in the Meeting Tent. No one must go in until Aaron comes out. So Aaron will perform the acts to remove sins from himself and his family so they will belong to the Lord. Then he will remove the sins of all the people of Israel so they will belong to the Lord. [18]Afterwards he will go out to the altar that is before the Lord. And he will make the altar ready for service to the Lord. Aaron will take some of the bull's blood and some of the goat's blood. He will put it on the corners of the altar on all sides. [19]Then he will sprinkle some of the blood with his finger. He will sprinkle it on the

altar seven times. In this way Aaron will make the altar holy for the Lord. And it will be clean from all the sins of the people of Israel.

[20]"Aaron will make the Most Holy Place, the Meeting Tent and the altar clean. Then he will bring the goat alive to the Lord. [21]He will put both his hands on the head of the living goat. Then he will confess all the sins and crimes of Israel over the goat. In this way Aaron will put the people's sins on the goat's head. Then he will send the goat away into the desert. A man who has been appointed will lead the goat away. [22]So the goat will carry all the people's sins on itself. It will go to a lonely place in the desert. The man who leads the goat will let it loose there.

[23]"Then Aaron will enter the Meeting Tent. He will take off the linen clothes. (He had put them on before he went into the Most Holy Place.) He must leave these clothes there. [24]He will wash his whole body with water in a holy place. Then he will put on his ordinary clothes again. He will come out and offer the whole burnt offering for himself. And he will offer the whole burnt offering for the people. He will remove sins from himself and the people so they will belong to the Lord. [25]Then he will burn the fat of the sin offering on the altar.

[26]"The person who led the goat into the desert must wash his clothes. Then he must wash his whole body with water. After that, he may come back into the camp.

[27]"The bull and goat for the sin offerings must be taken outside the camp. The blood from these animals was brought into the Most Holy Place. It was to make the Holy Place ready for service to the Lord. The priests will burn the animals' skins, bodies and intestines in the fire. [28]Then the one who burns them must wash his clothes. And he must wash

his whole body with water. After that, he may come back into the camp.

²⁹"This law will always continue for you: on the tenth day of the seventh month, you must not eat. You must not do any work. The travellers or foreigners living with you must not work either. ³⁰On this day the priests make you clean so you will belong to the Lord again. All your sins will be removed. ³¹This is a very important day of rest for you. And you must not eat. This law will continue for ever.

³²"So the appointed priest will perform the acts for making things ready for service to the Lord. He is the priest on whom oil was poured. He is appointed to take his father's place. That priest must put on the holy linen clothes. ³³He must make the Most Holy Place ready for service to the Lord. He must make the Meeting Tent and the altar ready for service to the Lord. He must remove the sins of himself and all the people of Israel so they will belong to the Lord. ³⁴That law for removing the sins of the Israelites so they will belong to the Lord will continue for ever. You will do these things once a year."

So they did the things the Lord had commanded Moses.

Offering Sacrifices

17 The Lord said to Moses, ²"Speak to Aaron, his sons and all the people of Israel. Tell them: 'This is what the Lord has commanded: ³an Israelite might sacrifice an ox, a lamb or a goat. He might kill it inside the camp or outside it. ⁴But he should have brought the animal to the entrance to the Meeting Tent.^d He should have given the animal as a gift to the Lord. If he didn't, he is guilty of killing. He must be separated from his people. ⁵This rule is so people will bring their sacrifices to the Lord. They have been sacrificing in the open fields. But they must bring those animals to the Lord at the entrance of the

Meeting Tent. They must bring them to the priest and offer them as fellowship offerings. ⁶Then the priest will sprinkle the blood from those animals on the Lord's altar. It is near the entrance to the Meeting Tent. And the priest will burn the fat from those animals on the altar. This smell will be pleasing to the Lord. ⁷They must not offer any more sacrifices to their goat idols. They have chased after those other gods. In that way they have acted like prostitutes.^d These rules will continue for people from now on'.

⁸"Tell the people this: 'Someone might offer a burnt offering or sacrifice. He might be a citizen of Israel. Or he might be a traveller or foreigner living with you. ⁹That person must take his sacrifice to the entrance to the Meeting Tent. There he may offer it to the Lord. If he does not do this, he must be separated from his people.

¹⁰" 'I will be against anyone who eats blood. It does not matter if it is a citizen of Israel or a foreigner living with you. I will separate that person from his people. ¹¹This is because the life of the body is in the blood. And I have given you rules for pouring that blood on the altar. You must do this to remove your sins so you will belong to the Lord. It is the blood that removes the sins from your life so you will belong to the Lord. ¹²So I tell the people of Israel this: "None of you may eat blood. And no foreigner living among you may eat blood."

¹³" 'Someone may catch a wild animal or bird that can be eaten. The person may be a citizen of Israel or a foreigner living among you. He must pour the blood on the ground and cover it with earth. ¹⁴This is because if blood is still in the meat, the animal's life is still in it. So I give this command to the people of Israel: "Don't eat meat that still has blood in it. Anyone who eats blood must be separated from his people."

¹⁵" 'Someone may eat an animal that

died by itself. Or he may eat an animal that was killed by another animal. The person may be a citizen of Israel or a foreigner living among you. If he eats the animal, he will be unclean until evening. He must wash his clothes and whole body with water. [16]If he does not wash his clothes and bathe his body, he will be guilty of sin'."

Rules About Sexual Relations

18 The Lord said to Moses, [2]"Tell the people of Israel: 'I am the Lord your God. [3]In the past you lived in Egypt. You must not do what was done in that country. And you must not do as they do in the land of Canaan where I am bringing you. Do not follow their customs. [4]You must obey my rules and follow them. I am the Lord your God. [5]Obey my laws and rules. A person who obeys my laws and rules will live because of them. I am the Lord.

[6]" 'You must never have sexual relations with your close relatives. I am the Lord.

[7]" 'You must not shame your father by having sexual relations with your mother. She is your mother. Do not have sexual relations with her. [8]You must not have sexual relations with your father's wife. That would shame your father.

[9]" 'You must not have sexual relations with your sister. She may be the daughter of your father or your mother. It doesn't matter if she was born in your house or somewhere else.

[10]" 'You must not have sexual relations with your granddaughter. She may be your son's daughter or your daughter's daughter. That would bring shame on you.

[11]" 'If your father and his wife have a daughter, she is your sister. You must not have sexual relations with her.

[12]" 'You must not have sexual relations with your father's sister. She is your father's close relative. [13]You must not have sexual relations with your mother's sister. She is your mother's close relative. [14]You must not have sexual relations with the wife of your father's brother. This would shame him. His wife is your aunt.

[15]" 'You must not have sexual relations with your daughter-in-law. She is your son's wife. Do not have sexual relations with her.

[16]" 'You must not have sexual relations with your brother's wife. That would shame your brother.

[17]" 'You must not have sexual relations with both a woman and her daughter. And do not have sexual relations with this woman's granddaughter. She may be the daughter of her son or her daughter. They are her close relatives. It is evil to do this.

[18]" 'While your wife is still living, you must not take her sister as another wife. Do not have sexual relations with her.

[19]" 'You must not go near a woman to have sexual relations with her during her monthly period. She is unclean[d] during this time.

[20]" 'You must not have sexual relations with your neighbour's wife and make yourself unclean with her.

[21]" 'You must not give any of your children to be sacrificed to Molech.[d] This will show that you do not respect your God. I am the Lord.

[22]" 'You must not have sexual relations with a man as you would a woman. That is a hated sin.

[23]" 'You must not have sexual relations with an animal and make yourself unclean with it. Also a woman must not have sexual relations with an animal. It is not natural.

[24]" 'Don't make yourself unclean by any of these wrong things. I am forcing nations out of their countries because they did these sins. And I am giving their land to you. [25]The land has become unclean. So I punished it for its sins. And the land is throwing out those people who live there.

26" 'You must obey my laws and rules. You must not do any of these hated sins. These rules are for the citizens of Israel. They are also for the people who live with you. 27The people who lived in the land before you did all these hated things. So the land became unclean. 28If you do these things, you will also make the land unclean. And it will throw you out as it threw out the nations before you. 29Anyone who does these hated sins must be separated from his people. 30The people who lived in the land before you have done these hated sins. But you must not do them. You must obey my laws. Don't make yourself unclean by these hated sins. I am the Lord your God'."

Other Laws

19 The Lord said to Moses, 2"Tell all the people of Israel: 'I am the Lord your God. You must be holy because I am holy.

3" 'Each person among you must respect his mother and father. And you must keep my Sabbaths.d I am the Lord your God.

4" 'Do not worship idols. Do not make statues or gods for yourselves. I am the Lord your God.

5" 'You may sacrifice a fellowship offering to the Lord. If you do, you must offer it so you will be accepted. 6You may eat it the same day you offer it. And you may also eat it on the next day. But if any is left on the third day, you must burn it up. 7If any of it is eaten on the third day, it is unclean.d It will not be accepted. 8Anyone who eats it then will be guilty of sin. This is because he did not respect the holy things that belong to the Lord. He must be separated from his people.

9" 'You harvest your crops on your land. But do not harvest all the way to the corners of your fields. If grain falls onto the ground, don't gather it up. 10Don't pick all the grapes in your vineyards. And don't pick up the grapes that fall to the ground. You must leave those things for poor people. You must also leave them for people travelling through your country. I am the Lord your God.

11" 'You must not steal. You must not cheat people. You must not lie to each other. 12You must not make a false promise by my name. If you do that, you will show that you don't respect your God. I am the Lord.

13" 'You must not cheat your neighbour. You must not rob him. You must not keep a hired worker's salary all night until morning. 14You must not curse a deaf man. And you must not put something in front of a blind person to make him fall. But you must respect your God. I am the Lord.

15" 'Be fair in your judging. You must not show special favour to poor people or great people. You must be fair when you judge your neighbour. 16You must not spread false stories against other people. You must not do anything that would put your neighbour's life in danger. I am the Lord.

17" 'You must not hate your brother in your heart. If your neighbour does something wrong, tell him about it. If you do not, you will be partly to blame. 18Forget about the wrong things people do to you. You must not try to get even. Love your neighbour as you love yourself. I am the Lord.

19" 'Obey my laws. You must not mate two different kinds of cattle. You must not sow your field with two different kinds of seed. You must not wear clothing made from two different kinds of material mixed together.

20" 'A man might have sexual relations with a slave girl of another man. But this slave girl has not been bought or given her freedom. If this happens, there must be punishment. But they are not to be put to death. This is because the woman was not free. 21The man must bring a male sheep as his penalty offering. He must bring it to the Lord at the entrance to the Meeting Tent.*d* ²²The priest will offer the male sheep as a penalty offering before the Lord. It will be for the man's sin. The priest will perform the acts to remove the sins of the man so he will belong to the Lord. Then the man will be forgiven for his sin.

²³" 'In the future you will enter your country. You will plant many kinds of trees for food. After planting a tree, wait three years before using its fruit. ²⁴In the fourth year the fruit from the tree will be the Lord's. It will be a holy offering of praise to him. ²⁵Then in the fifth year, you may eat the fruit from the tree. The tree will then produce more fruit for you. I am the Lord your God.

²⁶" 'You must not eat anything with the blood in it.

" 'You must not try to tell the future by signs or black magic.

²⁷" 'You must not cut the hair on the sides of your heads. And you must not cut the edges of your beard. ²⁸You must not cut your body to show sadness for someone who died. Do not put tattoo marks on yourselves. I am the Lord.

²⁹" 'You must not make your daughter become a prostitute.*d* That only shows you do not respect her. If you do this, the country will be filled with all kinds of sin.

³⁰" 'Obey the laws about Sabbaths. You must respect my Most Holy Place. I am the Lord.

³¹" 'Do not go to mediums*d* or fortune-tellers for advice. If you do, you will become unclean. I am the Lord your God.

³²" 'Show respect to old people. Stand up when they come into the room. Show respect also to your God. I am the Lord.

³³" 'Do not mistreat foreigners living in your country. ³⁴Treat them just as you treat your own citizens. Love foreigners as you love yourselves, because you were foreigners once. That

was in Egypt. I am the Lord your God.

³⁵" 'Be fair when you judge people. And be fair when you measure and weigh things. ³⁶Your weighing baskets should be the right size. And your jars should hold the right amount of liquid. Your weights and balances should weigh correctly. I am the Lord your God. I brought you out of the land of Egypt.

³⁷" 'Remember all my laws and rules, and obey them. I am the Lord'."

Warnings About Various Sins

20 The Lord said to Moses, ²"You must also tell the people of Israel these things: 'A person in your country might give one of his children to Molech.*d* That person must be killed. It doesn't matter if he is a citizen or a foreigner living in Israel. You must throw stones at him and kill him. ³I will be against him. I will separate him from his people. This is because he gave his children to Molech. He showed that he did not respect my holy name. And he made my Holy Place unclean.*d* ⁴The people of the community might ignore that person. They might not kill the one who gave his children to Molech. ⁵But I will be against him and his family. I will separate him from his people. I will do this to anyone who is unfaithful to me and who worships Molech.

⁶" 'I will be against anyone who goes to mediums*d* and fortune-tellers for advice. He is being unfaithful to me. So I will separate him from his people.

⁷" 'Be my holy people. Be holy because I am holy. I am the Lord your God. ⁸Remember and obey my laws. I am the Lord, and I have made you holy.

⁹" 'Anyone who curses his father or mother must be put to death. He has cursed his father or mother. So he must be punished.

Punishments for Sexual Sins

¹⁰" 'A man might have sexual relations with his neighbour's wife. If he does, both the man and the woman are guilty of adultery.ᵈ So they must be put to death. ¹¹A man might have sexual relations with his father's wife. If he does, both the man and his father's wife must be put to death. They have brought it on themselves. That man has shamed his father.

¹²" 'A man might have sexual relations with his daughter-in-law. If he does, both of them must be put to death. What they have done is not natural. It must be punished.

¹³" 'A man might have sexual relations with another man as a man does with a woman. If he does, these two men have done a hated sin. They must be put to death. They have brought it on themselves.

¹⁴" 'A man might have sexual relations with both a woman and her mother. This is evil. The people must burn that man and the two women in fire. Do this so that your people will not be evil.

¹⁵" 'A man might have sexual relations with an animal. If he does, he must be put to death. And you must also kill the animal. ¹⁶A woman might have sexual relations with an animal. If she does, you must kill the woman and the animal. They must be put to death. They have brought it on themselves.

¹⁷" 'It is shameful for a brother to marry his sister and to have sexual relations with her. In front of everyone they must both be separated from their people. The man has shamed his sister. And he is guilty of sin.

¹⁸" 'A man might have sexual relations with a woman during her monthly period. If he does, both the woman and the man must be separated from their people. They sinned because they showed the source of her blood.

¹⁹" 'Do not have sexual relations with your mother's sister or your father's sister. That would shame a close relative. Both of you are guilty of this sin.

²⁰" 'A man must not have sexual relations with his uncle's wife. That would shame his uncle. That man and his uncle's wife would die without children. They are guilty of sin.

²¹" 'It is unclean for a man to marry his brother's wife. That man has shamed his brother. They would have no children.

²²" 'Remember all my laws and rules, and obey them. I am leading you to your own land. If you obey my laws and rules, that land will not throw you out. ²³I am forcing the people who live there out of that country ahead of you. Because they did all these sins I have hated them. Do not live the way those people lived.

²⁴" 'I have told you that you will get their land. I will give it to you as your very own. It is a land where much food grows. I am the Lord your God. I have set you apart from other people and made you my own. ²⁵So you must treat clean animals and birds differently from unclean animals. Do not make yourselves unclean by any of these unclean birds or animals or things that crawl on the ground. I have made them unclean for you. ²⁶I have set you apart from other people. So you must be holy to me. This is because I am the Lord, and I am holy.

²⁷" 'A man or woman who is a mediumᵈ or a fortune-teller must be put to death. You must kill them with stones. They have brought it on themselves'."

How Priests Must Behave

21 The Lord said to Moses, "Tell these things to Aaron's sons, the priests: 'A priest must not make himself uncleanᵈ by touching a dead person. ²But if the dead person was one of his close relatives, he may touch him. The priest may make him-

self unclean if the dead person is his mother or father, son or daughter, brother or ³unmarried sister. This sister is close to him because she has no husband. So the priest may make himself unclean for her if she dies. ⁴But a priest must not make himself unclean if the dead person was only related to him by marriage.

⁵" 'Priests must not shave their heads. They must not shave off the edges of their beards. They must not cut their bodies. ⁶Priests must be holy to their God. They must show respect for God's name. This is because they present the offerings made by fire to the Lord. This is the food of their God. So they must be holy.

⁷" 'A priest serves God in a special way. So he must not marry an unclean prostitute ᵈ or a divorced woman. ⁸Treat the priest in a special way. Think of him as holy. This is because he offers up the food of your God. I am the Lord. I make you holy. And I am holy.

⁹" 'If a priest's daughter makes herself unclean by becoming a prostitute, she shames her father. She must be burned with fire.

¹⁰" 'The high priest was chosen from among his brothers. The special olive oil used in appointing people and things to the service of the Lord was poured on his head. He was appointed to wear the priestly clothes. So he must not do things to show his sadness in public. He must not let his hair go uncombed. He must not tear his clothes. ¹¹He must not go into a house where there is a dead body. He must not make himself unclean, even if it is his own father or mother. ¹²The high priest must not go out of the Holy Place. If he does and becomes unclean, he would make God's Holy Place unclean. The special oil used in appointing priests was poured on the high priest's head. This separated him from the rest of the people. I am the Lord.

¹³" 'The high priest must marry a woman who is a virgin.ᵈ ¹⁴He must not marry a widow, a divorced woman or a prostitute. He must marry a virgin from his own people. ¹⁵This is so the people will respect his children as his own. I am the Lord. I have set the high priest apart for his special job'."

¹⁶The Lord said to Moses, ¹⁷"Tell Aaron: 'Some of your descendantsᵈ might have something wrong with them. If they do, they must never offer the special food of their God. ¹⁸Anyone who has something wrong with him must not serve as priest. And he must not bring sacrifices to me. These people cannot serve as priests: blind men, crippled men, men with damaged faces, deformed men, ¹⁹men with a crippled foot or hand, ²⁰hunchbacks, dwarfs, men who have something wrong with their eyes, men who have an itching disease or a skin disease or men who have damaged sex glands.

²¹" 'One of Aaron's descendantsᵈ might have something wrong with him. If he does, he cannot make the offerings made by fire to the Lord. He has something wrong with him. He cannot offer the food of his God. ²²But he is from the family of priests. So he may eat the most holy food. He may also eat the holy food. ²³But he may not go through the curtain into the Most Holy Place. He may not go near the altar. He has something wrong with him. He must not make my Holy Place unfit. I am the Lord. I make these things holy'."

²⁴So Moses told these things to Aaron, Aaron's sons and all the people of Israel.

22 The Lord said to Moses, ²"Tell Aaron and his sons: 'The people of Israel will give offerings to me. These offerings are holy, and they are mine. So you must respect these offerings. This will show that you respect my holy name. I am the Lord. ³The people of Israel made the offerings holy for me. One of your descendants[d] might be unclean[d] and touch the offerings. From now on, anyone who does must be separated from appearing before me. I am the Lord.

4" 'One of Aaron's descendants might have one of the harmful skin diseases. Or he might discharge a body fluid. He cannot eat the holy offerings until he becomes clean. He can become unclean from touching a dead body or from his own semen."[n] [5]He will become unclean if he touches any unclean crawling animal. He will become unclean if he touches an unclean person. It doesn't matter what made him unclean. [6]Anyone who touches those things will become unclean until evening. That person must not eat the holy offerings. But if he washes with water, he may eat the holy offerings. [7]He will be clean only after the sun goes down. Then he may eat the holy offerings. The offerings are his food.

[8]" 'A priest might find an animal that died by itself. Or he might find one that was killed by some other animal. He must not eat that dead animal. If he eats it, he will become unclean. I am the Lord.

[9]" 'The priests must keep all the rules I have given. That way they will not become guilty. If they are careful, they will not die. I am the Lord. I have made them holy. [10]Only people in a priest's family may eat the holy offerings. A visitor staying with the priest must not eat it. A hired worker must not eat it. [11]But the priest might buy a slave with his own money. If he does, that slave may eat the holy offerings. Slaves who were born in the priest's house may also eat the priest's food. [12]A priest's daughter might marry a person who is not a priest. If she does, she must not eat any of the holy offerings. [13]The husband of a priest's daughter might die. Or the daughter might become divorced. She might not have children to support her. So she might go back to her father's house where she lived as a child. If this happens, she may eat some of her father's food. But only people from a priest's family may eat this food.

[14]" 'Someone might eat some of the holy offering by mistake. That person must pay back the priest for that holy food. He must also pay the priest another one-fifth of the price of that food.

[15]" 'The people of Israel will give offerings to the Lord. These gifts become holy. So the priest must not treat these holy things as though they were not holy. [16]The priests might allow someone who is not a priest to eat the holy offerings. If they do, they are treating those offerings as though they were not holy. The person who eats will become guilty. He will have to pay for it. I am the Lord. I make them holy'."

[17]The Lord said to Moses, [18]"Tell Aaron and his sons and all the people of Israel: 'A citizen of Israel or a foreigner living in Israel might want to bring a whole burnt offering. It might be for some special promise he has made. Or it might be a special gift he wanted to give to the Lord. [19]If he does, he must bring a male animal. It must have nothing wrong with it. The gift might be a bull, a sheep or a goat. This is so that it might be accepted for him. [20]He must not bring an animal that has something wrong with it. It will not be accepted for him.

[21]" 'Someone might bring a fellowship offering to the Lord. That offering might be payment for a special promise the person made. Or it may be a special gift the person wanted to give the Lord. It might be a bull or a sheep. But it must be healthy. There must be nothing wrong with it. This is so it might be accepted for him. [22]You

---

semen A man's body fluid by which he can make a woman pregnant.

must not offer to the Lord any animal that is blind. It must not have broken bones or be crippled. It must not have running sores or any sort of skin disease. You must not offer any animals like these on the altar. They cannot be used as an offering by fire to the Lord. 23" 'Sometimes a bull or lamb is smaller than normal. Or it may not be perfectly formed. If someone wants to give that animal as a special gift to the Lord, it will be accepted. But it will not be accepted as payment for a special promise the person made. 24" 'An animal might have bruised, crushed, torn or cut sex glands. If it does, you must not offer that animal to the Lord in your own land. 25You must not take such animals from foreigners as sacrifices to the Lord. This is because the animals have been hurt in some way. They have something wrong with them. They will not be accepted for you.' "

26The Lord said to Moses, 27"When an ox, a sheep or a goat is born, it must stay seven days with its mother. But from the eighth day on, this animal will be accepted as a sacrifice. It may be offered by fire to the Lord. 28But you must not kill the animal and its mother on the same day. This rule is the same for an ox or a sheep.

29"You might want to offer some special offering of thanks to the Lord. But you must do it in a way that pleases the Lord. 30You must eat the whole animal that same day. You must not leave any of the meat for the next morning. I am the Lord.

31"Remember my commands and obey them. I am the Lord. 32Show respect for my holy name. You Israelites must remember that I am holy. I am the Lord. I have made you holy. 33I brought you out of Egypt. I became your God. I am the Lord."

Special Holidays

23 The Lord said to Moses, 2"Tell the people of Israel: 'You will announce the Lord's appointed feasts as holy meetings. These are my special feasts.

The Sabbath

3" 'There are six days for you to work. But the seventh day will be a special day of rest. It is a day for a holy meeting. You must not do any work. It is a Sabbath*d* to the Lord in all your homes.

The Passover and Unleavened Bread

4" 'These are the Lord's appointed feasts. You will announce the holy meetings at the times set for them. 5The Lord's Passover*d* is on the fourteenth day of the first month. It begins at twilight. 6The Feast*d* of Unleavened Bread begins on the fifteenth day of the same month. You will eat bread made without yeast for seven days. 7On the first day of this feast you will have a holy meeting. On that day you must not do any work. 8For seven days you will bring an offering made by fire to the Lord. There will be a holy meeting on the seventh day. And on that day you must not do any ordinary work'. "

The Feast of Harvests

9The Lord said to Moses, 10"Tell the people of Israel: 'You will enter the land I will give you. You will gather its harvest. At that time you must bring the first bundle of grain from your harvest to the priest. 11The priest will present the bundle before the Lord. Then it will be accepted for you. He will present the bundle on the day after the Sabbath.*d* 12" 'On the day when you present the bundle of grain, offer a male lamb. It must be one year old. There must be nothing wrong with it. It will be a burnt offering to the Lord. 13You must also offer a grain offering. It should be 4.5 litres of fine flour mixed with olive oil. It is an offering made by fire to the

Lord. Its smell will be pleasing to the Lord. You must also offer a litre of wine as a drink offering. 14First bring your offering to your God. Until you do this, do not eat the new grain, roasted grain or bread made from the new grain. This law will always continue for people from now on, wherever you live.

The Feast of Pentecost

15" 'Count seven weeks from the morning after the Sabbath.*d* (This is the Sabbath that you bring the bundle of grain to present as an offering.) 16On the fiftieth day, you will bring a new grain offering to the Lord. This is the first day after the seventh week. 17On that day bring two loaves of bread from your homes. That bread will be presented as an offering. Use yeast and 4.5 litres of flour to make those loaves of bread. They will be your gift to the Lord from the first wheat of your harvest.

18" 'Offer one bull, two male sheep and seven male lambs. The lambs must be one year old. There must be nothing wrong with them. Offer them with their grain offerings and drink offerings. They will be a burnt offering to the Lord. They will be an offering made by fire. And the smell will be pleasing to the Lord. 19You must also offer one male goat for a sin offering. You must offer two male, one-year-old lambs as a fellowship offering.

20" 'The priest will present the two lambs as an offering. He will present them with the bread from the first wheat of the harvest. They are holy to the Lord. They will belong to the priest. 21On that same day you will call a holy meeting. You must not do any work that day. This law will continue for you from now on, wherever you live.

22" 'You will harvest your crops on your land. But do not harvest all the way to the corners of your field. If grain falls onto the ground, don't gath-

er it up. Leave it for poor people and foreigners in your country. I am the Lord your God'."

Feast of Trumpets

23Again the Lord said to Moses, 24"Tell the people of Israel: 'On the first day of the seventh month you must have a special day of rest. There will be a holy meeting. Blow the trumpet for a special time of remembering. 25Do not do any work. And bring an offering made by fire to the Lord'."

The Day of Cleansing

26The Lord said to Moses, 27"The Day of Cleansing will be on the tenth day of the seventh month. There will be a holy meeting. You will give up eating and bring an offering made by fire to the Lord. 28Do not do any work on that day. This is because it is the Day of Cleansing. On that day the priests will go before the Lord. They will perform the acts to make you clean*d* so you will belong to the Lord.

29"If anyone refuses to give up food on this day, he must be separated from his people. 30If anyone works on this day, I will destroy him from among his people. 31You must not do any work at all. This law will continue for people from now on wherever you live. 32It will be a special day of rest for you. And you must not eat. You will start this special day of rest on the evening after the ninth day of the month. It will continue from that evening until the next evening."

The Feast of Shelters

33Again the Lord said to Moses, 34"Tell the people of Israel: 'On the fifteenth day of the seventh month is the Feast*d* of Shelters. This feast to the Lord will continue for seven days. 35There will be a holy meeting on the first day. Do not do any work. 36You will bring an offering made by fire to the Lord each day for seven days. On the eighth day you will have another holy meeting. And you will bring an offering made by fire to the Lord. This will be a holy meeting. Do not do any work.

37(" 'These are the Lord's special feasts. There will be holy meetings on these feast days. You will bring offerings made by fire to the Lord. They will be whole burnt offerings, grain offerings, sacrifices and drink offerings. You must bring these gifts at the right times. 38You must bring these offerings in addition to those for the Lord's Sabbath*d* days. You must offer them in addition to offerings you give as payment for special promises. They are also in addition to special offerings you want to give to the Lord.)

39" 'So on the fifteenth day of the seventh month, celebrate the Lord's festival for seven days. By then you will have gathered in the crops of the land. You must rest on the first day and the seventh day. 40On the first day you will take good fruit from the fruit trees. And you will take branches from palms, poplars and other leafy trees. You will celebrate before the Lord your God for seven days. 41Celebrate this festival to the Lord for seven days each year. This law will continue from now on. You will celebrate it in the seventh month. 42Live in shelters for seven days. All the people born in Israel must live in shelters. 43This is so that all your descendants*d* will know I made Israel live in shelters. It was during the time I brought them out of Egypt. I am the Lord your God'."

44So Moses told the people of Israel about all of the Lord's appointed feast days.

The Lampstand and the Holy Bread

24 The Lord said to Moses, 2"Command the people of Israel to bring you pure oil from crushed olives. That oil is for the lamps. These lamps must never go out. 3Aaron will keep the lamps burning in the Meeting Tent.*d* They will burn from evening until morning before the Lord. This will be in front of the curtain of the Ark*d* of God. This law will continue from now on. 4Aaron must always keep the lamps burning. They are on the lampstands of pure gold before the Lord.

5"Take fine flour and bake 12 loaves of bread with it. Use 4.5 litres of flour for each loaf. 6Put them in two rows on the golden table before the Lord. Six loaves will be in each row. 7Put pure incense*d* on each row. This is the memorial portion to take the place of the bread. It is an offering made by fire to the Lord. 8Every Sabbath*d* day Aaron will put the bread in order before the Lord. This agreement with the people of Israel will continue for ever. 9That bread will belong to Aaron and his sons. They will eat it in a holy place. This is because it is a most holy part of the offerings made by fire to the Lord. That bread is their share for ever."

The Man Who Cursed God

10Now there was a son of an Israelite woman and an Egyptian father. The son was walking among the Israelites. And a fight broke out in the camp between him and an Israelite. 11The son of the Israelite woman began cursing and speaking against the Lord. So the people took him to Moses. (The mother's name was Shelomith. She was the daughter of Debri from the family of Dan.) 12The people held him as a prisoner. They waited for the Lord's command to be made clear to them.

13Then the Lord said to Moses, 14"Take the one who spoke against me outside the camp. Then bring together all the people who heard him. They must put their hands on his head.ⁿ Then all the people must throw stones at him and kill him. ¹⁵Tell the people of Israel this: 'If anyone curses his God, he is guilty of sin. ¹⁶Anyone who speaks against the Lord must be put to death. All the people must kill him by throwing stones at him. Foreigners must be punished just like the person born in Israel. If someone speaks against the Lord, he must be put to death.

¹⁷" 'If someone kills another person, he must be put to death. ¹⁸Someone might kill an animal that belongs to another person. If he does, he must give that person another animal to take its place. ¹⁹And someone might cause an injury to his neighbour. If he does, the same kind of injury must be given back to him. ²⁰A broken bone must be paid for a broken bone, an eye for an eye and a tooth for a tooth. In the same way someone injures another person, so he must be injured in return. ²¹So anyone who kills another person's animal must give that person another animal to take its place. But the person who kills another person must be put to death.

²²" 'The law will be the same for the foreigner as for those from your own country. I am the Lord your God'."

²³Then Moses spoke to the people of Israel. And they took the person who had cursed outside the camp. Then they killed him with stones. So the people of Israel did as the Lord had commanded Moses.

The Time of Rest for the Land

25 The Lord spoke to Moses at Mount Sinai. He said, ²"Tell the people of Israel this: 'I will give you land. When you enter it, let it have a special time of rest. This will be to honour the Lord. ³You may plant seed in your field for six years. You may trim your vineyards for six years and bring in their fruits. ⁴But during the seventh year, you must let the land rest. This will be a special time to honour the Lord. You must not plant seed in your field or trim your vineyards. ⁵You must not cut the crops that grow by themselves after harvest. You must not gather the grapes from your vines that are not trimmed. The land will have a year of rest.

⁶" 'You may eat whatever the land produces during that year of rest. It will be food for your men and women servants. It will be food for your hired workers and the foreigners living in your country. ⁷It will also be food for your cattle and the wild animals of your land. Whatever the land produces may be eaten.

The Year of Jubilee

⁸" 'Count off seven groups of seven years. This will be 49 years. During that time there will be seven years of rest for the land. ⁹On the Day of Cleansing,ᵈ you must blow the horn of a male sheep. This will be on the tenth day of the seventh month. You must blow the horn through the whole country. ¹⁰Make the fiftieth year a special year. Announce freedom for all the people living in your country. This time will be called Jubilee.ⁿ Each of you will go back to his own property. And each of you will go back to his own family and family group. ¹¹The fiftieth year will be a special time for you to celebrate. Don't plant seeds. Don't harvest the crops that grow by themselves. Don't gather grapes from the vines that are not trimmed. ¹²That year is Jubilee. It will be a holy time for you. You may eat the crops that come from the field. ¹³In the year of Jubilee each person will go back to his own property.

¹⁴" 'Don't cheat your neighbour

---

put . . . head This shows that all these people were sharing in punishing the one who spoke against God.
Jubilee This word comes from the Hebrew word for a horn of a male sheep.

when you sell your land to him. And don't let him cheat you when you buy land from him. [15]You might want to buy your neighbour's land. If you do, count the number of years since the last Jubilee. Use that number to decide the right price. If he sells the land to you, count the number of years left for harvesting crops. Use that number to decide the right price. [16]If there are many years, the price will be high. If there are only a few years, lower the price. This is because your neighbour is really selling only a few crops to you. At the next Jubilee the land will again belong to his family. [17]You must not cheat each other. You must respect your God. I am the Lord your God.

[18]" 'Remember my laws and rules, and obey them. Then you will live safely in the land. [19]The land will give good crops to you. You will eat as much as you want. And you will live safely in the land.

[20]" 'But you might ask, "If we don't plant seeds or gather crops, what will we eat in the seventh year?" [21]Don't worry. I will send you a great blessing during the sixth year. That year the land will produce enough crops for three years. [22]When you plant in the eighth year, you will still be eating from the old crop. You will eat the old crop until the harvest of the ninth year.

Property Laws

[23]" 'The land really belongs to me. So you can't sell it for ever. You are only foreigners and travellers living for a time on my land. [24]People might sell their land. But the family will always get its land back. [25]A person in your country might become very poor. He might be so poor that he must sell his land. So his close relatives must come and buy it back for him. [26]A person might not have a close relative to buy back his land for him. But he might get enough money to buy it back himself. [27]He must

count the years since the land was sold. He must use that number to decide how much to pay for the land. Then he may buy it back. And the land will be his again. [28]But he might not find enough money to buy it back for himself. Then the one who bought it will keep it until the year of Jubilee.[d] But during that celebration, the land will go back to the first owner's family.

[29]" 'Someone may sell a home in a walled city. But, for a full year after he sold it, he has the right to buy it back. [30]But the owner might not buy back the house before a full year is over. If he doesn't, the house in the walled city will belong to the one who bought it. It will belong to his future sons. The house will not go back to the first owner at Jubilee. [31]But houses in small towns without walls are like open country. They can be bought back. And they must be returned to their first owner at Jubilee.

[32]" 'The Levites may always buy back their houses. This is true in the cities which belong to them. [33]Someone might buy a house from a Levite. But that house in the Levites' city will again belong to the Levites in the Jubilee. This is because houses in Levite cities belong to the people of Levi. The people of Israel gave these cities to the Levites. [34]Also the fields and pastures around the Levites' cities cannot be sold. Those fields belong to the Levites for ever.

Rules for Slave Owners

[35]" 'Someone from your country might become too poor to support himself. Help him to live among you as you would a stranger or foreigner. [36]Do not charge him any interest on money you loan to him. Respect your God. And let the poor man live among you. [37]Don't lend him money for interest. Don't try to make a profit from the food he buys. [38]I am the Lord your God. I brought you out of the land of Egypt. I did it to give the land of Ca-

naan to you and to become your God.
39" 'Someone from your country might become very poor. He might even sell himself as a slave to you. If he does, you must not make him work like a slave. 40He will be like a hired worker. And he will be like a visitor with you until the year of Jubilee.*d* 41Then he may leave you. He may take his children and go back to his family and the land of his ancestors. 42This is because the Israelites are my servants. I brought them out of slavery in Egypt. They must not become slaves again. 43You must not rule this person cruelly. You must respect your God.

44" 'You may buy men and women slaves from other nations around you. 45Also you may buy children as slaves. These children must come from the families of foreigners living in your land. These child slaves will belong to you. 46You may even pass these foreign slaves on to your children after you die. You can make them slaves for ever. But you must not rule cruelly over your own brothers, the Israelites.

47" 'A foreigner or visitor among you might become rich. And someone in your country might become poor. The poor man might sell himself as a slave to a foreigner living among you. Or he might sell himself to a member of a foreigner's family. 48The poor man has the right to be bought back and become free. One of his relatives may buy him back. 49His uncle or his uncle's son may buy him back. One of his close relatives may buy him back. Or if he gets enough money, he may pay the money himself. Then he will be free again.

50" 'How do you decide the price? You must count the years from the time he sold himself to the foreigner. And count up to the next year of Jubilee. Use that number to decide the price. This is because the person really only hired himself out for a cer-

tain number of years. 51There might still be many years before the year of Jubilee. If so, the person must pay back a large part of the price. 52There might only be a few years left until Jubilee. If so, the person must pay a small part of the first price. 53But he will live like a hired man with the foreigner every year. Don't let the foreigner rule cruelly over him.

54" 'That person will become free, even if no one buys him back. At the year of Jubilee, he and his children will become free. 55This is because the people of Israel are my servants. I brought them out of slavery in Egypt. I am the Lord your God.

Rewards for Obeying God

26 " 'Don't make idols for yourselves. Don't set up statues or memorials. Don't put stone statues in your land to bow down to. This is because I am the Lord your God.

2" 'Remember my Sabbaths,*d* and respect my Holy Place. I am the Lord. 3" 'Remember my laws and commands, and obey them. 4If you do these things, I will give you rains at the right season. The land will produce crops. And the trees of the field will produce their fruit. 5Your threshing*d* will continue until the grape harvest. And your grape harvest will continue until it is time to plant. Then you will have plenty to eat. You will live safely in your land. 6I will give peace to your country. You will lie down in peace. No one will make you afraid. I will keep harmful animals out of your country. And armies will not pass through your country.

7" 'You will chase your enemies and defeat them. You will kill them with your sword. 8Five of you will chase 100 men. And 100 of you will chase 10,000 men. You will defeat your enemies and kill them with your sword.

9" 'Then I will show kindness to you. I will let you have many children. I will keep my agreement with you.

¹⁰You will have enough crops to last for more than a year. You will harvest the new crops. And you will have to throw out the old crops to make room for the new ones. ¹¹Also I will place my Holy Tent*d* among you. I will not turn away from you. ¹²I will walk with you and be your God. And you will be my people. ¹³I am the Lord your God. You were slaves in Egypt. You were bent low from the heavy weights you carried as slaves. But I broke the heavy weights that were on your shoulders. I let you walk proudly again.

Punishment for Not Obeying God

¹⁴" 'But you must obey me. You must obey all my commands. ¹⁵If you refuse to obey all my laws and commands, you have broken our agreement. ¹⁶If you do that, I will cause terrible things to happen to you. I will cause you to have disease and fever. They will destroy your eyes and kill you. You will not have success when you plant your seed. And your enemy will eat your crops. ¹⁷I will be against you, and your enemies will defeat you. These enemies hate you. And they will rule over you. You will run away even when no one is chasing you.

¹⁸" 'If you still do not obey me, I will punish you seven times more for your sins. ¹⁹And I will also break the great cities that make you proud. The skies will not give rain. The earth will not produce crops. ²⁰You will work hard, but it will not help. Your land will not grow any crops. Your trees will not give their fruit.

²¹" 'If you still turn against me and refuse to obey me, I will beat you seven times harder. The more you sin, the more you will be punished. ²²I will send wild animals to attack you. They will take your children away from you. They will destroy your cattle. They will make you so few in number the roads will be empty.

²³" 'If you don't learn your lesson after all these things, and if you still turn against me, ²⁴I will also turn against you. I will punish you seven more times for your sins. ²⁵You broke my agreement, and I will punish you. I will bring armies against you. You will go into your cities for safety. But I will cause diseases to spread among you. Then your enemy will defeat you. ²⁶There will be very little bread to eat. Ten women will be able to cook all your bread in one oven. They will measure each piece of bread. You will eat, but you will still be hungry.

²⁷" 'If you still refuse to listen to me, and if you still turn against me, ²⁸I will really show my anger. I will punish you seven more times for your sins. ²⁹You will eat the bodies of your sons and daughters. ³⁰I will destroy your places where false gods are worshipped. I will cut down your incense*d* altars. I will pile your dead bodies on the lifeless forms of your idols. I will hate you. ³¹I will destroy your cities. I will make your holy places empty. I will not smell the pleasing smell of your offerings. ³²I will make the land empty. Your enemies who come to live in it will be shocked at it. ³³I will scatter you among the nations. I will pull out my sword and destroy you. Your land will become empty. Your cities will become waste. ³⁴You will be taken to your enemy's country. So your land will finally get its rest. It will enjoy its time of rest all the time it lies empty. ³⁵During the time the land is empty, it will rest. It will have the rest you should have given it while you lived in it.

³⁶" 'Those who are left alive will lose their courage in the land of their enemies. They will be frightened of everything. They will be frightened by even the sound of a leaf being blown by the wind. They will run as if someone were chasing them with a sword. They will fall even when no one is chasing them. ³⁷They will run as if

someone were chasing them with a sword. They will fall over each other, even though no one is chasing them. You will not be strong enough to stand up against your enemies. 38You will die among other nations. You will disappear in your enemies' countries. 39So those who are left alive will rot away in their enemies' countries. They will rot away because of their sins and their ancestors' sins.

There Is Always Hope

40" 'But perhaps the people will confess their sins and the sins of their ancestors. Perhaps they will admit they turned against me and sinned against me. 41That made me turn against them. So I sent them into the land of their enemies. These disobedient people might be sorry for what they did. They might accept punishment for their sin. 42If they do, I will remember my agreement with Jacob. I will remember my agreement with Isaac and Abraham. And I will remember the land. 43The land will be empty. It will enjoy its time of rest. Then those who are left alive will accept the punishment for their sins. They will learn that they were punished because they hated my laws. And they refused to obey my rules. 44They truly sinned. But if they come to me for help, I will not turn away from them. I will listen to them even in the land of their enemies. I will not completely destroy them. I will not break my agreement with them. This is because I am the Lord their God. 45For their good I will remember the agreement with their ancestors. I brought their ancestors out of the land of Egypt. I did it so I could become their God. The other nations saw these things. I am the Lord'."

46These are the laws, rules and teachings the Lord gave the people of Israel. He gave these laws to the Israelites through Moses. This was at Mount Sinai.

Promises Are Important

27 The Lord said to Moses, 2"Tell the people of Israel: 'Someone might make a special promise to the Lord. He might promise to give himself or another person as a servant to the Lord. That person will then begin to serve the Lord in a special way. The priest must set a certain price for that person. That is the price that would have to be paid to free the person from his special promise to the Lord. 3The price for a man 20 to 60 years old is about 0.6 kilograms of silver. (You must use the measure as set by the Holy Place.) 4The price for a woman 20 to 60 years old is about 345 grams of silver. 5The price for a man five to 20 years old is about 230 grams of silver. The price for a woman five to 20 years old is about 115 grams of silver. 6The price for a baby boy one month to five years old is about 55 grams of silver. For a baby girl the price is about 35 grams of silver. 7The price for a man 60 years old or older is about 170 grams of silver. The price for a woman 60 years old or older is about 115 grams of silver.

8" 'A person might be too poor to pay the price. If he is, bring him to the priest. The priest will decide how much money the person can afford to pay.

Gifts to the Lord

9" 'Some animals may be used as sacrifices to the Lord. If someone promises to bring one of these animals, it will become holy. 10That person must not try to put another animal in its place. He must not try to exchange it for something else. He must not try to exchange a good animal for a bad animal. And he must not exchange a bad animal for a good animal. If he tries to exchange animals, both animals will become holy. 11" 'Unclean*d* animals cannot be offered as sacrifices to the Lord. Someone might bring one of them to the Lord. If he does, that animal must be brought to the priest. ¹²The priest will decide a price for the animal. The price will be according to whether the animal is good or bad. If the priest decides a price, that is the price for the animal. ¹³If the person wants to buy back the animal, he must add an additional one-fifth to the price.

Value of a House

¹⁴" 'A person might give his house as holy to the Lord. If he does, the priest must decide its value. The price will be according to whether the house is good or bad. If the priest decides a price, that is the price for the house. ¹⁵But the person who gives the house might want to buy it back. If he does, he must add an additional one-fifth to the price. Then the house will belong to him again.

Value of Land

¹⁶" 'A person might give part of his fields to the Lord. The value of those fields will depend on how much seed is needed to plant them. It will cost about 0.6 kilograms of silver for each 220 litres of barley seed needed. ¹⁷The person might give his field at the year of Jubilee.ᵈ Then its value will be what the priest decides. ¹⁸But he might give his field after the Jubilee. If he does, the priest must decide the exact price. He must count the number of years to the next year of Jubilee. Then he will use that number to decide the exact price. ¹⁹The person who gave the field might want to buy it back. If he does, he must add one-fifth to that price. Then the field will belong to him again. ²⁰" 'If he does not buy back the field, it will always belong to the priest. If it is sold to someone else, the first person cannot buy it back. ²¹But the person might not buy back the land. If he

doesn't, at the year of Jubilee, it will remain holy to the Lord. It will belong to the priest for ever. It will become the property of the priests. ²²" 'Someone may give a field he has bought to the Lord. But it may not be a part of his family land. ²³If he gives a field, the priest must count the years to the next Jubilee. He must decide the price for the land. Then that land will belong to the Lord. ²⁴At the year of Jubilee, the land will go back to its first owner. It will go back to the family who sold the land.

²⁵" 'Use the measure as set by the Holy Place in paying these prices. It weighs 11.5 grams.

Value of Animals

²⁶" 'People may give cattle and sheep to the Lord. But if an animal is the first one born to its parent, it already belongs to the Lord. So people may not give these animals again. ²⁷If the animal is unclean,ᵈ the person must buy it back. The priest will decide the price of the animal. And the person must add one-fifth to that price. If he does not buy it back, the priest must sell it. He will sell it for the price he had decided. ²⁸" 'There is a special kind of gift that people give to the Lord. It may be a person, animal or field from the family property. That gift cannot be bought back or sold. It is most holy to the Lord. ²⁹" 'If a person is given for the purpose of being destroyed, he cannot be bought back. He must be put to death. ³⁰" 'One-tenth of all crops belongs to the Lord. This includes the crops from fields and the fruit from trees. That one-tenth belongs to the Lord. ³¹A person might want to get back his tenth. If he does, he must add one-fifth to its price and buy it back. ³²" 'The priest will take every tenth animal from a person's cattle or

sheep. It will belong to the Lord. 33The owner should not pick out the good animals from the bad. He should not exchange one animal for another. If he does exchange it, both animals will become holy. They cannot be bought back'."

34These are the commands the Lord commanded at Mount Sinai. They are for the people of Israel.

NUMBERS

Wandering in the Desert

The People of Israel Are Counted

1 The Lord spoke to Moses in the Meeting Tent.*d* This was in the Desert of Sinai. It was on the first day of the second month. This was in the second year after the people of Israel left Egypt. The Lord said to Moses: 2"Count all the people of Israel. List the name of each man with his family and family group. 3You and Aaron must count all the men of Israel 20 years old or older. They will serve in the army of Israel. List them by their divisions. 4One man from each tribe*d* will help you. He is to be the leader of his family. 5These are the names of the men who will help you:

from the tribe of Reuben—
 Elizur son of Shedeur;
6from the tribe of Simeon—
 Shelumiel son of Zurishaddai;
7from the tribe of Judah—
 Nahshon son of Ammina-
 dab;
8from the tribe of Issachar—
 Nethanel son of Zuar;
9from the tribe of Zebulun—
 Eliab son of Helon;
10from the tribe of Ephraim son
 of Joseph—Elishama son
 of Ammihud;
from the tribe of Manasseh
 son of Joseph—Gamaliel
 son of Pedahzur;
11from the tribe of Benjamin—
 Abidan son of Gideoni;
12from the tribe of Dan—
 Ahiezer son of Ammishad-
 dai;
13from the tribe of Asher—
 Pagiel son of Ocran;

14from the tribe of Gad—
 Eliasaph son of Deuel;
15from the tribe of Naphtali—
 Ahira son of Enan."

16All these men were chosen by the people to be leaders of their tribes. They were the leaders of their family groups.

17Moses and Aaron took these men who had been picked. 18And Moses and Aaron called all the people of Israel together. This was the first day of the second month. Then the people were listed by their families and family groups. All the men who were 20 years old or older were listed by name. 19Moses did exactly what the Lord had commanded. Moses listed the people while they were in the Desert of Sinai.

20The tribe of Reuben was counted. Reuben was the first son born to Israel. All the men 20 years old or older who were able to serve in the army were listed. They were each listed by name with their families and family groups. 21The tribe of Reuben totaled 46,500 men.

22The tribe of Simeon was counted. All the men 20 years old or older who were able to serve in the army were listed. They were each listed by name with their families and family groups. 23The tribe of Simeon totaled 59,300 men.

24The tribe of Gad was counted. All the men 20 years old or older who were able to serve in the army were listed. They were listed by name with their families and family groups. 25The tribe of Gad totaled 45,650 men.

26The tribe of Judah was counted. All the men 20 years old or older who were able to serve in the army were listed. They were listed by name with their families and family groups. 27The tribe of Judah totalled 74,600 men.

28The tribe of Issachar was counted. All the men 20 years old or older who were able to serve in the army were listed. They were listed by name with their families and family groups. 29The tribe of Issachar totalled 54,400 men.

30The tribe of Zebulun was counted. All the men 20 years old or older who were able to serve in the army were listed. They were listed by name with their families and family groups. 31The tribe of Zebulun totalled 57,400 men.

32The tribe of Ephraim was counted. (Ephraim was a son of Joseph.) All the men 20 years old or older who were able to serve in the army were listed. They were listed by name with their families and family groups. 33The tribe of Ephraim totalled 40,500 men.

34The tribe of Manasseh was counted. (Manasseh was also a son of Joseph.) All the men 20 years old or older who were able to serve in the army were listed. They were listed by name with their families and family groups. 35The tribe of Manasseh totalled 32,200 men.

36The tribe of Benjamin was counted. All the men 20 years old or older who were able to serve in the army were listed. They were listed by name with their families and family groups. 37The tribe of Benjamin totalled 35,400 men.

38The tribe of Dan was counted. All the men 20 years old or older who were able to serve in the army were listed. They were listed by name with their families and family groups. 39The tribe of Dan totalled 62,700 men.

40The tribe of Asher was counted. All the men 20 years old or older who were able to serve in the army were listed. They were listed by name with their families and family groups. 41The tribe of Asher totalled 41,500 men.

42The tribe of Naphtali was counted. All the men 20 years old or older who were able to serve in the army were listed. They were listed by name with their families and family groups. 43The tribe of Naphtali totalled 53,400 men.

44Moses, Aaron and the 12 leaders of Israel counted these men. There was one leader from each of the families. 45Every man of Israel 20 years old or older who was able to serve in the army was counted. Each man was listed with his family. 46The total number of men was 603,550.

47The families from the tribe of Levi were not listed with the others. 48The Lord had told Moses: 49"Do not count the tribe of Levi or include them with the other Israelites. 50But make the Levites responsible for the Holy Tent*d* of the Agreement. They must take care of it and everything that is with it. They must carry the Holy Tent and everything in it. They must take care of it and make their camp around it. 51Whenever the Holy Tent is moved, the Levites must take it down. Whenever it is set up, the Levites must do it. If anyone else goes near the Holy Tent, he will be put to death. 52The Israelites will make their camps in separate divisions, each man near his family flag. 53But the Levites must make their camp around the Holy Tent of the Agreement. Then I will not be angry with the Israelites. The Levites will take care of the Holy Tent of the Agreement."

54So the Israelites did everything the Lord commanded Moses.

The Camp Arrangement

2 The Lord said to Moses and Aaron: 2"The Israelites should make their camps around the Meeting Tent.*d* But they should not camp too close to it. Each person should camp under the flag of his division near the banner of his family group."

3The camp of Judah will be on the east side, where the sun rises. They will camp by divisions there under their flag. The leader of the people of Judah is Nahshon son of Amminadab. [4]There are 74,600 men in his division.

[5]Next to them the tribe[d] of Issachar will camp. The leader of the people of Issachar is Nethanel son of Zuar. [6]There are 54,400 men in his division.

[7]Next is the tribe of Zebulun. The leader of the people of Zebulun is Eliab son of Helon. [8]There are 57,400 men in his division.

[9]There are a total of 186,400 men in the camp of Judah. They are in their divisions. They will be the first to march out of camp.

[10]The divisions of the camp of Reuben will be south of the Holy Tent. They will camp under their flag. The leader of the people of Reuben is Elizur son of Shedeur. [11]There are 46,500 men in his division.

[12]Next to them the tribe of Simeon will camp. The leader of the people of Simeon is Shelumiel son of Zurishaddai. [13]There are 59,300 men in his division.

[14]Next is the tribe of Gad. The leader of the people of Gad is Eliasaph son of Deuel. [15]There are 45,650 men in his division.

[16]There are a total of 151,450 men in the camp of Reuben. They are in their divisions. They will be the second group to march out of camp.

[17]When the Levites move the Meeting Tent, they will be in between the other camps. The tribes will move in the same order as they camp. Each person will be with his family flag.

[18]The divisions of the camp of Ephraim will be on the west side. They will camp under their flag. The leader of the people of Ephraim is Elishama son of Ammihud. [19]There are 40,500 men in his division.

[20]Next to them the tribe of Manasseh will camp. The leader of the people of Manasseh is Gamaliel son of Pedahzur. [21]There are 32,200 men in his division.

[22]Next to them the tribe of Benjamin will camp. The leader of the people of Benjamin is Abidan son of Gideoni. [23]There are 35,400 men in his division.

[24]There are a total of 108,100 men in the camp of Ephraim. They are in their divisions. They will be the third group to march out of camp.

[25]The divisions of the camp of Dan will be on the north side. They will camp under their flag. The leader of the people of Dan is Ahiezer son of Ammishaddai. [26]There are 62,700 men in his division.

[27]Next to them the tribe of Asher will camp. The leader of the people of Asher is Pagiel son of Ocran. [28]There are 41,500 men in his division.

[29]Next is the tribe of Naphtali. The leader of the people of Naphtali is Ahira son of Enan. [30]There are 53,400 men in his division.

[31]There are 157,600 men in the camp of Dan. They will be the last to march out of camp. They will travel under their own flag.

[32]These are the Israelites who were counted by families. The total number of Israelites in the camps, counted by divisions, is 603,550. [33]Moses did not count the Levites among the other people of Israel. This is what the Lord had commanded.

[34]So the Israelites obeyed everything the Lord commanded Moses. They camped under their flags. Each person travelled with his family and family group.

Aaron's Family, the Priests

3 This is the family history of Aaron and Moses. This was at the time the Lord talked to Moses on Mount Sinai.

[2]Aaron had four sons. Nadab was the oldest. Then Aaron had Abihu, Eleazar and Ithamar. [3]Those were the names of Aaron's sons. They were appointed to serve as priests. [4]But Nadab and Abihu died when they

sinned in the presence of the Lord. They made an offering to the Lord in the Desert of Sinai. But they used the wrong kind of fire. They had no sons. So Eleazar and Ithamar served as priests during the lifetime of their father Aaron.

5The Lord said to Moses, 6"Bring the tribe*d* of Levi to Aaron the priest. They must help him. 7They will help him and all the Israelites at the Meeting Tent.*d* They will do the work of the Holy Tent. 8The Levites must take care of everything in the Meeting Tent. They will serve the people of Israel by doing the work in the Holy Tent. 9Give the Levites to Aaron and his sons. Of all the Israelites, the Levites are given completely to him. 10Appoint Aaron and his sons to serve as priests. Anyone else who comes near the holy things must be put to death."

11The Lord also said to Moses, 12"I am choosing the Levites from all the Israelites. They will take the place of all the firstborn*d* children of Israel. The Levites will be mine. 13All the firstborn are mine. When you were in Egypt, I killed all the firstborn children of the Egyptians. I took all the firstborn of Israel to be mine. Firstborn animals and children are mine. I am the Lord."

14The Lord again talked to Moses in the Desert of Sinai. The Lord said, 15"Count the Levites by families and family groups. Count every male one month old or older." 16So Moses obeyed the Lord and counted them all.

17Levi had three sons. Their names were Gershon, Kohath and Merari. 18The Gershonite family groups were Libni and Shimei. 19The Kohathite family groups were Amram, Izhar, Hebron and Uzziel. 20The Merarite family groups were Mahli and Mushi.

These were the family groups that belonged to the Levites.

21The family groups of Libni and Shimei belonged to Gershon. They were all the Gershonite family groups. 22They had 7,500 males one month or older. 23The Gershonite family groups camped on the west side, behind the Holy Tent. 24The leader of the families of Gershon was Eliasaph son of Lael. 25In the Meeting Tent the Gershonites were responsible for taking care of these things: the Holy Tent, its covering, the curtain at the entrance to the Meeting Tent, 26the curtains in the courtyard, the curtain at the entrance to the courtyard around the Holy Tent and the altar, the ropes and all the work connected with these things.

27The family groups of Amram, Izhar, Hebron and Uzziel belonged to Kohath. They were all the Kohathite family groups. 28They had 8,600 males one month old or older. They were responsible for taking care of the Holy Place. 29The Kohathite family groups camped south of the Holy Tent. 30The leader of the Kohathite families was Elizaphan son of Uzziel. 31They were responsible for the Holy Ark,*d* the table, the lampstand, the altars, the tools of the Holy Place, the curtain and all the work connected with these things. 32The main leader of the Levites was Eleazar son of Aaron, the priest. Eleazar was in charge of all those responsible for the Holy Place.

33The family groups of Mahli and Mushi belonged to Merari. They were all the Merarite family groups. 34They had 6,200 males one month old or older. 35The leader of the Merari families was Zuriel son of Abihail. They were to camp north of the Holy Tent. 36The Merarites were responsible for the frame of the Holy Tent, the braces, the posts, the bases and all the work connected with these things. 37They were also responsible for the posts in the courtyard around the Holy Tent and their bases, tent pegs and ropes.

38Moses, Aaron and his sons camped east of the Holy Tent. They were in front of the Meeting Tent. They were responsible for the Holy Place. They did this for the Israelites. Anyone else who came near the Holy Place was to be put to death.

39Moses and Aaron counted the Levite men. The Lord commanded this. There were 22,000 males one month old or older.

Levites Take the Place of the Firstborn Sons

40The Lord said to Moses, "Count all the firstborn*d* sons in Israel one month old or older. List their names. 41Take the Levites for me instead of the firstborn sons of Israel. Take the animals of the Levites instead of the firstborn animals from the rest of Israel. I am the Lord."

42So Moses did what the Lord commanded. Moses counted all the firstborn sons of the Israelites. 43He listed all the firstborn sons one month old or older. There were 22,273 names.

44The Lord also said to Moses, 45"Take the Levites instead of all the firstborn sons of the Israelites. And take the animals of the Levites instead of the animals of the other people. The Levites are mine. I am the Lord. 46There are 273 more firstborn sons than Levites. 47So collect 55 grams of silver for each of the 273 sons. Use the measure as set by the Holy Place. It weighs 9 grams. 48Give the silver to Aaron and his sons. It is the payment for the 273 Israelites."

49So Moses collected the money for the people the Levites could not replace. 50Moses collected the silver from the firstborn of the Israelites. He collected 15.5 kilograms of silver, using the measure set by the Holy Place. 51So Moses obeyed the Lord. When he had finished he gave the silver to Aaron and his sons.

The Jobs of the Kohath Family

4 The Lord said to Moses and Aaron, 2"Count the Kohathites among the Levites. Count them by family groups and families. 3Count the men from 30 to 50 years old. They will serve in the Meeting Tent.*d*

4"They are responsible for the most holy things in the Meeting Tent. 5When the Israelites move, Aaron and his sons must go into the Holy Tent. They are to take down the curtain. Then they must cover the Ark*d* of God with it. 6Over this they must put a covering made from fine leather. Then they must spread the solid blue cloth over it. And they must put the poles in the rings on the Holy Ark.

7"Then they must spread a blue cloth over the table. This is the table for the bread that shows we are in God's presence. They must put the plates, spoons, bowls and the jars for drink offerings on the table. They must leave the bread on the table. 8Then they must put a red cloth over all of these things. They must cover everything with fine leather. Then they must put the poles in place.

9"With a blue cloth they must cover the lampstand, its lamps, its wick trimmers and trays. They must cover all the jars for the oil used in the lamps. 10Then they must wrap everything in fine leather. They must put all these things on a frame for carrying them.

11"They must spread a blue cloth over the gold altar. Then they must cover it with fine leather. They must put its poles in place.

12"They must gather everything used for serving in the Holy Place. They must wrap them in a blue cloth. Then they must cover that with fine leather. They must put these things on a frame for carrying them.

13"They must clean the ashes off the bronze altar. Then they must spread a purple cloth over it. 14They must gather all the things used for serving at the altar. These are the pans for carrying the fire, meat forks, shovels and bowls. They must put them on the bronze altar. Then they must spread a covering of fine leather over it. They must put the carrying poles in the rings on the altar.

¹⁵"When the camp is ready to move, have Aaron and his sons cover all the holy things. Then the Kohathites may go in and carry away those things. This way they won't touch the holy things and die. It is the Kohathites' job to carry the things that are in the Meeting Tent.

¹⁶"Eleazar son of Aaron, the priest, will be responsible for the Holy Tent. And he is responsible for everything in it: the oil for the lamp, the sweet-smelling incense,*d* the continual grain offering and the oil used to appoint priests and things to the Lord's service."

¹⁷The Lord said to Moses and Aaron, ¹⁸"Don't let the Kohathites be destroyed from the Levites. ¹⁹Do this for the Kohathites. Then they may go near the Most Holy Place and not die. Aaron and his sons must go in and show each Kohathite what to do. And they must show each man what to carry. ²⁰The Kohathites must not enter and look at the holy things, even for a second. If they do, they will die."

The Jobs of the Gershon Family

²¹The Lord said to Moses, ²²"Count the Gershonites by families and family groups. ²³Count the men from 30 to 50 years old. Everyone has a job to do in the Meeting Tent.*d*

²⁴"This is what the Gershonite family groups must do and what they must carry. ²⁵They must carry the pieces of cloth of the Holy Tent*d* and Meeting Tent. They must also carry its covering and the covering made from fine leather. And they must carry the curtains for the entrance to the Meeting Tent. ²⁶They must carry the curtains

of the courtyard that goes around the Holy Tent and the altar. They must carry the curtain for the entry to the courtyard and the ropes and all the things used with the curtains. They must do everything connected with these things. ²⁷Aaron and his sons are in charge of what the Gershonites do or carry. You tell them what they are responsible for carrying. ²⁸This is the work of the Gershonite family group at the Meeting Tent. Ithamar son of Aaron, the priest, will direct their work.

The Jobs of the Merari Family

²⁹"Count the Merarite families and family groups. ³⁰Count the men from 30 to 50 years old. They will work at the Meeting Tent.*d* ³¹It is their job to carry the frame of the Meeting Tent, the crossbars, the posts and bases. ³²They must also carry the posts that go around the courtyard. They must carry the bases, tent pegs and ropes. And they must carry everything that is used with the poles around the courtyard. Tell each man exactly what to carry. ³³This is the work the Merarites will do for the Meeting Tent. Ithamar son of Aaron, the priest, will direct their work."

The Levite Families

³⁴Moses, Aaron and the leaders of Israel counted the Kohathites by families and family groups. ³⁵The men from 30 to 50 years old were to work at the Meeting Tent.*d* ³⁶The family group had 2,750 men. ³⁷This was the total of the Kohath family group who worked at the Meeting Tent. Moses and Aaron counted them as the Lord had commanded Moses.

³⁸Also, the Gershon family group was counted by families and family groups. ³⁹The men from 30 to 50 years old were given work at the Meeting Tent. ⁴⁰The families and family groups had 2,630 men. ⁴¹This was the total of the Gershon family group

who worked at the Meeting Tent. Moses and Aaron counted them as the Lord had commanded.

⁴²Also, the men in the families and family groups of the Merari family were counted. ⁴³The men from 30 to 50 years old were to work at the Meeting Tent. ⁴⁴The family group had 3,200 men. ⁴⁵This was the total of the Merari family group. Moses and Aaron counted them as the Lord had commanded Moses.

⁴⁶So Moses, Aaron and the leaders of Israel counted all the Levites. They counted them by families and family groups. ⁴⁷The men from 30 to 50 were given work at the Meeting Tent. They also carried the Tent. ⁴⁸The total number of these men was 8,580. ⁴⁹Each man was counted as the Lord had commanded Moses. Each man was given his work and told what to carry. This was as the Lord had commanded Moses.

Rules About Cleanliness

5 The Lord said to Moses, ²"Command the Israelites to send away from camp anyone with a harmful skin disease. Send away anyone who gives off body fluid. And send away anyone who has touched a dead body. ³Send both men and women away from camp. Then they won't spread the disease there. I am living among you." ⁴So Israel obeyed God's command. They sent those people outside the camp as the Lord had told Moses.

Paying for Doing Wrong

⁵The Lord said to Moses, ⁶"Tell the Israelites: 'When a man or woman does something wrong to another person, that is really sinning against God. That person is guilty. ⁷He must tell what he has done wrong. And he must fully pay for the wrong he has done. Then he must add one-fifth to it. And he must give it to the person he wronged. ⁸But that person may be dead. That person may not have any

close relatives to receive the payment. Then the one who did wrong owes the Lord. That person must pay the priest. The priest must sacrifice a male sheep to remove the wrong so that the person will belong to God. ⁹When an Israelite brings a holy gift, he should give it to the priest. ¹⁰No one has to give these holy gifts. But if someone does give them, they belong to the priest'."

Suspicious Husbands

¹¹Then the Lord said to Moses, ¹²"Tell the Israelites: 'A man's wife might be unfaithful to him. ¹³She might have sexual relations with another man. Her sin might be kept hidden from her husband. Her husband might not know about the wrong thing she did. Perhaps no one saw it, and she wasn't caught. ¹⁴But her husband might have feelings of jealousy whether she has sinned or not. ¹⁵He then should take her to the priest. The husband must also take an offering for her. This offering will be 2 litres of barley flour. He must not pour oil or incense*d* on it. This is a grain offering for jealousy. It is to find out if she is guilty.

¹⁶"The priest will bring in the woman and make her stand before the Lord. ¹⁷He will take some holy water in a clay jar. Then he will put some dirt from the floor of the Holy Tent into the water. ¹⁸The priest will make the woman stand before the Lord. Then he will loosen her hair. And he will hand her the grain offering for jealousy. He will hold the bitter water that brings a curse on her. ¹⁹The priest will tell her what the oath says will happen to her. He will ask her, "Has another man had sexual relations with you? Have you been unfaithful to your husband? If you haven't, then this water that brings a curse won't hurt you. ²⁰But what if you have been unfaithful to your husband? What if you have had sexual relations with a man besides

your husband?" ²¹The priest will tell her the curse that the oath will bring. He will say, "If you are guilty, the Lord will make the people curse you. Your stomach will get big, and you will not be able to have another baby. ²²This water that brings a curse will go inside you. Your stomach will get big, and you will not be able to have another baby."

" 'The woman must say, "I agree."

²³" 'The priest should write these curses on a scroll. Then he should wash the words off into the water. ²⁴Then he will make the woman drink the water that brings a curse. When she does, it may make her sick. ²⁵Then the priest will take the grain offering for jealousy from her. He will present it before the Lord. Then he will bring it to the altar. ²⁶Then the priest will take a handful of the grain. This is a memorial offering. He will burn it on the altar. After that he will make the woman drink the water. ²⁷He will make her drink it to see if she is not pure. He will know if she has sinned against her husband. When it goes into her, her stomach may get big. And she may not be able to have another baby. Her people will turn against her. ²⁸But if the woman has not sinned, she is pure. She is not guilty. She will be able to have more babies.

²⁹" 'So this is the teaching about jealousy. This is what to do when a woman is unfaithful to her husband. ³⁰It also should be done if the man gets jealous because he suspects his wife. The priest will have her stand before the Lord. Then he will do all these things. This is the teaching. ³¹If the husband is right, the woman will suffer'."

The Nazirites

6 The Lord said to Moses, ²"Tell the Israelites: 'A man or a woman might want to promise to belong to the Lord in a special way. This person

will be called a Nazirite. ³During this time, he must not drink wine or beer. He must not drink vinegar made from wine or beer. He must not even drink grape juice or eat grapes or raisins. ⁴While he is a Nazirite, he must not eat anything that comes from the grapevine. He must not even eat the seeds or the skin.

⁵" 'During the time he promised to belong to the Lord, he must not cut his hair. He must be holy until this special time is over. He must let his hair grow long. ⁶During his special time of belonging to the Lord, a Nazirite must not go near a dead body. ⁷Even if his own father, mother, brother or sister dies, he must not touch them. This would make him unclean.[d] He must still keep his promise to belong to God in a special way. ⁸While he is a Nazirite, he belongs to the Lord.

⁹" 'If he is next to someone who dies suddenly, his hair has been made unclean. This was part of his promise. So he must shave his head seven days later to be clean. ¹⁰Then on the eighth day, he must bring two doves or two young pigeons to the priest. The priest will be at the entrance to the Holy Tent.[d] ¹¹The priest will offer one as a sin offering. He will offer the other as a burnt offering. This removes sin so the man will belong to God. He had sinned because he was near a dead body. That same day he will again promise to let his hair grow for the Lord. ¹²He must give himself to the Lord for another special time. He must bring a male lamb a year old. It will be a penalty offering. The days of the special time before don't count. This is because he became unclean during his first special time.

¹³" 'This is the teaching for a Nazirite. When the promised time is over, he must go the entrance of the Meeting Tent.[d] ¹⁴There he will give his offerings to the Lord. He must offer a year-old male lamb as a burnt offering.

It must have nothing wrong with it. He must also offer a year-old female lamb as a sin offering. There must be nothing wrong with it. And he must bring a male sheep for a fellowship offering. There must be nothing wrong with it. 15He must also bring the grain offerings and drink offerings that go with them. And he must bring a basket of bread made without yeast. There must be loaves made with fine flour mixed with oil. And there must be wafers made without yeast spread with oil.

16" 'The priest will give these offerings to the Lord. He will make the sin offering and the burnt offering. 17Then he will kill the male sheep as a fellowship offering to the Lord. Along with it, he will present the basket of bread. He will also make the grain offering and the drink offering along with the fellowship offering.

18" 'The Nazirite must go to the entrance of the Meeting Tent. There he must shave off his hair that he grew for his promise. The hair will be put in the fire that is under the sacrifice on the fellowship offering.

19" 'After the Nazirite cuts off his hair, the priest will give him a boiled shoulder from the male sheep. From the basket he will also give him a loaf and a wafer. Both are made without yeast. 20Then the priest will present them to the Lord. This is an offering presented before the Lord. They are holy and belong to the priest. Also, he is to present the breast and the thigh from the male sheep to the Lord. They also belong to the priest. After that, the Nazirite may drink wine.

21" 'This is the teaching for the Nazirite promise. If a person makes the Nazirite promise, he must give all of these gifts to the Lord. If he promised to do more, he must keep his promise. That is also the teaching of the Nazirite promise'."

The Priests' Blessings

22The Lord said to Moses, 23"Tell Aaron and his sons, 'This is how you should bless the Israelites. Say to them:

24"May the Lord bless you and keep
    you.
25May the Lord show you his
    kindness.
May he have mercy on you.
26May the Lord watch over you
    and give you peace".'

27"So Aaron and his sons will bless the Israelites with my name. And I will bless them."

The Holy Tent

7 When Moses had finished setting up the Holy Tent,^{d} he gave it for service to the Lord. Moses poured olive oil on the Tent and on everything used in the Tent. He also poured oil on the altar and all its tools. In this way he prepared them for service to the Lord. 2Then the leaders of Israel made offerings. These were the heads of the families and leaders of each tribe.^{d} They were the men who counted the people. 3They brought to the Lord six covered carts and 12 oxen. Each leader gave an ox. Every two leaders gave a cart. They gave these to the Holy Tent.

4The Lord said to Moses, 5"Accept these gifts from the leaders. Use them in the work of the Meeting Tent. Give them to the Levites as they need them."

6So Moses accepted the carts and the oxen. He gave them to the Levites. 7He gave two carts and four oxen to the Gershonites. This is what they needed for their work. 8Then Moses gave four carts and eight oxen to the Merarites. This is what they needed for their work. Ithamar son of Aaron, the priest, directed the work of all of them. 9Moses did not give any oxen or carts to the Kohathites. They were to carry the holy things

on their shoulders. This was their job.
¹⁰The oil was poured on the altar.
Then the leaders brought their offerings to it to give to the Lord's service.
¹¹The Lord had already told Moses,
"Each day one leader must bring his gift. The gifts will make the altar ready for service to me."
¹²⁻⁸³Each of the 12 leaders brought these gifts. Each leader brought one silver plate that weighed about 1.5 kilograms. And each one brought one silver bowl that weighed about 0.8 kilograms. These weights were set by the Holy Place measure. Each bowl and plate were filled with fine flour mixed with oil. This was for a grain offering. Each leader also brought a large gold dish that weighed about 115 grams. It was filled with incense.ᵈ

Each leader also brought one young bull, one male sheep and one male lamb a year old. These were for a burnt offering. Each leader also brought one male goat for a sin offering. Each leader brought two oxen, five male sheep, five male goats and five male lambs a year old. All of these were sacrificed for a fellowship offering.

On the first day Nahshon son of Amminadab brought his gifts. He was the leader of the tribe of Judah.

On the second day Nethanel son of Zuar brought his gifts. He was the leader of the tribe of Issachar.

On the third day Eliab son of Helon brought his gifts. He was the leader of the tribe of Zebulun.

On the fourth day Elizur son of Shedeur brought his gifts. He was the leader of the tribe of Reuben.

On the fifth day Shelumiel son of Zurishaddai brought his gifts. He was the leader of the tribe of Simeon.

On the sixth day Eliasaph son of Deuel brought his gifts. He was the leader of the tribe of Gad.

On the seventh day Elishama son of Ammihud brought his gifts. He was the leader of the tribe of Ephraim.

On the eighth day Gamaliel son of Pedahzur brought his gifts. He was the leader of the tribe of Manasseh.

On the ninth day Abidan son of Gideoni brought his gifts. He was the leader of the tribe of Benjamin.

On the tenth day Ahiezer son of Ammishaddai brought his gifts. He was the leader of the tribe of Dan.

On the eleventh day Pagiel son of Ocran brought his gifts. He was the leader of the tribe of Asher.

On the twelfth day Ahira son of Enan brought his gifts. He was the leader of the tribe of Naphtali.

⁸⁴So these were all the gifts from the Israelite leaders. Moses then poured oil on the altar. And they brought their gifts to give the altar to the service of the Lord. They brought 12 silver plates, 12 silver bowls and 12 gold dishes. ⁸⁵Each silver plate weighed about 1.5 kilograms. And each bowl weighed about 0.8 kilograms. All the silver plates and silver bowls together weighed about 27 kilograms. This weight was set by the Holy Place measure. ⁸⁶The 12 gold dishes filled with incense weighed 115 grams each. Together the gold dishes weighed about 1.4 kilograms. ⁸⁷The total number of animals for the burnt offering was 12 bulls, 12 male sheep and 12 male lambs a year old. There was also a grain offering. And there were 12 male goats for a sin offering. ⁸⁸The total number of animals for the fellowship offering was 24 bulls, 60 male sheep, 60 male goats and 60 male lambs a year old. All these offerings were for giving the altar to the service of the Lord. This was after Moses had poured oil on it.

⁸⁹Moses went into the Meeting Tent to speak with the Lord. He heard the Lord speaking to him. The voice was coming from between the two gold creatures with wings. They were above the lid of the Arkᵈ of God. And the Lord spoke with him.

The Lampstand

8 The Lord said to Moses, [2]"Speak to Aaron. Tell him, 'Put the seven lamps where they can light the area in front of the lampstand'."

[3]Aaron did this. He put the lamps so they lighted the area in front of the lampstand. He obeyed the command the Lord gave Moses. [4]The lampstand was made from hammered gold. It was gold from its base to the flowers. It was made exactly the way the Lord had showed Moses.

The Levites

[5]The Lord said to Moses, [6]"Take the Levites away from the other Israelites and make them clean.[d] [7]This is what you should do to make them clean. Sprinkle the cleansing water on them. Have them shave their bodies and wash their clothes. Then they will be clean. [8]They must take a young bull and the grain offering that goes with it. The grain offering will be flour mixed with oil. Then take another young bull for a sin offering. [9]Bring the Levites to the front of the Meeting Tent.[d] And gather all the Israelites around. [10]Bring the Levites before the Lord. Then the Israelites should put their hands on them.[n] [11]Aaron will present the Levites before the Lord. They will be like an offering presented from the Israelites. Then the Levites will be ready to do the work of the Lord.

[12]"The Levites will put their hands on the bulls' heads. One bull will be a sin offering to the Lord. The other will be a burnt offering. This will remove the sins of the Levites so they will belong to God. [13]Make the Levites stand in front of Aaron and his sons. Then present the Levites as an offering to the Lord. [14]In this way you must set apart the Levites from the other Israelites. The Levites will be mine.

[15]"So make the Levites pure. And present them as an offering. Then they may come to work at the Meeting Tent. [16]They will be given to me from the Israelites. I have taken them for myself. They are mine instead of the firstborn[d] son of every Israelite woman. [17]Every firstborn male in Israel—man or animal—is mine. I killed all the firstborn in Egypt. So now I set them aside for myself. [18]I have taken the Levites instead of all the firstborn sons in Israel. [19]I have chosen the Levites from all the Israelite tribes. And I have given them to Aaron and his sons. They will serve all the Israelites at the Meeting Tent. They will help to remove the Israelites' sins so they will belong to God. Then no disaster will strike the Israelites when they approach the Holy Place."

[20]So Moses, Aaron and all the Israelites obeyed the Lord. They did with the Levites what the Lord commanded Moses to do. [21]The Levites made themselves clean and washed their clothes. Then Aaron presented them as an offering to the Lord. Aaron also removed their sins so they would be pure for the Lord. [22]After that, the Levites came to the Meeting Tent to work. Aaron and his sons told them what to do. They did with the Levites what the Lord commanded Moses to do.

[23]The Lord said to Moses, [24]"This command is for the Levites. Every man 25 years old or older must come to the Meeting Tent. They all have a job to do in the work there. [25]At the age of 50, he must retire from his job. He doesn't have to work again. [26]He may help his fellow Levites with their work at the Meeting Tent. But he must not do the work himself. This is the way you are to give the Levites their jobs."

put . . . them This showed that the people had a part in giving the Levites their special work.

The Passover

9 The Lord spoke to Moses in the Desert of Sinai. This was in the first month of the second year after the Israelites had left Egypt. This is what he said, [2]"Tell the Israelites to celebrate the Passover[d] at the appointed time. [3]That appointed time is the fourteenth day of this month. They should celebrate it at twilight. They must obey all the rules about it."

[4]So Moses told the Israelites to celebrate the Passover. [5]And so they did. It was in the Desert of Sinai at twilight. This was on the fourteenth day of the first month. The Israelites did everything just as the Lord commanded Moses.

[6]But some of the people could not celebrate the Passover on that day. They were unclean[d] because of a dead body. So they went to Moses and Aaron that day. [7]They said to Moses, "We are unclean because of a dead body. But why should we be kept from offering gifts to the Lord at this appointed time? Why can't we join the other Israelites?"

[8]Moses said to them, "Wait. I will find out what the Lord says about you."

[9]Then the Lord said to Moses, [10]"Tell the Israelites this: 'You or your descendants[d] might become unclean because of a dead body. Or, you might be away on a trip during the Passover. Still celebrate the Lord's Passover. [11]But celebrate it at twilight on the fourteenth day of the second month. Eat the lamb with bitter herbs and bread made without yeast. [12]Don't leave any of it until the next morning. Don't break any of its bones. When you celebrate the Passover, follow all the rules. [13]Anyone who is clean and is not away on a trip must eat the Passover. If he doesn't, he must be separated from his people. He did not give an offering to the Lord at the appointed time. He must be punished for his sin.

[14]" 'A foreigner among you may celebrate the Lord's Passover. But he must follow all the rules. You must have the same rules for foreigners as you have for yourselves'."

The Cloud Above the Tent

[15]On the day the Holy Tent[d] was set up, a cloud covered it. (The Holy Tent was also called the Tent of the Agreement.) From dusk until dawn the cloud above the Tent looked like fire. [16]The cloud stayed above the Tent. At night it looked like fire. [17]When the cloud moved from its place over the Tent, the Israelites moved. Wherever the cloud stopped, the Israelites camped. [18]So the Israelites moved at the Lord's command. And they camped at his command. While the cloud stayed over the Tent, they stayed in place. [19]Sometimes the cloud stayed over the Tent for a long time. The Israelites obeyed the Lord and did not move. [20]Sometimes the cloud was over it only a few days. At the Lord's command the people camped. And at his command they moved. [21]Sometimes the cloud stayed only from dusk until dawn. When the cloud lifted the next morning, the people moved. When the cloud lifted, day or night, the people moved. [22]The cloud might stay over the Tent for two days, a month or a year. As long as it stayed, the people would camp. But when the cloud lifted, they moved. [23]At the Lord's command the people camped. And at his command they moved. They obeyed the Lord's order that he commanded through Moses.

The Silver Trumpets

10 The Lord said to Moses, [2]"Make two trumpets of hammered silver. Use them to call the people together and to march out of camp. [3]When both trumpets are blown, the people should gather.

They should gather before you at the entrance to the Meeting Tent.*d* 4If you blow only one trumpet, the leaders should meet before you. 5When you blow the trumpets once, the tribes*d* camping on the east should move. 6When you blow them again, the tribes camping on the south should move. The sound will tell them to move. 7When you want to gather the people, blow the trumpets. But don't blow them the same way.

8"Aaron's sons, the priests, should blow the trumpets. This is a law for you and your descendants*d* from now on. 9You might be fighting an enemy who attacks you in your own land. Blow the trumpets. The Lord your God will remember you. He will save you from your enemies. 10Also blow your trumpets at happy times. Blow them during your feasts and at New Moon*d* festivals. Blow them over your burnt offerings and fellowship offerings. They will help you remember your God. I am the Lord your God."

The Israelites Move Camp

11The cloud lifted from the Tent*d* of the Agreement. This was on the twentieth day of the second month of the second year. 12So the Israelites moved from the Desert of Sinai. They moved until the cloud stopped in the Desert of Paran. 13This was their first time to move. They did it as the Lord had commanded Moses.

14The divisions from the camp of Judah moved first under their flag. Nahshon son of Amminadab was the commander. 15Nethanel son of Zuar was over the division of the tribe*d* of Issachar. 16Eliab son of Helon was over the division of the tribe of Zebulun. 17Then the Meeting Tent was taken down. The Gershonites and Merarites, who carried it, moved next.

18Then came the divisions from the camp of Reuben under their flag. Elizur son of Shedeur was the command-

er. 19Shelumiel son of Zurishaddai was over the division of the tribe of Simeon. 20Eliasaph son of Deuel was over the division of the tribe of Gad. 21Then came the Kohathites. They carried the holy things. The Holy Tent was to be set up before they arrived.

22Next came the divisions from the camp of Ephraim under their flag. Elishama son of Ammihud was the commander. 23Gamaliel son of Pedahzur was over the division of the tribe of Manasseh. 24Abidan son of Gideoni was over the division of the tribe of Benjamin.

25The last ones were the rear guard for all the tribes. These were the divisions from the camp of Dan under their flag. Ahiezer son of Ammishaddai was the commander. 26Pagiel son of Ocran was over the division of the tribe of Asher. 27Ahira son of Enan was over the division of the tribe of Naphtali. 28This was the order the Israelite divisions marched in when they moved.

29Hobab was the son of Reuel the Midianite. Reuel, who is also called Jethro, was Moses' father-in-law. Moses said to Hobab, "We are moving to the land God promised to give us. Come with us. We will be good to you. The Lord has promised good things to Israel."

30But Hobab answered, "No, I will not go. I will go back to my own land where I was born."

31But Moses said, "Please don't leave us. You know where we can camp in the desert. You can be our guide. 32Come with us. We will share with you all the good things the Lord gives us." 33So they left the mountain of the Lord. The Ark*d* of God went in front of the people. For three days they looked for a place to camp. 34The Lord's cloud was over them during the day when they left their camp.

35When the Holy Ark left the camp, Moses always said,

"Rise up, Lord!

Scatter your enemies.
Make those who are against you
    run from you."
36And when the Holy Ark was set
down, Moses always said,
"Return, Lord,
    to the thousands of people of
    Israel."

Fire from the Lord

11 The people complained to the
Lord about their troubles.
When he heard them, he became angry. Fire from the Lord burned among
the people. It burned the edge of the
camp. 2So the people cried out to Moses. He prayed to the Lord, and the
fire stopped burning. 3So that place
was called Taberah.n The people
named it that because the Lord's fire
had burned among them.

The 70 Older Leaders

4Some troublemakers among them
wanted better food. Soon all the Israelites began complaining. They said,
"We want meat! 5We remember the
fish we ate for free in Egypt. We also
had cucumbers, melons, leeks, onions
and garlic. 6But now we have lost our
appetite. We never see anything but
this manna!"

7The manna was like small white
seeds. 8The people would go to gather it. Then they ground it in handmills.
Or they crushed it between stones.
They cooked it in a pot or made cakes
with it. It tasted like bread baked with
olive oil. 9When the dew fell on the
camp each night, so did the manna.

10Moses heard every family crying.
They stood in the entrances of their
tents. The Lord became very angry.
And Moses got upset. 11He asked the
Lord, "Why have you brought me this
trouble? I'm your servant. What have
I done wrong? Why did you make me
responsible for all these people? 12I
am not the father of all these people.
I didn't give birth to them. Why do you

make me carry them to the land you
promised to our ancestors? Must I
carry them in my arms as a nurse carries a baby? 13Where can I get meat
for all these people? They keep crying
to me, 'We want meat!' 14I can't take
care of all these people alone. It is too
much for me. 15If you are going to
continue doing this to me, then kill me
now. If you like me, put me to death.
Then I won't have any more troubles."

16The Lord said to Moses, "Bring
me 70 of Israel's older leaders. Pick
men you know are leaders among the
people. Bring them to the Meeting
Tent.d Have them stand there with
you. 17I will come down and speak
with you there. I will take some of the
Spiritd that is in you. And I will give it
to them. They will help you care for
the people. Then you will not have to
care for them alone.

18"Tell the people this: 'Make yourselves holy. Tomorrow you will eat
meat. The Lord heard you cry, "We
want meat! We were better off in
Egypt!" So now the Lord will give you
meat to eat. 19You will not eat it for
just one, two, five, ten or even
twenty days. 20You will eat that meat
for a whole month. You will eat it until it comes out of your nose. You will
hate it. This is because you have
rejected the Lord. He is here with
you. But you have cried to him. You
said, "Why did we ever leave
Egypt?" ' "

21Moses said, "Lord, here are
600,000 men standing around me.
And you say, 'I will give them enough
meat to eat for a month!' 22If we killed
all the sheep and cattle, that would not
be enough. If we caught all the fish in
the sea, that would not be enough."

23But the Lord said to Moses, "Do
you think I'm weak? You will see if I
can do what I say."

24So Moses went out to the people.

Taberah This name means "burning".

He told them what the Lord had said. Moses gathered 70 of the older leaders together. He had them stand around the Tent. 25Then the Lord came down in the cloud and spoke to Moses. The Lord took some of the Spirit Moses had. And he gave it to the 70 leaders. With the Spirit in them, they prophesied,[d] but just that one time.

26Two men named Eldad and Medad were also listed as leaders. But they did not go to the Tent. They stayed in the camp. The Spirit was given to them. So they prophesied in the camp. 27A young man ran to Moses. He said, "Eldad and Medad are prophesying in the camp."

28Joshua son of Nun said, "Moses, my master, stop them!" (Since he was a young boy, Joshua had been Moses' assistant.)

29But Moses answered, "Are you afraid for me? I wish all the Lord's people could prophesy. I wish the Lord would give his Spirit to all of them!" 30Then Moses and the leaders of Israel went back to the camp.

The Quails Come

31The Lord sent a strong wind from the sea. It blew quail into the area all around the camp. The quail were about 0.9 metres above the ground. There were quail a day's walk in any direction. 32The people went out and gathered quail. They gathered all that day, that night and the next day. Everyone gathered at least 2,160 litres. Then they spread them around the camp. 33But the Lord became very angry. He gave the people a terrible sickness. This came while the meat was still in their mouths. 34So the people named that place Kibroth Hattaavah.[n] They named it that because there they buried those who wanted other food.

35From Kibroth Hattaavah the people went to stay at Hazeroth.

Miriam and Aaron Speak Against Moses' Wife

12 Miriam and Aaron began to talk against Moses, who had married a Cushite. 2They said to themselves, "Is Moses the only one the Lord speaks through? Doesn't he speak through us?" And the Lord heard this.

3(Now Moses was very humble. He was the least proud person on earth.)

4So the Lord suddenly spoke to Moses, Aaron and Miriam. He said, "All three of you come to the Meeting Tent[d] now." So they went. 5The Lord came down in a pillar of cloud. He stood at the entrance to the Tent. He called to Aaron and Miriam, and they both came near. 6He said, "Listen to my words:

When a prophet[d] is among you,
    I, the Lord, will show myself to
        him in visions.
    I will speak to him in dreams.
7But this is not true with my
        servant Moses.
    I trust him to lead all my
        people.
8I speak face to face with him.
    I speak clearly, not with hidden
        meanings.
    He has even seen the form of
        the Lord.
You should be afraid
    to speak against my servant
        Moses."

9The Lord was very angry with them, but he left.

10The cloud lifted from the Tent. Then Aaron turned toward Miriam. She was as white as snow. She had a harmful skin disease. 11Aaron said to Moses, "Please, my master, forgive us for our foolish sin. 12Don't let her be like a baby who is born dead.

Kirbroth Hattaavah This name in Hebrew means "graves of craving".

(Sometimes a baby is born with half of its flesh eaten away.)"

13So Moses cried out to the Lord, "God, please heal her!"

14The Lord answered Moses, "If her father had spat in her face, she would have been shamed for seven days. So put her outside the camp for seven days. After that, she may come back." 15So Miriam was shut outside of the camp for seven days. And the people did not move on until she came back.

16After that, the people left Hazeroth. And they camped in the Desert of Paran.

The Spies Explore Canaan

13 The Lord said to Moses, 2"Send men to explore the land of Canaan. I will give that land to the Israelites. Send one leader from each tribe."d

3So Moses obeyed the Lord's command. He sent the Israelite leaders out from the Desert of Paran. 4These are their names: from the tribe of Reuben, Shammua son of Zaccur; 5from the tribe of Simeon, Shaphat son of Hori; 6from the tribe of Judah, Caleb son of Jephunneh; 7from the tribe of Issachar, Igal son of Joseph; 8from the tribe of Ephraim, Hoshea son of Nun; 9from the tribe of Benjamin, Palti son of Raphu; 10from the tribe of Zebulun, Gaddiel son of Sodi; 11from the tribe of Manasseh (a tribe of Joseph), Gaddi son of Susi; 12from the tribe of Dan, Ammiel son of Gamalli; 13from the tribe of Asher, Sethur son of Michael; 14from the tribe of Naphtali, Nahbi son of Vophsi; 15from the tribe of Gad, Geuel son of Maki.

16These are the names of the men Moses sent to explore the land. (Moses gave Hoshea son of Nun the new name Joshua.)

17Moses sent them to explore Canaan. He said, "Go through southern Canaan and then into the mountains. 18See what the land looks like. Are the people who live there strong or weak? Are there a few or many? 19What kind of land do they live in? Is it good or bad? What about the towns they live in — do they have walls, or are they open like camps? 20What about the soil? Is it fertile or poor? Are there trees there? Try to bring back some of the fruit from that land." (It was the season for the first grapes.)

21So they went up and explored the land. They went from the Desert of Zin all the way to Rehob by Lebo Hamath. 22They went through the southern area to Hebron. That is where Ahiman, Sheshai and Talmai lived. They were the descendantsd of Anak.d (The city of Hebron had been built seven years before Zoan in Egypt.) 23In the Valley of Eshcol, they cut off a branch of a grapevine. It had one bunch of grapes on it. They carried that branch on a pole between two of them. They also got some pomegranatesd and figs. 24They called that place the Valley of Eshcol.n That is because the Israelites cut off the bunch of grapes there. 25After 40 days of exploring the land, the men returned to the camp.

26They came back to Moses and Aaron and all the Israelites at Kadesh. This was in the Desert of Paran. The men reported to them and showed everybody the fruit from the land. 27They told Moses, "We went to the land where you sent us. It is a land where much food grows! Here is some of its fruit. 28But the people who live there are strong. Their cities are walled and large. We even saw some Anakites there. 29The Amalekites live in the southern area. The Hittites, Jebusites and Amorites live in the mountains. The Canaanites live near the sea and along the Jordan River."

Eshcol This name in Hebrew means "bunch".

³⁰Then Caleb told the people near Moses to be quiet. Caleb said, "We should go up and take the land for ourselves. We can do it."

³¹But the men who had gone with him said, "We can't attack those people. They are stronger than we are." ³²And those men gave the Israelites a bad report about the land they explored. They said, "The land would eat us up. All the people we saw are very tall. ³³We saw the Nephilim^d people there. (The Anakites come from the Nephilim people.) We felt like grasshoppers. And we looked like grasshoppers to them."

The People Complain Again

14 That night all the people in the camp began crying loudly. ²All the Israelites complained against Moses and Aaron. All the people said to them, "We should have died in Egypt. Or we should have died in the desert. ³Why is the Lord bringing us to this land? We will be killed with swords. Our wives and children will be taken away. We would be better off going back to Egypt." ⁴They said to each other, "Let's get a leader and go back to Egypt."

⁵Then Moses and Aaron bowed face down in front of all the Israelites gathered there. ⁶Joshua son of Nun and Caleb son of Jephunneh were among those who had explored the land. They tore their clothes. ⁷They said to all of the Israelites, "The land we went to explore is very good. ⁸If the Lord is pleased with us, he will lead us into that land. He will give us that land where much food grows. ⁹Don't turn against the Lord! Don't be afraid of the people in that land! We will chew them up. They have no protection, but we have the Lord. So don't be afraid of them."

¹⁰Then all the people talked about killing them with stones. But the glory of the Lord appeared at the Meeting Tent^d to the Israelites. ¹¹The Lord said to Moses, "How long will these people ignore me? How long will it be before they believe me? I have done miracles^d among them. ¹²I will give them a terrible sickness. I will destroy them. But I will make you into a great nation. It will be stronger than they are."

¹³Then Moses said to the Lord, "The Egyptians will hear about it! You brought these people from there by your great power. ¹⁴And the Egyptians will tell this to those who live in this land. They have already heard about you, Lord. They know that you are with your people. And they know you were seen face to face. They know your cloud stays over your people. They know you lead your people with that cloud during the day and with fire at night. ¹⁵The nations have heard about your power. If you put to death your people all at once, the nations will talk. They will say, ¹⁶'The Lord was not able to bring them into the land he promised them. So he killed them in the desert.'

¹⁷"So show your strength now, my Lord. Do what you said. You said: ¹⁸'The Lord doesn't become angry quickly. The Lord has great love. The Lord forgives sin and law breaking. He has great mercy. But the Lord does not forget to punish guilty people. When parents sin, he will also punish their children. He will punish their grandchildren, great-grandchildren and great-great-grandchildren'. ¹⁹Show your great love. Forgive these people's sin. Forgive them as you have from the time they left Egypt until now."

²⁰The Lord answered, "I have forgiven them as you asked. ²¹But, as surely as I live, I make this promise. As surely as my glory fills the whole earth, I make this promise. ²²All these men saw my glory. They saw the miracles I did in Egypt and in the desert. But they disobeyed me and tested me ten times. ²³So not one will see the

land I promised to their ancestors. No one who angered me will see that land. ²⁴But my servant Caleb has a different spirit. He follows me completely. So I will bring him into the land he has already seen. And his children will own that land. ²⁵The Amalekites and the Canaanites are living in the valleys. So leave tomorrow and go back. Follow the desert road toward the Gulf of Aqaba."

The Lord Punishes the People

²⁶The Lord said to Moses and Aaron, ²⁷"How long will these evil people complain about me? I have heard these Israelites' grumbling and complaining. ²⁸So tell them, 'This is what the Lord says. I heard what you said. As surely as I live, I will do those things to you. ²⁹You will die in this desert. Every one of you who is 20 years old or older and who was counted with the people will die. You complained against me, the Lord. ³⁰Not one of you will enter and live in the land I promised to you. Only Caleb son of Jephunneh and Joshua son of Nun will go in. ³¹You said that your children would be taken away. But I will bring them into the land. They will enjoy what you refused. ³²As for you, you will die in this desert. ³³Your children will be shepherds here for 40 years. They will suffer because you were not loyal. They will suffer until you lie dead in the desert. ³⁴For 40 years you will suffer for your sins. That is a year for each of the 40 days you explored the land. You will know me as your enemy'. ³⁵I, the Lord, have spoken. I will certainly do these things to all these evil people. They have come together against me. So they will all die here in this desert."

³⁶The men Moses had sent to explore the land had returned. They had spread complaints among all the Israelites. They had given a bad report about the land. ³⁷They were responsible for the bad report. So the Lord

killed them with a terrible sickness. ³⁸Only two of the men did not die. They were Joshua son of Nun and Caleb son of Jephunneh.

³⁹When Moses told these things to the Israelites, they were very sad. ⁴⁰Early the next morning they started to go towards the beginning of the mountains. They said, "We have sinned. We will go where the Lord told us."

⁴¹But Moses said, "Why are you disobeying the Lord's command? You will not win! ⁴²Don't go. The Lord is not with you. You will be beaten by your enemies. ⁴³You will run into the Amalekites and Canaanites. They will kill you with swords. You have turned away from the Lord. He will not be with you."

⁴⁴But they were proud. They went towards the beginning of the mountains. But Moses and the Ark*ᵈ* of God with the Lord did not leave the camp. ⁴⁵The Amalekites and the Canaanites who lived in those mountains came down. And they attacked the Israelites. They beat them back all the way to Hormah.

Rules About Sacrifices

15 The Lord said to Moses, ²"Speak to the people of Israel. Say to them, 'You will enter a land that I am giving you as a home. ³There give the Lord offerings made by fire. These may be from your herds or flocks. And the smell will be pleasing to the Lord. These offerings may be burnt offerings or sacrifices for special promises. They may be offerings which are gifts to the Lord. Or they may be festival offerings. ⁴And the one who brings his offering shall also give the Lord a grain offering. It should be 2 litres of fine flour mixed with 1 litre of olive oil. ⁵Each time you offer a lamb as a burnt offering or sacrifice, also prepare a litre of wine. This is a drink offering.

⁶" 'If you are giving a male sheep,

also prepare a grain offering. It should be 4.5 litres of fine flour mixed with 1.2 litres of olive oil. [7]Also prepare 1.2 litres of wine. This is a drink offering. Offer it to the Lord. Its smell is pleasing to him.

[8]" 'You might prepare a young bull as a burnt offering or sacrifice. This might be for a fellowship offering or for a special promise to the Lord. [9]Bring a grain offering with the bull. It should be 6.5 litres of fine flour mixed with 2 litres of olive oil. [10]Also bring 2 litres of wine as a drink offering. This offering is made by fire. And its smell will be pleasing to the Lord. [11]Prepare each bull or male sheep, lamb or young goat this way. [12]Do this for every one of the animals you bring.

[13]" 'All citizens must do these things in this way. And the smell of their offerings by fire will be pleasing to the Lord. [14]From now on foreigners will live among you. They will make offerings by fire so the smell will be pleasing to the Lord. They must offer them the same way you do. [15]The law is the same for you and for foreigners. It will be a law from now on. You and the foreigners are alike before the Lord. [16]The teachings and rules are the same for you and for the foreigners among you'."

[17]The Lord said to Moses, [18]"Tell the Israelites: 'You are going to another land. I am taking you there. [19]When you eat the food there, offer part of it to the Lord. [20]Offer a loaf of bread from the first of your grain. That will be your offering from the threshing[d] floor. [21]From now on offer to the Lord the first part of your grain.

[22]" 'Now what if you forget to obey any of these commands the Lord gave Moses? [23]These are the Lord's commands given to you through Moses. They began the day the Lord gave them to you. And they will continue from now on. [24]But you might forget to obey one of these commands. The people might not remember the com-

mand. Then all the people must offer a young bull as a burnt offering. Its smell is pleasing to the Lord. By law you must also give the grain offering and the drink offering with it. And you must bring a male goat as a sin offering.

[25]" 'The priest will remove that sin for all the Israelites so they will belong to God. They are forgiven. They didn't know they were sinning. For the wrong they did they brought offerings to the Lord. They brought an offering by fire and a sin offering. [26]All of the people of Israel and the foreigners living among them will be forgiven. No one meant to do wrong.

[27]" 'Just one person might sin without meaning to. He must bring a year-old female goat for a sin offering. [28]The priest will remove the sin of the person who sinned without meaning to. That person will belong to the Lord again. He will be forgiven. [29]The same teaching is for everyone who sins without meaning to. It is the same for those born Israelites and for foreigners living among you.

[30]" 'But anyone who sins on purpose is against the Lord. That person must be separated from his people. It is the same for someone born among you or a foreigner. [31]That person has turned against the Lord's word. He has not obeyed the Lord's commands. He must surely be separated from the others. He is guilty'."

A Man Worked on the Sabbath

[32]This happened when the Israelites were still in the desert. They found a man gathering wood on the Sabbath[d] day. [33]Those who found him gathering wood brought him to Moses and Aaron and all the people. [34]They held the man under guard. They did not know what to do with him. [35]Then the Lord said to Moses, "The man must die. All the people must kill him with stones outside the camp." [36]So the people took him outside the camp. They

killed him with stones as the Lord commanded Moses.

The Tassels

37The Lord said to Moses, 38"Speak to the Israelites. Tell them this: 'Tie several pieces of thread together. And tie them to the corners of your clothes. Put a blue thread in each one of these tassels. Wear them from now on. 39You will have these tassels to look at. They will remind you of the Lord's commands. Then you will obey them. And you won't follow what your bodies want and what your eyes wish for. 40Remember to obey all my commands. Then you will be God's holy people. 41I am the Lord your God. I brought you out of Egypt to be your God. I am the Lord your God'."

Korah, Dathan, Abiram and On

16 Korah, Dathan, Abiram and On turned against Moses. (Korah was the son of Izhar. Izhar was the son of Kohath, and Kohath was the son of Levi. Dathan and Abiram were brothers, the sons of Eliab. And On was the son of Peleth.) Dathan, Abiram and On were from the tribe*d* of Reuben. 2These four men gathered 250 other Israelite men and came to challenge Moses. They were well-known leaders chosen by the community. 3They came as a group to speak to Moses and Aaron. The men said, "You have gone too far. All the people are holy. Every one of them is holy. And the Lord is with them. So why do you put yourselves above all the people?"

4When Moses heard this, he bowed face down. 5Then he said to Korah and all his followers: "Tomorrow morning the Lord will show who belongs to him. The Lord will bring the one who is holy near to him. The Lord will bring to himself the person he chooses. 6So Korah, you and all your followers do this: get some pans for burning incense.*d* 7Tomorrow put fire

and incense in them. Then take them before the Lord. He will choose the man who is holy. You Levites have gone too far."

8Moses also said to Korah, "Listen, you Levites. 9The God of Israel has separated you from the rest of the Israelites. He brought you near to himself. You do the work in the Lord's Holy Tent.*d* You stand before all the Israelites and serve them. Isn't that enough? 10The Lord has brought you and all your fellow Levites near to himself. Now you want to be priests. 11You and your followers have joined together against the Lord. Your complaint is not against Aaron."

12Then Moses called Dathan and Abiram, the sons of Eliab. But they said, "We will not come! 13You have brought us out of a land where much food grows. You brought us to the desert to kill us. And now you want to order us around. 14You haven't brought us into a land where much food grows. You haven't given us any land with fields and vineyards. Will you put out the eyes of these men? No! We will not come!"

15Then Moses became very angry. He said to the Lord, "Don't accept their gifts. I have not taken anything from them, not even a donkey. I have not done wrong to any of them."

16Then Moses said to Korah, "You and all your followers must stand before the Lord tomorrow. And Aaron will stand there with you and them. 17Each of you must take your pan and put incense in it. Present these 250 pans before the Lord. You and Aaron must also present your pans." 18So each man got his pan and put burning incense in it. Then they stood with Moses and Aaron at the entrance to the Meeting Tent. 19Korah gathered all his followers who were against Moses and Aaron. And they stood at the entrance to the Meeting Tent. Then the glory of the Lord appeared to everyone.

²⁰The Lord said to Moses and Aaron, ²¹"Move away from these men. In a minute I will destroy them."

²²But Moses and Aaron bowed face down. They cried out, "God, you are the God over the spirits of all people. Please don't be angry with this whole group. Only one man has really sinned."

²³Then the Lord said to Moses, ²⁴"Tell everyone to move away from the tents of Korah, Dathan and Abiram."

²⁵Moses stood and went to Dathan and Abiram. The older leaders of Israel followed him. ²⁶Moses warned the people, "Move away from the tents of these evil men! Don't touch anything of theirs. If you do, you will be destroyed because of their sins." ²⁷So they moved away from the tents of Korah, Dathan and Abiram. Dathan and Abiram were standing outside their tents with their wives, children and little babies.

²⁸Then Moses said, "Now you will know that the Lord has sent me to do all these things. It was not my idea. ²⁹If these men die a normal death—the way men usually die—then the Lord did not really send me. ³⁰But if the Lord does something new, you will know they have insulted the Lord. The earth will open and swallow them. Alive, they will go to where the dead are. And everything that belongs to them will go with them."

³¹When Moses finished saying these things, the ground under the men opened up. ³²The earth seemed to open its mouth and swallow them. All their families, all Korah's men and everything they owned went down. ³³They were buried alive, going to where the dead are. And everything they owned went with them. Then the earth closed over them. They died and were gone from the community. ³⁴The people of Israel around them heard their screams. They ran away and said, "The earth will swallow us, too!"

³⁵Then a fire came down from the Lord. It destroyed the 250 men who had presented the incense.

³⁶The Lord said to Moses, ³⁷"Tell Eleazar son of Aaron, the priest, to take all the incense pans out of the fire. Have him scatter the coals. But the incense pans are still holy. ³⁸These men sinned and lost their lives. Take their pans and hammer them into flat sheets. Cover the altar with them. They are holy because they were presented to the Lord. It will be a sign to the Israelites."

³⁹So Eleazar the priest gathered all the bronze pans. These were the pans brought by the men who were burned up. Eleazar had the pans hammered into flat sheets to put on the altar. ⁴⁰This is what the Lord had commanded him through Moses. These sheets were to remind the Israelites that only descendants^d of Aaron should burn incense before the Lord. Anyone else would die like Korah and his followers.

Aaron Saves the People

⁴¹The next day all the Israelites complained against Moses and Aaron. They said, "You have killed the Lord's people."

⁴²The people gathered to complain against Moses and Aaron. But when they turned toward the Meeting Tent,^d the cloud covered it. The glory of the Lord appeared. ⁴³Then Moses and Aaron went in front of the Meeting Tent.

⁴⁴The Lord said to Moses, ⁴⁵"Move away from these people. In a minute I am going to destroy them." So Moses and Aaron bowed face down.

⁴⁶Then Moses said to Aaron, "Get your pan. Put fire from the altar and incense^d in it. Hurry to the people and remove their sin. The Lord is angry with them. The sickness has already started." ⁴⁷So Aaron did as Moses

said. He ran to the middle of all the people. The sickness had already started among them. So Aaron offered the incense to remove their sin. [48]He stood between the living and the dead. And the sickness stopped there. [49]But 14,700 people died from that sickness. There were also those who died because of Korah. [50]Then Aaron went back to Moses at the entrance to the Meeting Tent. The terrible sickness had been stopped.

Aaron's Walking Stick Buds

17 The Lord said to Moses, [2]"Speak to the people of Israel. Get 12 staffs from them. Get one from the leader of each tribe.[d] Write the name of each man on his staff. [3]On the staff from Levi, write Aaron's name. There must be one staff for the head of each tribe. [4]Put them in the Meeting Tent.[d] Place them in front of the Ark[d] of God, where I meet with you. [5]I will choose one man. His staff will begin to grow leaves. And I will stop the Israelites from always complaining against you."

[6]So Moses spoke to the Israelites. Each of the 12 leaders gave him a staff. And Aaron's staff was among them. [7]Moses put them before the Lord in the Tent of the Agreement.

[8]The next day Moses entered the Tent. He saw that Aaron's stick had grown leaves. (It stood for the family of Levi.) It had even budded, blossomed and produced almonds. [9]So Moses brought out to the Israelites all the staffs from the Lord's presence. They all looked, and each man took back his staff.

[10]Then the Lord said to Moses, "Put Aaron's staff back. Put it in front of the Ark of God. It will be a sign to these people who are always turning against me. This will stop their complaining against me. Now they won't die." [11]So Moses obeyed what the Lord commanded him.

[12]The people of Israel said to Moses, "We are going to die! We are lost. We are all lost! [13]Anyone who even comes near the Holy Tent of the Lord will die. Will we all die?"

The Work of the Priests and Levites

18 The Lord said to Aaron, "You, your sons and your family are now responsible for any wrongs done against the Holy Place. You and your sons are responsible for any wrongs done against the priests. [2]Bring with you your fellow Levites from your tribe.[d] They will help you and your sons serve in the Tent[d] of the Agreement. [3]They are under your control. They will do all the work that needs to be done in the Tent. But they must not go near the things in the Holy Place or near the altar. If they do, both you and they will die. [4]They will join you. They will take care of the Meeting Tent. They must do the work at the Tent. No one else may come near you.

[5]"You must take care of the Holy Place and the altar. Then I won't become angry with the Israelites again. [6]I myself chose your fellow Levites from among the Israelites. They are a gift given for you to the Lord. Their work is at the Meeting Tent. [7]But only you and your sons may serve as priests. Only you may serve at the altar or go behind the curtain. I am giving you this gift of serving as a priest. Anyone else who comes near the Holy Place will be put to death."

[8]Then the Lord said to Aaron, "I myself make you responsible for the offerings given to me. All the holy offerings that the Israelites give to me, I give to you. They are for you and your sons as your share. They will be your continual portion. [9]Your share of the holy offerings is that part which is not burned. The people will bring me gifts as most holy offerings. These are grain or sin or penalty offerings.

These will be set apart for you and your sons. ¹⁰You must eat it in a most holy place. Any male may eat it. But you must respect it as holy.

¹¹"I also give you the offerings the Israelites present to me. I give these to you and your sons and daughters. This is your share. Anyone in your family who is clean^d may eat it.

¹²"And I give you all the best olive oil and all the best new wine and grain. This is what the Israelites give to me, the Lord. These are the first things they harvest. ¹³They bring to the Lord all the first things they harvest. They will be yours. Anyone in your family who is clean may eat these things.

¹⁴"Everything in Israel that is given to the Lord is yours. ¹⁵The first one born to any family will be offered to the Lord. This is true for both men and animals. And that will be yours. But you must make a payment for every firstborn^d son and every firstborn animal that is unclean. ¹⁶When they are one month old, you must make a payment for them. The cost will be 55 grams of silver as set by the Holy Place measure.

¹⁷"But you must not make a payment for the firstborn ox or sheep or goat. Those animals are holy. Sprinkle their blood on the altar and burn their fat. This is an offering made by fire. The smell is pleasing to the Lord. ¹⁸But the meat will be yours. Also the breast that is presented and the right thigh will be yours. ¹⁹Anything the Israelites present as holy gifts I, the Lord, give to you. It goes to you, your sons and daughters. It is your continual portion. This is a lasting promise before the Lord to you and your children for ever."

²⁰The Lord also said to Aaron, "You will not inherit any of the land. And you will not own any land among the other people. I will be yours. Out of all the Israelites, only you will inherit me.

²¹"The people of Israel will give a tenth of what they make. I will give that tenth to the Levites. This is their payment for the work they do serving at the Meeting Tent. ²²But the other Israelites must never go near the Meeting Tent. If they do, they will die for their sin. ²³Only the Levites should work in the Meeting Tent. They are responsible for any sins against it. This is a rule from now on. The Levites will not get any land among the other Israelites. ²⁴But the Israelites will give a tenth of everything they make to me. And I will give that tenth to the Levites. That is why I said about the Levites: 'They will not get any land among the Israelites'."

²⁵The Lord said to Moses, ²⁶"Speak to the Levites. Tell them: 'You will receive a tenth of everything the Israelites make. I give that to you. But you must give a tenth of that back to the Lord. ²⁷I will accept your offering just as much as I accept the offerings from others. They give new grain or new wine. ²⁸In this way you will present an offering to the Lord as the other Israelites do. You will receive a tenth from the Israelites. Then you will give a tenth of that to Aaron the priest as the Lord's share. ²⁹Choose the best and holiest part from what you are given. This is the portion you must give to the Lord'.

³⁰"Say to the Levites: 'When you present the best it will be accepted as much as the grain and wine from the other people. ³¹You and your families may eat all that is left anywhere. This is your pay for your work in the Meeting Tent. ³²And if you always give the best part to the Lord, you will never be guilty. If you do not sin against the holy offerings of the Israelites, you will not die'."

The Offering for Cleansing

19 The Lord said to Moses and Aaron, ²"These are the teachings that the Lord commanded. Tell the Israelites to get a young red cow. It must not have anything wrong with it. It must not have been worked. ³Give the cow to Eleazar the priest. He will take it outside the camp and kill it. ⁴Then Eleazar the priest must put some of the blood on his finger. He must sprinkle it seven times towards the front of the Meeting Tent.*d* ⁵Then the whole cow must be burned while he watches. The skin, the meat, the blood and the intestines must all be burned. ⁶Then the priest must take a cedar stick, a hyssop branch and a red string. He must throw them onto the burning cow. ⁷Then the priest must wash himself and his clothes with water. After that, he may come back into the camp. But he will be unclean*d* until evening. ⁸The man who burns the cow must wash himself and his clothes in water. He will be unclean until evening.

⁹"Then someone who is clean will collect the ashes from the cow. He will put them in a clean place outside the camp. The Israelites will use these ashes in a special ceremony to cleanse away sin. ¹⁰The man who collected the cow's ashes must wash his clothes. He will be unclean until evening. This is a lasting rule. It is for the Israelites and for the foreigners among them.

¹¹"Whoever touches a dead body will be unclean for seven days. ¹²He must wash himself with special cleansing water. He must do this on the third day and on the seventh day. Then he will be clean. But if he does not wash himself on the third day and the seventh day, he cannot be clean. ¹³Whoever touches a dead body is unclean. If he stays unclean and goes to the Lord's Holy Tent, it becomes unclean. So he must be separated from Israel. If the cleansing water is not sprinkled on him, he will stay unclean.

¹⁴"This is the teaching about someone who dies in his tent. Anyone in the tent or who enters it will be un-

clean for seven days. ¹⁵And every open jar or pot without a cover becomes unclean. ¹⁶If anyone touches someone who was killed by a sword or who died a natural death, he is unclean. If he touches a human bone or a grave, he is unclean. He will be unclean for seven days.

¹⁷"So you must use the ashes from the burnt offering to make that person clean again. Pour fresh water over the ashes into a jar. ¹⁸A clean person must take a hyssop branch and dip it into the water. Then he must sprinkle it over the tent and its objects. And he must sprinkle the people who were there. He must sprinkle anyone who touched a bone or the body of someone who was killed. He must sprinkle anyone who touched a dead person or a grave. ¹⁹Then someone who is clean must sprinkle this water on the unclean person. He must do this on the third day and on the seventh day. On the seventh day that person becomes clean. He must wash his clothes and take a bath. He will be clean that evening. ²⁰If anyone who is unclean does not become clean, he must be separated from the community. He was not sprinkled with the cleansing water. He stays unclean. He could make the Holy Tent unclean. ²¹This is a lasting rule. Whoever sprinkles the cleansing water must also wash his clothes. Anyone who touches the water will be unclean until evening. ²²Anyone the unclean person touches becomes unclean. And whoever touches him will be unclean until evening."

Water from the Rock

20 In the first month all the people of Israel arrived at the Desert of Zin. They stayed at Kadesh. There Miriam died and was buried. ²There was no water for the people. So they came together against Moses and Aaron. ³They argued with Moses. They said, "We should have died in

front of the Lord as our brothers did. ⁴Why did you bring the Lord's people into this desert? Are we and our animals to die here? ⁵Why did you bring us from Egypt to this terrible place? It has no grain, figs or pomegranates.ᵈ And there's no water to drink!"

⁶So Moses and Aaron left the people. Then they went to the entrance of the Meeting Tent.ᵈ They bowed face down. And the glory of the Lord appeared to them. ⁷The Lord said to Moses, ⁸"You and your brother Aaron should gather the people. Also take your staff. Speak to that rock in front of them. Then water will flow from it. Give that water to the people and their animals."

⁹So Moses took the staff from in front of the Lord. He did as the Lord had said. ¹⁰He and Aaron gathered the people in front of the rock. Then Moses said, "Now listen to me, you complainers! Do you want us to bring water out of this rock?" ¹¹Then Moses lifted his hand and hit the rock twice with his staff. Water began pouring out. And the people and their animals drank it.

¹²But the Lord said to Moses and Aaron, "You did not believe me. You did not honour me as holy before the people. So you will not lead them into the land I will give them."

¹³These are the waters of Meribah.ⁿ Here the Israelites argued with the Lord. And the Lord showed them he was holy.

Edom Will Not Let Israel Pass

¹⁴From Kadesh, Moses sent messengers to the king of Edom. He said, "Your brothers, the Israelites, say to you: You know about all the troubles we have had. ¹⁵Our ancestors went down into Egypt. And we lived there for many years. The people of Egypt were cruel to our ancestors. ¹⁶But we cried out to the Lord. He heard us and sent us an angel to bring us out of Egypt.

"Now we are here at Kadesh, a town on the edge of your land. ¹⁷Please let us pass through your country. We will not touch any fields of grain or vineyards. We will not drink water from the wells. We will travel only along the king's road. We will not turn right or left until we have passed through your country."

¹⁸But the king of Edom answered: "You may not pass through here. If you try, I will come and meet you with swords."

¹⁹The Israelites answered: "We will go along the main road. If our animals drink any of your water, we will pay for it. We only want to walk through. That's all."

²⁰But he answered: "You may not pass through here."

Then the Edomites went out to meet the Israelites with a large and powerful army. ²¹The Edomites refused to let them pass through their country. So the Israelites turned back.

Aaron Dies

²²All the Israelites moved from Kadesh to Mount Hor. ²³It was near the border of Edom. The Lord said to Moses and Aaron, ²⁴"Aaron will die. He will not enter the land that I'm giving to the Israelites. This is because you both acted against my command at the waters of Meribah. ²⁵Take Aaron and his son Eleazar up on Mount Hor. ²⁶Take off Aaron's special clothes and put them on his son Eleazar. Aaron will die there. He will join his ancestors."

²⁷Moses obeyed the Lord's command. They climbed up Mount Hor. All the people saw them go. ²⁸Moses took off Aaron's clothes. He put them on Aaron's son Eleazar. Then Aaron died there on top of the mountain. And

Meribah This name in Hebrew means "argument".

Moses and Eleazar came back down the mountain. 29Then all the people learned that Aaron was dead. So everyone in Israel cried for him for 30 days.

War with the Canaanites

21 The Canaanite king of Arad lived in the southern area. He heard that the Israelites were coming on the road to Atharim. So he attacked them and captured some of them. 2Then the Israelites made this promise to the Lord: "If you will help us defeat these people, we will completely destroy their cities." 3The Lord listened to the Israelites. And he let them defeat the Canaanites. The Israelites completely destroyed the Canaanites and their cities. So the place was named Hormah."

The Bronze Snake

4The Israelites left Mount Hor and went on the road toward the Gulf of Aqaba. They did this to go around the country of Edom. But the people became impatient on the way. 5They grumbled at God and Moses. They said, "Why did you bring us out of Egypt? We will die in this desert! There is no bread! There is no water! And we hate this terrible food!"

6So the Lord sent them poisonous snakes. They bit the people, and many of the Israelites died. 7The people came to Moses and said, "We sinned when we grumbled at you and the Lord. Pray that the Lord will take away these snakes." So Moses prayed for the people.

8The Lord said to Moses, "Make a bronze snake. And put it on a pole. If anyone is bitten, he should look at it. Then he will live." 9So Moses made a bronze snake. And he put it on a pole. Then when a snake bit anyone, he looked at the bronze snake and lived.

The Journey to Moab

10The Israelites went and camped at Oboth. 11They went from Oboth to Iye Abarim. This was in the desert east of Moab. 12From there they went and camped in the Zered Valley. 13From there they went and camped across the Arnon. This was in the desert just inside the Amorite country. The Arnon is the border between the Moabites and the Amorites. 14That is why the Book of the Wars of the Lord says:

". . . and Waheb in Suphah, and
    the ravines,
    the Arnon, 15and the slopes of
    the ravines
that lead to the settlement of Ar.
    These places are at the border
    of Moab."

16The Israelites went from there to Beer. A well is there where the Lord said to Moses, "Gather the people. I will give them water."

17Then the Israelites sang this song:
"Pour out water, well!
    Sing about it.
18Princes dug this well.
    Important men made this hole.
    With their sceptres d and poles,
    they dug it."

The people went from the desert to Mattanah. 19From Mattanah they went to Nahaliel and on to Bamoth. 20From Bamoth they went to the valley of Moab. There the top of Mount Pisgah looks over the desert.

Sihon and Og

21The people of Israel sent messengers to Sihon, king of the Amorites. They said to him, 22"Let us pass through your country. We will not go through any fields of grain or vineyards. We will not drink water from the wells. We will travel only along the king's road. We will stay on it until

---

Hormah This name in Hebrew means "completely destroyed".

we have passed through your country."

²³But King Sihon would not let the Israelites pass through his country. He gathered his army together. They marched out to meet Israel in the desert. At Jahaz they fought the Israelites. ²⁴Israel killed the king. Then they captured his land from the Arnon River to the Jabbok River. They took the land as far as the Ammonite border. That border was strongly defended. ²⁵Israel captured all the Amorite cities and lived in them. They took Heshbon and all the towns around it. ²⁶Heshbon was the city where Sihon, the Amorite king, lived. In the past he had fought with the king of Moab. Sihon had taken all the land as far as the Arnon.

²⁷That is why the poets say:
"Come to Heshbon
  and rebuild it.
Rebuild Sihon's city.
²⁸A fire began in Heshbon.
  Flames came from Sihon's city.
It destroyed Ar in Moab.
  It burned the Arnon highlands.
²⁹How terrible for you, Moab!
  The people of Chemosh[d] are
    ruined.
His sons ran away.
  His daughters were captured
    by Sihon, king of the Amorites.
³⁰But we defeated those Amorites.
  We ruined their towns from
    Heshbon to Dibon.
We destroyed them as far as
    Nophah, near Medeba."

³¹So Israel lived in the land of the Amorites.

³²Moses sent spies to the town of Jazer. Then they captured the towns around it. They forced out the Amorites who lived there.

³³Then the Israelites went up the road toward Bashan. Og, the king of Bashan, and his army marched out to meet the Israelites. They fought at Edrei. ³⁴The Lord said to Moses, "Don't

be afraid of him. I will hand him, his whole army and his land over to you. Do to him what you did to Sihon, the Amorite king who lived in Heshbon."

³⁵So the Israelites killed Og and his sons and all his army. No one was left alive. And they took his land.

Balaam and Balak

22 Then the people of Israel went to the plains of Moab. They camped near the Jordan River across from Jericho.

²Balak son of Zippor saw everything the Israelites had done to the Amorites. ³And Moab was scared of so many Israelites. Truly, Moab was terrified by them.

⁴The Moabites said to the older leaders of Midian, "This mob will take everything around us. It will be like an ox eating grass."

Balak son of Zippor was the king of Moab at this time. ⁵He sent messengers to Balaam son of Beor at Pethor. It was near the Euphrates River in the land of Amaw. Balak said, "A nation has come out of Egypt. They cover the land. They have camped next to me. ⁶They are too powerful for me. So come and put a curse on them. Maybe then I can defeat them and make them leave the area. I know that if you bless someone, the blessings happen. And if you put a curse on someone, it happens."

⁷The leaders of Moab and Midian went with payment in their hands. They found Balaam. Then they told him what Balak had said.

⁸Balaam said to them, "Stay here for the night. I will tell you what the Lord tells me." So the Moabite leaders stayed with him.

⁹God came to Balaam and asked, "Who are these men with you?"

¹⁰Balaam said to God, "The king of Moab, Balak son of Zippor, sent them. He sent me this message: ¹¹'A nation has come out of Egypt. They cover the land. So come and put a

curse on them. Then maybe I can fight them and force them out of my land'."

¹²But God said to Balaam, "Do not go with them. Don't put a curse on those people. I have blessed them."

¹³The next morning Balaam awoke and said to Balak's leaders, "Go back to your own country. The Lord will not let me go with you."

¹⁴So the Moabite leaders went back to Balak. They said, "Balaam refused to come with us."

¹⁵So Balak sent other leaders. He sent more leaders this time. And they were more important. ¹⁶They went to Balaam and said, "Balak son of Zippor says this: Please don't let anything stop you from coming to me. ¹⁷I will pay you well. I will do what you say. Come and put a curse on these people for me."

¹⁸But Balaam answered Balak's servants, "King Balak could give me his palace full of silver and gold. But I cannot disobey the Lord my God in anything, great or small. ¹⁹You stay here tonight as the other men did. I will find out what more the Lord tells me."

²⁰That night God came to Balaam. He said, "These men have come to ask you to go with them. Go. But only do what I tell you."

Balaam and His Donkey

²¹Balaam got up the next morning. He put a saddle on his donkey. Then he went with the Moabite leaders. ²²But God became angry because Balaam went. So the angel of the Lord stood in the road to stop Balaam. Balaam was riding his donkey. And he had two servants with him. ²³The donkey saw the angel of the Lord standing in the road. The angel had a sword in his hand. So the donkey left the road and went into the field. Balaam hit the donkey to force her back on the road. ²⁴Later, the angel of the Lord stood on a narrow path between two vineyards. There were walls on both sides. ²⁵Again the donkey saw the an-

gel of the Lord. So the donkey walked close to one wall. This crushed Balaam's foot against the wall. So he hit her again.

²⁶The angel of the Lord went ahead again. The angel stood at a narrow place. It was too narrow to turn left or right. ²⁷The donkey saw the angel of the Lord. So she lay down under Balaam. Balaam was very angry and hit her with his stick. ²⁸Then the Lord made the donkey talk. She said to Balaam, "What have I done to make you hit me three times?"

²⁹Balaam answered the donkey, "You have made me look foolish! I wish I had a sword in my hand! I would kill you right now!"

³⁰But the donkey said to Balaam, "I am your very own donkey. You have ridden me for years. Have I ever done this to you before?"

"No", Balaam said.

³¹Then the Lord let Balaam see the angel. The angel of the Lord was standing in the road with his sword drawn. Then Balaam bowed face down on the ground.

³²The angel of the Lord asked Balaam, "Why have you hit your donkey three times? I have stood here to stop you. What you are doing is wrong. ³³The donkey saw me. She turned away from me three times. If she had not turned away, I would have killed you by now. But I would let her live."

³⁴Then Balaam said to the angel of the Lord, "I have sinned. I did not know you were standing in the road to stop me. If I am wrong, I will go back."

³⁵The angel of the Lord said to Balaam, "Go with these men. But say only what I tell you." So Balaam went with Balak's leaders.

³⁶Balak heard that Balaam was coming. So he went out to meet him at Ar in Moab. It was beside the Arnon, at the edge of his country. ³⁷Balak said to Balaam, "I had asked you before to come quickly. Why didn't you come to

me? I am able to reward you well."

38But Balaam answered, "I have come to you now. But I can't say just anything. I can only say what God tells me to say."

39Then Balaam went with Balak to Kiriath Huzoth. 40Balak offered cattle and sheep as a sacrifice. He gave some meat to Balaam and the leaders with him.

41The next morning Balak took Balaam to Bamoth Baal. From there he could see the edge of the Israelite camp.

Balaam's First Message

23 Balaam said, "Build me seven altars here. And prepare seven bulls and seven male sheep for me." 2Balak did what Balaam asked. Then they offered a male sheep and a bull on each of the altars.

3Then Balaam said to Balak, "Stay here beside your burnt offering. I will go. Maybe the Lord will come to me. I will tell you whatever he shows me." Then Balaam went to a higher place.

4God came to Balaam there. Balaam said to him, "I have prepared seven altars. And I have offered a bull and a male sheep on each altar."

5The Lord told Balaam what he should say. Then the Lord said, "Go back to Balak and give him this message."

6So Balaam went back to Balak. Balak and all the leaders of Moab were still standing beside his burnt offering. 7Then Balaam gave them this message:

"Balak brought me here from Aram.
    The king of Moab brought me from the eastern mountains.
Balak said, 'Come, put a curse on the people of Jacob for me.
    Come, wish evil on the people of Israel'.
8But God has not cursed them.
    So I cannot curse them.

The Lord has not wished evil on them.
    So I cannot wish evil on them.
9I see them from the mountains.
    I see them from the hills.
I see a people who live alone.
    They think they are different from other nations.
10No one can number the people of Jacob.
    No one can count a quarter of Israel.
Let me die like a good man.
    Let me end up like them!"

11Balak said to Balaam, "What have you done to me? I brought you here to curse my enemies. But you have only blessed them!"

12But Balaam answered, "I must say what the Lord tells me to say."

Balaam's Second Message

13Then Balak said to him, "Come with me to another place. There you can also see the people. But you can only see part of them, not all of them. Curse them for me from there." 14So Balak took Balaam to the field of Zophim. This was on top of Mount Pisgah. There Balak built seven altars. And he offered a bull and a male sheep on each altar.

15So Balaam said to Balak, "Stay here by your burnt offering. I will meet with God over there."

16So the Lord came to Balaam. He told Balaam what to say. Then he said, "Go back to Balak and say such and such."

17So Balaam went to Balak. Balak and the leaders of Moab were standing beside his burnt offering. Balak asked him, "What did the Lord say?"

18Then Balaam gave this message:
"Stand up, Balak, and listen.
    Hear me, son of Zippor.
19God is not a man. He will not lie.
    God is not a human being. He does not change his mind.
What he says he will do, he does.
    What he promises, he keeps.

²⁰He told me to bless them.
So I cannot change the blessing.
²¹He has found no wrong in the
people of Jacob.
He saw no fault in Israel.
The Lord their God is with them.
They praise their King.
²²God brought them out of Egypt.
They are as strong as a wild ox.
²³No tricks will work on the people
of Jacob.
No magic works against Israel.
People now say this about them,
'Look what God has done!'
²⁴The people are strong like a
lioness.
They get up like a lion.
Lions don't rest until they have
eaten.
They drink their enemies'
blood."

²⁵Then Balak said to Balaam, "You
haven't cursed these people. So at
least, don't bless them!"

²⁶Balaam answered Balak, "I told
you before. I can only do what the
Lord tells me."

Balaam's Third Message

²⁷Then Balak said to Balaam,
"Come, I will take you to another
place. Maybe God will be pleased. He
may let you curse them from there."
²⁸So Balak took Balaam to the top of
Peor. This mountain looks over the
desert.

²⁹Balaam told Balak, "Build me sev-
en altars here. Then prepare for me
seven bulls and seven male sheep."
³⁰Balak did what Balaam asked. He offered a bull and a male sheep on each
altar.

24 Balaam saw that the Lord
wanted to bless Israel. So Balaam did not try to use any magic. He
looked toward the desert. ²Balaam
saw the Israelites camped in their
tribes.ᵈ Then the Spiritᵈ of God entered him. ³And Balaam gave this
message:

"This is the message of Balaam
son of Beor.
This is the message of a man
who sees clearly.
⁴This is the message of a man who
hears the words of God.
I see a vision from the
All-Powerful One.
My eyes are open as I fall
before him.
⁵Your tents are beautiful, people of
Jacob!
So are your homes, Israel!
⁶Your tents spread out like valleys.
They are like gardens beside a
river.
They are like spices planted by
the Lord.
They are like cedar trees
growing by the water.
⁷Israel's water buckets will always
be full.
Their crops will have plenty of
water.
Their king will be greater than
Agag.
Their kingdom will be very
great.
⁸God brought them out of Egypt.
They are as strong as a wild ox.
They will defeat their enemies.
They will break their enemies'
bones.
They will shoot them with
arrows.
⁹Like a lion, they lie waiting to
attack.
No one would wake a sleeping
lion.
Anyone who blesses you will be
blessed.
And anyone who curses you will
be cursed."

¹⁰Then Balak was angry with Balaam. Balak pounded his fist. He said
to Balaam, "I called you here to curse
my enemies. But you have blessed
them three times. ¹¹Now go home! I
said I would pay you well. But the
Lord has made you lose your reward."

¹²Balaam said to Balak, "You sent messengers to me. I told them, ¹³'Balak could give me his palace filled with silver and gold. But I still cannot go against the Lord's commands. I could not do anything, good or bad, on my own. I must say what the Lord says'. ¹⁴Now I am going back to my own people. But I will tell you what these people will do to your people in the future."

Balaam's Final Message

¹⁵Then Balaam gave his final message:
"This is the message of Balaam
      son of Beor.
This is the message of a man
      who sees clearly.
¹⁶This is the message of a man who
      hears the words of God.
I know the Most High God.
I see a vision from the
      All-Powerful One.
My eyes are open as I fall
      before him.
¹⁷I see someone who will come
      some day.
I see someone who will come,
      but not soon.
A star will come from Jacob.
A ruler will rise from Israel.
He will crush the heads of the
      Moabites.
He will smash the skulls of the
      sons of Sheth.
¹⁸Edom will be conquered.
His enemy Edom will be
      conquered.
But Israel will grow wealthy.
¹⁹The descendants⁴ of Jacob will
      beat them down.
The Israelites will destroy those
      left in the city."

²⁰Then Balaam saw Amalek and gave this message:
"Amalek was the most important
      nation.
But Amalek will be destroyed at
      last."

²¹Then Balaam saw the Kenites and gave this message:
"Your home is safe.
It is like a nest on a cliff.
²²But you Kenites will be burned
      up.
Assyria will keep you captive."

²³Then Balaam gave this message:
"No one can live when God does
      this.
²⁴   Ships will sail from the shores of
      Cyprus.
They will defeat Assyria and
      Eber.
But they will also be
      destroyed."

²⁵Then Balaam got up and returned home. Balak also went on his way.

Israel at Peor

25 The people of Israel were still camped at Acacia. The men began sinning sexually with Moabite women. ²The women invited them to the sacrifices to their false gods. The Israelites ate food there and worshipped these gods. ³So the Israelites began to worship Baal⁴ of Peor. And the Lord was very angry with them.

⁴The Lord said to Moses, "Get all the leaders of the people. Then kill them in open daylight in the presence of the Lord. Then the Lord will not be angry with the people of Israel."

⁵So Moses said to Israel's judges, "Each of you must put to death your men who have become worshippers of Baal of Peor."

⁶Moses and the Israelites were gathered at the entrance to the Meeting Tent.⁴ They were crying there. Then an Israelite man brought a Midianite woman to his brothers. This was in plain sight of Moses and all the people. ⁷Phinehas son of Eleazar, the son of Aaron, the priest, saw this. So he left the meeting and got his spear. ⁸He followed the Israelite into his tent. And he drove his spear through both the Israelite man and the Midianite

woman. Then the terrible sickness among the Israelites stopped. [9]This sickness had killed 24,000 people.

[10]The Lord said to Moses, [11]"Phinehas son of Eleazar, the son of Aaron, the priest, has saved the Israelites from my anger. He is like I am in his concern for the people. He tried to save my honour among them. So I will not kill the Israelites. [12]So tell Phinehas that I am making my peace agreement with him. [13]He and all his descendants[d] will have an agreement. They will always be priests. This is because he had great concern for the honour of his God. He removed the sins of the Israelites so they would belong to God."

[14]The Israelite man who was killed with the Midianite woman was named Zimri son of Salu. He was the leader of a family in the tribe[d] of Simeon. [15]And the name of the Midianite woman who was put to death was Cozbi daughter of Zur. Zur was the chief of a Midianite family.

[16]The Lord said to Moses, [17]"The Midianites are your enemies. You should kill them. [18]They have already made you their enemies. They tricked you at Peor. Then there was Cozbi, the daughter of a Midianite leader. She was the woman who was killed when the sickness came. It came because the people were worshipping a false god at Peor."

The People Are Counted

26 After the great sickness, the Lord spoke to Moses and Eleazar son of Aaron, the priest. He said, [2]"Count all the people of Israel by families. Count all the men who are 20 years old or older. They will serve in the army of Israel." [3]Moses and Eleazar the priest spoke to the people. They were on the plains of Moab near the Jordan River, across from Jericho. They said, [4]"Count the men 20 years old or older. This is what the Lord commanded Moses."

Here are the Israelites who came out of Egypt:

[5]The tribe[d] of Reuben was counted. Reuben was the first son born to Israel. From Hanoch came the Hanochite family group. From Pallu came the Palluite family group. [6]From Hezron came the Hezronite family group. From Carmi came the Carmite family group. [7]These were the family groups of Reuben. The total number of men was 43,730.

[8]The son of Pallu was Eliab. [9]Eliab's sons were Nemuel, Dathan and Abiram. Dathan and Abiram were the leaders who turned against Moses and Aaron. They followed Korah when he turned against the Lord. [10]The earth opened up and swallowed them and Korah. They died when the fire burned up the 250 men. This was a warning. [11]But the children of Korah did not die.

[12]These were the family groups in the tribe of Simeon. From Nemuel came the Nemuelite family group. From Jamin came the Jaminite family group. From Jakin came the Jakinite family group. [13]From Zerah came the Zerahite family group. From Shaul came the Shaulite family group. [14]These were the family groups of Simeon. The total number of men was 22,200.

[15]These were the family groups in the tribe of Gad. From Zephon came the Zephonite family group. From Haggi came the Haggite family group. From Shuni came the Shunite family group. [16]From Ozni came the Oznite family group. From Eri came the Erite family group. [17]From Arodi came the Arodite family group. From Areli came the Arelite family group. [18]These were the family groups of Gad. The total number of men was 40,500.

[19]Two of Judah's sons, Er and Onan, died in Canaan.

20These were the family groups in the tribe of Judah. From Shelah came the Shelanite family group. From Perez came the Perezite family group. From Zerah came the Zerahite family group. 21These were the family groups from Perez. From Hezron came the Hezronite family group. From Hamul came the Hamulite family group. 22These were the family groups of Judah. The total number of men was 76,500.

23These were the family groups in the tribe of Issachar. From Tola came the Tolaite family group. From Puah came the Puthite family group. 24From Jashub came the Jashubite family group. From Shimron came the Shimronite family group. 25These were the family groups of Issachar. The total number of men was 64,300.

26These were the family groups in the tribe of Zebulun. From Sered came the Seredite family group. From Elon came the Elonite family group. From Jahleel came the Jahleelite family group. 27These were the family groups of Zebulun. The total number of men was 60,500.

28These were the family groups of Joseph through Manasseh and Ephraim.

29These were the family groups of Manasseh. From Makir came the Makirite family group. (Makir was the father of Gilead.) From Gilead came the Gileadite family group. 30These were the family groups that came from Gilead. From Iezer came the Iezerite family group. From Helek came the Helekite family group. 31From Asriel came the Asrielite family group. From Shechem came the Shechemite family group. 32From Shemida came the Shemidaite family group. From Hepher came the Hepherite family group. 33(Zelophehad son of Hepher had no sons. He had only daughters. Their names were Mahlah, Noah, Hoglah, Milcah and Tirzah.) 34These were the family groups of Manasseh.

The total number of men was 52,700.

35These were the family groups in the tribe of Ephraim. From Shuthelah came the Shuthelahite family group. From Beker came the Bekerite family group. From Tahan came the Tahanite family group. 36This was the family group from Shuthelah. From Eran came the Eranite family group. 37These were the family groups of Ephraim. The total number of men was 32,500. These are the family groups that came from Joseph.

38These were the family groups in the tribe of Benjamin. From Bela came the Belaite family group. From Ashbel came the Ashbelite family group. From Ahiram came the Ahiramite family group. 39From Shupham came the Shuphamite family group. From Hupham came the Huphamite family group. 40These were the family groups from Bela through Ard and Naaman. From Ard came the Ardite family group. From Naaman came the Naamite family group. 41These were the family groups of Benjamin. The total number of men was 45,600.

42This was the family group in the tribe of Dan. From Shuham came the Shuhamite family group. That was the family of Dan. 43The total number of men in the Shuhamite family group of Dan was 64,400.

44These were the family groups in the tribe of Asher. From Imnah came the Imnite family group. From Ishvi came the Ishvite family group. From Beriah came the Beriite family group. 45These were the family groups that came from Beriah. From Heber came the Heberite family group. From Malkiel came the Malkielite family group. 46(Asher also had a daughter named Serah.) 47These were the family groups of Asher. The total number of men was 53,400.

48These were the family groups in the tribe of Naphtali. From Jahzeel came the Jahzeelite family group. From Guni came the Gunite family group. ⁴⁹From Jezer came the Jezerite family group. From Shillem came the Shillemite family group. ⁵⁰These were the family groups of Naphtali. The total number of men was 45,400. ⁵¹So the total number of the men of Israel was 601,730.

⁵²The Lord said to Moses, ⁵³"Divide the land among these people by the number of names. ⁵⁴A large tribe will get more land. And a small tribe will get less land. The amount of land each tribe gets will depend on the number of its people. ⁵⁵Divide the land by drawing lots.ᵈ And the land each tribe gets will be named for that tribe. ⁵⁶Divide the land by drawing lots. Divide it between large and small groups."

⁵⁷The tribe of Levi was also counted. These were the family groups of Levi. From Gershon came the Gershonite family group. From Kohath came the Kohathite family group. From Merari came the Merarite family group. ⁵⁸These also were Levite family groups: the Libnite family group, the Hebronite family group, the Mahlite family group, the Mushite family group and the Korahite family group. (Kohath was the ancestor of Amram. ⁵⁹Amram's wife was named Jochebed. She was from the tribe of Levi. She was born in Egypt. She and Amram had two sons, Aaron and Moses, and their sister Miriam. ⁶⁰Aaron was the father of Nadab, Abihu, Eleazar and Ithamar. ⁶¹But Nadab and Abihu died. They died because they made an offering before the Lord with the wrong kind of fire.)

⁶²The total number of male Levites one month old or older was 23,000. But these men were not counted with the other Israelites. They did not receive any of the land that the Lord gave the other Israelites.

⁶³Moses and Eleazar the priest counted all these people. They counted the Israelites on the plains of Moab across the Jordan River from Jericho. ⁶⁴Moses and Aaron the priest had counted the Israelites in the Desert of Sinai. But no one Moses counted on the plains of Moab was in the first counting. ⁶⁵The Lord had told the Israelites they would all die in the desert. The only two left were Caleb son of Jephunneh and Joshua son of Nun.

Zelophehad's Daughters

27 Zelophehad was the son of Hepher. Hepher was the son of Gilead. Gilead was the son of Makir. Makir was the son of Manasseh. Zelophehad's daughters belonged to the family groups of Manasseh son of Joseph. The daughters' names were Mahlah, Noah, Hoglah, Milcah and Tirzah. ²They went to the entrance of the Meeting Tent.ᵈ There they stood before Moses, Eleazar the priest, the leaders and all the people. They said, ³"Our father died in the desert. He was not one of Korah's followers who came against the Lord. Our father died because of his own sin. But he had no sons. ⁴Our father's name will die out because he had no sons. Give us property among our father's relatives."

⁵So Moses brought their case to the Lord. ⁶The Lord said to him, ⁷"The daughters of Zelophehad are right. They should get what their father owned. Give them property among their father's relatives.

⁸"Tell the Israelites, 'If a man dies and has no son, then everything he owned should go to his daughter. ⁹If he has no daughter, then everything he owned should go to his brothers. ¹⁰If he has no brothers, then everything he owned should go to his father's brothers. ¹¹If his father had no brothers, then everything he owned should go to the nearest relative in his family group. This should be a rule among the people of Israel because the Lord has given this command to Moses'."

Joshua Is the New Leader

¹²Then the Lord said to Moses, "Climb this mountain in the Abarim Mountains. Look at the land I have given to the Israelites. ¹³After you have seen it, you will die as your brother Aaron did. ¹⁴You both acted against my command in the Desert of Zin. You did not honour me as holy before the people at the waters of Meribah." (This was at Meribah in Kadesh in the Desert of Zin.)

¹⁵Moses said to the Lord, ¹⁶"The Lord is the God of the spirits of all people. May he choose a good leader for these people. ¹⁷He must go in and out before them. He must lead them out like sheep and bring them in. The Lord's people must not be like sheep without a shepherd."

¹⁸So the Lord said to Moses, "Take Joshua son of Nun. My Spirit[d] is in him. Put your hand on him. ¹⁹Have him stand before Eleazar the priest and all the people. Then give him his orders as they watch. ²⁰Let him share your honour. Then all the Israelites will obey him. ²¹He must stand before Eleazar the priest. And Eleazar will get advice from the Lord by using the Urim.[d] At his command all the Israelites will go out. At his command they will all come in."

²²Moses did what the Lord told him. Moses had Joshua stand before Eleazar the priest and all the people. ²³Then Moses put his hands on him and gave him orders. This was just as the Lord had told him.

Daily Offerings

28 The Lord said to Moses, ²"Give this command to the Israelites. Tell them: 'Bring me food offerings made by fire. The smell is pleasing to me. Be sure to bring them at the right time'. ³Say to them: 'These are the offerings you must bring to the Lord. Bring two year-old lambs as a burnt offering each day.

They must have nothing wrong with them. ⁴Offer one lamb in the morning and the other lamb at twilight. ⁵Also bring a grain offering of 2 litres of fine flour. It must be mixed with 1 litre of oil from pressed olives. ⁶This is the daily burnt offering which began at Mount Sinai. The smell is pleasing to the Lord. ⁷Offer 1 litre of wine with each lamb as a drink offering. Pour it out to the Lord at the Holy Place. ⁸Offer the second lamb at twilight. As in the morning, also give a grain offering and a drink offering. This offering is made by fire. Its smell is pleasing to the Lord.

Sabbath Offerings

⁹" 'On the Sabbath[d] day you must give two year-old lambs. They must have nothing wrong with them. Also give a drink offering and a grain offering. The grain offering must be 4.5 litres of fine flour mixed with olive oil. ¹⁰This is the burnt offering for the Sabbath. It is in addition to the daily burnt offering and drink offering.

Monthly Offerings

¹¹" 'On the first day of each month bring a burnt offering to the Lord. This will be two young bulls, one male sheep and seven male lambs a year old. They all must have nothing wrong with them. ¹²Give a grain offering with each bull. It must be 6.5 litres of fine flour mixed with olive oil. Also give a grain offering with the male sheep. It must be 4.5 litres of fine flour mixed with olive oil. ¹³Also give a grain offering with each lamb. It must be 2 litres of fine flour mixed with olive oil. This is a burnt offering. And its smell is pleasing to the Lord. ¹⁴The drink offering with each bull will be 2 litres of wine. With the male sheep it will be 1.2 litres. And with each lamb it will be 1 litre of wine. This is the burnt offering that must be offered each month of the year. ¹⁵Besides the daily burnt offerings and drink offerings,

bring a sin offering to the Lord. It must be one male goat.

Passover

16" 'The Lord's Passover^d will be on the fourteenth day of the first month. ^{17}The Feast^d of Unleavened Bread begins on the fifteenth day of that month. It lasts for seven days. You may eat only bread made without yeast. ^{18}Have a holy meeting on the first day of the festival. Don't work that day. ^{19}Bring these burnt offerings to the Lord: two young bulls, one male sheep and seven male lambs a year old. They all must have nothing wrong with them. ^{20}Also give a grain offering with each bull. It must be six litres of fine flour mixed with olive oil. Give a grain offering with the male sheep. It must be 4 litres of fine flour mixed with oil. ^{21}Give a grain offering with each of the seven lambs. It must be 2 litres of fine flour mixed with oil. ^{22}Bring one goat as a sin offering. It will remove your sins so you will belong to God. ^{23}Bring these offerings in addition to the burnt offerings you give every morning. ^{24}So bring food offerings each day for seven days. The offering is made by fire. And its smell is pleasing to the Lord. Do it in addition to the daily burnt offering and its drink offering. ^{25}On the seventh day have a holy meeting. Don't work that day.

Feast of Weeks

26" 'On the day of first fruits^d offer new grain to the Lord. This is during the Feast^d of Weeks. Have a holy meeting. Don't work that day. ^{27}Give this burnt offering to the Lord: two young bulls, one male sheep and seven male lambs a year old. This smell is pleasing to the Lord. ^{28}Also give a grain offering with each bull. It must be 6 litres of fine flour mixed with oil. With the male sheep, it must be 4 litres of flour. ^{29}With each of the seven lambs offer 2 litres of flour.

^{30}Offer one male goat to remove your sins so you will belong to God. ^{31}Bring these offerings and their drink offerings. These are in addition to the daily burnt offering and its grain offering. The animals must have nothing wrong with them.

Feast of Trumpets

29 " 'Have a holy meeting on the first day of the seventh month. Don't work on that day. That is the day you blow the trumpets. ^{2}Bring these burnt offerings to the Lord: one young bull, one male sheep and seven male year-old lambs. They all must have nothing wrong with them. Their smell will be pleasing to the Lord. ^{3}Give a grain offering with the bull. It must be 6.5 litres of fine flour mixed with oil. With the male sheep offer 4.5 litres. ^{4}And with each of the seven lambs offer 2 litres. ^{5}Offer one male goat for a sin offering. It will remove your sins so you will belong to God. ^{6}These offerings are in addition to the monthly and daily burnt offerings. Their grain offerings and drink offerings must be done as you have been told. These offerings are made by fire to the Lord. And their smell is pleasing to him.

The Day of Cleansing

7" 'Have a holy meeting on the tenth day of the seventh month. On that day do not eat and do not work. ^{8}Bring these burnt offerings to the Lord: one young bull, one male sheep and seven male lambs a year old. They all must have nothing wrong with them. The smell will be pleasing to the Lord. ^{9}Give a grain offering with the bull. It must be 6.5 litres of fine flour mixed with oil. With the male sheep it must be 4.5 litres. ^{10}And with each of the seven lambs it must be 2 litres. ^{11}Offer one male goat as a sin offering. This will be in addition to the sin offering which removes your sins. It will also be in addition to the daily burnt offering with its grain offering and the drink offerings.

Feast of Tents

¹²" 'Have a holy meeting on the fifteenth day of the seventh month. Do not work on that day. Celebrate a festival to the Lord for seven days. ¹³Give these burnt offerings to the Lord: 13 young bulls, two male sheep and 14 male lambs a year old. They all must have nothing wrong with them. The smell is pleasing to the Lord. ¹⁴Also offer a grain offering with each of the 13 bulls. It must be 6 litres of fine flour mixed with oil. With each of the two male sheep it must be 4 litres. ¹⁵And with each of the 14 lambs it must be 2 litres. ¹⁶Offer one male goat as a sin offering. This must be in addition to the daily burnt offering with its grain and drink offerings.

¹⁷" 'On the second day of this festival give an offering. Offer 12 bulls, two male sheep and 14 male lambs a year old. They all must have nothing wrong with them. ¹⁸Bring the grain and drink offerings for the bulls, sheep and lambs. ¹⁹Offer one male goat as a sin offering. This must be in addition to the daily burnt offering with its grain and drink offerings.

²⁰" 'On the third day offer 11 bulls, two male sheep and 14 male lambs a year old. They all must have nothing wrong with them. ²¹Bring the grain and drink offerings for the bulls, sheep and lambs. ²²Offer one male goat as a sin offering. This must be in addition to the daily burnt offering with its grain and drink offerings.

²³" 'On the fourth day offer ten bulls, two male sheep and 14 male lambs a year old. They all must have nothing wrong with them. ²⁴Bring the grain and drink offerings for the bulls, sheep and lambs. ²⁵Offer one male goat as a sin offering. This must be in addition to the daily burnt offering with its grain and drink offerings.

²⁶" 'On the fifth day offer nine bulls, two male sheep and 14 male lambs a year old. They all must have nothing wrong with them. ²⁷Bring the grain and drink offerings for the bulls, sheep and lambs. ²⁸Offer one male goat as a sin offering. This must be in addition to the daily burnt offering with its grain and drink offerings.

²⁹" 'On the sixth day offer eight bulls, two male sheep and 14 male lambs a year old. They all must have nothing wrong with them. ³⁰Bring the grain and drink offerings for the bulls, sheep and lambs. ³¹Offer one male goat as a sin offering. This must be in addition to the daily burnt offering with its grain and drink offerings.

³²" 'On the seventh day offer seven bulls, two male sheep and 14 male lambs a year old. They all must have nothing wrong with them. ³³Bring the grain and drink offerings for the bulls, sheep and lambs. ³⁴Offer one male goat as a sin offering. This must be in addition to the daily burnt offering with its grain and drink offerings.

³⁵" 'On the eighth day have a closing meeting. Do not work on that day. ³⁶Bring a burnt offering. Its smell will be pleasing to the Lord. Offer one bull, one male sheep and seven male lambs a year old. They all must have nothing wrong with them. ³⁷Bring the grain and drink offerings for the bull, male sheep and lambs. ³⁸Offer one male goat as a sin offering. This must be in addition to the daily burnt offering with its grain and drink offerings.

³⁹" 'At your festivals you should bring these to the Lord: your burnt offerings, grain offerings, drink offerings and fellowship offerings. These are in addition to other promised offerings and special gifts you want to give to the Lord'."

⁴⁰Moses told the Israelites everything the Lord had commanded him.

Special Promises

30 Moses spoke with the leaders of the Israelite tribes.ᵈ He told

them these commands from the Lord.
²"A person might make a promise to the Lord. He might promise to do something special. If he does, he must keep his promise. He must do what he said. ³A young woman still living at home might make a promise to the Lord. She might pledge to do something special. ⁴Her father might hear about the promise or pledge and say nothing. Then she must do what she promised. She must keep her pledge. ⁵But when her father hears about the promise or pledge, he might not allow it. Then the promise or pledge does not have to be kept. Her father would not allow them. So the Lord will free her from her promise.

⁶"A woman might make a pledge or a careless promise and then get married. ⁷Her husband might hear about it and say nothing. Then she must keep her promise or the pledge she made. ⁸But when her husband hears about it, he might not allow it. He cancels her pledge or the careless promise she made. The Lord will free her from keeping it.

⁹"A widow or divorced woman might make a promise. She must do whatever she promised.

¹⁰"A woman might make a promise or pledge while she was married. ¹¹When her husband hears about it, he might say nothing. He might not stop her. Then she must keep her promise or pledge. ¹²But when her husband hears about it, he might cancel it. Then she does not have to do what she said. Her husband has cancelled it. The Lord will free her from it. ¹³A woman's husband may make her keep or cancel any promise or pledge she has made. ¹⁴But her husband might say nothing to her about it for several days. Then she must keep her promises. If he hears about them and says nothing, she must keep her promises. ¹⁵But he might cancel them long after he heard about them. Then he is responsible if she breaks her promise."

¹⁶These are commands that the Lord gave to Moses. They are for husbands and wives. And they are for fathers with daughters living at home.

Israel Attacks the Midianites

31 The Lord spoke to Moses. He said, ²"Pay back the Midianites for what they did to the Israelites. After that you will die."

³So Moses said to the people, "Get some men ready for war. The Lord will use them to pay back the Midianites. ⁴Send to war 1,000 men from each of the tribes^d of Israel." ⁵So 12,000 men got ready for war. There were 1,000 men from each tribe. ⁶Moses sent those 1,000 men from each tribe to war. Phinehas son of Eleazar the priest was with them. He took with him the holy things and the trumpets. ⁷They fought the Midianites as the Lord had commanded Moses. And they killed every Midianite man. ⁸Among those they killed were Evi, Rekem, Zur, Hur and Reba. They were the five kings of Midian. They also killed Balaam son of Beor with a sword.

⁹The Israelites captured the Midianite women and children. They also took all their flocks, herds and goods. ¹⁰Then they burned all the Midianite towns and camps. ¹¹They took all the people and animals and goods. ¹²Then they went back to Moses and Eleazar the priest and all the Israelites. They brought back the captives, the animals and the goods. The camp was on the plains of Moab near the Jordan River. This was across from Jericho.

¹³Moses, Eleazar the priest and all the leaders of the people went outside the camp to meet them. ¹⁴Moses was angry with the army officers who returned from war. He was angry with those commanders over 1,000 men and those over 100 men.

¹⁵He asked them, "Why did you let the women live? ¹⁶They were the ones who followed Balaam's advice.

They turned the Israelites from the Lord at Peor. Then a terrible sickness struck the Lord's people. ¹⁷Kill all the Midianite boys. Kill all the Midianite women who have had sexual relations. ¹⁸But save the girls for yourselves who have not had sexual relations with a man.

¹⁹"All you men who killed anyone or touched a dead body must stay outside the camp for seven days. On the third and seventh days you and your captives must make yourselves clean.ᵈ ²⁰You must clean all your clothes. And you must clean anything made of leather, wool or wood."

²¹Then Eleazar the priest spoke to the soldiers who had gone to war. He said, "These are the teachings that the Lord gave to Moses. ²²Put any gold, silver, bronze, iron, tin or lead into the fire. ²³Put into the fire anything that will not burn. Then wash those things with the cleansing water. Then they will be clean. If something cannot stand the fire, wash it with the water. ²⁴On the seventh day wash your clothes. Then you will be clean. After that you may come into the camp."

Dividing the Goods

²⁵The Lord said to Moses, ²⁶"You, Eleazar the priest and the leaders should take a count. Count the goods, the men and the animals that were taken. ²⁷Then divide those things between the soldiers who went to war and the rest of the people. ²⁸Tax the soldiers who went to war. The Lord's share is one thing out of every 500 things. This includes people, cattle, donkeys, sheep or goats. ²⁹Take it from the soldiers' half. And give it to Eleazar the priest. It is the Lord's share. ³⁰And from the people's half, take one thing out of every 50. This includes people, cattle, donkeys, sheep, goats or other animals. Give that to the Levites. They take care of the Lord's Holy Tent."ᵈ ³¹So Moses

and Eleazar did as the Lord commanded Moses.

³²There remained from what the soldiers had taken 675,000 sheep, ³³72,000 cattle, ³⁴61,000 donkeys ³⁵and 32,000 women. These were the women who had not had sexual relations with a man. ³⁶The soldiers who went to war got 337,500 sheep. ³⁷They gave 675 of the sheep to the Lord. ³⁸They got 36,000 cattle. They gave 72 of them to the Lord. ³⁹They got 30,500 donkeys. They gave 61 of them to the Lord. ⁴⁰They got 16,000 people. And they gave 32 of them to the Lord. ⁴¹Moses gave the Lord's share to Eleazar the priest. This was what the Lord had commanded him.

⁴²Moses separated the people's half from the soldiers' half. ⁴³The people got 337,500 sheep, ⁴⁴36,000 cattle, ⁴⁵30,500 donkeys ⁴⁶and 16,000 people. ⁴⁷From the people's half Moses took one thing out of every 50 for the Lord. This included the animals and the people. Then he gave them to the Levites. They took care of the Lord's Holy Tent. This was what the Lord had commanded Moses.

⁴⁸Then the officers of the army came to Moses. They were the commanders of 1,000 men and commanders of 100 men. ⁴⁹They told Moses, "We, your servants, have counted our soldiers under our command. Not one of them is missing. ⁵⁰So we have brought the Lord a gift. We have brought the gold things that each of us found: arm bands, bracelets, signetᵈ rings, earrings and necklaces. These are to remove our sins so we will belong to the Lord."

⁵¹So Moses and Eleazar the priest took the gold things from them. ⁵²The commanders of 1,000 men and the commanders of 100 men gave the Lord the gold. All of it together weighed about 190 kilograms. ⁵³Each soldier had taken something for himself. ⁵⁴Moses and Eleazar the priest took the gold from the commanders of

1,000 men and the commanders of 100 men. Then they put it in the Meeting Tent.*d* It was a memorial before the Lord for the people of Israel.

The Tribes East of the Jordan

32 The people of Reuben and Gad had many cattle. They saw that the lands of Jazer and Gilead were good for cattle. ²So they came to Moses, Eleazar the priest and the leaders of the people. ³⁻⁴They said, "We, your servants, have many cattle. The Lord has captured for the Israelites a land that is good for cattle. This is the land around Ataroth, Dibon, Jazer, Nimrah, Heshbon, Elealeh, Sebam, Nebo and Beon. ⁵If it pleases you, we would like this land to be given to us. Don't make us cross the Jordan River."

⁶Moses told the people of Gad and Reuben, "Shall your brothers go to war while you stay behind? ⁷You will discourage the Israelites. They will not want to go over to the land the Lord has given them. ⁸Your ancestors did the same thing. From Kadesh Barnea I sent them to look at the land. ⁹They went as far as the Valley of Eshcol. They saw the land. And they discouraged the Israelites from going into the land the Lord had given them. ¹⁰The Lord became very angry that day. He made this promise: ¹¹None of the people who came from Egypt and who are 20 years old or older will see this land. I promised it to Abraham, Isaac and Jacob. But these people have not followed me completely. ¹²Only Caleb son of Jephunneh the Kenizzite and Joshua son of Nun followed the Lord completely.'

¹³"The Lord was very angry with Israel. So he made them wander in the desert for 40 years. Finally all the people who had sinned against him had died. ¹⁴And now you are acting just like your fathers! You sinful people are making the Lord even more angry with Israel. ¹⁵If you stop following the Lord, it will add to their stay in the desert. So you will destroy all these people."

¹⁶But the Reubenites and Gadites came up to Moses. They said, "We will build pens for our animals. And we will build cities for our wives and children here. ¹⁷Then our families will be in strong, walled cities. They will be safe from the people who live in this land. Then we will prepare for war. We will help the other Israelites get their land. ¹⁸We will not return home until every Israelite has received his land. ¹⁹We won't take any of the land west of the Jordan River. Our part of the land is east of the Jordan."

²⁰So Moses told them, "You must do these things. You must go before the Lord into battle. ²¹You must cross the Jordan River armed. The Lord will force out the enemy. ²²After the Lord helps us take the land, you may return home. You will have done your duty to the Lord and Israel. Then you may have this land as your own.

²³"But if you don't do these things, you will be sinning against the Lord. And know for sure that you will be punished for your sin. ²⁴Build cities for your wives and children and pens for your animals. But then you must do what you promised."

²⁵The Gadites and Reubenites said to Moses, "We are your servants. We will do what you, our master, command. ²⁶Our wives, children and all our cattle will stay in the cities of Gilead. ²⁷But we, your servants, will prepare for battle. We will go over and fight for the Lord, as you have said."

²⁸So Moses gave orders about them to Eleazar the priest. And he gave them to Joshua son of Nun and the leaders of the tribes*d* of Israel. ²⁹Moses said to them, "The Gadites and Reubenites will prepare for battle. They will cross the Jordan River with you. They will go before the Lord and help you take the land. If they do that, give them the land of Gilead for their own. ³⁰But if they do not go over

armed, they will not receive it. Their land will be in Canaan with you."

31The Gadites and Reubenites answered, "We are your servants. We will do as the Lord said. 32We will cross over into Canaan. We will go before the Lord ready for battle. But our land will be east of the Jordan River."

33So Moses gave that land to the Gadites, Reubenites and the eastern half-tribe of Manasseh. (Manasseh was Joseph's son.) That land had been the kingdom of Sihon, the king of the Amorites. And it included the kingdom of Og, king of Bashan. It also included all the cities and the land around them.

34The Gadites rebuilt the cities of Dibon, Ataroth, Aroer, 35Atroth Shophan, Jazer, Jogbehah, 36Beth Nimrah and Beth Haran. These were strong, walled cities. And they built sheep pens.

37The Reubenites built Heshbon, Elealeh, Kiriathaim, 38Nebo, Baal Meon and Sibmah. They renamed Nebo and Baal Meon when they rebuilt them.

39The descendants*d* of Makir son of Manasseh went and captured Gilead. They forced out the Amorites who were there. 40So Moses gave Gilead to the family of Makir son of Manasseh. And they settled there. 41Jair son of Manasseh went out and captured the small towns there. He called them the Towns of Jair. 42Nobah went and captured Kenath and the small towns around it. Then he named it Nobah after himself.

Israel's Journey from Egypt

33 These are the places the Israelites went as Moses and Aaron led them out of Egypt in divisions. 2At the Lord's command Moses recorded the places they went. These are the places they went.

3On the fifteenth day of the first month, they left Rameses. That was the day after the Passover.*d* The Isra-

elites marched out boldly in front of all the Egyptians. 4The Egyptians were burying their firstborn*d* sons. The Lord had killed them. He showed that the gods of Egypt were false.

5The Israelites left Rameses and camped at Succoth.

6They left Succoth and camped at Etham. It was at the edge of the desert.

7They left Etham and went back to Pi Hahiroth. This was east of Baal Zephon. They camped near Migdol.

8They left Pi Hahiroth. They walked through the sea into the desert. After going three days through the Desert of Etham, they camped at Marah.

9They left Marah and went to Elim. There were 12 springs of water and 70 palm trees where they camped.

10They left Elim and camped near the Red Sea.*d*

11They left the Red Sea and camped in the Desert of Sin.

12They left the Desert of Sin and camped at Dophkah.

13They left Dophkah and camped at Alush.

14They left Alush and camped at Rephidim. The people had no water to drink there.

15They left Rephidim and camped in the Desert of Sinai.

16They left the Desert of Sinai and camped at Kibroth Hattaavah.

17They left Kibroth Hattaavah and camped at Hazeroth.

18They left Hazeroth and camped at Rithmah.

19They left Rithmah and camped at Rimmon Perez.

20They left Rimmon Perez and camped at Libnah.

21They left Libnah and camped at Rissah.

22They left Rissah and camped at Kehelathah.

23They left Kehelathah and camped at Mount Shepher.

²⁴They left Mount Shepher and camped at Haradah.

²⁵They left Haradah and camped at Makheloth.

²⁶They left Makheloth and camped at Tahath.

²⁷They left Tahath and camped at Terah.

²⁸They left Terah and camped at Mithcah.

²⁹They left Mithcah and camped at Hashmonah.

³⁰They left Hashmonah and camped at Moseroth.

³¹They left Moseroth and camped at Bene Berak Jaakan.

³²They left Bene Berak Jaakan and camped at Hor Haggidgad.

³³They left Hor Haggidgad and camped at Jotbathah.

³⁴They left Jotbathah and camped at Abronah.

³⁵They left Abronah and camped at Ezion Geber.

³⁶They left Ezion Geber and camped at Kadesh in the Desert of Zin.

³⁷They left Kadesh and camped at Mount Hor. This was on the border of Edom. ³⁸Aaron the priest obeyed the Lord and went up Mount Hor. There he died. He died on the first day of the fifth month. This was in the fortieth year after the Israelites left Egypt. ³⁹Aaron was 123 years old when he died on Mount Hor.

⁴⁰The king of Arad lived in the southern area of Canaan. He heard that the Israelites were coming.

⁴¹The people left Mount Hor and camped at Zalmonah.

⁴²They left Zalmonah and camped at Punon.

⁴³They left Punon and camped at Oboth.

⁴⁴They left Oboth and camped at Iye Abarim. This was on the border of Moab.

⁴⁵They left Iye Abarim and camped at Dibon Gad.

⁴⁶They left Dibon Gad and camped at Almon Diblathaim.

⁴⁷They left Almon Diblathaim and camped in the mountains of Abarim, near Nebo.

⁴⁸They left the mountains of Abarim and camped on the plains of Moab. This was near the Jordan River across from Jericho. ⁴⁹They camped along the Jordan on the plains of Moab. Their camp went from Beth Jeshimoth to Abel Acacia.

⁵⁰On the plains of Moab by the Jordan River across from Jericho, the Lord spoke to Moses. He said, ⁵¹"Speak to the Israelites. Tell them, 'Cross the Jordan River and go into Canaan. ⁵²Force out the people who live there. Destroy all of their carved statues. Destroy their metal idols. Wreck all of their places of worship. ⁵³Take over the land and settle there. I have given this land to you to own. ⁵⁴Throw lots*d* to divide up the land by family groups. Give larger portions to larger family groups. Give smaller portions to smaller family groups. The land will be given as the lots decide. Each tribe*d* will get its own land.

⁵⁵" 'But if you don't force those people out of the land, they will bring you trouble. They will be like sharp hooks in your eyes. They will be like thorns in your sides. They will bring trouble to the land where you live. ⁵⁶I will punish you as I had planned to punish them.' "

The Borders of Canaan

34 The Lord said to Moses, ²"Give this command to the people of Israel: 'You will soon enter Canaan. It will be yours. These shall be the borders. ³On the south you will get part of the Desert of Zin. This is near the border of Edom. On the east side your southern border will start at the south end of the Dead Sea.*d* ⁴It will cross south of Scorpion Pass. It will go through the Desert of Zin and south of Kadesh Barnea. Then it will

go to Hazar Addar and over to Azmon.
5From Azmon it will go to the brook of
Egypt. It will end at the Mediterranean Sea.

6" 'Your western border will be the
Mediterranean Sea.

7" 'Your northern border will begin
at the Mediterranean Sea and go to
Mount Hor. 8From Mount Hor it will
go to Lebo Hamath. Then it will go to
Zedad. 9Then the border will go to
Ziphron and end at Hazar Enan. This
will be your northern border.

10" 'Your eastern border will begin
at Hazar Enan and go to Shepham.
11From Shepham the border will go
east of Ain to Riblah. It will go along
the hills east of Lake Galilee. 12Then
the border will go down along the
Jordan River. It will end at the Dead
Sea.

" 'These are the borders around
your country'."

13So Moses gave this command to
the Israelites: "This is the land you
will receive. Throw lots*d* to divide it
among the nine and a half tribes.*d* The
Lord commanded that it should be
theirs. 14The tribes of Reuben and
Gad and the eastern half-tribe of Manasseh have already received their
land. 15These two and a half tribes received land east of the Jordan River. It
is across from Jericho."

16Then the Lord said to Moses,
17"These are the men who will divide
the land: Eleazar the priest and Joshua
son of Nun. 18Also take one leader
from each tribe. They will divide the
land. 19These are the names of the
leaders: from the tribe of Judah, Caleb
son of Jephunneh; 20from the tribe of
Simeon, Shemuel son of Ammihud;
21from the tribe of Benjamin, Elidad
son of Kislon; 22from the tribe of Dan,
Bukki son of Jogli; 23from the tribe of
Manasseh son of Joseph, Hanniel son
of Ephod; 24from the tribe of Ephraim
son of Joseph, Kemuel son of Shiph-
tan; 25from the tribe of Zebulun, Elizaphan son of Parnach; 26from the tribe

of Issachar, Paltiel son of Azzan;
27from the tribe of Asher, Ahihud son
of Shelomi; 28from the tribe of Naphtali, Pedahel son of Ammihud."

29The Lord commanded these men
to divide the land of Canaan among the
Israelites.

The Levites' Towns

35 The Lord spoke to Moses on
the plains of Moab. This was
across from Jericho by the Jordan River. He said, 2"Command the Israelites
to give the Levites cities to live in.
These will be cities in the land they
receive. Also give the Levites the
pastureland around these cities.
3Then the Levites will have cities
where they may live. And they will
have pastureland for their cattle,
sheep and other animals. 4The pastureland you give the Levites will extend 450 metres from the city wall.
5Also measure 900 metres in each direction from the city wall. Measure
900 metres east of the city. Measure 900 metres south of the city.
Measure 900 metres west of the city.
And measure 900 metres north of
the city. The city will be in the centre.
This will be pastureland for the Levites' cities.

Cities of Safety

6"Six of the cities you give the Levites will be cities of safety.*d* A person
might accidentally kill someone. If he
does, he may run to one of those cities
for safety. You must also give 42 other cities to the Levites. 7Give the Levites a total of 48 cities and their
pastures. 8The larger tribes*d* of Israel
must give more cities. The smaller
tribes must give fewer cities. Each
tribe must give some of its cities
to the Levites. The number of
cities they give will depend on the
size of their land."

9Then the Lord said to Moses,
10"Tell the Israelites these things:
'You will cross the Jordan River and go

into Canaan. [11]You must choose cities to be cities of safety. If a person accidentally kills someone, he may run to them for safety. [12]There he will be safe from the dead person's relative who has the duty of punishing the killer. He will not die before he is judged in court. [13]The six cities you give will be cities of safety. [14]Give three cities east of the Jordan River. And give three cities in Canaan as cities of safety. [15]These six cities will be places of safety for citizens of Israel. And they will be for foreigners and other people living with you. Any of these people may run to one of these cities if he accidentally kills someone.

[16]" 'If a person uses an iron weapon to kill someone, he is a murderer. He must be put to death. [17]A person might take a rock that could kill someone. If he kills a person with it, he is a murderer. He must be put to death. [18]A person might pick up a piece of wood that could kill someone. If he kills someone with it, he is a murderer. He must be put to death. [19]A relative of the dead person must put the murderer to death. When he finds the murderer, he must kill him. [20]A person might push someone and kill him. Or he might throw something at someone and kill him. [21]Or he might hit someone with his hand and kill him. If he did that from hate, he is a murderer. He must be put to death. A relative of the dead person must kill the murderer when he finds him.

[22]" 'But a person might suddenly push someone. He did not hate the person. Or he might accidentally throw something and hit someone. [23]Or he might drop a rock that could kill someone. It might fall on someone he did not see. And it might kill that person. He didn't plan to hurt anyone. He didn't hate the person he killed. [24]If that happens, the community must decide what to do. They must decide between the relative of the dead person and the killer. Here are

the rules. [25]They must protect the killer from the dead person's relative. They must send the killer back to the city of safety that he ran to. He must stay there until the high priest dies. The high priest had the holy oil poured on him.

[26]" 'That man must never go outside the limits of his city of safety. [27]If a relative of the dead person finds him outside the city, the relative may kill him. He will not be guilty of murder. [28]The killer must stay in his city of safety until the high priest dies. After the high priest dies, he may go back to his own land.

[29]" 'These laws are for you from now on, wherever you live.

[30]" 'A killer may be put to death only if he is a murderer. And there must be witnesses. No one may be put to death with only one witness.

[31]" 'A murderer should die. Don't take money to spare his life. He must be put to death.

[32]" 'A person might run to a city of safety. Don't take money to let him go back home before the high priest dies.

[33]" 'Don't let murder spoil your land. There is only one way to remove the sin of killing an innocent person. The murderer must be put to death. [34]I am the Lord. I live among the Israelites. I live in that land with you. So do not spoil it with murder'."

Land for Zelophehad's Daughters

36 The leaders of Gilead's family group went to talk to Moses and the leaders of the families of Israel. (Gilead was the son of Makir. Makir was Manasseh's son, and Manasseh was Joseph's son.) [2]They said, "The Lord commanded you, our master, to give the land to the Israelites by throwing lots.[d] And the Lord commanded you to give the land of Zelophehad, our brother, to his daughters. [3]His daughters may marry men from other tribes[d] of Israel. Then that land will leave our family. The people of the other tribes will get that land. So we will lose some of our land. [4]The time of Jubilee[d] will come for the Israelites. Then their land will go to other tribes. It will go to the tribes of the people they marry. So their land will be taken away from us. And that was land we received from our fathers."

[5]Then Moses gave the Israelites this command from the Lord: "These men from the tribe of Joseph are right. [6]This is the Lord's command to Zelophehad's daughters: You may marry anyone you wish from your own tribe. [7]In this way the Israelites' land will not pass from tribe to tribe. Each Israelite will keep the land in the tribe that belonged to his ancestors. [8]A woman who inherits her father's land may marry. But she must marry someone from her own tribe. In this way every

Israelite will keep the land that belonged to his ancestors. [9]The land must not pass from tribe to tribe. Each Israelite tribe will keep the land it received from its ancestors."

[10]Zelophehad's daughters obeyed the Lord's command to Moses.

[11]So Zelophehad's daughters—Mahlah, Tirzah, Hoglah, Milcah and Noah—married their cousins. These were their father's relatives. [12]Their husbands were from the tribe of Manasseh son of Joseph. So their land stayed in their father's family group and tribe.

[13]These were the laws and commands that the Lord gave to the Israelites. He gave them through Moses. The Israelites were on the plains of Moab by the Jordan River, across from Jericho.

DEUTERONOMY

Moses' Last Message to Israel

Moses Talks to the Israelites

1 This is the message Moses gave the people of Israel. They were in the desert east of the Jordan River. They were in the Jordan Valley near Suph, between Paran and the towns of Tophel, Laban, Hazeroth and Dizahab. ²(The trip from Mount Sinai to Kadesh Barnea on the Mount Edom road takes 11 days.) ³But it was now 40 years after the Israelites had left Egypt. On the first day of the eleventh month, Moses spoke to the people. He told them everything the Lord had commanded him to tell them. ⁴This was after the Lord had defeated Sihon and Og. Sihon was king of the Amorite people and lived in Heshbon. Og was king of Bashan and lived in Ashteroth and Edrei.

⁵Now the Israelites were east of the Jordan River in the land of Moab. There Moses began to explain what God had commanded. Moses said:

⁶The Lord our God spoke to us at Mount Sinai. He said, "You have stayed long enough at this mountain. ⁷Get ready. Go to the mountain country of the Amorites. Go to all the places around there — the Jordan Valley, the mountains, the western slopes, the southern area, the seacoast, the land of Canaan and Lebanon. Go as far as the great river, the Euphrates. ⁸See, I have given you this land. Go in and take it for yourselves. The Lord promised it to your ancestors — Abraham, Isaac and Jacob and their descendants."ᵈ

Moses Appoints Leaders

⁹At that time I said, "I am not able to take care of you by myself. ¹⁰The Lord your God has made you grow in number. There are as many of you as there are stars in the sky. ¹¹I pray that the Lord, the God of your ancestors, will give you a thousand times more people. That's what he promised. ¹²But I cannot take care of your problems, your troubles and your arguments by myself. ¹³So choose some men from each tribe.ᵈ Choose wise men who have understanding and experience. I will make them leaders over you."

¹⁴And you said, "That's a good thing to do."

¹⁵So I took the wise and experienced leaders of your tribes. And I made them your leaders. I appointed commanders over 1,000 people, over 100 people, over 50 people and over ten people. I made them officers over your tribes. ¹⁶Then I told your judges, "Listen to the arguments between your people. Judge fairly between two Israelites or between an Israelite and a foreigner. ¹⁷When you judge, be fair to everyone. Don't act as if one person is more important than another. Don't be afraid of anyone, because your decision comes from God. Bring the hard cases to me. I will judge them." ¹⁸At that time I told you everything you must do.

Spies Enter the Land

¹⁹Then, as the Lord our God commanded us, we left Mount Sinai. We went towards the mountain country of the Amorite people. We went through that large and terrible desert you saw. Then we came to Kadesh Barnea. ²⁰Then I said to you, "You have now come to the mountain country of the

Amorites. The Lord our God will give us this land. 21Look, there it is! Go up. Take it. The Lord, the God of your ancestors, told you to do this. So don't be afraid. Don't worry."

22Then all of you came to me. You said, "Let's send men before us to spy out the land. They can come back and tell us the way we should go. They can tell us about the cities we will find."

23I thought that was a good idea. So I chose 12 of your men, one for each tribe.*d* 24They left and went up to the mountains. They came to the Valley of Eshcol and explored it. 25They took some of the fruit from that land. And they brought it down to us. They said, "It is a good land that the Lord our God is giving us."

Israel Refuses to Enter

26But you refused to go. You would not obey the command of the Lord your God. 27You grumbled in your tents. You said, "The Lord hates us. He brought us out of Egypt just to give us to the Amorites. They will destroy us. 28Where can we go now? The spies we sent have made us afraid. They said, 'The people there are bigger and taller than we are. The cities are big. They have walls up to the sky. And we saw the Anakites*d* there!'"

29Then I said to you, "Don't be frightened. Don't be afraid of those people. 30The Lord your God will go ahead of you. He will fight for you as he did in Egypt. You saw him do it. 31And in the desert you saw how the Lord your God carried you. He was like a man carrying his son. And he has brought you safely all the way to this place."

32But you still did not trust the Lord your God. 33As you moved, he went before you. He found places for you to camp. He went before you in a fire at night and in a cloud during the day. He showed you which way to go.

34When the Lord heard what you said, he was angry. He made a promise. He said, 35"I promised a good land to your ancestors. But none of you evil people will see it. 36Only Caleb son of Jephunneh will see it. I will give him and his descendants*d* the land he walked on. I will do this because he followed me completely."

37Because of you, the Lord was also angry with me. He said to me, "You won't enter the land either. 38But your assistant, Joshua son of Nun, will go there. Encourage Joshua, because he will lead Israel to take the land for their own."

39The Lord said to us, "You said your babies would be captured. But they will go into the land. They are too young to know right from wrong. So I will give the land to them. And they will take it for their own. 40But you must turn around. Follow the desert road toward the Gulf of Aqaba."

41Then you said to me, "We have sinned against the Lord. But now we will go up and fight, as the Lord our God commanded us." Then all of you put on weapons. You thought it would be easy to go into the mountains.

42But the Lord said to me, "Tell them not to go up there and fight. I will not be with them. Their enemies will defeat them."

43So I told you, but you would not listen. You would not obey the Lord's command. You were proud. So you went on up into the mountains. 44The Amorites who lived there came out and fought you. They chased you like bees. They defeated you from Edom to Hormah. 45So you came back and cried to the Lord. But the Lord did not hear you. He refused to listen to you. 46So you stayed in Kadesh a long time.

Israel Wanders in the Desert

2 Then we turned around. And we travelled on the desert road towards the Gulf of Aqaba. That is what the Lord had told me to do. We trav-

elled through the mountains of Edom for many days.

²Then the Lord said to me, ³"You have travelled through these mountains long enough. Turn north. ⁴Tell the people this: 'You will soon go through the land of Edom. This land belongs to your relatives, the descendants^d of Esau. They will be afraid of you. But be very careful. ⁵Don't go to war against them. I am not giving you any of their land—not even a foot of it. I have given the mountains of Edom to Esau as his own. ⁶You must pay them in silver for any food you eat or water you drink'."

⁷The Lord your God has blessed everything you have done. He has protected you while you travelled through this large desert. The Lord your God has been with you for these 40 years. You have had everything you needed.

⁸So we passed by our relatives, the people of Esau who lived in Edom. We turned off the Jordan Valley road. It comes from the towns of Elath and Ezion Geber. And we travelled along the desert road of Moab.

The Land of Ar

⁹Then the Lord said to me, "Don't bother the people of Moab. Don't go to war against them. I am not giving you any of their land. I have given Ar to the descendants^d of Lot." ¹⁰(The Emites lived in Ar before. They were strong people, and there were many of them. They were very tall, like the Anakites.^d ¹¹The Emites were thought to be Rephaites,^d like the Anakites. But the Moabite people called them Emites. ¹²The Horites also lived in Edom before. But the people of Esau forced them out. They destroyed the Horites and took their place. That is also what Israel did in the land the Lord gave them as their own.)

¹³And the Lord said to me, "Now get up and cross the Zered Valley." So

we crossed the valley. ¹⁴It had been 38 years since we left Kadesh Barnea until we crossed the Zered Valley. By then, all the fighting men from that time had died. This is what the Lord had promised would happen. ¹⁵The Lord had continued to destroy them until they were all gone from the camp. ¹⁶Now the last of those fighting men had died.

¹⁷Then the Lord said to me, ¹⁸"Today you must go by Ar, on the border of Moab. ¹⁹When you come near the people of Ammon, don't bother them. Don't go to war against them. I am not giving you their land. I have given that land to the descendants^d of Lot."

²⁰(That land was also thought to be a land of Rephaites. Those people used to live there. But the Ammonites called them Zamzummites. ²¹They were strong people, and there were many of them. They were very tall, like the Anakites. The Lord went before the Ammonites and destroyed the Zamzummites. The Ammonites forced them out of the land and took their place. ²²The Lord did the same thing for the descendants of Esau. They lived in Edom. He destroyed the Horites. The Edomites forced them out of the land and took their place. And they live there to this day. ²³The Caphtorite people came from Crete. They destroyed the Avvites. The Avvites lived in towns all the way to Gaza. But the Caphtorites destroyed them and took their place.)

Fighting the Amorites

²⁴The Lord said, "Get up. Cross the Arnon Ravine. See, I am giving you the power to defeat Sihon the Amorite. He is king of Heshbon. I am giving you his land. So fight against him and begin taking his land. ²⁵Today I will begin to make all the people in the world afraid of you. They will hear reports about you. And they will shake with fear. They will be terrified of you."

26I sent messengers from the desert of Kedemoth to Sihon king of Heshbon. They offered him peace. They said, 27"Let us pass through your country. We will stay on the road. We will not turn right or left. 28We will pay you in silver for any food we eat or water we drink. We only want to walk through your country. 29The descendants*d* of Esau in Edom let us go through their land. So did the Moabites in Ar. We want to cross the Jordan River into the land the Lord our God has given us." 30But Sihon king of Heshbon would not let us pass. The Lord your God had made him stubborn. The Lord wanted you to defeat Sihon. And now this has happened.

31The Lord said to me, "See, I have begun to give Sihon and his country to you. Begin taking the land as your own."

32Then Sihon and all his army came out. And they fought us at Jahaz. 33But the Lord our God gave Sihon to us. We defeated him, his sons and all his army. 34We captured all his cities. We completely destroyed them, the men, women and children. We left no one alive. 35But we kept the cattle and valuable things from the cities for ourselves. 36We defeated Aroer on the edge of the Arnon Ravine. And we defeated the town in the ravine, and even Gilead. No town was too strong for us. The Lord our God gave us all of them. 37But you did not go near the land of the Ammonites. You did not go near the shores of the Jabbok River. You did not go near the towns in the mountains. This was what the Lord our God had commanded.

The Battle at Bashan

3 Then we turned and went up the road toward Bashan. Og king of Bashan and all his army came out to fight us at Edrei. 2The Lord said to me, "Don't be afraid of Og. I will hand him, his whole army and his land over

to you. Do to him what you did to Sihon king of the Amorites, who ruled in Heshbon."

3So the Lord our God gave us Og king of Bashan and all his army. We defeated them and left no one alive. 4Then we captured all of Og's cities. We captured all 60 of them. We took the whole area of Argob, Og's kingdom in Bashan. 5All these were strong cities. They had high walls and gates with bars. And there were also many small towns with no walls. 6We completely destroyed them. We destroyed them just like the cities of Sihon king of Heshbon. We killed all the men, women and children. 7But we kept all the cattle and valuable things from the cities for ourselves.

8So at that time we took the land east of the Jordan River. We took it from these two Amorite kings. It went from the Arnon Ravine to Mount Hermon. 9(Hermon is called Sirion by the Sidonian people. The Amorites call it Senir.) 10We captured all the cities on the high plain and all of Gilead. We took all of Bashan as far as Salecah and Edrei. These were towns in Og's kingdom of Bashan. 11(Only Og king of Bashan was left of the few Rephaites.*d* His bed was made of iron. It was more than 4 metres long and 2 metres wide! It is still in the Ammonite city of Rabbah.)

The Land Is Divided

12At that time we took this land to be our own. I gave the people of Reuben and Gad the land from Aroer by the Arnon Ravine. And I gave them half of the mountain country of Gilead and the cities in it. 13To the eastern half-tribe*d* of Manasseh I gave the rest of Gilead. And I gave them all of Bashan, the kingdom of Og. (The area of Argob in Bashan was called the land of the Rephaites.*d* 14Jair, a descendant*d* of Manasseh, took the whole area of Argob. It went to the border of the Geshurites and Maacathites. That land was named for Jair. So even today Bashan is called the Towns of Jair.) [15]I gave Gilead to Makir. [16]I gave the Reubenites and the Gadites the land that begins at Gilead. It goes from the Arnon Ravine to the Jabbok River. (The middle of the Arnon is the border.) The Jabbok River is the Ammonite border. [17]The border on the west was the Jordan River in the Jordan Valley. It goes from Lake Galilee to the Dead Sea[d] west of Mount Pisgah.

[18]At that time I gave you this command: "The Lord your God has given you this land as your own. Now your fighting men must take their weapons. And you must lead the other Israelites across the river. [19]Your wives, your young children and your cattle may stay here. I know you have many cattle. They may stay here in the cities I have given you. [20]Some day your Israelite relatives will also have a place to rest. They will receive the land the Lord your God has given them. It is on the other side of the Jordan River. After that, you may each return to the land I have given you."

[21]Then I gave this command to Joshua: "You have seen for yourself what the Lord your God has done to these two kings. The Lord will do the same thing to all the kingdoms where you are going. [22]Don't be afraid of them. The Lord your God will fight for you."

Moses Cannot Enter the Land

[23]Then I begged the Lord: [24]"Lord God, you have begun to show me, your servant, how great you are. You have great strength. No other god in heaven or earth can do the powerful things you do. There is no other god like you. [25]Please let me cross the Jordan River. I want to see the beautiful mountains and Lebanon."

[26]But the Lord was angry with me because of you. He would not listen to me. The Lord said to me, "That's enough. Don't talk to me any more about it. [27]Climb to the top of Mount Pisgah. Look west, north, south and east. You can look at the land. But you will not cross the Jordan River. [28]Appoint Joshua. Help him be brave and strong. He will lead the people across the river. He will give them the land that they are to inherit. You can only look at it." [29]So we stayed in the valley opposite Beth Peor.

Moses Tells Israel to Obey

4 Now, Israel, listen to the laws and commands I will teach you. Obey them so you will live. Then you will go over and take the land. The Lord, the God of your ancestors, is giving it to you. [2]Don't add to these commands. And don't leave anything out. But obey the commands of the Lord your God that I give you.

[3]You have seen for yourselves what the Lord did at Baal Peor. The Lord your God destroyed everyone among you who followed Baal[d] in Peor. [4]But you continued to follow the Lord your God. So you are still alive today.

[5]Look, I have taught you the laws and rules the Lord my God commanded me. Now you can obey the laws in the land you are entering. It is the land you will own. [6]Obey these laws carefully. This will show the other nations that you have wisdom and understanding. They will hear about these laws. And they will say, "This great nation of Israel is wise and understanding." [7]No other nation is as great as we are. Their gods do not come near them. But the Lord our God comes near when we pray to him. [8]And no other nation has such good teachings and commands. I am giving them to you today.

[9]But be careful! Watch out. Don't forget the things that you have seen. Don't forget them as long as you live. Teach them to your children and grandchildren. [10]Remember the day you stood before the Lord your God at

Mount Sinai. He said to me, "Bring the people together to listen to what I say. Then they will respect me as long as they live in the land. And they will teach these things to their children." ¹¹Then you came and stood at the bottom of the mountain. It blazed with fire that reached to the sky. Black clouds made it very dark. ¹²Then the Lord spoke to you from the fire. You heard the sound of words. But you did not see him. There was only a voice. ¹³The Lord told you about his agreement. It was the Ten Commandments. And he told you to obey them. Then he wrote them on two stone tablets. ¹⁴Then the Lord commanded me to teach you the laws and rules. You must obey them in the land you will own when you cross the Jordan River.

Laws About Idols

¹⁵The Lord spoke to you from the fire at Mount Sinai. But you did not see him. So watch yourselves carefully! ¹⁶Don't sin by making idols of any kind. Don't make statues of men or women. ¹⁷Don't make statues of animals on earth or birds that fly in the air. ¹⁸Don't make statues of anything that crawls on the ground. Don't make statues of fish in the water below. ¹⁹When you look up at the sky, you see the sun, moon and stars. You can see everything in the sky. But don't bow down and worship them. The Lord your God has made these things for all people everywhere. ²⁰Egypt tested you like a furnace for melting iron. The Lord brought you out of Egypt. And he made you his very own people, as you are now.

²¹The Lord was angry with me because of you. He made a strong promise that I would not cross the Jordan River. I could not go into the good land the Lord your God is giving you to own. ²²I will die here in this land. I will not cross the Jordan. But you will soon go across and take that good land. ²³Be careful. Don't forget the agreement of the Lord your God that he made with you. Don't make any idols for yourselves. The Lord your God has commanded you not to do that. ²⁴The Lord your God is a jealous God. He is like a fire that burns things up.

²⁵You will live in the land a long time. You will have children and grandchildren. Even after that, don't do evil things. Don't make any kind of idol. Don't do what the Lord says is evil. That will make him angry. ²⁶I will ask heaven and earth to speak against you that day. Then you will quickly be removed from this land. You are crossing the Jordan River to take the land. But you will not live there long after that. You will be completely destroyed. ²⁷The Lord will scatter you among the other nations. Only a few of you will be left alive. And those few will be in other nations where the Lord will send you. ²⁸There you will worship gods made by men. They will be made of wood and stone. They cannot see, hear, eat or smell. ²⁹But even there you can look for the Lord your God. And you will find him if you look. But you must look for him with your whole being. ³⁰It will be hard when all these things happen to you. But after that you will come back to the Lord your God. You will obey him. ³¹The Lord your God is a merciful God. He will not leave you or destroy you. He will not forget the agreement he made with your ancestors. He made that agreement sure with his strong promise.

The Lord Is Great

³²Nothing like this has ever happened before! Look at the past, long before you were even born. Go all the way back to when God made man on the earth. Look from one end of heaven to the other. Nothing like this has ever been heard of! ³³No other people have ever heard God speak from a fire

and still lived. But you have. ³⁴No other god has ever taken for himself one nation out of another. But the Lord your God did this for you in Egypt. He did it right before your own eyes. He did it with tests, signs, miracles,ᵈ war and great sights. He did it by his great power and strength.

³⁵He showed you things so you would know that the Lord is God. There is no other God besides him. ³⁶He spoke to you from heaven to teach you. He showed you his great fire on earth. And you heard him speak from the fire. ³⁷The Lord loved your ancestors. That is why he chose you, their descendants.ᵈ He brought you out of Egypt himself by his great strength. ³⁸He forced nations out of their land ahead of you. And these nations were bigger and stronger than you were. But the Lord brought you into their land and gave it to you to own. And this land is yours today.

³⁹Know and believe today that the Lord is God. He is God in heaven above and on the earth below. There is no other god! ⁴⁰Obey his laws and commands, which I am giving you today. Obey them so that things will go well for you and your children. Then you will live a long time in this land. The Lord your God is giving it to you for ever.

Cities of Safety

⁴¹Moses chose three cities east of the Jordan River. ⁴²A person who killed someone accidentally could go there. He did not hate the person he killed. So he could save his life by running to one of these cities. ⁴³These were the cities: Bezer in the desert high plain was for the Reubenites; Ramoth in Gilead was for the Gadites; Golan in Bashan was for the Manassites.

The Law Moses Gave

⁴⁴These are the teachings Moses gave to the people of Israel. ⁴⁵They are the rules, commands and laws he gave them when they came out of Egypt. ⁴⁶They were in the valley near Beth Peor. That is east of the Jordan River in the land of Sihon. Sihon was king of the Amorites. He ruled in Heshbon. He was defeated by Moses and the Israelites as they came out of Egypt. ⁴⁷The Israelites captured his land. They also took the land of Og king of Bashan. These were the two Amorite kings east of the Jordan River. ⁴⁸This land went from Aroer to Mount Hermon. Aroer is on the edge of the Arnon Ravine. ⁴⁹It included all the Jordan Valley east of the Jordan River. And it went as far as the Dead Seaᵈ below Mount Pisgah.

The Ten Commandments

5 Moses called all the people of Israel together and said: Listen, Israel, to the commands and laws I give you today. Learn them and obey them carefully. ²The Lord our God made an agreement with us at Mount Sinai. ³He did not make this agreement with our ancestors. He made it with us. He made it with all of us who are alive here today. ⁴The Lord spoke to you face to face. He spoke from the fire on the mountain. ⁵(At that time I stood between you and the Lord. I told you what the Lord said. You were afraid of the fire. So you would not go up on the mountain.) The Lord said:

⁶"I am the Lord your God. I brought you out of the land of Egypt where you were slaves.

⁷"You must not have any other gods except me.

⁸"You must not make for yourselves any idols. Don't make something that looks like anything in the sky above or on the earth below or in the water below the land. ⁹You must not worship or serve any idol. This is because I, the Lord your God, am a jealous God. A person may sin against me and hate me. I will punish his children, even his grandchildren and

great-grandchildren. ¹⁰But I will be very kind to thousands who love me and obey my commands.

¹¹"You must not use the name of the Lord your God thoughtlessly. The Lord will punish anyone who is guilty and misuses his name.

¹²"Keep the Sabbath*ᵈ* as a holy day. The Lord your God has commanded you to do this. ¹³You may work and get everything done during six days each week. ¹⁴But the seventh day is a day of rest to honour the Lord your God. On that day no one may do any work: not you, your son or daughter, or your men or women slaves. Neither your ox, your donkey nor any of your animals may work. The foreigners living in your cities may not work. That way your servants may rest as you do. ¹⁵Remember that you were slaves in Egypt. The Lord your God brought you out of Egypt by his great power and strength. So the Lord your God has commanded you to rest on the Sabbath day.

¹⁶"Honour your father and your mother. The Lord your God has commanded you to do this. Then you will live a long time. And things will go well for you in the land. The Lord your God is going to give you this land.

¹⁷"You must not murder anyone.

¹⁸"You must not be guilty of adultery.*ᵈ*

¹⁹"You must not steal.

²⁰"You must not tell lies about your neighbour in court.

²¹"You must not want to take your neighbour's wife. You must not want to take your neighbour's house or land. You must not want to take his men or women slaves. You must not want to take his ox or his donkey. You must not want to take anything that belongs to your neighbour."

²²The Lord gave these commands to all of you on the mountain. He spoke them in a loud voice out of the fire. He spoke from the cloud and the deep darkness. He did not say any-

thing else. Then he wrote them on two stone tablets. And he gave them to me.

²³You heard the voice from the darkness. The mountain was blazing with fire. Then all your older leaders and leaders of your tribes*ᵈ* came to me. ²⁴And you said, "The Lord our God has shown us his glory and majesty. We have heard his voice from the fire. Today we have seen that a person can live even if God speaks to him. ²⁵But now, we will die! This great fire will burn us up. And we will die if we hear the Lord our God speak any more. ²⁶No human being has ever heard the living God speaking from a fire and still lived. But we have. ²⁷Moses, you go near and listen to everything the Lord our God says. Then you tell us what the Lord our God tells you. We will listen and obey."

²⁸The Lord heard what you said to me. And he said to me, "I have heard what the people said to you. Everything they said was good. ²⁹I wish their hearts would always respect me. I wish they would always obey my commands. Then things would go well for them and their children for ever! ³⁰"Go and tell the people to return to their tents. ³¹But you stay here with me. I will give you all the commands, rules and laws. Teach the people to obey them in the land I am giving them to own."

³²So be careful. Do what the Lord your God has commanded you. You must follow the commands exactly. ³³Live the way the Lord your God has commanded you. Then you will live and be successful. You will live a long time in the land you will own.

The Command to Love God

6 These are the commands, rules and laws of the Lord your God. He told me to teach them to you. Obey them in the land you are crossing the Jordan River to own. ²You, your children and grandchildren must respect

the Lord your God. You must do this as long as you live. Obey all his rules and commands I give you. Then you will live a long time. ³Listen, Israel, and carefully obey these laws. Then all will go well for you. You will become a great nation in a land where much food grows. The Lord, the God of your ancestors, has promised it to you.

⁴Listen, people of Israel! The Lord is our God. He is the only Lord. ⁵Love the Lord your God with all your heart, soul and strength. ⁶Always remember these commands I give you today. ⁷Teach them to your children. Talk about them when you sit at home and walk along the road. Talk about them when you lie down and when you get up. ⁸Write them down and tie them to your hands as a sign. Tie them on your forehead to remind you. ⁹Write them on your doors and gates.

¹⁰The Lord your God will bring you into the land. He promised it to your ancestors, to Abraham, Isaac and Jacob. He will give it to you. The land has large, growing cities you did not build. ¹¹The houses there are full of good things that you did not buy. They have wells you did not dig. There are vineyards and olive trees you did not plant. You will eat as much as you want. ¹²But be careful! Do not forget the Lord. He brought you out of the land of Egypt where you were slaves.

¹³Respect the Lord your God. Serve only him. Make your promises in his name. ¹⁴Do not worship other gods as the people around you do. ¹⁵The Lord your God is a jealous God. He is present with you. If you worship other gods, he will become angry with you. And he will destroy you from the earth. ¹⁶Do not test the Lord your God as you did at Massah. ¹⁷Be sure to obey the commands of the Lord your God. Obey the rules and laws he has given you. ¹⁸Do what the Lord says is good and right. Then things will go well for you. Then you may go in and take the good land the Lord promised to your ancestors. ¹⁹He will force all your enemies out as you go in. This is what the Lord has said.

²⁰In the future your son will ask you, "What do the laws, commands and rules the Lord our God gave us mean?" ²¹Tell him, "We were slaves to the king of Egypt. But the Lord brought us out of Egypt by his great power. ²²The Lord showed us great and terrible signs and miracles.*ᵈ* He did them to Egypt, the king and his whole family. ²³The Lord brought us out of Egypt. He led us here. And he will give us the land he promised our ancestors. ²⁴The Lord ordered us to obey all these commands. And we must respect the Lord our God. Then we will always do well and stay alive as we are today. ²⁵The right thing for us to do is this: obey all these rules in the presence of the Lord our God. He has commanded it."

God's People

7 The Lord your God will bring you into the land. You are entering that land to own it. As you go in, he will force out these nations: the Hittites, Girgashites, Amorites, Canaanites, Perizzites, Hivites and Jebusites. These seven nations are stronger than you. ²The Lord your God will hand these nations over to you. You will defeat them. You must destroy them completely. Do not make a peace treaty with them. Do not show them any mercy. ³Do not marry any of them. Don't let your daughters marry their sons. And don't let your sons marry their daughters. ⁴Those people will turn your children away from me. Your children will begin serving other gods. The Lord will be very angry with you. And he will quickly destroy you. ⁵This is what you must do to those people: tear down their altars. Smash their holy stone pillars. Cut down their Asherah*ᵈ* idols and burn their idols in the fire. ⁶You are holy

people. You belong to the Lord your God. He has chosen you from all the people on earth. You are his very own.

7The Lord did not care for you and choose you because there were many of you. You are the smallest nation of all. 8But the Lord chose you because he loved you. And he kept his promise to your ancestors. So he brought you out of Egypt by his great power. He brought you back from the land of slavery. He bought you back from the power of the king of Egypt. 9So know that the Lord your God is God. He is the faithful God. He will keep his agreement of love for a thousand lifetimes. He does this for people who love him and obey his commands. 10But he will pay back those people who hate him. He will destroy them. And he will not be slow to pay back those who hate him. 11So be careful to obey the commands, rules and laws I give you today.

12Pay attention to these laws. Obey them carefully. Then the Lord your God will keep his agreement and show his love to you. He promised your ancestors he would. 13He will love and bless you. He will make the number of your people grow. He will bless you with children. He will bless your fields with good crops. He will give you grain, new wine and oil. He will bless your cows with calves and your sheep with lambs. This is the way it will be in the land he promised your ancestors he would give you. 14You will be blessed more than any other people. Every husband and wife will have children. All your cattle will have calves. 15The Lord will take away all disease from you. You will not have the terrible diseases that were in Egypt. But he will give them to your enemies. 16You must destroy all the people the Lord your God hands over to you. Do not feel sorry for them. Do not worship their gods. They will trap you. 17You might say to yourselves,

"These nations are stronger than we are. We can't force them out." 18But don't be afraid of them. Remember what the Lord your God did to all of Egypt and its king. 19You saw for yourselves the troubles, signs and miracles[d] he did. You saw how the Lord's great power and strength brought you out of Egypt. The Lord your God will do the same thing to all the nations you now fear. 20The Lord your God will also send hornets to attack them. Even those who are alive and hiding from you will die. 21Don't be afraid of them. The Lord your God is with you. He is a great God and people are afraid of him. 22The Lord your God will force those nations out of the land. They will leave little by little ahead of you. Don't destroy them all at once. Otherwise, the wild animals will grow too many in number. 23But the Lord your God will hand those nations over to you. He will confuse them until they are destroyed. 24The Lord will help you defeat their kings. The world will forget who they were. No one will be able to stop you. You will destroy them all. 25Burn up their idols in the fire. Do not wish for the silver and gold on them. Don't take it for yourselves, or you will be trapped by it. The Lord your God hates it. 26Do not bring one of those hated things into your house. If you do, you will be completely destroyed along with it. Hate and reject those things. They must be completely destroyed.

Remember the Lord

8 Carefully obey every command I give you today. Then you will live and grow in number. And you will enter and own the land the Lord promised your ancestors. 2Remember how the Lord your God has led you in the desert for these 40 years. He took away your pride. He tested you. He wanted to know what was in your heart. He wanted to know if you

would obey his commands. ³He took away your pride. He let you get hungry. Then he fed you with manna.*d* Manna was something neither you nor your ancestors had ever seen. This was to teach you that a person does not live only by eating bread. But a person lives by everything the Lord says. ⁴During these 40 years, your clothes did not wear out. And your feet did not swell. ⁵Know in your heart that the Lord your God corrects you. He corrects you as a father does his son.

⁶Obey the commands of the Lord your God. Live as he has commanded you and respect him. ⁷The Lord your God is bringing you into a good land. The land has rivers and pools of water. Springs flow in the valleys and hills. ⁸The land has wheat and barley, vines, fig trees, pomegranates,*d* olive oil and honey. ⁹It is a land where you will have plenty of food. You will have everything you need there. The rocks are iron. You can dig copper out of the hills.

¹⁰You will have all you want to eat. Then praise the Lord your God. He has given you a good land. ¹¹Be careful not to forget the Lord your God. Do not fail to obey his commands, laws and rules. I am giving them to you today. ¹²You will eat all you want. You will build nice houses and live in them. ¹³Your herds of cattle and flocks of sheep will grow large. You will have more silver and gold. You will have more of everything. ¹⁴Then your heart will become proud. You will forget the Lord your God. He brought you out of the land of Egypt, where you were slaves. ¹⁵He led you through the large and terrible desert. It was dry and had no water. It had poisonous snakes and stinging insects. He gave you water from a solid rock. ¹⁶He gave you manna to eat in the desert. Manna was something your ancestors had never seen. He did this to take away your pride and to test

you. He did it so things would go well for you in the end. ¹⁷You might say to yourself, "I am rich because of my own strength and power." ¹⁸But remember the Lord your God! It is he who gives you the power to become rich. He keeps the agreement he promised to your ancestors. So it is today.

¹⁹Never forget the Lord your God. Do not follow other gods. Do not worship them. Do not bow down to them. If you do, I warn you today that you will be destroyed. ²⁰The Lord destroyed the other nations for you. And you can be destroyed the same way if you do not obey the Lord your God.

The Lord Will Be with Israel

9 Listen, Israel. You will soon cross the Jordan River. You will go in to force out nations that are bigger and stronger than you. They have large cities with walls up to the sky. ²The people there are Anakites.*d* They are strong and tall. You know about them. You have heard it said: "No one can stop the Anakites." ³But today remember that the Lord your God goes in before you. He will destroy them like a fire that burns things up. He will defeat them ahead of you. And you will force them out. You will destroy them quickly. It will happen just as the Lord has said.

⁴The Lord your God will force those nations out ahead of you. After that, don't say to yourself, "The Lord brought me here. I own this land because I am so good." No! It is because these nations are evil. That is why the Lord will force them out ahead of you. ⁵You are going in to own the land. But it is not because you are good and honest. It is because these nations are evil. That is why the Lord your God will force them out ahead of you. The Lord will keep his promise to your ancestors, to Abraham, Isaac and Jacob. ⁶The Lord your God is giving you this good land to own. But know this: it is

not because you are good. You are a stubborn people.

Remember the Lord's Anger

7Remember this. Do not forget it. You made the Lord your God angry in the desert. You would not obey the Lord from the day you left Egypt until you arrived here. 8At Mount Sinai you made the Lord angry. He was angry enough to destroy you. 9I went up on the mountain to receive the stone tablets. The tablets were the agreement the Lord had made with you. I stayed on the mountain for 40 days and 40 nights. I did not eat bread or drink water. 10The Lord gave me two stone tablets. God had written on them with his own finger. On them were all the commands of the Lord. He gave them to you on the mountain out of the fire. This was on the day you were gathered there.

11Then the 40 days and 40 nights were over. And the Lord gave me the two stone tablets. Those tablets had the agreement on them. 12Then the Lord told me, "Get up. Go down quickly from here. The people you brought out from Egypt are ruining themselves. They have quickly turned away from what I commanded. They have made an idol for themselves."

13The Lord said to me, "I have watched these people. They are very stubborn! 14Leave me alone so I can destroy them. I will make the whole world forget who they are. Then I will make another nation from you. It will be bigger and stronger than they are."

15So I turned and came down the mountain. The mountain was burning with fire. And the two stone tablets with the agreement were in my hands. 16When I looked, I saw you had sinned against the Lord your God. You had made an idol in the shape of a calf. You had quickly turned away from what the Lord had told you to do. 17So I took the two stone tablets and threw them down. I broke them into pieces right in front of you.

18Then I again bowed face down on the ground before the Lord. I did this for 40 days and 40 nights. I did not eat bread or drink water. You had sinned by doing what the Lord said was evil. You made him angry. 19I was afraid of the Lord's anger and rage. He was angry enough with you to destroy you. But the Lord listened to me again. 20And the Lord was angry enough with Aaron to destroy him. But then I prayed for Aaron, too. 21I took that sinful calf idol you had made. And I burned it in the fire. I crushed it into a powder like dust. And I threw the dust into a stream that flowed down the mountain.

22You also made the Lord angry at Taberah, Massah and Kibroth Hattaavah. 23Then the Lord sent you away from Kadesh Barnea. He said, "Go up and take the land I have given you." But you would not obey the command of the Lord your God. You did not trust him or obey him. 24You have refused to obey the Lord as long as I have known you.

25The Lord had said he would destroy you. So I threw myself down in front of him for those 40 days and 40 nights. 26I prayed to the Lord. I said, "Lord God, do not destroy your people. They are your own people. You freed them and brought them out of Egypt by your great power and strength. 27Remember your servants Abraham, Isaac and Jacob. Don't look at how stubborn these people are. Don't look at their sin and evil. 28Otherwise, Egypt will say, 'The Lord was not able to take his people into the land he promised them. He hated them. So he took them into the desert to kill them'. 29But they are your people, Lord. They are your own people. You brought them out of Egypt with your great power and strength."

New Stone Tablets

10 At that time the Lord said to me, "Cut two stone tablets like the first ones. Then come up to me on the mountain. Also make a wooden box. ²I will write on the tablets the same words that were on the first tablets, which you broke. Put the new tablets in the box."

³So I made the box out of acacia wood. And I cut out two stone tablets like the first ones. Then I went up on the mountain. I had the two tablets in my hands. ⁴The Lord wrote the same things on these tablets he had written before. He wrote the Ten Commandments. He had told them to you on the mountain from the fire. This was on the day you were gathered there. And the Lord gave them to me. ⁵Then I turned and came down the mountain. I put the tablets in the box I had made. That is what the Lord had commanded. The tablets are still there in the box.

⁶(The people of Israel went from the wells of the Jaakanites to Moserah. There Aaron died and was buried. Aaron's son Eleazar became priest in Aaron's place. ⁷From Moserah they went to Gudgodah. From Gudgodah they went to Jotbathah, a place with streams of water. ⁸At that time the Lord chose the tribe*d* of Levi. They were to carry the Ark*d* of God with the Lord. They were to serve the Lord. They were to bless the people in the Lord's name. They still do this today. ⁹That is why the Levites did not receive any land to own. Instead, they received the Lord himself as their gift. This is what the Lord your God told them.)

¹⁰I stayed on the mountain 40 days and 40 nights just like the first time. And the Lord listened to me this time also. He did not want to destroy you. ¹¹The Lord said to me, "Go. Lead the people. They will go in and take the land I promised their ancestors."

What the Lord Wants You To Do

¹²Now, Israel, this is what the Lord wants you to do. Respect the Lord your God. Do what he has told you to do. Love him. Serve the Lord your God with your whole being. ¹³And obey the Lord's commands and laws. I am giving them to you today for your own good.

¹⁴The Lord owns the world and everything in it. The heavens, even the highest heavens, are his. ¹⁵But the Lord cared for and loved your ancestors. And he chose you, their descendants.*d* He chose you over all the other nations. And it is this way today. ¹⁶Give yourselves to serving the Lord. Do not be stubborn any longer. ¹⁷The Lord your God is God of all gods. He is the Lord of all lords. He is the great God. He is strong and wonderful. He does not take sides. And he will not be talked into doing evil. ¹⁸He helps orphans and widows. He loves foreigners. He gives them food and clothes. ¹⁹You also must love foreigners, because you were foreigners in Egypt. ²⁰Respect the Lord your God and serve him. Be loyal to him. Make your promises in his name. ²¹You should praise him. He is your God. He has done great and wonderful things for you. You have seen them with your own eyes. ²²There were only 70 of your ancestors when they went down to Egypt. Now the Lord your God has made you as many as the stars in the sky.

Great Things Israel Saw

11 Love the Lord your God. Obey his orders, rules, laws and commands. ²Remember today it was not your children who saw and felt the correction of the Lord your God. They did not see his majesty, his power and his strength. ³They did not see his signs and the things he did in Egypt to the king and his whole country. ⁴They did not see what he did to the Egyptian army, its horses and chariots. He drowned them in the Red Sea[d] when they were chasing you. The Lord ruined them for ever. [5]They did not see what he did for you in the desert until you arrived here. [6]They did not see what he did to Dathan and Abiram, the sons of Eliab the Reubenite. The ground opened up and swallowed them, their families and their tents. And it swallowed up everyone who stood with them in Israel. [7]It was you who saw all these great things the Lord has done.

[8]So obey all the commands I am giving you today. Then you will be strong. Then you can go in and take the land you are going to own. [9]Then you will live a long time in that land. The Lord promised to give it to your ancestors and their descendants.[d] It is a land where much food grows. [10]The land you are going to take is not like Egypt, where you were. There you had to plant your seed. Then you had to water it, like a vegetable garden, by using your feet. [11]But you will soon cross the Jordan River and take the land. It is a land of hills and valleys. It drinks rain from heaven. [12]It is a land the Lord your God loves. His eyes are on it continually. He watches it from the beginning of the year to the end.

[13]Carefully obey the commands I am giving you today. Love the Lord your God. Serve him with your whole being. [14]Then he will send rain on your land at the right time, in the autumn and spring. You will be able to gather your grain, new wine and oil. [15]He will put grass in the fields for your cattle. You will have plenty to eat.

[16]Be careful. Don't be fooled. Don't turn away and serve other gods. Don't worship them. [17]If you do, the Lord will become angry with you. He will shut the heavens so it will not rain. Then the land will not grow crops. And you will soon die in the good land the Lord is giving you. [18]Remember my words in your hearts and souls. Write them down and tie them to your hands as a sign. Tie them on your foreheads to remind you. [19]Teach them well to your children. Talk about them when you sit at home and walk along the road. Talk about them when you lie down and when you get up. [20]Write them on your doors and gates. [21]Then both you and your children will live a long time in the land. This is the land the Lord promised your ancestors. You will live there for as long as the skies are above the earth.

[22]Be careful to obey every command I am giving you to follow. Love the Lord your God. Do what he has told you to do. And be loyal to him. [23]Then the Lord will force all those nations out of the land ahead of you. And you will take the land from nations that are bigger and stronger than you. [24]Everywhere you step will be yours. Your land will go from the desert to Lebanon. And it will go from the Euphrates River to the Mediterranean Sea. [25]No one will be able to stop you. The Lord your God will do what he promised. He will make the people afraid everywhere you go.

[26]See, today I am letting you choose a blessing or a curse. [27]You will be blessed if you obey the commands of the Lord your God. I am giving them to you today. [28]But you will be cursed if you disobey the commands of the Lord your God. So do not disobey the commands I am giving you today. Do not worship other gods you do not know. [29]The Lord your God will bring you into the land you will own. Then you are to announce the blessings from Mount Gerizim. Announce the curses from Mount Ebal. [30]These mountains are on the other side of the Jordan River. They are west, towards the sunset. They are near the great trees of Moreh. They are in the land of the Canaanites who live in the Jordan Valley opposite Gilgal. [31]You will

soon cross the Jordan River. You will enter and take the land the Lord your God is giving you. You will take it over and live there. ³²Then be careful to obey all the commands and laws I am giving you.

The Place for Worship

12 These are the commands and laws you must carefully obey in the land the Lord your God is giving you. Obey them as long as you live in the land. ²You will inherit the lands of these nations. You must completely destroy all the places where they serve their gods. These places are on high mountains and hills and under every green tree. ³Tear down their altars. Smash their holy stone pillars. Burn their Asherah*d* idols. Cut down their idols. Destroy their names from those places.

⁴Don't worship the Lord your God that way. ⁵But look for the place the Lord your God will choose. He will choose a place among your tribes*d* where he is to be worshipped. Go there. ⁶Bring to that place your burnt offerings and sacrifices. Bring a tenth of what you gain and your special gifts. Bring what you have promised and the special gifts you want to give the Lord. And bring the first animals born to your herds and flocks.

⁷There you will be together with the Lord your God. There you and your families will eat. And you will enjoy all the good things for which you have worked. The Lord your God has blessed you.

⁸Do not worship the way we have been doing today. Each person does what he thinks is right. ⁹You have not yet come to a resting place. The Lord your God will give you your own land. ¹⁰But you will soon cross the Jordan River. And you will live in the land the Lord your God is giving you to own. And he will give you rest from all your enemies. You will live in safety. ¹¹Then the Lord your God will choose

a place where he is to be worshipped. To that place you must bring everything I tell you: your burnt offerings and sacrifices, your offerings of a tenth of what you gain, your special gifts and all your best things you promised to the Lord. ¹²There rejoice before the Lord your God. Everyone should rejoice: you, your sons and daughters, your male and female servants, and the Levites from your towns, who have no land of their own. ¹³Be careful. Don't sacrifice your burnt offerings just anywhere you please. ¹⁴Offer them only in the place the Lord will choose. He will choose a place in one of your tribes. And there you must do everything I am commanding you.

¹⁵But you may kill your animals in any of your towns. And you may eat as much of the meat as you want. Eat it as if it were a deer or a gazelle. This is the blessing the Lord your God is giving you. Anyone, clean*d* or unclean, may eat this meat. ¹⁶But do not eat the blood. Pour it out on the ground like water. ¹⁷Do not eat in your own towns what belongs to the Lord: one-tenth of your grain, new wine or oil; the first animals born to your herds or flocks; whatever you have promised to give; the special gifts you want to give to the Lord, or any other gifts. ¹⁸Eat these things when you are together with the Lord. Eat them in the place the Lord your God chooses to be worshipped. Everyone must do this: you, your sons and daughters, your male and female servants, and the Levites from your towns. Rejoice in the Lord's presence about the things you have worked for. ¹⁹Be careful not to forget the Levites as long as you live in the land.

²⁰The Lord your God will enlarge your country as he has promised. And you will want some meat. You will say, "I want some meat." Eat as much meat as you want. ²¹The Lord your God will choose a place where he is to

be worshipped. But it may be too far away from you. If it is, you may kill animals from your herds and flocks. The Lord has given them to you. I have commanded that you may do this. You may eat as much of them as you want in your own towns. ²²Eat them as you would eat gazelle or deer meat. Both clean and unclean people may eat this meat. ²³But be sure you don't eat the blood. The life is in the blood. Don't eat the life with the meat. ²⁴Don't eat the blood. Pour it out on the ground like water. ²⁵Don't eat it. Then things will go well for you and your children. You will be doing what the Lord says is right.

²⁶Take your holy things and the things you have promised to give. And go to the place the Lord will choose. ²⁷Present your burnt offerings on the altar of the Lord your God. Offer both the meat and the blood. The blood of your sacrifices should be poured beside the altar. But you may eat the meat. ²⁸Be careful to obey all the rules I am giving you. Then things will always go well for you and your children. You will be doing what the Lord your God says is good and right.

²⁹You will enter the land and take it away from the nations there. The Lord your God will destroy those nations ahead of you. You will force them out and live in their land. ³⁰They will be destroyed for you. Be careful not to be trapped by asking about their gods. Don't say, "How do these nations worship? I will do the same." ³¹Don't worship the Lord your God that way. The Lord hates the evil ways they worship their gods. They even burn their sons and daughters as sacrifices to their gods!

³²Be sure to do everything I have commanded you. Do not add anything to it. And do not take anything away from it.

False Prophets

13 A prophet[d] or someone who tells the future with dreams might come to you. He might say he will show you a miracle[d] or a sign. ²The miracle or sign might even happen. Then he might say, "Let's serve other gods." (These are gods you have not known.) "And let's worship them." ³But you must not listen to that prophet or dreamer. The Lord your God is testing you. He is finding out if you love him with your whole being. ⁴Serve only the Lord your God. Respect him. Keep his commands and obey him. Serve him and be loyal to him. ⁵That prophet or dreamer must be killed. He said you should turn against the Lord your God. The Lord brought you out of Egypt. He saved you from the land where you were slaves. That prophet tried to turn you from doing what the Lord your God commanded you to do. You must get rid of the evil among you.

⁶Some relative might try to lead you to serve other gods. It might be your brother, your son or daughter or the wife you love. Or it might be a close friend. He might say, "Let's go and worship other gods." (These are gods that neither you nor your ancestors have known. ⁷They are gods of the people who live around you. Some are nearby, and some are far away. They are from one end of the land to the other.) ⁸Do not give in to him. Do not listen. Do not feel sorry for him. Do not let him go free or protect him. ⁹You must put him to death. You must be the first one to start to kill him. Then everyone else must join in. ¹⁰You must throw stones at him until he dies. He tried to turn you away from the Lord your God. The Lord brought you out of the land of Egypt, where you were slaves. ¹¹Then everyone in Israel will hear about this. And they will be afraid. No one among

you will ever do such an evil thing again.

Cities to Destroy

12The Lord your God is giving you cities in which to live. You might hear something about one of them. Someone might say 13that evil men have moved in among you. And they might lead the people of that city away from God. They might say, "Let's go and worship other gods." (These are gods you have not known.) 14Then you must ask about it. Look into the matter and check carefully. It might be true. It may be proved that a terrible thing has happened among you. 15If it has, then you must kill with a sword everyone who lives in that city. Destroy the city completely. Kill everyone in it, as well as the animals, with a sword. 16Gather up everything those people owned. Put it in the middle of the city square. Then completely burn the city and everything they owned. It will be a burnt offering to the Lord your God. That city should never be rebuilt. Let it be ruined for ever. 17Don't keep any of the things found in that city for yourselves. Then the Lord will not be angry any more. He will give you mercy. He will feel sorry for you. And he will make your nation grow larger. He promised this to your ancestors. 18You will have obeyed the Lord your God. You will be keeping all his commands. I am giving them to you today. And you will be doing what the Lord says is right.

God's Special People

14 You are the children of the Lord your God. When someone dies, do not cut yourselves or shave your heads to show your sadness. 2You are holy people. You belong to the Lord your God. He has chosen you from all the people on earth to be his very own.

3Do not eat anything the Lord hates. 4These are the animals you

may eat: ox, sheep, goats, 5deer, gazelle, roe deer, wild goats, ibex, antelope and mountain sheep. 6You may eat any animal that has a split hoof and chews the cud.d 7But you may not eat camels, rabbits or rock badgers. These animals chew the cud, but their feet are not divided. So they are uncleand for you. 8Pigs are also unclean for you. They have split hoofs, but they do not chew the cud. Do not eat their meat or touch their dead bodies.

9There are many things that live in the water. You may eat anything that has fins and scales. 10But do not eat anything that does not have fins and scales. It is unclean for you.

11You may eat any clean bird. 12But do not eat these birds: eagles, vultures, black vultures, 13red kites, falcons, any kind of kite, 14any kind of raven, 15horned owls, screech owls, seagulls, any kind of hawk, 16little owls, great owls, white owls, 17desert owls, ospreys, cormorants, 18storks, any kind of heron, hoopoes or bats.

19All insects with wings are unclean for you. Do not eat them. 20Other things with wings are clean. You may eat them.

21Do not eat anything you find that is already dead. You may give it to a foreigner living in your town. He may eat it. Or you may sell it to a foreigner. But you are holy people. You belong to the Lord your God.

Do not cook a baby goat in its mother's milk.

Giving One-Tenth

22Be sure to save one-tenth of all your crops each year. 23Take it to the place the Lord your God will choose where he is to be worshipped. There you will be together with the Lord. There eat the tenth of your grain, new wine and oil. And eat the animals born first to your herds and flocks. Then you will learn to respect the Lord your God always. 24But the place the Lord will choose to be worshipped might be too far away. And he may have blessed you so much you cannot carry a tenth. [25]If so, exchange your one-tenth for silver. Then take the silver with you to the place the Lord your God shall choose. [26]Use the silver to buy anything you wish. You may buy cattle, sheep, wine, beer or anything you wish. Then you and your family will eat and celebrate there before the Lord your God. [27]Do not forget the Levites in your town. They have no land of their own among you.

[28]At the end of every third year, everyone should bring one-tenth of that year's crop. Store it in your towns. [29]This is for the Levites so they may eat and be full. (They have no land of their own among you.) It is also for strangers, orphans and widows who live in your towns. All of them may eat and be full. Then the Lord your God will bless you and all the work you do.

The Special Seventh Year

15 At the end of every seven years, you must forget about collecting what people owe you. [2]This is how you must do it: everyone who has lent money must forget the loan. He must not make his neighbour or brother pay it back. This is the Lord's time for cancelling what people owe. [3]You may make a foreigner pay what he owes you. But you must not collect what your brother owes you. [4]But there should be no poor people among you. The Lord your God will richly bless you in the land he is giving you to own. [5]He will bless you if you obey him completely. But you must be careful to obey all the commands I am giving you today. [6]The Lord your God will bless you as he promised. You will lend to other nations. But you will not need to borrow from them. You will rule over many nations. But none will rule over you.

[7]There might be a poor man among you. He might be in one of the towns of the land the Lord your God is giving you. Do not be selfish or greedy towards your poor brother. [8]But give freely to him. Freely lend him whatever he needs. [9]Beware of evil thoughts. Don't think, "The seventh year is near. It's the year to forget what people owe." You might be mean to your needy brother. You might not give him anything. Then he will complain to the Lord about you. And the Lord will find you guilty of sin. [10]Give freely to the poor person. Do not wish that you didn't have to give. The Lord your God will bless your work and everything you touch. [11]There will always be poor people in the land. So I command you to give freely to your brothers. Give freely to the poor and needy in your land.

Letting Slaves Go Free

[12]One of your own people might sell himself to you as a slave. It may be a Hebrew man or woman. That person will serve you for six years. The seventh year you must let him go free. [13]And when you let him go, don't send him away without anything. [14]Give him some of your sheep, your grain and your wine. Give to him as the Lord has given to you. [15]Remember that you were slaves in Egypt. And the Lord your God saved you. That is why I am commanding this to you today.

[16]But your slave might say to you, "I don't want to leave you." He might love you and your family. He might have a good life with you. [17]If he does this, stick an awl[n] through his ear into the door. He will be your slave for life. Also do this to a woman slave. [18]Do not think of it as a hard thing when you let your slave go free. After all, he served you six years. You paid him only half what a hired person

awl A tool like a big needle with a handle at one end.

would cost. The Lord your God will bless you in everything you do.

Rules About Firstborn Animals

¹⁹Save all the first male animals born to your herds and flocks. They are for the Lord your God. Do not work the first calf born to your oxen. And do not cut off the wool from the first lamb born to your sheep. ²⁰Each year you and your family are to eat these animals. Eat them in the presence of the Lord your God. Eat them in the place he will choose to be worshipped. ²¹An animal might have something wrong with it. It might be crippled or blind. It might have some other thing wrong with it. Do not sacrifice it to the Lord your God. ²²But you may eat that animal in your own town. Both clean*d* and unclean people may eat it. It would be like eating a gazelle or a deer. ²³But don't eat its blood. Pour it out on the ground like water.

The Passover

16 Celebrate the Passover*d* of the Lord your God during the month of Abib.*d* It was during Abib that he brought you out of Egypt at night. ²Offer a sacrifice for the Passover to the Lord your God. It should be an animal from your flock or herd. Offer it at the place the Lord will choose to be worshipped. ³Do not eat it with bread made with yeast. But for seven days eat bread made without yeast. This is the bread of suffering because you left Egypt in a hurry. So all your life you will remember the time you left Egypt. ⁴There must be no yeast anywhere in your land for seven days. Offer the sacrifice on the evening of the first day. Eat all the meat before morning. Do not leave it overnight.

⁵Do not offer the Passover sacrifice in just any town the Lord your God gives you. ⁶Offer it in the place he will choose to be worshipped. Offer it in the evening as the sun goes down.

That is when you left Egypt. ⁷Roast the meat. Then eat it at the place the Lord your God will choose. The next morning go back to your tents. ⁸Eat bread made without yeast for six days. On the seventh day have a special meeting for the Lord your God. Do not work that day.

Feast of Weeks

⁹Count seven weeks from the time you begin to harvest the grain. ¹⁰Then celebrate the Feast*d* of Weeks for the Lord your God. Bring him an offering as a special gift to him. Give to him just as he has blessed you. ¹¹Rejoice before the Lord your God. Rejoice at the place he will choose to be worshipped. Everybody should rejoice: you, your sons and daughters, your male and female servants, the Levites in your town, the strangers, orphans and widows living among you. ¹²Remember that you were slaves in Egypt. And carefully obey all these laws.

Feast of Shelters

¹³Celebrate the Feast*d* of Shelters for seven days. Do it after you have gathered your harvest from the threshing*d* floor and winepress.*d* ¹⁴Everybody should rejoice at your Feast: you, your sons and daughters, your male and female servants, the Levites and strangers who live in your towns, orphans and widows in your towns. ¹⁵Celebrate the Feast to the Lord your God for seven days. Celebrate it at the place he will choose. The Lord your God will bless all your harvest. He will bless all the work you do. And you will be completely happy.

¹⁶All your men must come before the Lord three times a year. They must come to the place he will choose. They must come at these times: the Feast*d* of Unleavened Bread, the Feast*d* of Weeks and the Feast of Shelters. No man should come before the Lord without a gift. ¹⁷Each of you

must bring a gift. It should show how much the Lord your God has blessed you.

Judges for the People

18Appoint judges and officers for your tribes.*d* Appoint them in every town the Lord your God is giving you. And they must judge the people fairly. 19Do not judge unfairly or take sides. Do not let people pay you to make wrong decisions. That kind of payment makes wise people seem blind. And it changes the words of good people. 20Always do what is right. Then you will live and own the land the Lord your God is giving you.

God Hates Idols

21Do not set up a wooden Asherah*d* idol next to the altar you build for the Lord your God. 22And do not set up holy stone pillars. The Lord your God hates them.

17 An ox or sheep might have something wrong with it. Do not offer it as a sacrifice to the Lord your God. He would hate that.

2A man or woman might be found doing something evil in one of the towns the Lord gave you. That man or woman is breaking his agreement with the Lord. 3That person may have served other gods. He may have bowed down to them, to the sun or moon or stars of the sky. I have commanded that should not be done. 4If someone has told you about it, you must look into the matter. It might be true. A terrible thing may have happened in Israel. 5If it is true, take the man or woman who has done the evil thing to the city gate. Throw stones at that person until he dies. 6There must be two or three witnesses that he did it. Then the person should be put to death. But if there is only one witness, the person should not be put to death. 7The witnesses must be the first to throw stones at the person.

Then everyone else will follow. You must get rid of the evil among you.

Courts of Law

8Some cases that come before you may be too difficult to judge. It may be a case of murder, quarrelling or attack. Take these cases to the place the Lord your God will choose. 9Go to the priests who are Levites. And go to the judge who is on duty at that time. Ask them about the case, and they will decide. 10You must follow the decision they give you. They will be at the place the Lord your God will choose. Be careful to do everything they tell you. 11Follow the teachings they give you. Do whatever they decide. Do exactly what they tell you. 12The person who does not show respect for the judge or priest must be put to death. They are there serving the Lord your God. You must get rid of that evil from Israel. 13Then everyone will hear about this. And they will be afraid. They will not show disrespect any more.

Choosing a King

14You will enter the land the Lord your God is giving you. You will take it as your own and live in it. Then you will say, "Let's appoint a king over us like the nations all around us." 15Be sure to appoint over you the king the Lord your God chooses. He must be one of your own people. Do not appoint a foreigner as your king. He is not a fellow Israelite. 16The king must not have too many horses for himself. He must not send people to Egypt to get more horses. The Lord has told you, "Don't return that way again." 17The king must not have many wives. If he does, his heart will be led away from God. He must not have too much silver and gold.

18When he becomes king, he should write a copy of the teachings on a scroll for himself. He should copy it from the priests and Levites. 19He should keep it with him all the time. He should read from it every day of his life. Then he will learn to respect the Lord his God. And he will obey all the teachings and commands. 20He should not think he is better than his brothers. He must not stop obeying the law in any way. Then he and his descendants*d* will rule the kingdom for a long time.

Shares for Priests and Levites

18 The priests are from the tribe*d* of Levi. That tribe will not receive a share of the land with the Israelites. They will eat the offerings made to the Lord by fire. That is their share. 2They will not inherit any of the land like their brothers. They will inherit the Lord himself. This is what he promised them.

3When you offer a bull or sheep as a sacrifice, you must share with the priests. Give them the shoulder, the cheeks and the inner organs. 4Give them the first of your grain, new wine and oil. Give them the first wool you cut from your sheep. 5The Lord your God has chosen the priests and their descendants*d* out of all your tribes. They are to stand and serve the Lord always.

6A Levite might move from one of your towns anywhere in Israel where he lives. He is sincere and comes to the place the Lord will choose. 7He may serve the Lord his God. He will be like his fellow Levites who serve there before the Lord. 8They all will have an equal share of the food. This is separate from what he has received from the sale of family possessions.

Do Not Follow Other Nations

9You will enter the land the Lord your God is giving you. But don't learn to do the terrible things the other nations do. 10Don't let anyone among you offer his son or daughter as a sacrifice in the fire. Don't let anyone use magic or witchcraft.*d* No one should

try to explain the meaning of signs. 11Don't let anyone try to control others with magic. Don't let them be mediums*d* or try to talk with the spirits of dead people. 12The Lord hates anyone who does these things. The other nations do these things. That is why the Lord your God will force them out of the land ahead of you. 13You must be innocent in the presence of the Lord your God.

The Lord's Special Prophet

14The nations you will force out listen to people who use magic and witchcraft.*d* But the Lord your God will not let you do those things. 15The Lord your God will give you a prophet*d* like me. He will be one of your own people. Listen to him. 16This is what you asked the Lord your God to do. You were gathered at Mount Sinai. You said, "Don't make us listen to the voice of the Lord our God again. Don't make us look at this terrible fire any more. We will die."

17So the Lord said to me, "What they have said is good. 18So I will give them a prophet like you. He will be one of their own people. I will tell him what to say. And he will tell them everything I command. 19This prophet will speak for me. Anyone who does not listen when he speaks will answer to me. 20But a prophet might say something I did not tell him to say. And he might say he is speaking for me. Or a prophet might speak in the name of other gods. That prophet must be killed."

21You might be thinking, "How can we know if a message is not from the Lord?" 22What a prophet says in the name of the Lord might not happen. If it doesn't, it is not the Lord's message. That prophet was speaking his own ideas. Don't be afraid of him.

Cities of Safety

19 The Lord your God is giving you land that belongs to other

nations. He will destroy those nations. You will force them out and live in their cities and houses. ²Then choose three cities. They must be in the middle of the land the Lord your God is giving you to own. ³Build roads to those cities. And divide the land the Lord is giving you into three parts. Then someone who kills another person may run to these cities.

⁴This is the rule for someone who kills another person. He may run to one of these cities to save his life. But he must have killed his neighbour without meaning to kill him. He did not hate his neighbour. ⁵A man might go into the forest with his neighbour to cut wood. The man swings his axe to cut down a tree. But the axe head flies off the handle. It hits his neighbour and kills him. The man who killed him may run to one of these cities to save his life. ⁶Otherwise, the dead man's relative who has the duty of punishing a murderer might be angry and chase him. And the relative might catch him if the city is far away. The relative might kill the man. But the man should not be killed because he did not mean to kill his neighbour. ⁷This is why I command you to choose these three cities.

⁸⁻⁹Carefully obey all these laws I'm giving you today. Love the Lord your God. Always do what he wants you to do. Then the Lord your God will enlarge your land as he promised your ancestors. He will give you the whole land he promised to them. After that, choose three more cities of safety. ¹⁰This is so that innocent people will not be killed in your land. The Lord your God is giving it to you to own. By doing this you will not be guilty of murder.

¹¹But a person might hate his neighbour. And he might hide and wait for him. He might attack and kill him and then run to one of these cities for safety. ¹²The older leaders of his own city should send for him. They should bring him back from the city of safety. And they should hand him over to the relative who has the duty of punishing the murderer. ¹³Give him no mercy. You must remove from Israel the guilt of murdering innocent people. Then things will go well for you.

¹⁴Do not move the stone that marks the border of your neighbour's land. People long ago set them in place. They mark what you inherit in the land the Lord your God is giving you to own.

Rules About Witnesses

¹⁵One witness is not enough to accuse a man of a crime or sin. A case must be proved by two or three witnesses.

¹⁶A witness might lie and accuse a person of a crime. ¹⁷The two people who are arguing must stand before the Lord. They must stand before the priests and judges who are on duty. ¹⁸The judges must check the matter carefully. The witness might be a liar. He might be lying about his fellow Israelite. ¹⁹If so, he must be punished as he wanted his brother punished. You must get rid of the evil among you. ²⁰The rest of the people will hear about this and be afraid. No one among you will ever do such an evil thing again. ²¹Give him no mercy. A life must be paid for a life. It must be an eye for an eye, a tooth for a tooth, a hand for a hand, a foot for a foot.

Laws for War

20 When you go to war against your enemies, you might see horses and chariots. Their army might be bigger than yours. But don't be afraid of them. The Lord your God will be with you. He brought you out of Egypt. ²The priest must come and speak to the army before you go into battle. ³He should say, "Listen, Israel! Today you are going into battle against your enemies. Don't lose your courage or be afraid. Don't panic or be frightened. ⁴The Lord your God goes with you. He will fight for you against your enemies. And he will save you from them."

⁵The officers should say to the army, "Has anyone built a new house but not given it to God? He may go home. He might die in battle. Then someone else would get to give his house to God. ⁶Has anyone planted a vineyard and not begun to enjoy it? He may go home. He might die in battle. Then someone else would enjoy his vineyard. ⁷Is any man engaged to a woman and not yet married to her? He may go home. He might die in battle. Then someone else would marry her." ⁸Then the officers should also say, "Is anyone here afraid? Has anyone lost his courage? He may go home. Then he will not cause others to lose their courage, too." ⁹When the officers finish speaking to the army, they should appoint commanders to lead it.

¹⁰You will march up to attack a city. First, make them an offer of peace. ¹¹They might accept your offer and open their gates to you. If that happens, all the people of that city will become your slaves. They will work for you. ¹²But they might not make peace with you. They might fight you in battle. Then you should surround that city. ¹³The Lord your God will give you the city. Then kill all the men with your swords. ¹⁴You may take everything else in the city for yourselves. Take the women and children and animals. And you may use these things the Lord your God gives you from your enemies. ¹⁵Do this to all the cities that are far away. They do not belong to the nations nearby.

¹⁶But leave nothing alive in the cities of the land. This is the land the Lord your God is giving you. ¹⁷Completely destroy these people: the Hittites, Amorites, Canaanites, Perizzites, Hivites and Jebusites. The Lord your God has commanded you to do this. ¹⁸Otherwise, they will teach you what they do for their gods. And if you do these terrible things, you will sin against the Lord your God.

¹⁹You might surround and attack a city for a long time, trying to capture it. But do not destroy its trees with an axe. You can eat the fruit from the trees. Do not cut them down. These trees are not the enemy. So don't make war against them. ²⁰But you may cut down trees that you know are not fruit trees. You may use them to build devices to attack the city walls. You may do this until the city is captured.

A Person Found Murdered

21 Someone might be found murdered. He might be lying in a field in the land the Lord your God is giving you to own. And no one knows who killed him. ²Your older leaders and judges should go to where he was found. And they should measure how far it is to the nearby cities. ³The older leaders of the city nearest the body are responsible. They must take a young cow that has never worked or worn a yoke.ᵈ ⁴And they must lead her down to a valley. It must never have been ploughed or planted. It must have a stream flowing through it. There they must break the young cow's neck. ⁵The priests should come forward. They are the sons of Levi. They have been chosen by the Lord your God. They are to serve and give blessings in the Lord's name. And they are to decide cases of quarrelling and attacks. ⁶Then all the older leaders of the city nearest the murdered man should wash their hands. They should do it over the young cow whose neck was broken in the valley. ⁷They should declare: "We did not kill this man. And we did not see it happen. ⁸Lord, remove this sin of your people Israel. You have saved them. Don't blame your people, the Israelites, for this innocent man's murder."

And so the murder will be paid for. ⁹Then you will have removed from yourselves the guilt of murdering an innocent person. You will be doing what the Lord says is right.

Captive Women as Wives

¹⁰You will go to war against your enemies. The Lord will help you defeat them. You will take them captive. ¹¹You might see a beautiful woman among the captives. And you might be attracted to her. You may take her as your wife. ¹²Bring her into your home. She must shave her head and cut her nails. ¹³She must change out of the clothes she was wearing when you captured her. And she must live in your house and cry for her parents for a month. After that, you may marry her. You will be her husband, and she will be your wife. ¹⁴But you might not be pleased with her. Then let her go anywhere she wants. You must not sell her for money. You must not make her a slave. You have taken away her honour.

The Oldest Son

¹⁵A man may have two wives. He might love one wife but not the other. Both wives might have sons by him. But the older son might be the son of the wife he does not love. ¹⁶Someday that man must will his property to his sons. But he must not give the son of the wife he loves what belongs to the older son. The older son is the son of the wife the man does not love. ¹⁷He must agree to give the older son two shares of everything he owns. The older son is from the wife he does not love. That son was the first to prove his father could have children. So he has the rights that belong to the older son.

Sons Who Refuse to Obey

¹⁸A man might have a son who is stubborn. The son turns against his father and mother and doesn't obey

them. He will not listen when they correct him. ¹⁹His parents must take him to the older leaders at the city gate. ²⁰They will say to the leaders, "Our son is stubborn and turns against us. He will not obey us. He eats too much. And he is always drunk." ²¹Then all the men in his town must throw stones at him until he dies. Get rid of the evil among you. All the people of Israel will hear about this and be afraid.

Other Laws

²²A man might be guilty of a sin worthy of death. He must be put to death and his body displayed on a tree. ²³But don't leave his body hanging on the tree overnight. Be sure to bury him that same day. Anyone whose body is displayed on a tree is cursed by God. You must not ruin the land the Lord your God is giving you to own.

22 You might see your fellow Israelite's ox or sheep wandering away. Don't ignore it. Take it back to its owner. ²The owner might not live close to you. Or you might not know who he is. Then take the animal home with you. Keep it until the owner comes looking for it. Then give it back to him. ³Do the same thing if you find his donkey or coat or anything he lost. Don't just ignore it.

⁴You might see your fellow Israelite's donkey or ox fallen on the road. Don't ignore it. Help him get it up.

⁵A woman must not wear men's clothes. And a man must not wear women's clothes. The Lord your God hates anyone who does that.

⁶You might find a bird's nest by the road. It might be in a tree or on the ground. And the mother bird might be sitting on the young birds or eggs. Do not take the mother bird with the young birds. ⁷You may take the young birds. But you must let the mother bird go free. Then things will go well for you. And you will live a long time. ⁸When you build a new house, build

a wall around the roof. *n* Then you will not be guilty of murder if someone falls off the roof.

⁹Don't plant two different kinds of seeds in your vineyard. Otherwise, both crops will be ruined.

¹⁰Don't plough with an ox and a donkey tied together.

¹¹Don't wear clothes made of wool and linen woven together.

¹²Tie several pieces of thread together. Then put these tassels on the four corners of your coat.

Marriage Laws

¹³A man might marry a girl and have sexual relations with her. But he might decide that he does not like her. ¹⁴So he might lie about her and give her a bad name. He might say, "I married this woman. But when I had sexual relations with her, I did not find that she was a virgin." *d* ¹⁵Then the girl's parents must bring proof that she was a virgin. They must bring it to the older leaders at the city gate. ¹⁶The girl's father will say to the leaders, "I gave my daughter to this man to be his wife. But now he does not want her. ¹⁷This man has told lies about my daughter. He has said, 'I did not find your daughter to be a virgin'. But here is the proof that my daughter was a virgin." Then her parents are to show the sheet to the city leaders. ¹⁸Then the leaders must take the man and punish him. ¹⁹They must make him pay about one and a quarter kilograms of silver. The silver will go to the girl's father. This is because the man has given an Israelite girl a bad name. The girl must continue to be the man's wife. And he may not divorce her as long as he lives.

²⁰But the things the husband said about his wife might be true. And there might be no proof that she was

a virgin. ²¹If so, the girl must be brought to the door of her father's house. Then the men of the town must put her to death by throwing stones at her. She has done a disgraceful thing in Israel. She had sexual relations before she was married. You must get rid of the evil among you.

²²A man might be found having sexual relations with another man's wife. Both the woman and the man who had sexual relations with her must die. Get rid of this evil from Israel.

²³A man might meet a virgin in a city and have sexual relations with her. But she might be engaged to another man. ²⁴You must take both of them to the city gate. Put them both to death by throwing stones at them. Kill the girl because she was in a city and did not scream for help. And kill the man for having sexual relations with another man's wife. You must get rid of the evil among you.

²⁵But a man might meet a girl out in the country. He might force her to have sexual relations with him. But she might be engaged to another man. Only the man who had sexual relations with her must be put to death. ²⁶Don't do anything to the girl. She has not done a sin worthy of death. This is like the person who attacks and murders his neighbour. ²⁷The man found the engaged girl in the country. And she screamed. But no one was there to save her.

²⁸A man might meet a virgin who is not engaged to be married. He might force her to have sexual relations with him. And people might find out about it. ²⁹The man must pay the girl's father about two-thirds of a kilogram of silver. He must also marry the girl because he has dishonoured her. And he may never divorce her for as long as he lives.

---

roof In Bible times houses were built with flat roofs. The roof was used for drying things such as flax and fruit. It was also used as an extra room, as a place for worship and as a place to sleep in the summer.

30A man must not marry his father's wife. He must not dishonour his father in this way.

The Lord's People

23 No man who has had part of his sex organ cut off may come into the worship meeting of the Lord's people.

2No one born to parents who were forbidden by law to marry may come into the meeting to worship the Lord. His descendants for ten generations may not come in either.

3No Ammonite or Moabite may come into the meeting to worship the Lord. And none of their descendants for ten generations may come in. 4This is because the Ammonites and Moabites did not give you bread and water when you came out of Egypt. And they hired Balaam to put a curse on you. He was the son of Beor from Pethor in North West Mesopotamia. 5But the Lord your God would not listen to Balaam. He turned the curse into a blessing for you. The Lord your God loves you. 6Don't wish for their peace or success as long as you live.

7Don't hate Edomites. They are your relatives. Don't hate Egyptians, because you were foreigners in their country. 8The great-grandchildren of these two peoples may come into the meeting to worship the Lord.

Keeping the Camp Clean

9When you are camped in time of war, keep away from unclean*d* things. 10A man might become unclean during the night. If he does, he must go outside the camp and not come back. 11But when evening comes, he must wash himself. At sunset he may come back into the camp.

12Choose a place outside the camp where people may go to relieve themselves. 13Carry a stick with you. When you relieve yourself, dig a hole. Cover up your dung. 14The Lord your God moves around through your camp. He will protect you. He will help you defeat your enemies. So the camp must be holy. The Lord must not see anything unclean among you. Then he will not leave you.

Other Laws

15An escaped slave might come to you. Do not hand him over to his master. 16Let the slave live with you anywhere he likes. He may live in any town he chooses. Do not mistreat him.

17No Israelite man or woman must ever become a temple prostitute.*d* 18Do not bring a male or female prostitute's pay to the Temple*d* of the Lord your God to pay what you have promised to the Lord. The Lord your God hates prostitution.

19You may loan your fellow Israelite money or food or anything else. But don't make him pay back more than what you loaned him. 20You may charge a foreigner, but not a fellow Israelite. Then the Lord your God will bless everything you do. He will bless you in the land you are entering to take as your own.

21You might make a promise to give something to the Lord your God. Do not be slow to pay it. The Lord your God demands it from you. Do not be guilty of sin. 22But if you do not make the promise, you will not be guilty. 23You must do whatever you say you will do. You chose to make the promise to the Lord your God.

24You might go into your neighbour's vineyard. You may eat as many grapes as you wish. But do not fill your basket with his grapes. 25You might go into your neighbour's grainfield. You may pick grain with your hands. But you must not cut down his grain with your sickle.

24 A man might marry a woman. But he might decide she doesn't please him. He has found something bad about her. He writes out divorce papers for her. He gives them to her and sends her away from his house. ²After she leaves his house, she goes and marries another man. ³But her second husband does not like her either. So he writes out divorce papers for her. He gives them to her and sends her away from his house. Or the second husband might die. ⁴In either case, her first husband who divorced her must not marry her again. She has become unclean.*d* The Lord would hate this. Don't bring this sin into the land the Lord your God is giving you to own.

⁵A man who has just married must not be sent to war. And he must not be given any other duty. He should be free to stay home for a year to make his new wife happy.

⁶A man might owe you something. But do not take his two stones for grinding grain — not even the upper one — in place of what he owes. This is how he makes his living.

⁷A man might kidnap a fellow Israelite. He might make him a slave or sell him. The kidnapper must be killed. You must get rid of the evil among you.

⁸Be careful when someone has a harmful skin disease. Do exactly what the priests, the Levites, teach you. Be careful to do what I have commanded them. ⁹Remember what the Lord your God did to Miriam on your way out of Egypt.

¹⁰You might make a loan to your neighbour. But don't go into his house to get something in place of it. ¹¹Stay outside. Let the man himself go in and get what he promised you. ¹²A poor man might give you his coat to show he will pay the loan back. But don't keep his coat overnight. ¹³Give his coat back to him at sunset. He needs his coat to sleep in. He will thank you. And the Lord your God will see that you have done a good thing.

¹⁴Don't cheat a hired servant who is poor and needy. He might be a fellow Israelite. Or he might be a foreigner living in one of your towns. ¹⁵Pay him each day before sunset. He is poor and needs the money. Otherwise, he may complain to the Lord about you. And you will be guilty of sin.

¹⁶Fathers must not be put to death when their children do wrong. And children must not be put to death when their fathers do wrong. Each person must die for his own sin.

¹⁷Do not be unfair to a foreigner or an orphan. Don't take a widow's coat in place of a loan. ¹⁸Remember that you were slaves in Egypt. And the Lord your God saved you from there. That is why I am commanding you to do this.

¹⁹You might be gathering your harvest in the field. You might forget a bundle of grain. Don't go back and get it. Leave it there for foreigners, orphans and widows. Then the Lord your God can bless everything you do. ²⁰You may beat your olive trees to knock the olives off. But don't beat the trees a second time. Leave what is left for foreigners, orphans and widows. ²¹You may harvest the grapes in your vineyard. But don't pick the vines a second time. Leave what is left for foreigners, orphans and widows. ²²Remember that you were slaves in Egypt. That is why I am commanding you to do this.

25 Two people may have an argument. They should go to the court. And the judges will decide the case. They will declare one person to be right. And they will punish the one who is guilty. ²The guilty person might have to be punished with a beating. If so, the judge will make him lie down. They will beat him in front of the judge. The number of lashes should match the crime. ³But don't hit him more than 40 times. If he is beaten more than that, it would disgrace him before others.

⁴When an ox is working in the grain,

do not cover its mouth to keep it from eating.

⁵Two brothers might be living together. One of them might die without having a son. His widow must not marry someone outside her husband's family. Her husband's brother must marry her. This is his duty for her as a brother-in-law. ⁶The first son she has must be named after the dead brother. Then his name will not be forgotten in Israel.

⁷But a man might not want to marry his brother's widow. Then she should go to the older leaders at the town gate. And she should say, "My brother-in-law will not carry on his brother's name in Israel. He refuses to do his duty for me."

⁸Then the older leaders of the town must call for the man and talk to him. But he might be stubborn and say, "I don't want to marry her."

⁹If he does, the woman must go up to him in front of the leaders. She must take off one of his sandals. She must spit in his face and say, "This is for the man who won't continue his brother's family!" ¹⁰Then that man's family shall be known in Israel as the Family of the Unsandalled.

¹¹Two men might be fighting. And one man's wife comes to save her husband from his attacker. And she grabs the attacker by his sex organs. ¹²You must cut off her hand. Give her no mercy.

¹³Don't carry two sets of weights with you, one heavy and one light. ¹⁴Don't have two different sets of measures in your house, one large and one small. ¹⁵You must have true and honest weights and measures. Then you will live a long time in the land the Lord your God is giving you. ¹⁶The Lord your God hates anyone who is dishonest and uses dishonest measures.

¹⁷Remember what the Amalekites did to you when you came out of Egypt. ¹⁸You were tired and worn out. And they met you on the road. They killed all those lagging behind. They were not afraid of God. ¹⁹The Lord your God will give you rest from all the enemies around you. It will be in the land he is giving you to own. Then you shall destroy any memory of the Amalekites on the earth. Do not forget!

The First Harvest

26 Soon you will go into the land the Lord your God is giving you to own. You will take it over and live in it. ²Then you must take some of the first harvest of crops. It will grow from the land the Lord your God is giving you. Put the food in a basket. Then go to the place where the Lord your God will choose to be worshipped. ³Say to the priest on duty at that time, "Today I declare this before the Lord your God. I have come into the land the Lord promised to give us. He promised this to our ancestors." ⁴The priest will take your basket. He will set it down in front of the altar of the Lord your God. ⁵Then you shall announce before the Lord your God: "My father was a wandering Aramean. He went down to Egypt. He stayed there with only a few people. But they became a great, powerful and large nation there. ⁶But the Egyptians were cruel to us. They made us suffer and work very hard. ⁷So we prayed to the Lord, the God of our ancestors. He heard us. He saw our trouble, hard work and suffering. ⁸Then the Lord brought us out of Egypt. He did it with his great power and strength. He used great terrors, signs and miracles.ᵈ ⁹Then he brought us to this place. He gave us this land where much food grows. ¹⁰Now I bring you part of the first harvest from this land. Lord, you have given me this land." Then place the basket before the Lord your God. And bow down before him. ¹¹Then you and the Levites and foreigners among you

should rejoice. The Lord your God has given good things to you and your family.

¹²Bring a tenth of all your harvest in the third year. This is the year to give a tenth of your harvest. Give it to the Levites, foreigners, orphans and widows. Then they may eat in your towns and be full. ¹³Then say to the Lord your God, "I have taken out of my house the part of my harvest that belongs to God. I have given it to the Levites, foreigners, orphans and widows. I have done everything you commanded me. I have not broken your commands. And I have not forgotten any of them. ¹⁴I have not eaten any of the holy part while I was in sorrow. I have not removed any of it while I was unclean.ᵈ I have not offered it for dead people. I have obeyed you, the Lord my God. I have done everything you commanded me. ¹⁵So look down from heaven, your holy home. Bless your people Israel. And bless the land you have given us. You promised it to our ancestors. It is a land where much food grows."

Obey the Lord's Commands

¹⁶Today the Lord your God commands you to obey all these rules and laws. Be careful to do them with your whole being. ¹⁷Today you have said that the Lord is your God. You have promised to do what he wants you to do. You have promised to keep his rules, commands and laws. You have said you will obey him. ¹⁸And today the Lord has said that you are his very own people. He has promised it. But you must obey his commands. ¹⁹The Lord will make you greater than all the other nations he made. He will give you praise, fame and honour. And you will be a holy people to the Lord your God. This is what he said.

The Law Written on Stones

27 Moses and the older leaders of Israel commanded the people.

They said, "Keep all the commands I have given you today. ²Soon you will cross the Jordan River. You will go into the land the Lord your God is giving you. On that day set up some large stones. Cover them with plaster. ³When you cross over, write all the words of these teachings on them. Then you may enter the land the Lord your God is giving you. It is a land where much food grows. It is just as the Lord, the God of your ancestors, promised. ⁴After you have crossed the Jordan River, set up these stones. Set them on Mount Ebal as I command you today. And cover them with plaster. ⁵Build an altar of stones there to the Lord your God. But don't use any iron tool to cut the stones. ⁶Build the altar of the Lord your God with stones from the field. Offer burnt offerings on it to the Lord your God. ⁷Offer fellowship offerings there. Eat them and rejoice before the Lord your God. ⁸Then write clearly all the words of these teachings on the stones."

Curses of the Law

⁹Then Moses and the Levites, who are the priests, spoke to all Israel. They said, "Be quiet, Israel. Listen! Today you have become the people of the Lord your God. ¹⁰Obey the Lord your God. Keep his commands and laws that I give you today."

¹¹That day Moses also gave the people this command:

¹²You will cross the Jordan River. Then these tribesᵈ must stand on Mount Gerizim to bless the people: Simeon, Levi, Judah, Issachar, Joseph and Benjamin. ¹³And these tribes must stand on Mount Ebal to announce the curses: Reuben, Gad, Asher, Zebulun, Dan and Naphtali.

¹⁴The Levites will say to all the people of Israel in a loud voice:

¹⁵"Anyone will be cursed who makes an idol or statue and secretly sets it up. The Lord hates idols made by man."

Then all the people will say, "Amen!"

¹⁶"Anyone will be cursed who dishonours his father or his mother."

Then all the people will say, "Amen!"

¹⁷"Anyone will be cursed who moves the stone that marks his neighbour's border."

Then all the people will say, "Amen!"

¹⁸"Anyone will be cursed who leads a blind person away from the road."

Then all the people will say, "Amen!"

¹⁹"Anyone will be cursed who is unfair to foreigners, orphans or widows."

Then all the people will say, "Amen!"

²⁰"A man will be cursed who has sexual relations with his father's wife. It is a dishonour to his father."

Then all the people will say, "Amen!"

²¹"Anyone will be cursed who has sexual relations with an animal."

Then all the people will say, "Amen!"

²²"A man will be cursed who has sexual relations with his sister. She may be his father's daughter or his mother's daughter."

Then all the people will say, "Amen!"

²³"A man will be cursed who has sexual relations with his mother-in-law."

Then all the people will say, "Amen!"

²⁴"Anyone will be cursed who kills his neighbour secretly."

Then all the people will say, "Amen!"

²⁵"Anyone will be cursed who takes money to murder an innocent person."

Then all the people will say, "Amen!"

²⁶"Anyone will be cursed who does not agree with the words of these teachings and does not obey them."

Then all the people will say, "Amen!"

Blessings for Obeying

28 You must completely obey the Lord your God. And you must carefully follow all his commands I am giving you today. Then the Lord your God will make you greater than any other nation on earth. ²Obey the Lord your God. Then all these blessings will come and stay with you:

³You will be blessed in the city. You will be blessed in the country.

⁴Your children will be blessed. Your crops will be blessed. Your cattle will be blessed with calves and your sheep with lambs.

⁵Your basket and your kitchen will be blessed.

⁶You will be blessed when you come in and when you go out.

⁷The Lord will let you defeat the enemies that come to fight you. They will attack you from one direction. But they will run from you in seven directions.

⁸The Lord your God will bless you with full barns. He will bless everything you do. He will bless the land he is giving you.

⁹The Lord will make you his holy people, as he promised. But you must obey his commands. You must do what he wants you to do. ¹⁰Then everyone on earth will see that you are the Lord's people. They will be afraid of you. ¹¹The Lord will make you rich. You will have many children. Your cattle will have many calves. Your land will give good crops. It is the land that the Lord promised your ancestors he would give to you.

¹²The Lord will open up his storehouse. The skies will send rain on your land at the right time. And he will bless everything you do. You will lend to other nations. But you will not need to borrow from them. ¹³The Lord will make you like the head and not like

the tail. You will be at the top and not at the bottom. But you must obey the commands of the Lord your God that I am giving you today. Be careful to keep them. [14]Do not disobey anything I command you today. Do exactly as I command. Do not follow other gods or serve them.

Curses for Disobeying

[15]But you might not obey the Lord your God. You might not carefully follow all his commands and laws I am giving you today. Then all these curses will come upon you and stay:

[16]You will be cursed in the city. You will be cursed in the country.

[17]Your basket and your kitchen will be cursed.

[18]Your children will be cursed. Your crops will be cursed. The calves of your cattle will be cursed. And the lambs of your flocks will be cursed.

[19]You will be cursed when you go in and when you go out.

[20]The Lord will send you curses, confusion and punishment in everything you do. You will be destroyed. You will suddenly be ruined. You did wrong when you left him. [21]The Lord will give you terrible diseases. He will destroy you from the land you are going to take. [22]The Lord will punish you with disease, fever, swelling, heat, no rain, plant diseases and mildew.[d] Then you will die. [23]The sky above will look like bronze. And the ground below will be like iron. [24]The Lord will turn the rain into dust and sand. It will fall from the skies until you are destroyed.

[25]The Lord will let your enemies defeat you. You will attack them from one direction. But you will run from them in seven directions. And you will become a thing of horror among all the kingdoms on earth. [26]Your dead bodies will be food for all the birds and wild animals. There will be no one to scare them away. [27]The Lord will punish you with boils like those the Egyp-

tians had. You will have bad growths, sores and itches that can't be cured. [28]The Lord will give you madness, blindness and a confused mind. [29]You will have to feel around in the daylight like a blind man. You will fail in everything you do. People will hurt you and steal from you every day. There will be no one to save you.

[30]You will be engaged to a woman. But another man will force her to have sexual relations with him. You will build a house. But you will not live in it. You will plant a vineyard. But you will not get its grapes. [31]Your ox will be killed before your eyes. But you will not eat any of it. Your donkey will be taken away from you. And it will not be brought back. Your sheep will be given to your enemies. And no one will rescue them. [32]Your sons and daughters will be given to another nation. You will grow tired looking for them every day. But there is nothing you can do. [33]People you don't know will eat the crops your land and hard work have produced. You will be mistreated and abused all your life. [34]The things you see will cause you to go mad. [35]The Lord will give you sore boils on your knees and legs. They cannot be cured. They will go from the soles of your feet to the top of your head.

[36]The Lord will send you and your king away to a nation you do not know. There you will serve other gods made of wood and stone. [37]You will become a hated thing to the nations where the Lord sends you. They will laugh at you and make fun of you.

[38]You will plant much seed in your field. But your harvest will be small. Locusts[d] will eat the crop. [39]You will plant vineyards and work hard in them. But you will not pick the grapes or drink the wine. The worms will eat them. [40]You will have olive trees in all your land. But you will not get any olive oil. The olives will drop off the trees. [41]You will have sons and daugh-

ters. But you will not be able to keep them. They will be taken captive. ⁴²Locusts will destroy all your trees and crops.

⁴³The foreigners who live among you will get stronger and stronger. And you will get weaker and weaker. ⁴⁴Foreigners will lend money to you. But you will not be able to lend to them. They will be like the head. And you will be like the tail.

⁴⁵All these curses will come upon you. They will chase you and catch you and destroy you. This will happen because you did not obey the Lord your God. You did not keep the commands and laws he gave you. ⁴⁶The curses will be signs and miracles*d* to you and your descendants*d* for ever. ⁴⁷You had plenty of everything. But you did not serve the Lord your God with joy and a pure heart. ⁴⁸So you will serve the enemies the Lord sends against you. You will be hungry, thirsty, naked and poor. The Lord will put a load on you until he has destroyed you.

The Curse of an Enemy Nation

⁴⁹The Lord will bring a nation against you from far away. It will be from the end of the world. The nation will swoop down like an eagle. You won't understand their language. ⁵⁰They will look mean. They will not respect old people or feel sorry for the young. ⁵¹They will eat the calves from your cattle and the harvest of your field. And you will be destroyed. They will not leave you any grain, new wine or oil. They will not leave you any calves from your herds or lambs from your flocks. You will be ruined. ⁵²That nation will surround and attack all your cities. You trust in your high, strong walls. But they will fall down. That nation will surround all your cities everywhere in the land the Lord your God is giving you. ⁵³Your enemy will surround you. Those people will make you starve.

You will eat your own babies. You will eat the bodies of the sons and daughters the Lord gave you. ⁵⁴Even the most gentle and kind man among you will become cruel. He will be cruel to his brother, his wife whom he loves and his children who are still alive. ⁵⁵He will not even give them any of the flesh of his children he is eating. It will be all he has left. Your enemy will surround you. Those people will make you starve in all your cities. ⁵⁶The most gentle and kind woman among you will become cruel. She is so gentle and kind she would hardly even walk on the ground. But she will be cruel to her husband whom she loves. And she will be cruel to her son and daughter. ⁵⁷She will give birth to a baby. But she will plan to eat the baby and what comes after the birth itself. She will eat them while the enemy surrounds the city. Those people will make you starve in all your cities.

⁵⁸Be careful to obey everything in these teachings. They are written in this book. You must respect the glorious and wonderful name of the Lord your God. ⁵⁹The Lord will give terrible diseases to you and your descendants.*d* You will have long and serious diseases. You will have long and miserable sicknesses. ⁶⁰And the Lord will give you all the diseases of Egypt that you dread. And the diseases will stay with you. ⁶¹The Lord will also give you every disease and sickness not written in this Book of the Teachings. Then you will be destroyed. ⁶²You people may have outnumbered the stars. But only a few of you will be left. You did not obey the Lord your God. ⁶³Once the Lord was happy with you. He gave you good things. He made you grow in number. But now the Lord will be happy to ruin and destroy you. You will be removed from the land you are entering to own.

⁶⁴Then the Lord will scatter you among the nations. He will scatter you from one end of the earth to the other.

There you will serve other gods of wood and stone. They are gods that neither you nor your ancestors have known. ⁶⁵You will have no rest among those nations. You will have no place that is yours. The Lord will make your mind worried, your sight weak and your soul sad. ⁶⁶You will live with danger. You will be afraid night and day. You will not be sure that you will live. ⁶⁷In the morning you will say, "I wish it were evening." And in the evening you will say, "I wish it were morning." Terror will be in your heart because of the things you have seen. ⁶⁸The Lord will send you back to Egypt in ships. I, Moses, said you would never go back to Egypt. And there you will try to sell yourselves as slaves to your enemies. But no one will buy you.

The Agreement in Moab

29 The Lord commanded Moses to make an agreement with the Israelites in Moab. This agreement was in addition to the agreement he had made with them at Mount Sinai. ²Moses called all the Israelites together. And he said to them:

You have seen everything the Lord did to the king of Egypt. You saw what he did to the king's leaders and to the whole country. ³With your own eyes you saw the great troubles, signs and miracles.^d ⁴But to this day the Lord has not given you a mind that understands. You don't really understand what you see with your eyes or hear with your ears. ⁵The Lord led you through the desert for 40 years. During that time neither your clothes nor sandals wore out. ⁶You ate no bread. You drank no wine or beer. This was so you would understand that he is the Lord your God.

⁷You came to this place. Then Sihon king of Heshbon and Og king of Bashan came out to fight us. But we defeated them. ⁸We captured their land. And we gave it to the Reubenites, the Gadites and the eastern half-tribe^d of Manasseh to own.

⁹You must carefully obey everything in this agreement. Then you will succeed in everything you do. ¹⁰Today you are all standing here before the Lord your God. Here are your leaders and important men. Your older leaders, officers and all the other men of Israel are here. ¹¹Here are your wives and children and the foreigners who live among you. They chop your wood and carry your water. ¹²You are all here to enter into an agreement and a promise with the Lord your God. The Lord is making this agreement with you today. ¹³This will make you today the Lord's own people. He will be your God. This is what he told you. He promised it to your ancestors Abraham, Isaac and Jacob. ¹⁴But the Lord is not just making this agreement and its promises with you. ¹⁵You are standing here before the Lord your God today. But he is also making it with those who are not here today.

¹⁶You know how we lived in Egypt. You know how we passed through the countries when we came here. ¹⁷You saw their hated idols made of wood, stone, silver and gold. ¹⁸Make sure no man, woman, family group or tribe among you leaves the Lord. Don't let them go and serve the gods of those nations. That would be like a plant that grows bitter, poisonous fruit.

¹⁹That kind of person might hear these curses. But he blesses himself. And he thinks, "I will be safe. I will continue doing what I want to do." That person might destroy all of your land, both wet and dry. ²⁰The Lord will not forgive that person. His anger will be like a burning fire against that man. All the curses written in this book will come on him. And the Lord will destroy any memory of him on the earth. ²¹The Lord will separate him from all the tribes of Israel for punishment. All the curses of the agreement

will happen to him. They are written in this Book of the Teachings.

²²Your children who will come after you will see this. And foreigners from faraway lands will see this. They will see the disasters that come to this land. And they will see the diseases the Lord will send on it. They will say, ²³"The land is nothing but burning cinders and salt. Nothing is planted. Nothing grows. Nothing blooms. It is like Sodom and Gomorrah, and Admah and Zeboiim. The Lord destroyed them because he was very angry." ²⁴All the other nations will ask, "Why has the Lord done this to the land? Why is he so angry?" ²⁵And the answer will be, "It is because the people broke the agreement of the Lord, the God of their ancestors. He made it with them when he brought them out of Egypt. ²⁶They went and served other gods. They bowed down to gods they did not even know. The Lord did not allow that. ²⁷So the Lord became very angry at the land. And he brought all the curses on it that are written in this book. ²⁸The Lord became angry and furious with them. So he took them out of their land. And he put them in another land where they are today."

²⁹There are some things the Lord our God has kept secret. But there are some things he has let us know. These things belong to us and our children for ever. It is so we will do everything in these teachings.

The Israelites Will Return

30 All these blessings and curses I have said will happen to you. The Lord your God will send you away to other nations. There you will think about these things. ²Then you and your children will return to the Lord your God. And you will obey him with your whole being. You will obey everything I command you today. ³Then the Lord your God will give you back your riches. He will feel sorry for

you. And he will bring you back again from the nations where he sent you. ⁴He may send you to the ends of the earth. But he will gather you. He will bring you back from there. ⁵He will bring you back to the land that belonged to your ancestors. It will be yours. He will give you success. And there will be more of you than there were of your ancestors. ⁶The Lord your God will prepare you and your descendants^d to serve him. You will love him with your whole being. Then you will live. ⁷The Lord your God will put all these curses on your enemies. They hate you and are cruel to you. ⁸And you will again obey the Lord. You will keep all his commands that I give you today. ⁹The Lord your God will make you successful in everything you do. You will have many children. Your cattle will have many calves. Your fields will produce good crops. He will again be happy with you, just as he was with your ancestors. ¹⁰But you must obey the Lord your God. You must obey his commands and rules that are written in this Book of the Teachings. You must follow the Lord your God with your whole being.

Life or Death

¹¹This command I give you today is not too hard for you. It is not beyond what you can do. ¹²It is not up in heaven. You do not have to ask, "Who will go up to heaven and get it for us? Then we can obey it and keep it." ¹³It is not on the other side of the sea. You do not have to ask, "Who will go across the sea and get it? Who will tell it to us? Then we can keep it." ¹⁴No, the word is very near you. It is in your mouth and in your heart. So, you may obey it.

¹⁵Look, today I offer you life and success, death and destruction. ¹⁶I command you today to love the Lord your God. Do what he wants you to do. Keep his commands, his rules and his laws. Then you will live and grow

in number. And the Lord your God will bless you in the land you are going to take as your own.

¹⁷But you might turn away from the Lord. You might not obey him. You might be led to bowing down and serving other gods. ¹⁸I tell you today that you will be destroyed. And you will not live long in the land you are crossing the Jordan River to enter and own.

¹⁹Today I ask heaven and earth to be witnesses. I am offering you life or death, blessings or curses. Now, choose life! Then you and your children may live. ²⁰Love the Lord your God. Obey him. Stay close to him. He is your life. And he will let you live many years in the land. This is the land he promised to give your ancestors Abraham, Isaac and Jacob.

Joshua Takes Moses' Place

31 Then Moses went and spoke these words to all the Israelites: ²"I am now 120 years old. I cannot lead you any more. The Lord told me I would not cross the Jordan River. ³The Lord your God will lead you across himself. He will destroy those nations for you. You will take over their land. Joshua will also lead you across. This is what the Lord has said. ⁴The Lord will do to these nations what he did to Sihon and Og. They were the kings of the Amorites. He destroyed them and their land. ⁵The Lord will give those nations to you. Do to them everything I told you. ⁶Be strong and brave. Don't be afraid of them. Don't be frightened. The Lord your God will go with you. He will not leave you or forget you."

⁷Then Moses called Joshua and spoke to him in front of the people. Moses said, "Be strong and brave. Lead these people into the land the Lord promised to give their ancestors. Help the people take it as their own. ⁸The Lord himself will go before you. He will be with you. He will not

leave you or forget you. Don't be afraid. Don't worry."

Moses Writes the Teachings

⁹So Moses wrote down the teachings. He gave them to the priests and all the older leaders of Israel. The priests are the sons of Levi. They carried the Ark*ᵈ* of God with the Lord. ¹⁰⁻¹¹Then Moses commanded them: "Read these teachings for all Israel to hear. Do it at the end of every seven years. That is the year to forget what people owe. Do it during the Feast*ᵈ* of Shelters. All the Israelites will come to appear before the Lord your God. They will stand at the place the Lord will choose. ¹²Gather all the people: the men, women, children and foreigners living in your towns. Then they can listen and learn to respect the Lord your God. Then they can carefully obey everything in this law. ¹³Their children do not know this law. They must hear it. They must learn to respect the Lord your God for as long as they live in the land. It is the land you are crossing the Jordan River to own."

The Lord Calls Moses and Joshua

¹⁴The Lord said to Moses, "Soon you will die. Get Joshua and come to the Meeting Tent.*ᵈ* I will command him." So Moses and Joshua went to the Meeting Tent.

¹⁵The Lord appeared at the Meeting Tent in a cloud. The cloud stood over the entrance of the Tent. ¹⁶And the Lord said to Moses, "You will soon die. Then these people will not be loyal to me. They will worship the foreign gods of the land they are entering. They will leave me. And they will break the agreement I made with them. ¹⁷Then I will become very angry at them. I will leave them. I will turn away from them. And they will be destroyed. Many terrible things will happen to them. Then they will say,

'God is not with us. That is why these terrible things are happening'. ¹⁸I will turn away from them then. They have done wrong. They have turned to other gods.

¹⁹"Now write down this song. And teach it to the Israelites. Then have them sing it. It will testify against them. ²⁰I will bring them into the land I promised to their ancestors. It is a land where much food grows. They will eat as much as they want and get fat. But then they will turn to other gods and serve them. They will reject me and break my agreement. ²¹Then many troubles and terrible things will happen to them. And this song will testify against them. The song will not be forgotten by their descendants.^d I know what they plan to do, even before I take them into the land I promised them." ²²So Moses wrote down the song that day. And he taught it to the Israelites.

²³Then the Lord gave this command to Joshua son of Nun: "Be strong and brave. Lead the people of Israel to the land I promised them. And I will be with you."

²⁴Moses wrote all the words of the teachings in a book. ²⁵Then he gave a command to the Levites. They carried the Ark^d of God with the Lord. ²⁶He said, "Take this Book of the Teachings. Put it beside the Ark of God with the Lord your God. It must stay there as a witness against you. ²⁷I know how stubborn and disobedient you are. You have disobeyed the Lord while I am alive and with you. You will disobey even more after I die! ²⁸Gather all the older leaders of your tribes^d and all your officers. I will say these things for them to hear. And I will ask heaven and earth to testify against them. ²⁹I know that after I die you will become completely evil. You will turn away from the commands I have given you. Then terrible things will happen to you in the future. You will do what the Lord says is evil. You

will make him angry with the idols you have made."

Moses' Song

³⁰And Moses spoke this whole song for all the people of Israel to hear:

32 Hear, heavens, and I will speak.
Listen, earth, to what I say.
²My teaching will drop like rain.
My words will fall like dew.
They will be like showers on the grass.
They will pour down like rain on young plants.
³I will announce the name of the Lord.
Praise God because he is great!
⁴He is like a rock. What he does is perfect.
He is always fair.
He is a faithful God who does no wrong.
He is right and fair.

⁵They have done evil against him.
To their shame they are no longer his children.
They are an evil and lying people.
⁶This is not the way to repay the Lord.
You are foolish and unwise.
He is your Father and Maker.
He made you and formed you.

⁷Remember the old days.
Think of the years already passed.
Ask your father. He will tell you.
Ask your older leaders. They will inform you.
⁸The Most High God gave the nations their lands.
He divided up the human race.
He set up borders for the people.
He even numbered the Israelites.
⁹The Lord took his people as his share.

The people of Jacob were his
very own.

¹⁰He found them in a desert.
It was a windy, empty land.
He surrounded them and brought
them up.
He guarded them as those he
loved very much.
¹¹He was like an eagle building its
nest.
It flutters over its young.
It spreads its wings to catch
them.
It carries them on its feathers.
¹²The Lord alone led them.
There were no foreign gods
among them.

¹³The Lord brought them to the
heights of the land.
He fed them the fruit of the
fields.
He gave them honey from the
rocks.
He brought oil from the solid
rock.
¹⁴There were milk curds from the
cows and milk from the
sheep.
There were fat sheep and goats.
There were sheep and goats from
Bashan.
There was the best of the
wheat.
You drank the juice of grapes.

¹⁵Israel grew fat and kicked.
They were fat and full and
firm.
They left the God who made
them.
They rejected the Rock*d* who
saved them.
¹⁶They made God jealous with
foreign gods.
They made him angry with
hated idols.
¹⁷They made sacrifices to demons,*d*
not God.
They were gods they had never
known.

They were new gods from
nearby.
Your ancestors did not fear
them.
¹⁸You left God who is the Rock,
your Father.
You forgot the God who gave
you birth.

¹⁹The Lord saw this and rejected
them.
His sons and daughters had
made him angry.
²⁰He said, "I will turn away from
them.
I will see what will happen to
them.
They are evil people.
They are unfaithful children.
²¹They used things that are not
gods to make me jealous.
They used worthless idols to
make me angry.
So I will use those who are not a
nation to make them jealous.
I will use a nation that does not
understand to make them
angry.
²²My anger has started a fire.
It burns down to where the
dead are.
It will burn up the ground and its
crops.
And it will set fire to the
mountains.

²³"I will pile troubles upon them.
I will shoot my arrows at them.
²⁴They will be starved and sick.
They will be destroyed by
terrible diseases.
I will send them vicious animals
and gliding, poisonous snakes.
²⁵In the streets the sword will kill.
In their homes there will be
terror.
Young men and women will die.
So will babies and grey-haired
men.
²⁶I will scatter them as I said.
And no one will remember
them.

²⁷But I didn't want their enemy to boast.
Their enemy might misunderstand.
They might say, 'We have won! The Lord has done none of this'."

²⁸Israel has no sense.
They do not understand.
²⁹I wish they were wise and understood this.
I wish they could see what will happen to them.
³⁰One person cannot chase 1,000 people.
And two people cannot fight 10,000.
This only happens if the Lord has sold them.
Their Rock would have to give them up.
³¹The rock of these people is not like our Rock.
Our enemies agree to that.
³²Their vine comes from Sodom.
Their fields are like Gomorrah.
Their grapes are full of poison.
Their bunches of grapes are bitter.
³³Their wine is like snake poison, like the deadly poison of cobras.

³⁴"I have been saving this.
I have it locked in my storehouses.
³⁵I will punish those who do wrong. I will repay them.
In time their foot will slip.
Their day of trouble is near.
And their punishment will come quickly."

³⁶The Lord will defend his people.
He will have mercy on his servants.
He will see that their strength is gone.
He will see that nobody is left, slaves or free.
³⁷Then he will say, "Where are their gods?

Where is the rock they trusted?
³⁸Who ate the fat from their sacrifices?
Who drank the wine of their drink offering?
Let those gods come to help you! Let them protect you!

³⁹"Now you will see that I am the one God!
There is no god but me.
I send life and death.
I can hurt, and I can heal.
No one can escape from me.
⁴⁰I raise my hand toward heaven and make this promise:
As surely as I live for ever,
⁴¹I will sharpen my flashing sword.
And I will take it in my hand to judge.
I will punish my enemies.
I will pay back those who hate me.
⁴²My arrows will be covered with their blood.
My sword will eat their flesh.
The blood will flow from those who are killed and the captives.
The heads of the enemy leaders will be cut off."

⁴³Be happy, nations, with his people.
He will repay you for the blood of his servants.
He will punish his enemies.
And he will remove the sin of his land and people.

⁴⁴Moses came with Joshua son of Nun. And they spoke all the words of this song for the people to hear. ⁴⁵When Moses had finished speaking these words to all Israel, ⁴⁶he said to them: "Pay attention to all the words I have said to you today. Command your children to obey carefully everything in these teachings. ⁴⁷These should not be unimportant words for you. They mean life for you! By these words you will live a long time in the

land you are crossing the Jordan River to own."

Moses Goes Up to Mount Nebo

⁴⁸The Lord spoke to Moses again that same day. He said, ⁴⁹"Go up the Abarim Mountains. Go to Mount Nebo in the country of Moab. It is across from Jericho. Look at the land of Canaan. I am giving it to the Israelites to own. ⁵⁰You will die on that mountain that you climb. This is how your brother Aaron died on Mount Hor. ⁵¹You both sinned against me at the waters of Meribah Kadesh. That is in the Desert of Zin. You did not honour me as holy there among the Israelites. ⁵²So now you will only look at the land from far away. You will not enter the land I am giving the people of Israel."

Moses Blesses the People

33 Moses, the man of God, gave this blessing to the Israelites before he died. ²He said:

"The Lord came from Mount
        Sinai.
    He rose like the sun from
        Edom.
    He showed his greatness from
        Mount Paran.
He came with thousands of
        angels.
    He came from the southern
        mountains.
³The Lord surely loves his people.
    He takes care of all those who
        belong to him.
    They bow down at his feet.
    And they are taught by him.
⁴Moses gave us the teachings.
    They belong to the people of
        Jacob.
⁵The Lord became king of Israel.
    The leaders of the people
        gathered then.
    The tribes*d* of Israel came
        together.

⁶"Let the people of Reuben live
        and not die.
    But let the people be few."

⁷Moses said this about the people of
Judah:
    "Lord, listen to Judah's prayer.
    Bring them back to their people.
    They defend themselves with their
        hands.
    Help them fight their enemies!"

⁸Moses said this about the people of
Levi:
    "Lord, your Thummim and Urim*d*
        belong
    to Levi whom you love.
Lord, you tested him at Massah.
    You argued with him at the
        waters of Meribah.
⁹He said about his father and
        mother,
    'I don't care about them'.
He did not recognise his brothers.
    He did not know his children.
But he protected your word.
    And he guarded your
        agreement.
¹⁰He teaches your laws to the
        people of Jacob
    and your teachings to the people
        of Israel.
He burns incense*d* before you.
    And he makes whole burnt
        offerings on your altar.
¹¹Lord, make them strong.
    Be pleased with the work they
        do.
Defeat those who attack them.
    Don't let their enemies rise up
        again."

¹²Moses said this about the people
of Benjamin:
    "The Lord's loved ones will lie
        down in safety.
    The Lord protects them all day
        long.
    The ones the Lord loves rest
        with him."

¹³Moses said this about the people
of Joseph:

"May the Lord bless their land
  with the best fruits.
Send rain from heaven above.
And bring the water from the
  springs below.
14Let the sun produce the best
  fruits.
  Let each month bring its best
  fruits.
15Let the old mountains give the
  finest crops.
  And let the everlasting hills give
  the best fruits.
16Let the full earth give the best
  fruits.
  Let the Lord who lived in the
  burning bush be pleased.
May these blessings rest on the
  head of Joseph.
May they rest on the forehead
  of the one who was
  separated from his brothers.
17Joseph has the majesty of a
  firstborn*d* bull.
  He is as strong as a wild ox.
He will stab other nations,
  even those nations far away.
These are the ten thousands of
  Ephraim.
And these are the thousands of
  Manasseh."

18Moses said this about the people
of Zebulun:
"Be happy when you go out,
  Zebulun.
  And be happy in your tents,
  Issachar.
19They will call the people to the
  mountain.
  And there they will offer the
  right sacrifices.
They will do well from all that is
  in the sea.
  And they will do well from the
  treasures hidden in the sand
  on the shore."

20Moses said this about the people
of Gad:
"Praise God who gives Gad more
  land!

Gad lives there like a lion.
He tears off arms and heads.
21They chose the best land for
  themselves.
They received a large share,
  like that given to an officer.
When the leaders of the people
  gathered,
  the people of Gad did what the
  Lord said was right.
And they judged Israel fairly."

22Moses said this about the people
of Dan:
"Dan is like a lion's cub,
  who jumps out of Bashan."

23Moses said this about the people
of Naphtali:
"Naphtali enjoys the Lord's special
  kindnesses.
They are full of his blessings.
Their land goes south to Lake
  Galilee."

24Moses said this about the people
of Asher:
"Asher is the most blessed of the
  sons.
He should be his brothers'
  favourite.
Let him bathe his feet in olive
  oil.
25Your gates will have locks of iron
  and bronze.
You will be strong as long as
  you live.

26"There is no one like the God of
  Israel.
He rides through the skies to
  help you.
He rides on the clouds in his
  majesty.
27The everlasting God is your place
  of safety.
His arms will hold you up for
  ever.
He will force your enemy out
  ahead of you.
He will say, 'Destroy the
  enemy!'

²⁸The people of Israel will lie down
    in safety.
Jacob's spring is theirs alone.
Theirs is a land full of grain and
    wine.
There the skies drop their dew.
²⁹Israel, you are blessed!
No one else is like you.
You are a people saved by the
    Lord.
He is your shield and helper.
He is your glorious sword.
Your enemies will be afraid of
    you.
You will walk all over their holy
    places."

Moses Dies

34 Then Moses climbed up Mount
Nebo. He went from the plains
of Moab to the top of Mount Pisgah.
It is across from Jericho. From there
the Lord showed him all the land. He
could see from Gilead to Dan. ²He
could see all of Naphtali and the lands
of Ephraim and Manasseh. He could
see all the land of Judah as far as the
Mediterranean Sea. ³He could see the
southern desert and the whole Valley
of Jericho up to Zoar. Jericho is called
the city of palm trees. ⁴Then the Lord
said to Moses, "This is the land I
promised to Abraham, Isaac and Jacob. I said to them, 'I will give this
land to your descendants'.ᵈ I have let
you look at it, Moses. But you will not
cross over there."

⁵Then Moses, the servant of the
Lord, died there in Moab. It was as
the Lord had said. ⁶The Lord buried
Moses in Moab in the valley opposite
Beth Peor. But even today no one
knows where his grave is. ⁷Moses
was 120 years old when he died. His
eyes were not weak. And he was still
strong. ⁸The Israelites cried for Moses for 30 days. They stayed in the
plains of Moab until the time of sadness was over.

⁹Joshua son of Nun was then filled
with wisdom. Moses had put his
hands on Joshua. So the Israelites listened to Joshua. And they did what
the Lord had commanded Moses.

¹⁰There has never been another
prophetᵈ like Moses. The Lord knew
Moses face to face. ¹¹The Lord sent
Moses to do signs and miraclesᵈ in
Egypt. He did them to the king, to all
his officers and to the whole land of
Egypt. ¹²Moses had great power. He
did wonderful things for all the Israelites to see.

JOSHUA

Israel Conquers the Promised Land

God's Command to Joshua

1 Moses was the servant of the Lord. Joshua son of Nun was Moses' assistant. After Moses died, the Lord said to Joshua: [2]"My servant Moses is dead. Now you and all these people go across the Jordan River. Go into the land I am giving to the people of Israel. [3]I promised Moses I would give you this land. So I will give you every place you go in the land. [4]All the land from the desert in the south to Lebanon in the north will be yours. All the land from the great river, the Euphrates, in the east, to the Mediterranean Sea in the west will be yours. This includes the land of the Hittites. [5]Just as I was with Moses, so I will be with you. No one will be able to stop you all your life. I will not leave you. I will never leave you alone.

[6]"Joshua, be strong and brave! You must lead these people so they can take their land. This is the land I promised their fathers I would give them. [7]Be strong and brave. Be sure to obey all the teachings my servant Moses gave you. If you follow them exactly, you will be successful in everything you do. [8]Always remember what is written in the Book of the Teachings. Study it day and night. Then you will be sure to obey everything that is written there. If you do this, you will be wise and successful in everything. [9]Remember that I commanded you to be strong and brave. So don't be afraid. The Lord your God will be with you everywhere you go."

Joshua's Orders to the People

[10]So Joshua gave orders to the officers of the people. He said, [11]"Go through the camp and tell the people, 'Get your supplies ready. Three days from now you will cross the Jordan River. You will go and take the land the Lord your God is giving you'."

[12]Then Joshua spoke to the people of Reuben, Gad and the eastern half-tribe[d] of Manasseh. Joshua said, [13]"Remember what Moses, the servant of the Lord, told you. He said the Lord your God would give you rest. And he said the Lord would give you this land. [14]Now the Lord has given you this land east of the Jordan River. Your wives, your children and your animals may stay here. But your fighting men must dress for war and cross the Jordan River ahead of your brothers. You must help your brothers. [15]The Lord has given you a place to rest. He will do the same for your brothers. But you must help them until they take the land. This is the land the Lord their God is giving them. Then you may return to your own land east of the Jordan River. That is the land that Moses, the servant of the Lord, gave you."

[16]Then the people answered Joshua, "Anything you command us to do, we will do. Any place you send us, we will go. [17]Just as we fully obeyed Moses, we will obey you. We ask only that the Lord your God be with you just as he was with Moses. [18]Then, if anyone refuses to obey your commands or turns against you, he will be put to death. Just be strong and brave!"

Spies Sent to Jericho

2 Joshua son of Nun secretly sent out two spies from Acacia. Joshua

said to them, "Go and look at the land. Look closely at the city of Jericho."

So the men went to Jericho. They went to the house of a prostitute[d] and stayed there. This woman's name was Rahab.

[2]Someone told the king of Jericho, "Some men from Israel have come here tonight. They are spying out the land."

[3]So the king of Jericho sent this message to Rahab: "Bring out the men who came to you and entered your house. They have come to spy out our whole land."

[4]Now the woman had hidden the two men. She said, "They did come here. But I didn't know where they came from. [5]In the evening, when it was time to close the city gate, they left. I don't know where they went. Go quickly. Maybe you can catch them." [6](But the woman had taken the men up to the roof.[n] She had hidden them there under stalks of flax.[d] She had spread the flax out there to dry.) [7]So the king's men went out looking for the spies from Israel. They went to the places where people cross the Jordan River. The city gate was closed just after the king's men left the city.

[8]The spies were ready to sleep for the night. So Rahab went to the roof and talked to them. [9]She said, "I know the Lord has given this land to your people. You frighten us very much. Everyone living in this land is terribly afraid of you. [10]We are afraid because we have heard how the Lord helped you. We heard how he dried up the Red Sea[d] when you came out of Egypt. We heard how you destroyed Sihon and Og. They were the two Amorite kings who lived east of the Jordan. [11]When we heard this, we became very frightened. Now our men are afraid to fight you. This is because the Lord your God rules the heavens above and the earth below! [12]So now, make me a promise before the Lord. Promise that you will show kindness to my family just as I showed you kindness. Give me some proof that you will do this. [13]Promise me you will allow my family to live. Save my father, mother, brothers, sisters and all of their families from death."

[14]The men agreed. They said, "We will trade our lives for your lives. Don't tell anyone what we are doing. When the Lord gives us our land, we will be kind to you. You may trust us."

[15]The house Rahab lived in was built on the city wall. So she used a rope to let the men down through a window. [16]She said to them, "Go into the hills. The king's men will not find you there. Hide there for three days. After the king's men return, you may go on your way."

[17]The men said to her, "You must do as we say. If not, we cannot be responsible for keeping our promise. [18]You are using a red rope to help us escape. When we return to this land, you must tie it in the window through which you let us down. Bring your father, mother, brothers and all your family into your house. [19]We can keep everyone safe who stays in this house. If anyone in your house is hurt, we will be responsible. If anyone goes out of your house and is killed, it is his own fault. We cannot be responsible for him. [20]But you must not tell anyone about this agreement. If you do, we are free from it."

[21]Rahab answered, "I agree to this." So she sent them away, and they left. Then she tied the red rope in the window.

[22]The men left and went into the hills. There they stayed for three

---

roof In Bible times houses were built with flat roofs. The roof was used for drying things such as flax and fruit. It was also used as an extra room, as a place for worship and as a place to sleep in the summer.

days. The king's men looked for them all along the road. But after three days, the king's men returned to the city without finding them. 23Then the two men started back to Joshua. They left the hills and crossed the river. They went to Joshua son of Nun and told him everything that had happened to them. 24They said to Joshua, "The Lord surely has given us all of the land. All the people in that land are terribly afraid of us."

Crossing the Jordan

3 Early the next morning Joshua and all the people of Israel left Acacia. They travelled to the Jordan River and camped there before crossing it. 2After three days the officers went through the camp. 3They gave orders to the people. They said, "You will see the priests and Levites carrying the Ark*d* of God with the Lord your God. Then you should leave where you are and follow it. 4That way you will know which way to go. You have never travelled this way before. But do not follow too closely. Stay about a thousand yards behind the Ark of God."

5Then Joshua told the people, "Make yourselves holy for the Lord. Tomorrow the Lord will do amazing things among you."

6Joshua said to the priests, "Take the Ark of God. Cross over the river ahead of the people." So the priests lifted the Holy Ark and carried it ahead of the people.

7Then the Lord said to Joshua, "Today I will begin to make you a great man to all the Israelites. So the people will know I am with you just as I was with Moses. 8The priests will carry the Ark of God. Tell them this: 'Go to the edge of the Jordan River and stand in the water'."

9Then Joshua said to the people of Israel, "Come here. Listen to the words of the Lord your God. 10Here is proof that the living God is with you.

Here is proof that he will drive out the Canaanites, Hittites, Hivites, Perizzites, Girgashites, Amorites and the Jebusites. 11This is the proof: the Ark of God will go ahead of you into the Jordan River. It is the Agreement with the Lord of the whole world. 12Now choose 12 men from among you. Choose one from each of the 12 tribes*d* of Israel. 13The priests will carry the Holy Ark of the Lord, the Master of the whole world. They will carry it into the Jordan ahead of you. When they enter the water, the river will stop flowing. The water will be stopped. It will stand up in a heap as if a dam were there."

14So the priests carried the Ark of God. And the people left the place where they had camped. Then they started across the Jordan River. 15During harvest the Jordan is flooded. So the river was at its fullest. The priests who were carrying the Holy Ark came to the edge of the river. And they stepped into the water. 16Just at that moment, the water stopped flowing. It stood up in a heap a great distance away at Adam. This is a town near Zarethan. The water flowing down to the Sea of Arabah (the Dead Sea*d*) was completely cut off. So the people crossed the river near Jericho. 17The ground there became dry. The priests carried the Ark of God with the Lord to the middle of the river and stopped. They waited there while all the people of Israel walked across. They crossed the Jordan River on dry land.

Rocks to Remind the People

4 All the people finished crossing the Jordan. Then the Lord said to Joshua, 2"Choose 12 men from among the people. Choose one from each tribe.*d* 3Tell the men to get 12 large rocks from the middle of the river. Take them from where the priests stood. Carry the rocks and put them down where you stay tonight."

⁴So Joshua chose one man from each tribe. Then he called the 12 men together. ⁵He said to them, "Go out into the river where the Holy Ark*d* of the Lord your God is. Each of you should find one large rock. There will be one rock for each tribe of Israel. Carry the rock on your shoulder. ⁶They will be a sign among you. In the future your children will ask you, 'What do these rocks mean?' ⁷Tell them the Lord stopped the water from flowing in the Jordan. When the Holy Ark of the Agreement with the Lord crossed the river, the water was stopped. These rocks will help the Israelites remember this for ever."

⁸So the Israelites obeyed Joshua. They carried 12 rocks from the middle of the Jordan River. There was one rock for each of the 12 tribes of Israel. They did this the way the Lord had commanded Joshua. They carried the rocks with them. And they put them down where they made their camp. ⁹Joshua also put 12 rocks in the middle of the Jordan River. He put them where the priests had stood while carrying the Holy Ark of the Lord. These rocks are still there today.

¹⁰The Lord had commanded Joshua to tell the people what to do. It was what Moses had said Joshua must do. So the priests carrying the Holy Ark continued standing in the middle of the river until everything was done. And the people hurried across the river. ¹¹The people finished crossing the river. Then the priests carried the Holy Ark of the Lord to the other side. As they carried it, the people watched. ¹²The men from the tribes of Reuben, Gad and the eastern half-tribe of Manasseh obeyed what Moses had told them. They were prepared for war. So they crossed the river ahead of the other people. ¹³About 40,000 soldiers were prepared for war. They passed before the Lord as they marched across the river. Then they went toward the plains of Jericho to go to war.

¹⁴That day the Lord made Joshua a great man to all the Israelites. They respected Joshua all his life, just as they had respected Moses.

¹⁵Then the Lord spoke to Joshua. ¹⁶He said, "Command the priests to bring the Ark of God out of the river." ¹⁷So Joshua commanded the priests, "Come up out of the Jordan."

¹⁸So the priests carried the Ark of God with the Lord out of the river. As soon as their feet touched dry land, the water began flowing again. The river again overflowed its banks. It was just as it had been before they crossed.

¹⁹The people crossed the Jordan on the tenth day of the first month. They camped at Gilgal, east of Jericho. ²⁰They carried with them the 12 rocks taken from the Jordan. And Joshua set them up at Gilgal. ²¹Then he spoke to the Israelites. He said, "In the future your children will ask you, 'What do these rocks mean?' ²²Tell them, 'Israel crossed the Jordan River on dry land. ²³The Lord your God caused the water to stop flowing. The river was dry until the people finished crossing it. The Lord did the same thing for us at the Jordan that he did for the people at the Red Sea.*d* Remember that he stopped the water at the Red Sea so we could cross. ²⁴The Lord did this so all people would know he has great power. Then they will always respect the Lord your God'."

5 So the Lord dried up the Jordan River until the Israelites had crossed it. Now all the kings of the Amorites west of the Jordan heard about it. And the Canaanite kings living by the Mediterranean Sea heard about it. They were very scared. After that they were too afraid to face the Israelites.

The Israelites Are Circumcised

²At that time the Lord spoke to Joshua. He said, "Make knives from

flint stones. Circumcise[d] the Israelites again." [3]So Joshua made knives from flint stones. Then he circumcised the Israelites at Gibeath Haaraloth.

[4]This is why Joshua circumcised the men: after the Israelites left Egypt, all the men old enough to serve in the army died. They died in the desert on the way out of Egypt. [5]The men who had come out of Egypt had been circumcised. But many were born in the desert on the trip from Egypt. They had not been circumcised. [6]The Israelites had moved about in the desert for 40 years. During that time all the fighting men who had left Egypt had died. This was because they had not obeyed the Lord. So the Lord swore they would not see the land. This was the land he had promised their ancestors to give them. It was a land where much food grows. [7]So their sons took their places. But none of the sons born on the trip from Egypt had been circumcised. So Joshua circumcised them. [8]After all the Israelites had been circumcised, they stayed in camp until they were healed.

[9]Then the Lord said to Joshua, "As slaves in Egypt you were ashamed. But today I have removed that shame." So Joshua named that place Gilgal. And it is still named Gilgal today.

[10]The people of Israel were still camped at Gilgal on the plains of Jericho. It was there, on the evening of the fourteenth day of the month, they celebrated the Passover[d] Feast. [11]The next day after the Passover, the people ate some of the food grown on that land: bread made without yeast and roasted grain. [12]The day they ate this food, the manna[d] stopped coming. The Israelites no longer got the manna from heaven. They ate the food grown in the land of Canaan that year.

[13]Joshua was near Jericho. He looked up and saw a man standing in front of him. The man had a sword in his hand. Joshua went to him and asked, "Are you a friend or an enemy?"

[14]The man answered, "I am neither one. I have come as the commander of the Lord's army."

Then Joshua bowed face down on the ground. He asked, "Does my master have a command for me, his servant?"

[15]The commander of the Lord's army answered, "Take off your sandals. The place where you are standing is holy." So Joshua did.

The Fall of Jericho

6 Now the people of Jericho were afraid because the Israelites were near. So they closed the city gates and guarded them. No one went into the city. And no one came out.

[2]Then the Lord spoke to Joshua. He said, "Look, I have given you Jericho, its king and all its fighting men. [3]March around the city with your army once every day. Do this for six days. [4]Have seven priests carry trumpets made from horns of male sheep. Tell them to march in front of the Holy Ark.[d] On the seventh day march around the city seven times. On that day tell the priests to blow the trumpets as they march. [5]They will make one long blast on the trumpets. When you hear that sound, have all the people give a loud shout. Then the walls of the city will fall. And the people will go straight into the city."

[6]So Joshua son of Nun called the priests together. He said to them, "Carry the Ark of God with the Lord. Tell seven priests to carry trumpets and march in front of it." [7]Then Joshua ordered the people, "Now go! March around the city. The soldiers with weapons should march in front of the Ark of God with the Lord."

[8]So Joshua finished speaking to the people. Then the seven priests began marching before the Lord. They carried the seven trumpets and blew

them as they marched. The priests carrying the Ark of God with the Lord followed them. ⁹The soldiers with weapons marched in front of the priests. And armed men walked behind the Holy Ark. They were blowing their trumpets. ¹⁰But Joshua had told the people not to give a war cry. He said, "Don't shout. Don't say a word until the day I tell you. Then shout!" ¹¹So Joshua had the Holy Ark of the Lord carried around the city one time. Then they went back to camp for the night.

¹²Early the next morning Joshua got up. And the priests carried the Holy Ark of the Lord again. ¹³The seven priests carried the seven trumpets. They marched in front of the Holy Ark of the Lord, blowing their trumpets. The soldiers with weapons marched in front of them. Other soldiers walked behind the Holy Ark of the Lord. All this time the priests were blowing their trumpets. ¹⁴So on the second day they marched around the city once. Then they went back to camp. They did this every day for six days.

¹⁵On the seventh day they got up at dawn. They marched around the city seven times. They marched just as they had on the days before. But on that day they marched around the city seven times. ¹⁶The seventh time around the priests blew their trumpets. Then Joshua gave the command: "Now, shout! The Lord has given you this city! ¹⁷The city and everything in it are to be destroyed as an offering to the Lord. Only Rahab the prostitute[d] and everyone in her house should remain alive. They must not be killed. This is because Rahab hid the two spies we sent out. ¹⁸Don't take any of the things that are to be destroyed as an offering to the Lord. If you take them and bring them into our camp, then you yourselves will be destroyed. You will also bring trouble to all of Israel. ¹⁹All the silver and gold

and things made from bronze and iron belong to the Lord. They must be saved for him."

²⁰When the priests blew the trumpets, the people shouted. At the sound of the trumpets and the people's shout, the walls fell. And everyone ran straight into the city. So the Israelites defeated that city. ²¹They completely destroyed every living thing in the city. They killed men and women, young and old. They killed cattle, sheep and donkeys.

²²Joshua spoke to the two men who had spied out the land. Joshua said, "Go into the prostitute's house. Bring her out. And bring out all the people who are with her. Do this because of the promise you made to her." ²³So the two men went into the house and brought out Rahab. They also brought out her father, mother, brothers and all those with her. They put all of her family in a safe place outside the camp of Israel.

²⁴Then Israel burned the whole city and everything in it. But they did not burn the things made from silver, gold, bronze and iron. These were saved for the Lord. ²⁵Joshua saved Rahab the prostitute, her family and all who were with her. He let them live. This was because Rahab had helped the men he had sent to spy out Jericho. Rahab still lives among the Israelites today.

²⁶Then Joshua made this important promise. He said:
"Anyone who tries to rebuild this
     city of Jericho
  will be punished by a curse from
     the Lord.
The man who lays the foundation
     of this city
  will lose his oldest son.
The man who sets up the gates
  will lose his youngest son."

²⁷So the Lord was with Joshua. And Joshua became famous through all the land.

The Sin of Achan

7 But the people of Israel did not obey the Lord. There was a man from the tribe*d* of Judah named Achan. (He was the son of Carmi and grandson of Zimri, who was the son of Zerah.) Achan kept some of the things that were to be given to the Lord. So the Lord became very angry at the Israelites.

²Joshua sent some men from Jericho to Ai. (Ai was near Beth Aven, east of Bethel.) He told them, "Go to Ai and spy out the area." So the men went to spy on Ai.

³Later they came back to Joshua. They said, "There are only a few men in Ai to fight against us. So we will not need all our people to defeat them. Send 2,000 or 3,000 men to fight there. There is no need to send all of our people." ⁴So about 3,000 men went to Ai. But the people of Ai beat them badly. ⁵The people of Ai chased the Israelites. They chased them from the city gate all the way to where stones were cut from the ground. They killed about 36 Israelites as they went down the hill. When the Israelites saw this, they became very afraid.

⁶Then Joshua tore his clothes to show how upset he was. He bowed face down on the ground before the Ark*d* of the Lord. And he stayed there until evening. The leaders of Israel did the same thing. They also threw dust on their heads to show they were upset. ⁷Then Joshua said, "Lord God, you brought our people across the Jordan River. Why did you bring us this far and then let the Amorites destroy us? We should have been happy to stay on the other side of the Jordan. ⁸Lord, there is nothing I can say now. Israel has been beaten by the enemy. ⁹The Canaanites and all the other people in this country will hear about this. They will surround and kill all of us!

Then what will you do for your own great name?"

¹⁰The Lord said to Joshua, "Stand up! Why are you down on your face? ¹¹The Israelites have sinned. They have broken the agreement I commanded them to obey. They took some of the things I commanded them to destroy. They have stolen from me. They have lied. They have taken those things for themselves. ¹²That is why the Israelites cannot face their enemies. They turn away from the fight and run. I have commanded that they be destroyed. You must destroy everything I commanded you to destroy. I will not help you any more unless you do this.

¹³"Now go! Have the people make themselves holy for me. Tell them, 'Set yourselves apart to the Lord for tomorrow. The Lord, the God of Israel, says some of you are keeping things he commanded you to destroy. You will never defeat your enemies until you throw away those things.

¹⁴"Tomorrow morning you must all stand before the Lord. All the tribes will stand before him. The Lord will choose one tribe. And that tribe must stand alone before him. Then the Lord will choose one family group from that tribe. And that family group must stand alone before him. Then the Lord will choose one family from that family group. And it must stand alone before him. Then the Lord will look at that family man by man. ¹⁵The man who is keeping what should have been destroyed will himself be destroyed by fire. And everything he owns will be destroyed with him. He has broken the agreement with the Lord. He has done a disgraceful thing among the people of Israel!' "

¹⁶Early the next morning Joshua led all of Israel before the Lord. All of the tribes stood before him. And the Lord chose the tribe of Judah. ¹⁷So all the family groups of Judah stood before

the Lord. The Lord then chose the family group of Zerah. And all the families of Zerah stood before the Lord. Then the family of Zimri was chosen. [18]And Joshua told all the men in that family to come before the Lord. The Lord chose Achan son of Carmi. (Carmi was the son of Zimri. And Zimri was the son of Zerah.)

[19]Then Joshua said to Achan, "My son, you should tell the truth. Confess to the Lord, the God of Israel. Tell me what you did. Don't try to hide anything from me."

[20]Achan answered, "It is true! I have sinned against the Lord, the God of Israel. This is what I did: [21]among the things I saw was a beautiful coat from Babylonia. And I saw about two kilograms of silver and nearly a kilogram of gold. I wanted these things very much for myself. So I took them. You will find them buried in the ground under my tent. The silver is under the coat."

[22]So Joshua sent some men to the tent. They ran to the tent and found the things hidden there. The silver was under the coat. [23]The men brought them out of the tent. Then they took them to Joshua and all the Israelites. They spread them out on the ground before the Lord. [24]Then Joshua and all the people led Achan son of Zerah to the Valley of Trouble. They also took the silver, the coat and the gold. They took Achan's sons, daughters, cattle, donkeys, sheep, tent and everything he owned. [25]Joshua said, "I don't know why you caused so much trouble for us. But now the Lord will bring trouble to you." Then all the people threw stones at Achan until he died. They also killed his family with stones. Then the people burned them. [26]They piled rocks over Achan's body. And those rocks are still there today. That is why it is called the Valley of Trouble. After this the Lord was no longer angry.

Ai Is Destroyed

8 Then the Lord said to Joshua, "Don't be afraid. Don't give up. Lead all your fighting men to Ai. I will help you defeat the king of Ai. I am giving you his people, his city and his land. [2]You will do to Ai and its king what you did to Jericho and its king. Only this time you may take all the wealth. You may keep it for yourselves. Now tell some of your soldiers to set up an ambush behind the city."

[3]So Joshua led his whole army toward Ai. Then he chose 30,000 of his best fighting men. He sent these men out at night. [4]Joshua gave them these orders: "Listen carefully. You must set up an ambush behind the city. Don't go far from it. Continue to watch and be ready. [5]I and the men who are with me will march toward the city. The men in the city will come out to fight us. Then we will turn and run away from them as we did before. [6]They will chase us away from the city. They will think we are running away from them as we did before. When we run away, [7]come out from your ambush and take the city. The Lord your God will give you the power to win. [8]After you take the city, burn it. See to it! You have your orders."

[9]Then Joshua sent them to their place of ambush to wait. They went to a place between Bethel and Ai, to the west of Ai. But Joshua stayed the night with his people.

[10]Early the next morning Joshua gathered his men together. He and the older leaders of Israel led them to Ai. [11]All of the soldiers who were with Joshua marched to Ai. They stopped in front of the city and made camp north of Ai. There was a valley between them and the city. [12]Then Joshua chose about 5,000 men. He set them in ambush in the area west of the city between Bethel and Ai. [13]So the people took their positions. The main camp was north of the city. The other

men were hiding to the west. That night Joshua went down into the valley.

¹⁴Now the king of Ai saw the army of Israel. So he and his people got up early the next morning and hurried out to fight them. They went out to a place east of the city. The king did not know soldiers were waiting in ambush behind the city. ¹⁵Joshua and all the men of Israel let the army of Ai push them back. Then they ran east toward the desert. ¹⁶The men in Ai were called to chase Joshua and his men. So they left the city and went after them. ¹⁷All the men of Ai and Bethel chased the army of Israel. The city was left open. Not a man stayed to protect it.

¹⁸Then the Lord said to Joshua, "Hold your spear toward Ai. I will give you that city." So Joshua held his spear toward the city of Ai. ¹⁹The men of Israel who were in ambush saw this. They quickly came out of their hiding place and hurried toward the city. They entered the city and took control of it. Then they quickly set it on fire.

²⁰When the men of Ai looked back, they saw smoke rising from their city. At the same time the men of Israel stopped running. They turned against the men of Ai. The men of Ai could not escape in any direction. ²¹Joshua and all his men saw that the army had taken control of the city. They saw the smoke rising from it. So they stopped running and turned to fight the men of Ai. ²²The men who were in ambush also came out of the city to help with the fight. The men of Ai were caught between the armies of Israel. The Israelites fought until not one of the men of Ai was left alive. None of the enemy escaped. ²³But the king of Ai was left alive. And Joshua's men brought him to Joshua.

A Review of the Fighting

²⁴During the fighting the army of Israel chased the men of Ai into the fields and desert. So the Israelites killed all of them in the fields and desert. Then they went back to Ai and killed everyone there. ²⁵All the people of Ai died that day, 12,000 men and women. ²⁶Joshua had held his spear toward Ai. It was a sign to his people to destroy the city. And Joshua held out his spear until all the people of Ai were destroyed. ²⁷The people of Israel kept the animals for themselves. They also kept the other things the people of Ai had owned. This is what the Lord told them to do when he gave Joshua the commands.

²⁸Then Joshua burned the city of Ai. It became an empty pile of ruins. And it is still like that today. ²⁹Joshua hung the king of Ai on a tree. He left him hanging there until evening. At sunset Joshua told his men to take the king's body down from the tree. He told them to throw it down at the city gate. Then they covered it with rocks. That pile of rocks is still there today.

³⁰Then Joshua built an altar for the Lord, the God of Israel. He built it on Mount Ebal, as ³¹Moses, the Lord's servant, had commanded. Joshua built the altar as it was explained in the Book of the Teachings of Moses. The altar was made from stones that were not cut. No tool was ever used on them. The Israelites offered burnt offerings to the Lord on that altar. They also offered fellowship offerings. ³²There Joshua wrote the teachings of Moses on stones. He did this for all the people of Israel to see. ³³The older leaders, officers, judges and all the Israelites were there. They were standing around the Ark[d] of God with the Lord. They stood before the priests, the Levites who had carried the Holy Ark. Israelites and non-Israelites were all standing there. Half of the people stood in front of Mount Ebal. The other half stood in front of Mount Gerizim. This was the way the Lord's servant Moses had earlier commanded the people to be blessed.

[34]Then Joshua read all the words of the teachings. He read the blessings and the curses. He read them exactly as they were written in the Book of the Teachings. [35]All the Israelites were gathered together. All the women and children were there. All the non-Israelites living with the Israelites were there. Joshua read every command that Moses had given.

The Gibeonite Trickery

9 All the kings west of the Jordan River heard about these things. These were the kings of the Hittites, Amorites, Canaanites, Perizzites, Hivites and Jebusites. They lived in the mountains and on the western mountain slopes. They also lived along the whole Mediterranean Sea coast. [2]All these kings gathered to fight Joshua and the Israelites.

[3]The people of Gibeon heard how Joshua had defeated Jericho and Ai. [4]So they decided to trick the Israelites. They gathered old leather wine bags that were cracked and mended. They put them on the backs of their donkeys. They also put old sacks on their donkeys. [5]The men put old sandals on their feet and wore old clothes. They took some dry, mouldy bread. [6]Then they went to Joshua in the camp near Gilgal.

The men spoke to Joshua and the men of Israel. They said, "We have travelled from a faraway country. Make a peace agreement with us."

[7]The men of Israel said to these Hivites, "Perhaps you live near us. How can we make a peace agreement with you?"

[8]The Hivites said to Joshua, "We are your servants."

But Joshua asked, "Who are you? Where do you come from?"

[9]The men answered, "We are your servants. We have come from a far country. We came because we heard of the fame of the Lord your God. We heard about what he has done. We

heard about everything he did in Egypt. [10]We heard that he defeated the two kings of the Amorites. They were from the east side of the Jordan River: Sihon king of Heshbon and Og king of Bashan who was king in Ashtaroth. [11]So our older leaders and our people spoke to us. They said, 'Take food for your journey. Go and meet the Israelites. Tell them, "We are your servants. Make a peace agreement with us".'

[12]"Look at our bread. When we left home it was warm and fresh. But now it is dry and mouldy. [13]Look at our leather winebags. When we left home they were new and filled with wine. Now they are cracked and old. Look at our clothes and sandals. The long journey has almost destroyed them."

[14]The men of Israel tasted the bread. But they did not ask the Lord what to do. [15]So Joshua agreed to make peace with the Gibeonites. He agreed to let them live. The leaders of the Israelites made a promise to keep the agreement.

[16]Three days later the Israelites learned that the Gibeonites lived nearby. [17]So the Israelites went to where they lived. On the third day the Israelites came to their cities. The cities were Gibeon, Kephirah, Beeroth and Kiriath Jearim. [18]But the Israelites did not attack those cities. They had made a promise to them before the Lord, the God of Israel.

All the Israelites grumbled against the leaders who had made the agreement. [19]But the leaders answered, "We have given our promise before the Lord, the God of Israel. We cannot attack them now. [20]This is what we must do. We must let them live. We cannot hurt them, or God's anger will be against us. We would be breaking the promise we made to them. [21]So let them live. But they will cut wood and carry water for our people." So the leaders kept their promise of peace to them.

²²Joshua called for the Gibeonites. He said, "Why did you lie to us? Your land was near our camp. But you told us you were from a far country. ²³Now, you will be placed under a curse. You will be our slaves. You will have to cut wood and carry water for the people of the house of God."

²⁴The Gibeonites answered Joshua, "We lied to you because we were afraid you would kill us. We heard that God commanded his servant Moses to give you all of this land. And God told you to kill all the people who lived in the land. That is why we did this. ²⁵Now you can decide what to do with us. You can do anything to us that you think is right."

²⁶So Joshua saved their lives. He did not allow the Israelites to kill them. ²⁷But Joshua made the Gibeonites slaves to the Israelites. They cut wood and carried water for the Israelites. And they did it for the altar of the Lord—wherever he chose it to be. They are still doing this today.

The Sun Stands Still

10 At this time Adoni-Zedek was the king of Jerusalem. He heard that Joshua had defeated Ai and completely destroyed it. He learned that Joshua had done the same thing to Jericho and its king. The king also learned that the Gibeonites had made a peace agreement with Israel. And they lived very near Jerusalem. ²So Adoni-Zedek and his people were very afraid because of this. Gibeon was not a little town like Ai. It was a large city. It was as big as a city that had a king. All its men were good fighters. ³So Adoni-Zedek king of Jerusalem sent a message to Hoham king of Hebron. He also sent it to Piram king of Jarmuth, Japhia king of Lachish, and Debir king of Eglon. The king of Jerusalem begged these men, ⁴"Come with me and help me attack Gibeon. Gibeon has made a peace agreement with Joshua and the Israelites."

⁵Then these five Amorite kings joined their armies. They were the kings of Jerusalem, Hebron, Jarmuth, Lachish and Eglon. These armies went to Gibeon, surrounded it and attacked it.

⁶The Gibeonites sent a message to Joshua in his camp at Gilgal. The message said: "We are your servants. Don't let us be destroyed. Come quickly and help us! Save us! All the Amorite kings from the mountains have joined their armies. They are fighting against us."

⁷So Joshua marched out of Gilgal with his whole army. His best fighting men were with him. ⁸The Lord said to Joshua, "Don't be afraid of those armies. I will allow you to defeat them. None of them will be able to defeat you."

⁹Joshua and his army marched all night to Gibeon. So Joshua surprised them when he attacked. ¹⁰The Lord confused those armies when Israel attacked. So Israel defeated them in a great victory. They chased them from Gibeon on the road going to Beth Horon. The army of Israel killed men all the way to Azekah and Makkedah. ¹¹They chased the enemy down the road from Beth Horon to Azekah. While they were chasing them, the Lord threw large hailstones on them from the sky. Many of the enemy were killed by the hailstones. More men were killed by the hailstones than the Israelites killed with their swords.

¹²That day the Lord allowed the Israelites to defeat the Amorites. And that day Joshua stood before all the people of Israel and said to the Lord:
"Sun, stand still over Gibeon.
Moon, stand still over the Valley of Aijalon."
¹³So the sun stood still.
And the moon stopped
until the people defeated their enemies.

These words are written in the Book of Jashar.

The sun stopped in the middle of the sky. It waited to go down for a full day. [14]That has never happened at any time before that day or since. That was the day the Lord listened to a man. Truly the Lord was fighting for Israel!

[15]After this, Joshua and his army went back to the camp at Gilgal.

[16]During the fight the five kings ran away. They hid in a cave near Makkedah. [17]But someone found them hiding in the cave and told Joshua. [18]So he said, "Cover the opening to the cave with large rocks. Put some men there to guard it. [19]But don't stay there yourselves. Continue chasing the enemy. Continue attacking them from behind. Don't let them get to their cities safely. The Lord your God has given you the victory over them."

[20]So Joshua and the Israelites killed the enemy. But a few were able to get back to their strong, walled cities. [21]After the fighting, Joshua's men came back safely to him at Makkedah. No one was brave enough to say a word against the Israelites.

[22]Joshua said, "Move the rocks that are covering the opening to the cave. Bring those five kings out to me." [23]So Joshua's men brought the five kings out of the cave. They were the kings of Jerusalem, Hebron, Jarmuth, Lachish and Eglon. [24]They brought the five kings out to Joshua. He called all his men to come to that place. He said to the commanders of his army, "Come here! Put your feet on the necks of these kings." So they came close and put their feet on their necks.

[25]Then Joshua said to his men, "Be strong and brave! Don't be afraid. I will show you what the Lord will do to the enemies you will fight in the future." [26]Then Joshua killed the five kings. He hung their bodies on five trees. And he left them hanging on the trees until evening.

[27]At sunset Joshua told his men to take the bodies down from the trees. Then they threw their bodies into the same cave where they had been hiding. They covered the opening to the cave with large rocks. They are still there today.

[28]That day Joshua defeated Makkedah. He killed the king and completely destroyed all the people in that city. He killed them as an offering to the Lord. There was no one left alive. He did the same thing to the king of Makkedah as he had done to the king of Jericho.

Defeating Southern Cities

[29]Then Joshua and all the Israelites travelled from Makkedah. They went to Libnah and attacked it. [30]The Lord allowed them to defeat it and its king. They killed every person in the city. No one was left alive. And they did the same thing to that king as they had done to the king of Jericho.

[31]Then Joshua and all the Israelites left Libnah and went to Lachish. They camped around Lachish and attacked it. [32]The Lord allowed them to defeat Lachish. On the second day Joshua defeated it. The Israelites killed everyone in that city. This was the same thing they had done to Libnah. [33]During this same time Horam king of Gezer came to help Lachish. But Joshua also defeated him and his army. There was no one left alive.

[34]Then Joshua and all the Israelites went from Lachish to Eglon. They camped around Eglon and attacked it. [35]That day they captured Eglon. They killed all its people and completely destroyed everything in it as an offering to the Lord. This is the same thing they had done to Lachish.

[36]Then Joshua and the Israelites went from Eglon to Hebron and attacked it. [37]They captured it and all the little towns near it. The Israelites killed everyone in Hebron. No one was left alive there. This was the

same thing they had done to Eglon. They completely destroyed the city and all its people as an offering to the Lord.

³⁸Then Joshua and the Israelites went back to Debir and attacked it. ³⁹They captured that city, its king and all the little towns near it. They completely destroyed everyone in Debir as an offering to the Lord. No one was left alive there. Israel did to Debir and its king the same thing they had done to Libnah and its king. This was what they had done to Hebron.

⁴⁰So Joshua defeated all the kings of the cities of these areas: the mountains, southern Canaan, the western mountain slopes and the eastern mountain slopes. The Lord, the God of Israel, had told Joshua to completely destroy all the people as an offering to the Lord. So he left no one alive in those places. ⁴¹Joshua captured all the cities from Kadesh Barnea to Gaza. And he captured all the cities from Goshen to Gibeon. ⁴²He captured all these cities and their kings on one trip. He did it because the Lord, the God of Israel, was fighting for Israel. ⁴³Then Joshua and all the Israelites returned to their camp at Gilgal.

Defeating Northern Kings

11 Jabin king of Hazor heard about all that had happened. He sent messages to Jobab king of Madon, to the king of Shimron and to the king of Acshaph. ²He sent one to the kings in the northern mountains. Jabin also sent a message to the kings in the Jordan Valley south of Lake Galilee and in the western mountain slopes. He sent a message to the king of Naphoth Dor in the west. ³Jabin also sent one to the kings of the Canaanites in the east and in the west. He sent messages to the Amorites, Hittites, Perizzites and Jebusites in the mountains. Jabin also sent one to the Hivites. They lived below Mount Hermon in the area of Mizpah. ⁴So the armies of all these kings

came together. There were many fighting men, horses and chariots. It was a huge army. It looked as if there were as many men as grains of sand on the seashore.

⁵All of these kings met together at the Waters of Merom. They joined their armies together into one camp. They made plans to fight against the Israelites.

⁶Then the Lord said to Joshua, "Don't be afraid of them. At this time tomorrow I will allow you to defeat them. You will kill all of them. You will cripple their horses and burn all their chariots."

⁷So Joshua and his whole army surprised the enemy. They attacked them at the Waters of Merom. ⁸The Lord allowed Israel to defeat them. They chased them to Greater Sidon, Misrephoth Maim and the Valley of Mizpah in the east. Israel fought until none of the enemy was left alive. ⁹Joshua did what the Lord told him to do. He cut the legs of their horses and burned their chariots.

¹⁰Then Joshua went back and captured the city of Hazor. He killed the king of Hazor. (Hazor had been the leader of all the kingdoms that fought against Israel.) ¹¹Israel killed everyone in Hazor. They completely destroyed them. There was nothing left alive. Then they burned Hazor itself.

¹²Joshua captured all of these cities. He killed all of their kings. He completely destroyed everything in these cities. He did this the way Moses, the servant of the Lord, had commanded. ¹³But the Israelites did not burn any cities that were built on their hills, except Hazor. That city alone was burned by Joshua. ¹⁴The people of Israel kept for themselves everything they found in the cities. They kept all the animals they found. But they killed all the people there. They did not leave anyone alive. ¹⁵Long ago the Lord had commanded his servant Moses to do this. Then Moses had com-

manded Joshua to do it. So Joshua obeyed God. He did everything the Lord had commanded Moses.

¹⁶So Joshua defeated all the people in the land. He had control of the mountains and the area of southern Canaan. He controlled all the areas of Goshen, the western mountain slopes and the Jordan Valley. He controlled the mountains of Israel and all the hills near them. ¹⁷Joshua controlled all the land from Mount Halak near Edom to Baal Gad. Baal Gad was in the Valley of Lebanon, below Mount Hermon. Joshua captured all the kings in the land and killed them. ¹⁸He fought against them for many years. ¹⁹The people of only one city in all the land had made a peace agreement with Israel. They were the Hivites living in Gibeon. All the other cities were defeated in war. ²⁰The Lord made those people stubborn so they would fight against Israel. This way he could completely destroy them without mercy. This is what the Lord had commanded Moses to do.

²¹Now Joshua fought the Anakites^d who lived in the mountains of Hebron, Debir, Anab, Judah and Israel. And he completely destroyed them and their towns. ²²There were no Anakites left living in the land of the Israelites. Only a few Anakites were left in Gaza, Gath and Ashdod. ²³Joshua took control of all the land of Israel. This was what the Lord had told Moses to do long ago. He gave the land to Israel because he had promised it to them. Then Joshua divided the land among the tribes^d of Israel. The fighting had finally ended. And there was peace in the land.

Kings Defeated by Israel

12 The Israelites took control of the land east of the Jordan River. They now had all the land from the Arnon Ravine to Mount Hermon. And they had all the land along the eastern side of the Jordan Valley. Here are all the kings the Israelites defeated to take this land:

²Sihon was the king of the Amorites. He lived in the city of Heshbon. He ruled the land from Aroer at the Arnon Ravine to the Jabbok River. His land started in the middle of the ravine. This was their border with the Ammonites. Sihon ruled over half the land of Gilead. ³He also ruled over the eastern side of the Jordan Valley from Lake Galilee to the Dead Sea.^d And he ruled from Beth Jeshimoth south to the hills of Pisgah.

⁴Og king of Bashan was one of the last of the Rephaites.^d He ruled the land in Ashtaroth and Edrei. ⁵He ruled over Mount Hermon, Salecah and all the area of Bashan. His land ended where the people of Geshur and Maacah lived. Og also ruled half the land of Gilead. It stopped at the border of Sihon king of Heshbon.

⁶The Lord's servant Moses and the Israelites defeated all these kings. And Moses gave that land to the tribes^d of Reuben and Gad and to the eastern half-tribe of Manasseh. This land was to be their own.

⁷The Israelites also defeated kings in the land that was west of the Jordan River. Joshua led the people in this land. He gave the people this land and divided it among the 12 tribes. This was the land that was promised to them. It was between Baal Gad in the Valley of Lebanon and Mount Halak near Edom. ⁸This included the mountains, the western mountain slopes and the Jordan Valley. It also included the eastern mountain slopes, the desert and southern Canaan. This was the land where the Hittites, Amorites, Canaanites, Perizzites, Hivites and Jebusites had lived. The people of Israel defeated the king of each of the following cities: ⁹Jericho, Ai (near Bethel), ¹⁰Jerusalem, Hebron, ¹¹Jarmuth, Lachish, ¹²Eglon, Gezer, ¹³Debir, Geder, ¹⁴Hormah, Arad, ¹⁵Libnah, Adullam, ¹⁶Makkedah,

Bethel, [17]Tappuah, Hepher, [18]Aphek, Lasharon, [19]Madon, Hazor, [20]Shimron Meron, Acshaph, [21]Taanach, Megiddo, [22]Kedesh, Jokneam in Carmel, [23]Dor (in Naphoth Dor), Goyim in Gilgal, and [24]Tirzah.

The total number of kings was 31.

Land Still to Be Taken

13 When Joshua was very old, the Lord spoke to him. He said, "Joshua, you have grown old. But there is still much land for you to take. [2]You have not yet taken the land of Geshur and the land of the Philistines. [3]You have not yet taken the area from the Shihor River at the border of Egypt to Ekron in the north. That belongs to the Canaanites. You must still defeat the five Philistine leaders. They are at Gaza, Ashdod, Ashkelon, Gath and Ekron. You must also defeat the Avvites. [4]They live south of the Canaanite land. [5]You have not yet defeated the Gebalites. And there is also the area of Lebanon east of Baal Gad below Mount Hermon to Lebo Hamath.

[6]"The Sidonians are living in the hill country from Lebanon to Misrephoth Maim. But I will force out all of them ahead of the Israelites. Be sure to remember this land when you divide the land among the Israelites. Do this as I told you.

[7]"Now divide the land among the nine tribes[d] and the western half-tribe of Manasseh."

Dividing the Land

[8]The eastern half-tribe[d] of Manasseh and the tribes of Reuben and Gad had received their land. The Lord's servant Moses gave them the land east of the Jordan River. [9]Their land started at Aroer at the Arnon Ravine. It continued to the town in the middle of the ravine. And it included the whole plain from Medeba to Dibon. [10]All the towns that Sihon king of the Amorites ruled were in that land. He

ruled in the city of Heshbon. The land continued to the area where the Ammonites lived. [11]Gilead was also there. And the area where the people of Geshur and Maacah lived was in that land. All of Mount Hermon and all of Bashan as far as Salecah was included. [12]All the kingdom of Og king of Bashan was in that land. In the past he ruled in Ashtaroth and Edrei. Og was one of the last of the Rephaites.[d] In the past Moses had defeated them and had taken their land. [13]The Israelites did not force out the people of Geshur and Maacah. They still live among the Israelites today.

[14]The tribe of Levi was the only one that did not get any land. Instead, they were to be given all the burned sacrifices made to the Lord, the God of Israel. That is what the Lord had promised them.

[15]Moses had given each family group from the tribe of Reuben some land. This is the land they were given: [16]It was the land from Aroer near the Arnon Ravine to the town of Medeba. This included the whole plain and the town in the middle of the ravine. [17]The land continued to Heshbon. It included all the towns on the plain. These towns were Dibon, Bamoth Baal and Beth Baal Meon. [18]They included Jahaz, Kedemoth, Mephaath, [19]Kiriathaim, Sibmah and Zereth Shahar on the hill in the valley. [20]They also included Beth Peor, the hills of Pisgah and Beth Jeshimoth. [21]So that land included all the towns on the plain and all the area that Sihon the king of the Amorites had ruled. He ruled from the town of Heshbon. But Moses had defeated him and the leaders of the Midianites. Those leaders included Evi, Rekem, Zur, Hur and Reba. All these leaders fought together with Sihon. And they lived in that country. [22]The Israelites killed many people during the fighting. They also killed Balaam of Beor. He tried to use magic to tell the future. [23]The land given to

Reuben stopped at the shore of the Jordan River. So the land given to the family groups of Reuben included all these towns and their fields that were listed.

24This is the land Moses gave to the tribe of Gad. He gave it to all the family groups: 25he gave them the land of Jazar and all the towns of Gilead. He also gave them half the land of the Ammonites. It went as far as Aroer near Rabbah. 26It included the area from Heshbon to Ramath Mizpah and Betonim. It included the area from Mahanaim to the land of Debir. 27The land included the valley, Beth Haram, Beth Nimrah, Succoth and Zaphon. All the other land Sihon king of Heshbon had ruled was also included in it. This is the land on the east side of the Jordan River. It continued to the end of Lake Galilee. 28All this is the land Moses gave to the tribe of Gad. It included all the towns that were listed. Moses gave it to all the family groups.

29This is the land Moses had given to the eastern half-tribe of Manasseh. Half of all the family groups in the tribe of Manasseh were given this land. 30The land started at Mahanaim. It included all of Bashan and the land ruled by Og king of Bashan. It also included all the towns of Jair in Bashan. There were 60 cities in all. 31It also included half of Gilead, Ashtaroth and Edrei. (These were the cities where Og king of Bashan had ruled.) All this land had been given to the family of Makir son of Manasseh. Half of all his sons had been given this land.

32Moses had given this land to these tribes on the plains of Moab. It was across the Jordan River east of Jericho. 33But Moses had given no land to the tribe of Levi. The Lord, the God of Israel, promised that he himself would be the gift for the Levites.

14 Eleazar the priest, Joshua son of Nun and the leaders of all the tribes of Israel decided what land to give to the people. 2The Lord had commanded Moses long ago how he wanted the people to choose their land. The people of the nine-and-a-half tribes threw lots*d* to decide which land they would receive. 3Moses had already given the two-and-a-half tribes their land east of the Jordan River. But the tribe of Levi was not given any land like the others. 4The sons of Joseph had divided into two tribes — Manasseh and Ephraim. The tribe of Levi was not given any land. It was given only some towns in which to live. It was also given pastures for its animals. 5The Lord had told Moses how to give the land to the tribes of Israel. The Israelites divided the land as the Lord had commanded.

Caleb's Land

6One day some men from the tribe*d* of Judah went to Joshua at Gilgal. One of those men was Caleb son of Jephunneh the Kenizzite. He said to Joshua, "You remember what the Lord said at Kadesh Barnea. He was speaking to the prophet Moses about you and me. 7Moses, the Lord's servant, sent me to look at the land where we were going. I was 40 years old then. When I came back, I told Moses what I thought about the land. 8The other men who went with me told the people things that made them afraid. But I fully believed the Lord would allow us to take the land. 9So that day Moses promised me, 'The land where you went will become your land. Your children will own it for ever. I will give you that land because you fully believed in the Lord, my God'.

10"Now then, the Lord has kept his promise. He has kept me alive for 45 years from the time he said this to Moses. During that time we all wandered in the desert. Now here I am, 85 years old. 11I am still as strong today as I was the day Moses sent me out. I am just as ready to fight now as I was then. 12So give me the mountain country the Lord promised me that day long ago. Back then you heard that the Anakite[d] people lived there. And the cities were large and well protected. But now with the Lord helping me, I will force them out, just as the Lord said."

[13]Joshua blessed Caleb son of Jephunneh. He gave him the city of Hebron as his own. [14]And Hebron still belongs to the family of Caleb son of Jephunneh the Kenizzite. It still belongs to his people because he had faith. He obeyed the Lord, the God of Israel. [15](In the past it was called Kiriath Arba. It was named after the greatest man among the Anakites. He was named Arba.)

After this there was peace in the land.

Land for Judah

15 The land that was given to the tribe[d] of Judah was divided among all the family groups. It went all the way to the Desert of Zin in the far south, at the border of Edom.

[2]The southern border of Judah's land started at the south end of the Dead Sea.[d] [3]It went south of Scorpion Pass to Zin. From there it passed to the south of Kadesh Barnea. It continued past Hezron to Addar. From Addar it turned and went to Karka. [4]It continued to Azmon, the brook of Egypt and then to the Mediterranean Sea. This was the southern border.

[5]The eastern border was the shore of the Dead Sea. It went as far as the area where the Jordan River flowed into the sea.

The northern border started at the area where the Jordan River flowed into the Dead Sea. [6]Then it went to Beth Hoglah and continued north of Beth Arabah. It continued to the stone of Bohan. Bohan was the son of Reuben. [7]Then the northern border went through the Valley of Achor to Debir. There it turned toward the north and went to Gilgal. Gilgal is

across from the road that goes through the mountain of Adummim. It is on the south side of the ravine. The border continued along the waters of En Shemesh. It stopped at En Rogel. [8]Then it went through the Valley of Ben Hinnom. This is next to the southern side of the Jebusite city. (That city was called Jerusalem.) There the border went to the top of the hill on the west side of Hinnom Valley. This was at the northern end of the Valley of Giants. [9]From there it went to the spring of the Waters of Nephtoah. Then it went to the cities near Mount Ephron. There it turned and went toward Baalah. (Baalah is also called Kiriath Jearim.) [10]At Baalah the border turned west and went toward Mount Edom. It continued along the north side of Mount Jearim (also called Kesalon) and came to Beth Shemesh. From there it went past Timnah. [11]Then it went to the hill north of Ekron. From there it turned toward Shikkeron and went past Mount Baalah. It continued on to Jabneel and ended at the sea.

[12]The Mediterranean Sea was the western border. Inside these borders lived the family groups of Judah.

[13]The Lord had commanded Joshua to give Caleb son of Jephunneh part of the land in Judah. So he gave Caleb the land God had commanded. He gave him the town of Kiriath Arba, also called Hebron. (Arba was the father of Anak.[d]) [14]Caleb forced out the three Anakite families living in Hebron. Those families were Sheshai, Ahiman and Talmai. They were descendants[d] of Anak. [15]Then he fought against the people living in Debir. (In the past Debir had been called Kiriath Sepher.) [16]Caleb said, "I want a man to attack and capture Kiriath Sepher. I will give him Acsah, my daughter, as a wife." [17]Othniel son of Kenaz defeated the city. So Caleb gave his daughter Acsah to Othniel to be his wife. [18]Acsah wanted Othniel

to ask her father Caleb for more land.

So Acsah went to her father. When she got off her donkey, Caleb asked her, "What do you want?"

19Acsah answered, "I would like a special favour. The land you gave me is very dry. So also give me land with springs of water on it."

So Caleb gave her land with springs of water on the upper and lower part of it.

20The tribe of Judah got the land God had promised them. Each family group got part of the land.

21The tribe of Judah got all the towns in the southern part of Canaan. These towns were near the border of Edom. Here is a list of the towns: Kabzeel, Eder, Jagur, 22Kinah, Dimonah, Adadah, 23Kedesh, Hazor and Ithnan; 24Ziph, Telem, Bealoth, 25Hazor Hadattah and Kerioth Hezron (also called Hazor); 26Amam, Shema, Moladah, 27Hazar Gaddah, Heshmon and Beth Pelet; 28Hazar Shual, Beersheba, Biziothiah, 29Baalah, Iim, Ezem, 30Eltolad, Kesil and Hormah; 31Ziklag, Madmannah, Sansannah, 32Lebaoth, Shilhim, Ain and Rimmon. There were 29 towns and all their fields.

33The tribe of Judah got these towns in the western mountain slopes: Eshtaol, Zorah, Ashnah, 34Zanoah, En Gannim, Tappuah and Enam; 35Jarmuth, Adullam, Socoh, Azekah, 36Shaaraim, Adithaim and Gederah (also called Gederothaim). There were 14 towns and all their fields.

37Judah was also given these towns in the western mountain slopes: Zenan, Hadashah, Migdal Gad, 38Dilean, Mizpah, Joktheel, 39Lachish, Bozkath and Eglon; 40Cabbon, Lahmas, Kitlish, 41Gederoth, Beth Dagon, Naamah and Makkedah. There were 16 towns and all their fields.

42Judah was also given these towns in the western mountain slopes: Libnah, Ether, Ashan, 43Iphtah, Ashnah, Nezib, 44Keilah, Aczib and Mareshah. There were nine towns and all their fields.

45The tribe of Judah also got the town of Ekron and all the small towns and fields near it. 46They also got the area west of Ekron and all the fields and towns near Ashdod. 47Ashdod and all the small towns around it were part of the land of Judah. They also got the fields and towns around Gaza. Their land continued to the brook of Egypt. And it went on along the coast of the Mediterranean Sea.

48The tribe of Judah was also given these towns in the mountains: Shamir, Jattir, Socoh, 49Dannah and Kiriath Sannah (also called Debir); 50Anab, Eshtemoh, Anim, 51Goshen, Holon and Giloh. There were 11 towns and all their fields.

52They were also given these towns in the mountains: Arab, Dumah, Eshan, 53Janim, Beth Tappuah and Aphekah; 54Humtah, Kiriath Arba (also called Hebron) and Zior. There were nine towns and all their fields.

55Judah was also given these towns in the mountains: Maon, Carmel, Ziph, Juttah, 56Jezreel, Jokdeam, Zanoah, 57Kain, Gibeah and Timnah. There were ten towns and all their fields.

58They were also given these towns in the mountains: Halhul, Beth Zur, Gedor, 59Maarath, Beth Anoth and Eltekon. There were six towns and all their fields.

60The people of Judah were also given the two towns of Rabbah and Kiriath Baal (also called Kiriath Jearim).

61Judah was given towns in the desert. Here are those towns: Beth Arabah, Middin, Secacah, 62Nibshan, the City of Salt and En Gedi. There were six towns and all their fields.

63The army of Judah was not able to force out the Jebusites living in Jerusalem. So the Jebusites still live among the people of Judah in Jerusalem to this day.

Land for Ephraim and Manasseh

16 This is the land the tribe*d* of Joseph received. It started at the Jordan River near Jericho. It continued to the waters of Jericho, just east of the city. The border went up from Jericho to the mountains of Bethel. ²Then it continued from Bethel (also called Luz) to the Arkite border at Ataroth. ³From there it went west to the border of the Japhletites. It continued to the area of the Lower Beth Horon. Then it went to Gezer and ended at the sea. ⁴So Manasseh and Ephraim received their land. They were sons of Joseph.

⁵This is the land that was given to the family groups of Ephraim: Their border started at Ataroth Addar in the east. It went to Upper Beth Horon ⁶and then to the sea. From Micmethath it turned eastwards toward Taanath Shiloh and continued eastwards to Janoah. ⁷Then it went down from Janoah to Ataroth and to Naarah. It continued until it touched Jericho and stopped at the Jordan River. ⁸The border went from Tappuah west to Kanah Ravine and went to the sea. This is all the land that was given to the Ephraimites. Each family group in the tribe got a part of this land. ⁹Many of the border towns of Ephraim were actually within Manasseh's borders. But the people of Ephraim got those towns and their fields. ¹⁰The Ephraimites could not force the Canaanites to leave Gezer. So the Canaanites still live among the Ephraimites today. But they became slaves of the Ephraimites.

17 Then land was given to the tribe of Manasseh. He was Joseph's first son. Manasseh's first son was Makir, the father of Gilead. Makir was a great soldier. So the lands of Gilead and Bashan were given to his family. ²Land was also given to the other family groups of Manasseh. They were Abiezer, Helek, Asriel, Shechem, Hepher and Shemida. These were all the other sons of Manasseh son of Joseph.

³Zelophehad was the son of Hepher. Hepher was the son of Gilead. Gilead was the son of Makir, and Makir was the son of Manasseh. But Zelophehad had no sons. He had five daughters. The daughters were named Mahlah, Noah, Hoglah, Milcah and Tirzah. ⁴The daughters went to Eleazar the priest. They also went to Joshua son of Nun and all the leaders. They said, "The Lord told Moses to give us land like the men received." So Eleazar obeyed the Lord and gave the daughters some land. These daughters received land just as the brothers of their father did. ⁵So the tribe of Manasseh had ten sections of land west of the Jordan River. They also had two more sections, Gilead and Bashan. These sections were on the other side of the Jordan River. ⁶The daughters of Manasseh got land just as the sons did. Gilead was given to the rest of the families of Manasseh.

⁷The lands of Manasseh were in the area between Asher and Micmethath. This is near Shechem. The border went south to the En Tappuah area. ⁸The land of Tappuah belonged to Manasseh. But the town of Tappuah did not. It was along the border of Manasseh's land and belonged to the sons of Ephraim. ⁹The border of Manasseh continued south to Kanah Ravine. The cities in this area of Manasseh belonged to Ephraim. Manasseh's border was on the north side of the ravine and went to the sea. ¹⁰The land to the south belonged to Ephraim. And the land to the north belonged to Manasseh. The Mediterranean Sea was the western border. The border touched Asher's land on the north. And it touched Issachar's land on the east.

¹¹In the areas of Issachar and Asher, the people of Manasseh owned

Beth Shan and its small towns. They also owned Ibleam and its small towns. And they owned all the people who lived in Dor and its small towns. They owned the people in Naphoth Dor and its small towns. And they owned all the people who lived in Taanach and its small towns. Manasseh also owned the people in Megiddo and its small towns. ¹²Manasseh was not able to defeat those cities. So the Canaanites continued to live there. ¹³But the Israelites grew strong. When this happened, they forced the Canaanites to work for them. But they did not force them to leave the land.

¹⁴The people from the tribes of Joseph spoke to Joshua. They said, "You gave us only one area of land. But we are many people. Why did you give us only one part of all the land the Lord gave his people?"

¹⁵And Joshua answered them, "You have many people. Go up to the forest. Make a place for yourselves to live there. This is in the land of the Perizzites and the Rephaites.ᵈ The mountain country of Ephraim is too small for you."

¹⁶The people of Joseph said, "It is true. The mountain country of Ephraim is not enough for us. But the land where the Canaanites live is dangerous. They are skilled fighters. They have powerful weapons in Beth Shan and all the small towns in that area. And they are also in the Valley of Jezreel."

¹⁷Then Joshua spoke to the people of Joseph — to Ephraim and to Manasseh. He said, "But there are many of you. And you have great power. You should be given more than one share of land. ¹⁸You also will have the mountain country. It is a forest. But you can cut down the trees and make it a good place to live. And you will own all of it. You will force the Canaanites to leave the land. You can defeat them even though they have powerful weapons and are strong."

The Rest of the Land Divided

18 All of the Israelites gathered together at Shiloh. There they set up the Meeting Tent.ᵈ The Israelites controlled that country. They had defeated all the enemies there. ²But there were still seven tribesᵈ of Israel that had not yet received the land God had promised them.

³So Joshua said to the Israelites: "Why do you wait so long to take your land? The Lord, the God of your fathers, has given this land to you. ⁴So each tribe should choose three men. I will send them out to study the land. They will describe in writing the land their tribe wants as its share. Then they will come back to me. ⁵They will divide the land into seven parts. The people of Judah will keep their land in the south. The people of Joseph will keep their land in the north. ⁶But you should divide the land into seven parts. Describe the seven parts in writing. Then bring what you have written to me. We will let the Lord our God decide which tribe will get which land. ⁷But the Levites do not get any part of these lands. They are priests, and their work is to serve the Lord. Gad, Reuben and the eastern half-tribe of Manasseh have received the land promised to them. They are on the east side of the Jordan River. Moses, the servant of the Lord, gave it to them."

⁸So the men who were chosen started into the land. Their plan was to describe it in writing and take it back to Joshua. Joshua told them, "Go and study the land. Describe it in writing. Then come back to me. Then I will ask the Lord to choose the land you should get. We will do this here in Shiloh." ⁹So the men left and went into the land. They studied it and described it in writing for Joshua. They studied each town. They saw that the land had seven parts. They described it in writing and then came back to

Joshua. He was still at the camp at Shiloh. ¹⁰Then Joshua asked the Lord to help. He threw lots*d* to choose the lands that should be given to each tribe.

Land for Benjamin

¹¹The first part of the land was given to the tribe*d* of Benjamin. Each family group in the tribe of Benjamin received some land. They were given the land between the land of Judah and the land of Joseph. This is the land chosen for Benjamin:

¹²The northern border started at the Jordan River. It went along the northern edge of Jericho. Then it went west into the mountains. That boundary continued until it was just east of Beth Aven. ¹³From there it went south to Luz (also called Bethel). Then it went down to Ataroth Addar. Ataroth Addar is on the hill south of Lower Beth Horon.

¹⁴There is a hill to the south of Beth Horon. At this hill the border turned and went south near the western side of the hill. It went to Kiriath Baal (also called Kiriath Jearim). This is a town where people of Judah lived. It was the western border.

¹⁵The southern border started near Kiriath Jearim and went to the Waters of Nephtoah. ¹⁶Then it went down to the bottom of the hill. This was near the Valley of Ben Hinnom. It was the north side of the Valley of Rephaim. The border continued down the Hinnom Valley just south of the Jebusite city to En Rogel. ¹⁷There it turned north and went to En Shemesh. It continued to Geliloth near the Adummim Pass in the mountains. Then it went down to the great Stone of Bohan. Bohan was the son of Reuben. ¹⁸The border continued to the northern part of Beth Arabah. Then it went down into the Jordan Valley. ¹⁹From there it went to the northern part of Beth Hoglah. It ended at the north shore of the Dead Sea.*d* This is where the Jordan River flows into the sea. This was the southern border.

²⁰The Jordan River was the border on the eastern side. So this was the land given to the family groups of Benjamin. These were the borders on all sides.

²¹Each family group of Benjamin received some of this land. And these are the cities they owned: Jericho, Beth Hoglah, Emek Keziz, ²²Beth Arabah, Zemaraim and Bethel; ²³Avvim, Parah, Ophrah, ²⁴Kephar Ammoni, Ophni and Geba. There were 12 towns and all their villages.

²⁵The tribe of Benjamin also owned Gibeon, Ramah and Beeroth. ²⁶They owned Mizpah, Kephirah, Mozah, ²⁷Rekem, Irpeel and Taralah. ²⁸They also owned Zelah, Haeleph, the Jebusite city (Jerusalem), Gibeah and Kiriath. There were 14 towns and all their villages. All these areas are the lands the tribe of Benjamin was given.

Land for Simeon

19 The second part of the land was given to the tribe*d* of Simeon. Each family group received some of the land. It was inside the area of Judah. ²They received Beersheba (also called Sheba), Moladah, ³Hazar Shual, Balah, Ezem, ⁴Eltolad, Bethul and Hormah. ⁵They also received Ziklag, Beth Marcaboth, Hazar Susah, ⁶Beth Lebaoth and Sharuhen. There were 13 towns and all their fields.

⁷They also received the towns of Ain, Rimmon, Ether and Ashan. There were four towns and all their fields. ⁸They also received all the very small areas with people living in them as far as Baalath Beer. (This is the same as Ramah in southern Canaan.) So these were the lands given to the tribe of Simeon. Each family group received some of the land. ⁹The land of the Simeonites was taken from part of the land of Judah. Judah had much more land than they needed. So the Simeonites received part of their land.

Land for Zebulun

[10]The third part of the land was given to the tribe[d] of Zebulun. Each family group of Zebulun received some of the land. The border of Zebulun went as far as Sarid. [11]Then it went west to Maralah and came near Dabbesheth. Then it went near Jokneam. [12]Then it turned to the east. It went from Sarid to the area of Kisloth Tabor. From there it went on to Daberath and to Japhia. [13]It continued eastwards to Gath Hepher and Eth Kazin. Then it ended at Rimmon. Then the border turned and went toward Neah. [14]At Neah it turned again and went to the north. It went to Hannathon and continued to the Valley of Iphtah El. [15]Inside this border were the cities of Kattath, Nahalal, Shimron, Idalah and Bethlehem. There were 12 towns and all their fields.

[16]So these are the towns and the areas that were given to Zebulun. Each family group received some of the land.

Land for Issachar

[17]The fourth part of the land was given to the tribe[d] of Issachar. Each family group of Issachar received some of the land. [18]Their land included Jezreel, Kesulloth, Shunem, [19]Hapharaim, Shion and Anaharath; [20]Rabbith, Kishion, Ebez, [21]Remeth, En Gannim, En Haddah and Beth Pazzez.

[22]The border of their land touched the area called Tabor, Shahazumah and Beth Shemesh. It stopped at the Jordan River. There were 16 towns and their fields.

[23]These cities and towns were part of the land that was given to the tribe of Issachar. Each family group received part of this land.

Land for Asher

[24]The fifth part of the land was given to the tribe[d] of Asher. Each family group of Asher received some of the land. [25]Their land included Helkath, Hali, Beten, Acshaph, [26]Allammelech, Amad and Mishal.

The western border touched Mount Carmel and Shihor Libnath. [27]Then it turned toward the east. It went to Beth Dagon. It touched Zebulun and the Valley of Iphtah El. Then it went north of Beth Emek and Neiel. It passed north to Cabul. [28]Then it went to Abdon, Rehob, Hammon and Kanah. It continued to Greater Sidon. [29]Then the border went back south toward Ramah. It continued to the strong, walled city of Tyre. Then it turned and went toward Hosah. It ended at the sea. This was in the area of Aczib, [30]Ummah, Aphek and Rehob. There were 22 towns and their fields.

[31]These cities and their fields were part of the land that was given to the tribe of Asher. Each family group in that tribe received some of this land.

Land for Naphtali

[32]The sixth part of the land was given to the tribe[d] of Naphtali. Each family group of Naphtali received some of the land. [33]The border of their land started at the large tree in the area of Zaanannim. This is near Heleph. Then it went through Adami Nekeb and Jabneel. It continued to the area of Lakkum and ended at the Jordan River. [34]Then it went to the west through Aznoth Tabor. It stopped at Hukkok. It went to the area of Zebulun on the south. And it went to the area of Asher on the west. It went to Judah, at the Jordan River, on the east. [35]There were some strong, walled cities inside these borders. Those cities were Ziddim, Zer, Hammath, Rakkath and Kinnereth; [36]Adamah, Ramah, Hazor, [37]Kedesh, Edrei and En Hazor; [38]Iron, Migdal El, Horem, Beth Anath and Beth Shemesh. There were 19 towns and all their fields.

[39]The cities and the towns around them were in the land that was given

to the tribe of Naphtali. Each family group in that tribe got some of this land.

Land for Dan

40The seventh part of the land was given to the tribe*d* of Dan. Each family group of Dan received some of the land. 41Their land included Zorah, Eshtaol, Ir Shemesh, 42Shaalabbin, Aijalon and Ithlah; 43Elon, Timnah, Ekron, 44Eltekeh, Gibbethon, Baalath, 45Jehud, Bene Berak and Gath Rimmon; 46Me Jarkon, Rakkon and the area near Joppa.

47(But the Danites had trouble taking their land. There were strong enemies there. And the Danites could not easily defeat them. So the Danites went and fought against Leshem. They defeated Leshem and killed the people who lived there. So the Danites lived in the town of Leshem. They changed its name to Dan because he was the father of their tribe.) 48All of these cities and towns were given to the tribe of Dan. Each family group got part of this land.

Land for Joshua

49So the Israelite leaders finished dividing the land and giving it to the different tribes.*d* After they had finished, all the Israelites decided to give Joshua son of Nun some land, too. This was land that had been promised to him. 50The Lord had commanded that he be given this land. So they gave Joshua the town of Timnath Serah in the mountains of Ephraim. This was the town that Joshua told them he wanted. So he built up the town and lived there.

51So all of these lands were given to the different tribes of Israel. Eleazar the priest, Joshua son of Nun and the leaders of each tribe worked together. They divided up the land while they were at Shiloh. They met before the Lord at the entrance to the Meet-

ing Tent*d* to do this. Now they had finished dividing the land.

Cities of Safety

20 Then the Lord said to Joshua: 2"Tell the Israelites to choose the special cities of safety.*d* This is what I had Moses command you to do. 3A person might kill someone accidentally and without meaning to kill him. He may go to a city of safety to hide. There he will be safe from the relative who has the duty of punishing a murderer.

4"This is what he must do. When he runs to one of those cities, he must stop at the entrance gate. He must stand there and tell the leaders of the people what has happened. Then they will allow him to enter the city. They will give him a place to live among them. 5But the one who is chasing him might follow him to that city. If this happens, the leaders of the city must not give him up. They must protect the person who came to them for safety. They must protect him because he killed that person accidentally. He was not angry and did not decide ahead of time to kill the person. 6He should stay in the city until he has been judged by the court there. And he should stay until the high priest dies. Then he may go back to his own home in the town from which he ran away."

7So the Israelites chose some cities to be cities of safety. These cities were: Kedesh in Galilee in the mountains of Naphtali; Shechem in the mountains of Ephraim; Kiriath Arba (also called Hebron) in the mountains of Judah; 8Bezer on the east side of the Jordan River near Jericho in the desert in the land of Reuben; Ramoth in Gilead in the land of Gad; and Golan in Bashan in the land of Manasseh. 9Any Israelite or anyone living among them who killed someone accidentally was included. He was to be allowed to run to one of these cities of safety. Then he could be safe there and would not be killed by the relative who had the duty of punishing a murderer. He would be judged by the court in that city.

Towns for the Levites

21 The heads of the Levite families went to talk to Eleazar the priest. They also talked to Joshua son of Nun and to the heads of the families of all the tribes^d of Israel. ²This happened at the town of Shiloh in the land of Canaan. The heads of the Levite families said to them, "The Lord commanded Moses that you give us towns where we may live. And he commanded that you give us pastures." ³So the Israelites obeyed this commandment of the Lord. They gave the Levite people these towns and pastures: ⁴The Kohath family groups were part of the tribe of Levi. Some of the Levites in the Kohath family groups were from the family of Aaron the priest. To these Levites were given 13 towns. These towns were in the areas that belonged to Judah, Simeon and Benjamin. ⁵The other family groups of Kohath were given ten towns. These ten towns were in the areas of Ephraim, Dan and West Manasseh.

⁶The people from the Gershon groups were given 13 towns. They were in the land that belonged to Issachar, Asher, Naphtali and the eastern half-tribe of Manasseh in Bashan.

⁷The family groups of Merari were given 12 towns. These 12 towns were in the area that belonged to Reuben, Gad and Zebulun.

⁸So the Israelites gave the Levites these towns and the pastures around them. They did this to obey the commandment that the Lord had given Moses.

⁹These are the names of the towns that came from the lands of Judah and Simeon. ¹⁰The first choice of towns was given to the Kohath family groups of the Levites. ¹¹They gave them Kiri-

ath Arba (also called Hebron) and all its pastures. This was in the mountains of Judah. (Arba was the father of Anak.^d) ¹²But the fields and the small towns around the city of Kiriath Arba had been given to Caleb son of Jephunneh.

¹³So they gave the city of Hebron to the descendants^d of Aaron. (Hebron was a city of safety.^d) They also gave them these towns: Libnah, ¹⁴Jattir, Eshtemoa, ¹⁵Holon, Debir, ¹⁶Ain, Juttah and Beth Shemesh. They also gave them all the pastures that were around these towns. There were nine towns given to these two groups.

¹⁷They also gave the people of Aaron cities that belonged to the tribe of Benjamin. These cities were Gibeon, Geba, ¹⁸Anathoth and Almon. They gave them these four towns and all the pastures around them.

¹⁹So these towns were given to the priests. These priests were from the family of Aaron. The total number of towns with their pastures was 13.

²⁰The other Kohathite family groups of the Levites were given these towns from the tribe of Ephraim: ²¹they gave them the city of Shechem from the mountains of Ephraim. (Shechem was a city of safety.) They also gave them Gezer, ²²Kibzaim and Beth Horon. There were four towns and their pastures.

²³The tribe of Dan gave them Eltekeh, Gibbethon, ²⁴Aijalon and Gath Rimmon. There were four towns and their pastures.

²⁵The western half-tribe of Manasseh gave them Taanach and Gath Rimmon. They were also given all the pastures around these two towns.

²⁶So this was ten more towns and all the pastures around the towns. These were given to the rest of the Kohathite family groups.

²⁷The Gershonite family groups of the Levite tribe were given these towns: The eastern half-tribe of Manasseh gave them Golan in Bashan.

(Golan was a city of safety.) Manasseh also gave them Be Eshtarah. All the pastures around these two towns were also given to the Gershonites.

28The tribe of Issachar gave them Kishion, Daberath, 29Jarmuth and En Gannim. Issachar also gave them all the pastures around these four towns.

30The tribe of Asher gave them Mishal, Abdon, 31Helkath and Rehob. All the pastures around these four towns were also given to them.

32The tribe of Naphtali gave them Kedesh in Galilee. (Kedesh was a city of safety.) Naphtali also gave them Hammoth Dor and Kartan. All the pastures around these two towns were also given to the Gershonites.

33So the Gershonite family groups received 13 towns. They also received all the pastures around these towns.

34The Merarite family groups (the rest of the Levites) were given these towns: the tribe of Zebulun gave them Jokneam, Kartah, 35Dimnah and Nahalal. All the pastures around these four towns were also given to the Merarites.

36The tribe of Reuben gave them Bezer, Jahaz, 37Kedemoth and Mephaath. All the pastures around these four towns were also given to the Merarites.

38The tribe of Gad gave them Ramoth in Gilead. (Ramoth was a city of safety.) They also gave them Mahanaim, 39Heshbon and Jazer. Gad also gave them all the pastures around these four towns.

40So the total number of towns given to the Merarite family groups was 12.

41A total of 48 towns with their pastures were given to the Levites. All these towns were in the land controlled by the Israelites. 42Each town had pastures around it.

43So the Lord kept the promise he had made to the Israelites. He gave the people all the land he had prom-ised. The people took the land and lived there. 44The Lord allowed them to have peace on all sides of their land. This is what he had promised to their people who lived long ago. None of their enemies defeated them. The Lord allowed the Israelites to defeat every enemy. 45He kept every promise he had made to the Israelites. No promises failed. Each one came true.

Three Tribes Go Home

22 Then Joshua called a meeting of all the people from the tribes of Reuben, Gad and the eastern half-tribe of Manasseh. 2He said to them, "You have obeyed everything Moses told you to do. He was a servant of the Lord. And also, you have obeyed all my commands. 3All this time you have supported all the other Israelites. You have been careful to obey all the commands the Lord your God gave you. 4The Lord your God promised to give the Israelites peace. Now he has kept his promise. Now you may go back to your homes. You may go to the land that Moses, the Lord's servant, gave you. It is the land on the east side of the Jordan River. 5But continue to obey the teachings Moses gave you. That law is to love the Lord your God and obey his commands. Continue to follow him and serve him the very best you can."

6Then Joshua said goodbye to them, and they left. They went away to their homes. 7Moses had given the land of Bashan to the eastern half-tribe of Manasseh. Joshua gave land on the west side of the Jordan River to the western half-tribe of Manasseh. And he sent them to their homes. He blessed them. 8He said, "Go back to your homes and your riches. You have many animals, silver, gold, bronze and iron. And you have many beautiful clothes. Also, you have taken many things from your enemies. You should divide these among yourselves."

9So the people from the tribes of

Reuben, Gad and the eastern half-tribe of Manasseh left the other Israelites. They left Shiloh in Canaan and went back towards Gilead. This was their own land. Moses gave it to them as the Lord had commanded.

¹⁰The people of Reuben, Gad and the eastern half-tribe of Manasseh travelled to Geliloth. This was near the Jordan River in the land of Canaan. There they built a beautiful altar. ¹¹But the other Israelites still at Shiloh heard about the altar these three tribes had built. They heard that the altar was at the border of Canaan at Geliloth. It was near the Jordan River on Israel's side. ¹²All the Israelites became very angry at these three tribes. They met together and decided to fight them.

¹³So the Israelites sent some men to talk to the people of Reuben, Gad and the eastern half-tribe of Manasseh. The leader of these men was Phinehas son of Eleazar the priest. ¹⁴They also sent one leader of each of the ten tribes at Shiloh. Each of these men was a leader of his family group of Israelites.

¹⁵So these men went to Gilead. They went to talk to the people of Reuben, Gad and the eastern half-tribe of Manasseh. The men said to them: ¹⁶"All the Israelites ask you: 'Why did you turn against the God of Israel? Why did you build an altar for yourselves? You know that this is against God's law. ¹⁷Remember what happened at Peor? We still suffer today because of that sin. Because of it, God caused many of the Israelites to become very sick. ¹⁸And now are you doing the same thing? Are you turning against the Lord? Will you refuse to follow the Lord?

" 'If you don't stop what you're doing, the Lord will be angry with everyone in Israel. ¹⁹Your land may not be a good enough place to worship. If not, come over into our land. The Lord's Tent is in our land. You may

have some of our land and live there. But don't turn against the Lord by building another altar. We already have the altar of the Lord our God. ²⁰Remember Achan son of Zerah. He refused to obey the command about what must be completely destroyed. That one man broke God's law, but all the Israelites were punished. Achan died because of his sin. But many other people also died'."

²¹The people from Reuben, Gad and the eastern half-tribe of Manasseh answered them. They said: ²²"The Lord is our God! Again we say that the Lord is our God! God knows why we did this. We want you to know also. You can judge what we did. If you believe we have done something wrong, you may kill us. ²³If we broke God's law, we ask the Lord himself to punish us. Do you think we built this altar to offer burnt offerings? And did we build it to use for offerings of grain and fellowship? ²⁴No! We did not build it for that reason. We feared that some day your people would not accept us as part of your nation. Then they might say, 'You cannot worship the Lord,' the God of Israel. ²⁵God gave you land on the other side of the Jordan River. It separates us from you people of Reuben and Gad. You cannot worship the Lord'. So we feared that your children might make our children stop worshipping the Lord.

²⁶"So we decided to build this altar. But we did not plan to use it for burning sacrifices and making offerings. ²⁷It was really to show our people that we worship the same God as you. This altar is proof to you and us. And it will prove to all our children who will come after us that we worship the Lord. We give our whole burnt offerings, grain and fellowship offerings to the Lord. This was to keep your children from saying that our children could not worship the Lord. ²⁸"In the future your children might

say that we do not belong to Israel. Then our children could say, 'Look! Our fathers who lived before us made an altar. It is exactly like the Lord's altar. We do not use it for sacrifices. This altar shows that we are part of Israel'.

²⁹"Truly, we don't want to be against the Lord. We don't want to stop following him. We know the only true altar is the one in front of the Holy Tent.^d It belongs to the Lord our God."

³⁰Phinehas the priest and the ten leaders heard these things. They listened to the people of Reuben, Gad and Manasseh. And they were pleased. ³¹So Phinehas, son of Eleazar the priest, spoke. He said, "Now we know the Lord is with us. And we know you didn't turn against him. We're happy that the Israelites will not be punished by the Lord."

³²Then Phinehas and the leaders went home. They left the people of Reuben and Gad in Gilead. And they went back to Canaan. There they told the Israelites what had happened. ³³They were also pleased. They were happy and thanked God. And they decided not to fight against the people of Reuben and Gad. They decided not to destroy those lands.

³⁴And the people of Reuben and Gad gave the altar a name. They called it Proof that We Believe that the Lord Is God.

Joshua Says Goodbye

23 The Lord gave Israel peace from their enemies around them. He made Israel safe. Many years passed, and Joshua became very old. ²So he called a meeting of all the older leaders, heads of families, judges and officers of the Israelites. He said, "I am now very old. ³You have seen what the Lord has done to our enemies. He did it to help us. The Lord your God fought for you. ⁴Remember that your people have been given their land. It's the land between the Jordan River and the Mediterranean Sea in the west. It's the land I promised to give you. But you don't control that land yet. ⁵The Lord your God will make the people living there leave. You will enter the land. And the Lord will force them out ahead of you. He has promised you this.

⁶"Be strong. You must be careful to obey everything the Lord has commanded. Obey everything written in the Book of the Teachings of Moses. Do exactly as it says. ⁷There are still some people living among us who are not Israelites. They worship their own gods. Don't become friends with them. Don't serve or worship their gods. ⁸You must continue to follow the Lord your God. You have done this in the past. And you must continue to do it.

⁹"The Lord has helped you defeat many great and powerful nations. He has forced them to leave ahead of you. No nation has been able to defeat you. ¹⁰With his help, one Israelite could defeat a thousand enemies. This is because the Lord your God fights for you, as he promised to do. ¹¹So you must be careful to love the Lord your God.

¹²"Don't turn away from the way of the Lord. Don't become friends with these people who are not part of Israel. Don't marry them. If you do become their friends, ¹³the Lord your God will not help you defeat your enemies. So they will become like traps for you. They will cause you pain like a whip on your back and thorns in your eyes. And none of you will be left in this good land the Lord your God has given you.

¹⁴"It's almost time for me to die. You know and fully believe that the Lord has done great things for you. You know that he has not failed in any of his promises. He has kept every promise he has given. ¹⁵Every good

promise that the Lord your God made has come true. And in the same way, his other promises will come true. He promised that evil will come to you. He will destroy you from this good land that he gave you. [16]This will happen if you don't keep your agreement with the Lord your God. You will lose this land if you go and serve other gods. You must not worship them. If you do, the Lord will become very angry with you. Then none of you will be left in this good land he has given you."

24 Then all the tribes[d] of Israel met together at Shechem. Joshua called them all together there. Then he called the older leaders, heads of families, judges and officers of Israel. These men stood before God.

[2]Then Joshua spoke to all the people. He said, "Here's what the Lord, the God of Israel, says to you: 'A long time ago your ancestors lived on the other side of the Euphrates River. I am talking about men like Terah, the father of Abraham and Nahor. They worshipped other gods. [3]But I, the Lord, took your ancestor Abraham out of the land on the other side of the river. I led him through the land of Canaan. And I gave him many children. I gave him his son Isaac. [4]And I gave Isaac two sons named Jacob and Esau. I gave the land around the mountains of Edom to Esau. But Jacob and his sons went down to Egypt. [5]Then I sent Moses and Aaron to Egypt. I caused many terrible things to happen to the Egyptians. Then I brought you people out. [6]When I brought your fathers out of Egypt, they came to the Red Sea.[d] And the Egyptians chased them. There were chariots and men on horses. [7]So the people asked me, the Lord, for help. And I caused great trouble to come to the Egyptians. I caused the sea to cover them. You yourselves saw what I did to the army

of Egypt. After that, you lived in the desert for a long time.

[8]" 'Then I brought you to the land of the Amorites. This was east of the Jordan River. They fought against you, but I gave you the power to defeat them. I destroyed them before you. Then you took control of that land. [9]But the king of Moab, Balak son of Zippor, prepared to fight against the Israelites. The king sent for Balaam son of Beor to curse you. [10]But I, the Lord, refused to listen to Balaam. So he asked for good things to happen to you! He blessed you many times. I saved you and brought you out of his power.

[11]" 'Then you travelled across the Jordan River and came to Jericho. The people in the city of Jericho fought against you. Also, the Amorites, Perizzites, Canaanites, Hittites, Girgashites, Hivites and Jebusites fought against you. But I allowed you to defeat them all. [12]While your army travelled forward, I sent hornets ahead of them. These hornets made the people leave before you came. So you took the land without using your swords and bows. [13]It was I, the Lord, who gave you that land. I gave you land where you did not have to work. I gave you cities that you did not have to build. And now you live in that land and in those cities. You eat from vineyards and olive trees. But you did not have to plant them'."

[14]Then Joshua spoke to the people. He said, "Now you have heard the Lord's words. So you must respect the Lord and serve him fully and sincerely. Throw away the false gods that your people worshipped. That happened on the other side of the Euphrates River and in Egypt. Now you must serve the Lord. [15]But perhaps you don't want to serve the Lord. You must choose for yourselves today. You must decide whom you will serve. You may serve the gods that your people worshipped when they

lived on the other side of the Euphrates River. Or you may serve the gods of the Amorites who lived in this land. As for me and my family, we will serve the Lord."

¹⁶Then the people answered, "No! We will never stop following the Lord. We will never serve other gods! ¹⁷We know it was the Lord our God who brought our people out of Egypt. We were slaves in that land. But the Lord did great things for us there. He brought us out. He protected us while we travelled through other lands. ¹⁸Then he helped us defeat the people living in these lands. He helped us defeat the Amorites who lived here. So we will continue to serve the Lord because he is our God."

¹⁹Then Joshua said, "You will not be able to serve the Lord well enough. He is a holy God. And he is a jealous God. If you turn against him and sin, he will not forgive you. ²⁰If you leave the Lord and serve other gods, he will cause great trouble to come to you. The Lord has been good to you. But if you turn against him, he will destroy you."

²¹But the people said to Joshua, "No! We will serve the Lord."

²²Then Joshua said, "Look around at yourselves and the people with you here. Do you all know and agree that you have chosen to serve the Lord? Are you all witnesses to this?"

The people answered, "Yes, it's true! We all see that we have chosen to serve the Lord."

²³Then Joshua said, "Now throw away the false gods that you have among you. Love the Lord, the God of Israel, with all your heart."

²⁴Then the people said to Joshua, "We will serve the Lord our God. We will obey him."

²⁵On that day Joshua made an agreement for the people. He made

the agreement a law for them to follow. This happened at Shechem. ²⁶Joshua wrote these things in the Book of the Teachings of God. Then he found a large stone. He put the stone under the oak tree near the Lord's Holy Tent.^d

²⁷Then Joshua said to all the people, "See this stone! It will help you remember what we did today. It was here when the Lord was speaking to us today. It will help you remember what happened. It will stop you from turning against your God."

Joshua Dies

²⁸Then Joshua told the people to go back to their homes. And everyone went back to his own land.

²⁹After that, Joshua son of Nun died. He was 110 years old. ³⁰And they buried him in his own land at Timnath Serah. This was in the mountains of Ephraim, north of Mount Gaash.

³¹The Israelites had served the Lord during the time Joshua was living. And after he died, they continued to serve the Lord. They continued to serve him while their older leaders were still alive. These were the leaders who had seen what the Lord had done for the Israelites.

Joseph Comes Home

³²When the Israelites left Egypt, they carried the bones of Joseph with them. They buried them at Shechem, in the land Jacob had bought from the sons of Hamor. (Hamor was the father of Shechem.) Jacob had bought the land for 100 pieces of silver. This land belonged to Joseph's children.

³³And Eleazar son of Aaron died. He was buried at Gibeah in the mountains of Ephraim. Gibeah had been given to Eleazar's son Phinehas.

JUDGES
Great Leaders Rescue Israel

The Men of Judah Fight the Canaanites

1 Joshua died. Then the people of Israel prayed to the Lord. They said, "Who will be first to go and fight for us against the Canaanite people?"

²The Lord said to them, "The tribe*d* of Judah will go. I have given them the power to take this land."

³The men of Judah asked for help from the men of Simeon, their relatives. The men of Judah said, "Come and help us fight the Canaanites for our land. If you do, we will go and help you fight for your land." So the men of Simeon went with them.

⁴The Lord gave the men of Judah the victory over the Canaanites and the Perizzites. The men of Judah defeated 10,000 men at the city of Bezek. ⁵There they found Adoni-Bezek, the ruler of the city, and fought him. The men of Judah defeated the Canaanites and the Perizzites. ⁶So Adoni-Bezek ran away. But the men of Judah chased him. When they caught him, they cut off his thumbs and big toes.

⁷Then Adoni-Bezek said, "I cut off the thumbs and big toes of 70 kings. And those kings had to eat scraps that fell from my table. Now God has paid me back for what I did to them." The men of Judah took Adoni-Bezek to Jerusalem, and he died there.

⁸Then the men of Judah fought against Jerusalem and captured it. They used their swords to kill the people of Jerusalem. And they burned the city.

⁹Later, they went down to fight against more of the Canaanites. Some of the Canaanites lived in the moun-tains. Others lived in the dry country to the south. And still others lived in the western mountain slopes. ¹⁰Then the men of Judah went to fight against the Canaanites in the city of Hebron. (Hebron used to be called Kiriath Arba.) The men of Judah defeated the descendants*d* of Sheshai, Ahiman and Talmai.

Caleb and His Daughter

¹¹Then the men of Judah left Hebron. They went to the city of Debir to fight against the people there. (Debir used to be called Kiriath Sepher.) ¹²Before attacking the city, Caleb said, "I want a man to attack and capture the city of Kiriath Sepher. I will give him Acsah, my daughter, as a wife." ¹³Caleb had a younger brother named Kenaz. Kenaz had a son named Othniel. Othniel captured the city of Kiriath Sepher. So Caleb gave his daughter Acsah to Othniel to be his wife. ¹⁴When Acsah came to Othniel, he told her to ask her father for some land. So she got down from her donkey, and Caleb said, "What do you want?"

¹⁵Acsah answered Caleb, "Do me a favour. You have put me in the dry land of southern Judah. Give me some land with springs of water." So Caleb gave her the upper and lower springs of water.

Fights with the Canaanites

¹⁶The Kenite people left Jericho, the city of palm trees. They went with the men of Judah. The Kenites went to the Desert of Judah to live with the people there. This was in southern Judah near the city of Arad. (The Ke-

nites were from the family of Moses' father-in-law.) ¹⁷Some Canaanite people also lived in the city of Zephath. So the men of Judah and the men of Simeon, their relatives, defeated those Canaanites. They completely destroyed the city. So they called the city Hormah.ⁿ ¹⁸The men of Judah captured Gaza, Ashkelon and Ekron and all the lands around them.

¹⁹The Lord was on the side of the men of Judah. They took the land in the mountains. But they could not force out the people living on the plain. This was because those people had iron chariots. ²⁰As Moses had promised, Hebron was given to Caleb. Caleb forced out the three sons of Anak.ᵈ ²¹But the people of Benjamin could not make the Jebusite people leave Jerusalem. Since that time the Jebusites have lived with the Benjaminites in Jerusalem.

²²The men of Joseph went to fight against the city of Bethel. The Lord was on their side. ²³They sent some spies to Bethel. (Bethel used to be called Luz.) ²⁴The spies saw a man coming out of the city. They said to him, "Show us a way into the city. If you help us, we will be kind to you." ²⁵The man showed the spies the way into the city. The men of Joseph killed the people in Bethel. But the man who helped them and his family were allowed to go free. ²⁶He went to the land where the Hittite people lived, and he built a city. He named the city Luz, and it is called that today.

²⁷There were Canaanites living in the cities of Beth Shan, Taanach, Dor, Ibleam, Megiddo and the small towns around them. The people of Manasseh did not force those people out of their towns. The Canaanites were determined to stay there. ²⁸Later, the people of Israel grew strong. They forced the Canaanites to work as slaves for them. But the Israelites did not make all the Canaanites leave their land. ²⁹There were Canaanites living in Gezer. And the people of Ephraim did not make all of those Canaanites leave their land. So the Canaanite people continued to live in Gezer with the people of Ephraim. ³⁰Some Canaanites lived in the cities of Kitron and Nahalol. The people of Zebulun did not make them leave their land. They stayed and lived with the people of Zebulun. But Zebulun made them work as slaves.

³¹The people of Asher did not make the Canaanites leave the cities of Acco, Sidon, Ahlab, Aczib, Helbah, Aphek and Rehob. ³²The people of Asher did not make them leave their land. So the Canaanites continued to live with the people of Asher. ³³The people of Naphtali did not make the people leave the cities of Beth Shemesh and Beth Anath. So the people of Naphtali continued to live with the Canaanites in those cities. Those people worked as slaves for the people of Naphtali. ³⁴The Amorites forced the Danites back into the mountains. The Amorites would not let them come down to live in the plain. ³⁵The Amorites were determined to stay in Mount Heres, Aijalon and Shaalbim. But the Israelites grew stronger. Then they made the Amorites work as slaves for them. ³⁶The land of the Amorites was from Scorpion Pass to Sela and beyond it.

The Angel of the Lord at Bokim

2 The angel of the Lord went up from Gilgal to Bokim. He spoke to the people of Israel there and said: "I brought you up from Egypt. I led you to the land I promised to give to your ancestors. I said, 'I will never break my agreement with you. ²But in return, you must not make an agreement with the people who live in this

Hormah Hormah sounds like the Hebrew word meaning "to destroy completely".

land. You must destroy their altars'. But you did not obey me. How could you do this? [3]Now I will tell you this: 'I will not force out the people in this land. They will become your enemies. Their gods will become a trap for you'."

[4]After the angel gave Israel this message from the Lord, they cried loudly. [5]So they named the place Bokim.[n] There they offered sacrifices to the Lord.

Joshua Dies

[6]Then Joshua told the people they could go home. So each one went to take his own share of the land. [7]The people of Israel served the Lord as long as Joshua was alive. They continued serving the Lord during the lifetimes of the older leaders who lived on after Joshua. These men had seen all the great things the Lord had done for Israel. [8]Joshua son of Nun was the servant of the Lord. Joshua died at the age of 110. [9]So the Israelites buried him in the land he had been given. That land was at Timnath Heres. It was in the mountains of Ephraim, north of Mount Gaash.

The People Disobey

[10]After those people had died, their children grew up. They did not know the Lord or what he had done for Israel. [11]So they did evil and worshipped the Baal[d] idols. They did what the Lord said was wrong. [12]The Lord had brought the people of Israel out of Egypt. And the ancestors of these people had worshipped the Lord. But the Israelites stopped following the Lord. They began to worship the gods of the people who lived around them. That made the Lord angry. [13]The Israelites stopped following the Lord and worshipped Baal and Ashtoreth.[d]

[14]The Lord was angry with the people of Israel. So he let robbers attack them and take their possessions. He let their enemies who lived around them defeat them. They could not protect themselves from their enemies. [15]When the Israelites went out to fight, they always lost. They lost because the Lord was not on their side. The Lord had sworn to them this would happen. So the Israelites suffered very much.

God Chooses Judges

[16]Then the Lord chose leaders called judges.[n] These leaders saved the people of Israel from the robbers. [17]But the Israelites did not listen to their judges. They were not faithful to God. They followed other gods instead. In the past the people of Israel obeyed the Lord's commands. But now the Israelites stopped obeying the Lord. [18]Many times the enemies of Israel hurt the Israelites. So the Israelites would cry for help. And each time the Lord felt sorry for them. Each time he sent a judge to save them from their enemies. The Lord was with those judges. [19]But when each judge died, the Israelites again sinned and worshipped the false gods. They became worse than their ancestors. The Israelites were very stubborn; they refused to change their evil ways.

[20]So the Lord became angry with the Israelites. He said, "These people have broken the agreement I made with their ancestors. They have not listened to me. [21]So I will no longer defeat the nations who were left when Joshua died. [22]I will use those nations to test Israel. I will see if Israel keeps the Lord's commands as their ancestors did." [23]In the past the Lord had permitted those nations to stay in the

---

Bokim This name means "crying".

judges They were not judges in courts of law, but leaders of the people in times of emergency.

land. He did not quickly force them out. He did not help Joshua's army defeat them.

3 These are the nations the Lord did not force to leave. He wanted to test the Israelites who had not fought in the wars to take Canaan. ²The only reason the Lord left those nations in the land was to teach the descendants*d* of the Israelites. He wanted to teach the people who had not fought in those wars how to fight. ³These are the nations: the five rulers of the Philistines, all the Canaanites, the people of Sidon and the Hivites. The Hivites lived in the Lebanon mountains from Mount Baal Hermon to Lebo Hamath. ⁴Those nations were in the land to test the Israelites. The Lord wanted to see if Israel would obey the commands he had given to their ancestors by Moses.

⁵The people of Israel lived with the Canaanites, Hittites, Amorites, Perizzites, Hivites and Jebusites. ⁶The Israelites began to marry the daughters of those people. And the Israelites allowed their daughters to marry the sons of those people. Israel served the gods of those people.

Othniel, the First Judge

⁷The people of Israel did what the Lord said was wrong. They forgot about the Lord their God. Instead, they served the idols of Baal*d* and Asherah.*d* ⁸The Lord was angry with Israel. He allowed Cushan-Rishathaim king of North West Mesopotamia to rule over the Israelites. They were under that king's rule for eight years. ⁹Then Israel cried to the Lord. So the Lord sent a man to save them. He was Othniel son of Kenaz. (Kenaz was Caleb's younger brother.) Othniel saved the Israelites. ¹⁰The Spirit*d* of the Lord entered Othniel. And he became Israel's judge and went to war. The Lord helped him to defeat Cushan-Rishathaim king of North West Mesopotamia. ¹¹So the land was at peace for 40 years. Then Othniel son of Kenaz died.

Ehud, the Judge

¹²Again the people of Israel did what the Lord said was wrong. So the Lord gave Eglon king of Moab power to defeat Israel. This was because of the evil Israel did. ¹³Eglon got the Ammonite people and the Amalekite people to join him. Then he attacked Israel and took Jericho, the city of palm trees. ¹⁴The people of Israel were under the rule of Eglon king of Moab for 18 years.

¹⁵So the people cried to the Lord. And he sent a man to save them. That man was Ehud, who was left-handed. Ehud was the son of Gera from the people of Benjamin. Israel sent Ehud to give Eglon king of Moab the payment he demanded. ¹⁶Ehud made a sword for himself. The sword had two edges and was about 0.5 metres long. He tied the sword to his right upper leg under his clothes. ¹⁷So Ehud came to Eglon king of Moab and gave him the payment he demanded. Eglon was a very fat man. ¹⁸After he had given Eglon the payment, Ehud sent home the men who had carried it. ¹⁹When he passed the statues near the city Gilgal, he turned around. Ehud said to Eglon, "I have a secret message for you, King Eglon."

The king said, "Be quiet!" Then he sent all of his servants out of the room. ²⁰Ehud went to King Eglon. Eglon was now sitting alone in the room on top of his summer palace.

Ehud said, "I have a message from God for you." As the king stood up from his chair, ²¹Ehud reached with his left hand. He took out the sword that was tied to his right upper leg. Then he stabbed the sword deep into the king's belly! ²²The sword went into Eglon's belly so far that even the handle sank in. And the blade came out of his back. The king's fat covered the whole sword. So Ehud left the sword in Eglon. [23]He went out of the room and closed and locked the doors behind him.

[24]The servants returned just after Ehud left. They found the doors to the room locked. So they thought the king was relieving himself. [25]They waited for a long time. Finally they became worried because he still had not opened the doors. So they got the key and unlocked them. When they entered, they saw their king lying dead on the floor!

[26]While the servants were waiting, Ehud had escaped. He passed by the statues and went to Seirah. [27]When he arrived there, he blew a trumpet in the mountains of Ephraim. The people of Israel heard it and went down from the hills with Ehud leading them.

[28]He said to them, "Follow me! The Lord has helped us to defeat our enemies, the people of Moab." So Israel followed Ehud. They took control of the places where the Jordan River could easily be crossed. Israel did not allow the Moabites to come across the Jordan River. [29]Israel killed about 10,000 strong and able men from Moab. Not one Moabite man escaped. [30]So that day Moab was forced to be under the rule of Israel. And there was peace in the land for 80 years.

Shamgar, the Judge

[31]After Ehud, another man saved Israel. His name was Shamgar, son of Anath. Shamgar killed 600 Philistines with a sharp stick used to guide oxen.

Deborah, the Woman Judge

4 After Ehud died, the people of Israel again did what the Lord said was wrong. [2]So he let Jabin, a king of Canaan, defeat Israel. Jabin ruled in the city of Hazor. Sisera was the commander of Jabin's army. Sisera lived in Harosheth Haggoyim. [3]He had 900 iron chariots and was very cruel to the people of Israel for 20 years. So they cried to the Lord for help.

[4]There was a prophetess[d] named Deborah. She was the wife of Lappidoth. She was judge of Israel at that time. [5]Deborah would sit under the Palm Tree of Deborah. This was between the cities of Ramah and Bethel, in the mountains of Ephraim. And the people of Israel would come to her to settle their arguments.

[6]Deborah sent a message to a man named Barak. He was the son of Abinoam. Barak lived in the city of Kedesh, which is in the area of Naphtali. Deborah said to Barak, "The Lord, the God of Israel, commands you: 'Go and gather 10,000 men of Naphtali and Zebulun. Lead them to Mount Tabor. [7]I will make Sisera, the commander of Jabin's army, come to you. Sisera, his chariots and his army will meet you at the Kishon River. I will help you to defeat Sisera there'."

[8]Then Barak said to Deborah, "I will go if you will go with me. But if you will not go with me, I won't go."

[9]"Of course I will go with you," Deborah answered. "But you will not get credit for the victory. The Lord will let a woman defeat Sisera." So Deborah went with Barak to Kedesh. [10]At Kedesh, Barak called the people of Zebulun and Naphtali together. From them, he gathered 10,000 men to follow him. Deborah went with Barak also.

[11]Now Heber the Kenite had left the other Kenite people. (The Kenites were descendants[d] of Hobab, Moses' brother-in-law.) Heber had put up his tent by the great tree in Zaanannim. This is near Kedesh.

[12]Then Sisera was told that Barak son of Abinoam had gone up to Mount Tabor. [13]So Sisera gathered his 900 iron chariots and all the men with him. They went from Harosheth Haggoyim to the Kishon River.

[14]Then Deborah said to Barak, "Get up! Today is the day the Lord will help you defeat Sisera. You know the Lord has already cleared the way for you."

So Barak led 10,000 men down from Mount Tabor. ¹⁵He and his men attacked Sisera and his men. During the battle the Lord confused Sisera and his army and chariots. So Barak and his men used their swords to defeat Sisera's army. But Sisera left his chariot and ran away on foot. ¹⁶Barak and his men chased Sisera's chariots and army to Harosheth Haggoyim. They used their swords to kill all of Sisera's men. Not one of them was left alive.

¹⁷But Sisera himself ran away. He came to the tent where Jael lived. She was the wife of Heber, one of the Kenite family groups. Heber's family was at peace with Jabin king of Hazor. ¹⁸Jael went out to meet Sisera. She said to him, "Come into my tent, master! Come in. Don't be afraid." So Sisera went into Jael's tent, and she covered him with a rug.

¹⁹Sisera said to Jael, "I am thirsty. Please give me some water to drink." So she opened a leather bag in which she kept milk and gave him a drink. Then she covered him up.

²⁰Then Sisera said to Jael, "Go and stand at the entrance to the tent. If anyone comes and asks you, 'Is anyone here?' say, 'No'."

²¹But Jael, the wife of Heber, took a tent peg and a hammer. She quietly went to Sisera. Since he was very tired, he was sleeping. She hammered the tent peg through the side of Sisera's head and into the ground! And so Sisera died.

²²Then Barak came by Jael's tent, chasing Sisera. Jael went out to meet him and said, "Come. I will show you the man you are looking for." So Barak entered her tent. There Sisera lay dead, with the tent peg in his head.

²³On that day God defeated Jabin king of Canaan in the sight of Israel. ²⁴Israel became stronger and stronger against Jabin king of Canaan. Finally, they destroyed him.

The Song of Deborah

5 On that day Deborah and Barak son of Abinoam sang this song:

²"The leaders led Israel.
  The people volunteered to go to
    battle.
  Praise the Lord!
³Listen, kings.
  Pay attention, rulers!
I myself will sing to the Lord.
I will make music to the Lord,
    the God of Israel.

⁴"Lord, in the past you came from
    Edom.
  You marched from the land of
    Edom,
and the earth shook.
  The skies rained,
  and the clouds dropped water.
⁵The mountains shook before the
    Lord, the God of Mount
    Sinai.
  They shook before the Lord,
    the God of Israel!

⁶"In the days of Shamgar son of
    Anath,
  in the days of Jael, the main
    roads were empty.
  Travellers went on the back
    roads.
⁷There were no warriors in Israel
    until I, Deborah, arose.
  I arose to be a mother to Israel.
⁸At that time they chose to follow
    new gods.
  Because of this, enemies fought
    us at our city gates.
No one could find a shield or a
    spear
  among the 40,000 men of Israel.
⁹My heart is with the commanders
    of Israel.
  They volunteered freely from
    among the people.
Praise the Lord!
¹⁰"You who ride on white donkeys
  and sit on saddle blankets,
    listen!

And you who walk along the
road, listen!
11Listen to the sound of the singers
at the watering holes.
There they tell about the victories
of the Lord.
They tell about the victories of
the Lord's warriors in Israel.
Then the Lord's people went
down to the city gates.
12"Wake up, wake up, Deborah!
Wake up, wake up, sing a song!
Get up, Barak!
Go and capture your enemies,
son of Abinoam!

13"Then the men who were left
came down to the important
leaders.
The Lord's people came down
to me with strong men.
14They came from Ephraim in the
mountains of Amalek.
Benjamin was among the people
who followed you.
From the family group of Makir in
West Manasseh, the
commanders came down.
And from Zebulun came those
men who lead with an
officer's staff.
15The princes of Issachar were with
Deborah.
The people of Issachar were
loyal to Barak.
They followed him into the
valley.
The Reubenites thought hard
about what they would do.
16Why did you stay by the
sheepfold?
Was it to hear the music played
for your sheep?
The Reubenites thought hard
about what they would do.
17The people of Gilead stayed east
of the Jordan River.
People of Dan, why did you stay
by the ships?
The people of Asher stayed at the
seashore.

They stayed at their safe
harbours.
18But the people of Zebulun risked
their lives.
So did the people of Naphtali on
the battlefield.

19"The kings came, and they fought.
At that time the kings of Canaan
fought
at Taanach, by the waters of
Megiddo.
But they took away no silver or
possessions of Israel.
20The stars fought from heaven.
From their paths, they fought
Sisera.
21The Kishon River swept Sisera's
men away,
that old river, the Kishon River.
March on, my soul, with strength!
22Then the horses' hoofs beat the
ground.
Galloping, galloping go Sisera's
mighty horses.
23'May the town of Meroz be
cursed,' said the angel of the
Lord.
'Bitterly curse its people,
because they did not come to help
the Lord.
They did not fight the strong
enemy.'

24"May Jael, the wife of Heber the
Kenite,
be blessed above all women who
live in tents.
25Sisera asked for water,
but Jael gave him milk.
In a bowl fit for a ruler,
she brought him cream.
26Jael reached out and took the tent
peg.
Her right hand reached for the
workman's hammer.
And she hit Sisera! She smashed
his head!
She crushed and pierced the
side of his head!
27At Jael's feet he sank.
He fell, and he lay there.

At her feet he sank. He fell.
Where Sisera sank, there he
    fell, dead!
28"Sisera's mother looked out
    through the window.
  She looked through the curtains.
  She asked, 'Why is Sisera's
    chariot so late in coming?'
  Why are sounds of his chariots'
    horses delayed?'
29The wisest of her servant ladies
    answer her.
  And Sisera's mother says to
    herself,
30'Surely they are taking the
    possessions of the people
    they defeated!
  Surely they are dividing those
    things among themselves!
  A girl or two is being given to
    each soldier.
  Maybe Sisera is taking pieces of
    dyed cloth.
  Maybe they are even taking
    pieces of dyed, embroidered
    cloth for the necks of the
    victors!'
31"Let all your enemies die this
    way, Lord!
  But let all the people who love
    you
    be powerful like the rising sun!"

So there was peace in the land for
40 years.

The Midianites Attack Israel

6 Again the people of Israel did what
the Lord said was wrong. So for
seven years the Lord let the people of
Midian rule Israel. 2The Midianites
were very powerful and were cruel to
the Israelites. So the Israelites made
hiding places in the mountains. They
also hid in caves and safe places.
3Whenever the Israelites planted
crops, the Midianites, Amalekites and
other peoples from the east would
come and attack them. 4These people
camped in the land. And they destroyed the crops that the Israelites
had planted. They did this as far as the
land near Gaza. The people left nothing for Israel to eat. They left them no
sheep, cattle or donkeys. 5The Midianites came up and camped in the
land. They brought their tents and
their animals with them. They were
like swarms of locusts!d There were
so many people and camels they could
not be counted. These people came
into the land to ruin it. 6Israel became
very poor because of the Midianites.
So the Israelites cried out to the Lord
for help.
  7The Israelites cried out to the Lord
for help against the Midianites. 8So
the Lord sent a prophetd to them. The
prophet said, "This is what the Lord,
the God of Israel, says: I brought you
out of Egypt, the land of slavery. 9I
saved you from the people of Egypt.
And I saved you from all the people of
Canaan. I forced them out of their
land. And I gave it to you. 10Then I
said to you, 'I am the Lord your God.
You will live in the land of the Amorites, but you must not worship their
gods'. But you did not obey me."

The Angel of the Lord Visits Gideon

11The angel of the Lord came and
sat down under an oak tree at Ophrah.
The oak tree belonged to Joash, who
was one of the Abiezrite people. Joash
was the father of Gideon. Gideon was
separating some wheat from the
chaffd in a winepress.d Gideon did this
to keep the wheat from the Midianites. 12The angel of the Lord appeared
to Gideon and said, "The Lord is with
you, mighty warrior!"
  13Then Gideon said, "Pardon me,
sir. If the Lord is with us, why are we
having so many troubles? Our ancestors told us he did miracles.d They
told us the Lord brought them out of
Egypt. But now he has left us. He has
allowed the Midianites to defeat us."
  14The Lord turned to Gideon and

said, "You have the strength to save the people of Israel. Go and save them from the Midianites. I am the one who is sending you."

¹⁵But Gideon answered, "Pardon me, Lord. How can I save Israel? My family group is the weakest in Manasseh. And I am the least important member of my family."

¹⁶The Lord answered him, "I will be with you. It will seem as if you are fighting only one man."

¹⁷Then Gideon said to the Lord, "If you are pleased with me, give me proof. Show me that it is really you talking with me. ¹⁸Please wait here. Do not go away until I come back to you. Let me bring my offering and set it in front of you."

And the Lord said, "I will wait until you come back."

¹⁹So Gideon went in and cooked a young goat. He also took about 20 litres of flour and made bread without yeast. Then he put the meat into a basket. And he put the broth from the boiled meat into a pot. He brought out the meat, the broth and the bread without yeast. He brought the food to the angel of the Lord. Gideon gave it to him under the oak tree.

²⁰The angel of God said to Gideon, "Put the meat and the bread without yeast on that rock over there. Then pour the broth on them." And Gideon did as he was told. ²¹The angel of the Lord had a stick in his hand. He touched the meat and the bread with the end of the stick. Then fire jumped up from the rock! The meat and the bread were completely burned up! And the angel of the Lord disappeared! ²²Then Gideon understood he had been talking to the angel of the Lord. So Gideon cried, "Lord God! I have seen the angel of the Lord face to face!"

²³But the Lord said to Gideon, "Calm down! Don't be afraid! You will not die!"

²⁴So Gideon built an altar there to worship the Lord. Gideon named the altar The Lord Is Peace. It still stands at Ophrah, where the Abiezrites live.

Gideon Tears Down the Altar of Baal

²⁵That same night the Lord spoke to Gideon. The Lord said, "Take the bull that belongs to your father and a second bull seven years old. Pull down your father's altar to Baal.ᵈ Cut down the Asherahᵈ idol beside it. ²⁶Then build an altar to the Lord your God. Build it on this high ground. Lay its stones in the right order. Then kill and burn the bull on this altar. Use the wood from the Asherah idol to burn your offering."

²⁷So Gideon got ten of his servants. And he did what the Lord had told him to do. But Gideon was afraid that his family and the men of the city might see him. So he did it at night, not in the daytime.

²⁸The men of the city got up the next morning. They saw that the altar for Baal had been destroyed! And they saw that the Asherah idol beside it had been cut down! They also saw the altar Gideon had built. And they saw the bull that had been sacrificed on it. ²⁹The men of the city looked at each other and asked, "Who did this?" They asked many questions and looked for the person who had done those things.

Someone told them, "Gideon son of Joash did this."

³⁰So they said to Joash, "Bring your son out. He has pulled down the altar of Baal. He has cut down the Asherah idol beside it. So your son must die!" ³¹But Joash spoke to the angry crowd around him. He said, "Are you going to take Baal's side? Are you going to defend Baal? Anyone who takes Baal's side will be killed by morning! If Baal is a god, let him fight for himself. It's his altar that has been pulled down." ³²So on that day Gideon got the name Jerub-Baal. The name

means "let Baal fight against him". They named him this because Gideon pulled down Baal's altar.

Gideon Defeats Midian

³³All the Midianites, the Amalekites and other peoples from the east joined together. They came across the Jordan River and camped in the Valley of Jezreel. ³⁴But the Spirit*d* of the Lord entered Gideon! Gideon blew a trumpet to call the Abiezrites to follow him. ³⁵He sent messengers to all of Manasseh. The people of Manasseh were called to follow Gideon. Gideon also sent messengers to the people of Asher, Zebulun and Naphtali. They also went up to meet Gideon and his men.

³⁶Then Gideon said to God, "You said you would help me save Israel. ³⁷I will put some wool on the threshing*d* floor. Let there be dew only on the wool. But let all of the ground be dry. Then I will know what you said is true. I will know that you will use me to save Israel." ³⁸And that is just what happened. Gideon got up early the next morning and squeezed the wool. He got a full bowl of water from the wool. ³⁹Then Gideon said to God, "Don't be angry with me. Let me ask just one more thing. Please let me make one more test. Let the wool be dry while the ground around it gets wet with dew." ⁴⁰That night God did that very thing. Just the wool was dry, but the ground around it was wet with dew.

7 Early in the morning Jerub-Baal and all his men set up their camp at the spring of Harod. (Jerub-Baal is also called Gideon.) The Midianites were camped north of them. The Midianites were camped in the valley at the bottom of the hill called Moreh. ²Then the Lord said to Gideon, "You have too many men to defeat the Midianites. I don't want the Israelites to brag that they saved themselves. ³So now, announce to the people, 'Anyone who is afraid may leave Mount Gilead. He may go back home'." And 22,000 men went back home. But 10,000 remained.

⁴Then the Lord said to Gideon, "There are still too many men. Take the men down to the water, and I will test them for you there. If I say, 'This man will go with you', he will go. But if I say, 'That one will not go with you', he will not go."

⁵So Gideon led the men down to the water. There the Lord said to him, "Separate them. Those who drink water by lapping it up like a dog will be in one group. Those who bend down to drink will be in the other group." ⁶There were 300 men who used their hands to bring water to their mouths. They lapped it as a dog does. All the rest got down on their knees to drink.

⁷Then the Lord said to Gideon, "I will save you, using the 300 men who lapped the water. And I will allow you to defeat Midian. Let all the other men go to their homes." ⁸So Gideon sent the rest of Israel to their homes. But he kept 300 men. He took the jars and the trumpets of those who went home.

Now the camp of Midian was in the valley below Gideon. ⁹That night the Lord spoke to Gideon. He said, "Get up. Go down and attack the camp of the Midianites. I will allow you to defeat them. ¹⁰But if you are afraid to go down, take your servant Purah with you. ¹¹When you come to the camp of Midian, you will hear what they are saying. Then you will not be afraid to attack the camp."

Gideon Is Encouraged

So Gideon and his servant Purah went down to the edge of the enemy camp. ¹²The Midianites, the Amalekites and all the peoples from the east were camped in that valley. There were so many of them they seemed like locusts.*d* They had so many camels no one could count them. There were as many as there are grains of sand on the seashore!

¹³When Gideon came to the enemy camp, he heard a man talking. That man was telling his friend about a dream. He was saying, "Listen, I dreamed that a loaf of barley bread rolled into the camp of Midian. It hit the tent so hard that the tent turned over and fell flat!"

¹⁴The man's friend said, "Your dream is about the sword of Gideon son of Joash, a man of Israel. God will let Gideon defeat Midian and the whole army!"

¹⁵When Gideon heard about the dream and what it meant, he worshipped God. Then Gideon went back to the camp of Israel. He called out to them, "Get up! The Lord has defeated the army of Midian for you!" ¹⁶Then Gideon divided the 300 men into three groups. He gave each man a trumpet and an empty jar. A burning torch was inside each jar.

¹⁷Gideon told the men, "Watch me and do what I do. When I get to the edge of the camp, do what I do. ¹⁸Surround the enemy camp. I and everyone with me will blow our trumpets. When we blow our trumpets, you blow your trumpets, too. Then shout, 'For the Lord and for Gideon!'"

Midian Is Defeated

¹⁹So Gideon and the 100 men with him came to the edge of the enemy camp. They came just after the enemy had changed guards. It was during the middle watch of the night. Then Gideon and his men blew their trumpets and smashed their jars. ²⁰All three groups of Gideon's men blew their trumpets and smashed their jars. They held the torches in their left hands and the trumpets in their right hands. Then they shouted, "A sword for the Lord and for Gideon!" ²¹Each of Gideon's men stayed in his place around the camp. But inside the

camp, the men of Midian began shouting and running away.

²²When Gideon's 300 men blew their trumpets, the Lord caused all the men of Midian to fight each other with their swords! The enemy army ran away to the city of Beth Shittah. It is towards Zererah. They ran as far as the border of the city of Abel Meholah. It is near the city of Tabbath. ²³Then men of Israel from Naphtali, Asher and all of Manasseh were called out to chase the Midianites. ²⁴Gideon sent messengers through all the mountains of Ephraim. They said, "Come down and attack the Midianites. Take control of the Jordan River as far as Beth Barah. Do this before the Midianites can get to the river and cross it."

So they called out all the men of Ephraim. They took control of the Jordan River as far as Beth Barah. ²⁵The men of Ephraim captured two princes of Midian named Oreb and Zeeb. The men of Ephraim killed Oreb at the rock of Oreb. They killed Zeeb at the winepress*d* of Zeeb. And they continued chasing the Midianites. They cut off the heads of Oreb and Zeeb and took them to Gideon. He was now east of the Jordan River.

8 The men of Ephraim asked Gideon, "Why did you treat us this way? Why didn't you call us when you went to fight against Midian?" They were very angry at Gideon.

²But he answered them, "I have not done as well as you! The small part you did was better than all that my people of Abiezer did. ³God allowed you to capture Oreb and Zeeb, the princes of Midian. How can I compare what I did with what you did?" When the men of Ephraim heard Gideon's answer, they were not as angry any more.

Gideon Captures Two Kings

⁴Then Gideon and his 300 men came to the Jordan River. They were

tired, but they chased the enemy across to the other side. ⁵Gideon said to the men of Succoth, "Please give my soldiers some bread. They are very tired. I am chasing Zebah and Zalmunna, the kings of Midian."

⁶But the leaders of Succoth said, "Why should we give your soldiers bread? You haven't caught Zebah and Zalmunna yet."

⁷Then Gideon said, "The Lord will help me capture Zebah and Zalmunna. After that, I will whip your skin with thorns and briers from the desert."

⁸Gideon left Succoth and went to the city of Peniel. He asked the men there for food. It was just as he had asked the men of Succoth. And the men of Peniel gave him the same answer as the men of Succoth. ⁹So Gideon said to the men of Peniel, "After I win the victory, I will come back here. And I will pull down this tower."

¹⁰Zebah and Zalmunna and their army were in the city of Karkor. Their army had about 15,000 men. They were all who were left of the army of the peoples of the east. Already 120,000 soldiers of that army had been killed. ¹¹Gideon used the road of those who live in tents. This road is east of Nobah and Jogbehah. Gideon attacked the enemy army when they did not expect it. ¹²Zebah and Zalmunna, the kings of Midian, ran away. But Gideon chased and captured them. Gideon and his men defeated the enemy army.

¹³Then Gideon son of Joash returned from the battle. He and his men returned by the Pass of Heres. ¹⁴Gideon captured a young man from Succoth and asked him some questions. The young man wrote down for Gideon the names of 77 men. They were the officers and older leaders of Succoth.

Gideon Punishes Succoth

¹⁵Then Gideon came to Succoth. He said to the men of that city, "Here are Zebah and Zalmunna. You made fun of me by saying, 'Why should we give bread to your tired men? You have not caught Zebah and Zalmunna yet'." ¹⁶So Gideon took the older leaders of the city. He punished them with thorns and briers from the desert. ¹⁷He also pulled down the tower of Peniel. Then he killed the men in that city.

¹⁸Gideon spoke to Zebah and Zalmunna. He said, "You killed some men on Mount Tabor. What were those men like?"

Zebah and Zalmunna answered, "They were like you. Each one of them seemed like a prince."

¹⁹Gideon said, "Those were my brothers, my mother's sons. As surely as the Lord lives, I would not kill you if you had spared them." ²⁰Then Gideon turned to Jether, his oldest son. Gideon said to him, "Kill them." But Jether was only a boy and was afraid. So he did not take out his sword.

²¹Then Zebah and Zalmunna said to Gideon, "Come on. Kill us yourself. As the saying goes, 'It takes a man to do a man's job'." So Gideon got up and killed Zebah and Zalmunna. Then he took the decorations off their camels' necks.

Gideon Makes an Idol

²²The people of Israel said to Gideon, "You saved us from the Midianites. So now, rule over us. We want you, your son and your grandson to rule over us."

²³But Gideon told them, "The Lord will be your ruler. I will not rule over you. And my son will not rule over you." ²⁴He said, "I want you to do this one thing for me. I want each of you to give me a gold earring from the things you took in the fighting." (The Ishmaelite men wore gold earrings. And some Ishmaelites had been defeated in the battle.)

²⁵So the people of Israel said to Gid-

eon, "We will gladly give you what you want." So they put a coat down on the ground. Each man threw an earring onto the coat. ²⁶The gold earrings weighed about 20 kilograms. This did not include the weight of the other gifts the people gave to Gideon. They gave him decorations, necklaces and purple robes. These were things that the kings of Midian had worn. The people also gave him chains from the camels of the kings of Midian. ²⁷Gideon used the gold to make an idol. He put the idol in his hometown of Ophrah. All the people of Israel were unfaithful to God and worshipped the idol. It became a trap that caused Gideon and his family to sin.

The Death of Gideon

²⁸So Midian was forced to be under the rule of Israel. Midian did not cause trouble any more. And the land had peace for 40 years, as long as Gideon was alive.

²⁹Gideon son of Joash went to his home to live. ³⁰He had 70 sons of his own. He had many sons because he had many wives. ³¹Gideon had a slave woman^d who lived in Shechem. He also had a son by her. He named that son Abimelech. ³²So Gideon son of Joash died at a good old age. He was buried in the tomb of Joash, his father. That tomb is in Ophrah, where the Abiezrites live.

³³As soon as Gideon died, the people of Israel were again unfaithful to God. They followed the Baal^d gods. They made Baal-of-the-Agreement their god. ³⁴The Israelites did not remember the Lord their God. He had saved them from all their enemies who were living all around them. ³⁵And Jerub-Baal, also called Gideon, had done many good things for Israel. But Israel was not kind to the family of Gideon for these things.

Abimelech Becomes King

9 Abimelech son of Jerub-Baal, also called Gideon, went to his uncles. They lived in the city of Shechem. He said to his uncles and all of his mother's family group, ²"Ask the leaders of Shechem this question: 'Is it better for you to be ruled by the 70 sons of Jerub-Baal or to be ruled by only one man?' Remember, I am your relative."

³Abimelech's uncles spoke to all the leaders of Shechem. They asked them that question. All the leaders decided to follow Abimelech. They said, "He is our brother." ⁴So the leaders of Shechem gave Abimelech about a kilogram of silver. The silver was from the temple of the god Baal^d-of-the-Agreement. Abimelech used the silver to hire some worthless, reckless men. They followed Abimelech wherever he went. ⁵Abimelech went to Ophrah, the hometown of his father. There Abimelech murdered his 70 brothers. They were the sons of Abimelech's father, Gideon. He killed them all on one stone. But Gideon's youngest son, Jotham, hid from Abimelech and escaped. ⁶Then all of the leaders of Shechem and Beth Millo came together. They gathered beside the great tree at the stone pillar in Shechem. There they made Abimelech their king.

Jotham's Story

⁷When Jotham heard this, he went and stood on the top of Mount Gerizim. Jotham shouted to the people: "Listen to me, you leaders of Shechem. Then God may listen to you! ⁸One day the trees decided to appoint a king to rule over them. They said to the olive tree, 'You be king over us!' ⁹"But the olive tree said, 'Men and gods are honoured by my oil. Should I stop making it just to go and sway over the other trees?'

¹⁰"Then the trees said to the fig tree, 'Come and be our king!'

¹¹"But the fig tree answered, 'Should I stop making my sweet and good fruit? Should I stop just to go and sway over the other trees?'

¹²"Then the trees said to the vine, 'Come and be our king!'

¹³"But the vine answered, 'My wine makes men and gods happy. Should I stop making it just to go and sway over the trees?'

¹⁴"Then all the trees said to the thornbush, 'Come and be our king'.

¹⁵"But the thornbush said to the trees, 'If you really want to appoint me king over you, come and find shelter in my shade! But if you do not want to do this, let fire come out of the thornbush. Let the fire burn up the cedars of Lebanon!'

¹⁶"Now, were you completely honest and sincere when you made Abimelech king? Have you been fair to Gideon and his family? Have you treated Gideon as you should? ¹⁷Remember, my father fought for you. He risked his life to save you from the power of the Midianites. ¹⁸But now you have turned against my father's family. You have killed my father's 70 sons on one stone. You have made Abimelech king over the people of Shechem. He is the son of my father's slave girl! You have made Abimelech king just because he is your relative. ¹⁹So then, if you have been honest and sincere to Gideon and his family today, be happy with Abimelech as your king. And may he be happy with you! ²⁰But if you have not acted right, may fire come out of Abimelech! May that fire completely burn you leaders of Shechem and Beth Millo! Also may fire come out of the leaders of Shechem and burn up Abimelech!"

²¹Then Jotham ran away. He escaped to the city of Beer. He lived there because he was afraid of his brother Abimelech.

Abimelech Fights Against Shechem

²²Abimelech ruled Israel for three years. ²³Then God sent an evil spirit to make trouble between Abimelech and the leaders of Shechem. So the leaders of Shechem turned against him. ²⁴Abimelech had killed Gideon's 70 sons. They were Abimelech's own brothers. And the leaders of Shechem had helped him kill them. So God sent the evil spirit to punish them. ²⁵The leaders of Shechem were against Abimelech then. They put men on the hill tops. These men attacked and robbed everyone who went by. Abimelech was told about these attacks.

²⁶A man named Gaal and his brothers moved into Shechem. He was the son of Ebed. The leaders of Shechem decided to trust and follow Gaal. ²⁷The people of Shechem went out to the vineyards to pick grapes. They walked on the grapes to make wine. Then they had a feast in the temple of their god. The people ate and drank and cursed Abimelech. ²⁸Then Gaal son of Ebed said, "We are the men of Shechem. Why should we obey Abimelech? Who does he think he is? Isn't Abimelech one of Gideon's sons? Didn't Abimelech make Zebul his officer? We should not obey Abimelech! We should obey the men of Hamor, Shechem's father. Why should we obey Abimelech? ²⁹If you made me commander of these people, I would get rid of Abimelech! I would say to him, 'Get your army ready and come out to battle!'"

³⁰Now Zebul was the ruler of Shechem. He heard what Gaal son of Ebed said. And Zebul became very angry. ³¹He sent messengers to Abimelech in the city of Arumah. The message said, "Gaal son of Ebed and Gaal's brothers have come to Shechem. Gaal is turning the city against you! ³²So now you and your men should get up in the night. Then go

and lie in the fields outside the city. [33]When the sun comes up in the morning, attack the city. Gaal and his men will come out to fight you. Then do what you can to them."

[34]So Abimelech and all his soldiers got up during the night. They went near Shechem and separated into four groups. There they hid. [35]Gaal son of Ebed went out and was standing at the entrance to the city gate. As he was standing there, Abimelech and his soldiers came out of their hiding places.

[36]When Gaal saw the soldiers, he said to Zebul, "Look! There are people coming down from the mountains!"

But Zebul said, "You are seeing the shadows of the mountains. The shadows just look like people."

[37]But again Gaal said, "Look, there are people coming down from the centre of the land. And there is a group coming from the fortune-tellers' tree!"

[38]Zebul said to Gaal, "Where is your boasting now? You said, 'Who is Abimelech? Why should we obey him?' You made fun of these men. Now go out and fight them."

[39]So Gaal led the men of Shechem out to fight Abimelech. [40]Abimelech and his men chased them. Many of Gaal's men were killed before they could get back to the city gate. [41]Then Abimelech stayed at Arumah. Zebul forced Gaal and his brothers to leave Shechem.

[42]The next day the people of Shechem went out to the fields. Abimelech was told about it. [43]So he separated his men into three groups. And he hid them in the fields. When he saw the people coming out of the city, he jumped up and attacked them. [44]Abimelech and his group ran to the entrance gate to the city. The other two groups ran out to the people in the fields and killed them. [45]Abime-

lech and his men fought the city of Shechem all day. They captured it and killed its people. Then Abimelech tore down the city. And he threw salt[n] over the ruins so nothing would ever grow there.

The Tower of Shechem

[46]The people who lived at the nearby Tower of Shechem heard what had happened to Shechem. So the leaders gathered in the safest room of the temple of the god Baal[d]-of-the-Agreement. [47]Abimelech heard that all the leaders of the Tower of Shechem had gathered there. [48]So he and all his men went up to Mount Zalmon, near Shechem. Abimelech took an axe and cut some branches. Then he put them on his shoulders. He said to all his men with him, "Hurry! Do what I have done!" [49]So all those men cut branches and followed Abimelech. They piled the branches against the safest room of the temple. Then they set them on fire and burned the people in the room. So all the people who lived at the Tower of Shechem also died. There were about 1,000 men and women.

Abimelech's Death

[50]Then Abimelech went to the city of Thebez. He surrounded the city, attacked it and captured it. [51]But inside the city was a strong tower. All the men and women of that city ran to the tower. When they got inside, they locked the door behind them. Then they climbed up to the roof of the tower. [52]Abimelech came to the tower and attacked it. He went up to the door of the tower to set it on fire. [53]As Abimelech came near, a woman dropped a large stone for grinding grain on his head. The stone crushed Abimelech's skull. [54]He quickly called to the officer who carried his armour. He said,

salt The salt would keep crops from growing there.

"Take out your sword and kill me. I don't want people to say, 'A woman killed Abimelech'." So the officer stabbed Abimelech, and he died. 55When the people of Israel saw Abimelech was dead, they all returned home.

56In that way God punished Abimelech for all the evil he had done. Abimelech had sinned against his own father by killing his 70 brothers. 57God also punished the men of Shechem for the evil they had done. So the curse Jotham had spoken came true. (Jotham was the youngest son of Gideon.)

Tola, the Judge

10 After Abimelech died, another judge came to save the people of Israel. He was Tola son of Puah. (Puah was the son of Dodo.) Tola was from the people of Issachar. He lived in the city of Shamir in the mountains of Ephraim. 2Tola was a judge for Israel for 23 years. Then he died and was buried in Shamir.

Jair, the Judge

3After Tola died, Jair became judge. He lived in the region of Gilead. He was a judge for Israel for 22 years. 4Jair had 30 sons, who rode 30 donkeys. These 30 sons controlled 30 towns in Gilead. These towns are called the Towns of Jair to this day. 5Jair died and was buried in the city of Kamon.

The Ammonites Trouble Israel

6Again the Israelites did what the Lord said was wrong. They worshipped the Baal[d] and Ashtoreth[d] idols. They also worshipped the gods of the peoples of Aram, Sidon, Moab and Ammon. And they worshipped the gods of the Philistines. The Israelites left the Lord and stopped serving him. 7So the Lord became angry with them. He allowed the Philistines and the Ammonites to defeat them. 8In

the same year those people destroyed the Israelites who lived east of the Jordan River. This is in the region of Gilead, where the Amorites lived. The Israelites suffered for 18 years. 9The Ammonites then crossed the Jordan River to fight the people of Judah, Benjamin and Ephraim. The Ammonites caused much trouble to the people of Israel. 10So the Israelites cried out to the Lord, "We have sinned against you. We left our God and worshipped the Baal idols."

11The Lord answered the Israelites, "You cried to me when the Egyptians, the Amorites, the Ammonites and the Philistines hurt you. I saved you from these people. 12You cried to me when the Sidonians, Amalekites and Maonites hurt you. I also saved you from those people. 13But you have left me. You have worshipped other gods. So I refuse to save you again! 14You have chosen those gods. So go and call to them for help. Let them save you when you are in trouble!"

15But the people of Israel said to the Lord, "We have sinned. Do to us whatever you want, but please save us today!" 16Then the Israelites threw away the foreign gods among them. And they worshipped the Lord again. So he felt sorry for them when he saw their suffering.

17The Ammonite people gathered for war and camped in Gilead. The Israelites gathered and camped at Mizpah. 18The leaders of the people of Gilead said, "Who will lead us to attack the people of Ammon? He will become the head of all those who live in Gilead."

Jephthah Is Chosen as Leader

11 Jephthah was from the people of Gilead. He was a strong soldier. His father was named Gilead, and his mother was a prostitute.[d] 2Gilead's wife had several sons. When they grew up, they forced Jephthah to leave his home. They said to him,

"You will not get any of our father's property. You are the son of another woman." ³So Jephthah ran away from his brothers. He lived in the land of Tob. There some worthless men began to follow Jephthah.

⁴After a time the Ammonite people fought against Israel. ⁵The Ammonites made war against Israel. At that time the older leaders of Gilead came to Jephthah. They wanted him to come back to Gilead. ⁶They said to him, "Come and lead our army so we can fight the Ammonites."

⁷But Jephthah said to them, "Didn't you hate me? You forced me to leave my father's house! Why are you coming to me now that you are in trouble?"

⁸The older leaders of Gilead said to Jephthah, "That is the reason we come to you now. Please come with us and fight against the Ammonites! You will be the ruler over everyone who lives in Gilead."

⁹Then Jephthah answered, "Suppose you take me back to Gilead to fight the Ammonites. If the Lord helps me win, I will be your ruler."

¹⁰The older leaders of Gilead said to him, "The Lord is listening to everything we are saying. We promise to do all that you tell us to do." ¹¹So Jephthah went with the older leaders of Gilead. The people made him their leader and commander of their army. Jephthah repeated all of his words in front of the Lord at Mizpah.

Jephthah Sends Messengers to the Ammonite King

¹²Jephthah sent messengers to the king of the Ammonites. The messengers asked the king, "What have you got against Israel? Why have you come to attack our land?"

¹³The king of the Ammonites answered the messengers of Jephthah. He said, "We are fighting Israel because you took our land when you came up from Egypt. You took our

land from the Arnon River to the Jabbok River to the Jordan River. Now tell the people of Israel to give our land back to us in peace."

¹⁴Jephthah sent the messengers to the Ammonite king again. ¹⁵They took this message:

"This is what Jephthah says: Israel did not take the land of the people of Moab or Ammon. ¹⁶When the people of Israel came out of Egypt, they went into the desert. They went to the Gulf of Aqaba and then to Kadesh. ¹⁷Israel sent messengers to the king of Edom. They asked, 'Let the people of Israel go across your land'. But the king of Edom didn't let us. We sent the same message to the king of Moab. But he would not let us go across his land either. So the Israelites stayed at Kadesh.

¹⁸"Then the Israelites went into the desert. They went around the borders of the lands of Edom and Moab. Israel walked east of the land of Moab. They camped on the other side of the Arnon River. It was the border of the land of Moab. They did not cross it to go into the land of Moab.

¹⁹"Then Israel sent messengers to Sihon king of the Amorites. Sihon was the king of the city of Heshbon. The messengers asked Sihon, 'Let the people of Israel pass through your land. We want to go to our land'. ²⁰But Sihon would not let the Israelites cross his land. He gathered all of his people and camped at Jahaz. Then the Amorites fought with Israel.

²¹"But the Lord, the God of Israel, helped the Israelites to defeat Sihon and his army. All the land of the Amorites became the property of Israel. ²²So Israel took all the land of the Amorites. It went from the Arnon River to the Jabbok River. It also went from the desert to the Jordan River.

²³"It was the Lord, the God of Israel, who forced out the Amorites ahead of the people of Israel. So do you think you can make the people of Israel

leave this land? 24Surely you can live in the land which your god Chemosh*d* has given you. So we will live in the land the Lord our God has given us! 25"Are you any better than Balak son of Zippor? He was the king of Moab. Did he ever quarrel or fight with the people of Israel? 26For 300 years the Israelites have lived in Heshbon and Aroer and the towns around them. They have lived for 300 years in all the cities along the Arnon River. Why have you not taken these cities back in all that time? 27I have not sinned against you. But you are sinning against me by making war on me! May the Lord, the Judge, decide whether the Israelites or Ammonites are right."

28But the king of the Ammonites ignored this message from Jephthah.

Jephthah's Promise

29Then the Spirit*d* of the Lord entered Jephthah. Jephthah passed through Gilead and Manasseh. He came to the city of Mizpah in Gilead. From there, Jephthah passed through to the land of the Ammonites. 30Jephthah made a promise to the Lord. He said, "If you will let me defeat the Ammonites, 31I will give you a burnt offering. I will sacrifice the first thing that comes out of my house to meet me when I return from the victory. It will be the Lord's."

32Then Jephthah went over to fight the Ammonites. The Lord helped him defeat them. 33Jephthah defeated them from the city of Aroer to the area of Minnith. He defeated them as far as the city of Abel Keramim. He defeated 20 cities in this area. The defeat was great. So the Ammonites were defeated by the Israelites.

34When Jephthah returned home to Mizpah, his daughter came out to meet him. She was playing a tambourine*d* and dancing. She was his only child. Jephthah did not have any other sons or daughters. 35When Jephthah saw his daughter, he tore his clothes to show how upset he was. He said, "My daughter! You have made me so sad! This is because I have made a promise to the Lord, and I cannot break it!"

36Then his daughter said, "Father, you made a promise to the Lord. So do to me just what you promised. The Lord helped you defeat your enemies, the Ammonites." 37Then she said, "But let me do one thing. Let me be alone for two months to go to the mountains. I will never marry. So let me and my friends go and cry together."

38Jephthah said, "Go." He sent her away for two months. She and her friends stayed in the mountains. There they cried for her because she would never marry. 39After two months she returned to her father. Jephthah did to her what he promised to the Lord. Now Jephthah's daughter had never had a husband.

So this became a custom in Israel. 40Every year the women of Israel would go out for four days. They did this to remember the daughter of Jephthah from Gilead.

Jephthah and Ephraim

12 The men of Ephraim called all their soldiers together. Then they crossed the river to the town of Zaphon. They said to Jephthah, "Why didn't you call us to help you fight the Ammonites? We will burn your house down with you in it!"

2Jephthah answered them, "My people and I fought a great battle against the Ammonites. I called you, but you didn't come to help me. 3I saw that you would not help me. So I risked my own life! I went over to fight against the Ammonites. The Lord helped me to defeat them. Now why have you come to fight against me today?"

4Then Jephthah called the men of Gilead together. They fought the men of Ephraim. The men of Gilead attacked them because the Ephraimites had insulted them. They had said, "You men of Gilead are nothing but deserters from Ephraim and Manasseh." [5]The men of Gilead captured the crossing places of the Jordan River. Those places led to the country of Ephraim. A man from Ephraim trying to escape would say, "Let me cross the river." Then the men of Gilead would ask him, "Are you from Ephraim?" If he said, "No", [6]they would say to him, "Say the word 'Shibboleth'." The men of Ephraim could not say that word correctly. They pronounced it "Sibboleth". If the man from Ephraim said, "Sibboleth", the men of Gilead would kill him at the crossing place. So 42,000 men from Ephraim were killed at that time.

[7]Jephthah was a judge for the people of Israel for six years. Then Jephthah, the man from Gilead, died. He was buried in a town in Gilead.

Ibzan, the Judge

[8]After Jephthah died, Ibzan was a judge for Israel. He was from Bethlehem. [9]He had 30 sons and 30 daughters. He let his daughters marry men who were not in his family group. And he brought 30 women who were not in his tribe to be wives for his sons. Ibzan judged Israel for seven years. [10]Then he died and was buried in Bethlehem.

Elon, the Judge

[11]After Ibzan died, Elon was a judge for Israel. He was from the tribe[d] of Zebulun. He judged Israel for ten years. [12]Then Elon, the man of Zebulun, died. He was buried in the city of Aijalon in the land of Zebulun.

Abdon, the Judge

[13]After Elon died, Abdon was a judge for Israel. He was the son of Hillel. Abdon was from the city of Pirathon. [14]He had 40 sons and 30 grandsons, who rode on 70 donkeys. He judged Israel for eight years. [15]Then Abdon son of Hillel died. He was buried in Pirathon in the land of Ephraim. This is in the mountains where the Amalekites lived.

The Birth of Samson

13 Again the people of Israel did what the Lord said was wrong. So he let the Philistines rule over them for 40 years.

[2]There was a man named Manoah from the city of Zorah. Manoah was from the tribe[d] of Dan. He had a wife, but she could not have children. [3]The angel of the Lord appeared to Manoah's wife. He said, "You have not been able to have children. But you will become pregnant and have a son! [4]Don't drink wine or beer. Don't eat anything that is unclean.[d] [5]You will become pregnant and have a son. You must never cut his hair because he will be a Nazirite.[d] He will be given to God from birth. He will begin the work of saving Israel from the power of the Philistines."

[6]Then Manoah's wife went to him and told him what had happened. She said, "A man from God came to me. He looked like an angel from God. His appearance was frightening. I didn't ask him where he was from. And he didn't tell me his name. [7]But he said to me, 'You will be pregnant and will have a son. Don't drink wine or beer. Don't eat anything that is unclean. The reason is that the boy will be a Nazirite to God. He will be that from his birth until the day of his death'."

[8]Then Manoah said a prayer to the Lord: "Lord, I beg you to let the man of God come to us again. Let him teach us what we should do for the boy who will be born to us."

[9]God heard Manoah's prayer. The angel of God came to Manoah's wife again. This was while she was sitting in a field. But her husband Manoah was not with her. [10]So she ran to tell

him, "He is here! The man who appeared to me the other day is here!"

¹¹Manoah got up and followed his wife. When he came to the man, he said, "Are you the man who spoke to my wife?"

The man said, "I am."

¹²So Manoah asked, "When what you say happens, what kind of life should the boy live? What should he do?"

¹³The angel of the Lord said, "Your wife must do everything I told her to do. ¹⁴She must not eat anything that grows on a grapevine. She must not drink any wine or beer. She must not eat anything that is unclean. She must do everything I have commanded her to do."

¹⁵Manoah said to the angel of the Lord, "We would like you to stay awhile. We want to cook a young goat for you."

¹⁶The angel of the Lord answered, "Even if I stay awhile, I would not eat your food. But if you want to prepare something, offer a burnt offering to the Lord." (Manoah did not understand that the man was really the angel of the Lord.)

¹⁷Then Manoah asked the angel of the Lord, "What is your name? We want to know. Then we may honour you when what you have said really happens."

¹⁸The angel of the Lord said, "Why do you ask my name? It is too wonderful for you to understand." ¹⁹Then Manoah sacrificed a young goat on a rock. He also offered some grain as a gift to the Lord. The Lord did an amazing thing. Manoah and his wife watched what happened. ²⁰The flames went up to the sky from the altar. As the fire burned, the angel of the Lord went up to heaven in the fire! When Manoah and his wife saw that, they bowed face down on the ground. ²¹The angel of the Lord did not appear to them again. Then Manoah understood that the man was really the an-

gel of the Lord. ²²Manoah said, "We have seen God! Surely we will die because of this!"

²³But his wife said to him, "The Lord does not want to kill us. If he wanted to kill us, he would not have accepted our burnt offering or grain offering. He would not have shown us all these things. And he would not have told us all this."

²⁴So the woman gave birth to a boy. She named him Samson. Samson grew, and the Lord blessed him. ²⁵The Spirit[d] of the Lord began to work in Samson. This was while he was in the city of Mahaneh Dan. It is between the cities of Zorah and Eshtaol.

Samson's Marriage

14 Samson went down to the city of Timnah. There he saw a young Philistine woman. ²When he returned home, he said to his father and mother, "I saw a Philistine woman in Timnah. I want you to get her for me. I want to marry her."

³His father and mother answered, "Surely there is a woman from Israel you can marry. Do you have to marry a woman from the Philistines? The Philistines are not even circumcised."[d]

But Samson said, "Get that woman for me! She is the one I want!" ⁴(Samson's parents did not know that the Lord wanted this to happen. He was looking for a way to start a fight with the Philistines. They were ruling over Israel at this time.) ⁵Samson went down with his father and mother to Timnah. They went as far as the vineyard near there. Suddenly, a young lion came roaring toward Samson! ⁶The Spirit[d] of the Lord entered Samson with great power. Samson tore the lion apart with his bare hands. For him it was as easy as tearing apart a young goat. But Samson did not tell his father or mother what he had done. ⁷Then he went down to the city.

There he talked to the Philistine woman, and he liked her.

⁸Several days later Samson went back to marry her. On his way he went over to look at the body of the dead lion. He found a swarm of bees in it. They had made some honey. ⁹Samson got some of the honey with his hands. He walked along eating it. When he came to his parents, he gave some to them. They ate it, too. But Samson did not tell them he had taken the honey from the body of the dead lion.

¹⁰Samson's father went down to see the Philistine woman. The custom was for the bridegroom to give a feast. So Samson gave a feast. ¹¹When the people saw him, they sent 30 men to be with him.

Samson's Riddle

¹²Then Samson said to the 30 men, "Let me tell you a riddle. This feast will last for seven days. Try to find the answer during that time. If you can, I will give you 30 linen shirts. I will also give you 30 changes of clothes. ¹³But if you can't tell me the answer, you must pay me. You must give me 30 linen shirts and 30 changes of clothes."

So they said, "Tell us your riddle. We want to hear it."

¹⁴Samson said,

"Out of the eater comes
    something to eat.
Out of the strong comes
    something sweet."

The 30 men tried for three days to figure it out. But they could not find the answer.

¹⁵On the fourthⁿ day, they came to Samson's wife. They said, "Did you invite us here to make us poor? Trick your husband into telling us the answer to the riddle. If you don't, we will burn you and everyone in your father's house!"

¹⁶So Samson's wife went to him and began crying. She said, "You hate me! You don't really love me! You told my people a riddle, but you won't tell me the answer."

Samson said, "I haven't even told my father or mother. Why should I tell you?"

¹⁷Samson's wife cried for the rest of the seven days of the feast. So he finally gave her the answer on the seventh day. He told her because she kept bothering him. Then she told her people the answer to the riddle.

¹⁸Before sunset on the seventh day of the feast, the Philistine men had the answer. They came to Samson and said,

"What is sweeter than honey?
What is stronger than a lion?"

Then Samson said to them,

"If you had not ploughed with my
    little cow,
you would not have solved my
    riddle!"

¹⁹The Spiritᵈ of the Lord entered Samson and gave him great power. Samson went down to the city of Ashkelon. He killed 30 of their men and took all their clothes and property. He gave those clothes to the men who had answered his riddle. Then he went to his father's house very angry. ²⁰And Samson's wife was given to his best man at the wedding.

Samson Troubles the Philistines

15 At the time of the wheat harvest, Samson went to visit his wife. He took a young goat with him. He said, "I'm going to my wife's room." But her father would not let Samson go in.

²He said to Samson, "I thought you really hated your wife. So I gave her to the best man from the wedding.

---

fourth The Hebrew word is "seventh". Some old translations say "fourth", which fits the order of events better.

Her younger sister is more beautiful. Take her."

³But Samson said to him, "Now I have a good reason to hurt you Philistines. No one will blame me!" ⁴So Samson went out and caught 300 foxes. He took two foxes at a time and tied their tails together. Then he tied a torch to the tails of each pair of foxes. ⁵Samson lit the torches. Then he let the foxes loose in the grainfields of the Philistines. In this way he burned up their standing grain and the piles of grain. He also burned up their vineyards and their olive trees.

⁶The Philistines asked, "Who did this?"

Someone told them, "Samson, the son-in-law of the man from Timnah, did. He did this because his father-in-law gave his wife to his best man."

So the Philistines burned Samson's wife and her father to death. ⁷Then Samson said to the Philistines, "Since you did this, I will hurt you, too! I won't stop until I pay you back!" ⁸Samson attacked the Philistines and killed many of them. Then he went down and stayed in a cave. It was in the rock of Etam.

⁹Then the Philistines went up and camped in the land of Judah. They stopped near a place named Lehi. ¹⁰The men of Judah asked them, "Why have you come here to fight us?"

They answered, "We have come to make Samson our prisoner. We want to pay him back for what he did to our people."

¹¹Then 3,000 men of Judah went to the cave in the rock of Etam. They said to Samson, "What have you done to us? Don't you know that the Philistines rule over us?"

Samson answered, "I only paid them back for what they did to me!"

¹²Then they said to him, "We have come to tie you up. We will give you to the Philistines."

Samson said to them, "Promise me you will not hurt me yourselves."

¹³The men from Judah said, "We agree. We will just tie you up and give you to the Philistines. We will not kill you." So they tied Samson with two new ropes. Then they led him up from the cave in the rock. ¹⁴When Samson came to the place named Lehi, the Philistines came to meet him. They were shouting for joy. Then the Spirit^d of the Lord entered Samson and gave him great power. The ropes on him became weak like strings that had been burned. They fell off his hands! ¹⁵Samson found a jawbone of a donkey that had just died. He took it and killed 1,000 men with it!

¹⁶Then Samson said,

"With a donkey's jawbone
   I have made donkeys out of them.
With a donkey's jawbone
   I have killed 1,000 men!"

¹⁷When he had finished speaking, he threw away the jawbone. So that place was named Ramath Lehi.^{n}

¹⁸Samson was very thirsty. So he cried out to the Lord. He said, "I am your servant. You gave me this great victory. Do I have to die of thirst now? Do I have to be captured by people who are not circumcised?"^{d} ¹⁹Then God opened up a hole in the ground at Lehi, and water came out. When Samson drank that water, he felt better. He felt strong again. So he named that spring Caller's Spring. It is still there in Lehi to this day.

²⁰So Samson judged Israel for 20 years. That was in the days of the Philistines.

Samson Goes to the City of Gaza

16 One day Samson went to Gaza. He saw a prostitute^d there. He went in to spend the night with her. ²Someone told the people of Gaza, "Samson has come here!" So they

---

Ramath Lehi   This name means Jawbone Hill.

surrounded the place and hid and waited for him. Remaining very quiet, they stayed near the city gate all night. They said to each other, "When dawn comes, we will kill Samson!"

³But Samson only stayed with the prostitute until midnight. Then he got up and took hold of the doors and the two posts of the city gate. He tore them loose, along with the bar. Then he put them on his shoulders. And he carried them to the top of the hill that faces the city of Hebron!

Samson and Delilah

⁴After this, Samson fell in love with a woman named Delilah. She lived in the Valley of Sorek. ⁵The kings of the Philistines went to Delilah. They said, "Try to find out what makes Samson so strong. Try to trick him into telling you. Find out how we could capture him and tie him up. Then we will be able to control him. If you do this, each one of us will give you 13 kilograms of silver."

⁶So Delilah said to Samson, "Tell me why you are so strong. How could someone tie you up and take control of you?"

⁷Samson answered, "Someone would have to tie me up. He would have to use seven new bowstrings that have not been dried. If he did that, I would be as weak as any other man."

⁸Then the kings of the Philistines brought seven new bowstrings to Delilah. They had not been dried. She tied Samson with them. ⁹Some men were hiding in another room. Delilah said to Samson, "Samson, the Philistines are about to capture you!" But Samson easily broke the bowstrings. They broke like pieces of string burned in a fire. So the Philistines did not find out the secret of Samson's strength.

¹⁰Then Delilah said to Samson,

"You've made me look foolish. You lied to me. Please tell me. How could someone tie you up?"

¹¹Samson said, "They would have to tie me with new ropes that have not been used before. Then I would become as weak as any other man."

¹²So Delilah took new ropes and tied Samson. Some men were hiding in another room. Then she called out to him, "Samson, the Philistines are about to capture you!" But he broke the ropes as easily as if they were threads.

¹³Then Delilah said to Samson, "Until now, you have made me look foolish. You have lied to me. Tell me how someone could tie you up."

He said, "Use the loom.ⁿ Weave the seven braids of my hair into the cloth. Tighten it with a pin. Then I will become as weak as any other man."

Then Samson went to sleep. So Delilah wove the seven braids of his hair into the cloth. ¹⁴Then she fastened it with a pin.

Again she called out to him, "Samson, the Philistines are about to capture you!" Samson woke up and pulled up the pin and the loom with the cloth.

¹⁵Then Delilah said to him, "How can you say, 'I love you', when you don't even trust me? This is the third time you have made me look foolish. You haven't told me the secret of your great strength." ¹⁶She kept bothering Samson about his secret day after day. He became so tired of it he felt he was going to die!

¹⁷So he told her everything. He said, "I have never had my hair cut. I have been set apart to God as a Naziriteᵈ since I was born. If someone shaved my head, then I would lose my strength. I would become as weak as any other man."

¹⁸Delilah saw that he had told her everything sincerely. So she sent a message to the kings of the Philis-

---

loom   A machine for weaving cloth from thread.

tines. She said, "Come back one more time. He has told me everything." So the kings of the Philistines came back to Delilah. They brought the silver they had promised to give her. ¹⁹Delilah got Samson to go to sleep. He was lying in her lap. Then she called in a man to shave off the seven braids of Samson's hair. In this way she began to make him weak. And Samson's strength left him.

²⁰Then she called out to him, "Samson, the Philistines are about to capture you!"

He woke up and thought, "I'll get loose as I did before and shake myself free." But he did not know that the Lord had left him.

²¹Then the Philistines captured Samson. They tore out his eyes. And they took him down to Gaza. They put bronze chains on him. They put him in prison and made him grind grain. ²²But his hair began to grow again.

Samson Dies

²³The kings of the Philistines gathered to celebrate. They were going to offer a great sacrifice to their god Dagon.ᵈ They said, "Our god has given us Samson our enemy." ²⁴When they saw him, they praised their god. They said,

"This man destroyed our country.
  He killed many of us!
But our god helped us
  capture our enemy."

²⁵The people were having a good time at the celebration. They said, "Bring Samson out to perform for us." So they brought Samson from the prison. He performed for them. They made him stand between the pillars of the temple of Dagon. ²⁶A servant was holding his hand. Samson said to him, "Let me feel the pillars that hold up the temple. I want to lean against

them." ²⁷Now the temple was full of men and women. All the kings of the Philistines were there. There were about 3,000 men and women on the roof.ⁿ They watched Samson perform. ²⁸Then Samson prayed to the Lord. He said, "Lord God, remember me. God, please give me strength one more time. Let me pay these Philistines back for putting out my two eyes!" ²⁹Then Samson held the two centre pillars of the temple. These two pillars supported the whole temple. He braced himself between the two pillars. His right hand was on one, and his left hand was on the other. ³⁰Samson said, "Let me die with these Philistines!" Then he pushed as hard as he could. And the temple fell on the kings and all the people in it. So Samson killed more of the Philistines when he died than when he was alive.

³¹Samson's brothers and his whole family went down to get his body. They brought him back and buried him in the tomb of Manoah, his father. That tomb is between the cities of Zorah and Eshtaol. Samson was a judge for the people of Israel for 20 years.

Micah's Idols

17 There was a man named Micah. He lived in the mountains of Ephraim. ²He said to his mother, "You remember the 13 kilograms of silver that were taken from you. I heard you say a curse about it. I have the silver with me. I took it."

His mother said, "The Lord bless you, my son!"

³Micah gave the 13 kilograms of silver to his mother. Then she said, "I will give this silver to the Lord. I will have my son make a carved idol and an idol of melted silver. So I will give the silver back to you."

⁴So he gave the silver back to his

---

roof In Bible times houses were built with flat roofs. The roof was used for drying things such as flax and fruit. It was also used as an extra room, as a place for worship and as a place to sleep in the summer.

mother. She took about 2 kilograms of the silver and gave it to a silversmith. He used it to make a carved idol and an idol of melted silver. The idols were put in Micah's house. ⁵Micah had a temple for worshipping idols. He made a robe*d* for a priest and some household idols. Then Micah chose one of his sons to be his priest. ⁶At that time the Israelites did not have a king. So everyone did what he thought was right.

⁷There was a young man who was a Levite.*"* He was from the city of Bethlehem in the land of Judah. He had been living with the people of Judah. ⁸He left Bethlehem to look for another place to live. On his way he came to Micah's house. It was in the mountains of Ephraim. ⁹Micah asked him, "Where have you come from?"

He answered, "I'm a Levite from Bethlehem in Judah. I'm looking for a place to live."

¹⁰Then Micah said to him, "Live with me. Be my father and my priest. I will give you 100 grams of silver each year. I will also give you clothes and food." So the Levite went in. ¹¹The young Levite agreed to live with Micah. He became like one of Micah's own sons. ¹²Micah made him a priest. And he lived in Micah's house. ¹³Then Micah said, "Now I know the Lord will be good to me. I know this because I have a Levite as my priest!"

Dan's Family Captures Laish

18 At that time the Israelites did not have a king. The people of Dan were still looking for a land where they could live. They wanted a land of their own. The other tribes*d* of Israel already had their own lands. But the Danites did not yet have their own land. ²So they chose five soldiers from all their family groups. These five men were from the cities of Zorah and Esh-

taol. They sent the men to spy out and explore the land. They were told, "Go, explore the land."

So they came to the mountains of Ephraim. They came to Micah's house, where they spent the night. ³When they came near Micah's house, they recognised the voice of the young Levite.*"* So they stopped at Micah's house. They asked the young Levite, "Who brought you to this place? What are you doing here? Why are you here?"

⁴He told them what Micah had done for him. "He has hired me. I am his priest."

⁵They said to him, "Please ask God something for us. Will our search for a place to live be successful?"

⁶The priest said to them, "Go in peace. The Lord is pleased with your journey."

⁷So the five men left. They came to the city of Laish. They saw that the people there lived in safety. They were like the people of Sidon. They lived in peace and were not afraid of others. They had plenty of everything. They lived a long way from the Sidonians. And they had no dealings with anyone else.

⁸The five men went back to Zorah and Eshtaol. Their relatives asked them, "What did you find?"

⁹They answered, "We have seen the land, and it is very good. We should attack them. Aren't you going to do something? Don't wait! Let's go and take that land! ¹⁰When you go, you will see there is plenty of land. There is plenty of everything! The people are not expecting an attack. Surely God has given that land to us!"

¹¹So 600 men of Dan left Zorah and Eshtaol. They were ready for war. ¹²On their way they stopped near the city of Kiriath Jearim in Judah. They set up camp there. That is why the

Levite The Levites were the only ones God had appointed as priests.

place is named Mahaneh Dan[n] to this very day. It is west of Kiriath Jearim. [13]From there they travelled on to the mountains of Ephraim. Then they came to Micah's house.

[14]So the five men who had explored the land around Laish spoke. They said to their relatives, "There is a robe[d] for a priest in one of these houses. There are also household gods, a carved idol and an idol of melted silver. You know what to do." [15]So they stopped at the Levite's house. This was also Micah's house. And they greeted the Levite. [16]The 600 men of Dan stood at the gate entrance. They wore their weapons of war. [17]The five spies went into the house. They took the carved idol, the robe for a priest, the household idols and the silver idol. The priest and the 600 men ready for war stood by the gate entrance.

[18]When the spies went into Micah's house and took the carved image, the robe for a priest, the household idols and the silver idol, the priest asked them, "What are you doing?"

[19]They answered, "Be quiet! Don't say a word. Come with us. Be our father and our priest. Is it better for you to be a priest for the people in one man's house? Or is it better for you to be a priest for a tribe[d] and family group in Israel?" [20]This made the Levite happy. So he took the robe for a priest, the household idols and the carved idol. And he went with the men of Dan. [21]They left Micah's house. They put their little children, their animals and everything they owned in front of them.

[22]The men of Dan went a long way from Micah's house. Then the men who lived near Micah were called out. They chased the men of Dan and caught up with them. [23]The men with Micah shouted at the men of Dan. The

men of Dan turned around. They said to Micah, "What's the matter with you? Why have you called out your men to fight?"

[24]Micah answered, "You took my idols! I made those idols. You have also taken my priest. What do I have left? How can you ask me, 'What's the matter?'"

[25]The men of Dan answered, "You should not argue with us. Some of our men have hot tempers. If you shout at us, they might attack you. You and your family might be killed." [26]Then the men of Dan went on their way. Micah knew they were too strong for him. So he turned and went back home.

[27]So the men of Dan took what Micah had made. They also took his priest and went on to Laish. They attacked those peaceful people. The people of Laish had not expected an attack. The men of Dan killed them with their swords. Then they burned the city. [28]There was no one to save the people of Laish. They lived too far from Sidon. And they had no dealings with anyone else. Laish was in a valley near Beth Rehob.

The people of Dan rebuilt the city in that place. And they lived there. [29]They changed the name of Laish to Dan. They named it after their ancestor Dan. He was one of the sons of Israel.

[30]The people of Dan set up the idols in the city of Dan. They made Jonathan son of Gershom their priest. Gershom was the son of Moses. Jonathan and his sons were priests for the tribe of Dan. They served as priests until the Israelites were taken captive. [31]The people of Dan worshipped the idols Micah had made. They worshipped them as long as the Holy Tent[d] of God was in Shiloh.

Mahaneh Dan This name means "the camp of Dan".

A Levite and His Servant

19 At that time the people of Israel did not have a king.

There was a Levite who lived in the faraway part of the mountains of Ephraim. He had taken a slave woman.*d* She was from the city of Bethlehem in the land of Judah. ²But she was unfaithful to him. She left him and went back to her father's house. It was in Bethlehem in Judah. She stayed there for four months. ³Then her husband went to ask her to come back to him. He took with him his servant and two donkeys. The Levite came to her father's house. And she invited the Levite to come in. Her father was happy to see him. ⁴The father-in-law, the young woman's father, asked him to stay. So he stayed for three days. He ate, drank and slept there.

⁵On the fourth day they got up early in the morning. The Levite was getting ready to leave. But the woman's father said to his son-in-law, "Refresh yourself by eating something. Then you may go." ⁶So the two men sat down to eat and drink together. After that, the father said to him, "Please stay tonight. Relax and enjoy yourself." ⁷When the man got up to go, his father-in-law asked him to stay. So he stayed again that night. ⁸On the fifth day the man got up early in the morning to leave. The woman's father said, "Refresh yourself. Wait until this afternoon." So the two men ate together.

⁹Then the Levite, his slave woman and his servant got up to leave. His father-in-law, the young woman's father, said, "It's almost night. The day is almost gone. So spend the night here and enjoy yourself. Tomorrow morning you may get up early and go on your way home." ¹⁰But the Levite did not want to stay another night. He took his two saddled donkeys and his slave woman. He travelled towards the city of Jebus. (Jebus is another name for Jerusalem.)

¹¹The day was almost over. They were near Jebus. So the servant said to his master, "Let's stop at this city. It's the city of the Jebusite people. Let's spend the night here." ¹²But his master said, "No. We won't go inside a strange city. Those people are not Israelites. We will go on to the city of Gibeah." ¹³Then he said, "Come on. Let's try to make it to Gibeah or Ramah. We can spend the night in one of those cities." ¹⁴So they went on. And the sun went down as they came near Gibeah. Gibeah belongs to the tribe*d* of Benjamin. ¹⁵So they stopped there to spend the night. They came to the public square in the middle of the city and sat down. But no one invited them home to spend the night.

¹⁶That evening an old man came into the city from his work in the fields. His home was in the mountains of Ephraim. But now he was living in Gibeah. (The men of Gibeah were from the tribe of Benjamin.) ¹⁷He saw the traveller, the Levite, in the public square. He asked, "Where are you going? Where did you come from?" ¹⁸The Levite answered, "We are travelling from Bethlehem in Judah. We're going to my home. I'm from a faraway part of the mountains of Ephraim. I have been to Bethlehem in Judah. Now I am going to the Holy Tent*d* of the Lord. No one has invited me to stay in his house. ¹⁹We already have straw and food for our donkeys. There is bread and wine for me, the young woman and my servant. We don't need anything."

²⁰The old man said, "You are welcome to stay at my house. Let me give you anything you need. But don't spend the night in the public square." ²¹So the old man took the Levite into his house. He fed their donkeys, and they washed their feet. Then he gave them something to eat and drink.

22While they were enjoying themselves, some wicked men of the city surrounded the house. They beat on the door. They shouted to the old man who owned the house. They said, "Bring out the man who came to your house. We want to have sexual relations with him."

23The owner of the house went outside. And he said to them, "No, my friends. Don't be so evil. This man is a guest in my house. Don't do this terrible thing! 24Look, here is my daughter. She has never had sexual relations before. And here is the man's slave woman. I will bring them out to you now. Do anything you want with them. But don't do such a terrible thing to this man."

25But the men would not listen to him. So the Levite took his slave woman and sent her outside to them. They had sexual relations with her even though she didn't want to. They treated her very badly all night long. Then, at dawn, they let her go. 26She came back to the house where her master was staying. She fell down at the door and lay there until daylight.

27In the morning the Levite got up. He opened the door of the house. He went outside to go on his way. But there lay his slave woman. She had fallen down at the doorway of the house. Her hands were on the doorsill. 28Then the Levite said to her, "Get up; let's go." But she did not answer. So he put her on his donkey and went home.

29When the Levite got home, he took a knife and cut his slave woman into 12 parts. Then he sent a part to each of the areas where the people of Israel lived. 30Everyone who saw this said, "Nothing like this has ever happened before. It has never happened since the people of Israel came out of

Egypt. Think about it. Tell us what to do."

The War Between Israel and Benjamin

20 So all the Israelites joined together. They came to stand before the Lord in the city of Mizpah. They came from as far away as the cities of Dan and Beersheba.[n] Even the Israelites from the land of Gilead were there. 2The leaders of all the tribes[d] of Israel were there. They took their places in the meeting of the people of God. There were 400,000 soldiers with swords. 3(The people of Benjamin heard that the Israelites had gone up to Mizpah.) Then the Israelites said to the Levite, "Tell us how this evil thing happened."

4So the husband of the murdered woman answered: "My slave woman[d] and I came to Gibeah in Benjamin to spend the night. 5During the night the men of Gibeah came after me. They surrounded the house and wanted to kill me. They had sexual relations with my slave woman even though she didn't want to. And she died! 6So I took her and cut her into parts. Then I sent one part to each area of Israel's land. I did it because the people of Benjamin have done this wicked and terrible thing in Israel. 7Now, all you men of Israel, speak up. Tell us what you have decided we should do."

8Then all the people stood up at the same time. They said, "None of us will go home. Not one of us will go back to his house! 9Now this is what we will do to Gibeah. We will throw lots[d] so that God can show us what to do. 10We will choose ten men from each 100 men. They will be from all the tribes of Israel. And we will choose 100 men from each 1,000. We will choose 1,000 men from each 10,000. These men will find supplies

Dan . . . Beersheba Dan was the city farthest north in Israel. Beersheba was the city farthest south. So this means all the people of Israel.

for the army. Then the army will go to the city of Gibeah of Benjamin. They will repay those people for the terrible thing they have done in Israel." ¹¹So all the men of Israel gathered against the city. They all agreed about what they were doing.

¹²The tribes of Israel sent men to all the family groups of Benjamin with a message. They said, "What is this evil thing some of your men have done? ¹³Give up the evil men in Gibeah so that we can put them to death. We must remove this evil from Israel."

But the Benjaminites would not listen to their relatives, the people of Israel. ¹⁴The Benjaminites left their own cities and met at Gibeah. They went to fight against the Israelites. ¹⁵In only one day the Benjaminites got 26,000 soldiers together. These soldiers were trained with swords. They also had 700 chosen men from Gibeah. ¹⁶700 of these trained soldiers were left-handed. Each of these left-handed soldiers could sling a stone at a hair and not miss!

¹⁷The Israelites, except for the Benjaminites, gathered 400,000 fighting men. These 400,000 men used swords and were trained soldiers.

¹⁸The Israelites went up to the city of Bethel. They asked God, "Which tribe shall be first to attack the Benjaminites?"

The Lord answered, "Judah shall go first."

¹⁹The next morning the Israelites got up. They made a camp near Gibeah. ²⁰Then the men of Israel went out to fight the Benjaminites. The Israelites got into battle position at Gibeah. ²¹Then the Benjaminites came out of Gibeah. They killed 22,000 Israelites during the battle that day. ²²⁻²³The Israelites went before the Lord. They cried until evening. They asked the Lord, "Shall we go to fight our relatives, the Benjaminites, again?"

The Lord answered, "Go up and fight them." The men of Israel en-couraged each other. So they took the same battle positions they had taken the first day.

²⁴The Israelites brought their battle lines against the Benjaminites the second day. ²⁵The Benjaminites came out of Gibeah to attack the Israelites. This time, the Benjaminites killed 18,000 Israelites. All of these Israelites had been trained with swords.

²⁶Then the Israelites went up to Bethel. There they sat down and cried to the Lord. They went without food all day until evening. They also brought burnt offerings and fellowship offerings to the Lord. ²⁷The Israelites asked the Lord a question. (In those days the Ark[d] of God with God was there at Bethel. ²⁸A priest named Phinehas served before the Ark of God. He was the son of Eleazar, who was the son of Aaron.) The people of Israel asked, "Shall we again go to fight against our relatives the Benjaminites? Or shall we stop fighting?"

The Lord answered, "Go, because tomorrow I will help you defeat them."

²⁹Then the Israelites hid some men all around Gibeah. ³⁰They went to fight against the Benjaminites at Gibeah on the third day. They got into position for battle, as they had done before. ³¹Then the Benjaminites came out of the city to fight them. The Israelites backed up and led the Benjaminites away from the city. The Benjaminites began to kill some of the Israelites as they had done before. About 30 men from Israel were killed. Some of them were killed in the fields and some on the roads. One road led to Bethel. Another road led to Gibeah.

³²The Benjaminites said, "We are winning as before!"

But the Israelites said, "Let's run. Let's trick them into going further away from their city and onto the roads."

³³All the men of Israel moved from

their places. They got into battle positions at a place named Baal Tamar. Then the Israelites ran out from their hiding places west of Gibeah. ³⁴10,000 of the best trained soldiers from the army of Israel attacked Gibeah. The battle was very hard. The Benjaminites did not know disaster was about to come to them. ³⁵The Lord used the Israelites to defeat the Benjaminites. On that day the Israelites killed 25,100 Benjaminites. All these men were armed with swords. ³⁶Then the Benjaminites saw that they were defeated.

The men of Israel had moved back. They backed up because they were depending on the surprise attack. They had set it up near Gibeah. ³⁷The men in hiding rushed into Gibeah. They spread out and killed everyone in the city with their swords. ³⁸Now the men of Israel had made a plan with the men in hiding. The men in the surprise attack were to send up a signal. It was to be a big cloud of smoke from the city. ³⁹So the army of Israel turned around in the battle.

The Benjaminites had killed about 30 Israelites. They were saying, "We are winning, as in the first battle!" ⁴⁰But then the big cloud of smoke began to rise from the city. The Benjaminites turned around and saw it. The whole city was full of smoke that went up into the sky. ⁴¹Then the Israelites turned and began to fight. The Benjaminites were terrified. Now they knew that disaster was coming to them. ⁴²So the Benjaminites ran away from the Israelites. They ran towards the desert. But they could not escape the battle. And the Israelites who came out of the cities killed them. ⁴³They surrounded the Benjaminites and chased them. They caught them in the area east of Gibeah. ⁴⁴So 18,000 brave and strong Benjaminite fighters were killed. ⁴⁵The Benjaminites ran towards the desert. They ran to a place called the rock of Rimmon. But the Israelites killed 5,000 Benjaminites along the roads. They kept chasing them as far as a place named Gidom. And they killed 2,000 more Benjaminites there.

⁴⁶On that day 25,000 Benjaminites were killed. All of them had fought bravely with swords. ⁴⁷But 600 Benjaminites ran to the rock of Rimmon in the desert. They stayed there for four months. ⁴⁸Then the men of Israel went back to the land of Benjamin. They killed the people in every city. They also killed the animals. They destroyed everything they could find. And they burned every city they found.

Wives for the Men of Benjamin

21 At Mizpah the men of Israel had made a promise. This was their promise: "Not one of us will let his daughter marry a man from the tribeᵈ of Benjamin."

²The people went to the city of Bethel. There they sat before God until evening, crying loudly. ³They said, "Lord, you are the God of Israel. Why has this terrible thing happened to us? Why has one tribe of Israel been taken away?"

⁴Early the next day the people built an altar. They put burnt offerings and fellowship offerings to God on it.

⁵Then the Israelites asked, "Did any tribe of Israel not come here to meet with us before the Lord?" They asked this question because they had made a great promise. They had promised that anyone who did not meet with them at Mizpah would be killed.

⁶The Israelites felt sorry for their relatives, the Benjaminites. They said, "Today one tribe has been separated from Israel. ⁷We made a promise before the Lord. We will not allow our daughters to marry a Benjaminite. How can we make sure that the men of Benjamin will have wives?" ⁸Then they asked, "Which one of the tribes

of Israel did not come here to Mizpah?" They found that no one from the city of Jabesh Gilead was there. 9The people of Israel counted everyone, but no one from Jabesh Gilead was there.

10So the whole group of Israelites sent 12,000 soldiers to Jabesh Gilead. They told the soldiers to kill the people in Jabesh Gilead with their swords. Even the women and children were to be killed.

11"This is what you must do: kill every man in Jabesh Gilead. Also kill every woman who has had sexual relations with a man." 12The soldiers found 400 young women in Jabesh Gilead who had never had sexual relations with a man. They brought these women to the camp at Shiloh in Canaan.

13Then the whole group of Israelites sent a message to the men of Benjamin. They offered to make peace with them. The men of Benjamin were at the rock of Rimmon. 14So the men of Benjamin came back at that time. The Israelites gave them the women from Jabesh Gilead who had not been killed. But there were not enough women for all of them.

15The people of Israel felt sorry for the Benjaminites. This was because the Lord had separated the tribes of Israel. 16The older leaders of the Israelites spoke. They said, "The women of Benjamin have been killed. Where can we get wives for the men of Benjamin who are still alive? 17These men must have children to continue their families. This is so a tribe in Israel will

not die out. 18But we cannot allow our daughters to marry them. We have made this promise: 'Anyone who gives a wife to a man of Benjamin is cursed'. 19We have an idea! There is a yearly festival of the Lord at Shiloh. Shiloh is north of the city of Bethel. It is east of the road that goes from Bethel to Shechem. And it is south of the city of Lebonah."

20So the older leaders told the men of Benjamin about their idea. They said, "Go and hide in the vineyards. 21Watch for the young women from Shiloh to come out. They will come to join the dancing. Then run out from the vineyards. Each of you take one of the young Shiloh women and go to the land of Benjamin. 22The fathers or brothers of those young women will come to us. They will complain, but we will say: 'Be kind to the men of Benjamin. We did not get wives for Benjamin during the war. And you did not give the women to the men from Benjamin. So you are not guilty'."

23So that is what the Benjaminites did. While the young women were dancing, each man caught one of them. They took them away and married them. Then they went back to the land God had given them. They rebuilt their cities and lived there.

24Then the Israelites went home. They went to their own tribes and family groups. They went to their own land that God had given them.

25In those days the Israelites did not have a king. Everyone did what he thought was right.

RUTH

The Story of a Girl from Moab

1 ¹⁻²Long ago the judges[n] ruled Israel. During their rule, there was a time in the land when there was not enough food to eat. A man named Elimelech left Bethlehem in Judah and moved to the country of Moab. He took his wife and his two sons with him. His wife was named Naomi, and his two sons were named Mahlon and Kilion. These people were from the Ephrathah district around Bethlehem in Judah. The family travelled to Moab and lived there.

³Later, Naomi's husband, Elimelech, died. So only Naomi and her two sons were left. ⁴These sons married women from Moab. The name of one wife was Orpah. The name of the other wife was Ruth. Naomi and her sons lived in Moab about ten years. ⁵Then Mahlon and Kilion also died. So Naomi was left alone without her husband or her two sons.

⁶While Naomi was in Moab, she heard that the Lord had taken care of his people. He had given food to them in Judah. So Naomi got ready to leave Moab and go back home. The wives of Naomi's sons also got ready to go with her. ⁷So they left the place where they had lived and started back on the way to the land of Judah. ⁸But Naomi said to her two daughters-in-law, "Go back home. Each of you go to your own mother's house. You have been very kind to me and to my sons who are now dead. I hope the Lord will also be kind to you in the same way. ⁹I hope the Lord will give you another home and a new husband."

Then Naomi kissed the women and they began to cry out loud. ¹⁰Her daughters-in-law said to her, "No. We will go with you to your people."

¹¹But Naomi said, "My daughters, go back to your own homes. Why do you want to go with me? I cannot give birth to more sons to give you new husbands. ¹²So go back to your own homes. I am too old to have another husband. But even if I had another husband tonight and if I had more sons, it wouldn't help! ¹³Would you wait until the babies were grown into men? Would you live for so many years without husbands? Don't do this thing. My life is much too sad for you to share. This is because the Lord is against me!"

¹⁴The women cried together again. Then Orpah kissed Naomi goodbye, but Ruth held on to her.

¹⁵Naomi said, "Look, your sister-in-law is going back to her own people and her own gods. Go back with her."

Ruth Stays with Naomi

¹⁶But Ruth said, "Don't ask me to leave you! Don't beg me not to follow you! Every place you go, I will go. Every place you live, I will live. Your people will be my people. Your God will be my God. ¹⁷And where you die, I will die. And there I will be buried. I ask the Lord to punish me terribly if I do not keep this promise: only death will separate us."

¹⁸Naomi saw that Ruth had made up her mind to go with her. So Naomi stopped arguing with her. ¹⁹Naomi and Ruth went on until they came to the town of Bethlehem. When the two

---

judges They were not judges in courts of law, but leaders of the people in times of emergency.

women entered Bethlehem, all the people became very excited. The women of the town said, "Is this Naomi?"

²⁰But Naomi told the people, "Don't call me Naomi.ⁿ Call me Mara,ⁿ because God All-Powerful has made my life very sad. ²¹When I left, I had all I wanted. But now, the Lord has brought me home with nothing. So why should you call me Naomi when the Lord has spoken against me? God All-Powerful has given me much trouble."

²²So Naomi and her daughter-in-law Ruth, the woman from Moab, came back from Moab. They came to Bethlehem at the beginning of the barley harvest.

Ruth Meets Boaz

2 Now there was a rich man living in Bethlehem whose name was Boaz. Boaz was one of Naomi's close relatives from Elimelech's family.

²One day Ruth, the woman from Moab, said to Naomi, "Let me go to the fields. Maybe someone will be kind and let me gather the grain he leaves in his field."

Naomi said, "Go, my daughter."

³So Ruth went to the fields. She followed the workers who were cutting the grain. And she gathered the grain that they had left. It just so happened that the field belonged to Boaz. He was a close relative from Elimelech's family.

⁴When Boaz came from Bethlehem, he spoke to his workers: "The Lord be with you!"

And the workers answered, "May the Lord bless you!"

⁵Then Boaz spoke to his servant who was in charge of the workers. He asked, "Whose girl is that?"

⁶The servant answered, "She is the Moabite woman who came with Naomi from the country of Moab. ⁷She said, 'Please let me follow the workers and gather the grain that they leave on the ground'. She came and has remained here. From morning until just now, she has stopped only a few moments to rest in the shelter."

⁸Then Boaz said to Ruth, "Listen, my daughter. Stay here in my field to gather grain for yourself. Do not go to any other person's field. Continue following behind my women workers. ⁹Watch to see which fields they go to and follow them. I have warned the young men not to bother you. When you are thirsty, you may go and drink. Take water from the water jugs that the servants have filled."

¹⁰Then Ruth bowed low with her face to the ground. She said to Boaz, "I am a stranger. Why have you been so kind to notice me?"

¹¹Boaz answered her, "I know about all the help you have given to Naomi, your mother-in-law. You helped her even after your husband died. You left your father and mother and your own country. You came to this nation where you did not know anyone. ¹²The Lord will reward you for all you have done. You will be paid in full by the Lord, the God of Israel. You have come to him as a little bird finds shelter under the wings of its mother."

¹³Then Ruth said, "You are very kind to me, sir. You have said kind words to me, your servant. You have given me hope. And I am not even good enough to be one of your servants."

¹⁴At mealtime Boaz told Ruth, "Come here! Eat some of our bread. Here, dip your bread in our vinegar."

So Ruth sat down with the workers. Boaz gave her some roasted grain. Ruth ate until she was full, and there was some food left over. ¹⁵Ruth rose

---

Naomi This name means "happy" or "pleasant".
Mara This name means "bitter" or "sad".

and went back to work. Then Boaz told his servants, "Let her gather even around the bundles of grain. Don't tell her to go away. ¹⁶Drop some full heads of grain for her. Let her gather that grain, and don't tell her to stop."

¹⁷So Ruth gathered grain in the field until evening. Then she separated the grain from the chaff.ᵈ There was about 10 kilograms of barley. ¹⁸Ruth carried the grain into town. And her mother-in-law saw what she had gathered. Ruth also gave her the food that was left over from lunch.

¹⁹Naomi asked her, "Where did you gather all this grain today? Where did you work? Blessed be the man who noticed you!"

Ruth told her about the one whose field she had worked in. She said, "The man I worked with today is named Boaz."

²⁰Naomi told her daughter-in-law, "The Lord bless him! The Lord still continues to be kind to all people—the living and the dead!" Then Naomi told Ruth, "Boaz is one of our close relatives,ⁿ one who will take care of us."

²¹Then Ruth said, "Boaz also told me to come back and continue working. He said, 'Keep close by my servants until they have finished the harvest'."

²²Then Naomi said to her daughter-in-law Ruth, "It is good for you to continue working with his women servants. If you work in another field, someone might hurt you." ²³So Ruth continued working closely with the women servants of Boaz. She gathered grain until the barley harvest was finished. She also worked there through the end of the wheat harvest. And Ruth continued to live with Naomi, her mother-in-law.

Naomi's Plan

3 Then Naomi, Ruth's mother-in-law, said to her, "My daughter, I must find a suitable home for you. That would be good for you. ²Now Boaz is our close relative.ⁿ You worked with his women servants. Tonight he will be working at the threshingᵈ floor. ³Go and wash yourself and put on perfume. Change your clothes, and go down to the threshing floor. But don't let him see you until he has finished eating and drinking. ⁴Then he will lie down. Watch him so you will know the place where he lies down. Go there and lift the cover off his feetⁿ and lie down. He will tell you what you should do."

⁵Then Ruth answered, "I will do everything you say."

⁶So Ruth went down to the threshing floor. She did all her mother-in-law told her to do. ⁷After eating and drinking, Boaz was in a good mood. He went to lie down beside the pile of grain. Then Ruth went to him quietly. She lifted the cover from his feet and lay down.

⁸About midnight Boaz woke up suddenly and rolled over. He was startled! There was a woman lying near his feet! ⁹Boaz asked, "Who are you?"

She said, "I am Ruth, your servant girl. Spread your cover over me because you are the one who is to take care of me."

¹⁰Then Boaz said, "The Lord bless you, my daughter. Your kindness to me is greater than the kindness you showed to Naomi in the beginning. You didn't look for a young man to marry, either rich or poor. ¹¹Now, my daughter, don't be afraid. I will do everything you ask. All the people in our town know you are a very good woman. ¹²And it is true, I am a relative who

---

close relatives In Bible times the closest relative could marry a widow without children so that she could have children. He would care for this family, but they and their property would not belong to him. They would belong to the dead husband.

lift . . . feet This showed Ruth was asking him to be her husband.

is to take care of you. But there is a man who is a closer relative to you than I. [13]But stay here tonight. In the morning we will see if he will take care of you. If he decides to take care of you, that is fine. If he refuses to take care of you, I myself will marry you. Then I will buy back Elimelech's land for you. As surely as the Lord lives, I promise to do this. So lie here until morning."

[14]So Ruth lay near his feet until the morning. She rose while it was still too dark to be recognised. Boaz said to his servants, "Don't tell anyone that the woman came here to the threshing[d] floor." [15]Then Boaz said to Ruth, "Bring me your shawl. Now, hold it open."

So Ruth held her shawl open, and Boaz poured six portions of barley into it. Boaz then put it on her back, and she went to the city.

[16]Ruth went to the home of her mother-in-law, and Naomi asked, "How did you do, my daughter?"

So Ruth told Naomi everything that Boaz did for her. [17]She said, "Boaz gave me these six portions of barley. He said, 'You must not go home without a gift for your mother-in-law'."

[18]Naomi answered, "Ruth, my daughter, wait until you hear what happens. Boaz will not rest until he has finished doing what he should do this day."

Boaz Marries Ruth

4 Boaz went to the city gate. He sat there until the close relative he had mentioned passed by. Boaz called to him, "Come here, friend! Sit down here!" So the man came over and sat down. [2]Boaz gathered ten of the old men who were leaders of the city. He told them, "Sit down here!" So they sat down.

[3]Then Boaz spoke to the close relative. He said, "Naomi has come back from the country of Moab. She wants to sell the piece of land that belonged

to our relative Elimelech. [4]So I decided to say this to you: If you want to buy back the land, then buy it! Buy it in front of the people who live here and in front of the older leaders of my people. If you don't want to buy it, tell me. I am the only person after you who can buy back the land. If you don't buy it back, I will."

And the close relative said, "I will buy back the land."

[5]Then Boaz said, "When you buy the land from Naomi, you must marry Ruth, the dead man's wife. She is the woman from Moab. That way, the land will stay in her dead husband's family."

[6]The close relative answered, "Then I can't buy back the land. If I did, I might lose what I can pass on to my own sons. I cannot buy the land back. So you buy it yourself."

[7]Long ago in Israel when people traded or bought back something, one person took off his sandal and gave it to the other person. This was their proof of purchase.

[8]So the close relative said, "Buy the land yourself." And then he took off his sandal.

[9]Then Boaz spoke to the older leaders and to all the people. He said, "You are witnesses today of what I am buying from Naomi. I am buying everything that belonged to Elimelech and Kilion and Mahlon. [10]I am also taking Ruth as my wife. She is the Moabite who was the wife of Mahlon. I am doing this so her dead husband's property will stay with his family. This way, his name will not be separated from his family and his land. You are witnesses this day."

[11]So all the people and older leaders who were at the city gate said, "We are witnesses. This woman will be coming into your home. We hope the Lord will make her like Rachel and Leah. They had many children. So the people of Israel grew in number. May you become powerful in the district of

Ephrathah. May you become famous in Bethlehem! [12]Tamar gave birth to Judah's son Perez.[n] In the same way, may the Lord give you many children through Ruth. And may your family be great like his."

[13]So Boaz took Ruth and married her. The Lord let her become pregnant, and she gave birth to a son. [14]The women told Naomi, "Praise the Lord who gave you this grandson. And may he become famous in Israel. [15]He will give you new life. And he will take care of you in your old age. This happened because of your daughter-in-law. She loves you. And she is better for you than seven sons. She has given birth to your grandson."

[16]Naomi took the boy, held him in her arms and cared for him. [17]The neighbours gave the boy his name. These women said, "This boy was born for Naomi." The neighbours named him Obed. Obed was Jesse's father. And Jesse was the father of David.

[18]This is the family history of Perez. Perez was the father of Hezron. [19]Hezron was the father of Ram. Ram was the father of Amminadab. [20]Amminadab was the father of Nahshon. Nahshon was the father of Salmon. [21]Salmon was the father of Boaz. Boaz was the father of Obed. [22]Obed was the father of Jesse, and Jesse was the father of David.

Perez One of Boaz's ancestors.

1 SAMUEL

Samuel and King Saul

Samuel's Birth

1 There was a man named Elkanah son of Jeroham. He was from Ramathaim in the mountains of Ephraim. Elkanah was from the family of Zuph. (Jeroham was Elihu's son. Elihu was Tohu's son. And Tohu was the son of Zuph from the family group of Ephraim.) [2]Elkanah had two wives. One was named Hannah, and the other was named Peninnah. Peninnah had children, but Hannah had none.

[3]Every year Elkanah left his town Ramah and went up to Shiloh. There he worshipped the Lord of heaven's armies and offered sacrifices to him. Shiloh was where Hophni and Phinehas served as priests of the Lord. They were the sons of Eli. [4]When Elkanah offered sacrifices, he always gave a share of the meat to his wife Peninnah. He also gave shares of the meat to her sons and daughters. [5]But Elkanah always gave a special share of the meat to Hannah. He did this because he loved Hannah and because the Lord had made Hannah unable to have children. [6]Peninnah would upset Hannah and make her feel bad. She did this because the Lord had made Hannah unable to have children. [7]This happened every year when they went up to the Tent[d] of the Lord at Shiloh. Peninnah would upset Hannah until Hannah would cry and not eat anything. [8]Her husband Elkanah would say to her, "Hannah, why are you crying? Why won't you eat? Why are you sad? Don't I mean more to you than ten sons?"

[9]Once, after they had eaten their meal in Shiloh, Hannah got up. Now Eli the priest was sitting on a chair near the entrance to the Lord's Holy Tent. [10]Hannah was very sad. She cried much and prayed to the Lord. [11]She made a promise. She said, "Lord of heaven's armies, see how bad I feel. Remember me! Don't forget me. If you will give me a son, I will give him back to you all his life. And no one will ever use a razor to cut his hair."[n]

[12]While Hannah kept praying, Eli watched her mouth. [13]She was praying in her heart. Her lips moved, but her voice was not heard. So Eli thought she was drunk. [14]He said to her, "Stop getting drunk! Throw away your wine!"

[15]Hannah answered, "No, master, I have not drunk any wine or beer. I am a woman who is deeply troubled. I was telling the Lord about all my problems. [16]Don't think of me as an evil woman. I have been praying because of my many troubles and much sadness."

[17]Eli answered, "Go in peace. May the God of Israel give you what you asked of him."

[18]Hannah said, "I want to be pleasing to you always." Then she left and ate something. She was not sad any more.

[19]Early the next morning Elkanah's family got up and worshipped the Lord. Then they went back home to Ramah. Elkanah had sexual relations with his wife Hannah. And the Lord remembered her. [20]So Hannah became pregnant, and in time she gave

---

And . . . hair People who made special promises not to cut their hair or to drink wine or beer were called Nazirites. These people gave their lives to the Lord. See Numbers 6:1-5.

birth to a son. She named him Samuel." She said, "His name is Samuel because I asked the Lord for him."

Hannah Gives Samuel to God

21Every year Elkanah went to Shiloh to offer sacrifices. He went to keep the promise he had made to God. He brought his whole family with him. So once again he went up to Shiloh. 22But Hannah did not go with him. She told him, "When the boy is old enough to eat solid food, I will take him to Shiloh. Then I will give him to the Lord. He will become a Nazirite.*d* He will always live there at Shiloh." 23Elkanah, Hannah's husband, said to her, "Do what you think is best. You may stay home until the boy is old enough to eat. May the Lord do what you have said." So Hannah stayed at home to nurse her son until he was old enough to eat.

24When Samuel was old enough to eat, Hannah took him to the Tent*d* of the Lord at Shiloh. She also took a three-year-old bull, 10 kilograms of flour and a leather bag filled with wine. 25They killed the bull for the sacrifice. Then Hannah brought Samuel to Eli. 26She said to Eli, "As surely as you live, my master, I am the same woman who stood near you praying to the Lord. 27I prayed for this child. The Lord answered my prayer and gave him to me. 28Now I give him back to the Lord. He will belong to the Lord all his life." And he worshipped the Lord there.

Hannah Gives Thanks

2 Hannah said:

"The Lord has filled my heart
  with joy.
I feel very strong in the Lord.
I can laugh at my enemies.
I am glad because you have
  helped me!

2"There is no one holy like the
  Lord.
There is no God but you.
There is no Rock*d* like our God.

3"Don't continue boasting.
Don't speak proud words.
The Lord is a God who knows
  everything.
He judges what people do.

4"The bows of warriors break,
but weak people become strong.
5Those who once had plenty of
  food now must work for
  food.
But people who once were
  hungry now grow fat on
  food.
The woman who was unable to
  have children now has had
  seven.
But the woman who had many
  sons now is sad.

6"The Lord causes people to die,
and he causes them to live.
He brings people down to where
  the dead are,
and he raises them to life again.
7The Lord makes people poor,
and he makes people rich.
He makes people humble,
and he makes people great.
8The Lord raises the poor up from
  the dust,
and he picks needy people up
  from the ashes.
He lets the poor sit with princes.
He lets them sit on a throne of
  honour.
"The foundations of the earth
  belong to the Lord.
The Lord set the world upon
  them.
9He protects his holy people.
But those who do evil will be
  silenced in darkness.
Their power will not help them
  win.

Samuel This name sounds like the Hebrew word for "God heard".

¹⁰The Lord destroys his enemies.
He will thunder in heaven
against them.
The Lord will judge all the earth.
He will give power to his king.
He will make his appointed king
strong."

Eli's Evil Sons

¹¹Then Elkanah went home to Ramah. But the boy continued to serve the Lord under Eli the priest.
¹²Now Eli's sons were evil men. They did not care about the Lord. ¹³This is what the priests would do to the people: every time someone brought a sacrifice, the meat would be cooked in a pot. The priest's servant would then come with a fork in his hand. The fork had three prongs. ¹⁴He would plunge the fork into the pot or the kettle. Whatever the fork brought out of the pot belonged to the priest. This is how they treated all the Israelites who came to Shiloh to offer sacrifices. ¹⁵But even before the fat was burned, the priest's servant would come to the person offering sacrifices. The servant would say, "Give the priest some meat to roast. The priest won't accept boiled meat from you. He will only accept raw meat."
¹⁶But the man who offered the sacrifice might say, "Let the fat be burned up first as usual. Then you may take anything you want."
If so, the priest's servant would answer, "No, give me the meat now. If you don't, I'll take it by force."
¹⁷The Lord saw that the sin of the servants was very great. They did not show respect for the offerings made to the Lord.

Samuel Grows Up

¹⁸But Samuel obeyed the Lord. He wore a linen holy robe.^d ¹⁹Every year Samuel's mother would make a little coat for him. She would take it to him when she went to Shiloh. She went

there with her husband for the sacrifice. ²⁰Eli would bless Elkanah and his wife. Eli would say, "May the Lord repay you with children through Hannah. They will take the place of the boy Hannah prayed for and gave back to the Lord." Then Elkanah and Hannah would go home. ²¹The Lord was kind to Hannah. She became the mother of three sons and two daughters. And the boy Samuel grew up serving the Lord.
²²Now Eli was very old. He heard about everything his sons were doing to all the Israelites. He also heard about how his sons had sexual relations with the women who served at the entrance to the Meeting Tent.^d ²³Eli said to his sons, "The people here tell me about the evil you do. Why do you do these evil things? ²⁴No, my sons. The Lord's people are saying bad things about you. ²⁵If someone sins against another person, God can help him. But if he sins against the Lord himself, no one can help him!" But Eli's sons would not listen to him. This was because the Lord had decided to put them to death.
²⁶The boy Samuel kept growing. He pleased God and the people.
²⁷A man of God came to Eli. He said, "This is what the Lord says: 'I clearly showed myself to the family of your ancestor Aaron. This was when they were slaves to the king of Egypt. ²⁸I chose them from all the tribes^d of Israel to be my priests. I wanted them to go up to my altar, to burn incense^d and to wear the holy robe. I also let the family of your ancestor have part of all the offerings sacrificed by the Israelites. ²⁹So why don't you respect the sacrifices and gifts? You honour your sons more than me. You become fat on the best parts of the meat the Israelites bring to me'.
³⁰"Here's what the Lord, the God of Israel, says: 'I promised that your family and your ancestor's family

Exodus 25:8
"The people must build a holy place for
me. Then I can live among them."

Deuteronomy 7:1
The Lord your God will bring you into the
land . . . to own it.

Ruth 2:6
"From morning until just now, she has stopped only a few minutes to rest in the shelter."

would serve me for ever'. But now the Lord says this: 'That will never be! I will honour those who honour me. But I will take honour away from those who do not honour me. ³¹The time is coming when I will destroy the descendants*d* of both you and your ancestors. No man will grow old in your family. ³²You will see trouble in my house. Good things will be done to Israel. But there will never be an old man in your family. ³³I will save one man to serve as priest at my altar. He will wear out his eyes and use up his strength. The rest of your descendants will die by the sword.

³⁴" 'I will give you a sign. Both your sons, Hophni and Phinehas, will die on the same day. ³⁵I will choose a loyal priest for myself. He will listen to me and do what I want. I will make his family strong. He will always serve before my appointed king. ³⁶Then everyone left in your family will come and bow down before him. They will beg for a little money or a little food. They will say, "Please give me a job as priest so I can have food to eat" '."

God Calls Samuel

3 The boy Samuel served the Lord under Eli. In those days the Lord did not speak directly to people very often. There were very few visions. ²Eli's eyes were so weak he was almost blind. One night he was lying in bed. ³Samuel was also in bed in the Lord's Holy Tent.*d* The Ark*d* of God was in the Holy Tent. God's lamp was still burning.

⁴Then the Lord called Samuel. Samuel answered, "I am here!" ⁵He ran to Eli and said, "I am here. You called me."

But Eli said, "I didn't call you. Go back to bed." So Samuel went back to bed.

⁶The Lord called again, "Samuel!"

Samuel again went to Eli and said, "I am here. You called me."

Again Eli said, "I didn't call you. Go back to bed."

⁷Samuel did not yet know the Lord. The Lord had not spoken directly to him yet.

⁸The Lord called Samuel for the third time. Samuel got up and went to Eli. He said, "I am here. You called me."

Then Eli realised the Lord was calling the boy. ⁹So he told Samuel, "Go to bed. If he calls you again, say, 'Speak, Lord. I am your servant, and I am listening'." So Samuel went and lay down in bed.

¹⁰The Lord came and stood there. He called as he had before. He said, "Samuel, Samuel!"

Samuel said, "Speak, Lord. I am your servant, and I am listening."

¹¹The Lord said to Samuel, "See, I am going to do something in Israel. It will shock those who hear about it. ¹²At that time I will do to Eli and his family everything I promised. I will not stop until I have finished. ¹³I told Eli I would punish his family for ever. I will do it because Eli knew his sons were evil. They spoke against me, but he did not control them. ¹⁴So here is what I promised Eli's family: 'Your guilt will never be removed by sacrifice or offering'."

¹⁵Samuel lay down until morning. Then he opened the doors of the Tent*d* of the Lord. He was afraid to tell Eli about the vision. ¹⁶But Eli said to him, "Samuel, my son!"

Samuel answered, "I am here."

¹⁷Eli asked, "What did the Lord say to you? Don't hide it from me. May God punish you terribly if you hide from me anything he said to you." ¹⁸So Samuel told Eli everything. He did not hide anything from him. Then Eli said, "He is the Lord. Let him do what he thinks is best."

¹⁹The Lord was with Samuel as he grew up. He did not let any of Samuel's messages fail to come true. ²⁰Then all Israel, from Dan to Beer-

sheba,[n] knew Samuel was a prophet[d] of the Lord. [21]And the Lord continued to show himself to Samuel at Shiloh. He also showed himself to Samuel through his word.

4 News about Samuel spread through all of Israel.

The Philistines Capture the Ark of God

At that time the Israelites went out to fight the Philistines. The Israelites camped at Ebenezer, and the Philistines camped at Aphek. [2]The Philistines went to meet the Israelites in battle. And as the battle spread, the Philistines defeated the Israelites. They killed about 4,000 soldiers of the Israelite army. [3]Then some Israelite soldiers went back to their camp. The older leaders of Israel asked, "Why did the Lord let the Philistines defeat us? Let's bring the Ark[d] of God with the Lord here from Shiloh. In this way God will go with us into battle. He will save us from our enemies."

[4]So the people sent men to Shiloh. They brought back the Ark of God with the Lord of heaven's armies. Eli's two sons, Hophni and Phinehas, were there with the Holy Ark.

[5]The Ark of God with the Lord came into the camp. And all the Israelites gave a great shout of joy. It made the ground shake. [6]The Philistines heard Israel's shout. They asked, "What's all this shouting in the Hebrew camp?"

Then the Philistines found out that the Holy Ark of the Lord had come into the Hebrew camp. [7]They were afraid and said, "A god has come into the Hebrew camp! We're in trouble! This has never happened before! [8]How terrible it will be for us! Who can save us from these powerful gods? They are the ones who struck the Egyptians with all kinds of disasters in the desert. [9]Be brave, Philistines! Fight like men! In the past they were our slaves. So fight like men, or you will become their slaves."

[10]So the Philistines fought hard and defeated the Israelites. Every Israelite soldier ran away to his own home. It was a great defeat for Israel, because 30,000 Israelite soldiers were killed. [11]The Holy Ark of God was taken by the Philistines. And Eli's two sons, Hophni and Phinehas, were killed.

[12]That same day a man from the tribe[d] of Benjamin ran from the battle. He tore his clothes and put dust on his head to show his great sadness. [13]When he arrived in Shiloh, Eli was by the side of the road. Eli was sitting there in a chair, watching. He was worried about the Holy Ark of God. When the Benjaminite entered Shiloh, he told the bad news. Then all the people in town cried loudly. [14]Eli heard the crying and asked, "What's all this noise?"

The Benjaminite ran to Eli and told him what had happened. [15]Eli was now 98 years old, and he was blind. [16]The Benjaminite told him, "I have come from the battle. I ran all the way here today."

Eli asked, "What happened, my son?"

[17]The Benjaminite answered, "Israel ran away from the Philistines. The Israelite army has lost many soldiers. Your two sons are both dead. And the Philistines have taken the Holy Ark of God."

[18]When he mentioned the Holy Ark of God, Eli fell backwards off his chair. He fell beside the gate and broke his neck, because he was old and fat. And Eli died. He had led Israel for 40 years.

Dan to Beersheba Dan was the city farthest north in Israel. Beersheba was the city farthest south. So this means all the people of Israel.

The Glory Is Gone

[19]Eli's daughter-in-law, the wife of Phinehas, was pregnant. It was nearly time for her baby to be born. She heard the news that the Holy Ark[d] of God had been taken. She heard also that Eli, her father-in-law, and Phinehas, her husband, were both dead. So she began to give birth to her child. The child was born, but the mother had much trouble in giving birth. [20]As she was dying, the women who helped her give birth said, "Don't worry! You've given birth to a son!" But she did not answer or pay attention. She named the baby Ichabod.[n] [21]She named him Ichabod and said, "Israel's glory is gone." She said this because the Holy Ark of God had been taken. It was also because her father-in-law and husband were dead. [22]She said, "Israel's glory is gone, because the Holy Ark of God has been taken away."

Trouble for the Philistines

5 After the Philistines had captured the Holy Ark[d] of God, they took it from Ebenezer to Ashdod. [2]They carried it into Dagon's[d] temple and put it next to Dagon. [3]The people of Ashdod rose early the next morning. They found that Dagon had fallen on his face on the ground. He was lying before the Holy Ark of the Lord. So the people of Ashdod put Dagon back in his place. [4]The next morning the people of Ashdod rose from sleep. And again they found Dagon on the ground! He had fallen down before the Holy Ark of the Lord. His head and hands had broken off and were lying in the doorway. Only his body was still in one piece. [5]So, even today, Dagon's priests and others who enter his temple at Ashdod refuse to step on the doorsill.

[6]The Lord punished the people of Ashdod and their neighbours. He gave them much trouble. He gave them growths on their skin. [7]The people of Ashdod saw what was happening. They said, "The Holy Ark of the God of Israel can't stay with us. God is punishing us and Dagon our god." [8]The people of Ashdod called all five Philistine kings together. They asked them, "What should we do with the Holy Ark of the God of Israel?"

The rulers answered, "Move the Holy Ark of the God of Israel to Gath." So the Philistines moved it to Gath.

[9]But after they had moved it to Gath, the Lord punished that city also. He made the people very afraid. God troubled both old and young people in Gath. He caused them to have growths on their skin. [10]Then the Philistines sent the Holy Ark of God to Ekron.

But when it came into Ekron, the people of Ekron yelled. They said, "Why are you bringing the Holy Ark of the God of Israel to our city? Do you want to kill us and our people?" [11]The people of Ekron called all the kings of the Philistines together. They said to the kings, "Send the Holy Ark of the God of Israel back to its place. Do it before it kills us and our people!" They were very afraid. God's punishment was very terrible there. [12]The people who did not die were troubled with growths on their skin. So the people of Ekron cried loudly to heaven.

The Holy Ark of God Is Sent Home

6 The Philistines kept the Holy Ark[d] of God in their land seven months. [2]Then they called for their priests and magicians. They said, "What should we do with the Holy Ark of the Lord? Tell us how to send it back home!"

[3]The priests and magicians answered them. They said, "If you send

back the Holy Ark of the God of Israel, don't send it away empty. You must offer a penalty offering so the God of Israel will forgive your sins. Then you will be healed. When God has forgiven you, he will stop punishing you."

⁴The Philistines asked, "What kind of penalty offering should we send to Israel's God?"

The priests and magicians answered, "Make five gold models of the growths on your skin. Also make five gold models of rats. The number of models must be the same as the number of Philistine kings. This is because the same sickness has come on you and your kings. ⁵Make models of the growths and the rats that are ruining the country. Give them to Israel's God and honour him. Then maybe Israel's God will stop punishing you, your gods and your land. ⁶Don't be stubborn like the king of Egypt and the Egyptians. God punished them terribly. That is why the Egyptians let the Israelites leave Egypt.

⁷"You must build a new cart. And get two cows that have just had calves. These must be cows that have never had yokes*ᵈ* on their necks. Then hitch the cows to the cart. Take the calves home. Don't let them follow their mothers. ⁸Put the Holy Ark of the Lord on the cart. And put the gold models in a box beside the Holy Ark. They are your penalty offerings for God to forgive your sins. Send the cart straight on its way. ⁹Watch the cart. It may go toward Beth Shemesh in Israel's own land. If so, the Lord has given us this great sickness. But it may not go toward Beth Shemesh. Then we will know that Israel's God has not punished us. We will know that our sickness just happened by chance."

¹⁰The Philistines did what the priests and magicians said. They took two cows that had just had calves. They hitched them to the cart. But they kept their calves at home. ¹¹They put the Holy Ark of the Lord on the cart. And they put the box with the gold rats and models of growths on the cart. ¹²Then the cows went straight toward Beth Shemesh. They stayed on the road, mooing all the way. They did not turn right or left. The Philistine kings followed the cows as far as the border of Beth Shemesh.

¹³Now the people of Beth Shemesh were harvesting their wheat in the valley. They looked up and saw Holy Ark of the Lord. They were very happy to see it again. ¹⁴The cart came to the field belonging to Joshua of Beth Shemesh. The cart stopped in this field near a large rock. The people of Beth Shemesh chopped up the wood of the cart. Then they killed the cows and sacrificed them to the Lord. ¹⁵The Levites took down the Holy Ark of the Lord. They also took down the box that had the gold models. They put both on the large rock. That day the people of Beth Shemesh offered whole burnt offerings and made sacrifices to the Lord. ¹⁶The five Philistine kings watched them do all these things. Then they went back to Ekron the same day.

¹⁷The Philistines sent these gold models of the growths. They were penalty offerings to the Lord for their sins. They sent one model for each Philistine town. These towns were Ashdod, Gaza, Ashkelon, Gath and Ekron. ¹⁸And the Philistines also sent gold models of rats. The number of rats was the same as the number of towns belonging to the Philistine kings. These towns included strong, walled cities and country villages. The large rock on which they put the Holy Ark of the Lord is still there. It is in the field of Joshua of Beth Shemesh.

¹⁹But some of the men of Beth Shemesh looked into the Holy Ark of the Lord. So God killed 70 of them. The people of Beth Shemesh cried because the Lord had punished them so

terribly. [20]They said, "Who can stand before the Lord, this holy God? Where can the Holy Ark go from here?"

[21]Then they sent messengers to the people of Kiriath Jearim. The messengers said, "The Philistines have brought back the Holy Ark of the Lord. Come down and take it to your city."

7 The men of Kiriath Jearim came and took the Holy Ark of the Lord. They took it to Abinadab's house on a hill. There they made Abinadab's son Eleazar holy for the Lord so he could guard the Holy Ark.

The Lord Saves the Israelites

[2]The Holy Ark[d] stayed at Kiriath Jearim a long time — 20 years in all. And the people of Israel began to follow the Lord again. [3]Samuel spoke to the whole group of Israel. He said, "If you're turning back to the Lord with all your hearts, you must remove your foreign gods. You must remove your idols of Ashtoreth.[d] You must give yourselves fully to the Lord and serve only him. Then he will save you from the Philistines."

[4]So the Israelites put away their idols of Baal[d] and Ashtoreth. And they served only the Lord.

[5]Samuel said, "All Israel must meet at Mizpah. I will pray to the Lord for you." [6]So the Israelites met together at Mizpah. They drew water from the ground and poured it out before the Lord. They did not eat that day. They confessed, "We have sinned against the Lord." And Samuel served as judge of Israel at Mizpah.

[7]The Philistines heard the Israelites were meeting at Mizpah. So the Philistine kings came up to attack them. When the Israelites heard they were coming, they were afraid. [8]They said to Samuel, "Don't stop praying to the Lord our God for us! Ask the Lord to save us from the Philistines!" [9]Then Samuel took a baby lamb. He offered the lamb to the Lord as a whole burnt offering. He called to the Lord for Israel's sake. And the Lord answered him.

[10]While Samuel was burning the offering, the Philistines came near. They were going to attack Israel. But the Lord thundered against the Philistines with loud thunder. They were so frightened they became confused. So the Israelites defeated the Philistines in battle. [11]The men of Israel ran out of Mizpah and chased the Philistines. They went almost to Beth Car, killing the Philistines along the way.

Peace Comes to Israel

[12]After this happened Samuel took a stone. He set it up between Mizpah and Shen. He named the stone Ebenezer.[n] Samuel said, "The Lord has helped us to this point." [13]So the Philistines were defeated. They did not enter the Israelites' land again.

The Lord was against the Philistines all Samuel's life. [14]Earlier the Philistines had taken towns from the Israelites. But the Israelites won them back, from Ekron to Gath. They also took back from the Philistines the neighbouring lands of these towns. There was peace also between Israel and the Amorites.

[15]Samuel continued as judge of Israel all his life. [16]Every year he went from Bethel to Gilgal to Mizpah. He judged the Israelites in all these towns. [17]But Samuel always went back to Ramah, where his home was. He also judged Israel there. And there he built an altar to the Lord.

Israel Asks for a King

8 When Samuel became old, he made his sons judges for Israel. [2]His first son was named Joel, and his second son was named Abijah. Joel

---

Ebenezer This name means "stone of help".

and Abijah were judges in Beersheba. ³But Samuel's sons did not live as he did. They tried to get money dishonestly. They took money secretly to be dishonest in their judging.

⁴So all the older leaders came together and met Samuel at Ramah. ⁵They said to him, "You're old, and your sons don't live as you do. Give us a king to rule over us like all the other nations."

⁶When the older leaders said that, Samuel was not pleased. He prayed to the Lord. ⁷The Lord told Samuel, "Listen to whatever the people say to you. They have not rejected you. They have rejected me from being their king. ⁸They are doing as they have always done. When I took them out of Egypt, they left me. They served other gods. They are doing the same to you. ⁹Now listen to the people. But give them a warning. Tell them what the king who rules over them will do."

¹⁰Samuel answered those who had asked him for a king. He told them all the words of the Lord. ¹¹Samuel said, "If you have a king ruling over you, this is what he will do. He will take your sons. He will make them serve with his chariots and his horses. They will run in front of the king's chariot. ¹²The king will make some of your sons commanders over 1,000 men or over 50 men. He will make some of your other sons plough his ground and reap his harvest. He will take others to make weapons of war and equipment for his chariots. ¹³This king will take your daughters. Some of your daughters will make perfume. Others will cook and bake for him. ¹⁴He will take your best fields, vineyards and olive groves. He will give them to his servants. ¹⁵He will take one-tenth of your grain and grapes and give it to his officers and servants. ¹⁶He will take your men servants and girl servants. He will take your best cattle and your

donkeys. He will use them all for his own work. ¹⁷He will take one-tenth of your flocks. And you yourselves will become his slaves. ¹⁸When that time comes, you will cry out because of the king you chose. The Lord will not answer you then."

¹⁹But the people would not listen to Samuel. They said, "No! We want a king to rule over us. ²⁰Then we will be the same as all the other nations. Our king will judge us. He will go with us and fight our battles."

²¹Samuel heard all that the people said. Then he repeated all their words to the Lord. ²²The Lord answered, "You must listen to them. Give them a king."

Then Samuel told the people of Israel, "Everyone go back to his town."

Saul Looks for His Father's Donkeys

9 Kish, son of Abiel, was from the tribe ᵈ of Benjamin. He was an important man. (Abiel was the son of Zeror and the grandson of Becorath, who was the son of Aphiah of Benjamin.) ²Kish had a son named Saul. Saul was a fine young man. There was no Israelite better than he. Saul stood a head taller than any other man in Israel.

³Now the donkeys of Saul's father, Kish, were lost. So Kish said to Saul, his son, "Take one of the servants. Go and look for the donkeys." ⁴Saul went through the mountains of Ephraim. And he went through the land of Shalisha. But he and the servant could not find the donkeys. They went into the land of Shaalim, but the donkeys were not there. They went through the land of Benjamin. But they still did not find the donkeys. ⁵They arrived in the area of Zuph. Saul said to his servant, "Let's go back. My father will stop thinking about the donkeys. He will start worrying about us."

⁶But the servant answered, "A man

of God is in this town. People respect him because everything he says comes true. Let's go into the town now. Maybe he can tell us something about the journey we have taken."

[7]Saul said to his servant, "If we go into the town, what can we give him? The food in our bags is gone. We have no gift to give him. Do we have anything at all to give him?"

[8]Again the servant answered Saul. "Look, I have 3 grams of silver. Give it to the man of God. Then he will tell us about our journey." [9](In the past, someone in Israel might want to ask something from God. If so, he would say, 'Let's go to the seer'.[d] We call the person a man of God today. But in the past he was called a 'seer.')

[10]Saul said to his servant, "That is a good idea. Come, let's go." So they went towards the town where the man of God was.

[11]Saul and the servant were going up the hill to the town. On the way they met some young women coming out to get water. Saul and the servant asked them, "Is the seer here?"

[12]The young women answered, "Yes, he's here. He's ahead of you. Hurry now. He has just come to our town today. This is because the people will offer a sacrifice at the place of worship. [13]When you enter the town, you will find him. He will be there before he goes up to the place of worship to eat. The people will not begin eating until the seer comes. He must bless the sacrifice. After that, the guests will eat. Go now, and you should find him."

Saul Meets Samuel

[14]Saul and the servant went up to the town. Just as they entered the town, they saw Samuel. He was on his way up to the place of worship. So he was coming out of the city towards them.

[15]The day before Saul came, the Lord had told Samuel: [16]"About this time tomorrow I will send you a man. He will be from Benjamin. You must appoint him as leader over my people Israel. He will save my people from the Philistines. I have seen the suffering of my people. I have listened to their cry."

[17]When Samuel first saw Saul, the Lord spoke to Samuel. He said, "This is the man I told you about. He will rule my people."

[18]Saul came near Samuel at the gate. Saul said, "Please tell me where the seer's[d] house is."

[19]Samuel answered, "I am the seer. Go ahead of me to the place of worship. Today you and your servant are to eat with me. Tomorrow morning I will send you home. And I will answer all your questions. [20]Don't worry about the donkeys you lost three days ago. They have been found. Israel now wants you and all your father's family."

[21]Saul answered, "But I am from the tribe[d] of Benjamin. It's the smallest tribe in Israel. And my family group is the smallest in the tribe of Benjamin. Why do you say Israel wants me?"

[22]Then Samuel took Saul and his servant into a large room. He gave them a chief place at the table. About 30 guests were there. [23]Samuel said to the cook, "Bring the meat I gave you. It's the portion I told you to set aside."

[24]So the cook took the thigh and put it on the table in front of Saul. Samuel said, "This is the meat saved for you. Eat it because it was set aside for you for this special time. As I said, 'I have invited the people'. " So Saul ate with Samuel that day.

[25]After they finished eating, they came down from the place of worship. They went to the town. Then Samuel

talked with Saul on the roof[n] of his house. [26]At dawn they got up, and Samuel called to Saul on the roof. He said, "Get up, and I will send you on your way." So Saul got up. He went out of the house with Samuel. [27]Saul, his servant and Samuel were getting near the edge of the city. Samuel said to Saul, "Tell the servant to go on ahead of us. I have a message from God for you."

Samuel Appoints Saul

10 Samuel took a jar of olive oil. He poured the oil on Saul's head. He kissed Saul and said, "The Lord has appointed you to be leader of his people Israel. You will rule over the people of the Lord. You will save them from their enemies all around. This will be the sign that the Lord has appointed you as leader of his people. [2]After you leave me today, you will meet two men. They will be near Rachel's tomb on the border of Benjamin at Zelzah. They will say to you, 'The donkeys you were looking for have been found. But now your father has stopped thinking about his donkeys. He is worrying about you. He is asking, 'What will I do about my son?'

[3]"Then you will go on until you reach the great tree at Tabor. There three men will meet you. They will be on their way to worship God at Bethel. One man will be carrying three young goats. The second man will be carrying three loaves of bread. And the third one will have a leather bag full of wine. [4]They will greet you and offer you two loaves of bread. You will accept the bread from them. [5]Then you will go to Gibeah of God. There is a Philistine camp there. When you come near this town, a group of prophets[d] will come out. They will be coming from the place of worship

playing harps, tambourines,[d] flutes and lyres.[d] They will be prophesying. [6]The Spirit[d] of the Lord will enter you with power. You will prophesy with these prophets. You will be changed into a different man. [7]After these signs happen, do whatever you find to do. God will help you.

[8]"Go ahead of me to Gilgal. I will come down to you. Then I will offer whole burnt offerings and fellowship offerings. But you must wait seven days. Then I will come and tell you what to do."

Saul Made King

[9]When Saul turned to leave Samuel, God changed Saul's heart. All these signs came true that day. [10]When Saul and his servant arrived at Gibeah, Saul met a group of prophets.[d] The Spirit[d] of God entered him, and he prophesied with the prophets. [11]People who had known Saul before saw him prophesying with the prophets. They asked each other, "What has happened to Kish's son? Is even Saul one of the prophets?"

[12]A man who lived there said, "Who is the father of these prophets?" This became a famous saying: "Is even Saul one of the prophets?" [13]When Saul finished prophesying, he went to the place of worship.

[14]Saul's uncle asked him and his servant, "Where have you been?"

Saul said, "We were looking for the donkeys. When we couldn't find them, we went to talk to Samuel."

[15]Saul's uncle asked, "Please tell me. What did Samuel say to you?"

[16]Saul answered, "He told us the donkeys had already been found." But Saul did not tell his uncle what Samuel had said about his becoming king.

[17]Samuel called all the people of Israel to meet with the Lord at Mizpah.

---

roof In Bible times houses were built with flat roofs. The roof was used for drying things such as flax and fruit. It was also used as an extra room, as a place for worship and as a place to sleep in the summer.

¹⁸He said, "This is what the Lord, the God of Israel, says: 'I led Israel out of Egypt. I saved you from Egypt's control. And I saved you from other kingdoms that were troubling you'. ¹⁹But now you have rejected your God. He saves you from all your troubles and problems. But you said, 'No! We want a king to rule over us'. Now come, stand before the Lord in your tribes*d* and family groups."

²⁰Samuel brought all the tribes of Israel near, and the tribe of Benjamin was chosen. ²¹Samuel had them pass by in family groups, and Matri's family was chosen. Then he had each man of Matri's family pass by, and Saul son of Kish was chosen. But when they looked for Saul, they could not find him. ²²Then they asked the Lord, "Has Saul come here yet?"

The Lord said, "Yes. He's hiding behind the baggage."

²³So they ran and brought him out. When Saul stood among the people, he was a head taller than anyone else. ²⁴Then Samuel said to the people, "See the man the Lord has chosen. There is no one like him among all the people."

Then the people shouted, "Long live the king!"

²⁵Samuel explained the rights and duties of the king. He wrote the rules in a book and put the book before the Lord. Then he told the people to go to their homes.

²⁶Saul also went to his home in Gibeah. God touched the hearts of certain brave men who went along with him. ²⁷But some troublemakers said, "How can this man save us?" They hated Saul and refused to bring gifts to him. But Saul kept quiet.

Nahash Troubles Jabesh Gilead

11 About a month later Nahash the Ammonite and his army surrounded the city of Jabesh in Gilead. All the people of Jabesh said to Nahash, "Make a treaty with us. And we will serve you."

²But he answered, "I will make a treaty with you. But I will only do it if I'm allowed to tear out the right eye of each of you. Then all Israel will be ashamed!"

³The older leaders of Jabesh said to Nahash, "Let us have seven days. We will send messengers through all Israel. If no one comes to help us, we will give ourselves up to you."

⁴The messengers came to Gibeah where Saul lived. When they told the people the news, the people cried loudly. ⁵Saul had finished ploughing in the fields with his oxen. He was coming home when he heard the people crying. He asked, "What's wrong with the people? Why are they crying?" Then they told Saul what the messengers from Jabesh had said. ⁶When Saul heard their words, God's Spirit*d* entered him with power. Saul became very angry. ⁷So he took a pair of oxen and cut them into pieces. Then he gave the pieces of the oxen to messengers. He ordered them to carry the pieces through all the land of Israel.

The messengers made an announcement to the people. They said, "This is what will happen to the oxen of anyone who does not follow Saul and Samuel." So the people became very afraid of the Lord. They all came together as if they were one person. ⁸Saul gathered the people together at Bezek. There were 300,000 men from Israel and 30,000 men from Judah.

⁹They spoke to the messengers who had come. They said, "Tell the people at Jabesh Gilead this: 'Before the day becomes hot tomorrow, you will be saved'." So the messengers went and reported this to the people at Jabesh. They were very happy. ¹⁰The people said to Nahash the Am-

monite, "Tomorrow we will give our-selves up to you. Then you can do anything you want to us."

¹¹The next morning Saul divided his soldiers into three groups. At dawn they entered the Ammonite camp and they defeated the Ammonites before the heat of the day. The Ammonites who were left alive were scattered. Not even two of them were still to-gether.

¹²Then the people said to Samuel, "Who was it that didn't want Saul as king? Bring them here, and we will kill them!"

¹³But Saul said, "No! No one will be put to death today. The Lord has saved Israel today!"

¹⁴Then Samuel said to the people, "Come, let's go to Gilgal. At Gilgal we will again promise to obey the king." ¹⁵All the people went to Gilgal. And there, before the Lord, the people made Saul king. They offered fellow-ship offerings to the Lord. Saul and all the Israelites had a great celebration.

Samuel's Farewell Speech

12 Samuel said to all Israel, "I have done everything you wanted me to do. I have put a king over you. ²Now you have a king to lead you. I am old and grey, and my sons are here with you. I have been your leader since I was young. ³Here I am. If I have done anything wrong, you must testify against me. Do this before the Lord and his appointed king. Did I steal anyone's ox or don-key? Did I hurt or cheat anyone? Did I ever secretly take money to pretend not to see something wrong? If I did any of these things, I will make it right."

⁴The Israelites answered, "You have not cheated us. You have not hurt us. You have not taken anything unfairly from anyone."

⁵Samuel said to them, "The Lord is a witness to what you have said. His appointed king is also a witness today. They are both witnesses that you did not find anything wrong in me."

"He is our witness," they said.

⁶Then Samuel said to the people, "The Lord is our witness. He chose Moses and Aaron. He brought your ancestors out of Egypt. ⁷Now, stand there. And I will talk with you about all the good things the Lord did for you and your ancestors.

⁸"After Jacob entered Egypt, his descendants*d* cried to the Lord for help. So the Lord sent Moses and Aaron. They took your ancestors out of Egypt and brought them to live in this place.

⁹"But they forgot the Lord their God. So he let them become the slaves of Sisera. He was the com-mander of the army of Hazor. The Lord let them become the slaves of the Philistines and the king of Moab. They all fought against your ances-tors. ¹⁰Then your ancestors cried to the Lord. They said, 'We have sinned. We have left the Lord. We served the Baals*d* and the Ashtoreths.*d* But now save us from our enemies, and we will serve you'. ¹¹The Lord sent Gideon, who is also called Jerub-Baal. And he sent Barak, Jephthah and Samuel. Then he saved you from your enemies around you. And you lived in safety. ¹²But then you saw Nahash king of the Ammonites coming against you. You said, 'No! We want a king to rule over us!' ¹³Now here is the king you chose. The Lord has put him over you. ¹⁴You must honour the Lord and serve him. You must obey his commands. Both you and the king ruling over you must follow the Lord your God. If you do, it will be well with you. ¹⁵But if you don't obey the Lord, and if you fight against his commands, he will be against you. He will do to you what he did to your ancestors.

¹⁶"Now stand still and see the great thing the Lord will do before your eyes. ¹⁷It is now the time of the wheat

harvest.ⁿ I will pray for the Lord to send thunder and rain. Then you will know what an evil thing you did against the Lord when you asked for a king."

¹⁸Then Samuel prayed to the Lord. That same day the Lord sent thunder and rain. And the people became very afraid of the Lord and Samuel. ¹⁹They said to Samuel, "Pray to the Lord your God for us, your servants! Don't let us die! We've added to all our sins the evil of asking for a king."

²⁰Samuel answered, "Don't be afraid. It's true that you did wrong. But don't turn away from the Lord. Serve the Lord with all your heart. ²¹Idols are of no use. So don't worship them. They can't help you or save you. They are useless! ²²For his own sake, the Lord won't leave his people. Instead, he was pleased to make you his own people. ²³I will surely not stop praying for you. If I did, I would be sinning against the Lord. I will teach you what is good and right. ²⁴But you must honour the Lord. You must always serve him with all your heart. Remember the wonderful things he did for you! ²⁵But if you are stubborn and do evil, God will sweep you and your king away."

13 Saul was 30 years old when he became king. He was king over Israel for 42 years.ⁿ ²Saul chose 3,000 men from Israel. There were 2,000 men who stayed with him at Michmash in the mountains of Bethel, and 1,000 men stayed with Jonathan at Gibeah in Benjamin. Saul sent the other men in the army back home.

³Jonathan attacked the Philistine camp in Geba, and the other Philistines heard about it. Saul said, "Let the Hebrew people hear what happened." So he told the men to blow trumpets through all the land of Israel. ⁴All the Israelites heard the news. The men said, "Saul has defeated the Philistine camp. Now the Philistines really hate us!" Then the Israelites were called to join Saul at Gilgal.

⁵The Philistines gathered to fight Israel. They had 3,000ⁿ chariots and 6,000 men to ride in the chariots. Their soldiers were many in number, like the grains of sand on the seashore. The Philistines went and camped at Michmash which is east of Beth Aven. ⁶The Israelites saw that they were in trouble. So they went to hide in caves and bushes. They also hid among the rocks and in pits and wells. ⁷Some Hebrews even went across the Jordan River to the land of Gad and Gilead.

But Saul stayed at Gilgal. All the men in his army were shaking with fear. ⁸Saul waited seven days, because Samuel had said he would meet him then. But Samuel did not come to Gilgal. And the soldiers began to leave.

⁹So Saul said, "Bring me the whole burnt offering and the fellowship offerings." Then Saul offered the whole burnt offering. ¹⁰Just as he finished, Samuel arrived. Saul went to meet him.

¹¹Samuel asked, "What have you done?"

Saul answered, "I saw the soldiers leaving me, and you were not here. The Philistines were gathering at Michmash. ¹²Then I thought, 'The Philistines will come against me at Gilgal. And I haven't asked for the Lord's approval'. So I forced myself to offer the whole burnt offering."

¹³Samuel said, "You acted foolishly! You haven't obeyed God's command. If you had obeyed him, God would

---

time . . . harvest This was a dry time in the summer when no rains fell.
Saul . . . years This is how the verse is worded in some early Greek copies. The Hebrew is not clear here.
3,000 Some Greek copies say 3,000. The Hebrew copies say 30,000.

make your kingdom continue in Israel for ever. [14]But now your kingdom will not continue. The Lord has looked for the kind of man he wants. The Lord has appointed him to become ruler of his people. He is doing this because you haven't obeyed his command."

[15]Then Samuel left Gilgal and went to Gibeah in Benjamin. The rest of the army followed Saul into battle. Saul counted the men still with him, and there were about 600.

Hard Times for Israel

[16]Saul and his son Jonathan stayed in Geba in the land of Benjamin. The soldiers with them also stayed there. The Philistines made their camp at Michmash. [17]Three groups went out from their camp to attack. One group went on the Ophrah road in the land of Shual. [18]The second group went on the Beth Horon road. And the third group went on the border road. It overlooked the Valley of Zeboim toward the desert.

[19]The whole land of Israel had no blacksmith. This is because the Philistines had said, "The Hebrews might make swords and spears." [20]So all the Israelites went down to the Philistines. They went to have their ploughs, hoes, axes and sickles sharpened. [21]The Philistine blacksmiths charged about 8 grams of silver for sharpening ploughs and hoes, and 4 grams of silver for sharpening picks, axes and the sticks used to guide oxen.

[22]So when the battle came, the soldiers with Saul and Jonathan had no swords or spears. Only Saul and his son Jonathan had them.

Israel Defeats the Philistines

[23]A group from the Philistine army had gone out to the mountain pass at Michmash.

14 One day Jonathan, Saul's son, spoke to the officer who carried his armour. Jonathan said,

"Come, let's go over to the Philistine camp on the other side." But Jonathan did not tell his father.

[2]Saul was sitting under a pomegranate[d] tree at the threshing[d] floor near Gibeah. He had about 600 men with him. [3]One man was Ahijah, who was a son of Ichabod's brother Ahitub. Ichabod was the son of Phinehas, Eli's son. Eli was the Lord's priest in Shiloh. He wore the holy robe.[d] No one knew Jonathan had left.

[4]There was a steep slope on each side of the pass. Jonathan planned to go through the pass to the Philistine camp. The cliff on one side was named Bozez. The other cliff was named Seneh. [5]One cliff faced north toward Michmash. The other faced south toward Geba.

[6]Jonathan said to his officer who carried his armour, "Come. Let's go to the camp of those men who are not circumcised.[d] Maybe the Lord will help us. It doesn't matter if we have many people, or just a few. Nothing can keep the Lord from giving us victory."

[7]The officer who carried Jonathan's armour said to him, "Do whatever you think is best. Go ahead. I'm with you."

[8]Jonathan said, "Then come. We will cross over to the Philistines. We will let them see us. [9]They may say to us, 'Stay there until we come to you'. If they do, we will stay where we are. We won't go up to them. [10]But they may say, 'Come up to us'. If so, we will climb up. And the Lord will allow us to defeat them. This will be the sign for us."

[11]Both Jonathan and his officer let the Philistines see them. The Philistines said, "Look! The Hebrews are crawling out of the holes they were hiding in!" [12]The Philistines in the camp shouted to Jonathan and his officer, "Come up to us. We'll teach you a lesson!"

Jonathan said to his officer, "Climb up behind me. The Lord has given the

Philistines to Israel!" [13]So Jonathan climbed up, using his hands and feet. His officer climbed just behind him. Jonathan cut down the Philistines as he went, and his officer killed them as he followed behind Jonathan. [14]In that first fight Jonathan and his officer killed about 20 Philistines.

[15]All the Philistine soldiers panicked. Those in the camp and those in the raiding party were frightened. The ground itself shook! God caused the panic.

[16]Saul's guards were at Gibeah in the land of Benjamin. They saw the Philistine soldiers running in every direction. [17]Saul said to his army, "Check and find out who has left our camp." When they checked, they learned that Jonathan and his officer were gone.

[18]So Saul said to Ahijah the priest, "Bring the Holy Ark[d] of God." (At that time it was with the Israelites.) [19]While Saul was talking to the priest, the confusion in the Philistine camp was growing. Then Saul said to Ahijah, "Stop. There's no time to pray now!"

[20]Then Saul and the army with him gathered and entered the battle. They found the Philistines confused, even striking each other with their swords! [21]Earlier, there were Hebrews who had served the Philistines and had stayed in their camp. They now joined the Israelites with Saul and Jonathan. [22]All the Israelites hidden in the mountains of Ephraim heard that the Philistine soldiers were running away. They too joined the battle and chased the Philistines. [23]So the Lord saved the Israelites that day, and the battle moved on past Beth Aven.

Saul Makes Another Mistake

[24]The men of Israel were miserable that day. This was because Saul had made an oath for all of them. He had said, "No one should eat food before evening and before I finish defeating my enemies. If he does, he will be cursed!" So no Israelite soldier ate food.

[25]Now the army went into the woods. There was some honey on the ground. [26]They came to where the honey was. But no one took any because they were afraid of the oath. [27]But Jonathan had not heard the oath Saul had put on the people. So Jonathan dipped the end of his stick into the honey. He pulled out the honey and ate it. Then he felt better. [28]So one of the soldiers told Jonathan, "Your father made an oath for all the soldiers. He said any man who eats today will be cursed! That's why they are weak."

[29]Jonathan said, "My father has made trouble for the land! See how much better I feel after just tasting a little of this honey! [30]It would have been much better for the men to eat the food they took from their enemies today. We could have killed many more Philistines!"

[31]That day the Israelites defeated the Philistines from Michmash to Aijalon. After they did this, they were very tired. [32]They had taken sheep, cattle and calves from the Philistines. Now they were so hungry they killed the animals on the ground and ate them. But the blood was still in the animals! [33]Someone said to Saul, "Look! The men are sinning against the Lord. They're eating meat that still has blood in it!"

Saul said, "You have sinned! Roll a large stone over here now!" [34]Then he said, "Go to the men. Tell them that each person must bring his ox and sheep to me. They must kill and eat their ox and sheep here. Don't sin against the Lord. Don't eat meat with the blood still in it."

That night everyone brought his animals and killed them there. [35]Then Saul built an altar to the Lord. It was the first altar Saul had built to the Lord.

³⁶Saul said, "Let's go after the Philistines tonight. Let's take what they own. We won't let any of them live!"

The men answered, "Do whatever you think is best."

But the priest said, "Let's ask God."

³⁷So Saul asked God, "Should I chase the Philistines? Will you let us defeat them?" But that day God did not answer Saul. ³⁸That is why Saul said to all the leaders of his army, "Come here. Let's find what sin has been done today. ³⁹As surely as the Lord lives, even if my son Jonathan did the sin, he must die." But no one in the army answered.

⁴⁰Then Saul said to all the Israelites, "You stand on this side. I and my son Jonathan will stand on the other side."

The men answered, "Do whatever you think is best."

⁴¹Then Saul prayed to the Lord, the God of Israel, "Give me the right answer."

And Saul and Jonathan were chosen by throwing lots.ᵈ The other men went free. ⁴²Saul said, "Throw the lot. It will show if it is I or Jonathan my son who is guilty." And Jonathan was chosen.

⁴³Saul said to Jonathan, "Tell me what you have done."

So Jonathan told Saul, "I only tasted a little honey from the end of my stick. And must I die now?"

⁴⁴Saul said, "Jonathan, if you don't die, may God punish me terribly."

⁴⁵But the soldiers said to Saul, "Must Jonathan die? Never! He is responsible for saving Israel today! As surely as the Lord lives, not even a hair of his head will fall to the ground! Today Jonathan fought against the Philistines with God's help!" So the army saved Jonathan, and he did not die.

⁴⁶Then Saul stopped chasing the Philistines, and they went back to their own land.

Saul Fights Israel's Enemies

⁴⁷When Saul became king over Israel, he fought against Israel's enemies all around. He fought Moab, the Ammonites, Edom, the king of Zobah and the Philistines. Everywhere Saul went he defeated Israel's enemies. ⁴⁸He became strong. He fought bravely and defeated the Amalekites. He saved Israel from the enemies who had taken what the Israelites owned.

⁴⁹Saul's sons were Jonathan, Ishvi and Malki-Shua. His older daughter was named Merab. His younger daughter was named Michal. ⁵⁰Saul's wife was Ahinoam daughter of Ahimaaz. The commander of his army was Abner son of Ner. Ner was Saul's uncle. ⁵¹Saul's father Kish and Abner's father Ner were sons of Abiel.

⁵²All Saul's life he fought hard against the Philistines. When he saw strong or brave men, he took them into his army.

Saul Rejected as King

15 Samuel said to Saul, "The Lord sent me to appoint you king over Israel. Now listen to his message. ²This is what the Lord of heaven's armies says: 'The Israelites came out of Egypt. But the Amalekites tried to stop them from going to Canaan. I saw what they did. ³Now go, attack the Amalekites. Destroy everything that belongs to them as an offering to the Lord. Don't let anything live. Put to death men and women, children and small babies. Kill the cattle and sheep, camels and donkeys'."

⁴So Saul called the army together at Telaim. There were 200,000 soldiers and 10,000 men from Judah. ⁵Then Saul went to the city of Amalek and set up an ambush in the ravine. ⁶He said to the Kenites, "Go away. Leave the Amalekites so that I won't destroy you with them. You showed kindness to the Israelites when they came out

of Egypt." So the Kenites moved away from the Amalekites.

[7]Then Saul defeated the Amalekites. He fought them all the way from Havilah to Shur, at the border of Egypt. [8]He took Agag king of the Amalekites alive, and killed all of Agag's army with the sword. [9]But Saul and the army let Agag live. They also let the best sheep, fat cattle and lambs live. They let every good animal live. They did not want to destroy them. But when they found an animal that was weak or useless, they killed it.

[10]Then the Lord spoke his word to Samuel: [11]"Saul has stopped following me. And I am sorry I made him king. He has not obeyed my commands." Samuel was upset, and he cried out to the Lord all night long.

[12]Early the next morning Samuel got up and went to meet Saul. But the people told Samuel, "Saul has gone to Carmel. He has put up a monument in his own honour. Now he has gone down to Gilgal."

[13]Then Samuel came to Saul. And Saul said, "May the Lord bless you! I have obeyed the Lord's commands."

[14]But Samuel said, "Then why do I hear cattle mooing and sheep bleating?"

[15]Saul answered, "The soldiers took them from the Amalekites. They saved the best sheep and cattle to offer as sacrifices to the Lord your God. But we destroyed all the other animals."

[16]Samuel said to Saul, "Stop! Let me tell you what the Lord said to me last night."

Saul answered, "Tell me."

[17]Samuel said, "Once you didn't think much of yourself. But now you have become the leader of the tribes[d] of Israel. The Lord appointed you to be king over Israel. [18]And he told you to do something. He said, 'Go and destroy those evil people, the Amalekites. Make war on them until all of them are dead'. [19]Why didn't you obey

the Lord? Why did you take the best things? Why did you do what the Lord said was wrong?"

[20]Saul said, "But I did obey the Lord. I did what the Lord told me to do. I destroyed all the Amalekites. And I brought back Agag their king. [21]The soldiers took the best sheep and cattle to sacrifice to the Lord your God at Gilgal."

[22]But Samuel answered,
"What pleases the Lord more:
    burnt offerings and sacrifices or
        obedience?
It is better to obey God than to
    offer a sacrifice.
It is better to listen to God than
    to offer the fat of male
    sheep.
[23]Refusing to obey is as bad as the
    sin of sorcery.[d]
Being stubborn is as bad as the
    sin of worshipping idols.
You have rejected the Lord's
    command.
For this reason, he now rejects
    you as king."

[24]Then Saul said to Samuel, "I have sinned. I didn't obey the Lord's commands. I didn't do what you told me. I was afraid of the people, and I did what they said. [25]Now I beg you, forgive my sin. Come back with me so I may worship the Lord."

[26]But Samuel said to Saul, "I won't go back with you. You refused the Lord's command. And now he rejects you as king of Israel."

[27]As Samuel turned to leave, Saul caught his robe, and it tore. [28]Samuel said to him, "The Lord has torn the kingdom of Israel from you today. He has given it to one of your neighbours. He has given it to one better than you. [29]The Lord is the Eternal One of Israel. He does not lie or change his mind. He is not a man. So he does not change his mind as men do."

[30]Saul answered, "I have sinned. But please honour me in front of my people's older leaders. Please honour

me in front of the Israelites. Come back with me so that I may worship the Lord your God." ³¹So Samuel went back with Saul, and Saul worshipped the Lord.

³²Then Samuel said, "Bring me Agag king of the Amalekites."

Agag came to Samuel in chains. Yet Agag thought, "Surely the threat of death has passed."

³³Samuel said to him, "Your sword caused mothers to be without their children. Now your mother will have no children." And Samuel cut Agag to pieces before the Lord at Gilgal.

³⁴Then Samuel left and went to Ramah. But Saul went up to his home in Gibeah. ³⁵And Samuel never saw Saul again all the rest of his life. But he was sorry for Saul. And the Lord was very sorry he had made Saul king of Israel.

Samuel Goes to Bethlehem

16 The Lord said to Samuel, "How long will you continue to feel sorry for Saul? I have rejected him as king of Israel. Fill your container with olive oil and go. I am sending you to Jesse who lives in Bethlehem. I have chosen one of his sons to be king."

²But Samuel said, "If I go, Saul will hear the news. And he will try to kill me."

The Lord said, "Take a young calf with you. Say, 'I have come to offer a sacrifice to the Lord'. ³Invite Jesse to the sacrifice. Then I will show you what to do. You must appoint the one I show you."

⁴Samuel did what the Lord told him to do. When he arrived at Bethlehem, the older leaders of Bethlehem shook with fear. They met him and asked, "Are you coming in peace?"

⁵Samuel answered, "Yes, I come in peace. I have come to make a sacrifice to the Lord. Make yourselves holy for the Lord and come to the sacrifice with me." Then he made Jesse and his

sons holy for the Lord, and he invited them to come to the sacrifice.

⁶When they arrived, Samuel saw Eliab. Samuel thought, "Surely the Lord has appointed this person standing here before him."

⁷But the Lord said to Samuel, "Don't look at how handsome Eliab is. Don't look at how tall he is. I have not chosen him. God does not see the same way people see. People look at the outside of a person, but the Lord looks at the heart."

⁸Then Jesse called Abinadab and told him to pass by Samuel. But Samuel said, "The Lord has not chosen this man either." ⁹Then Jesse had Shammah pass by. But Samuel said, "No, the Lord has not chosen this one." ¹⁰Jesse had seven of his sons pass by Samuel. But Samuel said to him, "The Lord has not chosen any of these."

¹¹Then he asked Jesse, "Are these all the sons you have?"

Jesse answered, "I still have the youngest son. He is out taking care of the sheep."

Samuel said, "Send for him. We will not sit down to eat until he arrives."

¹²So Jesse sent and had his youngest son brought in. He was a fine boy, tanned and handsome.

The Lord said to Samuel, "Go! Appoint him. He is the one."

¹³So Samuel took the container of olive oil. Then he poured oil on Jesse's youngest son to appoint him in front of his brothers. From that day on, the Lord's Spirit*d* entered David with power. Samuel then went back to Ramah.

David Serves Saul

¹⁴But the Lord's Spirit*d* had gone out of Saul. And an evil spirit from the Lord troubled him.

¹⁵Saul's servants said to him, "See, an evil spirit from God is troubling you. ¹⁶Give us the command. We will look for someone who can play the

harp. When the evil spirit from the Lord enters you, he will play. Then the evil spirit will leave you alone, and you will feel better."

17So Saul said to his servants, "Find someone. If he plays well, bring him to me."

18One of the servants said, "Jesse of Bethlehem has a son who plays the harp. I have seen him play it. He is a brave man and fights well. He is a good speaker and handsome. And the Lord is with him."

19Then Saul sent messengers to Jesse. The message said, "Send me your son David, who is with the sheep." 20So Jesse loaded a donkey with bread and a leather bag full of wine. He also took a young goat. He sent them all with his son David to Saul.

21When David came to Saul, he began to serve him. Saul loved David very much, and David became the officer who carried Saul's armour. 22Saul sent a message to Jesse. He said, "Let David stay and serve me. I like him."

23When the evil spirit from God entered Saul, David would take his harp and play. Then the evil spirit would go out of him, and Saul would feel relief. He would feel better again.

David and Goliath

17 The Philistines gathered their armies for war. They met at Socoh in Judah. Their camp was at Ephes Dammim between Socoh and Azekah. 2Saul and the Israelites gathered in the Valley of Elah and camped there. They took their positions to fight the Philistines. 3The Philistines controlled one hill, the Israelites controlled another. The valley was between them.

4The Philistines had a champion fighter named Goliath. He was from Gath. He was nearly 3 metres tall. He came out of the Philistine camp. 5He had a bronze helmet on his head, and

he wore a coat of scale armour. It was made of bronze and weighed about 60 kilograms. 6He wore bronze protectors on his legs and he had a small spear of bronze tied on his back. 7The wooden part of his larger spear was like a weaver's rod. And its blade weighed about 7 kilograms. The officer who carried his shield walked in front of him.

8Goliath stood and shouted to the Israelite soldiers, "Why have you taken positions for battle? I am a Philistine, and you are Saul's servants! Choose a man and send him to fight me. 9If he can fight and kill me, we will become your servants. But if I defeat and kill him, you will become our servants." 10Then he said, "Today I stand and dare the army of Israel! Send one of your men to fight me!" 11When Saul and the Israelites heard the Philistine's words, they were very afraid.

12Now David was the son of Jesse, an Ephrathite. Jesse was from Bethlehem in Judah. He had eight sons. In Saul's time Jesse was an old man. 13His three oldest sons followed Saul to the war. The first son was Eliab, the second son was Abinadab, and the third son was Shammah. 14David was the youngest son. Jesse's three oldest sons followed Saul. 15But David went back and forth from Saul to Bethlehem. There he took care of his father's sheep.

16The Philistine Goliath came out every morning and evening. He stood before the Israelite army. This continued for 40 days.

17Now Jesse said to his son David, "Take this 18 litres of cooked grain and ten loaves of bread. Take them to your brothers in the camp. 18Also take ten pieces of cheese. Give them to the commander of your brothers' group of 1,000 soldiers. See how your brothers are. Bring back something to show me they are all right. 19Your brothers are with Saul and the army in the Valley of Elah. They are fighting against the Philistines."

²⁰Early in the morning David left the sheep with another shepherd. He took the food and left as Jesse had told him. When David arrived at the camp, the army was leaving. They were going out to their battle positions. The soldiers were shouting their war cry. ²¹The Israelites and Philistines were lining up their men to face each other in battle.

²²David left the food with the man who kept the supplies. Then he ran to the battle line and talked to his brothers. ²³While he was talking with them, Goliath came out. He was the Philistine champion from Gath. He shouted things against Israel as usual, and David heard it. ²⁴When the Israelites saw Goliath, they were very much afraid and ran away.

²⁵They said, "Look at this man Goliath. He keeps coming out to speak against Israel. The king will give much money to the man who kills Goliath. He will also give his daughter in marriage to whoever kills him. And his father's family will not have to pay taxes in Israel."

²⁶David asked the men who stood near him, "What will be done to reward the man who kills this Philistine? What will be done for whoever takes away the shame from Israel? Goliath is a Philistine. He is not circumcised.ᵈ Why does he think he can speak against the armies of the living God?"

²⁷The Israelites told David what they had been saying. They said, "This is what will be done for the man who kills Goliath."

²⁸David's oldest brother Eliab heard David talking with the soldiers. He became angry with David. He asked David, "Why did you come here? Who's taking care of those few sheep of yours in the desert? I know you are proud. Your attitude is very poor. You came down here just to watch the battle!"

²⁹David asked, "Now what have I done wrong? Can't I even talk?" ³⁰He then turned to other people and asked the same questions. And they gave him the same answer as before. ³¹Some men heard what David said and told Saul. Then Saul ordered David to be sent to him.

³²David said to Saul, "Don't let anyone be discouraged. I, your servant, will go and fight this Philistine!"

³³Saul answered, "You can't go out against this Philistine and fight him. You're only a boy. Goliath has been a warrior since he was a young man."

³⁴But David said to Saul, "I, your servant, have been keeping my father's sheep. When a lion or bear came and took a sheep from the flock, ³⁵I would chase it. I would attack it and save the sheep from its mouth. When it attacked me, I caught it by its fur. I would hit it and kill it. ³⁶I, your servant, have killed both a lion and a bear! Goliath, the Philistine who is not circumcised, will be like the lion or bear I killed. He will die because he has stood against the armies of the living God. ³⁷The Lord saved me from a lion and a bear. He will also save me from this Philistine."

Saul said to David, "Go, and may the Lord be with you." ³⁸Saul put his own clothes on David. He put a bronze helmet on David's head and armour on his body. ³⁹David put on Saul's sword and tried to walk around. But he was not used to all the armour Saul had put on him.

He said to Saul, "I can't go in this. I'm not used to it." Then David took it all off. ⁴⁰He took his stick in his hand, and he chose five smooth stones from a stream. He put them in his pouch and held his sling in his hand. Then he went to meet Goliath.

⁴¹At the same time, the Philistine was coming closer to David. The man who held his shield walked in front of him. ⁴²Goliath looked at David. He saw that David was only a boy, tanned

and handsome. He looked down at David with disgust. ⁴³He said, "Do you think I am a dog, that you come at me with a stick?" He used his gods' names to curse David. ⁴⁴He said to David, "Come here. I'll feed your body to the birds of the air and the wild animals!"

⁴⁵But David said to him, "You come to me using a sword, a large spear and a small spear. But I come to you in the name of the Lord of heaven's armies. He's the God of the armies of Israel! You have spoken out against him. ⁴⁶Today the Lord will give you to me. I'll kill you, and I'll cut off your head. Today I'll feed the bodies of the Philistine soldiers to the birds of the air and the wild animals. Then all the world will know there is a God in Israel! ⁴⁷Everyone gathered here will know the Lord does not need swords or spears to save people. The battle belongs to him! And he will help us defeat all of you."

⁴⁸As Goliath came near to attack him, David ran quickly to meet him. ⁴⁹He took a stone from his pouch. He put it into his sling and slung it. The stone hit the Philistine on his forehead and sank into it. Goliath fell face down on the ground.

⁵⁰So David defeated the Philistine with only a sling and a stone! He hit him and killed him. He did not even have a sword in his hand. ⁵¹David ran and stood beside the Philistine. He took Goliath's sword out of its holder and killed him. Then he cut off Goliath's head.

When the Philistines saw that their champion was dead, they turned and ran. ⁵²The men of Israel and Judah shouted and started chasing the Philistines. They chased them all the way to the entrance to the city of Gath. And they chased them to the gates of Ekron.

Many of the Philistines died. Their bodies lay on the Shaaraim road as far as Gath and Ekron. ⁵³The Israelites returned after chasing the Philistines. Then they took many things from the Philistine camp. ⁵⁴David took Goliath's head to Jerusalem. He also put Goliath's weapons in his own tent.

⁵⁵Saul had watched David go out to meet Goliath. Saul spoke to Abner, commander of the army. He said, "Abner, who is that young man's father?"

Abner answered, "As surely as you live, my king, I don't know."

⁵⁶The king said, "Find out whose son he is."

⁵⁷When David came back from killing Goliath, Abner brought him to Saul. David still held Goliath's head. ⁵⁸Saul asked him, "Young man, who is your father?"

David answered, "I am the son of your servant Jesse of Bethlehem."

Saul Fears David

18 When David finished talking with Saul, Jonathan felt very close to David. He loved David as much as he loved himself. ²Saul kept David with him from that day on. He did not let David go home to his father's house. ³Jonathan made an agreement with David. He did this because he loved David as much as himself. ⁴He took off his coat and gave it to David. He also gave David his uniform, including his sword, bow and belt.

⁵Saul sent David to fight in different battles. And David was very successful. Then Saul put David over the soldiers. When he did this, Saul's officers and all the other people were pleased.

⁶After David had killed the Philistine, he and the men returned home. Women came out from all the towns of Israel to meet King Saul. They sang songs of joy, danced and played tambourines*ᵈ* and stringed instruments. ⁷As they played, they sang,

"Saul has killed thousands of his enemies.

But David has killed tens of thousands!"

⁸The women's song upset Saul, and he became very angry. He thought, "The women say David has killed tens of thousands of enemies. But they say I killed only thousands of enemies. The only thing left for him to have is the kingdom!" ⁹So Saul watched David closely from then on. He was jealous of him.

¹⁰The next day an evil spirit from God entered Saul with power. And he prophesied*d* in his house. David was playing the harp as he usually did. But Saul had a spear in his hand. ¹¹He raised the spear and thought, "I'll pin David to the wall." But David got away from him twice.

¹²The Lord was with David but had left Saul. So Saul was afraid of David. ¹³He sent David away from him. He made David commander of 1,000 soldiers. So David led them in battle. ¹⁴He had great success in everything he did because the Lord was with him. ¹⁵Saul saw that David was very successful. And he became even more afraid of David. ¹⁶But all the people of Israel and Judah loved David. This was because he led them well in battle.

Saul's Daughter and David

¹⁷Saul said to David, "You're a brave soldier. And you fight the Lord's battles. Here is my older daughter Merab. I will let you marry her." Saul had decided, "I won't have to kill David. The Philistines will do that!"

¹⁸But David said, "I am not good enough for this honour. And my family is not important enough for me to become the king's son-in-law." ¹⁹So when the time came for Saul's daughter Merab to marry David, Saul gave her instead to Adriel of Meholah.

²⁰Now Saul's other daughter Michal loved David. When they told Saul about Michal loving David, he was pleased. ²¹He thought, "I will let Michal marry David. Then she will become a trap for him. And the Philistines will defeat him." So Saul said to David a second time, "You may become my son-in-law."

²²And Saul gave an order to his servants. He told them, "Speak to David in private. Say, 'Look, the king is pleased with you. His servants like you. You should become his son-in-law'."

²³Saul's servants said these words to David. But David answered, "Do you think it is easy to become the king's son-in-law? I'm only a poor man. Nobody knows me."

²⁴Then Saul's servants told him what David had said. ²⁵Saul said, "Say to David, 'The king doesn't want you to pay a large price for the bride. All he wants is 100 Philistine foreskins. Then he will be even with his enemies'." Saul planned to let the Philistines kill David.

²⁶Saul's servants told David these words. David was pleased that he could become the king's son-in-law. ²⁷So he and his men went out and killed 200 Philistines. David took all their foreskins and brought them to Saul. He wanted to become the king's son-in-law. Then Saul gave him his daughter Michal for his wife. ²⁸Saul saw that the Lord was with David. He also saw that his daughter Michal loved David. ²⁹So he became even more afraid of David. And he was David's enemy all his life.

³⁰The Philistine commanders continued to go out to fight the Israelites. But every time, David defeated them. He had more success than Saul's officers. And he became famous.

Saul Plans to Kill David

19 Saul told his son Jonathan and all his servants to kill David. But Jonathan cared very much for David. ²So he warned David, "My father

Saul is looking for a chance to kill you. Watch out in the morning. Hide in a secret place. ³I will go out and stand with my father in the field where you are hiding. I'll talk to him about you. Then I'll let you know what I find out."

⁴Jonathan talked to Saul his father. He said good things about David. Jonathan said, "You are the king. Don't do wrong to your servant David. He did nothing wrong to you. What he did has helped you greatly. ⁵David risked his life when he killed Goliath the Philistine. The Lord won a great victory for all Israel. You saw it, and you were happy. Why would you do wrong against David? He's innocent. There's no reason to kill him!"

⁶Saul listened to Jonathan. Then he made this promise: "As surely as the Lord lives, David won't be put to death."

⁷So Jonathan called to David. He told David everything that had been said. And he brought David to Saul. So David was with Saul as before.

⁸When war broke out again, David went out to fight the Philistines. He defeated them, and they ran away from him.

⁹But once again an evil spirit from the Lord entered Saul. He was sitting in his house, and he had his spear in his hand. David was playing the harp. ¹⁰Saul tried to pin David to the wall with his spear. But David moved away from him. So Saul's spear went into the wall. And David ran away that night.

¹¹Saul sent men to David's house. They watched it, wanting to kill him in the morning. But Michal, David's wife, warned him. She said, "Tonight you must run away to save your own life. If you don't, you will be killed tomorrow morning." ¹²Then she let David down out of a window. So he ran away and escaped. ¹³Then Michal took an idol and laid it on the bed. She covered it with clothes and put goats' hair at its head.

¹⁴Saul sent messengers to take David prisoner. But Michal said, "He is sick."

¹⁵The men went and told Saul, but he sent them back to see David. He told them, "Bring him to me on his bed so I can kill him."

¹⁶But when the messengers entered David's house, they found it was just an idol on the bed. Its hair was goats' hair.

¹⁷Saul said to Michal, "Why did you trick me this way? You let my enemy go. He has run away!"

Michal answered Saul, "David told me if I did not help him escape, he would kill me."

¹⁸After David had escaped from Saul, he went to Samuel at Ramah. He told Samuel everything Saul had done to him. Then David and Samuel went to Naioth and stayed there. ¹⁹Saul heard that David was in Naioth at Ramah. ²⁰So he sent men to capture him. But they met a group of prophets*ᵈ* prophesying. Samuel was leading this group and was standing there. The Spirit*ᵈ* of God entered Saul's men, and they also prophesied. ²¹Saul heard the news. So he sent other men, but they also prophesied. Then he sent men a third time, but they also prophesied. ²²Finally, Saul himself went to Ramah. He came to the well at Secu. He asked, "Where are Samuel and David?"

The people answered, "In Naioth at Ramah."

²³Then Saul went to Naioth at Ramah. But the Spirit of God also entered him. And he walked on, prophesying until he came to Naioth at Ramah. ²⁴He took off his robes and prophesied in front of Samuel. He lay that way all day and all night. That is why people ask, "Is even Saul one of the prophets?"

David and Jonathan

20 Then David ran away from Naioth in Ramah. He went to Jonathan and asked, "What have I done? What is my crime? How have I sinned against your father so that he's trying to kill me?"

2Jonathan answered, "No! You won't die! See, my father doesn't do anything without first telling me. It doesn't matter if it is very important or just a small thing. Why would he refuse to tell me he wants to kill you? No, it's not true!"

3But David took an oath. He said, "Your father knows very well that I'm your friend. He has said to himself, 'Jonathan must not know about it. If he knows, he will tell David'. But as surely as the Lord lives and as you live, I am very close to death!"

4Jonathan said to David, "I'll do anything you want me to do."

5So David said, "Look, tomorrow is the New Moon*d* festival. I am supposed to eat with the king. But let me hide in the field until the third evening. 6Your father may notice I am gone. If he does, tell him, 'David begged me to let him go to his home town of Bethlehem. Every year at this time, his family group offers a sacrifice'. 7If your father says, 'Fine', I am safe. But if he becomes angry, you can believe he wants to hurt me. 8Jonathan, be kind to me, your servant. You have made an agreement with me before the Lord. If I am guilty, you may kill me yourself! Why hand me over to your father?"

9Jonathan answered, "No, never! If I learn that my father plans to harm you, I will warn you!"

10David asked, "Who will let me know if your father answers you unkindly?"

11Then Jonathan said, "Come, let's go out into the field." So Jonathan and David went together into the field.

12Jonathan said to David, "I promise this before the Lord, the God of Israel: at this same time the day after tomorrow, I will find out how my father feels. If he feels good towards you, I'll send word to you. I'll let you know. 13But my father may mean to hurt you. If so, I will let you know and send you away safely. May the Lord punish me terribly if I don't do this. And may the Lord be with you as he has been with my father. 14But show me the kindness of the Lord as long as I live. Do this so that I may not die. 15You must not stop showing your kindness to my family. Don't do this, even when the Lord has destroyed all your enemies from the earth."

16So Jonathan made an agreement with David. He said, "May the Lord punish David's enemies." 17And Jonathan asked David to repeat his promise of love for him. He did this because he loved David as much as he loved himself.

18Jonathan said to David, "Tomorrow is the New Moon festival. Your seat will be empty: so my father will notice you're gone. 19On the third day go to the place where you hid when this trouble began. Wait by the rock Ezel. 20On the third day I will shoot three arrows to the side of the rock. I will shoot as if I am shooting at a target. 21Then I will send a boy and tell him to go and find the arrows. I may say to him, 'Look, the arrows are on this side of you. Bring them here'. If so, you may come out of hiding. You may do this as surely as the Lord lives because you are safe. There is no danger. 22But I may say to the boy, 'Look, the arrows are beyond you'. If I do, you must go, because the Lord has sent you away. 23Remember what we talked about. The Lord is a witness between you and me for ever."

24So David hid in the field. And when the New Moon festival came, the king sat down to eat. 25He sat where he always sat, near the wall. Jonathan sat across from him, and Abner sat next to him. But David's place was empty. 26That day Saul said nothing. He thought, "Maybe something has happened to David so that he is unclean."*d* ²⁷But the next day was the second day of the month, and David's place was empty again. So Saul said to Jonathan, "Why hasn't the son of Jesse come to the festival yesterday or today?"

²⁸Jonathan answered, "David begged me to let him go to Bethlehem. ²⁹He said, 'Let me go, because our family has a sacrifice in the town. And my brother has ordered me to be there. Now if I am your friend, please let me go and see my brothers'. That is why he has not come to the king's table.'"

³⁰Then Saul became very angry with Jonathan. He said, "You son of an evil and disobedient woman! I know you are on the side of David, son of Jesse! You bring shame on yourself and on your mother who gave birth to you. ³¹As long as Jesse's son lives, you'll never be king or have a kingdom. Now send for David and bring him to me. He must die!"

³²Jonathan asked his father, "Why should David be killed? What wrong has he done?" ³³Then Saul threw his spear at Jonathan, trying to kill him. So Jonathan knew that his father really wanted to kill David. ³⁴Jonathan was very angry and left the table. That second day of the month he refused to eat. He was upset about what his father wanted to do to David.

³⁵The next morning Jonathan went out to the field. He went to meet David as they had agreed. He had a young boy with him. ³⁶Jonathan said to the boy, "Run and find the arrows I shoot." When he ran, Jonathan shot an arrow beyond him. ³⁷The boy ran to the place where Jonathan's arrow fell. But Jonathan called, "The arrow is beyond you!" ³⁸Then he shouted, "Hurry! Go quickly! Don't stop!" The boy picked up the arrow and brought it back to his master. ³⁹(The boy knew

nothing about what this meant. Only Jonathan and David knew.) ⁴⁰Then Jonathan gave his weapons to the boy. He told him, "Go back to town."

⁴¹When the boy left, David came out from the south side of the rock. He bowed face down on the ground before Jonathan. He did this three times. Then David and Jonathan kissed each other. They cried together, but David cried the most.

⁴²Jonathan said to David, "Go in peace. We have promised by the Lord that we will be friends. We said, 'The Lord will be a witness between you and me, and between our descendants*d* for ever'." Then David left, and Jonathan went back to town.

David Goes to See Ahimelech

21 David went to Nob to see Ahimelech the priest. Ahimelech shook with fear when he saw David. He asked David, "Why are you alone? Why is no one with you?"

²David answered him, "The king gave me a special order. He told me, 'No one must know about the work I am sending you to do. And no one must know what I told you to do'. I told my men where to meet me. ³Now, what food do you have with you? Give me five loaves of bread or anything you find."

⁴The priest said to David, "I don't have any plain bread here. But I do have some holy bread*n* here. You may eat it if your men have kept themselves from women."

⁵David answered, "Women have been kept from us. My men always keep their bodies holy, even when we do ordinary work. And this is especially true when the work is holy."

⁶There was no bread except the bread made holy for the Lord. So the priest gave David the bread that showed the people were in the pres-

---

holy bread This was the bread that showed the people were in the presence of God. Normally only the priests should eat this bread.

ence of God. This was the bread the priests had taken from the holy table before the Lord. Each day they took this bread away and put hot bread in its place.

7Now one of Saul's servants was there that day. He had been held there before the Lord. He was Doeg the Edomite, the chief of Saul's shepherds.

8David asked Ahimelech, "Do you have a spear or sword here? The king's business was very important. I had to leave quickly, and I didn't bring my sword or any other weapon."

9The priest answered, "The sword of Goliath the Philistine is here. He is the one you killed in the Valley of Elah. His sword is wrapped in a cloth. It is behind the holy robe.*d* If you want it, you may take it. There's no other sword here but that one."

David said, "There is no other sword like Goliath's. Give it to me."

David Goes to Gath

10That day David ran away from Saul. He went to Achish king of Gath. 11But the servants of Achish said to him, "This is David king of the Israelites. He's the man the Israelite women sing about when they dance. They sing:

'Saul has killed thousands of his enemies.
But David has killed tens of thousands'."

12David paid attention to these words. And he was very much afraid of Achish king of Gath. 13So he pretended to be insane in front of Achish and his servants. While he was with them, he acted like a madman. He made marks on the doors of the gate. He let spit run down his beard.

14Achish said to his servants, "Look at the man! He's insane! Why do you bring him to me? 15I have enough madmen. I don't need you to bring him

here to act like this in front of me! Don't leave him in my house!"

David at Adullam and Mizpah

22 David left Gath and escaped to the cave of Adullam. His brothers and other relatives heard that he was there, and they went to see him. 2Many people joined David. All those who were in trouble, who owed money or who were unsatisfied gathered around him, and he became their leader. He had about 400 men with him.

3From there David went to Mizpah in Moab. He spoke to the king of Moab. He said, "Please let my father and mother come and stay with you. Let them stay until I learn what God is going to do for me." 4So he left them with the king of Moab. And they stayed with the king as long as David was hiding in the protected place.

5But the prophet*d* Gad said to David, "Don't stay in the protected place. Go to the land of Judah." So David left and went to the forest of Hereth.

Saul Destroys Ahimelech's Family

6Saul heard that David and his men had been seen. He sat under the tamarisk tree on the hill at Gibeah. All his officers were standing around him. He had a spear in his hand. 7Saul said to them, "Listen, men of Benjamin! Do you think the son of Jesse will give all of you fields and vineyards? Will David make you commanders over thousands of men or hundreds of men? 8You have all made plans against me! No one tells me when my son makes an agreement with the son of Jesse! No one cares about me! No one tells me my son has encouraged my servant to ambush me! And David is doing this now!"

9Doeg the Edomite was standing there with Saul's officers. He said, "I saw the son of Jesse. He came to see Ahimelech son of Ahitub at Nob.

¹⁰Ahimelech prayed to the Lord for David. He also gave him food. And he gave him the sword of Goliath the Philistine."

¹¹Then the king sent for the priest Ahimelech son of Ahitub. He sent for all of Ahimelech's relatives who were priests at Nob. And they all came to the king. ¹²Saul said to Ahimelech, "Listen now, son of Ahitub."

Ahimelech answered, "Yes, master."

¹³Saul said, "Why have you and Jesse's son made plans against me? You gave him bread and a sword! You prayed to God for him. David is waiting to attack me. He is doing this now!"

¹⁴Ahimelech answered, "David is very loyal to you. You have no other servant who is as loyal as David. He is your own son-in-law and captain of your bodyguards. All the people in your house respect him. ¹⁵That was not the first time I prayed to God for David. Not at all! Don't blame me or any of my relatives. We are your servants. I know nothing about what is going on."

¹⁶But the king said, "Ahimelech, you and all your relatives must die!" ¹⁷Then he told the guards at his side, "Go and kill the priests of the Lord. Do this because they are on David's side. They knew he was running away, but they didn't tell me!"

But the king's officers refused to hurt the priests of the Lord.

¹⁸Then the king ordered Doeg, "Go and kill the priests." So Doeg the Edomite went and killed the priests. That day he killed 85 men who wore the linen holy robe.ᵈ ¹⁹He also killed the people of Nob, the city of the priests. With the sword he killed men, women, children and small babies. And he killed cattle, donkeys and sheep.

²⁰But Abiathar escaped. He was a son of Ahimelech, who was the son of Ahitub. Abiathar ran away and joined David. ²¹He told David that Saul had killed the Lord's priests. ²²Then David told him, "Doeg the Edomite was there at Nob that day. I knew he would surely tell Saul. So I am responsible for the death of all your father's family. ²³The man who wants to kill you also wants to kill me. Stay with me. Don't be afraid. You will be safe with me."

David at Keilah

23 Someone told David, "Look, the Philistines are fighting against Keilah. They are robbing grain from the threshingᵈ floors."

²David asked the Lord, "Should I go and fight these Philistines?"

The Lord answered him, "Go. Attack them, and save Keilah."

³But David's men said to him, "We're afraid here in Judah. We will be much more afraid if we go to Keilah where the Philistine army is."

⁴David again asked the Lord. And the Lord answered, "Go down to Keilah. I will help you defeat the Philistines." ⁵So David and his men went to Keilah. They fought the Philistines and took their cattle. David killed many Philistines and saved the people of Keilah. ⁶(Now Abiathar son of Ahimelech had brought the holy robeᵈ with him. He brought it when he came to David at Keilah.)

Saul Chases David

⁷Someone told Saul that David was now at Keilah. Saul said, "God has given David to me! He has trapped himself because he has entered a town with gates and bars." ⁸Saul called all his army together for battle. They prepared to go down to Keilah to attack David and his men.

⁹David learned Saul was making evil plans against him. So he said to Abiathar the priest, "Bring the holy robe."ᵈ ¹⁰David prayed, "Lord, God of Israel, I have heard about Saul's plans. He is coming to Keilah to de-

stroy the town because of me. [11]Will the people of Keilah give me to Saul? Will Saul come to Keilah, as I heard? Lord, God of Israel, tell me, your servant!"

The Lord answered, "Saul will come down."

[12]Again David asked, "Will the people of Keilah give me and my men to Saul?"

The Lord answered, "They will."

[13]So David and his men left Keilah. There were about 600 men who went with him. And they kept moving from place to place. When Saul found that David had escaped from Keilah, he did not go there.

[14]David stayed in the protected places in the desert. He also stayed in the hills of the Desert of Ziph. Every day Saul looked for David. But the Lord did not let him take David.

[15]David was at Horesh in the Desert of Ziph. He was afraid because Saul was coming to kill him. [16]But Saul's son Jonathan went to David at Horesh. He helped David have stronger faith in God. [17]Jonathan told him, "Don't be afraid. My father won't touch you. You will become king of Israel, and I will be second to you. Even my father Saul knows this." [18]The two of them made an agreement before the Lord. Then Jonathan went home. But David stayed at Horesh.

[19]The people from Ziph went to Saul at Gibeah. They told him, "David is hiding in our land. He's at the protected places of Horesh. They are on the hill of Hakilah, south of Jeshimon. [20]Now, our king, come down any time you want. It's our duty to give David to you."

[21]Saul answered, "The Lord bless you for helping me. [22]Go and learn more about him. Find out where he is staying. Find out who has seen him there. I have heard that he is clever. [23]Find all the hiding places he uses. And come back and tell me everything. Then I'll go with you. If David is in the area, I will find him. I will track him down among all the families in Judah."

[24]So they went back to Ziph ahead of Saul. David and his men were in the Desert of Maon.[n] This was in the desert area south of Jeshimon. [25]Saul and his men went to look for David. But people warned David that Saul was looking for him. David then went down to a rock and stayed in the Desert of Maon. Saul heard that David had gone there. So he went after him into the Desert of Maon.

[26]Saul was going along one side of the mountain. David and his men were on the other side. They were hurrying to get away from Saul. Saul and his soldiers were closing in on David and his men. [27]But a messenger came to Saul. He said, "Come quickly! The Philistines are attacking our land!" [28]So Saul stopped chasing David and went to fight the Philistines. That is why people call this place Rock of Parting. [29]David left the Desert of Maon and lived in the protected places of En Gedi.

David Shames Saul

24 Now Saul had chased the Philistines away. Then he was told, "David is in the Desert of En Gedi." [2]So he chose 3,000 men from all Israel. He took these men and began looking for David and his men. They looked near the Rocks of the Wild Goats.

[3]Saul came to the sheep pens beside the road. A cave was there, and he went in to relieve himself. Now David and his men were hiding far back in the cave. [4]The men said to David, "Today is the day the Lord talked about! The Lord told you, 'I will give your enemy to you. You can do anything you want with him'."

Maon Some early Greek copies say "Maon". The Hebrew copies say "Paran".

Then David crawled near Saul. He cut off a corner of Saul's robe. But Saul did not notice him. [5]Later David felt guilty because he had cut off a corner of Saul's robe. [6]He said to his men, "May the Lord keep me from doing such a thing to my master! Saul is the Lord's appointed king. I should not do anything against him, because he is the Lord's appointed king!" [7]David used these words to stop his men. He did not let them attack Saul. Then Saul left the cave and went his way.

[8]When David came out of the cave, he shouted to Saul, "My master and king!" Saul looked back, and David bowed face down on the ground. [9]He said to Saul, "Why do you listen when people say, 'David plans to harm you'? [10]You have seen something with your own eyes today. You have seen how the Lord put you in my power in the cave. But I refused to kill you. I was merciful to you. I said, 'I won't harm my master, because he is the Lord's appointed king'. [11]My father, look at this piece of your robe in my hand! I cut off the corner of your robe, but I didn't kill you. Now understand and know I am not planning any evil against you. I did nothing wrong to you, but you are hunting me to kill me. [12]May the Lord judge between us. And may he punish you for the wrong you have done to me! But I won't fight you. [13]There is an old saying: 'Evil things come from evil people'. So I won't hurt you. [14]Whom is the king of Israel coming out against? Whom are you chasing? You're not chasing someone who will hurt you! It's as if you are chasing a dead dog or a flea. [15]May the Lord be our judge and decide between you and me. May the Lord support me and show that I am right. May he save me from you!"

[16]David finished saying these words. Then Saul asked, "Is that your voice, David my son?" And he cried loudly. [17]He said, "You are right, and I am wrong. You have been good to me. But I have done wrong to you. [18]You told me what good things you did. The Lord brought me to you, but you did not kill me. [19]If a man finds his enemy, he won't send him away with goodness, will he? May the Lord reward you because you were good to me today. [20]I know you will surely be king. You will rule the kingdom of Israel. [21]Now make a promise to me. Promise in the name of the Lord that you will not kill my descendants.[d] Promise me that you won't wipe out my name from my father's family."

[22]So David made the promise to Saul. Then Saul went back home. David and his men went up to the protected place.

David and Nabal

25 Now Samuel died. All the Israelites met and had a time of sadness for him. They buried him at his home in Ramah.

Then David moved to the Desert of Maon.[n] [2]A man in Maon who had land at Carmel was very rich. He had 3,000 sheep and 1,000 goats. He was cutting the wool off his sheep at Carmel. [3]His name was Nabal, and he was a descendant[d] of Caleb. His wife was named Abigail. She was a wise and beautiful woman. But Nabal was cruel and mean.

[4]David was in the desert. He heard that Nabal was cutting the wool from his sheep. [5]So he sent ten young men. He told them, "Go to Nabal at Carmel. Greet him for me. [6]Say to Nabal, 'May you and your family have good health! And may all who belong to you have good health. [7]I have heard that you are cutting the wool from your sheep. When your shepherds were with us, we did nothing wrong to them. All the time your shepherds were at Carmel, we stole nothing from them. [8]Ask

Maon Some early Greek copies say "Maon". The Hebrew copies say "Paran".

your servants, and they will tell you. We come at a happy time. So for this reason, be kind to my young men. Please give them anything you can find for them. Please do this for your son David'." [9]When the men arrived, they gave the message to Nabal. But Nabal insulted them. [10]He answered them, "Who is David? Who is this son of Jesse? Many slaves are running away from their masters today! [11]I have bread and water. And I have meat that I killed for my servants who cut the wool. But I won't give it to men I don't know."

[12]David's men went back and told him all Nabal had said. [13]Then David said to them, "Put on your swords!" So they put on their swords, and David put on his also. About 400 men went with David. But 200 men stayed with the supplies.

[14]One of Nabal's servants spoke to Abigail, Nabal's wife. He said, "David sent messengers from the desert to greet our master. But Nabal insulted them. [15]These men were very good to us. They did nothing wrong to us. They stole nothing from us during all the time we were out in the field with them. [16]Night and day they protected us. They were like a wall around us while we were with them caring for the sheep. [17]Now think about it, and decide what you can do. Terrible trouble is coming to our master and all his family. Nabal is such a wicked man that no one can even talk to him."

[18]Abigail hurried. She took 200 loaves of bread, two leather bags full of wine and five cooked sheep. She took 17 litres of cooked grain, 100 cakes of raisins and 200 cakes of pressed figs. She put all these on donkeys. [19]Then she told her servants, "Go on. I'll follow you." But she did not tell her husband.

[20]Abigail rode her donkey and came down into the mountain ravine. There she met David and his men coming down toward her.

[21]David had just said, "It's been useless! I watched over Nabal's property in the desert. I made sure none of his sheep were missing. I did good to him, but he has paid me back with evil. [22]May God punish me terribly if I let just one of Nabal's family live until tomorrow."

[23]When Abigail saw David, she quickly got off her donkey. She bowed face down on the ground before David. [24]She lay at David's feet. She said, "My master, let the blame be on me! Please let me talk to you! Listen to what I say. [25]My master, don't pay attention to this worthless man Nabal. He is the same as his name. His name means 'fool', and he is truly foolish. But I, your servant, didn't see the men you sent. [26]The Lord has kept you from killing and punishing people yourself. As surely as the Lord lives and as surely as you live, may your enemies become like Nabal! [27]I have brought a gift to you. Please give it to the men who follow you. [28]Please forgive my wrong. The Lord will certainly let your family have many kings. He will do this because you fight his battles. As long as you live, people will find nothing bad in you. [29]A man might chase you to kill you. But the Lord your God will keep you alive. He will throw away your enemies' lives as he would throw a stone from a sling. [30]The Lord will keep all his promises about good things for you. He will make you leader over Israel. [31]Then you won't feel guilty. You won't have problems about killing innocent people and punishing them yourself. Please remember me when the Lord brings you success."

[32]David answered Abigail, "Praise the Lord, the God of Israel. He sent you to meet me. [33]May you be blessed for your wisdom. You have

kept me from killing or punishing people today. ³⁴As surely as the Lord, the God of Israel, lives, he has kept me from hurting you. If you hadn't come quickly to meet me, no one belonging to Nabal would have lived until tomorrow."

³⁵Then David accepted Abigail's gifts. He told her, "Go home in peace. I have heard your words, and I will do what you have asked."

Nabal's Death

³⁶When Abigail went back to Nabal, he was in the house. He was eating like a king. He was very drunk and in a good mood. So she told him nothing until the next morning. ³⁷In the morning he was not drunk. Then his wife told him everything. His heart failed him, and he became like a stone. ³⁸About ten days later the Lord struck Nabal and caused him to die.

³⁹When David heard that Nabal was dead, he said, "Praise the Lord! Nabal insulted me, but the Lord has supported me! He has kept me from doing wrong. And the Lord caused Nabal to die because he did wrong."

Then David sent a message to Abigail. He asked her to become his wife. ⁴⁰His servants went to Carmel and spoke to Abigail. They said, "David sent us to take you so you can become his wife."

⁴¹Abigail bowed face down on the ground. She said, "I am your servant. I'm ready to serve you. I'm ready to wash the feet of my master's servants." ⁴²Abigail quickly got on a donkey and went with David's messengers. She had five maids following her. And she became David's wife.

⁴³David also had married Ahinoam of Jezreel. So they were both David's wives. ⁴⁴Saul's daughter Michal was also David's wife. But Saul had given her to Paltiel son of Laish. Paltiel was from Gallim.

David Shames Saul Again

26 The people of Ziph went to see Saul at Gibeah. They said to him, "David is hiding on the hill of Hakilah opposite Jeshimon."

²So Saul went down to the Desert of Ziph. His 3,000 chosen men of Israel went with him. They looked for David in the Desert of Ziph. ³Saul made his camp on the hill of Hakilah, beside the road opposite Jeshimon. But David stayed in the desert. He heard Saul had followed him. ⁴So David sent out spies and learned that Saul had come to Hakilah.

⁵Then David went to the place where Saul had camped. He saw where Saul and Abner son of Ner were sleeping. Abner was the commander of Saul's army. Saul was sleeping in the middle of the camp with all the army around him.

⁶David talked to Ahimelech the Hittite and Abishai son of Zeruiah. Abishai was Joab's brother. He asked them, "Who will go down into Saul's camp with me?"

Abishai answered, "I'll go with you."

⁷So that night David and Abishai went into Saul's camp. Saul was asleep in the middle of the camp. His spear was stuck in the ground near his head. Abner and the army were sleeping around Saul. ⁸Abishai said to David, "Today God has let you defeat your enemy! Let me pin Saul to the ground with the spear. I'll only do it once! I won't hit him twice."

⁹But David said to Abishai, "Don't kill Saul! No one can harm the Lord's appointed king and still be innocent! ¹⁰As surely as the Lord lives, the Lord himself will punish Saul. Maybe Saul will die naturally. Or maybe he will go into battle and be killed. ¹¹But may the Lord keep me from harming his appointed king! Now pick up the spear and water jug that are near Saul's head. Then let's go."

¹²So David took the spear and water jug that were near Saul's head. They left, and no one saw them. No one knew about it or woke up. The Lord had made them stay asleep.

¹³David crossed over to the other side of the hill. He stood on top of the mountain far from Saul's camp. David's and Saul's camps were far apart. ¹⁴David shouted to the army and to Abner son of Ner, "Answer me, Abner!"

Abner answered, "Who is calling for the king? Who are you?"

¹⁵David said, "You're the greatest man in Israel. Isn't that true? Then why didn't you guard your master the king? Someone came into your camp to kill your master the king! ¹⁶What you have done is not good. As surely as the Lord lives, you and your men should die. You haven't guarded your master, the Lord's appointed king. Look! Where are the king's spear and water jug that were near his head?"

¹⁷Saul knew David's voice. He said, "Is that your voice, David my son?"

David answered, "Yes, it is, my master and king." ¹⁸David also said, "Why are you chasing me, my master? What wrong have I done? What evil am I guilty of? ¹⁹My master and king, listen to me. If the Lord caused you to be angry with me, let him accept an offering. But if men caused you to be angry with me, let the Lord curse them! They have made me leave the land the Lord gave me. They have told me, 'Go and serve other gods'. ²⁰Now don't let me die far away from the Lord's presence. The king of Israel has come out looking for a flea! You're like a man hunting a partridge in the mountains!"

²¹Then Saul said, "I have sinned. Come back, David my son. Today you respected my life. So I will not try to hurt you. I have acted foolishly. I have made a big mistake."

²²David answered, "Here is your spear. Let one of your young men come here and get it. ²³The Lord rewards every man for the things he does right and for his loyalty to him. The Lord put you into my power today. But I wouldn't harm the Lord's appointed king. ²⁴I respected your life today. Surely, in the same way, the Lord will respect my life. Surely he will save me from all trouble."

²⁵Then Saul said to David, "You are blessed, my son David. You will do great things and succeed."

So David went on his way, and Saul went back home.

David and the Philistines

27 But David thought to himself, "Saul will catch me some day. The best thing I can do is escape to the land of the Philistines. Then he will give up looking for me in Israel. That way I can get away from him."

²So David and his 600 men left Israel. They went to Achish son of Maoch. Achish was king of Gath. ³David, his men and their families made their home in Gath with Achish. David had his two wives with him. Their names were Ahinoam of Jezreel and Abigail of Carmel. Abigail was the widow of Nabal. ⁴Now Saul was told that David had run away to Gath. So he stopped looking for him.

⁵Then David said to Achish, "If you are pleased with me, give me a place in one of the country towns. I can live there. I don't need to live in the royal city with you."

⁶That day Achish gave David the town of Ziklag. That is why Ziklag has belonged to the kings of Judah ever since. ⁷David lived in the Philistine land a year and four months.

⁸David and his men went to raid the people of Geshur, Girzi and Amalek. (These people had lived for a long time in the land that reached to Shur and Egypt.) ⁹When David fought them, he killed all the men and women. He took sheep, cattle, donkeys,

camels and clothes. Then he returned to Achish.

[10]Many times Achish would ask David, "Where did you go raiding today?" And David would tell him that he had gone to the southern part of Judah. Or he would say he had gone to the territory of the Jerahmeelites or of the Kenites. [11]David never brought a man or woman alive to Gath. He thought, "If we bring anyone alive, he may tell Achish, 'This is what David really did'." David did this all the time he lived in the Philistine land. [12]Achish trusted David. He said to himself, "David's own people, the Israelites, now hate David very much. So David will serve me for ever."

Saul and the Witch of Endor

28 Later, the Philistines gathered their armies to fight against Israel. Achish said to David, "You understand that you and your men must join with me in my army."

[2]David answered, "Certainly! Then you can see for yourself what I, your servant, can do!"

Achish said, "Fine, I'll make you my bodyguard for life."

[3]Now Samuel was dead, and all the Israelites had shown their sadness for him. They had buried Samuel in his hometown of Ramah.

And Saul had forced out the mediums[d] and fortune-tellers from the land of Israel.

[4]The Philistines came together and made camp at Shunem. Saul gathered all the Israelites and made camp at Gilboa. [5]When he saw the Philistine army, he was afraid. His heart pounded with fear. [6]He prayed to the Lord, but the Lord did not answer him through dreams, Urim[d] or prophets.[d] [7]Then Saul said to his servants, "Find me a woman who is a medium. I'll go and ask her what will happen."

His servants answered, "There is a medium in Endor."

[8]Then Saul put on other clothes so no one would know who he was. At night Saul and two of his men went to see the woman. Saul said to her, "Talk to a spirit for me. Call up the person I name."

[9]But the woman said to him, "Surely you know what Saul has done. He has forced the mediums and fortune-tellers out from the land of Israel. You are trying to trap me and kill me."

[10]Saul made a promise to the woman in the name of the Lord. He said, "As surely as the Lord lives, you won't be punished for doing this."

[11]The woman asked, "Whom do you want me to bring up for you?"

He answered, "Bring up Samuel."

[12]When the woman saw Samuel, she screamed loudly. She said, "Why have you tricked me? You are Saul!"

[13]The king said to the woman, "Don't be afraid! What do you see?"

The woman said, "I see a spirit coming up out of the ground."

[14]Saul asked, "What does he look like?"

The woman answered, "An old man wearing a coat is coming up."

Then Saul knew it was Samuel, and he bowed face down on the ground.

[15]Samuel asked Saul, "Why have you disturbed me by bringing me up?"

Saul said, "I am greatly troubled. The Philistines are fighting against me. God has left me. He won't answer me any more, either by prophets or in dreams. That's why I called you. I want you to tell me what to do."

[16]Samuel said, "The Lord has left you. He has become your enemy. So why do you call on me? [17]He has done what he said he would do. He said these things through me. He has torn the kingdom out of your hands. He has given it to one of your neighbours, David. [18]You did not obey the Lord. You did not show the Amalekites how angry he was with them. That's why he has done this to you today. [19]The Lord will give both Israel and you to the Philistines. Tomorrow you and

your sons will be with me. The Lord will let the Philistines defeat the army of Israel."

²⁰Saul quickly fell to the ground and lay there. He was afraid because of what Samuel had said. He was also very weak because he had eaten nothing all that day and night.

²¹Then the woman came to Saul. She saw that he was really frightened. She said, "Look, I, your servant, have obeyed you. I have risked my life and done what you told me to do. ²²Now please listen to me. Let me give you some food. Then you may eat and have enough strength to go on your way."

²³But Saul refused. He said, "I won't eat."

His servants joined the woman in asking him to eat. And he listened to them. So he got up from the ground and sat on the bed.

²⁴The woman had a fat calf at the house. She quickly killed it. She took some flour and mixed dough with her hands. Then she baked some bread without yeast. ²⁵She put the food before them, and they ate. Then that same night they got up and left.

David Goes Back to Ziklag

29 The Philistines gathered all their soldiers at Aphek. Israel camped by the spring at Jezreel. ²The Philistine kings were marching with their groups of 100 and 1,000 men. David and his men were marching at the back with Achish. ³The Philistine commanders asked, "What are these Hebrews doing here?"

Achish told them, "This is David. He was an officer to Saul king of Israel. But he has been with me for over a year now. I have found nothing wrong in David since the time he left Saul and came to me."

⁴But the Philistine commanders were angry with Achish. They said, "Send David back! He must go back to the city you gave him. He can't go with us into battle. If he's here, we'll have an enemy in our own camp. He would please his king by killing our own men. ⁵David is the one the Israelites sing about in their dances:

'Saul has killed thousands of his enemies.
But David has killed tens of thousands'."

⁶So Achish called David. He said to him, "As surely as the Lord lives, you are loyal. I would be pleased to have you serve in my army. Since the day you came to me, I have found no wrong in you. But the Philistine kings don't trust you. ⁷Go back in peace. Don't do anything to displease the Philistine kings."

⁸David asked, "What wrong have I done? What evil have you found in me from the day I came to you until now? Why won't you allow me to fight your enemies, my lord and king?"

⁹Achish answered, "I know you are as pleasing to me as an angel from God. But the Philistine commanders have said, 'David can't go with us into battle'. ¹⁰Early in the morning you and your master's servants, the Israelites, should go back. Go back to the city I gave you. Leave as soon as the sun comes up."

¹¹So David and his men got up early in the morning. They went back to the country of the Philistines. And the Philistines went up to Jezreel.

David's War with the Amalekites

30 On the third day David and his men arrived at Ziklag. The Amalekites had raided southern Judah and Ziklag. They had attacked Ziklag and burned it. ²They took the women and everyone in Ziklag as prisoners, both young and old. But they did not kill any of the people. They only took them away.

³When David and his men came to Ziklag, they found the town had been burned. Their wives, sons and daugh-

ters had been taken as prisoners. ⁴Then David and his army cried loudly until they were too weak to cry any more. ⁵David's two wives had also been taken. They were Ahinoam of Jezreel and Abigail the widow of Nabal from Carmel. ⁶The men in the army were threatening to kill David with stones. This upset David very much. Each man was sad and angry because his sons and daughters had been taken as prisoners. But David found strength in the Lord his God. ⁷David said to Abiathar the priest, "Bring me the holy robe."ᵈ

⁸Then David prayed to the Lord. He said, "Should I chase the people who took our families? Will I catch them?"

The Lord answered, "Chase them. You will catch them. You will succeed in saving your families."

⁹David and the 600 men with him came to the Besor Ravine. Some of the men stayed there. ¹⁰David and 400 men kept up the chase. The other 200 men stayed behind because they were too tired and weak to cross the ravine.

¹¹David's men found an Egyptian in a field. They took him to David. They gave the Egyptian some water to drink and some food to eat. ¹²They gave him a piece of a fig cake and two clusters of raisins. He felt better after eating. He had not eaten any food or drunk any water for three days and nights.

¹³David asked him, "Who is your master? Where do you come from?"

He answered, "I'm an Egyptian. I'm the slave of an Amalekite. Three days ago my master left me, because I became sick. ¹⁴We attacked the southern area of the Kerethites. We attacked the land of Judah and the southern area belonging to Caleb. We burned Ziklag, as well."

¹⁵David asked him, "Will you lead me to the people who took our families?"

He answered, "Yes, if you will make a promise to me before God. Promise that you won't kill me or give me back to my master. Then I will take you to them."

¹⁶So the Egyptian led David to the Amalekites. They were lying around on the ground, eating and drinking. They were celebrating with the things they had taken from the land of the Philistines and from Judah. ¹⁷David fought them from sunset until evening the next day. None of them escaped, except 400 young men who rode off on their camels. ¹⁸David got his two wives back. He also got back everything the Amalekites had taken. ¹⁹Nothing was missing. David brought back everything: the young and old people, the sons and daughters, the valuable things and everything the Amalekites had taken. ²⁰David took all the sheep and cattle. His men made these animals go in front. They said, "They are David's prize."

²¹Then David came to the 200 men who had been too tired and weak to follow him. He had made them stay at the Besor Ravine. They came out to meet David and the army with him. When he came near, the men at the ravine greeted David and his army.

²²But there were evil men and troublemakers in the group that followed David. They said, "These 200 men didn't go with us. So we won't give them any of the things we took. But each man may take his wife and children and go."

²³David answered, "No, my brothers. Don't do that after what the Lord has given us. He has given us the enemy who attacked us. ²⁴Who will listen to what you say? The share will be the same for the man who stayed with the supplies as for the man who went into battle. All will share alike." ²⁵David made this an order and rule for Israel. This order and rule continues even today.

²⁶David arrived in Ziklag. Then he sent some of the things he had taken

from the Amalekites to his friends, the leaders of Judah. He said, "Here is a present for you from the things we took from the Lord's enemies."

²⁷David sent some things from the Amalekites to the leaders in Bethel, Ramoth in the southern part of Judah, Jattir, ²⁸Aroer, Siphmoth, Eshtemoa ²⁹and Racal. He also sent some to the leaders of the cities of the Jerahmeelites and the Kenites, ³⁰to Hormah, Bor Ashan, Athach ³¹and Hebron. He sent some things to the people in all the other places where he and his men had been.

The Death of Saul

31 The Philistines fought against Israel, and the Israelites ran away from them. Many Israelites were killed at Mount Gilboa. ²The Philistines fought hard against Saul and his sons. They killed his sons Jonathan, Abinadab and Malki-Shua. ³The fighting became bad around Saul. When the archers shot at him, he was badly wounded. ⁴He said to the officer who carried his armour, "Pull out your sword and kill me. Then those uncircumcised[d] men won't make fun of me and kill me." But Saul's officer refused, because he was afraid. So Saul took his own sword and threw himself on it. ⁵The officer saw that Saul was dead. So he threw himself on his own sword. And he died with Saul. ⁶So

Saul, his three sons and the officer who carried his armour died together that day.

⁷Now there were Israelites who lived on the other side of Jezreel Valley, and some lived across the Jordan River. They saw how the Israelite army had run away, and they saw that Saul and his sons were dead. So they left their cities and ran away. Then the Philistines came and lived there.

⁸The next day the Philistines came to take all the valuable things from the dead soldiers. They found Saul and his three sons dead on Mount Gilboa. ⁹They cut off Saul's head and took off his armour. Then they sent men to tell the news through all the land of the Philistines. They told it in the temple of their idols and to their people. ¹⁰They put Saul's armour in the temple of the Ashtoreths.[d] They also hung his body on the wall of Beth Shan.

¹¹The people living in Jabesh Gilead heard what the Philistines had done to Saul. ¹²So the brave soldiers of Jabesh marched all night and came to Beth Shan. They took the bodies of Saul and his sons off the wall of Beth Shan. Then they took them to Jabesh. There the people of Jabesh burned the bodies. ¹³They took their bones and buried them under the tamarisk tree in Jabesh. Then the people of Jabesh gave up eating for seven days.

2 SAMUEL

David, the Greatest King

David Learns About Saul's Death

1 Now Saul was dead. And after David had defeated the Amalekites, he returned to Ziklag. He stayed there two days. ²On the third day a young man came to Ziklag. He came from Saul's camp. To show his sadness his clothes were torn, and he had earth on his head. He came and bowed face down on the ground before David.

³David asked him, "Where did you come from?"

The man answered him, "I escaped from the Israelite camp."

⁴David asked him, "What happened? Please tell me!"

The man answered, "The people have run away from the battle. Many of them have fallen dead. Saul and his son Jonathan are dead also."

⁵David said to him, "How do you know Saul and his son Jonathan are dead?"

⁶The young man answered, "I happened to be on Mount Gilboa. There I saw Saul leaning on his spear. The Philistine chariots and the men riding in them were coming closer to Saul. ⁷When he looked back and saw me, he called to me. I answered him, 'Here I am!'

⁸"Then Saul asked me, 'Who are you?'

"I told him, 'I am an Amalekite'.

⁹"Then Saul said to me, 'Please come here and kill me. I am badly hurt and am almost dead already'.

¹⁰"So I went over and killed him. He had been hurt so badly I knew he couldn't live. Then I took the crown from his head and the bracelet from

his arm. I have brought them here to you, my master."

¹¹Then David tore his clothes to show his sorrow. And all the men with him did also. ¹²They were very sad and cried. They did not eat until evening. They cried for Saul and his son Jonathan. And they cried for the Israelites who had been killed with swords.

David Orders the Amalekite Killed

¹³David asked the young man who brought the report, "Where are you from?"

The young man answered, "I am the son of a foreigner. I am an Amalekite."

¹⁴David asked him, "Why were you not afraid to kill the Lord's appointed king?"

¹⁵Then David called one of his men. David told him, "Go! Kill the Amalekite!" So the Israelite killed the Amalekite. ¹⁶David had said to the Amalekite, "You are responsible for your own death. You have spoken against yourself! You said, 'I have killed the Lord's appointed king'. "

David's Song About Saul and Jonathan

¹⁷David sang a funeral song about Saul and his son Jonathan. ¹⁸David ordered that the people of Judah be taught this song. It is called "The Bow". This song is written in the Book of Jashar:

¹⁹"Israel, your leaders have been
    killed on the hills.
  How the mighty men have fallen
    in battle!

20Don't tell it in Gath.
> Don't announce it in the streets
> of Ashkelon.
If you do, the daughters of the
> Philistines will be happy.
> The daughters of the Philistines
> will rejoice.

21"May there be no dew or rain on
> the mountains of Gilboa.
> May their fields produce no
> grain.
This is because there the mighty
> warrior's shield was
> dishonoured.
> Saul's shield was no longer
> rubbed with oil.
22Jonathan's bow killed its share of
> enemies.
> And Saul's sword killed its
> share, too.
Their weapons are stained with
> the blood of dead men.
Their weapons have stabbed the
> flesh of strong men.

23"We loved Saul and Jonathan.
> We enjoyed them while they
> lived.
> Saul and Jonathan are together
> even in death.
They were faster than eagles.
They were stronger than lions.

24"You daughters of Israel, cry for
> Saul.
Saul clothed you with red
> dresses.
He put gold decorations on your
> dresses.

25"How the mighty men have fallen
> in battle!
> Jonathan is dead on Gilboa's
> hills.
26I cry for you, my brother
> Jonathan.
> I enjoyed your friendship so
> much.
Your love to me was wonderful,
> more wonderful than the love of
> women.

27"How the mighty men have fallen
> in battle!
> The weapons of war are gone."

David Is Made King of Judah

2 Later, David prayed to the Lord. David said, "Should I go up to any of the cities of Judah?"

The Lord said to David, "Go."

David asked, "Where should I go?"

The Lord answered, "To Hebron."

2So David went up to Hebron with his two wives. One was Ahinoam from Jezreel. The other was Abigail, the widow of Nabal in Carmel. 3David also brought his men and their families. They all made their homes in the cities of Hebron. 4Then the men of Judah came to Hebron. They appointed David king over Judah.

They told David that the men of Jabesh Gilead had buried Saul. 5So David sent messengers to the men of Jabesh Gilead. They told David's message to the men in Jabesh: "The Lord bless you. You have shown kindness to your master Saul by burying him. 6May the Lord now be kind and true to you. I will also be kind to you because you have done this. 7Now be strong and brave. Saul your master is dead. The people of Judah have appointed me their king."

War Between Judah and Israel

8Now Abner son of Ner was the commander of Saul's army. Abner took Saul's son Ish-Bosheth to Mahanaim. 9There Abner made him king of Gilead, Ashuri, Jezreel, Ephraim, Benjamin and all Israel. 10Saul's son Ish-Bosheth was 40 years old when he became king over Israel. He ruled for two years. But the people of Judah followed David. 11David was king in Hebron for seven years and six months.

12Abner son of Ner and the servants of Ish-Bosheth son of Saul left Mahanaim. They went to Gibeon. 13Joab son of Zeruiah and David's men also went there. They met Abner and Ish-Bosheth's men at the pool of Gibeon. Abner's group sat on one side of the pool. Joab's group sat on the other side.

14Abner said to Joab, "Let's have the young men get up and have a contest here."

Joab said, "Yes, let them have a contest."

15Then the young men got up. The two groups counted their men for the contest. Twelve men were chosen from the people of Benjamin for Ish-Bosheth son of Saul. Twelve men were chosen from David's men. 16Each man grabbed his enemy's head. Then he stabbed his enemy's side with a knife. And the men fell down together. So that place in Gibeon is called The Field of the Sharp Knives. 17That day the contest became a terrible battle. And David's men defeated Abner and the Israelites.

Abner Kills Asahel

18Zeruiah's three sons, Joab, Abishai and Asahel, were there. Now Asahel was a fast runner. He was as fast as a deer in the field. 19Asahel chased Abner, going straight towards him. 20Abner looked back and asked, "Are you Asahel?"

Asahel said, "Yes, I am."

21Then Abner said to Asahel, "Turn to your right or left. Catch one of the young men and take his armour." But Asahel refused to stop chasing him.

22Abner again said to Asahel, "Stop chasing me! If you don't stop, I'll have to kill you! Then I won't be able to face your brother Joab again!"

23But Asahel refused to stop chasing Abner. So Abner used the back end of his spear. He stabbed it into Asahel's stomach, and the spear came out of his back. Asahel died right there. Everyone stopped when they came to the place where Asahel's body lay.

24But Joab and Abishai continued chasing Abner. The sun was going down when they arrived at the hill of Ammah. This is near Giah on the way to the empty land near Gibeon. 25The men of Benjamin came to Abner. They all stood together at the top of the hill.

26Abner shouted to Joab, "Must the sword kill for ever? Surely you must know this will only end in sadness! Tell the people to stop chasing their own brothers!"

27Then Joab said, "If you had not said anything, the people would have chased their brothers until morning. This is as sure as God is alive." 28Then Joab blew a trumpet, and his people stopped chasing the Israelites. They did not try to fight them any more.

29Abner and his men marched all night through the Jordan Valley. They crossed the Jordan River. After marching all day, they arrived at Mahanaim.

30Joab came back after he had stopped chasing Abner. Then Joab gathered the people together. Asahel and 19 of David's men were missing. 31But David's men had killed 360 Benjaminites who had followed Abner. 32David's men took Asahel and buried him. They put him in the tomb of his father at Bethlehem. Then Joab and his men marched all night. The sun came up as they reached Hebron.

3 There was a long war between the people who supported Saul's family and those who supported David's family. The supporters of David's family became stronger and stronger, and the supporters of Saul's family became weaker and weaker.

David's Sons

2Sons were born to David at Hebron. The first son was Amnon. Amnon's mother was Ahinoam from Jezreel. 3The second son was Kileab. Kileab's mother was Abigail, the widow of Nabal from Carmel. The third son was Absalom. Absalom's mother was Maacah daughter of Talmai. Talmai was king of Geshur. ⁴The fourth son was Adonijah. His mother was Haggith. The fifth son was Shephatiah. His mother was Abital. ⁵The sixth son was Ithream. His mother was Eglah, David's wife. These sons were born to David at Hebron.

Abner Joins David

⁶Abner made himself a main leader among the supporters of Saul. He did this during the war between the supporters of Saul's family and the supporters of David's family.

⁷Now Saul had once had a slave woman*d* named Rizpah. She was the daughter of Aiah. Ish-Bosheth said to Abner, "Why did you have sexual relations with my father's slave woman?"

⁸Abner was very angry because of what Ish-Bosheth said. Abner said, "I have been loyal to Saul and his family and friends! I didn't hand you over to David. I am not a traitor working for Judah! But now you are saying I did something wrong with this woman! ⁹May God punish me terribly if I don't help David. I will make sure that what God promised does happen! ¹⁰I will take the kingdom from the family of Saul. I will make David king of Israel and Judah! He will rule from Dan to Beersheba."*n*

¹¹Ish-Bosheth couldn't say anything to Abner. He was too afraid of Abner.

¹²Then Abner sent messengers to David. Abner said, "Who is going to rule the land? Make an agreement with me, and I will help you become the king of all Israel."

¹³David answered, "Good! I will make an agreement with you. But I ask you one thing. I will not meet with you unless you bring Saul's daughter Michal to me." ¹⁴Then David sent messengers to Saul's son Ish-Bosheth. David said, "Give me my wife Michal. She was promised to me. I killed 100 Philistines to get her."

¹⁵So Ish-Bosheth sent men to take Michal from her husband. He was Paltiel son of Laish. ¹⁶Michal's husband went with her, crying as he followed her to Bahurim. But Abner said to Paltiel, "Go back home." So he went home.

¹⁷Abner sent a message to the older leaders of Israel. He said, "You have been wanting to make David your king. ¹⁸Now do it! The Lord has spoken about David. The Lord said, 'I will save my people the Israelites. I will save them from the Philistines and all their enemies. I will do this through my servant David.'"

¹⁹Abner also said these things to the people of Benjamin. He then went to Hebron to tell David what the Benjaminites and Israel wanted to do. ²⁰Abner came with 20 men to David at Hebron. There David prepared a feast for them. ²¹Then Abner said to David, "My master and king, I will go and bring all the Israelites to you. Then they will make an agreement with you. You will rule over all Israel as you wanted." So David let Abner go, and he left in peace.

Abner's Death

²²Just then Joab and David's men came from a battle. They had many valuable things they had taken from the enemy. David had let Abner leave in peace. So he was not with David at Hebron. ²³Joab and all his army arrived at Hebron. The army said to Joab, "Abner son of Ner came to King David, and David let him leave in peace."

²⁴Joab came to the king and said, "What have you done? Abner came to

---

Dan to Beersheba Dan was the city farthest north in Israel. Beersheba was the city farthest south. So this means all the people of Israel.

you. Why did you let him go? Now he's gone. 25You know Abner son of Ner! He came to trick you! He came to learn about everything you are doing!"

26Then Joab left David and sent messengers after Abner. They brought Abner back from the well of Sirah. But David did not know this. 27When Abner arrived at Hebron, Joab took him aside into the gateway. Joab acted as though he wanted to talk with him in private. But Joab stabbed Abner in the stomach, and Abner died. Abner had killed Joab's brother Asahel. So Joab killed Abner to pay him back.

28Later David heard the news. He said, "My kingdom and I are innocent for ever. We did not kill Abner son of Ner. The Lord knows this. 29Joab and his family are responsible for this. I hope many troubles will come to his family. May his family always have someone with sores or with a harmful skin disease. May they always have someone who must lean on a crutch. May some of his family be killed in war. May they always have someone without food to eat."

30(Joab and his brother Abishai had killed Abner, because he had killed their brother Asahel. This was in the battle at Gibeon.)

31Then David spoke to Joab and to all the people with Joab. He said, "Tear your clothes and put on rough cloth to show how sad you are. Cry for Abner." King David himself followed behind the body of Abner. 32So they buried Abner in Hebron. David and all the people cried at Abner's grave.

33King David sang this funeral song for Abner.

"Did Abner die like a foolish man?
34   His hands were not tied.
   His feet were not in chains.
   He fell as a person falls before evil
      men."

Then all the people cried again for Abner. 35They came to encourage David to eat while it was still day. But he made a promise. He said, "May God punish me terribly if I eat bread or any other food before the sun sets!"

36All the people saw what happened. They agreed with what the king was doing. 37That day all the people of Judah and all the Israelites understood. They knew it was not David who had killed Abner son of Ner.

38David said to his officers, "You know that a very important leader died today in Israel. 39Even though I am the appointed king, I am weak today. These sons of Zeruiah are too strong for me. May the Lord give them the punishment they should have."

Ish-Bosheth's Death

4 Ish-Bosheth son of Saul heard that Abner had died at Hebron. Then Ish-Bosheth and all Israel became very frightened. 2Two men who were captains in Saul's army came to Ish-Bosheth. One man was named Baanah, and the other was named Recab. They were the sons of Rimmon of Beeroth, who was a Benjaminite. (The town Beeroth belonged to the tribe^d of Benjamin.) 3The people of Beeroth ran away to Gittaim. And they still live there today.

4(Now Jonathan son of Saul had a son who was crippled in both feet. His name was Mephibosheth. He was five years old when the news came from Jezreel that Saul and Jonathan were dead. Mephibosheth's nurse picked him up and ran away. But as she hurried to leave, he fell and became crippled.)

5Recab and Baanah, sons of Rimmon, were from Beeroth. They went to Ish-Bosheth's house at noon. 6-7They came into the middle of the house. Recab and Baanah came as if they were going to get some wheat. Ish-Bosheth was lying on his bed in his bedroom. Recab and Baanah stabbed him in the stomach. Then they cut off his head and took it with them. They travelled all night through the Jordan Valley. ⁸When they arrived at Hebron, they gave his head to David. They said to the king, "Here is the head of Ish-Bosheth son of Saul. He was your enemy. He tried to kill you! Today the Lord has paid back Saul and his family for what they did to you!"

⁹David answered Recab and his brother Baanah sons of Rimmon of Beeroth. David said, "As surely as the Lord lives, he has saved me from all trouble! ¹⁰Once a man thought he was bringing me good news. He told me, 'Look! Saul is dead!' But I took hold of him and killed him at Ziklag. That was the reward I gave him for his news! ¹¹So even more I must require your death. This is because evil men have killed an innocent man. And he was on his own bed in his own house!"

¹²So David commanded his men to kill Recab and Baanah. Then they cut off the hands and feet of Recab and Baanah. They hung their hands and feet over the pool of Hebron. Then they took Ish-Bosheth's head and buried it in Abner's tomb at Hebron.

David Is Made King of Israel

5 Then all the tribes*d* of Israel came to David at Hebron. They said to him, "Look, we are your own family. ²In the past Saul was king over us. But you were the one leading us in battle for Israel. The Lord said to you, 'You will be like a shepherd for my people, the Israelites. You will become their ruler.'"

³All the older leaders of Israel came to King David at Hebron. He made an agreement with them in Hebron in front of the Lord. Then they poured oil on David to make him king over Israel.

⁴David was 30 years old when he became king. He ruled for 40 years. ⁵He was king over Judah in Hebron for seven years and six months, and he was king over all Israel and Judah in Jerusalem for 33 years.

⁶The king and his men went to Jerusalem to attack the Jebusites who lived there. The Jebusites said to David, "You can't come into our city. Even our people who are blind and crippled can stop you." They said this because they thought David could not enter their city. ⁷But David did take the city of Jerusalem with its strong walls. It became the City of David.

⁸That day David said to his men, "To defeat the Jebusites you must go through the water tunnel. Then you can reach those 'crippled' and 'blind' enemies. This is why people say, 'The blind and the crippled cannot enter the palace.'"

⁹So David lived in the city with its strong walls. He called it the City of David. David built more buildings around it. He began where the land was filled in on the east side of the city. He also built more buildings inside the city. ¹⁰He became stronger and stronger, because the Lord of heaven's armies was with him.

¹¹Hiram king of the city of Tyre sent messengers to David. He also sent cedar logs, carpenters and men to cut stone. They built a palace for David. ¹²Then David knew the Lord really had made him king of Israel. And he knew the Lord had made his kingdom very important. This was because the Lord loved his people, the Israelites.

¹³In Jerusalem David took for himself more slave women*d* and wives. This was after he moved there from Hebron. More sons and daughters were born to David. ¹⁴These are the names of the sons born to David in Jerusalem: Shammua, Shobab, Nathan, Solomon, ¹⁵Ibhar, Elishua, Nepheg, Japhia, ¹⁶Elishama, Eliada and Eliphelet.

David Defeats the Philistines

¹⁷Now the Philistines heard that Da-

vid had been made king over Israel. So all the Philistines went to look for him. But when David heard the news, he went down to a safe place. [18]So the Philistines came and camped in the Valley of Rephaim. David asked the Lord, "Should I attack the Philistines? Will you help me defeat them?"

[19]The Lord said to David, "Go! I will certainly help you defeat them."

[20]So David went to Baal Perazim and defeated the Philistines there. David said, "Like a flood of water, the Lord has broken through my enemies." So David named the place Baal Perazim.[n] [21]The Philistines left their idols behind at Baal Perazim, and David and his men carried these idols away.

[22]Once again the Philistines came and camped at the Valley of Rephaim. [23]David prayed to the Lord. This time the Lord told David, "Don't attack the Philistines from the front. Instead, go around them. Attack them opposite the balsam trees. [24]You will hear the sound of marching in the tops of the balsam trees. Then you must act quickly. I, the Lord, will have gone ahead of you and defeated the Philistine army." [25]So David did what the Lord commanded. He defeated the Philistines and chased them all the way from Gibeon to Gezer.

The Holy Ark Is Brought to Jerusalem

6 David again gathered all the chosen men of Israel. There were 30,000 of them. [2]Then David and all his people went to Baalah in Judah.[n] They took the Holy Ark[d] of God from Baalah in Judah and moved it to Jerusalem. The Holy Ark is called by the Name, the name of the Lord of heaven's armies. His throne is between the gold creatures with wings that are on the Holy Ark. [3]David's men put the Holy Ark of God on a new cart. Then they brought the Holy Ark out of Abinadab's house on the hill. Uzzah and Ahio, sons of Abinadab, led the new cart. [4]This cart had the Holy Ark of God on it. Ahio was walking in front of it. [5]David and all the Israelites were playing all kinds of musical instruments before the Lord. They were made of pine wood. There were lyres,[d] harps, tambourines,[d] rattles and cymbals.

[6]When David's men came to the threshing[d] floor of Nacon, the oxen stumbled. The Holy Ark of God began to fall off the cart. So Uzzah reached out and took hold of it. [7]The Lord was angry with Uzzah and killed him. Uzzah had not honoured God when he touched the Holy Ark. So Uzzah died there beside it. [8]David was angry because the Lord had killed Uzzah. So that place is called The Punishment of Uzzah even today.

[9]David was afraid of the Lord that day. He said, "How can the Holy Ark of the Lord come to me now?" [10]So David would not move the Holy Ark of the Lord to be with him in Jerusalem. Instead, he took it to the house of Obed-Edom, a man from Gath. [11]The Holy Ark of the Lord stayed in Obed-Edom's house for three months. And the Lord blessed Obed-Edom and all his family.

[12]The people told David, "The Lord has blessed the family of Obed-Edom. And all his things are blessed. This is because the Holy Ark of God is there." So David went and brought it up from Obed-Edom's house to Jerusalem with joy. [13]When the men carrying the Holy Ark of the Lord had walked six steps, David sacrificed a bull and a fat calf. [14]Then David danced with all his might before the Lord. He had on a holy linen robe.[d] [15]David and all the Israelites shouted

---

Baal Perazim This name means "the Lord breaks through".
Baalah in Judah Another name for Kiriath Jearim.

with joy. They blew the trumpets as they brought the Holy Ark of the Lord to the city.

¹⁶Saul's daughter Michal was looking out of the window. She watched as the Holy Ark of the Lord came into the city. When she saw David jumping and dancing before the Lord, she hated him.

¹⁷David put up a tent for the Holy Ark. Then the Israelites put it in its place inside the tent. David offered whole burnt offerings and fellowship offerings before the Lord. ¹⁸When David finished offering the whole burnt offerings and the fellowship offerings, he blessed the people in the name of the Lord of heaven's armies. ¹⁹David gave a loaf of bread, a cake of dates and a cake of raisins to everyone. He gave them to all the Israelites, both men and women. Then all the people went home.

²⁰David went back to bless the people in his home. But Saul's daughter Michal came out to meet him. She said, "The king of Israel did not honour himself today! You took off your clothes in front of the servant girls of your officers. You were like a foolish man who takes off his clothes without shame!"

²¹Then David said to Michal, "I did it before the Lord. The Lord chose me, not your father. He didn't choose anyone from Saul's family. The Lord appointed me to be leader of his people, the Israelites. So I will celebrate in front of the Lord. ²²Maybe I will lose even more honour. And you may think little of me. But the girls you talk about will honour me!"

²³And Saul's daughter Michal had no children to the day she died.

David Wants to Build a Temple

7 King David was living in his palace, and the Lord gave him peace from all his enemies around him. ²David said to Nathan the prophet,ᵈ "Look, I am living in a palace made of cedar wood. But the Holy Arkᵈ of God is still kept in a tent!"

³Nathan said to the king, "Go and do what you really want to do. The Lord is with you."

⁴But that night the Lord spoke his word to Nathan. The Lord said, ⁵"Go and tell my servant David, 'This is what the Lord says: You are not the person to build a house for me to live in. ⁶I did not live in a house when I brought the Israelites out of Egypt. I have been moving around all this time with a tent as my home. ⁷I have continued to move with the tribesᵈ of Israel. But I have never asked their leaders who take care of them to build me a house of cedar wood'.

⁸"You must tell my servant David, 'This is what the Lord of heaven's armies says: I took you from the pasture when you were following the sheep. I took you to become leader of my people, the Israelites. ⁹I have been with you everywhere you have gone. I have defeated your enemies for you. I will make you as famous as any of the great men on the earth. ¹⁰Also I will choose a place for my people, the Israelites. I will plant them so they can live in their own home. They will not be bothered any more. Wicked people will no longer make them suffer as they have in the past. ¹¹Wicked people continued to do this even when I appointed judges. But I will give you peace from all your enemies. I also tell you that I will make your descendantsᵈ kings of Israel after you.

¹²" 'Your days will come to an end, and you will die. At that time I will make one of your sons the next king. ¹³He will build a templeᵈ for me. I will make his kingdom strong for ever. ¹⁴I will be his father, and he will be my son. When he sins, I will use other people to punish him. They will be my whips. ¹⁵But I will not stop loving him. I took away my love and kindness from Saul. I removed Saul when I turned to you. ¹⁶But your family and

your kingdom will continue for ever before me. Your rule will last for ever'."

[17]Nathan told David everything he had heard.

David Prays to God

[18]Then King David went in the tent and sat in front of the Lord. David said, "Lord God, why have you made me so important to you? Why have you made my family important? [19]But that was not enough for you, Lord God. You have also said these kind things about my future family. I am your servant. Lord God, this is not the usual way you talk to people.

[20]"What more can I say to you? Lord God, you love me, your servant, so much! [21]You have done this wonderful thing because you said you would. You have done it because you wanted to. And you have decided to let me know all these great things. [22]This is why you are great, Lord God! There is no one like you. There is no God except you. We have heard all this ourselves! [23]And there are no others like your people, the Israelites. They are the one nation on earth that God chose to be his people. You used them to make your name well known. You did great and wonderful miracles[d] for them. You went ahead of them and forced other nations and their gods out of the land. You freed your people from slavery in Egypt. [24]You made the people of Israel your very own people for ever. And, Lord, you became their God.

[25]"Now, Lord God, keep the promise you made about my family and me, your servant. Do what you have promised. [26]Then you will be honoured for ever. And people will say, 'The Lord of heaven's armies is God over Israel!' And the family of your servant David will continue before you.

[27]"Lord of heaven's armies, the God of Israel, you have shown things

to me. You have said, 'I will make your family great'. So I, your servant, am brave enough to pray to you. [28]Lord God, you are God, and your words are true. And you have promised these good things to me, your servant. [29]Please, bless my family. Let it continue before you for ever. Lord God, you have said these wonderful things. With your blessing let my family be blessed for ever."

David Wins Many Wars

8 Later, David defeated the Philistines, and he took control of their capital city.

[2]He also defeated the people of Moab. He forced them to lie on the ground. Then he used a rope to measure them. When two men were measured, David ordered them killed. But every third man was allowed to live. So the people of Moab became servants of David. They gave him the payments he demanded.

[3]As David went to take control again at the Euphrates River, he defeated Hadadezer. Hadadezer son of Rehob was king of Zobah. [4]David took from Hadadezer 1,700 men who rode in his chariots. He also captured 20,000 foot soldiers. David crippled all but 100 of the chariot horses. He saved those horses to pull chariots.

[5]Arameans from Damascus came to help Hadadezer king of Zobah. But David defeated those 22,000 Arameans. [6]Then David put groups of soldiers in Damascus in Aram. The Arameans became David's servants and gave him the payments he demanded. The Lord gave David victory everywhere he went.

[7]David took the shields of gold that had belonged to Hadadezer's officers. He brought them to Jerusalem. [8]David also took many things made of bronze from Tebah and Berothai. (They were cities that had belonged to Hadadezer.)

[9]Toi, king of Hamath heard that Da-

vid had defeated all the army of Had-adezer. [10]So Toi sent his son Joram to greet and congratulate King David. Joram congratulated David for defeating Hadadezer. (Hadadezer had fought wars against Toi before.) Joram brought things made of silver, gold and bronze. [11]David took these things and gave them to the Lord. He also had given other silver and gold to the Lord. He had taken it from the nations he had defeated. [12]These nations were Edom, Moab, Ammon, Philistia and Amalek. David also defeated the king of Zobah who was Hadadezer son of Rehob.

[13]David was famous after he returned from the Valley of Salt. There he had defeated 18,000 Arameans. [14]David put groups of soldiers through all the land of Edom. All the people of Edom became servants for him. The Lord gave David victory everywhere he went.

[15]David was king over all Israel. His decisions were fair and right for all his people. [16]Joab son of Zeruiah was commander over the army. Jehoshaphat son of Ahilud was the recorder. [17]Zadok son of Ahitub and Ahimelech son of Abiathar were priests. Seraiah was the royal assistant. [18]Benaiah son of Jehoiada was over the Kerethites and Pelethites, the king's bodyguards. And David's sons were important leaders.

David Helps Saul's Family

9 David asked, "Is there anyone still left in Saul's family? I want to show kindness to this person for Jonathan's sake!"

[2]Now there was a servant named Ziba from Saul's family. So David's servants called Ziba to him. King David said to him, "Are you Ziba?"

He answered, "Yes, I am Ziba, your servant."

[3]The king asked, "Is there anyone left in Saul's family? I want to show God's kindness to this person."

Ziba answered the king, "Jonathan has a son still living. He is crippled in both feet."

[4]The king asked Ziba, "Where is this son?"

Ziba answered, "He is at the house of Makir son of Ammiel in Lo Debar."

[5]Then King David had servants bring Jonathan's son from the house of Makir son of Ammiel in Lo Debar. [6]Mephibosheth, Jonathan's son, came before David and bowed face down on the floor.

David said, "Mephibosheth!"

Mephibosheth said, "I am your servant."

[7]David said to him, "Don't be afraid. I will be kind to you for your father Jonathan's sake. I will give you back all the land of your grandfather Saul. And you will always be able to eat at my table."

[8]Mephibosheth bowed to David again. Mephibosheth said, "You are being very kind to me, your servant! And I am no better than a dead dog!"

[9]Then King David called Saul's servant Ziba. David said to him, "I have given your master's grandson everything that belonged to Saul and his family. [10]You, your sons and your servants will farm the land for Mephibosheth. You will harvest the crops. Then your master's grandson will have food to eat. But Mephibosheth, your master's grandson, will always be able to eat at my table."

(Now Ziba had 15 sons and 20 servants.) [11]Ziba said to King David, "I am your servant. I will do everything my master, the king, commands me."

So Mephibosheth ate at David's table as if he were one of the king's sons. [12]Mephibosheth had a young son named Mica. Everyone in Ziba's family became Mephibosheth's servants. [13]Mephibosheth was crippled in both feet. He lived in Jerusalem and always ate at the king's table.

War with the Ammonites and Arameans

10 Later Nahash king of the Ammonites died. His son Hanun became king after him. ²David said, "Nahash was kind to me. So I will be kind to his son Hanun." So David sent his officers to comfort Hanun about his father's death.

David's servants went to the land of the Ammonites. ³But the important men of Ammon spoke to Hanun, their master. They said, "Do you think David wants to honour your father by sending men to comfort you? No! David sent them to study the city and to spy it out. They plan to capture it!" ⁴So Hanun took David's officers and shaved off half their beards to shame them. He cut their clothes off at the hips to insult them. Then he sent them away.

⁵When the people told David, he sent messengers to meet his officers. He did this because these men were very ashamed. King David said, "Wait at Jericho until your beards have grown back. Then come back to Jerusalem."

⁶Now the Ammonites saw that they had become David's enemies. So they hired 20,000 Aramean foot soldiers from Beth Rehob and Zobah. They also hired the king of Maacah with 1,000 men, and they hired 12,000 men from Tob.

⁷David heard about this. So he sent Joab with the whole army of warriors. ⁸The Ammonites came out and got ready for the battle. They stood at the city gate. The Arameans from Zobah and Rehob and the men from Tob and Maacah were out in the field. They were standing away from the Ammonites.

⁹Joab saw that there were enemies both in front of him and behind him. So he chose some of the best men from the Israelites. He got them ready for battle against the Arameans. ¹⁰Then Joab gave the other men to his brother Abishai to lead against the Ammonites. ¹¹Joab said to Abishai, "If the Arameans are too strong for me, come and help me. If the Ammonites are too strong for you, I will come and help you. ¹²Be strong. Let us fight bravely for our people and for the cities of our God. The Lord will do what he decides is right."

¹³Then Joab and his men attacked the Arameans, and they ran away. ¹⁴When the Ammonites saw that the Arameans were running away, they ran away from Abishai and went back to their city. So Joab returned from the battle with the Ammonites and came to Jerusalem.

¹⁵The Arameans saw that the Israelites had defeated them. So they came together into one big army. ¹⁶Hadadezer sent messengers to bring the Arameans who lived on the other side of the Euphrates River. These Arameans went to Helam. Their leader was Shobach, the commander of Hadadezer's army.

¹⁷When David heard about this, he gathered all the Israelites together. They crossed over the Jordan River and went to Helam. There the Arameans prepared for battle and attacked. ¹⁸But David defeated the Arameans, and they ran away from the Israelites. David killed 700 Aramean chariot drivers and 40,000 Aramean horsemen. He also killed Shobach, the commander of the Aramean army.

¹⁹The kings who served Hadadezer saw that the Israelites had defeated them. So they made peace with the Israelites and served them. And the Arameans were afraid to help the Ammonites again.

David and Bathsheba

11 In the spring the kings would go out to war. So in the spring David sent out Joab, his servants and all the Israelites. They destroyed the Ammonites and attacked the city of

Rabbah. But David stayed in Jerusalem. [2]One evening David got up from his bed. He walked around on the roof[n] of his palace. While he was on the roof, he saw a woman bathing. She was very beautiful. [3]So David sent his servants to find out who she was. A servant answered, "That woman is Bathsheba daughter of Eliam. She is the wife of Uriah the Hittite." [4]David sent messengers to bring Bathsheba to him. When she came to him, he had sexual relations with her. (Now Bathsheba had purified herself from her monthly period.) Then she went back to her house. [5]But Bathsheba became pregnant. She sent word to David, saying, "I am pregnant."

[6]David sent this message to Joab: "Send Uriah the Hittite to me." So Joab sent Uriah to David. [7]Uriah came to David, and David asked him how Joab was, how the soldiers were and how the war was going. [8]Then David said to Uriah, "Go home and rest."

So Uriah left the palace. The king also sent a gift to him. [9]But Uriah did not go home. He slept outside the door of the palace. He slept there as all the king's officers did.

[10]The officers told David, "Uriah did not go home."

Then David said to Uriah, "You came from a long trip. Why didn't you go home?"

[11]Uriah said to him, "The Holy Ark[d] and the soldiers of Israel and Judah are staying in tents. My master Joab and his officers are camping out in the fields. It isn't right for me to go home to eat and drink and have sexual relations with my wife!"

[12]David said to Uriah, "Stay here today. Tomorrow I'll send you back to the battle." So Uriah stayed in Jerusalem that day and the next. [13]Then David called Uriah to come to see him. Uriah ate and drank with David. David made Uriah drunk, but he still did not go home. That evening Uriah went to sleep with the king's officers outside the king's door.

[14]The next morning David wrote a letter to Joab and sent it by Uriah. [15]In the letter David wrote, "Put Uriah in the front lines where the fighting is worst. Then leave him there alone. Let him be killed in battle."

[16]Joab watched the city and saw where its strongest defenders were. He put Uriah there. [17]The men of the city came out to fight against Joab. Some of David's men were killed. And Uriah the Hittite was one of them.

[18]Then Joab sent a report to David about everything that had happened in the war. [19]Joab told the messenger, "Tell King David what happened in the war. [20]After you finish, the king may become angry. He may ask you, 'Why did you go so near the city to fight? Didn't you know they would shoot arrows from the city wall? [21]Do you remember who killed Abimelech son of Jerub-Besheth?[n] It was a woman on the city wall. She threw a large stone for grinding grain on Abimelech. She killed him there in Thebez. Why did you go so near the wall?' If King David asks that, you must answer, 'Your servant Uriah the Hittite also died'."

[22]The messenger went in and told David everything Joab had told him to say. [23]The messenger told David, "The men of Ammon were winning. They came out and attacked us in the field. But we fought them back to the city gate. [24]The men on the city wall shot arrows at your servants. Some of

---

roof In Bible times houses were built with flat roofs. The roof was used for drying things such as flax and fruit. It was also used as an extra room, as a place for worship and as a place to sleep in the summer.

Jerub-Besheth Another name for Gideon.

your men were killed. Your servant Uriah the Hittite also died."

²⁵David said to the messenger, "Say this to Joab: 'Don't be upset about this. The sword kills everyone the same. Make a stronger attack against the city and capture it'. Encourage Joab with these words."

²⁶When Bathsheba heard that her husband was dead, she cried for him. ²⁷After she finished her time of sadness, David sent servants to bring her to his house. She became David's wife and gave birth to his son. But the Lord did not like what David had done.

David's Son Dies

12 The Lord sent Nathan to David. When Nathan came to David, Nathan said, "There were two men in a city. One man was rich, but the other was poor. ²The rich man had very many sheep and cattle. ³But the poor man had nothing except one little female lamb he had bought. The poor man fed the lamb. It grew up with him and his children. It shared his food and drank from his cup. It slept in his arms. The lamb was like a daughter to him.

⁴"Then a traveller stopped to visit the rich man. The rich man wanted to give food to the traveller. But he didn't want to take one of his own sheep or cattle to feed the traveller. Instead, he took the lamb from the poor man. The rich man killed the lamb and cooked it for his visitor."

⁵David became very angry at the rich man. He said to Nathan, "As surely as the Lord lives, the man who did this should die! ⁶He must pay for the lamb four times for doing such a thing. He had no mercy!"

⁷Then Nathan said to David, "You are the man! This is what the Lord, the God of Israel, says: 'I appointed you king of Israel. I saved you from Saul. ⁸I gave you his kingdom and his wives. And I made you king of Israel and Judah. And if that had not been

enough, I would have given you even more. ⁹So why did you ignore the Lord's command? Why did you do what he says is wrong? You killed Uriah the Hittite with the sword of the Ammonites! And you took his wife to become your wife! ¹⁰So there will always be people in your family who will be killed by a sword. This is because you showed that you did not respect me! And you took the wife of Uriah the Hittite!'

¹¹"This is what the Lord says: 'I am bringing trouble to you from your own family. While you watch, I will take your wives from you. And I will give them to someone who is very close to you. He will have sexual relations with your wives, and everyone will know it. ¹²You had sexual relations with Bathsheba in secret. But I will do this so all the people of Israel can see it'."

¹³Then David said to Nathan, "I have sinned against the Lord."

Nathan answered, "The Lord has taken away your sin. You will not die. ¹⁴But what you did caused the Lord's enemies to lose all respect for him. For this reason the son who was born to you will die."

¹⁵Then Nathan went home. And the Lord caused the son of David and Bathsheba, Uriah's widow, to become very sick. ¹⁶David prayed to God for the baby. David refused to eat or drink. He went into his house and stayed there. He lay on the ground all night. ¹⁷The older leaders of David's family came to him. They tried to pull him up from the ground. But he refused to get up. And he refused to eat food with them.

¹⁸On the seventh day the baby died. David's servants were afraid to tell him that the baby was dead. They said, "Look, we tried to talk to David while the baby was alive. But he refused to listen to us. If we tell him the baby is dead, he may harm himself."

¹⁹But David saw his servants whispering. Then he understood that the

baby was dead. So he asked them, "Is the baby dead?"

They answered, "Yes, he is dead."

[20]Then David got up from the floor. He washed himself, put lotions on himself and changed his clothes. Then he went into the Lord's house to worship. After that, he went home and asked for something to eat. His servants gave him some food, and he ate.

[21]David's servants said to him, "Why are you doing this? When the baby was still alive, you refused to eat. You cried. But when the baby died, you got up and ate food."

[22]David said, "While the baby was still alive, I refused to eat, and I cried. I thought, 'Who knows? Maybe the Lord will feel sorry for me and let the baby live'. [23]But now the baby is dead. So why should I go without food? I can't bring him back to life. Some day I will go to him. But he cannot come back to me."

[24]Then David comforted Bathsheba his wife. He slept with her and had sexual relations with her. She became pregnant again and had another son. David named the boy Solomon. The Lord loved Solomon. [25]The Lord sent word through Nathan the prophet[d] to name the baby Jedidiah.[n] This was because the Lord loved the child.

David Captures Rabbah

[26]Now Joab fought against Rabbah, a city of the Ammonites. And he was about to capture the royal city. [27]Joab sent messengers to David and said, "I have fought against Rabbah. I have captured its water supply. [28]Now bring the other soldiers together and attack this city. Capture it before I capture it myself. If I capture this city, it will be called by my name!"

[29]So David gathered all the army and went to Rabbah. He fought against Rabbah and captured it. [30]David took the crown off their king's head. It was gold and weighed about 35 kilograms. It also had gems in it. They put the crown on David's head. And David took many valuable things out of the city. [31]He also brought out the people of the city. He made them work with saws, iron picks and axes, and forced them to build with bricks. David did this to all the Ammonite cities. Then David and all his army went back to Jerusalem.

Amnon and Tamar

13 Now David had a son named Absalom and a son named Amnon. Absalom had a beautiful sister named Tamar. And Amnon loved her. [2]Tamar was a virgin.[d] Amnon did not think he should do anything bad to her. But he wanted her very much. He made himself sick just thinking about her.

[3]Amnon had a friend named Jonadab son of Shimeah. (Shimeah was David's brother.) Jonadab was a very clever man. [4]He asked Amnon, "Why do you look so sad day after day? You are the king's son! Tell me what's wrong!"

Amnon told him, "I love Tamar. But she is the sister of my half-brother Absalom."

[5]Jonadab said to Amnon, "Go to bed. Act as if you are sick. Then your father will come to see you. Tell him, 'Please let my sister Tamar come in and give me food to eat. Let her make the food in front of me. Then I will see it and eat it from her hand'."

[6]So Amnon lay down in bed and acted as if he were sick. King David came in to see him. Amnon said to him, "Please let my sister Tamar come in. Let her make two of her special cakes for me while I watch. Then I will eat them from her hands."

[7]David sent messengers to Tamar in the palace. They told her, "Go to your brother Amnon's house and make some food for him." [8]So Tamar

Jedidiah This name means "loved by the Lord".

went to her brother Amnon's house. He was in bed. Tamar took some dough and pressed it together with her hands. She made some special cakes while Amnon watched. Then she baked them. ⁹Next she took the pan and took out the cakes for Amnon. But he refused to eat.

He said to his servants, "All of you, leave me alone!" So all his servants left the room. ¹⁰Amnon said to Tamar, "Bring the food into the inner room. Then I'll eat from your hand."

Tamar took the cakes she had made, and she brought them to her brother Amnon in the inner room. ¹¹She went to him so he could eat from her hands. But Amnon grabbed her. He said, "Sister, come and have sexual relations with me."

¹²Tamar said to him, "No, brother! Don't force me! This should never be done in Israel! Don't do this shameful thing! ¹³I could never get rid of my shame! And you will become like the shameful fools in Israel! Please talk with the king. He will let you marry me."

¹⁴But Amnon refused to listen to her. He was stronger than she was. So he forced her to have sexual relations with him. ¹⁵After that, Amnon hated Tamar. He hated her much more than he had loved her before. Amnon said to her, "Get up and leave!"

¹⁶Tamar said to him, "No! Sending me away would be an even greater evil. That would be an worse than what you've already done!"

But he refused to listen to her. ¹⁷He called his young servant back in. Amnon said, "Get this girl out of here right now! Lock the door after her." ¹⁸So his servant led her out of the room and he bolted the door after her.

Now Tamar was wearing a special robe with long sleeves. The king's virgin daughters wore this kind of robe. ¹⁹To show how upset she was Tamar took ashes and put them on her head.

She tore her special robe. She put her hand on her head and went away, crying loudly.

²⁰Absalom, Tamar's brother, said to her, "Has Amnon, that brother of yours, forced you to have sexual relations with him? He is your brother. So for now, sister, be quiet. Don't let this upset you so much!" So Tamar lived in her brother Absalom's house. She was sad and lonely.

²¹When King David heard the news, he was very angry. ²²Absalom did not say a word, good or bad, to Amnon. He hated Amnon for forcing his sister Tamar to have sexual relations with him.

Absalom's Revenge

²³Two years later Absalom had some men come to Baal Hazor, near Ephraim. They were to cut the wool from his sheep. Absalom invited all the king's sons to come also. ²⁴Absalom went to the king and said, "I have men coming to cut the wool. Please come with your officers and join me."

²⁵King David said to Absalom, "No, my son. We won't all go. It would be too much trouble for you." Absalom begged David to go. David did not go, but he did give his blessing.

²⁶Absalom said, "If you don't want to go, then please let my brother Amnon go with me."

King David asked Absalom, "Why should he go with you?"

²⁷Absalom kept begging David. Finally, David let Amnon and all the king's sons go with Absalom.

²⁸Then Absalom gave a command to his servants. He said, "Watch Amnon. When he is drunk, I will tell you, 'Kill Amnon'. Right then, kill him! Don't be afraid. I have commanded you! Be strong and brave!" ²⁹So Absalom's young men killed Amnon as Absalom commanded. But all of David's other sons got on their mules and escaped.

³⁰While the king's sons were on their way, the news came to David.

The message was, "Absalom has killed all of the king's sons! Not one of them is left alive!" [31]King David tore his clothes and lay on the ground to show his sadness. All his servants standing nearby tore their clothes also.

[32]Jonadab was the son of Shimeah, David's brother. Jonadab said to David, "Don't think all the young men, your sons, are killed. No, only Amnon is dead! Absalom planned this because Amnon forced his sister Tamar to have sexual relations with him. [33]My master and king, don't think that all of the king's sons are dead. Only Amnon is dead!"

[34]In the meantime Absalom had run away.

There was a guard standing on the city wall. He saw many people coming from the other side of the hill. [35]So Jonadab said to King David, "Look, I was right! The king's sons are coming!"

[36]As soon as Jonadab had said this, the king's sons arrived. They were crying loudly. David and all his servants began crying also. They all cried very much. [37]David cried for his son every day.

But Absalom ran away to Talmai[n] son of Ammihud. Talmai was king of Geshur. [38]After Absalom ran away to Geshur, he stayed there for three years. [39]When King David got over Amnon's death, he missed Absalom greatly.

Joab Sends a Wise Woman to David

14 Joab, son of Zeruiah, knew that King David missed Absalom very much. [2]So Joab sent messengers to Tekoa to bring a wise woman from there. Joab said to her, "Please pretend to be very sad for someone. Put on clothes to show your sadness. Don't put lotion on yourself. Act like a

woman who has been crying many days for someone who died. [3]Go to the king. Talk to him using the words that I tell you." Then Joab told the wise woman what to say.

[4]So the woman from Tekoa talked to the king. She bowed face down on the ground to show respect. She said, "My king, help me!"

[5]King David asked her, "What is the matter?"

The woman said, "I am a widow. My husband is dead. [6]I had two sons. They were out in the field fighting. No one was there to stop them. So one son killed the other son. [7]Now all the family group is against me. They said to me, 'Bring the son who killed his brother. Then we will kill him for killing his brother. That way we will also get rid of the one who would receive what belonged to his father'. My son is like the last spark of a fire. He is all I have left. If they kill him, my husband's name and property will be gone from the earth."

[8]Then the king said to the woman, "Go home. I will take care of this for you."

[9]The woman of Tekoa said to him, "Let the blame be on me. My father's family and I are to blame, my master and king. But you and your throne are innocent."

[10]King David said, "Bring me anyone who says anything bad to you. Then he won't bother you again."

[11]The woman said, "Please promise in the name of the Lord your God. Then my relative who has the duty of punishing a murderer won't add to the destruction. And he won't kill my son."

David said, "As surely as the Lord lives, no one will hurt your son. Not even one hair from your son's head will fall to the ground."

[12]The woman said, "Let me say

Talmai He was Absalom's grandfather.

something to you, my master and king."

The king said, "Speak."

¹³Then the woman said, "Why have you planned this? It is against the people of God. When you say this, you show that you are guilty. You have not brought back your son whom you forced to leave home. ¹⁴We will all die some day. We're like water spilled on the ground. No one can gather it back. But God doesn't take away life. Instead, he plans ways that those who have been sent away will not have to stay away from him! ¹⁵My master and king, I came to say this to you because the people have made me afraid! I thought, 'Let me talk to the king. Maybe he will do what I ask. ¹⁶Maybe he will listen. Perhaps he will save me from the man who wants to kill both me and my son. That man is trying to keep us from getting what God gave us'.

¹⁷"Now I say, 'May the words of my master the king give me rest. Like an angel of God, you know what is good and what is bad. May the Lord your God be with you!'"

¹⁸Then King David said, "You must answer the question I will ask you."

The woman said, "My master the king, please ask your question."

¹⁹The king said, "Did Joab tell you to say all these things?"

The woman answered, "As you live, my master the king, you are right. Your servant Joab did tell me to say these things. ²⁰Joab did it so you would see things differently. My master, you are wise like an angel of God. You know everything that happens on earth."

Absalom Returns to Jerusalem

²¹The king said to Joab, "Look, I will do what I promised. Now please bring back the young man Absalom."

²²Joab bowed face down on the ground. He blessed the king. Then he said, "Today I know you are pleased with me. I know because you have done what I asked."

²³Then Joab got up and went to Geshur and brought Absalom back to Jerusalem. ²⁴But King David said, "Absalom must go to his own house. He may not come to see me." So Absalom went to his own house. He did not go to see the king.

²⁵Now Absalom was greatly praised for his handsome appearance. No man in Israel was as handsome as Absalom. No blemish was on him from his head to his foot. ²⁶At the end of every year, Absalom would cut the hair on his head. He cut it because it became too heavy. He would weigh it, and it would weigh more than 2 kilograms by the royal measure.

²⁷Absalom had three sons and one daughter. His daughter's name was Tamar. She was a beautiful woman.

²⁸So Absalom lived in Jerusalem for two full years without seeing King David. ²⁹Then Absalom sent for Joab. Absalom wanted to send Joab to the king. But Joab would not come. Absalom sent a message a second time. But Joab still refused to come. ³⁰Then Absalom said to his servants, "Look, Joab's field is next to mine. He has barley growing there. Go and burn it." So Absalom's servants set fire to Joab's field.

³¹Then Joab went to Absalom's house. Joab said to him, "Why did your servants burn my field?"

³²Absalom said to Joab, "I sent a message to you, asking you to come here. I wanted to send you to the king. I wanted you to ask him why he brought me home from Geshur. It would have been better for me to stay there! Now let me see the king. If I have sinned, he can kill me!"

³³So Joab went to the king and told him Absalom's words. The king called for Absalom, and Absalom came. He bowed face down on the ground before the king, and the king kissed him.

Absalom Plans to Take David's Kingdom

15 After this, Absalom got a chariot and horses for himself. He got 50 men to run before him. [2]Absalom would get up early and stand near the city gate.[n] If anyone had a problem he wanted the king to settle, he would come here. When he came, Absalom would call to the man. Absalom would say, "What city are you from?"

The man would answer, "I'm from one of the tribes[d] of Israel."

[3]Then Absalom would say to him, "Look, your claims are right. But the king has no one to listen to you." [4]Absalom would also say, "I wish someone would make me judge in this land! Then I could help everyone who comes with a problem. I could help him get a fair decision for his problem!"

[5]People would come near Absalom to bow to him. When they did, Absalom would reach out his hand and take hold of them. Then he would kiss them. [6]Absalom did that to all the Israelites who came to King David for decisions. In this way, Absalom won the hearts of all Israel.

[7]After four years Absalom said to King David, "Please let me go to Hebron. I want to carry out my promise that I made to the Lord. [8]I made it while I was living in Geshur in Aram. I said, 'If the Lord takes me back to Jerusalem, I will worship him in Hebron'."

[9]The king said, "Go in peace."

So Absalom went to Hebron. [10]But he sent secret messengers through all the tribes of Israel. They told the people, "When you hear the trumpets, say this: 'Absalom has become the king at Hebron!'"

[11]Absalom had invited 200 men to go with him. So they went from Jeru-salem with him. But they didn't know what he was planning. [12]Ahithophel was one of the people who advised David. He was from the town of Giloh. While Absalom was offering sacrifices, he called Ahithophel to come from his home town of Giloh. So Absalom's plans were working very well. More and more people began to support him.

[13]A man came in to tell the news to David. The man said, "The Israelites are beginning to follow Absalom."

[14]Then David spoke to all his officers who were with him in Jerusalem. He said, "We must leave quickly! If we don't, we won't be able to get away from Absalom. We must hurry before he catches us. He would destroy us and kill the people of Jerusalem."

[15]The king's officers said to him, "We will do anything you say."

[16]The king set out with everyone in his house. But he left ten slave women[d] to take care of the palace. [17]The king left with all his people following him. They stopped at the last house. [18]All the king's servants passed by him. All the Kerethites and Pelethites, the king's bodyguards, passed by him. All those from Gath, the 600 men who had followed him, passed by him.

[19]The king spoke to Ittai, a man from Gath. He said, "Why are you also going with us? Turn back and stay with King Absalom. You are a foreigner. This is not your homeland. [20]Only a short time ago you came to join me. Today should I make you go with us to other places? I don't even know where I'm going. Turn back, and take your brothers with you. May kindness and loyalty be shown to you."

[21]But Ittai said to the king, "As surely as the Lord lives and as you live, I will stay with you. I'll be with

---

city gate People came here to conduct business. Public meetings and court cases were also held here.

you wherever you are. I'll be with you whether it means life or death."

²²David said to Ittai, "Go, march on." So Ittai from Gath and all his people with their children marched on. ²³All the people cried loudly as everyone passed by. King David also crossed the Kidron Valley. Then all the people went on to the desert. ²⁴Zadok and all the Levites with him were carrying the Ark*d* of the Agreement with God. They set down the Holy Ark, and Abiathar offered sacrifices until all the people had left the city.

²⁵The king said to Zadok, "Take the Holy Ark of God back into the city. If the Lord is pleased with me, he will bring me back. He will let me see both it and Jerusalem again. ²⁶But if the Lord says he is not pleased with me, I am ready. He can do what he wants with me."

²⁷The king also said to Zadok the priest, "You are a seer.*d* Go back to the city in peace. Take your son Ahimaaz and Abiathar's son Jonathan with you. ²⁸I will wait near the crossings into the desert until I hear from you." ²⁹So Zadok and Abiathar took the Holy Ark of God back to Jerusalem and stayed there.

³⁰David went up the Mount of Olives*d* crying as he went. He covered his head and went barefoot. All the people with David covered their heads also, and they were crying as they went. ³¹Someone told David, "Ahithophel is one of the people with Absalom who made secret plans against you."

So David prayed, "Lord, please make Ahithophel's advice foolish."

³²David came to the top of the mountain. This was where he used to worship God. Hushai the Arkite came to meet him. Hushai's coat was torn, and there was dirt on his head to show how sad he was. ³³David said to Hushai, "If you go with me, you will be just one more person to take care of. ³⁴But if you return to the city, you can

make Ahithophel's advice useless. Tell Absalom, 'I am your servant, my king. In the past I served your father. But now I will serve you'. ³⁵The priests Zadok and Abiathar will be with you. You must tell them everything you hear in the king's palace. ³⁶Zadok's son Ahimaaz and Abiathar's son Jonathan are with them. Send them to tell me everything you hear." ³⁷So David's friend Hushai entered Jerusalem. About that time, Absalom also arrived there.

Ziba Meets David

16 David passed a short way over the top of the Mount of Olives.*d* There Ziba, Mephibosheth's servant, met David. Ziba had two donkeys with saddles on them. They carried 200 loaves of bread, 100 cakes of raisins and 100 cakes of figs. They also carried leather bags full of wine. ²The king asked Ziba, "What are these things for?"

Ziba answered, "The donkeys are for your family to ride. The bread and cakes of figs are for the servants to eat. And the wine is for anyone to drink who becomes weak in the desert."

³The king asked, "Where is Mephibosheth?"

Ziba answered him, "Mephibosheth is staying in Jerusalem. He thinks, 'Today the Israelites will give me my father's kingdom back to me!'"

⁴Then the king said to Ziba, "All right. Everything that belonged to Mephibosheth, I now give to you!"

Ziba said, "I bow to you. I hope I will always be able to please you."

Shimei Curses David

⁵As King David came to Bahurim, a man came out from there. He was from Saul's family group. His name was Shimei son of Gera. Shimei came out, cursing David as he came. ⁶He began throwing stones at David and his officers. But the people and sol-

diers gathered all around David. [7]Shimei cursed David. He said, "Get out, get out, you murderer, you troublemaker. [8]The Lord is punishing you for the people you killed in Saul's family! You took Saul's place as king! But now the Lord has given the kingdom to your son Absalom! Now you are ruined because you are a murderer!"

[9]Abishai son of Zeruiah said to the king, "Why should this dead dog curse you, the king? Let me go over and cut off his head!"

[10]But the king answered, "This does not concern you, sons of Zeruiah! If he is cursing me because the Lord told him to, who can question him?"

[11]David also said to Abishai and all his officers, "My own son is trying to kill me! This man is a Benjaminite and has more right to kill me! Leave him alone. Let him curse me. The Lord told him to do this. [12]Maybe the Lord will see my misery. Then maybe he will repay me with something good for the curses Shimei says today!"

[13]So David and his men went on down the road. But Shimei kept following David. Shimei walked on the hillside on the other side of the road. He kept cursing David and throwing stones and earth at him. [14]The king and all his people arrived at the Jordan. They were very tired, so they rested there.

[15]Meanwhile, Absalom, Ahithophel and all the men of Israel arrived at Jerusalem. [16]David's friend Hushai the Arkite came to Absalom. He said to Absalom, "Long live the king! Long live the king!"

[17]Absalom asked, "Why are you not loyal to your friend David? Why didn't you leave Jerusalem with your friend?"

[18]Hushai said, "I belong to the one chosen by the Lord and by these people and all the men of Israel. I will stay with you. [19]In the past I served your father. So whom should I serve now? David's son! I will serve you."

Ahithophel's Advice

[20]Absalom said to Ahithophel, "Please tell us what we should do."

[21]Ahithophel said, "Your father left behind some of his slave women[d] who give birth to his children. He left them here to take care of the palace. Have sexual relations with them. Then all the Israelites will hear that your father is your enemy. And all your people will be encouraged to give you more support." [22]So they put up a tent for Absalom on the flat roof[n] of the palace. Everyone in Israel could see it. And Absalom had sexual relations with his father's slave women.

[23]At that time people thought Ahithophel's advice was as reliable as God's own word. Both David and Absalom thought it was that reliable.

17 Ahithophel said to Absalom, "Let me choose 12,000 men. I'll chase David tonight. [2]I'll catch him while he is tired and weak. I'll frighten him so all his people will run away. But I'll kill only King David. [3]Then I'll bring everyone back to you. If the man you are looking for is dead, everyone else will return safely." [4]This plan seemed good to Absalom and to all the leaders of Israel.

[5]But Absalom said, "Now call Hushai the Arkite. I also want to hear what he says." [6]So Hushai came to Absalom. Absalom said to him, "This is the plan Ahithophel gave. Should we follow it? If not, tell us."

[7]Hushai said to Absalom, "Ahithophel's advice is not good this time." [8]Hushai added, "You know your father and his men are strong. They are as

---

roof In Bible times houses were built with flat roofs. The roof was used for drying things such as flax and fruit. It was also used as an extra room, as a place for worship and as a place to sleep in the summer.

angry as a bear that is robbed of its cubs. Your father is a skilled fighter. He won't stay all night with the people. ⁹He is probably already hiding in a cave or some other place. If your father attacks your men first, people will hear the news. And they will think, 'Absalom's followers are losing!' ¹⁰Then even the men who are as brave as a lion will become frightened. This is because all the Israelites know your father is a fighter. They know his men are brave!

¹¹"This is what I suggest: Gather all the Israelites from Dan to Beersheba.ⁿ There will be as many people as grains of sand by the sea. Then you yourself must go into the battle. ¹²We will catch David where he is hiding. We will fall on him as dew falls on the ground. We will kill him and all of his men. No one will be left alive. ¹³What if David escapes into a city? Then all the Israelites will bring ropes to that city. We'll pull that city into the valley. There won't be even a small stone left there!"

¹⁴Absalom and all the Israelites said, "The advice of Hushai the Arkite is better than that of Ahithophel." They said this because the Lord had planned to destroy the good advice of Ahithophel. In this way the Lord could bring disaster on Absalom.

¹⁵Hushai told these things to Zadok and Abiathar, the priests. He told them what Ahithophel had suggested to Absalom and the older leaders of Israel. He also reported to them what he himself had suggested. Hushai said, ¹⁶"Quickly! Send a message to David. Tell him not to stay tonight at the crossings into the desert. Tell him to cross over the Jordan River at once. If he crosses the river, he and all his people won't be caught."

¹⁷Jonathan and Ahimaaz were waiting at En Rogel. They did not want to be seen going into the town. So a servant girl would go out to them and give them messages. Then Jonathan and Ahimaaz would go and tell King David.

¹⁸But a boy saw Jonathan and Ahimaaz and told Absalom. So Jonathan and Ahimaaz ran away quickly. They went to a man's house in Bahurim. He had a well in his courtyard, and they climbed down into it. ¹⁹The man's wife spread a sheet over the opening of the well. Then she covered it with grain. No one could tell that Jonathan and Ahimaaz were hiding there.

²⁰Absalom's servants came to the woman at the house. They asked, "Where are Ahimaaz and Jonathan?"

She said to them, "They have already crossed the brook."

Absalom's servants then went to look for Jonathan and Ahimaaz. But they could not find them. So they went back to Jerusalem.

²¹After Absalom's servants had left, Jonathan and Ahimaaz climbed out of the well. Then they went to tell King David. They said, "Hurry, cross over the river! Ahithophel has said these things against you!" ²²So David and all his people crossed the Jordan River. By dawn, everyone had crossed the Jordan.

²³Now Ahithophel saw that the Israelites did not accept his advice. So he saddled his donkey and went to his home town. He gave orders for his family and property. Then he hanged himself. After Ahithophel died, he was buried in his father's tomb.

War Between David and Absalom

²⁴David arrived at Mahanaim, and Absalom and all his Israelites crossed over the Jordan River. ²⁵Now Absalom had made Amasa captain of the army instead of Joab. Amasa was the son of a man named Jether the Ishma-

---

Dan to Beersheba Dan was the city farthest north in Israel. And Beersheba was the city farthest south. So this means all the people of Israel.

elite. Amasa's mother was Abigail daughter of Nahash and sister of Zeruiah. Zeruiah was Joab's mother. ²⁶Absalom and the Israelites camped in the land of Gilead.

²⁷Shobi, Makir and Barzillai were at Mahanaim when David arrived. Shobi son of Nahash was from the Ammonite town of Rabbah. Makir son of Ammiel was from Lo Debar, and Barzillai was from Rogelim in Gilead. ²⁸They brought beds, bowls and clay pots. They brought wheat, barley, flour, roasted grain, beans and small peas. ²⁹They also brought honey and milk curds, sheep, and cheese made from cows' milk. They brought these things for David and his people. They had said, "The people have become hungry and tired and thirsty in the desert."

18 David counted his men. He chose commanders over groups of 1,000 and commanders over groups of 100. ²He sent the troops out in three groups. Joab commanded one-third of the men. Joab's brother Abishai son of Zeruiah commanded another third. And Ittai from Gath commanded the last third. King David said to them, "I will also go with you."

³But the men said, "No! You must not go with us! If we run away in the battle, Absalom's men won't care. Even if half of us are killed, Absalom's men won't care. But you're worth 10,000 of us! It is better for you to stay in the city. Then, if we need help, you can send it."

⁴The king said to his people, "I will do what you think is best." So the king stood at the side of the gate as the army went out. They went out in groups of 100 and 1,000.

⁵The king gave a command to Joab, Abishai and Ittai. He said, "Be gentle with young Absalom for my sake." Everyone heard the king's orders about Absalom to the commanders.

⁶David's army went out into the field against Absalom's Israelites. They fought in the forest of Ephraim. ⁷There David's army defeated the Israelites. Many died that day—20,000 men. ⁸The battle spread through all the country. But that day more men died in the forest than in the fighting.

Absalom Dies

⁹Then Absalom happened to meet David's troops. As Absalom was riding his mule, it went under a large oak tree. The branches were thick, and Absalom's head got caught in the tree. His mule ran out from under him. So Absalom was left hanging above the ground. ¹⁰When one of the men saw it happen, he told Joab. He said, "I saw Absalom hanging in an oak tree!"

¹¹Joab said to him, "You saw him? Why didn't you kill him and let him fall to the ground? I would have given you a belt and ten pieces of silver!"

¹²The man answered, "I wouldn't try to hurt the king's son. I wouldn't even if you gave me a thousand pieces of silver. We heard the king's command to you, Abishai and Ittai. The king said, 'Be careful not to hurt young Absalom'. ¹³If I had killed him, the king would have found out. And you would not have protected me!"

¹⁴Joab said, "I won't waste time here with you!" Now Absalom was still alive in the oak tree. So Joab took three spears and stabbed him in the heart. ¹⁵Ten young men who carried Joab's armour also gathered around Absalom. They struck him and killed him.

¹⁶Then Joab blew the trumpet. So the troops stopped chasing Absalom's Israelites. ¹⁷Joab's men took Absalom's body. They threw it into a large pit in the forest. Then they filled the pit with many stones. All the Israelites who followed Absalom ran away and went home.

¹⁸When Absalom was alive, he had put up a pillar in the King's Valley. It

was a monument to himself. He said, "I have no son to keep my name alive." So he named the pillar after himself. That pillar is called Absalom's Monument even today.

¹⁹Ahimaaz son of Zadok spoke to Joab. He said, "Let me run and take the news to King David. I'll tell him the Lord has destroyed the enemy for him."

²⁰Joab answered Ahimaaz, "No, you are not the one to take the news today. You may do it another time. But do not take it today, because the king's son is dead."

²¹Then Joab said to a man from Cush, "Go. Tell the king what you have seen." The Cushite bowed to Joab and ran to tell David.

²²But Ahimaaz son of Zadok begged Joab again. He said, "No matter what happens, please let me go, along with the Cushite!"

Joab said, "Son, why do you want to carry the news? You won't get any reward for the news you bring!"

²³Ahimaaz answered, "No matter what happens, I will run."

So Joab said to Ahimaaz, "Run!" Then Ahimaaz ran by way of the Jordan Valley and passed the Cushite.

²⁴Now David was sitting between the inner and outer gates of the city. The watchman went up to the roof by the gate walls. As he looked up, he saw a man running alone. ²⁵He shouted to tell King David.

The king said, "If he is alone, he is bringing good news!"

The man came nearer and nearer to the city. ²⁶Then the watchman saw another man running. The watchman called to the gatekeeper, "Look! Another man is running alone!"

The king said, "He is also bringing good news!"

²⁷The watchman said, "I think the first man runs like Ahimaaz son of Zadok."

The king said, "Ahimaaz is a good man. He must be bringing good news!"

²⁸Then Ahimaaz called a greeting to the king. He bowed face down on the ground to the king. He said, "Praise the Lord your God! The Lord has defeated the men who were against you, my king."

²⁹The king asked, "Is young Absalom all right?"

Ahimaaz answered, "When Joab sent me, I saw some great excitement. But I don't know what it was."

³⁰Then the king said, "Step over here and wait." So Ahimaaz stepped aside and stood there.

³¹Then the Cushite arrived. He said, "Master and king, hear the good news! Today the Lord has punished the people who were against you!"

³²The king asked the Cushite, "Is young Absalom all right?"

The Cushite answered, "May your enemies be like that young man. May all who come to hurt you be like that young man!"

³³Then the king knew Absalom was dead. He was very upset. He went to the room over the city gate and cried. As he went, he cried out, "My son Absalom, my son Absalom! I wish I had died for you. Absalom, my son, my son!"

Joab Scolds David

19 People told Joab, "Look, the king is crying. He is very sad because of Absalom." ²David's army had won the battle that day. But it became a very sad day for all the people. This was because they heard, "The king is very sad for his son." ³The people came into the city quietly. They were like people who had been defeated in battle and had run away. ⁴The king covered his face and cried loudly, "My son Absalom! Absalom, my son, my son!"

⁵Then Joab went into the king's house. He said to the king, "Today you have shamed all your men. They

saved your life today! They saved the lives of your sons, daughters, wives and slave women. *d* [6]You have shamed them because you love those who hate you. And you hate those people who love you. Today you've made it clear that your commanders and men mean nothing to you. What if Absalom had lived and all of us were dead? I can see you would be very pleased. [7]Now go out and encourage your servants. I swear by the Lord that if you don't go out, no man will be left with you by tonight! That will be worse than all the troubles you have had from your youth until today."

[8]So the king went to the city gate. *n* The news spread that the king was at the gate. So everyone came to see him.

David Goes Back to Jerusalem

All the Israelites who had followed Absalom had run away to their homes. [9]People in all the tribes *d* of Israel began to argue. They said, "The king saved us from the Philistines and our other enemies. But he left the country because of Absalom. [10]We appointed Absalom to rule us, but now he has died in battle. We should make David the king again."

[11]King David sent a message to Zadok and Abiathar, the priests. David said, "Speak to the older leaders of Judah. Say, 'Even in my house I have heard what all the Israelites are saying. So why are you the last tribe to bring the king back to his palace? [12]You are my brothers, my own family. Then why are you the last tribe to bring back the king?' [13]And say to Amasa, 'You are part of my own family. May God punish me terribly if I don't make you commander of the army in Joab's place!' "

[14]David touched the hearts of all the people of Judah. They agreed as if they were one man. They sent a message to the king. They said, "Return with all your men." [15]Then the king returned as far as the Jordan River. The men of Judah came to Gilgal to meet him. They wanted to bring the king across the Jordan River.

[16]Shimei son of Gera was a Benjaminite. He lived in Bahurim. He hurried down with the men of Judah to meet King David. [17]With Shimei came 1,000 Benjaminites. Ziba, the servant from Saul's family, also came. He brought his 15 sons and 20 servants with him. They all hurried to the Jordan River to meet the king. [18]The people went across the Jordan River to help bring the king's family back to Judah. They did whatever the king wanted. As the king was about to cross the river, Shimei son of Gera came to him. Shimei bowed face down on the ground in front of the king. [19]He said to the king, "My master, don't hold me guilty. Don't remember the wrong things I did when you left Jerusalem! Don't hold it against me. [20]I know I have sinned. That is why I am the first person from Joseph's family to come down and meet you today, my master and king!"

[21]But Abishai son of Zeruiah said, "Shimei should die. He cursed you, the Lord's appointed king!"

[22]David said, "This does not concern you, sons of Zeruiah! Today you're against me! No one will be put to death in Israel today. Today I know I am king over Israel!" [23]Then the king said to Shimei, "You won't die." The king made this promise to Shimei.

[24]Mephibosheth, Saul's grandson, also went down to meet King David. Mephibosheth had not cared for his feet, cut his beard or washed his clothes while David was gone. He had not done this from the time the king

---

city gate People came here to conduct business. Public meetings and court cases were also held here.

had left Jerusalem until he returned safely. ²⁵Mephibosheth came from Jerusalem to meet the king. The king asked him, "Mephibosheth, why didn't you go with me?"

²⁶He answered, "My master, my servant Ziba tricked me! I said to Ziba, 'I am crippled. So saddle a donkey. Then I will ride it so I can go with the king'. ²⁷But he lied about me to you. You, my master and king, are like an angel from God. Do what you think is good. ²⁸You could have killed all my grandfather's family. Instead, you put me with the people who eat at your own table. So I don't have a right to ask anything more from the king!"

²⁹The king said to him, "Don't say anything more. I have decided that you and Ziba may divide the land."

³⁰Mephibosheth said to the king, "Let Ziba take all the land. I'm just happy that my master the king has arrived in peace at his own house."

³¹Barzillai of Gilead came down from Rogelim to cross the Jordan River with the king. ³²Now Barzillai was a very old man. He was 80 years old. He had taken care of the king when David was staying at Mahanaim. Barzillai could do this, because he was very rich. ³³David said to Barzillai, "Cross the river with me. Come with me to Jerusalem, and I will take care of you."

³⁴But Barzillai answered the king, "Do you know how old I am? Do you think I can go with you to Jerusalem? ³⁵I am 80 years old! I am too old to taste what I eat or drink. I am too old to hear the voices of men and women singers. Why should you be bothered with me? ³⁶I am not worthy of a reward from you. But I will cross the Jordan River with you. ³⁷Then please let me go back so I may die in my own city. Let me die near the grave of my father and mother. But here is Kimham. Let him go with you, my master and king. Do with him whatever you want."

³⁸The king answered, "Kimham will go with me. I will do for him anything you wish. And I will do anything for you that you wish." ³⁹The king kissed Barzillai and blessed him. Then Barzillai returned home. And the king and all the people crossed the Jordan.

⁴⁰When the king crossed the Jordan to Gilgal, Kimham went with him. All the troops of Judah and half the troops of Israel led David across the river.

⁴¹Soon all the men of Israel came to the king. They said to him, "Our brothers, the men of Judah, stole you away. They brought you and your family across the Jordan River with your men! Why did they do this?"

⁴²All the men of Judah answered the Israelites, "We did this because the king is our close relative. Why are you angry about it? We have not eaten food at the king's expense! He did not give us any gifts!"

⁴³The men of Israel answered the people of Judah, "We have ten tribes in the kingdom. So we have more right to David than you do! But you ignored us! We were the first ones to talk about bringing our king back!"

But the men of Judah spoke even more unkindly than the men of Israel.

Sheba Leads Israel Away from David

20 It happened that a troublemaker named Sheba son of Bicri was there. Sheba was from the tribe[d] of Benjamin. He blew the trumpet and said:

"We have no share in David!
We have no part in the son of Jesse!
People of Israel, let's go to our own homes!"

²So all the Israelites left David and followed Sheba son of Bicri. But the men of Judah stayed with their king all the way from the Jordan River to Jerusalem.

³David came to his palace in Jerusalem. Earlier he had left there ten of his

slave women[d] who gave birth to his children. He had left them there to take care of the palace. Now he put them in a house where they would be guarded. They were kept there for the rest of their lives. David gave them food, but he did not have sexual relations with them. They lived like widows until they died.

⁴The king said to Amasa, "Tell the men of Judah to meet with me in three days. And you must also be here." ⁵So Amasa went to call the men of Judah together. But he took longer than the time the king had told him.

⁶David said to Abishai, "Sheba son of Bicri is more dangerous to us than Absalom was. Take my men and chase him. Hurry before he finds strong, walled cities. If he gets there, he will escape from us." ⁷So Joab's men, the Kerethites and the Pelethites, who were the king's bodyguards, and all the soldiers went with Abishai. They went out from Jerusalem to chase Sheba son of Bicri.

⁸When Joab and the army came to the great rock at Gibeon, Amasa came out to meet them. Joab was wearing his uniform. At his waist he wore a belt. It held his sword in its sheath. As Joab stepped forward, his sword fell out of its sheath. ⁹Joab asked Amasa, "Brother, is everything all right with you?" Then with his right hand he took Amasa by the beard to kiss him. ¹⁰Amasa did not guard against the sword that was in Joab's hand. So Joab pushed the sword into Amasa's stomach. This caused Amasa's insides to spill on the ground. Joab did not have to stab Amasa again. He was already dead. Then Joab and his brother Abishai continued to chase Sheba son of Bicri.

¹¹One of Joab's young men stood by Amasa's body. The young man said, "Everyone who is for Joab and David should follow Joab!" ¹²Amasa lay in the middle of the road, covered with his own blood. The young man saw that everyone was stopping to look at the body. So he dragged Amasa's body from the road and laid it in a field. Then he put a cloth over it. ¹³After Amasa's body was taken off the road, all the men followed Joab. They went with him to chase Sheba son of Bicri.

¹⁴Sheba went through all the tribes of Israel to Abel Beth Maacah. All the Berites also came together and followed him. ¹⁵So Joab and his men came to Abel Beth Maacah and surrounded it. They piled earth up against the city wall so they could attack it, and they began digging under the city walls to make them fall down.

¹⁶But a wise woman shouted out from the city. She said, "Listen! Listen! Tell Joab to come here. I want to talk to him!"

¹⁷So Joab came near her. She asked him, "Are you Joab?"

He answered, "Yes, I am."

Then she said, "Listen to what I say!"

Joab said, "I'm listening."

¹⁸Then the woman said, "In the past people would say, 'Ask for advice at Abel'. Then the problem would be solved. ¹⁹I am one of the peaceful, loyal people of Israel. You are trying to destroy an important city of Israel. Why must you destroy what belongs to the Lord?"

²⁰Joab answered, "May I not destroy or ruin anything. ²¹That is not what I want. But there is a man here from the mountains of Ephraim. He is named Sheba son of Bicri. He has turned against King David. If you will bring him to me, I will leave the city alone."

The woman said to Joab, "His head will be thrown over the wall to you."

²²Then the woman spoke very wisely to all the people of the city. They cut off the head of Sheba son of Bicri. Then they threw it over the wall to Joab. So he blew the trumpet, and the army left the city. Every man re-

turned home. And Joab went back to the king in Jerusalem.

[23]Joab was commander of all the army of Israel. Benaiah son of Jehoiada led the Kerethites and Pelethites, the king's bodyguards. [24]Adoniram led the men who were forced to do hard work. Jehoshaphat son of Ahilud was the recorder. [25]Sheba was the royal assistant. Zadok and Abiathar were the priests, [26]and Ira the Jairite was David's priest.

The Gibeonites Punish Saul's Family

21 During the time David was king, there was a time of hunger. It continued for three years. So David prayed to the Lord.

The Lord answered, "Saul and his family of murderers are the reason for this time of hunger. It has come because Saul killed the Gibeonites." [2](Now the Gibeonites were not Israelites. They were a group of Amorites who were left alive. The Israelites had promised not to hurt the Gibeonites. But Saul was very eager to help the people of Israel and Judah. So he tried to kill all the Gibeonites.)

King David called the Gibeonites together and talked to them. [3]He asked them, "What can I do for you? What can I do to take away Israel's sin so you can bless the Lord's people?"

[4]The Gibeonites said to David, "Saul and his family don't have enough silver and gold to pay for what they did! And we don't have the right to kill anyone in Israel."

Then David asked, "What do you want me to do for you?"

[5]The Gibeonites said to him, "Saul made plans against us. He tried to destroy all our people who are left in the land of Israel. [6]Saul was the Lord's chosen king. So bring seven of his sons to us. Then we will kill them and hang them on stakes. We will put them in front of the Lord at Gibeah, Saul's home town."

The king said, "I will give them to you." [7]But the king protected Jonathan's son Mephibosheth. (Jonathan was Saul's son.) David did this because of the promise he had made to Jonathan in the Lord's name. So the king did not let them hurt Mephibosheth. [8]But the king did take Armoni and Mephibosheth,[n] sons of Rizpah and Saul. (Rizpah was the daughter of Aiah.) And the king took the five sons of Saul's daughter Merab. Adriel was the father of Merab's five sons. (Adriel was the son of Barzillai the Meholathite.) [9]David gave these seven sons to the Gibeonites. Then the Gibeonites killed them and hung them on stakes on a hill before the Lord. All seven sons died together. They were put to death during the first days of the harvest season. (The barley harvest was just beginning.)

[10]Aiah's daughter Rizpah took the rough cloth that was worn to show sadness. Then she put it on a rock for herself. She stayed there from the beginning of the harvest until the rain fell on her sons' bodies. During the day she did not let the birds of the sky touch her sons' bodies. At night she did not let the wild animals touch them.

[11]People told David what Aiah's daughter Rizpah, Saul's slave woman,[d] was doing. [12]Then David took the bones of Saul and Jonathan from the men of Jabesh Gilead. (They had taken these bones secretly from the public square of Beth Shan. The Philistines had hung the bodies of Saul and Jonathan there after they had killed Saul at Gilboa.) [13]David brought the bones of Saul and his son Jonathan from Gilead. Then the people gathered the bodies of Saul's seven sons who were hung on stakes. [14]The people buried the bones of Saul and his

---

Mephibosheth This is not Jonathan's son but another man with the same name.

son Jonathan at Zela in Benjamin. They buried them in the tomb of Saul's father Kish. The people did everything the king commanded. Then God answered the prayers of the people in the land.

Wars with the Philistines

[15]Again there was war between the Philistines and Israel. David and his men went out to fight the Philistines. But David became tired and weak. [16]Ishbi-Benob was one of the sons of Rapha.[d] His bronze spearhead weighed about 3.5 kilograms. Ishbi-Benob had a new sword, and he planned to kill David. [17]But Abishai son of Zeruiah killed the Philistine. So he saved David's life.

Then David's men made a promise to David. They said, "Never again will you go out with us to battle. If you were killed, Israel would lose its greatest leader."

[18]Later, at Gob, there was another battle with the Philistines. Sibbecai the Hushathite killed Saph, another one of the sons of Rapha.

[19]Later, there was another battle at Gob with the Philistines. Elhanan son of Jaare-Oregim from Bethlehem killed Goliath[n] from Gath. Goliath's spear was as large as a weaver's rod.

[20]At Gath another battle took place. A very large man was there. He had six fingers on each hand and six toes on each foot. He had 24 fingers and toes in all. This man also was one of the sons of Rapha. [21]When he challenged Israel, Jonathan killed him. Jonathan was the son of Shimeah, David's brother.

[22]These four men were sons of Rapha from Gath. They all were killed by David and his men.

David's Song of Praise

22 David sang this song to the Lord. He sang it when the Lord had saved him from Saul and all his other enemies. [2]He said:

"The Lord is my rock, my place of safety, my Saviour.
[3]My God is my rock.
I can run to him for safety.
He is my shield and my saving strength.
The Lord is my high tower and my place of safety.
The Lord saves me from those who want to harm me.
[4]I will call to the Lord.
He is worthy of praise.
And I will be saved from my enemies.

[5]"The waves of death came around me.
The deadly rivers overwhelmed me.
[6]The ropes of death wrapped around me.
The traps of death were before me.
[7]In my trouble I called to the Lord.
I cried out to my God.
From his temple he heard my voice.
My call for help reached his ears.

[8]"The earth trembled and shook.
The foundations of heaven began to shake.
They shook because the Lord was angry.
[9]Smoke came out of his nose.
Burning fire came out of his mouth.
Burning coals went before him.
[10]He tore open the sky and came down.
Dark clouds were under his feet.
[11]He rode a creature with wings and flew.
He flew on the wings of the wind.

Goliath In 1 Chronicles 20:5 he is called Lahmi brother of Goliath.

¹²He made darkness his shelter
    around him,
  surrounded by fog and clouds.
¹³Out of the brightness of his
    presence
came flashes of lightning.
¹⁴The Lord thundered from heaven.
  The Most High God raised his
    voice.
¹⁵He shot his arrows and scattered
    his enemies.
  His bolts of lightning confused
    them with fear.
¹⁶The Lord spoke strongly.
  The wind blew from his nose.
  The valleys of the sea appeared.
  The foundations of the earth
    were seen.

¹⁷"The Lord reached down from
    above and took me.
  He pulled me from the deep
    water.
¹⁸He saved me from my powerful
    enemies.
  Those who hated me were too
    strong for me.
¹⁹They attacked me at my time of
    trouble.
  But the Lord supported me.
²⁰He took me to a safe place.
  Because he delights in me, he
    saved me.

²¹"The Lord spared me because I
    did what was right.
  Because I have not done evil, he
    has rescued me.
²²I have followed the ways of the
    Lord.
  I have not done evil by turning
    from my God.
²³I remember all his laws.
  I have not broken his rules.
²⁴I have kept myself innocent before
    him.
  I have kept myself from doing
    evil.
²⁵The Lord rescued me because I
    did what was right.

I did what the Lord said was
    right.
²⁶"Lord, you are loyal to those who
    are loyal.
  You are good to those who are
    good.
²⁷You are pure to those who are
    pure.
  But you are against those who
    are bad.
²⁸You save those who are not
    proud.
  But you make humble those who
    are proud.
²⁹Lord, you give light to my lamp.
  The Lord brightens the
    darkness around me.
³⁰With your help, I can attack an
    army.
  With God's help, I can jump
    over a wall.
³¹"The ways of God are without
    fault.
  The Lord's words are pure.
  He is a shield to those who trust
    him.
³²Who is God? Only the Lord.
  Who is the Rock?*d* Only our
    God.
³³God is my protection.
  He makes my way free from
    fault.
³⁴He makes me like a deer, which
    does not stumble.
  He helps me stand on the steep
    mountains.
³⁵He trains my hands for battle.
  So my arms can bend a bronze
    bow.
³⁶You protect me with your saving
    shield.
  You have stooped to make me
    great.
³⁷You give me a better way to live.
  So I live as you want me to.
³⁸I chased my enemies and
    destroyed them.
  I did not stop till they were
    destroyed.
³⁹I destroyed and crushed them,

so they couldn't rise up again.
They fell beneath my feet.
⁴⁰You gave me strength in battle.
You made my enemies bow
before me.
⁴¹You made my enemies turn back.
I destroyed those who hated
me.
⁴²They called for help,
but no one came to save them.
They called to the Lord,
but he did not answer them.
⁴³I beat my enemies into pieces.
They were like dust on the
ground.
I pounded them out and walked on
them
like mud in the streets.

⁴⁴"You saved me when my people
attacked me.
You kept me as the leader of
nations.
People I never knew serve me.
⁴⁵Foreigners obey me.
As soon as they hear me, they
obey me.
⁴⁶They all become afraid.
They tremble in their hiding
places.

⁴⁷"The Lord lives!
May my Rock be praised!
Praise God, the Rock, who
saves me!
⁴⁸God gives me victory over my
enemies.
He brings people under my rule.
⁴⁹He frees me from my enemies.

"You set me over those who hate
me.
You saved me from cruel men.
⁵⁰So I will praise you, Lord, among
the nations.
I will sing praises to your name.
⁵¹The Lord gives great victories to
his king.
He is loyal to his appointed king,
to David and his descendants*d*
for ever."

David's Last Words

23 These are the last words of David:

"This is the message of David son
of Jesse.
The man made great by the
Most High God speaks.
He is the appointed king of the
God of Jacob.
He is the sweet singer of Israel.

²"The Lord's Spirit*d* spoke through
me.
His word was on my tongue.
³The God of Israel spoke.
The Rock*d* of Israel said to me:
'The person who rules fairly over
people,
the person who rules with
respect for God,
⁴he is like the morning light at
dawn.
He is like a morning without
clouds.
He is like sunshine after a rain.
The sunshine makes the tender
grass grow out of the
ground'.

⁵"This is how God has cared for
my family.
God made a lasting agreement
with me,
good in every way and strong.
This agreement is my salvation.
This agreement is all I want.
Truly, the Lord will make it
grow.

⁶"But all evil people will be thrown
away like thorns.
People cannot hold on to thorns.
⁷Anyone who touches them
uses a tool of iron or a spear.
They will be thrown in the fire
and burned where they lie."

David's Army

⁸These are the names of David's
warriors:

Josheb-Basshebeth, the Tahkemonite, was head of the Three.[n] He killed 800 men at one time.

[9]Next there was Eleazar son of Dodai the Ahohite. Eleazar was one of the three soldiers who were with David when they challenged the Philistines. The Philistines were gathered for battle, and the Israelites drew back. [10]But Eleazar stayed where he was. He fought the Philistines until he was so tired he could not let go of his sword. The Lord gave a great victory to the Israelites that day. The people came back after Eleazar had won the battle. But they came only to take weapons and armour from the enemy. [11]Next there was Shammah son of Agee the Hararite. The Philistines came together to fight. They stood where there was a field full of small peas. Israel's troops ran away from the Philistines. [12]But Shammah stood in the middle of the field. He fought for the field and killed the Philistines. And the Lord gave a great victory.

[13]Once, three of the Thirty, David's chief soldiers, came down to him during harvest. Now David was at the cave of Adullam. The Philistine army had camped in the Valley of Rephaim. [14]At that time David was in a protected place, and some of the Philistine soldiers were in Bethlehem. [15]David had a strong desire for some water. He said, "Oh, I wish someone would get me water from the well near the city gate of Bethlehem!" [16]So the three warriors broke through the Philistine army. They took water out of the well near the city gate of Bethlehem. Then they took it to David. But he refused to drink it. He poured it out on the ground before the Lord. [17]David said, "Lord, I can't drink this! It would be like drinking the blood of the men who risked their lives!" So David refused to drink the water. These were the brave things that the three warriors did.

[18]Abishai was the brother of Joab son of Zeruiah. He was captain of the Three. Abishai used his spear against 300 enemies and killed them. He became as famous as the Three. [19]Abishai received even more honour than the Three. He became their commander. But he was not a member of them.

[20]Benaiah son of Jehoiada was a brave fighter from Kabzeel. He did many brave things. He killed two of the best soldiers from Moab. He also went down into a pit when it was snowing. There he killed a lion. [21]Benaiah killed a big Egyptian. The Egyptian had a spear in his hand. But Benaiah only had a club. Benaiah grabbed the spear from the Egyptian's hand. Then Benaiah killed him with his own spear. [22]These were the brave things that Benaiah son of Jehoiada did. He was as famous as the Three. [23]He received more honour than the Thirty. But he did not become a member of the Three. David made him leader of his bodyguard.

The Thirty Chief Soldiers

[24]The following men were among the Thirty:

Asahel the brother of Joab;
Elhanan son of Dodo from Bethlehem;
[25]Shammah the Harodite;
Elika the Harodite;
[26]Helez the Paltite;
Ira son of Ikkesh (from Tekoa);
[27]Abiezer the Anathothite;
Mebunnai the Hushathite;
[28]Zalmon the Ahohite;
Maharai the Netophathite;
[29]Heled son of Baanah the Netophathite;

Three These were David's most powerful soldiers. See 1 Chronicles 11:11.

Ithai son of Ribai from Gibeah of the land of Benjamin;
[30]Benaiah the Pirathonite;
Hiddai from the ravines of Gaash;
[31]Abi-Albon the Arbathite;
Azmaveth the Barhumite;
[32]Eliahba the Shaalbonite;
the sons of Jashen;
Jonathan [33]son of Shammah the Hararite;
Ahiam son of Sharar the Hararite;
[34]Eliphelet son of Ahasbai the Maacathite;
Eliam son of Ahithophel the Gilonite;
[35]Hezro the Carmelite;
Paarai the Arbite;
[36]Igal son of Nathan of Zobah;
the son of Hagri;
[37]Zelek the Ammonite;
Naharai the Beerothite, who carried the armour of Joab son of Zeruiah;
[38]Ira the Ithrite;
Gareb the Ithrite
[39]and Uriah the Hittite.

There were 37 in all.

David Counts His Army

24 The Lord was angry with Israel again. He caused David to turn against the Israelites. David said, "Go, count the people of Israel and Judah."

[2]King David spoke to Joab, the commander of the army. David said, "Go through all the tribes[d] of Israel. Go from Dan to Beersheba[n] and count the people. Then I will know how many there are."

[3]But Joab said to the king, "May the Lord your God give you 100 times more people. And may you live to see this happen. But why do you want to do this?"

[4]But the king very strongly commanded Joab and the commanders of the army. So they left the king to count the people of Israel.

[5]After crossing the Jordan River, they camped near Aroer. They camped on the south side of the city in the ravine. They went through Gad and on to Jazer. [6]Then they went to Gilead and the land of Tahtim Hodshi. Next they went to Dan Janai and around to Sidon. [7]They went to the strong, walled city of Tyre. They also went to all the cities of the Hivites and Canaanites. Finally, they went to southern Judah, to Beersheba. [8]After nine months and 20 days, they had gone through all the land. Then they came back to Jerusalem.

[9]Joab gave the list of the people to the king. There were 800,000 men in Israel who could use the sword, and there were 500,000 men in Judah.

[10]David felt ashamed after he had counted the people. He said to the Lord, "I have sinned greatly in what I have done! Lord, I beg you, forgive my sin! I have been very foolish."

[11]Before David got up in the morning, the Lord spoke his word to Gad. He was a prophet[d] and David's seer.[d] [12]The Lord told Gad, "Go and tell David, 'This is what the Lord says: I offer you three choices. Choose one for me to do to you'."

[13]Gad went to David and told him. Gad said, "Choose one of these three things. Should three years of hunger come to you and your land? Or should your enemies chase you for three months? Or should there be three days of disease in your country? Think about it. Then decide which of these things I should tell the Lord who sent me."

[14]David said to Gad, "I am really in trouble. But the Lord is very merciful.

Dan to Beersheba Dan was the city farthest north in Israel. Beersheba was the city farthest south. So this means all the people of Israel.

So let the Lord punish us. Don't let my punishment come from people!"

¹⁵So the Lord sent disease on Israel. It began in the morning, and it continued until the chosen time to stop. From Dan to Beersheba 70,000 people died. ¹⁶The angel raised his arm toward Jerusalem to destroy it also. But the Lord felt very sorry about the terrible things that had happened. He said to the angel who was destroying the people, "That's enough! Put down your arm!" At this time the angel of the Lord was by the threshing^d floor of Araunah the Jebusite.

¹⁷David saw the angel that killed the people. Then he said to the Lord, "I've sinned! I've done wrong! But these people only followed me like sheep! They did nothing wrong! Please let your punishment be against me and my father's family!"

¹⁸That day Gad came to David. Gad told him, "Go and build an altar to the Lord. Build it on the threshing floor of Araunah the Jebusite." ¹⁹So David did what Gad told him to do. He obeyed the Lord's command and went to see Araunah.

²⁰Araunah looked and saw the king and his servants coming to him. So he went out and bowed face down on the ground. ²¹He said, "Why has my master the king come to me?"

David answered, "To buy the threshing floor from you. I want to build an altar to the Lord. Then the disease will stop."

²²Araunah said to David, "My master and king, you may take anything you want for a sacrifice. Here are some oxen for the whole burnt offering. Here are the threshing boards and the yokes^d for the wood! ²³My king, I give everything to you!" Araunah also said to the king, "May the Lord your God be pleased with you!"

²⁴But the king answered Araunah, "No. I will pay you for the land. I won't offer to the Lord my God burnt offerings which cost me nothing!"

So David bought the threshing floor and the oxen for 50 pieces of silver. ²⁵Then he built an altar to the Lord there. And he offered whole burnt offerings and fellowship offerings. Then the Lord answered his prayer for the country. And the disease in Israel stopped.

1 KINGS

The Kingdom Is Divided

Adonijah Tries to Become King

1 At this time King David was very old. His servants covered him with blankets, but he could not keep warm. ²So they said to him, "We will find a young woman to care for you. She will lie close to you and keep you warm." ³So the king's servants looked everywhere in Israel for a beautiful young woman. They found a girl named Abishag from the Shunammite people. They brought her to the king. ⁴The girl was very beautiful. She cared for the king and served him. But King David did not have sexual relations with her.

⁵⁻⁶Adonijah was King David and Haggith's son. He was born next after Absalom. He was a very handsome man. He said, "I will be the king." So he got chariots and horses for himself, and he got 50 men to run ahead of him. Now David had never interfered with him by questioning what he did. ⁷Adonijah talked with Joab son of Zeruiah. He also talked with Abiathar the priest. They told him they would help him. ⁸But several men did not join Adonijah. These men were Zadok the priest, Benaiah son of Jehoiada, Nathan the prophet,ᵈ Shimei, Rei and King David's special guard.

⁹Then Adonijah killed some sheep, cows and fat calves for sacrifices. He made these sacrifices at the Stone of Zoheleth near the spring, En Rogel. He invited all his brothers, the other sons of King David, to come. He invited all the rulers and leaders of Judah also. ¹⁰But Adonijah did not invite Nathan the prophet, Benaiah, his father's special guard or his brother Solomon.

¹¹When Nathan heard about this, he went to Bathsheba. She was the mother of Solomon. Nathan asked her, "Have you heard what Adonijah, Haggith's son, is doing? He has made himself king. And our real king, David, does not know it. ¹²Your life and the life of your son Solomon may be in danger. But I will tell you how to save yourselves. ¹³Go to King David and say to him, 'My master and king, you made a promise to me. You promised that my son Solomon would be the king after you. You said he would rule on your throne. So why has Adonijah become king?' ¹⁴While you are still talking to him, I will come in. I will tell the king that what you have said about Adonijah is true."

¹⁵So Bathsheba went in to see the king in his bedroom. He was now very old. Abishag, the girl from Shunam, was caring for him there. ¹⁶Bathsheba bowed down before the king.

He asked, "What do you want?"

¹⁷She answered, "My master, you made a promise to me in the name of the Lord your God. You said, 'Your son Solomon will become king after me. He will rule on my throne'. ¹⁸But now Adonijah has become king. And you did not know it. ¹⁹Adonijah has killed many cows, fat calves and sheep for sacrifices. And he has invited all your sons. He also has invited Abiathar the priest and Joab the commander of your army. But he did not invite Solomon, your son who serves you. ²⁰My master and king, all the people of Israel are watching you. They are waiting for you to decide who will be king after you. ²¹As soon as you die, Solomon and I will be treated as criminals."

²²While Bathsheba was still talking

with the king, Nathan the prophet arrived. ²³The servants told the king, "Nathan the prophet is here." So Nathan went to the king and bowed face down on the ground before him.

²⁴Then Nathan said, "My master and king, have you said that Adonijah will be the king after you? Have you decided he will rule on your throne after you? ²⁵Today he has sacrificed many cows, fat calves and sheep. And he has invited all your other sons, the commanders of the army and Abiathar the priest. Right now they are eating and drinking with him. They are saying, 'Long live King Adonijah!' ²⁶But he did not invite me, Zadok the priest, Benaiah son of Jehoiada or your son Solomon. ²⁷Did you do this? We are your servants. Why didn't you tell us whom you chose to be the king after you?"

David Makes Solomon King

²⁸Then King David said, "Tell Bathsheba to come in!" So she came in and stood before the king.

²⁹Then the king said, "The Lord has saved me from all trouble. As surely as he lives, I make this promise to you. ³⁰Today I will do what I promised you in the past. I made that promise in the name of the Lord, the God of Israel. I promised that your son Solomon would be king after me. I promised he would rule on my throne after me."

³¹Then Bathsheba bowed face down on the ground before the king. She said, "Long live my master King David!"

³²Then King David said, "Tell Zadok the priest, Nathan the prophet[d] and Benaiah son of Jehoiada to come in here." So they came before the king. ³³Then the king said to them, "Take my servants with you and put my son Solomon on my own mule. Take him down to the spring called Gihon. ³⁴There Zadok the priest and Nathan the prophet should pour olive oil on him and make him king over Israel.

Blow the trumpet and shout, 'Long live King Solomon!' ³⁵Then come back here with him. He will sit on my throne and rule in my place. I have chosen him to be the ruler over Israel and Judah."

³⁶Benaiah son of Jehoiada answered the king, "This is good! And may your God make it happen. ³⁷The Lord has always helped you, our king. Let the Lord also help Solomon. And let King Solomon be an even greater king than you."

³⁸So Zadok the priest, Nathan the prophet and Benaiah son of Jehoiada went down. The Kerethites and Pelethites, the king's bodyguards, went with them. They put Solomon on King David's mule and went with him to the spring called Gihon. ³⁹Zadok the priest took with him the container of olive oil from the Holy Tent.[d] He poured the olive oil on Solomon's head to show he was the king. Then they blew the trumpet, and all the people shouted, "Long live King Solomon!" ⁴⁰All the people followed Solomon into the city. They were playing flutes and shouting for joy. They made so much noise the ground shook.

⁴¹At this time Adonijah and all the guests with him were finishing their meal. They heard the sound from the trumpet. Joab asked, "What does all that noise from the city mean?"

⁴²While Joab was speaking, Jonathan son of Abiathar the priest arrived. Adonijah said, "Come in! You are an important man. So you must be bringing good news."

⁴³But Jonathan answered, "No! Our master King David has made Solomon the new king. ⁴⁴King David sent Zadok the priest, Nathan the prophet, Benaiah son of Jehoiada and all the king's bodyguards with him. They put Solomon on the king's own mule. ⁴⁵And Zadok the priest and Nathan the prophet poured olive oil on Solomon at Gihon to make him king. Then they went into the city, shouting with joy.

Now the whole city is excited. That is the noise you hear. [46]Solomon has now become the king. [47]All the king's officers have come to tell King David that he has done a good thing. They are saying, 'May your God make Solomon even more famous than you. And may your God make Solomon an even greater king than you'." Jonathan continued, "And King David bowed down on his bed to worship God. [48]He said, 'Praise the Lord, the God of Israel. Today he has made one of my sons the king and allowed me to see it'."

[49]Then all of Adonijah's guests were afraid, and they left quickly. [50]Adonijah was also afraid of Solomon. So he went and took hold of the corners of the altar.[n] [51]Then someone told Solomon, "Adonijah is afraid of you. He is at the altar, holding on to its corners. He says, 'Tell King Solomon to promise me today that he will not kill me'."

[52]So Solomon answered, "Adonijah must show that he is a man of honour. If he does, I promise that he will not lose even a hair from his head. But if he does anything wrong, he will die." [53]Then King Solomon sent some men to get Adonijah. They brought him to King Solomon. So Adonijah came before King Solomon and bowed down. Then Solomon said, "Go home".

The Death of David

2 It was almost time for David to die. So he talked to Solomon and gave him his last commands. [2]David said, "My time to die is near. Be a good and strong leader. [3]Obey everything that the Lord commands. Follow the commands he has given us. Obey all his laws, and do what he told us. Obey what is written in the teachings of Moses. If you do these things, you will be successful in all you do and

wherever you go. [4]And if you obey the Lord, he will keep the promise he made to me. He promised: 'Your descendants[d] must live as I tell them. They must have complete faith in me. If they do this, then a man from your family will always be king over the people of Israel'.

[5]"Also, you remember what Joab son of Zeruiah did to me. He killed the two commanders of Israel's armies. He killed Abner son of Ner and Amasa son of Jether. He killed them as if he and they were at war. But this was in a time of peace. He killed innocent men, and their blood got on his belt and sandals. [6]You should punish him in the way you think is wisest. (But do not let him die peacefully of old age.)

[7]"Be kind to the children of Barzillai of Gilead. Allow them to eat at your table. They helped me when I ran away from your brother Absalom.

[8]"And remember, Shimei son of Gera is here with you. He is from the people of Benjamin in Bahurim. Remember he cursed me the day I went to Mahanaim. Then he came down to meet me at the Jordan River. I promised him before the Lord, 'Shimei, I will not kill you'. [9]But you should not leave him unpunished. You are a wise man. You will know what to do to him. But you must be sure he is killed."

[10]Then David died and was buried with his ancestors in Jerusalem. [11]He had ruled over Israel for 40 years. Seven years were in Hebron, and 33 years were in Jerusalem.

Solomon Takes Control as King

[12]Now Solomon became king after David, his father. And he was in control of his kingdom.

[13]At this time Adonijah son of Haggith went to Bathsheba, Solomon's

---

corners of the altar If a person were innocent of a crime, he could run into the Holy Place. If he held on to the corners of the altar there, he would not be punished. The corners looked like horns.

mother. Bathsheba asked, "Do you come in peace?"

Adonijah answered, "Yes. This is a peaceful visit. ¹⁴I have something to say to you."

"You may speak," she said.

¹⁵Adonijah said, "You remember that at one time the kingdom was mine. All the people of Israel thought I was their king. But things changed. Now my brother is the king because the Lord chose him. ¹⁶So now I have one thing to ask you. Please do not refuse me."

Bathsheba answered, "What do you want?"

¹⁷Adonijah said, "I know King Solomon will do anything you ask him. So please ask him to give me Abishag the Shunammite woman to be my wife."

¹⁸"Very well," she answered. "I will speak to the king for you."

¹⁹So Bathsheba went to King Solomon to talk to him for Adonijah. When Solomon saw her, he stood up to meet her. Then he bowed down to her and sat on the throne. He told some servants to bring another throne for his mother. Then she sat down at his right side.

²⁰Bathsheba said to him, "I have one small thing to ask you. Please do not refuse me."

The king answered, "Ask, mother. I will not refuse you."

²¹So she said, "Allow Abishag the Shunammite woman to marry your brother Adonijah."

²²King Solomon answered his mother, "Why do you ask me to give him Abishag? Why don't you ask for him to become the king also since he is my older brother? Abiathar the priest and Joab son of Zeruiah will support him!"

²³Then King Solomon made a promise in the name of the Lord. He said, "I promise Adonijah will pay for asking me this! May God punish me terribly if it doesn't cost Adonijah his life! ²⁴The Lord has given me the throne that belonged to my father David. The Lord has kept his promise and given the kingdom to me and my people. As surely as the Lord lives, Adonijah will die today!" ²⁵So King Solomon gave orders to Benaiah son of Jehoiada. And he went out and killed Adonijah.

²⁶Then King Solomon said to Abiathar the priest, "I should kill you. But I will allow you to go back to your home in Anathoth. I will not kill you now because you helped to carry the Holy Ark^d of the Lord God while marching with my father David. And I know you shared in all of the hard times with my father." ²⁷So Solomon removed Abiathar from being a priest to the Lord. This happened as the Lord had said it would. He had said this about the priest Eli and his family in Shiloh.

²⁸When Joab heard about this, he was afraid. He had supported Adonijah, but not Absalom. So Joab ran to the Tent^d of the Lord and took hold of the corners of the altar.^n ²⁹Someone told King Solomon that Joab had run to the Tent of the Lord and was beside the altar. So Solomon ordered Benaiah to go and kill him.

³⁰Benaiah went into the Tent of the Lord and said to Joab, "The king says, 'Come out!' "

But Joab answered, "No, I will die here."

So Benaiah went back to the king and told him what Joab had said. ³¹Then the king commanded Benaiah, "Do as he says! Kill him there and bury him. Then my family and I will be free of the guilt of Joab. Joab is guilty of killing innocent people. ³²He killed two men who were much better than he was. They were Abner son of Ner

---

corners of the altar If a person were innocent of a crime, he could run into the Holy Place. If he held on to the corners of the altar there, he would not be punished. The corners looked like horns.

and Amasa son of Jether. Abner was the commander of Israel's army, and Amasa was the commander of Judah's army. My father David did not know that he killed them. So the Lord will pay him back for those men he killed. ³³He and his family will be for ever guilty for their deaths. But there will be peace from God for David, his descendants,^d his family and his rule for ever."

³⁴So Benaiah son of Jehoiada killed Joab, and he was buried near his home in the desert. ³⁵Solomon then made Benaiah son of Jehoiada commander of the army in Joab's place. Solomon also made Zadok the new high priest in Abiathar's place.

³⁶Next the king sent for Shimei. The king said to him, "Build a house for yourself here in Jerusalem. Live in the house, and don't leave the city. ³⁷If you leave and go past the Kidron Valley, someone will kill you. And it will be your own fault."

³⁸So Shimei answered the king, "What you have said is good. I will obey you, my master and king." So Shimei lived in Jerusalem for a long time.

³⁹But three years later two of Shimei's slaves ran away. They went to Achish king of Gath. He was the son of Maacah. Shimei heard that his slaves were in Gath. ⁴⁰So he put his saddle on his donkey and left. He went to Achish at Gath to find his slaves. When he found them there, he brought them back to his home.

⁴¹Someone told Solomon that Shimei had gone from Jerusalem to Gath and had returned. ⁴²So Solomon sent for Shimei. Solomon said, "I made you promise in the name of the Lord not to leave Jerusalem. I warned you that if you went anywhere else you would die. And you agreed to what I said. You said you would obey me. ⁴³Why did you break your promise to the Lord? Why did you not obey my command? ⁴⁴You know the many wrong things you did against my father David. Now the Lord will punish you for those wrongs. ⁴⁵But the Lord will bless me. He will make the rule of David safe before the Lord for ever."

⁴⁶Then the king ordered Benaiah to kill Shimei, and he did. Now Solomon was in full control of his kingdom.

Solomon Asks for Wisdom

3 Solomon made an agreement with the king of Egypt by marrying his daughter. Solomon brought her to Jerusalem. At this time Solomon was still building his palace and the Temple^d of the Lord. He was also building a wall around Jerusalem. ²The Temple had not yet been finished. So people were still offering animal sacrifices at altars in many places of worship. ³Solomon showed that he loved the Lord. He did this by following the commands his father David had given him. But Solomon still used the many places of worship to offer sacrifices and to burn incense.^d

⁴King Solomon went to Gibeon to offer a sacrifice. He went there because it was the most important place of worship. He offered 1,000 burnt offerings on that altar. ⁵While he was at Gibeon, the Lord came to him in a dream during the night. God said, "Ask for anything you want. I will give it to you."

⁶Solomon answered, "You were very kind to your servant, my father David. He obeyed you. He was honest and lived right. And you showed great kindness to him when you allowed his son to be king after him. ⁷Lord my God, you have allowed me to be king in my father's place. But I am like a little child. I do not have the wisdom I need to do what I must do. ⁸I, your servant, am here among your chosen people. There are too many of them to count. ⁹So I ask that you give me wisdom. Then I can rule the people in the right way. Then I will know the difference between right and

wrong. Without wisdom, it is impossible to rule this great people of yours."

¹⁰The Lord was pleased that Solomon had asked him for this. ¹¹So God said to him, "You did not ask for a long life. And you did not ask for riches for yourself. You did not ask for the death of your enemies. Since you asked for wisdom to make the right decisions, ¹²I will give you what you asked. I will give you wisdom and understanding. Your wisdom will be greater than anyone has had in the past. And there will never be anyone in the future like you. ¹³Also, I will give you what you did not ask for. You will have riches and honour. During your life no other king will be as great as you. ¹⁴I ask you to follow me and obey my laws and commands. Do this as your father David did. If you do, I will also give you a long life."

¹⁵Then Solomon woke up. He knew that God had talked to him in the dream. Then he went to Jerusalem and stood before the Ark^d of the Agreement with the Lord. There he gave burnt offerings and fellowship offerings to the Lord. After that, he gave a feast for all of his leaders and officers.

Solomon Makes a Wise Decision

¹⁶One day two women who were prostitutes^d came to Solomon. They stood before him. ¹⁷One of the women said, "My master, this woman and I live in the same house. I gave birth to a baby while she was there with me. ¹⁸Three days later this woman also gave birth to a baby. No one else was in the house with us. There were only the two of us. ¹⁹One night this woman rolled over on her baby, and it died. ²⁰So during the night she took my son from my bed while I was asleep. She carried him to her bed. Then she put the dead baby in my bed. ²¹The next morning I got up to feed my baby. But I saw that he was dead! Then I looked

at him more closely. I saw that he was not my son."

²²But the other woman said, "No! The living baby is my son. The dead baby is yours!"

But the first woman said, "No! The dead baby is yours, and the living one is mine!" So the two women argued before the king.

²³Then King Solomon said, "Each of you says the living baby is your own. And each of you says the dead baby belongs to the other woman."

²⁴Then King Solomon sent his servants to get a sword. When they brought it to him, ²⁵he said, "Cut the living baby into two pieces. Give each woman half of the baby."

²⁶The real mother of the living child was full of love for her son. She said to the king, "Please, my master, don't kill him! Give the baby to her!"

But the other woman said, "Neither of us will have him. Cut him into two pieces!"

²⁷Then King Solomon said, "Give the baby to the first woman. Don't kill him. She is the real mother."

²⁸When the people of Israel heard about King Solomon's decision, they respected him very much. They saw he had wisdom from God to make the right decisions.

Solomon's Officers

4 King Solomon ruled over all Israel. ²These are the names of his leading officers:

Azariah son of Zadok was the priest;

³Elihoreph and Ahijah, sons of Shisha, recorded what happened in the courts;

Jehoshaphat son of Ahilud recorded the history of the people;

⁴Benaiah son of Jehoiada was commander of the army;

Zadok and Abiathar were priests;

⁵Azariah son of Nathan was in charge of the district governors;

Zabud son of Nathan was a priest and adviser to the king;

6Ahishar was responsible for everything in the palace;

Adoniram son of Abda was in charge of the slaves.

7Solomon placed 12 governors over the districts of Israel. They had to gather food from their districts. Then they were to give it to the king and his family. Each governor was responsible for giving food to the king one month of each year. 8These are the names of the 12 governors:

Ben-Hur was governor over the mountain country of Ephraim.

9Ben-Deker was governor over Makaz, Shaalbim, Beth Shemesh and Elon Bethhanan.

10Ben-Hesed was governor over Arubboth, Socoh and Hepher.

11Ben-Abinadab was governor over Naphoth Dor. (He was married to Taphath, daughter of Solomon.)

12Baana son of Ahilud was governor over Taanach, Megiddo and all of Beth Shan next to Zarethan. (This was below Jezreel from Beth Shan to Abel Meholah across Jokmeam.)

13Ben-Geber was governor over Ramoth in Gilead. (He was governor over all the Towns of Jair in Gilead. Jair was the son of Manasseh. Ben-Geber was also over the district of Argob in Bashan. It had 60 large, walled cities with bronze bars on their gates.)

14Ahinadab son of Iddo was governor over Mahanaim.

15Ahimaaz was governor over Naphtali. (He was married to Basemath daughter of Solomon.)

16Baana son of Hushai was governor over Asher and Aloth.

17Jehoshaphat son of Paruah was governor over Issachar.

18Shimei son of Ela was governor over Benjamin.

19Geber son of Uri was governor over Gilead. (Gilead was the country where Sihon king of the Amorite people lived. Og king of Bashan also lived there.) But Geber was the only governor over the district.

Solomon's Kingdom

20There were many people in Judah and Israel. There were as many people as there were grains of sand on the seashore. The people ate, drank and were happy. 21Solomon ruled over all the kingdoms from the Euphrates River to the land of the Philistine people. His kingdom went as far as the border of Egypt. These countries brought Solomon the payments he demanded, and they obeyed him all his life.

22Solomon needed much food each day to feed himself and all the people who ate at his table. It took 6,000 litres of fine flour and 12,000 litres of meal. 23It also took ten cows that were fed good grain, 20 cows that were raised in the fields and 100 sheep. And it took three different kinds of deer and fat birds.

24Solomon ruled over all the countries west of the Euphrates River. This was the land from Tiphsah to Gaza. And Solomon had peace on all sides of his kingdom. 25During Solomon's life Judah and Israel, from Dan to Beersheba,n lived in peace. Each man was able to sit under his own fig trees and grapevines.

26Solomon had 4,000 stalls for his chariot horses, and he had 12,000 chariot soldiers. 27Each month one of the district governors gave King Solomon all the food he needed. This was enough for every person who ate at the king's table. The governors made sure he had everything he needed. 28They also gave the king enough barley and straw for the chariot and work

Dan to Beersheba Dan was the city farthest north in Israel. Beersheba was the city farthest south. So this means all the people of Israel.

horses. Each person brought this grain to the required places.

Solomon's Wisdom

29God gave great wisdom to Solomon. Solomon could understand many things. His wisdom was as hard to measure as the sand on the seashore. 30His wisdom was greater than the wisdom of all the men in the East. And his wisdom was greater than all the wisdom of the men in Egypt. 31He was wiser than any other man on earth. He was even wiser than Ethan the Ezrahite. He was wiser than Heman, Calcol and Darda. They were the sons of Mahol. King Solomon became famous in all the countries around Israel and Judah. 32During his life King Solomon spoke 3,000 wise teachings. He also knew 1,005 songs. 33He taught about many different kinds of plants. He taught about everything from the great cedar trees of Lebanon to the hyssop that grows out of the walls. He also taught about animals, birds, crawling things and fish. 34People from all nations came to listen to King Solomon's wisdom. The kings of all nations sent them to listen to him. These kings had heard of Solomon's wisdom.

Solomon Prepares to Build the Temple

5 Now King Hiram was the king of Tyre. He had always been a friend of David. Hiram heard that Solomon had been made king in David's place. So he sent his messengers to Solomon. 2Then Solomon sent this message back to King Hiram: 3"You remember that my father David had to fight many wars with the countries around him. So he was never able to build a temple for worship to the Lord his God. David was waiting until the Lord allowed him to defeat all his enemies. 4But now the Lord my God has given me peace. There is peace on all sides of my country. I have no ene-

mies now. My people are in no danger.

5"The Lord made a promise to my father David. The Lord said, 'I will make your son king after you. And he will build a temple for worship to me'. Now, I plan to build that temple for worship to the Lord my God. 6And so I ask for your help. Send your men to cut down cedar trees for me from Lebanon. My servants will work with yours. I will pay your servants whatever wages you decide. We don't have anyone who can cut down trees as well as the people of Sidon can."

7When Hiram heard what Solomon asked, he was very happy. He said, "I thank the Lord today! He has given David a wise son to rule over this great nation!" 8Then Hiram sent back this message to Solomon: "I received the message you sent. I will give you all the cedar and pine trees you want. 9My servants will bring them down from Lebanon to the sea. There I will tie them together. Then I will float them down the shore to the place you choose. There I will separate the logs, and you can take them away. In return you will give food to all those who live with me." 10So Hiram gave Solomon as much cedar and pine as he wanted. 11And Solomon gave Hiram about 2,000 tons of wheat each year. It was to feed all those who lived with Hiram. And Solomon gave him about 400,000 litres of pure olive oil every year.

12The Lord gave wisdom to Solomon as he had promised. And there was peace between Hiram and Solomon. These two kings made a treaty between themselves.

13King Solomon forced 30,000 men of Israel to help in this work. 14He put a man named Adoniram over them. Solomon sent a group of 10,000 men each month to Lebanon. So each group worked in Lebanon one month. Then it went home for two months. 15Solomon forced 80,000 men to work in the hill country, cutting stone, and he had 70,000 men to carry the stones. ¹⁶There were also 3,300 men who directed the workers. ¹⁷King Solomon commanded them to cut large blocks of fine stone. These were to be used for the foundation of the Temple.*d* ¹⁸Solomon's and Hiram's builders and the men from Byblos carved the stones. They prepared the stones and the logs for building the Temple.

Solomon Builds the Temple

6 So Solomon began to build the Temple.*d* This was 480 years after the people of Israel had left Egypt. (This was the fourth year of King Solomon's rule over Israel.) It was the second month, the month of Ziv. ²The Temple was 27 metres long and 9 metres wide. It was 13.5 metres high. ³The porch in front of the main room of the Temple was 4.5 metres deep and 9 metres wide. The room ran along the front of the Temple itself. Its width was equal to the width of the Temple. ⁴There were narrow windows in the Temple. These windows were narrow on the outside and larger on the inside. ⁵Then Solomon built some side rooms against the walls of the main room of the Temple. These rooms were built on top of each other. ⁶The rooms on the bottom floor were 2.3 metres wide. The rooms on the middle floor were 2.7 metres wide. The rooms above that were 3.2 metres wide. The Temple wall which made the side of each room was thinner than the wall in the room below. The rooms were pushed against the wall but did not have their main beams built into the wall.

⁷The stones were prepared at the same place they were cut from the ground. Only these stones were used to build the Temple. So there was no noise of hammers, axes or any other iron tools at the Temple.

⁸The entrance to the bottom rooms built beside the Temple was on the south side. From there, stairs went up to the second floor rooms. And from there, they went on to the third floor rooms. ⁹Solomon put a roof made from beams and cedar boards on the Temple. So he finished building the Temple. ¹⁰He also finished building the bottom floor that was beside the Temple. It was 2.3 metres high. It was attached to the Temple by cedar beams.

¹¹The Lord spoke his word to Solomon: ¹²"Obey all my laws and commands. If you do, I will do for you what I promised your father David. ¹³And I will live among the children of Israel in this Temple you are building. I will never leave the people of Israel."

¹⁴So Solomon finished building the Temple. ¹⁵The inside walls were covered from floor to ceiling with cedar boards. The floor was made from pine boards. ¹⁶A room 9 metres long was built in the back part of the Temple. It was divided from the rest of the Temple by cedar boards reaching from floor to ceiling. It was called the Most Holy Place. ¹⁷The main room, the room in front of the Most Holy Place, was 18 metres long. ¹⁸Inside the Temple was cedar. It was carved with pictures of flowers and plants. Everything inside was covered with cedar. So a person could not see the stones of the wall. ¹⁹He prepared the inner room at the back of the Temple to keep the Ark*d* of the Agreement with the Lord. ²⁰This inner room was about 9 metres long, high and wide. Solomon covered this room with pure gold. He built an altar of cedar and covered it also. ²¹He covered the inside of the Temple with pure gold. And he placed gold chains across the front of the inner room. It was covered with gold. ²²So all the inside of the Temple was covered with gold. Also the altar in the Most Holy Place was covered with gold.

23Solomon made two creatures with wings from olive wood. Each creature was 4.5 metres tall. They were put in the Most Holy Place. 24Each creature had two wings. Each wing was 2.3 metres long. So it was 4.5 metres from the end of one wing to the end of the other wing. 25The creatures were the same size and shape, 26and each was 4.5 metres tall. 27These creatures were put beside each other in the Most Holy Place. Their wings were spread out. So one creature's wing touched one wall. The other creature's wing touched the other wall. And their wings touched each other in the middle of the room. 28The two creatures were covered with gold.

29All the walls around the Temple were carved. They were carved with pictures of creatures with wings, palm trees and flowers. This was true for both the main room and the inner room. 30The floors of both rooms were covered with gold.

31Doors made from olive wood were put at the entrance to the Most Holy Place. The doors were made to fit into an area with five sides. 32Creatures with wings, palm trees and flowers were carved on the two olive wood doors. Then the doors were covered with gold. And the creatures and the palm trees were covered with gold. 33At the entrance to the main room there was a door frame. It was square and was made of olive wood. 34Two doors were made from pine. Each door had two parts so that the doors folded. 35The doors were covered with pictures of creatures with wings, palm trees and flowers. And all of the carvings were covered with gold. The gold was smoothed over the carvings.

36The inner courtyard was built and enclosed with walls. The walls were made of three rows of cut stones and one row of cedar boards.

37Work began on the Temple in Ziv, the second month. This was during the fourth year that Solomon ruled over Israel. 38The Temple was finished during the eleventh year in which Solomon ruled. It was finished in the eighth month, the month of Bul. It was finished exactly as it was planned. Solomon had worked seven years to build the Temple.

Solomon's Palace

7 King Solomon also built a palace for himself. It took him 13 years to finish building it. 2He built the Palace of the Forest of Lebanon. It was 45 metres long, 22.5 metres wide and 13.7 metres high. It had four rows of cedar columns. They supported the cedar beams. 3The ceiling was covered with cedar above the beams. There were 45 beams on the roof, with 15 beams in each row. 4Windows were placed in three rows facing each other. 5All the doors were square. The three doors at each end faced each other.

6Solomon also built the porch of pillars. It was 22.5 metres long and 13.7 metres wide. Along the front of the porch, there was a covering supported by pillars.

7Solomon also built a throne room where he judged people. He called this the Hall of Justice. The room was covered with cedar from the floor to the ceiling. 8The palace where Solomon was to live was behind the Hall of Justice. And it was built like the Hall of Justice. Solomon also built the same kind of palace for his wife. She was the daughter of the king of Egypt.

9All these buildings were made with blocks of carefully cut fine stone. Then they were trimmed with a saw in the front and back. These fine stones went from the foundations of the buildings to the top of the walls. Even the courtyard was made with blocks of stone. 10The foundations were made with large blocks of fine stone. Some of the stones were 4.5 metres long.

Others were 3.6 metres long. ¹¹On top of those stones there were other cut blocks of fine stone and cedar beams. ¹²The palace courtyard, the courtyard inside the Temple*d* and the porch to the Temple were surrounded by walls. All of these walls had three rows of cut stone blocks and one row of cedar beams.

The Temple Is Completed Inside

¹³King Solomon sent to Tyre and had Huram brought to him. ¹⁴Huram's mother was a widow from the tribe*d* of Naphtali. His father was from Tyre and had been skilled in making things from bronze. Huram was also very skilled and experienced in bronze work. So he came to King Solomon. And he did all the bronze work Solomon wanted.

¹⁵He made two bronze pillars. Each one was 8.2 metres tall and 5.5 metres around. ¹⁶He also made two bronze capitals*d* that were 2.3 metres tall. He put them on top of the pillars. ¹⁷Then he made a net of seven chains for each capital. They covered the capitals on top of the two pillars. ¹⁸Then he made two rows of bronze pomegranates*d* to go on the nets. They were to cover the capitals at the top of the pillars. ¹⁹The capitals on top of the pillars in the porch were shaped like lilies. They were 2 metres tall. ²⁰The capitals were on top of both pillars. They were above the bowl-shaped section and next to the nets. At that place there were 200 pomegranates in rows all around the capitals. ²¹Huram put these two bronze pillars at the porch of the Temple.*d* He named the south pillar He Establishes, and he named the north pillar In Him Is Strength. ²²The capitals on top of the pillars were shaped like lilies. So the work on the pillars was finished.

²³Then Huram made a large round bowl from bronze, which was called the Sea. It was 13.7 metres around. It was 4.6 metres across and 2.3 metres deep. ²⁴There was a rim around the outer edge of the bowl. Under this rim there were two rows of bronze plants surrounding the bowl. There were ten plants in every 45 centimetres. They were made in one piece with the bowl. ²⁵The bowl rested on the backs of 12 bronze bulls. They faced outward from the centre of the bowl. Three bulls faced north, three faced east, three faced south and three faced west. ²⁶The sides of the bowl were 10 centimetres thick. The rim was like the rim of a cup or like a lily blossom. The bowl held about 40,000 litres.

²⁷Then Huram made ten bronze stands. Each one was 1.8 metres long and wide and 1.4 metres high. ²⁸The stands were made from square sides, which were put on frames. ²⁹On the sides were bronze lions, bulls and creatures with wings. On the frames above and below the lions and bulls there were designs of flowers hammered into the bronze. ³⁰Each stand had four bronze wheels with bronze axles. At the corners there were bronze supports for a large bowl. The supports had designs of flowers. ³¹There was a frame on top of the bowls. It was 45 centimetres high above the bowls. The opening of the bowl was round, 68 centimetres deep. There were designs carved into the bronze on the frame. The frame was square, not round. ³²The four wheels were under the frame. They were 68 centimetres high. The axles between the wheels were made as one piece with the stand. ³³The wheels were like a chariot's wheels. Everything on the wheels was made of bronze. The axles, rims, spokes and hubs were made of bronze.

³⁴The four supports were on the four corners of each stand. They were made as one piece with the stand. ³⁵There was a strip of bronze around the top of each stand. It was 22 centimetres deep. It was made as one

piece with the stand. ³⁶The sides of the stand and the frames were totally covered with carvings. They were carved with pictures of creatures with wings, lions and palm trees. There were also flowers carved all around. ³⁷So this is the way Huram made the ten stands. The bronze for each stand was melted and poured into a mould. So all of the stands were the same size and shape.

³⁸Huram also made ten bronze bowls. There was one bowl for each of the ten stands. Each bowl was 1.8 metres across and could hold nearly 900 litres. ³⁹Huram put five of the stands on the south side of the Temple. And he put the other five stands on the north side. He put the large bowl in the southeast corner of the Temple. ⁴⁰Huram also made bowls, shovels and small bowls.

So Huram finished making everything King Solomon wanted him to make. Here is a list of what Huram made for the Temple of the Lord:
⁴¹two pillars;
  two large bowls for the capitals on top of the pillars;
  two nets to cover the two large bowls for the capitals on top of the pillars;
⁴²400 pomegranates for the two nets (there were two rows of pomegranates for each net covering the bowls for the capitals on top of the pillars);
⁴³ten stands with a bowl on each stand;
⁴⁴the large bowl with 12 bulls under it;
⁴⁵the pots, shovels, small bowls and all the dishes for the Temple of the Lord.

Huram made everything King Solomon wanted. They were all made from polished bronze. ⁴⁶The king ordered these things to be made near the Jordan River between Succoth and Zarethan. They were made by melting and pouring bronze into clay moulds. ⁴⁷Solomon never weighed the bronze used to make these things. There was too much to weigh. So the total weight of all the bronze was never known.

⁴⁸Solomon also commanded that many things be made of gold for the Temple:
  the golden altar;
  the golden table which held the bread that shows God's people are in his presence;
⁴⁹the lampstands of pure gold (five on the right side and five on the left side in front of the Most Holy Place);
  the gold flowers, lamps and tongs;
⁵⁰the pure gold bowls, wick trimmers, small bowls, pans and dishes used to carry coals;
  the hinges for the doors of the Most Holy Place and the main room of the Temple.

⁵¹So the work King Solomon did for the Temple of the Lord was finished. David, Solomon's father, had saved silver, gold and other articles for the Temple. So Solomon brought these things into the Temple. And he put them into the treasuries of the Temple of the Lord.

The Holy Ark Is Brought into the Temple

8 Then King Solomon called for all the leaders of Israel to come to him in Jerusalem. He called for the older leaders, the heads of the tribes^d and the leaders of the families. He wanted them to bring the Ark^d of God with the Lord from the older part of the city. ²So all the men of Israel came together with King Solomon. This was during a festival in the month of Ethanim. That is the seventh month. ³All of the older leaders of Israel ar-

rived. Then the priests took up the Holy Ark. [4]They carried the Holy Ark of the Lord, the Meeting Tent[d] and the holy things in it. The Levites helped the priests carry these things. [5]King Solomon and all the people of Israel gathered before the Ark of God. They sacrificed so many sheep and cattle no one could count them all. [6]Then the priests put the Ark of God with the Lord in its right place. This was inside the Most Holy Place in the Temple.[d] The Ark of God was put under the wings of the golden creatures. [7]The wings of the creatures were spread out over the place of the Holy Ark. So they covered it and its carrying poles. [8]The carrying poles were very long. Anyone standing in the Holy Place in front of the Most Holy Place could see the ends of the poles. But no one could see them from outside the Holy Place. The poles are still there today. [9]The only things inside the Holy Ark were two stone tablets.[n] Moses had put them in the Holy Ark at Mount Sinai. That was where the Lord made his agreement with the Israelites after they came out of Egypt. [10]When the priests left the Holy Place, the cloud filled the Temple of the Lord. [11]The priests could not continue their work. This was because the Temple was filled with the glory of the Lord.

Solomon Speaks to the People

[12]Then Solomon said, "The Lord said he would live in a dark cloud. [13]Lord, I have truly built a wonderful Temple[d] for you. It is a place for you to live for ever."

[14]While all the people of Israel were standing there, King Solomon turned to them and blessed them. [15]Then he prayed: "Praise the Lord, the God of Israel. He himself has done what he promised to my fa-

ther David. The Lord told my father, [16]'I brought my people Israel out of Egypt. But I have not yet chosen a city in any tribe[d] of Israel where a temple will be built for worshipping me. But I have chosen David to rule over my people Israel'.

[17]"My father David wanted to build a temple for worshipping the Lord, the God of Israel. [18]But the Lord said to my father David, 'I know you want to build a temple for worshipping me. And this is good. [19]But you are not the one to build the temple. It will be your son, who comes from your own body. He is the one who will build my temple'.

[20]"So the Lord has kept the promise that he gave. I am the king now in place of David my father. Now I rule Israel as the Lord promised. And I have built the Temple for worshipping the Lord, the God of Israel. [21]I have made a place in the Temple for the Holy Ark. Inside that Ark is the agreement the Lord made with our ancestors. He made that agreement when he brought them out of Egypt."

Solomon's Prayer

[22]Then Solomon stood facing the Lord's altar. All of the people of Israel were standing behind him. He spread out his hands and looked toward the sky. [23]He said:

"Lord, God of Israel, there is no god like you. There is no god like you in heaven above or on the earth below. You make agreements with your people because you love them. And you keep your agreements with those who truly follow you. [24]You have kept the promise you made to your servant David, my father. You made that promise with your own mouth. And with your great power you have made it come true today. [25]Now Lord, God of Israel, keep the other promises you made to your servant David, my fa-

---

stone tablets They were the two tablets on which God wrote the Ten Commandments.

ther. You said, 'Your sons must be careful to obey me as you have obeyed me. If they do this, there will always be someone from your family ruling Israel'. 26Again, Lord, God of Israel, I ask you. Please continue to keep that promise you made to my father.

27"But, God, can you really live here on the earth? Even the sky and the highest place in heaven cannot contain you. Certainly this house which I have built cannot contain you either. 28But please listen to my prayer and my request. I am your servant, and you are the Lord my God. Hear this prayer I am praying to you today. 29In the past you said, 'I will be worshipped there'. So please watch over this Temple*d* night and day. Hear the prayer I pray to you here. 30Hear my prayers and the prayers of your people Israel. Please hear us when we pray facing this place. Hear us from your home in heaven. And when you hear us, forgive us.

31"If a person does something wrong against someone else, he will be brought to the altar in this Temple. If he swears an oath that he is not guilty, 32then hear in heaven. Judge the man. Punish the guilty person for what he has done. And declare that the innocent person is not guilty.

33"Sometimes your people of Israel will sin against you. Because of this their enemies will defeat them. Then the people will come back to you and praise you. They will pray to you in this Temple. 34Please hear them in heaven. Forgive the sins of your people Israel. Allow them to have their land again. This is the land you gave to their ancestors.

35"Sometimes when they sin against you, you will stop the rain from falling on their land. Then they will pray, facing this place. They will praise you. They will stop sinning when you make them suffer. 36When this happens,

please hear their prayer in heaven. Then forgive the sins of your servant. And forgive the sins of the people of Israel. Teach them to do what is right. Then please send rain to this land you gave them.

37"At times the land will become so dry that no food will grow. Or, a great sickness will spread among the people. Sometimes all the crops will be destroyed by locusts*d* or grasshoppers. Your people will be attacked in their cities by their enemies. Your people will become sick. 38When any of these things happen, the people will become truly sorry. If anyone of your people Israel spreads his hands in prayer toward this Temple, 39please hear his prayer. Hear it from your home in heaven. Then forgive the people and help them. Only you know what people are really thinking. So judge each person, and do to him what is right. 40Do this so your people will respect you all the time they live in this land. This is the land you gave to our ancestors.

41-42"People who are not Israelites, who come from other lands, will hear about your greatness and power. They will come from far away to pray at this Temple. 43Please hear their prayers from your home in heaven. Please do whatever they ask you. Then people everywhere will know you and respect you, as your people in Israel do. Then everyone will know I built this Temple for worship to you.

44"Sometimes you will command your people to go and fight against their enemies. Then your people will pray to you facing this city which you have chosen. They will pray facing the Temple I have built for your worship. 45When they pray, hear their prayers from your home in heaven. Then help them.

46"Everyone sins. So your people will also sin against you. And you will become angry with your people. You will let their enemies defeat them. Their enemies will make them prisoners and carry them away to their own countries. ⁴⁷Your people might be sorry for their sins when they are held as prisoners in another country. Perhaps they will be sorry and pray to you in the land where they are held as prisoners. They might say, 'We have sinned and done wrong'. ⁴⁸They may truly turn back to you in the land of their enemies. Perhaps they will pray to you, facing this land you gave their fathers. They may pray to you, facing this city you have chosen. They may face this Temple I have built for your worship. ⁴⁹If they do, then please hear them from your home in heaven. Hear their prayers and do what is right. ⁵⁰Forgive your people of all their sins. And forgive them for turning against you. Make those who have taken them as prisoners show them mercy. ⁵¹Remember that they are your people. Remember that you brought them out of Egypt. It was as if you pulled them out of a blazing furnace!

⁵²"Please give your attention to my prayers. And please give your attention to the prayers of your people Israel. Listen to their prayers whenever they ask you for help. ⁵³You chose them from all the nations on earth to be your very own people. This is what you promised through Moses your servant. You promised it when you brought our ancestors out of Egypt, Lord God."

⁵⁴Solomon prayed this prayer to the Lord. He had been kneeling in front of the altar. And his arms had been raised toward heaven. When Solomon finished praying, he stood up. ⁵⁵Then, in a loud voice, he blessed all the people of Israel. Solomon said: ⁵⁶"Praise the Lord! He promised he would give rest to his people Israel. And he has given us rest! The Lord has kept all the good promises he gave through his servant Moses. ⁵⁷I ask that the Lord our God be with us. May he be with us as he was with our ancestors. May he never leave us. ⁵⁸May he cause us to turn to him and follow him. May we obey all the laws and commands he gave our ancestors. ⁵⁹I ask that the Lord our God always remember this prayer. I pray that he will help his servant and his people Israel. I pray he will help us every day as we need it. ⁶⁰Then all the people of the world will know the Lord is the only true God. ⁶¹So you must fully obey the Lord our God. You must follow all his laws and commands. You must continue to obey in the future as you do now."

Sacrifices Are Offered

⁶²Then King Solomon and all Israel with him offered sacrifices to the Lord. ⁶³Solomon killed 22,000 cattle and 120,000 sheep. These were fellowship offerings. In this way the king and the Israelites showed they had given the Temple[d] to the Lord.

⁶⁴Also that day King Solomon made the courtyard before the Temple holy. He offered whole burnt sacrifices and grain offerings. He also offered the fat from the fellowship offerings. He had to make these offerings in the courtyard. This was because the bronze altar before the Lord was too small. It could not hold all the offerings.

⁶⁵So King Solomon and all the people of Israel also celebrated the other festival that came at that time. People came from as far away as Lebo Hamath in the north. And they came from as far as the brook of Egypt in the south. A great many people were there. They ate, drank and rejoiced before the Lord for a total of 14 days. ⁶⁶On the following day Solomon sent the people home. So they blessed the king and went home. They were happy because of all the good things the Lord had done for his servant David and for his people, Israel.

The Lord Appears to Solomon Again

9 So Solomon finished building the Temple[d] of the Lord and his royal palace. Solomon finished building everything he wanted to build. [2]Then the Lord appeared to him again. This was just as he had done before, in Gibeon. [3]The Lord said to him: "I have heard your prayer. I have heard what you asked me to do. You built this Temple. And I have made it a holy place. So I will be worshipped there for ever. I will watch over it and protect it always.

[4]"But you must serve me as your father David did. He was fair and sincere. You must obey my laws and do everything I command. [5]If you do these things, I will allow your family to rule Israel for ever. I made this promise to your father David. I told him that someone from his family would always be king over Israel.

[6]"But you and your children must follow me. You must obey the laws and commands I have given you. You must not go off to serve or worship other gods. [7]If you do, I will force Israel to leave the land I have given them. I made the Temple holy for people to worship me there. But if you don't obey me, I will tear it down. Then Israel will become a bad example, a joke, to other people. [8]If the Temple is destroyed, everyone who sees it will be shocked. They will make fun of you and ask, 'Why did the Lord do this? Why did he do this terrible thing to this land and this Temple?' [9]Other people will answer, 'This happened because they left the Lord their God. He brought their ancestors out of Egypt. But they decided to follow other gods. They worshipped and served those gods. That is why the Lord brought all this disaster to them'."

Solomon's Other Activities

[10]By the end of 20 years, King Solomon had built the Temple[d] of the Lord. And he had built the royal palace. [11]At that time King Solomon gave 20 towns in Galilee to Hiram king of Tyre. Solomon did this because Hiram had helped with the buildings. Hiram had given him all the cedar, pine and gold he wanted. [12]So Hiram travelled from Tyre to see the towns Solomon had given him. When Hiram saw them, he was not pleased. [13]He asked, "What are these towns you have given me, my brother?" So he named that land the Land of Cabul.[n] And it is still called that today. [14]Hiram had sent to King Solomon about 4 tons of gold.

[15]King Solomon had forced slaves to build the Temple and the palace. Then he had them fill in the land on the east side of the city. And he had them build the wall around Jerusalem. He also had them rebuild the cities of Hazor, Megiddo and Gezer. [16](In the past the king of Egypt had attacked Gezer and captured it. He had burned it and killed the Canaanites who lived there. Then he gave it to his daughter as a wedding present. His daughter married Solomon. [17]So Solomon rebuilt it.) He also built the cities of Lower Beth Horon, [18]Baalath and Tadmor, which is in the Judean desert. [19]King Solomon also built cities where he could store grain and supplies. And he built cities for his chariots and chariot soldiers. Solomon built whatever he wanted in Jerusalem, Lebanon and everywhere he ruled.

[20]There were people in the land who were not Israelites. There were some Amorites, Hittites, Perizzites, Hivites and Jebusites. [21]The Israelites had not been able to destroy them from the land. So Solomon forced them to work for him as slaves. And

---

Cabul This name sounds like the Hebrew word for "worthless".

they are still slaves today. ²²But Solomon did not force any Israelites to be his slaves. The Israelites were his soldiers, government leaders, officers, captains and chariot commanders and drivers.

²³There were 550 supervisors over Solomon's projects. They were supervisors over the men who did the work.

²⁴The daughter of the king of Egypt moved from the old part of Jerusalem to the palace. This was the palace Solomon had built for her. Then Solomon filled in the land on the east side of the city.

²⁵Three times each year Solomon offered whole burnt offerings and fellowship offerings on the altar. This is the altar he had built for the Lord. Solomon also burned incense*d* before the Lord. So he finished the work on the Temple.

²⁶Solomon also built ships at Ezion Geber. This town is near Elath. It is on the shore of the Gulf of Aqaba, in the land of Edom. ²⁷King Hiram had sailors who knew much about the sea. So he sent them to serve in Solomon's ships with Solomon's men. ²⁸Solomon's ships sailed to Ophir. From there they brought back more than 14 tons of gold to King Solomon.

The Queen of Sheba Visits Solomon

10 Now the queen of Sheba heard about Solomon's fame. So she came to test him with hard questions. ²She travelled to Jerusalem with a very large group of servants. There were many camels carrying spices, jewels and much gold. She came to Solomon and talked with him about all that she had in mind. ³Solomon answered all her questions. Nothing was too hard for him to explain to her. ⁴The queen of Sheba learned that Solomon was very wise. She saw the palace he had built. ⁵She saw his many officers and the food on his table. She

saw the palace servants and their good clothes. She was shown the servants who served him at feasts. And she was shown the whole burnt offerings he made in the Temple*d* of the Lord. All these things amazed her.

⁶So she said to King Solomon, "I heard in my own country about your achievements and wisdom. And all of it is true. ⁷I could not believe it then. But now I have come and seen it with my own eyes. I was not told even half of it! Your wisdom and wealth are much greater than I had heard. ⁸Your men and officers are very lucky! In always serving you, they are able to hear your wisdom! ⁹Praise the Lord your God! He was pleased to make you king of Israel. The Lord has constant love for Israel. So he made you king to keep justice and to rule fairly."

¹⁰Then the queen of Sheba gave the king more than 4 tons of gold. She also gave him many spices and jewels. No one since that time has brought more spices into Israel than the queen of Sheba gave King Solomon.

¹¹(Hiram's ships brought gold from Ophir. They also brought from there a large amount of juniper wood and jewels. ¹²Solomon used the juniper wood to build supports for the Temple of the Lord and the palace. He also used it to make harps and lyres*d* for the musicians. Such fine juniper wood has not been brought in or seen since that time.)

¹³King Solomon gave the queen of Sheba many gifts. He gave her gifts that a king would give to another ruler. Then he gave her whatever else she wanted and asked for. After this, she and her servants went back to her own country.

Solomon's Wealth

¹⁴Every year King Solomon received about 23 tons of gold. ¹⁵Besides that he also received gold from the traders and merchants, and from

the kings of Arabia and governors of the land.

16King Solomon made 200 large shields of hammered gold. Each shield contained about 3.5 kilograms of gold. 17He also made 300 smaller shields of hammered gold. They each contained nearly 2 kilograms of gold. The king put them in the Palace of the Forest of Lebanon.

18Then King Solomon built a large throne of ivory. And he covered it with pure gold. 19There were six steps leading up to the throne. The back of the throne was round at the top. There were armrests on both sides of the chair, and beside each armrest was a statue of a lion. 20Twelve lions stood on the six steps. There was one lion at each end of each step. Nothing like this had ever been made for any other kingdom. 21All of Solomon's drinking cups were made of gold. All of the dishes in the Palace of the Forest of Lebanon were pure gold. Nothing was made from silver. In Solomon's time people did not think silver was valuable.

22King Solomon also had many trading ships at sea, along with Hiram's ships. Every three years the ships returned. They brought back gold, silver, ivory, apes and baboons.

23So Solomon had more riches and wisdom than all the other kings on earth. 24People everywhere wanted to see King Solomon. They wanted to hear the wisdom God had given him. 25Every year everyone who came brought a gift. They brought things made of gold and silver, along with clothes, weapons, spices, horses and mules.

26So Solomon had many chariots and horses. He had 1,400 chariots and 12,000 chariot soldiers. He kept some in special cities for the chariots. And he kept some with him in Jerusalem. 27In Jerusalem silver was as common as stones while Solomon was king. Cedar trees were as common as the

fig trees growing on the mountain slopes. 28Solomon brought in horses from Egypt and Kue. His traders bought them in Kue and brought them to Israel. 29A chariot from Egypt cost about 600 pieces of silver, and a horse cost about 150 pieces of silver. The traders also sold horses and chariots to the kings of the Hittites and the Arameans.

Solomon's Many Wives

11 But King Solomon loved many women who were not from Israel. He loved the daughter of the king of Egypt. He also loved women of the Moabites, Ammonites, Edomites, Sidonians and Hittites. 2The Lord had told the Israelites, "You must not marry people of other nations. If you do, they will cause you to follow their gods." But Solomon fell in love with these women. 3He had 700 wives who were from royal families. He also had 300 slave womend who gave birth to his children. His wives caused him to turn away from God. 4As Solomon grew old, his wives caused him to follow other gods. He did not follow the Lord completely as his father David had done. 5Solomon worshipped Ashtoreth,d the goddess of the people of Sidon. And he worshipped Molech,d the hated god of the Ammonites. 6So Solomon did what the Lord said was wrong. He did not follow the Lord completely as his father David had done.

7On a hill east of Jerusalem, Solomon built two places for worship. He built a place to worship Chemosh,d the hated god of the Moabites. And he built a place to worship Molech, the hated god of the Ammonites. 8Solomon did the same thing for all of his foreign wives. So they burned incensed and gave sacrifices to their gods.

9The Lord had appeared to Solomon twice. But Solomon turned away from following the Lord, the God of Israel.

So the Lord was angry with him.
[10]The Lord had commanded Solomon
not to follow other gods. But Solomon
did not obey the Lord's command.
[11]So the Lord said to Solomon, "You
have chosen to break your agreement
with me. You have not obeyed my
commands. So I promise I will tear
your kingdom away from you. I will
give it to one of your officers. [12]But I
will not take it away while you are
alive. This is because of my love for
your father David. I will tear it away
from your son when he becomes king.
[13]But I will not tear away all the kingdom from him. I will leave him one
tribe[d] to rule. I will do this because of
David, my servant. And I will do it because of Jerusalem, the city I have
chosen."

Solomon's Enemies

[14]Now Hadad was a member of the
family of the king of Edom. And the
Lord caused Hadad the Edomite to
become Solomon's enemy. [15]Earlier,
David had defeated Edom. Joab, the
commander of David's army, went
into Edom to bury the dead. While he
was there, he killed all the males.
[16]Joab and all the Israelites stayed in
Edom for six months. During that
time they killed every male in Edom.
[17]But at that time Hadad was only a
young boy. So he ran away to Egypt
with some of his father's officers.
[18]They left Midian and went to Paran.
In Paran other men joined them. Then
they all went to Egypt to see the king.
He gave Hadad a house, some land
and food to eat.
[19]The king liked Hadad so much he
gave Hadad a wife. She was the sister
of Tahpenes, the king's wife. [20]They
had a son named Genubath. Queen
Tahpenes allowed him to grow up in
the royal palace. So he grew up with
the king's own children.
[21]While he was in Egypt, Hadad
heard that David had died. He also
heard that Joab, the commander of the

army, was dead. So Hadad said to the
king, "Let me go home. Let me return
to my own country."
[22]But the king said, "Why do you
want to go back to your own country?
What haven't I given you here?"
Hadad answered, "Nothing. But
please, let me go."
[23]God also caused another man to
be an enemy to Solomon. This man
was Rezon son of Eliada. Rezon had
run away from his master, Hadadezer
king of Zobah. [24]After David defeated
the army of Zobah, Rezon gathered
some men. He became the leader of a
small army. They went to Damascus
and settled there, and Rezon became
king of Damascus. [25]Rezon ruled
Aram, and he hated Israel. So he was
an enemy of Israel all the time Solomon was alive. Rezon and Hadad
caused some trouble for Israel.
[26]Jeroboam, son of Nebat, was one
of Solomon's officers. Jeroboam was
one of the Ephraimite people. He was
from the town of Zeredah. His mother
was a widow named Zeruah. He
turned against the king.
[27]This is the story of how Jeroboam
turned against the king. Solomon was
filling in the land on the east side of
Jerusalem. He was also repairing the
wall of Jerusalem. It was the city of
David, his ancestor. [28]Jeroboam was a
capable man. Solomon saw that this
young man was a good worker. So
Solomon put him over all the workers
from the tribes[d] of Ephraim and Manasseh.
[29]One day Jeroboam was leaving Jerusalem. Ahijah, the prophet[d] from
Shiloh, met him on the road. Ahijah
was wearing a new coat. The two men
were alone out in the country. [30]Ahi-
jah took his new coat and tore it into
12 pieces. [31]Then he said to Jeroboam, "Take ten pieces of this coat for
yourself. The Lord, the God of Israel,
says: 'I will tear the kingdom away
from Solomon. Then I will give you
ten tribes. [32]But I will allow the family

of David to control one tribe. I will do this for my servant David and for Jerusalem. Jerusalem is the city I have chosen from all the tribes of Israel. ³³I will do this because Solomon has stopped following me. He worships the Sidonian god Ashtoreth*d* and the Moabite god Chemosh.*d* He also worships Molech,*d* the Ammonite god. Solomon has not obeyed me. He has not done what I said is right. He has not obeyed my laws and commands. He is not living the way his father David lived.

³⁴" 'But I will not take all the kingdom away from Solomon. I will let him rule all his life. I will do this because of my servant David. I chose David, and he obeyed all my commands and laws. ³⁵But I will take the kingdom away from his son. Jeroboam, I will allow you to rule over the ten tribes. ³⁶I will allow Solomon's son to continue to rule over one tribe. I will do this so that David, my servant, will always have a king before me in Jerusalem. It is the city where I chose to be worshipped. ³⁷But I will make you rule over everything you want. You will rule over all of Israel. ³⁸I will always be with you if you do what I say is right. You must obey all my commands. If you obey my laws and commands as David did, I will be with you. I will make your family a family of kings, as I did for David. I will give Israel to you. ³⁹I will punish David's children because of this. But I will not punish them for ever'."

Solomon's Death

⁴⁰Solomon tried to kill Jeroboam. But Jeroboam ran away to Egypt. He went to Shishak king of Egypt. And Jeroboam stayed there until Solomon died. ⁴¹Everything else Solomon did is written down. He showed much wisdom. It is written in the book of the history of Solomon. ⁴²Solomon ruled in Jerusalem over all Israel for 40 years. ⁴³Then he died and was buried in Jerusalem, the city of David, his father. And his son Rehoboam became king after him.

Israel Turns Against Rehoboam

12 Rehoboam went to Shechem because all the Israelites had gone there to make him king. ²Jeroboam son of Nebat was still in Egypt. He had gone there to escape from Solomon. When Jeroboam heard about Rehoboam being made king, Jeroboam returned from Egypt. ³So the people sent for him. Then he and the people went to Rehoboam. They said to Rehoboam, ⁴"Your father forced us to work very hard. Now, make it easier for us. Don't make us work as hard as your father did. Then we will serve you."

⁵Rehoboam answered, "Come back to me in three days. Then I will answer you." So the people left.

⁶Some of the older leaders had helped Solomon make decisions during his lifetime. So King Rehoboam asked them what he should do. He said, "How do you think I should answer these people?"

⁷They answered, "You should be like a servant to them today. Serve them, and give them a kind answer. If you do, they will serve you always."

⁸But Rehoboam did not listen to this advice. He asked the young men who had grown up with him. They advised him in making decisions. ⁹Rehoboam said, "The people said, 'Don't make us work as hard as your father did'. How do you think I should answer them? What is your advice?"

¹⁰The young men answered, "Those people came to you and said, 'Your father forced us to work very hard. Now make our work easier'. So you should tell them, 'My little finger is bigger than my father's whole body. ¹¹My father forced you to work hard. But I will make you work even harder!

My father beat you with whips. But I will beat you with whips that have sharp points'."

[12]Rehoboam had told the people, "Come back to me in three days." So after three days all the people returned to Rehoboam. [13]At that time King Rehoboam spoke cruel words to them. He did not listen to the advice that the older leaders had given him. [14]He did what the young men had told him to do. Rehoboam said, "My father forced you to work hard. So I will give you even more work. My father beat you with whips. But I will beat you with whips that have sharp points." [15]So the king did not do what the people wanted. The Lord caused this to happen. He did this to keep the promise he had made to Jeroboam son of Nebat. He had made this promise through Ahijah, the prophet[d] from Shiloh.

[16]All the people of Israel saw that the new king refused to listen to them. So they said to the king,

"We have no share in David!
We have no part in the son of Jesse!
People of Israel, let's go to our own homes!
Let David's son rule his own people!"

So the Israelites went home. [17]But Rehoboam still ruled over the Israelites who lived in the towns of Judah.

[18]Adoniram was in charge of the people who were forced to work. King Rehoboam sent him to the people. But they threw stones at him until he died. But King Rehoboam ran to his chariot and escaped to Jerusalem. [19]Since then, Israel has been against the family of David.

[20]All the Israelites heard that Jeroboam had returned. So they called him to a meeting, and they made him king over all Israel. But the tribe[d] of Judah continued to follow the family of David.

[21]When Rehoboam arrived in Jeru-

salem, he gathered the tribes of Judah and Benjamin. This was an army of 180,000 men. Rehoboam wanted to fight against the people of Israel. He wanted to take back his kingdom.

[22]But God spoke his word to Shemaiah, a man of God. The Lord said, [23]"Talk to Solomon's son Rehoboam, the king of Judah. Talk also to all the people of Judah and Benjamin and to the rest of the people. [24]Say to them, 'The Lord says you must not go to war against your brothers, the Israelites. Every one of you should go home. I made all these things happen!'" So the men in Rehoboam's army obeyed the Lord's command. They all went home as the Lord had commanded.

[25]Then Jeroboam made Shechem a very strong city. It is in the mountains of Ephraim. And Jeroboam lived there. He also went to the city of Peniel and made it stronger.

Jeroboam Builds Golden Calves

[26]Jeroboam said to himself, "The kingdom will probably go back to David's family. [27]The people will continue going to the Temple[d] of the Lord in Jerusalem. If they do, they will want to be ruled again by Rehoboam. Then they will kill me and follow Rehoboam king of Judah.

[28]King Jeroboam asked his men for advice. So he made two golden calves. He said to the people, "It is too hard for you to go to Jerusalem to worship. Israel, here are your gods who brought you out of Egypt." [29]King Jeroboam put one golden calf in the city of Bethel, and he put the other in the city of Dan. [30]And this became a very great sin. The people travelled as far as Dan to worship the calf there.

[31]Jeroboam built temples on the places of worship. He chose priests from all the people. (He did not choose priests only from the tribe of Levi.) [32]And he started a new festival

It was the fifteenth day of the eighth month. This was like the festival in Judah. During that time the king offered sacrifices on the altar. He offered sacrifices to the calves in Bethel he had made. He also chose priests in Bethel to serve at the places of worship he had made. 33So Jeroboam chose his own time for a festival for the Israelites. It was the fifteenth day of the eighth month. During that time he offered sacrifices on the altar he had built in Bethel. So he set up a festival for the Israelites. And he offered sacrifices on the altar.

The Man of God Speaks Against Bethel

13 The Lord commanded a man of God from Judah to go to Bethel. When he arrived, Jeroboam was standing by the altar to offer a sacrifice. 2The Lord had commanded the man of God to speak against the altar. The man said, "Altar, the Lord says to you: 'David's family will have a son named Josiah. He will kill the priests of the places of worship. They now make their sacrifices on you. But Josiah will sacrifice those priests on you. Human bones will be burned on you'." 3The man of God gave proof that these things would happen. He said, "This is God's sign that this will happen. This altar will break apart. And the ashes on it will fall on to the ground."

4King Jeroboam heard what the man of God said about the altar in Bethel. So Jeroboam raised his hand from the altar and pointed at the man. "Capture him!" he said. But when the king said this, his arm became paralysed. He could not move it. 5Also, the altar broke into pieces. All its ashes fell onto the ground. This was the sign the Lord had told the man of God to give. 6Then the king said to the man of God, "Please pray to the Lord your God for me. Ask him to heal my arm." So the man of God prayed to the

Lord. And the king's arm was healed. It became as it was before.

7Then the king said to the man of God, "Please come home and eat with me. I will give you a gift."

8But the man of God answered the king, "I will not go home with you! Even if you gave me half of your kingdom, I would not go! I will not eat or drink anything in this place. 9The Lord commanded me not to eat or drink anything. He also commanded me not to return on the same road by which I came." 10So he travelled on a different road. He did not return on the same road by which he had come to Bethel.

11Now there was an old prophet[d] living in Bethel. His sons came and told him what the man of God had done there that day. They told their father what he had said to King Jeroboam. 12The father asked, "Which road did he use when he left?" So his sons showed him which road the man of God from Judah had taken. 13The prophet told his sons to put a saddle on his donkey. So they saddled the donkey, and he left.

14He went after the man of God. He found the man sitting under an oak tree. The prophet asked, "Are you the man of God who came from Judah?"

The man answered, "Yes, I am."

15So the prophet said, "Please come home and eat with me."

16But the man of God answered, "I can't go home with you. I can't eat or drink with you in this place. 17The Lord said to me, 'You must not eat or drink anything there. And you must not return on the same road by which you came'."

18Then the old prophet said, "But I also am a prophet like you." Then he told a lie. He said, "An angel from the Lord came to me. He told me to bring you to my home. He said you should eat and drink with me." 19So the man of God went to the old prophet's house. And he ate and drank with him there.

20While they were sitting at the table, the Lord spoke his word to the old prophet. 21The old prophet cried out to the man of God from Judah. He said, "The Lord said you did not obey him! He said you did not do what the Lord your God commanded you. 22The Lord commanded you not to eat or drink anything in this place. But you came back and ate and drank. So your body will not be buried in your family grave."

23The man of God finished eating. Then the prophet put a saddle on his donkey for him. And the man left. 24As he was travelling on the road home, a lion attacked and killed him. His body lay on the road. The donkey and the lion stood near it. 25Some men were travelling on that road. They saw the body and the lion standing near it. So they went to the city where the old prophet lived. And they told what they had seen.

26The old prophet who had brought the man of God back heard about what had happened. He said, "It is the man of God who did not obey the Lord's command. So the Lord sent a lion to kill him. The Lord said he would do this."

27Then the prophet said to his sons, "Put a saddle on my donkey." So they did. 28The old prophet went out and found the body lying on the road. The donkey and the lion were still standing near it. The lion had not eaten the body. And it had not hurt the donkey. 29So the prophet put the body on his donkey. And he carried it back to the city. There he would have a time of sadness for him and bury him. 30The prophet buried the body in his own family grave. And he was sad for the man of God. He said, "Oh, my brother."

31So the prophet buried the body. Then he said to his sons, "When I die, bury me in this same grave. Put my bones next to his. 32Through him the Lord spoke against the altar at Bethel. And he spoke against the places of worship in the towns of Samaria. And what the Lord spoke through him will certainly come true."

33But King Jeroboam did not stop doing evil things. He continued to choose priests for the places of worship from all the people. Anyone who wanted to be a priest for the places of worship was allowed. 34In this way the kingdom of Jeroboam sinned. And that sin caused its ruin and destruction from the earth.

Jeroboam's Son Dies

14 At that time Jeroboam's son Abijah became very sick. 2So Jeroboam said to his wife, "Go to Shiloh. Go to see the prophet*d* Ahijah. He is the one who said I would become king of Israel. But dress yourself so people won't know you are my wife. 3Give the prophet ten loaves of bread, some cakes and a jar of honey. Then ask him what will happen to our son, and he will tell you." 4So the king's wife did as he said. She went to Ahijah's home in Shiloh.

Now Ahijah was very old and had become blind. 5But the Lord had said to him, "Jeroboam's son is sick. So Jeroboam's wife is coming to ask you about him. When she arrives, she will pretend to be someone else." Then the Lord told Ahijah what to say.

6When Ahijah heard her walking to the door, he said, "Come in, wife of Jeroboam. Why are you pretending to be someone else? I have bad news for you. 7Go back and tell Jeroboam that this is what the Lord, the God of Israel, says: 'Jeroboam, I chose you from among all the people of Israel. I made you the leader of my people. 8I took the kingdom away from David's family and gave it to you. But you are not like my servant David. He always obeyed my commands. He followed me with all his heart. He did only the things I said were right. ⁹But you have done more evil things than anyone who ruled before you. You have stopped following me. You have made other gods and idols of metal. This has made me very angry. ¹⁰So I will bring disaster to the family of Jeroboam. I will kill all of the men in your family, both slaves and free men. I will destroy your family as completely as fire burns up manure. ¹¹Anyone from your family who dies in the city will be eaten by dogs, and anyone from your family who dies in the fields will be eaten by the birds. The Lord has spoken!' "

¹²Then Ahijah said to Jeroboam's wife, "Now go home. When you enter your city gate, your son will die. ¹³All Israel will be sad for him and bury him. He will be the only one of Jeroboam's family who will be buried. This is because he is the only one in Jeroboam's family who pleased the Lord, the God of Israel.

¹⁴"The Lord will put a new king over Israel. That king will destroy Jeroboam's family. This will happen soon. ¹⁵Then the Lord will punish Israel. The people of Israel will be like grass moving in the water. The Lord will pull up Israel from this good land. This is the land he gave to their ancestors. But he will scatter Israel beyond the Euphrates River. This will happen because the Lord is angry with the people. They made him angry when they made idols to worship Asherah.ᵈ ¹⁶Jeroboam sinned, and then he made the people of Israel sin. So the Lord will let the people of Israel be defeated."

¹⁷Then Jeroboam's wife travelled back to Tirzah. When she entered her home, the boy died. ¹⁸They buried him. And all Israel had a time of sadness for him. This happened as the Lord said it would. The Lord had said these things through his servant, the prophet Ahijah.

¹⁹Everything else Jeroboam did is written down. He fought wars and continued to rule the people. It is all written in the book of the history of the kings of Israel. ²⁰Jeroboam ruled as king for 22 years. Then he died, and his son Nadab became king in his place.

The Death of Rehoboam

²¹Solomon's son Rehoboam was 41 years old when he became king of Judah. His mother was Naamah from the land of Ammon. Rehoboam ruled in Jerusalem for 17 years. (The Lord had chosen that city from all the land of Israel. He chose to be worshipped there.)

²²The people of Judah did what the Lord said was wrong. The people's sins made the Lord very angry at them. They made the Lord even more angry than their ancestors had done. ²³The people built stone pillars and places to worship false gods and Asherahᵈ idols. They built them on every high hill and under every green tree. ²⁴There were even male prostitutesᵈ at the places of worship to the gods. The people who had lived in the land before the Israelites had done many evil things, and God had taken the land away from them. Now the people of Judah were doing the same evil things.

²⁵During the fifth year Rehoboam was king, Shishak attacked Jerusalem. Shishak was king of Egypt. ²⁶He took the treasures from the Templeᵈ of the Lord and the king's palace. He took everything, even the gold shields Solomon had made. ²⁷So King Rehoboam made bronze shields to put in their place. He gave them to the men who were guarding the palace gates. ²⁸Whenever the king went to the Temple of the Lord, the guards carried the shields. After they were finished, they put the shields back in the guardroom.

²⁹Everything else King Rehoboam did is written down. It is in the book of the history of the kings of Judah.

30Rehoboam and Jeroboam were always warring with each other. 31Rehoboam died and was buried with his ancestors in Jerusalem. His mother was Naamah from Ammon. And Rehoboam's son Abijah became king in his place.

Abijah King of Judah

15 Abijah became king of Judah. This was during the eighteenth year that Jeroboam son of Nebat ruled Israel. 2And Abijah ruled in Jerusalem for three years. His mother was Maacah daughter of Abishalom. 3He did all the same sins his father before him had done. Abijah was not faithful to the Lord his God. In this way he was not like David, his great-grandfather. 4Because the Lord had loved David, the Lord gave Abijah a kingdom in Jerusalem, and allowed him to have a son to be king after him. The Lord also kept Jerusalem safe. 5David had always done what the Lord said was right. All his life he had always obeyed the Lord's commands. There was only one time that David did not obey the Lord. This was when he sinned against Uriah the Hittite.

6Now there was war between Abijah and Jeroboam during Abijah's lifetime. 7Everything else Abijah did is written down. It is in the book of the history of the kings of Judah. During the time that Abijah ruled, there was war between Abijah and Jeroboam. 8And Abijah died and was buried in Jerusalem. Abijah's son Asa became king in his place.

Asa King of Judah

9During the twentieth year Jeroboam was king of Israel, Asa became king of Judah. 10Asa ruled in Jerusalem for 41 years. His grandmother's name was Maacah. She was the daughter of Abishalom.

11Asa did what the Lord said was right. This was as his ancestor David had done. 12There were male prostitutes[d] at the places where false gods were worshipped. Asa forced them to leave the country. He also took away the idols that his ancestors had made. 13His grandmother Maacah had made a terrible Asherah[d] idol. So Asa removed her from being queen. He cut down this idol and burned it in the Kidron Valley. 14Asa was faithful to the Lord all his life. But he did not destroy the places where false gods were worshipped. 15Asa and his father had given some things to God. They had given gifts of gold, silver and other objects. Asa put all these things in the Temple.[d]

16There was war between Asa and Baasha king of Israel. 17Baasha fought against Judah. He wanted to stop people from leaving or entering Asa's country, Judah. So he made the city of Ramah very strong.

18Then Asa took all the silver and gold from the treasuries of the Temple of the Lord and his own palace. He gave it to his officers. And he sent them to Ben-Hadad king of Aram. (Ben-Hadad was the son of Tabrimmon, the son of Hezion.) Ben-Hadad was ruling in the city of Damascus. 19Asa sent this message: "My father and your father had a peace agreement. I am sending you a gift of gold and silver. Break your treaty with Baasha king of Israel so that he will leave my land."

20Ben-Hadad agreed with King Asa. So he sent his army to fight against the towns of Israel. He defeated the towns of Ijon, Dan and Abel Bethmaacah, and all the land near Lake Galilee and the area of Naphtali. 21Baasha heard about these attacks. So he stopped building up Ramah and returned to Tirzah. 22Then King Asa gave an order to all the people of Judah. Everyone had to help. They carried away all the stones and wood Baasha had been using in Ramah. King Asa used those things to build up

Geba and Mizpah. (Geba was in the land of Benjamin.)

23Everything else Asa did is written down. His victories and the cities he built are written down. They are in the book of the history of the kings of Judah. When he became old, he got a disease in his feet. 24Then Asa died. And he was buried with his ancestors in Jerusalem. It was the city of David, his ancestor. Then Jehoshaphat, Asa's son, became king in his place.

Nadab King of Israel

25Nadab son of Jeroboam became king of Israel. This was during the second year Asa was king of Judah. Nadab was king of Israel for two years. 26He did what the Lord said was wrong. Jeroboam had caused the people of Israel to sin. Nadab sinned in the same way his father Jeroboam had sinned.

27Baasha son of Ahijah was from the tribe*d* of Issachar. He made plans to kill Nadab. Nadab and all Israel were attacking the Philistine town of Gibbethon. So Baasha killed Nadab there. 28This happened during Asa's third year as king of Judah. Baasha became the next king of Israel.

Baasha King of Israel

29As soon as Baasha became king, he killed all of Jeroboam's family. He left no one in Jeroboam's family alive. This happened as the Lord had said it would. The Lord had said this through his servant Ahijah from Shiloh. 30It happened because King Jeroboam had sinned very much. And he had caused the people of Israel to sin. Jeroboam had made the Lord, the God of Israel, very angry.

31Everything else Nadab did is written down. It is in the book of the history of the kings of Israel. 32There was war between Asa king of Judah and Baasha king of Israel all the time they were kings.

33Baasha son of Ahijah became king

of Israel. This was during Asa's third year as king of Judah. Baasha ruled in Tirzah for 24 years. 34But Baasha did what the Lord said was wrong. Jeroboam had caused the people of Israel to sin. And Baasha sinned in the same way Jeroboam had sinned.

16 Then Jehu son of Hanani spoke the word of the Lord against King Baasha. 2The Lord said, "You were nothing. Then I took you and made you a leader over my people Israel. But you have followed the ways of Jeroboam. You have caused my people Israel to sin. Their sins have made me angry. 3So, Baasha, I will destroy you and your family. I will do to you what I did to the family of Jeroboam son of Nebat. 4Anyone from your family who dies in the city will be eaten by dogs. And anyone from your family who dies in the fields will be eaten by birds."

5Everything else Baasha did and all his victories are written down. They are in the book of the history of the kings of Israel. 6So Baasha died and was buried in Tirzah. His son Elah became king in his place.

7The Lord spoke his word through the prophet*d* Jehu son of Hanani. The Lord's message was against Baasha and his family. Baasha had done many things the Lord said were wrong. This made the Lord very angry. Baasha did the same things that Jeroboam's family had done before him. The Lord was also angry because Baasha killed all of Jeroboam's family.

Elah King of Israel

8Elah son of Baasha became king of Israel. This was during Asa's twenty-sixth year as king of Judah. Elah ruled in Tirzah for two years.

9Zimri was one of Elah's officers. He commanded half of Elah's chariots. But Zimri made plans against Elah.

Elah was in Tirzah, getting drunk at Arza's home. (Arza was the man in charge of the palace at Tirzah.) 10So

Zimri went into Arza's house and killed Elah. This was during Asa's twenty-seventh year as king of Judah. Then Zimri became king of Israel in Elah's place.

Zimri King of Israel

11As soon as Zimri became king, he killed all of Baasha's family. He did not let any man of Baasha's family or friends live. 12So Zimri destroyed all of Baasha's family. This happened as the Lord had said it would. The Lord had spoken this against Baasha through the prophet[d] Jehu. 13This happened because of all the sins of Baasha and his son Elah. They sinned and caused the people of Israel to sin. They also made the Lord, the God of Israel, angry because they had made worthless idols.

14Everything else Elah did is written down. It is in the book of the history of the kings of Israel.

15So Zimri became king of Israel. This was during Asa's twenty-seventh year as king of Judah. Zimri ruled in Tirzah for seven days. This is what happened:

The army of Israel was camped near Gibbethon, a Philistine town. 16The men in the camp heard that Zimri had made secret plans against the king, and that Zimri had killed him. So that day in the camp they made Omri king over Israel. (Omri was commander of the army.) 17Omri and all the Israelites left Gibbethon and attacked Tirzah. 18Zimri saw that the city had been captured. He went into the palace and set it on fire. He burned the palace and himself with it. 19So Zimri died because he had sinned. He did what the Lord said was wrong. Jeroboam had caused the people of Israel to sin. And Zimri sinned in the same way Jeroboam had sinned.

20Everything else Zimri did is written down. It is in the book of the history of the kings of Israel. The story of

how Zimri turned against King Elah is also written there.

Omri King of Israel

21The people of Israel were divided into two groups. Half of the people wanted Tibni to be king. He was the son of Ginath. The other half of the people wanted Omri. 22But Omri's followers were stronger than the followers of Tibni son of Ginath. So Tibni died, and Omri became king.

23Omri became king of Israel. This was during the thirty-first year that Asa was king of Judah. And Omri ruled Israel for 12 years. For six of those years he ruled in the town of Tirzah. 24Omri bought the hill of Samaria from Shemer. He paid about 6000 pieces of silver for it. Omri built a city on that hill and called it Samaria after the name of its earlier owner, Shemer.

25But Omri did what the Lord said was wrong. He did more evil than all the kings who were before him. 26Jeroboam son of Nebat had caused the people of Israel to sin. And Omri sinned in the same way Jeroboam had sinned. So the Israelites made the Lord, the God of Israel, very angry. He was angry because they worshipped worthless idols.

27Everything else Omri did and all his successes are written down. They are all in the book of the history of the kings of Israel. 28So Omri died and was buried in Samaria. His son Ahab became king in his place.

Ahab King of Israel

29So Ahab son of Omri became king of Israel. This was during Asa's thirty-eighth year as king of Judah. Ahab ruled Israel in the town of Samaria for 22 years. 30Ahab did many things that the Lord said were wrong. He did more evil than any of the kings before him. 31He sinned in the same ways that Jeroboam son of Nebat had sinned. But he did even worse things. He married Jezebel daughter of Ethbaal. (Ethbaal was king of the city of Sidon.) Then Ahab began to serve Baal[d] and worship him. [32]He built a temple in Samaria for worshipping Baal. And he put an altar there for Baal. [33]Ahab also made an idol for worshipping Asherah.[d] He did more things to make the Lord, the God of Israel, angry than all the other kings before him.

[34]During the time of Ahab, Hiel from Bethel rebuilt the town of Jericho. It cost Hiel the life of Abiram, his oldest son, to begin work on the city. And it cost the life of Segub, his youngest son, to build the city gates. The Lord had said, through Joshua, that this would happen.[n] (Joshua was the son of Nun.)

Elijah Stops the Rain

17 Now Elijah was a prophet[d] from the town of Tishbe in Gilead. Elijah said to King Ahab, "I serve the Lord, the God of Israel. As surely as the Lord lives, I tell you the truth. No rain or dew will fall during the next few years unless I command it."

[2]Then the Lord spoke his word to Elijah: [3]"Leave this place. Go east and hide near Kerith Ravine. It is east of the Jordan River. [4]You may drink from the brook. And I have commanded ravens to bring you food there." [5]So Elijah did what the Lord told him to do. He went to Kerith Ravine, east of the Jordan, and lived there. [6]The birds brought Elijah bread and meat every morning and every evening. And he drank water from the brook. [7]After a while the brook dried up because there was no rain. [8]Then the Lord spoke his word to Elijah, [9]"Go to Zarephath in Sidon. Live there. I have commanded a widow there to take care of you."

[10]So Elijah went to Zarephath. When he reached the town gate, he saw a widow there. She was gathering wood for a fire. Elijah asked her, "Would you bring me a little water in a cup? I would like to have a drink." [11]As she was going to get his water, Elijah said, "Please bring me a piece of bread, too."

[12]The woman answered, "As surely as the Lord your God lives, I tell you the truth. I have no bread. I have only a handful of flour in a jar and a little olive oil in a jug. I came here to gather some wood. I will take it home and cook our last meal. My son and I will eat it and then die from hunger."

[13]Elijah said to her, "Don't worry. Go home and cook your food as you have said. But first make a small loaf of bread from the flour you have. Bring it to me. Then cook something for yourself and your son. [14]The Lord, the God of Israel, says, 'That jar of flour will never become empty. The jug will always have oil in it. This will continue until the day the Lord sends rain to the land'."

[15]So the woman went home. And she did what Elijah told her to do. So Elijah, the woman and her son had enough food every day. [16]The jar of flour and the jug of oil were never empty. This happened just as the Lord, through Elijah, said it would.

Elijah Brings a Boy Back to Life

[17]Some time later the son of the woman who owned the house became sick. He grew worse and worse. Finally he stopped breathing. [18]So the woman said to Elijah, "You are a man of God. What have you done to me? Did you come here to remind me of my sin? Did you come here to kill my son?"

[19]Elijah said to her, "Give me your son." So Elijah took the boy from her and carried him upstairs. Elijah laid the boy on the bed in the room where

The Lord . . . happen When Joshua destroyed Jericho, he said whoever rebuilt the city would lose his oldest and youngest sons. See Joshua 6:26.

he was staying. [20]Then he prayed to the Lord. He said, "Lord my God, this widow is letting me stay in her house. Why have you done this terrible thing to her? Why have you caused her son to die?" [21]Then Elijah lay on top of the boy three times. Elijah prayed to the Lord, "Lord my God, let this boy live again!"

[22]The Lord answered Elijah's prayer. The boy began breathing again, and he was alive. [23]Elijah carried the boy downstairs. He gave the boy to his mother and said, "See! Your son is alive!"

[24]The woman said to Elijah, "Now I know you really are a man from God. I know that the Lord truly speaks through you!"

Elijah and the Prophets of Baal

18 During the third year without rain, the Lord spoke his word to Elijah. The Lord said, "Go and meet King Ahab. I will soon send rain." [2]So Elijah went to meet Ahab.

By this time there was no food in Samaria. [3]So King Ahab sent for Obadiah. Obadiah was in charge of the king's palace. (Obadiah was a true follower of the Lord. [4]At one time Jezebel was killing all the Lord's prophets.[d] So Obadiah took 100 of them and hid them in two caves. He put 50 in one cave and 50 in another cave and brought them food and water.) [5]King Ahab said to Obadiah, "Let's look at every spring and valley in the land. Maybe we can find enough grass to keep our horses and mules alive. Then we will not have to kill our animals." [6]So each one chose a part of the country to search. Ahab went in one direction, and Obadiah went in another direction.

[7]While Obadiah was walking along, Elijah met him. Obadiah knew who Elijah was. So he bowed down to the ground before Elijah. He said, "Elijah? Is it really you, master?"

[8]Elijah answered, "Yes. Go and tell your master the king that I am here."

[9]Then Obadiah said, "If I tell Ahab that, he will kill me! I have done nothing wrong that I should be killed! [10]As surely as the Lord your God lives, the king has looked everywhere for you! He has sent people to every country to look for you. If the ruler said you were not there, that was not enough. Ahab then forced the ruler to swear you could not be found in his country. [11]Now you want me to go to my master and tell him, 'Elijah is here'? [12]The Spirit[d] of the Lord may carry you to some other place after I leave. If I go and tell King Ahab you are here, he will come. If he doesn't find you, he will kill me! I have followed the Lord since I was a boy. [13]Haven't you heard what I did? When Jezebel was killing the Lord's prophets, I hid 100 of them. I put 50 prophets in one cave and 50 prophets in another. I brought them food and water. [14]Now you want me to go and tell the king you are here. He will kill me!"

[15]Elijah answered, "I serve the Lord of heaven's armies. As surely as the Lord lives, I will stand before Ahab today."

[16]So Obadiah went to Ahab and told him where Elijah was. Then Ahab went to meet Elijah.

[17]When he saw Elijah, he said, "Is it you—the biggest troublemaker in Israel?"

[18]Elijah answered, "I have not caused trouble in Israel. You and your father's family have caused all this trouble. You have not obeyed the Lord's commands. You have followed the Baals.[d] [19]Now tell all Israel to meet me at Mount Carmel. Also bring the 450 prophets of Baal there. And bring the 400 prophets of Asherah,[d] who eat at Jezebel's table."

[20]So Ahab called all the Israelites and those prophets to Mount Carmel. [21]Elijah stood before the people. He said, "How long will you try to serve both Baal and the Lord? If the Lord is

the true God, follow him. But if Baal is the true God, follow him!"

But the people said nothing.

22Elijah said, "I am the only prophet of the Lord here. But there are 450 prophets of Baal. 23So bring two bulls. Let the prophets of Baal choose one bull. Let them kill it and cut it into pieces. Then let them put the meat on the wood. But they are not to set fire to it. Then I will do the same with the other bull. And I will put it on the wood. But I will not set fire to it. 24You prophets of Baal, pray to your god. And I will pray to the Lord. The god who answers the prayer will set fire to his wood. He is the true God."

All the people agreed that this was a good idea.

25Then Elijah said to the prophets of Baal, "There are many of you. So you go first. Choose a bull and prepare it. Pray to your god, but don't start the fire."

26So they took the bull that was given to them and prepared it. They prayed to Baal from morning until noon. They shouted, "Baal, answer us!" But there was no sound. No one answered. They danced around the altar they had built.

27At noon Elijah began to make fun of them. He said, "Pray louder! If Baal really is a god, perhaps he is thinking. Or perhaps he is busy or travelling! Perhaps he is sleeping so you will have to wake him!" 28So the prophets prayed louder. They cut themselves with swords and spears until their blood flowed. (This was the way they worshipped.) 29The afternoon passed, and the prophets continued to act wildly. They continued until it was time for the evening sacrifice. But no voice was heard. Baal did not answer. No one paid attention.

30Then Elijah said to all the people, "Now come to me." So they gathered around him. Elijah rebuilt the altar of the Lord because it had been torn down. 31He took 12 stones. He took one stone for each of the 12 tribes.d These 12 tribes were named for the 12 sons of Jacob. (Jacob was the man the Lord had called Israel.) 32Elijah used these stones to rebuild the altar in honour of the Lord. Then he dug a small ditch around it. It was big enough to hold nearly 15 litres of seed. 33Elijah put the wood on the altar. He cut the bull into pieces and laid them on the wood. Then he said, "Fill four jars with water. Put the water on the meat and on the wood."

34Then Elijah said, "Do it again." And they did it again.

Then he said, "Do it a third time." And they did it the third time. 35So the water ran off of the altar and filled the ditch.

36It was time for the evening sacrifice. So the prophet Elijah went near the altar. He prayed, "Lord, you are the God of Abraham, Isaac and Israel. I ask you now to prove that you are the God of Israel, and that I am your servant. Show these people that you commanded me to do all these things. 37Lord, answer my prayer. Show these people that you, Lord, are God. Then the people will know that you are bringing them back to you."

38Then fire from the Lord came down. It burned the sacrifice, the wood, the stones and the ground around the altar. It also dried up the water in the ditch. 39When all the people saw this, they fell down to the ground. They cried, "The Lord is God! The Lord is God!"

40Then Elijah said, "Capture the prophets of Baal! Don't let any of them run away!" So the people captured all the prophets. Then Elijah led them down to Kishon Valley. There he killed all the prophets.

The Rain Comes Again

41Then Elijah said to Ahab, "Now, go, eat and drink. A heavy rain is coming." 42So King Ahab went to eat and drink. At the same time Elijah climbed to the top of Mount Carmel. There he bent down to the ground with his head between his knees.

⁴³Then Elijah said to his servant, "Go and look towards the sea." The servant went and looked. He said, "I see nothing."

Elijah told him to go and look again. This happened seven times. ⁴⁴The seventh time, the servant said, "I see a small cloud. It's the size of a man's fist. It's coming from the sea."

Elijah told the servant, "Go to Ahab. Tell him to get his chariot ready and to go home now. If he doesn't leave now, the rain will stop him."

⁴⁵After a short time the sky was covered with dark clouds. The wind began to blow. Then a heavy rain began to fall. Ahab got into his chariot and started back to Jezreel. ⁴⁶The Lord gave his power to Elijah. Elijah tightened his clothes around him. Then he ran ahead of King Ahab all the way to Jezreel.

Elijah at Mount Sinai

19 King Ahab told Jezebel every-thing Elijah had done. Ahab told her how Elijah had killed all the proph-ets*d* with a sword. ²So Jezebel sent a messenger to Elijah. Jezebel said, "By this time tomorrow I will kill you. I will kill you as you killed those prophets. If I don't succeed, may the gods pun-ish me terribly."

³When Elijah heard this, he was afraid. So he ran away to save his life. He took his servant with him. When they came to Beersheba in Judah, Eli-jah left his servant there. ⁴Then Elijah walked for a whole day into the desert. He sat down under a bush and asked to die. Elijah prayed, "I have had enough, Lord. Let me die. I am no better than my ancestors." ⁵Then Eli-jah lay down under the tree and slept.

Suddenly an angel came to him and touched him. The angel said, "Get up and eat." ⁶Elijah saw near his head a loaf baked over coals and a jar of wa-

ter. So he ate and drank. Then he went back to sleep.

⁷Later the Lord's angel came to him a second time. The angel touched him and said, "Get up and eat. If you don't, the journey will be too hard for you." ⁸So Elijah got up and ate and drank. The food made him strong enough to walk for 40 days and nights. He walked to Mount Sinai, the mountain of God. ⁹There Elijah went into a cave and stayed all night.

Then the Lord spoke his word to him: "Elijah! Why are you here?" ¹⁰Elijah answered, "Lord, God of heaven's armies, I have always served you the best I could. But the people of Israel have broken their agreement with you. They have de-stroyed your altars. They have killed your prophets with swords. I am the only prophet left. And now they are trying to kill me, too!"

¹¹Then the Lord said to Elijah, "Go. Stand in front of me on the mountain. I will pass by you." Then a very strong wind blew. It caused the moun-tains to break apart. It broke apart large rocks in front of the Lord. But the Lord was not in the wind. After the wind, there was an earthquake. But the Lord was not in the earth-quake. ¹²After the earthquake, there was a fire. But the Lord was not in the fire. After the fire, there was a quiet, gentle voice. ¹³When Elijah heard it, he covered his face with his coat. He went out and stood at the entrance to the cave.

Then a voice said to him, "Elijah! Why are you here?" ¹⁴Elijah answered, "Lord, God of heaven's armies, I have always served you the best I could. But the people of Israel have broken their agreement with you. They have de-stroyed your altars. They have killed your prophets with swords. I am the only prophet left. And now they are trying to kill me, too."

¹⁵The Lord said to him, "Go back on

the road that leads to the desert around Damascus. Enter that city. There pour olive oil on Hazael to make him king over Aram. [16]Then pour oil on Jehu son of Nimshi to make him king over Israel. Next, pour oil on Elisha son of Shaphat from Abel Meholah. He will be a prophet in your place. [17]Jehu will kill anyone who escapes from Hazael's sword. And Elisha will kill anyone who escapes from Jehu's sword. [18]But I have left 7,000 people living in Israel. Those 7,000 have never bowed down before Baal.[d] Their mouths have never kissed his idol."

Elisha Becomes a Prophet

[19]So Elijah left there and found Elisha son of Shaphat. He was ploughing a field with a team of oxen. There were 11 teams ahead of him. Elisha was ploughing with the twelfth team of oxen. Elijah came up to Elisha. Elijah took off his coat and put it on Elisha. [20]Then Elisha left his oxen and ran to follow Elijah. Elisha said, "Let me kiss my father and my mother good bye. Then I will go with you."

Elijah answered, "All right, go back. I won't stop you."

[21]So Elisha went back. He took his pair of oxen and killed them. He used the wooden yoke[d] for the fire. Then he cooked the meat and gave it to the people, and they ate it. Then Elisha went and followed Elijah and became his helper.

Ben-Hadad and Ahab Go to War

20 Now Ben-Hadad was king of Aram. He gathered together all his army. There were 32 kings with their horses and chariots. They went with him and surrounded Samaria and attacked it. [2]The king sent messengers into the city to Ahab king of Israel. [3]This was his message: "Ben-Hadad says, 'You must give me your silver and gold and the best of your wives and children'."

[4]Ahab king of Israel answered, "My master and king, I agree to what you say. I and everything I have belongs to you."

[5]Then the messengers came to Ahab again. They said, "Ben-Hadad says, 'I told you before that you must give me your silver and gold, your wives and your children. [6]About this time tomorrow I am going to send my men to you. They are to search everywhere in your palace. And they are to search the homes of the men who rule under you. My men will take anything they want'."

[7]So Ahab called a meeting of all the older leaders of his country. He said, "Ben-Hadad is looking for trouble. First he said I had to give him my wives, my children, my silver and my gold. I agreed to that."

[8]But the older leaders and all the people said, "Pay no attention to him. Don't do what he says."

[9]So Ahab said to Ben-Hadad's messengers, "Tell my master the king this: 'I will do what you said at first. But I will not obey your second command'." So King Ben-Hadad's men carried the message back to him.

[10]Then Ben-Hadad sent another message to Ahab: "I will completely destroy Samaria. There won't even be enough left for each of my men to get a handful of dust. May the gods punish me terribly if I don't do this!"

[11]Ahab answered, "Tell Ben-Hadad this: 'The man who puts on his armour should not boast too soon. It's the man who lives long enough to take it off who has the right to boast'."

[12]Now Ben-Hadad was drinking in his tent with the other rulers. The messengers came and gave him the message from Ahab. Ben-Hadad commanded his men to prepare to attack the city. So they moved into their places for the battle.

[13]At the same time a prophet[d] came to Ahab, king of Israel. The prophet said, "Ahab, the Lord says to you, 'Do you see that big army? I will let you

defeat it today. Then you will know that I am the Lord'."

¹⁴Ahab said, "Who will you use to defeat them?"

The prophet answered, "The Lord says, 'The young officers of the district governors will defeat them'."

Then the king asked, "Who will command the main army?"

The prophet answered, "You will."

¹⁵So Ahab gathered the young officers of the district governors. There were 232 of them. Then he called together the army of Israel. There were 7,000 of them.

¹⁶At noon Ben-Hadad and the 32 rulers helping him were getting drunk in their tents. At this time Ahab attacked them. ¹⁷The young officers of the district governors attacked first.

Ben-Hadad's scouts told him that soldiers were coming from Samaria. ¹⁸So Ben-Hadad said, "They may be coming to fight. Or they may be coming to ask for peace. In either case capture them alive."

¹⁹The young officers of the district governors led the attack. The army of Israel followed them. ²⁰Then each officer of Israel killed the man who came against him. So the men from Aram ran away as Israel chased them. But Ben-Hadad king of Aram escaped on a horse with some of his horsemen. ²¹Ahab king of Israel led the army. He captured the Arameans' horses and chariots. So King Ahab caused a great defeat of the Aramean army.

²²Then the prophet went to Ahab king of Israel and said, "The king of Aram will attack you again next spring. So you should go home now and make your army stronger. Make plans to defend yourself."

²³The officers of Ben-Hadad king of Aram said to him, "The gods of Israel are mountain gods. Since we fought in a mountain area, Israel won. So let's fight them on the flat land. Then we will win. ²⁴This is what you should do. Don't allow the 32 rulers to command

the armies. Put commanders in their places. ²⁵Gather an army like the one that was destroyed. Gather as many horses and chariots as it had. We will fight the Israelites on flat land. Then we will win." Ben-Hadad agreed with their advice and did what they said.

²⁶The next spring Ben-Hadad gathered the people of Aram. He went to Aphek to fight against Israel. ²⁷The Israelites also prepared for war. They marched out to meet the Arameans and camped opposite them. They looked like two small groups of goats. But the Arameans covered the area.

²⁸A man of God came to the king of Israel with this message: "The Lord says, 'The people of Aram say that I, the Lord, am a god of the mountains. They think I am not a god of the valleys. So I will allow you to defeat this big army. Then you will know I am the Lord'."

²⁹The armies were camped across from each other for seven days. On the seventh day the battle began. The Israelites killed 100,000 Aramean soldiers in one day. ³⁰The rest of them ran away to the city of Aphek. There a city wall fell on 27,000 of them. Ben-Hadad also ran away to the city and hid in a room.

³¹His officers said to him, "We have heard that the kings of Israel are merciful. Let's dress in rough cloth to show our sadness. And let's wear ropes on our heads as a sign of surrender. Then let's go to the king of Israel. Maybe he will let you live."

³²So they dressed in rough cloth and wore ropes on their heads. Then they went to the king of Israel. They said, "Your servant Ben-Hadad says, 'Please let me live.'"

Ahab answered, "Is he still alive? He is my brother."

³³Now Ben-Hadad's men had wanted a sign from Ahab. They wanted to know he would not kill Ben-Hadad. So when Ahab called Ben-Hadad his

brother, they quickly said, "Yes! Ben-Hadad is your brother."

Ahab said, "Bring him to me." When Ben-Hadad came, Ahab asked him to join him in the chariot.

[34]Ben-Hadad said to him, "Ahab, I will give you back the towns my father took from your father. And you may put shops in Damascus, as my father did in Samaria."

Ahab said, "If you agree to this, I will allow you to go free." So the two kings made a peace agreement. Then Ahab let Ben-Hadad go free.

A Prophet Speaks Against Ahab

[35]One of the prophets[d] told another prophet, "Hit me!" He told him to do this because the Lord had commanded it. But the other prophet refused. [36]So the first prophet said, "You did not obey the Lord's command. So a lion will kill you as soon as you leave me." When the second prophet left, a lion found him and killed him.

[37]The first prophet went to another man and said, "Hit me, please!" So the man hit him and hurt him. [38]Then the prophet wrapped his face in a cloth. This way no one could tell who he was. Then he went and waited by the road for the king. [39]As Ahab king of Israel passed by, the prophet called out to him. The prophet said, "I went to fight in the battle. One of our men brought an enemy soldier to me. Our man said, 'Guard this man. If he runs away, you will have to give your life in his place. Or, you will have to pay a fine of 3000 pieces of silver.' [40]But I became busy doing other things. So the man ran away."

The king of Israel answered, "You have said what the punishment is. You must do what the man said."

[41]Then the prophet quickly took the cloth from his face. When the king of Israel saw him, he knew he was one of the prophets. [42]Then the prophet said to the king, "This is what the Lord says: 'You set free the man I said

should die. So your life will be taken in his place. And the lives of your people will be taken in place of the lives of his people'."

[43]Then the king went back to his palace in Samaria. He was angry and upset.

Naboth's Vineyard

21 A man named Naboth owned a vineyard. It was in Jezreel, near the palace of Ahab king of Israel. [2]One day Ahab said to Naboth, "Give me your vineyard. It is near my palace. I want to make it into a vegetable garden. I will give you a better vineyard in its place. Or, if you prefer, I will pay you what it is worth."

[3]Naboth answered, "May the Lord keep me from ever giving my land to you. It belongs to my family."

[4]So Ahab went home, angry and upset. He did not like what Naboth from Jezreel had said. (Naboth had said, "I will not give you my family's land.") So Ahab lay down on his bed. He turned his face to the wall and refused to eat.

[5]His wife, Jezebel, came in. She asked him, "Why are you upset? Why do you refuse to eat?"

[6]Ahab answered, "I talked to Naboth, the man from Jezreel. I said, 'Sell me your vineyard. Or, if you prefer, I will give you another vineyard for it'. But Naboth refused."

[7]Jezebel answered, "Is this how you rule as king over Israel? Get out of bed. Eat something. Cheer up. I will get Naboth's vineyard for you."

[8]So Jezebel wrote some letters and signed Ahab's name to them. And she used his own seal[d] to seal them. Then she sent them to the older leaders and important men who lived in Naboth's town. [9]The letter she wrote said: "Declare a day during which the people are to give up eating. Call the people together. And give Naboth a place of honour among them. [10]Seat two troublemakers across from him. Have them say they heard Naboth speak

against God and the king. Then take Naboth out of the city and kill him with stones."

^{11}So the older leaders and important men of Jezreel obeyed Jezebel's command. ^{12}They declared a special day. On that day the people were to give up eating. They called the people together, and put Naboth in a place of honour before the people. ^{13}Then two troublemakers sat across from Naboth. They said they had heard Naboth speak against God and the king. So the people carried Naboth out of the city and killed him with stones. ^{14}Then the leaders sent a message to Jezebel. It said, "Naboth has been killed."

^{15}When Jezebel heard that Naboth had been killed, she told Ahab. She said, "Naboth of Jezreel is dead. Now you may go and take for yourself his vineyard you wanted." ^{16}When Ahab heard that Naboth was dead, he left. He went to the vineyard to take it for his own.

^{17}At this time the Lord spoke his word to Elijah. (Elijah was the prophet^d from Tishbe.) The Lord said, ^{18}"Go to Ahab king of Israel, who rules in Samaria. He is at Naboth's vineyard to take it as his own. ^{19}Tell Ahab that I, the Lord, say to him, 'Ahab! You have murdered Naboth and have taken his land. So I tell you this! In the same place that Naboth died, you will also die. The dogs that licked up Naboth's blood will lick up your blood in the same place!'"

^{20}When Ahab saw Elijah, he said, "So you have found me, my enemy!"

Elijah answered, "Yes, I have found you. You have always chosen to do what the Lord says is wrong. ^{21}So the Lord says to you, 'I will destroy you. I will kill you and every male in your family, both slave and free. ^{22}Your family will be like the family of King Jeroboam son of Nebat. And it will be like the family of King Baasha son of Ahijah. Both of these families were

completely destroyed. I will do this to you because you have made me angry. And you have caused the people of Israel to sin'.

^{23}"And the Lord also says, 'Dogs will eat the body of Jezebel in the city of Jezreel'.

^{24}"Anyone in your family who dies in the city will be eaten by dogs. Anyone who dies in the fields will be eaten by birds."

^{25}There was no one like Ahab. No one had so often chosen to do what the Lord said was wrong. His wife Jezebel influenced him to do evil. ^{26}Ahab sinned terribly by worshipping idols. This was the same thing the Amorite people did. So the Lord took their land away from them and gave it to the people of Israel.

^{27}After Elijah finished speaking, Ahab tore his clothes. He put on rough cloth and refused to eat. He even slept in the rough cloth. He did this to show how sad and upset he was.

^{28}The Lord spoke his word to Elijah from Tishbe: ^{29}"I see that Ahab is now sorry for what he has done. So I will not cause the trouble to come to him during his life. I will wait until his son is king. Then I will bring this trouble to Ahab's family."

The Death of Ahab

22 For three years there was peace between Israel and Aram. ^{2}During the third year Jehoshaphat king of Judah went to visit Ahab king of Israel.

^{3}At this same time Ahab asked his officers, "Remember that the king of Aram took Ramoth in Gilead from us? Why have we done nothing to get it back?" ^{4}So Ahab asked King Jehoshaphat, "Will you go with us? Will you fight against the army of Aram at Ramoth in Gilead?"

Jehoshaphat answered, "I will go with you. My soldiers and my horses are ready to join with your army. ^{5}But first we should ask the Lord to guide us."

[6]So Ahab called the prophets[d] together. There were about 400 men. He asked them, "Should I go to war against the army of Aram at Ramoth in Gilead? Or should I wait?"

The prophets answered, "Go, because the Lord will let you defeat them."

[7]But Jehoshaphat asked, "Isn't there a prophet of the Lord here? Let's ask him what we should do."

[8]King Ahab answered, "There is one other prophet. We could ask the Lord through him. But I hate him. When he prophesies, he never says anything good about me. He always says something bad. He is Micaiah, Imlah's son."

Jehoshaphat said, "King Ahab, you shouldn't say that!"

[9]So Ahab king of Israel told one of his officers to bring Micaiah to him at once.

[10]Ahab king of Israel and Jehoshaphat king of Judah had on their royal robes. They were sitting on their thrones at the threshing[d] floor. This was near the entrance to the gate of Samaria. All the prophets were standing before them, speaking messages from the Lord. [11]One of the prophets was Zedekiah son of Kenaanah. He had made some iron horns. He said to Ahab, "This is what the Lord says, 'You will use these horns to fight the Arameans, and you will destroy them'."

[12]All the other prophets said the same thing. They said, "Attack Ramoth in Gilead and win. The Lord will let you defeat the Arameans."

[13]The messenger who had gone to get Micaiah found him. He said to Micaiah, "All the other prophets are saying the king will succeed. You should agree with them. Give the king a good answer."

[14]But Micaiah answered, "As surely as the Lord lives, I can tell him only what the Lord tells me."

[15]Then Micaiah came to Ahab. The king asked him, "Micaiah, should we attack Ramoth in Gilead or not?"

Micaiah answered, "Attack and win! The Lord will let you defeat them."

[16]But Ahab said to Micaiah, "Tell me only the truth in the name of the Lord. How many times do I have to tell you this?"

[17]So Micaiah answered, "I saw the army of Israel. They were scattered over the hills like sheep without a shepherd. The Lord said, 'They have no leader. They should go home and not fight'."

[18]Then Ahab king of Israel said to Jehoshaphat, "I told you! This prophet never says anything good about me. He only says bad things about me."

[19]But Micaiah continued to speak. He said, "Hear the message from the Lord: I saw the Lord sitting on his throne. His heavenly army was standing near him on his right and on his left. [20]The Lord said, 'Who will trick Ahab into attacking Ramoth in Gilead? Do this so he will go and be killed'.

"The spirits did not agree about what they should do. [21]Then one spirit came and stood before the Lord. He said, 'I will trick him'.

[22]"The Lord asked, 'How will you trick Ahab?'

"The spirit answered, 'I will go to Ahab's prophets. I will make them tell lies'.

"So the Lord said, 'You will succeed in tricking him. Go and do it'."

[23]Micaiah said, "Ahab, this has now happened. The Lord has caused your prophets to lie to you. The Lord has decided that great trouble should come to you."

[24]Then Zedekiah son of Kenaanah went up to Micaiah and hit him in the face. Zedekiah said, "Do you really believe the Lord's spirit has left me and is now speaking through you?"

25Micaiah answered, "You will find out on the day you go to hide in an inside room."

26Then Ahab king of Israel ordered, "Take Micaiah. Send him to Amon, the governor of the city, and to Joash, the king's son. 27Tell them I said to put Micaiah in prison. Give him only bread and water for food. Keep him there until I come home from the battle."

28Micaiah said, "Ahab, if you come back safely from battle, the Lord has not spoken through me. Remember my words, all you people."

29So Ahab king of Israel and Jehoshaphat king of Judah went to Ramoth in Gilead. 30Ahab said to Jehoshaphat, "I will go into battle. But I will change my appearance so that no one will recognise me. But you wear your royal clothes." So Ahab changed his appearance and went into battle.

31The king of Aram had 32 chariot commanders. He ordered them, "Don't fight with anyone but the king of Israel. It doesn't matter if they are important or unimportant." 32When these commanders saw Jehoshaphat, they thought he was the king of Israel. So they turned to attack him. But Jehoshaphat began shouting. 33Then the commanders saw he was not Ahab. So they stopped chasing him. 34A soldier shot an arrow without aiming at anyone. But he hit Ahab king of Israel. The arrow hit him in a place not covered by his armour. King Ahab said to his chariot driver, "Turn the chariot around. Take me out of the battle. I am hurt!" 35The battle continued all day. King Ahab was in his chariot, leaning against it to hold himself up. He was facing the Arameans. His blood flowed down and covered the bottom of the chariot. That evening he died. 36Near sunset a cry went out through the army of Israel: "Each man go back to his own country and city."

37So in that way King Ahab died. His body was carried to Samaria and buried there. 38The men cleaned Ahab's chariot at a pool in Samaria. This was a pool where prostitutes*d* bathed. And the dogs licked King Ahab's blood from the chariot. These things happened as the Lord had said they would.

39Everything else Ahab did is written down. It is in the book of the history of the kings of Israel. That book also tells about the palace Ahab built and decorated with ivory, and about the cities he built. 40So Ahab died, and his son Ahaziah became king in his place.

Jehoshaphat King of Judah

41Jehoshaphat son of Asa became king of Judah. This was during Ahab's fourth year as king over Israel. 42Jehoshaphat was 35 years old when he became king. And he ruled in Jerusalem for 25 years. His mother was the daughter of Shilhi. She was named Azubah. 43Jehoshaphat was good like his father before him. He did what the Lord said was right. But Jehoshaphat did not destroy the places where false gods were worshipped. So the people continued offering sacrifices and burning incense*d* there. 44Jehoshaphat was at peace with the king of Israel. 45Jehoshaphat fought many wars. These wars and his successes are written down. They are in the book of the history of the kings of Judah. 46There were prostitutes*d* in the places where false gods were worshipped. Jehoshaphat's father, Asa, had not forced all of them out. But Jehoshaphat forced the rest of them to leave.

47During this time the land of Edom had no king. It was ruled by a governor.

48King Jehoshaphat built trading ships to sale to Ophir for gold. But the ships were destroyed at Ezion Geber. So they never set sail. 49Ahaziah son of Ahab went to help Jehoshaphat. Ahaziah said he would give Jehoshaphat some men to sail with his men. But Jehoshaphat refused.

⁵⁰Jehoshaphat died and was buried with his ancestors. He was buried in Jerusalem, the city of David, his ancestor. And his son Jehoram became king.

Ahaziah King of Israel

⁵¹Ahaziah son of Ahab became king of Israel in Samaria. This was during Jehoshaphat's seventeenth year as king over Judah. Ahaziah ruled Israel for two years. ⁵²Ahaziah did what the Lord said was wrong. He did the same things his father Ahab, his mother Jezebel and Jeroboam son of Nebat had done. All these rulers led the people of Israel into more sin. ⁵³Ahaziah worshipped and served the god Baal.*ᵈ* So Ahaziah made the Lord, the God of Israel, very angry. In these ways Ahaziah did what his father had done.

2 KINGS

Two Kingdoms Are Destroyed

Elijah and King Ahaziah

1 After Ahab died, Moab broke away from Israel's rule. ²Ahaziah fell down through the wooden bars in his upstairs room in Samaria. He was badly hurt. He sent messengers and told them, "Go. Ask Baal-Zebub god of Ekron if I will get well from my injuries."

³But the Lord's angel said to Elijah the Tishbite, "Get up. Go and meet the messengers sent by the king of Samaria. Say to them, 'Why are you going to ask questions of Baal-Zebub god of Ekron? Is it because you think there is no God in Israel?' ⁴So this is what the Lord says: 'You will not get up from the bed you are lying on. You will die'." Then Elijah left.

⁵The messengers came back to Ahaziah. He asked them, "Why have you come back?"

⁶They said, "A man came to meet us. He said, 'Go back to the king who sent you. Tell him what the Lord says: "Why do you send men to ask questions of Baal-Zebub god of Ekron? Is it because you think there is no God in Israel? This is why you will not get up from your bed. You will die."'"

⁷Ahaziah asked them, "What did the man look like who met you and told you this?"

⁸They answered, "He wore a hairy coat and had a leather belt around his waist."

Ahaziah said, "It was Elijah the Tishbite."

⁹Then he sent a captain with his 50 men to Elijah. The captain went to Elijah, who was sitting on top of the hill. He said to Elijah, "Man of God, the king says, 'Come down!'"

¹⁰Elijah answered the captain, "I am a man of God. So let fire come down from heaven and burn up you and your 50 men." Then fire came down from heaven. It burned up the captain and his 50 men.

¹¹Ahaziah sent another captain and 50 men to Elijah. The captain said to him, "Man of God, this is what the king says: 'Come down quickly!'"

¹²Elijah answered, "I am a man of God. So let fire come down from heaven and burn up you and your 50 men!" Then fire came down from heaven. It burned up the captain and his 50 men.

¹³Ahaziah sent a third captain with his 50 men. The third captain came and fell down on his knees before Elijah. He begged Elijah, "Man of God, I ask you. Please let my life and the lives of your 50 servants be valuable to you! ¹⁴See, fire came down from heaven. It burned up the first two captains of 50 with all their men. But now, let my life be valuable to you."

¹⁵The Lord's angel said to Elijah, "Go with him. Don't be afraid of him." So Elijah got up and went with him to see the king.

¹⁶Elijah told Ahaziah, "This is what the Lord says: 'You have sent messengers to ask questions of Baal-Zebub god of Ekron. Is it because you think there is no God in Israel to ask? Because of this, you will not get up from your bed. You will die'." ¹⁷So he died, just as the Lord, through Elijah, had said he would.

Joram became king in Ahaziah's place. This was during the second year Jehoram son of Jehoshaphat was king of Judah. Joram ruled because Ahaziah had no son to take his place.

18The other things Ahaziah did are written down. They are in the book of the history of the kings of Israel.

Elijah Is Taken to Heaven

2 It was near the time for the Lord to take Elijah. He was going to take him by a whirlwind up into heaven. Elijah and Elisha were at Gilgal. 2Elijah said to Elisha, "Please stay here. The Lord has told me to go to Bethel."

But Elisha said, "As the Lord lives, and as you live, I won't leave you." So they went down to Bethel. 3A group of the prophets[d] at Bethel came to Elisha. They said to him, "Do you know the Lord will take your master away from you today?"

Elisha said, "Yes, I know. But don't talk about it."

4Elijah said to him, "Stay here, because the Lord has sent me to Jericho."

But Elisha said, "As the Lord lives, and as you live, I won't leave you."

So they went to Jericho. 5A group of the prophets at Jericho came to Elisha. They said, "Do you know that the Lord will take your master away from you today?"

Elisha answered, "Yes, I know. But don't talk about it."

6Elijah said to Elisha, "Stay here. The Lord has sent me to the Jordan River."

Elisha answered, "As the Lord lives, and as you live, I won't leave you."

So the two of them went on. 7Fifty men from a group of the prophets came. They stood far from where Elijah and Elisha were by the Jordan. 8Elijah took off his coat. Then he rolled it up and hit the water. The water divided to the right and to the left.

Then Elijah and Elisha crossed over on dry ground.

9After they had crossed over, Elijah said to Elisha, "What can I do for you before I am taken from you?"

Elisha said, "Leave me a double share of your spirit."[n]

10Elijah said, "You have asked a hard thing. But if you see me when I am taken from you, it will be yours. If you don't, it won't happen."

11Elijah and Elisha were still walking and talking. Then a chariot and horses of fire appeared. The chariot and horses of fire separated Elijah from Elisha. Then Elijah went up to heaven in a whirlwind. 12Elisha saw it and shouted, "My father! My father! The chariots of Israel and their horsemen!" Elisha could not see him any more. Elisha grabbed his own clothes and tore them to show how sad he was.

13He picked up Elijah's coat that had fallen from him. Then Elisha returned and stood on the bank of the Jordan. 14Elisha hit the water with Elijah's coat. He said, "Where is the Lord, the God of Elijah?" When he hit the water, it divided to the right and to the left. Then Elisha crossed over.

15A group of the prophets at Jericho were watching. They said, "Elisha now has the spirit Elijah had." They came to meet him. And they bowed down to the ground before him. 16They said to him, "There are 50 strong men with us! Please let them go and look for your master. Maybe the Spirit[d] of the Lord has taken Elijah up and set him down. He may be on some mountain or in some valley."

But Elisha answered, "No. Don't send them."

17The group of prophets begged Elisha until he hated to refuse them any more. Then he said, "Send them." So

Leave ... spirit By law, the first son in a family would inherit a double share of his father's possessions. Elisha is asking to inherit a share of his master's power. He is not asking for twice as much power as Elijah had.

they sent 50 men who looked for three days. But they could not find Elijah. 18Then they came back to Elisha at Jericho where he was staying. He said to them, "I told you not to go, didn't I?"

Elisha Makes the Water Pure

19The men of the city said to Elisha, "Look, master, this city is a nice place to live. You can see that. But the water is bad. That's why the land cannot grow crops."
20Elisha said, "Bring me a new bowl and put salt in it." So they brought it to him.
21Then Elisha went out to the spring of water and threw the salt in it. He said, "This is what the Lord says: 'I have healed this water. From now on it won't cause death. And it won't keep the land from growing crops'."
22The water was healed. It is still good today. It happened just as Elisha had said.

Young People Make Fun of Elisha

23From there Elisha went up to Bethel. On the way some young men came out of the city. They made fun of Elisha. They said to him, "Go up, you baldhead! Go up, you baldhead!" 24Elisha turned around and looked at them. He put a curse on them in the name of the Lord. Then two female bears came out of the woods. They tore to pieces 42 of the young men. 25Then Elisha left and went on to Mount Carmel. From there he went back to Samaria.

War Between Israel and Moab

3 Joram son of Ahab became king over Israel at Samaria. He began to rule in Jehoshaphat's eighteenth year as king of Judah. Joram ruled 12 years. 2Joram did what the Lord said was wrong. But he was not like his father and mother. He removed the stone pillars his father had made for Baal.d 3But he continued to do the same sins Jeroboam son of Nebat had done. Jeroboam had caused the people of Israel to sin. And Joram did not stop doing these same sins.

4Mesha king of Moab raised sheep. He had to give 100,000 lambs and the wool of 100,000 male sheep to the king of Israel. 5But when Ahab died, the king of Moab turned against the king of Israel. 6So King Joram went out from Samaria and gathered all Israel. 7He sent messengers to Jehoshaphat king of Judah. He said, "The king of Moab has turned against me. Will you go with me against Moab in battle?"

Jehoshaphat said, "I will go with you. I am ready to join you. My soldiers and my horses are ready to join with your army."

8Jehoshaphat asked, "Which way should we go to attack?"

Joram answered, "Through the Desert of Edom."

9So the king of Israel went with the king of Judah and the king of Edom. They marched seven days. There was no more water for the army or for their animals that were with them. 10The king of Israel said, "How terrible this is! Has the Lord called us three kings together so the Moabites can defeat us?"

11But Jehoshaphat asked, "Is there a prophetd of the Lord here? We can ask the Lord through a prophet."

An officer of the king of Israel answered, "Elisha son of Shaphat is here. He was Elijah's servant."

12Jehoshaphat said, "He speaks the Lord's truth." So the king of Israel and Jehoshaphat and the king of Edom went down to see Elisha.

13Elisha spoke to the king of Israel. He said, "I have nothing to do with you! Go to the prophets of your father and to the prophets of your mother!"

The king of Israel said to Elisha, "No. The Lord has called us three kings together to let the Moabites defeat us."

[14]Elisha said, "I serve the Lord of heaven's armies. As surely as he lives, I tell you the truth. I wouldn't even look at you or notice you if Jehoshaphat king of Judah were not here. I respect him! [15]Now bring me someone who plays the harp."

While the harp was being played, the Lord gave Elisha power. [16]Then Elisha said, "The Lord says to dig holes in the valley. [17]He says that you won't see wind or rain. But the valley will be filled with water. Then you, your cattle and other animals will drink. [18]This is easy for the Lord to do. He will also let you defeat Moab. [19]You will destroy every strong, walled city and every important town. You will cut down every good tree. You will stop up all springs of water. You will ruin every good field with rocks."

[20]The next morning, about the time the sacrifice was offered, there was water! It came from the direction of Edom and filled the valley.

[21]All the Moabites had heard that the kings had come up to fight against them. They gathered everyone old enough to put on armour. And they waited at the border. [22]But when the Moabites got up early in the morning, the sun was shining on the water. They saw the water across from them. It looked as red as blood. [23]The Moabites said, "This is blood! Surely the kings have fought and killed each other! Come, Moabites, let's take what is valuable from the dead bodies!"

[24]The Moabites came to the camp of the Israelites. But the Israelites came out and fought them until they ran away. The Israelites went on into the land to fight the Moabites. [25]They tore down the cities. They threw rocks on every good field and filled it. They stopped up all the springs of water. And they cut down all the good trees. Kir Hareseth was the only city with its stones still in place. But the men with slings surrounded Kir Hareseth and conquered it, too.

[26]The king of Moab saw that the battle was too strong for him. So he took 700 men with swords to break through to the king of Edom. But they could not break through. [27]Then the king of Moab took his oldest son, who would have become king after him. And he offered his son as a burnt offering on the wall. So there was great anger against the Israelites. They left and went back to their own land.

A Widow Asks Elisha for Help

4 The wife of a man from a group of the prophets[d] came to Elisha. She said, "Your servant, my husband, is dead! You know he honoured the Lord. But now the man he owes money to is coming to take my two boys. He will make them his slaves!"

[2]Elisha answered, "How can I help you? Tell me, what do you have in your house?"

The woman said, "I don't have anything there except a pot of oil."

[3]Then Elisha said, "Go and get empty jars from all your neighbours. Don't ask for just a few. [4]Then you must go into your house and close the door. Only you and your sons will be there. Then pour oil into all the jars. Set the full ones to one side."

[5]She left Elisha and shut the door. Only she and her sons were in the house. As they brought the jars to her, she poured the oil. [6]When the jars were all full, she said to her son, "Bring me another jar."

But he said, "There are no more jars." Then the oil stopped flowing.

[7]She went and told Elisha. Elisha said to her, "Go. Sell the oil and pay what you owe. You and your sons can live on what is left."

The Shunammite Woman

[8]One day Elisha went to Shunem.

An important woman lived there. She begged Elisha to stay and eat. So every time Elisha passed by, he stopped there to eat. [9]The woman said to her husband, "I know that Elisha is a holy man of God. He passes by our house all the time. [10]Let's make a small room on the roof.[n] Let's put a bed in the room for Elisha. And we can put a table, a chair and a lampstand there. Then when he comes by, he can stay there."

[11]One day Elisha came to the woman's house. He went to his room and rested. [12]He said to his servant Gehazi, "Call the Shunammite."

When the servant called her, she stood in front of him. [13]Elisha told his servant, "Now say to her, 'You have gone to all this trouble for us. What can I do for you? Do you want me to speak to the king or the commander of the army for you?'"

The woman answered, "I live among my own people."

[14]Elisha said, "But what can we do for her?"

Gehazi answered, "She has no son, and her husband is old."

[15]Then Elisha said, "Call her." So he called her, and she stood in the doorway. [16]Then Elisha said, "About this time next year, you will hold a son in your arms."

The woman said, "No, master, man of God. Don't lie to me!"

[17]But the woman became pregnant. And she gave birth to a son at that time the next year as Elisha had told her.

[18]The child grew. One day he went out to his father, who was with the men harvesting grain. [19]The boy said to his father, "My head! My head!"

The father said to his servant, "Carry him to his mother!" [20]The servant took him to his mother. He lay on his mother's lap until noon. Then he died. [21]She took him up and laid him on Elisha's bed. Then she shut the door and went out.

[22]She called to her husband. She said, "Send me one of the servants and one of the donkeys. Then I can go quickly to the man of God and come back."

[23]The woman's husband said, "Why do you want to go to him today? It isn't the New Moon[d] or the Sabbath[d] day."

She said, "It will be all right."

[24]Then she saddled the donkey and said to her servant, "Lead on. Don't slow down for me unless I tell you."

[25]So she went to Elisha at Mount Carmel.

He saw her coming from far away. So he said to his servant Gehazi, "Look, there's the Shunammite woman! [26]Run to meet her! Say to her, 'Are you all right? Is your husband all right? Is the child all right?'"

She answered, "Everything is all right."

[27]Then she came to Elisha at the hill. She caught hold of his feet. Gehazi came near to pull her away. But Elisha said to him, "Let her alone. She's very upset, and the Lord has not told me about it. He has hidden it from me."

[28]She said, "Master, I didn't tell you I wanted a son. I told you, 'Don't fool me'."

[29]Then Elisha said to Gehazi, "Get ready. Take my walking stick in your hand and go quickly. If you meet anyone, don't greet him. If anyone greets you, don't answer him. Lay my walking stick on the face of the boy."

[30]But the child's mother said, "As surely as the Lord lives and as you live, I won't leave you!" So he got up and followed her.

---

roof In Bible times houses were built with flat roofs. The roof was used for drying things such as flax and fruit. It was also used as an extra room, as a place for worship and as a place to sleep in the summer.

³¹Gehazi went on ahead. He laid the walking stick on the child's face. But the child did not talk or move. Then Gehazi went back to meet Elisha. He told Elisha, "The child has not awakened."

³²Elisha came to the house and went in. There was the child, lying dead on his bed. ³³When Elisha entered the room, he shut the door. Only he and the child were in the room. Then Elisha prayed to the Lord. ³⁴He went to the bed and lay on the child. He put his mouth on the child's mouth. He put his eyes on the child's eyes and his hands on the child's hands. He stretched himself out on top of the child. Then the child's skin became warm. ³⁵Elisha turned away and walked around the room. Then he went back and put himself on the child again. Then the child sneezed seven times and opened his eyes.

³⁶Elisha called Gehazi and said, "Call the Shunammite!" And he did. When she came, Elisha said, "Pick up your son." ³⁷She came in and fell at Elisha's feet. She bowed face down to the floor. Then she picked up her son and went out.

Elisha and the Poison

³⁸Elisha came to Gilgal again. There was a time of hunger in the land. A group of prophets*d* was sitting in front of him. He said to his servant, "Put the large pot on the fire. Boil some stew for these men."

³⁹One of them went out into the field to gather plants. He found a wild vine. He picked fruit from the vine and filled his robe with it. Then he came and cut up the fruit into the pot. But they did not know what kind of fruit it was. ⁴⁰Then they poured out the stew for the men to eat. But when they began to eat it, they shouted out, "Man of God! There's death in the pot!" They could not eat it.

⁴¹Elisha told them to bring some flour. Then he threw it into the pot.

He said, "Pour it out for the people to eat." And there was nothing harmful in the pot.

Elisha Multiplies Bread

⁴²A man from Baal Shalishah came to Elisha. He brought 20 loaves of barley bread from the first harvest to Elisha. He also brought fresh grain in his sack. Then Elisha said, "Give it to the people to eat."

⁴³Elisha's servant said, "How can I feed 100 men with so little?"

But Elisha said, "Give the bread to the people to eat. This is what the Lord says: 'They will eat and will have food left over'." ⁴⁴Then he gave it to them. The people ate and had food left over, as the Lord had said.

Naaman Is Healed

5 Naaman was commander of the army of the king of Aram. He was a great man to his master. He had much honour because the Lord had used him to give victory to Aram. He was a mighty and brave man. But he had a harmful skin disease.

²The Arameans had gone out to steal from the Israelites. And they had taken a little girl as a captive from Israel. This little girl served Naaman's wife. ³She said to her mistress, "I wish that my master would meet the prophet*d* who lives in Samaria. He would heal Naaman of his disease."

⁴Naaman went to the king. He told him what the girl from Israel had said. ⁵The king of Aram said, "Go now. And I will send a letter to the king of Israel." So Naaman left and took about 375 kilograms of silver. He also took about 75 kilograms of gold and ten changes of clothes with him. ⁶He brought the letter to the king of Israel. It read, "I am sending my servant Naaman to you. I'm sending him so you can heal him of his skin disease."

⁷The king of Israel read the letter. Then he tore his clothes to show how upset he was. He said, "I'm not God!

I can't kill and make alive again! Why does this man send someone with a harmful skin disease for me to heal? You can see that the king of Aram is trying to start trouble with me!"

⁸Elisha, the man of God, heard that the king of Israel had torn his clothes. So he sent a message to the king. It said, "Why have you become so upset that you tore your clothes? Let Naaman come to me. Then he will know there is a prophet in Israel!" ⁹So Naaman went with his horses and chariots to Elisha's house. And he stood outside the door.

¹⁰Elisha sent a messenger to Naaman. The messenger said, "Go and wash in the Jordan River seven times. Then your skin will be healed, and you will be clean."

¹¹Naaman became angry and left. He said, "I thought Elisha would surely come out and stand before me. I thought he would call on the name of the Lord his God. I thought he would wave his hand over the place and heal the disease! ¹²Abana and Pharpar, the rivers of Damascus, are better than all the waters of Israel! Why can't I wash in them and become clean?" So Naaman went away very angry.

¹³But Naaman's servants came near and talked to him. They said, "My father, if the prophet had told you to do some great thing, wouldn't you have done it? Doesn't it make more sense just to do what Elisha told you to do? After all, he only said, 'Wash, and you will be clean'." ¹⁴So Naaman went down and dipped in the Jordan seven times. He did just as Elisha had said. Then Naaman's skin became new again. It was like the skin of a little boy. And Naaman was clean!

¹⁵Naaman and all his group came back to Elisha. He stood before Elisha and said, "Look. I now know there is no God in all the earth except in Israel! Now please accept a gift from me."

¹⁶But Elisha said, "I serve the Lord. As surely as the Lord lives, I won't accept anything." Naaman urged him to take the gift, but he refused.

¹⁷Then Naaman said, "If you won't take the gift, then please give me some soil. Give me as much as two of my mules can carry. From now on I'll not offer any burnt offering or sacrifice to any other gods. I'll only offer sacrifices to the Lord. ¹⁸But let the Lord pardon me for this: my master goes into the temple of Rimmon*ⁿ* to worship. When he goes, he will lean on my arm. Then I must bow in that temple. May the Lord pardon me when I do that."

¹⁹Elisha said to him, "Go in peace."

Naaman left Elisha and went a short way. ²⁰Gehazi was the servant of Elisha the man of God. Gehazi thought, "My master has not accepted what Naaman the Aramean brought. As surely as the Lord lives, I'll run after him. I'll get something from him." ²¹So he went after him.

Naaman saw someone running after him. So he got off the chariot to meet Gehazi. He said, "Is everything all right?"

²²Gehazi said, "Everything is all right. My master has sent me. He said, 'Two young men just came to me. They are from the group of the prophets in the mountains of Ephraim. Please give them 34 kilograms of silver and two changes of clothes'."

²³Naaman said, "Please take 70 kilograms." He urged Gehazi to take it. He tied 70 kilograms of silver in two bags with two changes of clothes. Then he gave them to two of his servants. They carried them for Gehazi. ²⁴When they came to the hill, Gehazi took these things from Naaman's servants. And he put them in the house. He let Naaman's servants go, and they left.

²⁵Then he came in and stood before

---

temple of Rimmon The place where the Aramean people worshiped the false god Rimmon.

his master. Elisha said to him,
"Where have you been, Gehazi?"

Gehazi said, "I didn't go anywhere."

²⁶But Elisha said to him, "My spirit
was with you. I knew when the man
turned from his chariot to meet you.
This isn't a time to receive money,
clothes, olives and grapes. It isn't a
time to receive sheep, oxen, male
servants and female servants. ²⁷Naa-
man's skin disease will come on you
and your children for ever." When
Gehazi left Elisha, he had the disease.
He was as white as snow.

An Axe Head Floats

6 The group of the prophets*d* said to
Elisha, "The place where we
meet with you is too small for us.
²Let's go to the Jordan River. There
every man can get a pole. And let's
build a place there to live."

Elisha said, "Go."

³One of them said, "Please go with
us."

Elisha said, "I will go." ⁴So he went
with them. When they arrived at the
Jordan, they cut down some trees.
⁵As one man was cutting down a tree,
the head of his axe fell into the water.
He yelled, "Oh, my master! I borrowed that axe!"

⁶Elisha asked, "Where did it fall?"
The man showed Elisha the place.
Then Elisha cut down a stick and
threw it into the water. It made the
iron head float. ⁷Elisha said, "Pick up
the axe head." Then the man reached
out and took it.

Elisha and the Blinded Arameans

⁸The king of Aram was at war with
Israel. He had a council meeting with
his officers. He said, "I will set up my
camp in this place."

⁹But Elisha sent a message to the
king of Israel. It said, "Be careful!
Don't pass that place. The Arameans
are going down there!"

¹⁰The king of Israel checked the
place about which Elisha had warned

him. Elisha warned him several times.
So the king added guards in those
places.

¹¹The king of Aram was angry about
this. He called his officers together.
He said to them, "Tell me who of us
is working for the king of Israel."

¹²One of the officers of the king of
Aram said, "Not us, my master and
king. It's Elisha, the prophet*d* from Israel. He can tell you what you speak
even in your bedroom."

¹³The king said, "Go and find him.
Then I can send men and catch him."

The servants came back and reported, "He is in Dothan."

¹⁴Then the king sent horses, chariots and a large army to Dothan. They
arrived at night and surrounded the
city.

¹⁵The servant of Elisha got up early.
When he went out, he saw an army
with horses and chariots all around
city. The servant said to Elisha, "Oh,
my master, what can we do?"

¹⁶Elisha said, "Don't be afraid. The
army that fights for us is larger than
the one against us."

¹⁷Then Elisha prayed, "Lord, open
my servant's eyes. Let him see."

The Lord opened the eyes of the
young man. And he saw that the
mountain was full of horses and chariots of fire all around Elisha.

¹⁸As the enemy came down towards
Elisha, he prayed to the Lord. He
said, "Make these people blind." So
the Lord made the Aramean army
blind, as Elisha had asked.

¹⁹Elisha said to them, "This is not
the right road. This is not the right
city. Follow me. I'll take you to the
man you are looking for." Then Elisha
led them to Samaria.

²⁰After they entered Samaria, Elisha said, "Lord, open these men's
eyes so they can see." So the Lord
opened their eyes. And the Aramean
army saw that they were inside the
city of Samaria!

²¹The king of Israel saw the Arame-

an army. He said to Elisha, "My father, should I kill them? Should I kill them?"

²²Elisha answered, "Don't kill them. You wouldn't kill people whom you captured with your sword and bow. Give them food and water. And let them eat and drink. Then let them go home to their master." ²³So he prepared a great feast for the Aramean army. They ate and drank. Then the king sent them away. They went home to their master. The soldiers of Aram did not come any more into the land of Israel.

A Time of Hunger

²⁴Later, Ben-Hadad king of Aram gathered all his army. He went to surround and attack Samaria. ²⁵There was a time of terrible hunger in Samaria. It was so bad that a donkey's head was sold for about a kilogram of silver. Half of a pint of dove's dung sold for about 55 grams of silver.

²⁶The king of Israel was passing by on the wall. A woman yelled out to him, "Help me, my master and king!"

²⁷The king said, "If the Lord doesn't help you, how can I? Can I get help from the threshing[d] floor or from the winepress?"[d] ²⁸Then the king said to her, "What is your trouble?"

She answered, "This woman said to me, 'Give up your son so we can eat him today. Then we will eat my son tomorrow'. ²⁹So we boiled my son and ate him. Then the next day I said to her, 'Give up your son so we can eat him'. But she had hidden him."

³⁰When the king heard the woman's words, he tore his clothes to show how upset he was. He walked along the wall. The people looked and saw he had on rough cloth under his clothes. This was to show his sadness. ³¹He said, "The head of Elisha son of Shaphat will be taken from his body today! May God punish me terribly if this doesn't happen!"

³²The king sent a messenger to Eli-

sha. Elisha was sitting in his house. And the older leaders were sitting with him. But before the messenger arrived, Elisha spoke to them. He said, "See, this murderer is sending men to take off my head. When the messenger arrives, shut the door. Hold it and don't let him in. The sound of his master's feet is behind him."

³³While Elisha was still talking with the leaders, the king came. He said, "This trouble has come from the Lord. Why should I wait for the Lord any longer?"

7 Elisha said, "Listen to the Lord's word. This is what he says: 'About this time tomorrow 7 litres of fine flour will be sold for about 11 grams of silver. And 13 litres of barley will be sold for about 11 grams of silver. This will happen at the gate of Samaria.'"

²Then the officer who was close to the king answered Elisha. He said, "Even if the Lord opened windows in heaven, that couldn't happen."

Elisha said, "Because you have said that, you will see it with your eyes. But you will not eat any of it."

³There were four men with a harmful skin disease at the entrance to the city gate. They said to each other, "Why do we sit here until we die? ⁴A time of hunger is in the city. So if we go into the city, we will die there. If we stay here, we will die. So let's go to the Aramean camp. If they let us live, we will live. If they kill us, then we die."

⁵So they got up at twilight. And they went to the Aramean camp. But when they arrived, no one was there. ⁶The Lord had caused the Aramean army to hear the sound of chariots, horses and a large army. They had said to each other, "The king of Israel has hired the Hittite and Egyptian kings to attack us!" ⁷So they ran away in the twilight. They left their tents, horses and donkeys. They left the camp standing and ran for their lives.

⁸The men with the skin disease came to the edge of the camp. Then they went into one of the tents. They ate and drank. They carried silver, gold and clothes out of the camp and hid them. Then they came back and entered another tent. They carried things from this tent and hid them, also. ⁹Then they said to each other, "We're doing wrong. Today we have good news, but we are keeping silent. If we wait until the sun comes up, we'll be punished. Let's go now and tell the people in the king's palace."

¹⁰So they went and called to the gatekeepers of the city. They said, "We went to the Aramean camp. But no one is there. We didn't hear anyone. The horses and donkeys were still tied up, and the tents were still standing." ¹¹Then the gatekeepers shouted out and told the people in the palace.

¹²So the king got up in the night. He said to his officers, "I'll tell you what the Arameans are doing to us. They know we are hungry. They have gone out of the camp to hide in the field. They're saying, 'When the Israelites come out of the city, we'll capture them alive. Then we'll enter the city'."

¹³One of his officers answered, "Let some men take five horses still left in the city. These men are like all the Israelites who are left. They are also about to die. Let's send them to see what has happened."

¹⁴So the men took two chariots with horses. The king sent them after the Aramean army. He told them, "Go and see what has happened." ¹⁵The men followed the Aramean army as far as the Jordan River. The road was full of clothes and equipment. The Arameans had thrown these things away as they had hurried away. So the messengers came back and told the king. ¹⁶Then the people went out and took valuable things from the Aramean camp. So 7 litres of fine flour were sold for 11 grams of silver. And 13 litres of barley were sold for 11 grams of silver. It happened just as the Lord had said.

¹⁷The king chose the officer who was close to him to guard the gate. But the people ran over the officer so that he died. This happened just as the man of God had told the king. Elisha had said it when the king came to his house. ¹⁸He had said, "13 litres of barley and 7 litres of fine flour will each sell for 11 grams of silver. It will happen about this time tomorrow at the gate of Samaria."

¹⁹But the officer had answered, "Even if the Lord opened windows in heaven, that couldn't happen." And Elisha had told him, "Because you have said that, you will see it with your eyes. But you won't eat any of it." ²⁰It happened to the officer just that way. The people ran over him in the gate, and he died.

The Shunammite Regains Her Land

8 Elisha talked to the woman whose son he had brought back to life. He said, "Get up and go with your family. Stay any place you can. This is because the Lord has called for a time of hunger. It will last seven years." ²So the woman got up and did as the man of God said. She left with her family. And they stayed in the land of the Philistines for seven years. ³After seven years she came back from the land of the Philistines. She went to beg the king for her house and land back. ⁴The king was talking with Gehazi. He was the servant of the man of God. The king had said to Gehazi, "Please tell me all the great things Elisha has done." ⁵Now Gehazi was telling the king how Elisha had brought a dead person back to life. Just then the woman whose son Elisha had brought back to life came and begged the king for her house and land.

Gehazi said, "My master and king,

this is the woman. And this is the son Elisha brought back to life."

⁶The king asked the woman, and she told him about it. Then the king chose an officer to help her. The king said, "Give the woman everything that is hers. Give her all the money made from her land from the day she left until now."

Ben-Hadad Is Killed

⁷Elisha went to Damascus. Now Ben-Hadad king of Aram was sick. Someone told him, "The man of God has come here."

⁸Then the king said to Hazael, "Take a gift in your hand and go and meet him. Ask the Lord through him if I will get well from my sickness."

⁹So Hazael went to meet Elisha. He took with him a gift. It was 40 camels loaded with every good thing in Damascus. He came and stood before Elisha. Hazael said, "Your son Ben-Hadad king of Aram sent me to you. He asks if he will get well from his sickness."

¹⁰Then Elisha said to Hazael, "Go and tell Ben-Hadad, 'You will surely get well'. But the Lord has told me he will really die." ¹¹Elisha stared at Hazael until Hazael felt ashamed. Then Elisha cried.

¹²Hazael asked, "Why are you crying, master?"

Elisha answered, "Because I know what evil you will do to the Israelites. You will burn their strong, walled cities with fire. You will kill their young men with swords. You will throw their babies to the ground. You will split open their pregnant women."

¹³Hazael said, "I, your servant, am only a dog. How could I do such things?"

Elisha answered, "The Lord has shown me that you will be king over Aram."

¹⁴Then Hazael left Elisha and came to his master. Ben-Hadad said to Hazael, "What did Elisha say to you?"

Hazael answered, "He told me that you will surely get well." ¹⁵But the next day Hazael took a blanket and dipped it in water. Then he put it over Ben-Hadad's face, and he died. So Hazael became king in Ben-Hadad's place.

Jehoram King of Judah

¹⁶Jehoram son of Jehoshaphat became king of Judah. This was during Joram's fifth year as king of Israel. Joram was the son of Ahab. ¹⁷Jehoram was 32 years old when he began to rule. He ruled eight years in Jerusalem. ¹⁸But Jehoram followed the ways of the kings of Israel. This was just as the family of Ahab had done. It was because Ahab's daughter was Jehoram's wife. Jehoram did what the Lord said was wrong. ¹⁹But the Lord would not destroy Judah because of his servant David. The Lord had promised that David and his children would always have a kingdom.

²⁰In Jehoram's time Edom broke away from Judah's rule. The people of Edom chose their own king. ²¹So Jehoram and all his chariots went to Zair. At night the Edomites came around him and his chariot commanders. Jehoram got up and attacked the Edomites. But his army ran away to their tents. ²²So the Edomites broke away from the rule of Judah. And they are still separate today. At the same time Libnah also broke away from Judah's rule.

²³The other acts of Jehoram and all the things he did are written down. They are in the book of the history of the kings of Judah. ²⁴Jehoram died and was buried with his ancestors in Jerusalem. Jehoram's son Ahaziah ruled in his place.

²⁵Ahaziah son of Jehoram became king of Judah. This was during Joram's twelfth year as king of Israel. Joram was the son of Ahab. ²⁶Ahaziah was 22 years old when he became king. He ruled one year in Jerusalem. His

mother's name was Athaliah. She was a granddaughter of Omri king of Israel. [27]Ahaziah followed the ways of Ahab's family. He did what the Lord said was wrong, as Ahab's family had done. He did this because he was a son-in-law in Ahab's family.

[28]Ahaziah went with Joram son of Ahab to Ramoth in Gilead. There they fought against Hazael king of Aram. The Arameans wounded Joram. [29]So King Joram returned to Jezreel to heal from the injuries. (He had been wounded by the Arameans at Ramoth. This was when he fought Hazael king of Aram.) And Ahaziah son of Jehoram king of Judah went down to see Joram. He went to see Joram son of Ahab at Jezreel because he had been wounded.

Jehu Is Chosen King

9 Elisha called a man from the group of the prophets.[d] Elisha said, "Tighten your clothes around you. And take this small bottle of olive oil in your hand. Go to Ramoth in Gilead. [2]When you arrive, find Jehu son of Jehoshaphat. Jehoshaphat is the son of Nimshi. Go in and make Jehu get up from among his brothers. Take him to an inner room. [3]Take the bottle and pour the oil on Jehu's head. Say, 'This is what the Lord says: I have appointed you king over Israel'. Then open the door and run away. Don't wait!"

[4]So the young man, the prophet, went to Ramoth in Gilead. [5]When he arrived, he saw the officers of the army sitting together. He said, "Commander, I have a message for you."

Jehu asked, "For which one of us?"

The young man said, "For you, commander."

[6]Jehu got up and went into the house. Then the young prophet poured the olive oil on Jehu's head. He said to Jehu, "This is what the Lord of Israel says: 'I have appointed you king over the Lord's people, Israel. [7]You must destroy the family of Ahab your master. I will punish Jezebel for the deaths of my servants the prophets. And I will punish her for all the Lord's servants who were murdered. [8]So all Ahab's family will die. I will not let any male child in Ahab's family live in Israel. It does not matter if he is a slave or a free person. [9]I will make Ahab's family like the family of Jeroboam son of Nebat. They will be like the family of Baasha son of Ahijah. [10]The dogs will eat Jezebel in the portion of land at Jezreel. And no one will bury her'."

Then the young prophet opened the door and ran away.

[11]Jehu went back to his master's officers. One of them said to Jehu, "Is everything all right? Why did this crazy man come to you?"

Jehu answered, "You know the man and how he talks."

[12]They answered, "That's not true! Tell us."

Jehu said, "He said, 'This is what the Lord says: I have appointed you to be king over Israel.'"

[13]Then the officers hurried. Each man took off his own coat. They put them on the stairs for Jehu. Then they blew the trumpet. They said, "Jehu is king!"

Joram and Ahaziah Are Killed

[14]So Jehu son of Jehoshaphat made plans against Joram. (Jehoshaphat was the son of Nimshi.) Now Joram and all Israel had been defending Ramoth in Gilead from Hazael king of Aram. [15]But King Joram had to return to Israel to heal from the injuries the Arameans had given him. He received these injuries when he fought against Hazael king of Aram.

Jehu said, "If you agree with this, don't let anyone leave the city. They might tell the news in Jezreel." [16]Then he got into his chariot and set out for Jezreel. Joram was resting there. And Ahaziah king of Judah had gone down to see him.

[17]The lookout was standing on the

watchtower in Jezreel. He saw Jehu's troops coming. He said, "I see some soldiers!"

Joram said, "Take a horseman and send him to meet them. Tell him to ask, 'Do you bring good news?' "

¹⁸So the horseman rode out to meet Jehu. The horseman said, "This is what the king says: 'Do you bring good news?' "

Jehu said, "That's none of your business! Come along behind me."

The lookout reported, "The messenger reached them. But he is not coming back."

¹⁹So Joram sent out a second horseman. This rider came to Jehu's group and said, "This is what the king says: 'Do you bring good news?' "

Jehu answered, "That's none of your business! Come along behind me."

²⁰The lookout reported, "The second man reached them. But he is not coming back. The man in the chariot is driving like Jehu son of Nimshi. He drives as if he were crazy!"

²¹Joram said, "Get my chariot ready." Then the servant got Joram's chariot ready. Joram and Ahaziah king of Judah went out. Each king went in his own chariot to meet Jehu. And they met him at the property of Naboth the Jezreelite.

²²When Joram saw Jehu, he said, "Do you bring good news, Jehu?"

Jehu answered, "There will never be any good news as long as your mother Jezebel worships idols and uses witchcraft."ᵈ

²³Joram turned the horses to run away. He yelled to Ahaziah, "It's a trick, Ahaziah!"

²⁴Then Jehu drew his bow and shot Joram between his shoulders. The arrow went through Joram's heart. And he fell down in his chariot.

²⁵Jehu ordered Bidkar, his chariot officer, "Pick up Joram's body. Throw

it into the field of Naboth the Jezreelite. Remember when you and I rode together with Joram's father Ahab. The Lord made this prophecyᵈ against him: ²⁶'Yesterday I saw the blood of Naboth and his sons, says the Lord. So I will punish Ahab in his field, says the Lord'. So take Joram's body and throw it into the field, as the Lord has said."

²⁷When Ahaziah king of Judah saw this, he ran away towards Beth Haggan. Jehu chased him, saying, "Shoot Ahaziah, too!" Ahaziah was wounded in his chariot on the way up to Gur near Ibleam. Ahaziah got as far as Megiddo but died there. ²⁸His servants carried his body in a chariot to Jerusalem. They buried him with his ancestors in his tomb in Jerusalem. ²⁹(Ahaziah had become king over Judah in Joram's eleventh year as king. Joram was the son of Ahab.)

Death of Jezebel

³⁰When Jehu came to Jezreel, Jezebel heard about it. She put paint on her eyes and fixed her hair. Then she looked out the window. ³¹Jehu entered the city gate. And Jezebel said, "Have you come in peace, you Zimri,ⁿ you who killed your master?"

³²Jehu looked up at the window. He said, "Who is on my side? Who?" Two or three eunuchsᵈ looked out from the window at Jehu. ³³Jehu said to them, "Throw her down!" So they threw Jezebel down. And the horses ran over her body. Some of her blood splashed on the wall and on the horses.

³⁴Jehu went into the house and ate and drank. Then he said, "Now see about this cursed woman. Bury her, because she is a king's daughter."

³⁵The men went to bury Jezebel. But they could not find her body. They could only find the skull, feet and palms of her hands. ³⁶So they came

Zimri He was the man who killed Elah and the family of Baasha. Read 1 Kings 16:8-12.

back and told Jehu. Then Jehu said, "The Lord said this through his servant Elijah the Tishbite: 'The dogs will eat the body of Jezebel in the portion of land at Jezreel. 37Her body will be like manure on the field in the land at Jezreel. Then people cannot say that the body is Jezebel's'."

Families of Ahab and Ahaziah Killed

10 Ahab's family had 70 sons in Samaria. Jehu wrote letters and sent them to Samaria. He sent them to the officers and older leaders of Jezreel. He also sent them to the guardians of the sons of Ahab. Jehu said, 2"You have chariots, horses and a city with strong walls. You also have weapons. When you get this letter, 3choose the best and most worthy person among your master's sons. Make him king. Then fight for your master's family."

4But the officers and older leaders of Jezreel were very frightened. They said, "The two kings could not stop Jehu. So, surely we can't either."

5The palace manager, the city governor, the older leaders and the guardians sent a message to Jehu. They said, "We are your servants. We will do everything you tell us to do. We won't make any man king. Do whatever you think is best."

6Then Jehu wrote a second letter. It said, "If you are on my side and will obey me, cut off the heads of your master's sons. And come to me at Jezreel tomorrow about this time."

Now there were 70 sons of the king's family. They were with the leading men of the city who were their guardians. 7The leaders received the letter. Then they took the king's sons and killed all 70 of them. They put their heads in baskets. And they sent them to Jehu at Jezreel. 8The messenger came to Jehu. He told Jehu, "They have brought the heads of the king's sons!"

Then Jehu said, "Lay the heads in two piles at the city gate until morning."

9In the morning, Jehu went out and stood before the people. He said to them, "You are innocent. Look, I made plans against my master. I killed him. But who killed all these? 10You should know that nothing the Lord said will fail. Everything the Lord said about Ahab's family will come true. The Lord has spoken through his servant Elijah. And the Lord has done what he said." 11So Jehu killed everyone of Ahab's family in Jezreel who was still alive. He also killed all Ahab's leading men, close friends and priests. No one was left alive who had helped Ahab.

12Then Jehu left and went to Samaria. He went on the road to Beth Eked of the Shepherds. 13There Jehu met some relatives of Ahaziah king of Judah. Jehu said, "Who are you?"

They answered, "We are relatives of Ahaziah. We have come down to visit the families of the king and the king's mother."

14Then Jehu said, "Take them alive!" So they captured Ahaziah's relatives alive. But they killed them at the well near Beth Eked. There were 42 of them. Jehu did not leave anyone alive.

15After Jehu left there, he met Jehonadab son of Recab. He was on his way to meet Jehu. Jehu greeted him and said, "Are you as good a friend to me as I am to you?"

Jehonadab answered, "Yes, I am."

Jehu said, "If you are, then give me your hand." So Jehonadab gave him his hand, and Jehu pulled him into the chariot. 16Jehu said, "Come with me. You can see how strong my feelings are for the Lord." So Jehu had Jehonadab ride in his chariot.

17When Jehu came to Samaria, he killed all of Ahab's family. He did this until he had destroyed all of those who were left. Jehu did what the Lord had told Elijah would happen.

Baal Worshippers Killed

18Then Jehu gathered all the people together. He said to them, "Ahab served Baald a little. But Jehu will serve Baal much. 19Now call for me all Baal's prophets and priests. Call all the people who worship Baal. Don't let anyone miss this meeting. I have a great sacrifice for Baal. Anyone who is not there will not remain alive." But Jehu was tricking them so he could destroy the worshippers of Baal. 20He said, "Prepare a holy meeting for Baal." So they announced the meeting. 21Then Jehu sent word through all Israel. All the worshippers of Baal came. Not one stayed home. They came into the temple of Baal. The temple was filled from one side to the other.

22Jehu spoke to the man who kept the robes. He said, "Bring out robes for all the worshippers of Baal." So he brought out robes for them. 23Then Jehu and Jehonadab son of Recab went into the temple of Baal. Jehu said to the worshippers of Baal, "Look around. Be sure there are no servants of the Lord with you. Be sure there are only people here who worship Baal." 24So the worshippers of Baal went in to offer sacrifices and burnt offerings.

But Jehu had 80 men waiting outside. He told them, "Don't let anyone escape. If you let anyone escape, you must pay with your own life."

25Jehu finished offering the burnt offering. Then he spoke to the guards and the captains. He said, "Go in and kill the worshippers of Baal! Don't let anyone come out." So the guards and captains killed the worshippers of Baal with the sword. They threw the bodies of the worshippers of Baal out. Then they went to the inner rooms of the temple. 26They brought out the pillars of the temple of Baal and

burned them. 27Then they tore down the stone pillar of Baal. They also tore down the temple of Baal. They made it into a sewage pit, and it is still one today.

28So Jehu destroyed Baal worship in Israel. 29But he did not stop doing the sins Jeroboam son of Nebat had done. Jeroboam had caused Israel to sin. They worshipped the golden calves in Bethel and Dan.

30The Lord said to Jehu, "You have done well. You have done what I said was right. You have done to the family of Ahab as I wanted. Your descendantsd as far as your great-great-grandchildren will be kings of Israel." 31But Jehu was not careful to keep the teachings of the Lord with all his heart. He did not stop doing the same sins Jeroboam had done. Jeroboam had caused Israel to sin.

32At that time the Lord began to make Israel smaller. Hazael defeated the Israelites in all the land of Israel. 33He took all the land on the east side of the Jordan. This was the land of Gilead. (It was the region of Gad, Reuben and Manasseh.) He took land from Aroer by the Arnon Ravine through Gilead to Bashan.

34The other things Jehu did are written down. Everything he did and all his victories are recorded. They are in the book of the history of the kings of Israel. 35Jehu died and was buried in Samaria. Jehu's son Jehoahaz became king in his place. 36Jehu was king over Israel in Samaria for 28 years.

Athaliah and Joash

11 Now Ahaziah's mother, Athaliah, saw that her son was dead. Then she killed all the royal family. 2But Jehosheba took Joash, Ahaziah's son. She stole him from among the other sons of the king who were about to be murdered. (Jehosheba was King Jehoram's daughter and Ahaziah's sister.) She put Joash and his nurse in a bedroom. She hid Joash from Athali-

ah. So he was not killed. [3]He was hidden with her in the Temple[d] of the Lord for six years. During that time Athaliah ruled the land.

[4]In the seventh year Jehoiada sent for the commanders of groups of 100 men. He sent for guards and the Carites, the royal bodyguards. He brought them together in the Temple of the Lord. Then he made an agreement with them. There, in the Temple of the Lord, he made them promise loyalty. Then he showed them the king's son. [5]He commanded them, "This is what you must do. A third of you who come in on the Sabbath[d] will guard the king's palace. [6]Another third of you will be at the Sur Gate. And another third will be at the gate behind the guard. This way you will guard the Temple. [7]Two groups will go off duty on the Sabbath. They must protect the Temple of the Lord for the king. [8]All of you must stand around the king. Each man must have his weapon in his hand. If anyone comes near, kill him. Stay close to the king when he goes out and when he comes in."

[9]The commanders over 100 men obeyed everything Jehoiada the priest had commanded. Each one took his men who were beginning their Sabbath duty. Each one also took those who were ending their Sabbath duty. Both groups came to Jehoiada the priest. [10]And he gave spears and shields to the commanders. They used to belong to King David. They were kept in the Temple of the Lord.

Joash Becomes King

[11]Then each of the guards took his place. Each man had his weapon in his hand. There were guards from the south side of the Temple[d] to the north side. They stood by the altar and the Temple and around the king. [12]Jehoiada brought out the king's son. He put the crown on Joash. Then he gave Joash a copy of the Agreement with the Lord. They appointed him king and poured olive oil on him. They clapped their hands and said, "Long live the king!"

[13]Athaliah heard the noise of the guards and the people. So she came to the people at the Temple of the Lord. [14]She looked, and there was the king. He was standing by the pillar, as the custom was. The officers and trumpeters were standing beside him. All the people of the land were very happy and were blowing trumpets. Then Athaliah tore her clothes to show how upset she was. She screamed, "Traitors! Traitors!"

[15]Jehoiada the priest gave orders to the commanders of 100 men who led the army. He said, "Surround her with soldiers. Kill with a sword anyone who follows her." He said this because he had said, "Don't put Athaliah to death in the Temple of the Lord." [16]So they caught her when she came to where the horses enter the palace grounds. There she was put to death.

[17]Then Jehoiada made an agreement. It was between the Lord and the king and the people. They agreed to be the Lord's special people. He also made an agreement between the king and the people. [18]All the people of the land went to the temple of Baal[d] and tore it down. They smashed the altars and idols into small pieces. And they killed Mattan, the priest of Baal, in front of the altars.

Then Jehoiada the priest placed guards at the Temple of the Lord. [19]He took with him the commanders of 100 men and the Carites, the royal bodyguards. He took the guards and all the people of the land. Together they took the king out of the Temple of the Lord. They went into the palace through the gate of the guards. Then the king sat on the royal throne. [20]So all the people of Judah were very happy. And Jerusalem had peace because Athaliah had been put to death with the sword at the palace.

²¹Joash was seven years old when he became king.

12 Joash became king of Judah in Jehu's seventh year as king of Israel. Joash ruled for 40 years in Jerusalem. His mother's name was Zibiah. She was from Beersheba. ²Joash did what the Lord said was right all the time Jehoiada the priest taught him. ³But the places where false gods were worshipped were not removed. The people still made sacrifices and burned incense*d* there.

The Temple to Be Repaired

⁴Joash said to the priests, "Take all the money brought as offerings to the Temple*d* of the Lord. This includes the money each person owes in taxes. It also includes the money each person promises or brings to the Lord because he wants to. ⁵Each priest must take the money from the people he serves. Then the priests must repair any damage they find in the Temple."

⁶But by the twenty-third year of Joash the priests still had not repaired the Temple. ⁷So King Joash called for Jehoiada the priest and the other priests. He said to them, "Why are you not repairing the damage of the Temple? Don't take any more money from the people you serve. But hand over the money for the repair of the Temple." ⁸The priests agreed not to take any more money from the people. And they agreed not to repair the Temple themselves.

⁹But Jehoiada the priest took a box and made a hole in the top of it. Then he put it by the altar. It was on the right side as the people came into the Temple of the Lord. The priests guarding the doorway put all the money brought to the Temple of the Lord into the box.

¹⁰Each time the priests saw that the box was full of money, the king's royal assistant and the high priest came. They counted the money that had been brought to the Temple of the Lord. Then they put it into bags. ¹¹Next they weighed the money. They gave it to the men who were in charge of the work on the Temple. With it they paid the carpenters and the builders who worked on the Temple of the Lord. ¹²They also paid the stoneworkers and stonecutters. They used the money to buy timber and cut stone. The money was used to repair the damage of the Temple of the Lord. It paid for everything.

¹³The money brought into the Temple of the Lord was not used to make silver cups. It was not used for wick trimmers, bowls or trumpets. And it wasn't used for any gold or silver vessels. ¹⁴They paid the money to the workers. And the workers used it to repair the Temple of the Lord. ¹⁵They did not make the men tell how the money was spent. This was because the men were honest. ¹⁶The money from the penalty offerings and sin offerings was not brought into the Temple of the Lord. It belonged to the priests.

Joash Saves Jerusalem

¹⁷About this time Hazael king of Aram attacked Gath and captured it. Then he went to attack Jerusalem. ¹⁸But Joash king of Judah took all the holy things his ancestors had given. His ancestors were the kings of Judah—Jehoshaphat, Jehoram and Ahaziah. He also took his own holy things. He took the gold that was found in the treasuries of the Temple*d* of the Lord. And he took the gold from the palace. Joash sent all this treasure to Hazael king of Aram. Then Hazael turned away from Jerusalem.

¹⁹Everything else Joash did is written down. It is in the book of the history of the kings of Judah. ²⁰His officers made plans against him. They killed him at Beth Millo on the road to Silla. ²¹The officers who killed him were Jozabad son of Shimeath and Jehozabad son of Shomer. Joash was buried

with his ancestors in Jerusalem. And Amaziah, his son, became king in his place.

Jehoahaz King of Israel

13 Jehoahaz son of Jehu became king over Israel in Samaria. This was during Joash's twenty-third year as king of Judah. Joash was the son of Ahaziah. And Jehoahaz ruled 17 years. ²He did what the Lord said was wrong. Jehoahaz did the same sins Jeroboam son of Nebat had done. Jeroboam had caused Israel to sin. And Jehoahaz did not stop doing these same sins. ³So the Lord was angry with Israel. And he gave them into the power of Hazael king of Aram and his son Ben-Hadad.

⁴Then Jehoahaz begged the Lord, and the Lord listened to him. The Lord had seen the troubles of Israel. He saw how terribly the king of Aram was treating the Israelites. ⁵So he gave Israel a man to save them. And they escaped from the Arameans. So the Israelites lived in their own homes as they had before. ⁶But the Israelites still did not stop doing the same sins that the family of Jeroboam had done. He had caused Israel to sin. They continued doing those sins. The Asherah*d* idol also was left standing in Samaria.

⁷Nothing was left of Jehoahaz's army except 50 horsemen, 10 chariots and 10,000 foot soldiers. The king of Aram had destroyed them. He had made them like dust at the time of threshing.*d*

⁸Everything else Jehoahaz did and all his victories are written down. They are in the book of history of the kings of Israel. ⁹Jehoahaz died and was buried in Samaria. His son Jehoash became king in his place.

Jehoash King of Israel

¹⁰Jehoash son of Jehoahaz became king of Israel in Samaria. This was during Joash's thirty-seventh year as king of Judah. Jehoash ruled 16 years.

¹¹He did what the Lord said was wrong. He did not stop doing the same sins Jeroboam son of Nebat had done. Jeroboam had caused Israel to sin. And Jehoash continued to do the same thing. ¹²Everything else he did and all his victories are written down. This includes his war against Amaziah king of Judah. All this is written in the book of the history of the kings of Israel. ¹³Jehoash died, and Jeroboam took his place on the throne. Jehoash was buried in Samaria with the kings of Israel.

The Death of Elisha

¹⁴At this time Elisha became sick. (Later, he died from this illness.) Jehoash king of Israel went to Elisha and cried for him. Jehoash said, "My father, my father! The chariots of Israel and their horsemen!"

¹⁵Elisha said to Jehoash, "Take a bow and arrows." So he took a bow and arrows. ¹⁶Then Elisha said to him, "Put your hand on the bow." So Jehoash put his hand on the bow. Then Elisha put his hands on the king's hands. ¹⁷Elisha said, "Open the east window." So Jehoash opened the window. Then Elisha said, "Shoot," and Jehoash shot. Elisha said, "The Lord's arrow of victory over Aram! You will defeat the Arameans at Aphek until you destroy them."

¹⁸Elisha said, "Take the arrows." So Jehoash took them. Then Elisha said to him, "Hit the ground." So Jehoash hit the ground three times. Then he stopped. ¹⁹The man of God was angry with him. Elisha said, "You should have hit five or six times! Then you would have defeated Aram until you had completely destroyed it! But now you will defeat it only three times."

²⁰So Elisha died and was buried.

At that time groups of Moabites would rob the land in the springtime. ²¹Once the Israelites were burying a man. Suddenly they saw a group of

Moabites coming. The Israelites threw the dead man into Elisha's grave. When the man touched Elisha's bones, the man came back to life. And he stood up on his feet.

War with Aram

²²During all the days Jehoahaz was king, Hazael king of Aram troubled Israel. ²³But the Lord was kind to the Israelites. He had mercy on them. And he helped them because of his agreement with Abraham, Isaac and Jacob. He did not destroy them or reject them.

²⁴Hazael king of Aram died. And his son Ben-Hadad became king in his place. ²⁵During a war Hazael had taken some cities from Jehoahaz, Jehoash's father. But now Jehoash took back those cities from Hazael's son Ben-Hadad. He defeated Ben-Hadad three times and took back the cities of Israel.

Amaziah King of Judah

14 Amaziah son of Joash became king of Judah. This was during the second year Jehoash son of Jehoahaz was king of Israel. ²Amaziah was 25 years old when he became king. He ruled 29 years in Jerusalem. His mother was Jehoaddin. She was from Jerusalem. ³Amaziah did what the Lord said was right. Amaziah did everything his father Joash had done. But he did not do as David his ancestor had done. ⁴The places where false gods were worshipped were not removed. The people still sacrificed and burned incense^d there.

⁵Amaziah took strong control of the kingdom. Then he put the officers to death who had killed his father the king. ⁶But he did not put to death the children of the murderers. This is because of the rule written in the Book of the Teachings of Moses. The Lord had commanded: "Fathers must not

be put to death when their children do wrong. And children must not be put to death when their fathers do wrong. Each person must die for his own sins."ⁿ

⁷Amaziah killed 10,000 Edomites in the Valley of Salt. In a battle Amaziah took the city of Sela. He called it Joktheel, and it is still called that today.

⁸Amaziah sent messengers to Jehoash son of Jehoahaz. (Jehoahaz was the son of Jehu, king of Israel.) The message read, "Come, let's meet face to face in battle."

⁹Then Jehoash king of Israel answered Amaziah king of Judah. Jehoash said, "A little thornbush in Lebanon sent a message to a big cedar tree in Lebanon. It said, 'Let your daughter marry my son'. But then a wild animal from Lebanon came by. It walked on and crushed the thornbush. ¹⁰Yes, you have defeated Edom. But you have become proud because of your victory over Edom. Stay at home and brag! Don't ask for trouble by fighting me. If you do, you and Judah will be defeated."

¹¹But Amaziah would not listen. So Jehoash king of Israel went to attack. He and Amaziah king of Judah faced each other in battle at Beth Shemesh in Judah. ¹²Israel defeated Judah. Every man of Judah ran away to his home. ¹³At Beth Shemesh, Jehoash king of Israel captured Amaziah king of Judah. Amaziah was the son of Joash, who was the son of Ahaziah. Then Jehoash went to Jerusalem. He broke down the wall of Jerusalem from the Gate of Ephraim to the Corner Gate. This part of the wall was about 180 metres long. ¹⁴Then he took all the gold and silver and everything in the Temple^d of the Lord. And he took the treasuries of the palace. He also took some hostages and returned to Samaria.

¹⁵The other acts of Jehoash and his

"**Fathers . . . sins.**" See Deuteronomy 24:16.

victories are written down. This includes his war against Amaziah king of Judah. All this is in the book of the history of the kings of Israel. [16]Jehoash died and was buried in Samaria with the kings of Israel. And his son Jeroboam became king in his place.

[17]Amaziah son of Joash was king of Judah. He lived 15 years after Jehoash king of Israel died. Jehoash was the son of Jehoahaz. [18]The other things Amaziah did as king are written down. They are in the book of the history of the kings of Judah. [19]The people made plans in Jerusalem against Amaziah. So he ran away to the town of Lachish. But they sent men after him to Lachish and killed him. [20]They brought his body back on horses. And he was buried with his ancestors in Jerusalem, the City of David.

[21]Then all the people of Judah chose Azariah[n] to be king. He became king in place of his father Amaziah. Azariah was 16 years old. [22]He rebuilt the town of Elath and made it part of Judah again. He did this after Amaziah died.

Jeroboam King of Israel

[23]Jeroboam son of Jehoash became king of Israel in Samaria. This was during the fifteenth year Amaziah was king of Judah. (Amaziah was the son of Joash.) And Jeroboam ruled 41 years. [24]He did what the Lord said was wrong. Jeroboam son of Nebat had caused Israel to sin. And Jeroboam son of Jehoash did not stop doing the same sins. [25]Jeroboam won back Israel's border from Lebo Hamath to the Dead Sea.[d] This happened as the Lord of Israel had said. He said it through his servant Jonah son of Amittai. He was the prophet[d] from Gath Hepher. [26]The Lord had seen how the Israelites, both slave and free, were suffering terribly. No one was left who could help Israel. [27]But the Lord had not said that he would completely

destroy Israel from the world. So he saved the Israelites through Jeroboam son of Jehoash.

[28]Everything else Jeroboam did is written down. All his victories are recorded. He won back Damascus and Hamath for Israel. (They had belonged to Judah.) All this is written in the book of the history of the kings of Israel. [29]Jeroboam died and was buried with his ancestors, the kings of Israel. Jeroboam's son Zechariah became king in his place.

Azariah King of Judah

15 Azariah[n] son of Amaziah became king of Judah. This was during Jeroboam's twenty-seventh year as king of Israel. [2]Azariah was 16 years old when he became king. He ruled 52 years in Jerusalem. His mother was named Jecoliah, and she was from Jerusalem. [3]He did what the Lord said was right. He obeyed God just as his father Amaziah had done. [4]But the places where false gods were worshipped were not removed. So the people still made sacrifices and burned incense[d] there.

[5]The Lord struck Azariah with a harmful skin disease. He had this disease until the day he died. He lived in a separate house. Jotham, the king's son, was in charge of the palace. He governed the people of the land.

[6]All the other things Azariah did are written down. They are in the book of the history of the kings of Judah. [7]Azariah died and was buried near his ancestors in Jerusalem. And his son Jotham became king in his place.

Zechariah King of Israel

[8]Zechariah son of Jeroboam was king over Israel in Samaria. He ruled for six months. This was during Azariah's thirty-eighth year as king of Judah. [9]Zechariah did what the Lord said was wrong. He did just as his ances-

---

Azariah Also called Uzziah in 2 Chronicles.

tors had done. Jeroboam son of Nebat had caused the people of Israel to sin. And Zechariah did not stop doing the same sins.

¹⁰Shallum son of Jabesh made plans against Zechariah. He killed Zechariah in Ibleam. And Shallum became king in Zechariah's place. ¹¹The other acts of Zechariah are written down. They are in the book of the history of the kings of Israel. ¹²Now the Lord had told Jehu: "Your sons down to your great-great-grandchildren will be kings of Israel." And the Lord's word came true.

Shallum King of Israel

¹³Then Shallum son of Jabesh became king. This was during Uzziah's thirty-ninth year as king of Judah. Shallum ruled for a month in Samaria. ¹⁴Then Menahem son of Gadi came up from Tirzah to Samaria. He attacked Shallum son of Jabesh in Samaria. He killed him and became king in Shallum's place. ¹⁵The other acts of Shallum and his secret plans are written down. They are in the book of the history of the kings of Israel.

Menahem King of Israel

¹⁶Menahem started out from Tirzah and attacked Tiphsah. He destroyed the city and the area nearby. This was because the people had refused to open the city gate for him. So he defeated them and ripped open all their pregnant women. ¹⁷Menahem son of Gadi became king over Israel. This was during Azariah's thirty-ninth year as king of Judah. And Menahem ruled ten years in Samaria. ¹⁸He did what the Lord said was wrong. Jeroboam son of Nebat had caused Israel to sin. And all the time Menahem was king, he did not stop doing the same sins.

¹⁹Pul king of Assyria came to attack the land. Menahem gave him about 34 tons of silver. This was so Pul would support Menahem and make his hold on the kingdom stronger. ²⁰Menahem raised the money by taxing all the rich men of Israel. He taxed each man about 0.6 kilograms of silver. Then he gave the money to the king of Assyria. So the king of Assyria left and did not stay in the land.

²¹Everything else Menahem did is written down. It is in the book of the history of the kings of Israel. ²²Then Menahem died. And his son Pekahiah became king in his place.

Pekahiah King of Israel

²³Pekahiah son of Menahem became king over Israel in Samaria. This was during Azariah's fiftieth year as king of Judah. Pekahiah ruled two years. ²⁴He did what the Lord said was wrong. Jeroboam son of Nebat had caused Israel to sin. And Pekahiah did not stop doing the same sins. ²⁵Pekah son of Remaliah was one of Pekahiah's captains. He made plans against Pekahiah. He took 50 men of Gilead with him and killed Pekahiah. They killed him, Argob and Arieh in the palace at Samaria. Then Pekah became king in Pekahiah's place.

²⁶Everything else Pekahiah did is written down. It is in the book of the history of the kings of Israel.

Pekah King of Israel

²⁷Pekah son of Remaliah became king over Israel in Samaria. This was during Azariah's fifty-second year as king of Judah. And Pekah ruled 20 years. ²⁸He did what the Lord said was wrong. Jeroboam son of Nebat had caused Israel to sin. And Pekah did not stop doing the same sins. ²⁹Tiglath-Pileser, also called Pul, was king of Assyria. He attacked while Pekah was king of Israel. Tiglath-Pileser captured the cities of Ijon, Abel Beth Maacah, Janoah, Kedesh and Hazor. He also captured Gilead and Galilee. And he captured all the land of Naphtali. He sent the people from these places away to Assyr-

ia. ³⁰Then Hoshea son of Elah made plans against Pekah son of Remaliah. Hoshea attacked and killed Pekah. Then he became king in Pekah's place. This was during the twentieth year Jotham son of Uzziah was king. ³¹Everything else Pekah did is written down. It is in the book of the history of the kings of Israel.

Jotham King of Judah

³²Then Jotham son of Uzziah became king of Judah. This was during the second year Pekah son of Remaliah was king of Israel. ³³Jotham was 25 years old when he became king. He ruled 16 years in Jerusalem. His mother's name was Jerusha daughter of Zadok. ³⁴Jotham did what the Lord said was right. He obeyed God just as his father Uzziah had done. ³⁵But the places where false gods were worshipped were not removed. And the people still made sacrifices and burned incense*d* there. Jotham rebuilt the Upper Gate of the Temple*d* of the Lord. ³⁶The other things Jotham did while he was king are written down. They are in the book of the history of the kings of Judah. ³⁷At that time the Lord began to send Rezin king of Aram against Judah. He also sent Pekah son of Remaliah against them. ³⁸Jotham died and was buried with his ancestors in Jerusalem. It was the city of David, his ancestor. And Jotham's son Ahaz became king in his place.

Ahaz King of Judah

16 Ahaz was the son of Jotham king of Judah. Ahaz became king of Judah in the seventeenth year Pekah was king of Israel. Pekah was the son of Remaliah. ²Ahaz was 20 years old when he became king. He ruled 16 years in Jerusalem. He was not like his ancestor David. He did not do what the Lord his God said was right. ³Ahaz did the same things the kings of Israel had done. He even sacrificed his sons by burning them in the fire. He did the same hated sins as the other nations had done. And the Lord had forced these nations out of the land ahead of the Israelites. ⁴Ahaz offered sacrifices and burned incense*d* at the places where false gods were worshipped. And he did this on the hills and under every green tree.

⁵Rezin king of Aram and Pekah king of Israel came up to Jerusalem to attack it. (Pekah was the son of Remaliah.) They surrounded Ahaz but could not defeat him. ⁶At that time Rezin king of Aram took back the city of Elath for Aram. He forced out all the people of Judah. Then Edomites moved into Elath. And they still live there today.

⁷Ahaz sent messengers to Tiglath-Pileser king of Assyria. Ahaz said, "I am your servant. Come and save me from the king of Aram and the king of Israel. They are attacking me." ⁸Ahaz took the silver and gold that was in the Temple*d* of the Lord. He also took the treasuries of the palace. He sent these as a gift to the king of Assyria. ⁹So the king of Assyria listened to Ahaz. He attacked Damascus and captured it. Then he sent all the people of Damascus to Kir. And he killed Rezin.

¹⁰Then King Ahaz went to Damascus to meet Tiglath-Pileser king of Assyria. Ahaz saw an altar at Damascus. He sent plans and a pattern of this altar to Uriah the priest. ¹¹So Uriah the priest built an altar. It was just like the plans King Ahaz had sent him from Damascus. Uriah finished the altar before King Ahaz came back from Damascus. ¹²When the king arrived from Damascus, he saw the altar. He went near and offered sacrifices on it. ¹³He burned his burnt offerings and grain offerings. He poured out his drink offering. He also sprinkled the blood of his fellowship offerings on the altar.

¹⁴Ahaz moved the bronze altar that was before the Lord at the front of the Temple. It was between Ahaz's altar

and the Temple of the Lord. He put it on the north side of his altar. [15]King Ahaz gave a command to Uriah the priest. Ahaz said, "Burn the morning burnt offering and the evening grain offering on the large altar. Also offer the king's burnt offering and his grain offering. Offer the whole burnt offering for all the people of the land. And offer their grain offering and drink offering. Sprinkle on the altar all the blood of the burnt offering and of the sacrifice. But I will use the bronze altar to ask questions of God." [16]Uriah the priest did everything King Ahaz commanded him to do.

[17]Then King Ahaz took off the side panels from the bases. He took the washing bowls off the top of the bases. He also took the large bowl, which was called the Sea, off the bronze bulls that held it up. And he put it on a stone base. [18]Ahaz took away the platform for the royal throne. It had been built at the Temple. He also took away the outside entrance for the king. He did these things because of the king of Assyria.

[19]The other things Ahaz did as king are written down. They are in the book of the history of the kings of Judah. [20]Ahaz died and was buried with his ancestors in Jerusalem. Ahaz's son Hezekiah became king in his place.

Hoshea, Last King of Israel

17 Hoshea son of Elah became king over Israel. This was during Ahaz's twelfth year as king of Judah. Hoshea ruled in Samaria nine years. [2]He did what the Lord said was wrong. But he was not as bad as the kings of Israel who had ruled before him.

[3]Shalmaneser king of Assyria came to attack Hoshea. Hoshea had been Shalmaneser's servant. He had made the payments to Shalmaneser that he had demanded. [4]But the king of Assyria found out that Hoshea had made plans against him. Hoshea had sent messengers to So, the king of Egypt. And Hoshea had stopped giving Shalmaneser the payments he demanded. In the past Hoshea had paid him every year. So the king put Hoshea in prison. [5]Then the king of Assyria came and attacked all the land of Israel. He surrounded Samaria and attacked it for three years. [6]He defeated Samaria in the ninth year Hoshea was king. He took the Israelites away to Assyria. He settled some of them in Halah. Some were made to settle in Gozan on the Habor River. Others were settled in the cities of the Medes.

Israelites Punished for Sin

[7]All these things happened because the Israelites had sinned against the Lord their God. He had brought them out of Egypt. He had rescued them from the power of the king of Egypt. But the Israelites had honoured other gods. [8]They lived like the nations the Lord had forced out of the land ahead of them. They also lived as the evil kings had shown them. [9]They secretly sinned against the Lord their God. They built places in all their cities where false gods were worshipped. They built them everywhere from the watchtower to the strong, walled city. [10]They put up stone pillars for worshipping false gods. And they put up Asherah[d] idols on every high hill and under every green tree. [11]The Israelites burned incense[d] everywhere false gods were worshipped. The nations who lived there before them had done this. And the Lord had forced them out of the land. The Israelites did wicked things that made the Lord angry. [12]They served idols. And the Lord had said, "You must not do this." [13]The Lord used every prophet[d] and seer[d] to warn Israel and Judah. He said, "Stop your evil ways. Obey my commands and laws. Follow all the teachings that I commanded your ancestors to obey. I sent you this law through my servants the prophets."

¹⁴But the people would not listen. They were stubborn, just as their ancestors had been. Their ancestors did not believe in the Lord their God. ¹⁵They rejected the Lord's laws and the agreement he had made with their ancestors. And they refused to listen to his warnings. They worshipped useless idols and became useless themselves. They did what the nations around them did. And the Lord had warned them not to do this. ¹⁶The people disobeyed all the commands of the Lord their God. They made statues of two calves from melted metal. And they made an Asherah idol. They worshipped all the stars of heaven and served Baal.*d* ¹⁷They sacrificed their sons and daughters in the fire. And they tried to find out the future by magic and witchcraft.*d* They always chose to do what the Lord said was wrong. And this made him angry. ¹⁸So he was very angry with the people of Israel. He removed them from his presence. Only the tribe*d* of Judah was left.

Judah Is Also Guilty

¹⁹But even Judah did not obey the commands of the Lord their God. They did what the Israelites had done. ²⁰So the Lord rejected all the people of Israel. He punished them and let people destroy them. He threw them out of his presence. ²¹The Lord separated them from the family of David. And the Israelites made Jeroboam son of Nebat their king. Jeroboam led the Israelites away from following the Lord. He caused them to sin greatly. ²²So they continued to do all the sins Jeroboam did. They did not stop doing these sins ²³until the Lord removed the people from his presence. This was just as he had said he would do. He had said this through all his servants the prophets.*d* So the Israelites were taken out of their land to Assyria. And they have been there to this day.

The Beginning of the Samaritan People

²⁴The king of Assyria brought people from Babylon, Cuthah, Avva, Hamath and Sepharvaim. He put them in the cities of Samaria to replace the Israelites. These people took over Samaria and lived in the cities. ²⁵At first they did not worship the Lord. So he sent lions among them. The lions killed some of them. ²⁶The king of Assyria was told this. It was said, "You sent foreigners into the cities of Samaria. They do not know the law of the god of the land. This is why that land's god has sent lions among them. The lions are killing them because they don't know what the god wants." ²⁷Then the king of Assyria gave a command. He said, "You took Samaria's priests away. Send back one of the priests to live there. Let him teach them what the god wants." ²⁸So one of the priests who had been carried away from Samaria returned. He came to live in Bethel. And he taught the people how to worship the Lord.

²⁹But each nation made gods of its own. They put them in the cities where they lived. They put them in the temples where false gods were worshipped. These temples had been made by the Samaritans. ³⁰The men from Babylon made Succoth Benoth their god. The men from Cuthah worshipped Nergal. The men of Hamath worshipped Ashima. ³¹The Avvites worshipped Nibhaz and Tartak. And the Sepharvites burned their children in the fire. They sacrificed them to Adrammelech and Anammelech, the gods of Sepharvaim. ³²They also worshipped the Lord. But they chose priests for the places where false gods were worshipped. The priests were chosen from among themselves. And they made sacrifices for the people. ³³The people worshipped the Lord but also served their own gods. They served their gods as the nations did

from which they had been brought. [34]Even today they do as they did in the past. They do not worship the Lord. They do not obey his rules and commands. They do not obey the teachings or the commands of the Lord. He gave these commands to the children of Jacob, whom the Lord had named Israel. [35]The Lord had made an agreement with them. He had commanded them, "Do not worship other gods. Do not bow down to them or serve them. Do not give sacrifices to them. [36]Worship the Lord who brought you up out of the land of Egypt. He did it with great power and strength. Bow to the Lord and make sacrifices to him. [37]Obey the rules, orders and the teachings. Obey the commands the Lord wrote for you. Obey and always do them. Do not worship other gods. [38]Do not forget the agreement I made with you. And do not worship other gods. [39]Instead worship the Lord your God. He will save you from all your enemies."

[40]But the Israelites did not listen. They kept on doing the same things they had done before. [41]So these nations worshipped the Lord but served their idols. And their children and grandchildren still do as their ancestors did.

Hezekiah King of Judah

18 Hezekiah son of Ahaz king of Judah became king. This was during the third year Hoshea son of Elah was king of Israel. [2]Hezekiah was 25 years old when he became king. And he ruled 29 years in Jerusalem. His mother's name was Abijah daughter of Zechariah. [3]Hezekiah did what the Lord said was right. He did just as his ancestor David had done. [4]He removed the places where false gods were worshipped. He broke the stone pillars they worshipped. He cut down the Asherah[d] idols. Also the Israelites had been burning incense[d] to the bronze snake made by Moses. (It

was called Nehushtan.) But Hezekiah broke it into pieces.

[5]Hezekiah trusted in the Lord, the God of Israel. There was no one like him among all the kings of Judah. There was no king like him, before him or after him. [6]Hezekiah was loyal to the Lord. He did not stop following the Lord. He obeyed the commands the Lord had given Moses. [7]And the Lord was with Hezekiah. He had success in everything he did. He turned against the king of Assyria and stopped serving him. [8]Hezekiah defeated the Philistines all the way to Gaza and its borders. He defeated them everywhere, from the watchtower to the strong, walled city.

The Assyrians Capture Samaria

[9]Shalmaneser king of Assyria surrounded Samaria and attacked it. This was in the fourth year Hezekiah was king. And it was the seventh year Hoshea son of Elah was king of Israel. [10]After three years the Assyrians captured Samaria. This was in the sixth year Hezekiah was king. And it was Hoshea's ninth year as king of Israel. [11]The king of Assyria took the Israelites away to Assyria. He put them in Halah and in Gozan on the Habor River. He also put them in the cities of the Medes. [12]This happened because they did not obey the Lord their God. They broke his agreement. They did not obey all that Moses, the Lord's servant, had commanded. They would not listen to the commands or do them.

Assyria Attacks Judah

[13]During Hezekiah's fourteenth year as king, Sennacherib king of Assyria attacked Judah. He attacked all the strong, walled cities of Judah and defeated them. [14]Then Hezekiah king of Judah sent a message to the king of Assyria at Lachish. He said, "I have done wrong. Leave me alone. Then I will pay anything you demand of me."

So the king of Assyria told Hezekiah how much to pay. It was about 10 tons of silver and 1 ton of gold. [15]Hezekiah gave him all the silver that was in the Temple[d] of the Lord. And he gave him all the silver in the palace treasuries. [16]Hezekiah cut off all the gold that covered the doors of the Temple of the Lord. He also removed the gold from the doorposts. Hezekiah had put gold on these doors himself. He gave it all to the king of Assyria.

Assyria Troubles Hezekiah

[17]The king of Assyria sent out his supreme commander, his chief officer and his field commander. They went with a large army from Lachish to King Hezekiah in Jerusalem. When they came near the waterway from the upper pool, they stopped. The upper pool is on the road to the Washerman's Field. [18]They called for the king. So Eliakim, Shebna and Joah went out to meet them. Eliakim son of Hilkiah was the palace manager. Shebna was the royal assistant. And Joah son of Asaph was the recorder.

[19]The field commander said to them, "Tell Hezekiah this:

" 'The great king, the king of Assyria, says: You have nothing to trust in to help you. [20]You say you have battle plans and power for war. But your words mean nothing. Whom are you trusting for help so that you turn against me? [21]Look, you are depending on Egypt to help you. Egypt is like a splintered walking stick. If you lean on it for help, it will stab you and hurt you. The king of Egypt will hurt those who depend on him. [22]You might say, "We are depending on the Lord our God." But Hezekiah destroyed the Lord's altars and the places of worship. Hezekiah told Judah and Jerusalem, "You must worship only at this one altar in Jerusalem."

[23]" 'Now make an agreement with my master, the king of Assyria: I will give you 2,000 horses if you can find enough men to ride them. [24]You cannot defeat one of my master's least important officers. So why do you depend on Egypt to give you chariots and horsemen? [25]I have not come to attack and destroy this place without an order from the Lord. The Lord himself told me to come to this country and destroy it'."

[26]Then Eliakim son of Hilkiah, Shebna and Joah spoke to the field commander. They said, "Please speak to us in the Aramaic language. We understand it. Don't speak to us in Hebrew because the people on the city wall can hear you."

[27]But the commander said, "No. My master did not send me to tell these things only to you and your king. My master sent me to tell them also to those people sitting on the wall. They will have to eat their own dung and drink their own urine like you."

[28]Then the commander stood and shouted loudly in the Hebrew language. He said, "Listen to the word from the great king, the king of Assyria! [29]The king says you should not let Hezekiah fool you. Hezekiah can't save you from my power. [30]Don't let Hezekiah talk you into trusting the Lord. Hezekiah says, 'The Lord will surely save us. This city won't be given over to the king of Assyria'.

[31]"Don't listen to Hezekiah. The king of Assyria says, 'Make peace with me. Come out of the city to me. Then everyone will be free to eat the fruit from his own grapevine and fig tree. Everyone will be free to drink water from his own well. [32]Then I will come and take you to a land like your own. It is a land with grain and new wine. It has bread and vineyards. It is a land of olives and honey. Then you can choose to live and not to die!'

"Don't listen to Hezekiah. He is fooling you when he says, 'The Lord will save us'. [33]The god of any other nation has not saved his people from the power of the king of Assyria. [34]Where are the gods of Hamath and Arpad? Where are the gods of Sepharvaim, Hena and Ivvah? They did not save Samaria from my power. [35]Not one of all the gods of these countries has saved his people from me. Then the Lord cannot save Jerusalem from my power."

[36]The people were silent. They didn't answer the commander at all. This was because King Hezekiah had ordered, "Don't answer him."

[37]Then Eliakim, Shebna and Joah tore their clothes to show how upset they were. (Eliakim son of Hilkiah was the palace manager. Shebna was the royal assistant. And Joah son of Asaph was the recorder.) The three men went to Hezekiah and told him what the field commander had said.

Jerusalem Will Be Saved

19 When King Hezekiah heard the message, he tore his clothes. And he put on rough cloth to show how sad he was. Then he went into the Temple[d] of the Lord. [2]Hezekiah sent Eliakim, Shebna and the older priests to Isaiah. Eliakim was the palace manager, and Shebna was the royal assistant. The men were all wearing the rough cloth when they came to Isaiah. He was a prophet,[d] the son of Amoz. [3]These men told Isaiah, "This is what Hezekiah says: Today is a day of sorrow and punishment and disgrace. It is sad, as when a child should be born, but the mother is not strong enough to give birth to it. [4]The king of Assyria sent his field commander to make fun of the living God. Maybe the Lord your God will hear what the commander said. Maybe the Lord your God will punish him for what he said. So pray for the few people of Israel who are left alive."

[5]When Hezekiah's officers came to Isaiah, [6]he said to them, "Tell your master this: The Lord says, 'Don't be afraid of what you have heard. Don't be frightened by the words the servants of the king of Assyria said against me. [7]Listen! I am going to put a spirit in the king of Assyria. He will hear a report that will make him return to his own country. And I will cause him to die by the sword there'."

[8]The field commander heard that the king of Assyria had left Lachish. So the commander left and found the king fighting against the city of Libnah.

[9]The king received a report that Tirhakah was coming to attack him. Tirhakah was the Cushite king of Egypt. When the king of Assyria heard this, he sent messengers to Hezekiah. The king said: [10]"Say this to Hezekiah king of Judah: Don't be fooled by the god you trust. Don't believe him when he says Jerusalem will not be defeated by the king of Assyria. [11]You have heard what the kings of Assyria have done. They have completely defeated every country. Do not think you will be saved. [12]The gods of those people did not save them. My ancestors destroyed them. My ancestors defeated the cities of Gozan, Haran and Rezeph. They defeated the people of Eden living in Tel Assar. [13]Where are the kings of Hamath and Arpad? Where is the king of the city of Sepharvaim? Where are the kings of Hena and Ivvah?"

Hezekiah Prays to the Lord

[14]Hezekiah received the letter from the messengers and read it. Then he went up to the Temple[d] of the Lord. Hezekiah spread the letter out before the Lord. [15]And he prayed to the Lord: "Lord, God of Israel, your throne is between the gold creatures with wings! Only you are God of all the kingdoms of the earth. You made the heavens and the earth. [16]Hear, Lord, and listen. Open your eyes, Lord, and see. Listen to the word Sennacherib has said to insult the liv-

ing God. ¹⁷It is true, Lord. The kings of Assyria have destroyed these countries and their lands. ¹⁸These kings have thrown the gods of these nations into the fire. But they were only wood and rock statues that men made. So the kings have destroyed them. ¹⁹Now, Lord our God, save us from the king's power. Then all the kingdoms of the earth will know that you, Lord, are the only God."

God Answers Hezekiah

²⁰Then Isaiah son of Amoz sent a message to Hezekiah. Isaiah said, "The Lord, the God of Israel, says this: I have heard your prayer to me about Sennacherib king of Assyria. ²¹So this is what the Lord has said against Sennacherib:

'The people of Jerusalem
     hate you and make fun of you.
The people of Jerusalem
     laugh at you as you run away.
²²You have insulted me and spoken
          against me.
     You have raised your voice
          against me.
     You have a proud look on your
          face.
     You disobey me, the Holy One
          of Israel!
²³You have used your messengers
          to insult the Lord.
     You have said, "I have many
          chariots.
     With them I have gone to the tops
          of the mountains.
     I have climbed the highest
          mountains of Lebanon.
     I have cut down its tallest cedars.
     I have cut down its best pine
          trees.
     I have reached its farthest places.
     I have gone to its best forests.
²⁴I have dug wells in foreign
          countries.
     I have drunk water there.
     By the soles of my feet,
     I have dried up all the rivers of
          Egypt."

²⁵" 'King of Assyria, surely you
          have heard.
     Long ago I, the Lord, planned
          these things.
     Long ago I planned them.
     Now I have made them happen.
     I allowed you to turn those
          strong, walled cities
     into piles of rocks.
²⁶The people living in those cities
          were weak.
     They were frightened and put to
          shame.
     They were like grass in the field.
     They were like tender, young
          grass.
     They were like grass that grows
          on the housetop.
     It is burned by the wind before
          it can grow.

²⁷" 'I know when you rest and when
          you come and go.
     I know how you speak against
          me.
²⁸You speak strongly against me.
     And I have heard your proud
          words.
     So I will put my hook in your
          nose.
     And I will put my bit in your
          mouth.
     Then I will force you to leave my
          country
     the same way that you came'.

²⁹"Then the Lord said, 'Hezekiah, I will give you this sign:
     This year you will eat the grain
          that grows wild.
     And the second year you will eat
          what grows wild from that.
     But in the third year, plant grain
          and harvest it.
     Plant vineyards and eat their
          fruit.
³⁰Some of the people in the family
          of Judah
     will be saved.
     Like plants that take root,
     they will grow strong and have
          many children.

31A few people will come out of
Jerusalem alive.
There will be a few from Mount
Zion[d] who will live.
The strong love of the Lord of
heaven's armies
will cause this to happen'.

32"So this is what the Lord says
about the king of Assyria:
'He will not enter this city.
He will not even shoot an arrow
here.
He will not fight against it with
shields.
He will not build a ramp to
attack the city walls.
33He will return to his country the
same way he came.
He will not enter this city,'
says the Lord.
34The Lord says, 'I will defend and
save this city.
I will do this for myself and for
David, my servant'."

35That night the angel of the Lord
went out. He killed 185,000 men in
the Assyrian camp. The people got up
early the next morning. And they saw
all the dead bodies! 36So Sennacherib
king of Assyria took his men and left.
He went back to Nineveh and stayed
there. 37One day Sennacherib was worshipping in the temple of his god Nis-
roch. While he was there, his sons
Adrammelech and Sharezer killed him
with a sword. Then they escaped to
the land of Ararat. So Sennacherib's
son Esarhaddon became king of Assyria.

Hezekiah's Illness

20 At that time Hezekiah became
very sick. He was almost dead.
The prophet[d] Isaiah son of Amoz went
to see him. Isaiah told him, "This is
what the Lord says: You are going to
die. So you should give your last orders to everyone. You will not get
better."

2Hezekiah turned toward the wall
and prayed to the Lord. He said,
3"Lord, please remember that I have
always obeyed you. I have given myself completely to you. I have done
what you said was right." And Hezekiah cried loudly.

4Before Isaiah had left the middle
courtyard, the Lord spoke his word to
Isaiah: 5"Go back and tell Hezekiah,
the leader of my people: 'This is what
the Lord, the God of your ancestor
David, says: I have heard your
prayer. And I have seen your tears.
So I will heal you. Three days from
now you will go up to the Temple[d] of
the Lord. 6I will add 15 years to your
life. I will save you and this city from
the king of Assyria. And I will protect
the city for myself and for my servant
David'."

7Then Isaiah said, "Make a paste
from figs." So they made it and put it
on Hezekiah's boil. And he got better.

8Hezekiah asked Isaiah, "What will
be the sign that the Lord will heal me?
What is the sign that I will go up to the
Temple[d] of the Lord on the third
day?"

9Isaiah said, "The Lord will do what
he says. This is the sign from the Lord
to show you: Do you want the shadow
to go forward ten steps? Or do you
want it to go back ten steps?"

10Hezekiah answered, "It's easy for
the shadow to go forward ten steps.
Instead, let it go back ten steps."

11Then Isaiah the prophet called to
the Lord. And the Lord brought the
shadow back ten steps. It went back
up the stairway of Ahaz that it had
gone down.

Messengers from Babylon

12At that time Merodach-Baladan,
son of Baladan, was king of Babylon.
He sent letters and a gift to Hezekiah.
He did this because he had heard that
Hezekiah had been sick. 13Hezekiah
was happy to see the messengers. So
he showed them what was in his

storehouses: the silver, gold, spices and expensive perfumes. He showed them his swords and shields. He showed them all his wealth. He showed them everything in his palace and his kingdom.

¹⁴Then Isaiah the prophet*d* went to King Hezekiah. Isaiah asked him, "What did these men say? Where did they come from?"

Hezekiah said, "They came from a faraway country. They came to me from Babylon."

¹⁵So Isaiah asked him, "What did they see in your palace?"

Hezekiah said, "They saw everything in my palace. I showed them all my wealth."

¹⁶Then Isaiah said to Hezekiah, "Listen to the words of the Lord: ¹⁷'In the future everything in your palace will be taken away to Babylon. Everything your ancestors have stored up until this day will be taken away. Nothing will be left,' says the Lord. ¹⁸'Some of your own children will be taken away. Those who will be born to you will be taken away. And they will become eunuchs*d* in the palace of the king of Babylon'."

¹⁹Hezekiah told Isaiah, "These words from the Lord are good." He said this because he thought, "There will be peace and security while I am king."

²⁰Everything else Hezekiah did is written down. All his victories are written down. And his work on the tunnel and the pool is recorded. (These were for bringing water into the city.) They are all written in the book of the history of the kings of Judah. ²¹Then Hezekiah died. And his son Manasseh became king in his place.

Manasseh King of Judah

21 Manasseh was 12 years old when he became king. And he was king 55 years in Jerusalem. His mother's name was Hephzibah. ²He did what the Lord said was wrong. He did the hated things the other nations had done. And the Lord had forced these nations out of the land ahead of the Israelites. ³Manasseh's father, Hezekiah, had destroyed the places where false gods were worshipped. But Manasseh rebuilt them. He built altars for Baal.*d* And he made an Asherah*d* idol as Ahab king of Israel had done. Manasseh worshipped all the stars of heaven and served them. ⁴The Lord had said about the Temple,*d* "I will be worshipped in Jerusalem." But Manasseh built altars in the Temple of the Lord. ⁵He built altars to worship the stars in the two courtyards of the Temple of the Lord. ⁶He burned his own son as a sacrifice. He practised magic and told the future by explaining signs and dreams. He got advice from mediums*d* and fortunetellers. He did many things that the Lord said were wrong. And this made the Lord angry.

⁷Manasseh carved an Asherah idol and put it in the Temple. The Lord had spoken to David and his son Solomon about the Temple. He had said, "I will be worshipped in this Temple and in Jerusalem for ever. I have chosen Jerusalem from all the tribes*d* of Israel. ⁸I will never again make the Israelites wander out of the land I gave their ancestors. But they must obey everything I have commanded them. And they must obey all the teachings my servant Moses gave them." ⁹But the people did not listen. Manasseh led them to do wrong. They did more evil than the nations the Lord had destroyed ahead of the Israelites.

¹⁰The Lord spoke through his servants the prophets.*d* He said, ¹¹"Manasseh king of Judah has done these hated things. He has done more evil than the Amorites before him. Manasseh also has caused Judah to sin with his idols. ¹²So this is what the Lord, the God of Israel, says: 'I will bring much trouble on Jerusalem and Judah.

Anyone who hears about it will be shocked. [13]I will stretch the measuring line of Samaria over Jerusalem. And the plumb line[d] used against Ahab's family will be used on Jerusalem. I will wipe out Jerusalem as a man wipes a dish. He wipes it and turns it upside down. [14]I will go away from the rest of my people who are left. I will give them to their enemies. They will be robbed by all their enemies. [15]My people did what I said was wrong. They have made me angry from the day their ancestors left Egypt until now'."

[16]Manasseh also killed many innocent people. He filled Jerusalem from one end to the other with their blood. This was besides the sin he caused Judah to do. He caused Judah to do what the Lord said was wrong.

[17]The other things Manasseh did as king are written down, even the sin he did. They are in the book of the history of the kings of Judah. [18]Manasseh died and was buried in the garden of his own palace. It is the garden of Uzza. Then Manasseh's son Amon became king in his place.

Amon King of Judah

[19]Amon was 22 years old when he became king. He was king for two years in Jerusalem. His mother's name was Meshullemeth daughter of Haruz. She was from Jotbah. [20]Amon did what the Lord said was wrong. He did as his father Manasseh had done. [21]Amon lived in the same way his father had lived. He worshipped the idols his father had worshipped. And he bowed down before them. [22]Amon rejected the Lord, the God of his ancestors. He did not follow the ways of the Lord.

[23]Amon's officers made plans against him and killed him in his palace. [24]Then the people of Judah killed all those who had made plans to kill King Amon. And they made his son Josiah king in his place.

[25]Everything else Amon did is written down. It is in the book of the history of the kings of Judah. [26]He was buried in his grave in the garden of Uzza. And his son Josiah became king in his place.

Josiah King of Judah

22 Josiah was eight years old when he became king. He ruled 31 years in Jerusalem. His mother's name was Jedidah daughter of Adaiah. Adaiah was from Bozkath. [2]Josiah did what the Lord said was right. He did good things as his ancestor David had done. Josiah did not stop doing what was right.

[3]In Josiah's eighteenth year as king, he sent Shaphan to the Temple[d] of the Lord. Shaphan was the son of Azaliah, who was the son of Meshullam. Shaphan was the royal assistant. Josiah said, [4]"Go up to Hilkiah the high priest. Have him empty out the money the gatekeepers have gathered from the people. This is the money they have brought into the Temple of the Lord. [5]Have him give the money to the supervisors of the work on the Temple. They must pay the men who work to repair the Temple of the Lord. [6]The workers are carpenters, builders and stoneworkers. Also use the money to buy timber and cut stone to repair the Temple. [7]They do not need to report how they use the money given to them. They are working honestly."

The Book of the Law Is Found

[8]Hilkiah the high priest said to Shaphan the royal assistant, "I've found the Book of the Teachings. It was in the Temple[d] of the Lord." He gave it to Shaphan, who read it.

[9]Then Shaphan the royal assistant went to the king and reported to Josiah, "Your officers have paid out the money that was in the Temple of the Lord. They have given it to the workers and supervisors at the Temple."

[10]Then Shaphan the royal assistant told the king, "Hilkiah the priest has given me a book." And Shaphan read from the book to the king.

[11]The king heard the words of the Book of the Teachings. Then he tore his clothes to show how upset he was. [12]He gave these orders to Hilkiah the priest and Ahikam son of Shaphan. He also gave them to Acbor son of Micaiah, Shaphan and Asaiah. Shaphan was the royal assistant. And Asaiah was the king's servant. These were the orders: [13]"Go and ask the Lord about the words in the book that has been found. Ask for me and for all the people and for all Judah. The Lord's anger is burning against us because our ancestors did not obey the words of this book. They did not do all the things written for us to do!"

[14]So Hilkiah the priest, Ahikam, Acbor, Shaphan and Asaiah left. They went to talk to Huldah the prophetess.[d] She was the wife of Shallum son of Tikvah, the son of Harhas. Harhas took care of the king's clothes. Huldah lived in Jerusalem, in the new area of the city.

[15]She said to them, "This is what the Lord, the God of Israel, says: tell the man who sent you to me, [16]'This is what the Lord says: I will bring trouble to this place and to the people living here. It is in the words of the book which the king of Judah has read. [17]The people of Judah have left me. They have burned incense[d] to other gods. They have made me angry by all the idols they have made. My anger burns against this place like a fire. It will not be put out'. [18]Tell the king of Judah, who sent you to ask the Lord, 'This is what the Lord, the God of Israel, says about the words you heard: [19]You heard my words against this place and its people. You became sorry in the Lord's presence for what you had done. I said they would become cursed and would be destroyed. Then you tore your clothes to show how up-

set you were. And you cried in my presence. This is why I have heard you, says the Lord. [20]So I will cause you to die. You will be buried in peace. You won't see all the trouble I will bring to this place'."

So they took her message back to the king.

The People Hear the Law

23 Then the king gathered all the older leaders of Judah and Jerusalem together. [2]He went up to the Temple[d] of the Lord. All the men from Judah and Jerusalem went with him. The priests, prophets[d] and all the people—from the least important to the most important—went with him. He read to them all the words of the Book of the Agreement. That book was found in the Temple of the Lord. [3]The king stood by the pillar. He made an agreement in the presence of the Lord. He agreed to follow the Lord and obey his commands, rules and laws with his whole being. He agreed to do what was written in this book. Then all the people promised to obey the agreement.

Josiah Destroys the Places for Idol Worship

[4]The king gave a command to Hilkiah the high priest. He also gave it to the priests of the next rank and the gatekeepers. He told them to bring out of the Temple of the Lord everything made for Baal,[d] Asherah[d] and all the stars of heaven. Then Josiah burned them outside Jerusalem in the fields of the Kidron Valley. And he carried the ashes to Bethel. [5]The kings of Judah had chosen priests for these gods. These priests burned incense[d] on the places where false gods were worshipped. These places were in the cities of Judah and the towns around Jerusalem. The priests burned incense to Baal, the sun and the moon. And they burned incense to the planets and all the stars of heaven.

But Josiah took those priests away. [6]He removed the Asherah idol from the Temple of the Lord. He took it outside Jerusalem to the Kidron Valley. There he burned it and beat it into dust. And he threw the dust on the graves of the common people. [7]Then he tore down the houses of the male prostitutes[d] who were in the Temple of the Lord. This was where the women did weaving for Asherah.

[8]King Josiah brought all the false priests from the cities of Judah. He made the places where false gods were worshipped impure. This is where the priests had burned incense. These places of worship were everywhere, from Geba to Beersheba. He destroyed the places of worship at the entrance to the Gate of Joshua. (Joshua was the ruler of the city.) This gate was on the left side of the city gate. [9]The priests at the places where false gods were worshipped were not allowed to serve at the Lord's altar in Jerusalem. But they could eat bread made without yeast with their brothers.

[10]Topheth was in the Valley of Ben Hinnom. Josiah made it impure so no one could sacrifice his son or daughter to Molech.[d] [11]Judah's kings had placed horses at the front door of the Temple of the Lord. This was in the courtyard near the room of Nathan-Melech, an officer. These horses were for the worship of the sun. But Josiah removed them. Then he burned the chariots that were for sun worship. [12]The kings of Judah had also built altars on the roof[n] of the upstairs room of Ahaz. Josiah broke down these altars. He also broke down the altars Manasseh had made. These were in the two courtyards of the Temple of the Lord. He smashed

them to pieces. Then he threw their dust into the Kidron Valley. [13]King Josiah made impure the places east of Jerusalem where false gods were worshipped. These were south of the Mount of Olives.[n] Solomon king of Israel had built these places. One was for Ashtoreth,[d] the hated goddess of the Sidonians. One was for Chemosh,[d] the hated god of Moab. And one was for Molech, the hated god of the Ammonites. [14]Josiah smashed into pieces the stone pillars they worshipped. He cut down the Asherah idols. And he covered the places with human bones.

[15]Josiah also broke down the altar at Bethel. This was the place of worship Jeroboam son of Nebat had made. Jeroboam had caused Israel to sin. Josiah burned that place. He broke the stones of the altar to pieces. Then he beat them into dust. And he burned the Asherah idol. [16]When he turned around, he saw the graves on the mountain. He had the bones taken from the graves. Then he burned the bones on the altar to make it impure. This happened as the Lord had said it would through the man of God.

[17]Josiah asked, "What is that monument to the dead I see?"

The people of the city answered, "It's the grave of the man of God who came from Judah. This prophet announced the things you have done against the altar of Bethel."

[18]Josiah said, "Leave the grave alone. No person may move this man's bones." So they left his bones. And they left the bones of the prophet who had come from Samaria.

[19]The kings of Israel had built temples for worshipping false gods in the cities of Samaria. That had caused the Lord to be angry. Josiah removed all

---

roof In Bible times houses were built with flat roofs. The roof was used for drying things such as flax and fruit. It was also used as an extra room, as a place for worship and as a place to sleep in the summer.

Mount of Olives Literally, "The Mountain of Ruin".

those temples. He did the same things as he had done at Bethel. [20]Josiah killed all the priests of those places of worship. He killed them on the altars. And he burned human bones on the altars. Then he went back to Jerusalem.

The Passover Is Brought Back

[21]The king gave a command to all the people. He said, "Celebrate the Passover[d] to the Lord your God. Do it as it is written in this Book of the Agreement." [22]No Passover like this one had been celebrated since the judges led Israel. Nor had one like it happened while there were kings of Israel and kings of Judah. [23]This Passover was celebrated to the Lord in Jerusalem. It was the eighteenth year of King Josiah's rule.

[24]Josiah destroyed the mediums,[d] fortune-tellers, house gods and idols. He destroyed all the hated gods seen in the land of Judah and Jerusalem. He did this to obey the words of the teachings. They were written in the book Hilkiah the priest had found in the Temple[d] of the Lord. [25]There was no king like Josiah before or after him. He obeyed the Lord with all his heart, soul and strength. He followed all the Teachings of Moses.

[26]Even so, the Lord did not stop his strong and terrible anger. His anger burned against Judah. It was because of all that Manasseh had done to make him angry. [27]The Lord said, "I have taken Israel away. I will do the same to Judah. I will take them out of my sight. I will reject Jerusalem which I chose. I will take away the Temple about which I said, 'I will be honoured there'."

[28]Everything else Josiah did is written down. It is in the book of the history of the kings of Judah.

[29]While Josiah was king, Neco king of Egypt went to help the king of Assyria. Neco was at the Euphrates River. King Josiah marched out to fight against Neco. But at Megiddo, Neco faced Josiah and killed him. [30]Josiah's servants carried his body in a chariot from Megiddo. They brought him to Jerusalem and buried him in his own grave. Then the people of Judah chose Josiah's son Jehoahaz. They poured olive oil on him to appoint him king in his father's place.

Jehoahaz King of Judah

[31]Jehoahaz was 23 years old when he became king. And he was king in Jerusalem for three months. His mother's name was Hamutal. She was the daughter of Jeremiah from Libnah. [32]Jehoahaz did what the Lord said was wrong. He did just as his ancestors had done.

[33]King Neco took Jehoahaz prisoner at Riblah in the land of Hamath. He did this so Jehoahaz could not rule in Jerusalem. Neco made the people of Judah pay about 3.4 tons of silver and about 34 kilograms of gold.

[34]King Neco made Josiah's son Eliakim the king in place of Josiah his father. Then Neco changed Eliakim's name to Jehoiakim. But Neco took Jehoahaz to Egypt, and he died there. [35]Jehoiakim gave King Neco the silver and gold he demanded. But Jehoiakim taxed the land so he could pay the king. He took silver and gold from the people of the land. The amount he took from each person depended on how much he had.

Jehoiakim King of Judah

[36]Jehoiakim was 25 years old when he became king. He was king in Jerusalem for 11 years. His mother's name was Zebidah daughter of Pedaiah. She was from Rumah. [37]Jehoiakim did what the Lord said was wrong, just as his ancestors had done.

24 While Jehoiakim was king, Nebuchadnezzar king of Babylon attacked the land of Judah. So Jehoiakim became Nebuchadnezzar's servant for three years. Then Jehoiakim turned against Nebuchadnezzar. And he broke away from his rule. [2]The Lord sent men from Babylon, Aram, Moab and Ammon against Jehoiakim. He sent them to destroy Judah. This happened the way the Lord had said it would through his servants the prophets.[d]

[3]The Lord commanded this to happen to the people of Judah. He did it to remove them from his presence. This was because of all the sins Manasseh had done. [4]He had killed many innocent people. He had filled Jerusalem with their blood. And the Lord would not forgive these sins.

[5]The other things that happened while Jehoiakim was king and all that he did are written down. They are in the book of the history of the kings of Judah. [6]Jehoiakim died, and his son Jehoiachin became king in his place.

[7]The king of Egypt did not come out of his land again. This was because of the king of Babylon. He had captured all that belonged to the king of Egypt. He took all the land from the brook of Egypt to the Euphrates River.

Jehoiachin King of Judah

[8]Jehoiachin was 18 years old when he became king. He was king three months in Jerusalem. His mother's name was Nehushta daughter of Elnathan. She was from Jerusalem. [9]Jehoiachin did what the Lord said was wrong, just as his father had done.

[10]At that time the officers of Nebuchadnezzar king of Babylon came up to Jerusalem. They surrounded the city and attacked it. [11]Nebuchadnezzar himself came to the city while his officers were attacking it. [12]Jehoiachin king of Judah surrendered to the king of Babylon. Jehoiachin's mother, servants, leaders and officers also surrendered. Then the king of Babylon made Jehoiachin a prisoner. This was

in the eighth year Nebuchadnezzar was king. [13]Nebuchadnezzar took all the treasures from the Temple[d] of the Lord. He also removed the treasures from the palace. He took all the gold objects Solomon king of Israel had made for the Temple. This happened as the Lord had said it would. [14]Nebuchadnezzar took away all the people of Jerusalem. This included all the leaders and all the wealthy people. He also took all the craftsmen and metal workers. There were 10,000 prisoners in all. Only the poorest people in the land were left. [15]Nebuchadnezzar carried away Jehoiachin to Babylon. He took the king's mother and his wives. He also took the officers and leading men of the land. They were taken captive from Jerusalem to Babylon. [16]The king of Babylon also took all 7,000 soldiers. These men were all strong and able to fight in war. And 1,000 craftsmen and metal workers were taken, too. Nebuchadnezzar took them as prisoners to Babylon. [17]He made Mattaniah king in Jehoiachin's place. Mattaniah was Jehoiachin's uncle. He also changed Mattaniah's name to Zedekiah.

Zedekiah King of Judah

[18]Zedekiah was 21 years old when he became king. And he was king in Jerusalem for 11 years. His mother's name was Hamutal daughter of Jeremiah.[n] She was from Libnah. [19]Zedekiah did what the Lord said was wrong, just as Jehoiakim had done. [20]All this happened in Jerusalem and Judah because the Lord was angry with them. Finally, he threw them out of his presence.

The Fall of Jerusalem

Zedekiah turned against the king of Babylon.

25 Then Nebuchadnezzar king of Babylon marched against Jeru-

Jeremiah This is not the prophet Jeremiah, but a different man with the same name.

salem with his whole army. This happened during Zedekiah's ninth year, tenth month and tenth day as king. He made a camp around the city. Then he built devices all around the city walls to attack it. ²The city was under attack until Zedekiah's eleventh year as king. ³By the ninth day of the fourth month, the hunger was terrible in the city. There was no food for the people to eat. ⁴Then the city wall was broken through. And the whole army ran away at night. They went through the gate between the two walls by the king's garden. The Babylonians were still surrounding the city. Zedekiah and his men ran towards the Jordan Valley. ⁵But the Babylonian army chased King Zedekiah. They caught up with him in the plains of Jericho. All of his army was scattered from him. ⁶So they captured Zedekiah and took him to the king of Babylon at Riblah. There he passed sentence on Zedekiah. ⁷They killed Zedekiah's sons as he watched. Then they put out his eyes. They put bronze chains on him and took him to Babylon.

⁸Nebuzaradan was the commander of the king's special guards. This officer of the king of Babylon came to Jerusalem. This was on the seventh day of the fifth month. This was in Nebuchadnezzar's nineteenth year as king of Babylon. ⁹Nebuzaradan set fire to the Temple*d* of the Lord and the palace. He also set fire to all the houses of Jerusalem. Every important building was burned.

¹⁰The whole Babylonian army broke down the walls around Jerusalem. That army was led by the commander of the king's special guards. ¹¹Nebuzaradan, the commander of the guards, took captive the people left in Jerusalem. And he took captive those who had surrendered to the king of Babylon. The rest of the people were also taken away. ¹²But the commander left behind some of the poorest

people of the land. They were to take care of the vineyards and fields.

¹³The Babylonians broke up the bronze pillars, the bronze stands and the large bronze bowl, which was called the Sea. These were in the Temple of the Lord. Then they carried the bronze to Babylon. ¹⁴They also took the pots, shovels, wick trimmers, dishes and all the bronze objects. These were used to serve in the Temple. ¹⁵The commander of the king's special guards took away the pans for carrying hot coals. He also took the bowls and everything made of pure gold or silver. ¹⁶There was so much bronze that it could not be weighed. There were two pillars and the large bronze bowl. There were also the movable stands which Solomon had made for the Temple of the Lord. ¹⁷Each pillar was about 8.2 metres high. The bronze capital*d* on top of the pillar was about 1.4 metres high. It was decorated with a net design and bronze pomegranates*d* all around it. The other pillar also had a net design. It was like the first pillar.

Judah Is Taken Prisoner

¹⁸The commander of the guards took some prisoners. He took Seraiah the chief priest, Zephaniah the priest next in rank, and the three doorkeepers. ¹⁹The commander also took other people who were still in the city. He took the officer in charge of the fighting men. He also took five people who advised the king. And he took the royal assistant who selected people for the army. And he took 60 other men who were in the city. ²⁰Nebuzaradan, the commander, took all these people. And he brought them to the king of Babylon at Riblah. ²¹There at Riblah, in the land of Hamath, the king had them killed. So the people of Judah were led away from their country as captives.

Gedaliah Becomes Governor

[22]Nebuchadnezzar king of Babylon left some people in the land of Judah. He appointed Gedaliah son of Ahikam as governor. (Ahikam was the son of Shaphan.)

[23]The army captains and their men heard that the king of Babylon had made Gedaliah governor. So they all came to Gedaliah at Mizpah. They were Ishmael son of Nethaniah and Johanan son of Kareah. Also there were Seraiah son of Tanhumeth the Netophathite, Jaazaniah son of the Maacathite and their men. [24]Then Gedaliah made promises to these army captains and their men. He said, "Don't be afraid of the Babylonian officers. Live in the land and serve the king of Babylon. Then everything will go well for you."

[25]Ishmael was the son of Nethaniah. Nethaniah was the son of Elishama from the king's family. In the seventh month Ishmael came with ten men and killed Gedaliah. They also killed the men of Judah and Babylon who were with Gedaliah at Mizpah. [26]Then all the people, from the least important to the most important, ran away to Egypt. The army leaders also went. This was because they were afraid of the Babylonians.

Jehoiachin Is Set Free

[27]Jehoiachin king of Judah was held in Babylon for 37 years. In the thirty-seventh year Evil-Merodach became king of Babylon. He let Jehoiachin out of prison on the twenty-seventh day of the twelfth month. [28]Evil-Merodach spoke kindly to Jehoiachin. He gave Jehoiachin a seat of honour. It was above the seats of the other kings who were with him in Babylon. [29]So Jehoiachin put away his prison clothes. For the rest of his life, he ate at the king's table. [30]Every day the king gave Jehoiachin an allowance. This lasted as long as he lived.

1 CHRONICLES

Israel's History from Adam to David

From Adam to Abraham

1 Adam was the father of Seth. Seth was the father of Enosh. Enosh was the father of Kenan. ²Kenan was the father of Mahalalel. Mahalalel was the father of Jared. Jared was the father of Enoch. ³Enoch was the father of Methuselah. Methuselah was the father of Lamech. And he was the father of Noah.

⁴The sons of Noah were Shem, Ham and Japheth.

⁵Japheth's sons were Gomer, Magog, Madai, Javan, Tubal, Meshech and Tiras.

⁶Gomer's sons were Ashkenaz, Riphath and Togarmah.

⁷Javan's sons were Elishah, Tarshish, Kittim[n] and Rodanim.

⁸Ham's sons were Cush, Mizraim,[n] Put and Canaan.

⁹Cush's sons were Seba, Havilah, Sabta, Raamah and Sabteca.

Raamah's sons were Sheba and Dedan.

¹⁰Cush was the father of Nimrod. Nimrod grew up to become a mighty warrior on the earth.

¹¹Mizraim was the father of the people living in Lud, Anam, Lehab and Naphtuhim.

¹²Mizraim was also the father of the people living in Pathrus, Casluh and Crete. (The Philistine people came from Casluh.)

¹³Canaan's first child was Sidon. Canaan was also the father of the Hittites, ¹⁴Jebusites, Amorites and the Girgashites. ¹⁵He was the father of the Hivites, Arkites, Sinites, ¹⁶Arvadites, Zemarites and the Hamathites.

¹⁷Shem's sons were Elam, Asshur, Arphaxad, Lud and Aram.

Aram's sons were Uz, Hul, Gether and Meshech.

¹⁸Arphaxad was the father of Shelah. Shelah was the father of Eber.

¹⁹Eber had two sons. One son was named Peleg.[n] He was named this because the people on the earth were divided into different languages during his life. Peleg's brother was named Joktan.

²⁰Joktan was the father of Almodad, Sheleph, Hazarmaveth, Jerah, ²¹Hadoram, Uzal and Diklah. ²²He was also the father of Obal, Abimael, Sheba, ²³Ophir, Havilah and Jobab. All these were Joktan's sons. ²⁴The family line went from Shem to Abraham. It included Shem, Arphaxad, Shelah, ²⁵Eber, Peleg, Reu, ²⁶Serug, Nahor, Terah ²⁷and Abram, who is called Abraham.

Abraham's Family

²⁸Abraham's sons were Isaac and Ishmael.

²⁹These were the sons of Isaac and Ishmael. Ishmael's first son was Nebaioth. Ishmael's other sons were Kedar, Adbeel, Mibsam, ³⁰Mishma, Dumah, Massa, Hadad, Tema, ³¹Jetur, Naphish and Kedemah. These were Ishmael's sons. ³²Keturah was Abraham's slave woman.[d] She gave birth to Zimran, Jokshan, Medan, Midian, Ishbak and Shuah.

Kittim His descendants were the people of Cyprus.
Mizraim This is another name for Egypt.
Peleg This name sounds like the Hebrew word for "divided".

Jokshan's sons were Sheba and Dedan.

³³Midian's sons were Ephah, Epher, Hanoch, Abida and Eldaah. All these people were descendants^d of Keturah.

³⁴Abraham was the father of Isaac. Isaac's sons were Esau and Israel. ³⁵Esau's sons were Eliphaz, Reuel, Jeush, Jalam and Korah.

³⁶Eliphaz's sons were Teman, Omar, Zepho, Gatam, Kenaz, Timna and Amalek.

³⁷Reuel's sons were Nahath, Zerah, Shammah and Mizzah.

The Edomites from Seir

³⁸Seir's sons were Lotan, Shobal, Zibeon, Anah, Dishon, Ezer and Dishan.

³⁹Lotan's sons were Hori and Homam. Lotan had a sister named Timna.

⁴⁰Shobal's sons were Alvan, Manahath, Ebal, Shepho and Onam. Zibeon's sons were Aiah and Anah. ⁴¹Anah's son was Dishon.

Dishon's sons were Hemdan, Eshban, Ithran and Keran.

⁴²Ezer's sons were Bilhan, Zaavan and Akan.

Dishan's sons were Uz and Aran.

The Kings of Edom

⁴³There were kings ruling in Edom before there were kings in Israel. Bela son of Beor was king of Edom. Bela's city was named Dinhabah.

⁴⁴When Bela died, Jobab son of Zerah became king. Jobab was from Bozrah.

⁴⁵When Jobab died, Husham became king. He was from Teman.

⁴⁶When Husham died, Hadad son of Bedad became king. Hadad's city was named Avith. Hadad defeated Midian in the country of Moab.

⁴⁷When Hadad died, Samlah became king. He was from Masrekah.

⁴⁸When Samlah died, Shaul became king. He was from Rehoboth by the River.

⁴⁹When Shaul died, Baal-Hanan son of Acbor became king.

⁵⁰When Baal-Hanan died, Hadad became king. Hadad's city was named Pau. Hadad's wife was named Mehetabel, and she was Matred's daughter. Matred was the daughter of Me-Zahab. ⁵¹Then Hadad died.

The leaders of the family groups of Edom were Timna, Alvah, Jetheth, ⁵²Oholibamah, Elah, Pinon, ⁵³Kenaz, Teman, Mibzar, ⁵⁴Magdiel and Iram. These were the leaders of Edom.

Israel's Family

2 The sons of Israel, also called Jacob, were Reuben, Simeon, Levi, Judah, Issachar, Zebulun, ²Dan, Joseph, Benjamin, Naphtali, Gad and Asher.

Judah's Family

³Judah's sons were Er, Onan and Shelah. A Canaanite woman, the daughter of Shua, was their mother. Judah's first son, Er, did what the Lord said was wicked. So the Lord put him to death. ⁴Judah's daughter-in-law Tamar gave birth to Perez and Zerah. Judah was the father. So Judah had five sons.

⁵Perez's sons were Hezron and Hamul.

⁶Zerah had five sons. They were Zimri, Ethan, Heman, Calcol and Darda.

⁷Carmi's son was Achan. He caused trouble for Israel because he took things that had been given to the Lord to be destroyed.

⁸Ethan's son was Azariah.

⁹Hezron's sons were Jerahmeel, Ram and Caleb.

¹⁰Ram was Amminadab's father. And Amminadab was Nahshon's father. Nahshon was the leader of the people of Judah. ¹¹Nahshon was the father of Salmon. Salmon was the father of

Boaz. [12]Boaz was the father of Obed. Obed was the father of Jesse. [13]Jesse's first son was Eliab. His second son was Abinadab. His third son was Shimea. [14]His fourth son was Nethanel. His fifth son was Raddai. [15]Jesse's sixth son was Ozem, and his seventh son was David. [16]Their sisters were Zeruiah and Abigail. Zeruiah's three sons were Abishai, Joab and Asahel. [17]Abigail was the mother of Amasa. Amasa's father was an Ishmaelite named Jether.

Caleb's Family

[18]Caleb son of Hezron had children by his wife Azubah and by Jerioth. Caleb and Azubah's sons were Jesher, Shobab and Ardon. [19]When Azubah died, Caleb married Ephrath. They had a son named Hur. [20]Hur was the father of Uri. Uri was the father of Bezalel.

[21]Later, when Hezron was 60 years old, he married the daughter of Makir. Makir was Gilead's father. Hezron had sexual relations with Makir's daughter, and she had a son named Segub. [22]Segub was the father of Jair. Jair controlled 23 cities in the country of Gilead. [23](But Geshur and Aram captured the towns of Jair. They also captured Kenath and the small towns around it. There were 60 towns in all.) All these were descendants[d] of Makir, the father of Gilead.

[24]After Hezron died in Caleb Ephrathah, his wife Abijah had his son. He was named Ashur. Ashur became the father of Tekoa.

Jerahmeel's Family

[25]Jerahmeel was Hezron's first son. Jerahmeel's sons were Ram, Bunah, Oren, Ozem and Ahijah. Ram was Jerahmeel's first son. [26]Jerahmeel had another wife, who was named Atarah. She was the mother of Onam.

[27]Jerahmeel's first son, Ram, had sons. They were Maaz, Jamin and Eker.

[28]Onam's sons were Shammai and Jada.

Shammai's sons were Nadab and Abishur.

[29]Abishur's wife was named Abihail. Abishur and Abihail's sons were Ahban and Molid.

[30]Nadab's sons were Seled and Appaim. Seled died without having children.

[31]Appaim's son was Ishi. Ishi was the father of Sheshan.

Sheshan was the father of Ahlai.

[32]Jada was Shammai's brother. Jada's sons were Jether and Jonathan. Jether died without having children.

[33]Jonathan's sons were Peleth and Zaza.

These were Jerahmeel's descendants.[d]

[34]Sheshan did not have any sons, only daughters. He had a servant from Egypt named Jarha. [35]Sheshan let his daughter marry his servant Jarha. Then she had a son named Attai.

[36]Attai was the father of Nathan. Nathan was the father of Zabad. [37]Zabad was the father of Ephlal. Ephlal was the father of Obed. [38]Obed was the father of Jehu. Jehu was the father of Azariah. [39]Azariah was the father of Helez. Helez was the father of Eleasah. [40]Eleasah was the father of Sismai. Sismai was the father of Shallum. [41]Shallum was the father of Jekamiah. And Jekamiah was the father of Elishama.

Caleb's Family

[42]Caleb was Jerahmeel's brother. Caleb's first son was Mesha. Mesha was the father of Ziph. And his son Mareshah was the father of Hebron.

[43]Hebron's sons were Korah, Tappuah, Rekem and Shema. [44]Shema was the father of Raham. Raham was the father of Jorkeam. Rekem was the father of Shammai. [45]Shammai's son was Maon. Maon was the father of Beth Zur.

[46]Caleb's slave woman[d] was named

Ephah. She was the mother of Haran, Moza and Gazez. Haran was the father of Gazez. 47Jahdai's sons were Regem, Jotham, Geshan, Pelet, Ephah and Shaaph. 48Caleb had another slave woman named Maacah. She was the mother of Sheber and Tirhanah. 49She was also the mother of Shaaph and Sheva. Shaaph was the father of Madmannah. Sheva was the father of Macbenah and Gibea. Caleb's daughter was Acsah.

50-51These were Caleb's descendants:*d* Caleb's son Hur was the first son of his mother Ephrathah. Hur's sons were Shobal, Salma and Hareph. Shobal was the father of Kiriath Jearim. Salma was the father of Bethlehem. And Hareph was the father of Beth Gader.

52Shobal was the father of Kiriath Jearim. These were Shobal's descendants: Haroeh, half the Manahathites, 53and the family groups of Kiriath Jearim. Shobal was also the ancestor of the Ithrites, Puthites, Shumathites and the Mishraites. The Zorathites and the Eshtaolites came from the Mishraite people.

54Salma's descendants were Bethlehem, the Netophathites, Atroth Beth Joab, half the Manahathites and the Zorites. 55His descendants were also the families who lived at Jabez. These were the people who wrote and copied important papers. These people were the Tirathites, Shimeathites and Sucathites. They were from the Kenite family group who came from Hammath. He was the father of the people living in Recab.

David's Family

3 These are David's sons who were born in Hebron. David's first son was Amnon. Amnon's mother was Ahinoam from the town of Jezreel. David's second son was Daniel. His mother was Abigail from Carmel. 2David's third son was Absalom. His mother was Maacah, the daughter of Talmai king of Geshur. David's fourth son was Adonijah. His mother was Haggith. 3David's fifth son was Shephatiah. His mother was Abital. David's sixth son was Ithream. David's wife Eglah was his mother. 4These six sons of David were born to him in Hebron. David ruled there seven years and six months.

David ruled in Jerusalem 33 years. 5These were David's children who were born in Jerusalem: David and Bathsheba, Ammiel's daughter, had four children. They were Shammua, Shobab, Nathan and Solomon. 6-8David's other nine children were Ibhar, Elishua, Eliphelet, Nogah, Nepheg, Japhia, Elishama, Eliada and Eliphelet. 9Those are all of David's sons, except for those born to his slave women.*d* David also had a daughter named Tamar.

The Kings of Judah

10Solomon's son was Rehoboam. Rehoboam's son was Abijah. Abijah's son was Asa. Asa's son was Jehoshaphat. 11Jehoshaphat's son was Jehoram. Jehoram's son was Ahaziah. Ahaziah's son was Joash. 12Joash's son was Amaziah. Amaziah's son was Azariah. Azariah's son was Jotham. 13Jotham's son was Ahaz. Ahaz's son was Hezekiah. Hezekiah's son was Manasseh. 14Manasseh's son was Amon. Amon's son was Josiah.

15These were Josiah's sons: Josiah's first son was Johanan. His second son was Jehoiakim. His third son was Zedekiah. His fourth son was Shallum.

16Jehoiakim was followed by Jehoiachin. Jehoiachin was followed by Zedekiah.

David's Descendants After the Babylonian Captivity

17Jehoiachin was taken as a prisoner. His sons were Shealtiel, 18Malkiram, Pedaiah, Shenazzar, Jekamiah, Hoshama and Nedabiah.

¹⁹Pedaiah's sons were Zerubbabel and Shimei.

Zerubbabel's sons were Meshullam and Hananiah. Their sister was Shelomith. ²⁰Zerubbabel also had five other sons. Their names were Hashubah, Ohel, Berekiah, Hasadiah and Jushab-Hesed.

²¹Hananiah's descendants[d] were Pelatiah and Jeshaiah, and the sons of Rephaiah, Arnan, Obadiah and Shecaniah.

²²Shecaniah's son was Shemaiah. Shemaiah's sons were Hattush, Igal, Bariah, Neariah and Shaphat. There were six in all.

²³Neariah had three sons. They were Elioenai, Hizkiah and Azrikam.

²⁴Elioenai had seven sons. They were Hodaviah, Eliashib, Pelaiah, Akkub, Johanan, Delaiah and Anani.

Other Family Groups of Judah

4 Judah's descendants[d] were Perez, Hezron, Carmi, Hur and Shobal.

²Reaiah was Shobal's son. Reaiah was the father of Jahath. Jahath was the father of Ahumai and Lahad. They were the family groups of the Zorathite people.

³⁻⁴Hur was the oldest son of Caleb and his wife Ephrath. Hur was the leader of Bethlehem. Hur's three sons were Etam, Penuel and Ezer. Etam's sons were Jezreel, Ishma and Idbash. They had a sister named Hazzelelponi. Penuel was the father of Gedor. Ezer was the father of Hushah.

⁵Tekoa's father was Ashhur. Ashhur had two wives named Helah and Naarah.

⁶The sons of Ashhur and Naarah were Ahuzzam, Hepher, Temeni and Haahashtari. These were the descendants of Naarah.

⁷Helah's sons were Zereth, Zohar, Ethnan ⁸and Koz. Koz was the father of Anub and Hazzobebah. He was also the father of the Aharhel family group. Aharhel was the son of Harum.

⁹There was a man named Jabez. He was respected more than his brothers. His mother named him Jabez[n] because she said, "I was in much pain when I gave birth to him." ¹⁰Jabez prayed to the God of Israel. Jabez said, "Please do good things for me. Please give me more land. Stay with me, and don't let anyone hurt me. Then I won't have any pain." And God did what Jabez had asked.

¹¹Kelub was Shuhah's brother. Kelub was the father of Mehir. Mehir was the father of Eshton. ¹²Eshton was the father of Beth Rapha, Paseah and Tehinnah. Tehinnah was the father of the people from the town of Nahash. These people were from Recah.

¹³The sons of Kenaz were Othniel and Seraiah.

Othniel's sons were Hathath and Meonothai. ¹⁴Meonothai was the father of Ophrah.

Seraiah was the father of Joab. Joab was the ancestor of the people from Craftsmen's Valley. It is called Craftsmen's Valley because the people living there were craftsmen.

¹⁵Caleb was Jephunneh's son. Caleb's sons were Iru, Elah and Naam. Elah's son was Kenaz.

¹⁶Jehallelel's sons were Ziph, Ziphah, Tiria and Asarel.

¹⁷⁻¹⁸Ezrah's sons were Jether, Mered, Epher and Jalon. Mered married Bithiah, the daughter of the king of Egypt. The children of Mered and Bithiah were Miriam, Shammai and Ishbah. Ishbah was the father of Eshtemoa. Mered also had a wife from Judah. She gave birth to Jered, Heber and Jekuthiel. Jered became the father of Gedor. Heber became the father of Soco. And Jekuthiel became the father of Zanoah.

¹⁹Hodiah's wife was Naham's sister.

Jabez This name in Hebrew sounds like the word for "pain".

The sons of Hodiah's wife were Eshtemoa and the father of Keilah. Keilah was from the Garmite people. And Eshtemoa was from the Maacathite people. 20Shimon's sons were Amnon, Rinnah, Ben-Hanan and Tilon.

Ishi's sons were Zoheth and Ben-Zoheth.

21-22Shelah was Judah's son. Shelah's sons were Er, Laadah, Jokim, the men from Cozeba, Joash and Saraph. Er was the father of Lecah. Laadah was the father of Mareshah and the family groups of linen workers at Beth Ashbea. Joash and Saraph ruled in Moab and Jashubi Lehem. The writings about this family are very old. 23These sons of Shelah made things from clay. They lived in Netaim and Gederah. They stayed there and worked for the king.

Simeon's Children

24Simeon's sons were Nemuel, Jamin, Jarib, Zerah and Shaul. 25Shaul's son was Shallum. Shallum's son was Mibsam. Mibsam's son was Mishma. 26Mishma's son was Hammuel. Hammuel's son was Zaccur. Zaccur's son was Shimei. 27Shimei had 16 sons and six daughters. But his brothers did not have many children. So there were not as many people in their family group as there were in Judah. 28Shimei's children lived in Beersheba, Moladah, Hazar Shual, 29Bilhah, Ezem and Tolad. 30They also lived in Bethuel, Hormah, Ziklag, 31Beth Marcaboth, Hazar Susim, Beth Biri and Shaaraim. They lived in these cities until David became king. 32The five villages near these cities were Etam, Ain, Rimmon, Token and Ashan. 33There were also other villages as far away as Baalath. This is where they lived. And they wrote the history of their family.

34-38This is the list of men who were leaders of their family groups. There were Meshobab, Jamlech, Joshah son of Amaziah, Joel and Jehu son of Joshibiah. (Joshibiah was the son of Seraiah, who was the son of Asiel.) There were also Elioenai, Jaakobah, Jeshohaiah, Asaiah, Adiel, Jesimiel, Benaiah and Ziza. (Ziza was the son of Shiphi, who was the son of Allon. Allon was the son of Jedaiah, who was the son of Shimri. And Shimri was the son of Shemaiah.)

These men's families grew to be very large. 39They went to the area outside the city of Gedor to the east side of the valley. They went there to look for pasture for their sheep. 40They found good pastures with plenty of grass. The land was open country and peaceful and quiet. Ham's descendants*d* had lived there in the past.

41These men listed above came to Gedor while Hezekiah was king of Judah. They fought against the Hamite people and destroyed their tents. They also fought against the Meunite people who lived there and completely destroyed them. So there are no Meunites there even today. Then these men began to live there, because there was pasture for their sheep. 42Ishi's sons, Pelatiah, Neariah, Rephaiah and Uzziel, led 500 of the Simeonite people. They attacked the people living in the mountains of Edom. 43They killed the few Amalekite people who were still alive. From that time until now these Simeonites have lived in Edom.

Reuben's Children

5 Reuben was Israel's first son. Reuben should have received the special privileges of the oldest son. But he had sexual relations with his father's slave woman.*d* So those special privileges were given to Joseph's sons. (Joseph was a son of Israel.) In the family history Reuben's name is not listed as the first son. 2Judah became stronger than his brothers. And a leader came from his family. But Jo-

seph's family received the privileges that belonged to the oldest son. ³Reuben was the first son born to Israel. Reuben's sons were Hanoch, Pallu, Hezron and Carmi.

⁴These were the children of Joel: Shemaiah was Joel's son. Gog was Shemaiah's son. Shimei was Gog's son. ⁵Micah was Shimei's son. Reaiah was Micah's son. Baal was Reaiah's son. ⁶Beerah was Baal's son. Beerah was a leader of the tribe_d of Reuben. Tiglath-Pileser king of Assyria captured Beerah and took him away.

⁷Joel's brothers and all his family groups are listed just as they are written in their family histories: Jeiel was the first, then Zechariah ⁸and Bela. (Bela was the son of Azaz. Azaz was Shema's son. Shema was Joel's son.) They lived in the area of Aroer all the way to Nebo and Baal Meon. ⁹Bela's people lived to the east. Their land went as far as the edge of the desert, which is beside the Euphrates River. They lived there because they had too many cattle for the land of Gilead.

¹⁰When Saul was king, Bela's people fought a war against the Hagrite people. And they defeated the Hagrites. Then Bela's people lived in the tents that had belonged to the Hagrites. They lived in all the area east of Gilead.

Gad's Children

¹¹The people from the tribe_d of Gad lived near the Reubenite people. The Gadites lived in the area of Bashan all the way to Salecah. ¹²Joel was the main leader in Bashan. Shapham was the second leader. Then Janai and Shaphat were leaders.

¹³The seven relatives in their families were Michael, Meshullam, Sheba, Jorai, Jacan, Zia and Eber. ¹⁴They were the descendants_d of Abihail. Abihail was Huri's son. Huri was Jaroah's son. Jaroah was Gilead's son. Gilead was Michael's son. Michael was Jeshishai's son. Jeshishai was Jahdo's

son. Jahdo was the son of Buz. ¹⁵Ahi was Abdiel's son. Abdiel was Guni's son. Ahi was the leader of their family.

¹⁶The Gadite people lived in Gilead, Bashan and in the small towns around Bashan. They also lived on all the pasturelands in the Plain of Sharon all the way to the borders.

¹⁷All these people's names were written in the family history of Gad. This was done during the time Jotham was king of Judah and Jeroboam was king of Israel.

Soldiers Skilled in War

¹⁸There were 44,760 fighters from the tribes_d of Reuben and Gad and the eastern half-tribe of Manasseh. They were brave men who could use shields and swords. They could use their bows well. They were skilled in war. ¹⁹They started a war against the Hagrites and the people of Jetur, Naphish and Nodab. ²⁰The men from the tribes of Manasseh, Reuben and Gad prayed to God in the war. They asked God to help them. So he helped them because they trusted him. He allowed them to defeat the Hagrites. And they also defeated all those who were with the Hagrites. ²¹They took the animals that belonged to the Hagrites. They took 50,000 camels, 250,000 sheep and 2,000 donkeys. They also captured 100,000 people. ²²Many Hagrites were killed. This is because God helped the people of Reuben, Gad and Manasseh. Then they lived there until Babylon captured them and took them away.

The Eastern Half-Tribe of Manasseh

²³There were many people in the eastern half-tribe_d of Manasseh. They lived in the area of Bashan all the way to Baal Hermon, Senir and Mount Hermon.

²⁴These were the family leaders: Epher, Ishi, Eliel, Azriel, Jeremiah, Hodaviah and Jahdiel. They were all

strong, brave and famous men. And they were leaders in their families. 25But they sinned against the God that their ancestors had worshipped. They began worshipping the gods of the people in that land. And those were the people God was destroying. 26So the God of Israel made Pul king of Assyria want to go to war. Pul was also called Tiglath-Pileser. He captured the people of Reuben, Gad and the eastern half-tribe of Manasseh. And he took them away to Halah, Habor, Hara and near the Gozan River. And they have lived there from that time until this day.

Levi's Children

6 Levi's sons were Gershon, Kohath and Merari. 2Kohath's sons were Amram, Izhar, Hebron and Uzziel. 3Amram's children were Aaron, Moses and Miriam.

Aaron's sons were Nadab, Abihu, Eleazar and Ithamar. 4Eleazar was the father of Phinehas. Phinehas was the father of Abishua. 5Abishua was the father of Bukki. Bukki was the father of Uzzi. 6Uzzi was the father of Zerahiah. Zerahiah was the father of Meraioth. 7Meraioth was the father of Amariah. Amariah was the father of Ahitub. 8Ahitub was the father of Zadok. Zadok was the father of Ahimaaz. 9Ahimaaz was the father of Azariah. Azariah was the father of Johanan. 10Johanan was the father of Azariah. (Azariah was a priest in the Temple*d* Solomon built in Jerusalem.) 11Azariah was the father of Amariah. Amariah was the father of Ahitub. 12Ahitub was the father of Zadok. Zadok was the father of Shallum. 13Shallum was the father of Hilkiah. Hilkiah was the father of Azariah. 14Azariah was the father of Seraiah. Seraiah was the father of Jehozadak.

15Jehozadak was forced to leave his home when the Lord sent Judah and Jerusalem into captivity. That was when Nebuchadnezzar captured them and took them away.

16Levi's sons were Gershon, Kohath and Merari.

17The names of Gershon's sons were Libni and Shimei.

18Kohath's sons were Amram, Izhar, Hebron and Uzziel.

19Merari's sons were Mahli and Mushi.

This is a list of the family groups of Levi. They are listed by the name of the father of each group.

20Gershon's son was Libni. Libni's son was Jehath. Jehath's son was Zimmah. 21Zimmah's son was Joah. Joah's son was Iddo. Iddo's son was Zerah. And Zerah's son was Jeatherai.

22Kohath's son was Amminadab. Amminadab's son was Korah. Korah's son was Assir. 23Assir's son was Elkanah. Elkanah's son was Ebiasaph. Ebiasaph's son was Assir. 24Assir's son was Tahath. Tahath's son was Uriel. Uriel's son was Uzziah, and Uzziah's son was Shaul.

25Elkanah's sons were Amasai and Ahimoth. 26Ahimoth's son was Elkanah. Elkanah's son was Zophai. Zophai's son was Nahath. 27Nahath's son was Eliab. Eliab's son was Jeroham. Jeroham's son was Elkanah, and Elkanah's son was Samuel.

28Samuel's sons were Joel, the first son, and Abijah, the second son.

29Merari's son was Mahli. Mahli's son was Libni. Libni's son was Shimei. Shimei's son was Uzzah. 30Uzzah's son was Shimea. Shimea's son was Haggiah, and Haggiah's son was Asaiah.

The Temple Musicians

31David chose some men to be in charge of the music in the house of the Lord. They began their work after the Ark*d* of God was put there. 32They served by making music at the Holy Tent.*d* (It is also called the Meeting Tent.) And they served until Solomon built the Temple*d* of the Lord in Jerusalem. They followed the rules for their work.

33These are the musicians and their sons:

From Kohath's family there was Heman the singer. Heman was Joel's son. Joel was Samuel's son. 34Samuel was Elkanah's son. Elkanah was Jeroham's son. Jeroham was Eliel's son. Eliel was Toah's son. 35Toah was Zuph's son. Zuph was Elkanah's son. Elkanah was Mahath's son. Mahath was Amasai's son. 36Amasai was Elkanah's son. Elkanah was Joel's son. Joel was Azariah's son. Azariah was Zephaniah's son. 37Zephaniah was Tahath's son. Tahath was Assir's son. Assir was Ebiasaph's son. Ebiasaph was Korah's son. 38Korah was Izhar's son. Izhar was Kohath's son. Kohath was Levi's son. Levi was Israel's son.

39There was Heman's helper Asaph. Asaph's group stood by Heman's right side. Asaph was Berekiah's son. Berekiah was Shimea's son. 40Shimea was Michael's son. Michael was Baaseiah's son. Baaseiah was Malkijah's son. 41Malkijah was Ethni's son. Ethni was Zerah's son. Zerah was Adaiah's son. 42Adaiah was Ethan's son. Ethan was Zimmah's son. Zimmah was Shimei's son. 43Shimei was Jahath's son. Jahath was Gershon's son. Gershon was Levi's son.

44Merari's family were the helpers of Heman and Asaph. Merari's family stood by Heman's left side. In this group was Ethan son of Kishi. Kishi was Abdi's son. Abdi was Malluch's son. 45Malluch was Hashabiah's son. Hashabiah was Amaziah's son. Amaziah was Hilkiah's son. 46Hilkiah was Amzi's son. Amzi was Bani's son. Bani was Shemer's son. 47Shemer was Mahli's son. Mahli was Mushi's son. Mushi was Merari's son. Merari was Levi's son.

48The other Levites served by doing their own special work in the Holy Tent. It is the house of God. 49Aaron and his descendants[d] offered the sacrifices on the altar of burnt offering. They also burned the incense on the altar of incense. They offered the sacrifices that removed the Israelites' sins so they could belong to God. They did all the work in the Most Holy Place. They followed all the laws that Moses, God's servant, had commanded.

50These were Aaron's sons: Eleazar was Aaron's son. Phinehas was Eleazar's son. Abishua was Phinehas' son. 51Bukki was Abishua's son. Uzzi was Bukki's son. Zerahiah was Uzzi's son. 52Meraioth was Zerahiah's son. Amariah was Meraioth's son. Ahitub was Amariah's son. 53Zadok was Ahitub's son. Ahimaaz was Zadok's son.

Land for the Levites

54These are the places where Aaron's descendants[d] lived. Aaron's descendants from the Kohath family group were given this land to live in. They received the first share of the land that was given to the Levites.

55They were given the city of Hebron in Judah and the pastures around it. 56But the fields farther from the city were given to Caleb son of Jephunneh. And the villages near Hebron were given to Caleb. 57So the descendants of Aaron were given Hebron. It was one of the cities of safety.[n] They also received the cities of Libnah, Jattir, Eshtemoa, 58Hilen, Debir, 59Ashan, Juttah and Beth Shemesh. They received all these cities and the pastures around them. 60They also received cities from the tribe of Benjamin. They received Gibeon, Geba, Alemeth, Anathoth and their pastures.

---

cities of safety A person who had accidentally killed someone could go to one of the six cities of safety. There he would receive protection and a fair trial.

The Kohath family groups received a total of 13 cities.

⁶¹The rest of the Kohath family group was given ten cities. These cities were from the family groups of the western half-tribe*d* of Manasseh. The cities were chosen by throwing lots.*d*

⁶²The Gershon family group received 13 cities. They were from the tribes of Issachar, Asher, Naphtali and the part of Manasseh living in Bashan.

⁶³The Merari family group received 12 cities from the tribes of Reuben, Gad and Zebulun. Those cities were chosen by throwing lots.

⁶⁴So the Israelites gave these cities and their pastures to the Levites. ⁶⁵The cities from the tribes of Judah, Simeon and Benjamin were chosen by throwing lots. They are the cities named above.

⁶⁶Some of the Kohath family groups received cities and pastures from the tribe of Ephraim. ⁶⁷They received Shechem in the mountains of Ephraim. It was one of the cities of safety. They also received the cities of Gezer, ⁶⁸Jokmeam, Beth Horon, ⁶⁹Aijalon and Gath Rimmon. They received the cities and the pastures around them.

⁷⁰The rest of the people in the Kohath family group received cities from the western half-tribe of Manasseh. They received the cities of Aner and Bileam and their pastures.

⁷¹From the eastern half-tribe of Manasseh, the Gershon family received towns and pastures. They received Golan in Bashan, Ashtaroth and the pastures around them.

⁷²⁻⁷³From the tribe of Issachar, the Gershon family received towns and pastures. They received Kedesh, Daberath, Ramoth, Anem and their pastures.

⁷⁴⁻⁷⁵From the tribe of Asher, the Gershon family received towns and pastures. They received Mashal, Ab-

don, Hukok, Rehob and their pastures.

⁷⁶From the tribe of Naphtali, the Gershon family received towns and pastures. They received Kedesh in Galilee, Hammon, Kiriathaim and their pastures.

⁷⁷The rest of the Levites, the people from the Merari family, also received towns and pastures. They received Jokneam, Kartah, Rimmono and Tabor from the tribe of Zebulun. They also received the pastures around those cities.

⁷⁸⁻⁷⁹From the tribe of Reuben, the Merari family received towns and pastures. They received Bezer in the desert, Jahzah, Kedemoth, Mephaath and their pastures. (The tribe of Reuben lived east of the Jordan River, across from Jericho.)

⁸⁰⁻⁸¹From the tribe of Gad, the Merari family received towns and pastures. They received Ramoth in Gilead, Mahanaim, Heshbon, Jazer and their pastures.

Issachar's Children

7 Issachar had four sons. Their names were Tola, Puah, Jashub and Shimron.

²Tola's sons were Uzzi, Rephaiah, Jeriel, Jahmai, Ibsam and Samuel. They were leaders of their families. In the family history of Tola's descendants,*d* 22,600 men were listed as fighting men. This was during the time David was king.

³Uzzi's son was Izrahiah.

Izrahiah's sons were Michael, Obadiah, Joel and Isshiah. All five of them were leaders. ⁴Their family history shows they had 36,000 men ready to serve in the army. This was because they had many women and children.

⁵The records of the family groups of Issachar show there were 87,000 fighting men.

Benjamin's Children

⁶Benjamin had three sons. Their

names were Bela, Beker and Jediael. [7]Bela had five sons. Their names were Ezbon, Uzzi, Uzziel, Jerimoth and Iri. They were leaders of their families. Their family history shows they had 22,034 fighting men.

[8]Beker's sons were Zemirah, Joash, Eliezer, Elioenai, Omri, Jeremoth, Abijah, Anathoth and Alemeth. They all were Beker's sons. [9]Their family history listed the family leaders and 20,200 fighting men.

[10]Jediael's son was Bilhan.

Bilhan's sons were Jeush, Benjamin, Ehud, Kenaanah, Zethan, Tarshish and Ahishahar. [11]All these sons of Jediael were leaders of their families. They had 17,200 fighting men ready to serve in the army.

[12]The Shuppites and Huppites were descendants[d] of Ir. And the Hushites were descendants of Aher.

Naphtali's Children

[13]Naphtali's sons were Jahziel, Guni, Jezer and Shillem. They were Bilhah's grandsons.

Manasseh's Children

[14]These are Manasseh's descendants:[d] Manasseh had an Aramean slave woman.[d] She was the mother of Asriel and Makir. Makir was Gilead's father. [15]Makir took a wife from the Huppites and Shuppites. His sister was named Maacah. His second son was named Zelophehad. Zelophehad had only daughters. [16]Makir's wife Maacah had a son whom she named Peresh. Peresh's brother was named Sheresh. Sheresh's sons were Ulam and Rakem.

[17]Ulam's son was Bedan.

These were the sons of Gilead. Gilead was Makir's son. Makir was Manasseh's son. [18]Makir's sister Hammoleketh gave birth to Ishhod, Abiezer and Mahlah.

[19]The sons of Shemida were Ahian, Shechem, Likhi and Aniam.

Ephraim's Children

[20]These are the names of Ephraim's descendants.[d] Ephraim's son was Shuthelah. Shuthelah's son was Bered. Bered's son was Tahath. Tahath's son was Eleadah. Eleadah's son was Tahath. [21]Tahath's son was Zabad. Zabad's son was Shuthelah.

Ezer and Elead went to Gath to steal the people's cows and sheep. So some men who grew up in that city killed Ezer and Elead. [22]Their father Ephraim cried for them many days. And his family came to comfort him. [23]Then he had sexual relations with his wife again. She became pregnant and gave birth to a son. Ephraim named his son Beriah[n] because of the bad things that had happened to his family. [24]Ephraim's daughter was Sheerah. She built Lower Beth Horon and Upper Beth Horon and Uzzen Sheerah.

[25]Rephah was Ephraim's son. Resheph was Rephah's son. Telah was Resheph's son. Tahan was Telah's son. [26]Ladan was Tahan's son. Ammihud was Ladan's son. Elishama was Ammihud's son. [27]Nun was Elishama's son. Joshua was the son of Nun.

[28]Ephraim's descendants lived in these lands and cities: Bethel and the villages near it, Naaran on the east, Gezer and the villages near it on the west, and Shechem and the villages near it. These villages went all the way to Ayyah and its villages. [29]Along the borders of Manasseh's land were the towns of Beth Shan, Taanach, Megiddo and Dor. There were also villages near them. The descendants of Joseph son of Israel lived in these towns.

Asher's Children

[30]Asher's sons were Imnah, Ishvah,

Beriah This name sounds like the Hebrew word for "trouble".

Ishvi and Beriah. Their sister was Serah.
[31]Beriah's sons were Heber and
Malkiel. Malkiel was Birzaith's father.
[32]Heber was the father of Japhlet,
Shomer and Hotham and their sister
Shua.
[33]Japhlet's sons were Pasach, Bim-
hal and Ashvath. They were Japhlet's
children.
[34]Japhlet's brother was Shomer.
Shomer's sons were Rohgah, Hubbah
and Aram.
[35]Shomer's brother was Hotham.
Hotham's sons were Zophah, Imna,
Shelesh and Amal.
[36]Zophah's sons were Suah, Harne-
pher, Shual, Beri, Imrah, [37]Bezer,
Hod, Shamma, Shilshah, Ithran and
Beera.
[38]Jether's sons were Jephunneh,
Pispah and Ara.
[39]Ulla's sons were Arah, Hanniel
and Rizia.
[40]All these men were descendants
of Asher. They were leaders of their
families. They were powerful warriors and outstanding leaders. Their
family history lists that they had
26,000 soldiers ready to serve in the
army.

The Family History of King Saul

8 Benjamin was the father of Bela.
Bela was Benjamin's first son.
Ashbel was his second son. Aharah
was his third son. [2]Nohah was Benjamin's fourth son, and Rapha was his
fifth son.
[3]Bela's sons were Addar, Gera,
Abihud, [4]Abishua, Naaman, Ahoah,
[5]Gera, Shephuphan and Huram.
[6]These were the descendants[d] of
Ehud. They were leaders of their families in Geba. They were forced to
leave their homes and move to Manahath. [7]Ehud's descendants were Naaman, Ahijah and Gera. Gera forced
them to leave their homes. He was
the father of Uzza and Ahihud.
[8-11]Shaharaim and his wife Hushim

had sons named Abitub and Elpaal. In
Moab Shaharaim divorced his wives
Hushim and Baara. Shaharaim and his
wife Hodesh had these children: Jobab, Zibia, Mesha, Malcam, Jeuz, Sa-
kia and Mirmah. These sons were
leaders of their families.
[12-13]Elpaal's sons were Eber, Mi-
sham, Shemed, Beriah and Shema.
Shemed built the towns of Ono and
Lod and the villages around them. Beriah and Shema were leaders of the
families living in Aijalon. These sons
forced the people who lived in Gath to
leave.
[14]Beriah's sons were Ahio, Sha-
shak, Jeremoth, [15]Zebadiah, Arad,
Eder, [16]Michael, Ishpah and Joha.
[17]Elpaal's sons were Zebadiah, Meshullam, Hizki, Heber, [18]Ishmerai, Iz-
liah and Jobab.
[19]Shimei's sons were Jakim, Zicri,
Zabdi, [20]Elienai, Zillethai, Eliel, [21]Ada-
iah, Beraiah and Shimrath.
[22]Shashak's sons were Ishpan,
Eber, Eliel, [23]Abdon, Zicri, Hanan,
[24]Hananiah, Elam, Anthothijah, [25]Iph-
deiah and Penuel.
[26]Jeroham's sons were Shamsherai,
Shehariah, Athaliah, [27]Jaareshiah, Elijah and Zicri.
[28]The family histories show that all
these men were leaders of their families. They lived in Jerusalem.
[29]Jeiel lived in the town of Gibeon,
where he was the leader. His wife was
named Maacah. [30]Jeiel's first son was
Abdon. His other sons were Zur,
Kish, Baal, Ner, Nadab, [31]Gedor,
Ahio, Zeker [32]and Mikloth. Mikloth
was the father of Shimeah. These
sons also lived near their relatives in
Jerusalem.
[33]Ner was the father of Kish. Kish
was the father of Saul. And Saul was
the father of Jonathan, Malki-Shua,
Abinadab and Esh-Baal.
[34]Jonathan's son was Merib-Baal.
Merib-Baal was Micah's father.
[35]Micah's sons were Pithon, Melech, Tarea and Ahaz. [36]Ahaz was the

father of Jehoaddah. Jehoaddah was the father of Alemeth, Azmaveth and Zimri. Zimri was the father of Moza. [37]Moza was the father of Binea. Raphah was Binea's son. Eleasah was Raphah's son. And Azel was Eleasah's son.

[38]Azel had six sons. Their names were Azrikam, Bokeru, Ishmael, Sheariah, Obadiah and Hanan. All these were Azel's sons.

[39]Azel's brother was Eshek. Eshek's first son was Ulam. Jeush was his second son, and Eliphelet was his third son. [40]Ulam's sons were mighty warriors who could use a bow and arrow well. They had many sons and grandsons. There were 150 of them in all.

All these men were Benjamin's descendants.

9 The names of all the people of Israel were listed in their family histories. Those family histories were put in the book of the kings of Israel.

The People in Jerusalem

The people of Judah were captured and forced to go to Babylon. This is because they were not faithful to God. [2]The first people to come back and live in their own lands and towns were some Israelites, priests, Levites and Temple[d] servants.

[3]People from the tribes[d] of Judah, Benjamin, Ephraim and Manasseh lived in Jerusalem. This is a list of those people.

[4]There was Uthai son of Ammihud. (Ammihud was Omri's son. Omri was Imri's son. Imri was Bani's son. Bani was a descendant[d] of Perez. Perez was Judah's son.)

[5]Of the Shilonite people there were Asaiah and his sons. Asaiah was the oldest son in his family.

[6]Of the Zerahite people there were Jeuel and other relatives of Zerah. There were 690 of them in all.

[7]From the tribe of Benjamin there was Sallu son of Meshullam. (Meshullam was Hodaviah's son. Hodaviah was Hassenuah's son.) [8]There was also Ibneiah son of Jeroham and Elah son of Uzzi. (Uzzi was Micri's son.) And there was Meshullam son of Shephatiah. (Shephatiah was Reuel's son, and Reuel was Ibnijah's son.) [9]The family history of Benjamin lists 956 people living in Jerusalem. All these men were leaders of their families.

[10]Of the priests there were Jedaiah, Jehoiarib, Jakin and [11]Azariah son of Hilkiah. (Hilkiah was Meshullam's son. Meshullam was Zadok's son. Zadok was Meraioth's son. Meraioth was Ahitub's son. Ahitub was the officer who was responsible for the Temple of God.) [12]Also there was Adaiah son of Jeroham. (Jeroham was Pashhur's son, and Pashhur was Malkijah's son.) And there was Maasai son of Adiel. (Adiel was Jahzerah's son. Jahzerah was Meshullam's son. Meshullam was Meshillemith's son, and Meshillemith was Immer's son.) [13]There were 1,760 priests. They were leaders of their families. They were responsible for serving in the Temple of God.

[14]Of the Levites there was Semaiah son of Hasshub. (Hasshub was Azrikam's son. Azrikam was Hashabiah's son. Hashabiah was from the family of Merari.) [15]There were also Bakbakkar, Heresh, Galal and Mattaniah son of Mica. (Mica was Zicri's son. Zicri was Asaph's son.) [16]There was also Obadiah son of Shemaiah. (Shemaiah was Galal's son, and Galal was Jeduthun's son.) And there was Berekiah son of Asa. (Asa was Elkanah's son. Elkanah lived in the villages of the Netophathite people.)

[17]Of the gatekeepers there were Shallum, Akkub, Talmon, Ahiman and their relatives. Shallum was their leader. [18]These gatekeepers from the tribe of Levi still stand next to the King's Gate on the east side of the

city. ¹⁹Shallum was Kore's son. Kore was Ebiasaph's son. Ebiasaph was Korah's son. Shallum and his relatives from the family of Korah were gatekeepers. They were responsible for guarding the gates of the Temple. Their ancestors had also been responsible for guarding the entrance to the Temple. ²⁰In the past Phinehas was in charge of the gatekeepers. He was Eleazar's son. The Lord was with Phinehas. ²¹Zechariah was the gatekeeper at the entrance to the Temple. He was the son of Meshelemiah. ²²In all, 212 men were chosen to guard the gates. Their names were written in their family histories in their villages. David and Samuel the seer[d] chose these men because they were dependable. ²³The gatekeepers and their descendants had the responsibility of guarding the gates of the Temple of the Lord. (The Temple took the place of the Holy Tent.[d]) ²⁴There were gatekeepers on all four sides of the Temple: east, west, north and south. ²⁵The gatekeepers' relatives who lived in the villages had to come and help them at certain times. Each time they came they helped the gatekeepers for seven days. ²⁶Because they were dependable, four gatekeepers were made the leaders of all the gatekeepers. They were Levites. They were responsible for the rooms and treasures in the Temple of God. ²⁷They stayed up all night guarding the Temple of God. And they opened it every morning. ²⁸Some of the gatekeepers were responsible for the tools and dishes used in the Temple services. They counted these tools and dishes when people took them out. And they counted them when people brought them back. ²⁹Other gatekeepers were chosen to take care of the things in the Holy Place. They also took care of the flour, wine, oil, incense[d] and spices. ³⁰But some of the priests took care of mixing the spices. ³¹There was a Levite named Mattithiah. Because he was dependable, he had the job of baking the bread used for the offerings. He was Shallum's first son. Shallum was from the family of Korah. ³²Some of the gatekeepers had the job of preparing the special bread. This was the bread that was put on the table every Sabbath.[d] These people were from the Kohath family.

³³Some of the Levites were musicians in the Temple. The leaders of these families stayed in the rooms of the Temple. They were on duty day and night. So they did not do other work in the Temple.

³⁴These are the leaders of the Levite families. Their names were listed in their family histories. They lived in Jerusalem.

The Family History of King Saul

³⁵Jeiel lived in the town of Gibeon, where he was the leader. His wife was named Maacah. ³⁶Jeiel's first son was Abdon. His other sons were Zur, Kish, Baal, Ner, Nadab, ³⁷Gedor, Ahio, Zechariah and Mikloth. ³⁸Mikloth was Shimeam's father. Jeiel's family lived near their relatives in Jerusalem.

³⁹Ner was Kish's father. Kish was Saul's father. And Saul was the father of Jonathan, Malki-Shua, Abinadab and Esh-Baal. ⁴⁰Jonathan's son was Merib-Baal. Merib-Baal was Micah's father.

⁴¹Micah's sons were Pithon, Melech, Tahrea and Ahaz. ⁴²Ahaz was Jadah's father. Jadah was the father of Alemeth, Azmaveth and Zimri. Zimri was Moza's father. ⁴³Moza was Binea's father. Rephaiah was Binea's son. Eleasah was Rephaiah's son, and Azel was Eleasah's son.

⁴⁴Azel had six sons. Their names were Azrikam, Bokeru, Ishmael, Sheariah, Obadiah and Hanan. They were Azel's sons.

The Death of King Saul

10 The Philistine people fought against the people of Israel. The Israelites ran away from them. And many Israelites were killed on Mount Gilboa. ²The Philistines continued chasing Saul and his sons. And they killed Saul's sons Jonathan, Abinadab and Malki-Shua. ³The fighting became heavy around Saul. The archers shot him with their arrows and wounded him.

⁴Then Saul said to the officer who carried his armour, "Pull out your sword and kill me. If you don't, these men who are not circumcised will come and hurt me." But the officer was afraid. So he refused to kill Saul. Then Saul took his own sword and fell on it. ⁵The officer saw that Saul was dead. So he fell on his own sword and died. ⁶So Saul and three of his sons died. All his family died together.

⁷The Israelites living in the valley saw that their army had run away. And they saw that Saul and his sons were dead. So they left their towns and ran away. Then the Philistines came and lived in those towns.

⁸The next day the Philistines came to take valuable things from the dead bodies. On Mount Gilboa they found the bodies of Saul and his sons. ⁹The Philistines stripped Saul's body. And they took his head and his armour. They sent messengers through all their country to tell the news to their idols and their people. ¹⁰The Philistines put Saul's armour in the temple of their idols. And they hung his head in the temple of Dagon.ᵈ

¹¹All the people living in Jabesh Gilead heard what the Philistines had done to Saul. ¹²So all the brave men from Jabesh Gilead went and got the bodies of Saul and his sons. They brought them to Jabesh Gilead. Then they buried the bones of Saul and his sons under the large tree in Jabesh. And they gave up eating for seven days.

¹³Saul died because he was not faithful to the Lord. He did not obey the Lord. He even went to a mediumᵈ and asked her for advice. ¹⁴He did this instead of asking the Lord for help. This is why the Lord put Saul to death and gave the kingdom to Jesse's son David.

David Becomes King

11 All the people of Israel came to David at the town of Hebron. They said, "We are your people. ²Even when Saul was king, you were the man who led Israel in battle. The Lord your God spoke to you. He said, 'David, you will be the shepherd of my people, the people of Israel. You will become their leader'."

³All the leaders of Israel came to King David at Hebron. He made an agreement with them before the Lord in Hebron. The leaders poured olive oil on David to appoint him king over Israel. The Lord had promised this would happen. He had made this promise through Samuel.

David Defeats Jerusalem

⁴David and all the Israelites went to the city of Jerusalem. At that time Jerusalem was called Jebus. The people living there were named Jebusites. ⁵They said to David, "You can't get inside our city." But David captured their strong city of Jerusalem, the City of David.

⁶David had said, "The person who leads the attack against the Jebusites will become the commander over all my army." Joab son of Zeruiah led the attack. So he became the commander of the army.

⁷Then David made his home in the strong, walled city. That is why it was named the City of David. ⁸David rebuilt the city. He started where the land was filled in and went to the wall that was around the city. Joab repaired the other parts of the city. ⁹David became more and more powerful.

And the Lord of heaven's armies was with him.

David's Mighty Warriors

[10]This is a list of the leaders over David's warriors. These warriors helped make David's kingdom strong. All the people of Israel also supported David's kingdom. These heroes and all the people of Israel made David king. This happened as the Lord had promised.

[11]This is a list of David's warriors: Jashobeam was from the Hacmonite people. He was the leader of the Three,[n] David's most powerful soldiers. He used his spear to fight 300 men at one time. And he killed them all.

[12]Next was Eleazar. He was one of the Three. Eleazar was Dodai's son. Dodai was from the Ahohite people. [13]Eleazar was with David at Pas-Dammim. The Philistines came there to fight the Israelites. There was a field of barley at that place. The Israelites ran away from the Philistines. [14]But they stopped in the middle of that field and fought the Philistines. And they killed the Philistines. The Lord gave Israel a great victory.

[15]Three of the 30 leaders went to David. He was at the rock by the cave near Adullam. At the same time a group from the Philistine army was camped in the Valley of Rephaim. [16]David was in a protected place at that time. The Philistine army was staying in the town of Bethlehem. [17]David had a strong desire for some water. He said, "Oh, I wish someone would get me water from the well near the city gate of Bethlehem!" [18]So the Three fought their way through the Philistine army. And they took water out of the well near the city gate in Bethlehem. Then they took it back to David. But he refused to drink it. He poured it out before the Lord.

[19]David said, "May God keep me from drinking this water! It would be like drinking the blood of the men who risked their lives to bring me this water." So David refused to drink it. These were the brave things the Three did.

[20]Abishai brother of Joab was the leader of the Three. Abishai fought 300 men with his spear and killed them. He became as famous as the Three. [21]He was more honoured than the Three. He became their commander even though he was not one of them.

[22]Benaiah son of Jehoiada was a brave fighter from Kabzeel. Benaiah did many brave things. He killed two of the best warriors from Moab. He also went down into a pit when it was snowing. There he killed a lion. [23]Benaiah also killed an Egyptian who was about two and a half metres tall. The Egyptian had a spear as large as a weaver's rod. Benaiah had a club. But he grabbed the spear from the Egyptian's hand. And he used the Egyptian's own spear to kill him. [24]These were the things Benaiah son of Jehoiada did. Benaiah became as famous as the Three. [25]He received more honour than the Thirty, David's most powerful soldiers. But he did not become a member of the Three. David chose Benaiah to be the leader of his bodyguards.

[26]These were also mighty warriors:
Asahel brother of Joab;
Elhanan son of Dodo from Bethlehem;
[27]Shammoth from the Harorites;
Helez from the Pelonites;
[28]Ira son of Ikkesh from Tekoa;
Abiezer from the Anathothites;
[29]Sibbecai from the Hushathites;

Three Or maybe "Thirty". These were David's most powerful soldiers. See 2 Samuel 23:8.

Ilai from the Ahohites;
30Maharai from the Netophathites;
Heled son of Baanah from the
Netophathites;
31Ithai son of Ribai from Gibeah
in Benjamin.
Benaiah from the Piratho-
nites;
32Hurai from the ravines of Gaash;
Abiel from the Arbathites;
33Azmaveth from the Baharu-
mites;
Eliahba from the Shaalbo-
nites;
34the sons of Hashem from the
Gizonites;
Jonathan son of Shagee from
the Hararites;
35Ahiam son of Sacar from the
Hararites;
Eliphal son of Ur;
36Hepher from the Mekerath-
ites;
Ahijah from the Pelonites;
37Hezro from the Carmelites;
Naarai son of Ezbai;
38Joel brother of Nathan;
Mibhar son of Hagri;
39Zelek from the Ammonites;
Naharai, from the Beroth-
ites, the officer who carried the armour for Joab
son of Zeruiah;
40Ira from the Ithrites;
Gareb from the Ithrites;
41Uriah from the Hittites;
Zabad son of Ahlai;
42Adina son of Shiza the Reubenite, who was the leader
of the Reubenites, and his
30 soldiers;
43Hanan son of Maacah;
Joshaphat from the Mith-
nites;
44Uzzia from the Ashterath-
ites;
Shama and Jeiel sons of Hotham from the Aroer;
45Jediael son of Shimri;

Joha, Jediael's brother, from
the Tizites;
46Eliel from the Mahavites;
Jeribai and Joshaviah, Elna-
am's sons;
Ithmah from the Moabites;
47Eliel, Obed and Jaasiel from
the Mezobaites.

Warriors Join David

12 These were the men who came
to David at Ziklag. David was
hiding from Saul son of Kish at that
time. These were the men who
helped David in battle. 2They came
with bows for weapons. They could
use either their right or left hands to
shoot arrows or to sling rocks. They
were Saul's relatives from the tribe[d]
of Benjamin. 3Ahiezer was their leader. And there was Joash. (Ahiezer and
Joash were Shemaah's sons. He was
from the town of Gibeah.) There were
also Jeziel and Pelet the sons of Azmaveth. There were Beracah and Jehu
from the town of Anathoth. 4And
there was Ishmaiah from the town of
Gibeon. Ishmaiah was one of the Thirty. In fact, he was the leader of the
Thirty. There were Jeremiah, Jahaziel, Johanan and Jozabad from Gederah. 5There were Eluzai, Jerimoth,
Bealiah and Shemariah. There was
Shephatiah from Haruph. 6There
were Elkanah, Isshiah, Azarel, Joezer
and Jashobeam. They were from the
family group of Korah. 7And there
were Joelah and Zebadiah the sons of
Jeroham. They were from the town of
Gedor.
8Part of the people of Gad joined
David at his protected place in the
desert. They were brave warriors
trained for war. They were skilled
with shields and spears. They were as
fierce as lions. And they could run as
fast as gazelle[d] over the hills.
9Ezer was the leader of Gad's army.
Obadiah was second in command. Eliab was third. 10Mishmannah was
fourth, and Jeremiah was fifth. 11Attai

was sixth, and Eliel was seventh. [12]Johanan was eighth, and Elzabad was ninth. [13]Jeremiah was tenth, and Macbannai was eleventh in command.

[14]They were the commanders of the army from Gad. The weakest of these leaders was in charge of 100 soldiers. The strongest was in charge of 1,000 soldiers. [15]They crossed the Jordan River and chased away the people living in the valleys. They chased them to the east and to the west. This happened in the first month of the year when the Jordan floods the valley.

[16]Other people from the tribes[d] of Benjamin and Judah also came to David at his protected place. [17]David went out to meet them. He said to them, "If you have come peacefully to help me, I welcome you. Join me. But you might have come to turn me over to my enemies, even though I have done nothing wrong. If you do this, the God of our fathers will see this and punish you."

[18]Then the Spirit[d] entered Amasai, the leader of the Thirty. Amasai said:

"We belong to you, David.
We are with you, son of Jesse.
Success, success to you.
Success to those who help you,
    because your God helps you."

So David welcomed these men. He made them leaders of his army.

[19]Some of the men from Manasseh also joined David. They joined him when he went with the Philistines to fight Saul. But David and his men did not really help the Philistines. After talking about it, the Philistine leaders decided to send David away. They said, "If David goes back to his master Saul, we will be killed!" [20]The men from Manasseh joined David when he went to Ziklag. These were the men: Adnah, Jozabad, Jediael, Michael, Jozabad, Elihu and Zillethai. Each of these men was a leader of 1,000 men from Manasseh. [21]All these men of Manasseh were brave soldiers.

They helped David fight against groups of men who went around the country robbing people. These soldiers became commanders in David's army. [22]Every day more men joined David. So his army became large. It was like the army of God.

Others Join David at Hebron

[23]These are the numbers of the men who joined David at Hebron. They came ready for battle. They came to help turn the kingdom of Saul over to David. The Lord had said this would happen.

[24]There were 6,800 men with their weapons from the people of Judah. They carried shields and spears.

[25]There were 7,100 men from the people of Simeon. They were warriors ready for war.

[26]There were 4,600 men from the people of Levi. [27]Jehoiada, a leader from Aaron's family, was in that group. There were 3,700 with him. [28]Zadok was also in that group. He was a strong young warrior. He came with 22 leaders from his family.

[29]There were 3,000 men from the people of Benjamin. They were Saul's relatives. And most of them had remained loyal to Saul's family until then.

[30]There were 20,800 men from the people of Ephraim. They were brave warriors. They were famous men in their own family groups.

[31]There were 18,000 men from the western half-tribe of Manasseh. Each man was especially chosen to make David king.

[32]There were 200 leaders from the family of Issachar. They knew what Israel should do. And they knew the right time to do it. Their relatives were with them and under their command.

[33]There were 50,000 men from the people of Zebulun. They were trained soldiers. They were trained to use ev-

ery kind of weapon of war. They followed David completely.

³⁴There were 1,000 officers from the people of Naphtali. They had 37,000 men with them who carried shields and spears.

³⁵There were 28,600 men from the people of Dan. They were ready for war.

³⁶There were 40,000 trained soldiers from the people of Asher. They were ready for war.

³⁷There were 120,000 men from the east side of the Jordan River. They were from the people of Reuben, Gad and the eastern half-tribe of Manasseh. They had every kind of weapon.

³⁸All these fighting men were ready to go to war. They came to Hebron fully agreed to make David king of all Israel. All the other Israelites also agreed to make David king. ³⁹The men spent three days there with David. They ate and drank, because their relatives had prepared food for them. ⁴⁰Also, their neighbours brought food. They came from as far as the areas belonging to Issachar, Zebulun and Naphtali. They brought food on donkeys, camels, mules and oxen. They brought much flour, fig cakes, raisins, wine, oil, cows and sheep. This was because the people of Israel were very happy.

Bringing Back the Holy Ark

13 David talked with all the officers of his army. He talked with the commanders of 100 men and the commanders of 1,000 men. ²Then David called the people of Israel together. He said, "If you think it is a good idea, and if it is what the Lord our God wants, let's send a message. Let's send it to our fellow Israelites in all the areas of Israel. Let's also send it to the priests and Levites living with them in their towns and pastures. Tell them to come and join us. ³Let's bring the Holy Ark*d* of our God back to us.

We did not use it to ask God for help while Saul was king." ⁴So all the people agreed with David. They all thought it was the right thing to do. ⁵So David gathered all the Israelites from the Shihor River in Egypt to Lebo Hamath. They were to bring the Holy Ark of God back from the town of Kiriath Jearim. ⁶David and all the Israelites with him went to Baalah of Judah. (Baalah is another name for Kiriath Jearim.) They went there to get the Holy Ark of God the Lord. His throne is between the golden creatures with wings on the Holy Ark. It is called by the Lord's name.

⁷The people moved the Holy Ark of God from Abinadab's house. They put it on a new cart. And Uzzah and Ahio guided the cart. ⁸David and all the Israelites were celebrating with all their strength before God. They were singing and playing harps, lyres,*d* tambourines,*d* cymbals and trumpets.

⁹They came to the threshing*d* floor of Kidon. The oxen pulling the cart stumbled. And Uzzah reached out his hand to steady the Holy Ark. ¹⁰The Lord became very angry with Uzzah. And he killed Uzzah because Uzzah had touched the Holy Ark. So Uzzah died there in the presence of God.

¹¹David became angry because the Lord had punished Uzzah in his anger. So even today that place is called the Punishment of Uzzah.

¹²David was afraid of God that day. David asked, "How can I bring the Holy Ark of God home to me?" ¹³So David did not take the Holy Ark with him to Jerusalem. Instead, he took it to the house of Obed-Edom of Gath. ¹⁴The Holy Ark of God stayed with Obed-Edom's family in his house for three months. And the Lord blessed Obed-Edom's family and everything he owned.

David's Kingdom Grows

14 Hiram king of the city of Tyre sent messengers to David. He also sent cedar logs, stonecutters and carpenters. He sent them to build a palace for David. ²Then David knew that the Lord really had made him king of Israel. And he knew the Lord had made his kingdom very important. The Lord did this because he loved his people, the Israelites.

³David married more women in Jerusalem. And he had more sons and daughters. ⁴These are the names of David's children born in Jerusalem: Shammua, Shobab, Nathan, Solomon, ⁵Ibhar, Elishua, Elpelet, ⁶Nogah, Nepheg, Japhia, ⁷Elishama, Beeliada and Eliphelet.

David Defeats the Philistines

⁸The Philistine people heard that David had been appointed king of all Israel. So all the Philistines went to look for him. When David heard about it, he went out to fight them. ⁹The Philistines had attacked and robbed the people in the Valley of Rephaim. ¹⁰David asked God, "Should I go and attack the Philistines? Will you let me defeat them?"

The Lord answered him, "Go. I will let you defeat them."

¹¹So David and his men went up to the town of Baal Perazim. There he defeated the Philistines. David said, "Like a flood of water, God has broken through my enemies. He has done this through me." So that place was named Baal Perazim.ⁿ ¹²The Philistines had left their idols there. So David ordered his men to burn them.

¹³Soon the Philistines attacked the people in the valley again. ¹⁴So David prayed to God again, and God answered him. God said, "Don't attack the Philistines from the front. Instead, go around them. Attack them in front of the balsam trees. ¹⁵You will hear the sound of marching in the tops of the balsam trees. Then quickly attack

the Philistines. I, God, will have gone out before you to defeat the Philistine army." ¹⁶David did what God commanded him to do. So David and his men defeated the Philistine army. They killed the Philistines all the way from Gibeon to Gezer.

¹⁷So David became famous in all the countries. And the Lord made all nations afraid of David.

The Holy Ark Is Brought to Jerusalem

15 David built houses for himself in Jerusalem. Then he built a place for the Holy Arkᵈ of God. And he set up a tent for it. ²Then David said, "Only the Levites may carry the Holy Ark of God. The Lord chose them to carry the Holy Ark of the Lord. He chose them to serve him forever."

³David called all the people of Israel to come to Jerusalem. He wanted to bring the Holy Ark of the Lord to the place he had made for it. ⁴David called together the descendantsᵈ of Aaron and the Levites. ⁵There were 120 people from Kohath's family group. Uriel was their leader. ⁶There were 220 people from Merari's family group. Asaiah was their leader. ⁷There were 130 people from Gershon's family group. Joel was their leader. ⁸There were 200 people from Elizaphan's family group. Shemaiah was their leader. ⁹There were 80 people from Hebron's family group. Eliel was their leader. ¹⁰There were 112 people from Uzziel's family group. Amminadab was their leader.

¹¹Then David asked the priests Zadok and Abiathar to come to him. He also asked these Levites to come: Uriel, Asaiah, Joel, Shemaiah, Eliel and Amminadab. ¹²David said to them, "You are the leaders of the families of Levi. You and the other Levites must give yourselves for service

---

Baal Perazim This name means "the Lord breaks through".

to the Lord. Then bring up the Holy Ark of the Lord, the God of Israel. Bring it to the place I have made for it. ¹³The last time we did not ask the Lord how to carry it. You Levites didn't carry it. So the Lord our God punished us."

¹⁴Then the priests and Levites prepared themselves for service to the Lord. They did this so they could carry the Holy Ark of the Lord, the God of Israel. ¹⁵The Levites used special poles to carry the Holy Ark of God on their shoulders. This was the way Moses had commanded. They carried it just as the Lord had said they should.

¹⁶David told the leaders of the Levites to appoint their brothers as singers. The singers were to play their lyres,ᵈ harps and cymbals. And they were to sing happy songs.

¹⁷So the Levites appointed Heman and his relatives Asaph and Ethan. Heman was Joel's son. Asaph was Berekiah's son. And Ethan, from the Merari family group, was Kushaiah's son. ¹⁸There was also a second group of Levites. They were Zechariah, Jaaziel, Shemiramoth, Jehiel, Unni, Eliab, Benaiah, Maaseiah, Mattithiah, Eliphelehu, Mikneiah, Obed-Edom and Jeiel. They were the Levite guards.

¹⁹The singers Heman, Asaph and Ethan played bronze cymbals. ²⁰Zechariah, Jaaziel, Shemiramoth, Jehiel, Unni, Eliab, Maaseiah and Benaiah played the high-pitched lyres. ²¹Mattithiah, Eliphelehu, Mikneiah, Obed-Edom, Jeiel and Azaziah played the low-pitched harps. ²²The Levite leader Kenaniah was in charge of the singing. He had this job because he was very good at singing.

²³Berekiah and Elkanah were two of the guards for the Ark of God. ²⁴The priests Shebaniah, Joshaphat, Nethanel, Amasai, Zechariah, Benaiah and Eliezer had the job of blowing trumpets. They did this in front of the Ark of God. Obed-Edom and Jehiah were also guards for the Ark of God.

²⁵David, the leaders of Israel, and the commanders went to get the Ark of the Agreement with the Lord. Each of the commanders was over a group of 1,000 soldiers. They all went to bring the Holy Ark from Obed-Edom's house. And they were very happy. ²⁶God helped the Levites who carried the Ark of the Agreement with the Lord. So they sacrificed seven bulls and seven male sheep. ²⁷All the Levites who carried the Holy Ark wore robes of fine linen. Kenaniah, the man in charge of the singing, and all the singers wore robes of fine linen. David wore a robe of fine linen. And he also wore a holy robeᵈ of fine linen. ²⁸So all the people of Israel brought up the Ark of the Agreement with the Lord. They shouted and blew sheep horns and trumpets. They played cymbals, lyres, and harps.

²⁹So the Ark of the Agreement with the Lord entered Jerusalem. As it entered, Saul's daughter Michal watched from a window. When she saw King David dancing and celebrating, she hated him.

16 They brought the Holy Ark of God and put it inside the tent. This was the tent David had set up for it. Then they offered burnt offerings and fellowship offerings to God. ²David finished giving the burnt offerings and fellowship offerings. Then he used the Lord's name to bless the people. ³He gave a loaf of bread, some dates and raisins to every Israelite man and woman.

⁴Then David appointed some of the Levites to serve before the Holy Ark of the Lord. They had the job of leading the worship. They gave thanks and praise to the Lord, the God of Israel. ⁵Asaph was the leader. He played the cymbals. Zechariah was second to him. The other Levites were Jaaziel, Shemiramoth, Jehiel, Mattithiah, Eliab, Benaiah, Obed-

Edom and Jeiel. They played the lyres and harps. [6]Benaiah and Jahaziel were priests. They blew the trumpets regularly before the Ark of God with God. [7]That day David first gave Asaph and his relatives the job of singing praises to the Lord.

David's Song of Thanks

[8]Give thanks to the Lord and pray to him.
Tell the nations what he has done.
[9]Sing to him. Sing praises to him.
Tell about all the wonderful things he has done.
[10]Be glad that you are his.
Let those who ask the Lord for help be happy.
[11]Depend on the Lord and his strength.
Always go to him for help.
[12]Remember the wonderful things he has done.
Remember his miracles[d] and his decisions.
[13]You are the descendants[d] of Israel, the Lord's servant.
You are the children of Jacob, his chosen people.

[14]He is the Lord our God.
His laws are for all the world.
[15]He will keep his agreement for ever.
He will keep his promises always.
[16]He will keep the agreement he made with Abraham.
He will keep the promise he made to Isaac.
[17]The Lord made it a law for the people of Jacob.
He made it an agreement with Israel to last for ever.
[18]The Lord said, "I will give you the land of Canaan. The promised land will belong to you."

[19]Then God's people were few in number.
They were strangers in the land.
[20]They went from one nation to another.
They went from one kingdom to another.
[21]But the Lord did not let anyone hurt them.
He warned kings not to harm them.
[22]He said, "Don't hurt my chosen people.
Don't harm my prophets."[d]

[23]Sing to the Lord, all the earth.
Every day tell how he saves us.
[24]Tell the nations about the Lord's glory.
Tell all peoples about his wonderful works.
[25]The Lord is great; he should be praised.
He should be honoured more than all the gods.
[26]All the gods of the nations are only idols.
But the Lord made the skies.
[27]The Lord has glory and majesty.
He has power and joy in his Temple.[d]

[28]Praise the Lord, all nations on earth.
Praise the Lord's glory and power.
[29]Praise the Lord for the glory of his name.
Bring your offering to him.
Worship the Lord because he is holy.
[30]The whole earth should tremble before the Lord.
The earth is set, and it cannot be moved.
[31]Let the skies rejoice and the earth be glad.
Let people everywhere say, "The Lord is king!"
[32]Let the sea and everything in it shout.
Let the fields and everything in them show their joy.

33Then the trees of the forest will
sing.
They will sing with joy before
the Lord.
They will sing because the Lord
is coming to judge the
world.
34Thank the Lord because he is
good.
His love continues for ever.
35Say to him, "Save us, God our
Saviour.
Bring us back and save us from
the nations.
Then we will thank you.
Then we will gladly praise you."
36Praise the Lord, the God of
Israel,
for ever and for ever.

All the people said, "Amen" and
"Praise the Lord".

37Then David left Asaph and the
other Levites there in front of the
Ark*d* of God with the Lord. They were
to serve there every day. 38David also
left Obed-Edom and 68 other Levites
to serve with them. Hosah and Obed-
Edom son of Jeduthun were guards.
39David left Zadok the priest and the
other priests who served with him in
front of the Tent of the Lord. This
was at the place of worship in Gibeon.
40Every morning and evening they offered burnt offerings on the altar of
burnt offerings. They did this to follow
the rules written in the Teachings of
the Lord. These were the Teachings
he had given Israel. 41With them were
Heman and Jeduthun and other Levites. They were chosen by name to
sing praises to the Lord because the
Lord's love continues for ever. 42He-
man and Jeduthun also had the job of
playing the trumpets and cymbals.
They also played other musical instruments when songs were sung to God.
Jeduthun's sons guarded the gates.
43Then all the people left. Each person went to his own home. And David
also went home to bless his family.

God's Promise to David

17 David moved into his palace.
Then he said to Nathan the
prophet, "Look, I am living in a palace
made of cedar. But the Ark*d* of God
with the Lord sits in a tent."
2Nathan answered David, "Do what
you want to do. God is with you."
3But that night God spoke his word
to Nathan. God said, 4"Go and tell my
servant David: 'This is what the Lord
says: David, you are not the person to
build a house for me to live in. 5From
the time I brought Israel out of Egypt
until now I have not lived in a house.
I have moved from one tent site to another. I have gone from one place to
another. 6I have moved with the Israelites to different places. I commanded leaders to take care of my people.
I never said to any of those leaders,
"Why haven't you built me a house of
cedar?" '
7"Now, tell my servant David: 'The
Lord of heaven's armies says: I took
you from the pasture and from tending
the sheep. I made you king of my people Israel. 8I have been with you everywhere you have gone. I have killed
your enemies for you. Now I will
make you one of the most famous men
on earth. 9I will give this place to my
people Israel. I will settle them here.
Then they will have a home of their
own. They won't be bothered any
more. Evil people won't hurt them as
they have done since the first. 10Evil
people have hurt them since I chose
leaders for my people Israel. I will also
defeat all your enemies.
" 'I tell you that the Lord will make
your descendants*d* kings of Israel after you. 11When you die and join your
ancestors, I will let your child be the
new king. He will be one of your own
sons. And I will make his kingdom
strong. 12He will build a house for me.
And I will let his family rule for ever.
13I will be his father, and he will be my
son. I took away my love from Saul,

who ruled before you. But I will never stop loving your son. ¹⁴I will put him in charge of my house and kingdom for ever. His family will rule for ever'."

¹⁵Nathan told David everything God had said in this vision.

David's Prayer

¹⁶Then King David went in and sat in front of the Lord. David said, "Lord God, why have you made me so important to you? Why have you made my family important? ¹⁷But that was not enough for you, God. You have also said these kind things about my future family. I am your servant. Lord God, you have treated me like a very important man.

¹⁸"What more can I say to you? You have done so much for me, your servant. You love me so much. ¹⁹Lord, you have done this wonderful thing for me for my sake. And you have done it because you wanted to. You have let me know all these great promises.

²⁰"There is no one like you, Lord. There is no God except you. We have heard all this ourselves. ²¹There is no one like your people, the Israelites. It is the one nation on earth that God chose to be his people. You used them to make your name well-known. You did great and wonderful things for them. You went ahead of them and forced other nations out of the land. You freed your people from slavery in Egypt. ²²You made the people of Israel your very own people for ever. And, Lord, you became their God.

²³"Lord, you made this promise about my family and me, your servant. Now, keep your promise for ever. Do what you have promised. ²⁴Then people will know you and honour you for ever. And people will say, 'The Lord of heaven's armies, the God over Israel, is Israel's God!' And the family of your servant David will continue before you.

²⁵"My God, you have told me that you would make my family great. So I,

your servant, am brave enough to pray to you. ²⁶Lord, you are God. You have promised these good things to me, your servant. ²⁷You have chosen to bless my family. Let it continue before you for ever. Lord, you have blessed my family. So it will be blessed for ever."

David Defeats Nations

18 Later, David attacked the Philistine people and defeated them. He took Gath and the small towns around it from the Philistines. ²Then David defeated the country of Moab. So the Moabites became David's servants. And they brought the payments he demanded from them.

³David also fought against Hadadezer king of Zobah. David fought Hadadezer's army all the way to the town of Hamath. He did this because Hadadezer tried to spread his kingdom all the way to the Euphrates River. ⁴David took from Hadadezer 1,000 chariots and 7,000 chariot drivers. And he took 20,000 soldiers on foot. David also crippled most of Hadadezer's horses used for pulling chariots. He saved only 100 of the chariot horses.

⁵The Aramean people from Damascus came to help Hadadezer king of Zobah. But David killed 22,000 of them. ⁶Then David put camps of troops in Damascus in Aram. The Arameans became David's servants and brought him the payments he demanded. So the Lord gave David victory everywhere he went.

⁷David took the gold shields from Hadadezer's army leaders. And he brought them to Jerusalem. ⁸David also took much bronze from the towns of Tebah and Cun. These towns belonged to Hadadezer. Later, Solomon used this bronze to make things for the Temple:ᵈ the large bronze bowl, which was called the Sea, the pillars and other bronze things.

⁹Toi was king of the city of Hamath. He heard that David had defeated the

whole army of Hadadezer king of Zobah. [10]So Toi sent his son Hadoram to greet King David. Hadoram also congratulated David for fighting and defeating Hadadezer. Hadadezer had been at war with Toi before. Hadoram gave David all kinds of things made of gold, silver and bronze. [11]King David gave these things to the Lord. David had done the same thing with the silver and gold he had taken from these nations: Edom, Moab, the Ammonites, the Philistines and Amalek.

[12]Abishai son of Zeruiah killed 18,000 Edomite people in the Valley of Salt. [13]Abishai also put camps of troops in Edom. And all the Edomites became David's servants. The Lord gave David victory everywhere he went.

David's Important Officers

[14]David was king over all of Israel. He did what was right and fair for everyone. [15]Joab son of Zeruiah was commander of David's army. Jehoshaphat son of Ahilud was the recorder. [16]Zadok son of Ahitub and Ahimelech son of Abiathar were priests. Shavsha was the royal assistant. [17]Benaiah was responsible for leading the Kerethites and Pelethites, the king's bodyguards. Benaiah was Jehoiada's son. And David's sons were important officers. They served at King David's side.

David Fights the Ammonites

19 Nahash was king of the Ammonite people. When Nahash died, his son became the king. [2]David said, "Nahash was kind to me. So I will be kind to Hanun son of Nahash." Then David sent a group to comfort Hanun about the death of his father.

David's men went to comfort Hanun in the country of Ammon. [3]But the Ammonite leaders said to Hanun, "Don't be fooled. David didn't send these men to comfort you. They are not here to honour your dead father. David sent his men to spy on you and

your land. He wants to destroy your country." [4]So Hanun arrested David's men. To shame them he cut off their beards and cut off their clothes at the hips. Then he sent them away.

[5]David's men were too ashamed to go home. Some people came to David and told him what had happened to his men. So he sent messengers to meet them. He said, "Stay in Jericho until your beards have grown back. Then come home."

[6]The Ammonite people saw they had caused David to hate them. So Hanun and the Ammonites sent about 34 tons of silver to hire chariots and chariot drivers. They hired Arameans from North West Mesopotamia, Aram Maacah and Zobah. [7]The Ammonites hired 32,000 chariots and chariot drivers. They also hired the king of Maacah and his army. So he and his army came and set up camp near the town of Medeba. The Ammonites themselves came out of their towns and got ready for battle.

[8]David heard about this. So he sent out Joab and the whole army of Israel. [9]The Ammonites came out and got ready for battle. They were near the city gate. The kings who had come to help stayed out in the fields by themselves.

[10]Joab saw that there were enemy troops in front of him and behind him. So Joab chose some of the best soldiers of Israel. And he sent them out to fight the Arameans. [11]Joab put the rest of the army of Israel under the command of Abishai, his brother. Then they went out to fight the Ammonites. [12]Joab said to Abishai, "The Arameans may be too strong for me. If they are, then you must help me. Or, the Ammonites may be too strong for you. If they are, then I will help you. [13]Let's be strong. We must fight bravely for our people and the cities of our God. The Lord will do what he thinks is right."

[14]Then Joab and the army with him

went to attack the Arameans. And the Arameans ran away from them. ¹⁵The Ammonite army saw that the Arameans were running away. So they also ran away from Abishai and his army. The Ammonites went back inside their city. And Joab went back to Jerusalem.

¹⁶The Arameans saw that Israel had defeated them. So they sent messengers to bring other Arameans from east of the Euphrates River. Shophach the commander of Hadadezer's army led them.

¹⁷When David heard about this, he gathered all the Israelites. And he led them across the Jordan River. He lined them up for battle, facing the Arameans. And they attacked the Arameans. ¹⁸But the Arameans ran away from the Israelites. David and his army killed 7,000 Aramean chariot drivers. And they killed 40,000 Aramean foot soldiers. They also killed Shophach, the commander of the Aramean army.

¹⁹Hadadezer's officers saw that Israel had defeated them. So they made peace with David. They became his servants. So the Arameans refused to help the Ammonites again.

Joab Destroys the Ammonites

20 In the spring Joab led the army of Israel out to battle. This was the time of year when kings went out to battle. But David stayed in Jerusalem. The army of Israel destroyed the land of Ammon. Then they went to the city of Rabbah. They surrounded it and attacked it until they destroyed it. ²David took the crown from the head of their king.ⁿ That gold crown weighed about 34 kilograms. And it had valuable gems in it. The crown was put on David's head. Then David took many valuable things from the

city. ³David brought out the people from Rabbah. And he forced them to work with saws, iron picks and axes. David did the same thing to all the Ammonite towns. Then David and all the army returned to Jerusalem.

Philistine Giants Are Killed

⁴Later, war broke out between Israel and the Philistines at Gezer. At this time Sibbecai from Hushah killed Sippai. Sippai was one of the descendantsᵈ of the Rephaites.ᵈ So those Philistines were defeated.

⁵Another time, the Israelites again fought the Philistines. Elhanan son of Jair killed Lahmi, the brother of Goliath. Goliath was from the town of Gath. Lahmi's spear was as large as a weaver's rod.

⁶Later, the Israelites fought another war with the Philistines at Gath. In this town there was a very large man. He had six fingers on each hand and six toes on each foot. So he had 24 fingers and toes in all. He also was a descendant of Rapha.ᵈ ⁷When he made fun of Israel, Jonathan killed him. Jonathan was the son of Shimea, David's brother.

⁸These Philistines were descendants of Rapha from Gath. David and his men killed them.

David Counts Israel

21 Satan was against Israel. He encouraged David to count the people of Israel. ²So David gave an order to Joab and the commanders of the troops. He said, "Go and count all the Israelites. Count everyone from Beersheba to Dan."ⁿ Then tell me so I will know how many people there are."

³But Joab answered, "May the Lord make the nation 100 times as large. My master the king, all the Israelites

---

king Or, "Milcom", the god of the Ammonite people.
Beersheba to Dan Beersheba was the city farthest south in Israel. Dan was the city farthest north. So this means all the people of Israel.

are your servants. Why do you want to do this, my master? You will make Israel guilty of sin."

⁴But King David made Joab follow his order. So Joab left and went through all Israel, counting the people. Then he returned to Jerusalem. ⁵He told David how many people there were. In Israel there were 1,100,000 men who could use a sword. And there were 470,000 men in Judah who could use a sword. ⁶But Joab did not count the tribes*d* of Levi and Benjamin. He didn't count them because he didn't like King David's order. ⁷David had done something God had said was wrong. So God punished Israel.

⁸Then David said to God, "I have done something very foolish. It was a terrible sin. Now, I beg you to forgive me, your servant."

⁹Gad was David's seer.*d* The Lord said to Gad, ¹⁰"Go and tell David: 'This is what the Lord says: I am going to give you three choices. Choose one, and I will punish you in that way'."

¹¹So Gad went to David and said to him, "This is what the Lord says: 'Choose which punishment you want. ¹²You may choose three years without enough food for the nation. Or choose three months of running from your enemies as they chase you with their swords. Or choose three days of punishment from the Lord. A terrible disease will spread through the country. The angel of the Lord will go through Israel destroying the people'. Now, David, decide which answer I will give to the Lord, who sent me."

¹³David said to Gad, "I am in trouble. I don't want some man to punish me. The Lord is very merciful. So let the Lord punish me."

¹⁴So the Lord sent a terrible disease on Israel, and 70,000 people died. ¹⁵God sent an angel to destroy Jerusalem. But when the angel started to destroy it, the Lord saw it and felt sorry.

So he said to the angel who was destroying, "That is enough! Stop!" The angel of the Lord was then standing at the threshing*d* floor of Araunah the Jebusite.

¹⁶David looked up and saw the angel of the Lord in the sky. The angel was holding his sword over Jerusalem. Then David and the older leaders bowed face down on the ground. They were wearing rough cloth to show their sadness. ¹⁷David said to God, "I am the one who sinned. I gave the order for the people to be counted. I have done wrong. These people are only sheep. What wrong have they done? Lord my God, punish me and my family. But stop the terrible disease that is killing your people."

¹⁸Then the angel of the Lord gave an order to Gad. He told Gad to tell David to build an altar to worship the Lord. It was to be at the threshing floor of Araunah the Jebusite. ¹⁹Gad told David these things from the Lord. So David went to Araunah's threshing floor.

²⁰Araunah was separating the straw from the wheat. When he turned around, he saw the angel. Araunah's four sons who were with him hid. ²¹David went to Araunah. When Araunah saw David, he left the threshing floor. He bowed face down on the ground before David.

²²David said to him, "Sell me your threshing floor. Then I can build an altar to worship the Lord here. Then the terrible disease will be stopped. Sell it to me for the full price."

²³Araunah said to David, "Take this threshing floor. You are my master the king. Do anything you want. Look, I will also give you oxen for the burnt offering. I will give you boards as wood for the fire. And I will give the wheat for the grain offering. I will give all this to you."

²⁴But King David answered Araunah, "No, I must pay the full price. I won't take anything that is yours and

give it to the Lord. I won't give an offering that costs me nothing."

²⁵So David paid Araunah about 7 kilograms of gold for the place. ²⁶David built an altar to worship the Lord there. He offered burnt offerings and fellowship offerings. David prayed to the Lord. And the Lord answered him by sending down fire from heaven. It came down on the altar of burnt offering. ²⁷Then the Lord commanded the angel to put his sword back into its holder.

²⁸David saw that the Lord had answered him on the threshing floor of Araunah. So he offered sacrifices to the Lord there. ²⁹The Holy Tent[d] and the altar of burnt offerings were in Gibeon. They were at the place of worship there. Moses had made the Holy Tent while the Israelites were in the desert. ³⁰But David could not go to the Holy Tent to speak with God. He was afraid of the angel of the Lord and his sword.

22 David said, "The Temple[d] of the Lord God will be built here. And the altar for burnt offerings for Israel will be built here."

David Makes Plans for the Temple

²So David gave an order for all foreigners living in Israel to be gathered together. From that group David chose stonecutters. Their job was to cut stones to be used in building the Temple[d] of God. ³David supplied a large amount of iron. It was used for making nails and hinges for the gate doors. He also supplied more bronze than could be weighed. ⁴And he supplied more cedar logs than could be counted. Much of the cedar had been brought to David by the people from Sidon and Tyre. ⁵David said, "We should build a great Temple for the Lord. It should be famous everywhere for its greatness and beauty. But my son Solomon is young. He hasn't yet learned what he needs to know. So I will prepare for the building of it." So David got many of the materials ready before he died.

⁶Then David called for his son Solomon. He told Solomon to build the Temple for the Lord, the God of Israel. ⁷David said to him, "My son, I wanted to build a temple for worshiping the Lord my God. ⁸But the Lord spoke his word to me, 'David, you have killed too many people. You have fought too many wars. So you cannot build a temple for worship to me. You have killed too many people. ⁹But, you will have a son. He will be a man of peace and rest. I will give him rest from all his enemies around him. His name will be Solomon.[n] And I will give Israel peace and quiet while he is king. ¹⁰Solomon will build a temple for worship to me. He will be my son, and I will be his father. I will make his kingdom strong. Someone from his family will rule Israel for ever'."

¹¹David also said, "Now, my son, may the Lord be with you. May you build a temple for the Lord your God, as he said you would. ¹²The Lord will make you the king of Israel. May the Lord give you wisdom and understanding. Then you will be able to obey the teachings of the Lord your God. ¹³Be careful to obey the rules and laws the Lord gave Moses for Israel. If you obey them, you will have success. Be strong and brave. Don't be afraid or discouraged.

¹⁴"Solomon, I have worked hard getting many of the materials for building the Temple of the Lord. I have supplied about 3,450 tons of gold. And I have supplied about 34,500 tons of silver. I have supplied so much bronze and iron it cannot be weighed. And I have supplied wood and stone. And you may add to them.

Solomon This name sounds like the Hebrew word for "peace".

¹⁵You have many workmen. You have stonecutters, stoneworkers and carpenters. You have men skilled in every kind of work. ¹⁶They are skilled in working with gold, silver, bronze and iron. You have more craftsmen than can be counted. Now begin the work. And may the Lord be with you."

¹⁷Then David ordered all the leaders of Israel to help his son Solomon. ¹⁸David said to them, "The Lord your God is with you. He has given you rest from our enemies. He helped me to defeat the people living around us. The Lord and his people are in control of this land. ¹⁹Now give yourself completely to obeying the Lord your God. Build the holy place of the Lord God. Build the Temple for worship to the Lord. Then bring the Ark*d* of the Agreement with the Lord into the Temple. And bring in the holy things that belong to God."

The Levites

23 David had lived long and was old. Then he made his son Solomon the new king of Israel. ²David gathered all the leaders of Israel, along with the priests and Levites. ³David counted the Levites who were 30 years old and older. In all, there were 38,000 Levites. ⁴David said, "Of these, 24,000 Levites will direct the work of the Temple*d* of the Lord. And 6,000 Levites will be officers and judges. ⁵And 4,000 Levites will be gatekeepers. And 4,000 Levites will praise the Lord with musical instruments. I made these instruments for them to use for praise."

⁶David separated the Levites into three groups. These groups were led by Levi's three sons: Gershon, Kohath and Merari.

The People of Gershon

⁷From the people of Gershon, there were Ladan and Shimei.

⁸Ladan had three sons. His first son

was Jehiel. His other sons were Zetham and Joel.

⁹Shimei's sons were Shelomoth, Haziel and Haran. These three sons were leaders of Ladan's families. ¹⁰Shimei had four sons. They were Jahath, Ziza, Jeush and Beriah. ¹¹Jahath was the first son, and Ziza was the second son. But Jeush and Beriah did not have many children. So they were counted as if they were one family.

The People of Kohath

¹²Kohath had four sons. They were Amram, Izhar, Hebron and Uzziel.

¹³Amram's sons were Aaron and Moses. Aaron and his descendants*d* were chosen to be special for ever. They were chosen to prepare the holy things for the Lord's service. They were to offer sacrifices before the Lord. They were to serve him as priests. They were to give blessings in the Lord's name for ever.

¹⁴Moses was the man of God. Moses' sons were counted as part of the tribe*d* of Levi. ¹⁵Moses' sons were Gershom and Eliezer. ¹⁶Gershom's first son was Shubael. ¹⁷Eliezer's first son was Rehabiah. Eliezer had no other sons, but Rehabiah had many sons.

¹⁸Izhar's first son was Shelomith.

¹⁹Hebron's first son was Jeriah. His second son was Amariah. Jahaziel was the third son. And Jekameam was the fourth son.

²⁰Uzziel's first son was Micah. And Isshiah was his second son.

The People of Merari

²¹Merari's sons were Mahli and Mushi. Mahli's sons were Eleazar and Kish. ²²Eleazar died without having sons. He had only daughters. Eleazar's daughters married their cousins, the sons of Kish. ²³Mushi's three sons were Mahli, Eder and Jerimoth.

The Levites' Work

²⁴These were Levi's descendants*d* listed by their families. They were the

leaders of families. Each person who was 20 years old or older was listed. They served in the Lord's Temple.[d] [25]David had said, "The Lord is the God of Israel. He has given rest to his people. He has come to live in Jerusalem for ever. [26]So the Levites don't need to carry the Holy Tent.[d] They don't need to carry any of the things used in its services any more." [27]David's last instructions were to count the Levites. All who were 20 years old and older were counted.

[28]The Levites had the job of helping Aaron's descendants. They helped in the service of the Temple of the Lord. They cared for the Temple courtyard and side rooms. They had the job of making all the holy things pure. Their job was to serve in the Temple of God. [29]They were responsible for putting the holy bread on the table. They also were responsible for the flour in the grain offerings. And they were responsible for the bread made without yeast. They were also responsible for the baking and mixing. And they did all the measuring. [30]The Levites also stood every morning and gave thanks and praise to the Lord. They also did this every evening. [31]The Levites offered all the burnt offerings to the Lord on the special days of rest. And they offered them at the New Moon[d] festivals and at all appointed feasts. They served before the Lord every day. They were to follow the rules for how many Levites should serve each time. [32]So the Levites took care of the Meeting Tent. They also took care of the Holy Place. And they helped their relatives, Aaron's descendants, with the services at the Temple of the Lord.

The Groups of the Priests

24 These were the groups of Aaron's sons:

Aaron's sons were Nadab, Abihu, Eleazar and Ithamar. [2]But Nadab and Abihu died before their father did.

And they had no sons. So Eleazar and Ithamar served as the priests. [3]David separated the family groups of Eleazar and Ithamar into two different groups. Each group had certain duties it had been given. Zadok and Ahimelech helped David. Zadok was a descendant[d] of Eleazar. And Ahimelech was a descendant of Ithamar. [4]There were more leaders from Eleazar's family than from Ithamar's. There were 16 leaders from Eleazar's family. And there were eight leaders from Ithamar's family. [5]Men were chosen from Eleazar's and Ithamar's families by throwing lots.[d] Some men from each family were chosen to be in charge of the Holy Place. And some men from each family were chosen to serve as priests.

[6]Shemaiah son of Nethanel was the secretary. He was from the tribe[d] of Levi. Shemaiah recorded the names of those descendants in front of King David and these officers: Zadok the priest, Ahimelech son of Abiathar, and the leaders of the families of the priests and Levites. The work was divided by lots among the families of Eleazar and Ithamar. The following men with their groups were chosen.

[7]The first one chosen was Jehoiarib. The second was Jedaiah. [8]The third was Harim. The fourth was Seorim. [9]The fifth was Malkijah. The sixth was Mijamin. [10]The seventh was Hakkoz. The eighth was Abijah. [11]The ninth was Jeshua. The tenth was Shecaniah. [12]The eleventh was Eliashib. The twelfth was Jakim. [13]The thirteenth was Huppah. The fourteenth was Jeshebeab. [14]The fifteenth was Bilgah. The sixteenth was Immer. [15]The seventeenth was Hezir. The eighteenth was Happizzez. [16]The nineteenth was Pethahiah. The twentieth was Jehezkel. [17]The twenty-first was Jakin. The twenty-second was Gamul. [18]The twenty-third was Delaiah. The twenty-fourth was Maaziah.

[19]These were the groups chosen to

serve in the Temple of the Lord. They obeyed the rules Aaron had given them. The Lord, the God of Israel, had given those rules to Aaron.

The Other Levites

20These are the names of the rest of Levi's descendants:*d*

Shubael was a descendant of Amram. And Jehdeiah was a descendant of Shubael.

21Isshiah was the first son of Rehabiah.

22From the Izhar family group, there was Shelomoth. And Jahath was a descendant of Shelomoth.

23Hebron's first son was Jeriah. Amariah was his second son. Jahaziel was his third son, and Jekameam was his fourth.

24Uzziel's son was Micah. Micah's son was Shamir. 25Isshiah was Micah's brother. Isshiah's son was Zechariah.

26Merari's descendants were Mahli and Mushi. Merari's son was Jaaziah. 27Jaaziah son of Merari had sons named Shoham, Zaccur and Ibri. 28Mahli's son was Eleazar. But Eleazar did not have any sons.

29Kish's son was Jerahmeel.

30Mushi's sons were Mahli, Eder and Jerimoth.

These are the Levites, listed by their families. 31They were chosen for special jobs by throwing lots.*d* They did this just as their relatives, the priests, had done. The priests were Aaron's descendants. They threw lots in front of King David, Zadok and Ahimelech. The leaders of the families of the priests and Levites were also there. The families of the oldest brother and the youngest brother were treated the same.

The Music Groups

25 David and the commanders of the army chose some men to preach. They chose some of the sons of Asaph, Heman and Jeduthun. They were to preach God's message and play harps, lyres*d* and cymbals. Here is a list of the men who served in this way:

2Asaph's sons who served were Zaccur, Joseph, Nethaniah and Asarelah. King David chose Asaph to preach. And Asaph directed his sons.

3Jeduthun's sons who served were Gedaliah, Zeri, Jeshaiah, Shimei, Hashabiah and Mattithiah. There were six of them, and Jeduthun directed them. He preached. And he used a harp to give thanks and praise to the Lord.

4Heman's sons who served were Bukkiah, Mattaniah, Uzziel, Shubael and Jerimoth. There were also Hananiah, Hanani, Eliathah, Giddalti and Romamti-Ezer. And there were Joshbekashah, Mallothi, Hothir and Mahazioth. 5All these men were sons of Heman, David's seer.*d* God promised to make Heman strong. So Heman had many sons. God gave him 14 sons and three daughters. 6Heman directed all his sons in making music for the Temple*d* of the Lord. They used cymbals, lyres and harps. That was their way of serving in the Temple of God. And King David was in charge of Asaph, Jeduthun and Heman. 7These men and their relatives from the Levites were trained in music. They were skilled in making music for the Lord. There were 288 of them. 8Everyone threw lots*d* to choose the time his family was to serve at the Temple. The young and the old had to throw lots. The teacher and the student had to throw lots.

9First, 12 men were chosen from Joseph, his sons and relatives. Joseph was from the family of Asaph.

Second, 12 men were chosen from Gedaliah, his sons and relatives.

10Third, 12 men were chosen from Zaccur, his sons and relatives.

11Fourth, 12 men were chosen from Izri, his sons and relatives.

12Fifth, 12 men were chosen from Nethaniah, his sons and relatives. 13Sixth, 12 men were chosen from Bukkiah, his sons and relatives. 14Seventh, 12 men were chosen from Jesarelah, his sons and relatives. 15Eighth, 12 men were chosen from Jeshaiah, his sons and relatives. 16Ninth, 12 men were chosen from Mattaniah, his sons and relatives. 17Tenth, 12 men were chosen from Shimei, his sons and relatives. 18Eleventh, 12 men were chosen from Azarel, his sons and relatives. 19Twelfth, 12 men were chosen from Hashabiah, his sons and relatives. 20Thirteenth, 12 men were chosen from Shubael, his sons and relatives. 21Fourteenth, 12 men were chosen from Mattithiah, his sons and relatives. 22Fifteenth, 12 men were chosen from Jerimoth, his sons and relatives. 23Sixteenth, 12 men were chosen from Hananiah, his sons and relatives. 24Seventeenth, 12 men were chosen from Joshbekashah, his sons and relatives. 25Eighteenth, 12 men were chosen from Hanani, his sons and relatives. 26Nineteenth, 12 men were chosen from Mallothi, his sons and relatives. 27Twentieth, 12 men were chosen from Eliathah, his sons and relatives. 28Twenty-first, 12 men were chosen from Hothir, his sons and relatives. 29Twenty-second, 12 men were chosen from Giddalti, his sons and relatives. 30Twenty-third, 12 men were chosen from Mahazioth, his sons and relatives. 31Twenty-fourth, 12 men were chosen from Romamti-Ezer, his sons and relatives.

The Gatekeepers

26 These are the groups of the gatekeepers.

From the family of Korah, there was Meshelemiah and his sons. (Meshelemiah son of Kore was from Asaph's family.) 2Meshelemiah had sons. Zechariah was his first son. Jediael was his second son. Zebadiah was his third son. Jathniel was his fourth son. 3Elam was his fifth son. Jehohanan was his sixth son, and Eliehoenai was his seventh son.

4There were also Obed-Edom and his sons. Obed-Edom's first son was Shemaiah. Jehozabad was his second son. Joah was his third son. Sacar was his fourth son. Nethanel was his fifth son. 5Ammiel was his sixth son. Issachar was his seventh son, and Peullethai was his eighth son. God had blessed Obed-Edom with children.

6Obed-Edom's son Shemaiah also had sons. They were leaders in their father's family because they were capable men. 7Shemaiah's sons were Othni, Rephael, Obed, Elzabad, Elihu and Semakiah. Elihu and Semakiah were skilled workers. 8All these men were Obed-Edom's descendants.d They and their sons and relatives were capable men. They were strong enough to do the work. Obed-Edom had 62 descendants in all.

9Meshelemiah had sons and relatives. They were skilled workers. In all, there were 18 sons and relatives.

10These are the gatekeepers from the Merari family. Hosah had sons. Shimri was chosen to be in charge. He was not the oldest son, but his father chose him to be in charge. 11Hilkiah was his second son. Tabaliah was his third son, and Zechariah was his fourth son. In all, Hosah had 13 sons and relatives.

12These were the leaders of the groups of the gatekeepers. They had jobs for serving in the Templed of the Lord. Their relatives also had jobs in the Temple. 13Each family was given a gate to guard. They were chosen by throwing lots.d Young and old threw lots.

14Meshelemiah was chosen by lot to guard the East Gate. Then lots were thrown for Meshelemiah's son Zechariah. He was a wise counsellor. He was chosen for the North Gate. 15Obed-Edom was chosen for the South Gate. And Obed-Edom's sons were chosen to guard the storehouse. 16Shuppim and Hosah were chosen for the West Gate. They also were to guard the Shalleketh Gate on the upper road.

Guards stood side by side with guards. 17Six Levites stood guard every day at the East Gate. Four Levites stood guard every day at the North Gate. Four Levites stood guard every day at the South Gate. And two Levites at a time guarded the storehouse. 18There were two guards at the western court. And there were four guards on the road to the court.

19These were the groups of the gatekeepers. They were from the families of Korah and Merari.

Other Leaders

20Other Levites were responsible for taking care of the treasuries of the Temple^d of God. They were also responsible for the places where the holy things were kept.

21Ladan was Gershon's son. Ladan was the ancestor of several family groups. Jehiel was a leader of one of the family groups. 22Jehiel's sons were Zetham and his brother Joel. They were responsible for the treasuries of the Temple of the Lord.

23Other leaders were chosen from the family groups of Amram, Izhar, Hebron and Uzziel. 24Shubael was the leader responsible for the treasuries of the Temple of the Lord. Shubael was the descendant^d of Gershom, who was Moses' son. 25These were Shubael's relatives from Eliezer: Eliezer's son Rehabiah, Rehabiah's son Jeshaiah, Jeshaiah's son Joram, Joram's son Zicri and Zicri's son Shelomith. 26Shelomith and his relatives

were responsible for everything that had been collected for the Temple. Things had been collected by King David and the heads of families. They had been collected by commanders of 1,000 men and of 100 men and other army commanders. 27They also gave some of the things they had taken in wars. They gave them to be used in repairing the Temple of the Lord. 28Shelomith and his relatives took care of all the holy things. Some had been given by Samuel the seer^d and Saul son of Kish. Some had been given by Abner son of Ner and Joab son of Zeruiah.

29Kenaniah was from the Izhar family. He and his sons worked outside the Temple. They worked as officers and judges in different places in Israel.

30Hashabiah was from the Hebron family. He and his relatives were responsible for the Lord's work and the king's business in Israel west of the Jordan River. There were 1,700 skilled men in Hashabiah's group. 31The history of the Hebron family shows that Jeriah was their leader. In David's fortieth year as king, the records were searched. Some capable men of the Hebron family were found living at Jazer in Gilead. 32Jeriah had 2,700 relatives who were skilled men. They were leaders of families. King David gave them the responsibility of directing the tribes^d of Reuben, Gad and the eastern half-tribe of Manasseh. They took care of the Lord's work and the king's business for them.

Army Divisions

27 This is the list of the Israelite people who served the king in the army. Each division was on duty one month each year. There were leaders of families, commanders of 100 men, commanders of 1,000 men and other officers. Each division had 24,000 men.

2Jashobeam son of Zabdiel was in

charge of the first division for the first month. There were 24,000 men in his division. ³He was one of the descendants[d] of Perez. Jashobeam was leader of all the army officers for the first month.

⁴Dodai was in charge of the division for the second month. He was from the Ahohites. Mikloth was a leader in the division. There were 24,000 men in Dodai's division.

⁵The third commander was Benaiah son of Jehoiada the priest. He was the commander for the third month. There were 24,000 men in Benaiah's division. ⁶He was the Benaiah who was one of the Thirty[n] soldiers. Benaiah was a brave warrior who led those men. Benaiah's son Ammizabad was in charge of Benaiah's division.

⁷The fourth commander was Asahel, the brother of Joab. He was the commander for the fourth month. Later, Asahel's son Zebadiah took his place as commander. There were 24,000 men in his division.

⁸The fifth commander was Shamhuth, from Izrah's family. He was the commander for the fifth month. There were 24,000 men in his division.

⁹The sixth commander was Ira son of Ikkesh. He was the commander for the sixth month. He was from the town of Tekoa. There were 24,000 men in his division.

¹⁰The seventh commander was Helez. He was the commander for the seventh month. He was from the Pelonites and a descendant of Ephraim. There were 24,000 men in his division.

¹¹The eighth commander was Sibbecai. He was the commander for the eighth month. He was from Hushah and was from Zerah's family. There were 24,000 men in his division.

¹²The ninth commander was Abiezer, from the town of Anathoth. He was the commander for the ninth month. He was from the tribe[d] of Benjamin. There were 24,000 men in his division.

¹³The tenth commander was Maharai. He was the commander for the tenth month. He was from Netophah and was from Zerah's family. There were 24,000 men in his division.

¹⁴The eleventh commander was Benaiah. He was the commander for the eleventh month. He was from Pirathon and was from the tribe of Ephraim. There were 24,000 men in his division.

¹⁵The twelfth commander was Heldai. He was the commander for the twelfth month. He was from Netophah and was from Othniel's family. There were 24,000 men in his division.

Leaders of the Tribes

¹⁶These were the leaders of the tribes[d] of Israel. Eliezer son of Zicri was over the tribe of Reuben. Shephatiah son of Maacah was over the tribe of Simeon. ¹⁷Hashabiah son of Kemuel was over the tribe of Levi. Zadok was over the people of Aaron. ¹⁸Elihu, one of David's brothers, was over the tribe of Judah. Omri son of Michael was over the tribe of Issachar. ¹⁹Ishmaiah son of Obadiah was over the tribe of Zebulun. Jerimoth son of Azriel was over the tribe of Naphtali. ²⁰Hoshea son of Azaziah was over the tribe of Ephraim. Joel son of Pedaiah was over the western half-tribe of Manasseh. ²¹Iddo son of Zechariah was over the eastern half-tribe of Manasseh. Jaasiel son of Abner was over the tribe of Benjamin. ²²Azarel son of Jeroham was over the tribe of Dan.

These were the leaders of the tribes of Israel.

²³The Lord had promised to make the Israelites as many as the stars in the sky. So David only counted the men who were 20 years old and older.

Thirty These were David's most powerful soldiers. See 2 Samuel 23:28.

24Joab son of Zeruiah began to count the people. But he did not finish. God became angry with Israel for counting the people. So the number of the people was not put in the history book about King David's rule.

The King's Directors

25Azmaveth son of Adiel was in charge of the royal storehouses.

Jonathan was in charge of the storehouses in the towns, villages and towers. He was the son of Uzziah.

26Ezri son of Kelub was in charge of the field workers. They farmed the land.

27Shimei was in charge of the vineyards. He was from the town of Ramah.

Zabdi was in charge of storing the wine that came from the vineyards. Zabdi was from Shepham.

28Baal-Hanan was in charge of the olive trees and sycamore trees in the western mountain slopes. He was from Geder.

Joash was in charge of storing the olive oil.

29Shitrai was in charge of the cows that fed in the Plain of Sharon. He was from Sharon.

Shaphat son of Adlai was in charge of the cows in the valleys.

30Obil was in charge of the camels. He was an Ishmaelite.

Jehdeiah was in charge of the donkeys. He was from Meronoth.

31Jaziz was in charge of the sheep. He was from the Hagrites.

All these men were the officers who took care of King David's property.

32Jonathan was David's uncle. He advised David. Jonathan was a wise man and a teacher of the law. Jehiel son of Hacmoni took care of the king's sons. 33Ahithophel advised the king. Hushai was the king's friend. He was from the Arkite people. 34Jehoiada and Abiathar later took Ahithophel's place in advising the king. Jehoiada was Be-

naiah's son. Joab was the commander of the king's army.

David's Plans for the Temple

28 David commanded all the leaders of Israel to come to Jerusalem. There were the leaders of the tribes*d* and the commanders of the divisions serving the king. There were the commanders of 1000 men and of 100 men. There were the leaders who took care of the property and animals that belonged to the king and his sons. There were the men over the palace, the powerful men and all the brave warriors.

2King David stood up and said, "Listen to me, my relatives and my people. I wanted to build a place to keep the Ark*d* of the Agreement with the Lord. I wanted it to be God's footstool. And I made plans to build a temple for worship to God. 3But God said to me, 'You must not build a temple for worship to me. You must not do that because you are a soldier. You have killed many men'.

4"But the Lord, the God of Israel, chose me from my whole family. He chose me to be king of Israel for ever. The Lord chose the tribe of Judah to be a leader. And from the people of Judah, he chose my father's family. And from that family God was pleased to make me king of Israel. 5The Lord has given me many sons. And from those sons he has chosen Solomon. Solomon will be the new king of Israel. Israel is the Lord's kingdom. 6The Lord said to me, 'Your son Solomon will build my Temple.*d* And he will build the area around it. This is because I have chosen Solomon to be my son. And I will be his father. 7He is obeying my laws and commands now. If he continues to obey them, I will make his kingdom strong for ever'."

8David said, "Now, in front of all Israel and God, I tell you these things: be careful to obey all the commands of the Lord your God. Then you may keep this good land. And you may pass it on to your descendants*d* for ever. ⁹"And you, my son Solomon, accept the God of your father. Serve him completely. Be happy to serve him. Do this because the Lord knows what is in every person's mind. He understands everything you think. If you go to him for help, you will get an answer. But if you turn away from the Lord, he will leave you for ever. ¹⁰Solomon, you must understand this. The Lord has chosen you to build the Temple as his holy place. Be strong and finish the job."

¹¹Then David gave his son Solomon the plans for building the Temple. Those plans were also for the porch around the Temple. They were for its buildings, its storerooms, its upper rooms and its inside rooms. They also were the plans for the place where the people's sins were removed. ¹²David gave him plans for everything he had in mind. David gave him plans for the courtyards around the Lord's Temple and all the rooms around it. He gave him plans for the Temple treasuries. And he gave him plans for the treasuries of the holy things used in the Temple. ¹³David gave Solomon directions for the groups of the priests and Levites. David told him about all the work of serving in the Temple of the Lord. He told him about the things to be used in the Temple service. ¹⁴Many things made of gold or silver would be used in the Temple. David told Solomon how much gold or silver should be used to make each thing. ¹⁵David told him how much gold to use for each gold lampstand and its lamps. He told him how much silver to use for each silver lampstand and its lamps. The different lampstands were to be used where needed. ¹⁶David told how much gold should be used for each table that held the holy bread. And he told how much silver should be used for the silver tables. ¹⁷He told how

much pure gold should be used to make the forks, bowls and pitchers. He told how much gold should be used to make each gold dish. He told how much silver should be used to make each silver dish. ¹⁸David told how much pure gold should be used for the altar of incense.*d* He also gave Solomon the plans for the chariot. This is where the golden creatures spread their wings over the Ark*d* of the Agreement with the Lord.

¹⁹David said, "All these plans were written with the Lord guiding me. He helped me understand everything in the plans."

²⁰David also said to his son Solomon, "Be strong and brave. Do the work. Don't be afraid or discouraged. The Lord God, my God, is with you. He will help you until all the work is finished. He will not leave you. You will build the Temple of the Lord. ²¹The groups of the priests and Levites are ready for all the work on the Temple of God. Every skilled worker is ready to help you with all the work. The leaders and all the people will obey every command you give."

Gifts for Building the Temple

29 King David spoke to all the Israelites who were gathered. He said, "God chose my son Solomon. Solomon is young and hasn't yet learned what he needs to know. But the work is important. This palace is not for people. It is for the Lord God. ²I have done my best to prepare for building the Temple*d* of God. I have given gold for the things made of gold. I have given silver for the things made of silver. I have given bronze for the things made of bronze. I have given iron for the things made of iron. I have given wood for the things made of wood. I have given onyx for the settings and turquoise. I have given gems of many different colours. I have given valuable stones and white marble. I have given a lot of all these

things. ³I have already given this for
the Temple. But now I am also giving
my own treasures of gold and silver.
I am doing this because I really want
the Temple of my God to be built. ⁴I
have given about 100 tons of pure gold
from Ophir. And I have given about
240 tons of pure silver. They will be
used to cover the walls of the buildings. ⁵They will also be used for all the
gold and silver work. Skilled men may
use the gold and silver to make things
for the Temple. Now, who is ready to
give himself to the service of the Lord
today?"

⁶The family leaders and the leaders
of the tribes of Israel gave their valuable things. The commanders of 1,000
men and of 100 men gave their valuable things. And the leaders responsible for the king's work gave their
valuable things. ⁷These are the things
they gave for the Temple of God:
about 170 tons of gold, about 340 tons
of silver, about 610 tons of bronze and
about 3400 tons of iron. ⁸People who
had valuable gems gave them to the
treasury of the Temple of the Lord.
Jehiel, from the Gershon family, took
care of the valuable gems. ⁹The leaders gave freely and completely to the
Lord. The people were happy to see
their leaders give so gladly. King David was also very happy.

David's Prayer

¹⁰David praised the Lord in front of
all of the people who were gathered.
He said:
"We praise you, Lord.
    You are the God of our father
        Israel.
    We praise you for ever and
        ever.
¹¹Lord, you are great and powerful.
    You have glory, victory and
        honour.
    Everything in heaven and on
        earth belongs to you.
    The kingdom belongs to you,
        Lord.

You are the ruler over
    everything.
¹²Riches and honour come from
    you.
    You rule everything.
You have the power and strength
    to make anyone great and
    strong.
¹³Now, our God, we thank you.
    And we praise your glorious
        name.

¹⁴"These things did not really come
    from me and my people.
    Everything comes from you.
    We have given you back what
        you gave us.
¹⁵We are like foreigners and
    strangers.
    All our ancestors were also
        foreigners and strangers.
    Our time on earth is like a
        shadow.
    There is no hope.
¹⁶Lord our God, we have gathered
    all this to build your Temple.
    We will build it for worship to
        you.
    But everything has come from
        you.
    Everything belongs to you.
¹⁷I know, my God, that you test
    people's hearts.
    You are happy when people do
        what is right.
    I was happy to give all these
        things.
    I gave with an honest heart.
    Your people gathered here are
        happy to give to you.
    I am happy to see their giving.
¹⁸Lord, you are the God of our
    ancestors.
    You are the God of Abraham,
        Isaac and Jacob.
    Please help your people to want
        to serve you always.
    And help them to want to obey
        you always.
¹⁹Give my son Solomon a strong
    desire to serve you.

Help him always obey your commands, laws and rules. Help him build the Temple for which I have prepared."

[20]Then David said to all the people who were gathered, "Praise the Lord your God." So they all praised the Lord, the God their ancestors worshipped. They bowed to the ground to give honour to the Lord and the king.

Solomon Becomes King

[21]The next day the people made sacrifices to the Lord. They offered burnt offerings to him. They offered 1,000 bulls, 1,000 male sheep and 1,000 male lambs. They also brought drink offerings. Many sacrifices were made for all the people of Israel. [22]That day the people ate and drank with much joy. And the Lord was with them.

And they made David's son Solomon king for the second time. They poured olive oil on Solomon to appoint him king. And they poured oil on Zadok to appoint him as priest. They did this in the presence of the Lord. [23]Then Solomon sat on the Lord's throne as king. He took his father David's place. Solomon was very successful. And all the people of Israel obeyed him. [24]All the leaders and soldiers and King David's sons accepted Solomon as king. They promised to obey him. [25]The Lord made Solomon great before all the Israelites. The Lord gave Solomon much honour. No king of Israel before Solomon had such honour.

David's Death

[26]David son of Jesse was king over all Israel. [27]He was king for 40 years. He ruled in the city of Hebron for 7 years. And he ruled in Jerusalem for 33 years. [28]David died when he was old. He had lived a good, long life. He had received many riches and honours. And David's son Solomon became king after him.

[29]Everything King David did as king, from beginning to end, is recorded. Those things are written in the records of Samuel the seer.[d] And they are in the records of Nathan the prophet and the records of Gad the seer. [30]Those writings tell what David did as king of Israel. They tell about his power and all that happened to him. And they tell what happened to Israel and all the kingdoms around them.

2 CHRONICLES

Israel's History from Solomon to the Captivity

Solomon Asks for Wisdom

1 Solomon was David's son, and he became a powerful king. This was because the Lord his God was with him. The Lord made Solomon very great.

²Solomon spoke to all the people of Israel. He spoke to the commanders of 100 men and of 1,000 men. He spoke to the judges, to every leader in all Israel and to the leaders of the families. ³Then Solomon and all the people gathered with him went to the place of worship. This was at the town of Gibeon. God's Meeting Tent*d* was there. Moses, the Lord's servant, had made that Tent in the desert. ⁴David had brought the Ark*d* of the Agreement with God from Kiriath Jearim to Jerusalem. David had made a place for it there. He had set up a tent for it in Jerusalem. ⁵Bezalel was Uri's son, and Uri was Hur's son. Bezalel had made a bronze altar. It was in Gibeon in front of the Holy Tent. So Solomon and the people worshipped the Lord there. ⁶Solomon went up to the bronze altar before the Lord at the Meeting Tent. He offered 1,000 burnt offerings on the altar.

⁷That night God appeared to Solomon. God said, "Solomon, ask for whatever you want me to give you."

⁸Solomon answered, "You have been very kind to my father David. You have chosen me to be the king in his place. ⁹Now, Lord God, may your promise to my father David come true. You have made me king of a very large nation. There are so many of them they are like the dust of the earth. ¹⁰Now give me wisdom and knowledge so I can lead these people in the right way. No one can rule them without your help."

¹¹God said to Solomon, "What you want is good. I have chosen you to be king of these people. You have not asked for wealth or riches or honour. You have not asked for your enemies to be killed. You have not asked for a long life. But you have asked for wisdom and knowledge to lead my people. ¹²So I will give you wisdom and knowledge. I will also give you more wealth, riches and honour than any king who has lived before you. And the kings who will live after you will not have as much."

¹³Then Solomon left the place of worship at Gibeon. He left the Meeting Tent and went back to Jerusalem. There King Solomon ruled over Israel.

Solomon's Wealth

¹⁴Solomon gathered horses and chariots. He had 1,400 chariots and 12,000 horses. He put some horses and chariots in the cities where the chariots were kept. And he kept some with him in Jerusalem. ¹⁵In Jerusalem, Solomon gathered a large amount of silver and gold. He got so much it was as common as rocks. He also gathered a large amount of cedar wood. It became as plentiful as the sycamore trees on the western mountain slopes. ¹⁶Solomon imported horses from Egypt and Kue. The king's traders bought the horses in Kue. ¹⁷They imported a chariot from Egypt for about 7 kilograms of silver. And they imported a horse for nearly 1.7 kilograms of silver. Then they sold the horses and chariots to all the kings of the Hittites and the Arameans.

Solomon Prepares for the Temple

2 Solomon decided to build a temple[d] as a place to worship the Lord. He also decided to build a palace for himself. [2]He chose 70,000 men to carry things. He chose 80,000 men to cut stone in the mountains. And he chose 3,600 men to direct the workers.

[3]Then Solomon sent a message to Hiram king of the city of Tyre. Solomon said:

Help me as you helped my father David. You sent him cedar logs so he could build himself a palace to live in. [4]I will build a temple as a place to worship the Lord my God. And I will give this temple to the Lord. There we will burn sweet-smelling spices in his presence. We will set out the bread that shows we are in God's presence. And we will burn sacrifices every morning and evening. We will worship him on Sabbath[d] days and New Moons.[d] And we will worship him on the other feast days the Lord our God has commanded us to celebrate. This is a rule for Israel to obey for ever.

[5]The temple I build will be great. This is because our God is greater than all gods. [6]But no one can really build a house for our God. Not even the highest of heavens can hold God. How then can I build a temple for him? I can only build a place to burn sacrifices to God.

[7]Now send me a man skilled in working with gold, silver, bronze and iron. He must know how to work with purple, red and blue thread. He must know how to make engravings. He will work with my skilled craftsmen in Judah and Jerusalem. These are the men my father David chose.

[8]Also send me cedar, pine and juniper logs from Lebanon. I know your servants are experienced at cutting down the trees in Lebanon. My servants will help them. [9]Send me a lot of wood. The temple I am going to build will be large and wonderful. [10]I will give your servants who cut the wood 4400 kilolitres of wheat. And I will give them 4400 kilolitres of barley, 440 kilolitres of wine and 440 kilolitres of oil.

[11]Then Hiram king of Tyre answered Solomon with this letter:

Solomon, the Lord loves his people. That is why he chose you to be their king.

[12]Hiram also said:

Praise the Lord, the God of Israel! He made heaven and earth! He gave King David a wise son. Solomon, you have wisdom and understanding. You will build a temple for the Lord and a palace for yourself.

[13]I will send you a skilled and wise man named Huram-Abi. [14]His mother was from the people of Dan. And his father was from Tyre. Huram-Abi has skill in working with gold, silver, bronze, iron, stone and wood. He has skill in working with purple, blue and red thread and expensive linen. And he is skilled in making engravings. He can make any design you show him. He will help your craftsmen and the craftsmen of your father David.

[15]Now send my servants the wheat, barley, oil and wine you promised. [16]We will cut as much wood from Lebanon as you need. We will use rafts to carry it by sea to Joppa. Then you may carry it to Jerusalem.

[17]Solomon counted all the foreigners living in Israel. This was after the time his father David had counted the

people. There were 153,600 foreigners in the country. [18]Solomon chose 70,000 of them to carry things. He chose 80,000 of them to cut stone in the mountains. And he chose 3,600 of them to direct the workers. They were to keep the people working.

Solomon Builds the Temple

3 Solomon began to build the Temple[d] of the Lord. He built it in Jerusalem on Mount Moriah. This was where the Lord had appeared to David, Solomon's father. Solomon built the Temple on the place David had prepared. This place was the threshing[d] floor of Araunah the Jebusite. [2]Solomon began building in the second month of the fourth year he ruled Israel.

[3]Solomon used these measurements for building the Temple of God. It was 27 metres long and 9 metres wide. (Solomon used the old measurement.) [4]The porch in front of the Temple was 9 metres long and high.

Solomon covered the inside of the porch with pure gold. [5]He put panels of pine on the walls of the main room. Then he covered them with pure gold. And he put designs of palm trees and chains in the gold. [6]He put gems in the Temple for beauty. And he used gold from Parvaim.[n] [7]Solomon put gold on the Temple's ceiling beams, doorposts, walls and doors. And he carved creatures with wings on the walls.

[8]Then Solomon made the Most Holy Place. It was 9 metres long and wide. It was as wide as the Temple. He covered its walls with about 21 tons of pure gold. [9]The gold nails weighed over half kilogram. Solomon also covered the upper rooms with gold.

[10]He made two creatures with wings for the Most Holy Place. He made them out of hot liquid gold.

[11]The wings of the gold creatures were spread out. Together, they were 9 metres across. One wing of one creature touched the Temple wall. The wing was 2.3 metres long. The creature's other wing touched a wing of the second creature. This wing was also 2.3 metres long. [12]One wing of the second creature touched the other side of the room. It was also 2.3 metres long. The second creature's other wing touched the first creature's wing. This wing was also 2.3 metres long. [13]Together, the creatures' wings were 9 metres across. The creatures stood on their feet. They looked inside towards the main room.

[14]Solomon made the curtain of blue, purple and red thread and expensive linen. And he put designs of creatures with wings in it.

[15]Solomon made two pillars to stand in front of the Temple. They were about 16 metres tall. The capital[d] of each pillar was over 2 metres tall. [16]Solomon made a net of chains. He put them on the tops of the pillars. He made 100 pomegranates[d] and put them on the chains. [17]Then Solomon put the pillars up in front of the Temple. One pillar stood on the south side. The other stood on the north. He named the south pillar He Establishes. And he named the north pillar In Him Is Strength.

Things for the Temple

4 Solomon made a bronze altar. It was 9 metres long and wide and 4.5 metres tall. [2]Then Solomon used melted bronze to make a large bowl, which was called the Sea. It was round and measured 4.5 metres across from edge to edge. It was over 2 metres tall, and it measured 13.5 metres around. [3]There were carvings of bulls under the rim of the bowl. There were

Parvaim There was much gold there. It may have been in the country of Ophir.

ten bulls in every 0.5 metre. They were put in two rows around the bowl when it was made.

⁴The bowl rested on 12 statues of bulls. Three bulls faced north, three faced west, three faced south and three faced east. The bowl was on top of them. They faced outward from the centre of the bowl. ⁵The bowl was 8 centimetres thick. Its rim was like the rim of a cup. It looked like a lily blossom. It could hold about 40,000 litres.

⁶Solomon made ten smaller bowls. He put five of them on the south side. And he put five of them on the north. They were to be used to wash the animals for the burnt offerings. But the large bowl was to be used by the priests for washing.

⁷Solomon made ten lampstands of gold, following the plans for them. He put them in the Temple.ᵈ He put five on the south side and five on the north.

⁸Solomon made ten tables and put them in the Temple. He put five on the south side and five on the north. And he used gold to make 100 other bowls.

⁹Solomon also made the priests' courtyard and the large courtyard. He made the doors that opened to the courtyard and covered them with bronze. ¹⁰Then he put the large bowl on the south side. He put it in the Temple's southeast corner.

¹¹He made the pots, shovels and bowls. So Huram finished his work for King Solomon on the Temple of God. He had made these things:

¹²two pillars;

two large bowls for the capitals on top of the pillars;

two nets to cover the two large bowls for the capitals on top of the pillars;

¹³400 pomegranatesᵈ for the two nets (there were two rows of pomegranates for each net cov-

ering the bowls for the capitals on top of the pillars);

¹⁴the stands with a bowl on each stand;

¹⁵the large bowl with 12 bulls under it;

¹⁶the pots, shovels, forks and all the things to go with them.

All the things Huram-Abi made King Solomon for the Temple of the Lord were made of polished bronze. ¹⁷King Solomon first had these things poured into clay moulds. The moulds were made in the plain of the Jordan between Succoth and Zarethan. ¹⁸Solomon had so many things made no one even tried to weigh all the bronze used.

¹⁹Solomon also made all the things for God's Temple. He made the gold altar. He made tables to hold the bread that shows we are in God's presence. ²⁰He made the lampstands and their lamps of pure gold. They were to burn in front of the Most Holy Place as planned. ²¹Solomon used pure gold to make the flowers, lamps and tongs. ²²He used pure gold to make the wick trimmers. He used pure gold for the bowls, pans and dishes used to carry coals. He used pure gold to make the doors for the Temple. And he used pure gold for the inside doors for the Most Holy Place and the doors for the main room.

5 Then all the work Solomon had done for the Temple of the Lord was finished. He brought in everything his father David had given for the Temple. He brought in all the silver and gold and all the furniture. And he put everything in the treasuries of God's Temple.

The Holy Ark Is Carried into the Temple

²Then Solomon called for all the leaders of Israel. He asked them to come to him in Jerusalem. He called

for all the older leaders, the heads of the tribes*d* and the leaders of the families. He wanted them to bring the Ark*d* of the Agreement with the Lord from the older part of the city. ³All the men of Israel came together with King Solomon. This was during the festival that was held in the seventh month.

⁴All the older leaders of Israel arrived. Then the Levites picked up the Holy Ark. ⁵The priests and the Levites carried the Ark of God. They also carried the Meeting Tent*d* and the holy things in it. ⁶King Solomon and all the Israelites met in front of the Ark of God. They sacrificed so many sheep and bulls no one could count them.

⁷Then the priests put the Ark of the Agreement with the Lord in its place. This was inside the Most Holy Place in the Temple.*d* They put it under the wings of the gold creatures. ⁸The wings of the creatures were spread out over the place for the Holy Ark. They covered it and its carrying poles. ⁹The carrying poles were very long. Anyone standing in the Holy Place in front of the Most Holy Place could see the ends of the poles. But no one could see the poles from outside the Holy Place. The poles are still there today. ¹⁰The only things inside the Holy Ark were two stone tablets.*n* Moses had put them in the Holy Ark at Mount Sinai. That was where the Lord made an agreement with the Israelites after they came out of Egypt.

¹¹Then all the priests left the Holy Place. All the priests from each group made themselves ready to serve the Lord. ¹²All the Levite musicians stood on the east side of the altar. They were Asaph, Heman, Jeduthun and all their sons and relatives. They were dressed in white linen and played cymbals, lyres*d* and harps. With them were 120 priests who blew trumpets.

¹³Those who blew the trumpets and those who sang together sounded like one person. They praised and thanked the Lord. They sang as they played their trumpets, cymbals and other instruments. They praised the Lord with this song:

"The Lord is good.

His love continues for ever."

Then the Temple of the Lord was filled with a cloud. ¹⁴The priests could not continue their work because of the cloud. This was because the Lord's glory filled the Temple of God.

6 Then Solomon said, "The Lord said he would live in the dark cloud. ²I have built a great Temple for you, Lord. It is a place for you to live for ever."

Solomon's Speech

³King Solomon turned around and blessed all the Israelites gathered in front of him. ⁴He said, "Praise the Lord, the God of Israel. He has done what he promised my father David. The Lord said, ⁵'I brought my people out of Egypt. But I have not yet chosen a city in any tribe*d* of Israel for my temple.*d* This is where I have chosen to be worshipped. I have not chosen a man to lead my people, the Israelites. ⁶But now I have chosen Jerusalem as the place I am to be worshipped. And I have chosen David to lead my people Israel'.

⁷"My father David wanted to build a temple as a place to worship the Lord, the God of Israel. ⁸But the Lord said to my father, 'David, it was good that you wanted to build a temple as a place to worship me. ⁹But you are not the one who will build the temple. Your own son will build my temple'. ¹⁰"Now the Lord has kept his promise. I have taken my father David's place. Now I am Israel's king. This is what the Lord promised. And I have built the Temple where the Lord, the

stone tablets They were the two stone tablets on which God wrote the Ten Commandments.

God of Israel, will be worshipped. [11]I have put the Ark[d] of God there. The agreement that the Lord made with the people of Israel is kept in the Holy Ark."

Solomon's Prayer

[12]Solomon stood in front of the Lord's altar. He was standing before all the people gathered there. Then he spread his arms out. [13]He had made a bronze platform. It was 2.3 metres long, high and wide. And he had placed it in the middle of the outer courtyard. Solomon stood on the platform. Then he kneeled in front of all the people of Israel who were gathered there. Solomon spread his hands out towards the sky. [14]He said, "Lord, God of Israel, there is no god like you in heaven or on earth. You keep your agreement of love with your servants who completely obey you. [15]You have kept your promise to my father David, your servant. With your words you made a promise. And with the work of your hands, you have made that promise come true today.

[16]"Now, Lord, God of Israel, also keep this promise you made to my father David, your servant. You said, 'David, you will always have someone from your family rule Israel. But this will happen only if they are careful to obey my teachings in everything they do. They must obey my teachings just as you have'. [17]Now, Lord, God of Israel, keep your promise. Let this promise to your servant David come true.

[18]"But, God, can you really live here on the earth with people? Not even the highest of heavens can hold you. And this Temple[d] I built cannot hold you. [19]But pay attention to my prayer and my cry for mercy. Lord my God, listen to my cry. Listen to the prayer I, your servant, pray to you. [20]I pray that you will watch over this Temple day and night. You said you would make this the place to worship you. I pray that you will hear my prayers when I pray facing this Temple. [21]Hear my prayers and the prayers of your people Israel. Hear us when we pray facing this Temple. Hear from your home in heaven. And when you hear our prayers, forgive us.

[22]"A person might do something wrong against someone else. The person who did the wrong will have to swear he is innocent. He will come to swear this before your altar in the Temple. [23]When he does this, listen from heaven and act. Judge your servants. Punish the one who did wrong. Make him suffer the same things he made others suffer. Prove that the person who has done right is innocent.

[24]"An enemy might defeat your people Israel because they have sinned against you. Then the people of Israel will return to you and say you are God. They will pray and beg you for help in this Temple. [25]When this happens, listen from heaven. Forgive the sin of your people, the Israelites. Bring them back into the land you gave to them and their ancestors.

[26]"The sky might not let it rain because your people have sinned against you. Then they will pray, facing this Temple. They will say you are God. They will stop doing their sin because you are punishing them. [27]When that happens, then listen from heaven. Forgive the sins of your servants, the Israelites. Then teach them the right way to live. And send rain on your land. This is the land you gave your people as their own.

[28]"There might be a time without food in the land. Or there might be terrible sicknesses, disease in the crops, mildew,[d] locusts[d] or grasshoppers. Or enemies might attack Israel's cities. There might be a disaster in Israel. [29]Then one of your people, an Israelite, will pray or cry for help. Each person knows his own trouble and

pain. He will spread his arms out, facing this Temple. 30When that happens, then listen from heaven, your home. Forgive and treat each person as he should be treated. You know what is in his heart. (Only you know what is in a person's heart.) 31Then the people will fear and obey you as long as they live in this land. This is the land you gave our ancestors.

32"A foreigner might come here from a country far away. He is not one of your people, the people of Israel. But he will come because he has heard about your greatness and power. He knows about the things you have done. When he comes and prays, facing this Temple, 33then listen. Listen from heaven, your home. And do what he asks you to do. Then all the peoples of the earth will know you and respect you, just as your people Israel do. And they will know that this Temple I built is for worshipping you.

34"You might send your people to fight their enemies. They will pray to you, facing this city you chose and the Temple I built for worshipping you. 35If they do, then listen from heaven to their prayer. Listen to their cry and help them.

36"People will sin against you. There is not a person who does not sin. And you will become angry with them. You will let an enemy defeat them. The enemy will capture them and take them away. It may be to a land far away or near. 37But then they will be sorry for what they have done. As captives in that land, they will cry out to you. They will say, 'We have sinned. We have done wrong and acted wickedly'. 38In the land where they are captives, they will come back to you. They will want to obey you completely. They will pray, facing their land, the land you gave to their ancestors. They will pray, facing the city you chose and the Temple I built for you. 39When this happens, listen from your home in heaven. Listen to their

cries and help them. Forgive your people who have sinned against you. 40"Now, my God, look at us. Listen to the prayers we will pray in this place. 41Now, rise, Lord God, and come
to your resting place.
Come with the Ark*d* of God that
shows your strength.
Let your priests receive your
salvation, Lord God.
And may your holy people be
happy because of your
goodness. 42Lord God, do not reject your
appointed one.
Remember your love for your
servant David."

The Temple Is Given to the Lord

7 When Solomon finished praying, fire came down from the sky. It burned up the burnt offering and the sacrifices. The Lord's glory filled the Temple.*d* 2The priests could not enter the Temple of the Lord because the Lord's glory filled it. 3All the people of Israel saw the fire come down from heaven. They also saw the Lord's glory on the Temple. Then they bowed down on the pavement with their faces to the ground. They worshipped and thanked the Lord. They said,
"The Lord is good.
His love continues for ever."
4Then King Solomon and all the Israelites offered sacrifices before the Lord. 5King Solomon offered a sacrifice of 22,000 cattle and 120,000 sheep. So the king and all the people gave the Temple for the worship of God. 6The priests stood ready to do their work. The Levites also stood with the instruments of the Lord's music. King David had made these instruments for praising the Lord. The priests and Levites were saying, "The Lord's love continues for ever." The priests, who stood across from the Levites, blew their trumpets. And all the Israelites were standing.

[7]Solomon made the middle part of the courtyard holy for the Lord. That courtyard is in front of the Temple of the Lord. There Solomon offered burnt offerings and the fat of the fellowship offerings. He used the middle of the courtyard because the bronze altar he had made could not hold everything. It couldn't hold the burnt offerings, grain offerings and fat.

[8]Solomon and all the Israelites celebrated the festival for seven days. There were many people. They came from as far away as Lebo Hamath. And they came all the way from the brook of Egypt. [9]They had given the altar for the worship of the Lord. And they celebrated that for seven days. Then they celebrated the festival for seven days. On the eighth day they had a meeting. [10]On the twenty-third day of the seventh month Solomon sent the people home. They were full of joy. They were happy because the Lord had been so good to David, Solomon and his people the Israelites.

The Lord Appears to Solomon

[11]Solomon finished the Temple[d] of the Lord and the king's palace. He had success in doing everything he planned in the Temple of the Lord and his own palace. [12]Then the Lord appeared to Solomon at night. The Lord said, "Solomon, I have heard your prayer. And I have chosen this place for myself to be a Temple for sacrifices. [13]"I may stop the sky from sending rain. I may command the locusts[d] to destroy the land. I may send sicknesses to my people. [14]Then my people, who are called by my name, will be sorry for what they have done. They will pray and obey me and stop their evil ways. If they do, I will hear them from heaven. I will forgive their sin, and I will heal their land. [15]Now I will see them. And I will listen to the prayers prayed in this place. [16]I have chosen this Temple and made it holy.

So I will be worshipped here for ever. Yes, I will always watch over it and love it.

[17]"Solomon, obey me as your father David did. Obey all I have commanded. Obey my laws and rules. [18]If you do, I will make your kingdom strong. This is the agreement I made with your father David. I told him, 'David, someone from your family will always be king in Israel'.

[19]"But you must not turn away from me. You must not stop obeying the laws and commands I gave you. You must not serve and worship other gods. [20]If you do, I will take the Israelites out of my land, the land I gave them. And I will leave this Temple that I have made holy. All the nations will make fun of it and speak evil about it. [21]This Temple is honoured now. But then, everyone who passes by will be surprised. They will say, 'Why has the Lord done this terrible thing to this land and this Temple?' [22]Then people will answer, 'It's because the Israelites left the Lord, the God their ancestors obeyed. He is the God who led them out of Egypt. But they accepted other gods and worshipped and served them. That is why the Lord brought this disaster on them'."

Solomon's Other Achievements

8 It took Solomon 20 years to build the Temple[d] of the Lord and his own palace. [2]Then Solomon rebuilt the towns that Hiram had given him. And Solomon sent Israelites to live in them. [3]Then he went to Hamath Zobah and captured it. [4]Solomon also built the town of Tadmor in the desert. He built all the towns in Hamath as towns for storing things. [5]He rebuilt the towns of Upper Beth Horon and Lower Beth Horon. He made them protected towns with strong walls, gates and bars in the gates. [6]He also rebuilt the town of Baalath. And he built all the other towns where he stored things. He built all the cities

where the chariots and horses were kept. Solomon built all he wanted in Jerusalem, Lebanon and in all the country he ruled.

⁷⁻⁸Many people who were not Israelites were left living in the country. These people were the Hittites, Amorites, Perizzites, Hivites and Jebusites. They were descendants*d* of the people that the Israelites had not destroyed. Solomon forced all of them to be slave workers. This is still true today. ⁹But Solomon did not force any of the Israelites to be slave workers. They were his fighting men. They were the commanders of his army officers, his chariots and his chariot drivers. ¹⁰Some of them were his most important officers. There were 250 of them to direct the people.

¹¹Solomon brought the daughter of the king of Egypt from the older part of Jerusalem. He brought her to the palace he had built for her. Solomon said, "My wife must not live in King David's palace. This is because the places where the Ark*d* of God has been are holy places."

¹²Then Solomon offered burnt offerings to the Lord on the Lord's altar. Solomon built that altar in front of the Temple porch. ¹³He offered sacrifices every day as Moses had commanded. Sacrifices were to be offered on the Sabbath*d* days, New Moons*d* and the three yearly feasts. The three yearly feasts were the Feast*d* of Unleavened Bread, the Feast of Weeks and the Feast of Shelters. ¹⁴Solomon followed his father David's instructions. Solomon chose the groups of priests for their service. He chose the Levites to lead the praise. And they were to help the priests do their daily work. And he chose the gatekeepers by their groups to serve at each gate. This is what David, the man of God, had commanded. ¹⁵They obeyed all of Solomon's commands to the priests and Levites. And they obeyed his commands about the treasuries.

¹⁶All Solomon's work was done. Everything was done as he had said from the day the Temple of the Lord was begun until it was finished. So the Temple was finished.

¹⁷Then Solomon went to the towns of Ezion Geber and Elath. They were near the Red Sea*d* in the country of Edom. ¹⁸Hiram sent to Solomon ships commanded by his own men. They were skilled sailors. Hiram's men went with Solomon's men to Ophir. And they brought back about 17 tons of gold to King Solomon.

The Queen of Sheba Visits Solomon

9 The queen of Sheba heard about Solomon's fame. So she came to Jerusalem to test him with hard questions. She had a very large group of people with her. She had camels that carried spices, much gold and many gems. She came to Solomon and talked with him about all her questions. ²And Solomon answered all her questions. Nothing was too hard for him to explain to her. ³The queen of Sheba saw that Solomon was very wise. She also saw the palace he had built. ⁴She saw the food on his table and his many officers. She saw the palace servants and their good clothes. She saw the servants who served Solomon his wine. And she saw their good clothes. She saw the burnt offerings he made in the Temple*d* of the Lord. All these things amazed her. ⁵So she said to King Solomon, "I heard in my own country about your achievements and wisdom. And all of it is true. ⁶I did not believe it then. But now I have come and seen it with my own eyes. Not even half of your great wisdom was told to me! You are much greater than I had heard. ⁷Your men and officers are very lucky! Since they are always serving you, they are able to hear your wisdom! ⁸Praise the Lord your God! He was pleased to make you

king. He has put you on his throne to rule for the Lord your God. Your God loves Israel and supports Israel for ever. So the Lord has made you king of Israel to keep law and order and to rule fairly."

9Then the queen of Sheba gave King Solomon about 4 tons of gold. She also gave him many spices and gems. No one had ever given such fine spices as she gave to King Solomon.

10Hiram's men and Solomon's men brought in gold from Ophir. They also brought in juniper wood and gems. 11King Solomon used the juniper wood to make steps for the Temple of the Lord and the palace. He also used it to make lyres*d* and harps for the singers. No one in Judah had ever seen such beautiful things as these.

12King Solomon gave the queen of Sheba everything she wanted and asked for. He gave her more than she had brought to him. Then she and her servants left and returned to their own country.

Solomon's Great Wealth

13The amount of gold that Solomon received in one year weighed about 23 tons. 14Besides that, he also received gold from merchants and traders. All the kings of Arabia and the rulers of the land also brought gold and silver to Solomon.

15King Solomon made 200 large shields from hammered gold. Each shield contained about 3.5 kilograms of hammered gold. 16Solomon also made 300 small shields of hammered gold. Each shield contained about 1.7 kilograms of gold. King Solomon put them in the Palace of the Forest of Lebanon.

17Then he built a large throne of ivory. And he covered it with pure gold. 18The throne had six steps on it. And it had a gold footstool on it. There were armrests on both sides of the chair. And beside each armrest was a

statue of a lion. 19Twelve lions stood on the six steps. There was one lion at each end of each step. Nothing like this had ever been made for any other kingdom. 20All King Solomon's drinking cups were made of gold. All of the dishes in the Palace of the Forest of Lebanon were pure gold. In Solomon's time people did not think silver was valuable. So nothing was made of silver. 21King Solomon had many ships that he sent out to trade. Hiram's men sailed Solomon's ships. Every three years the ships returned. They brought back gold, silver, ivory, apes and baboons.

22King Solomon had more riches and wisdom than all the other kings on earth. 23All the kings of the earth came to see Solomon. They wanted to hear the wisdom God had given him. 24Every year everyone who came brought a gift. They brought things made of silver and gold, clothes, weapons, spices, horses and mules.

25Solomon had 4,000 stalls to hold his horses and chariots. He had 12,000 horses. They were in special cities where chariots were kept. And he kept some with him in Jerusalem. 26Solomon was king over all the kings from the Euphrates River to the Philistine country to the border of Egypt. 27In Jerusalem silver was as common as stones while Solomon was king. Cedar trees were as common as the fig trees growing on the western mountain slopes. 28Solomon imported horses from Egypt and all other countries.

Solomon's Death

29The other things Solomon did as king, from the beginning to the end, are written down. They are in the writings of Nathan the prophet.*d* And they are in the prophecy of Ahijah and the visions of Iddo. Ahijah was from Shiloh. Iddo was a seer*d* who wrote about Jeroboam, Nebat's son. 30Solomon was king in Jerusalem over all Israel for 40 years. ³¹Then Solomon died and was buried in Jerusalem. This was the city of his father David. And Solomon's son Rehoboam became king in his place.

Rehoboam Acts Foolishly

10 Rehoboam went to Shechem because all the Israelites had gone there to make him king. ²Jeroboam son of Nebat was in Egypt. He had gone there to run away from King Solomon. Jeroboam heard that Rehoboam was going to be the new king. So he returned from Egypt. ³The people sent for Jeroboam. Then he and the people went to Rehoboam. They said to Rehoboam, ⁴"Your father forced us to work very hard. Now, make it easier for us. Don't make us work as hard as your father did. Then we will serve you."

⁵Rehoboam answered, "Come back to me in three days." So the people left.

⁶There were some older leaders who had helped Solomon make decisions during his lifetime. So King Rehoboam asked them what he should do. He said, "How do you think I should answer these people?"

⁷They answered, "Be kind to these people. Please them and give them a kind answer. If you do, they will serve you always."

⁸But Rehoboam did not listen to the advice the older leaders gave him. He talked with the young men who had grown up with him. They advised him in making decisions. ⁹Rehoboam asked them, "What is your advice? How should we answer these people? They said, 'Don't make us work as hard as your father did'."

¹⁰Then the young men who had grown up with him said, "The people said to you, 'Your father forced us to work very hard. Now make our work easier'. But you should tell those people, 'My little finger is thicker than my father's waist. ¹¹My father forced you

to work hard. But I will make you work even harder. My father beat you with whips. But I will beat you with whips that have sharp points'."

¹²King Rehoboam had told the people, "Come back to me in three days." So three days later Jeroboam and all the people returned to Rehoboam. ¹³Then King Rehoboam spoke to them in a cruel way. He did not take the advice of the older leaders. ¹⁴He followed the advice of the young men. He said, "My father forced you to work hard. But I will give you even more work. My father beat you with whips. But I will beat you with whips that have sharp points." ¹⁵So King Rehoboam did not do what the people wanted. God caused this to happen. He did this so the Lord could keep his promise to Jeroboam son of Nebat. The Lord had made this promise through Ahijah, a prophet[d] from Shiloh.

¹⁶The people of Israel saw that King Rehoboam did not listen to them. So they said to the king,

"We have no share in David.
We have no part in the son of Jesse.
People of Israel, let's go to our own homes!
Let David's son rule his own people."

So all the Israelites went home. ¹⁷But Rehoboam still ruled over the Israelites who lived in the towns of Judah. ¹⁸Adoniram was in charge of the people who were forced to work. Rehoboam sent him to the people. But they threw stones at Adoniram until he died. But King Rehoboam was able to run to his chariot and escape to Jerusalem. ¹⁹Since then, Israel has always turned against the family of David.

11 When Rehoboam came to Jerusalem, he gathered 180,000 of the best soldiers. They were from the people of Judah and Benjamin. He gathered them to fight Israel. He wanted to bring the kingdom back under his control. ²But the Lord spoke his word to Shemaiah, the man of God. The Lord said, ³"Shemaiah, talk to Solomon's son Rehoboam, the king of Judah. Talk also to all the Israelites living in Judah and Benjamin. Say to them, ⁴'The Lord says you must not go to war against your brothers. Every one of you should go home. I made all these things happen'." So King Rehoboam and his army obeyed the Lord's command. They turned back and did not attack Jeroboam.

Rehoboam Makes Judah Strong

⁵Rehoboam lived in Jerusalem. He built strong cities in Judah to defend it against attacks. ⁶He built up the cities of Bethlehem, Etam, Tekoa, ⁷Beth Zur, Soco, Adullam, ⁸Gath, Mareshah, Ziph, ⁹Adoraim, Lachish, Azekah, ¹⁰Zorah, Aijalon and Hebron. These were strong, walled cities in Judah and Benjamin. ¹¹When Rehoboam made those cities strong, he put commanders in them. He also put supplies of food, oil and wine in them. ¹²Also, Rehoboam put shields and spears in all the cities. So he made them very strong. Rehoboam kept the peoples and cities of Judah and Benjamin under his control.

¹³The priests and the Levites from all over Israel joined Rehoboam. ¹⁴The Levites even left their pasturelands and fields and came to Judah and Jerusalem. They did this because Jeroboam and his sons refused to let them serve as priests to the Lord. ¹⁵Jeroboam chose his own priests to serve in the places of worship. He chose his own priests for the goat and calf idols he had made. ¹⁶There were people from all the tribesᵈ of Israel who wanted to obey the Lord, the God of Israel. They went to Jerusalem with the Levites. They went to sacrifice to the Lord, the God of their fathers. ¹⁷These people made the kingdom of Judah strong. And they

supported Solomon's son Rehoboam for three years. During this time they lived the way David and Solomon had lived.

Rehoboam's Family

¹⁸Rehoboam married Mahalath. She was the daughter of Jerimoth and Abihail. Jerimoth was David's son. Abihail was Eliab's daughter, and Eliab was Jesse's son. ¹⁹Mahalath gave Rehoboam these sons: Jeush, Shemariah and Zaham. ²⁰Then Rehoboam married Absalom's daughter Maacah. And she gave Rehoboam these children: Abijah, Attai, Ziza and Shelomith. ²¹Rehoboam loved Maacah more than his other wives and slave women.ᵈ Rehoboam had 18 wives and 60 slave women. He was the father of 28 sons and 60 daughters.

²²Rehoboam chose Abijah to be the leader of his own brothers. He did this because he planned to make Abijah king. ²³Rehoboam acted wisely. He spread his sons through all the areas of Judah and Benjamin. He sent them to every strong, walled city. And he gave plenty of supplies to his sons. He also found wives for them.

Shishak Attacks Jerusalem

12 Rehoboam became a strong king. He also made his kingdom strong. Then he and the people of Judah stopped obeying the teachings of the Lord. ²Shishak was the king of Egypt. He attacked Jerusalem in the fifth year Rehoboam was king. This happened because Rehoboam and the people were unfaithful to the Lord. ³Shishak had 1,200 chariots and 60,000 horsemen. He brought troops of Libyans, Sukkites and Cushites from Egypt with him. There were so many they couldn't be counted. ⁴Shishak captured the strong, walled cities of Judah. And he came as far as Jerusalem.

⁵Then Shemaiah the prophetᵈ came

to Rehoboam and the leaders of Judah. They had gathered in Jerusalem because they were afraid of Shishak. Shemaiah said to them, "This is what the Lord says: 'You have left me. So now I will leave you to face Shishak alone'."

6Then the leaders of Judah and King Rehoboam were sorry for what they had done. They said, "The Lord does what is right."

7The Lord saw that they were sorry for what they had done. So the Lord spoke his word to Shemaiah. The Lord said, "The king and the leaders are sorry. So I will not destroy them but will save them soon. I will not use Shishak to punish Jerusalem in my anger. 8But the people of Jerusalem will become Shishak's servants. Then they may learn that serving me is different from serving the kings of other nations."

9Shishak king of Egypt attacked Jerusalem. He took the treasures from the Temple*d* of the Lord and from the king's palace. He took everything, even the gold shields Solomon had made. 10So King Rehoboam made bronze shields to take their place. He gave them to the commanders of the guards for the entrance to the king's palace. 11Whenever the king entered the Temple of the Lord, the guards went with him. They would carry the shields. Later, they would put them back in the guard room.

12When Rehoboam was sorry for what he had done, the Lord held his anger back. So the Lord did not fully destroy Rehoboam. There was some good in Judah.

13King Rehoboam made himself a strong king in Jerusalem. He was 41 years old when he became king. And he was king in Jerusalem for 17 years. Jerusalem is the city that the Lord chose from all the tribes*d* of Israel. He chose to be worshipped in Jerusalem. Rehoboam's mother was Naamah from the country of Ammon. 14Reho-

boam did evil things because he did not want to ask the Lord for help.

15The things Rehoboam did as king, from the beginning to the end, are written down. They are in the records of Shemaiah the prophet. And they are in the records of Iddo the seer.*d* These men wrote family histories. There were wars between Rehoboam and Jeroboam all the time they ruled. 16Rehoboam died and was buried in Jerusalem. Then Rehoboam's son Abijah became king.

Abijah King of Judah

13 Abijah became the king of Judah. This was during the eighteenth year Jeroboam was king of Israel. 2Abijah was king in Jerusalem for three years. Abijah's mother was Maacah daughter of Uriel. Uriel was from the town of Gibeah.

And there was war between Abijah and Jeroboam. 3Abijah led an army of 400,000 capable soldiers into battle. And Jeroboam prepared to fight him with 800,000 capable soldiers.

4Abijah stood on Mount Zemaraim in the mountains of Ephraim. He said, "Jeroboam and all Israel, listen to me! 5You should know this: the Lord, the God of Israel, gave David and his sons the right to be king over Israel for ever. God gave this right to David with an agreement which will last for ever. 6But Jeroboam turned against his master. Jeroboam was the son of Nebat, one of Solomon's officers. Solomon was David's son. 7Then worthless, evil men became friends with Jeroboam. They were against Rehoboam, Solomon's son. Rehoboam was young and didn't know what to do. So he could not stop them.

8"Now you people are making plans against the Lord's kingdom. The Lord's kingdom belongs to David's sons! There are many of you. And you have the gold calves Jeroboam made for you as gods. 9You have thrown out the Lord's priests and the Levites.

The priests are Aaron's sons. You have chosen your own priests as people in other countries do. Anyone who comes to make himself ready to serve the Lord with a young bull and seven male sheep can become a priest. He may become a priest of idols that are not gods. ¹⁰"But as for us, the Lord is our God. We have not left him. The priests who serve the Lord are Aaron's sons. And the Levites help the priests serve the Lord. ¹¹They offer burnt offerings and sweet-smelling incense*d* to the Lord every morning and evening. They also put the bread on the special table in the Temple.*d* And they light the lamps on the gold lampstand every evening. We obey the command of the Lord our God. But you have left the Lord. ¹²God himself is with us. He is our ruler, and his priests are with us. The priests blow the trumpet to call us to war against you. Men of Israel, don't fight against the Lord because you won't succeed. He is the God of your ancestors."

¹³But Jeroboam had sent some troops to sneak behind Abijah's army. So while Jeroboam was in front of Abijah's army, Jeroboam's soldiers were behind them. ¹⁴The soldiers in Abijah's army looked around. Then they saw Jeroboam's army attacking both in front and at the back. They cried out to the Lord. The priests blew the trumpets. ¹⁵Then the men of Judah gave a battle cry. When they shouted, God defeated Jeroboam and the army of Israel. They ran away from Abijah and the army of Judah. ¹⁶The men of Israel ran away from the men of Judah. God let the army from Judah defeat them. ¹⁷Abijah's army killed many of Israel's men. Of Israel's best men 500,000 were killed. ¹⁸So at that time the people of Israel were defeated. And the people of Judah won. They won because they depended on the Lord, the God of their ancestors.

¹⁹Abijah's army chased Jeroboam's army. Abijah's army captured from Jeroboam the towns of Bethel, Jeshanah and Ephron. They also captured the small villages near these towns. ²⁰Jeroboam never became strong again while Abijah was alive. The Lord struck Jeroboam, and he died. ²¹But Abijah became strong. He married 14 women. And he was the father of 22 sons and 16 daughters. ²²All the other things Abijah did as king are written down. What he said and did are recorded in what the prophet Iddo has written.

14 Abijah died and was buried in Jerusalem. Then Abijah's son Asa became king in his place. There was peace in the country for ten years in Asa's time.

Asa King of Judah

²Asa did what the Lord said was good and right. ³He removed the foreign altars used for idol worship. He removed the places where false gods were worshipped. He smashed the stone pillars that honoured false gods. And he tore down the Asherah*d* idols. ⁴Asa commanded the people of Judah to obey the Lord, the God their ancestors followed. Asa commanded them to obey the Lord's teachings and commandments. ⁵He also removed the places where false gods were worshipped and the incense altars from every town in Judah. So the kingdom had peace while Asa was king. ⁶Asa built strong, walled cities in Judah during the time of peace. He had no war in these years because the Lord gave him peace.

⁷Asa said to the people of Judah, "Let's build up these towns and put walls around them. Let's make towers, gates and bars in the gates. This country is ours because we have obeyed the Lord our God. We have tried to obey him, and he has given us peace all around." So they built and had success.

⁸Asa had an army of 300,000 men

from the people of Judah. And he had 280,000 men from the people of Benjamin. The men from Judah carried large shields and spears. The men from Benjamin carried small shields and bows and arrows. All these men were brave fighting men.

9Then Zerah from Cush came out to fight Asa's army. Zerah had a large army and 300 chariots. They came as far as the town of Mareshah. 10Asa went out to fight Zerah. Asa's army prepared for battle in the Valley of Zephathah at Mareshah.

11Asa called out to the Lord his God. He said, "Lord, only you can help weak people against the strong. Help us, Lord our God. We depend on you. We fight against this large army in your name. Lord, you are our God. Don't let anyone win against you."

12Then the Lord defeated the Cushites when Asa's army from Judah attacked them. And the Cushites ran away. 13Asa's army chased them as far as the town of Gerar. So many Cushites were killed that the army could not fight again. They were crushed by the Lord and his army. Asa and his army carried many valuable things away from the enemy. 14They destroyed all the towns near Gerar. The people living in these towns were afraid of the Lord. These towns had many valuable things. So Asa's army took these things away. 15Asa's army also attacked the camps where the shepherds lived. And they took many sheep and camels. Then they went back to Jerusalem.

Asa's Changes

15 The Spirit*d* of God entered Azariah son of Oded. 2Azariah went to meet Asa. Azariah said, "Listen to me, Asa and all you people of Judah and Benjamin. The Lord is with you when you are with him. If you obey the Lord, you will find him. But if you leave him, he will leave you. 3For a long time Israel was without

the true God. And they were without a priest to teach them and without the teachings. 4But when they were in trouble, they turned to the Lord again. He is the God of Israel. They looked for the Lord and found him. 5In those days no one could travel safely. There was much trouble in all the nations. 6One nation would destroy another nation. And one city would destroy another city. This happened because God troubled them with all kinds of trouble. 7But you should be strong. Don't give up, because you will get a reward for your good work."

8Asa felt brave when he heard these words and the message from Azariah. Azariah was the son of Oded the prophet.*d* So he removed the hated idols from all of Judah and Benjamin. And he removed them from the towns he had captured in the hills of Ephraim. He repaired the Lord's altar that was in front of the porch of the Temple*d* of the Lord.

9Then Asa gathered all the people from Judah and Benjamin. He also gathered the people of the tribes*d* of Ephraim, Manasseh and Simeon who were living in Judah. Many people came to Asa from Israel. They came because they saw that the Lord, Asa's God, was with him.

10Asa and these people gathered in Jerusalem. This was in the third month of the fifteenth year of Asa's rule. 11At that time they sacrificed to the Lord 700 bulls and 7,000 sheep and goats. Asa's army had taken these animals and other valuable things from their enemies. 12Then they made an agreement. They promised to obey the Lord with their whole being. He is the God their ancestors served. 13Anyone who refused to obey the Lord, the God of Israel, was to be killed. It did not matter if that person was important or unimportant. It did not matter if that person was a man or woman. 14Then Asa and the people made a promise before the Lord.

They shouted with a loud voice. They also blew on trumpets and sheep's horns. ¹⁵All the people of Judah were happy about the promise. They had promised with all their heart. They looked for God and found him. So the Lord gave them peace in all the country.

¹⁶King Asa also removed Maacah, his mother, from being queen mother. He did this because she had made an Asherah*d* idol, which the Lord hated. Asa cut down that idol and smashed it into pieces. Then he burned it in the Kidron Valley. ¹⁷The places of worship to false gods were not removed from Judah. Asa desired very much to obey the Lord all his life.

¹⁸And Asa put the holy gifts that he and his father had given into the Temple of God. These things were made of silver and gold.

¹⁹There was no more war until the thirty-fifth year of Asa's rule.

Asa's Last Years

16 In the thirty-sixth year of Asa's rule, Baasha king of Israel attacked Judah. He went to the town of Ramah and made it strong. He used it to keep people from going in or out of the country of Judah.

²Asa took silver and gold out of the treasuries of the Temple*d* of the Lord. And he took silver and gold out of his own palace. Then he sent it with messengers to Ben-Hadad king of Aram. Ben-Hadad was living in Damascus. Asa's message said: ³"Let's make an agreement between you and me. Let's make it like the agreement between your father and mine. See, I am sending you silver and gold. Now break your agreement with Baasha king of Israel. Then he will take his army away from my country."

⁴Ben-Hadad agreed with King Asa. So Ben-Hadad sent the commanders of his armies to attack the towns of Israel. These commanders defeated the towns of Ijon, Dan and Abel Beth Maacah. They also defeated all the towns in Naphtali where treasures were stored. ⁵When Baasha heard about this, he stopped building Ramah. He left his work. ⁶Then King Asa called all the men of Judah together. They went to Ramah and took away the rocks and wood that Baasha had used. And they used the rocks and wood to build up Geba and Mizpah.

⁷At that time Hanani the seer*d* came to Asa king of Judah. Hanani said to him, "You depended on the king of Aram to help you. You did not depend on the Lord your God. So the king of Aram's army escaped from you. ⁸The Cushites and Libyans had a large and powerful army. They had many chariots and horsemen. But you depended on the Lord to help you. So he let you defeat them. ⁹The Lord searches all the earth for people who have given themselves completely to him. He wants to make them strong. Asa, you did a foolish thing. From now on you will have wars."

¹⁰Asa was angry with Hanani the seer because of what he had said. Asa was so angry that he put Hanani in prison. Asa was cruel with some of the people at that same time.

¹¹The things Asa did as king, from the beginning to the end, are written down. They are in the book of the kings of Judah and Israel. ¹²In the thirty-ninth year of his rule, Asa got a disease in his feet. His disease was very bad. But he did not ask for help from the Lord. He only asked for help from the doctors. ¹³Then Asa died in the forty-first year of his rule. ¹⁴The people buried Asa in the tomb he had made for himself in Jerusalem. They laid him on a bed. It was filled with spices and different kinds of mixed perfumes. And they made a large fire to honour Asa.

Jehoshaphat King of Judah

17 Jehoshaphat, Asa's son, became king of Judah in Asa's place. Jehoshaphat made Judah strong so they could fight against Israel. ²He put troops in all the strong, walled cities of Judah. And he put troops in Judah and in the towns of Ephraim his father Asa had captured.

³The Lord was with Jehoshaphat because he did good things. He lived as his father Asa did when he first became king. Jehoshaphat did not ask for help from the Baal^d idols. ⁴He asked for help from the God his father had followed. He obeyed God's commands. He did not live as the people of Israel lived. ⁵The Lord made Jehoshaphat a strong king over Judah. All the people of Judah brought gifts to Jehoshaphat. So he had much wealth and honour. ⁶He wanted very much to obey the Lord. He also removed the places for worshipping false gods and the Asherah^d idols from Judah.

⁷Jehoshaphat sent his officers to teach in the towns of Judah. This happened in the third year of his rule. These officers were Ben-Hail, Obadiah, Zechariah, Nethanel and Micaiah. ⁸Jehoshaphat sent with them these Levites: Shemaiah, Nethaniah, Zebadiah, Asahel, Shemiramoth, Jehonathan, Adonijah, Tobijah and Tob-Adonijah. He also sent the priests Elishama and Jehoram. ⁹These leaders, Levites and priests taught the people in Judah. They took the Book of the Teachings of the Lord with them. And they went through all the towns of Judah and taught the people.

¹⁰The nations near Judah were afraid of the Lord. So they did not start a war against Jehoshaphat. ¹¹Some of the Philistines brought gifts and silver to Jehoshaphat as forced payments. Some Arabs brought him flocks. They brought him 7,700 male sheep and 7,700 goats.

¹²Jehoshaphat became more and more powerful. He built strong, walled cities and storage towns in Judah. ¹³He kept many supplies in the towns of Judah. And he kept trained soldiers in Jerusalem. ¹⁴These soldiers were listed by families.

From the families of Judah, these were the commanders of groups of 1,000 men: Adnah was the commander of 300,000 soldiers. ¹⁵Jehohanan was the commander of 280,000 soldiers. ¹⁶And Amasiah was the commander of 200,000 soldiers. Amasiah son of Zicri had volunteered to serve the Lord.

¹⁷These were the commanders from the families of Benjamin: Eliada had 200,000 soldiers who used bows and shields. Eliada was a brave soldier. ¹⁸And Jehozabad had 180,000 men armed for war.

¹⁹All these soldiers served King Jehoshaphat. The king also put other men in the strong, walled cities through all of Judah.

Micaiah Warns King Ahab

18 Jehoshaphat had much wealth and honour. He made an agreement with King Ahab through marriage.^{n} ²A few years later Jehoshaphat visited Ahab in Samaria. Ahab sacrificed many sheep and cattle as a great feast to honour Jehoshaphat and the people with him. He encouraged Jehoshaphat to attack Ramoth in Gilead. ³Ahab king of Israel asked Jehoshaphat king of Judah, "Will you go with me to attack Ramoth in Gilead?"

Jehoshaphat answered, "I will be with you. And my soldiers will be like your own soldiers. We will join you in the battle." ⁴Jehoshaphat also said to Ahab, "But first we should ask the Lord to guide us."

---

agreement . . . through marriage Jehoshaphat's son Jehoram married Athaliah, Ahab's daughter. See 2 Chronicles 21:6.

⁵So King Ahab called a meeting of the prophets.*ᵈ* There were 400 men. Ahab asked them, "Should we go to war against Ramoth in Gilead or not?"

They answered, "Go, because God will let you defeat it."

⁶But Jehoshaphat asked, "Is there a prophet of the Lord here? If there is, let's ask him what we should do."

⁷Then King Ahab said to Jehoshaphat, "There is one other prophet. We could ask the Lord through him. But I hate him. When he prophesies, he never says anything good about me. He always says something bad. He is Micaiah, Imlah's son."

Jehoshaphat said, "King Ahab, you shouldn't say that."

⁸So King Ahab told one of his officers to bring Micaiah to him at once.

⁹King Ahab of Israel and King Jehoshaphat of Judah had on their royal robes. They were sitting on their thrones at the threshing*ᵈ* floor. This was near the entrance to the gate of Samaria. All the prophets were speaking messages in front of the two kings. ¹⁰One of the prophets was Zedekiah son of Kenaanah. He had made some iron horns. He said to Ahab, "This is what the Lord says: 'You will use these horns to fight the Arameans. And you will destroy them'."

¹¹All the other prophets said the same thing. They said, "Attack Ramoth in Gilead and win. The Lord will let you defeat the Arameans."

¹²The messenger who had gone to get Micaiah found him. He said to Micaiah, "All the other prophets are saying the same thing. They are saying that King Ahab will win against the Arameans. You had better agree with them. Give the king a good answer."

¹³But Micaiah said, "As surely as the Lord lives, I can tell him only what my God says."

¹⁴Then Micaiah came to King Ahab. The king asked him, "Micaiah, should we attack Ramoth in Gilead or not?"

Micaiah answered, "Attack and win. You will defeat it."

¹⁵King Ahab said to Micaiah, "Tell me only the truth by the power of the Lord. How many times do I have to tell you this?"

¹⁶Then Micaiah answered, "I saw the army of Israel. They were scattered over the hills like sheep without a shepherd. The Lord said, 'They have no leaders. Let each one go home and not fight'."

¹⁷Then King Ahab of Israel said to Jehoshaphat, "I told you! This prophet never says anything good about me. He only says bad things about me."

¹⁸But Micaiah continued to speak. He said, "Hear the message from the Lord: I saw the Lord sitting on his throne. His heavenly army was standing on his right and on his left. ¹⁹The Lord said, 'Who will trick King Ahab of Israel into attacking Ramoth in Gilead? Do this so he will go and be killed'. The spirits did not agree about what they should do. ²⁰Then a spirit came and stood before the Lord. He said, 'I will trick him'. The Lord asked, 'How will you do it?' ²¹The spirit answered, 'I will go to Ahab's prophets. I will make them tell lies'. So the Lord said, 'You will succeed in tricking him. Go and do it'."

²²Micaiah said, "Ahab, this has now happened. The Lord has caused your prophets to lie to you. The Lord has decided that great trouble should come to you."

²³Then Zedekiah son of Kenaanah went up to Micaiah. And he slapped Micaiah in the face. Zedekiah said, "Do you really believe that the Lord's Spirit*ᵈ* has left me and is now speaking through you?"

²⁴Micaiah answered, "You will find out on the day you go to hide in an inside room."

²⁵Then King Ahab ordered, "Take Micaiah. Send him to Amon, the governor of the city, and to Joash, the king's son. ²⁶Tell them I said to put

Micaiah in prison. Give him only bread and water. Keep him there until I come back safely from the battle."

27Micaiah said, "Ahab, if you come back safely from the battle, the Lord has not spoken through me. Remember my words, all you people!"

Ahab Is Killed

28So Ahab king of Israel and Jehoshaphat king of Judah went to Ramoth in Gilead. 29King Ahab said to Jehoshaphat, "I will go into battle. But I will wear other clothes so no one will know who I am. But you wear your royal clothes." So King Ahab of Israel wore other clothes and went into battle.

30The king of Aram gave an order to his chariot commanders. He said, "Don't fight with anyone but the king of Israel. It doesn't matter if they are important or unimportant." 31When these commanders saw Jehoshaphat, they thought he was the king of Israel. So they turned to attack him. But Jehoshaphat called out, and the Lord helped him. God made the chariot commanders turn away from Jehoshaphat. 32When they saw he was not King Ahab, they stopped chasing him. 33By chance, a soldier shot an arrow. And it hit Ahab king of Israel. The arrow went in between the pieces of his armour. King Ahab said to his chariot driver, "Turn around and get me out of the battle. I've been wounded." 34The battle went on all day. King Ahab held himself up in his chariot. He faced the Arameans until evening. Then Ahab died at sunset.

19 Jehoshaphat king of Judah came back safely to his palace in Jerusalem. 2Jehu son of Hanani went out to meet him. Jehu was a seer.d He said to King Jehoshaphat, "Why did you help evil people? Why do you love those who hate the Lord? That is the reason the Lord is angry with you. 3But there is some good in you. You took the Asherahd idols out of this country. And you have wanted to obey God."

Jehoshaphat Chooses Judges

4Jehoshaphat lived in Jerusalem. He went out again to be with the people. He went from Beersheba to the mountains of Ephraim. He brought these people back to the Lord, the God their ancestors followed. 5Jehoshaphat appointed judges in all the land. He appointed judges for each of the strong, walled cities of Judah. 6Jehoshaphat said to them, "Be careful in what you do. This is because you are not judging for people but for the Lord. He will be with you when you make a decision. 7Now let each of you fear the Lord. Be careful in what you do because the Lord our God wants people to be fair. He wants all people to be treated the same. And he doesn't want people to accept money to change their judgments."

8And in Jerusalem Jehoshaphat appointed some of the Levites, priests and leaders of Israelite families to be judges. They were to decide cases about the law of the Lord. And they were to settle problems between the people who lived in Jerusalem. 9Jehoshaphat gave them commands. He said, "You must always serve the Lord completely. You must fear him. 10You will have cases about killing, about the teachings, commands, rules or some other law. These cases will come from your people living in the cities. In all these cases you must warn the people not to sin against the Lord. If you don't, the Lord will be angry with you and your people. But if you warn them, you won't be guilty. 11"Amariah is the leading priest. He will be over you in all cases about the Lord. Zebadiah son of Ishmael is a leader in the tribed of Judah. He will be over you in all cases about the king. Also, the Levites will serve as officers for you. Have courage. May the Lord be with those who do what is right."

Jehoshaphat Faces War

20 Later some people came to start a war with Jehoshaphat. They were the Moabites, Ammonites and some Meunites. [2]Some men came and told Jehoshaphat, "A large army is coming against you from Edom. They are coming from the other side of the Dead Sea.[d] They are already in Hazazon Tamar!" (Hazazon Tamar is also called En Gedi.) [3]Jehoshaphat was afraid. So he decided to ask the Lord what to do. He announced that no one in Judah should eat during this special time of prayer to God. [4]The people of Judah came together to ask the Lord for help. They came from every town in Judah to ask for his help.

[5]The people of Judah and Jerusalem met in front of the new courtyard in the Temple[d] of the Lord. Then Jehoshaphat stood up before them. [6]He said, "Lord, you are the God of our ancestors. You are the God in heaven. You rule over all the kingdoms of the nations. You have power and strength. No one can stand against you. [7]Our God, you forced out the people who lived in this land. You forced them out as your people Israel moved in. And you gave this land for ever to the descendants[d] of your friend Abraham. [8]They lived in this land and built a Temple for worshipping you. They said, [9]"Trouble may come to us. It may be war, punishment, sickness or a time of hunger. If it comes, we will stand before you and before this Temple where you have chosen to be worshipped. We will cry out to you when we are in trouble. Then you will hear and save us'.

[10]"But now here are men from Ammon, Moab and Edom. You wouldn't let the Israelites enter their lands when the Israelites came from Egypt. So the Israelites turned away and did not destroy them. [11]But see how they repay us for not destroying them! They have come to force us out of your land. And you gave us this land as our own. [12]Our God, punish those people. We have no power against this large army that is attacking us. We don't know what to do. So we look to you for help."

[13]All the men of Judah stood before the Lord. Their babies, wives and children were with them. [14]Then the Spirit[d] of the Lord entered Jahaziel. (Jahaziel was Zechariah's son. Zechariah was Benaiah's son. Benaiah was Jeiel's son, and Jeiel was Mattaniah's son.) Jahaziel was a Levite and a descendant of Asaph. He stood up in the meeting. [15]And he said: "Listen to me, King Jehoshaphat! Listen, all you people living in Judah and Jerusalem! The Lord says this to you: 'Don't be afraid or discouraged because of this large army. The battle is not your battle. It is God's battle. [16]Tomorrow go down there and fight those people. They will come up through the Pass of Ziz. You will find them at the end of the ravine that leads to the Desert of Jeruel. [17]You won't need to fight in this battle. Just stand strong in your places. You will see the Lord save you. Judah and Jerusalem, don't be afraid. Don't be discouraged. The Lord is with you. So go out against those people tomorrow'!"

[18]Jehoshaphat bowed face down on the ground. All the people of Judah and Jerusalem bowed down before the Lord. And they worshipped him. [19]Then some Levites from the Kohathite and Korahite people stood up and praised the Lord. They praised the God of Israel with very loud voices.

[20]Jehoshaphat's army went out into the Desert of Tekoa early in the morning. As they were starting out, Jehoshaphat stood and said, "Listen to me, people of Judah and Jerusalem! Have faith in the Lord your God. Then you will stand strong. Have faith in the Lord's prophets.[d] Then you will succeed." [21]Jehoshaphat listened to the

people's advice. Then he chose men to be singers to the Lord. They were to praise the Lord because he is holy and wonderful. They marched in front of the army. They said,

"Thank the Lord.
His love continues for ever."

22As they began to sing and praise God, the Lord set ambushes. He set them for the people of Ammon, Moab and Edom. They were the ones who came to attack Judah. And they were defeated. 23The men of Ammon and Moab started to attack the men from Edom. They killed and destroyed them. After they had killed the men from Edom, they killed each other.

24The men from Judah came to a place where they could see the desert. They looked at the enemy's large army. But they only saw dead bodies lying on the ground. No one had escaped. 25Jehoshaphat and his army came to take valuable things from the dead bodies. They found many supplies, much clothing, and other valuable things. There was more than they could carry away. There was so much it took three days to gather it all. 26On the fourth day Jehoshaphat and his army met in the Valley of Beracah. There they praised the Lord. That is why that place has been called the Valley of Beracah*n* to this day.

27Then Jehoshaphat led all the men from Judah and Jerusalem back to Jerusalem. The Lord had made them happy because their enemies were defeated. 28They entered Jerusalem with lyres,*d* harps and trumpets and went to the Temple of the Lord.

29All the kingdoms of the lands around them heard how the Lord had fought Israel's enemies. So they feared the Lord. 30So Jehoshaphat's kingdom was not at war. His God gave him peace from all the countries around him.

Jehoshaphat's Rule Ends

31Jehoshaphat ruled over the country of Judah. He was 35 years old when he began to rule. And he ruled 25 years in Jerusalem. His mother's name was Azubah daughter of Shilhi. 32Jehoshaphat lived as his father Asa had lived. He followed what Asa had done. He did what the Lord said was right. 33But the places where false gods were worshipped were not removed. And the people did not strongly desire to follow the God their ancestors had followed.

34The other things Jehoshaphat did as king, from the beginning to the end, are written down. They are in the writings of Jehu son of Hanani. These writings are in the book of the kings of Israel.

35Later, Jehoshaphat king of Judah made an agreement with Ahaziah king of Israel. It was wrong for him to do this. 36Jehoshaphat agreed with Ahaziah to build trading ships. They built them in the town of Ezion Geber. 37Then Eliezer son of Dodavahu spoke against Jehoshaphat. Eliezer was from the town of Mareshah. He said, "Jehoshaphat, because you joined with Ahaziah, the Lord will destroy what you have made." The ships were wrecked. So Jehoshaphat and Ahaziah could not send them out to trade.

21 Then Jehoshaphat died and was buried with his ancestors in Jerusalem. Jehoshaphat's son Jehoram became king in his place. 2Jehoram's brothers were Azariah, Jehiel, Zechariah, Azariahu, Michael and Shephatiah. They were the sons of Jehoshaphat king of Judah. 3Jehoshaphat gave his sons many gifts of silver, gold and valuable things. He also gave them strong, walled cities in Judah. But Jehoshaphat gave the kingdom to Jehoram because he was the first son.

Beracah This name means "blessing or praise".

Jehoram King of Judah

4Jehoram took control of his father's kingdom. Then he killed all his brothers with a sword. He also killed some of the leaders of Israel. 5He was 32 years old when he began to rule. And he ruled eight years in Jerusalem. 6He lived as the kings of Israel had lived. He lived as Ahab's family had lived. This was because he married Ahab's daughter. Jehoram did what the Lord said was wrong. 7But the Lord would not destroy David's family. This was because of the agreement he had made with David. The Lord had promised that one of David's descendants*d* would always rule.

8While Jehoram was king, Edom turned against Judah's rule. The people of Edom chose their own king. 9So Jehoram went to Edom with all his commanders and chariots. The Edomite army surrounded Jehoram and his chariot commanders. But Jehoram fought his way out at night. 10From then until now the country of Edom has fought against Judah.

At the same time the people of Libnah also turned against Jehoram. This happened because Jehoram left the Lord, the God his ancestors followed. 11Jehoram also had built places to worship false gods on the hills in Judah. He had led the people of Jerusalem into sinning. And he had led the people of Judah away from the Lord. 12Jehoram received a letter from Elijah the prophet. The letter said:

This is what the Lord says. He is the God your father David followed. The Lord says, "Jehoram, you have not lived as your father Jehoshaphat lived. You have not lived as Asa king of Judah lived. 13But you have lived as the kings of Israel lived. You have led the people of Judah and Jerusalem into sinning against God. That is what Ahab and his family did. You have killed your brothers. And

they were better than you. 14So now the Lord is about to punish your people terribly. He will punish your children, wives and everything you own. 15You will have a terrible disease in your intestines. It will become worse every day. Finally it will cause your intestines to come out."

16The Lord caused the Philistines and the Arabs to be angry with Jehoram. They lived near the Cushites. 17So the Philistines and Arabs attacked Judah. They took away all the wealth of Jehoram's palace, as well as his sons and wives. Only Jehoram's youngest son, Ahaziah, was left.

18After these things happened, the Lord gave Jehoram a disease in his intestines. It could not be cured. 19After he was sick for two years, Jehoram's intestines fell out because of the disease. He died in terrible pain. The people did not make a large fire to honour Jehoram as they had done for his ancestors.

20Jehoram was 32 years old when he became king. And he ruled eight years in Jerusalem. No one was sad when he died. He was buried in Jerusalem, but not in the graves for the kings.

Ahaziah King of Judah

22 The people of Jerusalem chose Ahaziah to be king in Jehoram's place. Ahaziah was Jehoram's youngest son. The robbers who had come with the Arabs to attack Jehoram's camp had killed all of Jehoram's older sons. So Ahaziah began to rule Judah. 2He was 22 years old when he began to rule. And he ruled one year in Jerusalem. His mother's name was Athaliah, a granddaughter of Omri. 3Ahaziah also lived as Ahab's family had lived. This was because his mother encouraged him to do wrong things. 4Ahaziah did what the Lord said was wrong. That is what Ahab's family had done. And they gave advice to Ahaziah after

his father died. Their bad advice led to his death. ⁵Ahaziah followed their advice when he went to fight King Hazael of Aram. King Joram of Israel, Ahab's son, went with him. They met Hazael at the town of Ramoth in Gilead. The Arameans wounded Joram in battle. ⁶So Joram returned to the town of Jezreel to get well. He was wounded at Ramoth when he fought Hazael king of Aram.

Then King Ahaziah of Judah, son of Jehoram, went to Jezreel. He went there to visit Joram son of Ahab because he was wounded.

⁷God caused Ahaziah's death when he went to visit Joram. Ahaziah arrived and went out with Joram to meet Jehu son of Nimshi. The Lord had appointed Jehu to destroy Ahab's family. ⁸While Jehu was punishing Ahab's family, he found the leaders of Judah. He also found Ahaziah's relatives who served Ahaziah. Jehu killed them all. ⁹Then Jehu looked for Ahaziah. Jehu's men caught him hiding in Samaria. So they brought him to Jehu. Then they killed and buried him. They said, "Ahaziah is a descendant[d] of Jehoshaphat. And Jehoshaphat obeyed the Lord with all his heart." No one in Ahaziah's family had the power to take control of the kingdom of Judah.

Athaliah Queen of Judah

¹⁰Now Ahaziah's mother, Athaliah, saw that her son was dead. Then she killed all the royal family in Judah. ¹¹But Jehosheba took Joash, Ahaziah's son. She stole him from among the other sons of the king. Those sons were going to be murdered. She put Joash and his nurse in a bedroom. Jehosheba was King Jehoram's daughter and Ahaziah's sister. She was also the wife of Jehoiada the priest. She hid Joash so Athaliah could not kill him. ¹²Joash was hidden with them in the Temple[d] of God for six years. During that time Athaliah ruled the land.

23 In the seventh year Jehoiada decided to do something. He made an agreement with the commanders of the groups of 100 men. These were the commanders: Azariah son of Jeroham, Ishmael son of Jehohanan, Azariah son of Obed, Maaseiah son of Adaiah, and Elishaphat son of Zicri. ²They went around in Judah and gathered the Levites from all the towns. They also gathered the leaders of the families of Israel. Then they went to Jerusalem. ³All the people together made an agreement with the king in the Temple of God.

Jehoiada said to them, "The king's son will rule. That is what the Lord promised about David's descendants.[d] ⁴Now this is what you must do: you priests and Levites go on duty on the Sabbath.[d] A third of you will guard the doors. ⁵A third of you will be at the king's palace. And a third of you will be at the Foundation Gate. All the other people will stay in the courtyards of the Temple of the Lord. ⁶Don't let anyone come into the Temple of the Lord. Only the priests and Levites who serve may come in. They may come because they have been made ready to serve the Lord. But all the other men must do the job the Lord has given them. ⁷The Levites must stay near the king. Every man must have his sword with him. If anyone tries to enter the Temple, kill him. You must stay with the king everywhere he goes."

⁸The Levites and all the people of Judah obeyed everything Jehoiada the priest had commanded. He did not excuse anyone from the groups of the priests. So each commander took the men who came on duty on the Sabbath with those who went off duty on the Sabbath. ⁹Jehoiada gave the commanders of the groups of 100 men the spears and the large and small shields. They had belonged to King David. They were kept in the Temple of God. ¹⁰Then Jehoiada told the men where

to stand. Every man had his weapon in his hand. They stood around the king, near the altar and the Temple. They stood from the south side of the Temple to the north side.

¹¹Jehoiada and his sons brought out the king's son. And they put the crown on him. They gave him a copy of the law. Then they appointed him king and poured olive oil on him. Then they shouted, "Long live the king!" ¹²Athaliah heard the noise of the people running and praising the king. So she went to them at the Temple of the Lord. ¹³She looked and saw the king standing by his pillar at the entrance. The officers and the men who blew trumpets were near him. All the people of the land were happy and blowing trumpets. The singers were playing musical instruments and leading praises. Then Athaliah tore her clothes to show how upset she was. She shouted, "Traitors! Traitors!"

¹⁴Jehoiada the priest sent out the commanders of 100 men who led the army. He said to them, "Surround her with soldiers and take her out of the Temple area. Kill with a sword anyone who follows her." He had said, "Don't put Athaliah to death in the Temple of the Lord." ¹⁵So they caught her when she came to the entrance of the Horse Gate near the palace. And they put her to death there.

¹⁶Then Jehoiada made an agreement with the people and the king. They agreed that they would be the Lord's special people. ¹⁷All the people went to the temple of Baal[d] and tore it down. They smashed the altars and idols there. And they killed Mattan the priest of Baal in front of the altars. ¹⁸Then Jehoiada chose the priests to be responsible for the Temple of the Lord. These priests were Levites. David had given them duties in the Temple of the Lord. They were to offer the burnt offerings to the Lord as the Teachings of Moses commanded. They offered the sacrifices with much

joy and singing as David had commanded. ¹⁹Jehoiada put guards at the gates of the Temple of the Lord. Then anyone who was unclean[d] in any way could not enter the Temple.

²⁰Jehoiada took with him the commanders of 100 men, the important men, the rulers of the people and all the people of the land. They brought the king down from the Temple of the Lord. They went through the Upper Gate into the palace. Then they seated the king on the throne. ²¹All the people of Judah were very happy. And Jerusalem had peace because Athaliah had been put to death with the sword.

Joash Rebuilds the Temple

24 Joash was seven years old when he became king. And he ruled 40 years in Jerusalem. His mother's name was Zibiah. She was from Beersheba. ²Joash did what the Lord said was right as long as Jehoiada the priest was alive. ³Jehoiada chose two wives for Joash. And Joash had sons and daughters.

⁴Later, Joash decided to repair the Temple[d] of the Lord. ⁵He called the priests and the Levites together. He said to them, "Go to the towns of Judah. Gather the money all the Israelites have to pay every year. Use it to repair the Temple of your God. Do this now." But the Levites did not hurry.

⁶So King Joash called Jehoiada the leading priest. Joash said to him, "Why haven't you made the Levites bring in the tax money from Judah and Jerusalem? Moses the Lord's servant and the people of Israel used that money for the Holy Tent."[d]

⁷In the past the sons of wicked Athaliah had broken into the Temple of God. They had used its holy things for worshipping the Baal[d] idols.

⁸King Joash commanded that a box for contributions be made. It was to be put outside, at the gate of the Temple of the Lord. ⁹Then the Levites

made an announcement in Judah and Jerusalem. They told the people to bring the tax money to the Lord. Moses the servant of God had made the Israelites give it while they were in the desert. ¹⁰All the officers and people were happy to give their money. They put it in the box until the box was full. ¹¹Then the Levites would take the box to the king's officers. They would see that it was full of money. Then the king's royal assistant and the leading priest's officer would come and take out the money. Then they would take the box back to its place. They did this often and gathered a lot of money. ¹²King Joash and Jehoiada gave the money to the people who worked on the Temple of the Lord. And they hired stoneworkers and carpenters to repair the Temple of the Lord. They also hired people to work with iron and bronze to repair the Temple.

¹³The people worked hard. And the work to repair the Temple went well. They rebuilt the Temple of God to be as it was before. And they made it stronger. ¹⁴When the workers finished, they brought the money that was left to King Joash and Jehoiada. They used that money to make things for the Temple of the Lord. They made things for the service in the Temple and for the burnt offerings. They also made bowls and other things from gold and silver. Burnt offerings were given every day in the Temple of the Lord while Jehoiada was alive.

¹⁵Jehoiada grew old. He had lived many years. Then he died when he was 130 years old. ¹⁶Jehoiada was buried in Jerusalem with the kings. He was buried there because he had done much good in Israel for God and his Temple.

Joash Does Evil

¹⁷After Jehoiada died, the officers of Judah came and bowed down to King Joash. The king listened to them. ¹⁸The king and these leaders stopped worshipping in the Temple*d* of the Lord. He is the God their ancestors obeyed. The king and the officers began to worship the Asherah*d* idols and other idols. Because they did wrong, God was angry with the people of Judah and Jerusalem. ¹⁹The Lord sent prophets*d* to the people to turn them back to him. The prophets warned them, but the people refused to listen.

²⁰Then the Spirit*d* of God entered Zechariah son of Jehoiada the priest. Zechariah stood before the people and said, "This is what God says: 'Why do you disobey the Lord's commands? You will not be successful. You have left the Lord. So the Lord has also left you'."

²¹But the king and his officers made plans against Zechariah. The king commanded them to kill Zechariah. So they threw stones at him in the Temple courtyard until he died. ²²King Joash did not remember Jehoiada's kindness to him. So Joash killed Zechariah, Jehoiada's son. Before Zechariah died, he said, "May the Lord see what you are doing and punish you."

²³At the end of the year, the Aramean army came against Joash. They attacked Judah and Jerusalem and killed all the leaders of the people. Then they sent all the valuable things to their king in Damascus. ²⁴The Aramean army came with only a small group of men. But the Lord let them defeat a very large army from Judah. He did this because the people of Judah had left the Lord. He is the God their ancestors followed. So Joash was punished. ²⁵When the Arameans left, Joash was badly wounded. His own officers made plans against him. They did this because he had killed Zechariah son of Jehoiada the priest. So they killed Joash in his own bed. He died and was buried in Jerusalem. But he was not buried in the graves of the kings.

26The officers who made plans against Joash were Jozabad and Jehozabad. Jozabad was the son of Shimeath, a woman from Ammon. And Jehozabad was the son of Shimrith, a woman from Moab. 27The story of Joash's sons, the great prophecies*d* against him, and how he rebuilt the Temple of God are written down. They are in the book of the kings. Joash's son Amaziah became king in his place.

Amaziah King of Judah

25 Amaziah was 25 years old when he became king. He ruled for 29 years in Jerusalem. His mother's name was Jehoaddin. She was from Jerusalem. 2Amaziah did what the Lord said was right. But he did not really want to obey the Lord. 3Amaziah took strong control of the kingdom. Then he put to death the officers who had murdered his father the king. 4But Amaziah did not put their children to death. He obeyed what was written in the Book of Moses. There the Lord commanded, "Fathers must not be put to death when their children do wrong. And children must not be put to death when their fathers do wrong. Each person must die for his own sins."*n*

5Amaziah gathered the people of Judah together. He grouped all the people of Judah and Benjamin by families. And he put commanders over groups of 1,000 and over groups of 100. He counted the men who were 20 years old and older. In all there were 300,000 soldiers ready to fight. They were skilled with spears and shields. 6Amaziah also hired 100,000 soldiers from Israel. He paid about 3.4 tons of silver for them. 7But a man of God came to Amaziah and said, "My king, don't let the army of Israel go with you. The Lord is not with Israel. He is not with the people from the tribes*d*

of Israel. 8You can make yourself strong for war. But God will defeat you. He has the power to help you or to defeat you."

9Amaziah said to the man of God, "But what about the 3.4 tons of silver I paid to the Israelite army?"

The man of God answered, "The Lord can give you much more than that!"

10So Amaziah sent the Israelite army back home to Israel. They were very angry with the people of Judah. And they went home angry.

11Then Amaziah became very brave and led his army to the Valley of Salt. It is in the country of Edom. There Amaziah's army killed 10,000 men from Edom. 12The army of Judah also captured 10,000 men. They took those men to the top of a cliff and threw them off. And they were broken to pieces.

13At the same time the Israelite army was robbing some towns in Judah. These troops were those that Amaziah had not let fight in the war. They robbed towns from Samaria to Beth Horon. They killed 3,000 people and took many valuable things from them.

14Amaziah came home after he had defeated the Edomites. He brought back the idols they worshipped. And he started to worship them also. He bowed down to them and offered sacrifices to them. 15The Lord was very angry with Amaziah. The Lord sent a prophet*d* to him. The prophet said, "Why have you asked their gods for help? They could not even save their own people from you!"

16As the prophet spoke, Amaziah said to him, "We never gave you the job of advising the king! Stop, or you will be killed."

The prophet stopped speaking. Then he said, "I know that God has decided to destroy you because you

"Fathers . . . sins." See Deuteronomy 24:16.

have done this. You did not listen to my advice."

¹⁷Amaziah king of Judah talked with his men who gave him advice. Then he sent a message to Jehoash son of Jehoahaz. (Jehoahaz was the son of Jehu king of Israel.) Amaziah said to Jehoash, "Come, let's meet face to face in battle."

¹⁸Then Jehoash king of Israel answered Amaziah king of Judah. Jehoash said, "A little thornbush in Lebanon sent a message to a big cedar tree in Lebanon. It said, 'Let your daughter marry my son'. But then a wild animal from Lebanon came by. It walked on and crushed the thornbush. ¹⁹You say to yourself that you have defeated Edom. You are proud, and you brag. But you stay at home! Don't ask for trouble by fighting me. If you do, you and Judah will be defeated."

²⁰But Amaziah would not listen. God caused this to happen. He planned to let Jehoash of Israel defeat Judah. This was because Judah asked for help from the gods of Edom. ²¹So Jehoash king of Israel went to attack. He and Amaziah king of Judah faced each other in battle at Beth Shemesh in Judah. ²²Israel defeated Judah. Every man of Judah ran away to his home. ²³At Beth Shemesh Jehoash king of Israel captured Amaziah king of Judah. (Amaziah was the son of Joash, who was the son of Ahaziah.) Then Jehoash brought him to Jerusalem. Jehoash broke down the wall of Jerusalem from the Gate of Ephraim to the Corner Gate. This part of the wall was about 180 metres long. ²⁴Then he took all the gold and silver and everything in the Temple[d] of God. Obed-Edom had taken care of these things. Jehoash also took the treasures from the king's palace. Then he took some hostages and returned to Samaria.

²⁵Amaziah son of Joash was king of

Judah. He lived 15 years after Jehoash king of Israel died. Jehoash was the son of Jehoahaz. ²⁶The other things Amaziah did as king, from the beginning to the end, are written down. They are in the book of the kings of Judah and Israel. ²⁷When Amaziah stopped obeying the Lord, the people in Jerusalem made plans against him. So he ran away to the town of Lachish. But they sent men after him to Lachish and killed him there. ²⁸They brought his body back on horses. And he was buried with his ancestors in Jerusalem.

Uzziah King of Judah

26 Then all the people of Judah chose Uzziah[n] to be king. He became king in place of Amaziah, his father. Uzziah was 16 years old. ²He rebuilt the town of Elath and made it part of Judah again. He did this after Amaziah died.

³Uzziah was 16 years old when he became king. And he ruled 52 years in Jerusalem. His mother's name was Jecoliah, and she was from Jerusalem. ⁴He did what the Lord said was right. He obeyed God just as his father Amaziah had done. ⁵Uzziah obeyed God while Zechariah was alive. Zechariah taught Uzziah how to respect and obey God. As long as Uzziah obeyed the Lord, God gave him success.

⁶Uzziah fought a war against the Philistine people. He tore down the walls around their towns of Gath, Jabneh and Ashdod. He built new towns near Ashdod and in other places among the Philistines. ⁷God helped Uzziah fight the Philistines, the Arabs living in Gur Baal and the Meunites. ⁸The Ammonites made payments Uzziah demanded. Uzziah was very powerful. So his name became famous all the way to the border of Egypt.

⁹Uzziah built towers in Jerusalem and made them strong. He built them

Uzziah Also called Azariah in 2 Kings.

at the Corner Gate, the Valley Gate and where the wall turned. ¹⁰He also built towers in the desert and dug many wells. He had many cattle on the western mountain slopes and in the plains. He had people who worked his fields and vineyards. They worked in the hills and in the fertile lands. Uzziah loved the land.

¹¹He had an army of trained soldiers. They were counted and put in groups by Jeiel the royal assistant and Maaseiah the officer. Hananiah, one of the king's commanders, was their leader. ¹²There were 2,600 leaders over the soldiers. ¹³They were in charge of an army of 307,500 men. The army fought with great power. And they helped the king against the enemy. ¹⁴Uzziah gave his army shields, spears, helmets, armour, bows and stones for their slings. ¹⁵In Jerusalem Uzziah made devices that were invented by clever men. These devices were put on the towers and corners of the city walls. They were used to shoot arrows and large rocks. So Uzziah became famous in faraway places. He had a great deal of help until he became powerful.

¹⁶But when Uzziah became strong, his pride caused him to be destroyed. He was unfaithful to the Lord his God. He went into the Temple*d* of the Lord to burn incense*d* on the altar for incense. ¹⁷Azariah and 80 other brave priests who served the Lord followed Uzziah into the Temple. ¹⁸They told Uzziah he was wrong. They said to him, "You don't have the right to burn incense to the Lord. Only the priests, Aaron's descendants,*d* should burn the incense. They have been made holy for the Lord to do this special duty. Leave this holy place. You have been unfaithful to God. The Lord God will not honour you for this."

¹⁹Uzziah was standing beside the altar for incense in the Temple of the Lord. He had in his hand a pan for burning incense. He was very angry

with the priests. As he was standing in front of the priests, a harmful skin disease broke out on his forehead. ²⁰Azariah the leading priest and all the other priests looked at him. They could see the harmful skin disease on his forehead. So they hurried him out of the Temple. Uzziah rushed out, because the Lord had punished him. ²¹So King Uzziah had the skin disease until the day he died. He had to live in a separate house. He could not enter the Temple of the Lord. His son Jotham was in charge of the palace. He governed the people of the land.

²²The other things Uzziah did as king were written down by the prophet Isaiah. Isaiah son of Amoz wrote about Uzziah's rule from beginning to end. ²³Uzziah died and was buried near his ancestors in a graveyard that belonged to the kings. This was because people said, "He had a harmful skin disease." And his son Jotham became king in his place.

Jotham King of Judah

27 Jotham was 25 years old when he became king. He ruled 16 years in Jerusalem. His mother's name was Jerusha daughter of Zadok. ²Jotham did what the Lord said was right. He obeyed God just as his father Uzziah had done. But Jotham did not enter the Temple*d* of the Lord to burn incense*d* as his father had. But the people continued doing wrong. ³Jotham rebuilt the Upper Gate of the Temple of the Lord. He did much building on the wall at the place named Ophel. ⁴He also built towns in the hill country of Judah. And he built walled cities and towers in the forests.

⁵Jotham also fought the king of the Ammonite people. And Jotham defeated the Ammonites. So each year for three years they gave Jotham about 3.4 tons of silver. They also gave him about 2200 kilolitres of wheat and about 2200 kilolitres of barley. ⁶Jo-

tham became powerful because he always obeyed the Lord his God.

⁷The other things Jotham did while he was king and all his wars are written down. They are in the book of the kings of Israel and Judah. ⁸Jotham was 25 years old when he became king. And he ruled 16 years in Jerusalem. ⁹Jotham died and was buried in Jerusalem. And Jotham's son Ahaz became king in his place.

Ahaz King of Judah

28 Ahaz was 20 years old when he became king. And he ruled 16 years in Jerusalem. He was not like his ancestor David. He did not do what the Lord said was right. ²Ahaz did the same things the kings of Israel had done. He made metal idols to worship Baal.ᵈ ³He burned incenseᵈ in the Valley of Ben Hinnom. He sacrificed his own sons by burning them in the fire. He did the same terrible sins as the other nations had done. And the Lord had forced these nations out of the land ahead of the Israelites. ⁴Ahaz offered sacrifices and burned incense at the places where false gods were worshipped. And he did this on the hills and under every green tree.

⁵So the Lord his God let the king of Aram defeat Ahaz. The Arameans defeated Ahaz and took many people of Judah as prisoners. The Arameans took them to Damascus.

The Lord also let Pekah king of Israel defeat Ahaz. Pekah's army killed many soldiers of Ahaz. ⁶Pekah was the son of Remaliah. Pekah's army killed 120,000 brave soldiers from Judah in one day. Pekah defeated them because they had left the Lord. He is the God their ancestors obeyed. ⁷Zicri was a warrior from Ephraim. He killed King Ahaz's son Maaseiah. He also killed Azrikam, the officer in charge of the palace and Elkanah, second in command to the king. ⁸The Israelite army captured 200,000 of their own relatives. They took women, sons and daughters and many valuable things from Judah. Then they carried them back to Samaria. ⁹But a prophetᵈ of the Lord named Oded was there. He met the Israelite army when it returned to Samaria. He said to them, "The Lord is the God your ancestors obeyed. He let you defeat Judah because he was angry with those people. But God has seen the cruel way you killed them. ¹⁰Now you plan to make the people of Judah and Jerusalem your slaves. But you also have sinned against the Lord your God. ¹¹Now listen to me. Send back your brothers and sisters whom you captured. Do this because the Lord is very angry with you."

¹²Then some of the leaders in Israel met the Israelite soldiers coming home from war. These leaders were Azariah son of Jehohanan, Berekiah son of Meshillemoth, Jehizkiah son of Shallum and Amasa son of Hadlai. ¹³They warned the soldiers, "Don't bring the prisoners from Judah here. If you do, we will be guilty of sin. That will make our sin and guilt even worse. And our guilt is already so much that the Lord is angry with Israel."

¹⁴So the soldiers left the prisoners and valuable things in front of the officers and people there. ¹⁵The leaders who were named took the prisoners. These four men got the clothes that the Israelite army had taken. And they gave them to these people who were naked. They gave the prisoners clothes, sandals, food, drink and medicine. They put the weak prisoners on donkeys. Then they took them back to their families in Jericho, the city of palm trees. Then they returned home to Samaria.

¹⁶⁻¹⁷At that same time the Edomites came again. They attacked Judah and carried away prisoners. So King Ahaz asked the king of Assyria for help. ¹⁸The Philistines also robbed the towns in the western mountain slopes

and in southern Judah. They captured the towns of Beth Shemesh, Aijalon, Gederoth, Soco, Timnah and Gimzo. They also captured the villages around them. Then the Philistines lived in those towns. ¹⁹The Lord brought trouble on Judah because of Ahaz their king. Ahaz had caused the people of Judah to sin. And he had been unfaithful to the Lord. ²⁰Tiglath-Pileser king of Assyria came to Ahaz. But he gave Ahaz trouble instead of help. ²¹Ahaz took some valuable things from the Temple^d of the Lord. He also took some from the king's palace and from the princes. Ahaz gave them to the king of Assyria, but it did not help.

²²In Ahaz's troubles he was even more unfaithful to the Lord. ²³He offered sacrifices to the gods the people of Damascus worshipped. These people had defeated him. So he thought, "The gods of the kings of Aram helped them. If I offer sacrifices to them, they will help me also." But this brought ruin to Ahaz and all Israel.

²⁴Ahaz gathered the things from the Temple of God and broke them into pieces. Then he closed the doors of the Temple of the Lord. He made altars and put them on every street corner in Jerusalem. ²⁵In every town in Judah, Ahaz made places for burning sacrifices to worship other gods. He made the Lord, the God his ancestors worshipped, very angry.

²⁶The other things Ahaz did as king, from the beginning to the end, are written down. They are in the book of the kings of Judah and Israel. ²⁷Ahaz died and was buried in the city of Jerusalem. But he was not buried in the graves of the kings of Israel. Ahaz's son Hezekiah became king in his place.

Hezekiah Purifies the Temple

29 Hezekiah was 25 years old when he became king. And he ruled 29 years in Jerusalem. His mother's name was Abijah daughter of Zechariah. ²Hezekiah did what the Lord said was right. He did just as his ancestor David had done.

³Hezekiah opened the doors of the Temple^d of the Lord and repaired them. He did this in the first month of the first year he was king. ⁴Hezekiah brought the priests and Levites together in a group. He met with them in the courtyard on the east side of the Temple. ⁵Hezekiah said, "Listen to me, Levites! Make yourselves ready for the Lord's service. And make the Temple of the Lord holy. He is the God your ancestors obeyed. Remove from the Temple the things that make it impure. ⁶Our ancestors were unfaithful to God. They did what the Lord said was wrong. They left the Lord. They stopped worshipping at the Temple where he lives. They rejected him. ⁷They shut the doors of the porch of the Temple. They let the fire go out in the lamps. They stopped burning incense^d and offering burnt offerings in the holy place to the God of Israel. ⁸So the Lord became very angry with the people of Judah and Jerusalem. And he punished them. Other peoples are frightened and shocked by what the Lord did to Judah and Jerusalem. They insult the people of Judah. You know these things are true. ⁹That is why our ancestors were killed in battle. That is why our sons, daughters and wives were taken prisoner. ¹⁰So now I, Hezekiah, have decided to make an agreement with the Lord, the God of Israel. Then he will not be angry with us any more. ¹¹My sons, don't waste any more time. The Lord chose you to serve him. You should serve him and burn incense to him."

¹²These are the Levites who started to work. From the Kohathite family there were Mahath son of Amasai and Joel son of Azariah. From the Merarite family there were Kish son of Abdi and Azariah son of Jehallelel. From the Gershonite family there

were Joah son of Zimmah and Eden son of Joah. ¹³From Elizaphan's family there were Shimri and Jeiel. From Asaph's family there were Zechariah and Mattaniah. ¹⁴From Heman's family there were Jehiel and Shimei. From Jeduthun's family there were Shemaiah and Uzziel.

¹⁵These Levites gathered their brothers together. Then they made themselves holy for service in the Temple. They obeyed the king's command that had come from the Lord. They went into the Temple of the Lord to purify it. ¹⁶The priests went into the Temple of the Lord to purify it. They took out all the unclean*d* things they found in the Temple of the Lord. And they put them in the Temple courtyard. Then the Levites took these things out to the Kidron Valley. ¹⁷They made the Temple holy for the Lord's service. They began on the first day of the first month. On the eighth day of the month, they came to the porch of the Temple. For eight more days they made the Temple of the Lord holy. They finished on the sixteenth day of the first month.

¹⁸Then they went to King Hezekiah. They said to him, "We have purified all the Temple of the Lord. We have purified the altar for burnt offerings and its things. We have purified the table for the holy bread and all its things. ¹⁹When Ahaz was king, he was unfaithful to God. He removed some things from the Temple. But we have put them back and made them holy for the Lord. They are now in front of the Lord's altar."

²⁰Early the next morning King Hezekiah gathered the leaders of the city. They went up to the Temple of the Lord. ²¹They brought seven bulls, seven male sheep, seven male lambs and seven male goats. These animals were an offering to remove the sin of the people and the kingdom of Judah. And this offering made the Temple ready for service to God. King Hezekiah commanded the priests to offer these animals on the Lord's altar. The priests were from the family of Aaron. ²²So the priests killed the bulls. Then they sprinkled the bulls' blood on the altar. They killed the male sheep and sprinkled their blood on the altar. Then they killed the lambs. And they sprinkled the lambs' blood on the altar. ²³Then the priests brought the male goats before the king and the people there. The goats were for the sin offering. The king and the people put their hands on the goats. ²⁴Then the priests killed the goats. They made a sin offering with the goats' blood on the altar. They did this to remove the sins of the Israelites so they would belong to the Lord. The king had said that the burnt offering and sin offering should be made for all Israel.

²⁵King Hezekiah put the Levites in the Temple of the Lord with cymbals, harps and lyres.*d* He did this as David, Gad and Nathan had commanded. (Gad was the king's seer,*d* and Nathan was a prophet.*d*) This command came from the Lord through his prophets. ²⁶So the Levites stood ready with David's instruments of music. And the priests stood ready with their trumpets. ²⁷Then Hezekiah gave the order to sacrifice the burnt offering on the altar. When the burnt offering began, the singing to the Lord also began. The trumpets were blown. And the musical instruments of David king of Israel were played. ²⁸All the people worshipped, the singers sang, and the trumpet players blew their trumpets. They did this until the burnt offering was finished.

²⁹When the sacrifices were finished, King Hezekiah and everyone with him bowed down and worshipped. ³⁰King Hezekiah and his officers ordered the Levites to praise the Lord. They were to use the words David and Asaph the seer used. They praised

God with joy. And they bowed down and worshipped.

31Then Hezekiah said, "Now you people of Judah have given yourselves to the Lord. Come near to the Temple of the Lord. Bring sacrifices and offerings to show thanks to the Lord." So the people brought sacrifices and offerings to show thanks to the Lord. Anyone who wanted to also brought burnt offerings. 32For burnt offerings they brought a total of 70 bulls, 100 male sheep and 200 lambs. All these animals were sacrificed as burnt offerings to the Lord. 33The offerings made holy for the Lord totalled 600 bulls and 3,000 sheep and goats. 34There were not enough priests to skin all the animals for the burnt offerings. So their relatives the Levites helped them. They helped until the work was finished and other priests could be made holy for the Lord's service. The Levites had been more careful to make themselves holy for the Lord's service than the priests. 35There were many burnt offerings. With them were the fat of fellowship offerings and drink offerings. So the service in the Temple of the Lord began again. 36And Hezekiah and the people were very happy. They were happy that God had made everything happen so quickly for his people.

Hezekiah Celebrates the Passover

30 King Hezekiah sent messages to all the people of Israel and Judah. He also wrote letters to the people of Ephraim and Manasseh. Hezekiah invited all these people to come to the Temple*d* of the Lord in Jerusalem. There they could celebrate the Passover*d* for the Lord, the God of Israel. 2King Hezekiah, his officers and all the people in Jerusalem agreed to celebrate the Passover in the second month. 3They could not celebrate it at the normal time. This was because not enough priests had made themselves ready to serve the Lord. And the people had not gathered yet in Jerusalem. 4This plan satisfied King Hezekiah and all the people. 5So they made an announcement everywhere in Israel, from Beersheba to Dan.*n* They told the people to come to Jerusalem. There they would celebrate the Passover for the Lord, the God of Israel. For a long time most of the people had not celebrated the Passover as the law commanded. 6So the messengers took letters from the king and his officers all through Israel and Judah. This is what the letters said:

People of Israel, come back to obeying the Lord. He is the God that Abraham, Isaac and Israel obeyed. Then God will come back to you who are still alive. You have escaped from the kings of Assyria. 7Don't be like your ancestors or your relatives. They turned against the Lord, the God their fathers obeyed. So the Lord caused other people to be disgusted with them. You know this is true. 8Don't be stubborn as your ancestors were. Obey the Lord willingly. Come to the Temple, which the Lord has made holy for his service for ever. Serve the Lord your God. Then he will not be angry with you. 9Come back and obey the Lord. Then the people who captured your relatives and children will be kind to them. They will let them return to this land. The Lord your God is kind and merciful. He will not turn away from you if you come back to him.

10The messengers went to every

Beersheba to Dan Dan was the city farthest north in Israel. Beersheba was the city farthest south. So this means all the people of Israel.

town in Ephraim and Manasseh. They went all the way to Zebulun. But the people laughed at the messengers and made fun of them. [11]But some men from Asher, Manasseh and Zebulun were sorry for what they had done and went to Jerusalem. [12]And God caused all the people of Judah to agree to obey King Hezekiah and his officers. Their command had come from the Lord.

[13]A large crowd came together in Jerusalem to celebrate the Feast[d] of Unleavened Bread. This was in the second month. [14]The people removed the altars and incense[d] altars to false gods in Jerusalem. And they threw them into the Kidron Valley.

[15]They killed the Passover lamb on the fourteenth day of the second month. The priests and the Levites were ashamed. So they made themselves holy for the Lord. They brought burnt offerings into the Temple of the Lord. [16]They took their regular places in the Temple as the Teachings of Moses the man of God commanded. The Levites gave the blood of the sacrifices to the priests. Then the priests sprinkled the blood on the altar. [17]Many people in the crowd had not made themselves holy for the Lord. So they were not permitted to kill the Passover lambs. So the Levites were responsible for killing the Passover lambs for everyone who was not clean.[d] The Levites made each lamb holy for the Lord. [18-19]Many people from Ephraim, Manasseh, Issachar and Zebulun had not purified themselves for the feast. But they ate the Passover even though it was against the law. So Hezekiah prayed for them. He said, "Lord, you are good. You are the Lord, the God our ancestors obeyed. Please forgive everyone who tries to obey you. Forgive them even if they did not make themselves clean as the rules of the Temple command." [20]The Lord listened to Hezekiah's prayer,

and he healed the people. [21]The Israelites in Jerusalem celebrated the Feast of Unleavened Bread for seven days. And they were very happy. The Levites and priests praised the Lord every day with loud music. [22]Some of the Levites understood well how to do their service for the Lord. And Hezekiah encouraged them. The people ate the feast for seven days. And they offered fellowship offerings. They praised the Lord, the God their ancestors worshipped.

[23]Then all the people agreed to stay seven more days. So they celebrated the Passover with joy for seven more days. [24]Hezekiah king of Judah gave 1,000 bulls and 7,000 sheep to the people. The officers gave 1,000 bulls and 10,000 sheep to the people. Many priests made themselves holy for the Lord. [25]All the people of Judah, the priests, the Levites, those who came from Israel, the foreigners from Israel and the foreigners living in Judah were very happy. [26]There was much joy in Jerusalem. There had not been a celebration like this since Solomon's time. He was the son of David and king of Israel. [27]The priests and Levites stood up and blessed the people. And God heard them because their prayer reached heaven, which is his holy home.

The Collection for the Priests

31 The Passover[d] celebration was finished. All the Israelites in Jerusalem went out to the towns of Judah. There they smashed the stone pillars used to worship false gods. They cut down the Asherah[d] idols. They destroyed the altars and places for worshipping false gods. They destroyed all of them in the areas of Judah, Benjamin, Ephraim and Manasseh. They destroyed everything used for worshipping the false gods. Then all the Israelites returned to their own towns and homes.

[2]King Hezekiah appointed groups of

priests and Levites for their special duties. They were to offer burnt offerings and fellowship offerings. They were to worship and to give thanks and praise at the gates where the Lord lives. [3]Hezekiah gave some of his own animals for the burnt offerings. Burnt offerings were given every morning and evening. They were also given on Sabbath[d] days and during New Moons[d] and other feasts commanded by the Lord's Teachings.

[4]Hezekiah commanded the people living in Jerusalem to give the priests and Levites the portion that belonged to them. Then the priests and Levites could give all their time to the Lord's Teachings. [5]Soon the king's command went out to the Israelites. And they gave quickly and freely. They gave the first portion of their grain, wine, oil and honey. They gave the first portion of everything they grew in their fields. They brought a large amount, one-tenth of everything. [6]The men of Israel and Judah who lived in Judah also gave. They brought one-tenth of their cattle and sheep. And they brought one-tenth of the holy things that were given to the Lord their God. They put all these things in piles. [7]The people began bringing their things in the third month. And they finished in the seventh month. [8]Hezekiah and his officers came and saw the piles. Then they praised the Lord and his people, the people of Israel. [9]Hezekiah asked the priests and Levites about the piles. [10]Azariah was the leading priest from Zadok's family. He answered Hezekiah, "Since the people began to bring their offerings to the Temple[d] of the Lord, we have had plenty to eat. We have had plenty left over. The Lord has blessed his people. So we have all this left over."

[11]Then Hezekiah commanded the priests to prepare the storerooms in the Temple of the Lord. So this was done. [12]Then the priests brought the offerings and the things given to the

Lord. They also brought the tenth of everything the people had given. All these things were put in the storerooms. Conaniah the Levite was in charge of these things. Conaniah's brother Shimei was second to him. [13]Conaniah and his brother Shimei were over these supervisors: Jehiel, Azaziah, Nahath, Asahel, Jerimoth, Jozabad, Eliel, Ismachiah, Mahath and Benaiah. King Hezekiah and Azariah the officer in charge of the Temple of God chose those men.

[14]Kore was in charge of the special gifts the people wanted to give to God. He was responsible for giving out the contributions made to the Lord and the holy gifts. Kore was the son of Imnah the Levite. Kore was the guard at the East Gate. [15]Eden, Miniamin, Jeshua, Shemaiah, Amariah and Shecaniah helped Kore. They served well in the towns where the priests lived. They gave from what was collected to the other groups of priests. They gave both to the young and the old.

[16]These men also gave from what was collected to the males three years old and older. These were males who had their names in the Levite family histories. They were to enter the Temple of the Lord for their daily service. Each group had its own responsibilities. [17]The priests were given their part of the collection. This was done by families, as listed in the family histories. The Levites 20 years old and older were given their part of the collection. This was done by their responsibilities and by their groups. [18]The Levites' babies, wives, sons and daughters also got part of the collection. This was done for all the Levites who were listed in the family histories. This was because the Levites always kept themselves ready to serve the Lord.

[19]Some of Aaron's descendants,[d] the priests, lived on the farmland near the towns. Some also lived in the

towns. Men were chosen by name to give part of the collection to these priests. All the males and those named in the family histories of the Levites received part of the collection.

²⁰This is what King Hezekiah did in Judah. He did what was good and right and obedient before the Lord his God. ²¹Hezekiah tried to obey God in his service of the Temple of God. He tried to obey God's teachings and commands. He gave himself fully to his work for God. So he had success.

Assyria Troubles Hezekiah

32 Hezekiah did all these things to serve the Lord. Sennacherib king of Assyria came to attack Judah. He and his army surrounded and attacked the strong, walled cities. He wanted to take them for himself. ²Hezekiah knew that Sennacherib had come to Jerusalem to attack it. ³So Hezekiah talked to his officers and army commanders. They decided to cut off the waters from the springs outside the city. So the officers and commanders helped Hezekiah. ⁴Many people came to help. They cut off all the springs and the stream that flowed through the land. They said, "The king of Assyria will not find much water when he comes here." ⁵Then Hezekiah made Jerusalem stronger. He rebuilt all the broken parts of the wall. And he built towers on the wall. He also built another wall outside the first one. And he made the area that was filled in on the east side of the old part of Jerusalem stronger. He made many weapons and shields.

⁶Hezekiah put army commanders over the people. He met with these commanders at the open place near the city gate. Hezekiah encouraged them, saying, ⁷"Be strong and brave. Don't be afraid or worried because of the king of Assyria or his large army. There is a greater power with us than with him. ⁸He only has men, but we

have the Lord our God. He will help us. He will fight our battles." The people were encouraged by the words of Hezekiah king of Judah.

⁹King Sennacherib of Assyria and all his army surrounded and attacked Lachish. Then he sent his officers to Jerusalem with a message. The message was for King Hezekiah of Judah and all the people of Judah in Jerusalem. This was the message:

¹⁰Sennacherib king of Assyria says this: "You have nothing to trust in to help you. It is no use for you to stay in Jerusalem under attack. ¹¹Hezekiah says to you, 'The Lord our God will save us from the king of Assyria'. But he is fooling you. If you stay in Jerusalem, you will die from hunger and thirst. ¹²Hezekiah himself removed your Lord's places of worship and altars. He told you people of Judah and Jerusalem that you must worship and burn incense*d* on only one altar.

¹³"You know what my ancestors and I have done to all the people in other nations. The gods of those nations could not save their people from my power. ¹⁴My ancestors destroyed those nations. None of their gods could save them from me. So your god cannot save you from my power. ¹⁵Do not let Hezekiah fool you or trick you. Do not believe him. No god of any nation or kingdom has been able to save his people from me or my ancestors. Your god is even less able to save you from me."

¹⁶Sennacherib's officers said worse things against the Lord God and his servant Hezekiah. ¹⁷King Sennacherib also wrote letters insulting the Lord, the God of Israel. This is what his letters said: "The gods of the other nations could not save their people from me. In the same way Hezekiah's god

won't be able to save his people from me." [18]Then the king's officers shouted out in Hebrew. They called out to the people of Jerusalem who were on the city wall. The officers wanted to scare the people away so they could capture Jerusalem. [19]They said evil things about the gods the people of the world worshipped. They are only things people have made with their hands. In the same way the officers said evil things about the God of Jerusalem.

[20]King Hezekiah and the prophet[d] Isaiah son of Amoz prayed to heaven about this. [21]Then the Lord sent an angel to the king of Assyria's camp. That angel killed all the soldiers, leaders and officers of the Assyrian army. So the king of Assyria returned to his own country in disgrace. He went into the temple of his god. There some of his own sons killed him with a sword.

[22]So the Lord saved Hezekiah and the people in Jerusalem. He saved them from Sennacherib king of Assyria and from all other people. The Lord took care of Hezekiah and the people of Jerusalem. [23]Many people brought gifts for the Lord to Jerusalem. They also brought valuable gifts to King Hezekiah of Judah. From then on all the nations respected Hezekiah.

Hezekiah Dies

[24]At that time Hezekiah became very sick. He was almost dead. He prayed to the Lord. And the Lord spoke to him and gave him a sign.[n] [25]But Hezekiah was proud. So he did not thank God for his kindness. So the Lord was angry with him and the people of Judah and Jerusalem. [26]But later Hezekiah and the people of Jerusalem were sorry and stopped being proud.

So the Lord did not punish them while Hezekiah was alive.

[27]Hezekiah had many riches and much honour. He made treasuries for his silver, gold, gems, spices, shields and other valuable things. [28]Hezekiah built storage buildings for grain, new wine and oil. He built stalls for all the cattle and pens for the sheep. [29]He also built many towns. He had many flocks of sheep and herds of cattle. God gave Hezekiah much wealth.

[30]It was Hezekiah who cut off the upper pool of the Gihon spring. He made those waters flow straight down on the west side of the older part of Jerusalem. And Hezekiah was successful in everything he did. [31]But one time the leaders of Babylon sent messengers to Hezekiah. They asked him about a strange sign[n] that had happened in the land. When they came, God left Hezekiah alone to test him. He wanted to know everything that was in Hezekiah's heart.[n]

[32]Hezekiah's love for the Lord and the other things he did as king are recorded. They are written in the vision of the prophet[d] Isaiah son of Amoz. This is in the book of the kings of Judah and Israel. [33]Hezekiah died and was buried on a hill. It is where the graves of David's ancestors are. All the people of Judah and Jerusalem honoured Hezekiah when he died. And Hezekiah's son Manasseh became king in his place.

Manasseh King of Judah

33 Manasseh was 12 years old when he became king of Judah. And he was king for 55 years in Jerusalem. [2]He did what the Lord said was wrong. He did the hated things the other nations had done. And the Lord

---

sign See Isaiah 38:1-18. It tells the story about the sign and how the Lord gave Hezekiah 15 more years to live.
God ... heart See 2 Kings 20:12-19.

had forced these nations out of the land ahead of Israel. [3]Manasseh's father, Hezekiah, had torn down the places where false gods were worshipped. But Manasseh rebuilt them. Manasseh also built altars for the Baal[d] gods and made Asherah[d] idols. He bowed down to the stars and worshipped them. [4]The Lord had said about the Temple,[d] "I will be worshipped in Jerusalem for ever." But Manasseh built altars for false gods in the Temple of the Lord. [5]He built altars to worship the stars in the two courtyards of the Temple of the Lord. [6]He burned his sons as sacrifices in the Valley of Ben Hinnom. He practised magic and witchcraft.[d] He told the future by explaining signs and dreams. He got advice from mediums[d] and fortune-tellers. He did many things the Lord said were wrong. And this made the Lord angry.

[7]He carved an idol and put it in the Temple of God. God had spoken to David and his son Solomon about the Temple. He had said, "I will be worshipped in this Temple and in Jerusalem for ever. I have chosen Jerusalem from all the tribes[d] of Israel. [8]I will never again make the Israelites leave the land I gave to their ancestors. But they must obey everything I commanded them. They must obey all the teachings, rules and commands I gave them through Moses." [9]But Manasseh led the people of Judah and Jerusalem to do wrong. They did more evil than the nations the Lord had destroyed ahead of the Israelites.

[10]The Lord spoke to Manasseh and his people, but they did not listen. [11]So the Lord brought the king of Assyria's army commanders to attack Judah. They captured Manasseh and put hooks in him. They put bronze chains on his hands. They made him their prisoner and took him to Babylon. [12]As Manasseh suffered, he begged the Lord his God for help. He became very sorry for what he had done before the God of his ancestors. [13]When Manasseh prayed, the Lord heard him and felt pity for him. So the Lord let him return to Jerusalem and to his kingdom. Then Manasseh knew that the Lord is the true God.

[14]After that happened, Manasseh rebuilt the outer wall for Jerusalem. It was in the valley on the west side of the Gihon spring. It went to the entrance of the Fish Gate and around the hill of Ophel. He also made the wall higher. Then he put commanders in all the strong, walled cities in Judah.

[15]Manasseh removed the idols of other nations. And he took the idol out of the Temple of the Lord. He removed all the altars he had built on the Temple hill and in Jerusalem. And he threw them out of the city. [16]Then he set up the Lord's altar. And he sacrificed on it fellowship offerings and offerings to show thanks to the Lord. Manasseh commanded all the people of Judah to serve the Lord, the God of Israel. [17]The people continued to offer sacrifices at the places of worship. But their sacrifices were only to the Lord their God. [18]The other things Manasseh did as king are written down. His prayer to his God is recorded. And what the seers[d] said to him in the name of the Lord, the God of Israel, is recorded. They are all in the book of the history of the kings of Israel. [19]Manasseh's prayer and God's pity for him are written down. Also all of Manasseh's sins and how he was unfaithful to the Lord are recorded. The places he built for worshipping false gods and for the Asherah[d] idols are recorded. He did all these things but later became sorry for them. They are all in the book of the seers. [20]Manasseh died and was buried in his palace. Then Manasseh's son Amon became king in his place.

Amon King of Judah

[21]Amon was 22 years old when he became king. And he was king for two

years in Jerusalem. ²²He did what the Lord said was wrong. He did as his father Manasseh had done. Amon worshipped and offered sacrifices to all the carved idols Manasseh had made. ²³Amon was not sorry for what he did wrong before the Lord. He was not sorry as his father Manasseh had been. Instead, Amon sinned even more.

²⁴Amon's officers made plans against him and killed him in his palace. ²⁵But the people of Judah killed all those who had made plans to kill King Amon. And they made his son Josiah to be king in his place.

Josiah King of Judah

34 Josiah was eight years old when he became king. He ruled 31 years in Jerusalem. ²He did what the Lord said was right. He did good things as his ancestor David had done. Josiah did not stop doing what was right.

³In his eighth year as king, Josiah began to obey the God his ancestor David had followed. This was while Josiah was still young. In his twelfth year as king, Josiah began to remove the false gods from Judah and Jerusalem. He destroyed the places for worshipping false gods. He removed the Asherah*d* idols and the wooden and metal idols. ⁴The people tore down the altars for the Baal*d* gods as Josiah directed. Then Josiah cut down the incense*d* altars that were above them. He broke up the Asherah idols and the wooden and metal idols. He beat them into powder. Then he sprinkled the powder on the graves of the people who had offered sacrifices to these gods. ⁵He burned the bones of their priests on their own altars. So Josiah removed idol worship from Judah and Jerusalem. ⁶He did the same for the towns in the areas of Manasseh, Ephraim and Simeon. He did this all the way to Naphtali. And he did the same for the ruins near these towns.

⁷Josiah broke down the altars and Asherah idols. Then he beat the idols into powder. He cut down all the incense altars in all of Israel. Then he went back to Jerusalem.

⁸In Josiah's eighteenth year as king, he made Judah and the Temple*d* pure again. He sent Shaphan son of Azaliah, Maaseiah the city leader and Joah son of Joahaz the recorder. They were to repair the Temple of the Lord, the God of Josiah. ⁹These men went to Hilkiah the high priest. They gave him the money the people had given for the Temple of God. The Levite doorkeepers had collected this money from the people of Manasseh, Ephraim and all the Israelites who were left alive. They also collected this money from all the people of Judah, Benjamin and Jerusalem. ¹⁰Then the Levites gave it to the men who directed the work on the Temple of the Lord. And these supervisors paid the workers that rebuilt and repaired the Temple. ¹¹They gave money to carpenters and builders to buy cut rocks and wood. The wood was used to rebuild the buildings and to make beams for them. The kings of Judah had let the buildings become ruins. ¹²The men did their work well. Their supervisors were Jahath, Obadiah, Zechariah and Meshullam. Jahath and Obadiah were Levites from the family of Merari. Zechariah and Meshullam were from the family of Kohath. These Levites were all skilled musicians. ¹³They were in charge of the workers who carried things and all the other workers. Some Levites worked as secretaries, officers and doorkeepers.

The Law Is Found

¹⁴The Levites brought out the money that was in the Temple*d* of the Lord. As they were doing this, Hilkiah the priest found the Book of the Lord's Teachings. These teachings had been given through Moses. ¹⁵Hil-

kiah said to Shaphan the royal assistant, "I've found the Book of the Teachings. It was in the Temple of the Lord!" He gave it to Shaphan.

¹⁶Then Shaphan took the book to the king and reported to Josiah: "Your officers are doing everything you told them to do. ¹⁷They have paid out the money that was in the Temple of the Lord. They have given it to the supervisors and the workers." ¹⁸Then Shaphan the royal assistant told the king, "Hilkiah the priest has given me a book." And Shaphan read from the book to the king.

¹⁹The king heard the words of the Teachings. Then he tore his clothes to show how upset he was. ²⁰He gave these orders to Hilkiah, Ahikam son of Shaphan. He also gave them to Acbor son of Micaiah, Shaphan and Asaiah. Shaphan was the royal assistant. And Asaiah was the king's servant. These were the orders: ²¹"Go and ask the Lord about the words in the book that was found. Ask for me and for the people who are left alive in Israel and Judah. The Lord is very angry with us because our ancestors did not obey the Lord's word. They did not do everything this book says to do."

²²So Hilkiah and those the king sent with him left. They went to talk to Huldah the prophetess.^d She was the wife of Shallum son of Tikvah, the son of Harhas. Harhas took care of the king's clothes. Huldah lived in Jerusalem, in the new area of the city.

²³She said to them, "This is what the Lord, the God of Israel, says: tell the man who sent you to me, ²⁴'This is what the Lord says: I will bring trouble to this place and to the people living here. I will bring all the curses that are written in the book that was read to the king of Judah. ²⁵The people of Judah have left me. They have burned incense^d to other gods. They have made me angry by all the bad

things they have made. So I will punish them in my anger. My anger will not be stopped'. ²⁶Tell the king of Judah who sent you to ask the Lord, 'This is what the Lord, the God of Israel, says about the words you heard: ²⁷You heard my words against this place and its people. And you became sorry for what you had done. You became sorry in my presence. You tore your clothes to show how upset you were. And you cried in my presence. This is why I have heard you, says the Lord. ²⁸So I will let you die. You will be buried in peace. You won't see all the trouble that I will bring to this place and the people living here'."

So they took her message back to the king.

²⁹Then the king gathered all the older leaders of Judah and Jerusalem together. ³⁰He went up to the Temple of the Lord. All the men from Judah and the people from Jerusalem went with him. The priests and the Levites and all the people — from the most important to the least important — went with him. He read to them all the words in the Book of the Agreement. That book was found in the Temple of the Lord. ³¹Then the king stood by his pillar. He made an agreement in the presence of the Lord. He agreed to follow the Lord and to obey his commands, rules and laws with his whole being. And he agreed to obey the words of the agreement written in this book. ³²Then Josiah made all the people in Jerusalem and Benjamin promise to accept the agreement. The people of Jerusalem obeyed the agreement of God, the God their ancestors obeyed.

³³And Josiah threw out the hated idols from all the land that belonged to the Israelites. He led everyone in Israel to serve the Lord their God. While Josiah lived, the people obeyed the Lord, the God their ancestors obeyed.

Josiah Celebrates the Passover

35 King Josiah celebrated the Passover[d] to the Lord in Jerusalem. The Passover lamb was killed on the fourteenth day of the first month. ²Josiah chose the priests to do their duties. And he encouraged them as they served in the Temple[d] of the Lord. ³The Levites taught the Israelites and were made holy for service to the Lord. Josiah said to them: "When David's son Solomon was king of Israel, he built the Temple. Put the Holy Ark[d] in that Temple. Do not carry it from place to place on your shoulders any more. Now serve the Lord your God and his people the Israelites. ⁴Prepare yourselves by your family groups for service. Do the jobs that King David and his son Solomon gave you to do.

⁵"Stand in the holy place with a group of the Levites. Do this for each family group of the people so you may help them. ⁶Kill the Passover lambs. Make yourselves holy to the Lord. And prepare the lambs for your relatives, the people of Israel. Do everything the Lord through Moses commanded us to do."

⁷Josiah gave the Israelites 30,000 sheep and goats to kill for the Passover sacrifices. He also gave them 3,000 cattle. They were all King Josiah's own animals.

⁸Josiah's officers also gave willingly to the people, the priests and the Levites. Hilkiah, Zechariah and Jehiel were the officers in charge of the Temple. They gave the priests 2,600 lambs and goats and 300 cattle for Passover sacrifices. ⁹Also Conianiah, his brothers Shemaiah and Nethanel, and Hashabiah, Jeiel and Jozabad gave the Levites animals. They gave 5,000 sheep and goats and 500 cattle for Passover sacrifices. These men were leaders of the Levites.

¹⁰When everything was ready for the Passover service, the priests and Levites went to their places. This is what the king had commanded. ¹¹The Passover lambs were killed. Then the Levites skinned the animals and gave the blood to the priests. The priests sprinkled the blood on the altar. ¹²Then they gave the animals for the burnt offerings to the different family groups. This was done so the burnt offerings could be offered to the Lord as the Law of Moses taught. They also did this with the cattle. ¹³The Levites roasted the Passover sacrifices over the fire as they were commanded. And they boiled the holy offerings in pots, kettles and pans. Then they quickly gave the meat to the people. ¹⁴After this was finished, the Levites prepared meat for themselves and for the priests. The priests were the descendants[d] of Aaron. The priests worked until night, offering the burnt offerings and burning the fat of the sacrifices.

¹⁵The Levite singers were from Asaph's family. They stood in the places King David had chosen for them. They were Asaph, Heman and Jeduthun, the king's seer.[d] The gatekeepers at each gate did not have to leave their places. This was because their fellow Levites had prepared everything for them for the Passover.

¹⁶So everything was done that day for the worship of the Lord. And it was done as King Josiah commanded. The Passover was celebrated, and the burnt offerings were offered on the Lord's altar. ¹⁷The Israelites who were there celebrated the Passover and the Feast[d] of Unleavened Bread for seven days. ¹⁸The Passover had not been celebrated like this in Israel since the prophet[d] Samuel was alive. None of the kings of Israel had ever celebrated a Passover like this. King Josiah, the priests and the Levites celebrated it. And the people of Judah and Israel who were there with the people of Jerusalem celebrated it.

¹⁹This Passover was celebrated in the eighteenth year Josiah was king.

The Death of Josiah

²⁰So Josiah did all this for the Temple.ᵈ After this, King Neco of Egypt led an army to attack Carchemish. It was a town on the Euphrates River. And Josiah marched out to fight against Neco. ²¹But Neco sent messengers to Josiah. They said, "King Josiah, there should not be war between us. I did not come to fight you, but my enemies. God told me to hurry, and he is on my side. So don't fight God, or he will destroy you."

²²But Josiah did not go away. He wore different clothes so no one would know who he was. He refused to listen to what Neco said at God's command. So Josiah went to fight on the plain of Megiddo. ²³In the battle King Josiah was shot by arrows. He told his servants, "Take me away. I am badly wounded." ²⁴So they took him out of his chariot. And they put him in another chariot he had brought to the battle. Then they took him to Jerusalem where he died. He was buried in the graves where his ancestors were buried. All the people of Judah and Jerusalem were very sad because he was dead.

²⁵Jeremiah wrote some sad songs about Josiah. Even to this day all the men and women singers remember and honour Josiah with these songs. It became a custom in Israel to sing these songs. They are written in the collection of sad songs.

²⁶⁻²⁷The other things Josiah did as king, from the beginning to the end, are written down. They are in the book of the kings of Israel and Judah. It tells how he loved the Lord and obeyed the Lord's teachings.

Jehoahaz King of Judah

36 The people of Judah chose Josiah's son Jehoahaz. They made him king in Jerusalem in his father's place.

²Jehoahaz was 23 years old when he became king. And he was king in Jerusalem for three months. ³Then King Neco of Egypt made Jehoahaz no longer a king in Jerusalem. Neco made the people of Judah pay about 3.4 tons of silver and about 34 kilograms of gold. ⁴The king of Egypt made Jehoahaz's brother Eliakim the king of Judah and Jerusalem. Then Neco changed Eliakim's name to Jehoiakim. But Neco took Eliakim's brother Jehoahaz to Egypt.

Jehoiakim King of Judah

⁵Jehoiakim was 25 years old when he became king. And he was king in Jerusalem for 11 years. He did what the Lord his God said was wrong. ⁶King Nebuchadnezzar of Babylon attacked Judah. He captured Jehoiakim and put bronze chains on him. Then Nebuchadnezzar took him to Babylon. ⁷Nebuchadnezzar took some of the things from the Templeᵈ of the Lord. And he took them to Babylon and put them in his own palace.

⁸The other things Jehoiakim did as king are written down. The hated things he did and everything he was guilty of doing are recorded. They are in the book of the kings of Israel and Judah. Jehoiakim's son Jehoiachin became king in his place.

Jehoiachin King of Judah

⁹Jehoiachin was 18 years old when he became king of Judah. And he was king in Jerusalem for three months and ten days. He did what the Lord said was wrong. ¹⁰In the spring King Nebuchadnezzar sent some servants to get Jehoiachin. They took him and some valuable treasures from the Templeᵈ of the Lord to Babylon. Then Nebuchadnezzar made Jehoiachin's relative Zedekiah the king of Judah and Jerusalem.

Zedekiah King of Judah

[11]Zedekiah was 21 years old when he became king of Judah. And he was king in Jerusalem for 11 years. [12]Zedekiah did what the Lord his God said was wrong. The prophet[d] Jeremiah spoke messages from the Lord. But Zedekiah did not obey.

Jerusalem Is Destroyed

[13]Zedekiah turned against King Nebuchadnezzar. Nebuchadnezzar had forced Zedekiah to promise to be loyal to him. And Zedekiah had promised, using God's name. But Zedekiah became stubborn. He refused to obey the Lord, the God of Israel. [14]Also, all the leaders of the priests and the people of Judah became more wicked. They followed the evil example of the other nations. The Lord had made the Temple[d] in Jerusalem holy. But the leaders made the Temple unholy.

The Fall of Jerusalem

[15]The Lord, the God of their ancestors, sent prophets[d] again and again to warn his people. He did this because he had pity for them and for his Temple. [16]But the people made fun of God's prophets. They hated God's messages. So they refused to listen to the prophets. Finally God became so angry with his people that he could not be stopped. [17]So God brought the king of Babylon to attack them. The king killed the young men even when they were in the Temple. He did not have mercy on the people. He killed both young men and women. He even killed the old men and those who were sick. God permitted Nebuchadnezzar to punish the people of Judah and Jerusalem. [18]Nebuchadnezzar carried away to Babylon all the things from the Temple of God, both large and small. He took all the treasures from the Temple of the Lord and from the king and his officers. [19]Nebuchadnezzar and his army set fire to God's Temple. They broke down Jerusalem's wall. And they burned all the palaces. They took or destroyed every valuable thing in Jerusalem.

[20]Nebuchadnezzar took captive to Babylon the people who were left alive. And he forced them to be slaves for him and his descendants.[d] They remained there as slaves until the Persian kingdom defeated Babylon. [21]And so what the Lord had told Israel through the prophet Jeremiah happened. The Lord had said that place would be an empty wasteland for 70 years. This happened to make up for the years of Sabbath rests[n] that the people had not kept.

[22]It was the first year Cyrus was king of Persia. The Lord caused Cyrus to write an announcement and send it everywhere in his kingdom. This happened so the Lord's message spoken by Jeremiah would come true.

[23]This is what Cyrus king of Persia says:

"The Lord, the God of heaven, has given all the kingdoms of the earth to me. And he has appointed me to build a Temple for him at Jerusalem in Judah. Now all of you who are God's people are free to go to Jerusalem. May the Lord your God be with you."

Sabbath rests The Law said that every seventh year the land was not to be farmed. See Leviticus 25:1-7.

EZRA

The Return from Captivity

Cyrus Helps the Captives Return

1 It was the first year Cyrus was king of Persia. The Lord caused Cyrus to write an announcement and send it everywhere in his kingdom. And he also put it in writing. This happened so the Lord's message spoken by Jeremiah would come true. The announcement said:

²This is what Cyrus king of Persia says:

The Lord, the God of heaven, has given all the kingdoms of the earth to me. And he has appointed me to build a Temple[d] for him at Jerusalem in Judah. ³Now all of you who are God's people are free to go to Jerusalem. May your God be with you. And you may build the Temple of the Lord. He is the God of Israel, who is in Jerusalem. ⁴Those who stay behind should support anyone who wants to go. Give them silver and gold, supplies and cattle. And give them special gifts for the Temple of God in Jerusalem.

⁵Then the family leaders of Judah and Benjamin got ready to go to Jerusalem. So did the priests and the Levites. They were going to Jerusalem to build the Temple of the Lord. God made all these people want to go. ⁶All their neighbours helped them. They gave them things made of silver and gold, along with supplies, cattle and valuable gifts. And they gave them the special gifts for the Temple. ⁷Also, King Cyrus brought out the bowls and pans that belonged in the Temple of the Lord. Nebuchadnezzar had taken them from Jerusalem. And he had put them in the temple of his own god. ⁸Cyrus king of Persia had Mithredath the treasurer get them out. So he made a list of the things for Sheshbazzar the prince of Judah.

⁹There were 30 gold dishes, 1,000 silver dishes, 29 silver pans, ¹⁰30 gold bowls, 410 matching silver bowls and 1,000 other pieces.

¹¹There was a total of 5,400 pieces of gold and silver. Sheshbazzar brought all these things along when the captives went from Babylon to Jerusalem.

The Captives Who Returned

2 These are the people of the area who returned from captivity. Nebuchadnezzar king of Babylon had taken them captive to Babylon. Now they returned to Jerusalem and Judah. Each one went back to his own town. ²These people returned with Zerubbabel, Jeshua, Nehemiah, Seraiah, Reelaiah, Mordecai, Bilshan, Mispar, Bigvai, Rehum and Baanah.

These are the men from Israel: ³the descendants[d] of Parosh—2,172; ⁴the descendants of Shephatiah—372; ⁵the descendants of Arah—775; ⁶the descendants of Pahath-Moab (through the family of Jeshua and Joab)—2,812; ⁷the descendants of Elam—1,254; ⁸the descendants of Zattu—945; ⁹the descendants of Zaccai—760; ¹⁰the descendants of Bani—642; ¹¹the descendants of Bebai—623; ¹²the descendants of Azgad—1,222; ¹³the descendants of Adonikam—666; ¹⁴the descendants of Bigvai—2,056; ¹⁵the descendants of Adin—454; ¹⁶the descendants of Ater (through the family of Hezekiah)—98; ¹⁷the descendants of Bezai—323;

¹⁸the descendants of Jorah — 112; ¹⁹the descendants of Hashum — 223; ²⁰the descendants of Gibbar — 95.

²¹These are the men from the town of Bethlehem — 123; ²²from Netophah — 56; ²³from Anathoth — 128; ²⁴from Azmaveth — 42; ²⁵from Kiriath Jearim, Kephirah and Beeroth — 743; ²⁶from Ramah and Geba — 621; ²⁷from Micmash — 122; ²⁸from Bethel and Ai — 223; ²⁹from Nebo — 52; ³⁰from Magbish — 156; ³¹from the other town of Elam — 1,254; ³²from Harim — 320; ³³from Lod, Hadid and Ono — 725; ³⁴from Jericho — 345; ³⁵from Senaah — 3,630.

³⁶These are the priests: the descendants of Jedaiah (through the family of Jeshua) — 973; ³⁷the descendants of Immer — 1,052; ³⁸the descendants of Pashhur — 1,247; ³⁹the descendants of Harim — 1,017.

⁴⁰These are the Levites: the descendants of Jeshua and Kadmiel (through the family of Hodaviah) — 74.

⁴¹These are the singers: the descendants of Asaph — 128.

⁴²These are the gatekeepers of the Temple:ᵈ the descendants of Shallum, Ater, Talmon, Akkub, Hatita and Shobai — 139.

⁴³These are the Temple servants: the descendants of Ziha, Hasupha, Tabbaoth, ⁴⁴Keros, Siaha, Padon, ⁴⁵Lebanah, Hagabah, Akkub, ⁴⁶Hagab, Shalmai, Hanan, ⁴⁷Giddel, Gahar, Reaiah, ⁴⁸Rezin, Nekoda, Gazzam, ⁴⁹Uzza, Paseah, Besai, ⁵⁰Asnah, Meunim, Nephussim, ⁵¹Bakbuk, Hakupha, Harhur, ⁵²Bazluth, Mehida, Harsha, ⁵³Barkos, Sisera, Temah, ⁵⁴Neziah and Hatipha.

⁵⁵These are the descendants of the servants of Solomon: the descendants of Sotai, Hassophereth, Peruda, ⁵⁶Jaala, Darkon, Giddel, ⁵⁷Shephatiah, Hattil, Pokereth-Hazzebaim and Ami. ⁵⁸The Temple servants and the descendants of the servants of Solomon numbered 392.

⁵⁹Some people came to Jerusalem from these towns: Tel Melah, Tel Harsha, Kerub, Addon and Immer. But they could not prove that their families came from the family of Israel. Here are their names and their number: ⁶⁰the descendants of Delaiah, Tobiah and Nekoda — 652.

⁶¹And these priests could not prove that their families came from Israel: the descendants of Hobaiah, Hakkoz and Barzillai. (He had married a daughter of Barzillai from Gilead and was called by her family name.)

⁶²These people searched for their family records. But they could not find them. So they could not be priests because they were thought to be unclean.ᵈ ⁶³The governor ordered them not to eat any of the food offered to God. First a priest had to settle this matter by using the Urim and Thummim.ᵈ

⁶⁴The total number of those who returned was 42,360. ⁶⁵This is not counting their 7,337 male and female servants. They also had 200 men and women singers with them. ⁶⁶They had 736 horses, 245 mules, ⁶⁷435 camels and 6,720 donkeys.

⁶⁸That group arrived at the Temple of the Lord in Jerusalem. Some of the leaders of families gave special offerings. Those offerings were given to rebuild the Temple of God. It would be on the same site as before. ⁶⁹Those people gave as much as they could to the treasury. It was to rebuild the Temple. They gave about 500 kilograms of gold, about 2800 kilograms of silver and 100 pieces of clothing for the priests.

⁷⁰All the Israelites settled in their home towns. The priests, Levites, singers, gatekeepers and temple servants, along with some of the other people, settled in their own towns.

Rebuilding the Altar

3 By the seventh month, the Israelites were settled in their home towns. They met together in

Jerusalem. [2]Then Jeshua son of Jozadak and his fellow priests joined Zerubbabel son of Shealtiel. They began to build the altar of the God of Israel. That's where they offered burnt offerings just as it is written in the Teachings of Moses. Moses was the man of God. [3]They were afraid of the people living around them. But they still built the altar where it had been before. They offered burnt offerings on it to the Lord morning and evening. [4]Then, to obey what was written, they celebrated the Feast[d] of Shelters. They offered the right number of sacrifices for each day of the festival. [5]After the Feast of Shelters, they had regular sacrifices every day. They had sacrifices for the New Moon[d] and all the festivals commanded by the Lord. Also there were special offerings brought as gifts to the Lord. [6]On the first day of the seventh month they began to bring burnt offerings to the Lord. But the foundation of the Lord's Temple[d] had not yet been laid.

Rebuilding the Temple

[7]Then they gave money to the stoneworkers and carpenters. They also gave food, wine and oil to the cities of Sidon and Tyre. This was so they would float cedar logs from Lebanon to the seacoast town of Joppa. Cyrus king of Persia had given permission for this.

[8]It was in the second year after their arrival at the Temple[d] of God in Jerusalem. In the second month Zerubbabel and Jeshua began the work. So did the rest of their fellow priests and Levites. And all who had returned from captivity to Jerusalem began to work. They chose Levites 20 years old and older to be in charge of the building of the Temple of the Lord. [9]These men were in charge of the work of building the Temple of God: Jeshua and his sons and brothers; Kadmiel and his sons who were the descendants of Hodaviah; and the sons of Henadad and their sons and brothers. They were all Levites.

[10]The builders finished laying the foundation of the Temple of the Lord. Then the priests, dressed in their robes, got trumpets. And the Levites, the sons of Asaph, had cymbals. They all took their places. They praised the Lord just as David king of Israel had said to do. [11]With praise and thanksgiving, they sang to the Lord:

"He is good;
   his love for Israel continues for
      ever."

And then all the people shouted loudly, "Praise the Lord! The foundation of his Temple has been laid." [12]But many of the older priests, Levites and family leaders cried aloud. They had seen the first Temple. Now they saw the foundation of this Temple. But most of the other people were shouting with joy. [13]The people made so much noise no one could tell the difference between the joyful shouting and the sad crying. It could be heard far away.

Enemies of the Rebuilding

4 The people of Judah and Benjamin had enemies. They heard that the returned captives were building a Temple[d] for the Lord, the God of Israel. [2]So the enemies came to Zerubbabel and the leaders of the families. The enemies said, "Let us help you build. We are like you. We want to worship your God. We have been offering sacrifices to him since the time of Esarhaddon. He was king of Assyria, and he brought us here."

[3]But Zerubbabel, Jeshua and the leaders of Israel answered, "No. You people will not help us build a Temple to our God. We will build it ourselves. It is for the Lord, the God of Israel. This is what King Cyrus, the king of Persia, commanded us to do."

[4]Then the people around them tried to discourage the people of Judah. They tried to make them afraid to

build. ⁵Their enemies hired others to delay the building plans. This went on during the time Cyrus was king of Persia. And it continued to the time Darius was king of Persia.

More Problems for the Builders

⁶When Xerxes became king, those enemies wrote a letter against the people of Judah and Jerusalem.

⁷Later Artaxerxes became king of Persia. Then Bishlam, Mithredath, Tabeel and those with them wrote a letter to Artaxerxes. The letter was written in the Aramaic language. ⁸Also Rehum the governor and Shimshai the governor's assistant wrote a letter. It was to Artaxerxes the king. And it was against Jerusalem. It said:

⁹This letter is from Rehum the governor, Shimshai the assistant and others. They are judges and important officers. They are over the men who came from Tripolis, Persia, Erech and Babylon. They are over the Elamite people of Susa. ¹⁰And they are over those whom the great and honourable Ashurbanipal forced out of their countries. He forced them to move and settle in the city of Samaria. And he forced them to settle in other places west of the Euphrates River.

¹¹(This is a copy of the letter they sent to Artaxerxes:)

To King Artaxerxes.
From your servants who live west of the Euphrates River.

¹²King Artaxerxes, you remember the Jews who came to us from you. You should know they have gone to Jerusalem. They are rebuilding that evil city that refuses to obey. They are fixing the walls and repairing the foundations of the buildings.

¹³Now, King Artaxerxes, you should know what could happen. If Jerusalem is built and its walls are fixed, Jerusalem will pay no taxes of any kind. Then the amount of money your government collects will be less. ¹⁴Since we must be loyal to the government, we don't want to see the king dishonoured. So we are writing to let the king know. ¹⁵We suggest you search the records of the kings who ruled before you. You will find out that the city of Jerusalem refuses to obey. It makes trouble for kings and areas controlled by Persia. Since long ago it has been a place where disobedience started. That is why it was destroyed. ¹⁶We want you to know this, King Artaxerxes. This city should not be rebuilt and its walls fixed. If it is, you will be left with nothing west of the Euphrates River.

¹⁷King Artaxerxes sent this answer:

To Rehum the governor and Shimshai the assistant. To all the people with them living in Samaria. And to those in other places west of the Euphrates.

Greetings.
¹⁸The letter you sent to us has been translated and read to me. ¹⁹I ordered the records to be searched, and it was done. We found that Jerusalem has a long history of disobedience to kings. It has been a place of problems and trouble. ²⁰Jerusalem has had powerful kings. They have ruled over the whole area west of the Euphrates. Taxes of all kinds have been paid to them. ²¹Now, give an order for those men to stop work. The city of Jerusalem will not be rebuilt until I say so.

22Make sure you do this. If it continues, it will hurt the government.

23A copy of the letter that King Artaxerxes sent was read. It was read to Rehum and Shimshai the assistant and the others. Then they quickly went to the Jews in Jerusalem. They forced them to stop building.

24So the work on the Temple^d of God in Jerusalem stopped. It stopped until the second year Darius was king of Persia.

Tattenai's Letter to Darius

5 Haggai and Zechariah son of Iddo were prophets.^d They prophesied to the Jews in Judah and Jerusalem. They prophesied in the name of the God of Israel. 2Then Zerubbabel son of Shealtiel and Jeshua son of Jozadak started working again. They worked to rebuild the Temple^d of God in Jerusalem. The prophets of God were there, helping them.

3At that time Tattenai was the governor west of the Euphrates. He and Shethar-Bozenai and others went to the Jews. They asked, "Who gave you permission to rebuild this Temple and fix these walls?" 4They also asked, "What are the names of these men working on this building?" 5But their God was watching over the older leaders of the Jews. The builders were not stopped until a report could go to King Darius. And then his written answer had to be received.

6This is a copy of the letter that Tattenai, Shethar-Bozenai and the others sent to King Darius. Tattenai was governor west of the Euphrates River. The other people were important officers west of the Euphrates. 7This is what the report they sent to him said:

To King Darius.

Greetings. May you have peace.

8King Darius, you should know that we went to the district of Judah. That is where the Temple of the great God is. The people there are building that Temple with large stones. They are putting timbers in the walls. The people are working very hard. And they are building very fast.

9We asked their older leaders, "Who gave you permission to rebuild this Temple and these walls?" 10We also asked for their names. We wrote down the names of their leaders so you would know who they are.

11This is the answer they gave to us: "We are the servants of the God of heaven and earth. We are rebuilding the Temple that a great king of Israel built. He finished it many years ago. 12But our ancestors made the God of heaven angry. So God let them be defeated by Nebuchadnezzar king of Babylon. He destroyed this Temple. And he took the people to Babylon as captives.

13"Later, Cyrus was in his first year as king of Babylon. He gave a special order for this Temple to be rebuilt. 14And Cyrus brought out things from the temple in Babylon. They were the gold and silver bowls and pans that came from the Temple of God. Nebuchadnezzar had taken them from the Temple in Jerusalem. And he had put them in the temple in Babylon.

"Then King Cyrus gave them to Sheshbazzar. He had appointed Sheshbazzar as governor. 15Cyrus said to him, 'Take these gold and silver bowls and pans. Put them back in the Temple in Jerusalem. And rebuild the Temple of God where it was'. 16So Sheshbazzar came. He laid the foundations of the Temple of God in Jerusalem. From that day until now the work has been going on. But it is not yet finished."

[17]Now, if the king wishes, let a search be made. Search the royal records of Babylon to see if King Cyrus gave such an order. See if he gave an order to rebuild this Temple in Jerusalem. Then let the king write to us and tell us what he has decided.

The Order of Darius

6 So King Darius gave an order to search the records. They were kept in the treasury in Babylon. [2]A scroll was found in the capital city, Ecbatana. It is in the area of Media. This is what was written on it:

Note:

[3]King Cyrus gave an order about the Temple[d] of God in Jerusalem. This was in the first year he was king. This was the order:

'Let the Temple be rebuilt. It will be a place to present sacrifices. Let its foundations be laid. The Temple should be 27 metres high and 27 metres wide. [4]It must have three layers of large stones, then one layer of timbers. The costs should be paid from the king's treasury. [5]The gold and silver things from the Temple of God should be put back in their places. Nebuchadnezzar took those things from the Temple in Jerusalem. And he brought them to Babylon. They are to be put back in the Temple of God in Jerusalem'.

[6]Now then, I, Darius, give this order to you, Tattenai, governor west of the Euphrates. And I give it to Shethar-Bozenai and all the officers of that area. Stay away from there. [7]Do not bother or interrupt the work on that Temple of God. Let the governor of the Jews and the older Jewish leaders

rebuild this Temple. Let them build it where it was before.

[8]Also, I order you to do this for those older leaders of the Jews. They are building this Temple. The cost of the building is to be fully paid from the royal treasury. The money will come from taxes collected west of the Euphrates River. Do this so the work will not stop. [9]Give those people anything they need. Give them young bulls, male sheep or male lambs for burnt offerings to the God of heaven. Give them wheat, salt, wine or olive oil. Give the priests in Jerusalem anything they ask for. Give it every day without fail. [10]Then they may offer sacrifices pleasing to the God of heaven. And they can pray for the life of the king and his sons.

[11]Also, I give this order: if anyone changes this order, a wood beam is to be pulled from his house. Drive one end of the beam through his body. And because he did this crime, make his house a pile of ruins. [12]God has chosen Jerusalem as the place he is to be worshipped. May he defeat any king or person who tries to change this order. May God destroy anyone who tries to destroy this Temple.

I, Darius, have given this order. Let it be obeyed quickly and carefully.

Completion of the Temple

[13]So, Tattenai, the governor west of the Euphrates, Shethar-Bozenai and the others obeyed. They carried out King Darius' order quickly and carefully. [14]So the older Jewish leaders continued to build. And they were successful because of the preaching of Haggai the prophet[d] and Zechariah son of Iddo. They finished building the Temple[d] as the God of Israel had said. It was also done to obey the kings Cy-

rus, Darius and Artaxerxes of Persia. ¹⁵The Temple was finished on the third day of the month Adar. It was the sixth year that Darius was king. ¹⁶Then the people of Israel celebrated. They gave the Temple to God to honour him. Everybody was happy: the priests, the Levites and the rest of the Jews who had returned from captivity. ¹⁷This is how they gave the Temple to God for worshipping him: they offered 100 bulls, 200 male sheep and 400 male lambs as sacrifices. And as an offering to forgive the sins of all Israel, they offered 12 male goats. That is one goat for each tribe^d in Israel. ¹⁸Then they put the priests and the Levites into their separate groups. Each group had a certain time to serve God in the Temple at Jerusalem. This was done just as it is written in the Book of Moses.

The Passover

¹⁹The Jews who returned from captivity celebrated the Passover.^d This was on the fourteenth day of the first month. ²⁰The priests and Levites had made themselves clean.^d The Levites killed the Passover lambs for all the Jews who had returned from captivity. They also did it for their relatives the priests and for themselves. ²¹So all the people of Israel who returned from captivity ate the Passover lamb. So did those who had given up the unclean ways of their non-Jewish neighbours. They worshipped the Lord, the God of Israel. ²²For seven days they celebrated the Feast^d of Unleavened Bread in a very joyful way. The Lord had made them happy by changing the mind of the King of Assyria. So the king had helped them in the work on the Temple of the God of Israel.

Ezra Comes to Jerusalem

7 After these thingsⁿ during the rule of Artaxerxes king of Persia,

Ezra came up from Babylon. Ezra was the son of Seraiah. Seraiah was the son of Azariah. Azariah was the son of Hilkiah. ²Hilkiah was the son of Shallum. Shallum was the son of Zadok. Zadok was the son of Ahitub. ³Ahitub was the son of Amariah. Amariah was the son of Azariah. Azariah was the son of Meraioth. ⁴Meraioth was the son of Zerahiah. Zerahiah was the son of Uzzi. Uzzi was the son of Bukki. ⁵Bukki was the son of Abishua. Abishua was the son of Phinehas. Phinehas was the son of Eleazar. Eleazar was the son of Aaron the high priest. ⁶This Ezra came to Jerusalem from Babylon. He was a teacher. He knew the Teachings of Moses well. The Teachings had been given by the Lord, the God of Israel. Ezra received everything he asked for from the king. This was because the Lord his God was helping him. ⁷In the seventh year of King Artaxerxes more Israelites came to Jerusalem. Among them were priests, Levites, singers, gatekeepers and Temple^d servants.

⁸Ezra also arrived in Jerusalem. It was the fifth month of Artaxerxes' seventh year as king. ⁹Ezra had left Babylon on the first day of the first month. And he arrived in Jerusalem on the first day of the fifth month. God was helping Ezra. ¹⁰Ezra had worked hard to know and obey the Teachings of the Lord. He also taught the rules and commands of the Lord to the Israelites.

Artaxerxes' Letter to Ezra

¹¹King Artaxerxes had given a letter to Ezra. Ezra was a priest and teacher. He taught about the commands and laws the Lord gave Israel. This is a copy of the letter:

¹²From Artaxerxes, king of kings. To Ezra the priest, a teacher of the Law of the God of heaven.

After these things There is a time period of about 60 years between chapters six and seven.

Greetings. [13]Now I give this order: any Israelite in my kingdom who wishes may go with you to Jerusalem. This includes priests and Levites. [14]Ezra, you are sent by the king and the seven people who advise him. You are to ask about how Judah and Jerusalem are obeying the Law of your God, which you are carrying with you. [15]Also take with you the silver and gold the king and those who advise him have given freely. It's for the God of Israel, whose Temple[d] is in Jerusalem. [16]Also take the silver and gold you receive from the area of Babylon. And take the offerings the Israelites and their priests have given as gifts to the Lord. They are for the Temple of their God in Jerusalem. [17]With this money buy bulls, male sheep and male lambs. Buy the grain offerings and drink offerings that go with those sacrifices. Then sacrifice them on the altar in the Temple of your God in Jerusalem.

[18]Then you and your fellow Jews may spend the silver and gold left over. Use it as you want and as God wishes. [19]Take to the God of Jerusalem all the things put in your care. They are for the worship in the Temple of your God. [20]And you may get anything else you need for the Temple of your God. Pay for it from the royal treasury.

[21]Now I, King Artaxerxes, give this order to all the men in charge of the treasury west of the Euphrates: Give Ezra anything he asks for right away. Ezra is a priest and a teacher of the Law of the God of heaven. [22]Give him up to 3400 kilograms of silver, 10000 kilograms of wheat, 2000 litres of wine and 2000 litres of olive oil. And give him as much salt as he wants. [23]Carefully give him what-

ever the God of heaven wants. Do it for the Temple of the God of heaven. We do not want God to be angry with the king and his sons. [24]Remember, you must not make these people pay taxes of any kind: priests, Levites, singers, gatekeepers, Temple servants and other workers in this Temple of God.

[25]And you, Ezra, use the wisdom you have from your God. Choose judges and lawmakers to rule the Jews west of the Euphrates. They know the laws of your God. And teach anyone who does not know them. [26]Whoever does not obey the law of your God or of the king must be punished. He will be killed or sent away. He will have his property taken away or be put in jail.

[27]Praise the Lord, the God of our ancestors. He caused the king to want to honour the Temple of the Lord in Jerusalem. [28]The Lord has shown me, Ezra, his love. He did this before the king, those who advise the king and the royal officers. The Lord my God was helping me. So I had courage. I gathered the leaders of Israel to return with me.

Leaders Who Returned with Ezra

8 These are the leaders of the family groups who returned with me. And it is a listing of those who were with them. They came back from Babylon during the rule of King Artaxerxes.

[2]From the descendants[d] of Phinehas, there was Gershom.

From the descendants of Ithamar, there was Daniel.

From the descendants of David, there was Hattush [3]of the descendants of Shecaniah.

From the descendants of Parosh, there was Zechariah. And 150 men came with him.

⁴From the descendants of Pahath-Moab, there was Eliehoenai son of Zerahiah, with 200 men.

⁵From the descendants of Zattu, there was Shecaniah son of Jahaziel, with 300 men.

⁶From the descendants of Adin, there was Ebed son of Jonathan, with 50 men.

⁷From the descendants of Elam, there was Jeshaiah son of Athaliah, with 70 men.

⁸From the descendants of Shephatiah, there was Zebadiah son of Michael, with 80 men.

⁹From the descendants of Joab, there was Obadiah son of Jehiel, with 218 men.

¹⁰From the descendants of Bani, there was Shelomith son of Josiphiah, with 160 men.

¹¹From the descendants of Bebai, there was Zechariah son of Bebai, with 28 men.

¹²From the descendants of Azgad, there was Johanan son of Hakkatan, with 110 men.

¹³From the descendants of Adonikam, these were the last ones: Eliphelet, Jeuel and Shemaiah. With them were 60 men.

¹⁴From the descendants of Bigvai, there were Uthai and Zaccur, with 70 men.

The Return to Jerusalem

¹⁵I, Ezra, called all those people together at the canal. It flows towards Ahava. We camped there for three days. I checked all the people and the priests. But I did not find any Levites. ¹⁶So I called these leaders: Eliezer, Ariel, Shemaiah, Elnathan, Jarib, Elnathan, Nathan, Zechariah and Meshullam. And I called Joiarib and Elnathan, who were teachers. ¹⁷I sent those men to Iddo, the leader at Casiphia. I told them what to say to Iddo and his relatives, who are the Templeᵈ servants in Casiphia. I sent them to bring servants to us for the Tem-

pleᵈ of our God. ¹⁸Our God was helping us. So Iddo's relatives gave us Sherebiah, a wise man from the descendants of Mahli. Mahli was the son of Levi. And Levi was the son of Israel. And they brought Sherebiah's sons and brothers. In all there were 18 men. ¹⁹And they brought to us Hashabiah and Jeshaiah from the descendants of Merari. And they also brought his brothers and nephews. In all there were 20 men. ²⁰They also brought 220 of the Temple servants. This is a group David and the officers had set up to help the Levites. All of those men were listed by name.

²¹There by the Ahava Canal, I announced we would all give up eating. We would make ourselves humble before our God. And we would ask God for a safe trip for ourselves, our children and all our possessions. ²²I was ashamed to ask the king for soldiers and horsemen. They could have protected us from enemies on the road. But we had said to the king, "Our God helps everyone who obeys him. But God is very angry with all who reject him." ²³So we gave up eating and prayed to our God about our trip. He answered our prayers.

²⁴Then I chose 12 of the priests who were leaders. They were Sherebiah and Hashabiah and ten of their relatives. ²⁵I weighed the offering of silver and gold. And I weighed the things given for the Temple of our God. I gave them to the 12 priests I had chosen. The king, the people who advised him, his officers and all the Israelites there with us had given these things for the Temple. ²⁶I weighed out and gave them about 22 tons of silver, about 70 kilograms of silver objects and about 70 kilograms of gold. ²⁷I gave them 20 gold bowls that weighed about 8.4 kilograms. And I gave them two fine pieces of polished bronze that were as valuable as gold.

²⁸Then I said to the priests, "You

and these things belong to the Lord for his service. The silver and gold are gifts to the Lord, the God of your ancestors. 29Guard these things carefully. In Jerusalem, weigh them in front of the leading priests, Levites and the leaders of the family groups of Israel. Do this in the rooms of the Temple of the Lord." 30So the priests and Levites took the silver, the gold and the special things that had been weighed out. They were to take them to the Temple of our God in Jerusalem.

31On the twelfth day of the first month we left the Ahava Canal. We started toward Jerusalem. Our God helped us. He protected us from enemies and robbers along the way. 32Then we arrived in Jerusalem. We rested there three days.

33On the fourth day we weighed out the silver, the gold and the special things in the Temple of our God. We handed them to the priest Meremoth son of Uriah. Eleazar son of Phinehas was with Meremoth. Also the Levites Jozabad son of Jeshua and Noadiah son of Binnui were with them. 34We checked everything by number and by weight. And the total weight was written down at that time.

35Then the captives who returned made burnt offerings to the God of Israel. They sacrificed 12 bulls for all Israel, 96 male sheep and 77 male lambs. All these animals were burned as sacrifices to the Lord. For a sin offering to the Lord there were 12 male goats. 36They took King Artaxerxes' orders to the royal officers and to the governors west of the Euphrates. Then these men gave help to the people and the Temple of God.

Ezra's Prayer

9 After these things had been done, the leaders came to me. They said, "Ezra, the Israelites, including the priests and Levites, have not kept themselves separate from the people around us. Those neighbours do evil things just as the Canaanites, Hittites, Perizzites, Jebusites, Ammonites, Moabites, Egyptians and Amorites did. 2The Israelite men and their sons have married the women of these non-Jewish people. They have mixed the people who belong to God with the people around them. The leaders and officers of Israel did this first. And they caused the rest of the Israelites to do this unfaithful thing."

3When I heard this, I angrily tore my robe and coat. I pulled hair from my head and beard and sat down in shock. 4Then everyone who trembled in fear at the word of the God of Israel gathered around me. This was because of the unfaithfulness of the captives who had returned. I sat there in shock until the evening sacrifice.

5Then, at the evening sacrifice, I got up from where I had shown my disgrace. My inner robe and coat were torn. And I fell on my knees with my hands spread out to the Lord my God. 6I prayed,

"My God, I am too ashamed and embarrassed to lift up my face to you. I am in disgrace because our sins are so many they are higher than our heads. Our sins even reach up to the sky. 7From the days of our ancestors until now, we have been very guilty. Because of our sins, we, our kings and priests have suffered punishment. We have been punished by the sword and captivity. Foreign kings have taken away our things and shamed us. It is that way today.

8"But now, for a short time, the Lord our God has been kind to us. He has let some of us come back from captivity. He has let us live in safety in his holy place. And so our God gives us hope and a little relief from our slavery. 9Even though we are slaves, our God has not left us. He caused the kings of Persia to be kind to us. He has given us new life. So we can rebuild the Temple*d* and repair its ruins.

And he has given us a wall to protect us in Judah and Jerusalem.

¹⁰"But now, our God, what can we say after you have done all this? We have disobeyed your commands. ¹¹You gave these commands through your servants the prophets.ᵈ You said, 'The land you are entering to own is ruined. The people living there have spoiled it by the evil they do. Their evil filled the land with uncleannessᵈ from one end to the other. ¹²So do not let your daughters marry their sons. And do not let their daughters marry your sons. Do not wish for their peace or success. Then you may be strong and eat the good things of the land. And then you can leave this land to your descendantsᵈ for ever'.

¹³"What has happened to us is our own fault. We have done evil things. Our guilt is great. But you, our God, have punished us less than we deserve. You have left a few of us alive. ¹⁴We should not again break your commands by allowing marriages with these wicked people. If we did, you would get angry enough to destroy us. Then none of us would be left alive. ¹⁵Lord, God of Israel, by your goodness a few of us are left alive today. We admit that we are guilty. None of us should be allowed to stand before you."

The People Confess Sin

10 Ezra was praying and confessing. He was crying and throwing himself down in front of the Temple.ᵈ A large group of Israelite men, women and children gathered around him. They were also crying loudly. ²Then Shecaniah son of Jehiel the Elamite spoke to Ezra. Shecaniah said, "We have been unfaithful to our God. We have been marrying women from the peoples around us. But even so, there is still hope for Israel. ³Now let us make an agreement before our God. We will send away all these women and their children. This is

your advice. It is also the advice of those who respect the commands of our God. Let it be done to obey his Teachings. ⁴Get up, Ezra. You are in charge. But we will support you. So have courage and do it."

⁵So Ezra got up. He made these people make a promise: the priests, the Levites and all the people of Israel. They promised to do what was suggested. ⁶Then Ezra left the Temple. He went to the room of Jehohanan son of Eliashib. While Ezra was there, he did not eat or drink. He was still sad about the unfaithfulness of the captives who had returned.

⁷Then an order was sent everywhere in Judah and Jerusalem. All the captives who had returned had to meet together in Jerusalem. ⁸Whoever did not come to Jerusalem within three days would lose his property. And he would no longer be a member of the community of the returned captives. That was the decision of the officers and older leaders.

⁹So within three days all the men of Judah and Benjamin gathered in Jerusalem. It was the twentieth day of the ninth month. All the people were sitting in the open place in front of the Temple. They were upset because of the meeting and because it was raining. ¹⁰Then Ezra the priest stood up and said to them, "You have been unfaithful. You have married non-Jewish women. You have made Israel more guilty. ¹¹Now, confess it to the Lord, the God of your ancestors. Do the Lord's will. Separate yourselves from the people living around you and from your non-Jewish wives."

¹²Then the whole group answered Ezra. They shouted, "Ezra, you're right! We must do what you say. ¹³But there are many people here. It's the rainy season. We can't stand outside. Also, this problem can't be solved in a day or two. We have sinned badly. ¹⁴Let our officers make a decision for the whole group. Then let everyone in

our towns who has married a non-Jewish woman meet with the older leaders and judges of each town. Let them meet at a planned time. Then the hot anger of our God will turn away from us." 15Only these men were against the plan: Jonathan son of Asahel, Jahzeiah son of Tikvah, Meshullam and Shabbethai the Levite. 16So the returned captives did what was suggested. Ezra the priest chose men who were leaders of the family groups. He named one from each family division. On the first day of the tenth month they sat down to study each case. 17By the first day of the first month, they had finished. They had dealt with all the men who had married non-Jewish women.

Those Guilty of Marrying Non-Jewish Women

18These are the descendantsᵈ of the priests who had married foreign women:

From the descendants of Jeshua son of Jozadak and Jeshua's brothers, there were Maaseiah, Eliezer, Jarib and Gedaliah. 19(They all promised to divorce their wives. Then each one brought a male sheep from the flock as a penalty offering.)

20From the descendants of Immer, there were Hanani and Zebadiah.

21From the descendants of Harim, there were Maaseiah, Elijah, Shemaiah, Jehiel and Uzziah.

22From the descendants of Pashhur, there were Elioenai, Maaseiah, Ishmael, Nethanel, Jozabad and Elasah.

23Among the Levites, there were Jozabad, Shimei, Kelaiah (also called Kelita), Pethahiah, Judah and Eliezer.

24Among the singers, there was Eliashib.

Among the gatekeepers, there were Shallum, Telem and Uri.

25And among the other Israelites, these married non-Jewish women:

From the descendants of Parosh, there were Ramiah, Izziah, Malkijah, Mijamin, Eleazar, Malkijah and Benaiah.

26From the descendants of Elam, there were Mattaniah, Zechariah, Jehiel, Abdi, Jeremoth and Elijah.

27From the descendants of Zattu, there were Elioenai, Eliashib, Mattaniah, Jeremoth, Zabad and Aziza.

28From the descendants of Bebai, there were Jehohanan, Hananiah, Zabbai and Athlai.

29From the descendants of Bani, there were Meshullam, Malluch, Adaiah, Jashub, Sheal and Jeremoth.

30From the descendants of Pahath-Moab, there were Adna, Kelal, Benaiah, Maaseiah, Mattaniah, Bezalel, Binnui and Manasseh.

31From the descendants of Harim, there were Eliezer, Ishijah, Malkijah, Shemaiah, Shimeon, 32Benjamin, Malluch and Shemariah.

33From the descendants of Hashum, there were Mattenai, Mattattah, Zabad, Eliphelet, Jeremai, Manasseh and Shimei.

34From the descendants of Bani, there were Maadai, Amram, Uel, 35Benaiah, Bedeiah, Keluhi, 36Vaniah, Meremoth, Eliashib, 37Mattaniah, Mattenai and Jaasu.

38From the descendants of Binnui, there were Shimei, 39Shelemiah, Nathan, Adaiah, 40Macnadebai, Shashai, Sharai, 41Azarel, Shelemiah, Shemariah, 42Shallum, Amariah and Joseph.

43From the descendants of Nebo, there were Jeiel, Mattithiah, Zabad, Zebina, Jaddai, Joel and Benaiah.

44All these men had married non-Jewish women. And some of them had children by these wives.

NEHEMIAH

Rebuilding the Walls of Jerusalem

Nehemiah's Prayer

1 These are the words of Nehemiah son of Hacaliah.

I, Nehemiah, was in the capital city of Susa. It was in the month of Kislev. This was in the twentieth year." [2]One of my brothers named Hanani came from Judah. Some other men were with him. I asked them about the Jews who lived through the captivity. And I also asked about Jerusalem.

[3]They answered, "Nehemiah, those who are left from the captivity are back in the area of Judah. But they are in much trouble and are full of shame. The wall around Jerusalem is broken down. And its gates have been burned."

[4]When I heard these things, I sat down and cried for several days. I was sad and did not eat food. I prayed to the God of heaven. [5]I said, "Lord, God of heaven, you are the great God who is to be respected. You keep your agreement of love with those who love you and obey your commands. [6]Listen carefully. Look at me. Hear the prayer your servant is praying to you day and night. I am praying for your servants, the people of Israel. I confess the sins we Israelites have done against you. My father's family and I have sinned against you. [7]We have been wicked towards you. We have not obeyed the commands, rules and laws you gave your servant Moses.

[8]"Remember what you taught your servant Moses. You said, 'If you are unfaithful, I will scatter you among the nations. [9]But if you come back to me and obey my commands, I will gather your people. I will gather them from the far ends of the earth. And I will bring them from captivity to where I have chosen to be worshipped'.

[10]"They are your servants and your people. You have saved them with your great strength and power. [11]Lord, listen carefully to my prayer. I am your servant. And listen to the prayers of your servants who love to honour you. Give me, your servant, success today. Allow this king to show kindness to me."

I was the one who served wine to the king.

Nehemiah Is Sent to Jerusalem

2 It was the month of Nisan. It was in the twentieth year King Artaxerxes was king. He wanted some wine. So I took some and gave it to the king. I had not been sad in his presence before. [2]So the king said, "Why does your face look sad? You are not sick. Your heart must be sad."

Then I was very afraid. [3]I said to the king, "May the king live for ever! My face is sad because the city where my ancestors are buried lies in ruins. And its gates have been destroyed by fire."

[4]Then the king said to me, "What do you want?"

First I prayed to the God of heaven. [5]Then I answered the king, "Send me to the city in Judah where my ancestors are buried. I will rebuild it. Do this if you are willing and if I have pleased you."

twentieth year This is probably referring to the twentieth year King Artaxerxes I ruled Persia.

⁶The queen was sitting next to the king. The king asked me, "How long will your trip take? When will you get back?" It pleased the king to send me. So I set a time.

⁷I also said to him, "If you are willing, give me letters for the governors west of the Euphrates River. Tell them to let me pass safely through their lands on my way to Judah. ⁸And may I have a letter for Asaph? He is the keeper of the king's forest. Tell him to give me timber. I will need it to make boards for the gates of the palace. It is by the Temple.ᵈ The wood is also for the city wall and the house I will live in." So the king gave me the letters. This was because God was showing kindness to me. ⁹So I went to the governors west of the Euphrates River. I gave them the king's letters. The king had also sent army officers and soldiers on horses with me.

¹⁰Sanballat the Horonite and Tobiah the Ammonite leader heard about this. They were upset that someone had come to help the Israelites.

Nehemiah Inspects Jerusalem

¹¹I went to Jerusalem and stayed there three days. ¹²Then at night I started out with a few men. I had not told anyone what God had caused me to do for Jerusalem. There were no animals with me except the one I was riding.

¹³It was night. I went out through the Valley Gate. I rode toward the Dragon Well and the Rubbish Gate. I was inspecting the walls of Jerusalem. They had been broken down. And the gates had been destroyed by fire. ¹⁴Then I rode on towards the Fountain Gate and the King's Pool. But there was not enough room for the animal I was riding to get through. ¹⁵So I went up the valley at night. I was inspecting the wall. Finally, I turned and went back in through the Valley Gate. ¹⁶The officers did not know where I had gone or what I was doing. I had

not yet said anything to the Jews, the priests, the important men or the officers. I had not said anything to any of the others who would do the work.

¹⁷Then I said to them, "You can see the trouble we have here. Jerusalem is a pile of ruins. And its gates have been burned. Come, let's rebuild the wall of Jerusalem. Then we won't be full of shame any longer." ¹⁸I also told them how God had been kind to me. And I told them what the king had said to me.

Then they answered, "Let's start rebuilding." So they began to work hard.

¹⁹But Sanballat the Horonite, Tobiah the Ammonite leader and Geshem the Arab heard about it. They made fun of us and laughed at us. They said, "What are you doing? Are you turning against the king?"

²⁰But I answered them, "The God of heaven will give us success. We are God's servants. We will start rebuilding. But you have no share in Jerusalem. You have no claim or past right to it."

Builders of the Wall

3 Eliashib the high priest and his fellow priests went to work. They rebuilt the Sheep Gate. They gave it to the Lord's service and set its doors in place. They worked as far as the Tower of the Hundred, and they gave it to the Lord's service. Then they went on to the Tower of Hananel. ²The men of Jericho built the part of the wall next to the priests. And Zaccur son of Imri built next to them.

³The sons of Hassenaah rebuilt the Fish Gate. They set the boards in place. And they put its doors, bolts and bars in place. ⁴Meremoth son of Uriah made repairs next to them. (Uriah was the son of Hakkoz.) Meshullam son of Berekiah worked next to Meremoth. (Berekiah was the son of Meshezabel.) And Zadok son of Baana worked next to Meshullam. ⁵The

men from Tekoa made repairs next to them. But the leading men of Tekoa would not work under their supervisors. ⁶Joiada son of Paseah and Meshullam son of Besodeiah repaired the Old Gate. They set its boards in place. And they put its doors, bolts and bars in place. ⁷Next to them, men from Gibeon and Mizpah made repairs. Melatiah was from Gibeon, and Jadon was from Meronoth. These places were ruled by the governor west of the Euphrates River. ⁸Next to them, Uzziel son of Harhaiah made repairs. He was a goldsmith. And next to him, Hananiah made repairs. He was one of the people who made perfume. These men rebuilt Jerusalem as far as the Broad Wall. ⁹The next part of the wall was repaired by Rephaiah son of Hur. He was ruler of half of the district of Jerusalem. ¹⁰Next to him, Jedaiah son of Harumaph made repairs. He worked opposite his own house. And next to him, Hattush son of Hashabneiah made repairs. ¹¹Malkijah son of Harim and Hasshub son of Pahath-Moab repaired another part of the wall. And they repaired the Tower of the Ovens. ¹²Next to them, Shallum son of Hallohesh made repairs. He was ruler of half of the district of Jerusalem. His daughters helped him.

¹³Hanun and the people of Zanoah repaired the Valley Gate. They rebuilt it and put its doors, bolts and bars in place. They also repaired the 500 metres of the wall to the Rubbish Gate.

¹⁴Malkijah son of Recab repaired the Rubbish Gate. He was ruler of the district of Beth Hakkerem. He rebuilt that gate and put its doors, bolts and bars in place.

¹⁵Shallun son of Col-Hozeh repaired the Fountain Gate. He was ruler of the district of Mizpah. He rebuilt it and put a roof over it. And he put its

doors, bolts and bars in place. He also repaired the wall of the Pool of Siloam. It is next to the King's Garden. He repaired the wall all the way to the steps. They went down from the older part of the city. ¹⁶Next to Shallun, Nehemiahⁿ son of Azbuk made repairs. He was ruler of half of the district of Beth Zur. He made repairs up to a place opposite the tombs of David. He made repairs as far as the man-made pool and the House of the Heroes.

¹⁷Next to him, the Levites made repairs. Some worked under Rehum son of Bani. Next to him, Hashabiah made repairs for his district. He was ruler of half of the district of Keilah. ¹⁸Next to him, Binnui son of Henadad and his Levites made repairs. Binnui was the ruler of the other half of the district of Keilah. ¹⁹Next to them, Ezer son of Jeshua worked. He was ruler of Mizpah. He repaired another part of the wall. He worked across from the way up to the storehouse for weapons. And he worked to the place where the wall turns. ²⁰Next to him, Baruch son of Zabbai worked very hard to repair another part of the wall. It went from the place where the wall turns to the entrance of the house of Eliashib. He was the high priest. ²¹Next to him, Meremoth son of Uriah worked. (Uriah was the son of Hakkoz.) He repaired another part of the wall. It went from the entrance to Eliashib's house to the far end of it.

²²Next to him worked the priests from the surrounding area. ²³Next to them, Benjamin and Hasshub made repairs in front of their own house. Next to them, Azariah son of Maaseiah made repairs beside his own house. (Maaseiah was the son of Ananiah.) ²⁴Next to him, Binnui son of Henadad repaired another part of the wall. It went from Azariah's house to the place where the wall turned. And

Nehemiah This is a different Nehemiah than the one who wrote this book.

it went to the corner. 25Palal son of Uzai worked across from the place where the wall turned. And he worked by the tower on the upper palace. That is near the courtyard of the king's guard. Next to Palal, Pedaiah son of Parosh made repairs. 26The Temple*d* servants lived on the hill of Ophel. They made repairs as far as a point opposite the Water Gate. They worked towards the east and the tower that extends from the palace. 27Next to them, the men of Tekoa made repairs. They worked on the wall from the great tower that extends from the palace to the wall of Ophel.

28The priests made repairs above the Horse Gate. Each worked in front of his own house. 29Next to them, Zadok son of Immer made repairs across from his own house. Next to him, Shemaiah son of Shecaniah made repairs. He was the guard of the East Gate. 30Next to him, Hananiah son of Shelemiah and Hanun, the sixth son of Zalaph, made repairs. They worked on another part of the wall. Next to them, Meshullam son of Berekiah made repairs. It was across from where he lived. 31Next to him, Malkijah made repairs. He was one of the goldsmiths. He worked as far as the house of the Temple servants and the traders. That is across from the Inspection Gate. And he worked as far as the room above the corner of the wall. 32The goldsmiths and the traders made repairs on another part of the wall. It was between the room above the corner of the wall and the Sheep Gate.

Those Against the Rebuilding

4 Sanballat heard we were rebuilding the wall. He was very angry, even furious. He made fun of the Jews. 2He said to his friends and the army of Samaria, "What are these weak Jews doing? They think they can rebuild the wall. They think they will

offer sacrifices. Maybe they think they can finish rebuilding it in only one day. They can't bring stones back to life. These are piles of rubble and ashes."

3Tobiah the Ammonite was next to Sanballat. Tobiah said, "A fox could climb up on what they are building. Even it could break down their stone wall."

4I prayed, "Hear us, our God. We are hated. Turn the insults of Sanballat and Tobiah back on their own heads. Let them be captured and taken away like valuables that are stolen. 5Do not hide their guilt. Do not take away their sins so you can't see them. The builders have seen them make you angry."

6So we rebuilt the wall until all of it went halfway up. The people were willing to work hard.

7But Sanballat, Tobiah, the Arabs, the Ammonites and the men from Ashdod were very angry. They heard that the repairs to Jerusalem's walls were continuing. And they heard that the holes in the wall were being closed. 8So they all made plans against Jerusalem. They planned to come and fight and stir up trouble. 9But we prayed to our God. And we appointed guards to watch for them day and night.

10The people of Judah said, "The workers are getting tired. There is too much dirt and rubble. We cannot rebuild the wall."

11And our enemies said, "The Jews won't know it or see us. But we will come among them and kill them. We will stop the work."

12Then the Jews who lived near our enemies came. They told us ten times, "Everywhere you turn, the enemy will attack us." 13So I put some of the people behind the lowest places along the wall. And I put some at the open places. I put families together with their swords, spears and bows. 14Then I looked around. I stood up and spoke to the important men, the leaders and the rest of the people. I said, "Don't be afraid of them. Remember the Lord. He is great and others are afraid of him. And fight for your brothers, your sons and daughters, your wives and your homes."

15Then our enemies heard that we knew about their plans. God had ruined their plans. So we all went back to the wall. Each person went back to his own work.

16From that day on, half my men worked on the wall. The other half was ready with spears, shields, bows and armour. The officers stood behind the people of Judah 17who were building the wall. Those who carried materials did their work with one hand. They carried a weapon in the other hand. 18Each builder wore his sword at his side as he worked. The man who blew the trumpet to warn the people stayed next to me.

19Then I spoke to the important men, the leaders and the rest of the people. I said, "This is a very big job. We are spreading out along the wall. We are far apart. 20So wherever you hear the sound of the trumpet, assemble there. Our God will fight for us."

21So we continued to work. Half the men held spears. We worked from sunrise till the stars came out. 22At that time I also said to the people, "Let every man and his helper stay inside Jerusalem at night. They can be our guards at night. And they can be workmen during the day." 23Neither I, my brothers, my men nor the guards with me ever took off our clothes. Each person carried his weapon even when he went for water.

Nehemiah Helps Poor People

5 The men and their wives complained loudly against their fellow Jews. 2Some of them were saying, "We have many sons and daughters in our families. To eat and stay alive, we need grain."

3Others were saying, "We are borrowing money to get grain. There is not much food. We might not be able to pay back the money we've borrowed. Then we will have to pay with our fields, vineyards and homes."

4And still others were saying, "We are having to borrow money. We have to pay the king's tax on our fields and vineyards. 5We are just like our fellow Jews. Our sons are like their sons. But we have to sell our sons and daughters as slaves. Some of our daughters have already been sold. But there is nothing we can do. Our fields and vineyards already belong to other people."

6When I heard their complaints about these things, I was very angry. 7I thought about it. Then I accused the important people and the leaders. I told them, "You are charging your own brothers too much interest." So I called a large meeting to deal with them. 8I said to them, "Our fellow Jews had been sold to non-Jewish nations. But, as much as possible, we have bought them back. Now you are making your fellow Jews sell themselves to us!" The leaders were quiet. They had nothing to say.

9Then I said, "What you are doing is not right. You should live in fear of God. Don't let our non-Jewish enemies shame us. 10I, my brothers and my men are also lending money and grain to the people. But stop charging them too much for these things! 11Give back their fields, vineyards, olive trees and houses right now. Also give them back the extra amount you charged them. That is the hundredth part of the money, grain, new wine and oil."

12They said, "We will give it back. And we will not demand anything more from them. We will do as you say."

Then I called for the priests. And I made the important men and leaders promise to do what they had said.

[13]Also I shook out the folds of my robe. I said, "In this way may God shake out every man who does not keep his promise. May God shake him out of his house. And may he shake him out of the things that are his. Let that man be shaken out and emptied!" Then the whole group said, "Amen". And they praised the Lord. So the people did what they had promised.

[14]I was appointed governor in the land of Judah. This was in the twentieth year of King Artaxerxes' rule. I was governor till his thirty-second year. So I was governor of Judah for 12 years. During that time neither my brothers nor I ate the food that was allowed for the governor. [15]But the governors before me placed a heavy load on the people. They took about 0.5 kilogram of silver from each person. And they took food and wine. The governors' helpers before me also controlled the people. But I did not do that because I feared God. [16]I worked on the wall. So did all my men who were gathered there. We did not buy any fields.

[17]Also, I fed 150 Jews and officers at my table. And I fed those who came from the nations around us. [18]This is what was prepared every day for me and those who ate with me: one ox, six good sheep, and birds. And every ten days there were all kinds of wine. But I never demanded the food that was allowed for the governor. This was because the people were already working very hard.

[19]Remember, my God, to be kind to me. Remember all the good I have done for these people.

More Problems for Nehemiah

6 Then Sanballat, Tobiah, Geshem the Arab and our other enemies heard that I had rebuilt the wall. There was not one gap in it. But I had not yet set the doors in the gates. [2]So Sanballat and Geshem sent me this message: "Come, Nehemiah, let's meet together in Kephirim on the plain of Ono."

But they were planning to harm me. [3]So I sent messengers to them saying: "I am doing a great work. I can't come down. I don't want the work to stop while I leave to meet you." [4]Sanballat and Geshem sent the same message to me four times. And I sent back the same answer each time.

[5]The fifth time Sanballat sent his helper to me with the message. And in his hand was an unsealed letter. [6]This is what was written:

A report is going around to all the nations. And Geshem says it is true. It says you and the Jews are planning to turn against the king. That's why you are rebuilding the wall. They say you are going to be their king. [7]They say you have appointed prophets[d] to announce in Jerusalem: "There is a king of Judah!" The king will hear about this. So come, let's discuss this together.

[8]So I sent him back this answer: "Nothing you are saying is really happening. You are just making it up in your own mind."

[9]Our enemies were trying to scare us. They were thinking, "They will get too weak to work. Then the wall will not be finished."

But I prayed, "God, make me strong."

[10]One day I went to the house of Shemaiah son of Delaiah. Delaiah was the son of Mehetabel. Shemaiah had to stay at home. He said, "Nehemiah, let's meet in the Temple[d] of God. Let's go inside the Temple and close the doors. Men are coming at night to kill you."

[11]But I said, "Should a man like me run away? Should I run into the Temple to save my life? I will not go." [12]I knew that God had not sent him. Tobiah and Sanballat had paid him to

prophesy against me. [13]They paid him to frighten me so I would do this and sin. Then they could give me a bad name to shame me.

[14]I prayed, "Remember Tobiah and Sanballat, my God. Remember what they have done. Also remember the prophetess Noadiah and the other prophets who have been trying to frighten me."

The Wall Is Finished

[15]So the wall of Jerusalem was completed. It was on the twenty-fifth day of the month of Elul. It took 52 days to rebuild. [16]Then all our enemies heard about it. And all the nations around us saw it. So they were shamed. They understood that the work had been done with the help of our God.

[17]Also in those days the important men of Judah sent many letters to Tobiah. And Tobiah answered them. [18]Many Jews had promised to be faithful to Tobiah. This was because Tobiah was the son-in-law of Shecaniah son of Arah. And Tobiah's son Jehohanan had married the daughter of Meshullam son of Berekiah. [19]Those important men kept telling me about the good things Tobiah was doing. Then they would tell Tobiah what I said about him. So Tobiah sent letters to frighten me.

7 After the wall had been rebuilt, I had set the doors in place. Then the gatekeepers, singers and Levites were chosen. [2]I put my brother Hanani, along with Hananiah, in charge of Jerusalem. Hananiah was commander of the palace. He was honest, and he feared God more than most men. [3]I said to them, "The gates of Jerusalem should not be opened until the sun is hot. While the gatekeepers are still on duty, have them shut and bolt the doors. Appoint people who live in Jerusalem as guards. Put some at guard posts and some near their own houses."

The Captives Who Returned

[4]The city was large and full of room. But there were few people in it. And the houses had not yet been rebuilt. [5]So my God caused me to gather the people. I gathered the important men, the leaders and the common people. This was so I could register them by families. I found the family history of those who had returned first. This is what I found written there:

[6]These are the people of the area who returned from captivity. Nebuchadnezzar king of Babylon had taken them captive. Now they returned to Jerusalem and Judah. Each one went back to his own town. [7]These people returned with Zerubbabel, Jeshua, Nehemiah, Azariah, Raamiah, Nahamani, Mordecai, Bilshan, Mispereth, Bigvai, Nehum and Baanah.

These are the men from Israel: [8]the descendants[d] of Parosh—2,172; [9]the descendants of Shephatiah—372; [10]the descendants of Arah—652; [11]the descendants of Pahath-Moab (through the family of Jeshua and Joab)—2,818; [12]the descendants of Elam—1,254; [13]the descendants of Zattu—845; [14]the descendants of Zaccai—760; [15]the descendants of Binnui—648; [16]the descendants of Bebai—628; [17]the descendants of Azgad—2,322; [18]the descendants of Adonikam—667; [19]the descendants of Bigvai—2,067; [20]the descendants of Adin—655; [21]the descendants of Ater (through Hezekiah)—98; [22]the descendants of Hashum—328; [23]the descendants of Bezai—324; [24]the descendants of Hariph—112; [25]the descendants of Gibeon—95.

[26]These are the men from the towns of Bethlehem and Netophah—188; [27]the men from Anathoth—128; [28]the men from Beth Azmaveth—42; [29]the men from Kiriath Jearim, Kephirah and Beeroth—743; [30]the men from Ramah and Geba—621; [31]the men from Michmash—122; [32]the

men from Bethel and Ai—123; [33]the men from the other Nebo—52; [34]the men from the other Elam—1,254; [35]the men from Harim—320; [36]the men from Jericho—345; [37]the men from Lod, Hadid and Ono—721; [38]the men from Senaah—3,930.

[39]These are the priests: the descendants of Jedaiah (through the family of Jeshua)—973; [40]the descendants of Immer—1,052; [41]the descendants of Pashhur—1,247; [42]the descendants of Harim—1,017.

[43]These are the Levites: the descendants of Jeshua (through Kadmiel through the family of Hodaviah)—74.

[44]These are the singers: the descendants of Asaph—148.

[45]These are the gatekeepers: the descendants of Shallum, Ater, Talmon, Akkub, Hatita and Shobai—138.

[46]These are the Temple[d] servants: the descendants of Ziha, Hasupha, Tabbaoth, [47]Keros, Sia, Padon, [48]Lebana, Hagaba, Shalmai, [49]Hanan, Giddel, Gahar, [50]Reaiah, Rezin, Nekoda, [51]Gazzam, Uzza, Paseah, [52]Besai, Meunim, Nephussim, [53]Bakbuk, Hakupha, Harhur, [54]Bazluth, Mehida, Harsha, [55]Barkos, Sisera, Temah, [56]Neziah and Hatipha.

[57]These are the descendants of the servants of Solomon: the descendants of Sotai, Sophereth, Perida, [58]Jaala, Darkon, Giddel, [59]Shephatiah, Hattil, Pokereth-Hazzebaim and Amon.

[60]The Temple servants and the descendants of the servants of Solomon totalled 392 people.

[61]Some people came to Jerusalem from these towns: Tel Melah, Tel Harsha, Kerub, Addon and Immer. But they could not prove that their families came from the family of Israel. Here are their names and their number: [62]the descendants of Delaiah, Tobiah and Nekoda—642.

[63]And these priests could not prove that their families came from Israel: the descendants of Hobaiah, Hakkoz and Barzillai. (He had married a daughter of Barzillai from Gilead and was called by her family name.)

[64]These people searched for their family records. But they could not find them. So they could not be priests because they were thought to be unclean.[d] [65]So the governor ordered them not to eat any of the food offered to God. First a priest had to settle this matter by using the Urim and Thummim.[d]

[66]The total number of those who returned was 42,360. [67]This is not counting their 7,337 male and female servants. They also had 245 men and women singers with them. [68]They had 736 horses, 245 mules, [69]435 camels and 6,720 donkeys.

[70]Some of the family leaders gave to the work. The governor gave to the treasury about 8 kilograms of gold. He also gave 50 bowls and 530 pieces of clothing for the priests. [71]Some of the family leaders gave about 168 kilograms of gold to the treasury for the work. They also gave about 1.3 tons of silver. [72]This is the total of what the other people gave: about 168 kilograms of gold, about a ton of silver and 67 pieces of clothing for the priests. [73]So these people all settled in their own towns: the priests, the Levites, the gatekeepers, the singers, the Temple servants and all the other people of Israel.

Ezra Reads the Teachings

By the seventh month the Israelites were settled in their own towns.

8 All the people of Israel gathered together in the square by the Water Gate. They asked Ezra the teacher to bring out the Book of the Teachings of Moses. These are the Teachings the Lord had given to Israel.

[2]So Ezra the priest brought out the Teachings for the crowd. This was on the first day of the seventh month. Men, women and all who could listen

and understand had gathered. [3]Ezra read the Teachings out loud. He read from early morning until noon. He was facing the square by the Water Gate. He read to the men, women and everyone who could listen and understand. All the people listened carefully to the Book of the Teachings.

[4]Ezra the teacher stood on a high wooden platform. It had been built just for this time. On his right were Mattithiah, Shema, Anaiah, Uriah, Hilkiah and Maaseiah. And on his left were Pedaiah, Mishael, Malkijah, Hashum, Hashbaddanah, Zechariah and Meshullam.

[5]Ezra opened the book. All the people could see him because he was above them. As he opened it, all the people stood up. [6]Ezra praised the Lord, the great God. And all the people held up their hands and said, "Amen! Amen!" Then they bowed down and worshipped the Lord with their faces to the ground.

[7]These Levites taught the people the Teachings as they stood there: Jeshua, Bani, Sherebiah, Jamin, Akkub, Shabbethai, Hodiah, Maaseiah, Kelita, Azariah, Jozabad, Hanan and Pelaiah. [8]They read the Book of the Teachings of God. They read so the people could understand. And they explained what it meant. Then the people understood what was being read.

[9]Then Nehemiah the governor and Ezra the priest and teacher spoke up. And the Levites who were teaching spoke up. They said to all the people, "This is a holy day to the Lord your God. Don't be sad or cry." All the people had been crying as they listened to the words of the Teachings.

[10]Nehemiah said, "Go and enjoy good food and sweet drinks. Send some to people who have none. To-

day is a holy day to the Lord. Don't be sad. The joy of the Lord will make you strong."

[11]The Levites helped calm the people. They said, "Be quiet. This is a holy day. Don't be sad."

[12]Then all the people went away to eat and drink. They sent some of their food to others. And they celebrated with great joy. They finally understood what they had been taught.

[13]On the second day of the month, the leaders of all the families met with Ezra the teacher. The priests and Levites also met with him. They gathered to study the words of the Teachings. [14]This is what they found written in the Teachings: the Lord had commanded through Moses that the people of Israel were to live in shelters. This was during the feast of the seventh month. [15]The people were supposed to preach this message. They were to spread it through all of their towns and in Jerusalem: "Go out into the mountains. Bring back branches from olive and wild olive trees, myrtle trees, palms and shade trees. Make shelters with them. It is written in the Law."

[16]So the people went out and got tree branches. They built shelters on their roofs[n] and in their courtyards. They built shelters in the courtyards of the Temple.[d] And they built them in the square by the Water Gate and the square next to the Gate of Ephraim. [17]The whole group that had come back from captivity built shelters. And they lived in them. The Israelites had not done this since the time of Joshua son of Nun. And they were very happy.

[18]Ezra read to them from the Book of the Teachings. He read every day, from the first day to the last. The people of Israel celebrated the feast for seven days. Then on the eighth

---

roofs In Bible times houses were built with flat roofs. The roof was used for drying things such as flax and fruit. It was also used as an extra room, as a place for worship and as a place to sleep in the summer.

day the people gathered as the law said.

Israel Confesses Sins

9 It was on the twenty-fourth day of that same month. The people of Israel gathered together. They did not eat. And they put on rough cloth and put dust on their heads. This was to show their sadness. ²Those people whose ancestors were from Israel had separated themselves from all foreigners. They stood and confessed their sins and their ancestors' sins. ³For a quarter of the day they stood where they were. And they read from the Book of the Teachings of the Lord their God. They spent another quarter of the day confessing their sins. And they worshipped the Lord their God. ⁴These Levites were standing on the stairs: Jeshua, Bani, Kadmiel, Shebaniah, Bunni, Sherebiah, Bani and Kanani. They called out to the Lord their God with loud voices. ⁵And these Levites spoke: Jeshua, Kadmiel, Bani, Hashabneiah, Sherebiah, Hodiah, Shebaniah and Pethahiah. They said, "Stand up and praise the Lord your God. He lives for ever and ever."

The People's Prayer

"Blessed be your wonderful name.
It is more wonderful than all
blessing and praise.
⁶You are the only Lord.
You made the heavens, even the
highest heavens.
You made all the stars.
You made the earth and
everything that is on it.
You made the seas and
everything that is in them.
You give life to everything.
The heavenly army worships you.

⁷"You are the Lord God.
You chose Abram.
You brought him out of Ur of the
Babylonians.
You named him Abraham.

⁸You found that he was faithful to
you.
So you made an agreement with
him.
You promised to give his
descendants*d* the land of the
Canaanites,
Hittites, Amorites,
Perizzites, Jebusites and
Girgashites.
You have kept your promise.
You are fair.

⁹"You saw our ancestors suffering
in Egypt.
You heard them cry out at the
Red Sea.*d*
¹⁰You did signs and miracles*d*
against the king of Egypt.
And you did them against all his
officers and all the people of
Egypt.
You knew how proud they were.
You made everyone know your
name.
And it is still known today.
¹¹You divided the sea in front of our
ancestors.
They walked through it on dry
ground.
But you threw the people chasing
them into the deep water.
They were like a stone being
thrown into mighty waters.
¹²You led our ancestors with a pillar
of cloud in the daytime.
And you led them with a pillar of
fire at night.
It lit the way
they were supposed to go.
¹³You came down to Mount Sinai.
You talked to our ancestors
from heaven.
You gave them fair rules and true
teachings.
You gave them good orders and
commands.
¹⁴You told them about your holy
Sabbath.*d*
You gave commands, orders and
teachings to them

through your servant Moses.

¹⁵When they were hungry, you gave
them bread from heaven.
When they were thirsty, you
brought them water from
the rock.
You told them to go into the land
and take it over.
You had promised to give it to
them.

¹⁶"But our ancestors were proud
and stubborn.
They did not obey your
commands.

¹⁷They refused to listen.
They forgot the miracles^d you
did for them.
They became stubborn and turned
against you.
They chose a leader to lead
them back to their slavery.
But you are a forgiving God.
You are kind and full of mercy.
You do not become angry quickly,
and you have great love.
So you did not leave them.

¹⁸Our ancestors even made an idol
of a calf for themselves.
They said, 'This is your god,
Israel.
It brought you up out of Egypt'.
They spoke against you.

¹⁹"You have great mercy.
So you did not leave them in the
desert.
During the day the pillar of cloud
guided them on their way.
And the pillar of fire led them at
night.
It lit the way they were
supposed to go.

²⁰You gave your good Spirit^d to
teach them.
You gave them manna^d to eat.
And you gave them water when
they were thirsty.

²¹You took care of them for 40
years in the desert.
They needed nothing.
Their clothes did not wear out.

And their feet did not swell.

²²"You gave them kingdoms and
nations.
You gave them more land.
They took over the country of
Sihon king of Heshbon.
And they took over the country
of Og king of Bashan.

²³You made their children as many
as the stars in the sky.
And you brought them into the
land.
This was where you had told
their fathers to enter and
take over.

²⁴So their children went into the
land and took over.
The Canaanites lived there.
But you defeated them for our
ancestors.
You handed over to them the
Canaanites, their kings and
the people of the land.
Our ancestors could do what
they wanted with them.

²⁵Our ancestors captured strong,
walled cities and fertile land.
They took over houses full of
good things.
They took over wells that were
already dug.
They took vineyards, olive trees
and many fruit trees.
They ate until they were full and
became fat.
They enjoyed your great
goodness.

²⁶"But they were disobedient and
turned against you.
They ignored your teachings.
Your prophets^d warned them to
come back to you.
But they killed those prophets.
And they spoke against you.

²⁷So you allowed their enemies to
defeat them.
Their enemies treated them
badly.
But in this time of trouble our
ancestors cried out to you.

And you heard from heaven.
You had great mercy.
You gave them saviours who
    saved them from the power
    of their enemies.
²⁸But as soon as they had rest,
    they again did what was evil.
So you left them to their enemies
    who ruled over them.
But they cried out to you again.
And you heard from heaven.
Because of your mercy, you
    saved them again and again.
²⁹You warned them to return to
    obeying your teachings.
But they were proud. They did
    not obey your commands.
If a man obeys your laws, he will
    live.
But they sinned against your
    laws.
They were stubborn and
    disobedient.
They would not listen.
³⁰You were patient with them for
    many years.
You warned them by your Spirit
    through the prophets.
But they did not pay attention.
So you allowed them to be
    defeated by other countries.
³¹But because your mercy is great,
    you did not kill them all.
You did not leave them.
You are a kind and merciful
    God.

³²"And so, our God, you are the
    great and mighty and
    wonderful God.
You keep your agreement of
    love.
Do not let all our trouble seem
    unimportant in your eyes.
This trouble has come to us, to
    our kings and to our leaders.
It has come to our priests and
    prophets.
It has come to our ancestors
    and all your people.

This trouble has come to us since
    the days of the kings of
    Assyria.
And it has lasted until today.
³³You have been fair in everything
    that has happened to us.
You have been loyal, but we
    have been wicked.
³⁴Our kings, leaders, priests and
    ancestors did not obey your
    teachings.
They did not pay attention to
    the commands and warnings
    you gave them.
³⁵Even when our ancestors were
    living in their kingdom,
    they did not serve you.
They were enjoying all the good
    things you had given them.
They were enjoying the land
    that was fertile and full of
    room.
But they did not stop their evil
    ways.
³⁶"Look, we are slaves today
    in the land you gave our
    ancestors.
They were to enjoy its fruit and
    its good things.
But look, we are slaves here.
³⁷The land's great harvest belongs
    to the kings you have put
    over us.
This is because of our sins.
Those kings rule over us and our
    cattle as they please.
And we are in much trouble.

The People's Agreement

³⁸"Because of all this, we are making an agreement in writing. Our leaders, Levites and priests are putting their seals^d on it."

10 These are the men who sealed
    the agreement:
Nehemiah the governor, son of Hacaliah, sealed it.
    These men also sealed it: Zedekiah, ²Seraiah, Azariah, Jeremiah, ³Pashhur, Amariah, Malkijah, ⁴Hattush,

Shebaniah, Malluch, [5]Harim, Meremoth, Obadiah, [6]Daniel, Ginnethon, Baruch, [7]Meshullam, Abijah, Mijamin, [8]Maaziah, Bilgai and Shemaiah. These are the priests.

[9]These are the Levites who sealed it: Jeshua son of Azaniah, Binnui of the sons of Henadad, Kadmiel, [10]and their fellow Levites: Shebaniah, Hodiah, Kelita, Pelaiah, Hanan, [11]Mica, Rehob, Hashabiah, [12]Zaccur, Sherebiah, Shebaniah, [13]Hodiah, Bani and Beninu.

[14]These are the leaders of the people who sealed the agreement: Parosh, Pahath-Moab, Elam, Zattu, Bani, [15]Bunni, Azgad, Bebai, [16]Adonijah, Bigvai, Adin, [17]Ater, Hezekiah, Azzur, [18]Hodiah, Hashum, Bezai, [19]Hariph, Anathoth, Nebai, [20]Magpiash, Meshullam, Hezir, [21]Meshezabel, Zadok, Jaddua, [22]Pelatiah, Hanan, Anaiah, [23]Hoshea, Hananiah, Hasshub, [24]Hallohesh, Pilha, Shobek, [25]Rehum, Hashabnah, Maaseiah, [26]Ahiah, Hanan, Anan, [27]Malluch, Harim and Baanah.

[28]The rest of the people took an oath. They were the priests, Levites, gatekeepers, singers and Temple[d] servants. And they were all those who separated themselves from foreigners to keep the Teachings of God. It was also their wives and their sons and daughters who could understand. [29]They joined their fellow Israelites and their leading men. They took an oath, which was tied to a curse in case they broke the oath. They promised to follow the Teachings of God, which they had been given through Moses the servant of God. These people also promised to obey all the commands, rules and laws of the Lord our Master.

[30]They said:

We promise not to let our daughters marry foreigners. And we promise not to let our sons marry their daughters. [31]The foreigners might bring goods or grain to sell on the Sabbath.[d] But we will not buy on the Sabbath day or any holy day. Every seventh year we will not plant. And that year we will forget all that people owe us.

[32]We will be responsible for obeying the commands. We will pay for the service of the Temple of our God. We will give about 4 grams of silver each year. [33]It is to pay for the bread that is set out on the table. It is to pay for the regular grain offerings and burnt offerings. It is for the offerings on the Sabbaths, New Moon[d] festivals and special feasts. It is for the holy offerings. And it is for the offerings to remove the sins of the Israelites so they will belong to God. It is for the work of the Temple of our God.

[34]We are the priests, the Levites and the people. We have thrown lots[d] to decide when each family must bring wood to the Temple. This is to be done at certain times each year. The wood is for burning on the altar of the Lord our God. We will do this as it is written in the Teachings. [35]We also will bring the first fruits from our crops. And we will bring the first fruits of every tree to the Temple each year.

[36]We will bring our firstborn[d] sons and cattle to the Temple. We will bring the firstborn of our herds and flocks. We will do this as it is written in the Teachings. We will bring them to the priests who are serving in the Temple. [37]We will bring things to the priests at the storerooms of the Temple. We will bring the first of our ground meal, our offerings, the fruit from all our trees and our new wine and oil. And we will bring a tenth of our crops to the Levites. The Levites will collect these things in all the towns

where we work. ³⁸A priest of Aaron's family must be with the Levites when they receive the tenth of the people's crops. The Levites must bring a tenth of all they receive to the Temple of our God. Then they will put it in the storerooms of the treasury. ³⁹The people of Israel and the Levites are to bring their gifts to the storerooms. These are the gifts of grain, new wine and oil. The things for the Temple are kept in the storerooms. It is also where the priests, who are serving, the gatekeepers and singers stay. We will not ignore the Temple of our God.

New People Move into Jerusalem

11 The leaders of Israel lived in Jerusalem. The rest of the people threw lots.^d One person out of every ten was to come and live in Jerusalem. It was the holy city. The other nine could stay in their own cities. ²The people blessed those who volunteered to live in Jerusalem.

³These are the area leaders who lived in Jerusalem. (Some people lived on their own land in the cities of Judah. These included Israelites, priests, Levites, Temple servants and descendants^d of Solomon's servants. ⁴Others from the families of Judah and Benjamin lived in Jerusalem.)

These are descendants of Judah who moved into Jerusalem. There was Athaiah son of Uzziah. (Uzziah was the son of Zechariah, who was the son of Amariah. Amariah was the son of Shephatiah, who was the son of Mahalalel. Mahalalel was a descendant of Perez.) ⁵There was also Masseiah son of Baruch. (Baruch was the son of Col-Hozeh, who was the son of Hazaiah. Hazaiah was the son of Adaiah, who was the son of Joiarib. Joiarib was the son of Zechariah, who was a descendant of Shelah.) ⁶All the descendants of Perez who lived in Je-

rusalem totalled 468 men. They were soldiers.

⁷These are descendants of Benjamin who moved into Jerusalem. There was Sallu son of Meshullam. (Meshullam was the son of Joed, who was the son of Pedaiah. Pedaiah was the son of Kolaiah, who was the son of Maaseiah. Maaseiah was the son of Ithiel, who was the son of Jeshaiah.) ⁸Following him were Gabbai and Sallai. All together there were 928 men. ⁹Joel son of Zicri was appointed over them. And Judah son of Hassenuah was second in charge of the new area of the city.

¹⁰These are the priests who moved into Jerusalem. There was Jedaiah son of Joiarib, Jakin ¹¹and Seraiah son of Hilkiah. (Hilkiah was the son of Meshullam, who was the son of Zadok. Zadok was the son of Meraioth, who was the son of Ahitub.) Seraiah was the supervisor in the Temple. ¹²And there were others with them who did the work for the Temple. All together there were 822 men. Also there was Adaiah son of Jeroham. (Jeroham was the son of Pelaliah, who was the son of Amzi. Amzi was the son of Zechariah, who was the son of Pashhur. Pashhur was the son of Malkijah.) ¹³And there were family heads with him. All together there were 242 men. Also there was Amashsai son of Azarel. (Azarel was the son of Ahzai, who was the son of Meshillemoth. Meshillemoth was the son of Immer.) ¹⁴And there were brave men with Amashsai. All together there were 128 men. Zabdiel son of Haggedolim was appointed over them.

¹⁵These are the Levites who moved into Jerusalem. There was Shemaiah son of Hasshub. (Hasshub was the son of Azrikam, who was the son of Hashabiah. Hashabiah was the son of Bunni.) ¹⁶And there were Shabbethai and Jozabad. They were two of the leaders of the Levites. They were in charge of the work outside the Tem-

ple. [17]There was Mattaniah son of Mica. (Mica was the son of Zabdi, who was the son of Asaph.) Mattaniah was the director. He led the people in thanksgiving and prayer. There was Bakbukiah, who was second in charge over his fellow Levites. And there was Abda son of Shammua. (Shammua was the son of Galal, who was the son of Jeduthun.) [18]All together 284 Levites lived in the holy city of Jerusalem.

[19]These are the gatekeepers who moved into Jerusalem. There were Akkub, Talmon and others with them. There was a total of 172 men. They guarded the city gates.

[20]The other Israelites, priests and Levites lived on their own land. They were in all the cities of Judah.

[21]The Temple servants lived on the hill of Ophel. Ziha and Gishpa were in charge of them.

[22]Uzzi son of Bani was appointed over the Levites in Jerusalem. (Bani was the son of Hashabiah, who was the son of Mattaniah. Mattaniah was the son of Mica.) Uzzi was one of Asaph's descendants. They were the singers. They were responsible for the service of the Temple. [23]The singers took orders from the king. Those orders told the singers what to do each day.

[24]Pethahiah son of Meshezabel was the king's spokesman. Meshezabel was a descendant of Zerah, the son of Judah.

[25]Some of the people of Judah lived in villages and their surrounding fields. Some lived in Kiriath Arba and its surroundings. Some lived in Dibon and its surroundings. Some lived in Jekabzeel and its surroundings. [26]Others lived in Jeshua, Moladah, Beth Pelet, [27]Hazar Shual, Beersheba and its surroundings. [28]Others were in Ziklag and Meconah and its surroundings. [29]Some people lived in En Rimmon, Zorah, Jarmuth, [30]Zanoah, Adullam and their villages. Some were

in Lachish and the fields around it. Some lived in Azekah and its surroundings. So they settled from Beersheba all the way to the Valley of Hinnom.

[31]The descendants of the Benjaminites from Geba lived in Michmash, Aija, Bethel and its surroundings. [32]They lived in Anathoth, Nob, Ananiah, [33]Hazor, Ramah and Gittaim. [34]They lived in Hadid, Zeboim, Neballat, [35]Lod, Ono and in the Valley of the Craftsmen.

[36]Some groups of the Levites from Judah settled in the land of Benjamin.

Priests and Levites

12 These are the priests and Levites who returned with Zerubbabel son of Shealtiel and with Jeshua. There were Seraiah, Jeremiah, Ezra, [2]Amariah, Malluch, Hattush, [3]Shecaniah, Rehum, Meremoth, [4]Iddo, Ginnethon, Abijah, [5]Mijamin, Moadiah, Bilgah, [6]Shemaiah, Joiarib, Jedaiah, [7]Sallu, Amok, Hilkiah and Jedaiah. They were the leaders of the priests and their relatives. This was in the days of Jeshua.

[8]The Levites were Jeshua, Binnui, Kadmiel, Sherebiah, Judah and also Mattaniah. He and his relatives were in charge of the songs of thanksgiving. [9]Bakbukiah and Unni, their relatives, stood across from them in the services.

[10]Jeshua was the father of Joiakim. Joiakim was the father of Eliashib. Eliashib was the father of Joiada. [11]Joiada was the father of Jonathan. And Jonathan was the father of Jaddua.

[12]In the days of Joiakim, these priests were the leaders of the families of priests. Meraiah was over Seraiah's family. Hananiah was over Jeremiah's family. [13]Meshullam was over Ezra's family. Jehohanan was over Amariah's family. [14]Jonathan was over Malluch's family. Joseph was over Shecaniah's family. [15]Adna was over Harim's family. Helkai was

over Meremoth's family. [16]Zechariah was over Iddo's family. Meshullam was over Ginnethon's family. [17]Zicri was over Abijah's family. Piltai was over Miniamin's and Moadiah's families. [18]Shammua was over Bilgah's family. Jehonathan was over Shemaiah's family. [19]Mattenai was over Joiarib's family. Uzzi was over Jedaiah's family. [20]Kallai was over Sallu's family. Eber was over Amok's family. [21]Hashabiah was over Hilkiah's family. Nethanel was over Jedaiah's family.

[22]The leaders of the families of the Levites and the priests were written down. This was in the days of Eliashib, Joiada, Johanan and Jaddua. They were written down while Darius the Persian was king. [23]The family leaders among the Levites were written down in the history book. These were only up to the time of Johanan son of Eliashib. [24]The leaders of the Levites were Hashabiah, Sherebiah, Jeshua son of Kadmiel and their relatives. Their relatives stood across from them. They gave praise and thanksgiving to God. One group answered the other group. That is what David, the man of God, had commanded.

[25]These were the gatekeepers who guarded the storerooms next to the gates: Mattaniah, Bakbukiah, Obadiah, Meshullam, Talmon and Akkub. [26]They served in the days of Joiakim son of Jeshua. (Jeshua was the son of Jozadak.) They also served in the days of Nehemiah the governor and Ezra the priest and teacher.

Giving of the Wall of Jerusalem

[27]The wall of Jerusalem was offered as a gift to God. The Levites were found in the places where they lived. And they were brought to Jerusalem to celebrate with joy the giving of the wall. They were to celebrate with songs of thanksgiving and with the music of cymbals, harps and lyres.[d] [28]They also brought together singers.

They came from all around Jerusalem and from the Netophathite villages. [29]They came from Beth Gilgal and the areas of Geba and Azmaveth. The singers had built villages for themselves around Jerusalem. [30]The priests and Levites made themselves pure. They also made the people, the gates and the wall of Jerusalem pure.

[31]I had the leaders of Judah go up on top of the wall. I appointed two large choruses to give thanks. One chorus went to the right on top of the wall. This was towards the Rubbish Gate. [32]Behind them went Hoshaiah and half the leaders of Judah. [33]Azariah, Ezra, Meshullam, [34]Judah, Benjamin, Shemaiah and Jeremiah also went. [35]Some priests with trumpets also went, along with Zechariah son of Jonathan. (Jonathan was the son of Shemaiah, who was the son of Mattaniah. Mattaniah was the son of Micaiah, who was the son of Zaccur. Zaccur was the son of Asaph.) [36]Zechariah's relatives also went. They were Shemaiah, Azarel, Milalai, Gilalai, Maai, Nethanel, Judah and Hanani. These men played the musical instruments of David, the man of God. Ezra the teacher walked in front of them. [37]They went from the Fountain Gate straight up the steps to the older part of the city. They went on to the slope of the wall. They went above the house of David to the Water Gate on the east.

[38]The second chorus went to the left. I followed them on top of the wall. Half the people were with me. We went from the Tower of the Ovens to the Broad Wall. [39]We went over the Gate of Ephraim to the Old Gate and the Fish Gate. We went to the Tower of Hananel and the Tower of the Hundred. We went as far as the Sheep Gate. We stopped at the Gate of the Guard.

[40]The two choruses took their places at the Temple.[d] Half of the leaders and I did the same. [41]These

priests were there with their trumpets: Eliakim, Maaseiah, Miniamin, Micaiah, Elioenai, Zechariah and Hananiah. [42]These people were also there: Maaseiah, Shemaiah, Eleazar, Uzzi, Jehohanan, Malkijah, Elam and Ezer. The choruses sang, led by Jezrahiah. [43]The people offered many sacrifices that day. They were happy because God made them very happy. The women and children were happy. The sound of happiness in Jerusalem could be heard far away.

[44]At that time the leaders appointed men to be in charge of the storerooms. These rooms were for the gifts, the first fruits and a tenth of what the people gained. The Teachings said they should bring a share for the priests and Levites. These were to come from the fields around the towns. The people of Judah were happy to do this for the priests and Levites who served. [45]They performed the service of their God. They had the service of purifying things. The singers and gatekeepers also did their jobs as David had commanded his son Solomon. [46]Earlier, in the time of David and Asaph, there was a leader of the singers. There were songs of praise and thanksgiving to God. [47]So it was in the days of Zerubbabel and Nehemiah. All the people of Israel gave something to the singers and gatekeepers. They also set aside things for the Levites. The Levites set aside things for the descendants[d] of Aaron.

Foreign People Are Sent Away

13 On that day they read the Book of Moses to the people. They found that it said no Ammonite or Moabite should ever be allowed in the meeting to worship. [2]The Ammonites and Moabites had not welcomed the Israelites with food and water. Instead, they hired Balaam to put a curse on Israel. (But our God turned the curse into a blessing.) [3]The people

heard this teaching. So they separated all foreigners from Israel.

Nehemiah Returns to Jerusalem

[4]Before that happened, Eliashib the priest was in charge of the Temple[d] storerooms. He was friendly with Tobiah. [5]Eliashib let Tobiah use one of the large storerooms. That storeroom had been used for grain offerings, incense[d] and other things for the Temple. It was also used to keep the tenth offerings of grain, new wine and olive oil. These belonged to the Levites, singers and gatekeepers. It had also been used for gifts for the priests.

[6]I was not in Jerusalem when this happened. I had gone back to Artaxerxes king of Babylon. I went back in the thirty-second year he was king. Finally I asked the king to let me leave. [7]I came to Jerusalem. Then I found out the evil thing Eliashib had done. He had let Tobiah have a room in the Temple courtyard. [8]I was very upset at this. I threw all of Tobiah's goods out of the room. [9]I ordered the rooms to be purified. And I brought back the things for God's Temple, the grain offerings and the incense.[d]

[10]Then I found out the people were not giving the Levites their shares. So the Levites and singers who served had gone back to their own farms. [11]So I argued with the officers. I said, "Why haven't you taken care of the Temple?" Then I gathered the Levites and singers. I put them back at their places.

[12]Then all the people of Judah brought a tenth of what they had gained in grain, new wine and olive oil. And they brought it to the storerooms. [13]I put these men in charge of the storerooms: Shelemiah the priest, Zadok the teacher and Pedaiah a Levite. I made Hanan son of Zaccur their helper. (Zaccur was the son of Mattaniah.) Everyone knew they were hon-

est men. They gave out the portions that went to their relatives.

¹⁴Remember me, my God, for this. Do not ignore my love for the Temple and its service.

¹⁵In those days I saw people in Judah working in the winepresses[d] on the Sabbath[d] day. People were bringing in grain and loading it on donkeys on the Sabbath day. People were bringing loads of wine, grapes and figs into Jerusalem on the Sabbath day. I warned them about selling food on that day. ¹⁶Men from the city of Tyre were living in Jerusalem. They brought in fish and other things. They sold them in Jerusalem on the Sabbath day to the people of Judah. ¹⁷I argued with the important men of Judah. I said to them, "What is this evil thing you are doing? You are ruining the Sabbath day. ¹⁸This is just what your ancestors did. So our God did terrible things to us and to this city. Now you are making him even more angry at Israel. You are ruining the Sabbath day."

¹⁹So I ordered the doors shut at sunset before the Sabbath. The gates were not to be opened until the Sabbath was over. I put my servants at the gates. So no load could come in on the Sabbath. ²⁰Once or twice traders and sellers of all kinds of goods spent the night outside Jerusalem. ²¹So I warned them. I said, "Why are you spending the night by the wall? If you do it again, I will force you away." After that, they did not come back on the Sabbath. ²²Then I ordered the Levites to purify themselves. I told them to go and guard the city gates. They were to make sure the Sabbath remained holy.

Remember me, my God, for this. Have mercy on me because of your great love.

²³In those days I saw men of Judah who had married women from Ashdod, Ammon and Moab. ²⁴Half their children were speaking the language of Ashdod or some other place. They couldn't speak the language of Judah. ²⁵I argued with those people. I put curses on them. I hit some of them and pulled out their hair. I forced them to make a promise to God. I said, "Do not let your daughters marry the sons of foreigners. Do not take the daughters of foreigners as wives for your sons or yourselves. ²⁶Foreign women made King Solomon of Israel sin. There was never a king like him in any of the nations. God loved Solomon. God made him king over all Israel. But foreign women made him sin. ²⁷And now you are not obedient when you do this evil thing. You are unfaithful to our God when you marry foreign wives."

²⁸Joiada was the son of Eliashib the high priest. One of Joiada's sons married a daughter of Sanballat the Horonite, who was not a Jew. So I forced Joiada's son away from me.

²⁹Remember them, my God. They made the priesthood unclean.[d] They made the agreement of the priests and Levites unclean.

³⁰So I purified them of everything that was foreign. I appointed duties for the priests and Levites. Each man had his own job. ³¹I also made sure wood was brought for the altar at regular times. And I made sure the first fruits were brought.

Remember, my God, to be kind to me.

ESTHER

Esther Saves Her People

Queen Vashti Disobeys the King

1 This is what happened during the time of King Xerxes. He was the king who ruled the 127 areas from India to Cush. ²In those days King Xerxes ruled from his capital city of Susa. ³In the third year of his rule, he gave a banquet. It was for all his important men and royal officers. The army leaders from the countries of Persia and Media were there. And the important men from all Xerxes' empire were there.

⁴The banquet lasted 180 days. All during that time King Xerxes was showing off the great wealth of his kingdom. And he was showing his own honour and greatness. ⁵When the 180 days were over, the king gave another banquet. It was held in the courtyard of the palace garden for seven days. It was for everybody in the palace at Susa, from the greatest to the least important. ⁶The courtyard had fine white curtains and purple drapes. These were tied to silver rings on marble pillars by white and purple cords. And there were gold and silver couches. These were on a floor set with tiles of white marble, shells and gems. ⁷Wine was served in gold cups of various kinds. And there was plenty of the king's wine because he was very generous. ⁸The king commanded that each guest be permitted to drink as much as he wished. He had told the wine servers to serve each man what he wanted.

⁹Queen Vashti also gave a banquet. It was for the women in the royal palace of King Xerxes.

¹⁰On the seventh day of the banquet, King Xerxes was very happy because he had been drinking much wine. He gave a command to the seven eunuchs*d* who served him. They were Mehuman, Biztha, Harbona, Bigtha, Abagtha, Zethar and Carcas. ¹¹He commanded them to bring him Queen Vashti, wearing her royal crown. She was to come to show her beauty to the people and important men. She was very beautiful. ¹²The eunuchs told Queen Vashti about the king's command. But she refused to come. Then the king became very angry. His anger was like a burning fire.

¹³It was a custom for the king to ask advice from experts about law and order. So King Xerxes spoke with the wise men. They would know the right thing to do. ¹⁴The wise men the king usually talked to were Carshena, Shethar, Admatha, Tarshish, Meres, Marsena and Memucan. They were seven of the important men of Persia and Media. These seven had special privileges to see the king. They had the highest rank in the kingdom.

¹⁵The king asked those men, "What does the law say must be done to Queen Vashti? She has not obeyed the command of King Xerxes, which the eunuchs took to her."

¹⁶Then Memucan spoke to the king and the other important men. He said, "Queen Vashti has not done wrong to the king alone. She has also done wrong to all the important men and all the people in all the empire of King Xerxes. ¹⁷All the wives of the important men of Persia and Media will hear about the queen's actions. Then they will no longer honour their husbands. They will say, 'King Xerxes commanded Queen Vashti to be brought to him. But she refused to come'.

¹⁸Today the wives of the important men of Persia and Media have heard about the queen's actions. And they will speak in the same way to their husbands. And there will be no end to disrespect and anger.

¹⁹"So, our king, if it pleases you, give a royal order. And let it be written in the laws of Persia and Media, which cannot be changed. The law should say Vashti is never again to enter the presence of King Xerxes. Also let the king give her place as queen to someone who is better than she is. ²⁰And let the king's order be announced everywhere in his large kingdom. Then all the women will respect their husbands, from the greatest to the least important."

²¹The king and his important men were happy with this advice. So King Xerxes did as Memucan suggested. ²²He sent letters to all the areas of the kingdom. A letter was sent to each area, written in its own form of writing. And a letter was sent to each group of people, written in their own language. These letters announced that each man was to be the ruler of his own family. Also, each family was to speak the language of the man.

Esther Is Made Queen

2 Later, King Xerxes was not so angry. Then he remembered Vashti and what she had done. And he remembered his order about her. ²Then the king's personal servants had a suggestion. They said, "Let a search be made for beautiful young virgins*d* for the king. ³Let the king choose supervisors in every area of his kingdom. Let them bring every beautiful young virgin to the palace at Susa. These women should be taken to the women's quarters and put under the care of Hegai. He is the king's eunuch*d* in charge of the women. And let beauty treatments be given to them. ⁴Then let the girl who most pleases the king become queen in place of

Vashti." The king liked this advice. So he did as they said.

⁵Now there was a Jewish man in the palace of Susa. His name was Mordecai son of Jair. Jair was the son of Shimei. And Shimei was the son of Kish. Mordecai was from the tribe*d* of Benjamin. ⁶Mordecai had been taken captive from Jerusalem by Nebuchadnezzar king of Babylon. Mordecai was part of the group taken into captivity with Jehoiachin king of Judah. ⁷Mordecai had a cousin named Hadassah, who had no father or mother. So Mordecai took care of her. Hadassah was also called Esther, and she had a very pretty figure and face. Mordecai had adopted her as his own daughter when her father and mother died.

⁸The king's command and order had been heard. And many girls had been brought to the palace in Susa. They had been put under the care of Hegai. When this happened, Esther was also taken to the king's palace. She was put into the care of Hegai, who was in charge of the women. ⁹Esther pleased Hegai, and he liked her. So Hegai quickly began giving Esther her beauty treatments and special food. He gave her seven servant girls chosen from the king's palace. Then Hegai moved Esther and her seven servant girls to the best part of the women's quarters.

¹⁰Esther did not tell anyone about her family or who her people were. Mordecai had told her not to. ¹¹Every day Mordecai walked back and forth near the courtyard. This was where the king's women lived. He wanted to find out how Esther was and what was happening to her.

¹²Before a girl could take her turn with King Xerxes, she had to complete 12 months of beauty treatments. These were ordered for the women. For six months she was treated with oil and myrrh.*d* And she spent six months with perfumes and cosmetics. ¹³Then she was ready to go to the

king. Anything she asked for was given to her. She could take it with her from the women's quarters to the king's palace. ¹⁴In the evening she would go to the king's palace. And in the morning she would return to another part of the women's quarters. There she would be placed under the care of a man named Shaashgaz. Shaashgaz was the king's eunuch in charge of the slave women.ᵈ The girl would not go back to the king again unless he was pleased with her. Then he would call her by name to come back to him.

¹⁵Esther daughter of Abihail, Mordecai's uncle, had been adopted by Mordecai. The time came for Esther to go to the king. She asked for only what Hegai suggested she should take. (Hegai was the king's eunuch who was in charge of the women.) And everyone who saw Esther liked her. ¹⁶So Esther was taken to King Xerxes in the royal palace. This happened in the tenth month, the month of Tebeth. It was in Xerxes' seventh year as king.

¹⁷And the king was pleased with Esther more than with any of the other girls. And he liked her more than any of the other virgins. So King Xerxes put a royal crown on Esther's head. And he made her queen in place of Vashti. ¹⁸Then the king gave a great banquet for Esther. He invited all his important men and royal officers. He announced a holiday in all the empire. And he was generous and gave everyone a gift.

Mordecai Discovers an Evil Plan

¹⁹Now Mordecai was sitting at the king's gate. This was when the virginsᵈ were gathered the second time. ²⁰And Esther had still not told anyone about her family or who her people were. That is what Mordecai had told her to do. She still obeyed Mordecai just as she had done when he was bringing her up.

²¹Now Bigthana and Teresh were two of the king's officers who guarded the doorway. While Mordecai was sitting at the king's gate, Bigthana and Teresh became angry at the king. And they began to make plans to kill King Xerxes. ²²But Mordecai found out about their plans and told Queen Esther. Then Queen Esther told the king. She also told him that Mordecai had found out about the evil plan. ²³When the report was investigated, it was found to be true. The two officers who had planned to kill the king were hanged. And all this was written down in the daily court record in the king's presence.

Haman Plans to Destroy the Jews

3 After these things happened, King Xerxes honoured Haman son of Hammedatha the Agagite. He gave Haman a new rank that was higher than all the important men. ²And all the royal officers at the king's gate would bow down and kneel before Haman. This was what the king had ordered. But Mordecai would not bow down, and he did not kneel.

³Then the royal officers at the king's gate asked Mordecai, "Why don't you obey the king's command?" ⁴And they said this to him every day. When he did not listen to them, they told Haman about it. They wanted to see if Haman would accept Mordecai's behaviour because Mordecai had told them that he was a Jew.

⁵Then Haman saw that Mordecai would not bow down to him or kneel before him. And he became very angry. ⁶He had been told who the people of Mordecai were. And he thought of himself as too important to try to kill only Mordecai. So he looked for a way to destroy all of Mordecai's people, the Jews, in all of Xerxes' kingdom.

⁷It was in the first month of the twelfth year of King Xerxes' rule. That is the month of Nisan. Pur (that

is, the lot*d*) was thrown before Haman. The lot was used to choose a day and a month. So the twelfth month, the month of Adar, was chosen.

⁸Then Haman said to King Xerxes, "There is a certain group of people in all the areas of your kingdom. They are scattered among the other people. They keep themselves separate. Their customs are different from those of all the other people. And they do not obey the king's laws. It is not right for you to allow them to continue living in your kingdom. ⁹If it pleases the king, let an order be given to destroy those people. Then I will pay 345 tons of silver to those who do the king's business. They will put it into the royal treasury."

¹⁰So the king took his signet*d* ring off and gave it to Haman. Haman son of Hammedatha, the Agagite, was the enemy of the Jews. ¹¹Then the king said to Haman, "The money and the people are yours. Do with them as you please."

¹²On the thirteenth day of the first month, the royal secretaries were called. They wrote out all of Haman's orders. They wrote to the king's governors and to the captains of the soldiers in each area. And they wrote to the important men of each group of people. The orders were written to each area in its own form of writing. And they were written to each group of people in their own language. They were written in the name of King Xerxes and sealed with his signet ring. ¹³Letters were sent by messengers to all the king's empire. They stated the king's order to destroy, kill and completely wipe out all the Jews. That meant young and old, women and little children, too. The order said to kill all the Jews on a single day. That was to be the thirteenth day of the twelfth month, which was Adar. And it said to take all the things that belonged to the Jews. ¹⁴A copy of the order was to be given out as a law in every area. It

was to be made known to all the people so that they would be ready for that day.

¹⁵The messengers set out, hurried by the king's command. At the same time the order was given in the palace at Susa. And the king and Haman sat down to drink. But the city of Susa was in confusion.

Mordecai Asks Esther to Help

4 Now Mordecai heard about all that had been done. To show how upset he was, he tore his clothes. Then he put on rough cloth and ashes. And he went out into the city crying loudly and very sadly. ²But Mordecai went only as far as the king's gate. This was because no one was allowed to enter that gate dressed in rough cloth. ³The king's order reached every area. And there was great sadness and loud crying among the Jews. They gave up eating and cried out loudly. Many Jews lay down on rough cloth and ashes to show how sad they were.

⁴Esther's servant girls and eunuchs*d* came to her and told her about Mordecai. Esther was very upset and afraid. She sent clothes for Mordecai to put on instead of the rough cloth. But he would not wear them. ⁵Then Esther called for Hathach. He was one of the king's eunuchs chosen by the king to serve her. Esther ordered him to find out what was bothering Mordecai and why.

⁶So Hathach went to Mordecai. Mordecai was in the city square in front of the king's gate. ⁷Then Mordecai told Hathach everything that had happened to him. And he told Hathach about the amount of money Haman had promised to pay into the king's treasury for the killing of the Jews. ⁸Mordecai also gave him a copy of the order to kill the Jews, which had been given in Susa. He wanted Hathach to show it to Esther and to tell her about it. And Mordecai told him to order Esther to go into the king's presence. He

Samuel 17:50
avid defeated the Philistine with only a
ng and a stone!

1 Kings 10:1-2
Now the Queen of Sheba heard about Solomon's fame . . . She travelled to Jerusalem with a very large group of servants.

2 Chronicles 3:1
Solomon began to build the Temple of the
Lord.

wanted her to beg for mercy and to plead with him for her people.

⁹Hathach went back and reported to Esther everything Mordecai had said. ¹⁰Then Esther told Hathach to say to Mordecai, ¹¹"All the royal officers and people of the royal areas know this: no man or woman may go to the king in the inner courtyard without being called. There is only one law about this. Anyone who enters must be put to death. But if the king holds out his gold sceptre,ᵈ that person may live. And I have not been called to go to the king for 30 days."

¹²And Esther's message was given to Mordecai. ¹³Then Mordecai gave orders to say to Esther: "Just because you live in the king's palace, don't think that out of all the Jews you alone will escape. ¹⁴You might keep quiet at this time. Then someone else will help and save the Jews. But you and your father's family will all die. And who knows, you may have been chosen queen for just such a time as this."

¹⁵Then Esther sent this answer to Mordecai: ¹⁶"Go and get all the Jews in Susa together. For my sake, give up eating. Do not eat or drink for three days, night and day. I and my servant girls will also give up eating. Then I will go to the king, even though it is against the law. And if I die, I die."

¹⁷So Mordecai went away. He did everything Esther had told him to do.

Esther Speaks to the King

5 On the third day Esther put on her royal robes. Then she stood in the inner courtyard of the king's palace, facing the king's hall. The king was sitting on his royal throne in the hall, facing the doorway. ²The king saw Queen Esther standing in the courtyard. When he saw her, he was very pleased. He held out to her the gold sceptreᵈ that was in his hand. So Esther went up to him and touched the end of the sceptre.

³Then the king asked, "What is it, Queen Esther? What do you want to ask me? I will give you as much as half of my kingdom."

⁴Esther answered, "My king, if it pleases you, come today with Haman to a banquet. I have prepared it for him."

⁵Then the king said, "Bring Haman quickly so we may do what Esther asks."

So the king and Haman went to the banquet Esther had prepared for them. ⁶As they were drinking wine, the king said to Esther, "Now, Esther, what are you asking for? I will give it to you. What is it you want? I will give you as much as half of my kingdom."

⁷Esther answered, "This is what I want and ask for. ⁸My king, I hope you are pleased with me. If it pleases you, give me what I ask for and do what I want. Come with Haman tomorrow to the banquet I will prepare for you. Then I will answer your question about what I want."

Haman's Plans Against Mordecai

⁹Haman left the king's palace that day happy and content. Then he saw Mordecai at the king's gate. And he saw that Mordecai did not stand up nor did he tremble with fear before him. So Haman became very angry with Mordecai. ¹⁰But he controlled his anger and went home.

Then Haman called his friends and Zeresh, his wife, together. ¹¹And he told them about how wealthy he was and how many sons he had. He also told them about all the ways the king had honoured him. And he told them how the king had placed him higher than his important men and his royal officers. ¹²"And that's not all", Haman added. "I'm the only person Queen Esther invited to come with the king to the banquet she gave. And tomorrow also the queen has asked me to be her guest with the king. ¹³But all this does not really make me happy. I'm not happy as long as I see that Jew Mordecai sitting at the king's gate."

¹⁴Then Haman's wife Zeresh and all his friends said, "Have a platform built to hang someone. Build it 25 metres high. And in the morning ask the king to have Mordecai hanged on it. Then go to the banquet with the king and be happy." Haman liked this suggestion. So he ordered the platform to be built.

Mordecai Is Honoured

6 That same night the king could not sleep. So he gave an order for the daily court record to be brought in and read to him. ²And it was found recorded that Mordecai had warned the king about Bigthana and Teresh. These men had planned to kill the king. They were two of the king's officers who guarded the doorway.

³Then the king asked, "What honour and reward have been given to Mordecai for this?"

The king's personal servants answered, "Nothing has been done for Mordecai."

⁴The king said, "Who is in the courtyard?" Now Haman had just entered the outer court of the king's palace. He had come to ask the king about hanging Mordecai on the platform he had prepared.

⁵The king's personal servants said, "Haman is standing in the courtyard."

So the king said, "Bring him in."

⁶So Haman came in. And the king asked him, "What should be done for a man that the king wants very much to honour?"

And Haman thought to himself, "Whom would the king want to honour more than me?" ⁷So he answered the king, "This is what you could do for the man you want very much to honour. ⁸Have the servants bring a royal robe that the king himself has worn. And also bring a horse with a royal crown on its head. The horse should be one the king himself has ridden. ⁹Then let the robe and the horse be given to one of the king's most important men. Let the servants put the robe on the man the king wants very much to honour. And let them lead him on the horse through the city streets. As they are leading him, let them announce: 'This is what is done for the man the king wants very much to honour'!"

¹⁰The king commanded Haman, "Go quickly. Take the robe and the horse just as you have said. And do all this for Mordecai the Jew who sits at the king's gate. Do not leave out anything that you have suggested."

¹¹So Haman took the robe and the horse. And he put the robe on Mordecai. Then he led him on horseback through the city streets. Haman announced before Mordecai: "This is what is done for the man the king wants very much to honour!"

¹²Then Mordecai went back to the king's gate. But Haman hurried home with his head covered. He was embarrassed and ashamed. ¹³He told his wife Zeresh and all his friends everything that had happened to him.

Haman's wife and the men who gave him advice said, "You are starting to lose power to Mordecai. Since he is a Jew, you cannot win against him. You will surely be ruined." ¹⁴While they were still talking, the king's eunuchsᵈ came to Haman's house. They made Haman hurry to the banquet Esther had prepared.

Haman Is Hanged

7 So the king and Haman went in to eat with Queen Esther. ²They were drinking wine. And the king said to Esther on this second day also, "What are you asking for? I will give it to you. What is it you want? I will give you as much as half of my kingdom."

³Then Queen Esther answered, "My king, I hope you are pleased with me. If it pleases you, let me live. This is what I ask. And let my people live, too. This is what I want. ⁴I ask this

because my people and I have been sold to be destroyed. We are to be killed and completely wiped out. If we had been sold as male and female slaves, I would have kept quiet. That would not be enough of a problem to bother the king."

⁵Then King Xerxes asked Queen Esther, "Who is he? Where is he? Who has done such a thing?"

⁶Esther said, "A man who is against us! Our enemy is this wicked Haman!"

Then Haman was filled with terror before the king and queen. ⁷The king was very angry. He got up, left his wine and went out into the palace garden. But Haman stayed inside to beg Queen Esther to save his life. He could see that the king had already decided to kill him.

⁸The king came back from the palace garden to the banquet hall. And he saw Haman falling on the couch where Esther was lying. The king said, "Will he even attack the queen while I am in the house?"

As soon as the king said that, servants came in and covered Haman's face. ⁹Harbona was one of the eunuchs[d] there serving the king. He said, "Look, a platform for hanging people stands near Haman's house. It is 25 metres high. This is the one Haman had prepared for Mordecai, who gave the warning that saved the king."

The king said, "Hang Haman on it!" ¹⁰So they hanged Haman on the platform he had prepared for Mordecai. Then the king was not so angry any more.

The King Helps the Jews

8 That same day King Xerxes gave Queen Esther everything Haman had left when he died. Haman had been the enemy of the Jews. And Mordecai came in to see the king. He came because Esther had told the king how he was related to her. ²Then the king took off his signet[d] ring, which he had taken back from Haman. And he gave it to Mordecai. Then Esther put Mordecai in charge of everything Haman had left when he died.

³Once again Esther spoke to the king. She fell at the king's feet and cried. She begged the king to stop the evil plan of Haman the Agagite. Haman had thought up the plan against the Jews. ⁴The king held out the gold sceptre[d] to Esther. Esther got up and stood in front of the king.

⁵She said, "My king, I hope you are pleased with me. And maybe it will please you to do this. You might think it is the right thing to do. And maybe you are happy with me. If so, let an order be written to cancel the letters Haman wrote. ⁶I could not stand to see that terrible thing happen to my people. I could not stand to see my family killed."

⁷King Xerxes answered Queen Esther and Mordecai the Jew. He said, "Because Haman was against the Jews, I have given his things to Esther. And my soldiers have hanged him. ⁸Now write another order in the king's name. Write it to the Jews as it seems best to you. Then seal the order with the king's signet[d] ring. No letter written in the king's name and sealed with his signet ring can be cancelled."

⁹At that time the king's secretaries were called. This was done on the twenty-third day of the third month, which is Sivan. The secretaries wrote out all of Mordecai's orders. They wrote to the Jews and to the governors and to the captains of the soldiers in each area. And they wrote to the important men of the 127 areas which reached from India to Cush. They wrote to each area in its own form of writing. And they wrote to each group of people in their own language. They also wrote to the Jews in their own form of writing and their own language. ¹⁰Mordecai wrote orders in

the name of King Xerxes. And he sealed the letters with the king's signet ring. Then he sent the king's orders by messengers on horses. The messengers rode fast horses, which were raised just for the king.

[11]These were the king's orders: the Jews in every city have the right to gather together to protect themselves. They have the right to destroy, kill and completely wipe out the army of any area or people who attack them. And they are to do the same to the women and children of that army. The Jews also have the right to take by force the property of the enemies. [12]The one day set for the Jews to do this was the thirteenth day of the twelfth month. This was the month of Adar. They were allowed to do this in all the empire of King Xerxes. [13]A copy of the king's order was to be sent out as a law in every area. It was to be made known to the people of every nation living in the kingdom. This was so the Jews would be ready on that set day. The Jews would be allowed to pay back their enemies.

[14]The messengers hurried out, riding on the royal horses. The king commanded those messengers to hurry. And the order was also given in the palace at Susa.

[15]Mordecai left the king's presence wearing royal clothes. They were blue and white. And he had on a large gold crown. He also had a purple robe made of the best linen. And the people of Susa shouted for joy. [16]It was a time of happiness, joy, gladness and honour for the Jews. [17]The king's order went to every area and city. And there was joy and gladness among the Jews. This happened in every area and city to which the king's order went. The Jews were having feasts and celebrating. And many people through all the empire became Jews. They did that because they were afraid of the Jews.

Victory for the Jews

9 The order the king had commanded was to be done on the thirteenth day of the twelfth month. That was the month of Adar. That was the day the enemies of the Jews had hoped to defeat them. But that was changed. So the Jews themselves defeated those who hated them. [2]The Jews met in their cities in all the empire of King Xerxes. They met in order to attack those who wanted to harm them. And no one was strong enough to fight against them. This was because all the other people living in the empire were afraid of the Jews. [3]And all the important men of the areas, the governors, captains of the soldiers, and the king's officers helped the Jews. They helped because they were afraid of Mordecai. [4]Mordecai was very important in the king's palace. He was famous in all the empire. This was because he was becoming a leader of more and more people.

[5]And, with their swords, the Jews defeated all their enemies, killing and destroying them. And the Jews did what they wanted with those people who hated them. [6]In the palace at Susa, they killed and destroyed 500 men. [7]They also killed these men: Parshandatha, Dalphon, Aspatha, [8]Poratha, Adalia, Aridatha, [9]Parmashta, Arisai, Aridai and Vaizatha. [10]They were the ten sons of Haman, son of Hammedatha, the enemy of the Jews. But the Jews did not take their belongings.

[11]And on that day the number of the men killed in the palace at Susa was reported to the king. [12]The king said to Queen Esther, "The Jews have killed and destroyed 500 men in the palace at Susa. And they have also killed Haman's ten sons. What have they done in the rest of the king's empire! Now what else are you asking? I will do it! And what else do you want? It will be done."

¹³Esther answered, "If it pleases the king, give the Jews in Susa permission to do this. Let them do again tomorrow what the king ordered for today. And let the bodies of Haman's ten sons be hanged on the platform built for hanging people to death."

¹⁴So the king ordered that it be done. A law was given in Susa, and the bodies of the ten sons of Haman were hanged. ¹⁵The Jews in Susa came together. It was on the fourteenth day of the month of Adar. And they killed 300 men in Susa. But they did not take their belongings.

¹⁶At that same time, the other Jews in the king's empire also met. This was to protect themselves and get rid of their enemies. And they killed 75,000 of those who hated them. But they did not take their belongings. ¹⁷This happened on the thirteenth day of the month of Adar. And on the fourteenth day the Jews rested. They made it a day of joyful feasting.

The Feast of Purim

¹⁸But the Jews in Susa met on the thirteenth and fourteenth days of the month of Adar. Then they rested on the fifteenth day. They made it a day of joyful feasting.

¹⁹This is why the Jews who live in the country and small villages celebrate on the fourteenth day. They keep the fourteenth day of the month of Adar as a day of joyful feasting. And it is also a day for giving presents to each other.

²⁰Mordecai wrote down everything that had happened. Then he sent letters to all the Jews in all the empire of King Xerxes. He sent letters to places far and near. ²¹Mordecai did this to have the Jews celebrate every year. They were to celebrate on the fourteenth and fifteenth days of the month of Adar. ²²It was to celebrate a time when the Jews got rid of their enemies. They were also to celebrate it as the month their sadness was turned to joy. It was the month when their crying for the dead was turned into celebration. Mordecai wrote letters to all the Jews. He told them to celebrate those days as days of joyful feasting. It was to be a time of giving food to each other. And it was a time of giving presents to the poor.

²³So the Jews agreed to do what Mordecai had written to them. And they agreed to hold the celebration every year. ²⁴Haman son of Hammedatha, the Agagite, was the enemy of all the Jews. He had made an evil plan against the Jews to destroy them. And Haman had thrown the pur (that is, the lotᵈ) to choose a day to ruin and destroy the Jews. ²⁵But when the king learned of the evil plan, he sent out written orders. This was so the evil plans Haman had made against the Jews would be used against him. And those orders said that Haman and his sons should be hanged on the platform for hanging. ²⁶So these days were called Purim. The name Purim comes from the word "pur" (the lot). ²⁷And so the Jews set up this custom. They and their descendantsᵈ would celebrate these two days every year. The Jews and all those who join them are to celebrate these two days. They should do it without fail every year. They should do it in the right way and at the time Mordecai had ordered them in the letter. ²⁸These two days should be remembered and celebrated from now on in every family. And they must be celebrated in every area and every city. These days of Purim should never stop being celebrated by the Jews. And the descendants of the Jews should always remember to celebrate these two days of Purim.

²⁹So Queen Esther daughter of Abihail, along with Mordecai the Jew, wrote this second letter about Purim. Using the power they had, they wrote to prove the first letter was true. ³⁰And Mordecai sent letters to all the Jews in the 127 areas of the kingdom

of Xerxes. Mordecai wrote a message of peace and truth. [31]He wrote to set up these days of Purim. They are to be celebrated at their chosen times. Mordecai the Jew and Queen Esther had sent out the order for the Jews. They had set up for themselves and their descendants these two days. They set them up so the Jews would give up eating and cry loudly. [32]Esther's letter showed that these practices about Purim were correct. They were written down in the records.

The Greatness of Mordecai

10 King Xerxes made people pay taxes. Even the cities far away on the seacoast had to pay taxes. [2]And all the great things that Xerxes did are written down. They tell of his power and strength. They are written in the record books of the kings of Media and Persia. Also written in those record books are all the things that Mordecai did. The king had made Mordecai a great man. [3]Mordecai the Jew was second in importance to King Xerxes. He was the most important man among the Jews. And his fellow Jews respected him very much. They respected Mordecai because he worked for the good of his people. And they respected him because he spoke up for the safety of all the Jews.

JOB

A Good Man Suffers

Job, the Good Man

1 A man named Job lived in the land of Uz. He was an honest man and innocent of any wrong. He honoured God and stayed away from evil. [2]Job had seven sons and three daughters. [3]He owned 7,000 sheep, 3,000 camels, 500 pairs of oxen and 500 female donkeys. And he had a large number of servants. He was the greatest man among all the people of the East.

[4]Job's sons took turns holding feasts in their homes. And they invited their sisters to eat and drink with them. [5]After a feast was over, Job would send and have them made clean.[d] Early in the morning Job would offer a burnt offering for each of them. He thought, "My children may have sinned and cursed God in their hearts." Job did this every time.

Satan Appears Before God

[6]One day the angels came to show themselves before the Lord. Satan also came with them. [7]The Lord said to Satan, "Where have you come from?"

Satan answered the Lord, "I have been wandering around the earth. I have been going back and forth in it."

[8]Then the Lord said to Satan, "Have you noticed my servant Job? No one else on earth is like him. He is an honest man and innocent of any wrong. He honours God and stays away from evil."

[9]But Satan answered God, "Job honours God for a good reason. [10]You have put a wall around him, his family and everything he owns. You have blessed the things he has done. So his flocks of sheep and herds of cattle are large. They almost cover the land. [11]But reach out your hand and destroy everything he has. Then he will curse you to your face."

[12]The Lord said to Satan, "All right, then. Everything Job has is in your power. But you must not touch Job himself." Then Satan left the Lord's presence.

[13]One day Job's sons and daughters were eating and drinking wine together. They were at the oldest brother's house. [14]A messenger came to Job and said, "The oxen were ploughing. And the donkeys were eating grass nearby. [15]And the Sabeans attacked and carried them away. They killed the servants with swords. And I am the only one who escaped to tell you!"

[16]The messenger was still speaking when another messenger came in. He said, "Lightning from God fell from the sky. It burned up the sheep and the servants. And I am the only one who escaped to tell you!"

[17]The second messenger was still speaking when another messenger came in. He said, "The Babylonians sent three groups of attackers. They swept down and stole your camels. They killed the servants. And I am the only one who escaped to tell you!"

[18]The third messenger was still speaking when another messenger came in. He said, "Your sons and daughters were eating and drinking wine together. They were at the oldest brother's house. [19]Suddenly a great wind came in from the desert. It struck all four corners of the house at once. The house fell in on your sons and daughters. And they are all dead. I am the only one who escaped to tell you!"

²⁰When Job heard this, he got up. To show how sad he was he tore his robe and shaved his head. Then he bowed down to the ground to worship God. ²¹He said:

"I was naked when I was born.
And I will be naked when I die.
The Lord gave these things to me. And he has taken them away.
Praise the name of the Lord."

²²In all this Job did not sin. He did not blame God.

Satan Appears Before God Again

2 On another day the angels came to show themselves before the Lord. And Satan also came with them. ²The Lord said to Satan, "Where have you come from?"

Satan answered the Lord, "I have been wandering around the earth. I have been going back and forth in it."

³Then the Lord said to Satan, "Have you noticed my servant Job? No one else on earth is like him. He is an honest man, innocent of any wrong. He honours God and stays away from evil. You caused me to ruin him for no good reason. But he continues to be without blame."

⁴"One skin for another!" Satan answered. "A man will give all he has to save his own life. ⁵But reach out your hand and destroy his own flesh and bones. Then he will curse you to your face."

⁶The Lord said to Satan, "All right, then. Job is in your power. But you must let him live."

⁷So Satan left the Lord's presence. And he put painful sores all over Job's body. They went from the top of his head to the soles of his feet. ⁸Then Job took a piece of broken pottery. And he used it to scrape himself. He sat in ashes to show how upset he was.

⁹Job's wife said to him, "Are you still trying to stay innocent? You should just curse God and die!"

¹⁰Job answered, "You are talking like a foolish woman. Should we take only good things from God and not trouble?" In all this Job did not sin in what he said.

Job's Three Friends

¹¹Now Job had three friends. They were Eliphaz the Temanite, Bildad the Shuhite and Zophar the Naamathite. These friends heard about the troubles that had happened to Job. So they agreed to meet and go to see Job. They wanted to show him they were upset for him, too. And they wanted to comfort him. ¹²They saw Job from far away. But he looked so different they almost didn't recognise him. They began to cry loudly. They tore their robes and put dirt on their heads to show how sad they were. ¹³Then they sat on the ground and stayed with Job seven days and seven nights. No one said a word to him. This was because they saw how much he was suffering.

Job Curses His Birth

3 After seven days Job spoke. He cursed the day he had been born. ²Job said:

³"Let the day I was born be destroyed.
And destroy the night when it was said, 'A boy is born!'
⁴Let that day turn to darkness.
Let God not even care about it.
Don't let light shine on that day.
⁵Let darkness and gloom have that day.
Let a cloud hide that day.
Let darkness cover its light.
⁶Let thick darkness capture that night.
Don't count it among the days of the year.
Don't put it in any of the months.
⁷Let that night be empty.
Let no shout of joy be heard in it.

⁸Let the people who curse days
curse that day.
They know how to wake up the
sea monster Leviathan.ᵈ
⁹Let that day's morning stars
become dark.
Let it wait for daylight, but don't
let it come.
Don't let it see the first light of
dawn.
¹⁰This is because it allowed me to
be born.
That day did not hide trouble
from my eyes.
¹¹"Why didn't I die as soon as I was
born?
Why didn't I die when I came
out of the womb?
¹²Why did my mother's knees
receive me?
Why did my mother's breasts
feed me?
¹³If they had not been there, I
would be lying dead in
peace.
I would be asleep and at rest.
¹⁴I would be asleep with kings and
wise men of the earth.
They built places for themselves
that are now ruined.
¹⁵I would be asleep with rulers who
had gold.
They filled their houses with
silver!
¹⁶Or why was I not buried like a
child born dead?
I wish I were like a baby who
never saw the light of day.
¹⁷In the grave the wicked stop
causing trouble.
And people who are tired are at
rest.
¹⁸In the grave there is rest for the
captives.
They no longer hear the shout
of the slave driver.
¹⁹People great and small are in the
grave.
And the slave is freed from his
master.

²⁰"Why is life given to those who
are in misery?
Why is it given to those who are
so unhappy?
²¹Some people want to die, but
death does not come.
They search for death more
than for hidden treasure.
²²They are very happy
when they get to the grave.
²³Life shouldn't be given to a man
who doesn't know what will
happen to him.
It shouldn't be given to a man
who feels trapped by God.
²⁴I make sad sounds as I eat.
My groans pour out like
water.
²⁵The thing I was afraid of has
happened to me.
And the thing I dreaded has
happened.
²⁶I have no peace. I have no
quietness.
I have no rest. I only have
trouble."

Eliphaz Speaks

4 Then Eliphaz the Temanite answered:

²"If someone tried to speak to
you, would you be upset?
I cannot keep from speaking.
³Think about how many people you
have taught.
Think about how you have made
weak hands strong.
⁴Your words have comforted those
who fell.
And you have given strength to
those who could not stand.
⁵But now trouble comes to you.
And you are discouraged.
Trouble hits you, and you are
terrified.
⁶You should trust in your respect
for God.
You should have hope because
you are innocent.

7"Think about this now: a person
    who has not done wrong will
    not die.
Honest people were never
    destroyed.
8I have noticed that people who
    plough evil
and plant trouble harvest it.
9God's breath destroys them.
    A blast of his anger kills them.
10The lions roar and growl.
    But the teeth of great lions are
    broken.
11The lion dies because he can't find
    an animal to eat.
So the cubs of the female lion
    are scattered.

12"A word was brought to me in
    secret.
My ears heard a whisper of it.
13It was during troublesome dreams
    in the night
when men are in deep sleep.
14I was shaking with fear.
    All my bones were shaking.
15A spirit glided past my face.
    The hair on my body stood up in
    fear.
16The spirit stopped,
    but I could not see what it was.
A shape stood before my eyes.
    And I heard a quiet voice.
17It said, 'Can a man be holy in the
    presence of God?
Can a man be pure before the
    one who made him?
18God does not trust his servants.
    He even blames his angels for
    mistakes.
19So he puts even more blame on
    people who live in clay
    houses.*
The foundations of these houses
    are made of dust.
They can be crushed more
    easily than a moth.
20Between dawn and sunset they
    are broken to pieces.

They are not noticed. They die
    and are gone for ever.
21The ropes of their tents are pulled
    up.
And they die without wisdom'.

5 "Call if you want to, but no one
    will answer you.
You can't turn to any of the holy
    ones.
2Foolish anger kills a person.
    And jealousy kills a weak-minded
    person.
3I have seen a fool have success
    like a tree taking root.
But suddenly his home was
    destroyed.
4His children are far away from
    safety.
They are crushed in court with
    no one to defend them.
5Hungry people eat this fool's
    harvest.
They even take what grew up
    among the thorns.
And thirsty people want his
    wealth.
6Hard times do not come up from
    the ground.
And trouble does not grow from
    the earth.
7But man is born to have trouble
    as surely as sparks fly upward.

8"But if I were you, I would call on
    God.
I would bring my problem before
    him.
9God does wonderful things that
    cannot be understood.
He does so many miracles[d] they
    cannot be counted.
10God gives rain to the earth.
    He sends water on the fields.
11God makes the humble person
    important.
He lifts to places of safety those
    who are sad.

clay houses This is probably talking about people's bodies.

¹²God ruins the plans of those who
     trick others.
   Then they have no success.
¹³He catches wise men in their own
     clever traps.
   And the plans of those who try
     to trick others are swept
     away.
¹⁴Darkness covers them up in the
     daytime.
   At noon they feel around in the
     dark.
¹⁵God saves needy people from
     their lies.
   He saves them from the harm
     done by powerful people.
¹⁶So the poor people have hope.
   And those who are unfair are
     silenced.

¹⁷"The person whom God corrects
     is happy.
   So do not hate being corrected
     by God All-Powerful.
¹⁸God hurts, but he also bandages
     up.
   He injures, but his hands also
     heal.
¹⁹He will save you from six
     troubles.
   Even seven troubles will not
     harm you.
²⁰God will buy you back from death
     in times of hunger.
   And in battle he will save you
     from death by the sword.
²¹You will be hidden from the
     tongue that hits like a whip.
   You will not need to be afraid
     when destruction comes.
²²You will laugh at destruction and
     hunger.
   You do not need to fear the wild
     animals.
²³This is because you will have an
     agreement with the animals
     born in the wild.
   And the wild animals will be at
     peace with you.
²⁴You will know that your tent is
     safe.

You will check the things you
     own and find nothing
     missing.
²⁵You will know that you will have
     many children.
   Your descendants⁴ will be as
     many as the blades of grass
     on the earth.
²⁶You will come to the grave with
     all your strength.
   You will be like bundles of grain
     gathered at the right time.

²⁷"We have checked this, and it is
     true.
   So hear it and decide what it
     means to you."

Job Answers Eliphaz

6 Then Job answered:
   ²"I wish my suffering could be
     weighed.
   And I wish my misery could be
     put on the scales.
³My sadness would be heavier than
     the sand of the seas.
   No wonder my words seem
     careless.
⁴The arrows of God All-Powerful
     are in me.
   My spirit drinks in their poison.
   God's terrors are gathered
     against me.
⁵A wild donkey does not bray when
     it has grass to eat.
   An ox is quiet when it has feed.
⁶Tasteless food is not eaten
     without salt.
   There is no flavour in the white
     part of an egg.
⁷I refuse to touch it.
   Such food makes me sick.

⁸"How I wish I might have what I
     ask for.
   How I wish God would give me
     what I hope for.
⁹I wish God would be willing to
     crush me
   and reach out his hand to
     destroy me.

¹⁰Then I would have this comfort.
    I would be glad even in this
        unending pain.
    I would know I did not reject
        the words of the Holy One.
¹¹"I do not have the strength to
        wait.
    There is nothing to hope for so
        how can I be patient?
¹²I do not have the strength of
        stone.
    My flesh is not bronze.
¹³I have no power to help myself.
    This is because success has
        been taken away from me.
¹⁴"They say, 'A man's friends
        should be kind to him when
        he is in trouble.
    This should be done even if he
        stops fearing God
        All-Powerful'.
¹⁵But my brothers cannot be
        counted on.
    They are like streams that do
        not flow regularly,
    streams that sometimes run
        over.
¹⁶They are like streams made dark
        by melting ice,
    that rise with melting snow.
¹⁷But they stop flowing when it is
        the dry season.
    They go away when it is hot.
¹⁸Groups of travellers turn away
        from their paths.
    They go into the desert and die.
¹⁹The groups of travellers from
        Tema look for water.
    The traders of Sheba who travel
        look hopefully.
²⁰They are upset because they had
        been sure.
    But when they arrive, they are
        disappointed.
²¹You also have been no help.
    You see something terrible, and
        you are afraid.
²²I have never said, 'Give me a gift.
    Use your wealth to pay my
        debt.

²³Save me from the enemy's power.
    Buy me back from the clutches
        of cruel people'.
²⁴"Teach me, and I will be quiet.
    Show me where I have been
        wrong.
²⁵Honest words are painful!
    But your arguments prove
        nothing.
²⁶Do you mean to correct what I
        say?
    Will you treat the words of a
        troubled man as if they were
        only wind?
²⁷You would even throw lots*d* for
        orphans.
    And you would trade away your
        friend.
²⁸"But now please look at me.
    I would not lie to your face.
²⁹Change your mind. Do not be
        unfair.
    Think again, because my
        innocence is being
        questioned.
³⁰What I am saying is not wicked.
    I can tell the difference between
        right and wrong.

7 "Man has a hard task on earth.
    His days are like those of a
        hired man.
²Man is like a slave wishing for the
        evening shadows.
    Or he is like a hired man who
        wants his pay.
³But I am given months that are
        empty.
    Nights of misery have been
        given to me.
⁴When I lie down, I think, 'How
        long is it until I get up?'
    The night is long, and I toss
        until dawn.
⁵My body is covered with worms
        and scabs.
    My skin is broken and full of
        running sores.

⁶"My days go by faster than a
        weaver moves his tool.

And they come to an end
  without hope.
[7]Remember, God, that my life is
  only as long as a breath.
My eyes will never see happy
  times again.
[8]Those who see me now will see
  me no more.
You will look for me, but I will
  be gone.
[9]A cloud disappears and is gone.
In the same way, a person who
  goes where the dead are
  does not return.
[10]He will never come back to his
  house again.
His place will not know him any
  more.
[11]"So I will not stay quiet.
I will speak out in the suffering
  of my spirit.
I will complain because I am so
  unhappy.
[12]I am not the sea or the sea
  monster.
So why have you set a guard
  over me?
[13]Sometimes I think my bed will
  comfort me.
Or I think my couch will stop
  my complaint.
[14]Then you frighten me with
  dreams.
You terrify me with visions.
[15]My throat prefers to be choked.
My bones welcome death.
[16]I hate my life. I don't want to live
  for ever.
Let me alone. My days have no
  meaning.
[17]"Why do you make man so
  important?
Why do you give him so much
  attention?
[18]Will you examine him every
  morning?
Why do you test him every
  moment?
[19]Will you never look away from
  me?

Will you not let me alone even
  long enough to swallow?
[20]If I have sinned, what have I done
  to you,
  you watcher of men?
Why have you made me your
  target?
Have I become a heavy load for
  you?
[21]Why don't you pardon my wrongs
  and forgive my sins?
I will soon lie down in the dust
  and die.
You will search for me, but I
  will be no more."

Bildad Speaks to Job

8 Then Bildad the Shuhite answered:

[2]"How long will you say such
  things?
Your words are no more than a
  strong wind.
[3]God does not twist fairness.
God All-Powerful does not make
  wrong what is right.
[4]Your children sinned against God.
And he punished them for their
  sins.
[5]But you should ask God for help.
Pray to God All-Powerful for
  mercy.
[6]You must be good and honest.
Then he will start doing
  something for you.
And he will bring you back
  where you belong.
[7]The place you began will seem
  unimportant
because your future will be so
  successful.

[8]"Ask old people
  and find out what their ancestors
  learned.
[9]We were only born yesterday and
  know nothing.
Our days on earth are like only
  a shadow.
[10]Those people will teach you and
  tell you.

They will tell you what they
    know.
[11]Papyrus[d] plants cannot grow tall
    where there is no wet land.
Reeds cannot grow tall without
    water.
[12]While they are still growing and
    not yet cut,
they will dry up more quickly
    than grass.
[13]That is what will happen to
    everyone who forgets God.
The hope of the person without
    God will be gone.
[14]What he trusts in is easily broken.
    It is as easily broken as a
    spider's web.
[15]He leans on the spider's web, but
    it breaks.
He holds on to it, but it does
    not hold him up.
[16]He is like a well-watered plant in
    the sunshine.
The plant spreads its roots all
    through the garden.
[17]It wraps its roots around a pile of
    rocks.
And it looks for a place among
    the stones.
[18]But the plant may be torn from its
    place.
Then that place rejects it and
    says, 'I never saw you'.
[19]Then its life dries up.
And other plants grow up from
    the soil in its place.

[20]"Surely God does not reject
    innocent men.
He does not give strength to
    those who do evil.
[21]God will yet fill your mouth with
    laughter.
And he will fill your lips with
    shouts of joy.
[22]Your enemies will be covered in
    shame.
And the tents of the wicked will
    be gone."

Job Answers Bildad

9 Then Job answered:
[2]"Yes, I know that this is true.
But how can man be right in the
    presence of God?
[3]A person might want to argue
    with God.
But he could not answer God
    one time out of a thousand.
[4]God's wisdom is deep, and his
    power is great.
No one can fight God without
    being hurt.
[5]God moves mountains without
    anyone knowing it.
He turns mountains over when
    he is angry.
[6]God shakes the earth out of its
    place.
And he makes the earth's
    foundations shake.
[7]God commands the sun not to
    shine.
He shuts off the light of the
    stars.
[8]God alone stretches out the skies.
And he walks on the waves of
    the sea.
[9]It is God who made the Bear,
    Orion and the Pleiades[n]
and the groups of stars in the
    southern sky.
[10]God does wonderful things that
    people cannot understand.
He does so many miracles[d] they
    cannot be counted.
[11]When he passes me, I cannot see
    him.
When he goes by me, I cannot
    recognise him.
[12]If God snatches something away,
    no one can stop him.
No one can say to him, 'What
    are you doing?'.
[13]God will not hold back his anger.
Even the helpers of the monster
    Rahab[d] lie at God's feet in
    fear.

Bear . . . Pleiades Names of well-known groups of stars.

¹⁴So how can I argue with God?
I cannot find words to argue
with him.
¹⁵Even if I was right, I could not
answer him.
I could only beg God, my Judge,
for mercy.
¹⁶I might call to him. But even if he
answered,
I still would not believe he
would listen to me.
¹⁷God would crush me with a
storm.
He would multiply my hurts for
no reason.
¹⁸He would not let me catch my
breath.
He would overwhelm me with
misery.
¹⁹When it comes to strength, God is
stronger than I.
And when it comes to justice,
no one can accuse him!
²⁰Even if I were right, my own
mouth would say I was
wrong.
If I were innocent, my mouth
would say I was guilty.

²¹"I am innocent.
But I don't think about myself.
I hate my own life.
²²It is all the same. That is why I
say,
'God destroys both the innocent
and the evil people'.
²³A whip may bring sudden death.
And God will laugh when good
people suffer.
²⁴When land falls into the hands of
evil people,
God covers the judges' faces so
they can't see it.
If it is not God who does this,
then who is it?

²⁵"My days go by faster than a
runner.
They fly away without my
seeing even a little joy.
²⁶They glide past like boats made of
papyrus*d* plants.

My days are like eagles that
swoop down on animals they
attack.
²⁷I might say, 'I will forget my
complaint.
I will change the look on my
face, and smile'.
²⁸But I will still dread all my
suffering.
I know you will hold me guilty.
²⁹I have already been found guilty.
So why should I struggle for no
reason?
³⁰I might wash myself with soap.
And I might even wash my
hands with strong soap.
³¹But you would push me into a
dirty pit.
And even my clothes would hate
me.

³²"God is not a man like me. So I
cannot answer him.
We cannot meet each other in
court.
³³I wish there was someone to
make peace between us.
I wish someone could decide our
case.
³⁴I wish someone could remove
God's punishment from me.
Then his terror would not
frighten me any more.
³⁵Then I could speak up without
being afraid of God.
But I am not able to do that.

10 "I hate my own life.
So I will complain without
holding back.
And I will speak because I am
so unhappy.
²I will say to God: Do not hold me
guilty.
But tell me what you have
against me.
³Does it make you happy to trouble
me?
Don't you care about me, the
work of your own hands?
Are you happy with the plans of
evil people?

4Do you have human eyes?
  Do you see as a man sees?
5Are your days like the days of
    man?
  Are your years like the years of
    a man?
6You look for evil I have done
  and search for my sin.
7But you know I am not guilty.
  And you know no one can save
    me from your power.
8"Your hands shaped me and made
    me.
  But now you turn around and
    destroy me.
9Remember that you moulded me
    like a piece of clay.
  Now will you turn me back into
    dust?
10You formed me in my mother's
    womb
  as cheese is formed from milk.
11You put skin and flesh on me like
    clothing.
  You sewed me together with
    bones and muscles.
12You gave me life and showed me
    kindness.
  And in your care you watched
    over my life.
13"But in your heart you hid other
    plans.
  I know this is what was in your
    mind:
14If I sinned, you would be watching
    me.
  You would not let my sin go
    unpunished.
15How terrible it will be for me if I
    am guilty!
  But even if I am right, I cannot
    lift my head.
  I am full of shame.
  It is as if I am drowning in my
    pain.
16If I hold up my head, you hunt me
    like a lion.
  And again you show your
    terrible power against me.

17You bring new witnesses against
    me.
  You increase your anger against
    me.
  Your armies come against me
    like waves of the sea.
18"So why did you allow me to be
    born?
  I wish I had died before anyone
    saw me.
19I wish I had never been born.
  Or I wish I had been carried
    straight from birth to the
    grave!
20My few days of life are almost
    over.
  Leave me alone so I can have a
    moment of joy.
21Soon I will leave and not return.
  I will go to the land of darkness
    and gloom.
22It is the land of darkest night.
  It is the land of gloom and
    confusion.
  Even the light is darkness
    there."

Zophar Speaks to Job

11 Then Zophar the Naamathite
   answered:
2"All these words should not go
    without an answer.
  Is this talker to be judged as
    right?
3Your talk should not make people
    be quiet.
  People should shame you when
    you make fun of God.
4You say to God, 'My teachings
    are right.
  And I am clean*d* in God's sight.'
5I wish God would speak.
  I wish he would open his lips to
    speak against you.
6I wish he would tell you the
    secrets of wisdom.
  This is because wisdom has two
    sides.
  Know this: God has even
    forgotten some of your sin.

7"Can you understand the secrets
of God?
Can you search the limits of the
God All-Powerful?
8God's limits are higher than the
heavens. You cannot reach
them!
They are deeper than where the
dead are. You cannot know
them!
9His limits are longer than the
earth
and wider than the sea.

10"God might come along and put
you in prison.
If he calls you into court, no one
can stop him.
11God knows which men are evil.
And when he sees evil, he
notices it.
12A stupid person cannot become
wise.
That is as impossible as a wild
donkey being born tame.

13"You must give your whole heart
to him.
You must hold out your hands to
him for help.
14Put away the sin that is in your
hand.
Let no evil live in your tent.
15Then you can lift up your face
without shame.
You can stand strong without
fear.
16You will forget your trouble.
You will remember your
troubles only as water that
has passed by.
17Your life will be as bright as the
noonday sun.
And darkness will seem like
morning.
18You will feel safe because there is
hope.
You will look around and rest in
safety.
19You will lie down, and no one will
make you afraid.

Many people will want favour
from you.
20But the wicked people will not be
able to see.
So they will not be able to find
the way to escape.
Their only hope will be to die."

Job Answers Zophar

12 Then Job answered:
2"You really think you are the
only wise people.
You think when you die wisdom
will die with you.
3But my mind is as good as yours.
You are not better than I am.
Everyone knows all these
things.
4My friends all laugh at me
when I call on God and expect
him to answer me.
They laugh at me even though I
am right and innocent!
5People who are comfortable don't
care that others have
trouble.
They think that people who are
in trouble should have more
troubles.
6The tents of robbers are not
bothered.
Those who make God angry are
safe.
They have their god in their
pocket.

7"But ask the animals, and they
will teach you.
Or ask the birds of the air, and
they will tell you.
8Speak to the earth, and it will
teach you.
Or let the fish of the sea tell
you.
9Every one of these knows
that the hand of the Lord has
done this.
10The life of every creature
and the breath of all people are
in God's hand.

11The ear tests words
  as the tongue tastes food.
12Older people are supposed to be
  wise.
  Long life is supposed to bring
  understanding.

13"But God has wisdom and power.
  He has good advice and
  understanding.
14What God tears down cannot be
  rebuilt.
  The man God puts in prison
  cannot be let out.
15If God holds back the waters,
  there is a time without rain.
  But if he lets the waters go,
  they flood the land.
16God is strong and victorious.
  Both the person who fools
  others and the one who is
  fooled belong to him.
17God leads wise men away as
  captives.
  He turns wise judges into fools.
18God takes the royal belt off of
  kings.
  And he dresses them like
  prisoners with only a cloth
  around their waist.
19He leads priests away as captives.
  He destroys the power of those
  who have been powerful.
20God makes trusted people be
  silent.
  And he takes away the wisdom
  of older leaders.
21God brings disgrace on important
  people.
  And he takes away the weapons
  of the strong.
22God uncovers the deep things of
  darkness.
  He brings dark shadows into the
  light.
23He makes nations great, and he
  destroys them.
  He makes nations large, and he
  scatters them.
24He takes understanding away from
  the leaders of the earth.

He makes them wander through
  a desert with no paths.
25They feel around in darkness with
  no light.
  God makes them stumble
  around like drunken people.

13 "My eyes have seen all this.
  My ears have heard and
  understood it.
2What you know, I also know.
  You are not better than I am.
3But I want to speak to God
  All-Powerful.
  I want to argue my case with
  God.
4But you smear me with lies.
  You are worthless doctors, all of
  you!
5I wish you would just stop talking.
  Then you would really be wise!
6Listen to my argument.
  Hear my lips begging.
7You should not speak for God by
  saying evil things.
  You cannot speak God's truth by
  telling lies.
8You should not unfairly choose his
  side against mine.
  You should not argue the case
  for God.
9You will not do well if he
  examines you.
  You cannot fool God as you
  might fool men.
10God would surely scold you
  if you unfairly took one person's
  side.
11His bright glory would scare you.
  You would be very much afraid
  of him.
12Your wise sayings are worth no
  more than ashes.
  Your arguments are as weak as
  clay.
13"Be quiet and let me speak.
  Then let things happen to me as
  they will.
14I will put myself in danger
  and take my life in my own
  hands.

¹⁵He will kill me. I have no hope."
But I still will defend my ways
to his face.
¹⁶This might really save me,
because a wicked man would not
be brave enough to come
before him.
¹⁷Listen carefully to what I say.
Let your ears hear what I say.
¹⁸See now, I have prepared my
case.
I know I will be proved right.
¹⁹No one can blame me for doing
wrong.
If someone can, I will be quiet
and die.

²⁰"God, please just give me these
two things.
Then I will not hide from you.
²¹Take your punishment away from
me.
And stop frightening me with
your terrors.
²²Then call me, and I will answer.
Or let me speak and you
answer.
²³How many evil things and sins
have I done?
Show me my wrong and my sin.
²⁴Don't hide your face from me.
Don't think of me as your
enemy.
²⁵Don't punish a leaf that is blown
by the wind.
Don't chase after dry chaff.ᵈ
²⁶You write down cruel things
against me.
You make me suffer for sins I
did when I was young.
²⁷You put my feet in chains.
You keep close watch on
everywhere I go.
And you mark the soles of my
feet.
²⁸So man wears out like something
rotten.
He is like clothing that has been
eaten by moths.

14 "All of us born to women
live only a few days and have
a lot of trouble.
²We grow up like flowers and then
dry up and go away.
We are like a passing shadow
that does not last.
³Lord, do you need to watch
someone like this?
Do you need to bring him before
you to be judged?
⁴I wish something cleanᵈ could
come from something
unclean.
But it never can!
⁵Our time is limited.
You have given us only so many
months to live.
You have set limits we cannot
go beyond.
⁶So look away from us and leave us
alone.
Leave us alone until we put in
our time like a hired man.

⁷"There is hope for a tree.
If you cut it down, it will grow
again.
It will keep sending out new
branches.
⁸Its roots may grow old in the
ground.
And its stump may die in the
dirt.
⁹But at the smell of water it will
bud.
It will put out new shoots like a
plant.
¹⁰But we die, and our bodies are
laid in the ground.
We take our last breath and are
gone.
¹¹Water disappears from a lake.
And a river loses its water and
dries up.
¹²In the same way we lie down and
do not rise again.
We will not get up or be
awakened

He . . . hope Or "Even if God kills me, I will still put my hope in him."

until the heavens disappear.

13"I wish you would hide me where
the dead are.
Hide me until your anger is
gone.
I wish you would set a time
and then remember me!
14If a man dies, will he live again?
I will wait, struggling hard
until things change for me.
15You will call, and I will answer
you.
You will desire the creature
your hands have made.
16Then you will count my steps.
But you will not keep track of
my sin.
17My wrongs will be closed up in a
bag.
And you will cover up my sin.

18"A mountain washes away and
crumbles.
And a rock can be moved from
its place.
19Water washes over stones and
wears them down.
And rushing waters wash away
the dirt.
In the same way, you destroy
my hope.
20You defeat man for ever, and he
is gone.
You change his appearance and
send him away.
21His sons are honoured, but he
does not know it.
His sons are disgraced, but he
does not see it.
22He only feels the pain of his body.
And he feels sorry only for
himself."

Eliphaz Answers Job

15 Then Eliphaz the Temanite answered:

2"A wise man would not answer
with empty words.
He would not fill his stomach
with hot, east wind.

3He would not argue with useless
words.
He would not make speeches
that have no value.
4But you even break down the
worship of God.
You stand in the way of those
who pray to him.
5Your sin teaches your mouth what
to say.
You use the same words as
people who trick others.
6It is your own mouth, not mine,
that shows you are wicked.
Your own lips speak as a
witness against you.

7"You are not the first man ever
born.
You were not born before the
hills were made.
8You cannot listen in on God's
secret advice.
You cannot limit wisdom to
yourself.
9You don't know any more than we
know.
You don't understand any more
than we understand.
10Old people with grey hair are on
our side.
They are men even older than
your father.
11The comfort God gives you is not
enough for you,
even when words are spoken
gently to you.
12Your heart has carried you away
from God.
Your eyes flash with anger.
13You speak out your anger against
God.
And these words pour out of
your mouth.

14"How can man be pure?
How can a person born to a
woman be good?
15God places no trust in his holy
ones.
Even the heavens are not pure
in his eyes.

16And man is even less than they
     are. He is terrible and
     rotten.
He drinks up evil as if it were
     water!
17"Job, listen to me, and I will tell
     you about it.
I will tell you what I have seen.
18These are things wise men have
     told.
Their fathers told them these
     things, and they have hidden
     nothing.
19(The land was given to their
     fathers only.
No foreigner lived among them.)
20The evil man suffers pain all his
     life.
The cruel man suffers during all
     the years saved up for him.
21Terrible sounds fill his ears.
When things seem to be going
     well, robbers attack him.
22The evil person gives up trying to
     escape from the darkness.
It has been decided that he will
     die by the sword.
23He wanders around. He will
     become food for vultures.
He knows death will soon come.
24Worry and suffering terrify him.
They overwhelm him. They
     seem like a king ready to
     attack.
25This is because he shakes his fist
     at God.
He tries to get his own way
     against God All-Powerful.
26He stubbornly charges at God
     with a thick, strong shield.
27"The evil person's face is covered
     with fat.
His waist is fat with flesh.
28He will live in towns that are
     ruined.
He will live in houses where no
     one lives.
They are houses that are
     crumbling into ruins.

29The evil person will no longer get
     rich. And the riches he has
     will not last.
The things he owns will no
     longer spread over the land.
30He will not escape the darkness.
A flame will dry up his branches.
God's breath will carry that evil
     person away.
31The evil person should not fool
     himself by trusting what is
     useless.
If he does, he will get nothing in
     return.
32His branch will dry up before it
     finishes growing.
It will not even become green.
33He will be like a vine whose
     grapes are pulled off before
     they are ripe.
He will be like an olive tree that
     loses its blossoms.
34People without God can produce
     nothing.
Fire will destroy the tents of
     people who take money to
     do evil.
35They plan trouble and give birth
     to evil.
Their hearts plan ways to trick
     people."

Job Answers Eliphaz

16 Then Job answered:
2"I have heard many things
     like these.
You are all painful comforters!
3Will your long, useless speeches
     never end?
What makes you keep on
     arguing?
4I also could speak as you do
     if you were in my place.
I could make great speeches
     against you.
And I could shake my head at
     you.
5But, instead, my words would
     encourage you.

I would speak words of comfort
   to bring you relief.

6"But if I speak, my pain does not
   become less.
And if I don't speak, it still does
   not go away.
7God, you have surely taken away
   my strength.
You have destroyed my whole
   family.
8You have made me thin and weak.
And people feel that this shows
   I have done wrong.
9God attacks me and tears me with
   anger.
He grinds his teeth at me.
My enemy stares at me with his
   angry eyes.
10People open their mouths to make
   fun of me.
They hit my cheeks to insult
   me.
They join together against me.
11God has turned me over to evil
   men.
He has thrown me into the
   clutches of the wicked.
12Everything was fine with me.
But then God broke me into
   pieces.
He held me by the neck and
   crushed me.
He has made me his target.
13   God's archers surround me.
He stabs my kidneys and has no
   mercy.
He spills my blood on the
   ground.
14Again and again God attacks me.
He runs at me like a soldier.

15"I have sewn rough cloth over
   my skin to show my
   sadness.
I have buried my face in the
   dust.
16My face is red from crying.
I have dark circles around my
   eyes.
17And yet my hands have never
   done anything cruel.

And my prayer is pure.
18"Earth, please do not cover up my
   blood.
Don't let my cry ever stop being
   heard!
19Even now I have one who speaks
   for me in heaven.
The one who is on my side is
   high above.
20The one who speaks for me is my
   friend.
While he does this, my eyes
   pour out tears to God.
21He begs God on behalf of a man
   as a man begs for his friend.

22"Only a few years will pass
   before I go on the journey from
   which I cannot return.

17 My spirit is broken.
   The days of my life are
   almost gone.
The grave is waiting for me.
2Those who laugh at me surround
   me.
I watch them insult me.

3"God, make me a promise.
No one else will make a promise
   for me.
4You have closed the minds of my
   friends so they do not
   understand.
So you will not let them win
   over me.
5A man might speak against his
   friends for money.
But if he does, the eyes of his
   children go blind.

6"God has caused people to use my
   name as a curse word.
People spit in my face.
7My sight has grown weak because
   of my sadness.
My body is so thin it's like a
   shadow.
8Honest people are upset about
   this.
Innocent people are upset with
   people who do wrong.

9But people who do right will
    continue to do right.
And those whose hands are not
    dirty with sin will grow
    stronger.
10"But, all of you, come and try
    again!
I do not find a wise man among
    you!
11My days are gone, and my plans
    have been destroyed.
The desires of my heart are also
    destroyed.
12These men think night is day.
When it is dark, they say, 'Light
    is near'.
13It might be that the only home I
    hope for is where the dead
    are.
I might spread out my bed in
    darkness.
14I might say to the grave, 'You are
    my father'.
And I might say to the worm,
    'You are my mother' or 'You
    are my sister'.
15If these things are true, I have no
    hope.
No one can see any hope for
    me.
16Hope will go down to the gates of
    death.
We will go down together into
    the dust."

Bildad Answers Job

18 Then Bildad the Shuhite an-
    swered:

2"When will you stop these
    speeches?
Be sensible, and then we can
    talk.
3You think of us as only cattle.
You think we are stupid.
4You tear yourself to pieces in your
    anger.
Does everyone have to leave
    the earth just for you?
Do the rocks have to be moved
    from their place for you?

5"The lamp of the wicked person
    will be put out.
The flame in his lamp will stop
    burning.
6The light in his tent will become
    dark.
The lamp by his side will go
    out.
7His footsteps will become weak
    and lose their strength.
He will fall into his own evil
    trap.
8His feet are caught in a net
    when he walks into its web.
9A trap will catch him by the heel.
And it will hold him tight.
10A trap for him is hidden on the
    ground.
It lies in his path.
11Terrible things startle him from
    every side.
They chase him at every step.
12Hunger takes away his strength.
Disaster is at his side.
13Disease eats away parts of his
    skin.
The signs of death begin to eat
    away at his arms and legs.
14The evil person is torn from the
    safety of his tent.
He is dragged off to Death, the
    King of Terrors.
15His tent is set on fire.
Burning sulphur is scattered
    over his home.
16His roots dry up below ground,
    and his branches above ground
    die.
17People on earth will not
    remember him.
His name will be forgotten in the
    land.
18He will be driven from the light
    into darkness.
He will be chased out of the
    world.
19He has no children or
    descendants[d] among his
    people.
No one will be left alive where
    he once lived.

²⁰People of the west are shocked at
    what has happened to him.
People of the east are very
    frightened.
²¹This is surely what will happen to
    the home of an evil person.
This is the place of one who
    does not know God."

Job Answers Bildad

19 Then Job answered:

²"How long will you hurt me
and crush me with your words?
³You have insulted me ten times
    now.
You attack me without shame.
⁴If I have sinned,
    it is my worry alone.
⁵Maybe you want to make
    yourselves look better than I
    do
so you can blame me for my
    suffering.
⁶Then know that God has wronged
    me.
He has pulled his net around
    me.

⁷"I shout, 'I have been wronged!'
But I get no answer.
I call loudly for help,
    but I receive no justice.
⁸God has blocked my way so I
    cannot pass.
He has covered my paths with
    darkness.
⁹He has taken away my honour.
He has removed the crown from
    my head.
¹⁰He beats me down on every side
    until I am gone.
He pulls up my hope as a tree is
    pulled up by its roots.
¹¹His anger burns against me.
And he treats me as one of his
    enemies.
¹²His armies gather.
They prepare a way to attack
    me.
They camp around my tent.

¹³"God has made my brothers my
    enemies.
My friends have become
    complete strangers.
¹⁴My relatives have gone away.
My friends have forgotten me.
¹⁵My guests and my women
    servants think of me as a
    stranger.
They look at me as if I were a
    foreigner.
¹⁶I call for my servant, but he does
    not answer.
I even beg him with my own
    mouth.
¹⁷My wife hates my breath.
My own family hates me.
¹⁸Even the little boys hate me.
When I leave, they talk about
    me.
¹⁹All my close friends hate me.
Even those I love have turned
    against me.
²⁰I am nothing but skin and bones.
I have escaped with only the
    skin of my teeth.
²¹Pity me, my friends. Pity me!
The hand of God has hit me.
²²Why do you chase me as God
    does?
Haven't you had enough of
    hurting my body?

²³"How I wish my words were
    written down.
I wish they were written on a
    scroll.
²⁴I wish they were carved with an
    iron pen into lead,
or carved into stone for ever!
²⁵I know that my Defender lives.
And in the end he will come to
    show that I am right.
²⁶Even after my skin has been
    destroyed,
in my flesh I will still see God.
²⁷I will see him myself.
I myself will see him with my
    own eyes.
How my heart wants that to
    happen!

28"You may say, 'We will continue
  to trouble Job.
The problem lies with him'.
29But you should be afraid of the
  sword yourselves.
God's anger will bring
  punishment by the sword.
Then you will know that there is
  judgement."

Zophar Answers

20 Then Zophar the Naamathite
answered:

2"My troubled thoughts cause me
  to answer.
I am very upset.
3I hear you criticise, and I am
  insulted.
But I understand how to answer
  you.

4"You know how it has been for a
  long time.
It has been this way since man
  was put on the earth.
5The happiness of an evil person is
  very short.
The joy of a person without God
  lasts only a moment.
6His pride may be as high as the
  heavens.
His head may touch the clouds.
7But he will be gone for ever, like
  his own dung.
People who knew him will say,
  'Where is he?'
8He will fly away like a dream.
He will not be found again.
He will be chased away like a
  vision in the night.
9Those who saw him will not see
  him again.
The place where he lived will
  see him no more.
10His children will have to make up
  for how he mistreated the
  poor.
He will have to give his wealth
  back with his own hands.
11He has the strength of his youth
  in his bones.

But it will lie with him in the
  dust of death.

12"Evil may taste sweet in the evil
  person's mouth.
He may hide it under his
  tongue.
13He cannot stand to let go of it.
So he keeps it in his mouth.
14But his food will turn sour in his
  stomach.
It will be like the poison of a
  snake inside him.
15He has swallowed riches, but he
  will spit them out.
God will make the evil person's
  stomach vomit them up.
16He will suck the poison of snakes.
The snake's poisonous fangs will
  kill him.
17He will not admire the sparkling
  streams
or the rivers flowing with honey
  and cream.
18He must give back what he
  worked for without eating it.
He will not enjoy the money he
  made from his trading.
19This is because he has troubled
  the poor people and left
  them with nothing.
He has taken houses he did not
  build.

20"The evil person has no rest from
  his desire.
Nothing escapes his selfishness.
21But nothing will be left for him to
  eat.
His riches will not continue.
22When he still has plenty, trouble
  will catch up to him.
Great misery will come down on
  him.
23The evil person may eat until his
  stomach is full.
But then God will send his
  burning anger against him.
God will send blows of
  punishment down on him like
  rain.

²⁴The evil person may run away
from an iron weapon.
But then a bronze arrow will
stab him.
²⁵He will pull the arrow out of his
back.
He will pull its point out of his
liver.
Terrors will come over him.
²⁶ Total darkness waits for his
treasure.
A fire not fanned by people will
destroy him.
That fire will burn up what is
left of his tent.
²⁷The heavens will show his guilt.
The earth will rise up against
him.
²⁸A flood will carry his house away.
The rushing waters will come on
the day of God's anger.
²⁹This is what God plans for evil
people.
This is what he has decided they
will receive."

Job Answers Zophar

21 Then Job answered:
²"Listen carefully to my
words.
Let this be the way you comfort
me.
³Be patient while I speak.
After I have finished, you may
continue to make fun of me
if you wish.

⁴"My complaint is not just against
people.
I have reason to be impatient.
⁵Look at me then and be shocked.
Put your hand over your mouth
in shock.
⁶When I think about this, I am
terribly afraid.
My body shakes!
⁷Why do evil people live a long
time?
They grow old and become
more powerful.

⁸They see their children become
strong around them.
They watch their children grow
up.
⁹Their homes are safe and without
fear.
God does not punish them.
¹⁰Their bulls never fail to mate.
Their cows have healthy calves.
¹¹Their children run and play like
flocks of lambs.
Their little ones dance about.
¹²They sing to the music of
tambourines*d* and harps.
The sound of the flute makes
them happy.
¹³Evil people enjoy success during
their lives.
Then they go down in peace to
where the dead are.
¹⁴But they say to God, 'Leave us
alone!
We don't want to know your
ways.
¹⁵Who is God All-Powerful that we
should serve him?
We would gain nothing by
praying to him'.
¹⁶But the wicked think they succeed
by their own strength.
Their way of thinking is not
godly.
¹⁷Yet how often is the lamp of evil
people turned off?
How often does trouble come to
them?
How often do they suffer the
punishment God plans in his
anger?
¹⁸How often are they like straw in
the wind
or like chaff*d* that is blown away
by a storm?
¹⁹It is said, 'God saves up a man's
punishment for the man's
children'.
God should punish the evil
person himself so he will
know it.
²⁰His eyes should see his own
destruction.

He should suffer the anger of God All-Powerful.

²¹He does not care about the family he leaves behind
when his life has come to an end.

²²"No one can teach knowledge to God.
He is the one who judges even the most important people.

²³One man dies while he still has all his strength.
He feels completely safe and comfortable.

²⁴His body was well fed.
And his bones were strong and healthy.

²⁵But another man dies with an unhappy heart.
He never had any happiness.

²⁶These two men are buried next to each other.
And worms cover both of them.

²⁷"I know very well what you are thinking.
I know your plans to do wrong to me.

²⁸You say about me, 'Now where is this great man's house?
And where are the tents where the evil men lived?'

²⁹You have never asked those who travel.
You have not listened to their stories.

³⁰On the day of God's anger and punishment,
it is the evil man who is spared.

³¹Who will accuse him to his face?
No one pays him back for the evil he has done.

³²He is carried to his grave.
And someone keeps watch over his tomb.

³³The earth in the valley will seem sweet to him.
Everybody follows after him.
Many people go before him.

³⁴"So you cannot comfort me with this nonsense.
Your answers are still only lies!"

Eliphaz Answers

22 Then Eliphaz the Temanite answered:

²"A man cannot be of any real use to God.
Even a wise man does him no good.

³It does not help God All-Powerful for you to be good.
He gains nothing if you are innocent.

⁴God does not punish you for respecting him.
He does not bring you into court for this.

⁵No! It is because your evil is without limits.
And your sins have no end.

⁶You took your brothers' things to pay a debt they didn't owe.
You took clothes from people and left them naked.

⁷You did not give water to tired people.
And you kept food away from the hungry.

⁸You were a powerful man who owned land.
You were honoured and lived in the land.

⁹But you sent widows away without giving them anything.
You even mistreated orphans.

¹⁰That is why traps are all around you.
That is why sudden danger frightens you.

¹¹That is why it is so dark you cannot see.
And that is why a flood of water covers you.

¹²"God is in the highest part of heaven.
See how high the highest stars are!

¹³But you say, 'God knows nothing.
 He cannot judge us through the
  dark clouds.
¹⁴Thick clouds cover him so he
  cannot see us.
 He walks around high up in the
  sky'.
¹⁵Are you going to stay on the old
  path
 where evil people walk?
¹⁶They were carried away before
  their time was up.
 Their foundations were washed
  away by a flood.
¹⁷They said to God, 'Leave us
  alone!
 God All-Powerful can do nothing
  to us'.
¹⁸But it was God who filled their
  houses with good things.
 He did this even though their
  way of thinking was not
  godly.
¹⁹"Good people can watch and be
  glad.
 Innocent people can laugh at
  them and say,
²⁰'Surely our enemies are
  destroyed.
 And fire burns up their wealth'.
²¹"Obey God, and then you will be
  at peace with him.
 This way you can be happy.
²²Accept teaching from his mouth.
 Keep his words in your heart.
²³If you return to God All-Powerful,
  you will be blessed again.
 Remove evil from your house.
²⁴Throw your gold nuggets into the
  dust.
 Throw your fine gold to the
  rocks in the ravines.
²⁵Then God All-Powerful will be
  your gold.
 He will be the best silver for
  you.
²⁶You will find pleasure in God
  All-Powerful.
 And you will look up to him.

²⁷You will pray to him, and he will
  hear you.
 And you will keep your promises
  to him.
²⁸Anything you decide will be done.
 And light will shine on your
  ways.
²⁹When terrible things happen to
  people, you will say, 'Have
  courage'.
 Then those who are humble will
  be saved.
³⁰Even the guilty will escape.
 They will be saved because your
  hands are clean."*d*

Job Answers

23 Then Job answered:
²"My complaint is still strong
  today.
 God's hand is heavy against me
  even though I am groaning.
³I wish I knew where to find God.
 I wish I could go to where he
  lives.
⁴I would present my case before
  him.
 I would fill my mouth with
  arguments.
⁵I would know the words of his
  answer.
 And I would think about what he
  would say.
⁶He would not come against me
  with great power.
 He would really listen to me.
⁷Then an honest person could
  present his case to God.
 And I would be saved for ever
  from my judge.
⁸"If I go to the east, God is not
  there.
 And if I go to the west, I do not
  see him there.
⁹When he is at work in the north, I
  catch no sight of him.
 And when he turns to the south,
  I cannot see him.
¹⁰But God knows the way that I
  take.

When he has tested me, I will
  come out pure as gold.
11My feet have closely followed his
  steps.
  I have stayed in his way without
  turning aside.
12I have never left the commands
  he has spoken.
  I have treasured his words more
  than my food.
13"But he is the only God.
  No one can come against him.
  He does anything he wants.
14He will do to me what he said he
  would do.
  And he has many plans like this.
15That is why I am so afraid before
  him.
  When I think of all this, I am
  afraid of him.
16God has made me afraid.
  God All-Powerful has made me
  terribly afraid.
17But I am cut off by the darkness,
  by the thick darkness that
  covers my face.

24 "I wish God All-Powerful
  would set a time for judging.
  People who know God look for
  such a day, but they do not
  see it.
2Wicked people take other people's
  land.
  They steal flocks of sheep and
  take them to new pastures.
3They chase away the orphan's
  donkey.
  And they take the widow's ox
  when she cannot pay what
  she owes.
4They push needy people off the
  path.
  So all the poor people of the
  land hide from them.
5The poor become like wild
  donkeys in the desert.
  They go about their job of
  finding food.
  The desert gives them food for
  their children.

6They gather hay and straw in the
  fields.
  And they pick up leftover grapes
  from the evil man's
  vineyard.
7They spend the night naked,
  because they have no
  clothes.
  They have nothing to cover
  themselves in the cold.
8They are soaked from mountain
  rains.
  They stay near the large rocks
  because they have no
  shelter.
9The child who has no father is
  grabbed from its mother's
  breast.
  They take a poor mother's baby
  to pay for what she owes.
10So the poor go around naked
  because they have no
  clothes.
  They carry bundles of grain for
  evil people, but they still go
  hungry.
11They crush olives to get oil.
  And they crush grapes in the
  winepresses,d but they still
  are thirsty.
12Dying people groan in the city.
  People who are injured cry out
  for help.
  But God accuses no one of
  doing wrong.
13"There are people who fight
  against the light.
  God's ways are strange to them.
  And they do not stay in the
  lighted path.
14When the light of day is gone, the
  murderer gets up.
  He kills poor and needy people.
  At night he goes about like a
  thief.
15The person who is guilty of
  adulteryd watches for the
  night.
  He thinks, 'No one will see me'.
  And he keeps his face covered.

¹⁶In the dark, evil people break into houses.
But in the daytime they shut themselves up in their own houses.
They want nothing to do with the light.
¹⁷Darkness is like morning to all these evil people.
They make friends with the terrors of darkness.

¹⁸"They are like foam floating on the water.
Their part of the land is cursed.
No one uses the road that goes by their vineyards.
¹⁹Heat and dryness quickly take away the melted snow.
In the same way, the place for the dead quickly takes away those who have sinned.
²⁰The evil person's mother will even forget him.
The worms will eat his body.
He will no longer be remembered.
So wickedness is broken in pieces like a stick.
²¹These evil men are unfair to women who cannot have children.
And they show no kindness to widows.
²²God drags away strong men by his power.
But even though they seem strong, they do not know how long they will live.
²³God may let these evil people feel safe.
But he is watching their ways.
²⁴For a little while they are important, and then they are gone.
They are made unimportant and gathered up like everyone else.
They are cut off like the tops of stalks of grain.
²⁵If this is not true, who can prove I am wrong?

And who can show that my words are worth nothing?"

Bildad Answers

25 Then Bildad the Shuhite answered:

²"God rules and must be honoured.
He set up order in his high heaven.
³No one can count God's armies.
His light shines on all people.
⁴So no man can be good in the presence of God.
No one born to a woman can be pure.
⁵Even the moon is not bright, and the stars are not pure in his eyes.
⁶Man is much less! He is like an insect.
He is only a worm!"

Job Answers Bildad

26 Then Job answered:

²"You are no help to a person who has no strength!
You have given no help to one whose arm is weak!
³You have given advice to me as if I had no wisdom!
This is not great wisdom you have shown!
⁴Who has helped you say these words?
And where did you get these words you speak?

⁵"The spirits of the dead beneath the waters shake.
And so do those that live in the waters.
⁶Death is naked before God.
Destruction is uncovered before him.
⁷God stretches the northern sky out over empty space.
And he hangs the earth on nothing.
⁸God wraps up the waters in his thick clouds.

But the clouds do not break
   under the weight of the
   water.
9God covers the face of the full
   moon.
He spreads his clouds over it.
10God draws the horizon like a
   circle on the water
   at the place where light and
   darkness meet.
11Heaven's foundations shake
   when he thunders at them.
12God's power controls the sea.
   By his wisdom he destroyed
   Rahab,d the sea monster.
13God breathes, and the sky
   becomes clear.
God's hand stabs the gliding
   snake.
14And these are only a small part of
   God's works.
We only hear a small whisper of
   him.
So who can understand God's
   thundering power?"

27 And Job continued speaking:
   2"As surely as God lives, he
   has taken away my rights.
God All-Powerful has made me
   unhappy.
3As long as I am alive
   and God's breath of life is in my
   nose,
4My lips will not speak evil.
   And my tongue will not tell
   lie.
5I will never agree you are right.
   Until I die, I will never stop
   saying I was innocent.
6I will hold tightly to the right
   things I said.
My sense of right and wrong
   does not bother me at all.
7"Let my enemies be like evil
   people.
Let them be like those who are
   not fair!
8What hope does a wicked person
   have when he dies?

He has no hope when God takes
   his life away.
9God will not listen to his cry
   when trouble comes to him.
10He will not find joy in God
   All-Powerful,
   even though he calls out to God
   all the time.
11"I will teach you about the power
   of God.
I will not hide the ways of God
   All-Powerful.
12You have all seen this yourselves.
   So why are we having all this
   talk that means nothing?
13"Here is what God has planned for
   evil people.
This is what cruel people will
   get from God All-Powerful:
14They may have many children, but
   the sword will kill them.
The children who are left will
   never have enough to eat.
15Then they will die and be buried.
   And the widows will not even
   cry for them.
16The evil person may heap up
   silver like piles of dirt.
He may have so many clothes
   they are like piles of clay.
17But good people will wear what
   the evil person has
   gathered.
And those who are not guilty of
   wrong will divide up his
   silver.
18The house the evil person builds
   is like a spider's web.
It is like a hut that a guard
   builds.
19The evil person is rich when he
   goes to bed, but he is rich
   for the last time.
When he opens his eyes,
   everything is gone.
20Fears come over him like a flood.
   A storm snatches him away in
   the night.
21The east wind will carry him
   away, and then he is gone.

It sweeps him out of his place.
²²The wind will hit the evil person
without mercy
as he tries to run away from its
power.
²³It will be as if the wind is clapping
its hands at him.
It will whistle at him as he runs
from his place.

28 "There are mines where
people dig silver.
And there are places where gold
is made pure.
²Iron is taken out of the ground.
And copper is melted out of
rocks.
³Miners bring light into the mines.
They search even the deepest
parts of the mines.
They look for metal in places of
thick darkness.
⁴Miners dig a tunnel far away from
where people live.
They dig it where people never
go.
They work far away from
people, swinging and
swaying from ropes.
⁵Food grows on top of the earth.
But below ground things are
changed as if by fire.
⁶Sapphires are found in rocks.
And the dust of the earth
contains gold.
⁷No hawk knows the path.
The falcon has not seen it.
⁸Proud animals have not walked on
this path.
And no lions cross over it.
⁹Men hit the rocks of flint.
They dig away at the bottom of
the mountains.
¹⁰Miners cut tunnels through the
rock.
They see all the treasures
there.
¹¹They search the places where
rivers begin.
And they bring things hidden
there out into the light.

¹²"But where can wisdom be found.
Where does understanding live?
¹³People do not understand the
value of wisdom.
It cannot be found among living
people.
¹⁴The deep ocean says, 'It's not in
me'.
The sea says, 'It's not in me'.
¹⁵Wisdom cannot be bought with the
best gold.
Its cost cannot be weighed in
silver.
¹⁶Wisdom cannot be bought with
fine gold.
It cannot be bought with
valuable onyx or sapphire
gems.
¹⁷Gold and crystal are not as
valuable as wisdom.
And you cannot buy it with
jewels of gold.
¹⁸Coral and jasper are not even
worth talking about.
The price of wisdom is much
greater than rubies.
¹⁹The topaz from Cush cannot
compare to wisdom.
It cannot even be bought with
the purest gold.
²⁰"So from where does wisdom
come?
And where does understanding
live?
²¹It is hidden from the eyes of
every living thing.
It is hidden even from the birds
of the air.
²²The places of destruction and
death say,
'We have only heard reports
about it'.
²³God understands the way to
wisdom.
And he is the only one who
knows where it lives.
²⁴This is because God sees to the
farthest parts of the earth.
And he sees everything under
the heavens.

25Wisdom began when God gave
power to the wind.
It was when he measured the
water and put limits on it.
26It was when God made rules for
the rain.
And he set a path for a
thunderstorm to follow.
27Then God looked at wisdom and
decided its worth.
He set wisdom up and tested
it.
28Then he said to man,
'The fear of the Lord is wisdom,
and to stay away from evil is
understanding'."

Job Continues

29 Job continued to speak:
2"How I wish for the months
that have passed.
I wish for the days when God
watched over me.
3I wish for the days when God's
lamp shone on my head.
And I wish for the time I walked
through darkness by his
light.
4I wish for the days when I was at
my strongest,
when God's close friendship
blessed my house.
5That was when my children were
all around me.
And God All-Powerful was still
with me.
6Life was so good. It was as if my
path were covered with
cream.
It was as if even the rocks
poured out streams of olive
oil for me.
7I would go to the city gate
and sit in the public square.
8When the young men saw me,
they would step out of my
way.
And the old men would stand up
in respect for me.
9The leading men stopped speaking

and covered their mouths with
their hands.
10The voices of the important men
were quiet.
It was as if each man's tongue
stuck to the roof of his
mouth.
11Anyone who heard me said good
things about me.
And those who saw me praised
me.
12This was because I saved the
poor who cried for help.
And I saved the orphan who had
no one to help him.
13The dying person blessed me.
And I made the widow's heart
sing.
14I put on right living as if it were
clothing.
I wore fairness as if it were my
robe and my turban.
15I tried to be eyes for the blind.
And I tried to be feet for those
who were crippled.
16I was like a father to needy
people.
And I took the side of strangers
when they were in trouble.
17I broke the fangs of evil people.
And I snatched from their teeth
the people they wanted to
hurt.
18"I thought, 'I will live for as many
days as there are grains of
sand.
And I will die in my own house.
19I will be like a tree whose roots
reach down to the water.
The dew will lie on the branches
all night.
20New honours will come to me
continually.
I will always have great
strength'.
21"People listened to me carefully.
They waited quietly for my
advice.
22After I finished speaking, they
spoke no more.

My words fell very gently on
their ears.

23They waited for me as they would
for rain.

They drank in my words as if
they were spring rain.

24I smiled at them when they
doubted.

And my approval was important
to them.

25I chose the right way for them
and was their leader.

I lived like a king among his
army.

I was like a person who gives
comfort to sad people.

30 "But now men who are
younger than I
make fun of me.

I would not have even let their
fathers
sit with my sheep dogs.

2Their hands had no strength to
help me.

They had even lost their
strength to work.

3They were thin from being hungry
and in need.

They wandered through the dry
and ruined land at night.

4They gathered desert plants by
the brush for food.

They even ate the root of the
broom tree.

5They were forced to live away
from other people.

People shouted at them as if
they were thieves.

6These young men had to live in
dried up stream beds.

They lived in caves and among
the rocks.

7They howled like animals out
among the bushes.

And they huddled together in
the brush.

8They are worthless people without
names.

They were forced to leave the
land.

9"Now they make fun of me with
songs.

My name has become a joke
among them.

10They hate me and stay far away
from me.

But they do not mind spitting in
my face.

11God has taken away my strength
and made me suffer.

So they attack me with all their
anger.

12On my right side they attack me
like a mob.

They lay traps for my feet.

They prepare to attack me.

13They break up my road.

They work to destroy me
without anyone stopping them.

14They go forward as if through a
hole in the wall.

They roll in among the ruins.

15Great fears overwhelm me.

They blow my honour away as if
by a great wind.

My safety disappears like a
cloud.

16"Now my life is almost over.

My days are full of suffering.

17At night my bones ache.

Gnawing pains never stop.

18In his great power God grabs hold
of my clothing.

He chokes me with the collar of
my coat.

19He throws me into the mud.

And I become like dirt and
ashes.

20"I cry out to you, God, but you
do not answer.

I stand up, but you just look at
me.

21You turn on me without mercy.

You attack me with your
powerful hand.

22You snatch me up and throw me
into the wind.

You toss me about in the storm.

23I know you will bring me down to
death.

You will bring me to the place
   where all living people must
   go.

24"Surely no one would hurt a
      ruined man
   when he cries for help in his
   time of trouble.
25I have cried for those who are in
   trouble.
   My soul has been very sad for
   poor people.
26But when I hoped for good, only
   evil came to me.
   When I looked for light,
   darkness came.
27I never stop being upset inside.
   Days of suffering are ahead of
   me.
28I have become black, but not by
   the sun.
   I stand up in public and cry for
   help.
29It is as if I have become a brother
      to wild dogs
   and a friend to ostriches.
30My skin becomes black and peels
   off.
   My body burns with fever.
31My harp is tuned for singing a sad
   song.
   And my flute is tuned for the
   sound of loud crying.

31 "But I made an agreement
      with my eyes
   not to look with desire at a girl.
2What has God above promised
      those who do this?
   What has God All-Powerful on
   high planned for them?
3It is ruin for the evil people.
   It is disaster for those who do
   wrong.
4God sees my ways,
   and he counts every step I take.

5"I have not been a dishonest
      person.
   I have not lied to others.
6Let God weigh me on honest
   scales.

Then he will know I have done
   nothing wrong.
7I have not turned away from doing
   what is right.
   My heart has not been led by
   my eyes to do wrong.
   My hands have not been made
   unclean.[d]
8If I have done these things, then
      let other people eat what I
      have planted.
   And let my crops be ploughed
   up.

9"I have not desired another
      woman.
   I have never waited at my
      neighbour's door to have
      sexual relations with his
      wife.
10If I have done these things, then
      let my wife grind another
      man's grain.
   And let other men have sexual
   relations with her.
11Sexual sin is shameful.
   It is a sin which must be
   punished.
12It is like a fire that burns and
   destroys for ever.
   It would destroy all I have.

13"I have been fair to my male and
      female slaves
   when they had a complaint
   against me.
14If I have not, how could I tell God
   what I did?
   What will I answer when God
      asks me to explain what I've
      done?
15God made me in my mother's
      womb, and he also made
      them.
   The same God formed both of
   us in our mothers' wombs.

16"I have never refused anything
   the poor wanted.
   I have never let widows give up
   hope while looking for help.

17I have not kept my food to
myself.
I have also given it to the
orphans.
18Since I was young, I have been
like a father to the orphans.
And from my birth I guided the
widows.
19I have not let a person die
because he had no clothes.
I have not let a needy person go
without a coat.
20That person's heart blessed me.
This was because I warmed him
with the wool of my sheep.
21I have never hurt an orphan
even when I knew I could win in
court.
22If I have, then let my arm fall off
my shoulder.
Let it be broken at the joint.
23This is because I dread
destruction from God.
I could not do such things
because I fear his majesty.

24"I have not put my trust in gold.
I have not said to pure gold,
'You are my safety'.
25I have not celebrated my great
wealth.
I have not celebrated that my
hands had gained riches.
26I have not thought about
worshipping the sun in its
brightness.
I have not admired the moon
moving in glory
27so that my heart was pulled away
from God.
My hand has never offered the
sun and moon a kiss of
worship.
28If I had, these also would have
been sins to be punished.
I would have been unfaithful to
God if I had done these
things.

29"I have not been happy when my
enemy was ruined.

I have not laughed when he had
trouble.
30I have not let my mouth sin
by cursing my enemy's life.
31The men of my house have always
said,
'Everyone has eaten all he
wants of Job's food'.
32No stranger ever had to spend the
night in the street.
I always let the traveller stay in
my home.
33I have not hidden my sin as other
men do.
I did not hide my guilt in my
heart.
34I was not so afraid of the crowd.
I did not keep quiet and stay
inside
because I feared being hated by
other families.
35("How I wish a court would hear
my case!
Here I sign my name to show I
have told the truth.
Now let God All-Powerful answer
me.
Let the one who is against me
write down what he accuses
me of.
36I would surely wear the writing on
my shoulder.
I would put it on like a crown.
37I would explain to God every step
I took.
I would come near to God like a
prince.)
38"My land did not cry out against
me.
Its ploughed rows were not wet
with tears.
39I did not take the land's harvest
without paying.
I did not break the spirit of
those who took care of the
land.
40If I did, then let thorns come up
instead of wheat.
And let weeds come up instead
of barley."

The words of Job are finished.

Elihu Speaks

32 These three men stopped answering Job. This is because Job was so sure he was right. ²But Elihu son of Barakel the Buzite became very angry with Job. (Elihu was from the family of Ram.) He was angry because Job claimed he was right instead of God. ³Elihu was also angry with Job's three friends. They had no answer to show that Job was wrong. And yet they continued to blame him. ⁴Now Elihu had waited before speaking to Job. This is because the three friends were older than he was. ⁵But when Elihu saw that the three men had nothing more to say, he became very angry.

⁶So Elihu son of Barakel the Buzite said this:

"I am young,
    and you are old.
That is why I was afraid
    to tell you what I know.
⁷I thought, 'Older people should
        speak.
    Those who have lived many
        years should teach wisdom'.
⁸But it is the spirit in a person that
        gives him understanding.
    It is the breath of God
        All-Powerful in him.
⁹It is not just older people who are
        wise.
    Older people are not the only
        ones who understand what is
        right.
¹⁰So I say, listen to me!
    I will also tell you what I know.
¹¹I waited while you spoke.
    I listened to your explanations.
I waited while you looked for
        words to use.
¹² I paid close attention to you.
But not one of you has proved Job
        wrong.
Not one of you has answered his
        arguments.

¹³Don't you say, 'We have found
        wisdom.
Only God will show Job to be
        wrong, not people'.
¹⁴Job has not spoken his words
        against me.
So I will not use your arguments
        to answer Job.
¹⁵"These three friends are defeated
        and have no more to say.
Words have failed them.
¹⁶Now they are standing there with
        no answer for Job.
Now that they are quiet, must I
        wait to speak?
¹⁷No, I also will speak.
    I will also tell what I know.
¹⁸I am full of words.
    And the spirit in me causes me
        to speak.
¹⁹I am like wine that has been
        bottled up.
    I am ready to burst like a new
        leather bag for holding wine.
²⁰I must speak. Then I will feel
        relief.
    I must open my mouth and
        answer.
²¹I will be fair to everyone.
    I will not flatter anyone.
²²I don't know how to flatter.
    If I did, God, my Maker, would
        quickly take me away.

33 "But now, Job, listen to my
        words.
Pay attention to everything I
        say.
²I open my mouth.
    I am ready to speak.
³My words come from an honest
        heart.
    I am sincere when I speak what
        I know.
⁴The Spirit*d* of God created me.
    The breath of God All-Powerful
        gave me life.
⁵Answer me if you can.
    Get yourself ready and stand
        before me.
⁶I am just like you before God.

I was also made out of clay.
⁷Don't be afraid of me.
I will not be hard on you.

⁸"But I heard what you have said.
I heard every word.
⁹You said, 'I am pure and without sin.
I am innocent and free from guilt.
¹⁰But God has found fault with me.
He considers me his enemy.
¹¹He locks my feet in chains.
He closely watches everywhere I go'.

¹²"But I tell you, you are not right in saying this.
God is greater than we are!
¹³Why do you accuse God of not answering man's complaints?
¹⁴God does speak — sometimes one way and sometimes another.
He speaks even though men may not understand it.
¹⁵God may speak in a dream or a vision of the night.
This is when men are in a deep sleep
and lying in their beds.
¹⁶He may speak in their ears
and frighten them with warnings.
¹⁷He warns them to turn away from doing wrong.
And he warns them not to be proud.
¹⁸God does this to save a man's soul from death.
He does it to keep him from dying.
¹⁹A man may be corrected while on his bed in great pain.
He may have continual pain in his very bones.
²⁰He may be in such pain that he even hates food.
He may hate even the very best meal.
²¹His body becomes so thin there is almost nothing left of it.

And his bones that were hidden by flesh now stick out.
²²His soul is near the place of death.
His life is almost over.

²³"But there may be an angel on his side.
The angel may be one out of a thousand who will speak for the man.
He will tell the man what he should do.
²⁴The angel will beg for mercy and say:
'Save this man from the place of death.
I have found a way to pay for his life'.
²⁵Then his body is made new like a child's body.
It will be returned to the way it was when he was young.
²⁶That person will pray to God, and God will listen to him.
He will see God's face and will shout with happiness.
And God will set things right for him again.
²⁷Then the man will say to other people,
'I sinned and twisted what was right.
But I did not receive the punishment I should have received.
²⁸God bought back my life from death.
And I will continue to enjoy life'.

²⁹"God does all these things to a man.
He does them two times or even three.
³⁰He does them so a person won't die as punishment for his sins.
He does it so the man may still enjoy life.

³¹"Job, pay attention and listen to me.

Be quiet, and I will speak.
³²If you have anything to say,
   answer me.
Speak up, because I want you to
   be shown as right.
³³But if you have nothing to say,
   then listen to me.
Be quiet, and I will teach you
   wisdom."

34 Then Elihu said:

²"Hear my words, you men
   who think you are wise.
Listen to me, you men who
   think you know a lot.
³The ear tests words
   as the tongue tastes food.
⁴Let's decide for ourselves what is
   right.
And let's learn together what is
   good.

⁵"Job says, 'I am not guilty.
But God has refused me a fair
   trial.
⁶Instead of getting a fair trial,
   I am called a liar.
I have been seriously hurt,
   even though I have not sinned'.
⁷There is no other man like Job.
He takes insults as if he were
   drinking water.
⁸He is around people who do evil.
He spends time with wicked
   men.
⁹This is because he says, 'It does
   not help a man
to try and please God'.

¹⁰"So listen to me, you who can
   understand.
God All-Powerful can never do
   wrong!
It is impossible for God to do
   evil.
¹¹God pays a person back for what
   he has done.
God gives him what his actions
   deserve.
¹²Truly God will never do wrong!
God All-Powerful will never
   twist what is right.

¹³No one chose God to rule over
   the earth.
No one put him in charge of the
   whole world.
¹⁴God could decide
   to take away his spirit and
     breath.
¹⁵If he did, all people would die
   together.
And they would all turn back
   into dust.

¹⁶"If you can understand, hear this.
Listen to what I have to say.
¹⁷Can anyone govern who hates
   what is right?
How can you blame God who is
   both fair and powerful?
¹⁸God is the one who says to kings,
   'You are worth nothing'.
And he says to important
   people, 'You are evil'.
¹⁹God is not better to princes than
   other people.
He is not better to rich people
   than poor people.
This is because he made them
   all with his own hands.
²⁰They can die in a moment, in the
   middle of the night.
The rich are struck down, and
   then they pass away.
Powerful people die without
   man's help.

²¹"God watches where people go.
He sees every step they take.
²²There is no dark place or deep
   shadow
where those who do evil can
   hide from God.
²³God does not need to watch
   people more closely.
He does not need men to
   come before him for judging.
²⁴Without asking questions, God
   breaks powerful people into
   pieces.
And he puts other people in
   their place.
²⁵This is because God knows what
   people do.

He defeats them in the night,
and they are crushed.
²⁶He punishes them for the evil
things they do.
He does it so that everyone else
can watch.
²⁷This is because they stopped
following God.
They did not care about any of
his ways.
²⁸God lets the cry of poor people
reach him.
He hears the cry of the needy.
²⁹But if God keeps quiet, who can
blame him?
If he hides his face, no one can
see him.
But God still rules over both men
and nations.
³⁰ He still keeps wicked men from
ruling.
And he keeps them from
trapping others.

³¹"But suppose such a man says to
God,
'I am guilty, but I will not sin
any more.
³²Teach me what I cannot see.
If I have done wrong, I will not
do it again'.
³³So, Job, should God reward you
the way you want
when you will not change your
heart and life?
You must decide, not I.
So tell me what you know.

³⁴"Men who understand speak.
And wise men who hear me
say,
³⁵'Job speaks without knowing what
is true.
His words show he does not
understand'.
³⁶I wish Job would be tested
completely
because he answered like an evil
man!
³⁷Job has sinned, and now he turns
against God.
He claps his hands as an insult.

And he speaks more and more
against God."

35 Then Elihu said:

²"Do you think this is fair?
You say, 'God will show that I
am right'.
³But you say to him, 'What good is
it to me?
I don't gain anything by not
sinning'.

⁴"I would like to answer you.
And I want to answer your
friends who are with you.
⁵Look up at the sky and see.
Look at the clouds so high
above you.
⁶If you sin, it does nothing to God.
Even if your sins are many, they
do nothing to God.
⁷If you are good, you give nothing
to God.
He receives nothing from your
hand.
⁸Your evil ways only hurt a man
like yourself.
And the good you do only helps
other human beings.

⁹"People cry out for help when
they are in trouble.
They beg for relief from
powerful people.
¹⁰But no one asks, 'Where is God,
my Maker?
He gives us songs in the night.
¹¹He makes us more clever than the
animals of the earth.
He makes us wiser than the
birds of the air'.
¹²God does not answer evil people
when they cry for help.
This is because they are too
proud.
¹³He does not listen to their useless
begging.
God All-Powerful pays no
attention to them.
¹⁴He will listen to you even less
when you say you do not see
him.

He will not listen when you say
    your case is before him
and you must wait for him.
¹⁵He will not listen when you say
    his anger never punishes
and that he doesn't notice evil.
¹⁶So Job is only speaking useless
    words.
He says many words without
    knowing what is true."

Elihu's Speech Continues

36 Elihu continued:

²"Listen to me a little longer.
Then I will show you
that there is more to be said for
    God's side.
³What I know comes from far
    away.
I will show that God, my Maker,
    is right.
⁴You can be sure that my words
    are not false.
One who really knows is with
    you.

⁵"God is powerful, but he does not
    hate people.
He is powerful and sure of what
    he wants to do.
⁶God will not keep evil people
    alive.
But he gives troubled people
    their rights.
⁷God does not stop watching over
    those who do right.
He sets them on thrones with
    kings.
And he lifts them up on high for
    ever.
⁸People may be bound in chains.
Or trouble may tie them up like
    ropes around them.
⁹But then God tells them what
    they have done.
He tells them they have sinned
    by being too proud.
¹⁰God makes them listen to his
    warning.
He commands them to change
    from doing evil.

¹¹If they obey and serve him,
the rest of their lives will be
    successful.
And the rest of their years will
    be happy.
¹²But if they do not listen,
they will die by the sword.
And they will die without
    knowing better.

¹³"People who have wicked hearts
    hold on to anger.
Even when God ties them down
    with trouble, they do not cry
    for help.
¹⁴They die while they are still
    young.
They die among the male
    prostitutes^d at the places of
    worship.
¹⁵But God will save suffering people
    by their suffering.
He gets them to listen through
    their pain.

¹⁶"God is gently calling you from
    the jaws of trouble.
He is calling you to an open
    place of freedom.
There he has set your table full
    of the best food.
¹⁷But now you are given the
    punishment evil people
    should have.
Now you are being punished.
¹⁸Be careful! Don't be led away
    from God by riches.
Don't let a promise of much
    money turn you away.
¹⁹Neither your wealth nor all your
    great strength
will keep you out of trouble.
²⁰Don't wish for the night.
That is when people are taken
    from their homes.
²¹Be careful not to turn to evil,
which you seem to want more
    than suffering.

²²"God does great things by his
    power.
No other teacher is like him.

²³No one has planned his ways for
  him.
No one has said to God, 'You
  have done wrong'.
²⁴Remember to praise his work.
Men sing about it.
²⁵Everybody has seen it.
People look at it from far off.
²⁶God is so great! He is greater
  than we can understand!
No one can discover how many
  years he has been alive.

²⁷"God takes up the drops of water
  from the earth.
And he turns them into drops of
  rain.
²⁸Then the rain pours down from
  the clouds.
And showers fall on people.
²⁹No one understands how God
  spreads out the clouds.
No one understands how he
  thunders from where he
  lives.
³⁰Watch how God scatters his
  lightning around him.
It even lights up the deepest
  parts of the sea.
³¹This is the way God governs the
  nations.
This is how he gives us enough
  food.
³²God fills his hands with lightning.
And he commands it to strike its
  target.
³³His thunder announces that a
  storm is coming.
Even the cattle show that the
  storm is coming.

37 "At the sound of his thunder,
     my heart pounds.
It is as if my heart will jump out
  of my chest.
²Listen! Listen to the thunder of
  God's voice.
Listen to the rumbling that
  comes from his mouth.
³He turns his lightning loose under
  the whole sky.

And he sends it to the farthest
  parts of the earth.
⁴After that you can hear the roar
  when he thunders with a great
  sound.
He does not hold back the flashing
  when his voice is heard.
⁵God's voice thunders in wonderful
  ways.
He does great things we cannot
  understand.
⁶God says to the snow, 'Fall on the
  earth'.
And he says to the rain shower,
  'Be a heavy rain'.
⁷With it, God stops everyone from
  working.
That way, everyone knows it is
  the work of God.
⁸The animals take cover from the
  rain.
They stay in their dens.
⁹The storm comes from where it
  was stored.
The cold comes from the strong
  winds.
¹⁰The breath of God makes ice.
And the wide waters become
  frozen.
¹¹God fills the clouds up with water.
And he scatters his lightning
  through them.
¹²At God's command they swirl
  around
over the whole earth.
They do whatever he
  commands.
¹³God uses the clouds to punish
  people
or to water his earth and show
  his love.

¹⁴"Job, listen to this.
Stop and notice God's miracles.ᵈ
¹⁵Do you know how God controls
  the clouds
and makes his lightning flash?
¹⁶Do you know how the clouds hang
  in the sky?
They are the miracles of God,
  who knows everything.

¹⁷You suffer in your clothes
  when the land is made quiet by
    the hot, south wind.
¹⁸You cannot stretch out the sky
    like God
  and make it look as hard as
    polished bronze.
¹⁹Tell us what we should say to
    God.
  We cannot get our arguments
    ready because we do not
    have enough understanding.
²⁰Should God be told that I want to
    speak?
  A man might try to speak to
    God, but he would surely be
    swallowed up.
²¹No one can look at the sun
  when it is bright in the sky
  after the wind has blown all the
    clouds away.
²²God comes out of the north in
    golden light.
  He comes in overwhelming
    greatness.
²³God All-Powerful is too high for
    us to reach.
  He has great strength.
  He is always right and never
    punishes unfairly.
²⁴That is why people honour God.
  He does not respect those who
    say they are wise."

The Lord Questions Job

38 Then the Lord answered Job
from the storm. He said:

²"Who is this that makes my
    purpose unclear
  by saying things that are not
    true?
³Be strong like a man.
  I will ask you questions,
  and you must answer me.
⁴Where were you when I made the
    earth's foundation?
  Tell me, if you understand.
⁵Who marked off how big it should
    be?
  Surely you know!

⁶What were the earth's foundations
    set on?
  Or who put its cornerstone[d] in
    place?
⁷Who did all this while the morning
    stars sang together?
  Who did this while the angels
    shouted with joy?

⁸"Who shut the doors to keep the
    sea in
  when it broke through and was
    born?
⁹This was when I made the clouds
    like a coat for the sea.
  And I wrapped the sea in dark
    clouds.
¹⁰It was when I put limits on the
    sea.
  And I put its doors and bars in
    place.
¹¹It was when I said to the sea,
    'You may come this far, but
    no farther.
  This is where your proud waves
    must stop'.

¹²"Have you ever given orders for
    morning to begin?
  Or have you shown the dawn
    where its place was?
¹³The dawn takes hold of earth by
    its edges
  and shakes evil people out
    of it.
¹⁴At dawn the earth changes like
    clay being pressed by a
    seal.[d]
  The hills and valleys stand out
    like folds in a coat.
¹⁵Light is not given to evil people.
  Their arm is raised to do harm,
    but it is broken.

¹⁶"Have you ever gone to where
    the sea begins?
  Or have you walked in the
    valleys under the sea?
¹⁷Have the gates of death been
    opened to you?
  Or have you seen the gates of
    the deep darkness?

18Do you understand the great
    width of the earth?
  Tell me, if you know all these
    things.
19"What is the path to light's home?
  And where does darkness live?
20Can you take them to their
    places?
  Do you know the way to their
    homes?
21Surely you know, if you were
    already born when all this
    happened!
  Have you lived that many
    years?

22"Have you ever gone into the
    storehouse where snow is
    kept?
  Or have you seen the
    storehouses for hail?
23I save the snow and hail for times
    of trouble.
  I save them for days of war and
    battle.
24How do you get to the place
    where light comes from?
  Or where is the place from
    which the east winds are
    scattered over the earth?
25Who cuts a waterway for the
    heavy rains?
  And who sets a path for the
    thunderstorm to follow?
26Who waters the land where no
    one lives?
  Who waters the desert that has
    no one in it?
27Who sends rain to satisfy the
    empty land
  so the grass begins to grow?
28Does the rain have a father?
  Who is father to the drops of
    dew?
29Who is the mother of the ice?
  Who gives birth to the frost
    from the sky?
30The waters become hard as
    stone.
  Even the surface of the deep
    ocean is frozen.

31"Can you tie up the stars of the
    Pleiades?
  Can you loosen the ropes of the
    stars in Orion?
32Can you bring out the stars at the
    right times?
  Or can you lead out the stars of
    the Bear with its cubs?
33Do you know the laws of the sky?
  Can you understand their rule
    over the earth?
34"Can you shout an order to the
    clouds
  and cover yourself with a flood
    of water?
35Can you send lightning bolts on
    their way?
  Do the flashes of lightning
    report to you and say, 'Here
    we are'?
36Who put wisdom inside the mind?
  Or who put understanding in the
    heart?
37Who has the wisdom to count the
    clouds?
  Who can pour water from the
    jars of heaven?
38Who can do this when the dust
    becomes hard
  and the clumps of earth stick
    together?

39"Do you hunt food for the female
    lion
  to satisfy the hunger of the
    young lions?
40Do you hunt for them while they
    lie in their dens
  or hide in the bushes waiting to
    attack?
41Who gives food to the birds
  when their young cry out to
    God?
  And who gives them food when
    they wander about without
    any?

39 "Do you know when the
    mountain goats give birth?
  Do you watch when the deer
    gives birth to her fawn?

²Do you count the months until
  they give birth?
Do you know when the time is
  right for them to give birth?
³They lie down, and their young
  are born.
Then the pain of giving birth is
  over.
⁴Their young ones grow and
  become strong in the wild
  country.
Then they leave their homes
  and do not come back.

⁵"Who let the wild donkey go free?
Who untied his ropes?
⁶I am the one who gave the
  donkey the desert as his
  home.
I gave him the desert lands as a
  place to live.
⁷The wild donkey laughs at the
  confusion in the city.
He does not hear the drivers
  shout.
⁸He roams the hills looking for
  pasture.
And he looks for anything green
  to eat.

⁹"Will the wild ox agree to serve
  you?
Will he stay by your feeding box
  at night?
¹⁰Can you hold him to the ploughed
  row with a harness?
Will he plough the valleys for
  you?
¹¹Will you depend on the wild ox for
  his great strength?
Will you leave your heavy work
  for him to do?
¹²Can you trust the ox to bring in
  your grain?
Will he gather it to your
  threshing*d* floor?

¹³"The wings of the ostrich flap
  happily.
But the ostrich's wings are not
  as beautiful as the feathers
  of the stork.

¹⁴The ostrich lays her eggs on the
  ground
and lets them warm in the
  sand.
¹⁵She does not stop to think that a
  foot might step on them and
  crush them.
She does not care that some
  animal might walk on them.
¹⁶The ostrich is cruel to her young,
  as if they were not even
  hers.
She does not care that her work
  is for nothing.
¹⁷This is because God did not give
  the ostrich wisdom.
God did not give her a share of
  good sense.
¹⁸But when the ostrich gets up to
  run, she is so fast
that she laughs at the horse and
  its rider.

¹⁹"Job, are you the one who gives
  the horse his strength?
Or do you put a flowing mane
  on his neck?
²⁰Do you make the horse jump like
  a locust?*d*
He scares people with his proud
  snorting.
²¹He paws wildly, enjoying his
  strength.
And he charges into the battle.
²²He laughs at fear and is afraid of
  nothing.
He will not run away from the
  sword.
²³The bag of arrows rattles against
  the horse's side.
It is there with the flashing
  spears.
²⁴With great excitement, the horse
  races over the ground.
He cannot stand still when he
  hears the trumpet.
²⁵When the trumpet blows, the
  horse snorts, 'Aha!'
He smells the battle from far
  away.

He hears the thunder of
commanders and the shouts
of battle.

26"Is it through your wisdom that
the hawk flies?
Is this why he spreads his wings
toward the south?
27Are you the one that commands
the eagle to fly
and build his nest so high?
28The eagle lives on a high cliff and
stays there at night.
The rocky peak is his protected
place.
29From there he looks for his food.
His eyes can see it from far
away.
30His young eat blood.
And where there is something
dead, the eagle is there."

40 The Lord said to Job:
2"Will the person who argues
with God All-Powerful
correct him?
Let the person who accuses
God answer him!"

3Then Job answered the Lord:
4"I am not worthy. I cannot answer
you anything.
I will put my hand over my
mouth.
5I spoke once, but I will not
answer again.
I even spoke twice, but I
will say nothing more."

6Then the Lord spoke to Job from
the storm:
7"Be strong, like a man.
I will ask you questions.
And you must answer me.
8Would you say that I am unfair?
Would you blame me to make
yourself look right?
9Are you as strong as God?
And can your voice thunder like
his?

10If so, then decorate yourself with
glory and beauty.
And put on honour and
greatness as if they were
clothing.
11Let your great anger punish.
Look at everyone who is proud
and make him feel
unimportant.
12Look at everyone who is proud
and bring him under your
control.
Crush the wicked wherever they
are.
13Bury them all in the ground together.
Cover their faces in the grave.
14If you can do that, then I myself
will praise you
because you are strong enough
to save yourself.

15"Look at the behemoth.ⁿ
I made him just as I made you.
He eats grass like an ox.
16Look at the strength he has in his
body.
The muscles of his stomach are
powerful!
17His tail extends like a cedar tree.
The muscles of his thighs are
woven together.
18His bones are like tubes of bronze
metal.
His legs are like bars of iron.
19He is one of the first of God's
works.
But God, his Maker, can
destroy him.
20The hills, where the wild animals
play,
provide food for him.
21He lies under the lotus plants
hidden by the tall grass in the
swamp.
22The lotus plants hide him in their
shadow.
The poplar trees by the streams
surround him.

behemoth A large land animal. It could refer to the hippopotamus, the elephant or a monster.

23If the river floods, he will not be
 afraid.
 He is not afraid even if the
  Jordan River rushes to his
  mouth.
24Can anyone blind his eyes and
  capture him?
 Can anyone put hooks in his
  nose?

41 "Can you catch the
  leviathan* on a fish-hook?
 Or can you tie his tongue down
  with a rope?
2Can you put a cord through his
  nose
 or put a hook in his jaw?
3Will he keep begging you for
  mercy?
 Will he speak to you with gentle
  words?
4Will he make an agreement with
  you?
 Will he let you take him as your
  slave for life?
5Can you make a pet of the
  leviathan as you would a
  bird?
 Or can you put him on a leash
  for your girls?
6Will traders try to bargain with
  you for him?
 Will they divide him up among
  the traders?
7Can you stick him with darts until
  his skin is full of them?
 Or can you fill his head with
  fishing spears?
8If you put one hand on him,
 you will never forget the battle.
 And you will never do it again!
9There is no hope of defeating
  him.
 Just seeing him overwhelms
  people.
10No one is brave enough to make
  him angry.
 So who would be able to stand
  up against me?

11No one has ever given me
  anything that I must pay
  back.
 Everything under heaven
  belongs to me.
12"I can silence his bragging.
 I can silence his brave words
  and powerful arguments.
13No one can tear off his outer hide.
 No one can poke through his
  double armour.
14No one can force open his great
  jaws.
 There are frightening teeth all
  around his jaws.
15He has rows of shields on his
  back.
 They are tightly sealed
  together.
16Each shield is so close to the next
  one
 that no air can go between
  them.
17They are joined strongly to one
  another.
 They hold on to each other and
  cannot be broken apart.
18When he snorts, flashes of light
  are thrown out.
 His eyes look like the light at
  dawn.
19Flames blaze from his mouth.
 Sparks of fire shoot out.
20Smoke pours out of his nose
 as if coming from a large pot
  over a hot fire.
21His breath sets coals on fire.
 And flames come out of his
  mouth.
22There is great strength in his
  neck.
 People are afraid and run away
  from him.
23The folds of his skin are tightly
  joined.
 They are set and cannot be
  moved.
24His chest is as hard as a rock.

leviathan Possibly a crocodile or a sea monster.

It is as hard as a stone used to
grind grain.
25Powerful creatures fear his
terrible looks.
They draw back in fear as he
moves.
26The sword that hits him does not
hurt him.
The darts and spears, small and
large, do not hurt him.
27He treats iron as if it were straw.
And he treats bronze metal as if
it were rotten wood.
28He does not run away from
arrows.
Stones from slings are like chaff*d*
to him.
29Clubs feel like pieces of straw to
him.
And he laughs when they shake
a spear at him.
30The underside of his body is like
broken pieces of pottery.
It leaves a trail in the mud like a
threshing*d* board.
31He makes the deep sea bubble
like a boiling pot.
And he stirs up the sea like a
pot of oil.
32When he swims, he leaves a
shining path in the water.
It makes the sea look as if it had
white hair.
33Nothing else on earth is equal to
him.
He is a creature without fear.
34He looks down on all those who
are too proud.
He is king over all proud
creatures."

Job Answers the Lord

42 Then Job answered the Lord:
2"I know that you can do all
things.
No plan of yours can be ruined.
3You asked, 'Who is this that made
my purpose unclear by
saying things that are not
true?'

Surely I talked about things I did
not understand.
I spoke of things too wonderful
for me to know.

4You said, 'Listen now, and I will
speak.
I will ask you questions.
And you must answer me'.
5My ears had heard of you before.
But now my eyes have seen
you.
6So now I hate myself.
I will change my heart and life
and sit in the dust and
ashes."

End of the Story

7After the Lord had said these
things to Job, he spoke to Eliphaz the
Temanite. The Lord said to him, "I
am angry with you and your two
friends. This is because you have not
said what is right about me. But my
servant Job did. 8So now take seven
bulls and seven male sheep. Go to my
servant Job. And offer a burnt offering
for yourselves. My servant Job will
pray for you. And I will listen to his
prayer. Then I will not punish you for
being foolish. You have not said what
is right about me. But my servant Job
did." 9So Eliphaz the Temanite did as
the Lord told him to do. Bildad the
Shuhite and Zophar the Naamathite
also did as the Lord said. And the
Lord listened to Job's prayer.

10After Job had prayed for his
friends, God gave him success again.
God gave Job twice as much as he had
owned before. 11Job's brothers and
sisters came to his house. Everyone
who had known him before came to
his house. And they all ate with him
there. They comforted Job and spoke
kindly to him. They made him feel better about the trouble the Lord had
brought on him. And each one gave
Job a piece of silver and a gold ring.
12The Lord blessed the last part of

Job's life even more than the first part. Job had 14,000 sheep and 6,000 camels. He had 1,000 pairs of oxen and 1,000 female donkeys. 13Job also had seven sons and three daughters. 14He named the first daughter Jemimah. The second daughter he named Keziah. And his third daughter he named Keren-Happuch. 15There were no other women in all the land as beautiful as Job's daughters. And their father Job gave them land to own along with their brothers.

16After this, Job lived 140 years. He lived to see his children, grandchildren, great-grandchildren and great-great-grandchildren. 17Then Job died. He was old and had lived many years.

PSALMS

The Songbook of Israel

Book 1

Two Ways to Live

1 Happy is the person who doesn't
listen to the wicked.
He doesn't go where sinners go.
He doesn't do what bad people
do.
²He loves the Lord's teachings.
He thinks about those teachings
day and night.
³He is strong, like a tree planted
by a river.
It produces fruit in season.
Its leaves don't die.
Everything he does will succeed.

⁴But wicked people are not like
that.
They are like useless chaff*d*
that the wind blows away.
⁵So the wicked will not escape
God's punishment.
Sinners will not worship God
with good people.
⁶This is because the Lord protects
good people.
But the wicked will be
destroyed.

God's Chosen King

2 Why are the nations so angry?
Why are the people making
useless plans?
²The kings of the earth prepare to
fight.
Their leaders make plans
together
against the Lord
and his appointed king.
³"Let's break the chains that hold
us prisoners.
Let's throw off the ropes that
tie us," the nations say.

⁴But the Lord in heaven laughs.
He makes fun of them.
⁵Then the Lord warns them.
He frightens them with his
anger.
⁶He says, "I have appointed my
own king!
He will rule in Jerusalem on my
holy mountain."

⁷Now I will tell you what the Lord
has declared:
He said to me, "You are my son.
Today I have become your
father.
⁸If you ask me, I will give you the
nations.
All the people on earth will be
yours.
⁹You will make them obey you by
punishing them with an iron
rod.
You will break them into pieces
like pottery."

¹⁰So, kings, be wise.
Rulers, learn this lesson.
¹¹Obey the Lord with great fear.
Be happy, but tremble.
¹²Show that you are loyal to his
son.
Otherwise you will be
destroyed.
He can quickly become angry.
But happy are those who trust
him for protection.

A Morning Prayer

David sang this when he ran away from
his son Absalom.

3 Lord, I have many enemies!
Many people have turned
against me.
²Many people are talking about me.

They say, "God won't rescue
   him."   *Selah*^d

³But, Lord, you are my shield.
  You are my wonderful God who
    gives me courage.
⁴I will pray to the Lord.
  And he will answer me from his
    holy mountain.   *Selah*

⁵I can lie down and go to sleep.
  And I will wake up again
  because the Lord protects me.
⁶Thousands of enemies may
    surround me.
  But I am not afraid.

⁷Lord, rise up!
  My God, come and save me!
  You have hit my enemies on the
    cheek.
  You have broken the teeth of
    the wicked.
⁸The Lord can save his people.
  Lord, bless your people.   *Selah*

An Evening Prayer

For the director of music. With stringed
instruments. A song of David.

4 Answer me when I pray to you,
    my God who does what is right.
Lift the load that I carry.
  Be kind to me and hear my
    prayer.

²People, how long will you turn my
    honour into shame?
  You love what is false, and you
    look for new lies.   *Selah*^d
³You know that the Lord has
    chosen for himself those
    who are loyal to him.
  The Lord listens when I pray to
    him.
⁴When you are angry, do not sin.
  Think about these things quietly
    as you go to bed.   *Selah*
⁵Do what is right as a sacrifice to
    the Lord.
  And trust the Lord.

⁶Many people ask,

"Who will give us anything
    good?
Lord, be kind to us."
⁷But you have made me very
    happy.
I am happier than they are,
  even with all their grain and
    wine.
⁸I go to bed and sleep in peace.
  Lord, only you keep me safe.

A Morning Prayer for Protection

For the director of music. For flutes.
A song of David.

5 Lord, listen to my words.
    Understand what I am thinking.
²Listen to my cry for help.
  My king and my God, I pray to
    you.
³Lord, every morning you hear my
    voice.
  Every morning, I tell you what I
    need.
  And I wait for your answer.

⁴You are not a God who is pleased
    with what is wicked.
  You do not live with those who
    do evil.
⁵Those people who make fun of
    you cannot stand before you.
  You hate all those who do
    wrong.
⁶You destroy liars.
  The Lord hates those who kill
    and trick others.

⁷Because of your great love,
  I can come into your Temple.^d
Because I fear and respect you,
  I can worship in your holy
    Temple.
⁸Lord, since I have many enemies,
  show me the right thing to do.
  Show me clearly how you want
    me to live.

⁹With their mouths my enemies do
    not tell the truth.
  In their hearts they want to
    destroy people.

Their throats are like open
graves.
They use their tongues for
telling lies.
10God, declare them guilty!
Let them fall into their own
traps.
Send them away because their
sins are many.
They have turned against you.
11But let everyone who trusts you
be happy.
Let them sing glad songs for
ever.
Protect those who love you.
They are happy because of you.
12Lord, you bless those who do
what is right.
You protect them like a soldier's
shield.

A Prayer for Mercy in Troubled Times

For the director of music. With stringed
instruments. By the sheminith.d
A song of David.

6 Lord, don't correct me when
you are angry.
Don't punish me when you are
very angry.
2Lord, be kind to me because I am
weak.
Heal me, Lord, because my
bones ache.
3I am very upset.
Lord, how long will it be?
4Lord, return and save me.
Save me because of your
kindness.
5Dead people don't remember you.
Those in the grave don't praise
you.
6I am tired of crying to you.
Every night my bed is wet with
tears.
My bed is soaked from my
crying.
7My eyes are weak from so much
crying.

They are weak from crying
about my enemies.
8Get away from me, all you who do
evil.
The Lord has heard my crying.
9The Lord has heard my cry for
help.
The Lord will answer my
prayer.
10All my enemies will be ashamed
and troubled.
They will turn and suddenly
leave in shame.

A Prayer for Fairness

A shiggaiond of David which he sang to
the Lord about Cush, from the tribe
of Benjamin.

7 Lord my God, I trust in you for
protection.
Save me and rescue me
from those who are chasing me.
2Otherwise, they will tear me apart
like a lion.
They will rip me to pieces, and
no one can save me.

3Lord my God, what have I done?
Have my hands done something
wrong?
4Have I done wrong to my friend?
Have I stolen from my enemy?
5If I have, let my enemy chase me
and capture me.
Let him trample me into the
dust.
Let him bury me in the ground.
                              Selahd

6Lord, rise up in your anger.
Stand up against my enemies'
anger.
Get up and demand fairness.
7Gather the nations around you,
and rule them from above.
8Lord, judge the people.
Lord, defend me.
Prove that I am right.
Show that I have done no
wrong, God Most High.
9God, you do what is right.

You know our thoughts and
feelings.
Stop those wicked actions done by
evil people.
And help those who do what is
right.

¹⁰God Most High protects me like a
shield.
He saves those whose hearts
are right.
¹¹God judges by what is right.
And God is always ready to
punish the wicked.
¹²If they do not change their lives,
God will sharpen his sword.
He will string his bow and take
aim.
¹³He has prepared his deadly
weapons.
He has made his flaming arrows.

¹⁴There are people who think up
evil.
They plan trouble and tell lies.
¹⁵They dig a hole to trap other
people.
But they will fall into it
themselves.
¹⁶They themselves will get into
trouble.
The violence they cause will
hurt only themselves.

¹⁷I praise the Lord because he does
what is right.
I sing praises to the name of the
Lord Most High.

God's Greatness and Man's Worth

For the director of music. By the
gittith.ᵈ A song of David.

8 Lord our Master,
your name is the most
wonderful name in all the
earth!
It brings you praise in heaven
above.
²You have taught children and
babies
to sing praises to you.

This is because of your
enemies.
And so you silence your enemies
and destroy those who try to
take revenge.

³I look at the heavens,
which you made with your
hands.
I see the moon and stars,
which you created.
⁴But why is man important to you?
Why do you take care of human
beings?
⁵You made man a little lower than
the angels.
And you crowned him with glory
and honour.
⁶You put him in charge of
everything you made.
You put all things under his
control:
⁷all the sheep, the cattle
and the wild animals,
⁸the birds in the sky,
the fish in the sea,
and everything that lives under
water.

⁹Lord our Master,
your name is the most
wonderful name in all the
earth!

Thanksgiving for Victory

For the director of music. To the tune
of "The Death of the Son".
A song of David.

9 I will praise you, Lord, with all
my heart.
I will tell all the miraclesᵈ you
have done.
²I will be happy because of you.
God Most High, I will sing
praises to your name.

³My enemies turn back.
They are overwhelmed and die
because of you.
⁴You have heard what I complained
to you about.

You sat on your throne and
judged by what was right.
⁵You spoke strongly against the
foreign nations
and destroyed the wicked
people.
You wiped out their names for
ever and ever.
⁶The enemy is gone for ever.
You destroyed their cities.
No one even remembers them.

⁷But the Lord rules for ever.
He sits on his throne to judge.
⁸The Lord will judge the world by
what is right.
He will decide what is fair for
the nations.
⁹The Lord defends those who
suffer.
He protects them in times of
trouble.
¹⁰Those who know the Lord trust
him.
He will not leave those who
come to him.

¹¹Sing praises to the Lord who is
king on Mount Zion.ᵈ
Tell the nations what he has
done.
¹²He remembers who the
murderers are.
He will not forget the cries of
those who suffer.
¹³Lord, be kind to me.
See how my enemies hurt me.
Do not let me go through the
gates of death.
¹⁴Then, at the gates of Jerusalem, I
will praise you.
I will rejoice because you saved
me.

¹⁵The nations have fallen into the pit
they dug.
Their feet are caught in the nets
they laid.
¹⁶The Lord has made himself known
by his fair decisions.
The wicked get trapped by what
they do.   Higgaion.ᵈ Selahᵈ

¹⁷Wicked people will go to the
grave.
So will all those who forget God.
¹⁸Those who have troubles will not
be forgotten.
The hopes of the poor will not
die.

¹⁹Lord, rise up and judge the
nations.
Don't let humans think they are
strong.
²⁰Teach them to fear you, Lord.
The nations must learn that they
are only human.   Selah

A Complaint About Evil People

10 Lord, why are you so far
away?
Why do you hide when there is
trouble?
²Proudly the wicked chase down
those who suffer.
The wicked set traps to catch
them.
³They boast about the things they
want.
They bless the greedy but hate
the Lord.
⁴The wicked people are too proud.
They do not look for God.
There is no room for God in
their thoughts.
⁵They always succeed.
They are far from keeping your
laws.
They make fun of their enemies.
⁶They say to themselves, "Nothing
bad will ever happen to me.
I will never be ruined."
⁷Their mouths are full of curses,
lies and threats.
They use their tongues for sin
and evil.
⁸They hide near the villages.
They look for innocent people to
kill.
They watch in secret for the
helpless.
⁹They wait in hiding like a lion.
They wait to catch poor people.

They catch the poor in nets.
¹⁰The poor are thrown down and
      crushed.
   They are defeated because the
      others are stronger.
¹¹The wicked think,
   "God has forgotten us.
   He doesn't see what is
      happening."

¹²Lord, rise up and punish the
      wicked.
   Don't forget those who need
      help.
¹³Why do wicked people hate God?
   They say to themselves, "God
      won't punish us."
¹⁴Lord, surely you see these cruel
      and evil things.
   Look at them and do something.
   People in trouble look to you for
      help.
   You are the one who helps the
      orphans.
¹⁵Break the power of wicked men.
   Punish them for the evil they
      have done.

¹⁶The Lord is King for ever and
      ever.
   Remove from your land those
      nations that do not worship
      you.
¹⁷Lord, you have heard what the
      poor people want.
   Do what they ask. Listen to
      them.
¹⁸Protect the orphans. Put an end
      to suffering.
   Then they will no longer be
      afraid of evil people.

A Statement About Trust in God

For the director of music. Of David.

11 I trust in the Lord for
      protection.
   So why do you say to me,
   "Fly like a bird to your
      mountain.
²Like hunters, the wicked string
      their bows.

They set their arrows on the
      bowstrings.
   They shoot from dark places
   at those who are honest.
³When all that is good falls apart,
   what can good people do?"

⁴The Lord is in his holy temple.
   The Lord sits on his throne in
      heaven.
   And he sees what people do.
   He keeps his eye on them.
⁵The Lord tests those who do
      right.
   But he hates the wicked and
      those who love to hurt
      others.
⁶He will send hot coals on the
      wicked.
   Burning sulphur and a whirlwind
      is what they will get.
⁷The Lord does what is right, and
      he loves justice.
   So honest people will see his
      face.

A Prayer Against Liars

For the director of music. By the
sheminith.ᵈ A song of David.

12 Save me, Lord, because the
      good people are all gone.
   No true believers are left on
      earth.
²Everyone lies to his neighbours.
   They say one thing and mean
      another.

³The Lord will stop those lying
      lips.
   He will cut off those boasting
      tongues.
⁴They say, "Our tongues will help
      us win.
   We can say what we wish. No
      one is our master."

⁵But the Lord says,
   "I will now rise up
   because the poor are being hurt.
   Because of the moans of the
      helpless,

I will give them the help they
   want."
6The Lord's words are pure.
   They are like silver purified by
     fire,
   like silver purified seven times
     over.

7Lord, keep us safe.
   Always protect us from such
     people.
8The wicked are all around us.
   Everyone loves what is wrong.

A Prayer for God to Be Near

For the director of music.
A song of David.

13 How long will you forget me,
     Lord?
   How long will you hide from
     me? For ever?
2How long must I worry?
   How long must I feel sad in my
     heart?
   How long will my enemy win
     over me?

3Lord, look at me.
   Answer me, my God.
   Tell me, or I will die.
4Otherwise my enemy will say, "I
     have won!"
   Those against me will rejoice
     that I've been defeated.

5I trust in your love.
   My heart is happy because you
     saved me.
6I sing to the Lord
   because he has taken care of
     me.

The Unbelieving Fool

For the director of music. Of David.

14 A wicked fool says to himself,
     "There is no God."
Fools are evil. They do terrible
   things.
None of them does anything
   good.

2The Lord looked down from
   heaven at all the people.
He looked to see if anyone was
   wise,
if anyone was looking to God for
   help.
3But all have turned away.
   Together, everyone has become
     evil.
None of them does anything
   good.

4Don't the wicked understand?
They destroy my people as if they
   were eating bread.
They do not ask the Lord for
   help.
5But the wicked are filled with
   terror
because God is with those who
   do what is right.
6The wicked upset the plans of the
   poor.
But the Lord will protect the
   poor.
7I pray that victory will come to
   Israel from Mount Zion!d
May the Lord give them back
   their riches.
Then the people of Jacob will
   rejoice.
And the people of Israel will be
   glad.

What God Demands

A song of David.

15 Lord, who may enter your
     Holy Tent?d
Who may live on your holy
   mountain?

2Only a person who is innocent
   and who does what is right.
He must speak the truth from his
   heart.
3 He must not tell lies about
   others.
He must do no wrong to his
   neighbours.
He must not gossip.

⁴He must not respect hateful
　　people.
He must honour those who
　　honour the Lord.
He must keep his promises to his
　　neighbour,
　　even when it hurts.
⁵He must not charge interest on
　　money he lends.
And he must not take money to
　　hurt innocent people.

Whoever does all these things will
　　never be destroyed.

The Lord Takes Care of His People

A miktam^d of David.

16 Protect me, God,
　　because I trust in you.
²I said to the Lord, "You are my
　　Lord.
Every good thing I have comes
　　from you."
³There are godly people in the
　　world.
I delight in them.
⁴But those who turn to idols will
　　have much pain.
I will not offer blood to those
　　idols.
I won't even speak their names.

⁵No, the Lord is all I need.
He takes care of me.
⁶My share in life has been
　　pleasant.
My part has been beautiful.

⁷I praise the Lord because he
　　guides me.
Even at night, I feel his leading.
⁸I keep the Lord before me
　　always.
Because he is close by my side
I will not be hurt.
⁹So I rejoice, and I am glad.
Even my body has hope.
¹⁰This is because you will not leave
　　me in the grave.

You will not let your holy one
　　rot.
¹¹You will teach me God's way to
　　live.
Being with you will fill me with
　　joy.
At your right hand I will find
　　pleasure for ever.

A Prayer for Protection

A prayer of David.

17 Lord, hear me begging for
　　fairness.
Listen to my cry for help.
Pay attention to my prayer.
I speak the truth.
²You will judge that I am right.
Your eyes can see what is true.
³You have examined my heart.
You have tested me all night.
You questioned me without finding
　　anything wrong.
I did not plan any evil.
⁴I have obeyed your commands.
I have not done what evil
　　people do.
⁵I have done what you told me
　　to do.
I have not failed.

⁶I call to you, God,
　　and you answer me.
Listen to me now.
Hear what I say.
⁷Your love is wonderful.
By your power you save
from their enemies those who
　　trust you.
⁸Protect me as you would protect
　　your own eye.
Protect me as a bird hides her
　　young under her wings.
⁹Keep me from the wicked who
　　attack me.
Protect me from my enemies
　　who surround me.
¹⁰They are selfish.
They boast about themselves.
¹¹They have chased me.
Now they surround me.

They plan to throw me to the
    ground.
12They are like lions ready to kill.
    Like lions, they sit in hiding.
13Lord, rise up and face the enemy.
    Throw them down.
Save me from the wicked
    with your sword.
14Lord, save me from them by your
    power.
    Their reward is in this life.
They have plenty of food.
    They have many sons.
They leave money to their
    children.
15Because I have lived right, I will
    see your face.
When I wake up, I will see your
    likeness and be satisfied.

A Song of Victory

For the director of music. By the Lord's
servant, David. David sang this song to
the Lord. He sang it when the Lord had
saved him from Saul and all his
other enemies.

18 I love you, Lord. You are my
    strength.

2The Lord is my rock, my
    protection, my Saviour.
My God is my rock.
    I can run to him for safety.
He is my shield and my saving
    strength, my high tower.
3I will call to the Lord.
    He is worthy of praise.
And I will be saved from my
    enemies.
4The ropes of death bound me.
    The deadly rivers overwhelmed
    me.
5The ropes of death wrapped
    around me.
    The traps of death were before
    me.
6In my trouble I called to the Lord.
    I cried out to my God for help.
From his temple he heard my
    voice.

My call for help reached his
    ears.
7The earth trembled and shook.
    The foundations of the
    mountains began to shake.
They shook because the Lord
    was angry.
8Smoke came out of his nose.
    Burning fire came out of his
    mouth.
Burning coals went before him.
9He tore open the sky and came
    down.
    Dark clouds were under his
    feet.
10He rode a creature with wings and
    flew.
    He flew on the wings of the
    wind.
11He made darkness his covering,
    his shelter around him,
    surrounded by fog and clouds.
12Out of the brightness of his
    presence came clouds.
    They came with hail and
    lightning.
13The Lord thundered from heaven.
    God Most High raised his voice.
    And there was hail and lightning.
14He shot his arrows and scattered
    his enemies.
    His many bolts of lightning
    confused them with fear.
15Lord, you spoke strongly.
    The wind blew from your nose.
The valleys of the sea appeared.
    The foundations of the earth
    were seen.
16The Lord reached down from
    above and took me.
    He pulled me from the deep
    water.
17He saved me from my powerful
    enemies.
    Those who hated me were too
    strong for me.
18They attacked me at my time of
    trouble.
    But the Lord supported me.
19He took me to a safe place.

Because he delights in me, he
saved me.

²⁰The Lord spared me because I did
what was right.
Because I have not done evil, he
has rewarded me.
²¹I have followed the ways of the
Lord.
I have not done evil by turning
away from my God.
²²I remember all his laws.
I have not broken his rules.
²³I am innocent before him.
I have kept myself from doing
evil.
²⁴The Lord rewarded me because I
did what was right.
I did what the Lord said was
right.

²⁵Lord, you are loyal to those who
are loyal.
You are good to those who are
good.
²⁶You are pure to those who are
pure.
But you are against those who
are bad.
²⁷You save those who are not
proud.
But you make humble those who
are proud.
²⁸Lord, you give light to my lamp.
My God brightens the darkness
around me.
²⁹With your help I can attack an
army.
With God's help I can jump over
a wall.

³⁰The ways of God are without
fault.
The Lord's words are pure.
He is a shield to those who trust
him.
³¹Who is God? Only the Lord.
Who is the Rock?^d Only our
God.
³²God is my protection.
He makes my way free from
fault.

³³He makes me like a deer, which
does not stumble.
He helps me stand on the steep
mountains.
³⁴He trains my hands for battle.
So my arms can bend a bronze
bow.
³⁵You protect me with your saving
shield.
You support me with your right
hand.
You have stooped to make me
great.
³⁶You give me a wide path on which
to walk.
My feet have not slipped.
³⁷I chased my enemies and caught
them.
I did not turn back till they were
destroyed.
³⁸I crushed them so they couldn't
rise up again.
They fell beneath my feet.
³⁹You gave me strength in battle.
You made my enemies bow
before me.
⁴⁰You made my enemies turn back.
I destroyed those who hated
me.
⁴¹They called for help,
but no one came to save them.
They called to the Lord,
but he did not answer them.
⁴²I beat my enemies into pieces.
They were like dust in the wind.
I poured them out like mud in
the streets.

⁴³You saved me when the people
attacked me.
You made me the leader of
nations.
People I never knew serve me.
⁴⁴As soon as they hear me, they
obey me.
Foreigners obey me.
⁴⁵They all become afraid.
They tremble in their hiding
places.
⁴⁶The Lord lives!
May my Rock be praised.

Praise the God who saves me!
⁴⁷God gives me victory over my
enemies.
He brings people under my rule.
⁴⁸He saves me from my enemies.

You set me over those who hate
me.
You saved me from cruel men.
⁴⁹So I will praise you, Lord, among
the nations.
I will sing praises to your name.
⁵⁰The Lord gives great victories to
his king.
He is loyal to his appointed king,
to David and his descendants*d*
for ever.

God's Works and Word

For the director of music.
A song of David.

19 The heavens tell the glory of
God.
And the skies announce what his
hands have made.
²Day after day they tell the story.
Night after night they tell it
again.
³They have no speech or words.
They don't make any sound to
be heard.
⁴But their message goes out
through all the world.
It goes everywhere on earth.
The sky is like a home for the
sun.
⁵ The sun comes out like a
bridegroom from his
bedroom.
It rejoices like an athlete eager
to run a race.
⁶The sun rises at one end of the
sky,
and it follows its path to the
other end.
Nothing hides from its heat.

⁷The Lord's teachings are perfect.
They give new strength.
The Lord's rules can be trusted.
They make plain people wise.

⁸The Lord's orders are right.
They make people happy.
The Lord's commands are pure.
They light up the way.
⁹It is good to respect the Lord.
That respect will last for ever.
The Lord's judgements are true.
They are completely right.
¹⁰They are worth more than gold,
even the purest gold.
They are sweeter than honey,
even the finest honey.
¹¹They tell your servant what to do.
Keeping them brings great
reward.

¹²No one can see all his own
mistakes.
Forgive me for my secret sins.
¹³Keep me from the sins that I want
to do.
Don't let them rule me.
Then I can be pure
and free from the greatest of
sins.

¹⁴I hope my words and thoughts
please you.
Lord, you are my Rock,*d* the
one who saves me.

A Prayer for the King

For the director of music.
A song of David.

20 May the Lord answer you in
times of trouble.
May the God of Jacob protect
you.
²May he send you help from his
Temple.*d*
May he support you from Mount
Zion.*d*
³May he remember all your
offerings.
May he accept all your
sacrifices.   *Selahd*
⁴May he give you what you want.
May all your plans succeed.
⁵We will shout for joy when you
succeed.

We will raise a flag in the name
of our God.
May the Lord give you all that
you ask for.

6Now I know the Lord helps his
appointed king.
He answers him from his holy
heaven.
He saves him with his strong
right hand.
7Some trust in chariots, others in
horses.
But we trust the Lord our God.
8They are overwhelmed and
defeated.
But we march forward and win.
9Lord, save the king!
Answer us when we call for
help.

Thanksgiving for the King

For the director of music.
A song of David.

21 Lord, the king rejoices
because of your strength.
He is so happy when you save
him!
2You gave the king what he
wanted.
You did not refuse what he
asked for.   Selahd
3You put good things before him.
You placed a gold crown on his
head.
4He asked you for life.
And you gave it to him.
His years go on and on.
5He has great glory because you
gave him victories.
You gave him honour and praise.
6You always gave him blessings.
You made him glad because you
were with him.
7The king truly trusts the Lord.
Because God Most High always
loves him,
he will not be overwhelmed.
8Your hand is against all your
enemies.

Those who hate you will feel
your power.
9When you appear, you will burn
them like wood in a furnace.
In your anger you will eat them
up.
Your fire will burn them up.
10You will destroy their families
from the earth.
Their children will not live.
11They made evil plans against
you.
But their traps won't work.
12You will make them turn their
backs
when you aim your arrows at
them.
13Be supreme, Lord, in your power.
We sing and praise your
greatness.

The Prayer of a Suffering Man

For the director of music. To the tune
of "The Doe of Dawn". A song of David.

22 My God, my God, why have
you left me alone?
You are too far away to save
me.
You are too far away to hear my
moans.
2My God, I call to you during the
day.
But you do not answer.
And I call at night.
I am not silent.

3You sit as the Holy One.
The praises of Israel are your
throne.
4Our ancestors trusted you.
They trusted you, and you
saved them.
5They called to you for help.
And they were rescued.
They trusted you.
And they were not disappointed.

6But I am like a worm instead of a
man.
Men make fun of me.
They look down on me.

7Everyone who looks at me laughs.
They stick out their tongues.
They shake their heads.
8They say, "Turn to the Lord for
help.
Maybe he will save you.
If he likes you,
maybe he will rescue you."

9You had my mother give birth to
me.
You made me trust you
while I was just a baby.
10I have leaned on you since the day
I was born.
You have been my God since
my mother gave birth to
me.
11So don't be far away from me.
Now trouble is near,
and there is no one to help.
12Men have surrounded me like
angry bulls.
The strong bulls of Bashan are
on every side.
13Like hungry, roaring lions
they open their jaws at me.
14My strength is gone
like water poured out on to the
ground.
All my bones are out of joint.
My heart is like wax.
It has melted inside me.
15My strength has dried up like a
piece of a broken pot.
My tongue sticks to the top of
my mouth.
You laid me in the dust of death.
16Evil men have surrounded me.
Like dogs they have trapped
me.
They have bitten my arms and
legs.
17I can count all my bones.
People look and stare at me.
18They divided my clothes among
them,
and they threw lots[d] for my
clothing.

19But, Lord, don't be far away.

You are my power. Hurry to
help me.
20Save me from the sword.
Save my life from the dogs.
21Rescue me from the lion's mouth.
Save me from the horns of the
bulls.

22Then I will tell my fellow
Israelites about you.
I will praise you when your
people meet to worship
you.
23Praise the Lord, all you who
worship him.
All you descendants[d] of Jacob,
honour him.
Fear him, all you Israelites.
24The Lord does not ignore
the one who is in trouble.
He doesn't hide from him.
He listens when the one in
trouble calls out to him.
25Lord, I praise you in the great
meeting of your people.
These worshippers will see me
do what I promised.
26Poor people will eat until they are
full.
Those who look to the Lord will
praise him.
May your hearts live for ever!
27People everywhere will remember
and will turn to the Lord.
All the families of the nations
will worship him.
28This is because the Lord is King.
He rules the nations.

29All the powerful people on earth
will eat and worship.
Everyone will bow down to
him.
30The people in the future will serve
him.
They will always be told about
the Lord.
31They will tell that he does what is
right.
People who are not yet born
will hear what God has done.

The Lord the Shepherd

A song of David.

23 The Lord is my shepherd.
I have everything I need.
²He gives me rest in green
  pastures.
He leads me to calm water.
³ He gives me new strength.
For the good of his name,
  he leads me on paths that are
  right.
⁴Even if I walk
  through the dark valley of death,
I will not be afraid
  because you are with me.
Your rod and your staff*ⁿ* comfort
  me.

⁵You prepare a meal for me
  in front of my enemies.
You pour oil on my head.*ⁿ*
  You give me more than I can
  hold.
⁶Surely your goodness and love will
  be with me
all my life.
And I will live in the house of the
  Lord for ever.

A Welcome for God into the Temple

A song of David.

24 The earth and everything in it
belong to the Lord.
The world and all its people
  belong to him.
²He built it on the waters.
He set it on the rivers.

³Who may go up on the mountain
  of the Lord?
Who may stand in his holy
  Temple?*ᵈ*
⁴Only those with clean hands and
  pure hearts.

They must not have worshipped
  idols.
They must not have made
  promises in the name of a
  false god.
⁵It is they who will receive a
  blessing from the Lord.
The God who saves them will
  declare them right.
⁶They try to follow God.
They look to the God of Jacob
  for help.   *Selahᵈ*

⁷Gates, open all the way.
Open wide, aged doors.
Then the glorious king will come
  in.
⁸Who is this glorious king?
The Lord, strong and mighty.
The Lord, the powerful warrior.
⁹Gates, open all the way.
Open wide, aged doors.
Then the glorious king will come
  in.
¹⁰Who is this glorious king?
The Lord of heaven's armies—
  he is the glorious king.   *Selah*

A Prayer for God to Guide

Of David.

25 Lord, I give myself to you.
² My God, I trust you.
Do not let me be disgraced.
  Do not let my enemies laugh at
  me.
³No one who trusts you will be
  disgraced.
But those who sin without
  excuse will be disgraced.

⁴Lord, tell me your ways.
Show me how to live.
⁵Guide me in your truth.
Teach me, my God, my Saviour.
I trust you all day long.
⁶Lord, remember your mercy and
  love.

---

staff The stick a shepherd uses to guide and protect his sheep.
pour oil . . . head This can mean that God gave him great wealth and blessed him.

You have shown them since long
     ago.
[7]Do not remember the sins
     and wrong things I did when I
     was young.
But remember to love me always
     because you are good, Lord.
[8]The Lord is good and right.
     He points sinners to the right
     way.
[9]He shows those who are not
     proud how to do right.
He teaches them his ways.
[10]All the Lord's ways are loving and
     true
for those who follow the
     demands of his agreement.
[11]For the sake of your name, Lord,
     forgive my many sins.
[12]Is there someone who worships
     the Lord?
The Lord will point him to the
     best way.
[13]He will enjoy a good life.
     His children will inherit the land.
[14]The Lord tells his secrets to
     those who respect him.
He tells them about his
     agreement.
[15]My eyes are always looking to the
     Lord for help.
He will keep me from any traps.
[16]Turn to me and be kind to me.
     I am lonely and hurting.
[17]My troubles have grown larger.
     Free me from my problems.
[18]Look at my suffering and troubles.
     Take away all my sins.
[19]Look at how many enemies I
     have!
See how much they hate me!
[20]Protect me and save me.
     I trust you.
Do not let me be disgraced.
[21]My hope is in you.
     So may goodness and honesty
     guard me.
[22]God, save Israel from all their
     troubles!

The Prayer of an Innocent Man

Of David.

26 Lord, defend me.
     I have lived an innocent life.
I trusted the Lord and never
     doubted.
[2]Lord, try me and test me.
     Look closely into my heart and
     mind.
[3]I see your love.
     I live by your truth.
[4]I do not spend time with liars.
     I do not make friends with
     people who hide their sin.
[5]I hate the company of evil people.
     I won't sit with the wicked.
[6]I wash my hands to show I am
     innocent.
I come to your altar, Lord.
[7]I raise my voice in praise.
     I tell of all the miracles[d] you
     have done.
[8]Lord, I love the Temple[d] where
     you live.
It is where your greatness is.
[9]Do not kill me with those sinners.
     Do not take my life with those
     murderers.
[10]Evil is in their hands.
     They do wrong for money.
[11]But I have lived an innocent life.
     So save me and be kind to me.
[12]I stand in a safe place.
     Lord, I praise you in the great
     meeting.

A Song of Trust in God

Of David.

27 The Lord is my light and the
     one who saves me.
I fear no one.
The Lord protects my life.
     I am afraid of no one.
[2]Evil people may try to destroy my
     body.
My enemies and those who hate
     me attack me.
But they are overwhelmed and
     defeated.

3If an army surrounds me,
I will not be afraid.
If war breaks out,
I will trust the Lord.
4I ask only one thing from the
Lord.
This is what I want:
Let me live in the Lord's house
all my life.
Let me see the Lord's beauty.
Let me look for him in his
Temple.[d]
5During danger he will keep me
safe in his shelter.
He will hide me in his Holy
Tent.[d]
Or he will keep me safe on a
high mountain.
6My head is higher
than my enemies around me.
I will offer joyful sacrifices in his
Holy Tent.
I will sing and praise the Lord.

7Lord, hear me when I call.
Be kind and answer me.
8My heart said of you, "Go,
worship him."
So I come to worship you, Lord.
9Do not turn away from me.
Do not turn your servant away
in anger.
You have helped me.
Do not push me away or leave me
alone,
God, my Saviour.
10If my father and mother leave me,
the Lord will take me in.
11Lord, teach me your ways.
Guide me to do what is right
because I have enemies.
12Do not let my enemies defeat me.
They tell lies about me.
They say they will hurt me.

13I truly believe
I will live to see the Lord's
goodness.
14Wait for the Lord's help.
Be strong and brave
and wait for the Lord's help.

A Prayer in Troubled Times

Of David.

28 Lord, my Rock,[d] I call out to
you for help.
Do not be deaf to me.
If you are silent,
I will be like those in the grave.
2Hear the sound of my prayer,
when I cry out to you for help.
I raise my hands
toward your Most Holy Place.
3Don't drag me away with the
wicked,
with those who do evil.
They say, "Peace" to their
neighbours.
But evil is in their hearts.
4Pay them back for what they have
done.
They have done evil.
Pay them back for what they have
done.
Give them their reward.
5They don't understand what the
Lord has done
or what he has made.
So he will knock them down
and not lift them up.

6Praise the Lord.
He heard my prayer for help.
7The Lord is my strength and
shield.
I trust him, and he helps me.
I am very happy.
And I praise him with my song.
8The Lord is powerful.
He gives power and victory to
his chosen one.
9Save your people.
Bless those who are your own.
Be their shepherd and carry
them for ever.

God in the Thunderstorm

A song of David.

29 Praise the Lord, you angels.
Praise the Lord's glory and
power.

²Praise the Lord for the glory of
  his name.
Worship the Lord because he is
  holy.

³The Lord's voice is heard over
  the sea.
The glorious God thunders.
The Lord thunders over the
  great ocean.
⁴The Lord's voice is powerful.
The Lord's voice is majestic.
⁵The Lord's voice breaks the
  trees.
The Lord breaks the cedars of
  Lebanon.
⁶He makes the land of Lebanon
  dance like a calf.
He makes Mount Hermon jump
  like a baby bull.
⁷The Lord's voice makes the
  lightning flash.
⁸The Lord's voice shakes the
  desert.
The Lord shakes the Desert of
  Kadesh.
⁹The Lord's voice shakes the oaks.
The leaves fall off the trees.
In his Temple*d* everyone says,
  "Glory to God!"

¹⁰The Lord controls the flood.
The Lord will be King for ever.
¹¹The Lord gives strength to his
  people.
The Lord blesses his people
  with peace.

Thanksgiving for Escaping Death

A song of David. A song for giving the
  Temple*d* to the Lord.

30 I will praise you, Lord,
  because you rescued me.
You did not let my enemies
  laugh at me.
²Lord, my God, I prayed to you.
And you healed me.
³You lifted me out of the grave.
You spared me from going down
  where the dead are.

⁴Sing praises to the Lord, you who
  belong to him.
Praise his holy name.
⁵His anger lasts only a moment.
But his kindness lasts for a
  lifetime.
Crying may last for a night.
But joy comes in the morning.

⁶When I felt safe, I said,
  "I will never fail."
⁷Lord, in your kindness you made
  my mountain safe.
But when you turned away, I
  was frightened.

⁸I called to you, Lord.
I asked you to have mercy on
  me.
⁹I said, "What good will it do if I
  die
or if I go down to the grave?
Dust cannot praise you.
It cannot speak about your
  truth.
¹⁰Lord, hear me and be merciful to
  me.
Lord, help me."

¹¹You changed my sorrow into
  dancing.
You took away my rough cloth,
  which shows sadness, and
  clothed me in happiness.
¹²I will sing to you and not be
  silent.
Lord, my God, I will praise you
  for ever.

A Prayer of Faith in Troubled Times

For the director of music.
A song of David.

31 Lord, I trust in you.
  Let me never be disgraced.
Save me because you do what is
  right.
²Listen to me.
Save me quickly.
Be my rock of protection,
  a strong city to save me.

³You are my rock and my
          protection.
     For the good of your name, lead
          me and guide me.
⁴Set me free from the trap they
          set for me.
     You are my protection.
⁵I give you my life.
     Save me, Lord, God of truth.

⁶I hate those who worship false
          gods.
     I trust only in the Lord.
⁷I will be glad because of your
          love.
     You saw my suffering.
     You knew my troubles.
⁸You have not let my enemies
          defeat me.
     You have set me in a safe
          place.

⁹Lord, have mercy. I am in misery.
     My eyes are weak from so
          much crying.
     My whole being is tired from
          grief.
¹⁰My life is ending in sadness.
     My years are spent in crying.
     My troubles are using up my
          strength.
     My bones are getting weaker.
¹¹Because of all my troubles, my
          enemies hate me.
     Even my neighbours look down
          on me.
     When my friends see me,
          they are afraid and run.
¹²I am like a piece of a broken pot.
     I am forgotten as if I were dead.
¹³I have heard many insults.
     Terror is all around me.
     They make plans against me.
     They want to kill me.

¹⁴Lord, I trust you.
     I have said, "You are my God."
¹⁵My life is in your hands.
     Save me from my enemies'
          grasp.
     Save me from those who are
          chasing me.

¹⁶Show your kindness to me, your
          servant.
     Save me because of your love.
¹⁷Lord, I called to you.
     So do not let me be disgraced.
     Let the wicked be disgraced.
     Let them lie silent in the grave.
¹⁸With pride and hatred
          they speak against the
          righteous.
     So shut their lying lips.

¹⁹How great is your goodness!
     You have stored it up for those
          who fear you.
     You do good things for those who
          trust you.
     You do this for all to see.
²⁰You protect them by your
          presence
          from what people plan against
          them.
     You keep them safe in your
          shelter
          from evil words.
²¹Praise the Lord.
     His love to me was wonderful
          when my city was attacked.
²²In my distress, I said,
     "God cannot see me!"
     But you heard my prayer
          when I cried out to you for help.
²³Love the Lord, all you who belong
          to him.
     The Lord protects those who
          truly believe.
     But he punishes the proud as
          much as they have sinned.
²⁴All you who put your hope in the
          Lord
          be strong and brave.

It Is Better to Confess Sin

A maskil^d of David.

32 Happy is the person
          whose sins are forgiven,
     whose wrongs are pardoned.
²Happy is the person
     whom the Lord does not
          consider guilty.

In that person there is nothing
false.

3When I kept things to myself,
I felt weak deep inside me.
I moaned all day long.
4Day and night
you punished me.
My strength was gone
as in the summer heat.   *Selah^d*
5Then I confessed my sins to you.
I didn't hide my guilt.
I said, "I will confess my sins to
the Lord."
And you forgave my guilt.   *Selah*

6For this reason, all who obey you
should pray to you while they
still can.
When troubles rise like a flood,
they will not reach them.
7You are my hiding place.
You protect me from my
troubles.
You fill me with songs of
salvation.   *Selah*

8The Lord says, "I will make you
wise. I will show you where
to go.
I will guide you and watch over
you.
9So don't be like a horse or
donkey.
They don't understand.
They must be led with bits and
reins,
or they will not come near you."

10Wicked people have many
troubles.
But the Lord's love surrounds
those who trust him.
11Good people, rejoice and be happy
in the Lord.
All you whose hearts are right,
sing.

Praise God Who Creates and Saves

33 Sing to the Lord, you who do
what is right.

Honest people should praise
him.
2Praise the Lord on the harp.
Make music for him on the
ten-stringed lyre.*^d*
3Sing a new song to him.
Play well and joyfully.

4God's word is true.
Everything he does is right.
5He loves what is right and fair.
The Lord's love fills the earth.

6The sky was made at the Lord's
command.
By the breath from his mouth,
he made all the stars.
7He gathered the water in the sea
into a heap.
He made the great ocean stay in
its place.
8All the earth should worship the
Lord.
The whole world should fear
him.
9He spoke, and it happened.
He commanded, and it
appeared.
10The Lord upsets the plans of
nations.
He ruins all their plans.
11But the Lord's plans will stand for
ever.
His ideas will last from now on.
12Happy is the nation whose God is
the Lord.
Happy are the people he chose
for his very own.
13The Lord looks down from
heaven.
He sees every person.
14From his throne he watches
everyone who lives on earth.
15He made their hearts.
He understands everything they
do.
16No king is saved by his great
army.
No warrior escapes by his great
strength.
17Horses can't bring victory.

They can't save by their
strength.
¹⁸But the Lord looks after those
who fear him.
He watches over those who put
their hope in his love.
¹⁹He saves them from death.
He spares their lives in times of
hunger.
²⁰So our hope is in the Lord.
He is our help, our shield to
protect us.
²¹We rejoice in him.
We trust his holy name.
²²Lord, show your love to us
as we put our hope in you.

Praise God Who Judges and Saves

David's song from the time he pretended
to be mad so Abimelech would send him
away. And David did leave.

34 I will praise the Lord at all
times.
His praise is always on my
lips.
²My whole being praises the
Lord.
The poor will hear and be
glad.
³Tell the greatness of the Lord
with me.
Let us praise his name together.

⁴I asked the Lord for help, and he
answered me.
He saved me from all that I
feared.
⁵Those who go to him for help are
happy.
They are never disgraced.
⁶This poor man called, and the
Lord heard him.
The Lord saved him from all his
troubles.
⁷The Lord saves those who fear
him.
His angel camps around them.

⁸Examine and see how good the
Lord is.

Happy is the person who trusts
the Lord.
⁹People who belong to the Lord,
fear him!
Those who fear him will have
everything they need.
¹⁰Even lions may become weak and
hungry.
But those people who go to the
Lord for help will have every
good thing.
¹¹Children, come and listen to me.
I will teach you to worship the
Lord.
¹²You must do these things
to enjoy life and have many
happy days.
¹³You must not say evil things.
You must not tell lies.
¹⁴Stop doing evil and do good.
Look for peace and work for it.

¹⁵The Lord sees the good people.
He listens to their prayers.
¹⁶But the Lord is against those who
do evil.
He makes the world forget
them.
¹⁷The Lord hears good people when
they cry out to him.
He saves them from all their
troubles.
¹⁸The Lord is close to the
broken-hearted.
He saves those whose spirits
have been crushed.

¹⁹People who do what is right may
have many problems.
But the Lord will solve them all.
²⁰He will protect their very bones.
Not one of them will be broken.
²¹Evil will kill the wicked people.
Those who hate good people will
be judged guilty.
²²But the Lord saves his servants'
lives.
No one who trusts him will be
judged guilty.

A Prayer for Help

Of David.

35 Lord, battle with those who
battle with me.
Fight against those who fight
against me.
[2]Pick up the shield and armour.
Rise up and help me.
[3]Lift up your spears, both large
and small,
against those who chase me.
Tell me, "I will save you."

[4]Make those who want to kill me
be ashamed and disgraced.
Make those who plan to harm me
turn back and run away.
[5]Make them like chaff[d] blown by
the wind.
Let the angel of the Lord chase
them away.
[6]Let their road be dark and
slippery
as the angel of the Lord chases
them.
[7]For no reason they spread out
their net to trap me.
For no reason they dug a pit for
me.
[8]So let ruin strike them suddenly.
Let them be caught in their own
nets.
Let them fall into the pit and
die.
[9]Then I will rejoice in the Lord.
I will be happy when he saves
me.
[10]Even my bones will say,
"Lord, who is like you?
You save the weak from the
strong.
You save the weak and poor
from robbers."

[11]Men without mercy stand up to
testify.
They ask me things I do not
know.
[12]They repay me with evil for the
good I have done.
They make me very sad.

[13]Yet when they were sick, I put on
rough cloth to show my
sadness.
I showed my sorrow by going
without food.
But my prayers were not
answered.
[14] I acted as if they were my
friends or brothers.
I bowed in sadness as if I were
crying for my mother.
[15]But when I was in trouble, they
gathered and laughed.
They gathered to attack before I
knew it.
They insulted me without
stopping.
[16]They made fun of me and were
cruel to me.
They ground their teeth at me
in anger.

[17]Lord, how long will you watch this
happen?
Save my life from their attacks.
Save me from these people who
are like lions.
[18]I will praise you in the great
meeting.
I will praise you among crowds
of people.
[19]Do not let my enemies laugh at
me.
They hate me for no reason.
Do not let them make fun of me.
They have no reason to hate
me.
[20]Their words are not friendly.
They think up lies about
peace-loving people.
[21]They speak against me.
They say, "Aha! We saw what
you did!"

[22]Lord, you have been watching. Do
not keep quiet.
Lord, do not leave me alone.
[23]Wake up! Come and defend me!
My God and Lord, fight for me!
[24]Lord my God, defend me with
your justice.
Don't let them laugh at me.

²⁵Don't let them think, "Aha! We
  got what we wanted!"
 Don't let them say, "We
  destroyed him."
²⁶Let them be ashamed and
  embarrassed.
 They were happy when I hurt.
 Cover them with shame and
  disgrace.
 They thought they were better
  than I was.
²⁷May my friends sing and shout for
  joy.
 May they always say, "Praise
  the greatness of the Lord.
 He loves to see his servants do
  well."
²⁸I will tell of your goodness.
 I will praise you every day.

Wicked Men and a Good God

For the director of music. Of David,
the servant of the Lord.

36 Sin speaks to the wicked man
  in his heart.
 He has no fear of or respect for
  God.
²He thinks too much of himself.
 He doesn't see his sin and hate
  it.
³His words are wicked lies.
 He is no longer wise or good.
⁴At night he makes evil plans.
 What he does leads to nothing
  good.
 He doesn't refuse things that
  are evil.
⁵Lord, your love reaches to the
  heavens.
 Your loyalty goes to the skies.
⁶Your goodness is as high as the
  mountains.
 Your justice is as deep as the
  great ocean.
 Lord, you protect both men and
  animals.
⁷God, your love is so precious!
 You protect people as a bird
  protects her young under
  her wings.

⁸They eat the rich food in your
  house.
 You let them drink from your
  river of pleasure.
⁹You are the giver of life.
 Your light lets us enjoy life.
¹⁰Continue to love those who know
  you.
 And continue to do good to
  those who are good.
¹¹Don't let proud people attack
  me.
 Don't let the wicked force me
  away.
¹²Those who do evil have been
  defeated.
 They are overwhelmed; they
  cannot do evil any longer.

God Will Reward Fairly

Of David.

37 Don't be upset because of
  evil people.
 Don't be jealous of those who do
  wrong.
²Like the grass, they will soon dry
  up.
 Like green plants, they will soon
  die away.

³Trust the Lord and do good.
 Live in the land and enjoy its
  safety.
⁴Enjoy serving the Lord.
 And he will give you what you
  want.
⁵Depend on the Lord.
 Trust him, and he will take care
  of you.
⁶Then your goodness will shine like
  the sun.
 Your fairness will shine like the
  noonday sun.
⁷Wait and trust the Lord.
 Don't be upset when others get
  rich
 or when someone else's plans
  succeed.
⁸Don't get angry.

Don't be upset; it only leads to
    trouble.
9Evil people will be sent away.
But people who trust the Lord
    will inherit the land.
10In a little while there will be no
    more wicked people.
You may look for them, but they
    will be gone.
11People who are not proud will
    inherit the land.
They will enjoy complete
    peace.
12The wicked make evil plans
    against good people.
They grind their teeth at them
    in anger.
13But the Lord laughs at the
    wicked.
He sees that their day is
    coming.
14The wicked draw their swords.
They bend their bows.
They try to kill the poor and
    helpless.
They want to kill those who are
    honest.
15But their swords will stab their
    own hearts.
Their bows will break.
16It's better to have little and be
    right
than to have much and be
    wrong.
17The power of the wicked will be
    broken.
But the Lord supports those
    who do right.
18The Lord watches over the lives
    of the innocent.
Their reward will last for ever.
19They will not be ashamed when
    trouble comes.
They will be full in times of
    hunger.
20But the wicked will die.
The Lord's enemies will be like
    the flowers of the fields.
They will disappear like smoke.

21The wicked people borrow but
    don't pay back.
But those who do right give
    freely to others.
22Those people the Lord blesses
    will inherit the land.
But those he curses will be sent
    away.

23When a man's steps follow the
    Lord,
God is pleased with his ways.
24If he stumbles, he will not fall,
because the Lord holds his
    hand.
25I was young, and now I am old.
But I have never seen the Lord
    leave good people helpless.
I have never seen their children
    begging for food.
26Good people always lend freely to
    others.
And their children are a
    blessing.
27Stop doing evil and do good.
Then you will live for ever.
28The Lord loves justice.
He will not leave those who
    worship him.
He will always protect them.
But the children of the wicked
    will die.
29Good people will inherit the
    land.
They will live in it for ever.
30A good person speaks with
    wisdom.
He says what is fair.
31The teachings of his God are in
    his heart.
He does not fail to keep them.
32The wicked watch for good
    people.
They want to kill them.
33The Lord will not take away his
    protection.
He will not judge good people
    guilty.

34Wait for the Lord's help
and follow him.
He will honour you and give you
the land.
And you will see the wicked
people sent away.

35I saw a wicked and cruel man.
He looked strong like a healthy
tree in good soil.
36But he died and was gone.
I looked for him, but he couldn't
be found.

37Think of the innocent person.
Watch the honest one.
The man who has peace
will have children to live after
him.
38But sinners will be destroyed.
In the end the wicked will die.

39The Lord saves good people.
He is their strong city in times
of trouble.
40The Lord helps them and saves
them.
He saves them from the wicked
because they trust in him for
protection.

A Prayer in Time of Sickness

A song of David to remember.

38 Lord, don't correct me when
you are angry.
Don't punish me when you are
very angry.
2Your arrows have wounded me.
Your hand has come down on
me.
3My body is sick from your
punishment.
Even my bones are not healthy
because of my sin.
4My guilt has overwhelmed me.
Like a load it weighs me down.

5My sores stink and become
infected
because I was foolish.

6I am bent over and bowed down.
I am sad all day long.
7I am burning with fever.
My whole body is sore.
8I am weak and faint.
I moan from the pain I feel.
9Lord, you know everything I
want.
My cries are not hidden from
you.
10My heart pounds, and my
strength is gone.
I am losing my sight.
11Because of my wounds, my
friends and neighbours leave
me alone.
My relatives stay far away.
12Some people set traps to kill me.
Those who want to hurt me plan
trouble.
All day long they think up lies.

13I am like a deaf man; I cannot
hear.
Like a mute, I cannot speak.
14I am like a person who does not
hear.
I have no answer to give.
15I trust you, Lord.
You will answer, my God and
Lord.
16I said, "Don't let them laugh at
me.
Don't let them boast when I am
defeated."
17I am about to die.
I cannot forget my pain.
18I confess my guilt.
I am troubled by my sin.
19My enemies are strong and
healthy.
Many people hate me for no
reason.
20They repay me with evil for the
good I did.
They lie about me because I try
to do good.

21Lord, don't leave me.
My God, don't go away.
22Quickly come and help me,
my Lord and Saviour.

Life Is Short

For the director of music. For Jeduthun.
A song of David.

39 I said, "I will be careful how I
act.
I will not sin by what I say.
I will be careful what I say
around wicked people."
2So I kept very quiet.
I didn't even say anything good.
But I became even more upset.
3I became very angry inside.
And the more I thought about it,
the angrier I became.
So I spoke:
4"Lord, tell me when the end will
come.
How long will I live?
Let me know how long I have.
5You have given me only a short
life.
My lifetime is like nothing to
you.
Everyone's life is only a breath.
Selah[d]
6A person is like a shadow moving
about.
All his work is for nothing.
He collects things, but he
doesn't know who will get
them.

7"So, Lord, what hope do I have?
You are my hope.
8Save me from all my sins.
Don't let wicked fools make fun
of me.
9I am quiet. I do not open my
mouth.
You are the one who has done
this.
10Stop punishing me.
Your beating is about to kill me.
11You correct and punish people for
their sins.
Like a moth, you destroy what
they love.
Everyone's life is only a breath.
Selah
12"Lord, hear my prayer.

Listen to my cry.
Do not ignore my tears.
I am like a visitor to you.
Like my ancestors, I'm only
here a short time.
13Leave me alone so I can be
happy.
Soon I will leave and be no
more."

Praise and Prayer for Help

For the director of music. A song
of David.

40 I waited patiently for the
Lord.
He turned to me and heard my
cry.
2He lifted me out of the pit of
destruction,
out of the sticky mud.
He stood me on a rock.
He made my feet steady.
3He put a new song in my mouth.
It was a song of praise to our
God.
Many people will see this and
worship him.
Then they will trust the Lord.

4Happy is the person
who trusts the Lord.
He doesn't turn to those who are
proud,
to those who worship false
gods.
5Lord our God, you have done
many miracles.[d]
Your plans for us are many.
If I tried to tell them all,
there would be too many to
count.

6You do not want sacrifices and
offerings.
But you have made a hole in my
ear
to show that my body and life
are yours.
You do not ask for burnt offerings
and offerings to take away sins.
7Then I said, "Look, I have come.

It is written about me in the
book.
8My God, I want to do what you
want.
Your teachings are in my heart."

9I will tell about your goodness in
the great meeting of your
people.
Lord, you know my lips are not
silent.
10I do not hide your goodness in my
heart.
I speak about your loyalty and
salvation.
I do not hide your love and truth
from the people in the great
meeting.

11Lord, do not hold back your
mercy from me.
Let your love and truth always
protect me.
12Troubles have gathered around
me.
There are too many to count.
My sins have caught me.
I cannot see a way to escape.
I have more sins than hairs on my
head.
I have lost my courage.
13Please, Lord, save me.
Hurry, Lord, to help me.
14People are trying to kill me.
Shame them and disgrace them.
People want to hurt me.
Let them run away in disgrace.
15People are making fun of me.
Let them be shamed into
silence.
16But let those who follow you
be happy and glad.
They love you for saving them.
May they always say, "Praise
the Lord!"

17Lord, I am poor and helpless.
But please remember me.
You are my helper and saviour.
My God, do not wait.

A Prayer in Time of Sickness

For the director of music.
A song of David.

41 Happy is the person who
thinks about the poor.
When trouble comes, the Lord
will save him.
2The Lord will protect him and
spare his life.
The Lord will bless him in the
land.
The Lord will not let his
enemies take him.
3The Lord will give him strength
when he is sick.
The Lord will make him well
again.

4I said, "Lord, be kind to me.
Heal me because I have sinned
against you."
5My enemies are saying bad things
about me.
They say, "When will he die and
be forgotten?"
6Some people come to see me.
But they lie.
They just come to get bad news.
Then they go and gossip.
7All my enemies whisper about me.
They think the worst about me.
8They say, "He has a terrible
disease.
He will never get out of bed
again."
9My best and truest friend ate at
my table.
Now even he has turned against
me.
10Lord, have mercy on me.
Give me strength so I can pay
them back.
11My enemies do not defeat me.
That's how I know you are
pleased with me.
12Because I am innocent, you
support me.
You will let me be with you for
ever.

¹³Praise the Lord, the God of
Israel.
He has always been,
and he will always be.
Amen and amen.

Book 2

Wishing to Be Near God

For the director of music. A maskil^d
of the sons of Korah.

42 A deer thirsts for a stream of
water.
In the same way, I thirst for
you, God.
²I thirst for the living God.
When can I go to meet him?
³Day and night, my tears have
been my food.
People are always saying,
"Where is your God?"
⁴When I remember these things,
I speak with a broken heart.
I used to walk with the crowd.
I led the happy crowd to God's
Temple,^d
with songs of praise.

⁵Why am I so sad?
Why am I so upset?
I should put my hope in God.
I should keep praising him,
My Saviour and ⁶my God.

I am very sad.
So I remember you while I am
in the land where the Jordan
River begins.
I will remember you while I am
near the Hermon mountains
and on the mountain of Mizar.
⁷Troubles have come again and
again.
They sound like waterfalls.
Your waves are crashing
all around me.
⁸The Lord shows his true love
every day.
At night I have a song,
and I pray to my living God.
⁹I say to God, my Rock,^d

"Why have you forgotten me?
Why am I sad
and troubled by my enemies?"
¹⁰My enemies' insults make me feel
as if my bones were broken.
They are always saying,
"Where is your God?"

¹¹Why am I so sad?
Why am I so upset?
I should put my hope in God.
I should keep praising him,
my Saviour and my God.

A Prayer for Protection

43 God, defend me.
Argue my case against those
who don't follow you.
Save me from liars and those
who do evil.
²God, you are my strength.
Why have you rejected me?
Why am I sad
and troubled by my enemies?
³Send me your light and truth.
They will guide me.
Lead me to your holy mountain.
Lead me to where you live.
⁴I will go to the altar of God,
to God who is my joy and
happiness.
I will praise you with a harp,
God, my God.

⁵Why am I so sad?
Why am I so upset?
I should put my hope in God.
I should keep praising him,
my Saviour and my God.

A Prayer for Help

For the director of music. A maskil^d
of the sons of Korah.

44 God, we have heard about
you.
Our ancestors told us
what you did in their days,
in days long ago.
²With your power you forced the
nations out of the land.
You placed our ancestors here.

You destroyed those other
   nations.
  But you made our ancestors
   grow strong.
3It wasn't their swords that took
   the land.
  It wasn't their power that gave
   them victory.
  But it was your great power and
   strength.
  You were with them because
   you loved them.

4My God, you are my King.
  Your commands led Jacob's
   people to victory.
5With your help we pushed back
   our enemies.
  In your name we walked over
   those who came against us.
6I don't trust my bow to help me.
  My sword can't save me.
7You saved us from Egypt.
  You made our enemies
   ashamed.
8We will praise God every day.
  We will praise your name for
   ever.   *Selah*[d]

9But you have rejected us and
   shamed us.
  You don't march with our armies
   any more.
10You let our enemies push us back.
  Our enemies have taken our
   wealth.
11You gave us away like sheep to be
   eaten.
  You scattered us among the
   nations.
12You sold your people for nothing.
  You made no profit on the sale.

13You made us a joke to our
   neighbours.
  The community laughs and
   makes fun of us.
14You made us a joke to the other
   nations.
  People shake their heads.
15I am always in disgrace.
  I am covered with shame.

16My enemy is getting even
   with insults and curses.
17All these things have happened to
   us,
  but we have not forgotten you.
  We have kept our agreement
   with you.
18Our hearts haven't turned away
   from you.
  We haven't stopped following
   you.
19But you crushed us in this place
   where wild dogs live.
  You covered us with deep
   darkness.

20We did not forget our God.
  We did not lift our hands in
   prayer to foreign gods.
21God would have known if we had.
  He knows what is in our hearts.
22But for you we are in danger of
   death all the time.
  People think we are worth no
   more than sheep to be
   killed.

23Wake up, Lord! Why are you
   sleeping?
  Get up! Don't reject us for ever.
24Why are you hidden from us?
  Have you forgotten our pain and
   troubles?

25We have been pushed down into
   the dust.
  We are flat on the ground.
26Get up and help us.
  Because of your love, save us.

A Song for the King's Wedding

For the director of music. To the tune
of "Lilies". A maskil.[d] A love song of
the sons of Korah.

45 Beautiful words fill my mind.
  I am speaking of royal things.
  My tongue is like the pen of a
   skilled writer.

2You are more handsome than
   anyone.
  You are a very good speaker.

God has blessed you for ever.
3Put on your sword, powerful
    warrior.
  Show your glory and majesty.
4In your majesty win the victory.
  Defend what is true and right.
  Your power will do amazing
    things.
5Your sharp arrows will enter
  the hearts of the king's enemies.
  Nations will be defeated before
    you.
6God, your throne will last for ever
    and ever.
  You will rule your kingdom with
    fairness.
7You love right and hate evil.
  So God has chosen you to rule
    those with you.
  Your God has given you much
    joy.
8Your clothes smell like myrrh,d
  aloesd and cassia.d
  From palaces of ivory
  music comes to make you
    happy.
9Kings' daughters are among your
    honoured women.
  Your bride stands at your right
    side
  wearing gold from Ophir.
10Listen to me, daughter. Look and
    pay attention.
  Forget your people and your
    father's family.
11The king loves your beauty.
  Because he is your master, you
    should obey him.
12People from the city of Tyre have
    brought a gift.
  Wealthy people will want to
    meet you.
13The princess is very beautiful.
  Her gown is woven with gold.
14In her beautiful clothes she is
    brought to the king.
  Her bridesmaids follow behind
    her.
  And they are also brought to
    him.

15They come with happiness and
    joy.
  They enter the king's palace.
16You will have sons to take the
    place of your ancestors.
  You will make them rulers
    through all the land.
17I will make your name famous
    from now on.
  People will praise you for ever
    and ever.

God Protects His People

For the director of music. By the
alamoth.d A song of the sons of Korah.

46 God is our protection and our
    strength.
  He always helps in times of
    trouble.
2So we will not be afraid if the
    earth shakes,
  or if the mountains fall into the
    sea.
3We will not fear even if the
    oceans roar and foam,
  or if the mountains shake at the
    raging sea.   Selahd

4There is a river which brings joy
    to the city of God.
  This is the holy place where
    God Most High lives.
5God is in that city, and so it will
    not be shaken.
  God will help her at dawn.
6Nations tremble, and kingdoms
    shake.
  God shouts, and the earth
    crumbles.

7The Lord of heaven's armies is
    with us.
  The God of Jacob is our
    protection.   Selah

8Come and see what the Lord has
    done.
  He has done amazing things on
    the earth.

⁹He stops wars everywhere on the
earth.
He breaks all bows and spears
and burns up the chariots with
fire.
¹⁰God says, "Be quiet and know
that I am God.
I will be supreme over all the
nations.
I will be supreme in the earth."

¹¹The Lord of heaven's armies is
with us.
The God of Jacob is our
protection.   *Selah*

God, the King of the World

For the director of music. A song of the
sons of Korah.

47 Clap your hands, all you
people.
Shout to God with joy.
²The Lord Most High is wonderful.
He is the great King over all the
earth!
³He defeated nations for us
and put them under our control.
⁴He chose the land we would
inherit.
We are the children of Jacob,
whom he loved.   *Selah*ᵈ

⁵God has risen with a shout of
joy.
The Lord has risen as the
trumpets sounded.
⁶Sing praises to God. Sing praises.
Sing praises to our King. Sing
praises.
⁷God is King of all the earth.
So sing a song of praise to
him.
⁸God is King over the nations.
God sits on his holy throne.
⁹The leaders of the nations meet
with the people of the God of
Abraham.
Even the leaders of the earth
belong to God.
He is supreme.

Jerusalem, the City of God

A song of the sons of Korah.

48 The Lord is great; he should
be praised
in the city of our God, on his
holy mountain.
²It is high and beautiful.
It brings joy to the whole world.
Mount Zionᵈ is like the high
mountains of the north.
It is the city of the Great King.
³God is within its palaces.
He is known as its protection.
⁴Kings joined together
and came together to attack the
city.
⁵But when they saw it, they were
amazed.
They ran away in fear.
⁶Fear took hold of them.
They hurt like a woman having a
baby.
⁷You destroyed the large trading
ships
with an east wind.

⁸First we heard.
And now we have seen that
God will always keep his city safe.
It is the city of the Lord of
heaven's armies,
the city of our God.   *Selah*ᵈ

⁹God, we come into your Temple.ᵈ
There we think about your love.
¹⁰God, your name is known
everywhere.
Everywhere on earth people
praise you.
Your right hand is full of
goodness.
¹¹Mount Zion is happy.
All the towns of Judah rejoice
because your decisions are fair.

¹²Walk around Jerusalem
and count its towers.
¹³Notice how strong they are. Look
at the palaces.

Then you will be able to tell
  your children about them.
¹⁴This God is our God for ever and
  ever.
He will guide us from now on.

Trusting Money Is Foolish

*For the director of music. A song of the
sons of Korah.*

49 Listen to this, all you nations.
  Listen, all you who live on
  earth.
²Listen, both great and small,
  rich and poor together.
³What I say is wise.
  My heart speaks with
  understanding.
⁴I will pay attention to a wise
  saying.
  I will explain my riddle on the
  harp.

⁵Why should I be afraid of bad
  days?
  Why should I fear when evil
  men surround me?
⁶They trust in their money.
  They boast about their riches.
⁷No one can buy back the life of
  another person.
  No one can pay God for his own
  life.
⁸The price of a life is high.
  No payment is ever enough.
⁹Do people live for ever?
  Don't they all face death?

¹⁰See, even wise men die.
  Fools and stupid people also die.
  They leave their wealth to
  others.
¹¹Their graves will always be their
  homes.
  They will live there from now
  on,
  even though they named places
  after themselves.
¹²Even rich people do not live for
  ever.
  Like the animals, people die.

¹³This is what will happen to people
  who trust in themselves.
  And this will happen to their
  followers who believe them.
                        *Selah*ᵈ
¹⁴Like sheep, they must die.
  And death will be their
  shepherd.
  Honest people will rule over them
  in the morning.
  Their bodies will rot in a grave
  far from home.
¹⁵But God will save my life.
  He will take me from the grave.
                        Selah

¹⁶Don't be afraid of a rich man
  because his house is more
  beautiful.
¹⁷He won't take anything to the
  grave.
  His wealth won't die with him.
¹⁸He was praised when he was
  alive.
  (And people may praise you
  when you succeed.)
¹⁹But he will go to where his
  ancestors are.
  He will never see light again.
²⁰Rich people with no understanding
  are just like animals that die.

God Wants True Worship

A song of Asaph.

50 The God of gods, the Lord,
  speaks.
  He calls the earth from the
  rising to the setting sun.
²God shines from Jerusalem,
  whose beauty is perfect.
³Our God comes, and he will not
  be silent.
  A fire burns in front of him,
  and a storm surrounds him.
⁴He calls to the sky and to the
  earth
  to see him judge his people.
⁵He says, "You who worship me,
  gather around.

You have made an agreement
　　with me, using a sacrifice."
[6]God is the judge.
Even the skies say he is right.
　　　　　　　　　　　　Selah[d]

[7]God says, "My people, listen to
　　me.
Israel, I will testify against you.
I am God, your God.
[8]I do not scold you for your
　　sacrifices.
You always bring me your burnt
　　offerings.
[9]But I do not need the bulls from
　　your stalls
or the goats from your pens.
[10]Every animal of the forest is
　　already mine.
The cattle on a thousand hills
　　are mine.
[11]I know every bird on the
　　mountains.
Every living thing in the fields is
　　mine.
[12]If I were hungry, I would not tell
　　you.
The earth and everything on it
　　are mine.
[13]I don't eat the meat of bulls
or drink the blood of goats.

[14]"Give an offering to show thanks
　　to God.
Give God Most High what you
　　have promised.
[15]Call to me in times of trouble.
I will save you, and you will
　　honour me."

[16]But God says to the wicked
　　people,
"Why do you talk about my
　　laws?
Why do you mention my
　　agreement?
[17]You hate my teachings.
You turn your back on what I
　　say.
[18]When you see a thief, you join
　　him.
You take part in adultery.[d]

[19]You don't stop your mouth from
　　speaking evil.
Your tongue makes up lies.
[20]You speak against your brother.
You lie about your mother's
　　son.
[21]I have kept quiet while you did
　　these things.
So you thought I was just like
　　you.
But I will scold you.
I will accuse you to your face.
[22]"Think about this, you people who
　　forget God.
Otherwise, I will tear you apart,
and no one will save you.
[23]Those people honour me
who give me offerings to show
　　thanks.
And I, God, will save those who
　　do that."

A Prayer for Forgiveness

For the director of music. A song
of David when the prophet[d] Nathan
came to David after David's sin
with Bathsheba.

51 God, be merciful to me
　　because you are loving.
Because you are always ready to
　　be merciful,
wipe out all my wrongs.
[2]Wash away all my guilt
and make me clean again.

[3]I know about my wrongs.
I can't forget my sin.
[4]You are the one I have sinned
　　against.
I have done what you say is
　　wrong.
So you are right when you speak.
You are fair when you judge me.
[5]I was brought into this world in
　　sin.
In sin my mother gave birth to
　　me.

[6]You want me to be completely
　　truthful.
So teach me wisdom.

7Take away my sin, and I will be
    clean.
Wash me, and I will be whiter
    than snow.
8Make me hear sounds of joy and
    gladness.
Let the bones you crushed be
    happy again.
9Turn your face from my sins.
Wipe out all my guilt.

10Create in me a pure heart,
    God.
Make my spirit right again.
11Do not send me away from
    you.
Do not take your Holy Spirit*d*
    away from me.
12Give me back the joy that comes
    when you save me.
Keep me strong by giving me a
    willing spirit.
13Then I will teach your ways to
    those who do wrong.
And sinners will turn back to
    you.

14God, save me from the guilt of
    murder.
God, you are the one who saves
    me.
I will sing about your goodness.
15Lord, let me speak
    so I may praise you.
16You are not pleased by sacrifices.
Otherwise, I would give them.
You don't want burnt offerings.
17The sacrifice God wants is a
    willing spirit.
God, you will not reject
a heart that is broken and sorry
    for its sin.

18Do whatever good you wish for
    Jerusalem.
Rebuild the walls of Jerusalem.
19Then you will be pleased with
    right sacrifices and whole
    burnt offerings.
And bulls will be offered on your
    altar.

God Will Punish the Proud

For the director of music. A maskil*d*
of David. When Doeg the Edomite came
to Saul and said to him, "David is in
Ahimelech's house."

52 Mighty warrior, why do you
    boast about the evil you do?
God's love will continue for
    ever.
2You think up evil plans.
Your tongue is like a sharp
    razor,
making up lies.
3You love wrong more than right
and lies more than truth. *Selahd*
4You love words that bite
and tongues that lie.

5But God will ruin you for ever.
He will grab you and throw you
    out of your tent.
He will tear you away from the
    land of the living. *Selah*
6Those who do right will see this
    and fear God.
They will laugh at you and say,
7"Look what happened to the man
    who did not depend on God.
Instead, he depended on his
    money.
He grew strong by his evil
    plans."

8But I am like an olive tree
    growing in God's Temple.*d*
I trust God's love
    for ever and ever.
9God, I will thank you for ever for
    what you have done.
With those who worship you, I
    will trust you because you
    are good.

The Unbelieving Fool

For the director of music. By the
mahalath.*d* A maskil*d* of David.

53 A wicked fool says to himself,
    "There is no God."
Fools are evil. They do terrible
    things.

None of them does anything
   good.

²God looked down from heaven at
   all the people.
He looked to see if anyone was
   wise,
if anyone was looking to God for
   help.
³But everyone has turned away.
Together, everyone has become
   evil.
None of them does anything
   good.

⁴Don't the wicked understand?
They destroy my people as if
   they were eating bread.
They have not asked God for
   help.
⁵The wicked became filled with
   terror
where there had been nothing to
   be terrified of.
God will scatter the bones of
   your enemies.
You will defeat them,
because God has rejected them.

⁶I pray that victory will come to
   Israel from Mount Zion!^d
May God give them back their
   riches.
Then the people of Jacob will
   rejoice.
And the people of Israel will be
   glad.

A Prayer for Help

For the director of music. With stringed
instruments. A maskil^d of David when
the Ziphites went to Saul and said, "We
think David is hiding among our people."

54 God, save me because of
   who you are.
By your strength show that I am
   innocent.
²Hear my prayer, God.
Listen to what I say.
³Strangers turn against me.
Cruel men want to kill me.

They do not care about God.
                              Selah^d

⁴See, God will help me.
The Lord will spare my life.
⁵Let my enemies be punished with
   their own evil.
Destroy them because you are
   loyal to me.

⁶I will offer a sacrifice as a special
   gift to you.
I will thank you, Lord, because
   you are good.
⁷You have saved me from all my
   troubles.
I have seen my enemies
   defeated.

A Prayer About a False Friend

For the director of music. With stringed
instruments. A maskil^d of David.

55 God, listen to my prayer.
   Do not ignore my prayer.
²Pay attention to me and answer
   me.
I am troubled and upset
³by what the enemy says
and how the wicked look at me.
They bring troubles down on me.
In anger they attack me.

⁴I am frightened inside.
The terror of death has attacked
   me.
⁵I am scared and shaking.
Terror grips me.
⁶I said, "I wish I had wings like a
   dove.
Then I would fly away and rest.
⁷I would wander far away.
I would stay in the desert. *Selah^d*
⁸I would hurry to my place of
   escape,
far away from the wind and
   storm."

⁹Lord, destroy and confuse their
   words.
I see violence and fighting in the
   city.

10Day and night they are all around
     its walls.
   Evil and trouble are everywhere
     inside.
11Destruction is everywhere in the
     city.
   Trouble and lying never leave its
     streets.

12It was not an enemy insulting me.
   I could stand that.
   It was not someone who hated
     me.
   I could hide from him.
13But it is you, a person like me.
   You were my companion and
     good friend.
14We had a good friendship.
   We went together to God's
     Temple.*d*

15Let death take away my enemies.
   Let them die while they are still
     young
   because evil lives with them.
16But I will call to God for help.
   And the Lord will save me.
17Morning, noon and night I am
     troubled and upset.
   But he will listen to me.
18Many are against me.
   But he keeps me safe in battle.
19God who lives for ever
   will hear me and punish them.
   But they will not change.
   They do not fear God.   *Selah*

20The one who was my friend
     attacks his friends.
   He breaks his promises.
21His words are slippery like butter.
   But war is in his heart.
   His words are smoother than oil,
   but they cut like knives.

22Give your worries to the Lord.
   He will take care of you.
   He will never let good people
     down.
23But, God, you will bring down
   the wicked to the grave.
   Murderers and liars will live

only half a lifetime.
But I will trust in you.

Trusting God for Help

For the director of music. To the tune
of "The Dove in the Distant Oak".
A miktam*d* of David when the Philistines
captured him in Gath.

56 God, be merciful to me
     because people are chasing
   me.
   The battle has pressed me all
     day long.
2My enemies have chased me all
     day.
   There are many of them fighting
     me.
3When I am afraid,
   I will trust you.
4I praise God for his word.
   I trust God. So I am not afraid.
   What can human beings do to me?

5All day long they twist my words.
   All their evil plans are against
     me.
6They wait. They hide.
   They watch my steps.
   They hope to kill me.
7God, do not let them escape.
   Punish the foreign nations in
     your anger.
8You have recorded my troubles.
   You have kept a list of my
     tears.
   Aren't they in your records?

9On the day I call for help, my
     enemies will be defeated.
   I know that God is on my side.
10I praise God for his word to me.
   I praise the Lord for his word.
11I trust in God. I will not be afraid.
   What can people do to me?
12God, I must keep my promises to
     you.
   I will give you my offerings to
     thank you.
13You have saved me from death.
   You have kept me from being
     defeated.

So I will walk with God
in light among the living.

A Prayer in Troubled Times

For the director of music. To the tune
of "Do Not Destroy". A miktam[d]
of David when he escaped from Saul
into a cave.

57 Be merciful to me, God. Be
merciful to me
because I come to you for
protection.
I will come to you as a bird comes
for protection under its
mother's wings
until the trouble has passed.

[2]I cry out to God Most High,
to the God who does everything
for me.
[3]He sends help from heaven and
saves me.
He punishes those who attack
me.   Selah[d]
God sends me his love and
truth.

[4]Enemies are like lions all around
me.
I must lie down among them.
Their teeth are like spears and
arrows.
Their tongues are as sharp as
swords.

[5]God is supreme over the skies.
His greatness covers the earth.

[6]They set a trap for me.
I am very worried.
They dug a pit in my path.
But they fell into it themselves.
Selah

[7]My heart is right, God. My heart
is right.
I will sing and praise you.
[8]Wake up, my soul.
Wake up, harp and lyre![d]
I will wake up the dawn.
[9]Lord, I will praise you among the
nations.

I will sing songs of praise about
you to all the nations.
[10]Your love is so great it reaches to
the skies.
Your truth reaches to the
clouds.
[11]God, you are supreme over the
skies.
Let your glory be over all the
earth.

Unfair Judges

For the director of music. To the tune
of "Do Not Destroy". A miktam[d]
of David.

58 Do you rulers really say what
is right?
Do you judge people fairly?
[2]No, in your heart you plan evil.
You think up violent crimes in
the land.
[3]From birth evil men start doing
bad things.
They tell lies and do wrong as
soon as they are born.
[4]They are like poisonous snakes,
like deaf cobras that can't hear.
[5]They cannot hear the music of the
snake charmer
no matter how well he plays for
them.

[6]God, break the teeth out of their
mouths!
Tear out the fangs of those
lions, Lord!
[7]Let them disappear like water that
flows away.
Let them be cut short like a
broken arrow.
[8]Let them be like snails that melt
as they move.
Let them be like a child born
dead who never saw the
sun.
[9]His anger will blow them away
alive.
It will happen faster than
burning thorns can heat a
pot.

¹⁰Good people will be glad when
　　they see him get even.
　They will wash their feet in the
　　blood of the wicked.
¹¹Then people will say,
　"There really are rewards for
　　doing what is right.
　There really is a God who
　　judges the world."

A Prayer for Protection

For the director of music. To the tune
of "Do Not Destroy". A miktam[d]
of David when Saul sent men to watch
David's house and to kill him.

59 God, save me from my
　　enemies.
　Protect me from those who
　　come against me.
²Save me from those who do evil.
　Save me from murderers.

³Look, men are waiting to attack
　　me.
　Cruel men attack me.
　But I have not sinned or done
　　wrong, Lord.
⁴I have done nothing wrong, but
　　they are ready to attack me.
　Wake up to help me and look.
⁵You are the Lord God of heaven's
　　armies, the God of Israel.
　Come and punish those people.
　Do not give those traitors any
　　mercy.　　　　　　　*Selah*[d]

⁶They come back at night.
　Like dogs they growl and roam
　　around the city.
⁷Notice what comes from their
　　mouths.
　Insults come from their lips.
　They say, "Who's listening?"
⁸But, Lord, you laugh at them.
　You make fun of all of them.

⁹God, my strength, I wait for you.
　God, you are my protection.
¹⁰My God loves me, and he will be
　　with me.
　He will help me defeat my
　　enemies.

¹¹Lord, our protector, do not kill
　　them.
　If you do, my people will forget.
　With your power scatter them
　　and defeat them.
¹²They sin by what they say.
　They sin with their words.
　They curse and tell lies.
　So let their pride trap them.
¹³Destroy them in your anger.
　Destroy them completely!
　Then they will know
　　that God rules over Israel
　and to the ends of the earth.
　　　　　　　　　　　　Selah

¹⁴They come back at night.
　Like dogs they growl
　　and roam around the city.
¹⁵They wander about looking for
　　food.
　And they howl if they do not
　　find enough.
¹⁶But I will sing about your
　　strength.
　In the morning I will sing about
　　your love.
　You are my protection,
　　my place of safety in times of
　　trouble.
¹⁷God, my strength, I will sing
　　praises to you.
　God, my protection, you are the
　　God who loves me.

A Prayer After a Defeat

For the director of music. To the tune
of "Lily of the Agreement". A miktam[d]
of David. For teaching. When David
fought the Arameans of North West
Mesopotamia and Zobah, and when Joab
returned and defeated 12,000 Edomites
at the Valley of Salt.

60 God, you have rejected us
　　and scattered us.
　You have been angry, but please
　　come back to us.
²You made the earth shake and
　　tore it open.
　Mend its breaks because it is
　　shaking.

3You have given your people trouble.
You made us unable to walk straight, like people drunk with wine.
4You have raised a banner to gather those who fear you.
Now they can escape the enemy. *Selah*[d]
5Answer us and save us by your power.
Then the people you love will be rescued.

6God has said from his Temple,[d]
"When I win, I will divide Shechem
and cut up the Valley of Succoth.
7Gilead and Manasseh are mine.
Ephraim is like my helmet.
Judah holds my royal sceptre.[d]
8Moab is like my washbowl.
I throw my sandals at Edom.
I shout at Philistia."

9Who will bring me to the strong, walled city?
Who will lead me to Edom?
10God, surely you have rejected us.
You do not go out with our armies.
11Help us fight the enemy.
Human help is useless.
12But we can win with God's help.
He will defeat our enemies.

A Prayer for Protection

For the director of music. With stringed instruments. Of David.

61 God, hear my cry.
Listen to my prayer.
2I call to you from the ends of the earth.
I am afraid.
Carry me away to a high mountain.
3You have been my protection, like a strong tower against my enemies.

4Let me live in your Holy Tent[d] for ever.
Protect me as a bird protects its young under its wings. *Selah*[d]
5God, you have heard my promises.
You have given me the things that belong to those who fear you.
6Give the king a long life.
Let him live many years.
7Let him rule in the presence of God for ever.
Protect him with your love and truth.
8Then I will praise your name for ever.
And every day I will keep my promises.

Trust Only in God

For the director of music. For Jeduthun. A song of David.

62 I wait patiently for God.
Only he can save me.
2He is my rock, who saves me.
He protects me like a strong, walled city.
I will not be defeated.

3How long will you attack me?
Will all of you throw me down?
I am like a leaning wall, like a fence ready to fall.
4You are planning to make me fall.
You enjoy telling lies about me.
With your mouth you bless me.
But in your heart you curse me. *Selah*[d]

5I wait patiently for God to save me.
Only he gives me hope.
6He is my rock, who saves me.
He protects me like a strong, walled city.
I will not be defeated.
7My honour and salvation come from God.
He is my mighty rock and my protection.

8People, trust God all the time.
Tell him all your problems.
God is our protection.   *Selah*

9People are only a breath.
Even the greatest men are just
a lie.
On the scales, they weigh
nothing.
Together they are only a breath.
10Do not trust in force.
Stealing is of no use.
Even if you gain more riches,
don't put your trust in them.

11God has said this,
and I have heard it over and
over:
God, you are strong.
12Lord, you are loving.
You reward a person for what
he does.

Wishing to Be Near God

A song of David when he was in the
desert of Judah.

63 God, you are my God.
I want to follow you.
My whole being
thirsts for you,
like a man in a dry, empty land
where there is no water.
2I have seen you in the Temple.*d*
I have seen your strength and
glory.
3Your love is better than life.
I will praise you.
4I will praise you as long as I live.
I will lift up my hands in prayer
to your name.
5I will be content as if I had eaten
the best foods.
My lips will sing. My mouth will
praise you.
6I remember you while I'm lying in
bed.
I think about you through the
night.
7You are my help.
Because of your protection, I
sing.

8I stay close to you.
You support me with your right
hand.

9Some people are trying to kill me.
But they will go down to the
grave.
10They will be killed with swords.
They will be eaten by wild dogs.
11But the king will rejoice in his
God.
All who make promises in his
name will praise him.
But the mouths of liars will be
shut.

A Prayer Against Enemies

For the director of music.
A song of David.

64 God, listen to my complaint.
I am afraid of my enemies.
Protect my life from them.
2Hide me from those wicked
people,
from that mob who does evil.
3They sharpen their tongues like
swords.
They shoot bitter words like
arrows.
4They hide and shoot at innocent
people.
They shoot suddenly and are not
afraid.
5They encourage each other to do
wrong.
They talk about setting traps.
They think no one will see
them.
6They plan wicked things and say,
"We have a perfect plan."
The mind of man is hard to
understand.

7But God will shoot them with
arrows.
They will suddenly be struck
down.
8Their own words will be used
against them.
All who see them will shake
their heads.

⁹Then everyone will fear God.
They will tell what God has
done.
They will learn from what he
has done.
¹⁰Good people will be happy in the
Lord.
They will find protection in him.
Let everyone who is honest
praise the Lord.

A Hymn of Thanksgiving

For the director of music.
A song of David.

65 God, you will be praised in
Jerusalem.
We will keep our promises to
you.
²You hear our prayers.
All people will come to you.
³Our guilt overwhelms us.
But you forgive our sins.
⁴Happy are the people you choose.
You have them stay in your
courtyards.
We are filled with good things in
your house,
your holy Temple.ᵈ
⁵You answer us in amazing ways,
God our Saviour.
People everywhere on the earth
and beyond the sea trust you.
⁶You made the mountains by your
strength.
You have great power.
⁷You stopped the roaring seas,
the roaring waves and the
uproar of the nations.
⁸Even those people at the ends of
the earth fear your
miracles.ᵈ
You are praised from where the
sun rises to where it sets.
⁹You take care of the land and
water it.
You make it very fertile.
The rivers of God are full of
water.

Grain grows because you make
it grow.
¹⁰You cause rain to fall on the
ploughed fields.
You soak them with water.
You soften the ground with rain.
And then you bless it.
¹¹You give the year a good harvest.
You load the wagons with many
crops.
¹²The desert is covered with grass.
The hills are covered with
happiness.
¹³The pastures are full of sheep.
The valleys are covered with
grain.
Everything shouts and sings for
joy.

Praise God for Answering Prayers

For the director of music.
A song of praise.

66 Everything on earth, shout
with joy to God!
²Sing about his glory!
Make his praise glorious!
³Say to God, "Your works are
amazing!
Your power is great.
Your enemies fall before you.
⁴All the earth worships you.
They sing praises to you.
They sing praises to your
name."   *Selah*ᵈ

⁵Come and see what God has
done.
See what amazing things he has
done for people.
⁶He turned the sea into dry land.
The people crossed the river on
foot.
So let us rejoice because of
what he did.
⁷He rules for ever with his power.
He keeps his eye on the
nations.
So people should not turn
against him.   *Selah*

⁸You people, praise our God.
   Loudly sing his praise.
⁹He protects our lives
   and does not let us be defeated.
¹⁰God, you have tested us.
   You have purified us like silver.
¹¹You let us be trapped.
   You put a heavy load on us.
¹²You let our enemies walk on our
   heads.
   We went through fire and flood.
   But you brought us to a place
   with good things.

¹³I will come to your Temple*d* with
   burnt offerings.
   I will give you what I promised.
¹⁴I promised to give you these
   things
   when I was in trouble.
¹⁵I will bring you offerings of fat
   animals.
   And I will offer male sheep,
   bulls and goats.   *Selah*

¹⁶All of you who fear God, come
   and listen.
   I will tell you what he has done
   for me.
¹⁷I cried out to him with my mouth.
   I praised him with my tongue.
¹⁸If I had known of any sin in my
   heart,
   the Lord would not have
   listened to me.
¹⁹But God has listened.
   He has heard my prayer.
²⁰Praise God.
   He did not ignore my prayer.
   He did not hold back his love
   from me.

Everyone Should Praise God

For the director of music. With stringed
instruments. A song of praise.

67 God, have mercy on us and
   bless us.
   Show your kindness to us. *Selah*ᵈ
²Then the world will learn your
   ways.

All nations will learn that you
   can save.

³God, the people should praise
   you.
   All people should praise you.
⁴The nations should be glad and
   sing
   because you judge people fairly.
   You guide all the nations on
   earth.   *Selah*
⁵God, the people should praise
   you.
   All people should praise you.

⁶The land has given its crops.
   God, our God, blesses us.
⁷God blesses us
   so people to the ends of the
   earth will fear him.

Praise God Who Saved the Nation

For the director of music.
A song of David.

68 Let God come and scatter his
   enemies.
   Let those who hate him run
   away.
²Blow them away as smoke
   is driven away by the wind.
   As wax melts before a fire,
   let the wicked be destroyed
   before God.
³But those who do right should be
   glad.
   They should rejoice before God.
   They should be happy and glad.

⁴Sing to God. Sing praises to his
   name.
   Prepare the way for him
   who rides through the desert.
   His name is the Lord.
   Rejoice before him.
⁵God is in his holy Temple.*d*
   He is a father to orphans.
   He defends the widows.
⁶God gives the lonely a home.
   He leads prisoners out with joy.
   But those who turn against God
   will live in a dry land.

⁷God, you led your people out.
  You marched through the
    desert.   *Selah*^d
⁸The ground shook,
  and the sky poured down rain
before God, the God of Mount
    Sinai,
  before God, the God of Israel.
⁹God, you sent much rain.
  You refreshed your tired land.
¹⁰Your people settled there.
  God, in your goodness
  you took care of the poor.

¹¹The Lord gave the command.
  And a great army told the news:
¹²"Kings and their armies run away.
  The women at home divide the
    wealth taken in war."
¹³Those who stayed behind by the
    sheepfold
  will get the riches taken in
    battle.
¹⁴God scattered kings
  like snow on Mount Zalmon.

¹⁵The mountains of Bashan are
    great mountains.
  Mount Bashan has many peaks.
¹⁶Why do you mountains with many
    peaks look down
  on Mount Zion,^d which God
    chose for his home?
  The Lord will live there for
    ever.
¹⁷God comes with millions of
    chariots.
  The Lord comes from Mount
    Sinai to his holy place.
¹⁸He went up to the heights.
  He led a parade of captives.
  He received the payment he
    demanded from the people,
  even from those who turned
    against him.
  And the Lord God will live
    there.

¹⁹Praise the Lord, day by day.
  God our Saviour helps us.   *Selah*
²⁰Our God is a God who saves us.

The Lord God saves us from
  death.

²¹God will crush his enemies' heads,
  the hairy skulls of those who
    continue to sin.
²²The Lord said, "I will bring the
    enemy back from Bashan.
  I will bring them back from the
    depths of the sea.
²³Then you can plunge your feet in
    their blood.
  And your dogs can lick their
    share."

²⁴God, people have seen your
    victory march.
  God my King marched into the
    holy place.
²⁵The singers are in front, and the
    instruments are behind.
  In the middle are the girls with
    the tambourines.^d
²⁶Praise God in the meeting place.
  Praise the Lord in the gathering
    of Israel.
²⁷There is the smallest tribe,^d
    Benjamin, leading them.
  And there are the leaders of
    Judah with their group.
  There also are the leaders of
    Zebulun and of Naphtali.

²⁸God, call up your power.
  Show the mighty power you
    have used for us before.
²⁹Kings will bring their wealth to
    you,
  to your Temple in Jerusalem.
³⁰Punish Egypt, the beast among
    the tall grass along the river.
  Punish the leaders of nations,
    those bulls among the cows.
  Then they will bring you their
    silver.
  Scatter those nations that love
    war.
³¹Messengers will come from Egypt
    with forced payment.
  The people of Cush will pray to
    God.

32Kingdoms of the earth, sing to
  God.
  Sing praises to the Lord.   *Selah*
33Sing to the one who rides through
  the skies, which are from
  long ago.
  He speaks with a thundering
  voice.
34Announce that God is powerful.
  He rules over Israel.
  His power is in the skies.
35God, you are wonderful in your
  Temple.
  The God of Israel gives his
  people strength and power.

  Praise God!

A Cry for Help

For the director of music. To the tune
of "Lilies". A song of David.

69 God, save me.
       The water has risen to my
  neck.
2I'm sinking down into the mud.
  There is nothing to stand on.
  I am in deep water.
  The flood covers me.
3I am tired from calling for help.
  My throat is sore.
  My eyes are tired from waiting
  for God to help me.
4There are more people who hate
  me for no reason
  than hairs on my head.
  Those who want to destroy me
  are powerful.
  My enemies are liars.
  They make me pay back
  what I did not steal.

5God, you know what I have done
  wrong.
  I cannot hide my guilt from you.
6Master, the Lord of heaven's
  armies,
  do not let those who hope in
  you be ashamed because of
  me.
  God of Israel,
  do not let your worshippers

be disgraced because of me.
7For you, I carry this shame.
  My face is covered with
  disgrace.
8I am like a stranger to my
  brothers.
  I am like a foreigner to my
  mother's sons.
9My strong love for your Temple*d*
  completely controls me.
  When people insult you, it hurts
  me.
10When I cry and go without food,
  they make fun of me.
11When I wear rough cloth to show
  my sadness,
  they joke about me.
12They make fun of me in public
  places.
  The drunkards make up songs
  about me.

13But I pray to you, Lord.
  I pray that you will accept me.
  God, because of your great love,
  answer me.
  You are truly able to save.
14Pull me from the mud.
  Do not let me sink.
  Save me from those who hate me
  and from the deep water.
15Do not let the flood drown me.
  Do not let the deep water
  swallow me.
  Do not let the grave close its
  mouth over me.
16Lord, answer me because your
  love is so good.
  Because of your great kindness,
  turn to me.
17Do not hide from me, your
  servant.
  I am in trouble. Hurry to help
  me!
18Come near and save me.
  Rescue me from my enemies.

19You see my shame and disgrace.
  You know all my enemies and
  what they have said.
20Insults have broken my heart.
  I am weak.

I looked for sympathy, but there
    was none.
I found no one to comfort me.
21They put poison in my food.
    They gave me vinegar to drink.
22Let their own feasts cause their
    ruin.
Let their feasts trap them and
    pay them back.
23Let their eyes be closed so they
    cannot see.
Let their backs be for ever
    weak from troubles.
24Pour your anger out on them.
    Show them how angry you are.
25May their place be empty.
Leave no one to live in their
    tents.
26They chase after those you have
    hurt.
They talk about the pain of
    those you have wounded.
27Charge them with crime after
    crime.
Do not let them have anything
    good.
28Wipe their names from the book
    of life.
Do not list them with those who
    do what is right.
29I am sad and hurting.
    God, save me and protect me.
30I will praise God in a song.
I will honour him by giving
    thanks.
31That will please the Lord more
    than offering him cattle.
It will please him more than the
    sacrifice of a bull with horns
    and hoofs.
32People who are not proud will see
    this and be glad.
Be encouraged, you who
    worship God.
33The Lord listens to those in need.
He does not look down on
    captives.
34Heaven and earth should praise
    him.

The seas and everything in them
    should also.
35God will save Jerusalem.
He will rebuild the cities of
    Judah.
Then people will live there and
    own the land.
36 The descendantsd of his
    servants will inherit that
    land.
Those who love him will live
    there.

A Cry for God to Help Quickly

For the director of music. A song
of David to help people remember.

70 God, save me.
    Lord, hurry to help me.
2People are trying to kill me.
    Shame them and disgrace them.
People want to hurt me.
    Let them run away in disgrace.
3People make fun of me.
    Stop them and make them
    ashamed.
4But let all the people who worship
    you
rejoice and be glad.
Let the people who love your
    salvation
always say, "Praise the
    greatness of God."
5I am poor and helpless.
    God, hurry to me.
You help me and save me.
    Lord, do not wait.

An Old Person's Prayer

71 In you, Lord, is my
    protection.
Never let me be ashamed.
2Because you do what is right,
    save and rescue me.
Listen to me and save me.
3Be my place of safety
    where I can always come.
Give the command to save me.
    You are my rock and my strong,
    walled city.

⁴My God, save me from the power
      of the wicked.
   Save me from the hold of evil
      and cruel people.
⁵Lord God, you are my hope.
   I have trusted you since I was
      young.
⁶I have depended on you since I
      was born.
   You have been my help from the
      day I was born.
   I will always praise you.

⁷I am an example to many people.
   You are my strong protection.
⁸I am always praising you.
   All day long I honour you.
⁹Do not reject me when I am old.
   Do not leave me when my
      strength is gone.
¹⁰My enemies have made plans
      against me.
   They meet together to kill me.
¹¹They say, "God has left him.
   Go after him and take him.
   No one will save him."

¹²God, don't be far off.
   My God, hurry to help me.
¹³Let them be ashamed.
   Destroy those who accuse me.
   They are trying to hurt me.
   Cover them with shame and
      disgrace.
¹⁴But I will always have hope.
   And I will praise you more and
      more.
¹⁵I will tell about how you do what
      is right.
   I will tell about your salvation all
      day long,
   even though it is more than I
      can tell.
¹⁶I will come and tell about your
      powerful works, Lord God.
   I will tell only about you and
      how you do what is right.

¹⁷God, you have taught me since I
      was young.
   Even until today I tell about the
      miracles[d] you do.

¹⁸Even though I am old and grey,
      do not leave me, God.
   I will tell the children about your
      power.
   I will tell those who will live
      after me about your might.

¹⁹God, your justice reaches to the
      skies.
   You have done great things.
   God, there is no one like you.
²⁰You have given me many troubles
      and bad times.
   But you will give me life again.
   When I am almost dead,
      you will keep me alive.
²¹You will make me greater than
      ever.
   And you will comfort me again.

²²I will praise you with the harp.
   I trust you, my God.
   I will sing to you with the lyre.[d]
   You are the Holy One of Israel.
²³I will shout for joy when I sing
      praises to you.
   You have saved me.
²⁴I will tell about your justice all day
      long.
   And those who want to hurt me
   will be ashamed and disgraced.

A Prayer for the King

Of Solomon.

72 God, give the king your good
      judgement
   and the king's son your
      goodness.
²Help him judge your people fairly.
   Help him decide what is right for
      the poor.
³Let there be peace on the
      mountains
   and goodness on the hills.
⁴Help him be fair to the poor.
   Help him save the needy
   and punish those who hurt
      them.

⁵Help him live as long as the sun
      shines.

Help him rule as long as the
  moon glows.
Let him be king from now on!
[6]Let him be like rain on the grass,
  like showers that water the
  earth.
[7]Let goodness be plentiful while he
  lives.
Let peace continue as long as
  there is a moon.
[8]Let his kingdom go from sea to
  sea,
  and from the Euphrates River to
  the ends of the earth.
[9]Let the people of the desert bow
  down to him.
And make his enemies lick the
  dust.
[10]Let the kings of Tarshish and the
  faraway lands
  bring him gifts.
Let the kings of Sheba and Seba
  bring their presents to him.
[11]Let all kings bow down to him.
Let all nations serve him.

[12]He will help the poor when they
  cry for help.
He will help the needy when no
  one else will help them.
[13]He will be kind to the weak and
  poor.
He will save their lives.
[14]He will save them from cruel
  people who try to hurt
  them.
Their lives are precious to him.

[15]Long live the king!
Let him receive gold from
  Sheba.
Let people always pray for him.
Let them bless him all day long.
[16]Let the fields grow plenty of
  grain.
Let the hills be covered with
  crops.
Let the land be as fertile as
  Lebanon.
Let the cities grow like the
  grass in a field.

[17]Let the king be famous for ever.
Let him be remembered as long
  as the sun shines.
Let the nations be blessed
  because of him.
And may they all bless him.

[18]Praise the Lord God, the God of
  Israel.
Only he does such miracles. [d]
[19]Praise his glorious name for ever.
Let his glory fill the whole
  world.
  Amen and amen.

[20]This ends the prayers of David son
of Jesse.

Book 3

Should the Wicked Be Rich?

A song of Asaph.

73 God is truly good to Israel,
  to those who have pure
  hearts.
[2]But I had almost stopped believing
  this truth.
I had almost lost my faith
[3]because I was jealous of proud
  people.
I saw wicked people doing well.

[4]They are not suffering.
They are healthy and strong.
[5]They don't have troubles like the
  rest of us.
They don't have problems like
  other people.
[6]So they wear pride like a
  necklace.
They put on violence as their
  clothing.
[7]They are looking for profits.
They do not control their selfish
  desires.
[8]They make fun of others and
  speak evil.
Proudly they speak of hurting
  others.
[9]They boast to the sky.

Their mouths gossip on the
earth.
¹⁰So their people turn to them
and give them whatever they
want.
¹¹They say, "How can God know?
What does God Most High
know?"
¹²These people are wicked,
always at ease and getting
richer.
¹³So why have I kept my heart
pure?
Why have I kept my hands from
doing wrong?
¹⁴I have suffered all day long.
I have been punished every
morning.

¹⁵God, if I had decided to talk about
this,
I would have let your people
down.
¹⁶I tried to understand all this.
But it was too hard for me to
see
¹⁷until I went to the Temple[d] of
God.
Then I understood what will
happen to them.
¹⁸You have put them in danger.
You cause them to be
destroyed.
¹⁹They are destroyed in a moment.
They are swept away by
terrors.
²⁰It will be like waking from a
dream.
Lord, when you come, they will
disappear.

²¹When my heart was sad and
I was angry,
²²I was senseless and stupid.
I acted like an animal towards
you.
²³But I am always with you.
You have held my hand.
²⁴You guide me with your advice.
And later you will receive me in
honour.
²⁵I have no one in heaven but you.

I want nothing on earth besides
you.
²⁶My mind and my body may
become weak.
But God is my strength.
He is mine for ever.

²⁷Those who are far from God will
die.
You destroy those who are
unfaithful.
²⁸But I am close to God, and that is
good.
The Lord God is my protection.
I will tell of all that you have
done.

A Nation in Trouble Prays

A maskil[d] of Asaph.

74 God, why have you rejected
us for so long?
Why are you angry with us, the
sheep of your pasture?
²Remember the people you bought
long ago.
You saved us. We are your very
own.
You live on Mount Zion.[d]
³Make your way through these old
ruins.
The enemy wrecked everything
in the Temple.[d]

⁴Those who were against you
shouted in your meeting
place.
They raised their flags there.
⁵They came with axes raised
as if to cut down a forest of
trees.
⁶They smashed the carved panels
with their axes and hatchets.
⁷They burned your Temple to the
ground.
They have made the place
where you live unclean.[d]
⁸They thought, "We will completely
crush them!"
They burned every place where
God was worshipped in the
land.

⁹We do not see any signs.
 There are no more prophets.
 And no one knows how long this
  will last.
¹⁰God, how much longer will the
  enemy make fun of you?
 Will they insult you for ever?
¹¹Why do you hold back your
  power?
 Bring your power out in the
  open and destroy them!

¹²God, you have been our king for a
  long time.
 You have saved this country.
¹³You split open the sea by your
  power.
 You broke the heads of the sea
  monster.
¹⁴You smashed the heads of the
  monster Leviathan.ᵈ
 You gave him to the desert
  creatures as food.
¹⁵You opened up the springs and
  streams.
 And you made the rivers run
  dry.
¹⁶Both the day and the night are
  yours.
 You made the sun and the
  moon.
¹⁷You made all the limits on the
  earth.
 You created summer and winter.

¹⁸Lord, remember how the enemy
  insulted you.
 Remember how those foolish
  people turned away from
  you.
¹⁹Do not give us, your doves, to
  those wild animals.
 Never forget your poor people.
²⁰Remember the agreement you
  made with us
 because violence fills every dark
  corner of this land.
²¹Do not let your suffering people
  be disgraced.
 The poor and helpless people
  praise you.

²²God, come and defend yourself.
 Remember the insults that come
  from those foolish people all
  day long.
²³Don't forget what your enemies
  said.
 Don't forget their roar as they
  rise against you always.

God the Judge

For the director of music. To the tune
of "Do Not Destroy". A song of Asaph.

75 God, we thank you.
 We thank you because you
  are near.
 We tell of the wonderful things
  you do.

²You say, "I set the time for trial.
 I will judge fairly.
³The earth with all its people may
  shake.
 I am the one who holds it
  steady. *Selah*ᵈ
⁴I say to those who are proud,
  'Don't boast'.
 I say to the wicked, 'Don't show
  your power.
⁵Don't try to use your power
  against heaven.
 Don't be stubborn'."

⁶No one from the east or the west
  or the desert can judge you.
⁷God is the judge.
 He judges one person as guilty,
  and another as innocent.
⁸The Lord holds a cup of anger in
  his hand.
 It is full of wine mixed with
  spices.
 He pours it out even to the last
  drop.
 And the wicked drink it all.

⁹I will tell about this for ever.
 I will sing praise to the God of
  Jacob.
¹⁰He will take all power away from
  the wicked.

But the power of good people
will grow.

The God Who Always Wins

For the director of music. With stringed
instruments. A song of Asaph.

76 People in Judah know God.
People in Israel know he is
great.
[2]He lives in Jerusalem.
His home is on Mount Zion.[d]
[3]There God broke the flaming
arrows,
the shields and swords of war.
Selah[d]

[4]God, how wonderful you are!
You are more wonderful than
the hills full of animals.
[5]The brave soldiers were stripped
as they lay asleep in death.
Not one warrior
had the strength to stop it.
[6]God of Jacob, when you spoke
strongly,
horses and riders fell dead.
[7]You should be feared.
Who can stand against you when
you are angry?
[8]From heaven you gave the
decision.
And the earth was afraid and
silent.
[9]God, you stood up to judge
and to save the people of the
earth who were not proud.
Selah
[10]People praise you for your anger
against evil.
Those who live through your
anger are stopped from
doing more evil.

[11]Keep your promises to the Lord
your God.
From all around gifts should
come to the God we
worship.
[12]God defeats great leaders.
The kings on earth fear him.

Remembering God's Help

For the director of music. For Jeduthun.
A song of Asaph.

77 I cry out loud to God.
I call to God, and he will hear
me.
[2]I looked for the Lord on the day
of trouble.
All night long I reached out my
hands.
I cannot be comforted.
[3]When I remember God, I become
upset.
When I think, I become afraid.
Selah[d]

[4]You keep my eyes from closing.
I am too upset to say anything.
[5]I keep thinking about the old days,
the years of long ago.
[6]At night I remember my songs.
I think, and I ask myself:
[7]"Will the Lord reject us for ever?
Will he never be kind to us
again?
[8]Is his love gone for ever?
Has he stopped speaking for all
time?
[9]Has God forgotten mercy?
Is he too angry to pity us?" *Selah*
[10]Then I said, "This is what makes
me sad:
For years the power of God
Most High was with us."

[11]I remember what the Lord did.
I remember the miracles[d] you
did long ago.
[12]I think about all the things you
did.
I think about what you have
done.
[13]God, your ways are holy.
No god is as great as our God.
[14]You are the God who did
miracles.
You showed people your power.
[15]By your power you have saved
your people,

the descendants[d] of Jacob and
Joseph.   *Selah*

16God, the waters saw you.
  They saw you and became
    afraid.
  The deep waters shook with
    fear.
17The clouds poured down their
    rain.
  The sky thundered.
  Your lightning flashed back and
    forth.
18Your thunder sounded in the
    whirlwind.
  Lightning lit up the world.
  The earth trembled and shook.
19You made a way through the sea
    and paths through the deep
    waters.
  But your footprints were not
    seen.
20You led your people like a flock of
    sheep.
  You led them by using Moses
    and Aaron.

God Saved Israel from Egypt

A maskil[d] of Asaph.

78 My people, listen to my
    teaching.
  Listen to what I say.
2I will speak using stories.
  I will tell things that have been
    secret since long ago.
3We have heard them and know
    them.
  Our fathers told them to us.
4We will not keep them from our
    children.
  We will tell those who come
    later
  about the praises of the Lord.
  We will tell about his power
    and the miracles[d] he has done.

5The Lord made an agreement
    with Jacob.
  He gave the teachings to Israel.
  And he commanded our ancestors

to teach them to their children.
6Then their children would know
    them,
  even their children not yet born.
  And they would tell their
    children.
7So they would all trust God.
  They would not forget what God
    had done.
  Instead, they would obey his
    commands.
8They would not be like their
    ancestors
  who were stubborn and
    disobedient.
  Their hearts were not loyal to
    God.
  They were not true to him.

9The men of Ephraim had bows for
    weapons.
  But they ran away on the day of
    battle.
10They didn't keep their agreement
    with God.
  They refused to live by his
    teachings.
11They forgot what he had done
    and the miracles he had shown
    them.
12He did miracles while their
    ancestors watched,
  in the fields of Zoan in Egypt.
13He divided the Red Sea[d] and led
    them through.
  He made the water stand up like
    a wall.
14He led them with a cloud by day.
  And he led them at night by the
    light of a fire.
15He split the rocks in the desert.
  And he gave them much water,
    as if it were from the deep
    ocean.
16He brought streams out of the rock.
  The water flowed down like
    rivers.
17But the people continued to sin
    against him.
  In the desert they turned
    against God Most High.

¹⁸They decided to test God
    by asking for the food they
    wanted.
¹⁹Then they spoke against God.
    They said, "Can God prepare
    food in the desert?
²⁰When he hit the rock, water
    poured out.
    Rivers flowed down.
    But can he give us bread also?
    Will he provide his people with
    meat?"
²¹When the Lord heard them, he
    was very angry.
    His anger was like fire to the
    people of Jacob.
    His anger grew against the
    people of Israel.
²²They had not believed God.
    They had not trusted him to
    save them.
²³But he gave a command to the
    clouds above.
    The doors of heaven opened.
²⁴He rained manna^d down on them
    to eat.
    He gave them grain from
    heaven.
²⁵So they ate the bread of angels.
    He sent them all the food they
    could eat.
²⁶He sent the east wind from
    heaven.
    He led the south wind by his
    power.
²⁷He rained meat on them like dust.
    The birds were as many as the
    sand of the sea.
²⁸He made the birds fall inside the
    camp,
    all around the tents.
²⁹So the people ate and became
    very full.
    God had given them what they
    wanted.
³⁰While they were still eating,
    and while the food was still in
    their mouths,
³¹God became angry with them.
    He killed some of the healthiest
    of them.

He struck down the best young
    men of Israel.
³²But they kept on sinning.
    They did not believe in spite of
    seeing the miracles.
³³So he ended their days without
    meaning
    and their years in terror.
³⁴Whenever he killed them, some
    would look to him for help.
    They would come back to God
    and follow him.
³⁵They would remember that God
    was their Rock,^d
    that God Most High had saved
    them.
³⁶But their words were false.
    Their tongues lied to him.
³⁷Their hearts were not really loyal
    to God.
    They did not keep his
    agreement.
³⁸Still God was merciful.
    He forgave their sins.
    He did not destroy them.
    Many times he held back his
    anger.
    He did not stir up all his anger.
³⁹He remembered that they were
    only human.
    They were like a wind that
    blows and does not come
    back.
⁴⁰They turned against God so often
    in the desert!
    There they made him very sad.
⁴¹Again and again they tested God.
    They brought pain to the Holy
    One of Israel.
⁴²They did not remember his power
    or the time he saved them from
    the enemy.
⁴³They forgot the signs he did in
    Egypt
    and his miracles in the fields of
    Zoan.
⁴⁴He turned the rivers to blood.
    So no one could drink the
    water.
⁴⁵He sent flies that bit the people.

He sent frogs that destroyed them.

46He gave their crops to grasshoppers
and what they worked for to locusts.[d]

47He destroyed their vines with hail
and their sycamore trees with sleet.

48He killed their animals with hail
and their cattle with lightning.

49He showed them his hot anger.
He sent his strong anger against them.
He sent his destroying angels.

50He found a way to show his anger.
He did not keep them from dying.
He let them die by a terrible disease.

51God killed all the firstborn[d] sons in Egypt,
the oldest son of each family of Ham.[n]

52But God led out his people like sheep.
He guided them like a flock through the desert.

53He led them to safety. They had nothing to fear.
But their enemies drowned in the sea.

54So God brought them to his holy land.
He brought them to the mountain country he took with his own power.

55He forced out the other nations.
And he had his people inherit the land.
He let the tribes[d] of Israel settle there in tents.

56But they tested God
and turned against the Most High.
They did not keep his rules.

57They turned away and sinned just like their ancestors.
They were like a crooked bow that does not shoot straight.

58They made God angry by building places to worship false gods.
They made him jealous with their idols.

59When God heard them, he became very angry.
And he rejected the people of Israel completely.

60He left his dwelling at Shiloh,
the tent where he lived among men.

61He let his Holy Ark[d] be captured.
He let the Holy Ark, which was his glory, be taken by enemies.

62He let his people be killed.
He was very angry with his children.

63The young men died by fire.
The young women had no one to marry.

64Their priests fell by the sword.
But their widows were not allowed to cry.

65Then the Lord got up as if he had been asleep.
He awoke like a man who was drunk with wine.

66He struck down his enemies.
He disgraced them for ever.

67But God rejected the family of Joseph.
He did not choose the tribe of Ephraim.

68Instead, he chose the tribe of Judah
and Mount Zion,[d] which he loves.

69And he built his Temple[d] high like the mountains.
Like the earth, he built it to last for ever.

70He chose David to be his servant.

Ham The people in Egypt were descendants of Ham, one of Noah's sons. See Genesis 10:6.

He took him from the sheep
pens.
71He brought him from tending the
sheep
so he could lead the flock, the
people of Jacob.
This flock was his own people,
the people of Israel.
72And David led them with an
innocent heart.
He guided them with skilful
hands.

The Nation Cries for Jerusalem

A song of Asaph.

79 God, nations have come
against your people.
They have ruined your holy
Temple.*d*
They have turned Jerusalem into
ruins.
2They have given the bodies of
your servants
as food to the wild birds.
They have given the bodies of
those who worship you
to the wild animals.
3They have spilled blood like water
all around Jerusalem.
No one was left to bury the
dead.
4We are a bad joke to the other
nations.
They laugh and make fun of us.

5Lord, how long will this last? Will
you be angry for ever?
How long will your jealousy burn
like a fire?
6Be angry with the nations that do
not know you.
Be angry with the kingdoms that
do not honour you.
7They have destroyed the people
of Jacob.
Those nations have destroyed
the people's land.
8Don't punish us for the sins of our
ancestors.
Show your mercy to us soon.

We are helpless!
9God our Saviour, help us
so people will praise you.
Save us and forgive our sins
so people will honour you.
10Why should the nations say,
"Where is their God?"
Tell the other nations in our
presence
that you punish those who kill
your servants.
11Hear the moans of the prisoners.
Use your great power
to save those sentenced to die.
12Repay those around us seven
times over
for their insults to you, Lord.
13We are your people, the sheep of
your flock.
We will thank you always.
For ever and ever we will praise
you.

A Prayer to Bring Israel Back

*For the director of music. To the tune
of "Lilies of the Agreement".
A song of Asaph.*

80 Shepherd of Israel, listen to
us.
You lead the people of Joseph
like a flock.
You sit on your throne between
the gold creatures with
wings.
Show your greatness 2to the
people of Ephraim, Benjamin
and Manasseh.
Use your strength.
Come and save us.

3God, take us back.
Show us your kindness so we
can be saved.

4Lord God of heaven's armies,
how long will you be angry
at the prayers of your people?
5You have fed your people tears.
You have made them drink many
tears.

⁶You made those around us fight
over us.
Our enemies make fun of us.

⁷God of heaven's armies, take us
back.
Show us your kindness so we
can be saved.

⁸You brought us out of Egypt as if
we were a vine.
You forced out other nations and
planted us in the land.
⁹You cleared the land for us.
Like a vine, we took root and
filled the land.
¹⁰We covered the mountains with
our shade.
We had limbs like the mighty
cedar tree.
¹¹Our branches reached the
Mediterranean Sea.
And our shoots went to the
Euphrates River.

¹²So why did you pull down our
walls?
Now everyone who passes by
steals from us.
¹³Like wild pigs they walk over us.
Like wild animals they feed on
us.

¹⁴God of heaven's armies, come
back.
Look down from heaven and
see.
Take care of us, your vine.
¹⁵ You planted this shoot with your
own hands.
You raised and strengthened this
child.
¹⁶Now it is cut down and burned
with fire.
You destroyed us by your angry
looks.
¹⁷Help the man you have chosen.
Make this human being strong
for your service.
¹⁸Then we will not turn away from
you.
Give us life again, and we will
call to you for help.

¹⁹Lord God of heaven's armies, take
us back.
Show us your kindness so we
can be saved.

A Song for a Holiday

For the director of music. By the
gittith.ᵈ A song of Asaph.

81 Sing for joy to God, our
strength.
Shout out loud to the God of
Jacob.
²Begin the music. Play the
tambourines.ᵈ
Play pleasant music on the harps
and lyres.ᵈ
³Blow the sheep's horn at the time
of the New Moon.ᵈ
Blow it when the moon is full,
when our feast begins.
⁴This is the law for Israel.
It is God's command to the
people of Jacob.
⁵He made this agreement with the
people of Joseph
when they went out of the land
of Egypt.

I heard a language I did not know,
saying:
⁶"I took the load off your
shoulders.
I let you put down your baskets.
⁷When you were in trouble, you
called, and I saved you.
I answered you with thunder.
I tested you at the waters of
Meribah. *Selah*ᵈ
⁸My people, listen. I am warning
you.
Israel, please listen to me!
⁹You must not have foreign gods
among you.
You must not worship any false
god.
¹⁰I, the Lord, am your God.
I brought you out of Egypt.
Open your mouth, and I will
feed you.

11"But my people did not listen to
me.
Israel did not want me.
12So I let them go their stubborn
way.
They followed their own advice.
13I wish my people would listen to
me.
I wish Israel would live my way.
14Then I would quickly defeat their
enemies.
I would turn my hand against
those who are against them.
15Those who hate the Lord would
bow before him.
Their punishment would
continue for ever.
16But I would give you the finest
wheat.
I would fill you with honey from
the rocks."

God Judges the Judges

A song of Asaph.

82 God is in charge of the great
meeting of his people.
He judges the rulers.
2He says, "How long will you
defend evil people?
How long will you show greater
kindness to the wicked?   *Selah^d*
3Defend the orphans and the weak.
Defend the rights of the poor
and suffering.
4Save the weak and helpless
from the power of the wicked.

5"You know nothing. You don't
understand.
You walk in the dark,
while the world is falling apart.
6I said, 'You are gods.
You are all sons of the Most
High God'.
7But you will die like any other
person.
You will die like all the leaders."

8God, come and judge the earth.
You own all the nations.

A Prayer Against the Enemies

A song of Asaph.

83 God, do not keep quiet.
God, do not be silent or still.
2Your enemies are making plans.
Those who hate you are getting
ready to attack.
3They are making plans against
your people.
They plan to hurt those you
love.
4They say, "Come, let's destroy
them as a nation.
Then no one will remember the
name 'Israel' any more."
5They are united in their plan.
These have made an agreement
against you:
6the families of Edom and the
Ishmaelites,
Moab and the Hagrites,
7the people of Byblos, Ammon,
Amalek,
Philistia and Tyre.
8Even Assyria has joined them
to help Ammon and Moab, the
descendants^d of Lot.   *Selah^d*

9God, do to them what you did to
Midian.
Do what you did to Sisera and
Jabin at the Kishon River.
10They died at Endor.
Their bodies rotted on the
ground.
11Do to their important leaders what
you did to Oreb and Zeeb.
Do to their princes what you did
to Zebah and Zalmunna.
12They said, "Let's take for
ourselves
the pasturelands that belong to
God."
13My God, make them like the
tumbleweed,
like chaff^d blown away by the
wind.
14Be like a fire that burns a forest
or like flames that blaze through
the hills.

15Chase them with your storm.
   Frighten them with your wind.
16Cover them with shame.
   Then people will look for you,
     Lord.
17Make them afraid and ashamed for
    ever.
   Disgrace them and destroy
    them.
18Then they will know that you are
    the Lord.
   They will know that only you
    are God Most High over all
    the earth.

Wishing to Be in the Temple

For the director of music.
By the gittith.d A song
of the sons of Korah.

84 Lord of heaven's armies,
how lovely is your Temple!d
2I want to be in
   the courtyards of the Lord's
    Temple.
My whole being wants
   to be with the living God.
3The sparrows have found a home.
   And the swallows have nests.
They raise their young near your
    altars,
   Lord of heaven's armies, my
    King and my God.
4Happy are the people who live at
   your Temple.
   They are always praising you.
              Selahd

5Happy are those whose strength
   comes from you.
   They want to travel to
    Jerusalem.
6As they pass through the Valley of
    Baca,
   they make it like a spring.
   The autumn rains fill it with
    pools of water.
7The people get stronger as they
    go.
   And everyone meets with God
    in Jerusalem.

8Lord God of heaven's armies,
   hear my prayer.
   God of Jacob, listen to me.   Selah
9God, look at our shield.
   Be kind to your appointed king.

10One day in the courtyards of your
    Temple is better
   than a thousand days anywhere
    else.
I would rather be a doorkeeper in
    the Temple of my God
   than live in the homes of the
    wicked.
11The Lord God is like our sun and
    shield.
   The Lord gives us kindness and
    glory.
He does not hold back anything
    good
   from those whose life is
    innocent.
12Lord of heaven's armies,
   happy are the people who trust
    you!

A Prayer for the Nation

For the director of music. A song of the
sons of Korah.

85 Lord, you have been kind to
your land.
You gave the people of Jacob
   back their riches.
2You forgave the guilt of the
    people.
   You covered all their sins. Selahd
3You stopped all your anger.
   You stopped your strong anger.

4God our Saviour, bring us back
    again.
   Stop being angry with us.
5Will you be angry with us for
    ever?
   Will you stay angry from now
    on?
6Won't you give us life again?
   Your people would rejoice in
    you.
7Lord, show us your love.
   Save us.

8I will listen to God the Lord.
  He has ordered peace for his
    people who worship him.
  Don't let them go back to
    foolishness.
9God will soon save those who
    respect him.
  And his greatness will be seen
    in our land.
10Love and truth will belong to
    God's people.
  Goodness and peace will be
    theirs.
11On earth people will be loyal to
    God.
  And God's goodness will shine
    down from heaven.
12The Lord will give his goodness.
  And the land will give its crops.
13Goodness will go before God
  and prepare the way for him.

A Cry for Help

A prayer of David.

86 Lord, listen to me and
    answer me.
  I am poor and helpless.
2Protect me, because I worship
    you.
  My God, save me, your
    servant.
  I trust in you.
3Lord, be merciful to me.
  I have called to you all day.
4Give happiness to me, your
    servant.
  Lord, I give my life to you.
5Lord, you are kind and forgiving.
  You have great love for those
    who call to you.
6Lord, hear my prayer.
  Listen when I ask for mercy.
7I call to you in times of trouble.
  You certainly will answer me.

8Lord, there is no god like you.
  There are no works like yours.
9Lord, all the nations you have
    made
  will come and worship you.

  They will honour you.
10You are great, and you do
    miracles.*d*
  Only you are God.

11Lord, teach me what you want me
    to do.
  And I will live by your truth.
  Teach me to respect you
    completely.
12Lord, my God, I will praise you
    with all my heart.
  I will honour your name for
    ever.
13You have great love for me.
  You have saved me from death.

14God, proud men turn against me.
  A gang of cruel men are trying
    to kill me.
  They do not respect you.
15But Lord, you are a God who
    shows mercy and is kind.
  You don't become angry quickly.
  You have great love and
    faithfulness.
16Turn to me and be merciful.
  Give me, your servant,
    strength.
  Save me, the son of your female
    servant.
17Show me a sign of your goodness.
  When my enemies look, they
    will be ashamed.
  You, Lord, have helped me and
    comforted me.

God Loves Jerusalem

A song of the sons of Korah.

87 The Lord built Jerusalem on
    the holy mountain.
2 He loves its gates
  more than any other place in
    Israel.
3City of God,
  wonderful things are said about
    you.   *Selah*d
4God says, "I will put Egypt and
    Babylonia
  on the list of nations that know
    me.

People from Philistia, Tyre and
Cush
will be born there."

5They will say about Jerusalem,
"This one and that one were
born there.
God Most High will strengthen
her."
6The Lord will keep a list of the
nations.
He will note, "This person was
born there."   *Selah*
7They will dance and sing,
"All good things come from
Jerusalem."

A Sad Complaint

A song of the sons of Korah. For the
director of music. By the mahalath
leannoth.*d* A maskil*d* of Heman
the Ezrahite.

88 Lord, you are the God who
saves me.
I cry out to you day and night.
2Accept my prayer.
Listen to my cry.

3My life is full of troubles.
I am nearly dead.
4They think I am on the way to my
grave.
I am like a man with no
strength.
5I have been left as dead,
like a body lying in a grave.
You don't remember dead people.
They are cut off from your
care.
6You have brought me close to
death.
I am almost in the dark place of
the dead.
7You have been very angry with
me.
All your waves crush me.   *Selah*d
8You have taken my friends away
from me.
You have made them hate me.
I am trapped and cannot escape.
9 My eyes are weak from crying.

Lord, I have prayed to you every
day.
I have lifted my hands in prayer
to you.
10Do you show your miracles*d* for
the dead?
Do their spirits rise up and
praise you?   *Selah*
11Will your love be told in the
grave?
Will your loyalty be told in the
place of death?
12Will your miracles be known in the
dark grave?
Will your goodness be known in
the land where the dead are
forgotten?

13But, Lord, I have called out to
you for help.
Every morning I pray to you.
14Lord, why do you reject me?
Why do you hide from me?
15I have been weak and dying since
I was young.
I suffer from your terrors, and I
am helpless.
16You have been angry with me.
Your terrors have destroyed
me.
17They surround me daily like a
flood.
They are all around me.
18You have taken away my loved
ones and friends.
Darkness is my only friend.

A Song About God's Loyalty

A maskil*d* of Ethan the Ezrahite.

89 I will always sing about the
Lord's love.
I will tell of his loyalty from now
on.
2I will say, "Your love continues
for ever.
Your loyalty goes on and on like
the sky."
3You said, "I made an agreement
with the man of my choice.

I made a promise to my servant
David.
⁴I told him, 'I will make your family
continue for ever.
Your kingdom will continue from
now on'."   *Selah*ᵈ

⁵Lord, the heavens praise you for
your miraclesᵈ
and for your loyalty in the
meeting of your holy ones.
⁶Who in heaven is equal to the
Lord?
None of the angels is like the
Lord.
⁷When the holy ones meet, it is
God they fear.
He is more frightening than all
who surround him.
⁸Lord God of heaven's armies, who
is like you?
Lord, you are powerful and
completely to be trusted.
⁹You rule the mighty sea.
You calm the stormy waves.
¹⁰You crushed the sea monster
Rahab.ᵈ
By your power you scattered
your enemies.
¹¹The skies and the earth belong to
you.
You made the world and
everything in it.
¹²You created the north and the
south.
Mount Tabor and Mount
Hermon sing for joy at your
name.
¹³Your arm has great power.
Your hand is strong. Your right
hand is lifted up.
¹⁴Your kingdom is built on what is
right and fair.
Love and truth are in all you do.

¹⁵Happy are the people who know
how to praise you.
Lord, let them live in the light
of your presence.
¹⁶In your name they rejoice all the
time.

They praise your goodness.
¹⁷You are their glorious strength.
In your kindness you honour our
king.
¹⁸Our king, our shield, belongs to
the Lord.
Our king belongs to the Holy
One of Israel.

¹⁹Once, in a vision, you spoke
to those who worship you.
You said, "I have given strength
to a warrior.
I have selected a young man
from my people.
²⁰I have found my servant David.
I appointed him by pouring holy
oil on him.
²¹I will steady him with my hand.
I will strengthen him with my
arm.
²²No enemy will make him give
forced payments.
Wicked people will not defeat
him.
²³I will crush his enemies in front of
him.
I will defeat those who hate him.
²⁴My loyalty and love will be with
him.
Through me he will be strong.
²⁵I will give him power over the sea
and control over the rivers.
²⁶He will say to me, 'You are my
father,
my God, the Rock,ᵈ the one
who saves me'.
²⁷I will make him my firstbornᵈ son.
He will be the greatest king on
earth.
²⁸My love will watch over him for
ever.
My agreement with him will
never end.
²⁹I will make his family continue.
His kingdom will last as long as
the skies.
³⁰"But his descendantsᵈ might reject
my teachings
and not follow my rules.
³¹They might break my laws

and disobey my commands.
³²Then I will punish their sins with a
rod
and their wrongs with a whip.
³³But I will not hold back my love
from David.
I will not stop being loyal.
³⁴I will not break my agreement.
I will not change what I have
said.
³⁵It is certain that I am a holy God.
So it is certain I will not lie to
David.
³⁶His family will continue for ever.
His kingdom will continue before
me like the sun.
³⁷It will last for ever, like the moon,
like a lasting witness in the
sky." *Selah*
³⁸But now, you have rejected your
appointed king.
You have been angry with him.
³⁹You have broken the agreement
with your servant.
You threw his crown to the
ground.
⁴⁰You have torn down all the city
walls.
You have turned his strong,
walled cities into ruins.
⁴¹Everyone who passes by steals
from him.
His neighbours insult him.
⁴²You have given strength to his
enemies.
You have made them all happy.
⁴³You have made his sword useless.
You did not help him stand in
battle.
⁴⁴You have kept him from winning.
You threw his throne to the
ground.
⁴⁵You have cut his life short.
You have covered him with
shame. *Selah*
⁴⁶Lord, how long will this go on?
Will you ignore us for ever?
How long will your anger burn
like a fire?
⁴⁷Remember how short my life is.

Why did you create us anyway?
⁴⁸What man alive will not die?
Can he escape the grave? *Selah*
⁴⁹Lord, where is your love from
times past?
With loyalty you promised it to
David.
⁵⁰Lord, remember how they
insulted your servant.
Remember how I have suffered
the insults of the nations.
⁵¹Lord, remember how your
enemies insulted you.
Remember how they insulted
your appointed king
wherever he went.
⁵²Praise the Lord for ever!
Amen and amen.

Book 4

God Is Eternal, and We Are Not

A prayer of Moses, the man of God.

90 Lord, you have been our home
since the beginning.
²Before the mountains were born,
and before you created the earth
and the world,
you are God.
You have always been, and you
will always be.
³You turn people back into dust.
You say, "Go back into dust,
human beings."
⁴To you, a thousand years
is like the passing of a day.
It passes like an hour in the
night.
⁵While people sleep, you take their
lives.
They are like weeds that grow
in the morning.
⁶In the morning they are fresh and
new.
But by evening they dry up and
die.
⁷We are destroyed by your anger.

We are terrified by your hot
   anger.
8You have put the evil we have
   done right in front of you.
You clearly see our secret sins.
9All our days pass while you are
   angry.
Our years end with a moan.
10Our lifetime is 70 years.
   If we are strong, we may live to
      be 80.
But the years are full of hard
   work and pain.
They pass quickly, and then we
   are gone.

11Who knows the full power of your
   anger?
   Your anger is as great as our
      fear of you should be.
12Teach us how short our lives
   really are
   so that we may be wise.

13Lord, how long before you return
   and show kindness to your
      servants?
14Fill us with your love every
   morning.
   Then we will sing and rejoice all
      our lives.
15We have seen years of trouble.
   Now give us joy as you gave us
      sorrow.
16Show your servants the wonderful
   things you do.
   Show your greatness to their
      children.
17Lord our God, be pleased with us.
   Give us success in what we do.
   Yes, give us success in what we
      do.

Safe in the Lord

91 Those who go to God Most
High for safety
will be protected by God
   All-Powerful.
2I will say to the Lord, "You are
   my place of safety and
   protection.

You are my God, and I trust
   you."

3God will save you from hidden
   traps
   and from deadly diseases.
4He will protect you like a bird
   spreading its wings over its
      young.
His truth will be like your
   armour and shield.
5You will not fear any danger by
   night
   or an arrow during the day.
6You will not be afraid of diseases
   that come in the dark
   or sickness that strikes at noon.
7At your side 1,000 people may
   die,
   or even 10,000 right beside you.
But you will not be hurt.
8You will only watch what happens.
   You will see the wicked
      punished.

9The Lord is your protection.
   You have made God Most High
      your place of safety.
10Nothing bad will happen to you.
   No disaster will come to your
      home.
11He has put his angels in charge of
   you.
   They will watch over you
      wherever you go.
12They will catch you with their
   hands.
   And you will not hit your foot on
      a rock.
13You will walk on lions and cobras.
   You will step on strong lions and
      snakes.

14The Lord says, "If someone loves
   me, I will save him.
   I will protect those who know
      me.
15They will call to me, and I will
   answer them.
   I will be with them in trouble.
   I will rescue them and honour
      them.

16I will give them a long, full life.
They will see how I can save."

Thanksgiving for God's Goodness

A song for the Sabbath[d] day.

92 It is good to praise the Lord,
to sing praises to God Most
High.
2It is good to tell of your love in
the morning
and of your loyalty at night.
3It is good to praise you with the
ten-stringed lyre[d]
and with the soft-sounding
harp.

4Lord, you have made me happy
by what you have done.
I will sing for joy about what
your hands have done.
5Lord, you have done such great
things!
How deep are your thoughts!
6Stupid people don't know these
things.
Fools don't understand.
7Wicked people grow like the
grass.
Evil people seem to do well.
But they will be destroyed for
ever.
8But, Lord, you will be honoured
for ever.
9Lord, surely your enemies,
surely your enemies will be
destroyed.
All who do evil will be scattered.
10But you have made me as strong
as a wild ox.
You have poured fine oils on
me.
11When I looked, I saw my
enemies.
I heard the cries of those who
are against me.
12But good people will grow like
palm trees.
They will be tall like the cedar
trees of Lebanon.

13They will be like trees planted in
the courtyards of the Lord.
They will grow strong in the
courtyards of our God.
14When they are old, they will still
produce fruit.
They will be healthy and fresh.
15They will say that the Lord is
good.
He is my Rock,[d] and there is no
wrong in him.

The Majesty of God

93 The Lord is king. He is
clothed with majesty.
The Lord is clothed in majesty
and armed with strength.
The world is set,
and it cannot be moved.
2Lord, your kingdom was set up
long ago.
You are everlasting.

3Lord, the seas rise up.
The seas raise their voice.
The seas lift up their pounding
waves.
4The sound of the water is loud.
The ocean waves are powerful.
But the Lord above is much
greater.
5Lord, your laws will stand for
ever.
Your Temple[d] will be holy for
evermore.

God Will Pay Back His Enemies

94 The Lord is a God who gives
people what they deserve.
God, show your greatness and
punish!
2Rise up, Judge of the earth.
Give the proud what they
deserve.
3How long will the wicked be
happy?
How long, Lord?

4They are full of proud words.
Those who do evil brag about
what they have done.

⁵Lord, they crush your people.
   They make your children suffer.
⁶They kill widows and foreigners.
   They murder orphans.
⁷They say, "The Lord doesn't see.
   The God of Jacob doesn't
     notice."

⁸You stupid ones among the
     people, pay attention.
   You fools, when will you
     understand?
⁹Can't the creator of ears hear?
   Can't the maker of eyes see?
¹⁰Won't the one who corrects
     nations punish you?
   Doesn't the teacher of men
     know everything?
¹¹The Lord knows what people
     think.
   He knows they are just a puff of
     wind.

¹²Lord, those you correct are
     happy.
   You give them your teachings.
¹³You give them rest from times of
     trouble
   until a grave is dug for the
     wicked.
¹⁴The Lord won't leave his people.
   He will not give up his children.
¹⁵Judgement will again be fair.
   And all who are honest will
     follow it.

¹⁶Who will help me fight against the
     wicked?
   Who will stand with me against
     those who do evil?
¹⁷If the Lord had not helped me,
   I would have died soon.
¹⁸I said, "I am about to be
     overwhelmed."
   But, Lord, your love kept me
     safe.
¹⁹I was very worried.
   But you comforted me and made
     me happy.

²⁰Crooked leaders cannot be your
     friends.

   They use the law to cause
     suffering.
²¹They join forces against people
     who do right.
   They sentence to death the
     innocent.
²²But the Lord protects me like a
     strong, walled city.
   My God is the rock of my
     protection.
²³God will pay them back for their
     sins.
   He will destroy them for their
     evil.
   The Lord our God will destroy
     them.

A Call to Praise and Obedience

95 Come, let's sing for joy to
    the Lord.
   Let's shout praises to the Rock*ᵈ*
     who saves us.
²Let's come to him with
     thanksgiving.
   Let's sing songs to him.
³The Lord is the great God.
   He is the great King over all
     gods.
⁴The deepest places on earth are
     his.
   And the highest mountains
     belong to him.
⁵The sea is his because he made it.
   He created the land with his
     own hands.

⁶Come, let's bow down and
     worship him.
   Let's kneel before the Lord who
     made us.
⁷He is our God.
   And we are the people he takes
     care of
   and the sheep that he tends.

Today listen to what he says:
⁸ "Do not be stubborn, as your
     ancestors were at Meribah,
   as they were that day at Massah
     in the desert.
⁹There your ancestors tested me.

They put me to the test even
    though they saw what I did.
[10]I was angry with those people for
    40 years.
I said, 'They are not loyal to
    me.
They have not understood my
    ways'.
[11]I was angry and made a promise,
'They will never enter my land
    of rest'."

Praise for God's Glory

96 Sing to the Lord a new song.
Sing to the Lord, all the
    earth.
[2]Sing to the Lord and praise his
    name.
Every day tell how he saves us.
[3]Tell the nations of his glory.
Tell all peoples the miracles[d] he
    does.

[4]The Lord is great; he should be
    praised.
He should be honoured more
    than all the gods.
[5]All the gods of the nations are
    only idols.
But the Lord made the skies.
[6]The Lord has glory and majesty.
He has power and beauty in his
    Temple.[d]

[7]Praise the Lord, all nations on
    earth.
Praise the Lord's glory and
    power.
[8]Praise the glory of the Lord's
    name.
Bring an offering and come into
    his Temple courtyards.
[9]Worship the Lord because he is
    holy.
The whole earth should tremble
    before the Lord.
[10]Tell the nations, "The Lord is
    king."
The earth is set, and it cannot
    be moved.
He will judge the people fairly.

[11]Let the skies rejoice and the earth
    be glad.
Let the sea and everything in it
    shout.
[12]Let the fields and everything in
    them show their joy.
Then all the trees of the forest
    will sing for joy.
[13] They will sing before the Lord
    because he is coming.
He is coming to judge the world.
He will judge the world with
    fairness
and the nations with truth.

A Hymn About God's Power

97 The Lord is king. Let the
earth rejoice.
Faraway lands should be glad.
[2]Thick, dark clouds surround him.
His kingdom is built on what is
    right and fair.
[3]A fire goes before him
and burns up his enemies all
    around.
[4]His lightning flashes in the sky.
When the people see it, they
    tremble.
[5]The mountains melt like wax
    before the Lord.
He is Lord of all the earth.
[6]The skies tell about his goodness.
And all the people see his glory.

[7]Those who worship idols should
    be ashamed.
They boast about their false
    gods.
All the gods should worship the
    Lord.
[8]When Jerusalem hears this, she is
    glad.
The towns of Judah rejoice.
They are happy because of your
    judgements, Lord.
[9]You are the Lord Most High over
    all the earth.
You are supreme over all gods.
[10]People who love the Lord should
    hate evil.

The Lord watches over those
  who follow him.
He frees them from the power
  of the wicked.
11Light shines on those who do
  right.
Joy belongs to those who are
  honest.
12Rejoice in the Lord, you who do
  right.
Praise his holy name.

The God of Power and Justice

A song.

98 Sing to the Lord a new song
   because he has done
   miracles.*d*
By his right hand and holy arm
  he has won the victory.
2The Lord has told of his power to
  save.
He has shown the other nations
  his victory for his people.
3He has remembered his love
  and his loyalty to the people of
    Israel.
All the ends of the earth have
    seen
  God's power to save.

4Shout with joy to the Lord, all the
    earth.
  Burst into songs and praise.
5Make music to the Lord with
    harps,
  with harps and the sound of
    singing.
6Blow the trumpets and the
    sheep's horns.
  Shout for joy to the Lord the
    King.

7Let the sea and everything in it
    shout.
  Let the world and everyone on
    it sing.
8Let the rivers clap their hands.
  Let the mountains sing together
    for joy.
9Let them sing before the Lord

because he is coming to judge
  the world.
He will judge the world fairly.
He will judge the nations with
  fairness.

God the Fair and Holy King

99 The Lord is king.
   Let the nations shake with
   fear.
He sits between the gold
  creatures with wings.
Let the earth shake.
2The Lord in Jerusalem is great.
He is supreme over all the
  nations.
3Let them praise your name.
It is great, holy and to be
  feared.

4The King is powerful and loves
  justice.
Lord, you made things fair.
You have done what is fair and
  right
  for the people of Jacob.
5Praise the Lord our God.
Worship at the Temple,*d* his
  footstool.
He is holy.

6Moses and Aaron were among his
  priests.
And Samuel was among his
  worshippers.
They called to the Lord,
  and he answered them.
7He spoke to them from the pillar
  of cloud.
They kept the rules and laws he
  gave them.

8Lord our God, you answered
  them.
You showed them that you are a
  forgiving God.
But you punished them for their
  wrongs.
9Praise the Lord our God.
Worship at his holy mountain.
The Lord our God is holy.

A Call to Praise God

A song of thanks.

100 Shout to the Lord, all the earth.
2 Serve the Lord with joy.
Come before him with singing.
3 Know that the Lord is God.
He made us, and we belong to him.
We are his people, the sheep he tends.
4 Come into his city with songs of thanksgiving.
Come into his courtyards with songs of praise.
Thank him, and praise his name.
5 The Lord is good. His love continues for ever.
His loyalty continues from now on.

A Promise to Rule Well

A song of David.

101 I will sing of love and fairness.
Lord, I will sing praises to you.
2 I will be careful to live an innocent life.
When will you come to me?
I will live an innocent life in my house.
3 I will not look at anything wicked.
I hate those who turn against you.
They will not be found near me.
4 Let those who want to do wrong stay away from me.
I will have nothing to do with evil.
5 If anyone secretly says things against his neighbour,
I will stop him.
I will not allow people
to be proud and look down on others.
6 I will look for trustworthy people
so I can live with them in the land.

Only those who live innocent lives will be my servants.
7 No one who is dishonest will live in my house.
No liars will stay around me.
8 Every morning I will destroy the wicked in the land.
I will rid the Lord's city of people who do evil.

A Cry for Help

A prayer of a person who is suffering. When he is discouraged he tells the Lord his complaints.

102 Lord, listen to my prayer.
Let my cry for help come to you.
2 Do not hide from me
in my time of trouble.
Pay attention to me.
When I cry for help, answer me quickly.
3 My life is passing away like smoke.
My bones are burned up with fire.
4 My heart is like grass
that has been cut and dried.
I forget to eat.
5 Because of my grief,
my skin hangs on my bones.
6 I am like a desert owl.
I am like an owl living among the ruins.
7 I lie awake.
I am like a lonely bird on a housetop.
8 All day long enemies insult me.
Those who make fun of me use my name as a curse.
9 I eat ashes as my food.
My tears fall into my drink.
10 Because of your great anger,
you have picked me up and thrown me away.
11 My days are like a passing shadow.
I am like dried grass.
12 But, Lord, you rule for ever.

Your fame continues from now
on.
13You will come and have mercy on
Jerusalem.
The time has now come to be
kind to her.
14Your servants love even her
stones.
They even care about her dust.
15Nations will fear the name of the
Lord.
All the kings on earth will
honour him.
16The Lord will rebuild Jerusalem.
There his glory will be seen.
17He will answer the prayers of the
needy.
He will not reject their prayers.
18Write these things for the future.
Then people who are not yet
born will praise the Lord.
19The Lord looked down from his
holy place above.
From heaven he looked down at
the earth.
20He heard the moans of the
prisoners.
And he freed those sentenced to
die.
21The name of the Lord will be
heard in Jerusalem.
His praise will be heard in
Jerusalem.
22People will come together.
Kingdoms will serve the Lord.

23God has made me tired of living.
He has cut short my life.
24So I said, "My God, do not take
me in the middle of my life.
Your years go on and on.
25In the beginning you made the
earth.
And your hands made the skies.
26They will be destroyed, but you
will remain.
They will all wear out like
clothes.
And, like clothes, you will change
them.

And they will be thrown away.
27But you never change.
And your life will never end.
28Our children will live in your
presence.
And their children will remain
with you."

Praise to the God of Love

Of David.

103 My whole being, praise
the Lord.
All my being, praise his holy
name.
2My whole being, praise the Lord.
Do not forget all his kindnesses.
3The Lord forgives me for all my
sins.
He heals all my diseases.
4He saves my life from the grave.
He loads me with love and
mercy.
5He satisfies me with good things.
He makes me young again, like
the eagle.

6The Lord does what is right and
fair
for all who are wronged by
others.
7He showed his ways to Moses
and his miracles*d* to the people
of Israel.
8The Lord shows mercy and is
kind.
He does not become angry
quickly, and he has great
love.
9He will not always scold us.
He will not be angry for ever.
10He has not punished us as our
sins should be punished.
He has not repaid us for the evil
we have done.
11As high as the sky is above the
earth,
so great is his love for those
who respect him.
12He has taken our sins away from
us

as far as the east is from the
west.
¹³The Lord has mercy on those who
fear him,
as a father has mercy on his
children.
¹⁴He knows how we were made.
He remembers that we are
dust.
¹⁵Human life is like grass.
We grow like a flower in the
field.
¹⁶After the wind blows, the flower
is gone.
There is no sign of where it
was.
¹⁷But the Lord's love for those who
fear him
continues for ever and ever.
And his goodness continues to
their grandchildren
¹⁸and to those who keep his
agreement
and who remember to obey his
orders.
¹⁹The Lord has set his throne in
heaven.
And his kingdom rules over
everything.
²⁰You who are his angels, praise the
Lord.
You are the mighty warriors
who do what he says.
Listen to what he says.
²¹You, his armies, praise the Lord.
You are his servants who do
what he wants.
²²Everything the Lord has made
should praise him in all the
places he rules.
My whole being, praise the Lord.

Praise to God Who Made the World

104 My whole being, praise
the Lord.
Lord my God, you are very
great.
You are clothed with glory and
majesty.

² You wear light like a robe.
You stretch out the skies like a
tent.
³ You build your room above the
clouds.
You make the clouds your chariot.
You ride on the wings of the
wind.
⁴You make the winds your
messengers.
Flames of fire are your
servants.
⁵You built the earth on its
foundations.
So it can never be moved.
⁶You covered the earth with
oceans.
The water was above the
mountains.
⁷But at your command, the water
rushed away.
When you gave your orders like
thunder, it hurried away.
⁸The mountains rose.
The valleys sank.
The water went to the places
you made for it.
⁹You set borders for the seas that
they cannot cross.
The water will never cover the
earth again.
¹⁰You make springs pour into the
ravines.
They flow between the
mountains.
¹¹They water all the wild animals.
The wild donkeys come there to
drink.
¹²Wild birds make nests by the
water.
They sing among the tree
branches.
¹³You water the mountains from
above.
The earth is full of the things
you made.
¹⁴You make the grass for cattle
and vegetables for the use of
man.

You make food grow from the
earth.
15You give us wine that makes
happy hearts.
And you give us olive oil that
makes our faces shine.
You give us bread that gives us
strength.
16The Lord's trees have plenty of
water.
They are the cedar trees of
Lebanon, which he planted.
17The birds make their nests there.
The stork's home is in the fir
trees.
18The high mountains belong to the
wild goats.
The rocks are hiding places for
the badgers.

19You made the moon to mark the
seasons.
And the sun always knows when
to set.
20You make it dark, and it becomes
night.
Then all the wild animals creep
around.
21The lions roar as they attack.
They look to God for food.
22When the sun rises, they leave.
They go back to their dens to
lie down.
23Then people go to work.
And they work until evening.

24Lord, you have made many
things.
With your wisdom you made
them all.
The earth is full of your riches.
25Look at the sea, so big and wide.
Its creatures large and small
cannot be counted.
26Ships travel over the ocean.
And there is the sea monster
Leviathan,d
which you made to play there.

27All these things depend on you
to give them their food at the
right time.

28When you give it to them,
they gather it up.
When you open your hand, they
are filled with good food.
29When you turn away from them,
they become frightened.
When you take away their breath,
they die and turn into dust.
30When you breathe on them,
they are created.
You make the land new again.

31May the glory of the Lord be for
ever.
May the Lord enjoy what he has
made.
32He just looks at the earth, and it
shakes.
He touches the mountains, and
they smoke.

33I will sing to the Lord all my life.
I will sing praises to my God as
long as I live.
34May my thoughts please him.
I am happy in the Lord.
35Let sinners be destroyed from the
earth.
Let the wicked people live no
longer.

My whole being, praise the Lord.
Praise the Lord.

God's Love for Israel

105 Give thanks to the Lord
and pray to him.
Tell the nations what he has
done.
2Sing to him. Sing praises to him.
Tell of all the wonderful things
he has done.
3Be glad that you are his.
Let those who ask the Lord for
help be happy.
4Depend on the Lord and his
strength.
Always go to him for help.
5Remember the wonderful things
he has done.
Remember his miraclesd and his
decisions.

[6]You are descendants[d] of his servant Abraham,
the children of Jacob, his chosen people.

[7]He is the Lord our God.
His laws are for all the world.

[8]He will keep his agreement for ever.
He will keep his promises always.

[9]He will keep the agreement he made with Abraham.
He will keep the promise he made to Isaac.

[10]He made it a law for the people of Jacob.
He made it an agreement with Israel to last for ever.

[11]The Lord said, "I will give you the land of Canaan.
The promised land will belong to you."

[12]Then God's people were few in number.
They were strangers in the land.

[13]They went from one nation to another.
They went from one kingdom to another.

[14]But the Lord did not let anyone hurt them.
He warned kings not to harm them.

[15]He said, "Don't hurt my chosen people.
Don't harm my prophets."[d]

[16]God ordered a time of hunger in the land.
And he destroyed all the food.

[17]Then he sent a man ahead of them.
It was Joseph, who was sold as a slave.

[18]They put chains around his feet and an iron ring around his neck.

[19]Then the time he had spoken of came.
The Lord's words proved that Joseph was right.

[20]The king of Egypt sent for Joseph and freed him.
The ruler of the people set him free.

[21]He made him the master of his house.
Joseph was in charge of his riches.

[22]He could order the princes as he wished.
He taught the older men to be wise.

[23]Then his father Israel came to Egypt.
Jacob, also called Israel, lived in Egypt.[n]

[24]The Lord made his people grow in number.
He made them stronger than their enemies.

[25]And he caused the Egyptians to hate his people.
They made plans against the Lord's servants.

[26]Then he sent his servant Moses, and Aaron, whom he had chosen.

[27]They did many signs among the Egyptians.
They worked miracles in Egypt.

[28]The Lord sent darkness and made the land dark.
But the Egyptians turned against what he said.

[29]So he changed their water into blood
and made their fish die.

[30]Then their country was filled with frogs.
They were even in the bedrooms of their rulers.

[31]The Lord spoke, and flies came.

Egypt Literally, "the land of Ham". Also in verse 27. The people in Egypt were descendants of Ham, one of Noah's sons. See Genesis 10:6.

Gnats were everywhere in the
country.
32He made hail fall like rain.
And he sent lightning through
their land.
33He struck down their grapevines
and fig trees.
He destroyed every tree in the
country.
34He spoke, and grasshoppers
came.
The locusts*d* were too many to
count.
35They ate all the plants in the land.
They ate what the earth
produced.
36The Lord also killed all the
firstborn*d* sons in the land,
the oldest son of each family.

37Then he brought his people
out,
and they carried with them
silver and gold.
Not one of his people stumbled.
38The Egyptians were glad when
they left
because the Egyptians were
afraid of them.
39The Lord covered them with a
cloud
and lit up the night with fire.
40When they asked, he brought
them quail.
He filled them with bread from
heaven.
41God split the rock, and water
flowed out.
It ran like a river through the
desert.
42He remembered his holy promise
to his servant Abraham.

43So God brought his people out
with joy.
He brought out his chosen ones
with singing.
44He gave them lands that belonged
to other nations.
They received what others had
worked for.

45This was so they would keep his
orders
and obey his teachings.
Praise the Lord!

Israel's Failure to Trust God

106 Praise the Lord!
Thank the Lord because
he is good.
His love continues for ever.
2No one can tell all the mighty
things the Lord has done.
No one can speak all his praise.
3Happy are those people who are
fair,
who do what is right at all
times.

4Lord, remember me when you are
kind to your people.
Help me when you save them.
5Let me see the good things you
do for your chosen people.
Let me be happy along with
your happy nation.
Let me join your own people in
praising you.

6We have sinned just as our
ancestors did.
We have done wrong. We have
done evil.
7Our ancestors in Egypt
did not learn from your
miracles.*d*
They did not remember all your
kindnesses.
So they turned against you at
the Red Sea.*d*
8But the Lord saved them for his
own sake,
to show his great power.
9He commanded the Red Sea, and
it dried up.
He led them through the deep
sea as if it were a desert.
10He saved them from those who
hated them.
He saved them from their
enemies.
11And the water covered their
enemies.

Not one of them escaped.
¹²Then the people believed what the
Lord said.
They sang praises to him.

¹³But they quickly forgot what he
had done.
They did not wait for his advice.
¹⁴They became greedy for food in
the desert.
And they tested God there.
¹⁵So he gave them what they
wanted.
But he also sent a terrible
disease among them.

¹⁶The people in the camp became
jealous of Moses
and of Aaron, the holy priest of
the Lord.
¹⁷Then the ground opened up and
swallowed Dathan.
It closed over Abiram's group.
¹⁸Then a fire burned among their
followers.
Flames burned up the wicked
people.

¹⁹The people made a gold calf at
Mount Sinai.
They worshipped a metal statue.
²⁰They exchanged their glorious
God
for a statue of a bull, which eats
grass.
²¹They forgot the God who saved
them,
who had done great things in
Egypt.
²²He did miracles in Egypt.ⁿ
He did amazing things by the
Red Sea.
²³So God said he would destroy
them.
But Moses, his chosen one,
stood before him.
He stopped God's anger from
destroying them.

²⁴Then they refused to go into the
beautiful land of Canaan.
They did not believe what God
promised.
²⁵They grumbled in their tents
and did not obey the Lord.
²⁶So he swore to them
that they would die in the
desert.
²⁷He said their children would be
killed by other nations
and that they would be scattered
among other countries.

²⁸They joined in worshipping Baalᵈ
at Peor.
They ate meat that had been
sacrificed to lifeless statues.
²⁹They made the Lord angry by
what they did.
So many people became sick
with a terrible disease.
³⁰But Phinehas prayed to the Lord,
and the disease stopped.
³¹The Lord will remember that
Phinehas did what was right.
And God will remember this
from now on.

³²The people also made the Lord
angry at Meribah.
And Moses was in trouble
because of them.
³³The people turned against the
Spiritᵈ of God.
So Moses spoke without
stopping to think.

³⁴The people did not destroy the
other nations
as the Lord had told them to do.
³⁵Instead, they mixed with the
other nations.
And they learned their customs.
³⁶They worshipped other nations'
idols.
And they were trapped by them.
³⁷They even killed their sons and
daughters

Egypt Literally, "the land of Ham". The people in Egypt were descendants of Ham, one of
Noah's sons. See Genesis 10:6.

as sacrifices to demons.*d*
38They killed innocent people.
They killed their own sons and
daughters
as sacrifices to the idols of
Canaan.
So the land was made unholy by
their blood.
39The people became unholy by
their sins.
They were unfaithful to God in
what they did.

40So the Lord became angry with
his people.
He hated his own children.
41He let other nations defeat them.
He let their enemies rule over
them.
42Their enemies were cruel to
them.
Their enemies kept them under
their power.
43The Lord saved his people many
times.
But they continued to turn
against him.
So they became even more
wicked.

44But God saw their misery.
He heard their cry.
45He remembered his agreement
with them.
And he felt sorry for them
because of his great love.
46He caused them to be pitied
by those who held them captive.

47Lord our God, save us.
Bring us back from other
nations.
Then we will thank you.
Then we will gladly praise you.

48Praise the Lord, the God of
Israel.
He always was and always will
be.
Let all the people say, "Amen!"

Praise the Lord!

Book 5

God Saves from Many Dangers

107 Thank the Lord because
he is good.
His love continues for ever.
2That is what the people the Lord
has saved should say.
They are the ones he has saved
from the enemy.
3He has gathered them from other
lands,
from east and west, north and
south.

4Some people had wandered in the
desert lands.
They found no city to live in.
5They were hungry and thirsty.
They were discouraged.
6In their misery they cried out to
the Lord.
And he saved them from their
troubles.
7He led them on a straight road
to a city where they could live.
8Let them give thanks to the Lord
for his love
and for the miracles*d* he does for
people.
9He satisfies the thirsty.
He fills up the hungry.

10Some sat in gloom and darkness.
They were prisoners suffering in
chains.
11They had turned against the
words of God.
They had refused the advice of
God Most High.
12So he broke their pride by hard
work.
They stumbled, and no one
helped.
13In their misery they cried out to
the Lord.
And he saved them from their
troubles.
14He brought them out of their
gloom and darkness.
He broke their chains.

15Let them give thanks to the Lord
for his love
and for the miracles he does for
people.
16He breaks down bronze gates.
And he cuts apart iron bars.

17Some became fools who turned
against God.
They suffered for the evil they
did.
18They refused to eat anything.
So they almost died.
19In their misery they cried out to
the Lord.
And he saved them from their
troubles.
20God gave the command and
healed them.
So they were saved from dying.
21Let them give thanks to the Lord
for his love
and for the miracles he does for
people.
22Let them offer sacrifices to thank
him.
With joy they should tell what
he has done.

23Others went out to sea in ships.
They did business on the great
oceans.
24They saw what the Lord could do.
They saw the miracles he did.
25He spoke, and a storm came up.
It blew up high waves.
26The ships tossed as high as the
sky and fell low in the
waves.
The storm was so bad the men
lost their courage.
27They stumbled and fell like men
who were drunk.
They did not know what to do.
28In their misery they cried out to
the Lord.
And he saved them from their
troubles.
29He made the storm be still.
He calmed the waves.
30They were happy that it was
quiet.

And God guided them to the
port they wanted.
31Let them give thanks to the Lord
for his love
and for the miracles he does for
people.
32Let them praise his greatness in
the meeting of the people.
They should praise him in the
meeting of the older leaders.

33He changed rivers into a desert,
and springs of water into dry
ground.
34He made fertile land salty
because the people there did
evil.
35He changed the desert into pools
of water
and dry ground into springs of
water.
36He had the hungry settle there.
They built a city to live in.
37They planted seeds in the fields
and vineyards.
And they had a good harvest.
38God blessed them, and they grew
in number.
Their cattle did not become
fewer.

39Because of disaster, troubles and
sadness,
their families grew smaller and
weaker.
40He showed he was displeased
with their important men.
He made them wander in a
pathless desert.
41But he lifted the poor out of their
suffering.
And he made their families grow
like flocks of sheep.
42Good people see this and are
happy.
But the wicked say nothing.

43Whoever is wise will remember
these things.
He will think about the love of
the Lord.

A Prayer for Victory

A song of David.

108 God, my heart is right.
I will sing and praise you
with all my being.
²Wake up, harp and lyre!*d*
I will wake up the dawn.
³Lord, I will praise you among the
nations.
I will sing songs of praise about
you to all the nations.
⁴Your love is so great that it is
higher than the skies.
Your truth reaches to the
clouds.
⁵God, you are supreme over the
skies.
Let your glory be over all the
earth.

⁶Answer us and save us by your
power.
Then the people you love will be
rescued.
⁷God has said from his Temple,*d*
"When I win, I will divide
Shechem
and cut up the Valley of
Succoth.
⁸Gilead and Manasseh are mine.
Ephraim is like my helmet.
Judah holds my royal sceptre.*d*
⁹Moab is like my washbowl.
I throw my sandals at Edom.
I shout at Philistia."

¹⁰Who will bring me to the strong,
walled city?
Who will lead me to Edom?
¹¹God, surely you have rejected
us.
You do not go out with our
armies.
¹²Help us fight the enemy.
Human help is useless.
¹³But we can win with God's
help.
He will defeat our enemies.

A Prayer Against an Enemy

For the director of music.
A song of David.

109 God, I praise you.
Do not be silent.
²Wicked people and liars have
spoken against me.
They have told lies about me.
³They have said hateful things
about me.
They attack me for no reason.
⁴They attacked me, even though I
loved them
and prayed for them.
⁵I was good to them, but they
repay me with evil.
I loved them, but they hate me
in return.

⁶They say about me, "Have the
Evil One work against him.
Let the devil accuse him.
⁷When he is judged, let him be
found guilty.
Let even his prayers show that
he is guilty.
⁸Let his life be cut short.
Let another man replace him as
leader.
⁹Let his children become orphans.
Let his wife become a widow.
¹⁰Make his children wander around,
begging for food.
Let them be forced out of the
ruins they live in.
¹¹Let the people he owes money to
take everything he owns.
Let strangers steal everything
he has worked for.
¹²Let no one show him love.
Let no one have mercy on his
children.
¹³Let all his descendants*d* die.
Let him be forgotten by people
who live after him.
¹⁴Let the Lord remember how
wicked his ancestors were.
Don't let the sins of his mother
be wiped out.

¹⁵Let the Lord always remember
 their sins.
 Then he will make people forget
  about them completely.

¹⁶"He did not remember to be
  loving.
 He hurt the poor, the needy and
  those who were sad
 until they were nearly dead.
¹⁷He loved to put curses on others.
 So let those same curses fall on
  him.
 He did not like to bless others.
 So do not let good things happen
  to him.
¹⁸He cursed others as often as he
  wore clothes.
 Cursing others filled his body
  and his life,
 like drinking water and using
  olive oil.
¹⁹So let curses cover him like
  clothes.
 Let them wrap around him like a
  belt."
²⁰May the Lord do these things to
  those who accuse me,
 to those who speak evil against
  me.

²¹But you, Lord God,
 be kind to me so others will
  know you are good.
 Because your love is good, save
  me.
²²I am poor and helpless.
 And I am very sad.
²³I am dying like an evening
  shadow.
 I am shaken off like a locust.ᵈ
²⁴My knees are weak from hunger.
 I have become thin.
²⁵My enemies insult me.
 They look at me and shake their
  heads.

²⁶Lord my God, help me.
 Because you are loving, save
  me.
²⁷Then they will know that you have
  saved me.

They will know it was your
 power, Lord.
²⁸They may curse me, but you
 bless me.
 They may attack me, but they
  will be disgraced.
 Then I, your servant, will be
  glad.
²⁹Let those who accuse me be
 disgraced.
 Let them be covered with
  shame like a coat.

³⁰I will thank the Lord very much.
 I will praise him in front of many
  people.
³¹He defends the helpless.
 He saved me from those who
  accuse me.

The Lord Appoints a King

A song of David.

110 The Lord said to my
 Master,
"Sit by me at my right side
until I put your enemies under
 your control."
²The Lord will make you king in
 Jerusalem over all nations.
And you will rule your enemies
 in their own countries.
³Your people will join you on the
 day you come to power.
You have been dressed in
 holiness from birth.
You have the freshness of a
 child.

⁴The Lord has made a promise
 and will not change his mind.
He said, "You are a priest for
 ever,
a priest like Melchizedek."

⁵The Lord is beside you to help
 you.
When he becomes angry, he will
 crush kings.
⁶He will judge those nations, filling
 them with dead bodies.

He will defeat rulers all over the world.
⁷The king will drink from the brook on the way.
Then he will be strengthened and win the battle.

Praise for God's Goodness

111 Praise the Lord!

I will thank the Lord with all my heart
in the meeting of his good people.
²The Lord does great things.
Those people who love them think about them.
³What he does is glorious and splendid.
His goodness continues for ever.
⁴His miracles^d are unforgettable.
The Lord is kind and merciful.
⁵He gives food to those who fear him.
He remembers his agreement for ever.
⁶He has shown his people his power
when he gave them the lands of other nations.
⁷Everything he does is good and fair.
All his orders can be trusted.
⁸They will continue for ever.
They were made true and right.
⁹He sets his people free.
He made his agreement everlasting.
He is holy and wonderful.
¹⁰Wisdom begins with respect for the Lord.
Those who obey his orders have good understanding.
He should be praised for ever.

Honest People Are Blessed

112 Praise the Lord!

Happy is the person who fears the Lord.

He loves what the Lord commands.
²His descendants^d will be powerful in the land.
The children of honest people will be blessed.
³His house will be full of wealth and riches.
His goodness will continue for ever.
⁴A light shines in the dark for honest people.
It shines for those who are good and kind and merciful.
⁵It is good to be kind and generous.
Whoever is fair in his business
⁶will never be defeated.
A good person will be remembered from now on.
⁷He won't be afraid of bad news.
He is safe because he trusts the Lord.
⁸That person is confident. He will not be afraid.
He will look down on his enemies.
⁹He gives freely to the poor.
The things he does are right and will continue for ever.
He will be given great honour.

¹⁰The wicked will see this and become angry.
They will grind their teeth in anger and then disappear.
The wishes of the wicked will come to nothing.

Praise for God's Kindness

113 Praise the Lord!

Praise him, you servants of the Lord.
Praise the name of the Lord.
²The Lord's name should be praised
now and for ever.
³The Lord's name should be praised

from where the sun rises to
where it sets.
⁴The Lord is supreme over all the
nations.
His glory reaches to the skies.

⁵No one is like the Lord our God.
He rules from heaven.
⁶He bends down to look
at the skies and the earth.
⁷The Lord lifts the poor from the
dirt.
He takes the helpless from the
ashes.
⁸And he seats them with princes,
the princes of his people.
⁹He gives children to the woman
who has none.
He makes her a happy mother.

Praise the Lord!

God Brought Israel from Egypt

114 The Israelites went out of
Egypt.
The people of Jacob left that
foreign country.
²Then Judah became God's holy
place.
Israel became the land he ruled.

³The Red Sea*d* looked and ran
away.
The Jordan River turned back.
⁴The mountains danced like sheep
and the hills like little lambs.
⁵Sea, why did you run away?
Jordan, why did you turn back?
⁶Mountains, why did you dance like
sheep?
Hills, why did you dance like
little lambs?

⁷Earth, shake with fear before the
Lord.
Tremble in the presence of the
God of Jacob.
⁸He turned a rock into a pool of
water.
He changed a hard rock into a
spring of water.

The One True God

115 It does not belong to us,
Lord.
The praise belongs to you
because of your love and loyalty.

²Why do the nations ask,
"Where is their God?"
³Our God is in heaven.
He does what he wants.
⁴Their idols are made of silver and
gold.
They are made by human hands.
⁵They have mouths, but they
cannot speak.
They have eyes, but they
cannot see.
⁶They have ears, but they cannot
hear.
They have noses, but they
cannot smell.
⁷They have hands, but they cannot
feel.
They have feet, but they cannot
walk.
And no sounds come from their
throats.
⁸The people who make idols and
trust them
are all like them.

⁹Family of Israel, trust the Lord.
He is your helper and your
protection.
¹⁰Family of Aaron, trust the Lord.
He is your helper and your
protection.
¹¹You people who fear the Lord
should trust him.
He is your helper and your
protection.

¹²The Lord remembers us and will
bless us.
He will bless the family of
Israel.
He will bless the family of
Aaron.
¹³The Lord will bless those who
fear him,
from the smallest to the
greatest.

14May the Lord give you many
children.
And may he give them children
also.
15May the Lord bless you.
He made heaven and earth.

16Heaven belongs to the Lord.
But he gave the earth to people.
17Dead people do not praise the
Lord.
Those in the grave are silent.
18But we will praise the Lord
now and for ever.

Praise the Lord!

Thanksgiving for Escaping Death

116 I love the Lord because he
listens
to my prayers for help.
2He paid attention to me.
So I will call to him for help as
long as I live.
3The ropes of death bound me.
The fear of death took hold of
me.
I was troubled and sad.
4Then I called out the name of the
Lord.
I said, "Please, Lord, save me!"

5The Lord is kind and does what is
right.
Our God is merciful.
6The Lord watches over the
foolish.
When I was helpless, he saved
me.
7I said to myself, "Relax,
because the Lord takes care of
you."
8Lord, you have saved me from
death.
You have stopped my eyes from
crying.
You have kept me from being
defeated.
9So I will walk with the Lord
in the land of the living.
10I believed, so I said,
"I am completely ruined."

11In my distress I said,
"All people are liars."

12What can I give the Lord
for all the good things he has
given to me?
13I will give him a drink offering for
saving me.
And I will pray to the Lord.
14In front of all his people,
I will give the Lord what I
promised.

15The death of one that belongs to
him
is precious to the Lord.
16Lord, I am your servant.
I am your servant and the son
of your female servant.
You have freed me from my
chains.
17I will give an offering to show
thanks to you.
And I will worship the Lord.
18In front of all his people,
I will give the Lord what I
promised.
19I will do this in the Temple^d
courtyards
in Jerusalem.

Praise the Lord!

A Hymn of Praise

117 All you nations, praise the
Lord.
All you people, praise him.
2The Lord loves us very much.
His truth is everlasting.

Praise the Lord!

Thanksgiving for Victory

118 Thank the Lord because
he is good.
His love continues for ever.
2Let the people of Israel say,
"His love continues for ever."
3Let the family of Aaron say,
"His love continues for ever."
4Let those who fear the Lord say,
"His love continues for ever."

⁵I was in trouble. So I called to the
  Lord.
  The Lord answered me and set
  me free.
⁶I will not be afraid because the
  Lord is with me.
People can't do anything to me.
⁷The Lord is with me to help me.
  I will see my enemies defeated.
⁸It is better to trust the Lord
  than to trust people.
⁹It is better to trust the Lord
  than to trust princes.

¹⁰All the nations surrounded me.
  But I defeated them in the name
  of the Lord.
¹¹They surrounded me on every
  side.
  But with the Lord's power, I
  defeated them.
¹²They surrounded me like a swarm
  of bees.
  But they died as quickly as
  thorns burn.
  By the Lord's power, I defeated
  them.
¹³They chased me until I was
  almost defeated.
  But the Lord helped me.
¹⁴The Lord gives me strength and
  makes me sing.
  He has saved me.

¹⁵Shouts of joy and victory
  come from the tents of those
  who do right:
  "The Lord has done powerful
  things."
¹⁶The power of the Lord has won
  the victory.
  With his power the Lord has
  done mighty things.

¹⁷I will not die, but live.
  And I will tell what the Lord has
  done.
¹⁸The Lord has taught me a hard
  lesson.
  But he did not let me die.

¹⁹Open for me the Temple*d* gates.

Then I will come in and thank
  the Lord.
²⁰This is the Lord's gate.
  Only those who are good may
  enter it.
²¹Lord, I thank you for answering
  me.
  You have saved me.

²²The stone that the builders did
  not want
  became the cornerstone.*d*
²³The Lord did this,
  and it is wonderful to us.
²⁴This is the day that the Lord has
  made.
  Let us rejoice and be glad today!

²⁵Please, Lord, save us.
  Please, Lord, give us success.
²⁶God bless the one who comes in
  the name of the Lord.
  We bless all of you from the
  Temple of the Lord.
²⁷The Lord is God.
  And he has shown kindness to
  us.
With branches in your hands, join
  the feast.
  Come to the corners of the
  altar.

²⁸You are my God, and I will thank
  you.
  You are my God, and I will
  praise your greatness.

²⁹Thank the Lord because he is
  good.
  His love continues for ever.

The Word of God

119 Happy are the people who
  live pure lives.
  They follow the Lord's
  teachings.
²Happy are the people who keep
  his rules.
  They ask him for help with their
  whole heart.
³They don't do what is wrong.
  They follow his ways.
⁴Lord, you gave your orders

to be followed completely.
⁵I wish I were more loyal
in meeting your demands.
⁶Then I would not be ashamed
when I think of your commands.
⁷When I learned that your laws are
fair,
I praised you with an honest
heart.
⁸I will meet your demands.
So please don't ever leave me.

⁹How can a young person live a
pure life?
He can do it by obeying your
word.
¹⁰With all my heart I try to obey
you, God.
Don't let me break your
commands.
¹¹I have taken your words to heart
so I would not sin against you.
¹²Lord, you should be praised.
Teach me your demands.
¹³My lips will tell of
all the laws you have spoken.
¹⁴I enjoy living by your rules
as people enjoy great riches.
¹⁵I think about your orders
and study your ways.
¹⁶I enjoy obeying your demands.
And I will not forget your word.

¹⁷Do good to me, your servant, so I
can live,
so I can obey your word.
¹⁸Open my eyes to see the
wonderful things
in your teachings.
¹⁹I am a stranger on earth.
Do not hide your commands
from me.
²⁰I want to study
your laws all the time.
²¹You scold proud people.
Those who ignore your
commands are cursed.
²²Don't let me be insulted and hated
because I obey your rules.
²³Even if princes speak against me,
I, your servant, will think about
your demands.

²⁴Your rules give me pleasure.
They give me good advice.
²⁵I am about to die.
Give me life, as you have
promised.
²⁶I told you about my life, and you
answered me.
Teach me your demands.
²⁷Help me understand your orders.
Then I will think about your
miracles.ᵈ
²⁸I am sad and tired.
Make me strong again as you
have promised.
²⁹Don't let me be dishonest.
Be kind to me by helping me
obey your teachings.
³⁰I have chosen to obey you.
I have obeyed your laws.
³¹I hold on to your rules.
Lord, do not let me be
disgraced.
³²I will obey your commands
because you have made me
happy.

³³Lord, teach me your demands.
Then I will obey them until the
end.
³⁴Help me understand, so I can
obey your teachings.
I will obey them with all my
heart.
³⁵Help me obey your commands
because that makes me happy.
³⁶Help me to want to obey your
rules
instead of selfishly wanting
riches.
³⁷Keep me from looking at
worthless things.
Let me live by your word.
³⁸Keep your promise to me, your
servant,
so you will be feared.
³⁹Take away the shame I fear.
Your laws are good.
⁴⁰How I want to follow your orders.
Give me life because of your
goodness.

⁴¹Lord, show me your love.
Save me as you have promised.
⁴²Then I will have an answer for
people who insult me.
I trust what you say.
⁴³Never keep me from speaking
your truth.
I depend on your fair laws.
⁴⁴I will obey your teachings
for ever and ever.
⁴⁵So I will live in freedom
because I want to follow your
orders.
⁴⁶I will discuss your rules with
kings.
And I will not be ashamed.
⁴⁷I enjoy obeying your commands.
I love them.
⁴⁸I praise your commands, which I
love.
And I think about your demands.

⁴⁹Remember your promise to me,
your servant.
It gives me hope.
⁵⁰When I suffer, this comforts
me:
your promise gives me life.
⁵¹Proud people make fun of me all
the time.
But I do not reject your
teachings.
⁵²I remember your laws from long
ago.
They comfort me, Lord.
⁵³I become angry with wicked
people.
They have not kept your
teachings.
⁵⁴I sing about your demands
wherever I live.
⁵⁵Lord, I remember you at night.
I will obey your teachings.
⁵⁶This is what I do:
I follow your orders.

⁵⁷Lord, you are my share in life.
I have promised to obey your
words.
⁵⁸I prayed to you with all my heart.
Be kind to me as you have
promised.

⁵⁹I thought about my life,
and I decided to obey your
rules.
⁶⁰I hurried and did not wait
to obey your commands.
⁶¹Wicked people have surrounded
me.
But I have not forgotten your
teachings.
⁶²In the middle of the night, I get
up to thank you
because your laws are right.
⁶³I am a friend to everyone who
fears you.
I am a friend to anyone who
follows your orders.
⁶⁴Lord, your love fills the earth.
Teach me your demands.

⁶⁵You have done good things for
me, your servant,
as you have promised, Lord.
⁶⁶Teach me wisdom and knowledge
because I trust your commands.
⁶⁷Before I suffered, I did wrong.
But now I obey your word.
⁶⁸You are good, and you do what is
good.
Teach me your demands.
⁶⁹Proud people have made up lies
about me.
But I will follow your orders
with all my heart.
⁷⁰Those people have no feelings,
but I love your teachings.
⁷¹It was good for me to suffer
so I would learn your demands.
⁷²Your teachings are worth more to
me
than thousands of pieces of gold
and silver.

⁷³You made me and formed me with
your hands.
Give me understanding so I can
learn your commands.
⁷⁴Let those who fear you rejoice
when they see me
because I put my hope in your
word.
⁷⁵Lord, I know that your laws are
right.

And it was right for you to
    punish me.
76Comfort me with your love,
    as you promised me, your
        servant.
77Have mercy on me so that I may
        live.
    I love your teachings.
78Make the proud people ashamed
        because they lied about me.
    But I will think about your
        orders.
79Let those who fear you come to
        me.
    They know your rules.
80Let me obey your demands
        perfectly.
    Then I will not be ashamed.

81I am weak from waiting for you to
        save me.
    But I trust your word.
82My eyes are tired from looking for
        your promise.
    When will you comfort me?
83Even though I am like a leather
        wine bag going up in smoke,
    I do not forget your demands.
84How long will I live?
    When will you judge those who
        are hurting me?
85Proud people have dug pits to trap
        me.
    They have nothing to do with
        your teachings.
86All of your commands can be
        trusted.
    Liars are hurting me. Help
        me!
87They have almost put me in the
        grave.
    But I have not rejected your
        orders.
88Give me life by your love
    so I can obey your rules.

89Lord, your word is everlasting.
    It continues for ever in heaven.
90Your loyalty will continue from
        now on.
    You made the earth, and it still
        stands.

91All things continue to this day
        because of your laws.
    All things serve you.
92If I had not loved your teachings,
    I would have died from my
        sufferings.
93I will never forget your orders
    because you have given me life
        by them.
94I am yours. Save me.
    I have wanted to know your
        orders.
95Wicked people are waiting to
        destroy me.
    But I will think about your rules.
96Everything I see has its limits.
    But your commands have none.

97How I love your teachings!
    I think about them all day long.
98Your commands make me wiser
        than my enemies
    because they are mine for ever.
99I am wiser than all my teachers
    because I think about your
        rules.
100I have more understanding than
        the older leaders
    because I follow your orders.
101I have avoided every evil way
    so I could obey your word.
102I haven't stopped obeying your
        laws
    because you yourself are my
        teacher.
103Your promises are so sweet to
        me.
    They are like honey to my
        mouth!
104Your orders give me
        understanding.
    So I hate lying ways.

105Your word is like a lamp for my
        feet
    and a light for my way.
106I will do what I have promised
    and obey your fair laws.
107I have suffered for a long time.
    Lord, give me life by your word.
108Lord, accept my willing praise.
    And teach me your laws.

109My life is always in danger.
But I haven't forgotten your
teachings.
110Wicked people have set a trap for
me.
But I haven't disobeyed your
orders.
111I will follow your rules for ever.
They make me happy.
112I will try to do what you demand
for ever, until the end.
113I hate people who are not
completely loyal to you.
But I love your teachings.
114You are my hiding place and my
shield.
I trust your word.
115Get away from me, you people
who do evil,
so I can keep my God's
commands.
116Support me as you promised so I
can live.
Don't let me be embarrassed
because of my hopes.
117Help me, and I will be saved.
I will always respect your
demands.
118You reject everyone who ignores
your demands.
Their lies mislead them.
119You throw away the wicked of
the world like rubbish.
So I will love your rules.
120I shake in fear of you.
I fear your laws.

121I have done what is fair and right.
Don't leave me to my enemies.
122Promise that you will help me,
your servant.
Don't let proud people hurt me.
123My eyes are tired from looking
for your salvation
and for your good promise.
124Show your love to me, your
servant.
Teach me your demands.
125I am your servant. Give me
wisdom
so I can understand your rules.

126Lord, it is time for you to do
something.
People have disobeyed your
teachings.
127I love your commands
more than the purest gold.
128I respect all your orders.
So I hate lying ways.
129Your rules are wonderful.
That is why I obey them.
130Learning your words gives
wisdom
and understanding for the
foolish.
131I want to learn your commands.
I am like a person breathing
hard and waiting impatiently.
132Look at me and have mercy on
me
as you do for those who love
you.
133Guide my steps as you promised.
Don't let any sin control me.
134Save me from harmful people.
Then I will obey your orders.
135Show your kindness to me, your
servant.
Teach me your demands.
136Tears stream from my eyes
because people do not obey
your teachings.

137Lord, you do what is right.
And your laws are fair.
138The rules you commanded are
right
and completely trustworthy.
139I am so upset I am worn out.
This is because my enemies
have forgotten your words.
140Your promises are proven.
I, your servant, love them.
141I am unimportant and hated.
But I have not forgotten your
orders.
142Your goodness continues for
ever.
And your teachings are true.
143I have had troubles and misery.
But I love your commands.
144Your rules are good for ever.

Help me understand so I can
live.
145Lord, I call to you with all my
heart.
Answer me,
and I will keep your demands.
146I call to you. Save me
so I can obey your rules.
147I wake up early in the morning
and cry out.
I trust your word.
148I stay awake all night
so I can think about your
promises.
149Listen to me because of your
love.
Lord, give me life by your laws.
150Those who love evil are near.
They are far from your
teachings.
151But, Lord, you are also near.
And all your commands are true.
152Long ago I learned from your
rules
that you made them to continue
for ever.

153See my suffering and save me
because I have not forgotten
your teachings.
154Argue my case and save me.
Let me live by your promises.
155Wicked people are far from being
saved
because they do not want to
obey your demands.
156Lord, you are very kind.
Give me life by your laws.
157Many enemies are after me.
But I have not rejected your
rules.
158I see those traitors, and I hate
them
because they do not obey what
you say.
159See how I love your orders.
Lord, give me life by your love.
160Your words are true from the
start.
And all your laws will be fair for
ever.

161Leaders attack me for no reason.
But I fear your law in my heart.
162I am as happy over your
promises
as if I had found a great
treasure.
163I hate and despise lies.
But I love your teachings.
164Seven times a day I praise you
for your fair laws.
165Those who love your teachings
will find true peace.
Nothing will defeat them.
166I am waiting for you to save me,
Lord.
I will obey your commands.
167I keep your rules.
I love them very much.
168I keep your orders and rules.
You know everything I do.

169Hear my cry to you, Lord.
Let your word help me
understand.
170Listen to my prayer.
Save me as you promised.
171Let me speak your praise.
You have taught me your
demands.
172Let me sing about your promises.
All your commands are fair.
173Always be ready to help me
because I have chosen to obey
your commands.
174I want you to save me, Lord.
I love your teachings.
175Let me live so I can praise you.
Your laws will help me.
176I have wandered like a lost
sheep.
Look for your servant because I
have not forgotten your
commands.

A Prayer of Someone Far
from Home

A song for going up to worship.

120 When I was in trouble, I
called to the Lord.

And he answered me.
2Lord, save me from liars
and from those who plan
evil.

3You who plan evil, what will God
do to you?
How will he punish you?
4He will punish you with the sharp
arrows of a warrior
and with burning coals of
wood.

5How terrible it is to live in the
land of Meshech.
I have to live among the people
of Kedar.
6I have lived too long
with people who hate peace.
7I want peace and try to talk
peace,
but they want war.

The Lord Guards His People

A song for going up to worship.

121 I look up to the hills.
But where does my help
come from?
2My help comes from the Lord.
He made heaven and earth.

3He will not let you be defeated.
He who guards you never
sleeps.
4He who guards Israel
never rests or sleeps.
5The Lord guards you.
The Lord protects you as the
shade protects you from the
sun.
6The sun cannot hurt you during
the day.
And the moon cannot hurt you
at night.
7The Lord will guard you from all
dangers.
He will guard your life.
8The Lord will guard you as you
come and go,
both now and for ever.

Happy People in Jerusalem

A song for going up to worship.
Of David.

122 I was happy when they
said to me,
"Let's go to the Templed of the
Lord."
2Jerusalem, we are standing
at your gates.

3Jerusalem is built as a city
where friends can come
together.
4The people from the tribesd go up
there.
The tribes belong to the Lord.
It is the rule to praise
the Lord at Jerusalem.
5There the descendantsd of David
set their thrones to judge the
people.

6Pray for peace in Jerusalem:
"May those who love her be
safe.
7May there be peace within her
walls
and safety within her strong
towers."
8To help my relatives and friends,
I repeat, "Let Jerusalem have
peace."
9For the sake of the Temple of the
Lord our God,
I hope goodness comes to her.

A Prayer for Mercy

A song for going up to worship.

123 Lord, I look up to you.
You live in heaven.
2Slaves depend on their masters.
And a female servant depends
on her mistress.
In the same way, we depend on
our God.
We wait for him to show us
mercy.
3Be kind to us, Lord. Be kind to
us
because we have been insulted.

4We have suffered many insults
　　from lazy people
and much cruelty from the
　　proud.

The Lord Saves His People

A song for going up to worship.
Of David.

124 What if the Lord had not
been on our side?
(Let Israel repeat this.)
2What if the Lord had not been on
　　our side
　　when men attacked us?
3When they were angry with us,
　　they would have swallowed us
　　alive.
4They would have been like a flood
　　drowning us.
　　They would have poured over
　　us like a river.
5　They would have swept us away
　　like a mighty stream.

6Praise the Lord.
　　He did not let them chew us up.
7We have escaped like a bird
　　from the hunter's trap.
　　The trap has been broken,
　　and we have escaped.
8Our help comes from the Lord,
　　who made heaven and earth.

God Protects Those Who Trust Him

A song for going up to worship.

125 Those who trust the Lord
are like Mount Zion.*d*
It sits unmoved for ever.
2The mountains surround
　　Jerusalem.
　　And the Lord surrounds his
　　people
　　now and for ever.

3The wicked will not rule
　　over those who do right.
　　If they did, the people who do
　　right
　　might use their power to do
　　evil.

4Lord, be good to those who are
　　good,
　　whose hearts are honest.
5But, Lord, when you punish those
　　who do evil,
　　also punish those who stop
　　following you.

Let there be peace in Israel.

Lord, Give Us Our Riches Back

A song for going up to worship.

126 When the Lord gave the
riches back to Jerusalem,
it seemed as if we were
　　dreaming.
2Then we were filled with laughter,
　　and we sang happy songs.
Then the other nations said,
　　"The Lord has done great things
　　for them."
3The Lord has done great things
　　for us,
　　and we are very glad.

4Lord, give us back our riches
　　again.
　　Do this as you bring streams to
　　the desert.
5Those who cry as they plant crops
　　will sing at harvest time.
6Those who cry
　　as they carry out the seeds
　　will return singing
　　and carrying bundles of grain.

All Good Things Come from God

A song for going up to worship.
Of Solomon.

127 If the Lord doesn't build
the house,
the builders are working for
　　nothing.
If the Lord doesn't guard the city,
　　the guards are watching for
　　nothing.
2It is no use for you to get up
　　early
　　and stay up late,
working for a living.

The Lord gives sleep to those
   he loves.
3Children are a gift from the Lord.
   Babies are a reward.
4Sons who are born to a young
     man
   are like arrows in the hand of a
     warrior.
5Happy is the man
   who has his bag full of arrows.
They will not be defeated
   when they fight their enemies in
     court.

The Happy Home

A song for going up to worship.

128 Happy are those who
     respect the Lord
and obey him.
2You will enjoy what you work for.
   You will be blessed with good
     things.
3Your wife will give you many
     children.
   She will be like a vine that
     produces a lot of fruit.
Your children will bring you much
     good.
   They will be like olive branches
     that produce many olives.
4This is how the man who respects
   the Lord
will be blessed.
5May the Lord bless you from
     Mount Zion.d
May you enjoy the good things
     of Jerusalem all your life.
6May you see your grandchildren.

Let there be peace in Israel.

A Prayer Against the Enemies

A song for going up to worship.

129 They have treated me
     badly all my life.
(Let Israel repeat this.)
2They have treated me badly all
   my life.

But they have not defeated me.
3Like farmers ploughing, they
     ploughed over my back,
making long wounds.
4But the Lord does what is right.
   He has set me free from those
     wicked people.

5Let those who hate Jerusalem
   be turned back in shame.
6Let them be like the grass on the
     roof.
It dries up before it has grown.
7There is not enough of it to fill a
     man's hand
   or to make into a bundle to fill
     his arms.
8Let those who pass by them not
     say,
"May the Lord bless you.
We bless you by the power of
     the Lord."

A Prayer for Mercy

A song for going up to worship.

130 Lord, I am in great
     trouble.
So I call out to you for help.
2Lord, hear my voice.
   Listen to my prayer for help.
3Lord, if you punished people for
     all their sins,
no one would be left.
4But you forgive us.
   So you are respected.

5I wait for the Lord to help me.
   I trust his word.
6I wait for the Lord to help me
   more than night-watchmen wait
     for the dawn,
more than night-watchmen wait
     for the dawn.
7People of Israel, put your hope in
     the Lord
because he is loving
and able to save.
8He will save Israel
   from all their sins.

Childlike Trust in God

A song for going up to worship.
Of David.

131 Lord, my heart is not
proud.
I don't look down on others.
I don't do great things,
and I can't do miracles.*d*
2But I am calm and quiet.
I am like a baby with its mother.
I am at peace, like a baby with
its mother.

3People of Israel, put your hope in
the Lord
now and for ever.

In Praise of the Temple

A song for going up to worship.

132 Lord, remember David
and all his suffering.
2He made a promise to the Lord.
He made a promise to the
Mighty God of Jacob.
3He said, "I will not go home to
my house.
I will not lie down on my bed.
4I will not close my eyes
or let myself sleep
5until I find a place for the Lord.
I want to provide a home for the
Mighty God of Jacob."

6We heard about the Ark*d* of God
in Bethlehem.
We found it at Kiriath Jearim.
7Let's go to the Lord's house.
Let's worship at his footstool.
8Rise, Lord, and come to your
resting place.
Come with the Holy Ark that
shows your strength.
9May your priests do what is right.
May your people sing for joy.
10For the sake of your servant
David,
do not reject your appointed
king.
11The Lord made a promise to
David.

It was a sure promise that he
will not take back.
He promised, "I will make one of
your descendants*d*
rule as king after you.
12But your sons must keep my
agreement
and the rules that I teach them.
Then their sons after them will
rule
on your throne for ever and
ever."

13The Lord has chosen Jerusalem.
He wants it for his home.
14He says, "This is my resting place
for ever.
Here is where I want to stay.
15I will bless her with plenty of
food.
I will fill her poor with food.
16I will let her priests receive
salvation.
And those who worship me will
really sing for joy.

17"I will make a king come from the
family of David.
I will provide my appointed one
descendants*d* to rule after
him.
18I will cover his enemies with
shame.
But his crown will shine."

The Love of God's People

A song for going up to worship.
Of David.

133 It is good and pleasant
when God's people live
together in peace!
2It is like having perfumed oil
poured on the priest's head
and running down his beard.
It ran down Aaron's beard
and on to the collar of his robes.
3It is like the dew of Mount
Hermon
falling on the hills of Jerusalem.
There the Lord gives his blessing
of life for ever.

Temple Guards, Praise the Lord

A song for going up to worship.

134 Praise the Lord, all you
servants of the Lord.
You serve at night in the
Temple*d* of the Lord.
²Raise your hands in the Temple
and praise the Lord.

³May the Lord bless you from
Mount Zion.*d*
He made heaven and earth.

God Saves, Idols Do Not

135 Praise the Lord!
Praise the name of the
Lord.
Praise him, you servants of the
Lord.
²Praise him, you who stand in the
Lord's Temple*d*
and in the Temple courtyards.
³Praise the Lord, because he is
good.
Sing praises to him, because it
is pleasant.

⁴The Lord has chosen the people
of Jacob for himself.
He has chosen the people of
Israel for his very own.
⁵I know that the Lord is great.
Our Lord is greater than all the
gods.
⁶The Lord does what he wants,
in heaven and on earth,
in the seas and the deep oceans.
⁷He brings the clouds from the
ends of the earth.
He sends the lightning with the
rain.
He brings out the wind from his
storehouses.

⁸He destroyed the firstborn*d* sons
in Egypt,
the firstborn of both men and
animals.
⁹He did many signs and miracles*d*
in Egypt.

He did amazing things to the
king and his servants.
¹⁰He defeated many nations
and killed powerful kings:
¹¹Sihon king of the Amorites,
Og king of Bashan
and all the kings of Canaan.
¹²Then he gave their land as a gift.
It was a gift to his people, the
Israelites.

¹³Lord, your name is everlasting.
Lord, you will be remembered
from now on.
¹⁴You defend your people.
You have mercy on your
servants.

¹⁵The idols of other nations are
made of silver and gold.
They are made by human
hands.
¹⁶They have mouths, but they
cannot speak.
They have eyes, but they
cannot see.
¹⁷They have ears, but they cannot
hear.
They have no breath in their
mouths.
¹⁸The people who make idols and
trust them
are all like them.

¹⁹Family of Israel, praise the Lord.
Family of Aaron, praise the
Lord.
²⁰Family of Levi, praise the Lord.
You people who fear the Lord
should praise him.
²¹You people of Jerusalem, praise
the Lord on Mount Zion.*d*
Praise the Lord!

God's Love Continues For Ever

136 Give thanks to the Lord
because he is good.
His love continues for ever.
²Give thanks to the God of all
gods.
His love continues for ever.

3Give thanks to the Lord of all
  lords.
His love continues for ever.

4Only he can do great miracles.*d*
His love continues for ever.
5With his wisdom he made the
  skies.
His love continues for ever.
6He spread out the earth on the
  seas.
His love continues for ever.
7He made the sun and the moon.
His love continues for ever.
8He made the sun to rule the day.
His love continues for ever.
9He made the moon and stars to
  rule the night.
His love continues for ever.

10He killed the firstborn*d* sons of the
  Egyptians.
His love continues for ever.
11He brought the people of Israel
  out of Egypt.
His love continues for ever.
12He did it with his great power and
  strength.
His love continues for ever.
13He parted the water of the Red
  Sea.*d*
His love continues for ever.
14He brought the Israelites through
  the middle of it.
His love continues for ever.
15But the king of Egypt and his
  army drowned in the Red
  Sea.
His love continues for ever.

16He led his people through the
  desert.
His love continues for ever.
17He defeated great kings.
His love continues for ever.
18He killed powerful kings.
His love continues for ever.
19He defeated Sihon king of the
  Amorites.
His love continues for ever.

20He defeated Og king of Bashan.
His love continues for ever.
21He gave their land as a gift.
His love continues for ever.
22It was a gift to his servants, the
  Israelites.
His love continues for ever.

23He remembered us when we
  were in trouble.
His love continues for ever.
24He freed us from our enemies.
His love continues for ever.
25He gives food to every living
  creature.
His love continues for ever.

26Give thanks to the God of heaven.
His love continues for ever.

Israelites in Captivity

137 By the rivers in Babylon
we sat and cried
when we remembered
  Jerusalem.
2On the poplar trees nearby
we hung our harps.
3Those who captured us asked us
  to sing.
Our enemies wanted happy
  songs.
They said, "Sing us a Temple*d*
  song from Jerusalem!"

4But we cannot sing songs about
  the Lord
while we are in this foreign
  country!
5Jerusalem, if I forget you,
let my right hand lose its skill.
6Let my tongue stick to the roof of
  my mouth
if I do not remember you.
Let these things happen if I do not
  think about Jerusalem
as my greatest joy.

7Lord, remember what the
  Edomites did
on the day Jerusalem fell.
They said, "Tear it down!
Tear it down to its foundations!"

8People of Babylon, you will be destroyed.
The people who pay you back will be happy.
They will punish you for what you did to us.
9They will grab your babies
and throw them against the rocks.

A Hymn of Thanksgiving

A song of David.

138 Lord, I will thank you with all my heart.
I will sing to you before the false gods.
2I will bow down facing your holy Temple.d
And I will thank you for your love and loyalty.
You have made your name and your word
greater than anything.
3On the day I called to you, you answered me.
You made me strong and brave.

4Lord, let all the kings of the earth praise you.
They have heard the words you speak.
5They will sing about what the Lord has done
because the Lord's glory is great.

6Though the Lord is supreme
he takes care of those who are not proud.
But he stays away from those who are proud.
7Lord, even when I have trouble all around me,
you will keep me alive.
When my enemies are angry,
you will reach down and save me by your power.
8Lord, you do everything for me.

Lord, your love continues for ever.
You made us. Do not leave us.

God Knows Everything

For the director of music.
A song of David.

139 Lord, you have examined me.
You know all about me.
2You know when I sit down and when I get up.
You know my thoughts before I think them.
3You know where I go and where I lie down.
You know about everything I do.
4Lord, even before I say a word,
you already know what I am going to say.
5You are all around me—in front and at the back.
You have put your hand on me.
6Your knowledge is amazing to me.
It is more than I can understand.

7Where can I go to get away from your Spirit?d
Where can I run from you?
8If I go up to the skies, you are there.
If I lie down where the dead are, you are there.
9If I rise with the sun in the east,
and settle in the west beyond the sea,
10even there you would guide me.
With your right hand you would hold me.
11I could say, "The darkness will hide me.
The light around me will turn into night."
12But even the darkness is not dark to you.
The night is as light as the day.
Darkness and light are the same to you.

13You made my whole being.
    You formed me in my mother's
        body.
14I praise you because you made me
    in an amazing and wonderful
    way.
What you have done is
    wonderful.
I know this very well.
15You saw my bones being formed
    as I took shape in my mother's
    body.
When I was put together there,
16   you saw my body as it was
        formed.
All the days planned for me
    were written in your book
    before I was one day old.

17God, your thoughts are precious
    to me.
They are so many!
18If I could count them,
    they would be more than all the
        grains of sand.
When I wake up,
    I am still with you.

19God, I wish you would kill the
    wicked!
Get away from me, you
    murderers!
20These men say evil things about
    you.
Your enemies use your name
    thoughtlessly.
21Lord, I hate those who hate you.
    I hate those who rise up against
        you.
22I feel only hate for them.
    They are my enemies.

23God, examine me and know my
    heart.
Test me and know my thoughts.
24See if there is any bad thing in
    me.
Lead me in the way you set
    long ago.

A Prayer for Protection

For the director of music.
A song of David.

140 Lord, rescue me from evil
people.
Save me from cruel men.
2They make evil plans.
They always start fights.
3They make their tongues sharp as
    a snake's.
Their words are like snake
    poison.   *Selah*d

4Lord, guard me from the power of
    wicked people.
Save me from cruel men
who plan to trip me up.
5Proud men have hidden a trap for
    me.
They have spread out a net
    beside the road.
They have set traps for me.
                          Selah

6I said to the Lord, "You are my
    God."
Lord, listen to my prayer for
    help.
7Lord God, my mighty saviour,
    you protect me in battle.
8Lord, do not give the wicked what
    they want.
Don't let their plans succeed,
or they will become proud. *Selah*

9Those around me have planned
    trouble.
Now let it come to them.
10Let burning coals fall on them.
Throw them into the fire
or into pits from which they
    cannot escape.
11Don't let liars settle in the land.
Let evil quickly hunt down cruel
    men.

12I know the Lord will get justice
    for the poor.
He will defend the needy in
    court.

13Good people will praise his name.
Honest people will live in his
presence.

A Prayer Not to Sin

A song of David.

141 Lord, I call to you. Come
quickly.
Listen to me when I call to you.
2Let my prayer be like incense*d*
placed before you.
Let my praise be like the
evening sacrifice.

3Lord, help me control my tongue.
Help me be careful about what I
say.
4Don't let me want to do evil
or join others in doing wrong.
Don't let me eat
with those who do evil.

5If a good man punished me, that
would be kind.
If he corrected me,
that would be like having
perfumed oil on my head.
I shouldn't refuse it.
But I pray against those who do
evil.
6 Let their leaders be thrown over
the cliffs.
Then people will know that I
have spoken the truth:
7"The ground is ploughed and
broken up.
In the same way, our bones
have been scattered at the
grave."

8Lord God, I look to you for help.
I trust in you. Don't let me
die.
9Protect me from the traps they
set for me
and from the net evil people
have spread.
10Let the wicked fall into their own
pits.
And let me pass by safely.

A Prayer for Safety

*A maskild of David when he was
in the cave. A prayer.*

142 I cry out to the Lord.
I pray to the Lord for
mercy.
2I pour out my problems to him.
I tell him my troubles.
3When I am afraid,
you, Lord, know the way out.
In the path where I walk,
a trap is hidden for me.
4Look around me and see.
No one cares about me.
I have no place of safety.
No one cares if I live.

5Lord, I cry out to you.
I say, "You are my protection.
You are all I want in this life."
6Listen to my cry
because I am helpless.
Save me from those who are
chasing me.
They are too strong for me.
7Free me from my prison.
Then I will praise your name.
Then the good people will
surround me
because you have taken care of
me.

A Prayer Not to Be Killed

A song of David.

143 Lord, hear my prayer.
Listen to my cry for
mercy.
Come to help me
because you are loyal and good.
2Don't judge me, your servant,
because no one alive is right
before you.
3My enemies are chasing me.
They have crushed me to the
ground.
They have made me live in
darkness
like those who are long dead.
4I am afraid.
My courage is gone.

⁵I remember what happened long
  ago.
I recall everything you have
  done.
I think about all you have made.
⁶I lift my hands to you in prayer.
As a dry land needs rain, I thirst
  for you.   *Selahᵈ*

⁷Lord, answer me quickly.
I am getting weak.
Don't turn away from me,
  or I will be like those who are
  dead.
⁸Tell me in the morning about your
  love.
I trust you.
Show me what I should do
  because my prayers go up to
  you.
⁹Lord, save me from my enemies.
I come to you for safety.
¹⁰Teach me to do what you want,
  because you are my God.
Let your good Spiritᵈ
  lead me on level ground.

¹¹Lord, let me live
  so people will praise you.
In your goodness
  save me from my troubles.
¹²In your love defeat my enemies.
Destroy all those who trouble
  me
  because I am your servant.

A Prayer for Victory

Of David.

144 Praise the Lord, my
      Rock.ᵈ
He trains me for war.
He trains me for battle.
²He gives me love and protects me
  like a strong, walled city.
He is my place of safety and my
  Saviour.
He is my shield and my
  protection.
He helps me rule my people.

³Lord, why is man important to
  you?
Why do you even think about a
  human being?
⁴A man is like a breath.
His life is like a passing shadow.

⁵Lord, tear open the sky and come
  down.
Touch the mountains so they
  will smoke.
⁶Send the lightning and scatter my
  enemies.
Shoot your arrows and force
  them away.
⁷Reach down from above.
Pull me out of this sea of
  enemies.
Rescue me from these
  foreigners.
⁸They are liars.
They are dishonest.

⁹God, I will sing a new song to
  you.
I will play to you on the
  ten-stringed harp.
¹⁰You give victory to kings.
You save your servant David
  from cruel swords.
¹¹Save me, rescue me from these
  foreigners.
They are liars.
They are dishonest.

¹²Let our sons in their youth
  grow like strong trees.
Let our daughters be
  like the decorated stones in the
  Temple.ᵈ
¹³Let our barns be filled
  with crops of all kinds.
Let our sheep in the fields have
  thousands and thousands of
  lambs.
¹⁴ Let our cattle be strong.
Let no one break in.
Let there be no war.
Let there be no screams in our
  streets.

15Happy are those who are like this.
Happy are the people whose
God is the Lord.

Praise to God the King

A song of praise. Of David.

145 I praise your greatness,
my God the King.
I will praise you for ever and
ever.
2I will praise you every day.
I will praise you for ever and
ever.
3The Lord is great. He is worthy
of our praise.
No one can understand how
great he is.

4Parents will tell their children
what you have done.
They will retell your mighty
acts,
5wonderful majesty and glory.
And I will think about your
miracles.*d*
6They will tell about the amazing
things you do.
I will tell how great you are.
7They will remember your great
goodness.
They will sing about your
fairness.
8The Lord is kind and shows
mercy.
He does not become angry
quickly but is full of love.
9The Lord is good to everyone.
He is merciful to all he has
made.
10Lord, everything you have made
will praise you.
Those who belong to you will
bless you.
11They will tell about the glory of
your kingdom.
They will speak about your
power.
12Then everyone will know what
powerful things you do.

They will know about the glory
and majesty of your
kingdom.
13Your kingdom will continue for
ever.
And you will be King from now
on.

The Lord will keep his promises.
With love he takes care of all he
has made.
14The Lord helps those who have
been defeated.
He takes care of those who are
in trouble.
15All living things look to you for
food.
And you give it to them at the
right time.
16You open your hand,
and you satisfy all living things.

17Everything the Lord does is right.
With love he takes care of all he
has made.
18The Lord is close to everyone
who prays to him,
to all who truly pray to him.
19He gives those who fear him what
they want.
He listens when they cry, and
he saves them.
20The Lord protects everyone who
loves him.
But he will destroy the wicked.

21I will praise the Lord.
Let everyone praise his holy
name for ever.

Praise God Who Helps the Weak

146 Praise the Lord!
My whole being, praise
the Lord.
2I will praise the Lord all my life.
I will sing praises to my God as
long as I live.

3Do not put your trust in princes
or other people, who cannot
save you.

⁴When people die, they are buried.
  Then all of their plans come to
    an end.
⁵Happy are those who are helped
    by the God of Jacob.
  Their hope is in the Lord their
    God.
⁶He made heaven and earth,
    the sea and everything in it.
  He remains loyal for ever.
⁷The Lord does what is fair for
    those who have been
    wronged.
  He gives food to the hungry.
  The Lord sets the prisoners
    free.
⁸ The Lord gives sight to the
    blind.
  The Lord lifts up people who are
    in trouble.
  The Lord loves those who do
    right.
⁹The Lord protects the foreigners.
  He defends the orphans and
    widows.
  But he overthrows the wicked.

¹⁰The Lord will be King for ever.
  Jerusalem, your God is
    everlasting.

  Praise the Lord!

Praise God Who Helps His People

147 Praise the Lord!
  It is good to sing praises
    to our God.
  It is good and pleasant to praise
    him.
²The Lord rebuilds Jerusalem.
  He brings back the scattered
    Israelites who were taken
    captive.
³He heals the broken-hearted.
  He bandages their wounds.

⁴He counts the stars
  and names each one.

⁵Our Lord is great and very
    powerful.
  There is no limit to what he
    knows.
⁶The Lord defends those who are
    not proud.
  But he throws the wicked to the
    ground.

⁷Sing praises to the Lord.
  Praise our God with harps.
⁸He fills the sky with clouds.
  He sends rain to the earth.
  He makes grass grow on the
    hills.
⁹He gives food to cattle
  and to the little birds that call.

¹⁰He is not pleased by the strength
    of a horse
  or the power of a man.
¹¹The Lord is pleased with those
    who fear him,
  with those who trust his love.

¹²Jerusalem, praise the Lord.
  Jerusalem, praise your God.
¹³He makes your city gates strong.
  He blesses the people inside.
¹⁴He brings peace to your country.
  He fills you with the finest
    grain.

¹⁵He gives a command to the earth,
  and it quickly obeys him.
¹⁶He spreads the snow like wool.
  He scatters the frost like ashes.
¹⁷He throws down hail like rocks.
  No one can stand the cold he
    sends.
¹⁸Then he gives a command, and it
    melts.
  He sends the breezes, and the
    waters flow.

¹⁹He gave his word to Jacob.
  He gave his laws and demands
    to Israel.
²⁰He didn't do this for any other
    nation.
  They don't know his laws.

  Praise the Lord!

The World Should Praise the Lord

148 Praise the Lord!
Praise the Lord from the
heavens.
Praise him high above the
earth.
2Praise him, all you angels.
Praise him, all you armies of
heaven.
3Praise him, sun and moon.
Praise him, all you shining
stars.
4Praise him, highest heavens
and you waters above the
sky.
5Let them praise the Lord
because they were created by
his command.
6He set them in place for ever and
ever.
He made a law that will never
end.

7Praise the Lord from the earth.
Praise him, you large sea
animals and all the oceans.
8Praise him, lightning and hail,
snow and clouds,
and stormy winds that obey
him.
9Praise him, mountains and all hills,
fruit trees and all cedar trees.
10Praise him, you wild animals and
all cattle,
small crawling animals and birds.
11Praise him, you kings of the earth
and all nations,
princes and all rulers of the
earth.
12Praise him, you young men and
women,
old people and children.

13Praise the Lord.
He alone is great.
He is greater than heaven and
earth.
14God has given his people a king.
He should be praised by all who
belong to him.

He should be praised by the
Israelites, the people closest
to his heart.

Praise the Lord!

Praise the God of Israel

149 Praise the Lord!
Sing a new song to the
Lord.
Sing his praise in the meeting of
his people.

2Let the Israelites be happy
because of God, their
Maker.
Let the people of Jerusalem
rejoice because of their
King.
3They should praise him with
dancing.
They should praise him with
tambourines*d* and harps.
4The Lord is pleased with his
people.
He saves those who are not
proud.
5Let those who worship him rejoice
in his glory.
Let them sing for joy even in
bed!

6Let them shout his praise
with their two-edged swords in
their hands.
7They will punish the nations.
They will defeat the people.
8They will put those kings in chains
and those important men in iron
bands.
9They will punish them as God has
written.
God is honoured by all who
worship him.

Praise the Lord!

Praise the Lord with Music

150 Praise the Lord!
Praise God in his Temple.*d*
Praise him in his mighty heaven.

²Praise him for his strength.
Praise him for his greatness.
³Praise him with trumpet
blasts.
Praise him with harps and
lyres.*d*
⁴Praise him with tambourines*d* and
dancing.

Praise him with stringed
instruments and flutes.
⁵Praise him with loud cymbals.
Praise him with crashing
cymbals.
⁶Let everything that breathes
praise the Lord.

Praise the Lord!

PROVERBS

Wise Teachings for God's People

Why Proverbs Is Important

1 These are the wise words of Solomon son of David. Solomon was king of Israel.

²They teach wisdom and
self-control.
They give understanding.
³They will teach you how to be
wise and self-controlled.
They will teach you what is
honest and fair and right.
⁴They give the ability to think to
those with little knowledge.
They give knowledge and good
sense to the young.
⁵Wise people should also listen to
them and learn even more.
Even clever people will find wise
advice in these words.
⁶Then they will be able to
understand wise words and
stories.
They will understand the words
of wise men and their
riddles.

⁷Knowledge begins with respect for
the Lord.
But foolish people hate wisdom
and self-control.

Warnings Against Evil

⁸My child, listen to your father's
teaching.
And do not forget your mother's
advice.
⁹Their teaching will beautify your
life.
It will be like flowers in your
hair or a chain around your
neck.

¹⁰My child, sinners will try to lead
you into sin.
But do not follow them.
¹¹They might say, "Come with us.
Let's ambush and kill someone.
Let's attack some harmless
person just for fun.
¹²Let's swallow them alive, as death
does.
Let's swallow them whole, as
the grave does.
¹³We will take all kinds of valuable
things.
We will fill our houses with what
we steal.
¹⁴Come and join us,
and we will share with you what
we steal."
¹⁵My child, do not go along with
them.
Do not do what they do.
¹⁶They run to do evil.
They are quick to kill.
¹⁷It is useless to spread out a net
right where the birds can see
it!
¹⁸These men are setting their own
trap.
They will only catch themselves!
¹⁹All greedy people end up this
way.
Greed takes away the life of the
greedy person.

Wisdom Speaks

²⁰Wisdom is like a good woman who
shouts in the street.
She raises her voice in the city
squares.
²¹She cries out in the noisy street.
She makes her speech at the
city gates:
²²"You foolish people! How long do
you want to stay foolish?
How long will you make fun of
wisdom?

How long will you hate
knowledge?
23Listen when I correct you.
I will tell you what's in my
heart.
I will tell you what I am
thinking.
24I called, but you refused to listen.
I held out my hand, but you paid
no attention.
25You did not follow my advice.
You did not want me to correct
you.
26So I will laugh when you are in
trouble.
I will make fun when disaster
happens to you.
27Disaster will come over you like a
storm.
Trouble will strike you like a
whirlwind.
Pain and trouble will overwhelm
you.
28"Then you will call out to me.
But I will not answer.
You will look for me.
But you will not find me.
29You rejected knowledge.
You did not choose to respect
the Lord.
30You did not accept my advice.
You rejected my correction.
31So you will get what you deserve.
You will get what you planned
for others.
32Fools wander away and get killed.
They are destroyed because
they do not care.
33But those who listen to me will
live in safety.
They will be safe, without fear
of being hurt."

Rewards of Wisdom

2 My child, believe what I say.
And remember what I command
you.
2Listen to wisdom.
Try with all your heart to gain
understanding.

3Cry out for wisdom.
Beg for understanding.
4Search for it as you would for
silver.
Hunt for it like hidden treasure.
5Then you will understand what it
means to respect the Lord.
Then you will begin to know
God.
6Only the Lord gives wisdom.
Knowledge and understanding
come from him.
7He stores up wisdom for those
who are honest.
Like a shield he protects those
who are innocent.
8He guards those who are fair to
others.
He protects those who are loyal
to him.
9Then you will understand what is
honest and fair and right.
You will understand what is
good to do.
10You will have wisdom in your
heart.
And knowledge will be pleasing
to you.
11Good sense will protect you.
Understanding will guard you.
12It will keep you from doing evil.
It will save you from people
whose words are bad.
13Such people do not do what is
right.
They do what is evil.
14They enjoy doing wrong.
They are happy to do what is
crooked and evil.
15What they do is wrong.
Their ways are dishonest.
16It will save you from the unfaithful
wife
who tries to lead you into
adulteryd with pleasing
words.
17Such women leave the husbands
they married when they
were young.

They forget the promise they
made before God.
¹⁸If you go to her house, you are on
your way to death.
What she does leads to death.
¹⁹No one who goes to her comes
back.
He will not continue to live.

²⁰But wisdom will help you be a
good person.
It will help you do what is right.
²¹Those who are honest will stay in
the land.
Those who are innocent will
remain in it.
²²But evil people will be removed
from the land.
The unfaithful will be thrown out
of it.

Advice to Children

3 My child, do not forget my
teaching.
Keep my commands in mind.
²Then you will live a long time.
And your life will be successful.

³Don't ever stop being kind and
truthful.
Let kindness and truth show in
all you do.
Write them down in your mind
as if on a tablet.
⁴Then you will be respected
and pleasing to both God and
men.

⁵Trust the Lord with all your
heart.
Don't depend on your own
understanding.
⁶Remember the Lord in everything
you do.
And he will give you success.

⁷Don't depend on your own
wisdom.
Respect the Lord and refuse to
do wrong.
⁸Then your body will be healthy.
And your bones will be strong.

⁹Honour the Lord by giving him
part of your wealth.
Give him the first fruits^d from all
your crops.
¹⁰Then your barns will be full.
And your wine barrels will
overflow with new wine.

¹¹My child, do not reject the Lord's
discipline.
And don't become angry when
he corrects you.
¹²The Lord corrects those he loves,
just as a father corrects the
child that he likes.

¹³Happy is the person who finds
wisdom.
And happy is the person who
gets understanding.
¹⁴Wisdom is worth more than silver.
It brings more profit than gold.
¹⁵Wisdom is more precious than
rubies.
Nothing you want is equal to it.
¹⁶With her right hand wisdom offers
you a long life.
With her left hand she gives you
riches and honour.
¹⁷Wisdom will make your life
pleasant.
It will bring you peace.
¹⁸As a tree makes fruit, wisdom
gives life to those who use
it.
Everyone who uses wisdom will
be happy.

¹⁹Using his wisdom, the Lord made
the earth.
Using his understanding, he set
the sky in place.
²⁰Using his knowledge, he made
rivers flow from
underground springs.
And he made the clouds drop
rain on the earth.

²¹My child, hold on to wisdom and
reason.
Don't let them out of your sight!
²²They will give you life.

Like a necklace, they will
  beautify your life.
23Then you will go on your way in
  safety.
And you will not get hurt.
24You won't need to be afraid when
  you lie down.
When you lie down, your sleep
  will be peaceful.
25You won't need to be afraid of
  trouble coming suddenly.
You won't need to fear the ruin
  that comes to the wicked.
26The Lord will keep you safe.
He will keep you from being
  trapped.

27Whenever you are able,
  do good to people who need
  help.
28If you have what your neighbour
  asks for,
don't say to him,
"Come back later. I will give it
  to you tomorrow."
29Don't make plans to hurt your
  neighbour.
He lives nearby and trusts you.
30Don't accuse a man for no good
  reason.
Don't accuse him if he has not
  harmed you.
31Don't be jealous of men who use
  violence.
And don't choose to be like
  them.
32The Lord hates those who do
  wrong.
But he is a friend to those who
  are honest.
33The Lord will put a curse on the
  evil person's house.
But he will bless the home of
  people who do what is right.
34The Lord laughs at those who
  laugh at him.
But he is kind to those who are
  not proud.
35Wise people will receive honour.
But foolish people will be
  disgraced.

Wisdom Is Important

4 My children, listen to your
  father's teaching.
Pay attention so you will
  understand.
2What I am telling you is good.
Do not forget what I teach you.
3I was once a young boy in my
  father's house.
I was like an only child to my
  mother.
4And my father taught me and said,
"Hold on to my words with all
  your heart.
Keep my commands and you will
  live.
5Get wisdom and understanding.
Don't forget or ignore my
  words.
6Use wisdom, and it will take care
  of you.
Love wisdom, and it will keep
  you safe.
7Wisdom is the most important
  thing. So get wisdom.
If it costs everything you have,
  get understanding.
8Believe in the value of wisdom,
  and it will make you great.
Use it, and it will bring honour
  to you.
9Like flowers in your hair, it will
  beautify your life.
Like a crown, it will make you
  look beautiful."

10My child, listen and accept what I
  say.
Then you will have a long life.
11I am guiding you in wisdom.
And I am leading you to do what
  is right.
12Nothing will hold you back.
You will not be overwhelmed.
13Always remember what you have
  been taught.
Don't let go of it.
Keep safe all that you have
  learned.
It is the most important thing in
  your life.

[14]Don't follow the ways of the wicked.
Don't do what evil people do.
[15]Avoid their ways. Don't go near what they do.
Stay away from them and keep on going.
[16]They cannot sleep until they do evil.
They cannot rest until they hurt someone.
[17]They fill themselves with wickedness and cruelty
as if they were eating bread and drinking wine.
[18]The way of the good person is like the light of dawn.
It grows brighter and brighter until it is full daylight.
[19]But the wicked are like those who stumble in the dark.
They can't even see what has hurt them.

[20]My child, pay attention to my words.
Listen closely to what I say.
[21]Don't ever forget my words.
Keep them deep within your heart.
[22]These words are the secret to life for those who find them.
They bring health to the whole body.
[23]Be very careful about what you think.
Your thoughts run your life.
[24]Don't use your mouth to tell lies.
Don't ever say things that are not true.
[25]Keep your eyes focused on what is right.
Keep looking straight ahead to what is good.
[26]Be careful what you do.
Always do what is right.
[27]Do not do anything unless it is right.
Stay away from evil.

Warning About Adultery

5 My son, pay attention to my wisdom.
Listen to my words of understanding.
[2]Be careful to use good sense.
Watch what you say.
[3]The words of another man's wife may seem sweet as honey.
Her words may be as pleasant as olive oil.
[4]But in the end she will bring you sorrow. She will cause you pain like a two-edged sword.
[5]She is on the way to death.
Her steps are headed straight to the grave.
[6]She gives no thought to life.
She does not know that her ways are wrong.
[7]Now, my sons, listen to me.
Don't ignore what I say.
[8]Stay away from such a woman.
Don't even go near the door of her house.
[9]If you do, you will give your riches to others.
And the best years of your life will be given to someone who is cruel.
[10]Strangers will enjoy your wealth.
And what you worked so hard for will go to someone else.
[11]You will groan at the end of your life.
Then your health will be gone.
[12]Then you will say, "I hated self-control!
I would not listen when I was corrected!
[13]I would not listen to my teachers.
I paid no attention to what they taught me.
[14]I have come very close to being completely ruined
in front of a whole group of people."
[15]Be faithful to your own wife.

She is like your own well of
    water from which you drink.
16You wouldn't drink from streams
    flowing in the city streets or
    squares.
So be satisfied with your wife,
    not those outside your home.
17These things are yours alone.
    Don't share them with
    strangers.
18Be happy with the wife
    you married when you were
    young.
She gives you joys
    as your fountain gives you
    water.
19She is as lovely and graceful as a
    deer.
Let her love always make you
    happy.
Let her love always hold you
    captive.
20My son, don't be held captive by a
    woman who takes part in
    adultery.*d*
Don't hold another man's wife.
21The Lord sees everything you do.
    He watches where you go.
22An evil man will be caught in his
    evil ways.
He will be tied up by his sins as
    if they were ropes.
23He will die because he does not
    control himself.
He will be held captive by his
    own foolishness.

Dangers of Being Foolish

6 My child, be careful about giving
    a guarantee for somebody
    else.
Be careful about promising to
    pay what someone else
    owes.
2You might get trapped by what
    you say.
You might be caught by your
    own words.

3My child, you might do this and
    be under somebody's
    control.
Then here is how to get free.
Go to your neighbour and don't be
    proud.
Beg him to free you from your
    promise.
4Don't go to sleep.
    Don't even rest your eyes.
5But free yourself like a deer
    running from a hunter.
Free yourself like a bird flying
    away from a trapper.
6Go and watch the ants, you lazy
    person.
Watch what they do and be
    wise.
7Ants have no commander.
    They have no leader or ruler.
8But they store up food in the
    summer.
They gather their supplies at
    harvest.
9How long will you lie there, you
    lazy person?
When will you get up from
    sleeping?
10You sleep a little; you take a nap.
    You fold your hands and rest.
11So you will be as poor as if you
    had been robbed.
You will have as little as if you
    had been held up.
12Some people are wicked and no
    good.
They go around telling lies.
13They wink with their eyes and
    signal with their feet.
They make signs with their
    fingers.
14They make evil plans in their
    hearts.
They are always causing
    trouble.
15So trouble will strike them in an
    instant.
Suddenly they will be hurt
    beyond cure.

16There are six things the Lord
    hates.
  There are seven things he
    cannot stand:
17   a proud look,
   a lying tongue,
   hands that kill innocent people,
18   a mind that thinks up evil
    plans,
   feet that are quick to do evil,
19   a witness who tells lies
   and a man who causes trouble
    among brothers.

Warning About Adultery

20My son, keep your father's
    commands.
  Don't forget your mother's
    teaching.
21Remember their words for ever.
  Let it be as if they were tied
    around your neck.
22They will guide you when you
    walk.
  They will guard you while you
    sleep.
  They will speak to you when
    you are awake.
23Their commands are like a lamp.
  Their teaching is like a light.
  And the correction that comes
    from them
  helps you have life.
24Such teaching will keep you from
    sinful women
  and from the pleasing words of
    another man's unfaithful
    wife.
25Don't want her because she is
    beautiful.
  Don't let her capture you by the
    way she looks at you.
26A prostitute*d* may leave you with
    only a loaf of bread.
  And a woman who takes part in
    adultery*d* may cost you your
    life.
27You cannot carry hot coals against
    your chest
  without burning your clothes.
28And you cannot walk on hot coals

without burning your feet.
29The same thing happens if you
    have sexual relations with
    another man's wife.
  Anyone who does so will be
    punished.

30People do not hate a thief
  when he steals because he is
    hungry.
31But if he is caught, he must pay
    back seven times what he
    stole.
  It may cost him everything he
    owns.
32A man who takes part in adultery
    doesn't have any sense.
  He will destroy himself.
33He will be beaten up and
    disgraced.
  And his shame will never go
    away.
34Jealousy makes a husband very
    angry.
  He will have no mercy when he
    gets even.
35He will accept no payment for the
    wrong.
  He will take no money, no
    matter how much it is.

The Woman of Adultery

7 My son, remember what I say.
  Treasure my commands.
2Obey my commands, and you will
    live.
  Protect my teachings as you
    would your own eyes.
3Remind yourself of them.
  Write them down in your mind
    as if on a tablet.
4Be good to wisdom as if she were
    your sister.
  Make understanding your closest
    friend.
5Wisdom and understanding will
    keep you away from
    adultery.*d*
  They will keep you away from
    the unfaithful wife and her
    pleasing words.

⁶I once was standing at the window
    of my house.
I looked out through the
    shutters.
⁷I saw some foolish, young men.
I noticed one of them who had
    no wisdom.
⁸He was walking down the street
    near the corner.
He was on the road leading to
    her house.
⁹It was the twilight of the evening.
The darkness of the night was
    just beginning.
¹⁰Then the woman approached
    him.
She was dressed like a
    prostitute*d*
and was planning to trick him.
¹¹She was a loud and stubborn
    woman.
She never stayed at home.
¹²She was always out in the streets
    or in the city squares.
She was always waiting around
    on the street corners.
¹³She grabbed him and kissed him.
Without shame she said to him,
¹⁴"I made my fellowship offering and
    have the meat at home.
I have kept my special
    promises.
¹⁵So I have come out to meet you.
I have been looking for you and
    have found you!
¹⁶I have covered my bed
    with coloured sheets from
    Egypt.
¹⁷I have made my bed smell sweet
    with myrrh,*d* aloes*d* and
    cinnamon.
¹⁸Come, let's make love until
    morning.
Let's enjoy each other's love!
¹⁹My husband is not home.
He has gone on a long trip.
²⁰He took a lot of money with him.
And he won't be home for
    weeks."
²¹By her clever words she made
    him give in.

By her pleasing words she led
    him into doing wrong.
²²All at once he followed her.
He was like an ox being led to
    the butcher.
He was like a deer caught in a
    trap.
²³ But quickly an arrow shot
    through his liver.
He was like a bird caught in a
    trap.
He didn't know that what he did
    would kill him.

²⁴Now, my sons, listen to me.
Pay attention to what I say.
²⁵Don't let yourselves be tricked by
    the woman who is guilty of
    adultery.
Don't join her in her evil actions.
²⁶She has ruined many good men.
Many have died because of her.
²⁷Going to her house is like taking
    the road to death.
That road leads down to where
    the dead are.

Listen to Wisdom

8 Like a person, wisdom calls out
    to you.
Understanding raises her voice.
²On the hilltops along the road
and at the crossroads, she
    stands calling.
³She stands beside the city gates.
At the entrances into the city,
    she calls out:
⁴"People, I'm calling out to you.
I am shouting to all people.
⁵You who do not know better, get
    the ability to think.
You who are foolish, get
    understanding.
⁶Listen. I have important things to
    say.
What I tell you is right.
⁷What I say is true.
I hate it when people speak evil.
⁸Everything I say is honest.
Nothing I say is crooked or
    false.

⁹People with good sense know that
what I say is true.
People with knowledge know
that my words are right.
¹⁰Choose my teachings instead of
silver.
Choose knowledge rather than
the finest gold.
¹¹Wisdom is more precious than
rubies.
Nothing you want is equal to it.

¹²"I am wisdom, and I have the
ability to think.
I also have knowledge and good
sense.
¹³If you respect the Lord, you also
will hate evil.
It is wise to hate pride and
bragging,
evil ways and lies.
¹⁴I have good sense and advice.
I have understanding and power.
¹⁵Kings use me to govern.
And rulers use me to make fair
laws.
¹⁶Princes use me to lead.
So do important men and all
good judges.
¹⁷I love those who love me.
Those who want me find me.
¹⁸Riches and honour are mine.
So are wealth and lasting
success.
¹⁹What I give is better than the
finest gold.
What I give is better than pure
silver.
²⁰I do what is right.
I do what is fair.
²¹I give wealth to those who love
me.
I fill them with treasures.

²²"I, wisdom, was with God when
he began his work.
This was before he made
anything else long ago.
²³I was appointed in the very
beginning,
even before the world began.

²⁴I began before there were oceans.
There were no springs
overflowing with water.
²⁵I began before the hills were
there.
The mountains had not even
been put in place.
²⁶God still had not made the earth
or fields.
He had not even made the first
dust of the earth.
²⁷I was there when God put the
skies in place,
when he stretched the horizon
over the oceans.
²⁸I was there when he made the
clouds above.
I was there when he put the
fountains in the oceans.
²⁹I was there when he ordered the
sea
not to go beyond the borders he
had set for it.
I was there when he laid the
earth's foundation.
³⁰I was like a child by his side.
I was happy every day
and enjoyed being in his
presence.
³¹I enjoyed the whole world.
And I was happy with all its
people.

³²"Now, my children, listen to me.
Those who follow my ways are
happy.
³³Listen to my teaching, and you
will be wise.
Do not ignore it.
³⁴Those who listen to me are
happy.
They stand watching at my door
every day.
They are at my open doorway,
wanting to be with me.
³⁵Whoever finds me finds life.
And the Lord will be pleased
with him.
³⁶Whoever does not find me hurts
himself.
Those who hate me love death."

Being Wise or Foolish

9 Wisdom has built her house.
She has made its seven
columns.
2She has prepared her food and
wine.
She has set her table.
3She has sent out her servant girls.
She calls out from the highest
place in the city.
4She says to those who are not
wise,
"Come in here, you foolish
people!
5Come and eat my food.
And drink the wine I have
prepared.
6Stop your foolish ways, and you
will live.
Be a person of understanding.

7"If you correct someone who
makes fun of wisdom, you
will get insulted.
If you correct an evil person,
you will get hurt.
8Do not correct someone who
makes fun of wisdom, or he
will hate you.
But correct a wise man, and he
will love you.
9Teach a wise man, and he will
become even wiser.
Teach a good man, and he will
learn even more.

10"Wisdom begins with respect for
the Lord.
And understanding begins with
knowing God, the Holy One.
11If you live wisely, you will live a
long time.
Wisdom will add years to your
life.
12The wise person is rewarded by
his wisdom.
But a person who makes fun of
wisdom will suffer for it."

13Foolishness is like a loud woman.
She does not have wisdom or
knowledge.
14She sits at the door of her house.
It is at the highest place in the
city.
15She calls out to those who are
passing by.
They are minding their own
business.
16She says to those who are not
wise,
"Come in here, you foolish
people!
17Stolen water is sweeter.
Stolen food tastes better."
18But these people don't know that
everyone dies who goes
there.
They don't realise that her
guests are deep in the
grave.

The Proverbs of Solomon

10 These are the wise words of
Solomon:

A wise son makes his father
happy.
But a foolish son makes his
mother sad.

2Riches gained by doing wrong
have no value.
But right living will save you
from death.

3The Lord does not let people who
live right go hungry.
But he does not let evil people
get what they hunger for.

4A lazy person will end up poor.
But a hard worker will become
rich.

5A son who gathers crops when
they are ready is wise.
But the son who sleeps through
the harvest is a disgrace.

6People who do what is right will
have rich blessings.
But the wicked will be
overwhelmed by violence.

⁷Good people will be remembered
  as a blessing.
But evil people will soon be
  forgotten.

⁸A wise person does what he is
  told.
But a talkative fool will be
  ruined.

⁹The honest person will live safely.
But the one who is dishonest
  will be caught.

¹⁰A wink may get you into trouble.
And foolish talk will lead to your
  ruin.

¹¹Like a fountain of water, the
  words of a good person give
  life.
But the words of the wicked
  contain nothing but violence.

¹²Hatred stirs up trouble.
But love forgives all wrongs.

¹³You can expect clever people to
  speak wisely.
But people without wisdom can
  expect to be punished.

¹⁴Wise people don't tell everything
  they know.
But a foolish person talks too
  much and is ruined.

¹⁵Having lots of money protects the
  rich.
But having no money destroys
  the poor.

¹⁶Good people are rewarded with
  life.
But evil people are paid back
  with punishment.

¹⁷The person who accepts
  correction is on the way to
  life.
But the person who ignores
  correction will be ruined.

¹⁸Whoever hides his hate is a liar.
Whoever tells lies is a fool.

¹⁹If you talk a lot, you are sure to
  sin.
If you are wise, you will keep
  quiet.

²⁰The words of a good person are
  like pure silver.
But an evil person's thoughts
  are worth little.

²¹A good person's words will help
  many others.
But a foolish person dies
  because he doesn't have
  wisdom.

²²The Lord's blessing brings wealth.
And with it comes no sorrow.

²³A foolish person enjoys doing
  wrong.
But a person with understanding
  enjoys doing what is wise.

²⁴An evil person will get what he
  fears most.
But a good person will receive
  what he wants most.

²⁵A storm will blow the evil person
  away.
But a good person will always
  be safe.

²⁶A lazy person brings trouble to
  the one he works for.
He bothers others like vinegar
  on the teeth or smoke in the
  eyes.

²⁷Whoever respects the Lord will
  have a long life.
But an evil person will have his
  life cut short.

²⁸A good person can look forward to
  happiness.
But an evil person can expect
  nothing.

²⁹The Lord will protect good
  people.
But he will ruin those who do
  evil.

³⁰Good people will always be safe.

But evil people will not remain
in the land.

³¹A good person says wise things.
But a liar's tongue will be
stopped.

³²Good people say the right thing.
But the wicked tell lies.

11 The Lord hates dishonest
scales.
But he is pleased with correct
weights.

²Pride leads only to shame.
It is wise not to be proud.

³Good people will be guided by
honesty.
But dishonesty will destroy
those who are not
trustworthy.

⁴Riches will not help when it's time
to die.
But doing what is right will save
you from dying too soon.

⁵The goodness of an innocent
person makes his life easier.
But a wicked person will be
destroyed by his
wickedness.

⁶Doing what is right brings
freedom to honest people.
But those who are not
trustworthy will be caught
by their own desires.

⁷When a wicked person dies, his
hope is gone.
The hopes he placed in his
riches will come to nothing.

⁸The good man is saved from
trouble.
It comes to the wicked instead.

⁹By his words an evil person can
destroy his neighbour.
But a good person will escape
by being clever.

¹⁰When good people succeed, the
city is happy.

When evil people die, there are
shouts of joy.

¹¹The influence of good people
makes a city great.
But the wicked can destroy it
with their words.

¹²A person without good sense finds
fault with his neighbour.
But a person with understanding
keeps quiet.

¹³A person who gossips can't keep
secrets.
But a trustworthy person can
keep a secret.

¹⁴Without leadership a nation will be
defeated.
But when many people give
advice, it will be safe.

¹⁵Whoever guarantees to pay what
somebody else owes will
suffer.
It is safer to avoid such
promises.

¹⁶A kind woman is respected.
But cruel men get wealth.

¹⁷A kind person is doing himself a
favour.
But a cruel person brings
trouble on himself.

¹⁸An evil person really gains nothing
from what he earns.
But a good person will surely be
rewarded.

¹⁹Those who are truly good will
live.
But those who chase after evil
will die.

²⁰The Lord hates those with evil
hearts.
But he is pleased with those
who are innocent.

²¹You can be sure that evil people
will be punished.
But those who do what is right
will not be punished.

²²A beautiful woman without good
    sense
    is like a gold ring in a pig's
    snout.

²³The wishes of those who do right
    will come true.
    But the hopes of the wicked will
    be defeated by God's anger.

²⁴Some people give much but get
    back even more.
    But others don't give what they
    should, and they end up
    poor.
²⁵A person who gives to others will
    get richer.
    Whoever helps others will
    himself be helped.

²⁶People curse someone who keeps
    all the grain for himself.
    But they bless a person who is
    willing to sell it.

²⁷Whoever looks for good will find
    kindness.
    But whoever looks for evil will
    find trouble.

²⁸Those who trust in riches will be
    ruined.
    But a good person will be as
    healthy as a green leaf.

²⁹Whoever brings trouble to his
    family will be left with
    nothing but the wind.
    And a foolish person will become
    a servant to the wise.

³⁰As a tree makes fruit, a good
    person gives life to others.
    The wise person shows others
    how to be wise.

³¹Good people will be rewarded on
    earth.
    So the wicked and the sinners
    will also be punished.

12 Anyone who loves learning
    accepts being corrected.
    But a person who hates being
    corrected is stupid.

²The Lord is pleased with a good
    person.
    But he will punish anyone who
    plans evil.

³Doing evil brings a person no
    safety at all.
    But a good person has safety
    and security.

⁴A good wife is like a crown for
    her husband.
    But a disgraceful wife is like a
    disease in his bones.

⁵The plans that good people make
    are fair.
    But the advice of the wicked will
    trick you.

⁶The wicked talk of killing people.
    But the words of good people
    will save them.

⁷Wicked people die and leave
    nothing behind.
    But a good man's family goes
    on.

⁸A wise person is praised.
    But a stupid person is not
    respected.

⁹A person might not be important
    but still have a servant.
    He is better off than someone
    who acts important but has
    no food.

¹⁰A good man takes care of his
    animals.
    But even the kindest acts of the
    wicked are cruel.

¹¹The person who works his land
    will have plenty of food.
    But the one who chases useless
    dreams isn't wise.

¹²Evil people want what other evil
    people have stolen.
    But good people want to give to
    others.

¹³Evil people are trapped by their
    evil talk.

But good people stay out of
  trouble.

14A person will be rewarded for
  what he says.
  And he will also be rewarded for
  what he does.

15A foolish person thinks he is doing
  right.
  But a wise person listens to
  advice.

16A foolish person quickly shows
  that he is upset.
  But a wise person ignores an
  insult.

17An honest witness tells the truth.
  But a dishonest witness tells
  lies.

18Careless words stab like a sword.
  But wise words bring healing.

19Truth will last for ever.
  But lies last only a moment.

20Those who plan evil mean to lie.
  But those who plan peace will
  be happy.

21No harm comes to a good person.
  But an evil person's life is full of
  trouble.

22The Lord hates those who tell
  lies.
  But he is pleased with those
  who do what they promise.

23A wise person keeps what he
  knows to himself.
  But a foolish person shows how
  foolish he is.

24Hard workers will become
  leaders.
  But those who are lazy will be
  slaves.

25Worry makes a person feel as if
  he is carrying a heavy load.
  But a kind word cheers a
  person.

26A good person takes advice from
  his friends.
  But an evil person is easily led
  to do wrong.

27A lazy person catches no food to
  cook.
  But a hard worker will have
  great wealth.

28Doing what is right is the way to
  life.
  But there is another way that
  leads to death.

13 A wise son takes his father's
     advice.
  But a person who makes fun of
  wisdom won't listen to
  correction.

2A person will be rewarded for
  what he says.
  But those who can't be trusted
  want only violence.

3Whoever is careful about what he
  says protects his life.
  But anyone who speaks without
  thinking will be ruined.

4The lazy person will not get what
  he wants.
  But a hard worker gets
  everything he wants.

5Good people hate what is false.
  But wicked people do shameful
  and disgraceful things.

6Doing what is right protects the
  honest person.
  But evil ruins the sinner.

7Some people pretend to be rich
  but really have nothing.
  Other people pretend to be poor
  but really are wealthy.

8A rich man may have to pay a
  ransom for his life.
  But a poor person will never
  have to face such a danger.

9Good people will live long like
  bright flames.

But the wicked will die like a
flame going out.

¹⁰Pride leads to arguments.
But those who take advice are
wise.

¹¹Money that comes easily
disappears quickly.
But money that is gathered little
by little will slowly grow.

¹²It is sad when you don't get what
you hoped for.
But when wishes come true, it's
like eating fruit from the
tree of life.

¹³Whoever rejects what he is taught
will pay for it.
But whoever does what he is
told will be rewarded.

¹⁴The teaching of a wise person
gives life.
It is like a fountain of water that
can save people from death.

¹⁵People with good understanding
will be liked.
But the lives of those who are
not trustworthy are hard.

¹⁶Every wise person acts with good
sense.
But a foolish person shows how
foolish he is.

¹⁷A wicked messenger brings
nothing but trouble.
But a trustworthy one makes
everything right.

¹⁸A person who refuses correction
will end up poor and
disgraced.
But a person who accepts
correction will be honoured.

¹⁹It is so good when wishes come
true.
But foolish people still refuse to
stop doing evil.

²⁰Whoever spends time with wise
people will become wise.

But whoever makes friends with
fools will suffer.

²¹Trouble always comes to sinners.
But good people enjoy success.

²²Good people's wealth will be
inherited by their
grandchildren.
And a sinner's wealth will be
saved for good people.

²³A poor man's field might have
plenty of food.
But unfair people steal it from
him.

²⁴If a person does not punish his
children, he does not love
them.
But the person who loves his
children is careful to correct
them.

²⁵Good people have enough to eat.
But the wicked will go hungry.

14 A wise woman strengthens
her family.
But a foolish woman destroys
hers by what she does.

²People who live good lives show
respect for the Lord.
But those who live evil lives
show no respect for him.

³A foolish person will be punished
for his proud words.
But a wise person's words will
protect him.

⁴When there are no oxen, there is
no food in the barn.
But with the strength of an ox,
much grain can be grown.

⁵A truthful witness does not lie.
But a false witness tells nothing
but lies.

⁶Those who make fun of wisdom
look for it but do not find it.
But the person with
understanding easily finds
knowledge.

⁷Stay away from a foolish person.
  You won't learn anything from
    him.

⁸What makes a person wise is
    understanding what to do.
  But what makes a person foolish
    is dishonesty.

⁹Foolish people don't care if they
    sin.
  But honest people work at being
    right with others.

¹⁰No one else can know your
    sadness.
  Strangers cannot share your joy.

¹¹The wicked person's house will be
    destroyed.
  But a good person's tent will
    still be standing.

¹²Some people think they are doing
    what's right.
  But what they are doing will
    really kill them.

¹³When someone is laughing, he
    may be sad inside.
  And when the laughter is over,
    there is sorrow.

¹⁴Evil people will be paid back for
    their evil ways.
  And good people will be
    rewarded for their good
    ones.

¹⁵A foolish person will believe
    anything.
  But a wise person thinks about
    what he does.

¹⁶A wise person is careful and stays
    out of trouble.
  But a foolish person is quick to
    act and careless.

¹⁷A person who quickly loses his
    temper does foolish things.
  But a person with understanding
    remains calm.

¹⁸Foolish people get nothing for
    their work but more
    foolishness.
  But wise people are rewarded
    with knowledge.

¹⁹Evil people will have to bow down
    to good people.
  The wicked will bow down at
    the door of those who do
    right.

²⁰The poor are rejected, even by
    their neighbours.
  But rich people have many
    friends.

²¹It is a sin to hate your neighbour.
  But being kind to the needy
    brings happiness.

²²Those who make evil plans will be
    ruined.
  But people love and trust those
    who plan to do good.

²³Those who work hard make a
    profit.
  But those who only talk will be
    poor.

²⁴Wise people are rewarded with
    wealth.
  But foolish people will only be
    rewarded with more
    foolishness.

²⁵A truthful witness saves lives.
  But a false witness is a traitor.

²⁶A person who respects the Lord
    will have security.
  And his children will be
    protected.

²⁷Respect for the Lord gives life.
  It is like a fountain of water that
    can save people from death.

²⁸A king is honoured when he has
    many people to rule.
  But a prince is ruined if he has
    none.

²⁹A person who does not quickly
   get angry shows that he has
   understanding.
   But a person who quickly loses
   his temper shows his
   foolishness.

³⁰Peace of mind means a healthy
   body.
   But jealousy will rot your bones.

³¹Whoever is cruel to the poor
   insults their Maker.
   But anyone who is kind to the
   needy honours God.

³²The wicked are ruined by their
   own evil.
   But those who do what is right
   are protected by their
   honesty.

³³The person who has
   understanding has wisdom.
   And even fools recognise it.

³⁴Doing what is right makes a nation
   great.
   But sin will bring disgrace to any
   people.

³⁵A king is pleased with a wise
   servant.
   But he will become angry with
   one who causes him shame.

15 A gentle answer will calm a
   person's anger.
   But an unkind answer will cause
   more anger.

²Wise people use knowledge when
   they speak.
   But fools speak only foolishness.

³The Lord's eyes see everything
   that happens.
   He watches both evil and good
   people.

⁴As a tree gives us fruit, healing
   words give us life.
   But evil words crush the spirit.

⁵A foolish person rejects his
   father's correction.

But anyone who accepts
   correction is wise.

⁶There is much wealth in the
   houses of good people.
   But evil people are paid only
   with trouble.

⁷With their words wise people
   spread knowledge.
   But there is no knowledge in the
   thoughts of the foolish.

⁸The Lord hates the sacrifice that
   the wicked person offers.
   But he is pleased with an honest
   person's prayer.

⁹The Lord hates what evil people
   do.
   But he loves those who do what
   is right.

¹⁰The person who stops doing what
   is right will really be
   punished.
   The one who hates to be
   corrected will die.

¹¹The Lord knows what is
   happening where the dead
   people are.
   So he can surely know what
   living people are thinking.

¹²A person who laughs at wisdom
   does not like to be
   corrected.
   He will not ask advice from the
   wise.

¹³Happiness makes a person smile.
   But sadness breaks a person's
   spirit.

¹⁴Clever people want more
   knowledge.
   But a foolish person just wants
   more foolishness.

¹⁵Every day is hard for those who
   suffer.
   But a happy heart makes it like
   a continual feast.

¹⁶It is better to be poor and respect
the Lord
than to be wealthy and have
much trouble.

¹⁷It is better to eat vegetables with
those who love you
than to eat meat with those who
hate you.

¹⁸A person who quickly gets angry
causes trouble.
But a person who controls his
temper stops a quarrel.

¹⁹A lazy person's life is as difficult
as walking through a patch
of thorns.
But an honest person's life is as
easy as walking down a
smooth highway.

²⁰A wise son makes his father
happy.
But a foolish person hates his
mother.

²¹A man without wisdom enjoys
being foolish.
But a man with understanding
does what is right.

²²Plans fail without good advice.
But plans succeed when you get
advice from many others.

²³People enjoy giving good answers!
Saying the right word at the
right time is so pleasing!

²⁴A wise person does things that
will make his life better.
He avoids whatever would cause
his death.

²⁵The Lord will tear down the proud
person's house.
But he will protect the property
of a widow.

²⁶The Lord hates evil thoughts.
But he is pleased with kind
words.

²⁷A greedy person brings trouble to
his family.

But the person who can't be
paid to do wrong will live.

²⁸Good people think before they
answer.
But the wicked simply give evil
answers.

²⁹The Lord does not listen to the
wicked.
But he hears the prayers of
those who do right.

³⁰Good news makes you feel better.
Your happiness will show in your
eyes.

³¹A wise person pays attention to
correction
that will improve his life.

³²A person who refuses correction
hates himself.
But a person who accepts
correction gains
understanding.

³³Respect for the Lord will teach
you wisdom.
If you want to be honoured, you
must not be proud.

16 People make plans in their
hearts.
But only the Lord can make
those plans come true.

²A person may believe he is doing
right.
But the Lord will judge his
reasons.

³Depend on the Lord in whatever
you do.
Then your plans will succeed.

⁴The Lord makes everything work
the way he wants it.
He even has a day of disaster
for evil people.

⁵The Lord hates those who are
proud.
You can be sure that they will
be punished.

[6]Love and truth bring forgiveness
       of sin.
    By respecting the Lord you will
       avoid evil.

[7]A person should live so that he
       pleases the Lord.
    If he does, even his enemies will
       make peace with him.

[8]It is better to be poor and do
       what is right
    than to be wealthy and be
       unfair.

[9]A person may think up plans.
    But the Lord decides what he
       will do.

[10]The words of a king are like a
       message from God.
    So his decisions should be fair.

[11]The Lord wants honest balances
       and scales to be used.
    He wants all weights to be
       honest.

[12]Kings hate those who do wrong
       because governments only last if
       they are fair.

[13]Kings are pleased with those who
       speak honest words.
    They value a person who speaks
       the truth.

[14]If a king becomes angry, he may
       put someone to death.
    So a wise man will try to keep
       peace.

[15]A king's kindness can give people
       life.
    His kindness is like a spring
       shower.

[16]It is better to get wisdom than
       gold.
    It is better to choose
       understanding than silver!

[17]A good person stays away from
       evil.
    A person who watches what he
       does protects his life.

[18]Pride will destroy a person.
    A proud attitude leads to ruin.

[19]It is better not to be proud and to
       be with those who suffer
    than to share stolen property
       with proud people.

[20]Whoever pays attention to what
       he is taught will succeed.
    And whoever trusts the Lord
       will be happy.

[21]A wise person is known for his
       understanding.
    He wins people to his side with
       pleasant words.

[22]Understanding is like a fountain of
       water which gives life to
       those who use it.
    But foolishness will cause foolish
       people to be punished.

[23]A wise person's mind tells him
       what to say.
    This helps him to teach others
       better.

[24]Pleasant words are like a
       honeycomb.
    They make a person happy and
       healthy.

[25]Some people think they are doing
       what's right.
    But in the end it causes them to
       die.

[26]The worker's hunger helps him.
    His desire to eat makes him
       work.

[27]An evil person makes evil plans.
    And his words are like a burning
       fire.

[28]An evil person causes trouble.
    And a person who gossips ruins
       friendships.

[29]A cruel man tricks his neighbour.
    He leads him to do wrong.

[30]Someone who winks at you is
       planning evil.

And the one who grins at you is
   about to do something
   wrong.
³¹Grey hair is like a crown of
   honour.
   You earn it by living a good life.

³²Patience is better than strength.
   Controlling your temper is
   better than capturing a city.

³³People throw lots*d* to make a
   decision.
   But the answer comes from the
   Lord.

17 It is better to eat a dry crust
   of bread in peace
   than to have a feast where there
   is quarrelling.

²A wise servant will rule over his
   master's disgraceful son.
   And he will even inherit a share
   of what the master leaves
   his sons.

³A hot furnace tests silver and
   gold.
   In the same way, the Lord tests
   a person's heart.

⁴An evil person listens to evil
   words.
   A liar pays attention to cruel
   words.

⁵If you make fun of the poor,
   you insult God, who made them.
   If you laugh at someone's trouble,
   you will be punished.

⁶Grandchildren are the reward of
   old people.
   And children are proud of their
   parents.

⁷Foolish people should not be
   proud.
   And rulers should not be liars!

⁸A person might think he can pay
   people and they will do
   anything he asks.

He thinks it will succeed every
   time.
⁹Whoever forgives someone's sin
   makes a friend.
   But the one who tells about the
   sin breaks up friendships.

¹⁰A wise man will learn more from a
   warning
   than a foolish person will learn
   from 100 lashings.

¹¹A disobedient person is only
   looking for trouble.
   So a cruel messenger will be
   sent against him.

¹²It is better to meet a bear robbed
   of her cubs
   than to meet a foolish person
   doing foolish things.

¹³If a person gives evil in return for
   good,
   his house will always be full of
   trouble.

¹⁴Starting a quarrel is like a leak in
   a dam.
   So stop the quarrel before a
   fight breaks out.

¹⁵The Lord hates both these things:
   letting guilty people go free and
   punishing those who are not
   guilty.

¹⁶It won't do a fool any good to try
   to buy wisdom.
   He doesn't really want to be
   wise.

¹⁷A friend loves you all the time.
   A brother is always there to
   help you.

¹⁸It is not wise to promise
   to pay what your neighbour
   owes.

¹⁹Whoever loves to quarrel loves to
   sin.
   Whoever is proud is asking for
   trouble.

²⁰A person with an evil heart will find no success.
And the person whose words are evil will get into trouble.

²¹It is sad to have a foolish son.
There is no joy in being the father of a fool.

²²A happy heart is like good medicine.
But a broken spirit drains your strength.

²³A wicked person secretly accepts money to do wrong.
Then there will be no fairness.

²⁴The person with understanding looks for wisdom.
But a foolish person lets his mind wander everywhere.

²⁵A foolish son makes his father sad.
And he causes his mother great sorrow.

²⁶It is not good to punish those who have done what is right.
Nor is it good to punish leaders for being honest.

²⁷The person who has knowledge says very little.
And a person with understanding stays calm.

²⁸Even a foolish person seems to be wise if he keeps quiet.
He appears to have understanding if he doesn't speak.

18 An unfriendly person cares only about himself.
He makes fun of all wisdom.

²A foolish person does not want to understand anything.
He only enjoys telling others what he thinks.

³Do something evil, and people won't like you.
Do something shameful, and they will make fun of you.

⁴Understanding people's words is as hard as getting water out of a deep well.
But understanding wisdom is as easy as getting water from a flowing stream.

⁵It is not good to honour the wicked.
Nor is it good to be unfair to the innocent.

⁶A fool's words start quarrels.
They make people want to give him a beating.

⁷A fool's words will ruin him.
He will be trapped by his own words.

⁸The words of a gossip are like tasty bits of food.
People take them all in.

⁹A person who doesn't work hard is just like a person who destroys things.

¹⁰The Lord is like a strong tower.
Those who do what is right can run to him for safety.

¹¹Rich people trust their wealth to protect them.
They think it is like the high walls of a city.

¹²People who are proud will be ruined.
But those who are not proud will be honoured.

¹³A person who answers without listening
is foolish and disgraceful.

¹⁴The will to live can get you through sickness.
But no one can live with a broken spirit.

¹⁵The mind of a clever person is ready to get knowledge.

The wise person listens to learn more.

¹⁶Taking a gift to an important person
will help get you in to see him.

¹⁷The first person to tell his side of a story seems right.
But that may change when somebody comes and asks him questions.

¹⁸Throwing lots*d* settles arguments.
It keeps the two sides from fighting.

¹⁹A brother who has been insulted is harder to win back than a walled city.
And arguments separate people like the barred gates of a palace.

²⁰What you say affects how you live.
You will be rewarded by how you speak.

²¹What you say can mean life or death.
Those who love to talk will be rewarded for what they say.

²²A man who finds a wife finds something good.
She shows that the Lord is pleased with him.

²³Poor people beg for mercy.
Rich people give rude answers.

²⁴Some friends may ruin you.
But a real friend will be more loyal than a brother.

19 It is better to be poor and honest
than to be foolish and tell lies.

²Enthusiasm without knowledge is not good.
If you act too quickly, you might make a mistake.

³A person's own foolishness ruins his life.

But in his mind he blames the Lord for it.

⁴Wealthy people are always finding more friends.
But the poor lose their friends.

⁵A witness who lies will be punished.
An untruthful person will not be left unpunished.

⁶Many people want to please a leader.
And everyone is friends with those who give gifts.

⁷A poor person's relatives avoid him.
Even his friends stay far away!
He runs after them, begging.
But they are gone.

⁸The person who gets wisdom is good to himself.
And the one who has understanding will succeed.

⁹A witness who lies will be punished.
An untruthful person will die.

¹⁰No foolish person should live in luxury.
No slave should rule over princes!

¹¹A wise person is patient.
He will be honoured if he ignores a wrong done against him.

¹²A king's anger scares people like the roar of a lion.
But his kindness is as pleasant as the dew on the grass.

¹³A foolish son will ruin his father.
And a quarrelling wife is as bothersome as dripping water.

¹⁴Houses and wealth are inherited from parents.
But a wise wife is a gift from the Lord.

¹⁵Lazy people sleep a lot.
  Idle people will go hungry.

¹⁶Whoever obeys the commands
    protects his life.
  Whoever is careless in what he
    does will die.

¹⁷Being kind to the poor is like
    lending to the Lord.
  The Lord will reward you for
    what you have done.

¹⁸Correct your son while there is
    still hope.
  Do not help him destroy himself.

¹⁹A person who is always getting
    angry will pay for it.
  If you help him, you will have to
    do it again and again.

²⁰Listen to advice and accept
    correction.
  Then in the end you will be
    wise.

²¹People can make many different
    plans.
  But only the Lord's plan will
    happen.

²²People want others to be loyal.
  So it is better to be poor than to
    be a liar.

²³Those who respect the Lord will
    live
  and be content, unbothered by
    trouble.

²⁴The lazy person may put his hand
    in the dish,
  but he won't lift the food to his
    mouth!

²⁵Whip a person who makes fun of
    wisdom, and then foolish
    people will learn how to
    think.
  Just correct a clever man, and
    he will gain knowledge.

²⁶A son who robs his father and
    sends away his mother

brings shame and disgrace on
    himself.

²⁷Don't stop listening to correction,
    my child.
  If you do, you will not obey
    what you have already
    learned.

²⁸An evil witness makes fun of
    fairness.
  And wicked people love what is
    evil.

²⁹People who make fun of wisdom
    will be punished.
  And the backs of foolish people
    will be beaten.

20 Wine and beer make people
    loud and uncontrolled.
  It is not wise to get drunk on
    them.

²A king's anger is like the roar of a
    lion.
  Making him angry may cost you
    your life.

³Foolish people are always getting
    into quarrels.
  But avoiding quarrels will bring
    you honour.

⁴A lazy farmer doesn't plough when
    he should.
  So at harvest time he has no
    crop.

⁵Understanding a person's thoughts
    is as hard as getting water
    from a deep well.
  But someone with understanding
    can find the wisdom there.

⁶Many people claim to be loyal.
  But it is hard to find someone
    who really can be trusted.

⁷The good person who lives an
    honest life
  is a blessing to his children.

⁸A king sits on his throne and
    judges people.
  He knows evil when he sees it.

9No one can say, "I am innocent.
I have never done anything
wrong."

10The Lord hates both these things:
dishonest weights and dishonest
measures.

11Even a child is known by his
behaviour.
His actions show if he is
innocent and good.

12The Lord has made both these
things:
ears that can hear and eyes that
can see.

13If you love to sleep, you will be
poor.
If you stay awake, you will have
plenty of food.

14The buyer says, "This is bad. It's
no good."
Then he goes away and brags
about what he bought.

15There is plenty of gold, and there
are many rubies.
But there are only a few people
who speak with knowledge.

16Take the coat of someone who
promises to pay what a
stranger owes.
Keep it until he pays the
stranger's bills.

17When a person gets food
dishonestly, it may taste
sweet at first.
But later he will feel as if he has
a mouth full of gravel.

18Get advice if you want your plans
to work.
If you go to war, get the advice
of others.

19Gossips can't keep secrets.
So avoid people who talk too
much.

20Whoever curses his father or
mother

will die like a light going out in
darkness.

21Wealth that is gained quickly in
the beginning
will do you no good in the end.

22Don't say, "I'll pay you back for
the evil you did."
Wait for the Lord. He will make
things right.

23The Lord hates dishonest weights.
And dishonest scales do not
please him.

24The Lord decides what a person
does.
So no one can understand what
his life is all about.

25It's dangerous to promise
something to God too
quickly.
After you've thought about it, it
may be too late.

26A wise king finds out who the evil
people are.
Then he punishes them.

27The Lord looks into a person's
feelings.
He searches through a person's
thoughts.

28Loyalty and truth keep a king in
power.
He continues to rule if he is
loyal.

29Young men are admired for their
strength.
Old men are honoured for their
experience.

30Hard punishment will get rid of
evil.
Whippings can change the evil
person's heart.

21 The Lord can control a king's
mind as easily as he controls
a river.
He can direct it as he pleases.

2A person may believe he is doing
  right.
But the Lord judges his reasons.

3Do what is right and fair.
That is more important to the
  Lord than animal sacrifices.

4Proud looks, proud thoughts
and evil actions are sin.

5Those who plan and work hard
  earn a profit.
But those who act too quickly
  become poor.

6Wealth that comes from telling lies
vanishes like a mist and leads to
  death.

7The violence of the wicked will
  destroy them
because they refuse to do what
  is right.

8Guilty people live dishonest lives.
But honest people do what is
  right.

9It is better to live in a corner on
  the roof*
than inside the house with a
  quarrelling wife.

10An evil person only wants to harm
  others.
His neighbour will get no mercy
  from him.

11Punish a person who makes fun of
  wisdom, and he will become
  wise.
But just teach a wise person,
  and he will get knowledge.

12God, who is always right, sees
  the house of the wicked.
And he brings about the ruin of
  every evil person.

13If you ignore the poor when they
  cry for help,

you also will cry for help and not
  be answered.

14A gift given secretly will calm an
  angry man.
A present given in secrecy will
  calm even great anger.

15When things are done fairly, good
  people are happy,
but evil people are frightened.

16A person who does not use
  understanding
will join the dead.

17Whoever loves pleasure will
  become poor.
Whoever loves wine and rich
  food will never be wealthy.

18Wicked people will suffer instead
  of good people.
And those who cannot be
  trusted will suffer instead of
  those who can.

19It is better to live alone in the
  desert
than with a quarrelling and
  complaining wife.

20Wise people store up the best
  foods and olive oil.
But a foolish person eats up
  everything he has.

21A person who tries to live right
  and be loyal
finds life, success and honour.

22A wise person can defeat a city
  full of strong men.
He can tear down the defences
  they trust.

23A person who is careful about
  what he says
keeps himself out of trouble.

24People who act with stubborn
  pride

roof In Bible times houses were built with flat roofs. The roof was used for drying things such
  as flax and fruit. It was also used as an extra room, as a place for worship and as a place
  to sleep in the summer.

are called "proud" and
"bragger".

25The lazy person's desire for sleep
will kill him
because he refuses to work.
26All day long the lazy person
wishes for more.
But the good person gives
without holding back.

27The Lord hates sacrifices made by
evil people,
particularly when they make
them for the wrong reasons.

28The words of a lying witness will
die.
But the words of an obedient
man will always be
remembered.

29A wicked person is stubborn.
But an honest person thinks
carefully about what he
does.

30There is no wisdom,
understanding or advice
that can succeed against the
Lord.

31You can get the horses ready for
battle.
But it is the Lord who gives the
victory.

22 Being respected is more
important than having great
riches.
To be well thought of is better
than owning silver or gold.

2The rich and the poor are alike
in that the Lord made them all.

3When a wise person sees danger
ahead, he avoids it.
But a foolish person keeps going
and gets into trouble.

4Respecting the Lord and not being
proud
will bring you wealth, honour
and life.

5The lives of evil people are like
paths covered with thorns
and traps.
People who protect themselves
don't have such problems.

6Train a child how to live the right
way.
Then even when he is old, he
will still live that way.

7The rich rule over the poor.
And borrowers become servants
to those who lend.

8A person who does evil things will
receive trouble in return.
Then he won't be cruel to
others any longer.

9A generous person will be blessed
because he shares his food with
the poor.

10Get rid of the person who makes
fun of wisdom.
Then fighting, quarrels and
insults will stop.

11A person who loves innocent
thoughts and kind words
will have even the king as a
friend.

12The Lord protects knowledge
from being lost.
But he destroys false words.

13The lazy person says, "There's a
lion outside!
I might get killed out in the
street!"

14The words of an unfaithful wife
are like a deep trap.
Those who make the Lord angry
will get caught by them.

15Every child is full of foolishness.
But punishment can get rid of it.

16The one who gets rich by being
cruel to the poor will
become poor.
And so will the one who gives
presents to the wealthy.

Other Wise Sayings

¹⁷Pay attention and listen to what wise people say.
Remember what I am teaching you.
¹⁸It will be good to keep these things in mind.
Be prepared to repeat them.
¹⁹I am teaching them to you now so that you will put your trust in the Lord.
²⁰I have written down 30 sayings for you.
They give knowledge and good advice.
²¹I am teaching you true and reliable words.
Then you can give true answers to anyone who asks.

²²Do not abuse poor people because they are poor.
And do not take away the rights of the needy in court.
²³The Lord will defend them in court.
And he will take the life of those who take away their rights.

²⁴Don't make friends with someone who easily gets angry.
Don't spend time with someone who has a bad temper.
²⁵If you do, you may learn to be like him.
Then you will be in real danger.

²⁶Don't promise to pay what someone else owes.
And don't give guarantees that you will pay what he owes.
²⁷If you cannot pay what he owes, your own bed will be taken and sold.

²⁸Don't move an old stone that shows where a person's land is.
These stones were set up by your ancestors.

²⁹Do you see a man skilled in his work?
That man will work for kings.
He won't have to work for ordinary people.

23 If you sit down to eat with a ruler,
notice the food that is in front of you.
²Control yourself if you have a big appetite.
³Don't be greedy for his fine foods.
He might use that rich food to trick you.

⁴Don't wear yourself out trying to get rich.
Be wise enough to control yourself.
⁵Wealth can vanish in the wink of an eye.
It seems to grow wings and fly away like an eagle in the sky.

⁶Don't eat the food of a selfish person.
Don't be greedy for his fine foods.
⁷A selfish person is always worrying
about how much the food costs.
He tells you, "Eat and drink".
But he doesn't really mean it.
⁸So you will feel like vomiting the little bit you have eaten.
And you will have wasted your kind words.

⁹Don't speak to a foolish person.
He will only ignore your wise words.

¹⁰Don't move an old stone that shows where somebody's land is.
And don't take fields that belong to orphans.
¹¹God, their defender, is strong.
He will take their side against you.

¹²Remember what you are taught.
And listen carefully to words of knowledge.

¹³Don't fail to punish a child.
If you spank him, you will keep
him from dying.
¹⁴If you punish him with a spanking,
you will save him from a fool's
death.

¹⁵My child, if you are wise,
then I will be happy.
¹⁶I will be so pleased
if you speak what is right.

¹⁷Don't envy sinners.
But always respect the Lord.
¹⁸If you do, you will have hope for
the future.
Your wishes will come true.

¹⁹Listen, my child, and be wise.
Keep your mind on what is
right.
²⁰Don't be one of those who drink
too much wine
or who eat too much food.
²¹Those who drink too much and
eat too much become poor.
They sleep too much and end up
wearing rags.

²²Listen to your father, who gave
you life.
And do not forget your mother
when she is old.
²³Learn the truth and never reject
it.
Get wisdom, self-control and
understanding.
²⁴The father of a good child is very
happy.
The person who has a wise son
is glad because of him.
²⁵Make your father and mother
happy.
Give your mother a reason to be
glad.

²⁶My son, pay attention to me.
And watch closely what I do.
²⁷A prostitute*d* is as dangerous as a
deep pit.
And an unfaithful wife is like a
narrow well.
²⁸They ambush you like robbers.

And they cause many men to be
unfaithful to their wives.

²⁹⁻³⁰Some people drink too much
wine.
They try out all the different
kinds of drinks.
So they have trouble. They are
sad.
They fight. They complain.
They have unnecessary bruises.
They have bloodshot eyes.
³¹Don't stare at the wine's pretty,
red colour.
It may sparkle in the cup.
It may go down your throat
smoothly.
³²But later it bites like a snake.
Like a snake, it poisons you.
³³Your eyes will see strange sights.
And your mind will be confused.
³⁴You will feel dizzy, as if you're out
on the stormy ocean.
You will feel as if you're on top
of a ship's sails.
³⁵You will think, "They hit me, but
I'm not hurt!
They have beaten me up, but I
don't remember it.
I wish I could wake up.
Then I would get another
drink."

24 Don't envy evil people.
Don't try to be friends with
them.
²In their minds they plan cruel
things.
And they always talk about
making trouble.

³It takes wisdom to have a good
family.
It takes understanding to make
it strong.
⁴It takes knowledge to fill a home
with rare and beautiful
treasures.

⁵A wise man has great power.
And a man who has knowledge
is very strong.

⁶So you need the advice of others
    when you go to war.
If you have many people to give
    advice, you will win.

⁷A foolish person cannot
    understand wisdom.
He has nothing to say in court.

⁸Whoever makes evil plans
    will be known as a
    troublemaker.
⁹Making foolish plans is sinful.
    And making fun of others is
    hateful.

¹⁰If you give up when trouble
    comes,
    it shows that you have very
    little strength.

¹¹Save those who are being led to
    their death.
    Rescue those who are about to
    be killed.
¹²You may say, "We don't know
    anything about this."
    But God knows what is in your
    mind, and he will notice.
He is watching you, and he will
    know.
He will pay each person back for
    what he has done.

¹³My child, eat honey because it is
    good.
    Honey from the honeycomb
    tastes sweet.
¹⁴In the same way, wisdom is
    pleasing to you.
    If you find it, you have hope for
    the future.
    Your wishes will come true.

¹⁵Don't be like the wicked and
    attack a good man's house.
    Don't rob the place where he
    lives.
¹⁶A good man may be bothered by
    trouble seven times, but he
    does not give up.
    But the wicked are
    overwhelmed by trouble.

¹⁷Don't be happy when your enemy
    is defeated.
    Don't be glad when he is
    overwhelmed.
¹⁸The Lord will notice and be
    displeased.
    Then the Lord may not be angry
    with him any more.

¹⁹Don't envy evil people.
    And don't be jealous of the
    wicked.
²⁰An evil person has nothing to
    hope for.
    The wicked will die like a flame
    that is put out.

²¹My child, respect the Lord and
    the king.
    Don't join those people who
    refuse to obey them.
²²The Lord and the king will quickly
    destroy such people.
    Those two can cause great
    trouble!

More Words of Wisdom

²³These are also wise sayings:

It is not good to take sides when
    you are the judge.
²⁴Don't say that the wicked have
    done right.
    People will curse you, and
    nations will hate you.
²⁵But things will go well for judges
    who punish the guilty.
    And they will receive good
    things from God.

²⁶An honest answer is as pleasing
    as a kiss on the lips.

²⁷First, you should work outside
    and prepare your fields.
    After that, you can start having
    your family.

²⁸Don't testify against your
    neighbour for no good
    reason.
    Don't say things that are false.
²⁹Don't say, "I'll get even with that
    man.

I'll do to him what he did to
me."

30I passed by a lazy person's field.
I went by the vineyard of a man
who had no sense.
31Thorns had grown up everywhere.
The ground was covered with
weeds.
And the stone walls had fallen
down.
32I thought about what I had seen.
I learned this lesson from what I
saw.
33You sleep a little; you take a nap.
You fold your hands and rest.
34Soon you will be poor, as if you
had been robbed.
You will have as little as if you
had been held up.

More Wise Sayings of Solomon

25 These are more wise sayings
of Solomon. They were copied
by the men of Hezekiah king of Judah.

2God is honoured for what he
keeps secret.
Kings are honoured for what
they can discover.

3No one can measure the height of
the skies or the depth of the
earth.
So also no one can understand
the mind of a king.
4Remove the scum from the silver.
Then the silver can be used by
the silversmith.
5Remove wicked people from the
king's presence.
Then his government will be
honest and last a long time.
6Don't brag to the king.
Don't act as if you are a great
man.
7It is better for him to promote
you to a higher job
than to give you a less important
position.

Because of something you have
seen,
8 do not quickly take someone to
court.
What will you do later
when your neighbour proves you
are wrong?

9If you have an argument with your
neighbour,
don't tell other people what was
said.
10Whoever hears it might say bad
things about you.
And you might not ever be
respected again.

11The right word spoken at the
right time
is as beautiful as gold apples in a
silver bowl.

12The warning of a wise person is
valuable to someone who
will listen.
It is worth as much as gold
earrings or fine gold
jewellery.

13A trustworthy messenger
refreshes those who send
him.
He is like the coolness of snow
in the summer time.

14People who brag about gifts they
never give
are like clouds and wind that
give no rain.

15With patience you can convince a
ruler.
And a gentle word can get
through to the hard-headed.

16If you find honey, don't eat too
much.
Too much of it will make you
sick.
17Don't go to your neighbour's
house too often.
Too much of you will make him
hate you.

¹⁸Anyone who lies about his
     neighbour
  hurts him as a club, a sword or
     a sharp arrow would.

¹⁹Don't trust unfaithful people when
     you are in trouble.
  It's like eating with a broken
     tooth or walking with a
     crippled foot.

²⁰Don't sing songs to someone who
     is sad.
  It's like taking off a coat on a
     cold day
  or pouring vinegar on soda.

²¹If your enemy is hungry, feed
     him.
  If he is thirsty, give him a drink.
²²Doing this will be like pouring
     burning coals on his head.
  And the Lord will reward you.

²³The north wind brings rain.
  In the same way, telling gossip
     brings angry looks.

²⁴It is better to live in a corner on
     the roof*
  than inside the house with a
     quarrelling wife.

²⁵Hearing good news from a
     faraway place
  is like having a cool drink when
     you are tired.

²⁶A good person who gives in to
     evil
  is like a muddy spring or a dirty
     well.

²⁷It is not good to eat too much
     honey.
  In the same way, it is not good
     to brag about yourself.

²⁸A person who does not control
     himself
  is like a city whose walls have
     been broken down.

26 It shouldn't snow in summer
     or rain at harvest.
  Neither should a foolish person
     ever be honoured.

²Curses will not harm someone
     who is innocent.
  They are like sparrows or
     swallows that fly around and
     never land.

³A whip is used to guide a horse,
     and a harness is used for a
     donkey.
  In the same way, a paddle is
     used on a foolish person to
     guide him.

⁴Don't give a foolish person a
     foolish answer.
  If you do, you will be just like
     him.

⁵But answer a foolish person as he
     should be answered.
  If you don't, he will think he is
     really wise.

⁶Don't send a message by a foolish
     person.
  That would be like cutting off
     your feet or drinking poison.

⁷A wise saying spoken by a fool
     does no good.
  It is like the legs of a crippled
     person.

⁸Giving honour to a foolish person
     does no good.
  It is like tying a stone in a
     catapult.

⁹A wise saying spoken by a fool
  is like a thorn stuck in the hand
     of a drunk.

roof In Bible times houses were built with flat roofs. The roof was used for drying things such as flax and fruit. It was also used as an extra room, as a place for worship and as a place to sleep in the summer.

¹⁰Someone might employ a foolish
        person or anyone just
        passing by.
   That employer is like an archer
        who shoots at anything he
        sees.

¹¹A dog eats what it vomits.
   And a foolish person repeats his
        foolishness.

¹²Some people think they are wise.
   There is more hope for a foolish
        person than for them.

¹³The lazy person says, "There's a
        lion in the road.
   There's a lion in the streets!"

¹⁴The lazy person is like a door that
        turns back and forth on its
        hinges.
   He stays in bed and turns over
        and over.

¹⁵The lazy person may put his hand
        in the dish.
   But he's too tired to lift the food
        to his mouth.

¹⁶The lazy person thinks he is wiser
        than seven people who give
        sensible answers.

¹⁷To grab a dog by the ears is
        asking for trouble.
   So is interfering in someone
        else's quarrel if you're just
        passing by.

¹⁸⁻¹⁹A person shouldn't trick his
        neighbour
   and then say, "I was just
        joking!"
   That is like a madman shooting
        deadly, burning arrows.

²⁰Without wood, a fire will go out.
   And without gossip, quarrelling
        will stop.

²¹Charcoal and wood keep a fire
        going.

In the same way, a quarrelsome
        person keeps an argument
        going.

²²The words of a gossip are like
        tasty bits of food.
   People take them all in.

²³Kind words from a wicked mind
        are like a shiny coating on a clay
        pot.

²⁴A person who hates you may fool
        you with his words.
   But in his mind he is planning
        evil.

²⁵His words are kind, but don't
        believe him.
   His mind is full of evil thoughts.
²⁶He hides his hate with lies.
   But his evil will be plain to
        everyone.

²⁷Whoever digs a deep trap for
        others will fall into it himself.
   Whoever tries to roll a boulder
        over others will be crushed
        by it.

²⁸A liar hates the people he hurts.
   And false praise can ruin others.

27 Don't brag about what will
        happen tomorrow.
   You don't really know what will
        happen then.

²Don't praise yourself. Let
        someone else do it.
   Let the praise come from a
        stranger and not from your
        own mouth.

³Stone is heavy, and sand is hard
        to carry.
   But the complaining of a foolish
        person causes more trouble
        than either.

⁴Anger is cruel. It destroys like a
        flood.
   But who can put up with
        jealousy!

⁵It is better to correct someone
        openly

than to love him and not show
  it.

6The slap of a friend can be trusted
    to help you.
  But the kisses of an enemy are
    nothing but lies.

7When someone is full, not even
    honey tastes good.
  But when he is hungry, even
    something bitter tastes
    sweet.

8A man who leaves his home
  is like a bird that leaves its nest.

9Perfume and oils make you happy.
  And good advice from a friend is
    sweet.

10Don't forget your friend or your
    father's friend.
  Don't always go to your brother
    for help when trouble
    comes.
  A neighbour close by is better
    than a brother far away.

11Be wise, my child, and you will
    make me happy.
  Then I can respond to any
    insult.

12When a wise person sees danger
    ahead, he avoids it.
  But a foolish person keeps going
    and gets into trouble.

13Take the coat of someone who
    promises to pay what a
    stranger owes.
  Keep it until he pays the
    stranger's bills.

14Don't greet your neighbour loudly
    early in the morning.
  He will think of it as a curse.

15A quarrelling wife is as
    bothersome
  as a continual dripping on a rainy
    day.
16Stopping her is like stopping the
    wind.

It's like trying to grab oil in your
  hand.

17Iron can sharpen iron.
  In the same way, people can
    help each other.

18The person who tends a fig tree
    will eat its fruit.
  And the person who takes care
    of his master will be
    honoured.

19As water shows you your face,
  so your mind shows you what
    kind of person you are.

20People will never stop dying and
    being destroyed.
  In the same way, people will
    never stop wanting more
    than they have.

21A hot furnace tests silver and
    gold.
  And people are tested by the
    praise they receive.

22Even if you ground up a foolish
    person like grain in a bowl,
  you couldn't remove his
    foolishness.

23Be sure you know how your
    sheep are doing.
  Pay close attention to the
    condition of your cattle.
24Riches will not continue for ever.
  Nor do governments continue
    for ever.
25Bring in the hay. Let the new
    grass appear.
  Gather the grass from the hills.
26Make clothes from the lambs'
    wool.
  Sell some goats to buy a field.
27There will be plenty of goat's milk
    to feed you and your family.
  It will make your servant girls
    healthy.

28 Evil people run even though
     no one is chasing them.
  But good people are as brave as
    a lion.

²When a country is disobedient, it
has one ruler after another.
But when it is led by a man with
understanding and
knowledge, it continues
strong.

³Rulers who are cruel to the poor
are like a hard rain that destroys
the crops.

⁴People who disobey what they
have been taught praise the
wicked.
But those who obey what they
have been taught are against
the wicked.

⁵Evil people do not understand
fairness.
But those who follow the Lord
understand it completely.

⁶It is better to be poor and
innocent
than to be rich and wicked.

⁷The son who obeys what he has
been taught
shows that he is wise.
But the son who makes friends
with those who have no
self-control
disgraces his father.

⁸Some people get rich by
overcharging others.
But their wealth will be given to
those who are kind to the
poor.

⁹If you refuse to obey what you
have been taught,
your prayers will not be heard.

¹⁰Those who lead honest people to
do wrong
will be ruined by their own evil.
But the innocent will be
rewarded with good things.

¹¹A rich man may think he is wise.
But a poor man who has
understanding knows the
rich man is wrong.

¹²When good people win, there is
great happiness.
But when the wicked get power,
everybody hides.

¹³If you hide your sins, you will not
succeed.
If you confess and reject them,
you will receive mercy.

¹⁴Those who always respect the
Lord will be happy.
But those who are stubborn will
get into trouble.

¹⁵A wicked ruler is as dangerous to
poor people
as a roaring lion or a charging
bear.

¹⁶A ruler who is cruel does not have
wisdom.
But the one who hates money
taken dishonestly will live a
long time.

¹⁷A man who is guilty of murder
will run until he dies.
So do not stop him.

¹⁸Innocent people will be kept safe.
But those who are dishonest will
suddenly be ruined.

¹⁹The person who works his land
will have plenty of food.
But the one who chases useless
dreams instead will end up
very poor.

²⁰A truthful man will have many
blessings.
But those eager to get rich will
be punished.

²¹It is not good for a judge to take
sides.
But some will sin for just a
piece of bread.

²²A selfish person is in a hurry to
get rich.
He does not realise his
selfishness will make him
poor.

23Those who correct others will
     later be liked
  more than those who give false
     praise.

24Some people rob their fathers or
     mothers
  and say, "It's not wrong".
  Such people are just like those
     who destroy things.

25A greedy person causes trouble.
  But the one who trusts the Lord
     will succeed.

26The person who trusts in himself
     is foolish.
  But the person who lives wisely
     will be kept safe.

27The person who gives to the poor
     will have everything he
     needs.
  But the one who ignores the
     poor will have many curses
     put on him.

28When the wicked get power,
     everybody hides.
  But when the wicked die, the
     good people do well.

29 Some people are still
     stubborn after they have
     been corrected many times.
  But they will suddenly be hurt
     beyond cure.

2When good people do well,
     everyone is happy.
  But when evil people rule,
     everyone groans.

3Whoever loves wisdom makes his
     father happy.
  But the one who makes friends
     with prostitutes*d* wastes his
     money.

4If a king is fair, he makes his
     country strong.
  But if he takes money
     dishonestly, he tears his
     country down.

5Anyone who gives false praise to
     his neighbour
  is setting a trap for him.

6An evil person is trapped by his
     own sin.
  But a good person can sing and
     be happy.

7Good people are concerned that
     the poor are treated fairly.
  But the wicked don't care.

8People who make fun of others
     cause trouble in a city.
  But wise people calm anger
     down.

9A wise man should not take a
     foolish person to court.
  The fool will only shout or laugh
     at him. There will be no
     peace.

10Murderers hate honest people.
  But those who do right try to
     protect them.

11A foolish person loses his temper.
  But a wise person controls his
     anger.

12If a ruler pays attention to lies,
  then all his officers will become
     wicked.

13The poor person and the cruel
     person are alike in this way:
  the Lord gave eyes to both of
     them.

14A king should judge poor people
     fairly.
  Then his government will
     continue for ever.

15Punishment and correction make a
     child wise.
  If he is left to do as he pleases,
     he will disgrace his mother.

16When there are many wicked
     people, there is much sin.
  But those who do right will see
     them destroyed.

¹⁷Correct your child, and you will be
proud of him.
He will give you pleasure.

¹⁸Where there is no word from
God, people are
uncontrolled.
But those who obey what they
have been taught are happy.

¹⁹Words alone cannot correct a
servant.
Even if he understands, he
won't respond.

²⁰Sometimes you see people who
speak too quickly.
There is more hope for a foolish
person than for them.

²¹Don't spoil your servant when he
is young.
If you do, he will bring you grief
later on.

²²An angry person causes trouble.
A person who easily gets angry
sins a lot.

²³A man's pride will ruin him.
But a person who is humble will
be honoured.

²⁴The partner of a thief is his own
worst enemy.
He has to testify in court, but
he is afraid to say anything.

²⁵Being afraid of people can get you
into trouble.
But if you trust the Lord, you
will be safe.

²⁶Many people want to be heard by
a ruler.
But fairness comes from the
Lord.

²⁷Good people hate those who are
dishonest.
And the wicked hate those who
are honest.

Wise Words from Agur

30 These are the words of Agur
son of Jakeh.

This is his message to Ithiel and
Ucal:

²"I am the most stupid person
there is.
I have no understanding.
³I have not learned to be wise.
And I don't know much about
God, the Holy One.
⁴Who has gone up to heaven and
come back down?
Who can hold the wind in his
hand?
Who can gather up the waters in
his coat?
Who has decided where the
ends of the earth will be?
What is his name? And what is his
son's name?
Surely, you know!

⁵"Every word of God can be
trusted.
He protects those who come to
him for safety.
⁶Do not add to his words.
If you do, he will correct you
and prove that you are a
liar.

⁷"I ask two things from you, Lord.
Don't refuse me before I die.
⁸Keep me from lying and being
dishonest.
And don't make me either rich
or poor.
Just give me enough food for
each day.
⁹If I have too much, I might reject
you.
I might say, 'I don't know the
Lord'.
If I am poor, I might steal.
Then I would disgrace the name
of my God.

¹⁰"Do not say bad things about a
servant to his master.
If you do, he will curse you, and
you will suffer for it.
¹¹"Some people curse their fathers.

And they do not bless their
mothers.

¹²Some people think they are pure.
But they are not really free from
evil.

¹³Some people have such a proud
look!
They look down on others.

¹⁴Some people have teeth like
swords.
It is as if their jaws are full of
knives.
They want to remove the poor
people from the earth.
They want to get rid of the
needy.

¹⁵"Greed has two daughters.
Their names are 'Give me. Give
me'.
There are three things that are
never satisfied.
There are really four that never
say, 'I've had enough!'

¹⁶These things are the cemetery,
the childless mother,
the land that never gets enough
rain,
and fire that never says, 'I've
had enough!'

¹⁷"Don't make fun of your father.
Don't refuse to obey your
mother.
If you do, your eye will be pecked
out by the birds of the
valley.
You will be eaten by hawks.

¹⁸"There are three things that are
too hard for me.
There are really four that I don't
understand:

¹⁹the way an eagle flies in the sky,
the way a snake slides over a
rock,
the way a ship sails on the sea
and the way a man acts with a
girl.

²⁰"This is the way a woman who
takes part in adultery*d* acts:
she sins and doesn't care.

She says, 'I haven't done
anything wrong'.

²¹"There are three things that make
the earth tremble.
There are really four that it
cannot stand:

²²a servant who becomes a king,
a foolish person who has plenty
to eat,

²³a hateful woman who gets married
and a maid who replaces her
mistress.

²⁴"There are four things on earth
that are small.
But they are very wise.

²⁵Ants are not very strong.
But they store up food in the
summer.

²⁶Rock badgers are not powerful
animals.
But they can live among the
rocks.

²⁷Locusts*d* have no king.
But they all go out in formation.

²⁸And lizards can be caught in the
hand.
But they are found even in
kings' palaces.

²⁹"There are three things that strut
proudly.
There are really four that walk
as if they are important.

³⁰Lions are the proudest animals.
They are strong and run from
nothing.

³¹Cockerels and male goats strut
proudly.
And so does a king when his
army is around him.

³²"You may have been foolish and
proud.
If you planned evil, cover your
mouth.

³³Stirring milk makes butter.
Twisting noses makes them
bleed.
And stirring up anger makes
trouble."

Wise Words of King Lemuel

31 These are the words of King Lemuel. This is the message his mother taught him:

2"My son, I gave birth to you.
You are the son I prayed for.
3Don't waste your strength on
women.
Don't waste your time on those
who ruin kings.

4"Kings should not drink wine,
Lemuel.
Rulers should not desire beer.
5If they drink, they might forget
the law.
They might keep the needy
from getting their rights.
6Give beer to people who are
dying.
And give wine to those who are
sad.
7Let them drink and forget their
need.
Then they won't remember their
misery any more.

8"Speak up for those who cannot
speak for themselves.
Defend the rights of all those
who have nothing.
9Speak up and judge fairly.
Defend the rights of the poor
and needy."

The Good Wife

10It is hard to find an excellent
wife.
She is worth more than rubies.
11Her husband trusts her
completely.
With her, he has everything he
needs.
12She does him good and not harm
for as long as she lives.
13She looks for wool and linen.
She likes to work with her
hands.
14She is like a trader's ship.
She goes far to get food.
15She gets up while it is still dark.
She prepares food for her
family.
She also feeds her servant
girls.
16She looks at a field and buys it.
With money she has earned, she
plants a vineyard.
17She does her work with energy.
Her arms are strong.
18She makes sure that what she
makes is good.
She works by her lamp late into
the night.
19She makes thread with her hands
and weaves her own cloth.
20She welcomes the poor.
She helps the needy.
21She does not worry about her
family when it snows.
They all have fine clothes to
keep them warm.
22She makes coverings for her bed.
Her clothes are made of linen
and other expensive
material.
23Her husband is recognised at the
city meetings.
He makes decisions as one of
the leaders of the land.
24She makes linen clothes and sells
them.
She provides belts to the
merchants.
25She is strong and is respected by
the people.
She looks forward to the future
with joy.
26She speaks wise words.
And she teaches others to be
kind.
27She watches over her family.
And she is always busy.
28Her children bless her.
Her husband also praises her.
29He says, "There are many
excellent wives,
but you are better than all of
them."

30Charm can fool you, and beauty can trick you.
But a woman who respects the Lord should be praised.

31Give her the reward she has earned.
She should be openly praised for what she has done.

ECCLESIASTES

A Wise Man Believes in God

1 These are the words of the Teacher. He is a son of David, king in Jerusalem.
²The Teacher says,
"Useless! Useless!
Completely useless!
All things are useless."

³What do people really gain
from all the hard work they do
here on earth?

Things Never Change

⁴People live, and people die.
But the earth continues for
ever.
⁵The sun rises, and the sun sets.
Then it hurries back to the place
where it rises again.
⁶The wind blows to the south.
Then it blows to the north.
It blows from one direction and
then another.
Then it turns around and
repeats the same pattern,
going nowhere.
⁷All the rivers flow to the sea.
But the sea never becomes full.
⁸Everything is boring.
It makes you so tired you don't
even want to talk about it.
Words come again and again to
our ears.
But we never can hear enough.
Nor can we ever really see all
we want to see.
⁹All things continue the way they
have been since the
beginning.
The same things will be done
that have always been done.
There is nothing new here on
earth.
¹⁰A person might say,

"Look, this is new!"
But really it has always been
here.
It was here before we were!
¹¹People don't remember what
happened long ago.
In the future, people will not
remember what happens
now.
And later, other people will not
remember what was done
before them.

Does Wisdom Bring Happiness?

¹²I, the Teacher, was king over Israel in Jerusalem. ¹³I decided to use my wisdom. I wanted to learn about everything that happens here on earth. I learned that God has given us terrible things to face here on earth. ¹⁴I looked at everything done here on earth. I saw that it is all a waste of time. It is like chasing the wind.

¹⁵If something is crooked,
you can't make it straight.
If something is missing,
you can't say it is there.

¹⁶I said to myself, "I have become very wise. I am now wiser than anyone who ruled Jerusalem before me. I know what wisdom and knowledge really are." ¹⁷So I decided to find out how wisdom and knowledge are better than foolish thinking. But I learned that trying to become wise is also like chasing the wind.

¹⁸With much wisdom comes much
disappointment.
The person who gains more
knowledge also gains more
sorrow.

Does "Having Fun" Bring Happiness?

2 I said to myself, "I will try having fun. I will enjoy myself." But I found that this is also useless. ²It is foolish to laugh all the time. Having fun gets nothing done. ³I decided to cheer myself up with wine. At the same time my mind was still thinking wisely. I wanted to find a way to enjoy myself. I wanted to see what was good for people to do during their few days of life.

Does Hard Work Bring Happiness?

⁴Then I did great things. I built houses, and I planted vineyards for myself. ⁵I planted gardens, and I made parks. I planted all kinds of fruit trees in them. ⁶I made pools of water for myself and I used them to water my growing trees. ⁷I bought men and women slaves. Slaves were also born in my house. I had large herds of cattle and flocks of sheep. I had more than anyone in Jerusalem before me. ⁸I also gathered silver and gold for myself. I took treasures from kings and other areas. I had men and women singers. I had all the wives a man could ever want. ⁹I became very famous. I was greater than anyone who had lived in Jerusalem before me. My wisdom helped me in all this.

¹⁰Anything I saw and wanted, I got
   for myself.
I did not miss any pleasure I
   desired.
I was pleased with everything I
   did.
And this pleasure was the
   reward for all my hard work.
¹¹But then I looked at what I had
   done.
I thought about all the hard
   work.
Suddenly I realised it was just a
   waste of time, like chasing
   the wind!

There is nothing to gain from
   anything we do here on
   earth.

Maybe Wisdom Is the Answer

¹²Then I began to think again about
   being wise.
And I thought also about being
   foolish and doing silly things.
But after all, what more can any
   king do?
He can only do what some other
   king has already done.
¹³I saw that being wise is certainly
   better than being foolish,
just as light is better than
   darkness.
¹⁴A wise man sees where he is
   going.
But a foolish person is like
   someone walking around in
   the dark.
Yet I saw that
   both the foolish person and the
   wise man end the same way.

¹⁵I thought to myself,
"What happens to a foolish person
   will happen to me, too.
So what do I get for being so
   wise?"
I said to myself,
"Being wise is also useless."
¹⁶The wise man and the foolish
   person
will both die!
People will not remember either
   one for ever.
In the future, both will be
   forgotten.

Is There Real Happiness in Life?

¹⁷So I hated life. It made me sad to think that everything here on earth is useless. It is like chasing the wind. ¹⁸I hated all the things I had worked for here on earth. I hated them because I must leave them to someone who will live after me. ¹⁹Someone else will control everything for which I worked so hard here on earth. And I don't know

if he will be wise or foolish. This is also useless. ²⁰So I became sad about all the hard work I had done here on earth. ²¹A person can work hard using all his wisdom, knowledge and skill. But he will die, and other people will get the things he worked for. They did not do the work, but they will get everything. This is also unfair and useless. ²²What does a person get for all his work and struggling here on earth? ²³All his life his work is full of pain and sorrow. Even at night his mind doesn't rest. This is also useless.

²⁴The best a person can do is eat, drink and enjoy his work. I saw that even this comes from God. ²⁵No one can eat or enjoy life without God. ²⁶If a person pleases God, God will give him wisdom, knowledge and joy. But the sinner will get only the work of gathering and storing wealth. Then he will have to give it to the one who pleases God. So all his work is useless. It is like chasing the wind.

There Is a Time for Everything

3 There is a right time for everything.
Everything on earth has its special season.
²There is a time to be born
and a time to die.
There is a time to plant
and a time to pull up plants.
³There is a time to kill
and a time to heal.
There is a time to destroy
and a time to build.
⁴There is a time to cry
and a time to laugh.
There is a time to be sad
and a time to dance.
⁵There is a time to throw away stones
and a time to gather them.
There is a time to hug
and a time not to hug.
⁶There is a time to look for something
and a time to stop looking for it.

There is a time to keep things
and a time to throw things away.
⁷There is a time to tear apart
and a time to sew together.
There is a time to be silent
and a time to speak.
⁸There is a time to love
and a time to hate.
There is a time for war
and a time for peace.

God Controls His World

⁹Does a person really gain anything from his work? ¹⁰I saw the hard work God has given us to do. ¹¹God has also given us a desire to know the future. God certainly does everything at just the right time. But we can never completely understand what he is doing. ¹²So I realise that the best thing for people is to be happy. They should enjoy themselves as long as they live. ¹³God wants everyone to eat and drink and be happy in his work. These are gifts from God. ¹⁴I know anything God does will continue for ever. People cannot add anything to what God has done. And they cannot take anything away from it. God does it this way to cause people to honour him.

¹⁵What happens now has also
happened in the past.
Things that will happen in the
future have also happened
before.
God makes the same things
happen again and again.

God Allows Unfairness

¹⁶I also saw this here on earth:
where there should have been
justice, there was evil.
Where there should have been
fairness, there was
wickedness.
¹⁷I certainly believe that
God has planned a time for every
thing and every action.

He will judge both good people
and bad people.

¹⁸But I decided that God leaves it
the way it is to test people. He wants
to show them they are just like animals. ¹⁹The same thing happens to animals and to people. They both have
the same breath. So they both die.
People are no better off than the animals. The lives of both are soon gone.
²⁰Both end up the same way. Both
came from dust. And both will go back
to dust. ²¹Who can be sure that the
spirit of man goes up to God? Or who
can be sure that the spirit of an animal
goes down into the ground? ²²So I saw
the best thing a person can do is to
enjoy his work. That is all he has. No
one can help a person see what will
happen in the future.

Is It Better to Be Dead?

4 Again I saw all the people who
were treated badly here on earth.
I saw their tears.
  I saw that they had no one to
    comfort them.
  Cruel people had all the power.
  There was no one to comfort
    the people they hurt.
²I decided that the dead
  are better off than the living.
³But those who have never been
  born
  are better off still.
  They have not seen the evil
    that is done here on earth.

Why Work So Hard?

⁴I realised the reason people work
hard and try to succeed: they are jealous of each other. This, too, is useless. It is like chasing the wind.

⁵Some say that it is foolish to fold
    your hands and do nothing.
  You will starve to death!
⁶Maybe so, but I say it is better to
    be content
  with what little you have.

Otherwise, you will always be
    struggling for more.
  That is like chasing the wind.

⁷Again I saw something here on
    earth that was senseless:
⁸I saw a person who had no family.
  He had no son or brother.
  He always worked hard.
  But he was never satisfied with
    what he had.
  He never asked himself, "For
    whom am I working so hard?
  Why don't I let myself enjoy
    life?"
  This also is very sad and
    senseless.

Friends and Family Give Strength

⁹Two people are better than one.
  They get more done by working
    together.
¹⁰If one person falls,
  the other can help him up.
  But it is bad for the person who is
    alone when he falls.
  No one is there to help him.
¹¹If two lie down together, they will
    be warm.
  But a person alone will not be
    warm.
¹²An enemy might defeat one
    person,
  but two people together can
    defend themselves.
  A rope that has three parts
    wrapped together
  is hard to break.

Fame and Power Are Useless

¹³A young person may be poor but
wise. He is better than a foolish, old
king who doesn't listen to advice. ¹⁴I
saw such a young person become
king. He had been born poor in the
kingdom. He had even gone to prison
before becoming king. ¹⁵I watched
some of the people who live on earth
follow him. They made him their king.
¹⁶Yes, a great many people followed

him at first. But later, they did not like him, either. So fame and power are shown to be useless. They are like chasing the wind.

Be Careful About Making Promises

5 Be careful when you go to worship at the Temple.[d] It is better to listen than to offer foolish sacrifices. People who do this don't even know they are doing wrong.

²Think before you speak.
  Be careful about what you
    promise to God.
God is in heaven,
  and you are on the earth.
So say only a few words to
  God.
³The saying is true: bad dreams
    come from too much
    worrying.
  So too many words come from
    foolish people.

⁴If you make a promise to God, don't be slow to keep it. God is not happy with foolish people. Give God what you promised. ⁵It is better not to promise anything than to promise something and not do it. ⁶So don't let your words cause you to sin. Also, don't say to the priest at the Temple, "I didn't mean what I promised!" If you do, God will become angry with your words. He will destroy everything you have worked for. ⁷Many empty promises are like many foolish dreams. They mean nothing. You should honour God.

Officers Cheat Each Other

⁸In some countries you will see poor people treated badly. They are not treated fairly or given their rights. Don't be surprised! One officer is cheated by a higher officer. They in turn are cheated by even higher officers. ⁹The wealth of the country is divided up among them all. Even the king makes sure he gets his share of the profits.

Wealth Cannot Buy Happiness

¹⁰The person who loves money
    will never have all the money he
      wants.
The person who loves wealth
    will not be satisfied when he
      gets it.
  This is also useless.
¹¹The more wealth a person has,
    the more friends he has to help
      him spend it.
So what does he really gain?
  He gains nothing except to look
    at his riches.
¹²A man who works hard sleeps in
    peace.
  It is not important if he has little
    or much to eat.
But a rich person worries about
    his wealth.
  He cannot sleep.

¹³I have seen something unfair here
    on earth:
  a person suffers harm from saving
    up his money.
¹⁴ Then he loses it all in a bad
      deal.
  So he has nothing
    to give to his son.
¹⁵A person comes into this world
    with nothing.
  And when he dies, he leaves
    with nothing.
In spite of all his hard work,
  he leaves exactly as he came.
¹⁶This, too, is unfair:
  he leaves exactly as he came.
So what does he gain from
    chasing the wind?
¹⁷All he gets are days filled with
    sadness and sorrow.
  He ends up sick, defeated and
    angry.

Enjoy Your Life's Work

¹⁸I have seen what is best for a person to do here on earth. He should eat

and drink and enjoy his work. This is because the life God has given him on earth is short. 19God gives some people the ability to enjoy the wealth and property he gives them. He also gives them the ability to accept their state in life and enjoy their work. 20Such people do not worry much about how short life is. This is because God keeps them busy with the things they love to do.

6 I have seen something else unfair here on earth. It causes serious problems for people. 2God gives some people great wealth, riches and honour. They have everything they want. But God does not let them enjoy such things. Someone else enjoys them instead. This is unfair and senseless. 3It is sad when a person can't enjoy the good things God gives him. Such a person might have 100 children. He might live a long time. But what good is it if he can't enjoy the good God gives him? I say a baby who is born dead is better off than he is. 4It is useless for such a baby to be born. It ends up in the darkness of the grave without even a name. 5That baby never saw the sun. It never knew anything. But it finds more rest than the person who never gets to enjoy the good things God gives him. 6Even if he lives 2,000 years, it is sad if a person can't enjoy the good things God gives him. After all, both he and the baby born dead go to the same place—the grave.

7A person works just to feed himself.
But he never seems to get enough to eat.
8In this way a wise man
is no better off than a foolish person.
Then, too, it does a poor man little good
to know how to get along in life.
9So it is better to be happy with what you have

than always to be wanting more.
Always wanting more is useless—like chasing the wind.

Who Can Understand God's Plan?

10Everything that happens was planned long ago.
A man is only what he was created to be.
It is useless to argue with God about it.
This is because God is more powerful than man is.
11The more you argue,
the more useless it is.
You gain nothing at all by arguing.

12A person has only a few days of life on the earth. His short life passes like a shadow. And who knows what is best for him while he lives? Who can tell him what will happen after his time on earth?

Some Benefits of Serious Thinking

7 It is better to have respect than good perfume.
The day a person dies is better than the day he was born.
2It is better to go to a funeral than to a party.
We all must die.
Everyone living should think about this.
3Sorrow is better than laughter.
Sadness has a good influence on you.
4A wise man thinks about death,
but a foolish person thinks only about having a good time.
5It is better to be criticised by a wise man
than to be praised by a foolish person.
6The laughter of foolish people is useless.
It is like heating a pot by burning straw.

There is a lot of fire but no
    heat.

7Even a wise man will become
    foolish
    if he lets money change his
    thinking.

8It is better to finish something
    than to start it.
It is better to be patient
    than to be proud.
9Don't become angry quickly,
    because getting angry is foolish.

10Don't ask, "Why was life better in
    the 'good old days'?"
It is not wise to ask such
    questions.

11Wisdom is as good to have as
    inheriting property.
It helps people see what to do.
12Wisdom is like money.
    They both help a person.
But wisdom is better than money,
    because it can save a person's
    life.

13Stop and think about everything
    that God causes to happen.
You cannot change a thing,
    even if you think it is wrong.
14When life is good, enjoy it.
    But when life is hard,
    remember:
God gives us good times and hard
    times.
And no one knows what
    tomorrow will bring.

It Is Impossible to Be Truly Good

15In my short life I have seen both
    of these:
I have seen good men die being
    good,
    and I have seen evil men living a
    long time.
16Don't try to be too right all the
    time.
Don't try to be too wise, either.
Why should you destroy yourself
    this way?

17Don't be too wicked,
    and don't be a foolish person.
You will die young if you do so.
18Try to avoid going too far in doing
    anything.
Those who honour God will
    avoid doing too much of
    anything.

19Wisdom gives a person strength.
One wise man is stronger than
    ten leaders in a city.

20Surely there is not a good man on
    earth
who always does good and
    never sins.

21Don't listen to everything people
    say.
You might hear your servant
    insulting you.
22You know that many times
    you also have insulted others.

23I used wisdom to test all these
    things.
I wanted to be wise,
    but it was too hard for me.
24I cannot understand why things
    are as they are.
It is too hard for anyone to
    understand.
25I studied and tried very hard to
    find wisdom.
I tried to find some meaning for
    everything.
I learned that it is foolish to be
    evil,
    and it is silly to act like a fool.

26I found that some women are
    worse than death.
They are as dangerous as traps.
Their love is like a net.
Their arms hold men like chains.
A man who follows God will run
    away from them,
but a sinner will be caught by
    them.

27The Teacher says, "This is what I
    learned:
I added all these things together

to see if I could find some
meaning for everything.
28I am still looking for it,
but I have not found it.
But I did discover that truly good
people are hard to find.
Such people are one in a million!
29One thing I have learned:
God made people good.
But people have found all kinds
of ways to be bad."

Obey the King

8 No one is like the wise man.
He can understand what things
mean.
His wisdom makes him happy.
It makes his sad face happy.

2I advise you always to obey the
king's command. Do this because you
made a promise to God. 3Don't be too
quick to leave the job the king gave
you. But don't support something that
is wrong. Remember, the king does
whatever he pleases. 4The king is the
highest power. No one can tell him
what to do.

5A person will be safe if he obeys
the king's command.
A wise man knows how to do
the right thing at the right
time.
6And there is a right time and a
right way for everything.
Yet people often have many
troubles.
7They do not know what the future
holds.
No one can tell them what will
happen.
8No one has the power to keep the
wind from blowing.
No one has the power to stop
his own death.
During war a soldier cannot go
home.
So also, the person who does
evil things will not get away
free.

Justice, Rewards and
Punishment

9I saw all of this as I studied. I considered all that is done here on earth.
And I saw men rule others and hurt
them. 10I saw evil people being buried. They used to go in and out of the
holy place. Good things were said
about them in the same towns where
they had done evil. This is senseless,
too.
11Sometimes people are not punished right away for the bad things
they do. That makes other people
want to do bad things, too. 12A sinner
might do a hundred evil things, and he
might live a long time. Even so, I
know it will be better for those who
honour God. They fear him, and he
sees it. 13And I also know it will not go
well for evil people. Their lives will be
like a brief shadow. They will not live
very long. 14But sometimes something senseless happens on earth. Bad
things happen to good people. Good
things happen to bad people. This is
truly senseless. 15So I decided it was
more important to enjoy life. The best
that people can do here on earth is to
eat, drink and enjoy life. These joys
will help people do the hard work God
gives them here on earth.

We Cannot Understand All
God Does

16I used my mind to learn about all
that happens on earth. I saw how busy
people are. They work day and night
and hardly ever sleep. 17I also saw all
that God has done. Nobody can understand what God does here on
earth. No matter how hard a person
tries to understand it, he cannot.
Even if a wise man says he understands, he really cannot. No one at all
can really understand it.

Is Death Fair?

9 I thought about something else
and tried hard to understand it. I

saw that God takes care of both good people and wise people and what they do. But no one knows if he will see good or bad times.

2Both good and bad things happen
    to everyone.
  They happen to those who are
      fair and to those who are
      wicked.
  They happen to those who are
      good and to those who are
      evil.
  They happen to those who
      sacrifice and to those who
      do not.
  The same things happen to a good
      person
    as happen to a sinner.
  The same things happen to a
      person who makes promises
      to God
    as to one who does not.

3This is something unfair that happens here on earth. The same things happen to everyone. So men's minds are full of evil and foolish thoughts while they live. After that, they join the dead. 4But anyone still alive has hope. Even a live dog is better off than a dead lion!

5The living know they will die.
  But the dead no longer think
      about such things.
  Dead people have no more
      reward.
  People forget them.
6After a person is dead,
  he can no longer show love or
      hate or jealousy.
  And he will never again share
      in the things that happen here
      on earth.

Enjoy Life While You Can

7So go and eat your food and enjoy
    it.
  Drink your wine and be happy.
  It is all right with God
      if you do this.

8Put on nice clothes
    and make yourself look good.
9Enjoy life with the wife you love. Enjoy all the days of this short life God has given you here on earth. It is all you have. So enjoy the work you have to do here on earth. 10Whatever work you do, do your best. This is because you are going to the grave. There is no working, no planning, no knowledge and no wisdom there.

Time and Chance

11I also realised something else here
      on earth that is senseless:
  the fast runner does not always
      win the race.
  The strong army does not
      always win the battle.
  The wise man does not always
      have food.
  The smart man does not always
      become wealthy.
  And the man with special skills
      does not always receive
      praise.
  Bad things happen to everyone.
12A person never knows what will
      happen to him next.
  He is like a fish caught in a cruel
      net.
  He is like a bird caught in a
      trap.
  In the same way, a person is
      trapped by bad things
      that suddenly happen to him.

Wisdom Does Not Always Win

13I also saw something wise happen here on earth. And it was very impressive to me. 14There was a small town with only a few people in it. A great king fought against it and put his armies all around it. 15Now there was a wise man in the town. He was poor, but he used his wisdom to save his town. But later on, everyone forgot about him. 16I still think wisdom is better than strength. But those people forgot about the poor man's wisdom.

And they stopped listening to what he said.

[17]The quiet words of a wise man
are better
than the shouts of a foolish
ruler.
[18]Wisdom is better than weapons of
war.
But one sinner can destroy
much good.

10 Dead flies will make even
perfume smell bad.
In the same way, a little
foolishness can ruin
a wise man's fame for wisdom.
[2]A wise man's heart leads him in
the right way.
But the heart of a foolish person
leads him in the wrong way.
[3]A foolish person is not wise.
It shows in everything that he
does.
Even as he walks along the road,
he shows everyone how stupid
he is.
[4]Don't leave your job
just because the ruler is angry
with you.
Remain calm.
It will help correct your
mistakes.

[5]Here is something else unfair that
happens here on earth.
It is the kind of mistake rulers
make:
[6]Foolish people are given important
positions
while rich people are given less
important ones.
[7]I have seen servants ride on
horses
while princes walk beside them
on foot.
[8]Anyone who digs a pit might fall
into it.
Anyone who knocks down a wall
might be bitten by a snake.
[9]Anyone who moves large stones
might be hurt by them.

And anyone who cuts logs might
get hurt while doing it.
[10]Cutting logs with a dull axe
makes you work harder.
A wise man will sharpen his axe.
In the same way, wisdom can
make any job easier.
[11]Someone might know how to
control snakes.
But what good is such wisdom if
the snake has already bitten
him?

[12]A wise man's words bring him
praise.
But a foolish person's words will
destroy him.
[13]A foolish person begins by saying
something foolish.
In the end he is saying even
sillier things.
[14]A foolish person talks too much
about what he will do.
No one knows the future.
No one can tell him what will
happen after he dies.
[15]A foolish person doesn't know
even the most obvious
things.
He can't even find his way back
to town.
So he has to wear himself out
working.

The Value of Work

[16]How terrible it will be for a
country
if its king is a child.
How terrible it will be for that
country
if its leaders have parties all the
time.
[17]A country is well off
if its king comes from a good
family.
It is good for a country
if its leaders control their eating
and drinking.
They should eat and drink for
strength,
not to get drunk.

¹⁸If a person is lazy and doesn't
    repair the roof,
  it will begin to fall.
If he refuses to mend it,
    the house will leak.

¹⁹A party makes you feel good,
  and wine makes you feel happy.
But both cost you a lot of money.

²⁰Don't say or think bad things
    about the king.
And don't say bad things about
    rich people even alone in
    your bedroom.
A little bird might report it to
    others.
A bird might fly to them and tell
    all you said.

Boldly Face the Future

11 Do good things everywhere
    you go."
After a while the good you do
    will return to help you.
²Invest what you have in several
    different businesses.
You don't know what bad things
    might happen on earth.

³If clouds are full of rain,
  they will pour water on the
    earth.
A tree can fall to the north or
    south,
but it will stay where it falls.
⁴If a person waits for perfect
    weather,
he will never plant his seeds.
And if he is afraid that every cloud
    will bring rain,
he will never harvest his crops.

⁵You don't know where the wind
    will blow.
And you don't know how a baby
    grows in its mother's body.
In the same way, God certainly
    made all things.
But you can't understand what
    he is doing.

⁶Begin planting early in the
    morning,
and don't stop working until
    evening.
This is because you don't know
    which things you do will
    succeed.
It is even possible that
    everything you do will
    succeed.

Serve God While You Are Young

⁷It is good to be alive
  to enjoy the light of day.
⁸A person ought to enjoy every
    day of his life.
This is true no matter how long
    he lives.
But he should also remember this:
  you will be dead much longer
    than you live.
After you are dead, you
    accomplish nothing.
⁹Young people, enjoy yourselves
    while you are young.
Be happy while you are young.
Do whatever your heart desires.
Do whatever you want to do.
But remember that God will judge
    you
for everything you do.
¹⁰So avoid sorrow and sadness.
Forget about all the bad things
    that happen to you.
This is because the joys of
    youth pass quickly away.

The Problems of Old Age

12 Remember your Creator
    while you are young.
Your old age is coming
  when you will have many
    troubles.
When that time comes,
  you won't have much to enjoy.
²When you become old,
  the light from the sun, moon and
    stars will seem dark to you.

Do good . . . go Literally, "Throw your bread upon the water."

It will seem as if the rain clouds
never go away.
³At that time your arms will lose
their strength.
Your strong legs will become
weak and bent.
Your teeth will fall out so you
cannot chew.
Your eyes will not see clearly.
⁴Your ears will be deaf to the noise
in the streets.
You will barely hear singing.
The sound of the millstone
grinding your grain will seem
very quiet.
But you'll wake up when a bird
first starts singing!
⁵You will fear high places,
and you will be afraid to go for a
walk because you may fall.
Your hair will become white like
the flowers on an almond
tree.
You will limp along like a
grasshopper when you walk.
Your desires will be gone.
Then you will go to your
everlasting home,
and people will go to your
funeral.
⁶Remember God before your life is
snapped like a silver chain.
Remember God before your life
is broken like a golden bowl.
It will be as useless as a broken
bucket at the spring.
It will be no good, like a broken
wheel at a water well.

⁷Your body will become part of the
dust of the earth again,
but your spirit will return to God
who gave it.

⁸Everything is useless!
The Teacher says that
everything is useless.

Conclusion

⁹The Teacher was very wise. He
taught the people what he knew. The
Teacher very carefully thought about,
studied and set in order many wise
teachings. ¹⁰The Teacher looked for
just the right words. He wrote teachings that are dependable and true.

¹¹Words from wise men are like
sharp sticks used to guide animals.
These words are like nails that have
been driven in firmly. They are wise
teachings that come from God the
Shepherd. ¹²So be careful, my son,
about other teachings. People are always writing books. And too much
study will make you very tired.

¹³Now, everything has been heard.
Here is my final advice:
honour God and obey his
commands.
This is the most important thing
people can do.
¹⁴God knows everything people do,
even the things done in secret.
He knows all the good and all the
bad.
He will judge everything people
do.

SONG OF SOLOMON

A Love Song

1 Solomon's Greatest Song.

The Woman Speaks to the Man She Loves

²Kiss me with the kisses of your
    mouth!
Your love is better than wine.
³The smell of your perfume is
    pleasant.
Your name is pleasant like
    expensive perfume!
That's why the young women
    love you.
⁴Take me with you; let's run.
The king takes me into his
    rooms.

Friends Speak to the Man

We will rejoice and be happy with
    you.
We praise your love more than
    wine.

The Woman Speaks

With good reason, the young
    women love you, my lover.
⁵I'm dark but lovely,
    women of Jerusalem.
I'm dark like the tents of Kedar,
    like the curtains of Solomon.
⁶Don't look at how dark I am,
    at how dark the sun has made
        me.
My brothers were angry with me.
They made me tend the
    vineyards.
So I haven't tended my own
    vineyard!
⁷Tell me, you whom I love,
    where do you feed your sheep?
Where do you make them rest
    at noon?

Why should I look for you near
    your friend's sheep?
Am I like a woman who wears a
    veil?ⁿ

The Man Speaks to the Woman

⁸You are the most beautiful of
    women.
Surely you know to follow the
    sheep.
Feed your young goats
    near the shepherds' tents.
⁹My darling, you are like a mare
    that pulls the king's chariots.
¹⁰Your cheeks are beautiful with
    ornaments.
Your neck is beautiful with
    jewels.
¹¹We will make for you gold
    earrings
    with silver hooks.

The Woman Speaks

¹²The smell of my perfume spreads
    out
    to the king on his couch.
¹³My lover is like a bag of myrrhᵈ
    that lies all night between my
        breasts.
¹⁴My lover is like a bunch of flowers
    from the vineyards at En Gedi.

The Man Speaks

¹⁵My darling, you are beautiful!
    Oh, you are beautiful!
Your eyes are like doves!

The Woman Answers the Man

¹⁶You are so handsome, my lover.
You are so pleasant!
Our bed is the grass.

veil This was the way a prostitute usually dressed.

¹⁷The boards of our house are cedar
    trees.
And the wood of our ceiling is
    juniper trees.

The Woman Speaks Again

2 I am a rose in the Plain of
    Sharon.
I am a lily in the valleys.

The Man Speaks Again

²Among the young women, my
    darling
is like a lily among thorns!

The Woman Answers

³Among young men, my lover
    is like an apple tree among the
    trees in the woods!
I enjoy sitting in his shadow.
His fruit is sweet to my taste.
⁴He brought me to the banquet
    room.
His banner over me is love.
⁵Strengthen me with raisins.
Refresh me with apples,
    because I am weak with love.
⁶My lover's left hand is under my
    head,
    and his right arm holds me tight!

The Woman Speaks to the Friends

⁷Women of Jerusalem, promise me
    by the gazelleᵈ and the deer.
Promise not to wake love.
Don't excite my feelings of love
    until I'm ready.

The Woman Speaks Again

⁸I hear my lover's voice.
He comes jumping across the
    mountains.
He comes skipping over the
    hills!
⁹My lover is like a gazelleᵈ or a
    young deer.
Look, he stands behind our wall.
He stares in through the windows,
    looking through the blinds.
¹⁰My lover spoke. He said to me,

"Get up, my darling.
Let's go away, my beautiful one.
¹¹Look, the winter is past.
The rains are over and gone.
¹²Blossoms appear through all the
    land.
The time has come to sing.
The cooing of doves is heard in
    our land.
¹³There are young figs on the fig
    trees.
The blossoms on the vines smell
    sweet.
Get up, my darling.
Let's go away, my beautiful
    one."

The Man Speaks

¹⁴My beloved is like a dove that
    hides in the cracks of the
    rock.
She hides in the secret places of
    the cliff.
Show me your face.
Let me hear your voice.
Your voice is very sweet,
    and your face is lovely.
¹⁵Catch the foxes for us—
    the little foxes that ruin the
    vineyards.
Our vineyards are in blossom.

The Woman Speaks

¹⁶My lover is mine, and I am his.
He feeds among the lilies
¹⁷until the day dawns
    and the shadows disappear.
Turn, my lover.
Be like a gazelleᵈ or a young
    deer
    on the rugged mountains.

The Woman Dreams

3 At night on my bed,
    I looked for the one I love.
I looked for him, but I could not
    find him.
²I will get up now. I will go around
    the city,
    in the streets and squares.
I will look for the one I love.

I looked for him, but I could not
find him.
[3]The watchmen found me as they
patrolled the city.
I asked, "Have you seen the
one I love?"
[4]As soon as I had left them
I found the one I love.
I held him. I would not let him go
until I had brought him to my
mother's house.
I brought him into the room
where I was born.

The Woman Speaks to the Friends

[5]Women of Jerusalem, promise me
by the gazelle[d] and the deer.
Promise not to wake love.
Don't excite my feelings of love
until I'm ready.
[6]Who is this coming out of the
desert
like a cloud of smoke?
Who is this that smells like
myrrh,[d] incense[d]
and other spices?
[7]Look, it's Solomon's couch[n]
with 60 soldiers around it.
They are the finest soldiers of
Israel.
[8]These soldiers all carry swords.
They have been trained in war.
Every man wears his sword at his
side.
He is ready for the dangers of
the night.
[9]King Solomon had a couch made
for himself.
It is made of wood from
Lebanon.
[10]He made its posts of silver
and its braces of gold.
The seat was covered with purple
cloth.
The women of Jerusalem wove
it with love.

[11]Women of Jerusalem, go out and
see King Solomon.
He is wearing the crown his
mother put on his head.
It was his wedding day,
when his heart was happy!

The Man Speaks to the Woman

4 How beautiful you are, my
darling!
Oh, you are beautiful!
Your eyes behind your veil are
like doves.
Your hair is like a flock of goats
streaming down Mount
Gilead.
[2]Your teeth are white like
newly-sheared sheep
just coming from their bath.
Each one has a twin.
None of them is alone.
[3]Your lips are like red silk thread.
Your mouth is lovely.
Your cheeks behind your veil
are like slices of a
pomegranate.[d]
[4]Your neck looks like David's
tower.
The tower was built with rows
of stones.
A thousand shields hang on its
walls.
Each shield belongs to a strong
soldier.
[5]Your breasts are like two fawns.
They are like twins of a
gazelle,[d]
eating among the lilies.
[6]Until the day dawns
and the shadows disappear,
I will go to that mountain of
myrrh.[d]
And I will go to that hill of
incense.[d]
[7]My darling, everything about you
is beautiful.
How perfect you are.

---

couch Something like a bed carried by slaves on which the king lay or sat while travelling.

⁸Come with me from Lebanon, my
bride.
Come with me from Lebanon.
Come from the top of Mount
Amana,
from the tops of Mount Senir
and Mount Hermon.
Come from the lions' dens
and from the leopards' hills.
⁹My sister, my bride,
you have thrilled my heart.
You have thrilled my heart
with a glance of your eyes,
with one jewel from your
necklace.
¹⁰Your love is so sweet, my sister,
my bride!
Your love is better than wine.
Your perfume smells better than
any spice.
¹¹My bride, your lips drip honey.
Honey and milk are under your
tongue.
Your clothes smell like the
cedars of Lebanon.
¹²My sister, my bride, you are like
a garden locked up.
You are like a spring with a wall
around it, a fountain that is
closed.
¹³Your limbs are like an orchard
of pomegranates and all the best
fruit.
It is filled with flowers and nard.ᵈ
¹⁴It also has saffron,ᵈ calamusᵈ and
cinnamon.
It is filled with trees of incense,
myrrh and aloesᵈ—
all the best spices.
¹⁵You are like a garden fountain—
a well of fresh water
flowing down from the
mountains of Lebanon.

The Woman Speaks
¹⁶Awake, north wind!
Come, you south wind!
Blow on my garden.
Let its sweet smells flow out.
Let my lover enter the garden.
And let him eat its best fruits.

The Man Speaks

5 I have entered my garden, my
sister, my bride.
I have gathered my myrrhᵈ with
my spice.
I have eaten my honeycomb and
my honey.
I have drunk my wine and my
milk.

The Friends Speak
Eat, friends, and drink.
Yes, drink deeply, lovers.

The Woman Dreams
²I sleep, but my heart is awake.
I hear my lover knocking.
"Open to me, my sister, my
darling,
my dove, my perfect one.
My head is wet with dew.
And my hair is wet with the
dampness of the night."
³I have taken off my garment.
I don't want to put it on again!
I have washed my feet.
I don't want to get them dirty
again!
⁴My lover put his hand through the
door opening.
I felt excited inside.
⁵I got up to open the door for my
lover.
Myrrhᵈ was dripping from my
hands.
Myrrh was flowing from my
fingers,
onto the handles of the lock.
⁶I opened the door for my lover.
But my lover had left. He was
gone.
When he had spoken, he had
taken my breath away.
I looked for him, but I could not
find him.
I called for him, but he did not
answer me.
⁷The watchmen found me
as they patrolled the city.
They hit me; they hurt me.

The guards on the wall took
  away my coat.
8I tell you, women of Jerusalem,
  if you find my lover,
  tell him I am weak with love.

The Friends Answer the Woman

9Is your lover better than other
    lovers,
  you, the most beautiful of
    women?
  Is your lover better than other
    lovers?
  Is that why you talk like this?

The Woman Answers the Friends

10My lover is clean and tanned.
  He's the best of 10,000 men.
11His head is like the finest gold.
  His hair is wavy and black like a
    raven.
12His eyes are like doves
  by springs of water.
  They seem to be bathed in cream.
  They are set like jewels.
13His cheeks are like garden beds of
    spices.
  They smell like mounds of
    perfume.
  His lips are like lilies
  flowing with myrrh.d
14His hands are like gold hinges,
  filled with jewels.
  His body is like smooth ivory
  covered with sapphires.
15His legs are like large marble
    posts,
  standing on bases of fine gold.
  He is tall like a cedar of
    Lebanon—
  like the best cedar trees.
16His mouth is sweet to kiss.
  I desire him very much.
  Yes, daughters of Jerusalem,
  this is my lover.
  This is my friend.

The Friends Speak to the Woman

6 Where has your lover gone,
  most beautiful of women?
  Which way did your lover turn?

We will look for him with you.

The Woman Answers the Friends

2My lover has gone down to his
    garden.
  He has gone to the garden beds
    of spices
  to feed in the gardens
  and to gather lilies.
3I belong to my lover.
  And my lover belongs to me.
  He feeds among the lilies.

The Man Speaks to the Woman

4My darling, you are as beautiful as
  the city of Tirzah.
  You are as lovely as the city of
    Jerusalem.
  You are as wonderful as an army
    flying flags.
5Turn your eyes from me.
  They excite me too much!
  Your hair is like a flock of goats
    streaming down Mount Gilead.
6Your teeth are white like sheep
  just coming from their bath.
  Each one has a twin.
  None of them is alone.
7Your cheeks behind your veil
  are like slices of a
    pomegranate.d
8There may be 60 queens and 80
    slave womend
  and so many girls you cannot
    count them.
9But there is only one like my
    dove, my perfect one.
  She is her mother's only
    daughter,
  the brightest of the one who
    gave her birth.
  The young women saw her and
    called her happy.
  The queens and the slave
    women also praised her.

The Young Women Praise
the Woman

10Who is that young woman?
  She shines out like the dawn.
  She's as pretty as the moon.

She's as bright as the sun.
And she's as wonderful
as an army flying flags.

The Man Speaks

¹¹I went down into the orchard of
nut trees.
I went to see the blossoms of
the valley.
I went to look for buds on the
vines,
to see if the pomegranate*d* trees
had bloomed.
¹²My desire for you makes me feel
like a prince in a chariot.

The Friends Call to the Woman

¹³Come back, come back, woman of
Shulam.
Come back, come back,
so we may look at you!

The Woman Answers the Friends

Why do you want to look at the
woman of Shulam
as you would at the dance of
two groups?

The Man Speaks to the Woman

7 Your feet are beautiful in
sandals,
you daughter of a prince.
Your round thighs are like jewels
shaped by an artist.
²Your navel is like a round drinking
cup
always filled with wine.
Your stomach is like a pile of
wheat
with lilies around it like a fence.
³Your breasts are like two fawns.
They are like twins of a
gazelle.*d*
⁴Your neck is like an ivory tower.
Your eyes are like the pools in
Heshbon
near the gate of Bath Rabbim.
Your nose is like a tower of
Lebanon
which looks toward Damascus.
⁵Your head is like Mount Carmel.

And your hair is like purple
cloth.
The king is captured in its folds.
⁶You are beautiful.
You are very pleasant.
My love, you are full of delights!
⁷You are tall like a palm tree.
Your breasts are like its bunches
of fruit.
⁸I said, "I will climb up the palm
tree.
I will take hold of its fruit."
Let your breasts be like bunches
of grapes.
Let the smell of your breath be
like apples.
⁹ And let your mouth be like the
best wine.

The Woman Speaks to the Man

Let this wine go down sweetly for
my lover.
May it flow gently past the lips
and teeth.
¹⁰I belong to my lover,
and he desires only me.
¹¹Come, my lover.
Let's go out into the country.
Let's spend the night in the
fields.
¹²Let's go early to the vineyards.
Let's see if the buds are on the
vines.
Let's see if the blossoms have
already opened
and if the pomegranates*d* have
bloomed.
There I will give you my love.
¹³The mandrake flowers give their
sweet smell.
And at our gates there are all
the best fruits.
I have saved them for you, my
lover,
the old delights and the new.

8 I wish you were like my brother
who was fed at my mother's
breasts!
If I found you outside,
I would kiss you.

And no one would look down on
me.
[2]I would lead you and bring you
to my mother's house.
She is the one who has taught
me.
I would give you a drink of spiced
wine
from my pomegranates.

The Woman Speaks to the Friends

[3]My lover's left hand is under my
head.
And his right arm holds me
tight!
[4]Women of Jerusalem, promise me.
Promise not to wake love.
Don't excite my feelings of love
until I'm ready.

The Friends Speak

[5]Who is this coming out of the
desert,
leaning on her lover?

The Man Speaks to the Woman

I woke you under the apple tree.
It was there that you were
born.
There your mother gave birth to
you.
[6]Put me like a seal on your heart,
like a seal on your arm.
Love is as strong as death.
Desire is as strong as the grave.
Love bursts into flames.
It burns like a very hot fire.
[7]Even much water cannot put out
the flame of love.
Floods cannot drown love.
If a man offered everything in his
house for love,
people would totally reject it.

The Woman's Brothers Speak

[8]We have a little sister,
and her breasts are not yet
grown.
What should we do for our sister
on the day she becomes
engaged?
[9]If she is a wall,
we will put silver towers on her.
If she is a door,
we will protect her with cedar
boards.

The Woman Speaks

[10]I am a wall,
and my breasts are like towers.
So I was to him,
as one who brings happiness.
[11]Solomon had a vineyard at Baal
Hamon.
He rented the vineyards for
others to tend.
Everyone who rented had to pay
a thousand pieces of silver for
the fruit.
[12]But my own vineyard is mine to
give.
Solomon, the thousand pieces
of silver are for you.
And two hundred are for those
who tend the fruit.

The Man Speaks to the Woman

[13]You who live in the gardens,
my friends are listening for your
voice.
Let me hear it!

The Woman Speaks to the Man

[14]Hurry, my lover.
Be like a gazelle[d]
or a young deer
on the mountains where spices
grow.

ISAIAH

God's Message in Troubled Times

1 This is the vision Isaiah son of Amoz saw. God showed Isaiah what would happen to Judah and Jerusalem. Isaiah saw these things while Uzziah, Jotham, Ahaz and Hezekiah were kings of Judah.

God Finds Fault with His People

2Heaven and earth, listen,
  because the Lord is speaking:
"I raised my children and helped
    them grow.
But they have turned against
    me.
3An ox knows its master.
  And a donkey knows where its
    owner feeds it.
But the people of Israel do not
    know me.
My people do not understand."

4Terrible times are coming for
    Israel, a nation of sin.
The people are loaded down
    with guilt.
They are like a group of children
    doing evil.
They are full of evil.
They have left the Lord.
They hate God, the Holy One of
    Israel.
They have turned away from
    him.

5Why should you continue to be
    punished?
Why do you continue to turn
    against him?
Your whole head is hurt.
And your whole heart is sick.
6There is no healthy spot
  from the bottom of your foot to
    the top of your head.
You are covered with wounds,
    hurts and open sores.

Your wounds are not cleaned and
    covered.
No medicine takes away the
    pain.
7Your land is ruined.
Your cities have been burned
    with fire.
While you watch,
  your enemies are stealing
    everything from your land.
Your land is ruined like a
    country destroyed by
    enemies.
8Jerusalem is left alone
  like an empty shelter in a
    vineyard.
It is like a hut left in a field of
    melons.
It is like a city surrounded by
    enemies.
9The Lord of heaven's armies
  allowed a few of our people to
    live.
Otherwise we would have been
    completely destroyed
like the cities of Sodom and
    Gomorrah.

10Jerusalem, your rulers are like
    those of Sodom.
Your people are like those of
    Gomorrah.
Hear the word of the Lord.
Listen to the teachings of our
    God!
11The Lord says,
"I do not want all these
    sacrifices you give me.
I have had enough of your
    sacrifices
of male sheep and fat from fine
    animals.
I am not pleased

by the blood of bulls, sheep and
goats.
12You come to meet with me.
But who asked you to do
all this running in and out?
13Don't continue bringing me
worthless sacrifices!
I hate the incense*d* you burn.
I can't stand your New Moons,*d*
Sabbaths*d* and other feast
days.
I can't stand the evil you do in
holding your holy meetings.
14I hate your New Moon feasts
and your other yearly feasts.
They have become like heavy
weights on me.
I am tired of carrying them.
15You will raise your arms in prayer
to me.
But I will refuse to look at you.
Even if you say many prayers,
I will not listen to you.
It's because your hands are full of
blood.
16Wash yourselves and make
yourselves clean.*d*
Stop doing the evil things I see
you do.
Stop doing wrong!
17 Learn to do good.
Be fair to other people.
Punish those who hurt others.
Help the orphans.
Stand up for the rights of
widows."

18The Lord says,
"Come, we will talk these things
over.
Your sins are red like deep red
cloth.
But they can be as white as
snow.
Your sins are bright red.
But you can be white like wool.
19If you will obey me,
you will eat good crops from the
land.
20But if you refuse to obey and if
you turn against me,

you will be destroyed by your
enemies' swords."
The Lord himself said these
things.

Jerusalem Is Not Loyal to God

21The city of Jerusalem once
followed the Lord.
But she is no longer loyal to the
Lord.
She used to be filled with fairness.
People there lived the way God
wanted.
But now, murderers live there.
22Jerusalem, you have become like
the scum left when silver is
purified.
You are like wine mixed with
water.
23Your rulers are rebels.
They are friends of thieves.
They all accept money for doing
wrong things.
They are paid to cheat people.
They don't try to help the
orphans.
And they don't listen to the
widows' needs.
24The Master, the Lord of heaven's
armies,
the Mighty One of Israel, says:
"You, my enemies, will not cause
me any more trouble.
I will pay you back for what you
did.
25I will turn against you.
I will clean away all your wrongs
as if with soap.
I will take all the worthless
things out of you.
26I will bring back judges as you had
long ago.
Your counsellors will be like the
ones you had in the
beginning.
Then you will be called the City
That Is Right with God.
You will be called the Loyal
City."

²⁷Because the Lord does what is
    fair,
  he will rescue Jerusalem.
Because the Lord does what is
    right,
  he will save her people who
    come back to him.
²⁸But sinners and those who turn
    against him will be
    destroyed.
  Those who have left the Lord
    will die.

²⁹"You will be ashamed
  because you have worshipped
    false gods under the oak
    trees.
  You will be disgraced
  because you have worshipped
    idols in your gardens.
³⁰You will be like an oak whose
    leaves are dying.
  You will be like a garden without
    water.
³¹Powerful people will be like small,
    dry pieces of wood.
  And what they do will be like
    sparks.
  The people and what they do will
    burn together.
  And no one will be able to stop
    that fire."

The Message About Jerusalem

2 Isaiah son of Amoz saw this mes-
    sage about Judah and Jerusalem.
²In the last days
  the mountain on which the Lord's
    Temple[d] stands
  will become the most important
    of all mountains.
  It will be raised above the hills.
  And people from all nations will
    come streaming to it.
³Many nations will come and say,
  "Come, let us go up to the
    mountain of the Lord.
  Let us go to the Temple of the
    God of Jacob.
  Then God will teach us his ways.
  And we will obey his teachings."

The Lord's teachings will go out
    from Jerusalem.
  The Lord's message will go out
    from Jerusalem.
⁴Then the Lord will settle
    arguments among many
    nations.
  He will make decisions for
    strong nations that are far
    away.
  Then the nations will make their
    swords into ploughs.
  They will make their spears into
    hooks for trimming trees.
  Nations will no longer fight other
    nations.
  They will not even train for war
    any more.
⁵Come, family of Jacob.
  We should follow the way of the
    Lord.

A Terrible Day Is Coming

⁶Lord, you have left your people,
    the family of Jacob.
  They have become filled with
    wrong ideas from people in
    the East.
  Your people try to tell the future
    like the Philistines.
  They have completely accepted
    those foreign ideas.
⁷Their land has been filled with
    silver and gold.
  There are a great many
    treasures there.
  Their land has been filled with
    horses.
  There are many chariots there.
⁸Their land is full of idols.
  The people worship these idols
    that they made with their
    own hands.
  They worship statues shaped by
    their fingers.
⁹People will not be proud any
    longer.
  They will bow low with shame.
  God, do not forgive them.
¹⁰Go into the caves of the cliffs.

Dig holes and hide in the
  ground.
Hide from the anger of the Lord
  and from his great power!
11Proud people will stop being
  proud.
They will bow low with shame.
At that time only the Lord will still
  be praised.

12The Lord of heaven's armies has a
  certain day planned.
On that day he will punish the
  proud and those who brag.
They will no longer be
  important.
13He will bring down the tall cedar
  trees from Lebanon.
He will destroy the great oak
  trees of Bashan.
14He will destroy all the tall
  mountains
  and the high hills.
15He will knock down every tall
  tower
  and every high, strong wall.
16He will sink all the trading ships.
  And he will destroy the beautiful
  ships.
17At that time proud people will
  stop being proud.
They will bow low with shame.
And at that time only the Lord will
  be praised.
18   But all the idols will be gone.

19People will run to caves in the
  rocky cliffs.
They will dig holes and hide in
  the ground.
They will hide from the anger of
  the Lord
  and his great power.
They will do this when the Lord
  stands to shake the earth.
20At that time people will throw
  away
  their gold and silver idols.
They made these idols for
  themselves to worship.
But they will throw them away
  to the bats and moles.

21Then the people will hide in caves
  and cracks in the rocks.
They will hide from the anger of
  the Lord
  and his great power.
They will do this when the Lord
  stands to shake the earth.

22You should stop trusting in people
  to save you.
People are only human.
They aren't able to help you.

God Will Punish Judah and Jerusalem

3 Understand what I am telling
  you.
The Master, the Lord of
  heaven's armies,
will take away everything Judah
  and Jerusalem need.
He will take away all the food
  and water.
2He will take away all the heroes
  and great soldiers.
He will take away all the judges,
  prophets,d
people who do magic and older
  leaders.
3He will take away the military
  leaders and government
  leaders.
He will take away the
  counsellors, the skilled
  craftsmen and those who try
  to tell the future.
4The Lord says, "I will cause
  young boys to be your
  leaders.
Foolish children will rule over
  you.
5Everyone will be against everyone
  else.
Young people will not respect
  older people.
Common people will not respect
  important people."
6At that time a man will grab one
  of his brothers
  from his own family and say,

"You have a coat. So you will be
    our leader.
You will be the leader over all
    these ruins."
[7]But that brother will stand up and
    say,
"I cannot help you.
I do not have food or clothes in
    my house.
You will not make me your
    leader."
[8]This will happen because
    Jerusalem has stumbled
and Judah has fallen.
The things they say and do are
    against the Lord.
They sin openly against the
    Lord.
[9]The look on their faces shows
    they are guilty of doing
    wrong.
Like the people of Sodom, they
    are proud of their sin.
They don't care who sees it.
How terrible it will be for them!
They have brought much trouble
    to themselves.

[10]Tell the good people that good
    things will happen to them.
They will receive a reward for
    the good they do.
[11]But how terrible it will be for
    wicked people!
They will be punished for all the
    wrong they have done.
[12]Children treat my people cruelly.
Women rule over them.
My people, your guides lead you
    in the wrong way.
They turn you away from what
    is right.

[13]The Lord takes his place in
    court.
He stands to judge the people.
[14]The Lord presents his case
    against the older leaders and
        other leaders of his people.
He says, "You have burned my
    vineyard.

Your houses are full of what you
    took from the poor.
[15]What gives you the right to crush
    my people?
How can you grind the faces of
    the poor into the dirt?"
The Master, the Lord of heaven's
    armies, said this.

A Warning to Women of Jerusalem

[16]The Lord says,
"The women of Jerusalem are
    proud.
They walk around with their heads
    held high.
They flirt with their eyes.
They take quick, short steps,
    making noise with their ankle
    bracelets."
[17]So the Lord will put sores on the
    heads of those women in
    Jerusalem.
He will make them lose all their
    hair.

[18]At that time the Lord will take
away everything that makes them
proud. He will take away their beautiful ankle bracelets, their headbands
and their necklaces shaped like the
moon. [19]He will take away their earrings, bracelets and veils. [20]He will
take away their scarves, ankle chains,
the cloth belts worn around their
waists, their bottles of perfume and
charms. [21]He will take away their signet[d] rings, nose rings, [22]their fine
robes, capes, shawls and purses.
[23]And he will take away their mirrors,
linen dresses, turbans and long
shawls.

[24]Instead of having sweet-smelling
    perfume, they will stink.
Instead of fine cloth belts, they
    will have ropes of captives
    to wear.
Instead of having their hair fixed
    in fancy ways, they will be
    bald.

Instead of fine clothes, they will
have rough clothes of
sadness.
Instead of having beauty, they
will have the brand of a
captive.
²⁵At that time your men will be
killed with swords.
Your heroes will die in war.
²⁶There will be crying and sadness
in the meeting places near
the city gates.
Jerusalem will be like a woman
who has lost everything and
sits on the ground.

4 At that time seven women
will grab one man.
They will say, "We will make our
own bread.
And we will make our own
clothes.
But please marry us!
Please, take away our shame."

The Branch of the Lord

²At that time the Lord's branch will
be very beautiful and great. The people still living in Israel will be proud of
what the land grows. ³All the people
who are still living in Jerusalem will be
called holy. This will be all the people
whose names are recorded among the
living in Jerusalem. ⁴The Lord will
wash away the filth from the women of
Jerusalem. He will wash the blood-
stains out of Jerusalem. He will clean
Jerusalem with the spirit of fairness
and the spirit of fire. ⁵As he did when
Israel left Egypt, the Lord will cover
them with a cloud of smoke during the
day. And he will cover them with a
bright, flaming fire at night. These
proofs will be over Mount Zion.ᵈ They
will be over every meeting of the people there. There will be a covering
over every person. ⁶This covering will
be a place of safety. It will protect the
people from the heat of the sun. It will
be a safe place to hide from the storm
and rain.

Israel, God's Special Field

5 Now I will sing a song to my
friend. This song is about his vineyard.
My friend had a vineyard
on a hill with very rich soil.
²He dug and cleared the field of
stones.
He planted the best grapevines
there.
And he built a tower in the middle
of it.
He cut out a winepressᵈ as well.
He hoped good grapes would
grow there.
But only bad grapes grew.

³My friend says, "You people living
in Jerusalem,
and you men of Judah,
judge between me and my
vineyard.
⁴What more could I have done for
my vineyard?
I did everything I could.
I hoped for good grapes to grow.
But why were there only bad
grapes?
⁵Now I will tell you
what I will do to my vineyard:
I will remove the hedge,
and it will be burned.
I will break down the stone wall,
and it will be walked on.
⁶I will ruin my field.
It will not be trimmed or hoed.
Weeds and thorns will grow
there.
I will command the clouds
not to rain on it."

⁷The vineyard belonging to the
Lord of heaven's armies
is the nation of Israel.
The garden that the Lord loves
is the men of Judah.
The Lord looked for justice, but
there was only killing.
The Lord hoped for right living,
but there were only cries of
pain.

⁸How terrible it will be for you who
add more houses to your
houses
and more fields to your fields.
Finally there is no room left for
other people.
Then you are left alone in the
land.

⁹The Lord of heaven's armies said
this to me:
"The fine houses will be
destroyed.
The large and beautiful houses
will be left empty.
¹⁰At that time a 25 hectare
vineyard will make only 20
litres of wine.
And 200 litres of seed will grow
only 10 litres of grain."

¹¹How terrible it will be for people
who rise early in the
morning
to look for strong drink.
They stay awake late at night,
becoming drunk with wine.
¹²At their parties they have lyres,*d*
harps,
tambourines,*d* flutes and wine.
They don't see what the Lord has
done.
They don't notice the work of
his hands.
¹³So my people will be captured and
taken away
because they don't really know
me.
All the great men will die of
hunger.
The common people will die of
thirst.
¹⁴So the place where the dead are
wants more and more
people.
It opens its mouth wide.
Jerusalem's important men will go
down into it.
And the common people will go
down into it.

¹⁵So the common people and the
great people will be
humbled.
Those who are proud will be
humbled.
¹⁶The Lord of heaven's armies will
receive glory by judging
fairly.
The holy God will show himself
holy by doing what is right.
¹⁷Then the sheep will go anywhere
they want.
Lambs will feed on the land that
rich people once owned.

¹⁸How terrible it will be for those
people!
They pull their guilt and sins
behind them
as people pull wagons with
ropes.
¹⁹They say, "Let's see God hurry.
Let's see him do his work soon.
We want to see it.
Let's see the plan of the Holy One
of Israel happen soon.
Then we would know what it
really is."

²⁰How terrible it will be for people
who call good things bad
and bad things good.
They think darkness is light
and light is darkness.
They think sour is sweet
and sweet is sour.

²¹How terrible it will be for people
who think they are wise.
They think they are clever.

²²How terrible it will be for people
who are famous for drinking
wine.
They are champions at mixing
drinks.
²³They take money to set the guilty
free.
But they don't allow good people
to be judged fairly.
²⁴They will be destroyed
just as fire burns straw or dry
grass.

They will be destroyed
like a plant whose roots rot
and whose flower dies and blows
away like dust.
They have refused to obey the
teachings of the Lord of
heaven's armies.
They hated the message from
the Holy God of Israel.
25So the Lord has become very
angry with his people.
And he has raised his hand to
punish them.
Even the mountains are
frightened.
Dead bodies lie in the streets
like rubbish.

But the Lord is still angry.
His hand is still raised to strike
down the people.

26God raises a banner for the
nations far away.
He is whistling to call those
people.
The enemy comes quickly!
27Not one of them becomes tired or
falls down.
Not one of them gets sleepy and
falls asleep.
Their weapons are close at hand.
Their sandal straps are not
broken.
28Their arrows are sharp.
All of their bows are ready to
shoot.
The horses' hoofs are hard as
rock.
Their chariot wheels move like a
whirlwind.
29Their shout is like the roar of a
lion.
It is loud like a young lion.
The enemy growls as they grab
their captives.
There is no one to stop them
from taking their captives
away.
30On that day they will roar
like the waves of the sea.
And when people look at the land,

they will see only darkness and
pain.
All light will become dark in this
thick cloud.

Isaiah Becomes a Prophet

6 In the year that King Uzziah died,
I saw the Lord. He was sitting on
a very high throne. His long robe filled
the Temple.*d* 2Burning heavenly creatures stood above him. Each creature
had six wings. They used two wings
to cover their faces. They used two
wings to cover their feet. And they
used two wings for flying. 3Each creature was calling to the others:
"Holy, holy, holy is the Lord of
heaven's armies.
His glory fills the whole earth."
4Their voices caused the frame
around the door to shake. The Temple filled with smoke.
5I said, "Oh, no! I will be destroyed.
I am not pure. And I live among people who are not pure. But I have seen
the King, the Lord of heaven's armies."
6On the altar there was a fire. One
of the burning heavenly creatures
used a pair of tongs to take a hot coal
from the fire. Then he flew to me with
the hot coal in his hand. 7The creature
touched my mouth with the hot coal.
Then he said, "Look. Your guilt is tak-
en away because this hot coal has
touched your lips. Your sin is taken
away."
8Then I heard the Lord's voice. He
said, "Whom can I send? Who will go
for us?"
So I said, "Here I am. Send me!"
9Then the Lord said, "Go and tell
this to the people:
'You will listen and listen, but you
will not understand.
You will look and look, but you
will not learn'.
10Make these people stubborn.
Make them not able to
understand what they hear
and see.

Otherwise, they might really
　　understand
what they see with their eyes
　　and hear with their ears.
They might really understand in
　　their minds.
If they did this, they would
　　come back to me and be
　　forgiven."

[11]Then I asked, "Lord, how long
should I do this?"
He answered,
"Do this until the cities are
　　destroyed
and the people are gone.
Do this until there are no people
　　left living in the houses.
Do this until the land is
　　destroyed and left empty.
[12]I will send the people far away.
And the land will be left empty.
[13]One-tenth of the people will be
　　left in the land.
But the land will be destroyed
　　again.
These people will be like an oak
　　tree.
When the tree is chopped down,
　　a stump is left.
The people who remain will be
　　like a stump that will sprout
　　again."

Trouble with Aram

7 Now Ahaz was the son of Jotham,
who was the son of Uzziah. When
Ahaz was king of Judah, Rezin and Pekah went up to Jerusalem to fight
against it. Rezin was king of Aram.
And Pekah son of Remaliah was king
of Israel. But they were not able to
defeat the city.
[2]A message was told to Ahaz king of
Judah. It said, "The armies of Aram
and Israel[n] have joined together."
When Ahaz heard this, he and the
people became very frightened. They
shook with fear like trees of the forest
blown by the wind.
[3]Then the Lord told Isaiah, "You
and your son Shear-Jashub should go
out and talk to Ahaz. Go to the place
where the water flows into the upper
pool. This is on the road to the Washerman's Field. [4]Tell Ahaz, 'Be careful.
Be calm, and don't be afraid. Don't let
those two men, Rezin and Remaliah's
son Pekah, scare you. Don't be afraid
of their anger and Aram's anger.
Those two men are as weak as two
barely burning sticks that are ready to
go out. [5]They have made plans against
you. They said, [6]"Let's fight against
Judah and tear it apart. We will divide
Judah for ourselves. We will make the
son of Tabeel the new king of Judah."
[7]But I, the Lord God, say
　　their plan will not succeed.
It will not happen.
[8]That is because Aram is led by
　　the city of Damascus.
And Damascus is led by its
　　weak king, Rezin.
Within 65 years Israel will no
　　longer be a nation.
[9]Israel is led by the city of
　　Samaria,
　　and Samaria is led by its weak
　　king, the son of Remaliah.
If your faith is not strong,
　　then you will not have strength
　　to last'."

Immanuel — God Is with Us

[10]Then the Lord spoke to Ahaz
again. [11]The Lord said, "Ask for a sign
to prove to yourself that these things
are true. It may be a sign from as deep
as the place where the dead are or as
high as the heavens."
[12]But Ahaz said, "I will not ask for
a sign. I will not test the Lord."
[13]Then Isaiah said, "Ahaz, descendant[d] of David, listen very carefully!
Isn't it bad enough that you wear out
the patience of people? Do you have

Israel Literally, "Ephraim". Isaiah often uses "Ephraim" to mean all of Israel.

to wear out the patience of my God also? [14]But the Lord himself will give you a sign: the virgin[n] will be pregnant. She will have a son, and she will name him Immanuel.[n] [15]He will be eating milk curds and honey when he learns to reject what is evil and to choose what is good. [16]You are afraid of the kings of Israel and Aram now. But before the child learns what is good and what is evil, the lands of Israel and Aram will be empty. [17]The Lord will bring some troubled times to you. Those troubles will come to your people and to the people of your father's family. The Lord will bring the king of Assyria to fight against you.

[18]"At that time the Lord will whistle to call for the Egyptians. And they will come like flies from the streams of Egypt. The Lord will call for the Assyrians. And they will come like bees from the land of Assyria. [19]These enemies will camp in the deep ravines and in the cliffs. They will camp by the thornbushes and watering holes. [20]The Lord will use Assyria to punish Judah. Assyria will be hired and used like a razor. It will be as if the Lord is shaving the hair from Judah's head and legs and is shaving off Judah's beard.

[21]"At that time a person will be able to keep only one young cow and two sheep alive. [22]There will be only enough milk for that person to eat milk curds. All who remain in the land will go back to eating only milk curds and honey. [23]In this land there are now vineyards that have 1,000 grapevines. These grapevines are worth about 11.5 kilograms of silver. But these fields will become full of weeds and thorns. [24]The land will become wild and useful only as a hunting ground. [25]People once worked and grew food on these hills. But at that time people will not go there. The land will be filled with weeds and thorns. Only sheep and cattle will go to those places."

Assyria Will Come Soon

8 The Lord told me, "Take a large scroll on which to write. Use a pen to write these words: 'Maher-Shalal-Hash-Baz'.[n] [2]I will gather some men to be reliable witnesses. They will be Uriah the priest and Zechariah son of Jeberekiah."

[3]Then I went to the prophetess.[d] She became pregnant and had a son. Then the Lord told me, "Name the boy Maher-Shalal-Hash-Baz. [4]The king of Assyria will take away all the wealth and possessions of Damascus and Samaria. This will happen before the boy learns to say 'my father' or 'my mother'."

[5]Again the Lord spoke to me. [6]He said,
"These people refuse to accept
    the slow-moving waters of the
    pool of Shiloah.
These people are terrified of
    Rezin
and Remaliah's son Pekah.
[7]So I, the Lord, will bring
    the king of Assyria and all his
    power against them.
They will come like a powerful
    flood of water from the
    Euphrates River.
The Assyrians will be like water
    rising over the banks of the
    river,
flowing over the land.
[8]That water will flow into Judah
    and pass through it.
It will rise to Judah's throat.
Immanuel, this army will spread
    its wings like a bird
until it covers your whole
    country."

virgin The Hebrew word means "a young woman". Often this meant a girl who was not married and had not yet had sexual relations with anyone.
Immanuel This name means "God is with us".
Maher-Shalal-Hash-Baz This name means "there will soon be looting and stealing".

⁹Be broken, all you nations.
  Be smashed to pieces.
Listen, all you faraway countries.
  Prepare for battle and be
    smashed to pieces!
  Prepare for battle and be
    smashed to pieces!
¹⁰Make your plans for the fight.
  But your plans will be defeated.
  Give orders to your armies.
  But your orders will be useless.
  This is because God is with us.

Warnings to Isaiah

¹¹The Lord spoke to me with his great power. He warned me not to follow the lead of the rest of the people. The Lord said,
¹²"People are saying that others
    make plans against them.
  You should not believe those
    things.
  Don't be afraid of the things they
    fear.
  Do not dread those things.
¹³But remember that the Lord of
    heaven's armies is holy.
  He is the one you should fear.
  He is the one you should dread.
¹⁴Then he would be a place of
    safety for you.
  But for the two families of
    Israel,
  he will be like a stone that causes
    people to stumble.
  He will be like a rock that
    makes them fall.
  He will be like a trap for the
    people of Jerusalem.
  He will catch them in his trap.
¹⁵Many people will fall over this
    rock.
  They will fall and be broken.
  They will be trapped and
    caught."
¹⁶Make an agreement.
  Seal up the teaching while my
    followers are watching.
¹⁷I will wait for the Lord to help
  us.

The Lord is ashamed of the
    family of Israel.
  I will trust the Lord.

¹⁸I am here. And with me are the children the Lord has given me. We are signs and proofs for the people of Israel. We have been sent by the Lord of heaven's armies. He lives on Mount Zion.ᵈ

¹⁹Some people say, "Ask the mediumsᵈ and fortune-tellers what to do. They whisper and mutter and ask dead people what to do." But I tell you that people should ask their God for help. Why should people who are still alive ask something from the dead? ²⁰You should follow the teachings and the agreement with the Lord. The mediums and fortune-tellers do not speak the word of the Lord. Their words are worth nothing.

²¹People will wander through the land troubled and hungry. When they become hungry, they will become angry. Then they will look up and curse their king and their God. ²²They will look around them at their land. And they will see only trouble and darkness and awful gloom. And they will be forced into the darkness.

A New Day Is Coming

9 But suddenly there will be no more gloom for the land that suffered. In the past God made the lands of Zebulun and Naphtali hang their heads in shame. But in the future that land will be made great. That land stretches from the way along the Mediterranean Sea to the land along the Jordan River. And it goes north to Galilee where the people who are not Israelites live.

²Now those people live in
    darkness.
  But they will see a great light.
  They live in a place that is very
    dark.
  But a light will shine on them.

³God, you will cause the nation to
    grow.
You will make the people happy.
And they will show their
    happiness to you.
It will be like the joy during
    harvest time.
It will be like the joy of people
    taking what they have won in
    war.
⁴Like the time you defeated
    Midian,
    you will take away their heavy
    load.
You will take away the heavy pole
    from their backs.
You will take away the rod the
    enemy uses to punish your
    people.
⁵Every boot that marched in battle
    will be destroyed.
Every uniform stained with
    blood will be destroyed.
They will be thrown into the
    fire.
⁶A child will be born to us.
God will give a son to us.
He will be responsible for
    leading the people.
His name will be Wonderful
    Counsellor, Powerful God,
Father Who Lives For Ever,
    Prince of Peace.
⁷Power and peace will be in his
    kingdom.
It will continue to grow.
He will rule as king on David's
    throne
and over David's kingdom.
He will make it strong,
    by ruling with goodness and fair
    judgment.
He will rule it for ever and ever.
The Lord of heaven's armies will
    do this
    because of his strong love for
    his people.

God Will Punish Israel

⁸The Lord sent a message against
    the people of Jacob.

That message says that God will
    judge Israel.
⁹Then everyone in Israel, even the
    leaders in Samaria,
will know that God punished
    them.
Those people, who are proud and
    who brag now, say this:
¹⁰"These bricks have fallen,
    but we will build again with cut
    stones.
These small trees have been
    chopped down.
But we will put great cedars
    there."
¹¹But the Lord will make the
    enemies of Rezin strong
    against them.
He will stir up their enemies
    against them.
¹²The Arameans come from the
    east
and the Philistines from the
    west.
They will eat up Israel with their
    armies.

But the Lord is still angry.
His hand is still raised to punish
    the people.

¹³But the people do not return to
    the one who struck them.
They do not follow the Lord of
    heaven's armies.
¹⁴So the Lord will cut off Israel's
    head and tail.
He will take away both the
    branch and stalk in one day.
¹⁵The older leaders and important
    men are the head.
The prophets*ᵈ* who speak lies
    are the tail.
¹⁶Those who lead the people lead
    them in the wrong direction.
And those who follow them will
    be destroyed.
¹⁷So the Lord is not happy with the
    young men.
He will not show mercy to the
    widows and orphans.

All the people are separated from
God and are very evil.
They all speak lies.

But the Lord is still angry.
His hand is still raised to strike
down the people.

¹⁸Evil is like a small fire.
First, it burns weeds and
thorns.
Next, it burns the larger bushes in
the forest.
They all go up in a column of
smoke.
¹⁹The Lord of heaven's armies is
angry.
So the land will be burned.
All the people will be burned in
that fire.
No one will try to save his
brother.
²⁰People will grab something on the
right,
but they will still be hungry.
They will eat something on the
left,
but they will not be filled.
Then each person will turn and
eat his own children.
²¹The people of Manasseh will fight
against the people of
Ephraim.
And Ephraim will fight against
Manasseh.
Then both of them will turn
against Judah.

But the Lord is still angry.
His hand is still raised to strike
down the people.

10 How terrible it will be for the
lawmakers who write evil
laws.
They write laws that make life
hard for people.
²They are not fair to the poor.
They rob my people of their
rights.
They allow people to steal from
widows

and to take from orphans what
they should get.
³Lawmakers, how will you explain
the things you have done?
What will you do when your
destruction comes from far
away?
Where will you run for help?
Where will you hide your money
and your riches then?
⁴You will have to bow down among
the captives.
You will fall down among the
dead bodies.

But the Lord is still angry.
His hand is still raised to strike
down the people.

God Will Punish Assyria

⁵God says, "How terrible it will be
for the king of Assyria.
I use him like a stick.
In anger I use Assyria like a
club.
⁶I send it to fight against a nation
that is separated from God.
I am angry with those people.
So I command Assyria to fight
against them.
Assyria will take their wealth from
them.
Judah will become like dirt for
them to walk on in the
streets.
⁷But Assyria's king doesn't
understand that I am using
him.
He doesn't know he is a tool for
me.
He only wants to destroy other
people.
He plans to destroy many
nations.
⁸The king of Assyria says to
himself,
'All of my commanders are like
kings.
⁹The city Calno is like the city
Carchemish.

And the city Hamath is like the
  city Arpad.
The city Samaria is like the city
  Damascus.
¹⁰I defeated those kingdoms that
  worship idols.
And those idols were more than
  the idols of Jerusalem and
  Samaria.
¹¹I defeated Samaria and her idols.
So I will also defeat Jerusalem
  and her idols'."

¹²The Lord will finish doing what he
planned to Mount Zion*d* and Jerusalem. Then he will punish Assyria. The
king of Assyria is very proud. His
pride made him do these bad things.
So God will punish him. ¹³The king of
Assyria says this:
"By my own power I have done
  these things.
By my wisdom I have defeated
  many nations.
I have taken their wealth.
And like a mighty one, I have
  taken their people.
¹⁴I have taken the riches of all these
  people,
like one who reaches into a
  bird's nest.
I have taken these nations,
  like a person taking eggs.
No one raised a hand against
  me.
No one opened his mouth to
  stop me."

¹⁵An axe is not better than the
  person who swings it.
A saw is not better than the
  person who uses it.
A stick cannot control the person
  who picks it up.
A club cannot pick up the
  person!
¹⁶So the Master, the Lord of
  heaven's armies,
will send a terrible disease
  against Assyria's soldiers.
The strength of Assyria will be
  burned up.

It will be like a fire burning until
  everything is gone.
¹⁷God, the Light of Israel, will be
  like a fire.
The Holy One will be like a
  flame.
He will be like a fire
  that suddenly burns the weeds
  and thorns.
¹⁸The fire burns away the great
  trees and rich farmlands.
It will destroy everything.
Things will be like a sick man
  who wastes away.
¹⁹Only a few trees will be left
  standing.
There will be so few even a
  child will be able to count
  them.

²⁰At that time some people will be
  left alive in Israel
  from the family of Jacob.
They will not continue to depend
  on the person who defeated
  them.
They will learn truly to depend on
  the Lord,
  the Holy One of Israel.
²¹The people who are left alive in
  Jacob's family
  will again follow the powerful
  God.
²²Israel, your people are very
  many.
They are like the grains of sand
  by the sea.
But only a few of them will be
  left alive to return to the
  Lord.
God has announced that he will
  destroy the land
  completely and fairly.
²³The Master, the Lord of heaven's
  armies, will certainly destroy
  this land.
He will destroy it as he has
  announced.

²⁴This is what the Master, the Lord
of heaven's armies, says:
"My people living in Jerusalem,

don't be afraid of the Assyrians.
They beat you with a rod.
   They raise a stick to hurt you,
      as Egypt did.
25But after a short time my anger
     will stop.
   Then I will turn my anger to
     destroying them."

26Then the Lord of heaven's armies
     will beat the Assyrians with
     a whip.
   He will defeat them as he
     defeated Midian at the rock
     of Oreb.
   He will raise his stick over the
     waters
     as he did in Egypt.
27Then the troubles that Assyria
     puts on you
   will be removed.
   The load they make you carry
     will be taken away.

Assyria Invades Israel

28The army of Assyria will enter
     near Aiath.
   They will walk through Migron.
   They will store their food in
     Michmash.
29The army will go over the pass.
   They will sleep at Geba.
   The people of Ramah will be
     afraid.
   The people at Gibeah of Saul
     will run away.
30Cry out, Bath Gallim!
   Laishah, listen!
   Poor Anathoth!
31The people of Madmenah are
     running away.
   The people of Gebim are hiding.
32This day the army will stop at
     Nob.
   And the army will shake their
     fist at Mount Zion,d
     at the hill of Jerusalem.

33Watch! The Master, the Lord of
     heaven's armies,

will chop them down like a great
     tree.
   He will do this with his great
     power.
Those who are great will be cut
     down.
   Those who are important will fall
     to the ground.
34The Lord will cut them down
     as a forest is cut down with an
     axe.
And the great trees of Lebanon
   will fall by the power of the
     Mighty One.

The King of Peace Is Coming

11 A branch will grow
    from a stump of a tree that
     was cut down.
So a new king will come
   from the family of Jesse.n
2The Spiritd of the Lord will rest
     upon that king.
   The Spirit gives him wisdom,
     understanding, guidance and
     power.
   And the Spirit teaches him to
     know and respect the Lord.
3This king will be glad to obey the
     Lord.
   He will not judge by the way
     things look.
   He will not judge by what people
     say.
4He will judge the poor honestly.
   He will be fair in his decisions
     for the poor people of the
     land.
   At his command evil people will be
     punished.
   By his words the wicked will be
     put to death.
5Goodness and fairness will give
     him strength.
   They will be like a belt around
     his waist.

6Then wolves will live in peace
     with lambs.

Jesse King David's father.

And leopards will lie down to
    rest with goats.
Calves, lions and young bulls will
    eat together.
And a little child will lead them.
⁷Cows and bears will eat together
    in peace.
Their young will lie down
    together.
Lions will eat hay as oxen do.
⁸A baby will be able to play near a
    cobra's hole.
A child will be able to put his
    hand into the nest of a
    poisonous snake.
⁹They will not hurt or destroy each
    other
on all my holy mountain.
The earth will be full of the
    knowledge of the Lord,
    as the sea is full of water.

¹⁰At that time the new king from the
family of Jesse will stand as a banner
for the people. The nations will come
together around him. And the place
where he lives will be filled with glory.
¹¹At that time the Lord will again
reach out and take his people who are
left alive. These are God's people who
are left alive in Assyria, North Egypt,
South Egypt, Cush, Elam, Babylonia,
Hamath and all the islands of the sea.

¹²God will raise a banner as a sign
    for all people.
He will gather the people of
    Israel who were forced from
    their country.
He will gather the scattered
    people of Judah
from all parts of the earth.
¹³At that time Israel will not be
    jealous any more.
Judah will have no enemies left.
Israel will not be jealous of Judah.
And Judah will not hate Israel.
¹⁴But Israel and Judah will attack
    the Philistines on the west.
Together they will take the
    riches from the people of the
    east.

They will conquer Edom and
    Moab.
And the people of Ammon will
    be under their control.
¹⁵The Lord will dry up
    the Red Sea^d of Egypt.
He will wave his arm over the
    Euphrates River.
He will dry it up with a
    scorching wind.
He will divide it into seven small
    rivers.
And people will be able to walk
    across them with their
    sandals on.
¹⁶So God's people who are left
    alive
will have a way to leave Assyria.
It will be like the time the
    Israelites
    went out of Egypt.

A Song of Praise to God

12 At that time you will say:
    "I praise you, Lord!
You were angry with me.
But you are not angry with me
    now!
You have comforted me.
²God is the one who saves me.
I trust him. I am not afraid.
The Lord, the Lord, gives me
    strength and makes me sing.
He has saved me."
³You will receive your salvation
    with joy.
You will take it as you would
    draw water from a well.

⁴At that time you will say,
"Praise the Lord, and worship
    him.
Tell everyone what he has done.
Tell them how great he is.
⁵Sing praise to the Lord, because
    he has done great things.
Let all the world know what he
    has done.
⁶Shout and sing for joy, you people
    of Jerusalem.

The Holy One of Israel does
    great things before your
    eyes."

God's Message to Babylon

13 God showed Isaiah son of
Amoz this message about
Babylon:
²Raise a flag on the bare mountain.
    Call out to the men.
Raise your hand to signal them.
Tell them to enter through the
    gates for important people.
³I myself have commanded those
    people
    whom I have separated as mine.
I have called those warriors to
    carry out my anger.
    They rejoice and are glad to do
    my will.

⁴Listen to the loud noise in the
    mountains.
    It sounds like many people.
Listen to the noise among the
    kingdoms.
    Nations are gathering together.
The Lord of heaven's armies is
    calling
    his army together for battle.
⁵This army is coming from a
    faraway land.
    It is coming from the edge of
    the horizon.
In anger the Lord is using this
    army like a weapon.
    And it will destroy the whole
    country.

⁶Cry, because the Lord's day of
    judging is near.
    God All-Powerful is sending
    destruction.
⁷People will be weak with fear.
    Their courage will melt away.
⁸Everyone will be afraid.
    Pain and hurt will grab them.
    They will hurt like a woman
    giving birth to a baby.
They will look at each other in
    fear.

Their faces will become red like
    fire.

⁹Look, the Lord's day of judging is
    coming.
    It will be a terrible day. God will
    be very angry,
and he will destroy the country.
God will destroy the sinners
    who live in the land.
¹⁰The stars will not show their light.
    The skies will be dark.
The sun will grow dark as it rises.
    And the moon will not give its
    light.

¹¹The Lord says, "I will punish the
    world for its evil.
I will punish wicked people for
    their sins.
I will cause the proud people to
    lose their pride.
I will destroy the pride of those
    who are cruel to others.
¹²People will be harder to find than
    pure gold.
    There will be fewer people than
    there is fine gold in Ophir.
¹³I will make the sky shake.
    And the earth will be moved
    from its place.
The Lord of heaven's armies will
    be very angry.
    His anger will burn at that time.

¹⁴"Then the people from Babylon
    will run away like hunted
    deer.
    They will run like sheep who
    have no shepherd.
Everyone will turn back to his
    own people.
    Each will run back to his own
    land.
¹⁵Anyone who is captured will be
    killed.
    Everyone who is caught will be
    killed with a sword.
¹⁶Their little children will be beaten
    to death as their parents
    watch.

Everything in their houses will
  be stolen.
And their wives will be raped.
[17]Look, I will cause the armies of
  Media to attack Babylon.
They do not care about silver.
They do not delight in gold.
[18]Their soldiers will shoot the young
  men with arrows.
The soldiers will show no mercy
  on the children.
They will not feel sorry for the
  little boys.
[19]Babylon is the most beautiful of all
  kingdoms.
The Babylonians are very proud
  of it.
But God will destroy it
  like Sodom and Gomorrah.
[20]No one will ever live there.
No one will settle there again.
No Arab will put his tent there.
No shepherd will bring his sheep
  there.
[21]Only animals from the desert will
  live there.
The houses of Babylon will be
  full of wild dogs.
Owls will live there.
Wild goats will leap about in the
  houses.
[22]Wolves will howl within the strong
  walls.
Wild dogs will bark in the
  beautiful buildings.
The end of Babylon is near.
Its time is almost over."

Israel Will Return Home

14 The Lord will again show mercy to the people of Jacob. The
Lord will again choose the people of
Israel. He will settle them in their own
land. Then non-Israelite people will
join the Israelites. The non-Israelite
people will become a part of the family
of Jacob. [2]Nations will take the Israelites back to their land. Those men and
women from the other nations will become slaves to Israel. In the past the
Israelites were their slaves. But now
the Israelites will defeat those nations
and rule over them.

The King of Babylon Will Fall

[3]The Lord will take away the Israelites' hard work, and he will comfort
them. They will no longer have to
work as slaves. [4]On that day Israel
will sing this song about the king of
Babylon:
The cruel king who ruled us is
  finished.
His rule is finished!
[5]The Lord breaks the sceptre[d] of
  evil rulers.
He takes away their power.
[6]The king of Babylon beat people
  in anger.
He beat them again and again.
He ruled the people in anger.
He kept on doing terrible things
  to the people.
[7]But now, the whole land rests and
  is quiet.
Now the people begin to sing.
[8]Even the pine trees are happy.
And the cedar trees of Lebanon
  rejoice.
They say, "The king has fallen.
No one will ever cut us down
  again."

[9]The place of the dead is excited
  to meet you when you come.
It wakes the spirits of the dead to
  greet you.
They were the leaders of the
  world.
It makes dead kings stand up from
  their thrones to greet you.
They were rulers of nations.
[10]All these leaders will make fun of
  you.
They will say,
"Now you are weak, as we are.
Now you are just like us."
[11]Your pride has been sent down to
  where the dead are.
The music from your harps goes
  with it.

Flies are spread out like your bed
 beneath you.
And worms cover your body like
 a blanket.

¹²King of Babylon, morning star,
 you have fallen from heaven,
even though you were as bright
 as the rising sun!
In the past all the nations on earth
 bowed down before you.
But now you have been cut
 down.
¹³You told yourself,
 "I will go up to heaven.
I will put my throne
 above God's stars.
I will sit on the mountain of the
 gods.
I will sit on the slopes of the
 sacred mountain.
¹⁴I will go up above the tops of the
 clouds.
I will be like God Most High."
¹⁵But you were brought down to
 the grave.
You were brought down to the
 deep places where the dead
 are.

¹⁶Those who see you stare at you.
 They think about what has
 happened to you.
They say, "Is this the same man
 who caused great fear on
 earth?
Is he the one who shook the
 kingdoms?
¹⁷Is this the man who turned the
 land into a desert?
Is he the one who destroyed its
 cities?
Is he the one who captured people
 in war
and would not let them go
 home?"

¹⁸Every king of the earth has been
 buried with honour.
Every king has his own grave.
¹⁹But you are thrown out of your
 grave,

like an unwanted branch is cut
 from a tree and thrown
 away.
You are covered by bodies
 that died in battle.
You have been thrown into a
 rocky pit.
And other soldiers walk on you.
²⁰ You will not be buried like other
 people.
This is because you ruined your
 own country.
And you killed your own people.
So your children will never
 be mentioned again.

²¹Prepare to kill his children.
 Kill them because their father is
 guilty.
They will never again take control
 of the earth.
They will never again fill the
 world with their cities.

²²The Lord of heaven's armies says
 this:
"I will fight against those people.
I will destroy Babylon and its
 people.
I will destroy its people and
 their descendants,"^d says
 the Lord.
²³"I will make Babylon fit only for
 owls.
It will become a swamp.
I will sweep Babylon as with a
 broom of destruction,"
says the Lord of heaven's
 armies.

God Will Punish Assyria

²⁴The Lord of heaven's armies has
made this promise:
 "These things will happen exactly
 as I planned them.
These things will happen exactly
 as I set them up.
²⁵I will destroy the king of Assyria
 in my country.
I will trample him on my
 mountains.

He put a heavy load on my
people.
But that weight will be
removed.

26"This is what I plan to do against
all the earth.
I will raise my hand to strike
down all nations."
27When the Lord of heaven's armies
makes a plan,
no one can stop it.
When the Lord raises his hand to
punish people,
no one can stop him.

God's Message to Philistia

28This message was given the year
King Ahaz died:
29Country of Philistia, don't be so
happy.
The king who beat you is now
dead.
But he is like a snake that will
give birth to another
dangerous snake.
The new king will be like a
quick, dangerous snake to
bite you.
30Even the poorest of my people
will be able to eat safely.
People in need will be able to lie
down in safety.
But I will kill your family with
hunger.
And all your people who are left
will die.

31People near the city gates, cry
out!
Philistines, be frightened!
A cloud of dust comes from the
north.
It is an army, full of men ready
to fight.
32What shall we tell the messengers
from Philistia?

Say that the Lord has made
Jerusalem strong.
Say that his poor people will go
there for safety.

God's Message to Moab

15 This is a message about Moab:
In one night armies took the
wealth from Ar in Moab.
That night the city was
destroyed.
In one night armies took the
wealth from Kir in Moab.
That night the city was
destroyed.
2The people of Dibon go to the
places of worship to cry.
The people of Moab cry for the
cities of Nebo and Medeba.
Everyone has shaved his head and
beard to show how sad he
is.
3In the streets at Moab they wear
rough cloth to show their
sadness.
On the roofs" and in the public
squares,
they are crying loudly.
4People in the cities Heshbon and
Elealeh cry out loud.
You can hear their voices far
away in the city Jahaz.
Even the soldiers are frightened.
They are shaking from fear.

5My heart cries with sorrow for
Moab.
Its people run away to Zoar for
safety.
They run to Eglath Shelishiyah.
People are going up the mountain
road to Luhith.
They are crying as they go.
People are going on the road to
Horonaim.
They cry out loud over their
destruction.

---

roofs In Bible times houses were built with flat roofs. The roof was used for drying things
such as flax and fruit. It was also used as an extra room, as a place for worship and as a
place to sleep in the summer.

⁶But the water of Nimrim has dried
up.
The grass has dried up.
All the plants are dead.
Nothing green is left.
⁷So the people gather up what they
have saved.
They carry those things and
cross the Ravine of the
Poplars.
⁸Crying is heard everywhere in
Moab.
Their crying is heard as far
away as the city Eglaim.
Their crying is heard as far
away as Beer Elim.
⁹The water of the city Dibon is full
of blood.
And I, the Lord, will bring even
more troubles to Dibon.
A few people living in Moab have
escaped the enemy.
But I will send lions to kill them.

16 Send the king of the land
the payment he demands.
Send a lamb from Sela through the
desert
to the mountain of Jerusalem.
²The women of Moab
try to cross the river Arnon.
They are like little birds
that have fallen from their nest.

³They say: "Help us.
Tell us what to do.
Protect us from our enemies
as shade protects us from the
noon sun.
Hide us because we are running
for safety!
Don't give us to our enemies.
⁴Let those of us who were forced
out of Moab live in your
land.
Hide us from our enemies."

The robbing of Moab will stop.
The enemy will be defeated.
The men who hurt others will
disappear from the land.
⁵Then a new loyal king will come.

This faithful king will be from
the family of David.
He will judge fairly.
He wants to do what is right.

⁶We have heard that the people of
Moab are proud
and very conceited.
They are very proud and angry.
But their boasting means
nothing.
⁷So the people of Moab will cry.
They will all be sad.
They will moan and groan
for the raisin cakes they had in
Kir Hareseth.
⁸But the fields of Heshbon and the
vines of Sibmah cannot grow
grapes.
Foreign rulers have destroyed
the grapevines.
The grapevines once spread as far
as the city of Jazer and into
the desert.
They had spread as far as the
sea.
⁹I cry with the people of Jazer
for the grapevines of Sibmah.
I will cry with the people of
Heshbon and Elealeh.
There will be no shouts of joy,
because there will be no harvest
or ripe fruit.
¹⁰There will be no joy and happiness
in the orchards.
There will be no songs or
shouts of joy in the
vineyards.
No one makes wine in the
winepresses.^d
I have put an end to shouts of
joy.
¹¹My heart cries for Moab like a
harp playing a funeral song.
I am very sad for Kir Hareseth.
¹²The people of Moab will go to
their places of worship.
They will try to pray.
But when they go to their temple
to pray,
they will not be able.

[13]The Lord said these things about Moab before. [14]And now the Lord says, "In three years all those people and what they are proud of will be hated. (This is three years as a hired helper would count time.) There will be a few people left, but they will be weak."

God's Message to Aram

17 This is the message for Damascus:

"The city of Damascus will be
    destroyed.
Only ruins will be left there.
[2]People will leave the cities of
    Aroer.
Flocks of sheep will wander
    freely in those empty towns.
There will be no one to bother
    them.
[3]The strong, walled cities of Israel
    will be destroyed.
The government in Damascus
    will end.
Those left alive of Aram will be
like the glory of Israel," says
    the Lord of heaven's armies.

[4]"At that time Israel's wealth will
    all be gone.
Israel will be like a man who has
    lost much weight from
    sickness.
[5]That time will be like the grain
    harvest in the Valley of
    Rephaim.
The workers cut the wheat.
Then they cut the heads of grain
    from the plants.
And they collect the grain.
[6]That time will also be like the
    olive harvest,
when a few olives are left.
Two or three olives are left in the
    top branches.
Four or five olives are left on
    full branches," says the
    Lord, the God of Israel.

[7]At that time people will look to
    God, their Maker.

Their eyes will see the Holy
    One of Israel.
[8]They will not trust the altars they
    have made.
They will not trust what their
    hands have made.
They will not respect the
    Asherah[d] idols
and altars they have made.

[9]In that day all their strong cities
will be empty. They will be like the
cities that the Hivites and the Amorites left. They left their cities when
the Israelites came to take the land.
Everything will be ruined.

[10]You have forgotten the God who
    saves you.
You have not remembered that
    God is your place of safety.
You plant the finest grapevines.
You plant grapevines from
    faraway places.
[11]You will plant your grapevines one
    day and try to make them
    grow.
The next day they will begin to
    grow.
But at harvest time everything
    will be dead.
A sickness will kill all the plants.

[12]Listen to the many people!
They are crying loud like the
    noise from the sea.
Listen to the noise!
The crying is like the crashing of
    great waves.
[13]The people roar like those waves.
But when God speaks harshly to
    them, they will run away.
They will be like chaff[d] on the hills
    being blown by the wind.
They will be like tumbleweeds
    blown away by a storm.
[14]At night the people will be very
    frightened.
Before morning, no one will be
    left.
So our enemies will come to our
    land,

but they will become nothing.

God's Message to Cush

18 How terrible it will be for the land beyond the rivers of Cush.

It is filled with the sound of wings.
2That land sends people across the sea.
They go on the water in boats made of reeds.

Quick messengers, go
to the people who are tall and smooth-skinned.
They are feared everywhere.
They are a powerful nation with strange speech.
They defeat the other nations.
Their land is divided by rivers.

3All you people of the world, look!
Everyone who lives in the world, look!
You will see a banner raised on a mountain.
You will hear a trumpet sound.
4The Lord said to me,
"I will quietly watch from where I live.
I will be like heat in the sunshine.
I will be like the dew in the heat of harvest time."
5The time will be after the flowers have bloomed and before the harvest.
The new grapes will be budding and growing.
Then the enemy will cut the plants with knives.
He will cut down the vines and take them away.
6They will be left for the birds of the mountains to eat.
They will be left for the wild animals to eat.
Birds will feed on them all summer.
And that winter wild animals will eat them."

7At that time gifts will be brought to the Lord of heaven's armies.
They will come from the people who are tall and smooth-skinned.
They are feared everywhere.
They are a powerful nation with strange speech.
Their land is divided by rivers.
These gifts will be brought to the place of the Lord of heaven's armies.
They will be brought to Mount Zion.d

God's Message to Egypt

19 The message about Egypt:
Look, the Lord is coming on a fast cloud.
He will enter Egypt.
And the idols of Egypt will tremble before him.
Egypt's courage will melt away.

2The Lord says, "I will cause the Egyptians to fight against themselves.
Men will fight with their brothers.
Neighbours will fight neighbours.
Cities will fight cities.
Kingdoms will fight kingdoms.
3The Egyptians will be afraid.
I will ruin their plans.
They will ask their idols and spirits of the dead what they should do.
They will ask their mediumsd and fortune-tellers."
4The Master, the Lord of heaven's armies, says,
"I will give Egypt to a hard master.
A powerful king will rule over them."

5The sea will become dry.
The water will disappear from the Nile River.
6The canals will stink.

The streams of Egypt will
  decrease and dry up.
All the water plants will rot.
7 All the plants along the banks of
    the Nile will die.
  Even the planted fields by the Nile
    will dry up, blow away and
    disappear.
8The fishermen, all those who
    catch fish from the Nile,
  will groan and cry.
  Those who depend on the Nile for
    food will be sad.
9All the people who make cloth
    from flax will be sad.
  Those who weave linen will lose
    hope.
10Those who weave cloth will be
    broken.
  All those who work for money
    will be sad.

11The officers of the city of Zoan
    are fools.
  The wise men who advise the
    king of Egypt give wrong
    advice.
  How can they say to him they are
    wise?
  How can they say they are from
    the old family of the kings?
12Egypt, where are your wise men?
  Let them show you
  what the Lord of heaven's armies
    has planned for Egypt.
13The officers of Zoan have been
    fooled.
  The leaders of Memphis have
    believed false things.
  So the leaders of Egypt
    lead her the wrong way.
14The Lord has made the leaders
    confused.
  They wander and lead Egypt in
    the wrong ways.
  They are like drunk people
    stumbling in their own
    vomit.
15There is nothing Egypt can do.
  No one in Egypt can help.

16In that day the people of Egypt
will be like frightened women. They
will be afraid of the Lord of heaven's
armies. He will raise his hand to strike
them down. 17The land of Judah will
bring fear to the people in Egypt. Anyone in Egypt who hears the name Judah will be afraid. This will happen
because the Lord of heaven's armies
has planned terrible things for Egypt.
18At that time five cities in Egypt will
speak Hebrew, the language of Canaan. They will promise to be loyal to
the Lord of heaven's armies. One of
these cities will be named the City of
Destruction. 19At that time there will
be an altar for the Lord in the middle
of Egypt. At the border of Egypt
there will be a monument to the Lord.
20This will be a sign. It will show that
the Lord of heaven's armies is powerful. When the people cry to the Lord
for help, he will send help. He will
send someone to save and defend the
people. He will rescue them from
those who hurt them.

21So the Lord will show himself to
the Egyptians. Then they will say he
is the Lord. They will serve God and
offer many sacrifices. They will make
promises to the Lord, and they will
keep them. 22The Lord will punish the
Egyptians. Then he will heal them.
They will come back to the Lord. He
will listen to their prayers and heal
them.

23At that time there will be a highway from Egypt to Assyria. Then
people from Assyria will go to Egypt.
And the Egyptians will go to Assyria.
The Egyptians and Assyrians will
worship God together. 24At that time
Israel, Assyria and Egypt will join together. This will be a blessing for the
earth. 25The Lord of heaven's armies
will bless them. He will say, "Egypt,
you are my people. Assyria, I made
you. Israel, I own you. You are all
blessed!"

Assyria Will Defeat Egypt and Cush

20 Sargon was the king of Assyria. He sent a military commander to Ashdod to attack that city. So the commander attacked and captured it. ²Then the Lord spoke through Isaiah son of Amoz. The Lord said, "Take the rough cloth off your body. Take your sandals off your feet." So Isaiah obeyed the Lord. He walked around without his clothes of rough cloth or his sandals.

³Then the Lord said, "Isaiah my servant has walked around without his clothes of rough cloth or his sandals for three years. This is a sign for Egypt and Cush. ⁴The king of Assyria will defeat Egypt and Cush. Assyria will take prisoners and lead them away from their countries. The old people and young people will be led away naked. They will go without clothes and without sandals. So the Egyptians will be shamed. ⁵People who looked to Cush for help will be afraid. People who were amazed by Egypt's glory will be shamed. ⁶Those people who live near the sea will say, 'We trusted those countries to help us. We ran to them so they would save us from the king of Assyria. But look at them. They have been captured. So how will we be able to escape?' "

God's Message to Babylon

21 The message about the Desert by the Sea:*

Disaster is coming from the
    desert.
It is coming like wind blowing in
    the south.
It is coming from a terrible
    country.
²I have seen a terrible vision.

I see traitors turning against
    you.
I see people stealing your wealth.

Elam, attack the people!
Media, surround the city and
    attack it!
I will bring an end to the pain
    the city causes.

³I saw those terrible things, and
    now I am in pain.
My pains are like the pains of
    giving birth.
What I hear makes me very
    afraid.
What I see causes me to shake
    with fear.
⁴I am worried,
    and I am shaking with fear.
My pleasant evening
    has become a night of fear.

⁵They set the table.
    They spread the rugs.
    They eat and drink!
Leaders, stand up.
    Prepare the shields for battle!

⁶The Lord said to me,
"Go. Have a man be a lookout for
    the city.
Have him report what he sees.
⁷If he sees chariots and teams of
    horses,
    donkeys or camels,
he should pay very close
    attention."

⁸Then the lookout called out,
"My Master, each day I stand in
    the watchtower watching.
Every night I have been on
    guard.
⁹Look. I see a man coming in a
    chariot
    with a team of horses."
The man gives back the answer,
"Babylon has fallen. It has fallen!
All the statues of her gods
    lie broken on the ground."

Desert by the Sea Probably Babylon.

¹⁰My people are crushed like grain
    on the threshing^d floor.
My people, I tell you what I
    have heard from the Lord.
He is the Lord of heaven's
    armies,
    the God of Israel.

God's Message to Edom

¹¹The message about Dumah:ⁿ
Someone calls to me from Edom.
He says, "Watchman, how much
    of the night is left?
Watchman, how much longer
    will it be night?"
¹²The watchman answered,
    "Morning is coming, but then
    night will come again.
If you have something to ask,
    then come back and ask."

God's Message to Arabia

¹³The message about Arabia:
A group of traders from Dedan
    spent the night near some trees
    in Arabia.
¹⁴   They gave water to thirsty
    travellers.
The people of Tema gave food
    to those who were escaping.
¹⁵They were running from swords.
    The swords were ready to kill.
They were running from bows
    ready to shoot.
They were running from a hard
    battle.

¹⁶This is what the Lord said to me:
"In one year all the glory of the country of Kedar will be gone. (This is a
year as a hired helper counts time.)
¹⁷At that time only a few of the ar-
chers will be left. Only a few of the
soldiers of Kedar will be left alive."
The Lord, the God of Israel, has spoken.

God's Message to Jerusalem

22 The message about the Valley
    of Vision:ⁿ
What is wrong with you people?
    Why are you on your roofs?ⁿ
²This city was a very busy city.
    It was full of noise and wild
    parties.
But your people have been killed,
    but not with swords.
    They did not die in battle.
³All your leaders ran away
    together.
But they all have been captured
    without using a bow.
All you who were captured
    tried to run away before the
    enemy came near.
⁴So I say, "Don't look at me.
    Let me cry loudly.
Don't hurry to comfort me
    about the destruction of
    Jerusalem."
⁵The Master, the Lord of heaven's
    armies, has chosen a special
    day.
There will be riots and
    confusion.
People will trample each other in
    the Valley of Vision.
The city walls will be knocked
    down.
The people will cry out to the
    mountain.
⁶The soldiers from Elam will take
    their bags of arrows.
Men in chariots and on horses
    will attack.
Kir will prepare their shields.
⁷Your nicest valleys will be filled
    with chariots.
Horsemen will be ordered to
    guard the gates of the city.
⁸   The walls protecting Judah will
    fall.

Dumah Another name for Edom.
Valley of Vision This probably means a valley near Jerusalem.
roofs In Bible times houses were built with flat roofs. The roof was used for drying things
    such as flax and fruit. It was also used as an extra room, as a place for worship and as a
    place to sleep in the summer.

At that time the people of
Jerusalem depended on
the weapons kept at the Palace
of the Forest.
9You saw that the walls of
Jerusalem
had many cracks that needed
repairing.
You stored up water in the
lower pool.
10You counted the houses of
Jerusalem.
You tore them down to mend
the walls with their stones.
11You made a pool between the two
walls.
It was to save water from the
old pool.
But you did not trust the God who
made these things.
You did not respect the One
who planned them long ago.

12The Master, the Lord of heaven's
armies, told the people
to cry and be sad.
He told them to shave their
heads and wear rough cloth.
13But look. The people are happy.
There are wild parties.
They kill the cattle and the sheep.
They eat the food and drink the
wine.
They say, "Let us eat and drink,
because tomorrow we will die."

14The Lord of heaven's armies said
to me: "You people will die before this
guilt is forgiven." The Master, the
Lord of heaven's armies, said this.

God's Message to Shebna

15This is what the Master, the Lord
of heaven's armies, says:
"Go to this servant Shebna.
He is the manager of the palace.
16Say to him, 'What are you doing
here?
Who said you could cut out a
tomb for yourself here?
Why are you preparing your tomb
in a high place?

Why are you carving out a tomb
from the rock?
17Look, mighty man! The Lord will
throw you away.
He will take firm hold of you.
18He will roll you tightly into a ball
and throw you into another
country.
There you will die.
Your fine chariots will remain
there.
You are a disgrace to your
master's house.
19I will force you out of your
important job here.
You will be thrown down from
your important place'.

20"At that time I will call for my servant Eliakim son of Hilkiah. 21I will
take your robe and put it on him. I will
give him your belt. I will give him the
important job you have. He will be like
a father to the people of Jerusalem and
the family of Judah. 22I will put the key
to the house of David around his neck.
If he opens a door, no one will be able
to close it. If he closes a door, no one
will be able to open it. 23He will be like
an honoured chair in his father's
house. I will make him strong like a
peg that is hammered into a strong
board. 24All the honoured and important things of his family will depend on
him. All the adults and little children
will depend on him. They will be like
bowls and jars hanging on him.

25"At that time," says the Lord of
heaven's armies, "the peg hammered
into the strong board will weaken. It
will break and fall. And everything
hanging on it will be destroyed." The
Lord says this.

God's Message to Lebanon

23 The message about Tyre:
You ships of Tarshish, cry!
The houses and harbour of Tyre
are destroyed.
This news came to the ships
from the land of Cyprus.

²Be silent, you who live on the
island of Tyre.
You merchants of Sidon, be
silent.
Seamen have made you rich.
³They travelled the sea to bring
grain from Egypt.
The men of Tyre brought grain
from the Nile Valley
and sold it to other nations.

⁴Sidon, be ashamed.
Strong city of the sea, be
ashamed. The sea says:
"I have not felt the pain of giving
birth.
I have not reared young men or
women."
⁵Egypt will hear the news about
Tyre.
And it will make Egypt hurt with
sorrow.

⁶You ships should return to
Tarshish.
You people living near the sea
should be sad.
⁷Look at your once happy city!
Look at your old, old city!
People from that city have
travelled
far away to live.
⁸Who planned Tyre's destruction?
Tyre made others rich.
Her merchants were treated like
princes.
Her traders were greatly
respected.
⁹It was the Lord of heaven's
armies who planned this!
He decided to make these proud
men unimportant.
He decided to disgrace those
who were greatly respected.
¹⁰Go through your land,
Tarshish, like the Nile goes
through Egypt.
There is no harbour for you
now!
¹¹The Lord has stretched his hand
over the sea.
He makes its kingdoms tremble.

He commands that Canaan's
places of safety be destroyed.
¹²The Lord said, "Sidon, you will
not rejoice any longer.
You are destroyed.
Even if you cross the sea to
Cyprus,
you will not find a place to
rest."
¹³Look at the land of the
Babylonians.
Babylonia is not a country now.
Assyria has made it a place for
wild animals.
Assyria built towers to attack it.
The soldiers took all the treasures
from its cities.
They turned it into ruins.
¹⁴So be sad, you trading ships.
Your place of safety is
destroyed.

¹⁵At that time people will forget
about Tyre for 70 years. That is the
length of a king's life. After 70 years,
Tyre will be like the prostitute*d* in this
song:

¹⁶"Oh woman, you are forgotten.
Take your harp and walk
through the city.
Play your harp well. Sing your
song often.
Then people will remember
you."

¹⁷After 70 years the Lord will deal
with Tyre. Tyre will again have trade.
It will be like a prostitute for all the
nations of the earth. ¹⁸The profits will
be saved for the Lord. Tyre will not
keep the money she earns. She will
give it to the people who serve the
Lord. So they will have plenty of food
and nice clothes.

God Will Punish the World

24 Look! The Lord will destroy
the earth and leave it empty.
He will ruin the surface of the
land and scatter its people.
²At that time the same thing will
happen to everyone:

to common people and priests,
to slaves and masters,
to women slaves and their
    women masters,
to buyers and sellers,
to those who borrow and those
    who lend,
and to bankers and those who
    owe the bank.
³The earth will be completely
    empty.
The wealth will all be taken.
This will happen because the
    Lord commanded it.
⁴The earth will dry up and die.
The world will grow weak and
    die.
The great leaders in this land
    will become weak.
⁵The people of the earth have
    ruined it.
They do not follow God's
    teachings.
They do not obey God's laws.
They break their agreement
    with God that was to last for
    ever.
⁶A curse will destroy the earth.
The people of the world are
    guilty.
So they will be burned up.
Only a few will be left.
⁷The new wine will be bad, and the
    grapevines will die.
People who were happy will be
    sad.
⁸The happy music of the
    tambourines*d* will end.
The happy sounds of wild
    parties will stop.
The joyful music from the harps
    will end.
⁹People will no longer sing while
    they drink their wine.
The beer will taste bitter to
    those who drink it.
¹⁰The ruined city will be empty.
People will hide behind closed
    doors.
¹¹People in the streets will ask for
    wine.

But joy will have turned to
    sadness.
All the happiness will have left.
¹²The city will be left in ruins.
Its gates will be smashed to
    pieces.
¹³This is what will happen all over
    the earth.
This will happen to all the
    nations.
The earth will be like an olive tree
    after the harvest.
It will be like the few grapes left
    on a vine after harvest.
¹⁴The people shout for joy.
From the west they praise the
    greatness of the Lord.
¹⁵People in the east, praise the
    Lord.
People in the islands of the sea,
praise the name of the Lord, the
    God of Israel.
¹⁶We hear songs from every part of
    the earth.
These songs praise God, the
    Righteous One.

But I said, "I am dying! I am
    dying!
How terrible it will be for me!
Traitors turn against people.
With their dishonesty, they turn
    against people."
¹⁷There are terrors, holes and traps
    for the people of the earth.
¹⁸Anyone who tries to escape from
    the sound of terror
will fall into a hole.
Anyone who climbs out of the hole
will be caught in a trap.
The clouds in the sky will pour
    out rain.
The foundations of the earth will
    shake.
¹⁹The earth will be broken up.
And the earth will split open.
The earth will shake violently.
²⁰The earth will stumble around like
    a man who is drunk.
It will shake like a hut in a
    storm.

Its sin is like a heavy weight on
its back.
The earth will fall and never rise
again.

21At that time the Lord will punish
the powers in the sky above
and the rulers on earth below.
22They will be gathered together.
They will be thrown into a pit as
prisoners.
They will be shut up in prison.
After much time they will be
punished.
23The moon will be embarrassed.
The sun will be ashamed.
This will happen because the Lord
of heaven's armies will rule
as king
on Mount Zion*d* in Jerusalem.
Jerusalem's leaders will see his
greatness.

A Song of Praise to God

25 Lord, you are my God.
I honour you and praise you.
You have done amazing things.
You have always done what you
said you would.
You have done what you planned
long ago.
2You have made the city a pile of
rocks.
You have destroyed her walls.
The city our enemies built with
strong walls is gone.
It will never be built again.
3People from powerful nations will
honour you.
Cruel people from strong cities
will fear you.
4You help the poor people.
You help the helpless when they
are in danger.
You are like a shelter from
storms.
You are like shade that protects
them from the heat.
The cruel people attack
like a rainstorm beating against
the wall.

5 The cruel people burn like the
heat in the desert.
But you, God, stop their violent
attack.
As a cloud cools a hot day,
Lord, you silence the songs of
those who have no mercy.

God's Banquet for His Servants

6The Lord of heaven's armies will
give a feast.
It will be on this mountain for all
people.
It will be a feast with the best
food and wine.
The meat and wine will be the
finest.
7On this mountain God will destroy
the veil that covers all nations.
This veil, called "death", covers
all peoples.
8But God will destroy death for
ever.
The Lord God will wipe away
every tear from every face.
God will take away the shame
of his people from the earth.
The Lord has spoken.

9At that time people will say,
"Our God is doing this!
We have trusted in him, and he
has come to save us.
We have been trusting our
Lord.
So we will rejoice and be happy
when he saves us."
10The Lord will protect Jerusalem.
But the Lord will crush our
enemy Moab.
Moab will be like straw that is
trampled down in the
manure.
11They will spread their arms in it
like a person who is swimming.
The Lord will bring down their
pride.
All the clever things they have
made will mean nothing.
12Moab's high walls protect them.

But the Lord will destroy these
    walls.
The Lord will throw them down
    on the ground.
The stones will lie in the dust.

A Song of Praise to God

26 At that time people will sing
    this song in Judah:
We have a strong city.
    God protects us with its strong
        walls and defences.
2Open the gates,
    and the good people will enter.
    They follow God's good way of
        living.
3You, Lord, give true peace.
    You give peace to those who
        depend on you.
    You give peace to those who
        trust you.
4So, trust the Lord always.
    Trust the Lord because he is
        our Rock[d] for ever.
5But the Lord will destroy the
    proud city.
    And he will punish the people
        living there.
    He will bring that high city down
        to the ground.
    He throws it down into the dust.
6Then those who were hurt by the
    city will walk on its ruins.
    Those who were made poor by
        the city will trample it under
        their feet.

7The path of life of the people who
    are right with God is level.
    Lord, you make the way of life
        smooth for those people.
8But, Lord, we are waiting
    for your way of justice.
Our souls want to remember
    you and your name.
9My soul wants to be with you at
    night.
    And my spirit wants to be with
        you at the dawn of every
        day.

When your way of justice comes
    to the land,
    people of the world will learn
        the right way of living.
10An evil person will not learn to do
    good
    even if you show him kindness.
He will continue doing evil, even if
    he lives in a good world.
He never sees the Lord's
    greatness.
11Lord, you are ready to punish
    those people.
    But they do not see that.
Lord, show them your strong love
    for your people.
    Then the evil people will be
        ashamed.
Burn them in the fire
    you have prepared for your
        enemies.
12Lord, all our success is because of
    what you have done.
    So give us peace.
13Lord, our God, other masters
    besides you have ruled us.
    But we honour only you.
14Those masters are now dead.
    Their ghosts will not rise from
        death.
You decided to destroy them.
    And you destroyed any memory
        of them.
15Lord, you multiplied the number
    of your people.
    You multiplied them and brought
        honour to yourself.
You made the borders of the land
    wide.
16Lord, people remember you when
    they are in trouble.
    They say quiet prayers to you
        when you punish them.
17Lord, when we are with you,
    we are like a woman giving birth
        to a baby.
    She cries and has pain from the
        birth.
18In the same way, we had pain.
    We gave birth, but only to wind.

We don't bring salvation to the
land.
We don't make new people for
the world.
19Your people have died, but they
will live again.
Their bodies will rise from
death.
Dead people in the ground,
get up and be happy!
The dew covering you is like the
dew of a new day.
The ground will give birth to the
dead buried in it.

Judgement: Reward or Punishment

20My people, go into your rooms.
Shut your doors behind you.
Hide in your rooms for a short
time.
Hide until God's anger is
finished.
21The Lord will leave his place.
He will punish the people of the
world for their sins.
The earth will show the blood of
the people who have been
killed.
It will not cover the dead any
longer.

27 At that time the Lord will
judge Leviathan,d the gliding
snake.
He will punish Leviathan, the
coiled snake.
The Lord will use his great
sword,
his hard and powerful sword.
He will kill the monster in the sea.

2In that day
people will sing about the
pleasant vineyard.
3"I, the Lord, will care for that
vineyard.
I will water it at the right time.
No one will hurt it.
I will guard it day and night.
4I am not angry.

If anyone builds a wall of
thornbushes in war,
I will march to it and burn it.
5But if anyone comes to me for
safety
and wants to make peace with
me,
he should come and make peace
with me."
6In the days to come, the people of
Jacob will be like a plant with
good roots.
Israel will grow like a plant
beginning to bloom.
Then the world will be filled
with their children.

God "Divorces" Israel

7The Lord has not hurt his people
as he hurt their enemies.
His people have not been killed
like those who tried to kill
them.
8The Lord will settle his argument
with Israel by sending it far
away.
Like a hot desert wind, he will
drive Israel away.
9This is how Israel's guilt will be
forgiven.
This is how its sins will be taken
away.
Israel will crush the rocks of the
altar to dust.
No statues or altars will be left
standing for the Asherahd
idols.
10At that time the strong, walled
city will be empty.
It will be like a desert.
Calves will eat grass there.
They will lie down there.
They will eat leaves from the
branches.
11The limbs will become dry and
break off.
Women will use them for
firewood.
The people refuse to understand.
So God will not comfort them.

Their Maker will not be kind to
them.

¹²At that time the Lord will begin
gathering his people one by one. He
will gather all his people from the Euphrates River to the brook of Egypt.
He will separate them from others as
grain is separated from chaff.^d ¹³Many
of my people are now lost in Assyria.
Some of my people have run away to
Egypt. But at that time a great trumpet will be blown. And all those people
will come back to Jerusalem. They will
bow down before the Lord on that
holy mountain.

Warnings to North Israel

28 How terrible it will be for
Samaria, the pride of Israel's
drunken people!
That beautiful crown of flowers
is just a dying plant.
It sits on a hill above a rich valley
where drunkards live.
²Look, the Lord has someone who
is strong and full of power.
That person will come like a
storm of hail and strong
wind.
He will come like a sudden flood
of water pouring over the
country.
He will throw Samaria down to
the ground.
³That city, the pride of Israel's
drunken people,
will be trampled underfoot.
⁴That beautiful crown of flowers is
just a dying plant.
It sits on a hill above a rich
valley.
That city will be like the first fig
of summer.
When a person sees it,
he quickly picks it and eats it.

⁵At that time the Lord of heaven's
armies
will be like a beautiful crown.
He will be like a wonderful crown
of flowers

for his people who are left alive.
⁶Then the Lord will give wisdom
to the judges who rule his
people.
The Lord will give strength
to those who battle at the city
gate.
⁷But now those leaders are drunk
with wine.
They stumble from drinking too
much beer.
The priests and prophets^d are
drunk with beer.
They are filled with wine.
They stumble from too much
beer.
The prophets are drunk when
they see their visions.
The judges stumble when they
make their decisions.
⁸Every table is covered with vomit.
There is not a clean place
anywhere.

⁹The Lord is trying to teach the
people a lesson.
He is trying to make them
understand his teachings.
But the people are like little
babies.
They are like babies who just
nursed at their mother's
breast.
¹⁰So they make fun of the Lord's
prophet and say:
"A command here, a command
there.
A rule here, a rule there.
A lesson here, a lesson there."
¹¹So the Lord will use strange
words and foreign languages
to speak to these people.
¹²God said to them,
"Here is a place of rest.
Let the tired people come and
rest.
This is the place of peace."
But the people would not listen.
¹³So the words of the Lord will be,
"A command here, a command
there.

A rule here, a rule there.
A lesson here, a lesson there."
They will fall back and will be
    defeated.
They will be trapped and
    captured.

14You who boast should listen to the
    Lord's message.
Pay attention, you leaders in
    Jerusalem.
15You say, "We have made an
    agreement with death.
We have a contract with death.
When punishment passes by,
    it won't hurt us.
We will be safe with our lies.
We will hide behind our tricks."

16Because of these things, this is
what the Lord God says:
"I will put a stone in the ground in
    Jerusalem.
This will be a tested stone.
Everything will be built on this
    important and precious rock.
Anyone who trusts in it will
    never be disappointed.
17I will use justice as a measuring
    line.
I will use goodness to measure
    by.
The lies you hide behind will be
    destroyed as if by hail.
They will be washed away as if
    in a flood.
18Your agreement with death will be
    erased.
Your contract with death will not
    help you.
When punishment comes,
    you will be crushed by it.
19Whenever punishment comes, it
    will take you away.
It will come morning after
    morning.
It will defeat you by day and by
    night.
Those who hear of this
    punishment will be terrified."
20You will be like the man who tried
    to sleep

on a bed that was too short for
    him.
And his blanket was too narrow
    to wrap around himself.
21The Lord will fight as he did at
    Mount Perazim.
He will be angry as he was in
    the Valley of Gibeon.
Then the Lord will do his work,
    his strange work.
He will finish his job, his strange
    job.
22Now, you must not make fun of
    these things.
If you do, the ropes around you
    will become tighter.
The Lord of heaven's armies has
    told me these things.
He has told me how the whole
    earth will be destroyed.

The Lord Punishes Fairly

23Listen closely to what I tell you.
Listen carefully to what I say.
24A farmer does not plough his field
    all the time.
He does not go on working the
    soil.
25He prepares the ground.
Then he plants the dill seed and
    scatters the cumin seed.
He plants the wheat in rows.
He plants barley in its special
    place,
and other wheat in its own field.
26His God teaches him
    and shows him the right way.
27A farmer doesn't use heavy
    boards to crush dill.
He doesn't use a wagon to crush
    cumin.
He uses a small stick to break
    open the dill.
With a stick he opens the cumin.
28The grain is ground to make
    bread.
People do not ruin it by crushing
    it for ever.
The farmer separates the wheat
    from the chaff[d] with his
    cart.

But he does not let his horses
  grind it.
²⁹This lesson comes from the Lord
  of heaven's armies.
He gives wonderful advice. He
  is very wise.

Warnings to Jerusalem

29 How terrible it will be for
  you, Jerusalem.
You are the city where David
  camped.
Her festivals have continued
  year after year.
²I will attack Jerusalem.
That city will be filled with
  sadness and crying.
It will be like an altar to me.
³I will put armies all around you,
  Jerusalem.
I will surround you with towers.
I will build devices around you
  to attack you.
⁴You will be pulled down and will
  speak from the ground.
I will hear your voice rising from
  the ground.
It will sound like the voice of a
  ghost.
Your words will come like a
  whisper from the dust.
⁵Your many enemies will become
  like fine dust.
The groups of cruel people will
  be like chaff*ᵈ* that is blown
  away.
Everything will happen very
  quickly.
6   The Lord of heaven's armies will
  come.
He will come with thunder,
  earthquakes and great
  noises.
He will come with storms,
  strong winds and a fire that
  destroys.
⁷Then all the nations that fight
  against Jerusalem
will be like a dream.

All the nations that surround and
  attack her
will be like a vision in the night.
⁸They will be like a hungry man
  who dreams he is eating.
But when he wakes up, he is
  still hungry.
They will be like a thirsty man
  who dreams he is drinking.
But when he wakes up, he is
  still weak and thirsty.
It will be the same way with all
  the nations
who fight against Mount Zion.*ᵈ*

⁹Be surprised and amazed.
Blind yourselves so that you
  cannot see.
Become drunk, but not from wine.
Trip and fall, but not from beer.
¹⁰The Lord has made you go into a
  deep sleep.
He has closed your eyes. (The
  prophets are your eyes.)
He has covered your heads.
  (The seers*ᵈ* are your heads.)

¹¹This vision is like the words of a
book that is closed and sealed. You
may give the book to someone who
can read. And you may tell that person
to read it. But he will say, "I can't read
the book. It is closed, and I can't open
it." ¹²Or you may give the book to
someone who cannot read. You may
tell him to read the book. But he will
say, "I can't read it because I don't
know how to read."

¹³The Lord says:
"These people say they love me.
They show honour to me with
  words.
But their hearts are far from
  me.
The honour they show me
  is nothing but human rules they
  have memorised.
¹⁴So I will continue to amaze these
  people
  by doing more and more
  miracles.*ᵈ*

Their wise men will lose their
    wisdom.
Their wise men will not be able
    to understand."

Warnings About Other Nations

15How terrible it will be for those
    who try
    to hide things from the Lord.
How terrible it will be for those
    who do their work in
    darkness.
They think no one will see them
    or know what they do.
16You are confused.
    You think the clay is equal to
    the potter.
You think that an object can tell
    the person who made it,
    "You didn't make me."
This is like a pot telling its maker,
    "You don't know anything."

A Better Time Is Coming

17In a very short time, Lebanon will
    become rich farmland.
And the rich farmland will seem
    like a forest.
18At that time the deaf will hear the
    words in a book.
Instead of having darkness and
    gloom, the blind will see.
19The Lord will make the poor
    people happy.
They will rejoice in the Holy
    One of Israel.
20Then the people without mercy
    will come to an end.
Those who do not respect God
    will disappear.
Those who enjoy doing evil will
    be gone.
21Those who lie about others in
    court will be gone.
Those who trap people in court
    will be gone.
Those who lie and take justice
    from innocent people in
    court will be gone.

22The Lord set Abraham free. This
Lord speaks to the family of Jacob.
"Now the people of Jacob will not
    be ashamed.
They will not be disgraced any
    longer.
23They will see all their children,
    the children I made with my
    hands.
And they will say my name is
    holy.
The people will agree that the
    Holy One of Jacob is holy.
They will respect the God of
    Israel.
24People who do wrong will now
    understand.
Those who complain will accept
    being taught."

Warnings to the Stubborn Nation

30 The Lord said,
    "How terrible it will be for
    these stubborn children.
They make plans, but they don't
    ask me to help them.
They make agreements with
    other nations, without asking
    my Spirit.d
They are adding more and more
    sins to themselves.
2They go down to Egypt for help,
    but they didn't ask me about it
    first.
They hope they will be saved by
    the king of Egypt.
They want Egypt to protect
    them.
3But hiding in Egypt will bring you
    only shame.
Egypt's protection will only
    disappoint you.
4Your officers have gone to Zoan.
    Your messengers have gone to
    Hanes.
5But they will be put to shame,
    because Egypt is useless to
    them.
Egypt will give no help and be of
    no use.

It will cause them only shame
and embarrassment."

God's Message to Judah

⁶This is the message about the animals in southern Judah:
Southern Judah is a dangerous
place.
It is full of lions and lionesses,
poisonous snakes and darting
snakes.
The messengers travel through
there with their wealth on
donkeys' backs.
They have put their treasure on
the backs of camels.
They carry them to a nation that
cannot help them.
⁷ They go to Egypt whose help is
useless.
So I call that country Rahab*d* the
Do-Nothing.

⁸Now write this on a sign for the
people.
Write this on a scroll.
Write these things for the days to
come.
Write them so they will last for
ever.
⁹These people are like children
who lie and refuse to obey.
They refuse to listen to the
Lord's teachings.
¹⁰They tell the seers,*d*
"Don't see any more visions!"
They say to the prophets,*d*
"Don't tell us the truth!
Say things that will make us feel
good.
See only good things for us.
¹¹Stop blocking our path.
Get out of our way.
Stop telling us
about God, the Holy One of
Israel."

¹²So this is what the Holy One of Israel says:
"You people have refused to
accept this message from
the Lord.

You depended on cruelty and
lies to help you.
¹³You are guilty of these things.
So you are like a high wall with
cracks in it.
It will fall suddenly and break
into small pieces.
¹⁴You will be like a clay jar that
breaks.
It breaks into many pieces.
Those pieces will be too small
to take coals from the fire
or to get water from a well."

¹⁵This is what the Lord God, the
Holy One of Israel, says:
"If you come back to me and trust
me, you will be saved.
If you will be calm and trust me,
you will be strong."
But you don't want to do that.
¹⁶You say, "No, we need horses to
run away on."
So you will run away on horses.
You say, "We will ride away on
fast horses."
So those who chase you will be
fast.
¹⁷One enemy will make threats,
and 1,000 of your men will run
away.
Five enemies will make threats,
and all of you will run from
them.
You will be left alone like a
flagpole on a hilltop.
You will be like a banner on a
hill.
¹⁸The Lord wants to show his
mercy to you.
He wants to rise and comfort
you.
The Lord is a fair God.
And everyone who waits for his
help will be happy.

God Will Help His People

¹⁹You people who live on Mount
Zion*d* in Jerusalem will not cry any
more. The Lord will hear your crying,
and he will comfort you. The Lord will

hear you, and he will help you. [20]The Lord has given you sorrow and hurt. It was like the bread and water you ate every day. But he is your teacher, and he will not continue to hide from you. You will see your teacher with your own eyes. [21]If you go the wrong way—to the right or to the left—you will hear a voice behind you. It will say, "This is the right way. You should go this way." [22]You have statues covered with silver and gold. But you will ruin them for further use. You will throw them away like filthy rags. You will say, "Go away!"

[23]At that time the Lord will send rain for you. You will plant seeds in the ground, and the ground will grow food for you. The harvest will be very great. You will have plenty of food in the fields for your animals. There will be large fields for your sheep. [24]Your oxen and donkeys will work the soil. They will have all the food they need. You will have to use shovels and pitchforks to spread all the food for your animals to eat. [25]Every mountain and hill will have streams filled with water. These things will happen after many people are killed and the towers are pulled down. [26]At that time the light from the moon will be bright like the sun. The light from the sun will be seven times brighter than now. The light from the sun in one day will be like a full week. These things will happen when the Lord bandages his broken people and heals the hurts he gave them.

[27]Look! The Lord comes from far
    away.
  His anger is like a fire with thick
      clouds of smoke.
  His mouth is filled with anger,
    and his tongue is like a burning
      fire.

[28]The Lord's breath is like a rushing
      river.
  It rises until it reaches the
      throat.
  He will judge the nations as if he
      is sifting them through the
      strainer of destruction.
  He will place in their mouths a
      bit that will lead them the
      wrong way.
[29]You will sing happy songs
    as on the nights you begin a
      festival.
  You will be happy as people
      listening to flutes
    as they go to the mountain of
      the Lord.
  The Lord is the Rock[d] of Israel.
[30]The Lord will cause all people to
      hear his great voice.
  He will cause them to see his
      powerful arm come down.
  It will come with anger like a
      great fire that burns
      everything.
  It will be like a great storm with
      heavy rain and hail.
[31]Assyria will be afraid when it
      hears the voice of the Lord.
  The Lord will beat Assyria with
      a rod.
[32]The Lord will punish Assyria with
      a rod.
  He will beat them to the music
      of tambourines[d] and harps.
  The Lord will fight against them
      with his mighty weapons.
[33]Topheth[n] has been made ready
      for a long time.
  It is ready for the king.
  It was made deep and wide.
  There is a lot of wood and
      fire there.
  And the Lord's breath will come
      like a stream of burning sulphur
      and burn it.

Topheth Gehenna; the Valley of Hinnom. Here people burned the bodies of criminals and animals, along with rubbish.

Warnings About Relying on Egypt

31 How terrible it will be for those people who go down to Egypt for help.
They think horses will save them.
They think their many chariots and strong horsemen will save them.
They don't trust God, the Holy One of Israel.
They don't ask the Lord for help.
²But it is the Lord who is wise and who can bring them trouble.
He does not change his warnings.
He will rise up and fight against the evil people.
And he will fight against those who try to help evil people.
³The Egyptians are only people and are not God.
Their horses are only animals and are not spirit.
The Lord will stretch out his arm, and the one who helps will stumble.
The people who wanted help will fall.
All of them will be destroyed together.

⁴The Lord says this to me:
"When a lion or a lion's cub kills an animal to eat,
it stands over the dead animal and roars.
A band of shepherds may be assembled against it.
But the lion will not be afraid of their yelling.
It will not be upset by their noise.
So the Lord of heaven's armies will come down
to fight on Mount Zion^d and on its hill.
⁵The Lord of heaven's armies will defend Jerusalem.

He will defend it like birds flying over their nests.
He will defend and save it.
He will 'pass over' and save Jerusalem."

⁶You children of Israel, come back to the God that you fought against. ⁷The time is coming when each of you will stop worshipping the idols of gold and silver that you made. You truly sinned when you made them.

⁸"Assyria will be defeated by a sword, but not the sword of a man.
Assyria will be destroyed, but not by a man's sword.
Assyria will run away from the sword of God.
But their young men will be caught and made slaves.
⁹They will panic, and their place of safety will be destroyed.
Their commanders will be terrified when they see God's battle flag."
The Lord said all these things.
The Lord's fire is in Jerusalem.
His furnace is in Jerusalem.

A Good Kingdom Is Coming

32 A king will rule in a way that brings justice.
Leaders will make fair decisions.
²Then each ruler will be like a shelter from the wind.
He will be like a safe place in a storm.
He will be like streams of water in a dry land.
He will be like a cool shadow from a large rock in a hot land.

³People will look to the king for help.
And they will truly listen to what he says.
⁴People who are now worried will be able to understand.

Those who cannot speak clearly
now will then be able to
speak clearly and quickly.
5Fools will not be called great
men.
People will not respect wicked
men.
6A fool says foolish things.
And in his mind he plans to do
evil things.
A fool wants to do things that are
wrong.
He says wrong things about the
Lord.
A fool does not feed the hungry.
He does not let thirsty people
drink water.
7The wicked man uses evil like a
tool.
He plans ways to take
everything from poor people.
He destroys the poor with lies,
even when the poor man is in
the right.
8But a good leader plans good
things to do.
And those good things make him
a good leader.

Hard Times Are Coming

9You women who are calm now,
stand up and listen to me.
You women who feel safe now,
hear what I say.
10You women feel safe now,
but after one year you will be
afraid.
There will be no grape harvest.
There will not be any summer
fruit to gather.
11Women, you are calm now, but
you should shake with fear.
Women, you feel safe now, but
you should tremble.
Take off your nice clothes.
Then put rough cloth around
your waist to show your
sadness.
12Beat your breasts in grief because
the fields that were pleasant
are now empty.

Cry because the vines that once
had fruit now have no more
grapes.
13Cry for the land of my people.
Cry because only thorns and
weeds grow there now.
Cry for the city that once was
happy.
And cry for all the houses that
once were filled with joy.
14The palace will be empty.
People will leave the noisy city.
Strong cities and towers will be
empty.
Wild donkeys will love to live
there. Sheep will go there to
eat.

Things Will Get Better

15This will continue until God puts
his Spirit[d] from above into
us.
Then the desert will be like a
fertile field.
And the fertile field will be like a
forest.
16Justice will be found even in the
desert.
And fairness will be found in the
fertile fields.
17That fairness will bring peace.
And fairness will bring calm and
safety for ever.
18My people will live in peaceful
places.
They will have safe homes.
They will live in calm places of
rest.
19Hail will destroy the forest.
And the city will be completely
destroyed.
20But you will be happy as you plant
seeds near every stream.
You will let your cattle and
donkeys wander freely.

Warnings to Assyria and Promises to God's People

33 How terrible it will be for you
who destroy others.

But you have not been
destroyed yet.
How terrible it will be for you,
traitor.
But no one has turned against
you yet.
When you stop destroying,
others will destroy you.
When you stop turning against
others,
they will turn against you.

2Lord, be kind to us.
We have waited for your help.
Lord, give us strength every
morning.
Save us when we are in trouble.
3Your powerful voice makes people
run away in fear.
Your greatness causes the
nations to run away.
4Like locusts,d your enemies will
take away the things you
stole in war.
Like locusts rushing about, they
will take your wealth.
5The Lord is very great. He lives
in a high place.
He fills Jerusalem with fairness
and justice.
6The Lord will be your safety.
He is full of salvation, wisdom
and knowledge.
Respect for the Lord is the
greatest treasure.
7See, brave men are crying out in
the streets.
Those who tried to bring peace
are crying loudly.
8There is no one on the roads.
No one is walking in the paths.
People have broken the
agreements they made.
People refuse to believe the
proof from witnesses.
No one respects other people.
9The land is sick and dying.
Lebanon is ashamed and dying.
The Plain of Sharon is dry like the
desert.

The trees of Bashan and Carmel
are dying.
10The Lord says, "Now, I will stand
up
and show my greatness.
Now, I will become important to
the people.
11You people do useless things.
These things are like hay and
straw.
A destructive wind will burn you
like fire.
12People will be burned until their
bones become like lime.
They will burn quickly like dry
thornbushes."

13You people in faraway lands, hear
what I have done.
You people who are near me,
learn about my power.
14The sinners in Jerusalem are
afraid.
The people who are separated
from God shake with fear.
They say, "Can any of us live
through this fire that
destroys?
Who can live near this fire that
burns on and on?"
15A person might do what is right.
He might speak what is right.
He might refuse to take money
unfairly.
He might refuse to take money
to hurt others.
He might not listen to plans of
murder.
He might refuse to think about
evil.
16This is the kind of person who will
be safe.
He will be protected as he
would be in a high, walled
city.
He will always have bread,
and he will not run out of water.
17Your eyes will see the king in his
beauty.
You will see the land that
stretches far away.

18You will think about the terror of
the past.
You will think, "Where is that
officer?
Where is the one who collected
the taxes?
Where is the officer in charge of
our defence towers?"
19You will not see those proud
people from other countries
any more.
No more will you hear their
strange language
that you couldn't understand.

God Will Protect Jerusalem

20Look at Jerusalem, the city of our
festivals.
Look at Jerusalem, that beautiful
place of rest.
It is like a tent that will never be
moved.
The pegs that hold her in place
will never be moved.
Her ropes will never be broken.
21There the Lord will be our Mighty
One.
That land is a place with
streams and wide rivers.
But there will be no enemy boats
on those rivers.
No powerful ship will sail on
those rivers.
22This is because the Lord is our
judge.
The Lord makes our laws.
The Lord is our king.
He will save us.
23You sailors from other lands,
hear:
The ropes on your boats hang
loose.
The mast is not held firm.
The sails are not spread open.
The Lord will give us your wealth.
There will be so much wealth
even the crippled people will
carry off a share.
24No one living in Jerusalem will
say, "I am sick."

The people who live there will
have their sins forgiven.

God Will Punish His Enemies

34 All you nations, come near
and listen.
Pay attention, you peoples!
The earth and all the people in it
should listen.
The world and everything in it
should listen.
2The Lord is angry with all the
nations.
He is angry with their armies.
He will destroy them and kill them
all.
3Their bodies will be thrown
outside.
The stink will rise from the
bodies,
and the blood will flow down the
mountains.
4The sun, moon and stars will
dissolve.
The sky will be rolled up like a
scroll.
The stars will fall
like dead leaves from a vine
or dried-up figs from a fig tree.
5The Lord's sword in the sky is
covered with blood.
It will cut through Edom.
He will destroy these people as
an offering to the Lord.
6The Lord's sword will be covered
with blood.
It will be covered with fat.
It is the blood from lambs and
goats.
It is the fat from the kidneys of
male sheep.
This is because the Lord decided
there will be a sacrifice in
Bozrah.
He has decided there will be
much killing in Edom.
7The oxen will be killed.
And the cattle and the strong
bulls will be killed.
The land will be filled with their
blood.

The earth will be covered with
their fat.

[8]The Lord has chosen a time for
punishment.
He has chosen a year when
people must pay for the
wrongs they did to
Jerusalem.
[9]Edom's rivers will be like hot tar.
The soil of Edom will be like
burning sulphur.
The land of Edom will be like
burning tar.
[10]The fires will burn night and day.
The smoke will rise from Edom
for ever.
Year after year that land will be
empty.
No one will ever travel through
that land again.
[11]Birds and small animals will own
that land.
Owls and ravens will live there.
God will make it an empty
wasteland.
It will have nothing left in it.
[12]The important men will have no
one left to rule them.
The leaders will all be gone.
[13]Thorns will take over the strong
towers.
Wild bushes will grow in the
walled cities.
Wild dogs will live there.
Owls will live in those homes.
[14]Desert animals will live with the
hyenas there.
And wild goats will call to their
friends.
Night animals will live there.
They will find a place of rest
there.
[15]Owls will nest there and lay eggs.
When the eggs open, the owls
will gather their young under
their wings.
Hawks will gather
with their own kind.
[16]Look at the Lord's scroll. Read
what is written there:

None of these will be missing.
Every one will have its mate.
God said he will gather them
together.
So his Spirit[d] will gather them
together.
[17]God has divided the land among
them.
And he has given them each
their land.
So they will own that land for
ever.
They will live there year after
year.

God Will Comfort His People

35 The desert and dry land will
become happy.
The desert will be glad and will
produce flowers.
Like a flower, [2]it will have many
blooms.
It will show its happiness, as if
it is shouting with joy.
It will be beautiful like the forest
of Lebanon.
It will be as beautiful as the hill
of Carmel and the Plain of
Sharon.
All people will see the glory of the
Lord.
They will see the splendour of
our God.

[3]Make the weak hands strong.
Make the weak knees strong.
[4]Say to people who are afraid and
confused,
"Be strong. Don't be afraid.
Look, your God will come,
and he will punish your enemies.
He will make them pay for the
wrongs they did.
He will come and save you."

[5]Then the blind people will see
again.
Then the deaf will hear.
[6]Crippled people will jump like
deer.
And those who can't talk now
will shout with joy.

Springs of water will flow in the
  desert.
Streams will flow in the dry
  land.
7The burning desert will have pools
  of water.
The dry ground will have
  springs.
Where wild dogs once lived,
  grass and water plants will
  grow.
8A road will be there.
  This highway will be called "The
  Road to Being Holy".
Evil people will not be allowed to
  walk on that road.
Only good people will walk on
  that road.
No fools will go on it.
9No lions will be there.
  No dangerous animals will be on
  that road.
They will not be found there.
That road will be for the people
  God saves.
10   The people the Lord has freed
  will return there.
They will enter Jerusalem with
  joy.
Their happiness will last for
  ever.
Their gladness and joy will fill
  them completely.
Sorrow and sadness will go far
  away.

The Assyrians Invade Judah

36 During Hezekiah's fourteenth
year as king, Sennacherib king
of Assyria attacked Judah. He attacked all the strong, walled cities of
Judah and defeated them. 2The king of
Assyria sent out his field commander.
He went with a large army from Lachish to King Hezekiah in Jerusalem.
When the commander came near the
waterway from the upper pool, he
stopped. The upper pool is on the
road to the Washerman's Field. 3Elia-
kim, Shebna and Joah went out to
meet him. Eliakim son of Hilkiah was

the palace manager. Shebna was the
royal assistant. Joah son of Asaph was
the recorder.
4The field commander said to them,
"Tell Hezekiah this:
" 'The great king, the king of Assyria, says: You have nothing to trust in
to help you. 5You say you have battle
plans and power for war. But your
words mean nothing. Whom are you
trusting for help so that you turn
against me? 6Look, you are depending
on Egypt to help you. Egypt is like
a splintered staff. If you lean on it
for help, it will stab you and hurt
you. The king of Egypt will hurt those
who depend on him. 7You might say,
"We are depending on the Lord our
God." But Hezekiah destroyed the
Lord's altars and the places of worship. Hezekiah told Judah and Jerusalem, "You must worship only at this
one altar."
8" 'Now make an agreement with
my master, the king of Assyria: I will
give you 2,000 horses if you can find
enough men to ride them. 9You cannot
defeat one of my master's least important officers. So why do you depend
on Egypt to give you chariots and
horsemen? 10I have not come to attack and destroy this country without
an order from the Lord. The Lord
himself told me to come to this country and destroy it'."
11Then Eliakim, Shebna and Joah
spoke to the field commander. They
said, "Please speak to us in the Aramaic language. We understand it.
Don't speak to us in Hebrew because
the people on the city wall can hear
you."
12But the commander said, "No.
My master did not send me to tell
these things only to you and your
king. My master sent me to tell them
also to those people sitting on the
wall. They will have to eat their own
dung and drink their own urine like
you."
13Then the commander stood and

shouted loudly in the Hebrew language. He said, "Listen to the words from the great king, the king of Assyria! ¹⁴The king says you should not let Hezekiah fool you. Hezekiah can't save you. ¹⁵Don't let Hezekiah talk you into trusting the Lord. Hezekiah says, 'The Lord will surely save us. This city won't be given over to the king of Assyria'.

¹⁶"Don't listen to Hezekiah. The king of Assyria says, 'Make peace with me. Come out of the city to me. Then everyone will be free to eat the fruit from his own grapevine and fig tree. Everyone will be free to drink water from his own well. ¹⁷Then I will come and take you to a land like your own. It is a land with grain and new wine. It has bread and vineyards'.

¹⁸"Don't let Hezekiah fool you. He says, 'The Lord will save us'. No god from any other nation has saved his people from the power of the king of Assyria. ¹⁹Where are the gods of Hamath and Arpad? Where are the gods of Sepharvaim? They did not save Samaria from my power. ²⁰Not one of all the gods of these countries has saved his people from me. So the Lord cannot save Jerusalem from my power."

²¹The people were silent. They didn't answer the commander at all. This was because King Hezekiah had ordered, "Don't answer him."

²²Then Eliakim, Shebna and Joah tore their clothes to show how upset they were. (Eliakim son of Hilkiah was the palace manager. Shebna was the royal assistant. Joah son of Asaph was the recorder.) The three men went to Hezekiah and told him what the field commander had said.

Hezekiah Asks God to Help

37 When King Hezekiah heard the message, he tore his clothes. And he put on rough cloth to show how sad he was. Then he went into the Temple*ᵈ* of the Lord. ²Hezekiah sent Eliakim, Shebna and the older priests to Isaiah. Eliakim was the palace manager, and Shebna was the royal assistant. The men were all wearing the rough cloth when they came to Isaiah. He was a prophet,*ᵈ* the son of Amoz. ³These men told Isaiah, "This is what Hezekiah says: Today is a day of sorrow and punishment and disgrace. It is sad, as when a child should be born, but the mother is not strong enough to give birth to it. ⁴The king of Assyria sent his field commander to make fun of the living God. Maybe the Lord your God will hear what the commander said. Maybe the Lord your God will punish him for what he said. So pray for the few people of Israel who are left alive."

⁵When Hezekiah's officers came to Isaiah, ⁶he said to them, "Tell your master this: The Lord says, 'Don't be afraid of what you have heard. Don't be frightened by the words the servants of the king of Assyria said against me. ⁷Listen! I am going to put a spirit in the king of Assyria. He will hear a report that will make him return to his own country. And I will cause him to die by the sword there'."

⁸The field commander heard that the king of Assyria had left Lachish. So the commander left and found the king fighting against the city of Libnah.

⁹The king received a report that Tirhakah was coming to attack him. Tirhakah was the Cushite king of Egypt. When the king of Assyria heard this, he sent messengers to Hezekiah. The king said: ¹⁰"Say this to Hezekiah king of Judah: 'Don't be fooled by the god you trust. Don't believe him when he says Jerusalem will not be defeated by the king of Assyria. ¹¹You have heard what the kings of Assyria have done. They have completely defeated every country. Do not think you will be saved. ¹²The gods of those people did not save

them. My ancestors destroyed them. My ancestors defeated the cities of Gozan, Haran and Rezeph. They defeated the people of Eden living in Tel Assar. [13]Where are the kings of Hamath and Arpad? Where is the king of the city of Sepharvaim? Where are the kings of Hena and Ivvah?'."

Hezekiah Prays to the Lord

[14]Hezekiah received the letter from the messengers and read it. Then he went up to the Temple[d] of the Lord. Hezekiah spread the letter out before the Lord. [15]And he prayed to the Lord: [16]"Lord of heaven's armies, you are the God of Israel. Your throne is between the gold creatures with wings. Only you are the God of all the kingdoms of the earth. You made the heavens and the earth. [17]Hear, Lord, and listen. Open your eyes, Lord, and see. Listen to all the words Sennacherib has said to insult the living God.

[18]"It is true, Lord. The kings of Assyria have destroyed all these countries and their lands. [19]These kings have thrown the gods of these nations into the fire. But they were only wood and rock statues that men made. So the kings have destroyed them. [20]Now, Lord our God, save us from the king's power. Then all the kingdoms of the earth will know that you, Lord, are the only God."

God Answers Hezekiah

[21]Then Isaiah son of Amoz sent a message to Hezekiah. Isaiah said, "The Lord, the God of Israel, says this: 'You prayed to me about Sennacherib king of Assyria. [22]So this is what the Lord has said against Sennacherib:

The people of Jerusalem
  hate you and make fun of you.
The people of Jerusalem
  laugh at you as you run away.
[23]You have insulted me and spoken
  against me.

You have raised your voice
  against me.
You have a proud look on your
  face.
You disobey me, the Holy One
  of Israel!
[24]You have used your messengers
  to insult the Lord.
You have said, "I have many
  chariots.
With them I have gone to the tops
  of the mountains.
I have climbed the highest
  mountains of Lebanon.
I have cut down its tallest cedars.
I have cut down its best pine
  trees.
I have gone to its greatest
  heights.
I have gone to its best forests.
[25]I have dug wells in foreign
  countries.
I have drunk water there.
By the soles of my feet,
I have dried up all the rivers of
  Egypt."

[26]" 'King of Assyria, surely you
  have heard.
Long ago I, the Lord, planned
  these things.
Long ago I planned them.
Now I have made them happen.
I allowed you to turn those
  strong, walled cities
  into piles of rocks.
[27]The people living in those cities
  were weak.
They were frightened and put to
  shame.
They were like grass in the field.
They were like tender, young
  grass.
They were like grass that grows
  on the housetop.
It is burned by the wind before
  it can grow.
[28]" 'I know when you rest and when
  you come and go.
I know how you speak against
  me.

29You speak strongly against me.
And I have heard your proud
words.
So I will put my hook in your
nose.
And I will put my bit in your
mouth.
Then I will force you to leave my
country
the same way that you came'.

30"Then the Lord said, 'Hezekiah, I
will give you this sign:
This year you will eat the grain
that grows wild.
And the second year you will eat
what grows wild from that.
But in the third year, plant grain
and harvest it.
Plant vineyards and eat their
fruit.
31The people left alive in the family
of Judah
will be saved.
Like plants that take root,
they will grow strong and have
many children.
32A few people will come out of
Jerusalem alive.
There will be a few from Mount
Zion*d* who will live.
The strong love of the Lord of
heaven's armies
will cause this to happen'.

33"So this is what the Lord says
about the king of Assyria:
'He will not enter this city.
He will not even shoot an arrow
here.
He will not fight against it with
shields.
He will not build a ramp to
attack the city walls.
34He will return to his country the
same way he came.
He will not enter this city,'
says the Lord.

35The Lord says, 'I will defend and
save this city.
I will do this for myself and for
David, my servant'."

36Then the angel of the Lord went
out. He killed 185,000 men in the Assyrian camp. When the people got up
early the next morning, they saw all
the dead bodies! 37So Sennacherib
king of Assyria left. He went back to
Nineveh and stayed there.
38One day Sennacherib was worshipping in the temple of his god Nis-
roch. While he was there, his sons
Adrammelech and Sharezer killed him
with a sword. Then they escaped to
the land of Ararat. So Sennacherib's
son Esarhaddon became king of Assyria.

Hezekiah's Illness

38 At that time Hezekiah became
very sick. He was almost dead.
The prophet*d* Isaiah son of Amoz went
to see him. Isaiah told him, "This is
what the Lord says: You are going to
die. So you should give your last orders to everyone. You will not get
well."
2Hezekiah turned toward the wall
and prayed to the Lord. 3He said,
"Lord, please remember that I have
always obeyed you. I have given myself completely to you. I have done
what you said was right." And Hezekiah cried loudly.
4Then the Lord spoke his word to
Isaiah: 5"Go to Hezekiah and tell him:
'This is what the Lord, the God of
your ancestor David, says: I have
heard your prayer. And I have seen
your tears. I will add 15 years to your
life. 6I will save you and this city from
the king of Assyria. I will defend this
city'."
21nThen Isaiah said, "Make a

Verses 21-22 These verses are generally found at the end of chapter 38. But the same story in 2 Kings 20:6-9 shows the events happened in this order.

paste from figs. Put it on Hezekiah's boil. Then he will get well."

²²Hezekiah asked Isaiah, "What will be the sign? What will show me that I will go up to the Temple[d] of the Lord?"

⁷Isaiah said, "The Lord will do what he says. This is the sign from the Lord to show you: ⁸The sun has made a shadow go down the stairway of Ahaz. I will make it go back ten steps." So the shadow made by the sun went back up the ten steps it had gone down.

⁹After Hezekiah king of Judah got well, he wrote this song:

¹⁰I said, "I am in the middle of my life.
Do I have to go through the gates where the dead are now?
Will I have the rest of my life taken away from me?"
¹¹I said, "I will not see the Lord in the land of the living again.
I will not again see the people who live on the earth.
¹²Like a shepherd's tent,
my home has been pulled down and taken from me.
I am finished like the cloth a weaver rolls up and cuts from the loom.[n]
In one day you brought me to this end.
¹³All night I cried loudly.
Like a lion, he crushed all my bones.
In one day you brought me to this end.
¹⁴I cried like a bird.
I moaned like a dove.
My eyes became tired as I looked to the heavens.
Lord, I have troubles. Please help me."

¹⁵What can I say?

The Lord told me what would happen and then made it happen.
I have had these troubles in my soul.
So now I will be humble all my life.
¹⁶Lord, because of you, men live.
Because of you, my spirit also lives.
You made me well and let me live.
¹⁷It was for my own good that I had such troubles.
Because you love me very much, you did not let me die.
You threw my sins far away.
¹⁸People in the place where the dead are cannot praise you.
Those who have died cannot sing praises to you.
Those who die don't trust you to help them.
¹⁹The people who are alive are the ones who praise you.
They praise you as I praise you today.
A father should tell his children that you provide help.

²⁰The Lord saved me.
So we will sing and play songs.
We will make music in the Temple of the Lord
all the days of our lives.

Messengers from Babylon

39 At that time Merodach-Baladan son of Baladan was king of Babylon. He sent letters and a gift to Hezekiah. He did this because he had heard that Hezekiah had been sick and was now well. ²Hezekiah was happy to see the messengers. So he showed them what was in his storehouses: the silver, gold, spices and expensive perfumes. He showed them his swords and shields. He showed them all his

loom A machine for weaving cloth from thread.

wealth. He showed them everything in his palace and in his kingdom.

³Then Isaiah the prophet*ᵈ* went to King Hezekiah. He asked Hezekiah, "What did these men say? Where did they come from?"

Hezekiah said, "They came from a faraway country. They came to me from Babylon."

⁴So Isaiah asked him, "What did they see in your palace?"

Hezekiah said, "They saw everything in my palace. I showed them all my wealth."

⁵Then Isaiah said to Hezekiah: "Listen to the words of the Lord of heaven's armies: ⁶'In the future everything in your palace will be taken away to Babylon. Everything your ancestors have stored up until this day will be taken away. Nothing will be left,' says the Lord. ⁷Some of your own children will be taken away. Those who will be born to you will be taken away. And they will become eunuchs*ᵈ* in the palace of the king of Babylon."

⁸Hezekiah told Isaiah, "These words from the Lord are good." He said this because he thought, "There will be peace and security while I am king."

Israel's Punishment Will End

40 Your God says,
"Comfort, comfort my people.
²Speak kindly to the people of
    Jerusalem.
Tell them
that their time of service is
    finished.
Tell them that they have paid
    for their sins.
Tell them that the Lord has
    punished Jerusalem
twice for every sin they did."

³This is the voice of a man who
    calls out:
"Prepare in the desert
    the way for the Lord.

Make the road in the dry lands
    straight for our God.
⁴Every valley should be raised up.
Every mountain and hill should
    be made flat.
The rough ground should be made
    level.
The rugged ground should be
    made smooth.
⁵Then the glory of the Lord will be
    shown.
All people together will see it.
The Lord himself said these
    things."

⁶A voice says, "Cry out!"
Then I said, "What shall I cry
    out?"
"Say all people are like the grass.
And all their strength is like the
    flowers of the field.
⁷The grass dies, and the flowers
    fall.
This is because the breath of
    the Lord blows on them.
Surely the people are like grass.
⁸The grass dies, and the flowers
    fall.
But the word of our God will
    live for ever."

⁹Jerusalem, you have good news to
    tell.
Go up on a high mountain.
Jerusalem, you have good news to
    tell.
Shout out loud the good news.
Shout it out and don't be afraid.
Say to the towns of Judah,
    "Here is your God."
¹⁰Look, the Lord God is coming
    with power.
He will use his power to rule all
    the people.
Look, he will bring reward for his
    people.
He will have their payment with
    him.
¹¹The Lord takes care of his people
    like a shepherd.
He gathers the people like lambs
    in his arms.

He carries them close to him.
He gently leads the mothers of
the lambs.

God Is Supreme

¹²Who has measured the oceans in
the palm of his hand?
Who has used his hand to
measure the sky?
Who has used a bowl to measure
all the dust of the earth?
Who has used scales to weigh
the mountains and hills?
¹³Who has known the mind of the
Lord?
Who has been able to give the
Lord advice?
¹⁴Whom did the Lord ask for help?
Who taught him the right way?
Who taught the Lord knowledge?
Who showed him the way to
understanding?

¹⁵The nations are like one small
drop in a bucket.
They are no more than the dust
on his measuring scales.
To him the islands are no more
than fine dust on his scales.
¹⁶All the trees in Lebanon are not
enough for the altar fires.
And all the animals in Lebanon
are not enough for burnt
offerings.
¹⁷Compared to the Lord all the
nations are worth nothing.
To him they are less than
nothing.

¹⁸Can you compare God to
anything?
Can you compare him to an
image of anything?
¹⁹An idol is formed by a man.
And another man covers it with
gold.
And he makes silver chains for
it.
²⁰A poor man cannot buy those
expensive statues.
So he finds a tree that will not
rot.

And he finds a skilled workman
to make it into an idol that will
not fall over.

²¹Surely you know. Surely you have
heard.
Surely in the beginning someone
told you.
Surely you understand how the
earth was created.
²²God sits on his throne above the
circle of the earth.
And compared to him, people
are like grasshoppers.
He stretches out the skies like a
piece of cloth.
He spreads them out like a tent
to sit under.
²³He makes rulers unimportant.
He makes the judges of this
world worth nothing.
²⁴They are like plants that are
placed in the ground.
They are like seeds that are
planted.
As soon as they begin to grow
strong,
he blows on them and they die.
The wind blows them away like
chaff.ᵈ

²⁵God, the Holy One, says, "Can
you compare me to anyone?
Is anyone equal to me?
²⁶Look up to the skies.
Who created all these stars?
He leads out all the army of
heaven one by one.
He calls all the stars by name.
He is very strong and full of
power.
So not one of them is missing.

²⁷People of Jacob, why do you
complain?
People of Israel, why do you
say,
"The Lord does not see what
happens to me.
He does not care if I am treated
fairly"?
²⁸Surely you know.

Surely you have heard.
The Lord is the God who lives for
  ever.
He created all the world.
He does not become tired or need
  to rest.
No one can understand how
  great his wisdom is.
²⁹The Lord gives strength to those
  who are tired.
He gives more power to those
  who are weak.
³⁰Even boys become tired and need
  to rest.
Even young men trip and fall.
³¹But the people who trust the Lord
  will become strong again.
They will be able to rise up as an
  eagle in the sky.
They will run without needing
  rest.
They will walk without becoming
  tired.

The Lord Will Help Israel

41 The Lord says, "Faraway
  countries, listen to me.
Let the nations become strong.
Come to me and speak.
We will meet together to decide
  who is right.

²"Who caused the man to come
  from the east?
Who gives the man victories
  everywhere he goes?
The one who brought him gives
  nations over to him.
He defeats kings for him.
The man uses his sword, and the
  kings become like dust.
He uses his bow, and they are
  blown away like chaff.^d
³He chases them and is never hurt.
He goes places where he has
  never been before.
⁴Who caused this to happen?
Who has controlled history since
  the beginning?
I, the Lord, am the one. I was
  here at the beginning.

And I will be here when all
  things are finished."

⁵All you faraway places, look and
  be afraid.
All you places far away on the
  earth, shake with fear.
Come close and listen to me.
⁶ The workers help each other.
They say to each other, "Be
  strong!"
⁷The man who carves wood
  encourages the man who
  works with gold.
The workman who smooths the
  metal with a hammer
  encourages the man who
  shapes the metal.
This last workman says, "This
  metal work is good."
He nails the statue to a base so
  it can't fall over.

Only the Lord Can Save Us

⁸The Lord says, "People of Israel,
  you are my servants.
People of Jacob, I chose you.
You are from the family of my
  friend Abraham.
⁹You were far away on the earth.
I called you from a faraway
  country.
I said, 'You are my servants'.
I have chosen you, and I have
  not turned against you.
¹⁰So don't worry, because I am with
  you.
Don't be afraid, because I am
  your God.
I will make you strong and will
  help you.
I will support you with my right
  hand that saves you.

¹¹"All those people who are angry
  with you
will be ashamed and disgraced.
Those who are against you
  will disappear and be lost.
¹²You will look for your enemies.
But you will not find them.
Those who fought against you

will vanish completely.
13I am the Lord your God.
I am holding your right hand.
And I tell you, 'Don't be afraid.
I will help you'.
14You few people of Israel who are
    left,
do not be afraid even though
    you are weak as a worm.
I myself will help you," says the
    Lord.
"I am the one who saves you,
    the Holy One of Israel.
15Look, I have made you like a
    threshing*d* board.
You are new, with many sharp
    teeth.
So you will walk on mountains and
    crush them.
You will make the hills like
    chaff.*d*
16You will throw them into the air.
And the wind will carry them
    away.
A windstorm will scatter them.
Then you will be happy in the
    Lord.
You will be proud of the Holy
    One of Israel.

17"The poor and needy people look
    for water.
But they can't find any.
Their tongues are dry with
    thirst.
But I, the Lord, will answer their
    prayers.
I, the God of Israel, will not
    leave them to die.
18I will make rivers flow on the dry
    hills.
I will make springs of water flow
    through the valleys.
I will change the desert into a lake
    of water.
I will change the dry land into
    springs of water.
19I will make trees grow in the
    desert.

There will be cedars, acacia,
    myrtle and olive trees.
I will put pine, fir and cypress
    trees
growing together in the desert.
20People will see these things and
    understand.
Together they will think
    carefully about these things.
They will know that the Lord's
    power did this.
They will know that the Holy
    One of Israel made these
    things."

The Lord Challenges False Gods

21The Lord says, "Present your
    case."
The Lord, the King of Jacob,
    says, "Tell me your
    arguments.
22Bring in your idols to tell us
    what is going to happen.
Have them tell us what happened
    in the beginning.
Then we will think about these
    things.
Then we will know how they
    will turn out.
Tell us what will happen in the
    future.
23   Tell us what is coming next.
Then we will believe that you
    are gods.
Do something, whether it is good
    or bad.
Make us afraid of you.
24You false gods are less than
    nothing.
You can't do anything.
Those who worship you should
    be hated."

25"I have brought someone to come
    out of the north.*n*
I have called by name a man
    from the east, and he knows
    me.

___
someone . . . north This probably means Cyrus, a king of Persia.

He walks on kings as if they were
   mud.
He walks on them as a potter
   walks on the clay.
26Who told us about this before it
   happened?
Who told us ahead of time so
   we could say, 'He was
   right'?
None of you told us anything.
None of you told us before it
   happened.
No one heard you tell of it.
27I, the Lord, was the first one to
   tell Jerusalem that the
   people were coming home.
I sent a messenger to Jerusalem
   with the good news.
28I look at the idols, but there is not
   one that can answer.
None of them can give advice.
None of them can answer my
   questions.
29Look, all these idols are false
   gods.
They cannot do anything.
They are worth nothing.

The Lord's Special Servant

42 "Here is my servant, the one
   I support.
He is the one I chose, and I am
   pleased with him.
I will put my Spirit[d] in him.
And he will bring justice to all
   nations.
2He will not cry out or yell.
He will not speak loudly in the
   streets.
3He will not break a crushed blade
   of grass.
He will not put out even a weak
   flame.
He will bring justice and find what
   is true.
4He will not lose hope or give up
   until he brings justice to the
   world.
And people far away will trust
   his teachings."

5God, the Lord, said these things.
He created the skies and
   stretched them out.
He spread out the earth and
   everything on it.
He gives life to all people on
   earth.
He gives life to everyone who
   walks on the earth.
6The Lord says, "I called you to do
   right.
And I will hold your hand.
I will protect you.
You will be the sign of my
   agreement with the people.
You will be a light to shine for
   all people.
7You will help the blind to see.
You will free those who are in
   prison.
You will lead those who live in
   darkness out of their prison.

8"I am the Lord. That is my name.
I will not give my glory to
   another.
I will not let idols take the
   praise that should be mine.
9The things I said would happen
   have happened.
And now I tell you about new
   things.
Before those things happen,
   I tell you about them.

A Song of Praise to the Lord

10Sing a new song to the Lord.
Sing his praise everywhere on
   the earth.
Praise him, you people who sail
   on the seas and you animals
   who live in them.
Praise him, you people living in
   faraway places.
11The deserts and their cities should
   praise him.
The settlements of Kedar should
   praise him.
The people living in Sela should
   sing for joy.

They should sing from the
    mountain tops.
¹²They should give glory to the
    Lord.
People in faraway lands should
    praise him.
¹³The Lord will march out like a
    strong soldier.
He will be excited like a man
    ready to fight a war.
He will shout out the battle cry.
And he will defeat his enemies.

¹⁴The Lord says, "For a long time I
    have said nothing.
I have been quiet and held
    myself back.
But now I will cry out.
I will strain like a woman giving
    birth to a child.
¹⁵I will destroy the hills and
    mountains.
I will dry up all the plants that
    grow there.
I will make the rivers become dry
    land.
I will dry up the pools of water.
¹⁶Then I will lead the blind along a
    way they never knew.
I will guide them along paths
    they have not known.
I will make the darkness become
    light for them.
And I will make the rough
    ground smooth.
These are the things I will do.
I will not leave my people.
¹⁷But some people trust in idols.
They say to their statues,
'You are our gods'.
Those people will be rejected in
    disgrace.

Israel Refused to Listen to God

¹⁸"You who are deaf, hear me.
You who are blind, look and
    see.
¹⁹No one is more blind than my
    servant Israel.
The messenger I send is the
    most deaf.

No one is more blind than the
    person I own.
No one is more blind than the
    servant of the Lord.
²⁰Israel, you have seen much, but
    you have not obeyed.
You have heard, but you refuse
    to listen."
²¹The Lord made his teachings
    wonderful.
He did this because he is good.
²²These people have been defeated
    and robbed.
They are trapped in pits.
They are locked up in prison.
Like robbers, enemies have taken
    them away.
There is no one to save them.
Enemies carried them off.
And no one said, "Bring them
    back."

²³Will any of you listen to this?
Will you listen carefully in the
    future?
²⁴Who let the people of Jacob be
    carried off?
Who let robbers take Israel
    away?
The Lord allowed this to happen
    because we sinned against him.
We did not live the way the Lord
    wanted us to live.
We did not obey his teaching.
²⁵So the Lord became very angry
    with us.
He brought terrible wars against
    us.
It was as if the people of Israel
    had fire all around them.
But they didn't know what was
    happening.
It was as if they were burning.
But they didn't pay any
    attention.

God Is Always with His People

43 Now this is what the Lord
    says.
He created you, people of Jacob.
He formed you, people of Israel.

He says, "Don't be afraid,
　　because I have saved you.
I have called you by name, and
　　you are mine.
2When you pass through the
　　waters, I will be with you.
When you cross rivers, you will
　　not drown.
When you walk through fire, you
　　will not be burned.
The flames will not hurt you.
3This is because I, the Lord, am
　　your God.
I, the Holy One of Israel, am
　　your Saviour.
I gave Egypt to pay for you.
I gave Cush and Seba to make
　　you mine.
4You are precious to me.
I give you honour, and I love
　　you.
So I will give other people in your
　　place.
I will give other nations to save
　　your life.
5So don't be afraid. I am with you.
I will gather your children from
　　the east.
I will gather you from the west.
6I will tell the north: Give my
　　people to me.
I will tell the south: Don't keep
　　my people in prison.
Bring my sons from far away.
Bring my daughters from
　　faraway places.
7Bring to me all the people who
　　are mine.
I made them for my glory.
I formed them; I made them."

Judah Is God's Witness

8Bring out the people who have
　　eyes but don't see.
Bring out those who have ears
　　but don't hear.
9All the nations should gather
　　together.
All the people should come
　　together.

Which of their gods said that this
　　would happen?
Which of their gods can tell what
　　happened in the beginning?
They should bring their witnesses
　　to prove they were right.
Then others will say, "It is
　　true."
10The Lord says, "You are my
　　witnesses.
You are the servant I chose.
I chose you so you would know
　　and believe me.
I chose you so you would
　　understand that I am the
　　true God.
There was no God before me,
　　and there will be no God after
　　me.
11I myself am the Lord.
I am the only Saviour.
12I myself have spoken to you,
　　saved you and told you
　　these things.
It was not some foreign god
　　among you.
You are my witnesses, and I am
　　God,"
　　says the Lord.
13　"I have always been God.
No one can save people from my
　　power.
When I do something, no one
　　can change it."

14This is what the Lord says.
He is the Holy One of Israel
　　who saves you.
He says, "I will send armies to
　　Babylon for you.
All the Babylonians will be
　　captured.
They will be taken away in the
　　ships they are proud of.
15I am the Lord, your Holy One.
I made Israel. I am your king."

God Will Save His People Again

16This is what the Lord says.
He is the one who made a road
　　through the sea.

Even through rough waters he
made a path for his people.
¹⁷He is the one who defeated the
chariots and horses.
He defeated the mighty armies.
They fell together, and they will
never rise again.
They were destroyed as a flame
is put out.
¹⁸The Lord says, "Forget what
happened before.
Do not think about the past.
¹⁹Look at the new thing I am going
to do.
It is already happening. Don't
you see it?
I will make a road in the desert.
I will make rivers in the dry
land.
²⁰Even the wild animals will be
thankful to me.
The wild dogs and owls will
honour me.
They will honour me when I put
water in the desert.
They will honour me when I
make rivers in the dry land.
I will do this to give water to my
people, the ones I chose.
21   These are the people I made.
And they will sing songs to
praise me.

²²"People of Jacob, you have not
called to me.
People of Israel, you have
become tired of me.
²³You have not brought your
sacrifices of sheep to me.
You have not honoured me by
bringing sacrifices to me.
I did not force you to give
sacrifices to me.
I did not force you to burn
incense*ᵈ* until you became
tired.
²⁴So you did not buy incense for
me.
You did not freely bring fat from
your sacrifices to me.

Instead you have weighed me
down with your many sins.
You have made me tired of your
many wrongs.
²⁵"I, I am the One who forgives all
your sins.
I do this to please myself.
I will not remember your sins.
²⁶But you should remind me.
Let's meet and decide what is
right.
Tell me what you have done and
show you are right.
²⁷Your first father sinned.
And your leaders have turned
against me.
²⁸So I will make your holy rulers
unholy.
And I will bring destruction on
the people of Jacob.
And I will let Israel be insulted."

The Lord Is the Only God

44 The Lord says, "People of
Jacob, you are my servants.
Listen to me!
People of Israel, I chose you."
²This is what the Lord says. He
made you.
He formed you when you were
in your mother's body.
And he will help you.
The Lord says, "People of Jacob,
my servants, don't be afraid.
Israel, I chose you.
³I will pour out water for the
thirsty land.
I will make streams flow on dry
land.
I will put my Spirit*ᵈ* into your
children.
My blessing will be like a stream
of water flowing over your
family.
⁴Your children will grow like a tree
in the grass.
They will be like poplar trees
growing beside streams of
water.

5One person will say, 'I belong to
the Lord'.
Another will use the name
Jacob.
Another will sign his name 'I am
the Lord's'.
And another will use the name
Israel."

6The Lord is the king of Israel.
The Lord of heaven's armies
saves Israel.
The Lord says, "I am the
beginning and the end.
I am the only God.
7There is no other God like me.
If there is, then that god should
come and prove it.
Who has announced coming events
from the beginning?
He should tell what will happen
in the future.
8Don't be afraid! Don't worry!
I have always told you what will
happen.
You are my witnesses.
There is no other God.
I know of no other Rock.[d] I am
the only One."

False Gods Are Useless

9Some people make idols, but they
are worth nothing.
People love them, but they are
useless.
Those people are witnesses for
the statues. But those
people cannot see.
They know nothing. They don't
know enough to be
ashamed.
10Who made these false gods?
Who made these useless idols?
11The workmen who made those
gods will be ashamed!
Those workmen are only
human.
If they all would come together,
they would all be ashamed and
afraid.

12One workman uses tools to heat
iron.
He works over hot coals.
He uses his hammer to beat the
metal and make a statue.
He uses his powerful arms.
But when he becomes hungry, he
loses his power.
If he does not drink water, he
becomes tired.
13Another workman uses a line and
a compass
to draw lines on the wood.
Then he uses his chisels to cut a
statue from wood.
He uses his calipers to measure
the statue.
This way, the workman makes the
wood look exactly like a
man.
And this statue of a man sits in
the house.
14A man cuts down cedar
or gets cypress or oak trees.
Those trees grew by their own
power in the forest.
Or he plants a pine tree, and
the rain makes it grow.
15Then he burns the tree.
He uses some of the wood for a
fire to keep himself warm.
He also starts a fire to bake his
bread.
But he uses part of the wood to
make a god. Then he
worships it!
He makes the idol and bows
down to it!
16The man burns half of the wood in
the fire.
He uses the fire to cook his
meat.
And he eats the meat until he is
full.
He burns the wood to keep
himself warm. He says,
"Good! Now I am warm. I can
see because of the fire's
light."

17But the man makes a statue from
the wood that is left. He
calls it his god.
He bows down to it and
worships it.
He prays to it and says,
"You are my god. Save me!"
18Those people don't know what
they are doing. They don't
understand!
It is as if their eyes are covered
so they can't see.
Their minds don't understand.
19They have not thought about
these things.
They don't understand.
They have never thought to
themselves,
"I burned half of the wood in the
fire.
I used the hot coals to bake my
bread.
I cooked and ate my meat.
And I used the wood that was left
to make this hated thing.
I am worshipping a block of
wood!"
20He doesn't know what he is doing.
His confused mind leads him the
wrong way.
He cannot save himself.
He cannot say, "This statue I
am holding is a false god."

The Lord Is the True God

21The Lord says, "People of Jacob,
remember these things!
People of Israel, remember you
are my servants.
I made you. You are my servants.
So Israel, I will not forget you.
22I have swept away your sins like a
big cloud.
I have removed your sins like a
cloud that disappears into
the air.
Come back to me because I saved
you."

23Skies, sing for joy because the
Lord did great things!
Earth, shout for joy, even in
your deepest parts!
Sing, you mountains, with thanks
to God.
Sing, too, you trees in the
forest!
The Lord saved the people of
Jacob!
The Lord showed his greatness
when he saved Israel.
24The Lord saved you.
He formed you while you were
still in your mother's body.
The Lord says, "I, the Lord,
made everything!
I alone stretched out the skies.
I spread out the earth by
myself.
25I show that the lying prophets'[d]
signs are false.
I make fools of those who do
magic.
I confuse even wise men.
They think they are clever, but
I make them look foolish.
26I make the messages of my
servants come true.
I make the advice of my
messengers come true.
I say to Jerusalem,
'People will live in you again!'
I say to the towns of Judah,
'You will be built again!'
I say to Jerusalem's ruins,
'I will repair you'.
27I tell the deep waters, 'Become
dry!
I will make your streams
become dry!'
28I say of Cyrus,[n] 'He is my
shepherd.
He will do all that I want him to
do.
He will say to Jerusalem, "You
will be built again!"

Cyrus A king of Persia. He ruled from about 550 to 530 B.C.

He will tell the Temple,[d] "Your
foundations will be
rebuilt" '."

God Chooses Cyrus to Free Israel

45 This is what the Lord says to
Cyrus, his appointed king:
"I hold your right hand.
I will help you defeat nations.
I will help you take other kings'
power away.
I will open doors for you
so city gates will not stop you.
[2]I will go before you.
And I will make the mountains
flat.
I will break down the bronze gates
of the cities.
I will cut through the iron bars
on the gates.
[3]I will give you the wealth that is
stored away.
And I will give you hidden
riches.
I will do this so you will know I
am the Lord.
I, the God of Israel, call you by
name.
[4]I do these things for my servants,
the people of Jacob.
I do these things for my chosen
people, the Israelites.
Cyrus, I call you by name.
I give you a title of honour even
though you don't know me.
[5]I am the Lord. There is no other
God.
I am the only God.
I will make you strong
even though you don't know me.
[6]I do these things so everyone will
know
there is no other God.
From the east to the west they
will know
I alone am the Lord.
[7]I made the light and the darkness.
I bring peace, and I cause
troubles.
I, the Lord, do all these things.

[8]"Sky above, make victory fall like
rain.
Clouds, pour down victory.
May the earth receive it.
May salvation grow.
May victory grow with it.
I, the Lord, have created it.
[9]"How terrible it will be for those
who argue with the God who
made them.
They are like one piece of
broken pottery among many
pieces.
The clay does not ask the potter,
'What are you doing?'
The thing that is made doesn't say
to its maker,
'You have no hands'.
[10]How terrible it will be for the child
who says to his father,
'Why are you giving me life?'
How terrible it will be for the child
who says to his mother,
'Why are you giving birth to
me?' "

[11]The Lord is the Holy One of
Israel, and its Maker.
He says this:
"You ask me about what will
happen.
You question me about my
children.
You give me orders about what
I have made.
[12]I made the earth.
And I made all the people living
on it.
With my own hands I stretched
out the skies.
I command all the armies in the
sky.
[13]I will bring Cyrus to do good
things.
And I will make his work easy.
Cyrus will rebuild my city,
and he will set my people free.
Cyrus has not been paid to do
these things.
The Lord of heaven's armies
says this."

14The Lord says,
"The things made in Egypt and
Cush
and the tall people of Seba
will come to you.
They will become yours.
The Sabeans will walk behind you.
They will come along in chains.
They will bow down before you.
They will pray to you, saying,
'God is with you.
And there is no other God'."

15You are a God that people cannot
see.
You are the God and Saviour of
Israel.
16All the people who make idols will
be put to great shame.
They will go off together in
disgrace.
17But Israel will be saved by the
Lord.
That salvation will continue for
ever.
Never again will Israel be put to
shame.

18The Lord created the heavens.
He is the God
who formed the earth.
He made the earth.
But he did not want it to be
empty.
He wanted life to be on the
earth.
This is what the Lord says:
"I am the Lord. There is no
other God.
19I did not speak in secret.
I did not hide my words
somewhere in a dark place.
I did not tell the family of Jacob
to look for me in empty places.
I am the Lord, and I speak the
truth.
I say what is right.

20"You people have escaped from
other nations.
So gather together and come
before me.

Come near together.
People who carry idols of wood
don't know what they are
doing.
They pray to a god who cannot
save them.
21Tell these people to come to me.
Let them talk about these things
together.
Who told you long ago that this
would happen?
Who told about it long ago?
I, the Lord, said these things.
There is no other God besides
me.
I am the only good God. I am the
Saviour.
There is no other God.

22"All people everywhere,
follow me and be saved.
I am God. There is no other
God.
23I will make a promise by my own
power.
And my promise is true.
What I say will not be changed.
I promise that everyone will bow
before me.
Everyone will promise to follow
me.
24People will say, 'Goodness and
power
come only from the Lord'."
Everyone who has been angry
with the Lord
will come to him and be
ashamed.
25But with the Lord's help, the
people of Israel
will be found to be good.
And they will praise him.

False Gods Are Useless

46 Bel[d] and Nebo[d] bow down.
Their idols are carried by
animals.
The statues are only heavy loads
that must be carried.
They only make people tired.

2These false gods will all bow
    down.
  They cannot save themselves.
  They will all be carried away like
    prisoners.

3"Family of Jacob, listen to me!
  All you people from Israel who
    are still alive, listen!
  I have carried you since you were
    born.
  I have taken care of you from
    your birth.
4Even when you are old, I will take
    care of you.
  Even when your hair has turned
    grey, I will take care of you.
  I made you and will take care of
    you.
  I will carry you, and I will save
    you.

5"Can you compare me to anyone?
  No one is equal to me or like
    me.
6Some people are rich with gold.
  They weigh their silver on the
    scales.
  They hire a goldsmith, and he
    makes it into a god.
  Then they bow down and
    worship it.
7They put it on their shoulders and
    carry it.
  They set it in its place, and
    there it stands.
  It cannot move from its place.
  People may yell at it, but it cannot
    answer.
  It cannot save people from their
    troubles.

8"Remember this, and do not
    forget it!
  Think about these things, you
    who turn against God.
9Remember what happened long
    ago.
  Remember that I am God.
    There is no other God.
  I am God. There is no one like
    me.

10From the beginning I told you
    what would happen in the
    end.
  A long time ago I told you
    things that have not yet
    happened.
  When I plan something, it
    happens.
  I do the things I want to do.
11I am calling a man from the east
    to carry out my plan.
  He will come like a hawk from a
    country far away.
  I will make what I have said come
    true.
  I will do what I have planned.
12Listen to me, you stubborn
    people.
  You are far from what is right.
13I will soon do the things that are
    right.
  I will bring salvation soon.
  I will save Jerusalem.
  And I will bring glory to Israel."

God Will Destroy Babylon

47 The Lord says, "City of
    Babylon,
  go down and sit in the dust.
  People of Babylon, sit on the
    ground.
  You are no longer the ruler.
  You will no longer be called
    tender or beautiful.
2 You must use large stones to
    grind grain into flour.
  Remove your veil and your nice
    skirts.
  Uncover your legs and cross the
    rivers.
3Men will see your nakedness.
  They will see your shame.
  I will punish you.
  I will punish every one of you."

4Our Saviour is named the Lord of
    heaven's armies.
  He is the Holy One of Israel.

5"Babylon, sit in darkness and say
    nothing.

You will no longer be called the
    queen of kingdoms.
6I was angry with my people.
So I rejected those people who
    belonged to me.
I gave them to you,
    but you showed them no mercy.
You even made the old people
    work very hard.
7You said, 'I will live for ever.
I will always be the queen'.
You did not think about these
    things.
You did not think about what
    would happen.
8"Now, listen, you lover of
    pleasure.
You think you are safe.
You tell yourself,
'I am the only important person.
I will never be a widow.
I will never lose my children'.
9Two things will happen to you
    suddenly in a single day.
You will lose your children and
    your husband.
These things will truly happen to
    you.
All your magic and powerful
    tricks
will not save you.
10You do evil things, but you feel
    safe.
You say, 'No one sees what I
    do'.
Your wisdom and knowledge
    have fooled you.
You say to yourself,
'I am God. No one is equal to
    me'.
11But troubles will come to you.
You will not know how to stop
    them.
Disaster will fall on you.
And you will not be able to keep
    it away.
You will be destroyed quickly.
You will not even see it coming.

12"Keep on using your tricks.
Continue doing all your magic.

You have done these things
    since you were young.
Maybe they will help you.
Maybe you will be able to scare
    someone.
13You are tired of the advice you
    have received.
So let those who study the sky
    come.
They tell the future by looking at
    the stars.
So let them save you from what
    is about to happen to you.
14But they are like straw.
Fire will quickly burn them up.
They cannot save themselves
    from the power of the fire.
They are not like coals that give
    warmth.
They are not like a fire you may
    sit beside.
15You have worked with these
    people.
They have been with you since
    you were young.
But they will not be able to help
    you.
Everyone will go his own way.
And there will be no one left to
    save you."

God Controls the Future

48 The Lord says, "Family of
    Jacob, listen to me.
You are called Israel.
You come from the family of
    Judah.
You use the Lord's name to make
    promises.
You praise the God of Israel,
    but you are not honest or
    sincere.
2You call yourselves people of the
    holy city.
You depend on the God of
    Israel.
He is named the Lord of
    heaven's armies.
3Long ago I told you what would
    happen.

I said these things and made
them known.
Suddenly I acted, and these
things happened.
4I did that because I knew you
were stubborn.
Your neck was like an iron
muscle.
It was as if your head were
made of bronze.
5So a long time ago I told you
about these things.
I told you about them before
they happened.
I did this so you couldn't say, 'My
idols did this.
My wooden and metal statues
made these things happen'.

6"You heard and saw all the things
that happened.
So you should tell this news to
others.
Now I will tell you about new
things.
These are hidden things that
you don't know yet.
7These things are happening now,
not long ago.
You have not heard about them
before today.
So you cannot say, 'We already
knew about that'.
8But you have not heard me. You
have not understood.
Even long ago you did not listen
to me.
I knew you would surely turn
against me.
You have fought against me
since you were born.
9But for my own sake I will be
patient.
People will praise me for not
becoming angry
and destroying you.
10I have made you pure, but not by
fire, as silver is made pure.

I have purified you by giving you
troubles.
11I do this for myself, for my own
sake.
I will not let people speak evil
against me.
I will not let some false god take
my glory.

Israel Will Be Free

12"People of Jacob, listen to me.
People of Israel, I have called
you to be my people.
I am God.
I am the beginning and the end.
13I made the earth with my own
hands.
With my right hand I spread out
the skies.
When I call them,
they come together before me.

14"All of you, come together and
listen.
None of the false gods said
these things would happen.
I, the Lord, have chosen someone
to attack the Babylonians.
He will carry out my wishes
against Babylon.
15I have spoken. I have called
him.[n]
I have brought him, and I will
make him successful.
16Come to me and listen to this.
From the beginning I have
spoken openly.
From the time it began, I was
there."

Now, the Lord God
has sent me with his Spirit.[d]

17The Lord is your close relative
who saves you, the Holy
One of Israel.
The Lord says,
"I am the Lord your God.
I teach you to do what is good.

him This probably refers to Cyrus king of Persia.

I lead you in the way you should
    go.
¹⁸If you had obeyed me,
    you would have had peace like a
        full-flowing river.
Good things would have flowed
    to you like the waves of the
        sea.
¹⁹You would have had many
    children.
They would have been as many
    as the grains of sand.
They would never have died out.
They would not have been
    destroyed."

²⁰My people, leave Babylon!
    Run from the Babylonians!
Tell this news with shouts of joy
    to the people.
    Spread it everywhere on earth.
Say, "The Lord has saved
    his servants, the people of
        Jacob."
²¹They did not become thirsty when
    he led them through the
        deserts.
He made water flow from a rock
    for them.
He split the rock,
    and water flowed out.

²²"There is no peace for evil
    people," says the Lord.

God Calls His Special Servant

49 All of you people in faraway
    places, listen to me.
Listen, all you nations far away.
Before I was born, the Lord called
    me to serve him.
The Lord named me while I was
    still in my mother's body.
²The Lord made my tongue like a
    sharp sword.
He hid me in the shadow of his
    hand.
The Lord made me like a sharp
    arrow.
He hid me in the quiver for his
    arrows.

³The Lord told me, "Israel, you
    are my servant.
I will show my glory through
    you."
⁴But I said, "I have worked hard
    for nothing.
I have used all my power, but I
    did nothing useful.
But the Lord will decide what my
    work is worth.
God will decide my reward."
⁵The Lord made me in the body of
    my mother
so I would be his servant.
He made me to lead the people of
    Jacob back to him.
He made me so that Israel
    might be gathered to him.
The Lord will honour me.
I will get my strength from my
    God.
⁶The Lord told me,
"You are an important servant to
    me.
You will bring back the tribesᵈ of
    Jacob.
You will bring back the people of
    Israel who are left alive.
But, more importantly, I will make
    you a light for all nations.
You will show people all over
    the world the way to be
        saved."

⁷The Lord is your close relative
    who saves you.
He is the Holy One of Israel.
He speaks to the one who is
    hated by the people.
·   He speaks to the servant of
        rulers.
The Lord says, "Kings will see
    you and stand to honour
        you.
Great leaders will bow down
    before you.
This is because the Lord can be
    trusted.
He is the Holy One of Israel,
    who has chosen you."

The Day of Salvation

8This is what the Lord says:
"At the right time I will hear your
    prayers.
On the day of salvation I will
    help you.
I will protect you.
And you will be the sign of my
    agreement with the people.
You will bring back the people to
    the land.
You will give the land that is
    now ruined back to its
    owners.
9You will tell the prisoners, 'Come
    out of your prison'.
You will tell those in darkness,
    'Come into the light'.
The people will eat beside the
    roads.
They will find food even on bare
    hills.
10They will not be hungry or
    thirsty.
Neither the hot sun nor the
    desert wind will hurt them.
The God who comforts them will
    lead them.
He will lead them by springs of
    water.
11I will make my mountains into
    roads for my people.
And the roads will be raised up.
12Look, people are coming to me
    from far away.
They are coming from the north
    and from the west.
They are coming from Aswan in
    southern Egypt."

13Heavens and earth, be happy.
    Mountains, shout with joy.
Be happy because the Lord
    comforts his people.
He will comfort those who
    suffer.

Jerusalem and Her Children

14But Jerusalem said, "The Lord
    has left me.
The Lord has forgotten me."

15The Lord answers, "Can a woman
    forget the baby she nurses?
Can she feel no kindness for the
    child she gave birth to?
Even if she could forget her
    children,
I will not forget you.
16See, I have written your name on
    my hand.
Jerusalem, I always think about
    your walls.
17Your children will soon return to
    you.
And the people who defeated
    you and destroyed you will
    leave.
18Look up and look around you.
All your children are gathering
    to return to you."
The Lord says, "As surely as I
    live,
your children will be like jewels.
You will be as proud of them as
    a bride is of her jewels.

19"You were destroyed and
    defeated.
Your land was made useless.
But now you will have more
    people than the land can
    hold.
And those people who destroyed
    you will be far away.
20Children were born to you while
    you were sad.
But they will say to you,
'This place is too small for us.
Give us a bigger place to live'.
21Then you will say to yourself,
'Who gave me all these children?
I was sad and lonely.
I was defeated and away from
    my people.
So who reared these children?
I was left all alone.
Where did all these children
    come from?'"

22This is what the Lord God says:
"See, I will lift my hand to signal
    the nations.

I will raise my banner for all
    people to see.
Then they will bring your sons
    back to you in their arms.
They will carry your daughters
    on their shoulders.
23Kings will teach your children.
Daughters of kings will take care
    of those children.
They will bow down before you.
They will kiss the earth at your
    feet.
Then you will know I am the
    Lord.
Anyone who trusts in me will
    not be disappointed."

24Can the wealth a soldier wins in
    war be taken away from
    him?
Can a prisoner be freed from a
    powerful soldier?
25But this is what the Lord says:
"The prisoners will be taken from
    the strong soldiers.
What the soldiers have taken
    will be saved.
I will fight your enemies.
I will save your children.
26I will force those who trouble you
    to eat their own flesh.
Their own blood will be the wine
    that makes them drunk.
Then everyone will know
I, the Lord, am the One who
    saves you.
I am the Powerful One of Jacob
    who saves you."

Israel Was Punished for Its Sin

50 This is what the Lord says:
"People of Israel, you say I
    divorced your mother.
Then where is the paper that
    proves it?
Or do you think I sold you to pay
    a debt?
No! It was because of the evil
    things you did that I sold
    you.

It was because of the times she
    turned against me that your
    mother was sent away.
2I came home and found no one
    there.
I called, but no one answered.
Do you think I am not able to
    save you?
Do I not have the power to save
    you?
Look, I need only to shout, and
    the sea becomes dry.
I change rivers into a desert.
Their fish rot because there is no
    water.
The fish die of thirst.
3I can make the skies dark.
I can make them black like
    clothes of sadness."

God's Servant Obeys

4The Lord God gave me the ability
    to teach.
He has taught me what to say
    to make the weak strong.
Every morning he wakes me.
He teaches me to listen like a
    student.
5The Lord God helps me learn.
And I have not turned against
    him.
I have not stopped following
    him.
6I offered my back to those who
    beat me.
I offered my cheeks to those
    who pulled my beard.
I won't hide my face from them
    when they make fun of me and
    spit at me.
7The Lord God helps me.
So I will not be ashamed.
I will be determined.
I know I will not be disgraced.
8The Lord shows that I am
    innocent, and he is close to
    me.
So who can accuse me?
If there is someone, let us go to
    court together.

If someone wants to prove I have
  done wrong,
  he should come and tell me.
9It is the Lord God who helps me.
  So who can prove me guilty?
  All those who try will become
    useless like old clothes.
  Moths will eat them.

10Who among you fears the Lord
    and obeys his servant?
  That person may walk in the dark
    and have no light.
  Then let him trust in the Lord.
  Let him depend on his God.
11But instead, some of you want to
    light your own fires.
  You want to make your own
    light.
  So, go, walk in the light of your
    fires.
  Trust your own light to guide
    you.
  But this is what you will receive
    from me:
  You will lie down in a place of
    pain.

Jerusalem Will Be Saved

51 The Lord says, "Listen to
  me,
  those of you who try to live
    good lives and follow the Lord.
  Look at the rock from which you
    were cut.
  Look at the stone quarry from
    which you were dug.
2Look at Abraham, your ancestor.
  Look at Sarah, who gave birth
    to your ancestors.
  Abraham had no children when I
    called him.
  But I blessed him and gave him
    many descendants.d
3So the Lord will comfort
    Jerusalem.
  He will show mercy to those
    who live in her ruins.
  He will change her deserts into a
    garden like Eden.

He will make her empty lands
  like the garden of the Lord.
People there will be very happy.
  They will give thanks and sing
    songs.

4"My people, listen to me.
  My nation, pay attention to
    me.
  I will give the people my
    teachings.
  And my decisions will be like a
    light to all people.
5I will soon show I do what is
    right.
  I will soon save you.
  I will use my power and judge
    all nations.
  All the faraway places are waiting
    for me.
  They wait for my power to help
    them.
6Look up to the heavens.
  Look around you at the earth
    below.
  The skies will disappear like
    clouds of smoke.
  The earth will become useless
    like old clothes.
  Its people will die like flies.
  But my salvation will continue for
    ever.
  My goodness will never end.

7"You people who know what is
    right should listen to me.
  You people who follow my
    teachings should hear what I
    say.
  Don't be afraid of the evil things
    people say.
  Don't be upset by their insults.
8Moths will eat those people as if
    they were clothes.
  Worms will eat them as if they
    were wool.
  But my goodness will continue for
    ever.
  My salvation will continue from
    now on."

⁹Wake up, wake up, and use your
   strength,
powerful Lord.
Wake up as you did in the old
   times.
Wake up as you did a long time
   ago.
With your own power, you cut
   Rahab*d* into pieces.
You killed that sea monster.
¹⁰You caused the sea to become
   dry.
You dried the waters of the
   deep ocean.
You made the deepest parts of the
   sea into a road.
Your people crossed over on
   that road and were saved.
¹¹The people the Lord has freed will
   return.
They will enter Jerusalem with
   joy.
Their happiness will last for
   ever.
They will have joy and gladness.
All sadness and sorrow will be
   gone far away.

¹²The Lord says, "I am the one
   who comforts you.
So why should you be afraid of
   people, who die?
Why should you fear people who
   die like the grass?
¹³Have you forgotten that the Lord
   made you?
He stretched out the skies.
He made the earth.
Why are you always afraid
   of those angry people who
   trouble you?
They want to destroy.
But where are those angry people
   now?
¹⁴ People in prison will soon be set
   free.
They will not die in prison.
They will have enough food.
¹⁵This is because I am the Lord
   your God.

I stir the sea and make the
   waves roar.
My name is the Lord of
   heaven's armies.
¹⁶I will give you the words I want
   you to say.
I will cover you with my hands
   and protect you.
I made the heavens and the earth.
And I say to Jerusalem, 'You are
   my people'."

God Punished Israel

¹⁷The Lord was very angry with
   you.
Your punishment was like wine
   in a cup.
The Lord made you drink that
   wine
until you stumbled.
¹⁸Jerusalem had many people.
But there was not a person to
   lead her.
Of all the people who grew up
   there,
no one was there to guide her.
¹⁹Troubles came to you in groups of
   two.
No one will feel sorry for you.
There was ruin and disaster, great
   hunger and fighting.
No one can comfort you.
²⁰Your people have become weak.
They fall down and lie on every
   street corner.
They are like animals caught in a
   net.
They have felt the full anger of
   the Lord.
They have heard God's angry
   shout.

²¹So listen to me, poor Jerusalem,
   you who are drunk but not from
   wine.
²²Your God will fight for his people.
This is what the Lord your God
   says:
"The punishment I gave you is
   like a cup of wine.

You drank it and could not walk
    straight.
I am taking that cup of my anger
    away from you.
You will never be punished by
    my anger again.
23I will now give that cup of
    punishment to those who
    gave you pain.
They told you,
    'Bow down so we can walk over
    you'.
They made your back like the
    ground for them to walk on.
You were like a street for them
    to travel on."

Jerusalem Will Be Saved

52 Wake up, wake up,
    Jerusalem!
Become strong!
Be beautiful again,
    holy city of Jerusalem.
The people who do not worship
    God and who are not pure
will not enter you again.
2Jerusalem, you once were a
    prisoner.
Now shake off the dust and
    stand up.
Jerusalem, you once were a
    prisoner.
But now free yourself from the
    chains around your neck.
3This is what the Lord says:
"You were not sold for a price.
So you will be saved without
    cost."
4This is what the Lord God says:
"First my people went down to
    Egypt to live.
Later Assyria made them
    slaves.
5"Now see what has happened,"
    says the Lord.
"Another nation has taken away
    my people for nothing.
This nation who rules them
    makes fun of me," says the
    Lord.

"All day long they speak against
    me.
6But this has happened so my
    people will know who I am.
They will know I am God.
And they will know that I am
    the one speaking to them."

7How beautiful is the person
    who comes over the mountains
    to bring good news.
How beautiful is the one who
    announces peace.
He brings good news
    and announces salvation.
How beautiful are the feet of the
    one who says to Jerusalem,
"Your God is king."
8Listen! Your guards are shouting.
They are all shouting for joy!
They all will see with their own
    eyes
when the Lord returns to
    Jerusalem.
9Jerusalem, your buildings are
    destroyed now.
But shout and rejoice together.
You can rejoice because the Lord
    has comforted his people.
He has saved Jerusalem.
10The Lord will show his holy
    power
to all the nations.
Then everyone on earth
    will see the salvation of our
    God.

11You people, leave, leave; get out
    of Babylon!
Touch nothing that is unclean.d
You men who carry the things
    used in worship,
leave there and make yourselves
    pure.
12You will not be forced to leave
    Babylon quickly.
You will not be forced to run
    away.
The Lord will go before you.
And the God of Israel will guard
    you from behind.

God's Suffering Servant

¹³The Lord says, "See, my servant
will act wisely.
People will greatly honour and
respect him.
¹⁴Many people were shocked when
they saw him.
His appearance was so changed
he did not look like a man.
His form was changed so much
they could barely tell he was
human.
¹⁵But now he will sprinkle many
people.
Kings will be amazed and shut
their mouths.
They will see the things they had
not been told about my
servant.
They will understand the things
they had not heard."

53 Who would have believed
what we heard?
Who saw the Lord's power in
this?
²He grew up like a small plant
before the Lord.
He was like a root growing in a
dry land.
He had no special beauty or form
to make us notice him.
There was nothing in his
appearance to make us
desire him.
³He was hated and rejected by
people.
He had much pain and suffering.
People would not even look at
him.
He was hated, and we didn't
even notice him.
⁴But he took our suffering on him
and felt our pain for us.
We saw his suffering.
We thought God was punishing
him.
⁵But he was wounded for the
wrong things we did.

He was crushed for the evil
things we did.
The punishment, which made us
well, was given to him.
And we are healed because of
his wounds.
⁶We all have wandered away like
sheep.
Each of us has gone his own
way.
But the Lord has put on him the
punishment
for all the evil we have done.
⁷He was beaten down and
punished.
But he didn't say a word.
He was like a lamb being led to be
killed.
He was quiet, as a sheep is
quiet while its wool is being
cut.
He never opened his mouth.
⁸Men took him away roughly and
unfairly.
He died without children to
continue his family.
He was put to death.
He was punished for the sins of
my people.
⁹He was buried with wicked men.
He died with the rich.
He had done nothing wrong.
He had never lied.
¹⁰But it was the Lord who decided
to crush him and make him
suffer.
So the Lord made his life a
penalty offering.
But he will see his descendants^d
and live a long life.
He will complete the things the
Lord wants him to do.
¹¹He will suffer many things in his
soul.
But then he will see life and be
satisfied.
My good servant will make many
people right with God.
He carried away their sins.

¹²For this reason I will make him a
  great man among people.
He will share in all things with
  those who are strong.
He willingly gave his life.
He was treated like a criminal.
But he carried away the sins of
  many people.
And he asked forgiveness for
  those who sinned.

People Will Return to Jerusalem

54 The Lord says, "Sing,
  Jerusalem.
You are like a woman who never
  gave birth to children.
Start singing and shout for joy.
You never felt the pain of giving
  birth to children.
But you will have more children
  than the woman who has a
  husband.
²Make your tent bigger.
  Stretch it out and make it wider.
  Do not hold back.
Make the ropes longer.
  Make its stakes stronger.
³Do this because you will begin
  growing very much.
Your children will take over
  other nations.
And they will again live in cities
  that once were destroyed.

⁴"Don't be afraid because you will
  not be ashamed.
Don't be embarrassed because
  you will not be disgraced.
You will forget the shame you felt
  earlier.
You will not remember the
  shame you felt when you
  lost your husband.
⁵This is because the God who
  made you is like your
  husband.
His name is the Lord of
  heaven's armies.
The Holy One of Israel is the one
  who saves you.

He is called the God of all the
  earth.
⁶You were like a woman whose
  husband left her.
And you were very sad.
You were like a wife who married
  young
and then her husband left her.
But the Lord called you to be
  his,"
says your God.
⁷God says, "I left you, but only for
  a short time.
But with great kindness I will
  bring you back again.
⁸I became very angry
and hid from you for a short
  time.
But I will show you mercy with
  kindness for ever,"
says the Lord your close
  relative who saves you.

⁹The Lord says, "This is like the
  time of Noah.
I promised then
  that I would never flood the
  world again.
In the same way, I promise
  I will not be angry with you or
  punish you again.
¹⁰The mountains may disappear,
  and the hills may come to an
  end.
But my love will never disappear.
My promise of peace will not
  come to an end,"
says the Lord who shows mercy
  to you.

¹¹"You poor city. Storms have hurt
  you,
and you have not been
  comforted.
But I will rebuild you using
  turquoise stones.
I will build your foundations with
  sapphires.
¹²I will use rubies to build your
  walls.
I will use shining jewels for the
  gates.

I will build all your outer walls
    from precious jewels.
13All your children will be taught by
    the Lord.
And they will have much peace.
14I will build you using fairness.
    You will be safe from those who
        would hurt you.
    So you will have nothing to fear.
    Nothing will come to make you
        afraid.
15I will not send anyone to attack
        you.
    And you will defeat those who
        do attack you.

16"See, I made the blacksmith.
    He fans the fire to make it
        hotter.
    And he makes the kind of tool
        he wants.
In the same way I have made the
    destroyer to destroy.
17   So no weapon that is used
        against you will defeat you.
    You will show that those who
        speak against you are
        wrong.
    These are the good things my
        servants receive.
    Their victory comes from me,"
        says the Lord.

God Gives What Is Good

55 The Lord says, "All you who
    are thirsty,
    come and drink.
    Those of you who do not have
        money,
        come, buy and eat!
    Come buy wine and milk.
        You don't need money; it will
            cost you nothing.
2Why spend your money on
        something that is not real
        food?
    Why work for something that
        doesn't really satisfy you?
    Listen closely to me, and you will
        eat what is good.

You will enjoy the food that
        satisfies your soul.
3Come to me and listen.
    Listen to me so you may live.
    I will make an agreement with you
        that will last for ever.
    I will give you the blessings I
        promised to David.
4I made David a witness of my
        power for all nations.
    I made him a ruler and
        commander of many nations.
5You will call for nations that you
        don't yet know.
    And these nations will run to
        you.
    This will happen because of the
        Lord your God.
    The Holy One of Israel honours
        you."

6So you should look for the Lord
        before it is too late.
    You should call to him while he
        is near.
7Evil people should stop being evil.
    They should stop thinking bad
        thoughts.
    They should return to the Lord,
        and he will have mercy on
        them.
    They should come to our God,
        because he will freely
        forgive them.

8The Lord says, "Your thoughts
        are not like my thoughts.
    Your ways are not like my
        ways.
9Just as the heavens are higher
        than the earth,
    so are my ways higher than
        your ways.
    And my thoughts are higher
        than your thoughts.
10Rain and snow fall from the sky.
    They don't return without
        watering the ground.
    They cause the plants to sprout
        and grow.
    And the plants make seeds for
        the farmer.

And from these seeds people
 have bread to eat.
[11]The words I say do the same
 thing.
They will not return to me
 empty.
They make the things happen that
 I want to happen.
They succeed in doing what I
 send them to do.

[12]"So you will go out with joy.
 You will be led out in peace.
The mountains and hills will burst
 into song before you.
All the trees in the fields will
 clap their hands.
[13]Large cypress trees will grow
 where thornbushes were.
Myrtle trees will grow where
 weeds were.
These things will be a reminder of
 the Lord's promise.
And this reminder will never be
 destroyed."

All Nations Will Obey the Lord

56 This is what the Lord says:
 "Give justice to all people.
Do what is right.
Do this because my salvation will
 come to you soon.
Soon everyone will know that I
 do what is right.
[2]The person who obeys the law
 about the Sabbath[d]
will be blessed.
And the person who does no evil
 will be blessed."

[3]Foreigners have joined the Lord.
 They should not say,
"The Lord will not accept me
 with his people."
The eunuch[d] should not say,
 "Because I cannot have children
 the Lord will not accept
 me."
[4]This is what the Lord says:
 "The eunuchs should obey the law
 about the Sabbath.
They should do what I want.

They should keep my
 agreement.
[5]If they do, I will make their names
 remembered
within my Temple[d] and its walls.
It will be better for them than
 children.
I will give them a name that will
 last for ever.
It will never be forgotten.
[6]Foreigners will join the Lord to
 serve him.
They will worship and love him.
They will worship him.
They will obey the law about the
 Sabbath.
They will keep the agreement
 with the Lord.
[7]I will bring these people to my
 holy mountain.
I will give them joy in my house
 of prayer.
The offerings and sacrifices
 they place on my altar will
 please me.
This is because my Temple will be
 called
a house for prayer for people
 from all nations."
[8]The Lord gathers the Israelites
 who were forced to leave
 their country.
This is what the Lord God says,
 "I will bring other people to those
 who are already gathered."

Israel's Leaders Are Evil

[9]All you animals of the field, come
 to eat.
All you animals of the forest,
 come to eat.
[10]The leaders who are to guard the
 people are blind.
They don't know what they are
 doing.
All of them are like quiet dogs.
 They don't know how to bark.
They lie down and dream.
 They love to sleep.
[11]They are like hungry dogs.
 They are never satisfied.

They are like shepherds
  who don't know what they are
    doing.
They each have gone their own
    way.
All they want to do is satisfy
  themselves.
12They say, "Come, let's drink
  some wine.
Let's drink all the beer we want.
And tomorrow we will do this
  again.
Or, maybe we will have even a
  better time."

Israel Does Not Follow God

57 Those right with God may
  die,
but no one pays attention.
Good people are taken away,
  but no one understands.
The people who live good lives are
  being taken away because of
    evil.
2 But they are given peace.
The people who live the way God
  wants them to
find rest in death.

3"Come here, you magicians!
Come here, you sons of
  prostitutes*d* and those who
  take part in adultery!*d*
4Whom are you making fun of?
Whom are you insulting?
At whom do you stick out your
  tongue?
You turn against God,
  and you are liars.
5You have sexual relations under
  every green tree
to worship your false gods.
You kill children in the ravines
  and sacrifice them in the rocky
    places.
6You take the smooth rocks from
  the ravines.
They are your portion.
You pour drink offerings on them
  to worship them.

You give grain offerings to
  them.
Do you think this makes me
  want to forgive you?
7You make your bed on every hill
  and mountain.
And there you offer sacrifices.
8You have hidden your idols
  behind your doors and
    doorposts.
You have left me, and you have
  uncovered yourself.
You have pulled back the covers
  and climbed into bed.
You have made an agreement with
  the ones whose beds you love.
And you have looked at their
  nakedness.
9You use your oils and perfumes
  to look nice for Molech.*d*
You have sent your messengers
  to faraway lands.
You even tried to send them to
  where the dead are.
10You have worked hard to do these
  things.
But you never gave up.
You found new strength.
So you did not grow weak.

11"Whom were you so afraid of
  that you lied to me?
You have not remembered me
  or even thought about me.
I have been quiet for a long time.
Is that why you are not afraid of
  me?
12I will tell about your 'goodness'
  and what you do.
And those things will do you no
  good.
13When you cry out for help,
  let the false gods you have
    gathered help you.
The wind will blow them all away.
Just a puff of wind will take
  them away.
But the person who depends on
  me will receive the land.
He will have my holy mountain."

The Lord Will Save His People

¹⁴The Lord says, "Build a road!
Build a road! Prepare the
way!
Make the way clear for my
people."
¹⁵God lives for ever and is holy.
He is high and lifted up, and he
says,
"I live in a high and holy place.
But I also live with people who
are sad and humble.
I give new life to those who are
humble.
I give new life to those whose
hearts are broken.
¹⁶I will not accuse for ever.
I will not always be angry.
If I continued to be angry, man's
life would grow weak.
Man, whom I created, would
die.
¹⁷I was angry because they were
dishonest in order to make
money.
I punished them and turned
away from them in anger.
But they continued to do evil.
¹⁸I have seen what they have done,
but I will heal them.
I will guide them and comfort
them.
And those who were sad will
praise me.
¹⁹I will give peace, real peace, to
those far and near.
And I will heal them," says the
Lord.
²⁰But evil people are like the angry
sea.
It cannot rest.
Its waves toss up waste and
mud.
²¹"There is no peace for evil
people," says my God.

How to Honour God

58 The Lord says, "Shout out
loud. Don't hold back.
Shout out loud like a trumpet.

Tell the people about the things
they have done against God.
Tell the family of Jacob about
their sins.
²Then they will come every day
looking for me.
And they will want to learn my
ways.
They will become a nation that
does what is right.
They will obey the commands of
their God.
They will ask me to judge them
fairly.
They will want God to be near
them.
³They say, 'To honour you we had
special days when we gave
up eating.
But you didn't see.
We humbled ourselves to honour
you.
But you didn't notice'."

But the Lord says, "You do what
pleases yourselves on these
special days.
And you are unfair to your
workers.
⁴On these special days when you
do not eat, you argue and
fight.
You hit each other with your
fists.
You cannot do these things as you
do now
and believe I will listen to your
prayers.
⁵This kind of special day is not
what I want.
This is not the way I want
people to be sorry for what
they have done.
I don't want people just to bow
their heads like a plant.
I don't want them to wear rough
cloth and lie in ashes to
show their sadness.
This is what you do on your
special days when you do
not eat.

But do you think this is what
the Lord wants?

6"I will tell you the kind of special
day I want.
I want you to free the people you
have put in prison unfairly.
Undo their chains.
Free those to whom you are
unfair.
Free them from their hard
labour.
7I want you to share your food
with hungry people.
I want you to bring poor,
homeless people into your
own homes.
When you see someone who has
no clothes, give him yours.
Don't refuse to help your own
relatives.
8If you do these things, your light
will shine like the dawn.
Then your wounds will quickly
heal.
Your God will walk before you,
and the glory of the Lord will
protect you from behind.
9Then you will call to the Lord, and
the Lord will answer you.
You will cry out to the Lord,
and he will say, 'Here I am'.

"You should stop making trouble
for others.
You should stop using cruel
words and pointing your
finger at others.
10You should feed those who are
hungry.
You should take care of the
needs of those who are
troubled.
Then your light will shine in the
darkness.
And you will be bright like
sunshine at noon.
11The Lord will always lead you.
He will satisfy your needs in dry
lands.
He will give strength to your
bones.

You will be like a garden that has
much water.
You will be like a spring that
never runs dry.
12Your people will rebuild the old
cities that are now in ruins.
You will rebuild the foundations
of these ancient cities.
You will be known for repairing
the broken places.
You will be known for rebuilding
the roads and houses.

13"You must obey God's law about
the Sabbath.d
You must not do what pleases
yourselves on that holy day.
You should call the Sabbath a
joyful day.
You should honour the Lord's
holy day.
You should honour it by not doing
whatever you please on that
day.
You should not say whatever
you please on that day.
14Then you will find joy in the Lord.
And I, the Lord, will carry you
to the high places above the
earth.
I will let you eat the crops of
the land your ancestor Jacob
had."
The Lord has said these things.

The Evil That People Do

59 Surely the Lord's power is
enough to save you.
He can hear you when you ask
him for help.
2It is your evil that has separated
you from your God.
Your sins cause him to turn away
from you.
And then he does not hear
you.
3With your hands you have killed
others.
Your fingers are covered with
blood from killing people.
With your lips you have lied.

With your tongue you say evil
  things.
4People take each other to court
  unfairly.
No one tells the truth in arguing
  his case.
They accuse each other falsely
  and tell lies.
They cause trouble and create
  more evil.
5They hatch evil like eggs from
  poisonous snakes.
If you eat one of those eggs,
  you will die.
And if you break one open, a
  poisonous snake comes out.
People tell lies as they would spin
  a spider's web.
6 The webs they make cannot be
  used for clothes.
You can't cover yourself with
  those webs.
The things they do are evil.
They use their hands to hurt
  others.
7They eagerly run to do evil.
They are always ready to kill
  innocent people.
They think evil thoughts.
Everywhere they go they cause
  ruin and destruction.
8They don't know how to live in
  peace.
There is no fairness in their
  lives.
They are dishonest.
Anyone who lives as they live
  will never have peace.

Israel's Sin Brings Trouble

9Fairness has gone far away.
Goodness is nowhere to be
  found.
We wait for the light, but there is
  only darkness now.
We hope for a bright light, but
  all we have is darkness.
10We are like blind people feeling
  our way along a wall.
We have to feel our way as if
  we had no eyes.

In the brightness of day we trip as
  if it were night.
We are like dead men among
  the strong.
11All of us growl like the bears.
We call out sadly like the doves.
We look for justice, but there isn't
  any.
We want to be saved, but
  salvation is far away.

12We have done many wrong things
  against our God.
Our sins show we are wrong.
We know we have turned against
  God.
We know the evil things we
  have done.
13We have sinned and turned
  against the Lord.
We have turned away from our
  God.
We have planned to hurt others
  and to disobey God.
We have planned and spoken
  lies.
14We have driven away justice.
We have kept away from what is
  right.
Truth is not spoken in the streets.
What is honest is not allowed to
  enter the city.
15Truth cannot be found anywhere.
And people who refuse to do
  evil are attacked.

The Lord looked and could not
  find any justice.
And he was displeased.
16He could not find anyone to help
  the people.
He was surprised that there was
  no one to help.
So the Lord used his own power
  to save the people.
His own goodness gave him
  strength.
17The Lord covered himself with
  goodness like armour.
He put on the helmet of
  salvation.

He put on the clothes of
    punishment.
And he put on the coat of his
    strong love.
[18]The Lord will pay back his
    enemies for what they have
    done.
He will show his anger to those
    who were against him.
He will punish the people in
    faraway places.
He will give them the
    punishment they should
    have.
[19]Then people from the west will
    fear the Lord.
People in the east will fear his
    glory.
The Lord will come quickly like a
    fast-flowing river,
    driven by the breath of the
    Lord.
[20]"Then a close relative who will
    save you will come to
    Jerusalem.
He will come to the people of
    Jacob who sinned but turned
    back to God,"
    says the Lord.

[21]The Lord says, "I will make an
agreement with these people. I promise that my Spirit[d] and my words that
I give you will never leave you. They
will be with your children and your
grandchildren. They will be with you
now and for ever."

Jerusalem Will Be Great

60 "Jerusalem, get up and shine.
    Your light has come.
The glory of the Lord shines on
    you.
[2]Darkness now covers the earth.
Deep darkness covers her
    people.
But the Lord shines on you,
    and people see his glory around
    you.

[3]Nations will come to your light.
Kings will come to the
    brightness of your sunrise.
[4]"Look around you.
People are gathering and coming
    to you.
They are your sons coming from
    far away.
And your daughters are coming
    with them.
[5]When you see them, you will
    shine with happiness.
You will be excited and full of
    joy.
The wealth of the nations across
    the seas will be given to
    you.
The riches of the nations will
    come to you.
[6]Herds of camels will cover your
    land.
Young camels will come from
    Midian and Ephah.
People will come from Sheba
    bringing gold and incense.[d]
And they will sing praises to the
    Lord.
[7]All the sheep from Kedar will be
    given to you.
The male sheep from Nebaioth
    will be brought to you.
They will be pleasing sacrifices on
    my altar.
And I will make my beautiful
    Temple[d] more beautiful.

[8]"The people are returning to you
    like clouds.
They are like doves flying to
    their nests.
[9]People in faraway lands are
    waiting for me.
The great trading ships will
    come first.
They are bringing your children
    from faraway lands.
And with them they bring silver
    and gold.
This will happen to honour the
    Lord your God.

He is the Holy One of Israel.
And he does wonderful things
    for you.

10"Jerusalem, foreigners will rebuild
    your walls.
Their kings will serve you.
When I was angry, I hurt you.
But now I want to be kind to
    you and comfort you.
11Your gates will always be open.
They will not be closed day or
    night
so the nations can bring their
    wealth to you.
And their kings will be led to
    you.
12If a nation or kingdom doesn't
    serve you,
it will be destroyed.
It will be completely ruined.

13"The great trees of Lebanon will
    be given to you.
Its pine, fir and cypress trees
    will come to you.
You will use these trees to make
    my Temple beautiful.
And I will give much honour to
    this place where I rest my
    feet.
14The people who have hurt you will
    bow down to you.
Those who hated you will bow
    down at your feet.
They will call you The City of the
    Lord.
They will call you Jerusalem,
    city of the Holy One of
    Israel.

15"You have been hated and left
    empty.
No one has even passed
    through.
But I will make you great from
    now on.
You will be a place of happiness
    for ever and ever.
16Nations will give you what you
    need.

It will be like a child drinking
    milk from its mother.
Then you will know that it is I,
    the Lord, who saves you.
You will know that the Powerful
    One of Jacob protects you.
17I will bring you gold in place of
    bronze.
I will bring you silver in place of
    iron.
I will bring you bronze in place of
    wood.
I will bring you iron in place of
    rocks.
I will change your punishment into
    peace.
And you will be ruled by what is
    right.
18There will be no more violence in
    your country.
It will not be ruined or destroyed.
You will name your walls
    Salvation.
And you will name your gates
    Praise.
19The sun will no longer be your
    light during the day.
The light from the moon will no
    longer be your light.
This is because the Lord will be
    your light for ever.
Your God will be your glory.
20Your sun will never set again.
Your moon will never be dark
    again.
This is because the Lord will be
    your light for ever.
And your time of sadness will
    end.
21All of your people will do what is
    right.
They will receive the earth for
    ever.
They are the plant I have planted.
I made them with my own hands
    to show my greatness.
22The smallest family will grow to a
    thousand.
The least important of you will
    become a powerful nation.

I am the Lord,
and when it is time, I will make
these things happen
quickly."

The Lord's Message of Freedom

61 The Lord God has put his
Spirit[d] in me.
This is because he has appointed
me to tell the good news to
the poor.
He has sent me to comfort
those whose hearts are
broken.
He has sent me to tell the
captives they are free.
He has sent me to tell the
prisoners that they are
released.
²He has sent me to announce the
time when the Lord will
show his kindness
and the time when our God will
punish evil people.
He has sent me to comfort all
those who are sad.
³He has sent me to the sorrowing
people of Jerusalem.
I will give them a crown to
replace their ashes.
I will give them the oil of gladness
to replace their sorrow.
I will give them clothes of praise
to replace their spirit of
sadness.
Then they will be called Trees of
Goodness.
They will be like trees planted
by the Lord and will show
his greatness.

⁴They will rebuild the old ruins.
They will build up the places
destroyed long ago.
They will repair the ruined cities
that were destroyed for so long.

⁵My people, foreigners will come
to tend your sheep.
People from other countries will
tend your vineyards.

⁶You will be called priests of the
Lord.
You will be named the servants
of our God.
You will have riches from all the
nations on earth.
And you will take pride in them.
⁷Instead of being ashamed, you will
receive twice as much
wealth.
Instead of being disgraced, you
will be happy because of
what you receive.
You will receive a double share of
the land.
So your happiness will continue
for ever.
⁸The Lord says, "I love justice.
I hate stealing and everything
that is wrong.
I will be fair and give my people
what they should have.
I will make an agreement with
them that will continue for
ever.
⁹Everyone in all nations will know
the children of my people.
And their children will be known
among the nations.
Anyone who sees them will know
that the Lord blesses them."

¹⁰The Lord makes me very happy.
All that I am rejoices in my
God.
The Lord has covered me with
clothes of salvation.
He has covered me with a coat
of goodness.
I am like a bridegroom dressed for
his wedding.
I am like a bride dressed in
jewels.
¹¹The earth causes plants to grow.
And a garden causes the seeds
planted there to grow.
In the same way the Lord God
will make what is right
grow strong.
He will make praise come from
all the nations.

New Jerusalem

62 Because I love Jerusalem, I
will continue to speak for
her.
For Jerusalem's sake I will not
stop speaking.
I will speak until her goodness
shines like a bright light.
I will speak until her salvation
burns bright like a flame.
²Jerusalem, the nations will see
your goodness.
All kings will see your honour.
Then you will have a new name.
The Lord himself will give you
that new name.
³You will be like a beautiful crown
in the Lord's hand.
You will be like a king's crown
in your God's hand.
⁴You will never again be called the
People that God Left.
Your land will never again be
called the Land that God
Destroyed.
You will be called the People God
Loves.
Your land will be called the
Bride of God.
This is because the Lord loves
you.
And your land will belong to him
as a bride belongs to her
husband.
⁵As a young man marries a woman,
so your children will marry your
land.
As a man is very happy about his
new wife,
so your God will be happy with
you.
⁶Jerusalem, I have put guards on
the walls to watch.
They must not be silent day or
night.
You people who remind the Lord
should never be quiet.
⁷You should not stop praying to the
Lord until he builds up
Jerusalem.

Don't stop until he makes
Jerusalem a city all people
will praise.
⁸The Lord has made a promise.
And by his power he will keep
his promise.
He said, "I will never again give
your grain
as food to your enemies.
I will not let your enemies drink
the wine
that you have worked to make.
⁹The person who gathers food will
eat it.
And he will praise the Lord.
The person who gathers the
grapes will drink the wine
in the courts of my Temple."ᵈ

¹⁰Go through, go through the gates!
Make the way ready for the
people.
Build up, build up the road!
Move all the stones off the road.
Raise the banner as a sign for the
people.
¹¹The Lord is speaking
to all the faraway lands:
"Tell the people of Jerusalem,
'Look, your Saviour is coming.
He is bringing your reward to
you.
He is bringing his payment with
him'."
¹²His people will be called the Holy
People.
They will be called the Saved
People of the Lord.
And Jerusalem will be called the
City God Wants.
It will be named the City God
Has Not Rejected.

The Lord Judges His People

63 Who is this coming from
Edom?
He comes from the city of
Bozrah dressed in red.
Who is this dressed in fine
clothes?

He marches forward with his
    great power.

He says, "I, the Lord, speak what
    is right.
I have the power to save you."

2Why are your clothes bright red
    as if you had walked on the
    grapes to make wine?

3The Lord answers, "I have
    walked in the winepress*d*
    alone.
No one among the nations
    helped me.
I was angry and walked on the
    nations.
I crushed them because of my
    anger.
Blood splashed on my clothes.
I stained all my clothing.
4I chose a time to punish people.
And the time has come for me
    to save my people.
5I looked around, but I saw no one
    to help me.
I was surprised that no one
    supported me.
So I used my own power to save
    my people.
My own anger supported me.
6While I was angry, I walked on
    the nations.
In my anger I punished them
    and poured their blood on the
    ground."

The Lord's Kindness to His People

7I will tell about the Lord's
    kindness.
And I will praise him for what
    he has done.
He has given many good things to
    us.
He has been very good to the
    people of Israel.
The Lord has shown mercy to
    us.
And he has been kind to us.

8The Lord said, "These are my
    people.
My children will not lie to me."
So the Lord saved them.
9When they suffered, he suffered
    also.
He sent his own angel to save
    them.
Because of his love and kindness,
    the Lord saved them.
Since long ago he has picked
    them up and carried them.
10But they turned against the Lord.
They made his Holy Spirit*d* very
    sad.
So the Lord became their enemy.
And he fought against them.

11But then his people remembered
    what happened long ago.
They remembered Moses.
Where is the Lord who brought
    the people through the sea?
Where is the one who brought
    them with the leaders of his
    people?
Where is the one
who put his Holy Spirit among
    them?
12The Lord led Moses by the right
    hand.
The Lord led him by his
    wonderful power.
The Lord divided the water before
    them so the people could
    walk through the sea.
And by this the Lord made his
    name famous for ever.
13The Lord led the people through
    the deep waters.
Like a horse walking through a
    desert,
the people did not stumble.
14Like cattle that go down to the
    valley,
the Spirit of the Lord led the
    people to a place of rest.
Lord, that is the way you led your
    people.
And by this you made your
    name wonderful.

A Prayer for Help

15Lord, look down from the heavens
and see.
  Look at us from your wonderful
  holy home in heaven.
Where is your strong love and
power?
Why are you keeping your love
and mercy from us?
16You are our father.
  Abraham doesn't know we are
  his children.
  Israel doesn't know who we
  are.
Lord, you are our father.
  You are called "the one who has
  always saved us."
17Lord, why are you making us
wander from your ways?
Why do you make us stubborn
so that we don't honour
you?
For our sake come back to us.
  We are your servants, and we
  belong to you.
18Your people had your Temple*d* for
a while.
  But now our enemies have
  walked on your holy place
  and crushed it.
19You have never ruled over some
people.
  They have never worn your
  name.
And we have become like those
people.

64 Tear open the skies and
come down to earth.
The mountains would tremble
before you.
2Be like a fire that burns twigs.
  Be like a fire that makes water
  boil.
Do this so that your enemies will
know who you are.
  Then all nations will shake with
  fear when they see you.
3You have done amazing things that
we did not expect.

You came down, and the
mountains trembled before
you.
4From long ago no one has ever
heard of a God like you.
No one has ever seen a God
besides you.
You help the people who trust
you.
5You help those who enjoy doing
good.
You help those who remember
how you want them to live.
But you were angry because we
sinned.
For a long time we disobeyed.
How will we be saved?
6All of us are dirty with sin.
All the right things we have
done are like filthy pieces of
cloth.
All of us are like dead leaves.
Like the wind our sins have
carried us away.
7No one worships you.
No one even asks you to help
us.
So you have turned away from
us.
And we are destroyed because
of our sins.

8But Lord, you are our father.
We are like clay, and you are
the potter.
Your hands made us all.
9Lord, don't continue to be angry
with us.
Don't remember our sins for
ever.
Please, look at us
because we are your people.
10Your holy cities are empty like the
desert.
Jerusalem is like a desert;
Jerusalem is destroyed.
11Our ancestors worshipped you
in our holy and wonderful
Temple.
But now it has been burned with
fire.

All our precious things have
   been destroyed.
12When you see these things, will
   you hold yourself back from
   helping us, Lord?
Will you be silent and punish us
   beyond what we can stand?

All People Will Learn About God

65 The Lord says, "I made
   myself known to people who
were not looking for me.
I was found by those who were
   not asking me for help.
I spoke to a nation that was not
   praying to me.
I said, 'Here I am. Here I am'.
2All day long I stood ready to
   accept
people who turned against me.
But the way they continue to live
   is not good.
They do anything they want to
   do.
3Right in front of me they continue
   to do things that make me
   angry.
They offer sacrifices to their
   false gods in their gardens.
They burn incense^d on altars of
   brick.
4They sit among the graves.
They spend their nights waiting
   to get messages from the
   dead.
They eat the meat of pigs.
Their pots are full of soup made
   from meat that is wrong to
   eat.
5But they tell others, 'Stay away.
   Don't come near me.
I am too holy for you'.
These people are like smoke in
   my nose.
Like a fire that burns all the
   time, they continue to make
   me angry.

6"Look, it is written here before
   me.

I will not be quiet. Instead, I
   will repay you in full.
I will punish you for what you
   have done.
7I will punish you for your sins and
   your ancestors' sins,"
says the Lord.
"They burned incense to false
   gods on the mountains.
They shamed me on those hills.
So I will punish them as they
   should be punished
for what they did."

8This is what the Lord says:
"When there is juice left in the
   grapes,
people do not destroy them.
They know there is good left in
   them.
I will do the same thing to my
   servants.
I will not completely destroy
   them.
9I will leave some of the children of
   Jacob.
Some of the people of Judah will
   receive my mountain.
I will choose the people who will
   live there.
My servants will live there.
10Then the Plain of Sharon will be a
   field for sheep.
The Valley of Achor will be a
   place for cattle to rest.
They will be for the people who
   want to follow me.

11"But you who left the Lord will be
   punished.
You forgot about my holy
   mountain.
You worship the false god Luck.
You hold religious feasts for the
   false god Fate.
12But I decide your fate, and I will
   punish you with my sword.
You will all be killed.
This is because I called you, but
   you refused to answer.
I spoke to you, but you wouldn't
   listen.

You did the things I said were
    evil.
    You chose to do things that
    displease me."

¹³So the Lord God said these
    things:
    "My servants will eat.
    But you evil people will be
    hungry.
My servants will drink.
    But you evil people will be
    thirsty.
My servants will be happy.
    But you evil people will be
    shamed.
¹⁴My servants will shout for joy
    because of the goodness of their
    hearts.
But you evil people will cry,
    because you will be sad.
    You will cry loudly because your
    spirits will be broken.
¹⁵Your names will be like curses to
    my servants.
    And the Lord God will put you
    to death.
    But he will call his servants by
    another name.
¹⁶People in the land who ask for
    blessings
    will ask for them from the
    faithful God.
People in the land who make a
    promise
    will promise in the name of the
    faithful God.
This is because the troubles of the
    past will be forgotten.
    I will make those troubles go
    away.

A New Time Is Coming

¹⁷"Look, I will make new heavens
    and a new earth.
    And people will not remember
    the past.
    They will not think about those
    things.
¹⁸My people will be happy for ever

because of the things I will
    make.
I will make a Jerusalem that is full
    of joy.
And I will make her people a
    delight.
¹⁹Then I will rejoice over Jerusalem.
    I will be delighted with my
    people.
There will never again be
    crying and sadness in that city.
²⁰There will never be a baby from
    that city
    who lives only a few days.
And there will never be an older
    person
    who doesn't have a long life.
A person who lives 100 years will
    be called young.
    And the person who dies before
    he is 100 will be thought of
    as a sinner.
²¹In that city the person who builds
    a house will live there.
    The person who plants
    vineyards will get to eat
    grapes.
²²No more will one person build a
    house and someone else live
    there.
    One person will not plant a
    garden and someone else eat
    its fruit.
My people will live a long time
    as trees live long.
My chosen people will live there
    and enjoy the things they make.
²³People will never again work for
    nothing.
    They will never again give birth
    to children who die young.
All my people will be blessed by
    the Lord.
    My people and their children will
    be blessed.
²⁴I will provide for their needs
    before they ask.
    I will help them while they are
    still asking for help.
²⁵Wolves and lambs will eat
    together in peace.

Lions will eat hay like oxen.
A snake on the ground will not
    hurt anyone.
They will not hurt or destroy each
    other
    on all my holy mountain,"
says the Lord.

God Will Judge All Nations

66 This is what the Lord says:
    "The skies are my throne.
The earth is my footstool.
So do you think you can build a
    house for me?
There is no place where I need
    to rest.
[2]My hand made all things.
All things are here because I
    made them,"
says the Lord.

"These are the people I am
    pleased with.
They are those who are not
    proud or stubborn.
They fear me and obey me.
[3]But those people who kill bulls as
    a sacrifice to me
are like those who kill men.
Those who kill sheep as a sacrifice
    to me
    are like those who break the
    necks of dogs.
Those who give me grain offerings
    are like those who offer me the
    blood of pigs."
Those who burn incense[d]
    are like those who worship
    idols.
These people choose their own
    ways—not mine.
    They love the terrible things
    they do.
[4]So I will punish them.
    I will punish them using what
    they fear most.
I called to them, but they did not
    listen.

I spoke to them, but they did
    not hear me.
They did things I said were evil.
    They chose to do things I did
    not like."

[5]You people who obey the words
    of the Lord,
    listen to what he says:
"Your brothers hated you.
    They turned against you
    because you followed me.
Your brothers said, 'When the
    Lord is honoured,
    we will come back and rejoice
    with you'.
But they will be punished.
[6]Listen to the loud noise coming
    from the city.
Hear the noise from the
    Temple.[d]
It is the Lord punishing his
    enemies.
He is giving them the
    punishment they should
    have.

[7]"A woman does not give birth
    before she feels the pain.
She does not give birth to a son
    before she feels the pain of
    birth.
[8]No one has ever heard of that
    happening.
No one has ever seen that
    happen.
In the same way no one ever saw
    a country begin in one day.
No one has ever heard of a new
    nation beginning in one day.
But Jerusalem will give birth to
    her children
    just as soon as she feels the
    birth pains.
[9]In the same way I will not cause
    pain
    without allowing something new
    to be born," says the Lord.
"If I cause you the pain,

dogs . . . pigs God did not want his people to offer dogs and pigs as sacrifices because they
    were unclean animals.

I will not stop you from giving
     birth to your new nation,"
     says your God.
10"Jerusalem, rejoice.
     All you people who love
          Jerusalem, be happy.
     Those of you who felt sad for
          Jerusalem
     should now feel happy with her.
11You will enjoy her good things and
          be satisfied
     as a child is nursed by its
          mother.
     You will receive her good things
          and enjoy her wealth."

12This is what the Lord says:

"I will give her peace that will
     flow to her like a river.
     The wealth of the nations will
          come flowing to her.
     Like babies you will be nursed and
          held in my arms.
     You will be bounced on my
          knees.
13I will comfort you
     as a mother comforts her child.
     You will be comforted in
          Jerusalem."

14When you see these things, you
     will be happy.
     You will grow like the grass.
     The Lord's servants will see his
          power.
     But the Lord's enemies will see
          his anger.
15Look, the Lord is coming with
     fire.
     The Lord's armies are coming
          with clouds of dust.
     He will punish those people with
          his anger.
     He will punish them with flames
          of fire.
16The Lord will judge the people
     with fire.
     He will destroy many people
          with his sword.
     He will kill many people.

17"These people make themselves
holy and pure to go to worship their
false gods in their gardens. They follow each other into their special gardens. They eat the meat of pigs and
rats and other hated things. But they
will all be destroyed together," says
the Lord.
     18"I know they have evil thoughts
and do evil things. So I am coming to
punish them. I will gather all nations
and all people. All people will come together and see my glory.
     19"I will put a mark on some of the
people. And I will send some of these
saved people to the nations. I will
send them to Tarshish, Libya, Lud
(the land of archers), Tubal, Greece
and all the faraway lands. These people have never heard about what I
have done. They have never seen my
glory. So the saved people will tell the
nations about my glory. 20And they
will bring all your fellow Israelites
from all nations. They will bring them
to my holy mountain in Jerusalem.
Your fellow Israelites will come on
horses, donkeys, camels and in chariots and wagons. They will be like the
grain offerings that the people bring in
clean containers to the Temple," says
the Lord. 21"And I will choose some of
these people to be priests and Levites," says the Lord.
     22"I will make new heavens and the
new earth. And they will last for
ever," says the Lord. "In the same
way, your names and your children
will always be with me. 23All people
will come to worship me. They will
come to worship me every Sabbath[d]
and every New Moon,"[d] says the
Lord. 24"They will go out and see
the dead bodies of the people who
sinned against me. The worms that
eat them will never die. The fires
that burn them will never stop. And
everyone will hate to see those bodies."

JEREMIAH
A Warning About Captivity

1 These are the words of Jeremiah son of Hilkiah. He belonged to the family of priests who lived in the town of Anathoth. That town is in the land that belongs to the tribe^d of Benjamin. ²The Lord spoke his word to Jeremiah. This happened during the thirteenth year that Josiah son of Amon was king of Judah. ³The Lord also spoke to Jeremiah while Jehoiakim son of Josiah was king of Judah. And the Lord spoke to Jeremiah during the 11 years and five months Zedekiah son of Josiah was king of Judah. After that, the people who lived in Jerusalem were taken away as captives out of their country.

God Calls Jeremiah

⁴The Lord spoke these words to me:
⁵"Before I made you in your
    mother's womb, I chose
    you.
Before you were born, I set you
    apart for a special work.
I appointed you as a prophet^d to
    the nations."

⁶Then I said, "But Lord God, I don't know how to speak. I am only a boy."

⁷But the Lord said to me, "Don't say, 'I am only a boy'. You must go everywhere that I send you. You must say everything I tell you to say. ⁸Don't be afraid of anyone, because I am with you. I will protect you," says the Lord.

⁹Then the Lord reached out with his hand and touched my mouth. He said to me, "See, I am putting my words in your mouth. ¹⁰Today I have put you in charge of nations and kingdoms. You will pull up and tear down, destroy and overthrow. You will build up and plant."

Two Visions

¹¹The Lord spoke this word to me: "Jeremiah, what do you see?"

I answered the Lord and said, "I see a stick of almond wood."

¹²The Lord said to me, "You have seen correctly! And I am watching to make sure my words come true."

¹³The Lord spoke his word to me again: "Jeremiah, what do you see?"

I answered the Lord and said, "I see a pot of boiling water. It is tipping over from the north!"

¹⁴The Lord said to me, "Disaster will come from the north. It will happen to all the people who live in this country. ¹⁵In a short time I will call all of the people in the northern kingdoms," said the Lord.
"Those kings will come and set up
    their thrones
    near the entrance of the gates of
        Jerusalem.
They will attack the city walls
    around Jerusalem.
They will attack all the cities in
    Judah.
¹⁶And I will announce my
    judgements against my
    people.
I will do this because of their
    evil in turning away from
    me.
They offered sacrifices to other
    gods.
And they worshipped idols they
    had made with their own
    hands.

¹⁷"Jeremiah, get ready. Stand up and speak to the people. Tell them ev-

erything I tell you to say. Don't be afraid of the people. If you are afraid of them, I will give you good reason to be afraid of them. [18]Today I am going to make you a strong city, an iron pillar, a bronze wall. You will be able to stand against everyone in the land: Judah's kings, officers, priests and the people of the land. [19]They will fight against you. But they will not defeat you. This is because I am with you, and I will save you!" says the Lord.

Israel Turns from God

2 The Lord spoke this word to me: [2]"Go and speak to the people of Jerusalem. Say to them: This is what the Lord says:

'When you were a young nation,
    you were faithful to me.
You loved me like a young
    bride.
You followed me through the
    desert.
It was a land that had never
    been planted.
[3]The people of Israel were holy to
    the Lord.
They were like the first fruits
    from his harvest.
Those who tried to hurt Israel
    were judged guilty.
Disasters happened to them',"
    says the Lord.

[4]Hear the word of the Lord, family
    of Jacob.
Hear the message, all you family
    groups of Israel.
[5]This is what the Lord says:
"I was fair to your ancestors.
    Why did they turn away from
    me?
Your ancestors worshipped
    useless idols.
And they became useless
    themselves.
[6]Your ancestors didn't say,
'The Lord brought us out of
    Egypt.

He led us through the desert.
He led us through a dry and
    rocky land.
He led us through a dark and
    dangerous land.
He led us where no one travels
    or lives.
But where is he now?'
[7]I brought you into a fertile land.
I did this so you could eat its
    fruit and produce.
But you came and made my land
    unclean.[d]
You made it a hated place.
[8]The priests didn't ask,
    'Where is the Lord?'
The people who know the
    teachings didn't know me.
The leaders turned against me.
The prophets[d] prophesied in the
    name of Baal.[d]
They worshipped useless idols.

[9]"So now I will again tell what I
    have against you," says the
    Lord.
"And I will tell what I have
    against your grandchildren.
[10]Go across the sea to the island of
    Cyprus and see.
Send someone to the land of
    Kedar to look closely.
See if there has ever been
    anything like this!
[11]Has a nation ever exchanged their
    old gods for new ones?
(Of course, their gods are not
    really gods at all.)
But my people have exchanged
    their glorious God
for idols worth nothing!
[12]Skies, be shocked at the things
    that have happened.
Shake with great fear!" says the
    Lord.
[13]"My people have done two sins.
They have turned away from me.
And I am the spring of living
    water.
And they have dug their own
    wells.

But they are broken wells that
cannot hold water.
¹⁴Have the people of Israel become
slaves?
Have they become like someone
who was born a slave?
Why was their wealth stolen?
¹⁵Enemies roar like lions at Israel.
They growl at Israel.
They have destroyed the land of
Israel.
The cities of Israel have been
burned,
and all the people have left.
¹⁶The men from the Egyptian cities
of Memphis and Tahpanhes
have disgraced you by shaving
the top of your head.
¹⁷You have brought this on
yourselves.
You turned away from me, the
Lord your God,
when I led you in the way.
¹⁸It did not help to go to Egypt
and drink from the Shihor River.
It did not help to go to Assyria
and drink from the Euphrates
River.
¹⁹Your evil will bring punishment to
you.
The wrong you have done will
teach you a lesson.
Think about it and understand.
It is a terrible evil to turn away
from the Lord your God.
It is wrong not to fear me,"
says the Lord, the Lord of
heaven's armies.
²⁰"A long time ago you refused to
obey me as an ox breaks its
yoke.ᵈ
You broke the ropes I used to
hold you to me.
You said to me, 'I will not serve
you!'
In fact, on every high hill
and under every green tree
you lay down as a prostitute.ᵈ
²¹I planted you as a special vine.
You were like very good seed.

How then did you turn
into a wild vine that grows bad
fruit?
²²You might wash yourself with
cleanser.
And you might use much soap.
But I can still see the stain of
your guilt," says the Lord
God.
²³"How can you say to me, 'I am
not guilty.
I have not worshipped the Baalᵈ
idols'?
Think about the things you did in
the valley.
Think about what you have
done.
You are like a she-camel in mating
season
that runs from place to place.
²⁴You are like a wild donkey that
lives in the desert.
At mating time she sniffs the
wind.
At that time no one can hold her
back.
Any male who chases her will
easily catch her.
At mating time, it is easy to find
her.
²⁵Don't run until your feet are bare
or until your throat is dry.
But you say, 'It's no use!
I love those other gods.
I must worship them!'
²⁶"A thief is ashamed when
someone catches him
stealing.
In the same way the family of
Israel is ashamed.
The kings and the officers,
the priests and the prophets are
ashamed.
²⁷They say to things of wood, 'You
are my father'.
They say to idols of stone, 'You
gave birth to me'.
Those people won't look at me.
They have turned their backs to
me.

But when they get into trouble,
they say,
'Come and save us!'
28Where are the idols you have
made for yourselves?
Let them come and save you
when you are in trouble!
People of Judah, you have as
many idols
as you have towns!

29"Why do you accuse me?
All of you have turned against
me," says the Lord.
30"I punished your people, but it did
not help.
They didn't come back when
they were punished.
You killed with your swords the
prophets who came to you.
You were like a dangerous lion.

31"People of Judah, pay attention to
the word of the Lord:
Have I been like a desert to the
people of Israel?
Have I been like a dark and
dangerous land to them?
Why do my people say, 'We are
free to wander.
We won't come to you any
more'?
32A young woman does not forget
her jewellery.
A bride does not forget the
decorations for her dress.
But my people have forgotten me
for more days than can be
counted!
33You really know how to chase
after love.
Even the worst women can
learn evil ways from you.
34You have blood on your clothes.
It is the blood of the poor and
innocent people.
You killed them,
but they weren't thieves you
had caught breaking in.
You do all these things,
35 but you say, 'I am innocent.
God is not angry with me'.

But I will judge you guilty of lying.
It is because you say, 'I have
not sinned'.
36It is so easy for you to change
your mind.
Assyria let you down.
And Egypt will let you down,
too.
37You will eventually leave that
place.
And, like captives, your hands
will be on your head.
You trusted those countries.
But you will not be helped by
them.
This is because the Lord has
rejected them.

Judah Is Unfaithful

3 "Now a man might divorce his
wife.
And she might leave him and
marry another man.
Should her first husband come
back to her again?
If he went back to her, the land
would become completely
unclean.d
But you have acted like a
prostituted with many lovers.
And now you want to come back
to me?" says the Lord.
2"Look up to the bare hill tops,
Judah.
Is there any place where you
have not been a prostitute?
You have sat by the road waiting
for lovers.
You sat there like an Arab in the
desert.
You made the land unclean.
This was because you did evil
and were like a prostitute.
3So the rain has not come.
There have not been any spring
rains.
But your face still looks like the
face of a prostitute.
You refuse even to be ashamed
of what you did.
4But now you are calling to me.

You say, 'My father, you have
   been my friend since I was
   young.
⁵Will you always be angry at me?
   Will your anger last for ever?'
Judah, you say this,
   but you do as much evil as you
   can!"

Judah and Israel Are Like Sisters

⁶When King Josiah was ruling Judah, the Lord spoke to me. He said: "Jeremiah, you saw what unfaithful Israel did. She was guilty of adultery.ᵈ She had idols on every hill and under every green tree. ⁷I said to myself, 'Israel will come back to me after she does this evil'. But she didn't come back to me. And Israel's wicked sister Judah saw what Israel did. ⁸Unfaithful Israel knew that I divorced her because of her adultery. But that didn't make her wicked sister Judah afraid. She also went out and acted like a prostitute!ᵈ ⁹And she didn't care that she was acting like a prostitute. So she made her country unclean.ᵈ She was guilty of adultery. This was because she worshipped idols made of stone and wood. ¹⁰Israel's wicked sister didn't come back to me with her whole heart. She only pretended to come back to me," says the Lord.

¹¹The Lord said to me, "Unfaithful Israel had a better excuse than wicked Judah. ¹²Go and speak this message towards the north:
'Come back, unfaithful people of
   Israel', says the Lord.
'I will stop frowning at you.
I am full of mercy', says the Lord.
'I will not be angry with you for
   ever.
¹³All you have to do is admit your
   sin.
You turned against the Lord
   your God.
You worshipped the false gods of
   other nations.
You worshipped them under
   every green tree.

You didn't obey me'," says the
   Lord.

¹⁴"Come back to me, you unfaithful people," says the Lord. "I am your husband. I will take one person from every city. And I will take two people from every family group. And I will bring you to Jerusalem. ¹⁵Then I will give you new rulers. They will be faithful to me. They will lead you with knowledge and understanding. ¹⁶In those days there will be many of you in the land," says the Lord. "At that time people will no longer say, 'I remember the Arkᵈ of God'. They won't even think about the Holy Ark any more. They won't even remember or miss it or make another one. ¹⁷At that time Jerusalem will be called The Throne of the Lord. All nations will come together in Jerusalem to show respect to the Lord. They will not follow their stubborn, evil hearts any more. ¹⁸In those days the family of Judah will join the family of Israel. They will come together from a land in the north. They will come to the land I gave to their ancestors.

¹⁹"I, the Lord, said,
'How happy I would be to treat
   you as sons!
I would be glad to give you a
   pleasant land.
It's a land more beautiful than
   that of any other nation'.
I thought you would call me
   'Father'
and not turn away from me.
²⁰But like a woman who is unfaithful
   to her husband,
family of Israel, you have been
   unfaithful to me," says the
   Lord.

²¹You can hear crying on the bare
   hill tops.
The people of Israel are crying
   and praying for mercy.
They have become very evil.
They have forgotten the Lord
   their God.

22"Come back to me, you unfaithful
    people of Israel.
Come back, and I will forgive
    you for being unfaithful."

"Yes, we will come to you.
You are the Lord our God.
23It was foolish to worship idols on
    the hills.
All the loud noises on the
    mountains were a lie.
Surely the salvation of Israel
    comes from the Lord our God.
24Since we were young, shameful
    gods have eaten up in
    sacrifice
everything our fathers worked
    for.
The shameful gods have taken our
    fathers' sheep and cattle.
They have taken our fathers'
    sons and daughters.
25Let us lie down in our shame.
And let our shame cover us like
    a blanket.
We have sinned against the Lord
    our God.
Both we and our fathers have
    sinned.
Since we were children and until
    now,
    we have not obeyed the Lord
    our God."

4 "If you will come back, Israel,
    then come back to me," says
    the Lord.
"Throw away your idols that I
    hate.
Don't wander away from me.
2Then you may say when you
    make a promise,
'As surely as the Lord lives'.
And you can say it in a truthful,
    honest and right way.
Then the nations will be blessed
    by the Lord.
And they will praise the Lord for
    what he has done."

3This is what the Lord says to the
men of Judah and Jerusalem:

"Plough your unploughed fields.
Don't plant seeds among the
    thorns.
4Give yourselves to the service of
    the Lord.
Decide to obey him.
Do this, men of Judah and
    people of Jerusalem.
If you don't, my anger will spread
    among you like a fire.
No one will be able to put it out
    because of the evil you have
    done.

Trouble from the North

5"Announce this message to Judah
    and say it in Jerusalem:
'Blow the trumpet throughout
    the country!'
Shout out loud and say,
'Come together!
Let's all escape to the strong,
    walled cities!'
6Raise the signal flag towards
    Jerusalem!
Run for your lives! And don't
    wait!
Do this because I am bringing
    disaster from the north.
It will be terrible destruction."

7A lion has come out of his den.
A destroyer of nations has
    begun to march.
He has left his home
    to destroy your land.
Your towns will be destroyed.
There will be no people left to
    live in them.
8So put on rough cloth,
    show how sad you are and cry
    loudly.
The terrible anger of the Lord
    has not turned away from us.

9"When this happens," says the
    Lord,
"the king and officers will lose
    their courage.
The priests will be terribly afraid.

And the prophets*d* will be shocked!"

¹⁰Then I, Jeremiah, said, "Lord God, you have tricked the people of Judah and Jerusalem. You said, 'You will have peace'. But now the sword is pointing at our throats!"

¹¹At that time this message will be given to Judah and Jerusalem: "A hot wind blows from the bare hill tops. It comes out of the desert toward the Lord's people. It is not like the gentle wind farmers use to separate grain from chaff.*d* ¹²It's a stronger wind than that. And it comes from the Lord. Now he will announce his judgement against the people of Judah."

¹³Look! The enemy rises up like a cloud.
His chariots come like a windstorm.
His horses are faster than eagles.
How terrible it will be for us!
We are ruined!
¹⁴People of Jerusalem, clean the evil from your hearts and be saved.
Don't continue making evil plans.
¹⁵A voice from Dan makes an announcement.
From the mountains of Ephraim someone brings bad news.
¹⁶"Report this to the nations.
Spread this news in Jerusalem:
'Enemies are coming from a faraway country.
They are shouting words of war against the cities of Judah.
¹⁷The enemy has surrounded Jerusalem as men guard a field.
This is because Judah turned against me'," says the Lord.
¹⁸"The way you have lived and acted
has brought this trouble to you.
This is your punishment.
How terrible it is!
The pain stabs your heart!"

Jeremiah's Cry

¹⁹Oh, how I hurt! How I hurt!
I am bent over in pain.
Oh, the torture in my heart!
My heart is pounding inside me.
I cannot keep quiet.
This is because I have heard the sound of the trumpet.
I have heard the words of war.
²⁰Disaster follows disaster.
The whole country has been destroyed.
My tents are destroyed in only a moment.
My curtains are torn down quickly.
²¹How long must I look at the war flag?
How long must I listen to the war trumpets?
²²The Lord says, "My people are foolish.
They do not know me.
They are stupid children.
They don't understand.
They are skilful at doing evil.
They don't know how to do good."

Disaster Is Coming

²³I looked at the earth.
It was empty and had no shape!
I looked at the sky.
And its light was gone.
²⁴I looked at the mountains,
and they were shaking!
All the hills were trembling.
²⁵I looked, and there were no people!
Every bird in the sky had flown away.
²⁶I looked, and the good, rich land had become a desert!
All its towns had been destroyed.
The Lord and his great anger has caused this.

²⁷This is what the Lord says:
"All the land will be ruined.

But I will not completely destroy
it.
²⁸So the people in the land will cry
loudly.
And the sky will grow dark.
This is because I have spoken and
will not change my mind.
I have made a decision, and I
will not change it."

²⁹The towns will hear the sound of
the horsemen and soldiers
with bows.
All the people will run away.
Some of them will hide in the
thick bushes.
Some will climb up into the
rocks.
All of the cities of Judah are
empty.
No one lives in them.
³⁰Judah, you destroyed nation, what
are you doing?
Why do you put on your finest
dress?
Why do you put on your gold
jewellery?
Why do you put on your
eye-shadow?
You make yourself beautiful, but
it is all useless.
Your lovers hate you.
They want to kill you.

³¹I hear a cry like a woman having a
baby.
It is a cry like a woman having
her first child.
It is the voice of Jerusalem
gasping for breath.
She lifts her hands in prayer and
says,
"Oh! I am about to faint.
They are about to murder
me!"

No One Is Right

5 The Lord says, "Walk up and
down the streets of
Jerusalem.

Look around and think about
these things.
Search the public squares of the
city.
See if you can find one person
who does honest things.
Find just one who searches for
the truth.
If you can, I will forgive this
city.
²The people say, 'As surely as the
Lord lives!'
But they don't really mean it."

³Lord, don't you look for truth in
people?
You hit the people of Judah.
But they didn't feel any pain.
You crushed them,
but they refused to learn what is
right.
They became more stubborn than
a rock.
They refused to turn back to
God.
⁴But I thought,
"These are only the poor,
foolish people.
They have not learned the way of
the Lord.
They do not know what their
God wants them to do.
⁵So I will go to the leaders of
Judah.
I will talk to them.
Surely they understand the way of
the Lord.
They know what God wants
them to do."
But the leaders had all joined
together to break away from
the Lord.
They broke their ties with him.
⁶So a lion from the forest will
attack them.
A wolf from the desert will kill
them.
A leopard is hiding and waiting for
them near their towns.
It will tear to pieces anyone who
comes out of the city.

This will happen because the people of Judah have sinned greatly.
They have wandered away from the Lord many times.

⁷The Lord said, "Tell me why I should forgive you.
Your children have left me.
They have made promises to idols that are not gods at all.
I gave your children everything they needed.
But they still were like an unfaithful wife to me.
They spent much time in houses of prostitutes.ᵈ
⁸They are like well-fed, male horses filled with sexual desire.
Each one wants another man's wife.
⁹Shouldn't I punish the people of Judah for doing these things?" says the Lord.
"I should give a nation such as this the punishment it deserves.

¹⁰"Go along and cut down Judah's vineyards.
But do not completely destroy them.
Cut off all her people as if they were branches.
Do it because they do not belong to the Lord.
¹¹The families of Israel and Judah have been completely unfaithful to me," says the Lord!

¹²Those people have lied about the Lord.
They have said, "The Lord will not do anything to us!
Nothing bad will happen to us.
We will never see war or hunger.
¹³The prophetsᵈ are like an empty wind.
The word of God is not in them.

Let these bad things they say happen to them."

¹⁴So this is what the Lord of heaven's armies says:
"The people said I would not punish them.
So, Jeremiah, the words I give you will be like fire.
And these people will be like wood the fire burns up.
¹⁵Listen, family of Israel," says the Lord.
"I will soon bring a nation from far away to attack you.
It is an old nation that has lasted a long time.
The people there speak a language you do not know.
You cannot understand what they say.
¹⁶Their arrows bring death.
All their men are strong warriors.
¹⁷They will eat your crops and your food.
They will eat your sons and daughters.
They will eat your flocks and herds.
They will eat your grapes and figs.
They will destroy with their swords
the strong, walled cities you trust in!

¹⁸"Yet even then", says the Lord, "I will not destroy you completely. ¹⁹The people of Judah will ask, 'Why has the Lord our God done this terrible thing to us?' Give them this answer: 'You have left the Lord. You have served foreign idols in your own land. So now you will serve foreigners in a land that does not belong to you!'

²⁰"Announce this message to the family of Jacob.
And tell it to the nation of Judah:

²¹Hear this message, you foolish
    people who have no sense.
You have eyes, but you don't
    really see.
You have ears, but you don't
    really listen.
²²Surely you are afraid of me," says
    the Lord.
"You should shake with fear in
    my presence.
I am the one who made the
    beaches to be a border for
    the sea.
They keep the water in its place
    for ever.
The waves may pound the beach,
    but they can't win over it.
The waves may roar,
but they cannot go beyond it.
²³But the people of Judah are
    stubborn and have turned
    against me.
They have turned aside and
    gone away from me.
²⁴They do not say to themselves,
'We should fear the Lord our
    God.
He gives us autumn and spring
    rains in their seasons.
He makes sure we have the
    harvest at the right time'.
²⁵But your evil has kept away both
    rain and harvest.
Your sins have kept you from
    enjoying good things.
²⁶There are wicked men among my
    people.
They are like men who make
    nets for catching birds.
But they set their traps to catch
    men instead of birds.
²⁷Like cages full of birds,
    their houses are full of lies.
They have become rich and
    powerful.
²⁸ They have grown big and fat.
There is no end to the evil things
    they do.
They won't plead the case of the
    orphan.

They won't help the poor be
    judged fairly.
²⁹Shouldn't I punish the people of
    Judah for doing these
    things?" says the Lord.
"I should give a nation such as
    this the punishment it
    deserves.
³⁰"A terrible and shocking thing
    has happened in the land of
    Judah:
³¹The prophets tell lies.
The priests take power into
    their own hands.
And my people love it this way.
But what will you do when the
    end comes?

Jerusalem Is Surrounded

6 "Run for your lives, people of
    Benjamin!
Run away from Jerusalem!
Blow the war trumpet in the town
    of Tekoa!
Raise the warning flag over the
    town of Beth Hakkerem!
Disaster is coming from the north.
    Terrible destruction is coming to
    you.
²Jerusalem, I will destroy you.
    You are fragile and gentle.
³Shepherds with their flocks will
    come against Jerusalem.
They will set up their tents all
    around her.
Each shepherd will take care of
    his own section."
⁴They say, "Get ready to fight
    against Jerusalem!
Get up! We will attack at noon!
But it is already getting late.
The evening shadows are
    growing long.
⁵So get up! We will attack at night.
We will destroy the strong
    towers of Jerusalem!"

⁶This is what the Lord of heaven's
armies says:
"Cut down the trees around
    Jerusalem.

Build an attack ramp to the top
  of Jerusalem's walls.
This city must be punished!
  Inside this city is nothing but
    slavery.
⁷Jerusalem pours out her evil
  as a well pours out its water.
The sounds of violence and
    destruction are heard within
    her.
I can see the sickness and hurts
    of Jerusalem.
⁸Listen to this warning, Jerusalem.
  If you don't listen, I will turn my
    back on you.
I will make your land an empty
    desert.
  No one will be able to live
    there!"

⁹This is what the Lord of heaven's
armies says:
"Gather the few people of Israel
  who are left alive.
Gather them as you would the
    last grapes on a grapevine.
Check each vine again,
  like someone who gathers
    grapes."

¹⁰To whom can I speak? Whom can
    I warn?
  Who will listen to me?
The people of Israel have closed
    ears!
  So they cannot hear my
    warnings.
They don't like the word of the
    Lord.
  They don't want to listen to
    it!
¹¹But I am full of the anger of the
    Lord.
  I am tired of holding it in.

"Pour out the Lord's anger on the
    children who play in the
    street.
Pour it out on the young men
    gathered together.
A husband and his wife will both
    be caught in his anger.

The very old people will be
    caught in it.
¹²Their houses will be turned over
    to others.
Their fields and wives will be
    given away.
I will raise my hand
  and punish the people of Judah,"
    says the Lord.
¹³"Everyone, from the least
    important to the greatest,
  is greedy for money.
Even the prophets*d* and priests
  all tell lies.
¹⁴They try to heal my people's
    serious injuries
  as if they were small wounds.
They say, 'It's all right, it's all
    right!'
  But really, it is not all right.
¹⁵They should be ashamed of the
    terrible way they act.
But they are not ashamed at all.
They don't even know how to
    blush about their sins.
So they will fall, along with
    everyone else.
They will be thrown to the
    ground when I punish
    them," says the Lord.

¹⁶This is what the Lord says:
"Stand where the roads cross and
    look.
Ask where the old way is.
Ask where the good way is, and
    walk on it.
  If you do, you will find rest for
    yourselves.
But you have said, 'We will not
    walk on the good way!'
¹⁷I chose watchmen to watch over
    you.
  I told you, 'Listen for the sound
    of the war trumpet!'
But you said, 'We will not
    listen'.
¹⁸So listen, all you nations.
  Pay attention, you witnesses.
Watch what I will do to the
    people of Judah.

¹⁹Hear this, people of the earth:
I am going to bring disaster to
    the people of Judah!
It will happen because of the evil
    they plan.
They have not listened to my
    messages.
They have rejected my
    teachings.
²⁰Why do you bring me offerings of
    incense^d from the land of
    Sheba?
Why do you bring me sweet-
    smelling cane from a
    faraway land?
Your burnt offerings will not be
    accepted.
Your sacrifices do not please
    me."

²¹So this is what the Lord says:
"I will put problems in front of
    Judah.
Fathers and sons will stumble
    over them.
Neighbours and friends will
    die."

²²This is what the Lord says:
"Look, an army is coming
    from the land of the north.
A great nation is coming
    from the far sides of the earth.
²³The soldiers carry bows and
    spears.
They are cruel and show no
    mercy.
They sound like the roaring ocean
    when they ride their horses.
That army is coming lined up for
    battle.
It is coming to attack you,
    Jerusalem."

²⁴We have heard the news about
    that army.
We are helpless from fear.
We feel trapped by our troubles.
We are in pain like a woman
    having a baby.
²⁵Don't go out into the fields.
Don't walk down the roads!

This is because the enemy has
    swords.
There is terror on every side.
²⁶My people, put on rough cloth
    and roll in the ashes to show
    how sad you are.
Cry loudly for those who are
    dead.
Cry as if your only son had died.
Do it because the destroyer
    will soon come against us.

²⁷"Jeremiah, I have made you like a
    worker who tests metal.
And my people are like the ore
    for the metal.
You must observe their ways.
And you must test them.
²⁸My people have turned against me
    and are stubborn.
They go around telling lies about
    people.
They are like bronze and iron,
    that became covered with rust.
²⁹The fire is fanned to make it
    hotter.
But the lead does not melt.
The pure silver does not come
    out.
And the evil is not removed
    from my people.
³⁰My people will be called rejected
    silver.
They will be given that name
    because the Lord has
    rejected them."

Jeremiah's Temple Sermon

7 This is the word that the Lord
    spoke to Jeremiah: ²"Stand at the
gate of the Temple.^{d} Preach this message there:
    " 'Hear the word of the Lord, all you
people of the nation of Judah! All you
who come through these gates to
worship the Lord, listen to this message! ³This is what the Lord of heav-
en's armies, the God of Israel, says:
Change your lives and do what is
right! If you do, I will let you live in
this place. ⁴Don't trust the lies that

some people say! They say, "This is the Temple of the Lord. This is the Temple of the Lord. This is the Temple of the Lord!" ⁵You must change your lives and do what is right. You must be fair to each other. ⁶You must not be hard on the strangers, the orphans and widows. Don't kill innocent people in this place! Don't follow other gods, or they will ruin your lives. ⁷If you do these things, I will let you live in this land. This is the land I gave to your ancestors to keep for ever.

⁸" 'But look! You are trusting lies. Such trust is useless. ⁹Will you steal and murder? Will you be guilty of adultery?ᵈ Will you falsely accuse other people? Will you worship the false god Baal?ᵈ And will you follow other gods you have not known? ¹⁰If you do that, do you think you can come before me? Can you stand in this place where I have chosen to be worshipped? Do you think you can say, "We are safe!"? Are you safe to do all these hated things? ¹¹This is the place where I have chosen to be worshipped. Is it nothing more to you than a hideout for robbers? I have been watching you, says the Lord!

¹²" 'You people of Judah, go now to the town of Shiloh. It was there that I first made a place to be worshipped. Go there and see what I did because of the evil things they had done. ¹³You people of Israel were doing all these evil things, says the Lord. I spoke to you again and again. But you did not listen to me. I called you, but you did not answer. ¹⁴So I will destroy the place where I have chosen to be worshipped in Jerusalem. You trust in that place. I gave it to you and your ancestors. But I will destroy it just as I destroyed Shiloh. ¹⁵I will push you away from me. I will do it just as I pushed away your brothers, the people of Israel!'

¹⁶"As for you, Jeremiah, don't pray for these people. Don't cry out for them or ask anything for them. Don't

beg me to help them. I will not listen to you. ¹⁷Don't you see what they are doing in the towns of Judah? Don't you see what they are doing in the streets of Jerusalem? ¹⁸This is what the people of Judah are doing: the children gather wood. The fathers use the wood to make a fire. The women make the dough for cakes of bread. And they offer them to the Queen Goddess.ᵈ They pour out drink offerings to worship other gods. They do this to make me angry. ¹⁹But I am not the one the people of Judah are really hurting, says the Lord. They are only hurting themselves. They are bringing shame upon themselves.

²⁰" 'So this is what the Lord says: I will pour out my anger on this place. I will pour it out on man and animal. I will pour out my anger on the trees in the field. And I will pour it out on the crops in the ground. My anger will be like a hot fire. And no one will be able to put it out.

Obedience Is More Than Sacrifice

²¹" 'This is what the Lord of heaven's armies, the God of Israel, says: Go and offer as many burnt offerings and sacrifices as you want! Eat the meat of those sacrifices yourselves! ²²I brought your ancestors out of Egypt. I spoke to them. But I did not give them commands only about burnt offerings and sacrifices. ²³I also gave them this command: obey me, and I will be your God and you will be my people. Do all that I command, and good things will happen to you. ²⁴But your ancestors did not listen or pay attention to me. They were stubborn and did whatever their evil hearts wanted. They went backwards, not forwards. ²⁵Since the day your ancestors left Egypt, I have sent you my servants, the prophets.ᵈ I sent them to you again and again. ²⁶But your ancestors did not listen or pay attention to me. They were very stubborn. And

they did more evil than their ancestors'.

27"Jeremiah, you will tell these things to the people of Judah. But they will not listen to you! You will call to them, but they will not answer you. 28So say to them, 'This is the nation that has not obeyed the Lord its God. These people do nothing when I correct them. They do not tell the truth. It has disappeared from their lips.

The Valley of Killing

29" 'Cut off your hair and throw it away. Go up to the bare hill top and cry. Do it because I, the Lord, have rejected these people. I have turned my back on them. And in my anger I will punish them! 30The people of Judah have done what I said was evil, says the Lord. They have set up their hated idols in the place where I have chosen to be worshipped. They have made it unclean!d 31The people of Judah have built places of worship at Topheth in the Valley of Ben Hinnom. There the people offered their own sons and daughters as sacrifices. This is something I never commanded. It never even entered my mind! 32So, I warn you. The days are coming, says the Lord, when people will not call this place Topheth. They will not call it the Valley of Ben Hinnom any more. They will call it the Valley of Killing. They will bury dead people in Topheth until there is no room to bury anyone else! 33Then the bodies of the dead will lie on top of the ground. They will become food for the birds of the sky. Wild animals will eat the bodies. There will be no one left alive to chase the birds or animals away. 34I will end the happy sounds of the bride and bridegroom. There will be no happy sounds in Judah or in the streets of Jerusalem. The land will become an empty desert!

8 " 'The Lord says: At that time the bones will be removed from the tombs. The bones of Judah's kings and

officers, priests and prophetsd and the people of Jerusalem will be removed. 2The bones will be spread on the ground under the sun, moon and stars the people loved and served. They went after these gods, searched them out and worshipped them. No one will gather up the bones and bury them. So they will be like dung thrown on the ground. 3I will force the people of Judah to leave their homes and their land. Those of this evil family who are not dead will wish they were dead, says the Lord'.

Sin and Punishment

4"Say to the people of Judah: 'This is what the Lord says:
When a man falls down, doesn't
    he get up again?
And when a man goes the
    wrong way, doesn't he come
    back again?
5Why, then, have the people of
    Judah gone the wrong way?
And why do the people of
    Jerusalem not turn back?
They believe their own lies.
    They refuse to turn around and
    come back.
6I have listened to them very
    carefully.
But they do not say what is
    right.
They do not feel sorry about their
    wicked ways.
The people don't think about the
    bad things they have done.
Each person goes his own way.
    He is like a horse charging into
    a battle.
7Even the birds in the sky
    know the right times to do
    things.
The storks, doves, swifts and
    thrushes
    know when it is time to migrate.
But my people don't know
    what the Lord wants them to
    do!

8" 'You keep saying, "We are wise.
This is because we have the
teachings of the Lord."
But actually, those who copy the
Scriptures
have written lies with their
pens.
9These wise men refused to listen
to the word of the Lord.
So they are not really wise at
all.
They will be ashamed.
They will be shocked and
trapped.
10So I will give their wives to other
men.
I will give their fields to new
owners.
Everyone, from the least
important to the greatest,
is greedy for money.
Even the prophets^d and priests
all tell lies.
11They try to heal my people's
serious injuries
as if they were small wounds.
They say, "It's all right, it's all
right!"
But really, it is not all right.
12They should be ashamed of the
terrible way they act.
But they are not ashamed at all.
They don't even know how to
blush about their sins.
So they will fall, along with
everyone else.
They will be thrown to the
ground when I punish them,
says the Lord.

13" 'I will take away their crops,
says the Lord.
There will be no grapes on the
vine.
There will be no figs on the fig
tree.
Even the leaves will dry up and
die.
I will take away what I gave
them!' "

14"Why are we just sitting here?

Let's get together!
We have sinned against the Lord.
So he has given us poisoned
water to drink.
Come, let's run to the strong,
walled cities.
The Lord our God has decided
that we must die.
So let's die there.
15We hoped to have peace.
But nothing good has come.
We hoped for a time when he
would heal us.
But only disaster has come!
16From the land of the tribe^d of
Dan,
the snorting of the enemy's
horses is heard.
The ground shakes from the
neighing of their large
horses.
They have come to destroy
the land and everything in it.
They have come to destroy
the city and all the people who
live there."

17"Look! I am sending poisonous
snakes to attack you.
These snakes cannot be
charmed.
They will bite you," says the
Lord.

Jeremiah's Sadness

18God, you are my comfort when I
am very sad.
You are my comfort when I'm
afraid.
19Listen to my people!
They are crying for help from a
faraway land.
They say, "Is the Lord still in
Jerusalem?
Is Jerusalem's king still there?"

But God says, "Why did the
people make me angry by
worshipping idols?
They worshipped their useless
foreign idols."

²⁰And the people say, "Harvest
time is over.
Summer has ended.
And we have not been saved."

²¹My people are crushed. So I am
crushed.
I cry loudly, and I am afraid for
them.
²²Surely there is a balm^d in the land
of Gilead.
Surely there is a doctor there.
So why aren't the hurts of my
people healed?

9 I wish my head were like a
spring of water.
And I wish my eyes were a
fountain of tears!
Then I could cry day and night
for my people who have been
killed.
²I wish I had a place in the
desert—
a house where travellers spend
the night.
Then I could leave my people.
I could go away from them.
This is because they are all
unfaithful to God.
They are all turning against
him.

Judah's Failures

³"They use their tongues like a
bow.
They shoot lies from their
mouths like arrows.
Lies, not truth,
have grown strong in the land.
They go from one evil thing to
another.
They do not know who I am,"
says the Lord.
⁴"Watch your friends.
Don't trust your own brothers.
This is because every brother is a
cheat.
And every friend tells lies about
you.
⁵Everyone lies to his friend.
No one speaks the truth.

The people of Judah have taught
their tongues to lie.
They become tired from sinning.
⁶Jeremiah, you live in the middle of
evil.
And lies follow lies.
The people have refused to know
me," says the Lord.

⁷So this is what the Lord of heav-
en's armies says:
"I will test the people of Judah as
a person tests metal in a
fire.
I have no other choice.
My people have sinned.
⁸Their tongues are like sharp
arrows.
Their mouths speak lies.
Everyone speaks nicely to his
neighbour.
But he is secretly planning to
attack him.
⁹Shouldn't I punish the people for
doing this?" says the Lord.
"Shouldn't I give them the
punishment they deserve?"

¹⁰I, Jeremiah, will cry loudly for the
mountains.
I will sing a funeral song for the
empty fields.
They are empty, and no one
passes through.
The mooing of cattle cannot be
heard.
The birds have flown away,
and the animals are gone.

¹¹"I, the Lord, will make the city of
Jerusalem a heap of ruins.
It will become a home for wild
dogs.
I will destroy the cities in the land
of Judah
so no one can live there."

¹²What man is wise enough to un-
derstand these things? Is there someone who has been taught by the Lord
who can explain them? Why was the
land ruined? Why has it been made

like an empty desert where no one goes?

¹³The Lord answered, "It is because Judah stopped following my teachings that I gave them. They have not obeyed me. They have not done what I told them to do. ¹⁴Instead, the people of Judah were stubborn. They followed the false god Baal.ᵈ Their fathers taught them to do this!" ¹⁵So this is what the Lord of heaven's armies, God of Israel, says: "I will soon make the people of Judah eat bitter food. I will make them drink poisoned water. ¹⁶I will scatter them through other nations. They will live in strange nations that they and their ancestors never knew about. I will chase the people of Judah with the sword until they are all killed."

¹⁷This is what the Lord of heaven's armies says:
"Now, think about these things!
Call for the women who cry at funerals.
Send for those women who are good at that job.
¹⁸Let them come quickly
and cry loudly for us.
Then our eyes will fill with tears.
And streams of water will come out of our eyes.
¹⁹The sound of loud crying is heard from Jerusalem:
'We are truly ruined!
We are truly ashamed!
We must leave our land,
because our houses are in ruins'."

²⁰Now, women of Judah, listen to the word of the Lord.
Open your ears to hear the words of his mouth.
Teach your daughters how to cry loudly.
Teach one another a funeral song!
²¹Death has climbed in through our windows.
It has entered our strong cities.

Death has taken away our children who play in the streets.
It has taken the young men who meet in the city squares.

²²Say, "This is what the Lord says:
'The dead bodies of men will lie in the open field like dung.
They will lie on the ground like grain a farmer has cut.
But there will be no one to gather them'."

²³This is what the Lord says:
"Wise men must not boast about their wisdom.
Strong men must not boast about their strength.
Rich men must not boast about their money.
²⁴But if someone wants to boast, let him boast about this:
let him boast that he understands and knows me.
Let him boast that I am the Lord.
Let him boast that I am kind and fair.
Let him boast that I do things that are right on earth.
This kind of boasting pleases me,"
says the Lord.

²⁵The Lord says, "The time is coming when I will punish all those who are circumcisedᵈ only in the flesh. ²⁶That is the people of Egypt, Judah, Edom, Ammon and Moab. I will also punish the desert people who cut their hair short. The men in all those countries have not given themselves to serving me. And the men of Israel do not give themselves to serving me."

The Lord and the Idols

10 Family of Israel, listen to what the Lord says to you. ²This is what he says:
"Don't live like the people from other nations.
Don't be afraid of special signs in the sky,

even though the other nations
  are afraid of them.
³The customs of other people are
  worth nothing.
  Their idols are nothing but wood
    from the forest.
  They are made by a worker
    with his chisel.
⁴They decorate their idols with
    silver and gold.
  With hammers and nails they
    fasten them down.
  That keeps them from falling
    over.
⁵Their idols are like scarecrows in
    melon fields.
  They cannot talk.
  They cannot walk.
  They must be carried.
  Do not be afraid of those idols.
  They can't hurt you.
  And they can't help you either!"

⁶Lord, there is no one like you.
  You are great.
  Your name is great and
    powerful.
⁷Everyone should respect you,
    King of all nations.
  You deserve their respect.
  There are many wise men among
    the nations.
  And there are wise men in all
    the kingdoms.
  But none of them are as wise as
    you.
⁸Those wise men are stupid and
    foolish.
  Their teachings come from
    worthless wooden idols.
⁹They use silver from Tarshish
    and gold from Uphaz.
  Their idols are made by craftsmen
    and goldsmiths.
  They put blue and purple clothes
    on the idols.
  All these things are made by
    skilled workers.
¹⁰But the Lord is the only true God.
  He is the only living God, King
    for ever.

The earth shakes when he is
    angry.
  The nations cannot stand up to
    his anger.

¹¹"Tell them this message: 'These
false gods did not make heaven and
earth. But they will be destroyed and
disappear from heaven and earth'."

¹²God made the earth by his power.
  He used his wisdom to build the
    world.
  He used his understanding to
    stretch out the skies.
¹³When he thunders, the waters in
    the skies roar.
  He makes clouds rise in the sky
    all over the earth.
  He sends lightning with the rain.
  He brings out the wind from his
    storehouses.

¹⁴People are so stupid and know so
    little.
  Goldsmiths are made ashamed
    by their idols.
  Those statues are only false gods.
  They have no breath in them.
¹⁵They are worth nothing.
  People make fun of them.
  When they are judged, they will
    be destroyed.
¹⁶But God, who is Jacob's Portion,ᵈ
    is not like the idols.
  God made everything.
  And he made Israel to be his
    special people.
  The Lord of heaven's armies is
    his name.

Destruction Is Coming
¹⁷Get everything you own and
    prepare to leave.
  You people of Judah are trapped
    in the city by your enemies.
¹⁸This is what the Lord says:
  "At this time I will throw out
    the people of Judah who live
    in this land.
  I will bring pain and trouble to
    them.

And they will really feel it."

19How terrible it will be for me
    because of my injury.
I am injured and cannot be
    healed.
Yet I told myself,
"This is my sickness; I must
    suffer through it."
20My tent is ruined.
All its ropes are broken.
My children have gone away and
    left me.
No one is left to put up my tent.
No one is left to set up a shelter
    for me.
21The shepherds are stupid.
They don't ask the Lord.
So they do not have success.
    Their flocks are scattered and
    lost.
22Listen! The news is coming.
The loud noise is coming from
    the north.
It will make the towns of Judah an
    empty desert.
They will become a home for
    wild dogs!

Jeremiah's Prayer

23Lord, I know that a person's life
    doesn't really belong to him.
No one can control his own life.
24Lord, correct me, but be fair.
Don't punish me in anger.
If you do, you will destroy me.
25Pour out your anger on other
    nations.
They do not know you.
They do not pray to you.
Those nations have destroyed
    Jacob's family.
They have eaten him up.
They destroyed his homeland.

The Agreement Is Broken

11 These are the words that the Lord spoke to Jeremiah: 2"Listen to the words of this agreement. Tell the people of Judah about it. Tell it to those living in Jerusalem. 3Tell them this is what the Lord, the God of Israel, says: 'Trouble will come to anyone who does not obey this agreement. 4I am talking about the agreement I made with your ancestors. I made it with them when I brought them out of Egypt. Egypt was like a furnace for melting iron!' I told them, 'Obey me and do everything I command you. If you do this, you will be my people. And I will be your God. 5Then I will keep the promise I made to your ancestors. I promised to give them a land where much food grows'. And you are living in that country today!"

I, Jeremiah, answered, "Amen, Lord."

6The Lord said this to me: "Prophesy[d] this message in the towns of Judah and in the streets of Jerusalem: 'Listen to the words of this agreement. Then obey them! 7I warned your ancestors to obey me when I brought them out of Egypt. I have warned them again and again to this very day! 8But your ancestors did not listen to me. They were stubborn and did what their own evil hearts wanted. The agreement says curses will come upon them if they don't obey it. So I made all those curses come upon them! I commanded them to obey the agreement, but they did not'."

9Then the Lord said to me, "I know the people of Judah and those living in Jerusalem have made secret plans. 10They are doing the same sins their ancestors did! Their ancestors refused to listen to my message. They followed and worshipped other gods. The families of Israel and Judah have broken the agreement I made with their ancestors. 11So this is what the Lord says: 'I will soon bring a disaster on the people of Judah. They will not be able to escape! And they will cry to me for help. But I will not listen to them! 12The people living in the towns of Judah and the city of Jerusalem will pray to their idols for help. They will burn incense[d] to their idols. But those idols will not be able to help when that terrible time comes! [13]The people of Judah have as many idols as there are towns in Judah. They have built many altars for worshipping that shameful god Baal.[d] There are as many altars as there are streets in Jerusalem!'

[14]"As for you, Jeremiah, don't pray for these people. Don't cry out for them or ask anything for them. I will not listen when they call to me in the time of their trouble.

[15]"What is my lover, Judah, doing in
   my Temple?[d]
She makes many evil plans.
Does she think animal sacrifices
   will stop her punishment?
When you do your evil, then you
   are happy."
[16]The Lord called you "a leafy olive
   tree,
   with beautiful fruit to look at."
But with a strong storm
   the Lord will set that tree on
   fire.
And its branches will be burned
   up.

[17]The Lord of heaven's armies planted you. And he has announced that disaster will come to you. This is because the families of Israel and Judah have done evil things. They have made him angry by offering sacrifices to Baal.

Evil Plans Against Jeremiah

[18]The Lord showed me that men were making plans against me. The Lord showed me what they were doing. So I knew they were against me. [19]Before this, I was like a gentle lamb waiting to be butchered. I did not know they had made plans against me. They said:
"Let us destroy the tree and its
   fruit!
Let's kill him!
Then people will forget him!"

[20]But, Lord of heaven's armies, you
   are a fair judge.
You know how to test people's
   hearts and minds.
I will tell you what I have against
   them.
And I will let you give them the
   punishment they should
   have!

[21]So the Lord speaks about the men from Anathoth who were planning to kill Jeremiah. Those men say, "Don't prophesy[d] in the name of the Lord. If you do, we will kill you!" [22]So this is what the Lord of heaven's armies says: "I will soon punish the men from Anathoth. Their young men will die in war. Their sons and daughters will die from hunger. [23]No one from the city of Anathoth will be left alive. I will cause a disaster to happen to them that year."

Jeremiah's First Complaint

12 Lord, if I complain to you,
   you are always right.
But I want to ask you about the
   justice you give.
Why are evil people successful?
Why do dishonest people have
   such easy lives?
[2]You have put the evil people here.
They are like plants with strong
   roots.
They grow and produce fruit.
With their mouths they speak well
   of you.
But their hearts are really far
   away from you.
[3]But you know my heart, Lord.
You see me and test my mind.
Drag the evil people away like
   sheep to be butchered.
Set them aside for the day of
   killing.
[4]How much longer will the land
   stay dried up?
How long will the grass in every
   field be dead?

The animals and birds in the land
  have died.
And it is because the people are
  evil.
Yet, they are saying,
  "God does not see what
    happens to us!"

God's Answer to Jeremiah

5"If you get tired racing against
  men,
  how can you race against
    horses?
You stumble in a country that is
  safe.
  What will you do in the thick
    thornbushes along the Jordan
    River?
6These men are your own
  brothers.
  Members of your own family are
    making plans against you.
People from your own family are
  crying out against you.
Don't trust them,
  even when they speak to you
    like friends!

7"I have left Israel.
I have left my people.
I have given the people I love
  to their enemies.
8My people have become
  like a lion in the forest to me.
They roar at me.
  So I hate them.
9My people have become to me
  like a speckled bird attacked by
    hawks.
Go, gather the wild animals!
  Bring them to get something to
    eat.
10Many shepherds will ruin my
  vineyards.
  They will walk on the plants in
    my field.
They will turn my beautiful field
  into an empty desert.
11They will turn my field into a
  desert.
  It will be wilted and dead.

The whole country is an empty
  desert.
This is because no one who
  lives there cares.
12Many soldiers will march over
  those barren hills.
  The Lord will use the armies to
    punish that land.
People from one end of the land
  to the other will be
    punished.
  No one will be safe.
13The people will plant wheat.
  But they will harvest only
    thorns.
They will work hard until they are
  very tired.
  But they will get nothing for all
    their work.
You will be ashamed of your poor
  harvest.
  The Lord's terrible anger has
    caused this."

14This is what the Lord said to me: "Here is what I will do to those wicked people who take the land I gave my people, the Israelites. I will pull them up and throw them out of their land. And I will pull up the people of Judah from among them. 15But after I pull them up, I will feel sorry for them. I will bring each person back to his own property. And I will bring him back to his own land. 16I want them to learn their lessons well. In the past they taught my people to use Baal's[d] name to make promises. Now I want them to learn to use my name! I want them to say, 'As surely as the Lord lives . . .' If they do, I will allow them to be successful. And I will let them live among my people. 17But a nation might not listen to my message. If it doesn't, I will pull it up completely and destroy it," says the Lord.

Jeremiah's Linen Belt

13 This is what the Lord said to me: "Go and buy a linen belt.

Then put it around your waist. Don't let the belt get wet."

²So I bought a linen belt, just as the Lord told me. And I put it around my waist. ³Then the Lord spoke his word to me a second time: ⁴"Take the belt you bought and are wearing. Go to Perath. Hide the belt there in a crack in the rocks." ⁵So I went to Perath and hid the belt there, just as the Lord told me.

⁶Many days later the Lord said to me, "Now go to Perath. Get the belt that I told you to hide there." ⁷So I went to Perath and dug up the belt. I took it from where I had hidden it. But now it was ruined. It was good for nothing.

⁸Then the Lord spoke his word to me. ⁹This is what the Lord said: "In the same way I will ruin the pride of the people of Judah and the great pride of Jerusalem. ¹⁰These evil people refuse to listen to my warnings. They stubbornly do only what they want to do. They follow other gods to serve and worship them. So they will become like this linen belt. They will be good for nothing. ¹¹A belt is wrapped tightly around a man's waist. In the same way I wrapped the families of Israel and Judah around me," says the Lord. "I did that so they would be my people. Then they would bring fame, praise and honour to me. But my people would not listen to me.

Warnings About Leather Wine Bags

¹²"Say to them: 'This is what the Lord, the God of Israel, says: All leather bags for holding wine should be filled with wine'. People will say to you: 'Of course, we know all wine bags should be filled with wine'. ¹³Then you will say to them, 'This is what the Lord says: I will make everyone in this land like a drunken man. I am talking about the kings who sit on David's throne. I am also talking about the priests and the prophets.ᵈ I am talking about all the people who live in Jerusalem. ¹⁴I will make the people of Judah stumble and smash into one another. Fathers and sons will fall into one another, says the Lord. I will not feel sorry or have pity for them. My mercy will not stop me from destroying them!'"

Threat of Slavery

¹⁵Listen and pay attention.
　　Don't be too proud.
　　The Lord has spoken to you.
¹⁶Honour the Lord your God.
　　Give him glory before he brings
　　　darkness.
Praise him before you fall
　　on the dark hills.
You hope for light.
　　But the Lord will turn it into
　　　thick darkness.
He will change it into deep
　　gloom.
¹⁷If you don't listen to the Lord,
　　I will cry secretly.
　　Your pride will cause me to cry.
I will cry painfully.
　　My eyes will overflow with
　　　tears.
　　This is because the Lord's
　　　people will be captured.

¹⁸Tell this to the king and queen
　　mother:
"Come down from your thrones.
Your beautiful crowns
　　have fallen from your heads."
¹⁹The cities in the desert of
　　　southern Judah are shut up.
　　No one can open them.
All Judah will be taken as captives
　　to a foreign land.
　　They will be carried away
　　　completely.

²⁰Jerusalem, look up and see.
　　Someone comes from the north.
Where is the flock God gave to
　　you to care for?
　　It is the flock you boasted
　　　about.

21What will you say when they
  appoint as your heads
  those you had thought were
  your friends?
Won't you have much pain and
  trouble?
Your pain will be like that of a
  woman having a baby.
22You might ask yourself,
  "Why has this happened to me?"
It happened because of your many
  sins.
  Because of your sins, your skirt
  was torn off
  and your body has been treated
  badly.
23A black man from Cush cannot
  change the colour of his
  skin.
  A leopard cannot change his
  spots.
In the same way, Jerusalem, you
  cannot change and do good.
You always do evil.
24"I will scatter you like chaff[d] that
  is blown away by the desert
  wind.
25This is what will happen to you.
  This is your part in my plans,"
  says the Lord.
"This will happen because you
  forgot me.
You have trusted in false gods.
26Jerusalem, I will pull your skirts
  up over your face.
  Everyone will see you, and you
  will be ashamed.
27I have seen the terrible things you
  have done.
  I know your acts of adultery[d]
  and your loud cries of
  desire.
I have seen you acting like a
  prostitute.[d]
I have seen you hated acts
  on the hills and in the fields.
How terrible it will be for you,
  Jerusalem.
  How long will you continue
  being unclean?"[d]

A Time Without Rain

14 These are the words that the
  Lord spoke to Jeremiah about
the time when there was no rain:
2"The nation of Judah cries.
  Her cities are dying.
They cry out for the land.
  A cry goes up to God from
  Jerusalem.
3The important men send their
  servants to get water.
  The servants go to the wells,
  but they find no water.
So they return with empty jars.
  They are ashamed and
  embarrassed.
They cover their heads in
  shame.
4The ground is dry and cracked
  open
  because no rain falls on the
  land.
The farmers are upset and sad.
  So they cover their heads in
  shame.
5Even the mother deer in the field
  leaves her fawn.
  She does this because there is
  no grass.
6Wild donkeys stand on the bare
  hills.
  They sniff the wind like wild
  dogs.
But their eyes are dull because
  there is no food."

7We know that we suffer because
  of our sins.
  Lord, do something to help us
  for the good of your name.
We have left you many times.
  We have sinned against you.
8God, you are the Hope of Israel.
  You have saved Israel in times
  of trouble.
But now you are like a stranger in
  the land.
  You are like a traveller who only
  stays one night.
9You seem like a man who has
  been attacked by surprise.

You seem like a warrior who is
   not able to save anyone.
But you are among us, Lord.
   And we are called by your
     name.
   So don't leave us without help!

¹⁰This is what the Lord says about
the people of Judah:
"They really love to wander from
   me.
   They don't stop themselves
     from leaving me.
So now I, the Lord, will not
     accept them.
   I will now remember the evil
     they do.
   I will punish them for their
     sins."

¹¹Then the Lord said this to me:
"Don't pray for good things to happen
to the people of Judah. ¹²Even if they
give up eating, I will not listen to their
prayers. Even if they offer burnt offerings and grain offerings to me, I will
not accept them. I will destroy the
people of Judah with war, hunger and
terrible diseases."

¹³But I said, "Oh! Lord God, the
false prophets^d keep telling the people
something different! They are saying,
'You will not suffer from an enemy's
sword. You will never suffer from
hunger. The Lord will give you peace
in this land'."

¹⁴Then the Lord said to me, "Those
prophets are prophesying lies in my
name. I did not send them. I did not
appoint them or speak to them. They
have been prophesying false visions,
idolatries and worthless magic. And
they have been prophesying their own
wishful thinking. ¹⁵So this is what I say
about the prophets who are prophesy-
ing in my name. I did not send them.
They said, 'No enemy with swords
will ever attack this country. There
will never be hunger in this land'.
Those prophets will die from hunger.
And an enemy's sword will kill them.
¹⁶And the people the prophets spoke

to will be thrown into the streets of
Jerusalem. They will die from hunger
and from an enemy's sword. No one
will be there to bury them. And no one
will bury their wives, their sons or
their daughters. I will punish them.

¹⁷"Speak this message to the people
of Judah:
'Let my eyes be filled with
     tears.
   I will cry night and day, without
     stopping.
I will cry for my people.
   They have received a terrible
     blow.
   They have been hurt very badly.
¹⁸If I go into the country,
   I see people killed by swords.
If I go into the city,
   I see much sickness because the
     people have no food.
Both the priests and the prophets
   have been taken to a foreign
     land'."

¹⁹Lord, have you completely
     rejected the nation of Judah?
   Do you hate Jerusalem?
Why have you hurt us so badly
     that we cannot be made well
     again?
We hoped for peace,
   but nothing good has come.
We looked for a time of healing,
   but only terror came.
²⁰Lord, we admit that we are very
     wicked.
   We admit that our ancestors did
     evil things.
   We have sinned against you.
²¹For your sake, do not hate us.
   Do not take away the honour
     from your glorious throne.
Remember your agreement with
     us.
   Do not break it.
²²Do foreign idols have the power
     to bring rain?
   Does the sky itself have the
     power to send down
     showers of rain?

No, it is you, Lord our God.
You are our only hope.
You are the one who made all
these things.

15 The Lord said to me: "I would
not feel sorry for the people of
Judah even if Moses and Samuel
prayed for them. Send the people
away from me! Tell them to go! ²They
might ask you, 'Where will we go?'
You tell them this: 'This is what the
Lord says:
Some people are meant to die.
And they will die.
Some are meant to die in war.
And they will die in war.
Some are meant to die from
hunger.
And they will die from hunger.
Some are meant to be taken away
as slaves to a foreign
country.
And they will become slaves in
that foreign country'.

³"I will send four kinds of destroy-
ers against them," says the Lord. "I
will send war to kill. I will send dogs
to drag the bodies away. I will send
birds of the air and wild animals. They
will eat and destroy the bodies. ⁴I will
make the people of Judah hated by everyone on earth. I will do this because
of what Manasseh did in Jerusalem.
(Manasseh son of Hezekiah was king
of the nation of Judah.)

⁵"Who will feel sorry for you,
Jerusalem?
Who will be sad and cry for
you?
Who will go out of his way to
ask how you are?
⁶Jerusalem, you have left me,"
says the Lord.
"You keep going farther and
farther away.
So I will take hold of you and
destroy you.
I am tired of holding back my
anger.

⁷I will separate the people of Judah
with my pitchfork.
I will scatter them at the city
gates of the land.
My people haven't changed their
ways.
So I will destroy them.
I will take away their children.
⁸Many women will lose their
husbands.
There will be more widows than
the sand of the sea.
I will bring a destroyer at
noontime
against the mothers of the
young men of Judah.
I will suddenly bring pain and fear
on the people of Judah.
⁹The enemy will attack.
I will still hand over to the
killers those who are left
alive from Judah.
A woman might have seven sons,
but they will all die.
She will cry until she becomes
weak and unable to breathe.
She will be upset and confused.
Her bright day will become dark
from sadness!" says the
Lord.

Jeremiah's Second Complaint

¹⁰Mother, I am sorry that you gave
birth to me.
I am the one who must accuse
and criticise the whole land.
I have not lent or borrowed
anything.
But everyone curses me.
¹¹The Lord said,
"I will save you for a good
reason.
I will make your enemies beg you
in times of disaster and trouble.
¹²No one can smash a piece of iron
or bronze.
I mean the kind of iron and
bronze that comes from the
north.
¹³The people of Judah have wealth
and treasures.

But I will freely give those
riches to others.
This is because the people of
Judah have sinned
throughout the country.
¹⁴I will make you slaves to your
enemies.
You will be slaves in a land that
you have never known.
My anger is like a hot fire.
And it will burn against you."

¹⁵Lord, you understand.
Remember me and take care of
me.
Punish for me the people who
are hurting me.
Don't destroy me while you
remain patient with them.
Think about the pain I suffer for
you, Lord.
¹⁶Your words came to me, and I
listened carefully to them.
Your words made me very
happy.
I was happy because I am called
by your name.
Your name is the Lord God of
heaven's armies.
¹⁷I never sat with the crowd
as they laughed and had fun.
I sat by myself because you were
there.
You filled me with anger at the
evil around me.
¹⁸I don't understand why my pain
has no end.
I don't understand why my
injury is not cured or healed!
Lord, will you be like a brook that
goes dry?
Will you be like a spring whose
water stops flowing?

¹⁹So this is what the Lord says:
"If you change your heart and
come back to me, I will take
you back.
Then you may serve me.
You must speak things that have
worth.

You must not speak useless
words.
Then you may speak for me.
Let the people of Judah turn to
you.
But you must not change and be
like them.
²⁰I will make you as strong as a wall
to this people.
You will be as strong as a wall
of bronze.
They will fight against you.
But they will not defeat you.
This is because I am with you.
I will rescue you and save you,"
says the Lord.
²¹"I will save you from these evil
people.
I will save you from these cruel
people."

The Day of Disaster

16 Then the Lord spoke his word
to me: ²"You must not get married. You must not have sons or
daughters in this place."

³The Lord says this about the sons
and daughters born in this land. And
he says this about the mothers and fathers of those children: ⁴"They will
die of terrible diseases. No one will
cry for them. No one will bury them.
Their bodies will lie on the ground like
dung. They will die in war, or they will
starve to death. Their dead bodies will
be food for the birds of the sky. And
they will be food for the wild animals."

⁵So this is what the Lord says: "Jer-
emiah, do not go into a house where
there is a funeral meal. Do not go
there to cry for the dead or to show
your sorrow. Do not do this because
I have taken back my blessing, my
love and my pity from these people,"
says the Lord. ⁶"Important people and
common people will die in the land of
Judah. No one will bury them or cry
for them. No one will cut himself for
them. And no one will shave his head
to show sorrow for them. ⁷No one will
bring food to the people who are cry-

ing for the dead. No one will comfort one whose mother or father has died. No one will offer a drink to comfort them.

⁸"Do not go into a house where the people are having a feast. Do not go there and sit down to eat and drink. ⁹This is what the Lord of heaven's armies, the God of Israel, says: I will soon stop the sounds of joy and gladness in this place! I will stop the happy sounds of brides and bridegrooms! This will happen during your lifetime.

¹⁰"You will tell the people of Judah these things. And they will ask you, 'Why has the Lord said these terrible things to us? What have we done wrong? What sin have we done against the Lord our God?'

¹¹"Then say to them: 'This is because your ancestors stopped following me', says the Lord. 'And they began to follow other gods. They served and worshipped other gods. Your ancestors left me. And they stopped obeying my teaching. ¹²But you have done even more evil than your ancestors. You are very stubborn. You do only what you want to do. You have not obeyed me. ¹³So I will throw you out of this country. You will go to a land that you and your ancestors never knew. There you can serve false gods day and night. I will not help you or show you any favours'.

¹⁴"People say, 'As surely as the Lord lives, who brought the people of Israel out of Egypt . . .' But the time is coming," says the Lord, "when people will not say this any more. ¹⁵They will say instead, 'As surely as the Lord lives, who brought the Israelites from the northern land and from all the countries where he had sent them . . .' And I will bring them back to the land I gave to their ancestors.

¹⁶"I will soon send for many fishermen to come to this land," says the Lord. "The fishermen will catch the people of Judah. After that, I will send for many hunters to come to this land.

Those hunters will hunt the people of Judah on every mountain and hill. And they will hunt Judah in the cracks of the rocks. ¹⁷I see everything they do. They cannot hide the things they do from me. Their sin is not hidden from my eyes! ¹⁸I will pay back the people of Judah for the evil they have done. I will punish them twice for every one of their sins. I will do this because they have made my land unclean.ᵈ They have done it with their hated idols. They have filled my country with them!"

¹⁹Lord, you are my strength and my
    protection.
  You are a safe place for me to
    run to in times of trouble.
The nations will come to you from
    all over the world.
  They will say, "Our fathers had
    only false gods.
  They worshipped useless idols
    that didn't help them.
²⁰Can people make gods for
    themselves?
  They will not really be gods!"

²¹The Lord says, "So I will teach
    those who make idols.
  Right now I will teach them
  about my power and my
    strength.
  Then they will know
    that my name is the Lord.

Judah's Guilty Heart

17 "The sin of the people of Judah is written with an iron tool.
  Their sins were cut into stone
    with a hard point.
  That stone is their hearts.
  Their sins were cut into the
    corners of their altars.
²Even their children remember
    their altars to idols and their
    Asherahᵈ idols.
  They remember the altars under
    the green trees
    and on the high hills.

³They remember the altars on my
  mountain and in the open
  country.
I will give your wealth and
  treasures
to other people.
And they will destroy the places
  of worship in your country.
You sinned by worshipping at
  those places.
⁴You will lose the land I gave you.
  And it is your own fault.
I will let your enemies take you as
  their slaves.
You will be slaves in a land you
  have never known.
This is because you have made
  my anger burn like a hot
  fire.
And it will burn for ever."

Trusting in Man or God

⁵This is what the Lord says:
"A curse will be placed on those
  who trust other people.
It will happen to those who
  depend on people for
  strength.
Those are the ones who have
  stopped trusting the Lord.
⁶They are like a bush in a desert.
  It grows in a land where no one
  lives.
It is in a hot and dry land with
  bad soil.
They don't know about the good
  things that God can give.

⁷"But the person who trusts in the
  Lord will be blessed.
The Lord will show him that he
  can be trusted.
⁸He will be strong, like a tree
  planted near water.
That tree has large roots that
  find the water.
It is not afraid when the days are
  hot.
Its leaves are always green.
It does not worry in a year when
  no rain comes.

That tree always produces
  fruit."

⁹"More than anything else, a
  person's mind is evil.
It cannot be healed.
No one truly understands it.
¹⁰But I am the Lord, and I can look
  into a person's heart.
I can test a person's mind.
So I can decide what each one
  deserves.
I can give each one the right
  payment for what he does."

¹¹Sometimes a bird will hatch an
  egg that it did not lay.
That bird is like the man who
  gets rich by cheating.
When that man's life is half
  finished, he will lose his
  riches.
At the end of his life, it will be
  clear he was a fool.

¹²From the beginning, our Temple*d*
  has been honoured
as a glorious throne for God.
¹³Lord, you are the hope of Israel.
  Those who leave you will be
  shamed.
A person who stops following the
  Lord will be like a name
  written in the dust.
That is because he has left the
  Lord.
The Lord is the spring of living
  water.

Jeremiah's Third Complaint

¹⁴Lord, heal me, and I will truly be
  healed.
Save me, and I will truly be
  saved.
Lord, you are the one I praise.
¹⁵The people of Judah keep asking
  me,
"Where is the word from the
  Lord?
Let's see that message come
  true!"

¹⁶Lord, I didn't run away from being
the shepherd you wanted.
I didn't want the terrible day to
come.
You know everything I have said.
You see all that is happening.
¹⁷Lord, don't bring terror to me.
I run to you for safety in times
of trouble.
¹⁸Make those who are hurting me
be ashamed.
But don't bring shame to me.
Let them be terrified,
but keep me from terror.
Bring the day of disaster on my
enemies.
Destroy them, and destroy them
again.

Keeping the Sabbath Holy

¹⁹This is what the Lord said to me:
"Go and stand at the People's Gate of
Jerusalem. This is where the kings of
Judah go in and out. And then go to all
the other gates of Jerusalem. ²⁰Say to
them there: 'Hear the word of the
Lord. Listen, kings of Judah. Listen,
all you people of Judah and all who
come through these gates into Jerusalem! ²¹This is what the Lord says: Be
careful not to carry a load on the Sab-
bath^d day. And don't bring it through
the gates of Jerusalem on the Sab-
bath. ²²Don't take a load out of your
houses on the Sabbath. Don't do any
work on that day. Keep the Sabbath
as a holy day. I gave this same command to your ancestors. ²³But your
ancestors did not listen. They did not
pay attention to me. They were very
stubborn. I punished them, but it
didn't do any good. They did not listen
to me. ²⁴But you must be careful to
obey me, says the Lord. You must not
bring a load through the gates of Jerusalem on the Sabbath. You must keep
the Sabbath as a holy day. You must
not do any work on that day.

²⁵" 'If you obey this command, this
is what will happen: kings who sit on
David's throne will come through the
gates of Jerusalem with their officers.
They will come riding in chariots and
on horses. The people of Judah and Jerusalem will be with them. And the
city of Jerusalem will have people liv-
ing in it for ever! ²⁶People will come to
Jerusalem from the villages around it
and from the towns of Judah. They will
come from the land of Benjamin. They
will come from the western mountain
slopes and from the mountains. And
they will come from southern Judah.
They will all bring burnt offerings,
sacrifices, grain offerings, incense^d
and offerings to show thanks to God.
They will bring these to the Temple^d
of the Lord. ²⁷But you must obey me
and keep the Sabbath day as a holy
day. You must not carry any loads into
Jerusalem on the Sabbath. If you do,
I will start a fire that cannot be put
out. It will start at the gates of Jerusalem. And it will burn until it burns
even the strong towers!' "

The Potter and the Clay

18 This is the word the Lord
spoke to Jeremiah: ²"Go down
to the potter's house. I will give you
my message there." ³So I went down
to the potter's house. I saw him working at the potter's wheel. ⁴He was
making a pot from clay. But something went wrong with it. So the potter used that clay to make another
pot. He used his hands to shape the
pot the way that he wanted it to be.

⁵Then the Lord spoke his word to
me: ⁶"Family of Israel, can't I do the
same thing with you?" says the Lord.
"You are like the clay in the potter's
hands. ⁷There may come a time when
I will speak about a nation or a kingdom. I might say I will pull that nation
up by its roots. Or I might say I will
pull that nation down and destroy it.
⁸But if the people of that nation are
sorry for the evil they have done, I
will change my mind. I will not
carry out my plans to bring disaster to
them. ⁹There may come another time

when I will speak about a nation. I might say that I will build up and plant that nation. ¹⁰But if I see it doing evil by not obeying me, I will change my mind. I will not carry out my plans to do good for them.

¹¹"So, say this to the people of Judah and those who live in Jerusalem: 'This is what the Lord says: I am preparing disaster for you right now. I am making plans against you. So stop doing the evil you are doing. Change your ways and do what is right'. ¹²But the people of Judah will answer, 'It won't do any good to try! We will continue to do what we want. Each of us will do what his stubborn, evil heart wants!' "

¹³So this is what the Lord says:
"Ask the people in other nations
    this question:
'Have you ever heard anything
    like this?'
The people of Israel have done a
    horrible thing.
¹⁴The snow on the mountains of
    Lebanon
never melts from the rocks.
Its cool, flowing streams
    do not dry up.
¹⁵But my people have forgotten
    me.
They make offerings to
    worthless idols.
This makes them stumble in what
    they do.
They stumble in the old ways of
    their ancestors.
They walk along back roads
and on poor highways.
¹⁶So Judah's country will become an
    empty desert.
People will not stop making fun
    of it.
They will shake their heads as
    they pass by.
They will be shocked at how the
    country was destroyed.
¹⁷I will scatter them before their
    enemies

as a strong east wind blows
    things away.
At that awful time they will not
    see me coming to help
    them.
They will see me leaving."

Jeremiah's Fourth Complaint

¹⁸Then the people said, "Come, let's make plans against Jeremiah. Surely the teaching of the law by the priest will not be lost. And the advice from the wise men will still be with us. We will still have the words of the prophets.ᵈ So let's ruin him by telling lies about him! We won't pay attention to anything he says."

¹⁹Lord, listen to me.
Listen to what my accusers are
    saying!
²⁰Good should not be paid back with
    evil.
But they have dug a pit in order
    to kill me.
Lord, remember that I stood
    before you
and asked you to do good things
    for these people.
I asked you to turn your anger
    away from them.
²¹So now, let their children starve.
Let their enemies defeat them
    with swords.
Let their wives lose their children
    and husbands.
Let the men from Judah be put
    to death.
Let the young men be killed in
    battle.
²²Let them cry out in their houses.
Bring an enemy against them
    suddenly.
Let all this happen because my
    enemies have dug a pit to
    trap me.
And they have hidden traps for
    me to step in.
²³Lord, you know
    about their plans to kill me.
Don't forgive their crimes.

Don't erase their sins.
Make them fall from their places.
Punish them while you are
   angry.

The Broken Jar

19 This is what the Lord said to me: "Go and buy a clay jar from a potter. ²Go out to the Valley of Ben Hinnom. Go near the front of the Potsherd Gate. Take some of the older leaders of the people and priests with you. There speak the words I tell you. ³Say, 'King of Judah and people of Jerusalem, listen to this message from the Lord. This is what the Lord of heaven's armies, the God of Israel, says: I will soon bring a disaster on this place! Everyone who hears about it will be amazed and full of fear. ⁴I will do this because the people of Judah have stopped following me. They have made this a place for foreign gods. They have burned sacrifices to other gods. They did not worship these gods long ago! Their ancestors didn't worship these gods. The kings of Judah filled this place with the blood of the innocent people. ⁵The kings of Judah have built places to worship Baal.ᵈ There they burn their sons in the fire to Baal. I did not speak about it or tell them to do that. I never even thought of such a thing. ⁶Now people call this place the Valley of Ben Hinnom or Topheth. But watch out! The days are coming, says the Lord, when people will call this place the Valley of Killing.

⁷" 'At this place I will ruin the plans of the people of Judah and Jerusalem. The enemy will chase them. And I will let the people of Judah be killed with swords. I will make their dead bodies food for the birds and wild animals. ⁸I will completely destroy this city. People will make fun of it and hiss at it.

And they will shake their heads when they pass by Jerusalem. They will be shocked when they see how the city was destroyed. ⁹An enemy army will surround the city. They will not let anyone go out to get food. The people will become so hungry they will eat the bodies of their own sons and daughters. And then they will begin to eat each other'."

¹⁰The Lord said, "While the people with you are watching, break that jar. ¹¹Then say this: 'The Lord of heaven's armies says: I will break this nation and this city just as someone breaks a clay jar. It cannot be put back together again. The dead people will be buried here in Topheth. We will bury bodies until there is no more room. ¹²This is what I will do to these people and to this place, says the Lord. I will make this city like Topheth. ¹³The houses in Jerusalem and the king's palaces will become as uncleanᵈ as this place, Topheth. This is because the people worshipped false gods on the roofsⁿ of their houses. They worshipped the stars and burned incenseᵈ to honour them. They gave drink offerings to false gods'."

¹⁴Then Jeremiah left Topheth where the Lord had told him to prophesy.ᵈ He went to the Lord's Temple,ᵈ stood in the courtyard and said to all the people: ¹⁵"This is what the Lord of heaven's armies, the God of Israel, says: 'I said I would bring disaster to Jerusalem and the villages around it. I will make it happen soon! This is because the people are very stubborn. They do not listen at all to what I say'."

Jeremiah and Pashhur

20 Pashhur son of Immer was a priest. He was the highest officer in the Templeᵈ of the Lord. He

---

roofs In Bible times houses were built with flat roofs. The roof was used for drying things such as flax and fruit. It was also used as an extra room, as a place for worship and as a place to sleep in the summer.

heard Jeremiah prophesying^d in the Temple courtyard. ²So he had Jeremiah the prophet beaten. And he had Jeremiah's hands and feet locked between large blocks of wood. This was at the Upper Gate of Benjamin of the Lord's Temple. ³The next day Pashhur took Jeremiah out from between the blocks of wood. Then Jeremiah said to him, "The Lord's name for you is not Pashhur. Now the Lord's name for you is Terror on Every Side. ⁴That is your name because this is what the Lord says: 'I will soon make you a terror to yourself and to all your friends. You will watch enemies killing your friends with swords. And I will give all the people of Judah to the king of Babylon. He will take them away as captives to Babylon. Then his army will kill them with swords. ⁵I will give all the wealth of this city to its enemies. I will give them its goods and its valuables. I will give the treasures of the kings of Judah to their enemies. The enemies will carry Judah and all its valuables off to Babylon. ⁶And Pashhur, you and everyone in your house will be taken away. You will be forced to go as a captive to Babylon. You will die and be buried there. Your friends you have prophesied lies to will also die and be buried in Babylon!'"

Jeremiah's Fifth Complaint

⁷Lord, you tricked me, and I was fooled.
　You are stronger than I am. So you won.
I have become a joke.
　Everyone makes fun of me all day long.
⁸Every time I speak, I shout.
　I am always shouting about violence and destruction.
I tell the people about the message I received from the Lord.
　But this only brings me insults.
　The people make fun of me all day long.

⁹Sometimes I say to myself,
　"I will forget about the Lord.
　I will not speak any more in his name."
But then the Lord's message becomes like a burning fire inside me.
It feels as if it burns deep within my bones.
I get tired of trying to hold the Lord's message inside me.
And finally, I cannot hold it in.
¹⁰I hear many people whispering about me:
　"Terror on every side!
　Let's tell the rulers about him."
My friends are all just waiting for me to make some mistake.
　They are saying,
"Perhaps we can trick Jeremiah.
　Then we can defeat him.
　Then we can pay him back."

¹¹But the Lord is with me like a strong warrior.
　So those who are chasing me will trip and fall.
　They will not defeat me.
They will be very disappointed and ashamed.
　Their shame will never be forgotten.

¹²Lord of heaven's armies, you test good people.
You look deeply into the heart and mind of a person.
I have told you my arguments against these people.
　So let me see you give them the punishment they deserve.

¹³Sing to the Lord!
　Praise the Lord!
He saves the life of the poor.
　He saves them from the power of wicked people.

Jeremiah's Sixth Complaint

¹⁴Let there be a curse on the day I was born.

Let there be no blessing on the
day when my mother gave
birth to me.
15Let there be a curse on the man
who brought my father the
news:
"You have a son!"
This made my father glad.
16Let that man be like the towns
the Lord destroyed without pity.
Let that man hear loud crying in
the morning.
And let him hear battle cries at
noon.
17This is because he did not kill me
before I was born.
Then my mother would have
been my grave.
I would never have been born.
18Why did I have to come out of my
mother's body?
All I have known is trouble and
sorrow.
And my life will end in shame.

God Rejects King Zedekiah's Request

21 This is the word that the Lord
spoke to Jeremiah. It came
when Zedekiah king of Judah sent
Pashhur son of Malkijah to Jeremiah.
He also sent the priest Zephaniah son
of Maaseiah. 2They said, "Ask the
Lord for us what will happen. We want
to know because Nebuchadnezzar
king of Babylon is attacking us. Perhaps the Lord will do miracles*d* for us
as he did in the past. Perhaps he will
make Nebuchadnezzar stop attacking
us and leave."

3But Jeremiah answered them,
"Tell King Zedekiah this: 4'Here is
what the Lord, the God of Israel,
says: You have weapons of war in
your hands. You are using them to defend yourselves against the king of
Babylon and the Babylonians. But I
will make those weapons useless. The
army from Babylon is all around the
outside of the city wall. Soon I will

bring that army into the centre of the
city. 5I myself will fight against you
with my great power and strength. I
am very angry with you. So I will fight
against you with my own powerful
arm. I will fight very hard against you
in my very great anger. 6I will kill everything living in Jerusalem — both
people and animals. They will die from
terrible diseases. 7Then, says the
Lord, I'll give Zedekiah king of Judah
to Nebuchadnezzar king of Babylon. I
will also give Zedekiah's officers to
Nebuchadnezzar. Some of the people
in Jerusalem will not die from the terrible diseases. Some will not die in
battle or from hunger. I will give them
also to Nebuchadnezzar king of Babylon. I will let those win who want to
kill the people of Judah. So the people
of Judah and Jerusalem will be killed in
war. Nebuchadnezzar will not show
any mercy or pity or feel sorry for
them!'

8"Also tell this to the people of Jerusalem: 'This is what the Lord says: I
will let you choose to live or die. 9Any-
one who stays in Jerusalem will die.
He will die in war or from hunger or
from a terrible disease. But anyone
who goes out of Jerusalem and surrenders to the Babylonians who are
around the city will live. Anyone who
leaves the city will save his life. 10I
have decided to make trouble for this
city and not to help it, says the Lord.
I will give it to the king of Babylon. He
will burn it with fire'.

11"Tell these things to Judah's royal
family: 'Hear the word of the Lord!
12Family of David, the Lord says
these things:
You must judge people fairly
every day.
Protect from criminals
the person who has been
robbed.
If you don't do that, I will become
very angry.
My anger will be like a fire that
no one can put out.

This will happen because you
    have done evil things.

13" 'Jerusalem, I am against you.
You sit on top of the mountain.
You sit over this valley, says the
    Lord.
You say, "No one can attack us.
No one can come into our
    strong city."
14But I will give you the punishment
    you deserve, says the Lord.
I will start a fire in your forests.
It will burn up everything around
    you!' "

Judgement Against Evil Kings

22 This is what the Lord says:
"Go down to the palace of the
king of Judah. Prophesy*d* this message
there: 2'Hear the word of the Lord,
king of Judah. You rule from David's
throne. You and your officers, listen
well! All of your people who come
through these gates, listen! 3This is
what the Lord says: Do what is fair
and right. Protect those who have
been robbed from those who robbed
them. Don't do any wrong to the orphans or widows. Don't hurt them.
Don't kill innocent people here. 4If you
carefully obey these commands, this
is what will happen: kings who sit on
David's throne will come through the
gates of this palace. They will come
with their officers and people. They
will all come riding in chariots and on
horses. 5But if you don't obey these
commands, this is what the Lord
says: I promise in my own name that
this king's palace will become a ruin'."

6This is what the Lord says about
the palace where the king of Judah
lives:
"This palace is tall like the forests
    of Gilead.
It is high like the mountains of
    Lebanon.
But I will truly make it like a
    desert.

It will be empty like towns
    where no one lives.
7I will send men to destroy the
    palace.
Each man will have his weapons
    with him.
They will cut up your strong,
    beautiful cedar beams.
And they will throw them into
    the fire.

8"People from many nations will
pass by this city. They will ask each
other, 'Why has the Lord done such a
terrible thing to Jerusalem? This was
such a great city'. 9And the answer
will be: 'It was because the people of
Judah stopped following the agreement with the Lord their God. They
worshipped and served other gods'."

Judgement Against Jehoahaz

10Don't cry for the king who has
    died. Don't cry loudly for
    him.
But cry painfully for the king
    who is being taken away
    from here.
Cry for him because he will never
    come back again.
He will never see his homeland
    again.

11This is what the Lord says about
Jehoahaz son of Josiah. Jehoahaz became king of Judah after his father
died. He has left this place. The Lord
says, "He will never come back again.
12He will die where those who captured him have taken him. He will not
see this land again."

Judgement Against Jehoiakim

13"How terrible it will be for him
    who builds his palace by
    doing evil.
He cheats people so he can build
    its upper rooms.
He is making his own people work
    for nothing.
He is not paying them for their
    work.

¹⁴He says, 'I will build a great
    palace for myself.
I will have large upper rooms'.
So he builds the palace with large
    windows.
He uses cedar wood for the
    walls.
And he paints it red.
¹⁵"Does having a lot of cedar in
    your house
    make you a great king?
Your father was satisfied to have
    food and drink.
He did what was right and fair.
So everything went well for him.
¹⁶He helped those who were poor
    and needy.
So everything went well for him.
That's what it means to know
    God," says the Lord.
¹⁷"But your eyes only look for what
    you can get dishonestly.
You are always thinking about
    getting more for yourself.
You are even willing to kill
      innocent people to get it.
You are making it hard for
    people.
You even steal things from
    them."
¹⁸So this is what the Lord says to Je-
hoiakim son of Josiah king of Judah:
    "The people of Judah will not cry
      loudly when Jehoiakim dies.
They will not say, 'Oh, my
    brother, I am so sad!
Oh, my sister, I am so sad!'
The people of Judah will not cry
    for him, saying:
'Oh, master, oh, my king'.
¹⁹The people of Jerusalem will bury
    him like a donkey.
They will just drag his body
    away.
Then they will throw it outside
    the gates of Jerusalem.
²⁰"Judah, go up to Lebanon and cry
    out.
Let your voice be heard in
    Bashan.

Cry out from Abarim.
All your friends are destroyed!
²¹Judah, when you were successful,
    I warned you.
But you refused to listen.
You have acted like this since you
    were young.
You have not obeyed me.
²²My punishment will come like a
    storm.
And it will blow all your
    shepherds away.
Your friends will be taken away
    as captives.
Then you will really be ashamed.
You will be disgraced because of
    all the wicked things you
    did.
²³King, you live in your palace.
You are cosy in your rooms of
    cedar.
But you will groan when your
    punishment comes.
You will hurt like a woman
    giving birth to a baby!

Judgement Upon Jehoiachin

²⁴"As surely as I live," says the
Lord, "I will do this to you, Jehoiachin
son of Jehoiakim king of Judah: even
if you were a signet^d ring on my right
hand, I would still pull you off. ²⁵Jehoi-
achin, I will give you to Nebuchadnez-
zar king of Babylon. And I will hand
you over to the Babylonians. Those
are the people you are afraid of because they want to kill you. ²⁶I will
throw you and your mother into an-
other country. Neither of you was
born there. But both of you will die
there. ²⁷You will want to come back.
But you will never be able to return."

²⁸Jehoiachin is like a broken pot
    someone has thrown away.
He is like something no one
    wants.
Why will Jehoiachin and his
    children be thrown out?
Why will they be thrown into a
    foreign land?

²⁹Land, land, land of Judah,
  hear the word of the Lord!
³⁰This is what the Lord says:
  "Write this down about Jehoiachin:
  He is a man who is to have no
    children.
  He will not be successful in his
    lifetime.
And none of his children will be
    successful.
  None of his children will sit on
    the throne of David.
  They will not rule in Judah."

The Evil Leaders

23 "How terrible it will be for the leaders of Judah. They are destroying my people. They are making them run in all directions," says the Lord. ²They are responsible for the people. And the Lord, the God of Israel, says to them: "You have made my people run away in all directions. You have forced them away. And you have not taken care of them. So I will punish you for the evil things you have done," says the Lord. ³"I sent my people to other countries. But I will gather my people who are left alive. And I will bring them back to their own country. When they are back in their own land, they will have many children. And they will grow in number. ⁴I will place new leaders over my people. They will take care of my people. And my people will not be afraid or terrified. None of them will be lost," says the Lord.

The Good Descendant

⁵"The days are coming," says the
    Lord,
  "when I will raise up a good
    descendantᵈ in David's
    family.
  This descendant will be a king
    who will rule in a wise way.
  And he will do what is fair and
    right in the land.
⁶In his time Judah will be saved.

  Israel will live in safety.
  This will be his name:
  The Lord Does What Is Right.
⁷"So the days are coming," says the Lord, "when people will not say: 'As surely as the Lord lives, who brought Israel out of Egypt . . .' ⁸But people will say something new: 'As surely as the Lord lives, who brought Israel from the land of the north and from all the countries where he had sent them away . . .' Then the people of Israel will live in their own land."

False Prophets

⁹A message to the prophets:ᵈ
My heart is broken.
  All my bones shake.
I'm like a man who is drunk.
  I'm like a man who has been
    overcome with wine.
This is because of the Lord
  and his holy words.
¹⁰The land of Judah is full of people
    who are guilty of adultery.ᵈ
  Because of this, the Lord cursed
    the land.
  And it has become very dry.
  The pastures have dried up.
The people are evil.
  They use their power in the
    wrong way.

¹¹"Both the prophets and the
    priests are evil.
  I have seen them doing evil
    things even in my own
    Temple,"ᵈ says the Lord.
¹²"So they will be in danger.
  They will be forced into
    darkness.
  There they will be defeated.
  I will bring disaster on them.
  At that time I will punish those
    prophets and priests," says
    the Lord.

¹³"I saw the prophets of Samaria
    do something wrong.
  I saw those prophets prophesy by
    the false god Baal.ᵈ

And they led my people, the
Israelites, away.
¹⁴And I have seen the prophets of
Jerusalem
do some terrible things.
These prophets are guilty of
adultery
and live by lies.
They encourage evil people to
keep on doing evil.
So the people don't stop sinning.
All of those people are like the
city of Sodom.
The people of Jerusalem are like
the city of Gomorrah to
me!"

¹⁵So this is what the Lord of heav-
en's armies says about the prophets:
"I will make those prophets eat
bitter food.
I will make them drink poisoned
water.
This is because the prophets of
Jerusalem spread wickedness
through the whole country."

¹⁶This is what the Lord of heaven's
armies says:
"Don't pay attention to the things
those prophets are saying to
you.
They are trying to fool you.
Those prophets talk of visions
from their own minds.
But they did not get their
visions from me.
¹⁷They say to those who hate me:
'The Lord says: You will have
peace'.
They say to those who are
stubborn and do as they
please:
'Nothing bad will happen to you!'
¹⁸But none of these prophets has
stood in the meeting of
angels.
None of them has seen or heard
the message of the Lord.
None of them has paid close
attention to the Lord's
message.

¹⁹Look, the punishment from the
Lord
will come like a storm.
His anger will be like a hurricane.
It will come crashing down on
the heads of those wicked
people.
²⁰The Lord's anger will not stop
until he has finished what he plans
to do.
When that day is over,
you will understand this clearly.
²¹I did not send those prophets,
but they ran to tell their
message.
I did not speak to them,
but they prophesied anyway.
²²But if they had stood in the
meeting of angels,
they would have told my
message to my people.
They would have turned the
people from their evil ways.
They would have turned them
from doing evil.

²³"I am a God who is near," says
the Lord.
"I am also a God who is far
away."
²⁴"No one can hide
where I cannot see him," says
the Lord.
"I fill all of heaven and earth,"
says the Lord.

²⁵"I have heard the prophets who
prophesy lies in my name. They say,
'I have had a dream! I have had a
dream!' ²⁶How long will this continue
in the minds of these lying prophets?
They prophesy from their own wishful
thinking. ²⁷They are trying to make
the people of Judah forget me. They
are doing this by telling each other
these dreams. They are trying to
make my people forget me in the
same way that their ancestors forgot
me. Their ancestors forgot me and
worshipped Baal. ²⁸Straw is not the
same thing as wheat!" says the Lord.
"If a prophet wants to tell about his

dreams, let him! But let the person who hears my message speak it truthfully! 29My message is like a fire," says the Lord. "It is like a hammer that smashes a rock!

30"So I am against the false prophets," says the Lord. "These prophets keep stealing words from each other. They say these words are from me. 31I am against the false prophets," says the Lord. "They use their own words and pretend it is a message from me. 32I am against the prophets who prophesy false dreams," says the Lord. "They mislead my people with their lies and false teachings! I did not send those prophets to teach the people. I never commanded them to do anything for me. They can't help the people of Judah at all," says the Lord.

The Sad Message from the Lord

33"The people of Judah, a prophet[d] or a priest may ask you: 'Jeremiah, what is the message from the Lord?' You will answer them and say, 'You are a heavy load to the Lord. And I will throw down this heavy load, says the Lord!' 34A prophet or a priest or one of the people might say, 'This is a message from the Lord!' That person has lied. So I will punish him and his whole family. 35This is what you will say to each other: 'What did the Lord answer?' or 'What did the Lord say?' 36But you will never again say, 'The message of the Lord'. This is because the only message you speak is your own words. You used to change the words of our God. He is the living God, the Lord of heaven's armies. 37This is how you speak to the prophets: 'What answer did the Lord give you?' or 'What did the Lord say?' 38But don't say, 'What was the message from the Lord?' If you use these words, the Lord will say this to you: You should not have called it a message from the Lord. I told you not to use those words. 39I will pick you up

like a heavy load. And I'll throw you away from me. I gave the city of Jerusalem to your ancestors and to you. But I will throw you and that city away from me. 40And I will make a disgrace of you for ever. You will never forget your shame."

The Good and Bad Figs

24 I saw a vision after Nebuchadnezzar king of Babylon had taken Jehoiachin son of Jehoiakim as a prisoner. Jehoiachin king of Judah and his officers were taken away from Jerusalem. They were taken to Babylon. Nebuchadnezzar also took away all the craftsmen and metalworkers of Judah. It was then that the Lord showed me these things: I saw two baskets of figs. They were arranged in front of the Temple[d] of the Lord. 2One of the baskets had very good figs in it. They were like figs that ripen early in the season. But the other basket had rotten figs. They were too rotten to eat.

3The Lord said to me, "What do you see, Jeremiah?"

I answered, "I see figs. The good figs are very good. But the rotten figs are too rotten to eat."

4Then the Lord spoke his word to me. 5This is what the Lord, the God of Israel, said: "I sent the people of Judah out of their country into Babylon. Those people will be like these good figs. I think of them as good. 6I will look after them. I will bring them back to the land of Judah. I will not tear them down. I will build them up. I will not pull them up. I will plant them so they can grow. 7I will make them want to know me. They will know that I am the Lord. They will be my people, and I will be their God. This is because they will return to me with their whole hearts.

8"But the bad figs are too rotten to eat," says the Lord. "Zedekiah king of Judah and his officers will be like those rotten figs. All the people from Jerusalem who are left alive will be like that. This will be true even if those people now live in Egypt. [9]I will make those people hated as an evil people by all the kingdoms of the earth. People will make fun of the people from Judah and tell jokes about them. People will point fingers at them. They will curse them everywhere I scatter them. [10]I will send war, hunger and disease against them. I will attack them until they have all been killed. Then they will no longer be in the land I gave to them and their ancestors."

A Summary of Jeremiah's Preaching

25 This is the message that came to Jeremiah concerning all the people of Judah. It came in the fourth year that Jehoiakim son of Josiah was king of Judah. This was the first year that Nebuchadnezzar was king of Babylon. [2]This is the message Jeremiah the prophet[d] spoke to all the people of Judah and Jerusalem: [3]The Lord has spoken his word to me again and again for these past 23 years. I have been a prophet since the thirteenth year of Josiah. Josiah was the son of Amon king of Judah. I have spoken messages from the Lord to you from that time until today. But you have not listened.

[4]The Lord has sent his servants the prophets to you over and over again. But you have not listened to them. You have not paid any attention to them. [5]They have said, "Stop your evil ways. Stop doing what is wrong. Do this so you can stay in the land. This is the land that the Lord gave to you and your ancestors long ago. He gave it to you to live in for ever. [6]Don't follow other gods to serve them or to worship them. You must not worship idols that are the work of someone's hands. That makes the Lord angry, and he will punish you."

[7]"But you did not listen to me," says the Lord. "You worshipped idols that were the work of someone's hands. That made me angry. So I punished you."

[8]So this is what the Lord of heaven's armies says: "You have not listened to my messages. [9]So I will soon send for all the peoples of the north," says the Lord. "I will soon send for my servant Nebuchadnezzar king of Babylon. I will bring them all against Judah and all the nations around you, too. I will completely destroy all those countries. I will leave them in ruins for ever. People will be shocked when they see how badly they will be destroyed. [10]I will bring an end to the sounds of joy and happiness. There will be no more happy sounds of brides and bridegrooms. I will take away the sound of people grinding meal. And I will take away the light of the lamp. [11]That whole area will be an empty desert. And these nations will be slaves of the king of Babylon for 70 years.

[12]"But when the 70 years have passed, I will punish the king of Babylon and his nation," says the Lord. "I will punish the Babylonians for their evil. I will make that land a desert for ever. [13]I have said that many terrible things will happen to Babylonia. All of them will happen. Jeremiah prophesied about those foreign nations. And the warnings are written in this book. [14]The Babylonians will have to serve many nations and many great kings. I will give them the punishment they deserve. They will be punished for all the things they do."

Judgement on the Nations

[15]The Lord, the God of Israel, said this to me: "My anger is like the wine in a cup. Take it from my hand. I am sending you to all the nations. Make them drink all of my anger from this cup. [16]They will drink my anger like wine. Then they will not be able to walk straight. They will act like madmen. They will do this because of the

war that I am going to send among them."

¹⁷So I took the cup from the Lord's hand. I went to those nations. And I made them drink from the cup. ¹⁸I poured this wine for the people of Jerusalem and the towns of Judah. I made the kings and officers of Judah drink from the cup. I did it so that they would become a ruin. People would be shocked when they saw how badly they were destroyed. People would insult them and speak evil of them. And it happened. Judah is like that now. ¹⁹I also made these people drink from that cup of my anger: the king of Egypt, his servants, his officers and all his people; ²⁰all the Arabs, and all the kings of the land of Uz; all the kings of the Philistines (the kings of the cities of Ashkelon, Gaza, Ekron and the people left at Ashdod); ²¹the people of Edom, Moab and Ammon; ²²all the kings of Tyre and Sidon; all the kings of the faraway countries; ²³the people of Dedan and Tema and Buz; all who cut their hair short; ²⁴all the kings of Arabia; and the kings of the people who live in the desert; ²⁵all the kings of Zimri, Elam and Media; ²⁶and all the kings of the north, near and far, one after the other. I made all the kingdoms on earth drink from the cup of the Lord's anger. But the king of Babylon will drink from this cup after all the others.

²⁷"Then say this to them: 'This is what the Lord of heaven's armies, the God of Israel, says: Drink this cup of my anger. Get drunk from it and vomit. Fall down and don't get up. Don't get up because I am sending a war to kill you!'

²⁸"They will refuse to take the cup from your hand. They will refuse to drink it. Then say this to them: 'The Lord of heaven's armies says this: You must drink from this cup. ²⁹I am already bringing disaster on Jerusalem. And it is the city that is called by

my name. And do you think you will not be punished? You will be punished! I am sending war on all the people of the earth, says the Lord of heaven's armies'.

³⁰"You will prophesy*d* against them with these words. Say to them:

'The Lord roars from heaven.
He shouts from his Holy
      Temple.*d*
He roars against his land.
He will shout like people who walk
      on grapes to make wine.
He will shout against all who live
      on the earth.
³¹The noise will spread all over the
      earth.
This is because the Lord is
      punishing all the nations.
He judges and tells what is wrong
      with all people.
And he is killing the evil people
      with a sword'," says the
Lord.

³²This is what the Lord of heaven's armies says:

"Disasters will soon spread
      from nation to nation.
They will come like a powerful
      storm
to all the faraway places on
      earth."

³³At that time the dead bodies will reach from one end of the earth to the other. No one will cry for them. No one will gather up their bodies and bury them. They will be left lying on the ground like dung.

³⁴Cry, you leaders! Cry out loud!
Roll around in the dust, leaders
      of the people!
It is now time for you to be killed.
You will fall and be scattered
      everywhere, like pieces of a
      broken jar.
³⁵There will be nowhere for the
      leaders to hide.
These leaders will not escape.
³⁶I hear the leaders shouting.

I hear the leaders of the people
crying loudly.
This is because the Lord is
destroying their land.
³⁷Those peaceful pastures will be
like an empty desert.
This happened because the Lord
is very angry.
³⁸The Lord, like a lion, has left his
den.
Their land has been destroyed.
It is because of his destroying
anger.
It is because of his fierce anger.

Jeremiah's Lesson at the Temple

26 This message came from the
Lord. It was during the first
year Jehoiakim son of Josiah was king
of Judah. ²This is what the Lord said:
"Jeremiah, stand in the courtyard of
the Temple^d of the Lord. Give this
message to all the people of the towns
of Judah. They are coming to worship
at the Temple of the Lord. Tell them
everything I tell you to say. Don't
leave out any part of my message.
³Perhaps they will listen and stop their
evil ways. I have plans to bring disaster on them because of the evil they
have done. But if they change, I will
change my mind about bringing disaster on them. ⁴Say to them: 'This is
what the Lord says: I gave my teachings to you. You must obey me and
follow my teachings. ⁵You must listen
to what my servants the prophets^d
say to you. I have sent prophets to
you again and again. But you did not
listen to them. ⁶If you don't obey me,
I will destroy my Temple in Jerusa-
lem. I will destroy it as I destroyed my
Holy Tent^d at Shiloh. People all over
the world will curse Jerusalem'."

⁷The priests, the prophets and all
the people heard Jeremiah. He said all
of these words in the Temple of the
Lord. ⁸Jeremiah finished speaking everything the Lord had commanded
him to say. Then the priests, prophets and all the people grabbed Jeremi-

ah. They said, "You must die! ⁹How
dare you prophesy such a thing in the
name of the Lord! How dare you say
that this Temple will be destroyed like
the one at Shiloh! How dare you say
that Jerusalem will become a desert
without anyone to live in it!" All the
people crowded around Jeremiah in
the Temple of the Lord.

¹⁰Now the officers of Judah heard
about what was happening. So they
came out of the king's palace and went
up to the Temple of the Lord. There
they took their places at the entrance
of the New Gate. ¹¹Then the priests
and prophets spoke to the officers and
all the other people. They said, "Jeremiah should be killed. He said bad
things about Jerusalem! You heard
him say it."

¹²Then Jeremiah spoke to all the of-
ficers of Judah and all the other people. He said, "The Lord sent me to
say these things about this Temple
and this city. Everything that you
have heard is from the Lord. ¹³Now
change your lives! You must start doing good things. You must obey the
Lord your God. If you do that, the
Lord will change his mind. He will not
bring on you the disaster he has told
you about. ¹⁴As for me, I am in your
power. Do to me what you think is
good and right. ¹⁵But if you kill me, be
sure of one thing. You will be guilty of
killing an innocent person. You will
make this city and everyone who lives
in it guilty, too! The Lord sent me to
you. The message you heard is from
the Lord!"

¹⁶Then the officers and all the peo-
ple spoke. They said to the priests
and the prophets, "Jeremiah must not
be killed. What he told us comes from
the Lord our God."

¹⁷Then some of the older leaders
stood up. They spoke to all the people. ¹⁸They said, "Micah the prophet
was from the city of Moresheth. He
was a prophet during the time Hezekiah was king of Judah. Micah said these

things to all the people of Judah: 'This is what the Lord of heaven's armies says:

Jerusalem will be ploughed like a field.

Jerusalem will become a pile of rocks.

The hill where the Temple stands will be covered with bushes'.

¹⁹"Hezekiah was the king of Judah. And he did not kill Micah. No one else in Judah killed him. You know that Hezekiah feared the Lord. He wanted to please the Lord. So the Lord changed his mind. He did not bring on Judah the disaster he had promised. If we hurt Jeremiah, we will bring a terrible disaster on ourselves!"

²⁰(Now there was another man who prophesied in the name of the Lord. His name was Uriah the son of Shemaiah. Uriah was from the city of Kiriath Jearim. He preached the same things against this city and land that Jeremiah did. ²¹King Jehoiakim, all his army officers and all the leaders of Judah heard Uriah preach. King Jehoiakim wanted to kill Uriah. But Uriah heard about it and was afraid. So he escaped to Egypt. ²²But King Jehoiakim sent Elnathan son of Acbor and some other men to Egypt. ²³They brought Uriah back from Egypt. Then they took him to King Jehoiakim. Jehoiakim ordered Uriah to be killed with a sword. His body was thrown into the burial place where poor people are buried.)

²⁴There was an important man named Ahikam son of Shaphan. Ahikam supported Jeremiah. So Ahikam kept Jeremiah from being killed by the people.

Nebuchadnezzar Is Made Ruler

27 The Lord spoke his word to Jeremiah. This happened when Zedekiah son of Josiah was king of Judah. ²This is what the Lord said to me: "Make a yokeᵈ out of straps and poles. Put it on the back of your neck.

³Then send messages to the kings of Edom, Moab, Ammon, Tyre and Sidon. Send the messages through the messengers of these kings. Those messengers have come to Jerusalem to see Zedekiah king of Judah. ⁴Tell them to give this message to their masters. Tell them, 'The Lord of heaven's armies, the God of Israel, says: "Tell your masters: ⁵I made the earth and everyone on it. I made all the animals on the earth. I did this with my great power and my strong arm. I can give the earth to anyone I want. ⁶Now I have given all these lands to Nebuchadnezzar king of Babylon. He is my servant. I will make even the wild animals obey him. ⁷All nations will serve Nebuchadnezzar and his son and grandson. Then the time will come for Babylon to be defeated. Many nations and great kings will make Babylon their servant.

⁸" ' "But now some nations or kingdoms might refuse to serve Nebuchadnezzar king of Babylon. They might refuse to be under his control. If that happens, I will punish that nation with war, hunger and terrible sickness, says the Lord. I will do it until I destroy that nation. I will use Nebuchadnezzar to destroy the nation that fights against him. ⁹So don't listen to your false prophets.ᵈ Don't listen to people who use magic to tell what will happen in the future. Don't listen to those who say they can tell what dreams mean. Don't listen to mediumsᵈ or magicians. They all tell you, 'You will not be slaves to the king of Babylon'. ¹⁰They are telling you lies! They will only cause you to be taken far from your homeland. I will force you to leave your homes. And you will die in another land. ¹¹But some nations will put themselves under the control of the king of Babylon. They will serve him. I will let those nations stay in their own country, says the Lord. The people from those nations

will live in their own land and farm it." ' "
¹²I gave the same message to Zedekiah king of Judah. I said, "You must put yourself under the control of the king of Babylon and serve him. If you serve him and his people, you will live. ¹³Why should you and your people die like those who do not serve the king of Babylon? Why should you die because of war, hunger and sickness? The Lord said this will happen. ¹⁴But the false prophets are saying this: 'You will never be slaves to the king of Babylon'. Don't listen to them because they are prophesying lies to you! ¹⁵'I did not send them,' says the Lord. 'They are prophesying lies. And they are saying the message is from me. So I will send Judah away. You will die! And those prophets who prophesy to you will die also'."

¹⁶Then I, Jeremiah, said to the priests and all the people, "This is what the Lord says: Those false prophets are saying that what the Babylonians took from the Temple^d of the Lord will be brought back soon. Don't listen to them! They are prophesying lies to you. ¹⁷Don't listen to those prophets. But serve the king of Babylon, and you will live. There is no reason for you to cause Jerusalem to become a ruin. ¹⁸They might be prophets and have the message from the Lord. If so, let them pray to the Lord of heaven's armies. Let them pray about the things that are still in the Temple of the Lord. Let them pray about the things that are still in the king's palace and in Jerusalem. Let them pray that all this will not be taken away to Babylon.

¹⁹"This is what the Lord of heaven's armies says about those things left in Jerusalem. In the Temple there are the pillars, the large bronze bowl, which is called the Sea, the stands that can be moved and other things. Nebuchadnezzar king of Babylon left them in Jerusalem. ²⁰Nebuchadnezzar did

not take these away when he took Jehoiachin king of Judah captive. Jehoiachin was the son of King Jehoiakim. Nebuchadnezzar also took other important people away from Judah and Jerusalem. ²¹This is what the Lord of heaven's armies, the God of Israel, says about the things left in the Temple of the Lord and in the king's palace and in Jerusalem: 'All of this will also be taken to Babylon. ²²And they will stay there until the day I go to get them,' says the Lord. 'Then I will bring them back and return them to this place'."

The False Prophet Hananiah

28 It was the fifth month of King Zedekiah's fourth year as king of Judah. This was at the beginning of the king's rule. At that time Hananiah the prophet^d spoke to me. He was the son of Azzur. And he was from the town of Gibeon. He was in the Temple^d of the Lord when he spoke to me. In front of the priests and all the people, Hananiah said: ²"The Lord of heaven's armies, the God of Israel, says: 'I will break the yoke^d the king of Babylon has put on Judah. ³Before two years are over, I will bring back everything that Nebuchadnezzar king of Babylon took from the Lord's Temple. ⁴I will also bring Jehoiachin son of Jehoiakim king of Judah back here. And I will bring back all the other people of Judah as captives to Babylon,' says the Lord. 'So I will break the yoke the king of Babylon put on Judah'."

⁵Then the prophet Jeremiah answered the prophet Hananiah. They were standing in the Temple^d of the Lord. The priests and all the people there could hear Jeremiah's answer. ⁶He said, "Amen! Let the Lord really do that! May the Lord make the message you prophesy come true. May the Lord bring everything from the Lord's Temple back from Babylon. And may he bring back to their homes

all the people who were taken as captives.

7"But listen to what I must say to you and all the people. 8There were prophets long before we became prophets, Hananiah. They prophesied that war, hunger and terrible sicknesses would come. They would come to many countries and great kingdoms. 9But a prophet might prophesy that we will have peace. The message of that prophet might come true. If it does, only then can he be recognised as one truly sent by the Lord!"

10Then the prophet Hananiah took the yoke off Jeremiah's neck and broke it. 11Hananiah said in front of all the people, "This is what the Lord says: 'In the same way I will break the yoke of Nebuchadnezzar king of Babylon. He put that yoke on all the nations of the world. But I will break it before two years are over'." After Hananiah had said that, Jeremiah left the Temple.

12Then the Lord spoke his word to Jeremiah. This was not long after the prophet Hananiah had broken the yoke off the prophet Jeremiah's neck. 13The Lord said, "Go and tell Hananiah, 'This is what the Lord says: You have broken a wooden yoke. But I will make a yoke of iron in the place of the wooden one! 14The Lord of heaven's armies, the God of Israel, says: I will put a yoke of iron on the necks of all these nations. I will do that to make them serve Nebuchadnezzar king of Babylon. And they will be slaves to him. I will even give Nebuchadnezzar control over the wild animals'."

15Then the prophet Jeremiah said to the prophet Hananiah, "Listen, Hananiah! The Lord did not send you. And you have made the people of Judah trust in lies. 16So this is what the Lord says: 'Soon I will remove you from the earth. You will die this year. This is

because you taught the people to turn against the Lord'."

17Hananiah died in the seventh month of that same year.

A Letter to the Jews in Babylon

29 Jeremiah the prophet[d] sent a letter to the people taken as captives to Babylon. He sent it to the older leaders who were among the captives, the priests and the prophets. And he sent it to all the other people Nebuchadnezzar had taken from Jerusalem to Babylon. 2(This letter was sent after all these people were taken away: Jehoiachin and the queen mother; the officers and leaders of Judah and Jerusalem; and the craftsmen and metalworkers.) 3Zedekiah king of Judah had sent Elasah son of Shaphan and Gemariah son of Hilkiah to King Nebuchadnezzar. So Jeremiah gave the letter to them to take to Babylon. This is what the letter said:

4This is what the Lord of heaven's armies, the God of Israel, says to all those people he sent away from Jerusalem as captives to Babylon: 5"Build houses and settle in the land. Plant gardens and eat the food you grow. 6Get married and have sons and daughters. Find wives for your sons. Let your daughters be married so they may also have sons and daughters. Have many children and grow in number in Babylon. Don't become fewer in number. 7Also do good things for the city where I sent you as captives. Pray to the Lord for the city where you are living. If there is peace in that city, you will have peace also." 8The Lord of heaven's armies, the God of Israel, says: "Don't let your prophets and the people who do magic fool you. Don't listen to their dreams. 9They are prophesying lies. And they are saying that their message is from me. But I did not send them," says the Lord.

[10]This is what the Lord says: "Babylon will be powerful for 70 years. After that time I will come to you who are living in Babylon. I will keep my promise to bring you back to Jerusalem. [11]I say this because I know what I have planned for you," says the Lord. "I have good plans for you. I don't plan to hurt you. I plan to give you hope and a good future. [12]Then you will call my name. You will come to me and pray to me. And I will listen to you. [13]You will search for me. And when you search for me with all your heart, you will find me! [14]I will let you find me," says the Lord. "And I will bring you back from your captivity. I forced you to leave this place. But I will gather you from all the nations. I will gather you from the places I have sent you as captives," says the Lord. "And I will bring you back to this place."

[15]You might say, "The Lord has given us prophets here in Babylon."

[16]But the Lord says this about the king who is sitting on David's throne now. And I'm also talking about all the other people still in Jerusalem. These are your relatives who did not go to Babylon with you. [17]The Lord of heaven's armies says: "I will soon send war, hunger and terrible diseases against those still in Jerusalem. I will make them like bad figs that are too rotten to eat. [18]I will chase them with war, hunger and terrible diseases. I will make them a hated people by all the kingdoms of the earth. People will speak evil of them. They will be shocked when they hear what has happened. And people will use them as a shameful example wherever I make them go. [19]This is because those in Jerusalem have not listened to my message," says the Lord. "I sent my message to them again and again. I used my servants, the prophets, to give my messages to them. But they did not listen," says the Lord.

[20]You captives, I forced you to leave Jerusalem and go to Babylon. So listen to the message from the Lord. [21]The Lord of heaven's armies says this about Ahab son of Kolaiah. And he says it about Zedekiah son of Maaseiah: "These two men have been prophesying lies to you. They have said that their message is from me. But I will hand over those two prophets to Nebuchadnezzar king of Babylon. And Nebuchadnezzar will kill them in front of you who are captives in Babylon. [22]Because of this, all the captives from Judah will use this curse: 'May the Lord treat you like Zedekiah and Ahab. The king of Babylon burned them with fire'. [23]They have done evil things among the people of Israel. They are guilty of adultery[d] with their neighbours' wives. They have also spoken lies. And they said those lies were a message from me, the Lord. I did not tell them to do that. I know what they have done. I am a witness!" says the Lord.

[24]Also give a message to Shemaiah. He is from the Nehelamite family. [25]The Lord of heaven's armies, the God of Israel, says: "Shemaiah, you sent letters to all the people in Jerusalem. And you sent letters to the priest Zephaniah son of Maaseiah. You also sent letters to all the priests. You sent those letters in your own name. [26]You said to Zephaniah, 'The Lord has made you priest in place of Jehoiada. You are to be in charge of the Temple[d] of the Lord. You should arrest any

madman who acts like a prophet. You should lock the hands and feet of that person between wooden blocks. And put iron rings around his neck. 27Now Jeremiah from Anathoth is acting like a prophet. So why haven't you arrested him? 28Jeremiah has sent this message to us in Babylon: You will be there for a long time. So build houses and settle down. Plant gardens and eat what you grow'."

29Zephaniah the priest read the letter to Jeremiah the prophet. 30Then the Lord spoke his word to Jeremiah: 31"Send this message to all the captives in Babylon: 'This is what the Lord says about Shemaiah the Nehelamite: Shemaiah has prophesied to you, but I did not send him. He has made you believe a lie. 32Because Shemaiah has done that, this is what the Lord says: I will soon punish Shemaiah the Nehelamite. He will not see the good things I will do for my people, says the Lord. None of his family will be left alive among the people. This is because he has taught the people to turn against me'."

Promises of Hope

30 These are the words that the Lord spoke to Jeremiah. 2The Lord, the God of Israel, said: "Jeremiah, write in a book all the words I have spoken to you. 3The days will come when I will make everything as good as it was before," says the Lord. "I will bring Israel and Judah back from captivity," says the Lord. "I will return them to the land I gave their ancestors. Then my people will own that land again!"

4The Lord spoke this message about the people of Israel and Judah: 5This is what the Lord said:
"We hear people crying from fear.
    They are afraid. There is no
        peace.
6Ask this question, and consider it:
    A man cannot have a baby.
So why do I see every strong man

holding his stomach in pain like a
    woman having a baby?
Why is everyone's face turning
    white like a dead man's face?
7This will be a terrible day!
    There will never be another
        time like this.
This is a time of great trouble for
    the people of Jacob.
But they will be saved from it."

8The Lord of heaven's armies says,
    "At that time
    I will break the yoke[d] from their
        necks.
And I will break the ropes holding
    them.
    Foreign people will never again
        make my people slaves!
9They will serve the Lord their
    God.
    And they will serve David their
        king.
    I will send that king to them.

10"So people of Jacob, my servants,
        don't be afraid!
    Israel, don't be frightened," says
        the Lord.
"I will save you from that faraway
        place where you are
        captives.
    I will save your family from that
        land.
The people of Jacob will be safe
        and have peace again.
    There will be no enemy to
        frighten them.
11I am with you and will save you,"
        says the Lord.
"I scattered you among those
        nations.
    Even if I completely destroy all
        those nations,
    I will not destroy you.
You will be punished fairly.
    But I will punish you."

12This is what the Lord said:
"You people have a wound that
        cannot be cured.
    Your injury will not heal.

¹³There is no one to argue your
　　case.
　There is no cure for your sores.
　So you will not be healed.
¹⁴All those nations who were your
　　friends have forgotten you.
　They don't care about you.
　I hurt you as an enemy would.
　I punished you very hard.
　I did this because your guilt was
　　so great.
　I did this because your sins
　　were so many.
¹⁵Why are you crying about your
　　injury?
　There is no cure for your pain.
　I, the Lord, did these things to
　　you because of your great
　　guilt.
　I did these things because of
　　your many sins.
¹⁶But those nations that destroyed
　　you will now be destroyed.
　Your enemies will become
　　captives.
　Those who stole from you will
　　have their own things stolen.
　Those who took things from you
　　in war will have their own
　　things taken.
¹⁷I will bring back your health.
　And I will heal your injuries,"
　　says the Lord.
　"This is because other people
　　forced you out from among
　　them.
　Those people said about you,
　　'No one cares about
　　Jerusalem!' "

¹⁸This is what the Lord said:
"I will make the tents of Jacob's
　　people as they used to be.
　And I will have pity on Israel's
　　houses.
　The city will be rebuilt on its hill
　　of ruins.
　And the king's palace will stand
　　in its proper place.
¹⁹People in those places will sing
　　songs of praise.

There will also be the sound of
　　laughter.
　I will give them many children.
　They will not become fewer in
　　number.
　I will bring honour to them.
　No one will look down on them.
²⁰Their descendants*d* will be like
　　they were in the old days.
　I will make their people strong
　　before me.
　And I will punish the nations who
　　have hurt them.
²¹One of their own people will lead
　　them.
　Their ruler will come from
　　among them.
　He will come near to me when I
　　invite him.
　Who would dare to come
　　uninvited?" says the Lord.
²²"So you will be my people,
　　and I will be your God."
²³The Lord was very angry.
　He punished the people.
　And the punishment came like a
　　storm.
　It came like a hurricane against
　　the evil people.
²⁴The Lord will stay angry
　　until he has finished punishing the
　　people.
　He will stay angry
　　until he has finished the punishment
　　he planned.
　When that day comes,
　　you will understand this.

The New Israel

31 The Lord says, "At that time I
　　will be God of all Israel's family
groups. And they will be my people."
²This is what the Lord says:
"Some of the people were not
　　killed by the enemy's sword.
　Those people will find help in
　　the desert.
　I have come to give rest to
　　Israel."

³And from far away the Lord appeared to his people. He said,

"I love you people
with a love that will last for
ever.
I became your friend
because of my love and
kindness.
⁴People of Israel, I will build you
up again,
and you will be rebuilt.
You will pick up your
tambourines*d* again.
You will dance with those who
are joyful.
⁵You will plant vineyards again
on the hills around Samaria.
The farmers will plant them
and enjoy their fruit.
⁶There will be a time when
watchmen in the mountains
of Ephraim shout this
message:
'Come, let's go up to Jerusalem
to worship the Lord our
God!' "

⁷This is what the Lord says:
"Be happy and sing for the people
of Jacob.
Shout for Israel, the greatest of
the nations.
Sing your praises and shout this:
'Lord, save your people!
Save those who are left alive
from the nation of Israel!'
⁸Look, I will bring Israel from the
country in the north.
I will gather them from the
faraway places on earth.
Some of the people are blind and
crippled.
Some of the women will be
pregnant and ready to give
birth.
A great many people will come
back.
⁹Those people will be crying as
they come back.
But they will pray as I bring
them back.
I will lead those people by
streams of water.

I will lead them on an even road
where they will not stumble.
This is because I am Israel's
father.
And Israel is my firstborn*d* son.

¹⁰"Nations, listen to the message
from the Lord.
Tell this message in the faraway
lands by the sea:
'The one who scattered the
people of Israel will bring
them back together.
And he will watch over his
people like a shepherd'.
¹¹The Lord will bring the people of
Jacob back.
The Lord will buy them back
from people stronger than
they were.
¹²The people of Israel will come to
the high points of Jerusalem.
There they will shout for joy.
Their faces will shine with
happiness about all the good
things from the Lord:
the grain, new wine, oil, young
sheep and cows.
They will be like a garden that has
plenty of water.
And the people of Israel will not
be troubled any more.
¹³Then young women of Israel will
be happy and dance.
The young men and old men will
also dance.
I will change their sadness into
happiness.
I will give them comfort and joy
instead of sadness.
¹⁴The priests will have more than
enough sacrifices.
And my people will be filled with
the good things I give
them!" says the Lord.

¹⁵This is what the Lord says:
"A sound was heard in Ramah.
It was painful crying and much
sadness.
Rachel cries for her children.
And she cannot be comforted,

because her children are dead!"

¹⁶But this is what the Lord says:
"Stop crying.
Don't let your eyes fill with
   tears.
You will be rewarded for your
   work!" says the Lord.
"The people will come back
   from their enemy's land.
¹⁷So there is hope for you!" says
   the Lord.
"Your children will come back to
   their own land.

¹⁸"I have heard Israel moaning:
'Lord, you punished me, and I
   have learned my lesson.
I was like a calf that had never
   been trained.
Renew me, and I will come back.
You truly are the Lord my God.
¹⁹Lord, I wandered away from you.
But I changed my heart and life.
Once I understood,
   I beat my breast with sorrow.
I am ashamed and disgraced
   because of the foolish things I
   did when I was young'.
²⁰"You know that Israel is my dear
   son.
I love that child.
Yes, I often speak against Israel,
   but I still remember him.
I love him very much.
And I want to comfort him,"
   says the Lord.

²¹"People of Israel, set up the road
   signs.
Put up the signs that show you
   the way home.
Watch the road.
Pay attention to the road on
   which you travel.
People of Israel, come home.
Come back to your towns.
²²You are an unfaithful daughter.
How long will you wander
   before you come home?
The Lord will make something
   new happen in the land:

A woman will go seeking a
   man."

²³The Lord of heaven's armies, the
God of Israel, says: "I will again do
good things for the people of Judah. At
that time the people in the land of Judah and its towns will again say: 'May
the Lord bless you. You are a righteous dwelling. You are a holy moun-
tain'. ²⁴People in all the towns of Judah
will live together in peace. Farmers
and those who move around with their
flocks will live together in peace. ²⁵I
will give rest and strength to those
who are weak and tired."

²⁶After hearing that, I, Jeremiah,
woke up and looked around. My sleep
had been very pleasant.

²⁷The Lord says, "The days are
coming when I will help the families of
Israel and Judah to grow. I will help
their children and animals to grow,
too. It will be like planting and caring
for a plant. ²⁸In the past I watched
over Israel and Judah, but I watched
for the time to pull them up. I tore
them down. I destroyed them. I
brought disaster to them. But now I
will watch over them to build them up
and make them strong," says the
Lord.

²⁹"At that time people will no longer
say:
'The fathers have eaten sour
   grapes.
And that caused the children to
   grind their teeth from the
   sour taste'.
³⁰But each person will die for his own
sin. The person who eats sour grapes
will grind his own teeth.

The New Agreement

³¹"Look, the time is coming," says
   the Lord,
"when I will make a new
   agreement.
It will be with the people of Israel
   and the people of Judah.

32It will not be like the agreement
  I made with their ancestors.
That was when I took them by
    the hand
  to bring them out of Egypt.
I was a husband to them,
  but they broke that agreement,"
    says the Lord.
33"I will make this agreement
  with the people of Israel," says
    the Lord.
"I will put my teachings in their
    minds.
  And I will write them on their
    hearts.
I will be their God,
  and they will be my people.
34People will no longer have to
    teach their neighbours and
    relatives
  to know the Lord.
This is because all people will
    know me,
  from the least to the most
    important," says the Lord.
"I will forgive them for the wicked
    things they did.
  I will not remember their sins
    any more."

The Lord Will Never Leave Israel

35This is what the Lord says:
The Lord makes the sun shine in
    the day.
  And he makes the moon and
    stars shine at night.
He stirs up the sea so that its
    waves crash on the shore.
  The Lord of heaven's armies is
    his name.
36"Only if these laws should ever fail,"
    says the Lord,
  "will Israel's descendantsd stop
    being a nation before me."

37This is what the Lord says:
"There's only one way that I will
    reject all the descendants of
    Israel.
  That is if people can measure
    the sky above.

It is if they can learn the secrets
    of the earth below.
Then I will reject them because of
    what they have done," says
    the Lord.

The New Jerusalem

38The Lord says, "The days are
coming when Jerusalem will be rebuilt
for me. Everything from the Tower of
Hananel to the Corner Gate will be rebuilt. 39The measuring line will stretch
from the Corner Gate straight to the
hill of Gareb. Then it will turn to the
place named Goah. 40There is the
whole valley where dead bodies and
ashes are thrown. It will be holy to the
Lord. And all the terraces out to the
Kidron Valley will be included. They
are on the east as far as the corner of
the Horse Gate. All that area will be
holy to the Lord. The city of Jerusalem will never again be torn down or
destroyed."

Jeremiah Buys a Field

32 This is the word the Lord
spoke to Jeremiah. It was in
the tenth year that Zedekiah was king
of Judah. The tenth year of Zedekiah
was the eighteenth year of Nebuchadnezzar. 2At that time the army of Babylon was surrounding Jerusalem.
Jeremiah was under arrest in the
courtyard of the guard. This courtyard was at the palace of the king of
Judah.
3Zedekiah king of Judah had put Jeremiah in prison there. Zedekiah had
asked, "Why have you prophesiedd
the things you have?" (Jeremiah had
said, "This is what the Lord says: 'I
will soon give the city of Jerusalem to
the king of Babylon. Nebuchadnezzar
will capture this city. 4Zedekiah king
of Judah will not escape from the army
of the Babylonians. But he will surely
be given to the king of Babylon. And
Zedekiah will speak to the king of Babylon face to face. Zedekiah will see
him with his own eyes. 5The king of

Babylon will take Zedekiah to Babylon. Zedekiah will stay there until I have punished him', says the Lord. 'If you fight against the Babylonians, you will not succeed'. ")

⁶While Jeremiah was prisoner, he said, "The Lord spoke his word to me. He said: ⁷Jeremiah, your cousin Hanamel will come to you soon. He is the son of your uncle Shallum. Hanamel will say to you, 'Jeremiah, you are my nearest relative. So buy my field near the town of Anathoth. It is your right and your responsibility to buy that field'.

⁸"Then it happened just as the Lord had said. My cousin Hanamel came to me in the courtyard of the guard. He said to me, 'Buy my field near Anathoth in the land of Benjamin. Buy that land for yourself. It is your right to buy it and own it'. So I knew this was a message from the Lord.

⁹"I bought the field at Anathoth from my cousin Hanamel. I weighed out 200 grams of silver for him. ¹⁰I signed the record that showed I now owned the field. And I had a copy of the record sealed up. Some men witnessed it and signed it also. And I weighed out the silver on the scales. ¹¹Then I took the sealed copy of the record of ownership. And I took the copy that was not sealed. ¹²And I gave them to Baruch son of Neriah. Neriah was the son of Mahseiah. The sealed copy of the record of ownership had all the demands and limits of my purchase. I gave this paper of ownership to Baruch. It was while my cousin Hanamel and the other witnesses were there. Those witnesses also signed the record of ownership. There were also many Jews sitting in the courtyard. And they saw me give the record of ownership to Baruch.

¹³"With all the people watching, I said to Baruch, ¹⁴'This is what the Lord of heaven's armies, the God of Israel, says: Take both copies of the record of ownership. Take both the

sealed copy and the copy that was not sealed. And put them in a clay jar. Do this so that they will last a long time. ¹⁵This is what the Lord of heaven's armies, the God of Israel, says: In the future my people will once again buy houses. They will also buy fields for grain and vineyards in the land of Israel'.

¹⁶"I gave the record of ownership to Baruch son of Neriah. Then I prayed to the Lord. I said: ¹⁷Oh, Lord God, you made the skies and the earth. You made them with your very great power. There is nothing too wonderful for you to do. ¹⁸Lord, you show love and kindness to thousands of people. But you also bring punishment to children for their fathers' sins. Great and powerful God, your name is the Lord of heaven's armies. ¹⁹You plan and do great things, Lord. You see everything that people do. You reward people for the way they live and for what they do. ²⁰Lord, you did miracles[d] and wonderful things in the land of Egypt. You have kept on doing them even until today. You did miracles in Israel and among the other nations. You have become well known. ²¹Lord, you used signs and miracles and brought your people, the Israelites, out of Egypt. You used your great power and strength to do those things. You brought great terror on everyone. ²²Lord, you gave this land to the people of Israel. This is the land you promised to their ancestors long ago. It's a land where much food grows. ²³The people of Israel came into this land and took it for their own. But those people did not obey you. They did not follow your teachings. They did not do the things you commanded. So you made all these terrible things happen to them.

²⁴"And now, the enemy has surrounded the city. They are building roads to the top of the walls. There will be war, hunger and terrible diseases. These will cause the city to be

handed over to the Babylonians. They are attacking the city now. Lord, you said this would happen. And now you see it is happening. ²⁵But now, Lord God, you are telling me, 'Buy the field with silver. Choose some men to watch while I purchase it'. You are telling me this while the Babylonian army is ready to capture the city."

²⁶Then the Lord spoke his word to Jeremiah: ²⁷"I am the Lord. I am the God of every person on the earth. You know that nothing is impossible for me. ²⁸So this is what I say: I will soon give the city of Jerusalem to the Babylonian army. And I will give it to Nebuchadnezzar king of Babylon. That army will capture the city. ²⁹The Babylonian army is already attacking the city of Jerusalem. They will soon enter the city and start a fire to burn down the city. They will also burn down the houses. The people of Jerusalem made me angry. They offered sacrifices to Baal[d] on the roofs[n] of their houses. And the people poured out drink offerings to other idols. ³⁰The people of Israel and Judah have done only the things I said were wrong. They have done this since they were young. They have made me angry by worshipping idols made with their own hands," says the Lord. ³¹"From the day Jerusalem was built until now, they have made me very angry. Jerusalem has made me so angry I must remove it from my sight. ³²I will destroy it. This is because of the evil the people of Israel and Judah have done. The people, their kings and officers have made me angry. Their priests and prophets have made me angry. All the men of Judah and the people of Jerusalem have made me angry. ³³They turned their backs to me. I tried to teach them again and again. But they wouldn't listen to me.

I tried to correct them, but they wouldn't listen. ³⁴They put their hated idols in the place where I have chosen to be worshipped. In this way they made it unclean.[d] ³⁵In the Valley of Ben Hinnom those people built places to worship Baal. They built them so that they could burn their sons and daughters as sacrifices to Molech.[d] But I never commanded them to do such a hated thing. I never even thought of it! This would make Judah sin.

³⁶"You are saying, 'There will be war, hunger and terrible diseases. So the city will be handed over to the king of Babylon'. But the Lord, the God of Israel, says: ³⁷I have forced the people of Israel and Judah to leave their land. I was very furious and angry with them. But I will gather them from the land where I forced them to go. I will bring them back to this place. I will let them live in peace and safety. ³⁸The people of Israel and Judah will be my people. And I will be their God. ³⁹I will make them want to be truly one people. They will have one goal. They will truly want to worship me all their lives. They will do this for their own good and for their children after them.

⁴⁰"I will make an agreement with them. This agreement will last for ever. And I will never turn away from them. I will always be good to them. I will make them want to respect me. Then they will never turn away from me. ⁴¹I will enjoy doing good to them. And I will surely plant them in this land and make them grow. I will do this with my whole being."

⁴²This is what the Lord says: "I have brought this great disaster to the people of Israel and Judah. In the same way I will bring good things to them. I promise to do good things for them. ⁴³You are saying, 'This land is

---

roofs In Bible times houses were built with flat roofs. The roof was used for drying things such as flax and fruit. It was also used as an extra room, as a place for worship and as a place to sleep in the summer.

an empty desert. There are no people or animals here. The Babylonian army defeated this country'. But in the future, people will once again buy fields in this land. [44]They will use their money and buy fields. They will sign and seal their agreements. People will witness their signing records of ownership. They will again buy fields in the land of Benjamin and in the area around Jerusalem. They will buy fields in the towns of Judah and in the mountains. They will buy them in the western mountain slopes and in southern Judah. This is because I will make everything as good as it once was," says the Lord.

The Promise of God

33 Now Jeremiah was still locked up in the courtyard of the guards. And the Lord spoke his word to him a second time: [2]"The Lord made the earth. He made it, and he keeps it safe. The Lord is his name. This is what the Lord says: [3]'Judah, pray to me, and I will answer you. I will tell you important secrets. You have never heard these things before'. [4]The Lord is the God of Israel. He says these things about the houses in Jerusalem and the royal palaces of Judah. They have been torn down to be used against the attack by the Babylonian army. [5]The Lord says, 'Some people will come to fight against the Babylonians. They will fill these houses with dead bodies. I killed those people in my hot anger. I have turned away from this city because of all the evil its people have done.

[6]"But then I will bring health and heal the people there. I will let them enjoy peace and safety. [7]I will make good things happen to Judah and Israel again. I will make them strong as in the past. [8]They sinned against me. But I will wash away that sin. They did evil and turned away from me, but I will forgive them. [9]Then Jerusalem will be a wonderful place! People who

live there will be happy. And people from all nations will praise it. This will happen because they will hear about the good things I am doing there. They will be surprised and shocked at the good things and peace I will bring to Jerusalem'.

[10]"You are saying, 'Our country is an empty desert. There are no people or animals living there'. It is now quiet in the streets of Jerusalem and in the towns of Judah. There are no people or animals there either. But it will be noisy there soon! [11]There will be sounds of joy and gladness. There will be the happy sounds of brides and bridegrooms. There will be the sounds of people bringing their offerings to the Temple[d] of the Lord. Their offerings will be to show thanks to the Lord. They will say,

'Praise the Lord of heaven's
    armies!
The Lord is good!
His love continues for ever!'

They will say this because I will again do good things for Judah. It will be as in the beginning," says the Lord.

[12]This is what the Lord of heaven's armies says: "This place is empty now. There are no people or animals living here. But there will be shepherds in all the towns of Judah. And there will be pastures where they let their flocks of sheep rest. [13]Shepherds will again count their sheep as the sheep walk in front of them. People will be counting their sheep all around the country. They will count them in the mountains and in the western mountain slopes. They will count them in southern Judah and the land of Benjamin. They will count them around Jerusalem and the other towns of Judah!"

The Good Branch

[14]The Lord says, "The time is coming when I will do the things I promised. I made a special promise to the people of Israel and Judah.

¹⁵In those days and at that time,
I will make a righteous branch
sprout from David's family.
He will do what is fair and right
in the land.
¹⁶At this time Judah will be saved.
The people of Jerusalem will live
in safety.
The branch will be named:
The Lord Does What Is Right."
¹⁷This is what the Lord says:
"Someone from David's family will always sit on the throne. And he will rule the family of Israel. ¹⁸And there will always be priests from the family of Levi. Those priests will always stand before me. And they will offer burnt offerings and grain offerings. And they will offer sacrifices to me."

¹⁹The Lord spoke his word to Jeremiah. ²⁰"This is what the Lord says: I have an agreement with day and night. I agreed that they will continue for ever. Day and night will always come at the right times. If you could change that agreement, ²¹you could also change my agreement with David and Levi. Only then would descendants^d from my servant David not be the kings on their thrones. And only then would the family of Levi not be priests serving me in the Temple.^d ²²But I will give many descendants to my servant David. And I will give them to the family group of Levi who serve me in the Temple. They will be as many as the stars in the sky that no one can count. And they will be as many as the grains of sand on the seashore that no one can count."

²³The Lord spoke his word to Jeremiah: ²⁴"Jeremiah, have you heard what the people are saying? They are saying: 'The Lord turned away from the two families of Israel and Judah. He chose those people. But now he doesn't think of them as a nation any more!' "

²⁵This is what the Lord says: "If I had not made my agreement with day and night, and if I had not made the laws for the sky and earth, ²⁶only then might I turn away from Jacob's descendants. And only then might I not let the descendants of David my servant rule over the descendants of Abraham, Isaac and Jacob. And I will be kind to those people. I will cause good things to happen to them again."

A Warning to Zedekiah

34 The Lord spoke his word to Jeremiah. It came when Nebuchadnezzar king of Babylon was fighting against Jerusalem and all the towns around it. Nebuchadnezzar had with him all his army. And he had the armies of all the kingdoms and peoples he ruled. ²This is what the Lord, the God of Israel, said: "Jeremiah, go to Zedekiah king of Judah and tell him: 'This is what the Lord says: I will hand the city of Jerusalem over to the king of Babylon very soon. And he will burn it down! ³You will not escape from the king of Babylon. You will surely be caught and given to him. You will see the king of Babylon with your own eyes. He will talk to you face to face. And you will go to Babylon. ⁴But, Zedekiah king of Judah, listen to the promise of the Lord. This is what the Lord says about you: You will not be killed with a sword. ⁵You will die in a peaceful way. People made funeral fires to honour your ancestors, who ruled before you. In the same way, people will make a funeral fire to honour you. They will cry for you. They will sadly say, "Ah, master!" I myself make this promise to you, says the Lord'."

⁶So Jeremiah the prophet^d gave the message from the Lord to Zedekiah in Jerusalem. ⁷This was while the army of the king of Babylon was fighting against Jerusalem. It was also fighting against the cities of Judah that had not been taken prisoners—Lachish and Azekah. These were the only strong, walled cities left in the land of Judah.

Slaves Are Free

[8]King Zedekiah had made an agreement with all the people in Jerusalem. He agreed to give freedom to all the Hebrew slaves. After Zedekiah had made that agreement, the Lord spoke his word to Jeremiah. [9]Everyone was supposed to free his Hebrew slaves. This included all male and female Hebrew slaves. No one was to keep a fellow Jew as a slave. [10]So the officers and all the people accepted this agreement. Everyone would free their male and female slaves. They would no longer keep them as slaves. So all the slaves were set free. [11]But after that, the people who had slaves changed their minds. So they took back the people they had set free. And they made them slaves again.

[12]Then the Lord spoke his word to Jeremiah: [13]"This is what the Lord, the God of Israel, says: I brought your ancestors out of Egypt where they were slaves. When I did that, I made an agreement with them. [14]I said to your ancestors: 'At the end of every seven years, each one of you must set his Hebrew slaves free. You might have a fellow Hebrew who has sold himself to you. You must let him go free after he has served you for six years'. But your ancestors did not listen or pay attention to me. [15]A short time ago you changed your hearts and did what is right. Each of you gave freedom to his fellow Hebrews who were slaves. And you even made an agreement before me. You made it in the place where I have chosen to be worshipped. [16]But now you have changed your minds. You have shown you do not honour me. Each of you has taken back the male and female slaves you had set free. You have forced them to become slaves again. [17]"So this is what the Lord says: You have not obeyed me. You have not given freedom to your fellow Hebrews. Because you have not kept the agreement, I will give freedom, says the Lord. I will give freedom to war. And I will give freedom to terrible diseases and to hunger to kill you. I will make you hated by all the kingdoms of the earth. [18]I will hand over the men who broke my agreement. They have not kept the promises they made before me. These men cut a calf into two pieces before me. And they walked between the two pieces.[n] [19]These people made the agreement before me: the leaders of Judah and Jerusalem; the officers of the court; the priests and all the people of the land. [20]So I will hand those people over to their enemies. I will hand them over to everyone who wants to kill them. Their bodies will become food for the birds of the air. And they will become food for the wild animals of the earth. [21]I will hand Zedekiah king of Judah and his officers over to their enemies. I will hand them over to everyone who wants to kill them. I will hand Zedekiah and his people over to the army of the king of Babylon. I will do this even though that army has left Jerusalem. [22]I will give the order, says the Lord, to bring the Babylonian army back to Jerusalem. That army will fight against Jerusalem. They will capture it, set it on fire and burn it down. I will destroy the towns in the land of Judah. And they will become empty ruins. No one will live there!"

The Recabite Family

35 When Jehoiakim son of Josiah was king of Judah, the Lord spoke his word to Jeremiah. This was his message: [2]"Jeremiah, go to the family of Recab. Invite them to come to one of the side rooms of the Temple[d] of the Lord. Offer them wine to drink."

---

they walked . . . pieces This showed that the men were willing to be killed, like this animal, if they did not keep their agreement.

³So I went to get Jaazaniah son of Jeremiah.ⁿ Jeremiah was the son of Habazziniah. And I gathered all of Jaazaniah's brothers and sons. I gathered the whole family of the Recabites together. ⁴Then I brought them into the Temple of the Lord. We went into the room of the sons of Hanan son of Igdaliah. Hanan was a man of God. The room was next to the one where the officers stay. It was over the room of Maaseiah son of Shallum. Maaseiah was the doorkeeper in the Temple. ⁵Then I put some bowls full of wine and some cups before the Recabite family. And I said to them, "Drink some wine."

⁶But the Recabite people answered, "We never drink wine. It is because of our ancestor Jonadab son of Recab. He gave us this command: 'You and your descendantsᵈ must never drink wine. ⁷Also you must never build houses, plant seeds or plant vineyards. You must never do any of those things. You must live only in tents. Then you will live a long time in the land where you are a wanderer'. ⁸So we Recabites have obeyed everything Jonadab our ancestor commanded us. We never drink wine. And our wives, sons and daughters never drink wine. ⁹We never build houses in which to live. And we never own fields or vineyards. And we never plant crops. ¹⁰We have lived in tents. And we have obeyed everything our ancestor Jonadab commanded us. ¹¹But Nebuchadnezzar king of Babylon attacked the country of Judah. We said to each other, 'Come, we must enter Jerusalem. This is so we can escape the Babylonian army and the Aramean army'. So we have stayed in Jerusalem."

¹²Then the Lord spoke his word to Jeremiah: ¹³"This is what the Lord of heaven's armies, the God of Israel, says: Jeremiah, go and tell the men of Judah and the people of Jerusalem:

'You should learn a lesson and obey my message', says the Lord. ¹⁴'Jonadab son of Recab ordered his sons not to drink wine. And that command has been obeyed. Until today the descendants of Jonadab obeyed their ancestor's command. They do not drink wine. But I am the Lord. I have given you messages again and again. But you did not obey me. ¹⁵I sent my servants the prophets to you again and again. They said to you, "Each of you must stop doing evil. You must change and be good. Do not follow other gods to serve them. If you obey me, you will live in the land I have given to you and your ancestors." But you have not listened or paid attention to my message. ¹⁶The descendants of Jonadab obeyed the commands that their ancestor gave them. But the people of Judah have not obeyed me'.

¹⁷"So the Lord God of heaven's armies, the God of Israel, says: 'I said many disasters would come to Judah and on everyone living in Jerusalem. I will soon bring every one of those disasters on them. I spoke to those people, but they refused to listen. I called out to them, but they did not answer me'."

¹⁸Then Jeremiah said to the Recabites, "This is what the Lord of heaven's armies, the God of Israel, says: 'You have obeyed the commands of your ancestor Jonadab. You have followed all of Jonadab's teachings. You have done everything he commanded'. ¹⁹So this is what the Lord of heaven's armies, the God of Israel, says: 'There will always be a descendant of Jonadab son of Recab to serve me'."

Jehoiakim Burns Jeremiah's Scroll

36 The Lord spoke his word to Jeremiah. This was during the fourth year that Jehoiakim son of Josiah was king of Judah. This was his

---

Jeremiah Not the prophet Jeremiah, but a different man with the same name.

message: [2]"Jeremiah, get a scroll. Write on it all the words I have spoken to you about Israel and Judah and all the nations. Write everything I have spoken to you since Josiah was king until now. [3]Perhaps the family of Judah will hear what disasters I am planning to bring on them. And perhaps they will stop doing wicked things. Then I will forgive them for the sins and the evil things they have done."

[4]So Jeremiah called for Baruch son of Neriah. Jeremiah spoke the messages the Lord had given him. And Baruch wrote those messages on the scroll. [5]Then Jeremiah said to Baruch, "I cannot go to the Temple[d] of the Lord. I must stay here. [6]So I want you to go to the Temple of the Lord. Go there on a day when the people are giving up eating. Read to all the people of Judah from the scroll. These people come into Jerusalem from the towns where they live. Read the messages from the Lord. Read the words that you wrote on the scroll as I spoke them to you. [7]Perhaps they will ask the Lord to help them. Perhaps each one will stop doing wicked things. The Lord has announced that he is very angry with them." [8]So Baruch son of Neriah did everything Jeremiah the prophet[d] told him to do. He read aloud the scroll that had the Lord's messages written on it. He read it in the Lord's Temple.

[9]It was the ninth month of the fifth year that Jehoiakim son of Josiah was king. A special time to give up eating was announced. All the people of Jerusalem were supposed to give up eating to honour the Lord. And everyone who had come into Jerusalem from the towns of Judah was supposed to give up eating. [10]At that time Baruch read the scroll that contained Jeremiah's words. Baruch read the scroll in the Temple of the Lord to all the people there. He was in the room of Gemariah son of Shaphan. Gemariah was a royal assistant. That room was in the upper courtyard at the entrance of the New Gate of the Temple.

[11]A man named Micaiah son of Gemariah, the son of Shaphan, heard all the messages from the Lord. Baruch read them from the scroll. [12]Micaiah went down to the royal assistant's room in the king's palace. All of the officers were sitting there: Elishama the royal assistant; Delaiah son of Shemaiah; Elnathan son of Acbor; Gemariah son of Shaphan; Zedekiah son of Hananiah; and all the other officers. [13]Micaiah told those officers everything he had heard Baruch read from the scroll.

[14]Then the officers sent a man named Jehudi son of Nethaniah to Baruch. (Nethaniah was the son of Shelemiah, who was the son of Cushi.) Jehudi said to Baruch, "Bring the scroll that you read to the people and come with me."

So Baruch son of Neriah took the scroll and went with Jehudi to the officers. [15]Then the officers said to Baruch, "Sit down and read the scroll to us."

So Baruch read the scroll to them. [16]When the officers heard all the words, they became afraid. And they looked at one another. They said to Baruch, "We must certainly tell the king about these words." [17]Then the officers asked Baruch, "Tell us, Baruch, where did you get these words you wrote on the scroll? Did you write down what Jeremiah said to you?"

[18]"Yes," Baruch answered. "Jeremiah spoke, and I wrote down all the words with ink on this scroll."

[19]Then the officers said to Baruch, "You and Jeremiah must go and hide. Don't tell anyone where you are hiding."

[20]Then the officers put the scroll in the room of Elishama the royal assistant. Then they went to the king in the courtyard and told him all about the scroll. [21]So King Jehoiakim sent Jehudi to get the scroll. Jehudi brought the

scroll from the room of Elishama the royal assistant. Then Jehudi read the scroll to the king. And he read it to all the officers who stood around the king. 22This happened in the ninth month of the year. So King Jehoiakim was sitting in the winter apartment. There was a fire burning in a small firepot in front of him. 23Jehudi began to read from the scroll. But after he had read three or four columns, the king cut those columns off the scroll with a pen knife. And he threw them into the firepot. Finally, the whole scroll was burned in the fire. 24King Jehoiakim and his servants heard the message from the scroll. But they were not frightened! They did not tear their clothes to show their sorrow. 25Elnathan, Delaiah and Gemariah tried to talk King Jehoiakim into not burning the scroll. But the king would not listen to them. 26Instead, the king ordered some men to arrest Baruch the secretary and Jeremiah the prophet. Those men were Jerahmeel son of the king, Seraiah son of Azriel and Shelemiah son of Abdeel. But the Lord had hidden Baruch and Jeremiah.

27The Lord spoke his word to Jeremiah. This happened after King Jehoiakim had burned the scroll. This was the scroll where Baruch had written all the words Jeremiah had spoken to him. The Lord said: 28"Jeremiah, get another scroll. Write all the words on it that were on the first scroll. That was the scroll that Jehoiakim king of Judah burned. 29Also say this to Jehoiakim king of Judah: 'This is what the Lord says: You burned that scroll. You said, "Why did Jeremiah write that the king of Babylon will come and destroy this land? Why did he say the king of Babylon will destroy both men and animals in it?" 30So the Lord says this about Jehoiakim king of Judah: Jehoiakim's descendants*d* will not sit on David's throne. When Jehoiakim dies, his body will be thrown out on the ground. It will be left out in the heat of the day. And it will also be left in the cold frost of the night. 31I, the Lord, will punish Jehoiakim and his children. And I will punish his servants. I will do this because they have done evil things. I have promised to bring disasters upon them. And I will bring them upon all the people in Jerusalem and Judah, just as I promised. This is because they have not listened to me'."

32So Jeremiah took another scroll and gave it to Baruch. Baruch son of Neriah was his secretary. As Jeremiah spoke, Baruch wrote on the scroll. He wrote the same words that were on the scroll that Jehoiakim king of Judah had burned in the fire. And many other words like those words were added to the second scroll.

Jeremiah in Prison

37 Nebuchadnezzar was king of Babylon. He appointed Zedekiah son of Josiah as king of Judah. Zedekiah took the place of Jehoiachin son of Jehoiakim. 2But Zedekiah, his servants and the people of Judah did not listen to the words of the Lord. The Lord had spoken his words through Jeremiah the prophet.*d*

3Now King Zedekiah sent Jehucal and Zephaniah with a message to Jeremiah the prophet. Jehucal was the son of Shelemiah. And Zephaniah the priest was the son of Maaseiah. This was the message: "Jeremiah, pray to the Lord our God for us."

4At that time Jeremiah had not yet been put into prison. So he was free to go anywhere he wanted. 5The army of the king of Egypt had marched from Egypt toward Judah. Now the Babylonian army had surrounded the city of Jerusalem so they could attack it. Then they had heard about the Egyptian army marching towards them. So the Babylonian army left Jerusalem to fight the Egyptian army.

6The Lord spoke his word to Jeremiah the prophet: 7"This is what the

Lord, the God of Israel, says: Jehucal and Zephaniah, I know Zedekiah king of Judah sent you to ask me questions. Tell this to King Zedekiah: 'The army of the king of Egypt marched out of Egypt. They came here to help you against the Babylonian army. But that army will go back to Egypt. [8]After that, the Babylonian army will come back here. And they will attack Jerusalem. Then the Babylonian army will take and burn Jerusalem'.

[9]"This is what the Lord says: People of Jerusalem, do not fool yourselves. Do not say to yourselves: 'The Babylonian army will surely leave us alone'. They will not! [10]You might defeat all of the Babylonian army that is attacking you. But there would still be a few injured men left in their tents. Even those injured men would come from their tents and burn down Jerusalem!"

[11]So the Babylonian army left Jerusalem. They left to fight the army of the king of Egypt. [12]Now Jeremiah wanted to travel from Jerusalem to his home in the land of Benjamin. He was going there to get his share of the property that belonged to his family. [13]Jeremiah got to the Benjamin Gate of Jerusalem. But then the captain in charge of the guards arrested him. The captain's name was Irijah son of Shelemiah son of Hananiah. So Irijah the captain arrested Jeremiah. Irijah said, "You are leaving us to join the Babylonian side!"

[14]Jeremiah said to Irijah, "That's not true! I am not leaving to join the Babylonians." But Irijah refused to listen to Jeremiah. So he arrested Jeremiah and took him to the officers of Jerusalem. [15]Those rulers were very angry with Jeremiah. They gave an order for him to be beaten. Then they put him in prison in the house of Jonathan the royal assistant. Jonathan's house had been made into a prison. [16]So those people put Jeremiah into a cell in a dungeon. And Jeremiah was there for a long time.

[17]Then King Zedekiah sent for Jeremiah and had him brought to the palace. Zedekiah talked to Jeremiah in private. He asked Jeremiah, "Is there any message from the Lord?"

Jeremiah answered, "Yes, there is a message from the Lord. Zedekiah, you will be handed over to the king of Babylon." [18]Then Jeremiah said to King Zedekiah, "What crime have I done against you? What crime have I done to your officers or the people of Jerusalem? Why have you thrown me into prison? [19]Where are your prophets now? Those prophets prophesied this message to you: 'The king of Babylon will not attack you or this land of Judah'. [20]But now, my master, king of Judah, please listen to me. And please do what I ask of you. Do not send me back to the house of Jonathan the royal assistant. If you do, I will die there!"

[21]So King Zedekiah gave orders for Jeremiah to be put under guard in the courtyard. And he ordered that Jeremiah be given bread from the street of the bakers. Jeremiah was to be given bread until there was no more bread in the city. So he stayed under guard in the courtyard.

Jeremiah Is Thrown into a Well

38 Some of the officers heard what Jeremiah was prophesying.[d] They were Shephatiah son of Mattan, Gedaliah son of Pashhur, Jehucal son of Shelemiah and Pashhur son of Malkijah. Jeremiah was telling all the people this message: [2]"This is what the Lord says: 'Everyone who stays in Jerusalem will die in war. Or he will die of hunger or terrible diseases. But everyone who surrenders to the Babylonian army will live. They will escape with their lives and live'. [3]And this is what the Lord says: 'This city of Jerusalem will surely be handed

over to the army of the king of Babylon. He will capture this city!' "

⁴Then the officers said to the king, "Jeremiah must be put to death! He is making the soldiers who are still in the city become discouraged. He is discouraging everyone by the things he is saying. He does not want good to happen to us. He wants to ruin the people of Jerusalem."

⁵King Zedekiah said to them, "Jeremiah is in your control. I cannot do anything to stop you!"

⁶So the officers took Jeremiah and put him into the well of Malkijah, the king's son. That well was in the courtyard of the guards. The officers used ropes to lower Jeremiah into the well. It did not have any water in it, only mud. And Jeremiah sank down into the mud.

⁷But Ebed-Melech heard that the officers had put Jeremiah into the well. Ebed-Melech was a Cushite, and he was a eunuch*d* in the palace. King Zedekiah was sitting at the Benjamin Gate. ⁸So Ebed-Melech left the palace and went to the king. Ebed-Melech said, ⁹"My master and king, the rulers have acted in an evil way. They have treated Jeremiah the prophet badly! They have thrown him into a well! They have left him there to die! When there is no more bread in the city, he will starve."

¹⁰Then King Zedekiah commanded Ebed-Melech the Cushite: "Ebed-Melech, take 30 men from the palace with you. Go and lift Jeremiah the prophet out of the well before he dies."

¹¹So Ebed-Melech took the men with him. And he went to a room under the storeroom in the palace. He took some old rags and worn-out clothes from that room. Then he let those rags down with some ropes to Jeremiah in the well. ¹²Ebed-Melech the Cushite said to Jeremiah, "Put these old rags and worn-out clothes under your arms. They will be pads for the ropes." So Jeremiah did as Ebed-Melech said. ¹³The men pulled Jeremiah up with the ropes and lifted him out of the well. And Jeremiah stayed under guard in the courtyard.

Zedekiah Questions Jeremiah

¹⁴Then King Zedekiah sent someone to get Jeremiah the prophet.*d* He had Jeremiah brought to the third entrance to the Temple*d* of the Lord. Then the king said to Jeremiah, "I am going to ask you something. Do not hide anything from me. But tell me everything honestly."

¹⁵Jeremiah said to Zedekiah, "If I give you an answer, you will probably kill me. And even if I give you advice, you will not listen to me."

¹⁶But King Zedekiah made a secret promise to Jeremiah. He said, "As surely as the Lord lives who has given us breath and life, I will not kill you. And I promise not to give you to the officers who want to kill you."

¹⁷Then Jeremiah said to Zedekiah, "This is what the Lord God of heaven's armies, the God of Israel, says: 'You must surrender to the officers of the king of Babylon. Then your life will be saved. And Jerusalem will not be burned down. And you and your family will live. ¹⁸You must not refuse to surrender to the officers of the king of Babylon. If you do, Jerusalem will be given to the Babylonian army. They will burn Jerusalem down. And you will not escape from them'."

¹⁹Then King Zedekiah said to Jeremiah, "I'm afraid of some of the Jews. They have already gone over to the side of the Babylonian army. I'm afraid the Babylonians may hand me over to them. And they will treat me badly."

²⁰But Jeremiah answered, "The Babylonians will not hand you over to the Jews. Obey the Lord by doing what I tell you. Then things will go well for you. And your life will be saved. ²¹But if you refuse to surrender to the Babylonians, the Lord has

shown me what will happen. ²²All the women left in the palace of the king of Judah will be brought out. They will be taken to the important officers of the king of Babylon. Your women will make fun of you with this song:

'Your good friends led you the
    wrong way and were
    stronger than you.
Those were friends that you
    trusted.
Your feet are stuck in the mud.
Your friends have left you'.

²³"All your wives and children will be brought out. They will be given to the Babylonian army. You yourself will not even escape from them. You will be taken prisoner by the king of Babylon. And Jerusalem will be burned down."

²⁴Then Zedekiah said to Jeremiah, "Do not tell anyone that I have been talking to you. If you do, you will die. ²⁵Those officers might find out that I talked to you. Then they will come to you and say, 'Tell us what you said to King Zedekiah. And tell us what King Zedekiah said to you. Don't keep any secrets from us. If you don't tell us everything, we will kill you'. ²⁶If they ask you, tell them this: 'I was begging the king not to send me back to Jonathan's house to die'."

²⁷The officers did come to question Jeremiah. So he told them everything the king had ordered him to say. Then the officers said no more to Jeremiah. This was because no one had heard what Jeremiah and the king had discussed.

²⁸So Jeremiah stayed under guard in the courtyard until the day Jerusalem was captured.

The Fall of Jerusalem

39 This is how Jerusalem was captured:

¹Nebuchadnezzar king of Babylon marched against Jerusalem with his whole army. He surrounded the city to attack it. This was during the tenth month of the ninth year Zedekiah was king of Judah. ²This lasted until the ninth day of the fourth month in Zedekiah's eleventh year. Then the city wall was broken through. ³And all the officers of the king of Babylon came into Jerusalem. They sat down at the Middle Gate. They were Nergal-Sharezer of the district of Samgar; Nebo-Sarsekim, a chief officer; Nergal-Sharezer, an important leader; and all the other important officers.

⁴When Zedekiah king of Judah and all his soldiers saw them, they ran away. They left Jerusalem at night and went out from the king's garden. They went through the gate that was between the two walls. Then they headed towards the Jordan Valley. ⁵But the Babylonian army chased them. They caught up with Zedekiah in the plains of Jericho. They captured him and took him to Nebuchadnezzar king of Babylon. Nebuchadnezzar was at Riblah in the land of Hamath. There Nebuchadnezzar passed his sentence on Zedekiah. ⁶There at Riblah the king of Babylon killed Zedekiah's sons as he watched. And Nebuchadnezzar killed all the important officers of Judah as Zedekiah watched. ⁷Then he put out Zedekiah's eyes. He put bronze chains on Zedekiah and took him to Babylon.

⁸The Babylonians set fire to the palace. And they set fire to the houses of the people of Jerusalem. And they broke down the walls around Jerusalem. ⁹Nebuzaradan was commander of the king's special guards. He took the people left in Jerusalem as captives. He also took those captives who had surrendered to him earlier. And he took the rest of the people of Jerusalem. He carried them all away to Babylon. ¹⁰But Nebuzaradan, commander of the guard, left some of the poor people of Judah behind. They were the people who owned nothing.

So on that day he gave them vineyards and fields.

¹¹Nebuchadnezzar had given these orders about Jeremiah through Nebuzaradan, commander of the guard: ¹²"Find Jeremiah and take care of him. Do not hurt him. Give him whatever he asks for." ¹³So these men sent for Jeremiah: Nebuzaradan, commander of the guards; Nebushazban, a chief officer; Nergal-Sharezer, an important leader; and all the other officers of the king of Babylon. ¹⁴They had Jeremiah taken out of the courtyard of the guard. They turned him over to Gedaliah son of Ahikam son of Shaphan. Gedaliah had orders to take Jeremiah back home. So they took him home, and he stayed among his own people.

¹⁵While Jeremiah was guarded in the courtyard, the Lord spoke his word to him: ¹⁶"Jeremiah, go and tell Ebed-Melech the Cushite this message: 'This is what the Lord of heaven's armies, the God of Israel, says: Very soon I will make my words about Jerusalem come true. They will come true through disaster, not through good times. You will see everything come true with your own eyes. ¹⁷But I will save you on that day, Ebed-Melech, says the Lord. You will not be handed over to the people you fear. ¹⁸I will surely save you, Ebed-Melech. You will not die from a sword. But you will escape and live. This will happen because you have trusted in me, says the Lord'."

Jeremiah Is Set Free

40 The Lord spoke his word to Jeremiah. This was after Nebuzaradan, commander of the guards, had set Jeremiah free at the city of Ramah. He had found Jeremiah in Ramah bound in chains. He was with all the captives from Jerusalem and Judah. They were being taken away to Babylon. ²When commander Nebuzaradan found Jeremiah, Nebuzaradan said

to him, "The Lord your God announced this disaster would come to this place. ³And now the Lord has done everything he said he would do. This disaster happened because the people of Judah sinned against the Lord. You people did not obey the Lord. ⁴But now I will set you free. I am taking the chains off your wrists. If you want to, come with me to Babylon. And I will take good care of you. But if you don't want to come, then don't. Look, the whole country is open to you." ⁵Before Jeremiah turned to leave, Nebuzaradan said, "Or go back to Gedaliah son of Ahikam, the son of Shaphan. The king of Babylon has chosen Gedaliah to be governor over the towns of Judah. Go and live with Gedaliah among the people. Or go anywhere you want."

Then Nebuzaradan gave Jeremiah some food and a present and let him go. ⁶So Jeremiah went to Gedaliah son of Ahikam at Mizpah. And Jeremiah stayed with him there. He lived among the people who were left behind in Judah.

The Short Rule of Gedaliah

⁷There were some officers and their men from the army of Judah. These men were still out in the open country. They heard that the king of Babylon had put Gedaliah son of Ahikam in charge. He was put in charge of the people who were left in the land: the men, women and children who were very poor. They were the ones who were not carried off to Babylon as captives. ⁸So these soldiers came to Gedaliah at Mizpah. They were Ishmael son of Nethaniah, and Johanan and Jonathan sons of Kareah. Also Seraiah son of Tanhumeth and the sons of Ephai the Netophathite came. And Jaazaniah son of the Maacathite and their men came.

⁹Gedaliah son of Ahikam, the son of Shaphan, made a promise to them. Gedaliah said, "Do not be afraid to

serve the Babylonians. Live in the land and serve the king of Babylon. Then everything will go well for you. [10]I myself will live in Mizpah. I will speak for you before the Babylonians who come here. You harvest the wine, the summer fruit and the oil. Put what you harvest in your storage jars. Live in the towns you control."

[11]Some Jews were in Moab, Ammon, Edom and other countries. They heard that the king of Babylon had left a few Jews alive in the land. And they heard the king of Babylon had chosen Gedaliah as governor over them. (Gedaliah was the son of Ahikam, the son of Shaphan.) [12]When the people of Judah heard this news, they came back to Judah. They came back to Gedaliah at Mizpah. They came from all the countries where they had been scattered. They gathered a large harvest of wine and summer fruit.

[13]Johanan son of Kareah came to Gedaliah at Mizpah. All the army officers of Judah still in the open country also came. [14]Johanan and the officers with him said to Gedaliah, "Don't you know that Baalis king of the Ammonite people wants you dead? He has sent Ishmael son of Nethaniah to kill you." But Gedaliah son of Ahikam did not believe them.

[15]Then Johanan son of Kareah spoke to Gedaliah in private at Mizpah. He said to Gedaliah, "Let me go and kill Ishmael son of Nethaniah. No one will know anything about it. We should not let Ishmael kill you. All the Jews gathered around you would be scattered to different countries again. Then the few people of Judah who are left alive would be lost."

[16]But Gedaliah son of Ahikam said to Johanan son of Kareah, "Do not kill Ishmael! The things you are saying about Ishmael are not true!"

41 In the seventh month Ishmael son of Nethaniah came to Gedaliah son of Ahikam. (Nethaniah was the son of Elishama.) Ishmael came with ten of his men to Mizpah. Now Ishmael was a member of the king's family. He had been one of the officers of the king of Judah. Ishmael and his men ate a meal with Gedaliah at Mizpah. [2]While they were eating together, Ishmael and his ten men got up. They killed Gedaliah son of Ahikam with a sword. Gedaliah was the man the king of Babylon had chosen as governor over Judah. [3]Ishmael killed all the Jews with Gedaliah at Mizpah, too. He also killed the Babylonian soldiers who were there with Gedaliah.

[4-5]The day after Gedaliah was murdered, 80 men came to Mizpah. They were bringing grain offerings and incense[d] to the Temple[d] of the Lord. Those 80 men had shaved off their beards, torn their clothes and cut themselves.[n] They came from Shechem, Shiloh and Samaria. None of them knew that Gedaliah had been murdered. [6]Ishmael son of Nethaniah went out from Mizpah to meet them. He cried as he walked. When he met them, he said, "Come with me to meet Gedaliah son of Ahikam." [7]So they went into Mizpah. Then Ishmael son of Nethaniah and his men killed 70 of them! They threw the bodies into a deep well. [8]But the ten men who were left alive said to Ishmael, "Don't kill us! We have wheat and barley. And we have oil and honey. We have hidden these things in a field." So Ishmael let those ten men alone. He did not kill them with the others. [9]Now the well where he had thrown the bodies had been made by King Asa. Asa had made the well as a part of his defences against Baasha king of Israel. But Ishmael son of Nethaniah put dead bodies in it until it was full.

---

shaved ... themselves The men did this to show they were sad about the Temple in Jerusalem being destroyed.

10Ishmael captured all the other people in Mizpah. He captured the king's daughters and all the other people who were left there. They were the people whom Nebuzaradan commander of the guard had chosen Gedaliah son of Ahikam to take care of. So Ishmael son of Nethaniah captured those people. And he started to cross over to the country of the Ammonites.

11Johanan son of Kareah heard about all the evil things Ishmael son of Nethaniah had done. All the army officers with him heard it, too. 12So Johanan and the army officers took their men and went to fight Ishmael son of Nethaniah. They caught him near the big pool of water at Gibeon. 13The captives Ishmael had taken saw Johanan and the army officers. And they became very happy. 14Then all the people Ishmael had taken captive turned around. They ran to Johanan son of Kareah. 15But Ishmael son of Nethaniah and eight of his men escaped from Johanan. And they ran away to the Ammonites.

16So Johanan son of Kareah and all his army officers saved the captives. Ishmael son of Nethaniah had murdered Gedaliah son of Ahikam. Then he had taken those people from Mizpah. Among those left alive were soldiers, women, children and court officers. Johanan brought them back from the town of Gibeon.

The Escape to Egypt

17-18Johanan and the other army officers were afraid of the Babylonians. The king of Babylon had chosen Gedaliah son of Ahikam to be governor of Judah. But Ishmael son of Nethaniah had murdered Gedaliah. So Johanan was afraid that the Babylonians would be angry. They decided to run away to Egypt. On the way they stayed at Geruth Kimham, near the town of Bethlehem.

42 While there, Johanan son of Kareah and Jezaniah son of Hoshaiah went to Jeremiah the prophet.d All the army officers went with Johanan and Jezaniah. All the people, from the least important to the greatest, all went along, too. 2They said to him, "Jeremiah, please listen to what we ask. Pray to the Lord your God. Pray for all the people left alive from the family of Judah. At one time there were many of us. You can see that there are few of us now. 3So pray that the Lord your God will tell us where we should go. And pray he will tell us what we should do."

4Then Jeremiah the prophet answered, "I understand what you want me to do. I will pray to the Lord your God as you have asked. I will tell you everything he says. I will not hide anything from you."

5Then the people said to Jeremiah, "We will do everything the Lord your God tells us. If we don't, may the Lord be a true and loyal witness against us. We know he will send you to tell us what to do. 6It does not matter if we like the message or not. We will obey the Lord our God. We are sending you to the Lord for a message from him. We will obey what he says. Then good things will happen to us."

7Ten days later the Lord spoke his word to Jeremiah. 8Then Jeremiah called for Johanan son of Kareah and the army officers who were with him. Jeremiah also called all the other people, from the least important to the greatest. 9Then Jeremiah said to them, "You sent me to ask the Lord for what you wanted. This is what the Lord, the God of Israel, says: 10'If you will stay in Judah, I will make you strong. I will not destroy you. I will plant you, and I will not pull you up. This is because I am sad about the disaster I brought on you. 11Now you are afraid of the king of Babylon. But don't be afraid of him. Don't be afraid of the king of Babylon', says the Lord.

'I am with you. I will save you. I will rescue you from his power. [12]I will be kind to you. And the king of Babylon will also treat you with mercy. He will bring you back to your land'.

[13]"But you might say, 'We will not stay in Judah'. If you say that, you will disobey the Lord your God. [14]Or you might say, 'No, we will go and live in Egypt. We will not be bothered with war there. We will not hear the trumpets of war. And in Egypt we will not be hungry'. [15]If you say that, listen to the message of the Lord. It is to you who are left alive from Judah. This is what the Lord of heaven's armies, the God of Israel, says: 'If you make up your mind to go and live in Egypt, these things will happen. [16]You are afraid of war. But it will defeat you in the land of Egypt. And you are worried about hunger. But you will be hungry in Egypt. You will die there. [17]Everyone who goes to live in Egypt will die in war. Or he will die from hunger or terrible disease. No one who goes to Egypt will live. No one will escape the terrible things I will bring to them'.

[18]"This is what the Lord of heaven's armies, the God of Israel, says: 'I showed my anger against Jerusalem. I punished the people who lived in Jerusalem. In the same way I will show my anger against you when you go to Egypt. Other nations will speak evil of you. People will be shocked by what has happened to you. You will become a swear word. People will insult you. And you will never see Judah again'.

[19]"You who are left alive in Judah, the Lord has told you, 'Don't go to Egypt'. I warn you today. [20]You are making a mistake that will cause your deaths. You sent me to the Lord your God. You said to me, 'Pray to the Lord our God for us. Tell us everything the Lord says, and we will do it'. [21]So today I have told you the message from the Lord. But you have not obeyed the Lord your God. You have

not done all that he sent me to tell you to do. [22]So now be sure you understand this: you want to go to live in Egypt. But you will die by war, hunger or terrible diseases."

43 So Jeremiah finished telling the people the message from the Lord their God. He told them everything the Lord their God had sent him to tell them.

[2]Azariah son of Hoshaiah, Johanan son of Kareah and some other men were too proud. They said to Jeremiah, "Jeremiah, you are lying! The Lord our God did not send you to say, 'You must not go to Egypt to live there'. [3]Baruch son of Neriah is causing you to be against us. He wants you to hand us over to the Babylonians. Then they will kill us. Or they will capture us and take us to Babylon."

[4]So Johanan, the army officers and all the people disobeyed the Lord's command. He had commanded them to stay in Judah. [5]But Johanan son of Kareah and the army officers took those who were left alive from Judah to Egypt. These were the people who had run away from the Babylonians to other countries. But they had come back to Judah. [6]Now Johanan and the army officers took the men, women and children. Among those people were the king's daughters. And they led them to Egypt. Nebuzaradan commander of the guard had put Gedaliah in charge of those people. (Gedaliah was the son of Ahikam son of Shaphan.) Johanan also took Jeremiah the prophet[d] and Baruch son of Neriah. [7]These people did not listen to the Lord. So they all went to Egypt to the town of Tahpanhes.

[8]In Tahpanhes the Lord spoke his word to Jeremiah: [9]"Take some large stones. Bury them in the clay in the brick pavement. This is in front of the king of Egypt's palace in Tahpanhes. Do this while the Jews are watching you. [10]Then say to them, 'This is what

the Lord of heaven's armies, the God of Israel, says: I will send for my servant, Nebuchadnezzar king of Babylon. And I will set his throne over these stones I have buried. He will spread his covering for shade above these stones. ¹¹He will come here and attack Egypt. He will bring death to those who are supposed to die. He will make prisoners of those who are to be taken captive. And he will bring war to those who are to be killed with a sword. ¹²Nebuchadnezzar will set fire to the temples of the gods of Egypt. He will burn those temples. And he will take the idols away. A shepherd wraps himself in his clothes. In the same way Nebuchadnezzar will wrap Egypt around him. Then he will safely leave Egypt. ¹³He will destroy the stone pillars in the temple of the sun god in Egypt. And he will burn down the temples of the gods of Egypt'."

Disaster in Egypt

44 Jeremiah received a message from the Lord. It was for all the Jews living in Egypt. It was for the Jews in Migdol, Tahpanhes, Memphis and southern Egypt. This was the message: ²"The Lord of heaven's armies, the God of Israel, says: You saw the terrible things I brought on Jerusalem and the towns of Judah. Those towns are empty ruins today. ³And it is because the people who lived there did evil. Those people burned incense*d* to other gods. And that made me angry! Your people and your ancestors did not worship those gods before. ⁴I sent my prophets*d* to them again and again. Those prophets were my servants. They spoke my message and said to the people, 'Don't do this terrible thing. The Lord hates you to worship other gods'. ⁵But they did not listen to the prophets. They did not pay attention. They did not stop doing evil things. They did not stop burning incense to other gods.

⁶So I showed my great anger against them. I punished the towns of Judah and the streets of Jerusalem. My anger made Jerusalem and the towns of Judah empty. They are only ruins and piles of stones today.

⁷"So the Lord of heaven's armies, the God of Israel, says: Why are you doing such great harm to yourselves by continuing to worship other gods? You are cutting off the men and women, children and babies from the family of Judah. So you leave yourselves without anyone from the family of Judah. ⁸Why do you want to make me angry by making idols? Why do you burn incense to the gods of Egypt, where you have come to live? You will destroy yourselves. Other nations will speak evil of you. And all the other nations on the earth will make fun of you. ⁹Have you forgotten about the evil things your ancestors did? And have you forgotten the evil the kings and queens of Judah did? Have you forgotten about the evil you and your wives did? They did these things in Judah and in the streets of Jerusalem. ¹⁰Even to this day the people of Judah are still too proud. They have not learned to respect me. And they have not followed my teachings. They have not obeyed the laws I gave you and your ancestors!

¹¹"So this is what the Lord of heaven's armies, the God of Israel, says: I am determined to bring disasters on you. I will destroy the whole family of Judah. ¹²There were a few left alive from Judah. They were determined to go to Egypt and settle there. But they will all die in Egypt. They will be killed in war or die from hunger. From the least important to the greatest, they will be killed in war or die from hunger. Other nations will speak evil about them. People will be shocked by what has happened to them. They will become a swear word. People will insult them. ¹³I will punish those people who have gone to live in Egypt. I will

use swords, hunger and terrible diseases to punish them. I will punish them just as I punished Jerusalem. [14]Of the people of Judah who were left alive and have gone to Egypt none will escape my punishment. They want to return to Judah and live there. But none of them will live to return to Judah. None of them will return to Judah, except a few people who escape."

[15]A large group of the people of Judah, who lived in southern Egypt, were meeting together. Among them were many women of Judah who lived in Egypt. They were burning incense to other gods, and their husbands knew it. All these people said to Jeremiah, [16]"We will not listen to the message from the Lord that you spoke to us. [17]We promised to make sacrifices to the Queen Goddess![d] And we will do everything we promised. We will burn incense and pour out drink offerings to worship her. We did that in the past. And our ancestors, kings and officers did that in the past. All of us did those things in the towns of Judah and in the streets of Jerusalem. At that time we had plenty of food. We were successful. Nothing bad happened to us. [18]But then we stopped making sacrifices to the Queen Goddess. And we stopped pouring out drink offerings to her. Since then we have had problems. Our people have been killed in war and by hunger."

[19]The women said, "Our husbands knew what we were doing. We had their permission to burn incense to the Queen Goddess! We had their permission to pour out drink offerings to her. Our husbands knew we were making cakes that looked like her and that we poured out drink offerings to her."

[20]Then Jeremiah spoke to all the people — men and women — who answered him. [21]He said to them, "The Lord remembered that you burned incense. You burned it in the towns of Judah and in the streets of Jerusalem. You and your ancestors, kings and officers did that. And the people of the land did that. The Lord remembered and thought about it. [22]Then he could not be patient with you any longer. He hated the terrible things you did. So he made your country an empty desert. No one lives there now. Other people curse that country. [23]All this happened because you burned incense to other gods. You sinned against the Lord. You did not obey him. You did not follow his teachings or the laws he gave you. You did not keep your part of the agreement. This disaster has happened. It is there for you to see."

[24]Then Jeremiah spoke to all those men and also to the women. He said, "People of Judah who are now in Egypt, hear the word of the Lord: [25]The Lord of heaven's armies, the God of Israel, says: You women did what you said you would do. You said, 'We will keep the promises we made. We promised to make sacrifices to the Queen Goddess. And we promised to pour out drink offerings to her'. So, go ahead. Do the things you promised you would do. Keep your promises. [26]But hear the word of the Lord. Listen, all you Jews living in Egypt. The Lord says, 'I use my great name and make this promise: the people of Judah now living in Egypt will never again use my name to make promises. They will never again say, "As surely as the Lord God lives . . ." [27]I am watching over them. I am not watching over them to take care of them, but to hurt them. The Jews who live in Egypt will die from swords or hunger until they are all destroyed. [28]Some people will escape being killed by the sword. They will come back to Judah from Egypt. But there will only be a very few who escape. Then, of the people of Judah who came to live in Egypt, those who are left alive will know. They will know whether my word or their word came true. [29]I will

give you a sign that I will punish you here in Egypt', says the Lord. 'Then you will know my promises to hurt you will really happen'. ³⁰This is what the Lord says: 'Hophra king of Egypt has enemies who want to kill him. I will hand over King Hophra to his enemies. I will do this just as I handed Zedekiah king of Judah over to Nebuchadnezzar king of Babylon. Nebuchadnezzar wanted to kill Zedekiah'.''

A Message to Baruch

45 It was the fourth year that Jehoiakim son of Josiah was king of Judah. Jeremiah the prophet*d* told these things to Baruch son of Neriah. And Baruch wrote them on a scroll. This is what Jeremiah said to Baruch: ²"This is what the Lord, the God of Israel, says to you: ³Baruch, you have said, 'How terrible it is for me! The Lord has given me sorrow along with my pain. I am tired because of my suffering. I cannot rest'."

⁴The Lord said, "Say this to Baruch: 'This is what the Lord says: I will tear down what I have built. And I will pull up what I have planted. I will do that everywhere in Judah. ⁵Baruch, you are looking for great things for yourself. Don't do that! Don't look for them because I will bring disaster on all the people. The Lord says these things! You will have to go many places. But I will let you escape alive wherever you go'."

Messages About the Nations

46 The Lord spoke this word to Jeremiah the prophet*d* about the nations:

²This message is about Egypt: this message is about the army of King Neco, king of Egypt. His army was defeated at the city of Carchemish on the Euphrates River. It was defeated by Nebuchadnezzar king of Babylon. This was in the fourth year that Jehoiakim son of Josiah was king of Judah. This is the Lord's message to Egypt:

³"Prepare your shields, large and small.
March out for battle!
⁴Harness the horses.
Soldiers, get on your horses!
Go to your places for battle.
Put on your helmets!
Polish your spears.
Put on your armour!
⁵What do I see?
That army is terrified.
The soldiers are running away.
Their warriors are defeated.
They run away quickly.
They don't look back.
There is terror on every side!"
says the Lord.
⁶"The fast runners cannot run away.
The strong soldiers cannot escape.
They will stumble and fall
in the north, by the Euphrates River.
⁷Who is this, rising up like the Nile River?
Who comes like that strong, fast river?
⁸Egypt rises up like the Nile River.
It is Egypt that comes like that strong, fast river.
Egypt says, 'I will rise up and cover the earth.
I will destroy cities and the people in them!'
⁹Horsemen, charge into battle!
Chariot drivers, drive hard!
March on, brave soldiers—
soldiers from Cush and Put who carry shields.
March on, soldiers from Lydia who use bows.
¹⁰"But that day belongs to the Master, the Lord of heaven's armies.
At that time he will give those people the punishment they deserve.
The sword will kill until it has finished.

The sword will kill until it has
satisfied its thirst for blood.
This is because the Master, the
Lord of heaven's armies, will
offer a sacrifice.
That sacrifice is Egypt's army in
the land of the north, by the
Euphrates River.
11"Go to Gilead and get some
balm.*d*
Go up, people of Egypt!
You will make up many medicines,
but you will not be healed.
12The nations will hear of your
shame.
Your cries will fill all the earth.
One warrior will run into another.
And both of them will fall down
together!"

13This is the message the Lord
spoke to Jeremiah the prophet.*d* This
message is about Nebuchadnezzar
king of Babylon as he came to attack
Egypt:
14"Announce this message in Egypt,
and prophesy it in Migdol.
Preach this message also in
Memphis and Tahpanhes:
'Get ready for war.
The battle is all around you'.
15Egypt, why will your warriors be
killed?
They cannot stand because the
Lord will push them down.
16Those soldiers will stumble again
and again.
They will fall over each other.
They will say, 'Get up. Let's go
back
to our own people and our
homeland.
We must get away from our
enemy's sword!'
17In their homelands those soldiers
will say,
'The king of Egypt is only a lot
of noise.
His time of glory is over!' "

18The King's name is the Lord of
heaven's armies.
He says, "As surely as I live,
a powerful leader will come.
He will be strong as great Mount
Tabor is higher than other
mountains.
He will be mighty as Mount
Carmel is higher than the
sea.
19People of Egypt, pack your things
to be taken away as captives.
This is because Memphis will be
destroyed.
The cities will be ruins, and no
one will live there.
20"Egypt is like a beautiful young
cow.
But a horsefly is coming
from the north to attack her.
21The hired soldiers in Egypt's army
are like fat calves.
They will all turn and run away
together.
They will not stand strong
against the attack.
Their time of destruction is
coming.
They will soon be punished.
22Egypt is like a hissing snake that
is trying to escape.
The enemy comes closer and
closer.
They will come against Egypt with
axes.
They are like men who cut
down trees.
23They will chop down Egypt's army
as if it were a great forest,"
says the Lord.
"There are more enemy soldiers
than locusts.*d*
There are too many soldiers to
count.
24The people of Egypt will be
ashamed.
They will be handed over to the
enemy from the north."

25The Lord of heaven's armies, the
God of Israel, says: "Very soon I will

punish Amon, the god of Thebes. And I will punish Egypt, her king and her gods. And I will punish the people who depend on the king. 26I will let all those people be defeated by their enemies. And those enemies want to kill them. I will give them to Nebuchadnezzar king of Babylon and his officers. But in the future, Egypt will live in peace as it once did," says the Lord.

A Message to Israel

27"People of Jacob, my servants,
don't be afraid.
Don't be frightened, Israel.
I will surely save you from those
faraway places.
I will save your children from
the lands where they are
captives.
The people of Jacob will have
peace and safety again.
And no one will make them
afraid.
28People of Jacob, my servants, do
not be afraid.
I am with you," says the Lord.
"I scattered you to many different
nations.
And I will completely destroy all
those nations.
But I will not completely destroy
you.
I will punish you fairly.
But I cannot let you escape your
punishment."

A Message About the Philistines

47 The Lord spoke his word to Jeremiah the prophet.d This message is about the Philistine people. It came before the king of Egypt attacked the city of Gaza.
2This is what the Lord says:
"See, the enemy is gathering in
the north like rising waters.
They will become like an
overflowing stream.

They will cover the whole country
like a flood.
They will cover the towns and
the people living in them.
Everyone living in that country
will cry for help.
The people will cry painfully.
3They will hear the sound of the
running horses.
They will hear the noisy
chariots.
They will hear the rumbling
chariot wheels.
Fathers will not help their children
to safety.
Those fathers will be too weak
to help.
4The time has come
to destroy all the Philistines.
It's time to destroy all who are
left alive
who could help Tyre and Sidon.
The Lord will soon destroy the
Philistines.
He will destroy those left alive
from the island of Crete.
5The people from Gaza will be sad
and shave their heads.
The people from Ashkelon will
be made silent.
Those left alive from the valley,
how long will you cut
yourselves?n

6"You cry, 'Sword of the Lord,
how long will you keep fighting?
Return to your holder.
Stop! Be still'.
7But how can the sword of the
Lord rest?
The Lord gave it a command.
The Lord has ordered it
to attack the city of Ashkelon
and the seacoast."

A Message About Moab

48 This message is about the country of Moab. This is what

sad and . . . yourselves? The people did these things to show their sadness.

the Lord of heaven's armies, the God of Israel, says:

"How terrible it will be for Nebo.
   It will be ruined.
The town of Kiriathaim will be
   disgraced and captured.
The strong city will be disgraced
   and shattered.
2Moab will not be praised again.
Men in the town of Heshbon
   plan Moab's defeat.
They say, 'Come, let us put an
   end to that nation!'
Town of Madmen, you will also be
   silenced.
   The sword will chase you.
3Listen to the cries from the town
   of Horonaim.
They are cries of much
   confusion and destruction.
4Moab will be broken up.
Her little children will cry for
   help.
5Moab's people go up the path to
   Luhith.
   They cry loudly as they go.
On the road down to the town of
   Horonaim,
   cries of pain and suffering can be
   heard.
6Run! Run for your lives!
Go like a bush being blown
   through the desert.
7You trust in the things you do and
   in your wealth.
   So you also will be captured.
The god Chemosh*d* will be taken
   into captivity.
And his priests and officers will
   be taken with him.
8The destroyer will come against
   every town.
   Not one town will escape.
The valley will be ruined.
   The high plain will be destroyed.
The Lord said this would
   happen.
9Spread salt*n* over the fields in
   Moab.

The country will be an empty
   desert.
Moab's towns will become empty.
   No one will live in them.
10A curse will be on anyone who
   doesn't do what the Lord
   says.
A curse will be on anyone who
   keeps back his sword from
   killing.

11"The people of Moab have never
   known trouble.
They are like wine left to settle.
They have never been poured like
   wine from one jar to
   another.
They have not been taken into
   captivity.
So they taste as they did before.
And their smell has not changed.
12A time is coming," says the Lord.
"And I will soon send men to
   pour you from your jars.
Those men will empty Moab's
   jars.
And they will smash their jugs.
13The people of Israel trusted that
   god in Bethel.
They were ashamed when there
   was no help.
In the same way Moab will be
   ashamed of their god
   Chemosh.

14"You cannot say, 'We are
   warriors!
We are brave men in battle!'
15The enemy will attack Moab and
   destroy their towns.
Their best young men will be
   killed!" says the King.
The King's name is the Lord of
   heaven's armies.
16"The end of Moab is near.
They will soon be destroyed.
17All you who live around Moab, cry
   for her.
All you who know about her, cry
   for her.

---

salt The salt would stop crops from growing there.

Say, 'The ruler's power is broken.
Moab's power and glory are
gone'.

18"You people living in Dibon, come
down from your place of
honour.
Sit on the dry ground.
This is because the destroyer of
Moab is coming against you.
And he will destroy your strong,
walled cities.
19You people living in Aroer,
stand next to the road and
watch.
See the man running away and the
woman escaping.
Ask them what happened.
20Moab will be ruined and filled with
shame.
Cry, Moab, cry out!
Announce at the Arnon River
that Moab is destroyed.
21People on the high plain have
been punished.
Judgement has come to these
towns:
Holon, Jahzah and Mephaath;
22   Dibon, Nebo and Beth
Diblathaim;
23   Kiriathaim, Beth Gamul and
Beth Meon;
24   Kerioth and Bozrah.
Judgement has come to all the
towns of Moab, far and
near.
25Moab's strength has been cut off.
Moab's arm is broken!" says the
Lord.

26"The people of Moab thought they
were greater than the Lord.
So punish Moab until they act as
if they are drunk.
Moab will fall and roll around in
their own vomit.
People will make fun of them.
27Moab, you made fun of Israel.
Israel was caught in the middle
of a gang of thieves.
You often spoke about Israel.

And you shook your head and
acted as if you were better
than Israel.
28People in Moab, leave your towns
empty.
Go and live among the rocks.
Be like a dove that makes its nest
at the entrance of a cave!
29"We have heard that the people of
Moab are proud
and very conceited.
They are proud and think they are
important.
They were very proud in their
hearts."
30The Lord says,
"I know Moab's quick anger, but
it is useless.
Moab's boasting accomplishes
nothing.
31So I cry sadly for Moab.
I cry out for everyone in Moab.
I moan for the men from Kir
Hareseth.
32I cry with the people of Jazer
for the grapevines of Sibmah.
In the past your vines spread all
the way to the sea.
They reached as far as the sea
of Jazer.
But the destroyer has taken
your fruit and grapes.
33Joy and happiness are gone
from the large fields of Moab.
I have stopped the flow of wine
from the winepresses.d
No one walks on the grapes
with shouts of joy.
There are shouts,
but not shouts of joy.
34"Their crying can be heard
from Heshbon to Elealeh and
Jahaz.
It can be heard from Zoar as far
away as Horonaim and
Eglath Shelishiyah.
Even the waters of Nimrim are
dried up.
35I will stop Moab

from making burnt offerings at
the places of worship.
I will stop them from burning
incense[d] to their gods," says
the Lord.

36"My heart cries for Moab like a
flute playing a funeral song.
It cries for the people from Kir
Hareseth.
Their money and riches have all
been taken away.
37Everyone has a shaved head.
Everyone's beard is cut off.
Everyone's hands are cut.
Everyone wears rough cloth
around his waist.[n]
38People are crying on every roof[n]
in Moab
and in every public square.
There is nothing but sadness
because I have broken Moab
like a jar no one wants," says
the Lord.
39"Moab is shattered! The people
are crying!
Moab turns away in shame!
People all around her make fun of
her.
The things that have happened fill
them with fear."

40This is what the Lord says:
"Look! An eagle is diving down
from the sky.
It spreads its wings over Moab.
41The towns of Moab will be
captured.
The strong, walled cities will be
defeated.
At that time Moab's warriors will
be frightened.
They will feel pain like a woman
who is having a baby.
42The nation of Moab will be
destroyed.

This is because they thought they
were greater than the Lord.
43Fear, deep pits and traps wait for
you,
people of Moab," says the Lord.
44"People will run from fear.
But they will fall into the pits.
Anyone who climbs out of the pits
will be caught in the traps.
I will bring the year of punishment
to Moab," says the Lord.

45"People have run from the
powerful enemy.
They ran to Heshbon for safety.
But fire started in Heshbon.
A blaze broke out in Sihon's
town.
And it burns the leaders of Moab.
It destroys those proud people.
46How terrible it will be for you,
Moab!
Chemosh's people are being
destroyed.
Your sons and daughters are being
taken away as captives.

47"But in days to come,
I will make good things happen
again to Moab," says the
Lord.

This ends the judgement on Moab.

A Message About Ammon

49 This message is about the Am-
monite people. This is what the
Lord says:
"Do you think that Israel has no
sons?
Do you think there is no one to
take the land when the
parents die?
Maybe that is why Molech[d] took
Gad's land.
Maybe that is why Molech's
people live in Gad's towns."

shaved head . . . waist The people did these things to show their sadness for those who had
died.
roof In Bible times houses were built with flat roofs. The roof was used for drying things such
as flax and fruit. It was also used as an extra room, as a place for worship and as a place
to sleep in the summer.

²The Lord says,
"The time will come when I will
    make
  the capital city of Rabbah
    Ammon hear the battle cry.
It will be a hill covered with ruins.
And the towns around it will be
    burned.
Those people forced Israel out of
    that land.
But now the people of Israel will
    force them out!" says the
    Lord.
³"People in Heshbon, cry because
    the town of Ai is destroyed!
Those who live in Rabbah
    Ammon, cry out!
Put on your rough cloth to show
    your sadness, and cry
    loudly.
Run here and there for safety
    inside the walls.
This is because the enemy will
    take Molech away as a
    captive.
They will also take away his
    priests and officers with him.
⁴You boast about your valleys.
You boast about the fruit in your
    valleys.
You are like an unfaithful child.
You believe your treasures will
    save you.
You think, 'Who would attack
    me?'
⁵I will bring terror on you
    from every side,"
  says the Master, the Lord of
    heaven's armies.
"You will all be forced away.
No one will be able to gather
    you.
⁶"But the time will come
    when I will make good things
    happen to the Ammonites
    again,"
  says the Lord.

A Message About Edom

⁷This message is about Edom. This
is what the Lord of heaven's armies
says:
"Is there no more wisdom in
    Teman?
Can the wise men of Edom no
    longer give good advice?
Have they lost their wisdom?
⁸You people living in Dedan,
  run away and hide in deep
    caves.
This is because I will punish
  the people of Esau with disaster
    for what they did.
⁹If workers came and picked the
    grapes from your vines,
  they would leave a few grapes
    behind.
If robbers came at night,
  they would steal only enough for
    themselves.
¹⁰But I will strip Esau bare.
I will find all their hiding places.
They will not be able to hide
    from me.
The children, relatives and
    neighbours will die.
¹¹Leave the orphans, and I will take
    care of them.
  Your widows also can trust in
    me."

¹²This is what the Lord says: "Some
people did not deserve to be punished. But they had to drink from the
cup of suffering anyway. People of
Edom, you deserve to be punished.
So you will not escape punishment.
You must drink from the cup of suffering." ¹³The Lord says, "I make this
promise in my own name. The city of
Bozrah will become a pile of ruins!
People will be shocked by what happened there. People will insult that
city and speak evil of it. And all the
towns around Bozrah will become ruins for ever."

¹⁴I have heard a message from the
    Lord.
  A messenger has been sent
    among the nations, saying,
"Gather your armies to attack it!

Get ready for battle!"

15"Soon I will make you the smallest
    of nations!
You will be greatly hated.
16Edom, you frightened other
    nations.
Your pride has fooled you.
You live in the hollow places of
    the cliff.
You live on the high places of
    the hills.
Even if you build your home as
    high as an eagle's nest,
I will bring you down from
    there!" says the Lord.

17"Edom will be destroyed.
People will be shocked to see
    the destroyed cities.
They will be amazed at the
    injuries.
18Edom will be destroyed like the
    cities of Sodom and
    Gomorrah
and the towns around them,"
    says the Lord.
"No one will live there!
No man will stay in Edom."

19"A lion will come from the thick
    bushes near the Jordan
    River.
And it will go into the rich
    pastures where people feed
    their flocks.
I am like that lion! I will suddenly
    chase Edom from their land.
Who is the one I have chosen to
    do this?
There is no one like me.
There is no one who can
    challenge me.
None of their leaders can stand
    up against me."

20So listen to what the Lord has
    planned to do against Edom.
Listen to what he has decided to
    do to the people in Teman.
The Lord will surely drag away
    the young ones of Edom.

Edom's pastures will surely be
    destroyed because of them.
21At the sound of Edom's fall, the
    earth will shake.
Their cry will be heard all the
    way to the Gulf of Aqaba.
22The Lord is like an eagle
    swooping down.
He is like an eagle spreading its
    wings over the city of
    Bozrah.
At that time Edom's soldiers will
    become very frightened.
They will be crying from fear
    like a woman having a baby.

A Message About Damascus

23This message is about the city of
Damascus:
"The towns of Hamath and Arpad
    are put to shame.
They are afraid because they
    have heard bad news.
They are discouraged.
They are troubled like the
    tossing sea.
24The city of Damascus has become
    weak.
The people want to run away.
The people are ready to panic.
The people feel pain and suffering
    like a woman having a baby.
25Damascus was the city of my joy.
Why have the people not left
    that famous city yet?
26Surely the young men will die in
    the public squares of that
    city.
All of her soldiers will be killed
    at that time," says the Lord
    of heaven's armies.
27"I will set fire to the walls of
    Damascus.
The fire will completely burn the
    strong cities of Ben-Hadad."

A Message About Kedar and Hazor

28This message is about the tribe[d]
of Kedar and the kingdoms of Hazor.
Nebuchadnezzar king of Babylon de-

feated them. This is what the Lord says:
"Go and attack the people of
    Kedar.
Destroy the people of the East.
29Their tents and flocks will be
    taken away.
Their tents and all their things
    will be carried off.
Their enemy will take away
    their goods and camels.
Men will shout to them,
    'Terror on every side!'

30"Run away quickly!
People in Hazor, find a good
    place to hide!" says the
    Lord.
"Nebuchadnezzar king of Babylon
    has made plans against you.
He has made plans to defeat
    you!

31"There is a nation that is
    comfortable.
It is sure that no one will defeat
    it," says the Lord.
"That nation does not have gates
    or fences to protect it.
Its people live alone.
Attack that nation!
32The enemy will steal their camels
    and their large herds of cattle.
I will scatter the Arabs to every
    part of the earth.
And I will bring disaster on them
    from everywhere," says the
    Lord.
33"Hazor will become a place where
    wild dogs live.
It will become an empty desert
    for ever.
No one will live there.
No man will stay in it."

A Message About Elam

34It was early in the time when Zedekiah was king of Judah. The Lord spoke this word to Jeremiah the prophet.d This message is about the nation of Elam.

35This is what the Lord of heaven's armies says:
"I will break Elam's bow.
I will break its strength.
36I will bring the four winds against
    Elam.
I will bring them from the four
    corners of the skies.
I will scatter the people of Elam
    everywhere the four winds
    blow.
And its captives will go to every
    nation.
37I will break Elam to pieces in front
    of their enemies.
The enemies want to destroy
    Elam.
I will bring disaster to Elam.
I will show them how angry I
    am!" says the Lord.
"I will send a sword to chase
    Elam.
It will chase them until I have
    killed them all.
38I will show Elam that I am king.
And I will destroy her king and
    her officers!" says the Lord.

39"But I will make good things
    happen to Elam again
in the future," says the Lord.

A Message About Babylon

50 This is the message the Lord spoke about Babylon and the Babylonian people. He spoke this message through Jeremiah the prophet.d
2"Announce this to the nations.
Lift up a banner and tell them.
Speak the whole message and
    say:
'Babylon will be captured.
The god Beld will be put to
    shame.
The god Markukd will be very
    afraid.
Babylon's idols will be put to
    shame.
Her idols will be filled with
    terror!'

³A nation from the north will attack
Babylon.
That nation will make Babylon
like an empty desert.
No people will live there.
Both men and animals will run
away from there."

⁴The Lord says, "At that time
the people of Israel and Judah
will be together.
They will cry and look for the
Lord their God.
⁵Those people will ask how to go
to Jerusalem.
They will start to go in that
direction.
They will come and join
themselves to the Lord.
They will make an agreement
that will last for ever.
It will be an agreement that will
never be forgotten.

⁶"My people have been like lost
sheep.
Their leaders have led them in
the wrong way.
Their leaders made them wander
around in the mountains and
hills.
They forgot where their resting
place was.
⁷Whoever found my people hurt
them.
And those enemies said, 'We did
nothing wrong.
Those people sinned against the
Lord, their true resting
place.
He was the God their fathers
trusted'.

⁸"Run away from Babylon.
Leave the land of the
Babylonians.
Be like the goats that lead the
flock.
⁹I will bring against Babylon
many nations from the north.

This group of nations will take
their places for war against
Babylon.
Babylon will be captured by
people from the north.
Their arrows are like trained
soldiers
who do not return from war
with empty hands.
¹⁰The enemy will take all the wealth
from the Babylonians.
Those enemy soldiers will get all
they want!" says the Lord.

¹¹"Babylon, you are excited and
happy.
You took my land.
You dance around like a young
cow in the grain.
Your laughter is like the
neighing of male horses.
¹²Your mother will be very
ashamed.
The woman who gave you birth
will be disgraced.
Babylonia will be the least
important of all the nations.
She will be an empty, dry
desert.
¹³The Lord will show his anger.
No people will live there.
Babylon will be completely
empty.
Everyone who passes by Babylon
will be afraid.
They will shake their heads
when they see how it has
been destroyed.

¹⁴"Take your positions for war
against Babylon,
all you soldiers with bows.
Shoot your arrows at Babylon! Do
not save any of them.
This is because Babylon has
sinned against the Lord.
¹⁵Soldiers around Babylon, shout
the war cry!
Babylon has surrendered. Her
towers have fallen.
Her walls have been torn down.

The Lord is giving them the
    punishment they deserve.
You nations should give Babylon
    what she deserves.
Do to her what she has done to
    others.
16Don't let the people from Babylon
    plant their crops.
Don't let them gather the
    harvest.
The soldiers of Babylon treated
    their captives cruelly.
Now, let everyone go back
    home!
Let everyone run to his own
    country.
17"The people of Israel are like a
    flock of sheep that are
    scattered.
They are like sheep that have
    been chased away by lions.
The first lion to eat them up
    was the king of Assyria.
The last lion to crush their bones
    was Nebuchadnezzar king of
    Babylon."

18So this is what the Lord of heaven's armies, the God of Israel, says:
"I will punish the king of Babylon
    and his country.
I will punish him as I punished
    the king of Assyria.
19But I will bring the people of
    Israel back to their own
    pasture.
They will eat on Mount Carmel
    and in Bashan.
They will eat and be full.
They will eat on the hills of
    Ephraim and Gilead."
20The Lord says,
"At that time people will try to
    find Israel's guilt.
But there will be no guilt.
People will try to find Judah's sins.
But no sins will be found.
This is because I am saving the
    few people left alive from
    Israel and Judah.
And I am forgiving their sins.

21"Attack the land of Merathaim.
Attack the people who live in
    Pekod.
Chase them, kill them and
    completely destroy them.
Do everything I commanded
    you!" says the Lord.
22"The noise of battle can be heard
    all over the country.
It is the noise of much
    destruction.
23Babylon was the hammer of the
    whole earth.
But how broken and shattered
    that hammer is now!
Babylon is truly the most ruined
    of all the nations.
24Babylon, I set a trap for you.
And you were caught before you
    knew it.
You fought against the Lord.
So you were found and taken
    prisoner.
25The Lord has opened up his
    storeroom.
He has brought out the weapons
    of his anger.
This is because the Lord God of
    heaven's armies has work to
    do.
He has work to do in the land of
    the Babylonians.
26Come against Babylon from far
    away.
Break open her storehouses of
    grain.
Pile up her dead bodies like big
    piles of grain.
Completely destroy Babylon
    and do not leave anyone alive.
27Kill all the young men in Babylon.
Let them be killed.
The time has come for their
    defeat.
How terrible it will be for them!
It is time for them to be
    punished.
28Listen to the people running from
    the country of Babylon!
They are telling Jerusalem

how the Lord our God is
  punishing Babylon as it
  deserves.
This is because Babylon
  destroyed his Temple.*d*

29"Call for the men who shoot
  arrows
to come against Babylon.
Tell them to surround the city.
Don't let anyone escape.
Pay her back for the bad things
  she has done.
Do to her what she has done to
  other nations.
Babylon acted with pride against
  the Lord,
  the Holy One of Israel.
30So Babylon's young men will be
  killed in the streets.
All her soldiers will die on that
  day," says the Lord.
31"Babylon, you are too proud. And
  I am against you,"
says the Master, the Lord of
  heaven's armies.
"This is because the time has
  come
for you to be punished.
32Proud Babylon will stumble and
  fall.
And no one will help her get up.
I will start a fire in her towns.
It will completely burn up
  everything around her."

33This is what the Lord of heaven's
armies says:
"The people of Israel
  and Judah are both slaves.
The enemy took them as
  prisoners.
And they won't let them go.
34But God is strong and will buy
  them back.
His name is the Lord of
  heaven's armies.
He will defend them with power
  so he can give rest to their land.
But he will not give rest to
  those living in Babylon."

35The Lord says,
"Let a sword kill the people living
  in Babylon!
Let a sword kill its officers and
  wise men!
36Let a sword kill its false
  prophets!*d*
They will become fools.
Let a sword kill Babylon's
  warriors!
They will be full of terror.
37Let a sword kill its horses and
  chariots.
Let a sword kill all the soldiers
  hired from other countries!
They will be like frightened
  women.
Let there be a sword against
  Babylon's treasures!
They will be taken away.
38Let there be a sword against its
  waters!
They will be dried up.
It is a land of idols.
Those idols will go mad with
  fear.

39"Babylon will never be filled with
  people again.
Desert animals and hyenas will
  live there.
Owls will live there.
But no people will live there ever
  again.
40God completely destroyed the
  cities of Sodom and
  Gomorrah
and the towns around them,"
  says the Lord.
"In the same way no people will
  live in Babylon.
No man will stay there.

41"Look! An army is coming from
  the north.
It comes from a powerful nation.
Many kings are coming together
  from all around the world.
42Their armies have bows and
  spears.
The soldiers are cruel and have
  no mercy.

The soldiers come riding on their
    horses.
And the sound is loud like the
    roaring sea.
They stand in their places, ready
    for battle.
They are ready to attack you,
    city of Babylon.
43The king of Babylon heard about
    those armies.
And he became helpless because
    of his fear.
His fear is like pain.
It is like the pain of a woman
    having a baby.

44"A lion will come from the thick
    bushes near the Jordan
    River.
It will go into the rich pastures
    where people feed their
    flocks.
I am like that lion! I will suddenly
    chase the people of Babylon
    from their land.
Who is the one I have chosen to
    do this?
There is no one like me.
There is no one who can
    challenge me.
None of their leaders can stand
    up against me."

45So listen to what the Lord has
    planned to do against
    Babylon.
Listen to what he has decided to
    do to the people in Babylon.
He will surely drag away the
    young ones of Babylon.
Babylon's pastures will be
    destroyed because of them.
46At the sound of Babylon's fall, the
    earth will shake.
People in all nations will hear
    about their destruction.

51 This is what the Lord says:
    "I will cause a destroying
    wind to blow.
It will blow against Babylon and
    the Babylonian people.

2I will send foreign people to
    destroy Babylon
like a wind that blows chaff*d*
    away.
Those people will make Babylon
    empty.
Armies will surround the city
    when disaster comes upon her.
3The Babylonian soldiers will not
    use their bows and arrows.
Those soldiers will not even put
    on their armour.
Don't feel sorry for the young
    men of Babylon.
Completely destroy her army.
4Babylon's soldiers will be killed in
    Babylon.
They will be badly injured in
    Babylon's streets.
5The Lord God of heaven's armies
    did not leave Israel and Judah
    alone.
They are fully guilty of leaving the
    Holy One of Israel.
But he has not left them.

6"Run away from Babylon!
Run to save your lives!
Don't stay and be killed because
    of Babylon's sins.
It is time for the Lord to punish
    Babylon.
Babylon will get the punishment
    it deserves.
7Babylon was like a gold cup in the
    Lord's hand.
It made the whole earth drunk.
The nations drank Babylon's wine.
So they went mad.
8Babylon will suddenly fall and be
    broken.
Cry for her!
Get balm*d* for her pain.
Perhaps she can be healed.
9"Foreigners in Babylon say, 'We
    tried to heal Babylon.
But she cannot be healed.
So let us leave her and each go to
    his own country.
Babylon's guilt is as high as the
    clouds.

Babylon's guilt reaches to the
sky'.

10"The people of Judah say, 'The
Lord has shown us to be
right.
Come, let us tell about it in
Jerusalem.
Let us tell about what the Lord
our God has done'.

11"Sharpen the arrows.
Pick up your shields!
The Lord has stirred up the kings
of the Medes.
He has stirred them up because
he wants to destroy
Babylon.
The Lord will give the people of
Babylon the punishment they
deserve.
This is because Babylon
destroyed his Temple*d* in
Jerusalem.
12Lift up a banner against the walls
of Babylon!
Bring more guards.
Put the watchmen in their places.
Get ready for a secret attack!
The Lord will do what he has
planned.
He will do what he said he
would do against the people
of Babylon.
13People of Babylon, you live near
much water.
You are rich with treasures.
But your end as a nation has
come.
It is time for you to be
destroyed.
14The Lord of heaven's armies has
promised in his own name:
'Babylon, I will surely fill you
with so many enemy soldiers
they will be like a swarm of
locusts.*d*
They will stand over you and
shout their victory'.

15"The Lord made the earth by his
power.

He used his wisdom to build the
world.
He used his understanding to
stretch out the skies.
16When he thunders, the waters in
the skies roar.
He makes clouds rise in the sky
all over the earth.
He sends lightning with the rain.
He brings out the wind from his
storehouses.

17"People are so stupid and know so
little.
Goldsmiths are made ashamed
by their idols.
Those statues are only false
gods.
They have no breath in them.
18They are worth nothing.
People make fun of them.
When they are judged, they will
be destroyed.
19But God, who is Jacob's Portion,*d*
is not like the idols.
God made everything.
And he made Israel to be his
special people.
The Lord of heaven's armies is
his name.

20"You are my war club.
You are my battle weapon.
I use you to smash nations.
I use you to destroy kingdoms.
21I use you to smash horse and
rider.
I use you to smash chariot and
driver.
22I use you to smash men and
women.
I use you to smash old men and
young men.
I use you to smash young men
and young women.
23I use you to smash shepherds and
flocks.
I use you to smash farmers and
oxen.
I use you to smash governors
and officers.

24"But I will pay Babylon back, and I will pay back all the Babylonians for all the evil things they did to Jerusalem," says the Lord.

25The Lord says,
"Babylon, you are a destroying mountain.
And I am against you.
You have destroyed the whole land.
I will put my hand out against you.
I will roll you off the cliffs.
I will make you a burned-out mountain.
26People will not find any rocks in Babylon big enough for cornerstones.*d*
People will not take any rocks from Babylon to use for the foundation of a building.
This is because your city will be just a pile of ruins for ever," says the Lord.

27"Lift up the banner in the land!
Blow the trumpet among the nations!
Get the nations ready for battle against Babylon.
Call these kingdoms to come and fight against Babylon:
Ararat, Minni and Ashkenaz.
Choose a commander to lead the army against Babylon.
Send so many horses that they are like a swarm of locusts.
28Get the nations ready for battle against Babylon.
Get the kings of the Medes ready.
Get their governors and all their officers ready.
Get all the countries they rule ready for battle against Babylon.
29The land shakes and moves as if in pain.
It will shake when the Lord does what he has planned to Babylon.

His plan is to make Babylon into an empty desert.
No one will live there.
30Babylon's warriors have stopped fighting.
They stay in their protected cities.
Their strength is gone.
They have become like frightened women.
Babylon's houses are burning.
The bars of her gates are broken.
31One messenger follows another.
Messenger follows messenger.
They announce to the king of Babylon
that his whole city has been captured.
32The river crossings have been captured.
The swamplands are burning.
All of Babylon's soldiers are terribly afraid."

33This is what the Lord of heaven's armies, the God of Israel, says:
"The city of Babylon is like a threshing*d* floor,
where people crush the grain at harvest time.
The time to harvest Babylon is coming soon."

34"Nebuchadnezzar king of Babylon has destroyed us.
In the past he took our people away.
And we became like an empty jar.
He was like a giant snake that swallowed us.
He ate everything until he was full of our best things.
Then he spat us out.
35Babylon did terrible things to hurt us.
Now let those things happen to Babylon,"
say the people of Jerusalem.
"The people of Babylon are guilty of killing our people.

Now let them be punished for
the evil they did," says
Jerusalem.

³⁶So this is what the Lord says:
"I will defend you, Judah.
I will make sure that Babylon is
punished.
I will dry up Babylon's sea.
And I will make her springs
become dry.
³⁷Babylon will become a pile of
ruins.
Wild dogs will live there.
People will be shocked by what
happened there.
No one lives there any more.
³⁸Babylon's people are like roaring
young lions.
They growl like baby lions.
³⁹While they are stirred up,
I will give a feast for them.
I will make them drunk.
They will shout and laugh.
And they will sleep for ever and
never wake up!" says the
Lord.
⁴⁰"I will take the people of Babylon
to be killed.
They will be like lambs,
like male sheep and goats
waiting to be killed.

⁴¹"How Babylon will be defeated!
The pride of the whole earth will
be taken captive.
People from other nations will be
shocked at what happened to
Babylon.
And the things they see will
make them afraid.
⁴²The sea will rise over Babylon.
Its roaring waves will cover her.
⁴³Babylon's towns will be ruined and
empty.
Babylon will become a dry,
desert land.
It will become a land where no
one lives.
People will not even travel
through Babylon.

⁴⁴I will punish the god Bel^d in
Babylon.
I will make him spit out what he
has swallowed.
Nations will no longer come to
Babylon.
And the wall around the city will
fall.

⁴⁵"Come out of Babylon, my people!
Run for your lives!
Run from the Lord's great
anger.
⁴⁶Don't lose courage.
Rumours will spread, but don't
be afraid.
One rumour comes this year, and
another comes the next
year.
There will be rumours of
terrible fighting in the
country.
There will be rumours of rulers
fighting against rulers.
⁴⁷The time will surely come
when I will punish the idols of
Babylon.
And the whole land will be
disgraced.
There will be many dead people
lying all around.
⁴⁸Then heaven and earth and all that
is in them
will shout for joy about Babylon.
They will shout because the army
came from the north
and fought against Babylon,"
says the Lord.

⁴⁹"Babylon killed people from Israel.
Babylon killed people from
everywhere on earth.
So Babylon must fall.
⁵⁰You people escaped being killed
with swords.
You must hurry and leave
Babylon.
Don't wait!
Remember the Lord in the
faraway land where you are.
And think about Jerusalem."

51"We people of Judah are
    disgraced.
  We have been insulted.
  We have been shamed.
  This is because strangers have
    gone into
    the holy places of the Lord's
    Temple!"*d*

52The Lord says, "The time is
    coming
  when I will punish the idols of
    Babylon.
  Wounded people will cry with
    pain
  all over that land.

53Babylon might grow until she
    touches the sky.
  She might make her cities
    strong.
  But I will send people to destroy
    that city," says the Lord.

54"We can hear people crying in
    Babylon.
  We hear the sound of people
    destroying things
  in the land of the Babylonians.

55The Lord will destroy Babylon.
  He will make the loud sounds of
    the city become silent.
  Enemies will come roaring in like
    ocean waves.
  People all around will hear that
    roar.

56The army will come and destroy
    Babylon.
  Babylon's soldiers will be taken
    captive.
  Their bows will be broken.
  This is because the Lord is a God
    who punishes people for the
    evil they do.
  He gives them the full
    punishment they deserve.

57I will make Babylon's rulers and
    wise men drunk.
  I will make her governors,
    officers and soldiers drunk,
    too.

Then they will sleep for ever and
    never wake up," says the
    King.
  His name is the Lord of
    heaven's armies.

58This is what the Lord of heaven's
armies says:
  "Babylon's thick wall will be pulled
    down.
  Her high gates will be burned.
  The people will work hard, but it
    won't help.
  Their work will only become fuel
    for the flames!"

A Message to Babylon

59This is the message that Jeremiah
the prophet*d* gave to the officer Seraiah. Seraiah was the son of Neriah,
who was the son of Mahseiah. Seraiah
went to Babylon with Zedekiah king of
Judah. This happened in the fourth
year Zedekiah was king of Judah.
60Jeremiah had written on a scroll all
the terrible things that would happen
to Babylon. He had written all these
words about Babylon. 61Jeremiah said
to Seraiah, "Go to Babylon. Be sure
to read this message so all the people
can hear you. 62Then say, 'Lord, you
have said that you will destroy this
place. You will destroy it so that no
people or animals will live in it. It will
be an empty ruin for ever'. 63After you
have finished reading this scroll, tie a
stone to it. And throw it into the
Euphrates River. 64Then say, 'In the
same way Babylon will sink. It will not
rise again. It will sink because of
the terrible things I will cause to
happen here. Her people will fall'."
  The words of Jeremiah end here.

The Fall of Jerusalem

52 Zedekiah was 21 years old
   when he became king. And he
was king in Jerusalem for 11 years.
His mother's name was Hamutal

daughter of Jeremiah.*ⁿ* She was from Libnah. ²Zedekiah did what the Lord said was wrong, just as Jehoiakim had done. ³All this happened in Jerusalem and Judah because the Lord was angry with them. Finally, he threw them out of his presence.

Zedekiah turned against the king of Babylon.

⁴Then Nebuchadnezzar king of Babylon marched against Jerusalem with his whole army. They made a camp around the city. Then they built devices all around the city walls to attack it. This happened during Zedekiah's ninth year, tenth month and tenth day as king. ⁵The city was under attack until Zedekiah's eleventh year as king.

⁶By the ninth day of the fourth month, the hunger was terrible in the city. There was no food for the people to eat. ⁷Then the city wall was broken through. And the whole army ran away at night. They went through the gate between the two walls by the king's garden. The Babylonians were still surrounding the city. Zedekiah and his men ran towards the Jordan Valley.

⁸But the Babylonian army chased King Zedekiah. They caught up with him in the plains of Jericho. All of his army was scattered from him. ⁹So they captured Zedekiah and took him to the king of Babylon at Riblah. Riblah is in the land of Hamath. There he passed sentence on Zedekiah. ¹⁰There at Riblah the king of Babylon killed Zedekiah's sons as he watched. The king also killed all the officers of Judah. ¹¹Then he put out Zedekiah's eyes. He put bronze chains on him and took him to Babylon. And the king kept Zedekiah in prison there until the day he died.

¹²Nebuzaradan was the commander of the king's special guards. This servant of the king of Babylon came to Jerusalem. This was on the tenth day of the fifth month. This was in Nebuchadnezzar's nineteenth year as king of Babylon. ¹³Nebuzaradan set fire to the Temple*ᵈ* of the Lord and the palace. He also set fire to all the houses of Jerusalem. Every important building was burned. ¹⁴The whole Babylonian army broke down the walls around Jerusalem. That army was led by the commander of the king's special guards. ¹⁵Nebuzaradan, the commander of the guards, took captive some of the poorest people. And he took those who were left in Jerusalem. He took captive those who had surrendered to the king of Babylon. And he took away the skilled craftsmen who were left in Jerusalem. ¹⁶But Nebuzaradan left behind the rest of the poorest people of the land. They were to take care of the vineyards and fields.

¹⁷The Babylonians broke up the bronze pillars, the bronze stands and the large bronze bowl, which was called the Sea. These were in the Temple of the Lord. Then they carried all the bronze to Babylon. ¹⁸They also took the pots, shovels, wick trimmers, bowls, dishes and all the bronze objects. They were used to serve in the Temple. ¹⁹The commander of the king's special guards took these things away: bowls, pans for carrying hot coals and large bowls; pots, lampstands, pans and bowls used for drink offerings. He took everything that was made of pure gold or silver.

²⁰There was so much bronze that it could not be weighed. There were two pillars. There was the large bronze bowl with the 12 bronze bulls under it. And there were the movable stands, which King Solomon had made for the Temple of the Lord.

²¹Each of the pillars was about 8.1 metres high. Each pillar was 5.5 metres around and hollow. The wall of

---

Jeremiah   This is not the prophet Jeremiah but a different man with the same name.

each pillar was 5 centimetres thick. ²²The bronze capital^d on top of the pillar was about 2.3 metres high. It was decorated with a net design and bronze pomegranates^d all around it. The other pillar also had pomegranates. It was like the first pillar. ²³There were 96 pomegranates on the sides of the pillars. There was a total of 100 pomegranates above the net design.

²⁴The commander of the guards took some prisoners. He took Seraiah the chief priest, Zephaniah the priest next in rank, and the three doorkeepers. ²⁵The commander also took other people who were still in the city. He took the officer in charge of the fighting men. He also took seven people who advised the king. He also took the royal assistant who selected people for the army. And he took 60 other men who were in the city. ²⁶Nebuzaradan, the commander, took all these people. And he brought them to the king of Babylon at Riblah. ²⁷There at Riblah, in the land of Hamath, the king had them killed.

So the people of Judah were led away from their country as captives.

²⁸This is how many people Nebuchadnezzar took away as captives: in the seventh year, 3,023 Jews; ²⁹in Nebuchadnezzar's eighteenth year, 832 people from Jerusalem; ³⁰in Nebuchadnezzar's twenty-third year, Nebuzaradan took 745 Jews as captives. Nebuzaradan was the commander of the king's special guards.

In all 4,600 people were taken captive.

Jehoiachin Is Set Free

³¹Jehoiachin king of Judah was in prison in Babylon for 37 years. That year Evil-Merodach became king of Babylon. He let Jehoiachin king of Judah out of prison that year. He set Jehoiachin free on the twenty-fifth day of the twelfth month. ³²Evil-Merodach spoke kindly to Jehoiachin. He gave Jehoiachin a seat of honour. It was above the seats of the other kings who were with him in Babylon. ³³So Jehoiachin put away his prison clothes. For the rest of his life, he ate at the king's table. ³⁴Every day the king of Babylon gave Jehoiachin an allowance. This lasted as long as he lived, until Jehoiachin died.

LAMENTATIONS

Sad Songs About Jerusalem

Jerusalem Cries Over Her Destruction

1 Jerusalem once was full of
people.
But now the city is empty.
Jerusalem once was a great city
among the nations.
But now she*n* has become like
a widow.
She was like a queen of all the
other cities.
But now she is a slave.

2She cries loudly at night.
Tears are on her cheeks.
There is no one to comfort her.
All her lovers are gone.
All her friends have turned against
her.
They have become her enemies.

3Judah has gone into captivity.
She has suffered and worked
hard.
She lives among other nations.
But she has found no rest.
Those who chased her caught her.
They caught her when she was
in trouble.

4The roads to Jerusalem are sad.
No one comes to Jerusalem for
the feasts.
No one passes through her gates.
And her priests groan.
Her young women are suffering.
And Jerusalem suffers terribly.

5Her enemies have become her
masters.
Her enemies enjoy the wealth
they have won.
The Lord is punishing her

for her many sins.
Her children have gone away.
They are captives of the enemy
in a foreign land.

6The beauty of Jerusalem
has gone away.
Her rulers are like deer
that cannot find food.
They are weak and have run away
from those who chased them.

7Jerusalem is suffering and
homeless.
She remembers all the precious
things
she had in the past.
She remembers when her people
were defeated by the
enemy.
There was no one to help her.
When her enemies saw her,
they laughed to see her ruined.

8Jerusalem sinned terribly.
So she has become unclean.*d*
Those who honoured her hate her
now
because they have seen her
nakedness.
Jerusalem groans
and turns away.

9Jerusalem made herself dirty by
her sins.
She did not think about what
would happen to her.
Her defeat was surprising.
There was no one to comfort
her.
She says, "Lord, see how I
suffer.
The enemy has won."

she   In this poem the city of Jerusalem is described as a woman.

¹⁰The enemy reached out and took
all her precious things.
She even saw foreigners
enter her Temple.*ᵈ*
Lord, you had commanded
that they should not enter the
meeting of your people.

¹¹All of Jerusalem's people are
groaning.
They are looking for bread.
They are giving away their
precious things for food
so they can stay alive.
The city says, "Look, Lord, and
see.
I am hated."

¹²Jerusalem says, "You who pass by
on the road don't seem to
care.
Come, look at me and see.
Is there any pain like mine?
Is there any pain like that he
has caused me?
The Lord has punished me
on the day of his great anger.

¹³"The Lord sent fire from above.
It went down into my bones.
He stretched out a net for my
feet.
He turned me back.
He made me sad and lonely.
I am weak all day.

¹⁴"He has noticed my sins.
They are tied together by his
hands.
They hang around my neck.
He has turned my strength into
weakness.
The Lord has let me be defeated
by those who are stronger than
I am.

¹⁵"The Lord has rejected
all my mighty men inside my
walls.
He brought an army against me
to destroy my young men.
As if in a winepress,*ᵈ* the Lord
has crushed

the capital city of Judah.

¹⁶"I cry about these things.
My eyes overflow with tears.
There is no one near to comfort
me.
There is no one who can give
me strength again.
My children are left sad and lonely
because the enemy has won."

¹⁷Jerusalem reaches out her hands,
but there is no one to comfort
her.
The Lord has commanded for the
people of Jacob
that their enemies surround
them.
Jerusalem has become unclean
like those around her.

¹⁸Jerusalem says, "The Lord is
right.
But I refused to obey him.
Listen, all you people.
Look at my pain.
My young women and men
have gone into captivity.

¹⁹"I called out to my friends,
but they turned against me.
My priests and my older leaders
have died in the city.
They were looking for food
so they could stay alive.

²⁰"Look at me, Lord. I am upset.
I am troubled.
My heart is troubled
because I have been so
stubborn.
Out in the streets, the sword
kills.
Inside the houses, death
destroys.

²¹"People have heard my groaning.
There is no one to comfort me.
All my enemies have heard of my
trouble.
They are happy that you have
done this to me.
Now bring that day you have
announced.

Let my enemies be like me.

22"Look at all their evil.
Do to them what you have done
to me
because of all my sins.
I groan over and over again,
and I am afraid."

The Lord Destroyed Jerusalem

2 Look how the Lord in his anger
has brought Jerusalem to shame.
He has thrown down the
greatness of Israel
from the sky to the earth.
He did not remember the
Temple,[d] his footstool,
on the day of his anger.

2The Lord swallowed up without
mercy
all the houses of the people of
Jacob.
In his anger he pulled down
the strong places of Judah.
He threw her kingdom and its
rulers
down to the ground in
dishonour.

3In his anger the Lord has
removed
all the strength of Israel.
He took away his power from
Israel
when the enemy came.
He burned against the people of
Jacob like a flaming fire
that burns up everything around
it.

4Like an enemy, the Lord prepared
to shoot his bow.
He took hold of his sword.
Like an enemy, he killed
all the good-looking people.
He poured out his anger like fire
on the tents of Jerusalem.

5The Lord has become like an
enemy.
He has swallowed up Israel.

He has swallowed up all her
palaces.
He has destroyed all her strong
places.
He has caused more moaning and
groaning
for Judah.

6He has destroyed his Temple as if
it were a garden tent.
He has destroyed the place
where he met with his
people.
The Lord has made Jerusalem
forget
the set feasts and Sabbath[d]
days.
He has rejected the king and the
priest
in his great anger.

7The Lord has rejected his altar
and abandoned his Temple.
He has given to the enemy
the walls of Jerusalem's palaces.
The enemy shouted in the Lord's
Temple
as if it were a feast day.

8The Lord planned to destroy
the wall around Jerusalem.
He marked the wall off with a
measuring line.
He did not stop himself from
destroying it.
He made the walls and defences
sad.
Together they have fallen.

9Jerusalem's gates have fallen to
the ground.
He destroyed and smashed the
bars of the gates.
Her king and her princes are sent
away among the nations.
The teaching of the Lord has
stopped.
The prophets[d] have not had
any visions from the Lord.

10The older leaders of Jerusalem
sit on the ground and are silent.
They pour dust on their heads

and put on rough cloth to show
how sad they are.
The young women of Jerusalem
bow their heads to the ground in
sorrow.

¹¹My eyes are weak from crying.
I am troubled.
I feel as if I have been poured out
on the ground
because my people have been
destroyed.
Children and babies are fainting
in the streets of the city.

¹²They say to their mothers,
"Where is some bread and
wine?"
They faint like wounded soldiers
in the streets of the city.
They die in their mothers' arms.

¹³What can I say about you,
Jerusalem?
What can I compare you to?
What can I say you are like?
How can I comfort you,
Jerusalem?
Your ruin is as big as the sea.
No one can heal you.

¹⁴Your prophets saw visions about
you.
But they were false and worth
nothing.
They did not expose your sins.
They did not keep you from
being captured.
The messages they preached to
you were false.
They fooled you.

¹⁵All who pass by on the road
clap their hands at you.
They make fun and shake their
heads
at Jerusalem.
They ask, "Is this the city that
people called
the most beautiful city,
the happiest city on earth?"

¹⁶All your enemies open their
mouths

to say things against you.
They make fun and grind their
teeth in anger.
They say, "We have swallowed
her up.
This is the day we were waiting
for.
We have finally seen it happen."

¹⁷The Lord has done what he
planned.
He has carried out the order
that he commanded long ago.
He has destroyed without mercy.
He has made your enemies
happy because of what
happened to you.
He has strengthened your
enemies.

¹⁸The people
cry out to the Lord.
Wall of Jerusalem,
let your tears flow
like a river day and night.
Do not stop.
Do not let your eyes rest.

¹⁹Get up, cry out in the night.
Cry all through the night.
Pour out your heart like water
in prayer to the Lord.
Lift up your hands in prayer to
him.
Pray for the life of your
children.
They are fainting with hunger
on every street corner.

²⁰Jerusalem says: "Look, Lord, and
see.
You have never done this to
anyone else.
Women eat their own babies,
the children they have cared for.
Priests and prophets
are killed in the Temple of the
Lord.

²¹"Young men and old men
lie on the ground in the streets
of the city.
My young women and young men

have been killed by the sword.
You, Lord, killed them on the day
    of your anger.
You killed them without mercy.

22"You invited terrors to come
    against me on every side.
It was as if you were inviting
    them to a feast.
No one escaped or remained alive
    on the day of the Lord's anger.
My enemy has killed
    those whom I gave birth to and
    brought up."

The Meaning of Suffering

3 I am a man who has seen the
    suffering
that comes from the rod of the
    Lord's anger.
2He led me
    into darkness, not light.
3He turned his hand against me
    again and again, all day long.

4He caused my flesh and skin to
    wear out.
He broke my bones.
5He surrounded me and attacked
    me
with sadness and grief.
6He made me sit in the dark,
like someone who has been dead
    a long time.

7He shut me in so I could not get
    out.
He put heavy chains on me.
8I cry out and beg for help.
But he ignores my prayer.
9He has blocked my way with
    stones.
He has made my life difficult.
10The Lord is like a bear ready to
    attack me.
He is like a lion in hiding.
11He led me the wrong way and
    tore me to pieces.
He left me without help.
12He prepared to shoot his bow.
He made me the target for his
    arrows.

13He shot me in the kidneys
    with the arrows from his
    quiver.
14I have become a joke to all my
    people.
All day long they make fun of
    me with songs.
15The Lord filled me with misery.
He filled me with suffering.

16The Lord broke my teeth with
    gravel.
He crushed me into the dirt.
17I have no more peace.
I have forgotten what happiness
    is.
18I said, "My strength is gone.
I have no more hope that the
    Lord will help me."

19Lord, remember my suffering and
    how I have no home.
Remember the misery and
    suffering.
20I remember them well.
And I am very sad.
21But I have hope
    when I think of this:

22The Lord's love never ends.
His mercies never stop.
23They are new every morning.
Lord, your loyalty is great.
24I say to myself, "The Lord is
    what I have left.
So I have hope."

25The Lord is good to those who
    put their hope in him.
He is good to those who look to
    him for help.
26It is good to wait quietly
    for the Lord to save.
27It is good for a man to work hard
    while he is young.

28He should sit alone and be quiet
    because the Lord has given him
    hard work to do.
29He should bow to the Lord with
    his face to the ground.
Maybe there is still hope.

Esther 7:7
Haman stayed inside
to beg Queen Esther
to save his life.

Psalm 133:1
It is good and pleasant when God's people
live together in peace!

Daniel 6:22
"My God sent his angel to close the lions' mouths."

Jonah 1:17
And the Lord caused a very big fish to
swallow Jonah.

30He should offer his cheek if
    someone wants to hit him.
He should be filled with shame.
31The Lord will not reject
    his people for ever.
32Although the Lord brings sorrow,
    he also has mercy.
His love is great.
33The Lord does not like to punish
    people
    or make them sad.

34The Lord sees if any prisoner of
    the earth
is crushed under his feet.
35He sees if someone is treated
    unfairly
before the Most High God.
36The Lord sees
    if someone is cheated in his case
    in court.

37Nobody can speak and have it
    happen
unless the Lord commands it.
38Both bad and good things
come by the command of the
    Most High God.
39No man should complain
    when he is punished for his sins.

40Let us examine and look at what
    we have done.
Then let us return to the Lord.
41Let us lift up our hands and pray
    from our hearts.
Let us say to God in heaven,
42"We have sinned and turned
    against you.
And you have not forgiven us.

43"You wrapped yourself in anger
    and chased us.
You killed us without mercy.
44You wrapped yourself in a cloud.
No prayer could get through.
45You made us like scum and
    rubbish
among the other nations.

46"All of our enemies
open their mouths and say
    things against us.

47We have been frightened and
    fearful.
We have been ruined and
    destroyed."
48Streams of tears flow from my
    eyes
because my people are
    destroyed.

49My tears flow continually,
    without stopping,
50until the Lord looks down
    and sees from heaven.
51I am sad when I see
    what has happened to all the
    women of my city.

52Those who are my enemies for no
    reason
    hunted me like a bird.
53They threw me alive into a pit.
They threw stones at me.
54Water came up over my head.
I said to myself, "I am going to
    die."

55I called out to you, Lord,
    from the bottom of the pit.
56You heard me calling, "Do not
    close your ears.
Do not ignore my cry for help."
57You came close when I called out
    to you.
You said, "Don't be afraid."

58Lord, you have taken my case. ·
You have given me back my life.
59Lord, you have seen how I have
    been wronged.
Now judge my case for me.
60You have seen how my enemies
    took revenge on me.
You have seen all their evil plans
    against me.

61Lord, you have heard their insults
    and all their evil plans against
    me.
62The words and thoughts of my
    enemies
are against me all the time.
63Look! In everything they do
    they make fun of me with songs.

⁶⁴Punish them as they should be
    punished, Lord.
Pay them back for what they
    have done.
⁶⁵Make them stubborn.
Put your curse on them.
⁶⁶Chase them in anger.
Destroy them from the Lord's
    earth.

The Attack on Jerusalem

4 See how the gold has lost its
    shine!
See how the good gold has
    changed!
The stones of the Temple[d] are
    scattered
at every street corner.

²The precious people of Jerusalem
    were more valuable than gold.
But now they are thought of as
    clay jars
made by the hands of a potter.

³Even wild dogs give their milk
    to feed their young.
But my people are cruel
    like ostriches in the desert.

⁴The baby is so thirsty
    that his tongue sticks to the roof
    of his mouth.
Children beg for bread.
    But no one breaks off a piece to
    share with them.

⁵Those who once ate fine foods
    are now starving in the streets.
The people who grew up wearing
    nice clothes
now pick through rubbish piles.

⁶My people have been punished
    more than Sodom was.
Sodom was destroyed suddenly.
No hands reached out to help
    her.

⁷Our princes were purer than
    snow.
They were whiter than milk.
Their bodies were redder than
    rubies.

Their faces shone like
    sapphires.
⁸But now they are blacker than
    coal.
No one even recognises them in
    the streets.
Their skin is stretched over their
    bones.
It is as dry as wood.

⁹Those people who were killed by
    the sword had it better
than those killed by hunger.
They starved in pain and died
because there was no food from
    the field.

¹⁰With their own hands kind women
    cooked their own children.
The children became food for their
    parents.
This happened when my people
    were destroyed.

¹¹The Lord turned loose all of his
    anger.
He poured out his strong anger.
He set fire to Jerusalem.
It burned down to the
    foundations.

¹²Kings of the earth and people of
    the world
could not believe it.
They could not believe that
    enemies
could come through the gates of
    Jerusalem.

¹³But it happened because her
    prophets[d] had sinned.
And her priests had done evil.
They killed in the city
    the people who did what was
    right.

¹⁴They wandered in the streets
    like blind men.
They became dirty with blood.
So no one could touch their
    clothes.

¹⁵"Go away! You are unclean,"[d]
    people shouted at them.

"Get away! Get away! Do not
touch us!"
So they left and wandered around.
The other nations said, "Don't
stay here."

¹⁶The Lord himself scattered them.
He did not look after them any
more.
He did not respect the priests.
He showed no mercy to the
older leaders.

¹⁷Also, our eyes grew tired
looking for help that never
came.
We kept watch from our towers
for a nation to save us.

¹⁸Our enemies hunted us
so we could not even walk in
the streets.
Our end came near. Our time was
up.
Our end came.

¹⁹The men who chased us
were faster than eagles in the
sky.
They chased us on to the
mountains.
They ambushed us in the
desert.

²⁰The Lord's appointed king, who
was our very breath,
was caught in their traps.
We had said of him, "We will be
protected by him
among the nations."

²¹Be happy and glad, people of
Edom,
you who live in the land of Uz.
But the Lord's anger is like a cup
of wine that you also will
have to drink.
Then you will get drunk on it
and make yourselves naked.

²²Your punishment is complete,
Jerusalem.
He will not keep you in captivity
any longer.

But the Lord will punish your
wrongs, people of Edom.
He will uncover your sins.

A Prayer to the Lord

5 Remember, Lord, what
happened to us.
Look and see our disgrace.
²Our land has been turned over to
strangers.
Our houses have been given to
foreigners.
³We have become orphans with no
father.
Our mothers have become like
widows.
⁴We have to buy the water we
drink.
We must pay for the wood for
our fires.
⁵They work us hard as if we were
animals with a yoke^d on our
necks.
We get tired and have no rest.
⁶We made an agreement with
Egypt
and with Assyria to get enough
food.
⁷Our ancestors sinned against you.
But they are gone.
Now we must suffer because of
their sins.
⁸Slaves have become our rulers.
There is no one who can save
us from them.
⁹We risk our lives to get our food
because there are men with
swords in the desert.
¹⁰Our skin is hot like an oven.
We burn with fever because of
the terrible hunger.
¹¹The enemy attacked the women
of Jerusalem
and the girls in the cities of
Judah.
¹²The enemy hung our princes by
the hands.
They do not honour our older
leaders.
¹³The young men grind grain at the
mill.

Boys stumble while carrying
　　loads of wood.
14The older leaders no longer sit at
　　the city gates.
The young men no longer make
　　music.
15We have no more joy in our
　　hearts.
Our dancing has turned into
　　sadness.
16The glory has gone from
　　Jerusalem.
How terrible it is for us because
　　we have sinned.
17Because of this we are afraid.
Because of these things our
　　eyes are dim.

18Mount Zion*d* is empty.
Now wild dogs wander around
　　it.
19But you rule for ever, Lord.
You will be King from now on.
20Why have you forgotten us for so
　　long?
Why have you left us for so
　　long?
21Bring us back to you, Lord. We
　　will return.
Make our days as they were
　　before.
22Or have you completely rejected
　　us?
Will your anger never end?

EZEKIEL

God's Message to the Captives

Ezekiel's Vision of Living Things

1 It was the thirtieth year, on the fifth day of the fourth month of our captivity. I, Ezekiel, was by the Kebar River in Babylon. I was among the people who had been carried away as captives from the land of Judah. The sky opened, and I saw visions of God. ²It was the fifth year that King Jehoiachin had been a prisoner. It was on the fifth day of the month. ³The Lord spoke his word to Ezekiel son of Buzi. This was in the land of the Babylonians by the Kebar River. There he felt the power of the Lord.

⁴When I looked, I saw a stormy wind coming from the north. There was a great cloud with a bright light around it. Fire was flashing out of it. And there was something that looked like glowing metal in the centre of the fire. ⁵Inside the cloud were what looked like four living creatures. They were shaped like men. ⁶Each of them had four faces. And each of them had four wings. ⁷Their legs were straight. Their feet were like a calf's hoofs. And they sparkled like polished bronze. ⁸The living creatures had men's hands. They were under their wings on their four sides. All four of them had faces and wings. ⁹And their wings touched each other. The living creatures did not turn when they moved. Each went straight ahead.

¹⁰Their faces looked like this: in front each living creature had the face of a man. Each one had the face of a lion on the right side. Each one had the face of an ox on the left side. And at the back each one had the face of an eagle. ¹¹This was what their faces looked like. Their wings were spread out above. Each had two wings that touched one of the other living creatures. Each living creature had two wings that covered its body. ¹²Each went straight ahead. Wherever the spirit would go, the living creatures would also go. When they went, they did not turn. ¹³The living creatures looked like burning coals of fire. They were like torches. Fire went back and forth among the living creatures. It was bright, and lightning flashed from it. ¹⁴The living creatures ran back and forth like bolts of lightning.

¹⁵Now I looked at the living creatures. And I saw a wheel on the ground by each of the living creatures with its four faces. ¹⁶The wheels and the way they were made were like this: they looked like sparkling chrysolite. All four of them looked the same. The wheels looked like one wheel crossways inside another wheel. ¹⁷When they moved, they went in any one of the four directions. They did not turn as they went. ¹⁸I saw the rims of the wheels. The rims were full of eyes all around.

¹⁹When the living creatures moved, the wheels moved beside them. When the living creatures were lifted up from the ground, the wheels also were lifted up. ²⁰Wherever the spirit would go, the living creatures would go. And the wheels were lifted up beside them. This is because the spirit of the living creatures was in the wheels. ²¹When the living creatures moved, the wheels moved. When the living creatures stopped, the wheels stopped. And when the living creatures were lifted from the ground, the wheels were lifted beside them. This

is because the spirit of the living creatures was in the wheels.

22Now there was something like a dome over the heads of the living creatures. It sparkled like ice and was frightening. 23And under the dome the wings of the living creatures were stretched out straight toward one another. Each living creature also had two wings covering its body. 24I heard the sound of their wings as they moved. It was like the roaring sound of the sea. It was like the voice of God All-Powerful. It was a roaring sound like a noisy army. When the living creatures stood still, they lowered their wings.

25And a voice came from above the dome over the heads of the living creatures. When the living creatures stood still, they lowered their wings. 26Now above the dome there was something that looked like a throne. It looked like a sapphire gem. And on the throne was a shape like a man. 27Then I noticed what he looked like from the waist up. He looked like glowing metal with fire inside it. And from his waist down he looked like fire. I saw a bright light all around him. 28The glow around him looked like the rainbow in the clouds on a rainy day. It seemed to look like the glory of the Lord. So when I saw it, I bowed face down on the ground. And I heard a voice speaking.

The Lord Speaks to Ezekiel

2 He said to me, "Human being, stand up on your feet. Then I will speak with you." 2While he spoke to me, the Spirit*d* entered me and put me on my feet. Then I heard the Lord speaking to me.

3He said, "Human being, I am sending you to the people of Israel. They are a nation of people who turned against me. They broke away from me. They and their ancestors have sinned against me until this very day. 4And I am sending you to people who

are stubborn. They do not obey. You will say this to them, 'This is what the Lord God says'. 5The people may listen, or they may not. They are a people who turn against me. But whatever they do, they will know that a prophet*d* has been among them. 6You, human being, don't be afraid of the people or their words. Thorny branches and thorns may be all around you. And you may live with insects that sting with poison. Don't be afraid of their words. Don't be afraid of their looks. They are a people who turn against me. 7But speak my words to them. They may listen, or they may not, because they turn against me. 8But you, human being, listen to what I say to you. Don't turn against me as those people do. Open your mouth and eat what I am giving you."

9I looked and saw a hand stretched out to me. A scroll was in the hand. 10The Lord opened the scroll in front of me. The scroll was written on the front and back. Funeral songs, sad writings and troubles were written on the scroll.

3 Then the Lord said to me, "Human being, eat what you find. Eat this scroll. Then go and speak to the people of Israel." 2So I opened my mouth, and the Lord gave me the scroll.

3The Lord said to me, "Human being, eat this scroll which I am giving you. Fill your stomach with it." Then I ate it. And it was sweet like honey in my mouth.

4Then the Lord said to me, "Human being, go to the people of Israel. Speak my words to them. 5You are not being sent to people whose speech you can't understand. Their language is not difficult. You are being sent to Israel. 6You are not being sent to many nations whose speech you can't understand. The language of Israel is not difficult. You are not being sent to people whose words you cannot understand. If I had sent you to them, they would have listened to you. ⁷But the people of Israel are not willing to listen to you. This is because they are not willing to listen to me. Yes, all the people of Israel are stubborn and will not obey. ⁸See, I have made you as stubborn as they are. You will be as hard as they are. ⁹I have made you as hard as a diamond, harder than stone. Don't be afraid of them. Don't be frightened by them. They are a people who turn against me."

¹⁰Also, the Lord said to me, "Human being, believe all the words that I will speak to you. And listen carefully. ¹¹Go to the captives, your people. And speak to them, whether they listen or not. Tell them, 'The Lord God says this'."

¹²Then the Spirit lifted me up. And I heard a loud rumbling sound behind me. A voice said, "Praise God in heaven." ¹³I heard the wings of the living creatures touching each other. And I heard the sound of the wheels by them. It was a loud rumbling sound. ¹⁴So the Spirit lifted me up and took me away. I was unhappy and angry. I felt the great power of the Lord. ¹⁵I came to the captives from Judah. They lived by the Kebar River at Tel Abib. I sat there seven days where these people lived. I was shocked.

Israel's Warning

¹⁶After seven days the Lord spoke his word to me again. He said, ¹⁷"Human being, I have made you a watchman for Israel. Whenever you hear a word from my mouth, warn them for me. ¹⁸When I say to an evil person, 'You will surely die', you must warn him. If you don't speak out to warn the evil person to leave his evil ways, he will die in his sin. But I will hold you responsible for his death. ¹⁹You must warn the evil person. Then if he does not turn from his wickedness or his evil ways, he will die because of his sin. But you will have saved yourself. ²⁰"Again, a person who does right

may turn away from his goodness. He may do evil. If I caused him to sin, he will die. Because you have not warned him, he will die because of his sin. And the good he did will not be remembered. But I will hold you responsible for his death. ²¹But if you do warn that good person not to sin, he may not sin. Then he will surely live. This is because he was warned. And you will save yourself."

²²Then I felt the power of the Lord there. He said to me, "Get up and go out to the plain. There I will speak to you." ²³So I got up and went out to the plain. I saw the glory of the Lord standing there. It was like the glory I saw by the Kebar River. And I bowed face down on the ground.

²⁴Then the Spirit^d entered me and made me stand on my feet. He spoke to me and said, "Go, shut yourself up in your house. ²⁵As for you, human being, the people will tie you up with ropes. They will tie you up, and you will not be able to go out among them. ²⁶Also, I will make your tongue stick to the roof of your mouth. Then you will be silent. And you will not be able to argue with the people, even though they turn against me. ²⁷But when I speak to you, I will open your mouth. And you will say, 'The Lord God says this'. Whoever will listen, let him listen. Whoever refuses, let him refuse. They are a people who turn against me.

The Map of Jerusalem

4 "Now, human being, get yourself a brick. Put it in front of you and draw a map of Jerusalem on it. ²Then surround it with an army. Build battle works against the city. Build a road of earth to the top of the city walls. Set up camps around it. Put heavy logs in place to break down the walls. ³Then get yourself an iron plate. Put it up like an iron wall between you and the city. Turn your face towards the city

as if to attack it. Then surround it and attack it. This is a sign to Israel.

4"Then lie down on your left side. Take the guilt of Israel on yourself. Their guilt will be on you for the number of days you lie on your left side. 5I have given you the same number of days as the years of the people's sin. So you will have the guilt of Israel's sin on you for 390 days.

6"When you have finished these 390 days, lie down a second time. This time lie on your right side. You will then have the guilt of Judah on you. I have given it to you for 40 days. This is a day for each year of their sin. 7Then you will turn your face towards the army attacking Jerusalem. With your arm bare, you will prophesy*d* against Jerusalem. 8I will put ropes on you so you cannot turn from one side to the other. This will last until you have finished the days of your attack on Jerusalem.

9"Take wheat, barley, beans, small peas and millet seeds. And put them in one bowl. Make them into bread for yourself. You will eat it the 390 days you lie on your side. 10You will eat 0.2 kilogram of food every day. You will eat it at set times. 11You will drink about 0.6 of a litre of water every day. Drink it at set times. 12Eat your food as you would eat a barley cake. Bake it over human dung where the people can see." 13Then the Lord said, "In the same way Israel will eat unclean*d* food. They will eat it among the nations where I force them to go."

14But I said, "No, Lord God! I have never been made unclean. From the time I was young until now I've never eaten anything that died by itself. And I've never eaten anything torn by animals. Unclean meat has never entered my mouth."

15"Very well," he said. "Then I will give you cow's dung instead of human dung. You may use it for your fire to bake your bread."

16Then the Lord said to me, "Human being, look! I am going to cut off the supply of bread to Jerusalem. They will eat the bread that is measured out to them. And they will worry as they eat it. They will drink water that is measured out to them. And they will be in shock as they drink it. 17This is because bread and water will be hard to find. And the people will be shocked at the sight of each other. They will become weak because of their sin.

Ezekiel Cuts His Hair

5 "Now, human being, take a sharp sword. Use it like a barber's razor to shave your head and beard. Then take scales and weigh and divide the hair. 2Burn one-third with fire when the days of the attack on Jerusalem are over. Burn it in the middle of the city. Then take one-third and cut it up with the knife all around the city. And scatter one-third to the wind. This is how I will chase them with a sword. 3Also take a few of these hairs and tie them in the folds of your clothes. 4Take a few more and throw them into the fire and burn them up. From there a fire will spread to all the people of Israel.

5"This is what the Lord says: This is Jerusalem. I have put her at the centre of the nations with countries all around her. 6But she has refused to obey my laws. She has been more evil than the nations. She has refused to obey my rules even more than those around her. The people of Jerusalem have rejected my laws and have not lived by my rules.

7"So this is what the Lord God says: You caused more confusion than the nations around you. You did not follow my rules or obey my laws. You have not even obeyed the laws of the nations around you.

8"So this is what the Lord God says: I myself am against you. I will punish you and the nations will watch. 9I will do things among you that I have not done before. I will never do anything like them again. I will do them because you do the things I hate. ¹⁰So fathers among you will eat their children. And children will eat their fathers. I will punish you. I will scatter to the winds all who are left alive. ¹¹So the Lord God says: As surely as I live, you have made my Temple*d* unclean.*d* You have done it with all your evil idols and the hated things you do. Because of this I will cut you off. I will have no pity. I will show no mercy. ¹²A third of you will die by disease or be destroyed by hunger inside your walls. A third will fall dead by the sword outside your walls. And a third I will scatter in every direction. I will chase them with a sword. ¹³Then my anger will come to an end. I will use it up against them. Then I will be satisfied. Then they will know that I, the Lord God, have spoken. After I have carried out my anger against them, they will know how strongly I felt.

¹⁴"I will make you a ruin. And I will make you a shame among the nations around you. All who pass by will see this. ¹⁵Then you will be shamed by the nations around you. They will make fun of you. You will be a warning to them. They will be terrified. This will happen when I punish you in my great anger. I, the Lord, have spoken. ¹⁶I will send a time of hunger to destroy you. Then I will make your hunger get even worse. I will cut off your supply of food. ¹⁷I will send a time of hunger and wild animals against you. They will kill your children. Disease and death will sweep through your people. I will bring the sword against you to kill you. I, the Lord, have spoken."

Prophecies Against the Mountains

6 Again the Lord spoke his word to me. The Lord said, ²"Human being, look towards the mountains of Israel. Prophesy*d* against them. ³Say, 'Mountains of Israel, listen to the

word of the Lord God. The Lord God says this to the mountains, the hills, the ravines and the valleys: I will bring a sword against you. I will destroy your places of idol worship. ⁴Your altars will be destroyed. Your incense*d* altars will be broken down. Your people will be killed in front of your idols. ⁵I will lay the dead bodies of the Israelites before their idols. And I will scatter your bones around your altars. ⁶In all the places you live, cities will become empty. And the places of idol worship will be ruined. Your altars will become lonely ruins. Your idols will be broken and brought to an end. Your incense altars will be cut down. And the things you made will be wiped out. ⁷Your people will be killed and fall among you. Then you will know that I am the Lord God.

⁸"'But I will leave some people alive. Some will not be killed by the nations when you are scattered among the foreign lands. ⁹Then those who have escaped will remember me. They will be living among the nations where they have been taken as captives. They will remember how I was hurt because they were unfaithful to me. They had turned away from me. They will remember how I was hurt because they desired to worship their idols. They will hate themselves because of the evil things they did that I hate. ¹⁰Then they will know that I am the Lord. I did not bring this terrible thing on them for no reason.

¹¹"'This is what the Lord God says: Clap your hands, stamp your feet. Say, "Oh!" because the people of Israel have done terrible things. So they will die by war, hunger and disease. ¹²The person who is far away will die by disease. The one who is nearby will die in war. The person who is still alive and has escaped these will die from hunger. So I will carry out my anger on them. ¹³Their people will lie dead among their idols around the altars. They will be on every high hill,

on all the mountain tops and under every green tree and leafy oak. These are the places where they offered sweet-smelling incense to their idols. Then you will know that I am the Lord. ¹⁴I will use my power against them. I will make the land empty and wasted from the desert to Diblah, wherever they live. Then they will know that I am the Lord'."

Ezekiel Tells of the End

7 Again the Lord spoke his word to me. He said: ²"Human being, the Lord says this to the land of Israel: An end! The end has come on the four corners of the land. ³Now the end has come for you. I will send my anger against you. I will judge you for the way you have lived. I will make you pay for your terrible actions. ⁴I will have no pity on you. I will not hold back punishment from you. I will make you pay for your ways and for your terrible actions. Then you will know that I am the Lord.

⁵"This is what the Lord God says: Disaster on top of disaster is coming. ⁶The end has come! The end has come! It has stirred itself up against you! Look! It has come! ⁷The end has come for you who live in the land! The time has come. The day of confusion is near. There will be no happy shouting on the mountains. ⁸Soon I will pour out my anger against you. I will carry out my anger against you. I will judge you for the way you have lived. I will make you pay for all the things you have done that I hate. ⁹I will show no pity. I will not hold back punishment. I will pay you back for the way you have lived and the terrible things you have done. Then you will know that I am the Lord who punishes.

¹⁰"Look, the day is here. It has come. Destruction has come. Violence has grown. There is more pride than ever. ¹¹Violence has grown into a weapon for punishing wickedness. None of the people will be left. None of that crowd, none of their wealth, and nothing of value will be left among them. ¹²The time has come. The day has arrived. Don't let the buyer be happy or the seller be sad. My burning anger is against the whole crowd. ¹³Sellers will not return to the land they have sold as long as they live. This is because the vision against all that crowd will not be changed. Because of their sins, no one will save his life. ¹⁴They have blown the trumpet, and everything is ready. But no one is going to the battle. My anger is against all that crowd.

¹⁵"The sword is outside. Disease and hunger are inside. The person who is in the field will die by the sword. Hunger and disease will destroy those in the city. ¹⁶Those who are left alive and who escape will be on the mountains. They will moan like doves of the valleys. Each person will groan about his own sin. ¹⁷All hands will hang weakly. All knees will become as weak as water. ¹⁸They will put on rough cloth to show how sad they are. They will tremble all over with fear. Their faces will show their shame. And all their heads will be shaved. ¹⁹The people will throw their silver into the streets. Their gold will be like rubbish. Their silver and gold will not save them from the Lord's anger. It will not satisfy their hunger or fill their stomachs. It was what caused them to fall into sin. ²⁰They were proud of their beautiful jewellery. They used it to make their idols, which I hate, and their evil statues. So I will turn their wealth into something they hate. ²¹And I will give it to the foreigners as treasures from war. I will give it to the evil people of the earth as treasure. These foreigners and evil people will dishonour the people's jewellery. ²²I will also turn away from the people of Israel. They will dishonour my treasured place. Then robbers will enter and dishonour it.

²³"Make chains for captives. The

land is full of bloody crimes. And the city is full of violence. ²⁴So I will bring the worst of the nations to take over the people's houses. I will also end the pride of the rich. And their holy places will be dishonoured. ²⁵When the people are suffering greatly, they will look for peace. But there will be none. ²⁶Disaster will come on top of disaster. Rumour will be added to rumour. Then they will try to get a vision from a prophet.ᵈ Even the teachings of God from the priest will be lost. And advice from the older leaders will also be lost. ²⁷The king will cry greatly. The prince will give up hope. The hands of the people who owned land will shake with fear. I will punish them for the way they have lived. The way they have judged others is the way I will judge them. Then they will know that I am the Lord'."

Ezekiel's Vision of Jerusalem

8 It was the sixth year, on the fifth day of the sixth month of our captivity. I was sitting in my house with the older leaders of Judah before me. There I felt the power of the Lord God. ²I looked and saw something that looked like a man. From his waist down he looked like fire. From his waist up he looked like bright glowing metal. ³He stretched out the shape of a hand. And he caught me by the hair on my head. The Spiritᵈ lifted me up between the earth and the sky. He took me in the visions of God to Jerusalem. He took me to the entrance to the north gate of the inner courtyard of the Temple.ᵈ The courtyard was where the idol was that caused God to be jealous. ⁴The glory of the God of Israel was there. It was like what I had seen on the plain.

⁵Then God said to me, "Human be-

ing, now look toward the north." So I looked up toward the north. I saw an altar to the north of the gate. The idol that caused God to be jealous was in the entrance.

⁶The Lord said to me, "Human being, do you see what they are doing? Do you see how many hated things the people of Israel are doing here? This will drive me far away from my Temple. But you will see things more hated than these."

⁷Then the Lord brought me to the entry of the courtyard. When I looked, I saw a hole in the wall. ⁸The Lord said to me, "Human being, dig through the wall." So I dug through the wall and saw an entrance.

⁹Then the Lord said to me, "Go in and see the terrible, evil things they are doing here." ¹⁰So I entered and looked. And I saw pictures of every kind of crawling thing. I saw awful beasts and all the idols of the people of Israel. They were carved on the wall all around. ¹¹Seventy of the older leaders of Israel were standing there. They were in front of these carvings and idols. Jaazaniah son of Shaphan stood with them. Each man had his pan for burning incenseᵈ in his hand. A sweet-smelling cloud of incense was rising.

¹²Then the Lord said to me, "Human being, have you seen what the older leaders of Israel are doing in the dark? Have you seen each man in the room of his own idol? They say, 'The Lord doesn't see us. The Lord has left the land'." ¹³And he said to me, "You will see even more terrible things that they are doing."

¹⁴Then the Lord brought me to the opening of the north gate of the Temple. And I saw women sitting there crying for Tammuz.ⁿ ¹⁵The Lord said to me, "Do you see, human being?

Tammuz Tammuz was a false god in Babylon. Every year people thought this god died when the plants died. After they cried for him, they believed he came back to life and the plants lived again.

You will see things even more terrible than these."

¹⁶Then the Lord brought me into the inner courtyard of the Temple. And I saw about 25 men. They were at the entrance to the Temple, between the porch and the altar. Their backs were turned to the Temple of the Lord. They faced east. They were worshipping the sun in the east.

¹⁷The Lord said to me, "Do you see, human being? Is it unimportant that the people of Judah are doing the terrible things they have done here? They have filled the land with violence. They continually make me angry. Look, they are insulting me in every way they can. ¹⁸So I will act in anger. I will have no pity. I will not show mercy. Even if they shout in my ears, I won't listen to them."

Vision of the Angels

9 The Lord shouted with a loud voice in my ears. He said, "You who are chosen to punish this city, come near. Bring your weapon in your hand." ²Then six men came from the direction of the upper gate, which faces north. Each had his powerful weapon in his hand. Among them was a man dressed in linen. At his side he had things to write with. The men went in and stood by the bronze altar.

³Then the glory of the God of Israel went up. It had been above the creatures with wings. It moved to the place in the Temple*d* where the door opened. Then the Lord called the man dressed in linen. He had the things to write with at his side. ⁴The Lord said to him, "Go through Jerusalem. Put a mark on the foreheads of the people who groan and cry about all the terrible things being done among them."

⁵As I listened, the Lord spoke to the other men. He said, "Go through the city behind the man dressed in linen and kill. Don't pity anyone. Don't show mercy. ⁶Kill and destroy old men, young men and women, little

children and older women. But don't touch anyone who has the mark on him. Start at my Temple." So they started with the older leaders who were in front of the Temple.

⁷And the Lord said to the men, "Make the Temple unclean.*d* Fill the courtyards with those who have been killed. Go out!" Then the men went out and killed the people in the city. ⁸While the men were killing the people, I was left alone. I bowed face down on the ground. I cried out, "Oh, Lord God! Will you destroy everyone left alive in Israel when you turn loose your anger on Jerusalem?"

⁹Then the Lord said to me, "The sin of the people of Israel and Judah is very great. The land is filled with people who murder. And the city is full of people who are not fair. The people say, 'The Lord has left the land. And the Lord does not see'. ¹⁰But I will have no pity. I will show no mercy. But I will bring their evil acts back on their heads."

¹¹Then the man dressed in linen reported to the Lord. He was the man who had things to write with at his side. He said, "I have done just as you have commanded me."

The Coals of Fire

10 Then I looked and saw the sky above the heads of the living creatures. I saw something like a sapphire gem. It looked like a throne. ²The Lord said to the man dressed in linen, "Go in between the wheels under the living creatures. And fill your hands with coals of fire from between the living creatures. Scatter the coals over the city."

As I watched, the man with linen clothes went in. ³Now the living creatures were standing on the south side of the Temple*d* when the man went in. And the cloud from the Lord filled the inner courtyard. ⁴Then the glory of the Lord went up from the living creatures. And it stood over the door of the Temple. The Temple was filled with the cloud. And the courtyard was full of the brightness from the glory of the Lord. ⁵The sound of the wings of the living creatures was heard all the way to the outer courtyard. It was like the voice of God All-Powerful when he speaks.

⁶The Lord commanded the man dressed in linen, "Take fire from between the wheels, from between the living creatures." Then the man went in and stood by a wheel. ⁷One living creature put out his hand to the fire that was among them. The living creature took some of the fire. And he put it in the hands of the man dressed in linen. The man took the fire and went out.

The Wheels and the Creatures

⁸Something that looked like a man's hand appeared under the wings of the living creatures. ⁹I saw the four wheels by the living creatures. One wheel was by each living creature. The wheels looked like shining chrysolite. ¹⁰All four wheels looked alike. Each looked like a wheel crossways inside another wheel. ¹¹When the wheels moved, they went in any of the directions that the four living creatures faced. The wheels did not turn about. The living creatures did not turn their bodies as they went. But they followed wherever their faces pointed. ¹²All their bodies, their backs, hands, wings and the wheels were full of eyes all over. Now each of the four living creatures had a wheel. ¹³I heard the wheels being called "whirling wheels". ¹⁴Each living creature had four faces. The first face was the face of a creature with wings. The second face was the face of a man. The third was the face of a lion. And the fourth was the face of an eagle.

¹⁵The living creatures flew up. They were the same living creatures I had seen by the Kebar River. ¹⁶And when the living creatures moved, the wheels moved by their sides. The living creatures lifted their wings to fly up from the ground. And the wheels did not leave their sides. ¹⁷When the living creatures stopped, the wheels stopped. When the creatures went up, the wheels went up also. This was because the spirit of the living creatures was in the wheels.

¹⁸Then the glory of the Lord left the door of the Temple*d* and stood over the living creatures. ¹⁹The living creatures spread their wings. And they flew up from the ground while I watched. As they went up, the wheels stayed by their sides. They stood where the east gate of the Temple of the Lord opened. The glory of the God of Israel was over them.

²⁰These are the living creatures I had seen under the God of Israel. This was by the Kebar River. I knew they were called cherubim. ²¹Each one had four faces. Each one had four wings. Things that looked like a man's hands were under their wings. ²²Their faces looked the same as the ones I had seen by the Kebar River. They each went straight ahead.

Prophecies Against Evil Leaders

11 The Spirit*d* lifted me up. And he brought me to the front gate of the Temple*d* of the Lord. This gate faces east. I saw 25 men where the gate opens. I saw Jaazaniah son of Azzur and Pelatiah son of Benaiah. They were leaders of the people. They were among these 25 men. ²Then the Lord said to me, "Human being, these are the men who plan evil. And they give wicked advice in this city of Jerusalem. ³They say, 'It is almost time for us to build houses. This city is like a cooking pot. And we are like the best meat'. ⁴So prophesy*d* against them. Prophesy, human being."

⁵Then the Spirit of the Lord entered me. He told me to say: "This is what the Lord says: You have said these things, people of Israel. But I know

what is going through your mind. ⁶You have killed many people in this city. You have filled its streets with their bodies.

⁷"So this is what the Lord God says: Those people you have killed and left in the middle of the city are like the best meat. And this city is like the cooking pot. But I will force you out of the city. ⁸You have feared the sword. But I will bring a sword against you, says the Lord God. ⁹I will force you out of the city. I will hand you over to strangers. I will surely punish you. ¹⁰You will die by the sword. I will punish you at the border of Israel. Then you will know that I am the Lord. ¹¹This city will not be your cooking pot. You will not be the best meat in the middle of the city. I will punish you at the border of Israel. ¹²Then you will know that I am the Lord. You did not live by my rules. You did not obey my laws. You did the same things that the nations around you do."

¹³As I prophesied, Pelatiah son of Benaiah died. Then I bowed face down on the ground. I shouted with a loud voice and said, "Oh no, Lord God! Will you completely destroy the Israelites who are left alive?"

Promise to Those Remaining

¹⁴The Lord spoke his word to me. He said, ¹⁵"Human being, the people still in Jerusalem have spoken about your relatives. And they have spoken about all the people of Israel who are captives with you. The people still in Jerusalem have said, 'They are far from the Lord. This land was given to us as our property'.

¹⁶"So say, 'This is what the Lord God says: I sent the people far away among the nations. I scattered them among the countries. But for a little while I have become a Temple*ᵈ* to them in the countries where they have gone'.

¹⁷"So say: 'This is what the Lord God says: I will gather you from the

nations. And I will bring you together from the countries where you have been scattered. Then I will give you back the land of Israel'.

¹⁸"They will come to this land. Then they will take away all the hated idols from the land. They will take all the terrible images from there. ¹⁹I will give them a desire to respect me completely. I will put a new way to think inside them. I will take out the stubborn heart like stone from their bodies. Then I will give them an obedient heart of flesh. ²⁰Then they will live by my rules. They will obey my laws and keep them. They will be my people, and I will be their God. ²¹But some people will want to serve their evil statues and hated idols. And I will pay them back for their evil ways, says the Lord God."

Ezekiel's Vision Ends

²²Then the living creatures lifted their wings. The wheels went beside them. And the glory of the God of Israel was above them. ²³The glory of the Lord went up from inside Jerusalem. And it stopped on the mountain on the east side of the city. ²⁴The Spirit*ᵈ* lifted me up. And he brought me to the captives who had been taken from Judah to Babylonia. He did this in a vision given by the Spirit of God. Then the vision I had seen ended. ²⁵And I told the things that the Lord had shown me. I told it to the captives from Judah.

Ezekiel Moves Out

12 Again the Lord spoke his word to me. He said: ²"Human being, you are living among a people who refuse to obey. They have eyes to see, but they do not see. They have ears to hear, but they do not hear. This is because they are a family that refuses to obey.

³"So, human being, pack your things as if you will be taken away captive. And walk away like a captive. Do

this in the daytime with the people watching. Move from your place to another with the people watching. Perhaps they will understand, even though they are a people who refuse to obey. ⁴Bring out the things you would pack as a captive. Do it during the day when the people are watching. At evening go out with the people watching. Go like those who are taken away as captives from their country. ⁵Dig a hole through the wall while they watch. Bring your things out through the hole. ⁶Lift them on to your shoulders with the people watching. Carry them out in the dark. Cover your face so you cannot see the ground. I have made you a sign to the people of Israel."

⁷I did these things as I was commanded. In the daytime I brought out my things. I was packed, ready to go away as a captive. Then in the evening I dug through the wall with my hands. I brought my things out in the dark. I carried them on my shoulders. And the people saw all this.

⁸Then in the morning the Lord spoke his word to me. He said: ⁹"Human being, Israel refuses to obey. Didn't those people ask you, 'What are you doing?'

¹⁰"Say to them, 'This is what the Lord God says: This message is about the king in Jerusalem. And it is about all the people of Israel who live there'. ¹¹Say, 'I am a sign to you'.

"The same things I have done will be done to the people in Jerusalem. They will be taken away from their country as captives. ¹²The king among them will put his things on his shoulder in the dark. And he will leave. The people will dig a hole through the wall to bring him out. He will cover his face so he cannot see the ground. ¹³But I will spread my net over him. He will be caught in my trap. Then I will bring him to Babylon in the land of the Babylonians. He will not see that land, but he will die there.

¹⁴All who are around the king I will scatter in every direction. I will scatter his helpers and all his army. I will chase them with a sword.

¹⁵"Then they will know that I am the Lord. I will scatter them among the nations. And I will spread them among the countries. ¹⁶But I will save a few of them from the sword. I will save a few from hunger and disease. Then they can tell about their hated actions among the nations where they go. Then they will know that I am the Lord."

The Lesson of Ezekiel's Shaking

¹⁷The Lord spoke his word to me. He said: ¹⁸"Human being, shake as you eat your food. Shake with fear as you drink your water. ¹⁹Then say to the people of the land: 'This is what the Lord God says about the people who live in Jerusalem in the land of Israel: They will eat their food with fear. And they will drink their water in shock. This is because their land will be made empty. This is because of the violence of the people who live in it. ²⁰And the cities where people live will become ruins. The land will become empty. Then you will know that I am the Lord'."

The Visions Will Come True

²¹The Lord spoke his word to me. He said: ²²"Human being, what is this saying you have in the land of Israel: 'The days go by and every vision comes to nothing?' ²³So say to them, 'This is what the Lord God says: I will make them stop saying this. Then nobody in Israel will use it any more'. But tell them, 'The time is near when every vision will come true. ²⁴There will be no more false visions or pleasing prophecies*ᵈ* inside the nation of Israel. ²⁵This is because I, the Lord God, will speak. What I say will be done. It will not be delayed. You are a people who refuse to obey. And in

your time I will say the word and do it, says the Lord God'."

²⁶The Lord spoke his word to me. He said: ²⁷"Human being, look! The people of Israel are saying this: 'The vision that Ezekiel sees is for a time many years from now. He is prophesying about times far away'.

²⁸"So say to them: 'The Lord God says this: None of my words will be delayed any more. What I have said will be done, says the Lord God'."

Ezekiel Speaks Against False Prophets

13 The Lord spoke his word to me. He said: ²"Human being, prophesy*d* against the prophets of Israel. Say to those who make up their own prophecies: 'Listen to the word of the Lord. ³This is what the Lord God says: How terrible it will be for the foolish prophets. They are the ones who follow their own ideas. And they have not seen a vision from me. ⁴People of Israel, your prophets have been like wild dogs hunting to kill and eat among ruins. ⁵Israel is like a house in ruins. But you have not gone up into the broken places. Your prophets have not repaired the wall. So how can Israel hold back the enemy in the battle on the Lord's day of judging? ⁶Your prophets see false visions. They prophesy lies. They say, "This is the message of the Lord." The Lord has not sent them. But they still hope their words will come true. ⁷You said, "This is the message of the Lord." But that is a false vision. Your prophecies are lies because I have not spoken.

⁸"So this is what the Lord God says: You prophets spoke things that are false. You saw visions that do not come true. That is why I am against you, says the Lord God. ⁹So I will punish the prophets who see false visions and prophesy lies. They will have no place among my people. Their names will not be written on the list of the people of Israel. They will not enter the land of Israel. Then you will know that I am the Lord God.

¹⁰"'It is because they led my people away. They said, "Peace!" but there is no peace. When the people build a weak wall, the prophets cover it with whitewash to make it look strong. ¹¹So tell those who cover a weak wall with whitewash that it will fall down. Rain will pour down. Hailstones will fall. And a stormy wind will break the wall down. ¹²When the wall has fallen, people will ask you, "Where is the whitewash you used on the wall?"

¹³"'So this is what the Lord God says: I will break the wall with a stormy wind. In my anger rain will pour down. And hailstones will destroy the wall. ¹⁴I will tear down the wall on which you put whitewash. I will level it to the ground. Then people will see the wall's foundation. And when the wall falls, you will be destroyed under it. Then you will know that I am the Lord. ¹⁵So I will carry out my anger on the wall and against those who covered it with whitewash. Then I will tell you, "The wall is gone. And those who covered it with whitewash are also gone. ¹⁶The prophets of Israel who prophesy to Jerusalem will be gone. And those who see visions of peace for Jerusalem will be gone also. There will be no peace, says the Lord God'."

False Women Prophets

¹⁷"Now, human being, reject the women among your people who make up their own prophecies.*d* Prophesy against them. ¹⁸Say, 'This is what the Lord God says: How terrible it will be for women who sew magic charms on their wrists. How terrible it will be for those who make veils of every length. These women do this to trap people. You ruin the lives of my people but try to save your own lives! ¹⁹And you have dishonoured me among my people. You have done it for handfuls of

barley and pieces of bread. You have killed people who should not die. And you have kept alive those who should die. You have done this by lying to my people. And my people are willing to listen to lies.

20" 'So this is what the Lord God says: I am against your magic charms. You use them to trap people as if they were birds. I will tear these charms off your arms. I will free those people you have trapped like birds. ²¹I will also tear off your veils. I will save my people from your hands. They will no longer be in your power. You will not trap them. Then you will know that I am the Lord. ²²By your lies you caused the heart of the person who did right to be sad. I did not make him sad. You have encouraged the evil person not to stop being evil. And that would have saved his life. ²³So you will not see any more false visions. You will not prophesy any more. And I will save my people from your power. Then you will know that I am the Lord'."

Stop Worshipping Idols

14 Some of the older leaders of Israel came to me and sat down before me. ²Then the Lord spoke his word to me. He said: ³"Human being, these men love to worship idols. They put up evil things that cause people to sin. Should I allow them to ask me for help? ⁴So speak to them. Tell them, 'This is what the Lord God says: Any person in Israel might want to worship idols. He might even put up evil things that cause people to sin. Then he might come to the prophet.ᵈ When he does, I, the Lord, will answer him. I will put him to death because he worshipped idols. ⁵Then I will win back my people Israel. They have left me because of all their idols'.

⁶"So say this to the people of Israel: 'This is what the Lord God says: Change your hearts and lives. Stop worshipping idols. Stop doing all the

things I hate. ⁷Any Israelite or any foreigner in Israel can separate himself from me. He can do this by wanting to worship idols. Or he can put up the things that cause people to sin. Then if he comes to the prophet to ask me questions, I, the Lord, will answer him myself. ⁸I will reject him. I will make him a sign and an example. I will separate him from my people. Then you will know that I am the Lord.

⁹" 'But the prophet may be tricked into giving a prophecy. Then it is because I, the Lord, have tricked that prophet to speak. Then I will use my power against him. I will destroy him from among my people Israel. ¹⁰The prophet will be as guilty as the one who asks him for help. They will both be responsible for their guilt. ¹¹Then the nation of Israel will not leave me any more. And they will not make themselves uncleanᵈ any more with all their sins. Then they will be my people. And I will be their God, says the Lord God'."

Jerusalem Will Not Be Spared

¹²The Lord spoke his word to me. He said: ¹³"Human being, sometimes the people of a country will sin against me by not being loyal. When that happens, I will use my power against them. I will cut off their supply of food. I will send them a time of hunger. I will destroy both their people and animals. ¹⁴Three great men like Noah, Daniel and Job might be in that country. But their goodness could save only themselves, says the Lord God.

¹⁵"I might even send wild animals into that land. They would leave the land empty and without children. Then no one would pass through it because of the animals. ¹⁶As surely as I live, says the Lord God, not even Noah, Daniel and Job could help. Even if they were in the land, they could not save their own sons or daughters. They could only save themselves.

And that country would remain empty.

17"Or, I might bring a war against that country. I might say, 'Let a war be fought in that land. Let it destroy its men and animals'. 18As surely as I live, says the Lord God, not even these three men could help. Even if they were in the land, they could not save their sons or daughters. They could only save themselves.

19"Or, I might cause a disease to spread in that country. I might pour out my anger against that country, destroying and killing people and animals. 20As surely as I live, says the Lord God, not even Noah, Daniel and Job could help. Even if they were in the land, they could not save their son or daughter. They could save only themselves because they did what was right.

21"This is what the Lord God says: I will send my four terrible punishments against Jerusalem. They are war, hunger, wild animals and disease. They will destroy people and animals from Jerusalem. 22But some people will escape. Some sons and daughters will be led out. They will come out to you. You will see how they live. Then you will be comforted after the disasters I have brought against Jerusalem. You will be comforted after all the things I will bring against it. 23You will be comforted when you see how they live. You will know there was a good reason for what I did to Jerusalem, says the Lord God."

Story of the Vine

15 The Lord spoke his word to me. He said: 2"Human being, what good is the wood of the vine? Is it better than the wood of a tree in the forest? 3Can wood be taken from the vine to make anything? Can you use it to make a peg on which to hang something? 4The vine is thrown into the fire for fuel. The fire burns up both ends and starts to burn the middle. Then is it useful for anything? 5When the vine was whole, it couldn't be made into anything. When the fire has burned it completely, it certainly cannot be made into anything."

6So this is what the Lord God says: "Out of all the trees in the forest, I gave the wood of the vine as fuel for fire. In the same way I have given up the people who live in Jerusalem. 7I will turn against them. They came through one fire. But fire will still destroy them. When I turn against them, you will know that I am the Lord. 8So I will make the land empty. This is because the people have not been loyal, says the Lord God."

The Lord's Kindness to Jerusalem

16 The Lord spoke his word to me. He said: 2"Human being, tell Jerusalem about her hated actions. 3Say, 'This is what the Lord God says to Jerusalem: Your beginnings and your ancestors were in the land of the Canaanites. Your father was an Amorite. And your mother was a Hittite. 4On the day you were born, your cord[n] was not cut. You were not washed with water for cleansing. You were not rubbed with salt. You were not wrapped in cloths. 5No one felt sorry for you. No one would do any of these things for you. No, you were thrown out into the open field. This is because you were hated on the day you were born.

6"Then I passed by and saw you kicking about in your blood. I said to you, "Live!" 7I made you grow like a plant in the field. You grew up and became tall. You grew up and became like a beautiful jewel. Your breasts formed. Your hair grew. But you were naked and without clothes.

---

cord The umbilical cord that gives the unborn baby food and air from its mother.

8" 'Later I passed by you and looked at you. I saw that you were at the time for love. So I spread my robe over you and covered your nakedness. I also made a marriage promise to you. I entered into an agreement with you. Then you became mine, says the Lord God.

9" 'Then I bathed you with water and washed all the blood off you. I put oil on you. 10I put beautiful clothes made with needlework on you. I put sandals of fine leather on your feet. I wrapped you in fine linen and covered you with silk. 11I put jewellery on you. I put bracelets on your arms and a necklace around your neck. 12I also put a ring in your nose and earrings in your ears. And I put a beautiful crown on your head. 13So you wore gold and silver. Your dress was made of fine linen, silk and beautiful needlework. You ate fine flour, honey and olive oil. You were very beautiful and became a queen. 14Then you became famous among the nations because you were so beautiful. Your beauty was perfect, because of the glory I gave you, says the Lord God.

Jerusalem Becomes a Prostitute

15" 'But you trusted in your beauty. You became a prostitute*d* because you were so famous. You had sexual relations with anyone who passed by. 16And you took some of your clothes and made your places of worship colourful. This is where you carried on your prostitution. These things should not have happened. They should never happen again. 17You also took your beautiful jewellery. It was made from gold and silver I had given you. Then you made male idols for yourselves. And you were a prostitute with them. 18Then you took your clothes with beautiful needlework and covered the idols. You gave my oil and incense*d* as an offering to them. 19Also, you took the bread I gave you. You took the fine flour, oil and honey I gave you to

eat. And you offered them before the false gods as a pleasing smell. This is what happened, says the Lord God.

20" 'Also, you took your sons and daughters who were my children. And you sacrificed them to idols as food. Your sexual sins were not enough for you. 21You killed my children and offered them up in fire to idols. 22You did all your hated acts and sexual sins. But you did not remember when you were young. At that time you were naked and had no clothes. You were left in your blood.

23" 'How terrible! How terrible it will be for you, says the Lord God. This is what you did after all these evil things. 24You built yourself a place to worship false gods. You made for yourself a place of worship in every city square. 25You built a place of worship at the head of every street. You made your beauty hateful. You offered your body for sex to anyone who passed by. Your sexual sins became worse and worse. 26You also had sexual relations with the Egyptians. They were your neighbours and partners in sexual sin. Your sexual sins became even worse. And they caused me to be angry. 27So then, I used my power against you. I took away some of your land. I let those who hated you defeat you. They were the Philistine women. Even they were ashamed of your evil ways. 28Also, you had sexual relations with the Assyrians because you could not be satisfied. You had sexual relations with them, but you still were not satisfied. 29You did even more sexual sins in the land of Babylonia. The Babylonians were traders. But you were not satisfied even with this.

30" 'Truly your will is weak, says the Lord God. You do all the things a stubborn prostitute does. 31You built your place to worship false gods at the beginning of every street. And you made places of worship in every city square. But you were not like a prostitute because you refused payment.

³²" 'You are a wife who is guilty of adultery.ᵈ You desire strangers instead of your husband. ³³Men pay prostitutes, but you pay all your lovers. You pay them to come to you. And they come from all around for sexual relations. ³⁴So you are different from other prostitutes. No one acts like a prostitute the same way you do. You give money, and no money is given to you. Yes, you are different.

The Prostitute Is Judged

³⁵" 'So, prostitute,ᵈ hear the word of the Lord. ³⁶This is what the Lord God says: You showed your riches to other countries. And you uncovered your body in your sexual sins with your lovers. And you even did it with all your hated idols. You killed your children and offered their blood to your idols. ³⁷So I will gather all your lovers with whom you found pleasure. Yes, I will gather all those you loved and those you hated. Yes, I will gather them against you from all around. I will strip you naked in front of them. Then they will be able to see your nakedness. ³⁸So I will punish you as judges punish women guilty of adultery.ᵈ I will punish you as murderers are punished. I will put you to death because I am angry and jealous. ³⁹I will also hand you over to your lovers. They will tear down your places of worship. They will destroy the places where you worship false gods. They will tear off your clothes and take away your jewellery. They will leave you naked and bare. ⁴⁰They will bring a crowd against you. They will throw stones at you and cut you into pieces with their swords. ⁴¹They will burn your houses with fire. They will punish you in front of many women. Then I will put an end to your sexual sins. And you will no longer pay your lovers. ⁴²Then I will rest from my anger against you. I will stop being jealous. I will be quiet and not angry any more.

⁴³" 'You didn't remember when you were young. So you have made me angry in all these ways. And I will repay you for what you have done, says the Lord God. Didn't you add sexual sins to all your other acts which I hate?

⁴⁴" 'Everyone who uses wise sayings will say this about you: "The daughter is like her mother." ⁴⁵You are like your mother. She hated her husband and children. You are also like your sisters. They hated their husbands and children. Your mother was a Hittite. And your father was an Amorite. ⁴⁶Now your older sister is Samaria. She lived north of you with her daughters. And your younger sister Sodom lived south of you with her daughters. ⁴⁷You followed their ways. And you did what they did. But you were even worse than they were in everything you did. ⁴⁸As surely as I live, says the Lord God, this is true. Your sister Sodom and her daughters never did what you and your daughters have done.

⁴⁹" 'This was the sin of your sister Sodom: she and her daughters were proud. They had plenty of food. They lived in great comfort. But she did not help the poor and needy. ⁵⁰So Sodom and her daughters were proud. And they did things I hate in front of me. So I got rid of them when I saw what they did. ⁵¹Also, Samaria did not do half the sins you do. You have done more hated things than they did. So you make your sisters look good because of all the hated things you have done. ⁵²You will suffer disgrace because you have provided an excuse for your sisters. They are more right than you are. Your sins were even more terrible than theirs. Be ashamed and suffer disgrace because you made your sisters seem right.

⁵³" 'But I will give Sodom and her daughters their riches back. I will give Samaria and her daughters their riches back. And with them I will also

give you back your riches. ⁵⁴But you will have to suffer disgrace. You will feel ashamed for all the things you have done. You even gave comfort to your sisters in their sins. ⁵⁵Your sisters are Sodom with her daughters and Samaria with her daughters. They will return to what they were before. You and your daughters will also return to what you were before. ⁵⁶You would not even mention your sister Samaria when you were proud. ⁵⁷Nor would you mention her before your evil was uncovered. And now the Edomite women and their neighbours say bad things about you. Even the Philistine women say bad things about you. Those around you hate you. ⁵⁸You will be punished for your sexual sins and actions that I hate, says the Lord.

God Keeps His Promises

⁵⁹" 'This is what the Lord God says: I will give you what you should have. You hated and broke the marriage agreement. ⁶⁰But I will remember my agreement I made with you when you were young. I will make an agreement that will continue for ever with you. ⁶¹Then you will remember what you have done. You will be ashamed when you receive your sisters — both your older and your younger sisters. I will give them to you like daughters. But it will not be because of my agreement with you. ⁶²I will set up my agreement with you. And you will know that I am the Lord. ⁶³You will remember and be ashamed. You will not open your mouth again because of your shame. This is because I will forgive you for all the things you have done, says the Lord God'."

The Eagle and the Vine

17 The Lord spoke his word to me. He said: ²"Human being, give a riddle. Tell a story to the people of Israel. ³Say, 'This is what the Lord God says: A great eagle came to Leb-

anon. He had great wings with long feathers of many different colours. The eagle took hold of the top of a cedar tree. ⁴He pulled off the top branch. And he brought it to a land of traders. The eagle planted it in a city of traders.

⁵" 'The eagle took a young plant from the land. And he planted it in a good field near plenty of water. He planted it to grow like a willow tree. ⁶The plant grew and became a low vine that spread over the ground. The vine's branches turned toward the eagle. The vine's roots were under the eagle. So the plant became a vine. And its branches grew, sending out leaves.

⁷" 'But there was another eagle with great wings and many feathers. The vine then bent its roots toward this eagle. The vine also sent out its branches toward the eagle so he could water it. The vine turned away from the area where it was planted. ⁸It was planted in a good field. It was by plenty of water so it could grow branches and give fruit. It could have become a fine vine'.

⁹"Say to them, 'This is what the Lord God says: The vine will not continue to grow. The first eagle will pull up the vine's roots and strip off its fruit. Then the vine will dry up. All its new leaves will dry up and die. It will not take a strong arm or many people to pull the vine up by its roots. ¹⁰It might be planted again. But it will not continue to grow. It will completely die when the east wind hits it. It will dry up in the area where it grew'."

Zedekiah Against Nebuchadnezzar

¹¹Then the Lord spoke his word to me. He said: ¹²"Say now to the people who refuse to obey: 'Do you know what these things mean?' Say: 'The king of Babylon came to Jerusalem. He took the king and important men of Jerusalem and brought them to Bab-

ylon. [13]Then he took a member of the family of the king of Judah. He made an agreement with him. The king of Babylon made this person promise to support him. The king also took away the leaders of Judah. [14]He did this to make the kingdom of Judah weak so it would not be strong again. Then the kingdom of Judah could continue only by keeping its agreement with the king of Babylon. [15]But the king of Judah turned against the king of Babylon. The king of Judah sent his messengers to Egypt. He asked the Egyptians for horses and many soldiers. Will the king of Judah succeed? Will the one who does such things escape? He cannot break the agreement and escape.

[16]" 'As surely as I live, says the Lord God, he will die in Babylon. He will die in the land of the king who made him king of Judah. The king of Judah hated his promise. He broke his agreement with the king of Babylon. [17]The king of Egypt will not help the king of Judah in the war. He will not help with his mighty army and many people. The Babylonians will build devices to attack the cities and to kill many people. [18]The king of Judah showed that he hated the promise by breaking the agreement. He promised to support Babylon, but he did all these things. So he will not escape.

[19]" 'So this is what the Lord God says: As surely as I live, this is true: I will pay back the king of Judah for hating my promise and breaking my agreement. [20]I will spread my net over him. He will be caught in my trap. Then I will bring him to Babylon. There I will judge him for the unfaithful acts he did against me. [21]And all the best of his soldiers who escape will die by the sword. Those who live will be scattered to every wind. Then you will know that I, the Lord, have spoken.

[22]" 'This is what the Lord God says: I myself will also take a young branch from the top of a cedar tree. And I will plant it. I will cut off a small twig. It will be from the top of the tree's young branches. I will plant it on a high and great mountain. [23]I will plant it on the high mountain of Israel. Then it will grow branches and give fruit. And it will become a great cedar tree. Birds of every kind will build nests in it. They will live in the shelter of the tree's branches. [24]Then all the trees of the field will know that I am the Lord. I am the one who brings down the high tree. I make the low tree tall. I dry up the green tree. And I make the dry tree grow. I am the Lord. I have spoken, and I will do it'."

God Is Fair

18 The Lord spoke his word to me. He said: [2]"What do you mean by using this saying about the land of Israel:

'The fathers have eaten sour
        grapes.
    And that caused the children to
        grind their teeth from the
        sour taste'?

[3]"As surely as I live, says the Lord God, this is true: you will not use this saying in Israel any more. [4]Every living thing belongs to me. The life of the father is mine. And the life of the son is mine. The person who sins will die.

[5]"There may be a good person. This person does what is fair and right. [6]He does not eat at the mountain places of worship. He does not look to the idols of Israel for help. He does not have sexual relations with his neighbour's wife. He does not have sexual relations with a woman during her time of monthly bleeding. [7]He does not mistreat anyone. But he returns what was given as a promise for a loan. He does not rob other people. He gives bread to hungry people. He gives clothes to those who have no clothes. [8]He does not lend money to get too much interest or profit. He keeps his hand from doing wrong. He

judges fairly between men. ⁹He lives by my rules and obeys my laws faithfully. The person who does all these things is good. He will surely live, says the Lord God.

¹⁰"But this person might have a wild son who murders people. This son may do any of these other bad things. ¹¹(But the father himself has not done any of these things.) This son eats at the mountain places of worship. He has sexual relations with his neighbour's wife. ¹²He mistreats the poor and needy. He steals things. He refuses to return what was promised for a loan. He looks to idols for help. He does things which I hate. ¹³He lends money for too much interest and profit. Will this son live? No, he will not live! He has done all these hated things. He will surely be put to death. He will be responsible for his own sins.

¹⁴"But this son might have a son who has seen the sins his father did. But after seeing them, he does not do those things. ¹⁵He does not eat at the mountain places of worship. He does not look to the idols of Israel for help. He does not have sexual relations with his neighbour's wife. ¹⁶He does not mistreat anyone. He does not keep something promised for a loan. He does not steal. But he gives bread to the hungry people. He gives clothes to people without clothes. ¹⁷He keeps his hand from doing wrong. He does not take too much interest or profit when he lends money. He obeys my laws and lives by my rules. He will not die for his father's sin. He will surely live. ¹⁸But his father took other people's money unfairly. He robbed his brother. He did what was wrong among his people. So he will die for his own sin.

¹⁹"But you ask, 'Why is the son not punished for the father's sin?' The son has done what is fair and right. He obeys all my rules. So he will surely live. ²⁰It is the person who sins that will die. The son will not be punished for the father's sin. The father will not be punished for the son's sin. The person who does right is responsible for his own goodness. The evil person is responsible for his own evil.

²¹"But the evil person might stop doing all the sins he has done. And he might obey all my rules and do what is fair and right. Then he will surely live. He will not die. ²²His sins will be forgotten. Now he does what is right. So he will live. ²³I do not really want the evil person to die, says the Lord God. I want him to stop his bad ways and live.

²⁴"But a person who does right might stop doing good and do wrong. And he might do the same hated things an evil person does. Will he live? All his good acts will be forgotten. This is because he became unfaithful. He has sinned. So he will die because of his sins.

²⁵"But you say, 'What the Lord does isn't fair'. Hear now, people of Israel. I am fair. It is what you do that is not fair! ²⁶A good person might stop doing good. He might do wrong and die because of it. He will die because he did wrong. ²⁷An evil person might stop doing the evil things he has done. And he might do what is fair and right. He will save his life. ²⁸He thought about it and stopped doing all the sins he had done. He will surely live. He will not die. ²⁹But the people of Israel still say, 'What the Lord does isn't fair'. People of Israel, I am fair. It is what you do that is not fair.

³⁰"So I will judge you, people of Israel. I will judge each person by what he does, says the Lord God. Change your hearts. Stop all your sinning. Then sin will not bring your ruin. ³¹Get rid of all the sins you have done. And get for yourselves a new heart and a new way to think. Why do you want to die, people of Israel? ³²I do not want anyone to die. So change your hearts and lives so you may live.

A Sad Song for Israel

19 "Sing a funeral song for the leaders of Israel. ²Say:

'Your mother was like a female lion.
She lay down among the young lions.
She had many cubs.
³She brought up one of her cubs.
And he became a strong lion.
He learned to tear the animals he hunted.
And he ate people.
⁴The nations heard about him.
He was trapped in their pit.
And they brought him with hooks to the land of Egypt.

⁵" 'The mother lion waited and saw that there was no hope for her cub.
So she took another one of her cubs
and made him a strong lion.
⁶This cub roamed among the lions.
He was now a strong lion.
He learned to tear the animals he hunted.
And he ate people.
⁷He destroyed their strong places.
He destroyed their cities.
The land and everything in it were terrified by the sound of his roar.
⁸Then the nations came against him from areas all around.
And they spread their net over him.
He was trapped in their pit.
⁹Then they put him into a cage with chains.
And they brought him to the king of Babylon.
They put him into prison.
Then his roar could not be heard again
on the mountains of Israel.

¹⁰" 'Your mother was like a vine in your vineyard.
It was planted beside the water.
The vine had many branches and gave much fruit
because there was plenty of water.
¹¹The vine had strong branches.
They were good enough for a king's sceptre.*d*
The vine became tall among the thick branches.
And it was seen because it was tall
with many branches.
¹²But it was pulled up by its roots in anger.
It was thrown down to the ground.
The east wind dried it up.
Its fruit was torn off.
Its strong branches were broken off.
They were burned up.
¹³Now the vine is planted in the desert,
in a dry and thirsty land.
¹⁴And fire has spread from the vine's main branch.
It has destroyed its fruit.
There is not a strong branch left on it
that could become a sceptre for a king'.

This is a funeral song. It is to be used as a funeral song."

Israel Has Refused God

20 It was the seventh year, in the fifth month of our captivity. It was the tenth day of the month. Some of the older leaders of Israel came to ask about the Lord. They sat down before me.

²The Lord spoke his word to me. He said: ³"Human being, speak to the older leaders of Israel. Say to them: 'This is what the Lord God says: Did you come to ask me questions? As surely as I live, I will not let you ask me questions'.

⁴"Will you judge them? Will you judge them, human being? Let them

know the hated things their fathers did. ⁵Say to them: 'This is what the Lord God says: I chose Israel and made a promise to the descendants*d* of Jacob. At that time I made myself known to them in Egypt. I promised them, "I am the Lord your God." ⁶At that time I promised them I would bring them out of Egypt. I promised to bring them into a land I had chosen for them. This is a land where much food grows. It is the best of all lands. ⁷I said to them, "Each one of you must throw away the hateful idols you have set your eyes on. Don't make yourselves unclean*d* with the idols of Egypt. I am the Lord your God."

⁸" 'But they turned against me and refused to listen to me. They did not throw away the hated idols which they saw and liked. They did not leave the idols of Egypt. Then I decided to pour out my anger against them in the land of Egypt. ⁹But I acted to show who I am. I did not allow myself to be dishonoured before the nations where the Israelites lived. I made myself known to the Israelites. I did this by bringing them out of Egypt while the nations were watching. ¹⁰So I took them out of Egypt and brought them into the desert. ¹¹I gave them my rules. I told them about my laws. If a person obeys them, he will live. ¹²I also gave them my Sabbaths.*d* They were to be a sign between us. Then they would know that I am the Lord. I make them holy.

¹³" 'But in the desert Israel turned against me. They did not follow my rules. They rejected my laws. But if a person obeys them, he will live. They dishonoured my Sabbaths. Then I decided to pour out my anger against them and destroy them in the desert. ¹⁴But I acted for the sake of my name. I did not allow it to be dishonoured before the nations. As the nations watched, I had brought the Israelites out of Egypt. ¹⁵But in the desert I had to make another promise to the Isra-

elites. I had to promise I would not bring them into the land I had given them. It is a land where much food grows. It is the best of all the lands. ¹⁶This is because they rejected my laws. They did not follow my rules. They dishonoured my Sabbaths. They would rather worship their idols. ¹⁷But I had pity on them. I did not destroy them. I did not put an end to them in the desert. ¹⁸I said to their children in the desert, "Don't live by the rules of your fathers. Don't obey their laws. Don't make yourselves unclean with their idols. ¹⁹I am the Lord your God. Live by my rules. Obey my laws and do them. ²⁰Keep my Sabbaths holy. They will be a sign between me and you. Then you will know that I am the Lord your God."

²¹" 'But the people turned against me. If a person obeys my laws, he will live. But they did not live by my rules. They were not careful to obey my laws. They dishonoured my Sabbaths. So I decided to pour out my anger against them. I decided to carry out my anger against them in the desert. ²²But I held back my anger. I acted for the sake of my name. Then my name would not be dishonoured with the nations watching. As the nations watched, I had brought the Israelites out from Egypt. ²³Also in the desert I had to make a promise to the Israelites. I had to promise to scatter them among the nations and spread them among the countries. ²⁴This is because they did not obey my laws. They had rejected my rules and dishonoured my Sabbaths. And they worshipped the idols of their ancestors. ²⁵I also allowed them to follow rules that were not good. And they followed laws by which they could not live. ²⁶I let the Israelites make themselves unclean by the gifts they brought to their false gods. They sacrificed their oldest children in the fire. This is how I shocked them so they would know that I am the Lord'.

²⁷"So, human being, speak to the people of Israel. Say to them, 'This is what the Lord God says: Your ancestors spoke against me by being unfaithful to me in this way: ²⁸I had brought them into the land I promised to give them. They saw every high hill and every leafy tree. There they offered their sacrifices to false gods. They brought offerings that made me angry. There, also, they burned their incense.ᵈ There they poured out their drink offerings. ²⁹Then I said to them: What is this place where you go to worship false gods?' " (It is still called High Place today.)

³⁰"So say to the people of Israel: 'This is what the Lord God says: Will you make yourselves unclean as your ancestors did? Will you be unfaithful and desire their hated idols? ³¹You offer your children as gifts to the false gods. You sacrifice them in the fire. You make yourselves unclean with all your idols even today. So, people of Israel, should I let you ask me questions? As surely as I live, says the Lord God, I will not accept questions from you.

³²" 'What you want will not come true. You say, "We want to be like the other nations and the people in other lands. We want to worship idols made of wood and stone." ³³As surely as I live, says the Lord God, I will rule you. I will rule you with my great power and strength and anger. ³⁴I will bring you out from the foreign nations. I will gather you from the lands where you are scattered. I will do this with my great power and strength and anger. ³⁵I will bring you among the nations as I brought your ancestors into the desert with Moses. There I will judge you face to face. ³⁶I will judge you the same way I judged your ancestors. That was in the desert of the land of Egypt. So I will judge you, says the Lord God. ³⁷I will take control of you. I will punish you by my agreement. ³⁸I will get rid of those who refuse to obey me and who turn against me. I will bring them out of the land where they are now living. But they will never enter the land of Israel. Then you will know that I am the Lord.

³⁹" 'This is what the Lord God says: People of Israel, go and serve your idols for now. But later you will listen to me. You will not continue to dishonour my holy name with your gifts and false gods. ⁴⁰My holy mountain is the high mountain of Israel. There all Israel will serve me in the land, says the Lord God. There I will accept you. There I will look for your offerings. I will look for the first harvest of your offerings and all your holy gifts. ⁴¹I will accept you like a pleasing smell. This will happen when I bring you out from the foreign nations. It will take place when I gather you from the lands where you are scattered. Then through you I will show how holy I am. The nations will see it. ⁴²When I bring you into the land of Israel, you will know that I am the Lord. I will bring you into the land I promised your ancestors. ⁴³There you will remember everything you did that made you unclean. Then you will hate yourselves for all the evil things you have done. ⁴⁴I will deal with you to show who I am. Then you will know I am the Lord, people of Israel. But it's not because of your evil ways or unclean actions, says the Lord God'."

⁴⁵Now the Lord spoke his word to me. He said: ⁴⁶"Human being, look towards the south. Prophesyᵈ against the south. Prophesy against the forest of the southern area. ⁴⁷Say to that forest: 'Hear the word of the Lord. This is what the Lord God says: I am ready to start a fire in you. The fire will destroy all your green trees and all your dry trees. The flame that burns will not be put out. All the land from south to north will be burned by the fire. ⁴⁸Then all the people will see that I,

the Lord, have started the fire. It will not be put out'."

⁴⁹Then I said, "Ah, Lord God! The people are saying about me, 'He is only telling stories'."

Babylon, the Lord's Sword

21 Then the Lord spoke his word to me. He said: ²"Human being, look towards Jerusalem and speak against their holy place. Prophesy*d* against the land of Israel. ³Say to Israel: 'This is what the Lord says: I am against you. I will pull my sword out of its holder. I will separate you from both wicked people and those who do right. ⁴I am going to separate the wicked and those who do right. So my sword will come out from its holder. And it will come against all people from south to north. ⁵Then all people will know that I, the Lord, have pulled my sword out from its holder. My sword will not go back in again'.

⁶"So, human being, groan with breaking heart and great sadness. Make these sad sounds in front of the people. ⁷They will ask you, 'Why do you make these sad sounds?' Then you will say, 'Because of the news that is coming. Every heart will melt with fear. All hands will become weak. Everyone will be afraid. All knees will become weak as water. Look, it is coming. It will happen, says the Lord God'."

⁸The Lord spoke his word to me. He said, ⁹"Human being, prophesy and say, 'This is what the Lord says:
A sword, a sword,
   made sharp and polished.
¹⁰It is made sharp for the killing.
   It is polished to flash like
      lightning.
" 'You are not happy about this horrible punishment by the sword. But my son, Judah, you did not change when you were only beaten with a rod.
¹¹The sword should be polished.

The sword is meant to be held
   in the hand.
It is made sharp and polished.
   It is made ready for the hand of
      the killer.
¹²Shout and yell, human being.
   This is because the sword is
      against my people.
   It is against all the rulers of
      Israel.
They will be killed by the sword,
   along with my people.
So beat your chest in sadness.
¹³" 'The test will come. And Judah, who is hated by the armies of Babylon, will not last, says the Lord God'.

¹⁴"So, human being, prophesy.
   And clap your hands.
Let the sword hit
   two or three times.
It is the sword for killing.
   It is the sword for much killing.
This sword surrounds the
   people.
¹⁵Their hearts will melt with fear.
   And many people will die.
I have placed the killing sword
   at all their gates.
Oh! The sword is made to flash
   like lightning.
   It is held, ready for killing.
¹⁶Sword, cut on the right side.
   Then cut on the left side.
Cut anywhere your blade is
   turned.
¹⁷I will also clap my hands.
   Then my anger will rest.
I, the Lord, have spoken."

Jerusalem to Be Destroyed

¹⁸The Lord spoke his word to me. He said: ¹⁹"Human being, mark two roads that the king of Babylon and his sword can follow. Both of these roads will start from the same country. And make signs where the road divides and one way goes toward the city. ²⁰One sign shows the road he can take with his sword to Rabbah. It is in the land of the Ammonites. And the other

sign shows the road he can take to Judah and Jerusalem. Jerusalem is protected with strong walls. 21The king of Babylon will come to where the road divides into two. He will use magic. He will throw lots*d* with arrows. He will ask questions of his family idols. He will look at the liver of a sacrificed animal to learn where he should go. 22The lots will tell him to go towards his right to Jerusalem. They will tell him these things: use logs to break down the city gates. Shout the battle cry and give the order to kill. Build a dirt road to the top of the walls and devices to attack the walls. 23The people of Jerusalem have made agreements with other nations to help them fight Babylon. So they will think this prediction is wrong. But the king of Babylon will remind them of their sin. And he will capture them.

24"So this is what the Lord God says: 'You have shown how sinful you are by turning against the Lord. Your sins are seen in all the things you do. So you will be taken captive by the enemy.

25" 'You unclean*d* and evil leader of Israel, you will be killed! The time of your final punishment has come. 26This is what the Lord God says: Take off the turban. Take off the crown. Things will change. Those who are important now will be made unimportant. And those who are unimportant now will be made important. 27A ruin! A ruin! I will make it a ruin! This place will not be rebuilt until the one comes who has a right to be king. Then I will give it to him'.

The Punishment of Ammon

28"And you, human being, prophesy*d* and say: 'This is what the Lord God says about the people of Ammon and their insults:

A sword, a sword
   is pulled out of its holder.
It is polished to kill and destroy.
   It will flash like lightning!

29Prophets*d* see false visions about you
  and prophesy lies about you.
The sword will be put on the necks
  of these evil people who are to be killed.
Their day has come.
The time of your final punishment has come.
30Put the sword back in its holder.
I will judge you in the place
  where you were created.
I will judge you in the land where you were born.
31I will pour out my anger against you.
I will breathe on you with the fire of my anger.
I will hand you over to cruel men
  who are skilled in destruction.
32You will be like fuel for the fire.
You will die in the land.
You will not be remembered.
I, the Lord, have spoken'."

The Sins of Jerusalem

22 The Lord spoke his word to me. He said: 2"And you, human being, will you judge? Will you judge the city of murderers? Then tell her about all her hated acts. 3You will say: 'This is what the Lord God says: You are a city that kills those who come to live there. You make yourself unclean*d* by making idols. 4You have become guilty of murder. And you have become unclean by the idols which you have made. So you have brought your time of punishment near. You have come to the end of your years. So I have made you a thing of shame to the nations. All lands will laugh at you. 5Those near and those far away will laugh at you. You will have a bad name. You will be full of confusion.

6" 'Jerusalem, see how each ruler of Israel in you has been trying to kill people. 7The people in you hate their fathers and mothers. They mistreat the foreigners in you. They wrong the orphans and widows in you. ⁸You hate my holy things. You dishonour my Sabbaths.ᵈ ⁹The men in you tell lies to cause the death of others. The people in you eat food offered to idols at the mountain places of worship. They do sexual sins in you. ¹⁰The people in you have sexual relations with their fathers' wives. The men in you have sexual relations with women who are unclean, during their time of monthly bleeding. ¹¹One person in you does a hated act with his neighbour's wife. Another has shamefully made his daughter-in-law unclean sexually. And another forces his half-sister to have sexual relations with him. ¹²The people in you take money to kill people. You take unfair interest and profits. You make profits by mistreating your neighbour. And you have forgotten me, says the Lord God.

¹³" 'So with my fists I will hit you who have stolen money and you who have murdered people. ¹⁴Will you still be brave and strong when I punish you? I, the Lord, have spoken, and I will act. ¹⁵I will scatter you among the nations. I will spread you through the countries. I will get rid of your uncleanness. ¹⁶But you, yourself, will be dishonoured in the sight of the nations. Then you will know that I am the Lord'."

Israel Is Worthless

¹⁷The Lord spoke his word to me. He said: ¹⁸"Human being, the people of Israel have become useless like scum to me. They are like the copper, tin, iron and lead left in the furnace. These are left when silver is purified by melting. ¹⁹So this is what the Lord God says: 'You have become useless like scum. I am going to gather you into Jerusalem. ²⁰People gather silver, copper, iron, lead and tin into a furnace. Then they melt it in a blazing fire. In the same way I will gather you

in my hot anger. I will put you in Jerusalem and melt you. ²¹I will gather you. And I will make you feel the heat of my anger. You will be melted in the fire. ²²Silver is melted in the furnace. In the same way you will be melted in the city. Then you will know that I, the Lord, have poured out my anger against you'."

Sins of the People

²³The Lord spoke his word to me. He said: ²⁴"Human being, say to the land, 'You are a land that has not had rain or showers in a day of anger'. ²⁵Israel's rulers make evil plans. They are like a roaring lion that tears the animal it has caught. They have destroyed lives. They have taken treasure and valuable things. They have caused many women to become widows. ²⁶Israel's priests do cruel things to my teachings. They do not honour my holy things. They make no difference between holy and unholy things. They teach that there is no difference between cleanᵈ and unclean things.ᵈ They do not remember my Sabbaths.ᵈ So I am dishonoured by them. ²⁷Jerusalem's leaders are like wolves tearing a dead animal. They have killed people for profit. ²⁸And the prophetsᵈ try to cover this up by false visions and by lying. They say, 'This is what the Lord God says' when the Lord has not spoken. ²⁹The people cheat others. They steal. They hurt people who are poor and needy. They cheat foreigners and don't treat them fairly.

³⁰"I looked for someone to build up the walls. I looked for someone to stand before me where the walls are broken to defend these people. Then I would not have to destroy them. But I did not find anyone. ³¹So I will let them see my anger. I will destroy them with an anger that is like fire. This is because of all the things they have done, says the Lord God."

Samaria and Jerusalem

23 The Lord spoke his word to me. He said: [2]"Human being, a woman had two daughters. [3]While they were young, they went to Egypt and became prostitutes.[d] They let men touch and hold their breasts. [4]The older girl was named Oholah, and her sister was named Oholibah. They were mine and had sons and daughters. Oholah is Samaria, and Oholibah is Jerusalem.

[5]"Samaria left me. She went to her lover, Assyria. The Assyrians were warriors. [6]They wore blue uniforms. And all of them — governors, commanders and horsemen — were handsome. [7]Samaria became a prostitute for all the important men in Assyria. And she made herself unclean[d] with all the idols of everyone she desired. [8]She continued the prostitution she began in Egypt. When she was young, she slept with men. They touched her breasts and had sexual relations with her.

[9]"So I gave her to her lovers, the Assyrians, that she wanted so badly. [10]They stripped her naked and took away her sons and daughters. Then they killed her with a sword. Women everywhere began talking about how she had been punished.

[11]"Her sister Jerusalem saw what happened to Samaria. And so Jerusalem became worse than her sister in her sexual desire and prostitution. [12]She also desired the Assyrians. All of them — governors, commanders, warriors dressed in uniform, and horsemen — were handsome. [13]I saw that both girls were alike. Both of them were prostitutes.

[14]"But Jerusalem went even further. She saw carvings of Babylonian men on a wall. They wore red [15]and had belts around their waists. They wore turbans on their heads. They all looked like chariot officers born in Babylonia. [16]When she saw them, she wanted to have sexual relations with them. So she sent messengers to them in Babylonia. [17]So these Babylonian men came and had sexual relations with her. They made her unclean. After that, she became sick of them. [18]But she continued her prostitution so that everyone knew about it. And I finally became sick of her, as I had of her sister. [19]But she remembered how she was a young prostitute in Egypt. So she took part in even more prostitution. [20]She wanted men who behaved like animals in their sexual desire. [21]In the same way you desired to do the sinful things you had done in Egypt. There men touched and held your young breasts.

God's Judgement on Jerusalem

[22]"So, Jerusalem, this is what the Lord God says: You have tired of your lovers. So now I will make them angry with you. And they will surround you. [23]Men from Babylon and all Babylonia and men from Pekod, Shoa and Koa will come against you. All the Assyrians will come against you. They are governors, commanders, chariot drivers and important men, all riding horses. [24]Those men will come with great armies. They will come with their weapons, chariots and wagons. They will surround you with large and small shields and with helmets. And I will hand you over to them for punishment. And they will punish you with their own kind of punishment. [25]Then you will see how strong my anger can be. They will punish you in their anger. They will cut off your noses and ears. They will take away your sons and daughters. Those who are left will be burned. [26]They will take off your clothes and steal your jewellery. [27]I will put a stop to the sinful life you began when you were in Egypt. You will not desire these things any more. And you will not remember Egypt any more.

[28]"This is what the Lord God says:

You became sick of your lovers. But I am giving you to those men you now hate. ²⁹They will treat you with hate and take away everything you worked for. They will leave you empty and naked. Everyone will know about the sinful things you did. Your sexual sins ³⁰have brought this on you. You have made yourselves unclean^d by worshipping their idols. ³¹You did the same things your sister did. So you will get the same punishment.

³²"This is what the Lord God says:
You will drink the same cup your
    sister did.
And that cup is deep and wide.
Everyone will make fun of you,
    because the cup is full.
³³It will make you miserable and
    drunk.
It is the cup of fear and ruin.
It is the cup of your sister
    Samaria.
³⁴You will drink everything in it.
    Then you will smash it
    and tear at your breasts.
I have spoken, says the Lord God.

³⁵"So this is what the Lord God says: You have forgotten me and turned your back on me. So you will be punished for your sexual sins."

Judgement on Samaria and Jerusalem

³⁶The Lord said to me: "Human being, will you judge Samaria and Jerusalem? Then show them their hated acts. ³⁷They are guilty of adultery^d and murder. They have taken part in adultery with their idols. They even offered their children as sacrifices in the fire. They were to be food for these idols. ³⁸They have also done this to me: they made my Temple^d unclean^d at the same time they dishonoured my Sabbaths.^d ³⁹They offered their children to their idols. Then they entered my Temple at that very time to dishonour it. That is what they did inside my Temple.

⁴⁰"They even sent for men from far away. A messenger was sent to them, and they came. The two sisters bathed themselves for them, painted their eyes and put on jewellery. ⁴¹They sat on a fine bed with a table set before it. They put my incense^d and my oil on the table.

⁴²"There was the noise of a reckless crowd in the city. Common people gathered, and drunkards were brought from the desert. They put bracelets on the hands of the two sisters. And they put beautiful crowns on their heads. ⁴³Then I said about the one who was worn out by her acts of adultery, 'Let them continue their sexual sins with her. She is nothing but a prostitute'.^d ⁴⁴They kept going to her as they would go to a prostitute. So they continued to go to Oholah, which was Samaria, and Oholibah, which was Jerusalem. These were the shameful women. ⁴⁵But men who do right will judge them as they judge women who take part in adultery. And they will judge them as they judge women who murder people. This is because Samaria and Jerusalem are guilty of adultery and murder.

⁴⁶"This is what the Lord God says: Bring together a mob against Samaria and Jerusalem. And hand them over to be frightened and robbed. ⁴⁷Let the mob kill them by throwing stones at them. Let the mob cut them down with their swords. Let them kill their sons and daughters and burn their houses with fire.

⁴⁸"So I will put an end to sexual sins in the land. Then all women will be warned. And they will not do the sexual sins you have done. ⁴⁹You will be punished for your sexual sins and the sin of worshipping idols. Then you will know that I am the Lord God."

The Pot and the Meat

24 The Lord spoke his word to me. It was in the ninth year, in the tenth month of our captivity. It was on the tenth day of the month. He said: ²"Human being, write for yourself this date, this very date. The king of Babylon has surrounded Jerusalem this very day. ³And tell a story to the people who refuse to obey me. Say to them: 'This is what the Lord God says:

Put on the pot. Put it on
    and pour water in it.
⁴Put in the pieces of meat.
Put in the best pieces — the legs
    and the shoulders.
Fill it with the best bones.
⁵ Take the best of the flock.
Pile wood under the pot.
Boil the pieces of meat
    until even the bones are cooked.

⁶" 'This is what the Lord God says:
How terrible it will be for the city
    of murderers!
How terrible it will be for the
    rusty pot!
Its rust will not go away!
Take the meat out of it, piece by
    piece.
Don't choose any special piece.

⁷" 'The blood from her killings is
    still in the city.
She poured the blood on the
    bare rock.
She did not pour it on the ground
    where dust would cover it.
⁸To stir up my anger and revenge,
I put the blood she spilled on
    the bare rock.
So it will not be covered.

⁹" 'So this is what the Lord God
says:
How terrible it will be for the city
    of murderers!
I will also pile the wood high for
    burning.
¹⁰Pile up the wood
    and light the fire.
Finish cooking the meat.
    Mix in the spices.
And let the bones burn.
¹¹Then set the empty pot on the
    coals.

It will become hot, and its
    copper sides will glow.
The dirty scum stuck inside it may
    then melt
    and its rust burn away.
¹²But efforts to clean the pot have
    failed.
Its heavy rust cannot be
    removed,
    even in the fire.

¹³" 'In your sinful action there is shame. I wanted to cleanse you, but you are still unclean.ᵈ You will never be cleansed from your sin until my anger against you is carried out.

¹⁴" 'I, the Lord, have spoken. The time has come for me to act. I will not hold back punishment. I will not feel pity. I will judge you by your ways and actions, says the Lord God'."

The Death of Ezekiel's Wife

¹⁵Then the Lord spoke his word to me. He said: ¹⁶"Human being, I am going to take your wife from you. She is the desire of your eyes. She will die suddenly. But you must not be sad or cry loudly for her. You must not shed any tears. ¹⁷Groan silently. Do not cry loudly for the dead. Tie on your turban, and put your sandals on your feet. Do not cover your face. And do not eat the food people eat when they are sad about a death."

¹⁸So I spoke to the people in the morning. Then my wife died in the evening. The next morning I did as I had been commanded. ¹⁹Then the people asked me, "Tell us, what do the things you are doing mean for us?" ²⁰Then I said to them, "The Lord spoke his word to me. He said, ²¹'Say to the people of Israel, This is what the Lord God says: I am going to dishonour my Temple.ᵈ You think it gives you strength. You are proud of it. You love to look at it. It makes you happy. But your sons and daughters that you left behind in Jerusalem will

fall dead by the sword. 22And you will do as I have done. You will not cover your face. You will not eat the food people eat when they are sad about a death. 23Your turbans will be on your heads. And your sandals will be on your feet. You will not cry loudly. But you will rot away in your sins. You will groan to each other. 24So Ezekiel will be a sign for you. You will do all the same things he did. When it happens, you will know that I am the Lord God'.

25"And as for you, human being, this is how it will be. I will take away the Temple that gives them strength. It makes them happy and proud. They love to look at it. It makes them happy. And I will take away their sons and daughters also. 26At that time the person who escapes will come to you. He will have information for you to hear. 27At that time your mouth will be opened. You will speak and be silent no more. So you will be a sign for them. Then they will know that I am the Lord."

Prophecy Against Ammon

25 The Lord spoke his word to me. He said: 2"Human being, look towards the people of Ammon and prophesy*d* against them. 3Say to them, 'Hear the word of the Lord God. This is what the Lord God says: You were glad when my Temple*d* was dishonoured. You were glad when the land of Israel was ruined. And you were glad when the people of Judah were taken away as captives. 4So I am going to give you to the people of the East to be theirs. They will set up their camps among you. They will make their homes among you. They will eat your fruit and drink your milk. 5And I will make the city of Rabbah a pasture for camels. And the land of Ammon will become a resting place for sheep. Then you will know that I am the Lord. 6This is what the Lord God says: You clapped your hands and stamped your feet. You are happy

about all the insults you have made against the land of Israel. 7So I will use my power against you. I will give you to the nations as if you were valuables taken in war. I will wipe you out of the lands so you will no longer be a nation. I will destroy you. And you will know that I am the Lord'."

Prophecy Against Moab and Edom

8"This is what the Lord God says: 'Moab and Edom say, "The people of Judah are like all the other nations." 9So I am going to take away the cities that protect Moab's borders. They are the best cities in that land. They are Beth Jeshimoth, Baal Meon and Kiriathaim. 10Then I will give Moab, along with the Ammonites, to the people of the East. They will take over these people. Then along with the Ammonites, Moab will not be a nation any more. 11So I will punish the people of Moab. And they will know that I am the Lord'."

Prophecy Against Edom

12"This is what the Lord God says: 'Edom took revenge on the people of Judah. And the Edomites became guilty because of it. 13So this is what the Lord God says: I will use my power against Edom. I will kill every man and animal in Edom. And I will destroy Edom all the way from Teman to Dedan. The Edomites will die in battle. 14I will take revenge on Edom through my people Israel. So the Israelites will do to Edom what my hot anger demands. Then the Edomites will know my revenge, says the Lord God'."

Prophecy Against Philistia

15"This is what the Lord God says: 'The Philistines have taken revenge with hateful hearts. Because of their strong hatred, they have tried to destroy Judah. 16So this is what the Lord God says: I will use my power against the Philistines. I will remove the Kerethites. I will destroy those people still alive on the coast of the Mediterranean Sea. [17]I will punish them in my anger until they have had enough. They will know that I am the Lord when I punish them'."

Prophecy Against Tyre

26 It was the eleventh year, on the first day of the month of our captivity. The Lord spoke his word to me. He said: [2]"Human being, the city of Tyre has spoken against Jerusalem: 'The city that traded with the nations is destroyed. Now we can be the trading centre. The city Jerusalem is ruined. Now we can make money'. [3]So this is what the Lord God says: I am against you, Tyre. I will bring many nations against you. They will come like the sea beating its waves on your island shores. [4]They will destroy the walls of Tyre and pull down her towers. I will also scrape away her ruins. I will make Tyre a bare rock. [5]Tyre will be an island where fishermen dry their nets. I have spoken, says the Lord God. The nations will steal valuable things from Tyre. [6]Also, her villages on the shore across from the island will be destroyed by war. Then they will know that I am the Lord.

Nebuchadnezzar to Attack Tyre

[7]"This is what the Lord God says: I will bring a king from the north against Tyre. He is Nebuchadnezzar king of Babylon, the greatest king. He will bring horses, chariots, horsemen and a great army. [8]He will fight a battle and destroy your villages on the shore across from the island. He will set up devices to attack you. He will build a road of earth to the top of the walls. He will raise his shields against you. [9]He will bring logs to pound through your city walls. And he will break down your towers with his iron bars. [10]His horses will be so many that they will cover you with their dust. Your walls will shake at the noise of horse-

men, wagons and chariots. The king of Babylon will enter your city gates. He will enter as men enter a city where the walls are broken through. [11]The hoofs of his horses will run over your streets. He will kill your people with the sword. Your strong pillars will fall down to the ground. [12]Also, his men will take away your riches. They will steal the things you sell. They will break down your walls and destroy your nice houses. They will throw your stones, wood and rubbish into the sea. [13]So I will stop your songs. The music of your harps will not be heard any more. [14]I will make you a bare rock. You will be a place for drying fishing nets. You will not be built again. This is because I, the Lord, have spoken, says the Lord God.

[15]"This is what the Lord God says to Tyre: The people who live along the coast will shake with fear when they hear your defeat. Those of you who are injured and dying will groan. [16]Then all the leaders of the coast will go down from their thrones. They will take off their beautiful needlework clothes. They will clothe themselves with fear. They will sit on the ground. They will shake with fear all the time. They will be shocked when they see you. [17]They will begin singing a funeral song about you. They will say to you:

'Tyre, you famous city, you have
    been destroyed!
Once seamen lived in you.
You and your people
    had great power on the seas.
All the people around you
    were afraid of you.
[18]Now the people who live by the
    coast
    will shake with fear on the day
    you fall.
The islands of the sea
    will be afraid because you have
    been defeated'.
[19]"This is what the Lord God says:

I will make you an empty city. You will
be like the cities that have no people
living in them. I will bring the deep
ocean waters over you. The Mediterranean Sea will cover you. [20]At that
time I will send you down to the place
of the dead. You will join the people
who died long ago. I will make you live
with the dead below the earth among
old ruined places. You will not come
back from there. People will never
live in you again. [21]Other people will
be afraid of what happened to you. It
will be the end of you. People will look
for you. But they will never find you
again, says the Lord God."

A Funeral Song for Tyre

27 The Lord spoke his word to
me. He said: [2]"Human being,
sing a funeral song for the city of
Tyre. [3]Speak to Tyre that is at the entrance to the Mediterranean Sea. For
the people of many lands along the
seacoast, Tyre is a place for trade.
'This is what the Lord God says:
   Tyre, you have said,
     "I am like a beautiful ship."
[4]You were at home on the high
     seas.
   Your builders have made your
     beauty perfect.
[5]Your builders made all your
     boards
   of fir trees from Mount Hermon.
   They have taken a cedar tree
     from Lebanon.
   They took it to make a ship's
     mast for you.
[6]They made your oars
     from oak trees in Bashan.
   They made your deck
     from cypress trees from the
     coast of Cyprus.
   Your deck has ivory set into it.
[7]Your sail of linen with designs
     sewed on it came from
     Egypt.

   Your sail became like a flag for
     you.
   Your cloth shades over the deck
     were blue and purple.
   They came from the island of
     Cyprus.
[8]Men from Sidon and Arvad used
     oars to row you.
   Tyre, your skilled men were the
     sailors on your deck.
[9]Workers of Byblos were on board
     ship with you.
   They caulked[n] your ship's
     seams.
   All the ships of the sea and their
     sailors
     came alongside to trade with
     you.

[10]" 'Men of Persia, Lydia and Put
     were soldiers in your army.
   They hung their shields and
     helmets on your walls.
   Their victories made you
     famous.
[11]Men of Arvad and Celicia
     guarded your city walls all
     around.
   Men of Gammad
     were in your watchtowers.
   They hung their shields around
     your walls.
   They made your beauty perfect.

[12]" 'Tarshish traded with you for
many kinds of things. They paid for
them with silver, iron, tin and lead.
[13]" 'People of Greece, Tubal and
Meshech traded with you. They traded slaves and bronze things for the
things you sell.
[14]" 'People of Beth Togarmah traded work horses, war horses and
mules for the things you sell.
[15]" 'People of Rhodes traded with
you. You sold your things to many
coastal lands. They paid you with
ivory tusks and valuable black wood.
[16]" 'Aram traded with you because

caulked Put something like tar between the boards of a ship to make it waterproof so it will not
sink.

you had so many good things to sell.
They traded turquoise, purple cloth
and cloth with designs sewed on.
They also traded fine linen, coral and
rubies for the things you sell.

17" 'Judah and Israel traded with
you. They paid for the things you sell
with wheat from Minnith. They also
paid with honey, olive oil and balm.*d*

18" 'Damascus traded with you be-
cause you had many good things.
They paid for them with wine from
Helbon and wool from Zahar.

19" 'The Greeks from Uzal traded
for the things you sold. They paid with
wrought iron, cassia*d* and sugar cane
for your good things.

20" 'Dedan traded saddle blankets to
you.

21" 'Arabia and all the rulers of Kedar traded with you. They traded
lambs, male sheep and goats to you.

22" 'The traders of Sheba and Raamah traded with you. They paid with
all the best spices, valuable gems and
gold.

23" 'Haran, Canneh, Eden and the
traders of Sheba, Asshur and Kilmad
traded with you. 24They paid with the
best clothes, blue cloth and cloth with
designs sewed on. They traded car-
pets of many colours and tightly
wound ropes.

25" 'Trading ships
    carried the things you sold.
You were like a ship full of heavy
        cargo
    in the middle of the sea.
26The men who rowed you
    brought you out into the high
        seas.
But the east wind has broken you
        to pieces
    in the middle of the sea.
27Your wealth, your trade and the
        things you sell will sink.
Your seamen, your sailors and
        your workers will sink.
Your traders, your soldiers,
    and everyone else on board

will sink into the sea.
    This will happen on the day your
        ship is wrecked.
28The people on the shore will
        shake with fear
    when your sailors cry out.
29All the men who row
    will leave their ships.
The seamen and the sailors of
        other ships
    will stand on the shore.
30They will cry loudly about you.
    They will cry very much.
They will throw dust on their
        heads.
    They will roll in ashes to show
        they are sad.
31They will shave their heads for
        you.
    And they will put on rough cloth
        to show they are upset.
They will cry very much for you.
    They will cry loudly.
32And in their loud crying
    they will sing a funeral song for
        you.
"No one was ever destroyed like
        Tyre,
    surrounded by the sea."
33The things you traded went out
        over the seas.
    You met the needs of many
        nations.
With your great wealth and things
        you sold,
    you made kings of the earth
        rich.
34But now you are broken by the
        sea.
    You have sunk to the bottom.
The things you sell and all your
        people
    have gone down with you.
35All those who live along the shore
    are shocked by what happened
        to you.
Their kings are terribly afraid.
    Their faces show their fear.
36The traders among the nations
    hiss at you.

You have come to a terrible
end.
And you are gone for ever'.''

Prophecy Against the King of Tyre

28 The Lord spoke his word to
me. He said: [2]"Human being,
say to the ruler of Tyre: 'This is what
the Lord God says:
You are too proud.
And you say, "I am a god.
I sit on the throne of a god
in the middle of the seas."
You think you are as wise as a
god.
But you are a man, not a god.
[3]You think you are wiser than
Daniel.
You think you can find out all
secrets.
[4]Through your wisdom and
understanding
you have made yourself rich.
You have gained gold and silver.
And you have saved it in your
storerooms.
[5]Through your great skill in
trading,
you have made your riches
grow.
You are too proud
because of your riches.

[6]" 'So this is what the Lord God
says:
You think you are wise
like a god.
[7]But I will bring foreign people
against you.
They will be the cruellest
nation.
They will pull out their swords
and destroy all that your wisdom
has built.
And they will dishonour your
greatness.
[8]They will kill you.
You will die a terrible death
like those who are killed at sea.
[9]While they are killing you,

you will not be able to say any
more, "I am a god."
You will be only a man, not a god,
when your murderers kill you.
[10]You will die like an unclean[d]
person.
Foreigners will kill you.

I have spoken, says the Lord God'.''

[11]The Lord spoke his word to me.
He said: [12]"Human being, sing a funeral song for the king of Tyre. Say to
him: 'This is what the Lord God says:
You were an example of what was
perfect.
You were full of wisdom and
perfect in beauty.
[13]You had a wonderful life,
like those in Eden, the garden of
God.
Every valuable gem was on you:
ruby, topaz and emerald,
yellow quartz, onyx and jasper,
sapphire, turquoise and
chrysolite.
Your jewellery was made of gold.
It was prepared on the day you
were created.
[14]I appointed a living creature to
guard you.
I put you on the holy mountain
of God.
You walked among the gems of
fire.
[15]Your life was right and good.
This was from the day you were
created,
until evil was found in you.
[16]Because you traded with countries
far away,
you learned to be cruel, and you
sinned.
So I threw you down in disgrace
from the mountain of God.
And the living creature who
guarded you
forced you out from among the
gems of fire.
[17]You became too proud
because of your beauty.
You ruined your wisdom

because of your greatness.
I threw you down to the ground.
Your example taught a lesson to
    other kings.
18You dishonoured your places of
    worship
through your many sins and
    dishonest trade.
So I set your city on fire.
And it burned up.
I turned you into ashes on the
    ground
for all those watching to see.
19All the nations who knew you
    are shocked about you.
Your punishment was so terrible.
And you are gone for ever'."

Prophecy Against Sidon

20The Lord spoke his word to me.
He said: 21"Human being, look toward
the city of Sidon and prophesy*d*
against her. 22Say: 'This is what the
Lord God says:
I am against you, Sidon.
    I will show my greatness among
        you.
Then people will know that I am
        the Lord
    when I have punished Sidon.
    I will show my holiness by
        defeating her.
23I will send diseases to Sidon,
    and blood will flow in her
        streets.
Those who are wounded in Sidon
    will fall dead.
She will be attacked from all
    sides.
Then they will know that I am the
    Lord.

God Will Help Israel

24" 'No more will neighbouring nations be like prickly branches or sharp
thorns to hurt Israel. Then they will
know that I am the Lord God.
25" 'This is what the Lord God says:
I will gather the people of Israel from
the nations where they are scattered.
I will show my holiness when the na-

tions see what I do to my people.
Then they will live in their own land —
the land I gave to my servant Jacob.
26Then they will live safely in the land.
They will build houses and plant vineyards. They will live in safety after I
have punished all the nations around
who hate them. Then they will know
that I am the Lord their God'."

Prophecy Against Egypt

29 It was the tenth year, in the
tenth month of our captivity. It
was on the twelfth day of the month.
The Lord spoke his word to me. He
said: 2"Human being, look toward the
king of Egypt. And prophesy*d* against
him and all Egypt. 3Say: 'This is what
the Lord God says:
I am against you, king of Egypt.
You are like a great crocodile
    that lies in the Nile River.
You say, "The Nile is mine.
I made it for myself."
4But I will put hooks in your jaws.
I will make the fish of the Nile
    stick to your sides.
I will pull you up out of your
    rivers,
with all the fish sticking to your
    sides.
5I will leave you in the desert.
I will leave you and all the fish
    from your rivers.
You will fall on the open field.
You will not be picked up or
    buried.
I have given you to the wild
    animals.
And I have given you to the
    birds of the sky for food.
6Then all the people who live in Egypt
will know that I am the Lord.
" 'Israel tried to lean on you for
help. But you were like a crutch made
out of a weak stalk of grass. 7When
their hands grabbed you, you splintered and tore open their shoulders.
When they leaned on you, you broke
and made all their backs twist.
8" 'So this is what the Lord God

says: I will cause an enemy to attack you. He will kill your men and animals. ⁹Then Egypt will become an empty desert. They will know that I am the Lord.

" 'This is because you said, "The Nile River is mine. And I have made it." ¹⁰So, I am against you. I am against your rivers. I will destroy the land of Egypt. It will be empty desert from Migdol in the north to Aswan in the south. It will be empty all the way to the southern border of Cush. ¹¹No man or animal will walk through it. No one will live in Egypt for 40 years. ¹²I will make the land of Egypt the emptiest country of all. And her cities will be the emptiest of all ruined cities for 40 years. And I will scatter the Egyptians among the nations. And I will spread them among the countries.

¹³" 'This is what the Lord God says: After 40 years I will gather Egypt from the nations where they have been scattered. ¹⁴I will bring back the Egyptian captives. I will make the Egyptians return to southern Egypt. They will return to the land that they came from. They will become a weak kingdom there. ¹⁵It will be the weakest kingdom. It will never again rule other nations. I will make it so weak it will never again rule over the nations. ¹⁶The Israelites will never again depend on Egypt. Egypt's punishment will remind the Israelites of their sin. They turned to Egypt for help and not to God. Then they will know that I am the Lord God'."

Egypt Is Given to Babylon

¹⁷It was the twenty-seventh year of our captivity, in the first month. It was on the first day of the month. The Lord spoke his word to me. He said: ¹⁸"Human being, Nebuchadnezzar king of Babylon made his army fight hard against Tyre. Every soldier's head was rubbed bare. Every shoulder was rubbed raw. But Nebuchadnezzar and his army gained nothing

from fighting Tyre. ¹⁹So this is what the Lord God says: I will give the land of Egypt to Nebuchadnezzar king of Babylon. And Nebuchadnezzar will take away Egypt's people. He will take Egypt's wealth and its valuable things as pay for his army. ²⁰I have given Nebuchadnezzar the land of Egypt. It is a reward for working hard to defeat Egypt for me. That is what the Lord God says.

²¹"On that day I will make Israel grow strong again. I will let you, Ezekiel, speak to them. Then they will know that I am the Lord God."

Egypt Will Be Punished

30 The Lord spoke his word to me. He said, ²"Human being, prophesy*ᵈ* and say, 'This is what the Lord God says:

Cry and say,
    "The terrible day is coming."
³The day is near.
    The Lord's day of judging is
        near.
    It is a cloudy day.
    It is a time when the nations will
        be judged.
⁴An enemy will attack Egypt.
    And Cush will tremble with fear.
When the killing begins in Egypt,
    her wealth will be taken away.
    Egypt's foundations will be torn
        down.

⁵Cush, Put, Lydia, Arabia, Libya and my people will die. All these who made an agreement with Egypt will fall dead in war.

⁶" 'This is what the Lord God says:
Those who fight on Egypt's side
    will fall.
The power she is proud of will
    go down.
The people in Egypt will fall dead
    in war
    from Migdol in the north to
        Aswan in the south,
    says the Lord God.
⁷They will be

the emptiest land.
Egypt's cities will be
  like other cities that lie in ruin.
⁸Then they will know that I am the
    Lord.
This will happen when I set fire
    to Egypt
and when all those nations on
    her side are crushed.
⁹" 'At that time I will send messengers in ships. They will frighten Cush which now feels safe. The people of Cush will tremble with fear when Egypt is punished. And that time is sure to come.
  ¹⁰" 'This is what the Lord God says:
I will destroy great numbers of
    people in Egypt.
I will do it through
    Nebuchadnezzar king of
    Babylon.
¹¹Nebuchadnezzar and his army
  are the cruellest army of any
    nation.
They will be brought in to
    destroy the land.
They will pull out their swords
    against Egypt.
They will fill the land with those
    they kill.
¹²I will make the streams of the
    Nile River become dry land.
Then I will sell the dry land to
    evil people.
I will destroy the land and
    everything in it.
I will do it through the power of
    strangers.

I, the Lord, have spoken.

Egypt's Idols Are Destroyed

  ¹³" 'This is what the Lord God says:
I will destroy the idols.
And I will take away the statues
    of false gods from the city of
    Memphis.
There will no longer be a leader in
    Egypt.
And I will spread fear through
    the land of Egypt.

¹⁴I will make southern Egypt
    empty.
I will start a fire in Zoan.
I will punish Thebes.
¹⁵And I will pour out my anger
    against Pelusium,
  the strong place of Egypt.
I will destroy great numbers of
    people in Thebes.
¹⁶I will set fire to Egypt.
Pelusium will be in great pain.
The walls of Thebes will be
    broken open.
And Memphis will have troubles
    every day.
¹⁷The young men of Heliopolis and
    Bubastis
  will fall dead in war.
And the people will be taken
    away as captives.
¹⁸In Tahpanhes the day will be dark
    when I break Egypt's power.
A cloud will cover Egypt.
And her villages will be captured
    and taken away.
¹⁹So I will punish Egypt.
And they will know I am the
    Lord'."

Egypt Becomes Weak

  ²⁰It happened in the eleventh year of our captivity, in the first month. It was on the seventh day of the month. The Lord spoke his word to me. He said: ²¹"Human being, I have broken the powerful arm of the king of Egypt. It has not been tied up so it will not get well. It has not been wrapped with a bandage. So his arm will not be strong enough to hold a sword in war. ²²So this is what the Lord God says: I am against the king of Egypt. I will break his arms. I will break both the strong arm and the broken arm. I will make the sword fall from his hand. ²³I will scatter the Egyptians among the nations. And I will spread them among the countries. ²⁴I will make the arms of the king of Babylon strong. I will put my sword in his hand. But I will break the arms of the king of Egypt.

Then he will cry out in pain as a wounded man cries out. 25So I will make the arms of the king of Babylon strong. But the arms of the king of Egypt will fall. Then they will know that I am the Lord. I will put my sword into the hand of the king of Babylon. And he will use the sword in war against Egypt. 26Then I will scatter the Egyptians among the nations. And I will spread them among the countries. And they will know that I am the Lord."

A Cedar Tree

31 It happened in the eleventh year of our captivity, in the third month. It was on the first day of the month. The Lord spoke his word to me. He said: 2"Human being, say to the king of Egypt and his people:
'No one was like you in your
    greatness.
3Assyria was once like a cedar tree
    in Lebanon.
It had beautiful branches that
    shaded the forest.
It was very tall.
Its top was among the clouds.
4Much water made the tree grow.
The deep springs of water made
    the tree tall.
Rivers flowed
    around the bottom of the tree.
They sent their streams
    to all other trees of the field.
5So the tree was taller
    than all the other trees of the
        field.
Its branches became long and big
    because of so much water.
6All the birds of the sky
    made their nests in the tree's
        branches.
And all the wild animals
    gave birth under the tree's
        branches.
All great nations
    lived in the tree's shade.
7So the tree was great and
    beautiful,

with its long branches.
Its roots reached down to many
    waters.
8The cedar trees in the garden of
        God
    were not as great as it was.
The pine trees
    did not have such great
        branches.
The plane trees
    did not have such branches.
No tree in the garden of God
    was as beautiful as this tree.
9I made it beautiful
    with many branches.
And all the trees of Eden in the
        garden of God
    wanted to be like it.

10" 'So this is what the Lord God says: The tree has grown tall. Its top has reached the clouds. And it has become proud of its height. 11So I have let a mighty ruler of the nations take care of the tree. The ruler will surely punish the tree. Because it is evil I will get rid of it. 12The cruellest foreign nation cut it down and left it. The tree's branches fell on the mountains and in all the valleys. Its broken branches were in all the ravines of the land. All the nations of the earth left the shade of that tree. 13The birds of the sky live on the fallen tree. The wild animals live among the tree's fallen branches. 14Then the trees that grow by the water will not be proud to be tall. They will not put their tops among the clouds. None of the trees that are watered well will grow that tall. They all are meant to die and go under the ground. They will be with those who have died and have gone down to where the dead are.

15" 'This is what the Lord God says: On the day when the tree went down to where the dead are, I made people cry loudly. I covered the deep springs and held back their rivers. And the great waters stopped flowing. I made Lebanon cry loudly for the great tree.

All the trees of the field dried up and died. ¹⁶I made the nations shake with fear at the sound of the tree falling. I brought the tree down to where the dead are. It went with those who go down to the grave. Then the trees of Eden and the best trees of Lebanon were comforted. All the well-watered trees were comforted in the earth below. ¹⁷But these trees also went down with the great tree to the place where the dead are. They went to join those who were killed in war. They had lived under the great tree's shade. They were its friends among the nations.

¹⁸" 'So no tree in Eden is equal to you in greatness and honour. But you will go down with the trees of Eden to the earth below. You will lie among unclean*d* people who were killed in war.

" 'This will happen to the king of Egypt and all his people, says the Lord God'."

A Funeral Song

32 It happened in the twelfth year, in the twelfth month of our captivity. It was on the first day of the month. The Lord spoke his word to me. He said: ²"Human being, sing a funeral song about the king of Egypt. Say to him:
'You are like a young lion among the nations.
You are like a crocodile in the seas.
You splash around in your streams.
And you stir up the waters with your feet.
You make the rivers muddy.

³" 'This is what the Lord God says:
I will spread my net over you.
And I will use a large group of people
to pull you up in my net.
⁴Then I will throw you on the land.
I will toss you into the open field.

I will let the birds of the sky rest on you.
And I will let the animals of the earth eat you until they are full.
⁵I will scatter your flesh on the mountains.
And I will fill the valleys with what is left of you.
⁶I will drench the land with your flowing blood.
I will soak the mountains,
and the ravines will be full of your flesh.
⁷I will make you disappear.
And I will cover the sky and make the stars dark.
I will cover the sun with a cloud.
And the moon will not shine.
⁸I will make all the shining lights in the sky
become dark over you.
I will bring darkness over your land,
says the Lord God.
⁹I will cause many people to be afraid
when I have another nation destroy you.
Nations you have not known will be afraid because of you.
¹⁰I will cause people to be shocked about you.
Their kings will tremble with fear because of you
when I swing my sword before them.
They will shake every moment on the day you fall.
Each king will be afraid for his own life.

¹¹" 'So this is what the Lord God says:
The sword of the king of Babylon will come on you.
¹²I will cause your people to fall by the swords of mighty soldiers.
They are the most terrible of all the nations.

They will destroy the pride of
  Egypt.
All Egypt's people will be
  destroyed.
13I will also destroy all Egypt's
  cattle
which live alongside many
  waters.
The foot of man will not stir the
  waters.
And the hoofs of cattle will not
  muddy them any more.
14So I will let the Egyptians' waters
  become quiet.
I will cause their rivers to run
  as smoothly as olive oil,
  says the Lord God.
15I will make the land of Egypt
  empty.
I will take everything that is in
  the land.
I will destroy all those who live in
  Egypt.
Then they will know that I am
  the Lord'.

16"This is the funeral song people
will sing for Egypt. The women of the
nations will sing it for Egypt. They will
sing a funeral song for Egypt and all its
people, says the Lord God."

Egypt to Be Destroyed

17It happened in the twelfth year of
our captivity. It was on the fifteenth
day of the month. The Lord spoke his
word to me. He said: 18"Human being,
cry for the people of Egypt. Bring
down Egypt, together with the wom-
en of the powerful nations. Bring
them down to the earth below. Bring
them down with those who go to the
place of the dead. 19Say to them: 'Are
you more beautiful than others? Go and
lie down in death with those who are
unclean'. d 20The Egyptians will fall
among those killed by war. Egypt is
going to be killed by the sword. The
enemy will drag her and all her people
away. 21The leaders of the mighty
ones will speak from the place of

death. They will say about the king of
Egypt and the nations which help him:
'The king and the nations which help
him have come down here. They lie
killed by the sword among those who
are unclean'.
22"Assyria and all its army lie dead
there. The graves of their soldiers are
all around. All were killed in war.
23Assyria's grave was put in the deep
parts of the place where the dead are.
And its army lies around its grave.
When they lived, they frightened people in the land of the living. But now all
of them have been killed in war.
24"The nation of Elam is there. And
all its army is around its grave. All of
them were killed in war. They had
frightened people on earth and were
unclean. So they went down to the
lowest parts of the place where the
dead are. And they must carry their
shame with those who go down to the
place where the dead are. 25A bed is
made for Elam with all those killed in
war. They will be in the place where
the dead are. The graves of her soldiers are all around her. Elam's people
are unclean. So they have been killed
in war. They also scared people who
live on earth. But they must also carry
their shame with those who go down
to where the dead are. Their graves
are with the rest who were killed.
26"Meshech and Tubal are there.
The graves of all their soldiers surround them. All of them are unclean.
So they have been killed in war. They
also frightened people who live on
earth. 27But they are not buried with
the other unclean soldiers who have
been killed in battle. They are not with
those who went where the dead are
with their weapons of war. These
soldiers had their swords laid under
their heads and their shields on their
bodies. People who live on earth
used to be afraid of these mighty soldiers.
28"You, king of Egypt, will be broken and lie among those who are un-

clean. You will be with those who were killed in war.

29"Edom is there also. Its kings and all its leaders are there. They were mighty. But now they lie in death with those killed in war. They will lie with those who are unclean. And they will be with those who go down to where the dead are.

30"All the rulers of the north are there. And all the Sidonians are there. Their strength frightened people. These rulers of the north and the Sidonians have gone down in shame with those who were killed. They are unclean, lying with those killed in war. They have carried their shame with those who go down to where the dead are.

31"The king of Egypt and his army will see these who have been killed in war. Then the king and all his army will be comforted for all his soldiers killed in war, says the Lord God. 32I made people who live on earth afraid of the king of Egypt. But he and his people will lie among those who are unclean. They will lie with those who were killed by the sword, says the Lord God."

Ezekiel Is Watchman for Israel

33 The Lord spoke his word to me. He said: 2"Human being, speak to your people. Say to them: 'I might bring a war against a land. The people of the land may choose one of their men. They may make him their watchman. 3This watchman might see the enemy coming to attack the land. And he will blow the trumpet and warn the people. 4A person might hear the sound of the trumpet, but do nothing. Then the enemy will come and kill him. That person will be responsible for his own death. 5He heard the sound of the trumpet. But he did not do anything. So he is to blame for his own death. If he had done something, he would have saved his own life. 6But the watchman might see the enemy coming to attack and not blow the trumpet. So the people are not warned. Then the enemy will come and kill one of them. That person has died because of his own sin. But I will punish the watchman for the person's death'.

7"As for you, human being, I have made you a watchman for Israel. If you hear a message from me, you must warn them for me. 8I might say to the wicked person: 'Wicked man, you will surely die'. But you might not speak to warn the evil person to stop doing evil. Then he will die while still a sinner. But I will punish you for his death. 9But you might warn a wicked person to stop doing evil. If he does not stop, he will die while still a sinner. But you have saved your life.

10"So you, human being, say to Israel: 'You have said: surely our lawbreaking and sins are hurting us. They will kill us. What can we do so we will live?' 11Say to them: 'The Lord God says: As surely as I live, this is true. I do not want a wicked person to die. I want him to stop doing evil and live. Turn back! Turn back from your wicked ways! You don't want to die, people of Israel'.

12"And you, human being, say to your people: 'The goodness of a good person will not save him when he sins. The evil of the wicked person will not cause him to be punished if he turns from it. A good person will not be able to live by the good he did earlier if he sins'. 13I might tell the good person, "You will surely live." But he might think he has done enough good and then do evil. Then none of the good things he did will be remembered. He will die because of the evil he has done. 14Or, I might say to the wicked person, "You will surely die." But he might turn from his sin and do what is right and honest. 15He returns what somebody gave him as a promise to repay a loan. He pays back what he stole. He lives by the rules that give life. He does not sin. Then that one will surely live. He will not die. ¹⁶He will not be punished for any of his sins. He now does what is right and fair. He will surely live.

¹⁷"But your people say: 'The way of the Lord is not fair'. But it is their own way that is not fair. ¹⁸The good person might turn from his goodness and do evil. Then he will die for his evil. ¹⁹But the wicked person might stop doing evil and do what is right and fair. Then he will live. ²⁰You still say: 'The way of the Lord is not fair'. Israel, I will judge each of you by his own ways."

The Fall of Jerusalem Explained

²¹It happened in the twelfth year of our captivity. It was on the fifth day of the tenth month. A person who had escaped from Jerusalem came to me. He said, "Jerusalem has been defeated." ²²Now I had felt the power of the Lord on me the evening before. The Lord had made me able to talk again. He did this before the person came to me in the morning. I could speak. I was not without speech any more.

²³Then the Lord spoke his word to me. He said: ²⁴"Human being, people who live in the ruins in the land of Israel are saying: 'Abraham was only one person. Yet he was given the land as his own. Surely the land has been given to us, who are many, as our very own'. ²⁵So say to them: 'This is what the Lord God says: You eat meat with the blood still in it. You ask your idols for help. You murder people. Should you then have the land as your very own? ²⁶You depend on your sword. You do terrible things which I hate. Each of you has sexual relations with his neighbour's wife. So should you have the land?'

²⁷"Say to them: 'This is what the Lord God says: As surely as I live, this is true. Those who are among the city ruins in Israel will be killed in war. Those who live in the country will be eaten by wild animals. People hiding in the strong places and caves will die of disease. ²⁸I will make the land an empty desert. The people's pride in the land's power will end. The mountains of Israel will become empty. No one will pass through them. ²⁹They will know that I am the Lord when I make the land an empty desert. This is because of the things they have done that I hate'.

³⁰"But as for you, human being, your people talk against you. They talk by the walls and in the doorways of houses. They say to each other: 'Come now, and hear the message from the Lord'. ³¹So they come to you as if they are still my people. They sit before you. They hear your words. But they will not do them. With their mouths they tell me they love me. But their hearts desire their selfish profits. ³²To your people you are nothing more than a singer who sings love songs. You are like one who has a beautiful voice. You are like one who plays a musical instrument well. They hear your words, but they will not do them.

³³"This will come true. It will surely happen. Then the people will know that a prophet*d* has been among them."

The Leaders Are like Shepherds

34 The Lord spoke his word to me. He said: ²"Human being, prophesy*d* against the leaders of Israel, who are like shepherds. Prophesy and say to them: 'This is what the Lord God says: How terrible it will be for the shepherds of Israel who feed only themselves! Why don't the shepherds feed the flock? ³You eat the milk curds from the sheep. You clothe yourselves with the wool from the sheep. You kill the fat sheep. But you do not feed the flock. ⁴You have not made the weak strong. You have not healed the sick. You have not put bandages on those that were hurt. You have not brought back those who strayed away. You have not searched for the lost. You ruled the sheep with cruel force. ⁵The sheep were scattered because there was no shepherd. Then they became food for every wild animal. ⁶My flock wandered over all the mountains and on every high hill. They were scattered over all the face of the earth. And no one searched or looked for them.

⁷" 'So, you shepherds, hear the word of the Lord. This is what the Lord God says: ⁸As surely as I live, my flock has been caught. It has become food for all the wild animals. This is because the flock has no shepherd. The shepherds did not search for my flock. No, they fed themselves instead of my flock. ⁹So, you shepherds, hear the word of the Lord. ¹⁰This is what the Lord God says: I am against the shepherds. I will blame them for what has happened to my sheep. I will not let them tend the flock any more. Then the shepherds will stop feeding themselves. And I will take my flock from their mouths. My sheep will no longer be their food.

¹¹" 'This is what the Lord God says: I, myself, will search for my sheep. I will take care of them. ¹²A shepherd will take care of his scattered flock when it is found. In the same way I will take care of my sheep. I will save them from all the places where they are scattered. I will do this on a cloudy and dark day. ¹³I will bring them out from the nations. I will gather them from the countries. I will bring them to their own land. I will pasture them on the mountains and in the ravines of Israel. And I will feed them in all the places where people live in the land. ¹⁴I will feed them in a good pasture. They will eat grass on the high mountains of Israel. They will lie down on good ground where they eat grass. They will eat in rich grassland on the mountains of Israel. ¹⁵I will feed my flock and lead them to rest, says the Lord God. ¹⁶I will search for the lost.

I will bring back those that were scattered. I will put bandages on those that were hurt. I will make the weak strong. I will destroy those sheep that are fat and strong. I will tend the sheep with fairness.

¹⁷" 'This is what the Lord God says: And as for you, my flock, I will judge between one sheep and another. I will judge between the male sheep and the male goats. ¹⁸Is it not enough for you to eat grass in the good land? Must you crush the rest of the grass with your feet? Is it not enough for you to drink clear water? Must you make the rest of the water muddy with your feet? ¹⁹Must my flock eat what you crush? And must they drink what you make muddy with your feet?

²⁰" 'So this is what the Lord God says to them: I, myself, will judge between the fat sheep and the thin sheep. ²¹You push with your side and with your shoulder. You knock down all the weak sheep with your horns. You do this until you have forced them away. ²²So I will save my flock. They will not be hurt any more. I will judge between one sheep and another. ²³Then I will put one shepherd over them, my servant David. He will feed them. He will tend them and will be their shepherd. ²⁴Then I, the Lord, will be their God. And my servant David will be a ruler among them. I, the Lord, have spoken.

²⁵" 'And I will make an agreement of peace with my sheep. I will remove harmful animals from the land. Then the sheep will live safely in the desert. And they will sleep in the woods without danger. ²⁶I will bless them and let them live around my hill. I will cause the rains to come when it is time for them. There will be showers to bless them. ²⁷Also the trees of the field will give their fruit. The land will give its harvest. And the sheep will be safe on their land. Then they will know that I am the Lord. I will break the bars of their captivity. And I will save them

from the power of those who made them slaves. ²⁸They will not be led captive by the nations again. The wild animals will not eat them. But they will live safely. No one will make them afraid. ²⁹I will give them a place famous for its good crops. Then they will no longer suffer from hunger in the land. They will not suffer the insults of other nations any more. ³⁰Then they will know that I, the Lord their God, am with them. The nation of Israel will know that they are my people, says the Lord God. ³¹And you, my sheep, are the sheep of my pasture. You are my people and I am your God, says the Lord God'."

Prophecy Against Edom

35 The Lord spoke his word to me. He said: ²"Human being, look toward Mount Edom and prophesy*d* against it. ³Say to it: 'This is what the Lord God says: I am against you, Mount Edom. I will stretch out my hand against you. And I will make you an empty desert. ⁴I will destroy your cities. And you will become empty. Then you will know that I am the Lord.

⁵" 'This is because you have always been an enemy of Israel. You let them be defeated in war when they were in trouble. It was the time of their final punishment. ⁶So the Lord God says, As surely as I live, I will let you be murdered. Murder will chase you. You did not hate murdering people, so murder will chase you. ⁷And I will make Mount Edom an empty ruin. And I will destroy everyone who goes in or comes out of it. ⁸I will fill its mountains with those who are killed. Those killed in war will fall on your hills. They will fall in your valleys and in all your ravines. ⁹I will make you a ruin for ever. No one will live in your cities. Then you will know that I am the Lord.

¹⁰" 'You said, "These two nations, Israel and Judah, and these two lands

will be ours. We will take them for our own." But the Lord was there. ¹¹So this is what the Lord God says: As surely as I live, this is true. I will treat you just as you treated them. When you were angry and jealous, you acted hatefully against them. I will punish you. And that is how I will show the Israelites who I am. ¹²Then you will know that I, the Lord God, have heard all your insults. Those insults were against the mountains of Israel. You said, "They have been ruined. They have been given to us to eat." ¹³You have not stopped your proud talk against me. I have heard you. ¹⁴This is what the Lord God says: All the earth will be happy when I make you an empty ruin. ¹⁵You were happy when the land of Israel was ruined. But I will do the same thing to you. Mount Edom and all Edom, you will become an empty ruin. Then you will know that I am the Lord God'."

Israel to Come Home

36 "Human being, prophesy*d* to the mountains of Israel and say: 'Mountains of Israel, hear the word of the Lord. ²This is what the Lord God says: The enemy has said this against you: "Now the old places to worship false gods have become ours." ' ³So prophesy and say: 'This is what the Lord God says: They have made you an empty ruin. They have crushed you from all around. You belonged to the other nations. People talked and whispered against you. ⁴So, mountains of Israel, hear the word of the Lord God. The Lord God speaks to the mountains, hills, ravines and valleys. And he speaks to the empty ruins and abandoned cities that have been robbed and laughed at by the other nations. ⁵This is what the Lord God says: I have spoken in hot anger against the other nations. I have spoken against Edom. The Edomites took my land for themselves. They did this with joy and with hate in their hearts. They forced out the people and took their pastureland'. ⁶So prophesy about the land of Israel. Say to the mountains, hills, ravines and valleys: 'This is what the Lord God says: I speak in my jealous anger. This is because you have suffered the insults of the nations. ⁷So this is what the Lord God says: I promise that the nations around you will also have to suffer insults.

⁸" 'But you, mountains of Israel, you will grow branches and fruit for my people. My people will soon come home. ⁹I am concerned about you. I am for you. You will be ploughed, and seed will be planted in you. ¹⁰I will multiply the people who live on you. All the people of Israel will come. The cities will have people living in them. The ruins will be rebuilt. ¹¹I will make the people and animals living on you increase in number. They will grow and be fruitful. You will have people living on you as you did before. I will make you better off than at the beginning. Then you will know that I am the Lord. ¹²I will cause my people Israel to walk on you. Then they will take you, and you will belong to them. You will never again take their children away from them.

¹³" 'This is what the Lord God says: People say about you: "You eat people and take children from your nation." ¹⁴You will not destroy people any more. You will not make your nation stumble any more, says the Lord God. ¹⁵I will not make you listen to insults from the nations any more. You will not suffer shame from them any more, says the Lord God'."

The Lord Acts for Himself

¹⁶The Lord spoke his word to me again. He said: ¹⁷"Human being, the nation of Israel were living in their own land. But they made it unclean*d* by their ways and the things they did. Their ways were like a woman's uncleanness in her time of monthly

bleeding. ¹⁸So I poured out my anger against them. I did it because of the murders they did in the land. And I did it because they made the land unclean with their idols. ¹⁹I scattered them among the nations. And they were spread through all the countries. I punished them for how they lived and the things they did. ²⁰They dishonoured my holy name in the nations where they went. The nations said about them: 'These are the people of the Lord. But they had to leave the land which he gave them'. ²¹But I felt bad about my holy name. The nation of Israel had dishonoured it among the nations where they went.

²²"So say to the people of Israel, 'This is what the Lord God says: Israel, I am going to act, but not for your sake. Israel, I will do something to help my holy name. You have dishonoured it among the nations where you went. ²³I will prove the holiness of my great name. It has been dishonoured among the nations. You have dishonoured it among these nations. But the nations will know that I am the Lord. I will prove myself holy before their eyes, says the Lord God.

²⁴" 'I will take you from the nations. I will gather you out of all the lands. And I will bring you back into your own land. ²⁵Then I will sprinkle clean water on you, and you will be clean. I will cleanse you from all your uncleanness and your idols. ²⁶Also, I will teach you to respect me completely. I will put a new way to think inside you. I will take out the stubborn heart like stone from your bodies. And I will give you an obedient heart of flesh. ²⁷I will put my Spirit*d* inside you. And I will help you to live by my rules. You will be careful to obey my laws. ²⁸Then you will live in the land I gave to your ancestors. So you will be my people, and I will be your God. ²⁹Also, I will save you from all your uncleanness. I will command the grain to come and grow. I will not allow a time of hunger

to hurt you. [30]I will multiply the harvest of the field. You will never again suffer shame among the nations because of hunger. [31]And you will remember your evil ways and the things you did that were not good. Then you will hate yourselves because of your sins and terrible acts that I hate. [32]I want you to know that I am not doing this for your sake, says the Lord God. Be ashamed and embarrassed about your ways, Israel.

[33]" 'This is what the Lord God says: This is what will happen on the day I cleanse you from all your sins: I will cause the cities to have people living in them again. And the destroyed places will be rebuilt. [34]The empty land will be ploughed. It will no longer be a ruin for everyone who passes by to see. [35]They will say: "This land was ruined. Now it has become like the garden of Eden. The cities were destroyed. They were empty and ruined. But now they are protected and have people living in them." [36]Then those nations still around you will know. They will know that I, the Lord, have rebuilt what was destroyed. And I have planted what was empty. I, the Lord, have spoken. And I will do it'.

[37]"This is what the Lord God says: I will again be asked by the people of Israel to do this thing for them. I will make their people grow to be as many as a flock of sheep. [38]They will be like the flocks brought to Jerusalem during her holy feasts. Her ruined cities will be filled with flocks of people. Then they will know that I am the Lord."

The Vision of Dry Bones

37 I felt the power of the Lord was on me. He brought me out by the Spirit[d] of the Lord. And he put me down in the middle of a valley. It was full of bones. [2]The Lord led me around among the bones. There were many bones on the bottom of the valley. I saw the bones were very dry. [3]Then he asked me, "Human being, can these bones live?"

I answered, "Lord God, only you know."

[4]The Lord said to me, "Prophesy[d] to these bones. Say to them, 'Dry bones, hear the word of the Lord. [5]This is what the Lord God says to the bones: I will cause breath to enter you. Then you will live. [6]I will put muscles on you. I will put flesh on you. I will cover you with skin. Then I will put breath in you, and you will live. Then you will know that I am the Lord'."

[7]So I prophesied as I was commanded. While I prophesied, there was a noise and a rattling. The bones came together, bone to bone. [8]I looked and saw muscles come on the bones. Flesh grew, and skin covered the bones. But there was no breath in them.

[9]Then the Lord said to me, "Prophesy to the wind.[n] Prophesy, human being, and say to the wind: 'This is what the Lord God says: Wind, come from the four winds. Breathe on these people who were killed so they can live again'." [10]So I prophesied as the Lord commanded me. And the breath came into them, and they came to life. They stood on their feet. They were a very large army.

[11]Then the Lord said to me: "Human being, these bones are like all the people of Israel. They say, 'Our bones are dried up, and our hope has gone. We are destroyed'. [12]So, prophesy, and say to them: 'This is what the Lord God says: My people, I will open your graves. And I will cause you to come up out of your graves. Then I will bring you into the land of Israel. [13]This is how you, my people, will know that I am the Lord. I will open your graves and cause you to come up

---

wind This Hebrew word could also mean "breath" or "spirit".

from them. [14]And I will put my Spirit inside you. You will come to life. Then I will put you in your own land. And you will know that I, the Lord, have spoken and done it, says the Lord'."

Judah and Israel Back Together

[15]The Lord spoke his word to me. He said, [16]"Human being, take a stick of wood. Write on it, 'For Judah and all the Israelites with him'. Then take another stick of wood. Write on it, 'The stick of Ephraim, for Joseph and all the Israelites with him'. [17]Then join them together into one stick. Then they will be one in your hand.

[18]"Your people will say to you, 'Explain to us what you mean by this'. [19]Tell them, 'This is what the Lord God says: I will take the stick which is for Joseph and the tribes[d] of Israel with him. This stick is in the hand of Ephraim. Then I will put it with the stick of Judah. And I will make them into one stick. And they will be one in my hand'. [20]Hold the sticks of wood on which you wrote these names. Hold them in your hands so the people can see them. [21]Say to the people: 'This is what the Lord God says: I will take the people of Israel from among the nations where they have gone. I will gather them from all around. I will bring them into their own land. [22]I will make them one nation in the land, on the mountains of Israel. One king will rule all of them. They will never again be two nations. They will not be divided into two kingdoms any more. [23]They will not continue to make themselves unclean[d] by their idols, their statues of gods which I hate or their sins. But I will save them from all the ways they sin and turn against me. And I will make them clean. Then they will be my people. And I will be their God.

[24]" 'And my servant David will be their king. They will all have one shepherd. They will live by my rules and obey my laws. [25]They will live on the

land I gave to my servant Jacob. It is the land in which your ancestors lived. They will all live on the land for ever: they, their children and their grandchildren. David my servant will be their king for ever. [26]And I will make an agreement of peace with them. It will be an agreement that continues for ever. I will put them in their land. I will make them grow in number. Then I will put my Temple[d] among them for ever. [27]The place where I live will be with them. I will be their God, and they will be my people. [28]When my Temple is among them for ever, the nations will know that I, the Lord, make Israel holy'."

Prophecy Against Gog

38 The Lord spoke his word to me. He said: [2]"Human being, turn toward Gog of the land of Magog. He is the chief ruler of the nations of Meshech and Tubal. Prophesy[d] against him. [3]Say, 'The Lord God says this: I am against you, Gog, chief ruler of Meshech and Tubal. [4]I will turn you around. I will put hooks in your jaws. And I will bring you out with all your army, horses and horsemen. All of them will be finely dressed. They will be a large army with large and small shields. All of them will have swords. [5]Persia, Cush and Put will be with them. All of them will have shields and helmets. [6]There will also be Gomer with all its troops. And there will be the nation of Togarmah from the far north. It will have all its troops. There will be many other nations with you.

[7]" 'Be prepared. Be prepared, you and all the armies that have come together to make you their commander. [8]After many days you will be called for service. After many years you will come into a land that has been rebuilt from war. The people in the land will be gathered from many nations to the mountains of Israel. Those mountains were empty for a long time. These people were brought out from the na-

tions. They will all be living in safety. ⁹And you will go up like a storm. You will be like a cloud covering the land. It will be you, all your troops and many nations with you.

¹⁰"'This is what the Lord God says: At that time ideas will come into your mind. You will think up an evil plan. ¹¹You will say, "I will march against a land of towns without walls. I will attack those who are at rest and live in safety. All of them live without city walls. They have no gate bars or gates. ¹²I will capture valuable things and take good things. I will turn my power against the rebuilt ruins that now have people living in them. I will go against these people who have been gathered from the nations. They have become rich with farm animals and property. They live at the centre of the world." ¹³Sheba, Dedan and the traders of Tarshish, with all its villages, will say this to you: "Did you come to capture valuable things? Did you bring your troops together to take things? Did you bring them to carry away silver and gold? Did you bring them to take away farm animals and property?"'

¹⁴"So prophesy, human being, and say to Gog: 'This is what the Lord God says: Now that my people Israel are living in safety, you will know about it. ¹⁵You will come from your place in the far north. And many people will be with you. All of them will ride on horses. You will be a large group with a mighty army. ¹⁶You will come against my people Israel like a cloud that covers the land. This will happen in the days to come. I will bring you against my land, Gog; then the nations will know me. They will see me show my greatness by what I do through you.

¹⁷"'This is what the Lord God says: You are the one about whom I spoke in past days. I spoke through my servants the prophets of Israel. These prophets of Israel prophesied for

many years. They said that I would bring you against them. ¹⁸This is what will happen: on the day Gog comes against the land of Israel, my anger will become very great, says the Lord God. ¹⁹With jealousy and great anger I tell you this. At that time there will surely be a great earthquake in Israel. ²⁰The fish of the sea and the birds of the sky will shake with fear before me. The wild animals and everything that crawls on the ground will shake with fear. And all the people on the earth will shake with fear before me. Also the mountains will be thrown down. And the cliffs will fall. Every wall will fall to the ground. ²¹And I will call for a war against Gog on all my mountains, says the Lord God. Every man's sword will be against his brother. ²²I will punish Gog with disease and death. I will send a heavy rain, with hailstones and burning sulphur on Gog. I will send it on his army and on the many nations with him. ²³Then I will show how great I am. I will show my holiness. And I will make myself known to the many nations that watch. Then they will know that I am the Lord'.

The Death of Gog and His Army

39 "Human being, prophesy against Gog and say: 'This is what the Lord God says: I am against you, Gog, chief ruler of Meshech and Tubal. ²I will turn you around and lead you. I will bring you from the far north. I will send you to attack the mountains of Israel. ³I will knock your bow out of your left hand. I will throw down your arrows from your right hand. ⁴You will fall dead on the mountains of Israel. You, all your troops and the nations with you will fall dead. I will let you be food for every bird that eats meat and every wild animal. ⁵You will die in the country. I have spoken, says the Lord God. ⁶I will send fire on Magog and those who live

in safety in the coastal lands. Then they will know that I am the Lord.

7" 'And I will make myself known among my people Israel. I will not let myself be dishonoured any more. Then the nations will know that I am the Lord. They will know I am the Holy One in Israel. 8It is coming! It will happen, says the Lord God. The day I talked about is coming.

9" 'Then those who live in the cities of Israel will go out. They will make fires with the enemy's weapons and burn them. They will burn both large and small shields. They will burn bows and arrows, war clubs and spears. They will use the weapons to burn in their fires for seven years. 10They won't need to take wood from the field or chop firewood from the forests. This is because they will make fires with the weapons. They will take the valuable things of those who took their valuable things. They will grab the things of those who grabbed their things, says the Lord God.

11" 'On that day I will give Gog a place to be buried in Israel. It will be the Valley of the Travellers, east of the Dead Sea.d It will block the road for travellers. This is because Gog and all his army will be buried there. People will call it The Valley of Gog's Army.

12" 'The people of Israel will be burying them for seven months to make the land cleand again. 13All the people of the land will bury them. The people of Israel will be honoured on the day of my victory, says the Lord God.

14" 'They will choose men to work through the land to make it clean. With others they will bury Gog's soldiers still lying dead on the ground. After the seven months are finished, they will still search. 15They will go through the land. If one person sees a human bone, he will put a marker by it. The sign will stay there until the gravediggers come. They will bury

the bone in The Valley of Gog's Army. 16A city will be there named Hamonah. So they will make the land clean again'.

17"Human being, this is what the Lord God says: Speak to every kind of bird and wild animal: 'Come together, come! Come together from all around to my sacrifice. I will prepare it for you. It is a great sacrifice on the mountains of Israel. Then you can eat flesh and drink blood. 18You will eat the flesh of mighty men. You will drink the blood of the rulers of the earth. You will do it as people eat all the fat animals from Bashan: male sheep, lambs, goats and bulls. 19You will eat and drink from my sacrifice which I have made ready for you. So you will eat fat until you are full. You will drink blood until you are drunk. 20At my table you will eat until you are full of horses and riders and all kinds of soldiers', says the Lord God.

21"And I will show my greatness among the nations. All the nations will feel my power when I punish them. 22From that day on the people of Israel will know that I am the Lord their God. 23And the nations will know Israel was taken away captive because they turned against me. So I turned away from them. And I let their enemies defeat them. All of them died in war. 24I punished them for their uncleannessd and their sins. I turned away from them.

25"So this is what the Lord God says: Now I will bring the people of Jacob back from captivity. I will have mercy on the whole nation of Israel. I will not let them dishonour me. 26The people will forget their shame. And they will forget how they rejected me. They will live in safety on their own land. No one will make them afraid. 27I will bring the people back from other lands. I will gather them from the lands of their enemies. That is how I will show that I am holy through my people. And many nations will see that

I am holy. [28]Then my people will know that I am the Lord their God. This is because I sent them into captivity among the nations. But then I brought them back to their own land. And I didn't leave any behind. [29]I will not turn away from them any more. I will put my Spirit[d] into the people of Israel, says the Lord God."

The New Temple

40 It was the twenty-fifth year of our captivity. It was at the beginning of the year, on the tenth day of the month. It was in the fourteenth year after Jerusalem was defeated. On that same day I felt the power of the Lord. He brought me to Jerusalem. [2]In the visions of God he brought me into the land of Israel. He put me on a very high mountain. On the south of the mountain there were some buildings that looked like a city. [3]The Lord took me closer to the buildings. I saw a man who looked as if he were made of bronze. He was standing in the gateway. He had a cord made of linen and a stick in his hand, both for measuring. [4]The man said to me, "Human being, look with your eyes and hear with your ears. And pay attention to all that I will show you. That's why you have been brought here. Tell the people of Israel all that you see."

The East Gate

[5]I saw a wall that surrounded the Temple.[d] The measuring stick in the man's hand was 3.5 metres long. So the man measured the wall. It was 3.5 metres thick and 3.5 metres high.

[6]Then the man went to the east gate. He went up its steps and measured the opening of the gate. It was more than 3.5 metres wide. [7]There were rooms for the guards. They were 3.5 metres long and 3.5 metres wide. The walls that came out between the guards' rooms were about

3 metres thick. And there was a gate next to the porch that faced the Temple. The opening of this gate was 3.5 metres wide.

[8]Then the man measured the porch of the gate. [9]It was about 4.5 metres deep. And its doors were 1.2 metres thick. The porch of the gate faced the Temple.

[10]There were three little rooms on each side of the last gate. These three rooms measured the same on each side. The walls between each room were the same thickness. [11]The man measured the width of the entrance to the gateway. It was 5 metres wide. The length of the gate was about 6.5 metres. [12]And there was a low wall about 0.5 metre high in front of each room. The rooms were 3.5 metres on each side. [13]The man measured the gateway from the roof of one room to the roof of the opposite room. It was about 12.5 metres from one door to the opposite door. [14]The man also measured the porch. It was about 30 metres wide. The courtyard was around the porch. [15]From the front of the outer side of the gate to the front of the porch of the inner side of the gate was 25 metres. [16]The rooms and porch had small windows on all sides. The windows were narrower on the side facing the gateway. Carvings of palm trees were on each inner wall of the rooms.

The Outer Courtyard

[17]Then the man brought me into the outer courtyard. I saw rooms and a pavement of stones. Thirty rooms were along the edge of the paved walkway. [18]The pavement ran alongside the gates. It was as long as the gates were wide. This was the lower pavement. [19]Then the man measured from the outer wall to the inner wall. The outer court between these two walls was 50 metres on the east and on the north.

The North Gate

20The man measured the length and width of the gate leading to the outer courtyard. It faced north. 21It had three rooms on each side. Its inner walls and its porch measured the same as the first gate. It was 25 metres long. And it was 12.5 metres wide. 22Its windows, porch and carvings of palm trees measured the same as the east gate. Seven steps went up to the gate. And the gate's porch was opposite them. 23The inner courtyard had a gate across from the northern gate like the one on the east. The man measured it and found it was 50 metres from inner gate to outer gate.

The South Gate

24Then the man led me south. I saw a gate facing south. He measured its inner walls and its porch. They measured the same as the other gates. 25The gate and its porch had windows all around like the other gates. It was 25 metres long and 12.5 metres wide. 26Seven steps went up to this gate. Its porch was in front of them. It had carvings of palm trees on its inner walls. 27A gate was on the south side of the inner courtyard. The man measured from gate to gate on the south side. It was 50 metres.

The Inner Courtyard

28Then the man brought me through the south gate to the inner courtyard. The inner south gate measured the same as the gates in the outer wall. 29The inner south gate's rooms, inner walls and porch measured the same as the gates in the outer wall. There were windows all around the gate and its porch. The gate was 25 metres long and 12.5 metres wide. 30Each porch of each inner gate was about 12.5 metres long and about 2.5 metres wide. 31The inner south gate's porch faced the outer courtyard. Carvings of palm trees were on its in-

side walls. Its stairway had eight steps.

32The man brought me into the inner courtyard on the east side. He measured the inner east gate. It measured the same as the other gates. 33The inner east gate's rooms, inside walls and porch measured the same as the other gates. Windows were all around the gate and its porch. The inner east gate was 25 metres long and 12.5 metres wide. 34Its porch faced the outer courtyard. Carvings of palm trees were on its inner walls on each side. Its stairway had eight steps.

35Then the man brought me to the inner north gate. He measured it. It measured the same as the other gates. 36Its rooms, inner walls and porch measured the same as the other gates. Windows were all around the gate. It was 25 metres long and 12.5 metres wide. 37Its porch faced the outer courtyard. Carvings of palm trees were on its inner walls on each side. And its stairway had eight steps.

Rooms for Preparing Sacrifices

38There was a room with a door that opened onto the porch of the inner north gate. In this room the priests washed animals for the burnt offerings. 39There were two tables on each side of the room. Animals for burnt offerings, sin offerings and penalty offerings were killed on these tables. 40On each side of the porch, outside the door to the room, were two tables. 41So four tables were on one side of the gate. And four tables were on the other side of the gate. In all there were eight tables on which the priests killed animals for sacrifices. 42There were four tables of cut stone for the burnt offering. These tables were about 1 metre long and 1 metre wide. And they were about 0.6 metre high. On these tables the priests put their tools. They used the tools to kill animals for burnt offerings and the other sacrifices. 43Double hooks 0.1 metre long were put up on all the walls. The flesh for the offering was put on the tables.

The Priests' Rooms

⁴⁴There were two rooms in the inner courtyard. One was beside the north gate. It faced south. The other room was beside the south gate. It faced north. ⁴⁵The man said to me, "The room which faces the south is for the priests. They serve in the Temple.ᵈ ⁴⁶And the room that faces north is for the priests who serve at the altar. These priests are descendantsᵈ of Zadok. They are the only descendants of Levi who can come near the Lord to serve him."

⁴⁷The man measured the Temple courtyard. It was a perfect square. It was 50 metres long and wide. The altar was in front of the Temple.

The Temple Porch

⁴⁸The man brought me to the porch of the Temple.ᵈ And he measured each wall of the porch. It was about 2.5 metres on each side. The gate was 7 metres wide. The walls of the gate were about 1.5 metres on each side. ⁴⁹The porch was 10 metres long and 6 metres wide. Ten steps went up to the porch. Pillars were by the walls, one on each side of the entrance.

The Holy Place of the Temple

41 The man brought me to the Holy Place. He measured its walls. They were 3.5 metres wide on each side. ²The entrance was 5 metres wide. The walls alongside the entrance were about 2.5 metres wide on each side. The man measured the Holy Place. It was 20 metres long and 10 metres wide.

³Then the man went inside. And he measured the walls of the doorway. Each was 1 metre wide. The doorway was 3 metres wide. The walls next to

it were more than 3.5 metres thick. ⁴Then the man measured the room at the end of the Holy Place. It was 10 metres long and 10 metres wide. The man said to me, "This is the Most Holy Place."

⁵Then the man measured the wall of the Temple.ᵈ It was 3.5 metres wide. The side rooms were 2 metres wide all around the Temple. ⁶The side rooms were on three different storeys, each above the other. There were 30 rooms on each storey. The side rooms had ledges on the wall all around. The rooms rested on the ledges but were not attached to the walls. ⁷The side rooms around the Temple were wider on each higher storey. So rooms were wider on the top storey. A stairway went up from the lowest storey to the highest through the middle storey.

⁸I also saw that the Temple had a raised base all around. It was the foundation for the side rooms and was 3.5 metres thick. ⁹The outer wall of the side rooms was about 2.5 metres thick. There was an open area between the side rooms of the Temple ¹⁰and the priests' rooms. It was 10 metres wide and went all around the Temple. ¹¹The doors of the side rooms led to a paved base around the outside of the Temple. One door faced north. And the other door faced south. The paved base was about 2.5 metres wide all around.

¹²There was a building facing the Temple courtyard at the west side. It was 35 metres wide. The wall of the building was about 2.5 metres thick all around. It was 45 metres long. ¹³Then the man measured the Temple. The Temple was 50 metres long. This included the courtyard with the building and its walls. It was all 50 metres long. ¹⁴Also the eastern front of the Temple and its courtyard was 50 metres wide.

¹⁵The man measured the length of

the building facing the courtyard on the west side, including its side rooms. Its walls from one side to the other were 50 metres.

The Holy Place, the Most Holy Place and the porch of the courtyard [16]had wood panels on the walls. By the doorway, the Temple had wood panels on the walls. The wood covered all the walls from the floor up to the windows. The windows were covered with crossed strips of wood.

[17]In the space above the entrance to the Most Holy Place there were carvings. And on the outside and all the walls around the Most Holy Place and the Holy Place were carvings. [18]The carvings were of creatures with wings and palm trees. A palm tree was between each carved creature. Every creature had two faces. [19]One was a man's face looking toward the palm tree on one side. The other was a lion's face looking toward the palm tree on the other side. They were carved all around the Temple wall. [20]This was from the floor to above the door. Palm trees and creatures with wings were carved on all the walls of the Holy Place. [21]The walls of the Holy Place were square. In front of the Most Holy Place was something that looked like [22]an altar of wood. It was more than 1.5 metres high and 1 metre wide. Its corners, base and sides were wood. The man said to me, "This is the table that is in the presence of the Lord." [23]Both the Holy Place and the Most Holy Place had double doors. [24]Each of the doors had two pieces that would swing open. [25]Palm trees and creatures with wings were also carved on the doors of the Holy Place. They were like those carved on the walls. And there was a wooden roof on the front Temple porch. [26]There were windows and palm trees on both side walls of the porch. The side rooms of the Temple were also covered by a roof.

The Priests' Room

42 Then the man led me north out into the outer courtyard. He led me to the rooms across from the Temple[d] courtyard. The outer wall was north of these rooms. [2]The building on the north side was 50 metres long and 25 metres wide. [3]There was 10 metres of the Temple courtyard between this building and the Temple. On the other side, this building faced the stone pavement of the outer courtyard. The building had rooms and balconies on three storeys. [4]There was a hallway on the north side of the rooms. It was 5 metres wide and 50 metres long. Doors led into the rooms from this hallway. [5]The top rooms were narrower. This was because the balconies took more space from them. The rooms on the first and second storeys of the building were wider. [6]The rooms were on three storeys. They did not have pillars like the pillars of the courtyards. So the top rooms were farther back than those on the first and second storeys. [7]There was a wall outside parallel to the rooms and to the outer courtyard. It ran in front of the rooms for 25 metres. [8]The row of rooms along the outer courtyard was 25 metres long. The rooms that faced the Temple were about 50 metres long. [9]The lower rooms had an entrance on the east end of the building. This was so a person could enter them from the courtyard.

[10]There were rooms on the south side, parallel to the wall of the outer courtyard. They faced the Temple courtyard. [11]These rooms had a hallway in front of them. They were like the rooms on the north. They had the same length and width. And the doors were the same. [12]The doors of the south rooms were like the doors of the north rooms. There was a door at the east end of a hall. This hall went to all the rooms.

[13]The man said to me, "The north and south rooms across from the Temple courtyard are holy rooms. There the priests who go near the Lord will eat the most holy offerings. There they will put the most holy offerings: the grain offerings, sin offerings and the penalty offerings. [14]The priests who enter the Holy Place must leave their serving clothes there. Then they may go into the outer courtyard. This is because these clothes are holy. The priests must put on other clothes. Then they may go to the part of the Temple which is for the people."

The Outside of the Temple

[15]The man finished measuring inside the Temple.[d] Then he brought me out through the east gate. He measured the area all around. [16]The man measured the east side with the measuring stick. It was 250 metres by the measuring stick. [17]He measured the north side. It was 250 metres by the measuring stick. [18]He measured the south side. It was 250 metres by the measuring stick. [19]He went around to the west side. And it measured 250 metres by the measuring stick. [20]So he measured the Temple on all four sides. The Temple had a wall all around it. It was 250 metres long and 250 metres wide. It separated the holy from that which is not holy.

The Lord Among His People

43 The man led me to the outer east gate. [2]And I saw the greatness of the God of Israel coming from the east. God's voice was like the roar of rushing water. His greatness made the earth shine. [3]I saw a vision. It was like the vision I had seen when the Lord came to destroy the city. It was also like the vision I had seen by the Kebar River. I bowed face down on the ground. [4]The greatness of the Lord came into the Temple[d] through the east gate.

[5]Then the Spirit[d] picked me up. And he brought me into the inner courtyard. There the Lord's greatness filled the Temple. [6]The man stood at my side. I heard someone speaking to me from inside the Temple. [7]The voice from the Temple said to me, "Human being, this is my throne. And this is the place my feet rest. I will live here among the Israelites for ever. The people of Israel will not make my holy name unclean[d] again. Neither the people nor their kings will make it unclean by their sexual sins. Nor will they make it unclean with the dead bodies of their kings. [8]They made my name unclean by putting their doorway next to my doorway. And they put their doorpost next to my doorpost. Only a wall separated me from them. When they did their acts that I hate, they made my holy name unclean. So I destroyed them in my anger. [9]Now let them stop their sexual sins. And let them take the dead bodies of their kings far away from me. Then I will live among them for ever.

[10]"Human being, tell the people of Israel about the Temple. Then they will be ashamed of their sins. Let them think about the plan of the Temple. [11]Then they will be ashamed of all they have done. Let them know the design of the Temple. Let them know how it is built. Show them its exits and entrances. Show them all its designs, all its rules and all its teachings. And write the rules as they watch. Do this so they can obey all the Temple's teachings and rules. [12]This is the teaching of the Temple: all the area around the top of the mountain is most holy. This is the teaching of the Temple.

The Altar

[13]"And these are the measurements of the altar, using the measuring stick. It is 56 centimetres long. The altar's

base is 56 centimetres high and 56 centimetres long. Its rim is about 24 centimetres around its edge. And the altar is this tall: ¹⁴from the ground up to the lower ledge, it measures 1 metre. It is 56 centimetres wide. It measures 2 metres from the smaller ledge to the larger ledge and is 56 centimetres wide. ¹⁵The place where the sacrifice is burned on the altar is 2 metres high. The four corners are shaped like horns and reach up above it. ¹⁶It is square. It is 6 metres long and 6 metres wide. ¹⁷The upper ledge is also square, 7 metres long and 7 metres wide. The border around it is 25 centimetres wide. Its base is 56 centimetres around. Its steps are on the east."

¹⁸Then the man said to me, "Human being, this is what the Lord God says: These are the rules for the altar. When it is built, use these rules to offer burnt offerings and sprinkle blood on it. ¹⁹You must give a young bull as a sin offering to the priests. These priests are the Levites from the family of Zadok. They come near me to serve me, says the Lord God. ²⁰Take some of the bull's blood and put it on the altar's four corners. Put it also on the four corners of the ledge. And put it on the border all around. This is how you will make the altar pure and ready for God's service. ²¹Then take the bull for the sin offering and burn it in the proper place in the Templeᵈ area. It will be outside the Holy Place.

²²"On the second day offer a male goat. It must have nothing wrong with it. It will be for a sin offering. The priests will make the altar pure and ready for God's service. They will do it the same way they did with the young bull. ²³When you have finished making the altar pure and ready, offer a young bull and a male sheep from the flock. They must also have nothing wrong with them. ²⁴You must offer them before the Lord. The priests will throw salt on them.

Then they will offer them as a burnt offering to the Lord.

²⁵"You must prepare a goat every day for seven days as a sin offering. Also, you must prepare a young bull and male sheep from the flock. They must have nothing wrong with them. ²⁶For seven days the priests will make the altar pure and ready for God's service. Then the priests will give the altar to God. ²⁷After these seven days, on the eighth day, the priests must present your offerings. They must offer your burnt offerings and your fellowship offerings on the altar. Then I will accept you, says the Lord God."

The Outer East Gate

44 Then the man brought me back to the outer east gate of the Templeᵈ area. The gate was shut. ²The Lord said to me, "This gate will stay shut. It will not be opened. No one may enter through it. This is because the Lord God of Israel has entered through it. So it must stay shut. ³Only the ruler himself may sit in the gateway to eat bread before the Lord. He must enter through the porch of the gateway and go out the same way."

⁴Then the man brought me through the outer north gate. He brought me to the front of the Temple. I looked and saw the greatness of the Lord. It was filling the Temple of the Lord. I bowed face down on the ground.

⁵The Lord said to me, "Human being, pay attention. See this with your eyes. And hear this with your ears. See and hear everything I tell you about all the rules and teachings of the Temple of the Lord. Pay attention to the entrance to the Temple and to all the exits from the Temple area. ⁶Then speak to those who refuse to obey. Say to the people of Israel, 'This is what the Lord God says: Stop doing all your acts that I hate, Israel! ⁷You brought foreigners into my Holy Place. They were not circumcisedᵈ in the flesh. They had not given them-

selves to serving me. You dishonoured my Temple when you offered me food, fat and blood. You broke my agreement by all your ways that I hate. [8]And you have not taken care of my holy things. You put foreigners in charge of my Temple. [9]This is what the Lord God says: Foreigners who are not circumcised in flesh and who do not give themselves to serving me may not enter my Temple. Even a foreigner living among the people of Israel may not enter.

[10]" 'Some Levites stopped obeying me when Israel left me and followed their idols. These Levites must be punished for their sin. [11]These Levites are to be servants in my Holy Place. They may guard the gates of the Temple. They may serve in the Temple. They may kill the animals for the burnt offering and the sacrifices for the people. They may stand before the people to serve them. [12]But these Levites helped the people worship their idols and caused the people of Israel to fall. So I have made this promise: they will be punished for their sin, says the Lord God. [13]They will not come near me to serve as priests. They will not come near any of my holy things or the most holy offerings. But they will be ashamed of the things they did that I hate. [14]But I will make them take care of the Temple. They will take care of everything that must be done in it.

[15]" 'But this is not true for priests who are Levites and descendants[d] of Zadok. They took care of my Holy Place when Israel left me. They may come near to serve me. They may stand in my presence. They will offer me the fat and blood of the animals they sacrifice, says the Lord God. [16]They are the only ones who may enter my Holy Place. They may come near my table to serve me. They may take care of the things I gave them.

[17]" 'When they enter the gates of the inner courtyard, they must wear linen robes. They must not wear wool to serve at the gates of the inner courtyard or in the Temple. [18]They will wear linen turbans on their heads and linen underclothes. They will not wear anything that makes them perspire. [19]At times they will go out into the outer courtyard to the people. But before they go, they must take off their serving clothes. They must put these clothes away in the holy rooms. And they must put on other clothes. Then they will not let their holy clothes hurt the people.

[20]" 'They must not shave their heads or let their hair grow long. They must keep the hair of their heads trimmed. [21]None of the priests may drink wine when they enter the inner courtyard. [22]The priests must not marry a widow or a divorced woman. They may marry only virgins[d] from the people of Israel. Or they may marry a widow of a priest. [23]They must teach my people the difference between what is holy and what is not holy. They must help my people know what is unclean[d] and what is clean.

[24]" 'In court they will act as judges. When they judge, they will follow my teachings. They must obey my laws and my rules at all my special feasts. They must keep my Sabbaths[d] holy.

[25]" 'They must not go near a dead person, making themselves unclean.[d] But they are allowed to make themselves unclean if the dead person is a relative. It might be his father, mother, son, daughter, brother or a sister who has not married. [26]After the priest has been made clean again, he must wait seven days. [27]Then he may go into the inner courtyard to serve in the Temple. But he must offer a sin offering for himself, says the Lord God.

[28]" 'These are the rules about the priests and their property: they will have me instead of property. You will not give them any land to own in Israel. I am what they will own. [29]They

will eat the grain offerings, sin offerings and penalty offerings. Everything Israel offers will be theirs. [30]And the best fruits of all the first harvests will be for the priests. And they will have all the special gifts offered to me. You will also give to the priests the first part of your grain that you grind. This will cause a blessing to come on your house. [31]The priests must not eat any bird or animal that died a natural death. And they must not eat one that has been torn by wild animals.

The Land Is Divided

45 " 'Divide the land for the Israelite tribes[d] by throwing lots.[d] At that time you will give a part of the land to belong to the Lord. It will be about 11 kilometres long and about 10 kilometres wide. All of this land will be holy. [2]An area of 250 metres square will be for the Temple.[d] There will be an open space around the Temple that is 25 metres wide. [3]In the holy area you will measure a part about 11 kilometres long and 5 kilometres wide. The Most Holy Place will be in this holy area. [4]This holy part of the land will be for the priests who serve in the Temple. This is where they come near to serve the Lord. It will be a place for the priests' houses. And it will be the place for the Temple. [5]Another area will be about 11 kilometres long and more than 5 kilometres wide. It will be for the Levites, who serve in the Temple. It will belong to them so they will have cities in which to live.

[6]'And you will give the city an area that is about 2.5 kilometres wide and about 11 kilometres long. It will be along the side of the holy area. It will belong to all the people of Israel.

[7]" 'The ruler will have land on both sides of the holy area and the city. On the west of the holy area, his land will reach to the Mediterranean Sea. On the east of the holy area, his land will reach to the eastern border. It will be as long as the land given to each tribe. [8]This land will be the ruler's property in Israel. So my rulers will not be cruel to my people any more. But they will give land to each tribe in the nation of Israel.

[9]" 'This is what the Lord God says: You have gone far enough, you rulers of Israel! Stop being cruel and hurting people. Do what is right and fair. Stop forcing my people out of their homes, says the Lord God. [10]You must have honest scales, an honest dry measurement and an honest liquid measurement. [11]The dry measure and the liquid measure will be the same: the liquid measure will always be a tenth of a homer.[n] The ephah will always be a tenth of a homer. The measurement they follow will be the homer. [12]The shekel[n] will be worth 20 gerahs. A mina will be worth 60 shekels.

Offerings and Holy Days

[13]" 'This is the gift you will offer: a sixth of an ephah from a homer of wheat; a sixth of an ephah from a homer of barley. [14]The amount of oil you are to offer is a tenth of a bath from each cor. (Ten baths make a homer and also make a cor.) [15]You should give one sheep from each flock of 200 from the watering places of Israel. They are to be offered with the grain offerings, burnt offerings and fellowship offerings. These offerings are to remove sins so you will belong to God, says the Lord God. [16]All people in the land will give this special offering for the ruler of Israel. [17]It will be the ruler's responsibility to supply the burnt offerings, grain offerings and drink offerings. These offerings will be given at the feasts and at the New

---

homer The Hebrew word means "donkey-load". It measured about 180 litres or 175 liquid litres. So an ephah was about 22 litres. And a bath was about 18 litres.
shekel In Ezekiel's time a shekel weighed about 11.5 grams.

Moons.[d] They will also be given on the Sabbaths[d] and at all the other feasts of Israel. The ruler will supply the sin offerings, grain offerings and fellowship offerings. These offerings are to pay for the sins of Israel.

18" 'This is what the Lord God says: On the first day of the first month take a young bull that has nothing wrong with it. Use it to make the Temple[d] pure and ready for God's service. 19The priest will take some of the blood from the sin offering. And he will put it on the doorposts of the Temple. He will put it on the four corners of the ledge of the altar. And he will put it on the posts of the gate of the inner courtyard. 20You will do the same thing on the seventh day of the month. You will do it for anyone who has sinned by accident or without knowing it. This is how you make the Temple pure and ready for God's service.

Passover Feast Offerings

21" 'On the fourteenth day of the first month you will celebrate the Feast[d] of Passover. It will be a feast of seven days when you eat bread made without yeast. 22On that day the ruler must offer a bull for himself and for all the people of the land. The bull will be a sin offering. 23During the seven days of the feast the ruler must offer seven bulls. And he must offer seven male sheep. The bulls and sheep must have nothing wrong with them. They will be burnt offerings to the Lord. The ruler will offer them every day of the seven days of the feast. He must also offer a male goat every day as a sin offering. 24The ruler must give as a grain offering 22 litres for each bull and 22 litres for each sheep. He must give 4.5 litres of olive oil for every 22 litres.

25" 'Beginning on the fifteenth day of the seventh month, you will celebrate the Feast[d] of Shelters. During the feast, the ruler will do the same

things for seven days. He will supply the sin offering, burnt offering, grain offering and the olive oil.

Rules for Worship

46 " 'This is what the Lord God says: The east gate of the inner courtyard will be shut on the six working days. But it will be opened on the Sabbath[d] day. And it will be open on the day of the New Moon.[d] 2The ruler will enter through the porch of the gateway. He will enter from outside and stand by the gatepost. Then the priests will offer the ruler's burnt offering and fellowship offerings. The ruler will worship at the entrance of the gate. Then he will go out. But the gate will not be shut until evening. 3The people of the land will worship at the entrance of that gateway. They will worship there in the presence of the Lord on the Sabbaths and New Moons. 4This is the burnt offering the ruler will offer to the Lord on the Sabbath day. It will be six male lambs that have nothing wrong with them. And it will be a male sheep that has nothing wrong with it. 5He must give 22 litres of grain offering with the male sheep. But he can give as much grain offering with the lambs as he pleases. He must also give 4.5 litres of olive oil for 22 litres of grain. 6On the day of the New Moon he must offer a young bull. It must have nothing wrong with it. He must also offer six lambs and a male sheep. They also must have nothing wrong with them. 7The ruler must give 22 litres of grain offering with the bull. And he must give the same with the male sheep. With the lambs, he can give as much grain as he pleases. But he must give 4.5 litres of olive oil for 22 litres of grain. 8And when the ruler enters, he must go in through the porch of the gateway. He must go out the same way.

9" 'The people of the land must come before the Lord at the special feasts. Anyone who enters through the north gate to worship must go out through the south gate. Anyone who enters through the south gate must go out through the north gate. No one will return the same way he entered. Each person will go out straight ahead. 10When the people go in, the ruler will go in with them. When they go out, the ruler will go out.

11" 'At the feasts and regular times of worship 22 litres of grain must be offered. It will be offered with a young bull. And 22 litres of grain must be offered with a male sheep. But with an offering of lambs, the ruler may give as much grain as he pleases. He should give 4.5 litres of olive oil for 22 litres of grain. 12The ruler may give an offering as a special gift to the Lord. It may be a burnt offering or fellowship offering. When he gives it to the Lord, the inner east gate will be opened for him. He must offer his burnt offering and his fellowship offerings as he does on the Sabbath*d* day. Then he will go out. After he has gone out, the gate will be shut.

13" 'Every morning you will give a year-old lamb that has nothing wrong with it. It will be for a burnt offering to the Lord every day. 14Also, you must offer a grain offering with the lamb every morning. With it you will give three and a third litres of grain and one and a third litres of olive oil. This is to make the fine flour moist. It will be a grain offering to the Lord. This is a rule that must be kept from now on. 15So they must always give the lamb, the grain offering and the olive oil every morning as a burnt offering.

Rules for the Ruler

16" 'This is what the Lord God says: The ruler might give a gift from his land to one of his sons. Then that land will belong to that son's children. It is their property from their family. 17But the ruler might give a gift from his land to one of his slaves. That land will be-

long to the slave only until the year of freedom. Then the land will go back to the ruler. Only the ruler's sons may keep a gift of land from the ruler. 18The ruler must not take any of the people's land. He must not force them out of their land. He must give his sons land from his own land. Then my people will not be scattered out of their own land'."

The Special Kitchens

19The man led me through the entrance at the side of the gateway. He led me to the priests' holy rooms that face north. There I saw a place at the west end. 20The man said to me, "This is where the priests will boil the meat of the penalty offering and sin offering. There the priests will bake the grain offering. Then they will not need to bring these offerings into the outer courtyard. That would hurt the people."

21Then the man brought me out to the outer courtyard. He led me to its four corners. In each corner of the courtyard was a smaller courtyard. 22Small courtyards were in the four corners of the courtyard. Each small courtyard was 23 metres long and 17 metres wide. All four corners measured the same. 23A stone wall was around each of the four small courtyards. Places for cooking were built in each of the stone walls. 24The man said to me, "These are the kitchens. The Temple*d* priests will boil the sacrifices for the people here."

The River from the Temple

47 The man led me back to the door of the Temple.*d* I saw water coming out from under the doorway that faces east. (The Temple faced east.) The water flowed down from the south end of the Temple. It was south of the altar. 2The man brought me out through the outer

north gate. And he led me around outside to the outer east gate. The water was coming out on the south side of the gate.

³The man went toward the east with a line in his hand. He measured about 460 metres. Then he led me through water that came up to my ankles. ⁴The man measured about 460 metres again. Then he led me through water that came up to my knees. Then he measured about 460 metres again. And he led me through water up to my waist. ⁵The man measured about 460 metres again. But it was now a river that I could not cross. The water had risen too high. It was deep enough for swimming. It was a river that no one could cross. ⁶The man asked me, "Human being, do you see this?"

Then the man led me back along the bank of the river. ⁷As I went back, I saw many trees on both sides of the water. ⁸The man said to me, "This water will flow toward the eastern areas. It will go down into the Jordan Valley. When the water enters the Dead Sea,ᵈ it will become fresh. ⁹And everywhere the river goes, there will be many animals and fish. Wherever this water goes the Dead Sea will become fresh. So where the river goes there will be many living things. ¹⁰Fishermen will stand by the sea. From En Gedi all the way to En Eglaim will become a place to spread fishing nets. There will be many kinds of fish in the Dead Sea. There will be as many kinds of fish as there are in the Mediterranean Sea. ¹¹But the swamps and marshes will not become fresh. They will be left for salt. ¹²All kinds of fruit trees will grow on both banks of the river. Their leaves will not dry and die. The trees will have fruit every month because the water for them comes from the Temple. The fruit from the trees will be for food. And their leaves will be for medicine."

Borders of the Land

¹³This is what the Lord God says: "These are the borders to divide the land among the 12 tribesᵈ of Israel. Joseph will have two parts of land. ¹⁴You will divide the land equally. I promised to give it to your ancestors. So this land will belong to you from your family.

¹⁵"This will be the border line of the land.

"On the north side it will start at the Mediterranean Sea. It will go by the Hethlon Road. This is where the road turns toward Lebo Hamath. And it will go to the cities of Zedad, ¹⁶Berothah and Sibraim. Sibraim is on the border between Damascus and Hamath. And it will go on to the city of Hazer Hatticon on the border of the country of Hauran. ¹⁷So the border line will go from the Mediterranean Sea east to the city of Hazar Enan. This is on the northern border of Damascus. And the country of Hamath will be on the north side of the border.

¹⁸"On the east side the border runs south from a point between Hauran and Damascus. It will go along the Jordan between Gilead and the land of Israel. It will continue to the city of Tamar on the Dead Sea.ᵈ This will be the east side of the land.

¹⁹"On the south side the border line will go east from Tamar. It will go all the way to the waters of Meribah Hadesh. Then it will run along the brook of Egypt to the Mediterranean Sea. This will be the south side of the land.

²⁰"On the west side the Mediterranean Sea will be the border line. It will go to a place across from Lebo Hamath. This will be the west side of your land.

²¹"So you will divide this land among the tribes of Israel. ²²You will divide it as a property for yourselves. And it will be for you and for the foreigners who live and have children among you. These foreigners will be like peo-

ple born in Israel. You will divide some land for them among the tribes of Israel. [23]In whatever tribe the foreigner lives, you will give him some land," says the Lord God.

Dividing the Land

48 "These are the names of the tribes.[d] Dan will have one share. It will begin at the northern border. It will go from the sea and over the Hethlon Road. It will follow the road to Lebo Hamath. It will go all the way to Hazar Enan. This is on the northern border of Damascus. It will stop there next to Hamath. This will be Dan's northern border from the east side to the Mediterranean Sea on the west side.

[2]"South of Dan's border, Asher will have one share. It will go from the east side to the west side.

[3]"South of Asher's border, Naphtali will have one share. It will go from the east side to the west side.

[4]"South of Naphtali's border, Manasseh will have one share. It will go from the east side to the west side.

[5]"South of Manasseh's border, Ephraim will have one share. It will go from the east side to the west side.

[6]"South of Ephraim's border, Reuben will have one share. It will go from the east side to the west side.

[7]"South of Reuben's border, Judah will have one share. It will go from the east side to the west side.

[8]"South of Judah's border will be the holy area which you are to give. It will be about 11 kilometres wide. It will be as long and wide as one of the tribes' shares. It will run from the east side to the west side. The Temple[d] will be in the middle of this area.

[9]"The share which you will give the Lord will be about 11 kilometres long and 5 kilometres wide. [10]The holy area will be divided among these people. For the priests on the north side, the land will measure about 11 kilometres. It will be 5 kilometres wide

on the west side and 5 kilometres wide on the east side. It will be about 11 kilometres on the south side. The Temple of the Lord will be in the middle of it. [11]This land is for the priests who are given to serve the Lord. They are the descendants[d] of Zadok who did my work. They did not leave me. The other Levites left me when Israel did. [12]This share from the holy portion of the land will be a gift for these priests. It will be next to the land of the Levites.

[13]"Alongside the land for the priests, the Levites will have a share. It will be about 11 kilometres long and 5 kilometres wide. Its full length will be about 11 kilometres. And its full width will be about 5 kilometres. [14]The Levites are not to sell or trade any of this land. They will not sell any of this best part of the land. It belongs to the Lord.

City Property

[15]"The rest of the land will be an area about 2.5 kilometres wide and 11 kilometres long. It will be for the other people's use. It will be for the city, for homes and for pastures. The city will be in the middle of it. [16]These are the city's measurements: the north side will be about 2 kilometres. The south side will be about 2 kilometres. The east side will be about 2 kilometres. And the west side will be about 2 kilometres. [17]The city's land for pastures will be about 145 metres on the north, 145 metres on the south, 145 metres on the east and 145 metres on the west. [18]Alongside the length of the holy area there will be left 5 kilometres on the east and 5 kilometres on the west. It will be used to grow food for the city workers. [19]The city workers will plough this land. The workers will be from all the tribes[d] of Israel. [20]This whole area will be square, 11 kilometres by 11 kilometres. You shall give to the Lord

the holy share along with the city property.

²¹"Land that is left over on both sides of the holy area and city property will belong to the ruler. That land will extend east of the holy area to the eastern border. And it will extend west of it to the Mediterranean Sea. Both of these areas run the length of the lands of the tribes. They belong to the ruler. The holy area with the Holy Place of the Temple*d* will be in the middle. ²²The Levites' land and the city property will be between the lands belonging to the ruler. The ruler's land will be between Judah's border and Benjamin's border.

The Other Tribes' Land

²³"Here is what the rest of the tribes will receive: Benjamin will have one share. It will go from the east side to the Mediterranean Sea on the west side.

²⁴"South of Benjamin's land, Simeon will have one share. It will go from the east side to the west side.

²⁵"South of Simeon's land, Issachar will have one share. It will go from the east side to the west side.

²⁶"South of Issachar's land, Zebulun will have one share. It will go from the east side to the west side.

²⁷"South of Zebulun's land, Gad will have one share. It will go from the east side to the west side.

²⁸"The southern border of Gad's land will go east from Tamar on the Dead Sea*d* to the waters of Meribah Kadesh. Then it will run along the brook of Egypt to the Mediterranean Sea.

²⁹"This is the land you will divide among the tribes of Israel. These are to be their shares," says the Lord God.

The Gates of the City

³⁰"These will be the outside borders of the city: The north side will measure more than 2 kilometres. ³¹There will be three gates facing north. They are Reuben's Gate, Judah's Gate and Levi's Gate. The city's gates will be named for the tribes*d* of Israel.

³²"The east side will measure more than 2 kilometres. There will be three gates facing east. They are Joseph's Gate, Benjamin's Gate and Dan's Gate.

³³"The south side will measure more than 2 kilometres. There will be three gates facing south. They are Simeon's Gate, Issachar's Gate and Zebulun's Gate.

³⁴"The west side will measure more than 2 kilometres. There will be three gates facing west. They are Gad's Gate, Asher's Gate and Naphtali's Gate.

³⁵"The city will measure about 12 kilometres around. From then on the name of the city will be The Lord God Is There."

DANIEL

The Life and Visions of Daniel

Daniel Taken to Babylon

1 Nebuchadnezzar king of Babylon came to Jerusalem and surrounded it with his army. This happened during the third year that Jehoiakim was king of Judah. ²The Lord allowed Nebuchadnezzar to capture Jehoiakim king of Judah. Nebuchadnezzar also took some of the things from the Temple*d* of God. He carried them to Babylonia and put them in the temple of his gods.

³Then King Nebuchadnezzar gave an order to Ashpenaz, his chief officer. He told Ashpenaz to bring some of the Israelite men into his house. He wanted them to be from important families. And he wanted those who were from the family of the king of Judah. ⁴King Nebuchadnezzar wanted only healthy, young, Israelite men. These men were not to have anything wrong with their bodies. They were to be handsome and well educated. They were to be able to learn and understand things. He wanted those who were able to serve in his palace. Ashpenaz was to teach them the language and writings of the Babylonians. ⁵The king gave the young men a certain amount of food and wine every day. That was the same kind of food that the king ate. They were to be trained for three years. Then the young men would become servants of the king of Babylon. ⁶Among those young men were some from the people of Judah. These were Daniel, Hananiah, Mishael and Azariah.

⁷Then Ashpenaz, the chief officer, gave them Babylonian names. Daniel's new name was Belteshazzar. Hananiah's was Shadrach. Mishael's was Meshach. And Azariah's new name was Abednego.

⁸Daniel decided not to eat the king's food and wine because that would make him unclean.*d* So he asked Ashpenaz for permission not to make himself unclean in this way.

⁹God made Ashpenaz want to be kind and merciful to Daniel. ¹⁰But Ashpenaz said to Daniel, "I am afraid of my master, the king. He ordered me to give you this food and drink. If you don't eat this food, you will begin to look worse than other young men your age. The king will see this. And he will cut off my head because of you."

¹¹Ashpenaz had ordered a guard to watch Daniel, Hananiah, Mishael and Azariah. ¹²Daniel said to the guard, "Please give us this test for ten days: don't give us anything but vegetables to eat and water to drink. ¹³Then after ten days compare us with the other young men who eat the king's food. See for yourself who looks healthier. Then you judge for yourself how you want to treat us, your servants."

¹⁴So the guard agreed to test them for ten days. ¹⁵After ten days they looked very healthy. They looked better than all of the young men who ate the king's food. ¹⁶So the guard took away the king's special food and wine. He gave Daniel, Hananiah, Mishael and Azariah vegetables instead.

¹⁷God gave these four men wisdom and the ability to learn. They learned many kinds of things people had written and studied. Daniel could also understand all kinds of visions and dreams.

¹⁸The end of the three years came. And Ashpenaz brought all of the

young men to King Nebuchadnezzar. [19]The king talked to them. He found that none of the young men were as good as Daniel, Hananiah, Mishael and Azariah. So those four young men became the king's servants. [20]Every time the king asked them about something important, they showed much wisdom and understanding. He found they were ten times better than all the fortune-tellers and magicians in his kingdom. [21]So Daniel continued to be the king's servant until the first year Cyrus was king.

Nebuchadnezzar's Dream

2 During Nebuchadnezzar's second year as king, he had some dreams. Those dreams bothered him, and he could not sleep. [2]So the king called for his fortune-tellers, magicians, wizards and wise men. The king wanted those men to tell him what he had dreamed. So they came in and stood in front of the king.

[3]Then the king said to them, "I had a dream that bothers me. I want to know what the dream means."

[4]Then the wise men answered the king in the Aramaic language. They said, "Our king, live for ever! We are your servants. Please tell us your dream. Then we will tell you what it means."

[5]Then King Nebuchadnezzar said to them, "No! You must tell me the dream. And then you must tell me what it means. If you don't do these things, I will have you torn apart. And I will turn your houses into piles of stones. [6]But if you tell me my dream and its meaning, I will reward you. I will give you gifts and great honour. So tell me the dream, and tell me what it means."

[7]Again the wise men said to the king, "Please, tell us the dream. And we will tell you what it means."

[8]King Nebuchadnezzar answered, "Now I know that you are trying to get more time. You know that I meant what I said. [9]If you don't tell me my dream, you will be punished. You have all agreed to tell me lies and wicked things. You are hoping things will change. Now, tell me the dream. Then I will know you can tell me what it really means!"

[10]The wise men answered the king. They said, "No one on earth can do what the king asks! Not even a great and powerful king has ever asked the fortune-tellers, magicians or wise men to do this. [11]The king is asking something that is too hard. Only the gods could tell the king this. But the gods do not live among people."

[12]When the king heard that, he became very angry. He gave an order for all the wise men of Babylon to be killed. [13]So King Nebuchadnezzar's order was announced. All the wise men were to be put to death. Men were sent to look for Daniel and his friends to kill them.

[14]Arioch was the commander of the king's guards. He was going to put to death the wise men of Babylon. But Daniel spoke to him with wisdom and skill. [15]Daniel asked, "Why did the king order such a terrible punishment?" Then Arioch explained everything to Daniel. [16]When Daniel heard the story, he went to King Nebuchadnezzar. Daniel asked him to give him some more time. Then he would tell the king what he had dreamed and what it meant.

[17]So Daniel went to his house. He explained the whole story to his friends Hananiah, Mishael and Azariah. [18]Daniel asked his friends to pray to the God of heaven. Daniel asked them to pray that God would show them mercy and help them understand this secret. Then Daniel and his friends would not be put to death with the other wise men of Babylon.

[19]During the night God explained the secret to Daniel in a vision. Then Daniel praised the God of heaven. [20]Daniel said:

"Praise God for ever and ever.
He has wisdom and power.
21He changes the times and seasons
of the year.
He takes away the power of
kings.
And he gives their power to
new kings.
He gives wisdom to people so
they become wise.
And he helps people learn and
know things.
22He makes known secrets that are
deep and hidden.
He knows what is hidden in
darkness,
and light lives with him.
23I thank you and praise you, God
of my ancestors.
You have given me wisdom and
power.
You told me what we asked of
you.
You told us about the king's
dream."

The Meaning of the Dream

24Then Daniel went to Arioch. King Nebuchadnezzar had chosen Arioch to put to death the wise men of Babylon. Daniel said to Arioch, "Don't put the wise men of Babylon to death. Take me to the king. I will tell him what his dream means."

25So very quickly Arioch took Daniel to the king. Arioch said to the king, "I have found a man among the captives from Judah. He can tell the king what his dream means."

26The king asked Daniel (also called Belteshazzar) a question. He asked, "Are you able to tell me what I dreamed and what it means?"

27Daniel answered, "No person can explain to the king the secret he has asked about. No wise man, magician or fortune-teller can do this. 28But there is a God in heaven who explains secret things. God has shown King Nebuchadnezzar what will happen at a later time. This is your dream. This is

the vision you saw while lying on your bed: 29my king, as you were lying there, you thought about things to come. God, who can tell people about secret things, showed you what is going to happen. 30God also told this secret to me. It is not because I have greater wisdom than other men. It is so that you, my king, may know what it means. In that way you will understand what went through your mind.

31"My king, in your dream you saw a large statue in front of you. It was huge, shiny and frightening. 32The head of the statue was made of pure gold. Its chest and arms were made of silver. Its middle and the upper part of its legs were made of bronze. 33The lower part of the legs were made of iron. Its feet were made partly of iron and partly of baked clay. 34While you were looking at the statue, you saw a rock cut free. But no human being touched the rock. It hit the statue on its feet of iron and clay and smashed them. 35Then the iron, clay, bronze, silver and gold broke to pieces at the same time. They became like chaff^d on a threshing^d floor in the summer time. The wind blew them away, and there was nothing left. Then the rock that hit the statue became a very large mountain. It filled the whole earth.

36"That was your dream. Now we will tell the king what it means. 37My king, you are the greatest king. God of heaven has given you a kingdom. He has given you power, strength and glory. 38God has given you power over people, wild animals and birds. Wherever they live, God has made you ruler over them all. King Nebuchadnezzar, you are the head of gold on that statue.

39"Another kingdom will come after you. But that kingdom will not be as great as yours. Next a third kingdom will rule over the earth. That is the bronze part. 40Then there will be a fourth kingdom, strong as iron. Iron crushes and smashes things to pieces.

In the same way the fourth kingdom will smash and crush all the other kingdoms.

41"You saw that the statue's feet and toes were partly baked clay and partly iron. That means the fourth kingdom will be a divided kingdom. It will have some of the strength of iron in it. As you saw, iron was mixed with clay. 42The toes of the statue were partly iron and partly clay. So the fourth kingdom will be partly strong like iron and partly breakable like clay. 43You saw the iron mixed with clay. But iron and clay don't mix completely together. In the same way the people of the fourth kingdom will be a mixture. Those people will not be united as one people.

44"During the time of those kings, the God of heaven will set up another kingdom. It will never be destroyed. And it will not be given to another group of people. This kingdom will crush all the other kingdoms. It will bring them to an end. But that kingdom itself will continue for ever.

45"King Nebuchadnezzar, you saw a rock cut from a mountain. But no human being touched it. The rock broke the iron, bronze, clay, silver and gold to pieces. In this way the great God showed you what will happen. The dream is true, and you can trust this explanation."

46Then King Nebuchadnezzar fell face down on the ground in front of Daniel. The king honoured him. He ordered that an offering and incense*d* be presented to Daniel. 47Then the king said to Daniel, "Truly I know your God is the greatest of all gods. And he is the Lord of all the kings. He tells people about things they cannot know. I know this is true. You were able to tell these secret things to me."

48Then the king gave Daniel an important position in his kingdom. And he gave many gifts to Daniel. Nebu-

chadnezzar made him ruler over the whole area of Babylon. And he put Daniel in charge of all the wise men of Babylon. 49Daniel asked the king to make Shadrach, Meshach and Abednego important leaders over the area of Babylon. And the king did as Daniel asked. Daniel himself became one of the important people who stayed at the royal court.

The Gold Idol and Blazing Furnace

3 Now King Nebuchadnezzar had a gold statue made. That statue was 27 metres high and 2.5 metres wide. He set up the statue on the plain of Dura in the area of Babylon. 2Then the king called the important leaders: the governors, assistant governors, captains of the soldiers, people who advised the king, keepers of the treasury, judges, rulers and all other officers in his kingdom. He wanted these men to come to the special service for the statue he had set up. 3So they all came for the special service. And they stood in front of the statue that King Nebuchadnezzar had set up. 4Then the man who made announcements for the king spoke in a loud voice. He said, "People, nations and men of every language, this is what you are commanded to do: 5you will hear the sound of the horns, flutes, lyres,*d* zithers,*n* harps, pipes and all the other musical instruments. When this happens, you must bow down and worship the gold statue. This is the one King Nebuchadnezzar has set up. 6Everyone must bow down and worship this gold statue. Anyone who doesn't will be quickly thrown into a blazing furnace."

7Now people, nations and men who spoke every language were there. And they heard the sound of the horns, flutes, lyres, zithers, pipes and all the other musical instruments. So

zithers Musical instruments with 30 to 40 strings.

they bowed down and worshipped the gold statue that King Nebuchadnezzar had set up.

[8]Then some Babylonians came up to the king. They began speaking against the men of Judah. [9]They said to King Nebuchadnezzar, "Our king, live for ever! [10]Our king, you gave a command. You said that everyone would hear the horns, lyres, zithers, harps, pipes and all the other musical instruments. Then they would have to bow down and worship the gold statue. [11]Anyone who wouldn't do this was to be thrown into a blazing furnace. [12]Our king, there are some men of Judah who did not pay attention to your order. You made them important officers in the area of Babylon. Their names are Shadrach, Meshach and Abednego. They do not serve your gods. And they do not worship the gold statue you have set up."

[13]Nebuchadnezzar became very angry. He called for Shadrach, Meshach and Abednego. So those men were brought to the king. [14]And Nebuchadnezzar said, "Shadrach, Meshach and Abednego, is it true that you do not serve my gods? And is it true that you did not worship the gold statue I have set up? [15]Now, you will hear the sound of the horns, flutes, lyres, zithers, harps, pipes and all the other musical instruments. And you must be ready to bow down and worship the statue I made. That will be good. But if you do not worship it, you will be thrown quickly into the blazing furnace. Then no god will be able to save you from my power!"

[16]Shadrach, Meshach and Abednego answered the king. They said, "Nebuchadnezzar, we do not need to defend ourselves to you. [17]You can throw us into the blazing furnace. The God we serve is able to save us from the furnace and your power. If he does this, it is good. [18]But even if God does not save us, we want you, our king, to know this: we will not serve your gods. We will not worship the gold statue you have set up."

[19]Then Nebuchadnezzar was furious with Shadrach, Meshach and Abednego. He ordered the furnace to be heated seven times hotter than usual. [20]Then he commanded some of the strongest soldiers in his army to tie up Shadrach, Meshach and Abednego. The king told the soldiers to throw them into the blazing furnace. [21]So Shadrach, Meshach and Abednego were tied up and thrown into the blazing furnace. They were still wearing their robes, trousers, turbans and other clothes. [22]The king was very angry when he gave the command. And the furnace was made very hot. The fire was so hot that the flames killed the strong soldiers who took Shadrach, Meshach and Abednego there. [23]Firmly tied, Shadrach, Meshach and Abednego fell into the blazing furnace.

[24]Then King Nebuchadnezzar was very surprised and jumped to his feet. He asked the men who advised him, "Didn't we tie up only three men? Didn't we throw them into the fire?" They answered, "Yes, our king." [25]The king said, "Look! I see four men. They are walking around in the fire. They are not tied up, and they are not burned. The fourth man looks like a son of the gods."

[26]Then Nebuchadnezzar went to the opening of the blazing furnace. He shouted, "Shadrach, Meshach and Abednego, come out! Servants of the Most High God, come here!"

So Shadrach, Meshach and Abednego came out of the fire. [27]When they came out, the princes, assistant governors, governors and royal advisers crowded around them. They saw that the fire had not harmed their bodies. Their hair was not burned. Their robes were not burned. And they didn't even smell of smoke.

[28]Then Nebuchadnezzar said, "Praise the God of Shadrach, Meshach and Abednego. Their God has

sent his angel and saved his servants from the fire! These three men trusted their God. They refused to obey my command. And they were willing to die rather than serve or worship any god other than their own. ²⁹So I now make this law: the people of any nation or language must not say anything against the God of Shadrach, Meshach and Abednego. Anyone who does will be torn apart. And his house will be turned into a pile of stones. No other god can save his people like this." ³⁰Then the king promoted Shadrach, Meshach and Abednego in the area of Babylon.

Nebuchadnezzar's Dream of a Tree

4 King Nebuchadnezzar sent a letter. It went to the people, nations and those who speak every language in all the world. The letter said:

I wish you great wealth!

²The Most High God has done miracles* and wonderful things for me. I am happy to tell you about these things.

³The things he has done are
    great.
  His miracles are mighty.
  His kingdom continues for
    ever.
  His rule will continue for all
    time.

⁴I, Nebuchadnezzar, was at my palace. I was happy and successful. ⁵I had a dream that made me afraid. As I was lying on my bed, I saw pictures and visions in my mind. Those things made me very afraid. ⁶So I gave an order. All the wise men of Babylon were to be brought to me. I wanted them to tell me what my dream meant. ⁷The fortune-tellers, magicians and wise men came. I told them about the dream. But those

men could not tell me what it meant.

⁸Finally, Daniel came to me. (I called him Belteshazzar to honour my god. The spirit of the holy gods is in him.) I told my dream to Daniel. ⁹I said, "Belteshazzar, you are the most important of all the fortune-tellers. I know that the spirit of the holy gods is in you. I know there is no secret that is too hard for you to understand. This was what I dreamed. Tell me what it means. ¹⁰These are the visions I saw while I was lying in my bed: I looked, and there in front of me was a tree. It was standing in the middle of the earth. The tree was very tall. ¹¹The tree grew large and strong. The top of the tree touched the sky. It could be seen from anywhere on earth. ¹²The leaves of the tree were beautiful. It had plenty of good fruit on it. On the tree was food for everyone. The wild animals found shelter under the tree. And the birds lived in its branches. Every animal ate from it.

¹³"I was looking at those things in the vision while lying on my bed. And then I saw a holy angel coming down from heaven. ¹⁴He spoke very loudly. He said, 'Cut down the tree, and cut off its branches. Strip off its leaves. Scatter its fruit around. Let the animals that are under the tree run away. Let the birds that were in its branches fly away. ¹⁵But let the stump and its roots stay in the ground. Put a band of iron and bronze around it. Let it stay in the field with the grass around it.

" 'Let the man become wet with dew. Let him live among the animals and plants of the earth. ¹⁶Let him not think like a man any longer. Let him have the mind of an animal for seven years.

17" 'Messengers gave this command. The holy ones declared the sentence. This is so all the people may know that the Most High God rules over the kingdoms of men. God gives those kingdoms to anyone he wants. And he chooses people to rule them who are not proud'.

18"That is what I, King Nebuchadnezzar, dreamed. Now Daniel, called Belteshazzar, tell me what the dream means. None of the wise men in my kingdom can explain it to me. But you can, because the spirit of the holy gods is in you."

Daniel Explains the Dream

19Then Daniel (also called Belteshazzar) was very quiet for a while. His thoughts made him afraid. So the king said, "Belteshazzar, do not let the dream or its meaning make you afraid."

Then Daniel, called Belteshazzar, answered the king. He said, "My master, I wish the dream were about your enemies. And I wish its meaning were for those who are against you! 20You saw a tree in your dream. The tree grew large and strong. Its top touched the sky. It could be seen from all over the earth. 21Its leaves were beautiful, and it had plenty of fruit. The fruit gave food for everyone. It was a home for the wild animals. And its branches were nesting places for the birds. That is the tree you saw. 22My king, you are that tree! You have become great and powerful. You are like the tall tree that touched the sky. And your power reaches to the far parts of the earth.

23"My king, you saw a holy angel coming down from heaven. He said, 'Cut down the tree and destroy it. But leave the stump and its roots in the ground. Put a band of iron and bronze around it. Leave it in the field with the grass. Let him become wet with dew. He will live like a wild animal for seven years'.

24"This is the meaning of the dream, my king. The Most High God has commanded these things to happen to my master the king: 25you will be forced away from people. You will live among the wild animals. People will feed you grass like an ox. And dew from the sky will make you wet. Seven years will pass, and then you will learn this lesson: the Most High God is ruler over the kingdoms of men. And the Most High God gives those kingdoms to anyone he wants.

26"The stump of the tree and its roots were to be left in the ground. This means your kingdom will be given back to you. This will happen when you learn that heaven rules your kingdom. 27So, my king, please accept my advice. I advise you to stop sinning and do what is right. Stop doing wicked things and be kind to poor people. Then you might continue to be successful."

The King's Dream Comes True

28All these things happened to King Nebuchadnezzar. 29Twelve months after the dream, King Nebuchadnezzar was walking on the roof[n] of his palace in Babylon. 30And he said, "Look at Babylon. I built this great city. It is my palace. I built this great

roof In Bible times houses were built with flat roofs. The roof was used for drying things such as flax and fruit. It was also used as an extra room, as a place for worship and as a place to sleep in the summer.

place by my power to show how great I am."

³¹The words were still in his mouth when a voice came from heaven. The voice said, "King Nebuchadnezzar, these things will happen to you: your royal power has been taken away from you. ³²You will be forced away from people. You will live with the wild animals. You will be fed grass like an ox. Seven years will pass before you learn this lesson: the Most High God rules over the kingdoms of men. And the Most High God gives those kingdoms to anyone he wants."

³³Those things happened quickly. Nebuchadnezzar was forced to go away from people. He began eating grass like an ox. He became wet from dew. His hair grew long like the feathers of an eagle. And his nails grew long like the claws of a bird.

³⁴Then at the end of that time, I, Nebuchadnezzar, looked up towards heaven. And I could think correctly again. Then I gave praise to the Most High God. I gave honour and glory to him who lives for ever.

God's rule is for ever.
His kingdom continues for
all time.
³⁵People on earth
are not truly important.
God does what he wants
with the powers of heaven
and the people on earth.
No one can stop his powerful
hand.
No one can question the
things he does.

³⁶So, at that time I could think correctly again. And God gave back my great honour and power as king. The people who advise me and the royal family came to

me for help again. I became king again. And I became even greater and more powerful than before. ³⁷Now I, Nebuchadnezzar, give praise and honour and glory to the King of heaven. Everything he does is right. He is always fair. And he is able to make proud people humble.

The Writing on the Wall

5 King Belshazzar gave a big banquet for 1,000 royal guests. And he drank wine with them. ²As Belshazzar was drinking his wine, he gave an order to his servants. He told them to bring the gold and silver cups that his ancestor Nebuchadnezzar had taken from the Temple*d* in Jerusalem. King Belshazzar wanted his royal guests to drink from those cups. He also wanted his wives and his slave women*d* to drink from them. ³So they brought the gold cups. They had been taken from the Temple of God in Jerusalem. And the king and his royal guests, his wives and his slave women drank from them. ⁴As they were drinking, they praised their gods. Those gods were made from gold, silver, bronze, iron, wood and stone.

⁵Then suddenly a person's hand appeared. The fingers wrote words on the plaster on the wall. This was near the lampstand in the royal palace. The king watched the hand as it wrote.

⁶King Belshazzar was very frightened. His face turned white, and his knees knocked together. He could not stand up because his legs were too weak. ⁷The king called for the magicians and wise men to be brought to him. He said to the wise men of Babylon, "I will give a reward to anyone who can read this writing and explain it. I will give him purple clothes fit for a king. I will put a gold chain around his neck. And I will make him the third highest ruler in the kingdom."

⁸So all the king's wise men came in. But they could not read the writing.

And they could not tell the king what it meant. [9]King Belshazzar became even more afraid. His face became even whiter. His royal guests were confused.

[10]Then the king's mother came into the banquet room. She had heard the voices of the king and his royal guests. She said, "My king, live for ever! Don't be afraid! Don't let your face be white with fear! [11]There is a man in your kingdom who has the spirit of the holy gods in him. In the days of your father, this man showed understanding, knowledge and wisdom. He was like the gods in these things. Your father, King Nebuchadnezzar, put this man in charge of all the wise men. He ruled over all the fortune-tellers, magicians and wise men. [12]The man I am talking about is named Daniel. The king gave him the name Belteshazzar. He was very clever, and he had knowledge and understanding. He could explain dreams and secrets. He could answer very hard problems. Call for Daniel. He will tell you what the writing on the wall means."

[13]So they brought Daniel to the king. The king said to him, "Is your name Daniel? Are you one of the captives my father the king brought from Judah? [14]I have heard that the spirit of the gods is in you. And I have heard that you are very clever and have knowledge and understanding. [15]The wise men and magicians were brought to me to read this writing on the wall. I wanted those men to explain to me what it means. But they could not explain it. [16]I have heard that you are able to explain what things mean. And you can find the answers to hard problems. Read this writing on the wall and explain it to me. If you can, I will give you purple clothes fit for a king, and I will put a gold chain around your neck. And you will become the third highest ruler in the kingdom."

[17]Then Daniel answered the king, "You may keep your gifts for yourself. Or you may give those rewards to someone else. I will read the writing on the wall for you. And I will explain to you what it means.

[18]"My king, the Most High God made your father Nebuchadnezzar a great, important and powerful king. [19]God made him very important. So all the people, nations and those who spoke every language were very afraid of Nebuchadnezzar. If he wanted a person to die, he put that person to death. And if he wanted a person to live, he let that person live. If he wanted to promote a person, he promoted him. And if he wanted a person to be unimportant, he made him unimportant.

[20]"But Nebuchadnezzar became too proud and stubborn. So he was taken off his royal throne. His glory was taken away. [21]Then Nebuchadnezzar was forced away from people. His mind became like the mind of an animal. He lived with the wild donkeys and was fed grass like an ox. He became wet with dew. These things happened to him until he learned his lesson: the Most High God rules over the kingdoms of men. And the Most High God sets anyone he wants over those kingdoms.

[22]"But, Belshazzar, you already knew these things. You are a descendant[d] of Nebuchadnezzar. But still you have not been sorry for what you have done. [23]Instead, you have turned against the Lord of heaven. You ordered the drinking cups from the Temple of the Lord to be brought to you. Then you and your royal guests drank wine from them. Your wives and your slave women also drank wine from them. You praised the gods of silver, gold, bronze, iron, wood and stone. They are not really gods. They cannot see or hear or understand anything. But you did not honour God. He is the One who has power over your life and everything you do. [24]So God sent the hand that wrote on the wall.

²⁵"These are the words that were written on the wall: 'Mene, mene, tekel, parsin'.

²⁶"This is what these words mean. Mene: God has counted the days until your kingdom will end. ²⁷Tekel: you have been weighed on the scales and found not good enough. ²⁸Parsin: your kingdom is being divided. It will be given to the Medes and the Persians."

²⁹Then Belshazzar gave an order for Daniel to be dressed in purple clothes. A gold chain was put around his neck. And he was announced to be the third highest ruler in the kingdom. ³⁰That very same night Belshazzar, king of the Babylonian people, was killed. ³¹A man named Darius the Mede became the new king. Darius was 62 years old.

Daniel and the Lions

6 Darius thought it would be a good idea to choose 120 governors. They would rule through all of his kingdom. ²And he chose three men as supervisors over those 120 governors. Daniel was one of these three supervisors. The king set up these men so that he would not be cheated. ³Daniel showed that he could do the work better than the other supervisors and the governors. Because of this, the king planned to put Daniel in charge of the whole kingdom. ⁴So the other supervisors and the governors tried to find reasons to accuse Daniel. But he went on doing the business of the government. And they could not find anything wrong with him. So they could not accuse him of doing anything wrong. Daniel was trustworthy. He was not lazy and did not cheat the king. ⁵Finally these men said, "We will never find any reason to accuse Daniel. But we must find something to complain about. It will have to be about the law of his God."

⁶So the supervisors and the governors went as a group to the king. They said: "King Darius, live for ever! ⁷The supervisors, assistant governors, governors, the people who advise you and the captains of the soldiers have all agreed on something. We think the king should make this law that everyone would have to obey: no one should pray to any god or man except to you, our king. This should be done for the next 30 days. Anyone who doesn't obey will be thrown into the lions' den. ⁸Now, our king, make the law. Write it down so it cannot be changed. The laws of the Medes and Persians cannot be cancelled." ⁹So King Darius made the law and had it written.

¹⁰When Daniel heard that the new law had been written, he went to his house. He went to his upstairs room. The windows of that room opened towards Jerusalem. Three times each day Daniel got down on his knees and prayed. He prayed and thanked God, just as he always had done.

¹¹Then those men went as a group and found Daniel. They saw him praying and asking God for help. ¹²So they went to the king. They talked to him about the law he had made. They said, "Didn't you write a law that says no one may pray to any god or man except you, our king? Doesn't it say that anyone who disobeys during the next 30 days will be thrown into the lions' den?"

The king answered, "Yes, I wrote that law. And the laws of the Medes and Persians cannot be cancelled."

¹³Then those men spoke to the king. They said, "Daniel is one of the captives from Judah. And he is not paying attention to the law you wrote. Daniel still prays to his God three times every day." ¹⁴The king became very upset when he heard this. He decided he had to save Daniel. He worked until sunset trying to think of a way to save him.

¹⁵Then those men went as a group to the king. They said, "Remember, our king, the law of the Medes and

Persians. It says that no law or command given by the king can be changed."

16So King Darius gave the order. They brought Daniel and threw him into the lions' den. The king said to Daniel, "May the God you serve all the time save you!" 17A big stone was brought. It was put over the opening of the lions' den. Then the king used his signet[d] ring to put his special seal[d] on the rock. And he used the rings of his royal officers to put their seals on the rock also. This showed that no one could move that rock and bring Daniel out. 18Then King Darius went back to his palace. He did not eat that night. He did not have any entertainment brought to entertain him. And he could not sleep.

19The next morning King Darius got up at dawn. He hurried to the lions' den. 20As he came near the den, he was worried. He called out to Daniel. He said, "Daniel, servant of the living God! Has your God that you always worship been able to save you from the lions?"

21Daniel answered, "My king, live for ever! 22My God sent his angel to close the lions' mouths. They have not hurt me, because my God knows I am innocent. I never did anything wrong to you, my king."

23King Darius was very happy. He told his servants to lift Daniel out of the lions' den. So they lifted him out and did not find any injury on him. This was because Daniel had trusted in his God.

24Then the king gave a command. The men who had accused Daniel were brought to the lions' den and thrown into it. Their wives and children were also thrown into it. The lions grabbed them before they hit the floor of the den. And the lions crushed their bones.

25Then King Darius wrote a letter. It was to all people and all nations, to those who spoke every language in the world:

I wish you great wealth.

26I am making a new law. This law is for people in every part of my kingdom. All of you must fear and respect the God of Daniel.

Daniel's God is the living God.
He lives for ever.
His kingdom will never be destroyed.
His rule will never end.
27God rescues and saves people.
God does mighty miracles[d] in heaven and on earth.
God saved Daniel from the power of the lions.

28So Daniel was successful during the time that Darius was king. This was also the time that Cyrus the Persian was king.

Daniel's Dream About Four Animals

7 In Belshazzar's first year as king of Babylon, Daniel had a dream. He saw visions as he was lying on his bed. Daniel wrote down what he had dreamed.

2Daniel said: "I saw my vision at night. In the vision the wind was blowing from all four directions. These winds made the sea very rough. 3I saw four huge animals come up from the sea. Each animal was different from the others.

4"The first animal looked like a lion. But it had wings like an eagle. I watched this animal until its wings were torn off. It was lifted from the ground so that it stood up on two feet like a man. And it was given the mind of a man.

5"And then I saw a second animal before me. It looked like a bear. It was raised up on one of its sides. And it had three ribs in its mouth between its teeth. It was told, 'Get up and eat all the meat you want!'

⁶"After that, I looked, and there before me was another animal. This animal looked like a leopard. And the leopard had four wings on its back. The wings looked like a bird's wings. This animal had four heads. It was given power to rule.

⁷"After that, in my vision at night I continued looking. There in front of me was a fourth animal. This animal looked cruel and terrible and very strong. It had large iron teeth. It crushed and ate what it killed. Then it walked on whatever was left. This fourth animal was different from all the animals I had seen before it. It had ten horns.

⁸"While I was thinking about the horns, another horn grew up among them. It was a little horn. It had eyes like a person's eyes. It also had a mouth. And the mouth was boasting. The little horn pulled out three of the other horns.

⁹"As I looked,
thrones were put in their places.
And God, who has been alive for
    ever, sat on his throne.
His clothes were white like snow.
And the hair on his head was
    white like wool.
His throne was made from fire.
And the wheels of his throne
    were blazing with fire.
¹⁰A river of fire was flowing
    from in front of him.
Many thousands of angels were
    serving him.
Millions of angels stood before
    him.
Court was ready to begin.
And the books were opened.

¹¹"I kept on looking because the little horn was boasting. I kept watching until finally the fourth animal was killed. Its body was destroyed, and it was thrown into the burning fire. ¹²(The power and rule of the other animals had been taken from them. But they were permitted to live for a certain period of time.)

¹³"In my vision at night I looked. There in front of me was someone who looked like a human being. He was coming with clouds in the sky. He came near God, who has been alive for ever. And he was led to God. ¹⁴The one who looked like a human being was given the power to rule. He was also given glory and royal power. All peoples, nations and men who spoke every language will serve him. His rule will last for ever. His kingdom will never be destroyed.

The Meaning of the Dream

¹⁵"I, Daniel, was worried. The visions that went through my mind frightened me. ¹⁶I came near one of those standing there. I asked him what all this meant.

"So he told me. He explained to me what these things meant. ¹⁷He said, 'The four great animals are four kingdoms. Those four kingdoms will come from the earth. ¹⁸But the people who belong to the Most High God will receive the power to rule. And they will have the power to rule for ever. They will have it from now on'.

¹⁹"Then I wanted to know what the fourth animal meant. It was different from all the other animals. It was very terrible. It had iron teeth and bronze claws. It was the animal that crushed and ate what it killed. And it walked on whatever was left. ²⁰I also wanted to know about the ten horns on its head. And I wanted to know about the little horn that grew there. It had pulled out three of the other ten horns. It looked greater than the others. And it had eyes and a mouth that kept boasting. ²¹As I watched, the little horn began making war against God's people. And the horn kept killing them ²²until God, who has been alive for ever, came. He judged in favour of the people who belong to the Most High God. And the

time came for them to receive the power to rule.

²³"And he explained this to me: 'The fourth animal is a fourth kingdom that will come on the earth. It will be different from all the other kingdoms. It will destroy people all over the world. It will walk on and crush the whole earth. ²⁴The ten horns are ten kings who will come from this fourth kingdom. After those ten kings are gone, another king will come. He will be different from the kings who ruled before him. He will defeat three of the other kings. ²⁵This king will say things against the Most High God. And he will hurt and kill God's people. He will try to change times and laws that have already been set. The people that belong to God will be in that king's power for three and a half years.

²⁶"'But the court will decide what should happen. And the power of the king will be taken away. His kingdom will be completely destroyed. ²⁷Then the people who belong to the Most High God will have the power to rule. They will rule over all the kingdoms under heaven with power and greatness. Their power to rule will last for ever. And people from all the other kingdoms will respect and serve them'.

²⁸"And that was the end of the dream. I, Daniel, was very afraid. My face became very white from fear. But I kept everything to myself."

Daniel's Vision

8 During the third year Belshazzar was king, I saw this vision. This was after the other one. ²In this vision I saw myself in the capital city of Susa. Susa is in the area of Elam. I was standing by the Ulai River. ³I looked up, and I saw a male sheep standing beside the river. It had two long horns. But one horn was longer than the other. The long horn was newer than the other horn. ⁴I watched the male sheep charge to the west. He

also charged to the north and the south. No animal could stand before him. And none could save another animal from his power. He did whatever he wanted. And he became very powerful.

⁵While I was thinking about this, I saw a male goat come from the west. This goat had one large horn that was easy to see. It was between his eyes. He crossed over the whole earth. But his feet did not touch the ground.

⁶That goat charged the male sheep with the two horns. This was the male sheep I had seen standing by the river. The goat was very angry. ⁷I watched the goat attack the male sheep. It broke the sheep's two horns. The sheep could not stop it. The goat knocked the sheep to the ground. Then the goat walked all over him. No one was able to save the sheep from the goat. ⁸So the male goat became very great. But when he was strong, his big horn broke off. Then four horns grew in place of the one big horn. Those four horns were easy to see. They pointed in four different directions.

⁹Then a little horn grew from one of those four horns. It became very big. It grew to the south and the east and towards the beautiful land of Judah. ¹⁰That little horn grew until it reached to the sky. It even threw some of the army of heaven to the ground. And it walked on them. ¹¹That little horn became very strong against God, the commander of heaven's armies. It stopped the daily sacrifices that were offered to the commander. The place where people worshipped the commander was pulled down. ¹²There was a turning away from God. Because of this the people stopped daily sacrifices. It was like throwing truth down to the ground. The horn was successful in everything it did.

¹³Then I heard an angel speaking. Another angel asked the first one, "How long will the things in this vision

last? The vision is about the daily sacrifices. It is about the turning away from God that brings destruction. It is about the Temple*d* being pulled down. It is about the army of heaven being walked on."

¹⁴He said to me, "This will happen for 2,300 evenings and mornings.ⁿ Then the holy place will be repaired."

¹⁵I, Daniel, saw this vision. And I tried to understand what it meant. Then someone who looked like a man suddenly stood before me. ¹⁶And I heard a man's voice calling from the Ulai River: "Gabriel, explain the vision to this man."

¹⁷Gabriel came to where I was standing. When he came close to me, I was very afraid. I bowed face down on the ground. But Gabriel said to me, "Human being, understand that this vision is about the time of the end."

¹⁸While Gabriel was speaking, I fell into a deep sleep. My face was on the ground. Then he touched me and lifted me to my feet. ¹⁹He said, "Now, I will explain the vision to you. I will tell you what will happen later, in the time of God's anger. Your vision was about the set time of the end.

²⁰"You saw a male sheep with two horns. Those horns are the kings of Media and Persia. ²¹The male goat is the king of Greece. The big horn between its eyes is the first king. ²²After that horn broke, four horns grew in its place. Those four horns are four kingdoms. Those four kingdoms will come from the nation of the first king. But they will not be as strong as the first king.

²³"When the end comes near for those kingdoms, a bold and cruel king will come. This king will tell lies. This will happen when many people have turned against God. ²⁴This king will be very powerful. But his power will not come from himself. He will cause terrible destruction. He will be success-

ful in everything he does. He will destroy powerful people and even God's people. ²⁵This king will use his wisdom to make lies successful. He will think that he is very important. He will destroy many people without warning. He will try to fight even God, the Prince of princes! But that cruel king will be destroyed. And it will not be human power that destroys him.

²⁶"The vision that has been shown to you about those times is true. But seal up the vision. Those things won't happen for a long time."

²⁷I, Daniel, became very weak. I was sick for several days after that vision. Then I got up and went back to work for the king. But I was very upset about the vision. I didn't understand what it meant.

Daniel's Prayer

9 These things happened during the first year Darius son of Xerxes was king. He was a descendant*d* of the Medes. ²During Darius' first year as king, I, Daniel, was reading the Scriptures.*d* In them I saw what the Lord told Jeremiah. He said Jerusalem would be an empty desert for 70 years.

³Then I turned to the Lord God. I prayed to him and asked him for help. I did not eat any food. To show how sad I was I put on rough cloth and sat in ashes. ⁴I prayed to the Lord my God. I told him about all of my sins. I said, "Lord, you are a great God. You cause fear and wonder. You keep your agreement of love with all who love you and obey your commands.

⁵"But we have sinned and done wrong. We have been wicked and turned against you. We have not obeyed your commands and laws. ⁶We did not listen to your servants, the prophets. They spoke for you to our kings, our leaders and our ances-

---

2,300 evenings and mornings This could mean 1,150 days or 2,300 days.

tors. They spoke to all the people of the land.

⁷"Lord, you are good and right. But we are full of shame today. The people of Judah and Jerusalem and all the people of Israel are ashamed. People near and far whom you scattered among many nations are ashamed. We were not loyal to you. ⁸Lord, we are all ashamed. Our kings and leaders and our fathers are ashamed. This is because we have sinned against you.

⁹"But, Lord our God, you show us mercy. You forgive us even though we have turned against you. ¹⁰We have not obeyed the Lord our God. We have not obeyed the teachings he gave us through his servants, the prophets. ¹¹All the people of Israel have disobeyed your teachings. They all have turned away and refused to obey you. So you brought on us the curses and promises of punishment written in the Teachings of Moses, the servant of God. These things have happened to us because we sinned against you.

¹²"God said these things would happen to us and our leaders. And he made them happen. You brought on us a great disaster. Nothing has ever been done here on earth like what was done to Jerusalem. ¹³All this disaster came to us just as it is written in the Teachings of Moses. But we still have not stopped sinning. We still do not pay attention to your truth. ¹⁴The Lord was ready to bring the disaster on us. This is because he is right in everything he does. But we still have not obeyed him.

¹⁵"Lord our God, you used your power and brought us out of Egypt. Because of that, your name is known even today. Lord, we have sinned. We have done wrong. ¹⁶Lord, you do the right things. So do not be angry with Jerusalem. Jerusalem is your city on your holy hill. All this has happened because of our sins and the evil things done by our ancestors. So now people

all around insult and make fun of Jerusalem and your people.

¹⁷"Now, our God, hear my prayers. I am your servant. Listen to my prayer for help. Do good things for your holy place that is in ruins. Do this for your sake. ¹⁸My God, pay attention and hear me. Open your eyes and see all the terrible things that have happened to us. See what has happened to the city that is called by your name. We do not ask these things because we are good. We ask because of your mercy. ¹⁹Lord, listen! Lord, forgive! Lord, hear us and do something! For your sake, don't wait! Your city and your people are called by your name."

Gabriel's Explanation

²⁰I was saying those things in my prayer to the Lord, my God. I was confessing my sins and the sins of the people of Israel. I was praying for God's holy hill. ²¹While I was still praying, Gabriel came to me. Gabriel was the person I had seen in my last vision. He came flying quickly to me about the time of the evening sacrifice. ²²Gabriel said to me, "Daniel, I have come to give you wisdom and to help you understand. ²³When you first started praying, an answer was given. And I came to tell you, because God loves you very much. So think about the message and understand the vision.

²⁴"God has ordered 490 years for your people and your holy city. These years are ordered for these reasons: to stop people from turning against God; to put an end to sin; to take away evil; to bring in goodness that continues for ever; to make the vision and prophecy*ᵈ* come true; and to appoint a most holy place.

²⁵"Learn and understand these things. A command will come to rebuild Jerusalem. The time from this command until the appointed leader comes will be 49 years and 434 years.

Jerusalem will be rebuilt with streets and a trench around it. But it will be built in times of trouble. [26]After the 434 years the appointed leader will be killed. He will have nothing. The people of the leader who is to come will destroy the city. They will also destroy the holy place. That end will come like a flood. War will continue until the end. God has ordered that place to be completely destroyed. [27]That leader will make an agreement with many people for seven years. He will put a stop to offerings and sacrifices after three and a half years. And the horrible thing that destroys will be placed on the highest point of the Temple.[d] But God has ordered him to be destroyed!"

Daniel's Vision of a Man

10 During Cyrus' third year as king of Persia, Daniel learned about these things. (Daniel's other name is Belteshazzar.) The message was true. It was about a great war. But Daniel understood it, because it was explained to him in a vision.

[2]At that time I, Daniel, was very sad for three weeks. [3]I did not eat any fancy food. I did not eat any meat or drink any wine. I did not use any perfumed oil. I did not do any of these things for three weeks.

[4]On the twenty-fourth day of the first month, I was standing beside the great Tigris River. [5]While standing there, I looked up. And I saw a man dressed in linen clothes. A belt made of fine gold was wrapped around his waist. [6]His body was like shiny yellow quartz. His face was bright like lightning, and his eyes were like fire. His arms and legs were shiny like polished bronze. His voice sounded like the roar of a crowd.

[7]I, Daniel, was the only person who saw the vision. The men with me did not see it. But they were badly frightened. They were so afraid they ran away and hid. [8]So I was left alone,

watching this great vision. I lost my strength. My face turned white like a dead person, and I was helpless. [9]Then I heard the man in the vision speaking. As I listened, I fell into a deep sleep. My face was on the ground.

[10]Then a hand touched me and set me on my hands and knees. I was so afraid that I was shaking. [11]The man in the vision said to me, "Daniel, God loves you very much. Think very carefully about the words I will speak to you. Stand up because I have been sent to you." And when he said this, I stood up. I was still shaking.

[12]Then the man said to me, "Daniel, do not be afraid. Some time ago you decided to try to get understanding. You wanted to be humble before God. Since that time God has listened to you. And I came to you because you have been praying. [13]But the prince of Persia has been fighting against me for 21 days. Then Michael, one of the most important angels, came to help me. He came because I had been left there with the king of Persia. [14]Now I have come to you, Daniel. I will explain to you what will happen to your people. The vision is about a time in the future."

[15]While he was speaking to me, I bowed face down. I could not speak. [16]Then one who looked like a man touched my lips. I opened my mouth and started to speak. I said to the one standing in front of me, "Master, I am upset and afraid. It is because of what I saw in the vision. I feel helpless. [17]Master, I am Daniel your servant. How can I talk with you! My strength is gone, and it is hard for me to breathe."

[18]The one who looked like a man touched me again. And he gave me strength. [19]He said, "Daniel, don't be afraid. God loves you very much. Peace be with you. Be strong now, be strong."

When he spoke to me, I became

stronger. Then I said, "Master, speak, since you have given me strength."

20So then he said, "Daniel, do you know why I have come to you? Soon I must go back to fight against the prince of Persia. When I go, the prince of Greece will come. 21But before I go, I must first tell you what is written in the Book of Truth. No one stands with me against them except Michael. He is the angel ruling over your people.

11 In the first year Darius the Mede was king, I stood up to support Michael. I supported him in his fight against the prince of Persia.

Kingdoms of the South and North

2"Now then, Daniel, I tell you the truth: three more kings will rule in Persia. Then a fourth king will come. He will be much richer than all the kings of Persia before him. He will use his riches to get power. And he will stir up everyone against the kingdom of Greece. 3Then a mighty king will come. He will rule with great power. He will do anything he wants. 4After that king has come, his kingdom will be broken up. It will be divided towards the four parts of the world. His kingdom will not go to his descendants.d And it will not have the power that he had. This is because his kingdom will be pulled up and given to other people.

5"The king of the South will become strong. But one of his commanders will become even stronger. He will begin to rule his own kingdom with great power. 6Then after a few years, the king of the South and the commander will become friends. The daughter of the king of the South will marry the king of the North. She will do this to bring peace. But she will not keep her power. And his family will not last. She, her husband, her child and those who brought her to that country will be killed.

7"But a person from her family will become king of the South. He will attack the armies of the king of the North. He will go into that king's strong, walled city. He will fight and win. 8He will take their gods and their metal idols. He will also take their valuable things made of silver and gold. He will take those things to Egypt. Then he will not bother the king of the North for a few years. 9Next, the king of the North will attack the king of the South. But he will be beaten back to his own country.

10"The sons of the king of the North will prepare for war. They will get a large army together. That army will move through the land very quickly, like a powerful flood. Later, that army will come back and fight. They will fight all the way to the strong, walled city of the king of the South. 11Then the king of the South will become very angry. He will march out to fight against the king of the North. The king of the North will have a large army. But he will lose the battle. 12The soldiers will be carried away. So the king of the South will be very proud. And he will kill thousands of soldiers from the northern army. But he will not continue to be successful. 13The king of the North will gather another army. That army will be larger than the first one. After several years he will attack. That army will be very large, and it will have plenty of weapons.

14"In those times many people will be against the king of the South. Some of your own people who love to fight will turn against the king of the South. They will think it is time for God's promises to come true. But it will not be the time yet. And they will fail. 15Then the king of the North will come. He will build roads of earth to the tops of the city walls. And he will capture a strong, walled city. The southern army will not have the power to fight back. Even their best soldiers will not be strong enough to stop the northern army. ¹⁶The king of the North will do whatever he wants. No one will be able to stand against him. He will gain power and control in the beautiful land of Israel. And he will have the power to destroy it. ¹⁷The king of the North will decide to use all his power to fight against the king of the South. He will make an agreement with the king of the South. The king of the North will give one of his daughters as a wife to the king of the South. He will do that so he can defeat the king of the South. But those plans will not succeed or help him. ¹⁸Then the king of the North will turn his attention to other places. He will take many cities along the coast of the Mediterranean Sea. But a commander will put an end to the pride of the king of the North. The commander will turn that pride back on him. ¹⁹After that happens the king of the North will go back to the strong, walled cities of his own country. But he will lose his power. That will be the end of him.

²⁰"The next king of the North will send out a tax collector. He will then have plenty of money. In a few years that ruler will be killed. But he will not die in anger or in a battle.

²¹"That ruler will be followed by a very cruel and hated man. He will not have the honour of being from a king's family. He will attack the kingdom when the people feel safe. He will take power by lying to the people. ²²He will sweep away in defeat large and powerful armies. He will even defeat a prince who made an agreement. ²³Many nations will make agreements with that cruel and hated ruler, but he will lie to them. He will gain much power, but only a few people will support him. ²⁴The richest areas will feel safe, but that cruel and hated ruler will attack them. And he will succeed where his ancestors did not. He will take things from the countries he defeated. And he will give those things

to his followers. He will plan to defeat and destroy strong cities. He will be successful, but only for a short time.

²⁵"That very cruel and hated ruler will have a large army. He will use it to stir up his strength and courage. He will attack the king of the South. The king of the South will get a large and very powerful army and get ready for war. But the people who are against him will make secret plans. And the king of the South will be defeated. ²⁶There were people who were supposed to be good friends of the king of the South. But they will try to destroy him. His army will be swept away in defeat. Many of his soldiers will be killed in battle. ²⁷Those two kings will want to hurt each other. They will sit at the same table and lie to each other, but it will not do either one any good. This is because God has set a time for their end to come. ²⁸The king of the North will go back to his own country with much wealth. Then he will decide to go against the holy agreement. He will do what he planned. Then he will go back to his own country.

²⁹"At the right time the king of the North will attack the king of the South again. But this time he will not be successful as he was before. ³⁰Ships from the west will come and fight against the king of the North. He will see those ships coming and be afraid. Then he will return and show his anger against God's people who obey the holy agreement. He will be good to those who have stopped obeying the holy agreement.

³¹"The king of the North will send his army. They will make the Temple*d* in Jerusalem unclean.*d* They will stop the people from offering the daily sacrifice. Then they will set up the horrible thing that destroys. ³²The king of the North will tell lies to God's people. Those who have not obeyed God will be ruined. But there will be some who know God and obey him. They will be strong and fight back.

33"Those who are wise will help the others understand what is happening. But some of them will be killed with swords. Some will be burned or taken captive. Some of them will have their homes and things taken away. These things will continue for many days. 34When the wise ones are suffering, they will get a little help. Many who join the wise ones will not love God. 35Some of the wise ones will be killed. But the hard times must come. This is so they can be made stronger and purer. They will be without faults until the time of the end comes. Then, at the right time, the end will come.

The King Who Praises Himself

36"The king of the North will do whatever he wants. He will boast about himself. He will praise himself and think he is even better than a god. He will say things against the God of gods that no one has ever heard. He will be successful until all the bad things have happened. What God has planned to happen will happen. 37That king of the North will not care about the gods his ancestors worshipped. He won't care about the god that women worship. He won't care about any god. Instead, he will make himself more important than any god. 38The king of the North will worship power and strength. His ancestors did not love power as he will. He will honour the god of power with gold and silver, expensive jewels and gifts. 39That king will attack strong, walled cities. He will do it with the help of a foreign god. He will give much honour to the people who join him. He will make them rulers in charge of many other people. He will make those rulers pay him for the land they rule.

40"At the time of the end, the king of the South will fight a battle against the king of the North. The king of the North will attack him. He will attack with chariots and soldiers on horses and many large ships. He will invade many countries and sweep through their lands like a flood. 41The king of the North will attack the beautiful land of Judah. He will defeat many countries. But Edom, Moab and the leaders of Ammon will be saved from him. 42The king of the North will show his power in many countries. Egypt will not escape. 43The king will get treasures of gold and silver. And he will get all the riches of Egypt. The Libyan and Nubian people will obey him. 44But the king of the North will hear news from the east and the north. And it will make him afraid and angry. He will go to destroy completely many nations. 45He will set up his royal tents. They will be between the sea and the beautiful mountain where the Temple[d] is built. But, finally, his end will come. There will not be anyone to help him when he dies.

The Time of the End

12 "Daniel, at that time Michael, the great prince, will stand up. (He is the one who protects your people.) There will be a time of much trouble. It will be the worst time since nations have been on earth. But your people will be saved. Everyone whose name is written in God's book will be saved. 2Many people who have already died will live again. Some of them will wake up to have life for ever. But some will wake up to find shame and disgrace for ever. 3The wise people will shine like the brightness of the sky. Those who teach others to live right will shine like stars for ever and ever.

4"But you, Daniel, close up the book and seal it. These things will happen at the time of the end. Many people will go here and there to find true knowledge."

5Then I, Daniel, looked, and I saw two other men. One was standing on my side of the river. And the other was standing on the far side. 6The man who was dressed in linen was standing over the water in the river. One of the two men spoke to him. He asked, "How long will it be before these amazing things come true?"

⁷The man dressed in linen who stood over the water raised his hands towards heaven. And I heard him make a promise. He used the name of God who lives for ever. He said, "It will be for three and a half years. The power of the holy people will finally be broken. Then all these things will come true."

⁸I heard the answer, but I did not really understand. So I asked, "Master, what will happen after all these things come true?"

⁹He answered, "Go your way, Dan-iel. The message is closed up and sealed until the time of the end. ¹⁰Many people will be made clean,ᵈ pure and spotless. But the wicked will continue to be wicked. And those wicked people will not understand these things. But the wise people will understand them.

¹¹"The daily sacrifice will be stopped. There will be 1,290 days from that time. Then the horrible thing that destroys will be set up. ¹²Those who wait for the end of the 1,335 days will be happy.

¹³"As for you, Daniel, go your way till the end. You will get your rest when you die. And at the end you will rise from the dead to get your reward."

HOSEA

Israel Acts like an Unfaithful Wife

1 The Lord spoke his word to Hosea son of Beeri. This was during the time that Uzziah, Jotham, Ahaz and Hezekiah were kings of Judah. During part of this time Jeroboam son of Jehoash was king of Israel.

Hosea's Wife and Children

2The Lord said to him, "Go, and marry a woman who will be unfaithful to you. She will give you children whose fathers are other men. Do this because people in this country have acted like an unfaithful wife toward the Lord." 3So Hosea married Gomer daughter of Diblaim. Gomer became pregnant and gave birth to Hosea's son.

4The Lord said to Hosea, "Name him Jezreel. This is because soon I will punish the family of Jehu for the people they killed at Jezreel. Then I will put an end to the kingdom of Israel. 5And I will also break the power of Israel's army in the Valley of Jezreel."

6Gomer became pregnant again and gave birth to a daughter. The Lord said to Hosea, "Name her Lo-Ruhamah.n This is because I will not pity Israel any more. I will no longer forgive them. 7But I will show pity to the people of Judah. I will save them. I will not use bows or swords, horses or horsemen, or weapons of war to save them. I, the Lord their God, will save them."

8After Gomer had finished nursing Lo-Ruhamah, she became pregnant again. And she gave birth to another son. 9The Lord said, "Name him Lo-Ammin because you are not my people. And I am not your God.

God's Promise to Israel

10"But the people of Israel will become like the grains of sand of the sea. You cannot measure or count them. Now it is said to Israel, 'You are not my people'. But later they will be called 'children of the living God'. 11Then the people of Judah and Israel will be joined together again. They will choose one leader for themselves. And again they will grow in their land. The day of Jezreel, when God plants, will be truly great.

2 "Your brothers and your sisters will be called 'my people' and 'you have been shown love'.

God Speaks About Israel

2"Plead with your mother.n
    Plead with her because she no
        longer acts like a wife to
        me.
    And I am not treated like her
        husband.
    Tell her to stop acting like a
        prostitute.d
    Tell her to stop behaving like an
        unfaithful wife.
3If she refuses, I will strip her
        naked.
    I will leave her bare like the day
        she was born.
    I will make her dry like a desert.
    I will make her like a land
        without water.
    I will kill her with thirst.

Lo-Ruhamah This name in Hebrew means "not pitied".
Lo-Ammi This name in Hebrew means "not my people".
mother This refers to the nation of Israel here.

⁴I will not take pity on her
    children.
They are the children of an
    unfaithful wife.
⁵Their mother has acted like a
    prostitute.
The one who became pregnant
    with them has acted
    disgracefully.
She said, 'I will chase after my
    lovers."
They give me food and water.
They give me wool and linen.
They give me wine and olive
    oil'.
⁶So I will block her road with
    thornbushes.
I will build a wall around her
so she cannot find her way.
⁷She will run after her lovers,
but she won't catch up to them.
She will look for them,
but she won't find them.
Then she will say, 'I will go back
    to my first husband."
Life was better for me then than
    it is now'.
⁸But she has not accepted that I
    was the one
who gave her grain, wine and
    oil.
I gave her much silver and gold,
but she used it to make statues
    of Baal.ᵈ

⁹"So I will take away my grain at
    harvest time.
And I will take away my wine
    when it is ready.
I will take back my wool and linen.
I gave her those things to cover
    her nakedness.
¹⁰So I will show her nakedness to
    her lovers.
No one will save her from my
    punishment.

¹¹I will put an end to all her
    celebrations:
her yearly festivals, her New
    Moonᵈ festivals and her
    Sabbaths.ᵈ
I will stop all of her special
    feasts.
¹²I will destroy her vines and fig
    trees.
She said they were her pay from
    her lovers.
I will turn them into a forest.
Wild animals will eat those
    plants.
¹³I will punish her for all the times
    she burned incenseᵈ to the
    Baals.
She put on her rings and
    jewellery.
Then she went chasing after her
    lovers.
But she has forgotten me!"
    says the Lord.

¹⁴"So I am going to attract her.
I will lead her into the desert
and speak tenderly to her.
¹⁵Then I will give her back her
    vineyards.
And I will make the Valley of
    Achorⁿ a door of hope.
Then she will respond as when
    she was young,
as when she came out of
    Egypt."

¹⁶The Lord says, "Then she will call
    me 'my husband'.
She will no longer call me 'my
    baal'.ⁿ
¹⁷I will never let her say the names
    of Baal again.
Then people won't use their
    names any more.
¹⁸At that time I will make an
    agreement for them.

lovers This refers to the nations surrounding Israel, who led Israel to worship false gods.
husband This refers to God here.
Achor This name in Hebrew means "trouble". It refers here to punishment as the way to
    blessing.
baal Another Hebrew word for husband. But it was the same word as the false god Baal.

It will be with the wild animals,
　　the birds and the crawling
　　things.
I will remove from the land
　　the bow and the sword and the
　　weapons of war.
Then my people will live in
　　safety.
[19]And I will make you my promised
　　bride for ever.
I will be good and fair.
I will show you my love and
　　mercy.
[20]I will be true to you as my
　　promised bride.
Then you will accept that I am
　　the Lord.

[21]"And at that time I will answer
　　you," says the Lord.
"I will speak to the skies.
And they will give rain to the
　　earth.
[22]The earth will produce grain, wine
　　and oil.
Much will grow because my
　　people are called
　　Jezreel–God plants.
[23]I will plant my people in the land.
I will show pity to the one I had
　　called 'not shown pity'.
I will say, 'You are my people'
　　to those I had called 'not my
　　people'.
And they will say to me, 'You
　　are our God'."

Hosea Buys Gomer Back

3 The Lord said to me, "Go, show
　your love to your wife again. She
has had other lovers and has been unfaithful to you. But you must keep on
loving her the way the Lord loves the
people of Israel. This is true even
though the Israelites worship other
gods. They love to eat the raisin
cakes."[n]

[2]So I bought Gomer for 170 grams
of silver and about 300 litres of barley.

[3]Then I told her, "You must wait for
me for many days. You must not be a
prostitute.[d] You must not be any other man's lover. I, in turn, will wait for
you."

[4]In the same way Israel will live
many days without a king or leader.
They will not have sacrifices or holy
stone pillars. They will be without the
holy robe[d] or an idol. [5]After this, the
people of Israel will return to the Lord
their God. They will follow the Lord
and the king from David's family. In
the last days they will come to the
Lord. And he will bless them.

The Lord's Word Against Israel

4 People of Israel, listen to the
　Lord's message.
The Lord says he has this
against you who live in this
　　country:
"The people are not true, not
　　loyal to God.
They do not even know him.
[2]They curse. They lie. They kill.
They steal.
They are guilty of adultery.[d]
They break all my laws.
One murder follows another.
[3]Because of this the land dries up,
　and all its people are dying off.
Even the wild animals are dying.
Even the birds of the air and the
　　fish of the sea are dying.

God's Case Against the Priests

[4]"No one should accuse
　or blame another person.
Don't blame the people, you
　　priests,
when they quarrel with you.
[5]You will be ruined one of these
　　days.
And your prophets[d] will be
　　ruined with you one of these
　　nights.
I will also destroy your mother,
　the nation of Israel.

raisin cakes This food may have been used in the feasts that honoured false gods.

[6]My people will be destroyed
  because they have no
    knowledge.
You priests have refused to learn,
  so I will refuse to let you be
    priests to me.
You have forgotten the teachings
    of your God
  so I will reject your children.
[7]The more priests there are,
  the more they sin against me.
I will take away their honour
  and give them nothing but
    shame.
[8]The priests live off the sin
    offerings of the people.
  So they want the people to sin
    more and more.
[9]The priests are as wrong as the
    people.
  I will punish them both for what
    they have done.
  I will repay them for the wrong
    they have done.

[10]"They will eat
  but not have enough.
They will have sexual relations
  with the prostitutes.[d]
But they will not have children.
This is because they left the
    Lord.

God's Case Against the People

[11]"Sexual sins, old wine and new
    wine
  take away my people's ability to
    understand.
[12]My people ask wooden idols for
    advice.
  They ask those sticks of wood
    to advise them!
Like prostitutes, they have chased
  after other gods.
They have left their own God.
[13]They make sacrifices on the tops
    of the mountains.
  They burn offerings on the hills,

under oaks, poplars and other
    trees.
  They think the shade under
    those trees is pleasant.
So your daughters become
    prostitutes.
  And your daughters-in-law are
    guilty of adultery.[d]

[14]"But I will not punish your
    daughters
  when they become prostitutes.
I will not punish your
    daughters-in-law
  for their sins of adultery.
I will not punish them
  because you yourselves have
    sexual relations with
    prostitutes.
You offer sacrifices with the
    temple prostitutes.
  You foolish people are
    destroying yourselves.

[15]"Israel, you act like a prostitute.
  But don't let Judah be guilty.
Don't go to sacrifice at Gilgal.
  Don't go up to give offerings at
    Beth Aven.[n]
Don't use the Lord's name to
    make promises.
  Don't say, 'As surely as the
    Lord lives...'
[16]The people of Israel are stubborn
  like a stubborn young cow.
How then can the Lord feed them
  like lambs in a meadow?
[17]Israel has chosen to worship
    idols.
  So, let them.
[18]Her rulers get drunk.
  Then they give themselves to
    being prostitutes.
They love these disgraceful
    things.
[19]They will be swept away as by a
    whirlwind.
  Their sacrifices will bring them
    only shame.

Gilgal and Beth Aven Cities in Israel where people worshipped false gods.

The Lord's Word Against the Leaders

5 "Listen, you priests.
Pay attention, people of Israel.
Listen, royal family.
You will all be judged.
You have been like a trap at
Mizpah.
You have been like a net spread
out at Mount Tabor.
[2]You have done many bad things.
So I will punish you all.
[3]I know all about Israel.
What they have done is not
hidden from me.
They all act like prostitutes.[d]
Israel has made itself unclean.[d]

[4]"And those bad things they have
done
keep them from returning to
their God.
They are determined to be
unfaithful to me.
They do not know the Lord.
[5]Israel's pride testifies against
them.
The people of Israel will stumble
because of their sin.
The people of Judah will also
stumble with them.
[6]The people will come to worship
the Lord.
They will come with their sheep
and cattle.
But they will not be able to find
him,
because he has left them.
[7]They have not been true to the
Lord.
Their children do not belong to
him.
So their false worship
will destroy them and their
land.

[8]"Blow the horn in Gibeah.
Blow the trumpet in Ramah.
Give the warning at Beth Aven.
Be first into battle, people of
Benjamin.

[9]A time of punishment is coming.
Israel will be destroyed.
I warn the tribes[d] of Israel
that this will surely happen.
[10]The leaders of Judah are like
thieves.
They try to steal the property of
others.
My punishment will overwhelm
them
like a flood of water.
[11]Israel will be crushed by the
punishments,
because they decided to follow
idols.
[12]I will destroy Israel
as a moth destroys clothing.
I will destroy Judah
as rot destroys wood.

[13]"Israel saw how weak she was.
Judah saw the wounds she
suffered.
So Israel turned to Assyria for
help.
She sent to the great king of
Assyria for help.
But he cannot heal you.
He cannot cure your wound.
[14]I will be like a lion to Israel.
I will be like a young lion to
Judah.
I will attack them
and tear them to pieces.
I will drag them off,
and no one will be able to save
them.
[15]Then I will go back to my place
until the people admit they are
guilty.
At that time they must look for
me.
In their trouble they must turn
to me."

The People Are Not Faithful

6 You people say,
"Come, let's go back to the
Lord.
He has hurt us, but he will heal
us.

He has wounded us, but he will bandage our wounds.
²In a short while he will put new life in us.
We will not have to wait long for him to raise us up.
Then we may live in his presence.
³Let's learn about the Lord.
Let's try hard to know who he is.
He will come to us
as surely as the dawn comes.
The Lord will come to us like the rain,
like the spring rain that waters the ground."

⁴The Lord says, "Israel, what should I do with you?
Judah, what should I do with you?
Your faithfulness is like a morning mist.
It lasts only as long as the dew in the morning.
⁵I have warned you by my prophets^d
that I will kill you and destroy you.
My judgements will flash forth like lightning against you.
⁶I want faithful love more than I want animal sacrifices.
I want people to know me more than I want burnt offerings.
⁷But you have broken the agreement as Adam did.
You have been unfaithful to me.
⁸Gilead is full of people who do evil.
It is covered with bloody footprints.
⁹Some of the priests are like robbers waiting in ambush.
They murder people on the way to Shechem.ⁿ

They do wicked crimes.
¹⁰I have seen horrible things in Israel.
The people are unfaithful to God, and Israel has become unclean.^d

¹¹"Judah, I have set a time to punish you also.

"I would like to give my people back their riches.

7 I would like to heal Israel.
But their sin can be seen by everyone.
The wickedness of Israel is too well-known.
They cheat one another.
They break into other people's houses.
There are robberies in the streets.
²It never enters their minds that I remember all their wicked deeds.
The bad things they do are all around,
and I can see their sins clearly.

Israel Destroys Her Rulers

³"They make the king happy with their wickedness.
They make their rulers glad with their lies.
⁴But all of them are traitors.
They are like an oven heated by a baker.
While he mixes the dough,
he does not stir up the flame.
⁵They hold a festival day for the king.
On that day the rulers become drunk with wine.
The king joins in with those who have made evil plans.
⁶They approach him with murder in mind.
Their hearts are like a hot oven.
All night long its fire is low.
When morning comes, it is fanned into flame.

Shechem A city of safety where men could go for protection.

⁷So all these people are as hot as
    an oven.
Like a fire they destroy their
    rulers.
Their kings fall one after another.
And no one calls on me.

Israel and the Other Nations

⁸"Israel mixes with other nations.
Israel is useless like a pancake
    cooked only on one side.
⁹Foreign nations are using up
    Israel's strength.
And Israel doesn't even know it.
Israel is weak and feeble, like an
    old man.
And they don't even know it.
¹⁰Israel's pride will cause their
    defeat.
They have had many troubles.
But they still do not turn to the
    Lord their God.
They do not look to him for
    help.
¹¹Israel has become like a silly
    pigeon.
The people have no
    understanding.
First they call to Egypt for help.
Then they run for help to
    Assyria.
¹²When they go, I will catch them
    as men catch birds in a net.
Then I will punish them
    as I have warned them.
¹³How terrible for them because
    they left me!
They will be destroyed because
    they turned against me.
I want to save them,
    but they have spoken lies
    against me.
¹⁴They do not call to me from their
    hearts.
They just lie on their beds and
    cry.
They come together to ask for
    grain and new wine,
but they really turn away from
    me.

¹⁵I trained them and gave them
    strength,
but they have made evil plans
    against me.
¹⁶They did not turn to the Most
    High God.
They are like a crooked bow
    that does not shoot straight.
Their leaders boast about their
    strength,
but they will be killed with
    swords.
Then the people in Egypt
    will laugh at them.

Israel Has Trusted Wrong Things

8 "Put the trumpet to your lips
    and give the warning!
The enemy swoops down on my
    people like an eagle.
The Israelites have broken my
    agreement.
They have turned against my
    teachings.
²They cry out to me,
    'Our God, we in Israel know
    you!'
³But Israel has rejected what is
    good.
So the enemy chases them.
⁴They chose their own kings
    without asking my permission.
They chose their own leaders,
    men I did not know.
They made their silver and gold
    into idols.
For all this they will be
    destroyed.
⁵I hate that calf-shaped idol.
I am very angry with the
    people.
How long will they remain
    unclean?ᵈ
⁶The idol is something a craftsman
    made.
It is not God.
Israel's calf-shaped idol
    will surely be smashed to
    pieces.

7"Israel's foolish plans are like
      planting the wind.
But they will harvest a
      whirlwind.
Her plans are like a stalk with no
      head of grain.
It produces nothing.
Even if it produces something,
      other nations would eat it.
8Israel is destroyed.
The people are mixed among
      the other nations.
They have become useless to
      me.
9Like a wild donkey,
      Israel has run to Assyria.
Israel has hired other nations to
      protect her.
10Although Israel is mixed among
      the nations,
I will gather them together.
They will become weaker and
      weaker
as they suffer under the great
      king of Assyria.
11"The more altars Israel built to
      remove sin,
the more they have become
      altars for sinning.
12They reject the many teachings I
      have written for them.
They act as if the teachings
      were strange and foreign to
      them.
13The Israelites offer sacrifices to
      me
and eat the meat.
But the Lord is not pleased with
      them.
He remembers the evil they
      have done.
And he will punish them for their
      sins.
They will be slaves again as
      they were in Egypt.
14The people of Israel have
      forgotten their Maker.
They trust in the palaces they
      have built.

And Judah trusts in her many
      strong, walled cities.
But I will send fire on their cities
and destroy their strong
      towers."

Israel's Punishment

9 Israel, do not rejoice.
Don't celebrate as the other
      nations do.
You have been unfaithful to your
      God.
You love the grain on your
      threshing*d* floors.
So you worship the gods who
      supposedly gave it.
2But there won't be enough grain
      to feed the people.
And there won't be enough wine
      to go around.
3The Israelites will not stay in the
      Lord's land.
Israel will return to being
      captives as they were in
      Egypt.
In Assyria they will eat food that
      they are not allowed to eat.
4The Israelites will not give
      offerings of wine to the
      Lord.
Their sacrifices will not please
      him.
Their sacrifices will be like food
      that is eaten at a funeral.
It is unclean,*d* and everyone who
      eats it becomes unclean.
Their food will only satisfy their
      hunger.
They cannot sacrifice it in the
      Temple.*d*
5What will you do then on the day
      of feasts
and on the festival days of the
      Lord?
6Even if the people are not
      destroyed,
Egypt will take them as
      captives.

Memphis A city in Syria famous for its tombs.
Gibeah The sins of the men of Gibeah caused a civil war. See Judges 19-21.

They will be buried in
        Memphis.*
Weeds will grow over their silver
        treasures.
Thorns will grow over their
        houses.
⁷Let Israel know this.
        The time of punishment has
            come.
        The time to pay for your sins
            has come.
You have sinned very much,
        and your hatred is great.
You think the prophet^d is a fool.
        You say the spiritual man is
            insane.
⁸The prophet is God's watchman
        to warn Israel of danger.
But everywhere he goes you set
        traps for him.
        You treat him as an enemy in
            God's own land.
⁹The men of Israel have become as
        sinful
        as the men of Gibeah* were.
The Lord will remember the evil
        things they have done.
        He will punish them for their
            sins.
¹⁰"When I found Israel,
        it was like finding grapes in the
            desert.
Your ancestors were like
        finding the first figs on the tree.
But when they came to Baal Peor,
        they began worshipping an idol.
        They became as disgusting as
            the thing they worshipped.
¹¹Israel's glory will fly away like a
        bird.
        There will be no more
            pregnancies, no more births,
            no more babies.
¹²But even if the Israelites bring up
        children,
        I will take them all away.
How terrible it will be for them

when I turn away from them!
¹³I have seen Israel, like Tyre,
        given a pleasant place.
But the people of Israel will soon
        bring out
        their children to be killed."
¹⁴Lord, give them what they should
        have.
        What will you give them?
Make their women unable to
        have children.
Give them breasts that cannot
        feed their babies.

¹⁵"The Israelites were wicked in
        Gilgal,
        so I began to hate them there.
Because of the sinful things they
        have done,
        I will force them to leave my
            land.
I will no longer love them.
        Their leaders have turned
            against me.
¹⁶Israel is like a sick plant.
        Its root is dying, and it has no
            fruit.
So the people will have no more
        children.
        And if they did, I would kill the
            children they love."

¹⁷God will reject them,
        because they have not obeyed
            him.
        They will wander among the
            nations.

Israel Will Pay for Sin

10 Israel is like a vine
        that produced plenty of fruit.
As the people became richer,
        they built more altars for idols.
As their land became better,
        they put up better stone pillars
            to honour false gods.
²Their heart was false.
        Now they must pay for their
            guilt.

Memphis A city in Egypt famous for its tombs.
Gibeah The sins of the men of Gibeah caused a civil war. See Judges 19—21.

The Lord will break down their
   altars.
   He will destroy their holy stone
      pillars.

³Then the Israelites will say, "We
      have no king,
   because we didn't honour the
      Lord.
But even if we had one,
   he couldn't do anything for us."
⁴They make many false promises.
   They make agreements they
      don't keep.
So people sue each other in court.
   They are like poisonous weeds
      growing in a ploughed field.
⁵The people from Israel are
      worried about
   the calf-shaped idol at Beth
      Aven.
The people and the priests will
      cry
   because their glorious idol is
      gone.
⁶It will be carried off as a payment
      that was demanded
   to the great king of Assyria.
Israel will be disgraced.
   The people will be ashamed of
      trusting that idol.
⁷The king of Israel will be carried
      off
   like a chip of wood floating on
      the water.
⁸The places of worship at Beth
      Aven will be destroyed.
   They are where Israel sins.
Thorns and weeds will grow
      up
   and cover their altars.
Then they will say to the
      mountains, "Cover us!"
   And they will say to the hills,
      "Fall on us!"

⁹"Israel, you have sinned since the
      time of Gibeah."
   The people there have continued
      sinning.

But war will surely overwhelm
      them,
   because of the evil they have
      done there.
¹⁰When I am ready,
   I will come to punish them.
Armies will come together against
      them.
   They will be punished for their
      many sins.
¹¹Israel is like a well-trained young
      cow
   that likes to thresh*ᵈ* grain.
But I will put a yoke*ᵈ* on her
      neck.
   I will make Israel work hard in
      the field.
Judah will plough.
   Israel will break up the ground.
¹²I said, 'Break new ground.
   Plant what is right.
Then you will harvest good things
   from your loyalty to me.
It is time for you to turn back to
   me, the Lord.
Do it until I come and pour out
   my goodness on you'.
¹³But you have planted evil.
   So you have harvested trouble.
You have trusted in your own
      power
   and your many soldiers.
Now you must live with the
      result of your lies.
¹⁴So your armies will hear the noise
      of battle.
   And all your strong, walled cities
      will be destroyed.
It will be like the time King
      Shalman
   destroyed Beth Arbel in battle.
Mothers and children were
      crushed to the ground
      together.
¹⁵The same will happen to you,
      people of Bethel,
   because you did so much evil.
When that time comes,
   the king of Israel will die.

Gibeah The sins of the men of Gibeah caused a civil war. See Judges 19–21.

God's Love for Israel

11 "When Israel was a child, I
loved him.
And I called my son out of
Egypt.
2But the more I called to the
people of Israel,
the further they went from
me.
They offered sacrifices to the
Baals.[d]
They burned incense[d] to the
idols.
3But it was I who taught Israel to
walk.
I took them by the arms.
But they did not understand
that I had healed them.
4I led them with cords of human
kindness,
with ties of love.
I lifted the yoke[d] from their neck.
I bent down and fed them.

5"The Israelites will become
captives again, as they were
in Egypt.
The king of Assyria will become
their king.
This is because they refuse to
turn to God.
6War will sweep through their
cities.
It will destroy them,
because of their wicked plans.
7My people have made up their
minds
to turn away from me.
The prophets[d] call them to turn to
me.
But none of them honours me at
all.

8"Israel, I don't want to give you
up.
I don't want to go away and
leave you.
I don't want to make you like
Admah.

I don't want to treat you like
Zeboiim.[n]
My heart beats for you.
My love for you stirs up my
pity.
9I won't punish you in my anger.
I won't destroy Israel again.
I am God and not man.
I am the Holy One, and I am
among you.
I will not come against you in
anger.
10I will call for my people like
a lion calling for its young.
My children will come and follow
me.
They will hurry to me from the
west.
11They will come swiftly
like birds from a captivity like
Egypt was,
and like doves from Assyria.
I will settle them again in their
homes,"
says the Lord.

The Lord Is Against Israel

12Israel has surrounded me with
lies.
The people of Israel have made
their secret plans.
And Judah turns against God,
the faithful Holy One.

12 What Israel does is as
useless as chasing the wind,
as dangerous as being in a
windstorm.
They tell more and more lies
and do more and more violence.
They make agreements with
Assyria,
and they send a gift of olive oil
to Egypt.
2The Lord also has some things
against Judah.
He will punish Israel for what
they have done.
He will give them what they
deserve.

Admah and Zeboiim Two other cities destroyed when God destroyed Sodom and Gomorrah.

³Their ancestor Jacob held on to
his brother's heel
while the two of them were
being born.
When Jacob grew to be a man,
he wrestled with God.
⁴He wrestled with the angel and
won.
Jacob cried and asked for his
blessing.
Later, God met with him at
Bethel
and spoke with him there.
⁵He is the Lord God of heaven's
armies.
He wants to be remembered as
the Lord.
⁶Like Jacob you must return to
him.
You must be loyal and true to
him.
You must do what is honest and
just.
You must always trust in him as
your God.

⁷The merchants use dishonest
scales.
They like to cheat people.
⁸The people of Israel boast that
they are rich.
They think that because they
are rich
no one will learn about their
sins.

⁹"But I am the Lord your God.
I brought you out of Egypt.
I will make you live in tents again
as you used to do in the desert.
¹⁰I spoke to the prophets*d*
and gave them many visions.
Through them, I taught my
lessons to you."

¹¹The people of Gilead are evil.
They are worth nothing.
People sacrifice bulls at Gilgal.
But their altars will become like
piles of stone in a ploughed field.
¹²Your ancestor Jacob fled to North
West Mesopotamia.

There he worked to get a wife.
He tended sheep to pay for her.
¹³Later the Lord used a prophet
to bring Jacob's descendants*d*
out of Egypt.
The Lord used a prophet
to take care of the Israelites.
¹⁴But the Israelites made the Lord
angry.
They killed other people.
They deserve to die for their
crimes.
The Lord will make them pay
for the disgraceful things they
have done.

The Final Word Against Israel

13 People used to fear the tribe*d*
of Ephraim.
They were important people in
Israel.
But they sinned by worshipping
Baal.*d*
So they must die.
²But they keep on sinning more
and more.
They make idols of their silver.
Those idols are cleverly made.
They are the work of a
craftsman.
Yet the people of Israel say to
each other,
"Kiss those calf idols and
sacrifice to them."
³So those people will be like the
morning dew.
They will disappear like the
morning mist.
They will be like chaff*d* blown
from the threshing*d* floor.
They will vanish away like
smoke rising from a
chimney.

⁴"I have been the Lord their God
since they were in the land of
Egypt.
They have really known no other
God except me.
I am the one who has saved
them.

5I cared for them in the desert
where it was hot and dry.
6I gave them food, and they
became full and satisfied.
But then they became proud and
forgot me.
7That is why I will be like a lion to
them.
I will be like a leopard waiting
by the road.
8I will attack like a bear robbed of
her cubs.
I will rip their bodies open.
I will devour them like a lion.
I will tear them apart like a wild
animal.
9"Israel, I will destroy you
for turning against me, your
helper.
10What good are your kings and
your leaders now?
Can they save you in any of
your towns?
You asked for them, saying,
'Give us a king and leaders'.
11So I gave you kings, but only in
anger.
And I took them away in my
great anger.
12The sins of Israel are on record.
They are filed away, waiting for
punishment.
13Israel has a chance to live again,
but the people are too foolish to
take it.
They are like an unborn baby
who won't come out of its
mother's womb.
14So I will not save them from the
place where the dead are.
I will not rescue them from
death.
I will call on death to hurt them.
I will call on the place where the
dead are to destroy them.
I will show them no mercy.
15Israel has become important
among the nations.
But the Lord will send a
destroyer from the east.

He will come like a wind from the
desert
that dries up all the springs and
wells of water.
He will destroy all their treasures,
everything of value.
16The nation of Israel will be
punished,
because it fought against God.
The people of Israel will die by
the sword.
Their children will be torn to
pieces.
And their pregnant women will
be ripped open."

Israel Returns to God

14 Israel, return to the Lord
your God.
Your sins have caused your ruin.
2Come back to the Lord
and say these words to him:
"Take away all our sin
and kindly receive us.
Then we will give you the praise
we promised you.
3Assyria cannot save us.
We will not trust in our horses.
We will not say again, 'Our gods',
to the things our hands have
made.
We are like orphans, but
you show mercy to us."

4The Lord says,
"I will forgive them for leaving
me.
I will love them freely.
I am not angry with them any
more.
5I will be like the dew to Israel.
It will blossom like a lily.
Like the cedar trees in Lebanon,
its roots will be firm.
6The people will be like spreading
branches.
They will be like the beautiful
olive trees.
They will be like the
sweet-smelling cedars in
Lebanon.

⁷The people of Israel will again live
        under my protection.
    They will grow like the grain.
    They will bloom like a vine.
        They will be as famous as the
        wine of Lebanon.
⁸Israel, have nothing to do with
        idols.
    I, the Lord, am the one who
        answers your prayers.
    I am the one who watches over
        you.

I am like a green pine tree.
    Your blessings come from me."

⁹A wise person will know these
        things.
    An understanding person will
        take them to heart.
    The Lord's ways are right.
    Good people live by following
        them,
    but those who turn against God
        die because of them.

JOEL

God Will Punish Judah

Locusts Destroy the Crops

1 The Lord spoke his word to Joel
son of Pethuel:

²Older leaders, listen to this
message.
Listen to me, all you people who
live in the land.
Nothing like this has ever
happened during your
lifetime.
Nothing like this has ever
happened during your
fathers' lifetimes.
³Tell your children about these
things.
And let your children tell their
children.
And let your grandchildren tell
their children.
⁴What the cutting locusts have not
eaten,
the swarming locusts have
eaten.
And what the swarming locusts
have left,
the hopping locusts have eaten.
And what the hopping locusts
have left,
the destroying locusts*ⁿ* have
eaten.

⁵Drunkards, wake up and cry!
All of you people who drink
wine, cry!
Cry because your sweet wine
has been taken away from you.
⁶A powerful nation has come into
my land.
It has too many soldiers to
count.

It has teeth like a lion.
And it has fangs like a female
lion.
⁷That army has eaten my
grapevines.
It has destroyed my fig trees.
It has eaten the bark off my
trees
and left the branches white.

⁸Cry as a young woman cries
when the man she was going to
marry is killed.
⁹There will be no more grain or
drink offerings
to offer in the Temple*ᵈ* of the
Lord.
Because of this, the priests,
the servants of the Lord,
cry.
¹⁰The fields are ruined.
Even the ground is dried
up.
The grain is destroyed.
The new wine is dried up.
And the olive oil runs out.
¹¹Be sad, farmers.
Cry loudly, you who grow
grapes.
Cry for the wheat and the barley.
Cry because the harvest in the
field is lost.
¹²The vines have become dry.
And the fig trees are dying.
The pomegranate*ᵈ* trees, the date
palm trees and the apple
trees have dried up.
All the trees in the field have
died.
And the happiness of the people
has died, too.

---

cutting . . . locusts These are different names for an insect like a large grasshopper. The
locust can quickly destroy trees, plants and crops. In this destruction by locusts, Joel sees
a warning. God will cause this type of destruction when he punishes his people.

¹³Priests, put on your rough cloth
and cry to show your
sadness.
Servants of the altar, cry out
loud.
Servants of my God,
sleep in your rough cloth to
show your sadness.
Cry because there will be no more
grain or drink offerings
to offer in the Temple of your
God.
¹⁴Call the people together.
Tell them there will be a time to
give up food.
Bring together the older leaders
and everyone who lives in the
land.
Bring them to the Temple of the
Lord your God.
And cry out to the Lord.
¹⁵This will be a terrible day!
The Lord's day of judging is
near.
At that time punishment will come
like an attack from God
All-Powerful.

¹⁶Our food is taken away
while we watch.
Joy and happiness are gone
from the Temple of our God.
¹⁷We planted seeds,
but they lie dry and dead in the
ground.
Our barns are empty and falling
down.
The store rooms for grain have
been broken down.
This is because the grain has
dried up.
¹⁸The animals are hungry and
groaning!
The herds of cattle wander
around confused.
They have no grass to eat.
Even the flocks of sheep suffer.
¹⁹Lord, I am calling to you for help.
Fire has burned up the open
pastures.

Flames have burned all the trees
in the field.
²⁰Wild animals also need your help.
The water in the streams has
dried up.
Fire has burned up the open
pastures.

The Coming Day of Judgement

2 Blow the trumpet in Jerusalem.
Shout a warning on my holy
mountain.
Let all the people who live in the
land shake with fear.
The Lord's day of judging is
coming.
The Lord's day of judging is
near.
²It will be a dark, gloomy day.
It will be a cloudy and black day.
Like the light at sunrise,
the great and powerful army will
spread over the mountains.
There has never been anything
like it before.
And there will never be anything
like it again.

³The army destroys the land
like a burning fire.
The land in front of them is like
the garden of Eden.
The land behind them is like an
empty desert.
Nothing will escape them.
⁴They look like horses.
They run like war horses.
⁵Listen to them!
It is like the noise of chariots
rumbling over the mountains.
It is like the noise of crackling
flames
burning dry stalks.
They are like a powerful army
lined up for battle.
⁶Before this army, nations shake
with fear.
Their faces become pale.
⁷The army charges ahead like
soldiers.

They climb over the walls like
  warriors.
They all march straight ahead.
  They do not move off their path.
8They do not run into each other.
  Each one walks in line.
They charge through all efforts to
    stop them
  and stay in line.
9They run into the city.
  They run along the tops of the
    walls.
They climb into the houses.
  They enter through windows
    like a thief.
10Before them, earth and sky
    shake.
  The sun and the moon become
    dark,
  and the stars stop shining.
11The Lord calls out orders loudly
    as he leads his army.
  That army obeys his commands.
  It is very large and powerful.
  The Lord's day of judging
    is an overwhelming and terrible
    day.
  No one can stand up against it.

Change Your Hearts

12The Lord says, "Now, come back
    to me with all your heart.
  Go without food, and cry and be
    sad."

13Tearing your clothes is not
    enough to show you are sad.
  Let your heart be broken.
  Come back to the Lord your God.
  He is kind and shows mercy.
  He doesn't become angry quickly.
  He has great love.
  He would rather forgive than
    punish.
14Who knows? Maybe the Lord will
    change his mind
  and leave behind a blessing for
    you.
  Then you may give grain and
    drink offerings
  to the Lord your God.

15Blow the trumpet in Jerusalem.
  Call for a special time of going
    without food.
  Call for a special meeting.
16Bring the people together.
  Make the meeting holy for the
    Lord.
  Bring together the older leaders.
  Bring together the children,
    even babies that still feed at
    their mothers' breasts.
  The bridegroom should come from
    his room.
  The bride should come from her
    bedroom.
17The priests, the Lord's servants,
    should cry.
  They should cry between the
    altar and entrance to the
    Temple.*d*
  They should say, "Lord, have
    mercy on your people.
  Don't let them be put to shame.
  Don't let other nations make fun
    of them.
  Don't let people in other nations
    ask,
  'Where is their God?'"

The Lord Restores the Land

18Then the Lord became concerned
    about his land.
  He felt sorry for his people.
19The Lord said to them:
  "I will send you grain, wine and
    olive oil.
  You will have plenty.
  No more will I shame you
    among the nations.
20I will force the army from the
    north to leave your land.
  I will force them into a dry,
    empty land.
  Their soldiers in front will be
    forced into the Dead Sea.*d*
  And those in the rear will be
    forced into the
    Mediterranean Sea.
  Their bodies will rot and stink
    because they did horrible
    things."

21But, land, don't be afraid.
Be happy and full of joy
because the Lord has begun to
do wonderful things.
22Wild animals, don't be afraid.
The open pastures will grow
grass.
The trees will grow fruit.
The fig trees and the vines will
grow much fruit.
23So be happy, people of Jerusalem.
Be joyful in the Lord your God.
He will do what is right
and will give you rain.
He will send the early rain
and the late rain for you, as
before.
24And the threshing[d] floors will be
full of wheat.
And the barrels will overflow
with wine and olive oil.

The Lord Speaks

25"I sent my great army against
you.
Those swarming locusts and the
hopping locusts,
the destroying locusts and the
cutting locusts[n] ate your
crops.
But I will pay you back
for those years of trouble.
26Then you will have plenty to eat.
You will be full.
You will praise the name of the
Lord your God.
He has done miracles[d] for you.
My people will never again be
shamed.
27Then you will know that I am
among the people of Israel.
You will know that I am the
Lord your God.
There is no other God.
My people will never be shamed
again.

28"After this,
I will give my Spirit[d] freely to all
kinds of people.
Your sons and daughters will
prophesy.[d]
Your old men will dream
dreams.
Your young men will see
visions.
29At that time I will give my Spirit
even to servants, both men and
women.
30I will show miracles
in the sky and on the earth:
blood, fire and thick smoke.
31The sun will become dark.
The moon will become red as
blood.
And then the Lord's
overwhelming and terrible
day of judging will come.
32Then anyone who asks the Lord
for help
will be saved.
Even on Mount Zion[d] and in
Jerusalem
there will be people who will be
saved.
This will happen just as the Lord
has said.
Those left alive after the day of
punishment
are the people whom the Lord
called.

Punishment for Judah's Enemies

3 "In those days and at that time,
I will give Judah and Jerusalem
back their riches.
2I will also gather all the nations
together.
I will bring them down into the
Valley of Judgement.
And there I will judge them.
Those nations scattered my own
people, Israel.

---

swarming . . . locusts These are different names for an insect like a large grasshopper. The
locust can quickly destroy trees, plants and crops. In this destruction by locusts, Joel sees
a warning. God will cause this type of destruction when he punishes his people.

They forced my people to live in
  other nations.
They divided up my land.
[3]They threw lots[d] for my people.
They traded boys for prostitutes.[d]
  And they sold girls to buy wine
  to drink.

[4]"Tyre and Sidon and all of you regions of Philistia! What do you have
against me? Are you punishing me for
something I did? Or are you doing
something to hurt me? Then I will
quickly do to you what you have done
to me. [5]You took my silver and gold.
You took my precious treasures and
put them in your temples. [6]You sold
the people of Judah and Jerusalem to
the Greeks. That way you could send
them far from their land.
[7]"You sent my people to that faraway place. But I will bring them
back. And I will do to you what you
have done to them. [8]I will sell your
sons and daughters to the people of
Judah. Then they will sell them to the
Sabean people far away." The Lord
said this.

God Judges the Nations

[9]Announce this among the nations:
  Prepare for war!
Wake up the soldiers!
Let all the men of war come
  near and attack.
[10]Make your ploughs into swords.
  Make spears from your hooks
  for trimming trees.
Let the weak say,
  "I am strong."
[11]All of you nations, hurry.
  Come together in that place.
Lord, send your strong soldiers
  to gather the nations.

[12]"Wake up, nations.
  Come to the Valley of
  Judgement.
There I will sit to judge

all the nations on every side.
[13]Cut them down like grain
  because the harvest is ripe with
  sin.
Come, walk on them as you would
  walk on grapes,
  because the winepress[d] is full.
The barrels are full of their sins
  and spilling over.
These people are so evil!"

[14]There are many people
  in the Valley of Decision.[n]
The Lord's day of judging is near
  in the Valley of Decision.
[15]The sun and the moon will
  become dark.
The stars will stop shining.
[16]The Lord will roar like a lion from
  Jerusalem.
His loud voice will sound like a
  growl from Jerusalem.
And the sky and the earth will
  shake.
But the Lord will be a safe place
  for his people.
He will be a strong place of
  safety for the people of
  Israel.

[17]"Then you will know that I am the
  Lord your God.
I stay in my holy Mount Zion.[d]
Jerusalem will become holy.
Strangers will never take over
  that city again.

A New Life Promised for Judah

[18]"On that day the mountains will be
  covered with grapes for
  sweet wine.
The hills will be covered with
  cows to give milk.
And water will flow through all
  the ravines of Judah.
A fountain will flow from the
  Temple[d] of the Lord.
It will give water to the valley of
  acacia trees.

Valley of Decision This is like the name "The Valley of Judgement" in 3:2 and 3:12.

¹⁹But Egypt will become empty.
  And Edom will become an
    empty desert.
  This is because they were cruel to
    the people of Judah.
  They killed innocent people in
    the land of Judah.

²⁰But there will always be people
    living in Judah.
  And people will live in Jerusalem
    from now on.
²¹Egypt and Edom killed my people.
  So I will definitely punish them."

The Lord lives in Jerusalem!

AMOS

God Warns Israel to Stop Sinning

1 Amos was one of the shepherds from the town of Tekoa. God showed him this vision about Israel. It was at the time Uzziah was king of Judah and Jeroboam son of Jehoash was king of Israel. This happened two years before the earthquake.

²Amos said,
"The Lord will roar like a lion
  from Jerusalem.
His loud voice will sound like a
  growl from Jerusalem.
The green pastures of the
  shepherds will become dry.
Even Mount Carmel will dry
  up."

Israel's Neighbours Are Punished

The People of Aram

³This is what the Lord says:
"For the many crimes Damascus
  is doing,
I will punish them.
They beat the people of Gilead
  with threshing*d* boards that had
  iron teeth.
⁴So I will send fire upon the house
  of Hazael.
That fire will destroy the strong
  towers of Ben-Hadad.
⁵I will break down the gate of
  Damascus.
I will destroy the king who is in
  the Valley of Aven.
I will also destroy the king of Beth
  Eden.
The people of Aram will be
  taken captive to the country
  of Kir," says the Lord.

The People of Philistia

⁶This is what the Lord says:

"For the many crimes Gaza is
  doing,
I will punish them.
They sold all the people of one
  area
  as slaves to Edom.
⁷So I will send a fire on the walls
  of Gaza.
That fire will destroy the city's
  strong towers.
⁸I will destroy the king of the city
  of Ashdod.
I will destroy the king of the
  city of Ashkelon.
Then I will turn against the people
  of the city of Ekron.
I will punish the Philistines until
  they are all dead," says the
  Lord God.

The People of Phoenicia

⁹This is what the Lord says:
"For the many crimes Tyre is
  doing,
I will punish them.
They sold all the people of one
  area
  as slaves to Edom.
They forgot the brotherly
  agreement they had made
  with Israel.
¹⁰So I will send fire on the walls of
  Tyre.
That fire will destroy the city's
  strong towers."

The People of Edom

¹¹This is what the Lord says:
"For the many crimes Edom is
  doing,
I will punish them.
They hunted down their brothers,
  the Israelites, with the
  sword.

They showed them no mercy.
The people of Edom were
    continually angry.
And they did not hold back their
    great anger.
[12] So I will send fire on the city of
    Teman.
That fire will even destroy the
    strong towers of Bozrah."[n]

The People of Ammon

[13] This is what the Lord says:
"For the many crimes Ammon is
    doing,
I will punish them.
They ripped open the pregnant
    women in Gilead.
They did this so they could take
    over that land
and make their own country
    larger.
[14] So I will send fire on the walls of
    Rabbah.
That fire will destroy the city's
    strong towers.
It will come during a day of battle.
There will be strong winds on a
    stormy day.
[15] Then their king and leaders will be
    captured.
They will all be taken away
    together," says the Lord.

The People of Moab

2 This is what the Lord says:
"For the many crimes Moab is
    doing,
I will punish them.
They burned the bones of the
    king of Edom into lime.
[2] So I will send fire on Moab.
And it will destroy the strong
    towers of the city of
    Kerioth.
The people of Moab will die in a
    great noise.
They will die in the middle of
    sounds of war and trumpets.

[3] So I will bring an end to the king
    of Moab.
And I will kill all its leaders with
    him," says the Lord.

The People of Judah

[4] This is what the Lord says:
"For the many crimes Judah is
    doing,
I will punish them.
They rejected the teachings of the
    Lord.
They did not keep his
    commands.
Their ancestors followed false
    gods.
And Judah followed those same
    gods.
[5] So I will send fire on Judah.
It will destroy the strong towers
    of Jerusalem."

Israel Is Punished

[6] This is what the Lord says:
"For the many crimes Israel is
    doing,
I will punish them.
For silver they sell people who
    have done nothing wrong.
They sell poor people for the
    price of a pair of sandals.
[7] They walk on poor people
as if they were dust.
They refuse to be fair to those
    who are suffering.
Fathers and sons have sexual
    relations with the same
    woman.
By doing this they ruin my holy
    name.
[8] As they worship at their altars,
    they lie down on clothes taken
    from poor people.
They make people pay money as
    punishment.
With that money they buy wine
    to drink in the house of their
    god.

Teman and Bozrah   Teman was in northern Edom, and Bozrah was in southern Edom. So this means the whole country will be destroyed.

9"But it was I who destroyed the
Amorites before them.
The Amorites were tall like
cedar trees and as strong as
oaks.
But I destroyed them completely.
10It was I who brought you from the
land of Egypt.
For 40 years I led you through
the desert.
I led you so I could give you the
land of the Amorites.
11I made some of your sons to be
prophets.*d*
I made some of your young men
to be Nazirites.*d*
People of Israel, isn't this true?"
says the Lord.
12"But you made the Nazirites drink
wine.
You told the prophets not to
prophesy my message.
13Now I will crush you
as a wagon loaded with grain
crushes anything beneath it.
14No one will escape, not even the
fastest runner.
Strong men will not be strong
enough.
Warriors will not be able to save
themselves.
15Soldiers with bows and arrows will
not stand and fight.
Even soldiers who run quickly
will not get away.
Soldiers on horses will not
escape alive.
16At that time even the bravest
warriors
will run away without their
armour," says the Lord.

Warning to Israel

3 Listen to this message that the
Lord has spoken against you, people of Israel. The message is against
the whole nation the Lord brought out
of Egypt.
2"I have chosen only you
out of all the families of the
earth.

So I will punish you
for all your sins."

3Two people will not walk together
unless they have agreed to do
this.
4A lion in the forest will roar
when he has caught an animal.
He does not growl in his den
when he has caught nothing.
5A bird will not fall into a trap
where there is no bait.
The trap will not spring shut
if there is nothing to catch.
6When a trumpet blows a warning,
the people tremble.
When trouble comes to a city,
the Lord has caused it.
7Before the Lord God does
anything,
he tells his servants the
prophets.*d*
8The lion has roared!
Who wouldn't be afraid?
The Lord God has spoken,
and I must prophesy his
message.

9Announce this to the strong
towers of Ashdod.
Announce it to the strong cities
of Egypt:
"Come to the mountains of
Samaria.
There you will see great
confusion.
You will see people hurting
others."

10"The people don't know how to do
what is right," says the
Lord.
"Their strong cities are filled
with treasures they took by
force from others."

11So this is what the Lord God says:
"An enemy will take over the
land.
He will pull down your strong
towers.
He will take the treasures you
hid in your strong cities."

¹²This is what the Lord says:
"A shepherd might save from a
   lion's mouth
only two leg bones or a scrap of
   an ear of his sheep.
In the same way only a few
   Israelites will be saved.
These people now sit on their
   beds in Samaria.
They sit on their couches."

¹³"You nations, listen to what I say
against the family of Israel. You are
my witnesses against them," says the
Lord God, the God of heaven's armies.

¹⁴"The people of Israel sinned, and
   I will punish them.
I will also destroy the altars at
   Bethel.
The corners of the altar will be
   cut off,
and they will fall to the ground.
¹⁵I will tear down the winter house,
   together with the summer
   house.
The houses decorated with ivory
   will be destroyed.
And the great houses will come
   to an end," says the Lord.

Israel Will Not Return

4 Listen to this message, you rich
women on the Mountain of
   Samaria.
You take things from the poor
   and crush people who are in
   need.
You tell your husbands,
   "Bring us money so we can
   drink!"
²The Lord God has promised this:
   "It is certain that I am a holy
   God.
So it is certain that the time will
   come
when some of you will be taken
   away by hooks.
The rest of you will be taken
   away with fish-hooks.
³You will go straight out of the city

through holes in the walls.
And you will be thrown on the
   rubbish dump," says the
   Lord.

⁴"Go to the city of Bethel and sin.
   Go to Gilgal and sin even more.
Offer your sacrifices every
   morning.
Bring one-tenth of your crops on
   the third day.
⁵Offer bread made with yeast as a
   sacrifice to show your
   thanks,
and boast about the offerings
   you bring to show thanks to
   the Lord.
Boast about these things,
   Israelites.
This is what you love to do,"
   says the Lord God.

⁶"I did not give you any food to
   eat.
There was not enough food in
   any of your towns.
But you did not come back to
   me," says the Lord.
⁷"I held back the rain from you
   three months before harvest
   time.
Then I let it rain on one city
   but not on another.
Rain fell on one field,
   but another field got none and
   dried up.
⁸People weak from thirst went
   from town to town for
   water.
But they could not get enough
   water to drink.
But you still did not come back
   to me," says the Lord.
⁹"I made your crops die from
   disease and mildew.^d
I destroyed your gardens and
   your vineyards.
Locusts^d ate your fig trees and
   olive trees.
But you still did not come back
   to me," says the Lord.
¹⁰"I sent disasters against you,

as I did to Egypt.
I killed your young men with
swords.
I also killed your horses.
I made you smell the stink from
all the dead bodies.
But you still did not come back
to me," says the Lord.
11"I destroyed some of you
as I destroyed Sodom and
Gomorrah.
You were like a burning stick
pulled from a fire.
But you still have not come back
to me," says the Lord.

12"So this is what I will do to you,
Israel.
And because I will do this to
you,
get ready to meet your God,
Israel."

13He is the one who makes the
mountains.
He creates the wind.
He makes his thoughts known to
man.
He changes the dawn into
darkness.
He walks over the mountains of
the earth.
His name is the Lord God of
heaven's armies.

Israel Needs to Repent

5 Listen to this funeral song that I
sing about you, people of Israel.
2"Israel has fallen.
It will not rise up again.
It was left alone in the land.
There is no one to lift it up."

3This is what the Lord God says:
"If 1,000 soldiers leave a city,
only 100 will return.
If 100 soldiers leave a city,
only ten will return."

4This is what the Lord says to the
nation of Israel:
"Come to me and live.
5 But do not look for Bethel.

Do not go to Gilgal,
and do not go down to
Beersheba.
The people of Gilgal will be taken
away as captives.
And Bethel will become
nothing."
6Come to the Lord and live.
If you don't, he will destroy the
descendantsd of Joseph as a
fire would.
The fire will burn,
but there will be no one to put it
out for Bethel.
7You change the justice of the
courts into something unfair.
You reject what is right.

8God is the one who made the star
groups Pleiades and Orion.
He changes darkness into the
morning light.
And he changes the day into the
dark night.
He calls for the waters of the sea
to pour out on the earth.
The Lord is his name.
9He destroys the protected city.
And he ruins the strong, walled
city.

10You hate those who speak in court
against evil.
And you hate those who tell the
truth.
11You walk on poor people.
You force them to give you
grain.
You have built fancy houses of cut
stone,
but you will not live in them.
You have planted beautiful
vineyards,
but you will not drink the wine
from them.
12It is because I know your many
crimes.
I know your terrible sins.
You hurt people who do right.
You accept money to do wrong.
You keep the poor from getting
justice in court.

¹³In such times the wise man will
      keep quiet,
   because it is a bad time.

¹⁴Try to do good, not evil.
   Then you will live.
And the Lord God of heaven's
      armies will be with you
   just as you say he is.
¹⁵Hate evil and love good.
   Be fair in the courts.
Perhaps the Lord God of heaven's
      armies will be kind
   to the people of Joseph who are
      left alive.

¹⁶This is what the Lord, the Lord
God of heaven's armies, says:
   "People will be crying in all the
      public places.
   They will be saying, 'Oh, no!' in
      the streets.
   They will call the farmers to
      come and weep.
   They will pay people to cry out
      loud for them.
¹⁷People will be crying in all the
      vineyards.
   This is because I will pass
      among you to punish you,"
   says the Lord.

The Lord's Day of Judging
¹⁸How terrible it will be for you who
      want
   the Lord's day of judging to
      come.
Why do you want that day to
      come?
   It will bring darkness for you,
      not light.
¹⁹It will be like a man who runs
      from a lion
   and meets a bear.
It will be like him going into his
      house
   and putting his hand on the wall.
And then a snake bites him.
²⁰So the Lord's day of judging will
      bring darkness, not light.
   It will be a time of sadness, not
      joy.

²¹The Lord says, "I hate your
      feasts.
   I cannot stand your religious
      meetings.
²²You offer me burnt offerings and
      grain offerings,
   but I won't accept them.
You bring the best fellowship
      offerings,
   but I will ignore them.
²³Take the noise of your songs
      away from here!
   I won't listen to the music of
      your harps.
²⁴But let justice flow like a river.
   Let goodness flow like a stream
      that never stops.

²⁵"People of Israel, you did not
      bring me sacrifices and
      offerings
   while you travelled in the desert
      for 40 years.
²⁶But now you will have to carry
      with you
   your king, the false god
      Sakkuth,
   and Kaiwan your idol
   and the idols of your other star
      gods you have made.
²⁷This is because I will send you
      away as captives beyond
      Damascus,"
   says the Lord. His name is God
      of heaven's armies.

Israel Will Be Destroyed

6 How terrible it will be for you
      who live comfortable lives
      in Jerusalem.
   How terrible for you who live on
      Mount Samaria and feel safe.
You think you are important
      people of the best nation in
      the world.
   The Israelites come to you for
      help.
²Go and look at the city of Calneh.
   From there go to the great city
      Hamath.

Go down to Gath of the
    Philistines.
Are you better than these
    kingdoms?
Are their lands larger than yours?
³You put off the day of punishment.
    But you bring near the day
        when you can do evil to
        others.
⁴You lie on beds decorated with
    ivory.
    You stretch out on your
        couches.
You eat tender lambs
    and fattened calves.
⁵You play your harps.
    Like David, you compose songs
        on musical instruments.
⁶You drink wine by the bowlful.
    You use the best perfumed
        lotions.
    But you are not sad over the
        ruin of Israel, Joseph's
        descendants.ᵈ
⁷So you will be some of the first
    ones taken as slaves.
    Your feasting and lying around
    will come to an end.

⁸The Lord God made this promise.
The Lord God of heaven's armies
says:
    "I hate the pride of the people of
        Israel.
    I hate their strong towers.
    So I will let the enemy take the
        city
    and everything in it."

⁹At that time there might be ten
people left alive in a house. But they
will also die. ¹⁰A relative and one who
is to prepare bodies for burial may
come to get the bodies. One of them
will take the bodies out to burn them.
He will call to the other and ask, "Are
there any other dead bodies with
you?"
    That person will answer, "No."

Then the one who asked will say,
"Hush! We must not speak the name
of the Lord."

¹¹The Lord has given the command.
    The large house will be broken
        into pieces.
    And the small house will be
        broken into bits.
¹²Horses do not run on rocks.
    People do not plough rocks with
        oxen.
    But you have changed fairness
        into poison.
    You have changed what is right
        into something wrong.
¹³You are happy that the town of Lo
        Debarⁿ was taken.
    You say, "We have taken
        Karnaimⁿ by our own
        strength."

¹⁴The Lord God of heaven's armies
        says,
    "Israel, I will bring a nation
        against you.
    It will bring trouble for you from
        Lebo Hamath in the north
    to the valley south of the Dead
        Sea."ᵈ

The Vision of Locusts

7 This is what the Lord God showed
me: he was forming a swarm of lo-
custs.ᵈ This was after the king had
taken his share of the first crop. The
second crop had just begun growing.
²The locusts ate all the crops in the
country. After that I said, "Lord God,
forgive us, I beg you! No one in Israel
could live through this. Israel is too
small already!"
    ³So the Lord felt sorry about this.
"This will not happen," said the Lord.

The Vision of Fire

⁴This is what the Lord God showed
me: the Lord God was calling for fire
to come to punish. The fire dried up

Lo Debar   This name means "nothing at all".
Karnaim   This name means "horns", a symbol of strength.

the deep water and destroyed the land. ⁵Then I cried out, "Lord God, stop, I beg you! No one in Israel could live through this. Israel is too small already."

⁶So the Lord felt sorry about this. "This will not happen either," said the Lord God.

The Vision of the Plumb Line

⁷This is what the Lord showed me: the Lord stood by a straight wall. He had a plumb line*d* in his hand. ⁸The Lord said to me, "Amos, what do you see?"

I said, "A plumb line."

Then the Lord said, "See, I will put a plumb line among my people Israel to show how crooked they are. I will not feel sorry for them any longer.

⁹"The places where Isaac's
    descendants*d* worship will be
    destroyed.
Israel's holy places will be
    turned into ruins.
And I will attack King
    Jeroboam's family with the
    sword."

Amaziah and Amos

¹⁰So Amaziah, a priest at Bethel, sent this message to Jeroboam king of Israel: "Amos is making evil plans against you with the people of Israel. He has been speaking so much that this land can't hold all his words. ¹¹Amos has said this:
'Jeroboam will die by the sword,
    and the people of Israel will be
    taken as captives
out of their own country'."

¹²Then Amaziah said to Amos, "Seer,*d* go, run away to Judah. Do your prophesying*d* and earn your living there. ¹³But don't prophesy any more here at Bethel. This is King Jeroboam's holy place. This is Israel's temple."

¹⁴Then Amos answered Amaziah, "I do not make my living as a prophet. And I am not a member of a group of prophets. I make my living as a shepherd. And I take care of sycamore trees. ¹⁵But the Lord took me away from tending the sheep. He said to me, 'Go, prophesy to my people, the Israelites'. ¹⁶So listen to the Lord's message. You tell me,
'Don't prophesy against Israel.
    And stop prophesying against
        the descendants of Isaac'.

¹⁷"Because you have said this, the Lord says:
'Your wife will become a
        prostitute*d* in the city.
Your sons and daughters will be
        killed with swords.
Other people will take your land
        and divide it among
        themselves.
And you will die in a foreign
        country.
The people of Israel will definitely
        be taken
    from their own land as
        captives'."

The Vision of Ripe Fruit

8 This is what the Lord showed me: a basket of ripe fruit. ²The Lord said to me, "Amos, what do you see?"

I said, "A basket of fruit from the end of the harvest."

Then the Lord said to me, "An end has come for my people, the Israelites. I will not overlook their sins any more.

³"On that day the palace songs will become funeral songs," says the Lord God. "There will be dead bodies thrown everywhere! Silence!"

⁴Listen to me you who walk on
        helpless people.
You are trying to destroy the
        poor people of this country.

⁵Your businessmen say,
"When will the New Moon*d*
Festival be over
so we can sell grain?
When will the Sabbath*d* be over
so we can bring out wheat to
sell?
We can charge them more
and give them less.
We can change the scales to
cheat the people.
⁶We will buy poor people for silver.
And we will buy needy people
for the price of a pair of
sandals.
We will even sell the wheat that
was swept up from the
floor."

⁷The Lord used his name, the Pride
of Jacob, to make a promise. He said,
"I will never forget what these people
have done.
⁸The whole land will shake because
of it.
Everyone who lives in the land
will cry for those who died.
The whole land will rise like the
Nile.
It will be shaken, and then it will
fall
like the Nile River in Egypt."

⁹The Lord God says:
"At that time I will cause the sun
to go down at noon.
I will make the earth dark on a
clear day.
¹⁰I will change your festivals into
days of crying for the dead.
All your songs will become
songs of sadness for the
dead.
I will make all of you wear rough
cloth to show your sadness.
You will shave your heads to
show sadness.

I will make that day like the crying
for the death of an only son.
Its end will be very painful."

¹¹The Lord God says: "The days
are coming
when I will cause a time of
hunger in the land.
The people will not be hungry for
bread or thirsty for water,
but they will be hungry for
words from the Lord.
¹²People will wander from the
Mediterranean Sea to the
Dead Sea.*d*
They will wander from the north
to the east.
They will search for the word of
the Lord,
but they won't find it.
¹³At that time the beautiful young
women and the young men
will become weak from thirst.
¹⁴They made promises by the idol in
Samaria.
They said, 'As surely as the god
of Dan lives . . .'
And they said, 'As surely as the
god of Beersheba*n* lives, we
promise . . .'
So they will fall
and never get up again."

Israel Will Be Destroyed

9 I saw the Lord standing by the altar. He said:
"Smash the top of the pillars
so that even the bottom of the
doors will shake.
Make the pillars fall on the
people's heads.
Anyone left alive I will kill with a
sword.
Not one person will get away.
No one will escape.
²If they dig down as deep as where
the dead are,
I will pull them up from there.

Dan . . . Beersheba Dan was the city farthest north in Israel, and Beersheba was the city farthest south.

If they climb up into the skies,
   I will bring them down from
      there.
[3]If they hide at the top of Mount
      Carmel,
   I will find them and take them
      away.
If they try to hide from me at the
      bottom of the sea,
   I will command a snake to bite
      them.
[4]If they are captured and taken
      away by their enemies,
   I will command the sword to kill
      them.
I will keep watch over them.
   But I will keep watch to give
      them trouble, not to do
      them good."

[5]The Master, the Lord of heaven's
      armies, will touch the land.
   And the land will shake.
   Then everyone who lives in the
      land will cry for the dead.
The whole land will rise like the
      Nile River.
   It will fall like the river of
      Egypt.
[6]The Lord built his upper rooms
      above the skies.
   He sets their foundations on the
      earth.
He calls for the waters of the
      sea.
   He pours them out on the land.
   The Lord is his name.

[7]The Lord says this:
"Israel, you are no different to me
      than the people of Cush.
I brought Israel out of the land of
      Egypt.
   I also brought the Philistines
      from Crete
   and the Arameans from Kir.
[8]I, the Lord God, am watching the
      sinful kingdom Israel.
I will destroy Israel
   from the earth's surface.
But I will not completely destroy

Jacob's descendants,"[d] says the
      Lord.
[9]"I am giving the command
   to scatter the nation of Israel
      among all nations.
   It will be like someone sifting
      flour.
   A person shakes flour through a
      sifter.
   The good flour falls through, but
      not the bad clumps.
[10]Sinners among my people
   will die by the sword.
All of them say,
   'Nothing bad will happen to
      us'.

The Lord Promises to Restore Israel

[11]"The kingdom of David is like a
      fallen tent.
   But in that day I will set it up
      again
   and mend its broken places.
I will rebuild its ruins.
   I will rebuild it as it was before.
[12]Then Israel will take over what is
      left of Edom
   and the other nations that
      belong to me,"
says the Lord.
   And he will make it happen.

[13]The Lord says, "The time is
      coming when there will be
      plenty of food.
A person will still be harvesting
      his crops
   when it's time to plough again.
A person will still be taking the
      juice from his grapes
   when it's time to plant again.
Sweet wine will drip from the
      mountains.
   And it will pour from the hills.
[14]I will bring my people Israel back
      from captivity.
   They will build the ruined cities
      again.
   And they will live in them.

They will plant vineyards and
    drink the wine from them.
They will plant gardens and eat
    their fruit.
15I will plant my people on their land.

And they will not be pulled out
    again
from the land which I have given
    them,"
says the Lord your God.

OBADIAH

God Will Punish Edom

The Lord Will Punish the Edomites

¹This is the vision of Obadiah.

This is what the Lord God says
about Edom:ⁿ
We have heard a message from
the Lord.
A messenger has been sent
among the nations, saying
"Let's go and attack Edom!"

The Lord Speaks to the Edomites

²"Look, I have made you only a
small nation.
Others do not respect you.
³But your pride has fooled you.
You live in the hollow places of
the cliff.
Your home is up high.
And you say to yourself,
'No one can bring me down to
the ground'.
⁴You fly high like the eagle.
You make your nest among the
stars.
But I will bring you down from
there," says the Lord.
⁵"You will really be ruined!
It would be better if thieves come
to you,
if robbers come by night.
They would steal only enough
for themselves.
Workers come and pick the
grapes from your vines.
But they would leave a few
grapes behind.
⁶But you, Edom, will really lose
everything!

People will find even your
hidden treasures!
⁷All the people who are your
friends
will force you out of the land.
The people who are at peace with
you
will trick you and defeat you.
They eat your bread with you
now,
but they are planning a trap for
you.
And you will not notice it."

⁸The Lord says, "On that day
I will surely destroy the wise
men from Edom.
I will destroy these men of
understanding from the
mountains of Edom.
⁹Then, city of Teman, your mighty
men will be afraid.
And everyone from the
mountains of Edom will be
killed.
¹⁰You did violence against your
relatives, the people of
Israel.
So you will be covered with
shame.
You will be destroyed for ever.
¹¹You stood aside without helping
while strangers carried Israel's
treasures away.
Foreigners entered Israel's city
gate.
They threw lotsᵈ to decide what
part of Jerusalem they would
take.
At that time you were like one
of those foreigners.

Edom The Edomites were the people who were descended from Esau, Jacob's twin brother.
They were enemies of the Israelites.

Commands that Edom Broke

¹²"Do not laugh at your brothers'
    trouble.
  Do not be happy when people
    destroy Judah.
  Do not boast about the cruel things
    done to them.
¹³Do not enter the city gate of my
    people
  in their time of trouble.
  Do not laugh at their problems
    in their time of trouble.
  Do not take their treasures
    in their time of trouble.
¹⁴Do not stand at the crossroads
    to destroy those who are trying
    to escape.
  Do not capture those who escape
    alive
  in a time of trouble.

The Nations Will Be Judged

¹⁵"The Lord's day of judging is
    coming soon
  to all the nations.
  You did evil things to other
    people.
  Those same things will happen
    to you.
  They will come back upon your
    own head.
¹⁶Because you joined the nations in
    robbing my Temple,ᵈ
  you drank my anger.
  So all the nations will drink my
    anger.
  They will be punished so much
    that they will disappear.
¹⁷But on Mount Zionᵈ some will be
    left alive.
  The mountain will be a holy
    place.
  The people of Jacob will take back
    their land.

They will take it from those who
    took it from them.
¹⁸The people of Jacob, the
    Israelites, will be like a fire.
  And the people of Joseph will be
    like a flame.
  But the people of Esau, the
    Edomites, will be like dry
    stalks.
  The people of Jacob will set
    these stalks on fire.
  They will burn up the Edomites.
  Then there will be no one left of
    the people of Esau."
  This will happen because the Lord
    has said it.

¹⁹Then God's people will regain
    southern Judah from Edom,
    the mountain of Esau.
  They will take back the western
    mountain slopes
  from the Philistines.
  They will regain the lands of
    Ephraim and Samaria.
  And Benjamin will take over
    Gilead.
²⁰People from Israel once were
    forced to leave their homes.
  But at that time they will take
    the land of the Canaanites.
  They will take it all the way to
    Zarephath.
  People from Judah were once
    forced to leave Jerusalem
  and live in Sepharad.
  But at that time they will take
    back
  the cities of southern Judah.
²¹Powerful warriors will go up on
    Mount Zion.
  There they will rule the people
    living on Edom's mountain.
  And the kingdom will belong to
    the Lord.

JONAH

A Prophet Runs from God

God Calls and Jonah Runs

1 The Lord spoke his word to Jonah son of Amittai: ²"Get up, go to the great city of Nineveh and preach against it. I see the evil things they do."

³But Jonah got up to run away from the Lord. He went to the city of Joppa. There he found a ship that was going to the city of Tarshish. Jonah paid for the trip and went aboard. He wanted to go to Tarshish to run away from the Lord.

⁴But the Lord sent a great wind on the sea. This wind made the sea very rough. So the ship was in danger of breaking apart. ⁵The sailors were afraid. Each man cried to his own god. The men began throwing the cargo into the sea. This would make the ship lighter so it would not sink.

But Jonah had gone down into the ship to lie down. He fell fast asleep. ⁶The captain of the ship came and said, "Why are you sleeping? Get up! Pray to your god! Perhaps your god will pay attention to us. Perhaps he will save us!"

⁷Then the men said to each other, "Let's throw lots*d* to see who caused these troubles to happen to us."

So the men threw lots. The lot showed that the trouble had happened because of Jonah. ⁸Then the men said to Jonah, "Tell us what you have done. Why has this terrible thing happened to us? What is your job? Where do you come from? What is your country? Who are your people?"

⁹Then Jonah said to them, "I am a Hebrew. I fear the Lord, the God of heaven. He is the God who made the sea and the land."

¹⁰Then the men were very afraid. They asked Jonah, "What terrible thing did you do?" They knew Jonah was running away from the Lord because Jonah had told them.

¹¹The wind and the waves of the sea were becoming much stronger. So the men said to Jonah, "What should we do to you to make the sea calm down?"

¹²Jonah said to them, "Pick me up, and throw me into the sea. Then it will calm down. I know it is my fault that this great storm has come on you."

¹³Instead, the men tried to row the ship back to the land. But they could not. The wind and the waves of the sea were becoming much stronger.

Jonah's Punishment

¹⁴So the men cried to the Lord, "Lord, please don't let us die because of taking this man's life. Please don't think we are guilty of killing an innocent man. Lord, you have caused all this to happen. You wanted it this way." ¹⁵Then the men picked up Jonah and threw him into the sea. So the sea became calm. ¹⁶Then they began to fear the Lord very much. They offered a sacrifice to the Lord. They also made promises to him.

¹⁷And the Lord caused a very big fish to swallow Jonah. Jonah was in the stomach of the fish for three days and three nights.

2 While Jonah was in the stomach of the fish, he prayed to the Lord his God. Jonah said,

²"I was in danger.
So I called to the Lord,
  and he answered me.
I was about to die.
  So I cried to you,

and you heard my voice.
³You threw me into the sea.
  I went down, down into the
    deep sea.
The water was all around me.
  Your powerful waves flowed
    over me.
⁴I said, 'I was driven out of your
    presence.
But I hope to see your Holy
    Temple*d* again'.
⁵The waters of the sea closed over
    me.
  I was about to die.
The deep sea was all around me.
  Seaweed wrapped around my
    head.
⁶I went down to where the
    mountains of the sea start to
    rise.
  I thought I was locked in this
    prison for ever.
But you saved me from death,
    Lord my God.
⁷"When my life had almost gone,
  I remembered the Lord.
Lord, I prayed to you.
  And you heard my prayers in
    your Holy Temple.

⁸"People who worship useless idols
    give up their loyalty to you.
⁹Lord, I will praise and thank you
    while I give sacrifices to you.
  I will make promises to you.
    And I will do what I promise.
Salvation comes from the Lord!"

¹⁰Then the Lord spoke to the fish.
And the fish spat Jonah out of its stomach onto the dry land.

God Calls and Jonah Obeys

3 Then the Lord spoke his word to
Jonah again. The Lord said, ²"Get
up. Go to the great city Nineveh.
Preach against it what I tell you."

³So Jonah obeyed the Lord. He got
up and went to Nineveh. It was a very
large city. It took a person three days
just to walk across it. ⁴Jonah entered

the city. When he had walked for one
day, he preached to the people. He
said, "After 40 days, Nineveh will be
destroyed!"

⁵The people of Nineveh believed in
God. They announced that they would
stop eating for a while. They put on
rough cloth to show how sad they
were. All the people in the city wore
the cloth. People from the most important to the least important did this.

⁶When the king of Nineveh heard
this news, he got up from his throne.
He took off his robe. He covered himself with rough cloth and sat in ashes
to show how upset he was.

⁷He made an announcement and
sent it through the city. The announcement said:

By command of the king and his
important men: no person or animal should eat anything. No herd
or flock will be allowed to taste
anything. Do not let them eat
food or drink water. ⁸But every
person and animal should be covered with rough cloth. People
should cry loudly to God. Everyone must turn away from his evil
life. Everyone must stop doing
harm. ⁹Perhaps God will change
his mind. Perhaps he will stop being angry. Then we will not die.

¹⁰God saw what the people did. He
saw that they had stopped doing evil
things. So God changed his mind and
did not do what he had warned. He did
not punish them.

God's Mercy Makes Jonah Angry

4 But Jonah was very unhappy that
God did not destroy the city. He
was angry. ²He complained to the
Lord and said, "I knew this would happen. I knew it when I was still in my
own country. It is why I quickly ran
away to Tarshish. I knew that you are
a God who is kind and shows mercy.
You don't become angry quickly. You
have great love. I knew you would

rather forgive than punish them. ³So now I ask you, Lord, please kill me. It is better for me to die than to live."

⁴Then the Lord said, "Do you think it is right for you to be angry?"

⁵Jonah went out and sat down east of the city. There he made a shelter for himself. And he sat there in the shade. He was waiting to see what would happen to the city. ⁶The Lord made a plant grow quickly up over Jonah. This made a cool place for him to sit. And it helped him to be more comfortable. Jonah was very pleased to have the plant for shade. ⁷The next day the sun rose. And God sent a worm to attack the plant. Then the plant died.

⁸When the sun was high in the sky, God sent a hot east wind to blow. The sun became very hot on Jonah's head. And he became very weak. He wished he were dead. Jonah said, "It is better for me to die than to live."

⁹But God said this to Jonah: "Do you think it is right for you to be angry because of the plant?"

Jonah answered, "It is right for me to be angry! I will stay angry until I die!"

¹⁰And the Lord said, "You showed concern for that plant. But you did not plant it or make it grow. It appeared in the night, and the next day it died. ¹¹Then surely I can show concern for the great city Nineveh. There are many animals in that city. And there are more than 120,000 people living there. Those people simply do not know right from wrong!"

MICAH

Assyria Will Punish Israel and Judah

Samaria and Israel to Be Punished

1 Jotham, Ahaz and Hezekiah were kings of Judah. During the time they were kings, the word of the Lord came to Micah, who was from Moresheth. He saw these visions about Samaria and Jerusalem.

²Hear this, all you nations.
  Listen, all you who live on the
    earth.
The Lord God will come from his
    Holy Temple.*d*
He will come as a witness
    against you.
³See, the Lord is coming out of his
    place in heaven.
He is coming down to walk on
    the tops of the mountains.
⁴The mountains will melt under him
    like wax in a fire.
The valleys will crack open
    as if split by water raging down
    a mountain.
⁵This is because of Jacob's sin.
It is because of the sins of the
    nation of Israel.
Who is responsible for Jacob's sin?
    Samaria!
Who is responsible for Judah's
    worshipping idols?
    Jerusalem!

The Lord Speaks

⁶"So I will make Samaria a pile of
    ruins in the open country.
It will be like a place for planting
    vineyards.

I will pour Samaria's stones down
    into the valley.
And I will destroy her down to
    her foundations.
⁷All her idols will be broken into
    pieces.
All the gifts to her idols will be
    burned with fire.
I will destroy all her idols.
This is because Samaria earned
    her money by being
    unfaithful to me.
So this money will be carried off
    by other people who are not
    faithful to me."

Micah's Great Sadness

⁸I will moan and cry because of this
    evil.
I will go around barefoot and
    without clothes.
I will cry loudly like the wild
    dogs.
I will cry like the ostriches.
⁹I will do this because Samaria's
    wound cannot be healed.
Her destruction will spread to
    Judah.
It will reach the city gate of my
    people.
It will come all the way to
    Jerusalem.
¹⁰Don't tell it in Gath.*n*
Don't cry in Acco.*n*
Cry and roll in the dust
    at Beth Ophrah.*n*
¹¹Pass on your way, naked and
    ashamed,
    you who live in Shaphir.*n*

Gath This name sounds like the Hebrew word for "tell".
Acco This name sounds like the Hebrew word for "cry".
Beth Ophrah This name means "house of dust".
Shaphir This name means "beautiful".

Those who live in Zaanan[n]
won't come out to help you.
The people in Beth Ezel[n] will
cry,
but they will not give you any
support.
[12]Those who live in Maroth[n]
will be anxious for good news to
come.
This is because trouble will come
from the Lord.
It will come all the way to the
gate of Jerusalem.
[13]You people living in Lachish,[n]
harness the fastest horse to the
chariot.
Jerusalem's sins started in you.
This is because you followed in
Israel's sins.
[14]So you must give farewell gifts
to Moresheth[n] in Gath.
The houses in Aczib[n] will be false
help
to the kings of Israel.
[15]I will bring an enemy against you
who live in Mareshah.[n]
He will take what you own.
The leaders Israel boasts about
will hide in the cave at Adullam.
[16]Cut off your hair to show you are
sad.
Cry for the children you love.
Make yourself bald like the eagle,
because your children will be
forced to live in a foreign
land.

The Evil Plans of People

2 How terrible it will be for people
who plan wickedness.
They lie on their beds and make
evil plans.

When the morning light comes,
they do the things they
planned.
They do them just because they
have the power to do so.
[2]They want fields; so they take
them.
They want houses; so they take
them.
They cheat a man and take his
house.
They cheat a man and take his
property.

[3]That is why the Lord says:
"Look, I am planning trouble
against such people.
You won't be able to save
yourselves.
You will no longer walk proudly,
because it will be a terrible
time.
[4]At that time people will make fun
of you.
They will sing this sad song
about you:
'We are completely ruined.
The Lord has taken away our
land.
Yes, he has taken our land away
from us.
He has divided our fields among
our enemies!'"
[5]So you will have no land for
people to measure.
They will not throw lots[d] to
divide the land among the
Lord's people.

Micah Is Asked Not to Prophesy

[6]People say, "Don't prophesy[d] to
us!

Zanaan This name sounds like the Hebrew word for "come out".
Beth Ezel This name means "house by the side of another", suggesting help or support.
Maroth This name sounds like the Hebrew word for "sad" or "miserable".
Lachish This name sounds like the Hebrew word for "horses".
Moresheth This may be a word play on the word "engaged", referring to a farewell gift to a bride.
Aczib This name means "lie" or "trick".
Mareshah This name sounds like the Hebrew word for a person who captures other cities and lands.

Don't say those bad things about
us!
Nothing like that will happen to
us!"

⁷But I must say this, people of
Jacob.
The Lord is becoming angry
about what you have done.
If you lived good lives,
I could speak kind words to you.
⁸But recently, my people have
become my enemy.
You take the coats from people
who pass by.
They think they are safe.
But you rob them
as if they were prisoners of war.
⁹You've forced the women of my
people
from their nice houses.
You've taken my glory
from their children for ever.
¹⁰Get up and leave.
This is not your promised place
of rest any more.
You have made this place
unclean.ᵈ
It is doomed to destruction.
¹¹But you people want a false
prophet
who will tell you nothing but
lies.
You want one who promises to
prophesy good things for
you
if you give him wine and beer.
He's just the prophet for you.

The Lord Promises to Rescue His People

¹²"Yes, people of Jacob, I will bring
all of you together.
I will bring together all those left
alive in Israel.
I'll put them together like sheep in
a pen,
like a flock in its pasture.
Then the place will be filled with
many people.
¹³Someone will open the way and
lead the people out.

The people will break through
the gate and leave the city
where they were held
captive.
Their king will go out in front of
them.
The Lord will lead his people."

The Leaders of Israel Are Guilty of Evil

3 Then I said,
"Listen, leaders of the people of
Jacob.
Listen, you rulers of the nation
of Israel.
You should know how to decide
cases fairly.
² But you hate good and love evil.
You skin my people alive.
You tear the flesh off their
bones.
³You are destroying my people.
You skin them and break their
bones.
You chop them up in pieces
like meat to put in the pot.
⁴Then you will pray to the Lord,
but he won't answer you.
He will hide his face from you,
because you have done evil."

⁵The Lord says this about the
prophetsᵈ who teach his people the
wrong way of living:
"If someone gives these prophets
food to eat,
they shout, 'Peace!'
But if he doesn't give them food,
they prepare for war against
him.
⁶So it will become like night to the
prophets.
They won't have any visions
from the Lord.
It will become dark for them.
They won't be able to tell what
will happen in the future.
The sun is about to set for the
prophets.
Their days will become dark.
⁷The seersᵈ will be ashamed.

The people who see the future
will be embarrassed.
Yes, all of them will cover their
mouths.
This is because there will be no
answer from God."

Micah Is an Honest Prophet of God

8But the Lord's Spirit*d* has filled
me
with power and strength to
preach fairness.
I will tell the people of Jacob how
they have turned against
God.
I will tell the people of Israel
how they have done wrong.
9Leaders of Jacob and rulers of
Israel,
listen to me.
You hate fairness.
You destroy what is right.
10You build Jerusalem by murdering
people.
You build it with the sins you
do.
11The judges in Jerusalem take
money
to decide who wins in court.
The priests in Jerusalem only
teach for pay.
The prophets*d* only look into the
future when they get paid.
But yet those leaders say,
"The Lord is with us.
Nothing bad will happen to us."
12Because of you,
Jerusalem will be ploughed like a
field.
Jerusalem will become a pile of
rocks.
The hill on which the Temple*d*
stands will be covered with
bushes.

The Mountain of the Lord

4 In the last days
the mountain on which the
Lord's Temple*d* stands
will become the most important
of all mountains.
It will be raised above the hills.
People from other nations will
come streaming to it.
2Many nations will come and say,
"Come, let us go up to the
mountain of the Lord.
Let us go to the Temple of the
God of Jacob!
Then God will teach us his ways.
And we will obey his teachings."
The Lord's teachings will go out
from Jerusalem.
The word of the Lord will go
out from Jerusalem.
3The Lord will settle arguments
among many nations.
He will decide between strong
nations that are far away.
Then the nations will make their
swords into ploughs.
They will make their spears into
hooks for trimming trees.
Nations will no longer fight other
nations.
They will not even train for war
any more.
4Everyone will sit under his own
vine and fig tree.
No one will make them afraid.
This is because the Lord of
heaven's armies has said it.
5All other nations follow their own
gods,
but we will follow the Lord our
God for ever and ever.
6The Lord says, "At that time,
I will bring back to me the
crippled.
I will bring back to Jerusalem
those who were sent away.
I will bring back to me those
who were hurt.
7I will keep alive those who were
crippled.
I will make a strong nation of
those who were sent away.
The Lord will be their king in
Mount Zion*d* for ever.

[8]And you, watchtower of the
flocks," strong city of
Jerusalem,
you will be a kingdom as in the
past.
Jerusalem, the right to rule will
come again to you."

Why the Israelites Must Go to Babylon

[9]Now, why do you cry so loudly?
Is your king gone?
Have you lost your leader?
You are in pain like a woman
trying to give birth.
[10]People of Jerusalem, be in pain.
Be like a woman trying to give
birth.
Now you must leave the city
and live in the field.
You will go to Babylon.
But you will be saved from that
place.
The Lord will go there
and take you back from your
enemies.

[11]But now many nations
have come to fight against you.
They say, "Let's destroy
Jerusalem
and be proud we have defeated
her."
[12]But they don't know
what the Lord is thinking.
They don't understand his plan for
them.
He will crush them like a bundle
of grain on the threshing[d]
floor.

[13]"Get up and crush them, people of
Jerusalem.
I will make you strong as if you
had horns of iron.
I will make you strong as if you
had hoofs of bronze.
You will beat many nations into
small pieces.

You will give their wealth to the
Lord.
You will give their treasure to
the Lord of all the earth."

5 So, strong city, gather your
soldiers together.
We are surrounded and
attacked.
The enemy will swing his club.
He will hit the leader of Israel in
the face.

The Ruler to Be Born in Bethlehem

[2]"But you, Bethlehem Ephrathah,
are one of the smallest towns in
Judah.
But from you will come one who
will rule Israel for me.
He comes from very old times,
from days long ago."

[3]The Lord will leave his people in
Babylon
until Jerusalem, who is in labour,
gives birth to her children.
Then his brothers who are in
captivity will return.
They will come back to the
people of Israel living in
Judah.
[4]Then the ruler of Israel will stand
and take care of his people.
He will lead them with the Lord's
power.
He will lead them in the
wonderful name of the Lord
his God.
They will live in safety.
And his greatness will be known
all over the earth.
[5] He will bring peace.

Rescue and Punishment

The Assyrian army will come into
our country.
They will destroy our large
houses.

---

watchtower . . . flocks This probably means a part of Jerusalem. The leaders would be like
shepherds in a tower watching their sheep.

But we will choose seven or eight
leaders.
They will shepherd our people.
⁶They will destroy the Assyrians
with their swords.
They will conquer the land of
Assyria with their swords
drawn.
The Assyrians will come into our
land.
They will come within our
borders.
But the leaders of Israel
will save us from them.

⁷Then the people of Jacob who are
left alive
will be like dew from the Lord
to many people.
They will be like rain which does
not wait for man.
They will be like showers which
do not wait for human
beings.
⁸Those left alive of Jacob's people
will be scattered among the
nations.
They will be among many
peoples.
They will be like a lion among the
animals of the forest.
They will be like a young lion
going through the flock.
He steps on what is in his way.
No one can save the nations
from God's people.
⁹So you will raise your fist in
victory over your enemies,
and you will destroy them.

¹⁰The Lord says, "At that time,
I will take your horses from
you.
I will destroy your chariots.
¹¹I will destroy the walled cities in
your country.
I will tear down all your
defences.
¹²You will no longer be able to do
witchcraft.ᵈ
You will not have anyone who
can tell the future.

¹³I will destroy your statues of false
gods.
I will tear down the stone pillars
you worship.
You will no longer worship
what your hands have made.
¹⁴I will destroy the Asherahᵈ idols.
I will destroy your cities.
¹⁵Some people won't obey me.
I will show my anger and punish
them."

The Lord's Complaint

6 Now hear what the Lord says:
"Get up; plead your case in
front of the mountains.
Let the hills hear your story.
²Mountains, listen to the Lord's
complaint.
Foundations of the earth, listen
to the Lord.
The Lord has a complaint against
his people.
He will prove that Israel is
wrong."

³The Lord says, "My people, did I
do something wrong to you?
How did I make you tired of
me?
Tell me.
⁴I brought you from the land of
Egypt.
I freed you from slavery.
I sent Moses, Aaron and Miriam
to you.
⁵My people, remember
the evil plans of Balak king of
Moab.
Remember what Balaam son of
Beor told Balak.
Remember what happened from
Acacia to Gilgal.
Then you will know the Lord
does what is right!"

⁶You say, "What can I bring with
me
when I come before the Lord?
What can I bring
when I bow before God on high?

Should I come before the Lord
　　with burnt offerings,
　with year-old calves?
⁷Will the Lord be pleased with
　　1,000 male sheep?
　Will he be pleased with 10,000
　　rivers of oil?
　Should I give my first child for the
　　evil I have done?
　Should I give my very own child
　　for my sin?"
⁸The Lord has told you what is
　　good.
　He has told you what he wants
　　from you:
　Do what is right to other people.
　Love being kind to others.
　And live humbly, trusting your
　　God.

⁹The voice of the Lord shouts to
　　the city.
　The wise person honours the
　　Lord.
　So pay attention to the rod of
　　punishment.
　Pay attention to the One who
　　threatens to punish.
¹⁰Can the Lord forget that the
　　wicked still hide
　treasures they have stolen?
　Do they still cheat others?
　I curse their false measure!
¹¹Can I forgive people who cheat
　　others
　with wrong weights and scales?
¹²The rich men in the city
　　still do cruel things.
　The people still tell lies.
　　They do not tell the truth.
¹³So I have started to punish you.
　I will destroy you because of
　　your sins.
¹⁴You will eat, but you won't
　　become full.
　You will still be hungry and
　　empty.
　You will store up but save
　　nothing.

What you store up the sword
　　will destroy.
¹⁵You will plant,
　　but you won't harvest.
　You will squeeze your olives,
　　but you won't get any oil from
　　them to put on your skin.
　You will crush the grapes,
　　but you will not drink the wine.
¹⁶This is because you obey the
　　wicked laws of King Omri.
　You do all the evil that Ahab's
　　family does.
　You follow their teachings.
　So I will let you be destroyed.
　The people in your city will be
　　laughed at.
　Other nations will make fun of
　　you.

Micah Is Upset at the Evil that People Do

7 Poor me! I am like a hungry
　　man.
　And all the summer fruit has
　　been picked.
　There are no grapes left to eat.
　There are none of the early figs
　　I love.
²All of the faithful people are
　　gone.
　There is not one good person
　　left in this country.
　Everyone is waiting to kill
　　someone.
　Everyone is trying to trap his
　　brother.
³People are good at doing evil with
　　both hands.
　Rulers ask for money.
　And judges' decisions are bought
　　for a price.
　Rich people make their wishes
　　known.
　They all join in their evil plans.
⁴Even the best of them is like a
　　thornbush.
　Even the most upright of them is
　　worse than a thornbush.

Your watchmen[n] warned you
    about this day.
Now it has come.
Now you will be punished.
    Your punishment will amaze
    you.
5Don't trust your neighbour.
    Don't even trust a friend.
Be careful what you say,
    even to your wife.
6A son will not honour his father.
    A daughter will turn against her
    mother.
A daughter-in-law will fight with
    her mother-in-law.
A person's enemies will be
    members of his own family.

The Lord's Kindness

7Israel says, "I will look to the
    Lord for help.
I will wait for God to save
    me.
My God will hear me.
8Enemy, don't laugh at me.
I have fallen, but I will get up
    again.
I sit in the shadow of trouble
    now.
But the Lord will be a light for
    me.
9I sinned against the Lord.
    So he was angry with me.
But he will defend my case in
    court.
He will do what is right for me.
Then he will bring me out into the
    light.
I will see him set things right.
10Then my enemies will see this,
    and they will be ashamed.
My enemies said to me,
    'Where is the Lord your God?'
Now I will laugh at them.
They will fall down defeated,
    like the mud people walk
    on."

The Jews to Return

11The time will come when your
    walls will be built again.
At that time your country will
    grow.
12Your people will come back to
    your land.
They will come from Assyria
    and the cities of Egypt.
They will come from the countries
    between the river of Egypt and
    the Euphrates River.
They will come from the countries
    between the Mediterranean Sea
    in the west and the
    mountains in the east.
13The rest of the earth will be
    ruined.
This is because of what the
    people who lived in it did.

A Prayer to God

14So shepherd your people with
    your stick.
Tend the flock of people who
    belong to you.
That flock now lives alone in the
    desert,
but there is fertile pasture
    nearby.
Let them feed in Bashan and
    Gilead
as they did long ago.

15The Lord says, "I did many
    miracles[d] when I brought
    you out of Egypt.
I will show you more miracles
    like that."

16The nations will see those
    miracles.
Then they will no longer boast
    about their power.
They will be amazed and put their
    hands over their mouths.
They will refuse to listen.
17They will crawl in the dust like a
    snake.

---

watchmen Another name for a prophet. The prophets were like guards who stood on a city's wall. They watched for trouble coming from far away.

They will shake with fear.
They will crawl on the ground
like insects crawling from their
holes.
They will come trembling to you,
Lord our God.
They will tremble in fear before
you.
¹⁸There is no God like you.
You forgive people who are
guilty of sin.
You don't look at the sins of your
people
who are left alive.

You, Lord, will not stay angry for
ever.
You enjoy being kind.
¹⁹Lord, you will have mercy on us
again.
You will conquer our sins.
You will throw away all our sins
into the deepest sea.
²⁰You will be true to the people of
Jacob!
You will be kind to the people of
Abraham.
You will do what you promised
to our ancestors long ago.

NAHUM

God Will Punish Assyria

1 This is the message for the city of Nineveh.ⁿ This is the vision of Nahum, who was from the town of Elkosh.

The Lord Is Angry with Nineveh

²The Lord is a jealous God who
  gives punishment.
The Lord punishes wicked
  people and is filled with
  anger.
The Lord punishes those who are
  against him.
He stays angry with his
  enemies.
³The Lord does not become angry
  quickly.
His power is great.
The Lord will not let the guilty
  go unpunished.
Where the Lord goes, whirlwinds
  and storms show his power.
The clouds are the dust that his
  feet kick up.
⁴The Lord speaks to the sea and
  makes it dry.
He dries up all the rivers.
The areas of Bashan and Carmel
  dry up.
And the flowers of Lebanon die.
⁵He shakes the mountains
  and makes the hills melt away.
The earth trembles when he
  comes.
The world and all who live in it
  shake with fear.
⁶No one can stay alive when the
  Lord is angry with him.
No one can survive his strong
  anger.
His anger is poured out like fire.

He smashes rocks that are in his
  path.
⁷The Lord is good.
He gives protection in times of
  trouble.
He knows who trusts in him.
⁸But he will completely destroy the
  city of Nineveh.
An army will come like a rushing
  flood.
The Lord will chase his enemies
  until he kills them.
⁹The Lord will completely destroy
  the plans that are made against
  him.
Trouble will not come a second
  time.
¹⁰Those people will be like tangled
  thorns
or like people drunk from their
  wine.
They will be destroyed quickly
  like dry weeds.
¹¹Someone has come from Nineveh.
He makes evil plans against the
  Lord.
And he gives wicked advice.

¹²This is what the Lord says:
"Assyria is strong and has many
  people,
but it will be defeated and
  brought to an end.
Judah, I have punished you, my
  people,
but I will punish you no more.
¹³Now I will free you from their
  control.
And I will tear away the chains
  with which they hold you."

Nineveh The capital city of the country of Assyria. Nahum uses Nineveh to stand for all of Assyria.

[14]The Lord has given you this
command, Nineveh:
"You will not have descendants[d]
to carry on your name.
I will destroy the idols and metal
images
that are in the temple of your
gods.
I will dig your grave
because you are wicked."

[15]Look, there on the hills,
someone is bringing good news!
He is announcing peace!
Celebrate your feasts, people of
Judah.
And do what you promised to
God.
The wicked will not attack you
again.
They have been completely
destroyed.

Nineveh Will Be Defeated

2 The destroyer[n] is coming to
attack you, Nineveh.
Guard the defences.
Watch the road.
Get ready.
Gather all your strength!
[2]Destroyers have destroyed God's
people
and ruined their vines.
But the Lord will make the people
of Jacob
and the people of Israel great
again.

[3]The shields of the soldiers are
red.
The army is dressed in red.
The metal on the chariots flashes
when they are ready to attack.
Their horses are excited.
[4]The chariots race through the
streets.
They rush back and forth
through the city squares.

They look like torches.
They run like lightning.
[5]He[n] calls his officers,
but they fall down on the way.
They hurry to the city wall.
The shield is put into place.
[6]The river gates are thrown open.
And the palace is destroyed.
[7]It has been announced that the
people of Nineveh
will be captured and carried
away.
The slave girls moan like doves.
They beat their breasts because
they are sad.
[8]Nineveh is like a pool.
And its water is draining away.
"Stop! Stop!" the people yell.
But no one turns back.
[9]Take the silver!
Take the gold!
There is no end to the treasure.
There is wealth of every kind.
[10]Nineveh is robbed, ruined and
destroyed.
The people lose their courage.
Their knees knock with fear.
Stomachs ache. And everyone's
face grows pale from fright.

[11]Where is the lions'[n] den?
Where do they feed their
young?
Where did the lion, lioness and
cubs go?
Where were they not afraid?
[12]The lion killed enough for his
cubs.
He killed it for his mate.
He filled his cave with the animals
he caught.
He filled his den with what he
had killed.

[13]"I am against you, Nineveh,"
says the Lord of heaven's
armies.

---

destroyer The Babylonians, the Scythians and the Medes destroyed Nineveh.
He This probably means the king of Assyria.
lions' The symbol of Assyria was the lion.

"I will burn up your chariots in
  smoke.
And I will kill your young lions
  with a sword.
I will stop you from hunting
  down others on the earth.
Your messengers' voices
  will no longer be heard."

It Will Be Terrible for Nineveh

3 How terrible it will be for the
  city which has killed so
  many.
It is full of lies.
It is full of stolen things from
  other countries.
It is always hurting or killing
  somebody.
²Hear the sound of whips.
  Listen to the wheels.
Hear horses galloping
  and chariots bouncing along!
³Soldiers on horses are charging.
  Their swords are shining.
  Their spears are gleaming!
There are many bodies.
  Dead people are piled up.
There are too many to count.
  People fall over the dead bodies.
⁴The city was like a prostitute.ᵈ
  She was charming and a lover of
    magic.
She made nations slaves with her
    evil ways
  and her witchcraft.ᵈ

⁵"I am against you, Nineveh," says
    the Lord of heaven's
    armies.
  "I will pull your dress up over
    your face.
I will show the nations your
    nakedness.
And I will show the kingdoms
    your shame.
⁶I will throw earth on you.
I will make a fool of you.
People will see you and make
    fun of you.

⁷Everyone who sees you will run
    away and say,
  'Nineveh is in ruins. Who will
    cry for her?'
Nineveh, I cannot find anyone to
    comfort you."

⁸Nineveh, you are no better than
    Thebes.ⁿ
  She sits by the Nile River
    with water all around her.
The river was her defence.
  The waters were like a wall
    around her.
⁹Cush and Egypt gave her endless
    strength.
  Put and Libya supported her.
¹⁰But Thebes was captured.
  And she went into captivity.
Her little children were beaten to
    death
  at every street corner.
Lotsᵈ were thrown for her
    important men.
And all of her leaders were put
    in chains.

¹¹Nineveh, you will be drunk, too.
  You will hide.
You will look for a place safe
    from the enemy.
¹²All your defences are like fig trees
    with ripe fruit.
  When the tree is shaken, the
    figs fall into the mouth of the
    eater.
¹³Look at your soldiers.
  They are all women!
The gates of your land
  are wide open for your
    enemies.
Fire has burned the bars of
    those gates.

¹⁴Get enough water before the
    attack begins.
  Make your defences strong!
Make the bricks.
  Mix the mortar.
  Repair the wall!

Thebes A great city in Egypt.

¹⁵There the fire will burn you up.
    The sword will kill you.
    Like grasshoppers eating crops,
        the battle will completely
        destroy you.
    Grow in number like hopping
        locusts.ᵈ
    Grow in number like swarming
        locusts!
¹⁶Your traders are more than the
        stars in the sky,
    but like locusts, they strip the
        land and then fly away.
¹⁷Your guards are like locusts.
    Your officers are like swarms of
        locusts
    that settle in the walls on a cold
        day.

But when the sun comes up they
        fly away.
    And no one knows where they
        have gone.
¹⁸King of Assyria, your rulers are
        asleep.
    Your important men lie down to
        rest.
    Your people have been scattered
        on the mountains.
    And there is no one to bring
        them back.
¹⁹Nothing can heal your wound.
    Your injury will not heal.
    Everyone who hears about you
        applauds
    because everyone has felt your
        endless cruelty.

HABAKKUK

Learning How to Trust God

1 This is the message that was given to Habakkuk the prophet.*d*

Habakkuk Complains

²Lord, I continue to ask for help.
How long will you ignore me?
I cry out to you about violence,
but you do not save us!
³Why do you let me see wrong things?
Why do you put up with evil?
People are destroying things and hurting others while I am looking.
They are arguing and fighting.
⁴People are not forced to obey the teachings.
No one receives a fair trial.
Evil people gain while good people lose.
The judges no longer make fair decisions.

The Lord Answers

⁵"You and your people, look at the nations!
Watch them and be amazed.
I will do something in your lifetime that will amaze you.
You won't believe it even when you are told about it.
⁶I will use the Babylonian people to punish the evil people.
The Babylonians are cruel and powerful fighters.
They march across the earth.
They take lands that don't belong to them.
⁷The Babylonians frighten other people.
They do what they want to do.
They are good only to themselves.

⁸Their horses are faster than leopards
and more cruel than wolves at sunset.
Their horse soldiers attack quickly.
They come from places that are far away.
They attack quickly, like an eagle swooping down for food.
⁹ They all come to fight.
Their armies march quickly like a whirlwind in the desert.
Their prisoners are as many as the grains of sand.
¹⁰The Babylonian soldiers laugh at kings.
They make fun of rulers.
They laugh at all the strong, walled cities.
They build roads of earth up to the top of the walls.
They capture the cities.
¹¹Then they leave like the wind and move on.
They are guilty of worshipping their own strength."

Habakkuk Complains Again

¹²Lord, you are the Lord who lives for ever.
You are my God, my holy God.
You will not let those who trust you die.
Lord, you have chosen the Babylonians to punish people.
Our Rock,*d* you created them to punish the people.
¹³Your eyes are too good to look at evil.
You cannot stand to see people do wrong.

So how can you put up with those
    evil people?
  How can you be quiet when
      wicked people defeat people
      who are better than they
      are?
14You treat people like fish in the
      sea.
  You treat them like sea animals
      without a leader.
15The enemy catches all of them
      with hooks.
  He catches them in his net.
  He drags them in.
  He is glad that he has caught
      them.
16The enemy offers sacrifices to his
      net.
  He burns incense^d to worship it.
  This is because his net lets him
      live like a rich man.
  His net lets him enjoy the best
      food.
17Will he keep on taking riches with
      his net?
  Will he go on destroying people
      without showing mercy?

2 I will stand like a guard to
      watch.
  I will stand on the tower.
  I will wait to see what the Lord
      will say to me.
  I will wait to learn how to
      answer his complaint.

The Lord Answers

  2The Lord answered me:
  "Write down what I show you.
  Write it clearly on stone tablets
      so whoever reads it can run to
      tell others.
3It is not yet time for the message
      to come true,
  but that time is coming soon.
  The message will come true.
  It may seem like a long time
      before it happens,
  but be patient and wait for
      it.

These things will happen.
  They will not be delayed.
4See, the nation that is evil and
      trusts in itself will fail.
  But those who do right because
      they trust in God will live.

5"Wine can trick a person.
  In the same way the
      Babylonians are fooled by
      their pride.
  Their desire for wealth is like a
      grave's desire for death.
  They always want more and
      more.
  And, like death, they collect other
      nations for themselves.
  They make them their own
      people.
6But all the nations the Babylonians
      have hurt will laugh at them.
  They will make fun of the
      Babylonians.
  They will say, 'How terrible it will
      be for the nation that steals
      many things.
  How long will that nation get
      rich by forcing others to pay
      them?'

7"One day the people you have
      taken money from will turn
      against you.
  They will realise what is
      happening and make you
      shake with fear.
  Then they will hurt you.
8You have stolen from many
      nations.
  So the people who are left will
      take much from you.
  This is because you have killed
      many people.
  You have destroyed countries
      and cities and everyone in
      them.

9"How terrible it will be for the
      nation that becomes rich by
      doing wrong.

They do those things to live in a
  safe place.
They think they will be safe
  from harm.
10You have made plans to destroy
  many people.
This has made your own houses
  ashamed of you.
Because of it, you will lose your
  lives.
11The stones of the walls will cry
  out against you.
Even the wooden boards that
  support the roof will agree
  that you are wrong.

12"How terrible it will be for the
  nation that kills people to
  build a city.
How terrible for that nation that
  wrongs others to start a
  town.
13The Lord of heaven's armies will
  send fire
to destroy what those people
  have built.
All the nations' work will be for
  nothing.
14Then people everywhere will
  know the Lord's greatness.
This news will spread like water
  covering the sea.

15"How terrible for the nation that
  becomes angry and makes
  others suffer.
In anger they knock other
  people to the ground.
And they treat them as if they
  are naked and drunk.
16You Babylonians will receive the
  Lord's anger, not respect.
This anger will be like a cup of
  poison in the Lord's right
  hand.
You will taste this anger and fall to
  the ground like a drunk
  person.
You will drink from this cup.
You will receive disgrace, not
  respect.

17You hurt many people in Lebanon.
  Now you will be hurt.
You killed many animals there.
  And now you must be afraid.
You will be afraid because of what
  you did
to those cities and the people
  who lived in them.

The Message About Idols

18"An idol does no good, because a
  man made it.
It is only a statue that teaches
  lies.
The person who made it expects
  his own work to help him.
But it can't even speak!
19How terrible it will be for the
  nation that says to a wooden
  statue, 'Come to life!'
How terrible it will be when this
  nation says to a stone that
  cannot speak, 'Get up!'
These things cannot tell them
  what to do.
That idol is only a statue
  covered with gold and silver.
There is no life in it.
20The Lord is in his Holy Temple.d
So all the earth should be silent
  in his presence."

Habakkuk's Prayer

3 This is the prayer of Habakkuk the
  prophet,d on shigionoth.d

2Lord, I have heard the news
  about you.
Lord, I am amazed at the
  powerful things you have
  done.
Do great things once again in our
  time.
Make those things happen again
  in our own days.
Even when you are angry,
  remember to be gentle with us.

3God is coming from Teman in the
  south.

The Holy One comes from
    Mount Paran.*   *Selah*^d
The Lord's greatness covers the
    heavens.
His praise fills the earth.
⁴He is like a bright light.
    Rays of light shine from his
        hand.
    And there he hides his power.
⁵Sickness goes before him,
    and fever follows behind him.
⁶The Lord stands and shakes the
        earth.
    He looks, and the nations shake
        with fear.
The mountains, which stood for
    ages, break into pieces.
    The old hills fall down.
    God has always done this.

⁷I saw that the tents of Cushan
    were in trouble.
    The tents of Midian trembled.
⁸Lord, were you angry at the
        rivers?
    Were you angry at the streams?
Were you angry with the sea
    when you rode your horses and
        chariots to victory?*
⁹You uncovered your bow.
    You commanded many arrows to
        be brought to you.   *Selah*
You split the earth with rivers.
¹⁰ The mountains saw you and
        shook with fear.
    The rushing water flowed by.
    The sea made a loud noise,
    and its waves rose high.
¹¹The sun and moon stood still in
        the sky.
    They stopped when they saw
        the flash of your flying
        arrows.
    They stopped when they saw
        the gleam of your shining
        spear.

¹²In anger you marched on the
        earth.
    In anger you punished the
        nations.
¹³You came to save your people.
    You came to save your chosen
        one.
    You crushed the leader of the
        wicked ones.
    You took everything away from
        them.   *Selah*
¹⁴With the enemy's own spear you
        stabbed the leader of his
        army.
    His soldiers rushed out like a
        storm to scatter us.
    They were happy as if
        they were robbing the poor
        people in secret.
¹⁵But you marched through the sea
        with your horses,
    stirring the great waters.

¹⁶I hear these things, and my body
        trembles.
    My lips tremble when I hear the
        sound.
My bones feel weak.
    My legs shake.

But I will wait patiently for the
        day of disaster.
    That day is coming to the people
        who attack us.
¹⁷Fig trees may not grow figs.
    There may be no grapes on the
        vines.
There may be no olives growing
        on the trees.
There may be no food growing
        in the fields.
There may be no sheep in the
        pens.
    There may be no cattle in the
        barns.
¹⁸But I will still be glad in the
        Lord.

Teman . . . Paran God is seen as again coming from the direction of Mount Sinai. He came
    from Sinai when he rescued his people from Egypt.
sea . . . victory This is probably talking about the Israelites crossing the Red Sea.

I will rejoice in God my Saviour.
¹⁹The Lord God gives me my
    strength.
He makes me like a deer, which
    does not stumble.

He leads me safely on the steep
    mountains.

For the director of music. On my
stringed instruments.

ZEPHANIAH

God Will Judge the World

1 This is the message of the Lord that came through Zephaniah. It came while Josiah son of Amon was king of Judah. Zephaniah was the son of Cushi, who was the son of Gedaliah. Gedaliah was the son of Amariah, who was the son of Hezekiah.

The Lord's Judgement

2"I will destroy everything
  on earth," says the Lord.
3"I will destroy the people and
    animals.
  I will destroy the birds in the air
  and the fish of the sea.
  I will ruin the evil people.
  I will remove all the people from
    the earth," says the Lord.

The Future of Judah

4"I will punish Judah
  and all the people living in
    Jerusalem.
  I will remove from this place
  all signs of Baal*d* and his priests.
5I will destroy those who worship
  the stars from the roofs.*n*
  I will destroy those who worship
    and make promises
  by both the Lord and the god
    Molech.*d*
6I will destroy those who turned
    away from the Lord.
  They stopped following the Lord
    and consulting him.
7Be silent before the Lord God.
  His day for judging people is
    coming soon.
  The Lord has prepared to sacrifice
    Judah.

He has appointed the invited
  guests to feast on Judah.
8On that day the Lord will sacrifice
    Judah.
  I, the Lord, will punish the
    princes and the king's sons.
And I will punish all
  those who wear foreign clothes.
9On that day I will punish those
  who worship Dagon.*d*
  I will punish those who hurt
    others
  and tell lies in the temples of
    their gods.

10"On that day this will happen,"
    says the Lord.
"A cry will be heard at the Fish
    Gate.
  A wail will come from the new
    area of the city.
  A loud crash will echo from the
    hills.
11The people living in the market
    area will wail.
  All the merchants will be dead.
  All the silver traders will be
    gone.
12At that time I, the Lord, will
    search Jerusalem with lamps.
  I will punish those who are
    settled and satisfied with
    themselves.
  They are like wine left to settle.
  They think, 'The Lord never does
    anything.
  He won't help us or punish us'.
13Their wealth will be stolen.
  Their houses will be destroyed.
  They may build houses,

roofs In Bible times houses were built with flat roofs. The roof was used for drying things such as flax and fruit. It was also used as an extra room, as a place for worship and as a place to sleep in the summer.

but they will never live in them.
They may plant vineyards,
  but they will never drink any
    wine from them.

The Lord's Day of Judging

14"The Lord's day of judging is
    coming soon.
  That great day is near and
    coming fast.
  The cry will be very sad on that
    day.
  Even soldiers will cry.
15That day will be a day of anger.
  It will be a day of terror and
    trouble.
  It will be a day of destruction and
    ruin.
  It will be a day of darkness and
    gloom.
  It will be a day of clouds and
    blackness.
16It will be a day of alarms and
    battle cries.
  'Attack the strong, walled cities!
  Attack the corner towers!'
17I will make life hard on the
    people.
  They will walk around like blind
    men.
  This is because they have
    sinned against the Lord.
  Their blood will be poured out like
    dust.
  And their bodies will be dumped
    like rubbish.
18On that day God will show his
    anger.
  Then neither their silver nor
    gold will save them.
  The Lord's anger will be like fire.
  And the whole world will be
    burned up.
  Suddenly he will bring an end
    to everyone on earth."

God Asks People to Change

2 Gather together,
    you unwanted people.
2Do it before it's too late.

Do it before you are blown away
    like chaff.ᵈ
Do it before the Lord's terrible
    anger reaches you.
Do it before the day of the
    Lord's anger comes to you.
3All you who are not proud, come
    to the Lord.
  You who obey his laws, come to
    him.
  Do what is right. Learn to be
    humble.
  Maybe you will escape
  on the day the Lord shows his
    anger.

Philistia Will Be Punished

4No one will be left in the city of
    Gaza.
  The city of Ashkelon will be
    destroyed.
  Ashdod will be empty by noon.
  And the people of Ekron will be
    chased away.
5How terrible it will be for you who
    live by the Mediterranean
    Sea,
    you Philistines!
  This message from the Lord is for
    you,
    people of Canaan, land of the
    Philistines.

"I will destroy you.
  No one will be left."
6You live in the land by the
    Mediterranean Sea.
  It will be a place for shepherds
    and sheep.
7Your land will belong to the
    descendantsᵈ of Judah who
    are left alive.
  There they will let their sheep
    eat grass.
  At night they will sleep
    in the houses of Ashkelon.
  The Lord their God will come to
    be with them.
  He will give them back their
    riches.

Moab and Ammon Will Be Punished

8"I heard the country of Moab
insult my people.
The country of Ammon
threatened to take their
land."
9So the Lord of heaven's armies,
the God of Israel, says,
"As surely as I live,
Moab will be destroyed like
Sodom.
Ammon will be destroyed like
Gomorrah."
Their land will be covered with
weeds and salt.
It will be destroyed for ever.
Those of my people who are left
alive will take whatever they
want from them.
Those who are left from my
nation will take their
land."
10This is what Moab and Ammon
get for being proud.
This will happen because they
insulted and made fun of the
people of the Lord of
heaven's armies.
11Those people will be afraid of the
Lord.
He will destroy all the gods of
the earth.
Then those people in faraway
places
will worship the Lord in their
own countries.

Cush and Assyria Will Be Destroyed

12"You Cushites also
will be killed by my sword."
13Then the Lord will turn against
the north
and punish Assyria.
He will destroy Nineveh.
It will be dry like a desert.

14Sheep and goats will lie down
there.
Wild animals will live there.
The owls and crows will sit
on the stone pillars that are left
standing.
Their calls will be heard through
the windows.
Rubbish will be in the doorways.
The wooden boards of the
buildings will be gone.
15This is the happy and safe city.
It thinks there is no one else as
strong as it is,
but that city will be destroyed.
Only animals will stay there.
Those who pass by will make
fun
and shake their fists.

Jerusalem Will Be Punished

3 How terrible it will be for
Jerusalem that hurts its own
people.
It's a wicked, stubborn city.
2Her people don't listen.
They can't be taught to do right.
They don't trust the Lord.
They don't worship their God.
3Their officers are like roaring
lions.
Their rulers are like hungry
wolves that attack in the
evening.
In the morning nothing is left of
those they attacked.
4Their prophets*d* are proud.
They cannot be trusted.
Their priests don't respect holy
things.
They break God's teachings.
5But the Lord is good, and he is
there in that city.
He does no wrong.
Every morning he governs the
people fairly.
Every day he can be trusted by
his people.

Sodom and Gomorrah Two cities God destroyed because the people were so evil.

But evil people are not ashamed
of the bad things they do.

6"I have destroyed other nations.
Their towers have fallen.
I made their streets empty.
No one goes there any more.
Their cities are ruined.
No one lives there any more.
7I said, 'Maybe now Jerusalem will
respect me.
Maybe now my people will let
me teach them to do what is
right'.
Then the place where they lived
would not be destroyed.
Then I would not have punished
them.
They got up early in order to do
evil.
Everything they did was bad.
8Just wait," says the Lord.
"Some day I will hold court and
be the judge.
I will gather nations.
I will assemble kingdoms.
I will pour out my anger on them.
My anger will be very strong.
My anger will be like fire.
And the whole world will be
burned up.

A New Day for God's People

9"Then I will make the people of all
nations speak a pure
language.
All of them will speak the name
of the Lord.
And they will worship me
together.
10People will come from where the
Nile River begins.
My scattered people will come
with gifts for me.
11Then Jerusalem will not be
ashamed
of the wrongs done against me.
I will remove from this city
those who like to boast.
There will never be any more
proud people

on my holy mountain in
Jerusalem.
12Only the meek and humble will
stay in my city.
And they will trust in the Lord.
13Those who are left alive of Israel
won't do wrong.
They won't tell lies.
They won't trick people with
their words.
They will be like sheep that eat
and lie down.
No one will bother them."

A Happy Song

14Sing, Jerusalem.
Israel, shout for joy!
Jerusalem, be happy.
Rejoice with all your heart.
15The Lord has stopped punishing
you.
He has sent your enemies away.
The King of Israel, the Lord, is
with you.
You will never again be afraid of
being harmed.
16On that day Jerusalem will be told,
"Don't be afraid, city of
Jerusalem.
Don't be so discouraged that
you can't do anything.
17The Lord your God is with you.
The mighty One will save you.
The Lord will be happy with
you.
You will rest in his love.
He will sing and be joyful about
you."

18"I will take away the sadness
planned for you.
It would have made you very
ashamed.
19At that time I will punish
all those who harmed you.
I will save my people who are
hurt.
I will gather my people who are
scattered.

I will give them praise and honour
in every place where they were
disgraced.
20At that time I will gather you.
At that time I will bring you
back home.

I will give you honour and praise
from people everywhere.
That will happen when I give you
back your riches.
You will see this with your own
eyes," says the Lord.

HAGGAI

The Temple Is Rebuilt

It Is Time to Build the Temple

1 The prophet[d] Haggai spoke the word of the Lord to Zerubbabel and to Joshua. Zerubbabel son of Shealtiel was governor of Judah. Joshua son of Jehozadak was high priest. This message came in the second year that Darius was king of Persia. It came on the first day of the sixth month of that year. This was the message:

2"This is what the Lord of heaven's armies says: 'The people say the right time has not come to rebuild the Temple[d] of the Lord'."

3Then Haggai the prophet spoke the word of the Lord: 4"The Temple is still in ruins. Is it right for you to be living in fancy houses?"

5This is why the Lord of heaven's armies says: "Think about what you have done. 6You have planted much, but you harvest little. You eat, but you do not become full. You drink, but you are still thirsty. You put on clothes, but you are not warm enough. You earn money, but then you lose it all. It is as if you put it into a purse full of holes."

7This is what the Lord of heaven's armies says: "Think about what you have done. 8Go up to the mountains. Bring back wood and build the Temple. Then I will be pleased with it and be honoured," says the Lord. 9The Lord of heaven's armies says: "You look for much, but you find little. When you bring it home, I destroy it. Why? Because you are busy working on your own houses. But my house is still in ruins! 10Because of what you have done, the sky holds back its rain. And the ground holds back its crops.[d] 11I have called for a dry time in the land. There will be no rain in the mountains for the grain, new wine and olive oil. It will be a dry time for the plants which the earth produces. It will be a dry time for men and farm animals. The dry time will make your hard work useless."

12Zerubbabel was the son of Shealtiel. And Joshua, the high priest, was the son of Jehozadak. Zerubbabel and Joshua obeyed the Lord their God. And they obeyed the message from Haggai the prophet. All the rest of the people who were left alive also obeyed. This was because they realised that the Lord their God had sent Haggai. And they feared the Lord.

13The Lord sent a message to Haggai, the Lord's messenger. Haggai gave this message to the people. He said: "The Lord says, 'I am with you'." 14The Lord made Zerubbabel and Joshua excited about building the Temple. Zerubbabel son of Shealtiel was the governor of Judah. Joshua son of Jehozadak was the high priest. The Lord made all the rest of the people who were left alive excited, too. They came and worked on the Temple of their God, the Lord of heaven's armies. 15They began on the twenty-fourth day of the sixth month. This was in the second year that Darius was king of Persia.

The Beauty of the Temple

2 The Lord spoke his word through Haggai the prophet[d] on the twenty-first day of the seventh month. This is what the Lord said: 2"Speak to Zerubbabel son of Shealtiel, governor of Judah. Speak also to Joshua son of Jehozadak, the high

priest. And speak to the rest of the people who were left alive. Say: ³'Do any of you who are still alive remember how beautiful the Temple*ᵈ* was before it was destroyed? What does it look like now? The truth is it means nothing to you!' ⁴But the Lord says: 'Zerubbabel, be brave. Joshua son of Jehozadak, the high priest, be brave. And all you people who live in the land, be brave', says the Lord. 'Work, because I am with you', says the Lord of heaven's armies. ⁵'I made a promise to you when you came out of Egypt. My Spirit*ᵈ* is still with you. So don't be afraid'.

⁶"This is what the Lord of heaven's armies says: 'In a short time I will shake the heavens and earth once again. And I will shake the sea and the dry land. ⁷I will shake all the nations. All the nations will bring their wealth. Then I will fill this Temple with glory', says the Lord of heaven's armies. ⁸'The silver is mine, and the gold is mine', says the Lord of heaven's armies. ⁹'The new Temple will be more beautiful than the one that was destroyed', says the Lord of heaven's armies. 'And in this place I will give peace to the people', says the Lord of heaven's armies."

¹⁰The Lord spoke his word to Haggai the prophet. This was on the twenty-fourth day of the ninth month. It was in the second year that Darius was king of Persia. This is what the Lord said: ¹¹"This is what the Lord of heaven's armies says: 'Ask the priests what the teachings say. ¹²A person might carry meat made holy for the Lord in the fold of his clothes. And that fold might touch bread, cooked food, wine, olive oil or some other food. Will the thing the fold touches be made holy for the Lord, too?' "

The priests answered, "No."

¹³Then Haggai said, "A person who touches a dead body will become unclean.*ᵈ* If he touches any of these foods, will it become unclean, too?"

The priests answered, "Yes. It would become unclean."

¹⁴Then Haggai answered, "The Lord says this: 'This is also true for the people of this nation. They are unclean, and everything they do with their hands is unclean to me. If these people offer something at the altar to me, it is also unclean.

¹⁵" 'Think about this from now on! Think about how it was before you started piling stones on top of stones. Think about how it was before you started building the Temple of the Lord. ¹⁶A person used to come to a pile of grain expecting to find 20 basketfuls. But there were only ten. And a person used to come to the wine vat to take out 50 jarfuls. But only 20 were there. ¹⁷I destroyed your work with diseases, mildew*ᵈ* and hail. But you still did not come to me'. The Lord says this. ¹⁸'It is the twenty-fourth day of the ninth month. On this day the people finished working on the foundation of the Temple of the Lord. From now on, think about these things: ¹⁹do you have seeds for your crops already in the barn? No! Your vines and trees are not giving fruit yet, either. You don't have any figs, pomegranates*ᵈ* or olives yet. But from now on I will bless you!' "

The Lord Makes a Promise to Zerubbabel

²⁰Then the Lord spoke his word a second time to Haggai. It was on the twenty-fourth day of the month. This is what the Lord said: ²¹"Tell Zerubbabel, the governor of Judah: 'I am going to shake the heavens and the earth. ²²I will destroy the foreign kingdoms. I will take away the power of the kingdoms of the nations. I will destroy the chariots and their riders. The horses will fall with their riders. People will kill each other with

swords'. [23]The Lord of heaven's armies says this: 'On that day I will take you, Zerubbabel son of Shealtiel, my servant'. The Lord says this: 'I will make you important like my signet[d] ring. This is because I have chosen you!' says the Lord of heaven's armies."

ZECHARIAH

Encouraging the People

The Lord Calls His People Back

1 It was the eighth month of the second year that Darius was king of Persia. The Lord spoke his word to the prophet*d* Zechariah son of Berekiah. Berekiah was the son of Iddo. The Lord said:

2"The Lord was very angry with your ancestors. 3So tell the people: This is what the Lord of heaven's armies says: Return to me, and I will return to you. 4Don't be like your ancestors. In the past the prophets spoke to them. They said: This is what the Lord of heaven's armies says: 'Stop your evil ways and evil actions'. But they wouldn't listen or pay attention to me, says the Lord. 5Your ancestors are dead. And those prophets didn't live for ever. 6I commanded my words and laws to my servants the prophets. They preached to your ancestors, who returned to me. They said, 'The Lord of heaven's armies did as he said he would. He punished us for the way we lived and for what we did'."

The Vision of the Horses

7It was on the twenty-fourth day of the eleventh month, which is called Shebat. It was Darius' second year as king. The Lord spoke his word to the prophet*d* Zechariah son of Berekiah. Berekiah was the son of Iddo.

8During the night I had a vision. I saw a man riding a red horse. He was standing among some myrtle trees in the ravine. Behind him were red, brown and white horses.

9I asked, "What are these, sir?"

The angel who was talking with me answered. He said, "I'll show you what they are."

10Then the man standing among the myrtle trees explained. He said, "They are the ones the Lord sent through all the earth."

11Then they spoke to the Lord's angel. He was standing among the myrtle trees. They said, "We have gone through all the earth. Everything is calm and quiet."

12Then the Lord's angel asked, "Lord of heaven's armies, how long before you show mercy to Jerusalem and the cities of Judah? You have been angry with them for 70 years now." 13Then the Lord answered the angel who was talking with me. His words were comforting and good.

14Then the angel told me, "Announce this: This is what the Lord of heaven's armies says: 'I have a strong love for Jerusalem. 15And I am very angry with the nations that feel so safe. I was only a little angry, but they made things worse for my people'.

16"So this is what the Lord says: 'I will return to Jerusalem with mercy. My Temple*d* will be rebuilt,' says the Lord of heaven's armies. 'And the measuring line will be used to rebuild Jerusalem'.

17"Also announce: This is what the Lord of heaven's armies says: 'My towns will be rich again. I will comfort Jerusalem again. I will still choose Jerusalem'."

The Vision of the Horns

18Then I looked up and saw four animal horns. 19I asked the angel who was talking with me, "What are these?"

He said, "These are the strong nations that scattered the people of Judah, Israel and Jerusalem."

²⁰Then the Lord showed me four craftsmen. ²¹I asked, "What are they coming to do?"

He answered, "They have come to scare and throw down the horns. Those horns scattered the people of Judah. No one could even lift up his head. The horns stand for the strong nations that attacked the people of Judah and scattered them."

The Vision of the Measuring Line

2 Then I looked up. And I saw a man holding a line for measuring things. ²I asked him, "Where are you going?"

He said to me, "I am going to measure Jerusalem. I will see how wide and how long it is."

³Then the angel who was talking with me left. And another angel came out to meet him. ⁴The second angel said to him, "Run and tell that young man this: 'Jerusalem will become a city without walls because there will be so many people and cattle in it. ⁵I will be a wall of fire around it', says the Lord. 'And I will be the glory within it'.

⁶"Hurry! Run away from Babylon. I have scattered you in all directions," says the Lord.

⁷"Hurry, people of Jerusalem! Escape from Babylon." ⁸This is what the Lord of heaven's armies says: "Whoever hurts you hurts what is precious to me."

So the Lord will honour me. And he will send me to speak against those nations who scattered you. ⁹"I will raise my hand against them. Their slaves will rob them."

Then you will know that the Lord of heaven's armies sent me.

¹⁰"Shout and be glad, Jerusalem. I am coming, and I will live among you," says the Lord. ¹¹"At that time people from many nations will come to the Lord. And they will become my peo-

ple. I will live among you. And you will know that the Lord of heaven's armies has sent me to you. ¹²Judah will be the Lord's special part of the holy land. And Jerusalem will be his chosen city again. ¹³Be silent, everyone. The Lord is coming out of the holy place where he lives."

The Vision of the High Priest

3 Then he showed me Joshua the high priest. He was standing in front of the Lord's angel. And Satan was standing by Joshua's right side to accuse him. ²The Lord said to Satan, "The Lord says you are guilty, Satan. The Lord who has chosen Jerusalem says you are guilty. This man was like a burning stick pulled from the fire."

³Joshua was standing in front of the angel. And Joshua was wearing dirty clothes. ⁴Then the angel spoke to those standing near him. He said, "Take those dirty clothes off Joshua."

Then the angel said to Joshua, "Look, I have taken away your sin. And I am giving you new clothes."

⁵Then I said, "Put a clean turban on his head." So they put a clean turban on his head. They dressed him while the Lord's angel stood there.

⁶Then the Lord's angel said to Joshua, "This is what the Lord of heaven's armies says: ⁷'Do as I tell you and serve me. Then you will be in charge of my Temple.ᵈ You will take care of my courtyards. And I will let you be with these angels who are standing here.

⁸"'Listen, high priest Joshua and the people with you. You stand for things that will happen. I am going to bring my servant called the Branch. ⁹Look, I put this stone in front of Joshua. The stone has seven sides. I will carve a message on it', says the Lord of heaven's armies. 'And in one day I will take away the sin of this land'.

¹⁰"The Lord of heaven's armies says, 'In that day, each of you will invite your neighbour to join you. And

you will sit together under your own grapevine and under your own fig tree'."

The Vision of the Lampstand

4 Then the angel who was talking with me came back. He woke me up as if I had been asleep. ²He asked me, "What do you see?"

I said, "I see a solid gold lampstand. There is a bowl at the top. And there are seven lamps. There are also seven places for wicks. ³There are two olive trees by it. One is on the right of the bowl. And one is on the left."

⁴I asked the angel who talked with me, "Sir, what are these?"

⁵The angel said, "Don't you know what they are?"

"No, sir," I said.

⁶Then he told me, "This is the message from the Lord to Zerubbabel: 'You will not succeed by your own strength or power. The power will come from my Spirit',ᵈ says the Lord of heaven's armies.

⁷"No mountain can stand in Zerubbabel's way. It will be flattened. Then he will bring out the topmost stone. There will be shouts of 'It's beautiful! It's beautiful!'"

⁸Then the Lord spoke his word to me again. He said: ⁹"Zerubbabel has laid the foundation of this Temple.ᵈ He will also complete it. Then you will know that the Lord of heaven's armies has sent me to you.

¹⁰"The people should not think that small beginnings are unimportant. They will be happy when they see Zerubbabel with tools, building the Temple.

"(These seven lamps stand for the eyes of the Lord. They look back and forth across the earth.)"

¹¹Then I asked the angel, "What are the two olive trees on the right and left of the lampstand?"

¹²I also asked him, "What are the two branches full of olives? The olive

oil flows through the two gold pipes to the lamps."

¹³He answered, "Don't you know what they are?"

"No, sir," I said.

¹⁴So he said, "They stand for two men. They have been appointed to serve the Lord of all the earth."

The Vision of the Flying Scroll

5 I looked up again. And I saw a flying scroll.

²The angel asked me, "What do you see?"

I answered, "I see a flying scroll. It is 9 metres long and 4.5 metres wide."

³And he said to me, "This is the curse that will go all over the land. One side says every thief will be sent away. The other side says everyone who makes false promises will be sent away. ⁴The Lord of heaven's armies says, 'I will send it to the houses of thieves. I will also send it to those who use my name to make false promises. The scroll will stay in that person's house. And it will destroy the house with its wood and stones'."

The Vision of the Woman

⁵Then the angel who was talking with me came forward. He said to me, "Look up and see what is coming."

⁶I asked, "What is it?"

He answered, "It is a measuring basket." He also said, "It stands for the people's sins in all the land."

⁷Then the lid made of lead was raised. There was a woman sitting in the basket. ⁸The angel said, "The woman stands for wickedness." Then he pushed her back into the basket. And he put the lid back down.

⁹Then I looked up. I saw two women. They had wind in their wings. Their wings were like those of a stork. They lifted up the basket into the sky.

¹⁰I spoke to the angel who was talk-

ing with me. I asked, "Where are they taking the basket?"

¹¹He answered, "They are going to Babylonia. They will build a temple for it. When the temple is ready, they will set the basket there in its place."

The Vision of the Four Chariots

6 I looked up again. I saw four chariots coming from between two mountains. They were mountains of bronze. ²Red horses pulled the first chariot. Black horses pulled the second chariot. ³White horses pulled the third chariot. And strong, spotted horses pulled the fourth chariot. ⁴I spoke to the angel who was talking with me. I asked, "What are these, sir?"

⁵He said, "These are going to the four directions on earth. They have just come from the presence of the Lord of the whole world. ⁶The chariot pulled by the black horses will go north. The white horses will go west. And the spotted horses will go south."

⁷The powerful horses were trying to go through all the earth. So he said, "Go through all the earth." And they did.

⁸Then he called to me, "Look. The horses that went north have calmed the Lord's anger that came from there to punish."

A Crown for Joshua

⁹The Lord spoke his word to me. He said: ¹⁰"Heldai, Tobijah and Jedaiah were captives in Babylon. Get silver and gold from them. Go that same day to the house of Josiah son of Zephaniah. ¹¹Make the silver and gold into a crown. And put it on the head of Joshua son of Jehozadak. Joshua is the high priest. ¹²Tell him this is what the Lord of heaven's armies says: 'There is a man whose name is the Branch. He will branch out from where he is.

He will build the Temple^d of the Lord. ¹³One man^n will build the Temple of the Lord. And the other^n will receive the honour of a king. One man will sit on his throne and rule. And the other will be a priest on his throne. And these two men will work together in peace'. ¹⁴The crown will be kept in the Temple of the Lord. It will remind Heldai, Tobijah, Jedaiah and Josiah son of Zephaniah of God's king. ¹⁵People living far away will come and build the Temple of the Lord. Then you will know the Lord of heaven's armies has sent me to you. This will happen if you completely obey the Lord your God."

The People Should Show Mercy

7 It was the fourth year of King Darius' rule. It was on the fourth day of the ninth month, which is called Kislev. The Lord spoke his word to Zechariah. ²The city of Bethel sent Sharezer, Regem-Melech and their men to ask the Lord a question. ³They went to the prophets^d and priests. They were at the Temple^d of the Lord of heaven's armies. The men said, "For years the fifth month of each year has been a special time for us. We have shown our sadness and gone without food in this month. Should we continue to do this?"

⁴The Lord of heaven's armies spoke his word to me. He said, ⁵"Tell the priests and the people in the country this: 'For 70 years you went without food and cried in the fifth and seventh months. But that was not really for me. ⁶And when you ate and drank, it was really for yourselves. ⁷The Lord used the earlier prophets to say the same thing. Jerusalem and the surrounding towns were at peace and wealthy then. People lived in the southern area and the western mountain slopes'."

⁸And the Lord spoke his word to

One man This probably refers to Zerubbabel.
other This probably refers to Joshua.

Zechariah again: ⁹"This is what the Lord of heaven's armies says: 'Do what is right and fair. Be kind and merciful to each other. ¹⁰Don't hurt widows and orphans, foreigners or the poor. Don't even think of doing evil to somebody else'.

¹¹"But they refused to pay attention. They were stubborn and would not listen. ¹²They made their hearts as hard as rock. They would not listen to the teachings of the Lord of heaven's armies. And they would not hear his words through the earlier prophets. So the Lord of heaven's armies became very angry.

¹³"The Lord of heaven's armies says, 'When I called to them, they would not listen. So when they called to me, I would not listen. ¹⁴I scattered them like a hurricane to other countries. These were countries they did not know. This good land was left so ruined that no one could live there'."

The Lord Will Bless Jerusalem

8 The Lord of heaven's armies spoke his word to me again. ²This is what the Lord of heaven's armies says: "I have a very strong love for Jerusalem. My strong love for her is like a fire burning in me."

³This is what the Lord says: "I will return to Jerusalem. I will live in Jerusalem. Then it will be called the City of Truth. And the mountain of the Lord of heaven's armies will be called the Holy Mountain."

⁴This is what the Lord of heaven's armies says: "Old men and old women will again sit along Jerusalem's streets. Each will carry a cane because of his age. ⁵And the streets will be filled with boys and girls playing."

⁶This is what the Lord of heaven's armies says: "Those who are left alive then may think it is too difficult to happen. But it is not too difficult for me," says the Lord of heaven's armies. ⁷This is what the Lord of heaven's armies says: "I will save my people from

countries in the east and west. ⁸I will bring them back. And they will live in Jerusalem. They will be my people. And I will be their good and loyal God."

⁹This is what the Lord of heaven's armies says: "Be strong, you who are hearing these words today. The prophets spoke these words when the foundation was laid for the building of the Temple.ᵈ ¹⁰Before that time there was no money to hire men or animals. People could not safely come and go because of their enemies. I had turned everyone against his neighbour. ¹¹But I will not do to these people who are left alive what I did in the past," says the Lord of heaven's armies.

¹²"Their seeds will come up. Their grapevines will have fruit. The ground will give good crops. And the sky will send rain. I will give all this to those who are left alive. ¹³Judah and Israel, your names have been used as curses. But I will save you. And you will be a blessing. So don't be afraid. Be strong."

¹⁴This is what the Lord of heaven's armies says: "Your ancestors made me angry. So I planned to punish you. I had no mercy," says the Lord of heaven's armies. ¹⁵"But now I am planning to do good to Jerusalem and Judah. So don't be afraid. ¹⁶But do these things: tell each other the truth. In the courts judge with truth and complete fairness. ¹⁷Do not make plans to hurt your neighbours. And don't make false promises. I hate all these things," says the Lord.

¹⁸The Lord of heaven's armies spoke his word to me again. ¹⁹This is what the Lord of heaven's armies says: "You have special days when you give up eating. These days are in the fourth, fifth, seventh and tenth months. Those days will become good, joyful, happy feasts in Judah. But you must love truth and peace."

²⁰This is what the Lord of heaven's armies says: "Many people from

many cities will still come to Jerusalem. ²¹People from one city will say to those from another city, 'We are going to pray to the Lord. We want to ask the Lord of heaven's armies for help. Come and go with us'. ²²Many people and powerful nations will come to Jerusalem. They will worship the Lord of heaven's armies. They will pray to the Lord."

²³This is what the Lord of heaven's armies says: "At that time, ten men from different countries with different languages will come. They will take hold of one Jew by his coat. They will say to him, 'Let us go with you. We have heard that God is with you'."

Punishment on Israel's Enemies

9 This message is the word of the Lord.

The message is against the land of Hadrach.
And it is against the city of Damascus.
The tribes*d* of Israel and all people belong to the Lord.
²The Lord's message is also against the city of Hamath, which is on the border of the land of Hadrach.
The Lord's message is against Tyre and Sidon, with their skill.
³Tyre has built a strong, walled city.
The people have piled up silver like dust.
They have as much gold as mud in the streets.
⁴But the Lord will take away all she has.
He will destroy her power on the sea.
That city will be destroyed by fire.
⁵The city of Ashkelon will see it and be afraid.
The people of Gaza will shake with fear.

And the people of Ekron will lose hope.
No king will be left in Gaza.
And no one will live in Ashkelon any more.
⁶Foreigners will live in Ashdod.
And I will destroy the pride of the Philistines.
⁷I will stop them from drinking blood.
They will not eat any other forbidden food.
Those left alive will belong to God.
They will be leaders in Judah.
And Ekron will become part of my people like the Jebusites.
⁸I will protect my Temple*d* from armies who come and go.
No one will hurt my people again because now I am guarding it.

The King Is Coming

⁹Rejoice, people of Jerusalem.
Shout for joy, people of Jerusalem.
Your king is coming to you.
He does what is right, and he saves.
He is gentle and riding on a donkey.
He is on the colt of a donkey.
¹⁰I will take away the chariots from Ephraim
and the horses from Jerusalem.
The bows used in war will be broken.
The king will talk to the nations about peace.
His kingdom will go from sea to sea,
and from the Euphrates River to the ends of the earth.
¹¹My people, I made an agreement with you
and sealed it with the blood of sacrifices.
Because of this, I will set your prisoners free from captivity,
which is like a dry pit.

¹²You prisoners who have hope,
   return to your place of safety.
Today I am telling you
   that I will give you back twice
      as much as before.
¹³I will use Judah like a bow.
   And Ephraim will be like the
      arrows.
Jerusalem, I will use your men
   to fight the men of Greece.
   I will make you like the sword
      of a warrior.
¹⁴Then the Lord will appear to
      them.
   He will shoot his arrows like
      lightning.
The Lord God will blow the
      trumpet.
   And he will march in the storms
      of the south.
¹⁵The Lord of heaven's armies will
      protect them.
   They will destroy the enemy
      with catapults.
   They will drink and shout like
      drunken men.
   They will be filled like a bowl
      used for sprinkling blood at the
      corners of the altar.
¹⁶On that day the Lord their God
      will save them
   as if his people were sheep.
They will shine in his land
   like jewels in a crown.
¹⁷They will be so pretty and
      beautiful.
   The young men will grow strong
      on the grain.
   And the young women will grow
      strong on new wine.

The Lord's Promises

10 Ask the Lord for rain in the
      springtime.
   The Lord makes the clouds.
He sends the showers.
   And he gives everyone green
      fields.
²Idols tell lies.
   Fortune-tellers see false visions.

They tell about false dreams.
   The comfort they give is worth
      nothing.
So the people are like lost sheep.
   They are abused because there
      is no shepherd.

³The Lord says, "I am angry at my
      shepherds.
   I will punish the leaders.
I, the Lord of heaven's armies,
      will care
for my flock, which is the people
      of Judah.
   I will make them like my proud
      war horses.
⁴From Judah will come the
      cornerstone^d
   and the tent peg.
From him will come the battle
      bow.
   From him will come every ruler.
⁵They will be like soldiers
   marching to battle through
      muddy streets.
The Lord is with them.
   So they will fight and defeat the
      horsemen.

⁶"I will strengthen the people of
      Judah.
   And I will save the people of
      Joseph.
I will bring them back
   because I care for them.
It will be as though
   I had never left them.
I am the Lord their God,
   and I will answer their calls for
      help.
⁷The people of Ephraim will be
      strong like soldiers.
   They will be glad as when they
      have drunk wine.
Their children will see it and
      rejoice.
   They will be happy in the Lord.
⁸I will call my people
   and gather them together.
   I will save them.
And there will be as many of
   them as there used to be.

⁹I have scattered them among the
nations.
But in those faraway places,
they will remember me.
They and their children will live
and return.
¹⁰I will bring them back from Egypt.
I will gather them from Assyria.
I will bring them to Gilead and
Lebanon.
There won't be enough room in
the land for them all.
¹¹They will come through their sea
of trouble.
The waves of the sea will be
calm.
And the Nile River will dry up.
I will defeat Assyria's pride.
I will destroy Egypt's power
over other countries.
¹²I will make my people strong.
And they will live as I say,"
says the Lord.

11 Lebanon, open your gates
so fire may burn your cedar
trees."
²Cry, pine trees, because the
cedar has fallen.
The tall trees are ruined.
Cry, oaks in Bashan,
because the mighty forest has
been cut down.
³Listen to the shepherds crying.
Their rich pastures are
destroyed.
Listen to the lions roaring.
The thick bushes near the
Jordan River are ruined.

⁴This is what the Lord my God
says: "Feed the sheep that are about
to be killed. ⁵Their buyers kill them
and are not punished. Those who sell
them say, 'Praise the Lord. I am rich'.
Even the shepherds don't feel sorry
for their sheep. ⁶Even I don't feel sorry any more for the people of this
country," says the Lord. "I will let ev-

eryone be under the power of his
neighbour and king. They will bring
trouble to the country. And I will not
stop them."
⁷So I fed the sheep about to be
killed, particularly the weakest ones.
Then I took two sticks. I called one
Favour. I called the other Union. And
I fed the sheep. ⁸In one month I got
rid of three shepherds. The flock hated me, and I got impatient with them.
⁹I said, "I will no longer take care of
you like a shepherd. Let those that
are dying die. Let those that are to be
destroyed be destroyed. Let those
that are left eat each other."
¹⁰Then I broke the stick named Favour. This broke the agreement God
made with his people. ¹¹That day it
was broken. Those weak sheep were
watching me. They knew this message was from the Lord.
¹²Then I said, "If you want to pay
me, then pay me. If not, then don't."
So they paid me 30 pieces of silver.
¹³The Lord said to me, "Throw the
money to the potter." That is how little they thought I was worth.ⁿ So I
threw the money to the potter in the
Templeᵈ of the Lord.
¹⁴Then I broke the second stick
named Union. This broke the tie between Judah and Israel.
¹⁵Then the Lord said to me, "Become a foolish shepherd again. ¹⁶I am
going to get a new shepherd for the
country. He will not care for the dying
sheep. He will not look for the young
ones. He will not heal the injured
ones. He will not feed the healthy. But
he will eat the best sheep and tear off
their hoofs.

¹⁷"How terrible it will be for the
useless shepherd.
He abandoned the flock.
May war destroy his power and
wisdom.

trees In this poem, trees, bushes and animals stand for leaders of countries around Judah.
worth This was a small amount. It was about the price paid for a slave.

May his power become useless.
May his wisdom be taken
away."

Jerusalem Will Be Saved

12 This message is the word of the Lord to Israel. The Lord stretched out the skies. He laid the foundations of the earth. He put man's spirit in him. And the Lord says this: 2"I will make Jerusalem like a cup of poison to the nations around her. They will come and attack Jerusalem and Judah. 3One day all the nations on earth will come together to attack Jerusalem. But I will make Jerusalem like a heavy rock. Anyone who tries to move it will get hurt. 4At that time I will scare every horse. And its rider will panic," says the Lord. "I will watch over Judah. But I will blind all the horses of the enemies. 5Then the leaders of Judah will say to themselves, 'The people of Jerusalem are strong. This is because the Lord of heaven's armies is their God'.

6"At that time I will make the leaders of Judah like a fire burning a stack of wood. They will be like a fire burning straw. They will destroy all the people around them left and right. But Jerusalem will remain safe.

7"The Lord will save the people of Judah first. Then the people in Jerusalem, David's city, won't have more honour than Judah. 8At that time the Lord will protect the people in Jerusalem. Then even the weakest of them will be strong like David. And the family of David will be like God. They will be like an angel of the Lord leading the people. 9At that time I will go to destroy all the nations that attack Jerusalem.

Crying for the One They Stabbed

10"I will give David's family and people in Jerusalem a spirit of kindness and mercy. They will look at me, the one they have stabbed. And they will cry like someone crying over the

death of an only child. They will be as sad as someone who has lost a first-born[d] son. 11At that time there will be much crying in Jerusalem. It will be like the crying for Hadad Rimmon in the plain of Megiddo. 12The land will cry. Each family will cry alone. The family of David and their wives will cry. The family of Nathan and their wives will cry. 13The family of Levi and their wives will cry. The family of Shimei and their wives will cry. 14And all the rest of the families and their wives will cry.

13 "At that time a fountain will be opened. It will be for David's descendants[d] and for the people of Jerusalem. It will cleanse them of their sins and wrongs."

2The Lord of heaven's armies says, "At that time I will get rid of the names of the idols from the land. No one will remember them any more. I will also remove the prophets[d] and unclean[d] spirits. 3A person might continue to prophesy. If he does, his own father and mother will tell him, 'You have told lies using the Lord's name. So you must die'. When he prophesies, his own parents should stab him.

4"At that time the prophets will be ashamed of their visions and prophecies. They won't wear the prophet's clothes made of hair to trick people. 5They will say, 'I am not a prophet. I am a farmer. I have been a farmer since I was young'. 6But someone will ask, 'What are the deep cuts on your body?' And he will answer, 'I was hurt at my friend's house'.

The Shepherd Is Killed

7"Sword, hit the shepherd.
    Attack the man who is my
      friend,"
  says the Lord of heaven's
    armies.
"Kill the shepherd,
  and the sheep will scatter.
  I will punish the little ones."

[8]The Lord says, "Two-thirds of the
   people
   through all the land will die.
   And one-third will be left.
[9]I will test the ones left with fire.
   I will purify them like silver.
   I will test them like gold.
Then they will call on me.
   And I will answer them.
I will say, 'You are my people'.
   And they will say, 'The Lord is
   our God'."

The Day of Punishment

14 The Lord's day of judging is
coming. The wealth you have
taken will be divided among you.

[2]I will bring all the nations together
to fight Jerusalem. They will capture
the city and rob the houses. The
women will be attacked. Half the people will be taken away as captives. But
the rest won't be taken from the city.

[3]Then the Lord will go to war
against those nations. He will fight as
in a day of battle. [4]On that day he will
stand on the Mount of Olives,[d] east of
Jerusalem. The Mount of Olives will
split in two. A deep valley will run east
and west. Half the mountain will move
north. And half will move south. [5]You
will run through this mountain valley
to the other side. You will run as you
ran from the earthquake. That was
when Uzziah was king of Judah. Then
the Lord my God will come. And all
the holy ones will be with him.

[6]On that day there will be no light,
cold or frost. [7]There will be no other
day like it. The Lord knows when it
will come. There will be no day or
night. Even at evening it will still be
light.

[8]At that time fresh water will flow
from Jerusalem. Half of it will flow
east to the Dead Sea.[d] And half of it
will flow west to the Mediterranean
Sea. It will flow summer and winter.

[9]Then the Lord will be king over the
whole world. At that time there will be
only one Lord. And his name will be
the only name.

[10]All the land south of Jerusalem
from Geba to Rimmon will be turned
into a plain. Jerusalem will be raised
up, but it will stay in the same place.
The city will reach from the Benjamin
Gate to the First Gate to the Corner
Gate. It will go from the Tower of
Hananel to the king's winepresses.[d]
[11]People will live there. It will never
be destroyed again. Jerusalem will be
safe.

[12]But the Lord will punish the nations that fought against Jerusalem.
He will bring a terrible disease on
them. Their flesh will rot away while
they are still standing up. Their eyes
will rot in their sockets. And their
tongues will rot in their mouths. [13]At
that time the Lord will cause panic.
Everybody will grab his neighbour.
They will attack each other. [14]The
people of Judah will fight in Jerusalem.
And the wealth of the nations around
them will be collected. There will be
lot of gold, silver and clothes. [15]A
similar disease will strike the horses,
mules, camels and donkeys. All the
animals in the camps will have the disease.

[16]Some of the people who came to
fight Jerusalem will be left alive. They
will come back to Jerusalem year after
year. They will come to worship the
King, the Lord of heaven's armies.
They will celebrate the Feast[d] of Shelters. [17]Some people from the nations
might not go to Jerusalem. They
might not worship the King, the Lord
of heaven's armies. Then rain will not
fall on their land. [18]The Egyptians
might not go to Jerusalem. They
might not celebrate the Feast of Shelters. Then the Lord will send them
the same terrible disease as he sent
the other nations. [19]This will be the
punishment. It will be for Egypt and
any nation which does not go to
celebrate the Feast of Shelters.

[20]At that time the horses' bells will

have written on them: holy to the Lord. The cooking pots in the Temple*d* of the Lord will be like the holy altar bowls. [21]Every pot in Jerusalem and Judah will be holy to the Lord of heaven's armies. And everyone who offers sacrifices will be able to cook in them. At that time there will not be any traders in the Temple of the Lord of heaven's armies.

MALACHI

God Tells Israel to Be Loyal

1 This message is the word of the Lord. It is given to Israel through Malachi.

God Loves Israel

[2]The Lord said, "I love you."

But you ask, "How have you loved us?"

The Lord said, "Esau and Jacob were brothers. I loved Jacob, [3]but I hated Esau. I destroyed his mountain country. I left his land to the wild dogs of the desert."

[4]The people of Edom might say, "We were destroyed. But we will go back and rebuild the ruins."

But the Lord of heaven's armies says, "If they rebuild them, I will destroy them. People will say, 'Edom is the Wicked Country. The Lord is always angry with the Edomites'. [5]You will see these things with your own eyes. You will say, 'The Lord is great, even outside the borders of Israel!' "

The Priests Don't Respect God

[6]The Lord of heaven's armies says, "A child honours his father. A servant honours his master. I am a father. So why don't you honour me? I am a master. So why don't you respect me? You priests do not respect me.

"But you ask, 'How have we shown you disrespect?'

[7]"You have shown it by bringing unclean[d] sacrifices to my altar.

"But you ask, 'What makes them unclean?'

"They are unclean because you don't show respect for my altar. [8]You bring blind animals as sacrifices, and that is wrong. You bring crippled and sick animals. That is wrong. Try giving them to your governor. Would he be pleased with you? He wouldn't accept you," says the Lord of heaven's armies.

[9]"Now ask God to be kind to you. But he won't accept you with such offerings," says the Lord of heaven's armies.

[10]"I wish one of you would close the Temple[d] doors. Then you would not light useless fires on my altar! I am not pleased with you. I will not accept your gifts," says the Lord of heaven's armies. [11]"From the east to the west I will be honoured among the nations. Everywhere they will bring incense[d] and clean offerings to me. I will be honoured among the nations," says the Lord of heaven's armies.

[12]"But you don't honour me. You say of the Lord's altar, 'It is unclean. The food has no worth'. [13]You say, 'We are tired of doing this'. And you sniff at it in disgust," says the Lord of heaven's armies.

"And you bring hurt, crippled and sick animals. You bring them as gifts. But I won't accept them from you," says the Lord. [14]"The cheat will be cursed. He has an animal in his flock. He promises to offer it. But then he offers me an animal that has something wrong with it. I am a great king," says the Lord of heaven's armies. "I am feared by all the nations.

Rules for Priests

2 "Priests, this command is for you. [2]Listen to me. Pay attention to what I say. Honour my name," says the Lord of heaven's armies. "If you don't, I will send a curse on you. I will curse your blessings. I have already cursed them because you don't pay attention to what I say.

³"I will punish your descendants.ᵈ I will smear your faces with the rubbish from your feasts. And you will be thrown away with it. ⁴Then you will know why I am giving you this command. It is so that my agreement with Levi will continue," says the Lord of heaven's armies. ⁵"My agreement for priests was with the tribeᵈ of Levi. I promised them life and peace. And I gave these to them so they would honour me. They did honour me and fear me. ⁶They taught the true teachings. They spoke no lies. With peace and honesty they did what I said they should do. They kept many people from sinning.

⁷"A priest should teach what he knows. People should learn the teachings from him because he is the messenger of the Lord of heaven's armies. ⁸But you priests have stopped obeying me. With your teachings you have caused many people to do wrong. You have broken the agreement with the tribeᵈ of Levi!" says the Lord of heaven's armies. ⁹"You have not been careful to do what I say. You take sides in court cases. So I have caused you to be hated and disgraced in front of everybody."

Judah Was Not Loyal to God

¹⁰We all have the same father. The same God made us. So why do people break their promises to each other? They don't respect the agreement that our ancestors made with God. ¹¹The people of Judah have broken their promises. They have done something God hates in Israel and Jerusalem. The people of Judah did not respect the Templeᵈ that the Lord loves. The men of Judah married the women who worship foreign gods. ¹²The man who does this might bring offerings to the Lord of heaven's armies. But the Lord will still separate him from the community of Israel.

¹³This is another thing you do. You cover the Lord's altar with your tears. You cry and moan because the Lord does not accept your offerings. He is not pleased with what you bring. ¹⁴You ask, "Why?" It is because the Lord sees how you treated the wife you married when you were young. You broke your promise with her. She was your partner. You promised yourself to her. ¹⁵God made husbands and wives to become one body and one spirit for his purpose. This is so they would have children who are true to God. So be careful. Do not break your promise with the wife you married when you were young.

¹⁶The Lord God of Israel says, "I hate divorce. And I hate people who do cruel things as easily as they put on clothes," says the Lord of heaven's armies. So be careful. And do not break your trust.

The Special Day of Judging

¹⁷You have tired the Lord with what you say.

You ask, "How have we tired him?"

You did it by saying, "God thinks anyone who does evil is good. And he is pleased with them." Or you asked, "Where is the God who is fair?"

3 The Lord of heaven's armies says, "I will send my messenger. He will prepare the way for me to come. Suddenly, the Lord you are looking for will come to his Temple.ᵈ The messenger of the agreement, whom you want, will come." ²No one can live through that time. No one can survive when he comes. He will be like a purifying fire. He will be like strong soap. ³He will be like someone who heats and purifies silver. He will purify the Levites. He will make them pure like gold and silver. Then they will bring offerings to the Lord in the right way. ⁴And he will accept the offerings from Judah and Jerusalem. It will be as it was in the past. ⁵The Lord of heaven's armies says, "Then I will come to you and judge you. I will testify against those who take part in evil

magic, adultery[d] and lying. I will testify against those who cheat workers of their pay and who cheat widows and orphans. And I will testify against those who are unfair to foreigners. These people do not respect me.

Stealing from God

[6]"I am the Lord. I do not change. So you descendants[d] of Jacob have not been destroyed. [7]Like your ancestors before you, you have disobeyed my rules. You have not kept them. Return to me. Then I will return to you," says the Lord of heaven's armies.

"But you ask, 'How can we return?'

[8]"Should a man rob God? But you rob me.

"You ask, 'How have we robbed you?'

"You have robbed me in your offerings and the tenth of your crops. [9]So a curse is on you because the whole nation has robbed me. [10]Bring to the storehouse a tenth of what you produce. Then there will be food in my house. Test me in this," says the Lord of heaven's armies. "I will open the windows of heaven for you. I will pour out more blessings than you have room for. [11]I will stop the insects so they won't eat your crops. The grapes won't fall from your vines before they are ready to pick," says the Lord of heaven's armies. [12]"All the nations will call you blessed. You will have a pleasant country," says the Lord of heaven's armies.

The Lord's Promise of Mercy

[13]The Lord says, "You have said terrible things about me.

"But you ask, 'What have we said about you?'

[14]"You have said, 'It is useless to serve God. It did no good to obey his laws. And it did no good to show the Lord of heaven's armies that we are sorry for what we did. [15]So we say that proud people are happy. Evil people succeed. They challenge God and get away with it'."

[16]Then those who honoured the Lord spoke with each other. The Lord listened and heard them. The names of those who honoured the Lord and respected him were written in a book. The Lord will remember them.

[17]The Lord of heaven's armies says, "They belong to me. On that day they will be my very own. A father shows mercy to his son who serves him. In the same way I will show mercy to my people. [18]You will again see the difference between good and evil people. You will see the difference between those who serve God and those who don't.

The Day of the Lord's Judging

4 "There is a day coming that will be like a hot furnace. All the proud and evil people will be like straw. On that day they will be completely burned up. Not a root or branch will be left," says the Lord of heaven's armies. [2]"But for you who honour me, goodness will shine on you like the sun. There will be healing in its rays. You will jump around, like calves freed from their stalls. [3]Then you will crush the wicked. They will be like ashes under your feet. I will do this on that day," says the Lord of heaven's armies.

[4]"Remember the teaching of Moses my servant. I gave those laws and rules to him at Mount Sinai. They are for all the Israelites.

[5]"But I will send Elijah the prophet[d] to you. He will come before that great and terrible day of the Lord's judging. [6]Elijah will help fathers love their children. And he will help the children love their fathers. Otherwise, I will come and put a curse on the land."

THE NEW TESTAMENT

THE NEW TESTAMENT

CONTENTS

THE NEW TESTAMENT

Matthew	1109	1 Timothy	1393
Mark	1156	2 Timothy	1399
Luke	1185	Titus	1403
John	1233	Philemon	1406
Acts	1267	Hebrews	1407
Romans	1312	James	1422
1 Corinthians	1332	1 Peter	1427
2 Corinthians	1350	2 Peter	1433
Galatians	1362	1 John	1437
Ephesians	1369	2 John	1442
Philippians	1376	3 John	1443
Colossians	1381	Jude	1444
1 Thessalonians	1386	Revelation	1446
2 Thessalonians	1390		

MATTHEW

Matthew Tells the Jews About Jesus

The Family History of Jesus

1 This is the family history of Jesus Christ. He came from the family of David. David came from the family of Abraham.

2 Abraham was the father[n] of Isaac.

Isaac was the father of Jacob.

Jacob was the father of Judah and his brothers.

3 Judah was the father of Perez and Zerah.

(Their mother was Tamar.)

Perez was the father of Hezron.

Hezron was the father of Ram.

4 Ram was the father of Amminadab.

Amminadab was the father of Nahshon.

Nahshon was the father of Salmon.

5 Salmon was the father of Boaz.

(Boaz's mother was Rahab.)

Boaz was the father of Obed.

(Obed's mother was Ruth.)

Obed was the father of Jesse.

6 Jesse was the father of King David.

David was the father of Solomon.

(Solomon's mother had been Uriah's wife.)

7 Solomon was the father of Rehoboam.

Rehoboam was the father of Abijah.

Abijah was the father of Asa.

8 Asa was the father of Jehoshaphat.

Jehoshaphat was the father of Jehoram.

Jehoram was the ancestor of Uzziah.

9 Uzziah was the father of Jotham.

Jotham was the father of Ahaz.

Ahaz was the father of Hezekiah.

10 Hezekiah was the father of Manasseh.

Manasseh was the father of Amon.

Amon was the father of Josiah.

11 Josiah was the grandfather of Jehoiachin and his brothers.

(This was at the time that the people were taken to Babylon.)

12 After they were taken to Babylon: Jehoiachin was the father of Shealtiel.

Shealtiel was the grandfather of Zerubbabel.

13 Zerubbabel was the father of Abiud.

Abiud was the father of Eliakim.

Eliakim was the father of Azor.

14 Azor was the father of Zadok.

Zadok was the father of Akim.

Akim was the father of Eliud.

15 Eliud was the father of Eleazar.

Eleazar was the father of Matthan.

Matthan was the father of Jacob.

16 Jacob was the father of Joseph.

Joseph was the husband of Mary, and Mary was the mother of Jesus.

Jesus is called the Christ.[d]

17 So there were 14 generations from Abraham to David. There were 14 generations from David until the time when the people were taken to Babylon. And there were 14 genera-

---

father "Father" in Jewish lists of ancestors can sometimes mean grandfather or more distant relative.

tions from the time when the people were taken to Babylon until Christ was born.

The Birth of Jesus Christ

[18]The mother of Jesus Christ was Mary. And this is how the birth of Jesus came about. Mary was engaged to marry Joseph. But before they married, she learned that she was going to have a baby. She was pregnant by the power of the Holy Spirit.[d] [19]Mary's husband, Joseph, was a good man. He did not want to disgrace her in public, so he planned to divorce her secretly.

[20]While Joseph thought about this, an angel of the Lord came to him in a dream. The angel said, "Joseph, descendant[d] of David, don't be afraid to take Mary as your wife. The baby in her is from the Holy Spirit. [21]She will give birth to a son. You will name the son Jesus.[n] Give him that name because he will save his people from their sins."

[22]All this happened to make clear the full meaning of what the Lord had said through the prophet:[d] [23]"The virgin[d] will be pregnant. She will have a son, and they will name him Immanuel."[n] This name means "God is with us."

[24]When Joseph woke up, he did what the Lord's angel had told him to do. Joseph married Mary. [25]But he did not have sexual relations with her until she gave birth to a son. And Joseph named the son Jesus.

Wise Men Come to Visit Jesus

2 Jesus was born in the town of Bethlehem in Judea during the time when Herod was king. After Jesus was born, some wise men from the east came to Jerusalem. [2]They asked, "Where is the baby who was born to be the king of the Jews? We saw his star in the east. We have come to worship him."

[3]When King Herod heard about this new king of the Jews, he was troubled. And all the people in Jerusalem were worried too. [4]Herod called a meeting of all the leading priests and teachers of the law. He asked them where the Christ[d] would be born. [5]They answered, "In the town of Bethlehem in Judea. The prophet[d] wrote about this in the Scriptures:[d]

[6]'But you, Bethlehem, in the land
    of Judah,
  you are important among the
    rulers of Judah.
A ruler will come from you.
  He will be like a shepherd for
    my people, the Israelites'."

Micah 5:2

[7]Then Herod had a secret meeting with the wise men from the east. He learned from them the exact time they first saw the star. [8]Then Herod sent the wise men to Bethlehem. He said to them, "Go and look carefully to find the child. When you find him, come and tell me. Then I can go and worship him too."

[9]The wise men heard the king and then left. They saw the same star they had seen in the east. It went before them until it stopped above the place where the child was. [10]When the wise men saw the star, they were filled with joy. [11]They went to the house where the child was and saw him with his mother, Mary. They bowed down and worshipped the child. They opened the gifts they had brought for him. They gave him treasures of gold, frankincense,[d] and myrrh.[d] [12]But God warned the wise men in a dream not to go back to Herod. So they went home to their own country by a different way.

Jesus The name Jesus means "salvation".
"The virgin . . . Immanuel." Quotation from Isaiah 7:14.

Jesus' Parents Take Him to Egypt

[13]After they left, an angel of the Lord came to Joseph in a dream. The angel said, "Get up! Take the child and his mother and escape to Egypt. Herod will start looking for the child to kill him. Stay in Egypt until I tell you to return."

[14]So Joseph got up and left for Egypt during the night with the child and his mother. [15]Joseph stayed in Egypt until Herod died. This was to make clear the full meaning of what the Lord had said through the prophet.[d] The Lord said, "I called my son out of Egypt."[n]

Herod Kills the Baby Boys

[16]When Herod saw that the wise men had tricked him, he was very angry. So he gave an order to kill all the baby boys in Bethlehem and in all the area around Bethlehem who were two years old or younger. This was in keeping with the time he learned from the wise men. [17]So what God had said through the prophet[d] Jeremiah came true:

[18]"A sound was heard in Ramah.
    It was painful crying and much
        sadness.
Rachel cries for her children,
    and she cannot be comforted,
    because her children are dead."

                              Jeremiah 31:15

Joseph and Mary Return

[19]After Herod died, an angel of the Lord came to Joseph in a dream. This happened while Joseph was in Egypt. [20]The angel said, "Get up! Take the child and his mother and go to Israel. The people who were trying to kill the child are now dead."

[21]So Joseph took the child and his mother and went to Israel. [22]But he heard that Archelaus was now king in Judea. Archelaus became king when his father Herod died. So Joseph was afraid to go there. After being warned in a dream, he went to the area of Galilee. [23]He went to a town called Nazareth and lived there. And so what God had said through the prophets[d] came true: "He will be called a Nazarene."[n]

The Work of John the Baptist

3 About that time John the Baptist[d] came and began preaching in the desert area of Judea. [2]John said, "Change your hearts and lives because the kingdom of heaven is coming soon." [3]John the Baptist is the one Isaiah the prophet[d] was talking about. Isaiah said:
    "This is a voice of a man
        who calls out in the desert:
    'Prepare the way for the Lord.
        Make the road straight for
            him'."
                              Isaiah 40:3

[4]John's clothes were made from camel's hair. He wore a leather belt around his waist. For food, he ate locusts[d] and wild honey. [5]Many people went to hear John preach. They came from Jerusalem and all Judea and all the area around the Jordan River. [6]They told of the sins they had done, and John baptised them in the Jordan River.

[7]Many of the Pharisees[d] and Sadducees[d] came to the place where John was baptising people. When John saw them, he said: "You are all snakes! Who warned you to run away from God's anger that is coming? [8]You must do the things that show that you have really changed your hearts and lives. [9]And don't think that you can say to yourselves, 'Abraham is our father'. I tell you that God could make children for Abraham from these

"I called . . . Egypt." Quotation from Hosea 11:1.
Nazarene A person from the city of Nazareth, a name probably meaning "branch" (see Isaiah 11:1).

rocks. [10]The axe is now ready to cut down the trees. Every tree that does not produce good fruit will be cut down and thrown into the fire.[n]

[11]"I baptise you with water to show that your hearts and lives have changed. But there is one coming later who is greater than I am. I am not good enough to carry his sandals. He will baptise you with the Holy Spirit[d] and with fire. [12]He will come ready to clean the grain. He will separate the good grain from the chaff.[d] He will put the good part of the grain into his barn. And he will burn the chaff with a fire that cannot be put out."[n]

Jesus Is Baptised by John

[13]At that time Jesus came from Galilee to the Jordan River. He came to John and wanted John to baptise him. [14]But John tried to stop him. John said, "Why do you come to me to be baptised? I should be baptised by you!"

[15]Jesus answered, "Let it be this way for now. We should do all things that are right." So John agreed to baptise Jesus.

[16]Jesus was baptised and came up out of the water. Heaven opened, and he saw God's Spirit[d] coming down on him like a dove. [17]And a voice spoke from heaven. The voice said, "This is my Son and I love him. I am very pleased with him."

The Temptation of Jesus

4 Then the Spirit[d] led Jesus into the desert to be tempted by the devil. [2]Jesus ate nothing for 40 days and nights. After this, he was very hungry. [3]The devil came to Jesus to tempt him. The devil said, "If you are the Son of God, tell these rocks to become bread."

[4]Jesus answered, "It is written in the Scriptures,[d] 'A person does not live only by eating bread. But a person lives by everything the Lord says'."[n]

[5]Then the devil led Jesus to the holy city of Jerusalem. He put Jesus on a very high place of the Temple.[d] [6]The devil said, "If you are the Son of God, jump off. It is written in the Scriptures,

'He has put his angels in charge of
    you.
They will catch you with their
    hands.
And you will not hit your foot on a
    rock'."   *Psalm 91:11-12*

[7]Jesus answered him, "It also says in the Scriptures, 'Do not test the Lord your God'."[n]

[8]Then the devil led Jesus to the top of a very high mountain. He showed Jesus all the kingdoms of the world and all the great things that are in those kingdoms. [9]The devil said, "If you will bow down and worship me, I will give you all these things."

[10]Jesus said to the devil, "Go away from me, Satan! It is written in the Scriptures, 'You must worship the Lord your God. Serve only him!'"[n]

[11]So the devil left Jesus. And then some angels came to Jesus and helped him.

Jesus Begins Work in Galilee

[12]Jesus heard that John had been put in prison. So Jesus went back to Galilee. [13]He left Nazareth and went and lived in Capernaum, a town near Lake Galilee. Capernaum is in the area near Zebulun and Naphtali. [14]Jesus did this

---

The axe . . . fire. This means that God is ready to punish his people who do not obey him.
He will . . . out. This means that Jesus will come to separate the good people from the bad people, saving the good and punishing the bad.
'A person . . . says'. Quotation from Deuteronomy 8:3.
'Do . . . God'. Quotation from Deuteronomy 6:16.
'You . . . him!' Quotation from Deuteronomy 6:13.

to make what the prophet[d] Isaiah had said come true:

15"Land of Zebulun and land of
   Naphtali
are on the way to the sea.
They are along the Jordan River.
This is Galilee where the
   non-Jewish people live.
16These people who live in darkness
   will see a great light.
They live in a place that is very
   dark.
But a light will shine on them."

   Isaiah 9:1-2

Jesus Chooses Some Followers

17From that time Jesus began to preach, saying, "Change your hearts and lives, because the kingdom of heaven is coming soon."

18Jesus was walking by Lake Galilee. He saw two brothers, Simon (called Peter) and Simon's brother Andrew. The brothers were fishermen, and they were fishing in the lake with a net. 19Jesus said, "Come and follow me. I will make you fishermen for men." 20At once Simon and Andrew left their nets and followed him.

21Jesus continued walking by Lake Galilee. He saw two other brothers, James and John, the sons of Zebedee. They were in a boat with their father Zebedee, preparing their nets to catch fish. Jesus told them to come with him. 22At once they left the boat and their father, and they followed Jesus.

Jesus Teaches and Heals People

23Jesus went everywhere in Galilee. He taught in the synagogues[d] and preached the Good News[d] about the kingdom of heaven. And he healed all the people's diseases and sicknesses. 24The news about Jesus spread all over Syria, and people brought all the sick to him. These sick people were suffering from different kinds of diseases and pain. Some were suffering very great pain, some had demons,[d] some were epileptics,[n] and some were paralysed. Jesus healed all of them. 25Many people followed him. They came from Galilee, the Ten Towns,[n] Jerusalem, Judea, and the land across the Jordan River.

Jesus Teaches the People

5 Jesus saw the crowds who were there. He went up on a hill and sat down. His followers came to him. 2Jesus taught the people and said:
3"Those people who know they
   have great spiritual needs
   are happy.
The kingdom of heaven belongs
   to them.
4Those who are sad now are
   happy.
God will comfort them.
5Those who are humble are happy.
The earth will belong to them.
6Those who want to do right more
   than anything else are
   happy.
God will fully satisfy them.
7Those who give mercy to others
   are happy.
Mercy will be given to them.
8Those who are pure in their
   thinking are happy.
They will be with God.
9Those who work to bring peace
   are happy.
God will call them his sons.
10Those who are treated badly for
   doing good are happy.
The kingdom of heaven belongs
   to them.
11"People will say bad things about you and hurt you. They will lie and say all kinds of evil things about you be-

---

epileptics People with a disease that causes them sometimes to lose control of their bodies, and maybe faint, shake strongly, or not be able to move.
Ten Towns In Greek, called "Decapolis". It was an area east of Lake Galilee that once had ten main towns.

cause you follow me. But when they do these things to you, you are happy. 12Rejoice and be glad. You have a great reward waiting for you in heaven. People did the same evil things to the prophets*d* who lived before you.

You Are like Salt and Light

13"You are the salt of the earth. But if the salt loses its salty taste, it cannot be made salty again. It is good for nothing. It must be thrown out for people to walk on.

14"You are the light that gives light to the world. A city that is built on a hill cannot be hidden. 15And people don't hide a light under a bowl. They put the light on a lampstand. Then the light shines for all the people in the house. 16In the same way, you should be a light for other people. Live so that they will see the good things you do. Live so that they will praise your Father in heaven.

The Importance of the Law

17"Don't think that I have come to destroy the law of Moses or the teaching of the prophets.*d* I have not come to destroy their teachings but to do what they said. 18I tell you the truth. Nothing will disappear from the law until heaven and earth are gone. The law will not lose even the smallest letter or the smallest part of a letter until all has happened. 19Whoever refuses to obey any command and teaches other people not to obey that command will be the least important in the kingdom of heaven. But whoever obeys the law and teaches other people to obey the law will be great in the kingdom of heaven. 20I tell you that you must do better than the teachers of the law and the Pharisees.*d* If you are not better than they are, you will not enter the kingdom of heaven.

Jesus Teaches About Anger

21"You have heard that it was said to our people long ago, 'You must not murder anyone.'*n* Anyone who murders another will be judged'. 22But I tell you, if you are angry with your brother, you will be judged. And if you say bad things to your brother, you will be judged by the Jewish council. And if you call your brother a fool, then you will be in danger of the fire of hell.

23"So when you offer your gift to God at the altar, and you remember that your brother has something against you, 24leave your gift there at the altar. Go and make peace with him. Then come and offer your gift.

25"If your enemy is taking you to court, become friends with him quickly. You should do that before you go to court. If you don't become his friend, he might turn you over to the judge. And the judge might give you to a guard to put you in jail. 26I tell you that you will not leave that jail until you have paid everything you owe.

Jesus Teaches About Sexual Sin

27"You have heard that it was said, 'You must not be guilty of adultery'.*n* 28But I tell you that if anyone looks at a woman and wants to sin sexually with her, then he has already done that sin with the woman in his mind. 29If your right eye causes you to sin, then take it out and throw it away. It is better to lose one part of your body than to have your whole body thrown into hell. 30If your right hand causes you to sin, then cut it off and throw it away. It is better to lose one part of your body than for your whole body to go into hell.

Jesus Teaches About Divorce

31"It was also said, 'Anyone who divorces his wife must give her a writ-

'You . . . anyone'. Quotation from Exodus 20:13; Deuteronomy 5:17.
'You . . . adultery'. Quotation from Exodus 20:14; Deuteronomy 5:18.

ten divorce paper'.[n] [32]But I tell you that anyone who divorces his wife is causing his wife to be guilty of adultery.[d] The only reason for a man to divorce his wife is if she has sexual relations with another man. And anyone who marries that divorced woman is guilty of adultery.

Make Promises Carefully

[33]"You have heard that it was said to our people long ago, 'When you make a promise, don't break your promise. Keep the promises that you make to the Lord'.[n] [34]But I tell you, never make an oath. Don't make an oath using the name of heaven, because heaven is God's throne. [35]Don't make an oath using the name of the earth, because the earth belongs to God. Don't make an oath using the name of Jerusalem, because that is the city of the great King. [36]And don't even say that your own head is proof that you will keep your oath. You cannot make one hair on your head become white or black. [37]Say only 'yes' if you mean 'yes', and say only 'no' if you mean 'no'. If you must say more than 'yes' or 'no', it is from the Evil One.

Don't Fight Back

[38]"You have heard that it was said, 'An eye for an eye, and a tooth for a tooth'.[n] [39]But I tell you, don't stand up against an evil person. If someone slaps you on the right cheek, then turn and let him slap the other cheek too. [40]If someone wants to sue you in court and take your shirt, then let him have your coat too. [41]If a soldier forces you to go with him one mile, then go with him two miles. [42]If a person asks you for something, then give it to him. Don't refuse to give to a person who wants to borrow from you.

Love All People

[43]"You have heard that it was said, 'Love your neighbour[n] and hate your enemies'. [44]But I tell you, love your enemies. Pray for those who hurt you. [45]If you do this, then you will be true sons of your Father in heaven. Your Father causes the sun to rise on good people and on bad people. Your Father sends rain to those who do good and to those who do wrong. [46]If you love only the people who love you, then you will get no reward. Even the tax collectors do that. [47]And if you are nice only to your friends, then you are no better than other people. Even people without God are nice to their friends. [48]So you must be perfect, just as your Father in heaven is perfect.

Jesus Teaches About Giving

6 "Be careful! When you do good things, don't do them in front of people to be seen by them. If you do that, then you will have no reward from your Father in heaven.

[2]"When you give to the poor, don't be like the hypocrites.[d] They blow trumpets before they give so that people will see them. They do that in the synagogues[d] and on the streets. They want other people to honour them. I tell you the truth. Those hypocrites already have their full reward. [3]So when you give to the poor, give very secretly. Don't let anyone know what you are doing. [4]Your giving should be done in secret. Your Father can see what is done in secret, and he will reward you.

Jesus Teaches About Prayer

[5]"When you pray, don't be like the hypocrites.[d] They love to stand in the synagogues[d] and on the street cor-

---

'Anyone . . . divorce paper'. Quotation from Deuteronomy 24:1.
'When . . . Lord'. Quotation from Leviticus 19:12; Numbers 30:2; Deuteronomy 23:21.
'An eye . . . tooth'. Quotation from Exodus 21:24; Leviticus 24:20; Deuteronomy 19:21.
'Love your neighbour' Quotation from Leviticus 19:18.

ners and pray loudly. They want people to see them pray. I tell you the truth. They already have their full reward. ⁶When you pray, you should go into your room and close the door. Then pray to your Father who cannot be seen. Your Father can see what is done in secret, and he will reward you.

⁷"And when you pray, don't be like those people who don't know God. They continue saying things that mean nothing. They think that God will hear them because of the many things they say. ⁸Don't be like them. Your Father knows the things you need before you ask him. ⁹So when you pray, you should pray like this:

'Our Father in heaven,
we pray that your name will
    always be kept holy.
¹⁰We pray that your kingdom will
    come.
We pray that what you want will
    be done,
    here on earth as it is in heaven.
¹¹Give us the food we need for each
    day.
¹²Forgive the sins we have done,
    just as we have forgiven those
    who did wrong to us.
¹³Do not cause us to be tested;
    but save us from the Evil One'.
¹⁴Yes, if you forgive others for the things they do wrong, then your Father in heaven will also forgive you for the things you do wrong. ¹⁵But if you don't forgive the wrongs of others, then your Father in heaven will not forgive the wrong things you do.

Jesus Teaches About Worship

¹⁶"When you give up eating,ⁿ don't put on a sad face like the hypocrites.ᵈ They make their faces look strange to show people that they are giving up eating. I tell you the truth, those hypocrites already have their full reward.

¹⁷So when you give up eating, comb your hair and wash your face. ¹⁸Then people will not know that you are giving up eating. But your Father, whom you cannot see, will see you. Your Father sees what is done in secret, and he will reward you.

God Is More Important than Money

¹⁹"Don't store treasures for yourselves here on earth. Moths and rust will destroy treasures here on earth. And thieves can break into your house and steal the things you have. ²⁰So store your treasure in heaven. The treasures in heaven cannot be destroyed by moths or rust. And thieves cannot break in and steal that treasure. ²¹Your heart will be where your treasure is.

²²"The eye is a light for the body. If your eyes are good, then your whole body will be full of light. ²³But if your eyes are evil, then your whole body will be full of darkness. And if the only light you have is really darkness, then you have the worst darkness.

²⁴"No one can be a slave to two masters. He will hate one master and love the other. Or he will follow one master and refuse to follow the other. So you cannot serve God and money at the same time.

Don't Worry

²⁵"So I tell you, don't worry about the food you need to live. And don't worry about the clothes you need for your body. Life is more important than food. And the body is more important than clothes. ²⁶Look at the birds in the air. They don't plant or harvest or store food in barns. But your heavenly Father feeds the birds. And you know that you are worth much more than the birds. ²⁷You can-

---

give up eating This is called "fasting". The people would give up eating for a special time of prayer and worship to God. It was also done to show sadness.

not add any time to your life by worrying about it.

²⁸"And why do you worry about clothes? Look at the flowers in the field. See how they grow. They don't work or make clothes for themselves. ²⁹But I tell you that even Solomon with his riches was not dressed as beautifully as one of these flowers. ³⁰God clothes the grass in the field like that. The grass is living today, but tomorrow it is thrown into the fire to be burned. So you can be even more sure that God will clothe you. Don't have so little faith! ³¹Don't worry and say, 'What will we eat?' or 'What will we drink?' or 'What will we wear?' ³²All the people who don't know God keep trying to get these things. And your Father in heaven knows that you need them. ³³The thing you should want most is God's kingdom and doing what God wants. Then all these other things you need will be given to you. ³⁴So don't worry about tomorrow. Each day has enough trouble of its own. Tomorrow will have its own worries.

Be Careful About Judging Others

7 "Don't judge other people, and you will not be judged. ²You will be judged in the same way that you judge others. And the forgiveness you give to others will be given to you.

³"Why do you notice the little piece of dust that is in your brother's eye, but you don't notice the big piece of wood that is in your own eye? ⁴Why do you say to your brother, 'Let me take that little piece of dust out of your eye'? Look at yourself first! You still have that big piece of wood in your own eye. ⁵You are a hypocrite!ᵈ First, take the wood out of your own eye. Then you will see clearly enough to take the dust out of your brother's eye.

⁶"Don't give holy things to dogs. Don't throw your pearls before pigs. Pigs will only trample on them. And the dogs will only turn to attack you.

Ask God for What You Need

⁷"Continue to ask, and God will give to you. Continue to search, and you will find. Continue to knock, and the door will open for you. ⁸Yes, everyone who continues asking will receive. He who continues searching will find. And he who continues knocking will have the door opened for him.

⁹"What would you do if your son asks for bread? Which of you would give him a stone? ¹⁰Or if your son asks for a fish, would you give him a snake? ¹¹Even though you are bad, you know how to give good gifts to your children. So surely your heavenly Father will give good things to those who ask him.

The Most Important Rule

¹²"Do for other people the same things you want them to do for you. This is the meaning of the law of Moses and the teaching of the prophets.ᵈ

The Way to Heaven Is Hard

¹³"Enter through the narrow gate. The road that leads to hell is a very easy road. And the gate to hell is very wide. Many people enter through that gate. ¹⁴But the gate that opens the way to true life is very small. And the road to true life is very hard. Only a few people find that road.

People Know You by Your Actions

¹⁵"Be careful of false prophets.ᵈ They come to you and look gentle like sheep. But they are really dangerous like wolves. ¹⁶You will know these people because of the things they do. Good things don't come from bad people, just as grapes don't come from thorn bushes. And figs don't come from thorny weeds. ¹⁷In the same way, every good tree produces good fruit, and bad trees produce bad fruit. ¹⁸A good tree cannot produce bad

fruit, and a bad tree cannot produce good fruit. ¹⁹Every tree that does not produce good fruit is cut down and thrown into the fire. ²⁰You will know these false prophets by what they produce.

²¹"Not everyone who says that I am his Lord will enter the kingdom of heaven. The only people who will enter the kingdom of heaven are those who do the things that my Father in heaven wants. ²²On the last day many people will say to me, 'You are our Lord! We spoke for you. And through you we forced out demons*d* and did many miracles'.*d* ²³Then I will tell them clearly, 'Get away from me, you who do evil. I never knew you'.

Two Kinds of People

²⁴"Everyone who hears these things I say and obeys them is like a wise man. The wise man built his house on rock. ²⁵It rained hard and the water rose. The winds blew and hit that house. But the house did not fall, because the house was built on rock. ²⁶But the person who hears the things I teach and does not obey them is like a foolish man. The foolish man built his house on sand. ²⁷It rained hard, the water rose, and the winds blew and hit that house. And the house fell with a big crash."

²⁸When Jesus finished saying these things, the people were amazed at his teaching. ²⁹Jesus did not teach like their teachers of the law. He taught like a person who had authority.

Jesus Heals a Sick Man

8 When Jesus came down from the hill, great crowds followed him. ²Then a man sick with a harmful skin disease came to Jesus. The man bowed down before him and said,

"Lord, you have the power to heal me if you want."

³Jesus touched the man and said, "I want to heal you. Be healed!" And immediately the man was healed from his skin disease. ⁴Then Jesus said to him, "Don't tell anyone about what happened. But go and show yourself to the priest.*n* And offer the gift that Moses commanded*n* for people who are made well. This will show people that you are healed."

Jesus Heals a Soldier's Servant

⁵Jesus went to the city of Capernaum. When he entered the city, an army officer came to Jesus and begged for help. ⁶The officer said, "Lord, my servant is at home in bed. He can't move his body and is in much pain."

⁷Jesus said to the officer, "I will go and heal him."

⁸The officer answered, "Lord, I am not good enough for you to come into my house. All you need to do is command that my servant be healed, and he will be healed. ⁹I myself am a man under the authority of other men. And I have soldiers under my command. I tell one soldier, 'Go', and he goes. I tell another soldier, 'Come', and he comes. I say to my servant, 'Do this', and my servant obeys me."

¹⁰When Jesus heard this, he was amazed. He said to those who were with him, "I tell you the truth. This man has more faith than any other person I have found, even in Israel. ¹¹Many people will come from the east and from the west. They will sit and eat with Abraham, Isaac, and Jacob in the kingdom of heaven. ¹²And those people who should have the kingdom will be thrown outside into the darkness. In that place people will cry and grind their teeth with pain."

---

show . . . priest The law of Moses said a priest must say when a Jew who had a harmful skin disease was well.
Moses commanded Read about this in Leviticus 14:1-32.

[13]Then Jesus said to the officer, "Go home. Your servant will be healed just as you believed he would." And at that same time his servant was healed.

Jesus Heals Many People

[14]Jesus went to Peter's house. There Jesus saw that Peter's mother-in-law was in bed with a high fever. [15]Jesus touched her hand, and the fever left her. Then she stood up and began to serve Jesus.

[16]That evening people brought to Jesus many who had demons.[d] Jesus spoke and the demons left them. Jesus healed all the sick. [17]He did these things to make what Isaiah the prophet[d] had said come true:

"He took our suffering on him.
    And he felt our pain for us."
                              Isaiah 53:4

People Want to Follow Jesus

[18]When Jesus saw the crowd around him, he told his followers to go to the other side of the lake. [19]Then a teacher of the law came to Jesus and said, "Teacher, I will follow you wherever you go."

[20]Jesus said to him, "The foxes have holes to live in. The birds have nests to live in. But the Son of Man[d] has no place where he can rest his head."

[21]Another man, one of Jesus' followers, said to Jesus, "Lord, let me go and bury my father first."

[22]But Jesus said to him, "Follow me, and let the people who are dead bury their own dead."

Jesus Stops a Storm

[23]Jesus got into a boat, and his followers went with him. [24]A very bad storm arose on the lake. The waves covered the boat. But Jesus was sleeping. [25]The followers went to Jesus and woke him. They said, "Lord, save us! We will drown!"

[26]Jesus answered, "Why are you afraid? You don't have enough faith." Then Jesus got up and gave a command to the wind and the sea. The wind stopped, and the sea became very calm.

[27]The men were amazed. They said, "What kind of man is this? Even the wind and the sea obey him!"

Jesus Heals Two Men with Demons

[28]Jesus arrived at the other side of the lake in the country of the Gadarene[n] people. There, two men came to Jesus. They had demons[d] in them. These men lived in the burial caves. They were so dangerous that people could not use the road by those caves. [29]The two men came to Jesus and shouted, "What do you want with us, Son of God? Did you come here to punish us before the right time?"

[30]Near that place there was a large herd of pigs feeding. [31]The demons begged Jesus, "If you make us leave these men, please send us into that herd of pigs."

[32]Jesus said to them, "Go!" So the demons left the men and went into the pigs. Then the whole herd of pigs ran down the hill into the lake and were drowned. [33]The men who were caring for the pigs ran away and went into town. They told about all of this and what had happened to the men who had demons. [34]Then the whole town went out to see Jesus. When they saw him, they begged him to leave their area.

Jesus Heals a Paralysed Man

9 Jesus got into a boat and went back across the lake to his own town. [2]Some people brought to Jesus a man who was paralysed. The man was lying on his mat. Jesus saw that these people had great faith, so he said to the paralysed man, "Be happy, young man. Your sins are forgiven."

Gadarene From Gadara, an area southeast of Lake Galilee.

³Some of the teachers of the law heard this. They said to themselves, "This man speaks as if he were God — that is blasphemy!"[n]

⁴Jesus knew what they were thinking. So he said, "Why are you thinking evil thoughts? ⁵Which is easier: to tell this paralysed man, 'Your sins are forgiven', or to tell him, 'Stand up and walk'? ⁶But I will prove to you that the Son of Man[d] has power on earth to forgive sins." Then Jesus said to the paralysed man, "Stand up. Take your mat and go home." ⁷And the man stood up and went home. ⁸The people saw this and were amazed. They praised God for giving power like this to men.

Jesus Chooses Matthew

⁹When Jesus was leaving, he saw a man named Matthew. Matthew was sitting in the tax office. Jesus said to him, "Follow me." And Matthew stood up and followed Jesus.

¹⁰Jesus had dinner at Matthew's house. Many tax collectors and "sinners" came and ate with Jesus and his followers. ¹¹The Pharisees[d] saw this and asked Jesus' followers, "Why does your teacher eat with tax collectors and 'sinners'?"

¹²Jesus heard the Pharisees ask this. So he said, "Healthy people don't need a doctor. Only the sick need a doctor. ¹³Go and learn what this means: 'I want faithful love more than I want animal sacrifices'.[n] I did not come to invite good people. I came to invite sinners".

Jesus Is Not like Other Jews

¹⁴Then the followers of John[n] came to Jesus. They said to Jesus, "We and

the Pharisees[d] often give up eating.[n] But your followers don't. Why?"

¹⁵Jesus answered, "The friends of the bridegroom are not sad while he is with them. But the time will come when the bridegroom will leave them. Then his friends are sad, and they will give up eating.

¹⁶"When someone sews a patch over a hole in an old coat, he never uses a piece of cloth that is not yet shrunk. If he does, the patch will shrink and pull away from the coat. Then the hole will be worse. ¹⁷Also, people never pour new wine into old leather bags for holding wine. If they do, the old bags will break. The wine will spill, and the wine bags will be ruined. But people always pour new wine into new wine bags. Then the wine and the wine bags will continue to be good."

Jesus Gives Life to a Dead Girl and Heals a Sick Woman

¹⁸While Jesus was saying these things, a ruler of the synagogue[d] came to him. The ruler bowed down before Jesus and said, "My daughter has just died. But come and touch her with your hand, and she will live again."

¹⁹So Jesus stood up and went with the ruler. Jesus' followers went too. ²⁰Then a woman who had been bleeding for 12 years came behind Jesus and touched the edge of his coat. ²¹She was thinking, "If I can touch his coat, then I will be healed."

²²Jesus turned and saw the woman. He said, "Be happy, dear woman. You are made well because you believed." And the woman was healed at once.

²³Jesus continued along with the ruler and went into the ruler's house. Jesus saw people there who play mu-

---

blasphemy Saying things against God.
'I want . . . sacrifices'. Quotation from Hosea 6:6.
John John the Baptist, who preached to people about Christ's coming (Matthew 3, Luke 3).
give up eating This is called "fasting". The people would give up eating for a special time of prayer and worship to God. It was also done to show sadness.

sic for funerals. And he saw many people there crying. [24]Jesus said, "Go away. The girl is not dead. She is only asleep." But the people laughed at Jesus. [25]After the crowd had been put outside, Jesus went into the girl's room. He took her hand, and she stood up. [26]The news about this spread all around the area.

Jesus Heals More People

[27]When Jesus was leaving there, two blind men followed him. They cried out, "Show kindness to us, Son of David!"[d]

[28]Jesus went inside, and the blind men went with him. He asked the men, "Do you believe that I can make you see again?"

They answered, "Yes, Lord."

[29]Then Jesus touched their eyes and said, "You believe that I can make you see again. So this will happen." [30]Then the men were able to see. But Jesus warned them very strongly, saying, "Don't tell anyone about this." [31]But the blind men left and spread the news about Jesus all around that area.

[32]When the two men were leaving, some people brought another man to Jesus. This man could not talk because he had a demon[d] in him. [33]Jesus forced the demon to leave the man. Then the man who couldn't talk was able to speak. The crowd was amazed and said, "We have never seen anything like this in Israel."

[34]But the Pharisees[d] said, "The leader of demons is the one that gives him power to force demons out."

[35]Jesus travelled through all the towns and villages. He taught in their synagogues[d] and told people the Good News[d] about the kingdom. And he healed all kinds of diseases and sicknesses. [36]He saw the crowds of people and felt sorry for them because they were worried and helpless. They were like sheep without a shepherd. [37]Jesus said to his followers, "There are many people to harvest, but there are only a few workers to help harvest them. [38]God owns the harvest. Pray to him that he will send more workers to help gather his harvest."[n]

Jesus Sends Out His Apostles

10 Jesus called his 12 followers together. He gave them power to drive out evil spirits and to heal every kind of disease and sickness. [2]These are the names of the 12 apostles:[d] Simon (also called Peter) and his brother Andrew; James son of Zebedee, and his brother John; [3]Philip and Bartholomew; Thomas and Matthew, the tax collector; James son of Alphaeus, and Thaddaeus; [4]Simon the Zealot[d] and Judas Iscariot. Judas is the one who turned against Jesus.

[5]These 12 men he sent out with the following order: "Don't go to the non-Jewish people. And don't go into any town where the Samaritans[d] live. [6]But go to the people of Israel. They are like sheep that are lost. [7]When you go, preach this: 'The kingdom of heaven is coming soon'. [8]Heal the sick. Give dead people life again. Heal those who have harmful skin diseases. Force demons[d] to leave people. I give you these powers freely. So help other people freely. [9]Don't carry any money with you—gold or silver or copper. [10]Don't carry a bag. Take for your trip only the clothes and sandals you are wearing. Don't take a walking stick. A worker should be given the things he needs.

[11]"When you enter a city or town, find some worthy person there and stay in his home until you leave. [12]When you enter that home, say, 'Peace be with you'. [13]If the people there welcome you, let your peace stay there. But if they don't welcome

---

"There are . . . harvest." As a farmer sends workers to harvest the grain, Jesus sends his followers to bring people to God.

you, take back the peace you wished for them. [14]And if a home or town refuses to welcome you or listen to you, then leave that place. Shake its dust off your feet.[n] [15]I tell you the truth. On the Judgement Day it will be worse for that town than for the towns of Sodom and Gomorrah.[n]

Jesus Warns His Apostles

[16]"Listen! I am sending you out, and you will be like sheep among wolves. So be as clever as snakes. But also be like doves and do nothing wrong. [17]Be careful of people. They will arrest you and take you to court. They will whip you in their synagogues.[d] [18]Because of me you will be taken to stand before governors and kings. You will tell them and the non-Jewish people about me. [19]When you are arrested, don't worry about what to say or how you should say it. At that time you will be given the things to say. [20]It will not really be you speaking. The Spirit of your Father will be speaking through you. [21]"Brothers will turn against their own brothers and give them over to be killed. Fathers will turn against their own children and give them to be killed. Children will fight against their own parents and have them killed. [22]All people will hate you because you follow me. But the person who continues strong until the end will be saved. [23]When you are treated badly in one city, go to another city. I tell you the truth. You will not finish going through all the cities of Israel before the Son of Man[d] comes.

[24]"A student is not better than his teacher. A servant is not better than his master. [25]A student should be satisfied to become like his teacher. A servant should be satisfied to become like his master. If the head of the family is called Beelzebul,[d] then the other members of the family will be called worse names!

Fear God, Not People

[26]"So don't be afraid of those people. Everything that is hidden will be shown. Everything that is secret will be made known. [27]I tell you these things in the dark, but I want you to tell them in the light. I speak these things only to you, but you should tell them to everyone. [28]Don't be afraid of people. They can only kill the body. They cannot kill the soul. The only one you should fear is the One who can destroy the body and the soul in hell. [29]When birds are sold, two small birds cost only a penny. But not even one of the little birds can die without your Father's knowing it. [30]God even knows how many hairs are on your head. [31]So don't be afraid. You are worth much more than many birds.

Tell People About Your Faith

[32]"If anyone stands before other people and says he believes in me, then I will say that he belongs to me. I will say this before my Father in heaven. [33]But if anyone stands before people and says he does not believe in me, then I will say that he does not belong to me. I will say this before my Father in heaven.

[34]"Don't think that I have come to bring peace to the earth. I did not come to bring peace, but a sword. [35]I have come to make this happen:

'A son will be against his father,
    a daughter will be against her
        mother,
a daughter-in-law will be against
        her mother-in-law.
[36] A person's enemies will be
        members of his own family'.
                                    Micah 7:6

[37]"Whoever loves his father or mother more than he loves me is not

---

Shake . . . feet. A warning. It showed that they had finished talking to these people.
Sodom and Gomorrah Two cities that God destroyed because the people were so evil.

worthy to be my follower. Whoever loves his son or daughter more than he loves me is not worthy to be my follower. 38Whoever is not willing to die on a cross and follow me is not worthy of me. 39Whoever tries to hold on to his life will give up true life. Whoever gives up his life for me will hold on to true life. 40Whoever accepts you also accepts me. And whoever accepts me also accepts the One who sent me. 41Whoever meets a prophet*d* and accepts him will receive the reward of a prophet. And whoever accepts a good man because that man is good will receive the reward of a good man. 42Whoever helps one of these little ones because they are my followers will truly get his reward. He will get his reward even if he only gave my follower a cup of cold water."

Jesus and John the Baptist

11 Jesus finished telling these things to his 12 followers. Then he left there and went to the towns in Galilee to teach and preach.

2John the Baptist*d* was in prison, but he heard about the things Christ was doing. So John sent some of his followers to Jesus. 3They asked Jesus, "Are you the man who John said was coming, or should we wait for another one?"

4Jesus answered, "Go back to John and tell him about the things you hear and see: 5The blind can see. The crippled can walk. People with harmful skin diseases are healed. The deaf can hear. The dead are raised to life. And the Good News*d* is told to the poor. 6The person who does not lose faith because of me is blessed."

7As John's followers were leaving, Jesus began talking to the people about John. Jesus said, "What did you go out to the desert to see? A reed*n* blown by the wind? No. 8Really, what did you go out to see? A man dressed in fine clothes? No. Those people who wear fine clothes live in kings' palaces. 9So what did you go out to see? A prophet?*d* Yes, and I tell you, John is more than a prophet. 10This was written about John in the Scriptures:*d*

'I will send my messenger ahead
    of you.
He will prepare the way for
    you'. *Malachi 3:1*

11I tell you the truth: John the Baptist is greater than any other man who has ever lived. But even the least important person in the kingdom of heaven is greater than John. 12Since the time John the Baptist came until now, the kingdom of heaven has been going forwards in strength. People using force have been trying to take the kingdom. 13All the prophets and the law of Moses spoke until the time John came. They told about the things that would happen. 14And if you will believe the things the law and the prophets said, then you will believe that John is Elijah. The law and the prophets said he would come. 15You people who hear me, listen!

16"What can I say about the people who live today? What are they like? They are like children sitting in the market place. One group calls to the other,

17'We played music for you, but you
        did not dance;
    we sang a sad song, but you did
        not cry'.

18John came, and he did not eat like other people or drink wine. And people say, 'He has a demon'.*d* 19The Son of Man*d* came, eating and drinking wine, and people say, 'Look at him! He eats too much and drinks too much. He is a friend of tax collectors and "sinners".' But wisdom is proved to be right by the things it does."

Jesus Warns Unbelievers

20Then Jesus criticised the cities

---

reed It means that John was not weak like grass blown by the wind.

where he did most of his miracles.[d] He criticised them because the people there did not change their lives and stop sinning. [21]Jesus said, "How terrible for you, Korazin! How terrible for you, Bethsaida! I did many miracles in you. If those same miracles had happened in Tyre and Sidon,[n] then the people there would have changed their lives a long time ago. They would have worn rough cloth and put ashes on themselves to show that they had changed. [22]But I tell you, on the Judgement Day it will be worse for you than for Tyre and Sidon. [23]And you, Capernaum,[n] will you be lifted up to heaven? No. You will be thrown down to the depths. I did many miracles in you. If those same miracles had happened in Sodom,[n] its people would have stopped sinning, and it would still be a city today. [24]But I tell you it will be worse for you on the Judgement Day than for Sodom."

Jesus Offers Rest to People

[25]Then Jesus said, "I thank you, Father, Lord of heaven and earth. I praise you because you have hidden these things from the people who are wise and clever. But you have shown them to those who are like little children. [26]Yes, Father, this is what you really wanted.

[27]"My Father has given me all things. No one knows the Son—only the Father knows the Son. And no one knows the Father—only the Son knows the Father. And the only people who will know about the Father are those whom the Son chooses to tell.

[28]"Come to me, all of you who are tired and have heavy loads. I will give you rest. [29]Accept my work and learn from me. I am gentle and humble in spirit. And you will find rest for your souls. [30]The work that I ask you to accept is easy. The load I give you to carry is not heavy."

Jesus Is Lord of the Sabbath

12 About that same time, Jesus was walking through some fields of grain on a Sabbath[d] day. His followers were with him, and they were hungry. So they began to pick the grain and eat it. [2]The Pharisees[d] saw this, and they said to Jesus, "Look! Your followers are doing something that is against the Jewish law to do on the Sabbath day."

[3]Jesus answered, "Have you not read what David did when he and the people with him were hungry? [4]David went into God's house. He and those with him ate the bread that was made holy for God. It was against the law for them to eat that bread. Only the priests were allowed to eat it. [5]And have you not read in the law of Moses that on every Sabbath day the priests in the Temple[d] break this law about the Sabbath day? But the priests are not wrong for doing that. [6]I tell you that there is something here that is greater than the Temple. [7]The Scripture[d] says, 'I want faithful love more than I want animal sacrifices'.[n] You don't really know what those words mean. If you understood them, you would not judge those who have done nothing wrong.

[8]"The Son of Man[d] is Lord of the Sabbath day."

Jesus Heals a Man's Crippled Hand

[9]Jesus left there and went into their synagogue.[d] [10]In the synagogue,

---

Tyre and Sidon Towns where wicked people lived.
Korazin, Bethsaida, Capernaum Towns by Lake Galilee where Jesus preached to the people.
Sodom City that God destroyed because the people were so evil.
'I . . . sacrifices'. Quotation from Hosea 6:6.

there was a man with a crippled hand. Some Jews there were looking for a reason to accuse Jesus of doing wrong. So they asked him, "Is it right to heal on the Sabbath*d* day?"*n*

[11]Jesus answered, "If any of you has a sheep, and it falls into a ditch on the Sabbath day, then you will take the sheep and help it out of the ditch. [12]Surely a man is more important than a sheep. So the law of Moses allows people to do good things on the Sabbath day."

[13]Then Jesus said to the man with the crippled hand, "Let me see your hand." The man put his hand out, and the hand became well again, the same as the other hand. [14]But the Pharisees*d* left and made plans to kill Jesus.

Jesus Is God's Chosen Servant

[15]Jesus knew what the Pharisees*d* were doing, so he left that place. Many people followed him, and he healed all who were sick. [16]But Jesus warned the people not to tell who he was. [17]He did these things to make what Isaiah the prophet*d* had said come true:

[18]"Here is my servant whom I have chosen.
I love him, and I am pleased with him.
I will put my Spirit*d* in him.
Then he will tell how I will judge all people fairly.
[19]He will not argue or shout.
No one will hear his voice in the streets.
[20]He will not break a crushed blade of grass.
He will not put out even a weak flame.
He will continue until he makes fair judgement win the victory.
[21] In him will the nations find hope."   *Isaiah 42:1-4*

Jesus' Power Is from God

[22]Then some people brought a man to Jesus. This man was blind and could not talk, because he had a demon.*d* Jesus healed the man, and the man could talk and see. [23]All the people were amazed. They said, "Perhaps this man is the Son of David!"*d*

[24]The Pharisees*d* heard the people saying this. The Pharisees said, "Jesus uses the power of Beelzebul*d* to force demons out of people. Beelzebul is the ruler of demons."

[25]Jesus knew what the Pharisees were thinking. So he said to them, "Every kingdom that is fighting against itself will be destroyed. And every city that is divided will fall. And every family that is divided cannot succeed. [26]So if Satan forces out his own demons, then Satan is divided, and his kingdom will not continue. [27]You say that I use the power of Satan when I force out demons. If that is true, then what power do your people use when they force out demons? So your own people prove that you are wrong. [28]But if I use the power of God's Spirit*d* to force out demons, this shows that the kingdom of God has come to you.

[29]"If anyone wants to enter a strong man's house and steal his things, first he must tie up the strong man. Then he can steal the things from the strong man's house.

[30]"If anyone is not with me, then he is against me. He who does not work with me is working against me. [31]So I tell you, people can be forgiven for every sin they do. And people can be forgiven for every bad thing they say. But if anyone speaks against the Holy Spirit, then he will not be forgiven. [32]Anyone who says things against the Son of Man*d* can be forgiven. But anyone who says things against the Holy Spirit will not be

forgiven. He will not be forgiven now or in the future.

People Know You by Your Words

33"If you want good fruit, you must make the tree good. If your tree is not good, then it will have bad fruit. A tree is known by the kind of fruit it produces. 34You snakes! You are evil people! How can you say anything good? The mouth speaks the things that are in the heart. 35A good person has good things in his heart. And so he speaks the good things that come from his heart. But an evil person has evil in his heart. So he speaks the evil things that come from his heart. 36And I tell you that people will have to explain about every careless thing they have said. This will happen on the Judgement Day. 37The words you have said will be used to judge you. Some of your words will prove you right, but some of your words will prove you guilty."

The Leaders Ask for a Miracle

38Then some of the Pharisees*d* and teachers of the law answered Jesus. They said, "Teacher, we want to see you work a miracle*d* as a sign."

39Jesus answered, "Evil and sinful people are the ones who want to see a miracle for a sign. But no sign will be given to them. The only sign will be what happened to the prophet*d* Jonah. 40Jonah was in the stomach of the big fish for three days and three nights. In the same way, the Son of Man*d* will be in the grave three days and three nights. 41And on the Judgement Day the men from Nineveh*n* will stand up with you people who live today. They will show that you are guilty because when Jonah preached to them, they were sorry and changed their lives. And I tell you that someone greater

than Jonah is here! 42On the Judgement Day, the Queen of the South*n* will stand up with you people who live today. She will show that you are guilty because she came from far away to listen to Solomon's wise teaching. And I tell you that someone greater than Solomon is here!

People Today Are Full of Evil

43"When an evil spirit comes out of a man, it travels through dry places looking for a place to rest. But it finds no place to rest. 44So the spirit says, 'I will go back to the home I left'. When the spirit comes back to the man, the spirit finds the home still empty. The home is swept clean and made neat. 45Then the evil spirit goes out and brings seven other spirits even more evil than it is. Then all the spirits go into the man and live there. And that man has even more trouble than he had before. It is the same way with the evil people who live today."

Jesus' True Family

46While Jesus was talking to the people, his mother and brothers stood outside. They wanted to talk to him. 47Someone told Jesus, "Your mother and brothers are waiting for you outside. They want to talk to you."

48He answered, "Who is my mother? Who are my brothers?" 49Then he pointed to his followers and said, "See! These people are my mother and my brothers. 50My true brothers and sisters and mother are those who do the things that my Father in heaven wants."

A Story About Planting Seed

13 That same day Jesus went out of the house and sat by the lake. 2Large crowds gathered around

---

Nineveh The city where Jonah preached to warn the people. Read Jonah 3.
Queen of the South The Queen of Sheba. She travelled 1,000 miles to learn God's wisdom from Solomon. Read 1 Kings 10:1-13.

him. So Jesus got into a boat and sat, while the people stayed on the shore. ³Then Jesus used stories to teach them many things. He said: "A farmer went out to plant his seed. ⁴While he was planting, some seed fell by the road. The birds came and ate all that seed. ⁵Some seed fell on rocky ground, where there wasn't enough soil. That seed grew very fast, because the ground was not deep. ⁶But when the sun rose, the plants dried up because they did not have deep roots. ⁷Some other seed fell among thorny weeds. The weeds grew and choked the good plants. ⁸Some other seed fell on good ground where it grew and became grain. Some plants made 100 times more grain. Other plants made 60 times more grain, and some made 30 times more grain. ⁹You people who hear me, listen!"

Why Jesus Used Stories to Teach

¹⁰The followers came to Jesus and asked, "Why do you use stories to teach the people?"

¹¹Jesus answered, "Only you can know the secret truths about the kingdom of heaven. Other people cannot know these secret truths. ¹²The person who has something will be given more. And he will have all he needs. But the person who does not have much, even what he has will be taken from him. ¹³This is why I use stories to teach the people: they see, but they don't really see. They hear, but they don't really understand. ¹⁴So they show that the things Isaiah said about them are true:

'You will listen and listen, but you will not understand.
You will look and look, but you will not learn.
¹⁵For these people have become stubborn.
They do not hear with their ears.

And they have closed their eyes.
Otherwise they might really understand
what they see with their eyes
and hear with their ears.
They might really understand in their minds.
If they did this, they would come back to me and be forgiven'. *Isaiah 6:9-10*

¹⁶But you are blessed. You understand the things you see with your eyes. And you understand the things you hear with your ears. ¹⁷I tell you the truth. Many prophets*d* and good people wanted to see the things that you now see, but they did not see them. And many prophets and good people wanted to hear the things that you now hear, but they did not hear them.

Jesus Explains the Seed Story

¹⁸"So listen to the meaning of that story about the farmer. ¹⁹What is the seed that fell by the road? That seed is like the person who hears the teaching about the kingdom but does not understand it. The Evil One comes and takes away the things that were planted in that person's heart. ²⁰And what is the seed that fell on rocky ground? That seed is like the person who hears the teaching and quickly accepts it with joy. ²¹But he does not let the teaching go deep into his life. He keeps it only a short time. When trouble or persecution comes because of the teaching he accepted, then he quickly gives up. ²²And what is the seed that fell among the thorny weeds? That seed is like the person who hears the teaching but lets worries about this life and love of money stop that teaching from growing. So the teaching does not produce fruit*n* in that person's life. ²³But what is the seed that fell on the good ground?

produce fruit To produce fruit means to have in your life the good things God wants.

That seed is like the person who hears the teaching and understands it. That person grows and produces fruit, sometimes 100 times more, sometimes 60 times more, and sometimes 30 times more."

A Story About Wheat and Weeds

24Then Jesus told them another story. He said, "The kingdom of heaven is like a man who planted good seed in his field. 25That night, when everyone was asleep, his enemy came and planted weeds among the wheat. Then the enemy went away. 26Later, the wheat grew and heads of grain grew on the wheat plants. But at the same time the weeds also grew. 27Then the man's servants came to him and said, 'You planted good seed in your field. Where did the weeds come from?' 28The man answered, 'An enemy planted weeds'. The servants asked, 'Do you want us to pull up the weeds?' 29The man answered, 'No, because when you pull up the weeds, you might also pull up the wheat. 30Let the weeds and the wheat grow together until the harvest time. At harvest time I will tell the workers this: first gather the weeds and tie them together to be burned. Then gather the wheat and bring it to my barn'."

Stories of Mustard Seed and Yeast

31Then Jesus told another story: "The kingdom of heaven is like a mustard seed. A man plants the seed in his field. 32That seed is the smallest of all seeds. But when it grows, it is one of the largest garden plants. It becomes a tree, big enough for the wild birds to come and make nests in its branches."

33Then Jesus told another story: "The kingdom of heaven is like yeast that a woman mixes into a big bowl of flour. The yeast makes all the dough rise."

34Jesus used stories to tell all these things to the people. He always used stories to teach people. 35This is as the prophet[d] said:

"I will speak using stories;
I will tell things that have been
secret since the world was
made."　　　*Psalm 78:2*

Jesus Explains About the Wheat and Weeds

36Then Jesus left the crowd and went into the house. His followers came to him and said, "Explain to us the meaning of the story about the weeds in the field."

37Jesus answered, "The man who planted the good seed in the field is the Son of Man.[d] 38The field is the world. And the good seed is all of God's children in the kingdom. The weeds are those people who belong to the Evil One. 39And the enemy who planted the bad seed is the devil. The harvest time is the end of the world. And the workers who gather are God's angels.

40"The weeds are pulled up and burned in the fire. It will be this way at the end of the world. 41The Son of Man will send out his angels. They will gather out of his kingdom all who cause sin and all who do evil. 42The angels will throw them into the blazing furnace. There the people will cry and grind their teeth with pain. 43Then the good people will shine like the sun in the kingdom of their Father. You people who hear me, listen!

Stories of a Treasure and a Pearl

44"The kingdom of heaven is like a treasure hidden in a field. One day a man found the treasure, and then he hid it in the field again. The man was very happy to find the treasure. He went and sold everything that he owned to buy that field.

45"Also, the kingdom of heaven is like a man looking for fine pearls. 46One day he found a very valuable pearl. The man went and sold everything he had to buy that pearl.

A Story of a Fishing Net

47"Also, the kingdom of heaven is like a net that was put into the lake. The net caught many different kinds of fish. 48When it was full, the fishermen pulled the net to the shore. They sat down and put all the good fish in baskets. Then they threw away the bad fish. 49It will be this way at the end of the world. The angels will come and separate the evil people from the good people. 50The angels will throw the evil people into the blazing furnace. In that place the people will cry and grind their teeth with pain."

51Jesus asked his followers, "Do you understand all these things?"

They answered, "Yes, we understand."

52Then Jesus said to them, "So every teacher of the law who has been taught about the kingdom of heaven is like the owner of a house. He has both new things and old things saved in his house. And he brings out both those new things and old things."

Jesus Goes to His Home Town

53When Jesus finished teaching with these stories, he left there. 54He went to the town where he grew up. He taught the people in the synagogue,*d* and they were amazed. They said, "Where did this man get this wisdom and this power to do miracles?*d* 55He is only the son of the carpenter. And his mother is Mary. His brothers are James, Joseph, Simon and Judas. 56And all his sisters are here with us. So where does this man get all these things?" 57And the people refused to accept Jesus.

But Jesus said to them, "A prophet*d* is honoured everywhere except in his own town or in his own home."

58The people there did not believe in Jesus. So Jesus did not do many miracles there.

How John the Baptist Was Killed

14 At that time Herod, the ruler of Galilee, heard the reports about Jesus. 2So Herod said to his servants, "Jesus is really John the Baptist.*d* He has risen from death. That is why he is able to do these miracles."*d*

3Sometime before this, Herod had arrested John, tied him up, and put him into prison. Herod did this because of Herodias. Herodias was the wife of Philip, Herod's brother. 4Herod arrested John because he told Herod: "It is not right for you to have Herodias." 5Herod wanted to kill John, but he was afraid of the people. They believed that John was a prophet.*d*

6On Herod's birthday, the daughter of Herodias danced for Herod and his guests. Herod was very pleased with her, 7so he promised he would give her anything she wanted. 8Herodias told her daughter what to ask for. So she said to Herod, "Give me the head of John the Baptist here on a platter." 9King Herod was very sad. But he had promised to give her anything she wanted, and the people eating with him had heard his promise. So Herod ordered that what she asked for be done. 10He sent men to the prison to cut off John's head. 11And the men brought John's head on a platter and gave it to the girl. She took it to her mother, Herodias. 12John's followers came and got his body and buried it. Then they went and told Jesus what happened.

More than 5,000 People Fed

13When Jesus heard what happened to John, Jesus left in a boat. He went to a lonely place by himself. But when the crowds heard about it, they followed him on foot from the towns. 14When Jesus arrived, he saw a large crowd. He felt sorry for them and healed those who were sick.

15Late that afternoon, his followers

came to Jesus and said, "No one lives in this place. And it is already late. Send the people away so they can go to the towns and buy food for themselves."

¹⁶Jesus answered, "They don't need to go away. You give them some food to eat."

¹⁷The followers answered, "But we have only five loaves of bread and two fish."

¹⁸Jesus said, "Bring the bread and the fish to me." ¹⁹Then he told the people to sit down on the grass. He took the five loaves of bread and the two fish. Then he looked to heaven and thanked God for the food. Jesus divided the loaves of bread. He gave them to his followers, and they gave the bread to the people. ²⁰All the people ate and were satisfied. After they finished eating, the followers filled 12 baskets with the pieces of food that were not eaten. ²¹There were about 5,000 men there who ate, as well as women and children.

Jesus Walks on the Water

²²Then Jesus made his followers get into the boat. He told them to go ahead of him to the other side of the lake. Jesus stayed there to tell the people they could go home. ²³After he said good bye to them, he went alone up into the hills to pray. It was late, and Jesus was there alone. ²⁴By this time, the boat was already far away on the lake. The boat was having trouble because of the waves, and the wind was blowing against it.

²⁵Between three and six o'clock in the morning, Jesus' followers were still in the boat. Jesus came to them. He was walking on the water. ²⁶When the followers saw him walking on the water, they were afraid. They said, "It's a ghost!" and cried out in fear.

²⁷But Jesus quickly spoke to them. He said, "Have courage! It is I! Don't be afraid."

²⁸Peter said, "Lord, if that is really you, then tell me to come to you on the water."

²⁹Jesus said, "Come."

And Peter left the boat and walked on the water to Jesus. ³⁰But when Peter saw the wind and the waves, he became afraid and began to sink. He shouted, "Lord, save me!"

³¹Then Jesus reached out his hand and caught Peter. Jesus said, "Your faith is small. Why did you doubt?"

³²After Peter and Jesus were in the boat, the wind became calm. ³³Then those who were in the boat worshipped Jesus and said, "Truly you are the Son of God!"

³⁴After they crossed the lake, they came to the shore at Gennesaret. ³⁵The people there saw Jesus and knew who he was. So they told people all around there that Jesus had come. They brought all their sick to him. ³⁶They begged Jesus to let them just touch the edge of his coat to be healed. And all the sick people who touched it were healed.

Obey God's Law Not Men's

15 Then some Pharisees[d] and teachers of the law came to Jesus from Jerusalem. They asked him, ²"Why do your followers not obey the rules given to us by the great people who lived before us? Your followers don't wash their hands before they eat!"

³Jesus answered, "And why do you refuse to obey God's command so that you can follow those rules you have? ⁴God said, 'Honour your father and mother'.[n] And God also said, 'Anyone who says cruel things to his father or mother must be put to death'.[n]

'Honour ... mother'. Quotation from Exodus 20:12; Deuteronomy 5:16.
'Anyone ... death'. Quotation from Exodus 21:17.

[5]But you say that a person can tell his father or mother, 'I have something I could use to help you. But I will not use it for you. I will give it to God'. [6]You teach that person not to honour his father. You teach that it is not important to do what God said. You think that it is more important to follow the rules you have. [7]You are hypocrites![d] Isaiah was right when he spoke about you:

[8]"These people show honour to me
    with words,
  but their hearts are far from me.
[9]Their worship of me is worthless.
  The things they teach are
    nothing
  but human rules they have
    memorised'."   *Isaiah 29:13*

[10]Jesus called the crowd to him. He said, "Listen and understand what I am saying. [11]It is not what a person puts into his mouth that makes him unclean.[d] It is what comes out of his mouth that makes him unclean."

[12]Then his followers came to Jesus and asked, "Do you know that the Pharisees are angry because of what you said?"

[13]Jesus answered, "Every plant that my Father in heaven has not planted himself will be pulled up by the roots. [14]Stay away from the Pharisees. They are blind leaders. And if a blind man leads another blind man, then both men will fall into a ditch."

[15]Peter said, "Explain the story to us."

[16]Jesus said, "You still have trouble understanding? [17]Surely you know that all the food that enters the mouth goes into the stomach. Then that food goes out of the body. [18]But what a person says with his mouth comes from the way he thinks. And these are the things that make him unclean. [19]Out of his mind come evil thoughts, murder, adultery,[d] sexual sins, stealing, lying, and saying bad things against other people. [20]These things make a person unclean. But eating with unwashed hands does not make him unclean."

Jesus Helps a Non-Jewish Woman

[21]Jesus left that place and went to the area of Tyre and Sidon. [22]A Canaanite woman from that area came to Jesus. The woman cried out, "Lord, Son of David,[d] please help me! My daughter has a demon,[d] and she is suffering very much."

[23]But Jesus did not answer the woman. So the followers came to Jesus and begged him, "Tell the woman to go away. She is following us and shouting."

[24]Jesus answered, "God sent me only to the lost sheep, the people of Israel."

[25]Then the woman came to Jesus again. She bowed before him and said, "Lord, help me!"

[26]Jesus answered, "It is not right to take the children's bread and give it to the dogs."

[27]The woman said, "Yes, Lord, but even the dogs eat the pieces of food that fall from their masters' table."

[28]Then Jesus answered, "Woman, you have great faith! I will do what you asked me to do." And at that moment the woman's daughter was healed.

Jesus Heals Many People

[29]Then Jesus left that place and went to the shore of Lake Galilee. He went up on a hill and sat there.

[30]Great crowds came to Jesus. They brought their sick with them: the lame, the blind, the crippled, the dumb and many others. They put them at Jesus' feet, and he healed them. [31]The crowd were amazed when they saw that people who could not speak were able to speak again. The crippled were made strong again. Those who could not walk were able to walk again. The blind were able to see again. And they praised the God of Israel for this.

More than 4,000 People Fed

[32]Jesus called his followers to him and said, "I feel sorry for these people. They have been with me for three days, and now they have nothing to eat. I don't want to send them away hungry. They might faint while going home."

[33]His followers asked him, "Where can we get enough bread to feed all these people? We are far away from any town."

[34]Jesus asked, "How many loaves of bread do you have?"

They answered, "We have seven loaves and a few small fish."

[35]Jesus told the people to sit on the ground. [36]He took the seven loaves of bread and the fish and gave thanks to God for the food. Then Jesus divided the food and gave it to his followers. They gave the food to the people. [37]All the people ate and were satisfied. After this, the followers filled seven baskets with the pieces of food that were not eaten. [38]There were about 4,000 men there who ate, besides women and children. [39]After they had eaten, Jesus told the people to go home. He got into the boat and went to the area of Magadan.

The Leaders Ask for a Miracle

16 The Pharisees[d] and Sadducees[d] came to Jesus. They wanted to trap him. So they asked him to show them a miracle[d] to prove that he was from God.

[2]Jesus answered, "When you see the sunset, you know what the weather will be. If the sky is red, then you say we will have good weather. [3]And in the morning if the sky is dark and red, then you say that it will be a rainy day. You see these signs in the sky, and you know what they mean. In the same way, you see the things that are happening now. But you don't know

their meaning. [4]Evil and sinful people ask for a miracle as a sign. But they will have no sign—only the sign of Jonah."[n] Then Jesus left them and went away.

Guard Against Wrong Teachings

[5]Jesus and his followers went across the lake. But the followers forgot to bring bread. [6]Jesus said to them, "Be careful! Guard against the yeast of the Pharisees[d] and the Sadducees."[d]

[7]The followers discussed the meaning of this. They said, "Did Jesus say this because we forgot to bring bread?"

[8]Jesus knew that they were talking about this. So he asked them, "Why are you talking about not having bread? Your faith is small. [9]You still don't understand? Remember the five loaves of bread that fed the 5,000 people? And remember that you filled many baskets with bread after the people finished eating? [10]And remember the seven loaves of bread that fed the 4,000 people? Remember that you filled many baskets then also? [11]So I was not talking to you about bread. Why don't you understand that? I am telling you to be careful and guard against the yeast of the Pharisees and the Sadducees." [12]Then the followers understood what Jesus meant. He was not telling them to guard against the yeast used in bread. He was telling them to guard against the teaching of the Pharisees and the Sadducees.

Peter Says Jesus Is the Christ

[13]Jesus went to the area of Caesarea Philippi. He said to his followers, "I am the Son of Man.[d] Who do the people say I am?"

[14]They answered, "Some people say you are John the Baptist.[d] Others say you are Elijah. And others say that

---

sign of Jonah Jonah's three days in the big fish are like Jesus' three days in the tomb. The story about Jonah is in the book of Jonah.

you are Jeremiah or one of the prophets."[d]

15Then Jesus asked them, "And who do you say I am?"

16Simon Peter answered, "You are the Christ,[d] the Son of the living God."

17Jesus answered, "You are blessed, Simon son of Jonah. No person taught you that. My Father in heaven showed you who I am. 18So I tell you, you are Peter.[n] And I will build my church on this rock. The power of death will not be able to defeat my church. 19I will give you the keys of the kingdom of heaven. The things you don't allow on earth will be the things that God does not allow. The things you allow on earth will be the things that God allows." 20Then Jesus warned his followers not to tell anyone that he was the Christ.

Jesus Says that He Must Die

21From that time on Jesus began telling his followers that he must go to Jerusalem. He explained that the older Jewish leaders, the leading priests, and the teachers of the law would make him suffer many things. And he told them that he must be killed. Then, on the third day, he would be raised from death.

22Peter took Jesus aside and began to criticise him. Peter said, "God save you from those things, Lord! Those things will never happen to you!"

23Then Jesus said to Peter, "Go away from me, Satan![n] You are not helping me! You don't care about the things of God. You care only about things that men think are important."

24Then Jesus said to his followers, "If anyone wants to follow me, he must say 'no' to the things he wants. He must be willing even to die on a cross, and he must follow me. 25Whoever wants to save his life will give up true life. And whoever gives up his life for me will have true life. 26It is worth nothing for a man to have the whole world if he loses his soul. He could never pay enough to buy back his soul. 27The Son of Man[d] will come again with his Father's glory and with his angels. At that time, he will reward everyone for what he has done. 28I tell you the truth. There are some people standing here who, before they die, will see the Son of Man coming with his kingdom."

Jesus with Moses and Elijah

17 Six days later, Jesus took Peter, James, and John the brother of James up on a high mountain. They were all alone there. 2While they watched, Jesus was changed. His face became bright like the sun. And his clothes became white as light. 3Then two men were there, talking with him. The men were Moses and Elijah.[n]

4Peter said to Jesus, "Lord, it is good that we are here. If you want, I will put three tents here—one for you, one for Moses, and one for Elijah."

5While Peter was talking, a bright cloud covered them. A voice came from the cloud. The voice said, "This is my Son and I love him. I am very pleased with him. Obey him!"

6The followers with Jesus heard the voice. They were so frightened that they fell to the ground. 7But Jesus went to them and touched them. He said, "Stand up. Don't be afraid." 8When the followers looked up, they saw Jesus was now alone.

9When Jesus and the followers were coming down the mountain, Jesus

---

Peter The Greek name "Peter", like the Aramaic name "Cephas", means "rock".
Satan Name for the devil, meaning "the enemy". Jesus means that Peter was talking like Satan.
Moses and Elijah Two of the most important Jewish leaders in the past.

commanded them, "Don't tell anyone about the things you saw on the mountain. Wait until the Son of Man[d] has been raised from death. Then you may tell."

[10]The followers asked Jesus, "Why do the teachers of the law say that Elijah must come first, before the Christ[d] comes?"

[11]Jesus answered, "They are right to say that Elijah is coming. And it is true that Elijah will make everything the way it should be. [12]But I tell you, Elijah has already come. People did not know who he was. They did to him everything they wanted to do. It will be the same with the Son of Man. Those same people will make the Son of Man suffer." [13]Then the followers understood that Jesus was talking about John the Baptist.[d]

Jesus Heals a Sick Boy

[14]Jesus and his followers went back to the crowd. A man came to Jesus and bowed before him. [15]The man said, "Lord, please help my son. He has epilepsy[n] and is suffering very much. He often falls into the fire or into the water. [16]I brought him to your followers, but they could not cure him."

[17]Jesus answered, "You people have no faith. Your lives are all wrong. How long must I stay with you? How long must I continue to be patient with you? Bring the boy here." [18]Jesus gave a strong command to the demon[d] inside the boy. Then the demon came out, and the boy was healed.

[19]The followers came to Jesus when he was alone. They said, "Why couldn't we force the demon out?"

[20]Jesus answered, "You were not able to drive out the demon because your faith is too small. I tell you the truth. If your faith is as big as a mustard seed,[n] you can say to this mountain, 'Move from here to there'. And the mountain will move. All things will be possible for you." [21] [n]

Jesus Talks About His Death

[22]Later, the followers met together in Galilee. Jesus said to them, "The Son of Man[d] will be given into the control of some men. [23]They will kill him, but on the third day he will be raised from death." And the followers were filled with sadness.

Jesus Talks About Paying Taxes

[24]Jesus and his followers went to Capernaum. There some men came to Peter. They were the men who collected the Temple[d] tax. They asked, "Does your teacher pay the Temple tax?"

[25]Peter answered, "Yes, Jesus pays the tax."

Peter went into the house where Jesus was. Before Peter could speak, Jesus said to him, "The kings on the earth collect different kinds of taxes. But who are the people who pay the taxes? Are they the king's children? Or do others pay the taxes? What do you think?"

[26]Peter answered, "Other people pay the taxes."

Jesus said to Peter, "Then the children of the king don't have to pay taxes. [27]But we don't want to make these tax collectors angry. So go to the lake and fish. After you catch the first fish, open its mouth. Inside its mouth you will find a coin. Take that coin and give it to the tax collectors. That will pay the tax for you and me."

---

epilepsy A disease that causes a person sometimes to lose control of his body, and maybe faint, shake strongly, or not be able to move.
mustard seed This seed is very small, but the plant grows taller than a man.
Verse 21 Some Greek copies add verse 21: "That kind of spirit comes out only if you use prayer and give up eating."

Who Is the Greatest?

18 At that time the followers came to Jesus and asked, "Who is greatest in the kingdom of heaven?"

²Jesus called a little child to him. He stood the child before the followers. ³Then he said, "I tell you the truth. You must change and become like little children. If you don't do this, you will never enter the kingdom of heaven. ⁴The greatest person in the kingdom of heaven is the one who makes himself humble like this child.

⁵"Whoever accepts a little child in my name accepts me. ⁶If one of these little children believes in me, and someone causes that child to sin, then it will be very bad for that person. It would be better for him to have a large stone tied around his neck and be drowned in the sea. ⁷How terrible for the people of the world because of the things that cause them to sin. Such things will happen. But how terrible for the one who causes them to happen. ⁸If your hand or your foot causes you to sin, cut it off and throw it away. It is better for you to have only part of your body but have life for ever. That is much better than to have two hands and two feet but be thrown into the fire that burns for ever. ⁹If your eye causes you to sin, take it out and throw it away. It is better for you to have only one eye but have life for ever. That is much better than to have two eyes but be thrown into the fire of hell.

A Lost Sheep

¹⁰"Be careful. Don't think these little children are worth nothing. I tell you that they have angels in heaven who are always with my Father in heaven. ¹¹ *n*

¹²"If a man has 100 sheep, but one of the sheep gets lost, he will leave the other 99 sheep on the hill. He will go to look for the lost sheep. ¹³And if he finds it, he is happier about that one sheep than about the 99 that were never lost. I tell you the truth. ¹⁴In the same way, your Father in heaven does not want any of these little children to be lost.

When a Person Sins Against You

¹⁵"If your brother sins against you, go and tell him what he did wrong. Do this in private. If he listens to you, then you have helped him to be your brother again. ¹⁶But if he refuses to listen, then go to him again and take one or two other people with you. 'Every case may be proved by two or three witnesses'. *n* ¹⁷If he refuses to listen to them, then tell it to the church. If he refuses to listen to the church, then treat him as you would one who does not believe in God. Treat him as if he were a tax collector.

¹⁸"I tell you the truth. The things you don't allow on earth will be the things God does not allow. The things you allow on earth will be the things that God allows.

¹⁹"Also, I tell you that if two of you on earth agree about something, then you can pray for it. And the thing you ask for will be done for you by my Father in heaven. ²⁰This is true because if two or three people come together in my name, I am there with them."

An Unforgiving Servant

²¹Then Peter came to Jesus and asked, "Lord, when my brother sins against me, how many times must I forgive him? Should I forgive him as many as seven times?"

²²Jesus answered, "I tell you, you must forgive him more than seven times. You must forgive him even if he does wrong to you 77 times.

²³"The kingdom of heaven is like a king who decided to collect the money

---

Verse 11 Some Greek copies add verse 11: "The Son of Man came to save lost people."
'Every . . . witnesses'. Quotation from Deuteronomy 19:15.

his servants owed him. ²⁴So the king began to collect his money. One servant owed him several million pounds. ²⁵But the servant did not have enough money to pay his master, the king. So the master ordered that everything the servant owned should be sold, even the servant's wife and children. The money would be used to pay the king what the servant owed.

²⁶"But the servant fell on his knees and begged, 'Be patient with me. I will pay you everything I owe'. ²⁷The master felt sorry for his servant. So the master told the servant he did not have to pay. He let the servant go free.

²⁸"Later, that same servant found another servant who owed him a few pounds. The servant grabbed the other servant around the neck and said, 'Pay me the money you owe me!'

²⁹"The other servant fell on his knees and begged him, 'Be patient with me. I will pay you everything I owe'.

³⁰"But the first servant refused to be patient. He threw the other servant into prison until he could pay everything he owed. ³¹All the other servants saw what happened. They were very sorry. So they went and told their master all that had happened.

³²"Then the master called his servant in and said, 'You evil servant! You begged me to forget what you owed. So I told you that you did not have to pay anything. ³³I had mercy on you. You should have had the same mercy on that other servant'. ³⁴The master was very angry, and he put the servant in prison to be punished. The servant had to stay in prison until he could pay everything he owed.

³⁵"This king did what my heavenly Father will do to you if you do not forgive your brother from your heart."

Jesus Teaches About Divorce

19 After Jesus said all these things, he left Galilee. He went into the area of Judea on the other side of the Jordan River. ²Large crowds followed Jesus, and he healed them there.

³Some Pharisees[d] came to Jesus and tried to trick him. They asked, "Is it right for a man to divorce his wife for any reason he chooses?"

⁴Jesus answered, "Surely you have read in the Scriptures[d] that when God made the world, 'he made them male and female'.[n] ⁵And God said, 'So a man will leave his father and mother and be united with his wife. And the two people will become one body'.[n] ⁶So the two are not two, but one. God joined the two people together. No person should separate them."

⁷The Pharisees asked, "Why then did Moses give a command for a man to divorce his wife by giving her divorce papers?"

⁸Jesus answered, "Moses allowed you to divorce your wives because you refused to accept God's teaching. But divorce was not allowed in the beginning. ⁹I tell you that anyone who divorces his wife and marries another woman is guilty of adultery.[d] The only reason for a man to divorce and marry again is if his first wife has sexual relations with another man."

¹⁰The followers said to him, "If that is the only reason a man can divorce his wife, then it is better not to marry."

¹¹Jesus answered, "Not everyone can accept this truth about marriage. But God has made some able to accept it. ¹²There are different reasons why some men cannot marry. Some men were born without the ability to become fathers. Others were made that way later in life by other people.

'he made ... female'. Quotation from Genesis 1:27 or 5:2.
'So ... body'. Quotation from Genesis 2:24.

And other men have given up marriage because of the kingdom of heaven. But the person who can marry should accept this teaching about marriage." [n]

Jesus Welcomes Children

[13]Then the people brought their little children to Jesus so that he could put his hands on them [n] and pray for them. When his followers saw this, they told the people to stop bringing their children to Jesus. [14]But Jesus said, "Let the little children come to me. Don't stop them, because the kingdom of heaven belongs to people who are like these children." [15]After Jesus put his hands on the children, he left there.

A Rich Young Man's Question

[16]A man came to Jesus and asked, "Teacher, what good thing must I do to have life for ever?"

[17]Jesus answered, "Why do you ask me about what is good? Only God is good. But if you want to have life for ever, obey the commands."

[18]The man asked, "Which commands?"

Jesus answered, " 'You must not murder anyone. You must not be guilty of adultery. [d] You must not steal. You must not tell lies about your neighbour in court. [19]Honour your father and mother.' [n] Love your neighbour as you love yourself'. " [n]

[20]The young man said, "I have obeyed all these things. What else do I need to do?"

[21]Jesus answered, "If you want to be perfect, then go and sell all the things you own. Give the money to the poor. If you do this, you will have

a treasure in heaven. Then come and follow me!"

[22]But when the young man heard this, he became very sad because he was very rich. So he left Jesus.

[23]Then Jesus said to his followers, "I tell you the truth. It will be very hard for a rich person to enter the kingdom of heaven. [24]Yes, I tell you that it is easier for a camel to go through the eye of a needle than for a rich person to enter the kingdom of God."

[25]When the followers heard this, they were very surprised. They asked, "Then who can be saved?"

[26]Jesus looked at them and said, "This is something that men cannot do. But God can do all things."

[27]Peter said to Jesus, "We left everything we had and followed you. So what will we have?"

[28]Jesus said to them, "I tell you the truth. When the new age comes, the Son of Man [d] will sit on his great throne. And all of you who followed me will also sit on 12 thrones. And you will judge the 12 tribes [d] of Israel. [29]And everyone who has left houses, brothers, sisters, father, mother, children, or farms to follow me will get much more than he left. And he will have life for ever. [30]Many who have the highest place in life now will have the lowest place in the future. And many who have the lowest place now will have the highest place in the future.

A Story About Vineyard Workers

20 "The kingdom of heaven is like a man who owned some land. One morning, he went out very early to hire some people to work in his vineyard. [2]The man agreed to pay the

---

But . . . marriage. This may also mean, "The person who can accept this teaching about not marrying should accept it."
put his hands on them Showing that Jesus gave special blessings to these children.
'You . . . mother.' Quotation from Exodus 20:12-16; Deuteronomy 5:16-20.
'Love . . . yourself'. Quotation from Leviticus 19:18.

workers one silver coin" for working that day. Then he sent them into the vineyard to work. ³About nine o'clock the man went to the marketplace and saw some other people standing there, doing nothing. ⁴So he said to them, 'If you go and work in my vineyard, I will pay you what your work is worth'. ⁵So they went to work in the vineyard. The man went out again about twelve o'clock and again at three o'clock. Both times he hired people to work in his vineyard. ⁶About five o'clock the man went to the marketplace again. He saw others standing there. He asked them, 'Why did you stand here all day doing nothing?' ⁷They answered, 'No one gave us a job'. The man said to them, 'Then you can go and work in my vineyard'.

⁸"At the end of the day, the owner of the vineyard said to the foreman, 'Call the workers and pay them. Start by paying the last people I hired. Then pay all of them, ending with the workers I hired first'.

⁹"The workers who were hired at five o'clock came to get their pay. Each worker received one silver coin. ¹⁰Then the workers who were hired first came to get their pay. They thought they would be paid more than the others. But each one of them also received one silver coin. ¹¹When they got their silver coin, they complained to the man who owned the land. ¹²They said, 'Those people were hired last and worked only one hour. But you paid them the same as you paid us. And we worked hard all day in the hot sun'. ¹³But the man who owned the vineyard said to one of those workers, 'Friend, I am being fair to you. You agreed to work for one silver coin. ¹⁴So take your pay and go. I want to give the man who was hired last the same pay that I gave

you. ¹⁵I can do what I want with my own money. Are you jealous because I am good to those people?'

¹⁶"So those who have the last place now will have the first place in the future. And those who have the first place now will have the last place in the future."

Jesus Talks About His Own Death

¹⁷Jesus was going to Jerusalem. His 12 followers were with him. While they were on the way, Jesus gathered the followers together and spoke to them privately. He said to them, ¹⁸"We are going to Jerusalem. The Son of Manᵈ will be turned over to the leading priests and the teachers of the law. They will say that he must die. ¹⁹They will give the Son of Man to the non-Jewish people. They will laugh at him and beat him with whips, and then they will kill him on a cross. But on the third day after his death, he will be raised to life again."

A Mother Asks Jesus a Favour

²⁰Then the wife of Zebedee came to Jesus. Her sons were with her. The mother bowed before Jesus and asked him to do something for her.

²¹Jesus asked, "What do you want?"

She said, "Promise that one of my sons will sit at your right side in your kingdom. And promise that the other son will sit at your left side."

²²But Jesus said, "You don't understand what you are asking. Can you accept the kind of suffering that I must suffer?"ⁿ

The sons answered, "Yes, we can!"

²³Jesus said to them, "Truly you will suffer the same things that I will suffer. But I cannot choose who will sit at

---

silver coin A Roman denarius. One coin was the average pay for one day's work.
accept ... suffer Literally, "drink the cup that I must drink". Jesus used the idea of drinking from a cup to mean accepting the terrible things that would happen to him.

my right side or my left side. Those places belong to those for whom my Father has prepared them."

24The other ten followers heard this and were angry with the two brothers.

25Jesus called all the followers together. He said, "You know that the rulers of the non-Jewish people love to show their power over the people. And their important leaders love to use all their authority. 26But it should not be that way among you. If one of you wants to become great, then he must serve the rest of you like a servant. 27If one of you wants to become first, then he must serve the rest of you like a slave. 28So it is with the Son of Man.d The Son of Man did not come for other people to serve him. He came to serve others. The Son of Man came to give his life to save many people."

Jesus Heals Two Blind Men

29When Jesus and his followers were leaving Jericho, a great many people followed Jesus. 30There were two blind men sitting by the road. The blind men heard that Jesus was going by, so they shouted, "Lord, Son of David,d please help us!"

31All the people criticised the blind men. They told them to be quiet. But the blind men shouted more and more, "Lord, Son of David, please help us!"

32Jesus stopped and said to the blind men, "What do you want me to do for you?"

33They answered, "Lord, we want to be able to see."

34Jesus felt sorry for the blind men. He touched their eyes, and at once they were able to see. Then the men followed Jesus.

Jesus Enters Jerusalem as a King

21 Jesus and his followers were coming closer to Jerusalem. But first they stopped at Bethphage at the hill called the Mount of Olives.d From there Jesus sent two of his followers into the town. 2He said to them, "Go to the town you can see there. When you enter it, you will find a donkey tied there with its colt. Untie them and bring them to me. 3If anyone asks you why you are taking the donkeys, tell him, 'The Master needs them. He will send them back soon'."

4This was to make clear the full meaning of what the prophetd said:
5"Tell the people of Jerusalem,
'Your king is coming to you.
He is gentle and riding on a
    donkey.
He is on the colt of a donkey'."
Isaiah 62:11; Zechariah 9:9

6The followers went and did what Jesus told them to do. 7They brought the donkey and the colt to Jesus. They laid their coats on the donkeys, and Jesus sat on them. 8Many people spread their coats on the road before Jesus. Others cut branches from the trees and spread them on the road. 9Some of the people were walking ahead of Jesus. Others were walking behind him. All the people were shouting,
"Praisen to the Son of David!d
God bless the One who comes in
    the name of the Lord!
Psalm 118:26
Praise to God in heaven!"

10Then Jesus went into Jerusalem. The city was filled with excitement. The people asked, "Who is this man?"

11The crowd answered, "This man is Jesus. He is the prophet from the town of Nazareth in Galilee."

Praise Literally, "Hosanna", a Hebrew word used at first in praying to God for help. At this time it was probably a shout of joy used in praising God or his Messiah.

Jesus Goes to the Temple

[12]Jesus went into the Temple.[d] He threw out all the people who were buying and selling there. He turned over the tables that belonged to the men who were exchanging different kinds of money. And he upset the benches of those who were selling doves. [13]Jesus said to all the people there, "It is written in the Scriptures,[d] 'My Temple will be a house where people will pray'.[n] But you are changing God's house into a 'hideout for robbers'."[n]

[14]The blind and crippled people came to Jesus in the Temple, and Jesus healed them. [15]The leading priests and the teachers of the law saw that Jesus was doing wonderful things. They saw the children praising him in the Temple. The children were saying, "Praise[n] to the Son of David."[d] All these things made the priests and the teachers of the law very angry.

[16]They asked Jesus, "Do you hear the things these children are saying?"

Jesus answered, "Yes. Haven't you read in the Scriptures, 'You have taught children and babies to sing praises'?"[n]

[17]Then Jesus left and went out of the city to Bethany, where he spent the night.

The Power of Faith

[18]Early the next morning, Jesus was going back to the city. He was very hungry. [19]He saw a fig tree beside the road. Jesus went to it, but there were no figs on the tree. There were only leaves. So Jesus said to the tree, "You will never again have fruit!" The tree immediately dried up.

[20]His followers saw this and were amazed. They asked, "How did the fig tree dry up so quickly?"

[21]Jesus answered, "I tell you the truth. If you have faith and do not doubt, you will be able to do what I did to this tree. And you will be able to do more. You will be able to say to this mountain, 'Go, mountain, fall into the sea'. And if you have faith, it will happen. [22]If you believe, you will get anything you ask for in prayer."

Leaders Doubt Jesus' Authority

[23]Jesus went to the Temple.[d] While he was teaching there, the leading priests and the older leaders of the people came to Jesus. They said to him, "Tell us! What authority do you have to do these things? Who gave you this authority?"

[24]Jesus answered, "I will ask you a question, too. If you answer me, then I will tell you what authority I have to do these things. [25]Tell me: when John baptised people, did that come from God or from man?"

The priests and the leaders argued about Jesus' question. They said to each other, "If we answer, 'John's baptism was from God', then Jesus will say, 'Then why didn't you believe John?' [26]But if we say, 'It was from man', we are afraid of what the people will do because they all believe that John was a prophet."[d]

[27]So they answered Jesus, "We don't know."

Then Jesus said, "Then I won't tell you what authority I have to do these things!

A Story About Two Sons

[28]"Tell me what you think about this: there was a man who had two sons. He went to the first son and

---

'My Temple . . . pray'. Quotation from Isaiah 56:7.

'hideout for robbers'. Quotation from Jeremiah 7:11.

Praise Literally, "Hosanna", a Hebrew word used at first in praying to God for help. At this time it was probably a shout of joy used in praising God or his Messiah.

'You . . . praises' Quotation from the Septuagint (Greek) version of Psalm 8:3.

said, 'Son, go and work today in my vineyard'. ²⁹The son answered, 'I will not go'. But later the son decided he should go, and he went. ³⁰Then the father went to the other son and said, 'Son, go and work today in my vineyard'. The son answered, 'Yes, sir, I will go and work'. But he did not go. ³¹Which of the two sons obeyed his father?"

The priests and leaders answered, "The first son."

Jesus said to them, "I tell you the truth. The tax collectors and the prostitutes*d* will enter the kingdom of God before you do. ³²John came to show you the right way to live. And you did not believe him. But the tax collectors and prostitutes believed John. You saw this, but you still refused to change and believe him.

God Sends His Son

³³"Listen to this story: there was a man who owned a vineyard. He put a wall around the vineyard and dug a hole for a winepress.*d* Then he built a tower. He leased the land to some farmers and left for a trip. ³⁴Later, it was time for the grapes to be picked. So the man sent his servants to the farmers to get his share of the grapes. ³⁵But the farmers grabbed the servants, beat one, killed another, and then killed a third servant with stones. ³⁶So the man sent some other servants to the farmers. He sent more servants than he sent the first time. But the farmers did the same thing to the servants that they had done before. ³⁷So the man decided to send his son to the farmers. He said, 'The farmers will respect my son'. ³⁸But when the farmers saw the son, they said to each other, 'This is the owner's son. This vineyard will be his. If we kill him, then his vineyard will be ours!' ³⁹So the farmers grabbed the son, threw him out of the vineyard, and killed him. ⁴⁰So what will the owner of the vineyard do to these farmers when he comes?"

⁴¹The priests and leaders said, "He will surely kill those evil men. Then he will lease the vineyard to some other farmers. They will give him his share of the crop at harvest time."

⁴²Jesus said to them, "Surely you have read this in the Scriptures:*d*

'The stone that the builders did
    not want
    became the cornerstone.*d*
The Lord did this,
    and it is wonderful to us'.
                    Psalm 118:22-23

⁴³"So I tell you that the kingdom of God will be taken away from you. It will be given to people who do the things God wants in his kingdom. ⁴⁴The person who falls on this stone will be broken. But if the stone falls on him, he will be crushed."

⁴⁵The leading priests and the Pharisees*d* heard these stories that Jesus told. They knew he was talking about them. ⁴⁶They wanted to arrest him, but they were afraid of the people, because the people believed that Jesus was a prophet.*d*

A Story About a Wedding Feast

22 Jesus used stories to tell other things to the people. He said, ²"The kingdom of heaven is like a king who prepared a wedding feast for his son. ³The king invited some people to the feast. When the feast was ready, the king sent his servants to tell the people to come. But they refused to come to the feast.

⁴"Then the king sent other servants. He said to them, 'Tell those who have been invited that my feast is ready. I have killed my best bulls and calves for the dinner. Everything is ready. Come to the wedding feast'.

⁵"But the people refused to listen to the servants. They went to do other things. One went to work in his field, and another went to his business. ⁶Some of the other people grabbed

the servants, beat them, and killed them. [7]The king was very angry. He sent his army to kill the people who had killed his servants. And the army burned their city.

[8]"After that, the king said to his servants, 'The wedding feast is ready. I invited those people, but they were not worthy to come. [9]So go to the street corners and invite everyone you see. Tell them to come to my feast'. [10]So the servants went into the streets. They gathered all the people they could find, both good and bad. And the wedding hall was filled with guests.

[11]"Then the king came in to see all the guests. He saw a man there who was not dressed in the right clothes for a wedding. [12]The king said, 'Friend, how were you allowed to come in here? You are not wearing the right clothes for a wedding'. But the man said nothing. [13]So the king told some servants, 'Tie this man's hands and feet. Throw him out into the darkness. In that place, people will cry and grind their teeth with pain'.

[14]"Yes, many people are invited. But only a few are chosen."

The Pharisees Try to Trap Jesus

[15]Then the Pharisees[d] left the place where Jesus was teaching. They made plans to trap Jesus with a question. [16]They sent some of their own followers and some men from the group called Herodians.[n] These men said, "Teacher, we know that you are an honest man. We know that you teach the truth about God's way. You are not afraid of what other people think about you. All men are the same to you. [17]So tell us what you think. Is it right to pay taxes to Caesar[d] or not?"

[18]But Jesus knew that these men were trying to trick him. So he said, "You hypocrites![d] Why are you trying to trap me? [19]Show me a coin used for paying the tax." The men showed him a silver coin.[n] [20]Then Jesus asked, "Whose picture is on the coin? And whose name is written on the coin?"

[21]The men answered, "Caesar's."

Then Jesus said to them, "Give to Caesar the things that are Caesar's. And give to God the things that are God's."

[22]The men heard what Jesus said, and they were amazed. They left him and went away.

Sadducees Try to Trick Jesus

[23]That same day some Sadducees[d] came to Jesus. (Sadducees believe that no person will rise from death.) The Sadducees asked Jesus a question. [24]They said, "Teacher, Moses told us that a married man might die without having children. Then his brother must marry the widow and have children for him. [25]There were seven brothers among us. The first one married but died. He had no children. So his brother married the widow. [26]Then the second brother also died. The same thing happened to the third brother and all the other brothers. [27]The woman was last to die. [28]But all seven men had married her. So when people rise from death, whose wife will she be?"

[29]Jesus answered, "You don't understand because you don't know what the Scriptures[d] say. And you don't know about the power of God. [30]When people rise from death, there will be no marriage. People will not be married to each other. They will be like the angels in heaven. [31]Surely you have read what God said to you about the rising from death? [32]God said, 'I am the God of Abraham, the God of

---

Herodians A political group that followed Herod and his family.
silver coin A Roman denarius. One coin was the average pay for one day's work.

Isaac, and the God of Jacob'.[n] God is the God of living people, not dead people."

33All the people heard this. They were amazed at Jesus' teaching.

The Most Important Command

34The Pharisees[d] learned that the Sadducees[d] could not argue with Jesus' answers to them. So the Pharisees met together. 35One Pharisee was an expert in the law of Moses. That Pharisee asked Jesus a question to test him. 36The Pharisee asked, "Teacher, which command in the law is the most important?"

37Jesus answered, " 'Love the Lord your God with all your heart, soul and mind'.[n] 38This is the first and most important command. 39And the second command is like the first: 'Love your neighbour as you love yourself'.[n] 40All the law and the writings of the prophets[d] depend on these two commands."

Jesus Questions the Pharisees

41While the Pharisees[d] were together, Jesus asked them a question. 42He asked, "What do you think about the Christ?[d] Whose son is he?"

The Pharisees answered, "The Christ is the Son of David."[d]

43Then Jesus said to them, "Then why did David call him 'Lord'? David was speaking by the power of the Holy Spirit.[d] David said,

44'The Lord said to my Lord:
    Sit by me at my right side,
    until I put your enemies under
        your control.'   Psalm 110:1
45David calls the Christ 'Lord'. So how can he be David's son?"

46None of the Pharisees could answer Jesus' question. And after that day no one was brave enough to ask Jesus any more questions.

Jesus Accuses the Leaders

23 Then Jesus spoke to the crowds and to his followers. Jesus said, 2"The teachers of the law and the Pharisees[d] have the authority to tell you what the law of Moses says. 3So you should obey and follow whatever they tell you. But their lives are not good examples for you to follow. They tell you to do things, but they don't do the things themselves. 4They make strict rules and try to force people to obey them. But they themselves will not try to follow any of those rules.

5"The reason they do good things is so other people will see them. They make the boxes[n] of Scriptures[d] that they wear bigger and bigger. And they make their special prayer clothes very long so that people will notice them. 6Those Pharisees and teachers of the law love to have the most important seats at the feasts. And they love to have the most important seats in the synagogues.[d] 7They love people to show respect to them in the marketplaces. And they love to have people call them 'Teacher'.

8"But you must not be called 'Teacher'. You are all brothers and sisters together. You have only one Teacher. 9And don't call any person on earth 'Father'. You have one Father. He is in heaven. 10And you should not be called 'Master'. You have only one Master, the Christ.[d] 11He who serves you as a servant is the greatest among you. 12Whoever makes himself great will be made humble. Whoever makes himself humble will be made great.

'I am . . . Jacob'.   Quotation from Exodus 3:6.
'Love . . . mind'.   Quotation from Deuteronomy 6:5.
'Love . . . yourself'.   Quotation from Leviticus 19:18.
boxes   Small leather boxes containing four important Scriptures. Some Jews tied these to the forehead and left arm, probably to show they were very religious.

¹³"How terrible for you, teachers of the law and Pharisees! You are hypocrites!ᵈ You close the door for people to enter the kingdom of heaven. You yourselves don't enter, and you stop others who are trying to enter. ¹⁴ ⁿ

¹⁵"How terrible for you, teachers of the law and Pharisees! You are hypocrites! You travel across land and sea to find one person who will follow your ways. When you find that person, you make him more fit for hell than you are.

¹⁶"How terrible for you, teachers of the law and Pharisees! You guide the people, but you are blind. You say, 'If anyone swears by the Templeᵈ when he makes a promise, that means nothing. But if anyone swears by the gold that is in the Temple, then he must keep that promise'. ¹⁷You are blind fools! Which is greater: the gold or the Temple? The Temple makes that gold holy. ¹⁸And you say, 'If anyone swears by the altar when he makes a promise, that means nothing. But if he swears by the gift on the altar, then he must keep his promise'. ¹⁹You are blind! Which is greater: the gift or the altar? The altar makes the gift holy. ²⁰The person who swears by the altar is really using the altar and also everything on the altar. ²¹And the person who uses the Temple to make a promise is really using the Temple and also everything in the Temple. ²²The person who uses heaven to make a promise is also using God's throne and the One who sits on that throne.

²³"How terrible for you, teachers of the law and Pharisees! You are hypocrites! You give to God one-tenth of everything you earn — even your mint, dill, and cumin.ⁿ But you don't obey the really important teachings of the law — being fair, showing mercy, and being loyal. These are the things you should do, as well as those other things. ²⁴You guide the people, but you are blind! You are like a person who picks a fly out of his drink and then swallows a camel!ⁿ

²⁵"How terrible for you, teachers of the law and Pharisees! You are hypocrites! You wash the outside of your cups and dishes. But inside they are full of things that you got by cheating others and pleasing only yourselves. ²⁶Pharisees, you are blind! First make the inside of the cup clean and good. Then the outside of the cup can be truly clean.

²⁷"How terrible for you, teachers of the law and Pharisees. You are hypocrites! You are like tombs that are painted white. Outside, those tombs look fine. But inside, they are full of the bones of dead people, and all kinds of unclean things are there. ²⁸It is the same with you. People look at you and think you are good. But on the inside you are full of hypocrisy and evil.

²⁹"How terrible for you, teachers of the law and Pharisees! You are hypocrites! You build tombs for the prophets.ᵈ You show honour to the graves of people who lived good lives. ³⁰And you say, 'If we had lived during the time of our fathers, we would not have helped them kill the prophets'. ³¹But you give proof that you are children of those people who murdered the prophets. ³²And you will complete the sin that your fathers started!

³³"You are snakes! A family of poisonous snakes! You will not escape God. You will all be judged guilty and be sent to hell! ³⁴So I tell you this: I

Verse 14 Some Greek copies add verse 14: "How terrible for you, teachers of the law and Pharisees. You are hypocrites. You take away widows' houses, and you make long prayers so that people can see you. So you will have a worse punishment."

mint, dill, and cumin Small plants grown in gardens and used for spices. Only very religious people would be careful enough to give a tenth of these plants.

You . . . camel! Meaning, "You worry about the smallest mistakes but commit the biggest sin."

am sending to you prophets and wise men and teachers. You will kill some of these people. You will nail some of them to crosses. You will beat some of them in your synagogues. You will chase them from town to town. [35]So you will be guilty for the death of all the good people who have been killed on earth. You will be guilty for the murder of that good man Abel. And you will be guilty for the murder of Zechariah[n] son of Berakiah. He was murdered when he was between the Temple and the altar. [36]I tell you the truth. All of these things will happen to you people who are living now.

Jesus Feels Sorry for Jerusalem

[37]"Jerusalem, Jerusalem! You kill the prophets[d] and kill with stones those men God sent to you. Many times I wanted to help your people! I wanted to gather them together as a hen gathers her chicks under her wings. But you did not let me. [38]Now your home will be left completely empty. [39]I tell you, you will not see me again until that time when you will say, 'God bless the One who comes in the name of the Lord'. "[n]

The Temple Will Be Destroyed

24 Jesus left the Temple[d] and was walking away. But his followers came to show him the Temple's buildings. [2]Jesus asked, "Do you see all these buildings? I tell you the truth. Every stone will be thrown down to the ground. Not one stone will be left on another."

[3]Later, Jesus was sitting on the Mount of Olives.[d] His followers came to be alone with him. They said, "Tell us when these things will happen. And what will happen to show us that it is time for you to come again and for the world to end?"

[4]Jesus answered: "Be careful that no one fools you. [5]Many people will come in my name. They will say, 'I am the Christ'.[d] And they will fool many people. [6]You will hear about wars and stories of wars that are coming. But don't be afraid. These things must happen before the end comes. [7]Nations will fight against other nations. Kingdoms will fight against other kingdoms. There will be times when there is no food for people to eat. And there will be earthquakes in different places. [8]These things are like the first pains when something new is about to be born.

[9]"Then men will arrest you and hand you over to be hurt and kill you. They will hate you because you believe in me. [10]At that time, many who believe will lose their faith. They will turn against each other and hate each other. [11]Many false prophets[d] will come and cause many people to believe false things. [12]There will be more and more evil in the world. So most people will stop showing their love for each other. [13]But the person who continues to be strong until the end will be saved. [14]The Good News[d] about God's kingdom will be preached in all the world, to every nation. Then the end will come.

[15]"Daniel the prophet spoke about 'the horrible thing that destroys'.[n] You will see this terrible thing standing in the holy place." (You who read this should understand what it means.) [16]"At that time, the people in Judea should run away to the mountains. [17]If a person is on the roof[n] of

---

Abel ... Zechariah In the Hebrew Old Testament, the first and last men to be murdered.
God ... Lord Quotation from Psalm 118:26.
'horrible ... destroys'. Mentioned in Daniel 9:27; 12:11 (cf. Daniel 11:31).
roof In Bible times houses were built with flat roofs. The roof was used for drying things such as flax and fruit. It was also used as an extra room, as a place for worship and as a place to sleep in the summer.

his house, he must not go down to get anything out of his house. [18]If a person is in the field, he must not go back to get his coat. [19]At that time, it will be hard for women who are pregnant or have nursing babies! [20]Pray that it will not be winter or a Sabbath[d] day when these things happen and you have to run away. [21]This is because at that time there will be much trouble. There will be more trouble than has ever happened since the beginning of the world. And nothing as bad as that will ever happen again. [22]God has decided to make that terrible time short. If that time were not made short, then no one would go on living. But God will make that time short to help the people he has chosen. [23]At that time, someone might say to you, 'Look, there is the Christ!' Or another person might say, 'There he is!' But don't believe them. [24]False Christs and false prophets will come and perform great things and miracles.[d] They will do these things to the people God has chosen. They will fool them, if that is possible. [25]Now I have warned you about this before it happens.

[26]"If people tell you, 'The Christ is in the desert'—don't go there. If they say, 'The Christ is in the inner room'—don't believe it. [27]When the Son of Man[d] comes, he will be seen by everyone. It will be like lightning flashing in the sky that can be seen everywhere. [28]Wherever there is a dead body, there the vultures will gather.

[29]"Soon after the trouble of those days, this will happen:

'The sun will grow dark.

And the moon will not give its
        light.

The stars will fall from the sky.

And everything in the sky will
        be changed'.   *Isaiah 13:10; 34:4*

[30]"At that time, there will be something in the sky that shows the Son of Man is coming. All the peoples of the world will cry. They will see the Son of Man coming on clouds in the sky. He will come with great power and glory. [31]He will use a loud trumpet to send his angels all around the earth. They will gather his chosen people from every part of the world.

[32]"The fig tree teaches us a lesson. When its branches become green and soft, and new leaves begin to grow, then you know that summer is near. [33]So also, when you see all these things happening, you will know that the time is near, ready to come. [34]I tell you the truth. All these things will happen while the people of this time are still living! [35]The whole world, earth and sky, will be destroyed, but the words I have said will never be destroyed!

When Will Jesus Come Again?

[36]"No one knows when that day or time will be. Even the Son and the angels in heaven don't know. Only the Father knows. [37]When the Son of Man[d] comes, it will be the same as what happened during Noah's time. [38]In those days before the flood, people were eating and drinking. They were marrying and giving their children to be married. They were still doing those things until the day Noah entered the boat. [39]They knew nothing about what was happening. But then the flood came, and all those people were destroyed. It will be the same when the Son of Man comes. [40]Two men will be working together in the field. One man will be taken and the other left. [41]Two women will be grinding grain with a hand mill.[n] One woman will be taken and the other will be left.

[42]"So always be ready. You don't know the day your Lord will come. [43]Remember this: if the owner of the house knew what time a thief was coming, then the owner would be

mill Two large, round, flat rocks used for grinding grain to make flour.

ready for him. The owner would watch and not let the thief enter his house. ⁴⁴So you also must be ready. The Son of Man will come at a time you don't expect him.

⁴⁵"Who is the wise and trusted servant? The master trusts one servant to give the other servants their food at the right time. ⁴⁶When the master comes and finds the servant doing his work, the servant will be very happy. ⁴⁷I tell you the truth. The master will choose that servant to take care of everything the master owns. ⁴⁸But what will happen if the servant is evil and thinks his master will not come back soon? ⁴⁹Then that servant will begin to beat the other servants. He will feast and get drunk with others like him. ⁵⁰And the master will come when the servant is not ready and is not expecting him. ⁵¹Then the master will punish that servant. He will send him away to be among the hypocrites.ᵈ There people will cry and grind their teeth with pain.

A Story About Ten Girls

25 "At that time the kingdom of heaven will be like ten girls who went to wait for the bridegroom. They took their lamps with them. ²Five of the girls were foolish and five were wise. ³The five foolish girls took their lamps, but they did not take more oil for the lamps to burn. ⁴The wise girls took their lamps and more oil in jars. ⁵The bridegroom was very late. All the girls became sleepy and went to sleep.

⁶"At midnight someone cried out, 'The bridegroom is coming! Come and meet him!' ⁷Then all the girls woke up and got their lamps ready. ⁸But the foolish girls said to the wise, 'Give us some of your oil. Our lamps are going out'. ⁹The wise girls answered, 'No! The oil we have might not be enough for all of us. Go to the people who sell oil and buy some for yourselves'.

¹⁰"So the five foolish girls went to buy oil. While they were gone, the bridegroom came. The girls who were ready went in with the bridegroom to the wedding feast. Then the door was closed and locked.

¹¹"Later the others came back. They called, 'Sir, sir, open the door to let us in'. ¹²But the bridegroom answered, 'I tell you the truth, I don't know you'.

¹³"So always be ready. You don't know the day or the time the Son of Manᵈ will come.

A Story About Three Servants

¹⁴"The kingdom of heaven is like a man who was going to another place for a visit. Before he left, he talked with his servants. The man told them to take care of his things while he was gone. ¹⁵He decided how much each servant would be able to care for. He gave one servant five bags of money. He gave another servant two bags of money. And he gave a third servant one bag of money. Then the man left. ¹⁶The servant who got five bags went quickly to invest the money. The five bags of money earned five more. ¹⁷It was the same with the servant who had two bags of money. He invested the money and earned two more. ¹⁸But the servant who got one bag of money went out and dug a hole in the ground. Then he hid his master's money in the hole.

¹⁹"After a long time the master came home. He asked the servants what they did with his money. ²⁰The servant who got five bags of money brought five more bags to the master. The servant said, 'Master, you trusted me to care for five bags of money. So I used your five bags to earn five more'. ²¹The master answered, 'You did well. You are a good servant who can be trusted. You did well with small things. So I will let you care for much greater things. Come and share my happiness with me'.

²²"Then the servant who got two

bags of money came to the master. The servant said, 'Master, you gave me two bags of money to care for. So I used your two bags to earn two more'. ²³The master answered, 'You did well. You are a good servant who can be trusted. You did well with small things. So I will let you care for much greater things. Come and share my happiness with me'.

²⁴"Then the servant who got one bag of money came to the master. The servant said, 'Master, I knew that you were a hard man. You harvest things you did not plant. You gather crops where you did not sow any seed. ²⁵So I was afraid. I went and hid your money in the ground. Here is the bag of money you gave me'. ²⁶The master answered, "You are a bad and lazy servant! You say you knew that I harvest things I did not plant, and that I gather crops where I did not sow any seed? ²⁷So you should have put my money in the bank. Then, when I came home, I would get my money back with interest'.

²⁸"So the master told his other servants, 'Take the bag of money from that servant and give it to the servant who has ten bags of money. ²⁹Everyone who uses what he has will get more. He will have much more than he needs. But the one who does not use what he has will have everything taken away from him'. ³⁰Then the master said, 'Throw that useless servant outside, into the darkness! There people will cry and grind their teeth with pain'.

The King Will Judge All People

³¹"The Son of Man*d* will come again in his great glory. All his angels will come with him. He will be King and sit on his great throne. ³²All the people of the world will be gathered before him. Then he will separate them into two groups as a shepherd separates the sheep from the goats. ³³The Son of Man will put the sheep, the good peo-

ple, on his right and the goats, the bad people, on his left.

³⁴"Then the King will say to the good people on his right, 'Come. My Father has given you his blessing. Come and receive the kingdom God has prepared for you since the world was made. ³⁵I was hungry, and you gave me food. I was thirsty, and you gave me something to drink. I was alone and away from home, and you invited me into your house. ³⁶I was without clothes, and you gave me something to wear. I was sick, and you cared for me. I was in prison, and you visited me'.

³⁷"Then the good people will answer, 'Lord, when did we see you hungry and give you food? When did we see you thirsty and give you something to drink? ³⁸When did we see you alone and away from home and invite you into our house? When did we see you without clothes and give you something to wear? ³⁹When did we see you sick or in prison and care for you?'

⁴⁰"Then the King will answer, 'I tell you the truth. Anything you did for any of my people here, you also did for me'.

⁴¹"Then the King will say to those on his left, 'Go away from me. God has said that you will be punished. Go into the fire that burns for ever. That fire was prepared for the devil and his helpers. ⁴²I was hungry, and you gave me nothing to eat. I was thirsty, and you gave me nothing to drink. ⁴³I was alone and away from home, and you did not invite me into your house. I was without clothes, and you gave me nothing to wear. I was sick and in prison, and you did not care for me'.

⁴⁴"Then those people will answer, 'Lord, when did we see you hungry or thirsty? When did we see you alone and away from home? Or when did we see you without clothes or sick or in prison? When did we see these things and not help you?'

⁴⁵"Then the King will answer, 'I tell you the truth. Anything you refused to do for any of my people here, you refused to do for me'.

⁴⁶"These people will go off to be punished for ever. But the good people will go to live for ever."

The Plan to Kill Jesus

26 After Jesus finished saying all these things, he told his followers, ²"You know that the day after tomorrow is the day of the Passover[d] Feast. On that day the Son of Man[d] will be given to his enemies to be killed on a cross."

³Then the leading priests and the older Jewish leaders had a meeting at the palace of the high priest. The high priest's name was Caiaphas. ⁴At the meeting, they planned to set a trap to arrest Jesus and kill him. ⁵But they said, "We must not do it during the feast. The people might cause a riot."

A Woman with Perfume for Jesus

⁶Jesus was in Bethany. He was at the house of Simon, who had a harmful skin disease. ⁷While Jesus was there, a woman came to him. She had an alabaster[d] jar filled with expensive perfume. She poured this perfume on Jesus' head while he was eating.

⁸His followers saw the woman do this and were upset. They asked, "Why waste that perfume? ⁹It could be sold for a great deal of money, and the money could be given to the poor."

¹⁰But Jesus knew what happened. He said, "Why are you troubling this woman? She did a very beautiful thing for me. ¹¹You will always have the poor with you. But you will not always have me. ¹²This woman poured perfume on my body to prepare me for burial. ¹³I tell you the truth. The Good News[d] will be told to people in all the world. And in every place where it is preached, what this woman has done

will be told. And people will remember her."

Judas Becomes an Enemy of Jesus

¹⁴Then one of the 12 followers went to talk to the leading priests. This was the follower named Judas Iscariot. ¹⁵He said, "I will give Jesus to you. What will you pay me for doing this?" The priests gave Judas 30 silver coins. ¹⁶After that, Judas waited for the best time to give Jesus to the priests.

Jesus Eats the Passover Feast

¹⁷On the first day of the Feast[d] of Unleavened Bread, the followers came to Jesus. They said, "We will prepare everything for you to eat the Passover[d] Feast. Where do you want to have the feast?"

¹⁸Jesus answered, "Go into the city to a certain man. Tell him that the Teacher says, 'The chosen time is near. I will have the Passover Feast with my followers at your house'." ¹⁹The followers did what Jesus told them to do, and they prepared the Passover Feast.

²⁰In the evening Jesus was sitting at the table with his 12 followers. ²¹They were all eating. Then Jesus said, "I tell you the truth. One of you 12 will turn against me."

²²This made the followers very sad. Each one said to Jesus, "Surely, Lord, I am not the one who will turn against you. Am I?"

²³Jesus answered, "The man who has dipped his hand with me into the bowl is the one who will turn against me. ²⁴The Son of Man[d] will die. The Scriptures[d] say this will happen. But how terrible it will be for the person who gives the Son of Man to be killed. It would be better for him if he had never been born."

²⁵Then Judas said to Jesus, "Teacher, surely I am not the one. Am I?"

2

(Judas is the one who would give Jesus to his enemies.)

Jesus answered, "Yes, it is you."

The Lord's Supper

26While they were eating, Jesus took some bread. He thanked God for it and broke it. Then he gave it to his followers and said, "Take this bread and eat it. This bread is my body."

27Then Jesus took a cup. He thanked God for it and gave it to the followers. He said, "Every one of you drink this. 28This is my blood which begins the new agreement that God makes with his people. This blood is poured out for many to forgive their sins. 29I tell you this: I will not drink of this fruit of the vine* again until that day when I drink it new with you in my Father's kingdom."

30They sang a hymn. Then they went out to the Mount of Olives.*

Jesus' Followers Will All Leave Him

31Jesus told the followers, "Tonight you will lose your faith because of me. It is written in the Scriptures:*

'I will kill the shepherd,

and the sheep will scatter'.

Zechariah 13:7

32But after I rise from death, I will go ahead of you into Galilee."

33Peter said, "All the other followers may lose their faith because of you. But I will never lose my faith."

34Jesus said, "I tell you the truth. Tonight you will say you don't know me. You will say this three times before the cock crows."

35But Peter said, "I will never say that I don't know you! I will even die with you!" And all the other followers said the same thing.

Jesus Prays Alone

36Then Jesus went with his followers to a place called Gethsemane. He said to them, "Sit here while I go over there and pray." 37He told Peter and the two sons of Zebedee to come with him. Then Jesus began to be very sad and troubled. 38He said to Peter and the two sons of Zebedee, "My heart is full of sorrow and breaking with sadness. Stay here with me and watch."

39Then Jesus walked a little further away from them. He fell to the ground and prayed, "My Father, if it is possible, do not give me this cup* of suffering. But do what you want, not what I want." 40Then Jesus went back to his followers and found them asleep. Jesus said to Peter, "You men could not stay awake with me for one hour? 41Stay awake and pray for strength against temptation. Your spirit wants to do what is right. But your body is weak."

42Then Jesus went away a second time. He prayed, "My Father, if it is not possible for this painful thing to be taken from me, and if I must do it, then I pray that what you want will be done."

43Then Jesus went back to the followers. Again he found them asleep, because their eyes were heavy. 44So Jesus left them and went away one more time and prayed. This third time he prayed, he said the same thing.

45Then Jesus went back to the followers and said, "You are still sleeping and resting? The time has come for the Son of Man* to be given to sinful people. 46Get up. We must go. Here comes the man who has turned against me."

Jesus Is Arrested

47While Jesus was still speaking, Judas came up. Judas was one of the 12

---

fruit of the vine Product of the grapevine; this may also be translated "wine".
cup Jesus is talking about the bad things that will happen to him. Accepting these things will be very hard, like drinking a cup of something that tastes very bitter.

followers. He had many people with him. They had been sent from the leading priests and the older leaders of the people. They carried swords and clubs. ⁴⁸Judas had planned to give them a signal. He had said, "The man I kiss is Jesus. Arrest him." ⁴⁹At once Judas went to Jesus and said, "Greetings, Teacher!" Then Judas kissed him.

⁵⁰Jesus answered, "Friend, do the thing you came to do."

Then the men came and grabbed Jesus and arrested him. ⁵¹When that happened, one of Jesus' followers reached for his sword and pulled it out. The follower struck the servant of the high priest with the sword and cut off his ear.

⁵²Jesus said to the man, "Put your sword back in its place. All who use swords will be killed with swords. ⁵³Surely you know I could ask my Father, and he would give me more than 12 armies of angels. ⁵⁴But this thing must happen this way so that it will be as the Scriptures*ᵈ* say."

⁵⁵Then Jesus said to the crowd, "You came to get me with swords and clubs as if I were a criminal. Every day I sat in the Temple*ᵈ* teaching. You did not arrest me there. ⁵⁶But all these things have happened so that it will be as the prophets*ᵈ* wrote." Then all of Jesus' followers left him and ran away.

Jesus Before the Jewish Leaders

⁵⁷Those men who arrested Jesus led him to the house of Caiaphas, the high priest. The teachers of the law and the older Jewish leaders were gathered there. ⁵⁸Peter followed Jesus but did not go near him. He followed Jesus to the courtyard of the high priest's house. He sat down with the guards to see what would happen to Jesus.

⁵⁹The leading priests and the Jewish council tried to find something false against Jesus so that they could kill him. ⁶⁰Many people came and told lies

about him. But the council could find no real reason to kill Jesus. Then two people came and said, ⁶¹"This man said, 'I can destroy the Temple*ᵈ* of God and build it again in three days'."

⁶²Then the high priest stood up and said to Jesus, "Aren't you going to answer? Don't you have something to say about their charges against you?" ⁶³But Jesus said nothing.

Again the high priest said to Jesus, "You must swear to this. I command you by the power of the living God to tell us the truth. Tell us, are you the Christ,*ᵈ* the Son of God?"

⁶⁴Jesus answered, "Yes, I am. But I tell you, in the future you will see the Son of Man*ᵈ* sitting at the right hand of God, the Powerful One. And you will see him coming in clouds in the sky."

⁶⁵When the high priest heard this, he was very angry. He tore his clothes and said, "This man has said things that are against God! We don't need any more witnesses. You all heard him say these things against God. ⁶⁶What do you think?"

The people answered, "He is guilty, and he must die."

⁶⁷Then the people there spat in Jesus' face and beat him with their fists. Others slapped Jesus. ⁶⁸They said, "Prove to us that you are a prophet,*ᵈ* you Christ! Tell us who hit you!"

Peter Says He Doesn't Know Jesus

⁶⁹At that time, Peter was sitting in the courtyard. A servant girl came to him and said, "You were with Jesus, that man from Galilee."

⁷⁰But Peter said that he was never with Jesus. He said this to all the people there. Peter said, "I don't know what you are talking about."

⁷¹Then he left the courtyard. At the gate, another girl saw him. She said to the people there, "This man was with Jesus of Nazareth."

⁷²Again, Peter said that he was nev-

er with Jesus. Peter said, "I swear that I don't know this man Jesus!"

[73]A short time later, some people standing there went to Peter. They said, "We know you are one of those men who followed Jesus. We know this because of the way you talk."

[74]Then Peter began to curse. He said, "May a curse fall on me if I'm not telling the truth. I don't know the man." After Peter said this, a cock crowed. [75]Then he remembered what Jesus had told him: "Before the cock crows, you will say three times that you don't know me." Then Peter went outside and cried painfully.

Jesus Is Taken to Pilate

27 Early the next morning, all the leading priests and older leaders of the people decided to kill Jesus. [2]They tied him, led him away, and turned him over to Pilate, the governor.

Judas Kills Himself

[3]Judas saw that they had decided to kill Jesus. Judas was the one who gave Jesus to his enemies. When Judas saw what happened, he was very sorry for what he had done. So he took the 30 silver coins back to the priests and the leaders. [4]Judas said, "I sinned. I gave you an innocent man to be killed."

The leaders answered, "What is that to us? That's your problem, not ours."

[5]So Judas threw the money into the Temple.[d] Then he went off and hanged himself.

[6]The leading priests picked up the silver coins in the Temple. They said, "Our law does not allow us to keep this money with the Temple money. This money has paid for a man's death." [7]So they decided to use the coins to buy a field called Potter's Field. This field would be a place to bury strangers who died while visiting

Jerusalem. [8]That is why that field is still called the Field of Blood. [9]So the thing came true that Jeremiah the prophet[d] had said: "They took 30 silver coins. That is how little the Israelites thought he was worth. [10]They used those 30 silver coins to buy the potter's field, as the Lord commanded me."[n]

Pilate Questions Jesus

[11]Jesus stood before Pilate the governor. Pilate asked him, "Are you the King of the Jews?"

Jesus answered, "Yes, I am."

[12]When the leading priests and the older leaders accused Jesus, he said nothing.

[13]So Pilate said to Jesus, "Don't you hear these people accusing you of all these things?"

[14]But Jesus said nothing in answer to Pilate. Pilate was very surprised at this.

Pilate Tries to Free Jesus

[15]Every year at the time of Passover[d] the governor would free one person from prison. This was always a person the people wanted to be set free. [16]At that time there was a man in prison who was known to be very bad. His name was Barabbas. [17]All the people gathered at Pilate's house. Pilate said, "Which man do you want me to free: Barabbas, or Jesus who is called the Christ?"[d] [18]Pilate knew that the people gave Jesus to him because they were jealous.

[19]Pilate said these things while he was sitting on the judge's seat. While he was sitting there, his wife sent a message to him. The message said, "Don't do anything to that man. He is not guilty. Today I had a dream about him, and it troubled me very much."

[20]But the leading priests and older leaders told the crowd to ask for Bar-

"They . . . commanded me." See Zechariah 11:12-13 and Jeremiah 32:6-9.

abbas to be freed and for Jesus to be killed.

²¹Pilate said, "I have Barabbas and Jesus. Which do you want me to set free for you?"

The people answered, "Barabbas!" ²²Pilate asked, "What should I do with Jesus, the one called the Christ?"

They all answered, "Kill him on a cross!"

²³Pilate asked, "Why do you want me to kill him? What wrong has he done?"

But they shouted louder, "Kill him on a cross!"

²⁴Pilate saw that he could do nothing about this, and a riot was starting. So he took some water and washed his hands[n] in front of the crowd. Then he said, "I am not guilty of this man's death. You are the ones who are causing it!"

²⁵All the people answered, "We will be responsible. We accept for ourselves and for our children any punishment for his death."

²⁶Then Pilate freed Barabbas. Pilate told some of the soldiers to beat Jesus with whips. Then he gave Jesus to the soldiers to be killed on a cross.

²⁷Pilate's soldiers took Jesus into the governor's palace. All the soldiers gathered around Jesus. ²⁸They took off his clothes and put a red robe on him. ²⁹Then the soldiers used thorny branches to make a crown. They put this crown of thorns on Jesus' head. They put a stick in his right hand. Then the soldiers bowed before Jesus and made fun of him. They said, "Hail, King of the Jews!" ³⁰They spat on Jesus. Then they took his stick and hit him on the head many times. ³¹After they finished making fun of Jesus, the soldiers took off the robe and put his own clothes on him again. Then they led Jesus away to be killed on a cross.

Jesus Is Killed on a Cross

³²The soldiers were going out of the city with Jesus. They forced another man to carry the cross to be used for Jesus. This man was Simon, from Cyrene. ³³They all came to the place called Golgotha. (Golgotha means the Place of the Skull.) ³⁴At Golgotha, the soldiers gave Jesus wine to drink. This wine was mixed with gall.[n] He tasted the wine but refused to drink it. ³⁵The soldiers nailed Jesus to a cross. They threw lots[d] to decide who would get his clothes. ³⁶The soldiers sat there and continued watching him. ³⁷They put a sign above Jesus' head with the charge against him written on it. The sign read: "THIS IS JESUS, THE KING OF THE JEWS." ³⁸Two robbers were nailed to crosses beside Jesus, one on the right and the other on the left. ³⁹People walked by and insulted Jesus. They shook their heads, ⁴⁰saying, "You said you could destroy the Temple[d] and build it again in three days. So save yourself! Come down from that cross, if you are really the Son of God!"

⁴¹The leading priests, the teachers of the law, and the older Jewish leaders were also there. These men made fun of Jesus ⁴²and said, "He saved other people, but he can't save himself! People say he is the King of Israel! If he is the King, then let him come down now from the cross. Then we will believe in him. ⁴³He trusts in God. So let God save him now, if God really wants him. He himself said, 'I am the Son of God'." ⁴⁴And in the same way, the robbers who were being killed on crosses beside Jesus also insulted him.

Jesus Dies

⁴⁵At noon the whole country became dark. This darkness lasted for

---

washed his hands He did this as a sign to show that he wanted no part in what the people did.
gall Probably a drink of wine mixed with drugs to help a person feel less pain.

three hours. [46]About three o'clock Jesus cried out in a loud voice, "Eli, Eli, lema sabachthani?" This means, "My God, my God, why have you left me alone?"

[47]Some of the people standing there heard this. They said, "He is calling Elijah."

[48]Quickly one of them ran and got a sponge. He filled the sponge with vinegar and tied it to a stick. Then he used the stick to give the sponge to Jesus to drink from it. [49]But the others said, "Don't bother him. We want to see if Elijah will come to save him."

[50]Again Jesus cried out in a loud voice. Then he died.

[51]Then the curtain in the Temple[n] split into two pieces. The tear started at the top and tore all the way down to the bottom. Also, the earth shook and rocks broke apart. [52]The graves opened, and many of God's people who had died were raised from death. [53]They came out of the graves after Jesus was raised from death. They went into the holy city, and many people saw them.

[54]The army officer and the soldiers guarding Jesus saw this earthquake and everything else that happened. They were very frightened and said, "He really was the Son of God!"

[55]Many women were standing at a distance from the cross, watching. These were women who had followed Jesus from Galilee to care for him. [56]Mary Magdalene, and Mary the mother of James and Joseph, and the mother of James and John were there.

Jesus Is Buried

[57]That evening a rich man named Joseph came to Jerusalem. He was a follower of Jesus from the town of Arimathea. [58]Joseph went to Pilate and asked to have Jesus' body. Pilate gave orders for the soldiers to give it to Joseph. [59]Then Joseph took the body and wrapped it in a clean linen cloth. [60]He put Jesus' body in a new tomb that he had cut in a wall of rock. He rolled a very large stone to block the entrance of the tomb. Then Joseph went away. [61]Mary Magdalene and the other woman named Mary were sitting near the tomb.

The Tomb of Jesus Is Guarded

[62]That day was the day called Preparation[d] Day. The next day, the leading priests and the Pharisees[d] went to Pilate. [63]They said, "Sir, we remember that while that liar was still alive he said, 'After three days I will rise from death'. [64]So give the order for the tomb to be guarded closely till the third day. His followers might come and steal the body. Then they could tell the people that he has risen from death. That lie would be even worse than the first one."

[65]Pilate said, "Take some soldiers and go and guard the tomb the best way you know." [66]So they all went to the tomb and made it safe from thieves. They did this by sealing the stone in the entrance and then putting soldiers there to guard it.

Jesus Rises from Death

28 The day after the Sabbath[d] day was the first day of the week. At dawn on the first day, Mary Magdalene and another woman named Mary went to look at the tomb.

[2]At that time there was a strong earthquake. An angel of the Lord came down from heaven. The angel went to the tomb and rolled the stone away from the entrance. Then he sat on the stone. [3]He was shining as bright as lightning. His clothes were white as snow. [4]The soldiers guarding

---

curtain in the Temple A curtain divided the Most Holy Place from the other part of the Temple. That was the special building in Jerusalem where God commanded the Jews to worship him.

the tomb were very frightened of the angel. They shook with fear and then became like dead men.

⁵The angel said to the women, "Don't be afraid. I know that you are looking for Jesus, the one who was killed on the cross. ⁶But he is not here. He has risen from death as he said he would. Come and see the place where his body was. ⁷And go quickly and tell his followers. Say to them: 'Jesus has risen from death. He is going into Galilee. He will be there before you. You will see him there'." Then the angel said, "Now I have told you."

⁸The women left the tomb quickly. They were afraid, but they were also very happy. They ran to tell Jesus' followers what had happened. ⁹Suddenly, Jesus met them and said, "Greetings." The women came up to Jesus, took hold of his feet, and worshipped him. ¹⁰Then Jesus said to them, "Don't be afraid. Go and tell my brothers to go on to Galilee. They will see me there."

The Soldiers Report to the Jewish Leaders

¹¹The women went to tell Jesus' followers. At the same time, some of the soldiers who had been guarding the tomb went into the city. They went to tell the leading priests everything that had happened. ¹²Then the priests met with the older Jewish leaders and made a plan. They paid the soldiers a large amount of money. ¹³They said to the soldiers, "Tell the people that Jesus' followers came during the night and stole the body while you were asleep. ¹⁴If the governor hears about this, we will satisfy him and save you from trouble." ¹⁵So the soldiers kept the money and obeyed the priests. And that story is still spread among the Jews even today.

Jesus Talks to His Followers

¹⁶The 11 followers went to Galilee. They went to the mountain where Jesus told them to go. ¹⁷On the mountain they saw Jesus and worshipped him. But some of them did not believe that it was really Jesus. ¹⁸Then Jesus came to them and said, "All power in heaven and on earth is given to me. ¹⁹So go and make followers of all people in the world. Baptise them in the name of the Father and the Son and the Holy Spirit.ᵈ ²⁰Teach them to obey everything that I have told you. You can be sure that I will be with you always. I will continue with you until the end of the world."

MARK

Mark Tells About the Power of Jesus

John Prepares for Jesus

1 This is the beginning of the Good News[d] about Jesus Christ, the Son of God,[n] [2]as the prophet[d] Isaiah wrote:

"I will send my messenger ahead
  of you.
He will prepare your way."
  Malachi 3:1
[3]"There is a voice of a man who
  calls out in the desert:
'Prepare the way for the Lord.
Make the road straight for
  him'."
  Isaiah 40:3
[4]John was baptising people in the desert. He preached a baptism of changed hearts and lives for the forgiveness of sins. [5]All the people from Judea and Jerusalem were going out to John. They told about the sins they had done. Then they were baptised by him in the Jordan River. [6]John wore clothes made from camel's hair and had a leather belt around his waist. He ate locusts[d] and wild honey. [7]This is what John preached to the people: "There is one coming later who is greater than I. I am not good enough even to kneel down and untie his sandals. [8]I baptise you with water. But the one who is coming will baptise you with the Holy Spirit."[d]

Jesus Is Baptised

[9]At that time Jesus came from the town of Nazareth in Galilee to the place where John was. John baptised Jesus in the Jordan River. [10]When Jesus was coming up out of the water, he saw heaven open. The Holy Spirit[d] came down on him like a dove. [11]A voice came from heaven and said: "You are my Son and I love you. I am very pleased with you."

[12]Then the Spirit sent Jesus into the desert alone. [13]He was in the desert 40 days and was there with the wild animals. While he was in the desert, he was tempted by Satan. Then angels came and took care of Jesus.

Jesus Chooses Some Followers

[14]After John was put in prison, Jesus went into Galilee and preached the Good News[d] from God. [15]Jesus said, "The right time has come. The kingdom of God is near. Change your hearts and lives and believe the Good News!"

[16]When Jesus was walking by Lake Galilee, he saw Simon[n] and Simon's brother, Andrew. They were fishermen and were throwing a net into the lake to catch fish. [17]Jesus said to them, "Come and follow me. I will make you fishermen for men." [18]So Simon and Andrew immediately left their nets and followed him.

[19]Jesus continued walking by Lake Galilee. He saw two more brothers, James and John, the sons of Zebedee. They were in their boat, preparing their nets to catch fish. [20]Their father Zebedee and the men who worked for him were in the boat with the brothers. When Jesus saw the brothers, he called them to come with him. They left their father and followed Jesus.

Jesus Removes an Evil Spirit

[21]Jesus and his followers went to Capernaum. On the Sabbath[d] day

---

the Son of God Some Greek copies omit these words.
Simon Simon's other name was Peter.

Jesus went to the synagogue[d] and began to teach. [22]The people there were amazed at his teaching. He did not teach like their teachers of the law. He taught like a person who had authority. [23]While he was in the synagogue, a man was there who had an evil spirit in him. The man shouted, [24]"Jesus of Nazareth! What do you want with us? Did you come to destroy us? I know who you are—God's Holy One!"

[25]Jesus said strongly, "Be quiet! Come out of the man!" [26]The evil spirit made the man shake violently. Then the spirit gave a loud cry and came out of him.

[27]The people were amazed. They asked each other, "What is happening here? This man is teaching something new. And he teaches with authority. He even gives commands to evil spirits, and they obey him." [28]And the news about Jesus spread quickly everywhere in the area of Galilee.

Jesus Heals Many People

[29]Jesus and his followers left the synagogue.[d] They all went at once with James and John to the home of Simon[n] and Andrew. [30]Simon's mother-in-law was sick in bed with a fever. The people there told Jesus about her. [31]So Jesus went to her bed, took her hand, and helped her up. Immediately the fever left her, and she was healed. Then she began serving them.

[32]That night, after the sun went down, the people brought to Jesus all who were sick. They also brought those who had demons[d] in them. [33]The whole town gathered at the door of the house. [34]Jesus healed many who had different kinds of sickness. He also forced many demons to leave people. But he would not allow

the demons to speak, because they knew who he was.

[35]Early the next morning, Jesus woke and left the house while it was still dark. He went to a place to be alone and pray. [36]Later, Simon and his friends went to look for Jesus. [37]They found him and said, "Everyone is looking for you!"

[38]Jesus answered, "We should go somewhere else, to other towns around here. Then I can preach there too. That is the reason I came." [39]So he travelled everywhere in Galilee. He preached in the synagogues and forced demons to leave people.

Jesus Heals a Sick Man

[40]A man who had a harmful skin disease came to Jesus. The man fell to his knees and begged Jesus, "I know that you can heal me if you will."

[41]Jesus felt sorry for the man. So he touched him and said, "I want to heal you. Be healed!" [42]At once the disease left the man, and he was healed.

[43]Jesus told the man to go at once. But Jesus warned him strongly, [44]"Don't tell anyone about what I did for you, but go and show yourself to the priest. And offer a gift to God because you have been healed. Offer the gift that Moses commanded.[n] This will show the people that you are healed." [45]The man left there, but he told everyone he saw that Jesus had healed him. So the news about Jesus spread. That is the reason Jesus could not enter a town if people saw him. He stayed in places where nobody lived. But people came from all the towns to wherever he was.

Jesus Heals a Paralysed Man

2 A few days later, Jesus came back to Capernaum. The news spread that he was home. [2]So many people gathered to hear him preach that the

---

Simon Simon's other name was Peter.
Moses commanded Read about this in Leviticus 14:1-32.

house was full. There was nowhere to stand, not even outside the door. Jesus was teaching them. [3]Some people came, bringing a paralysed man to Jesus. Four of them were carrying the paralysed man. [4]But they could not get to Jesus because of the crowd. So they went to the roof above Jesus and made a hole in the roof. Then they lowered the mat with the paralysed man on it. [5]Jesus saw that these men had great faith. So he said to the paralysed man, "Young man, your sins are forgiven."

[6]Some of the teachers of the law were sitting there. They saw what Jesus did, and they said to themselves, [7]"Why does this man say things like that? He is saying things that are against God. Only God can forgive sins."

[8]At once Jesus knew what these teachers of the law were thinking. So he said to them, "Why are you thinking these things? [9]Which is easier: to tell this paralysed man, 'Your sins are forgiven', or to tell him, 'Stand up. Take your mat and walk'? [10]But I will prove to you that the Son of Man[d] has authority on earth to forgive sins." So Jesus said to the paralysed man, [11]"I tell you, stand up. Take your mat and go home." [12]Immediately the paralysed man stood up. He took his mat and walked out while everyone was watching him.

The people were amazed and praised God. They said, "We have never seen anything like this!"

[13]Jesus went to the lake again. A crowd followed him there, and he taught them. [14]While he was walking beside the lake, he saw a tax collector named Levi son of Alphaeus. Levi was sitting in the tax office. Jesus said to him, "Follow me". And Levi stood up and followed Jesus.

[15]Later that day, Jesus ate at Levi's house. There were many tax collectors and "sinners" eating there with Jesus and his followers. Many people like this followed Jesus. [16]The teachers of the law who were Pharisees[d] saw Jesus eating with the tax collectors and "sinners". They asked his followers, "Why does he eat with tax collectors and 'sinners'?"

[17]Jesus heard this and said to them, "Healthy people don't need a doctor. It is the sick who need a doctor. I did not come to invite good people. I came to invite sinners."

Jesus' Followers Are Criticised

[18]One day the followers of John[n] and the Pharisees[d] were giving up eating.[n] Some people came to Jesus and said, "John's followers and the followers of the Pharisees give up eating, but your followers don't. Why?"

[19]Jesus answered, "When there is a wedding, the friends of the bridegroom are not sad while he is with them. They do not give up eating while the bridegroom is still there. [20]But the time will come when the bridegroom will leave them. Then the friends will be sad and will give up eating.

[21]"When a person sews a patch over a hole on an old coat, he never uses a piece of cloth that is not yet shrunk. If he does, the patch will shrink and pull away from the coat. Then the hole will be worse. [22]Also, no one ever pours new wine into old leather bags for holding wine. If he does, the new wine will break the bags, and the wine will be ruined along with the bags for the wine. People always put new wine into new leather bags."

Jesus Is Lord of the Sabbath

[23]On the Sabbath[d] day, Jesus was

John John the Baptist who preached to the Jews about Christ's coming (Mark 1:4-8).
giving up eating This is called "fasting". The people would give up eating for a special time of prayer and worship to God. It was also done to show sadness.

walking through some grainfields. His followers were with him and picked some grain to eat. ²⁴The Pharisees^d saw this and said to Jesus, "Why are your followers doing what is not lawful on the Sabbath?"

²⁵Jesus answered, "You have read what David did when he and those with him were hungry and needed food. ²⁶It was during the time of Abiathar the high priest. David went into God's house and ate the bread that was made holy for God. The law of Moses says that only priests may eat that bread. But David also gave some of the bread to those who were with him."

²⁷Then Jesus said to the Pharisees, "The Sabbath day was made to help people. They were not made to be ruled by the Sabbath day. ²⁸The Son of Man^d is Lord even of the Sabbath."

Jesus Heals a Man's Crippled Hand

3 Another time when Jesus went into a synagogue,^d a man with a crippled hand was there. ²Some people there wanted to see Jesus do something wrong so they could accuse him. They watched him closely to see if he would heal the man on the Sabbath^d day.

³Jesus said to the man with the crippled hand, "Stand up here in front of everyone."

⁴Then Jesus asked the people, "Which is right on the Sabbath day: to do good, or to do evil? Is it right to save a life or to destroy one?" But they said nothing to answer him.

⁵Jesus was angry as he looked at the people. But he felt very sad because they were stubborn. Then he said to the man, "Let me see your hand." The man put his hand out for Jesus, and it was healed. ⁶Then the Pharisees^d left and began making plans with

the Herodiansⁿ about a way to kill Jesus.

Many People Follow Jesus

⁷Jesus left with his followers for the lake. A large crowd from Galilee followed him. ⁸Also many people came from Judea, from Jerusalem, from Idumea, from the lands across the Jordan River, and from the area of Tyre and Sidon. They came because they had heard about all the things Jesus was doing. ⁹Jesus saw the crowds. So he told his followers to get a boat ready for him. He wanted the boat so that the many people would not crowd themselves against him. ¹⁰He had healed many people. So all the sick were pushing toward him to touch him. ¹¹Some had evil spirits in them. When the evil spirits saw Jesus, they fell down before him and shouted, "You are the Son of God!" ¹²But Jesus strongly commanded the spirits not to tell who he was.

Jesus Chooses His 12 Apostles

¹³Then Jesus went up on a hill and called some men to come to him. These were the men Jesus wanted, and they went up to him. ¹⁴Jesus chose 12 men and called them apostles.^d He wanted these 12 to be with him, and he wanted to send them to other places to preach. ¹⁵He also wanted them to have the power to force demons^d out of people. ¹⁶These are the 12 men he chose: Simon (Jesus gave him the name Peter); ¹⁷James and John, the sons of Zebedee (Jesus gave them the name Boanerges, which means "Sons of Thunder"); ¹⁸Andrew, Philip, Bartholomew, Matthew, Thomas, James the son of Alphaeus, Thaddaeus, Simon the Zealot,^d ¹⁹and Judas Iscariot. Judas is the one who gave Jesus to his enemies.

Herodians A political group that followed Herod and his family.

People Say Jesus Has a Devil

²⁰Then Jesus went back home. But again a crowd gathered. There were so many people that Jesus and his followers could not eat. ²¹His family heard about all these things. They went to get him because people were saying that Jesus was out of his mind. ²²And the teachers of the law from Jerusalem were saying, "Beelzebul[d] is living inside him! He uses power from the ruler of demons[d] to force demons out."

²³So Jesus called the people together and used stories to teach them. He said, "Satan will not force his own demons out of people. ²⁴A kingdom that fights against itself cannot continue, ²⁵and a family that is divided cannot continue. ²⁶And if Satan is against himself and fights against his own people, then he cannot continue. And that is the end of Satan. ²⁷If a person wants to enter a strong man's house and steal his things, first he must tie up the strong man. Then the thief can steal the things from the strong man's house. ²⁸I tell you the truth. All sins that people do can be forgiven. And all the bad things people say against God can be forgiven. ²⁹But any person who says bad things against the Holy Spirit[d] will never be forgiven. He is guilty of a sin that continues for ever."

³⁰Jesus said this because the teachers of the law said that Jesus had an evil spirit inside him.

Jesus' True Family

³¹Then Jesus' mother and brothers arrived. They stood outside and sent someone in to tell him to come out. ³²Many people were sitting around Jesus. They said to him, "Your mother and brothers are waiting for you outside."

³³Jesus asked, "Who is my mother? Who are my brothers?" ³⁴Then Jesus looked at those sitting around him. He said, "Here are my mother and my brothers! ³⁵My true brother and sister and mother are those who do the things God wants."

A Story About Planting Seed

4 Another time Jesus began teaching by the lake. A great crowd gathered around him. So he got into a boat and went out on the lake. All the people stayed on the shore close to the water. ²Jesus used many stories to teach them. He said, ³"Listen! A farmer went out to plant his seed. ⁴While the farmer was planting, some seed fell by the road. The birds came and ate all that seed. ⁵Some seed fell on rocky ground where there wasn't much soil. The seed grew very fast there because the ground was not deep. ⁶But when the sun rose, the plants withered. The plants died because they did not have deep roots. ⁷Some other seed fell among thorny weeds. The weeds grew and choked the good plants. So those plants did not make grain. ⁸Some other seed fell on good ground. In the good ground, the seed began to grow. It grew and made a crop of grain. Some plants made 30 times more grain, some 60 times more grain, and some 100 times more grain."

⁹Then Jesus said, "You people who hear me, listen!"

Jesus Tells Why He Used Stories

¹⁰Later, when Jesus was alone, the 12 apostles[d] and others around him asked him about the stories.

¹¹Jesus said, "Only you can know the secret truth about the kingdom of God. But to other people I tell everything by using stories. ¹²I do this so that:

'They will look and look, but they
    will not learn.
They will listen and listen, but
    they will not understand.
If they did learn and understand,
    they would come back to me
      and be forgiven'." *Isaiah 6:9-10*

Jesus Explains the Seed Story

[13]Then Jesus said to the followers, "Do you understand this story? If you don't, then how will you understand any story? [14]The farmer is like a person who plants God's teaching in people. [15]Sometimes the teaching falls on the road. This is like some people. They hear the teaching of God. But Satan quickly comes and takes away the teaching that was planted in them. [16]Others are like the seed planted on rocky ground. They hear the teaching and quickly accept it with joy. [17]But they don't allow the teaching to go deep into their lives. They keep it only a short time. When trouble or persecution comes because of the teaching, they quickly give up. [18]Others are like the seed planted among the thorny weeds. They hear the teaching. [19]But then other things come into their lives: worries, the love of money, and wanting all kinds of other things. These things stop the teaching from growing. So that teaching does not produce fruit* in their lives. [20]Others are like the seed planted in the good ground. They hear the teaching and accept it. Then they grow and produce fruit — sometimes 30 times more, sometimes 60 times more, and sometimes 100 times more."

Use What You Have

[21]Then Jesus said to them, "Do you hide a lamp under a bowl or under a bed? No! You put the lamp on a lampstand. [22]Everything that is hidden will be made clear. Every secret thing will be made known. [23]You people who hear me, listen!

[24]"Think carefully about the things you hear. The way you give to others is the way God will give to you. But God will give you more than you give. [25]The person who has something will be given more. But the person who does not have much, even what he has will be taken from him."

Jesus Uses a Story About Seed

[26]Then Jesus said, "The kingdom of God is like a man who plants seed in the ground. [27]The seed comes up and grows night and day. It doesn't matter whether the man is asleep or awake; the seed still grows. The man does not know how it grows. [28]Without any help, the earth produces grain. First the plant grows, then the head, and then all the grain in the head. [29]When the grain is ready, the man cuts it. This is the harvest time."

A Story About Mustard Seed

[30]Then Jesus said, "How can I show you what the kingdom of God is like? What story can I use to explain it? [31]The kingdom of God is like a mustard seed. The mustard seed is the smallest seed you plant in the ground. [32]But when you plant this seed, it grows and becomes the largest of all garden plants. It produces large branches. Even the wild birds can make nests in it and be protected from the sun."

[33]Jesus used many stories like these to teach them. He taught them all that they could understand. [34]He always used stories to teach them. But when he and his followers were alone together, Jesus explained everything to them.

Jesus Stops a Storm

[35]That evening, Jesus said to his followers, "Come with me across the lake." [36]He and the followers left the people there. They went in the boat that Jesus was already sitting in. There were also other boats with them. [37]A very strong wind came up on the lake. The waves began coming over the sides and into the boat. It was almost full of water. [38]Jesus was

produce fruit To produce fruit means to have in your life the good things God wants.

at the back of the boat, sleeping with his head on a pillow. The followers went to him and woke him. They said, "Teacher, do you care about us? We will drown!"

[39]Jesus stood up and commanded the wind and the waves to stop. He said, "Quiet! Be still!" Then the wind stopped, and the lake became calm.

[40]Jesus said to his followers, "Why are you afraid? Do you still have no faith?"

[41]The followers were very afraid and asked each other, "What kind of man is this? Even the wind and the waves obey him!"

A Man with Demons Inside Him

5 Jesus and his followers went across the lake to the region of the Gerasene people. [2]When Jesus got out of the boat, a man came to him from the caves where dead people were buried. This man, who lived in the caves, had an evil spirit living in him. [3]No one could tie him up, not even with a chain. [4]Many times people had used chains to tie the man's hands and feet. But he always broke the chains off. No one was strong enough to control him. [5]Day and night he would wander around the burial caves and on the hills, screaming and cutting himself with stones. [6]While Jesus was still far away, the man saw him. He ran to Jesus and knelt down before him. [7-8]Jesus said to the man, "You evil spirit, come out of that man."

But the man shouted in a loud voice, "What do you want with me, Jesus, Son of the Most High God? I beg you, promise God that you will not punish me!"

[9]Then Jesus asked the man, "What is your name?"

The man answered, "My name is Legion," because I have many spirits

in me." [10]The man begged Jesus again and again not to send the spirits out of that area.

[11]A large herd of pigs was eating on a hill near there. [12]The evil spirits begged Jesus, "Send us to the pigs. Let us go into them." [13]So Jesus allowed them to do this. The evil spirits left the man and went into the pigs. Then the herd of pigs rushed down the hill into the lake and were drowned. There were about 2,000 pigs in that herd.

[14]The men who took care of the pigs ran away. They went to the town and to the countryside, telling everyone about this. So people went out to see what had happened. [15]They came to Jesus and saw the man who had had the many evil spirits. The man was sitting there, clothed and in his right mind. The people were frightened. [16]Some people were there who saw what Jesus had done. They told the others what had happened to the man who had the demons[d] living in him. And they also told about the pigs. [17]Then the people began to beg Jesus to leave their area.

[18]Jesus was getting ready to leave in the boat. The man who was freed from the demons begged to go with him.

[19]But Jesus would not allow the man to go. Jesus said, "Go home to your family and friends. Tell them how much the Lord has done for you and how he has had mercy on you." [20]So the man left and told the people in the Ten Towns[n] about the great things Jesus had done for him. All the people were amazed.

Jesus Gives Life to a Dead Girl and Heals a Sick Woman

[21]Jesus went in the boat back to the other side of the lake. There, a large

---

Legion Means very many. A legion was about 5,000 men in the Roman army.

Ten Towns In Greek, called "Decapolis". It was an area east of Lake Galilee that once had ten main towns.

crowd gathered around him. ²²A ruler from the synagogue,*d* named Jairus, came to that place. Jairus saw Jesus and bowed before him. ²³The ruler begged Jesus again and again. He said, "My little daughter is dying. Please come and put your hands on her. Then she will be healed and will live." ²⁴So Jesus went with the ruler, and many people followed Jesus. They were pushing very close around him.

²⁵A woman was there who had been bleeding for the past 12 years. ²⁶She had suffered very much. Many doctors had tried to help her. She had spent all the money she had, but she was not improving. She was getting worse. ²⁷When the woman heard about Jesus, she followed him with the people and touched his coat. ²⁸The woman thought, "If I can even touch his coat, that will be enough to heal me." ²⁹When she touched his coat, her bleeding stopped. She could feel in her body that she was healed.

³⁰At once Jesus felt power go out from him. So he stopped and turned around. Then he asked, "Who touched my clothes?"

³¹The followers said, "There are so many people pushing against you! And you ask, 'Who touched me?'"

³²But Jesus continued looking around to see who had touched him. ³³The woman knew that she was healed. So she came and bowed at Jesus' feet. Shaking with fear, she told him the whole story. ³⁴Jesus said to the woman, "Dear woman, you are made well because you believed. Go in peace. You will have no more suffering."

³⁵Jesus was still speaking to her when some men came from the house of Jairus, the synagogue ruler. The men said, "Your daughter is dead. There is now no need to bother the teacher."

³⁶But Jesus paid no attention to what the men said. He said to the synagogue ruler, "Don't be afraid; only believe."

³⁷Jesus let only Peter, James, and John the brother of James go with him to Jairus's house. ³⁸They came to the house of the synagogue ruler, and Jesus found many people there crying loudly. There was much confusion. ³⁹Jesus entered the house and said to the people, "Why are you crying and making so much noise? This child is not dead. She is only asleep." ⁴⁰But they only laughed at Jesus. He told all the people to leave. Then he went into the room where the child was. He took the child's father and mother and his three followers into the room with him. ⁴¹Then he took hold of the girl's hand and said to her, "Talitha, koum!" (This means, "Little girl, I tell you to stand up!") ⁴²The girl stood right up and began walking. (She was 12 years old.) The father and mother and the followers were amazed. ⁴³Jesus gave the father and mother strict orders not to tell people about this. Then he told them to give the girl some food.

Jesus Goes to His Home Town

6 Jesus left there and went back to his home town. His followers went with him. ²On the Sabbath*d* day he taught in the synagogue.*d* Many people heard him and were amazed. They said, "Where did this man get these teachings? What is this wisdom that has been given to him? And where did he get the power to work miracles?*d* ³He is only the carpenter. His mother is Mary. He is the brother of James, Joseph, Judas, and Simon. And his sisters are here with us." The people did not accept Jesus.

⁴Jesus said to them, "Other people give honour to a prophet.*d* But in his own town with his own people and in his own home, a prophet does not receive honour." ⁵Jesus was not able to work many miracles there. The only miracles he did were to heal some sick people by putting his hands on them.

[6]Jesus was amazed that they had no faith.

Then Jesus went to other villages in that area and taught. [7]He called the 12 followers together and sent them out in groups of two. He gave them authority over evil spirits. [8]This is what Jesus told them: "Take nothing for your trip except a walking stick. Take no bread, no bag, and no money in your pockets. [9]Wear sandals, and take only the clothes you are wearing. [10]When you enter a house, stay there until you leave that place. [11]If any town refuses to accept you or its people refuse to listen to you, then leave that town. Shake its dust off your feet.[n] This will be a warning to them."

[12]The followers went out and preached to the people to change their hearts and lives. [13]The followers forced many demons[d] out and poured olive oil on many sick people and healed them.

How John the Baptist Was Killed

[14]King Herod heard about Jesus, because Jesus was now well-known. Some people said, "He is John the Baptist.[d] He is risen from death. That is the reason he can work these miracles."[d]

[15]Others said, "He is Elijah."[n]

Other people said, "Jesus is a prophet.[d] He is like the prophets who lived long ago."

[16]Herod heard all these things about Jesus. He said, "I killed John by cutting off his head. Now he has been raised from death!"

[17]Herod himself had ordered his soldiers to arrest John, and John was put in prison. Herod did this to please his wife, Herodias. Herodias was the wife of Philip, Herod's brother. But then Herod married her. [18]John told Herod that it was not lawful for him to be married to his brother's wife. [19]So Herodias hated John and wanted to kill him. But she could not because of Herod. [20]Herod was afraid to kill John because he knew John was a good and holy man. So Herod protected John. Also, Herod enjoyed listening to John preach. But John's preaching always bothered him.

[21]Then the perfect time came for Herodias to cause John's death. It happened on Herod's birthday. Herod gave a dinner party for the most important government leaders, the commanders of his army, and the most important people in Galilee. [22]The daughter of Herodias came to the party and danced. When she danced, Herod and the people eating with him were very pleased.

So King Herod said to the girl, "I will give you anything you want." [23]He promised her, "Anything you ask for I will give to you. I will even give you half of my kingdom."

[24]The girl went to her mother and asked, "What should I ask the king to give me?"

Her mother answered, "Ask for the head of John the Baptist."[d]

[25]Quickly the girl went back to the king. She said to him, "Please give me the head of John the Baptist. Bring it to me now on a platter."

[26]The king was very sad. But he had promised to give the girl anything she wanted. And the people eating there with him had heard his promise. So Herod could not refuse what she asked. [27]Immediately the king sent a soldier to bring John's head. The soldier went and cut off John's head in the prison [28]and brought it back on a platter. He gave it to the girl, and the girl gave it to her mother. [29]John's followers heard about what happened. So they came and got John's body and put it in a tomb.

Shake . . . feet A warning. It showed that they had finished talking to these people.
Elijah A man who spoke for God. He lived hundreds of years before Christ.

More than 5,000 People Fed

[30]The apostles[d] that Jesus had sent out to preach returned. They gathered around him and told him about all the things they had done and taught. [31]Crowds of people were coming and going. Jesus and his followers did not even have time to eat. He said to them, "Come with me. We will go to a quiet place to be alone. There we will get some rest."

[32]So they went in a boat alone to a place where there were no people. [33]But many people saw them leave and recognised them. So people from all the towns ran to the place where Jesus was going. They got there before Jesus arrived. [34]When he landed, he saw a great crowd waiting. Jesus felt sorry for them, because they were like sheep without a shepherd. So he taught them many things.

[35]It was now late in the day. Jesus' followers came to him and said, "No one lives in this place. And it is already very late. [36]Send the people away. They need to go to the farms and towns around here to buy some food to eat."

[37]But Jesus answered, "You give them food to eat."

They said to him, "We can't buy enough bread to feed all these people! We would all have to work a month to earn enough money to buy that much bread!"

[38]Jesus asked them, "How many loaves of bread do you have now? Go and see."

When they found out, they came to him and said, "We have five loaves and two fish."

[39]Then Jesus said to the followers, "Tell all the people to sit in groups on the green grass." [40]So all the people sat in groups. They sat in groups of 50 or groups of 100. [41]Jesus took the five loaves and two fish. He looked up to heaven and thanked God for the bread. He divided the bread and gave it to his followers for them to give to the people. Then he divided the two fish among them all. [42]All the people ate and were satisfied. [43]The followers filled 12 baskets with the pieces of bread and fish that were not eaten. [44]There were about 5,000 men there who ate.

Jesus Walks on the Water

[45]Then Jesus told his followers to get into the boat and go to Bethsaida on the other side of the lake. Jesus said that he would come later. He stayed there to tell the people they could go home. [46]After sending them away, he went into the hills to pray.

[47]That night, the boat was in the middle of the lake. Jesus was alone on the land. [48]He saw the followers working hard to row the boat because the wind was blowing against them. At some time between three and six o'clock in the morning, Jesus came to them, walking on the water. He continued walking until he was almost past the boat. [49]But when his followers saw him walking on the water, they thought he was a ghost and cried out. [50]They all saw him and were terrified. But Jesus spoke to them and said, "Have courage! It is I! Do not be afraid." [51]Then he got into the boat with them. And the wind became calm. The followers were greatly amazed. [52]They had seen Jesus make more bread from the five loaves. But they did not understand what it meant. Their minds were closed.

[53]When they had crossed the lake, they came to shore at Gennesaret. They tied the boat there. [54]When they got out of the boat, the people saw Jesus and immediately recognised him. [55]They ran to tell others everywhere in that area that Jesus was there. They brought sick people on mats to every place Jesus went. [56]Jesus went into towns and cities and farms around that area. And everywhere he went, the people brought

the sick to the marketplaces. They begged him to let them just touch the edge of his coat. And all who touched him were healed.

Obey God's Law Not Men's

7 Some Pharisees[d] and some teachers of the law came from Jerusalem. They gathered around Jesus. [2]They saw that some of Jesus' followers ate food with hands that were not clean.[d] ("Not clean" means that they did not wash their hands in the way the Pharisees said people must. [3]The Pharisees and all the Jews never eat before washing their hands in this special way. They do this to follow the teaching given to them by their great people who lived before them. [4]And when the Jews buy something in the market, they never eat it until they have washed it in a special way. They also follow other rules of their great people who lived before them. They follow rules about the washing of cups, pitchers, and pots.)

[5]The Pharisees and the teachers of the law said to Jesus, "Your followers don't follow the rules given to us by our great people who lived before us. Your followers eat their food with hands that are not clean. Why do they do this?"

[6]Jesus answered, "You are all hypocrites![d] Isaiah was right when he spoke about you. Isaiah wrote,

'These people show honour to me
    with words.
But their hearts are far from
    me.
[7]Their worship of me is worthless.
The things they teach are
    nothing
but human rules they have
    memorised'.   *Isaiah 29:13*
[8]You have stopped following the commands of God. Now you only follow the teachings of men."

[9]Then Jesus said to them: "You think you are clever! You ignore the commands of God so that you can follow your own teachings! [10]Moses said, 'Honour your father and mother'.[n] Then Moses also said, 'Anyone who says cruel things to his father or mother must be put to death'.[n] [11]But you teach that a person can say to his father or mother, 'I have something I could use to help you. But I will not use it for you. I will give it to God'. [12]You are telling that person that he does not have to do anything for his father or mother. [13]So you are teaching that it is not important to do what God said. You think that it is more important to follow your own rules, which you teach people. And you do many things like that."

[14]Jesus called the people to him again. He said, "Every person should listen to me and understand what I am saying. [15]There is nothing a person puts into his body that makes him unclean. A person is made unclean by the things that come out of him." [16][n]

[17]When Jesus left the people and went inside, his followers asked him about this story. [18]Jesus said, "Do you still have trouble understanding? Surely you know that nothing that enters a man from the outside can make him unclean. [19]Food does not go into a person's mind. Food goes into his stomach. Then that food goes out of his body." (When Jesus said this, he meant that there is no food that is unclean for people to eat.)

[20]And Jesus said, "The things that come out of a man are the things that make him unclean. [21]All these evil things begin inside a person, in his mind: evil thoughts, sexual sins, stealing, murder, adultery,[d] [22]selfishness,

---

'Honour your father and mother'. Quotation from Exodus 20:12; Deuteronomy 5:16.
'Anyone . . . death'. Quotation from Exodus 21:17.
Verse 16 Some Greek copies add verse 16: "You people who hear me, listen!"

doing bad things to other people, lying, doing sinful things, jealousy, saying bad things about people, pride, and foolish living. [23]All these evil things come from within a person. These things make a person unclean."

Jesus Helps a Non-Jewish Woman

[24]Jesus left that place and went to the area around Tyre. He went into a house and did not want anyone to know he was there. But Jesus could not stay hidden. [25]A woman heard that he was there. Her little daughter had an evil spirit in her. So the woman quickly came to Jesus and fell at his feet. [26]She was not Jewish. She was Greek, born in Phoenicia, in Syria. She begged Jesus to force the demon[d] out of her daughter.

[27]Jesus told the woman: "It is not right to take the children's bread and give it to the dogs. First let the children eat all they want."

[28]She answered, "That is true, Lord. But the dogs under the table can eat the pieces of food that the children don't eat."

[29]Then Jesus said, "That is a very good answer. You may go. The demon has left your daughter."

[30]The woman went home and found her daughter lying in bed. The demon was gone.

Jesus Heals a Deaf Man

[31]Then Jesus left the area around Tyre. He went through Sidon to Lake Galilee, to the area of the Ten Towns.[n] [32]While he was there, some people brought a man to him. This man was deaf and could not talk. The people begged Jesus to put his hand on the man to heal him.

[33]Jesus led the man away from the crowd, to be alone with him. Jesus put his fingers in the man's ears. Then Jesus spat and touched the man's tongue. [34]Jesus looked up to heaven and took a deep breath. He said to the man, "Ephphatha!" (This means, "Be opened".) [35]When Jesus did this, the man was able to hear. He was also able to use his tongue, and he spoke clearly.

[36]Jesus commanded the people not to tell anyone about what happened. But the more he commanded them, the more they told about it. [37]They were really amazed. They said, "Jesus does everything well. He makes the deaf hear! And those who can't talk—Jesus makes them able to speak."

More than 4,000 People Fed

8 Another time there was a great crowd with Jesus. They had nothing to eat. So Jesus called his followers to him. He said, [2]"I feel sorry for these people. They have been with me for three days, and now they have nothing to eat. [3]I cannot send them home hungry. If they leave without eating, they will faint on the way home. Some of them live a long way from here."

[4]Jesus' followers answered, "But we are far away from any towns. Where can we get enough bread to feed all these people?"

[5]Jesus asked, "How many loaves of bread do you have?"

They answered, "We have seven loaves."

[6]Jesus told the people to sit on the ground. Then he took the seven loaves and gave thanks to God. Jesus divided the bread and gave the pieces to his followers. He told them to pass out the bread to the people, and they did so. [7]The followers also had a few small fish. Jesus gave thanks for the fish and told his followers to give the fish to the people. [8]All the people ate

---

Ten Towns In Greek, called "Decapolis". It was an area east of Lake Galilee that once had ten main towns.

and were satisfied. Then the followers filled seven baskets with the pieces of food that were not eaten. [9]There were about 4,000 men who ate. After they had eaten, Jesus told them to go home. [10]Then he went in a boat with his followers to the area of Dalmanutha.

The Leaders Ask for a Miracle

[11]The Pharisees[d] came to Jesus and asked him questions. They wanted to trap him. So they asked Jesus to do a miracle[d] to show that he was from God. [12]Jesus sighed deeply. He said, "Why do you people ask for a miracle as proof? I tell you the truth. No miracle will be given to you." [13]Then Jesus left the Pharisees. He went in the boat to the other side of the lake.

Guard Against Wrong Teachings

[14]The followers had only one loaf of bread with them in the boat. They had forgotten to bring more bread. [15]Jesus warned them, "Be careful! Guard against the yeast of the Pharisees[d] and the yeast of Herod."

[16]Among themselves, his disciples discussed the meaning of this. They said, "He said this because we have no bread."

[17]Jesus knew what his followers were talking about. So he asked them, "Why are you talking about having no bread? You still don't see or understand? Are your minds closed? [18]You have eyes, but you don't really see. You have ears, but you don't really listen. Remember what I did before, when we did not have enough bread? [19]I divided five loaves of bread for 5,000 people. Remember how many baskets you filled with pieces of food that were not eaten?"

They answered, "We filled 12 baskets."

[20]"And remember that I divided seven loaves of bread for 4,000 peo-

ple. Remember how many baskets you filled with pieces of food that were not eaten?"

They answered, "We filled seven baskets."

[21]Then Jesus said to them, "You remember these things I did, but you still don't understand?"

Jesus Heals a Blind Man

[22]Jesus and his followers came to Bethsaida. Some people brought a blind man to Jesus and begged him to touch the man. [23]So Jesus took the blind man's hand and led him out of the village. Then he spat on the man's eyes. He put his hands on the blind man and asked, "Can you see now?"

[24]The man looked up and said, "Yes, I see people, but they look like trees walking around."

[25]Again Jesus put his hands on the man's eyes. Then the man opened his eyes wide. His eyes were healed, and he was able to see everything clearly. [26]Jesus told him to go home, saying, "Don't go into the town."

Peter Says Jesus Is the Christ

[27]Jesus and his followers went to the towns around Caesarea Philippi. While they were travelling, Jesus asked them, "Who do people say I am?"

[28]They answered, "Some people say you are John the Baptist.[d] Others say you are Elijah.[n] And others say that you are one of the prophets."[d]

[29]Then Jesus asked, "Who do you say I am?"

Peter answered, "You are the Christ."[d]

[30]Jesus ordered his followers, "Don't tell anyone who I am."

[31]Then Jesus began to teach them that the Son of Man[d] must suffer many things. He taught that the Son of Man would not be accepted by the older Jewish leaders, the leading priests,

Elijah A man who spoke for God. He lived hundreds of years before Christ.

and the teachers of the law. He taught that the Son of Man must be killed and then rise from death after three days. [32]Jesus told them plainly what would happen. Then Peter took Jesus aside and began to criticise him. [33]But Jesus turned and looked at his followers. Then he criticised Peter and said, "Go away from me, Satan![n] You don't care about the things of God. You care only about things men think are important."

[34]Then Jesus called the crowd to him, along with his followers. He said, "If anyone wants to follow me, he must say 'no' to the things he wants. He must be willing to die on a cross, and he must follow me. [35]Whoever wants to save his life will give up true life. But whoever gives up his life for me and for the Good News[d] will have true life for ever. [36]It is worth nothing for a person to have the whole world, if he loses his soul. [37]A person could never pay enough to buy back his soul. [38]The people who live now are living in a sinful and evil time. If anyone is ashamed of me and my teaching, then I will be ashamed of him. I will be ashamed of him when I come with the glory of my Father and the holy angels."

9 Then Jesus said to the people, "I tell you the truth. Some of you standing here will see the kingdom of God come with power before you die."

Jesus with Moses and Elijah

[2]Six days later Jesus took Peter, James, and John and went up on a high mountain. They were all alone there. While these followers watched, Jesus was changed. [3]His clothes became shining white, whiter than any person could make them. [4]Then two men appeared, talking with Jesus. The men were Moses and Elijah.[n]

[5]Peter said to Jesus, "Teacher, it is good that we are here. We will put three tents here—one for you, one for Moses, and one for Elijah." [6]Peter did not know what to say, because he and the others were so frightened.

[7]Then a cloud came and covered them. A voice came from the cloud. The voice said, "This is my Son, and I love him. Obey him!"

[8]Then Peter, James, and John looked around, but they saw only Jesus there alone with them.

[9]As Jesus and his followers were walking back down the mountain, he commanded them, "Don't tell anyone about the things you saw on the mountain. Wait till the Son of Man[d] rises from death. Then you may tell."

[10]So the followers obeyed Jesus and said nothing about what they had seen. But they discussed what Jesus meant about rising from death.

[11]They asked Jesus, "Why do the teachers of the law say that Elijah must come first?"

[12]Jesus answered, "They are right to say that Elijah must come first. Elijah makes all things the way they should be. But why does the Scripture[d] say that the Son of Man will suffer much and that people will treat him as if he were nothing? [13]I tell you that Elijah has already come. And people did to him whatever they wanted to do. The Scriptures said this would happen to him."

Jesus Heals a Sick Boy

[14]Then Jesus, Peter, James, and John went to the other followers. They saw a great crowd around them. The teachers of the law were arguing with them. [15]But when the crowd saw

---

Satan Name for the devil meaning "the enemy". Jesus means that Peter was talking like Satan.
Moses and Elijah Two of the most important Jewish leaders in the past.

Jesus, they were surprised and ran to welcome him.

[16]Jesus asked, "What are you arguing about with the teachers of the law?"

[17]A man answered, "Teacher, I brought my son to you. He has a spirit from the devil in him. This spirit stops him from talking. [18]The spirit attacks him and throws him on the ground. My son foams at the mouth, grinds his teeth, and becomes very stiff. I asked your followers to force the evil spirit out, but they couldn't."

[19]Jesus answered, "You people don't believe! How long must I stay with you? How long must I go on being patient with you? Bring the boy to me!"

[20]So the followers brought him to Jesus. As soon as the evil spirit saw Jesus, it attacked the boy. He fell down and rolled on the ground, foaming from his mouth.

[21]Jesus asked the boy's father, "How long has this been happening?"

The father answered, "Since he was very young. [22]The spirit often throws him into a fire or into water to kill him. If you can do anything for him, please have pity on us and help us."

[23]Jesus said to the father, "You said, 'If you can!' All things are possible for him who believes."

[24]Immediately the father cried out, "I do believe! Help me to believe more!"

[25]Jesus saw that a crowd was running there to see what was happening. So he spoke to the evil spirit, saying, "You deaf and dumb spirit—I command you to come out of this boy and never enter him again!"

[26]The evil spirit screamed and caused the boy to fall on the ground again. Then the spirit came out. The boy looked as if he were dead. And many people said, "He is dead!" [27]But Jesus took hold of the boy's hand and helped him to stand up.

[28]Jesus went into the house. His followers were alone with him there. They said, "Why couldn't we force that evil spirit out?"

[29]Jesus answered, "That kind of spirit can only be forced out by prayer."

Jesus Talks About His Death

[30]Then Jesus and his followers left that place and went through Galilee. Jesus did not want anyone to know where he was [31]because he wanted to teach his followers alone. He said to them, "The Son of Man[d] will be given to men who will kill him. After three days, he will rise from death." [32]But the followers did not understand what Jesus meant. And they were afraid to ask.

Who Is the Greatest?

[33]Jesus and his followers went to Capernaum and went into a house there. Then Jesus said to them, "What were you arguing about on the road?" [34]But the followers did not answer, because their argument on the road was about which one of them was the greatest.

[35]Jesus sat down and called the 12 apostles[d] to him. He said, "If anyone wants to be the most important, then he must be last of all and servant of all."

[36]Then Jesus took a small child and had him stand among them. He took the child in his arms and said, [37]"If anyone accepts children like these in my name, then he is also accepting me. And if he accepts me, then he is also accepting the One who sent me."

Anyone Not Against Us Is For Us

[38]Then John said, "Teacher, we saw a man using your name to force demons[d] out of a person. We told him to stop, because he does not belong to our group."

[39]Jesus said, "Don't stop him. Anyone who uses my name to do powerful

things will not say evil things about me. [40]He who is not against us is with us. [41]I tell you the truth. If anyone helps you by giving you a drink of water because you belong to the Christ,[d] then he will truly get his reward.

[42]"If one of these little children believes in me, and someone causes that child to sin, then it will be very bad for him. It would be better for him to have a large stone tied around his neck and be drowned in the sea. [43]If your hand causes you to sin, cut it off. It is better for you to lose part of your body but have life for ever. That is much better than to have two hands and go to hell. In that place the fire never goes out. [44] n [45]If your foot causes you to sin, cut it off. It is better for you to lose part of your body but have life for ever. That is much better than to have two feet and be thrown into hell. [46] n [47]If your eye causes you to sin, take it out. It is better for you to have only one eye but have life for ever. That is much better than to have two eyes and be thrown into hell. [48]In hell the worm does not die; the fire is never stopped. [49]Every person will be salted with fire.

[50]"Salt is good. But if the salt loses its salty taste, then you cannot make it salty again. So, be full of goodness. And have peace with each other."

Jesus Teaches About Divorce

10 Then Jesus left that place. He went into the area of Judea and across the Jordan River. Again, crowds came to him. And Jesus taught them as he always did.

[2]Some Pharisees[d] came to Jesus and tried to trick him. They asked, "Is it right for a man to divorce his wife?"

[3]Jesus answered, "What did Moses command you to do?"

[4]They said, "Moses allowed a man to write out divorce papers and send her away."[n]

[5]Jesus said, "Moses wrote that command for you because you refused to accept God's teaching. [6]But when God made the world, 'he made them male and female'.[n] [7]So a man will leave his father and mother and be united with his wife. [8]And the two people will become one body'.[n] So the people are not two, but one. [9]God has joined the two people together. So no one should separate them."

[10]Later, the followers and Jesus were in the house. They asked Jesus again about the question of divorce. [11]He answered, "Anyone who divorces his wife and marries another woman is guilty of adultery[d] against her. [12]And the woman who divorces her husband and marries another man is also guilty of adultery."

Jesus Accepts Children

[13]Some people brought their small children to Jesus so he could touch them. But his followers told the people to stop bringing their children to him. [14]When Jesus saw this, he was displeased. He said to them, "Let the little children come to me. Don't stop them. The kingdom of God belongs to people who are like these little children. [15]I tell you the truth. You must accept the kingdom of God as a little child accepts things, or you will never enter it." [16]Then Jesus took the children in his arms. He put his hands on them and blessed them.

A Rich Young Man's Question

[17]Jesus started to leave, but a man

Verse 44 Some Greek copies of Mark add verse 44, which is the same as verse 48.
Verse 46 Some Greek copies of Mark add verse 46, which is the same as verse 48.
"Moses . . . away." Quotation from Deuteronomy 24:1.
'he made . . . female'. Quotation from Genesis 1:27.
'So . . . body'. Quotation from Genesis 2:24.

ran to him and fell on his knees before Jesus. The man asked, "Good teacher, what must I do to get the life that never ends?"

18Jesus answered, "Why do you call me good? No one is good except God alone. 19You know the commands: 'You must not murder anyone. You must not be guilty of adultery.d You must not steal. You must not tell lies about your neighbour in court. You must not cheat. Honour your father and mother'. "u

20The man said, "Teacher, I have obeyed all these commands since I was a boy."

21Jesus looked straight at the man and loved him. Jesus said, "There is still one more thing you need to do. Go and sell everything you have, and give the money to the poor. You will have a reward in heaven. Then come and follow me."

22He was very sad to hear Jesus say this, and he left. The man was sad because he was very rich.

23Then Jesus looked at his followers and said, "How hard it will be for those who are rich to enter the kingdom of God!"

24The followers were amazed at what Jesus said. But he said again, "My children, it is very hard to enter the kingdom of God! 25And it will be very hard for a rich person to enter the kingdom of God. It would be easier for a camel to go through the eye of a needle!"

26The followers were even more amazed and said to each other, "Then who can be saved?"

27Jesus looked straight at them and said, "This is something that men cannot do. But God can do it. God can do all things."

28Peter said to Jesus, "We left everything to follow you!"

29Jesus said, "I tell you the truth. Everyone who has left his home,

brothers, sisters, mother, father, children, or fields for me and for the Good Newsd 30will get a hundred times more than he left. Here in this world he will have more homes, brothers, sisters, mothers, children, and fields. And with those things, he will also suffer for his belief. But in the age that is coming he will have life for ever. 31Many who have the highest place now will have the lowest place in the future. And those who have the lowest place now will have the highest place in the future."

Jesus Talks About His Own Death

32Jesus and the people with him were on the road to Jerusalem. Jesus was leading the way. The followers were amazed, but those who followed behind them were afraid. Jesus took the 12 apostlesd aside and talked with them alone. He told them what would happen in Jerusalem. 33He said, "We are going to Jerusalem. The Son of Mand will be given to the leading priests and teachers of the law. They will say that he must die. They will give him to the non-Jewish people, 34who will laugh at him and spit on him. They will beat him with whips and kill him. But on the third day after his death, he will rise to life again."

Two Followers Ask Jesus a Favour

35Then James and John, sons of Zebedee, came to Jesus. They said, "Teacher, we want to ask you to do something for us."

36Jesus asked, "What do you want me to do for you?"

37They answered, "You will have glory in your kingdom. Let one of us sit at your right, and let one of us sit at your left."

38Jesus said, "You don't understand what you are asking. Can you drink

'You . . . mother'. Quotation from Exodus 20:12-16; Deuteronomy 5:16-20.

the cup that I must drink? And can you be baptised with the same kind of baptism that I must have?"[n]

[39]They answered, "Yes, we can!"

Jesus said to them, "You will drink the same cup that I will drink. And you will be baptised with the same baptism that I must have. [40]But I cannot choose who will sit at my right or my left. These places are for those for whom they are prepared."

[41]The ten followers heard this. They began to be angry with James and John.

[42]Jesus called all the followers together. He said, "The non-Jewish people have men they call rulers. You know that those rulers love to show their power over the people. And their important leaders love to use all their authority. [43]But it should not be that way among you. If one of you wants to become great, then he must serve you like a servant. [44]If one of you wants to become the most important, then he must serve all of you like a slave. [45]In the same way, the Son of Man[d] did not come to be served. He came to serve. The Son of Man came to give his life to save many people."

Jesus Heals a Blind Man

[46]Then they came to the town of Jericho. As Jesus was leaving there with his followers and a large crowd, a blind beggar named Bartimaeus (son of Timaeus) was sitting by the road. [47]He heard that Jesus from Nazareth was walking by. The blind man cried out, "Jesus, Son of David,[d] please help me!"

[48]Many people scolded the blind man and told him to be quiet. But he shouted more and more, "Son of David, please help me!"

[49]Jesus stopped and said, "Tell the man to come here."

So they called the blind man. They said, "Cheer up! Get to your feet. Jesus is calling you." [50]The blind man stood up quickly. He left his coat there and went to Jesus.

[51]Jesus asked him, "What do you want me to do for you?"

The blind man answered, "Teacher, I want to see again."

[52]Jesus said, "Go. You are healed because you believed." At once the man was able to see again, and he followed Jesus on the road.

Jesus Enters Jerusalem as a King

11 Jesus and his followers were coming closer to Jerusalem. They came to the towns of Bethphage and Bethany near the Mount of Olives.[d] There Jesus sent two of his followers. [2]He said to them, "Go to the town you see there. When you enter it, you will find a colt tied which no one has ever ridden. Untie it and bring it here to me. [3]If anyone asks you why you are doing this, tell him, 'The Master needs the colt. He will send it back soon'."

[4]The followers went into the town. They found a colt tied in the street near the door of a house, and they untied it. [5]Some people were standing there and asked, "What are you doing? Why are you untying that colt?" [6]The followers answered the way Jesus told them to answer, and the people let them take the colt.

[7]The followers brought the colt to Jesus. They put their coats on the colt, and Jesus sat on it. [8]Many people spread their coats on the road. Others cut branches in the fields and spread the branches on the road. [9]Some of the people were walking ahead of Jesus. Others were following him. All of them were shouting,

---

Can you . . . have? Jesus was asking if they could suffer the same terrible things that would happen to him.

"Praise[n] God!
God bless the One who comes in
the name of the Lord!
Psalm 118:26

[10]God bless the kingdom of our
father David!
That kingdom is coming!
Praise to God in heaven!"

[11]Jesus entered Jerusalem and went
into the Temple.[d] When he had looked
at everything, and since it was already
late, he went out to Bethany with the
12 apostles.[d]

[12]The next day as Jesus was leaving
Bethany, he was hungry. [13]He saw a
fig tree in leaf. So he went to the tree
to see if it had any figs on it. But he
found no figs, only leaves. It was not
the right season for figs to grow. [14]So
Jesus said to the tree, "May no one
ever eat fruit from you again." Jesus'
followers heard him say this.

Jesus Goes to the Temple

[15]Jesus returned to Jerusalem and
went into the Temple.[d] He began to
throw out those who were buying and
selling things there. He overturned
the tables that belonged to the men
who were exchanging different kinds
of money. And he turned over the
benches of the men who were selling
doves. [16]Jesus refused to allow anyone to carry goods through the Temple courts. [17]Then Jesus taught the
people. He said, "It is written in the
Scriptures,[d] 'My Temple will be a
house where people from all nations
will pray'.[n] But you are changing
God's house into a 'hideout for robbers'."[n]

[18]The leading priests and the teachers of the law heard all this. They began trying to find a way to kill Jesus.

They were afraid of him because all
the people were amazed at his teaching. [19]That night, Jesus and his followers left the city.

The Power of Faith

[20]The next morning, Jesus was
passing by with his followers. They
saw the fig tree, and it was dry and
dead, even to the roots. [21]Peter remembered the tree and said to Jesus,
"Teacher, look! Yesterday, you
cursed the fig tree. Now it is dry and
dead!"

[22]Jesus answered, "Have faith in
God. [23]I tell you the truth. You can
say to this mountain, 'Go, mountain,
fall into the sea'. And if you have no
doubts in your mind and believe that
the thing you say will happen, then
God will do it for you. [24]So I tell you
to ask for things in prayer. And if you
believe that you have received those
things, then they will be yours.
[25]When you are praying, and you remember that you are angry with another person about something, then
forgive him. If you do this, then your
Father in heaven will also forgive your
sins." [26][n]

Leaders Doubt Jesus' Authority

[27]Jesus and his followers went again
to Jerusalem. Jesus was walking in the
Temple.[d] The leading priests, the
teachers of the law, and the older Jewish leaders came to him. [28]They said
to him, "Tell us! What authority do
you have to do these things? Who
gave you this authority?"

[29]Jesus answered, "I will ask you
one question. You answer it. Then I
will tell you whose authority I use to
do these things. [30]Tell me: when John

Praise Literally, "Hosanna", a Hebrew word used at first in praying to God for help, but at
this time it was probably a shout of joy used in praising God or his Messiah.
'My Temple . . . pray'. Quotation from Isaiah 56:7.
'hideout for robbers'. Quotation from Jeremiah 7:11.
Verse 26 Some early Greek copies add verse 26: "But if you don't forgive other people, then
your Father in heaven will not forgive your sins."

baptised people, was that from God or from man? Answer me!"

[31]They argued about Jesus' question. They said to each other, "If we answer, 'John's baptism was from God', then Jesus will say, 'Then why didn't you believe John?' [32]But if we say, 'From man', then the people will be against us." (These leaders were afraid of the people. All the people believed that John was a prophet.[d])

[33]So the leaders answered Jesus, "We don't know."

Jesus said, "Then I will not tell you what authority I use to do these things."

God Sends His Son

12 Jesus used stories to teach the people. He said, "A man planted a vineyard. He put a wall around it and dug a hole for a winepress.[d] Then he built a tower. He leased the vineyard to some farmers and left for a trip. [2]Later, it was time for the grapes to be picked. So the man sent a servant to the farmers to get his share of the grapes. [3]But the farmers grabbed the servant and beat him. They sent him away with nothing. [4]Then the man sent another servant. They hit him on the head and showed no respect for him. [5]So the man sent another servant. They killed this servant. The man sent many other servants. The farmers beat some of them and killed others.

[6]"The man had one person left to send, his son whom he loved. He sent him last of all, saying, 'The farmers will respect my son'.

[7]"But they said to each other, 'This is the owner's son. This vineyard will be his. If we kill him, then it will be ours'. [8]So they took the son, killed him, and threw him out of the vineyard.

[9]"So what will the man who owns the vineyard do? He will go to the vineyard and kill those farmers. Then he will give the vineyard to other farmers. [10]Surely you have read this Scripture:[d]

'The stone that the builders did
    not want
    became the cornerstone.[d]
[11]The Lord did this,
    and it is wonderful to us'."

                                    Psalm 118:22-23

[12]The Jewish leaders knew that the story was about them. So they wanted to find a way to arrest Jesus, but they were afraid of the people. So the leaders left him and went away.

The Leaders Try to Trap Jesus

[13]Later, the Jewish leaders sent some Pharisees[d] and some men from the group called Herodians[n] to Jesus. They wanted to catch Jesus saying something wrong. [14]They came to him and said, "Teacher, we know that you are an honest man. You are not afraid of what other people think about you. All men are the same to you. And you teach the truth about God's way. Tell us: is it right to pay taxes to Caesar?[d] Should we pay them, or not?"

[15]But Jesus knew what these men were really trying to do. He said, "Why are you trying to trap me? Bring me a silver coin. Let me see it." [16]They gave Jesus a coin, and he asked, "Whose picture is on the coin? And whose name is written on it?"

They answered, "Caesar's."

[17]Then Jesus said to them, "Give to Caesar the things that are Caesar's. And give to God the things that are God's." The men were amazed at what Jesus said.

Sadducees Try to Trick Jesus

[18]Then some Sadducees[d] came to Jesus. (Sadducees believe that no person will rise from death.) The Sadducees asked Jesus a question. [19]They said, "Teacher, Moses wrote that a

Herodians A political group that followed Herod and his family.

man's brother might die. He leaves a wife but no children. Then that man must marry the widow and have children for the dead brother. [20]There were seven brothers. The first brother married but died. He had no children. [21]So the second brother married the widow. But he also died and had no children. The same thing happened with the third brother. [22]All seven brothers married her and died. None of the brothers had any children. The woman was last to die. [23]But all seven brothers had married her. So at the time people rise from death, whose wife will the woman be?"

[24]Jesus answered, "Why did you make this mistake? Is it because you don't know what the Scriptures[d] say? Or is it because you don't know about the power of God? [25]When people rise from death, there will be no marriage. People will not be married to each other but will be like angels in heaven. [26]Surely you have read what God said about people rising from death. In the book in which Moses wrote about the burning bush,[n] it says that God told Moses this: 'I am the God of Abraham, the God of Isaac, and the God of Jacob'.[n] [27]God is the God of living people, not dead people. You Sadducees are wrong!"

The Most Important Command

[28]One of the teachers of the law came to Jesus. He heard Jesus arguing with the Sadducees[d] and the Pharisees.[d] He saw that Jesus gave good answers to their questions. So he asked Jesus, "Which of the commands is most important?"

[29]Jesus answered, "The most important command is this: 'Listen, people of Israel! The Lord our God, he is the only Lord. [30]Love the Lord your God. Love him with all your heart, all your soul, all your mind, and all your strength'.[n] [31]The second most important command is this: 'Love your neighbour as you love yourself'.[n] These two commands are the most important commands."

[32]The man answered, "That was a good answer, Teacher. You were right when you said these things. God is the only Lord, and there is no other God besides him. [33]A person must love God with all his heart, all his mind, and all his strength. And he must love his neighbour as he loves himself. These commands are more important than all the animals and sacrifices we offer to God."

[34]Jesus saw that the man answered him wisely. So Jesus said to him, "You are close to the kingdom of God." And after that, no one was brave enough to ask Jesus any more questions.

[35]Jesus was teaching in the Temple.[d] He asked, "Why do the teachers of the law say that the Christ[d] is the son of David? [36]David himself, speaking by the Holy Spirit,[d] said:

'The Lord said to my Lord:
　Sit by me at my right side,
　until I put your enemies under
　　your control'.　　　*Psalm 110:1*

[37]David himself calls the Christ 'Lord'. So how can the Christ be David's son?" The large crowd listened to Jesus with pleasure.

[38]Jesus continued teaching. He said, "Beware of the teachers of the law. They like to walk around wearing clothes that look important. And they love people to show respect to them in the marketplaces. [39]They love to have the most important seats in the synagogues.[d] And they love to have the most important seats at the feasts. [40]They cheat widows and steal

---

burning bush Read Exodus 3:1-12 in the Old Testament.
'I am . . . Jacob'. Quotation from Exodus 3:6.
'Listen . . . strength'. Quotation from Deuteronomy 6:4-5.
'Love . . . yourself'. Quotation from Leviticus 19:18.

their homes. Then they try to make themselves look good by saying long prayers. God will punish these people terribly."

True Giving

41Jesus sat near the Temple[d] money box where people put their gifts. He watched the people put in their money. Many rich people gave large sums of money. 42Then a poor widow came and gave two very small copper coins. These coins were not worth even a penny.

43Jesus called his followers to him. He said, "I tell you the truth. This poor widow gave only two small coins. But she really gave more than all those rich people. 44The rich have plenty; they gave only what they did not need. This woman is very poor, but she gave all she had. And she needed that money to help her live."

The Temple Will Be Destroyed

13 Jesus was leaving the Temple.[d] One of his followers said to him, "Look, Teacher! This Temple has beautiful buildings with very big stones."

2Jesus said, "Do you see all these great buildings? Every stone will be thrown to the ground. Not one stone will be left on another."

3Later, Jesus was sitting on the Mount of Olives.[d] He was alone with Peter, James, John, and Andrew. They could all see the Temple. They asked Jesus, 4"Tell us, when will all these things happen? And what will show us that the time has come for them to happen?"

5Jesus said to them: "Be careful that no one fools you. 6Many people will come and use my name. They will say, 'I am the One'. And they will fool many. 7You will hear about wars and stories of wars that are coming. But don't be afraid. These things must happen before the end comes. 8Nations will fight against other nations. Kingdoms will fight against other kingdoms. There will be times when there is no food for people to eat. And there will be earthquakes in different places. These things are like the first pains when something new is about to be born.

9"You must be careful. People will arrest you and take you to court. They will beat you in their synagogues.[d] You will be forced to stand before kings and governors, to tell them about me. This will happen to you because you follow me. 10But before these things happen, the Good News[d] must be told to all people. 11When you are arrested and judged, don't worry about what you should say. Say the things God gives you to say at that time. It will not really be you speaking. It will be the Holy Spirit.[d]

12"Brothers will turn against their own brothers and give them over to be killed. Fathers will turn against their own children and give them over to be killed. Children will fight against their own parents and cause their parents to be killed. 13All people will hate you because you follow me. But the person who continues to be strong until the end will be saved.

14"You will see 'the horrible thing that destroys'.[n] You will see this thing standing in the place where it should not be." (You who read this should understand what it means.) "At that time, the people in Judea should run away to the mountains. 15If a person is on the roof[n] of his house, he must not go down to take anything

---

'**horrible . . . destroys.'** Mentioned in Daniel 9:27; 12:11 (cf. Daniel 11:31).
roof In Bible times houses were built with flat roofs. The roof was used for drying things such as flax and fruit. It was also used as an extra room, as a place for worship and as a place to sleep in the summer.

out of his house. [16]If a person is in the field, he must not go back to get his coat. [17]At that time, it will be hard for women who are pregnant or have nursing babies. [18]Pray that these things will not happen in winter. [19]This is because those days will be full of trouble. There will be more trouble than there has ever been since the beginning, when God made the world. And nothing as bad will ever happen again. [20]God has decided to make that terrible time short. If that time were not made short, then no one would go on living. But God will make that time short to help his special people whom he has chosen. [21]At that time, someone might say to you, 'Look, there is the Christ!'[d] Or another person might say, 'There he is!' But don't believe them. [22]False Christs and false prophets[d] will come and perform great wonders and miracles.[d] They will do these things to the people God has chosen. They will do these things to try to fool them, if that is possible. [23]So be careful. For I have warned you about all this before it happens.

[24]"During the days after this trouble comes,

'The sun will grow dark.
And the moon will not give its
        light.
[25]The stars will fall from the sky.
And everything in the sky will
        be changed'.   *Isaiah 13:10; 34:4*

[26]"Then people will see the Son of Man[d] coming in clouds with great power and glory. [27]The Son of Man will send his angels all around the earth. They will gather his chosen people from every part of the earth.

[28]"The fig tree teaches us a lesson: when its branches become green and soft, and new leaves begin to grow, then you know that summer is near. [29]So also when you see all these things happening, then you will know that the time is near, ready to come. [30]I tell you the truth. All these things

will happen while the people of this time are still living. [31]The whole world, earth and sky, will be destroyed, but the words I have said will never be destroyed.

[32]"No one knows when that day or time will be. The Son and the angels in heaven don't know. Only the Father knows. [33]Be careful! Always be ready! You don't know when that time will be. [34]It is like a man who goes on a trip. He leaves his house and lets his servants take care of it. He gives each servant a special job to do. One servant has the work of guarding the door. The man tells this servant always to be watchful. This is what I am now telling you. [35]You must always be ready. You don't know when the owner of the house will come back. He might come in the evening, or at midnight, or in the early morning, or when the sun rises. [36]He might come back quickly. If you are always ready, then he will not find you sleeping. [37]I tell you this, and I say this to everyone: 'Be ready!' "

The Plan to Kill Jesus

14 It was now only two days before the Passover[d] and the Feast[d] of Unleavened Bread. The leading priests and teachers of the law were trying to find a way to use some trick to arrest Jesus and kill him. [2]But they said, "We must not do it during the feast. The people might cause a riot."

A Woman with Perfume for Jesus

[3]Jesus was in Bethany. He was at dinner in the house of Simon, who had a harmful skin disease. While Jesus was there, a woman came to him. She had an alabaster[d] jar filled with very expensive perfume, made of pure nard.[d] The woman opened the jar and poured the perfume on Jesus' head.

[4]Some of those who were there saw this and became angry. They complained to each other, saying, "Why

waste that perfume? [5]It was worth a full year's work. It could be sold, and the money could be given to the poor." They spoke to the woman sharply.

[6]Jesus said, "Don't bother the woman. Why are you troubling her? She did a beautiful thing for me. [7]You will always have the poor with you. You can help them whenever you want. But you will not always have me. [8]This woman did the only thing she could do for me. She poured perfume on my body. She did this before I die to prepare me for burial. [9]I tell you the truth. The Good News[d] will be told to people in all the world. And in every place it is preached, what this woman has done will be told. And people will remember her."

Judas Becomes an Enemy of Jesus

[10]One of the 12 followers, Judas Iscariot, went to talk to the leading priests. Judas offered to give Jesus to them. [11]The leading priests were pleased about this. They promised to pay Judas money. So he waited for the best time to give Jesus to them.

Jesus Eats the Passover Feast

[12]It was now the first day of the Feast[d] of Unleavened Bread. This was a time when the Jews always sacrificed the Passover[d] lambs. Jesus' followers came to him. They said, "We will go and prepare everything for the Passover Feast. Where do you want to eat the feast?"

[13]Jesus sent two of his followers and said to them, "Go into the city. A man carrying a jar of water will meet you. Follow him. [14]He will go into a house. Tell the owner of the house, 'The Teacher asks that you show us the room where he and his followers can eat the Passover Feast'. [15]The owner will show you a large room upstairs.

This room is ready. Prepare the food for us there."

[16]So the followers left and went into the city. Everything happened as Jesus had said. So they prepared the Passover Feast.

[17]In the evening, Jesus went to that house with the 12. [18]While they were all eating, Jesus said, "I tell you the truth. One of you will give me to my enemies — one of you eating with me now."

[19]The followers were very sad to hear this. Each one said to Jesus, "I am not the one, am I?"

[20]Jesus answered, "The man who is against me is one of the 12. He is the one who dips his bread into the bowl with me. [21]The Son of Man[d] must go and die. The Scriptures[d] say this will happen. But how terrible it will be for the person who gives the Son of Man to be killed. It would be better for that person if he had never been born."

The Lord's Supper

[22]While they were eating, Jesus took some bread. He thanked God for it and broke it. Then he gave it to his followers and said, "Take it. This bread is my body."

[23]Then Jesus took a cup. He thanked God for it and gave it to the followers. All the followers drank from the cup.

[24]Then Jesus said, "This is my blood which begins the new agreement that God makes with his people. This blood is poured out for many. [25]I tell you the truth. I will not drink of this fruit of the vine[n] again until that day when I drink it new in the kingdom of God."

[26]They sang a hymn and went out to the Mount of Olives.[d]

Jesus' Followers Will All Leave Him

[27]Then Jesus told the followers,

---

fruit of the vine Product of the grapevine; this may also be translated "wine".

"You will all lose your faith in me. It is written in the Scriptures:[d]

'I will kill the shepherd,
and the sheep will scatter'.

Zechariah 13:7

28But after I rise from death, I will go ahead of you into Galilee."

29Peter said, "All the other followers may lose their faith. But I will not."

30Jesus answered, "I tell you the truth. Tonight you will say you don't know me. You will say this three times before the cock crows twice."

31But Peter answered strongly, "I will never say that I don't know you! I will even die with you!" And all the other followers said the same thing.

Jesus Prays Alone

32Jesus and his followers went to a place called Gethsemane. He said to his followers, "Sit here while I pray." 33Jesus told Peter, James, and John to come with him. Then Jesus began to be very sad and troubled. 34He said to them, "I am full of sorrow. My heart is breaking with sadness. Stay here and watch."

35Jesus walked a little further away from them. Then he fell on the ground and prayed. He prayed that, if possible, he would not have this time of suffering. 36He prayed, "Abba,[n] Father! You can do all things. Let me not have this cup[n] of suffering. But do what you want, not what I want."

37Then Jesus went back to his followers. He found them asleep. He said to Peter, "Simon, why are you sleeping? You could not stay awake with me for one hour? 38Stay awake and pray that you will not be tempted. Your spirit wants to do what is right, but your body is weak."

39Again Jesus went away and prayed the same thing. 40Then he went back to the followers. Again he found them asleep because their eyes were very heavy. And they did not know what to say to Jesus.

41After Jesus prayed a third time, he went back to his followers. He said to them, "You are still sleeping and resting? That's enough! The time has come for the Son of Man[d] to be given to sinful people. 42Get up! We must go. Here comes the man who has turned against me."

Jesus Is Arrested

43While Jesus was still speaking, Judas came up. Judas was one of the 12 followers. He had many people with him. They were sent from the leading priests, the teachers of the law, and the older Jewish leaders. Those with Judas had swords and clubs.

44Judas had planned a signal for them. He had said, "The man I kiss is Jesus. Arrest him and guard him while you lead him away." 45So Judas went to Jesus and said, "Teacher!" and kissed him. 46Then the men grabbed Jesus and arrested him. 47One of the followers standing near drew his sword. He struck the servant of the high priest with the sword and cut off his ear.

48Then Jesus said, "You came to get me with swords and clubs as if I were a criminal. 49Every day I was with you teaching in the Temple.[d] You did not arrest me there. But all these things have happened to make the Scriptures[d] come true." 50Then all of Jesus' followers left him and ran away.

51A young man, wearing only a linen cloth, was following Jesus. The people also grabbed him. 52But the cloth he was wearing came off, and he ran away naked.

Abba Name that a child called his father.
cup Jesus is talking about the bad things that will happen to him. Accepting these things will be very hard, like drinking a cup of something that tastes very bitter.

Jesus Before the Leaders

⁵³The people who arrested Jesus led him to the house of the high priest. All the leading priests, the older Jewish leaders, and the teachers of the law were gathered there. ⁵⁴Peter followed far behind and entered the courtyard of the high priest's house. There he sat with the guards, warming himself by the fire.

⁵⁵The leading priests and all the Jewish council tried to find something that Jesus had done wrong so they could kill him. But the council could find no proof against him. ⁵⁶Many people came and told false things about him. But all said different things—none of them agreed.

⁵⁷Then some men stood up and lied about Jesus. They said, ⁵⁸"We heard this man say, 'I will destroy this Temple*d* that men made. And three days later, I will build another Temple—a Temple not made by men'." ⁵⁹But even the things these men said did not agree.

⁶⁰Then the high priest stood before them and said to Jesus, "Aren't you going to answer the charges these men bring against you?" ⁶¹But Jesus said nothing. He did not answer.

The high priest asked Jesus another question: "Are you the Christ,*d* the Son of the blessed God?"

⁶²Jesus answered, "I am. And in the future you will see the Son of Man*d* sitting at the right side of the Powerful One. And you will see the Son of Man coming on clouds in the sky."

⁶³When the high priest heard this, he was very angry. He tore his clothes and said, "We don't need any more witnesses! ⁶⁴You all heard him say these things against God. What do you think?"

They all said that Jesus was guilty and should be killed. ⁶⁵Some of the people there spat at Jesus. They cov-

ered his eyes and hit him with their fists. They said, "Prove that you are a prophet!"*d* Then the guards led Jesus away and beat him.

Peter Says He Doesn't Know Jesus

⁶⁶Peter was still in the courtyard when a servant girl of the high priest came there. ⁶⁷She saw Peter warming himself at the fire. She looked closely at him.

Then the girl said, "You were with Jesus, that man from Nazareth."

⁶⁸But Peter said that he was never with Jesus. He said, "I don't know or understand what you are talking about." Then Peter left and went toward the entrance of the courtyard.*n*

⁶⁹The servant girl saw Peter there. Again she said to the people who were standing there, "This man is one of those who followed Jesus." ⁷⁰Again Peter said that it was not true.

A short time later, some people were standing near Peter. They said, "We know you are one of those who followed Jesus. You are from Galilee, too."

⁷¹Then Peter began to curse. He said, "I swear that I don't know this man you're talking about!"

⁷²As soon as Peter said this, the cock crowed the second time. Then Peter remembered what Jesus had told him: "Before the cock crows twice, you will say three times that you don't know me." Then Peter was very sad and began to cry.

Pilate Questions Jesus

15 Very early in the morning, the leading priests, the older Jewish leaders, the teachers of the law, and all the Jewish council decided what to do with Jesus. They tied him, led him away, and turned him over to Pilate, the governor.

Verse 68 Many Greek copies add: "And the cock crowed."

[2]Pilate asked Jesus, "Are you the king of the Jews?"

Jesus answered, "Yes, I am."

[3]The leading priests accused Jesus of many things. [4]So Pilate asked Jesus another question. He said, "You can see that these people are accusing you of many things. Why don't you answer?"

[5]But Jesus still said nothing. Pilate was very surprised at this.

Pilate Tries to Free Jesus

[6]Every year at the Passover[d] time the governor would free one person from prison. He would free any person the people wanted him to free. [7]At that time, there was a man named Barabbas in prison. He was a rebel and had committed murder during a riot. [8]The crowd came to Pilate and asked him to free a prisoner as he always did.

[9]Pilate asked them, "Do you want me to free the king of the Jews?" [10]Pilate knew that the leading priests had given Jesus to him because they were jealous of Jesus. [11]And the leading priests had persuaded the people to ask Pilate to free Barabbas, not Jesus.

[12]Pilate asked the crowd again, "So what should I do with this man you call the king of the Jews?"

[13]They shouted, "Kill him on a cross!"

[14]Pilate asked, "Why? What wrong has he done?"

But they shouted louder and louder, "Kill him on a cross!"

[15]Pilate wanted to please the crowd. So he freed Barabbas for them. And Pilate told the soldiers to beat Jesus with whips. Then he gave Jesus to the soldiers to be killed on a cross.

[16]Pilate's soldiers took Jesus into the governor's palace (called the Praetorium). They called all the other soldiers together. [17]They put a purple robe on Jesus. Then they used thorny branches to make a crown. They put it on his head. [18]Then they called out to him, "Hail, King of the Jews!" [19]The soldiers beat Jesus on the head many times with a stick. They also spat on him. Then they made fun of him by bowing on their knees and worshipping him. [20]After they had finished making fun of him, the soldiers took off the purple robe and put his own clothes on him again. Then they led Jesus out of the palace to be killed on a cross.

Jesus Is Killed on a Cross

[21]There was a man from Cyrene coming from the fields to the city. The man was Simon, the father of Alexander and Rufus. The soldiers forced Simon to carry the cross for Jesus. [22]They led Jesus to the place called Golgotha. (Golgotha means the Place of the Skull.) [23]At Golgotha the soldiers tried to give Jesus wine to drink. This wine was mixed with myrrh.[d] But he refused to drink it. [24]The soldiers nailed Jesus to a cross. Then they divided his clothes among themselves. They threw lots[d] to decide which clothes each soldier would get.

[25]It was nine o'clock in the morning when they nailed Jesus to the cross. [26]There was a sign with the charge against Jesus written on it. The sign read: THE KING OF THE JEWS. [27]They also put two robbers on crosses beside Jesus, one on the right, and the other on the left. [28][n] [29]People walked by and insulted Jesus. They shook their heads, saying, "You said you could destroy the Temple[d] and build it again in three days. [30]So save yourself! Come down from that cross!"

[31]The leading priests and the teachers of the law were also there. They

---

Verse 28 Some Greek copies add verse 28: "And the Scripture came true that says, 'They put him with criminals'."

made fun of Jesus just as the other people did. They said among themselves, "He saved other people, but he can't save himself. ³²If he is really the Christ,ᵈ the king of Israel, then let him come down from the cross now. We will see this, and then we will believe in him." The robbers who were being killed on the crosses beside Jesus also insulted him.

Jesus Dies

³³At noon the whole country became dark. This darkness lasted for three hours. ³⁴At three o'clock Jesus cried in a loud voice, "Eloi, Eloi, lama sabachthani." This means, "My God, my God, why have you left me alone?"

³⁵Some of the people standing there heard this. They said, "Listen! He is calling Elijah."

³⁶One man there ran and got a sponge. He filled the sponge with vinegar and tied it to a stick. Then he used the stick to give the sponge to Jesus to drink from it. The man said, "We should wait now and see if Elijah will come to take him down from the cross."

³⁷Then Jesus cried in a loud voice and died.

³⁸When Jesus died, the curtain in the Templeⁿ split into two pieces. The tear started at the top and tore all the way to the bottom. ³⁹The army officer that was standing there before the cross saw what happened when Jesus died. The officer said, "This man really was the Son of God!"

⁴⁰Some women were standing at a distance from the cross, watching. Some of these women were Mary Magdalene, Salome, and Mary the mother of James and Joseph. (James was her youngest son.) ⁴¹These were the women who followed Jesus in Galilee and cared for him. Many other women were also there who had come with Jesus to Jerusalem.

Jesus Is Buried

⁴²This was Preparationᵈ Day. (That means the day before the Sabbathᵈ day.) It was becoming dark. ⁴³A man named Joseph from Arimathea was brave enough to go to Pilate and ask for Jesus' body. Joseph was an important member of the Jewish council. He was one of the people who wanted the kingdom of God to come. ⁴⁴Pilate wondered if Jesus was already dead. Pilate called the army officer who guarded Jesus and asked him if Jesus had already died. ⁴⁵The officer told Pilate that he was dead. So Pilate told Joseph he could have the body. ⁴⁶Joseph bought some linen cloth, took the body down from the cross and wrapped it in the linen. He put the body in a tomb that was cut in a wall of rock. Then he closed the tomb by rolling a very large stone to cover the entrance. ⁴⁷And Mary Magdalene and Mary the mother of Joseph saw the place where Jesus was laid.

Jesus Rises from Death

16 The day after the Sabbathᵈ day, Mary Magdalene, Mary the mother of James, and Salome bought some sweet-smelling spices to put on Jesus' body. ²Very early on that day, the first day of the week, the women were on their way to the tomb. It was soon after sunrise. ³They said to each other, "There is a large stone covering the entrance of the tomb. Who will move the stone for us?"

⁴Then the women looked and saw that the stone had already been moved. The stone was very large, but it had been moved away from the entrance. ⁵The women entered the tomb

---

curtain in the Temple A curtain divided the Most Holy Place from the other part of the Temple. That was the special building in Jerusalem where God commanded the Jews to worship him.

and saw a young man wearing a white robe. He was sitting on the right side, and the women were afraid.

6But the man said, "Don't be afraid. You are looking for Jesus from Nazareth, the one who was killed on a cross. He has risen from death. He is not here. Look, here is the place they laid him. 7Now go and tell his followers and Peter, 'Jesus is going into Galilee. He will be there before you. You will see him there as he told you before'."

8The women were confused and shaking with fear. They left the tomb and ran away. They did not tell anyone about what happened, because they were afraid.*n*

Some Followers See Jesus

9Jesus rose from death early on the first day of the week. He showed himself first to Mary Magdalene. Once in the past, he had forced seven demons*d* to leave Mary. 10After Mary saw Jesus, she went and told his followers. They were very sad and were crying. 11But Mary told them that Jesus was alive. She said that she had seen him, but the followers did not believe her.

12Later, Jesus showed himself to two of his followers while they were walking in the country. But Jesus did not look the same as before. 13These followers went back to the others

and told them what had happened. Again, the followers did not believe them.

Jesus Talks to the Apostles

14Later Jesus showed himself to the 11 followers while they were eating. He criticised them because they had little faith. They were stubborn and refused to believe those who had seen him after he had risen from death.

15Jesus said to the followers, "Go everywhere in the world. Tell the Good News*d* to everyone. 16Anyone who believes and is baptised will be saved. But he who does not believe will be judged guilty. 17And those who believe will be able to do these things as proof: they will use my name to force demons*d* out of people. They will speak in languages*n* they never learned. 18They will pick up snakes without being hurt. And they will drink poison without being hurt. They will touch the sick, and the sick will be healed."

19After the Lord Jesus said these things to the followers, he was carried up into heaven. There, Jesus sat at the right side of God. 20The followers went everywhere in the world and told the Good News to people. And the Lord helped them. The Lord proved that the Good News they told was true by giving them power to work miracles.*d*

Verse 8 Some early Greek copies end the book with verse 8.
languages This can also be translated "tongues".

LUKE

Luke Tells the Non-Jews About Jesus

Luke Writes About Jesus' Life

1 To Theophilus:
Many have tried to give a history of the things that happened among us. [2]They have written the same things that we learned from others—the people who saw those things from the beginning and served God by telling people his message. [3]I myself studied everything carefully from the beginning, your Excellency.[n] I thought I should write it out for you. So I put it in order in a book. [4]I write these things so that you can know that what you have been taught is true.

Zechariah and Elizabeth

[5]During the time Herod ruled Judea, there was a priest named Zechariah. He belonged to Abijah's group.[n] Zechariah's wife came from the family of Aaron. Her name was Elizabeth. [6]Zechariah and Elizabeth truly did what God said was good. They did everything the Lord commanded and told people to do. They were without fault in keeping his law. [7]But Zechariah and Elizabeth had no children. Elizabeth could not have a baby; and both of them were very old.

[8]Zechariah was serving as a priest before God for his group. It was his group's time to serve. [9]According to the custom of the priests, he was chosen to go into the Temple[d] of the Lord and burn incense.[d] [10]There were a great many people outside praying at the time the incense was offered. [11]Then, on the right side of the incense table, an angel of the Lord came and stood before Zechariah. [12]When

he saw the angel, Zechariah was confused and frightened. [13]But the angel said to him, "Zechariah, don't be afraid. Your prayer has been heard by God. Your wife, Elizabeth, will give birth to a son. You will name him John. [14]You will be very happy. Many people will be happy because of his birth. [15]John will be a great man for the Lord. He will never drink wine or beer. Even at the time John is born, he will be filled with the Holy Spirit.[d] [16]He will help many people of Israel return to the Lord their God. [17]He himself will go first before the Lord. John will be powerful in spirit like Elijah. He will make peace between fathers and their children. He will bring those who are not obeying God back to the right way of thinking. He will make people ready for the coming of the Lord."

[18]Zechariah said to the angel, "How can I know that what you say is true? I am an old man, and my wife is old, too."

[19]The angel answered him, "I am Gabriel. I stand before God. God sent me to talk to you and to tell you this good news. [20]Now, listen! You will not be able to talk until the day these things happen. You will lose your speech because you did not believe what I told you. But these things will really happen."

[21]Outside, the people were still waiting for Zechariah. They were surprised that he was staying so long in the Temple. [22]Then Zechariah came outside, but he could not speak to them. So they knew that he had seen

---

Excellency This word was used to show respect to an important person like a king or ruler.
Abijah's group The Jewish priests were divided into 24 groups. See 1 Chronicles 24.

a vision in the Temple. Zechariah could not speak. He could only make signs to them. ²³When his time of service as a priest was finished, he went home.

²⁴Later, Zechariah's wife, Elizabeth, became pregnant. She did not go out of her house for five months. Elizabeth said, ²⁵"Look what the Lord has done for me! My people were ashamed[n] of me, but now the Lord has taken away that shame."

The Virgin Mary

²⁶⁻²⁷During Elizabeth's sixth month of pregnancy, God sent the angel Gabriel to a virgin[d] who lived in Nazareth, a town in Galilee. She was engaged to marry a man named Joseph from the family of David. Her name was Mary. ²⁸The angel came to her and said, "Greetings! The Lord has blessed you and is with you."

²⁹But Mary was very confused by what the angel said. Mary wondered, "What does this mean?"

³⁰The angel said to her, "Don't be afraid, Mary, because God is pleased with you. ³¹Listen! You will become pregnant. You will give birth to a son, and you will name him Jesus. ³²He will be great, and people will call him the Son of the Most High. The Lord God will give him the throne of King David, his ancestor. ³³He will rule over the people of Jacob for ever. His kingdom will never end."

³⁴Mary said to the angel, "How will this happen? I am a virgin!"

³⁵The angel said to Mary, "The Holy Spirit[d] will come upon you, and the power of the Most High will cover you. The baby will be holy. He will be called the Son of God. ³⁶Now listen! Elizabeth, your relative, is very old. But she is also pregnant with a son. Everyone thought she could not have a baby, but she has been pregnant for

six months. ³⁷God can do everything!"

³⁸Mary said, "I am the servant girl of the Lord. Let this happen to me as you say!" Then the angel went away.

Mary's Visit

³⁹Mary got up and went quickly to a town in the mountains of Judea. ⁴⁰She went to Zechariah's house and greeted Elizabeth. ⁴¹When Elizabeth heard Mary's greeting, the unborn baby inside Elizabeth jumped. Then Elizabeth was filled with the Holy Spirit.[d] ⁴²She cried out in a loud voice, "God has blessed you more than any other woman. And God has blessed the baby which you will give birth to. ⁴³You are the mother of my Lord, and you have come to me! Why has something so good happened to me? ⁴⁴When I heard your voice, the baby inside me jumped with joy. ⁴⁵You are blessed because you believed what the Lord said to you would really happen."

Mary Praises God

⁴⁶Then Mary said,
"My soul praises the Lord;
⁴⁷ my heart is happy because God
    is my Saviour.
⁴⁸I am not important, but God has
    shown his care for me, his
    servant girl.
From now on, all people will say
    that I am blessed,
⁴⁹ because the Powerful One has
    done great things for me.
His name is holy.
⁵⁰God will always give mercy
    to those who worship him.
⁵¹God's arm is strong.
He scatters the people who are
    proud
and think great things about
    themselves.
⁵²God brings down rulers from their
    thrones,

ashamed The Jews thought it was a disgrace for women not to have children.

and he raises up the humble.
⁵³God fills the hungry with good
    things,
    but he sends the rich away with
    nothing.
⁵⁴God has helped his people Israel
    who serve him.
    He gave them his mercy.
⁵⁵God has done what he promised
    to our ancestors,
    to Abraham and to his children
    for ever."

⁵⁶Mary stayed with Elizabeth for
about three months and then returned
home.

The Birth of John

⁵⁷When it was time for Elizabeth to
give birth, she had a boy. ⁵⁸Her neighbours and relatives heard how good
the Lord was to her, and they rejoiced.
    ⁵⁹When the baby was eight days old,
they came to circumcise*d* him. They
wanted to name him Zechariah because this was his father's name.
⁶⁰But his mother said, "No! He will be
named John."
    ⁶¹The people said to Elizabeth, "But
no one in your family has this name!"
⁶²Then they made signs to his father,
"What would you like to name him?"
    ⁶³Zechariah asked for something to
write on. Then he wrote, "His name
is John." Everyone was surprised.
⁶⁴Then Zechariah could talk again. He
began to praise God. ⁶⁵And all their
neighbours became alarmed. In all the
mountains of Judea people continued
talking about all these things. ⁶⁶The
people who heard about these things
wondered about them. They thought,
"What will this child be?" They said
this because the Lord was with him.

Zechariah Praises God

⁶⁷Then Zechariah, John's father,
was filled with the Holy Spirit.*d* He
told the people what would happen:
⁶⁸"Let us thank the Lord, the God
    of Israel.

God has come to help his people
    and has given them freedom.
⁶⁹God has given us a powerful
    Saviour
    from the family of God's servant
    David.
⁷⁰God said that he would do this.
    He said it through his holy
    prophets*d* who lived long
    ago.
⁷¹God will save us from our
    enemies
    and from the power of all those
    who hate us.
⁷²God said he would give mercy to
    our fathers.
    And he remembered his holy
    promise.
⁷³God promised Abraham, our
    father,
⁷⁴   that he would free us from the
    power of our enemies,
    so that we could serve him
    without fear.
⁷⁵We will be righteous and holy
    before God as long as we
    live.

⁷⁶"Now you, child, will be called a
    prophet of the Most High
    God.
    You will go first before the Lord
    to prepare the people for his
    coming.
⁷⁷You will make his people know
    that they will be saved.
    They will be saved by having
    their sins forgiven.
⁷⁸With the loving mercy of our
    God,
    a new day from heaven will
    shine upon us.
⁷⁹God will help those who live in
    darkness,
    in the fear of death.
    He will guide us into the path that
    goes toward peace."

⁸⁰And so the child grew up and became strong in spirit. John lived away
from other people until the time when
he came out to preach to Israel.

The Birth of Jesus

2 At that time, Augustus Caesar[d] sent an order to all people in the countries that were under Roman rule. The order said that they must list their names in a register. [2]This was the first registration[n] taken while Quirinius was governor of Syria. [3]And everyone went to their own towns to be registered.

[4]So Joseph left Nazareth, a town in Galilee. He went to the town of Bethlehem in Judea. This town was known as the town of David. Joseph went there because he was from the family of David. [5]Joseph registered with Mary because she was engaged to marry him. (Mary was now pregnant.) [6]While Joseph and Mary were in Bethlehem, the time came for her to have the baby. [7]She gave birth to her first son. There were no rooms left in the inn. So she wrapped the baby in cloths and laid him in a box where animals are fed.

Some Shepherds Hear About Jesus

[8]That night, some shepherds were in the fields nearby watching their sheep. [9]An angel of the Lord stood before them. The glory of the Lord was shining around them, and suddenly they became very frightened. [10]The angel said to them, "Don't be afraid, because I am bringing you some good news. It will be a joy to all the people. [11]Today your Saviour was born in David's town. He is Christ,[d] the Lord. [12]This is how you will know him: you will find a baby wrapped in cloths and lying in a feeding box."

[13]Then a very large group of angels from heaven joined the first angel. All the angels were praising God, saying:

[14]"Give glory to God in heaven,
   and on earth let there be peace
      to the people who please
         God."

[15]Then the angels left the shepherds and went back to heaven. The shepherds said to each other, "Let us go to Bethlehem and see this thing that has happened. We will see this thing the Lord told us about."

[16]So the shepherds went quickly and found Mary and Joseph. [17]And the shepherds saw the baby lying in a feeding box. Then they told what the angels had said about this child. [18]Everyone was amazed when they heard what the shepherds said to them. [19]Mary hid these things in her heart; she continued to think about them. [20]Then the shepherds went back to their sheep, praising God and thanking him for everything that they had seen and heard. It was just as the angel had told them.

[21]When the baby was eight days old, he was circumcised,[d] and he was named Jesus. This name had been given by the angel before the baby began to grow inside Mary.

Jesus Is Presented in the Temple

[22]The time came for Mary and Joseph to do what the law of Moses taught about being made pure.[n] They took Jesus to Jerusalem to present him to the Lord. [23]It is written in the law of the Lord: "Give every firstborn[d] male to the Lord."[n] [24]Mary and Joseph also went to offer a sacrifice, as the law of the Lord says: "You must sacrifice two doves or two young pigeons."[n]

Simeon Sees Jesus

[25]A man named Simeon lived in Je-

---

registration Census. A counting of all the people and the things they own.
pure The law of Moses said that 40 days after a Jewish woman gave birth to a baby, she must be cleansed by a ceremony at the Temple. Read Leviticus 12:2-8.
"Give ... Lord." Quotation from Exodus 13:2.
"You ... pigeons." Quotation from Leviticus 12:8.

rusalem. He was a good man and very religious. He was waiting for the time when God would help Israel. The Holy Spirit[d] was in him. [26]The Holy Spirit told Simeon that he would not die before he saw the Christ[d] promised by the Lord. [27]The Spirit led Simeon to the Temple.[d] Mary and Joseph brought the baby Jesus to the Temple to do what the law said they must do. [28]Then Simeon took the baby in his arms and thanked God:

[29]"Now, Lord, you can let me, your servant,
   die in peace as you said.
[30]I have seen your Salvation[n] with
   my own eyes.
[31] You prepared him before all
   people.
[32]He is a light for the non-Jewish
   people to see.
He will bring honour to your
   people, the Israelites."

[33]Jesus' father and mother were amazed at what Simeon had said about him. [34]Then Simeon blessed them and said to Mary, "Many in Israel will fall and many will rise because of this child. He will be a sign from God that many people will not accept. [35]The things they think in secret will be made known. And the things that will happen will make your heart sad, too."

Anna Sees Jesus

[36]Anna, a prophetess,[d] was there at the Temple.[d] She was from the family of Phanuel in the tribe[d] of Asher. Anna was very old. She had once been married for seven years. [37]Then her husband died and she lived alone. She was now 84 years old. Anna never left the Temple. She worshipped God by going without food and praying day and night. [38]She was standing there at that time, thanking God. She talked about Jesus to all who were waiting for God to free Jerusalem.

Joseph and Mary Return Home

[39]Joseph and Mary finished doing everything that the law of the Lord commanded. Then they went home to Nazareth, their own town in Galilee. [40]The little child began to grow up. He became stronger and wiser, and God's blessings were with him.

Jesus As a Boy

[41]Every year Jesus' parents went to Jerusalem for the Passover[d] Feast. [42]When Jesus was 12 years old, they went to the feast as they always did. [43]When the feast days were over, they went home. The boy Jesus stayed behind in Jerusalem, but his parents did not know it. [44]Joseph and Mary travelled for a whole day. They thought that Jesus was with them in the group. Then they began to look for him among their family and friends, [45]but they did not find him. So they went back to Jerusalem to look for him there. [46]After three days they found him. Jesus was sitting in the Temple[d] with the religious teachers, listening to them and asking them questions. [47]All who heard him were amazed at his understanding and wise answers. [48]When Jesus' parents saw him, they were amazed. His mother said to him, "Son, why did you do this to us? Your father and I were very worried about you. We have been looking for you."

[49]Jesus asked, "Why did you have to look for me? You should have known that I must be where my Father's work is!" [50]But they did not understand the meaning of what he said.

[51]Jesus went with them to Nazareth and obeyed them. His mother was still thinking about all that had happened. [52]Jesus continued to learn more and more and to grow physically. People liked him, and he pleased God.

Salvation Simeon was talking about Jesus. The name Jesus means "salvation".

The Preaching of John

3 It was the fifteenth year of the rule of Tiberius Caesar.[d] These men were under Caesar: Pontius Pilate was the ruler of Judea. Herod was the ruler of Galilee. Philip, Herod's brother, was the ruler of Iturea and Trachonitis. And Lysanias was the ruler of Abilene. [2]Annas and Caiaphas were the high priests. At this time, a command from God came to John son of Zechariah. John was living in the desert. [3]He went all over the area around the Jordan River and preached to the people. He preached a baptism of changed hearts and lives for the forgiveness of their sins. [4]As it is written in the book of Isaiah the prophet:[d]

"This is a voice of a man
    who calls out in the desert:
'Prepare the way for the Lord.
Make the road straight for him.
[5]Every valley should be filled in.
    Every mountain and hill should
        be made flat.
Roads with turns should be made
        straight,
    and rough roads should be made
        smooth.
[6]And all people will know about the
        salvation of God!' "

Isaiah 40:3-5

[7]Crowds of people came to be baptised by John. He said to them, "You poisonous snakes! Who warned you to run away from God's anger that is coming? [8]You must do the things that will show that you really have changed your hearts. Don't say, 'Abraham is our father'. I tell you that God can make children for Abraham from these rocks here. [9]The axe is now ready to cut down the trees. Every tree that does not produce good fruit will be cut down and thrown into the fire."[n]

[10]The people asked John, "What should we do?"

[11]John answered, "If you have two shirts, share with the person who does not have one. If you have food, share that too."

[12]Even tax collectors came to John to be baptised. They said to John, "Teacher, what should we do?"

[13]John said to them, "Don't take more taxes from people than you have been ordered to take."

[14]The soldiers asked John, "What about us? What should we do?"

John said to them, "Don't force people to give you money. Don't lie about them. Be satisfied with the pay you get."

[15]All the people were hoping for the Christ[d] to come, and they wondered about John. They thought, "Maybe he is the Christ."

[16]John answered everyone, "I baptise you with water, but there is one coming later who can do more than I can. I am not good enough to untie his sandals. He will baptise you with the Holy Spirit[d] and with fire. [17]He will come ready to clean the grain. He will separate the good grain from the chaff.[d] He will put the good part of the grain into his barn. Then he will burn the chaff with a fire that cannot be put out."[n] [18]And John continued to preach the Good News,[d] saying many other things to encourage the people.

[19]But John spoke against Herod, the governor, because of his sin with Herodias, the wife of Herod's brother. John also criticised Herod for the many other evil things Herod did. [20]So Herod did another evil thing: he put John in prison.

Jesus Is Baptised by John

[21]When all the people were being baptised by John, Jesus also was bap-

---

The axe . . . fire. This means that God is ready to punish his people who do not obey him.
He will . . . out. This means that Jesus will come to separate the good people from the bad people, saving the good and punishing the bad.

tised. While Jesus was praying, heaven opened and [22]the Holy Spirit[d] came down on him. The Spirit was in the form of a dove. Then a voice came from heaven and said, "You are my Son and I love you. I am very pleased with you."

The Family History of Jesus

[23]When Jesus began to teach, he was about 30 years old. People thought that Jesus was Joseph's son. Joseph was the son[n] of Heli. [24]Heli was the son of Matthat. Matthat was the son of Levi. Levi was the son of Melki. Melki was the son of Jannai. Jannai was the son of Joseph. [25]Joseph was the son of Mattathias. Mattathias was the son of Amos. Amos was the son of Nahum. Nahum was the son of Esli. Esli was the son of Naggai. [26]Naggai was the son of Maath. Maath was the son of Mattathias. Mattathias was the son of Semein. Semein was the son of Josech. Josech was the son of Joda. [27]Joda was the son of Joanan. Joanan was the son of Rhesa. Rhesa was the son of Zerubbabel. Zerubbabel was the grandson of Shealtiel. Shealtiel was the son of Neri. [28]Neri was the son of Melchi. Melchi was the son of Addi. Addi was the son of Cosam. Cosam was the son of Elmadam. Elmadam was the son of Er. [29]Er was the son of Joshua. Joshua was the son of Eliezer. Eliezer was the son of Jorim. Jorim was the son of Matthat. Matthat was the son of Levi. [30]Levi was the son of Simeon. Simeon was the son of Judah. Judah was the son of Joseph. Joseph was the son of Jonam. Jonam was the son of Eliakim.

[31]Eliakim was the son of Melea. Melea was the son of Menna. Menna was the son of Mattatha. Mattatha was the son of Nathan. Nathan was the son of David. [32]David was the son of Jesse. Jesse was the son of Obed. Obed was the son of Boaz. Boaz was the son of Salmon. Salmon was the son of Nahshon. [33]Nahshon was the son of Amminadab. Amminadab was the son of Admin. Admin was the son of Arni. Arni was the son of Hezron. Hezron was the son of Perez. Perez was the son of Judah. [34]Judah was the son of Jacob. Jacob was the son of Isaac. Isaac was the son of Abraham. Abraham was the son of Terah. Terah was the son of Nahor. [35]Nahor was the son of Serug. Serug was the son of Reu. Reu was the son of Peleg. Peleg was the son of Eber. Eber was the son of Shelah. [36]Shelah was the son of Cainan. Cainan was the son of Arphaxad. Arphaxad was the son of Shem. Shem was the son of Noah. Noah was the son of Lamech. [37]Lamech was the son of Methuselah. Methuselah was the son of Enoch. Enoch was the son of Jared. Jared was the son of Mahalalel. Mahalalel was the son of Kenan. [38]Kenan was the son of Enosh. Enosh was the son of Seth. Seth was the son of Adam. Adam was the son of God.

Jesus Is Tempted by the Devil

4 Jesus, filled with the Holy Spirit,[d] returned from the Jordan River. The Spirit led Jesus into the desert [2]where the devil tempted Jesus for 40 days. Jesus ate nothing during that

---

son "Son" in Jewish lists of ancestors can sometimes mean grandson or more distant relative.

time. When those days were ended, he was very hungry.

³The devil said to Jesus, "If you are the Son of God, tell this rock to become bread."

⁴Jesus answered, "It is written in the Scriptures:ᵈ 'A person does not live only by eating bread'. "ⁿ

⁵Then the devil took Jesus and showed him all the kingdoms of the world in a moment of time. ⁶The devil said to Jesus, "I will give you all these kingdoms and all their power and glory. It has all been given to me, and I can give it to anyone I wish. ⁷If you worship me, all will be yours."

⁸Jesus answered, "It is written in the Scriptures: 'You must worship the Lord your God. Serve only him!' "ⁿ

⁹Then the devil led Jesus to Jerusalem and put him on a high place of the Temple.ᵈ He said to Jesus, "If you are the Son of God, jump off! ¹⁰It is written in the Scriptures:

'He has put his angels in charge of you.
They will watch over you'.
                              Psalm 91:11
¹¹'They will catch you with their hands.
And you will not hit your foot on a rock'."   *Psalm 91:12*

¹²Jesus answered, "But it also says in the Scriptures: 'Do not test the Lord your God'."ⁿ

¹³After the devil had tempted Jesus in every way, he went away to wait until a better time.

Jesus Teaches the People

¹⁴Jesus went back to Galilee with the power of the Holy Spirit.ᵈ Stories about Jesus spread all through the area. ¹⁵He began to teach in the synagogues,ᵈ and all the people praised him.

¹⁶Jesus travelled to Nazareth,

where he had grown up. On the Sabbathᵈ day he went to the synagogue as he always did. Jesus stood up to read. ¹⁷The book of Isaiah the prophetᵈ was given to him. He opened the book and found the place where this is written: ¹⁸"The Spirit of the Lord is in me.

This is because God chose me
    to tell the Good Newsᵈ to
    the poor.
God sent me to tell the prisoners
    of sin that they are free,
and to tell the blind that they
    can see again.   *Isaiah 61:1*
God sent me to free those who
    have been treated unfairly,
                              Isaiah 58:6
¹⁹ and to announce the time when
    the Lord will show kindness
    to his people."   *Isaiah 61:2*

²⁰Jesus closed the book, gave it back, and sat down. Everyone in the synagogue was watching Jesus closely. ²¹He began to speak to them. He said, "While you heard these words just now, they were coming true!"

²²All the people praised Jesus. They were amazed at the beautiful words he spoke. They asked, "Isn't this Joseph's son?"

²³Jesus said to them, "I know that you will tell me the old saying: 'Doctor, heal yourself'. You want to say, 'We heard about the things you did in Capernaum. Do those things here in your own town!' " ²⁴Then Jesus said, "I tell you the truth. A prophet is not accepted in his own town. ²⁵What I say is true. During the time of Elijah it did not rain in Israel for three and a half years. There was no food anywhere in the whole country. And there were many widows in Israel during that time. ²⁶But Elijah was sent to none of those widows. He was sent only to a widow in Zarephath, a town in Sidon. ²⁷And there were many with

'A person . . . bread'. Quotation from Deuteronomy 8:3.
'You . . . him!' Quotation from Deuteronomy 6:13.
'Do . . . God'. Quotation from Deuteronomy 6:16.

a harmful skin disease living in Israel during the time of the prophet Elisha. But none of them were healed except Naaman, who was from the country of Syria."

²⁸When all the people in the synagogue heard these things, they became very angry. ²⁹They got up and forced Jesus out of town. The town was built on a hill. They took Jesus to the edge of the hill and wanted to throw him off. ³⁰But Jesus walked through the crowd and went on his way.

Jesus Removes an Evil Spirit

³¹Jesus went to Capernaum, a city in Galilee. On the Sabbath*d* day, Jesus taught the people. ³²They were amazed at his teaching, because he spoke with authority. ³³In the synagogue*d* there was a man who had an evil spirit from the devil inside him. The man shouted in a loud voice, ³⁴"Jesus of Nazareth! What do you want with us? Did you come here to destroy us? I know who you are — God's Holy One!"

³⁵But Jesus warned the evil spirit to stop. He said, "Be quiet! Come out of the man!" The evil spirit threw the man down to the ground before all the people. Then the evil spirit left the man and did not hurt him.

³⁶The people were amazed. They said to each other, "What does this mean? With authority and power he commands evil spirits, and they come out." ³⁷And so the news about Jesus spread to every place in the whole area.

Jesus Heals Many People

³⁸Jesus left the synagogue*d* and went to Simon's*n* house. Simon's mother-in-law was very sick with a high fever. They asked Jesus to do something to help her. ³⁹He stood very close to her and commanded the

fever to leave. It left her immediately, and she got up and began serving them.

⁴⁰When the sun went down, the people brought their sick to Jesus. They had many different diseases. Jesus put his hands on each sick person and healed every one of them. ⁴¹Demons*d* came out of many people. The demons would shout, "You are the Son of God." But Jesus gave a strong command for the demons not to speak. They knew Jesus was the Christ.*d*

⁴²At daybreak, Jesus went to a place to be alone, but the people looked for him. When they found him, they tried to keep him from leaving. ⁴³But Jesus said to them, "I must tell the Good News*d* about God's kingdom to other towns, too. This is why I was sent." ⁴⁴Then Jesus kept on preaching in the synagogues*d* of Judea.

Jesus' First Followers

5 One day Jesus was standing beside Lake Galilee. Many people were pressing all around him. They wanted to hear the word of God. ²Jesus saw two boats at the shore of the lake. The fishermen had left them and were washing their nets. ³Jesus got into one of the boats, the one which belonged to Simon.*n* Jesus asked Simon to push off a little from the land. Then Jesus sat down in the boat and continued to teach the people on the shore.

⁴When Jesus had finished speaking, he said to Simon, "Take the boat into deep water. If you will put your nets in the water, you will catch some fish."

⁵Simon answered, "Master, we worked hard all night trying to catch fish, but we caught nothing. But you say to put the nets in the water; so I will." ⁶The fishermen did as Jesus told them. And they caught so many fish

that the nets began to break. [7]They called to their friends in the other boat to come and help them. The friends came, and both boats were filled so full that they were almost sinking.

[8-9]The fishermen were all amazed at the many fish they caught. When Simon Peter saw what had happened, he bowed down before Jesus and said, "Go away from me, Lord. I am a sinful man!" [10]James and John, the sons of Zebedee, were amazed too. (James and John were Simon's partners.)

Jesus said to Simon, "Don't be afraid. From now on you will be fishermen for men." [11]When the men brought their boats to the shore, they left everything and followed Jesus.

Jesus Heals a Sick Man

[12]Once Jesus was in a town where a very sick man lived. The man was covered with a harmful skin disease. When he saw Jesus, he bowed before Jesus and begged him, "Lord, heal me. I know you can if you want to."

[13]Jesus said, "I want to. Be healed!" And Jesus touched the man. Immediately the disease disappeared. [14]Then Jesus said, "Don't tell anyone about what happened. But go and show yourself to the priest.[n] And offer a gift to God for your healing as Moses commanded.[n] This will prove to everyone that you are healed."

[15]But the news about Jesus was spreading more and more. Many people came to hear Jesus and to be healed of their sicknesses. [16]But Jesus often slipped away to other places to be alone so that he could pray.

Jesus Heals a Paralysed Man

[17]One day Jesus was teaching the people. The Pharisees[d] and teachers

of the law were there, too. They had come from every town in Galilee and from Judea and Jerusalem. The Lord was giving Jesus the power to heal people. [18]There was a man who was paralysed. Some men were carrying him on a mat. They tried to bring him in and put him down before Jesus. [19]But because there were so many people there, they could not find a way to Jesus. So the men went up on the roof and made a hole in the ceiling. They lowered the mat so that the paralysed man was lying right before Jesus. [20]Jesus saw that these men believed. So he said to the sick man, "Friend, your sins are forgiven."

[21]The Jewish teachers of the law and the Pharisees thought to themselves, "Who is this man? He is saying things that are against God! Only God can forgive sins."

[22]But Jesus knew what they were thinking. He said, "Why do you have thoughts like that in your hearts? [23]Which is easier: to tell this paralysed man, 'Your sins are forgiven', or to tell him, 'Stand up and walk'? [24]But I will prove to you that the Son of Man[d] has authority on earth to forgive sins." So Jesus said to the paralysed man, "I tell you, stand up! Take your mat and go home."

[25]Then the man stood up before the people there. He picked up his mat and went home, praising God. [26]All the people were totally amazed and began to praise God. They were filled with much respect and said, "Today we have seen amazing things!"

Levi Follows Jesus

[27]After this, Jesus went out and saw a tax collector named Levi sitting in the tax office. Jesus said to him, "Follow me!" [28]Levi got up, left everything, and followed Jesus.

show . . . priest The law of Moses said a priest must say when a Jew with a harmful skin disease was well.
Moses commanded Read about this in Leviticus 14:1-32.

²⁹Then Levi gave a big dinner for Jesus. The dinner was at Levi's house. At the table there were many tax collectors and other people, too. ³⁰But the Pharisees[d] and the men who taught the law for the Pharisees began to complain to the followers of Jesus. They said, "Why do you eat and drink with tax collectors and 'sinners'?" ³¹Jesus answered them, "Healthy people don't need a doctor. It is the sick who need a doctor. ³²I have not come to invite good people. I have come to invite sinners to change their hearts and lives!"

Jesus Answers a Question

³³They said to Jesus, "John's followers often give up eating[n] and pray, just as the Pharisees[d] do. But your followers eat and drink all the time." ³⁴Jesus said to them, "When there is a wedding, you cannot make the friends of the bridegroom give up eating while he is still with them. ³⁵But the time will come when he will be taken away from them. Then his friends will give up eating." ³⁶Jesus told them this story: "No one takes cloth off a new coat to cover a hole in an old coat. If he does, he ruins the new coat, and the cloth from the new coat will not be the same as the old cloth. ³⁷People never pour new wine into old leather bags for holding wine. If they do, the new wine will break the bags, and the wine will spill out. Then the leather bags for holding wine will be ruined. ³⁸People always put new wine into new leather bags. ³⁹No one after drinking old wine wants new wine because he says, 'The old wine is better'."

Jesus Is Lord over the Sabbath

6 One Sabbath[d] day Jesus was walking through some grainfields. His followers picked the heads of grain, rubbed them in their hands, and ate them. ²Some Pharisees[d] said, "Why are you doing that? It is against the law of Moses to do that on the Sabbath day." ³Jesus answered, "Haven't you read about what David did when he and those with him were hungry? ⁴David went into God's house. He took the bread that was made holy for God and ate it. And he gave some of the bread to the people with him. This was against the law of Moses. It says that only priests can eat that bread." ⁵Then Jesus said to the Pharisees, "The Son of Man[d] is Lord of the Sabbath day."

Jesus Heals a Man's Crippled Hand

⁶On another Sabbath[d] day Jesus went into the synagogue[d] and was teaching. A man with a crippled right hand was there. ⁷The teachers of the law and the Pharisees[d] were watching to see if Jesus would heal on the Sabbath day. They wanted to see Jesus do something wrong so that they could accuse him. ⁸But he knew what they were thinking. He said to the man with the crippled hand, "Get up and stand before these people." The man got up and stood there. ⁹Then Jesus said to them, "I ask you, which is it right to do on the Sabbath day: to do good, or to do evil? Is it right to save a life or to destroy one?" ¹⁰Jesus looked around at all of them. He said to the man, "Let me see your hand." The man stretched out his hand, and it was completely healed. ¹¹The Pharisees and the teachers of the law became very angry. They said to each other, "What can we do to Jesus?"

Jesus Chooses His Apostles

¹²At that time Jesus went off to a

---

give up eating This is called "fasting". The people would give up eating for a special time of prayer and worship to God. It was also done to show sadness.

mountain to pray. He stayed there all night, praying to God. [13]The next morning, Jesus called his followers to him. He chose 12 of them, whom he named "apostles".[d] They were [14]Simon (Jesus named him Peter) and Andrew, Peter's brother; James and John, Philip and Bartholomew; [15]Matthew, Thomas, James son of Alphaeus, and Simon (called the Zealot[d]), [16]Judas son of James and Judas Iscariot. This Judas was the one who gave Jesus to his enemies.

Jesus Teaches and Heals

[17]Jesus and the apostles[d] came down from the mountain. Jesus stood on level ground where there was a large group of his followers. Also, there were many people from all around Judea, Jerusalem, and the seacoast cities of Tyre and Sidon. [18]They all came to hear Jesus teach and to be healed of their sicknesses. He healed those who were troubled by evil spirits. [19]All the people were trying to touch Jesus, because power was coming from him and healing them all!

[20]Jesus looked at his followers and said,

"Poor people, you are happy,
  because God's kingdom belongs
    to you.
[21]You people who are now hungry
    are happy,
  because you will be satisfied.
You people who are now crying
    are happy,
  because you will laugh with joy.

[22]"You are happy when people hate you and are cruel to you. You are happy when they say that you are evil because you belong to the Son of Man.[d] [23]At that time be full of joy, because you have a great reward in heaven. Their fathers were cruel to the prophets[d] in the same way these people are cruel to you.

[24]"But how terrible it will be for you who are rich,

because you have had your easy
    life.
[25]How terrible it will be for you who
    are full now,
  because you will be hungry.
How terrible it will be for you who
    are laughing now,
  because you will be sad and cry.

[26]"How terrible when all people say only good things about you. Their fathers always said good things about the false prophets.

Love Your Enemies

[27]"I say to you who are listening to me, love your enemies. Do good to those who hate you. [28]Ask God to bless those who say bad things to you. Pray for those who are cruel to you. [29]If anyone slaps you on one cheek, let him slap the other cheek too. If someone takes your coat, do not stop him from taking your shirt. [30]Give to everyone who asks you. When a person takes something that is yours, don't ask for it back. [31]Do for other people what you want them to do for you. [32]If you love only those who love you, should you get some special praise for doing that? No! Even sinners love the people who love them! [33]If you do good only to those who do good to you, should you get some special praise for doing that? No! Even sinners do that! [34]If you lend things to people, always hoping to get something back, should you get some special praise for that? No! Even sinners lend to other sinners so that they can get back the same amount! [35]So love your enemies. Do good to them, and lend to them without hoping to get anything back. If you do these things, you will have a great reward. You will be sons of the Most High God. Yes, because God is kind even to people who are ungrateful and full of sin. [36]Show mercy just as your father shows mercy.

Look at Yourselves

37"Don't judge other people, and you will not be judged. Don't accuse others of being guilty, and you will not be accused of being guilty. Forgive other people, and you will be forgiven. 38Give, and you will receive. You will be given much. It will be poured into your hands — more than you can hold. You will be given so much that it will spill into your lap. The way you give to others is the way God will give to you."

39Jesus told them this story: "Can a blind man lead another blind man? No! Both of them will fall into a ditch. 40A student is not better than his teacher. But when the student has fully learned all that he has been taught, then he will be like his teacher.

41"Why do you notice the little piece of dust that is in your brother's eye, but you don't see the big piece of wood that is in your own eye? 42You say to your brother, 'Brother, let me take that little piece of dust out of your eye'. Why do you say this? You cannot see that big piece of wood in your own eye! You are a hypocrite!*d* First, take the piece of wood out of your own eye. Then you will see clearly to take the dust out of your brother's eye.

Two Kinds of Fruit

43"A good tree does not produce bad fruit. Also, a bad tree does not produce good fruit. 44Each tree is known by its fruit. People don't gather figs from thorn bushes. And they don't get grapes from bramble bushes. 45A good person has good things saved up in his heart. And so he brings good things out of his heart. But an evil person has evil things saved up in his heart. So he brings out bad things. A person speaks the things that are in his heart.

Two Kinds of People

46"Why do you call me, 'Lord, Lord', but do not do what I say? 47Everyone who comes to me and listens to my words and obeys 48is like a man building a house. He digs deep and lays his foundation on rock. The floods come, and the water tries to wash the house away. But the flood cannot move the house, because the house was built well. 49But the one who hears my words and does not obey is like a man who builds his house on the ground without a foundation. When the floods come, the house quickly falls down. And that house is completely destroyed."

Jesus Heals a Soldier's Servant

7 When Jesus finished saying all these things to the people, he went to Capernaum. 2In Capernaum there was an army officer. He had a servant who was so sick he was nearly dead. The officer loved the servant very much. 3When the officer heard about Jesus, he sent some older Jewish leaders to him. The officer wanted the leaders to ask Jesus to come and heal his servant. 4The men went to Jesus and begged him saying, "This officer is worthy of your help. 5He loves our people, and he built us a synagogue."*d*

6So Jesus went with the men. He was getting near the officer's house when the officer sent friends to say, "Lord, you don't need to come into my house. I am not good enough for you to be under my roof. 7That is why I did not come to you myself. You only need to say the word, and my servant will be healed. 8I, too, am a man under the authority of other men, and I have soldiers under my command. I tell one soldier, 'Go', and he goes. And I tell another soldier, 'Come', and he comes. And I say to my servant, 'Do this', and my servant obeys me."

9When Jesus heard this, he was amazed. He turned to the crowd following him and said, "I tell you, this is the greatest faith I have seen anywhere, even in Israel."

¹⁰The men who had been sent to Jesus went back to the house. There they found that the servant was healed.

Jesus Brings a Man Back to Life

¹¹The next day Jesus went to a town called Nain. His followers and a large crowd were travelling with him. ¹²When he came near the town gate, he saw a funeral. A mother, who was a widow, had lost her only son. A large crowd from the town was with the mother while her son was being carried out. ¹³When the Lord saw her, he felt very sorry for her. Jesus said to her, "Don't cry." ¹⁴He went up to the coffin and touched it. The men who were carrying it stopped. Jesus said, "Young man, I tell you, get up!" ¹⁵And the son sat up and began to talk. Then Jesus gave him back to his mother.

¹⁶All the people were amazed. They began praising God. They said, "A great prophet*d* has come to us! God is taking care of his people."

¹⁷This news about Jesus spread through all Judea and into all the places around there.

John Asks a Question

¹⁸John's followers told him about all these things. He called for two of his followers. ¹⁹He sent them to the Lord to ask, "Are you the One who is coming, or should we wait for another?"

²⁰So the men came to Jesus. They said, "John the Baptist*d* sent us to you with this question: 'Are you the One who is coming, or should we wait for another?'"

²¹At that time, Jesus healed many people of their sicknesses, diseases, and evil spirits. He healed many blind people so that they could see again. ²²Then Jesus said to John's followers,

"Go and tell John the things that you saw and heard here. The blind can see. The crippled can walk. People with a harmful skin disease are healed. The deaf can hear, and the dead are given life. And the Good News*d* is told to the poor. ²³The person who does not lose faith is blessed!"

²⁴When John's followers left, Jesus began to tell the people about John: "What did you go out into the desert to see? A reed*n* blown by the wind? ²⁵What did you go out to see? A man dressed in fine clothes? No. People who have fine clothes live in kings' palaces. ²⁶But what did you go out to see? A prophet?*d* Yes, and I tell you, John is more than a prophet. ²⁷This was written about John:

'I will send my messenger ahead
    of you.
He will prepare the way for
    you'.   *Malachi 3:1*

²⁸I tell you, John is greater than any other man ever born. But even the least important person in the kingdom of God is greater than John."

²⁹(When the people heard this, they all agreed that God's teaching was good. Even the tax collectors agreed. These were people who were already baptised by John. ³⁰But the Pharisees*d* and teachers of the law refused to accept God's plan for themselves; they did not let John baptise them.)

³¹Then Jesus said, "What shall I say about the people of this time? What are they like? ³²They are like children sitting in the marketplace. One group of children calls to the other group and says,

'We played music for you, but you
    did not dance.
We sang a sad song, but you did
    not cry'.

³³John the Baptist came and did not eat like other people or drink wine. And you say, 'He has a demon*d* in

---

reed It means that John was not weak like grass blown by the wind.

Matthew 2:6
A ruler will come from you.
He will be like a shepherd
for my people, the Israelites."

Mark 1:10-11
When Jesus was coming up out of the
water . . . the Holy Spirit came down on
Him like a dove.

Luke 4:24
I tell you the truth. A prophet is not accepted in his own town.

him'. ³⁴The Son of Man*ᵈ* came eating like other people and drinking wine. And you say, 'Look at him! He eats too much and drinks too much wine! He is a friend of the tax collectors and "sinners"!' ³⁵But wisdom is shown to be right by the things it does."

Simon the Pharisee

³⁶One of the Pharisees*ᵈ* asked Jesus to eat with him. Jesus went into the Pharisee's house and sat at the table. ³⁷A sinful woman in the town learned that Jesus was eating at the Pharisee's house. So she brought an alabaster*ᵈ* jar of perfume. ³⁸She stood at Jesus' feet, crying, and began to wash his feet with her tears. She dried his feet with her hair, kissed them many times and rubbed them with the perfume. ³⁹The Pharisee who asked Jesus to come to his house saw this. He thought to himself, "If Jesus were a prophet,*ᵈ* he would know that the woman who is touching him is a sinner!"

⁴⁰Jesus said to the Pharisee, "Simon, I have something to say to you." Simon said, "Teacher, tell me."

⁴¹Jesus said, "There were two men. Both men owed money to the same banker. One man owed the banker 500 silver coins.*ⁿ* The other man owed the banker 50 silver coins. ⁴²The men had no money; so they could not pay what they owed. But the banker told the men that they did not have to pay him. Which one of the two men will love the banker more?"

⁴³Simon, the Pharisee, answered, "I think it would be the one who owed him the most money."

Jesus said to Simon, "You are right." ⁴⁴Then Jesus turned towards the woman and said to Simon, "Do you see this woman? When I came into your house, you gave me no water for my feet. But she washed my feet with her tears and dried my feet

with her hair. ⁴⁵You did not kiss me, but she has been kissing my feet since I came in! ⁴⁶You did not rub my head with oil, but she rubbed my feet with perfume. ⁴⁷I tell you that her many sins are forgiven. This is clear because she showed great love. But the person who has only a little to be forgiven will feel only a little love."

⁴⁸Then Jesus said to her, "Your sins are forgiven."

⁴⁹The people sitting at the table began to think to themselves, "Who is this man? How can he forgive sins?"

⁵⁰Jesus said to the woman, "Because you believed, you are saved from your sins. Go in peace."

The Group with Jesus

8 The next day, while Jesus was travelling through some cities and small towns, he preached and told the Good News*ᵈ* about God's kingdom. The 12 apostles*ᵈ* were with him. ²There were also some women with him who had been healed of sicknesses and evil spirits. One of the women was Mary, called Magdalene, from whom seven demons*ᵈ* had gone out. ³Also among the women were Joanna, the wife of Chuza (Herod's helper), Susanna, and many other women. These women used their own money to help Jesus and his apostles.

A Story About Planting Seed

⁴A great crowd gathered. People were coming to Jesus from every town. He told them this story:

⁵"A farmer went out to plant his seed. While he was planting, some seed fell beside the road. People walked on the seed, and the birds ate all this seed. ⁶Some seed fell on rock. It began to grow but then died because it had no water. ⁷Some seed fell among thorny weeds. This seed grew, but later the weeds choked the good plants. ⁸And some seed fell on

silver coins A Roman denarius. One coin was the average pay for one day's work.

good ground. This seed grew and made 100 times more grain."

Jesus finished the story. Then he called out, "You people who hear me, listen!"

[9]Jesus' followers asked him, "What does this story mean?"

[10]Jesus said, "You have been chosen to know the secret truths of the kingdom of God. But I use stories to speak to other people. I do this so that:

'They will look, but they may not see.
They will listen, but they may not understand'.   *Isaiah 6:9*

[11]"This is what the story means: The seed is God's teaching. [12]What is the seed that fell beside the road? It is like the people who hear God's teaching, but then the devil comes and takes it away from their hearts. So they cannot believe the teaching and be saved. [13]What is the seed that fell on rock? It is like those who hear God's teaching and accept it gladly. But they don't have deep roots. They believe for a while, but then trouble comes. They stop believing and turn away from God. [14]What is the seed that fell among the thorny weeds? It is like those who hear God's teaching, but they let the worries, riches, and pleasures of this life keep them from growing. So they never produce good fruit. [15]And what is the seed that fell on the good ground? That is like those who hear God's teaching with a good, honest heart. They obey God's teaching and patiently produce good fruit.

Use What You Have

[16]"No one lights a lamp and then covers it with a bowl or hides it under a bed. Instead, he puts the lamp on a lampstand so that those who come in will have enough light to see. [17]Everything that is hidden will become clear. Every secret thing will be made known. [18]So be careful how you listen.

The person who has something will be given more. But to the person who has nothing, this will happen: even what he thinks he has will be taken away from him."

Jesus' True Family

[19]Jesus' mother and brothers came to see him. There was such a crowd that they could not get to him. [20]Someone said to Jesus, "Your mother and your brothers are standing outside. They want to see you."

[21]Jesus answered them, "My mother and my brothers are those who listen to God's teaching and obey it!"

Jesus Stops a Storm

[22]One day Jesus and his followers got into a boat. He said to them, "Come with me across the lake." And so they started across. [23]While they were sailing, Jesus fell asleep. A big storm blew up on the lake. The boat began to fill with water, and they were in danger.

[24]The followers went to Jesus and woke him. They said, "Master! Master! We will drown!"

Jesus got up and gave a command to the wind and the waves. The wind stopped, and the lake became calm. [25]Jesus said to his followers, "Where is your faith?"

The followers were afraid and amazed. They said to each other, "What kind of man is this? He commands the wind and the water, and they obey him!"

A Man with Demons Inside Him

[26]Jesus and his followers sailed across the lake from Galilee to the area where the Gerasene people live. [27]When Jesus got out of the boat, a man from the town came to Jesus. This man had demons[d] inside him. For a long time he had worn no clothes. He lived in the burial caves, not in a house. [28]When he saw Jesus, he cried

out and fell down before him. The man said with a loud voice, "What do you want with me, Jesus, Son of the Most High God? Please don't punish me!" ²⁹He said this because Jesus had commanded the evil spirit to come out of him. Many times it had taken hold of him. He had been kept under guard and chained hand and foot. But he had broken his chains and had been driven by the demon out into the desert.

³⁰Jesus asked him, "What is your name?"

The man answered, "Legion".ⁿ (He said his name was "Legion" because many demons were in him.) ³¹The demons begged Jesus not to send them into eternal darkness.ⁿ ³²On the hill there was a large herd of pigs eating. The demons begged Jesus to allow them to go into the pigs. So Jesus allowed them to do this. ³³Then the demons came out of the man and went into the pigs. The herd of pigs ran down the hill and into the lake. All the pigs drowned.

³⁴The men who took care of the pigs ran away. They told about this in the town and the countryside. ³⁵And people went to see what had happened. They came to Jesus and found the man sitting there at Jesus' feet. The man was clothed and in his right mind because the demons had gone. But the people were frightened. ³⁶The men who saw these things happen told the others all about how Jesus had made the man well. ³⁷All the people of the Gerasene country asked Jesus to go away. They were all very afraid. So Jesus got into the boat and went back to Galilee.

³⁸The man that Jesus had healed begged to go with him. But Jesus sent him away, saying, ³⁹"Go back home and tell people what God did for you." So the man went all over town telling how much Jesus had done for him.

Jesus Gives Life to a Dead Girl and Heals a Sick Woman

⁴⁰When Jesus got back to Galilee, a crowd welcomed him. Everyone was waiting for him. ⁴¹A man named Jairus came to Jesus. Jairus was a ruler of the synagogue.ᵈ He bowed down at Jesus' feet and begged him to come to his house. ⁴²Jairus had only one daughter. She was 12 years old, and she was dying.

While Jesus was on his way to Jairus' house, the people were crowding all around him. ⁴³A woman was there who had been bleeding for 12 years. She had spent all her money on doctors, but no doctor was able to heal her. ⁴⁴The woman came up behind Jesus and touched the edge of his coat. At that moment, her bleeding stopped. ⁴⁵Then Jesus said, "Who touched me?"

All the people said they had not touched Jesus. Peter said, "Master, the people are all around you and are pushing against you."

⁴⁶But Jesus said, "Someone did touch me! I felt power go out from me." ⁴⁷When the woman saw that she could not hide, she came forward, shaking. She bowed down before Jesus. While all the people listened, she told why she had touched him. Then, she said, she was healed immediately. ⁴⁸Jesus said to her, "Dear woman, you are healed because you believed. Go in peace."

⁴⁹While Jesus was still speaking, someone came from the house of the synagogue ruler and said to the ruler, "Your daughter has died! Don't bother the teacher now."

⁵⁰When Jesus heard this, he said to Jairus, "Don't be afraid. Just believe, and your daughter will be well."

⁵¹Jesus went to the house. He let only Peter, John, James, and the girl's father and mother go inside with him.

"Legion" Means very many. A legion was about 5,000 men in the Roman army.
eternal darkness Literally, "the abyss", something like a pit or a hole that has no end.

⁵²All the people were crying and feeling sad because the girl was dead. But Jesus said, "Don't cry. She is not dead; she is only sleeping."

⁵³The people laughed at Jesus because they knew that the girl was dead. ⁵⁴But Jesus took her by the hand and called to her, "My child, stand up!" ⁵⁵Her spirit came back into her, and she stood up immediately. Jesus said, "Give her something to eat." ⁵⁶The girl's parents were amazed. Jesus told them not to tell anyone about what happened.

Jesus Sends Out the Apostles

9 Jesus called the 12 apostles*d* together. He gave them power to heal sicknesses and power over all demons.*d* ²Jesus sent the apostles out to tell about God's kingdom and to heal the sick. ³He said to them, "When you travel, don't take a walking stick. Also, don't carry a bag, or food, or money. Take for your trip only the clothes you are wearing. ⁴When you go into a house, stay there until it is time to leave. ⁵If the people in the town will not welcome you, go outside the town and shake the dust off of your feet.*n* This will be a warning to them."

⁶So the apostles went out. They travelled through all the towns. They told the Good News*d* and healed people everywhere.

Herod Is Confused About Jesus

⁷Herod, the governor, heard about all these things that were happening. He was confused because some people said, "John the Baptist*d* is risen from death." ⁸Others said, "Elijah has come to us." And still others said, "One of the prophets*d* from long ago has risen from death." ⁹Herod said, "I cut off John's head. So who is this man I hear these things about?" And Herod kept trying to see Jesus.

More than 5,000 People Fed

¹⁰When the apostles*d* returned, they told Jesus all the things they had done on their trip. Then Jesus took them away to a town called Bethsaida. There, Jesus and his apostles could be alone together. ¹¹But the people learned where Jesus went and followed him. Jesus welcomed them and talked with them about God's kingdom. He healed those who needed to be healed.

¹²Late in the afternoon, the 12 apostles came to Jesus and said, "No one lives in this place. Send the people away. They need to find food and places to sleep in the towns and countryside around here."

¹³But Jesus said to them, "You give them something to eat."

They said, "We have only five loaves of bread and two fish. Do you want us to go and buy food for all these people?" ¹⁴(There were about 5,000 men there.)

Jesus said to his followers, "Tell the people to sit in groups of about 50 people."

¹⁵So the followers did this, and all the people sat down. ¹⁶Then Jesus took the five loaves of bread and two fish. He looked up to heaven and thanked God for the food. Then Jesus divided the food and gave it to the followers to give to the people. ¹⁷All the people ate and were satisfied. And there was a lot of food left. Twelve baskets were filled with pieces of food that were not eaten.

Jesus Is the Christ

¹⁸Once when Jesus was praying alone, his followers came together there. Jesus asked them, "Who do the people say I am?"

¹⁹They answered, "Some say you are John the Baptist.*d* Others say you

shake . . . feet A warning. It showed that they had finished talking to these people.

are Elijah.ⁿ And others say you are
one of the prophets*d* from long ago
who has come back to life."

²⁰Then Jesus asked, "And who do
you say I am?"

Peter answered, "You are the
Christ*d* from God."

²¹Jesus warned them not to tell anyone. Then he said, ²²"The Son of
Man*d* must suffer many things. He will
be rejected by the older Jewish leaders, the leading priests, and the
teachers of the law. The Son of Man
will be killed. But after three days he
will be raised from death."

²³Jesus went on to say to all of
them, "If anyone wants to follow me,
he must say 'no' to the things he
wants. Every day he must be willing
even to die on a cross, and he must
follow me. ²⁴Whoever wants to save
his life will lose it. And whoever gives
his life for me will save it. ²⁵It is worth
nothing for a man to have the whole
world, if he himself is destroyed or
lost. ²⁶If anyone is ashamed of me and
my teaching, then Iⁿ will be ashamed
of him. I will be ashamed of him at the
time I come with my glory and with
the glory of the Father and the holy
angels. ²⁷I tell you the truth. Some of
you people standing here will see the
kingdom of God before you die."

Jesus with Moses and Elijah

²⁸About eight days after Jesus said
these things, he took Peter, James,
and John and went up on a mountain to
pray. ²⁹While Jesus was praying, his
face was changed, and his clothes became shining white. ³⁰Then two men
were talking with Jesus. The men
were Moses and Elijah.ⁿ ³¹They appeared in heavenly glory, talking with
Jesus about his death which would
happen in Jerusalem. ³²Peter and the
others were asleep. But they woke up

and saw the glory of Jesus. They also
saw the two men who were standing
with him. ³³When Moses and Elijah
were about to leave, Peter said,
"Master, it is good that we are here.
We will put three tents here — one for
you, one for Moses, and one for Elijah." (Peter did not know what he was
saying.)

³⁴While Peter was saying these
things, a cloud came down all around
them. Peter, James, and John became
afraid when the cloud covered them.
³⁵A voice came from the cloud. The
voice said, "This is my Son. He is the
One I have chosen. Obey him."

³⁶When the voice finished speaking,
only Jesus was there. Peter, James,
and John said nothing. At that time
they told no one about what they had
seen.

Jesus Heals a Sick Boy

³⁷The next day, Jesus, Peter,
James, and John came down from the
mountain. A large crowd met Jesus.
³⁸A man in the crowd shouted to
Jesus, "Teacher, please come and
look at my son. He is the only child I
have. ³⁹An evil spirit comes into my
son, and then he shouts. He loses
control of himself, and he foams at the
mouth. The evil spirit keeps on hurting him and almost never leaves him.
⁴⁰I begged your followers to make the
evil spirit leave my son, but they could
not do it."

⁴¹Jesus answered, "You people who
live now have no faith. Your lives are
all wrong. How long must I be with
you and be patient with you?" Then
Jesus said to the man, "Bring your son
here."

⁴²While the boy was coming, the demon*d* threw him on the ground. The
boy lost control of himself. But Jesus
gave a strong command to the evil

Elijah A man who spoke for God. He lived hundreds of years before Christ.
I Literally, "the Son of Man."
Moses and Elijah Two of the most important Jewish leaders in the past.

spirit. Then the boy was healed, and Jesus gave him back to his father. 43All the people were amazed at the great power of God.

Jesus Talks About His Death

The people were all wondering about the things Jesus did. But he said to his followers, 44"Don't forget the things I tell you now: the Son of Man*d* will be handed over into the control of men." 45But the followers did not understand what Jesus meant. The meaning was hidden from them so that they could not understand it. But they were afraid to ask Jesus about what he said.

The Most Important Person

46Jesus' followers began to have an argument about which one of them was the greatest. 47Jesus knew what they were thinking. So he took a little child and stood the child beside him. 48Then Jesus said, "If anyone accepts a little child like this in my name, then he accepts me. And when he accepts me, he accepts the One who sent me. He who is least among you all — he is the greatest."

Anyone Not Against Us Is for Us

49John answered, "Master, we saw someone using your name to force demons*d* out of people. We told him to stop because he does not belong to our group."

50Jesus said to him, "Don't stop him. If a person is not against you, then he is for you."

A Samaritan Town

51The time was coming near when Jesus would leave and be taken to heaven. He was determined to go to Jerusalem 52and sent some men ahead of him. The men went into a town in Samaria to make everything ready for Jesus. 53But the people there would not welcome him because he was going toward Jerusalem. 54James and John, the followers of Jesus, saw this. They said, "Lord, do you want us to call fire down from heaven and destroy those people?"*n* 55But Jesus turned and scolded them.*n* 56Then he and his followers went to another town.

Following Jesus

57They were all going along the road. Someone said to Jesus, "I will follow you anywhere you go."

58Jesus answered, "The foxes have holes to live in. The birds have nests to live in. But the Son of Man*d* has no place to rest his head."

59Jesus said to another man, "Follow me!"

But the man said, "Lord, first let me go and bury my father."

60But Jesus said to him, "Let the people who are dead bury their own dead! You must go and tell about the kingdom of God."

61Another man said, "I will follow you, Lord, but first let me go and say good bye to my family."

62Jesus said, "Anyone who begins to plough a field but keeps looking back is of no use in the kingdom of God."

Jesus Sends the 72 Men

10 After this, the Lord chose 72*n* others. He sent them out in pairs. He sent them ahead of him into every town and place where he planned to go. 2He said to them, "There are a great many people to

---

Verse 54 Here, some Greek copies add: ". . . as Elijah did."
Verse 55 Here, some copies add: "And Jesus said, 'You don't know what kind of spirit you belong to. 56The Son of Man did not come to destroy the souls of men but to save them'."
72 Many Greek copies read 70.

harvest. But there are only a few workers to harvest them. God owns the harvest. Pray to God that he will send more workers to help gather his harvest. ³You can go now. But listen! I am sending you, and you will be like sheep among wolves. ⁴Don't carry a purse, a bag, or sandals. Don't stop to talk with people on the road. ⁵Before you go into a house, say, 'Peace be with this house'. ⁶If a peaceful man lives there, your blessing of peace will stay with him. If the man is not peaceful, then your blessing of peace will come back to you. ⁷Stay in the peaceful house. Eat and drink what the people there give you. A worker should be given his pay. Don't move from house to house. ⁸If you go into a town and the people welcome you, eat what they give you. ⁹Heal the sick who live there. Tell them, 'The kingdom of God is soon coming to you!' ¹⁰But if you go into a town, and the people don't welcome you, then go out into the streets of that town. Say to them, ¹¹'Even the dust from your town that sticks to our feet we wipe off against you.ⁿ But remember that the kingdom of God is coming soon'. ¹²I tell you, on the Judgement Day it will be worse for the people of that town than for the people of Sodom.ⁿ

Jesus Warns Unbelievers

¹³"How terrible for you, Korazin! How terrible for you, Bethsaida! I did many miraclesᵈ in you. If those same miracles had happened in Tyre and Sidon,ⁿ those people would have changed their lives and stopped sinning long ago. They would have worn rough cloth and put ashes on themselves to show that they had changed.

¹⁴But on the Judgement Day it will be worse for you than for Tyre and Sidon. ¹⁵And you, Capernaum,ⁿ will you be lifted up to heaven? No! You will be thrown down to the depths!

¹⁶"He who listens to you is really listening to me. He who refuses to accept you is really refusing to accept me. And he who refuses to accept me is refusing to accept the One who sent me."

Satan Falls

¹⁷When the 72ⁿ men came back from their trip, they were very happy. They said, "Lord, even the demonsᵈ obeyed us when we used your name!"

¹⁸Jesus said to the men, "I saw Satan falling like lightning from the sky. ¹⁹Listen! I gave you power to walk on snakes and scorpions. I gave you more power than the Enemy has. Nothing will hurt you. ²⁰You should be happy, but not because the spirits obey you. You should be happy because your names are written in heaven."

Jesus Prays to the Father

²¹Then the Holy Spiritᵈ made Jesus rejoice. He said, "I thank you, Father, Lord of heaven and earth, because you have hidden these things from the people who are wise and clever. But you have shown them to those who are like little children. Yes, Father, you did this because this is what you really wanted.

²²"My Father has given me all things. No one knows the Son—only the Father knows. And only the Son knows the Father. The only people who will know about the Father are those whom the Son chooses to tell."

---

dust . . . you A warning. It showed that they had finished talking to these people.
Sodom City that God destroyed because the people were so evil.
Tyre and Sidon Towns where wicked people lived.
Korazin, Bethsaida, Capernaum Towns by Lake Galilee where Jesus preached to the people.
72 Many Greek copies read 70.

²³Then Jesus turned to his followers and said privately, "You are blessed to see what you now see! ²⁴I tell you, many prophets[d] and kings wanted to see what you now see. But they did not see these things. And many prophets and kings wanted to hear what you now hear. But they did not hear these things."

The Good Samaritan

²⁵Then a teacher of the law stood up. He was trying to test Jesus. He said, "Teacher, what must I do to get life for ever?"

²⁶Jesus said to him, "What is written in the law? What do you read there?"

²⁷The man answered, "Love the Lord your God. Love him with all your heart, all your soul, all your strength, and all your mind."[n] Also, "You must love your neighbour as you love yourself."[n]

²⁸Jesus said to him, "Your answer is right. Do this and you will have life for ever."

²⁹But the man wanted to show that the way he was living was right. So he said to Jesus, "And who is my neighbour?"

³⁰To answer this question, Jesus said, "A man was going down the road from Jerusalem to Jericho. Some robbers attacked him. They tore off his clothes and beat him. Then they left him lying there, almost dead. ³¹It happened that a Jewish priest was going down that road. When the priest saw the man, he walked by on the other side of the road. ³²Next, a Levite[n] came there. He went over and looked at the man. Then he walked by on the other side of the road. ³³Then a Sa-maritan[n] travelling down the road came to where the hurt man was lying. He saw the man and felt very sorry for him. ³⁴The Samaritan went to him and poured olive oil and wine[n] on his wounds and bandaged them. He put the hurt man on his own donkey and took him to an inn. At the inn, the Samaritan took care of him. ³⁵The next day, the Samaritan brought out two silver coins[n] and gave them to the innkeeper. The Samaritan said, 'Take care of this man. If you spend more money on him, I will pay it back to you when I come again'."

³⁶Then Jesus said, "Which one of these three men do you think was a neighbour to the man who was attacked by the robbers?"

³⁷The teacher of the law answered, "The one who helped him."

Jesus said to him, "Then go and do the same thing he did!"

Mary and Martha

³⁸While Jesus and his followers were travelling, Jesus went into a town. A woman named Martha let Jesus stay at her house. ³⁹Martha had a sister named Mary. Mary was sitting at Jesus' feet and listening to him teach. ⁴⁰Martha became angry because she had so much work to do. She went in and said, "Lord, don't you care that my sister has left me alone to do all the work? Tell her to help me!"

⁴¹But the Lord answered her, "Martha, Martha, you are getting worried and upset about too many things. ⁴²Only one thing is important. Mary has chosen the right thing, and it will never be taken away from her."

"Love ... mind." Quotation from Deuteronomy 6:5.
"You ... yourself." Quotation from Leviticus 19:18.
Levite Levites were men from the tribe of Levi who helped the Jewish priests with their work in the Temple. Read 1 Chronicles 23:24-32.
Samaritan Samaritans were people from Samaria. These people were part Jewish, but the Jews did not accept them as true Jews. Samaritans and Jews hated each other.
olive oil and wine Oil and wine were used like medicine to soften and clean wounds.
silver coins A Roman denarius. One coin was the average pay for one day's work.

Jesus Teaches About Prayer

11 Once Jesus was praying in a place. When he had finished, one of his followers said to him, "John taught his followers how to pray. Lord, please teach us how to pray, too."

²Jesus said to them, "When you pray, say:

'Father, we pray that your name
  will always be kept holy.
We pray that your kingdom will
  come.
³Give us the food we need for each
  day.
⁴Forgive us the sins we have done,
  because we forgive every
    person who has done wrong
    to us.
And do not cause us to be
  tested'."

Continue to Ask

⁵⁻⁶Then Jesus said to them, "Suppose one of you went to your friend's house at midnight and said to him, 'A friend of mine has come into town to visit me, but I have nothing for him to eat. Please lend me three loaves of bread'. ⁷Your friend inside the house answers, 'Don't bother me! The door is already locked. My children and I are in bed. I cannot get up and give you the bread now'. ⁸I tell you, perhaps friendship is not enough to make him get up to give you the bread. But he will surely get up to give you what you need if you continue to ask. ⁹So I tell you, continue to ask, and God will give to you. Continue to search, and you will find. Continue to knock, and the door will open for you. ¹⁰Yes, if a person continues asking, he will receive. If he continues searching, he will find. And if he continues knocking, the door will open for him. ¹¹What would you fathers do if your son asks you for a fish? Would any of you give him a snake? ¹²Or, if your son asks for

an egg, would you give him a scorpion? ¹³Even though you are bad, you know how to give good things to your children. So surely your heavenly Father knows how to give the Holy Spirit*d* to those who ask him."

Jesus' Power Is from God

¹⁴Once Jesus was sending a demon*d* out of a man who could not talk. When the demon came out, the man was able to speak. The people were amazed. ¹⁵But some of them said, "Jesus uses the power of Beelzebul*d* to force demons out of people. Beelzebul is the ruler of demons."

¹⁶Other people wanted to test Jesus. They asked him to give them a sign from heaven. ¹⁷But Jesus knew what they were thinking. So he said to them, "Every kingdom that is divided and fights against itself will be destroyed. And a family that fights against itself will break apart. ¹⁸So if Satan is fighting against himself, then how will his kingdom last? You say that I use the power of Beelzebul to force out demons. ¹⁹But if I use the power of Beelzebul to force out demons, then by what power do your people force out demons? So your own people prove that you are wrong. ²⁰But if I use the power of God to force out demons, the kingdom of God has come to you!

²¹"When a strong man with many weapons guards his own house, then the things in his house are safe. ²²But suppose a stronger man comes and defeats him. The stronger man will take away the weapons that the first man trusted to keep his house safe. Then the stronger man will do what he wants with the first man's things.

²³"If anyone is not with me, he is against me. He who does not work with me is working against me.

The Empty Man

²⁴"When an evil spirit comes out of

a person, it travels through dry places, looking for a place to rest. But that spirit finds no place to rest. So it says, 'I will go back to the home I left'. 25When the spirit comes back to that person, it finds that home swept clean and made neat. 26Then the evil spirit goes out and brings seven other spirits more evil than itself. Then all the evil spirits go into that person and live there. And he has even more trouble than he had before."

People Who Are Truly Blessed

27When Jesus was saying these things, a woman in the crowd spoke out. She said to Jesus, "Your mother is blessed because she gave birth to you and nursed you."

28But Jesus said, "Those who hear the teaching of God and obey it — they are the ones who are truly blessed."

Give Us Proof!

29The crowd grew larger. Jesus said, "The people who live today are evil. They ask for a miracle*d* as a sign from God. But they will have no sign — only the sign of Jonah.*n* 30Jonah was a sign for those people who lived in Nineveh. In the same way the Son of Man*d* will be a sign for the people of this time. 31On the Judgement Day the Queen of the South*n* will stand up with the men who live now. She will show that they are guilty because she came from far away to listen to Solomon's wise teaching. And I tell you that someone greater than Solomon is here! 32On the Judgement Day the men of Nineveh will stand up with the people who live now. And they will show that you are guilty, because when Jonah preached to those people, they changed their hearts and lives.

And I tell you that someone greater than Jonah is here!

Be a Light for the World

33"No one takes a light and puts it under a bowl or hides it. Instead, he puts the light on a lampstand so that the people who come in can see. 34Your eye is a light for the body. If your eyes are good, then your whole body will be full of light. But if your eyes are evil, then your whole body will be full of darkness. 35So be careful! Don't let the light in you become darkness. 36If your whole body is full of light, and none of it is dark, then you will shine bright, as when a lamp shines on you."

Jesus Accuses the Pharisees

37After Jesus had finished speaking, a Pharisee*d* asked Jesus to eat with him. So Jesus went in and sat at the table. 38But the Pharisee was surprised when he saw that Jesus did not wash his hands*n* before the meal. 39The Lord said to him, "You Pharisees clean the outside of the cup and the dish. But inside you are full of greed and evil. 40You are foolish. The same One who made what is outside also made what is inside. 41So give what is in your cups and dishes to the poor. Then you will be fully clean. 42But how terrible for you Pharisees! You give God one-tenth of even your mint, your rue, and every other plant in your garden. But you forget to be fair to other people and to love God. These are the things you should do. And you should also continue to do those other things — like giving one-tenth. 43How terrible for you Pharisees, because you love to get the most important seats in the syna-

---

sign of Jonah Jonah's three days in the big fish are like Jesus' three days in the tomb.
Queen of the South The Queen of Sheba. She travelled 1,000 miles to learn God's wisdom from Solomon. Read 1 Kings 10:1-3.
wash his hands This was a Jewish religious custom that the Pharisees thought was very important.

gogues.*d* And you love people to show respect to you in the marketplaces. ⁴⁴How terrible for you, because you are like hidden graves. People walk on them without knowing it."

Jesus Talks to Teachers of the Law

⁴⁵One of the teachers of the law said to Jesus, "Teacher, when you say these things, you are insulting us, too."

⁴⁶Jesus answered, "How terrible for you, you teachers of the law! You make strict rules that are very hard for people to obey. But you yourselves don't even try to follow those rules. ⁴⁷How terrible for you, because you build tombs for the prophets.*d* But these are the prophets that your fathers killed! ⁴⁸And now you show that you approve of what your fathers did. They killed the prophets, and you build tombs for the prophets! ⁴⁹This is why in his wisdom God said, 'I will send prophets and apostles*d* to them. Some of my prophets and apostles will be killed, and others will be treated cruelly'. ⁵⁰So you who live now will be punished for the deaths of all the prophets who were killed since the beginning of the world. ⁵¹You will be punished for the killing of Abel and for the killing of Zechariah.*n* Zechariah was killed between the altar and the Temple.*d* Yes, I tell you that you people who live now will be punished for them all.

⁵²"How terrible for you, you teachers of the law. You have hidden the key to learning about God. You yourselves would not learn, and you stopped others from learning, too."

⁵³When Jesus was leaving, the teachers of the law and the Pharisees*d* began to give him trouble, asking him questions about many things. ⁵⁴They were trying to catch Jesus saying something wrong.

Don't Be Like the Pharisees

12 Many thousands of people had gathered. There were so many people that they were stepping on each other. Before Jesus spoke to them, he said to his followers, "Be careful of the yeast of the Pharisees.*d* They are hypocrites.*d* ²Everything that is hidden will be shown. Everything that is secret will be made known. ³The things you say in the dark will be told in the light. The things you have whispered in an inner room will be shouted from the top of the house."

Fear Only God

⁴Then Jesus said to the people, "I tell you, my friends, don't be afraid of people. People can kill the body, but after that they can do nothing more to hurt you. ⁵I will show you the One to fear. You should fear him who has the power to kill you and also to throw you into hell. Yes, he is the One you should fear.

⁶"When five sparrows are sold, they cost only two pennies. But God does not forget any of them. ⁷Yes, God even knows how many hairs you have on your head. Don't be afraid. You are worth much more than many sparrows.

Don't Be Ashamed of Jesus

⁸"I tell you, if anyone stands before others and says that he believes in me, then I will say that he belongs to me. I will say this before the angels of God. ⁹But if anyone stands before others and says he does not believe in me, then I will say that he does not belong to me. I will say this before the angels of God.

¹⁰"If a person says something against the Son of Man,*d* he can be forgiven. But a person who says bad

---

Abel . . . Zechariah In the Hebrew Old Testament, the first and last men to be murdered.

things against the Holy Spirit[d] will not be forgiven.

[11]"When men bring you into the synagogues[d] before the leaders and other important men, don't worry about how to defend yourself or what to say. [12]At that time the Holy Spirit will teach you what you must say."

Jesus Warns Against Selfishness

[13]One of the men in the crowd said to Jesus, "Teacher, tell my brother to divide with me the property our father left us."

[14]But Jesus said to him, "Who said that I should be your judge or decide how to divide the property between you two?" [15]Then Jesus said to them, "Be careful and guard against all kinds of greed. A man's life is not measured by the many things he owns."

[16]Then Jesus used this story: "There was a rich man who had some land, which grew a good crop of food. [17]The rich man thought to himself, 'What will I do? I have no place to keep all my crops'. [18]Then he said, 'I know what I will do. I will tear down my barns and build bigger ones! I will put all my grain and other goods together in my new barns. [19]Then I can say to myself, I have enough good things stored to last for many years. Rest, eat, drink, and enjoy life!'

[20]"But God said to that man, 'Foolish man! Tonight you will die. So who will get those things you have prepared for yourself?'

[21]"This is how it will be for anyone who stores things up only for himself and is not rich towards God."

Don't Worry

[22]Jesus said to his followers, "So I tell you, don't worry about the food you need to live. Don't worry about the clothes you need for your body. [23]Life is more important than food. And the body is more important than clothes. [24]Look at the birds. They don't plant or harvest. They don't

save food in houses or barns. But God takes care of them. And you are worth much more than birds. [25]None of you can add any time to your life by worrying about it. [26]If you cannot do even the little things, then why worry about the big things? [27]Look at the wild flowers. See how they grow. They don't work or make clothes for themselves. But I tell you that even Solomon, the great and rich king, was not dressed as beautifully as one of these flowers. [28]God clothes the grass in the field like that. That grass is living today, but tomorrow it will be thrown into the fire. So you know how much more God will clothe you. Don't have so little faith! [29]Don't always think about what you will eat or what you will drink. Don't worry about it. [30]All the people in the world are trying to get those things. Your Father knows that you need them. [31]The thing you should seek is God's kingdom. Then all the other things you need will be given to you.

Don't Trust in Money

[32]"Don't fear, little flock. Your Father wants to give you the kingdom. [33]Sell the things you have and give to the poor. Get for yourselves purses that don't wear out. Get the treasure in heaven that never runs out. Thieves can't steal it in heaven, and moths can't destroy it. [34]Your heart will be where your treasure is.

Always Be Ready

[35]"Be ready! Be dressed for service and have your lamps shining. [36]Be like servants who are waiting for their master to come home from a wedding party. The master comes and knocks. The servants immediately open the door for him. [37]Those servants will be blessed when their master comes home, because he sees that his servants are ready and waiting for him. I tell you the truth. The master will dress himself to serve and tell the servants to sit at the table. Then the

master will serve them. ³⁸Those servants might have to wait until midnight or later for their master. But they will be happy when he comes in and finds them still waiting.

³⁹"Remember this: if the owner of the house knew what time a thief was coming, then the owner would not allow the thief to enter his house. ⁴⁰So you also must be ready! The Son of Man*d* will come at a time when you don't expect him!"

Who Is the Trusted Servant?

⁴¹Peter said, "Lord, did you tell this story for us or for all people?"

⁴²The Lord said, "Who is the wise and trusted servant? Who is the servant the master trusts to give the other servants their food at the right time? ⁴³When the master comes and finds his servant doing the work he gave him, that servant will be very happy. ⁴⁴I tell you the truth. The master will choose that servant to take care of everything the master owns. ⁴⁵But what will happen if the servant is evil and thinks that his master will not come back soon? That servant will begin to beat the other servants, men and women. He will eat and drink and get drunk. ⁴⁶Then the master will come when that servant is not ready. It will be a time when the servant is not expecting him. Then the master will cut him in pieces and send him away to be with the others who don't obey.

⁴⁷"The servant who knows what his master wants but is not ready or does not do what the master wants will be beaten with many blows! ⁴⁸But the servant who does not know what his master wants and does things that should be punished will be beaten with few blows. Everyone who has been given much will be responsible for much. Much more will be expected from the one who has been given more."

Jesus Causes Division

⁴⁹Jesus continued speaking, "I came to set fire to the world. I wish it were already burning! ⁵⁰I must be baptised with a different kind of baptism.*n* I feel very troubled until it is over. ⁵¹Do you think that I came to give peace to the world? No! I came to divide the world! ⁵²From now on, a family with five people will be divided, three against two, and two against three. ⁵³A father and son will be divided: the son will be against his father. The father will be against his son. A mother and her daughter will be divided: the daughter will be against her mother. The mother will be against her daughter. A mother-in-law and her daughter-in-law will be divided: the daughter-in-law will be against her mother-in-law. The mother-in-law will be against her daughter-in-law."

Understanding the Times

⁵⁴Then Jesus said to the people, "When you see clouds coming up in the west, you say, 'It's going to rain'. And soon it begins to rain. ⁵⁵When you feel the wind begin to blow from the south, you say, 'It will be a hot day'. And you are right. ⁵⁶Hypocrites!*d* You can understand the weather. Why don't you understand what is happening now?

Settle Your Problems

⁵⁷"Why can't you decide for yourselves what is right? ⁵⁸When someone is suing you, and you are going with him to court, try hard to settle it on the way. If you don't settle it, he may take you to the judge. The judge might turn you over to the officer. And the officer might throw you into jail. ⁵⁹You will not get out of there until

I . . . baptism. Jesus was talking about the suffering he would soon go through.

they have taken everything you have."

Change Your Hearts

13 At that time some people were there with Jesus. They told him about what had happened to some people from Galilee. Pilate[n] killed those people while they were worshipping. He mixed their blood with the blood of the animals they were sacrificing to God. [2]Jesus answered, "Do you think this happened to them because they were more sinful than all others from Galilee? [3]No, they were not! But if all of you don't change your hearts and lives, then you will be destroyed as they were! [4]What about those 18 people who died when the tower of Siloam fell on them? Do you think they were more sinful than all the others who live in Jerusalem? [5]They were not! But I tell you, if you don't change your hearts and lives, then you will all be destroyed too!"

The Useless Tree

[6]Jesus told this story: "A man had a fig tree planted in his vineyard. He came looking for some fruit on the tree, but he found none. [7]So the man said to his servant who took care of his vineyard, 'I have been looking for fruit on this tree for three years, but I never find any. Cut it down! Why should it waste the ground?' [8]But the servant answered, 'Master, let the tree have one more year to produce fruit. Let me dig up the soil around it and put on some fertiliser. [9]Maybe the tree will produce fruit next year. If the tree still doesn't produce fruit, then you can cut it down'."

Jesus Heals on the Sabbath

[10]Jesus was teaching in one of the synagogues[d] on the Sabbath[d] day. [11]In the synagogue there was a woman who had an evil spirit in her. This spirit had made the woman a cripple for 18 years. Her back was always bent; she could not stand up straight. [12]When Jesus saw her, he called her over and said, "Woman, your sickness has left you!" [13]Jesus put his hands on her. Immediately she was able to stand up straight and began praising God.

[14]The synagogue leader was angry because Jesus healed on the Sabbath day. He said to the people, "There are six days for work. So come to be healed on one of those days. Don't come for healing on the Sabbath day."

[15]The Lord answered, "You people are hypocrites![d] All of you untie your work animals and lead them to drink water every day — even on the Sabbath day! [16]This woman that I healed is our Jewish sister. But Satan has held her for 18 years. Surely it is not wrong for her to be freed from her sickness on a Sabbath day!" [17]When Jesus said this, all the men who were criticising him were ashamed. And all the people were happy with the wonderful things Jesus was doing.

Stories of Mustard Seed and Yeast

[18]Then Jesus said, "What is God's kingdom like? What can I compare it with? [19]God's kingdom is like the seed of the mustard plant.[n] A man plants this seed in his garden. The seed grows and becomes a tree. The wild birds build nests on its branches."

[20]Jesus said again, "What can I compare God's kingdom with? [21]It is like yeast that a woman mixes into a big bowl of flour. The yeast makes all the dough rise."

The Narrow Door

[22]Jesus was teaching in every town and village. He continued to travel towards Jerusalem. [23]Someone said to

---

Pilate Pontius Pilate was the Roman governor of Judea from A.D. 26 to A.D. 36.
mustard plant The seed is very small, but the plant grows taller than a man.

Jesus, "Lord, how many people will be saved? Only a few?"

Jesus said, [24]"Try hard to enter through the narrow door that opens the way to heaven! Many people will try to enter there, but they will not be able. [25]A man gets up and closes the door of his house. You can stand outside and knock on the door. You can say, 'Sir, open the door for us!' But he will answer, 'I don't know you! Where did you come from?' [26]Then you will say, 'We ate and drank with you. You taught in the streets of our town'. [27]But he will say to you, 'I don't know you! Where did you come from? Go away from me! All of you do evil!' [28]You will see Abraham, Isaac, Jacob, and all the prophets[d] in God's kingdom. But you will be thrown outside. Then you will cry and grind your teeth with pain. [29]People will come from the east, west, north, and south. They will sit down at the table in the kingdom of God. [30]Those who have the lowest place in life now will have the highest place in the future. And those who have the highest place now will have the lowest place in the future."

Jesus Will Die in Jerusalem

[31]At that time some Pharisees[d] came to Jesus and said, "Go away from here! Herod wants to kill you!"

[32]Jesus said to them, "Go and tell that fox Herod, 'Today and tomorrow I am forcing demons[d] out of people and finishing my work of healing. Then, on the third day, I will reach my goal'. [33]Yet I must be on my way today and tomorrow and the next day. Surely it cannot be right for a prophet[d] to be killed anywhere except in Jerusalem.

[34]"Jerusalem, Jerusalem! You kill the prophets. You kill with stones those men that God has sent you. Many times I wanted to help your people. I wanted to gather them to-

gether as a hen gathers her chicks under her wings. But you did not let me. [35]Now your home will be left completely empty. I tell you, you will not see me again until that time when you will say, 'God bless the One who comes in the name of the Lord'."[n]

Is It Right to Heal on the Sabbath?

14 On a Sabbath[d] day, Jesus went to the home of a leading Pharisee[d] to eat with him. The people there were all watching Jesus very closely. [2]A man with dropsy[n] was brought before Jesus. [3]Jesus said to the Pharisees and teachers of the law, "Is it right or wrong to heal on the Sabbath day?" [4]But they would not answer his question. So Jesus took the man, healed him, and sent him away. [5]Jesus said to the Pharisees and teachers of the law, "If your son or ox falls into a well on the Sabbath day, will you not pull him out quickly?" [6]And they could not answer him.

Don't Make Yourself Important

[7]Then Jesus noticed that some of the guests were choosing the best places to sit. So Jesus told this story: [8]"When someone invites you to a wedding feast, don't take the most important seat. The host may have invited someone more important than you. [9]And if you are sitting in the most important seat, the host will come to you and say, 'Give this man your seat'. Then you will begin to move down to the last place. And you will be very embarrassed. [10]So when you are invited, go and sit in a seat that is not important. Then the host will come to you and say, 'Friend, move up here to a more important place!' Then all the other guests will respect you. [11]Everyone who makes himself great will be made humble. But the

'God . . . Lord'.   Quotation from Psalm 118:26.
dropsy   A sickness that causes the body to swell larger and larger.

person who makes himself humble will be made great."

You Will Be Rewarded

[12]Then Jesus said to the man who had invited him, "When you give a lunch or a dinner, don't invite only your friends, brothers, relatives, and rich neighbours. At another time they will invite you to eat with them. Then you will have your reward. [13]Instead, when you give a feast, invite the poor, the crippled, the lame and the blind. [14]Then you will be blessed, because they cannot pay you back. They have nothing. But you will be rewarded when the good people rise from death."

A Story About a Big Banquet

[15]One of the men sitting at the table with Jesus heard these things. The man said to Jesus, "The people who will eat a meal in God's kingdom are blessed."

[16]Jesus said to him, "A man gave a big banquet and invited many people. [17]When it was time to eat, the man sent his servant to tell the guests, 'Come! Everything is ready!'

[18]"But all the guests said they could not come. Each man made an excuse. The first one said, 'I have just bought a field, and I must go and look at it. Please excuse me'. [19]Another man said, 'I have just bought five pairs of oxen; I must go and try them. Please excuse me'. [20]A third man said, 'I just got married; I can't come'. [21]So the servant returned. He told his master what had happened. Then the master became angry and said, 'Go at once into the streets and alleys of the town. Bring in the poor, the crippled, the blind, and the lame'. [22]Later the servant said to him, 'Master, I did what you told me to do, but we still have places for more people'. [23]The master said to the servant, 'Go out to the roads and country lanes. Tell the people there to come. I want my house to

be full! [24]None of those men that I invited first will ever eat with me!' "

You Must First Plan

[25]Large crowds were travelling with Jesus. He turned and said to them, [26]"If anyone comes to me but loves his father, mother, wife, children, brothers, or sisters more than he loves me, then he cannot be my follower. A person must love me more than he loves himself! [27]If anyone is not willing to die on a cross when he follows me, then he cannot be my follower. [28]If you wanted to build a tower, you would first sit down and decide how much it would cost. You must see if you have enough money to finish the job. [29]If you don't do that, you might begin the work, but you would not be able to finish. And if you could not finish it, then all who would see it would laugh at you. [30]They would say, 'This man began to build but was not able to finish!'

[31]"If a king is going to fight against another king, first he will sit down and plan. If the king has only 10,000 men, he will plan to see if he is able to defeat the other king who has 20,000 men. [32]If he cannot defeat the other king, then he will send some men to speak to the other king and ask for peace. [33]In the same way, you must give up everything you have to follow me. If you don't, you cannot be my follower!

Don't Lose Your Influence

[34]"Salt is a good thing. But if the salt loses its salty taste, then it is worth nothing. You cannot make it salty again. [35]It is no good for the soil or for manure. People throw it away.

"You people who hear me, listen!"

A Lost Sheep and a Lost Coin

15 Many tax collectors and "sinners" came to listen to Jesus. [2]The Pharisees[d] and the teachers of the law began to complain: "Look!

This man welcomes sinners and even eats with them!"

³Then Jesus told them this story: ⁴"Suppose one of you has 100 sheep, but he loses one of them. Then he will leave the other 99 sheep alone and go out and look for the lost sheep. The man will keep on searching for the lost sheep until he finds it. ⁵And when he finds it, the man is very happy. He puts it on his shoulders ⁶and goes home. He calls to his friends and neighbours and says, 'Be happy with me because I found my lost sheep!' ⁷In the same way, I tell you there is much joy in heaven when one sinner changes his heart. There is more joy for that one sinner than there is for 99 good people who don't need to change.

⁸"Suppose a woman has ten silver coins," but she loses one of them. She will light a lamp and clean the house. She will look carefully for the coin until she finds it. ⁹And when she finds it, she will call her friends and neighbours and say, 'Be happy with me because I have found the coin that I lost!' ¹⁰In the same way, there is joy before the angels of God when one sinner changes his heart."

The Son Who Left Home

¹¹Then Jesus said, "A man had two sons. ¹²The younger son said to his father, 'Give me my share of the property'. So the father divided the property between his two sons. ¹³Then the younger son gathered up all that was his and left. He travelled far away to another country. There he wasted his money in foolish living. ¹⁴He spent everything that he had. Soon after that, the land became very dry, and there was no rain. There was not enough food to eat anywhere in the country. The son was hungry and needed money. ¹⁵So he got a job with one of the citizens there. The man sent the son into the fields to feed pigs. ¹⁶The son was so hungry that he was willing to eat the food the pigs were eating. But no one gave him anything. ¹⁷The son realised that he had been very foolish. He thought, 'All of my father's servants have plenty of food. But I am here, almost dying with hunger. ¹⁸I will leave and return to my father. I'll say to him: Father, I have sinned against God and have done wrong to you. ¹⁹I am not good enough to be called your son. But let me be like one of your servants'. ²⁰So the son left and went to his father.

"While the son was still a long way off, his father saw him coming. He felt sorry for his son. So the father ran to him, and hugged and kissed him. ²¹The son said, 'Father, I have sinned against God and have done wrong to you. I am not good enough to be called your son'. ²²But the father said to his servants, 'Hurry! Bring the best clothes and put them on him. Also, put a ring on his finger and sandals on his feet. ²³And get our fat calf and kill it. Then we can have a feast and celebrate! ²⁴My son was dead, but now he is alive again! He was lost, but now he is found!' So they began to celebrate.

²⁵"The older son was in the field. As he came closer to the house, he heard the sound of music and dancing. ²⁶So he called to one of the servants and asked, 'What does all this mean?' ²⁷The servant said, 'Your brother has come back. Your father killed the fat calf to eat because your brother came home safely!' ²⁸The older son was angry and would not go in to the feast. So his father went out and begged him to come in. ²⁹The son said to his father, 'I have served you like a slave for many years! I have always obeyed your commands, but you never even killed a young goat for me to have a feast with my friends. ³⁰But your other son has wasted all your money on

silver coins A Roman denarius. One coin was the average pay for one day's work.

prostitutes.[d] Then he comes home, and you kill the fat calf for him!' [31]The father said to him, 'Son, you are always with me. All that I have is yours. [32]We had to celebrate and be happy because your brother was dead, but now he is alive. He was lost, but now he is found'."

True Wealth

16 Jesus also said to his followers, "Once there was a rich man. He had a manager to take care of his business. Later, the rich man learned that his manager was cheating him. [2]So he called the manager in and said to him, 'I have heard bad things about you. Give me a report of what you have done with my money. You can't be my manager any longer!' [3]Later, the manager thought to himself, 'What will I do? My master is taking my job away from me! I am not strong enough to dig ditches. I am too proud to beg. [4]I know! I'll do something so that when I lose my job, people will welcome me into their homes'.

[5]"So the manager called in everyone who owed the master any money. He said to the first man, 'How much do you owe my master?' [6]The man answered, 'I owe him 3000 litres of olive oil'. The manager said to him, 'Here is your bill; sit down quickly and make the bill less. Write 1500 litres'. [7]Then the manager said to another man, 'How much do you owe my master?' The man answered, 'I owe him 36,000 litres of wheat'. Then the manager said to him, 'Here is your bill; you can make it less. Write 28,000 litres'. [8]Later, the master praised the dishonest manager for being clever. Yes, worldly people are smarter with their own kind than spiritual people are.

[9]"I tell you, make friends for yourselves using worldly riches. Then, when those things are gone, you will be welcomed in that home that contin-

ues for ever. [10]Whoever can be trusted with small things can also be trusted with large things. Whoever is dishonest in little things will be dishonest in large things too. [11]If you cannot be trusted with worldly riches, then you will not be trusted with the true riches. [12]And if you cannot be trusted with the things that belong to someone else, then you will not be given things of your own.

[13]"No servant can serve two masters. He will hate one master and love the other. Or he will follow one master and refuse to follow the other. You cannot serve both God and money."

God's Law Cannot Be Changed

[14]The Pharisees[d] were listening to all these things. They made fun of Jesus because they all loved money. [15]Jesus said to them, "You make yourselves look good in front of people. But God knows what is really in your hearts. The things that are important to people are worth nothing to God.

[16]"God wanted the people to live by the law of Moses and the writings of the prophets.[d] But ever since John[n] came, the Good News[d] about the kingdom of God is being told. Now everyone is trying hard to get into the kingdom. [17]Even the smallest part of a letter in the law cannot be changed. It would be easier for heaven and earth to pass away.

Divorce and Remarriage

[18]"If a man divorces his wife and marries another woman, he is guilty of adultery.[d] And the man who marries a divorced woman is also guilty of adultery."

The Rich Man and Lazarus

[19]Jesus said, "There was a rich man who always dressed in the finest clothes. He lived in luxury every day. [20]There was also a very poor man

John John the Baptist, who preached to people about Christ's coming (Matthew 3, Luke 3).

named Lazarus, whose body was covered with sores. Lazarus was often placed at the rich man's gate. 21He wanted to eat only the small pieces of food that fell from the rich man's table. And the dogs would come and lick his sores! 22Later, Lazarus died. The angels took Lazarus and placed him in the arms of Abraham.*d* The rich man died, too, and was buried. 23But he was sent to where the dead are and had much pain. The rich man saw Abraham far away with Lazarus in his arms. 24He called, 'Father Abraham, have mercy on me! Send Lazarus to me so that he can dip his finger in water and cool my tongue. I am suffering in this fire!' 25But Abraham said, 'My child, remember when you lived? You had all the good things in life, but all the bad things happened to Lazarus. Now Lazarus is comforted here, and you are suffering. 26Also, there is a big pit between you and us. No one can cross over to help you. And no one can leave there and come here'. 27The rich man said, 'Then please send Lazarus to my father's house on earth! 28I have five brothers. Lazarus could warn my brothers so that they will not come to this place of pain'. 29But Abraham said, 'They have the law of Moses and the writings of the prophets*d* to read; let them learn from them!' 30The rich man said, 'No, father Abraham! If someone came to them from the dead, they would believe and change their hearts and lives'. 31But Abraham said to him, 'No! If your brothers won't listen to Moses and the prophets, then they won't listen to someone who comes back from death'."

Sin and Forgiveness

17 Jesus said to his followers, "Things will surely happen that cause people to sin. But how terrible for the one who causes them to hap-

pen. 2It would be better for him to be thrown into the sea with a large stone around his neck than to cause one of these weak people to sin. 3So be careful!

"If your brother sins, tell him he is wrong. But if he is sorry and stops sinning, forgive him. 4If your brother sins against you seven times in one day, but he says that he is sorry each time, then forgive him."

How Big Is Your Faith?

5The apostles*d* said to the Lord, "Give us more faith!"

6The Lord said, "If your faith is as big as a mustard seed,*n* then you can say to this mulberry tree, 'Dig yourself up and plant yourself in the sea!' And the tree will obey you.

Be Good Servants

7"Suppose one of you has a servant who has been ploughing the ground or caring for the sheep. When the servant comes in from working in the field, would you say, 'Come in and sit down to eat'? 8No, you would say to your servant, 'Prepare something for me to eat. Then get yourself ready and serve me. When I finish eating and drinking, then you can eat'. 9The servant does not get any special thanks for doing what his master told him to do. 10It is the same with you. When you do everything you are told to do, you should say, 'We don't deserve any special thanks. We have only done the work we should do'."

Be Thankful

11Jesus was on his way to Jerusalem. Travelling from Galilee to Samaria, 12he came into a small town. Ten men met him there. These men did not come close to Jesus, because they all had a harmful skin disease. 13But they called to him, "Jesus! Master! Please help us!"

mustard seed This seed is very small, but the plant grows taller than a man.

[14]When Jesus saw the men, he said, "Go and show yourselves to the priests."[n]

While the ten men were going, they were healed. [15]When one of them saw that he was healed, he went back to Jesus. He praised God in a loud voice. [16]Then he bowed down at Jesus' feet and thanked him. (This man was a Samaritan.[d]) [17]Jesus asked, "Ten men were healed; where are the other nine? [18]Is this Samaritan the only one who came back to thank God?" [19]Then Jesus said to him, "Stand up and go on your way. You were healed because you believed."

God's Kingdom Is Within You

[20]Some of the Pharisees[d] asked Jesus, "When will the kingdom of God come?"

Jesus answered, "God's kingdom is coming, but not in a way that you will be able to see with your eyes. [21]People will not say, 'Look, God's kingdom is here!' or, 'There it is!' No, God's kingdom is within you."

[22]Then Jesus said to his followers, "The time will come when you will want very much to see one of the days of the Son of Man.[d] But you will not be able to see it. [23]People will say to you, 'Look, there he is!' or, 'Look, here he is!' Stay where you are; don't go away and search.

When Jesus Comes Again

[24]"The Son of Man[d] will come again. On the day he comes he will shine like lightning, which flashes across the sky and lights it up from one side to the other. [25]But first, the Son of Man must suffer many things and be rejected by the people of this time. [26]When the Son of Man comes again, it will be as it was when Noah lived. [27]In the time of Noah, people were eating, drinking, and getting married even on the day when Noah entered the boat. Then the flood came and killed all the people. [28]It will be the same as during the time of Lot. Those people were eating, drinking, buying, selling, planting, and building. [29]They were doing these things even on the day Lot left Sodom.[n] Then fire and sulphur rained down from the sky and killed them all. [30]This is exactly how it will be when the Son of Man comes again.

[31]"On that day, if a man is on his roof, he will not have time to go inside and get his things. If a man is in the field, he cannot go back home. [32]Remember what happened to Lot's wife?[n] [33]Whoever tries to keep his life will give up true life. But whoever gives up his life will have true life. [34]At the time when I come again, there may be two people sleeping in one bed. One will be taken and the other will be left. [35]There may be two women grinding grain together. One will be taken and the other will be left." [36][n]

[37]The followers asked Jesus, "Where will this be, Lord?"

Jesus answered, "People can always find a dead body by looking for the vultures."

God Will Answer His People

18 Then Jesus used this story to teach his followers that they should always pray and never lose hope. [2]"Once there was a judge in a town. He did not care about God. He also did not care what people thought

show . . . priests The law of Moses said a priest must say when a Jew with a harmful skin disease became well.
Sodom City that God destroyed because the people were so evil.
Lot's wife A story about what happened to Lot's wife is found in Genesis 19:15-17,26.
Verse 36 A few Greek copies add verse 36: "Two men will be in the same field. One man will be taken, but the other will be left behind."

about him. [3]In that same town there was a widow who kept coming to this judge. She said, 'There is a man who is not being fair to me. Give me my rights!' [4]But the judge did not want to help the widow. After a long time, he thought to himself, 'I don't care about God. And I don't care about what people think. [5]But this widow is bothering me. I will see that she gets her rights, or she will bother me until I am worn out!'"

[6]The Lord said, "Listen to what the bad judge said. [7]God's people cry to him night and day. God will always give them what is right, and he will not be slow to answer them. [8]I tell you, God will help his people quickly! But when the Son of Man[d] comes again, will he find those on earth who believe in him?"

Being Right with God

[9]There were some people who thought that they were very good and looked down on everyone else. Jesus used this story to teach them: [10]"One day there was a Pharisee[d] and a tax collector. Both went to the Temple[d] to pray. [11]The Pharisee stood alone, away from the tax collector. When the Pharisee prayed, he said, 'God, I thank you that I am not as bad as other people. I am not like men who steal, cheat, or take part in adultery.[d] I thank you that I am better than this tax collector. [12]I give up eating[n] twice a week, and I give one-tenth of everything I earn!'

[13]"The tax collector stood at a distance. When he prayed, he would not even look up to heaven. He beat on his chest because he was so sad. He said, 'God, have mercy on me. I am a sinner!' [14]I tell you, when this man went home, he was right with God. But the Pharisee was not right with

God. Everyone who makes himself great will be made humble. But everyone who makes himself humble will be made great."

Who Will Enter God's Kingdom?

[15]Some people brought their small children to Jesus so that he could touch them. When the followers saw this, they told the people not to do it. [16]But Jesus called the little children to him and said to his followers, "Let the little children come to me. Don't stop them, because the kingdom of God belongs to people who are like these little children. [17]I tell you the truth. You must accept God's kingdom like a little child, or you will never enter it!"

A Rich Man's Question

[18]A Jewish leader asked Jesus, "Good Teacher, what must I do to get the life that continues for ever?"

[19]Jesus said to him, "Why do you call me good? Only God is good. [20]You know the commands: 'You must not be guilty of adultery.[d] You must not murder anyone. You must not steal. You must not tell lies about your neighbour in court. Honour your father and mother'."[n]

[21]But the leader said, "I have obeyed all these commands since I was a boy!"

[22]When Jesus heard this, he said to him, "But there is still one more thing you need to do. Sell everything you have and give the money to the poor. You will have a reward in heaven. Then come and follow me!" [23]But when the man heard this, he became very sad because he was very rich.

[24]When Jesus saw that the man was sad, he said, "It will be very hard for rich people to enter the kingdom of God! [25]It would be easier for a camel to go through the eye of a needle than

---

give up eating This is called "fasting". The people would give up eating for a special time of prayer and worship to God. It was also done to show sadness.
'You . . . mother'. Quotation from Exodus 20:12-16; Deuteronomy 5:16-20.

for a rich person to enter the kingdom of God!"

Who Can Be Saved?

26When the people heard this, they asked, "Then who can be saved?"

27Jesus answered, "God can do things that are not possible for men to do!"

28Peter said, "Look, we left everything we had and followed you!"

29Jesus said, "I tell you the truth. Everyone who has left his house, wife, brothers, parents, or children for God's kingdom 30will get much more than he left. He will receive many times more in this life. And after he dies, he will live with God for ever."

Jesus Will Rise from Death

31Then Jesus talked to the 12 apostles*d* alone. He said to them, "Listen! We are going to Jerusalem. Everything that God told the prophets*d* to write about the Son of Man*d* will happen! 32He will be turned over to the non-Jewish people. They will laugh at him, insult him, and spit on him. 33They will beat him with whips and then kill him. But on the third day after his death, he will rise to life again." 34The apostles tried to understand this, but they could not; the meaning was hidden from them.

Jesus Heals a Blind Man

35Jesus was coming near the city of Jericho. There was a blind man sitting beside the road, begging for money. 36When he heard the people coming down the road, he asked, "What is happening?"

37They told him, "Jesus, the one from Nazareth, is coming here."

38The blind man cried out, "Jesus, Son of David!*d* Please help me!"

39The people who were in front, leading the group, told the blind man to be quiet. But the blind man shouted

more and more, "Son of David, please help me!"

40Jesus stopped and said, "Bring the blind man to me!" When he came near, Jesus asked him, 41"What do you want me to do for you?"

He said, "Lord, I want to see again."

42Jesus said to him, "Then see! You are healed because you believed."

43At once the man was able to see, and he followed Jesus, thanking God. All the people who saw this praised God.

Zacchaeus

19 Jesus was going through the city of Jericho. 2In Jericho there was a man named Zacchaeus. He was a wealthy, very important tax collector. 3He wanted to see who Jesus was, but he was too short to see above the crowd. 4He ran ahead to a place where he knew Jesus would come. He climbed a sycamore tree so he could see Jesus. 5When Jesus came to that place, he looked up and saw Zacchaeus in the tree. He said to him, "Zacchaeus, hurry and come down! I must stay at your house today."

6Zacchaeus came down quickly. He was pleased to have Jesus in his house. 7All the people saw this and began to complain, "Look at the kind of man Jesus stays with. Zacchaeus is a sinner!"

8But Zacchaeus said to the Lord, "I will give half of my money to the poor. If I have cheated anyone, I will pay that person back four times more!"

9Jesus said, "Salvation has come to this house today. This man truly belongs to the family of Abraham. 10The Son of Man*d* came to find lost people and save them."

A Story About Three Servants

11Jesus travelled closer to Jerusalem. Some of the people thought that God's kingdom would appear soon. 12Jesus knew that the people thought this, so he told them this story: "A very important man was preparing to go to a country far away to be made a king. Then he planned to return home and rule his people. [13]So the man called ten of his servants together. He gave a bag of money[n] to each servant. He said, 'Do business with this money till I get back'. [14]But the people in the kingdom hated the man. So they sent a group to follow him and say, 'We don't want this man to be our king!'

[15]"But the man became king. When he came home, he said, 'Call those servants who have my money. I want to know how much they earned with it'.

[16]"The first servant came and said, 'Sir, I earned ten bags of money with the one bag you gave me!' [17]The king said to the servant, 'Fine! You are a good servant. I see that I can trust you with small things. So now I will let you rule over ten of my cities'.

[18]"The second servant said, 'Sir, with your one bag of money I earned five bags!' [19]The king said to this servant, 'You can rule over five cities'.

[20]"Then another servant came in. The servant said to the king, 'Sir, here is your bag of money. I wrapped it in a piece of cloth and hid it. [21]I was afraid of you because you are a hard man. You even take money that you didn't earn and gather food that you didn't plant'. [22]Then the king said to the servant, 'You evil servant! I will use your own words to condemn you. You said that I am a hard man. You said that I even take money that I didn't earn and gather food that I didn't plant. [23]If that is true, then you should have put my money in the bank. Then, when I came back, my money would have earned some interest'.

[24]"Then the king said to the men who were watching, 'Take the bag of money away from this servant and give it to the servant who earned ten bags of money'. [25]They said to the king, 'But sir, that servant already has ten bags of money!' [26]The king said, 'The one who uses what he has will get more. But the one who does not use what he has will have everything taken away from him. [27]Now where are my enemies who didn't want me to be king? Bring them here and kill them before me'."

Jesus Enters Jerusalem as a King

[28]After Jesus said this, he went on towards Jerusalem. [29]Jesus came near Bethphage and Bethany, towns near the hill called the Mount of Olives.[d] Then he sent out two of his followers. [30]He said, "Go into the town you can see there. When you enter it, you will find a colt tied there. No one has ever ridden this colt. Untie it, and bring it here to me. [31]If anyone asks you why you are taking it, say, 'The Master needs it'."

[32]The two followers went into town. They found the colt just as Jesus told them. [33]The followers untied it, but the owners of the colt came out. They asked the followers, "Why are you untying our colt?"

[34]The followers answered, "The Master needs it." [35]So they brought it to Jesus. They threw their coats on the colt's back and put Jesus on it. [36]As Jesus rode toward Jerusalem, the followers spread their coats on the road before him.

[37]Jesus was coming close to Jerusalem. He was already near the bottom of the Mount of Olives. The whole crowd of followers was very happy. They began shouting praise to God for

---

bag of money One bag of money was a Greek "mina". One mina was enough money to pay a person for working three months.

all the powerful works they had seen. They said,

38"God bless the king who comes in the name of the Lord!

There is peace in heaven and glory to God!"   *Psalm 118:26*

39Some of the Pharisees*d* said to Jesus, "Teacher, tell your followers not to say these things!"

40But Jesus answered, "I tell you, if my followers don't say these things, then the stones will cry out."

Jesus Cries for Jerusalem

41Jesus came near Jerusalem. He saw the city and began to cry for it. 42Jesus said to Jerusalem, "I wish you knew today what would bring you peace! But you can't know it, because it is hidden from you. 43A time is coming when your enemies will build a wall around you and will hold you in on all sides. 44They will destroy you and all your people. Not one stone of your buildings will be left on another. All this will happen because you did not know the time when God came to save you."

Jesus Goes to the Temple

45Jesus went into the Temple.*d* He began to throw out the people who were selling things there. 46He said, "It is written in the Scriptures,*d* 'My Temple will be a house where people will pray'.*n* But you have changed it into a 'hideout for robbers'!"*n*

47Jesus taught in the Temple every day. The leading priests, the teachers of the law, and some of the leaders of the people wanted to kill Jesus. 48But all the people were listening closely to him and were interested in all the things he said. So the leading priests, the teachers of the law, and the leaders did not know how they could kill him.

Jewish Leaders Question Jesus

20 One day Jesus was in the Temple,*d* teaching the people and telling them the Good News.*d* The leading priests, teachers of the law, and older Jewish leaders came up to talk with him. 2They said, "Tell us! What authority do you have to do these things? Who gave you this authority?"

3Jesus answered, "I will ask you a question too. Tell me: 4when John baptised people, did that come from God or from man?"

5The priests, the teachers of the law, and the Jewish leaders all talked about this. They said to each other, "If we answer, 'John's baptism was from God', then Jesus will say, 'Then why did you not believe John?' 6But if we say, 'John's baptism was from man', then all the people will kill us with stones because they believe that John was a prophet."*d* 7So they answered, "We don't know the answer."

8So Jesus said to them, "Then I will not tell you by what authority I do these things!"

God Sends His Son

9Then Jesus told the people this story: "A man planted a vineyard. The man leased the land to some farmers. Then he went away for a long time. 10Later, it was time for the grapes to be picked. So the man sent a servant to those farmers to get his share of the grapes. But they beat the servant and sent him away with nothing. 11Then he sent another servant. They beat this servant too. They showed no respect for him and sent him away with nothing. 12So the man sent a third servant. The farmers hurt this servant badly and threw him out. 13The owner of the vineyard said, 'What will I do now? I will send my son whom I

'My Temple . . . pray'. Quotation from Isaiah 56:7.
'hideout for robbers' Quotation from Jeremiah 7:11.

love very much. Maybe they will respect him!' 14When they saw the son, they said to each other, 'This is the owner's son. This vineyard will be his. If we kill him, then it will be ours!' 15So the farmers threw the son out of the vineyard and killed him.

"What will the owner of this vineyard do? 16He will come and kill those farmers! Then he will give the vineyard to other farmers."

The people heard this story. They said, "No! Let this never happen!"

17But Jesus looked at them and said, "Then what does this verse mean:

'The stone that the builders did
    not want
became the cornerstone'?*d*

Psalm 118:22

18Everyone who falls on that stone will be broken. If that stone falls on you, it will crush you!"

19The teachers of the law and the priests heard this story that Jesus told. They knew the story was about them. So they wanted to arrest Jesus at once. But they were afraid of what the people would do.

The Leaders Try to Trap Jesus

20So they waited for the right time to get Jesus. They sent some spies who acted as if they were good men. They wanted to trap Jesus in what he said so they could hand him over to the authority and power of the governor. 21So the spies asked Jesus, "Teacher, we know that what you say and teach is true. You teach the same to all people. You always teach the truth about God's way. 22Tell us, is it right that we pay taxes to Caesar*d* or not?"

23But Jesus knew that these men were trying to trick him. He said, 24"Show me a coin. Whose name is on the coin? And whose picture is on it?" They said, "Caesar's."

25Jesus said to them, "Then give to Caesar the things that are Caesar's. And give to God the things that are God's."

26The men were amazed at his answer. They could say nothing. They were not able to trap Jesus in anything he said before the people.

Sadducees Try to Trick Jesus

27Some Sadducees*d* came to Jesus. (Sadducees believe that people will not rise from death.) They asked, 28"Teacher, Moses wrote that a man's brother might die. He leaves a wife but no children. Then that man must marry the widow and have children for his dead brother. 29Once there were seven brothers. The first brother married, but died. He had no children. 30Then the second brother married the widow, and he died. 31And the third brother married the widow, and he died. The same thing happened with all the other brothers. They all died and had no children. 32The woman was the last to die. 33But all seven brothers married her. So when people rise from death, whose wife will the woman be?"

34Jesus said to the Sadducees, "On earth, people marry each other. 35But those who will be worthy to be raised from death and live again will not marry. 36In that life they are like angels and cannot die. They are children of God, because they have been raised from death. 37Moses clearly showed that the dead are raised to life. When Moses wrote about the burning bush,*n* he said that the Lord is 'the God of Abraham, the God of Isaac, and the God of Jacob'.*n* 38God is the God of living people, not dead people. All people are alive to God."

39Some of the teachers of the law said, "Teacher, your answer was

---

burning bush Read Exodus 3:1-12 in the Old Testament.
'the God of . . . Jacob'. These words are taken from Exodus 3:6.

good." 40No one was brave enough to ask him another question.

Is the Christ the Son of David?

41Then Jesus said, "Why do people say that the Christ*d* is the Son of David?*d* 42In the book of Psalms, David himself says:

'The Lord said to my Lord:
   Sit by me at my right side,
43until I put your enemies under
      your control'.*n*   *Psalm 110:1*
44David calls the Christ 'Lord'. But the Christ is also the son of David. How can both these things be true?"

Jesus Accuses the Leaders

45While all the people were listening, Jesus said to his followers, 46"Be careful of the teachers of the law. They like to walk around wearing clothes that look important. And they love people to show respect to them in the marketplaces. They love to have the most important seats in the synagogues*d* and at the feasts. 47But they cheat widows and steal their houses. Then they try to make themselves look good by saying long prayers. God will punish these men very much."

True Giving

21 Jesus saw some rich people putting their gifts into the Temple*d* money box.*n* 2Then Jesus saw a poor widow. She put two small copper coins into the box. 3He said, "I tell you the truth. This poor widow gave only two small coins. But she really gave more than all those rich people. 4The rich have plenty; they gave only what they did not need. This woman is very poor, but she gave all she had. And she needed that money to live on."

The Temple Will Be Destroyed

5Some of the followers were talking about the Temple*d* and how it was decorated with beautiful stones and gifts offered to God.

6But Jesus said, "The time will come when all that you see here will be destroyed. Every stone will be thrown down to the ground. Not one stone will be left on another!"

7Some followers asked Jesus, "Teacher, when will these things happen? What will show us that it is time for them to take place?"

8Jesus said, "Be careful! Don't be fooled. Many people will come using my name. They will say, 'I am the Christ'*d* and, 'The right time has come!' But don't follow them. 9When you hear about wars and riots, don't be afraid. These things must happen first. Then the end will come later."

10Then he said to them, "Nations will fight against other nations. Kingdoms will fight against other kingdoms. 11There will be great earthquakes, sicknesses, and other terrible things in many places. In some places there will be no food for the people to eat. Fearful events and great signs will come from heaven.

12"But before all these things happen, people will arrest you and treat you cruelly. They will judge you in their synagogues*d* and put you in jail. You will be forced to stand before kings and governors. They will do all these things to you because you follow me. 13But this will give you an opportunity to tell about me. 14Don't worry about what you will say. 15I will give you the wisdom to say things so that none of your enemies will be able to show that you are wrong. 16Even your parents, brothers, relatives and friends will turn against you. They will kill some of you. 17All people will hate you because you follow me. 18But none of these things can really harm you. 19You will save yourselves by

---

until . . . control Literally, "until I make your enemies a footstool for your feet".
money box A special box in the Jewish place for worship where people put their gifts to God.

continuing strong in your faith through all these things.

Jerusalem Will Be Destroyed

[20]"When you see armies all around Jerusalem, then you will know that it will soon be destroyed. [21]At that time, the people in Judea should run away to the mountains. The people in Jerusalem must get out. If you are near the city, don't go in! [22]These are the days of punishment to make all that is written in the Scriptures come true.[d] [23]At that time, it will be hard for women who are pregnant or have nursing babies! Great trouble will come upon this land, and God will be angry with these people. [24]Some will be killed by the sword and taken as prisoners to all nations. Jerusalem will be crushed by non-Jewish people until their time is over.

Don't Fear

[25]"Amazing things will happen to the sun, moon, and stars. On earth, nations will be afraid because of the roar and fury of the sea. They will not know what to do. [26]People will be so afraid they will faint. They will wonder what is happening to the whole world. Everything in the sky will be changed. [27]Then people will see the Son of Man[d] coming in a cloud with power and great glory. [28]When these things begin to happen, don't fear. Look up and hold your heads high because the time when God will free you is near!"

My Words Will Live For Ever

[29]Then Jesus told this story: "Look at the fig tree and all the other trees. [30]When their leaves appear, you know that summer is near. [31]In the same way, when you see all these things happening, then you will know that God's kingdom is coming very soon. [32]"I tell you the truth. All these things will happen while the people of this time are still living! [33]The whole world, earth and sky, will be de-stroyed; but the words I have said will never be destroyed!

Be Ready All the Time

[34]"Be careful! Don't spend your time feasting and drinking. Or don't be too busy with worldly things. If you do that, you will not be able to think straight. And then that day might come when you are not ready. [35]It will close like a trap on all people on earth. [36]So be ready all the time. Pray that you will be strong enough to escape all these things that will happen. And pray that you will be able to stand before the Son of Man."[d]

[37]During the day, Jesus taught the people in the Temple.[d] At night he went out of the city and stayed on the Mount of Olives.[d] [38]Every morning all the people got up early to go to the Temple to listen to him.

Plans to Kill Jesus

22 It was almost time for the Jewish Feast[d] of Unleavened Bread, called the Passover[d] Feast. [2]The leading priests and teachers of the law were trying to find a way to kill Jesus. But they were afraid of the people.

[3]One of Jesus' 12 apostles[d] was named Judas Iscariot. Satan entered Judas, and he went to [4]the leading priests and some of the soldiers who guarded the Temple.[d] He talked to them about a way to give Jesus to them. [5]They were pleased and promised to give Judas money. [6]Judas agreed. Then he waited for the best time to turn Jesus over to them without the crowd knowing it.

Preparation of the Passover Meal

[7]The Day of Unleavened[d] Bread came. This was the day the Passover[d] lambs had to be sacrificed. [8]Jesus said to Peter and John, "Go and prepare the Passover meal for us to eat." [9]They asked, "Where do you want us to prepare it?"

Jesus said to them, [10]"Listen! After you go into the city, you will see a man carrying a jar of water. Follow him into the house that he enters. [11]Tell the person who owns that house, 'The Teacher asks that you please show us the room where he and his followers may eat the Passover meal'. [12]Then he will show you a large room upstairs. This room is ready for you. Prepare the Passover meal there."

[13]So Peter and John left. Everything happened as Jesus had said. So they prepared the Passover meal.

The Lord's Supper

[14]When the time came, Jesus and the apostles[d] were sitting at the table. [15]He said to them, "I wanted very much to eat this Passover[d] meal with you before I die. [16]I will never eat another Passover meal until it is given its true meaning in the kingdom of God."

[17]Then Jesus took a cup. He gave thanks to God for it and said, "Take this cup and give it to everyone here. [18]I will not drink again from the fruit of the vine[n] until God's kingdom comes."

[19]Then Jesus took some bread. He thanked God for it, broke it, and gave it to the apostles. Then Jesus said, "This bread is my body that I am giving for you. Do this to remember me." [20]In the same way, after supper, Jesus took the cup and said, "This cup shows the new agreement that God makes with his people. This new agreement begins with my blood which is poured out for you."[n]

Who Will Turn Against Jesus?

[21]Jesus said, "One of you will turn against me. His hand is by my hand on the table. [22]The Son of Man[d] will do what God has planned. But how terrible it will be for that man who gives the Son of Man to be killed."

[23]Then the apostles[d] asked each other, "Which one of us would do that to Jesus?"

Be Like a Servant

[24]Then the apostles[d] began to argue about which one of them was the most important. [25]But Jesus said to them, "The kings of the world rule over their people. Men who have authority over others are called 'very important'. [26]But you must not be like that. The greatest among you should be like the youngest, and the leader should be like the servant. [27]Who is more important: the one sitting at the table or the one serving him? You think the one at the table is more important. But I am like a servant among you!

[28]"You men have stayed with me through many struggles. [29]My Father has given me the power to rule. I also give you authority to rule with me. [30]You will eat and drink at my table in my kingdom. You will sit on thrones and judge the 12 tribes[d] of Israel.

Don't Lose Your Faith!

[31]"Satan has asked to test all of you as a farmer tests his wheat. Simon, Simon, [32]I have prayed that you will not lose your faith! Help your brothers to be stronger when you come back to me."

[33]But Peter said to Jesus, "Lord, I am ready to go to prison with you. I will even die with you!"

[34]But Jesus said, "Peter, before the cock crows tonight, you will say you don't know me. You will say this three times!"

Be Ready for Trouble

[35]Then Jesus said to the apostles,[d] "When I sent you out without money,

---

fruit of the vine Product of the grapevine; this may also be translated "wine".
Verse 20 A few Greek copies do not have the last part of verse 19 and all of verse 20.

a bag, or sandals, did you need anything?"

They said, "No."

[36]He said to them, "But now if you have money or a bag, carry that with you. If you don't have a sword, sell your coat and buy one. [37]The Scripture[d] says, 'He was treated like a criminal'.[n] This scripture must have its full meaning. It was written about me, and it is happening now."

[38]The followers said, "Look, Lord, here are two swords!"

He said to them, "That's enough."

Jesus Prays Alone

[39-40]Jesus left the city and went to the Mount of Olives.[d] His followers went with him. (Jesus went there often.) He said to his followers, "Pray for strength against temptation."

[41]Then Jesus went about a stone's throw away from them. He kneeled down and prayed, [42]"Father, if it is what you want, then let me not have this cup[n] of suffering. But do what you want, not what I want." [43]Then an angel from heaven appeared to him to help him. [44]Jesus was full of pain; he prayed even more. Sweat dripped from his face as if he were bleeding. [45]When he had finished praying, he went to his followers. They were asleep. (Their sadness had made them very tired.) [46]Jesus said to them, "Why are you sleeping? Get up and pray for strength against temptation."

Jesus Is Arrested

[47]While Jesus was speaking, a crowd came up. One of the 12 apostles[d] was leading them. He was Judas. He came close to Jesus so that he could kiss him.

[48]But Jesus said to him, "Judas, are you using the kiss to give the Son of Man[d] to his enemies?"

[49]The followers of Jesus were standing there too. They saw what was happening. They said to Jesus, "Lord, should we use our swords?" [50]And one of them did use his sword. He cut off the right ear of the servant of the high priest.

[51]Jesus said, "Stop!" Then he touched the servant's ear and healed him.

[52]Those who came to arrest Jesus were the leading priests, the soldiers who guarded the Temple,[d] and the older Jewish leaders. Jesus said to them, "Why did you come out here with swords and sticks? Do you think I am a criminal? [53]I was with you every day in the Temple. Why didn't you try to arrest me there? But this is your time — the time when darkness rules."

Peter Says He Doesn't Know Jesus

[54]They arrested Jesus and took him away. They brought him into the house of the high priest. Peter followed them, but he did not go near Jesus. [55]The soldiers started a fire in the middle of the courtyard and sat together. Peter sat with them. [56]A servant girl saw Peter sitting there near the light. She looked closely at Peter's face and said, "This man was also with him!"

[57]But Peter said this was not true. He said, "Girl, I don't know him."

[58]A short time later, another person saw Peter and said, "You are also one of them."

But Peter said, "Man, I am not!"

[59]About an hour later, another man insisted, "It is true! This man was with him. He is from Galilee!"

[60]But Peter said, "Man, I don't know what you are talking about!"

Immediately, while Peter was still

'He ... criminal'. Quotation from Isaiah 53:12.

cup Jesus is talking about the bad things that will happen to him. Accepting these things will be hard, like drinking a cup of something that tastes very bitter.

speaking, a cock crowed. [61]Then the Lord turned and looked straight at Peter. And Peter remembered what the Lord had said: "Before the cock crows tonight, you will say three times that you don't know me." [62]Then Peter went outside and cried with much pain in his heart.

The People Laugh at Jesus

[63-64]Some men were guarding Jesus. They made fun of him like this: they covered his eyes so that he could not see them. Then they hit him and said, "Prove that you are a prophet,[d] and tell us who hit you!" [65]The men said many cruel things to Jesus.

Jesus Before the Leaders

[66]When day came, the older leaders of the people, the leading priests, and the teachers of the law came together. They led Jesus away to their highest court. [67]They said, "If you are the Christ,[d] then tell us that you are!"

Jesus said to them, "If I tell you I am the Christ, you will not believe me. [68]And if I ask you, you will not answer. [69]But beginning now, the Son of Man[d] will sit at the right hand of the powerful God."

[70]They all said, "Then are you the Son of God?"

Jesus said to them, "Yes, you are right when you say that I am."

[71]They said, "Why do we need witnesses now? We ourselves heard him say this!"

Governor Pilate Questions Jesus

23 Then the whole group stood up and led Jesus to Pilate.[n] [2]They began to accuse Jesus. They told Pilate, "We caught this man telling things that were confusing our people. He says that we should not pay taxes to Caesar.[d] He calls himself the Christ,[d] a king."

[3]Pilate asked Jesus, "Are you the king of the Jews?"

Jesus answered, "Yes, that is right."

[4]Pilate said to the leading priests and the people, "I find nothing wrong with this man."

[5]They said again and again, "But Jesus is making trouble with the people! He teaches all around Judea. He began in Galilee, and now he is here!"

Pilate Sends Jesus to Herod

[6]Pilate heard this and asked if Jesus was from Galilee. [7]If so, Jesus was under Herod's authority. Herod was in Jerusalem at that time; so Pilate sent Jesus to him. [8]When Herod saw Jesus, he was very glad. He had heard about Jesus and had wanted to meet him for a long time. Herod was hoping to see Jesus work a miracle.[d] [9]Herod asked Jesus many questions, but Jesus said nothing. [10]The leading priests and teachers of the law were standing there. They were shouting things against Jesus. [11]Then Herod and his soldiers made fun of Jesus. They dressed him in a kingly robe and then sent him back to Pilate. [12]In the past, Pilate and Herod had always been enemies. But on that day they became friends.

Jesus Must Die

[13]Pilate called all the people together with the leading priests and the Jewish leaders. [14]He said to them, "You brought this man to me. You said that he was making trouble among the people. But I have questioned him before you all, and I have not found him guilty of the things you say. [15]Also, Herod found nothing wrong with him; he sent him back to us. Look, he has done nothing for which he should die.

Pilate   Pontius Pilate was the Roman governor of Judea from A.D. 26 to A.D. 36.

[16]So, after I punish him, I will let him go free." [17] [n]

[18]But all the people shouted, "Kill him! Let Barabbas go free!" [19](Barabbas was a man who was in prison because he started a riot in the city. He was guilty of murder.)

[20]Pilate wanted to let Jesus go free. So he told this to the crowd. [21]But they shouted again, "Kill him! Kill him on a cross!"

[22]A third time Pilate said to them, "Why? What wrong has he done? I can find no reason to kill him. So I will have him punished and set him free."

[23]But they continued to shout. They demanded that Jesus be killed on the cross. Their yelling became so loud that [24]Pilate decided to give them what they wanted. [25]They wanted Barabbas to go free, the man who was in jail for starting a riot and for murder. Pilate let Barabbas go free and gave Jesus to them to be killed.

Jesus Is Killed on a Cross

[26]The soldiers led Jesus away. At that time, there was a man coming into the city from the fields. His name was Simon, and he was from the city of Cyrene. The soldiers forced Simon to carry Jesus' cross and walk behind him.

[27]A large crowd of people were following Jesus. Some of the women were sad and crying. [28]But Jesus turned and said to them, "Women of Jerusalem, don't cry for me. Cry for yourselves and for your children too! [29]The time is coming when people will say, 'Happy are the women who cannot have children! Happy are the women who have no babies to nurse'.

[30]Then people will say to the mountains, 'Fall on us!' And they will say to the hills, 'Cover us!' [31]If they act like this now when life is good, what will happen when bad times come?"[n]

[32]There were also two criminals led out with Jesus to be killed. [33]Jesus and the two criminals were taken to a place called the Skull. There the soldiers nailed Jesus to his cross. They also nailed the criminals to their crosses, one beside Jesus on the right and the other beside Jesus on the left. [34]Jesus said, "Father, forgive them. They don't know what they are doing."[n]

The soldiers threw lots[d] to decide who would get his clothes. [35]The people stood there watching. The Jewish leaders made fun of Jesus. They said, "If he is God's Chosen One, the Christ,[d] then let him save himself. He saved other people, didn't he?"

[36]Even the soldiers made fun of him. They came to Jesus and offered him some vinegar. [37]They said, "If you are the king of the Jews, save yourself!" [38](At the top of the cross these words were written: "THIS IS THE KING OF THE JEWS.")

[39]One of the criminals began to shout insults at Jesus: "Aren't you the Christ? Then save yourself! And save us too!"

[40]But the other criminal stopped him. He said, "You should fear God! You are getting the same punishment as he is. [41]We are punished justly; we should die. But this man has done nothing wrong!" [42]Then this criminal said to Jesus, "Jesus, remember me when you come into your kingdom!"

[43]Then Jesus said to him, "Listen! What I say is true: today you will be with me in paradise!"[n]

Verse 17 A few Greek copies add verse 17: "Every year at the Passover Feast, Pilate had to release one prisoner to the people."

If . . . come? Literally, "If they do these things in the green tree, what will happen in the dry?"

Verse 34 Some early Greek copies do not have this part of the verse.

paradise A place where good people go when they die.

Jesus Dies

[44]It was about noon, and the whole land became dark until three o'clock in the afternoon. [45]There was no sun! The curtain in the Temple[n] was torn into two pieces. [46]Jesus cried out in a loud voice, "Father, I give you my life." After Jesus said this, he died.

[47]The army officer there saw what happened. He praised God, saying, "I know this was a good man!"

[48]Many people had gathered there to watch this thing. When they saw what happened, they returned home. They beat their chests because they were so sad. [49]Those who were close friends of Jesus were there. Some were women who had followed Jesus from Galilee. They all stood far away from the cross and watched.

Joseph of Arimathea

[50-51]A man from the Jewish town of Arimathea was there, too. His name was Joseph. He was a good, religious man. He wanted the kingdom of God to come. Joseph was a member of the Jewish council, but he had not agreed when the other leaders decided to kill Jesus. [52]Joseph went to Pilate to ask for the body of Jesus. [53]So Joseph took the body down from the cross and wrapped it in cloth. Then he put Jesus' body in a tomb that was cut in a wall of rock. This tomb had never been used before. [54]This was late on Preparation[d] Day. When the sun went down, the Sabbath[d] day would begin. [55]The women who had come from Galilee with Jesus followed Joseph. They saw the tomb and saw inside where the body of Jesus was laid. [56]Then the women left to prepare perfumes and spices.

On the Sabbath day they rested, as the law of Moses commanded.

Jesus Rises from Death

24 Very early on the first day of the week, the women came to the tomb where Jesus' body was laid. They brought the spices they had prepared. [2]They found that the stone had been rolled away from the entrance of the tomb. [3]They went in, but they did not find the body of the Lord Jesus. [4]While they were wondering about this, two men in shining clothes suddenly stood beside them. [5]The women were very afraid; they bowed their heads to the ground. The men said to the women, "Why are you looking for a living person here? This is a place for the dead. [6]Jesus is not here. He has risen from death! Do you remember what he said in Galilee? [7]He said that the Son of Man[d] must be given to evil men, be killed on a cross, and rise from death on the third day." [8]Then the women remembered what Jesus had said.

[9]The women left the tomb and told all these things to the 11 apostles[d] and the other followers. [10]These women were Mary Magdalene, Joanna, Mary the mother of James, and some other women. The women told the apostles everything that had happened at the tomb. [11]But they did not believe the women. It sounded like nonsense. [12]But Peter got up and ran to the tomb. He looked in, but he saw only the cloth that Jesus' body had been wrapped in. Peter went away to be alone, wondering about what had happened.

On the Road to Emmaus

[13]That same day two of Jesus' followers were going to a town named Emmaus. It is about 11 kilometres from Jerusalem. [14]They were talking about everything that had happened. [15]While they were discussing these

---

curtain in the Temple A curtain divided the Most Holy Place from the other part of the Temple. This was the special building in Jerusalem where God commanded the Jews to worship him.

things, Jesus himself came near and began walking with them. [16](They were not allowed to recognise Jesus.) [17]Then he said, "What are these things you are talking about while you walk?"

The two followers stopped. Their faces were very sad. [18]The one named Cleopas answered, "You must be the only one in Jerusalem who does not know what just happened there."

[19]Jesus said to them, "What are you talking about?"

The followers said, "It is about Jesus of Nazareth. He was a prophet[d] from God to all the people. He said and did many powerful things. [20]Our leaders and the leading priests gave him up to be judged and killed. They nailed him to a cross. [21]But we were hoping that he would free the Jews. It is now the third day since this happened. [22]And today some women among us told us some amazing things. Early this morning they went to the tomb, [23]but they did not find his body there. They came and told us that they had seen a vision of angels. The angels said that Jesus was alive! [24]So some of our group went to the tomb, too. They found it just as the women said, but they did not see Jesus."

[25]Then Jesus said to them, "You are foolish and slow to realise what is true. You should believe everything the prophets said. [26]They said that the Christ[d] must suffer these things before he enters his glory." [27]Then Jesus began to explain everything that had been written about himself in the Scriptures.[d] He started with Moses, and then he talked about what all the prophets had said about him.

[28]They came near the town of Emmaus, and Jesus acted as if he did not plan to stop there. [29]But they begged him, "Stay with us. It is late; it is almost night." So he went in to stay with them.

[30]Jesus sat down with them and took some bread. He gave thanks for the food and divided it. Then he gave it to them. [31]And then, they were allowed to recognise Jesus. But when they saw who he was, he disappeared. [32]They said to each other, "When Jesus talked to us on the road, it felt like a fire burning in us. It was exciting when he explained the true meaning of the Scriptures."

[33]So the two followers got up at once and went back to Jerusalem. There they found the 11 apostles[d] and others gathered. [34]They were saying, "The Lord really has risen from death! He showed himself to Simon." [35]Then the two followers told what had happened on the road. They talked about how they recognised Jesus when he divided the bread.

Jesus Appears to His Followers

[36]While the two followers were telling this, Jesus himself stood among those gathered. He said to them, "Peace be with you."

[37]They were fearful and terrified. They thought they were seeing a ghost. [38]But Jesus said, "Why are you troubled? Why do you doubt what you see? [39]Look at my hands and my feet. It is I myself! Touch me. You can see that I have a living body; a ghost does not have a body like this."

[40]After Jesus said this, he showed them his hands and feet. [41]The followers were amazed and very happy. They still could not believe it. Jesus said to them, "Do you have any food here?" [42]They gave him a piece of cooked fish. [43]While the followers watched, Jesus took the fish and ate it.

[44]He said to them, "Remember when I was with you before? I said that everything written about me must happen — everything in the law of Moses, the books of the prophets,[d] and the Psalms."

[45]Then Jesus opened their minds so

that they could understand the Scriptures.[d] [46]He said to them, "It is written that the Christ[d] would be killed and rise from death on the third day. [47-48]You saw these things happen— you are witnesses. You must tell people to change their hearts and lives. If they do this, their sins will be forgiven. You must start at Jerusalem and preach these things in my name to all nations. [49]Listen! My Father has promised you something; I will send it to you. But you must stay in Jerusa-

lem until you have received that power from heaven."

Jesus Goes Back to Heaven

[50]Jesus led his followers out of Jerusalem almost to Bethany. He raised his hands and blessed them. [51]While he was blessing them, he was separated from them and carried into heaven. [52]They worshipped him and then went back to the city very happy. [53]They stayed in the Temple[d] all the time, praising God.

JOHN

John Tells About Jesus, the Son of God

Christ Comes to the World

1 Before the world began, there was the Word.[n] The Word was with God, and the Word was God. [2]He was with God in the beginning. [3]All things were made through him. Nothing was made without him. [4]In him there was life. That life was light for the people of the world. [5]The Light shines in the darkness. And the darkness has not overpowered the Light.

[6]There was a man named John[n] who was sent by God. [7]He came to tell people about the Light. Through him all people could hear about the Light and believe. [8]John was not the Light, but he came to tell people about the Light. [9]The true Light was coming into the world. The true Light gives light to all.

[10]The Word was in the world. The world was made through him, but the world did not know him. [11]He came to the world that was his own. But his own people did not accept him. [12]But some people did accept him. They believed in him. To them he gave the right to become children of God. [13]They did not become his children in the human way. They were not born because of the desire or wish of some man. They were born of God.

[14]The Word became a man and lived among us. We saw his glory — the glory that belongs to the only Son of the Father. The Word was full of grace and truth. [15]John told about him. He said, "This is the One I was talking about. I said, 'The One who comes after me is greater than I am. He was living before me'."

[16]The Word was full of grace and truth. From him we all received more and more blessings. [17]The law was given through Moses, but grace and truth came through Jesus Christ. [18]No man has ever seen God, but God the only Son is very close to the Father.[n] And the Son has shown us what God is like.

John Tells People About Jesus

[19]The Jews in Jerusalem sent some priests and Levites to John.[n] The Jews sent them to ask, "Who are you?"

[20]John spoke freely and did not refuse to answer. He said clearly, "I am not the Christ."[d]

[21]So they asked him, "Then who are you? Are you Elijah?"[n]

He answered, "No, I am not Elijah."

Then they asked, "Are you the Prophet?"[n]

He answered, "No, I am not the Prophet."

[22]Then they said, "Who are you? Give us an answer to tell those who sent us. What do you say about yourself?"

Word The Greek word is "logos", meaning any kind of communication. It could be translated "message". Here, it means Christ. Christ was the way God told people about himself.
John John the Baptist, who preached to people about Christ's coming (Matthew 3, Luke 3).
but . . . Father This could be translated, "but the only Son of God is very close to the Father."
Also, some Greek copies say, "but the only Son is very close to the Father."
Elijah A man who spoke for God. He lived hundreds of years before Christ.
Prophet They probably meant the prophet that God told Moses he would send (Deuteronomy 18:15-19).

23John told them in the words of the prophet Isaiah:

"I am the voice of a man
    calling out in the desert:
'Make the road straight for the
    Lord'."   *Isaiah 40:3*

24In the group of Jews who were sent, there were some Pharisees.*d* 25They said to John: "You say you are not the Christ. You say you are not Elijah or the Prophet. Then why do you baptise people?"

26John answered, "I baptise people with water. But there is one here with you that you don't know. 27He is the One who comes after me. I am not good enough to untie the strings of his sandals."

28This all happened at Bethany on the other side of the Jordan River. This is where John was baptising people.

29The next day John saw Jesus coming toward him. John said, "Look, the Lamb of God.*n* He takes away the sins of the world! 30This is the One I was talking about. I said, 'A man will come after me, but he is greater than I am, because he was living before me'. 31Even I did not know who he was. But I came baptising with water so that the people of Israel could know who he is."

32-33Then John said, "I did not know who the Christ was. But God sent me to baptise with water. And God told me, 'You will see the Spirit*d* come down and rest on a man. That man is the One who will baptise with the Holy Spirit'." John said, "I saw the Spirit come down from heaven. The Spirit looked like a dove and rested on him. 34I have seen this happen. So I tell people: 'He is the Son of God'."

The First Followers of Jesus

35The next day John*n* was there

again with two of his followers. 36He saw Jesus walking by and said, "Look, the Lamb of God!"*n*

37The two followers heard John say this. So they followed Jesus. 38Jesus turned and saw them following him. He asked, "What do you want?"

They said, "Rabbi, where are you staying?" ("Rabbi" means "Teacher".)

39Jesus answered, "Come with me and you will see." So the two men went with Jesus. They saw the place where Jesus was staying and stayed there with him that day. It was then about four o'clock.

40These two men followed Jesus after they heard about him from John. One of the men was Andrew. He was Simon Peter's brother. 41The first thing Andrew did was to find his brother, Simon. He said to Simon, "We have found the Messiah." ("Messiah" means "Christ".*d*)

42Then Andrew took Simon to Jesus. Jesus looked at Simon and said, "You are Simon son of John. You will be called Cephas." ("Cephas" means "Peter".*n*)

43The next day Jesus decided to go to Galilee. He found Philip and said to him, "Follow me." 44Philip was from the town of Bethsaida, where Andrew and Peter lived. 45Philip found Nathanael and told him, "Remember that Moses wrote in the law about a man who was coming, and the prophets*d* also wrote about him. We have found him. He is Jesus, the son of Joseph. He is from Nazareth."

46But Nathanael said to Philip, "Nazareth! Can anything good come from Nazareth?"

Philip answered, "Come and see." 47Jesus saw Nathanael coming toward him. He said, "Here is truly a

---

Lamb of God Name for Jesus. Jesus is like the lambs that were offered as a sacrifice to God.
John John the Baptist, who preached to people about Christ's coming (Matthew 3, Luke 3).
Peter The Greek name "Peter", like the Aramaic name "Cephas", means "rock".

person of Israel. There is nothing false in him."

[48]Nathanael asked, "How do you know me?"

Jesus answered, "I saw you when you were under the fig tree. That was before Philip told you about me."

[49]Then Nathanael said to Jesus, "Teacher, you are the Son of God. You are the King of Israel."

[50]Jesus said to Nathanael, "You believe in me because I told you I saw you under the fig tree. But you will see greater things than that!" [51]And Jesus said to them, "I tell you the truth. You will all see heaven open. You will see 'angels of God going up and coming down'[n] on the Son of Man."[d]

The Wedding at Cana

2 Two days later there was a wedding in the town of Cana in Galilee. Jesus' mother was there. [2]Jesus and his followers were also invited to the wedding. [3]When all the wine was gone, Jesus' mother said to him, "They have no more wine."

[4]Jesus answered, "Dear woman, why come to me? My time has not yet come."

[5]His mother said to the servants, "Do whatever he tells you to do."

[6]In that place there were six stone water jars. The Jews used jars like these in their washing ceremony.[n] Each jar held about 100 litres.

[7]Jesus said to the servants, "Fill the jars with water." So they filled the jars to the top.

[8]Then he said to them, "Now take some out and give it to the master of the feast."

So the servants took the water to the master. [9]When he tasted it, the water had become wine. He did not know where the wine came from. But the servants who brought the water knew. The master of the wedding called the bridegroom [10]and said to him, "People always serve the best wine first. Later, after the guests have been drinking a lot, they serve the cheaper wine. But you have saved the best wine till now."

[11]So in Cana of Galilee, Jesus did his first miracle.[d] There he showed his glory, and his followers believed in him.

Jesus in the Temple

[12]Then Jesus went to the town of Capernaum with his mother, brothers and his followers. They all stayed in Capernaum for a few days. [13]But it was almost time for the Jewish Passover[d] Feast. So Jesus went to Jerusalem. [14]In the Temple[d] he found men selling cattle, sheep, and doves. He saw others sitting at tables, exchanging money. [15]Jesus made a whip out of cords. Then he forced all these men, with the sheep and cattle, to leave the Temple. He turned over the tables and scattered the money of the men who were exchanging it. [16]Then he said to those who were selling pigeons, "Take these things out of here! Don't make my Father's house a place for buying and selling!"

[17]When this happened the followers remembered what was written in the Scriptures:[d] "My strong love for your Temple completely controls me."[n]

[18]The Jews said to Jesus, "Show us a miracle[d] for a sign. Prove that you have the right to do these things."

[19]Jesus answered, "Destroy this temple, and I will build it again in three days."

[20]The Jews answered, "Men worked 46 years to build this Temple!

'angels . . . down' These words are from Genesis 28:12.
washing ceremony The Jews washed themselves in special ways before eating, before worshipping in the Temple, and at other special times.
"My . . . me." Quotation from Psalm 69:9.

Do you really believe you can build it again in three days?"

²¹(But the temple Jesus meant was his own body. ²²After Jesus was raised from death, his followers remembered that Jesus had said this. Then they believed the Scripture*d* and the words Jesus said.)

²³Jesus was in Jerusalem for the Passover Feast. Many people believed in him because they saw the miracles he did. ²⁴But Jesus did not trust himself to them because he knew them all. ²⁵He did not need anyone to tell him about people. Jesus knew what was in a person's mind.

Jesus and Nicodemus

3 There was a man named Nicodemus who was one of the Pharisees.*d* He was an important Jewish leader. ²One night Nicodemus came to Jesus. He said, "Teacher, we know that you are a teacher sent from God. No one can do the miracles*d* you do, unless God is with him."

³Jesus answered, "I tell you the truth. Unless a person is born again, he cannot be in God's kingdom."

⁴Nicodemus said, "But if a man is already old, how can he be born again? He cannot enter his mother's body again. So how can he be born a second time?"

⁵But Jesus answered, "I tell you the truth. Unless a person is born from water and the Spirit,*d* he cannot enter God's kingdom. ⁶A person's body is born from his human parents. But a person's spiritual life is born from the Spirit. ⁷Don't be surprised when I tell you, 'You must all be born again'. ⁸The wind blows where it wants to go. You hear the wind blow. But you don't know where the wind

comes from or where it is going. It is the same with every person who is born from the Spirit."

⁹Nicodemus asked, "How can all this be possible?"

¹⁰Jesus said, "You are an important teacher in Israel. But you still don't understand these things? ¹¹I tell you the truth. We talk about what we know. We tell about what we have seen. But you don't accept what we tell you. ¹²I have told you about things here on earth, but you do not believe me. So certainly you will not believe me if I tell you about the things of heaven! ¹³The only one who has ever gone up to heaven is the One who came down from heaven—the Son of Man.*d*

¹⁴"Moses lifted up the snake in the desert.*n* It is the same with the Son of Man. The Son of Man must be lifted up too. ¹⁵Then everyone who believes in him can have eternal life.

¹⁶"For God loved the world so much that he gave his only Son. God gave his Son so that whoever believes in him may not be lost, but have eternal life. ¹⁷God did not send his Son into the world to judge the world guilty, but to save the world through him. ¹⁸He who believes in God's Son is not judged guilty. He who does not believe has already been judged guilty, because he has not believed in God's only Son. ¹⁹People are judged by this fact: I am the Light from God that has come into the world. But men did not want light. They wanted darkness because they were doing evil things. ²⁰Everyone who does evil hates the light. He will not come to the light because it will show all the evil things he has done. ²¹But he who follows the true way comes to the light. Then the light will show that the things he has done were done through God."

Moses . . . desert The people of Israel were dying from snake bites. God told Moses to put a brass snake on a pole. The people who looked at the snake were healed (Numbers 21:4-9).

Jesus and John the Baptist

22After this, Jesus and his followers went into the area of Judea. There Jesus stayed with his followers and baptised people. 23John was also baptising in Aenon, near Salim, because there was plenty of water there. People were going there to be baptised. 24(This was before John was put into prison.)

25Some of John's followers had an argument with a Jew about religious washing.*n* 26So they came to John and said, "Teacher, remember the man who was with you on the other side of the Jordan River, the one you spoke about? He is baptising, and everyone is going to him."

27John answered, "A man can get only what God gives him. 28You yourselves heard me say, 'I am not the Christ.*d* I am only the one God sent to prepare the way for him'. 29The bride belongs only to the bridegroom. The friend who helps the bridegroom waits and listens for him. He is glad when he hears the bridegroom's voice. That is the same pleasure I have. And my time of joy is now here. 30He must become greater. And I must become less important.

The One Who Comes from Heaven

31"The One who comes from above is greater than all. He who is from the earth belongs to the earth and talks about things on the earth. But the One who comes from heaven is greater than all. 32He tells what he has seen and heard, but no one accepts what he says. 33The person who accepts what he says has proved that God is true. 34God sent him, and he tells the things that God says. God gives him the Spirit*d* fully. 35The Father loves the Son and has given him power over everything. 36He who believes in the Son has eternal life. But he who does not obey the Son will never have that life. God's anger stays with him."

Jesus and a Samaritan Woman

4 The Pharisees*d* heard that Jesus was getting and baptising more followers than John. 2(But really Jesus himself did not baptise people. His followers did the baptising.) Jesus knew that the Pharisees had heard about him. 3So he left Judea and went back to Galilee. 4On the way he had to go through the country of Samaria.

5In Samaria Jesus came to the town called Sychar. This town is near the field that Jacob gave to his son Joseph. 6Jacob's well was there. Jesus was tired from his long trip, so he sat down beside the well. It was about six o'clock in the evening. 7A Samaritan*d* woman came to the well to get some water. Jesus said to her, "Please give me a drink." 8(This happened while Jesus' followers were in town buying some food.)

9The woman said, "I am surprised that you ask me for a drink. You are a Jew and I am a Samaritan." (Jews are not friends with Samaritans.*n*)

10Jesus said, "You don't know what God gives. And you don't know who asked you for a drink. If you knew, you would have asked me, and I would have given you living water."

11The woman said, "Sir, where will you get that living water? The well is very deep, and you have nothing to get water with. 12Are you greater than Jacob, our father? Jacob is the one who gave us this well. He drank from it himself. Also, his sons and flocks drank from this well."

13Jesus answered, "Every person

---

religious washing The Jews washed themselves in special ways before eating, before worshipping in the Temple, and at other special times.

Jews . . . Samaritans This can also be translated "Jews don't use things that Samaritans have used".

who drinks this water will be thirsty again. [14]But whoever drinks the water I give will never be thirsty again. The water I give will become a spring of water flowing inside him. It will give him eternal life."

[15]The woman said to him, "Sir, give me this water. Then I will never be thirsty again. And I will not have to come back here to get more water."

[16]Jesus told her, "Go and get your husband and come back here."

[17]The woman answered, "But I have no husband."

Jesus said to her, "You are right to say you have no husband. [18]Really you have had five husbands. But the man you live with now is not your husband. You told the truth."

[19]The woman said, "Sir, I can see that you are a prophet.[d] [20]Our fathers worshipped on this mountain. But you Jews say that Jerusalem is the place where people must worship."

[21]Jesus said, "Believe me, woman. The time is coming when you will not have to be in Jerusalem or on this mountain to worship the Father. [22]You Samaritans worship what you don't understand. We Jews understand what we worship. Salvation comes from the Jews. [23]The time is coming when the true worshippers will worship the Father in spirit and truth. That time is now here. And these are the kinds of worshippers the Father wants. [24]God is spirit. Those who worship God must worship in spirit and truth."

[25]The woman said, "I know that the Messiah is coming." (Messiah is the One called Christ.[d]) "When the Messiah comes, he will explain everything to us."

[26]Then Jesus said, "He is talking to you now. I am he."

[27]Just then his followers came back from town. They were surprised be-cause they saw Jesus talking with a woman. But none of them asked, "What do you want?" or "Why are you talking with her?"

[28]Then the woman left her water jar and went back to town. She said to the people, [29]"A man told me everything I have ever done. Come and see him. Perhaps he is the Christ!" [30]So the people left the town and went to see Jesus.

[31]While the woman was away, the followers were begging him, "Teacher, eat something!"

[32]But Jesus answered, "I have food to eat that you know nothing about."

[33]So the followers asked themselves, "Has somebody already brought Jesus some food?"

[34]Jesus said, "My food is to do what the One who sent me wants me to do. My food is to finish the work that he gave me to do. [35]You say, 'Four more months to wait before we gather the grain'. But I tell you, open your eyes. Look at the fields that are ready for harvesting now. [36]Even now, the one who harvests the crop is being paid. He is gathering crops for eternal life. So now the one who plants can be happy along with the one who harvests. [37]It is true when we say, 'One person plants, but another harvests the crop'. [38]I sent you to harvest a crop that you did not work for. Others did the work, and you get the profit from their work."[n]

[39]Many of the Samaritans in that town believed in Jesus. They believed because of what the woman said: "He told me everything I have ever done." [40]The Samaritans came to Jesus and begged him to stay with them. So he stayed there two days. [41]Many more believed because of the things he said.

[42]They said to the woman, "First we believed in Jesus because of what you told us. But now we believe be-

---

Look at ... their work. As a farmer sends workers to harvest grain, Jesus sends his followers out to bring people to God.

cause we heard him ourselves. We know that this man really is the Saviour of the world."

Jesus Heals an Officer's Son

⁴³Two days later, Jesus left and went to Galilee. ⁴⁴(Jesus had said before that a prophet*d* is not respected in his own country.) ⁴⁵When Jesus arrived in Galilee, the people there welcomed him. They had seen all the things he did at the Passover*d* Feast in Jerusalem. They had been at the Passover Feast, too.

⁴⁶Jesus went to visit Cana in Galilee again. This is where Jesus had changed the water into wine. One of the king's important officers lived in the city of Capernaum. This man's son was sick. ⁴⁷The man heard that Jesus had come from Judea and was now in Galilee. He went to Jesus and begged him to come to Capernaum and heal his son. His son was almost dead. ⁴⁸Jesus said to him, "You people must see signs and miracles*d* before you will believe in me."

⁴⁹The officer said, "Sir, come before my child dies."

⁵⁰Jesus answered, "Go. Your son will live."

The man believed what Jesus told him and went home. ⁵¹On the way the man's servants came and met him. They told him, "Your son is well."

⁵²The man asked, "What time did my son begin to get well?"

They answered, "It was about one o'clock yesterday when the fever left him."

⁵³The father knew that one o'clock was the exact time that Jesus had said, "Your son will live." So the man

and all the people of his house believed in Jesus.

⁵⁴That was the second miracle that Jesus did after coming from Judea to Galilee.

Jesus Heals a Man at a Pool

5 Later Jesus went to Jerusalem for a special Jewish feast. ²In Jerusalem there is a pool with five covered porches. In the Jewish language*n* it is called Bethesda.*n* This pool is near the Sheep Gate. ³Many sick people were lying on the porches beside the pool. Some were blind, some were crippled, and some were paralysed.*n* ⁵There was a man lying there who had been sick for 38 years. ⁶Jesus saw the man and knew that he had been sick for a very long time. So Jesus asked him, "Do you want to be well?"

⁷The sick man answered, "Sir, there is no one to help me get into the pool when the water starts moving. I try to be the first one into the water. But when I try, someone else always goes in before I can."

⁸Then Jesus said, "Stand up. Pick up your mat and walk." ⁹And immediately the man was well. He picked up his mat and began to walk.

The day all this happened was a Sabbath*d* day. ¹⁰So the Jews said to the man who had been healed, "Today is the Sabbath. It is against our law for you to carry your mat on the Sabbath day."

¹¹But he answered, "The man who made me well told me, 'Pick up your mat and walk'."

¹²Then they asked him, "Who is the man who told you to pick up your mat and walk?"

¹³But the man who had been healed

Jewish language Aramaic, the language of the Jews in the first century.
Bethesda Also called Bethsaida or Bethzatha, a pool of water north of the Temple in Jerusalem.
Verse 3 Some Greek copies add "and they waited for the water to move". A few later copies add verse 4: "Sometimes an angel of the Lord came down to the pool and stirred up the water. After the angel did this, the first person to go into the pool was healed of any sickness he had."

did not know who it was. There were many people in that place, and Jesus had left.

[14]Later, Jesus found the man at the Temple.[d] Jesus said to him, "See, you are well now. But stop sinning or something worse may happen to you!"

[15]Then the man left and went back to the Jews. He told them that Jesus was the one who had made him well.

[16]Jesus was doing this on the Sabbath day. So the Jews began to do bad things to him. [17]But Jesus said to them, "My Father never stops working. And so I work, too."

[18]This made the Jews try harder to kill him. They said, "First Jesus was breaking the law about the Sabbath day. Then he said that God is his own Father! He is making himself equal with God!"

Jesus Has God's Authority

[19]But Jesus said, "I tell you the truth. The Son can do nothing alone. The Son does only what he sees his Father doing. The Son does whatever the Father does. [20]The Father loves the Son, and the Father shows the Son all the things he himself does. But the Father will show the Son greater things than this to do. Then you will all be amazed. [21]The Father raises the dead and gives them life. In the same way, the Son gives life to those he wants to. [22]Also, the Father judges no one. But the Father has given the Son power to do all the judging. [23]God did this so that all people will respect the Son the same way they respect the Father. He who does not respect the Son does not respect the Father. The Father is the One who sent the Son.

[24]"I tell you the truth. Whoever hears what I say and believes in the One who sent me has eternal life. He will not be judged guilty. He has already left death and has entered into life. [25]I tell you the truth. The time is coming and is already here when the dead will hear the voice of the Son of God. And those who hear will have life. [26]Life comes from the Father himself. So the Father has allowed the Son to give life. [27]And the Father has given the Son the power to judge because he is the Son of Man.[d] [28]Don't be surprised at this. A time is coming when all who are dead and in their graves will hear his voice. [29]Then they will come out of their graves. Those who did good will rise and have life for ever. But those who did evil will rise to be judged guilty.

Jesus Is God's Son

[30]"I can do nothing alone. I judge only the way I am told, so my judgement is right. I don't try to please myself. I try to please the One who sent me.

[31]"If I tell people about myself, then they will not accept what I say about myself. [32]But there is another who tells about me. And I know that the things he says about me are true. [33]"You have sent men to John.[n] And he has told you about the truth. [34]But I don't need a man to tell about me. I tell you this so that you can be saved. [35]John was like a burning and shining lamp. And you were happy to enjoy his light for a while.

[36]"But I have a proof about myself that is greater than that of John. The things I do are my proof. These are the things my Father gave me to do. They show that the Father sent me. [37]And the Father who sent me has given proof about me himself. You have never heard his voice. You have never seen what he looks like. [38]His teaching does not live in you because you don't believe in the One that the Father sent. [39]You carefully study the Scriptures[d] because you think that they give you eternal life. Those are the same Scriptures that tell about me! [40]But you refuse to come to me to have that life.

John John the Baptist; who preached to people about Christ's coming (Matthew 3, Luke 3).

41"I don't want praise from men. 42But I know you—I know that you don't have God's love in you. 43I have come from my Father—I speak for him. But you don't accept me. But when another person comes, speaking only for himself, you will accept him. 44You like to have praise from each other. But you never try to get the praise that comes from the only God. So how can you believe? 45Don't think that I will stand before the Father and say that you are wrong. Moses is the one who says that you are wrong. And he is the one that you hoped would save you. 46If you really believed Moses, you would believe me because Moses wrote about me. 47But you don't believe what Moses wrote. So how can you believe what I say?"

More than 5,000 People Fed

6 After this, Jesus went across Lake Galilee (or, Lake Tiberias). 2Many people followed him because they saw the miracles[d] he did to heal the sick. 3Jesus went up on a hill and there sat down with his followers. 4It was almost the time for the Jewish Passover[d] Feast.

5Jesus looked up and saw a large crowd coming toward him. He said to Philip, "Where can we buy bread for all these people to eat?" 6(Jesus asked Philip this question to test him. Jesus already knew what he planned to do.)

7Philip answered, "We would all have to work a month to buy enough bread for each person here to have only a little piece."

8Another follower there was Andrew. He was Simon Peter's brother. Andrew said, 9"Here is a boy with five loaves of barley bread and two little fish. But that is not enough for so many people."

10Jesus said, "Tell the people to sit down." This was a very grassy place. There were about 5,000 men who sat down there. 11Then Jesus took the loaves of bread. He thanked God for the bread and gave it to the people who were sitting there. He did the same with the fish. He gave them as much as they wanted.

12They all had enough to eat. When they had finished, Jesus said to his followers, "Gather the pieces of fish and bread that were not eaten. Don't waste anything." 13So they gathered up the pieces that were left. They filled 12 large baskets with the pieces that were left of the five barley loaves.

14The people saw this miracle that Jesus did. They said, "He must truly be the Prophet[n] who is coming into the world." 15Jesus knew that the people planned to come and take him by force and make him their king. So he left and went into the hills alone.

Jesus Walks on the Water

16That evening Jesus' followers went down to Lake Galilee. 17It was dark now and Jesus had not yet come to them. The followers got into a boat and started across the lake to Capernaum. 18By now a strong wind was blowing, and the waves on the lake were getting bigger. 19They rowed the boat about four or five kilometres. Then they saw Jesus walking on the water, coming toward the boat. The followers were afraid. 20But Jesus said to them, "Don't be afraid. It is I." 21Then they were glad to take him into the boat. At once the boat came to land at the place where they wanted to go.

The People Seek Jesus

22The next day came. Some people had stayed on the other side of the lake. They knew that Jesus had not gone in the boat with his followers but

Prophet They probably meant the prophet that God told Moses he would send (Deuteronomy 18:15-19).

that they had left without him. And they knew that only one boat had been there. 23But then some boats came from Tiberias. They landed near the place where the people had eaten the bread after the Lord had given thanks. 24The people saw that Jesus and his followers were not there now. So they got into boats and went to Capernaum. They wanted to find Jesus.

Jesus, the Bread of Life

25The people found Jesus on the other side of the lake. They asked him, "Teacher, when did you come here?"

26Jesus answered, "Are you looking for me because you saw me do miracles?d No! I tell you the truth. You are looking for me because you ate the bread and were satisfied. 27Earthly food spoils and ruins. So don't work to get that kind of food. But work to get the food that stays good always and gives you eternal life. The Son of Mand will give you that food. God the Father has shown that he is with the Son of Man."

28The people asked Jesus, "What are the things God wants us to do?"

29Jesus answered, "The work God wants you to do is this: to believe in the One that God sent."

30So the people asked, "What miracle will you do? If we can see a miracle, then we will believe you. What will you do? 31Our fathers ate the mannad in the desert. This is written in the Scriptures:d 'God gave them bread from heaven to eat'."n

32Jesus said, "I tell you the truth. Moses was not the one who gave you bread from heaven. But my Father gives you the true bread from heaven. 33God's bread is the One who comes down from heaven and gives life to the world."

34The people said, "Sir, give us this bread always."

35Then Jesus said, "I am the bread that gives life. He who comes to me will never be hungry. He who believes in me will never be thirsty. 36But as I told you before, you have seen me, and still you don't believe. 37The Father gives me my people. Every one of them will come to me, and I will always accept them. 38I came down from heaven to do what God wants me to do. I did not come to do what I want to do. 39I must not lose even one of those that God has given me, but I must raise them up on the last day. This is what the One who sent me wants me to do. 40Everyone who sees the Son and believes in him has eternal life. I will raise him up on the last day. This is what my Father wants."

41The Jews began to complain about Jesus. They complained because he said, "I am the bread that comes down from heaven." 42The Jews said, "This is Jesus. We know his father and mother. He is only Joseph's son. How can he say, 'I came down from heaven'?"

43But Jesus answered, "Stop complaining to each other. 44The Father is the One who sent me. No one can come to me unless the Father draws him to me. And I will raise him up on the last day. 45It is written in the prophets,d 'God will teach all the people'.n Everyone who listens to the Father and learns from him comes to me. 46No one has seen the Father except the One who is from God. Only he has seen the Father. 47I tell you the truth. He who believes has eternal life. 48I am the bread that gives life. 49Your ancestors ate the manna in the desert. But still they died. 50Here is the bread that comes down from heaven. If anyone eats this bread, he will never die. 51I am the living bread

'God gave . . . eat.' Quotation from Psalm 78:24.
'God . . . people.' Quotation from Isaiah 54:13.

that came down from heaven. If anyone eats this bread, he will live for ever. This bread is my flesh. I will give my flesh so that the people in the world may have life."

52Then the Jews began to argue among themselves. They said, "How can this man give us his flesh to eat?"

53Jesus said, "I tell you the truth. You must eat the flesh of the Son of Man. And you must drink his blood. If you don't do this, then you won't have real life in you. 54He who eats my flesh and drinks my blood has eternal life. I will raise him up on the last day. 55My flesh is true food. My blood is true drink. 56Whoever eats my flesh and drinks my blood lives in me, and I live in him. 57The Father sent me. The Father lives, and I live because of the Father. So he who eats me will live because of me. 58I am not like the bread our ancestors ate. They ate that bread, but still they died. I am the bread that came down from heaven. He who eats this bread will live for ever." 59Jesus said all these things while he was teaching in the synagogue[d] in Capernaum.

The Words of Eternal Life

60The followers of Jesus heard this. Many of them said, "This teaching is hard. Who can accept it?"

61Jesus knew that his followers were complaining about this. So he said, "Does this teaching bother you? 62If so will it also bother you to see the Son of Man[d] going back to the place where he came from? 63It is not the flesh that gives a person life. It is the spirit that gives life. The words I told you are spirit, and so they give life. 64But some of you don't believe." (Jesus knew who did not believe. He knew this from the beginning. And he knew who would turn against him.) 65Jesus said, "That is the reason I said, 'If the Father does not let a person come to me, then he cannot come'."

66After Jesus said this, many of his followers left him. They stopped following him.

67Jesus asked the 12 followers, "Do you want to leave, too?"

68Simon Peter answered Jesus, "Lord, where would we go? You have the words that give eternal life. 69We believe in you. We know that you are the Holy One from God."

70Then Jesus answered, "I chose all 12 of you. But one of you is a devil." 71Jesus was talking about Judas, the son of Simon Iscariot. Judas was one of the 12. But later he was going to turn against Jesus.

Jesus and His Brothers

7 After this, Jesus travelled around Galilee. He did not want to travel in Judea, because the Jews there wanted to kill him. 2It was time for the Jewish Feast[d] of Shelters. 3So Jesus' brothers said to him, "You should leave here and go to Judea. Then your followers there can see the miracles[d] you do. 4Anyone who wants to be well known does not hide what he does. If you are doing these things, show yourself to the world." 5(Even Jesus' brothers did not believe in him.)

6Jesus said to his brothers, "The right time for me has not yet come. But any time is right for you. 7The world cannot hate you. But it hates me, because I tell about the evil things it does. 8So you go to the feast. I will not go now. The right time for me has not yet come." 9After saying this, Jesus stayed in Galilee.

10So Jesus' brothers left to go to the feast. When they had gone, Jesus went, too. But he did not let people see him. 11At the feast the Jews were looking for him. They said, "Where is that man?"

12There was a large crowd of people there. Many of them were whispering to each other about Jesus. Some said, "He is a good man."

Others said, "No, he fools the people." [13]But no one was brave enough to talk about Jesus openly. They were afraid of the Jews.

Jesus Teaches at the Feast

[14]The feast was about half over. Then Jesus went to the Temple[d] and began to teach. [15]The Jews were amazed. They said, "This man has never studied in school. How did he learn so much?"

[16]Jesus answered, "The things I teach are not my own. My teaching comes from him who sent me. [17]If anyone chooses to do what God wants, then he will know that my teaching comes from God. He will know that this teaching is not my own. [18]He who teaches his own ideas is trying to get honour for himself. But he who tries to bring honour to the one who sent him—that person speaks the truth. There is nothing false in him. [19]Moses gave you the law,[n] but none of you obey that law. Why are you trying to kill me?"

[20]The people answered, "A demon[d] has come into you. We are not trying to kill you."

[21]Jesus said to them, "I did one miracle,[d] and you are all amazed. [22]Moses gave you the law about circumcision.[d] (But really Moses did not give you circumcision. Circumcision came from our ancestors.) And yet you circumcise a baby on a Sabbath[d] day. [23]This shows that a baby can be circumcised on a Sabbath day to obey the law of Moses. So why are you angry at me for healing a person's whole body on the Sabbath day? [24]Stop judging by the way things look! Be fair, and judge by what is really right."

Is Jesus the Christ?

[25]Then some of the people who lived in Jerusalem said, "This is the man they are trying to kill. [26]But he is

teaching where everyone can see and hear him. And no one is trying to stop him. Perhaps the leaders have decided that he really is the Christ.[d] [27]But we know where this man is from. And when the real Christ comes, no one will know where he comes from."

[28]Jesus was still teaching in the Temple.[d] He cried out, "Yes, you know me, and you know where I am from. But I have not come by my own authority. I was sent by the One who is true. You don't know him. [29]But I know him. I am from him, and he sent me."

[30]When Jesus said this, the people tried to take him. But no one was able to touch him. It was not yet the right time. [31]But many of the people believed in Jesus. They said, "When the Christ comes, will he do more miracles[d] than this man has done?"

Some Leaders Try to Arrest Jesus

[32]The Pharisees[d] heard the crowd whispering these things about Jesus. So the leading priests and the Pharisees sent some Temple[d] guards to arrest him. [33]Then Jesus said, "I will be with you a little while longer. Then I will go back to the One who sent me. [34]You will look for me, but you will not find me. And you cannot come where I am."

[35]The Jews said to each other, "Where will this man go so we cannot find him? Will he go to the Greek cities where our people live? Will he teach the Greek people there? [36]This man says, 'You will look for me but you will not find me'. He also says, 'You cannot come where I am'. What does this mean?"

Jesus Talks About the Spirit

[37]The last day of the feast came. It was the most important day. On that day Jesus stood up and said in a loud

---

law Moses gave God's people the law that God gave him on Mount Sinai (Exodus 34:29-32).

voice, "If anyone is thirsty, let him come to me and drink. [38]If a person believes in me, rivers of living water will flow out from his heart. This is what the Scripture[d] says." [39]Jesus was talking about the Holy Spirit.[d] The Spirit had not yet been given because Jesus had not yet been raised to glory. But later, those who believed in Jesus would receive the Spirit.

The People Argue About Jesus

[40]The people heard these things that Jesus said. Some of them said, "This man really is the Prophet."[n]

[41]Others said, "He is the Christ."[d]

Still others said, "The Christ will not come from Galilee. [42]The Scripture[d] says that the Christ will come from David's family. And the Scripture says that the Christ will come from Bethlehem, the town where David lived." [43]So the people did not agree with each other about Jesus. [44]Some of them wanted to arrest him, but no one was able to touch him.

The Leaders Won't Believe

[45]The Temple[d] guards went back to the leading priests and the Pharisees.[d] The priests and the Pharisees asked, "Why didn't you bring Jesus?"

[46]The Temple guards answered, "The things he says are greater than the words of any man!"

[47]The Pharisees answered, "So Jesus has fooled you too! [48]Have any of the leaders or the Pharisees believed in him? No! [49]But those people, who know nothing about the law, are under God's curse!"

[50]But Nicodemus was there in that group. He was the one who had gone to see Jesus before.[n] Nicodemus said, [51]"Our law does not judge a man

without hearing him. We cannot judge him until we know what he has done."

[52]They answered, "Are you from Galilee too? Study the Scriptures.[d] You will learn that no prophet[d] comes from Galilee."

[53]And everyone left and went home.[n]

The Woman Caught in Adultery

8 Jesus went to the Mount of Olives.[d] [2]But early in the morning he went back to the Temple.[d] All the people came to Jesus, and he sat and taught them. [3]The teachers of the law and the Pharisees[d] brought a woman there. She had been caught in adultery.[d] They forced the woman to stand before the people. [4]They said to Jesus, "Teacher, this woman was caught having sexual relations with a man who is not her husband. [5]The law of Moses commands that we kill with stones every woman who does this. What do you say we should do?" [6]They were asking this to trick Jesus so that they could have some charge against him.

But Jesus knelt down and started writing on the ground with his finger. [7]They continued to ask Jesus their question. So he stood up and said, "Is there anyone here who has never sinned? The person without sin can throw the first stone at this woman." [8]Then Jesus knelt down again and wrote on the ground.

[9]Those who heard Jesus began to leave one by one. The older men left first, and then the others. Jesus was left there alone with the woman. She was standing before him. [10]Jesus stood up again and asked her, "Woman, all of those people have gone. Has no one judged you guilty?"

Prophet They probably meant the prophet God told Moses he would send (Deuteronomy 18:15-19).

But Nicodemus ... before The story about Nicodemus going and talking to Jesus is in John 3:1-21.

Verse 53 Some early Greek manuscripts do not contain 7:53—8:11.

¹¹She answered, "No one has judged me, sir."

Then Jesus said, "So I don't judge you either. You may go now, but don't sin again."

Jesus Is the Light of the World

¹²Later, Jesus talked to the people again. He said, "I am the light of the world. The person who follows me will never live in darkness. He will have the light that gives life."

¹³But the Pharisees*d* said to Jesus, "When you talk about yourself, you are the only one to say these things are true. We cannot accept these things you say."

¹⁴Jesus answered, "Yes, I am saying these things about myself, but they are true. I know where I came from. And I know where I am going. You don't know where I came from or where I am going. ¹⁵You judge me the way you would judge any man. I don't judge anyone. ¹⁶But if I judge, my judging is true. When I judge, I am not alone. The Father who sent me is with me. ¹⁷Your own law says that when two witnesses say the same thing, then you must accept what they say. ¹⁸I am one of the witnesses who speaks about myself. And the Father who sent me is my other witness."

¹⁹They asked, "Where is your father?"

Jesus answered, "You don't know me or my Father. But if you knew me, then you would know my Father, too." ²⁰Jesus said these things while he was teaching in the Temple.*d* He was near the place where the money that the people give is kept. But no one arrested him. The right time for Jesus had not yet come.

The People Misunderstand Jesus

²¹Again, Jesus said to the people, "I will leave you. You will look for me, but you will die in your sins. You cannot come where I am going."

²²So the Jews asked, "Will Jesus kill himself? Is that why he said, 'You cannot come where I am going'?"

²³But Jesus said, "You people are from here below, but I am from above. You belong to this world, but I don't belong to this world. ²⁴So I told you that you would die in your sins. Yes, you will die in your sins if you don't believe that I am he."

²⁵They asked, "Then who are you?"

Jesus answered, "I am what I have told you from the beginning. ²⁶I have many things to say about you and to judge you for. But I tell people only the things I have heard from the One who sent me. And he speaks the truth."

²⁷The people did not understand that Jesus was talking to them about the Father. ²⁸So Jesus said to them, "You will lift up the Son of Man.*d* Then you will know that I am he. You will know that these things I do are not by my own authority. You will know that I say only what the Father has taught me. ²⁹The One who sent me is with me. I always do what is pleasing to him. So he has not left me alone." ³⁰While Jesus was saying these things, many people believed in him.

Freedom from Sin

³¹So Jesus said to the Jews who believed in him, "If you continue to obey my teaching, you are truly my followers. ³²Then you will know the truth. And the truth will make you free."

³³The Jews answered, "We are Abraham's children. And we have never been slaves. So why do you say that we will be free?"

³⁴Jesus answered, "I tell you the truth. Everyone who lives in sin is a slave to sin. ³⁵A slave does not stay with a family for ever, but a son belongs to the family for ever. ³⁶So if the Son makes you free, then you will be truly free. ³⁷I know you are Abraham's children. But you want to kill me because you don't accept my teaching. ³⁸I am telling you what my

Father has shown me. But you do what your father has told you."

³⁹They answered, "Our father is Abraham."

Jesus said, "If you were really Abraham's children, you would do the things that Abraham did. ⁴⁰I am a man who has told you the truth which I heard from God. But you are trying to kill me. Abraham did nothing like that. ⁴¹So you are doing the things that your own father did."

But the Jews said, "We are not like children who never knew who their father was. God is our Father. He is the only Father we have."

⁴²Jesus said to them, "If God were really your Father, you would love me. I came from God and now I am here. I did not come by my own authority. God sent me. ⁴³You don't understand what I say because you cannot accept my teaching. ⁴⁴Your father is the devil. You belong to him and want to do what he wants. He was a murderer from the beginning. He was against the truth, for there is no truth in him. He is a liar, and he is like the lies he tells. He is the father of lies. ⁴⁵But I speak the truth. That is why you don't believe me. ⁴⁶Can any of you prove that I am guilty of sin? If I am telling the truth, why don't you believe me? ⁴⁷He who belongs to God accepts what God says. But you don't accept what God says, because you don't belong to God."

Jesus and Abraham

⁴⁸The Jews answered, "We say you are a Samaritan!ᵈ We say a demonᵈ has come into you. Are we not right?"

⁴⁹Jesus answered, "I have no demon in me. I give honour to my Father, but you dishonour me. ⁵⁰I am not trying to get honour for myself. There is One who wants this honour for me, and he is the judge. ⁵¹I tell you the truth. If anyone obeys my teaching, he will never die."

⁵²The Jews said to Jesus, "Now we

know that you have a demon in you! Even Abraham and the prophetsᵈ died. But you say, 'Whoever obeys my teaching will never die'. ⁵³Do you think that you are greater than our father Abraham? Abraham died. And the prophets died, too. Who do you think you are?"

⁵⁴Jesus answered, "If I give honour to myself, that honour is worth nothing. The One who gives me honour is my Father. And you say that he is your God. ⁵⁵But you don't really know him. I know him. If I said I did not know him, then I would be a liar as you are liars. But I do know him, and I obey what he says. ⁵⁶Your father Abraham was very happy that he would see my day. He saw that day and was glad."

⁵⁷The Jews said to him, "What? You have seen Abraham! You are not even 50 years old!"

⁵⁸Jesus answered, "I tell you the truth. Before Abraham was born, I am!" ⁵⁹When Jesus said this, the people picked up stones to throw at him. But Jesus hid himself, and then he left the Temple.ᵈ

Jesus Heals a Man Born Blind

9 As Jesus was walking along, he saw a man who had been born blind. ²His followers asked him, "Teacher, whose sin caused this man to be born blind—his own sin or his parents' sin?"

³Jesus answered, "It is not this man's sin or his parents' sin that caused him be blind. This man was born blind so that God's power could be shown in him. ⁴While it is day time, we must continue doing the work of the One who sent me. The night is coming. And no one can work at night. ⁵While I am in the world, I am the light of the world."

⁶After Jesus said this, he spat on the ground and made some mud with it. He put the mud on the man's eyes. ⁷Then he told the man, "Go and wash

in the Pool of Siloam." (Siloam means Sent.) So the man went to the pool. He washed and came back. And he was able to see.

8Some people had seen this man begging before. They and the man's neighbours said, "Look! Is this the same man who always sits and begs?"

9Some said, "Yes! He is the one." But others said, "No, he's not the same man. He only looks like him."

So the man himself said, "I am the man."

10They asked, "What happened? How did you get your sight?"

11He answered, "The man named Jesus made some mud and put it on my eyes. Then he told me to go to Siloam and wash. So I went and washed and came back seeing."

12They asked him, "Where is this man?"

The man answered, "I don't know."

Pharisees Question the Healing

13Then the people took to the Phariseesd the man who had been blind. 14The day Jesus had made mud and healed his eyes was a Sabbathd day. 15So now the Pharisees asked the man, "How did you get your sight?"

He answered, "He put mud on my eyes. I washed, and now I can see."

16Some of the Pharisees were saying, "This man does not keep the Sabbath day. He is not from God!"

Others said, "But a man who is a sinner can't do miraclesd like these." So they could not agree with each other.

17They asked the man again, "What do you say about him? It was your eyes he opened."

The man answered, "He is a prophet."d

18The Jews did not believe that he had been blind and could now see again. So they sent for the man's parents 19and asked them, "Is this your son? You say that he was born blind. Then how does he see now?"

20His parents answered, "We know that this is our son, and we know that he was born blind. 21But we don't know how he can see now. We don't know who opened his eyes. Ask him. He is old enough to answer for himself." 22His parents said this because they were afraid of the Jews. The Jews had already decided that anyone who said that Jesus was the Christd would be put out of the synagogue.d 23That is why his parents said, "He is old enough. Ask him."

24So for the second time, the Jewish leaders called the man who had been blind. They said, "You should give God the glory by telling the truth. We know that this man is a sinner."

25He answered, "I don't know if he is a sinner. But one thing I do know. I was blind, and now I can see."

26The Jewish leaders asked, "What did he do to you? How did he make you see again?"

27He answered, "I have already told you that. But you would not listen to me. Why do you want to hear it again? Do you want to become his followers, too?"

28Then they insulted him and said, "You are his follower. We are followers of Moses. 29We know that God spoke to Moses. But we don't even know where this man comes from!"

30The man answered, "This is a very strange thing. You don't know where he comes from, and yet he opened my eyes. 31We all know that God does not listen to sinners. But God listens to anyone who worships and obeys him. 32Nobody has ever heard of anyone giving sight to a man born blind. 33If this man was not from God, he could do nothing."

34They answered, "You were born full of sin! Are you trying to teach us?" And they threw the man out.

Spiritual Blindness

35Jesus heard that they had thrown him out. So Jesus found him and said,

"Do you believe in the Son of Man?"[d]

[36]He asked, "Who is the Son of Man, sir? Tell me, so I can believe in him!"

[37]Jesus said to him, "You have already seen him. The Son of Man is the one talking with you now."

[38]He said, "Yes, Lord, I believe!" Then the man bowed and worshipped Jesus.

[39]Jesus said, "I came into this world so that the world could be judged. I came so that the blind[n] could see and so that those who see will become blind."

[40]Some of the Pharisees[d] were near Jesus. When they heard him say this, they asked, "What? Are you saying that we are blind, too?"

[41]Jesus said, "If you were really blind, you would not be guilty of sin. But now that you say you can see, your guilt remains."

The Shepherd and His Sheep

10 Jesus said, "I tell you the truth. The man who does not enter the sheep fold by the door, but climbs in some other way, is a thief and a robber. [2]The one who enters by the door is the shepherd of the sheep. [3]The man who guards the door opens it for him. And the sheep listen to the voice of the shepherd. He calls his own sheep, using their names, and he leads them out. [4]He brings all of his sheep out. Then he goes ahead of them and leads them. They follow him because they know his voice. [5]But they will never follow a stranger. They will run away from him because they don't know his voice." [6]Jesus told the people this story, but they did not understand what it meant.

Jesus Is the Good Shepherd

[7]So Jesus said again, "I tell you the truth. I am the door for the sheep. [8]All the people who came before me were

thieves and robbers. The sheep did not listen to them. [9]I am the door. The person who enters through me will be saved. He will be able to come in and go out and find pasture. [10]A thief comes to steal and kill and destroy. But I came to give life—life in all its fullness.

[11]"I am the good shepherd. The good shepherd gives his life for the sheep. [12]The worker who is paid to keep the sheep is different from the shepherd who owns them. So when the worker sees a wolf coming, he runs away and leaves the sheep alone. Then the wolf attacks the sheep and scatters them. [13]The man runs away because he is only a paid worker. He does not really care for the sheep.

[14-15]"I am the good shepherd. I know my sheep, as the Father knows me. And my sheep know me, as I know the Father. I give my life for the sheep. [16]I have other sheep that are not in this flock here. I must bring them also. They will listen to my voice, and there will be one flock and one shepherd. [17]The Father loves me because I give my life. I give my life so that I can take it back again. [18]No one takes it away from me. I give my own life freely. I have the right to give my life, and I have the right to take it back. This is what my Father commanded me to do."

[19]Again the Jews did not agree with each other because of these words Jesus said. [20]Many of them said, "A demon[d] has come into him and made him mad. Why listen to him?"

[21]But others said, "A man who is mad with a demon does not say things like this. Can a demon open the eyes of the blind?"

[22]The time came for the Feast[d] of Dedication at Jerusalem. This was during the winter. [23]Jesus was walking in the Temple[d] in Solomon's Porch.[d] [24]The Jews gathered around

---

blind Jesus is talking about people who are spiritually blind, not physically blind.

him and said, "How long will you make us wonder about you? If you are the Christ,*d* then tell us plainly."

Jesus Is the Son of God

25Jesus answered, "I have told you already, but you did not believe. I do miracles*d* in my Father's name. Those miracles show who I am. 26But you don't believe because you are not my sheep. 27My sheep listen to my voice. I know them, and they follow me. 28I give them eternal life, and they will never die. And no person can steal them out of my hand. 29My Father gave my sheep to me. He is greater than all, and no person can steal my sheep out of my Father's hand. 30The Father and I are one."

31Again the Jews picked up stones to kill Jesus. 32But Jesus said to them, "I have done many good works from the Father. Which of these good works are you killing me for?"

33The Jews answered, "We are not killing you for any good work you did. But you say things that are against God. You are only a man, but you say you are the same as God!"

34Jesus answered, "It is written in your law that God said, 'I have said you are gods!'*n* 35This Scripture*d* called those people gods, the people who received God's message. And Scripture is always true. 36So why do you say that I speak against God because I said, 'I am God's Son'? I am the one God chose and sent into the world. 37If I don't do what my Father does, then don't believe me. 38But if I do what my Father does, even though you don't believe in me, believe what I do. Then you will know and understand that the Father is in me and I am in the Father."

39The Jews tried to take Jesus again, but he escaped from them.

40Then Jesus went back across the Jordan River to the place where John*n*

had first baptised. Jesus stayed there, 41and many people came to him. They said, "John never did a miracle. But everything John said about this man is true." 42And in that place many believed in Jesus.

The Death of Lazarus

11 There was a man named Lazarus who was sick. He lived in the town of Bethany, where Mary and her sister Martha lived. 2Mary is the woman who later put perfume on the Lord and wiped his feet with her hair. Mary's brother was Lazarus, the man who was now sick. 3So Mary and Martha sent someone to tell Jesus, "Lord, the one you love is sick."

4When Jesus heard this he said, "This sickness will not end in death. It is for the glory of God. This has happened to bring glory to the Son of God." 5Jesus loved Martha and her sister and Lazarus. 6But when he heard that Lazarus was sick, he stayed where he was for two more days. 7Then Jesus said to his followers, "Let us go back to Judea."

8The followers said, "But Teacher, the Jews there tried to kill you with stones. That was only a short time ago. Now you want to go back there?"

9Jesus answered, "Are there not 12 hours in the day? If anyone walks in the daylight, he will not stumble because he can see by this world's light. 10But if anyone walks at night he stumbles because there is no light to help him see."

11After Jesus said this, he added, "Our friend Lazarus has fallen asleep. But I am going there to wake him."

12The followers said, "But Lord, if he can sleep, he will get well."

13Jesus meant that Lazarus was dead. But Jesus' followers thought that he meant Lazarus was really sleeping. 14So then Jesus said plainly, "Lazarus is dead. 15And I am glad for

---

John John the Baptist, who preached to people about Christ's coming (Matthew 3, Luke 3). **'I . . . gods.'** Quotation from Psalm 82:6.

your sakes that I was not there so that you may believe. But let us go to him now."

¹⁶Then Thomas (the one called Didymus) said to the other followers, "Let us go, too. We will die with him."

Jesus in Bethany

¹⁷Jesus arrived in Bethany. There he learned that Lazarus had already been dead and in the tomb for four days. ¹⁸Bethany was about three kilometres from Jerusalem. ¹⁹Many Jews had come there to comfort Martha and Mary about their brother.

²⁰Martha heard that Jesus was coming, and she went out to meet him. But Mary stayed at home. ²¹Martha said to Jesus, "Lord, if you had been here, my brother would not have died. ²²But I know that even now God will give you anything you ask."

²³Jesus said, "Your brother will rise and live again."

²⁴Martha answered, "I know that he will rise and live again in the resurrectionⁿ on the last day."

²⁵Jesus said to her, "I am the resurrection and the life. He who believes in me will have life even if he dies. ²⁶And he who lives and believes in me will never die. Martha, do you believe this?"

²⁷Martha answered, "Yes, Lord. I believe that you are the Christ,^d the Son of God. You are the One who was coming to the world."

Jesus Cries

²⁸After Martha said this, she went back to her sister Mary. She talked to Mary alone. Martha said, "The Teacher is here and he is asking for you." ²⁹When Mary heard this, she got up quickly and went to Jesus. ³⁰Jesus had not yet come into the town. He was still at the place where Martha had met him. ³¹The Jews were with Mary in the house, comforting

her. They saw Mary stand and leave quickly. They followed her, thinking that she was going to the tomb to cry there. ³²But Mary went to the place where Jesus was. When she saw him, she fell at his feet and said, "Lord, if you had been here, my brother would not have died."

³³Jesus saw that Mary was crying and that the Jews who came with her were crying, too. Jesus felt very sad in his heart and was deeply troubled. ³⁴He asked, "Where did you bury him?"

"Come and see, Lord," they said.

³⁵Jesus cried.

³⁶So the Jews said, "See how much he loved him."

³⁷But some of them said, "If Jesus healed the eyes of the blind man, why didn't he keep Lazarus from dying?"

Jesus Raises Lazarus

³⁸Again Jesus felt very sad in his heart. He came to the tomb. The tomb was a cave with a large stone covering the entrance. ³⁹Jesus said, "Move the stone away."

Martha said, "But, Lord, it has been four days since he died. There will be a bad smell." Martha was the sister of the dead man.

⁴⁰Then Jesus said to her, "Didn't I tell you that if you believed, you would see the glory of God?"

⁴¹So they moved the stone away from the entrance. Then Jesus looked up and said, "Father, I thank you that you heard me. ⁴²I know that you always hear me. But I said these things because of the people here around me. I want them to believe that you sent me." ⁴³After Jesus said this, he cried out in a loud voice, "Lazarus, come out!" ⁴⁴The dead man came out. His hands and feet were wrapped with pieces of cloth, and he had a cloth around his face.

---

resurrection Being raised from death to live again.

Jesus said to them, "Take the cloth off him and let him go."

The Leaders Plan to Kill Jesus

[45]There were many Jews who had come to visit Mary. They saw what Jesus did. And many of them believed in him. [46]But some of the Jews went to the Pharisees.[d] They told the Pharisees what Jesus had done. [47]Then the leading priests and Pharisees called a meeting of the Jewish council. They asked, "What should we do? This man is doing many miracles.[d] [48]If we let him continue doing these things, everyone will believe in him. Then the Romans will come and take away our Temple[d] and our nation."

[49]One of the men there was Caiaphas. He was the high priest that year. Caiaphas said, "You people know nothing! [50]It is better for one man to die for the people than for the whole nation to be destroyed. But you don't realise this."

[51]Caiaphas did not think of this himself. He was high priest that year. So he was really prophesying[d] that Jesus would die for the Jewish nation [52]and for God's scattered children. This would bring them all together and make them one.

[53]That day the Jewish leaders started planning to kill Jesus. [54]So Jesus no longer travelled openly among the Jews. He left there and went to a place near the desert. He went to a town called Ephraim and stayed there with his followers.

[55]It was almost time for the Jewish Passover[d] Feast. Many from the country went up to Jerusalem before the Passover. They went to do the special things to make themselves pure. [56]The people looked for Jesus. They stood in the Temple and were asking each other, "Is he coming to the Feast? What do you think?" [57]But the leading priests and the Pharisees had given orders about Jesus. They said that if anyone knew where Jesus was, he must tell them. Then they could arrest Jesus.

Jesus with Friends in Bethany

12 Six days before the Passover[d] Feast, Jesus went to Bethany, where Lazarus lived. (Lazarus is the man Jesus raised from death.) [2]There they had a dinner for Jesus. Martha served the food. Lazarus was one of the people eating with Jesus. [3]Mary brought in half a litre of very expensive perfume made from pure nard.[d] She poured the perfume on Jesus' feet, and then she wiped his feet with her hair. And the sweet smell from the perfume filled the whole house.

[4]Judas Iscariot, one of Jesus' followers, was there. (He was the one who would later turn against Jesus.) Judas said, [5]"This perfume was worth 300 silver coins.[n] It should have been sold and the money given to the poor." [6]But Judas did not really care about the poor. He said this because he was a thief. He was the one who kept the money box, and he often stole money from it.

[7]Jesus answered, "Leave her alone. It was right for her to save this perfume for today—the day for me to be prepared for burial. [8]The poor will always be with you, but you will not always have me."

The Plot Against Lazarus

[9]A large crowd of Jews heard that Jesus was in Bethany. So they went there to see not only Jesus but also Lazarus. Lazarus was the one Jesus raised from death. [10]So the leading priests made plans to kill Lazarus, too. [11]Because of Lazarus many Jews were leaving them and believing in Jesus.

---

silver coin One coin, a denarius, was the average pay for one day's work.

Jesus Enters Jerusalem

12The next day a great crowd in Jerusalem heard that Jesus was coming there. These were the people who had come to the Passover*d* Feast. 13They took branches of palm trees and went out to meet Jesus. They shouted,

"Praise*n* God!
God bless the One who comes in
     the name of the Lord!
God bless the King of Israel!"
                                        Psalm 118:25-26

14Jesus found a colt and sat on it. This was as the Scripture*d* says,
15"Don't be afraid, people of
     Jerusalem!
Your king is coming.
He is sitting on the colt of a
     donkey."   *Zechariah 9:9*

16The followers of Jesus did not understand this at first. But after Jesus was raised to glory, they remembered that this had been written about him. And they remembered that they had done these things to him.

People Tell About Jesus

17There had been many people with Jesus when he raised Lazarus from death and told him to come out of the tomb. Now they were telling others about what Jesus did. 18Many people went out to meet Jesus, because they had heard about this miracle.*d* 19So the Pharisees*d* said to each other, "You can see that nothing is going right for us. Look! The whole world is following him."

Jesus Talks About His Death

20There were some Greek people, too, who came to Jerusalem to worship at the Passover*d* Feast. 21They went to Philip. (Philip was from Bethsaida, in Galilee.) They said, "Sir, we would like to see Jesus." 22Philip told

Andrew. Then Andrew and Philip told Jesus.

23Jesus said to them, "The time has come for the Son of Man*d* to receive his glory. 24I tell you the truth. A grain of wheat must fall to the ground and die. Then it makes many seeds. But if it never dies, it remains only a single seed. 25The person who loves his life will give up true life. But the person who hates his life in this world will keep true life for ever. 26Whoever serves me must follow me. Then my servant will be with me everywhere I am. My Father will honour anyone who serves me.

27"Now I am very troubled. What should I say? Should I say, 'Father, save me from this time'? No, I came to this time so that I could suffer. 28Father, bring glory to your name!"

Then a voice came from heaven, "I have brought glory to it, and I will do it again."

29The crowd standing there heard the voice. They said it was thunder. But others said, "An angel has spoken to him."

30Jesus said, "That voice was for you, not for me. 31Now is the time for the world to be judged. Now the ruler of this world will be thrown down. 32I will be lifted up from the earth. And when this happens, I will draw all people toward me." 33Jesus said this to show how he would die.

34The crowd said, "We have heard from the law that the Christ*d* will live for ever. So why do you say, 'The Son of Man must be lifted up'? Who is this 'Son of Man'?"

35Then Jesus said, "The light will be with you for a little longer. So walk while you have the light. Then the darkness will not catch you. He who walks in the darkness does not know where he is going. 36So believe in the light while you still have it. Then you

---

Praise Literally, "Hosanna", a Hebrew word used at first in praying to God for help, but at this time it was probably a shout of joy used in praising God or his Messiah.

will become sons of light." When Jesus had said this, he left and hid himself from them.

Some Don't Believe in Jesus

37Though Jesus had done many miracles[d] before the people, they still did not believe in him. 38This was to make clear the full meaning of what Isaiah the prophet[d] said:

"Lord, who believed the things we
  told them?
Who has seen the Lord's
  power?"   *Isaiah 53:1*

39This is why the people could not believe: Isaiah also said,

40"He has blinded their eyes.
  He has closed their minds.
This is so that they will not see
    with their eyes
  nor understand in their minds.
This is so they will not
  come back to me and be
    forgiven."   *Isaiah 6:10*

41Isaiah said this because he saw Jesus' glory and spoke about him.

42But many people believed in Jesus, even many of the Jewish leaders. But because of the Pharisees,[d] they did not say that they believed in him. They were afraid that they would be put out of the synagogue.[d] 43They loved praise from men more than praise from God.

44Then Jesus cried out, "He who believes in me is really believing in the One who sent me. 45He who sees me sees the One who sent me. 46I have come as light into the world. I came so that whoever believes in me would not stay in darkness.

47"If anyone hears my words and does not obey them, I do not judge him. For I did not come to judge the world, but to save the world. 48There is a judge for the one who refuses to believe in me and does not accept my words. The word I have taught will be his judge on the last day. 49The things I taught were not from myself. The Father who sent me told me what to

say and what to teach. 50And I know that eternal life comes from what the Father commands. So whatever I say is what the Father told me to say."

Jesus Washes His Followers' Feet

13 It was almost time for the Jewish Passover[d] Feast. Jesus knew that it was time for him to leave this world and go back to the Father. He had always loved those who were his own in the world, and he loved them all the way to the end.

2Jesus and his followers were at the evening meal. The devil had already persuaded Judas Iscariot to turn against Jesus. (Judas was the son of Simon.) 3Jesus knew that the Father had given him power over everything. He also knew that he had come from God and was going back to God. 4So during the meal Jesus stood up and took off his outer clothing. Taking a towel, he wrapped it around his waist. 5Then he poured water into a bowl and began to wash the followers' feet. He dried them with the towel that was wrapped around him.

6Jesus came to Simon Peter. But Peter said to Jesus, "Lord, are you going to wash my feet?"

7Jesus answered, "You don't understand what I am doing now. But you will understand later."

8Peter said, "No! You will never wash my feet."

Jesus answered, "If I don't wash your feet, then you are not one of my people."

9Simon Peter answered, "Lord, after you wash my feet, wash my hands and my head, too!"

10Jesus said, "After a person has had a bath, his whole body is clean. He needs only to wash his feet. And you men are clean,[d] but not all of you." 11Jesus knew who would turn against him. That is why Jesus said, "Not all of you are clean."

12When he had finished washing

their feet, he put on his clothes and sat down again. Jesus asked, "Do you understand what I have just done for you? 13You call me 'Teacher' and 'Lord'. And this is right, because that is what I am. 14I, your Lord and Teacher, have washed your feet. So you also should wash each other's feet. 15I did this as an example for you. So you should do as I have done for you. 16I tell you the truth. A servant is not greater than his master. A messenger is not greater than the one who sent him. 17If you know these things, you will be happy if you do them.

18"I am not talking about all of you. I know those I have chosen. But what the Scripture*d* said must happen: 'The man who ate at my table has now turned against me'.*n* 19I am telling you this now before it happens. Then when it happens you will believe that I am he. 20I tell you the truth. Whoever accepts anyone I send also accepts me. And whoever accepts me also accepts the One who sent me."

Jesus Talks About His Death

21After Jesus said this, he was very troubled. He said openly, "I tell you the truth. One of you will turn against me."

22The followers all looked at each other. They did not know whom Jesus was talking about. 23One of the followers was sitting*n* next to Jesus. This was the follower Jesus loved. 24Simon Peter made signs to him to ask Jesus who it was that he was talking about.

25That follower leaned closer to Jesus and asked, "Lord, who is it that will turn against you?"

26Jesus answered, "I will dip this bread into the dish. The man I give it to is the man who will turn against me." So Jesus took a piece of bread. He dipped it and gave it to Judas Iscar-iot, the son of Simon. 27As soon as Judas took the bread, Satan entered him. Jesus said to Judas, "The thing that you will do—do it quickly!" 28None of the men at the table understood why Jesus said this to Judas. 29He was the one who kept the money box. So some of the followers thought that Jesus was telling Judas to buy what was needed for the feast. Or they thought that Jesus wanted Judas to give something to the poor.

30Judas accepted the bread Jesus gave him and immediately went out. It was night.

31When Judas was gone, Jesus said, "Now the Son of Man*d* receives his glory. And God receives glory through him. 32If God receives glory through him, then God will give glory to the Son through himself. And God will give him glory quickly."

33Jesus said, "My children, I will be with you only a little longer. You will look for me. And what I told the Jews, I tell you now: where I am going you cannot come.

34"I give you a new command: love each other. You must love each other as I have loved you. 35All people will know that you are my followers if you love each other."

Peter Will Say He Doesn't Know Jesus

36Simon Peter asked Jesus, "Lord, where are you going?"

Jesus answered, "Where I am going you cannot follow now. But you will follow later."

37Peter asked, "Lord, why can't I follow you now? I am ready to die for you!"

38Jesus answered, "Will you really die for me? I tell you the truth. Before the cock crows, you will say three times that you don't know me."

'The man . . . me.' Quotation from Psalm 41:9.
sitting Literally, "lying". The people of that time ate lying down and leaning on one arm.

Jesus Comforts His Followers

14 Jesus said, "Don't let your hearts be troubled. Trust in God. And trust in me. [2]There are many rooms in my Father's house. I would not tell you this if it were not true. I am going there to prepare a place for you. [3]After I go and prepare a place for you, I will come back. Then I will take you to be with me so that you may be where I am. [4]You know the way to the place where I am going."

[5]Thomas said to Jesus, "Lord, we don't know where you are going. So how can we know the way?"

[6]Jesus answered, "I am the way. And I am the truth and the life. The only way to the Father is through me. [7]If you really knew me, then you would know my Father, too. But now you do know him, and you have seen him."

[8]Philip said to him, "Lord, show us the Father. That is all we need."

[9]Jesus answered, "I have been with you a long time now. Do you still not know me, Philip? He who has seen me has seen the Father. So why do you say, 'Show us the Father'? [10]Don't you believe that I am in the Father and the Father is in me? The words I say to you don't come from me. The Father lives in me, and he is doing his own work. [11]Believe me when I say that I am in the Father and the Father is in me. Or believe because of the miracles[d] I have done. [12]I tell you the truth. He who believes in me will do the same things that I do. He will do even greater things than these because I am going to the Father. [13]And if you ask for anything in my name, I will do it for you. Then the Father's glory will be shown through the Son. [14]If you ask me for anything in my name, I will do it.

The Promise of the Holy Spirit

[15]"If you love me, you will do the things I command. [16]I will ask the Father, and he will give you another Helper.[n] He will give you this Helper to be with you for ever. [17]The Helper is the Spirit[d] of truth. The world cannot accept him because it does not see him or know him. But you know him. He lives with you and he will be in you.

[18]"I will not leave you all alone like orphans. I will come back to you. [19]In a little while the world will not see me any more, but you will see me. Because I live, you will live, too. [20]On that day you will know that I am in my Father. You will know that you are in me and I am in you. [21]He who knows my commands and obeys them is the one who loves me. And my Father will love him who loves me. I will love him and will show myself to him."

[22]Then Judas (not Judas Iscariot) said, "But, Lord, why do you plan to show yourself to us, but not to the world?"

[23]Jesus answered, "If anyone loves me, then he will obey my teaching. My Father will love him, and we will come to him and make our home with him. [24]He who does not love me does not obey my teaching. This teaching that you hear is not really mine. It is from my Father, who sent me.

[25]"I have told you all these things while I am with you. [26]But the Helper will teach you everything. He will cause you to remember all the things I told you. This Helper is the Holy Spirit whom the Father will send in my name.

[27]"I leave you peace. My peace I give you. I do not give it to you as the world does. So don't let your hearts be troubled. Don't be afraid. [28]You heard me say to you, 'I am going, but

---

Helper "Counsellor", or "Comforter". Jesus is talking about the Holy Spirit.

I am coming back to you'. If you loved me, you should be happy that I am going back to the Father because he is greater than I am. ²⁹I have told you this now, before it happens. Then when it happens, you will believe. ³⁰I will not talk with you much longer. The ruler of this world is coming. He has no power over me. ³¹But the world must know that I love the Father. So I do exactly what the Father told me to do.

"Come now, let us go."

Jesus Is Like a Vine

15 "I am the true vine; my Father is the gardener. ²He cuts off every branch of mine that does not produce fruit. And he trims and cleans every branch that produces fruit so that it will produce even more fruit. ³You are already clean*d* because of the words I have spoken to you. ⁴Remain in me, and I will remain in you. No branch can produce fruit alone. It must remain in the vine. It is the same with you. You cannot produce fruit alone. You must remain in me.

⁵"I am the vine, and you are the branches. If a person remains in me and I remain in him, then he produces much fruit. But without me he can do nothing. ⁶If anyone does not remain in me, then he is like a branch that is thrown away. That branch dies. People pick up dead branches, throw them into the fire, and burn them. ⁷Remain in me and follow my teachings. If you do this, then you can ask for anything you want, and it will be given to you. ⁸You should produce much fruit and show that you are my followers. This brings glory to my Father. ⁹I loved you as the Father loved me. Now remain in my love. ¹⁰I have obeyed my Father's commands, and I remain in his love. In the same way, if you obey my commands, you will remain in my love. ¹¹I have told you

these things so that you can have the same joy I have. I want your joy to be the fullest joy.

¹²"This is my command: love each other as I have loved you. ¹³The greatest love a person can show is to die for his friends. ¹⁴You are my friends if you do what I command you. ¹⁵I don't call you servants now. A servant does not know what his master is doing. But now I call you friends because I have made known to you everything I heard from my Father. ¹⁶You did not choose me; I chose you. And I gave you this work, to go and produce fruit. I want you to produce fruit that will last. Then the Father will give you anything you ask for in my name. ¹⁷This is my command: love each other.

Jesus Warns His Followers

¹⁸"If the world hates you, remember that it hated me first. ¹⁹If you belonged to the world, then it would love you as it loves its own. But I have chosen you out of the world. So you don't belong to it. That is why the world hates you. ²⁰Remember what I told you: a servant is not greater than his master. If people did wrong to me, they will do wrong to you, too. And if they obeyed my teaching, they will obey yours, too. ²¹They will do all this to you because of me. They don't know the One who sent me. ²²If I had not come and spoken to them, they would not be guilty of sin. But now they have no excuse for their sin. ²³He who hates me also hates my Father. ²⁴I did works among them that no one else has ever done. If I had not done those works, they would not be guilty of sin. But now they have seen what I did, and yet they have hated both me and my Father. ²⁵But this happened so that what is written in their law would be true: 'They hated me for no reason'.*n*

'They . . . reason' These words could be from Psalm 35:19 or Psalm 69:4.

26"I will send you the Helper[n] from the Father. He is the Spirit of truth who comes from the Father. When he comes, he will tell about me. 27And you also must tell people about me because you have been with me from the beginning.

16 "I have told you these things to keep you from giving up. 2People will put you out of their synagogues.[d] Yes, the time is coming when whoever kills you will think that he is offering service to God. 3They will do this because they have not known the Father and they have not known me. 4I have told you these things now. So when the time comes, you will remember that I warned you.

The Work of the Holy Spirit

"I did not tell you these things at the beginning, because I was with you then. 5Now I am going back to the One who sent me. But none of you asks me, 'Where are you going?' 6Your hearts are filled with sadness because I have told you these things. 7But I tell you the truth. It is better for you that I go away. When I go away I will send the Helper[n] to you. If I do not go away, then the Helper will not come. 8When the Helper comes, he will prove to the people of the world the truth about sin, about being right with God, and about judgement. 9He will prove to them about sin, because they don't believe in me. 10He will prove to them that I am right with God, because I am going to the Father. You will not see me any more. 11And the Helper will prove to them the truth about judgement, because the ruler of this world is already judged.

12"I have many more things to say to you, but they are too much for you now. 13But when the Spirit[d] of truth comes he will lead you into all truth. He will not speak his own words. He will speak only what he hears and will tell you what is to come. 14The Spirit of truth will bring glory to me. He will take what I have to say and tell it to you. 15All that the Father has is mine. That is why I said that the Spirit will take what I have to say and tell it to you.

Sadness Will Become Happiness

16"After a little while you will not see me. And then after a little while you will see me again."

17Some of the followers said to each other, "What does Jesus mean when he says, 'After a little while you will not see me, and then after a little while you will see me again'? And what does he mean when he says, 'Because I am going to the Father'?" 18They also asked, "What does he mean by 'a little while'? We don't understand what he is saying."

19Jesus saw that the followers wanted to ask him about this. So Jesus said to the followers, "Are you asking each other what I meant when I said, 'After a little while you will not see me. And then after a little while you will see me again'? 20I tell you the truth. You will cry and be sad, but the world will be happy. You will be sad, but your sadness will become joy. 21When a woman gives birth to a baby, she has pain, because her time has come. But when her baby is born, she forgets the pain. She forgets because she is so happy that a child has been born into the world. 22It is the same with you. Now you are sad. But I will see you again and you will be happy. And no one will take away your joy. 23In that day you will not ask me for anything. I tell you the truth. My Father will give you anything you ask for in my name. 24You have never asked for anything in my name. Ask and you will receive. And your joy will be the fullest joy.

Helper "Counsellor", or "Comforter". Jesus is talking about the Holy Spirit.

Victory over the World

25"I have told you these things, using words that hide the meaning. But the time will come when I will not use words like that to tell you things. I will speak to you in plain words about the Father. 26In that day you will ask the Father for things in my name. I am saying that I will not need to ask the Father for you. 27No! The Father himself loves you. He loves you because you have loved me. And he loves you because you have believed that I came from God. 28I came from the Father into the world. Now I am leaving the world and going back to the Father."

29Then the followers of Jesus said, "You are speaking clearly to us now. You are not using words that are hard to understand. 30We can see now that you know all things. You can answer a person's question even before he asks it. This makes us believe that you came from God."

31Jesus answered, "So now you believe? 32Listen to me. A time is coming when you will be scattered. Each of you will be scattered to his own home. That time is now here. You will leave me. I will be alone. But I am never really alone. Why? Because the Father is with me.

33"I told you these things so that you can have peace in me. In this world you will have trouble. But be brave! I have defeated the world!"

Jesus Prays for His Followers

17 After Jesus said these things he looked towards heaven. Jesus prayed, "Father, the time has come. Give glory to your Son so that the Son can give glory to you. 2You gave the Son power over all people so that the Son could give eternal life to all those people you have given to him. 3And this is eternal life: that men can know you, the only true God, and that men can know Jesus Christ, the One you sent. 4I have finished the work you gave me to do. I have brought you glory on earth. 5And now, Father, give me glory with you. Give me the glory I had with you before the world was made.

6"You gave me some men from the world. I have shown them what you are like. Those men belonged to you, and you gave them to me. They have obeyed your teaching. 7Now they know that everything you gave me comes from you. 8I gave these men the teachings that you gave me. They accepted those teachings. They know that I truly came from you. 9I pray for them now. I am not praying for the people in the world. But I am praying for those men you gave me, because they are yours. 10All I have is yours, and all you have is mine. And my glory is shown through these men. 11Now I am coming to you. I will not stay in the world now. But these men are still in the world. Holy Father, keep them safe. Keep them safe by the power of your name (the name you gave me), so that they will be one, the same as you and I are one. 12While I was with them, I kept them safe. I kept them safe by the power of your name — the name you gave me. I protected them. And only one of them, the one who is going to hell, was lost. He was lost so that what was said in the Scripture*d* would happen.

13"I am coming to you now. But I pray these things while I am still in the world. I say these things so that these men can have my joy. I want them to have all of my joy. 14I have given them your teaching. And the world has hated them. The world hated these men, because they don't belong to the world, just as I don't belong to the world. 15I am not asking you to take them out of the world. But I am asking that you keep them safe from the Evil One. 16They don't belong to the world, just as I don't belong to the world. 17Make them ready for your service through your truth. Your teaching is truth. [18]I have sent them into the world, just as you sent me into the world. [19]I am making myself ready to serve. I do this for them so that they can truly be ready for your service.

[20]"I pray for these men. But I am also praying for all people who will believe in me because of the teaching of these men. [21]Father, I pray that all people who believe in me can be one. You are in me and I am in you. I pray that these people can also be one in us, so that the world will believe that you sent me. [22]I have given these people the glory that you gave me. I gave them this glory so that they can be one, just as you and I are one. [23]I will be in them and you will be in me. So they will be completely one. Then the world will know that you sent me. And the world will know that you loved these people just as you loved me.

[24]"Father, I want those you have given me to be with me in every place I am. I want them to see my glory. This is the glory you gave me because you loved me before the world was made. [25]Father, you are the One who is good. The world does not know you, but I know you. And these people know that you sent me. [26]I showed them what you are like. And again I will show them what you are like. Then they will have the same love that you have for me. And I will live in them."

Jesus Is Arrested

18 When Jesus finished praying, he left with his followers. They went across the Kidron Valley. On the other side there was a garden of olive trees. Jesus and his followers went there.

[2]Judas knew where this place was, because Jesus met there often with his followers. Judas was the one who turned against Jesus. [3]So Judas led a group of soldiers to the garden. Judas also brought some guards from the leading priests and the Pharisees.[d] They were carrying torches, lanterns, and weapons.

[4]Jesus knew everything that would happen to him. Jesus went out and asked, "Who is it you are looking for?"

[5]The men answered, "Jesus from Nazareth."

Jesus said, "I am Jesus." (Judas, the one who turned against Jesus, was standing there with them.) [6]When Jesus said, "I am Jesus," the men moved back and fell to the ground.

[7]Jesus asked them again, "Who is it you are looking for?"

They said, "Jesus of Nazareth."

[8]Jesus said, "I told you that I am he. So if you are looking for me, then let these other men go." [9]This happened so that the words Jesus said before might come true: "I have not lost any of the men you gave me."

[10]Simon Peter had a sword. He took out the sword and struck the servant of the high priest, cutting off his right ear. (The servant's name was Malchus.) [11]Jesus said to Peter, "Put your sword back. Shall I not drink of the cup[n] the Father has given me?"

Jesus Is Brought Before Annas

[12]Then the soldiers with their commander and the Jewish guards arrested Jesus. They tied him [13]and led him first to Annas. Annas was the father-in-law of Caiaphas, the high priest that year. [14]Caiaphas was the one who had told the Jews that it would be better if one man died for all the people.

Peter Says He Doesn't Know Jesus

[15]Simon Peter and another one of Jesus' followers went along after

cup Jesus is talking about the bad things that will happen to him. Accepting these things will be very hard, like drinking a cup of something that tastes very bitter.

Jesus. This follower knew the high priest. So he went with Jesus into the high priest's courtyard. [16]But Peter waited outside near the door. The follower who knew the high priest came back outside. He spoke to the girl at the door and brought Peter inside. [17]The girl at the door said to Peter, "Aren't you also one of that man's followers?"

Peter answered, "No, I am not!"

[18]It was cold, so the servants and guards had built a fire. They were standing around it and warming themselves. Peter was standing with them, warming himself.

The High Priest Questions Jesus

[19]The high priest asked Jesus questions about his followers and his teaching. [20]Jesus answered, "I have spoken openly to everyone. I have always taught in synagogues[d] and in the Temple,[d] where all the Jews come together. I never said anything in secret. [21]So why do you question me? Ask the people who heard my teaching. They know what I said."

[22]When Jesus said this, one of the guards standing there hit him. The guard said, "Is that the way you answer the high priest?"

[23]Jesus answered him, "If I said something wrong, then say what was wrong. But if what I said is true, why do you hit me?"

[24]Then Annas sent Jesus to Caiaphas, the high priest. Jesus was still tied.

Peter Says Again He Doesn't Know Jesus

[25]Simon Peter was standing and warming himself. They said to him, "Aren't you one of that man's followers?"

Peter denied it and said, "No, I am not."

[26]One of the servants of the high priest was there. This servant was a relative of the man whose ear Peter had cut off. The servant said, "Didn't I see you with him in the garden?"

[27]Again Peter said it wasn't true. Just then a cockerel crowed.

Jesus Is Brought Before Pilate

[28]Then the Jews led Jesus from Caiaphas' house to the Roman governor's palace. It was early in the morning. The Jews would not go inside the palace. They did not want to make themselves unclean,[n] because they wanted to eat the Passover[d] meal. [29]So Pilate went outside to them. He asked, "What charges do you bring against this man?"

[30]They answered, "He is a criminal. That is why we brought him to you."

[31]Pilate said to the Jews, "Take him yourselves and judge him by your own law."

They answered, "But we are not allowed to put anyone to death." [32](This happened so that what Jesus had said about how he would die would come true.)

[33]Then Pilate went back inside the palace. He called Jesus to him and asked, "Are you the king of the Jews?"

[34]Jesus said, "Is that your own question, or did others tell you about me?"

[35]Pilate answered, "I am not a Jew. It was your own people and their leading priests who brought you before me. What have you done wrong?"

[36]Jesus said, "My kingdom does not belong to this world. If it belonged to this world, my servants would fight so that I would not be given over to the Jews. But my kingdom is from another place."

[37]Pilate said, "So you are a king!"

Jesus answered, "You say that I am

unclean Going into a non-Jewish place would make them unfit to eat the Passover Feast, according to Jewish law.

a king. That is true. I was born for this: to tell people about the truth. That is why I came into the world. And everyone who belongs to the truth listens to me."

³⁸Pilate said, "What is truth?" After he said this, he went out to the Jews again. He said to them, "I can find nothing to charge against this man. ³⁹But it is your custom that I free one prisoner to you at the time of the Passover. Do you want me to free this 'King of the Jews'?"

⁴⁰They shouted back, "No, not him! Let Barabbas go free!" (Barabbas was a robber.)

19 Then Pilate ordered that Jesus be taken away and whipped. ²The soldiers used some thorny branches to make a crown. They put this crown on Jesus' head and put a purple robe around him. ³Then they came to Jesus many times and said, "Hail, King of the Jews!" They hit Jesus in the face.

⁴Again Pilate came out and said to the Jews, "Look! I am bringing Jesus out to you. I want you to know that I find nothing I can charge against him." ⁵Then Jesus came out, wearing the crown of thorns and the purple robe. Pilate said to the Jews, "Here is the man!"

⁶When the leading priests and the Jewish guards saw Jesus they shouted, "Kill him on a cross! Kill him on a cross!"

But Pilate answered, "Take him and nail him to a cross yourselves. I find nothing I can charge against him."

⁷The Jews answered, "We have a law that says he should die, because he said he is the Son of God."

⁸When Pilate heard this, he was even more afraid. ⁹He went back inside the palace and asked Jesus, "Where are you from?" But Jesus did not answer him. ¹⁰Pilate said, "You refuse to speak to me? Don't you

know that I have power to set you free and power to have you killed on a cross?"

¹¹Jesus answered, "The only power you have over me is the power given to you by God. The man who gave me to you is guilty of a greater sin."

¹²After this, Pilate tried to let Jesus go free. But the Jews cried out, "Anyone who makes himself king is against Caesar. If you let this man go free, you are not Caesar's friend."

¹³Pilate heard what the Jews were saying. So he brought Jesus out to the place called The Stone Pavement. (In the Jewish language ⁿ the name is Gabbatha.) Pilate sat down on the judge's seat there. ¹⁴It was about six o'clock in the morning on Preparation ᵈ Day of Passover ᵈ week. Pilate said to the Jews, "Here is your king!"

¹⁵The Jews shouted, "Take him away! Take him away! Kill him on a cross!"

Pilate asked them, "Do you want me to kill your king on a cross?"

The leading priests answered, "The only king we have is Caesar!"

¹⁶So Pilate gave Jesus to them to be killed on a cross.

Jesus Is Killed on a Cross

The soldiers took charge of Jesus. ¹⁷Carrying his own cross, Jesus went out to a place called The Place of the Skull. (In the Jewish language ⁿ this place is called Golgotha.) ¹⁸There they nailed Jesus to the cross. They also put two other men on crosses, one on each side of Jesus with Jesus in the middle. ¹⁹Pilate wrote a sign and put it on the cross. It read: "JESUS OF NAZARETH, THE KING OF THE JEWS." ²⁰The sign was written in the Jewish language, in Latin, and in Greek. Many of the Jews read the sign, because this place where they killed Jesus was near the city. ²¹The leading Jewish priests said to Pilate, "Don't write,

Jewish language Aramaic, the language of the Jews in the first century.

'The King of the Jews'. But write, 'This man said, I am the King of the Jews'."

²²Pilate answered, "What I have written, I have written!"

²³After the soldiers nailed Jesus to the cross, they took his clothes. They divided them into four parts. Each soldier got one part. They also took his long shirt. It was all one piece of cloth, woven from top to bottom. ²⁴So the soldiers said to each other, "We should not tear this into parts. We should throw lots[d] to see who will get it." This happened to give full meaning to the Scripture:[d]

"They divided my clothes among them.

And they threw lots[d] for my clothing."   *Psalm 22:18*

So the soldiers did this.

²⁵Jesus' mother stood near his cross. His mother's sister was also standing there, with Mary the wife of Clopas, and Mary Magdalene. ²⁶Jesus saw his mother. He also saw the follower he loved standing there. He said to his mother, "Dear woman, here is your son." ²⁷Then he said to the follower, "Here is your mother." From that time on, this follower took her to live in his home.

Jesus Dies

²⁸After this, Jesus knew that everything had been done. To make the Scripture[d] come true, he said, "I am thirsty."[n] ²⁹There was a jar full of vinegar there, so the soldiers soaked a sponge in it. Then they put the sponge on a branch of a hyssop plant and lifted it to Jesus' mouth. ³⁰Jesus tasted the vinegar. Then he said, "It is finished." He bowed his head and died.

³¹This day was Preparation[d] Day. The next day was a special Sabbath[d] day. The Jews did not want the bodies to stay on the cross on the Sabbath day. So they asked Pilate to order that the legs of the men be broken[n] and the bodies be taken away. ³²So the soldiers came and broke the legs of the first man on the cross beside Jesus. Then they broke the legs of the man on the other cross beside Jesus. ³³But when the soldiers came to Jesus, they saw that he was already dead. So they did not break his legs, ³⁴but one of the soldiers stuck his spear into Jesus' side. At once blood and water came out. ³⁵(The one who saw this happen has told about it. The things he says are true. He knows that he tells the truth. He told about it so that you also can believe.) ³⁶These things happened to make the Scripture come true: "Not one of his bones will be broken."[n] ³⁷And another Scripture said, "They will look at the one they have stabbed."[n]

Jesus Is Buried

³⁸Later, a man named Joseph from Arimathea asked Pilate if he could take the body of Jesus. (Joseph was a secret follower of Jesus, because he was afraid of the Jews.) Pilate gave his permission. So Joseph came and took Jesus' body away. ³⁹Nicodemus went with Joseph. Nicodemus was the man who earlier had come to Jesus at night. He brought about 35 kilograms of spices. This was a mixture of myrrh[d] and aloes.[d] ⁴⁰These two men took Jesus' body and wrapped it with the spices in pieces of linen cloth. (This is how the Jews bury people.) ⁴¹In the place where Jesus was killed,

"I am thirsty."   Read Psalms 22:15; 69:21.
broken The breaking of the men's bones would make them die sooner.
"Not one . . . broken." Quotation from Psalm 34:20. The idea is from Exodus 12:46; Numbers 9:12.
"They . . . stabbed." Quotation from Zechariah 12:10.

there was a garden. In the garden was a new tomb where no one had ever been buried. [42]The men laid Jesus in that tomb because it was near, and the Jews were preparing to start their Sabbath[d] day.

Jesus' Tomb Is Empty

20 Early on the first day of the week, Mary Magdalene went to the tomb. It was still dark. Mary saw that the large stone had been moved away from the tomb. [2]So Mary ran to Simon Peter and the other follower (the one Jesus loved). Mary said, "They have taken the Lord out of the tomb. We don't know where they have put him."

[3]So Peter and the other follower started for the tomb. [4]They were both running, but the other follower ran faster than Peter. So the other follower reached the tomb first. [5]He bent down and looked in. He saw the strips of linen cloth lying there, but he did not go in. [6]Then following him came Simon Peter. He went into the tomb and saw the strips of linen lying there. [7]He also saw the cloth that had been around Jesus' head. The cloth was folded up and laid in a different place from the strips of linen. [8]Then the other follower, who had reached the tomb first, also went in. He saw and believed. [9](These followers did not yet understand from the Scriptures[d] that Jesus must rise from death.)

Jesus Appears to Mary Magdalene

[10]Then the followers went back home. [11]But Mary stood outside the tomb, crying. While she was still crying, she bent down and looked inside the tomb. [12]She saw two angels dressed in white. They were sitting where Jesus' body had been, one at the head and one at the feet.

[13]They asked her, "Woman, why are you crying?"

She answered, "They have taken away my Lord. I don't know where they have put him." [14]When Mary said this, she turned around and saw Jesus standing there. But she did not know that it was Jesus.

[15]Jesus asked her, "Woman, why are you crying? Whom are you looking for?"

Mary thought he was the gardener. So she said to him, "Did you take him away, sir? Tell me where you put him, and I will get him."

[16]Jesus said to her, "Mary."

Mary turned toward Jesus and said in the Jewish language,[n] "Rabboni." (This means Teacher.)

[17]Jesus said to her, "Don't hold me. I have not yet gone up to the Father. But go to my brothers and tell them this: 'I am going back to my Father and your Father. I am going back to my God and your God'."

[18]Mary Magdalene went and said to the followers, "I have seen the Lord!" And she told them what Jesus had said to her.

Jesus Appears to His Followers

[19]It was the first day of the week. That evening the followers were together. The doors were locked, because they were afraid of the Jews. Then Jesus came and stood among them. He said, "Peace be with you!" [20]After he said this, he showed them his hands and his side. The followers were very happy when they saw the Lord.

[21]Then Jesus said again, "Peace be with you! As the Father sent me, I now send you." [22]After he said this, he breathed on them and said, "Receive the Holy Spirit.[d] [23]If you forgive anyone his sins, they are forgiven. If you don't forgive them, they are not forgiven."

Jewish language Aramaic, the language of the Jews in the first century.

Jesus Appears to Thomas

24Thomas (called Didymus) was not with the followers when Jesus came. Thomas was one of the 12. 25The other followers told Thomas, "We have seen the Lord."

But Thomas said, "I will not believe it until I see the nail marks in his hands. And I will not believe until I put my finger where the nails were and put my hand into his side."

26A week later the followers were in the house again. Thomas was with them. The doors were locked, but Jesus came in and stood among them. He said, "Peace be with you!" 27Then he said to Thomas, "Put your finger here. Look at my hands. Put your hand here in my side. Stop doubting and believe."

28Thomas said to him, "My Lord and my God!"

29Then Jesus told him, "You believe because you see me. Those who believe without seeing me will be truly happy."

Why John Wrote This Book

30Jesus did many other miracles[d] in front of his followers that are not written in this book. 31But these are written so that you can believe that Jesus is the Christ,[d] the Son of God. Then, by believing, you can have life through his name.

Jesus Appears to Seven Followers

21 Later, Jesus showed himself to his followers by Lake Galilee.[n] This is how it happened. 2Some of the followers were together. They were Simon Peter, Thomas (called Didymus), Nathanael from Cana in Galilee, the two sons of Zebedee, and two other followers. 3Simon Peter said, "I am going out to fish."

The other followers said, "We will go with you." So they went out and got into the boat. They fished that night but caught nothing.

4Early the next morning Jesus stood on the shore. But the followers did not know that it was Jesus. 5Then he said to them, "Friends, have you caught any fish?"

They answered, "No".

6He said, "Throw your net into the water on the right side of the boat, and you will find some." So they did this. They caught so many fish that they could not pull the net back into the boat.

7The follower whom Jesus loved said to Peter, "It is the Lord!" When Peter heard him say this, he wrapped his coat around himself. (Peter had taken his clothes off.) Then he jumped into the water. 8The other followers went to shore in the boat, dragging the net full of fish. They were not very far from shore, only about 100 metres. 9When the followers stepped out of the boat and onto the shore, they saw a fire of hot coals. There were fish on the fire, and there was bread.

10Then Jesus said, "Bring some of the fish that you caught."

11Simon Peter went into the boat and pulled the net to the shore. It was full of big fish. There were 153. Even though there were so many, the net did not tear. 12Jesus said to them, "Come and eat." None of the followers dared ask him, "Who are you?" They knew it was the Lord. 13Jesus came and took the bread and gave it to them. He also gave them the fish.

14This was now the third time that Jesus showed himself to his followers after he was raised from death.

Jesus Talks to Peter

15When they had finished eating, Jesus said to Simon Peter, "Simon,

Lake Galilee Literally, "Sea of Tiberias".

son of John, do you love me more than these?"

He answered, "Yes, Lord, you know that I love you."

Jesus said, "Take care of my lambs."

[16]Again Jesus said, "Simon, son of John, do you love me?"

He answered, "Yes, Lord, you know that I love you."

Jesus said, "Take care of my sheep."

[17]A third time he said, "Simon, son of John, do you love me?"

Peter was hurt because Jesus asked him the third time, "Do you love me?" Peter said, "Lord, you know everything. You know that I love you!"

He said to him, "Take care of my sheep. [18]I tell you the truth. When you were younger, you tied your own belt and went where you wanted. But when you are old, you will put out your hands and someone else will tie them. They will take you where you don't want to go." [19](Jesus said this to show how Peter would die to give glory to God.) Then Jesus said to Peter, "Follow me!"

[20]Peter turned and saw that the follower Jesus loved was walking behind them. (This was the follower who had leaned against Jesus at the supper and had said, "Lord, who will turn against you?") [21]When Peter saw him behind them he asked Jesus, "Lord, what about him?"

[22]Jesus answered, "Perhaps I want him to live until I come back. That should not be important to you. You follow me!"

[23]So a story spread among the brothers that this follower would not die. But Jesus did not say that he would not die. He only said, "Perhaps I want him to live until I come back. That should not be important to you."

[24]That follower is the one who is telling these things. He is the one who has now written them down. We know that what he says is true.

[25]There are many other things that Jesus did. If every one of them were written down, I think the whole world would not be big enough for all the books that would be written.

ACTS

The Good News of Jesus Spreads

Luke Writes Another Book

1 To Theophilus,
The first book I wrote was about everything that Jesus did and taught. ²I wrote about the whole life of Jesus, from the beginning until the day he was taken up into heaven. Before this, Jesus talked to the apostles*d* he had chosen. With the help of the Holy Spirit,*d* Jesus told them what they should do. ³After his death, he showed himself to them and proved in many ways that he was alive. The apostles saw Jesus during the 40 days after he was raised from death. He spoke to them about the kingdom of God. ⁴Once when he was eating with them, he told them not to leave Jerusalem. He said, "The Father has made you a promise which I told you about before. Wait here to receive this promise. ⁵John baptised people with water, but in a few days you will be baptised with the Holy Spirit."

Jesus Is Taken Up into Heaven

⁶The apostles*d* were all together. They asked Jesus, "Lord, are you at this time going to give the kingdom back to Israel?"

⁷Jesus said to them, "The Father is the only One who has the authority to decide dates and times. These things are not for you to know. ⁸But the Holy Spirit*d* will come to you. Then you will receive power. You will be my witnesses — in Jerusalem, in all of Judea, in Samaria, and in every part of the world."

⁹After he said this, as they were watching, he was lifted up. A cloud hid him from their sight. ¹⁰As he was going, they were looking into the sky.

Suddenly, two men wearing white clothes stood beside them. ¹¹They said, "Men of Galilee, why are you standing here looking into the sky? You saw Jesus taken away from you into heaven. He will come back in the same way you saw him go."

A New Apostle Is Chosen

¹²Then they went back to Jerusalem from the Mount of Olives.*d* (This mountain is about a kilometre from Jerusalem.) ¹³When they entered the city, they went to the upstairs room where they were staying. Peter, John, James, Andrew, Philip, Thomas, Bartholomew, Matthew, James son of Alphaeus, Simon (known as the Zealot*d*), and Judas son of James were there. ¹⁴They all continued praying together. Some women, including Mary the mother of Jesus, and Jesus' brothers were also there with the apostles.

¹⁵During this time there was a meeting of the believers. (There were about 120 of them.) Peter stood up and said, ¹⁶⁻¹⁷"Brothers, in the Scriptures*d* the Holy Spirit*d* said through David that something must happen. The Spirit was talking about Judas, one of our own group, who served together with us. The Spirit said that Judas would lead men to arrest Jesus. ¹⁸Judas bought a field with the money he got for his evil act. (But Judas fell to his death, his body burst open, and all his intestines poured out.) ¹⁹Everyone in Jerusalem learned about this. This is why they named the field Akeldama. (In their language Akeldama means "field of blood".) ²⁰In the Book of Psalms, this is written:
'May his place be empty.

Leave no one to live in it.'

Psalm 69:25

And it is also written:

'Let another man replace him as leader'.   *Psalm 109:8*

21-22"So now a man must join us and become a witness of Jesus' being raised from death. He must be one of the men who were part of our group during all the time the Lord Jesus was with us. He must have been with us from the time John began to baptise people until the day when Jesus was taken up from us to heaven."

23They put the names of two men before the group. One was Joseph Barsabbas, who was also called Justus. The other was Matthias. 24-25The apostles prayed, "Lord, you know the minds of everyone. Show us which one of these two you have chosen to do this work. Judas turned away from it and went where he belongs. Lord, show us which one should take his place as an apostle!"*d* 26Then they used lots*d* to choose between them, and the lots showed that Matthias was the one. So he became an apostle with the other 11.

The Coming of the Holy Spirit

2 When the day of Pentecost*d* came, they were all together in one place. 2Suddenly a noise came from heaven. It sounded like a strong wind blowing. This noise filled the whole house where they were sitting. 3They saw something that looked like flames of fire. The flames were separated and stood over each person there. 4They were all filled with the Holy Spirit,*d* and they began to speak different languages.*n* The Holy Spirit was giving them the power to speak these languages.

5There were some religious Jews staying in Jerusalem who were from every country in the world. 6When they heard this noise, a crowd came together. They were all surprised, because each one heard them speaking in his own language. 7They were completely amazed at this. They said, "Look! Aren't all these men that we hear speaking from Galilee?*n* 8But each of us hears them in his own language. How is this possible? We are from different places: 9Parthia, Media, Elam, Mesopotamia, Judea, Cappadocia, Pontus, Asia, 10Phrygia, Pamphylia, Egypt, the areas of Libya near Cyrene, Rome 11(both Jews and those who had become Jews), Crete and Arabia. But we hear these men telling in our own languages about the great things God has done!" 12They were all amazed and confused. They asked each other, "What does this mean?"

13But others were making fun of them, saying, "They have had too much wine."

Peter Speaks to the People

14But Peter stood up with the 11 apostles.*d* In a loud voice he spoke to the crowd: "My fellow Jews, and all of you who are in Jerusalem, listen to me. Pay attention to what I have to say. 15These men are not drunk, as you think; it is only nine o'clock in the morning! 16But Joel the prophet*d* wrote about what is happening here today:

17'God says: In the last days
   I will give my Spirit*d* freely to all
      kinds of people.
Your sons and daughters will
      prophesy.*d*
Your old men will dream
      dreams.
Your young men will see
      visions.
18At that time I will give my Spirit

---

languages This can also be translated "tongues".
from Galilee The people were surprised because the men from Galilee were speaking other languages and not their own.

even to my servants, both men
and women.
And they will prophesy.
[19]I will show miracles[d]
in the sky and on the earth:
blood, fire and thick smoke.
[20]The sun will become dark.
The moon will become red as
blood.
And then the great and glorious
day of the Lord will come.
[21]Then anyone who asks the Lord
for help
will be saved'.   *Joel 2:28-32*

[22]"Men of Israel, listen to these
words: Jesus from Nazareth was a
very special man. God clearly showed
this to you by the miracles,[d] wonders,
and signs God did through him. You all
know this, because it happened right
here among you. [23]Jesus was given to
you, and you killed him. With the help
of evil men you nailed him to a cross.
But God knew all this would happen.
This was God's plan which he had
made long ago. [24]God raised Jesus
from death. God set him free from the
pain of death. Death could not hold
him. [25]For David said this about him:
'I keep the Lord before me
always.
Because he is close by my side,
I will not be hurt.
[26]So I am glad, and I rejoice.
Even my body has hope.
[27]This is because you will not leave
me in the grave.
You will not let your Holy One
rot.
[28]You will teach me God's way to
live.
Being with you will fill me with
joy'.   *Psalm 16:8-11*
[29]"Brothers, I can tell you truly
about David, our ancestor. He died
and was buried. His grave is still here
with us today. [30]David was a prophet[d]
and knew what God had said. God had

promised David that he would make a
person from David's family a king just
as he was.[n] [31]David knew this before
it happened. That is why he said:
'He was not left in the grave.
His body did not rot',
David was talking about the Christ[d]
rising from death. [32]So Jesus is the
One whom God raised from death!
And we are all witnesses to this. [33]Jesus
was lifted up to heaven and is now at
God's right side. The Father has giv-
en the Holy Spirit[d] to Jesus as he
promised. So now Jesus has poured
out that Spirit. This is what you see
and hear. [34]David was not the one
who was lifted up to heaven. But he
said:
'The Lord said to my Lord:
Sit by me at my right side,
[35]until I put your enemies under
your control'.[n]   *Psalm 110:1*
[36]"So, all the people of Israel should
know this truly: God has made Jesus
both Lord and Christ. He is the man
you nailed to the cross!"

[37]When the people heard this, they
were sick at heart. They asked Peter
and the other apostles, "What shall
we do?"

[38]Peter said to them, "Change your
hearts and lives and be baptised, each
one of you, in the name of Jesus Christ
for the forgiveness of your sins. And
you will receive the gift of the Holy
Spirit. [39]This promise is for you. It is
also for your children and for all who
are far away. It is for everyone the
Lord our God calls to himself."

[40]Peter warned them with many
other words. He begged them, "Save
yourselves from the evil of today's
people!" [41]Then those people who accepted what Peter said were baptised. About 3,000 people were added
to the number of believers that day.
[42]They spent their time learning the
apostles' teaching. And they contin-

God . . . was. See 2 Samuel 7:13; Psalm 132:11.
until . . . control Literally, "until I make your enemies a footstool for your feet".

ued to share, to break bread,*n* and to pray together.

The Believers Share

[43]The apostles*d* were doing many miracles*d* and signs. And everyone felt great respect for God. [44]All the believers stayed together. They shared everything. [45]They sold their land and the things they owned. Then they divided the money and gave it to those people who needed it. [46]The believers met together in the Temple*d* every day. They all had the same purpose. They broke bread in their homes, happy to share their food with joyful hearts. [47]They praised God, and all the people liked them. More and more people were being saved every day; the Lord was adding those people to the group of believers.

Peter Heals a Crippled Man

3 One day Peter and John went to the Temple.*d* It was three o'clock in the afternoon. This was the time for the daily prayer service. [2]There, at the Temple gate called Beautiful Gate, was a man who had been crippled all his life. Every day he was carried to this gate to beg. He would ask for money from the people going into the Temple. [3]The man saw Peter and John going into the Temple and asked them for money. [4]Peter and John looked straight at him and said, "Look at us!" [5]The man looked at them; he thought they were going to give him some money. [6]But Peter said, "I don't have any silver or gold, but I do have something else I can give you: by the power of Jesus Christ from Nazareth — stand up and walk!" [7]Then Peter took the man's right hand and lifted him up. Immediately the man's feet and ankles became strong. [8]He jumped up, stood on his feet, and be-

gan to walk. He went into the Temple with them, walking and jumping, and praising God. [9-10]All the people recognised him. They knew he was the crippled man who always sat by the Beautiful Gate begging for money. Now they saw this same man walking and praising God. The people were amazed. They could not understand how this could happen.

Peter Speaks to the People

[11]The man was holding on to Peter and John. All the people were amazed and ran to Peter and John at Solomon's Porch.*d* [12]When Peter saw this, he said to them, "Men of Israel, why are you surprised? You are looking at us as if it were our own power that made this man walk. Do you think this happened because we are good? No! [13]The God of Abraham, Isaac and Jacob, the God of our ancestors, gave glory to Jesus, his servant. But you gave him up to be killed. Pilate decided to let him go free. But you told Pilate you did not want Jesus. [14]He was pure and good, but you said you did not want him. You told Pilate to give you a murderer*n* instead of Jesus. [15]And so you killed the One who gives life! But God raised him from death. We are witnesses to this. [16]It was the power of Jesus that made this crippled man well. This happened because we trusted in the power of Jesus. You can see this man, and you know him. He was made completely well because of trust in Jesus. You all saw it happen!

[17]"Brothers, I know you did those things to Jesus because you did not understand what you were doing. Your leaders did not understand either. [18]God said this would happen. He said through the prophets*d* that his Christ*d* would suffer and die. And now God has made these things come true

---

break bread This may mean a meal as in verse 46, or the Lord's Supper, the special meal Jesus told his followers to eat to remember him (Luke 22:14-20).
murderer Barabbas, the man the Jews asked Pilate to set free instead of Jesus (Luke 23:18).

in this way. [19]So you must change your hearts and lives! Come back to God, and he will forgive your sins. [20]Then the Lord will give you times of spiritual rest. He will give you Jesus, the One he chose to be the Christ. [21]But Jesus must stay in heaven until the time comes when all things will be made right again. God told of this time long ago when he spoke through his holy prophets. [22]Moses said, 'The Lord your God will give you a prophet like me. He will be one of your own people. You must obey everything he tells you. [23]Anyone who does not obey him will die, separated from God's people'.[n] [24]Samuel, and all the other prophets who spoke for God after Samuel, told of this time now. [25]You have received what the prophets talked about. You have received the agreement God made with your ancestors. He said to your father Abraham, 'Through your descendants[d] all the nations on the earth will be blessed'.[n] [26]God has raised up his servant and sent him to you first. He sent Jesus to bless you by turning each of you away from doing evil things."

Peter and John at the Council

4 While Peter and John were speaking to the people, a group of men came up to them. There were Jewish priests, the captain of the soldiers that guarded the Temple,[d] and some Sadducees.[d] [2]They were upset because the two apostles[d] were teaching the people. Peter and John were preaching that people will rise from death through the power of Jesus. [3]The Jewish leaders grabbed Peter and John and put them in jail. It was already night, so they kept them in jail until the next day. [4]But many of those who heard Peter and John preach believed the things they said. There were now about 5,000 men in the group of believers.

[5]The next day the Jewish leaders, the older Jewish leaders, and the teachers of the law met in Jerusalem. [6]Annas the high priest, Caiaphas, John, and Alexander were there. Everyone from the high priest's family was there. [7]They made Peter and John stand before them. The Jewish leaders asked them: "By what power or authority did you do this?"

[8]Then Peter was filled with the Holy Spirit.[d] He said to them, "Rulers of the people and you older leaders, [9]are you questioning us about a good thing that was done to a crippled man? Are you asking us who made him well? [10]We want all of you and all the Jewish people to know that this man was made well by the power of Jesus Christ from Nazareth! You nailed him to a cross, but God raised him from death. This man was crippled, but he is now well and able to stand here before you because of the power of Jesus! [11]Jesus is

'the stone[n] that you builders did not want.

It has become the cornerstone'.[d]

Psalm 118:22

[12]Jesus is the only One who can save people. His name is the only power in the world that has been given to save people. And we must be saved through him!"

[13]The Jewish leaders saw that Peter and John were not afraid to speak. They understood that these men had no special training or education. So they were amazed. Then they realised that Peter and John had been with Jesus. [14]They saw the crippled man standing there beside the two apostles. They saw that the man was healed. So they could say nothing

---

'The Lord . . . people' Quotation from Deuteronomy 18:15,19 and Leviticus 23:39.
'Through . . . blessed' Quotation from Genesis 22:18; 26:24.
stone A symbol meaning Jesus.

against them. [15]The Jewish leaders told them to leave the meeting. Then the leaders talked to each other about what they should do. [16]They said, "What shall we do with these men? Everyone in Jerusalem knows that they have done a great miracle![d] We cannot say it is not true. [17]But we must warn them not to talk to people any more using that name. Then this thing will not spread among the people."

[18]So they called Peter and John in again. They told them not to speak or to teach at all in the name of Jesus. [19]But Peter and John answered them, "What do you think is right? What would God want? Should we obey you or God? [20]We cannot keep quiet. We must speak about what we have seen and heard." [21-22]The Jewish leaders could not find a way to punish them because all the people were praising God for what had been done. (This miracle was a proof from God. The man who was healed was more than 40 years old!) So the Jewish leaders warned the apostles again and let them go free.

The Believers' Prayer

[23]Peter and John left the meeting of Jewish leaders and went to their own group. They told them everything that the leading priests and the older Jewish leaders had said to them. [24]When the believers heard this, they prayed to God with one purpose. They prayed, "Lord, you are the One who made the sky, the earth, the sea, and everything in the world. [25]Our father David was your servant. With the help of the Holy Spirit[d] he said:

'Why are the nations so angry?
Why are the people making
    useless plans?
[26]The kings of the earth prepare to
    fight.
Their leaders make plans
    together

against the Lord
    and against his Christ'.[d]
                Psalm 2:1-2

[27]These things really happened when Herod, Pontius Pilate, the non-Jewish people, and the Jewish people all came together against Jesus here in Jerusalem. Jesus is your holy Servant. He is the One you made to be the Christ. [28]These people made your plan happen; it happened because of your power and your will. [29]And now, Lord, listen to what they are saying. They are trying to make us afraid! Lord, we are your servants. Help us to speak your word without fear. [30]Help us to be brave by showing us your power; make sick people well, give proofs, and make miracles[d] happen by the power of Jesus, your holy servant."

[31]After they had prayed, the place where they were meeting was shaken. They were all filled with the Holy Spirit,[d] and they spoke God's word without fear.

The Believers Share

[32]The group of believers were joined in their hearts, and they had the same spirit. No person in the group said that the things he had were his own. Instead, they shared everything. [33]With great power the apostles[d] were telling people that the Lord Jesus was truly raised from death. And God blessed all the believers greatly. [34]They all received the things they needed. Everyone that owned fields or houses sold them. They brought the money [35]and gave it to the apostles. Then each person was given the things he needed.

[36]One of the believers was named Joseph. The apostles called him Barnabas. (This name means "one who encourages".) He was a Levite, born in Cyprus. [37]Joseph owned a field. He sold it, brought the money, and gave it to the apostles.

Ananias and Sapphira

5 A man named Ananias and his wife Sapphira sold some land. ²But he gave only part of the money to the apostles.ᵈ He secretly kept some of it for himself. His wife knew about this, and she agreed to it. ³Peter said, "Ananias, why did you let Satan rule your heart? You lied to the Holy Spirit.ᵈ Why did you keep part of the money you received for the land for yourself? ⁴Before you sold the land, it belonged to you. And even after you sold it, you could have used the money any way you wanted. Why did you think of doing this? You lied to God, not to men!" ⁵⁻⁶When Ananias heard this, he fell down and died. Some young men came in, wrapped up his body, carried it out, and buried it. And everyone who heard about this was filled with fear.

⁷About three hours later his wife came in. She did not know what had happened. ⁸Peter said to her, "Tell me how much money you got for your field. Was it this much?"

Sapphira answered, "Yes, that was the price."

⁹Peter said to her, "Why did you and your husband agree to test the Spirit of the Lord? Look! The men who buried your husband are at the door! They will carry you out." ¹⁰At that moment Sapphira fell down by his feet and died. The young men came in and saw that she was dead. They carried her out and buried her beside her husband. ¹¹The whole church and all the others who heard about these things were filled with fear.

Proofs from God

¹²The apostlesᵈ did many signs and miraclesᵈ among the people. And they would all meet together on Solomon's Porch.ᵈ ¹³None of the others dared to stand with them. All the people were saying good things about them. ¹⁴More and more men and women be-

lieved in the Lord and were added to the group of believers. ¹⁵As Peter was passing by, the people brought their sick into the streets. They put their sick on beds and mats so at least Peter's shadow might fall on them. ¹⁶Crowds came from all the towns around Jerusalem. They brought their sick and those who were bothered by evil spirits. All of them were healed.

The Apostles Obey God

¹⁷The high priest and all his friends (a group called the Sadduceesᵈ) became very jealous. ¹⁸They took the apostlesᵈ and put them in jail. ¹⁹But during the night, an angel of the Lord opened the doors of the jail. He led the apostles outside and said, ²⁰"Go and stand in the Temple.ᵈ Tell the people everything about this new life." ²¹When the apostles heard this, they obeyed and went into the Temple. It was early in the morning, and they began to teach.

The high priest and his friends arrived. They called a meeting of the Jewish leaders and all the important older men of the Jews. They sent some men to the jail to bring the apostles to them. ²²When the men went to the jail, they could not find the apostles. So they went back and told the Jewish leaders about this. ²³They said, "The jail was closed and locked. The guards were standing at the doors. But when we opened the doors, the jail was empty!" ²⁴Hearing this, the captain of the Temple guards and the leading priests were confused. They wondered, "What will happen because of this?"

²⁵Then someone came and told them, "Listen! The men you put in jail are standing in the Temple. They are teaching the people!" ²⁶Then the captain and his men went out and brought the apostles back. But the soldiers did not use force, because they were afraid that the people would kill them with stones.

27The soldiers brought the apostles to the meeting and made them stand before the Jewish leaders. The high priest questioned them. 28He said, "We gave you strict orders not to go on teaching in that name. But look what you have done! You have filled Jerusalem with your teaching. You are trying to make us responsible for this man's death."

29Peter and the other apostles answered, "We must obey God, not men! 30You killed Jesus. You hung him on a cross. But God, the same God our ancestors had, raised Jesus up from death! 31Jesus is the One whom God raised to be on his right side. God made Jesus our Leader and Saviour. God did this so that all Jews could change their hearts and lives and have their sins forgiven. 32We saw all these things happen. The Holy Spirit*d* also proves that these things are true. God has given the Spirit to all who obey him."

33When the Jewish leaders heard this, they became very angry and wanted to kill them. 34A Pharisee*d* named Gamaliel stood up in the meeting. He was a teacher of the law, and all the people respected him. He ordered the apostles to leave the meeting for a little while. 35Then he said to them, "Men of Israel, be careful of what you are planning to do to these men! 36Remember when Theudas appeared? He said that he was a great man, and about 400 men joined him. But he was killed. And all his followers were scattered. They were able to do nothing. 37Later, a man named Judas came from Galilee at the time of the registration.*n* He led a group of followers, too. He was also killed, and all his followers were scattered. 38And so now I tell you: stay away from these men. Leave them alone. If their plan comes from men, it will fail. 39But if it is from God, you will not be able to stop them. You might even be fighting against God himself!"

The Jewish leaders agreed with what Gamaliel said. 40They called the apostles in again. They beat the apostles and told them not to speak in the name of Jesus again. Then they let them go free. 41The apostles left the meeting full of joy because they were given the honour of suffering disgrace for Jesus. 42The apostles did not stop teaching people. Every day in the Temple and in people's homes they continued to tell the Good News — that Jesus is the Christ.*d*

Seven Men Are Chosen

6 More and more people were becoming followers of Jesus. But during this same time, the Greek-speaking followers had an argument with the other Jewish followers. The Greek-speaking Jews said that their widows were not getting their share of the food that was given out every day. 2The 12 apostles*d* called the whole group of followers together. They said, "It is not right for us to stop our work of teaching God's word in order to serve tables. 3So, brothers, choose seven of your own men. They must be men who are good. They must be full of wisdom and full of the Spirit.*d* We will put them in charge of this work. 4Then we can use all our time to pray and to teach the word of God."

5The whole group liked the idea. So they chose these seven men: Stephen (a man with great faith and full of the Holy Spirit), Philip,*n* Procorus, Nicanor, Timon, Parmenas, and Nicolas (a man from Antioch who had become a Jew). 6Then they put these men before the apostles. The apostles

registration Census. A counting of all the people and the things they own.
Philip Not the apostle named Philip.

prayed and laid their hands on[n] the men.

[7]The word of God was reaching more and more people. The group of followers in Jerusalem became larger and larger. A great number of the Jewish priests believed and obeyed.

Stephen Is Arrested

[8]Stephen was richly blessed by God. God gave him the power to do great miracles[d] and signs among the people. [9]But some Jews were against him. They belonged to a synagogue[d] of Free Men[n] (as it was called). (This synagogue was also for Jews from Cyrene and from Alexandria.) Jews from Cilicia and Asia were also with them. They all came and argued with Stephen.

[10]But the Spirit[d] was helping him to speak with wisdom. His words were so strong that the Jews could not argue with him. [11]So they paid some men to say, "We heard him say things against Moses and against God!"

[12]This upset the people, the older Jewish leaders, and the teachers of the law. They came to Stephen, grabbed him and brought him to a meeting of the Jewish leaders. [13]They brought in some men to tell lies about Stephen. They said, "This man is always saying things against this holy place and the law of Moses. [14]We heard him say that Jesus from Nazareth will destroy this place. He also said that Jesus will change the things that Moses told us to do." [15]All the people in the meeting were watching Stephen closely. His face looked like the face of an angel.

Stephen's Speech

[7] The high priest said to Stephen, "Are these things true?"

[2]Stephen answered, "Brothers and fathers, listen to me. Our glorious God appeared to Abraham, our ancestor. Abraham was in Mesopotamia before he lived in Haran. [3]God said to Abraham, 'Leave your country and your relatives. Go to the land I will show you'.[n] [4]So Abraham left the country of Chaldea and went to live in Haran. After Abraham's father died, God sent him to this place where you now live. [5]God did not give Abraham any of this land, not even a foot of it. But God promised that he would give him and his descendants[d] this land. (This was before Abraham had any descendants.) [6]This is what God said to him: 'Your descendants will be strangers in a land they don't own. The people there will make them slaves. And they will do cruel things to them for 400 years. [7]But I will punish the nation where they are slaves. Then your descendants will leave that land. Then they will worship me in this place'.[n] [8]God made an agreement with Abraham; the sign for this agreement was circumcision.[d] And so when Abraham had his son Isaac, Abraham circumcised him when he was eight days old. Isaac also circumcised his son Jacob. And Jacob did the same for his sons, the 12 ancestors[n] of our people.

[9]"These sons became jealous of Joseph. They sold him to be a slave in Egypt. But God was with him. [10]Joseph had many troubles there, but God saved him from all those troubles. The king of Egypt liked Joseph and respected him because of the wis-

---

laid their hands on Here, doing this showed that these men were given a special work of God.
Free Men Jews who had been slaves or whose fathers had been slaves, but were now free.
'Leave . . . you' Quotation from Genesis 12:1.
'Your descendants . . . place' Quotation from Genesis 15:13-14 and Exodus 12.
12 ancestors Important ancestors of the Jews; the leaders of the 12 Jewish tribes.

dom that God gave him. The king made him governor of Egypt. He put Joseph in charge of all the people in his palace.

11"Then all the land of Egypt and of Canaan became so dry that nothing would grow there. This made the people suffer greatly. The sons could not find anything to eat. 12But when Jacob heard that there was grain in Egypt, he sent his sons, our ancestors, there. This was their first trip to Egypt. 13Then they went there a second time. This time, Joseph told his brothers who he was. And the king learned about Joseph's family. 14Then Joseph sent some men to invite Jacob, his father, to come to Egypt. He also invited all his relatives (75 persons altogether). 15So Jacob went down to Egypt, where he and his sons died. 16Later their bodies were moved to Shechem and put in a grave there. (It was the same grave that Abraham had bought in Shechem from the sons of Hamor for a sum of money.)

17"The number of people in Egypt grew large. There were more and more of our people there. (The promise that God made to Abraham was soon to come true.) 18Then a new king began to rule Egypt. He did not know who Joseph was. 19This king tricked our people and was cruel to our ancestors. He forced them to put their babies outside to die. 20This was the time when Moses was born. He was a fine child. For three months Moses was cared for in his father's house. 21When they put Moses outside, the king's daughter took him. She raised him as if he were her own son. 22The Egyptians taught Moses all the things they knew. He was a powerful man in the things he said and did.

23"When Moses was about 40 years old, he thought it would be good to visit his brothers, the people of Israel. 24Moses saw an Egyptian doing wrong to a Jew. So he defended the Jew and punished the Egyptian for hurting him. Moses killed the Egyptian. 25Moses thought that his fellow Jews would understand that God was using him to save them. But they did not understand. 26The next day, Moses saw two Jewish men fighting. He tried to make peace between them. He said, 'Men, you are brothers! Why are you hurting each other?' 27The man who was hurting the other man pushed Moses away. He said, 'Who made you our ruler and judge? 28Are you going to kill me as you killed the Egyptian yesterday?'n 29When Moses heard him say this, he left Egypt. He went to live in the land of Midian where he was a stranger. While Moses lived in Midian, he had two sons.

30"After 40 years Moses was in the desert near Mount Sinai. An angel appeared to him in the flames of a burning bush. 31When Moses saw this, he was amazed. He went near to look closer at it. Moses heard the Lord's voice. 32The Lord said, 'I am the God of your ancestors. I am the God of Abraham, Isaac and Jacob'.n Moses began to shake with fear and was afraid to look. 33The Lord said to him, 'Take off your sandals. You are standing on holy ground. 34I have seen the troubles my people have suffered in Egypt. I have heard their cries. I have come down to save them. And now, Moses, I am sending you back to Egypt'.n

35"This Moses was the same man the Jews said they did not want. They had said to him, 'Who made you our ruler and judge?'n Moses is the same man God sent to be a ruler and sav-

'Who . . . yesterday?' Quotation from Exodus 2:14.
'I am . . . Jacob' Quotation from Exodus 3:6.
'Take . . . Egypt' Quotation from Exodus 3:5-10.
'Who . . . judge?' Quotation from Exodus 2:14.

iour, with the help of an angel. This was the angel Moses saw in the burning bush. ³⁶So Moses led the people out of Egypt. He worked miracles*d* and signs in Egypt, at the Red Sea,*d* and then in the desert for 40 years. ³⁷This is the same Moses that said to the Jewish people: 'God will give you a prophet*d* like me. He will be one of your own people'.*n* ³⁸This is the same Moses who was with the gathering of the Jews in the desert. He was with the angel that spoke to him at Mount Sinai, and he was with our ancestors. He received commands from God that give life, and he gave those commands to us.

³⁹"But our fathers did not want to obey Moses. They rejected him. They wanted to go back to Egypt again. ⁴⁰They said to Aaron, 'Moses led us out of Egypt. But we don't know what has happened to him. So make us gods who will lead us'.*n* ⁴¹So the people made an idol that looked like a calf. Then they brought sacrifices to it. The people were proud of what they had made with their own hands! ⁴²But God turned against them. He did not try to stop them from worshipping the sun, moon and stars. This is what is written in the book of the prophets: God says,

'People of Israel, you did not bring
    me sacrifices and offerings
  while you travelled in the desert
    for 40 years.
⁴³But now you will have to carry
    with you
  the tent to worship the false god
    Molech*d*
  and the idols of the star god
    Rephan that you made to
    worship.
This is because I will send you
    away beyond Babylon'.
                            Amos 5:25-27

⁴⁴"The Holy Tent*d* where God spoke to our fathers was with the Jews in the desert. God told Moses how to make this Tent. He made it like the plan God showed him. ⁴⁵Later, Joshua led our fathers to capture the lands of the other nations. Our people went in, and God drove the other people out. When our people went into this new land, they took with them this same Tent. They received this Tent from their fathers and kept it until the time of David. ⁴⁶God was very pleased with David. He asked God to let him build a house for him, the God of Jacob. ⁴⁷But Solomon was the one who built the Temple.*d*

⁴⁸"But the Most High does not live in houses that men build with their hands. This is what the prophet says:
⁴⁹'Heaven is my throne.
  The earth is my footstool.
So do you think you can build a
    house for me? says the
    Lord.
  There is no place where I need
    to rest.
⁵⁰Remember, I made all these
    things!' "
                            Isaiah 66:1-2

⁵¹Stephen continued speaking: "You stubborn Jewish leaders! You have not given your hearts to God! You won't listen to him! You are always against what the Holy Spirit*d* is trying to tell you. Your ancestors were like this, and you are just like them! ⁵²Your fathers tried to hurt every prophet who ever lived. Those prophets said long ago that the Righteous One would come. But your fathers killed them. And now you have turned against the Righteous One and killed him. ⁵³You received the law of Moses, which God gave you through his angels. But you don't obey it!"

Stephen Is Killed

⁵⁴When the Jewish leaders heard

'God . . . people' Quotation from Deuteronomy 18:15.
'Moses . . . us' Quotation from Exodus 32:1.

Stephen saying all these things, they became very angry. They were so angry that they were grinding their teeth at Stephen. [55]But Stephen was full of the Holy Spirit.[d] He looked up to heaven and saw the glory of God. He saw Jesus standing at God's right side. [56]He said, "Look! I see heaven open. And I see the Son of Man[d] standing at God's right side!"

[57]Then the Jewish leaders all shouted loudly. They covered their ears with their hands and all ran at Stephen. [58]They took him out of the city and threw stones at him until he was dead. The men who told lies against Stephen left their coats with a young man named Saul. [59]While they were throwing stones, Stephen prayed, "Lord Jesus, receive my spirit!" [60]He fell on his knees and cried in a loud voice, "Lord, do not hold this sin against them!" After Stephen said this, he died.

8 Saul agreed that the killing of Stephen was a good thing.

Trouble for the Believers

[2-3]Some religious men buried Stephen. They cried very loudly for him. On that day the Jews began trying to hurt the church in Jerusalem. The Jews made them suffer very much. Saul was also trying to destroy the church. He went from house to house. He dragged out men and women and put them in jail. All the believers, except the apostles,[d] went to different places in Judea and Samaria. [4]And everywhere they were scattered, they told people the Good News.[d]

Philip Preaches in Samaria

[5]Philip[n] went to the city of Samaria and preached about the Christ.[d] [6]The people there heard Philip and saw the miracles[d] he was doing. They all listened carefully to the things he said. [7]Many of these people had evil spirits in them. But Philip made the evil spirits leave them. The spirits made a loud noise when they came out. There were also many weak and crippled people there. Philip healed them, too. [8]So the people in that city were very happy.

[9]But there was a man named Simon in that city. Before Philip came there, Simon had practised magic. He amazed all the people of Samaria with his magic. He boasted and called himself a great man. [10]All the people — the least important and the most important — paid attention to what Simon said. They said, "This man has the power of God, called 'the Great Power'!" [11]Simon had amazed them with his magic tricks so long that the people became his followers. [12]But Philip told them the Good News[d] about the kingdom of God and the power of Jesus Christ. Men and women believed Philip and were baptised. [13]Simon himself believed and was baptised. He stayed very close to Philip. When he saw the miracles and the very powerful things that Philip did, Simon was amazed.

[14]The apostles[d] were still in Jerusalem. They heard that the people of Samaria had accepted the word of God. So they sent Peter and John to them. [15]When Peter and John arrived, they prayed that the Samaritan believers might receive the Holy Spirit.[d] [16]These people had been baptised in the name of the Lord Jesus. But the Holy Spirit had not yet entered any of them. [17]Then, when the two apostles began laying their hands on[n] the people, they received the Holy Spirit. [18]Simon saw that the Spirit was giv-

---

Philip Not the apostle named Philip.
laying their hands on Here, doing this showed that these men were given a special work of God.

en to people when the apostles laid their hands on them. So he offered the apostles money. [19]He said, "Give me also this power so that when I lay my hands on a person, he will receive the Holy Spirit."

[20]Peter said to him, "You and your money should both be destroyed! You thought you could buy God's gift with money. [21]You cannot share with us in this work. Your heart is not right before God. [22]Change your heart! Turn away from this evil thing you have done. Pray to the Lord. Maybe he will forgive you for thinking this. [23]I see that you are full of bitter jealousy and ruled by sin."

[24]Simon answered, "Both of you pray for me to the Lord. Pray that the things you have said will not happen to me!"

[25]Then the two apostles told the people the things they had seen Jesus do. And after the apostles had given the message of the Lord, they went back to Jerusalem. On the way, they went through many Samaritan towns and preached the Good News to the people.

Philip Teaches an Ethiopian

[26]An angel of the Lord spoke to Philip.[n] The angel said, "Get ready and go south. Go to the road that leads down to Gaza from Jerusalem — the desert road." [27]So Philip got ready and went. On the road he saw a man from Ethiopia, a eunuch.[d] He was an important officer in the service of Candace, the queen of the Ethiopians. He was responsible for taking care of all her money. He had gone to Jerusalem to worship, and [28]now he was on his way home. He was sitting in his chariot and reading from the book of Isaiah, the prophet.[d] [29]The Spirit[d]

said to Philip, "Go to that chariot and stay near it."

[30]So Philip ran toward the chariot. He heard the man reading from Isaiah, the prophet. Philip asked, "Do you understand what you are reading?"

[31]He answered, "How can I understand? I need someone to explain it to me!" Then he invited Philip to climb in and sit with him. [32]The verse of Scripture[d] that he was reading was this:

"He was like a sheep being led to
    be killed.
He was quiet, as a sheep is
    quiet while its wool is being
    cut.
He said nothing.
[33] He was shamed and was treated
    unfairly.
He died without children to
    continue his family.
His life on earth has ended."
                                    Isaiah 53:7-8

[34]The officer said to Philip, "Please tell me, who is the prophet talking about? Is he talking about himself or about someone else?" [35]Philip began to speak. He started with this same Scripture and told the man the Good News[d] about Jesus.

[36]While they were travelling down the road, they came to some water. The officer said, "Look! Here is water! What is stopping me from being baptised?" [37][n] [38]Then the officer commanded the chariot to stop. Both Philip and the officer went down into the water, and Philip baptised him. [39]When they came up out of the water, the Spirit of the Lord took Philip away; the officer never saw him again. The officer continued on his way home, full of joy. [40]But Philip appeared in a city called Azotus and preached the Good News in all the towns on the way from Azotus to Caesarea.

Philip Not the apostle named Philip.
Verse 37 Some late copies of Acts add verse 37: "Philip answered, 'If you believe with all your heart, you can'. The officer said, 'I believe that Jesus Christ is the Son of God'."

Saul Is Converted

9 In Jerusalem Saul was still trying to frighten the followers of the Lord by saying he would kill them. So he went to the high priest [2]and asked him to write letters to the synagogues[d] in the city of Damascus. Saul wanted the high priest to give him the authority to find people in Damascus who were followers of Christ's Way. If he found any there, men or women, he would arrest them and bring them back to Jerusalem.

[3]So Saul went to Damascus. As he came near the city, a bright light from heaven suddenly flashed around him. [4]Saul fell to the ground. He heard a voice saying to him, "Saul, Saul! Why are you doing things against me?"

[5]Saul said, "Who are you, Lord?"

The voice answered, "I am Jesus. I am the One you are trying to hurt. [6]Get up now and go into the city. Someone there will tell you what you must do."

[7]The men travelling with Saul stood there, but they said nothing. They heard the voice, but they saw no one. [8]Saul got up from the ground. He opened his eyes, but he could not see. So the men with Saul took his hand and led him into Damascus. [9]For three days Saul could not see, and he did not eat or drink.

[10]There was a follower of Jesus in Damascus named Ananias. The Lord spoke to Ananias in a vision, "Ananias!"

Ananias answered, "Here I am, Lord."

[11]The Lord said to him, "Get up and go to the street called Straight Street. Find the house of Judas.[n] Ask for a man named Saul from the city of Tarsus. He is there now, praying. [12]Saul has seen a vision. In it a man named Ananias comes to him and lays his hands on him. Then he sees again."

[13]But Ananias answered, "Lord, many people have told me about this man and the terrible things he did to your people in Jerusalem. [14]Now he has come here to Damascus. The leading priests have given him the power to arrest everyone who worships you."

[15]But the Lord said to Ananias, "Go! I have chosen Saul for an important work. He must make me known to non-Jews, to kings, and to the people of Israel. [16]I will show him how much he must suffer for my name."

[17]So Ananias went to the house of Judas. He laid his hands on Saul and said, "Brother Saul, the Lord Jesus sent me. He is the one you saw on the road on your way here. He sent me so that you can see again and be filled with the Holy Spirit."[d] [18]Immediately, something that looked like fish scales fell from Saul's eyes. He was able to see again! Then Saul got up and was baptised. [19]After eating some food, his strength returned.

Saul Preaches in Damascus

Saul stayed with the followers of Jesus in Damascus for a few days. [20]Soon he began to preach about Jesus in the synagogues,[d] saying, "Jesus is the Son of God!"

[21]All the people who heard him were amazed. They said, "This is the man who was in Jerusalem. He was trying to destroy those who trust in this name! He came here to do the same thing. He came here to arrest the followers of Jesus and take them back to the leading priests."

[22]But Saul became more and more powerful. His proofs that Jesus is the Christ[d] were so strong that the Jews in Damascus could not argue with him.

Saul Escapes from Damascus

[23]After many days, the Jews made

Judas This is not either of the apostles named Judas.

plans to kill Saul. 24They were watching the city gates day and night. They wanted to kill him, but Saul learned about their plan. 25One night some followers of Saul helped him leave the city. They lowered him in a basket through an opening in the city wall.

Saul in Jerusalem

26Then Saul went to Jerusalem. He tried to join the group of followers, but they were all afraid of him. They did not believe that he was really a follower. 27But Barnabas accepted Saul and took him to the apostles.*d* Barnabas told them that Saul had seen the Lord on the road. He explained how the Lord had spoken to Saul. Then he told them how boldly Saul had preached in the name of Jesus in Damascus.

28And so Saul stayed with the followers. He went everywhere in Jerusalem, preaching boldly in the name of Jesus. 29He would often talk and argue with the Jews who spoke Greek. But they were trying to kill him. 30When the brothers learned about this, they took Saul to Caesarea. From there they sent him to Tarsus.

31The church everywhere in Judea, Galilee, and Samaria had a time of peace. With the help of the Holy Spirit,*d* the group became stronger. The believers showed that they respected the Lord by the way they lived. Because of this, the group of believers grew larger and larger.

Peter Heals Aeneas

32As Peter was travelling through all the area, he visited God's people who lived in Lydda. 33There he met a paralysed man named Aeneas. Aeneas had not been able to leave his bed for the past eight years. 34Peter said to him, "Aeneas, Jesus Christ heals you. Stand up and make your bed!" Aeneas stood up immediately. 35All the people living in Lydda and on the Plain of Sharon saw him. These people turned to the Lord.

Peter in Joppa

36In the city of Joppa there was a follower named Tabitha. (Her Greek name, Dorcas, means "a deer".) She was always doing good and helping the poor. 37While Peter was in Lydda, Tabitha became sick and died. Her body was washed and put in a room upstairs. 38The followers in Joppa heard that Peter was in Lydda. (Lydda is near Joppa.) So they sent two men to Peter. They begged him, "Hurry, please come to us!" 39Peter got ready and went with them. When he arrived, they took him to the upstairs room. All the widows stood around Peter, crying. They showed him the shirts and coats that Tabitha had made when she was still alive. 40Peter sent everyone out of the room. He kneeled and prayed. Then he turned to the body and said, "Tabitha, stand up!" She opened her eyes, and when she saw Peter, she sat up. 41He gave her his hand and helped her up. Then he called the saints*d* and the widows into the room. He showed them Tabitha; she was alive! 42People everywhere in Joppa learned about this, and many believed in the Lord. 43Peter stayed in Joppa for many days with a man named Simon who was a leatherworker.

Peter and Cornelius

10 At Caesarea there was a man named Cornelius. He was an officer in the Italian group of the Roman army. 2Cornelius was a religious man. He and all the other people who lived in his house worshipped the true God. He gave much of his money to the poor and prayed to God often. 3One afternoon about three o'clock, Cornelius saw a vision clearly. In the vision an angel of God came to him and said, "Cornelius!"

4Cornelius stared at the angel. He became afraid and said, "What do you want, Lord?"

The angel said, "God has heard your prayers. He has seen what you give to the poor. And God remembers you. [5]Send some men now to Joppa to bring back a man named Simon. Simon is also called Peter. [6]Simon is staying with a man, also named Simon, who is a leatherworker. He has a house beside the sea." [7]Then the angel who spoke to Cornelius left. Cornelius called two of his servants and a soldier. The soldier was a religious man who worked for Cornelius. [8]Cornelius explained everything to these three men and sent them to Joppa.

[9]The next day as they came near Joppa, Peter was going up to the roof[n] to pray. It was about noon. [10]Peter was hungry and wanted to eat. But while the food was being prepared, he had a vision. [11]He saw heaven opened and something coming down. It looked like a big sheet being lowered to earth by its four corners. [12]In it were all kinds of animals, reptiles, and birds. [13]Then a voice said to Peter, "Get up, Peter; kill and eat."

[14]But Peter said, "No, Lord! I have never eaten food that is unholy or unclean."[d]

[15]But the voice said to him again, "God has made these things clean. Don't call them 'unholy'!" [16]This happened three times. Then the sheet was taken back to heaven.

[17]While Peter was wondering what this vision meant, the men Cornelius sent had found Simon's house. They were standing at the gate. [18]They asked, "Is Simon Peter staying here?"

[19]Peter was still thinking about the vision. But the Spirit[d] said to him, "Listen! Three men are looking for you. [20]Get up and go downstairs. Go with them and don't ask questions. I have sent them to you."

[21]So Peter went down to the men.

He said, "I am the man you are looking for. Why have you come here?"

[22]They said, "A holy angel spoke to Cornelius, an army officer. He is a good man; he worships God. All the Jewish people respect him. The angel told Cornelius to ask you to his house so that he can hear what you have to say." [23]Peter asked the men to come in and spend the night.

The next day Peter got ready and went with them. Some of the brothers from Joppa joined him. [24]On the following day they came to Caesarea. Cornelius was waiting for them. He had called together his relatives and close friends. [25]When Peter entered, Cornelius met him. He fell at Peter's feet and worshipped him. [26]But Peter helped him up, saying, "Stand up! I too am only a man." [27]Peter went on talking with Cornelius as they went inside. There Peter saw many people together. [28]He said, "You people understand that it is against our Jewish law for a Jew to associate with or visit anyone who is not a Jew. But God has shown me that I should not call any person 'unholy' or 'unclean'. [29]That is why I did not argue when I was asked to come here. Now, please tell me why you sent for me."

[30]Cornelius said, "Four days ago, I was praying in my house. It was at this same time—three o'clock in the afternoon. Suddenly, there was a man standing before me wearing shining clothes. [31]He said, 'Cornelius! God has heard your prayer. He has seen what you give to the poor. And God remembers you. [32]So send some men to Joppa and ask Simon Peter to come. Peter is staying in the house of a man, also named Simon, who is a leatherworker. His house is beside the sea'. [33]So I sent for you immediately, and it was very good of you to

---

roof In Bible times houses were built with flat roofs. The roof was used for drying things such as flax and fruit. It was also used as an extra room, as a place for worship and as a place to sleep in the summer.

come. Now we are all here before God to hear everything the Lord has commanded you to tell us."

Peter's Speech

³⁴Peter began to speak: "I really understand now that to God every person is the same. ³⁵God accepts anyone who worships him and does what is right. It is not important what country a person comes from. ³⁶You know that God has sent his message to the people of Israel. That message is the Good News*d* that peace has come through Jesus Christ. Jesus is the Lord of all people! ³⁷You know what has happened all over Judea. It began in Galilee after John*ⁿ* preached to the people about baptism. ³⁸You know about Jesus from Nazareth. God made him the Christ*d* by giving him the Holy Spirit*d* and power. You know how Jesus went everywhere doing good. He healed those who were ruled by the devil, for God was with Jesus. ³⁹We saw all the things that Jesus did in Judea and in Jerusalem. But they killed him by nailing him to a cross. ⁴⁰Yet, on the third day, God raised Jesus to life and caused him to be seen. ⁴¹But he was not seen by all the people. Only the witnesses that God had already chosen saw him, and we are those witnesses. We ate and drank with him after he was raised from death. ⁴²He told us to preach to the people and to tell them that he is the one whom God chose to be the judge of the living and the dead. ⁴³Everyone who believes in Jesus will be forgiven. God will forgive his sins through Jesus. All the prophets*d* say this is true."

Non-Jews Receive the Holy Spirit

⁴⁴While Peter was still saying this, the Holy Spirit*d* came down on all those who were listening. ⁴⁵The Jew-

ish believers who came with Peter were amazed that the gift of the Holy Spirit had been given even to the non-Jewish people. ⁴⁶These Jewish believers heard them speaking in different languages*ⁿ* and praising God. Then Peter said, ⁴⁷"Can anyone keep these people from being baptised with water? They have received the Holy Spirit just as we did!" ⁴⁸So Peter ordered that they be baptised in the name of Jesus Christ. Then they asked Peter to stay with them for a few days.

Peter Returns to Jerusalem

11 The apostles*d* and the believers in Judea heard that non-Jewish people had accepted God's teaching too. ²But when Peter came to Jerusalem, some Jewish believers argued with him. ³They said, "You went into the homes of people who are not Jews and are not circumcised!*d* You even ate with them!"

⁴So Peter explained the whole story to them. ⁵He said, "I was in the city of Joppa. While I was praying, I had a vision. In the vision, I saw something which looked like a big sheet coming down from heaven. It was being lowered to earth by its four corners. It came down very close to me, and ⁶I looked inside it. I saw animals, wild beasts, reptiles, and birds. ⁷I heard a voice say to me, 'Get up, Peter. Kill and eat'. ⁸But I said, 'No, Lord! I have never eaten anything that is unholy or unclean'.*d* ⁹But the voice from heaven answered again, 'God has made these things clean. Don't call them unholy!' ¹⁰This happened three times. Then the whole thing was taken back to heaven. ¹¹Right then three men came to the house where I was staying. They were sent to me from Caesarea. ¹²The Spirit*d* told me to go with them without doubting. These six believers

---

John John the Baptist, who preached to people about Christ's coming (Matthew 3, Luke 3).
languages This can also be translated "tongues".

here also went with me. We went to the house of Cornelius. [13]He told us about the angel he saw standing in his house. The angel said to him, 'Send some men to Joppa and invite Simon Peter to come. [14]He will speak to you. The things he will say will save you and all your family'. [15]When I began my speech, the Holy Spirit came on them just as he came on us at the beginning. [16]Then I remembered the words of the Lord. He said, 'John baptised in water, but you will be baptised in the Holy Spirit!' [17]God gave to them the same gift that he gave to us who believed in the Lord Jesus Christ. So could I stop the work of God? No!"

[18]When the Jewish believers heard this, they stopped arguing. They praised God and said, "So God is allowing the non-Jewish people also to turn to him and live."

The Good News Comes to Antioch

[19]Many of the believers were scattered by the terrible things that happened after Stephen was killed. Some of them went to places as far away as Phoenicia, Cyprus, and Antioch. They were telling the message to others, but only to Jews. [20]Some of these believers were men from Cyprus and Cyrene. When they came to Antioch, they spoke also to Greeks, telling them the Good News[d] about the Lord Jesus. [21]The Lord was helping the believers. And a large group of people believed and turned to the Lord.

[22]The church in Jerusalem heard about all of this, so they sent Barnabas to Antioch. [23-24]Barnabas was a good man, full of the Holy Spirit[d] and full of faith. When he reached Antioch and saw how God had blessed the people, he was glad. He encouraged all the believers in Antioch. He told them, "Never lose your faith. Always obey the Lord with all your hearts." Many people became followers of the Lord. [25]Then Barnabas went to the city of Tarsus to look for Saul. [26]When he found Saul, he brought him to Antioch. And for a whole year Saul and Barnabas met with the church. They taught many people there. In Antioch the followers were called Christians for the first time.

[27]About that time some prophets[d] came from Jerusalem to Antioch. [28]One of them was named Agabus. He stood up and spoke with the help of the Holy Spirit. He said, "A very hard time is coming to the whole world. There will be no food for people to eat." (This happened when Claudius ruled.) [29]The followers all decided to help their brothers who lived in Judea. Each one planned to send them as much as he could. [30]They gathered the money and gave it to Barnabas and Saul, who brought it to the elders[d] in Judea.

Herod Agrippa Hurts the Church

12 During that same time King Herod began to do terrible things to some who belonged to the church. [2]He ordered James, the brother of John, to be killed by the sword. [3]Herod saw that the Jews liked this, so he decided to arrest Peter, too. (This happened during the time of the Feast[d] of Unleavened Bread.) [4]After Herod arrested Peter, he put him in jail and handed him over to be guarded by 16 soldiers. Herod planned to bring Peter before the people for trial after the Passover[d] Feast. [5]So Peter was kept in jail. But the church kept on praying to God for him.

Peter Leaves the Jail

[6]The night before Herod was to bring him to trial, Peter was sleeping. He was between two soldiers, bound with two chains. Other soldiers were guarding the door of the jail. [7]Suddenly, an angel of the Lord stood there. A light shined in the room. The angel touched Peter on the side and woke

him up. The angel said, "Hurry! Get up!" And the chains fell off Peter's hands. [8]The angel said to him, "Get dressed and put on your sandals." And so Peter did this. Then the angel said, "Put on your coat and follow me." [9]So the angel went out, and Peter followed him. Peter did not know if what the angel was doing was real. He thought he might be seeing a vision. [10]They went past the first and the second guard. They came to the iron gate that separated them from the city. The gate opened itself for them. They went through the gate and walked down a street. And the angel suddenly left him.

[11]Then Peter realised what had happened. He thought, "Now I know that the Lord really sent his angel to me. He rescued me from Herod and from all the things the Jewish people thought would happen."

[12]When he realised this, he went to the home of Mary. She was the mother of John. (John was also called Mark.) Many people were gathered there, praying. [13]Peter knocked on the outside door. A servant girl named Rhoda came to answer it. [14]She recognised Peter's voice, and she was very happy. She even forgot to open the door. She ran inside and told the group, "Peter is at the door!"

[15]They said to her, "You are insane!" But she kept on saying that it was true. So they said, "It must be Peter's angel."

[16]Peter continued to knock. When they opened the door, they saw him and were amazed. [17]Peter made a sign with his hand to tell them to be quiet. He explained how the Lord led him out of the jail. And he said, "Tell James and the other believers what happened." Then he left to go to another place.

[18]The next day the soldiers were very upset. They wondered what had happened to Peter. [19]Herod looked everywhere for Peter but could not find him. So he questioned the guards and ordered that they be killed.

The Death of Herod Agrippa

Later Herod moved from Judea and went to the city of Caesarea, where he stayed for a while. [20]Herod was very angry with the people of Tyre and Sidon. But the people of those cities all came in a group to Herod. They were able to get Blastus, the king's personal servant, on their side. They asked Herod for peace because their country got its food from his country.

[21]On a chosen day Herod put on his royal robes. He sat on his throne and made a speech to the people. [22]They shouted, "This is the voice of a god, not a man!" [23]Herod did not give the glory to God. So an angel of the Lord caused him to become sick. He was eaten by worms and died.

[24]God's message continued to spread and reach more and more people.

[25]After Barnabas and Saul finished their task in Jerusalem, they returned to Antioch. John, also called Mark, was with them.

Barnabas and Saul Are Chosen

13 In the church at Antioch there were these prophets[d] and teachers: Barnabas, Simeon (also called Niger), Lucius (from the city of Cyrene), Manaen (who had grown up with Herod, the ruler) and Saul. [2]They were all worshipping the Lord and giving up eating.[n] The Holy Spirit[d] said to them, "Give Barnabas and Saul to me to do a special work. I have chosen them for it."

[3]So they gave up eating and prayed.

---

giving up eating This is called "fasting". The people would give up eating for a special time of prayer and worship to God. It was also done to show sadness.

They laid their hands on[n] Barnabas and Saul and sent them out.

Barnabas and Saul in Cyprus

[4]Barnabas and Saul were sent out by the Holy Spirit.[d] They went to the city of Seleucia. From there they sailed to the island of Cyprus. [5]When they came to Salamis, they preached the Good News[d] of God in the Jewish synagogues.[d] John Mark was with them to help.

[6]They went across the whole island to Paphos. In Paphos they met a Jew who was a magician. His name was Bar-Jesus. He was a false prophet,[d] [7]who always stayed close to Sergius Paulus, the governor. Sergius Paulus was a clever man. He asked Barnabas and Saul to come to him, because he wanted to hear the message of God. [8]But Elymas, the magician, was against them. (Elymas is the name for Bar-Jesus in the Greek language.) He tried to stop the governor from believing in Jesus. [9]But Saul was filled with the Holy Spirit. (Saul's other name was Paul.) He looked straight at Elymas [10]and said, "You son of the devil! You are an enemy of everything that is right! You are full of evil tricks and lies. You are always trying to change the Lord's truths into lies! [11]Now the Lord will touch you, and you will be blind. For a time you will not be able to see anything—not even the light from the sun."

Then everything became dark for Elymas. He walked around, trying to find someone to lead him by the hand. [12]When the governor saw this, he believed. He was amazed at the teaching about the Lord.

Paul and Barnabas Leave Cyprus

[13]Paul and those with him sailed away from Paphos. They came to Perga, in Pamphylia. But John Mark left them and returned to Jerusalem. [14]They continued their trip from Perga and went to Antioch, a city in Pisidia. On the Sabbath[d] day they went into the synagogue[d] and sat down. [15]The law of Moses and the writings of the prophets[d] were read. Then the leaders of the synagogue sent a message to Paul and Barnabas: "Brothers, if you have any message that will encourage the people, please speak!"

[16]Paul stood up. He raised his hand and said, "Men of Israel and you other people who worship God, please listen! [17]The God of the people of Israel chose our ancestors. He made the people great during the time they lived in Egypt. He brought them out of that country with great power. [18]And he was patient with them for 40 years in the desert. [19]God destroyed seven nations in the land of Canaan and gave the land to his people. [20]All this happened in about 450 years.

"After this, God gave them judges until the time of Samuel the prophet. [21]Then the people asked for a king. God gave them Saul son of Kish. Saul was from the tribe[d] of Benjamin. He was king for 40 years. [22]After God took him away, God made David their king. This is what God said about him: 'I have found David son of Jesse. He is the kind of man I want. He will do all that I want him to do'. [23]So God has brought one of David's descendants[d] to Israel to be their Saviour.[d] That descendant is Jesus. And God promised to do this. [24]Before Jesus came, John[n] preached to all the people of Israel. He told them about a baptism of changed hearts and lives. [25]When he was finishing his work, he said, 'Who do you think I am? I am not the Christ.[d] He is coming later. I am not worthy to untie his sandals'.

---

laid their hands on Here, this was a sign to show that these men were given a special work of God.

John John the Baptist, who preached to people about Christ's coming (Matthew 3, Luke 3).

26"Brothers, sons in the family of Abraham, and you non-Jews who worship God, listen! The news about this salvation has been sent to us. 27Those who live in Jerusalem and their leaders did not realise that Jesus was the Saviour. They did not understand the words that the prophets wrote, which are read every Sabbath*d* day. But they made them come true when they said Jesus was guilty. 28They could not find any real reason for Jesus to die, but they asked Pilate to have him killed. 29They did to him all that the Scriptures*d* had said. Then they took him down from the cross and laid him in a tomb. 30But God raised him up from death! 31After this, for many days, the people who had gone with Jesus from Galilee to Jerusalem saw him. They are now his witnesses to the people. 32We tell you the Good News*d* about the promise God made to our ancestors. 33We are their children, and God has made this promise come true for us. God did this by raising Jesus from death. We read about this also in Psalm 2:

'You are my Son.
　Today I have become your
　　Father'. *Psalm 2:7*

34God raised Jesus from death. He will never go back to the grave and become dust. So God said:

'I will give you the holy and sure
　blessings
　that I promised to David'.
Isaiah 55:3

35But in another place God says:

'You will not let your Holy One
　rot in the grave'. *Psalm 16:10*

36David did God's will during his lifetime. Then he died and was buried with his fathers. And his body did rot in the grave! 37But the One God raised from death did not rot in the grave. 38-39Brothers, you must understand what we are telling you: you can have forgiveness of your sins through Jesus. The law of Moses could not free you from your sins. But everyone who believes is free from all sins through him. 40Be careful! Don't let what the prophets said happen to you:

41'Listen, you people who doubt!
　You can wonder, and then die.
I will do something in your lifetime
　that will amaze you.
You won't believe it even when
　you are told about it!' "
Habakkuk 1:5

42While Paul and Barnabas were leaving the synagogue, the people asked them to tell them more about these things on the next Sabbath. 43After the meeting, many Jews followed Paul and Barnabas from that place. With the Jews there were many who had changed to the Jewish religion and worshipped God. Paul and Barnabas were persuading them to continue trusting in God's kindness.

44On the next Sabbath day, almost all the people in the city came to hear the word of the Lord. 45Seeing the crowd, the Jews became very jealous. They said insulting things and argued against what Paul said. 46But Paul and Barnabas spoke very boldly. They said, "We must speak the message of God to you first. But you refuse to listen. You are judging yourselves not worthy of having eternal life! So we will now go to the people of other nations! 47This is what the Lord told us to do. The Lord said:

'I have made you a light for the
　non-Jewish nations.
You will show people all over
　the world the way to be
　　saved'." *Isaiah 49:6*

48When the non-Jewish people heard Paul say this, they were happy. They gave honour to the message of the Lord. And many of the people believed the message. They were the ones chosen to have life for ever.

49And so the message of the Lord was spreading through the whole country. 50But the Jews stirred up some of the important religious women and the leaders of the city against

Paul and Barnabas. They started trouble against Paul and Barnabas and drove them out of their area. [51]So Paul and Barnabas shook the dust off their feet[n] and went to Iconium. [52]But the followers were filled with joy and the Holy Spirit.[d]

Paul and Barnabas in Iconium

14 In Iconium, Paul and Barnabas went as usual to the Jewish synagogue.[d] They spoke so well that a great many Jews and Greeks believed. [2]But some of the Jews who did not believe excited the non-Jewish people and turned them against the believers. [3]But Paul and Barnabas stayed in Iconium a long time and spoke bravely for the Lord. The Lord showed that their message about his grace was true by giving them the power to work miracles[d] and signs. [4]But some of the people in the city agreed with the Jews. Others believed the apostles.[d] So the city was divided.

[5]Some non-Jewish people, some Jews, and some of their rulers wanted to harm Paul and Barnabas by killing them with stones. [6]When Paul and Barnabas learned about this, they went to Lystra and Derbe, cities in Lycaonia, and to the areas around those cities. [7]They announced the Good News[d] there, too.

Paul in Lystra and Derbe

[8]In Lystra there sat a man who had been born crippled; he had never walked. [9]This man was listening to Paul speak. Paul looked straight at him and saw that the man believed God could heal him. [10]So he cried out, "Stand up on your feet!" The man jumped up and began walking around. [11]When the crowds saw what Paul did, they shouted in their own Lycaonian language. They said, "The gods have become like men! They have come down to us!" [12]And the people began to call Barnabas "Zeus".[n] They called Paul "Hermes",[n] because he was the main speaker. [13]The temple of Zeus was near the city. The priest of this temple brought some bulls and flowers to the city gates. The priest and the people wanted to offer a sacrifice to Paul and Barnabas. [14]But when the apostles,[d] Barnabas and Paul, understood what they were about to do, they tore their clothes in anger. Then they ran in among the people and shouted, [15]"Men, why are you doing these things? We are only men, human beings like you! We are bringing you the Good News.[d] We are telling you to turn away from these worthless things and turn to the true living God. He is the One who made the sky, the earth, the sea, and everything that is in them. [16]In the past, God let all the nations do what they wanted. [17]Yet he did things to prove he is real: He shows kindness to you. He gives you rain from heaven and crops at the right times. He gives you food and fills your hearts with joy." [18]Even with these words, they were barely able to keep the crowd from offering sacrifices to them.

[19]Then some Jews came from Antioch and Iconium. They persuaded the people to turn against Paul. And so they threw stones at Paul and dragged him out of town. They thought that they had killed him. [20]But the followers gathered around him, and he got up and went back into the town. The next day, he and Barnabas left and went to the city of Derbe.

The Return to Antioch in Syria

[21]Paul and Barnabas told the Good News[d] in Derbe and many became fol-

---

shook . . . feet A warning. It showed that they had finished talking to these people.
"Zeus" The Greeks believed in many gods. Zeus was their most important god.
"Hermes" The Greeks believed he was a messenger for the other gods.

lowers. Paul and Barnabas returned to Lystra, Iconium, and Antioch. ²²In those cities they made the followers of Jesus stronger. They helped them to stay in the faith. They said, "We must suffer many things to enter God's kingdom." ²³They chose elders*d* for each church, by praying and giving up eating.*n* These elders were men who had trusted the Lord. So Paul and Barnabas put them in the Lord's care.

²⁴Then they went through Pisidia and came to Pamphylia. ²⁵They preached the message in Perga, and then they went down to Attalia. ²⁶And from there they sailed away to Antioch. This is where the believers had put them into God's care and had sent them out to do this work. And now they had finished the work.

²⁷When they arrived in Antioch, they gathered the church together. Paul and Barnabas told them all about what God had done with them. They told how God had made it possible for the non-Jews to believe! ²⁸And they stayed there a long time with the followers.

The Meeting at Jerusalem

15 Then some men came to Antioch from Judea. They began teaching the non-Jewish brothers: "You cannot be saved if you are not circumcised.*d* Moses taught us to do this." ²Paul and Barnabas were against this teaching and argued with the men about it. So the group decided to send Paul, Barnabas, and some other men to Jerusalem. There they could talk more about this with the apostles*d* and elders.*d*

³The church helped the men leave on the trip. They went through the countries of Phoenicia and Samaria, telling all about how the non-Jewish people had turned to God. This made all the believers very happy. ⁴When they arrived in Jerusalem, the apostles, the elders, and the church welcomed them. Paul, Barnabas, and the others told of all the things that God had done with them. ⁵But some of the believers who had belonged to the Pharisee*d* group came forward. They said, "The non-Jewish believers must be circumcised. We must tell them to obey the law of Moses!"

⁶The apostles and the elders gathered to study this problem. ⁷There was a long debate. Then Peter stood up and said to them, "Brothers, you know what happened in the early days. God chose me from among you to preach the Good News*d* to the non-Jewish people. They heard the Good News from me, and they believed. ⁸God, who knows the thoughts of all men, accepted them. He showed this to us by giving them the Holy Spirit,*d* just as he did to us. ⁹To God, those people are not different from us. When they believed, he made their hearts pure. ¹⁰So now why are you testing God? You are putting a heavy load around the necks of the non-Jewish brothers. It is a load that neither we nor our fathers were able to carry. ¹¹But we believe that we and they too will be saved by the grace of the Lord Jesus!"

¹²Then the whole group became quiet. They listened to Paul and Barnabas speak. Paul and Barnabas told about all the miracles*d* and signs that God did through them among the non-Jewish people. ¹³After they finished speaking, James spoke. He said, "Brothers, listen to me. ¹⁴Simon has told us how God showed his love for the non-Jewish people. For the first time he has accepted them and made them his people. ¹⁵The words of the prophets*d* agree with this too: ¹⁶'After these things I will return.

---

giving up eating This is called "fasting". The people would give up eating for a special time of prayer and worship to God. It was also done to show sadness.

The kingdom of David is like a
fallen tent.
But I will rebuild it.
And I will again build its ruins.
And I will set it up.
17Then those people who are left
alive may ask the Lord for
help.
And all people from other
nations may worship me,
says the Lord.
And he will make it happen.
18 And these things have been
known for a long time'.

Amos 9:11-12

19"So I think we should not bother
the non-Jewish brothers who have
turned to God. 20Instead, we should
write a letter to them. We should tell
them these things: Do not eat food
that has been offered to idols. (This
makes the food unclean.*d*) Do not take
part in any kind of sexual sin. Do not
taste blood. Do not eat animals that
have been strangled. 21They should
not do these things, because there are
still men in every city who teach
the law of Moses. For a long time the
words of Moses have been read in the
synagogue*d* every Sabbath*d* day."

Letter to Non-Jewish Believers

22The apostles,*d* the elders,*d* and
the whole church decided to send
some of their men with Paul and Barnabas to Antioch. They chose Judas
Barsabbas and Silas, who were respected by the believers. 23They sent
the following letter with them:

From the apostles and elders,
your brothers.
To all the non-Jewish brothers
in Antioch, Syria and Cilicia:
Dear Brothers,
24We have heard that some of
our men have come to you and
said things that trouble and upset
you. But we did not tell them to

do this! 25We have all agreed to
choose some men and send them
to you. They will be with our dear
friends Barnabas and Paul—
26men who have given their lives
to serve our Lord Jesus Christ.
27So we have sent Judas and Silas
with them. They will tell you the
same things. 28It has pleased the
Holy Spirit*d* that you should not
have a heavy load to carry, and
we agree. You need to do only
these things: 29do not eat any
food that has been offered to
idols. Do not taste blood. Do not
eat any animals that have been
strangled. Do not take part in any
kind of sexual sin. If you stay
away from these things, you will
do well.
Good bye.

30So the men left Jerusalem and
went to Antioch. There they gathered
the church and gave them the letter.
31When they read it, they were very
happy because of the encouraging letter. 32Judas and Silas were also prophets,*d* who said many things to
encourage the believers and make
them stronger. 33After some time Judas and Silas were sent off in peace by
the believers. They went back to
those who had sent them. 34 *n*
35But Paul and Barnabas stayed in
Antioch. They and many others
preached the Good News*d* and taught
the people the message of the Lord.

Paul and Barnabas Separate

36After some time, Paul said to Barnabas, "We preached the message of
the Lord in many towns. We should go
back to all those towns to visit the believers and see how they are doing."
37Barnabas wanted to take John
Mark with them too. 38But John Mark
had left them at Pamphylia; he did not
continue with them in the work. So

Verse 34 Some Greek copies add verse 34: ". . .but Silas decided to remain there."

Paul did not think it was a good idea to take him. [39]Paul and Barnabas had a serious argument about this. They separated and went different ways. Barnabas sailed to Cyprus and took Mark with him. [40]But Paul chose Silas and left. The believers in Antioch put Paul into the Lord's care. [41]And he went through Syria and Cilicia, giving strength to the churches.

Timothy Goes with Paul and Silas

16 Paul came to Derbe and Lystra. A follower named Timothy was there. Timothy's mother was Jewish and a believer. His father was a Greek.

[2]The brothers in Lystra and Iconium respected Timothy and said good things about him. [3]Paul wanted Timothy to travel with him. But all the Jews living in that area knew that Timothy's father was Greek. So Paul circumcised[d] Timothy to please the Jews. [4]Paul and the men with him travelled from town to town. They gave the decisions made by the apostles[d] and elders[d] in Jerusalem for the people to obey. [5]So the churches became stronger in the faith and grew larger every day.

Paul Is Called Out of Asia

[6]Paul and the men with him went through the areas of Phrygia and Galatia. The Holy Spirit[d] did not let them preach the Good News[d] in the country of Asia. [7]When they came near the country of Mysia, they tried to go into Bithynia. But the Spirit of Jesus did not let them. [8]So they passed by Mysia and went to Troas. [9]That night Paul had a vision. In the vision, a man from Macedonia came to him. The man stood there and begged, "Come over to Macedonia. Help us!" [10]After Paul had seen the vision, we immediately prepared to leave for Macedonia. We understood that God had called us to tell the Good News to those people.

Lydia Becomes a Christian

[11]We left Troas in a ship, and we sailed straight to the island of Samothrace. The next day we sailed to Neapolis.[n] [12]Then we went by land to Philippi, the leading city in that part of Macedonia. It is also a Roman colony.[n] We stayed there for several days.

[13]On the Sabbath[d] day we went outside the city gate to the river. There we thought we would find a special place for prayer. Some women had gathered there, so we sat down and talked with them. [14]There was a woman named Lydia from the city of Thyatira. Her job was selling purple cloth. She worshipped the true God. The Lord opened her mind to pay attention to what Paul was saying. [15]She and all the people in her house were baptised. Then Lydia invited us to her home. She said, "If you think I am truly a believer in the Lord, then come and stay in my house." And she persuaded us to stay with her.

Paul and Silas in Jail

[16]Once, while we were going to the place for prayer, a servant girl met us. She had a special spirit[n] in her. She earned a lot of money for her owners by telling fortunes. [17]This girl followed Paul and us. She said loudly, "These men are servants of the Most High God! They are telling you how you can be saved!" [18]She kept this up for many days. This bothered Paul, so he turned and said to the spirit, "By the power of Jesus Christ, I command you to come

---

Neapolis City in Macedonia. It was the first city Paul visited on the continent of Europe.
Roman colony A town begun by Romans with Roman laws, customs and privileges.
spirit This was a spirit from the devil. It caused her to say she had special knowledge.

out of her!" Immediately, the spirit came out.

[19]The owners of the servant girl saw this. These men knew that now they could not use her to make money. So they grabbed Paul and Silas and dragged them before the city rulers in the marketplace. [20]Here they brought Paul and Silas to the Roman rulers and said, "These men are Jews and are making trouble in our city. [21]They are teaching things that are not right for us as Romans to do."

[22]The crowd joined the attack against them. The Roman officers tore the clothes of Paul and Silas and had them beaten with rods again and again. [23]Then Paul and Silas were thrown into jail. The jailer was ordered to guard them carefully. [24]When he heard this order, he put them far inside the jail. He pinned down their feet between large blocks of wood.

[25]About midnight Paul and Silas were praying and singing songs to God. The other prisoners were listening to them. [26]Suddenly, there was a big earthquake. It was so strong that it shook the foundation of the jail. Then all the doors of the jail broke open. All the prisoners were freed from their chains. [27]The jailer woke up and saw that the jail doors were open. He thought that the prisoners had already escaped. So he got his sword and was about to kill himself.[n] [28]But Paul shouted, "Don't hurt yourself! We are all here!"

[29]The jailer told someone to bring a light. Then he ran inside. Shaking with fear, he fell down before Paul and Silas. [30]Then he brought them outside and said, "Men, what must I do to be saved?"

[31]They said to him, "Believe in the Lord Jesus and you will be saved—

you and all the people in your house." [32]So Paul and Silas told the message of the Lord to the jailer and all the people in his house. [33]At that hour of the night the jailer took Paul and Silas and washed their wounds. Then he and all his people were baptised immediately. [34]After this the jailer took Paul and Silas home and gave them food. He and his family were very happy because they now believed in God.

[35]The next morning, the Roman officers sent the police to tell the jailer, "Let these men go free!"

[36]The jailer said to Paul, "The officers have sent an order to let you go free. You can leave now. Go in peace."

[37]But Paul said to the police, "They beat us in public without a trial, even though we are Roman citizens.[n] And they threw us in jail. Now they want to make us go away quietly. No! Let them come themselves and bring us out!"

[38]The police told the Roman officers what Paul said. When the officers heard that Paul and Silas were Roman citizens, they were afraid. [39]So they came and told Paul and Silas they were sorry. They took Paul and Silas out of jail and asked them to leave the city. [40]So when they came out of the jail, they went to Lydia's house. There they saw some of the believers and encouraged them. Then they left.

Paul and Silas in Thessalonica

17 Paul and Silas travelled through Amphipolis and Apollonia and came to Thessalonica. In that city there was a Jewish synagogue.[d] [2]Paul went into the synagogue as he always did. On each Sabbath[d] day for three weeks, Paul talked with the Jews about the Scriptures.[d] [3]He explained and proved that the Christ[d] must die

---

kill himself He thought the leaders would kill him for letting the prisoners escape.
Roman citizens Roman law said that Roman citizens must not be beaten before they had a trial.

and then rise from death. He said, "This Jesus I am telling you about is the Christ." ⁴Some of the Jews were convinced and joined Paul and Silas. Many of the Greeks who worshipped the true God and many of the important women joined them.

⁵But the Jews became jealous. They got some evil men from the marketplace, formed a mob and started a riot. They ran to Jason's house, looking for Paul and Silas. The men wanted to bring Paul and Silas out to the people. ⁶But they did not find them. So they dragged Jason and some other believers to the leaders of the city. The people were yelling, "These men have made trouble everywhere in the world. And now they have come here too! ⁷Jason is keeping them in his house. All of them do things against the laws of Caesar.ᵈ They say that there is another king called Jesus."

⁸When the people and the leaders of the city heard these things, they became very upset. ⁹They made Jason and the others put up a sum of money. Then they let the believers go free.

Paul and Silas Go to Berea

¹⁰That same night the believers sent Paul and Silas to Berea. There Paul and Silas went to the Jewish synagogue.ᵈ ¹¹These Jews were better than the Jews in Thessalonica. They were eager to hear the things Paul and Silas said. These Jews in Berea studied the Scripturesᵈ every day to find out if these things were true. ¹²So, many of them believed. Many important Greek men and women also believed. ¹³But when the Jews in Thessalonica learned that Paul was preaching the word of God in Berea, they came there, too. They upset the people and made trouble. ¹⁴So the be-

lievers quickly sent Paul away to the coast. But Silas and Timothy stayed in Berea. ¹⁵The men who took Paul went with him to Athens. Then they carried a message from Paul back to Silas and Timothy. It said, "Come to me as soon as you can."

Paul in Athens

¹⁶Paul was waiting for Silas and Timothy in Athens. He was troubled because he saw that the city was full of idols. ¹⁷In the synagogue,ᵈ he talked with the Jews and the Greeks who worshipped the true God. He also talked every day with people in the marketplace.

¹⁸Some of the Epicurean and Stoic philosophersⁿ argued with him. Some of them said, "This man doesn't know what he is talking about. What is he trying to say?" Paul was telling them the Good Newsᵈ of Jesus' rising from death. They said, "He seems to be telling us about some other gods." ¹⁹They got Paul and took him to a meeting of the Areopagus.ⁿ They said, "Please explain to us this new idea that you have been teaching. ²⁰The things you are saying are new to us. We want to know what this teaching means." ²¹(All the people of Athens and those from other countries always used their time talking about all the newest ideas.)

²²Then Paul stood before the meeting of the Areopagus. He said, "Men of Athens, I can see that you are very religious in all things. ²³I was going through your city, and I saw the things you worship. I found an altar that had these words written on it: "TO A GOD WHO IS NOT KNOWN". You worship a god that you don't know. This is the God I am telling you about! ²⁴He is the God who made the whole world and every-

---

Epicurean and Stoic philosophers Philosophers were those who searched for truth. Epicureans believed that pleasure, especially pleasures of the mind, were the goal of life. Stoics believed that life should be without feelings of joy or grief.
Areopagus A council or group of important leaders in Athens. They were like judges.

thing in it. He is the Lord of the land and the sky. He does not live in temples that men build! 25This God is the One who gives life, breath, and everything else to people. He does not need any help from them. He has everything he needs. 26God began by making one man. From him came all the different people who live everywhere in the world. He decided exactly when and where they must live. 27God wanted them to look for him and perhaps search all around for him and find him. But he is not far from any of us: 28'We live in him. We walk in him. We are in him'. Some of your own poets have said: 'For we are his children'. 29We are God's children. So, you must not think that God is like something that people imagine or make. He is not like gold, silver, or rock. 30In the past, people did not understand God, but God ignored this. But now, God tells everyone in the world to change his heart and life. 31God has decided on a day that he will judge all the world. He will be fair. He will use a man to do this. God chose that man long ago. And God has proved this to everyone by raising that man from death!"

32When the people heard about Jesus being raised from death, some of them laughed. They said, "We will hear more about this from you later." 33So Paul went away from them. 34But some of the people believed Paul and joined him. One of those who believed was Dionysius, a member of the Areopagus. Also a woman named Damaris and some others believed.

Paul in Corinth

18 Later, Paul left Athens and went to Corinth. 2Here he met a Jew named Aquila. Aquila was born in the country of Pontus. But Aquila and his wife, Priscilla, had recently moved to Corinth from Italy. They left Italy because Claudius*n* commanded that all Jews must leave Rome. Paul went to visit Aquila and Priscilla. 3They were tentmakers, just as he was. He stayed with them and worked with them. 4Every Sabbath*d* day he talked with the Jews and Greeks in the synagogue.*d* Paul tried to persuade these people to believe in Jesus.

5Silas and Timothy came from Macedonia and joined Paul in Corinth. After this, Paul used all his time telling people the Good News.*d* He showed the Jews that Jesus is the Christ.*d* 6But they would not accept Paul's teaching and said some evil things. So he shook off the dust from his clothes.*n* He said to them, "If you are not saved, it will be your own fault! I have done all I can do! After this, I will go only to non-Jewish people!" 7Paul left the synagogue and moved into the home of Titius Justus. It was next to the synagogue. This man worshipped the true God. 8Crispus was the leader of that synagogue. He and all the people living in his house believed in the Lord. Many others in Corinth also listened to Paul. They too believed and were baptised.

9During the night, Paul had a vision. The Lord said to him, "Don't be afraid! Continue talking to people and don't be quiet! 10I am with you. No one will hurt you because many of my people are in this city." 11Paul stayed there for a year and a half, teaching God's word to the people.

Paul Is Brought Before Gallio

12Gallio became the governor of the country of Southern Greece. At that time, some of the Jews came together against Paul and took him to the court. 13They said to Gallio, "This man is teaching people to worship God in a way that is against our law!"

Claudius The emperor (ruler) of Rome, A.D. 41-54.
shook . . . clothes This was a warning. It showed that Paul had finished talking to the Jews.

[14]Paul was about to say something, but Gallio spoke to the Jews. Gallio said, "I would listen to you Jews if you were complaining about a crime or some wrong. [15]But the things you are saying are only questions about words and names — arguments about your own name. So you must solve this problem yourselves. I don't want to be a judge of these things!" [16]Then Gallio made them leave the court.

[17]Then they all grabbed Sosthenes. (Sosthenes was now the leader of the synagogue.[d]) They beat him there before the court. But this did not bother Gallio.

Paul Returns to Antioch

[18]Paul stayed with the believers for many more days. Then he left and sailed for Syria. Priscilla and Aquila went with him. At Cenchrea, Paul cut off his hair.[n] This showed that he had made a promise to God. [19]Then they went to Ephesus, where Paul left Priscilla and Aquila. While Paul was there, he went into the synagogue[d] and talked with the Jews. [20]When they asked him to stay with them longer, he refused. [21]He left them, but he said, "I will come back to you again if God wants me to." And so he sailed away from Ephesus.

[22]Paul landed at Caesarea. Then he went and gave greetings to the church in Jerusalem. After that, Paul went to Antioch. [23]He stayed there for a while and then left and went through the countries of Galatia and Phrygia. He travelled from town to town in these countries, giving strength to all the followers.

Apollos in Ephesus and Corinth

[24]A Jew named Apollos came to Ephesus. He was born in the city of Alexandria. He was an educated man who knew the Scriptures[d] well. [25]He had been taught about the Lord. He was always very excited when he spoke and taught the truth about Jesus. But the only baptism that Apollos knew about was the baptism that John[n] taught. [26]Apollos began to speak very boldly in the synagogue,[d] and Priscilla and Aquila heard him. So they took him to their home and helped him better understand the way of God. [27]Now Apollos wanted to go to the country of Southern Greece, so the believers helped him. They wrote a letter to the followers there, asking them to accept him. These followers had believed in Jesus because of God's grace. When Apollos went there, he helped them very much. [28]He argued very strongly with the Jews before all the people. Apollos clearly proved that the Jews were wrong. Using the Scriptures, he proved that Jesus is the Christ.[d]

Paul in Ephesus

19 While Apollos was in Corinth, Paul was visiting some places on the way to Ephesus. There he found some followers. [2]Paul asked them, "Did you receive the Holy Spirit[d] when you believed?"

They said, "We have never even heard of a Holy Spirit!"

[3]So he asked, "What kind of baptism did you have?"

They said, "It was the baptism that John[n] taught."

[4]Paul said, "John's baptism was a baptism of changed hearts and lives. He told people to believe in the One who would come after him. That One is Jesus."

[5]When they heard this, they were baptised in the name of the Lord Jesus. [6]Then Paul laid his hands on

---

cut ... hair Jews did this to show that the time of a special promise to God was finished.
John John the Baptist, who preached to people about Christ's coming (Matthew 3, Luke 3).

them,[n] and the Holy Spirit came upon them. They began speaking different languages[n] and prophesying.[d] [7]There were about 12 men in this group.

[8]Paul went into the synagogue[d] and spoke out boldly for three months. He talked with the Jews and persuaded them to accept the things he said about the kingdom of God. [9]But some of the Jews became stubborn and refused to believe. These Jews said evil things about the Way of Jesus. All the people heard these things. So Paul left them and took the followers with him. He went to a place where a man named Tyrannus had a school. There Paul talked with people every day [10]for two years. Because of his work, every Jew and Greek in the country of Asia heard the word of the Lord.

The Sons of Sceva

[11]God used Paul to do some very special miracles.[d] [12]Some people took handkerchiefs and clothes that Paul had used and put them on the sick. When they did this, the sick were healed and evil spirits left them.

[13-14]But some Jews also were travelling around and making evil spirits go out of people. The seven sons of Sceva were doing this. (Sceva was a leading Jewish priest.) These Jews tried to use the name of the Lord Jesus to force the evil spirits out. They would say, "By the same Jesus that Paul talks about, I order you to come out!"

[15]But once an evil spirit said to these Jews, "I know Jesus, and I know about Paul, but who are you?"

[16]Then the man, who had the evil spirit in him, jumped on these Jews. He was much stronger than all of them. He beat them and tore their clothes off, so they ran away from the house. [17]All the people in Ephesus, Jews and Greeks, learned about this. They were filled with fear. And the people gave great honour to the Lord Jesus. [18]Many of the believers began to confess openly and tell all the evil things they had done. [19]Some of them had used magic. These believers brought their magic books and burned them before everyone. Those books were worth about 50,000 silver coins.[n]

[20]So in a powerful way the word of the Lord kept spreading and growing.

Paul Plans a Trip

[21]After these things, Paul made plans to go to Jerusalem. He planned to go through the countries of Macedonia and Southern Greece, and then on to Jerusalem. He said, "After I have been to Jerusalem, I must also visit Rome." [22]Paul sent Timothy and Erastus, two of his helpers, ahead to Macedonia. He himself stayed in Asia for a while.

Trouble in Ephesus

[23]But during that time, there was some serious trouble in Ephesus about the Way of Jesus. [24]There was a man named Demetrius, who worked with silver. He made little silver models that looked like the temple of the goddess Artemis.[n] The men who did this work made much money. [25]Demetrius had a meeting with these men and some others who did the same kind of work. He told them, "Men, you know that we make a lot of money from our business. [26]But look at what this man Paul is doing! He has con-

laid his hands on them Here, doing this was a sign to show that Paul had God's authority or power to give these people special powers of the Holy Spirit.
languages This can also be translated "tongues".
50,000 silver coins Probably drachmas. One coin was enough to pay a man for working one day.
Artemis A Greek goddess that the people of Asia Minor worshipped.

vinced and turned away many people in Ephesus and in almost all of Asia! He says the gods that men make are not real. [27]There is a danger that our business will lose its good name. But there is also another danger: people will begin to think that the temple of the great goddess Artemis is not important! Her greatness will be destroyed. And Artemis is the goddess that everyone in Asia and the whole world worships."

[28]When the men heard this, they became very angry. They shouted, "Artemis, the goddess of Ephesus, is great!" [29]The whole city became confused. The people grabbed Gaius and Aristarchus. (These two men were from Macedonia and were travelling with Paul.) Then all the people ran to the theatre. [30]Paul wanted to go in and talk to the crowd, but the followers did not let him. [31]Also, some leaders of Asia were friends of Paul. They sent him a message, begging him not to go into the theatre. [32]Some people were shouting one thing, and some were shouting another. The meeting was completely confused. Most of the people did not know why they had come together. [33]The Jews put a man named Alexander in front of the people. Some of them had told him what to do. Alexander waved his hand because he wanted to explain things to the people. [34]But when they saw that Alexander was a Jew, they all began shouting the same thing. They continued shouting for two hours: "Great is Artemis of Ephesus!"

[35]Then the city clerk made the crowd be quiet. He said, "Men of Ephesus, everyone knows that Ephesus is the city that keeps the temple of the great goddess Artemis. All people know that we also keep her holy stone[n] that fell from heaven. [36]No one can say that this is not true. So you should be quiet. You must stop and think before you do anything. [37]You brought these men here, but they have not said anything evil against our goddess. They have not stolen anything from her temple. [38]We have courts of law, and there are judges. Do Demetrius and the men who work with him have a charge against anyone? They should go to the courts! That is where they can argue with each other! [39]Is there something else you want to talk about? It can be decided at the regular town meeting of the people. [40]I say this because some people might see this trouble today and say that we are rioting. We could not explain this because there is no real reason for this meeting." [41]After the city clerk said these things, he told the people to go home.

Paul in Macedonia and Greece

20 When the trouble stopped, Paul sent for the followers to come to him. He encouraged them and then told them good bye. Paul left and went to the country of Macedonia. [2]He said many things to strengthen the followers in the different places on his way through Macedonia. Then he went to Southern Greece. [3]He stayed there three months. He was ready to sail for Syria, but some Jews were planning something against him. So Paul decided to go back through Macedonia to Syria. [4]Some men went with him. They were Sopater son of Pyrrhus, from the city of Berea; Aristarchus and Secundus, from the city of Thessalonica; Gaius, from Derbe; and Timothy; and Tychicus and Trophimus, two men from the country of Asia. [5]These men went first, ahead of Paul, and waited for us at Troas. [6]We sailed from Philippi after the Feast[d] of Unleavened Bread and we met them in Troas five days later. We stayed there seven days.

---

holy stone Probably a meteorite or stone that the people thought looked like Artemis.

Paul's Last Visit to Troas

⁷On the first day of the week,ⁿ we all met together to break bread.ⁿ Paul spoke to the group. Because he was planning to leave the next day, he kept on talking till midnight. ⁸We were all together in a room upstairs, and there were many lamps in the room. ⁹A young man named Eutychus was sitting in the window. As Paul continued talking, Eutychus was falling into a deep sleep. Finally, he went sound asleep and fell to the ground from the third floor. When they picked him up, he was dead. ¹⁰Paul went down to Eutychus. He knelt down and put his arms around him. He said, "Don't worry. He is alive now." ¹¹Then Paul went upstairs again, broke bread, and ate. He spoke to them a long time, until it was early morning. Then he left. ¹²They took the young man home alive and were greatly comforted.

The Trip from Troas to Miletus

¹³We sailed for the city of Assos. We went first, ahead of Paul. He wanted to join us on the ship there. Paul planned it this way because he wanted to go to Assos by land. ¹⁴When he met us at Assos, we took him aboard and went to Mitylene. ¹⁵The next day, we sailed from Mitylene and came to a place near Chios. The next day, we sailed to Samos. A day later, we reached Miletus. ¹⁶Paul had already decided not to stop at Ephesus. He did not want to stay too long in the country of Asia. He was hurrying to be in Jerusalem on the day of Pentecost,ᵈ if that was possible.

The Elders from Ephesus

¹⁷Now from Miletus Paul sent to Ephesus and called for the eldersᵈ of the church. ¹⁸When they came to him, he said, "You know about my life from the first day I came to Asia. You know the way I lived all the time I was with you. ¹⁹The Jews plotted against me. This troubled me very much. But you know that I always served the Lord. I never thought of myself first, and I often cried. ²⁰You know I preached to you, and I did not hold back anything that would help you. You know that I taught you in public and in your homes. ²¹I warned both Jews and Greeks to change their lives and turn to God. And I told them all to believe in our Lord Jesus. ²²But now I must obey the Holy Spiritᵈ and go to Jerusalem. I don't know what will happen to me there. ²³I know only that in every city the Holy Spirit tells me that troubles and even jail wait for me. ²⁴I don't care about my own life. The most important thing is that I complete my mission. I want to finish the work that the Lord Jesus gave me — to tell people the Good Newsᵈ about God's grace.

²⁵"And now, I know that none of you will ever see me again. All the time I was with you, I was preaching the kingdom of God. ²⁶So today I can tell you one thing that I am sure of: if any of you should be lost, I am not responsible. ²⁷This is because I have told you everything God wants you to know. ²⁸Be careful for yourselves and for all the people God has given you. The Holy Spirit gave you the work of caring for this flock. You must be like shepherds to the church of God.ⁿ This is the church that God bought with his own death. ²⁹I know that after I leave, some men will come like wild

---

first day of the week Sunday, which for the Jews began at sunset on our Saturday. But if in this part of Asia a different system of time was used, then the meeting was on our Sunday night.

break bread Probably the Lord's Supper, the special meal that Jesus told his followers to eat to remember him (Luke 22:14-20).

of God Some Greek copies say, "of the Lord".

wolves and try to destroy the flock. [30]Also, men from your own group will rise up and twist the truth. They will lead away followers after them. [31]So be careful! Always remember this: for three years I never stopped warning each of you. I taught you night and day. I often cried over you.

[32]"Now I am putting you in the care of God and the message about his grace. That message is able to give you strength, and it will give you the blessings that God has for all his holy people. [33]When I was with you, I never wanted anyone's money or fine clothes. [34]You know that I always worked to take care of my own needs and the needs of those who were with me. [35]I showed you in all things that you should work as I did and help the weak. I taught you to remember the words of Jesus. He said, 'It is more blessed to give than to receive'."

[36]When Paul had said this, he knelt down with all of them and prayed. [37-38]And they all cried because Paul had said that they would never see him again. They put their arms around him and kissed him. Then they went with him to the ship.

Paul Goes to Jerusalem

21 We all said good bye to them and left. We sailed straight to Cos. The next day, we reached Rhodes, and from Rhodes we went to Patara. [2]There we found a ship that was going to Phoenicia. We went aboard and sailed away. [3]We sailed near the island of Cyprus. We could see it to the north, but we sailed on to Syria. We stopped at Tyre because the ship needed to unload its cargo there. [4]We found some followers in Tyre, and we stayed with them for seven days. Through the Holy Spirit[d] they warned Paul not to go to Jerusalem. [5]When we finished our visit, we left and continued our trip. All the fol-

lowers, even the women and children, came outside the city with us. We all knelt down on the beach and prayed. [6]Then we said good bye and got on the ship. The followers went back home. [7]We continued our trip from Tyre and arrived at Ptolemais. We greeted the believers there and stayed with them for a day. [8]We left Ptolemais and went to the city of Caesarea. There we went into the home of Philip and stayed with him. Philip had the work of telling the Good News.[d] He was one of the seven helpers.[n] [9]He had four unmarried daughters who had the gift of prophesying.[d] [10]After we had been there for some time, a prophet named Agabus arrived from Judea. [11]He came to us and borrowed Paul's belt. Then he used the belt to tie his own hands and feet. He said, "The Holy Spirit says, 'This is how the Jews in Jerusalem will tie up the man who wears this belt. Then they will give him to the non-Jewish people'."

[12]We all heard these words. So we and the people there begged Paul not to go to Jerusalem. [13]But he said, "Why are you crying and making me so sad? I am ready to be tied up in Jerusalem. And I am ready to die for the Lord Jesus!"

[14]We could not persuade him to stay away from Jerusalem. So we stopped begging him and said, "We pray that what the Lord wants will be done."

[15]After this, we got ready and started on our way to Jerusalem. [16]Some of the followers from Caesarea went with us. They took us to the home of Mnason, a man from Cyprus. Mnason was one of the first followers. They took us to his home so that we could stay with him.

Paul Visits James

[17]In Jerusalem the believers were glad to see us. [18]The next day, Paul went with us to visit James. All the el-

---

helpers The seven men chosen for a special work described in Acts 6:1-6.

ders[d] were there, too. [19]Paul greeted them and told them everything that God had done among the non-Jewish people through him. [20]When they heard this, they praised God. Then they said to Paul, "Brother, you can see that many thousands of Jews have become believers. But they think it is very important to obey the law of Moses. [21]These Jews have heard about your teaching. They heard that you tell the Jews who live among non-Jews to leave the law of Moses. They heard that you tell them not to circumcise[d] their children and not to obey Jewish customs. [22]What should we do? The Jewish believers here will learn that you have come. [23]So we will tell you what to do: four of our men have made a promise to God. [24]Take these men with you and share in their cleansing ceremony.[n] Pay their expenses. Then they can shave their heads.[n] Do this and it will prove to everyone that what they have heard about you is not true. They will see that you follow the law of Moses in your own life. [25]We have already sent a letter to the non-Jewish believers. The letter said: 'Do not eat food that has been offered to idols. Do not taste blood. Do not eat animals that have been strangled. Do not take part in any kind of sexual sin'."

[26]Then Paul took the four men with him. The next day, he shared in the cleansing ceremony. Then he went to the Temple.[d] Paul announced the time when the days of the cleansing ceremony would be finished. On the last day an offering would be given for each of the men.

[27]The seven days were almost over. But some Jews from Asia saw Paul at the Temple. They caused all the people to be upset, and they grabbed Paul. [28]They shouted, "Men of Israel, help us! This is the man who goes everywhere teaching things that are against the law of Moses, against our people, and against this Temple. And now he has brought some Greek men into the Temple. He has made this holy place unclean!"[d] [29](The Jews said this because they had seen Trophimus with Paul in Jerusalem. Trophimus was a man from Ephesus. The Jews thought that Paul had brought him into the Temple.)

[30]All the people in Jerusalem became very upset. They ran and took Paul and dragged him out of the Temple. The Temple doors were closed immediately. [31]The people were about to kill Paul. Now the commander of the Roman army in Jerusalem learned that there was trouble in the whole city. [32]Immediately he ran to the place where the crowd was gathered. He brought officers and soldiers with him, and the people saw them. So they stopped beating Paul. [33]The commander went to Paul and arrested him. He told his soldiers to tie Paul with two chains. Then he asked, "Who is this man? What has he done wrong?" [34]Some in the crowd were yelling one thing, and some were yelling another. Because of all this confusion and shouting, the commander could not learn what had happened. So he ordered the soldiers to take Paul to the army barracks. [35-36]The whole mob was following them. When the soldiers came to the steps, they had to carry Paul. They did this because the people were ready to hurt him. They were shouting, "Kill him!"

[37]The soldiers were about to take Paul into the army barracks. But he spoke to the commander, "May I say something to you?"

The commander said, "Do you speak Greek? [38]I thought you were the Egyptian who started some trouble against the government not long

---

cleansing ceremony The special things Jews did to end the Nazirite promise.
shave their heads The Jews did this to show that their promise was finished.

ago. He led 4,000 killers out to the desert."

³⁹Paul said, "No, I am a Jew from Tarsus in the country of Cilicia. I am a citizen of that important city. Please, let me speak to the people."

⁴⁰The commander gave permission, so Paul stood on the steps. He waved with his hand so that the people would be quiet. When there was silence, Paul spoke to them in the Jewish language.ⁿ

Paul Speaks to the People

22 Paul said, "Brothers and fathers, listen to me! I will make my defence to you." ²When the Jews heard him speaking the Jewish language,ⁿ they became very quiet. Paul said, ³"I am a Jew. I was born in Tarsus in the country of Cilicia. I grew up in this city. I was a student of Gamaliel.ⁿ He carefully taught me everything about the law of our ancestors. I was very serious about serving God, just as are all of you here today. ⁴I hurt the people who followed the Way of Jesus. Some of them were even killed. I arrested men and women and put them in jail. ⁵The high priest and the whole council of older Jewish leaders can tell you that this is true. These leaders gave me letters to the Jewish brothers in Damascus. So I was going there to arrest these people and bring them back to Jerusalem to be punished.

⁶"But something happened to me on my way to Damascus. It was about noon when I came near Damascus. Suddenly a bright light from heaven flashed all around me. ⁷I fell to the ground and heard a voice saying, 'Saul, Saul, why are you doing things against me?' ⁸I asked, 'Who are you, Lord?' The voice said, 'I am Jesus from Nazareth. I am the One you are trying to hurt'. ⁹The men who were

with me did not understand the voice. But they saw the light. ¹⁰I said, 'What shall I do, Lord?' The Lord answered, 'Get up and go to Damascus. There you will be told about all the things I have planned for you to do'. ¹¹I could not see, because the bright light had made me blind. So the men led me into Damascus.

¹²"There a man named Ananias came to me. He was a religious man; he obeyed the law of Moses. All the Jews who lived there respected him. ¹³Ananias came to me, stood by me, and said, 'Brother Saul, see again!' Immediately I was able to see him. ¹⁴Ananias told me, 'The God of our fathers chose you long ago. He chose you to know his plan. He chose you to see the Righteous One and to hear words from him. ¹⁵You will be his witness to all people. You will tell them about the things you have seen and heard. ¹⁶Now, why wait any longer? Get up, be baptised, and wash your sins away. Do this, trusting in him to save you'.

¹⁷"Later, I returned to Jerusalem. I was praying in the Temple,ᵈ and I saw a vision. ¹⁸I saw the Lord saying to me, 'Hurry! Leave Jerusalem now! The people here will not accept the truth about me'. ¹⁹But I said, 'Lord, they know that in every synagogueᵈ I put the believers in jail and beat them. ²⁰They also know that I was there when Stephen, your witness, was killed. I stood there and agreed that they should kill him. I even held the coats of the men who were killing him!' ²¹But the Lord said to me, 'Leave now. I will send you far away to the non-Jewish people'."

²²The crowd listened to Paul until he said this. Then they began shouting, "Kill him! Get him out of the world! A man like this should not be allowed to live!" ²³They shouted and

Jewish language Aramaic, the language of the Jews in the first century.
Gamaliel A very important teacher of the Pharisees, a Jewish religious group (Acts 5:34).

threw off their coats.ⁿ They threw dust into the air.ⁿ

24Then the commander ordered the soldiers to take Paul into the army barracks and beat him. The commander wanted to make Paul tell why the people were shouting against him like this. 25So the soldiers were tying him up, preparing to beat him. But Paul said to an officer there, "Do you have the right to beat a Roman citizenⁿ who has not been proved guilty?"

26When the officer heard this, he went to the commander and told him about it. The officer said, "Do you know what you are doing? This man is a Roman citizen!"

27The commander came to Paul and said, "Tell me, are you really a Roman citizen?"

He answered, "Yes."

28The commander said, "I paid a lot of money to become a Roman citizen."

But Paul said, "I was born a citizen."

29The men who were preparing to question Paul moved away from him immediately. The commander was frightened because he had already tied Paul, and Paul was a Roman citizen.

Paul Speaks to Jewish Leaders

30The next day the commander decided to learn why the Jews were accusing Paul. So he ordered the leading priests and the Jewish council to meet. The commander took Paul's chains off. Then he brought Paul out and stood him before their meeting.

23 Paul looked at the Jewish council and said, "Brothers, I have lived my life in a good way before God up to this day." 2Ananias,ⁿ the high priest, heard this and told the men who were standing near Paul to hit him on his mouth. 3Paul said to Ananias, "God will hit you too! You are like a dirty wall that has been painted white! You sit there and judge me, using the law of Moses. But you are telling them to hit me, and that is against the law."

4The men standing near Paul said to him, "You cannot talk like that to God's high priest! You are insulting him!"

5Paul said, "Brothers, I did not know this man was the high priest. It is written in the Scriptures,ᵈ 'You must not curse a leader of your people'."ⁿ

6Some of the men in the meeting were Sadducees,ᵈ and others were Pharisees.ᵈ So Paul shouted to them, "My brothers, I am a Pharisee and my father was a Pharisee! I am on trial here because I hope that people will rise from death!"

7When Paul said this, there was an argument between the Pharisees and the Sadducees. The group was divided. 8(The Sadducees believe that after people die, they cannot live again. The Sadducees also teach that there are no angels or spirits. But the Pharisees believe in them all.) 9So there was a great uproar. Some of the teachers of the law, who were Pharisees, stood up and argued, "We find nothing wrong with this man! Maybe an angel or a spirit did speak to him."

10The argument was beginning to turn into a fight. The commander was afraid that the Jews would tear Paul to pieces. So the commander told the soldiers to go down and take Paul

---

threw off their coats This showed that the Jews were very angry at Paul.
threw dust into the air This showed even greater anger.
Roman citizen Roman law said that Roman citizens must not be beaten before they had a trial.
Ananias This is not the same man as the one named Ananias in Acts 22:12.
'You . . . people.' Quotation from Exodus 22:28.

away and put him in the army barracks.

¹¹The next night the Lord came and stood by Paul. He said, "Be brave! You have told people in Jerusalem about me. You must do the same in Rome also."

¹²In the morning some of the Jews made a plan to kill Paul. They made a promise that they would not eat or drink anything until they had killed him. ¹³There were more than 40 Jews who made this plan. ¹⁴They went and talked to the leading priests and the older Jewish leaders. They said, "We have made a promise to ourselves that we will not eat or drink until we have killed Paul! ¹⁵So this is what we want you to do: send a message to the commander to bring Paul out to you. Tell him you want to ask Paul more questions. We will be waiting to kill him while he is on the way here."

¹⁶But Paul's nephew heard about this plan. He went to the army barracks and told Paul about it. ¹⁷Then Paul called one of the officers and said, "Take this young man to the commander. He has a message for him."

¹⁸So the officer brought Paul's nephew to the commander. The officer said, "The prisoner, Paul, asked me to bring this young man to you. He wants to tell you something."

¹⁹The commander led the young man to a place where they could be alone. The commander asked, "What do you want to tell me?"

²⁰The young man said, "The Jews have decided to ask you to bring Paul down to their council meeting tomorrow. They want you to think that they are going to ask him more questions. ²¹But don't believe them! There are more than 40 men who are hiding and waiting to kill Paul. They have all made a promise not to eat or drink until they have killed him! Now they are waiting for you to agree."

²²The commander sent the young man away. He said to him, "Don't tell anyone that you have told me about their plan."

Paul Is Sent to Caesarea

²³Then the commander called two officers. He said to them, "I need some men to go to Caesarea. Get 200 soldiers ready. Also, get 70 horsemen and 200 men with spears. Be ready to leave at nine o'clock tonight. ²⁴Get some horses for Paul to ride. He must be taken to Governor Felix safely." ²⁵And he wrote a letter that said:

²⁶From Claudius Lysias.

To the Most Excellent Governor Felix:

Greetings.

²⁷The Jews had taken this man, and they planned to kill him. But I learned that he is a Roman citizen, so I went with my soldiers and saved him. ²⁸I wanted to know why they were accusing him. So I brought him before their council meeting. ²⁹I learned that the Jews said Paul did some things that were wrong. But these charges were about their own laws. And no charge was worthy of jail or death. ³⁰I was told that some of the Jews were planning to kill Paul. So I sent him to you at once. I also told those Jews to tell you what they have against him.

³¹So the soldiers did what they were told. They took Paul and brought him to the city of Antipatris that night. ³²The next day the horsemen went with Paul to Caesarea. But the other soldiers went back to the army barracks in Jerusalem. ³³The horsemen came to Caesarea and gave the letter to the governor. Then they turned Paul over to him. ³⁴The governor read the letter. Then he asked Paul, "What area are you from?" He learned that Paul was from Cilicia. ³⁵He said, "I will hear your case when those who are against you come here too." Then the

governor gave orders for Paul to be kept under guard in the palace. (This building had been built by Herod.)

The Jews Accuse Paul

24 Five days later Ananias, the high priest, went to the city of Caesarea. With him were some of the older Jewish leaders and a lawyer named Tertullus. They had come to make charges against Paul before the governor. ²Paul was called into the meeting, and Tertullus began to accuse him, saying: "Most Excellent Felix! Our people enjoy much peace because of you, and many wrong things in our country are being made right through your wise help. ³We accept these things always and in every place. And we are thankful for them. ⁴But I do not want to take any more of your time. I beg you to be kind and listen to our few words. ⁵This man is a troublemaker. He makes trouble among the Jews everywhere in the world. He is a leader of the Nazarene*d* group. ⁶Also, he was trying to make the Temple*d* unclean,*d* but we stopped him.*n* ⁸You can decide if all these things are true. Ask him some questions yourself." ⁹The other Jews agreed and said that all of this was true.

¹⁰The governor made a sign for Paul to speak. So Paul said, "Governor Felix, I know that you have been a judge over this nation for a long time. So I am happy to defend myself before you. ¹¹I went to worship in Jerusalem only 12 days ago. You can learn for yourself that this is true. ¹²Those who are accusing me did not find me arguing with anyone in the Temple. I was not stirring up the people. And I was not making trouble in the Temple or in the synagogues*d* or in the city. ¹³They

cannot prove the things they are saying against me now. ¹⁴But I will tell you this: I worship the God of our ancestors as a follower of the Way of Jesus. The Jews say that the Way of Jesus is not the right way. But I believe everything that is taught in the law of Moses and that is written in the books of the Prophets.*d* ¹⁵I have the same hope in God that they have—the hope that all people, good and bad, will be raised from death. ¹⁶This is why I always try to do what I believe is right before God and men.

¹⁷"I was away from Jerusalem for several years. I went back there to bring money to my people and to offer sacrifices. ¹⁸I was doing this when they found me in the Temple. I had finished the cleansing ceremony. I had not made any trouble; no people were gathering around me. ¹⁹But some Jews from the country of Asia were there. They should be here, standing before you. If I have really done anything wrong, they are the ones who should accuse me. ²⁰Or ask these Jews here if they found any wrong in me when I stood before the Jewish council in Jerusalem. ²¹But I did say one thing when I stood before them: 'You are judging me today because I believe that people will rise from death!'"

²²Felix already understood much about the Way of Jesus. He stopped the trial and said, "When commander Lysias comes here, I will decide about your case." ²³Felix told the officer to keep Paul guarded. But he told the officer to give Paul some freedom and to let his friends bring what he needed.

Paul Speaks to Felix and His Wife

²⁴After some days Felix came with

Verse 6 Some Greek copies add 6b-8a: "And we wanted to judge him by our own law. ⁷But the officer Lysias came and used much force to take him from us. ⁸And Lysias commanded his people to come to you to accuse us."

his wife, Drusilla, who was a Jew. He asked for Paul to be brought to him. He listened to Paul talk about believing in Christ Jesus. ²⁵But Felix became afraid when Paul spoke about things like right living, self-control, and the time when God will judge the world. He said, "Go away now. When I have more time, I will call for you." ²⁶At the same time Felix hoped that Paul would give him some money. So he sent for Paul often and talked with him.

²⁷But after two years, Porcius Festus became governor. Felix was no longer governor, but he had left Paul in prison to please the Jews.

Paul Asks to See Caesar

25 Three days after Festus became governor, he went from Caesarea to Jerusalem. ²There the leading priests and the important Jewish leaders made charges against Paul before Festus. ³They asked Festus to do something for them. They wanted him to send Paul back to Jerusalem. (They had a plan to kill Paul on the way.) ⁴But Festus answered, "No! Paul will be kept in Caesarea. I will return there soon myself. ⁵Some of your leaders should go with me. They can accuse the man there in Caesarea, if he has really done something wrong."

⁶Festus stayed in Jerusalem another eight or ten days. Then he went back to Caesarea. The next day he told the soldiers to bring Paul before him. Festus was seated on the judge's seat ⁷when Paul came into the room. The Jews who had come from Jerusalem stood around him. They started making serious charges against Paul. But they could not prove any of them. ⁸This is what Paul said to defend himself: "I have done nothing wrong against the Jewish law, against the Temple,ᵈ or against Caesar!"ᵈ

⁹But Festus wanted to please the Jews. So he asked Paul, "Do you want to go to Jerusalem? Do you want me to judge you there on these charges?"

¹⁰Paul said, "I am standing at Caesar's judgment seat now. This is where I should be judged! I have done nothing wrong to the Jews; you know this is true. ¹¹If I have done something wrong and the law says I must die, I do not ask to be saved from death. But if these charges are not true, then no one can give me to them. No! I want Caesar to hear my case!"

¹²Festus talked about this with the people who advised him. Then he said, "You have asked to see Caesar; so you will go to Caesar!"

Paul Before King Agrippa

¹³A few days later King Agrippa and Bernice came to Caesarea to visit Festus. ¹⁴They stayed there for some time, and Festus told the king about Paul's case. Festus said, "There is a man that Felix left in prison. ¹⁵When I went to Jerusalem, the leading priests and the older Jewish leaders there made charges against him. They wanted me to sentence him to death. ¹⁶But I answered, 'When a man is accused of a crime, Romans do not hand him over just to please someone. The man must be allowed to face his accusers and defend himself against their charges'. ¹⁷So these Jews came here to Caesarea for the trial. And I did not waste time. The next day I sat on the judge's seat and commanded that the man be brought in. ¹⁸The Jews stood up and accused him. But they did not accuse him of any serious crime as I thought they would. ¹⁹The things they said were about their own religion and about a man named Jesus. Jesus died, but Paul said that he is still alive. ²⁰I did not know much about these things; so I did not ask questions. But I asked Paul, 'Do you want to go to Jerusalem and be judged there?' ²¹But he asked to be kept in Caesarea. He

wants a decision from the Emperor."
So I ordered that Paul be held until I
could send him to Caesar*d* in Rome."
²²Agrippa said to Festus, "I would
like to hear this man, too."

Festus said, "Tomorrow you will
hear him!"

²³The next day Agrippa and Bernice
appeared. They dressed and acted
like very important people. Agrippa
and Bernice, the army leaders, and
the important men of Caesarea went
into the judgement room. Then Festus
ordered the soldiers to bring Paul in.
²⁴Festus said, "King Agrippa and all
who are gathered here with us, you
see this man. All the Jewish people,
here and in Jerusalem, have complained to me about him. They shout
that he should not live any longer.
²⁵When I judged him, I could find nothing wrong. I found no reason to order
his death. But he asked to be judged
by Caesar. So I decided to send him.
²⁶But I have nothing definite to write
to the Emperor about him. So I have
brought him before all of you—
especially you, King Agrippa. I hope
that you can question him and give me
something to write. ²⁷I think it is foolish to send a prisoner to Caesar without saying what the charges are
against him."

Paul Defends Himself

26 Agrippa said to Paul, "You may
now speak to defend yourself."
Then Paul raised his hand and began
to speak. ²He said, "King Agrippa, I
will answer all the charges that the
Jews make against me. I think it is a
blessing that I can stand here before
you today. ³I am very happy to talk to
you, because you know so much about
all the Jewish customs and the things
that the Jews argue about. Please listen to me patiently.

⁴"All the Jews know about my whole
life. They know the way I lived from
the beginning in my own country and
later in Jerusalem. ⁵They have known
me for a long time. If they want to,
they can tell you that I was a good
Pharisee.*d* And the Pharisees obey
the laws of the Jewish religion more
carefully than any other group of Jewish people. ⁶Now I am on trial because
I hope for the promise that God made
to our ancestors. ⁷This is the promise
that the 12 tribes*d* of our people hope
to receive. For this hope the Jews
serve God day and night. My king, the
Jews have accused me because I hope
for this same promise! ⁸Why do any of
you people think it is impossible for
God to raise people from death?

⁹"I too thought I ought to do many
things against Jesus from Nazareth.
¹⁰And in Jerusalem I did many things
against God's people. The leading
priests gave me the power to put
many of them in jail. When they were
being killed, I agreed that it was a
good thing. ¹¹In every synagogue,*d* I
often punished them. I tried to make
them say evil things against Jesus. I
was so angry against them that I even
went to other cities to find them and
punish them.

¹²"One time the leading priests
gave me permission and the power to
go to Damascus. ¹³On the way there,
at noon, I saw a light from heaven.
The light was brighter than the sun. It
flashed all around me and the men who
were travelling with me. ¹⁴We all fell
to the ground. Then I heard a voice
speaking to me in the Jewish language." The voice said, 'Saul, Saul,
why are you doing things against me?
You are only hurting yourself by fighting me'. ¹⁵I said, 'Who are you, Lord?'
The Lord said, 'I am Jesus. I am the
One you are trying to hurt. ¹⁶Stand

Emperor The ruler of the Roman Empire, which was Europe, North Africa and the Middle
East.
Jewish language Aramaic, the language of the Jews in the first century.

up! I have chosen you to be my servant. You will be my witness—you
will tell people the things that you
have seen and the things that I will
show you. This is why I have come to
you today. [17]I will not let your own
people hurt you. And I will keep you
safe from the non-Jewish people too.
These are the people I am sending
you to. [18]I send you to open their eyes
that they may turn away from darkness to the light. I send you that they
may turn away from the power of Satan and turn to God. Then their sins
can be forgiven and they can have a
place with those people who have
been made holy by believing in me'.

[19]"King Agrippa, after I had this vision from heaven, I obeyed it. [20]I began telling people that they should
change their hearts and lives and turn
to God. I told them to do things to
show that they really had changed. I
told this first to those in Damascus,
then in Jerusalem and in every part of
Judea, and also to the non-Jewish people. [21]This is why the Jews took me
and were trying to kill me in the Temple.[d] [22]But God helped me and is still
helping me today. With God's help I
am standing here today and telling all
people what I have seen. But I am
saying nothing new. I am saying what
Moses and the prophets[d] said would
happen. [23]They said that the Christ[d]
would die and be the first to rise from
death. They said that the Christ would
bring light to the Jewish and non-
Jewish people."

Paul Tries to Persuade Agrippa

[24]While Paul was saying these
things to defend himself, Festus said
loudly, "Paul, you are out of your
mind! Too much study has driven you
insane!"

[25]Paul said, "Most Excellent Festus, I am not insane. My words are

true. They are not the words of a foolish man. [26]King Agrippa knows about
these things. I can speak freely to
him. I know that he has heard about all
of these things. They did not happen
in a corner. [27]King Agrippa, do you
believe what the prophets[d] wrote? I
know you believe!"

[28]King Agrippa said to Paul, "Do
you think you can persuade me to become a Christian in such a short
time?"

[29]Paul said, "Whether it is a short or
a long time, I pray to God that not only
you but every person listening to me
today would be saved and be like
me—except for these chains I have!"

[30]Then King Agrippa, Governor
Festus, Bernice, and all the people
sitting with them stood up [31]and left
the room. They were talking to each
other. They said, "There is no reason
why this man should die or be put in
jail." [32]And Agrippa said to Festus,
"We could let this man go free, but he
has asked Caesar[d] to hear his case."

Paul Sails for Rome

27 It was decided that we would
sail for Italy. An officer named
Julius, who served in the Emperor's[n]
army, guarded Paul and some other
prisoners. [2]We got on a ship and left.
The ship was from the city of Adra-
myttium and was about to sail to different ports in the country of Asia.
Aristarchus, a man from the city of
Thessalonica in Macedonia, went with
us. [3]The next day we came to Sidon.
Julius was very good to Paul. He gave
Paul freedom to go and visit his
friends, who took care of his needs.
[4]We left Sidon and sailed close to the
island of Cyprus because the wind was
blowing against us. [5]We went across
the sea by Cilicia and Pamphylia. Then
we came to the city of Myra, in Lycia.
[6]There the officer found a ship from

Emperor The ruler of the Roman Empire, which was Europe, North Africa and the Middle
East.

Alexandria that was going to Italy. So he put us on it.

[7]We sailed slowly for many days. We had a hard time reaching Cnidus because the wind was blowing against us. We could not go any farther that way. So we sailed by the south side of the island of Crete near Salmone. [8]We sailed along the coast, but the sailing was hard. Then we came to a place called Safe Harbours, near the city of Lasea.

[9]But we had lost a lot of time. It was now dangerous to sail, because it was already after the Day of Cleansing.[n] So Paul warned them, [10]"Men, I can see there will be a lot of trouble on this trip. The ship and the things in the ship will be lost. Even our lives may be lost!" [11]But the captain and the owner of the ship did not agree with Paul. So the officer did not believe Paul. Instead, the officer believed what the captain and owner of the ship said. [12]And that harbour was not a good place for the ship to stay for the winter. So most of the men decided that the ship should leave. The men hoped we could go to Phoenix. The ship could stay there for the winter. (Phoenix was a city on the island of Crete. It had a harbour which faced south west and north west.)

The Storm

[13]Then a good wind began to blow from the south. The men on the ship thought, "This is the wind we wanted, and now we have it!" So they pulled up the anchor. We sailed very close to the island of Crete. [14]But then a very strong wind named the "north-easter" came from the island. [15]This wind took the ship and carried it away. The ship could not sail against it. So we stopped trying and let the wind

blow us. [16]We went below a small island named Cauda. Then we were able to bring in the lifeboat, but it was very hard to do. [17]After the men took the lifeboat in, they tied ropes around the ship to hold it together. The men were afraid that the ship would hit the sandbanks of Syrtis.[n] So they lowered the sail and let the wind carry the ship. [18]The next day the storm was blowing us so hard that the men threw out some of the cargo. [19]A day later they threw out the ship's equipment. [20]For many days we could not see the sun or the stars. The storm was very bad. We lost all hope of staying alive—we thought we would die.

[21]The men had gone without food for a long time. Then one day Paul stood up before them and said, "Men, I told you not to leave Crete. You should have listened to me. Then you would not have all this trouble and loss. [22]But now I tell you to cheer up. None of you will die! But the ship will be lost. [23]Last night an angel from God came to me. This is the God I worship. I am his. [24]God's angel said, 'Paul, do not be afraid! You must stand before Caesar.[d] And God has given you this promise: He will save the lives of all those men sailing with you'. [25]So men, be cheerful! I trust in God. Everything will happen as his angel told me. [26]But we will go aground on an island."

[27]On the fourteenth night we were floating around in the Adriatic Sea.[n] The sailors thought we were close to land. [28]They threw a rope into the water with a weight on the end of it. They found that the water was 20 fathoms deep. They went a little farther and threw the rope in again. It was 15 fathoms deep. [29]The sailors were afraid that we would hit the

---

Day of Cleansing An important Jewish holy day in the Autumn. This was the time of year that bad storms happened on the sea.
Syrtis Shallow area in the sea near the Libyan coast.
Adriatic Sea The sea between Greece and Italy, including the central Mediterranean.

rocks, so they threw four anchors into the water. Then they prayed for daylight to come. 30Some of the sailors wanted to leave the ship, and they lowered the lifeboat. These sailors wanted the other men to think that they were throwing more anchors from the front of the ship. 31But Paul told the officer and the other soldiers, "If these men do not stay in the ship, your lives cannot be saved!" 32So the soldiers cut the ropes and let the lifeboat fall into the water.

33Just before dawn Paul began persuading all the people to eat something. He said, "For the past 14 days you have been waiting and watching. You have not eaten. 34Now I beg you to eat something. You need it to stay alive. None of you will lose even one hair off your heads." 35After he said this, Paul took some bread and thanked God for it before all of them. He broke off a piece and began eating. 36All the men felt better. They all started eating too. 37(There were 276 people on the ship.) 38We ate all we wanted. Then we began making the ship lighter by throwing the grain into the sea.

The Ship Is Destroyed

39When daylight came, the sailors saw land. They did not know what land it was, but they saw a bay with a beach. They wanted to sail the ship to the beach, if they could. 40So they cut the ropes to the anchors and left the anchors in the sea. At the same time, they untied the ropes that were holding the rudders. Then they raised the front sail into the wind and sailed toward the beach. 41But the ship hit a sandbank. The front of the ship stuck there and could not move. Then the big waves began to break the back of the ship to pieces.

42The soldiers decided to kill the prisoners so that none of them could swim away and escape. 43But Julius, the officer, wanted to let Paul live. He did not allow the soldiers to kill the prisoners. Instead he ordered everyone who could swim to jump into the water and swim to land. 44The rest used wooden boards or pieces of the ship. And this is how all the people made it safely to land.

Paul on the Island of Malta

28 When we were safe on land, we learned that the island was called Malta. 2It was raining and very cold. But the people who lived there were very good to us. They made us a fire and welcomed all of us. 3Paul gathered a pile of sticks for the fire. He was putting them on the fire when a poisonous snake came out because of the heat and bit him on the hand. 4The people living on the island saw the snake hanging from Paul's hand. They said to each other, "This man must be a murderer! He did not die in the sea, but Justice" does not want him to live." 5But Paul shook the snake off into the fire. He was not hurt. 6The people thought that Paul would swell up or fall down dead. The people waited and watched him for a long time, but nothing bad happened to him. So they changed their minds about Paul. Now they said, "He is a god!"

7There were some fields around there owned by a very important man on the island. His name was Publius. He welcomed us into his home and was very good to us. We stayed in his house for three days. 8Publius' father was very sick with a fever and dysentery." But Paul went to him and prayed. Then he put his hands on the man and healed him. 9After this, all the other sick people on the island came to Paul, and he healed them,

Justice The people thought there was a god named Justice who would punish bad people.
dysentery A sickness like diarrhoea.

too. ¹⁰⁻¹¹The people on the island gave us many honours. We stayed there three months. When we were ready to leave, they gave us the things we needed.

Paul Goes to Rome

We got on a ship from Alexandria. The ship had stayed on the island during the winter. On the front of the ship was the sign of the twin gods.ⁿ ¹²We stopped at Syracuse for three days and then left. ¹³From there we sailed to Rhegium. The next day a wind began to blow from the southwest, so we were able to leave. A day later we came to Puteoli. ¹⁴We found some believers there, and they asked us to stay with them for a week. Finally, we came to Rome. ¹⁵The believers in Rome heard that we were there. They came out as far as the Market of Appiusⁿ and the Three Innsⁿ to meet us. When Paul saw them, he was encouraged and thanked God.

Paul in Rome

¹⁶Then we arrived at Rome. There, Paul was allowed to live alone. But a soldier stayed with him to guard him.

¹⁷Three days later Paul sent for the Jewish leaders there. When they came together, he said, "Brothers, I have done nothing against our people. I have done nothing against the customs of our fathers. But I was arrested in Jerusalem and given to the Romans. ¹⁸The Romans asked me many questions. But they could find no reason why I should be killed. They wanted to let me go free, ¹⁹but the Jews there did not want that. So I had to ask to come to Rome to have my trial before Caesar.ᵈ But I have no charge to bring against my own people. ²⁰That is why I wanted to see you and talk with you. I am bound with this

chain because I believe in the hope of Israel."

²¹The Jews answered Paul, "We have received no letters from Judea about you. None of our Jewish brothers who have come from there brought news about you or told us anything bad about you. ²²We want to hear your ideas. We know that people everywhere are speaking against this religious group."

²³Paul and the Jews chose a day for a meeting. On that day many more of the Jews met with Paul at the place he was staying. Paul spoke to them all day long, explaining the kingdom of God to them. He tried to persuade them to believe these things about Jesus. He used the law of Moses and the writings of the prophetsᵈ to do this. ²⁴Some of the Jews believed what Paul said, but others did not. ²⁵So they argued, and the Jews were ready to leave. But Paul said one more thing to them: "The Holy Spiritᵈ spoke the truth to your fathers through Isaiah the prophet. He said,

²⁶'Go to this people and say:
You will listen and listen, but you
    will not understand.
You will look and look, but you
    will not learn.
²⁷For these people have become
    stubborn.
They don't hear with their ears.
And they have closed their
    eyes.
Otherwise, they might really
    understand
what they see with their eyes
and hear with their ears.
They might really understand in
    their minds.
If they did this, they would come
    back to me and be forgiven'.
                        Isaiah 6:9-10

²⁸"I want you Jews to know that

twin gods Statues of Castor and Pollux, gods in old Greek tales.
Market of Appius A town about 43 kilometres from Rome.
Three Inns A town about 48 kilometres from Rome.

God has also sent his salvation to the non-Jewish people. They will listen!"

²⁹ *n*

³⁰Paul stayed two full years in his own rented house. He welcomed all people who came and visited him. ³¹He preached about the kingdom of God and taught about the Lord Jesus Christ. He was very bold, and no one tried to stop him from speaking.

Verse 29 Some late Greek copies add verse 29: "After Paul said this, the Jews left. They were arguing very much with each other."

ROMANS

God's Plan to Save Us

1 From Paul, a servant of Christ Jesus. God called me to be an apostle[d] and chose me to tell the Good News.[d]

[2]God promised this Good News long ago through his prophets.[d] That promise is written in the Holy Scriptures.[d] [3-4]The Good News is about God's Son, Jesus Christ our Lord. As a man, he was born from the family of David. But through the Spirit[d] of holiness he was appointed to be God's Son with great power by rising from death. [5]Through Christ, God gave me the special work of an apostle. This was to lead people of all nations to believe and obey. I do this work for Christ. [6]And you who are in Rome are also called to belong to Jesus Christ.

[7]This letter is to all of you in Rome whom God loves and has called to be his holy people.

May God our Father and the Lord Jesus Christ show you kindness and give you peace.

A Prayer of Thanks

[8]First I want to say that I thank my God through Jesus Christ for all of you. I thank God because people everywhere in the world are talking about your great faith. [9-10]God knows that every time I pray I always mention you. God is the One I serve with my whole heart by telling the Good News[d] about his Son. I pray that I will be allowed to come to you, and this will happen if God wants it. [11]I want very much to see you, to give you some spiritual gift to make you strong. [12]I mean that I want us to help each other with the faith that we have.

Your faith will help me, and my faith will help you. [13]Brothers, I want you to know that I planned many times to come to you. But this has not been possible. I wanted to come so that I could help you grow spiritually. I wanted to help you as I have helped the other non-Jewish people.

[14]I must serve all people — Greeks and non-Greeks, the wise and the foolish. [15]That is why I want so much to preach the Good News to you in Rome.

[16]I am proud of the Good News. It is the power God uses to save everyone who believes — to save the Jews first, and also to save the non-Jews. [17]The Good News shows how God makes people right with himself. God's way of making people right with him begins and ends with faith. As the Scripture[d] says, "The person who is made right with God by faith will live for ever."[n]

All People Have Done Wrong

[18]God's anger is shown from heaven against all the evil and wrong things that people do. By their own evil lives they hide the truth. [19]God shows his anger because everything that may be known about God has been made clear. Yes, God has clearly shown them everything that may be known about him. [20]There are things about God that people cannot see — his eternal power and all the things that make him God. But since the beginning of the world those things have been easy to understand. They are made clear by what God has made. So people have no excuse for the bad things they

do. ²¹They knew God. But they did not give glory to God, and they did not thank him. Their thinking became useless. Their foolish minds were filled with darkness. ²²They said they were wise, but they became fools. ²³They gave up the glory of God who lives for ever. They traded that glory for the worship of idols made to look like earthly people. They traded God's glory for things that look like birds, animals, and snakes.

²⁴People were full of sin, wanting only to do evil. So God let them go their sinful way. They became full of sexual sin, using their bodies wrongly with each other. ²⁵They traded the truth of God for a lie and worshipped and served things that were made by man. But they did not worship and serve the God who made those things. God should be praised for ever. Amen.

²⁶Because people did those things, God left them and let them do the shameful things they wanted to do. Women stopped having natural sex and started having sex with other women. ²⁷In the same way, men stopped having natural sex and began wanting each other. Men did shameful things with other men. And in their bodies they received the punishment for those wrongs.

²⁸People did not think it was important to have a true knowledge of God. So God left them and allowed them to have their own worthless thinking. And so those people do the things that they should not do. ²⁹They are filled with every kind of sin, evil, selfishness, and hatred. They are full of jealousy, murder, fighting, lying, and thinking the worst about each other. They gossip ³⁰and say evil things about each other. They hate God. They are rude and conceited and boast about themselves. They invent ways of doing evil. They do not obey their parents. ³¹They are foolish, they

do not keep their promises, and they show no kindness or mercy to other people. ³²They know God's law says that those who live like this should die. But they continue to do these evil things. And they also feel that those who do these things are doing right.

You People Also Are Sinful

2 If you think that you can judge others, then you are wrong. You too are guilty of sin. You judge people, but you do the same bad things they do. So when you judge them, you are really judging yourself guilty. ²God judges those who do wrong things. And we know that God's judging is right. ³You judge those who do wrong, but you do wrong yourselves. Do you think you will be able to escape the judgement of God? ⁴God has been very kind to you, and he has been patient with you. God has been waiting for you to change. But you think nothing of his kindness. Perhaps you do not understand that God is kind to you so that you will change your hearts and lives. ⁵But you are hard and stubborn and refuse to change. So you are making your own punishment greater and greater on the day God shows his anger. On that day all people will see God's right judgements. ⁶God will reward or punish every person for what he has done. ⁷Some people live for God's glory, for honour, and for life that has no end. They live for those things by always continuing to do good. God will give life for ever to them. ⁸But other people are selfish and refuse to follow truth. They follow evil. God will give them his punishment and anger. ⁹He will give trouble and suffering to everyone who does evil — to the Jews first and also to the non-Jews. ¹⁰But God will give glory, honour, and peace to everyone who does good — to the Jews first and also to the non-Jews. ¹¹For God judges all people in the same way.

¹²People who have God's law and those who have never heard of the law are all the same when they sin. Those who do not have the law and are sinners will be lost. And, in the same way, people who have the law and are sinners will be judged by the law. ¹³Hearing the law does not make people right with God. The law makes people right with God only if they obey what the law says. ¹⁴(The non-Jews do not have the law. But when they freely do things that the law commands, then they are the law for themselves. This is true even though they do not have the law. ¹⁵They show that in their hearts they know what is right and wrong, just as the law commands. And they also show this by the way they feel about right and wrong. Sometimes their thoughts tell them they did wrong. And sometimes their thoughts tell them they did right.) ¹⁶All these things will happen on the day when God will judge the secret thoughts of people's hearts. The Good News[d] that I preach says that God will judge everyone through Christ Jesus.

The Jews and the Law

¹⁷What about you? You call yourself a Jew. You trust in the law of Moses and boast that you are close to God. ¹⁸You know what God wants you to do. And you know the things that are important because you have learned the law. ¹⁹You think you are a guide for the blind and a light for those who are in darkness. ²⁰You think you can show foolish people what is right and teach those who know nothing. You have the law; so you think you know everything and have all truth. ²¹You teach other people. So why don't you teach yourself? You tell others not to steal. But you yourselves steal. ²²You say that others must not take part in

adultery.[d] But you yourselves are guilty of that sin. You hate idols. But you steal from temples. ²³You boast about having God's law. But you bring shame to God by breaking his law. ²⁴It is written in the Scriptures:[d] "The non-Jews speak against God's name because of you Jews."[n]

²⁵If you follow the law, then your circumcision[d] has meaning. But if you break the law, then it is as if you were never circumcised. ²⁶The non-Jews are not circumcised. But if they do what the law says, then it is as if they were circumcised. ²⁷You Jews have the written law and circumcision, but you break the law. So those who are not circumcised in their bodies, but still obey the law, will show that you are guilty.

²⁸A person is not a true Jew if he is only a Jew in his physical body. True circumcision is not only on the outside of the body. ²⁹A person is a true Jew only if he is a Jew inside. True circumcision is done in the heart by the Spirit,[d] not by the written law. Such a person gets praise from God, not from other people.

3 So, do Jews have anything that other people do not have? Is there anything special about being circumcised? ²Yes, of course, there is in every way. The most important thing is this: God trusted the Jews with his teachings. ³It is true that some Jews were not faithful to God. But will that stop God from doing what he promised? ⁴No! God will continue to be true even when every person is false. As the Scriptures[d] say:

"So your words may be shown to
    be right.
You are fair when you judge
    me."   *Psalm 51:4*

⁵When we do wrong, that shows more clearly that God is right. So can we say that God is wrong to punish

"The non-Jews . . . Jews." Quotation from Isaiah 52:5; Ezekiel 36:20.

us? (I am talking as men might talk.) [6]No! If God could not punish us, then God could not judge the world.

[7]A person might say, "When I lie, it really gives God glory, because my lie shows God's truth. So why am I judged a sinner?" [8]It would be the same to say, "We should do evil so that good will come." Some people find fault with us and say that we teach this. Those who say such things about us are wrong, and they should be punished.

All People Are Guilty

[9]So are we Jews better than others? No! We have already said that Jews and non-Jews are the same. They are all guilty of sin. [10]As the Scriptures[d] say:

"There is no one without sin.
    None!
[11] There is no one who
        understands.
    There is no one who looks to
        God for help.
[12]All have turned away.
    Together, everyone has become
        evil.
    None of them does anything
        good."   *Psalm 14:1-3*
[13]"Their throats are like open
        graves.
    They use their tongues for
        telling lies."   *Psalm 5:9*
    "Their words are like snake's
        poison."   *Psalm 140:3*
[14] "Their mouths are full of cursing
        and hate."   *Psalm 10:7*
[15]"They are always ready to kill
        people.
[16] Everywhere they go they cause
        ruin and misery.
[17]They don't know how to live in
        peace."   *Isaiah 59:7-8*
[18] "They have no fear of or
        respect for God."   *Psalm 36:1*
[19]The law commands many things. We know that those commands are for those who are under the law. This

stops all excuses and brings the whole world under God's judgement, [20]because no one can be made right with God by following the law. The law only shows us our sin.

How God Makes People Right

[21]But God has a way to make people right with him without the law. And God has now shown us that way which the law and the prophets[d] told us about. [22]God makes people right with himself through their faith in Jesus Christ. This is true for all who believe in Christ, because all are the same. [23]All people have sinned and are not good enough for God's glory. [24]People are made right with God by his grace, which is a free gift. They are made right with God by being made free from sin through Jesus Christ. [25]God gave Jesus as a way to forgive sin through faith. And all of this is because of the blood of Jesus' death. This showed that God always does what is right and fair. God was right in the past when he was patient and did not punish people for their sins. [26]And God gave Jesus to show today that God does what is right. God did this so that he could judge rightly and also make right any person who has faith in Jesus.

[27]So do we have a reason to boast about ourselves? No! And why not? It is the way of faith that stops all boasting, not the way of following the law. [28]A person is made right with God through faith, not through what he does to follow the law. [29]Is God only the God of the Jews? Is he not also the God of the non-Jews? [30]Of course he is, for there is only one God. He will make Jews right with him by their faith. And he will also make non-Jews right with him through their faith. [31]So do we destroy the law by following the way of faith? No! Faith causes us to be what the law truly wants.

The Example of Abraham

4 So what can we say about Abraham,[n] the father of our people? What did he learn about faith? [2]If Abraham was made right by the things he did, then he had a reason to boast. But he could not boast before God. [3]The Scripture[d] says, "Abraham believed God. And that faith made him right with God."[n]

[4]When a person works, his pay is not given to him as a gift. He earns the pay he gets. [5]But a person cannot do any work that will make him right with God. So he must trust in God. Then God accepts his faith, and that makes him right with God. God is the One who can make even those who are evil right in his sight. [6]David said the same thing. He said that a person is truly blessed when God does not look at what he has done but accepts him as good:

[7]"Happy are they
   whose sins are forgiven,
   whose wrongs are pardoned.
[8]Happy is the person
   whom the Lord does not
     consider guilty."   *Psalm 32:1-2*

[9]Is this blessing only for those who are circumcised?[d] Or is it also for those who are not circumcised? We have already said that God accepted Abraham's faith, and that faith made him right with God. [10]So how did this happen? Did God accept Abraham before or after he was circumcised? God accepted him before his circumcision. [11]Abraham was circumcised later to show that God accepted him. His circumcision was proof that he was right with God through faith before he was circumcised. So Abraham is the father of all those who believe but are not circumcised. He is the father of all believers who are accepted as being

right with God. [12]And Abraham is also the father of those who have been circumcised. But it is not their circumcision that makes him their father. He is their father only if they live following the faith that our father Abraham had before he was circumcised.

God Keeps His Promise

[13]Abraham[n] and his descendants[d] received the promise that the whole world would belong to them. But Abraham did not receive that promise through the law. He received it because he was right with God through his faith. [14]If people could receive what God promised by following the law, then faith is worthless. And God's promise to Abraham is worthless, [15]because the law can only bring God's anger. But if there is no law, then there is nothing to disobey.

[16]So people receive God's promise by having faith. This happens so that the promise can be a free gift. And if the promise is a free gift, then all of Abraham's children can have that promise. The promise is not only for those people that live under the law of Moses. It is for anyone who lives with faith like Abraham. He is the father of us all. [17]As it is written in the Scriptures:[d] "I am making you a father of many nations."[n] This is true before God. Abraham believed in God—the God who gives life to the dead and decides that things will happen that have not yet happened.

[18]There was no hope that Abraham would have children. But Abraham believed God and continued hoping. And that is why he became the father of many nations. As God told him, "Your descendants will also be too many to count."[n] [19]Abraham was almost 100 years old, well past the age for hav-

---

Abraham Most respected ancestor of the Jews. Every Jew hoped to see Abraham.
"Abraham . . . God." Quotation from Genesis 15:6.
"I . . . nations." Quotation from Genesis 17:5.
"Your . . . count." Quotation from Genesis 15:5.

ing children. Also, Sarah could not have children. Abraham thought about all this. But his faith in God did not become weak. [20]He never doubted that God would keep his promise. Abraham never stopped believing. He grew stronger in his faith and gave praise to God. [21]Abraham felt sure that God was able to do the thing that God promised. [22]So, "God accepted Abraham's faith, and that made him right with God."[n] [23]Those words ("God accepted Abraham's faith") were written not only for Abraham. [24]They were written also for us. God will accept us also because we believe. We believe in the One who raised Jesus our Lord from death. [25]Jesus was given to die for our sins. And he was raised from death to make us right with God.

Right with God

5 We have been made right with God because of our faith. So we have peace with God through our Lord Jesus Christ. [2]Through our faith, Christ has brought us into that blessing of God's grace that we now enjoy. And we are happy because of the hope we have of sharing God's glory. [3]And we also have joy with our troubles because we know that these troubles produce patience. [4]And patience produces character, and character produces hope. [5]And this hope will never disappoint us, because God has poured out his love to fill our hearts. God gave us his love through the Holy Spirit,[d] whom God has given to us.

[6]Christ died for us while we were still weak. We were living against God, but at the right time, Christ died for us. [7]Very few people will die to save the life of someone else. Although perhaps for a good man someone might possibly die. [8]But Christ died for us while we were still sinners.

In this way God shows his great love for us.

[9]We have been made right with God by the blood of Christ's death. So through Christ we will surely be saved from God's anger. [10]I mean that while we were God's enemies, God made friends with us through the death of his Son. Surely, now that we are God's friends, God will save us through his Son's life. [11]And not only that, but now we are also very happy in God through our Lord Jesus Christ. Through Jesus we are now God's friends again.

Adam and Christ

[12]Sin came into the world because of what one man did. And with sin came death. And this is why all men must die—because all men sinned. [13]Sin was in the world before the law of Moses. But God does not judge people guilty of sin if there is no law. [14]But from the time of Adam to the time of Moses, everyone had to die. Adam died because he sinned by not obeying God's command. But even those who did not sin in the same way had to die.

Adam was like the One who was coming in the future. [15]But God's free gift is not like Adam's sin. Many people died because of the sin of that one man. But the grace that they received from God was much greater. Many people received God's gift of life by the grace of the one man, Jesus Christ. [16]After Adam sinned once, he was judged guilty. But the gift of God is different. God's free gift came after many sins. And the gift makes people right with God. [17]One man sinned, and so death ruled all people because of that one man. But now some people accept God's full grace and the great gift of being made right with him. They will surely have true life and rule through the one man, Jesus Christ.

[18]So one sin of Adam brought the

"God . . . God." Quotation from Genesis 15:6.

punishment of death to all people. But in the same way, one good act that Christ did makes all people right with God. And that brings true life for all. ¹⁹One man disobeyed God, and many became sinners. But in the same way, one man obeyed God, and many will be made right. ²⁰The law came to make people have more sin. But when people had more sin, God gave them more of his grace. ²¹Sin once used death to rule us. But God gave people more of his grace so that grace could rule by making people right with him. And this brings life for ever through Jesus Christ our Lord.

Dead to Sin but Alive in Christ

6 So do you think that we should continue sinning so that God will give us more and more grace? ²No! We died to our old sinful lives. So how can we continue living with sin? ³Did you forget that all of us became part of Christ when we were baptised? We shared his death in our baptism. ⁴So when we were baptised, we were buried with Christ and shared his death. We were buried with him so that we could live a new life, just as Christ was raised from death by the wonderful power of the Father.

⁵Christ died, and we have been joined with Christ by dying too. So we will also be joined with him by rising from death as he did. ⁶We know that our old life died with Christ on the cross. This was so that our sinful selves would have no power over us, and we would not be slaves to sin. ⁷Anyone who has died is made free from sin's control.

⁸If we died with Christ, we know that we will also live with him. ⁹Christ was raised from death. And we know that he cannot die again. Death has no power over him now. ¹⁰Yes, when Christ died, he died to defeat the power of sin once — enough for all time. He now has a new life, and his new life is with God. ¹¹In the same way, you

should see yourselves as being dead to the power of sin and alive with God through Christ Jesus.

¹²So, do not let sin control you in your life here on earth. You must not be ruled by the things your sinful self makes you want to do. ¹³Do not offer the parts of your body to serve sin. Do not use your bodies as things to do evil with, but offer yourselves to God. Be like people who have died and now live. Offer the parts of your body to God to be used for doing good. ¹⁴Sin will not be your master, because you are not under law but under God's grace.

Slaves of Righteousness

¹⁵So what should we do? Should we sin because we are under grace and not under law? No! ¹⁶Surely you know that when you give yourselves like slaves to obey someone, then you are really slaves of that person. The person you obey is your master. You can follow sin, or obey God. Sin brings spiritual death. But obeying God makes you right with him. ¹⁷In the past you were slaves to sin — sin controlled you. But thank God, you fully obeyed the things that were taught to you. ¹⁸You were made free from sin, and now you are slaves to goodness. ¹⁹I use this example because this is hard for you to understand. In the past you offered the parts of your body to be slaves to sin and evil. You lived only for evil. In the same way now you must give yourselves to be slaves of goodness. Then you will live only for God.

²⁰In the past you were slaves to sin, and goodness did not control you. ²¹You did evil things, and now you are ashamed of them. Those things only bring death. ²²But now you are free from sin and have become slaves of God. This brings you a life that is only for God. And this gives you life for ever. ²³When someone sins, he earns what sin pays — death. But God gives

us a free gift—life for ever in Christ Jesus our Lord.

An Example from Marriage

7 Brothers, all of you understand the law of Moses. So surely you know that the law rules over a person only while he is alive. ²For example, a woman must stay married to her husband as long as he is alive. But if her husband dies, then she is free from the law of marriage. ³But if she marries another man while her husband is still alive, the law says she is guilty of adultery.*d* But if her husband dies, then the woman is free from the law of marriage. So if she marries another man after her husband dies, she is not guilty of adultery.

⁴In the same way, my brothers, your old selves died, and you became free from the law through the body of Christ. Now you belong to someone else. You belong to the One who was raised from death. We belong to Christ so that we can be used in service to God. ⁵In the past, we were ruled by our sinful selves. The law made us want to do sinful things. And those sinful things we wanted to do controlled our bodies, so that the things we did were only bringing us death. ⁶In the past, the law held us like prisoners. But our old selves died, and we were made free from the law. So now we serve God in a new way, not in the old way with written rules. Now we serve God in the new way, with the Spirit.*d*

Our Fight Against Sin

⁷You might think that I am saying that sin and the law are the same thing. That is not true. But the law was the only way I could learn what sin meant. I would never have known what it means to want something wrong if the law had not said, "You must not want to take your neigh-

bour's things."*n* ⁸And sin found a way to use that command and cause me to want every kind of wrong thing. So sin came to me because of that command. But without the law, sin has no power. ⁹I was alive without the law before I knew the law. But when the law's command came to me, then sin began to live. ¹⁰And I died because of sin. The command was meant to bring life, but for me that command brought death. ¹¹Sin found a way to fool me by using the command. Sin used the command to make me die.

¹²So the law is holy, and the command is holy and right and good. ¹³Does this mean that something that is good brought death to me? No! Sin used something that is good to bring death to me. This happened so that I could see what sin is really like. The command was used to show that sin is something very evil.

The War Within Man

¹⁴We know that the law is spiritual. But I am not spiritual. Sin rules me as if I were its slave. ¹⁵I do not understand the things I do. I do not do the good things I want to do. And I do the bad things I hate to do. ¹⁶And if I do not want to do the bad things I do, then that means that I agree that the law is good. ¹⁷But I am not really the one who is doing these bad things. It is sin living in me that does these things. ¹⁸Yes, I know that nothing good lives in me—I mean nothing good lives in the part of me that is earthly and sinful. I want to do the things that are good. But I do not do them. ¹⁹I do not do the good things that I want to do. I do the bad things that I do not want to do. ²⁰So if I do things I do not want to do, then I am not the one doing those things. It is sin living in me that does those bad things.

²¹So I have learned this rule: when

"You . . . things." Quotation from Exodus 20:13,15-17.

I want to do good, evil is there with me. [22]In my mind, I am happy with God's law. [23]But I see another law working in my body. That law makes war against the law that my mind accepts. That other law working in my body is the law of sin, and that law makes me its prisoner. [24]What a miserable man I am! Who will save me from this body that brings me death? [25]God will. I thank him for saving me through Jesus Christ our Lord!

So in my mind I am a slave to God's law. But in my sinful self I am a slave to the law of sin.

Life in the Spirit

8 So now, those who are in Christ Jesus are not judged guilty. [2]I am not judged guilty because in Christ Jesus the law of the Spirit[d] that brings life made me free. It made me free from the law that brings sin and death. [3]The law was without power, because the law was made weak by our sinful selves. But God did what the law could not do. He sent his own Son to earth with the same human life that others use for sin. He sent his Son to be an offering to pay for sin. So God used a human life to destroy sin. [4]He did this so that we could be right as the law said we must be. Now we do not live following our sinful selves, but we live following the Spirit.

[5]Those who live following their sinful selves think only about things that their sinful selves want. But those who live following the Spirit are thinking about the things that the Spirit wants them to do. [6]If a person's thinking is controlled by his sinful self, then there is death. But if his thinking is controlled by the Spirit, then there is life and peace. [7]This is true because if a person's thinking is controlled by his sinful self, then he is against God. He refuses to obey God's law. And really

he is not able to obey God's law. [8]Those people who are ruled by their sinful selves cannot please God.

[9]But you are not ruled by your sinful selves. You are ruled by the Spirit, if that Spirit of God really lives in you. But if anyone does not have the Spirit of Christ, then he does not belong to Christ. [10]Your body will always be dead because of sin. But if Christ is in you, then the Spirit gives you life, because Christ made you right with God. [11]God raised Jesus from death. And if God's Spirit is living in you, then he will also give life to your bodies that die. God is the One who raised Christ from death. And he will give life through his Spirit that lives in you.

[12]So, my brothers, we must not be ruled by our sinful selves. We must not live the way our sinful selves want. [13]If you use your lives to do the wrong things your sinful selves want, then you will die spiritually. But if you use the Spirit's help to stop doing the wrong things you do with your body, then you will have true life.

[14]The true children of God are those who let God's Spirit lead them. [15]The Spirit that we received is not a spirit that makes us slaves again to fear. The Spirit that we have makes us children of God. And with that Spirit we say, "Father, dear Father."[n] [16]And the Spirit himself joins with our spirits to say that we are God's children. [17]If we are God's children, then we will receive the blessings God has for us. We will receive these things from God together with Christ. But we must suffer as Christ suffered, and then we will have glory as Christ has glory.

Our Future Glory

[18]We have sufferings now. But the sufferings we have now are nothing compared to the great glory that will

---

"Father, dear Father" Literally, "Abba, Father". Jewish children called their fathers "Abba".

be given to us. [19]Everything that God made is waiting with excitement for the time when God will show the world who his children are. The whole world is longing for that to happen. [20]Everything that God made was changed to become useless. This was not by its own wish. It happened because God wanted it. But there was this hope: [21]that everything God made would be set free from ruin. There was hope that everything God made would have the freedom and glory that belong to God's children.

[22]We know that everything God made has been waiting until now in pain, like a woman ready to give birth. [23]Not only the world, but we also have been waiting with pain inside us. We have the Spirit[d] as the first part of God's promise. So we are waiting for God to finish making us his own children. I mean we are waiting for our bodies to be made free. [24]We were saved, and we have this hope. If we see what we are waiting for, then that is not really hope. People do not hope for something they already have. [25]But we are hoping for something that we do not have yet. We are waiting for it patiently.

[26]Also, the Spirit helps us. We are very weak, but the Spirit helps us with our weakness. We do not know how to pray as we should. But the Spirit himself speaks to God for us, even begs God for us. The Spirit speaks to God with deep feelings that words cannot explain. [27]God can see what is in people's hearts. And he knows what is in the mind of the Spirit, because the Spirit speaks to God for his people in the way that God wants.

[28]We know that in everything God works for the good of those who love him. They are the people God called, because that was his plan. [29]God knew them before he made the world. And

God decided that they would be like his Son. Then Jesus would be the firstborn[n] of many brothers. [30]God planned for them to be like his Son. And those he planned to be like his Son, he also called. And those he called, he also made right with him. And those he made right, he also glorified.

God's Love in Christ Jesus

[31]So what should we say about this? If God is with us, then no one can defeat us. [32]God let even his own Son suffer for us. God gave his Son for us all. So with Jesus, God will surely give us all things. [33]Who can accuse the people that God has chosen? No one! God is the One who makes them right. [34]Who can say that God's people are guilty? No one! Christ Jesus died, but that is not all. He was also raised from death. And now he is on God's right side and is begging God for us. [35]Can anything separate us from the love Christ has for us? Can troubles or problems or sufferings? If we have no food or clothes, if we are in danger, or even if death comes—can any of these things separate us from Christ's love? [36]As it is written in the Scriptures:[d]

"For you we are in danger of
     death all the time.
People think we are worth no
     more than sheep to be
     killed."   *Psalm 44:22*

[37]But in all these things we have full victory through God who showed his love for us. [38-39]Yes, I am sure that nothing can separate us from the love God has for us. Not death, not life, not angels, not ruling spirits, nothing now, nothing in the future, no powers, nothing above us, nothing below us, or anything else in the whole world will ever be able to separate us from

---

firstborn Here this probably means that Christ was the first in God's family to share God's glory.

the love of God that is in Christ Jesus our Lord.

God and the Jewish People

9 I am in Christ, and I am telling you the truth. I do not lie. My feelings are ruled by the Holy Spirit,[d] and they tell me that I am not lying. [2]I have great sorrow and always feel much sadness for the Jewish people. [3]I wish I could help my Jewish brothers, my people. I would even wish that I were cursed and cut off from Christ if that would help them. [4]They are the people of Israel. They were God's chosen children. They have the glory of God and the agreements that God made between himself and his people. God gave them the law of Moses and the right way of worship. And God gave his promises to them. [5]They are the descendants[d] of our great ancestors, and they are the earthly family of Christ. Christ is God over all. Praise him for ever![n] Amen.

[6]I do not mean that God failed to keep his promise to them. But only some of the people of Israel are truly God's people.[n] [7]And only some of Abraham's[n] descendants are true children of Abraham. But God said to Abraham: "The descendants I promised you will be from Isaac."[n] [8]This means that not all of Abraham's descendants are God's true children. Abraham's true children are those who become God's children because of the promise God made to Abraham. [9]God's promise to Abraham was this: "At the right time I will return, and Sarah will have a son."[n] [10]And that is

not all. Rebekah also had sons. And those sons had the same father, our father Isaac. [11-12]But before the two boys were born, God told Rebekah, "The older will serve the younger."[n] This was before the boys had done anything good or bad. God said this before they were born so that the one chosen would be chosen because of God's own plan. He was chosen because he was the one God wanted to call, not because of anything he did. [13]As the Scripture[d] says, "I loved Jacob, but I hated Esau."[n]

[14]So what should we say about this? Is God unfair? In no way. [15]God said to Moses, "I will show kindness to anyone I want to show kindness. I will show mercy to anyone I want to show mercy."[n] [16]So God will choose the one he decides to show mercy to. And his choice does not depend on what people want or try to do. [17]The Scripture says to the king of Egypt: "I made you king so I might show my power in you. In this way my name will be talked about in all the earth."[n] [18]So God shows mercy where he wants to show mercy. And he makes stubborn the people he wants to make stubborn.

[19]So one of you will ask me: "If God controls the things we do, then why does he blame us for our sins? Who can fight his will?" [20]Do not ask that. You are only human. And human beings have no right to question God. An object cannot tell the person who made it, "Why did you make me like this?" [21]The man who makes a jar can make anything he wants to make. He

---

Christ . . . for ever! This can also mean, "May God, who rules over all things, be praised for ever!"

God's people Literally, "Israel", the people God chose to bring his blessings to the world.

Abraham Most respected ancestor of the Jews. Every Jew hoped to see Abraham.

"The descendants . . . Isaac." Quotation from Genesis 21:12.

"At . . . son." Quotation from Genesis 18:10,14.

"The older . . . younger." Quotation from Genesis 25:23.

"I . . . Esau." Quotation from Malachi 1:2-3.

"I . . . mercy." Quotation from Exodus 33:19.

"I . . . earth." Quotation from Exodus 9:16.

can use the same clay to make different things. He can make one thing for special use and another thing for daily use.

[22]It is the same way with what God has done. God wanted to show his anger and to let people see his power. But God patiently stayed with those people he was angry with—people who were ready to be destroyed. [23]God waited with patience so that he could make known his rich glory. He wanted to give that glory to the people who receive his mercy. He has prepared these people to have his glory, and [24]we are those people whom God called. He called us from the Jews and from the non-Jews. [25]As the Scripture says in Hosea:

"I will say, 'You are my people'
  to those I had called 'not my
  people'.
And I will show my love
  to those people I did not love."
                        Hosea 2:1,23
[26]"Now it is said to Israel,
  'You are not my people'.
But later they will be called
  'children of the living God'."
                        Hosea 1:10
[27]And Isaiah cries out about Israel:
"There are so many people of
  Israel.
They are like the grains of sand
  by the sea.
But only a few of them will be
  saved.
[28]For the Lord will quickly and
  completely punish the people
  on the earth."   *Isaiah 10:22-23*
[29]It is as Isaiah said:
"The Lord of heaven's armies
  allowed a few of our
  descendants to live.
Otherwise we would have been
  completely destroyed
like the cities of Sodom and
  Gomorrah."[n]   *Isaiah 1:9*

[30]So what does all this mean? It means this: the non-Jews were not trying to make themselves right with God. But they were made right with God because of their faith. [31]And the people of Israel tried to follow a law to make themselves right with God. But they did not succeed, [32]because they tried to make themselves right by the things they did. They did not trust in God to make them right. They fell over the stone that causes people to fall. [33]As it is written in the Scripture:

"I will put in Jerusalem a stone
  that causes people to
  stumble.
It is a rock that makes them fall.
Anyone who trusts in him will not
  be disappointed."
                  Isaiah 8:14; 28:16

10 Brothers, the thing I want most is for all the Jews to be saved. That is my prayer to God. [2]I can say this about them: they really try to follow God. But they do not know the right way. [3]They did not know the way that God makes people right with him. And they tried to make themselves right in their own way. So they did not accept God's way of making people right. [4]Christ ended the law, so that everyone who believes in him may be right with God.

[5]Moses writes about being made right by following the law. He says, "A person who does these things will have life for ever because of them."[n] [6]But this is what the Scripture says about being made right through faith: "Don't say to yourself, 'Who will go up into heaven?'" (That means, "Who will go up to heaven to get Christ and bring him down to earth?") [7]"And do not say, 'Who will go down into the world below?'" (That means, "Who will go down to get Christ and bring him up from death?") [8]This is what the Scripture says: "God's teaching is

Sodom, Gomorrah Two cities that God destroyed because the people were so evil.
"A person . . . them." Quotation from Leviticus 18:5.

near you; it is in your mouth and in your heart."[n] That is the teaching of faith that we tell. [9]If you use your mouth to say, "Jesus is Lord", and if you believe in your heart that God raised Jesus from death, then you will be saved. [10]We believe with our hearts, and so we are made right with God. And we use our mouths to say that we believe, and so we are saved. [11]As the Scripture says, "Anyone who trusts in him will never be disappointed."[n] [12]That Scripture says "anyone" because there is no difference between Jew and non-Jew. The same Lord is the Lord of all and gives many blessings to all who trust in him. [13]The Scripture says, "Anyone who asks the Lord for help will be saved."[n]

[14]But before people can trust in the Lord for help, they must believe in him. And before they can believe in the Lord, they must hear about him. And for them to hear about the Lord, someone must tell them. [15]And before someone can go and tell them, he must be sent. It is written, "How beautiful is the person who comes to bring Good News."[n]

[16]But not all the Jews accepted the good news. Isaiah said, "Lord, who believed what we told them?"[n] [17]So faith comes from hearing the Good News.[d] And people hear the Good News when someone tells them about Christ.

[18]But I ask: Didn't people hear the Good News? Yes, they heard — as the Scripture says:

"Their message went out through
    all the world.
It goes everywhere on earth."
                                    Psalm 19:4

[19]Again I ask: Didn't the people of Israel understand? Yes, they did understand. First, Moses says:

"I will use those who are not a
    nation to make you jealous.
I will use a nation that does not
    understand to make you
    angry."   *Deuteronomy 32:21*

[20]Then Isaiah is bold enough to say:

"I was found by those who were
    not asking me for help.
I made myself known to people
    who were not looking for
    me."   *Isaiah 65:1*

[21]But about Israel God says,

"All day long I stood ready to
    accept
people who disobey and are
    stubborn."   *Isaiah 65:2*

God Shows Mercy to All People

11 So I ask: Did God throw out his people? No! I myself am an Israelite. I am from the family of Abraham, from the tribe[d] of Benjamin. [2]God chose the Israelites to be his people before they were born. And God did not leave his people. Surely you know what the Scripture[d] says about Elijah, how he prayed to God against the people of Israel. Elijah said, [3]"They have killed your prophets,[d] and they have destroyed your altars. I am the only prophet left. And now they are trying to kill me, too."[n] [4]But what answer did God give Elijah? He said, "But I have left 7,000 people in Israel. Those 7,000 have never bowed down before Baal."[n] [5]It is the same now. There are a few people that God has chosen by his grace. [6]And if God chose them by grace, then it is not for the things they have done. If they could be made God's people by what they did, then God's

Verses 6-8 Quotations from Deuteronomy 9:4; 30:12-14; Psalm 107:26.
"Anyone ... disappointed." Quotation from Isaiah 28:16.
"Anyone ... saved." Quotation from Joel 2:32.
"How ... news." Quotation from Isaiah 52:7.
"Lord, ... them?" Quotation from Isaiah 53:1.
"They ... too." Quotation from 1 Kings 19:10,14.
"But ... Baal." Quotation from 1 Kings 19:18.

gift of grace would not really be a gift.
⁷So this is what has happened: the people of Israel tried to be right with God. But they did not succeed. But the ones God chose did become right with him. The others became hard and refused to listen to God. ⁸As it is written in the Scriptures:ᵈ

"God gave the people a dull mind
    so they could not
    understand."   *Isaiah 29:10*
"God closed their eyes so they
    could not see,
and God closed their ears so
    they could not hear.
This continues until today."
                        Deuteronomy 29:4

⁹And David says:

"Let their own feasts trap them
    and cause their ruin.
Let their feasts cause them to
    sin and be paid back.
¹⁰Let their eyes be closed so they
    cannot see.
Let their backs be for ever
    weak from troubles."
                        Psalm 69:22-23

¹¹So I ask: when the Jews fell, did that fall destroy them? No! But their mistake brought salvation to the non-Jews. This took place to make the Jews jealous. ¹²The Jews' mistake brought rich blessings for the world. And what the Jews lost brought rich blessings for the non-Jewish people. So surely the world will get much richer blessings when enough Jews become the kind of people God wants.

¹³Now I am speaking to you who are not Jews. I am an apostleᵈ to the non-Jews. So while I have that work, I will do the best I can. ¹⁴I hope I can make my own people jealous. That way, maybe I can help some of them to be saved. ¹⁵God turned away from the Jews. When that happened, God became friends with the other people in the world. So when God accepts the Jews, then surely that will bring to them life after death.

¹⁶If the first piece of bread is offered to God, then the whole loaf is made holy. If the roots of a tree are holy, then the tree's branches are holy too.

¹⁷Some of the branches from an olive tree have been broken off, and the branch of a wild olive tree has been joined to that first tree. You non-Jews are the same as that wild branch, and you now share the strength and life of the first tree, the Jews. ¹⁸So do not boast about those branches that were broken off. You have no reason to boast. Why? You do not give life to the root. The root gives life to you. ¹⁹You will say, "Branches were broken off so that I could be joined to their tree." ²⁰That is true. But those branches were broken off because they did not believe. And you continue to be part of the tree only because you believe. Do not be proud, but be afraid. ²¹If God did not let the natural branches of that tree stay, then he will not let you stay if you don't believe.

²²So you see that God is kind, but he can also be very strict. God punishes those who stop following him. But God is kind to you, if you continue following in his kindness. If you do not continue following him, you will be cut off from the tree. ²³And if the Jews will believe in God again, then God will accept the Jews back again. God is able to put them back where they were. ²⁴It is not natural for a wild branch to be part of a good tree. But you non-Jews are like a branch cut from a wild olive tree. And you were joined to a good olive tree. But those Jews are like a branch that grew from the good tree. So surely they can be joined to their own tree again.

²⁵I want you to understand this secret truth, brothers. This truth will help you understand that you do not know everything. The truth is this: part of Israel has been made stubborn. But that will change when many non-Jews have come to God. ²⁶And that is how all Israel will be saved. It is written in the Scriptures:

"The Saviour will come from
  Jerusalem;
he will take away all evil from
  the family of Jacob. *n*
²⁷And I will make this agreement
  with those people
when I take away their sins."

Isaiah 59:20-21; 27:9

²⁸The Jews refuse to accept the Good News,*d* so they are God's enemies. This has happened to help you non-Jews. But the Jews are still God's chosen people, and God loves them very much. He loves them because of the promises he made to their ancestors. ²⁹God never changes his mind about the people he calls and the things he gives them. ³⁰At one time you refused to obey God. But now you have received mercy, because those people refused to obey. ³¹And now the Jews refuse to obey, because God showed mercy to you. But this happened so that they also can receive mercy from God. ³²All people have refused to obey God. God has given them all over to their stubborn ways, so that God can show mercy to all.

Praise to God

³³Yes, God's riches are very great! God's wisdom and knowledge have no end! No one can explain the things God decides. No one can understand God's ways. ³⁴As the Scripture*d* says,
"Who has known the mind of the
  Lord?
Who has been able to give the
  Lord advice?" *Isaiah 40:13*
³⁵"No one has ever given God
  anything
that he must pay back." *Job 41:11*
³⁶Yes, God made all things. And everything continues through God and for God. To God be the glory for ever! Amen.

Give Your Lives to God

12 So brothers, since God has shown us great mercy, I beg you to offer your lives as a living sacrifice to him. Your offering must be only for God and pleasing to him. This is the spiritual way for you to worship. ²Do not change yourselves to be like the people of this world. But be changed within by a new way of thinking. Then you will be able to decide what God wants for you. And you will be able to know what is good and pleasing to God and what is perfect. ³God has given me a special gift. That is why I have something to say to everyone among you. Do not think that you are better than you are. You must see yourself as you really are. Decide what you are by the amount of faith God has given you. ⁴Each one of us has a body, and that body has many parts. These parts all have different uses. ⁵In the same way, we are many, but in Christ we are all one body. Each one is a part of that body. And each part belongs to all the other parts. ⁶We all have different gifts. Each gift came because of the grace that God gave us. If one has the gift of prophecy,*d* he should use that gift with the faith he has. ⁷If one has the gift of serving, he should serve. If one has the gift of teaching, he should teach. ⁸If one has the gift of encouraging others, he should encourage. If one has the gift of giving to others, he should give freely. If one has the gift of being a leader, he should try hard when he leads. If one has the gift of showing kindness to others, that person should do so with joy.

⁹Your love must be real. Hate what is evil. Hold on to what is good. ¹⁰Love each other like brothers and sisters. Give your brothers and sisters more honour than you want for yourselves. ¹¹Do not be lazy but work

---

Jacob Father of the 12 family groups of Israel, the people God chose to be his people.

hard. Serve the Lord with all your heart. [12]Be joyful because you have hope. Be patient when trouble comes. Pray at all times. [13]Share with God's people who need help. Bring strangers in need into your homes.

[14]Wish good for those who do bad things to you. Wish them well and do not curse them. [15]Be happy with those who are happy. Be sad with those who are sad. [16]Live together in peace with each other. Do not be proud, but make friends with those who seem unimportant. Do not think how clever you are.

[17]If someone does wrong to you, do not pay him back by doing wrong to him. Try to do what everyone thinks is right. [18]Do your best to live in peace with everyone. [19]My friends, do not try to punish others when they wrong you. Wait for God to punish them with his anger. It is written: "I am the One who punishes; I will pay people back,"[n] says the Lord. [20]But you should do this:

"If your enemy is hungry, feed him;
if your enemy is thirsty, give him a drink.
Doing this will be like pouring burning coals on his head."

Proverbs 25:21-22

[21]Do not let evil defeat you. Defeat evil by doing good.

Christians Should Obey the Law

13 All of you must obey the government rulers. No one rules unless God has given him the power to rule. And no one rules now without that power from God. [2]So if anyone is against the government, he is really against what God has commanded. And so he brings punishment on himself. [3]Those who do right do not have to fear the rulers. But people who do wrong must fear them. Do you want to be unafraid of the rulers? Then do what is right, and the ruler will praise you. [4]He is God's servant to help you. But if you do wrong, then be afraid. The ruler has the power to punish; he is God's servant to punish those who do wrong. [5]So you must obey the government. You must obey not only because you might be punished, but because you know it is the right thing to do.

[6]And this is also why you pay taxes. Rulers are working for God and give their time to their work. [7]Pay everyone, then, what you owe him. If you owe any kind of tax, pay it. Show respect and honour to them all.

Loving Others

[8]Do not owe people anything. But you will always owe love to each other. The person who loves others has obeyed all the law. [9]The law says, "You must not be guilty of adultery.[d] You must not murder anyone. You must not steal. You must not want to take your neighbour's things."[n] All these commands and all others are really only one rule: "Love your neighbour as you love yourself."[n] [10]Love never hurts a neighbour. So loving is obeying all the law.

[11]I say this because we live in an important time. Yes, it is now time for you to wake up from your sleep. Our salvation is nearer now than when we first believed. [12]The "night"[n] is almost finished. The "day"[n] is almost here. So we should stop doing things that belong to darkness and take up the weapons used for fighting in the light. [13]Let us live in a right way, like

---

"I . . . back,"   Quotation from Deuteronomy 32:35.
"You . . . things."   Quotation from Exodus 20:13-15,17.
"Love . . . yourself."   Quotation from Leviticus 19:18.
"night"   This is used as a symbol of the sinful world we live in. This world will soon end.
"day"   This is used as a symbol of the good time that is coming, when we will be with God.

people who belong to the day. We should not have wild parties or get drunk. There should be no sexual sins of any kind, no fighting or jealousy. [14]But clothe yourselves with the Lord Jesus Christ. Forget about satisfying your sinful self.

Do Not Criticise Other People

14 Do not refuse to accept into your group someone who is weak in faith. And do not argue with him about opinions. [2]One person believes that he can eat all kinds of food.[n] But if another man's faith is weak, then he believes he can eat only vegetables. [3]The one who knows that he can eat any kind of food must not feel that he is better than the one who eats only vegetables. And the person who eats only vegetables must not think that the one who eats all foods is wrong. God has accepted him. [4]You cannot judge another man's servant. His own master decides if he is doing well or not. And the Lord's servant will do well because the Lord helps him do well.

[5]One person thinks that one day is more important than another. And someone else thinks that every day is the same. Each one should be sure in his own mind. [6]The person who thinks one day is more important than other days is doing that for the Lord. And the one who eats all kinds of food is doing that for the Lord. Yes, he gives thanks to God for that food. And the man who refuses to eat some foods does that for the Lord, and he gives thanks to God. [7]For we do not live or die for ourselves. [8]If we live, we are living for the Lord. And if we die, we are dying for the Lord. So living or dying, we belong to the Lord.

[9]That is why Christ died and rose from death to live again. He did this so that he would be Lord over both the dead and the living. [10]So why do you judge your brother in Christ? And why do you think that you are better than he is? We will all stand before God, and he will judge us all. [11]Yes, it is written in the Scriptures:[d]

"Everyone will bow before me;
    everyone will say that I am God.
As surely as I live, these things
    will happen, says the Lord."

Isaiah 45:23

[12]So each of us will have to answer to God for what he has done.

Do Not Cause Others to Sin

[13]So we should stop judging each other. We must make up our minds not to do anything that will make a Christian brother sin. [14]I am in the Lord Jesus, and I know that there is no food that is wrong to eat. But if a person believes that something is wrong, then that thing is wrong for him. [15]If you hurt your brother's faith because of something you eat, then you are not really following the way of love. Do not destroy his faith by eating food that he thinks is wrong. Christ died for him. [16]Do not allow what you think is good to become what others say is evil. [17]In the kingdom of God, eating and drinking are not important. The important things are living right with God, peace, and joy in the Holy Spirit.[d] [18]Anyone who serves Christ by living this way is pleasing God and will be accepted by other people.

[19]So let us try to do what makes peace and helps one another. [20]Do not let the eating of food destroy the work of God. All foods are all right to eat, but it is wrong to eat food that causes someone else to sin. [21]It is better not to eat meat or drink wine or do anything that will cause your brother to sin.

[22]Your beliefs about these things

---

all . . . food The Jewish law said there were some foods Jews should not eat. When Jews became Christians, some of them did not understand they could now eat all foods.

should be kept secret between you and God. A person is blessed if he can do what he thinks is right without feeling guilty. [23]But if he eats something without being sure that it is right, then he is wrong because he did not believe that it was right. And if he does anything without believing that it is right, then it is a sin.

15 We who are strong in faith should help those who are weak. We should help them with their weaknesses, and not please only ourselves. [2]Let each of us please his neighbour for his good, to help him be stronger in faith. [3]Even Christ did not live to please himself. It was as the Scriptures[d] said: "When people insult you, it hurts me."[n] [4]Everything that was written in the past was written to teach us, so that we could have hope. That hope comes from the patience and encouragement that the Scriptures give us. [5]Patience and encouragement come from God. And I pray that God will help you all agree with each other the way Christ Jesus wants. [6]Then you will all be joined together, and you will give glory to God the Father of our Lord Jesus Christ. [7]Christ accepted you, so you should accept each other. This will bring glory to God. [8]I tell you that Christ became a servant of the Jews. This was to show that God's promises to the Jewish ancestors are true. [9]And he also did this so that the non-Jews could give glory to God for the mercy he gives to them. It is written in the Scriptures:

"So I will praise you among the
    non-Jewish people.
I will sing praises to your
    name."   *Psalm 18:49*
[10]The Scripture also says,
"Be happy, you non-Jews,
    together with God's people."
        Deuteronomy 32:43

[11]Again the Scripture says,
"All you non-Jews, praise the
    Lord.
All you people, sing praises to
    him."   *Psalm 117:1*
[12]And Isaiah says,
"A new king will come from
    Jesse's family.[n]
He will come to rule over the
    non-Jews;
and the non-Jews will have hope
    because of him."   *Isaiah 11:10*
[13]I pray that the God who gives hope will fill you with much joy and peace while you trust in him. Then your hope will overflow by the power of the Holy Spirit.[d]

Paul Talks About His Work

[14]My brothers, I am sure that you are full of goodness. I know that you have all the knowledge you need and that you are able to teach each other. [15]But I have written to you very openly about some things that I wanted you to remember. I did this because God gave me this special gift: [16]to be a minister of Christ Jesus to the non-Jewish people. I served God by teaching his Good News,[d] so that the non-Jewish people could be an offering that God would accept—an offering made holy by the Holy Spirit.[d]

[17]So I am proud of what I have done for God in Christ Jesus. [18]I will not talk about anything I did myself. I will talk only about what Christ has done through me in leading the non-Jewish people to obey God. They have obeyed God because of what I have said and done. [19]And they have obeyed God because of the power of miracles[d] and the great things they saw, and the power of the Holy Spirit. I preached the Good News from Jerusalem all the way around to Illyricum. And so I have finished that part of my work. [20]I always want to preach the

---

"When . . . me." Quotation from Psalm 69:9.
Jesse's family Jesse was the father of David, king of Israel. Jesus was from their family.

Good News in places where people have never heard of Christ. I do this because I do not want to build on the work that someone else has already started. ²¹But it is written in the Scriptures:*d*

"Those who were not told about
    him will see,
and those who have not heard
    about him will understand."

Isaiah 52:15

Paul's Plan to Visit Rome

²²That is why many times I was stopped from coming to you. ²³Now I have finished my work here. Since for many years I have wanted to come to you, ²⁴I hope to visit you on my way to Spain. I will enjoy being with you, and you can help me on my trip. ²⁵Now I am going to Jerusalem to help God's people. ²⁶The believers in Macedonia and Southern Greece were happy to give their money to help the poor among God's people at Jerusalem. ²⁷They were happy to do this, and really they owe it to them. These non-Jews have shared in the Jews' spiritual blessings. So they should use their material possessions to help the Jews. ²⁸I must be sure that the poor in Jerusalem get the money that has been given for them. After I do this, I will leave for Spain and stop and visit you. ²⁹I know that when I come to you, I will bring Christ's full blessing.

³⁰Brothers, I beg you to help me in my work by praying for me to God. Do this because of our Lord Jesus and the love that the Holy Spirit*d* gives us. ³¹Pray that I will be saved from the non-believers in Judea. And pray that this help I bring to Jerusalem will please God's people there. ³²Then, if God wants me to, I will come to you. I will come with joy, and together you

and I will have a time of rest. ³³The God who gives peace be with you all. Amen.

Greetings to the Christians

16 I recommend to you our sister Phoebe. She is a helper*n* in the church in Cenchrea. ²I ask you to accept her in the Lord in the way God's people should. Help her with anything she needs because she has helped me and many other people too.

³Give my greetings to Priscilla and Aquila, who work together with me in Christ Jesus. ⁴They risked their own lives to save my life. I am thankful to them, and all the non-Jewish churches are thankful to them as well. ⁵Also, greet for me the church that meets at their house.

Greetings to my dear friend Epenetus. He was the first person in the country of Asia to follow Christ. ⁶Greetings to Mary, who worked very hard for you. ⁷Greetings to Andronicus and Junias, my relatives, who were in prison with me. The apostles feel they are very important. They were believers in Christ before I was. ⁸Greetings to Ampliatus, my dear friend in the Lord. ⁹Greetings to Urbanus. He is a worker together with me for Christ. And greetings to my dear friend Stachys. ¹⁰Greetings to Apelles. He was tested and proved that he truly loves Christ. Greetings to all those who are in the family of Aristobulus. ¹¹Greetings to Herodion, my relative. Greetings to all those in the family of Narcissus who belong to the Lord. ¹²Greetings to Tryphena and Tryphosa. Those women work very hard for the Lord. Greetings to my dear friend Persis. She also has worked very hard for the Lord. ¹³Greetings to Rufus who is a special person in the Lord. Greetings to his

---

helper Literally, "deaconess". This might mean the same as one of the special women helpers in 1 Timothy 3:11.

mother, who has been a mother to me also. [14]Greetings to Asyncritus, Phlegon, Hermes, Patrobas, Hermas, and all the brothers who are with them. [15]Greetings to Philologus and Julia, Nereus and his sister, and Olympas. And greetings to all God's people with them. [16]Greet each other with a holy kiss. All of Christ's churches send greetings to you.

[17]Brothers, I ask you to look out for those who cause people to be against each other and who upset other people's faith. They are against the true teaching you learned. Stay away from them. [18]For such people are not serving our Lord Christ. They are only doing what pleases themselves. They use fancy talk and fine words to fool the minds of those who do not know about evil. [19]All the believers have heard that you obey. So I am very happy because of you. But I want you to be wise in what is good and innocent in what is evil.

[20]The God who brings peace will soon defeat Satan and give you power over him.

The grace of our Lord Jesus be with you.

[21]Timothy, a worker together with me, sends greetings, as well as Lucius, Jason, and Sosipater, my relatives.

[22]I am Tertius, and I am writing this letter from Paul. I send greetings to you in the Lord.

[23]Gaius is letting me and the whole church here use his home. He also sends greetings to you, as do Erastus and our brother Quartus. Erastus is the city treasurer here. [24] n

[25]Glory to God! God is the One who can make you strong in faith by the Good News[d] that I tell people and by the message about Jesus Christ. The message about Christ is the secret truth that was hidden for long ages past, but is now made known. [26]It has been made clear through the writings of the prophets.[d] And by the command of the eternal God it is made known to all nations, that they might believe and obey.

[27]To the only wise God be glory forever through Jesus Christ! Amen.

Verse 24 Some Greek copies add verse 24: "The grace of our Lord Jesus Christ be with all of you. Amen."

1 CORINTHIANS

Help for a Church with Problems

1 From Paul. I was called to be an apostle[d] of Christ Jesus because that is what God wanted. Also from Sosthenes, our brother in Christ.

2To the church of God in Corinth, to those people who have been made holy in Christ Jesus. You were called to be God's holy people with all people everywhere who trust in the name of the Lord Jesus Christ—their Lord and ours:

3Grace and peace to you from God our Father and the Lord Jesus Christ.

Paul Gives Thanks to God

4I always thank my God for you because of the grace that God has given you in Christ Jesus. 5In Jesus you have been blessed in every way, in all your speaking and in all your knowledge. 6The truth about Christ has been proved in you. 7So you have every gift from God while you wait for our Lord Jesus Christ to come again. 8Jesus will keep you strong until the end. He will keep you strong, so that there will be no wrong in you on the day our Lord Jesus Christ comes again. 9God is faithful. He is the One who has called you to share life with his Son, Jesus Christ our Lord.

Problems in the Church

10I beg you, brothers, in the name of our Lord Jesus Christ. I beg that all of you agree with each other, so that you will not be divided. I beg that you be completely joined together by having the same kind of thinking and the same purpose. 11My brothers, some people from Chloe's family have told me that there are arguments among you. 12This is what I mean: one of you says, "I follow Paul"; another says, "I follow Apollos"; another says, "I follow Peter"; and another says, "I follow Christ". 13Christ cannot be divided into different groups! Did Paul die on the cross for you? No! Were you baptised in the name of Paul? No! 14I am thankful that I did not baptise any of you except Crispus and Gaius. 15I am thankful, because now no one can say that you were baptised in my name. 16(I also baptised the family of Stephanas. But I do not remember that I myself baptised any others.) 17Christ did not give me the work of baptising people. He gave me the work of preaching the Good News,[d] and he sent me to preach the Good News without using words of worldly wisdom. If I used worldly wisdom to tell the Good News, the cross[n] of Christ would lose its power.

Christ Is God's Power and Wisdom

18The teaching about the cross seems foolish to those who are lost. But to us who are being saved it is the power of God. 19It is written in the Scriptures:[d]

"I will cause the wise men to lose
    their wisdom.
I will make the wise men unable
    to understand."   Isaiah 29:14

20Where is the wise person? Where is the educated person? Where is the

---

cross Paul uses the cross as a picture of the gospel, the story of Christ's death and rising from death to pay for men's sins. The cross, or Christ's death, was God's way to save men.

philosopher[n] of our times? God has made the wisdom of the world foolish. [21]The world did not know God through its own wisdom. So God chose to use the message that sounds foolish to save those who believe it. [22]The Jews ask for miracles[d] as proofs. The Greeks want wisdom. [23]But we preach Christ on the cross. This is a big problem to the Jews. And it seems foolish to the non-Jews. [24]But Christ is the power of God and the wisdom of God to those people God has called—Jews and Greeks. [25]Even the foolishness of God is wiser than men. Even the weakness of God is stronger than men.

[26]Brothers, look at what you were when God called you. Not many of you were wise in the way the world judges wisdom. Not many of you had great influence. Not many of you came from important families. [27]But God chose the foolish things of the world to shame the wise. He chose the weak things of the world to shame the strong. [28]And he chose what the world thinks is not important. He chose what the world hates and thinks is nothing. He chose these to destroy what the world thinks is important. [29]God did this so that no man can boast before him. [30]It is God who has made you part of Christ Jesus. Christ has become wisdom for us from God. Christ is the reason we are right with God and have freedom from sin; Christ is the reason we are holy. [31]So, as the Scripture[d] says, "If a person boasts, he should boast only about the Lord."[n]

The Message of Christ's Death

2 Dear brothers, when I came to you, I did not come as a proud man. I preached God's truth, but not with fancy words or a show of great learning. [2]I decided that while I was

with you I would forget about everything except Jesus Christ and his death on the cross. [3]When I came to you, I was weak and shook with fear. [4]My teaching and my speaking were not with wise words that persuade people. But the proof of my teaching was the power that the Spirit[d] gives. [5]I did this so that your faith would be in God's power, not in the wisdom of a man.

God's Wisdom

[6]Yet I speak wisdom to those who are mature. But this wisdom is not from this world or of the rulers of this world. (These rulers are losing their power.) [7]But I speak God's secret wisdom, which he has kept hidden. God planned this wisdom for our glory, before the world began. [8]None of the rulers of this world understood it. If they had, they would not have killed the Lord of glory on a cross. [9]But as it is written in the Scriptures:[d]

"no one has ever seen this.
No one has ever heard about it.
No one has ever imagined
what God has prepared for
those
who love him."   *Isaiah 64:4*

[10]But God has shown us these things through the Spirit.[d]

The Spirit knows all things, even the deep secrets of God. [11]It is like this: no one knows the thoughts that another person has. Only a person's spirit that lives in him knows his thoughts. It is the same with God. No one knows the thoughts of God. Only the Spirit of God knows God's thoughts. [12]We did not receive the spirit of the world, but we received the Spirit that is from God. We received this Spirit so that we can know all that God has given us. [13]When we speak, we do not use words taught to us by the wisdom that men have. We

---

philosopher Philosophers were those who searched for truth.
"If . . . Lord." Quotation from Jeremiah 9:24.

use words taught to us by the Spirit. We use spiritual words to explain spiritual things. [14]A person who is not spiritual does not accept the gifts that come from the Spirit of God. That person thinks they are foolish. He cannot understand the Spirit's gifts, because they can only be judged spiritually. [15]But the spiritual person is able to judge all things. Yet no one can judge him. The Scripture says:

[16]"Who has known the mind of the
    Lord?
  Who has been able to teach
    him?"   *Isaiah 40:13*

But we have the mind of Christ.

Following Men Is Wrong

3 Brothers, in the past I could not talk to you as I talk to spiritual people. I had to talk to you as I would to people of the world—babies in Christ. [2]The teaching I gave you was like milk, not solid food. I did this because you were not ready for solid food. And even now you are not ready. [3]You are still not spiritual. You have jealousy and arguing among you. This shows that you are not spiritual. You are acting like people of the world. [4]One of you says, "I follow Paul," and another says, "I follow Apollos." When you say things like this, you are acting like worldly people.

[5]Is Apollos important? No! Is Paul important? No! We are only servants of God who helped you believe. Each one of us did the work God gave us to do. [6]I planted the seed of the teaching in you, and Apollos watered it. But God is the One who made the seed grow. [7]So the one who plants is not important, and the one who waters is not important. Only God is important, because he is the One who makes things grow. [8]The one who plants and

the one who waters have the same purpose. And each will be rewarded for his own work. [9]We are workers together for God. And you are like a farm that belongs to God.

And you are a house that belongs to God. [10]Like an expert builder I built the foundation of that house. I used the gift that God gave me to do this. Others are building on that foundation. But everyone should be careful how he builds. [11]The foundation has already been built. No one can build any other foundation. The foundation that has already been laid is Jesus Christ. [12]Anyone can build on that foundation, using gold, silver, jewels, wood, grass, or straw. [13]But the work that each person does will be clearly seen, because the Day[n] will make it plain. That Day will appear with fire, and the fire will test every man's work. [14]If the building that a man puts on the foundation still stands, he will get his reward. [15]But if his building is burned up, he will suffer loss. The man will be saved, but it will be as if he escaped from a fire.

[16]You should know that you yourselves are God's temple. God's Spirit[d] lives in you. [17]If anyone destroys God's temple, God will destroy him, because God's temple is holy. You yourselves are God's temple.

[18]Do not fool yourselves. If anyone among you thinks he is wise in this world, he should become a fool. Then he can become truly wise, [19]because the wisdom of this world is foolishness to God. It is written in the Scriptures,[d] "He catches wise men in their own clever traps."[n] [20]It is also written in the Scriptures, "The Lord knows what people think. He knows they are just a puff of wind."[n] [21]So you should not boast about men. All things are yours: [22]Paul, Apollos and

---

Day The day Christ will come to judge all people and take his people home to live with him.
"He . . . traps." Quotation from Job 5:13.
"The Lord . . . wind." Quotation from Psalm 94:11.

Peter; the world, life, death, the present, and the future—all these things are yours. ²³And you belong to Christ, and Christ belongs to God.

Apostles of Christ

4 This is what people should think about us: we are servants of Christ. We are the ones God has trusted with his secret truths. ²A person who is trusted with something must show that he is worthy of that trust. ³I do not care if I am judged by you or if I am judged by any human court. I do not even judge myself. ⁴I know of no wrong that I have done. But this does not make me innocent. The Lord is the One who judges me. ⁵So do not judge before the right time; wait until the Lord comes. He will bring to light things that are now hidden in darkness. He will make known the secret purposes of people's hearts. Then God will give everyone the praise he should get.

⁶Brothers, I have used Apollos and myself as examples. I did this so that you could learn from us the meaning of the words, "Follow only what is written in the Scriptures."ᵈ Then you will not be proud of one man and hate another. ⁷Who says that you are better than others? Everything you have was given to you. And if this is so, why do you boast as if you got these things by your own power?

⁸You think you have everything you need. You think you are rich. You think you have become kings without us. I wish you really were kings! Then we could be kings together with you. ⁹But it seems to me that God has given me and the other apostlesᵈ the last place. We are like men sentenced to die. We are like a show for the whole world to see—angels and people. ¹⁰We are fools for Christ's sake. But you think you are very wise in Christ. We are weak, but you think you are strong. You receive honour, but we are hated. ¹¹Even now we still do not

have enough to eat or drink or enough clothes. We are often beaten. We have no homes. ¹²We work hard with our own hands for our food. People curse us, but we bless them. They hurt us, and we accept it. ¹³They say evil things against us, but we say only kind things to them. Even today, we are treated as though we are the rubbish of the world—the scum of the earth.

¹⁴I am not trying to make you feel ashamed. I am writing this to give you a warning as if you were my own dear children. ¹⁵For though you may have 10,000 teachers in Christ, you do not have many fathers. Through the Good Newsᵈ I became your father in Christ Jesus. ¹⁶So I beg you, please be like me. ¹⁷That is why I am sending Timothy to you. He is my son in the Lord. I love Timothy, and he is faithful. He will help you remember the way I live in Christ Jesus. This way of life is what I teach in all the churches everywhere.

¹⁸Some of you have become proud, thinking that I will not come to you again. ¹⁹But I will come very soon if the Lord wants me to. Then I will see what those who are proud can do, not what they say. ²⁰I want to see this because the kingdom of God is not talk but power. ²¹Which do you want: that I come to you with punishment, or that I come with love and gentleness?

Wickedness in the Church

5 Now, it is actually being said that there is sexual sin among you. And it is of such a bad kind that it does not happen even among those who do not know God. A man there has his father's wife. ²And still you are proud of yourselves! You should have been filled with sadness. And the man who did that sin should be put out of your group. ³My body is not there with you, but I am with you in spirit. And I have already judged the man who did

that sin. I judged him just as I would if I were really there. [4]Meet together as the people of our Lord Jesus. I will be with you in spirit, and you will have the power of our Lord Jesus with you. [5]Then give this man to Satan, so that his sinful self[n] will be destroyed. And then his spirit can be saved on the day of the Lord.

[6]Your boasting is not good. You know the saying, "Just a little yeast makes the whole batch of dough rise." [7]Take out all the old yeast so that you will be a new batch of dough. And you really are new dough without yeast. For Christ, our Passover[d] lamb, was killed to cleanse us. [8]So let us continue our feast, but not with the bread that has the old yeast. That old yeast is the yeast of sin and wickedness. But let us eat the bread that has no yeast. This is the bread of goodness and truth.

[9]I wrote to you in my letter that you should not associate with those who take part in sexual sin. [10]But I did not mean that you should not associate with the sinful people of this world. People of the world do take part in sexual sin, or they are selfish and they cheat each other, or they worship idols. But to get away from them you would have to leave this world. [11]I am writing to tell you that the person you must not associate with is this: anyone who calls himself a brother in Christ but who takes part in sexual sin, or is selfish, or worships idols, or lies about others, or gets drunk, or cheats people. Do not even eat with someone like that.

[12-13]It is not my business to judge those who are not part of the church. God will judge them. But you must judge the people who are part of the church. The Scripture[d] says, "You must get rid of the evil person among you."[n]

Judging Problems Among Christians

6 When one of you has something against a brother in Christ, why do you go to the judges in the law courts? Those people are not right with God. So why do you let them decide who is right? You should be ashamed! Why do you not let God's people decide who is right? [2]Surely you know that God's people will judge the world. So if you are to judge the world, then surely you are able to judge small things as well. [3]You know that in the future we will judge angels. So surely we can judge things in this life. [4]So if you have disagreements that must be judged, why do you take them to those who are not part of the church? They mean nothing to the church. [5]I say this to shame you. Surely there is someone among you wise enough to judge a complaint between two brothers in Christ. [6]But now one brother goes to court against another brother. And you let men who are not believers judge their case!

[7]The lawsuits that you have against each other show that you are already defeated. It would be better for you to let someone wrong you! It would be better for you to let someone cheat you! [8]But you yourselves do wrong and cheat! And you do this to your own brothers in Christ!

[9-10]Surely you know that the people who do wrong will not receive God's kingdom. Do not be fooled. These people will not receive God's kingdom: those who sin sexually, or worship idols, or take part in adultery,[d] or men who have sexual relations with other men, or steal, or are selfish, or get drunk, or lie about others, or cheat. [11]In the past, some of you were like that. But you were washed clean. You were made holy. And you were made right with God in the name of

---

sinful self Literally, "flesh". This could also mean his body.
"You . . . you." Quotation from Deuteronomy 17:7; 19:19; 22:21,24; 24:7.

the Lord Jesus Christ and by the Spirit of our God.

Use Your Bodies for God's Glory

[12]"I am allowed to do all things." But all things are not good for me to do. "I am allowed to do all things." But I must not do those things that will make me their slave. [13]"Food is for the stomach, and the stomach for food." Yes. But God will destroy them both. The body is not for sexual sin. The body is for the Lord, and the Lord is for the body. [14]By God's power God raised the Lord Jesus from death. And God will also raise us from death. [15]Surely you know that your bodies are parts of Christ himself. So I must never take parts of Christ and join them to a prostitute![d] [16]It is written in the Scriptures,[d] "The two people will become one body."[n] So you should know that a man who joins himself with a prostitute becomes one with her in body. [17]But the one who joins himself with the Lord is one with the Lord in spirit.

[18]So run away from sexual sin. Every other sin that a man does is outside his body. But the one who sins sexually sins against his own body. [19]You should know that your body is a temple for the Holy Spirit.[d] The Holy Spirit is in you. You have received the Holy Spirit from God. You do not own yourselves. [20]You were bought by God for a price. So honour God with your bodies.

About Marriage

7 Now I will discuss the things you wrote to me about. It is good for a man not to marry. [2]But sexual sin is a danger. So each man should have his own wife. And each woman should have her own husband. [3]The husband should give his wife all that she should have as his wife. And the wife should give her husband all that he should

have as her husband. [4]The wife does not have power over her own body. Her husband has the power over her body. And the husband does not have power over his own body. His wife has the power over his body. [5]Do not refuse to give your bodies to each other. But you might both agree to stay away from sexual relations for a time. You might do this so that you can give your time to prayer. Then come together again. This is so that Satan cannot tempt you in your weakness. [6]I say this to give you permission. It is not a command. [7]I wish everyone were like me. But each person has his own gift from God. One has one gift, another has another gift.

[8]Now for those who are not married and for the widows I say this: it is good for them to stay single as I am. [9]But if they cannot control their bodies, then they should marry. It is better to marry than to burn with sexual desire.

[10]Now I give this command for the married people. (The command is not from me; it is from the Lord.) A wife should not leave her husband. [11]But if she does leave, she must not marry again. Or she should go back to her husband. Also the husband should not divorce his wife.

[12]For all the others I say this (I am saying this, not the Lord): a brother in Christ might have a wife who is not a believer. If she will live with him, he must not divorce her. [13]And a woman might have a husband who is not a believer. If he will live with her, she must not divorce him. [14]The husband who is not a believer is made holy through his believing wife. And the wife who is not a believer is made holy through her believing husband. If this were not true, then your children would not be clean.[d] But now your children are holy.

[15]But if the person who is not a be-

"**The two . . . body.**" Quotation from Genesis 2:24.

liever decides to leave, let him leave. When this happens, the brother or sister in Christ is free. God called us to a life of peace. ¹⁶Wife, maybe you will save your husband; and husband, maybe you will save your wife. You do not know now what will happen later.

Live as God Called You

¹⁷But each one should continue to live the way God has given him to live—the way he was when God called him. This is a rule I make in all the churches. ¹⁸If a man was already circumcised*d* when he was called, he should not change his circumcision. If a man was without circumcision when he was called, he should not be circumcised. ¹⁹It is not important if a man is circumcised or not circumcised. The important thing is obeying God's commands. ²⁰Each one should stay the way he was when God called him. ²¹If you were a slave when God called you, do not let that bother you. But if you can be free, then become free. ²²The person who was a slave when the Lord called him is free in the Lord. He belongs to the Lord. In the same way, the one who was free when he was called is now Christ's slave. ²³You all were bought for a price. So do not become slaves of men. ²⁴Brothers, in your new life with God each one of you should continue the way you were when you were called.

Questions About Getting Married

²⁵Now I write about people who are not married. I have no command from the Lord about this, but I give my opinion. And I can be trusted, because the Lord has given me mercy. ²⁶This is a time of trouble. So I think that it is good for you to stay the way you are. ²⁷If you have a wife, then do not try to become free from her. If you are not married, then do not try to find a wife. ²⁸But if you decide to marry, this is not a sin. And it is not a sin for a girl who has never married to get married. But those who marry will have trouble in this life. And I want you to be free from this trouble.

²⁹Brothers, this is what I mean: we do not have much time left. So starting now, those who have wives should use their time to serve the Lord as if they had no wives. ³⁰Those who are sad should live as if they are not sad. Those who are happy should live as if they are not happy. Those who buy things should live as if they own nothing. ³¹Those who use the things of the world should live as if those things are not important to them. You should live like this, because this world, the way it is now, will soon be gone.

³²I want you to be free from worry. A man who is not married is busy with the Lord's work. He is trying to please the Lord. ³³But a man who is married is busy with things of the world. He is trying to please his wife. ³⁴He must think about two things—pleasing his wife and pleasing the Lord. A woman who is not married or a girl who has never married is busy with the Lord's work. She wants to give herself fully—body and soul—to the Lord. But a married woman is busy with things of the world. She is trying to please her husband. ³⁵I am saying this to help you. I am not trying to limit you. But I want you to live in the right way. And I want you to give yourselves fully to the Lord without giving your time to other things.

³⁶A man might think that he is not doing the right thing with the girl he is engaged to. The girl might be almost past the best age to marry. So he might feel that he should marry her. He should do what he wants. They should get married. It is no sin. ³⁷But another man might be more sure in his mind. There may be no need for marriage, so he is free to do what he wants. If he has decided in his own heart not to marry, he is doing the right thing. ³⁸So the man who marries

his girl does right. And the man who does not marry does even better.

³⁹A woman must stay with her husband as long as he lives. If the husband dies, she is free to marry any man she wants. But she must marry in the Lord. ⁴⁰The woman is happier if she does not marry again. This is my opinion, and I believe that I have God's Spirit.

About Food Offered to Idols

8 Now I will write about meat that is sacrificed to idols. We know that "we all have knowledge". Knowledge puffs you up with pride, but love builds up. ²Whoever thinks he knows something does not yet know anything as he should. ³But he who loves God is known by God.

⁴So this is what I say about eating meat sacrificed to idols: we know that an idol is really nothing in the world. And we know that there is only one God. ⁵It is really not important if there are things called gods, in heaven or on earth. (And there are many things that people call "gods" and "lords".) ⁶But for us there is only one God. He is our Father. All things came from him, and we live for him. And there is only one Lord—Jesus Christ. All things were made through Jesus, and we also have life through him.

⁷But not all people know this. Until now, some people have had the habit of worshipping idols. So now when they eat meat, they still feel as if it belongs to an idol. They are not sure that it is right to eat this meat. When they eat it, they feel guilty. ⁸But food will not make us closer to God. Refusing to eat does not make us less pleasing to God. And eating does not make us better in God's sight.

⁹But be careful with your freedom. Your freedom may cause those who are weak in faith to fall into sin. ¹⁰You

have "knowledge", so you might eat in an idol's temple.ⁿ Someone who is weak in faith might see you eating there. This would encourage him to eat meat sacrificed to idols. But he really thinks it is wrong. ¹¹So this weak brother is ruined because of your "knowledge". And Christ died for this brother. ¹²When you sin against your brothers in Christ like this and cause them to do what they feel is wrong, you are also sinning against Christ. ¹³So if the food I eat makes my brother fall into sin, I will never eat meat again. I will stop eating meat, so that I will not cause my brother to sin.

Paul Is like the Other Apostles

9 I am a free man. I am an apostle.^d I have seen Jesus our Lord. You people are all an example of my work in the Lord. ²Others may not accept me as an apostle, but surely you accept me. You are proof that I am an apostle in the Lord.

³Some people want to judge me. So this is the answer I give them: ⁴do we not have the right to eat and drink? ⁵Do we not have the right to bring a believing wife with us when we travel? The other apostles, the Lord's brothers, and Peter all do this. ⁶And are Barnabas and I the only ones who must work to earn our living? ⁷No soldier ever serves in the army and pays his own salary. No one ever plants a vineyard without eating some of the grapes himself. No person takes care of a flock of sheep without drinking some of the milk himself.

⁸This is not only what men think. God's law says the same thing. ⁹Yes, it is written in the law of Moses: "When an ox is working in the grain, do not cover its mouth and keep it from eating."ⁿ When God said this, was he thinking only about oxen? No.

idol's temple Building where a false god is worshipped.
"When an ox . . . eating." Quotation from Deuteronomy 25:4.

¹⁰He was really talking about us. Yes, that Scripture*d* was written for us. The one who ploughs and the one who works in the grain should hope to get some of the grain for their work. ¹¹We planted spiritual seed among you. So we should be able to harvest from you some things for this life. Surely this is not asking too much. ¹²Other men have the right to receive something from you. So surely we have this right, too. But we do not use this right. No, we put up with everything ourselves so that we will not stop anyone from obeying the Good News*d* of Christ. ¹³Surely you know that those who work at the Temple*d* get their food from the Temple. And those who serve at the altar get part of what is offered at the altar. ¹⁴It is the same with those who tell the Good News. The Lord has commanded that those who tell the Good News should get their living from this work.

¹⁵But I have not used any of these rights. And I am not writing this now to get anything from you. I would rather die than to have my reason for boasting taken away. ¹⁶Telling the Good News is not my reason for boasting. Telling the Good News is my duty — something I must do. And how bad it will be for me if I do not tell the Good News. ¹⁷If I preach because it is my own choice, I should get a reward. But I have no choice. I must tell the Good News. I am only doing the duty that was given to me. ¹⁸So what reward do I get? This is my reward: that when I tell the Good News I can offer it freely. In this way I do not use my right to be paid in my work for the Good News.

¹⁹I am free. I belong to no man. But I make myself a slave to all people. I do this to help save as many people as I can. ²⁰To the Jews I became like a Jew. I did this to help save the Jews. I myself am not ruled by the law. But to those who are ruled by the law I became like a person who is ruled by

the law. I did this to help save those who are ruled by the law. ²¹To those who are without the law I became like a person who is without the law. I did this to help save those people who are without the law. (But really, I am not without God's law — I am ruled by Christ's law.) ²²To those who are weak, I became weak so that I could help save them. I have become all things to all people. I did this so that I could save some of them in any way possible. ²³I do all this because of the Good News. I do it so that I can share in the blessings of the Good News.

²⁴You know that in a race all the runners run. But only one gets the prize. So run like that. Run to win! ²⁵All those who compete in the games use strict training. They do this so that they can win a crown. That crown is an earthly thing that lasts only a short time. But our crown will continue for ever. ²⁶So I do not run without a goal. I fight like a boxer who is hitting something — not just the air. ²⁷It is my own body that I hit. I make it my slave. I do this so that I myself will not be rejected after I have preached to others.

Don't Be like the Jews

10 Brothers, I want you to know what happened to our ancestors who followed Moses. They were all under the cloud, and they all went through the sea. ²They were all baptised as followers of Moses in the cloud and in the sea. ³They all ate the same spiritual food. ⁴And they all drank the same spiritual drink. They drank from that spiritual rock that was with them. That rock was Christ. ⁵But God was not pleased with most of them. They died in the desert.

⁶And these things that happened are examples for us. They should stop us from wanting evil things as those people did. ⁷Do not worship idols, as some of them did. It is written in the Scriptures:*d* "The people sat down to

eat and drink. Then they got up and sinned sexually."[n] [8]We should not take part in sexual sins, as some of them did. In one day 23,000 of them died because of their sins. [9]We should not test the Lord as some of them did. They were killed by snakes. [10]And do not complain as some of them did. They were killed by the angel that destroys.

[11]The things that happened to those people are examples. And they were written down to be warnings for us. For we live in a time when all these things of the past have reached their goal. [12]So anyone who thinks he is standing strong should be careful not to fall. [13]The only temptations that you have are the temptations that all people have. But you can trust God. He will not let you be tempted more than you can stand. But when you are tempted, God will also give you a way to escape that temptation. Then you will be able to stand it.

[14]So, my dear friends, stay away from worshipping idols. [15]I am speaking to you, as to intelligent people; judge for yourselves what I say. [16]We give thanks for the cup of blessing.[n] It is a sharing in the blood of Christ's death. And the bread that we break is a sharing in the body of Christ. [17]There is one loaf of bread. And we are many people. But we all share from that one loaf. So we are really one body.

[18]Think about the people of Israel: do not those who eat the sacrifices share in the altar? [19]I do not mean that the food sacrificed to an idol is something important. And I do not mean that an idol is anything at all. [20]But I say that what is sacrificed to idols is offered to demons,[d] not to God. And I do not want you to share anything

with demons. [21]You cannot drink the cup of the Lord and the cup of demons, too. You cannot share in the Lord's table and the table of demons, too. [22]Do we want to make the Lord jealous? We are not stronger than he is, are we?

How to Use Christian Freedom

[23]"We are allowed to do all things." Yes. But all things are not good for us to do. "We are allowed to do all things." Yes. But not all things help others grow stronger. [24]No one should try to do what will help only himself. He should try to do what is good for others.

[25]Eat any meat that is sold in the meat market. Do not ask questions about the meat to see if it is something you think is wrong to eat. [26]You can eat it, "because the earth and everything on it belong to the Lord."[n]

[27]Someone who is not a believer may invite you to eat with him. If you want to go, eat anything that is put before you. Do not ask questions to see if it is something you think might be wrong to eat. [28]But if anyone says to you, "That food was offered to idols," then do not eat it. Do not eat it because of that person who told you and because eating it would be something that might be thought wrong. [29]I don't mean that you think it is wrong. But the other person might think it is wrong. My own freedom should not be judged by what someone else thinks. [30]I eat the meal with thankfulness. And I do not want to be criticised because of something I thank God for.

[31]So if you eat, or if you drink, or if you do anything, do everything for the glory of God. [32]Never do anything that might make others do wrong—Jews,

"The people . . . sexually." Quotation from Exodus 32:6.
cup of blessing The cup of the fruit of the vine that Christians thank God for and drink at the Lord's Supper.
"because . . . Lord." Quotation from Psalms 24:1; 50:12; 89:11.

Greeks, or God's church. ³³I do the same thing. I try to please everybody in every way. I am not trying to do what is good for me. I try to do what is good for the most people. I do this so that they can be saved.

11 Follow my example, as I follow the example of Christ.

Being Under Authority

²I praise you because you remember me in everything. You follow closely the teachings that I gave you. ³But I want you to understand this: the head of every man is Christ. And the head of a woman is the man.ⁿ And the head of Christ is God. ⁴Every man who prophesiesᵈ or prays with his head covered brings shame to his head. ⁵But every woman who prays or prophesies should have her head covered. If her head is not covered, she brings shame to her head. She is the same as a woman who has her head shaved. ⁶If a woman does not cover her head, it is the same as cutting off all her hair. But it is shameful for a woman to cut off her hair or to shave her head. So she should cover her head. ⁷But a man should not cover his head, because he is made like God and is God's glory. But woman is man's glory. ⁸Man did not come from woman, but woman came from man. ⁹And man was not made for woman. Woman was made for man. ¹⁰So that is why a woman should have her head covered with something to show that she is under authority. And also she should do this because of the angels.

¹¹But in the Lord the woman is important to the man, and the man is important to the woman. ¹²This is true because woman came from man, but also man is born from woman. Really, everything comes from God. ¹³Decide this for yourselves: is it right for a woman to pray to God without something on her head? ¹⁴Even nature itself teaches you that wearing long hair is shameful for a man. ¹⁵But wearing long hair is a woman's honour. Long hair is given to the woman to cover her head. ¹⁶Some people may still want to argue about this. But I would add that neither we nor the churches of God accept any other practice.

The Lord's Supper

¹⁷In the things I tell you now I do not praise you. Your meetings hurt you more than they help you. ¹⁸First, I hear that when you meet together as a church you are divided. And I believe some of this. ¹⁹(It is necessary for there to be differences among you. That is the way to make it clear which of you are really doing right.) ²⁰When you all come together, you are not really eating the Lord's Supper.ⁿ ²¹This is because when you eat, each person eats without waiting for the others. Some people do not get enough to eat, while others have too much to drink. ²²You can eat and drink in your own homes! It seems that you think God's church is not important. You embarrass those who are poor. What should I tell you? Should I praise you for doing this? I do not praise you.

²³The teaching that I gave you is the same teaching that I received from the Lord: on the night when Jesus was handed over to be killed, he took bread ²⁴and gave thanks for it. Then he broke the bread and said, "This is my body; it is for you. Do this to remember me." ²⁵In the same way, after they ate, Jesus took the cup. He said, "This cup shows the new agreement from God to his people. This new agreement begins with the blood of my death. When you drink this, do it to remember me." ²⁶Every time you eat this bread and drink this cup, you

---

the man This could also mean "her husband".
Lord's Supper The meal Jesus told his followers to eat to remember him (Luke 22:14-20).

show others about the Lord's death until he comes. [27]So a person should not eat the bread or drink the cup of the Lord in a way that is not worthy of it. If he does he is sinning against the body and the blood of the Lord. [28]Everyone should look into his own heart before he eats the bread and drinks the cup. [29]If someone eats the bread and drinks the cup without recognising the body, then he is judged guilty by eating and drinking. [30]That is why many in your group are sick and weak. And many have died. [31]But if we judged ourselves in the right way, then God would not judge us. [32]But when the Lord judges us, he punishes us to show us the right way. He does this so that we will not be destroyed along with the world.

[33]So my brothers, when you come together to eat, wait for each other. [34]If anyone is too hungry, he should eat at home. Do this so that your meeting together will not bring God's judgement on you. I will tell you what to do about the other things when I come.

Gifts from the Holy Spirit

12 Now, brothers, I want you to understand about spiritual gifts. [2]You remember the lives you lived before you were believers. You let yourselves be influenced and led away to worship idols — things that have no life. [3]So I tell you that no one who is speaking with the help of God's Spirit says, "Jesus be cursed." And no one can say, "Jesus is Lord," without the help of the Holy Spirit.[d]

[4]There are different kinds of gifts; but they are all from the same Spirit. [5]There are different ways to serve; but all these ways are from the same Lord. [6]And there are different ways that God works in people; but all these ways are from the same God. God

works in us all in everything we do. [7]Something from the Spirit can be seen in each person, to help everyone. [8]The Spirit gives one person the ability to speak with wisdom. And the same Spirit gives another the ability to speak with knowledge. [9]The same Spirit gives faith to one person. And that one Spirit gives another gifts of healing. [10]The Spirit gives to another person the power to do miracles,[d] to another the ability to prophesy.[d] And he gives to another the ability to know the difference between good and evil spirits. The Spirit gives one person the ability to speak in different kinds of languages[n] and to another the ability to interpret those languages. [11]One Spirit, the same Spirit, does all these things. The Spirit decides what to give each person.

The Body of Christ

[12]A person's body is only one thing, but it has many parts. Yes, there are many parts to a body, but all those parts make only one body. Christ is like that too. [13]Some of us are Jews, and some of us are Greeks. Some of us are slaves, and some of us are free. But we were all baptised into one body through one Spirit.[d] And we were all made to share in the one Spirit.

[14]And a person's body has more than one part. It has many parts. [15]The foot might say, "I am not a hand. So I am not part of the body." But saying this would not stop the foot from being a part of the body. [16]The ear might say, "I am not an eye. So I am not part of the body." But saying this would not make the ear stop being a part of the body. [17]If the whole body were an eye, the body would not be able to hear. If the whole body were an ear, the body would not be able to smell anything. [18-19]If each part of the body were the same part, there would

---

languages This can also be translated "tongues".

be no body. But truly God put the parts in the body as he wanted them. He made a place for each one of them. [20]And so there are many parts, but only one body.

[21]The eye cannot say to the hand, "I don't need you!" And the head cannot say to the foot, "I don't need you!" [22]No! Those parts of the body that seem to be weaker are really very important. [23]And the parts of the body that we think are not worth much are the parts that we give the most care to. And we give special care to the parts of the body that we want to hide. [24]The more beautiful parts of our body need no special care. But God put the body together and gave more honour to the parts that need it. [25]God did this so that our body would not be divided. God wanted the different parts to care the same for each other. [26]If one part of the body suffers, then all the other parts suffer with it. Or if one part of our body is honoured, then all the other parts share its honour.

[27]All of you together are the body of Christ. Each one of you is a part of that body. [28]And in the church God has given a place first to apostles,[d] second to prophets,[d] and third to teachers. Then God has given a place to those who do miracles,[d] those who have gifts of healing, those who can help others, those who are able to lead, and those who can speak in different languages.[n] [29]Not all are apostles. Not all are prophets. Not all are teachers. Not all do miracles. [30]Not all have gifts of healing. Not all speak in different languages.[n] Not all interpret those languages. [31]But you should truly want to have the greater gifts.

Love

And now I will show you the best way of all.

13 I may speak in different languages[n] of men or even angels. But if I do not have love, then I am only a noisy bell or a ringing cymbal. [2]I may have the gift of prophecy;[d] I may understand all the secret things of God and all knowledge; and I may have faith so great that I can move mountains. But even if I have all these things, if I do not have love, then I am nothing. [3]I may give everything I own to feed the poor. And I may even give my body as an offering to be burned. But I gain nothing by doing these things if I do not have love.

[4]Love is patient and kind. Love is not jealous, it does not boast, and it is not proud. [5]Love is not rude, is not selfish, and does not become angry easily. Love does not remember wrongs done against it. [6]Love is not happy with evil, but is happy with the truth. [7]Love patiently accepts all things. It always trusts, always hopes, and always continues strong.

[8]Love never ends. There are gifts of prophecy,[d] but they will be ended. There are gifts of speaking in different languages,[n] but those gifts will end. There is the gift of knowledge, but it will be ended. [9]These things will end, because this knowledge and these prophecies we have are not complete. [10]But when perfection comes, the things that are not complete will end. [11]When I was a child, I talked like a child; I thought like a child; I made plans like a child. When I became a man, I stopped those childish ways. [12]It is the same with us. Now we see as if we are looking into a dark mirror. But at that time, in the future, we shall see clearly. Now I know only a part. But at that time I will know fully, as God has known me. [13]So these three things continue for ever: faith, hope and love. And the greatest of these is love.

---

languages This can also be translated "tongues".

Spiritual Gifts

14 Love, then, is what you should try for. And you should truly want to have the spiritual gifts. And the gift you should want most is to be able to prophesy.[d] 2I will explain why. One who has the gift of speaking in a different language[n] is not speaking to people. He is speaking to God. No one understands him—he is speaking secret things through the Spirit.[d] 3But one who prophesies is speaking to people. He gives people strength, encouragement, and comfort. 4The one who speaks in a different language is helping only himself. But the one who prophesies is helping the whole church. 5I would like all of you to have the gift of speaking in different kinds of languages. But more, I want you to prophesy. The person who prophesies is greater than the one who can only speak in different languages—unless someone is there who can explain what he says. Then the whole church can be helped.

6Brothers, will it help you if I come to you speaking in different languages? No! It will help you only if I bring you a new truth or some knowledge, or some prophecy, or some teaching. 7It is the same as with nonliving things that make sounds—like a flute or a harp. If different musical notes are not made clear, you will not know what song is being played. Each note must be played clearly for you to be able to understand the tune. 8And in a war, if the trumpet does not sound clearly, the soldiers will not know it is time to prepare for fighting. 9It is the same with you. The words you speak with your tongue must be clear. Unless you speak clearly, no one can understand what you are saying. You will be talking in the air! 10It is true that there are many kinds of speech in the world. And they all have meaning.

11So unless I understand the meaning of what someone says to me, I am a stranger to him, and he is a stranger to me. 12It is the same with you. You want spiritual gifts very much. So try most to have the gifts that help the church grow stronger.

13The one who has the gift of speaking in a different language should pray that he can also interpret what he says. 14If I pray in a different language, my spirit is praying, but my mind does nothing. 15So what should I do? I will pray with my spirit, but I will also pray with my mind. I will sing with my spirit, but I will also sing with my mind. 16You might be praising God with your spirit. But a person there without understanding cannot say "Amen"[n] to your prayer of thanks. He does not know what you are saying. 17You may be thanking God in a good way, but the other person is not helped.

18I thank God that my gift of speaking in different kinds of languages is greater than any of yours. 19But in the church meetings I would rather speak five words that I understand than thousands of words in a different language. I would rather speak with my understanding, so that I can teach others.

20Brothers, do not think like children. In evil things be like babies. But in your thinking you should be like full-grown men. 21It is written in the Scriptures:[d]

"I will use strange words and
       foreign languages
  to speak to these people.
But even then they will not
     listen."   *Isaiah 28:11-12*

That is what the Lord says.

22So the gift of speaking in different kinds of languages is a proof for those who do not believe, not for those who believe. And prophecy is for people

---

language This can also be translated "tongue".
"Amen" When a person says "Amen", it means he agrees with the things that were said.

who believe, not for those who do not believe. ²³Suppose the whole church meets together and everyone speaks in different languages. If some people come in who are without understanding or do not believe, they will say you are mad. ²⁴But suppose everyone is prophesying and someone comes in who does not believe or is without understanding. If everyone is prophesying, his sin will be shown to him, and he will be judged by all that he hears. ²⁵The secret things in his heart will be made known. So he will bow down and worship God. He will say, "Truly, God is with you."

Meetings Should Help the Church

²⁶So, brothers, what should you do? When you meet together, one person has a song. Another has a teaching. Another has a new truth from God. Another speaks in a different language,ⁿ and another person interprets that language. The purpose of all these things should be to help the church grow strong. ²⁷When you meet together, if anyone speaks in a different language, then it should be only two, or not more than three, who speak. They should speak one after the other. And someone else should interpret what they say. ²⁸But if there is no interpreter, then anyone who speaks in a different language should be quiet in the church meeting. He should speak only to himself and to God. ²⁹And only two or three prophetsᵈ should speak. The others should judge what they say. ³⁰And if a message from God comes to another person who is sitting, then the first speaker should stop. ³¹You can all prophesy one after the other. In this way all the people can be taught and encouraged. ³²The spirits of prophets are under the control of the prophets

themselves. ³³God is not a God of confusion but a God of peace.

This is true in all the churches of God's people. ³⁴Women should keep quiet in the church meetings. They are not allowed to speak. They must be under control. This is also what the law of Moses says. ³⁵If there is something the women want to know, they should ask their own husbands at home. It is shameful for a woman to speak in the church meeting. ³⁶Did God's teaching come from you? Or are you the only ones who have received that teaching?

³⁷If anyone thinks that he is a prophet or that he has a spiritual gift, then he should understand that what I am writing to you is the Lord's command. ³⁸If that person does not know this, then he is not known by God.

³⁹So my brothers, you should truly want to prophesy. And do not stop people from using the gift of speaking in different kinds of languages. ⁴⁰But let everything be done in a way that is right and orderly.

The Good News About Christ

15 Now, brothers, I want you to remember the Good Newsᵈ I brought to you. You received this Good News, and you continue strong in it. ²And you are saved by this Good News. But you must continue believing what I told you. If you do not, then you believed for nothing.

³I passed on to you what I received. And this was the most important: that Christ died for our sins, as the Scripturesᵈ say; ⁴that he was buried and was raised to life on the third day as the Scriptures say; ⁵and that he showed himself to Peter and then to the twelve apostles.ᵈ ⁶After that, Jesus showed himself to more than 500 of the believers at the same time. Most of them are still living today. But some have died. ⁷Then Jesus showed

language This can also be translated "tongue".

himself to James and later to all the apostles. [8]Last of all he showed himself to me — as to a person not born at the normal time. [9]All the other apostles are greater than I am. This is because I persecuted the church of God. And this is why I am not even good enough to be called an apostle. [10]But God's grace has made me what I am. And his grace to me was not wasted. I worked harder than all the other apostles. (But I was not really the one working. It was God's grace that was with me.) [11]So then it is not important if I preached to you or if the other apostles preached to you. We all preach the same thing, and this is what you believed.

We Will Be Raised from Death

[12]It is preached that Christ was raised from death. So why do some of you say that people will not be raised from death? [13]If no one will ever be raised from death, then Christ was not raised from death. [14]And if Christ was not raised, then our preaching is worth nothing. And your faith is worth nothing. [15]And also, we will be guilty of lying about God. Because we have preached about him by saying that he raised Christ from death. And if people are not raised from death, then God never raised Christ from death. [16]If the dead are not raised, Christ has not been raised either. [17]And if Christ has not been raised, then your faith is for nothing; you are still guilty of your sins. [18]And also, those in Christ who have already died are lost. [19]If our hope in Christ is for this life only, we should be pitied more than anyone else in the world.

[20]But Christ has truly been raised from death — the first one and proof that those who are asleep in death will also be raised. [21]Death comes to everyone because of what one man did.

But the rising from death also happens because of one man. [22]In Adam all of us die. In the same way, in Christ all of us will be made alive again. [23]But everyone will be raised to life in the right order. Christ was first to be raised. When Christ comes again, those who belong to him will be raised to life. [24]Then the end will come. Christ will destroy all rulers, authorities, and powers. And he will give the kingdom to God the Father. [25]Christ must rule until God puts all enemies under Christ's control. [26]The last enemy to be destroyed will be death. [27]The Scripture[d] says, "God put all things under his control."[n] When it says that "all things" are put under him, it is clear that this does not include God himself. God is the one putting everything under Christ's control. [28]After everything has been put under Christ, then the Son himself will be put under God. God is the One who put all things under Christ. And Christ will be put under God, so that God will be the complete ruler over everything.

[29]If the dead are never raised, then what will people do who are baptised for those who have died? If the dead are not raised at all, why are people baptised for them?

[30]And what about us? Why do we put ourselves in danger every hour? [31]I die every day. That is true, brothers, just as it is true that I boast about you in Christ Jesus our Lord. [32]If I fought wild animals in Ephesus only for human reasons, I have gained nothing. If the dead are not raised, then, "Let us eat and drink, because tomorrow we will die."[n]

[33]Do not be fooled: "Bad friends will ruin good habits." [34]Come back to your right way of thinking and stop sinning. I say this to shame you — some of you do not know God.

"God put ... control." Quotation from Psalm 8:6.
"Let us ... die." Quotation from Isaiah 22:13; 56:12.

What Kind of Body Will We Have?

35But someone may ask, "How are the dead raised? What kind of body will they have?" 36Those are stupid questions. When you plant something, it must die in the ground before it can live and grow. 37And when you plant it, what you plant does not have the same "body" that it will have later. What you plant is only a seed, maybe wheat or something else. 38But God gives it a body that he has planned for it. And God gives each kind of seed its own body. 39All things made of flesh are not the same kinds of flesh: people have one kind of flesh, animals have another kind, birds have another, and fish have another. 40Also there are heavenly bodies and earthly bodies. But the beauty of the heavenly bodies is one kind. The beauty of the earthly bodies is another kind. 41The sun has one kind of beauty. The moon has another beauty, and the stars have another. And each star is different in its beauty.

42It is the same with the dead who are raised to life. The body that is "planted" will ruin and decay. But that body is raised to a life that cannot be destroyed. 43When the body is "planted", it is without honour. But it is raised in glory. When the body is "planted", it is weak. But when it is raised, it has power. 44The body that is "planted" is a physical body. When it is raised, it is a spiritual body.

There is a physical body. And there is also a spiritual body. 45It is written in the Scriptures:*d* "The first man became a living person."*n* But the last Adam became a spirit that gives life. 46The spiritual man did not come first. It was the physical man who came first; then came the spiritual. 47The first man came from the dust of the earth. The second man came from

heaven. 48People belong to the earth. They are like the first man of earth. But those people who belong to heaven are like the man of heaven. 49We were made like the man of earth. So we will also be made like the man of heaven.

50I tell you this, brothers: flesh and blood cannot have a part in the kingdom of God. A thing that will die cannot have a part in something that never dies. 51But listen, I tell you this secret: we will not all die, but we will all be changed. 52It will only take a second. We will be changed as quickly as an eye blinks. This will happen when the last trumpet sounds. The trumpet will sound and those who have died will be raised to live for ever. And we will all be changed. 53This body that will decay must clothe itself with something that will never decay. And this body that dies must clothe itself with something that will never die. 54So this body that decays will clothe itself with that which never decays. And this body that dies will clothe itself with that which never dies. When this happens, then this Scripture will be made true:

"Death is destroyed for ever in
        victory."   *Isaiah 25:8*
55"Death, where is your victory?
    Death, where is your power to
        hurt?"   *Hosea 13:14*
56Death's power to hurt is sin. The power of sin is the law. 57But we thank God! He gives us the victory through our Lord Jesus Christ.

58So my dear brothers, stand strong. Do not let anything change you. Always give yourselves fully to the work of the Lord. You know that your work in the Lord is never wasted.

The Gift for Other Believers

16 Now I will write about the collection of money for God's peo-

ple. Do the same thing that I told the Galatian churches to do: ²on the first day of every week, each one of you should put aside as much money as you can from what you are blessed with. You should save it up, so that you will not have to collect money after I come. ³When I arrive, I will send some men to take your gift to Jerusalem. These will be men who you all agree should go. I will send them with letters of introduction. ⁴If it seems good for me to go also, these men will go along with me.

Paul's Plans

⁵I plan to go through Macedonia. So I will come to you after I go through there. ⁶Maybe I will stay with you for a time. I might even stay all winter. Then you can help me on my trip, wherever I go. ⁷I do not want to come to see you now, because I would have to leave to go on to other places. I hope to stay a longer time with you if the Lord allows it. ⁸But I will stay at Ephesus until Pentecost.ᵈ ⁹I will stay, because a good opportunity for a great and growing work has been given to me now. And there are many people working against me.

¹⁰Timothy might come to you. Try to make him feel comfortable with you. He is working for the Lord just as I am. ¹¹So none of you should refuse to accept Timothy. Help him on his trip in peace, so that he can come back to me. I am expecting him to come back with the brothers.

¹²Now about our brother Apollos: I strongly encouraged him to visit you with the other brothers. But he was sure that he did not want to go now. But when he has the opportunity, he will go to you.

Paul Ends His Letter

¹³Be careful. Continue strong in the faith. Have courage, and be strong. ¹⁴Do everything in love.

¹⁵You know that the family of Stephanas were the first believers in Southern Greece. They have given themselves to the service of God's people. I ask you, brothers, ¹⁶to follow the leading of people like these and anyone else who works and serves with them.

¹⁷I am happy that Stephanas, Fortunatus, and Achaicus have come. You are not here, but they have filled your place. ¹⁸They have given rest to my spirit and to yours. You should recognise the value of men like these.

¹⁹The churches in the country of Asia send greetings to you. Aquila and Priscilla greet you in the Lord. Also the church that meets in their house greets you. ²⁰All the brothers here send greetings. Give each other a holy kiss when you meet.

²¹I am Paul, and I am writing this greeting with my own hand.

²²If anyone does not love the Lord, then let him be separated from God— lost for ever!

Come, O Lord!

²³The grace of the Lord Jesus be with you.

²⁴My love be with all of you in Christ Jesus.

2 CORINTHIANS

Paul Answers Those Who Accuse Him

1 From Paul, an apostle[d] of Christ
Jesus. I am an apostle because
that is what God wanted.

Also from Timothy our brother in
Christ.

To the church of God in Corinth,
and to all of God's people in the whole
country of Southern Greece:

[2]Grace and peace to you from God
our Father and the Lord Jesus Christ.

Paul Gives Thanks to God

[3]Praise be to the God and Father of
our Lord Jesus Christ. God is the Father who is full of mercy. And he is the
God of all comfort. [4]He comforts us
every time we have trouble, so that
we can comfort others when they
have trouble. We can comfort them
with the same comfort that God gives
us. [5]We share in the many sufferings
of Christ. In the same way, much
comfort comes to us through Christ.
[6]If we have troubles, it is for your
comfort and salvation. If we have
comfort, then you also have comfort.
This helps you to accept patiently the
same sufferings that we have. [7]Our
hope for you is strong. We know that
you share in our sufferings. So we
know that you also share in the comfort we receive.

[8]Brothers, we want you to know
about the trouble we suffered in the
country of Asia. We had great burdens there that were greater than our
own strength. We even gave up hope
for life. [9]Truly, in our own hearts we
believed that we would die. But this
happened so that we would not trust
in ourselves. It happened so that we
would trust in God, who raises people
from death. [10]God saved us from
these great dangers of death. And he

will continue to save us. We have put
our hope in him, and he will save us
again. [11]And you can help us with your
prayers. Then many people will give
thanks for us — that God blessed us
because of their many prayers.

The Change in Paul's Plans

[12]This is what we are proud of, and
I can say with all my heart that it is
true: in all the things we have done in
the world, we have done everything
with an honest and pure heart from
God. And this is even more true in
what we have done with you. We did
this by God's grace, not by the kind of
wisdom the world has. [13]For we write
to you only what you can read and understand. And I hope that [14]as you
have understood some things about
us, you may come to know everything
about us. Then you can be proud of
us, as we will be proud of you on the
day our Lord Jesus Christ comes
again.

[15]I was very sure of all this. That is
why I made plans to visit you first.
Then you could be blessed twice. [16]I
planned to visit you on my way to
Macedonia. Then I planned to visit
you again on my way back. I wanted to
get help from you for my trip to Judea.
[17]Do you think that I made these plans
without really thinking? Or maybe you
think I make plans as the world does,
so that I say "Yes, yes", and at the
same time "No, no".

[18]But if you can believe God, then
you can believe that what we tell you
is never both "Yes" and "No". [19]The
Son of God, Jesus Christ, that Silas
and Timothy and I preached to you,
was not "Yes" and "No". In Christ it
has always been "Yes". [20]The "Yes"

to all of God's promises is in Christ. And that is why we say "Amen"*n* through Christ to the glory of God. [21]And God is the One who makes you and us strong in Christ. God made us his chosen people. [22]He put his mark on us to show that we are his. And he put his Spirit*d* in our hearts to be a guarantee for all he has promised.

[23]I tell you this, and I ask God to be my witness that this is true: the reason I did not come back to Corinth was that I did not want to punish or hurt you. [24]I do not mean that we are trying to control your faith. You are strong in faith. But we are workers with you for your own happiness.

2 So I decided that my next visit to you would not be another visit to make you sad. [2]If I make you sad, who will make me happy? Only you can make me happy — you whom I made sad. [3]I wrote you a letter for this reason: that when I came to you I would not be made sad by the people who should make me happy. I felt sure of all of you. I felt sure that you would share my joy. [4]When I wrote to you before, I was very troubled and unhappy in my heart. I wrote with many tears. I did not write to make you sad, but to let you know how much I love you.

Forgive the Sinner

[5]Someone there among you has caused sadness. He caused this not to me, but to all of you — I mean he caused sadness to all in some way. (I do not want to make it sound worse than it really is.) [6]The punishment that most of you gave him is enough for him. [7]But now you should forgive him and comfort him. This will keep him from having too much sadness and giving up completely. [8]So I beg you to show him that you love him. [9]This is why I wrote to you. I wanted to test you and see if you obey in everything.

[10]If you forgive someone, I also forgive him. And what I have forgiven — if I had anything to forgive — I forgave it for you, and Christ was with me. [11]I did this so that Satan would not win anything from us. We know very well what Satan's plans are.

Paul's Concern in Troas

[12]I went to Troas to preach the Good News*d* of Christ. The Lord gave me a good opportunity there. [13]But I had no peace because I did not find my brother Titus there. So I said good bye and went to Macedonia.

Victory Through Christ

[14]But thanks be to God, who always leads us in victory through Christ. God uses us to spread his knowledge everywhere like a sweet-smelling perfume. [15]Our offering to God is this: we are the sweet smell of Christ among those who are being saved and among those who are lost. [16]To those who are lost, we are the smell of death that brings death. But to those who are being saved, we are the smell of life that brings life. So who is able to do this work? [17]We do not sell the word of God for a profit as many other people do. But in Christ we speak the truth before God. We speak as men sent from God.

Servants of the New Agreement

3 Are we starting to boast about ourselves again? Do we need letters of introduction to you or from you, like some other people? [2]You yourselves are our letter, written on our hearts. It is known and read by everyone. [3]You show that you are a letter from Christ that he sent through us. This letter is not written with ink, but with the Spirit*d* of the living God. It is not written on stone

---

"Amen" When a person says "Amen", it means he agrees with the things that were said.

tablets.*ⁿ* It is written on human hearts.

⁴We can say this, because through Christ we feel sure before God. ⁵I do not mean that we are able to say that we can do this work ourselves. It is God who makes us able to do all that we do. ⁶God made us able to be servants of a new agreement from himself to his people. This new agreement is not a written law. It is of the Spirit. The written law brings death, but the Spirit gives life.

⁷The law that brought death was written in words on stone. It came with God's glory. Moses' face was so bright with glory that the people of Israel could not continue to look at his face. And that glory later disappeared. ⁸So surely the new way that brings the Spirit has even more glory. ⁹That law judged people guilty of sin, but it had glory. So surely the new way that makes people right with God has much greater glory. ¹⁰That old law had glory. But it really loses its glory when it is compared to the much greater glory of this new way. ¹¹If that law which disappeared came with glory, then this new way which continues for ever has much greater glory.

¹²We have this hope, so we are very brave. ¹³We are not like Moses. He put a covering over his face so that the people of Israel would not see it. The glory was disappearing, and Moses did not want them to see it end. ¹⁴But their minds were closed. Even today that same covering hides the meaning when they read the old agreement. That covering is taken away only through Christ. ¹⁵But even today, when they read the law of Moses, there is a covering over their minds. ¹⁶But when a person changes and follows the Lord, that covering is taken away. ¹⁷The Lord is the Spirit. And where the Spirit of the Lord is, there is freedom. ¹⁸Our faces, then, are not covered. We all show the Lord's glory, and we are being changed to be like him. This change in us brings more and more glory. And it comes from the Lord, who is the Spirit.

Preaching the Good News

4 God, with his mercy, gave us this work to do. So we don't give up. ²But we have turned away from secret and shameful ways. We use no trickery, and we do not change the teaching of God. We teach the truth plainly. This is how we show everyone who we are. And this is how they can know in their hearts what kind of people we are before God. ³The Good News*ᵈ* that we preach may be hidden. But it is hidden only to those who are lost. ⁴The devil who rules this world has blinded the minds of those who do not believe. They cannot see the light of the Good News—the Good News about the glory of Christ, who is exactly like God. ⁵We do not preach about ourselves. But we preach that Jesus Christ is Lord; and we preach that we are your servants for Jesus. ⁶God once said, "Let the light shine out of the darkness!" And this is the same God who made his light shine in our hearts. He gave us light by letting us know the glory of God that is in the face of Christ.

Spiritual Treasure in Clay Jars

⁷We have this treasure from God. But we are only like clay jars that hold the treasure. This shows that this great power is from God, not from us. ⁸We have troubles all around us, but we are not defeated. We do not know what to do, but we do not give up. ⁹We are persecuted, but God does not leave us. We are hurt sometimes, but we are not destroyed. ¹⁰We carry the death of Jesus in our own bodies, so that the life of Jesus can also be seen

---

stone tablets Meaning the law of Moses that was written on stone tablets (Exodus 24:12; 25:16).

in our bodies. [11]We are alive, but for Jesus we are always in danger of death. This is so that the life of Jesus can be seen in our bodies that die. [12]So death is working in us, but life is working in you.

[13]It is written in the Scriptures,[d] "I believed, so I spoke."[n] Our faith is like this, too. We believe, and so we speak. [14]God raised the Lord Jesus from death. And we know that God will also raise us with Jesus. God will bring us together with you, and we will stand before him. [15]All these things are for you. And so the grace of God is being given to more and more people. This will bring more and more thanks to God for his glory.

Living by Faith

[16]So we do not give up. Our physical body is becoming older and weaker, but our spirit inside us is made new every day. [17]We have small troubles for a while now, but they are helping us gain an eternal glory. That glory is much greater than the troubles. [18]So we set our eyes not on what we see but on what we cannot see. What we see will last only a short time. But what we cannot see will last for ever.

5 We know that our body—the tent we live in here on earth—will be destroyed. But when that happens, God will have a house for us to live in. It will not be a house made by men. It will be a home in heaven that will last for ever. [2]But now we are tired of this body. We want God to give us our heavenly home. [3]It will clothe us, and we will not be naked. [4]While we live in this body, we have burdens, and we complain. We do not want to be naked. We want to be clothed with our heavenly home. Then this body that dies will be fully covered with life. [5]This is what God made us for. And he has given us the Spirit[d] to be a guarantee for this new life.

[6]So we always have courage. We know that while we live in this body, we are away from the Lord. [7]We live by what we believe, not by what we can see. [8]So I say that we have courage. And we really want to be away from this body and be at home with the Lord. [9]Our only goal is to please God. We want to please him whether we live here or there. [10]For we must all stand before Christ to be judged. Each one will receive what he should get—good or bad—for the things he did when he lived in the earthly body.

Becoming Friends with God

[11]We know what it means to fear the Lord. So we try to help people accept the truth. God knows what we really are. And I hope that in your hearts you know, too. [12]We are not trying to prove ourselves to you again. But we are telling you about ourselves, so you will be proud of us. Then you will have an answer for those who are proud about things that can be seen. They do not care about what is in the heart. [13]If we are out of our minds, it is for God. If we have our right mind, then it is for you. [14]The love of Christ controls us. Because we know that One died for all. So all have died. [15]Christ died for all so that those who live would not continue to live for themselves. He died for them and was raised from death so that they would live for him.

[16]From this time on we do not think of anyone as the world does. It is true that in the past we thought of Christ as the world thinks. But we no longer think of him in that way. [17]If anyone belongs to Christ, then he is made new. The old things have gone; everything is made new! [18]All this is from God. Through Christ, God made peace between us and himself. And God gave us the work of bringing everyone into peace with him. [19]I mean

"I . . . spoke." Quotation from Psalm 116:10.

that God was in Christ, making peace between the world and himself. In Christ, God did not hold the world guilty of its sins. And he gave us this message of peace. [20]So we have been sent to speak for Christ. It is as if God is calling to you through us. We speak for Christ when we beg you to be at peace with God. [21]Christ had no sin. But God made him become sin. God did this for us so that in Christ we could become right with God.

6 We are workers together with God. So we beg you: do not let the grace that you received from God be for nothing. [2]God says,

"I heard your prayers at the right time,
and I gave you help on the day of salvation."   *Isaiah 49:8*

I tell you that the "right time" is now. The "day of salvation" is now.

[3]We do not want anyone to find anything wrong with our work. So we do nothing that will be a problem for anyone. [4]But in every way we show that we are servants of God: in accepting many hard things, in troubles, in difficulties, and in great problems. [5]We are beaten and thrown into prison. Men become upset and fight us. We work hard, and sometimes we get no sleep or food. [6]We show that we are servants of God by living a pure life, by our understanding, by our patience, and by our kindness. We show this by the Holy Spirit,[d] by true love, [7]by speaking the truth, and by God's power. We use our right living to defend ourselves against everything. [8]Some people honour us, but other people shame us. Some people say good things about us, but other people say bad things. Some people say we are liars, but we speak the truth. [9]We are not known, but we are well known. We seem to be dying, but look—we continue to live. We are punished, but we are not killed. [10]We

have much sadness, but we are always rejoicing. We are poor, but we are making many people rich in faith. We have nothing, but really we have everything.

[11]We have spoken freely to you in Corinth. We have opened our hearts to you. [12]Our feelings of love for you have not stopped. It is you that have stopped your feelings of love for us. [13]I speak to you as if you were my children. Do to us as we have done—open your hearts to us.

Warning About Non-Christians

[14]You are not the same as those who do not believe. So do not join yourselves to them. Good and bad do not belong together. Light and darkness cannot share together. [15]How can Christ and Belial, the devil, have any agreement? What can a believer have together with a non-believer? [16]The temple of God cannot have any agreement with idols. And we are the temple of the living God. As God said:
"I will live with them and walk with them. And I will be their God. And they will be my people."[n]

[17]"Leave those people,
and make yourselves pure, says the Lord.
Touch nothing that is unclean,[d]
and I will accept you."
    Isaiah 52:11; Ezekiel 20:34,41

[18]"I will be your father,
and you will be my sons and daughters,
says the Lord All-Powerful."
    2 Samuel 7:14; 7:8

7 Dear friends, we have these promises from God. So we should make ourselves pure—free from anything that makes body or soul unclean. We should try to become perfect in the way we live, because we respect God.

"**I . . . people.**" Quotation from Leviticus 26:11-12; Jeremiah 32:38; Ezekiel 37:27.

Paul's Joy

[2]Open your hearts to us. We have not done wrong to anyone. We have not ruined the faith of any person, and we have cheated no one. [3]I do not say this to blame you. I told you before that we love you so much that we would live or die with you. [4]I feel very sure of you. I am very proud of you. You give me much comfort. And in all of our troubles I have great joy.

[5]When we came into Macedonia, we had no rest. We found trouble all around us. We had fighting on the outside and fear on the inside. [6]But God comforts those who are troubled. And God comforted us when Titus came. [7]We were comforted by his coming and also by the comfort that you gave him. Titus told us about your wish to see me. He told us that you are very sorry for what you did. And he told me about your great care for me. When I heard this, I was much happier.

[8]Even if the letter I wrote you made you sad, I am not sorry I wrote it. I know it made you sad, and I was sorry for that. But it made you sad only for a short time. [9]Now I am happy, but not because you were made sad. I am happy because your sorrow made you change your hearts. You became sad in the way God wanted you to. So you were not hurt by us in any way. [10]Being sorry in the way God wants makes a person change his heart and life. This leads to salvation, and we cannot be sorry for that. But the kind of sorrow the world has will bring death. [11]You had the kind of sorrow God wanted you to have. Now see what this sorrow has brought you: it has made you very serious. It made you want to prove that you were not wrong. It made you angry and afraid. It made you want to see me. It made you care. It made you want the right thing to be done. You proved that you were not guilty in any part of the problem. [12]I wrote that letter, but not be-cause of the one who did the wrong. And it was not written because of the person who was hurt. But I wrote the letter so that you could see, before God, the great care that you have for us. [13]That is why we were comforted.

We were very comforted. And we were even happier to see that Titus was so happy. All of you made him feel much better. [14]I boasted to Titus about you. And you showed that I was right. Everything that we said to you was true. And you have proved that what we boasted about to Titus is true. [15]And his love for you is stron-ger when he remembers that you were all ready to obey. You welcomed him with respect and fear. [16]I am very happy that I can trust you fully.

Christian Giving

8 And now, brothers, we want you to know about the grace that God gave the churches in Macedonia. [2]They have been tested by great trou-bles. And they are very poor. But they gave much because of their great joy. [3]I can tell you that they gave as much as they were able. They gave even more than they could afford. No one told them to do it. [4]But they asked us again and again — they begged us to let them share in this service for God's people. [5]And they gave in a way that we did not expect: they first gave themselves to the Lord and to us. This is what God wants. [6]So we asked Titus to help you finish this special work of grace. He is the one who started this work. [7]You are rich in everything—in faith, in speaking, in knowledge, in truly wanting to help, and in the love you learned from us. And so we want you to be rich also in this gift of giving.

[8]I am not commanding you to give. But I want to see if your love is true love. I do this by showing you that others really want to help. [9]You know the grace of our Lord Jesus Christ. You know that Christ was rich, but for

you he became poor. Christ did this so that by his being poor you might become rich.

[10]This is what I think you should do: Last year you were the first to want to give. And you were the first who gave. [11]So now finish the work that you started. Then your "doing" will be equal to your "wanting to do". Give from what you have. [12]If you want to give, your gift will be accepted. Your gift will be judged by what you have, not by what you do not have. [13]We do not want you to have troubles while other people are at ease. We want everything to be equal. [14]At this time you have plenty. What you have can help others who are in need. Then later, when they have plenty, they can help you when you are in need. Then all will be equal. [15]As it is written in the Scriptures,[d] "The person who gathered more did not have too much. The person who gathered less did not have too little."[n]

Titus and His Companions

[16]I thank God because he gave Titus the same love for you that I have. [17]Titus accepted what we asked him to do. He wanted very much to go to you. This was his own idea. [18]We are sending with him the brother who is praised by all the churches. This brother is praised because of his service in preaching the Good News.[d] [19]Also, this brother was chosen by the churches to go with us when we deliver this gift of money. We are doing this service to bring glory to the Lord and to show that we really want to help.

[20]We are being careful so that no one will criticise us about the way we are handling this large gift. [21]We are trying to do what is right. We want to do what the Lord accepts as right and also what people think is right.

[22]Also, we are sending with them our brother who is always ready to help. He has proved this to us in many ways. And he wants to help even more now because he has much faith in you.

[23]Now about Titus—he is my partner who is working with me to help you. And about the other brothers—they are sent from the churches, and they bring glory to Christ. [24]So show these men that you really have love. Show them why we are proud of you. Then all the churches can see it.

Help for Fellow Christians

9 I really do not need to write to you about this help for God's people. [2]I know that you want to help. I have been boasting about this to the people in Macedonia. I have told them that you in Southern Greece have been ready to give since last year. And your wanting to give has made most of them here ready to give also. [3]But I am sending the brothers to you. I do not want our boasting about you in this to be for nothing. I want you to be ready, as I said you would be. [4]If any of the people from Macedonia come with me and find that you are not ready, we will be ashamed. We will be ashamed that we were so sure of you. (And you will be ashamed, too!) [5]So I thought that I should ask these brothers to go to you before we come. They will finish getting in order the gift you promised. Then the gift will be ready when we come, and it will be a gift you wanted to give—not a gift that you hated to give.

[6]Remember this: the person who plants a little will have a small harvest. But the person who plants a lot will have a big harvest. [7]Each one should give, then, what he has decided in his heart to give. He should not give if it makes him sad. And he should not give if he thinks he is forced to give. God loves the person who gives hap-

---

"The person . . . little." Quotation from Exodus 16:18.

pily. [8]And God can give you more blessings than you need. Then you will always have plenty of everything. You will have enough to give to every good work. [9]It is written in the Scriptures:[d]

"He gives freely to the poor.
The things he does are right and
will continue for ever."

Psalm 112:9

[10]God is the One who gives seed to the farmer. And he gives bread for food. And God will give you all the seed you need and make it grow. He will make a great harvest from your goodness. [11]God will make you rich in every way so that you can always give freely. And your giving through us will cause many to give thanks to God. [12]This service that you do helps the needs of God's people. It is also bringing more and more thanks to God. [13]This service you do is a proof of your faith. Many people will praise God because of it. They will praise God because you follow the Good News[d] of Christ — the gospel you say you believe. They will praise God because you freely share with them and with all others. [14]And when they pray, they will wish they could be with you. They will feel this because of the great grace that God has given you. [15]Thanks be to God for his gift that is too wonderful to explain.

Paul Defends His Ministry

10 I, Paul, am begging you with the gentleness and the kindness of Christ. Some people say that I am easy on you when I am with you and strict when I am away. [2]They think that we live in a worldly way. I plan to be very strict against them when I come. I beg you that when I come I will not need to use that same strictness with you. [3]We do live in the world. But we do not fight in the same way that the world fights. [4]We fight with weapons that are different from those the world uses. Our weapons

have power from God. These weapons can destroy the enemy's strong places. We destroy men's arguments. [5]And we destroy every proud thing that raises itself against the knowledge of God. We capture every thought and make it give up and obey Christ. [6]We are ready to punish anyone there who does not obey. But first we want you to obey fully.

[7]You must look at the facts before you. If anyone feels sure that he belongs to Christ, then he must remember that we belong to Christ just as he does. [8]It is true that we boast freely about the authority the Lord gave us. But he gave us this authority to strengthen you, not to hurt you. So I will not be ashamed of the boasting we do. [9]I don't want you to think that I am trying to scare you with my letters. [10]Some people say, "Paul's letters are powerful and sound important. But when he is with us, he is weak. And his speaking is nothing." [11]They should know this: we are not there with you now, so we say these things in letters. But when we are there with you, we will show the same authority that we show in our letters.

[12]We do not dare to put ourselves in the same group with those who think that they are very important. We do not compare ourselves to them. They use themselves to measure themselves, and they judge themselves by what they themselves are. This shows that they know nothing. [13]But we will not boast about things outside the work that was given us to do. We will limit our boasting to the work that God gave us. And this work includes our work with you. [14]We are not boasting too much. We would be boasting too much if we had not already come to you. But we have come to you with the Good News[d] of Christ. [15]We limit our boasting to the work that is ours. We do not boast in the work other men have done. We hope that your faith will continue to grow.

And we hope that you will help our work to grow much larger. [16]We want to tell the Good News in the areas beyond your city. We do not want to boast about work that has already been done in another man's area. [17]But, "If a person boasts, he should boast only about the Lord."[n] [18]It is not the one who says he is good who is accepted but the one that the Lord thinks is good.

Paul and the False Apostles

11 I wish you would be patient with me even when I am a little foolish. But you are already doing that. [2]I am jealous over you. And this jealousy comes from God. I promised to give you to Christ. He must be your only husband. I want to give you to Christ to be his pure bride. [3]But I am afraid that your minds will be led away from your true and pure following of Christ. This might happen just as Eve was tricked by the snake with his evil ways. [4]You are very patient with anyone who comes to you and preaches a different Jesus than the one we preached. You are very willing to accept a spirit or good news that is different from the Spirit[d] and Good News[d] that you received from us.

[5]I do not think that those "great apostles" are any better than I am. [6]I may not be a trained speaker, but I do have knowledge. We have shown this to you clearly in every way.

[7]I preached God's Good News to you without pay. I made myself unimportant to make you important. Do you think that was wrong? [8]I accepted pay from other churches. I took their money so that I could serve you. [9]If I needed something when I was with you, I did not trouble any of you. The brothers who came from Macedonia gave me all that I needed. I did not

allow myself to depend on you in any way. And I will never depend on you. [10]No one in Southern Greece will stop me from boasting about that. I say this with the truth of Christ in me. [11]And why do I not depend on you? Do you think it is because I do not love you? No. God knows that I love you.

[12]And I will keep on doing what I am doing now. I will continue because I want to stop those people from having a reason to boast. They would like to say that the work they boast about is the same as ours. [13]Such men are not true apostles.[d] They are workers who lie. And they change themselves to look like apostles of Christ. [14]This does not surprise us. Even Satan changes himself to look like an angel of light.[n] [15]So it does not surprise us if Satan's servants also make themselves look like servants who work for what is right. But in the end they will be punished for the things they do.

Paul Tells About His Sufferings

[16]I tell you again: No one should think that I am a fool. But if you think that I am a fool, then accept me as you would accept a fool. Then I can boast a little, too. [17]I boast because I feel sure of myself. But I am not talking as the Lord would talk. I am boasting like a fool. [18]Many people are boasting about their lives in the world. So I will boast, too. [19]You are wise, so you will gladly be patient with fools! [20]You are even patient with someone who orders you around and uses you! You are patient with those who trick you, or think they are better than you, or hit you in the face! [21]It is shameful to me to say this, but we were too "weak" to do those things to you!

But if anyone else is brave enough to boast, then I also will be brave and boast. (I am talking like a fool.) [22]Are

---

"If a person . . . Lord." Quotation from Jeremiah 9:24.
angel of light Messenger from God. The devil fools people so that they think he is from God.

they Hebrews?[n] So am I. Are they Israelites? So am I. Are they from Abraham's family? So am I. 23Are they serving Christ? I am serving him more. (I am insane to talk like this.) I have worked much harder than they. I have been in prison more often. I have been hurt more in beatings. I have been near death many times. 24Five times the Jews have given me their punishment of 39 lashes with a whip. 25Three different times I was beaten with rods. Once they tried to kill me with stones. Three times I was in ships that were wrecked, and one of those times I spent the night and the next day in the sea. 26I have gone on many travels. And I have been in danger from rivers, from thieves, from my own people, the Jews, and from those who are not Jews. I have been in danger in cities, in places where no one lives, and on the sea. And I have been in danger with false brothers. 27I have done hard and tiring work, and many times I did not sleep. I have been hungry and thirsty. Many times I have been without food. I have been cold and without clothes. 28Besides all this, there is on me every day the load of my concern for all the churches. 29I feel weak every time someone is weak. I feel upset every time someone is led into sin.

30If I must boast, I will boast about the things that show I am weak. 31God knows that I am not lying. He is the God and Father of the Lord Jesus Christ, and he is to be praised for ever. 32When I was in Damascus, the governor under King Aretas wanted to arrest me. So he put guards around the city. 33But my friends put me in a basket. Then they put the basket through a hole in the wall and lowered

me down. So I escaped from the governor.

A Special Blessing in Paul's Life

12 I must continue to boast. It will do no good, but I will talk now about visions and revelations[n] from the Lord. 2I know a man in Christ who was taken up to the third heaven. This happened 14 years ago. I do not know whether the man was in his body or out of his body. But God knows. 3-4And I know that this man was taken up to paradise.[n] I don't know if he was in his body or away from his body. But he heard things he is not able to explain. He heard things that no man is allowed to tell. 5I will boast about a man like that. But I will not boast about myself, except about my weaknesses. 6But if I wanted to boast about myself, I would not be a fool. I would not be a fool, because I would be telling the truth. But I will not boast about myself. I do not want people to think more of me than what they see me do or hear me say.

7But I must not become too proud of the wonderful things that were shown to me. So a painful problem[n] was given to me. This problem is a messenger from Satan. It is sent to beat me and keep me from being too proud. 8I begged the Lord three times to take this problem away from me. 9But the Lord said to me, "My grace is enough for you. When you are weak, then my power is made perfect in you." So I am very happy to boast about my weaknesses. Then Christ's power can live in me. 10So I am happy when I have weaknesses, insults, hard times, sufferings, and all kinds of troubles. All these things are for Christ. And I am happy, because

Hebrews A name for the Jews that some Jews were very proud of.
revelations Revelation is making known a truth that was hidden.
paradise A place where good people go when they die.
painful problem Literally, "thorn in the flesh".

when I am weak, then I am truly strong.

Paul's Love for the Christians

[11]I have been talking like a fool. But you made me do it. You are the ones who should say good things about me. I am worth nothing, but those "great apostles" are not worth any more than I am! [12]When I was with you, I did what proves that I am an apostle[d] — signs, wonders, and miracles.[d] And I did these things with much patience. [13]So you received everything that the other churches have received. Only one thing was different: I was not a burden to you. Forgive me for this!

[14]I am now ready to visit you the third time. And I will not be a burden to you. I want nothing from you, I only want you. Children should not have to save up to give to their parents. Parents should save to give to their children. [15]So I am happy to give everything I have for you. I will even give myself for you. If I love you more, will you love me less?

[16]It is clear that I was not a burden to you. But you think that I was sly and used lies to catch you. [17]Did I cheat you by using any of the men I sent to you? No, you know I did not. [18]I asked Titus to go to you. And I sent our brother with him. Titus did not cheat you, did he? No, you know that Titus and I did the same thing and with the same spirit.

[19]Do you think that we have been defending ourselves to you all this time? We have been speaking in Christ and before God. You are our dear friends. And everything that we do is to make you stronger. [20]I do this because I am afraid that when I come, you will not be what I want you to be. And I am afraid that I will not be what you want me to be. I am afraid that among you there may be arguing, jealousy, anger, selfish fighting, evil talk,

gossip, pride, and confusion. [21]I am afraid that when I come to you again, my God will make me ashamed before you. I may be saddened by many of those who have sinned. I may be saddened because they have not changed their hearts and have not turned away from their sexual sins and from the shameful things they have done.

Final Warnings and Greetings

13 I will come to you for the third time. And remember, "Every case must be proved by two or three witnesses."[n] [2]When I was with you the second time, I gave a warning to those who had sinned. Now I am away from you, and I give a warning to all the others. When I come to you again, I will not be easy on them. [3]You want proof that Christ is speaking through me. My proof is that he is not weak among you, but he is powerful. [4]It is true that he was weak when he was killed on the cross. But he lives now by God's power. It is true that we are weak in Christ. But for you we will be alive in Christ by God's power.

[5]Look closely at yourselves. Test yourselves to see if you are living in the faith. You know that Christ Jesus is in you — unless you fail the test. [6]But I hope you will see that we ourselves have not failed the test. [7]We pray to God that you will not do anything wrong. It is not important to see that we have passed the test. But it is important that you do what is right, even if it seems that we have failed. [8]We cannot do anything against the truth, but only for the truth. [9]We are happy to be weak, if you are strong. And we pray that you will grow stronger and stronger. [10]I am writing this while I am away from you. I am writing so that when I come I will not have to be harsh in my use of authority. The Lord gave me this authority to

---

"Every . . . witnesses." Quotation from Deuteronomy 19:15.

use to make you stronger, not to destroy you.

[11]Now, brothers, I say good bye. Try to be perfect. Do what I have asked you to do. Agree with each other, and live in peace. Then the God of love and peace will be with you.

[12]Give each other a holy kiss when you greet each other. [13]All of God's holy people send greetings to you.

[14]The grace of the Lord Jesus Christ, the love of God, and the fellowship of the Holy Spirit[d] be with you all.

GALATIANS

Christians Are Saved by Grace

1 From Paul, an apostle.*d*
I was not chosen to be an apostle by men. I was not sent from men. It was Jesus Christ and God the Father who made me an apostle. God is the One who raised Jesus from death. ²This letter is also from all the brothers who are with me.

To the churches in Galatia.*n*

³I pray that God our Father and the Lord Jesus Christ will be good to you and give you peace. ⁴Jesus gave himself for our sins to free us from this evil world we live in. This is what God the Father wanted. ⁵The glory belongs to God for ever and ever. Amen.

The Only Good News

⁶A short time ago God called you to follow him. He called you by his grace that came through Christ. But now I am amazed at you! You are already turning away and believing something different from the Good News.*d* ⁷Really, there is no other Good News. But some people are confusing you and want to change the Good News of Christ. ⁸We preached to you the Good News. So if we ourselves, or even an angel from heaven, preach to you something different from the Good News, he should be condemned! ⁹I said this before. Now I say it again: you have already accepted the Good News. If anyone tells you another way to be saved, he should be condemned!

¹⁰Do you think I am trying to make people accept me? No! God is the One I am trying to please. Am I trying to please men? If I wanted to please men, I would not be a servant of Christ.

Paul's Authority Is from God

¹¹Brothers, I want you to know that the Good News*d* I preached to you was not made by men. ¹²I did not get it from men, nor did any man teach it to me. Jesus Christ showed it to me.

¹³You have heard about my past life. I belonged to the Jewish religion. I hurt the church of God very much and tried to destroy it. ¹⁴I was becoming a leader in the Jewish religion. I did better than most other Jews of my age. I tried harder than anyone else to follow the old rules. These rules were the customs handed down by our ancestors.

¹⁵But God had special plans for me even before I was born. So he called me through his grace that I might ¹⁶tell the Good News about his Son to the non-Jewish people. So God told me about his Son. When God called me, I did not get advice or help from any man. ¹⁷I did not go to Jerusalem to see those who were apostles*d* before I was. But, without waiting, I went away to Arabia and later went back to Damascus.

¹⁸After three years I went to Jerusalem to meet Peter and stayed with him for 15 days. ¹⁹I met no other apostles, except James, the brother of the Lord. ²⁰God knows that these things I write are not lies. ²¹Later, I went to the areas of Syria and Cilicia.

²²In Judea the churches in Christ had never met me. ²³They had only heard this about me: "This man was

---

Galatia Probably the same country where Paul preached and began churches on his first missionary trip. Read the book of Acts, chapters 13 and 14.

1363 GALATIANS 2

trying to hurt us. But now he is preaching the same faith that he once tried to destroy." ²⁴And these believers praised God because of me.

Other Apostles Accepted Paul

2 After 14 years, I went to Jerusalem again, this time with Barnabas. I also took Titus with me. ²I went because God showed me that I should go. I met with those men who were the leaders of the believers. When we were alone, I told them the Good News*d* that I preach to the non-Jewish people. I did not want my past work and the work I am now doing to be wasted. ³Titus was with me. But Titus was not forced to be circumcised,*d* even though he was a Greek. ⁴We talked about this problem because some false brothers had come into our group secretly. They came in like spies to find out about the freedom we have in Christ Jesus. They wanted to make us slaves. ⁵But we did not agree with anything those false brothers wanted! We wanted the truth of the Good News to continue for you.

⁶Those men who seemed to be important did not change the Good News that I preach. (It doesn't matter to me if they were "important" or not. To God all men are the same.) ⁷But these leaders saw that God had given me special work, just as he had to Peter. God gave Peter the work of telling the Good News to the Jews. But God gave me the work of telling the Good News to the non-Jewish people. ⁸God gave Peter the power to work as an apostle*d* for the Jewish people. But he also gave me the power to work as an apostle for those who are not Jews. ⁹James, Peter, and John, who seemed to be the leaders, saw that God had given me this special grace. So they accepted Barnabas and me. They said, "Paul and Barnabas, we agree that you should go to the people who are not Jews. We will go to the Jews." ¹⁰They asked us to do only one

thing — to remember to help the poor. And this was something that I really wanted to do.

Paul Shows that Peter Was Wrong

¹¹When Peter came to Antioch, I was against him because he was wrong. ¹²This is what happened: when Peter first came to Antioch, he ate with the non-Jewish people. But then some Jewish men were sent from James. When they arrived, Peter stopped eating with the non-Jewish people and separated himself from them. He was afraid of the Jews who believe that all non-Jewish people must be circumcised.*d* ¹³So Peter was a hypocrite.*d* The other Jewish believers joined with him and were hypocrites, too. Even Barnabas was influenced by what these Jewish believers did. ¹⁴I saw what they did. They were not following the truth of the Good News.*d* So I spoke to Peter in front of them all. I said: "Peter, you are a Jew, but you are not living like a Jew. You are living like the non-Jewish people. So why do you now try to force the non-Jewish people to live like Jews?"

¹⁵We were not born as non-Jewish "sinners", but we were born as Jews. ¹⁶Yet we know that a person is not made right with God by following the law. No! It is trusting in Jesus Christ that makes a person right with God. So we, too, have put our faith in Christ Jesus, that we might be made right with God. And we are right with God because we trusted in Christ — not because we followed the law. For no one can be made right with God by following the law.

¹⁷We Jews came to Christ to be made right with God. So it is clear that we were sinners too. Does this mean that Christ makes us sinners? No! ¹⁸But I would really be wrong to begin teaching again those things of the law of Moses that I gave up. ¹⁹I stopped

living for the law. It was the law that put me to death. I died to the law so that I can now live for God. I was put to death on the cross with Christ. [20]I do not live any more—it is Christ living in me. I still live in my body, but I live by faith in the Son of God. He loved me and gave himself to save me. [21]This gift is from God, and it is very important to me. If the law could make us right with God, then Christ did not have to die.

Blessing Comes Through Faith

3 You people in Galatia were told very clearly about the death of Jesus Christ on the cross. But you were very foolish. You let someone trick you. [2]Tell me this one thing: how did you receive the Holy Spirit?[d] Did you receive the Spirit by following the law? No! You received the Spirit because you heard the Good News[d] and believed it. [3]You began your life in Christ by the Spirit. Now do you try to continue it by your own power? That is foolish. [4]You have experienced many things. Were all those experiences wasted? I hope not! [5]Does God give you the Spirit because you follow the law? No! Does God work miracles[d] among you because you follow the law? No! God gives you his Spirit and works miracles among you because you heard the Good News and believed it.

[6]The Scriptures[d] say the same thing about Abraham: "Abraham believed God, and God accepted Abraham's faith, and that faith made him right with God."[n] [7]So you should know that the true children of Abraham are those who have faith. [8]The Scriptures told what would happen in the future.

They said that God would make the non-Jewish people right through their faith. This Good News was told to Abraham beforehand, as the Scripture says: "All nations will be blessed through you."[n] [9]Abraham believed this, and because he believed, he was blessed. It is the same today. All who believe today are blessed just as Abraham was blessed. [10]But those who depend on following the law to make them right are under a curse because the Scriptures say, "Anyone will be cursed who does not always obey what is written in the Book of the Law!"[n] [11]So it is clear that no one can be made right with God by the law. The Scriptures say, "He who is right with God by faith will live." [12]The law does not use faith. It says, "A person who does these things will live for ever because of them."[n] [13]So the law put a curse on us, but Christ took away that curse. He changed places with us and put himself under that curse. It is written in the Scriptures, "Everyone whose body is displayed on a tree[n] is cursed." [14]Christ did this so that God's blessing promised to Abraham might come to the non-Jews. This blessing comes through Jesus Christ. Jesus died so that we could have the Spirit that God promised and receive this promise by believing.

The Law and the Promise

[15]Brothers, let me give you an example: think about an agreement that a person makes with another person. After that agreement is accepted by both people, no one can stop that agreement or add anything to it. [16]God made promises to Abraham and

---

"Abraham . . . God." Quotation from Genesis 15:6.
"All . . . you." Quotation from Genesis 12:3.
"Anyone . . . Law!" Quotation from Deuteronomy 27:26.
"A person . . . them." Quotation from Leviticus 18:5.
displayed on a tree Deuteronomy 21:22-23 says that when a person was killed for doing wrong, his body was hung on a tree to show shame. Paul means that the cross of Jesus was like that.

his descendant.*d* God did not say, "and to your descendants". That would mean many people. But God said, "and to your descendant". That means only one person; that person is Christ. [17]This is what I mean: God had an agreement with Abraham and promised to keep it. The law, which came 430 years later, cannot change God's promise to Abraham. [18]Can following the law give us what God promised? No! If this is so, it is not God's promise that brings us the blessings. Instead God freely gave his blessings to Abraham through the promise he had made.

[19]So what was the law for? The law was given to show the wrong things people do. It continued until the special descendant of Abraham came. God's promise was about this descendant. The law was given through angels who used Moses as a mediator*n* to give the law to men. [20]But a mediator is not needed when there is only one side. And God is only one.

The Purpose of the Law of Moses

[21]Does this mean that the law is against God's promises? Never! If there were a law that could give men life, then we could be made right by following that law. [22]But this is not true, because the Scriptures*d* showed that the whole world is bound by sin. This was so that the promise would be given through faith. And it is given to people who believe in Jesus Christ.

[23]Before this faith came, we were all held prisoners by the law. We had no freedom until God showed us the way of faith that was coming. [24]So the law was our master until Christ came. After Christ came, we could be made right with God through faith. [25]Now the way of faith has come, and we no longer live under the law.

[26-27]You were all baptised into Christ, and so you were all clothed with Christ. This shows that you are all children of God through faith in Christ Jesus. [28]Now, in Christ, there is no difference between Jew and Greek. There is no difference between slaves and free men. There is no difference between male and female. You are all the same in Christ Jesus. [29]You belong to Christ. So you are Abraham's descendants.*d* You receive all of God's blessings because of the promise that God made to Abraham.

4 I want to tell you this: while the one who will inherit his father's property is still a child, he is no different from a slave. It does not matter that the child owns everything. [2]While he is a child, he must obey those who are chosen to care for him. But when the child reaches the age set by his father, he is free. [3]It is the same for us. We were once like children. We were slaves to the useless rules of this world. [4]But when the right time came, God sent his Son. His Son was born of a woman and lived under the law. [5]God did this so that he could buy freedom for those who were under the law. His purpose was to make us his children.

[6]And you are God's children. That is why God sent the Spirit of his Son into your hearts. The Spirit*d* cries out, "Father, dear Father."*n* [7]So now you are not a slave; you are God's child, and God will give you what he promised, because you are his child.

Paul's Love for the Christians

[8]In the past you did not know God. You were slaves to gods that were not real. [9]But now you know the true God. Really, it is God who knows you. So why do you turn back to those weak and useless rules you followed before? Do you want to be slaves to those things again? [10]You still follow

---

mediator A person who helps one person talk to or give something to another person.
"Father, dear Father" Literally, "Abba, Father". Jewish children called their fathers "Abba".

teachings about special days, months, seasons, and years. [11]I am afraid for you. I fear that my work for you has been wasted.

[12]Brothers, I was like you; so I beg you to become like me. You were very good to me before. [13]You remember that I came to you the first time because I was sick. That was when I preached the Good News[d] to you. [14]Though my sickness was a trouble for you, you did not hate me or make me leave. But you welcomed me as an angel from God, as if I were Jesus Christ himself! [15]You were very happy then. Where is that joy now? I remember that you would have taken out your eyes and given them to me if that were possible. [16]Now am I your enemy because I tell you the truth?

[17]Those people[n] are working hard to persuade you. But this is not good for you. They want to persuade you to turn against us. They want you to follow only them. [18]It is good for people to show interest in you, but only if their purpose is good. This is always true. It is true when I am with you and when I am away. [19]My little children, again I feel pain for you as a mother feels when she gives birth. I will feel this until you truly become like Christ. [20]I wish I could be with you now. Then perhaps I could change the way I am talking to you. Now I do not know what to do about you.

The Example of Hagar and Sarah

[21]Some of you people still want to be under the law of Moses. Tell me, do you know what the law says? [22]The Scriptures[d] say that Abraham had two sons. The mother of one son was a slave woman. The mother of the other son was a free woman. [23]Abraham's son from the slave woman was born in the normal human way. But the son from the free woman was born because of the promise God made to Abraham.

[24]This makes a picture for us. The two women are like the two agreements between God and men. One agreement is the law that God made on Mount Sinai.[n] The people who are under this agreement are like slaves. The mother named Hagar is like that agreement. [25]She is like Mount Sinai in Arabia and is a picture of the earthly Jewish city of Jerusalem. This city is a slave, and all its people, the Jews, are slaves to the law. [26]But the heavenly Jerusalem which is above is like the free woman. She is our mother. [27]It is written in the Scriptures:

"Be happy, Jerusalem.
You are like a woman who never gave birth to children.
Start singing and shout for joy.
You never felt the pain of giving birth to children.
But you will have more children than the woman who has a husband."   *Isaiah 54:1*

[28]My brothers, you are God's children because of his promise, as Isaac was then. [29]The son who was born in the normal way treated the other son badly. It is the same today. [30]But what does the Scripture say? "Throw out the slave woman and her son! The son of the free woman will receive everything his father has. But the son of the slave woman will receive nothing."[n] [31]So, my brothers, we are not children of the slave woman. We are children of the free woman.

Keep Your Freedom

5 We have freedom now because Christ made us free. So stand strong. Do not change and go back

---

Those people They are the false teachers who were bothering the believers in Galatia (Galatians 1:7).
Mount Sinai Mountain in Arabia where God gave his laws to Moses (Exodus 19 and 20).
"Throw ... nothing." Quotation from Genesis 21:10.

into the slavery of the law. [2]Listen! I am Paul. I tell you that if you go back to the law by being circumcised,[d] then Christ is no good for you. [3]Again, I warn every man: if you allow yourselves to be circumcised, then you must follow all the law. [4]If you try to be made right with God through the law, then your life with Christ is over — you have left God's grace. [5]But we hope to be made right with God through faith, and we wait for this hope anxiously with the Spirit's[d] help. [6]When we are in Christ Jesus, it is not important if we are circumcised or not. The important thing is faith — the kind of faith that works through love.

[7]You were running a good race. You were obeying the truth. Who stopped you from following the true way? [8]Whatever way he used did not come from the One who chose you. [9]Be careful! "Just a little yeast makes the whole batch of dough rise." [10]But I trust in the Lord that you will not believe those different ideas. Someone is confusing you with such ideas. And he will be punished, whoever he is.

[11]My brothers, I do not teach that a man must be circumcised. If I teach circumcision, then why am I still being treated badly? If I still taught circumcision, my preaching about the cross would not be a problem. [12]I wish the people who are bothering you would castrate[n] themselves!

[13]My brothers, God called you to be free. But do not use your freedom as an excuse to do the things that please your sinful self. Serve each other with love. [14]The whole law is made complete in this one command: "Love your neighbour as you love yourself."[n] [15]If you go on hurting each other and tearing each other apart, be careful! You will completely destroy each other.

The Spirit and Human Nature

[16]So I tell you: live by following the Spirit.[d] Then you will not do what your sinful selves want. [17]Our sinful selves want what is against the Spirit. The Spirit wants what is against our sinful selves. The two are against each other. So you must not do just what you please. [18]But if you let the Spirit lead you, you are not under the law.

[19]The wrong things the sinful self does are clear: being sexually unfaithful, not being pure, taking part in sexual sins, [20]worshipping false gods, doing witchcraft,[d] hating, making trouble, being jealous, being angry, being selfish, making people angry with each other, causing divisions among people, [21]having envy, being drunk, having wild and wasteful parties, and doing other things like this. I warn you now as I warned you before: those who do these things will not be in God's kingdom. [22]But the Spirit gives love, joy, peace, patience, kindness, goodness, faithfulness, [23]gentleness, self-control. There is no law that says these things are wrong. [24]Those who belong to Christ Jesus have crucified their own sinful selves. They have given up their old selfish feelings and the evil things they wanted to do. [25]We get our new life from the Spirit. So we should follow the Spirit. [26]We must not be proud. We must not make trouble with each other. And we must not be jealous of each other.

Help Each Other

6 Brothers, someone in your group might do something wrong. You who are spiritual should go to him and help make him right again. You should do this in a gentle way. But be careful! You might be tempted to sin, too.

---

castrate To cut off part of the male sex organ. Paul uses this word because it is similar to "circumcision". Paul wanted to show that he is very upset with the false teachers.
"Love ... yourself." Quotation from Leviticus 19:18.

²Help each other with your troubles. When you do this, you truly obey the law of Christ. ³If anyone thinks that he is important when he is really not important, he is only fooling himself. ⁴He should not compare himself with others. Each person should judge his own actions. Then he can be proud for what he himself has done. ⁵Each person must be responsible for himself.

⁶Anyone who is learning the teaching of God should share all the good things he has with his teacher.

Life Is like Planting a Field

⁷Do not be fooled: you cannot cheat God. A person harvests only what he plants. ⁸If he plants to satisfy his sinful self, his sinful self will bring him eternal death. But if he plants to please the Spirit,ᵈ he will receive eternal life from the Spirit. ⁹We must not become tired of doing good. We will receive our harvest of eternal life at the right time. We must not give up! ¹⁰When we have the opportunity to help anyone, we should do it. But we should give special attention to those who are in the family of believers.

Paul Ends His Letter

¹¹I am writing this myself. See what large letters I use. ¹²Some men are trying to force you to be circumcised.ᵈ They do these things so that the Jews will accept them. They are afraid that they will be treated badly if they follow only the cross of Christ.ⁿ ¹³Those who are circumcised do not obey the law themselves, but they want you to be circumcised. Then they can boast about what they forced you to do. ¹⁴I hope I will never boast about things like that. The cross of our Lord Jesus Christ is my only reason for boasting. Through the cross of Jesus my world was crucified and I died to the world. ¹⁵It is not important if a man is circumcised or not circumcised. The important thing is being the new people God has made. ¹⁶Peace and mercy to those who follow this rule—to all of God's people.

¹⁷So do not give me any more trouble. I have scars on my body. These showⁿ I belong to Christ Jesus.

¹⁸My brothers, I pray that the grace of our Lord Jesus Christ will be with your spirit. Amen.

---

cross of Christ Paul uses the cross as a picture of the gospel, the story of Christ's death and rising from death to pay for men's sins. The cross, or Christ's death, was God's way to save men.

These show Many times Paul was beaten and whipped by people who were against him because he was teaching about Christ. The scars were from these beatings.

EPHESIANS

God Unites His People

1 From Paul, an apostle[d] of Christ Jesus. I am an apostle because that is what God wanted.

To God's holy people living in Ephesus, believers in Christ Jesus.

[2] Grace and peace to you from God our Father and the Lord Jesus Christ.

Spiritual Blessings in Christ

[3] Praise be to the God and Father of our Lord Jesus Christ. In Christ, God has given us every spiritual blessing in heaven. [4] In Christ, he chose us before the world was made. In his love he chose us to be his holy people — people without blame before him. [5] And before the world was made, God decided to make us his own children through Jesus Christ. That was what he wanted and what pleased him. [6] This brings praise to God because of his wonderful grace. God gave that grace to us freely, in Christ, the One he loves. [7] In Christ we are set free by the blood of his death. And so we have forgiveness of sins because of God's rich grace. [8] God gave us that grace fully and freely. God, with full wisdom and understanding, [9] let us know his secret purpose. This was what God wanted, and he planned to do it through Christ. [10] His goal was to carry out his plan when the right time came. He planned that all things in heaven and on earth would be joined together in Christ as the head.

[11] In Christ we were chosen to be God's people. God had already chosen us to be his people, because that is what he wanted. And God is the One who makes everything agree with what he decides and wants. [12] We are the first people who hoped in Christ.

And we were chosen so that we would bring praise to God's glory. [13] So it is with you. You heard the true teaching — the Good News[d] about your salvation. When you heard it, you believed in Christ. And in Christ, God put his special mark on you by giving you the Holy Spirit[d] that he had promised. [14] That Holy Spirit is the guarantee that we will get what God promised for his people. This will bring full freedom to the people who belong to God, to bring praise to God's glory.

Paul's Prayer

[15-16] That is why I always remember you in my prayers and always thank God for you. I have always done this since the time I heard about your faith in the Lord Jesus and your love for all God's people. [17] I always pray to the God of our Lord Jesus Christ — to the glorious Father. I pray that he will give you a spirit that will make you wise in the knowledge of God — the knowledge that he has shown you. [18] I pray that you will have greater understanding in your heart. Then you will know the hope that God has chosen to give us. I pray that you will know that the blessings God has promised his holy people are rich and glorious. [19] And you will know that God's power is very great for us who believe. That power is the same as the great strength [20] God used to raise Christ from death and put him at his right side in heaven. [21] God made Christ more important than all rulers, authorities, powers, and kings. Christ is more important than anything in this world or in the next world. [22] God put

everything under his power. And God made him the head over everything for the church. ²³The church is Christ's body. The church is filled with Christ, and Christ fills everything in every way.

From Death to Life

2 In the past your spiritual lives were dead because of your sins and the things you did wrong against God. ²Yes, in the past you lived the way the world lives. You followed the ruler of the evil powers that are above the earth. That same spirit is now working in those who refuse to obey God. ³In the past all of us lived like them. We lived trying to please our sinful selves. We did all the things our bodies and minds wanted. We should have suffered God's anger because of the way we were. We were the same as all other people.

⁴But God's mercy is great, and he loved us very much. ⁵We were spiritually dead because of the things we did wrong against God. But God gave us new life with Christ. You have been saved by God's grace. ⁶And he raised us up with Christ and gave us a seat with him in the heavens. He did this for those of us who are in Christ Jesus. ⁷He did this so that for all future time he could show the very great riches of his grace. He shows that grace by being kind to us in Christ Jesus. ⁸I mean that you have been saved by grace because you believe. You did not save yourselves. It was a gift from God. ⁹You cannot boast that you are saved by the work you have done. ¹⁰God has made us what we are. In Christ Jesus, God made us new people so that we would do good works. God had planned in advance those good works for us. He had planned for us to live our lives doing them.

One in Christ

¹¹You were born non-Jews. You are the people the Jews call "uncircumcised".ⁿ Those who call you "uncircumcised" call themselves "circumcised".ᵈ (Their circumcision is only something they themselves do to their bodies.) ¹²Remember that in the past you were without Christ. You were not citizens of Israel. And you had no part in the agreementsⁿ with the promise that God made to his people. You had no hope, and you did not know God. ¹³Yes, at one time you were far away from God. But now in Christ Jesus you are brought near to God through the blood of Christ's death. ¹⁴Because of Christ we now have peace. Christ made both Jews and non-Jews one people. They were separated as if there were a wall between them. But Christ broke down that wall of hate by giving his own body. ¹⁵The Jewish law had many commands and rules. But Christ ended that law. Christ's purpose was to make the two groups of people become one new people in him. By doing this Christ would make peace. ¹⁶Through the cross Christ ended the hatred between the two groups. And after Christ made the two groups to be one body, he wanted to bring them back to God. Christ did this with his death on the cross. ¹⁷Christ came and preached peace to you non-Jews who were far away from God. And he preached peace to those Jews who were near to God. ¹⁸Yes, through Christ we all have the right to come to the Father in one Spirit.ᵈ

¹⁹So now you non-Jews are not visitors or strangers. Now you are citizens together with God's holy people. You belong to God's family. ²⁰You believers are like a building that God owns. That building was built on the foundation of the apostlesᵈ and proph-

uncircumcised People not having the mark of circumcision as the Jews have.
agreements The agreements that God gave to his people in the Old Testament.

ets.*d* Christ Jesus himself is the most important stone*n* in that building. [21]That whole building is joined together in Christ. And Christ makes it grow and become a holy temple in the Lord. [22]And in Christ you, too, are being built together with the Jews. You are being built into a place where God lives through the Spirit.

Paul's Work for the Non-Jews

3 So I, Paul, am a prisoner of Christ Jesus. I am a prisoner for you who are not Jews. [2]Surely you know that God gave me this work through his grace to help you. [3]God let me know his secret plan. He showed it to me. I have already written a little about this. [4]And if you read what I wrote, then you can see that I truly understand the secret truth about the Christ.*d* [5]People who lived in other times were not told that secret truth. But now, through the Spirit,*d* God has shown that secret truth to his holy apostles*d* and prophets.*d* [6]This is that secret truth: that the non-Jews will receive what God has for his people, just as the Jews will. The non-Jews are together with the Jews as part of the same body. And they share together in the promise that God made in Christ Jesus. The non-Jews have all of this because of the Good News.*d*

[7]By God's special gift of grace, I became a servant to tell that Good News. God gave me that grace through his power. [8]I am the least important of all God's people. But God gave me this gift — to tell the non-Jewish people the Good News about the riches of Christ. Those riches are too great to understand fully. [9]And God gave me the work of telling all people about the plan for God's secret truth. That secret truth has been hidden in God since the beginning of time. God is the One who created ev-

erything. [10]His purpose was that through the church all the rulers and powers in the heavenly world will now know God's wisdom, which has so many forms. [11]This agrees with the purpose God had since the beginning of time. And God carried out his plan through Christ Jesus our Lord. [12]In Christ we can come before God with freedom and without fear. We can do this through faith in Christ. [13]So I ask you not to become discouraged because of the sufferings I am having for you. My sufferings bring honour to you.

The Love of Christ

[14]So I bow in prayer before the Father. [15]Every family in heaven and on earth gets its true name from him. [16]I ask the Father in his great glory to give you the power to be strong in spirit. He will give you that strength through his Spirit.*d* [17]I pray that Christ will live in your hearts because of your faith. I pray that your life will be strong in love and be built on love. [18]And I pray that you and all God's holy people will have the power to understand the greatness of Christ's love. I pray that you can understand how wide and how long and how high and how deep that love is. [19]Christ's love is greater than any person can ever know. But I pray that you will be able to know that love. Then you can be filled with the fullness of God.

[20]With God's power working in us, God can do much, much more than anything we can ask or think of. [21]To him be glory in the church and in Christ Jesus for all time, for ever and ever. Amen.

The Unity of the Body

4 I am in prison because I belong to the Lord. God chose you to be his people. I tell you now to live the way

---

most important stone Literally, "cornerstone". The first and most important stone in a building.

God's people should live. [2]Always be humble and gentle. Be patient and accept each other with love. [3]You are joined together with peace through the Spirit.[d] Do all you can to continue together in this way. Let peace hold you together. [4]There is one body and one Spirit. And God called you to have one hope. [5]There is one Lord, one faith, and one baptism. [6]There is one God and Father of everything. He rules everything. He is everywhere and in everything.

[7]Christ gave each one of us a special gift. Each one received what Christ wanted to give him. [8]That is why it says in the Scriptures,[d]

"When he went up to the heights,
    he led a parade of captives.
And he gave gifts to people."

Psalm 68:18

[9]When it says, "He went up", what does it mean? It means that he first came down to the earth. [10]So Jesus came down, and he is the same One who went up. He went up above all the heavens. Christ did that to fill everything with himself. [11]And Christ gave gifts to men—he made some to be apostles,[d] some to be prophets,[d] some to go and tell the Good News,[d] and some to have the work of caring for and teaching God's people. [12]Christ gave those gifts to prepare God's holy people for the work of serving. He gave those gifts to make the body of Christ stronger. [13]This work must continue until we are all joined together in the same faith and in the same knowledge about the Son of God. We must become like a mature person—we must grow until we become like Christ and have all his perfection.

[14]Then we will no longer be babies. We will not be tossed about like a ship that the waves carry one way and then another. We will not be influenced by every new teaching we hear from men who are trying to fool us. Those men make plans and try any kind of trick to fool people into following the wrong path. [15]No! We will speak the truth with love. We will grow up in every way to be like Christ, who is the head. [16]The whole body depends on Christ. And all the parts of the body are joined and held together. Each part of the body does its own work. And this makes the whole body grow and be strong with love.

The Way You Should Live

[17]In the Lord's name, I tell you this. I warn you: do not continue living like those who do not believe. Their thoughts are worth nothing. [18]They do not understand. They know nothing, because they refuse to listen. So they cannot have the life that God gives. [19]They have lost their feeling of shame. And they use their lives for doing evil. More and more they want to do all kinds of evil things. [20]But the things you learned in Christ were not like this. [21]I know that you heard about him, and you are in him; so you were taught the truth. Yes, the truth is in Jesus. [22]You were taught to leave your old self—to stop living the evil way you lived before. That old self becomes worse and worse because people are fooled by the evil things they want to do. [23]But you were taught to be made new in your hearts. [24]You were taught to become a new person. That new person is made to be like God—made to be truly good and holy.

[25]So you must stop telling lies. Tell each other the truth because we all belong to each other in the same body.[n] [26]When you are angry, do not sin. And do not go on being angry all day. [27]Do not give the devil a way to defeat you. [28]If a person is stealing, he must stop stealing and start working. He must use his hands for doing something good. Then he will have

Tell ... body. Quotation from Zechariah 8:16.

something to share with those who are poor.

²⁹When you talk, do not say harmful things. But say what people need — words that will help others become stronger. Then what you say will help those who listen to you. ³⁰And do not make the Holy Spirit*ᵈ* sad. The Spirit is God's proof that you belong to him. God gave you the Spirit to show that God will make you free when the time comes. ³¹Do not be bitter or angry or cross. Never shout angrily or say things to hurt others. Never do anything evil. ³²Be kind and loving to each other. Forgive each other just as God forgave you in Christ.

Living in the Light

5 You are God's children whom he loves. So try to be like God. ²Live a life of love. Love other people just as Christ loved us. Christ gave himself for us — he was a sweet-smelling offering and sacrifice to God.

³But there must be no sexual sin among you. There must not be any kind of evil or greed. Those things are not right for God's holy people. ⁴Also, there must be no evil talk among you. You must not speak foolishly or tell evil jokes. These things are not right for you. But you should be giving thanks to God. ⁵You can be sure of this: no one will have a place in the kingdom of Christ and of God if he does sexual sins, or does evil things, or is greedy. Anyone who is greedy is serving a false god.

⁶Do not let anyone fool you by telling you things that are not true. These things will bring God's anger on those who do not obey him. ⁷So have nothing to do with them. ⁸In the past you were full of darkness, but now you are full of light in the Lord. So live like children who belong to the light. ⁹Light brings every kind of goodness, right living, and truth. ¹⁰Try to learn what pleases the Lord. ¹¹Do not do the things that people in darkness do. That brings

nothing good. But do good things to show that the things done in darkness are wrong. ¹²It is shameful even to talk about what those people do in secret. ¹³But the light makes all things easy to see. ¹⁴And everything that is made easy to see can become light. This is why it is said:

"Wake up, sleeper!
 Rise from death,
 and Christ will shine on you."

¹⁵So be very careful how you live. Do not live like those who are not wise. Live wisely. ¹⁶I mean that you should use every chance you have for doing good, because these are evil times. ¹⁷So do not be foolish with your lives. But learn what the Lord wants you to do. ¹⁸Do not be drunk with wine. That will ruin you spiritually. But be filled with the Spirit.*ᵈ* ¹⁹Speak to each other with psalms, hymns, and spiritual songs. Sing and make music in your hearts to the Lord. ²⁰Always give thanks to God the Father for everything, in the name of our Lord Jesus Christ.

Wives and Husbands

²¹Be willing to obey each other. Do this because you respect Christ.

²²Wives, be under the authority of your husbands, as of the Lord. ²³The husband is the head of the wife, as Christ is the head of the church. The church is Christ's body — Christ is the Saviour of the body. ²⁴The church is under the authority of Christ. So it is the same with you wives. You should be under the authority of your husbands in everything.

²⁵Husbands, love your wives as Christ loved the church. Christ died for the church ²⁶to make it belong to God. Christ used the word to make the church clean by washing it with water. ²⁷Christ died so that he could give the church to himself like a bride in all her beauty. He died so that the church could be pure and without fault, with no evil or sin or any other

wrong thing in it. [28]And husbands should love their wives in the same way. They should love their wives as they love their own bodies. The man who loves his wife loves himself. [29]No person ever hates his own body, but feeds and takes care of it. And that is what Christ does for the church, [30]because we are parts of his body. [31]The Scripture says, "So a man will leave his father and mother and be united with his wife. And the two people will become one body."[n] [32]That secret truth is very important—I am talking about Christ and the church. [33]But each one of you must love his wife as he loves himself. And a wife must respect her husband.

Children and Parents

6 Children, obey your parents the way the Lord wants. This is the right thing to do. [2]The command says, "Honour your father and mother."[n] This is the first command that has a promise with it. [3]The promise is: "Then everything will be well with you, and you will have a long life on the earth."[n]

[4]Fathers, do not make your children angry, but raise them with the training and teaching of the Lord.

Slaves and Masters

[5]Slaves, obey your masters here on earth with fear and respect. And do that with a heart that is true, just as you obey Christ. [6]You must do more than obey your masters to please them only while they are watching you. You must obey them as you are obeying Christ. With all your heart you must do what God wants. [7]Do your work, and be happy to do it. Work as if you were serving the Lord, not as if you were serving only men. [8]Remember that the Lord will give a reward to everyone, slave or free, for doing good.

[9]Masters, in the same way, be good to your slaves. Do not say things to scare them. You know that the One who is your Master and their Master is in heaven. And that Master treats everyone alike.

Wear the Full Armour of God

[10]Finally, be strong in the Lord and in his great power. [11]Wear the full armour of God. Wear God's armour so that you can fight against the devil's evil tricks. [12]Our fight is not against people on earth. We are fighting against the rulers and authorities and the powers of this world's darkness. We are fighting against the spiritual powers of evil in the heavenly world. [13]That is why you need to put on God's full armour. Then on the day of evil you will be able to stand strong. And when you have finished the whole fight, you will still be standing. [14]So stand strong, with the belt of truth tied around your waist. And on your chest wear the protection of right living. [15]And on your feet wear the Good News[d] of peace to help you stand strong. [16]And also use the shield of faith. With that you can stop all the burning arrows of the Evil One. [17]Accept God's salvation to be your helmet. And take the sword of the Spirit[d]—that sword is the teaching of God. [18]Pray in the Spirit at all times. Pray with all kinds of prayers, and ask for everything you need. To do this you must always be ready. Never give up. Always pray for all God's people.

[19]Also pray for me. Pray that when I speak, God will give me words so that I can tell the secret truth of the Good News without fear. [20]I have the work of speaking that Good News. I

"So . . . body." Quotation from Genesis 2:24.
"Honour . . . mother." Quotation from Exodus 20:12; Deuteronomy 5:16.
"Then . . . earth." Quotation from Exodus 20:12; Deuteronomy 5:16.

am doing that now, here in prison. Pray that when I preach the Good News I will speak without fear, as I should.

Final Greetings

[21]I am sending to you Tychicus, our brother whom we love. He is a faithful servant of the Lord's work. He will tell you everything that is happening with me. Then you will know how I am and what I am doing. [22]That is why I am sending him. I want you to know how we are. I am sending him to encourage you.

[23]Peace and love with faith to you from God the Father and the Lord Jesus Christ. [24]God's grace to all of you who love our Lord Jesus Christ with love that never ends.

PHILIPPIANS

Serve Others with Joy

1 From Paul and Timothy, servants of Jesus Christ.

To all of God's holy people in Christ Jesus who live in Philippi. And to your elders[d] and deacons.[d]

[2]Grace and peace to you from God our Father and the Lord Jesus Christ.

Paul's Prayer

[3]I thank God every time I remember you. [4]And I always pray for all of you with joy. [5]I thank God for the help you gave me while I preached the Good News.[d] You helped from the first day you believed until now. [6]God began doing a good work in you. And he will continue it until it is finished when Jesus Christ comes again. I am sure of that.

[7]And I know that I am right to think like this about all of you. I am sure because I have you in my heart. All of you share in God's grace with me. You share in God's grace with me while I am in prison, while I am defending the Good News, and while I am proving the truth of the Good News. [8]God knows that I want to see you very much. I love all of you with the love of Christ Jesus.

[9]This is my prayer for you: that your love will grow more and more; that you will have knowledge and understanding with your love; [10]that you will see the difference between good and bad and choose the good; that you will be pure and without wrong for the coming of Christ; [11]that you will do many good things with the help of Christ to bring glory and praise to God.

Paul's Troubles Help the Work

[12]Brothers, I want you to know that what has happened to me has helped to spread the Good News.[d] [13]I am in prison because I am a believer in Christ. All the palace guards and everyone else knows this. [14]I am still in prison, but most of the believers feel better about this now. And so they are much braver about telling the Good News about Christ.

[15]It is true that some preach about Christ because they are jealous and bitter. But others preach about Christ because they want to help. [16]They preach because they have love, and they know that God gave me the work of defending the Good News. [17]But others preach about Christ because they are selfish. Their reason for preaching is wrong. They want to make trouble for me in prison.

[18]But I do not care if they make trouble for me. The important thing is that they are preaching about Christ. They should do it for the right reasons. But I am happy even if they do it for wrong reasons. And I will continue to be happy. [19]You are praying for me, and the Spirit of Jesus Christ helps me. So I know that this trouble will bring my freedom. [20]The thing I want and hope for is that I will not fail Christ in anything. I hope that I will have the courage now, as always, to show the greatness of Christ in my life here on earth. I want to do that if I die or if I live. [21]To me the only important thing about living is Christ. And even death would be profit for me. [22]If I continue living in the body, I will be able to work for the Lord. But what should I choose—living or dying? I do not know. [23]It is hard to choose between the two. I want to leave this life and be with Christ. That is much bet-

ter. ²⁴But you need me here in my body. ²⁵I know that you need me, and so I know that I will stay with you. I will help you grow and have joy in your faith. ²⁶You will be very happy in Christ Jesus when I am with you again.

²⁷Be sure that you live in a way that brings honour to the Good News of Christ. Then whether I come and visit you or am away from you, I will hear good things about you. I will hear that you continue strong with one purpose and that you work together as a team for the faith of the Good News. ²⁸And you will not be afraid of those who are against you. All of these things are proof from God that you will be saved and that your enemies will be lost. ²⁹God gave you the honour both of believing in Christ and suffering for Christ. Both these things bring glory to Christ. ³⁰When I was with you, you saw the struggles I had. And you hear about the struggles I am having now. You yourselves are having the same kind of struggles.

2 Does your life in Christ give you strength? Does his love comfort you? Do we share together in the Spirit?^d Do you have mercy and kindness? ²If so, make me very happy by having the same thoughts, sharing the same love, and having one mind and purpose. ³When you do things, do not let selfishness or pride be your guide. Be humble and give more honour to others than to yourselves. ⁴Do not be interested only in your own life, but be interested in the lives of others.

Be Unselfish like Christ

⁵In your lives you must think and act like Christ Jesus.
⁶Christ himself was like God in
    everything.
He was equal with God.
But he did not think that being
    equal with God was
    something to be held on to.

⁷He gave up his place with God
    and made himself nothing.
He was born to be a man
    and became like a servant.
⁸And when he was living as a man,
    he humbled himself and was fully
        obedient to God.
He obeyed even when it caused
    his death—death on a cross.
⁹So God raised Christ to the
    highest place.
God made the name of Christ
    greater than every other
    name.
¹⁰God wants every knee to bow to
    Jesus—
everyone in heaven, on earth,
    and under the earth.
¹¹Everyone will say, "Jesus Christ
        is Lord"
and bring glory to God the
    Father.

Be the People God Wants You to Be

¹²My dear friends, you have always obeyed. You obeyed God when I was with you. It is even more important that you obey now while I am not with you. Keep on working to complete your salvation, and do it with fear and trembling. ¹³Yes, God is working in you to help you want to do what pleases him. Then he gives you the power to do it.

¹⁴Do everything without complaining or arguing. ¹⁵Then you will be innocent and without anything wrong in you. You will be God's children without fault. But you are living with crooked and mean people all around you. Among them you shine like stars in the dark world. ¹⁶You offer to them the teaching that gives life. So when Christ comes again, I can be happy because my work was not wasted. I ran in the race and won.

¹⁷Your faith makes you offer your lives as a sacrifice in serving God. Perhaps I will have to offer my own blood with your sacrifice. But if that

happens, I will be happy and full of joy with all of you. [18]You also should be happy and full of joy with me.

Timothy and Epaphroditus

[19]I hope in the Lord Jesus to send Timothy to you soon. I will be happy to learn how you are. [20]I have no other person like Timothy. He truly cares for you. [21]Other people are interested only in their own lives. They are not interested in the work of Christ Jesus. [22]You know the kind of person Timothy is. You know that he has served with me in telling the Good News, [d] as a son serves his father. [23]I plan to send him to you quickly when I know what will happen to me. [24]I am sure that the Lord will help me to come to you soon.

[25]Epaphroditus is my brother in Christ. He works and serves with me in the army of Christ. When I needed help, you sent him to me. I think now that I must send him back to you [26]because he wants very much to see all of you. He is worried because you heard that he was sick. [27]Yes, he was sick, and nearly died. But God helped him and me too, so that I would not have more sadness. [28]So I want very much to send him to you. When you see him, you can be happy. And I can stop worrying about you. [29]Welcome him in the Lord with much joy. Give honour to people like Epaphroditus. [30]He should be honoured because he almost died for the work of Christ. He put his life in danger so that he could help me. This was help that you could not give me.

The Importance of Christ

3 My brothers, be full of joy in the Lord. It is no trouble for me to write the same things to you again, and it will help you to be more ready. [2]Be careful of those who do evil. They are like dogs. They demand that we

cut[n] the body. [3]But we are the ones who are truly circumcised.[d] We worship God through his Spirit.[d] We are proud to be in Christ Jesus. And we do not trust in ourselves or anything we can do. [4]Even if I am able to trust in myself, still I do not. If anyone thinks that he has a reason to trust in himself, he should know that I have greater reason for trusting in myself. [5]I was circumcised eight days after my birth. I am from the people of Israel and the tribe[d] of Benjamin. I am a Hebrew, and my parents were Hebrews. The law of Moses was very important to me. That is why I became a Pharisee.[d] [6]I was so enthusiastic that I tried to hurt the church. No one could find fault with the way I obeyed the law of Moses. [7]At one time all these things were important to me. But now I think those things are worth nothing because of Christ. [8]Not only those things, but I think that all things are worth nothing compared with the greatness of knowing Christ Jesus my Lord. Because of Christ, I have lost all those things. And now I know that all those things are worthless rubbish. This allows me to have Christ [9]and to belong to him. Now that I belong to Christ, I am right with God and this being right does not come from my following the law. It comes from God through faith. God uses my faith in Christ to make me right with him. [10]All I want is to know Christ and the power of his rising from death. I want to share in Christ's sufferings and become like him in his death. [11]If I have those things, then I have hope that I myself will be raised from death.

Continuing Towards Our Goal

[12]I do not mean that I am already as God wants me to be. I have not yet reached that goal. But I continue trying to reach it and to make it mine. Christ wants me to do that. That is

cut The word in Greek is like the word "circumcise", but it means "to cut completely off".

the reason Christ made me his. [13]Brothers, I know that I have not yet reached that goal. But there is one thing I always do: I forget the things that are past. I try as hard as I can to reach the goal that is before me. [14]I keep trying to reach the goal and get the prize. That prize is mine because God called me through Christ to the life above.

[15]All of us who have grown spiritually to be mature should think this way, too. And if there are things you do not agree with, God will make them clear to you. [16]But we should continue following the truth we already have.

[17]Brothers, all of you should try to follow my example and to copy those who live the way we showed you. [18]Many people live like enemies of the cross of Christ. I have often told you about them, and it makes me cry to tell you about them now. [19]The way they live is leading them to destruction. Instead of serving God, they do whatever their bodies want. They do shameful things, and they are proud of it. They think only about earthly things. [20]But our homeland is in heaven, and we are waiting for our Saviour, the Lord Jesus Christ, to come from heaven. [21]He will change our simple bodies and make them like his own glorious body. Christ can do this by his power. With that power he is able to rule all things.

What the Christians Are to Do

4 My dear brothers, I love you and want to see you. You bring me joy and make me proud of you. Continue following the Lord as I have told you.

[2]I ask Euodia and Syntyche to agree in the Lord. [3]And because you serve faithfully with me, my friend, I ask you to help these women to do this. They served with me in telling people the Good News.[d] They served together with Clement and others who worked with me. Their names are written in the book of life.[n]

[4]Be full of joy in the Lord always. I will say again, be full of joy.

[5]Let all men see that you are gentle and kind. The Lord is coming soon. [6]Do not worry about anything. But pray and ask God for everything you need. And when you pray, always give thanks. [7]And God's peace will keep your hearts and minds in Christ Jesus. The peace that God gives is so great that we cannot understand it.

[8]Brothers, continue to think about the things that are good and worthy of praise. Think about the things that are true and honourable and right and pure and beautiful and respected. [9]And do what you learned and received from me. Do what I told you and what you saw me do. And the God who gives peace will be with you.

Paul Thanks the Christians

[10]I am very happy in the Lord that you have shown your care for me again. You continued to care about me, but there was no way for you to show it. [11]I am telling you this, but it is not because I need anything. I have learned to be satisfied with the things I have and with everything that happens. [12]I know how to live when I am poor. And I know how to live when I have plenty. I have learned the secret of being happy at any time in everything that happens. I have learned to be happy when I have enough to eat and when I do not have enough to eat. I have learned to be happy when I have all that I need and when I do not have the things I need. [13]I can do all things through Christ because he gives me strength.

[14]But it was good that you helped me when I needed help. [15]You people in Philippi remember when I first

---

book of life God's book that has the names of all God's chosen people (Revelation 3:5; 21:27).

preached the Good News[d] there. When I left Macedonia, you were the only church that gave me help. [16]Several times you sent me things I needed when I was in Thessalonica. [17]Really, it is not that I want to receive gifts from you. But I want you to have the good that comes from giving. [18]And now I have everything, and more. I have all I need because Epaphroditus brought your gift to me. Your gift is like a sweet-smelling sacrifice offered to God. God accepts that sacrifice, and it pleases him. [19]My God will use his wonderful riches in Christ Jesus to give you everything you need. [20]Glory to our God and Father for ever and ever! Amen.

[21]Greet each of God's people in Christ. God's people who are with me send greetings to you. [22]All of God's people greet you. And those believers from the palace of Caesar[d] greet you, too.

[23]The grace of the Lord Jesus Christ be with you all.

COLOSSIANS

Only Christ Can Save People

1 From Paul, an apostle[d] of Christ Jesus. I am an apostle because that is what God wanted.

Also from Timothy, our brother.

[2]To the holy and faithful brothers in Christ that live in Colosse. Grace and peace from God our Father.

[3]In our prayers for you we always thank God, the Father of our Lord Jesus Christ. [4]We thank God because we have heard about the faith you have in Christ Jesus and the love you have for all of God's people. [5]You have this faith and love because of your hope, and what you hope for is saved for you in heaven. You learned about this hope when you heard the true teaching, the Good News[d] [6]that was told to you. Everywhere in the world that Good News is bringing blessings and is growing. This has happened with you, too, since you heard the Good News and understood the truth about the grace of God. [7]You learned about God's grace from Epaphras, whom we love. Epaphras works together with us and is a faithful servant of Christ for us. [8]He also told us about the love you have from the Holy Spirit.[d]

[9]Since the day we heard this about you, we have continued praying for you. We ask God that you will know fully what God wants. We pray that you will also have great wisdom and understanding in spiritual things. [10]Then you will live the kind of life that honours and pleases the Lord in every way. You will produce fruit in every good work and grow in the knowledge of God. [11]Then God will strengthen you with his own great power. And you will not give up when troubles come, but you will be patient. [12]Then you will joyfully give thanks to the Father. He has made you able to have all that he has prepared for his people who live in the light. [13]God made us free from the power of darkness, and he brought us into the kingdom of his dear Son. [14]The Son paid for our sins, and in him we have forgiveness.

The Importance of Christ

[15]No one has seen God, but Jesus is exactly like him. Christ ranks higher than all the things that have been made. [16]Through his power all things were made — things in heaven and on earth, things seen and unseen, all powers, authorities, lords, and rulers. All things were made through Christ and for Christ. [17]Christ was there before anything was made. And all things continue because of him. [18]He is the head of the body. (The body is the church.) Everything comes from him. And he is the first one who was raised from death. So in all things Jesus is most important. [19]God was pleased for all of himself to live in Christ. [20]And through Christ, God decided to bring all things back to himself again — things on earth and things in heaven. God made peace by using the blood of Christ's death on the cross.

[21]At one time you were separated from God. You were God's enemies in your minds because the evil deeds you did were against God. [22]But now Christ has made you God's friends again. He did this by his death while he was in the body, that he might bring you into God's presence. He brings you before God as people who are holy, with no wrong in you, and with nothing that God can judge you guilty of. [23]And Christ will do this if

you continue to believe in the Good News[d] you heard. You must continue strong and sure in your faith. You must not be moved away from the hope that Good News gave you. That same Good News has been told to everyone in the world. I, Paul, help in preaching that Good News.

Paul's Work for the Church

24I am happy in my sufferings for you. There are many things that Christ must still suffer through his body, the church. I am accepting my part of these things that must be suffered. I accept these sufferings in my body. I suffer for his body, the church. 25I became a servant of the church because God gave me a special work to do that helps you. My work is to tell fully the teaching of God. 26This teaching is the secret truth that was hidden since the beginning of time. It was hidden from everyone, but now it is made known to God's holy people. 27God decided to let his people know this rich and glorious truth which he has for all people. This truth is Christ himself, who is in you. He is our only hope for glory. 28So we continue to preach Christ to all men. We use all wisdom to warn and to teach everyone. We are trying to bring each one into God's presence as a mature person in Christ. 29To do this, I work and struggle, using Christ's great strength that works so powerfully in me.

2 I want you to know that I am trying very hard to help you. And I am trying to help those in Laodicea and others who have never seen me. 2I want them to be strengthened and joined together with love. I want them to be rich in the strong belief that comes from understanding. I mean I want you to know fully God's secret truth. That truth is Christ himself. 3And in him all the treasures of wisdom and knowledge are safely kept.

4I say this so that no one can fool you by arguments that seem good, but are false. 5I am not there with you, but my heart is with you. I am happy to see your good lives and your strong faith in Christ.

Continue to Live in Christ

6As you received Christ Jesus the Lord, so continue to live in him. 7Keep your roots deep in him and have your lives built on him. Be strong in the faith, just as you were taught. And always be thankful.

8Be sure that no one leads you away with false ideas and words that mean nothing. Those ideas come from men. They are the worthless ideas of this world. They are not from Christ. 9All of God lives in Christ fully (even when Christ was on earth). 10And in him you have a full and true life. He is ruler over all rulers and powers.

11In Christ you had a different kind of circumcision.[d] That circumcision was not done by hands. I mean, you were made free from the power of your sinful self. That is the kind of circumcision Christ does. 12When you were baptised, you were buried with Christ and you were raised up with Christ because of your faith in God's power. That power was shown when he raised Christ from death. 13You were spiritually dead because of your sins and because you were not free from the power of your sinful self. But God made you alive with Christ. And God forgave all our sins. 14We owed a debt because we broke God's laws. That debt listed all the rules we failed to follow. But God forgave us that debt. He took away that debt and nailed it to the cross. 15God defeated the spiritual rulers and powers. With the cross God won the victory and defeated them. He showed the world that they were powerless.

Don't Follow People's Rules

16So do not let anyone make rules for you about eating and drinking or

about a religious feast, a New Moon*d*
Festival, or a Sabbath*d* day. [17]In the
past, these things were like a shadow
of what was to come. But the new
things that were coming are found in
Christ. [18]Some enjoy acting as if they
were humble and love to worship angels. They are always talking about
the visions they have seen. Do not let
them tell you that you are wrong.
They are full of foolish pride because
of their human way of thinking. [19]They
do not keep themselves under the
control of Christ, the head. The whole
body depends on Christ. Because of
him all the parts of the body care for
each other and help each other. This
strengthens the body and holds it together. And so the body grows in the
way God wants.

[20]You died with Christ and were
made free from the worthless rules of
the world. So why do you act as if you
still belong to this world? I mean, why
do you follow rules like these:
[21]"Don't eat this", "Don't taste that",
"Don't touch that thing"? [22]These
rules are talking about earthly things
that are gone as soon as they are
used. They are only man-made commands and teachings. [23]These rules
seem to be wise. But they are only
part of a man-made religion. They
make people pretend not to be proud
and make them punish their bodies.
But they do not really control the evil
desires of the sinful self.

Your New Life in Christ

3 You were raised from death with
Christ. So aim at what is in heav-
en, where Christ is sitting at the right
hand of God. [2]Think only about the
things in heaven, not the things on
earth. [3]Your old sinful self has died,
and your new life is kept with Christ in

God. [4]Christ is your life. When he
comes again, you will share in his glory.

[5]So put all evil things out of your
life: sexual sinning, doing evil, letting
evil thoughts control you, wanting
things that are evil, and always selfishly wanting more and more. This
really means living to serve a false
god. [6]These things make God an-
gry.*n* [7]In your evil life in the past, you
also did these things.

[8]But now put these things out of
your life: anger, bad temper, doing or
saying things to hurt others, and using
evil words when you talk. [9]Do not lie
to each other. You have left your old
sinful life and the things you did before. [10]You have begun to live the new
life. In your new life you are being
made new. You are becoming like the
One who made you. This new life
brings you the true knowledge of
God. [11]In the new life there is no difference between Greeks and Jews.
There is no difference between those
who are circumcised*d* and those who
are not circumcised, or people that
are foreigners, or Scythians.*n* There
is no difference between slaves and
free people. But Christ is in all believers. And Christ is all that is important.

[12]God has chosen you and made you
his holy people. He loves you. So always do these things: show mercy to
others; be kind, humble, gentle, and
patient. [13]Do not be angry with each
other, but forgive each other. If
someone does wrong to you, then forgive him. Forgive each other because
the Lord forgave you. [14]Do all these
things; but most important, love each
other. Love is what holds you all together in perfect unity. [15]Let the
peace that Christ gives control your

These . . . angry Some Greek copies add: "against the people who do not obey God."
Scythians The Scythians were known as very wild and cruel people.

thinking. You were all called together in one body[n] to have peace. Always be thankful. [16]Let the teaching of Christ live in you richly. Use all wisdom to teach and strengthen each other. Sing psalms, hymns, and spiritual songs with thankfulness in your hearts to God. [17]Everything you say and everything you do should all be done for Jesus your Lord. And in all you do, give thanks to God the Father through Jesus.

Your New Life with Other People

[18]Wives, be under the authority of your husbands. This is the right thing to do in the Lord.

[19]Husbands, love your wives, and be gentle to them.

[20]Children, obey your parents in all things. This pleases the Lord.

[21]Fathers, do not nag your children. If you are too hard to please, they may want to stop trying.

[22]Slaves, obey your masters in all things. Do not obey just when they are watching you, to gain their favour. But serve them honestly, because you respect the Lord. [23]In all the work you are doing, work the best you can. Work as if you were working for the Lord, not for men. [24]Remember that you will receive your reward from the Lord, which he promised to his people. You are serving the Lord Christ. [25]But remember that anyone who does wrong will be punished for that wrong. And the Lord treats everyone the same.

4 Masters, give the things that are good and fair to your slaves. Remember that you have a Master in heaven.

What the Christians Are to Do

[2]Continue praying and keep alert. And when you pray, always thank God. [3]Also pray for us. Pray that God will give us an opportunity to tell people his message. Pray that we can preach the secret truth that God has made known about Christ. I am in prison because I preach this truth. [4]Pray that I can speak in a way that will make it clear as I should.

[5]Be wise in the way you act with people who are not believers. Use your time in the best way you can. [6]When you talk, you should always be kind and wise. Then you will be able to answer everyone in the way you should.

News About the People with Paul

[7]Tychicus is my dear brother in Christ. He is a faithful minister and servant with me in the Lord. He will tell you all the things that are happening to me. [8]That is why I am sending him. I want you to know how we are. I am sending him to encourage you. [9]I send him with Onesimus. Onesimus is a faithful and dear brother in Christ. He is one of your group. They will tell you all that has happened here.

[10]Aristarchus greets you. He is a prisoner with me. And Mark, the cousin of Barnabas, also greets you. (I have already told you what to do about Mark. If he comes, welcome him.) [11]Jesus, who is called Justus, also greets you. These are the only Jewish believers who work with me for the kingdom of God. They have been a comfort to me.

[12]Epaphras also greets you. He is a servant of Jesus Christ. And he is from your group. He always prays for you. He prays that you will grow to be spiritually mature and have everything that God wants for you. [13]I know that he has worked hard for you and the people in Laodicea and in Hierapolis. [14]Demas and our dear friend Luke, the doctor, greet you.

[15]Greet the brothers in Laodicea. And greet Nympha and the church

body   The spiritual body of Christ, meaning the church or his people.

that meets in her house. [16]After this letter is read to you, be sure that it is also read to the church in Laodicea. And you must read the letter that I wrote to Laodicea. [17]Tell Archippus,

"Be sure to do the work the Lord gave you."

[18]I, Paul, greet you and write this with my own hand. Remember me in prison. God's grace be with you.

1 THESSALONIANS

Paul Encourages New Christians

1 From Paul, Silas, and Timothy. To the church in Thessalonica, the church in God the Father and the Lord Jesus Christ. May God's grace and peace be yours.

The Faith of the Thessalonians

2We always remember you when we pray and thank God for all of you. 3When we pray to God our Father, we always thank him for the things you have done because of your faith. And we thank him for the work you have done because of your love. And we thank him that you continue to be strong because of your hope in our Lord Jesus Christ.

4Brothers, God loves you. And we know that he has chosen you to be his. 5We brought the Good News*d* to you. But we did not use only words. We brought the Good News with power, with the Holy Spirit,*d* and with sure knowledge that it is true. Also you know how we lived when we were with you. We lived that way to help you. 6And you became like us and like the Lord. You suffered much, but still you accepted the teaching with the joy that comes from the Holy Spirit. 7So you became an example to all the believers in Macedonia and Southern Greece. 8The Lord's teaching spread from you in Macedonia and Southern Greece. And your faith in God has become known everywhere. So we do not need to say anything about your faith. 9People everywhere are telling of the good way you accepted us when we were there with you. They tell about how you stopped worshiping idols and changed to serving the living and true God. 10And you changed to wait for God's Son to come from heav-en. God raised that Son from death. He is Jesus, who saves us from God's angry judgement that is sure to come.

Paul's Work in Thessalonica

2 Brothers, you know that our visit to you was not a failure. 2Before we came to you, we suffered in Philippi. People there insulted us. You know about that. And when we came to you, many people were against us. But our God helped us to be brave and to tell you his Good News.*d* 3Our message was a message to encourage you. We were not trying to lie. We had no evil plan. We were not trying to trick you. 4But we speak the Good News because God tested us and trusted us to do it. When we speak, we are not trying to please men. But we are trying to please God, who tests our hearts. 5You know that we never tried to influence you by saying nice things about you. We were not trying to get your money. We had no selfishness to hide from you. God knows that this is true. 6We were not looking for praise from you or anyone else. We are apostles*d* of Christ. When we were with you, we could have used our authority to make you do things.

7But we were very gentle with you. We were like a mother caring for her little children. 8Because we loved you, we were happy to share God's Good News with you. But not only that, we were also happy to share even our own lives with you. 9Brothers, I know that you remember how hard we worked. We worked night and day so that we would not burden any of you while we preached God's Good News to you.

[10]When we were with you, we lived in a holy and right way, without fault. You know that this is true, and God knows that this is true. [11]You know that we treated each of you as a father treats his own children. [12]We strengthened you, we comforted you, and we told you to live good lives for God. It is God who calls you to his glorious kingdom.

[13]Also, we always thank God because of the way you accepted his message. You heard his message from us, and you accepted it as the word of God, not the words of men. And it really is God's message. And that message works in you who believe. [14]Brothers, you have been like God's churches in Christ that are in Judea.[n] God's people suffered bad things from the other Jews there. And you suffered the same bad things from the people of your own country. [15]Those Jews killed both the Lord Jesus and the prophets.[d] And they forced us to leave that country. They do not please God. They are against all people. [16]They try to stop us from teaching the non-Jews so that they may be saved. But those Jews are adding more and more sins to the sins they already have. The anger of God has come to them at last.

Paul Wants to Visit Them Again

[17]Brothers, we were separated from you for a short time, but our thoughts were still with you. We wanted very much to see you, and tried very hard to do so. [18]I, Paul, tried to come many times, but Satan stopped us. [19]For you are our hope, our joy, and the crown we will be proud of when our Lord Jesus Christ comes. [20]Truly you are our glory and our joy.

3 We could not come to you, but it was very hard to wait any longer. So we decided to stay in Athens alone [2]and send Timothy to you. Timothy is our brother, who works with us for God. He helps us tell people the Good News[d] about Christ. We sent Timothy to strengthen and comfort you in your faith. [3]We sent him so that none of you would be upset by these troubles we have now. You yourselves know that we must have these troubles. [4]Even when we were with you, we told you that we all would have to suffer. And you know that it has happened the way we said. [5]This is why I sent Timothy to you, so that I could know about your faith. I sent him when I could not wait any longer. I was afraid that the devil had tempted you, and then our hard work would have been wasted.

[6]But Timothy now has come back to us from you and has brought us good news about your faith and love. He told us that you always remember us in a good way. He told us that you want to see us just as much as we want to see you. [7]So, brothers, we are comforted about you, because of your faith. We have much trouble and suffering, but still we are comforted. [8]For our life is really full if you stand strong in the Lord. [9]We have so much joy before our God because of you, and we thank him for you. But we cannot thank him enough for all the joy we feel. [10]And we continue praying with all our heart for you night and day. We pray that we can see you again and give you all the things you need to make your faith strong.

[11]We pray that our God and Father and our Lord Jesus will prepare the way for us to come to you. [12]We pray that the Lord will make your love grow more and more for each other and for all people. We pray that you will love others as we love you and [13]that your hearts will be made strong. Then you will be holy and without fault before our God and Fa-

---

Judea The Jewish land where Jesus lived and taught and where the church first began.

ther when our Lord Jesus comes with all his holy people.

A Life that Pleases God

4 Brothers, now I have some other things to tell you. We taught you how to live in a way that will please God. And you are living that way. Now we ask you and encourage you in the Lord Jesus to live that way more and more. ²You know what we told you to do by the authority of the Lord Jesus. ³God wants you to be holy and to stay away from sexual sins. ⁴He wants each one of you to learn how to take a wife*ⁿ* in a way that is holy and honourable. ⁵Don't use your body for sexual sin. The people who do not know God use their bodies for that. ⁶So do not wrong your brother or cheat him in this way. The Lord will punish people who do those things. We have already told you and warned you about that. ⁷God called us to be holy and does not want us to live in sin. ⁸So the person who refuses to obey this teaching is refusing to obey God, not man. And God is the One who gives us his Holy Spirit.*d*

⁹We do not need to write to you about having love for your brothers and sisters in Christ. God has already taught you to love each other. ¹⁰And truly you do love the brothers in all of Macedonia. Brothers, now we encourage you to love them more and more.

¹¹Do all you can to live a peaceful life. Take care of your own business. Do your own work. We have already told you to do these things. ¹²If you do, then people who are not believers will respect you. And you will not have to depend on others for what you need.

The Lord's Coming

¹³Brothers, we want you to know about those who have died. We do not want you to be sad as others who have no hope. ¹⁴We believe that Jesus died and that he rose again. So, because of Jesus, God will bring together with Jesus those who have died. ¹⁵What we tell you now is the Lord's own message. We who are living now may still be living when the Lord comes again. We who are living at that time will be with the Lord, but not before those who have already died. ¹⁶The Lord himself will come down from heaven. There will be a loud command with the voice of the archangel*ⁿ* and with the trumpet call of God. And those who have died and were in Christ will rise first. ¹⁷After that, those who are still alive at that time will be gathered up with them. We will be taken up in the clouds to meet the Lord in the air. And we will be with the Lord for ever. ¹⁸So comfort each other with these words.

Be Ready for the Lord's Coming

5 Now, brothers, we do not need to write to you about times and dates. ²You know very well that the day the Lord comes again will be a surprise like a thief that comes in the night. ³People will say, "We have peace and we are safe." At that time they will be destroyed quickly, as pains come quickly to a woman having a baby. And those people will not escape. ⁴But you, brothers, are not living in darkness. And so that day will not surprise you like a thief. ⁵You are all people who belong to the light. You belong to the day. We do not belong to the night or to darkness. ⁶So we should not be like other people. We should not be sleeping, but we should be awake and have self-control. ⁷Those who sleep, sleep at night. Those who get drunk, get drunk at night. ⁸But we belong to the day; so

learn ... wife This might also mean "learn to control your own body".
archangel The leader among God's angels or messengers.

we should control ourselves. We should wear faith and love to protect us. And the hope of salvation should be our helmet. [9]God did not choose us to suffer his anger, but to have salvation through our Lord Jesus Christ. [10]Jesus died for us so that we can live together with him. It is not important if we are alive or dead when Jesus comes. [11]So comfort each other and give each other strength, just as you are doing now.

Final Instructions and Greetings

[12]Now, brothers, we ask you to respect those people who work hard with you, who lead you in the Lord and teach you. [13]Respect them with a very special love because of the work they do with you.

Live in peace with each other. [14]We ask you, brothers, to warn those who do not work. Encourage the people who are afraid. Help those who are weak. Be patient with every person. [15]Be sure that no one pays back wrong for wrong. But always try to do what is good for each other and for all people.

[16]Always be happy. [17]Never stop praying. [18]Give thanks whatever happens. That is what God wants for you in Christ Jesus.

[19]Do not stop the work of the Holy Spirit.[d] [20]Do not treat prophecy[d] as if it were not important. [21]But test everything. Keep what is good. [22]And stay away from everything that is evil.

[23]We pray that God himself, the God of peace, will make you pure, belonging only to him. We pray that your whole self—spirit, soul, and body—will be kept safe and be without wrong when our Lord Jesus Christ comes. [24]The One who calls you will do that for you. You can trust him.

[25]Brothers, please pray for us. [26]Give all the brothers a holy kiss when you meet. [27]I tell you by the authority of the Lord to read this letter to all the brothers.

[28]The grace of our Lord Jesus Christ be with you.

2 THESSALONIANS

The Problems of New Christians

1 From Paul, Silas, and Timothy.
To the church in Thessalonica in God our Father and the Lord Jesus Christ.
²Grace and peace to you from God the Father and the Lord Jesus Christ.

Paul Talks About God's Judgement

³We must always thank God for you. And we should do this because it is right. It is right because your faith is growing more and more. And the love that every one of you has for each other is also growing. ⁴So we boast about you to the other churches of God. We tell them about the way you continue to be strong and have faith. You are being treated badly and are suffering many troubles, but you continue with strength and faith.

⁵This is proof that God is right in his judgement. God wants you to be worthy of his kingdom. Your suffering is for that kingdom. ⁶And God will do what is right. He will give trouble to those who trouble you. ⁷And he will give peace to all of you who are troubled and to us also. God will give us this help when the Lord Jesus is shown to us from heaven with his powerful angels. ⁸He will come from heaven with burning fire to punish those who do not know God. He will punish those who do not obey the Good News*d* of our Lord Jesus Christ. ⁹Those people will be punished with a destruction that continues for ever. They will not be allowed to be with the Lord, and they will be kept away from his great power. ¹⁰This will happen on the day when the Lord Jesus comes to receive glory with his holy people. And all the people who have believed will be amazed at Jesus. You will be in

that group of believers because you believed what we told you.

¹¹That is why we always pray for you. We ask our God to help you live the good way that he called you to live. The goodness you have makes you want to do good, and the faith you have makes you work. We pray that with his power God will help you do these things more and more. ¹²We pray all this so that the name of our Lord Jesus Christ can have glory in you. And you can have glory in him. That glory comes from the grace of our God and the Lord Jesus Christ.

Evil Things Will Happen

2 Brothers, we have something to say about the coming of our Lord Jesus Christ. We want to talk to you about that time when we will meet together with him. ²Do not become easily upset in your thinking or afraid if you hear that the day of the Lord has already come. Someone may say this in a prophecy*d* or in a message. Or you may read it in a letter that someone tells you came from us. ³Do not let any person fool you in any way. That day of the Lord will not come until the turning away from God happens. And that day will not come until the Man of Evil appears. He belongs to hell. ⁴He is against anything called God or anything that people worship. And the Man of Evil puts himself above anything called God or anything that people worship. And that Man of Evil even goes into God's Temple*d* and sits there. Then he says that he is God.

⁵I told you when I was with you that all this would happen. Do you not remember? ⁶And you know what is

Luke 8:54-55
Jesus took her by the hand and called to her, "My child, stand up!" Her spirit came back into her, and she stood up immediately.

Luke 22:19
Jesus took some bread. He thanked God
for it, broke it, and gave it to the apostles.

Luke 23:33
Jesus and the two criminals were taken to
a place called the Skull. There the
soldiers nailed Jesus to his cross.

stopping that Man of Evil now. He is being stopped now so that he will appear at the right time. ⁷The secret power of evil is already working in the world now. But there is one who is stopping that power. And he will continue to stop it until he is taken out of the way. ⁸Then that Man of Evil will appear. And the Lord Jesus will kill him with the breath that comes from his mouth and will destroy him with the glory of his coming. ⁹The Man of Evil will come by the power of Satan. He will have great power, and he will do many different false miracles,ᵈ signs, and wonders. ¹⁰He will use every kind of evil to trick those who are lost. They are lost because they refused to love the truth. (If they loved the truth, they would be saved.) ¹¹But they refused to love the truth; so God sends them something powerful that leads them away from the truth. He sends them that power so they will believe something that is not true. ¹²So all those who do not believe the truth will be judged guilty. They did not believe the truth, and they enjoyed doing evil.

You Are Chosen for Salvation

¹³Brothers, the Lord loves you. God chose you from the beginning to be saved. So we must always thank God for you. You are saved by the Spiritᵈ that makes you holy and by your faith in the truth. ¹⁴God used the Good Newsᵈ that we preached to call you to be saved. He called you so that you can share in the glory of our Lord Jesus Christ. ¹⁵So, brothers, stand strong and continue to believe the teachings we gave you. We taught you those things in our speaking and in our letter to you.

¹⁶⁻¹⁷We pray that the Lord Jesus Christ himself and God our Father will comfort you and strengthen you in every good thing you do and say. God loved us. Through his grace he gave us a good hope and comfort that continues for ever.

Pray for Us

3 And now, brothers, pray for us. Pray that the Lord's teaching will continue to spread quickly. And pray that people will give honour to that teaching, just as happened with you. ²And pray that we will be protected from bad and evil people. (Not all people believe in the Lord.)

³But the Lord is faithful. He will give you strength and protect you from the Evil One. ⁴The Lord makes us feel sure that you are doing the things we told you. And we know that you will continue to do those things. ⁵We pray that the Lord will lead your hearts into God's love and Christ's patience.

The Duty to Work

⁶Brothers, by the authority of our Lord Jesus Christ we command you to stay away from any believer who refuses to work. People who refuse to work are not following the teaching that we gave them. ⁷You yourselves know that you should live as we live. We were not lazy when we were with you. ⁸And when we ate another person's food, we always paid for it. We worked and worked so that we would not be a trouble to any of you. We worked night and day. ⁹We had the right to ask you to help us. But we worked to take care of ourselves so that we would be an example for you to follow. ¹⁰When we were with you, we gave you this rule: "If anyone will not work, he will not eat."

¹¹We hear that some people in your group refuse to work. They do nothing. And they busy themselves in other people's lives. ¹²We command those people to work quietly and earn their own food. In the Lord Jesus Christ we beg them to do this. ¹³Brothers, never become tired of doing good.

14If anyone does not obey what we tell you in this letter, then remember who he is. Do not associate with him. Then maybe he will feel ashamed. 15But do not treat him as an enemy. Warn him as a brother.

Final Words

16We pray that the Lord of peace will give you peace at all times and in every way. May the Lord be with all of you.

17I am Paul, and I end this letter now in my own handwriting. All my letters have this to show they are from me. This is the way I write.

18May our Lord Jesus Christ show all of you his grace.

1 TIMOTHY

Advice to a Young Preacher

1 From Paul, an apostle*d* of Christ Jesus, by the command of God our Saviour and Christ Jesus our hope.

²To Timothy, a true son to me because you believe.

Grace, mercy, and peace from God the Father and Christ Jesus our Lord.

Warning Against False Teaching

³I want you to stay in Ephesus. I asked you to do that when I went into Macedonia. Some people there in Ephesus are teaching false things. Stay there so that you can command them to stop. ⁴Tell them not to spend their time on stories that are not true and on long lists of names in family histories. These things only bring arguments; they do not help God's work. God's work is done by faith. ⁵The purpose of this command is for people to have love. To have this love they must have a pure heart, they must do what they know is right, and they must have true faith. ⁶Some people have wandered away from these things. They talk about things that are worth nothing. ⁷They want to be teachers of the law, but they do not know what they are talking about. They do not even understand what they say they are sure about.

⁸We know that the law is good if a man uses it correctly. ⁹We also know that the law is not made for good men. The law is made for people who are against the law and for those who refuse to follow the law. It is for people who are against God and are sinful, who are not holy and have no religion, who kill their fathers and mothers, who murder, ¹⁰who take part in sexual sins, men who have sexual relations with other men, those who sell slaves, who tell lies, who speak falsely, and who do anything against the true teaching of God. ¹¹That teaching is part of the Good News*d* that God gave me to tell. That glorious Good News is from the blessed God.

Thanks for God's Mercy

¹²I thank Christ Jesus our Lord because he trusted me and gave me this work of serving him. And he gives me strength. ¹³In the past I spoke against Christ and persecuted him and did all kinds of things to hurt him. But God showed mercy to me because I did not know what I was doing. I did those things when I did not believe. ¹⁴But the grace of our Lord was fully given to me. And with that grace came the faith and love that are in Christ Jesus.

¹⁵What I say is true, and you should fully accept it: Christ Jesus came into the world to save sinners. And I am the worst of those sinners. ¹⁶But I was given mercy. I was given mercy so that in me Christ Jesus could show that he has patience without limit. And he showed his patience with me, the worst of all sinners. Christ wanted me to be an example for those who would believe in him and have life for ever. ¹⁷Honour and glory to the King that rules for ever! He cannot be destroyed and cannot be seen. Honour and glory for ever and ever to the only God. Amen.

¹⁸Timothy, you are like a son to me. I am giving you a command that agrees with the prophecies*d* that were given about you in the past. I tell you this so that you can follow those prophecies and fight the good fight of faith. ¹⁹Continue to have faith and do what you know is right. Some people

have not done this. Their faith has been destroyed. ²⁰Hymenaeus and Alexander are men who have done that. I have given them to Satan so that they will learn not to speak against God.

Some Rules for Men and Women

2 First, I tell you to pray for all people. Ask God for the things people need, and be thankful to him. ²You should pray for kings and for all who have authority. Pray for the leaders so that we can have quiet and peaceful lives — lives full of worship and respect for God. ³This is good, and it pleases God our Saviour. ⁴God wants all people to be saved. And he wants everyone to know the truth. ⁵There is only one God. And there is only one way that people can reach God. That way is through Jesus Christ, who is also a man. ⁶Jesus gave himself to pay for the sins of all people. Jesus is proof that God wants all people to be saved. And that proof came at the right time. ⁷That is why I was chosen to tell the Good News*d* and was chosen to be an apostle.*d* (I am telling the truth. I am not lying.) I was chosen to teach the non-Jewish people to believe and to know the truth.

⁸I want men everywhere to pray. These men who lift up their hands in prayer must be holy. They must not be men who become angry and have arguments.

⁹I also want women to wear clothes that are right for them. They should dress with respect and right thinking. They should not use fancy braided hair or gold or pearls or expensive clothes to make themselves beautiful. ¹⁰But they should make themselves beautiful by doing good deeds. Women who say they worship God should make themselves beautiful in that way.

¹¹A woman should learn by listening quietly and being fully ready to obey. ¹²I do not allow a woman to teach a man or to have authority over a man. She must remain silent. ¹³For Adam was made first; Eve was made later. ¹⁴Also, Adam was not the one who was tricked by the devil. It was the woman who was tricked and became a sinner. ¹⁵But women will be saved through having children. They will be saved if they continue in faith, love, holiness, and self-control.

Leaders in the Church

3 What I say is true: if anyone wants to become an elder,*d* he is wanting a good work. ²An elder must be so good that people cannot rightly criticise him. He must have only one wife. He must have self-control and be wise. He must be respected by other people and must be ready to help people by accepting them into his home. He must be a good teacher. ³He must not drink too much wine, and he must not be a man who likes to fight. He must be gentle and peaceful. He must not love money. ⁴He must be a good leader of his own family so that his children obey him with full respect. ⁵(If a man does not know how to be a leader over his own family, he will not be able to take care of God's church.) ⁶But an elder must not be a new believer. A new believer might be too proud of himself. Then he would be judged guilty for his pride just as the devil was. ⁷An elder must also have the respect of people who are not in the church. Then he will not be criticised by others and caught in the devil's trap.

Helpers in the Church

⁸In the same way, deacons*d* must be men that people can respect. They must not say things they do not mean. They must not use their time drinking too much wine, and they must not be men who are always trying to get rich by cheating others. ⁹They must follow the faith that God made known to us and always do what they know is

right. [10]You should test those men first. If you find nothing wrong in them, then they can serve as deacons. [11]In the same way, the women[n] must have the respect of other people. They must not be women who repeat evil gossip about other people. They must have self-control and be women who can be trusted in everything. [12]Deacons must have only one wife. They must be good leaders of their children and their own families. [13]Those who serve well as deacons are making an honourable place for themselves. And they will feel very sure of their faith in Christ Jesus.

The Secret of Our Life

[14]I hope I can come to you soon. But I am writing these things to you now. [15]Then, even if I cannot come soon, you will know about the things that people must do in the family of God. That family is the church of the living God, the support and foundation of the truth. [16]Without doubt, the secret of our life of worship is great:

He was shown to us in a human
body,
proved right by the Spirit,[d]
and seen by angels.
He was preached to the nations,
believed in by the world,
and taken to heaven in glory.

A Warning About False Teachers

4 The Holy Spirit[d] clearly says that in the later times some people will stop believing the true faith. They will obey spirits that lie and will follow the teachings of demons.[d] [2]Such teachings come from hypocrites,[d] men who cannot see what is right and what is wrong. It is as if their understanding were destroyed by a hot iron. [3]They tell people that it is wrong to marry. And they tell people that there are

some foods that must not be eaten. But God made those foods, and the people who believe and who know the truth can eat those foods with thanks. [4]Everything that God made is good. Nothing that God made should be refused if it is accepted with thanks to God. [5]Everything God made is made holy by what God has said and by prayer.

Be a Good Servant of Christ

[6]Tell these things to the brothers. This will show that you are a good servant of Christ Jesus. You will show that you are made strong by the words of faith and good teaching that you have been following. [7]People tell silly stories that do not agree with God's truth. Do not follow what those stories teach. But teach yourself only to serve God. [8]Training your body helps you in some ways, but serving God helps you in every way. Serving God brings you blessings in this life and in the future life, too. [9]What I say is true, and you should fully accept it. [10]For this is why we work and struggle: we hope in the living God. He is the Saviour of all people. And in a very special way, he is the Saviour of all who believe in him.

[11]Command and teach these things. [12]You are young, but do not let anyone treat you as if you were not important. Be an example to show the believers how they should live. Show them with your words, with the way you live, with your love, with your faith, and with your pure life. [13]Continue to read the Scriptures[d] to the people, strengthen them, and teach them. Do these things until I come. [14]Remember to use the gift that you have. That gift was given to you through a prophecy[d] when the group of elders[d] laid their hands on[n] you. [15]Continue to do

---

women This might mean the wives of the deacons, or it might mean women who serve in the same way as deacons.
laid their hands on A sign to show that Timothy was being given a special work of God.

those things. Give your life to doing them. Then everyone can see that your work is progressing. [16]Be careful in your life and in your teaching. Continue to live and teach rightly. Then you will save yourself and those people who listen to you.

Rules for Living with Others

5 Do not speak angrily to an older man, but talk to him as if he were your father. Treat younger men like brothers. [2]Treat older women like mothers, and younger women like sisters. Always treat them in a pure way.

[3]Take care of widows who are all alone. [4]But if a widow has children or grandchildren, the first thing they need to learn is to do their duty to their own family. When they do this, they will be repaying their parents or grandparents. That pleases God. [5]If a widow is all alone and without help, then she puts her hope in God and prays night and day for God's help. [6]But the widow who uses her life to please herself is really dead while she is still living. [7]Tell the believers there to do these things so that no one can say they are doing wrong. [8]A believer should take care of his own relatives, especially his own family. If he does not do that, he has turned against the faith. He is worse than a person who does not believe in God.

[9]To be on your list of widows, a woman must be 60 years old or older. She must have been faithful to her husband. [10]She must be known as a woman who has done good works. By this, I mean good works such as raising her children, accepting visitors in her home, washing the feet of God's people, helping those in trouble, and using her life to do all kinds of good deeds.

[11]But do not put younger widows on that list. After they give themselves to Christ, they are often pulled away from him by their physical needs. And then they want to marry again. [12]And they will be judged for not doing what they first promised to do. [13]Also, those younger widows begin to waste their time going from house to house. They begin to gossip and busy themselves with other people's lives. They say things that they should not say. [14]So I want the younger widows to marry, have children, and take care of their homes. If they do this, then no enemy will have any reason to criticise them. [15]But some of the younger widows have already turned away to follow Satan.

[16]If any woman who is a believer has widows in her family, then she should care for them herself. The church should not have to care for them. Then the church will be able to care for the widows who have no living family.

[17]The elders[d] who lead the church well should receive great honour. Those who work hard by speaking and teaching especially should receive great honour. [18]For the Scripture[d] says, "When an ox is working in the grain, do not cover its mouth to keep it from eating."[n] And the Scripture also says, "A worker should be given his pay."[n]

[19]Do not listen to someone who accuses an elder, unless there are two or three other persons who say he did wrong. [20]Tell those who keep on sinning that they are wrong. Do this in front of the whole church so that the others will have a warning.

[21]Before God and Jesus Christ and the chosen angels, I command you to do these things. Be careful to do them without showing favour to anyone.

"When . . . eating." Quotation from Deuteronomy 25:4.
"A worker . . . pay." Quotation from Luke 10:7.

²²Think carefully before you lay your hands on" anyone for the Lord's service. Do not share in the sins of others. Keep yourself pure.

²³Timothy, stop drinking only water and drink a little wine. This will help your stomach, and you will not be sick so often.

²⁴The sins of some people are easy to see even before they are judged. But the sins of others are seen only later. ²⁵So also good deeds are easy to see. But even when they are not easy to see, they cannot stay hidden.

6 All who are slaves should show full respect to their masters. Then no one will speak against God's name and our teaching. ²Some slaves have masters who are believers. This means they are all brothers. But the slaves should not show their masters any less respect. They should serve their masters even better, because they are helping believers they love.

False Teaching and True Riches

You must teach and preach these things. ³If anyone has a different teaching, he does not accept the true teaching of our Lord Jesus Christ. And that teaching shows him the true way to serve God. ⁴The person who teaches falsely is full of pride and understands nothing. He is sick with a love for arguing and fighting about words. And that brings jealousy, quarrels, insults, and evil mistrust. ⁵And that also brings arguments from men who have evil minds. They have lost the truth. They think that serving God is a way to get rich.

⁶It is true that serving God makes a person very rich, if he is satisfied with what he has. ⁷When we came into the world, we brought nothing. And when we die, we can take nothing out. ⁸So, if we have food and clothes, we will be satisfied with that. ⁹Those who want to become rich bring temptation to

themselves. They are caught in a trap. They begin to want many foolish things that will hurt them, things that ruin and destroy people. ¹⁰The love of money causes all kinds of evil. Some people have left the true faith because they want to get more and more money. But they have caused themselves a great deal of sorrow.

Some Things to Remember

¹¹But you are a man of God. So you should stay away from all those things. Try to live in the right way, serve God, have faith, love, patience, and gentleness. ¹²Keeping your faith is like running a race. Try as hard as you can to win. Be sure you receive the life that continues for ever. You were called to have that life. And you confessed the great truth about Christ in a way that many people heard. ¹³Before God and Christ Jesus I give you a command. Christ Jesus confessed that same great truth when he stood before Pontius Pilate. And God gives life to everything. Now I tell you: ¹⁴do the things you were commanded to do. Do them without wrong or blame until the time when our Lord Jesus Christ comes again. ¹⁵God will make that happen at the right time. He is the blessed and only Ruler. He is the King of all kings and the Lord of all lords. ¹⁶God is the only One who never dies. He lives in light so bright that men cannot go near it. No one has ever seen God, or can see him. May honour and power belong to God for ever. Amen.

¹⁷Give this command to those who are rich with things of this world. Tell them not to be proud. Tell them to hope in God, not their money. Money cannot be trusted, but God takes care of us richly. He gives us everything to enjoy. ¹⁸Tell the rich people to do good and to be rich in doing good deeds. Tell them to be happy to give

---

lay your hands on A sign of giving authority or power to another person.

and ready to share. [19]By doing that, they will be saving a treasure for themselves in heaven. That treasure will be a strong foundation. Their future life can be built on that treasure. Then they will be able to have the life that is true life.

[20]Timothy, God has trusted you with many things. Keep those things safe. Stay away from people who say foolish things that are not from God. Stay away from those who argue against the truth. They use something they call "knowledge", but it is really not knowledge. [21]They say that they have that "knowledge", but they have left the true faith.

God's grace be with you.

2 TIMOTHY

Paul Encourages Timothy

1 From Paul, an apostle[d] of Christ Jesus by the will of God. God sent me to tell of the promise of life that is in Christ Jesus.

[2] To Timothy, a dear son to me. Grace, mercy, and peace to you from God the Father and Christ Jesus our Lord.

Encouragement for Timothy

[3] I always remember you in my prayers, day and night. And I thank God for you in these prayers. He is the God my ancestors served. And I serve him, doing what I know is right. [4] I remember that you cried for me. And I want very much to see you so that I can be filled with joy. [5] I remember your true faith. That kind of faith first belonged to your grandmother Lois and to your mother Eunice. And I know that you now have that same faith. [6] That is why I remind you to use the gift God gave you. God gave you that gift when I laid my hands on[n] you. Now let it grow, as a small flame grows into a fire. [7] God did not give us a spirit that makes us afraid. He gave us a spirit of power and love and self-control.

[8] So do not be ashamed to tell people about our Lord Jesus. And do not be ashamed of me. I am in prison for the Lord. But suffer with me for the Good News.[d] God gives us the strength to do that. [9] God saved us and made us his holy people. That was not because of anything we did ourselves but because of what he wanted and because of his grace. That grace was given to us through Christ Jesus before time

began. [10] It was not shown to us until our Saviour Christ Jesus came. Jesus destroyed death. And through the Good News, he showed us the way to have life that cannot be destroyed. [11] I was chosen to tell that Good News and to be an apostle[d] and a teacher. [12] And I suffer now because I tell the Good News. But I am not ashamed. I know Jesus, the One I have believed in. And I am sure that he is able to protect what he has trusted me with until that Day.[n] [13] Follow the true teachings you heard from me. Follow them as an example of the faith and love we have in Christ Jesus. [14] Protect the truth that you were given. Protect it with the help of the Holy Spirit[d] who lives in us.

[15] You know that everyone in the country of Asia has left me, even Phygelus and Hermogenes. [16] I pray that the Lord will show mercy to the family of Onesiphorus. He has often helped me and was not ashamed that I was in prison. [17] When he came to Rome, he looked for me until he found me. [18] I pray that the Lord will allow Onesiphorus to have mercy from the Lord on that Day. You know how many ways Onesiphorus helped me in Ephesus.

A Loyal Soldier of Christ Jesus

2 Timothy, you are like a son to me. Be strong in the grace that we have in Christ Jesus. [2] You and many others have heard what I have taught. You should teach the same thing to some people you can trust. Then they will be able to teach it to others. [3] Share in the troubles that we have.

---

laid . . . on A sign to show that Paul had power from God to give Timothy a special blessing.
Day The day Christ will come to judge all people and take his people to live with him.

Accept them like a true soldier of Christ Jesus. [4]A soldier wants to please his commanding officer, so he does not waste his time doing the things that most people do. [5]If an athlete is running a race, he must obey all the rules in order to win. [6]The farmer who works hard should be the first person to get some of the food that he grew. [7]Think about these things that I am saying. The Lord will give you the ability to understand all these things.

[8]Remember Jesus Christ. He is from the family of David. After Jesus died, he was raised from death. This is the Good News[d] that I preach, [9]and I am suffering because of that Good News. I am even bound with chains like a criminal. But God's teaching is not in chains. [10]So I patiently accept all these troubles. I do this so that those whom God has chosen can have the salvation that is in Christ Jesus. With that salvation comes glory that never ends.

[11]This teaching is true:

If we died with him,
   then we will also live with him.
[12]If we accept suffering,
   then we will also rule with him.
If we refuse to accept him,
   then he will refuse to accept us.
[13]If we are not faithful,
   he will still be faithful,
   because he cannot be false to
      himself.

A Worker Pleasing to God

[14]Continue teaching these things. And warn people before God not to argue about words. Arguing about words does not help anyone, and it ruins those who listen. [15]Do the best you can to be the kind of person that God will accept, and give yourself to him. Be a worker who is not ashamed of his work—a worker who uses the true teaching in the right way. [16]Stay away from those who talk about useless worldly things. That kind of talk will lead a person more and more away from God. [17]Their evil teaching will spread like a sickness inside the body. Hymenaeus and Philetus are men like that. [18]They have left the true teaching. They say that the rising from death of all men has already taken place. And those two men are destroying the faith of some people. [19]But God's strong foundation continues to stand. These words are written on that foundation: "The Lord knows those who belong to him."[n] And also these words are written on that foundation, "Everyone who says that he believes in the Lord must stop doing wrong."

[20]In a large house there are things made of gold and silver. But also there are things made of wood and clay. Some things are used for special purposes, and others are made for ordinary jobs. [21]If anyone makes himself clean[d] from evil things, he will be used for special purposes. He will be made holy, and the Master can use him. He will be ready to do any good work.

[22]Stay away from the evil things young people love to do. Try hard to live right and to have faith, love, and peace. Work for these things together with those who have pure hearts and who trust in the Lord. [23]Stay away from foolish and stupid arguments. You know that such arguments grow into bigger arguments. [24]And a servant of the Lord must not quarrel! He must be kind to everyone. He must be a good teacher. He must be patient. [25]The Lord's servant must gently teach those who do not agree with him. Maybe God will let them change their hearts so that they can accept the truth. [26]The devil has trapped them and causes them to do what he wants. But maybe they can wake up

"**The Lord . . . him.**" Quotation from Numbers 16:5.

and free themselves from the devil's trap.

The Last Days

3 Remember this! There will be many troubles in the last days. ²In those times people will love only themselves and money. They will boast and be proud. They will say evil things against others. They will not obey their parents. People will not be thankful or be the kind of people God wants. ³They will not have love for others. They will refuse to forgive others and will speak bad things. They will not control themselves. They will be cruel and will hate what is good. ⁴In the last days, people will turn against their friends. They will do foolish things without thinking. They will be conceited and proud. They will love pleasure. They will not love God. ⁵They will continue to act as if they serve God, but they will not really serve God. Stay away from those people. ⁶Some of them go into homes and get control of weak women who are full of sin. They are led to sin by the many evil desires they have. ⁷Those women always try to learn new teachings, but they are never able to understand the truth fully. ⁸Just as Jannes and Jambres were against Moses, these people are against the truth. They are people whose thinking has been confused. They have failed in trying to follow the faith. ⁹But they will not be successful in what they do. Everyone will see that they are foolish. That is what happened to Jannes and Jambres.

Obey the Teachings

¹⁰But you know all about me. You know what I teach and the way I live. You know my goal in life. You know my faith, my patience, and my love. You know that I never stop trying. ¹¹You know how I have been hurt and have suffered. You know all that happened to me in Antioch, Iconium, and Lystra. You know the hurts I suffered in those places. But the Lord saved me from all those troubles. ¹²Everyone who wants to live the way God wants, in Christ Jesus, will be hurt. ¹³People who are evil and cheat other people will go from bad to worse. They will fool others, but they will also be fooling themselves.

¹⁴But you should continue following the teachings that you learned. You know that these teachings are true. And you know you can trust those who taught you. ¹⁵You have known the Holy Scriptures*d* since you were a child. The Scriptures are able to make you wise. And that wisdom leads to salvation through faith in Christ Jesus. ¹⁶All Scripture is given by God and is useful for teaching and for showing people what is wrong in their lives. It is useful for correcting faults and teaching us how to live correctly. ¹⁷Using the Scriptures, the person who serves God will be ready and will have everything he needs to do every good work.

4 Before God and Jesus Christ I give you a command. Christ Jesus is the One who will judge all who are living and all who have died. Jesus has a kingdom, and he is coming again. So I give you this command: ²preach the Good News.*d* Be ready at all times. Tell people what they need to do, tell them when they are wrong, and encourage them. Do these things with great patience and careful teaching. ³The time will come when people will not listen to the true teaching. They will find more and more teachers who are pleasing to them, teachers who say the things they want to hear. ⁴They will stop listening to the truth. They will begin to follow the teaching in false stories. ⁵But you should control yourself at all times. When troubles come, accept them. Do the work of telling the Good News. Do all the duties of a servant of God.

⁶My life is being given as an offering

to God. The time has come for me to leave this life. [7]I have fought the good fight. I have finished the race. I have kept the faith. [8]Now, a crown is waiting for me. I will get that crown for being right with God. The Lord is the judge who judges rightly, and he will give me the crown on that Day.[n] He will give that crown not only to me but to all those who have waited with love for him to come again.

Personal Words

[9]Do your best to come to me as soon as you can. [10]Demas loved this world too much. He left me and went to Thessalonica. Crescens went to Galatia. And Titus went to Dalmatia. [11]Luke is the only one still with me. Get Mark and bring him with you when you come. He can help me in my work here. [12]I sent Tychicus to Ephesus. [13]When I was in Troas, I left my coat there with Carpus. So when you come, bring it to me. Also, bring my books, particularly the ones written on parchment.[n]

[14]Alexander the metalworker did many harmful things against me. The Lord will punish him for the things he did. [15]You should be careful that he does not hurt you too. He fought strongly against our teaching.

[16]The first time I defended myself, no one helped me. Everyone left me. I pray that God will forgive them. [17]But the Lord stayed with me. He gave me strength so that I could fully tell the Good News[d] to the non-Jews. The Lord wanted all the non-Jews to hear it. So I was saved from the lion's mouth. [18]The Lord will save me when anyone tries to hurt me. The Lord will bring me safely to his heavenly kingdom. Glory for ever and ever to the Lord. Amen.

Final Greetings

[19]Greet Priscilla and Aquila and the family of Onesiphorus. [20]Erastus stayed in Corinth. And I left Trophimus sick in Miletus. [21]Try as hard as you can to come to me before winter.

Eubulus sends greetings to you. Also Pudens, Linus, Claudia, and all the brothers in Christ greet you.

[22]The Lord be with your spirit. Grace be with you.

Day The day Christ will come to judge all people and take his people to live with him.
parchment Something like paper made from the skins of sheep and used for writing on.

TITUS

Paul Instructs Titus

1 From Paul, a servant of God and an apostle*d* of Jesus Christ. I was sent to help the faith of God's chosen people. I was sent to help them to know the truth. And that truth shows people how to serve God. ²That faith and that knowledge come from our hope for life for ever. God promised that life to us before time began, and God does not lie. ³At the right time God let the world know about that life through preaching. He trusted me with that work, and I preached because God our Saviour commanded me to.

⁴To Titus. You are like a true son to me in the faith we share.

Grace and peace to you from God the Father and Christ Jesus our Saviour.

Titus' Work in Crete

⁵I left you in Crete so that you could finish doing the things that still needed to be done. I left you there also so that you could choose men to be elders*d* in every town. ⁶To be an elder, a man must not be guilty of doing wrong. He must have only one wife. His children must be believers. They must not be known as children who are wild and who do not obey. ⁷An elder has the job of taking care of God's work. So he must not be guilty of doing wrong. He must not be a man who is proud and selfish or who becomes angry quickly. He must not drink too much wine. He must not be a person who likes to fight. And he must not be a person who always tries to get rich by cheating people. ⁸An elder must be ready to help others by accepting them into his home. He must love what is good. He must be wise. He must live right. He must be holy. And he must be able to control himself. ⁹An elder must faithfully follow the truth just as we teach it. He must be able to help people by using true and right teaching. And he must be able to show those who are against the true teaching that they are wrong.

¹⁰There are many people who refuse to obey — people who talk about worthless things and lead others into the wrong way. I am talking mostly about those who say that all non-Jews must be circumcised.*d* ¹¹These people must be stopped from talking. They are destroying whole families by teaching things that they should not teach. They teach them only to cheat people and make money. ¹²Even one of their own prophets from Crete said, "Cretan people are always liars. They are evil animals and lazy people who do nothing but eat." ¹³The words that prophet said are true. So tell those people that they are wrong. You must be strict with them. Then they will become strong in the faith ¹⁴and stop accepting Jewish stories. And they will stop following the commands of others who do not accept the truth. ¹⁵To those who are pure, all things are pure. But to those who are full of sin and do not believe, nothing is pure. The thinking of those people has become evil and their knowledge of what is right has been ruined. ¹⁶They say they know God, but the evil things they do show that they do not accept God. They are terrible people, they refuse to obey, and they are useless for doing anything good.

Following the True Teaching

2 You must speak things that make the true teaching attractive. ²Teach older men to have self-control, to be serious, and to be wise. They should be strong in faith, strong in love, and strong in patience.

³Also, teach older women to be holy in the way they live. Teach them not to speak against others or have the habit of drinking too much wine. They should teach what is good. ⁴In that way they can teach younger women to love their husbands and children. ⁵They can teach younger women to be wise and pure, to take care of their homes, to be kind, and to obey their husbands. Then no one will be able to criticise the teaching God gave us.

⁶In the same way, tell young men to be wise. ⁷You should do good deeds to be an example in every way for young men. When you teach, be honest and serious. ⁸And when you speak, speak the truth so that you cannot be criticised. Then anyone who is against you will be ashamed because there is nothing bad that he can say against us.

⁹And tell slaves to obey their masters at all times. They should try to please them and not argue with them. ¹⁰They should not steal from them. And they should show their masters that they can be fully trusted. Then, in everything they do they will make the teaching of God our Saviour attractive.

¹¹That is the way we should live, because God's grace has come. That grace can save every person. ¹²It teaches us not to live against God and not to do the evil things the world wants to do. That grace teaches us to live on earth now in a wise and right way—a way that shows that we serve God. ¹³We should live like that while we are waiting for the coming of our great God and Saviour Jesus Christ. He is our great hope, and he will come with glory. ¹⁴He gave himself for us;

he died to free us from all evil. He died to make us pure people who belong only to him—people who are always wanting to do good things.

¹⁵Tell everyone these things. You have full authority. So use that authority to strengthen the people and tell them what they should do. And do not let anyone treat you as if you were not important.

The Right Way to Live

3 Remind the believers to do these things: to be under the authority of rulers and government leaders, to obey them and be ready to do good, ²to speak no evil about anyone, to live in peace with all, to be gentle and polite to all people.

³In the past we were foolish people, too. We did not obey, we were wrong, and we were slaves to many things our bodies wanted and enjoyed. We lived doing evil and being jealous. People hated us and we hated each other. ⁴But then the kindness and love of God our Saviour was shown. ⁵He saved us because of his mercy, not because of good deeds we did to be right with God. He saved us through the washing that made us new people. He saved us by making us new through the Holy Spirit.ᵈ ⁶God poured out to us that Holy Spirit fully through Jesus Christ our Saviour. ⁷We were made right with God by His grace. And God gave us the Spirit so that we could receive the life that never ends. That is what we hope for.

⁸This teaching is true. And I want you to be sure that the people understand these things. Then those who believe in God will be careful to use their lives for doing good. These things are good and will help all people.

⁹Stay away from those who have foolish arguments, who talk about useless family histories, who make trouble and fight about what the law of Moses teaches. Those things are

worth nothing and will not help anyone. [10]If someone causes arguments, then give him a warning. If he continues to cause arguments, warn him again. If he still continues causing arguments, then do not be around him. [11]You know that such a person is evil and sinful. His sins prove that he is wrong.

Some Things to Remember

[12]I will send Artemas and Tychicus to you. When I send them, try hard to come to me at Nicopolis. I have decided to stay there this winter. [13]Zenas the lawyer and Apollos will be travelling from there. Do all that you can to help them on their way. Be sure that they have everything they need. [14]Our people must learn to use their lives for doing good deeds. They should do good to those in need. Then our people will not have useless lives.

[15]All who are with me greet you. Greet those who love us in the faith. Grace be with you all.

PHILEMON

A Slave Becomes a Christian

[1]From Paul, a prisoner for Jesus Christ, and from Timothy, our brother.

To Philemon, our dear friend and worker with us; [2]to Apphia, our sister; to Archippus, a worker with us; and to the church that meets in your home.

[3]Grace and peace to you from God our Father and the Lord Jesus Christ.

Philemon's Love and Faith

[4]I remember you in my prayers. And I always thank my God for you. [5]I hear about the love you have for all God's holy people and the faith you have in the Lord Jesus. [6]I pray that the faith you share will make you understand every blessing that we have in Christ. [7]My brother, you have shown love to God's people. You have made them feel happy. This has given me great joy and comfort.

Accept Onesimus as a Brother

[8]There is something that you should do. And because of your love in Christ, I feel free to order you to do it. [9]But because I love you, I am asking you instead. I, Paul, am an old man now, and a prisoner for Christ Jesus. [10]I am asking you a favour for my son Onesimus. He became my son while I was in prison. [11]In the past he was useless to you. But now he has become useful for both you and me.

[12]I am sending him back to you, and with him I am sending my own heart. [13]I wanted to keep him with me to help me while I am in prison for the Good News.[d] By helping me he would be serving you. [14]But I did not want to do anything without asking you first. Then any favour you do for me will be because you want to do it, not because I forced you to do it.

[15]Onesimus was separated from you for a short time. Maybe that happened so that you could have him back for ever — [16]not to be a slave, but better than a slave, to be a loved brother. I love him very much. But you will love him even more. You will love him as a man and as a brother in the Lord.

[17]If you think of me as your friend, then accept Onesimus back. Welcome him as you would welcome me. [18]If Onesimus has done anything wrong to you, charge that to me. If he owes you anything, charge that to me. [19]I, Paul, am writing this with my own hand. I will pay back anything Onesimus owes. And I will say nothing about what you owe me for your own life. [20]So, my brother, I ask that you do this for me in the Lord. Comfort my heart in Christ. [21]I write this letter, knowing that you will do what I ask you and even more.

[22]Also, please prepare a room for me to stay in. I hope that God will answer your prayers and I will be able to come to you.

Final Greetings

[23]Epaphras is a prisoner with me for Christ Jesus. He sends greetings to you. [24]And also Mark, Aristarchus, Demas, and Luke send greetings. They are workers together with me. [25]The grace of our Lord Jesus Christ be with your spirit.

HEBREWS

A Better Life Through Christ

God Spoke Through His Son

1 In the past God spoke to our ancestors through the prophets.[d] He spoke to them many times and in many different ways. [2]And now in these last days God has spoken to us through his Son. God has chosen his Son to own all things. And he made the world through the Son. [3]The Son reflects the glory of God. He is an exact copy of God's nature. He holds everything together with his powerful word. The Son made people clean from their sins. Then he sat down at the right side of God, the Great One in heaven. [4]The Son became much greater than the angels. And God gave him a name that is much greater than theirs.

[5]This is because God never said to any of the angels,

"You are my Son.
    Today I have become your
        Father."   *Psalm 2:7*
Nor did God say of any angel,
"I will be his Father,
    and he will be my Son."
                        2 Samuel 7:14

[6]And when God brings his firstborn Son into the world, he says,

"Let all God's angels worship
    him."[n]   *Psalm 97:7*

[7]This is what God said about the angels:

"God makes his angels become
    like winds.
He makes his servants become
    like flames of fire."
                        Psalm 104:4

[8]But God said this about his Son:

"God, your throne will last for
    ever and ever.
You will rule your kingdom with
    fairness.
[9]You love what is right and hate
    evil.
So God has chosen you to rule
    those with you.
Your God has given you much
    joy."   *Psalm 45:6-7*
[10]God also says,
"Lord, in the beginning you made
    the earth.
And your hands made the skies.
[11]They will be destroyed, but you
    will remain.
They will all wear out like
    clothes.
[12]You will fold them like a coat.
And, like clothes, you will
    change them.
But you never change.
    And your life will never end."
                        Psalm 102:25-27

[13]And God never said this to an angel:

"Sit by me at my right side
until I put your enemies under
    your control."[n]   *Psalm 110:1*

[14]All the angels are spirits who serve God and are sent to help those who will receive salvation.

Our Salvation Is Great

2 So we must be more careful to follow what we were taught. Then we will not be pulled away from the truth. [2]The teaching that God spoke through angels was shown to be true. And anyone who did not follow it or obey it received the punishment he

---

"Let . . . him." These words are found in Deuteronomy 32:43 in the Septuagint, the Greek version of the Old Testament, and in a Hebrew copy among the Dead Sea Scrolls.
until . . . control Literally, "until I make your enemies a footstool for your feet."

earned. ³The salvation that was given to us is very great. So surely we also will be punished if we live as if this salvation were not important. It was the Lord himself who first told about this salvation. And those who heard him proved to us that this salvation is true. ⁴God also proved it by using wonders, great signs, and many kinds of miracles.ᵈ And he proved it by giving people gifts through the Holy Spirit,ᵈ just as he wanted.

Christ Became like Men

⁵God did not choose angels to be the rulers of the new world that was coming. It is that future world we have been talking about. ⁶It is written somewhere in the Scriptures,ᵈ

"Why is man important to you?
    Why do you take care of the son
        of man?"
⁷For a short time you made him
        lower than the angels.
    But you crowned him with glory
        and honour.
⁸ You put all things under his
        control."   *Psalm 8:4-6*

If God put everything under his control, there was nothing left that he did not rule. But we do not yet see him ruling over everything. ⁹But we see Jesus! For a short time he was made lower than the angels. But now we see him wearing a crown of glory and honour because he suffered and died. Because of God's grace, he died for everyone. ¹⁰God is the One who made all things. And all things are for his glory. God wanted to have many sons share his glory. So God made perfect the One who leads people to salvation. He made Jesus a perfect Saviour through Jesus' suffering. ¹¹Jesus, who makes people holy, and those who are made holy are from

the same family. So he is not ashamed to call them his brothers. ¹²He says,

"Then, I will tell my fellow
        Israelites about you.
I will praise you when your
        people meet to worship
        you."   *Psalm 22:22*
¹³He also says,
    "I will trust in God."   *Isaiah 8:17*
And he also says,
    "I am here. And with me are the
        children that God has given
        me."   *Isaiah 8:18*
¹⁴These children are people with physical bodies. So Jesus himself became like them and had the same experiences they have. He did this so that, by dying, he could destroy the one who has the power of death. That one is the devil. ¹⁵Jesus became like men and died so that he could free them. They were like slaves all their lives because of their fear of death. ¹⁶Clearly, it is not angels that Jesus helps, but the people who are from Abraham.ⁿ ¹⁷For this reason Jesus had to be made like his brothers in every way. He became like men so that he could be their merciful and faithful high priest in service to God. Then Jesus could bring forgiveness for their sins. ¹⁸And now he can help those who are tempted. He is able to help because he himself suffered and was tempted.

Jesus Is Greater than Moses

3 So all of you, holy brothers, should think about Jesus. You were all called by God. God sent Jesus to us, and he is the high priest of our faith. ²And Jesus was faithful to God as Moses was. Moses did everything God wanted him to do in God's family. ³A man who is the head of a family receives more honour than others in the family. It is the same with Jesus. Jesus

---

son of man This can mean any, but the name "Son of Man" is often used to mean Jesus. When Jesus became a man, he showed what God planned for all people to be.
Abraham Most respected ancestor of the Jews. Every Jew hoped to see Abraham.

should have more honour than Moses.
⁴Every family has its head, but God is
the head of everything. ⁵Moses was
faithful in God's family as a servant.
He told what God would say in the future. ⁶But Christ is faithful as a Son
who is the head of God's family. And
we are God's family if we hold on to
our faith and are proud of the great
hope we have.

We Must Continue to Follow God

⁷So it is as the Holy Spirit*d* says:
"Today listen to what he says.
⁸ Do not be stubborn as in the
       past
    when you turned against God.
  There you tested God in the
       desert.
⁹ For 40 years in the desert your
       ancestors saw the things I
       did.
    But they tested me and my
       patience.
¹⁰I was angry with them.
    I said, 'They are not loyal to
       me.
    They have not understood my
       ways'.
¹¹So I was angry and made a
       promise.
    'They will never enter my land
       of rest'." *n*   *Psalm 95:7-11*
¹²So brothers, be careful that none
of you has an evil, unbelieving heart.
This will stop you from following the
living God. ¹³But encourage each other every day. Do this while it is "today". *n* Help each other so that none
of you will become hardened because
of sin and its tricks. ¹⁴We all share in
Christ. This is true if we keep till the
end the sure faith we had in the beginning. ¹⁵This is what the Scripture*d*
says:

"Today listen to what he says.
    Do not be stubborn as in the
       past
    when you turned against God."
                              Psalm 95:7-8
¹⁶Who heard God's voice and was
against him? It was all those people
Moses led out of Egypt. ¹⁷And whom
was God angry with for 40 years? He
was angry with those who sinned,
who died in the desert. ¹⁸And whom
was God talking to when he promised
that they would never enter and have
his rest? He was talking to those who
did not obey him. ¹⁹So we see that
they were not allowed to enter and
have God's rest because they did not
believe.

4 Now God has left us that promise
   that we may enter and have his
rest. Let us be very careful, then, so
that none of you will fail to get that
rest. ²The Good News*d* was preached
to us just as it was to them. But the
teaching they heard did not help them.
They heard it but did not accept it with
faith. ³We who have believed are able
to enter and have God's rest. As God
has said,
"So I was angry and made a
       promise.
    'They will never enter my land
       of rest'." *Psalm 95:11*
But God's work was finished from the
time he made the world. ⁴Somewhere
in the Scriptures*d* he talked about the
seventh day of the week: "And on the
seventh day God rested from all his
work." *n* ⁵And again in the Scripture
God said, "They will never enter my
land of rest."

⁶It is still true that some people will
enter and have God's rest. But those
who first heard the way to be saved
did not enter. They did not enter because they did not obey. ⁷So God

rest A place of rest God promised to give his people.
"today" This word is taken from verse 7. It means that it is important to do these things
    now.
"And . . . work." Quotation from Genesis 2:2.

planned another day, called "today". He spoke about that day through David a long time later. It is the same Scripture used before:

"Today listen to what he says.

Do not be stubborn." *Psalm 95:7-8*

[8]We know that Joshua[n] did not lead the people into that rest. We know this because God spoke later about another day. [9]This shows that the seventh-day rest[n] for God's people is still coming. [10]For anyone who enters and has God's rest will rest from his work as God did. [11]So let us try as hard as we can to enter God's rest. We must try hard so that no one will be lost by following the example of those who refused to obey.

[12]God's word is alive and working. It is sharper than a sword sharpened on both sides. It cuts all the way into us, where the soul and the spirit are joined. It cuts to the centre of our joints and our bones. And God's word judges the thoughts and feelings in our hearts. [13]Nothing in all the world can be hidden from God. Everything is clear and lies open before him. And to him we must explain the way we have lived.

Jesus Is Our High Priest

[14]We have a great high priest who has gone into heaven. He is Jesus the Son of God. So let us hold on to the faith we have. [15]For our high priest is able to understand our weaknesses. When he lived on earth, he was tempted in every way that we are, but he did not sin. [16]Let us, then, feel free to come before God's throne. Here there is grace. And we can receive mercy and grace to help us when we need it.

[5] Every high priest is chosen from among men. He is given the work of going before God for them. He must offer gifts and sacrifices for sins. [2]He himself is weak. So he is able to be gentle with those who do not understand and who are doing wrong things. [3]Because he is weak the high priest must offer sacrifices for his own sins. And then he offers sacrifices for the sins of the people.

[4]To be a high priest is an honour. But no one chooses himself for this work. He must be called by God as Aaron[n] was. [5]So also Christ did not choose himself to have the honour of being a high priest. But God chose him. God said to him,

"You are my Son;
   today I have become your
      Father." *Psalm 2:7*

[6]And in another Scripture[d] God says,

"You are a priest for ever,
   a priest like Melchizedek."[n]

Psalm 110:4

[7]While Jesus lived on earth, he prayed to God and asked God for help. He prayed with loud cries and tears to the One who could save him from death. And his prayer was heard because he left it all up to God. [8]Even though Jesus was the Son of God, he learned to obey by what he suffered. [9]And he became our perfect high priest. He gives eternal salvation to all who obey him. [10]And God made Jesus high priest, a priest like Melchizedek.

Warning Against Falling Away

[11]We have much to say about this. But it is hard to explain because you are so slow to understand. [12]You have

---

Joshua After Moses died, Joshua became leader of the Jewish people. Joshua led them into the land that God promised to give them.

seventh-day rest Literally, "sabbath rest", meaning a sharing in the rest that God began after he created the world.

Aaron Aaron was the first Jewish high priest. He was Moses' brother.

Melchizedek A priest and king who lived in the time of Abraham. (Read Genesis 14:17-24.)

had enough time so that by now you should be teachers. But you need someone to teach you again the first lessons of God's message. You still need the teaching that is like milk. You are not ready for solid food. [13]Anyone who lives on milk is still a baby. He knows nothing about right teaching. [14]But solid food is for those who are grown up. They have practised in order to know the difference between good and evil.

6 So let us go on to grown-up teaching. Let us not go back over the lessons we learned about Christ at the beginning. We should not start over again with teaching about turning from acts that lead to death and about believing in God. [2]We should not return to the teaching of baptisms,[n] of laying on of hands,[n] of the raising of the dead and eternal judgement. [3]And we will go on to grown-up teaching if God allows.

[4]Some people cannot be brought back again to a changed life. They were once in God's light. They enjoyed heaven's gift, and they shared in the Holy Spirit.[d] [5]They found out how good God's word is, and they received the powers of his new world. [6]And then they fell away from Christ! It is not possible to keep on bringing them back to a changed life again. For they are nailing the Son of God to a cross again and are shaming him in front of others.

[7]Some people are like land that gets plenty of rain. The land produces a good crop for those who work it, and it receives God's blessings. [8]Other people are like land that grows thorns and weeds and is worthless. It is in danger of being cursed by God. It will be destroyed by fire.

[9]Dear friends, we are saying this to you. But we really expect better things from you that will lead to your salvation. [10]God is fair. He will not forget the work you did and the love you showed for him by helping his people. And he will remember that you are still helping them. [11]We want each of you to go on with the same hard work all your lives. Then you will surely get what you hope for. [12]We do not want you to become lazy. Be like those who have faith and patience. They will receive what God has promised.

[13]God made a promise to Abraham. And as there is no one greater than God, he used himself when he swore to Abraham. [14]He said, "I will surely bless you and give you many descendants."[n] [15]Abraham waited patiently for this to happen. And he received what God promised.

[16]People always use the name of someone greater than themselves when they swear. The oath proves that what they say is true. And this ends all arguing about what they say. [17]God wanted to prove that his promise was true. He wanted to prove this to those who would get what he promised. He wanted them to understand clearly that his purposes never change. So God proved his promise by also making an oath. [18]These two things cannot change. God cannot lie when he makes a promise, and he cannot lie when he makes an oath. These things encourage us who came to God for safety. They give us strength to hold on to the hope we have been given. [19]We have this hope as an anchor for the soul, sure and strong. It enters behind the curtain in the Most Holy Place in heaven. [20]Jesus has gone in there ahead of us and for us. He has

---

baptisms The word here may refer to Christian baptism, or it may refer to the Jewish ceremonial washings.

laying . . . hands Putting the hands on people showed that they were being given some special work or some spiritual gift or blessing.

"I . . . descendants." Quotation from Genesis 22:17.

become the high priest for ever, a priest like Melchizedek. [n]

The Priest Melchizedek

7 Melchizedek[n] was the king of Salem and a priest for the Most High God. He met Abraham when Abraham was coming back after defeating the kings. When they met, Melchizedek blessed Abraham. [2]And Abraham gave Melchizedek a tenth of everything he had brought back from the battle. First, Melchizedek's name means "king of goodness". Also, he is king of Salem, which means "king of peace". [3]No one knows who Melchizedek's father or mother was. [n] No one knows where he came from. And no one knows when he was born or when he died. Melchizedek is like the Son of God; he continues being a priest for ever.

[4]You can see that Melchizedek was very great. Abraham, the great father, gave Melchizedek a tenth of everything that Abraham won in battle. [5]Now the law says that those in the tribe[d] of Levi who become priests must get a tenth from the people. The priests collect it from their own people, even though the priests and the people are both from the family of Abraham. [6]Melchizedek was not from the tribe of Levi. But he got a tenth from Abraham. And he blessed Abraham, the man who had God's promises. [7]And everyone knows that the more important person blesses the less important person. [8]Those priests get a tenth, but they are only men who live and then die. But Melchizedek, who got a tenth from Abraham, continues living, as the Scripture[d] says. [9]It is Levi who gets a tenth from the people. But we might even say that when Abraham paid Melchizedek a tenth, then Levi also paid it. [10]Levi

was not yet born. But Levi was in the body of his ancestor Abraham when Melchizedek met Abraham.

[11]The people were given the law[n] based on a system of priests from the tribe of Levi. But they could not be made spiritually perfect through that system of priests. So there was a need for another priest to come. I mean a priest like Melchizedek, not Aaron. [12]And when a different kind of priest comes, the law must be changed, too. [13]We are saying these things about Christ. He belonged to a different tribe. No one from that tribe ever served as a priest at the altar. [14]It is clear that our Lord came from the tribe of Judah. And Moses said nothing about priests belonging to that tribe.

Jesus Is like Melchizedek

[15]And this becomes even more clear. We see that another priest comes, who is like Melchizedek. [n] [16]He was not made a priest by human rules and laws. He became a priest through the power of his life, which continues for ever. [17]In the Scriptures,[d] this is said about him:

"You are a priest for ever,
   a priest like Melchizedek."

Psalm 110:4

[18]The old rule is now set aside because it was weak and useless. [19]The law of Moses could not make anything perfect. But now a better hope has been given to us. And with this hope we can come near to God.

[20]Also, it is important that God made an oath when he made Jesus high priest. When the others became priests, there was no oath. [21]But Christ became a priest with God's oath. God said:

"The Lord has made a promise
   and will not change his mind.

Melchizedek A priest and king who lived in the time of Abraham. (Read Genesis 14:17-24.)
No . . . was Literally, "Melchizedek was without father, without mother, without genealogy."
The . . . law This refers to the people of Israel who were given the law of Moses.

'You are a priest for ever'."
Psalm 110:4

[22]So this means that Jesus is the guarantee of a better agreement[n] from God to his people.

[23]Also, when one of the other priests died, he could not continue being a priest. So there were many priests. [24]But Jesus lives for ever. He will never stop serving as priest. [25]So he is always able to save those who come to God through him. He can do this, because he always lives, ready to help those who come before God.

[26]So Jesus is the kind of high priest that we need. He is holy; he has no sin in him. He is pure and not influenced by sinners. And he is raised above the heavens. [27]He is not like the other priests. They had to offer sacrifices every day, first for their own sins, and then for the sins of the people. But Christ does not need to do that. He offered his sacrifice only once and for all time. Christ offered himself! [28]The law chooses high priests who are men with all their weaknesses. But the word of God's oath came later than the law. It made God's Son to be the high priest. And that Son has been made perfect for ever.

Jesus Is Our High Priest

8 Here is the point of what we are saying: we do have a high priest who sits on the right side of God's throne in heaven. [2]Our high priest serves in the Most Holy Place. He serves in the true place of worship that was made by God, not by men.

[3]Every high priest has the work of offering gifts and sacrifices to God. So our high priest must also offer something to God. [4]If our high priest were now living on earth, he would not be a priest. I say this because there are already priests here who follow the law by offering gifts to God. [5]The work that they do as priests is only a dim copy of what is in heaven. For when Moses was ready to build the Holy Tent,[d] God warned him: "Be very careful to make everything by the plan I showed you on the mountain."[n] [6]But the priestly work that has been given to Jesus is much greater than the work that was given to the other priests. In the same way, the new agreement that Jesus brought from God to his people is much greater than the old one. And the new agreement is based on promises of better things.

[7]If there was nothing wrong with the first agreement,[n] there would be no need for a second agreement. [8]But God found something wrong with his people. He says:
"The time is coming, says the Lord,
    when I will make a new agreement.
It will be with the people of Israel
    and the people of Judah.
[9]It will not be like the agreement
    I made with their ancestors.
That was when I took them by the hand
    to bring them out of Egypt.
But they broke that agreement,
    and I turned away from them,
    says the Lord.
[10]In the future I will make this agreement
    with the people of Israel, says the Lord.
I will put my teachings in their minds.

agreement God gives a contract or agreement to his people. For the Jews, this agreement was the law of Moses. But now God has given a better agreement to his people through Christ.
"Be . . . mountain." Quotation from Exodus 25:40.
first agreement The contract God gave the Jewish people when he gave them the law of Moses.

And I will write them on their
hearts.
I will be their God,
and they will be my people.
11People will no longer have to
teach
their neighbours and relatives to
know the Lord.
This is because all will know me,
from the least to the most
important.
12I will forgive them for the wicked
things they did.
I will not remember their sins
any more."   *Jeremiah 31:31-34*

13God called this a new agreement, so he has made the first agreement old. And anything that is old and worn out is ready to disappear.

Worship Under the Old Agreement

9 The first agreement[n] had rules for worship. And it had a man-made place for worship. 2The Holy Tent[d] was set up for this. The first area in the Tent was called the Holy Place. In it were the lamp and the table with the bread that was made holy for God. 3Behind the second curtain was a room called the Most Holy Place. 4In it was a golden altar for burning incense.[d] Also there was the Holy Ark[d] that held the old agreement. The Holy Ark was covered with gold. Inside this Holy Ark was a golden jar of manna[d] and Aaron's rod — the rod that once grew leaves. Also in it were the stone tablets of the old agreement. 5Above the Holy Ark were the creatures with wings that showed God's glory. The wings of the creatures reached over the lid. But we cannot tell everything about these things now.

6Everything in the Tent was made ready in this way. Then the priests went into the first room every day to do their worship. 7But only the high priest could go into the second room, and he did that only once a year. He could never enter the inner room without taking blood with him. He offered that blood to God for himself and for the people's sins. These were sins people did without knowing that they were sinning. 8The Holy Spirit[d] uses this to show that the way into the Most Holy Place was not open. This was while the system of the old Holy Tent was still being used. 9This is an example for the present time. It shows that the gifts and sacrifices offered cannot make the worshipper perfect in his heart. 10These gifts and sacrifices were only about food and drink and special washings. They were rules for the body, to be followed until the time of God's new way.

Worship Under the New Agreement

11But Christ has come as the high priest of the good things we now have. The tent he entered is greater and more perfect. It is not made by men. It does not belong to this world. 12Christ entered the Most Holy Place only once — and for all time. He did not take with him the blood of goats and calves. His sacrifice was his own blood. He entered the Most Holy Place and set us free from sin for ever. 13The blood of goats and bulls and the ashes of a cow are sprinkled on the people who are unclean[d] and this makes their bodies clean again.

14How much more is done by the blood of Christ. He offered himself through the eternal Spirit[n] as a perfect sacrifice to God. His blood will

first agreement The contract God gave the Jewish people when he gave them the law of Moses.
Spirit This refers to the Holy Spirit; to Christ's own spirit; or to the spiritual and eternal nature of his sacrifice.

make our hearts clean from useless acts. We are made pure so that we may serve the living God. ¹⁵So Christ brings a new agreement from God to his people. Those who are called by God can now receive the blessings that God has promised. These blessings will last for ever. They can have those things because Christ died so that the people who lived under the first agreement could be set free from sin.

¹⁶When there is a will,ⁿ it must be proven that the man who wrote that will is dead. ¹⁷A will means nothing while the man is alive. It can be used only after he dies. ¹⁸This is why even the first agreement could not begin without blood to show death. ¹⁹First, Moses told all the people every command in the law. Next he took the blood of calves and mixed it with water. Then he used red wool and a branch of the hyssop plant to sprinkle the blood and water on the book of the law and on all the people. ²⁰He said, "This is the blood which begins the agreement that God commanded you to obey."ⁿ ²¹In the same way, Moses sprinkled the blood on the Holy Tentᵈ and over all the things used in worship. ²²The law says that almost everything must be made clean by blood. And sins cannot be forgiven without blood to show death.

Christ's Death Takes Away Sins

²³So the copies of the real things in heaven had to be made cleanᵈ by animal sacrifices. But the real things in heaven need much better sacrifices. ²⁴For Christ did not go into the Most Holy Place made by men. It is only a copy of the real one. He went into heaven itself. He is there now before God to help us. ²⁵The high priest enters the Most Holy Place once every

year. He takes with him blood that is not his own blood. But Christ did not go into heaven to offer himself many times. ²⁶Then he would have had to suffer many times since the world was made. But Christ came only once and for all time. He came at just the right time to take away all sin by sacrificing himself. ²⁷Everyone must die once. After a person dies, he is judged. ²⁸So Christ was offered as a sacrifice once to take away the sins of many people. And he will come a second time, but not to offer himself for sin. He will come again to bring salvation to those who are waiting for him.

10 The law is only an unclear picture of the good things coming in the future. It is not a perfect picture of the real things. The people under the law offered the same sacrifices every year. These sacrifices can never make perfect those who come near to worship God. ²If the law could make them perfect, the sacrifices would have already stopped. The worshippers would be made clean, and they would no longer feel guilty for their sins. ³These sacrifices remind them of their sins every year, ⁴because it is not possible for the blood of bulls and goats to take away sins.

⁵So when Christ came into the world, he said:
"You do not want sacrifices and
    offerings.
But you have prepared a body
    for me.
⁶You do not ask for burnt offerings
    and offerings to take away sins.
⁷Then I said, 'Look, I have come.
    It is written about me in the
    book.
My God, I have come to do
    what you want'." *Psalm 40:6-8*
⁸In this Scriptureᵈ he first said, "You do not want sacrifices and offerings.

will A legal document that shows how a person's money and property are to be distributed at the time of his death. This is the same word in Greek as "agreement" in verse 15.
"This . . . obey." Quotation from Exodus 24:8.

You do not ask for burnt offerings and offerings to take away sins." (These are all sacrifices that the law commands.) [9]Then he said, "Here I am. I have come to do what you want." So God ends the first system of sacrifices so that he can set up the new system. [10]Jesus Christ did what God wanted him to do. And because of this, we are made holy through the sacrifice of his body. Christ made this sacrifice only once, and for all time.

[11]Every day the priests stand and do their religious service. Again and again they offer the same sacrifices. But those sacrifices can never take away sins. [12]But Christ offered one sacrifice for sins, and it is good for ever. Then he sat down at the right side of God. [13]And now Christ waits there for his enemies to be put under his power. [14]With one sacrifice he made perfect for ever those who are being made holy.

[15]The Holy Spirit[d] also tells us about this. First he says:

[16]"In the future I will make this
        agreement[n]
    with the people of Israel, says
        the Lord.
I will put my teachings in their
        hearts.
And I will write them on their
        minds."   Jeremiah 31:33

[17]Then he says:

"Their sins and the evil things
    they do—
I will not remember any more."
                        Jeremiah 31:34

[18]And when these have been forgiven, there is no more need for a sacrifice for sins.

Continue to Trust God

[19]So, brothers, we are completely free to enter the Most Holy Place. We can do this without fear because of the blood of Jesus' death. [20]We can enter through a new way that Jesus opened for us. It is a living way. It leads through the curtain—Christ's body. [21]And we have a great priest over God's house. [22]So let us come near to God with a sincere heart and a sure faith. We have been cleansed and made free from feelings of guilt. And our bodies have been washed with pure water. [23]Let us hold firmly to the hope that we have confessed. We can trust God to do what he promised.

[24]Let us think about each other and help each other to show love and do good deeds. [25]You should not stay away from the church meetings, as some are doing. But you should meet together and encourage each other. Do this even more as you see the Day[n] coming.

[26]If we decide to go on sinning after we have learned the truth, there is no longer any sacrifice for sins. [27]There is nothing but fear in waiting for the judgement and the angry fire that will destroy all those who live against God. [28]Any person who refused to obey the law of Moses was found guilty from the proof given by two or three witnesses. He was put to death without mercy. [29]So what do you think should be done to a person who does not respect the Son of God? He looks at the blood of the agreement, the blood that made him holy, as no different from other men's blood. He insults the Spirit[d] of God's grace. Surely he should have a much worse punishment. [30]We know that God said, "I will punish those who do wrong. I will repay them."[n] And he also said, "The

---

agreement God gives a contract or agreement to his people. For the Jews, this agreement was the law of Moses. But now God has given a better agreement to his people through Christ.
Day The day Christ will come to judge all people and take his people to live with him.
"I ... them." Quotation from Deuteronomy 32:35.

Lord will judge his people."ⁿ ³¹It is a terrible thing to fall into the hands of the living God.

³²Remember those days in the past when you first learned the truth. You had a hard struggle with many sufferings, but you continued strong. ³³Sometimes you were hurt and persecuted before crowds of people. And sometimes you shared with those who were being treated that way. ³⁴You helped the prisoners. And you even had joy when all that you owned was taken from you. You were joyful because you knew that you had something better and more lasting.

³⁵So do not lose the courage that you had in the past. It has a great reward. ³⁶You must hold on, so you can do what God wants and receive what he has promised. ³⁷For in a very short time,

"The One who is coming will
   come.
He will not be late.
³⁸The person who is right with me
   will have life because of his
   faith.
But if he turns back with fear,
I will not be pleased with him."

Habakkuk 2:3-4

³⁹But we are not those who turn back and are lost. We are people who have faith and are saved.

Faith

11 Faith means being sure of the things we hope for. And faith means knowing that something is real even if we do not see it. ²People who lived in the past became famous because of faith.

³It is by faith we understand that the whole world was made by God's command. This means that what we see was made by something that cannot be seen.

⁴It was by faith that Abel offered God a better sacrifice than Cain did. God said he was pleased with the gifts Abel offered. So God called Abel a good man because of his faith. Abel died, but through his faith he is still speaking.

⁵It was by faith that Enoch was taken to heaven. He never died. He could not be found, because God had taken him away. Before he was taken, the Scriptureᵈ says that he was a man who truly pleased God. ⁶Without faith no one can please God. Anyone who comes to God must believe that he is real and that he rewards those who truly want to find him.

⁷It was by faith that Noah heard God's warnings about things that he could not yet see. He obeyed God and built a large boat to save his family. By his faith, Noah showed that the world was wrong. And he became one of those who are made right with God through faith.

⁸It was by faith that Abraham obeyed God's call to go to another place that God promised to give him. He left his own country, not knowing where he was to go. ⁹It was by faith that he lived in the country God promised to give him. He lived there like a visitor who did not belong. He lived in tents with Isaac and Jacob, who had received that same promise from God. ¹⁰Abraham was waiting for the cityⁿ that has real foundations—the city planned and built by God.

¹¹He was too old to have children, and Sarah was not able to have children. It was by faith that Abraham was made able to become a father. Abraham trusted God to do what he had promised. ¹²This man was so old that he was almost dead. But from him came as many descendants as there are stars in the sky. They are as many

"The Lord . . . people." Quotation from Deuteronomy 32:36; Psalm 135:14.
city The spiritual "city" where God's people live with him. Also called "the heavenly Jerusalem". (See Hebrews 12:22.)

as the grains of sand on the seashore that cannot be counted.

13All these great men died in faith. They did not get the things that God promised his people. But they saw them coming far in the future and were glad. They said that they were like visitors and strangers on earth. 14When people say such things, they show that they are looking for a country that will be their own country. 15If they had been thinking about that country they had left, they could have gone back. 16But those men were waiting for a better country—a heavenly country. So God is not ashamed to be called their God, for he has prepared a city for them.

17It was by faith that Abraham offered his son Isaac as a sacrifice. God made the promises to Abraham. But God tested him. And Abraham was ready to offer his own son as a sacrifice. 18God had said, "The descendants I promised you will be from Isaac."[n] 19Abraham believed that God could raise the dead. And really, it was as if Abraham brought Isaac back from death.

20It was by faith that Isaac blessed the future of Jacob and Esau. 21It was by faith that Jacob blessed each one of Joseph's sons. He did this while he was dying. Then he worshipped as he leaned on the top of his staff.

22It was by faith that Joseph spoke about the Israelites leaving Egypt while he was dying. He told them what to do with his body.

23It was by faith that Moses' parents hid him for three months after he was born. They saw that Moses was a beautiful baby. And they were not afraid to disobey the king's order.

24It was by faith that Moses, when he grew up, refused to be called the son of the king of Egypt's daughter. 25He chose to suffer with God's people instead of enjoying sin for a short time. 26He thought that it was better to suffer for the Christ[d] than to have all the treasures of Egypt. He was looking only for God's reward. 27It was by faith that Moses left Egypt. He was not afraid of the king's anger. Moses continued strong as if he could see the God that no one can see. 28It was by faith that Moses prepared the Passover[d] and spread the blood on the doors. It was spread so that the one who brings death would not kill the firstborn[d] sons of Israel.

29It was by faith that the people crossed the Red Sea as if it were dry land. The Egyptians also tried to do it, but they were drowned.

30It was by faith that the walls of Jericho fell. They fell after the people had marched around the walls of Jericho for seven days.

31It was by faith that Rahab, the prostitute,[d] welcomed the spies and was not killed with those who refused to obey God.

32Do I need to give more examples? I do not have time to tell you about Gideon, Barak, Samson, Jephthah, David, Samuel, and the prophets.[d] 33Through their faith they defeated kingdoms. They did what was right and received what God promised. They shut the mouths of lions, 34stopped great fires and were saved from being killed with swords. They were weak, and yet were made strong. They were powerful in battle and defeated other armies. 35Women received their dead relatives raised back to life. Others were tortured and refused to accept their freedom. They did this so that they could be raised from death to a better life. 36Some were laughed at and beaten. Others were tied and put into prison. 37They were killed with stones and they were cut in half. They were killed with swords. Some wore the skins of sheep and goats. They were poor,

"The descendants . . . Isaac."   Quotation from Genesis 21:12.

abused, and treated badly. [38]The world was not good enough for them! They wandered in deserts and mountains, living in caves and holes in the earth.

[39]All these people are known for their faith. But none of them received what God had promised. [40]God planned to give us something better. Then they would be made perfect, but only together with us.

Follow Jesus' Example

12 So we have many people of faith around us. Their lives tell us what faith means. So let us run the race that is before us and never give up. We should remove from our lives anything that would get in the way. And we should remove the sin that so easily catches us. [2]Let us look only to Jesus. He is the one who began our faith, and he makes our faith perfect. Jesus suffered death on the cross. But he accepted the shame of the cross as if it were nothing. He did this because of the joy that God put before him. And now he is sitting at the right side of God's throne. [3]Think about Jesus. He held on patiently while sinful men were doing evil things against him. Look at Jesus' example so that you will not get tired and stop trying.

God Is Like a Father

[4]You are struggling against sin, but your struggles have not yet caused you to be killed. [5]You have forgotten his encouraging words for his sons:

"My son, don't think the Lord's
    discipline of you is worth
        nothing.
And don't stop trying when the
    Lord corrects you.
[6]The Lord corrects those he loves.
And he punishes everyone he
    accepts as his child."
                    Proverbs 3:11-12

[7]So accept your sufferings as if they were a father's punishment. God does these things to you like a father pun-

ishing his sons. All sons are punished by their fathers. [8]If you are never punished (and every son must be punished), you are not true children and not really sons. [9]We have all had fathers here on earth who punished us. And we respected our fathers. So it is even more important that we accept punishment from the Father of our spirits. If we do this, we will have life. [10]Our fathers on earth punished us for a short time. They punished us in the way they thought was best. But God punishes us to help us, so that we can become holy as he is. [11]We do not enjoy punishment. Being punished is painful. But later, after we have learned from being punished, we have peace, because we start living in the right way.

Be Careful How You Live

[12]You have become weak. So make yourselves strong again. [13]Live in the right way so that you will be saved and your weakness will not cause you to be lost.

[14]Try to live in peace with all people. And try to live lives free from sin. If anyone's life is not holy, he will never see the Lord. [15]Be careful that no one fails to get God's grace. Be careful that no one becomes like a bitter weed growing among you. A person like that can ruin all of you. [16]Be careful that no one takes part in sexual sin. And be careful that no person is like Esau and never thinks about God. Esau was the oldest son, and he would have received everything from his father. But Esau sold all that for a single meal. [17]You remember that after Esau did this, he wanted to get his father's blessing. He wanted this blessing so much that he cried. But his father refused to give him the blessing, because Esau could find no way to change what he had done.

[18]You have not come to a mountain that can be touched and that is burning with fire. You have not come to dark-

ness, sadness and storms. [19]You have not come to the noise of a trumpet or to the sound of a voice. When the people of Israel heard the voice, they begged not to have to hear another word. [20]They did not want to hear the command: "If anything, even an animal, touches the mountain, it must be put to death with stones."[n] [21]What they saw was so terrible that Moses said, "I am shaking with fear."[n]

[22]But you have not come to that kind of place. The new place you have come to is Mount Zion.[n] You have come to the city of the living God, the heavenly Jerusalem. You have come to thousands of angels gathered together with joy. [23]You have come to the meeting of God's firstborn[n] children. Their names are written in heaven. You have come to God, the judge of all people. And you have come to the spirits of good people who have been made perfect. [24]You have come to Jesus, the One who brought the new agreement from God to his people. You have come to the sprinkled blood[n] that has a better message than the blood of Abel.[n]

[25]So be careful and do not refuse to listen when God speaks. They refused to listen to him when he warned them on earth. And they did not escape. Now God is warning us from heaven. So it will be worse for us if we refuse to listen to him. [26]When he spoke before, his voice shook the earth. But now he has promised, "Once again I will shake not only the earth but also the heavens."[n] [27]The words "once again" clearly show us that everything that was made will be

destroyed. These are the things that can be shaken. And only the things that cannot be shaken will remain.

[28]So let us be thankful because we have a kingdom that cannot be shaken. We should worship God in a way that pleases him. So let us worship him with respect and fear, [29]because our God is like a fire that burns things up.

13 Keep on loving each other as brothers in Christ. [2]Remember to welcome strangers into your homes. Some people have done this and have welcomed angels without knowing it. [3]Do not forget those who are in prison. Remember them as if you were in prison with them. Remember those who are suffering as if you were suffering with them.

[4]Marriage should be honoured by everyone. Husband and wife should keep their marriage pure. God will judge guilty those who take part in sexual sins. [5]Keep your lives free from the love of money. And be satisfied with what you have. God has said,

"I will never leave you;
I will never forget you."
Deuteronomy 31:6

[6]So we can feel sure and say,

"I will not be afraid because the
Lord is my helper.
People can't do anything to me."
Psalm 118:6

[7]Remember your leaders. They taught God's message to you. Remember how they lived and died, and copy their faith. [8]Jesus Christ is the same yesterday, today, and for ever.

[9]Do not let all kinds of strange teachings lead you into the wrong

---

"If . . . stones." Quotation from Exodus 19:12-13.
"I . . . fear." Quotation from Deuteronomy 9:19.
Mount Zion Another name for Jerusalem, here meaning the spiritual city of God's people.
firstborn The first son born in a Jewish family was given the most important place in the family and received special blessings. All of God's children are like that.
sprinkled blood The blood of Jesus' death.
Abel The son of Adam and Eve, who was killed by his brother Cain (Genesis 4:8).
"Once . . . heavens." Quotation from Haggai 2:6,21.

way. Your hearts should be strengthened by God's grace, not by obeying rules about foods. Obeying such rules does not help anyone.

[10]We have a sacrifice. But the priests who serve in the Holy Tent[d] cannot eat from it. [11]The high priest carries the blood of animals into the Most Holy Place. There he offers this blood for sins. But the bodies of the animals are burned outside the camp. [12]So Jesus also suffered outside the city. He died to make his people holy with his own blood. [13]So let us go to Jesus outside the camp. We should accept the same shame that Jesus had.

[14]Here on earth we do not have a city that lasts for ever. But we are looking for the city that we will have in the future. [15]So through Jesus let us always offer our sacrifice to God. This sacrifice is our praise, coming from lips that speak his name. [16]Do not forget to do good to others. And share with them what you have. These are the sacrifices that please God.

[17]Obey your leaders and be under their authority. These men are watching you because they are responsible for your souls. Obey them so that they will do this work with joy, not

sadness. It will not help you to make their work hard.

[18]Continue praying for us. We feel sure about what we are doing, because we always want to do the right thing. [19]And I beg you to pray that God will send me back to you soon.

[20-21]I pray that the God of peace will give you every good thing you need so that you can do what he wants. God is the One who raised from death our Lord Jesus, the Great Shepherd of the sheep. God raised him because of the blood of his death. His blood began the agreement that God made with his people. And this agreement is eternal. I pray that God, through Christ, will do in us what pleases him. And to Jesus Christ be glory for ever and ever. Amen.

[22]My brothers, I beg you to listen patiently to this message I have written to encourage you. This letter is not very long. [23]I want you to know that our brother Timothy has been let out of prison. If he arrives soon, we will both come to see you.

[24]Greet all your leaders and all of God's people. Those from Italy send greetings to you. [25]God's grace be with you all.

JAMES

How to Live as a Christian

1 From James, a servant of God and of the Lord Jesus Christ. To all of God's people who are scattered everywhere in the world: Greetings.

Faith and Wisdom

²My brothers, you will have many kinds of troubles. But when these things happen, you should be very happy. ³You know that these things are testing your faith. And this will give you patience. ⁴Let your patience show itself perfectly in what you do. Then you will be perfect and complete. You will have everything you need. ⁵But if any of you needs wisdom, you should ask God for it. God is generous. He enjoys giving to all people, so God will give you wisdom. ⁶But when you ask God, you must believe. Do not doubt God. Anyone who doubts is like a wave in the sea. The wind blows the wave up and down. ⁷⁻⁸He who doubts is thinking two different things at the same time. He cannot decide about anything he does. A person like that should not think that he will receive anything from the Lord.

True Riches

⁹If a believer is poor, he should be proud because God has made him spiritually rich. ¹⁰If he is rich, he should be proud because God has shown him that he is spiritually poor. The rich person will die like a wild flower in the grass. ¹¹The sun rises and becomes hotter and hotter. The heat makes the plants very dry, and the flower falls off. The flower was beautiful, but now it is dead. It is the same with a rich person. While he is still taking care of his business, he will die.

Temptation Is Not from God

¹²When a person is tempted and still continues strong, he should be happy. After he has proved his faith, God will reward him with life for ever. God promised this to all people who love him. ¹³When someone is being tempted, he should not say, "God is tempting me." Evil cannot tempt God, and God himself does not tempt anyone. ¹⁴It is the evil that a person wants that tempts him. His own evil desire leads him away and holds him. ¹⁵This desire causes sin. Then the sin grows and brings death.

¹⁶My dear brothers, do not be fooled about this. ¹⁷Every good action and every perfect gift is from God. These good gifts come down from the Creator of the sun, moon, and stars. God does not change like their shifting shadows. ¹⁸God decided to give us life through the word of truth. He wanted us to be the most important of all the things he made.

Listening and Obeying

¹⁹My dear brothers, always be willing to listen and slow to speak. Do not become angry easily. ²⁰Anger will not help you live a good life as God wants. ²¹So put out of your life every evil thing and every kind of wrong you do. Don't be proud but accept God's teaching that is planted in your hearts. This teaching can save your souls.

²²Do what God's teaching says; do not just listen and do nothing. When you only sit and listen, you are fooling yourselves. ²³A person who hears

God's teaching and does nothing is like a man looking in a mirror. [24]He sees his face, then goes away and quickly forgets what he looked like. [25]But the truly happy person is the one who carefully studies God's perfect law that makes people free. He continues to study it. He listens to God's teaching and does not forget what he has heard. Then he obeys what God's teaching says. When he does this, it makes him happy.

The True Way to Worship God

[26]A person might think he is religious. But if he says things he should not say, then he is just fooling himself. His "religion" is worth nothing. [27]Religion that God accepts is this: caring for orphans or widows who need help; and keeping yourself free from the world's evil influence. This is the kind of religion that God accepts as pure and good.

Love All People

2 My dear brothers, you are believers in our glorious Lord Jesus Christ. So never think that some people are more important than others. [2]Suppose someone comes into your church meeting wearing very nice clothes and a gold ring. At the same time a poor man comes in wearing old, dirty clothes. [3]You show special attention to the one wearing nice clothes. You say, "Please, sit here in this good seat." But you say to the poor man, "Stand over there", or "Sit on the floor by my feet!" [4]What are you doing? You are making some people more important than others. With evil thoughts you are deciding which person is better.

[5]Listen, my dear brothers! God chose the poor in the world to be rich in faith. He chose them to receive the

kingdom God promised to people who love him. [6]But you show no respect to the poor man. And you know that it is the rich who are always trying to control your lives. And they are the ones who take you to court. [7]They are the ones who say bad things against Jesus, who owns you.

[8]One law rules over all other laws. This royal law is found in the Scriptures:[d] "Love your neighbour as you love yourself."[n] If you obey this law, then you are doing right. [9]But if you are treating one person as if he were more important than another, then you are sinning. That royal law proves that you are guilty of breaking God's law. [10]A person might follow all of God's law. But if he fails to obey even one command, he is guilty of breaking all the commands in that law. [11]God said, "You must not be guilty of adultery."[dn] The same God also said, "You must not murder anyone."[n] So if you do not take part in adultery, but you murder someone, then you are guilty of breaking all of God's law. [12]You will be judged by the law that makes people free. You should remember this in everything you say and do. [13]Yes, you must show mercy to others, or God will not show mercy to you when he judges you. But the person who shows mercy can stand without fear when he is judged.

Faith and Good Works

[14]My brothers, if someone says he has faith, but does nothing, his faith is worth nothing. Can faith like that save him? [15]A brother or sister in Christ might need clothes or might need food. [16]And you say to him, "God be with you! I hope you stay warm and get plenty to eat." You say this, but you do not give that person the things he needs. Unless you help him, your

"Love . . . yourself." Quotation from Leviticus 19:18.
"You . . . adultery." Quotation from Exodus 20:14 and Deuteronomy 5:18.
"You . . . anyone." Quotation from Exodus 20:13 and Deuteronomy 5:17.

words are worth nothing. [17]It is the same with faith. If faith does nothing, then that faith is dead, because it is alone.

[18]Someone might say, "You have faith, but I do things. Show me your faith! Your faith does nothing. I will show you my faith by the things I do." [19]You believe there is one God. Good! But the demons[d] believe that, too! And they shake with fear.

[20]You foolish person! Must you be shown that faith that does nothing is worth nothing? [21]Abraham is our father. He was made right with God by the things he did. He offered his son Isaac to God on the altar. [22]So you see that Abraham's faith and the things he did worked together. His faith was made perfect by what he did. [23]This shows the full meaning of the Scripture[d] that says: "Abraham believed God, and God accepted Abraham's faith, and that faith made him right with God."[n] And Abraham was called "God's friend."[n] [24]So you see that a person is made right with God by the things he does. He cannot be made right by faith only.

[25]Another example is Rahab, who was a prostitute.[d] But she was made right with God by something she did: she helped the spies for God's people. She welcomed them into her home and helped them escape by a different road.

[26]A person's body that does not have a spirit is dead. It is the same with faith. Faith that does nothing is dead!

Controlling the Things We Say

3 My brothers, not many of you should become teachers. You know that we who teach will be judged more strictly than others. [2]We all make many mistakes. If there were a person who never said anything

wrong, he would be perfect. He would be able to control his whole body, too. [3]We put bits into the mouths of horses to make them obey us. We can control their whole bodies. [4]It is the same with ships. A ship is very big, and it is pushed by strong winds. But a very small rudder controls that big ship. The man who controls the rudder decides where the ship will go. The ship goes where the man wants. [5]It is the same with the tongue. It is a small part of the body, but it boasts about doing great things.

A big forest fire can be started with only a little flame. [6]And the tongue is like a fire. It is a whole world of evil among the parts of our bodies. The tongue spreads its evil through the whole body. It starts a fire that influences all of life. The tongue gets this fire from hell. [7]People can tame every kind of wild animal, bird, reptile, and fish, and they have tamed them. [8]But no one can tame the tongue. It is wild and evil. It is full of poison that can kill. [9]We use our tongues to praise our Lord and Father, but then we curse people. And God made them like himself. [10]Praises and curses come from the same mouth! My brothers, this should not happen. [11]Do good and bad water flow from the same spring? [12]My brothers, can a fig tree make olives? Can a grapevine make figs? No! And a well full of salty water cannot give good water.

True Wisdom

[13]Is there anyone among you who is truly wise and understanding? Then he should show his wisdom by living right. He should do good things without being proud. A wise person does not boast. [14]But if you are selfish and have bitter jealousy in your hearts, you have no reason to boast. Your boasting is a lie that hides the truth.

"Abraham . . . God." Quotation from Genesis 15:6.
"God's friend" These words about Abraham are found in 2 Chronicles 20:7 and Isaiah 41:8.

[15]That kind of "wisdom" does not come from God. That "wisdom" comes from the world. It is not spiritual. It is from the devil. [16]Where there is jealousy and selfishness, there will be confusion and every kind of evil. [17]But the wisdom that comes from God is like this: first, it is pure. Then it is also peaceful, gentle, and easy to please. This wisdom is always ready to help those who are troubled and to do good for others. This wisdom is always fair and honest. [18]When people work for peace in a peaceful way, they receive the good result of their good living.

Give Yourselves to God

4 Do you know where your fights and arguments come from? They come from the selfish desires that make war inside you. [2]You want things, but you do not have them. So you are ready to kill and are jealous of other people. But you still cannot get what you want. So you argue and fight. You do not get what you want because you do not ask God. [3]Or when you ask, you do not receive because the reason you ask is wrong. You want things only so that you can use them for your own pleasures.

[4]So, you people are not loyal to God! You should know that loving the world is the same as hating God. So if a person wants to be a friend of the world, he makes himself God's enemy. [5]Do you think the Scripture[d] means nothing? It says, "The Spirit[d] that God made to live in us wants us for himself alone."[n] [6]But God gives us even more grace, as the Scripture says,

"God is against the proud,
but he gives grace to the
humble."   *Proverbs 3:34*

[7]So give yourselves to God. Stand against the devil, and the devil will run away from you. [8]Come near to God, and God will come near to you. You are sinners. So clean sin out of your lives. You are trying to follow God and the world at the same time. Make your thinking pure. [9]Be sad, cry, and weep! Change your laughter into crying. Change your joy into sadness. [10]Don't be too proud before the Lord, and he will make you great.

You Are Not the Judge

[11]Brothers, do not say bad things about each other. If you say bad things about your brother in Christ or judge him, then you are saying bad things about the law he follows. You are also judging the law he follows. And when you are judging the law, you are not a follower of the law. You have become a judge! [12]God is the only One who makes laws, and he is the only Judge. He is the only One who can save and destroy. So it is not right for you to judge your neighbour.

Let God Plan Your Life

[13]Some of you say, "Today or tomorrow we will go to some city. We will stay there a year, do business, and make money." [14]But you do not know what will happen tomorrow! Your life is like a mist. You can see it for a short time, but then it goes away. [15]So you should say, "If the Lord wants, we will live and do this or that." [16]But now you are proud and you boast. All of this boasting is wrong. [17]And when a person knows the right thing to do, but does not do it, then he is sinning.

A Warning to the Rich

5 You rich people, listen! Cry and be very sad because of the trouble that will come to you. [2]Your riches will rot, and your clothes will be eaten by moths. [3]Your gold and silver will rust, and rust will be a proof that you were wrong. It will eat your bodies like fire.

"The Spirit . . . alone." These words may be from Exodus 20:5.

You saved your treasure for the last days. [4]Men worked in your fields, but you did not pay them. They harvested your crops and are crying out against you. Now the Lord of heaven's armies has heard their cries. [5]Your life on earth was full of rich living. You pleased yourselves with everything you wanted. You made yourselves fat, like an animal ready to be killed. [6]You showed no mercy to the innocent man. You murdered him. He cannot stand against you.

Be Patient

[7]Brothers, be patient until the Lord comes again. A farmer is patient. He waits for his valuable crop to grow from the earth. He waits patiently for it to receive the first rain and the last rain. [8]You, too, must be patient. Do not give up hope. The Lord is coming soon. [9]Brothers, do not complain against each other. If you do not stop complaining, you will be judged guilty. And the Judge is ready to come! [10]Brothers, follow the example of the prophets[d] who spoke for the Lord. They suffered many hard things, but they were patient. [11]We say they are happy because they were able to do this. You have heard about Job's patience. You know that after all his trouble, the Lord helped him. This shows that the Lord is full of mercy and is kind.

Be Careful What You Say

[12]My brothers, it is very important that you do not use an oath when you make a promise. Don't use the name of heaven, earth, or anything else to prove what you say. When you mean yes, say only "yes". When you mean no, say only "no". Do this so that you will not be judged guilty.

The Power of Prayer

[13]If one of you is having troubles, he should pray. If one of you is happy, he should sing praises. [14]If one of you is sick, he should call the church's elders.[d] The elders should pour oil on him[n] in the name of the Lord and pray for him. [15]And the prayer that is said with faith will make the sick person well. The Lord will heal him. And if he has sinned, God will forgive him. [16]Confess your sins to each other and pray for each other. Do this so that God can heal you. When a good man prays, great things happen. [17]Elijah was a man just like us. He prayed that it would not rain. And it did not rain on the land for three and a half years! [18]Then Elijah prayed again. And the rain came down from the sky, and the land grew crops again.

Saving a Soul

[19]My brothers, one of you may wander away from the truth. And someone may help him come back. [20]Remember this: anyone who brings a sinner back from the wrong way will save that sinner's soul from death. By doing this, that person will cause many sins to be forgiven.

pour oil on him Oil was used like medicine, so that is probably how the believers used it.

1 PETER

Encouragement for Suffering Christians

1 From Peter, an apostle[d] of Jesus
Christ.

To God's chosen people who are
away from their homes. You are scattered all around the countries of Pontus, Galatia, Cappadocia, Asia, and
Bithynia. [2]God planned long ago to
choose you by making you his holy
people. Making you holy is the Spirit's[d] work. God wanted you to obey
him and to be made clean by the
blood of the death of Jesus Christ.
Grace and peace be yours more and
more.

A Living Hope

[3]Praise be to the God and Father of
our Lord Jesus Christ. God has great
mercy, and because of his mercy he
gave us a new life. He gave us a living
hope because Jesus Christ rose from
death. [4]Now we hope for the blessings God has for his children. These
blessings are kept for you in heaven.
They cannot be destroyed or be
spoiled or lose their beauty. [5]God's
power protects you through your
faith, and it keeps you safe until your
salvation comes. That salvation is
ready to be given to you at the end of
time. [6]This makes you very happy.
But now for a short time different
kinds of troubles may make you sad.
[7]These troubles come to prove that
your faith is pure. This purity of faith
is worth more than gold. Gold can be
proved to be pure by fire, but gold can
be destroyed. But the purity of your
faith will bring you praise and glory
and honour when Jesus Christ comes
again. [8]You have not seen Christ, but
still you love him. You cannot see him
now, but you believe in him. You are

filled with a joy that cannot be explained. And that joy is full of glory.
[9]Your faith has a goal, to save your
souls. And you are receiving that
goal—your salvation.

[10]The prophets[d] searched carefully
and tried to learn about this salvation. They spoke about the grace that
was coming to you. [11]The Spirit[d] of
Christ was in the prophets. And the
Spirit was telling about the sufferings
that would happen to Christ and about
the glory that would come after those
sufferings. The prophets tried to learn
about what the Spirit was showing
them. They tried to learn when those
things would happen and what the
world would be like at that time. [12]It
was shown to them that their service
was not for themselves. It was for
you. They were serving you when
they told about the truths you have
now heard. The men who preached
the Good News[d] to you told you those
things. They did it with the help of the
Holy Spirit that was sent from heav-
en. These are truths that even the angels long to know about.

A Call to Holy Living

[13]So prepare your minds for service
and have self-control. All your hope
should be for the gift of grace that will
be yours when Jesus Christ comes
again. [14]In the past you did not understand, so you did the evil things you
wanted. But now you are children of
God who obey. So do not live as you
lived in the past. [15]But be holy in all
that you do, just as God is holy. God
is the One who called you. [16]It is written in the Scriptures:[d] "You must be
holy, because I am holy."[n]

"You must be . . . holy." Quotation from Leviticus 11:45; 19:2; 20:7.

[17]You pray to God and call him Father. And this Father judges each man's work equally. So while you are here on earth, you should live with respect for God. [18]You know that in the past you were living in a worthless way. You got that way of living from the people who lived before you. But you were saved from that useless life. You were bought, but not with something that can be destroyed like gold or silver. [19]You were bought with the precious blood of the death of Christ, who was like a pure and perfect [20]lamb. Christ was chosen before the world was made. But he was shown to the world in these last times for you. [21]You believe in God through Christ. God raised Christ from death and gave him glory. So your faith and your hope are in God.

[22]Now you have made yourselves pure by obeying the truth. Now you can have true love for your brothers. So love each other deeply with all your heart. [23]You have been born again. This new life did not come from something that dies, but from something that cannot die. You were born again through God's living message that continues for ever. [24]The Scripture says,

"All people are like the grass.
And all their strength is like the
    flowers of the field.
The grass dies and the flowers
    fall,
[25]but the word of the Lord will live
    for ever."   *Isaiah 40:6-8*
And this is the word that was preached to you.

Jesus Is the Living Stone

2 So then, get rid of all evil and all lying. Do not be a hypocrite.[d] Do not be jealous or speak evil of others. Put all these things out of your life. [2]As newborn babies want milk, you should want the pure and simple teaching. By it you can grow up and be saved. [3]For you have already examined and seen how good the Lord is.

[4]The Lord Jesus is the "stone"[n] that lives. The people of the world did not want this stone. But he was the stone God chose. To God he was worth much. So come to him. [5]You also are like living stones. Let yourselves be used to build a spiritual temple — to be holy priests who offer spiritual sacrifices to God. He will accept those sacrifices through Jesus Christ. [6]The Scripture[d] says:

"I will put a stone in the ground in
    Jerusalem.
Everything will be built on this
    important and precious rock.
Anyone who trusts in him
    will never be disappointed."
                        Isaiah 28:16

[7]This stone is worth a great deal to you who believe. But to the people who do not believe, he is

"the stone that the builders did
    not want.
It has become the
    cornerstone."[d]   *Psalm 118:22*
[8]To people who do not believe, he is
"a stone that causes people to
    stumble.
It is a rock that makes them
    fall."   *Isaiah 8:14*
They stumble because they do not obey what God says. This is what God planned to happen to them.

[9]But you are chosen people. You are the King's priests. You are a holy nation. You are a nation that belongs to God alone. God chose you to tell of the wonderful things he has done. He called you out of darkness into his wonderful light. [10]At one time you were not God's people, but now you are his people. In the past you had never received mercy, but now you have received God's mercy.

"stone" The most important stone in God's spiritual temple or house (his people).

Live for God

[11]Dear friends, you are like visitors and strangers in this world. So I beg you to stay away from the evil things your bodies want to do. These things fight against your soul. [12]People who do not believe are living all around you. They might say that you are doing wrong. So live good lives. Then they will see the good things you do, and they will give glory to God on the day when Christ comes again.

Obey Every Human Authority

[13]Obey the people who have authority in this world. Do this for the Lord. Obey the king, who is the highest authority. [14]And obey the leaders who are sent by the king. They are sent to punish those who do wrong and to praise those who do right. [15]So when you do good, you stop foolish people from saying stupid things about you. This is what God wants. [16]Live as free men. But do not use your freedom as an excuse to do evil. Live as servants of God. [17]Show respect for all people. Love the brothers and sisters of God's family. Respect God. Honour the king.

Follow Christ's Example

[18]Slaves, accept the authority of your masters. Do this with all respect. You should obey masters who are good and kind, and you should obey masters who are bad. [19]A person might have to suffer even when he has done nothing wrong. But if he thinks of God and bears the pain, this pleases God. [20]If you are punished for doing wrong, there is no reason to praise you for bearing punishment. But if you suffer for doing good, and you are patient, then that pleases God. [21]That is what you were called to do. Christ suffered for you. He gave you an example to follow. So you should do as he did.

[22]"He did no sin.
He never lied."   *Isaiah 53:9*

[23]People insulted Christ, but he did not insult them in return. Christ suffered, but he did not threaten. He let God take care of him. God is the One who judges rightly. [24]Christ carried our sins in his body on the cross. He did this so that we would stop living for sin and start living for what is right. And we are healed because of his wounds. [25]You were like sheep that went the wrong way. But now you have come back to the Shepherd and Protector of your souls.

Wives and Husbands

3 In the same way, you wives should accept the authority of your husbands. Then, if some husbands have not obeyed God's teaching, they will be persuaded to believe. You will not need to say a word to them. They will be persuaded by the way their wives live. [2]Your husbands will see the pure lives that you live with your respect for God. [3]It is not fancy hair, gold jewellery, or fine clothes that should make you beautiful. [4]No, your beauty should come from within you—the beauty of a gentle and quiet spirit. This beauty will never disappear, and it is worth a great deal to God. [5]It was the same with the holy women who lived long ago and followed God. They made themselves beautiful in this way. They accepted the authority of their husbands. [6]Sarah obeyed Abraham, her husband, and called him her master. And you women are true children of Sarah if you always do what is right and are not afraid.

[7]In the same way, you husbands should live with your wives in an understanding way. You should show respect to them. They are weaker than you. But God gives them the same blessing that he gives you—the grace that gives true life. Do this so that nothing will stop your prayers.

Suffering for Doing Right

[8]Finally, all of you should live together in peace. Try to understand each other. Love each other as brothers. Be kind and humble. [9]Do not do wrong to a person to pay him back for doing wrong to you. Or do not insult someone to pay him back for insulting you. But ask God to bless that person. Do this, because you yourselves were called to receive a blessing. [10]The Scripture[d] says,

"A person must do these things
    to enjoy life and have many,
        happy days.
He must not say evil things.
    He must not tell lies.
[11]He must stop doing evil and do
        good.
    He must look for peace and
        work for it.
[12]The Lord sees the good people.
    He listens to their prayers.
But the Lord is against
    those who do evil."   *Psalm 34:12-16*

[13]If you are always trying to do good, no one can really hurt you. [14]But you may suffer for doing right. Even if that happens, you are blessed. "Don't be afraid of the things they fear.
    Do not dread those things.
[15]But respect Christ as the holy
    Lord in your hearts."
                           Isaiah 8:12-13
Always be ready to answer everyone who asks you to explain about the hope you have. [16]But answer in a gentle way and with respect. Always feel that you are doing right. Then, those who speak evil of your good life in Christ will be made ashamed. [17]It is better to suffer for doing good than for doing wrong. Yes, it is better, if that is what God wants. [18]Christ himself died for you. And that one death paid for your sins. He was not guilty, but he died for those who are guilty. He did this to bring you all to God. His body was killed, but he was made alive

in the spirit. [19]And in the spirit he went and preached to the spirits in prison. [20]These were the spirits who refused to obey God long ago in the time of Noah. God was waiting patiently for them while Noah was building the boat. Only a few people — eight in all — were saved by water. [21]That water is like baptism that now saves you — not the washing of dirt from the body, but the promise made to God from a good heart. And this is because Jesus Christ was raised from death. [22]Now Jesus has gone into heaven and is at God's right side. He rules over angels, authorities, and powers.

Changed Lives

4 Christ suffered while he was in his body. So you should strengthen yourselves with the same way of thinking Christ had. The person who has suffered in his body is finished with sin. [2]Strengthen yourselves so that you will live your lives here on earth doing what God wants, not doing the evil things that people want. [3]In the past you wasted too much time doing what the non-believers like to do. You were guilty of sexual sins and had evil desires. You were getting drunk, you had wild and drunken parties, and you did wrong by worshipping idols. [4]Non-believers think it is strange that you do not do the many wild and wasteful things that they do. And so they insult you. [5]But they will have to explain about what they have done. They must explain to God who is ready to judge the living and the dead. [6]The Good News[d] was preached to those who are now dead. By their dying, they were judged like all men. But the Good News was preached to them so that they could live in the spirit as God lives.

Use God's Gifts Wisely

[7]The time is near when all things will end. So keep your minds clear,

and control yourselves. Then you will be able to pray. ⁸Most importantly, love each other deeply. Love has a way of not looking at others' sins. ⁹Open your homes to each other, without complaining. ¹⁰Each of you received a spiritual gift. God has shown you his grace in giving you different gifts. And you are like servants who are responsible for using God's gifts. So be good servants and use your gifts to serve each other. ¹¹Anyone who speaks should speak words from God. The person who serves should serve with the strength that God gives. You should do these things so that in everything God will be praised through Jesus Christ. Power and glory belong to him for ever and ever. Amen.

Suffering as a Christian

¹²My friends, do not be surprised at the painful things you are now suffering. These things are testing your faith. So do not think that something strange is happening to you. ¹³But you should be happy that you are sharing in Christ's sufferings. You will be happy and full of joy when Christ comes again in glory. ¹⁴When people insult you because you follow Christ, then you are blessed. You are blessed because the glorious Spirit,ᵈ the Spirit of God, is with you. ¹⁵Do not suffer for murder, theft, or any other crime, nor because you trouble other people. ¹⁶But if you suffer because you are a Christian, then do not be ashamed. You should praise God because you wear that name. ¹⁷It is time for judgement to begin, and it will begin with God's family. If that judging begins with us, what will happen to those people who do not obey the Good Newsᵈ of God?

¹⁸"It is very hard for a good person
    to be saved.
Then the wicked person and

the sinner will surely be lost!"ⁿ
¹⁹So then those who suffer as God wants them to should trust their souls to him. God is the One who made them, and they can trust him. So they should continue to do what is right.

The Flock of God

5 Now I have something to say to the eldersᵈ in your group. I am also an elder. I myself have seen Christ's sufferings. And I will share in the glory that will be shown to us. I beg you to ²take care of God's flock, his people, that you are responsible for. Watch over it because you want to, not because you are forced to do it. That is how God wants it. Do it because you are happy to serve, not because you want money. ³Do not be like a ruler over people you are responsible for. Be good examples to them. ⁴Then when Christ, the Head Shepherd, comes, you will get a crown. This crown will be glorious, and it will never lose its beauty.

⁵In the same way, younger men should be willing to be under older men. And all of you should be very humble with each other.

"God is against the proud,
    but he gives grace to the
        humble."   *Proverbs 3:34*
⁶So be humble under God's powerful hand. Then he will lift you up when the right time comes. ⁷Give all your worries to him, because he cares for you.

⁸Control yourselves and be careful! The devil is your enemy. And he goes around like a roaring lion looking for someone to eat. ⁹Refuse to give in to the devil. Stand strong in your faith. You know that your Christian brothers and sisters all over the world are having the same sufferings you have.

¹⁰Yes, you will suffer for a short time. But after that, God will make

---

"It . . . lost!" Quotation from Proverbs 11:31 in the Septuagint, the Greek version of the Old Testament.

everything right. He will make you strong. He will support you and keep you from falling. He is the God who gives all grace. He called you to share in his glory in Christ. That glory will continue for ever. [11]All power is his for ever and ever. Amen.

Final Greetings

[12]I wrote this short letter with the help of Silas. I know that he is a faith-ful brother in Christ. I wrote to comfort and encourage you. I wanted to tell you that this is the true grace of God. Stand strong in that grace.

[13]The church in Babylon sends you greetings. They were chosen the same as you. Mark, my son in Christ, also greets you. [14]Give each other a kiss of Christian love when you meet.

Peace to all of you who are in Christ.

2 PETER

Correcting False Teachings

1 From Simon Peter, a servant and apostle[d] of Jesus Christ.

To you who have received a faith as valuable as ours. You received that faith because our God and Saviour Jesus Christ is fair and does what is right.

[2]Grace and peace be given to you more and more. You will have grace and peace because you truly know God and Jesus our Lord.

God Has Given Us Blessings

[3]Jesus has the power of God. His power has given us everything we need to live and to serve God. We have these things because we know him. Jesus called us by his glory and goodness. [4]Through his glory and goodness, he gave us the very great and rich gifts he promised us. With those gifts you can share in being like God. And so the world will not ruin you with its evil desires.

[5]Because you have these blessings, you should try as much as you can to add these things to your lives: to your faith, add goodness; and to your goodness, add knowledge; [6]and to your knowledge, add self-control; and to your self-control, add the ability to hold on; and to your ability to hold on, add service for God; [7]and to your service for God, add kindness for your brothers and sisters in Christ; and to this kindness, add love. [8]If all these things are in you and are growing, they will help you never to be useless. They will help your knowledge of our Lord Jesus Christ make your lives better. [9]But if anyone does not have these things, he cannot see clearly. He is blind. He has forgotten that he was made clean from his past sins.

[10]My brothers, God called you and chose you to be his. Try hard to show that you really are God's chosen people. If you do all these things, you will never fall. [11]And you will be given a very great welcome into the kingdom of our Lord and Saviour Jesus Christ. That kingdom continues for ever.

[12]You know these things, and you are very strong in the truth. But I will always help you to remember these things. [13]I think it is right for me to help you remember while I am still living here on earth. [14]I know that I must soon leave this body. Our Lord Jesus Christ has shown me that. [15]I will try the best I can to help you remember these things always. I want you to be able to remember them even after I am gone.

We Saw Christ's Glory

[16]We have told you about the powerful coming of our Lord Jesus Christ. What we told you were not just clever stories that someone invented. But we saw the greatness of Jesus with our own eyes. [17]Jesus heard the voice of God, the Greatest Glory. That was when Jesus received honour and glory from God the Father. The voice said, "This is my Son, and I love him. I am very pleased with him." [18]We heard that voice. It came from heaven while we were with Jesus on the holy mountain.

[19]This makes us more sure about the message the prophets[d] gave. And it is good for you to follow closely what they said. Their message is like a light shining in a dark place. That light shines until the day begins and the morning star rises in your hearts. [20]Most of all, you must understand

this: no prophecy in the Scriptures[d] ever comes from the prophet's own interpretation. [21]No prophecy ever came from what a man wanted to say. But men led by the Holy Spirit[d] spoke words from God.

False Teachers

2 There used to be false prophets[d] among God's people, just as there are now. And you will have some false teachers in your group. They will secretly teach things that are wrong — teachings that will cause people to be lost. They will even refuse to accept the Master, Jesus, who bought their freedom. And so they will quickly destroy themselves. [2]Many will follow their evil ways and say evil things about the Way of truth. [3]Those false teachers only want your money. So they will use you by telling you what is not true. But God has already judged them guilty. And they will not escape the One who will destroy them.

[4]When angels sinned, God did not let them go free without punishment. God sent them to hell and put them in caves of darkness. They are being held there to be judged. [5]And God punished the evil people who lived long ago. He brought a flood to the world that was full of people who were against him. But God saved Noah and seven other people with him. Noah was a man who preached about being right with God. [6]And God also punished the evil cities of Sodom and Gomorrah.[n] He burned those cities until there was nothing left but ashes. He made those cities an example to show what will happen to those who are against God. [7]But God saved Lot from those cities. Lot, a good man, was troubled because of the dirty lives of evil people. [8](Lot was a good man, but he lived with evil people every day. His good heart was hurt by the evil things that he saw and heard.) [9]And so the Lord knows how to save those who serve him. He will save them when troubles come. And the Lord will hold evil people and punish them, while waiting for the Judgement Day. [10]That punishment is especially for those who live by doing the evil things their sinful selves want, and for those who hate the Lord's authority.

These false teachers do anything they want and boast about it. They are not afraid to say bad things about the glorious angels. [11]The angels are much stronger and more powerful than false teachers. But even the angels do not accuse them with insults before the Lord. [12]But these men say bad things about what they do not understand. They are like animals that act without thinking. These animals are born to be caught and killed. And, like wild animals, these false teachers will be destroyed. [13]They have caused many people to suffer; so they themselves will suffer. That is their pay for what they have done. They take pleasure in doing evil things openly. So they are like dirty spots and stains among you. They bring shame to you in the meals that you eat together. [14]Every time they look at a woman they want her. Their desire for sin is never satisfied. They lead weak people into the trap of sin. They have taught their hearts to be selfish. God will punish them. [15]These false teachers left the right road and lost their way. They followed the way that Balaam went. Balaam was the son of Beor, who loved being paid for doing wrong. [16]But a donkey told Balaam that he was sinning. And the donkey is an animal that cannot talk. But the donkey spoke with a man's voice and stopped the prophet's mad thinking.

[17]Those false teachers are like rivers that have no water. They are like clouds blown by a storm. A place in

Sodom and Gomorrah Two cities God destroyed because the people were so evil.

the blackest darkness has been kept for them. [18]They boast with words that mean nothing. By their evil desires they lead people into the trap of sin. They lead away people who are just beginning to escape from other people who live in error. [19]They promise them freedom, but they themselves are not free. They are slaves of things that will be destroyed. For a person is a slave of anything that controls him. [20]They were made free from the evil in the world by knowing our Lord and Saviour Jesus Christ. But if they return to evil things and those things control them, then it is worse for them than it was before. [21]Yes, it would be better for them to have never known the right way. That would be better than to know the right way and then to turn away from the holy teaching that was given to them. [22]What they did is like this true saying: "A dog eats what it throws up."[n] And, "After a pig is washed, it goes back and rolls in the mud."

Jesus Will Come Again

3 My friends, this is the second letter I have written to you. I wrote both letters to you to help your honest minds remember something. [2]I want you to remember the words that the holy prophets[d] spoke in the past. And remember the command that our Lord and Saviour gave us through your apostles.[d] [3]It is important for you to understand what will happen in the last days. People will laugh at you. They will live doing the evil things they want to do. [4]They will say, "Jesus promised to come again. Where is he? Our fathers have died. But the world continues the way it has been since it was made." [5]But they do not want to remember what happened long ago. God spoke and made heaven and earth. He made the earth from

water and with water. [6]Then the world was flooded and destroyed with water. [7]And that same word of God is keeping heaven and earth that we have now. They are being kept to be destroyed by fire. They are being kept for the Judgement Day and the destruction of all who are against God.

[8]But do not forget this one thing, dear friends: to the Lord one day is as a thousand years, and a thousand years is as one day. [9]The Lord is not slow in doing what he promised — the way some people understand slowness. But God is being patient with you. He does not want anyone to be lost. He wants everyone to change his heart and life.

[10]But the day the Lord comes again will be a surprise, like a thief. The skies will disappear with a loud noise. Everything in the skies will be destroyed by fire. And the earth and everything in it will be burned up.[n] [11]In that way everything will be destroyed. So what kind of people should you be? You should live holy lives and serve God. [12]You should wait for the day of God and look forward to its coming. When that day comes, the skies will be destroyed with fire, and everything in the skies will melt with heat. [13]But God made a promise to us. And we are waiting for what he promised — a new heaven and a new earth where goodness lives.

[14]Dear friends, we are waiting for this to happen. So try as hard as you can to be without sin and without fault. Try to be at peace with God. [15]Remember that we are saved because our Lord is patient. Our dear brother Paul told you the same thing when he wrote to you with the wisdom that God gave him. [16]Paul writes about this in all his letters. Sometimes there are things in Paul's letters that are hard to understand. And some people explain

---

"A dog . . . up." Quotation from Proverbs 26:11.
will be burned up Many Greek copies say, "will be found". One copy says, "will disappear".

these things falsely. They are igno-
rant and weak in faith. They also falsely explain the other Scriptures.*d* But
they are destroying themselves by
doing that.

¹⁷Dear friends, you already know
about this. So be careful. Do not let
those evil people lead you away by the
wrong they do. Be careful so that you
will not fall from your strong faith.
¹⁸But grow in the grace and knowledge of our Lord and Saviour Jesus
Christ. Glory be to him now and for
ever! Amen.

1 JOHN

Love One Another

1 We write to you now about something that has always existed.
We have heard.
We have seen with our own eyes.
We have watched,
and we have touched with our hands.
We write to you about the Word[n] that gives life. [2]He who gives life was shown to us. We saw him, and we can give proof about it. And now we tell you that he has life that continues for ever. The One who gives this life was with God the Father. God showed him to us. [3]Now we tell you what we have seen and heard because we want you to have fellowship with us. The fellowship we share together is with God the Father and his Son, Jesus Christ. [4]We write this to you so that you can be full of joy with us.

God Forgives Our Sins

[5]Here is the message we have heard from God and now tell to you: God is light,[n] and in him there is no darkness at all. [6]So if we say that we have fellowship with God, but we continue living in darkness, then we are liars. We do not follow the truth. [7]God is in the light. We should live in the light, too. If we live in the light, we share fellowship with each other. And when we live in the light, the blood of the death of Jesus, God's Son, is making us clean from every sin.

[8]If we say that we have no sin, we are fooling ourselves, and the truth is not in us. [9]But if we confess our sins, he will forgive our sins. We can trust God. He does what is right. He will make us clean from all the wrongs we have done. [10]If we say that we have not sinned, then we make God a liar. We do not accept God's true teaching.

Jesus Is Our Helper

2 My dear children, I write this letter to you so that you will not sin. But if anyone does sin, we have Jesus Christ to help us. He is the Righteous One. He defends us before God the Father. [2]Jesus is the way our sins are taken away. And Jesus is the way that all people can have their sins taken away, too.

[3]If we obey what God has told us to do, then we are sure that we truly know God. [4]If someone says, "I know God!" but does not obey God's commands, then he is a liar. The truth is not in him. [5]But if someone obeys God's teaching, then God's love has truly arrived at its goal in him. This is how we know that we are following God: [6]whoever says that God lives in him must live as Jesus lived.

The Command to Love Others

[7]My dear friends, I am not writing a new command to you. It is the same command you have had since the beginning. It is the teaching you have already heard. [8]But I am writing a new command to you. This command is true; you can see its truth in Jesus and in yourselves. The darkness is passing away, and the true light is already shining.

[9]Someone says, "I am in the

Word The Greek word is "logos", meaning any kind of communication. It could be translated "message". Here, it means Christ. Christ was the way God told people about himself.
light This word is used to show what God is like. It means goodness or truth.

light."[n] But if he hates his brother, he is still in the darkness. [10]Whoever loves his brother lives in the light, and there is nothing in him that will cause him to do wrong. [11]But whoever hates his brother is in darkness. He lives in darkness and does not know where he is going. The darkness has made him blind.

[12]I write to you, dear children,
    because your sins are forgiven
        through Christ.
[13]I write to you, fathers,
    because you know the One who
        existed from the beginning.
I write to you, young men,
    because you have defeated the
        Evil One.
[14]I write to you, children,
    because you know the Father.
I write to you, fathers,
    because you know the One who
        existed from the beginning.
I write to you, young men,
    because you are strong;
    the word of God lives in you,
    and you have defeated the Evil
        One.

[15]Do not love the world or the things in the world. If anyone loves the world, the love of the Father is not in him. [16]These are the evil things in the world: wanting things to please our sinful selves; wanting the sinful things we see; being too proud of the things we have. But none of those things comes from the Father. All of them come from the world. [17]The world is passing away. And everything that people want in the world is passing away. But the person who does what God wants lives for ever.

Reject the Enemies of Christ

[18]My dear children, the end is near! You have heard that the Enemy of Christ[d] is coming. And now many enemies of Christ are already here. So we know that the end is near. [19]Those enemies of Christ were in our group. But they left us. They did not really belong with us. If they were really part of our group, then they would have stayed with us. But they left. This shows that none of them really belonged with us.

[20]You have the gift[n] that the Holy One gave you. So you all know the truth. [21]Why do I write to you? Do I write because you do not know the truth? No, I write this letter because you do know the truth. And you know that no lie comes from the truth.

[22]So who is the liar? It is the person who says Jesus is not the Christ. A person who says Jesus is not the Christ is the enemy of Christ. He does not believe in the Father or in his Son. [23]If anyone does not believe in the Son, he does not have the Father. But whoever accepts the Son has the Father, too.

[24]Be sure that you continue to follow the teaching that you heard from the beginning. If you continue in that teaching, you will stay in the Son and in the Father. [25]And this is what the Son promised to us — life for ever.

[26]I am writing this letter about those people who are trying to lead you the wrong way. [27]Christ gave you a special gift. You still have this gift in you. So you do not need any other teacher. The gift he gave you teaches you about everything. This gift is true, not false. So continue to live in Christ, as his gift taught you.

[28]Yes, my dear children, live in him. If we do this, we can be without fear on the day when Christ comes back. We will not need to hide and be ashamed when he comes. [29]You know that Christ is righteous. So you know that all who do what is right are God's children.

light This word is used to show what God is like. It means goodness or truth.
gift This might mean the Holy Spirit. Or it might mean teaching or truth as in verse 24.

We Are God's Children

3 The Father has loved us so much! He loved us so much that we are called children of God. And we really are his children. But the people in the world do not understand that we are God's children, because they have not known him. ²Dear friends, now we are children of God. We have not yet been shown what we will be in the future. But we know that when Christ comes again, we will be like him. We will see him as he really is. ³Christ is pure. And every person who has this hope in Christ keeps himself pure like Christ.

⁴When a person sins, he breaks God's law. Yes, sinning is the same as living against God's law. ⁵You know that Christ came to take away sins. There is no sin in Christ. ⁶So the person who lives in Christ does not go on sinning. If he goes on sinning, he has never really understood Christ and has never known him.

⁷Dear children, do not let any person lead you the wrong way. Christ is righteous. To be like Christ, a person must do what is right. ⁸The devil has been sinning since the beginning. Anyone who continues to sin belongs to the devil. The Son of God came for this purpose: to destroy the devil's work.

⁹When God makes someone his child, that person does not go on sinning. The new life God gave that person stays in him. So he is not able to go on sinning, because he has become a child of God. ¹⁰So we can see who God's children are and who the devil's children are. Those who do not do what is right are not children of God, and anyone who does not love his brother is not a child of God.

We Must Love Each Other

¹¹This is the teaching you have heard from the beginning: we must love each other. ¹²Do not be like Cain who belonged to the Evil One. Cain killed his brother. He killed his brother because the things Cain did were evil, and the things his brother did were good.

¹³Brothers, do not be surprised when the people of this world hate you. ¹⁴We know that we have left death and have come into life. We know this because we love our brothers in Christ. Whoever does not love is still in death. ¹⁵Everyone who hates his brother is a murderer.* And you know that no murderer has eternal life in him. ¹⁶This is how we know what real love is: Jesus gave his life for us. So we should give our lives for our brothers. ¹⁷Suppose a believer is rich enough to have all that he needs. He sees his brother in Christ who is poor and does not have what he needs. What if the believer does not help the poor brother? Then the believer does not have God's love in his heart. ¹⁸My children, our love should not be only words and talk. Our love must be true love. And we should show that love by what we do.

¹⁹⁻²⁰This is the way we know that we belong to the way of truth. When our hearts make us feel guilty, we can still have peace before God. God is greater than our hearts, and he knows everything.

²¹My dear friends, if we do not feel that we are doing wrong, we can be without fear when we come to God. ²²And God gives us the things we ask for. We receive these things because we obey God's commands, and we do what pleases him. ²³This is what God commands: that we believe in his Son, Jesus Christ, and that we love each other, just as he commanded. ²⁴The person who obeys God's commands lives in God. And God lives in him.

Everyone . . . murderer. If a person hates his brother in Christ, then in his mind he has killed his brother. Jesus explained this sin to his followers (Matthew 5:21-26).

How do we know that God lives in us? We know because of the Spirit[d] God gave us.

Warning Against False Teachers

4 My dear friends, many false prophets[d] are in the world now. So do not believe every spirit. But test the spirits to see if they are from God. [2]This is how you can know God's Spirit:[d] one spirit says, "I believe that Jesus is the Christ who came to earth and became a man." That Spirit is from God. [3]Another spirit refuses to say this about Jesus. That spirit is not from God but is the spirit of the Enemy of Christ. You have heard that the Enemy of Christ is coming. And now he is already in the world.

[4]My dear children, you belong to God. So you have defeated them because God's Spirit, who is in you, is greater than the devil, who is in the world. [5]And they belong to the world. What they say is from the world, and the world listens to them. [6]But we are from God, and those who know God listen to us. But those who are not from God do not listen to us. That is how we know the Spirit that is true and the spirit that is false.

Love Comes from God

[7]Dear friends, we should love each other, because love comes from God. The person who loves has become God's child and knows God. [8]Whoever does not love does not know God, because God is love. [9]This is how God showed his love to us: he sent his only Son into the world to give us life through him. [10]True love is God's love for us, not our love for God. God sent his Son to be the way to take away our sins. [11]That is how much God loved us, dear friends! So we also must love each other. [12]No one has ever seen God. But if we love each other, God lives in us. If we love each other,

God's love has reached its goal. It is made perfect in us.

[13]We know that we live in God and God lives in us. We know this because God gave us his Spirit.[d] [14]We have seen that the Father sent his Son to be the Saviour of the world. That is what we teach. [15]If someone says, "I believe that Jesus is the Son of God," then God lives in him. And he lives in God. [16]And so we know the love that God has for us, and we trust that love.

God is love. Whoever lives in love lives in God, and God lives in him. [17]If God's love is made perfect in us, then we can be without fear on the day God judges us. We will be without fear, because in this world we are like him. [18]Where God's love is, there is no fear, because God's perfect love takes away fear. It is punishment that makes a person fear. So love is not made perfect in the person who has fear.

[19]We love because God first loved us. [20]If someone says, "I love God," but hates his brother, he is a liar. He can see his brother, but he hates him. So he cannot love God, whom he has never seen. [21]And God gave us this command: whoever loves God must also love his brother.

Faith in the Son of God

5 Everyone who believes that Jesus is the Christ[d] is God's child. The person who loves the Father also loves the Father's children. [2]How do we know that we love God's children? We know because we love God and we obey his commands. [3]Loving God means obeying his commands. And God's commands are not too hard for us. [4]Everyone who is a child of God has the power to win against the world. It is our faith that wins the victory against the world. [5]So the one who wins against the world is the person who believes that Jesus is the Son of God.

[6]Jesus Christ is the One who came

with water[n] and with blood.[n] He did not come by water only. He came by both water and blood. And the Spirit[d] says that this is true. The Spirit is the truth. [7]So there are three witnesses that tell us about Jesus: [8]the Spirit, the water, and the blood. These three witnesses agree. [9]We believe people when they say something is true. But what God says is more important. And he has told us the truth about his own Son. [10]Anyone who believes in the Son of God has the truth that God told us. Anyone who does not believe makes God a liar. He does not believe what God told us about his Son. [11]This is what God told us: God has given us eternal life, and this life is in his Son. [12]Whoever has the Son has life. But the person who does not have the Son of God does not have life.

We Have Eternal Life Now

[13]I write this letter to you who believe in the Son of God. I write so that you will know that you have eternal life now. [14]We can come to God with no doubts. This means that when we ask God for things (and those things agree with what God wants for us),

then God cares about what we say. [15]God listens to us every time we ask him. So we know that he gives us the things that we ask from him.

[16]Suppose someone sees his brother in Christ sinning (sin that does not lead to eternal death). That person should pray for his brother who is sinning. Then God will give the brother life. I am talking about people whose sin does not lead to eternal death. There is sin that leads to death. I do not mean that a person should pray about that sin. [17]Doing wrong is always sin. But there is sin that does not lead to eternal death.

[18]We know that anyone who is God's child does not continue to sin. The Son of God keeps him safe, and the Evil One cannot hurt him. [19]We know that we belong to God. But the Evil One controls the whole world. [20]And we know that the Son of God has come and has given us understanding. Now we can know God, the One who is true. And our lives are in that true God and in his Son, Jesus Christ. He is the true God, and he is eternal life. [21]So, dear children, keep yourselves away from false gods.

2 JOHN

Do Not Help False Teachers

¹From the Elder."

To the chosen lady" and to her children:

I love all of you in the truth." Also, all those who know the truth love you. ²We love you because of the truth—the truth that lives in us and will be with us for ever.

³Grace, mercy, and peace will be with us from God the Father and from his Son, Jesus Christ. And may we have these blessings in truth and love.

⁴I was very happy to learn about some of your children. I am happy that they are following the way of truth, as the Father commanded us. ⁵And now, dear lady, I tell you: we should all love each other. This is not a new command. It is the same command we have had from the beginning. ⁶And loving means living the way he commanded us to live. And God's command is this: that you live a life of love. You have heard this command from the beginning.

⁷Many false teachers are in the world now. They refuse to say that Jesus Christ came to earth and became a man. Anyone who refuses to say this is a false teacher and an enemy of Christ. ⁸Be careful! Do not lose the reward that you have worked for. Be careful, so that you will receive your full reward.

⁹A person must continue to follow only the teaching of Christ. If he goes beyond Christ's teaching, then he does not have God. But if he continues following the teaching of Christ, then he has both the Father and the Son. ¹⁰If someone comes to you, but does not bring this teaching, then do not accept him into your house. Do not welcome him. ¹¹If you accept him, you are helping him with his evil work.

¹²I have much to say to you, but I do not want to use paper and ink. Instead, I hope to come and visit you. Then we can be together and talk. That will make us very happy. ¹³The children of your chosen sister" send you their love.

Elder This is probably John the apostle. "Elder" means an older man. It can also mean a special leader in the church (as in Titus 1:5).

lady This might mean a woman. Or, in this letter, it might mean a church. If it is a church, then "her children" would be the people of the church.

truth The truth or "Good News" about Jesus Christ that joins all believers together.

sister Sister of the "lady" in verse 1. This might be another woman or another church.

3 JOHN

Help Christians Who Teach Truth

[1]From the Elder.*

To my dear friend Gaius whom I love in the truth:*

[2]My dear friend, I know your soul is doing well. I pray that you are doing fine in every way and that your health is good. [3]Some brothers in Christ came and told me about the truth in your life. They said that you are following the way of truth. This made me very happy. [4]It always gives me the greatest joy when I hear that my children are following the way of truth.

[5]My dear friend, it is good that you continue to help the brothers. You are helping those that you do not even know! [6]These brothers told the church about the love you have. Please help them to continue their mission. Help them in a way that will please God. [7]They started out on their mission to serve Christ. They did not accept any help from those who are not believers. [8]So we should help these brothers. And when we do, we share in their work for the truth.

[9]I wrote a letter to the church. But Diotrephes will not listen to what we say. He always wants to be their leader. [10]When I come, I will talk about what Diotrephes is doing. He lies and says evil things about us. But that is not all he does. He refuses to help those who are working to serve Christ. He also stops those who want to help the brothers and puts them out of the church.

[11]My dear friend, do not follow what is bad; follow what is good. He who does what is good is from God. But he who does evil has never known God. [12]Everyone says good things about Demetrius. And the truth agrees with what they say. Also, we say good about him. And you know that what we say is true.

[13]I have many things I want to tell you, but I do not want to use pen and ink. [14]I hope to visit you soon. Then we can be together and talk. [15]Peace to you. The friends here with me send their love. Please give our love to each one of the friends there.

Elder This is probably John the apostle. "Elder" means an older man. It can also mean a special leader in the church (as in Titus 1:5).

truth The truth or "Good News" about Jesus Christ that joins all believers together.

JUDE

Warnings About False Teachers

[1]From Jude, a servant of Jesus Christ and a brother of James.

To all who have been called by God. God the Father loves you, and you have been kept safe in Jesus Christ.

[2]All mercy, peace, and love be yours.

God Will Punish Sinners

[3]Dear friends, I wanted very much to write to you about the salvation we all share together. But I felt the need to write to you about something else: I want to encourage you to fight hard for the faith that God gave his holy people. God gave this faith once, and it is good for all time. [4]Some people have secretly entered your group. They have already been judged guilty for the things they are doing. Long ago the prophets[d] wrote about these people. They are against God. They have used the grace of our God in the wrong way — to do sinful things. They refuse to accept Jesus Christ, our only Master and Lord.

[5]I want to remind you of some things that you already know: remember that the Lord saved his people by bringing them out of the land of Egypt. But later the Lord destroyed all those who did not believe. [6]And remember the angels who had power but did not keep it. They left their own home. So the Lord has kept these angels in darkness. They are bound with everlasting chains, to be judged on the great day. [7]Also remember the cities of Sodom and Gomorrah[n] and the other towns around them. They acted as the angels who did not obey God.

Their towns were full of sexual sin and men having sexual relations with men. They suffer the punishment of eternal fire, as an example for all to see.

[8]It is the same with these people who have entered your group. They are guided by dreams. They make themselves dirty with sin. They reject God's authority and say bad things against the glorious angels. [9]Not even the archangel[n] Michael did this. He argued with the devil about who would have the body of Moses. Michael did not dare to accuse the devil with insults. He said, "The Lord punish you." [10]But these people say bad things about what they do not understand. They do understand some things. But they understand them not by thinking, but by feeling, the way dumb animals understand things. And these are the very things that destroy them. [11]It will be bad for them. They have followed the way that Cain went. To make money, they have given themselves to doing the wrong that Balaam did. They have fought against God as Korah did. And like Korah, they will be destroyed. [12]They are like dirty spots in the special meals you share together. They eat with you and have no fear. They take care only of themselves. They are clouds without rain. The wind blows them around. They are trees that have no fruit when it is time and are pulled out of the ground. So they are dead twice over. [13]They are like wild waves in the sea. These people do shameful things in the same way that waves make foam. They are like stars that wander in

Sodom and Gomorrah Two cities God destroyed because the people were so evil.
archangel The leader among God's angels or messengers.

the sky. A place in the blackest darkness has been kept for them for ever.

[14]Enoch, the seventh descendant[d] from Adam, said this about these people: "Look, the Lord is coming with thousands and thousands of his holy angels. [15]The Lord will judge every person. He is coming to judge everyone and to punish all who are against God. He will punish them for all the evil they have done against him. And he will punish the sinners who are against God. He will punish them for all the evil things they have said against him."

[16]These people always complain and blame others. They always do the evil things they want to do. They boast about themselves. The only reason they say good things about other people is to get what they want.

A Warning and Things to Do

[17]Dear friends, remember what the apostles[d] of our Lord Jesus Christ said before. [18]They said to you, "In the last times there will be people who laugh about God. They will do only what they want to do — things that are against God." [19]These are the people who divide you. They do only what their sinful selves want. They do not have the Spirit.[d]

[20]But dear friends, use your most holy faith to build yourselves up strong. Pray with the Holy Spirit. [21]Keep yourselves in God's love. Wait for the Lord Jesus Christ with his mercy to give you life for ever.

[22]Show mercy to people who have doubts. [23]Save them. Take them out of the fire. Show mercy mixed with fear to others. Hate even their clothes which are dirty from sin.

Praise God

[24]God is strong and can help you not to fall. He can bring you before his glory without any wrong in you and give you great joy. [25]He is the only God. He is the One who saves us. To him be glory, greatness, power, and authority through Jesus Christ our Lord for all time past, now, and for ever. Amen.

REVELATION

Christ Will Win over Evil

John Tells About This Book

1 This is the revelation[n] of Jesus Christ. God gave this revelation to Jesus, to show his servants what must soon happen. And Jesus sent his angel to show it to his servant John. [2]John has told everything that he has seen. It is the truth that Jesus Christ told him; it is the message from God. [3]The one who reads the words of God's message is happy. And the people who hear this message and do what is written in it are happy. The time is near when all of this will happen.

Jesus' Message to the Churches

[4]From John,

To the seven churches in the country of Asia:

Grace and peace to you from the One who is and was and is coming, and from the seven spirits before his throne, [5]and from Jesus Christ. Jesus is the faithful witness. He is first among those raised from death. He is the ruler of the kings of the earth.

He is the One who loves us. And he is the One who made us free from our sins with the blood of his death. [6]He made us to be a kingdom of priests who serve God his Father. To Jesus Christ be glory and power for ever and ever! Amen.

[7]Look, Jesus is coming with the clouds! Everyone will see him, even those who stabbed him. And all peoples of the earth will cry loudly because of him. Yes, this will happen! Amen.

[8]The Lord God says, "I am the Alpha and the Omega.[n] I am the One who is and was and is coming. I am the All-Powerful."

[9]I am John, and I am your brother in Christ. We are together in Jesus, and we share in these things: in suffering, in the kingdom, and in patience. I was on the island of Patmos[n] because I had preached God's message and the truth about Jesus. [10]On the Lord's Day the Spirit[d] took control of me. I heard a loud voice behind me that sounded like a trumpet. [11]The voice said, "Write what you see and send that book to the seven churches: to Ephesus, Smyrna, Pergamum, Thyatira, Sardis, Philadelphia, and Laodicea."

[12]I turned to see who was talking to me. When I turned, I saw seven golden lampstands. [13]I saw someone among the lampstands who was "like a Son of Man".[n] He was dressed in a long robe. He had a gold band around his chest. [14]His head and hair were white like wool, as white as snow. His eyes were like flames of fire. [15]His feet were like bronze that glows hot in a furnace. His voice was like the noise of flooding water. [16]He held seven stars in his right hand. A sharp two-edged sword came out of his mouth.

---

revelation A making known of truth that has been hidden.
Alpha and the Omega The first and last letters in the Greek alphabet. This means "the beginning and the end".
Patmos A small island in the Aegean Sea, near the coast of Asia Minor (modern Turkey).
"like ... Man" "Son of Man" is a name Jesus called himself. It showed he was God's Son, but he was also a man. See dictionary.

He looked like the sun shining at its brightest time.

[17]When I saw him, I fell down at his feet like a dead man. He put his right hand on me and said, "Do not be afraid! I am the First and the Last. [18]I am the One who lives. I was dead, but look: I am alive for ever and ever! And I hold the keys of death and where the dead are. [19]So write the things you see, what is now and what will happen later. [20]Here is the hidden meaning of the seven stars that you saw in my right hand and the seven golden lampstands that you saw. The seven lampstands are the seven churches. The seven stars are the angels of the seven churches.

To the Church in Ephesus

2 "Write this to the angel of the church in Ephesus:

"The One who holds the seven stars in his right hand and walks among the seven golden lampstands says this to you. [2]I know what you do. You work hard, and you never give up. I know that you do not accept evil people. You have tested those who say that they are apostles[d] but really are not. You found that they are liars. [3]You continue to serve me. You have suffered troubles for my name, and you have not given up.

[4]"But I have this against you: you have left the love you had in the beginning. [5]So remember where you were before you fell. Change your hearts and do what you did at first. If you do not change, I will come to you. I will take away your lampstand from its place. [6]But there is something you do that is right: you hate what the Nicolaitans[n] practise, as much as I.

[7]"Every person who has ears

should listen to what the Spirit[d] says to the churches. To him who wins the victory I will give the right to eat the fruit from the tree of life. This tree is in the garden of God.

To the Church in Smyrna

[8]"Write this to the angel of the church in Smyrna:

"The One who is the First and the Last says this to you. He is the One who died and came to life again. [9]I know your troubles. I know that you are poor, but really you are rich! I know the bad things that some people say about you. They say they are Jews, but they are not true Jews. They are a synagogue[d] that belongs to Satan. [10]Do not be afraid of what will happen to you. I tell you, the devil will put some of you in prison to test you. You will suffer for ten days. But be faithful, even if you have to die. If you are faithful, I will give you the crown of life.

[11]"Everyone who has ears should listen to what the Spirit[d] says to the churches. He who wins the victory will not be hurt by the second death.

To the Church in Pergamum

[12]"Write this to the angel of the church in Pergamum:

"The One who has the sharp two-edged sword says this to you. [13]I know where you live. You live where Satan has his throne. But you are true to me. You did not refuse to tell about your faith in me even during the time of Antipas. Antipas was my faithful witness who was killed in your city. Your city is where Satan lives.

[14]"But I have a few things

Nicolaitans This is the name of a religious group that followed false beliefs and ideas.

against you: you have some there who follow the teaching of Balaam. Balaam taught Balak how to cause the people of Israel to sin. They sinned by eating food offered to idols and by taking part in sexual sins. ¹⁵You also have some who follow the teaching of the Nicolaitans.ⁿ ¹⁶So change your hearts and lives! If you do not, I will come to you quickly and fight against them with the sword that comes out of my mouth.

¹⁷"Everyone who has ears should listen to what the Spiritᵈ says to the churches!

"I will give the hidden mannaᵈ to everyone who wins the victory. I will also give him a white stone with a new name written on it. No one knows this new name except the one who receives it.

To the Church in Thyatira

¹⁸"Write this to the angel of the church in Thyatira:

"The Son of God is saying these things. He is the One who has eyes that blaze like fire and feet like shining bronze. He says this to you: ¹⁹I know what you do. I know about your love, your faith, your service, and your patience. I know that you are doing more now than you did at first. ²⁰But I have this against you: you let that woman Jezebel do what she wants. She says that she is a prophetess.ᵈ But she is leading my people away with her teaching. Jezebel leads them to take part in sexual sins and to eat food that is offered to idols. ²¹I have given her time to change her heart and turn away from her sin. But she does not want to change. ²²And so I will throw her on a bed of suffering. And all those who

take part in adulteryᵈ with her will suffer greatly. I will do this now if they do not turn away from the wrongs she does. ²³I will also kill her followers. Then all the churches will know that I am the One who knows what people feel and think. And I will repay each of you for what you have done.

²⁴"But others of you in Thyatira have not followed her teaching. You have not learned what some call Satan's deep secrets. This is what I say to you: I will not put any other load on you. ²⁵Only continue the way you are until I come.

²⁶"I will give power to everyone who wins the victory and continues to the end to do what I want. I will give him power over the nations:

²⁷'You will make them obey you
   by punishing them with
   an iron rod.
You will break them into
   pieces like pottery'.
                    Psalm 2:9

²⁸This is the same power I received from my Father. I will also give him the morning star. ²⁹Everyone who has ears should listen to what the Spiritᵈ says to the churches.

To the Church in Sardis

3 "Write this to the angel of the church in Sardis:

"The One who has the seven spirits and the seven stars says this to you. I know what you do. People say that you are alive, but really you are dead. ²Wake up! Make yourselves stronger while you still have something left and before it dies completely. I have found that what you are doing is not good enough for my God. ³So

Nicolaitans This is the name of a religious group that followed false beliefs and ideas.

do not forget what you have received and heard. Obey it. Change your hearts and lives! You must wake up, or I will come to you and surprise you like a thief. And you will not know when I will come. [4]But you have a few there in Sardis who have kept themselves clean. They will walk with me. They will wear white clothes, because they are worthy. [5]He who wins the victory will be dressed in white clothes like them. I will not take away his name from the book of life. I will say that he belongs to me before my Father and before his angels. [6]Everyone who has ears should listen to what the Spirit[d] says to the churches.

To the Church in Philadelphia

[7]"Write this to the angel of the church in Philadelphia:

"The One who is holy and true says this to you. He holds the key of David. When he opens something, it cannot be closed. And when he closes something, it cannot be opened. [8]I know what you do. I have put an open door before you, and no one can close it. I know that you have a little strength. But you have followed my teaching. And you were not afraid to speak my name. [9]Listen! There is a synagogue[d] that belongs to Satan. Those in this synagogue say they are Jews, but they are liars. They are not true Jews. I will make them come before you and bow at your feet. They will know that I have loved you. [10]You have followed my teaching about not giving up. So I will keep you from the time of trouble that will come to the

whole world. This trouble will test those who live on earth. [11]"I am coming soon. Continue the way you are now. Then no one will take away your crown. [12]I will make the one who wins the victory a pillar in the temple of my God. He will never have to leave it. I will write on him the name of my God and the name of the city of my God. This city is the new Jerusalem.[n] It comes down out of heaven from my God. I will also write on him my new name. [13]Every person who has ears should listen to what the Spirit[d] says to the churches.

To the Church in Laodicea

[14]"Write this to the angel of the church in Laodicea:

"The Amen[n] is the One who is the faithful and true witness. He is the ruler of all that God has made. He says this to you: [15]I know what you do. You are not hot or cold. I wish that you were hot or cold! [16]But you are only warm—not hot, not cold. So I am ready to spit you out of my mouth. [17]You say you are rich. You think you have become wealthy and do not need anything. But you do not know that you are really miserable, pitiful, poor, blind, and naked. [18]I advise you to buy gold from me—gold made pure in fire. Then you can be truly rich. Buy from me clothes that are white. Then you can cover your shameful nakedness. Buy from me medicine to put on your eyes. Then you can truly see.

[19]"I correct and punish those whom I love. So be eager to do right. Change your hearts and

---

Jerusalem This name is used to mean the spiritual city God built for his people.
Amen Used here as a name for Jesus, it means to agree fully that something is true.

lives. [20]Here I am! I stand at the door and knock. If anyone hears my voice and opens the door, I will come in and eat with him. And he will eat with me.

[21]"He who wins the victory will sit with me on my throne. It was the same with me. I won the victory and sat down with my Father on his throne. [22]Everyone who has ears should listen to what the Spirit[d] says to the churches."

John Sees Heaven

4 After this I looked, and there before me was an open door in heaven. And I heard the same voice that spoke to me before. It was the voice that sounded like a trumpet. The voice said, "Come up here, and I will show you what must happen after this." [2]Then the Spirit[d] took control of me. There before me was a throne in heaven. Someone was sitting on the throne. [3]The One who sat on the throne looked like precious stones, like jasper and carnelian. All around the throne was a rainbow the colour of an emerald. [4]Around the throne there were 24 other thrones. There were 24 elders[n] sitting on the 24 thrones. The elders were dressed in white, and they had golden crowns on their heads. [5]Lightning flashes and noises of thunder came from the throne. Before the throne there were seven lamps burning. These lamps are the seven spirits of God. [6]Also before the throne there was something that looked like a sea of glass. It was clear like crystal.

Around the throne, on each side, there were four living things. These living things had eyes all over them, in front and behind. [7]The first living thing was like a lion. The second was like a calf. The third had a face like a man. The fourth was like a flying ea-

gle. [8]Each of these four living things had six wings. The living things were covered all over with eyes, inside and out. Day and night they never stop saying:

"Holy, holy, holy is the Lord God
    All-Powerful.
He was, he is, and he is
    coming."

[9]These living things give glory and honour and thanks to the One who sits on the throne. He is the One who lives for ever and ever. And every time the living things do this, [10]the 24 elders bow down before the One who sits on the throne. The elders worship him who lives for ever and ever. They put their crowns down before the throne and say:

[11]"Our Lord and God! You are
    worthy
to receive glory and honour and
    power.
You made all things.
Everything existed and was
    made
because you wanted it."

5 Then I saw a scroll in the right hand of the One sitting on the throne. The scroll had writing on both sides. It was kept closed with seven seals. [2]And I saw a powerful angel. He called in a loud voice, "Who is worthy to break the seals and open the scroll?" [3]But there was no one in heaven or on earth or under the earth who could open the scroll or look inside it. [4]I cried and cried because there was no one who was worthy to open the scroll or look inside. [5]But one of the elders said to me, "Do not cry! The Lion[n] from the tribe[d] of Judah has won the victory. He is David's descendant.[d] He is able to open the scroll and its seven seals."

[6]Then I saw a Lamb standing in the centre of the throne with the four living things around it. The elders were

---

24 elders Elder means "older". Here the elders probably represent God's people.
Lion Here refers to Christ.

also around the Lamb. The Lamb looked as if he had been killed. He had seven horns and seven eyes. These are the seven spirits of God that were sent into all the world. 7The Lamb came and took the scroll from the right hand of the One sitting on the throne. 8After he had taken the scroll, the four living things and the 24 elders bowed down before the Lamb. Each one of them had a harp. Also, they were holding golden bowls full of incense.*d* These bowls of incense are the prayers of God's holy people. 9And they all sang a new song to the Lamb:

"You are worthy to take the scroll
  and to open its seals,
because you were killed;
  and with the blood of your death
    you bought men for God
  from every tribe, language,
    people, and nation.
10You made them to be a kingdom
    of priests for our God.
  And they will rule on the earth."

11Then I looked, and I heard the voices of many angels. The angels were around the throne, the four living things, and the elders. There were thousands and thousands of angels — there were 10,000 times 10,000. 12The angels said in a loud voice:

"The Lamb who was killed is
    worthy
to receive power, wealth, wisdom
    and strength,
honour, glory, and praise!"

13Then I heard every living thing in heaven and on earth and under the earth and in the sea. I heard every thing in all these places, saying:

"All praise and honour and glory
    and power
  for ever and ever
to the One who sits on the throne
  and to the Lamb!"

14The four living things said, "Amen!" And the elders bowed down and worshipped.

6 Then I watched while the Lamb opened the first of the seven seals. I heard one of the four living things speak with a voice like thunder. It said, "Come!" 2I looked and there before me was a white horse. The rider on the horse held a bow, and he was given a crown. And he rode out, defeating the enemy. He rode out to win the victory.

3The Lamb opened the second seal. Then I heard the second living thing say, "Come!" 4Then another horse came out. This was a red horse. Its rider was given power to take away peace from the earth. He was given power to make people kill each other. And he was given a big sword.

5The Lamb opened the third seal. Then I heard the third living thing say, "Come!" I looked, and there before me was a black horse. Its rider held a pair of scales in his hand. 6Then I heard something that sounded like a voice. It came from where the four living things were. The voice said, "A litre of wheat for a day's pay. And three litres of barley for a day's pay. And do not damage the olive oil and wine!"

7The Lamb opened the fourth seal. Then I heard the voice of the fourth living thing say, "Come!" 8I looked, and there before me was a pale horse. Its rider was named death. Hades*n* was following close behind him. They were given power over a quarter of the earth. They were given power to kill people by war, by starving them, by disease, and by the wild animals of the earth.

9The Lamb opened the fifth seal. Then I saw some souls under the altar. They were the souls of those who had been killed because they were faithful to God's message and to the truth they had received. 10These

Hades The unseen world where the dead are.

souls shouted in a loud voice, "Holy and true Lord, how long until you judge the people of the earth and punish them for killing us?" [11]Then each one of these souls was given a white robe. They were told to wait a short time longer. There were still some of their brothers in the service of Christ who must be killed as they were. They were told to wait until all of this killing was finished.

[12]Then I watched while the Lamb opened the sixth seal. There was a great earthquake. The sun became black like rough black cloth. The full moon became red like blood. [13]The stars in the sky fell to the earth like figs falling from a fig tree when the wind blows. [14]The sky disappeared. It was rolled up like a scroll. And every mountain and island was moved from its place.

[15]Then all people hid in caves and behind the rocks on the mountains. There were the kings of the earth, the rulers, the generals, the rich people and the powerful people. Everyone, slave and free, hid himself. [16]They called to the mountains and the rocks, "Fall on us. Hide us from the face of the One who sits on the throne. Hide us from the anger of the Lamb! [17]The great day for their anger has come. Who can stand against it?"

The 144,000 People of Israel

7 After this I saw four angels standing at the four corners of the earth. The angels were holding the four winds of the earth. They were stopping the wind from blowing on the land or on the sea or on any tree. [2]Then I saw another angel coming from the east. This angel had the seal of the living God. He called out in a loud voice to the four angels. These were the four angels that God had given power to harm the earth and the sea. He said to the four angels, [3]"Do

not harm the land or the sea or the trees before we put the sign on the people who serve our God. We must put the sign on their foreheads." [4]Then I heard how many people were marked with the sign. There were 144,000. They were from every tribe[d] of the people of Israel.

[5]From the tribe of Judah 12,000 were marked with the sign,
from the tribe of Reuben 12,000,
from the tribe of Gad 12,000,
[6]from the tribe of Asher 12,000,
from the tribe of Naphtali 12,000,
from the tribe of Manasseh 12,000,
[7]from the tribe of Simeon 12,000,
from the tribe of Levi 12,000,
from the tribe of Issachar 12,000,
[8]from the tribe of Zebulun 12,000,
from the tribe of Joseph 12,000,
from the tribe of Benjamin 12,000.

The Great Crowd

[9]Then I looked, and there was a great number of people. There were so many people that no one could count them. They were from every nation, tribe,[d] people, and language of the earth. They were all standing before the throne and before the Lamb. They wore white robes and had palm branches in their hands. [10]They were shouting in a loud voice, "Salvation belongs to our God, who sits on the throne, and to the Lamb." [11]The elders[n] and the four living things were there. All the angels were standing around them and the throne. The angels bowed down on their faces before the throne and worshipped God. [12]They were saying, "Amen! Praise, glory, wisdom, thanks, honour, power, and strength belong to our God for ever and ever. Amen!"

[13]Then one of the elders asked me, "Who are these people in white robes? Where did they come from?" [14]I answered, "You know who they are, sir."

---

elders Elder means "older". Here the elders probably represent God's people.

And the elder said, "These are the people who have come out of the great suffering. They have washed their robes[n] with the blood of the Lamb. Now they are clean and white. [15]And they are before the throne of God. They worship God day and night in his temple. And the One who sits on the throne will protect them. [16]Those people will never be hungry again. They will never be thirsty again. The sun will not hurt them. No heat will burn them. [17]For the Lamb at the centre of the throne will be their shepherd. He will lead them to springs of water that give life. And God will wipe away every tear from their eyes."

The Seventh Seal

[8] The Lamb opened the seventh seal. Then there was silence in heaven for about half an hour. [2]And I saw the seven angels who stand before God. They were given seven trumpets.

[3]Another angel came and stood at the altar. This angel had a golden incense burner.[d] The angel was given a lot of incense to offer with the prayers of all God's holy people. The angel put this offering on the golden altar before the throne. [4]The smoke from the incense went up from the angel's hand to God. It went up with the prayers of God's people. [5]Then the angel filled the incense burner with fire from the altar and threw it on the earth. There were flashes of lightning, thunder and loud noises, and an earthquake.

The Seven Angels and Trumpets

[6]Then the seven angels who had the seven trumpets prepared to blow them.

[7]The first angel blew his trumpet. Then hail and fire mixed with blood was poured down on the earth. And a third of the earth and all the green grass and a third of the trees were burned up.

[8]The second angel blew his trumpet. Then something that looked like a big mountain burning with fire was thrown into the sea. And a third of the sea became blood. [9]And a third of the living things in the sea died, and a third of the ships were destroyed.

[10]The third angel blew his trumpet. Then a large star, burning like a torch, fell from the sky. It fell on a third of the rivers and on the springs of water. [11]The name of the star is Wormwood.[n] And a third of all the water became bitter. Many people died from drinking the water that was bitter.

[12]The fourth angel blew his trumpet. Then a third of the sun and a third of the moon and a third of the stars were hit. So a third of them became dark. A third of the day was without light.

[13]While I watched, I heard an eagle that was flying high in the air. The eagle said with a loud voice, "Trouble! Trouble! Trouble for those who live on the earth! The trouble will begin with the sounds of the trumpets that the other three angels are about to blow."

[9] Then the fifth angel blew his trumpet. And I saw a star fall from the sky to the earth. The star was given the key to the deep hole that leads down to the bottomless pit. [2]Then it opened the bottomless pit. Smoke came up from the hole like smoke from a big furnace. The sun and sky became dark because of the smoke from the hole. [3]Then locusts[d] came down to the earth out of the smoke.

washed their robes This means they believed in Jesus so that their sins could be forgiven by Christ's blood.
Wormwood Name of a very bitter plant, used here to give the idea of bitter sorrow.

They were given the power to sting like scorpions.*n* [4]They were told not to harm the grass on the earth or any plant or tree. They could harm only the people who did not have the sign of God on their foreheads. [5]These locusts were given the power to cause pain to the people for five months. But they were not given the power to kill anyone. And the pain they felt was like the pain that a scorpion gives when it stings a person. [6]During those days people will look for a way to die, but they will not find it. They will want to die, but death will run away from them.

[7]The locusts looked like horses prepared for battle. On their heads they wore things that looked like crowns of gold. Their faces looked like human faces. [8]Their hair was like women's hair, and their teeth were like lions' teeth. [9]Their chests looked like iron breastplates. The sound their wings made was like the noise of many horses and chariots hurrying into battle. [10]The locusts had tails with stingers like scorpions. The power they had to hurt people for five months was in their tails. [11]The locusts had a king who was the angel of the bottomless pit. His name in the Hebrew language is Abaddon. In the Greek language his name is Apollyon.*n*

[12]The first great trouble is past. There are still two other great troubles that will come.

[13]The sixth angel blew his trumpet. Then I heard a voice coming from the horns on the golden altar that is before God. [14]The voice said to the sixth angel who had the trumpet, "Free the four angels who are tied at the great river Euphrates." [15]These four angels had been kept ready for this hour and day and month and year. They were freed to kill a third of all people on the earth. [16]I heard how many troops on horses were in their army. There were 200,000,000.

[17]In my vision I saw the horses and their riders. They looked like this: they had breastplates that were fiery red, dark blue, and yellow like sulphur. The heads of the horses looked like heads of lions. The horses had fire, smoke, and sulphur coming out of their mouths. [18]A third of all the people on earth were killed by these three terrible things coming out of the horses' mouths: the fire, the smoke, and the sulphur. [19]The horses' power was in their mouths and also in their tails. Their tails were like snakes that have heads to bite and hurt people.

[20]The other people on the earth were not killed by these terrible things. But they still did not change their hearts and turn away from what they had made with their own hands. They did not stop worshipping demons*d* and idols made of gold, silver, bronze, stone, and wood—things that cannot see or hear or walk. [21]These people did not change their hearts and turn away from murder or evil magic, from their sexual sins or stealing.

The Angel and the Little Scroll

10 Then I saw another powerful angel coming down from heaven. He was dressed in a cloud and had a rainbow around his head. His face was like the sun, and his legs were like poles of fire. [2]The angel was holding a small scroll open in his hand. He put his right foot on the sea and his left foot on the land. [3]He shouted loudly like the roaring of a lion. When he shouted, the voices of seven thunders spoke. [4]The seven thunders spoke, and I started to write. But then I heard a voice from heaven. The voice said, "Do not write what the seven thunders said. Keep these things secret."

---

scorpions A scorpion is an insect that stings with a poison.
Abaddon, Apollyon Both names mean "Destroyer".

John 21:9-12
The followers . . . saw a fire of hot coals . . .
Jesus said to them, "Come and eat," . . .
They knew it was the Lord.

Acts 17:18
Paul was telling them the Good News
of Jesus' rising from death.

Acts 8:36
"Look! Here is water! What is stopping me from being baptised?"

⁵Then the angel I saw standing on the sea and on the land raised his right hand to heaven. ⁶He made a promise by the power of the One who lives for ever and ever. He is the One who made the skies and all that is in them. He made the earth and all that is in it, and he made the sea and all that is in it. The angel said, "There will be no more waiting! ⁷In the days when the seventh angel is ready to blow his trumpet, God's secret plan will be finished. This plan is the Good News*d* God told to his servants, the prophets."*d*

⁸Then I heard the same voice from heaven again. The voice said to me, "Go and take the open scroll that is in the angel's hand. This is the angel that is standing on the sea and on the land."

⁹So I went to the angel and asked him to give me the little scroll. He said to me, "Take the scroll and eat it. It will be sour in your stomach. But in your mouth it will be sweet as honey." ¹⁰So I took the little scroll from the angel's hand and I ate it. In my mouth it tasted sweet as honey. But after I had eaten it, it was sour in my stomach. ¹¹Then I was told, "You must prophesy*d* again about many peoples, nations, languages, and kings."

The Two Witnesses

11 Then I was given a measuring stick like a rod. I was told, "Go and measure the temple*n* of God and the altar, and count the number of people worshipping there. ²But do not measure the yard outside the temple. Leave it alone. It has been given to the people who are not Jews. They will walk on the holy city for 42 months. ³And I will give power to my two witnesses to prophesy*d* for 1,260 days. They will be dressed in rough cloth to show how sad they are."

⁴These two witnesses are the two olive trees and the two lampstands that stand before the Lord of the earth. ⁵If anyone tries to hurt the witnesses, fire comes from their mouths and kills their enemies. Anyone who tries to hurt them will die like this. ⁶These witnesses have the power to stop the sky from raining during the time they are prophesying. They have power to make the waters become blood. They have power to send every kind of trouble to the earth. They can do this as many times as they want.

⁷When the two witnesses have finished telling their message, the beast will fight against them. This is the beast that comes up from the bottomless pit. He will defeat them and kill them. ⁸The bodies of the two witnesses will lie in the street of the great city. This city is named Sodom*n* and Egypt. These names for the city have a special meaning. It is the city where the Lord was killed. ⁹Men from every race of people, tribe,*d* language, and nation will look at the bodies of the two witnesses for three and a half days. They will refuse to bury them. ¹⁰People who live on the earth will be happy because these two are dead. They will have parties and send each other gifts. They will do these things because these two prophets brought much suffering to those who live on the earth.

¹¹But after three and a half days, God put the breath of life into the two prophets again. They stood on their feet. Everyone who saw them was filled with fear. ¹²Then the two prophets heard a loud voice from heaven say, "Come up here!" And they went

---

temple God's house—the place where God's people worship and serve him. Here, John sees it pictured as the special building in Jerusalem where God commanded the Jews to worship him.

Sodom City that God destroyed because the people were so evil.

up into heaven in a cloud. Their enemies watched them go.

13At that same time there was a great earthquake. A tenth of the city was destroyed. And 7,000 people were killed in the earthquake. Those who did not die were very afraid. They gave glory to the God of heaven.

14The second great trouble is finished. The third great trouble is coming soon.

The Seventh Trumpet

15Then the seventh angel blew his trumpet. And there were loud voices in heaven. The voices said:

"The power to rule the world
    now belongs to our Lord and his
    Christ.*d*
And he will rule for ever and
    ever."

16Then the 24 elders*n* bowed down on their faces and worshipped God. These are the elders who sit on their thrones before God. 17They said:

"We give thanks to you, Lord God
    All-Powerful.
You are the One who is and
    who was.
We thank you because you have
    used your great power
    and have begun to rule!
18The people of the world were
    angry;
but now is the time for your
    anger.
Now is the time for the dead to
    be judged.
It is time to reward your servants
    the prophets*d*
and to reward your holy people,
    all who respect you, great and
    small.
It is time to destroy those who
    destroy the earth!"

19Then God's temple*n* in heaven

was opened. The Holy Ark*d* that holds the agreement that God gave to his people could be seen in his temple. Then there were flashes of lightning, noises, thunder, an earthquake, and a great hailstorm.

The Woman and the Dragon

12 And then a great wonder appeared in heaven. There was a woman who was clothed with the sun. The moon was under her feet. She had a crown of 12 stars on her head. 2The woman was pregnant. She cried out with pain because she was about to give birth. 3Then another wonder appeared in heaven. There was a giant red dragon. He had seven heads with seven crowns on each head. He also had ten horns. 4The dragon's tail swept a third of the stars out of the sky and threw them down to the earth. The dragon stood in front of the woman who was ready to give birth to a baby. He wanted to eat the woman's baby as soon as it was born. 5The woman gave birth to a son. He will rule all the nations with an iron sceptre.*d* But her child was taken up to God and to his throne. 6The woman ran away into the desert to a place God prepared for her. There she would be taken care of for 1,260 days.

7Then there was a war in heaven. Michael*n* and his angels fought against the dragon. The dragon and his angels fought back. 8But the dragon was not strong enough. He and his angels lost their place in heaven. 9He was thrown down out of heaven. (The giant dragon is that old snake called the devil or Satan. He leads the whole world the wrong way.) The dragon with his angels was thrown down to the earth.

24 elders Elder means "older". Here the elders probably represent God's people.
temple God's house—the place where God's people worship and serve him. John sees the heavenly temple pictured to be like the Temple of God's people in the Old Testament.
Michael The archangel—leader among God's angels or messengers (Jude 9).

¹⁰Then I heard a loud voice in heaven say:

"The salvation and the power and
the kingdom of our God
and the authority of his Christ[d]
have now come.
They have come because the
accuser of our brothers has
been thrown out.
He accused our brothers day
and night before our God.
¹¹And our brothers defeated him
by the blood of the Lamb's
death
and by the truth they preached.
They did not love their lives so
much
that they were afraid of death.
¹²So be happy, you heavens
and all who live there!
But it will be terrible for the earth
and the sea,
because the devil has come
down to you!
He is filled with anger.
He knows that he does not have
much time."

¹³The dragon saw that he had been thrown down to the earth. So he hunted down the woman who had given birth to the son. ¹⁴But the woman was given the two wings of a great eagle. Then she could fly to the place that was prepared for her in the desert. There she would be taken care of for three and a half years. There she would be away from the snake. ¹⁵Then the snake poured water out of its mouth like a river. He poured the water towards the woman, so that the flood would carry her away. ¹⁶But the earth helped her. The earth opened its mouth and swallowed the river that came from the mouth of the dragon. ¹⁷Then the dragon was very angry at the woman. He went off to make war against all her other children. Her children are those who obey God's commands and have the truth that Jesus taught.

¹⁸And the dragon stood on the seashore.

The Two Beasts

13 Then I saw a beast coming up out of the sea. It had ten horns and seven heads. There was a crown on each horn. A name against God was written on each head. ²This beast looked like a leopard, with feet like a bear's feet. He had a mouth like a lion's mouth. The dragon gave the beast all of his power and his throne and great authority. ³One of the heads of the beast looked as if it had been wounded and killed. But this death wound was healed. The whole world was amazed and followed the beast. ⁴People worshipped the dragon because he had given his power to the beast. And they also worshipped the beast. They asked, "Who is as powerful as the beast? Who can make war against him?"

⁵The beast was allowed to speak proud words and words against God. He was allowed to use his power for 42 months. ⁶He used his mouth to speak against God. He spoke against God's name, against the place where God lives, and against all those who live in heaven. ⁷He was given power to make war against God's holy people and to defeat them. He was given power over every tribe,[d] people, language, and nation. ⁸All who live on earth will worship the beast. These are all the people since the beginning of the world whose names are not written in the Lamb's book of life. The Lamb is the One who was killed.

⁹If anyone has ears, he should listen:
¹⁰If anyone is to be a prisoner,
then he will be a prisoner.
If anyone is to be killed with the
sword,
then he will be killed with the
sword.
This means that God's holy people must have patience and faith.

[11]Then I saw another beast coming up out of the earth. He had two horns like a lamb, but he talked like a dragon. [12]This beast stands before the first beast and uses the same power that the first beast has. He uses this power to make everyone living on earth worship the first beast. The first beast was the one that had the death wound that was healed. [13]The second one does great miracles.[d] He even makes fire come down from heaven to earth while people are watching. [14]This second beast fools those who live on earth. He fools them by the miracles he has been given the power to do. He does these miracles to serve the first beast. The second beast ordered people to make an idol to honour the first beast. This was the one that was wounded by the sword but did not die. [15]The second beast was given power to give life to the idol of the first one. Then the idol could speak and order all who did not worship it to be killed. [16]The second animal also forced all people, small and great, rich and poor, free and slave, to have a mark on their right hand or on their forehead. [17]No one could buy or sell without this mark. This mark is the name of the beast or the number of his name. [18]Whoever has understanding can find the meaning of the number. This requires wisdom. This number is the number of a man. His number is 666.

The Song of the Saved

14 Then I looked, and there before me was the Lamb. He was standing on Mount Zion.[n] There were 144,000 people with him. They all had his name and his Father's name written on their foreheads. [2]And I heard a sound from heaven like the noise of flooding water and like the sound of loud thunder. The sound I

heard was like people playing harps. [3]And they sang a new song before the throne and before the four living things and the elders.[n] The only ones who could learn the new song were the 144,000 who had been saved from the earth. No one else could learn the song. [4]These 144,000 are the ones who did not do sinful things with women. They kept themselves pure. They follow the Lamb everywhere he goes. These 144,000 were saved from among the people of the earth. They are the first people to be offered to God and the Lamb. [5]They were not guilty of telling lies. They are without fault.

The Three Angels

[6]Then I saw another angel flying high in the air. The angel had the eternal Good News[d] to preach to those who live on earth — to every nation, tribe,[d] language, and people. [7]The angel said in a loud voice, "Fear God and give him praise. The time has come for God to judge all people. Worship God. He made the heavens, the earth, the sea, and the springs of water."

[8]Then the second angel followed the first angel and said, "She is destroyed! The great city of Babylon is destroyed! She made all the nations drink the wine of her adultery[d] and of God's anger."

[9]A third angel followed the first two angels. This third angel said in a loud voice: "It will be bad for the person who worships the beast and his idol and gets the beast's mark on the forehead or on the hand. [10]He will drink the wine of God's anger. This wine is prepared with all its strength in the cup of God's anger. He will be put in pain with burning sulphur before the holy angels and the Lamb. [11]And the smoke from their burning pain will rise

---

Mount Zion Another name for Jerusalem, here meaning the spiritual city of God's people.
elders Elder means "older". Here the elders probably represent God's people.

for ever and ever. There will be no rest, day or night, for those who worship the beast and his idol or who get the mark of his name." [12]This means that God's holy people must be patient. They must obey God's commands and keep their faith in Jesus.

[13]Then I heard a voice from heaven. It said, "Write this: from now on, the dead who were in the Lord when they died are happy."

The Spirit[d] says, "Yes, that is true. They will rest from their hard work. The reward of all they have done stays with them."

The Earth Is Harvested

[14]I looked and there before me was a white cloud. Sitting on the white cloud was One who looked like a Son of Man.[n] He had a gold crown on his head and a sharp sickle[n] in his hand. [15]Then another angel came out of the temple. This angel called to the One who was sitting on the cloud, "Take your sickle and gather from the earth. The time to harvest has come. The fruit of the earth is ripe." [16]So the One that was sitting on the cloud swung his sickle over the earth. And the earth was harvested.

[17]Then another angel came out of the temple in heaven. This angel also had a sharp sickle. [18]And then another angel came from the altar. This angel had power over the fire. This angel called to the angel with the sharp sickle. He said, "Take your sharp sickle and gather the bunches of grapes from the earth's vine. The earth's grapes are ripe." [19]The angel swung his sickle over the earth. He gathered the earth's grapes and threw them into the great winepress[d] of God's anger. [20]The grapes were crushed in the winepress outside the city. And blood flowed out of the winepress. It rose as high as the heads of the horses for a distance of 300 kilometres.

The Last Troubles

15 Then I saw another wonder in heaven. It was great and amazing. There were seven angels bringing seven troubles. These are the last troubles, because after these troubles God's anger is finished.

[2]I saw what looked like a sea of glass mixed with fire. All of those who had won the victory over the beast and his idol and over the number of his name were standing by the sea. They had harps that God had given them. [3]They sang the song of Moses, the servant of God, and the song of the Lamb:

"You do great and wonderful
　　things,　　　　*Psalm 111:2*
Lord God, the God of heaven's
　　armies.　　　　*Amos 3:13*
Everything the Lord does is right
　　and true,　　　*Psalm 145:17*
　King of the nations.
[4]Everyone will respect you, Lord.
　　　　　　　　　Jeremiah 10:7
　They will honour you.
　Only you are holy.
　All people will come
　　and worship you.　*Psalm 86:9,10*
　This is because he is a faithful
　　God who does no wrong.
　He is right and fair."
　　　　　　　　Deuteronomy 32:4

[5]After this I saw the temple (the Tent[d] of the Agreement) in heaven. The temple was opened. [6]And the seven angels bringing the seven troubles came out of the temple. They were dressed in clean, shining linen. They wore golden bands tied around their chests. [7]Then one of the four living things gave seven golden bowls to the seven angels. The bowls were filled with the anger of God, who lives

---

Son of Man "Son of Man" is a name Jesus called himself. It showed he was God's Son, but he was also a man. See dictionary.

sickle A farming tool with a curved blade. It was used to harvest grain.

for ever and ever. [8]The temple was filled with smoke from the glory and the power of God. No one could enter the temple until the seven troubles of the seven angels were finished.

The Bowls of God's Anger

16 Then I heard a loud voice from the temple. The voice said to the seven angels, "Go and pour out the seven bowls of God's anger on the earth."

[2]The first angel left. He poured out his bowl on the land. Then ugly and painful sores came upon all those who had the mark of the beast and who worshipped his idol.

[3]The second angel poured out his bowl on the sea. Then the sea became blood like that of a dead man. Every living thing in the sea died.

[4]The third angel poured out his bowl on the rivers and the springs of water. And they became blood. [5]Then I heard the angel of the waters say to God:

"Holy One, you are the One who
    is and who was.
You are right to decide to punish
    these evil people.
[6]They have spilled the blood of
    your holy people and your
    prophets.[d]
Now you have given them blood
    to drink as they deserve."

[7]And I heard the altar say:

"Yes, Lord God All-Powerful,
    the way you punish evil people
        is right and fair."

[8]The fourth angel poured out his bowl on the sun. The sun was given power to burn the people with fire. [9]They were burned by the great heat, and they cursed the name of God. God is the One who had control over these troubles. But the people refused to change their hearts and lives and give glory to God.

[10]The fifth angel poured out his bowl on the throne of the beast. And darkness covered the beast's kingdom. People bit their tongues because of the pain. [11]They cursed the God of heaven because of their pain and the sores they had. But they refused to change their hearts and turn away from the evil things they did.

[12]The sixth angel poured out his bowl on the great river Euphrates. The water in the river was dried up. This prepared the way for the kings from the east to come. [13]Then I saw three evil spirits that looked like frogs. They came out of the mouth of the dragon, out of the mouth of the beast, and out of the mouth of the false prophet.[d] [14]These evil spirits are the spirits of demons.[d] They have power to do miracles.[d] They go out to the kings of the whole world. They go out to gather the kings for battle on the great day of God All-Powerful.

[15]"Listen! I will come as a thief comes! Happy is the person who stays awake and keeps his clothes with him. Then he will not have to go without clothes and be ashamed because he is naked."

[16]Then the evil spirits gathered the kings together to the place that is called Armageddon[n] in the Hebrew language.

[17]The seventh angel poured out his bowl into the air. Then a loud voice came out of the temple from the throne. The voice said, "It is finished!" [18]Then there were flashes of lightning, noises, thunder, and a big earthquake. This was the worst earthquake that has ever happened since people have been on earth. [19]The great city split into three parts. The cities of the nations were destroyed. And God did not forget to punish Babylon the Great. He gave that city the cup filled with the wine of his terrible anger. [20]Every island disappeared, and there were no more

---

Armageddon This word means "Hill of Megiddo", where many battles were fought long ago.

mountains. [21]Giant hailstones fell on people from the sky. The hailstones weighed about 50 kilograms each. People cursed God because of the hail. This trouble was a terrible thing.

The Woman on the Animal

17 One of the seven angels came and spoke to me. This was one of the angels that had the seven bowls. He said, "Come, and I will show you the punishment that will be given to the famous prostitute.[d] She is the one sitting over many waters. [2]The kings of the earth sinned sexually with her. And the people of the earth became drunk from the wine of her sexual sin."

[3]Then the angel carried me away by the Spirit[d] to the desert. There I saw a woman sitting on a red beast. He was covered with names against God written on him. He had seven heads and ten horns. [4]The woman was dressed in purple and red. She was shining with the gold, jewels, and pearls she was wearing. She had a golden cup in her hand. This cup was filled with evil things and the uncleanness of her sexual sin. [5]She had a title written on her forehead. This title has a hidden meaning. This is what was written:

THE GREAT BABYLON
MOTHER OF PROSTITUTES
AND THE EVIL THINGS OF THE EARTH

[6]I saw that the woman was drunk. She was drunk with the blood of God's holy people. She was drunk with the blood of those who were killed because of their faith in Jesus.

When I saw the woman, I was totally amazed. [7]Then the angel said to me, "Why are you amazed? I will tell you the hidden meaning of this woman and the beast she rides — the one with seven heads and ten horns. [8]The beast that you saw was once alive. He is not alive now. But he will be alive and come up out of the bottomless pit and go away to be destroyed. The

people who live on earth will be amazed when they see the beast. They will be amazed because he was once alive, is not alive now, but will come again. These are the people whose names have never been written in the book of life since the beginning of the world.

[9]"You need a wise mind to understand this. The seven heads on the beast are the seven hills where the woman sits. They are also seven kings. [10]Five of the kings have already died. One of the kings lives now. And the last king is coming. When he comes, he will stay only a short time. [11]The beast that was once alive but is not alive now is an eighth king. This eighth king also belongs to the first seven kings. And he will go away to be destroyed.

[12]"The ten horns you saw are ten kings. These ten kings have not yet begun to rule. But they will receive power to rule with the beast for one hour. [13]All ten of these kings have the same purpose. And they will give their power and authority to the beast. [14]They will make war against the Lamb. But the Lamb will defeat them, because he is Lord of lords and King of kings. He will defeat them with his chosen and faithful followers — the people that he has called."

[15]Then the angel said to me, "You saw the water where the prostitute sits. These waters are the many peoples, the different races, nations, and languages. [16]The beast and the ten horns you saw will hate the prostitute. They will take everything she has and leave her naked. They will eat her body and burn her with fire. [17]God made the ten horns want to carry out his purpose: they agreed to give the beast their power to rule. They will rule until what God has said is completed. [18]The woman you saw is the great city that rules over the kings of the earth."

Babylon Is Destroyed

18 Then I saw another angel coming down from heaven. This angel had great power. The angel's glory made the earth bright. ²The angel shouted in a powerful voice:
"The great city of Babylon is
    destroyed!
She has become a home for
    demons.*d*
She has become a city for every
    evil spirit,
a city for every unclean*d* and
    hated bird.
³All the peoples of the earth have
    drunk
    the strong wine of her sexual
        sin.
The kings of the earth have
    sinned sexually with her,
and the businessmen of the
    world have grown rich from
    the great wealth of her
    luxury."

⁴Then I heard another voice from heaven say:
"Come out of that city, my
    people,
    so that you will not share in her
        sins.
Then you will not receive the
    terrible things that will
    happen to her.
⁵The city's sins are piled up as high
    as the sky.
God has not forgotten the
    wrongs she has done.
⁶Give that city the same as she
    gave to others.
Pay her back twice as much as
    she did.
Prepare wine for her that is twice
    as strong
    as the wine she prepared for
        others.
⁷She gave herself much glory and
    rich living.
Give her that much suffering and
    sadness.

She says to herself, 'I am a queen
    sitting on my throne.
I am not a widow; I will never
    be sad'.
⁸So these terrible things will come
    to her in one day:
    death, crying, and great hunger.
She will be destroyed by fire,
    because the Lord God who
        judges her is powerful."

⁹The kings of the earth who sinned sexually with her and shared her wealth will see the smoke from her burning. Then they will cry and weep because of her death. ¹⁰They will be afraid of her suffering and stand far away. They will say:
"Terrible! How terrible, great
    city,
    powerful city of Babylon!
Your punishment has come in one
    hour!"

¹¹And the businessmen of the earth will cry and weep for her. They will be sad because now there is no one to buy the things they sell. ¹²They sell gold, silver, jewels, pearls, fine linen cloth, purple cloth, silk, and red cloth. They sell all kinds of citron wood and all kinds of things made from ivory, expensive wood, bronze, iron, and marble. ¹³They also sell cinnamon, spice, incense,*d* myrrh,*d* frankincense,*d* wine, and olive oil; fine flour, wheat, cattle, sheep, horses, and carriages. They sell the bodies and souls of men.

¹⁴They will say,
"Babylon, the good things you
    wanted are gone from you.
All your rich and fancy things have
    disappeared.
You will never have them
    again."
¹⁵The businessmen will be afraid of her suffering and stand far away from her. These are the men who became rich from selling those things to her. The men will cry and be sad. ¹⁶They will say:

"Terrible! How terrible for the
    great city!
She was dressed in fine linen,
    purple and red cloth.
She was shining with gold,
    jewels, and pearls!
¹⁷All these riches have been
    destroyed in one hour!"

Every sea captain, all those who
travel on ships, the sailors, and all the
people who earn money from the sea
stood far away from Babylon. ¹⁸They
saw the smoke from her burning.
They said loudly, "There was never a
city like this great city!" ¹⁹They threw
dust on their heads and cried to show
how sad they were. They said:

"Terrible! How terrible for the
    great city!
All the people who had ships on
    the sea
became rich because of her
    wealth!
But she has been destroyed in
    one hour!
²⁰Be happy because of this, heaven!
Be happy, God's holy people and
    apostles*d* and prophets!*d*
God has punished her because of
    what she did to you."

²¹Then a powerful angel picked up a
stone like a large stone for grinding
grain. The angel threw the stone into
the sea and said:

"That is how the great city of
    Babylon will be thrown
    down.
The city will never be found
    again.
²²The music of people playing harps
    and other instruments, flutes
    and trumpets,
will never be heard in you again.
No workman doing any job
will ever be found in you again.
The sound of grinding grain
will never be heard in you again.
²³The light of a lamp

will never shine in you again.
The voices of a bridegroom and
    bride
will never be heard in you again.
Your businessmen were the
    world's great men.
All the nations were tricked by
    your magic.
²⁴She is guilty of the death
    of the prophets and God's holy
    people
    and of all who have been killed
    on earth."

People in Heaven Praise God

19 After this I heard what sounded
like a great many people in
heaven. They were saying:
"Hallelujah!*n*
Salvation, glory, and power belong
    to our God.
² His judgements are true and
    right.
Our God has punished the
    prostitute.*d*
She is the one who made the
    earth evil with her sexual
    sin.
God has punished the prostitute to
    pay her for the death of his
    servants."

³Again they said:
"Hallelujah!
She is burning, and her smoke will
    rise for ever and ever."

⁴Then the 24 elders*n* and the four
living things bowed down. They worshipped God, who sits on the throne.
They said:
"Amen, Hallelujah!"

⁵Then a voice came from the
throne:
"Praise our God, all you who
    serve him!
Praise our God, all you who
    honour him, both small and
    great!"

⁶Then I heard what sounded like a

great many people. It sounded like the
noise of flooding water and like loud
thunder. The people were saying:
"Hallelujah!
    Our Lord God rules. He is the
      All-Powerful.
⁷Let us rejoice and be happy
    and give God glory!
Give God glory, because the
    wedding of the Lamb has
    come.
    And the Lamb's bride has made
      herself ready.
⁸Fine linen was given to the bride
    for her to wear.
    The linen was bright and clean."
(The fine linen means the good things
done by God's holy people.)
⁹Then the angel said to me, "Write
this: those who are invited to the wedding meal of the Lamb are happy!"
Then the angel said, "These are the
true words of God."
¹⁰Then I bowed down at the angel's
feet to worship him. But he said to
me, "Do not worship me! I am a servant like you and your brothers who
have the truth of Jesus. Worship God!
Because the truth about Jesus is the
spirit that gives all prophecy."ᵈ

The Rider on the White Horse

¹¹Then I saw heaven open. There
before me was a white horse. The rider on the horse is called Faithful and
True. He is right when he judges and
makes war. ¹²His eyes are like burning fire, and on his head are many
crowns. He has a name written on
him, but he is the only one who knows
the name. No other person knows the
name. ¹³He is dressed in a robe
dipped in blood. His name is the Word
of God. ¹⁴The armies of heaven were
following him on white horses. They
were dressed in fine linen, white and
clean. ¹⁵A sharp sword comes out of
the rider's mouth. He will use this
sword to defeat the nations. He will
rule them with a sceptreᵈ of iron. He
will crush out the wine in the wine-

pressᵈ of the terrible anger of God All-
Powerful. ¹⁶On his robe and on his leg
was written this name: "KING OF KINGS
AND LORD OF LORDS".
    ¹⁷Then I saw an angel standing in
the sun. The angel called with a loud
voice to all the birds flying in the sky,
"Come together for the great feast of
God. ¹⁸Come together so that you can
eat the bodies of kings and generals
and famous men. Come to eat the
bodies of the horses and their riders
and the bodies of all people—free,
slave, small, and great."
    ¹⁹Then I saw the beast and the
kings of the earth. Their armies were
gathered together to make war
against the rider on the horse and his
army. ²⁰But the beast was captured
and with him the false prophet.ᵈ This
false prophet was the one who did the
miraclesᵈ for the beast. The false
prophet had used these miracles to
trick those who had the mark of the
beast and worshipped his idol. The
false prophet and the beast were
thrown alive into the lake of fire that
burns with sulphur. ²¹Their armies
were killed with the sword that came
out of the mouth of the rider on the
horse. All the birds ate the bodies until they were full.

The 1,000 Years

20 I saw an angel coming down
from heaven. He had the key to
the bottomless pit. He also held a
large chain in his hand. ²The angel
grabbed the dragon, that old snake
who is the devil. The angel tied him up
for 1,000 years. ³Then he threw him
into the bottomless pit and closed it
and locked it over him. The angel did
this so that he could not trick the people of the earth any more until the
1,000 years were ended. After 1,000
years he must be set free for a short
time.
    ⁴Then I saw some thrones and peo-
ple sitting on them. They had been
given the power to judge. And I saw

the souls of those who had been killed because they were faithful to the truth of Jesus and the message from God. They had not worshipped the beast or his idol. They had not received the mark of the beast on their foreheads or on their hands. They came back to life and ruled with Christ for 1,000 years. 5(The others that were dead did not live again until the 1,000 years were ended.) This is the first raising of the dead. 6Blessed and holy are those who share in this first raising of the dead. The second death has no power over them. They will be priests for God and for Christ. They will rule with him for 1,000 years.

7When the 1,000 years are over, Satan will be set free from his prison. 8He will go out to trick the nations in all the earth—Gog and Magog. Satan will gather them for battle. There will be so many people that they will be like sand on the seashore. 9And Satan's army marched across the earth and gathered around the camp of God's people and the city that God loves. But fire came down from heaven and burned them up. 10And Satan, who tricked them, was thrown into the lake of burning sulphur with the beast and the false prophet.*d* There they will be punished day and night for ever and ever.

People of the World Are Judged

11Then I saw a great white throne and the One who was sitting on it. Earth and sky ran away from him and disappeared. 12And I saw the dead, great and small, standing before the throne. And the book of life was opened. There were also other books opened. The dead were judged by what they had done, which was writ-ten in the books. 13The sea gave up the dead who were in it. Death and Hades*n* gave up the dead who were in them. Each person was judged by what he had done. 14And Death and Hades were thrown into the lake of fire. This lake of fire is the second death. 15And if anyone's name was not found written in the book of life, he was thrown into the lake of fire.

The New Jerusalem

21 Then I saw a new heaven and a new earth. The first heaven and the first earth had disappeared. Now there was no sea. 2And I saw the holy city coming down out of heaven from God. This holy city is the new Jerusalem.*n* It was prepared like a bride dressed for her husband. 3I heard a loud voice from the throne. The voice said, "Now God's home is with men. He will live with them, and they will be his people. God himself will be with them and will be their God. 4He will wipe away every tear from their eyes. There will be no more death, sadness, crying, or pain. All the old ways are gone."

5The One who was sitting on the throne said, "Look! I am making everything new!" Then he said, "Write this, because these words are true and can be trusted."

6The One on the throne said to me: "It is finished! I am the Alpha and the Omega,*n* the Beginning and the End. I will give free water from the spring of the water of life to anyone who is thirsty. 7Anyone who wins the victory will receive this. And I will be his God, and he will be my son. 8But those who are cowards, who refuse to believe, who do evil things, who kill, who sin sexually, who do evil magic, who worship idols, and who tell lies—all these

Hades Where the dead are.
new Jerusalem The spiritual city where God's people live with him.
Alpha and the Omega The first and last letters in the Greek alphabet. This means "the beginning and the end".

will have a place in the lake of burning sulphur. This is the second death."

⁹One of the seven angels came to me. This was one of the angels who had the seven bowls full of the seven last troubles. He said, "Come with me. I will show you the bride, the wife of the Lamb." ¹⁰The angel carried me away by the Spirit^d to a very large and high mountain. He showed me the holy city, Jerusalem. It was coming down out of heaven from God. ¹¹It was shining with the glory of God. It was shining bright like a very expensive jewel, like a jasper. It was clear as crystal. ¹²The city had a great high wall with 12 gates. There were 12 angels at the gates. On each gate was written the name of one of the 12 tribes^d of Israel. ¹³There were three gates on the east, three on the north, three on the south, and three on the west. ¹⁴The walls of the city were built on 12 foundation stones. On the stones were written the names of the 12 apostles^d of the Lamb.

¹⁵The angel who talked with me had a measuring rod made of gold. He had this rod to measure the city, its gates, and its wall. ¹⁶The city was built in a square. Its length was equal to its width. The angel measured the city with the rod. The city was 12,000 stadia^n long, 12,000 stadia wide, and 12,000 stadia high. ¹⁷The angel also measured the wall. It was 144 cubits^n high, by man's measurement. That was the measurement the angel was using. ¹⁸The wall was made of jasper. The city was made of pure gold, as pure as glass. ¹⁹The foundation stones of the city walls had every kind of jewel in them. The first cornerstone was jasper, the second was sapphire, the third was chalcedony, the fourth was emerald, ²⁰the fifth was onyx, the sixth was carnelian, the seventh was chrysolite, the eighth was beryl, the ninth was topaz, the tenth was chrysoprase, the eleventh was jacinth, and the twelfth was amethyst. ²¹The 12 gates were 12 pearls. Each gate was made from a single pearl. The street of the city was made of pure gold. The gold was clear as glass.

²²I did not see a temple in the city. The Lord God All-Powerful and the Lamb are the city's temple. ²³The city does not need the sun or the moon to shine on it. The glory of God is its light, and the Lamb is the city's lamp. ²⁴By its light the people of the world will walk. The kings of the earth will bring their glory into it. ²⁵The city's gates will never be shut on any day, because there is no night there. ²⁶The greatness and the honour of the nations will be brought into it. ²⁷Nothing unclean^d will ever enter the city. No one who does shameful things or tells lies will ever go into it. Only those whose names are written in the Lamb's book of life will enter the city.

22 Then the angel showed me the river of the water of life. The river was shining like crystal. It flows from the throne of God and of the Lamb ²down the middle of the street of the city. The tree of life was on each side of the river. It produces fruit 12 times a year, once each month. The leaves of the tree are for the healing of all people. ³Nothing that God judges guilty will be in that city. The throne of God and of the Lamb will be there. And God's servants will worship him. ⁴They will see his face, and his name will be written on their foreheads. ⁵There will never be night again. They will not need the light of a lamp or the light of the sun. The Lord God will give them light. And they will rule like kings for ever and ever.

⁶The angel said to me, "These words are true and can be trusted.

---

stadia One stadion was a distance of about 200 metres. It was one-eighth of a Roman mile.
cubits A cubit is about half a metre, the length from the elbow to the tip of the little finger.

The Lord is the God of the spirits of the prophets.*d* He sent his angel to show his servants the things that must happen soon."

⁷"Listen! I am coming soon! He who obeys the words of prophecy in this book will be happy."

⁸I am John. I am the one who heard and saw these things. When I heard and saw them, I bowed down to worship at the feet of the angel who showed these things to me. ⁹But the angel said to me, "Do not worship me! I am a servant like you and your brothers the prophets. I am a servant like all those who obey the words in this book. Worship God!"

¹⁰Then the angel told me, "Do not keep secret the words of prophecy in this book. The time is near for all this to happen. ¹¹Whoever is doing evil, let him continue to do evil. Whoever is unclean, let him continue to be unclean. Whoever is doing right, let him continue to do right. Whoever is holy, let him continue to be holy.

¹²"Listen! I am coming soon! I will bring rewards with me. I will repay each one for what he has done. ¹³I am the Alpha and the Omega,*n* the First and the Last, the Beginning and the End.

¹⁴"Those who wash their robes*n* will be blessed. They will have the right to eat the fruit from the tree of life. They may go through the gates into the city. ¹⁵Outside the city are the evil people, those who do evil magic, who sin sexually, who murder, who worship idols, and who love lies and tell lies.

¹⁶"I, Jesus, have sent my angel to tell you these things for the churches. I am the descendant*d* from the family of David. I am the bright morning star."

¹⁷The Spirit*d* and the bride say, "Come!" Everyone who hears this should also say, "Come!" If anyone is thirsty, let him come; whoever wishes it may have the water of life as a free gift.

¹⁸I warn everyone who hears the words of the prophecy of this book: if anyone adds anything to these words, God will give him the troubles written about in this book. ¹⁹And if anyone takes away from the words of this book of prophecy, God will take away his share of the tree of life and of the holy city, which are written about in this book.

²⁰Jesus is the One who says that these things are true. Now he says, "Yes, I am coming soon."

Amen. Come, Lord Jesus!

²¹The grace of the Lord Jesus be with you all. Amen.

Alpha and the Omega The first and last letters in the Greek alphabet. This means "the beginning and the end".
wash their robes This means they believed in Jesus so that their sins could be forgiven by Christ's blood.

FEATURES

What is the Bible?   vii
How Do I Use My Bible?   viii
Invitation   ix
List of Maps   x
Dictionary   1471
Bible Diary   1503
Table of Weights and Measures   1504
When We Want . . .   1505
Forty Fascinating Questions   1506
Facts   1507
Answers to Forty Fascinating Questions   1508
The Miracles of Jesus   1509
Stories Jesus Told   1511
Paul's Journeys   1513
Pages for Personal Notes   1514

DICTIONARY

A

Aaron (AIR-ohn) was the older brother of Moses. He often spoke for Moses. Only men from Aaron's family could be priests. (Exodus 4–40; Numbers 1–25)

Abba (AB-uh) was a child's word for "father" in the Aramaic language. Early Christians used this word in speaking to God. This shows how close we can feel to him. (Mark 14:36; Romans 8:15; Galatians 4:6)

Abib (ah-BEEB) means "young ears of grain". It is the first month of the Jewish calendar and about the same time of year as our March or April. It is also called Nisan. (Exodus 13:4; 34:18; Deuteronomy 16:1)

Abraham (AY-brah-ham) was the most respected man in the Jewish nation. The Jews called him "father Abraham". He was known for his great faith. (Genesis 12-25; John 8:39; Romans 4:1,16; Hebrews 11:11,12)

Adam (AD-um) means "out of the earth". He was the first man God created. He was made from the dust of the ground. (Genesis 1–4; 1 Corinthians 15:45)

adultery (ah-DUL-ter-ee) is breaking a marriage promise by having sexual relations with someone other than your husband or wife. (Exodus 20:14; Mark 10:11,12; John 8:3-5)

agreement (uh-GREE-ment) is a contract or promise. It is sometimes called a covenant. God made agreements with his people. One agreement was the "Law of Moses". God has given a new agreement to his people through Christ in the New Testament. Hebrews 8-10 explains the differences between the two agreements. (Genesis 9: 9-17; Hebrews 9:15-22)

Agrippa (uh-GRIP-pah) See "Herod Agrippa II".

alabaster (AL-a-bas-ter) is a light-coloured stone with streaks or stripes through it. Perfume was often kept in beautiful containers made of alabaster. (Matthew 26:7; Luke 7:37)

alamoth (AL-a-moth) was probably a musical word. It may mean "like a flute" or "high-pitched". (Psalm 46)

aloes (AL-ohs) were oils from sweet-smelling sap of certain trees. They were used for perfume, medicine and to prepare bodies for burial. (Numbers 24:6; John 19:39)

ALTAR

altar (ALL-ter) was a place where sacrifices, gifts or prayers were offered to God. Altars were often made of earth, grass or rocks piled up in the shape of a table on which the gift could be placed. (Genesis 8:20; 22:9; 1 Kings 18:30-35; Matthew 5:23,24; James 2:21)

amen (AH-MEN) is a Hebrew word for "that is right". A person says "amen" to show he agrees

Anak/Anakites (A-nak/AN-uh-kites) The Anakites were named after their ancestor Anak. They were a group of people who lived in Canaan when the Israelites arrived. They were known as large, mean, fighting people. (Numbers 13:22,28,33; Deuteronomy 1:28; 2:10,11; 9:2; Joshua 11:21,22)

Andrew (AN-droo) was a fisherman and the brother of the apostle Peter. Andrew was also one of the 12 apostles of Jesus. (Mark 1:16-18; 3:14-19; John 1:40-44; Acts 1:13)

angel (AIN-jel) is a Greek word that means "messenger". Angels are heavenly beings. They can sometimes look like people. God used angels to help his people and to announce important events. (Genesis 21:17; 22:11-15; Matthew 25:41; Luke 2:8-15; Hebrews 1:14; 12:22; 13:2; 2 Peter 2:4)

Annas (AN-us) was a high priest of the Jews during Jesus' lifetime. He served as the high priest in Jerusalem from A.D. 7 to 14. (Luke 3:2; John 18:12-23; Acts 4:6) See also "priest".

apostle (uh-POS-'l) is a Greek word that means "someone who is sent off". Jesus gave the name to the 12 men he chose as his special followers. He sent them to tell the good news about him to the whole world. Later, after Judas killed himself, Matthias became an apostle. Paul was also called an apostle. (Matthew 10:1-4; Mark 3:14-19; Acts 1: 2-26; 1 Corinthians 15:8-10)

Aquila (AK-wi-lah) was a Jewish Christian from the city of Rome. He and his wife Priscilla (or Prisca) worked as tentmakers and travelled with Paul. When they were at home in Rome or working in Ephesus, the Christians worshipped in their home. (Acts 18:2,3,18,26; Romans 16:3-5; 1 Corinthians 16:19)

Aramaic (AR-uh-MAY-ik) was the language of the people in the nation of Aram. The Jews in the country of Palestine started speaking Aramaic when they were taken as slaves by the Babylonian people. Jesus probably spoke Aramaic. (2 Kings 18:26-28; John 19:20)

ark, Noah's In this Bible it is called Noah's boat. (Genesis 6:13,14; 1 Peter 3:20)

Ark of God or Holy Box is often called Ark of the Covenant. It was a special box made of acacia wood and gold. Gold creatures with wings covered the top. Inside were the stone tablets where the Ten Commandments were written.

Later, a pot of manna and Aaron's staff were also put into the Box. It was to remind the people of Israel of God's promise to be with them. In this Bible it is also called the Holy Ark or the Holy Ark of God. (Exodus 25:10-22; 26:34; Joshua 3:1-17; 2 Chronicles 35:3; Hebrews 9:4)

Asherah (ah-SHIR-ah) was the name of a false goddess of the people of Canaan. She was thought to be the wife of the false god Baal. (Judges 3:7; 1 Kings 15:13; 2 Kings 21:7; 2 Chronicles 15:16)

Ashtoreth (ASH-toh-reth) was the name of a false goddess of the Canaanites. (Judges 2:13; 1 Samuel

7:3; 12:10; 1 Kings 11:5,33)

Augustus Caesar (aw-GUS-tus-SEE-zer) or Caesar Augustus was the first Roman emperor. He was the ruler when Jesus was born. He was a nephew to the famous Julius Caesar. (Luke 2:1,2)

B

Baal was a false god of the Canaanites. (1 Kings 18:17-40; Jeremiah 11:13)

Babylonians (bab-e-LONE-e-unz) were the people from Babylonia. This was a land east of Israel. Their largest city was Babylon. When Nebuchadnezzar was their king, they took many of the people of Judah to Babylonia as captives. The Babylonians were sometimes called Chaldeans. (2 Kings 25:4-26; 2 Chronicles 36; Daniel 1-4)

balm (BAHM) was an oil from a plant used as a medicine to comfort and heal sore skin. (Genesis 37:25; Jeremiah 51:8)

baptise (BAP-tise) is from a Greek word that in New Testament times meant to dip or immerse. Baptism as practised by Christians was in water. Baptism reminds us of Jesus' death, burial and rising to live again. It shows our death to sin and our being raised to new life with Christ. (Acts 2:38,41; 8:36-39; 10:47; 16:15,33; 18:8; Romans 6:3,4)

Baptist (BAP-tist) means "someone who baptises". John, a relative of Jesus, was called this

because he baptised many people. (Matthew 3:11)

Barabbas (bah-RAB-us) means "son of a father". He was a robber who had murdered someone in Jerusalem. He was in jail when Jesus was on trial. It was the time of year when a criminal would be freed from prison. The people cried out to have Barabbas freed and Jesus killed on the cross. Pilate, the Roman governor, did as they demanded. (Matthew 27:16-26; Mark 15: 6-11)

Barnabas (BAR-nah-bus) means "one who encourages". The apostles gave this name to Joseph because he helped others. Barnabas, who was from Cyprus, often travelled with Paul to teach about Jesus. The journeys of Barnabas with Paul are told in Acts 13-15. (Acts 4:36,37; 11:22-26)

Bartholomew (bar-THOL-oh-mew) was one of the 12 apostles of Jesus. He may also have been called Nathanael. (Matthew 10:2,3; Luke 6:13-15; John 1:43-50)

beatitude (bee-A-ti-tyood) means "blessed" or "happy". This name is often used for Jesus' teaching in Matthew 5:3-12 and Luke 6:20-22. In these verses Jesus described a blessed or happy person.

Beelzebul (bee-EL-ze-bull), also spelled Beelzebub, came from the name Baal-Zebub. This was the name of the false god of the Philistines. In the New Testament Beelzebul is a name sometimes used for the devil. (Matthew 12:24; Mark 3:22,23)

Bel was a false god of the Babylonians. (Jeremiah 50:2)

believers (be-LEE-vers) is a word used in the New Testament to describe the followers of Jesus. (Acts 2:41-47; 5:14)

Bethlehem (BETH-le-hem) means "house of bread". It is a small town five miles from Jerusalem in the country of Judea. It was the home town of King David in the Old Testament. Jesus was born there. (1 Samuel 16:4; Matthew 2:1; Luke 2:15-18)

THE BIBLE

Bible (BY-bul) means "the book". The Bible is a group of books and letters that Christians accept as the word of God. It is divided into two parts. The Old Testament contains 39 books, and the New Testament contains 27 books. See also "Scriptures".

blasphemy (BLAS-feh-mee) is saying things against God. Jesus was often accused of blasphemy because he said he was the Son of God. The people who accused him did not understand that he really was God's Son. (Matthew 9:3; 26:65; John 10:36)

blessing (BLES-ing) is a good gift from God to his people. (Luke 6:28; 24:50,51; Acts 3:26; Hebrews 6:7; 1 Peter 3:9)

bread that shows we are in God's presence is also called Bread of the Presence, or showbread. It was a group of 12 loaves of bread that were kept on the table in the Holy Tent and later in the Temple. This special bread reminded the people that they were always in God's presence. (Exodus 25:30; Leviticus 24:5-9; Luke 6:1-4)

C

Caesar (SEE-zer) was the name of a famous Roman family. In New Testament times it was used as the title of the Roman emperors. (Luke 2:1; 3:1; 20:22-25) See "Augustus Caesar".

Caiaphas (KY-uh-fus) was the Jewish high priest from A.D. 18 to 36. He was one of those who planned to kill Jesus. (Matthew 26:57-68; John 11:49-53; 18:12-28)

calamus (KAH-lah-mus) is a sweet-tasting plant stalk probably like sugar cane. (Exodus 30:23; Jeremiah 6:20; Ezekiel 27:19)

capital is the top of a pillar. This top part of the pillar was usually decorated with beautiful carvings. (Amos 9:1; 1 Kings 7:16-20; 2 Kings 25:17)

cassia (CAS-e-uh) is a pleasant-smelling powder. Its odour is like that of the cinnamon plant. (Exodus 30:24; Psalm 45:8)

centurion (sen-TYUR-ree-un) was a Roman army officer who commanded 100 soldiers. (Matthew 8:5; 7:12)

Cephas (SEE-fus) See "Peter".

chaff (CHAHF) is the husk of a head of grain. Farmers must separate it from the good part of the grain. In Bible times they tossed the grain and chaff together into the air. Since the chaff is lighter, the wind blew it away and the good grain fell back to the threshing floor. (Job 21:18; Psalms 1:4; 35:5; Isaiah 29:5; 41:2) See "threshing floor".

CHARIOT

chariot (CHA-re-ut) was a kind of fast, two-wheeled cart usually pulled by two horses. It was used for battles, travelling and parades. (Genesis 46:29; Exodus 14:6; Acts 8:28-31)

Chemosh (KEE-mosh) was the name of a false god of the Moabites. (Numbers 21:29; Jeremiah 48:46)

Christ (KRYST) means "anointed (or chosen) one" in Greek. In Hebrew the word is "Messiah". Jesus is the Christ. He was chosen by God to save people from their sins. (Mark 8:29; 14:61,62; Luke 23:2; Acts 2:36; 17:3; 18:28)

Christian (KRIS-chun) means "belonging to Christ". Christ's followers are called Christians. (Acts 11:26; 26:28; 1 Peter 4:16)

church in the New Testament means a group of Christians. In those times the church often met in someone's home. (Matthew 16:18; Acts 2:47; 14:27; Romans 16:5)

circumcision (SIR-kum-SIH-zhun) This means to cut off the foreskin of the male sex organ. Each Jewish baby boy was circumcised on the eighth day after he was born. This act was done as a sign of the agreement God had made with his people, the Jews. Because of this, the Jews sometimes are called "the circumcision" and non-Jews are called "the uncircumcision". (Leviticus 12:3; John 7:22; Acts 7:8)

clean is used to describe the state of a person, animal or action that is pleasing to God. God called some animals clean and said they could be eaten. People who had not touched or eaten anything God said was unclean were called clean. Or, if they did not have a disease that made them unclean, they were called clean. They could live and serve God normally. (Genesis 7:2; Leviticus 20:25; Deuteronomy 14:3-20) See "unclean".

Cleansing, Day of is also called the Day of Atonement. It was the most special day of the year for the Israelites. No one worked or ate on that day. This was the one day of the year when the high priest could go into the Most Holy Place. Animals were sacrificed for the sins of the people. This was a sign to the people that they were cleansed from their sins for a year. Jews still celebrate this day today. It is called Yom Kippur. (Leviticus 16:1-34; 25:9)

confess (kun-FES) means to

admit that something is true. The New Testament teaches a believer to confess that Jesus is the Son of God. Christians are also told to confess their sins, to admit that they have done wrong. (Romans 10:9,10; Philippians 2:11; 1 John 1:9)

coral (KOR-al) is a type of limestone that forms in the ocean. Coral is usually a rich red or deep pink colour. It is used to make jewellery. (Job 28:18; Ezekiel 27:16)

cornerstone This was the most important stone at a corner in the base of a building. The cornerstone had to be perfect so the building's walls would be straight. The other stones were fitted against the cornerstone. Jesus is called the cornerstone of the new law. (Joshua 6:26; Job 38:6; Ephesians 2:20)

council (KOWN-s'l), or meeting, was the highest Jewish court in the days of Jesus. Its proper name was the "Sanhedrin". The men of the council sat in a half circle to hear the people who came to speak to them. The trials of Jesus and Stephen were held in front of this council. (Matthew 26:57-68; Acts 6:13-15)

covenant (KUV-eh-nant) See "agreement".

cross refers to a cruel way of killing criminals in New Testament times. The person was tied or nailed to two rough beams of wood nailed together in the shape of an "x" or a "t". Then, he was left hanging in a public place to die. Jesus was killed by the Roman soldiers this way. In the New Testament the word "cross" is often used to remind us that Christ's death on the cross was God's way of saving us from our sins. (John 19:17-31; 1 Corinthians 1:18-25; Galatians 6:12; Ephesians 2:15,16)

cud An animal that chews the cud chews its food and swallows it. Then it chews it a second time. (Leviticus 11:3)

D

Dagon (DAY-gon) was one of the false gods of the Philistines. (Judges 16:23; 1 Samuel 5:2-7; 1 Chronicles 10:10)

Daniel (DAN-yel) was a Hebrew captive taken to Babylon as a young man. He told Nebuchadnezzar what his dream meant. God also made him able to tell Belshazzar what the strange handwriting on the wall meant. When he was about 80 years old, Daniel was put in the lions' den by King Darius. But God saved him. (Daniel 1–6)

David (DAY-vid) was Israel's greatest king. Jesus is called the "Son of David" because he was born to members of David's family. (1 Samuel 1:16-31; Luke1:69; 2:4; 18:38; Acts 2:29-31; 13:22)

deacon (DEE-kun) is a Greek word meaning "servant". Deacons are people chosen to serve the church in special ways. The men named in Acts 6:1-6 may have been the first deacons. Deacons are described in 1 Timothy 3:8-13.

Dead Sea is a large lake at the south end of the Jordan River. The

Jordan and several small streams flow into it. But it has no outlet. And it is so salty that nothing lives in it. It is about 80 kilometres long and 16 kilometres wide. In Bible days it was often called the Salt Sea, the Eastern Sea or the Sea of the Arabah. (Genesis 14:3; Numbers 34:3,12; Joshua 3:16)

demon (DEE-mun) was an evil spirit from the devil. Sometimes a demon lived in a person. But Jesus has more power than demons and could make them come out of people. (Deuteronomy 32:17; Psalm 106:37; Matthew 12:22; Luke 8:26-39)

descendants (de-SEN-dants) are family members who are born to a person and his children. They would include grandchildren, great-grandchildren, great-great-grand-children and so on. (Genesis 12:7; Leviticus 21:21; Romans 4:18)

devil (DEV-'l) means "one who accuses". In the New Testament, the devil is often called Satan or Beelzebul. He is a spirit and the enemy of God and man. (Matthew 4:1-11; John 13:2; Ephesians 4:27; 6:10-17) See "Beelzebul".

disciple (dih-SYE-p'l) See "follower".

E

Edom (E-dum) means "red". Edom was also called Esau, the older son of Isaac. The land where Esau's descendants lived was named Edom. It was south of the Dead Sea. Seir is another name for the land of Edom. (Genesis 25:30; 36:8; 2 Samuel 8:14; Psalm 137:7;

Ezekiel 25:12-14; Obadiah 10-14)

ELDER

elder (EL-der) means "older". In the Old Testament this Bible uses elders, older leaders, to describe a special group of men who led God's people. In the New Testament elders are appointed leaders in the church. (Numbers 11:16; Acts 20:17-38; 1 Timothy 3:1-7; 1 Peter 5:1-4)

Elijah (e-LIE-juh) was a man who spoke for God in the Old Testament. He was a prophet about 800 years before Jesus was born. (1 Kings 17–21; 2 Kings 1–2; Matthew 16:14; 17:3,4; 27:47; Luke 1:17; James 5:17)

ephod (E-fod) See "robe, holy".

epistle (e-PIS-'l) is a Greek word meaning "letter". Many books of the New Testament were actually letters written to Christians in various cities. Some of these letters are Ephesians, Galatians, Romans, 1 and 2 Corinthians, Philippians and Colossians. (Colossians 4:16; 1 Thessalonians 5:27; 2 Thessalonians 3:17; 2 Peter 3:16)

Esau (E-saw) See "Edom".

eternal life (e-TER-nul LIFE) is the new kind of life promised to those who follow Jesus. It is living with a new help from God. It is also life that will never end. (John 3:16; 4:14; Galatians 2:20; 1 John 5:11-15)

eunuch (YOU-nuk) is a man who cannot have sexual relations.

In the Bible eunuchs were often high officers in royal palaces or armies. (2 Kings 9:32; Esther 2:3; Isaiah 56:3-5; Acts 8:26-40)

Eutychus (YOU-ti-cus) means "lucky". Eutychus was a young man in the city of Troas. As he was sitting in an upstairs window listening to Paul preach, he went to sleep. He fell out of the window and died. But Paul, by God's power, brought him back to life. (Acts 20:7-12)

Ezra (EZ-ra) was the leader of a group of Israelites who were allowed to return to Jerusalem from Babylon. He taught them to worship and serve God correctly. (Ezra 7–10; Nehemiah 8–9)

F

faith (FAYTH) is belief and trust. People who have great faith in God do what he says to do, even when they do not understand why. They do it because they believe in him and trust him. Faith in Jesus means believing he is the Son of God and trusting in him. (2 Chronicles 20:20; Isaiah 7:9; Habakkuk 2:4; Matthew 8:10; Luke 8:24,25; Romans 4:16-22; 5:1,2; Ephesians 4:13; Hebrews 11)

fasting (FAST-ing) means giving up food for a while. People sometimes fast during a special time of prayer and worship to God. Jesus fasted for 40 days before he began preaching. It was also done to show sadness. (2 Samuel 12:16-22; Ezra 8:23; Matthew 4:1-11; 6:16-

18; 9:14,15; Acts 12:2,3; 14:23)

feast (FEEST) is a special meal and celebration for a certain purpose. There were many different feasts in Bible times.

Feast of Dedication was an eight-day celebration for the Jews. It was a way of being thankful that the Temple had been cleansed again. This was done in 164 B.C. after the Greeks had spoiled and ruined it. The celebration is called Hanukkah today by the Jews. (John 10:22)

Feast of Harvest See "Feast of Weeks".

FEAST OF SHELTERS

Feast of Shelters is also called the Feast of Booths or Feast of Tabernacles. The people gathered fruit and lived in tent-like shelters for a week. This feast reminded them of how God had taken care of them when the Israelites left Egypt and lived in tents in the wilderness. (Exodus 23:14-17; Deuteronomy 16:13-17)

Feast of Unleavened Bread was also called Passover. It was held to remember how God helped the Israelites in Egypt. He saved them from the one that brings death, that passed over their families. And God led them out of slavery. For seven days they ate bread made without yeast and did only certain types of work. (Exodus 12:14-20; Numbers 28:16-25;

Deuteronomy 16:1-8) See "Passover Feast".

Feast of Weeks was also called Pentecost, the Feast of Harvest and the Day of First Fruits. It was held seven weeks and one day after Passover. This was a feast of thanksgiving for the summer harvest. (Exodus 34:22; Leviticus 23:15-22; Numbers 28:26-31; Deuteronomy 16:9-12; Acts 2) See "Pentecost".

Felix (FEE-lix) was the Roman governor of Judea from A.D. 52 to 54. He was a cruel ruler. He kept the apostle Paul in prison for two years to please the Jews who hated Jesus and Paul. His full name was Marcus Antonius Felix. (Acts 23:24–24:27)

fellowship (FEL-o-ship) is sharing friendship and love with others. Christians have a very special fellowship with God and his people. (Acts 2:42; 1 John 1:3-7)

Festus (FES-tus) was the governor of Judea after Felix. His full name was Porcius (POR-shus) Festus. He allowed Paul to go to Rome to be tried by Caesar. (Acts 24:27–25:27; 26:24-32)

firstborn (FIRST-born) is the oldest child in a family. The son born first to a Jewish family received a double share of his father's wealth. Then he became the leader of the family when his father died. The Israelite people were called God's firstborn because he gave them special privileges. Jesus was also called God's firstborn son. He is now ruling over all creation. (Genesis 35:23; Exodus 4:22; Psalm 89:27; Romans 8:29; Colossians 1:18; Hebrews 1:6)

first fruits (FIRST fruits) were the first and best crops and animals the Israelites raised. They were to give these to God. This showed that they knew everything really belonged to God. (Exodus 34:22-26; Leviticus 23:9-21; Numbers 28:26; Deuteronomy 18:4)

flax (FLAKS) is a plant used to make clothing and ropes. The inside of the plant was combed and spun into thread. Then it was woven into cloth. (Exodus 9:31; Joshua 2:6; Proverbs 31:13; Isaiah 19:9)

follower (FOL-o-wer) is a person who is learning from someone. Jesus' followers are those who believe and obey his teaching. Another word for "follower" is "disciple". During his ministry, Jesus chose 12 special followers and made them his apostles. (Matthew 15:32-39; John 19:38; Acts 6:1-7; 11:26)

forgiveness (for-GIV-ness) means to be pardoned and not punished for a wrong thing done. A sinner who is sorry for his sin and stops doing that sin will be forgiven when he comes to God. That person will not be punished. Christians are also to forgive others for wrong things done to them. (Genesis 50:17; Psalms 19:12; 32:1-5; 51:1-17; Matthew 6:12-15; 9:2-8; 18:21,22; Acts 8:22; Romans 4:7; 1 John 1:9)

frankincense (FRANK-in-sens) is a very expensive, sweet-smelling perfume. It comes from inside the terebinth tree that grows in the country of Arabia. Some wise men gave frankincense to Jesus when he was born. (Exodus 30:34; Matthew 2:11; Revelation 18:13)

G

Gabriel (GAY-bree-el) is God's angel who announced that John the Baptist and Jesus would be born. (Luke1:11-20,26-35)

Galilee (GAL-i-lee) was the country between the Jordan River and the Mediterranean Sea. It had lots of water and trees, and the land was good for growing grains like wheat and barley. Jesus grew up in the city of Nazareth in Galilee and, so, was often called "the Galilean". (Matthew 4:23-25; 21:11; John 2:1,2; 7:1,9,41)

Galilee, Lake (GAL-i-lee) is also called the "Sea of Galilee". It is really a lake 20 kilometres long and about 13 kilometres wide. Storms often come up very quickly on this lake. Jesus spent much time around Lake Galilee. (Matthew 4:18-22; 8:23-27; 14:22-36; John 6:1,2,16-21)

gazelle (gah-ZEL) is an animal of the antelope family. It is known for its beauty and speed. It is usually about 60 centimetres tall and a metre long. (Deuteronomy 12:15,22; 2 Samuel 2:18; Proverbs 6:5)

GAZELLE

Gentiles (JEN-tiles) means "nations". The Jews called anyone who was not a Jew a Gentile. The Jews thought all non-Jewish people were enemies. The Good News of Jesus is for all people, both Jews and non-Jewish people. (Acts 10:44-48; 11:18; 13:46-48; Romans 1;5; 11:11-13; Ephesians 3:6-8)

Gethsemane (geth-SEM-uh-nee) was a garden of olive trees just outside Jerusalem. It was at the bottom of the Mount of Olives. The night before Jesus was killed, he prayed in this garden. Jesus was there when Judas brought the soldiers to arrest him. (Matthew 26:36-50; Mark 14:32)

gittith (GIT-tith) is probably a musical word and may be a kind of musical instrument. (Psalms 8; 81; 84)

God is the One who made the world and everything in it. He is a spirit and does not have a body as man does. But people can know what God is like because he sent Jesus into the world to show them. God hates evil, but he loves his people so much that he let his Son die for them. God is the wisest and most powerful being in the universe. He has always been alive, and he will always be alive. He is love. Christians are called "children of God" because they have been given a spirit like God. (Genesis 1:1; Psalm 139:7-12; Isaiah 44:6; Matthew 5:9; John 4:24; 14:9; Romans 1:18; 5:8-11; 8:16; 11:36; Hebrews 1:1-4; 1 John 4:7-12)

Golgotha (GOL-goh-thuh) is an Aramaic word meaning "skull". The Latin word for it is "Calvary". This is the hill where Jesus was killed on the cross by the Roman soldiers. It may have been called "the place of the skull" because many people died there. Or it may have been called that because the hill looks like a giant skull. (Matthew 27:32-35; Mark 15:22-24; John 19:17,18)

Good News is also called the

gospel. In the New Testament, the Good News is that Jesus died for us on the cross, was buried in a tomb and came back to life. Because he did these things for us, we can be saved. That is good news. (Mark 1:1; Acts 20:24; Colossians 1:21-23; 2 Timothy 1:10) See "gospel".

gospel (GOS-p'l) means "good news". It refers to Jesus' life, death and rising to live again. The first four books of the New Testament are called the gospels because they tell the good news of what Jesus has done for us. (Philippians 1:5,7,12; 2 Thessalonians 1:8) See "Good News".

grace is God's kindness and love shown to us, even though we do not deserve them. Part of God's grace is his forgiveness. He forgives us for the wrong things we do. He even let Jesus take the punishment for our sins. (John 1:14; Acts 15:11; Romans 5:1,2,8; 1 Corinthians 15:10; 2 Corinthians 6:1,2; Ephesians 2:4,5,8; Titus 3:3-7; Hebrews 4:16)

Greek is the language of the people of Greece. The New Testament was first written in the Greek language. Also, a person from the country of Greece is called a Greek. (John 19:20; Acts 14:1; 16:1,3; 21:37; Colossians 3:11)

H

Hades (HAY-deez) is where the dead, both good and bad, are. (Acts 2:27,31; Revelation 1:18)

heart in the Bible usually means the mind or feelings. It is not talking about the physical heart that pumps blood through the body. (Deuteronomy 30:10-17; Psalm 26:2; Proverbs 15:13-15; Mark 12:30; Luke 2:19; 6:45; 12:34; Acts 2:46)

heaven (HEV-'n) is the home of God. In the New Testament it is said to be a place where there is no pain, no crying, no sadness, no night and no death. Jesus showed us his love by leaving heaven and coming to earth to die on a cross. God's people will live in heaven with him for ever. (John 3:13; 6:38-40; Acts 7:56; 2 Corinthians 5:1-10; 1 Peter 1:4; Revelation 21:4)

Hebrews (HEE-brooz) is another name for the Jewish people. The book of Hebrews is a letter written to Jewish Christians. (2 Corinthians 11:22; Philippians 3:5; Hebrews)

heir (AIR) is the person who is supposed to inherit what belongs to a relative. The heir usually receives these things when the relative dies. Because through Christ we can be adopted children of God, Christians are heirs of God's riches. (Genesis 15:3-4; 2 Samuel 14:7; Galatians 4:1)

hell is the home of the devil. It is the place of punishment for ever for those who turn against God. Hell is described in the

HELL

New Testament as a place of fire, pain, sorrow and sadness. (Matthew 23:33; 25:41; 2 Peter 2:4,9; Revelation 20:14,15; 21:8)

Herod (HEH-rud) was the name of

four different rulers in the New Testament:

Herod I (Herod the Great) was king of the country of Palestine from the year 40 B.C. until about 4 B.C. He tried to kill the baby Jesus because Jesus was called a "king". Herod thought Jesus was an earthly king and would take away his throne. (Matthew 2:1-16; Luke 1:5)

Herod Antipas was the son of Herod I. He had John the Baptist's head cut off. Later, Jesus was sent to this man for trial. He ruled from the year 4 B.C. to about A.D. 39. (Matthew 14:1; Mark 6:14; Luke 23:6)

Herod Agrippa I was the king of Palestine for about three years (A.D. 41-44). He was the grandson of Herod I. He had the apostle James killed and the apostle Peter arrested. He did it to please the Jews who hated Jesus' followers. Later, this man was eaten by worms and died because he let the people treat him like a god. (Acts 12:1-21)

Herod Agrippa II was king of Palestine from the year A.D. 48 to 93. He was a great-grandson to Herod I. He heard the apostle Paul speak. He sent Paul to Caesar for trial. (Acts 25:13,26; 26:1-32)

higgaion (hig-GI-on) is probably a musical word. It seems to mean "to meditate". So it may mean a time to think quietly during a song. (Psalm 9:16)

high priest was the most important religious leader of the Jewish people. He was often as important as the king. Caiaphas was the high priest when Jesus was killed. Annas was another high priest at that time. (Matthew 26:3,57; Acts 23:2-5)

holy (HO-lee) means pure, belonging to and willing to serve God. God's people are called "holy people". (Exodus 3:5; 22:31; 31:13; 1 Corinthians 1:2; Ephesians 1:4; Philemon 4; 1 Peter 1:15,16)

Holy Place This was a room in the Holy Tent and the Temple. The priests came to this room every day to burn candles and incense to the Lord. Each week fresh loaves of bread were placed on the table there. A curtain separated the Holy Place from the Most Holy Place. (Exodus 26:31-35; 31:11; Leviticus 6:30) See "bread that shows we are in God's presence".

Holy Spirit (HO-lee SPIH-rit) is one of the three persons of God. The other two persons are God the Father and God the Son (Jesus). The Holy Spirit helped the apostles do miracles. He led men to write God's word. The Holy Spirit lives in Christians today. He is also called the Spirit of Christ, the Spirit of God, and the Comforter. (Genesis 1:2; John 3:5-8; 16:13; Acts 2:1-4; 5:32; Romans 5:5; 8:9-16; 2 Peter 1:20,21)

Holy Tent See "Meeting Tent".

hypocrite (HIP-oh-krit) comes from the word for an actor on a stage. In the Bible it is a person who acts as if he is good but isn't. (Matthew 6:2,5,16; 7:3-5; Luke 13:15-17)

IDOL

idol (EYE-d'l) is a false god. The non-Jewish people often worshipped statues they made from wood, stone or metal. They worshipped these idols instead of the true God of heaven. (Leviticus 19:4; 2 Kings 17:12-17; Acts 7:40-43; 17:16-23; 1 Thessalonians 1:9)

incense (IN-sens) was a spice burned to make a sweet smell. This was done by the priests in the Meeting Tent and the Temple. A special altar was used to burn incense as worship to God. Since the smoke seemed to go up to God, this reminded people of prayer. (Exodus 30:1-10,34-38; Psalm 141:2; Luke 1:9; Revelation 8:3-4)

Isaac (EYE-zak) means "laughter". He was the son of Abraham and Sarah. He was named Isaac because Sarah laughed when the angel told her she would have a baby. She thought she was too old. God tested Abraham by asking him to offer Isaac as a sacrifice on an altar. When God saw that Abraham would obey him he saved Isaac's life. (Genesis 21–26; Mark 12:26; Hebrews 11:17-20)

Isaiah (i-ZY-uh) was one of the great prophets of the Old Testament. He often gave God's message to King Hezekiah. (2 Kings 19–20; Isaiah 6–9; 53)

Israel (IZ-ray-el) is a Hebrew word that means "he who wrestles with God". When Jacob struggled with an angel at Bethel, God named him Israel. The 12 tribes of the Jewish nation were descendants of Jacob. They were called Israelites. (Exodus 3:16-18; Psalm 73:1; Luke 1:68; Acts 2:36; 5:33-36)

J

Jacob (JAY-cub) was one of the sons of Isaac. He was the father of the 12 tribes of God's chosen people. He had 12 sons, and each son was the head of a tribe. (Genesis 25–36; Matthew 1:2; 8:11; John 4:6)

Jacob's Portion (JAY-cubs POR-shun) is a name for God. It means that God cares for Jacob's people, the Israelites. (Jeremiah 10:16; 51:19)

James was the name of several men in the New Testament:

James, the son of Zebedee, was an apostle of Jesus and a brother of the apostle John. He was killed by Herod Agrippa I. (Matthew 10:2; Mark 10:35,41; Acts 12:2)

James, the son of Alphaeus, was also one of Jesus' apostles. He may have been a cousin to Jesus. (Matthew 10:3)

James, the brother of Jesus, was a respected leader in the church in Jerusalem. He probably wrote the book of James in the New Testament. (Matthew 13:55; John 7:5; Acts 12:17; 21:18; Galatians 1:19).

Jeremiah (jer-eh-MY-ah) was a prophet who warned the people of

Judah. He told them they were disobeying God and would be punished. He had a very difficult life, but he stayed faithful to God. He lived to see Jerusalem destroyed and the people taken to Babylon. (2 Chronicles 35:25; 36:21,22; Jeremiah 1,2; 20:1-6; 28:5; 36–40)

Jerusalem (jeh-ROO-suh-lem) is sometimes called "Zion" or the "City of David". It was the greatest city of the country of Palestine. It was the centre of the Jewish religion because the Temple was there. Jesus was killed on the cross near Jerusalem. The city was destroyed by the Roman army in the year A.D. 70. Later, it was rebuilt in the same place by the Moslems and is a great city today in the Middle East. (2 Samuel 5:5,6; 2 Chronicles 36:14,19; Ezra 1:1-11; Luke 2:22-45; 13:34; 24:13,18, 33,47, 49; Acts 2:5,14) See "Zion".

Jesus (JEE-zus) means "saviour". He is the Son of God. He was born to Mary, a young Jewish woman. Mary was told by the angel Gabriel that she would have a baby boy. She was to name him "Jesus" because he would save his people from their sins. He is also called "Christ" and "Messiah". He lived a perfect life and never sinned. But he was killed by Roman soldiers on a cross near Jerusalem. Then, he came back to life and now lives in heaven with his father, God. He is one of the three persons of God. The other two persons are God the Father, and God the Holy Spirit. (Matthew 1:21; Luke 2:21; 3:23; John 20:19; Acts 1:19,36; 4:10; Philippians 2:10-11) See "Christ" and "Messiah".

Jesus was a common name among Jewish people, so there were other less important men in the New Testament named Jesus, too. (Colossians 4:11)

Jew (JOO) at first meant someone from the tribe of Judah. Judah was one of Jacob's 12 sons and the head of one of the 12 tribes of Israel. Later, the word Jew meant any person in any of the 12 tribes (Hebrews 1–13). A person who is not a Jew is called a Gentile or non-Jew. Jesus was a Jew. (Ezra 4:12; Matthew 2:2; 28:11-15; Acts 2:5; Romans 1:16; 10:12)

John was the name of several men in the New Testament:

John the Baptist was Jesus' relative and the son of Elizabeth and Zechariah the priest. He lived in the desert and ate locusts and wild honey. He preached that the Saviour, Jesus, was coming soon. Jesus came to John the Baptist to be baptised in the Jordan River. Herod Antipas had John killed by cutting off his head. (Matthew 3:1-17; 11:11-13; 14:3-12; Luke 1:13-17)

John, the apostle, was one of the sons of Zebedee. He and his brother James were fishermen. He wrote the gospel of John, the books of 1, 2 and 3 John and probably Revelation. He is sometimes referred to as "the one Jesus loved". John, Peter and James were Jesus' closest friends. (Mark 1:19,20; 9:2; 14:33,34; Acts 3:1-11; Revelation 1:1-4, 9)

John Mark See "Mark".

Jordan (JOR-d'n) is the only large river in the country of Palestine. It runs about 75 miles from Mount Hermon to the Dead Sea. It also makes two lakes — Lake Huleh and Lake Galilee. Jesus was baptised in the Jordan River near the city of Jericho. (Joshua 3:11-17; 2 Kings 5:10,14; Matthew 3:5-17)

Joseph (JOZ-uf) was the name of several men in the Bible:

Joseph, the son of Jacob, was one of the 12 sons of Israel. His two sons, Ephraim and Manasseh, each started a tribe. (Genesis 37–50; Exodus 1:5-8;13:19; Acts 7:10-14)

Joseph of Nazareth was the husband of Mary, Jesus' mother. He was a carpenter. He may have died when Jesus was a young man because he is not mentioned after Jesus' childhood. The New Testament says he was "a good man". (Matthew 1:18-24; 2:13-23)

Joseph of Arimathea took the body of Jesus down from the cross and buried it in a tomb he had dug for himself. He was a member of the Jewish religious court called the Sanhedrin. He was probably a Christian. (Matthew 27:57-60; Mark 15:43-46)

Jubilee (JOO-bih-lee) was a Jewish celebration that took place every 50 years. Israelites were to do three things: (1) give the soil a rest and not farm, (2) free Israelite slaves and (3) return land and houses to the first owners or their children. (Leviticus 25)

Judas Iscariot (JOO-dus is-CAH-ree-ut) was the apostle who turned against Jesus and handed him over to the Roman soldiers to be killed. For this he was paid only 30 pieces of silver, the price of a slave. Later, Judas killed himself. (Matthew 26:47-50; 27:3-5; John 13:26-30)

Jude (JOOD) was possibly a brother of Jesus and James. In Jesus' early ministry, Jude did not believe Jesus was the Son of God. Later, he believed and became a leader in Christ's church. He wrote the book of Jude in the New Testament. (John 7:5; Jude)

Judea (joo-DEE-uh) was the land of the Jews. It was a district in the country of Palestine. Both Jerusalem and Bethlehem were cities in Judea. John the Baptist began his preaching in the desert of Judea. (Matthew 2:1; Luke 1:5; 2:4; Acts 1:8)

judges (JUH-jez) were the leaders of Israel before Israel had kings. A judge decided who was guilty in court, led the army in battle and was in charge of the government, like a governor. Israel had 15 judges in all. (Judges 2:16-19; 1 Samuel 7:15-17)

Judgement Day (JUJ-ment DAY) is the day Christ will judge all people. He will take his followers to live with him for ever in heaven. Those who have followed the devil will be sent to live with him in hell for ever. (Matthew 11:20-24; Hebrews 9:27,28; 2 Peter 2:9,10; 3:7)

L

LAMB

lamb (LAM) is an animal that the Jews often offered as a sacrifice (gift) to God. Since Jesus died as a sacrifice for us, he is called the Lamb of God that takes away the sins of the world. (Genesis 4:4;22:7; Exodus 12:3-13; John 1:29,36; 1 Corinthians 5:7)

Lazarus (LAZ-uh-rus) was the name of two men in the New Testament:

Lazarus of Bethany was a brother to Mary and Martha. He was also a very dear friend of Jesus. When he died, Jesus brought him back to life. (John 11:1-45; 12:1-11)

Lazarus, the beggar, was the name of a person in a story Jesus told his followers. (Luke 16:19-31)

leprosy (LEH-prah-see) is a name for some bad skin diseases. A person with leprosy was called a leper and had to live outside the city. When other people came by, the lepers had to warn them by crying out, "Unclean! Unclean!" (Leviticus 13:45,46; 2 Kings 5:1-27; 2 Chronicles 26:19-23; Matthew 8:1-3; Luke 17:11-19)

Leviathan (le-VI-ah-than) was the name for a sea monster. Some people think it was a crocodile. (Job 3:8; 41:1; Psalm 74:14; Isaiah 27:1)

Levites (LEE-vites) were descendants of Levi, one of Jacob's sons. The priests all came from this tribe. But not all Levites were priests. Those who were not priests worked in the Meeting Tent or Temple in other ways. (Exodus 32:25-29; Numbers 1:47-53; 8:5-26; Deuteronomy 10:8-9; 18:1-8; 1 Kings 12:31; Luke 10:32)

lid on the Holy Ark is also called the mercy seat. This was the beautiful gold lid on the Ark of God. It had a gold creature with wings on each end of it. This Holy Ark was kept in the Most Holy Place of the Meeting Tent and later in the Temple. (Exodus 25:17-22; 26:34; Leviticus 16:2,14-16; Hebrews 9:5)

locust (LO-cust) is an insect that looks like a grasshopper. Locusts travel in large groups. They eat crops and other green plants. Locusts were sometimes eaten as food. (Exodus 10:4-19; Deuteronomy 28:38-42; Joel 1:4; Matthew 3:4)

lord means "master" or one who is in control. Jesus is called Lord because he rules over all the world and universe. Christians let Jesus be the Lord of their lives. (Acts 2:36; 21:12-14; Romans 10:9; 1 Corinthians 6:11; Colossians 3:17-24)

Lord's Prayer is the name often given to the model prayer Jesus taught his followers. (Matthew 6:9-13; Luke 11:1-4)

Lord's Supper is the meal Jesus' followers eat to remember how he died for them. The bread reminds us of his body. The fruit of the vine reminds us of his blood. The Lord's Supper also shows that

Jesus came back to life and now lives in heaven with God. (Matthew 26:26-30; Luke 22:14-20; 1 Corinthians 10:17; 11: 23-32)

lots were sticks, stones or pieces of bone thrown like dice to decide something. Often God controlled the result of the lots to let the people know what he wanted them to do. (Numbers 26:55,56; Proverbs 18:18; Jonah 1:7; Luke 1:9; 23:34; Acts 1:26)

Luke was a non-Jewish doctor who often travelled with the apostle Paul. He was a very educated man. He wrote the books of Luke and Acts in the New Testament. Luke tells many acts of Jesus that are not told in the other three gospels. (Colossians 4:14; 2 Timothy 4:11)

LYRE

lyre (LIRE) is a musical instrument with strings. It is similar to a harp, but smaller. (2 Samuel 6:5; 1 Chronicles 15:16-28; Psalms 33:2; 144:9; 150:3)

M

mahalath (mah-HAY-lath), or mahalath leannoth, was probably a musical word. It may have been the name of a tune, or it may mean to dance and shout. (Psalms 53:88)

manna (MAN-ah) means "what is it?" It was the white, sweet-tasting food God gave the people of Israel in the wilderness. It appeared on the ground during the night so they could gather it in the morning. (Exodus 16:13-35; Numbers 11:7-9; Joshua 5:12; Hebrews 9:4)

Marduk (MAR-dook) was a false god of the Babylonians. (Jeremiah 50:2)

Mark, sometimes called John Mark, was a cousin to Barnabas. Mark travelled with Paul and Barnabas on part of their first missionary journey. He also wrote the gospel of Mark. Christians met in the home of Mark's mother, Mary, to pray for Peter to be freed from prison.(Acts 12:12,25; 13:5,13; 15:36-41; Colossians 4:10; 2 Timothy 4:11)

Martha (MAR-thuh) was the sister of Mary and Lazarus. They lived in the village of Bethany, which is very near Jerusalem. Jesus often stayed in their home when he was in that area. Martha and her brother and sister loved Jesus very much. (Luke 10:38-41; John 11:1-39; 12:12)

martyr (MAR-ter) is a Greek word that means "witness". Being a witness means telling what you know about something. Later, martyr came to mean a person who was killed for being a witness. Stephen was the first Christian martyr. He was killed because he told people that Jesus is the Son of God. It is believed that all the apostles, except one, were martyrs for being witnesses about Jesus. (Acts 7:54-60; 12:2; 22:20; Revelation 2:13)

Mary is the name of several women in the New Testament:

Mary, the mother of Jesus, was a Jewish woman whom God chose to give birth to his only Son. This was a great honour and blessing from God. She married a man named Joseph. Mary stood at the foot of the cross when Jesus was killed. (Matthew 1:18-25; Luke 1:27-45; John 19:25-27)

Mary Magdalene was from the town of Magdala. She was a follower of Jesus. She watched the men put Jesus' body in the tomb. She was the first person to see Jesus after he came back to life. (Matthew 27:56,61; Mark 15:40,47; 16:1,9; John 20:1-18)

Mary of Bethany was the sister of Martha and Lazarus. She was a dear friend of Jesus. Mary sat at Jesus' feet and listened to him teach. Once she poured some expensive perfume on his feet and dried them with her hair. (Luke 10:39-42)

maskil (MAS-kil) is probably a description of the kind of song that some of the Psalms were. It appears with 13 of the Psalms. (Psalms 32; 42; 44; 45)

Matthew (MATH-you), also called Levi, was a tax collector. He was one of Jesus' 12 apostles. He wrote the gospel of Matthew. (Matthew 9: 9,10; 10:3)

medium (MEED-ee-um) means "go-between". This is a person who tries to help living people talk to the spirits of dead people. (Leviticus 19:31; Deuteronomy 18:11; 1 Samuel 28:3-9; 2 Kings 23:24; Isaiah 8:19,20)

Meeting Tent is often called the Tabernacle or Holy Tent. This was the special tent where the Israelites worshipped God. It was used from the time they left Egypt until Solomon built the Temple in Jerusalem. This tent was kept in the middle of their camp to remind them that God was always with them. (Exodus 25–27; 39:32–40:36; Numbers 8; 2 Chronicles 1:3-13; 5:5)

Melchizedek (mel-KIZ-ih-dek) means "king of righteousness". He was a priest and king who worshipped God in the time of Abraham. Jesus is now the Christian's king and high priest. In this way, Jesus is a priest and a king like Melchizedek. (Genesis 14:17-24; Hebrews 5:4-10; 7:1-17)

mercy (MUR-see) is kindness and forgiveness. God had mercy on us. He sent his only Son, Jesus, to die on the cross for our sins. We, too, are taught to have mercy on other people. God says he will be as merciful to us as we are to others. (Genesis 43:14; 2 Samuel 24:14; Matthew 5:7; Romans 11:32; James 2:13; 5:11; 1 Peter 2:10)

mercy seat See "lid on the Holy Ark".

Messiah (muh-SY-uh) is a Hebrew word for "appointed one" or "one chosen by God". The Greek word for Messiah is "Christ". Christians believe that Jesus is the Messiah or Christ. (John 1:41; 4:25)

miktam (MIK-tam) is probably a description of the kind of song some of the Psalms were. It may mean that it is a sad song or a song about danger. (Psalms 16; 56–60)

mildew (MIL-dyoo) is a growth

that appears on things that have been damp for a long time. (Leviticus 13:47-59; 14:33-54)

minister (MIN-i-ster) means "servant". It also means one who lives serving God and others. Christians are taught to minister to each other and to non-Christians. (Romans 15:16)

miracle (MYR-ih-k'l) is a Latin word that means "wonderful thing". It is a great event which can be done only by God's help. Miracles are special signs to show God's power. In the Old Testament God used miracles to rescue his people. Jesus did miracles to prove that he was God's Son. The Bible tells us of many miracles. The sick were healed, the blind were given sight, the crippled were able to walk and people could speak languages they had never studied. Sometimes people were even brought back to life after they had died. The best miracle was Jesus' coming back to life after he was killed on the cross. (Nehemiah 9:17; Psalm 77:11,14; Matthew 28:5-7; Luke 23:8; John 2:1-11; 3:2; 20:30,31; Acts 4:16-22; 8:13)

Molech (MO-lek) was a false god of the Canaanite people. Those who worshipped Molech often sacrificed their own children to him by burning them on altars. (Leviticus 18:21; 20:1-5; 2 Kings 23:10; Jeremiah 32:35)

mortar (MORE-tuh) has two meanings:

It can be a stone bowl where grain is ground into flour by pounding. Manna was ground up this way. (Numbers 11:8; Proverbs 27:22)

Mortar is also the sticky material that holds bricks together. It was often made of mud or clay. (Genesis 11:3; Exodus 1:14; Isaiah 41:25)

Moses (MO-zez) in Hebrew means "saved from the water". Moses led God's people out of the land of Egypt where they had been slaves for 400 years. Moses wrote the first five books of the Old Testament. On Mount Sinai God gave to Moses the law for the Israelite people. It is called "the Law of Moses". (Exodus 2–40; Numbers 1–26; Deuteronomy 27–34; John 1:17,45; 3:14; Hebrews 11:23,24; Revelation 15:3)

Most Holy Place was the inner and most special room in the Meeting Tent and the Temple. The Ark of God was kept here. Only the high priest could come into this room, and he could enter only once a year. This was when he sprinkled blood on the lid of the Holy Ark to remind the people that their sins needed to be forgiven. (Exodus 26:33,34; Leviticus 16:2-20; 1 Kings 6:16-35; Hebrews 9:3-25)

MOUNT OF OLIVES

Mount of Olives is a hill covered with olive trees near Jerusalem. The garden of Gethsemane is on one side of the Mount of Olives. Jesus was praying there when the Roman soldiers came to arrest him. Some of the same olive trees that were in the garden when Jesus was on earth may still be there today. (2 Samuel 15:30; Luke 22:39-52; Acts 1:12)

Mount Zion (ZI-on) at first meant one of the hills on which Jerusalem was built. Later Zion became another name for the whole city of Jerusalem. In the New Testament, Zion is also used as a name for heaven. (Psalms 48:2,11; 74:2; 78:68; Obadiah 17; Hebrews 12:22)

myrrh (MUR) was a sweet-smelling liquid taken from certain trees and shrubs. It was used as a perfume and as a pain reliever. It was one of the gifts the wise men gave Jesus when he was born. (Genesis 37:25; 43:11; Proverbs 7:17; Matthew 2:11; Mark 15:23; John 19:39)

N

nard was an expensive perfume. It was expensive because it had to be imported from India. (Song of Solomon 4:13; Mark 14:3; John 12:3)

Nazarene (NAZ-uh-reen) is a person from the town of Nazareth. Jesus grew up in Nazareth and was called a Nazarene. Sometimes Christians also were called Nazarenes, since they followed Jesus. (Matthew 2:23; Acts 24:5)

Nazirite (NAZ-e-rite) was a Jewish person who made a special promise to God. He was to serve God by following special rules. Samson and Samuel were Nazirites.

(Numbers 6:1-21; Judges 13:7; 16:17)

Nebo (NEE-boh) was the name of a Babylonian god. He was thought to be the god of writing and the son of Bel. (Isaiah 46:1)

Nebo was also the name of the mountain where Moses died, as well as a town nearby. (Numbers 32:3; Deuteronomy 34:1; Isaiah 15:2)

Nehemiah (nee-uh-MY-uh) was a servant of King Artaxerxes I of Persia. He got permission to take a group of Jews back to Jerusalem to rebuild its walls. Nehemiah was such a good leader that they finished the job even though they had many difficulties. (Nehemiah 1–12)

Nephilim (NEF-eh-lim) were a group of people who were famous for being large and strong. The ten spies who were afraid to enter Canaan had seen the Nephilim who lived there. (Genesis 6:4; Numbers 13:33)

NEW MOON

New Moon was a Jewish feast held on the first day of the month. It was celebrated with animal sacrifices and the blowing of trumpets. It was a way for the Israelites to dedicate the month to the Lord. (Numbers 10:10; 28:14; 1

Samuel 20:5,24; Psalm 81:3; Ezekiel 46:3-6; Colossians 2:16)

Noah (NO-uh) and his family were the only people of their time who served God. So God told them about the great flood that was coming. They built a large boat (often called an ark) about 450 feet long. Noah's family and every kind of animal were saved to start the world all over again. (Genesis 6–9; 1 Peter 3:20)

P

parable (PAR-uh-b'l) is a story that teaches a lesson by comparing two things. Jesus often used parables to teach the people. Some examples of parables can be found in Mark 12:1-12, Luke 10:29-37 and Luke 15:1-31.

Passover Feast (PASS-o-ver FEEST) was an important holy day for the Jews in the spring of each year. They ate a special meal on this day to remind them that God had freed them from being slaves in Egypt. Jesus was killed at Passover time. (Exodus 12:27; Numbers 9; Joshua 5:10; Matthew 26:2,17-19)

Paul is the Roman name for "Saul". Saul was a Jew, born in the city of Tarsus. He studied under Gamaliel, a famous teacher of God's law. At first, Paul tried to destroy Christ's church by putting Christians in jail and killing them. But Jesus appeared to him and changed his life completely. He was then called Paul. And he became an apostle and a great servant of God.

He travelled to many countries, teaching about Jesus. Paul wrote many of the books of the New Testament as letters to Christians in different cities, such as Romans, Colossians and Corinthians. (Acts 7:58-60; 9:1-31; Philippians 3:5-7)

Pentecost (PEN-tee-cost) means "fifty". Pentecost was a Jewish feast day celebrating the summer harvest. It took place 50 days after the Passover Feast. The apostles began telling the Good News on Pentecost after Jesus died. (Acts 2; 20:16; 1 Corinthians 16:8)

persecute (PUR-seh-cute) means to hurt people. Christians in the New Testament times were often persecuted. Saul persecuted Christians by dragging

PERSECUTE

them from their homes, putting them in jail and killing them. (Matthew 5:11,12; Acts 8:1-4; Galatians 6:12; 1 Peter 3:13-15)

Peter (PEE-ter) was a fisherman. He and his brother, Andrew, were the first two apostles Jesus chose. He was first named Simon, but Jesus changed his name to Cephas, which means "rock" in Aramaic. In Greek the name is Peter. Peter, James and John were Jesus' closest friends. Peter was the first to tell the Good News of Jesus to the non-Jewish people. Later in his life Peter wrote the New Testament books of 1 and 2 Peter. He probably died as a martyr for Christ. (Matthew 14:25-33; 16:13-18; Mark 14:27-39; Luke 22:54-62; John 20:1-6; Acts 3:1-26; 10:1-48)

pharaoh (FAIR-row) was the title given to the kings of Egypt. The word first meant "great house", meaning the palace where the king lived. Later it became the title of the king who lived in the great house. Pharaoh is also called "king of Egypt". (Genesis 40–47; Exodus 1–14; 2 Kings 23:29)

Pharisees (FA-rih-seez) means "the separate people". They were a Jewish religious group who followed the religious laws and customs very strictly. Jesus often spoke against the Pharisees for their religious teachings and traditions. Many of the Pharisees did not like Jesus because he did not follow all of their rules. (Matthew 5:20; 23:23-36; Mark 7:1-13; Luke 18:9-14)

Philip (FIL-ip) was the name of several men in the New Testament:

Philip, the apostle, was from the city of Bethsaida and was a friend of Peter and Andrew. He brought Nathanael to Jesus. (Matthew 10:2,3; John 1:43-48; 12:21; 14:8,9)

Philip, the evangelist, was a Greek-speaking Jew. He was one of the seven men chosen to serve in the church in Jerusalem. Later, he preached the Good News in many places. (Acts 6:1-6; 8:5-40; 21:8,9)

Philip, the tetrarch (ruler), was the son of Herod I and Cleopatra. He built the city of Caesarea Philippi. (Luke 3:1)

Philistines (FIL-ih-steyens) were Israel's enemies for many years. They had five strong cities near the Mediterranean Sea: Ashdod, Ashkelon, Ekron, Gath and Gaza. They worshipped several false gods. They were finally defeated by the Egyptians. (Judges 15-16; 1 Samuel 4:1-10; 6–7; 17–18; 1 Chronicles 18:1)

plumb line (PLUM LINE) is a string with a rock or other weight on one end. People used it to see if a wall was straight. The plumb line was sometimes used to mean that God was checking to see if his people were living right. This is just as they checked to see if a wall was built right. (2 Kings 21:13; Amos 7:7,8)

POMEGRANATE

pomegranate (POM-ee-gran-it) is a red fruit about the size of an apple. It has many seeds. Each seed has a pocket of sweet juice around it. (Exodus 28:33; 39:24; Numbers 13:23; Deuteronomy 8:8; 1 Samuel 14:2)

Pontius Pilate (PON-shus PIE-lut) means "armed with a spear". Pilate was the Roman govenor of Judea from A.D. 26 to 36. The Jews who wanted Jesus killed brought him to Pilate. He did not find Jesus guilty of any crime. But Pilate allowed the Jews to crucify Jesus because he was afraid of the people. (Luke 13:1; 23:1-52; Acts 3:13; 4:27; 1 Timothy 6:13)

Preparation Day (prep-a-RAY-shun DAY) was the day before the Sabbath day. On that day the Jews prepared or got everything ready for the Sabbath. (Luke 23:54; John 19:14,31)

priest (PREEST) in the Old Testament was a servant of God who worked in the Meeting Tent or Temple. Priests helped the people offer their gifts and sacrifices to God. Jesus is the Christian's high priest. He brings man and God together. Because of this all Christians are now priests. (Leviticus 21–22; Hebrews 7:26-28; 1 Peter 2:5,9; Revelation 1:5,6) See "high priest".

Priscilla (prih-SIL-uh) See "Aquila".

prophecy (PROH-feh-see) means "message". It is God speaking through chosen people called prophets. The Old Testament has many prophecies about the Saviour who was to come into the world. Jesus was the answer to these prophecies. (Ezekiel 12:26-28; 2 Peter 1:20,21; Revelation 22:18,19) See "prophet".

prophesy (PROH-fes-sy) is to speak a prophecy. See "prophecy".

prophet (PROH-fet) means "messenger" or one who speaks for someone else. With God's help, a prophet was able to tell the people God's message correctly. Sometimes prophets told what would happen in the future. A woman who spoke God's message was called a prophetess (2 Kings 22:14; Luke 2:36). Several books of the Old Testament were written by prophets, including Jeremiah, Amos, Jonah and Micah. (2 Kings 6:12-16; 17:12-13; Matthew 2:5,6; Luke 16:29-31; 24;25-27; Romans 1:2; 1 Corinthians 12:28,29; 1 Peter 1:10-12)

prophetess See "prophet".

prostitute (PROH-sti-tyou-t) is a person who sells his or her body for sexual relations with someone to whom he or she is not married. This is a sin. In the Old Testament God's people often worshipped other gods. God said this was acting like a prostitute. (Genesis 38:15; Exodus 34:15-16; Proverbs 23:27; Jeremiah 3:1-6; Hosea 3:3; 1 Corinthians 6:15)

proverbs (PROH-verbs) are wise sayings. They are usually short so they can be easily remembered. The Old Testament book of Proverbs contains many wise sayings. They tell how to live a good and happy life. (Book of Proverbs)

psalm (SAHM) means "song". The Book of Psalms is like a songbook. The Jews sang many of these psalms, particularly at special times. There are many musical directions in the Psalms, such as the tune or the instruments to be used. (Book of Psalms)

Q

Queen Goddess is another name for Ishtar, a goddess of the Babylonians. During Jeremiah's time some of the Israelites worshipped her. (Jeremiah 7:18; 44:17-25)

R

Rahab (RAY-hab) was the name of a make-believe dragon. In a well-known story, Rahab looked strong but was defeated. Egypt was sometimes called Rahab to show that it would be defeated as Rahab was. (Job 9:13; 26:12; Psalms 87:4; 89:10; Isaiah 30:7; 51:9)

Rahab was also the name of a woman in Jericho. She hid the Israelite spies and helped them escape. (Joshua 2:1-3; 6:17-25; Matthew 1:5; Hebrews 11:31; James 2:25)

Rapha (RAY-fa) was a leader of a group of people in Canaan. They may have been giants. The descendants of Rapha are called Rephaites. (Genesis 14:5; Deuteronomy 2:11; 2 Samuel 21:16-22)

Red Sea is sometimes called the Sea of Reeds. It is a large body of water between Africa and Arabia. At the northern end it has two parts, one on each side of the Sinai Peninsula. God used a miracle to divide these waters at the northern end on the west side. This meant the Israelites could walk across on dry land and escape from Egypt. (Exodus 13:17–15:22; Joshua 2:10; 4:23; Psalm 106:7-22)

repent (rih-PENT) means being sorry for doing something wrong and not continuing to do that wrong thing. To repent is to "change your heart and life". (2 Chronicles 32:26; Matthew 3:2; 4:17; Mark 1:15; Luke 15:7,10; Acts 2:38; 3:19)

Rephaites See "Rapha".

resurrection (REZ-uh-REK-shun) is a dead person's coming back to life. In the New Testament several people came back to life with God's help. Some of them were Lazarus (John 11:38-45),

Tabitha (Acts 9:36-42), the widow's son in the town of Nain (Luke 7:11-17), and Eutychus (Acts 20:8-12). Jesus, the Son of God, came back to life after being dead three days. This was the most important resurrection. His resurrection from death means we can be saved and live in heaven for ever. (Matthew 28:1-10; 1 Corinthians 15; 1 Peter 3:21,22)

revelation (rev-uh-LAY-shun) means to show plainly something that has been hidden. The last book in the New Testament is called the Revelation to John. God showed the apostle John what to write to Christians to give them hope and faith even though they were being persecuted. (2 Corinthians 12:1; Revelation 1:1-3)

robe, holy is often called the "ephod". This was a special type of clothing for the priests in the Old Testament. The holy robe for the high priest had gold and gems on it. The Urim and Thummim were attached to the holy robe. (Exodus 25; 28; 39) See "Thummim".

Rock is often used as a name for God. A large rock is strong and a good place to hide. God is strong and protects us from our enemies. (Genesis 49:24; Deuteronomy 32:4,15,18,30; 2 Samuel 22:32,47; Psalm 18:2,31,46)

S

Sabbath (SAB-uth) means "rest". It was the seventh day of the Jewish week, their day of worship to God. The Jews were not allowed to work on this day. Some Jews became angry with Jesus because he healed people on the Sabbath. They thought this was breaking the Old Testament law of the Sabbath. (Exodus 16:23-30; 20:8-11; Matthew 12:9-14; Luke 6:1-11; Acts 18:4; Colossians 2:16,17)

Sadducees (SAD-you-seez) were a Jewish religious group. They were rich and important men. They believed that only the first five books of the Old Testament were true. They did not believe in angels or life after death (resurrection). The Sadducees lost their power and importance after Jerusalem was destroyed by the Romans about the year A.D. 70. (Matthew 22:23-33; Acts 4:1,2; 5:17,18; 23:6-9)

safety, city of is sometimes called City of Refuge. In Bible times, someone who had accidentally killed another person could go to a city of safety for protection. As long as the person was in a city of safety, the dead person's relative could not punish him. There were six cities of safety. (Numbers 35:6-34; Joshua 20)

saffron (SAF-ron) is a purple flower. Parts of it are used as a spice. (Song of Solomon 4:14)

saint is another word for Christian. God has set Christians apart to serve him. They live to please God and be like him — pure and holy. (Acts 9:13,32,41; 26:10; Romans 1:7; 1 Corinthians 1:2; Ephesians 1:1)

Samaritan (suh-MAR-ih-t'n) was a person from the area of Samaria in Palestine. Samaria was between Galilee and Judea. These people were only part Jewish, so the Jews did not accept them. They hated the Samaritans. But Jesus showed love and concern for the Samaritans. One story that Jesus told is known as the story of "the good Samaritan". (Luke 10:30-37; John 4:1-42)

Samuel (SAM-you-el) was the last judge in Israel. God used him to choose both Saul and David as kings. (1 Samuel 1–3; 7–16)

Sanhedrin (san-HEE-drin) See "council".

Satan (SAY-t'n) in Hebrew means "enemy". It is a name for the devil, the enemy of God and man. (1 Chronicles 21:1; Job 1:6-9; Matthew 4:10; Luke 10:18,19; Acts 5:3; 26:18) See "devil".

Saul (SAWL) in the Old Testament was the first king of Israel (1 Samuel 9–31). Saul in the New Testament was a man whose name was changed to Paul. See "Paul".

saviour (SAVE-yur) is someone who saves people from danger. The name Jesus means "saviour". Jesus is the Saviour of the people of this world. His life, death and resurrection made it possible for people to be saved from death and punishment for their sins. (Luke 2:11; John 4:42; Ephesians 5:23; Philippians 3:20; Titus 1:4; 1 John 4:14)

SCEPTRE

sceptre (SEP-tur) is a wand or a rod that the king holds. It is a sign of his power. Some are long and thin. Others are short and flat like a paddle. Some of them are highly decorated with gold. (Esther 4:11; 5:2; 8:4; Psalm 2:9)

scribe is a Hebrew word that means to write, to count and to put in order. In New Testament times scribes were men who wrote copies of the Scriptures. They were very careful when they copied the words of God. To be sure they had not made a mistake in copying, they would count the number of letters on each line they wrote. Scribes were educated, and some of them served as secretaries, royal assistants and teachers. (Nehemiah 8:1; Jeremiah 36:26; Matthew 7:29; 15:1-9; 23:1-36; Luke 22:2)

Scriptures (SCRIP-churs) means "writings". They are the special writings of God's word for man. When the word Scriptures is used in the New Testament, it usually means the Old Testament. Later, it came to mean the whole Bible. (Daniel 9:2; Luke 24:27,32,45; Acts 8:32-35; 17:2,11; 2 Timothy 3:16; 2 Peter 1:20; 3:16) See "Bible".

scroll is a long roll of paper used for writing. In Bible times books were written on scrolls. These scrolls were rolled up from each end to the middle. They were made of papyrus (a plant) or parchment (an animal skin). Some scrolls were as long as 11.6 metres. (Numbers 5:23; Isaiah 8:1; Jeremiah 36; Luke 4:17-20; 2 Timothy 4:13; Revelation 5:1-5)

Sea of Galilee See "Galilee, Lake".

seal was a tool with a design or picture carved on it. Kings pressed this seal into wax which would be placed on important papers to close them. It was like a person's signature. If the seal was broken, it showed that someone else had looked at the papers. A seal also showed who owned something. Sometimes these seals were worn as rings. (1 Kings 21:8; Esther 8:8; 2 Corinthians 1:22) See "signet ring".

seer was another name for prophet (1 Samuel 9:9) See "prophet".

Selah (SEE-lah) is probably a musical direction and is used in the Psalms. It may mean to pause. The word was not intended to be spoken when reading the Psalm. (Psalms 3; 4; 9; 24)

sheminith (SHEM-e-nith) means "on the eighth". It is probably a musical word in the Psalms that means an octave. It may mean to use an instrument with eight strings. (1 Chronicles 15:21; Psalms 6; 12)

shepherd (SHEP-'rd) is a person who cares for and protects sheep. A shepherd loves his sheep and gives them food and water. He guides them to a quiet place to rest. He protects the sheep from wolves and other wild animals. A good shepherd will even die trying to protect his sheep.

Jesus is called the Good Shepherd because he loves and cares for his followers who are often called sheep. Jesus was willing to die for his followers to save them. (Psalm 23; Mark 6:34; John 10:1-30; 1 Peter 2:25; 5:4)

shiggaion/shigionoth (shi-GY-on/shigi-O-noth) could be musical words meaning a sad song. (Psalm

7; Habakkuk 3:1)

signet ring (SIG-net ring) was a ring worn by a king or other important person. It had his seal on it. He would stamp things with this ring to show that he owned them. The stamp was like a signature. (Genesis 41:42; Esther 3:10; 8:2-10; Daniel 6:17) See "seal".

Silas (SY-lus) is sometimes called Silvanus. He was a teacher in the church in Jerusalem who often travelled with Paul. He became one of Paul's most trusted helpers. He may have written down some of Peter's and Paul's letters for them. (Acts 15:22,30–17:16;18:5; 1 Thessalonians 1:1; 1 Peter 5:12)

Simeon (SIM-ee-un) is a name that means "God has heard". He was one of the 12 sons of Israel. (Genesis 29:33; 35:23)

Another Simeon was a godly man who lived in Jerusalem. When he saw the baby Jesus in the Temple, he knew that this child would save his people from their sins. He held the baby Jesus in his arms and said a prayer of thanks to God. (Luke 2:25-35)

Simon (SY-mun), sometimes called Simeon, is a name that means "God has heard". The apostle Peter was first named Simon. Other men named Simon are also mentioned in the New Testament:

Simon of Cyrene carried the cross of Jesus to the hill of Calvary. (Matthew 27:32)

Simon, the magician, tried to buy the power of the Holy Spirit to do miracles. (Acts 8:9-24)

Simon, the Zealot, was one of the 12 apostles. (Matthew 10:4)

Simon, the brother of Jesus (Matthew 13:55)

sin is a word, thought or act against the law of God. Sin is doing something God said not to do, or it could be not doing something he said to do. Jesus came to save us from being punished for our sins. (Psalm 32:2; Romans 3:23; 5:12; 1 Corinthians 15:3; Galatians 1:4; Hebrews 4:15,16; 1 John 1:8-10; 2:1,2)

Solomon (SOL-o-mon) was a son of David. He took his father's place as king. He was famous for his wisdom and for building the Temple in Jerusalem. (1 Kings 1–11; 2 Chronicles 1–11)

Solomon's Porch (SOL-o-mon's PORCH) was a covered courtyard on the east side of the Temple. People gathered here to sell animals and exchange money. Others met to discuss the Law of Moses. (1 Kings 7:6; John 10:23; Acts 3:11; 5:12)

Son of David was a name the Jews used for the Christ who was to save the world. This was because the Saviour was to come from the family of King David. Jesus was the "Son of David". (Matthew 9:27; 20:30; 21:9)

Son of Man was a name Jesus called himself. It showed that he was God's Son, but he was also a man. This title for Jesus comes from "one who looked like a human being" in Daniel 7:13-14. There Daniel prophesies about Jesus. (Matthew 24:30; 26:64; Mark 13:26; 14:62; Luke 21:27; 22:69)

sorcery (SOR-sir-ee) means trying to put magical spells on people or harming them by some kind of magic. The Bible warns against doing this. (Leviticus 19:26; Deuteronomy 18:14; 2 Kings 17:17)

soul (SOLE) is what makes a person alive. Sometimes the Bible writers used words like heart and soul to mean a person's whole being or the person himself. (Deuteronomy 4:29; Psalm 108:1; Matthew 10:28)

Spirit See "Holy Spirit".

spirit (SPIH-rit) is the part of man that was made to be like God because God is spirit. The New Testament also talks about evil spirits. (Isaiah 26:9; John 4:23,24; James 2:24-26) See "demons", "Holy Spirit" and "soul".

Stephen (STEE-ven) was one of the seven men chosen to serve the church in Jerusalem. The New Testament says he was a man who had great faith. He was able to do miracles. Stephen was the first martyr for Christ. The Jews killed him by throwing stones at him because he taught that Jesus was the Son of God. (Acts 6:5-15; 7:54-60; 22:20)

synagogue (SIN-uh-gog) is a Greek word that means "a meeting". By the first century, the Jews met in synagogues to read and study the Scriptures. The building was also used as the Jewish court and as a school. Both Jesus and Paul often went to the Jewish synagogues to teach and discuss the Scriptures. (Matthew 4:23; Luke 4:16,17; Acts 15:21; 17:1,10)

Syria (SIH-ree-uh) is a Hebrew word that means "plain". In New Testament times it was the area north of Galilee and east of the Mediterranean Sea. Damascus was its capital city. In Old Testament times, this country was called Aram. (1 Kings 11:25; 2 Kings 5:1; Matthew 4:24; 15:23)

TABERNACLE

tabernacle (TAB-er-NAK-'l) See "Meeting Tent".

tambourine (tam-buh-REEN) is a musical instrument that is beaten to keep rhythm. (Exodus 15:20; 1 Samuel 18:6; Psalm 81:2)

tax collector was a Jew hired by the Romans to collect taxes. Most people did not like tax collectors because they worked for the Romans and often cheated people. The apostle Matthew was a tax collector before he became an apostle. Zacchaeus was also a tax collector. (Matthew 9:10,11; 10:3; Luke 5:27; 19:1-8)

temple (TEM-p'l) is a building where people worship their gods. God told the Jewish people to worship him at the Temple in Jerusalem. This Temple had been built by King Solomon. It was later destroyed by the Babylonians. It was rebuilt by Zerubbabel. This Temple was destroyed by a Roman general, Pompey. Herod built a third Temple which was used in Jesus' time. (2 Chronicles 2–7; Ezra 3:10-12; Mark 11:15-17; Acts 7:47; 19:27)

The New Testament also speaks of a Christian's body as a temple. That is because God's Spirit lives in the Christian. (Acts 7:48;19:27; 1 Corinthians 6:19)

temptation (temp-TAY-shun) is the devil's trying to get us to do something wrong. God has promised to help us when we are tempted, so we can choose to do the right thing. (Matthew 4:1-11; 1 Corinthians 10:13; Hebrews 2:18; 4:15,16; James 1:12-14)

Tent See "Meeting Tent".

testament (TES-tuh-ment) See "agreement".

Thaddaeus (THAD-ee-us) was one of the 12 apostles. Little else is known about him. (Matthew 10:3; Mark 3:18)

Thomas (TOM-us), or Didymus, is a name that means "twin". He was one of Jesus' 12 apostles. His courage and love for Jesus are shown in John 11:16. Sometimes people call him "doubting Thomas". The other apostles told him Jesus had been raised from death. But Thomas did not believe it until he saw Jesus himself. (John 14:5-7; 20:24-29; 21:2)

threshing floor was a place where farmers separated grain from chaff. This was done by beating the stalks on the hard ground. Then they would throw it in the air and let the wind blow the chaff away. (Genesis 50:10; Judges 6:11; 2 Samuel 24:16-24) See "chaff".

Thummim (THUM-im) The

Urim and Thummim were something attached to the holy robe of the high priest. They may have been gems. They were used in some way to find out what God wanted the Israelites to do. (Exodus 28:30; Leviticus 8:8; Deuteronomy 33:8)

Tiberius Caesar (ty-BEER-ee-us SEE-zur) was the Roman emperor during the last half of Jesus' life. He ruled from A.D. 14 to 37. The city of Tiberias was named after him. (Luke 3:1)

Timothy (TIM-oh-thee) means "one who honours God". Timothy was a close friend and helper of the apostle Paul. He was the son of a Greek father and Jewish Christian mother. His mother Eunice and his grandmother Lois taught him the Scriptures. Paul wrote two letters, called 1 and 2 Timothy, to him. (Acts 16:1-3; 17:13-16; 1 Corinthians 4:17; 1 Thessalonians 3:1-6; 2 Timothy 1:2-5)

tithe (TIETH) means "tenth". In the Old Testament the Jewish people were told to give one-tenth of what they earned to God. (Leviticus 27:30-32; Malachi 3:8; Luke 11:42; 18:12)

Titus (TY-tus) was a trusted friend and helper of the apostle Paul. He often travelled with or for Paul. Paul wrote the book of Titus to him while Titus was on the island of Crete. (2 Corinthians 2:13; 7:6,7,13-15; 8:6,16,23; Titus 1:4,5)

tomb (TOOM) is a place where a dead person's body is buried. Some tombs were underground. More often, in biblical times they were dug out of the side of a huge rock or mountain. A large stone was then rolled in front of the tomb to seal it. (Genesis 50:5; Luke 23:53-55; 24:1,2; John 20:1-9; 11:38-41)

TOMB

transfiguration (tranz-fig-uh-RAY-shun) means "to change". Jesus was transfigured in front of Peter, James and John. Jesus had taken them up on a mountain with him. There his face and clothes began to shine brightly. God spoke to the apostles. He said that Jesus is his Son and that they should obey only him. (Matthew 17:1-9)

tribe was all the descendants of a certain person. The 12 tribes of Israel were the descendants of the 12 sons of Jacob, who was later named Israel. (Genesis 49:28; Joshua 3:12; 7:14)

U

uncircumcised See "circumcision".

unclean is used to describe the state of a person, animal or action that was not pleasing to God. In the Old Testament God said certain animals were unclean. They were not to be eaten. If a person disobeyed this (or some other rule about being clean), that person was called unclean. He could not serve God until he was made clean again. (Genesis 7:2; Leviticus 11–15; Romans 14:14) See "clean".

unleavened bread (un-LEV-'nd bred) is bread made without yeast. This kind of bread is like a flat, thin cracker because it does not rise when it is baked. God told the Jews to use unleavened bread for the Passover Feast. (Exodus 12:20; Matthew 26:17-29; Mark 14:12-25)

Unleavened Bread, Day of was the first day of the Feast of Unleavened Bread or Passover. (Luke 22:7)

Urim (YOUR-im) See "Thummim".

V

virgin (VUR-jin) is a woman or girl who has not had sexual relations. (Genesis 24:16; Deuteronomy 22:15-28; Isaiah 7:14; Matthew 1:23; Luke 1:34)

vision (VIH-zhun) is like a dream. A vision may come to a person when he is awake or asleep. God used visions to tell people what he wanted them to do, to teach them something or to let them know something that was going to happen. Peter had a vision of a sheet filled with animals. (Genesis 15:1; Daniel 2:19; Acts 9:10-12; 10:3-19; 11:5; 16:9,10; 18:9)

W

WINEPRESS

winepress was a pit where grapes were mashed to get the juice out. People stepped on the grapes. The juice ran out into another container. The winepress is sometimes used to describe how God will punish people. When they sinned terribly, God would allow enemy armies to defeat them as if they were grapes crushed in a winepress. (Deuteronomy 15:14; Judges 6:11; Lamentations 1:15)

wise men, or "magi", was a name for men who studied the stars. Some wise men followed a star from the East and brought gifts to Jesus when he was born. (Matthew 2:1-12)

witchcraft means using the power of the devil to do magic. (Deuteronomy 18:10; 2 Chronicles 33:6; Galatians 5:20)

witness (WIT-ness) is someone who tells what he has seen or what he knows. The apostles were witnesses for Christ because they told people that Jesus is the Son of God. (Acts 1:8,22; 2:32; 22:14,15)

woman, slave is also called a concubine. She was a woman who may have been captured by a man during a war. Or he may have bought her as a slave. She was like a second-class wife whose main purpose was to have children for him. (Genesis 36:12; 2 Chronicles 11:21)

word in the Bible often means God's message to us in the Scriptures. (1 Peter 1:24,25; 1 John 2:14) Jesus is called the "Word" because he shows us what God is like. (John 1:1-5,14)

Y

YOKE

yoke is a wooden frame that fits on the necks of animals to hold them together while working. Two oxen were often yoked together to pull a farmer's plough. The word yoke is also used to mean the work a person is to do. (Deuteronomy 21:3; 2 Chronicles 10:4-11; Matthew 11:29)

Z

Zealots (ZEL-ots) were a group of Jewish men who were also called "Enthusiasts". They hated the Romans for controlling their home country and planned to force them out. Simon, the apostle, was a Zealot. (Luke 6:15; Acts 1:13)

ZION

Zion (ZY-on) was a hill inside the city of Jerusalem. Later, the name Zion, or Sion, was used to mean all of Jerusalem. In the New Testament, Mount Zion is sometimes even used as a name for heaven. (Hebrews 12:22; Revelation 14:1)

Bible Diary

EVENT	CHARACTER(S)	PLACE	BOOK	DATE
Creation	God	In the beginning...	Gen 1-2	
Adam & Eve	Adam & Eve	Eden	Gen 3	
Cain kills Abel	Cain & Abel	Not in Eden!	Gen 4	
Tower of Babel		Babel	Gen 5	
Noah's Ark	Noah			
Abraham & Isaac	Abraham & Isaac	Moriah	Gen 22	
Jacob's dream	Jacob	Bethel	Gen 28	1800 B.C.
Joseph's technicolour coat	Joseph	Canaan	Gen 37	
Moses in the bulrushes	Moses	Egypt	Ex 2	
Moses & the burning bush	Moses	Hareb	Ex 3	
The seven plagues	Moses & Pharoah	Egypt	Ex 7-11	
The Passover	Moses & Aaron	Egypt	Ex 12	1400 B.C.
The Exodus	Moses		Ex 12	
Crossing the red sea	Moses		Ex 13-14	
Manna & quail	Desert of Sin		Ex 16	
The Ten Commandments	Moses	Mt. Sinai	Ex 20	
Crossing the Jordan	Joshua	Jordan	Josh 3	
The walls of Jericho fall	Joshua	Jericho	Josh 6	1200 B.C.
Gideon & the fleece	Gideon	Canaan	Judg 6-7	
Samson & Delilah	Samson	Canaan	Judg 13-16	
Samuel is called	Samuel	Israel	1 Sam 1-3	
David & Goliath	David & Goliath	Israel	1 Sam 17	1000 B.C.
David & Bathsheba	David & Bathsheba	Jerusalem	2 Sam 11	
Solomon builds the temple	Solomon	Israel	1 Kgs 6-7	900 B.C.
Writing on the wall	Daniel	Babylon	Dan 5	
Daniel in the lions' den	Daniel	Babylon	Dan 6	587 B.C.
Jonah is swallowed	Jonah	Nineveh	Jon 1	400 B.C.
Birth	Jesus		Mt 1-2	6 B.C.
Baptism	John & Jesus		Mk 1	
Temptation	Jesus		Lk 4	
Jairus' daughter	Jesus		Lk 8	
Feeding 5000	Jesus		Lk 9	
Calming the storm	Jesus & disciples		Mk 4	
Man with leprosy	Jesus		Mt 8	
Walking on water	Peter & Jesus		Mk 6	
Transfiguration	Jesus		Mt 17	
Withering fig tree	Jesus		Mt 21	
Triumphal entry	Jesus		Mk 11	
Jesus gets angry	Jesus		Jn 2	
Wedding of Cana	Jesus		Jn 2	
Bethesda Pool	Jesus		Jn 5	
The widow's two coins			Lk 21	
The Last Supper	Jesus & disciples		Mt 26	
Lazarus rises	Jesus & Lazarus		Jn 11	
Washing of feet	Jesus & disciples		Jn 13	
Garden of Gethsemane	Jesus		Mk 14	
Judas betrays Jesus	Judas, Jesus & the disciples		Lk 22	
Peter denies Jesus	Peter & Jesus		Mt 26	
The Crucifixion	Jesus		Mk 15	
The Resurrection	Jesus		Lk 24	
Baptism by fire	The disciples		Acts 2	
Conversion of Saul	Saul to Paul		Acts 9	
A new heaven & a new earth	John		Rev 21	100 A.D.

TABLE OF WEIGHTS AND MEASURES

METRIC CONVERSION

Linear Measurements

METRIC	IMPERIAL
1 centimetre =	0.4 inch
1 metre =	36 inches or 3 feet = 1 yard
1 kilometre =	0.6 mile

Land measure

1 hectare =	2.5 acres = 100 acres

Weights

1 gram =	0.035 ounce
1 kilogram =	2.2 pounds
1 ton =	2200 pounds

Liquid and dry measures

0.15 litre =	5 fluid ounces = 1 gill
0.5 litre =	1 pint
1.1 litres =	2 pints = 1 quart
4.5 litres =	1 gallon = 4 quarts
9 litres =	2 gallons = 1 peck
36 litres =	1 bushel = 4 pecks

Avoirdupois Weight

453 grams =	1 pound
6 kilograms =	14 pounds = 1 stone
1016 kilograms =	2240 pounds = 1 ton

The figures of this table are not mathematically precise; but merely give approximate amounts and lengths. Weights and measures differed during biblical times and different places and the units are not always consistent throughout the books. Further research may well bring to light more accurate details.

WHEN WE WANT . . .

to know how to pray — Matthew 6: 5-15.

to pray . . .

1. For our family — Ephesians 6:14
2. For our friends — Psalm 91

to stop . . .

1. Being afraid — Matthew 8: 23-27
2. Being worried — 1 Peter 5: 7
3. Being angry — Psalm 37
4. Being upset — 1 John 5: 10-13
5. Being sad — John 5: 24
6. Being lonely — Psalm 23
7. Being tempted — James 1: 2-6
8. Being depressed — 2 Corinthians 4: 7-9
9. Doubting — Mark 9: 17-27

to say thank you . . .

1. For being happy — Psalm 103
2. For being loved — 1 Chronicles 16: 8-11
3. For being chosen — Psalm 104

GOD WANTS . . .

Commitment — 2 Timothy 4: 1-8
Faith — Hebrews 11: 1-12
Love — 1 Corinthians 13: 1-13
— 1 John 3: 11-18
Obedience — Psalm 15
Praise — Psalm 146
Prayer — John 17
Repentance — Luke 15
Wisdom — Proverbs 3

FORTY FASCINATING QUESTIONS

Can you discover the answers to these questions about some interesting facts and stories from the Bible?

1. Who named all the animals in the world? (Genesis 2:19-20)
2. Who was the first musician? (Genesis 4:21)
3. Who was the oldest man that ever lived and how old was he? (Genesis 5:27)
4. Who was the first zoo keeper? (Genesis 7:13-17)
5. Who wrestled with God all night long? (Genesis 32:22-32)
6. Who had the first waterbed? (Exodus 2:1-10)
7. Who heard a bush talk? (Exodus 3:1-6)
8. Why did a donkey talk? (Numbers 22:21-34)
9. What colour was the rope used by Rahab to save the Israelite spies? (Joshua 2:18-19)
10. When did a river suddenly stop flowing? (Joshua 3:13-17)
11. When did a city's walls tumble down at the sound of trumpets? (Joshua 6:1-27)
12. When did the sun stand still in the sky? (Joshua 10:12-14)
13. When was an army too big to go into battle? (Judges 7:1-7)
14. What battle was won with torches and clay jars and without fighting? (Judges 7:19-24)
15. Who carried away the gates of a city? (Judges 16:3)
16. Who was the strongest man and what was the secret of his strength? (Judges 16:4-22)
17. Who killed a giant with just a stone? (1 Samuel 17:1-51)
18. Who fought a lion, a bear and a giant and won? (1 Samuel 17:33-51)
19. Who in the Bible saw a ghost? (1 Samuel 28:4-20)
20. Why did the very large man from Gath need special shoes and special gloves? (2 Samuel 21:20)
21. Who were David's "Three Musketeers"? (2 Samuel 23:8-12)
22. Who was the "biggest troublemaker" in Israel? (1 Kings 18:17)
23. Who was fed by ravens? (1 Kings 17:2-6)
24. Who was one of the first marathon runners? (1 Kings 18:41-46)
25. Who rode a whirlwind to heaven? (2 Kings 2:1-14)
26. When did an axehead float on water? (2 Kings 6:1-7)
27. Who was the youngest person to become king in the Bible? (2 Kings 22:1)
28. Why was Queen Esther afraid to go and see her husband, the king? (Esther 4:10-11)
29. Who built a gallows only to hang from it himself? (Esther 5:9-14;7:9-10)
30. On what did a mysterious message appear and who was the message for? (Daniel 5:1-31)
31. Who spent three days and nights inside a big fish and lived to tell about it? (Jonah 1-2)
32. What two people walked on top of water? (Matthew 14:22-33)
33. Who went fishing when they owed taxes to the temple? (Matthew 17:24-27)
34. How did four men get their crippled friend to Jesus so that he could heal him? (Mark 2:1-12)
35. What gift was both the smallest and most generous? (Mark 12:41-44)
36. What was poured on Jesus' head and cost a full year's pay? (Mark 14:3)
37. What was Jesus' first miracle?
38. How did a little boy feed 5,000 people with just his small lunch? (John 6:1-14)
39. Who escaped his enemies by being lowered over the city wall in a basket? (Acts 9:23-25)
40. Who fell out of a window during a sermon? (Acts 20:7-12)

FACTS

Read on . . . They are really quite interesting.

The Bible is a story of what God is doing in history.

The Old Testament gives us the growth of the human race from Adam and Eve to Abraham and Sarah.

The Bible links the Old Testament from Abraham through to Christ, through the stories of God's chosen race: the Jews.

The New Testament as expected starts from Jesus Christ to *now*, describing the history of the church.

Old Testament Books	New Testament Books
Law – five	Gospels – four
History – twelve	History – one
Poetry – six	Prophecy – one
Prophecy – sixteen	Letters – twenty-one

Quick Fax

- Did you know Jesus was actually born six years earlier than our calendars tell us?
- There are 31,102 verses in the Bible.
  How many do you know by heart?
- The longest chapter is Psalm 119.
- The shortest chapter is Psalm 117.
- The longest book in the Old Testament is Psalms.
- The longest book in the New Testament is Luke.
- Between chapters 6 and 7 of Ezra, both Confucius and Buddha died (516-458 B.C.)

- From Canaan it is . . .

St. Augustine said: "The New is in the Old contained,
The Old is in the New explained."

which means the Old Testament is the firm foundation built on by the New Testament which is the actual building.

ANSWERS TO FORTY FASCINATING QUESTIONS

1. The man called Adam.
2. Jubal was the first person to play the harp and flute.
3. Methuselah lived for 969 years.
4. Noah was the first zoo keeper.
5. Jacob wrestled all night.
6. Moses!
7. Moses.
8. Because Balaam went out with the Moabite leaders against God's wishes.
9. The rope was red.
10. The Jordan stopped flowing when the Ark of God was carried across.
11. Jericho city walls tumbled down when Joshua marched around them.
12. The day that the Lord allowed the Israelites to defeat the Amorites.
13. When Gideon was going to fight the Midianites.
14. The battle against the Midian army.
15. Samson tore up the gates and carried them away.
16. Samson. His secret was that he had never had his hair cut.
17. David killed Goliath.
18. David.
19. Saul.
20. The large man needed special gloves and shoes, because he had six fingers on each hand and six toes on each foot.
21. Josheb-Basshebeth, Eleazar and Shammah.
22. Elijah.
23. Elijah was fed by ravens.
24. Elijah, when he ran ahead of King Ahab to Jezreel.
25. Elijah went up to heaven in a whirlwind.
26. When a group of prophets met with Elisha by the river Jordan.
27. Josiah. He was eight when he became king.
28. Because the law stated that anyone who entered the inner courtyard without being called would be killed.
29. Haman.
30. The plastered wall of the royal palace. The words were for King Belshazzar.
31. Jonah lived to tell the tale.
32. Jesus and Peter walked on water.
33. Jesus and Peter.
34. The four men lowered the paralysed man through a hole they had made in the roof.
35. Two very small copper coins, which was all the poor woman had.
36. Nard. A very expensive perfume.
37. Jesus turned the water into wine during the wedding at Cana.
38. He shared his lunch of five loaves and two fish.
39. Saul.
40. Eutychus fell asleep and fell out of a window during Paul's sermon.

THE MIRACLES OF JESUS

Miracle	Scripture	Where performed
Power over nature		
Turns water to wine	John 2:1-11	Cana
First catch of fish	Luke 5:1-11	Sea of Galilee
Stills the storm	Matthew 8:23-27 Mark 4:35-41 Luke 8:22-25	Sea of Galilee
Feeds 5,000	Matthew 14:15-21 Mark 6:35-44 Luke 9:12-17 John 6:5-15	near Bethsaida
Walks on sea	Matthew 14:22-33 Mark 6:45-52 John 6:16-21	Sea of Galilee
Feeds 4,000	Matthew 15:32-39 Mark 8:1-9	near Bethsaida
Money from fish	Matthew 17:24-27	Capernaum
Withers fig tree	Matthew 21:17-22 Mark 11:12-14; 20-25	Jerusalem
Second catch of fish	John 21:1-14	Sea of Tiberias
Power over sickness		
Heals nobleman's son	John 4:46-54	Cana
Cures man with harmful skin disease	Matthew 8:1-4 Mark 1:40-45 Luke 5:12-15	Galilean city
Heals soldier's servant	Matthew 8:5-13 Luke 7:1-10	Capernaum
Heals Peter's mother-in-law	Matthew 8:14-17 Mark 1:29-31 Luke 4:38-89	Capernaum
Heals paralysed man	Matthew 9:1-8 Mark 2:1-12 Luke 5:17-26	Capernaum
Cures woman of bleeding	Matthew 9:20-22 Mark 5:25-34 Luke 8:43-48	Capernaum

Miracle	Scripture	Where performed

Power over sickness

Miracle	Scripture	Where performed
Gives blind their sight	Matthew 9:27-31	Capernaum
Heals crippled hand	Matthew 12:9-14 Mark 3:1-6 Luke 6:6-11	Galilee
Heals non-Jewish girl	Matthew 15:21-28 Mark 7:24-30	Tyre
Heals a deaf man who cannot talk	Mark 7:31-37	Decapolis
Heals a man at a pool	John 5:1-18	Bethsaida
Gives back sight	Mark 8:22-26	Bethsaida
Gives sight to a man born blind	John 9:1-41	Jerusalem
Heals man with dropsy	Luke 14:1-6	Jerusalem
Heals ten of harmful skin disease	Luke 17:11-19	Galilee
Replaces ear of high priest's servant	Luke 22:49-51 John 18:10-11	Garden of Gethsemane

Power over evil spirits

Miracle	Scripture	Where performed
Heals man who could not talk because of a demon	Matthew 9:32-34	Capernaum
Sends evil spirit from man	Mark 1:23-27 Luke 4:33-36	Capernaum
Heals man who was blind and could not talk	Matthew 12:22 Luke 11:14	Galilee
Heals child with demon	Matthew 17: 14-20 Mark 9:14-29	Mt. Tabor
Heals woman crippled for 18 years	Luke 13:10-17	Jerusalem

Power over death

Miracle	Scripture	Where performed
Raises Jairus' daughter	Matthew 9:18-26 Mark 5:35-43 Luke 8:41-42, 49-56	Capernaum
Raises widow's only son	Luke: 7:11-16	Nain
Raises Lazarus	John 11:1-45	Bethany

STORIES JESUS TOLD

Parable	Passage	Subject	Lesson
New winebags	Matthew 9:16-17	Jesus' message	Jesus has a new message from God
Farmer and the seed	Matthew 13:1-8 Mark 4:3-8 Luke 8:5-8	God's Word	We must hear and obey God's Word
Weeds	Matthew 13:24-30	God's people	The good and bad will be separated
Mustard seed	Matthew 13:31-32 Mark 4:30-32 Luke 13:18-19	God's people	Small beginnings can lead to big things
Yeast	Matthew 13:33 Luke 13:20-21	God's people	Small beginnings can lead to big things
Hidden treasure	Matthew 13:44	God's people	Choose what is truly valuable in life
Very valuable pearl	Matthew 13:45-46	God's people	Choose what is truly valuable in life
Fishing net	Matthew 13:47-50	God's people	The good and bad will be separated
Lost sheep	Matthew 18:12-14 Luke 15:3-7	God's love	God loves each person deeply
Servant who would not forgive	Matthew 18:23-25	God's people	We forgive because God forgave us
Workers in a vineyard	Matthew 20:1-16	Service	God rewards us generously
Two sons	Matthew 21:28-32	God's love	God welcomes the sinner who comes to Him
Evil renters	Matthew 21:33-46 Mark 12:1-12	Punishment	People who hate God's Son will be punished
Wedding dinner	Matthew 22:1-14	Punishment	People who do not accept God's invitation will be punished
Ten virgins	Matthew 25:1-13	Jesus' return	We must be ready when He comes back
Talents	Matthew 25:14-30	Service	We must use our abilities to serve God
Wise and evil servants	Matthew 24:45-51 Luke 12:42-48	Service	We are to serve God and others as we wait for Jesus to return
Two men who owed money	Luke 7:41-43	God's people	We love God more when we realise we are sinners
Good Samaritan	Luke 10:30-37	Service	Do good to all in need

Parable	Passage	Subject	Lesson
Friend at midnight	Luke 11:5-8	God's love	God is always willing to help
Unimportant seat at party	Luke 14:7-11	Humility	Don't be proud: let God reward
Lost coin	Luke 15:8-10	God's love	Each one is important to God
Son who left home	Luke 15:11-32	God's love	God forgives all who change their hearts and minds and return to Him
Clever manager	Luke 16:1-10	God's people	We are to use money to do good and prepare for the future
Rich man and Lazarus	Luke 16:19-31	Punishment	People who love money more than God are foolish
Unworthy servants	Luke 17:7-10	Service	Serve God because we are thankful
Unfair judge	Luke 18:1-8	God's love	God will answer our prayers if we ask Him
Pharisee and tax collector	Luke 18:9-14	God's love	Anyone who changes his heart and life can be forgiven
Bags of money	Luke 19:11-27	Service	Use our talents to serve God

PAUL'S MISSIONARY JOURNEYS

Acts and New Testament Letters

Crucifixion of Jesus	A.D.30	Paul's visit to Jerusalem (Acts 21)	A.D.57
Pentecost (Acts 2)	A.D.30	Paul's arrest (Acts 21-24)	A.D.57
Stephen martyred (Acts 7)	early A.D.35	Paul in prison	A.D.57-59
Paul converted	summer A.D.35	Paul's sea voyage to Rome	A.D.59-60
Paul in Damascus (Acts 9)	A.D.35-37	Paul's first Roman imprisonment	A.D.60-62
		Ephesians written	A.D.60
Paul to Jerusalem (Acts 9)	summer A.D.37	*Colossians written*	A.D.61
		Philemon written	A.D.61
Paul in Tarsus	A.D.37-43	*Philippians written*	A.D.62
Paul in Antioch	A.D.43-48	Paul released and travelling	A.D.62-64
		1 Timothy written	A.D.62
Paul's first missionary journey	A.D.48-49	Paul travels to Spain	A.D.64-66
Galatians written	A.D.49	*Titus written*	A.D.66
Jerusalem Council (Acts 15)	A.D.49	Paul in Greece	A.D.67
Paul's second missionary journey	A.D.50-52	Paul arrested and taken to Rome	A.D.67
1 Thessalonians written	A.D.51	*2 Timothy written*	A.D.67
2 Thessalonians written	A.D.51	Paul put to death in Rome	A.D.68
Paul's third missionary journey	A.D.53-57	City of Jerusalem destroyed	A.D.70
1 Corinthians written	A.D.56		
2 Corinthians written	A.D.56		
Romans written	A.D.57		

NOTES

NOTES

NOTES

NOTES

NOTES

The Exodus

The Holy Land Today

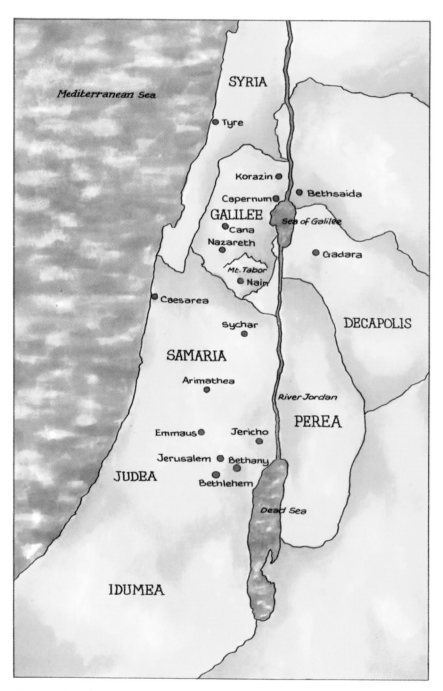

Palestine in the Life of Jesus

Paul's Journeys 1 and 2

Paul's Journeys 3 and 4

Revelation 7:9-10
There were so many people that no
one could count them. They were
from every nation, tribe, people, and
language of the earth.